CHAMBERS

OFFICIAL SCRABBLE

LISTS

International

CHAMBERS

OFFICIAL SCRABBLE® LISTS International

Compiled by
Allan Simmons
Darryl Francis

CHAMBERS

CHAMBERS
An imprint of Chambers Harrap Publishers Ltd
7 Hopetoun Crescent
Edinburgh, EH7 4AY

www.chambers.co.uk

First published by Chambers Harrap Publishers Ltd 2002

A CIP catalogue record for this book is available from the British Library.

ISBN 0550 10068 7

Designed and typeset by Chambers Harrap Publishers Ltd, Edinburgh
Printed in Great Britain by Clays Ltd, St Ives plc

Contributors

Compilers
Allan Simmons
Darryl Francis

Computer compilation
Peter Schwarz

Editor
Catherine Schwarz

Project Manager
Una McGovern

Prepress
Marina Karapanovic

Acknowledgement

The Compilers and Publisher would like to thank Mike Baron for developing the algorithm on which the top bonus stems are based and *The Wordbook* (1988), which played a part in the *Official Scrabble® Lists* project.

Contents

Hints xiv
Preface xv
Introduction xvii

Section One: Starter Lists
Introduction 1
Beginners' Starter Sets
Introduction 3
Starter Sets 4
Basic Words
Introduction 6
2-letter words 7
3-letter words 8
4-letter words 11
Light and Heavy Words
Introduction 20
Light words (many vowels) 20
Heavy words (many consonants) except -S extensions 25
Awkward Vowel Dumps
Introduction 27
Awkward vowel dumps – A's 27
Awkward vowel dumps – E's 28
Awkward vowel dumps – I's 28
Awkward vowel dumps – O's 29
Awkward vowel dumps – U's 29
Awkward Consonant Dumps
Introduction 31
Awkward consonant dumps – B's 31
Awkward consonant dumps – C's 31
Awkward consonant dumps – F's 31
Awkward consonant dumps – H's 32
Awkward consonant dumps – V's 32
Awkward consonant dumps – W's 32
Awkward consonant dumps – Y's 32
K and V Words
Introduction 35
K-words 35
V-words 38

High Scorers
Introduction 40
J-words 40
Q-words 43
X-words 46
Z-words 49

Section Two: Beginnings
Introduction 57
Useful Prefixes
Introduction 58
Words prefixed with AB- 59
Words prefixed with AD- 59
Words prefixed with AIR- 59
Words prefixed with BE- 59
Words prefixed with BI- 60
Words prefixed with COM- 61
Words prefixed with CON- 61
Words prefixed with DE- 61
Words prefixed with DIS- 62
Words prefixed with EM- 63
Words prefixed with EN- 63
Words prefixed with EX- 64
Words prefixed with FOOT- 64
Words prefixed with FOR- 65
Words prefixed with IM- 65
Words prefixed with IN- 65
Words prefixed with ISO- 66
Words prefixed with MAN- 66
Words prefixed with MIS- 67
Words prefixed with NON- 67
Words prefixed with OUT- 68
Words prefixed with OVER- 69
Words prefixed with PER- 69
Words prefixed with PRE- 70
Words prefixed with PRO- 70
Words prefixed with RE- 71
Words prefixed with RED- 73
Words prefixed with SEA- 73
Words prefixed with SUB- 73
Words prefixed with SUN- 74
Words prefixed with TRI- 74
Words prefixed with UN- 75

Words prefixed with UP- 77
Words prefixed with WAR- 77
5 to 8's
Introduction 79
5 to 8's 80

Section Three: Endings
Introduction 101
Useful Suffixes
Introduction 102
Words ending in -ABLE 103
Words ending in -AGE 103
Words ending in -ANCE 104
Words ending in -ANCY 104
Words ending in -ARCH 104
Words ending in -BACK 104
Words ending in -BALL 105
Words ending in -BAND 105
Words ending in -BIRD 105
Words ending in -DOM 105
Words ending in -EAUX 106
Words ending in -ENCE 106
Words ending in -ENCY 106
Words ending in -EST 106
Words ending in -ETTE 108
Words ending in -EUR 109
Words ending in -FISH 109
Words ending in -FORM 109
Words ending in -FUL 109
Words ending in -GEN 110
Words ending in -GRAM 110
Words ending in -HOLE 110
Words ending in -HOOD 110
Words ending in -HORN 111
Words ending in -IBLE 111
Words ending in -IFY 111
Words ending in -INGS 111
Words ending in -ISE 113
Words ending in -ISH 114
Words ending in -ISM 114
Words ending in -IST 115
Words ending in -ITY 116
Words ending in -IUM 116

Words ending in -KIN 117
Words ending in -LAND 117
Words ending in -LESS 117
Words ending in -LET 118
Words ending in -LIKE 118
Words ending in -LOGY 119
Words ending in -LY 119
Words ending in -MAN 122
Words ending in -MEN 122
Words ending in -NESS 123
Words ending in -OID 123
Words ending in -OR 124
Words ending in -OUS 125
Words ending in -OUT 125
Words ending in -SET 126
Words ending in -SHIP 126
Words ending in -SKIN 126
Words ending in -SMAN 126
Words ending in -SMEN 126
Words ending in -SOME 127
Words ending in -TIME 127
Words ending in -TION 127
Words ending in -URE 128
Words ending in -WARD 128
Words ending in -WARDS 128
Words ending in -WAY 128
Words ending in -WISE 129
Words ending in -WOOD 129
Words ending in -WORK 129
Words ending in -WORM 129
Words ending in -WORT 129
Words ending in -YARD 130
Unusual Vowel Endings
Introduction 131
Words ending in -A 131
Words ending in -I 136
Words ending in -O 138
Words ending in -U 140

Section Four: Variants
Introduction 143
Variants AE/E 144
Variants OE/E 145

Variants EI/IE 145
Variants -RE/-ER 146
Variants -ER/-OR 146
Variants -OUR/-OR 147
Variants -ABLE/-IBLE 148
Variants -SMAN/-MAN 148
Variants EN-/IN- 148
Variants -EY/-IE/-Y 149

Section Five: Bonus Word Lists
Introduction 153
Summary of 6-Letter Stems with ranking, keywords, combining letters and mnemonic 155
7-Letter Sets: from the top 250 6-letter stems 160
7-Letter Sets List: alphabetical 181
Summary of 7-Letter Stems with ranking, keywords, combining letters and mnemonic 189
8-Letter Sets: from the top 250 7-letter stems 193
8-Letter Sets List: alphabetical 207
Additional High-probability Words
Introduction 213
Additional bonus words (1 and 2 point tiles only)
7-letter words 214
8-letter words 214
Additional bonus words (with one 3 or 4 point tile)
7-letter words with one B 215
7-letter words with one C 216
7-letter words with one F 217
7-letter words with one H 218
7-letter words with one M 218
7-letter words with one P 219
7-letter words with one V 220
7-letter words with one W 221
7-letter words with one Y 221
8-letter words with one B 221
8-letter words with one C 222
8-letter words with one F 223
8-letter words with one H 224
8-letter words with one M 224
8-letter words with one P 225
8-letter words with one V 226
8-letter words with one W 227
8-letter words with one Y 227

AEIO Bonus Words
Introduction 229
AEIO bonus words (no U)
7-letter words 230
8-letter words 230
AEIO bonus words (with U)
7-letter words 232
8-letter words 232
Further Bonus Sets
Introduction 233
6-letter stems that combine with each vowel
6-letter stems – 2 vowels, no S 234
6-letter stems – 2 vowels, one S 235
6-letter stems that combine with AEIOU and Y only 238
6-letter stems that combine with AEIOU only 239

Section Six: Hooks and Blockers
Introduction 243
Hooks
Introduction 244
2-letter word hooks 245
3-letter word hooks 247
4-letter word hooks 254
5-letter word hooks 271
6-letter word hooks 292
7-letter word hooks 326
8-letter word hooks 362
Useful -S hooks
Introduction 372
Nounal adjectives ending in -ABLE 372
Nounal past tenses ending in -ED 372
Nounal adjectives ending in -IBLE 373
Words ending in -IC 373
Words ending in -ING 374
Words ending in -OID 377
Words ending in -(consonant) Y 378
Words ending in -S 378
Blockers
Introduction 379
2-letter word blockers 379
3-letter word blockers 379
4-letter word blockers 379

5-letter word blockers (except words ending in -ED, -J, -S, -X, -Y, -Z) 380
6-letter word blockers (except words ending in -ED, -J, -S, -X, -Y, -Z) 382

Section Seven: Anagrams
Introduction 387
7-Letter Anagrams 388
8-Letter Anagrams 492

Hints

Two's Company 7
Score or Strategy? 7
Tackling the Threes 10
Open Play 10
Fours Feeding 10
Think Big – Think Bonus 18
Practising with Plates 18
Suspicious Minds 19
Tile Turnover 19
Spreading the Words 19
Vowel Advice 24
Triple Tactics 24
Valuing the S and Blank 24
ING Addiction 24
Bonus Hunting 25
Looking at Hooks 25
Fishing 26
Mind Your Changing 26
Flashcards 29
Fighting Back 30
Passing Thoughts 30
Learn As You Play 30
Rack Balancing 33
Edging the Endgame 33
Combination Management 34
Unusual Clues 34
Knowing Non-Words 34
Q But No U 39
Managing the Big Four 55
Learning the J Q X Z Words 55
Do-it-Yourself 6-Letter Sets 56
Tile-Tracking 56

Preface

Official Scrabble® Lists International (OSLI) brings the invaluable resource of *Official Scrabble® Lists* (OSL) into line with the word list of *Official Scrabble® Words International* (OSWI). Whether you play Scrabble at an international level or you simply want to play with OSWI's increased vocabulary, OSLI is the ideal guide for increasing vocabulary and confidence.

The lists included are specifically structured to help Scrabble players learn more words and study for a variety of real-game situations. Over 30 panels containing hints on strategy, tactics and learning will also improve a Scrabble player's game. OSLI will help inspire players in every Scrabble situation.

The Publisher

Introduction

Official Scrabble® Lists International (OSLI) is the ideal companion to *Official Scrabble® Words International* (OSWI), which is the definitive authority for UK tournament and club players, as well as being the authority for many overseas organizations and tournaments, and for the World Scrabble® Championships.

This *International* edition of OSL is a unique and thorough collection derived from the wealth of words in OSWI, which is a combination of *Official Scrabble® Words*, 4th edition (based on *The Chambers Dictionary*, 1998) and the equivalent American word source (based on a number of American desk dictionaries). OSLI reflects the many new words that have been brought into play by this combination.

The words are organized into useful sections and lists to meet the needs of Scrabble players. The lists are an invaluable aid, acting as a convenient vocabulary-building guide for newcomers to the game and a specialist reference for the more experienced players.

The Starter section comprehensively covers the indispensable 2-, 3- and 4-letter words and the high-scoring words. There are lists to help players get out of tricky situations: words with many vowels; words with many consonants; words containing V, K, etc. Newer players should note the two pages of some 1,500 essential words at the beginning of the Starter Lists section as a crash-course on Scrabble vocabulary.

There is a section on Beginnings, including useful prefixes and even '5 to 8's', which are 3-letter extensions to 5-letter words; there is also a section on Endings, including useful suffixes and unusual vowel endings. Following these there is a section on Variants, which focuses on variant spellings. These are either words which look similar but have completely different meanings or alternative spellings of words which have the same meaning.

As players get a 50-point bonus for using all their tiles in one turn, a complete section is devoted to 7- and 8-letter Bonus Words. This includes the 250 most fruitful 6- and 7-letter combinations which yield thousands of likely 'bonuses', with suggested mnemonic phrases to help memorize the letters that go with each combination. In addition, there are lists of 6-letter sets which combine with all the vowels, as well as worthwhile high-probability bonus word lists.

Then comes the Hooks and Blockers section, which details the hook letters that can be added to the front or back of words from two to eight letters to form valid longer words. As well as normal examples like VOID to AVOID and ARSON to PARSON, there are some fascinating novelties to unearth, such as ZYGOSES to AZYGOSES, HOMELY to HOMELYN and even

MELINITE to GMELINITE, as well as common but often unthought-of extensions such as VINY to VINYL and UNFAIR to FUNFAIR. If you're feeling mean, the blockers list provides some great words to make life difficult for your opponent.

OSLI also of course contains anagrams, as every Scrabble book should. It lists every valid 7- and 8-letter word according to its constituent letters. Thousands of anagrams are there at your fingertips, from the exotic ALEMBIC/CEMBALI to the more down-to-earth OUTSIDE/TEDIOUS, and it even gives solutions to jumbles of letters such as AAAGMNR – what else but ANAGRAM!

As well as the many additional words now accommodated from OSWI, there have also been some enhancements. The layout of the Hooks section has been revised and additional useful -S hooks lists have been added. The mnemonic phrases for the Bonus Word stems have been overhauled to cover the many new bonus words and to make them more memorable. The Variants lists have been modified to enable a better focus on genuine variant spellings.

With lots of tips and hints on strategic secrets of success and learning words to help improve your vocabulary, what more could the Scrabble player want? OSLI is the ultimate Scrabble players' ready-reckoner.

Earlier *Official Scrabble® Lists* have certainly helped me prepare for tournament play, and over the years have been the backbone to my study for my British Matchplay Championship and UK Master titles, as well as helping me prepare for the 2001 World Championships. Many other Scrabble players have valued OSL, and this *International* edition will be widely welcomed.

Allan Simmons

Section One

Starter Lists

Introduction

This section contains a variety of 'starter' lists, a knowledge of which will give every player a firm foundation of useful Scrabble words. There are:

☆ a handy package of 1,500 or so particularly useful words to help newer players get started

☆ the basic words – a complete listing of all the valid 2-, 3- and 4-letter words

☆ words with many vowels ('light' words) and words with many consonants ('heavy' words) – ammunition for helping you to use up vowels or consonants when you have too many of them

☆ words containing more than one of the same vowel or consonant – awkward vowel dumps and awkward consonant dumps

☆ all the words up to five letters long containing a K or a V

☆ all the words up to eight letters long containing a J, Q, X or Z

Each of these lists has an introduction that describes it in more detail.

Beginners' Starter Sets

To help newer players to improve their game rapidly, the following two pages contain a selection of around 1,500 words specifically chosen for their usefulness and likelihood of occurring. The lists include:

List 1: 2-letter words

This list includes *all* the 2-letter words, which underlines how useful they are, especially for parallel plays.

List 2: 3-letter words

An extensive list of 3-letter words, excluding the very common that will be in most people's everyday vocabulary, and excluding the less useful words. Familiarity with some of the more unusual 3-letter words will improve your ability to score with fewer letters and give you a greater chance of extending 2-letter words on the board.

List 3: Vowel-heavy words

All the 4- and 5-letter words that contain no more than one consonant, excluding common words and those with JQXZ. These are essential for rapid resolution of racks abounding in vowels – one of the most common rack difficulties.

List 4: JQXZ words

A selection of words containing one of the power tiles, J, Q, X or Z, combined only with tiles having a value of less than 3. The more common everyday words have been excluded so that you can focus more easily on the words to learn. We have also excluded words that are -S, -ES, -D or -ED extensions of shorter words.

List 5: 7-letter words

Over two hundred 7-letter words that are most likely to crop up in the game. Some of these are common words, others more unusual, but all are worth being familiar with. They will help you achieve those 50-point bonus scores for playing all your tiles.

List 6: 8-letter words

It may seem strange to include 8-letter plays in a list for beginners, but a knowledge of just a few likely 8-letter words can be extremely useful for playing bonus words when there is no scope for 7's. It's important for newer players to 'think big' and explore the full spectrum of possibilities to improve scoring. For this reason, a hundred of the most likely 8-letter words have been selected. Some are common words, some more unusual, but all are likely to crop up more often than you might think.

List 1: 2-letter words

AA	AL	AX	CH	EE	ES	GU	IF	KO	MI	NO	OH	OS	PH	SO	UH	WE	YU
AB	AM	AY	DA	EF	ET	HA	IN	KY	MM	NU	OI	OU	PI	ST	UM	WO	ZO
AD	AN	BA	DE	EH	EX	HE	IO	LA	MO	NY	OM	OW	PO	TA	UN	XI	
AE	AR	BE	DI	EL	FA	HI	IS	LI	MU	OB	ON	OX	QI	TE	UP	XU	
AG	AS	BI	DO	EM	FY	HM	IT	LO	MY	OD	OO	OY	RE	TI	UR	YA	
AH	AT	BO	EA	EN	GI	HO	JO	MA	NA	OE	OP	PA	SH	TO	US	YE	
AI	AW	BY	ED	ER	GO	ID	KA	ME	NE	OF	OR	PE	SI	UG	UT	YO	

List 2: 3-letter words

AAH	BEL	DEV	ESS	GIS	IDS	KOW	MHO	NUR	PAM	REI	SOU	UKE	WOS
AAL	BEN	DEX	EST	GJU	IFF	KUE	MIB	NUS	PAP	REM	SOV	ULE	WOT
AAS	BEY	DEY	ETA	GOA	IFS	KYE	MIG	NYE	PAS	REN	SOX	ULU	WOW
ABA	BEZ	DIS	ETH	GOE	ILK	KYU	MIL	NYS	PAX	RES	SOY	UMM	WOX
ABB	BIO	DIT	EUK	GON	INS	LAC	MIM	OBA	PEC	RET	SUK	UMP	WUD
ABO	BIS	DIV	EWK	GOR	ION	LAH	MIR	OBE	PED	REW	SUQ	UNI	WUS
ABS	BIZ	DOB	EWT	GOS	IOS	LAM	MIS	OBI	PEH	REX	SUR	UNS	WYE
ABY	BOH	DOC	FAH	GOV	IRK	LAR	MIZ	OBO	PEP	REZ	SUS	UPO	WYN
ACH	BOK	DOD	FAP	GOX	ISH	LAS	MNA	OBS	PES	RHO	SWY	UPS	XIS
ADS	BON	DOH	FAS	GOY	ISM	LAT	MOA	OCA	PHI	RHY	SYE	URB	YAH
ADZ	BOR	DOL	FAW	GUB	ISO	LAV	MOC	OCH	PHO	RIF	SYN	URD	YAM
AFF	BOS	DOM	FAY	GUE	ITA	LEA	MOD	ODA	PHS	RIN	TAD	URE	YAR
AGA	BOT	DOO	FEH	GUL	JAG	LEE	MOE	ODS	PHT	RIT	TAE	UTA	YAW
AHA	BRO	DOP	FEM	GUP	JAK	LEK	MOG	OES	PIA	RIZ	TAI	UTE	YAY
AHS	BUR	DOR	FER	GUR	JAP	LEP	MOI	OFT	PIC	ROC	TAJ	UTS	YEA
AIA	BYS	DOS	FET	GUS	JEE	LES	MOL	OHM	PIR	ROK	TAK	UTU	YEH
AIN	CAM	DOW	FEU	GYP	JEU	LEV	MOM	OHO	PIS	ROM	TAM	UVA	YEP
AIS	CAW	DSO	FEY	HAE	JIN	LEW	MON	OHS	PIU	ROO	TAO	VAC	YEX
AIT	CAY	DUN	FID	HAH	JIZ	LEX	MOR	OIK	PIX	RUC	TAS	VAE	YGO
AKE	CEE	DUP	FIE	HAJ	JOE	LEY	MOS	OKA	POA	RUD	TAU	VAR	YID
ALA	CEL	DUX	FIL	HAN	JOR	LEZ	MOT	OKE	POH	RYA	TAV	VAS	YIN
ALB	CEP	DZO	FIZ	HAO	JOW	LIG	MOU	OLM	POI	SAB	TAW	VAU	YOD
ALP	CHE	EAN	FOH	HAP	JUD	LIN	MOY	OMS	POL	SAC	TAY	VAV	YOK
ALS	CHI	EAS	FON	HAW	JUN	LIS	MOZ	ONS	POM	SAE	TED	VAW	YOM
ALT	CID	EAU	FOP	HEH	JUS	LOD	MUN	OOF	POO	SAI	TEF	VEE	YON
AMA	CIG	ECH	FOU	HEP	KAB	LOR	MUS	OOH	POS	SAL	TEG	VEG	YOS
AMI	CIS	ECU	FOY	HES	KAE	LOS	MUT	OOM	POW	SAM	TEL	VIA	YOW
AMU	CIT	EDH	FRA	HET	KAF	LOX	MUX	OON	POX	SAN	TES	VID	YUG
ANA	CLY	EEK	FRO	HEW	KAI	LOY	NAE	OOP	POZ	SAR	TET	VIG	YUK
ANE	COL	EEN	FUB	HEX	KAM	LUD	NAH	OOR	PRE	SAX	TEW	VIM	YUM
ANI	COR	EFF	FUD	HIC	KAS	LUM	NAM	OOS	PSI	SAZ	THO	VIN	YUP
ANN	COS	EFS	FUG	HIE	KAT	LUR	NAS	OOT	PUH	SEC	TIC	VIS	YUS
ARB	COZ	EFT	FUM	HIN	KAW	LUV	NAT	OPE	PUL	SED	TID	VLY	ZAG
ARD	CUD	EHS	GAB	HOA	KAY	LUX	NAW	OPS	PUR	SEL	TIG	VOE	ZAP
ARF	CUM	EIK	GAD	HOC	KEA	LUZ	NEB	ORA	PUY	SEN	TIL	VOL	ZAX
ARS	CUR	ELD	GAE	HOH	KEB	LYE	NED	ORC	PYA	SER	TIS	VOR	ZEA
ARY	CUZ	ELL	GAL	HOI	KED	MAA	NEE	ORD	PYE	SEY	TOC	VOX	ZED
ATT	CWM	ELS	GAM	HON	KEF	MAC	NEF	ORF	PYX	SEZ	TOG	VUG	ZEE
AUF	DAE	ELT	GAN	HOO	KEN	MAE	NEK	ORS	QAT	SHA	TOR	VUM	ZEK
AVA	DAG	EME	GAR	HOS	KEP	MAG	NEP	ORT	QIS	SIB	TUI	WAB	ZEL
AVE	DAH	EMF	GAT	HOX	KET	MAK	NID	OSE	QUA	SIC	TUM	WAE	ZEX
AVO	DAK	EMS	GED	HOY	KEX	MAL	NIM	OUD	RAD	SIM	TUN	WAP	ZHO
AWA	DAL	ENE	GEE	HUE	KHI	MAM	NIS	OUK	RAH	SIS	TUP	WAT	ZIG
AWN	DAN	ENG	GEO	HUH	KIF	MAS	NIX	OUP	RAI	SKA	TUX	WAW	ZIN
AYS	DAP	ENS	GEY	HUI	KIR	MAW	NOB	OVA	RAJ	SMA	TWA	WEM	ZIT
AYU	DAS	EON	GHI	HUN	KOA	MAX	NOH	OWT	RAS	SNY	TYE	WEN	ZOA
AZO	DAW	ERE	GIB	HUP	KOB	MED	NOM	OXO	RAX	SOC	TYG	WEX	ZOS
BAC	DEB	ERF	GID	HYE	KOI	MEG	NON	OXY	REB	SOG	UDO	WEY	
BAH	DEE	ERG	GIE	HYP	KON	MEL	NOO	OYE	REC	SOH	UEY	WHA	
BAL	DEF	ERK	GIF	ICH	KOP	MEM	NOS	OYS	REE	SOL	UFO	WIS	
BAM	DEI	ERN	GIO	ICK	KOR	MES	NOX	PAC	REG	SOS	UGH	WIZ	
BAS	DEL	ERS	GIP	IDE	KOS	MEU	NOY	PAH	REH	SOT	UGS	WOK	

List 3: Vowel-heavy words

AEON	AITU	AMIE	AUTO	EINE	EUOI	ILIA	LUAU	ODEA	OOSE	UNAI	VIAE
AERO	AKEE	ANOA	AWEE	EMEU	EURO	INIA	MEOU	OGEE	OUZO	UNAU	
AGEE	ALAE	ASEA	CIAO	EOAN	EVOE	IOTA	MOOI	OHIA	PAUA	URAO	AALII
AGIO	ALEE	AULA	EALE	EPEE	HUIA	IURE	MOUE	OLEA	RAIA	UREA	ADIEU
AGUE	ALOE	AUNE	EAVE	ETUI	IDEE	KAIE	NAOI	OLEO	ROUE	UVAE	AECIA
AINE	AMIA	AURA	EIDE	EUGE	ILEA	LIEU	OBIA	OLIO	TOEA	UVEA	AERIE

AIDOI	AIOLI	AUDIO	AURAE	COOEE	LOOIE	MIAOU	OORIE	URAEI
AINEE	AREAE	AULOI	AUREI	EERIE	LOUIE	OIDIA	OURIE	

List 4: JQXZ words

AJEE	JOUR	JIGOT	AQUA	QUIST	LUXE	GALAX	TAXUS	TOZE	AZLON	NEEZE	ZIGAN
DJIN	JUGA	JINGO	QADI	QUOAD	NIXE	IXORA	TELEX	TREZ	AZOLE	NERTZ	ZLOTE
DOJO	JURA	JINNI	QAID	QUOIN	OXER	IXTLE	TEXAS	TZAR	AZOTE	OUZEL	ZOEAE
GAJO	JURE	JIRGA	QUAG	ROQUE	OXID	LAXER	UNSEX	ZATI	AZURE	RAZEE	ZOEAL
JAGG	RAJA	JODEL	QUAI	SQUEG	SEXT	LEXIS	UNTAX	ZEIN	AZURN	RAZOO	ZOIST
JANE	ROJI	JOTUN	QUAT	TALAQ	TAXA	NEXUS	XENIA	ZETA	DARZI	ROZET	ZONAE
JANN	SIJO	JOUAL	QUOD	TOQUE	ULEX	NIXIE	XENON	ZILA	DIAZO	ROZIT	ZONAL
JARL	SOJA	JUDAS	AQUAE	TRANQ	ADDAX	NOXAL	XERUS	ZILL	DIZEN	SADZA	ZONDA
JATO	AJUGA	JUGAL	EQUID	TUQUE	AUXIN	OXTER	XOANA	ZINE	GAZAL	SEAZE	ZOOEA
JEAN	DJINN	JUNTA	QANAT		AXIAL	RADIX		ZITE	GAZAR	SENZA	ZOOID
JEAT	GADJE	JUNTO	QUAIR	AXAL	AXILE	REDOX	ADZE	ZITI	GAZON	SIZAR	ZORIL
JEEL	GANJA	JURAL	QUALE	AXEL	AXION	REDUX	AZAN	ZOEA	GAZOO	SIZEL	ZORRO
JELL	GAUJE	JURAT	QUANT	AXIL	AXITE	SALIX	AZON	ZONA	GLITZ	SOZIN	
JEON	JAGER	JUREL	QUARE	AXON	AXOID	SEXER	DITZ	ZOON	GLOZE	TEAZE	
JETE	JAGIR	NINJA	QUATE	DIXI	AXONE	SEXTO	GEEZ	ZORI	GONZO	TOAZE	
JIAO	JAGRA	OUIJA	QUEAN	DOUX	DEXIE	SILEX	IZAR	ZULU	GRIZE	TOUZE	
JILL	JARTA	REJON	QUENA	EAUX	DIXIE	SIXER	LAZO	ADOZE	GROSZ	TOZIE	
JINN	JARUL	RIOJA	QUERN	EXON	DIXIT	SIXTE	LUTZ	AGAZE	IZARD	TROOZ	
JIRD	JELLO	SAJOU	QUINA	EXUL	DOXIE	SOREX	NAZE	AIZLE	LAZAR	ULZIE	
JOLE	JERID	SLOJD	QUINE	ILEX	EXEAT	TAXOL	ORZO	AZIDE	LEAZE	ZAIRE	
JOLL	JETON	SUJEE	QUINT	IXIA	EXINE	TAXON	RITZ	AZIDO	LOZEN	ZANTE	
JOTA	JEUNE		QUIRT	LANX	EXODE	TAXOR	RIZA	AZINE	NAZIR	ZERDA	

List 5: 7-letter words

ACETINS	DETRAIN	INGATES	NASTIER	SAINTED	TAMINES	URANITE	REALTIE	REGINAE
ANESTRI	EASTING	INGESTA	NASTIES	SALIENT	TANGIER	URINATE	SERIATE	AIRDATE
ANTIRED	EASTLIN	INGRATE	NATIVES	SALTINE	TANGIES	VAINEST	TAENIAE	AIRIEST
ANTISEX	EATINGS	INMATES	NATTIER	SAPIENT	TANKIES	WANIEST	ADONISE	AIRLINE
ANTSIER	ELASTIN	INSTATE	NITRATE	SATINED	TANSIES	WANTIES	AEOLIAN	ALUNITE
ARENITE	ENTAILS	INSTEAD	OTARINE	SATINET	TARTINE	ZANIEST	ANISOLE	AMNIOTE
ATEBRIN	ENTASIA	INTAKES	PAINTER	SEATING	TAURINE	ZEATINS	ANODISE	ANTLIAE
ATONIES	ENTASIS	INTREAT	PANTIES	SESTINA	TAWNIER	ETAERIO	DARIOLE	ARANEID
AUNTIES	ENTRAIL	ISATINE	PATINES	SEXTAIN	TAWNIES	AILERON	IODATES	AUDIENT
AWNIEST	ENTRAIN	ITERANT	PERTAIN	SHEITAN	TEARING	ALERION	ISOLATE	DENARII
BANTIES	ETAMINS	JANTIER	RAIMENT	SINUATE	TEASING	ALIENOR	OLEARIA	EROTICA
BASINET	ETESIAN	JANTIES	RATINES	SLAINTE	TENAILS	ANEROID	OUTEARN	GODETIA
BESAINT	FAINEST	KENTIAS	RATLINE	SPINATE	TERRAIN	ELATION	ROADIES	INEDITA
BESTAIN	FAINTER	KERATIN	RELIANT	STAINED	TERTIAN	ERASION	ROUTINE	IRISATE
CANIEST	FENITAR	LATRINE	REPAINT	STAINER	THERIAN	OARIEST	SODAINE	MORAINE
CANTIER	GAINEST	MAINEST	RESIANT	STANIEL	TINWARE	OTARIES	SOREDIA	NIOBATE
CERATIN	GENISTA	MANTIES	RETAINS	STANINE	TISANES	TOENAIL	TOADIES	RADIATE
CERTAIN	GRANITE	MINARET	RETINAE	STARNIE	TRAINED	GOATIER	ENATION	RAINOUT
CINEAST	GRATINE	NACRITE	RETINAL	STEARIN	TRAINEE	ORIGANE	ARENOSE	ROMAINE
CREATIN	HAIRNET	NAIFEST	RETINAS	STHENIA	TRAINER	AERIEST	ELOINER	TIARAED
CRINATE	INANEST	NAILSET	RETRAIN	TAENIAS	TRANNIE	ALIENER	ORDINEE	UNAIRED
DESTAIN	INEARTH	NAIVEST	RETSINA	TAJINES	TRENAIL	ATELIER	ROSEATE	URALITE
DETAINS	INERTIA	NARTJIE	RUINATE	TAMEINS	TSIGANE	LINEATE	TROELIE	URANIDE

List 6: 8-letter words

ABOITEAU	ARANEOUS	DEVIATOR	ERGATOID	IODINATE	OUTLEARN	SAUTOIRE	TOLERATE
ACIERATE	AREOLATE	DONATIVE	ERIONITE	JAROSITE	OUTRAISE	SEROTINE	TONALITE
ADROITER	ARTERIAL	DOUANIER	ETIOLATE	LITERATI	PAEONIES	SIDENOTE	TREENAIL
AEGIRINE	ATROPINE	EATERIES	ETOURDIE	LITERATO	RAINDATE	TAENIATE	TROTLINE
AEGIRITE	AURELIAN	EGESTION	FOEDARIE	METANOIA	RAISONNE	TAENIOID	UINTAITE
AERATION	AUROREAN	EGOITIES	IDEATION	NAUSEATE	RATOONER	TAILERON	UNEASIER
AEROLITE	DAINTIER	ELOIGNER	IDOLATER	NEGATION	REORDAIN	TAILORED	UREDINIA
AERONAUT	DELATION	ELONGATE	INAURATE	OILERIES	REORIENT	TAINTURE	URINATOR
AEROTONE	DENTALIA	ENDOSTEA	INERTIAE	ONERIEST	RETAINED	TENEBRIO	YEASTIER
ALEURONE	DENTARIA	ENTAILER	INERTIAL	ORANGIER	RETAINER	TENORITE	
ALIENATE	DERATION	ENTOILED	INFERIAE	ORIENTAL	RETIARII	TENTORIA	
ANOESTRA	DEROGATE	EQUATION	INTERIOR	ORIENTED	RETINOID	TERATOID	
ANTERIOR	DETAINEE	ERADIATE	INTERNAL	OUTEATEN	RITORNEL	THIOUREA	

Basic Words

The following lists contain all the valid 2-, 3- and 4-letter words. There are just over 6,500 words in these three lists, and while it is not essential to know all of them, it will certainly help your game to know as many as possible.

2-letter words

2-letter words, all 121 of which are listed here, can be considered as the backbone words of any Scrabble game. They are very important, not necessarily for the scores which they themselves achieve, but also for the scores of other words they enable to be played.

The 2-letter words:

☆ provide a means of playing words parallel to other words already on the board

☆ can resolve surplus vowel problems (they include AA, EE and OO)

☆ can squeeze scores out of tight board situations

☆ can open the board for future scoring opportunities

Also, many of the 2-letter words can have letters added before or after them, making valid 3-letter words. See Section Six (Hooks) for these.

Make a list of the 2-letter words that you are not familiar with and try to introduce them into your games. Top-flight Scrabble players will know all of these words and will also know most of their meanings!

3-letter words

3-letter words (there are over 1,200 of these here) are also important, as they:

☆ provide a means of discarding unwanted letters

☆ can squeeze scores out of difficult board situations

☆ provide a means of playing higher-scoring words (perhaps bonuses) by turning 2-letter words into 3-letter words

Try to familiarize yourself with some of the 3-letter words that you don't know, and see if you can play them in your games. Leading Scrabble players will be aware of most of the 3-letter words and will be able to call on them when they are needed. But many of the top players will occasionally be uncertain about some of them, possibly recalling FAY and FEY, but being unsure of FOY; they may know HAH and HOH, but could wonder about HEH and HUH.

4-letter words

There are almost 5,200 of these here. 4-letter words are less important than the 2- and 3-letter words, but they do still provide a useful pool of words to dip into for scoring or rack-balancing purposes.

2-LETTER WORDS

AA	AW	EA	FY	IS	MO	OI	PH	UG	YE
AB	AX	ED	GI	IT	MU	OM	PI	UH	YO
AD	AY	EE	GO	JO	MY	ON	PO	UM	YU
AE	BA	EF	GU	KA	NA	OO	QI	UN	ZO
AG	BE	EH	HA	KO	NE	OP	RE	UP	
AH	BI	EL	HE	KY	NO	OR	SH	UR	
AI	BO	EM	HI	LA	NU	OS	SI	US	
AL	BY	EN	HM	LI	NY	OU	SO	UT	
AM	CH	ER	HO	LO	OB	OW	ST	WE	
AN	DA	ES	ID	MA	OD	OX	TA	WO	
AR	DE	ET	IF	ME	OE	OY	TE	XI	
AS	DI	EX	IN	MI	OF	PA	TI	XU	
AT	DO	FA	IO	MM	OH	PE	TO	YA	

Hint

Two's Company

There are 121 2-letter words and they are all fundamental to the game. The importance of knowing all the 2-letter words can't be emphasized enough; they are vital for parallel word play and maximizing scoring on tight boards and should be learnt off by heart. Write out the complete list over and over again. Play a few solo games allowing yourself to 'cheat' by referring to the list, but don't rely on the lists for too long. If you don't exercise your memory you won't recall them during actual play.

Hint

Score or Strategy?

The highest-scoring move is not always the best play. Always consider lower-scoring alternatives that might be better for your strategy. A lower-scoring move might not give so many points away to your opponent, or might leave you with a better balance of letters on your rack, or might enable you to set yourself up for a good score the next turn. Losing 10 points one turn may provide an extra 20 points the following turn or, if your emphasis had been on rack balance rather than score, it may even yield a 50-point bonus play.

3-LETTER WORDS

AAH AAL AAS ABA ABB ABO ABS ABY ACE ACH ACT ADD ADO ADS ADZ AFF AFT AGA AGE AGO AHA AHS AIA AID AIL AIM AIN AIR AIS AIT AKE ALA ALB ALE ALL ALP ALS ALT AMA AMI AMP AMU ANA AND ANE ANI ANN ANT ANY APE APT ARB ARC ARD ARE ARF ARK ARM ARS ART ARY ASH ASK ASP ASS ATE ATT AUF AUK AVA AVE AVO AWA AWE AWL AWN AXE AYE AYS AYU AZO

BAA BAC BAD BAG BAH BAL BAM BAN BAP BAR BAS BAT BAY BED BEE BEG BEL BEN BET BEY BEZ BIB BID BIG BIN BIO BIS BIT BIZ BOA BOB BOD BOG BOH BOK BON BOO BOP BOR BOS BOT BOW BOX BOY BRA BRO BRR BUB BUD BUG BUM BUN BUR BUS BUT BUY BYE BYS

CAB CAD CAM CAN CAP CAR CAT CAW CAY CEE CEL CEP CHA CHE CHI CID CIG CIS CIT CLY COB COD COG COL CON COO COP COR COS COT COW COX COY COZ CRU CRY CUB CUD CUE CUM CUP CUR CUT CUZ CWM

DAB DAD DAE DAG DAH DAK DAL DAM DAN DAP DAS DAW DAY DEB DEE DEF DEI DEL DEN DEV DEW DEX DEY DIB DID DIE DIG DIM DIN DIP DIS DIT DIV DOB DOC DOD DOE DOG DOH DOL DOM DON DOO DOP DOR DOS DOT DOW DRY DSO DUB DUD DUE DUG DUI DUN DUO DUP DUX DYE DZO

EAN EAR EAS EAT EAU EBB ECH ECU EDH EEK EEL EEN EFF EFS EFT EGG EGO EHS EIK EKE ELD ELF ELK ELL ELM ELS ELT EME EMF EMS EMU END ENE ENG ENS EON ERA ERE ERF ERG ERK ERN ERR ERS ESS EST ETA ETH EUK EVE EWE EWK EWT EYE

FAB FAD FAG FAH FAN FAP FAR FAS FAT FAW FAX FAY FED FEE FEH FEM FEN FER FET FEU FEW FEY FEZ FIB FID FIE FIG FIL FIN FIR FIT FIX FIZ FLU FLY FOB FOE FOG FOH FON FOP FOR FOU FOX FOY FRA FRO FRY FUB FUD FUG FUM FUN FUR

GAB GAD GAE GAG GAL GAM GAN GAP GAR GAS GAT GAU GAY GED GEE GEL GEM GEN GEO GET GEY GHI GIB GID GIE GIF GIG GIN GIO GIP GIS GIT GJU GNU GOA GOB GOD GOE GON GOO GOR GOS GOT GOV GOX GOY GUB GUE GUL GUM GUN GUP GUR GUS GUT GUV GUY GYM GYP

HAD HAE HAG HAH HAJ HAM HAN HAO HAP HAS HAT HAW HAY HEH HEM HEN HEP HER HES HET HEW HEX HEY HIC HID HIE HIM HIN HIP HIS HIT HMM HOA HOB HOC HOD HOE HOG HOH HOI HON HOO HOP HOS HOT HOW HOX HOY HUB HUE HUG HUH HUI HUM HUN HUP HUT HYE HYP

ICE ICH ICK ICY IDE IDS IFF IFS ILK ILL IMP INK INN INS ION IOS IRE IRK ISH ISM ISO ITA ITS IVY

JAB JAG JAK JAM JAP JAR JAW JAY JEE JET JEU JEW JIB JIG JIN JIZ JOB JOE JOG JOR JOT JOW JOY JUD JUG JUN JUS JUT

KAB KAE KAF KAI KAM KAS KAT KAW KAY KEA KEB KED KEF KEG KEN KEP KET KEX KEY KHI KID KIF KIN KIP KIR KIT KOA KOB KOI KON KOP KOR KOS KOW KUE KYE KYU

LAB LAC LAD LAG LAH LAM LAP LAR LAS LAT LAV LAW LAX LAY LEA LED LEE LEG LEI LEK LEP LES LET LEU LEV LEW LEX LEY LEZ LIB LID LIE LIG LIN LIP LIS LIT LOB LOD LOG LOO LOP LOR LOS LOT LOW LOX LOY LUD LUG LUM LUR LUV LUX LUZ LYE LYM

MAA MAC MAD MAE MAG MAK MAL MAM MAN MAP MAR MAS MAT MAW MAX MAY MED MEG MEL MEM MEN MES MET MEU MEW MHO MIB MID MIG MIL MIM MIR MIS MIX MIZ MNA MOA MOB MOC MOD MOE MOG MOI MOL MOM MON MOO MOP MOR MOS MOT MOU MOW MOY MOZ MUD MUG MUM MUN MUS MUT MUX

NAB NAE NAG NAH NAM NAN NAP NAS NAT NAW NAY NEB NED NEE NEF NEK NEP NET NEW NIB NID NIE NIL NIM NIP NIS NIT NIX NOB NOD NOG NOH NOM NON NOO NOR NOS NOT

NOW NOX NOY NTH NUB NUN NUR NUS NUT NYE NYS

OAF OAK OAR OAT OBA OBE OBI OBO OBS OCA OCH ODA ODD ODE ODS OES OFF OFT OHM OHO OHS OIK OIL OKA OKE OLD OLE OLM OMS ONE ONS OOF OOH OOM OON OOP OOR OOS OOT OPE OPS OPT ORA ORB ORC ORD ORE ORF ORS ORT OSE OUD OUK OUP OUR OUT OVA OWE OWL OWN OWT OXO OXY OYE OYS

PAC PAD PAH PAL PAM PAN PAP PAR PAS PAT PAW PAX PAY PEA PEC PED PEE PEG PEH PEN PEP PER PES PET PEW PHI PHO PHS PHT PIA PIC PIE PIG PIN PIP PIR PIS PIT PIU PIX PLY POA POD POH POI POL POM POO POP POS POT POW POX POZ PRE PRO PRY PSI PST PUB PUD PUG PUH PUL PUN PUP PUR PUS PUT PUY PYA PYE PYX

QAT QIS QUA

RAD RAG RAH RAI RAJ RAM RAN RAP RAS RAT RAW RAX RAY REB REC RED REE REF REG REH REI REM REN REP RES RET REV REW REX REZ RHO RHY RIA RIB RID RIF RIG RIM RIN RIP RIT RIZ ROB ROC ROD ROE ROK ROM ROO ROT ROW RUB RUC RUD RUE RUG RUM RUN RUT RYA RYE

SAB SAC SAD SAE SAG SAI SAL SAM SAN SAP SAR SAT SAU SAW SAX SAY SAZ SEA SEC SED SEE SEG SEI SEL SEN SER SET SEW SEX SEY SEZ SHA SHE SHH SHY SIB SIC SIM SIN SIP SIR SIS SIT SIX SKA SKI SKY SLY SMA SNY SOB SOC SOD SOG SOH SOL SON SOP SOS SOT SOU SOV SOW SOX SOY SPA SPY SRI STY SUB SUD SUE SUI SUK SUM SUN SUP SUQ SUR SUS SWY SYE SYN

TAB TAD TAE TAG TAI TAJ TAK TAM TAN TAO TAP TAR TAS TAT TAU TAV TAW TAX TAY TEA TED TEE TEF TEG TEL TEN TES TET TEW THE THO THY TIC TID TIE TIG TIL TIN TIP TIS TIT TOC TOD TOE TOG TOM TON TOO TOP TOR TOT TOW TOY TRY TSK TUB TUG TUI TUM TUN TUP TUT TUX TWA TWO TWP TYE TYG

UDO UDS UEY UFO UGH UGS UKE ULE ULU UMM UMP UNI UNS UPO UPS URB URD URE URN USE UTA UTE UTS UTU UVA

VAC VAE VAN VAR VAS VAT VAU VAV VAW VEE VEG VET VEX VIA VID VIE VIG VIM VIN VIS VLY VOE VOL VOR VOW VOX VUG VUM

WAB WAD WAE WAG WAN WAP WAR WAS WAT WAW WAX WAY WEB WED WEE WEM WEN WET WEX WEY WHA WHO WHY WIG WIN WIS WIT WIZ WOE WOG WOK WON WOO WOP WOS WOT WOW WOX WRY WUD WUS WYE WYN

XIS

YAH YAK YAM YAP YAR YAW YAY YEA YEH YEN YEP YES YET YEW YEX YGO YID YIN YIP YOB YOD YOK YOM YON YOS YOU YOW YUG YUK YUM YUP YUS

ZAG ZAP ZAX ZEA ZED ZEE ZEK ZEL ZEX ZHO ZIG ZIN ZIP ZIT ZIZ ZOA ZOO ZOS ZUZ

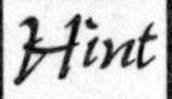

Tackling the Threes

To the uninitiated the number of allowable 3-letter words is quite daunting. However, if you ignore the everyday words the lists begin to become a little more manageable. Pay particular attention to those that can be made by extending 2-letter words (see the Hooks section) and those containing tiles worth three points or more. Write out those you don't know and try to learn the definitions.

Hint

Open Play

Most people play Scrabble to win, which is natural and should not be discouraged. However, if you are keen to improve your scoring power and vocabulary, try playing the occasional more open game. This will enable you to concentrate on strengthening your rack-balancing, bonus-spotting and hook-word skills. Here are a few tips on open play:

- ☆ Try to ensure vowels are next to premium squares to provide scoring opportunities for high-scoring consonants.
- ☆ Experiment with playing the first word to the left of the board to enable easier access to the otherwise awkward top left.
- ☆ Play conservatively and consider points per tile gained each move rather than points per move.
- ☆ Don't be afraid to open up the triple-word squares and equally don't think you have to take a triple-word square as soon as it is available.
- ☆ Change tiles if your rack gets imbalanced and the only moves available block the openings on the board.
- ☆ Whenever you get the opportunity start a game with a 3-letter word consisting of vowel-consonant-vowel played centrally to open up all four areas of the board, eg ADO, EGO, IRE, OCA, UDO.

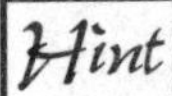

Fours Feeding

Very few top players are actually familiar with all the 4-letter words. The ones they tend to concentrate on are those that are formed from 3-letter words (see the Hooks section), those that contain the higher-scoring consonants, and those that are useful for sorting out those vowel problems. Work through the 4-letter list and highlight those you don't know, then play a solo game restricting yourself to just 4-letter words as far as you are able. Initially consult the list whilst playing but also try to play from memory. After a while oddities such as BAPU, COFT, DHAL and EUOI become second nature to your game, and impress your opponents!

4-LETTER WORDS

AAHS AALS ABAC ABAS ABBA ABBE ABBS ABED ABET ABID ABLE ABLY ABOS ABRI ABUT ABYE ABYS ACED ACER ACES ACHE ACHY ACID ACME ACNE ACRE ACTA ACTS ACYL ADAW ADDS ADIT ADOS ADRY ADZE AEON AERO AERY AESC AFAR AFFY AFRO AGAR AGAS AGED AGEE AGEN AGER AGES AGHA AGIN AGIO AGLY AGMA AGOG AGON AGUE AHED AHEM AHOY AIAS AIDE AIDS AILS AIMS AINE AINS AIRN AIRS AIRT AIRY AITS AITU

AJAR AJEE AKED AKEE AKES AKIN ALAE ALAN ALAP ALAR ALAS ALAY ALBA ALBE ALBS ALEC ALEE ALEF ALES ALEW ALFA ALGA ALIF ALIT ALKY ALLS ALLY ALMA ALME ALMS ALOD ALOE ALOW ALPS ALSO ALTO ALTS ALUM AMAH AMAS AMBO AMEN AMIA AMID AMIE AMIN AMIR AMIS AMLA AMMO AMOK AMPS AMUS AMYL ANAL ANAN ANAS ANCE ANDS ANES ANEW ANGA ANIL ANIS ANKH ANNA ANNO ANNS ANOA ANON ANOW ANSA ANTA

ANTE ANTI ANTS ANUS APAY APED APER APES APEX APOD APSE APTS AQUA ARAK ARAR ARBA ARBS ARCH ARCO ARCS ARDS AREA ARED AREG ARES ARET AREW ARFS ARIA ARID ARIL ARIS ARKS ARLE ARMS ARMY ARNA AROW ARSE ARTS ARTY ARUM ARVO ARYL ASAR ASCI ASEA ASHY ASKS ASPS ATAP ATES ATMA ATOC ATOK ATOM ATOP AUFS AUKS AULA AULD AUNE AUNT AURA AUTO AVAL AVAS AVER AVES AVID AVOS AVOW AWAY

AWDL AWED AWEE AWES AWLS AWNS AWNY AWOL AWRY AXAL AXED AXEL AXES AXIL AXIS AXLE AXON AYAH AYES AYIN AYRE AYUS AZAN AZON AZYM

BAAL BAAS BABA BABE BABU BABY BACH BACK BACS BADE BADS BAEL BAFF BAFT BAGS BAHT BAIL BAIT BAJU BAKE BALD BALE BALK BALL BALM BALS BALU BAMS BANC BAND BANE BANG BANI BANK BANS BANT BAPS BAPU BARB BARD BARE BARF BARK BARM BARN BARP BARS

BASE BASH BASK BASS BAST BATE BATH BATS BATT BAUD BAUK BAUR BAWD BAWL BAWN BAWR BAYE BAYS BAYT BEAD BEAK BEAM BEAN BEAR BEAT BEAU BECK BEDE BEDS BEDU BEEF BEEN BEEP BEER BEES BEET BEGO BEGS BEIN BELL BELS BELT BEMA BEND BENE BENI BENJ BENS BENT BERE BERG BERK BERM BEST BETA BETE BETH BETS BEVY BEYS BHEL BHUT BIAS BIBB BIBS BICE BIDE BIDS BIEN BIER BIFF BIGA BIGG

BIGS BIKE BILE BILK BILL BIMA BIND BINE BING BINK BINS BINT BIOG BIOS BIRD BIRK BIRL BIRR BISE BISH BISK BITE BITO BITS BITT BIZE BLAB BLAD BLAE BLAG BLAH BLAM BLAT BLAW BLAY BLEB BLED BLEE BLET BLEW BLEY BLIN BLIP BLOB BLOC BLOT BLOW BLUB BLUE BLUR BOAK BOAR BOAS BOAT BOBA BOBS BOCK BODE BODS BODY BOFF BOGS BOGY BOHS BOIL BOKE BOKO BOKS BOLA BOLD BOLE BOLL BOLO

BOLT BOMA BOMB BONA BOND BONE BONG BONK BONY BOOB BOOH BOOK BOOL BOOM BOON BOOR BOOS BOOT BOPS BORA BORD BORE BORN BORS BORT BOSH BOSK BOSS BOTA BOTH BOTS BOTT BOUK BOUN BOUT BOWL BOWR BOWS BOXY BOYG BOYO BOYS BOZO BRAD BRAE BRAG BRAN BRAS BRAT BRAW BRAY BRED BREE BREN BRER BREW BRIE BRIG BRIM BRIN BRIO BRIS BRIT BROD BROG BROO BROS BROW BRRR BRUT BUAT BUBA BUBO

BUBS BUCK BUDO BUDS BUFF BUFO BUGS BUHL BUHR BUIK BUKE BULB BULK BULL BUMF BUMP BUMS BUNA BUND BUNG BUNK BUNN BUNS BUNT BUOY BURA BURD BURG BURK BURL BURN BURP BURR BURS BURY BUSH BUSK BUSS BUST BUSY BUTE BUTS BUTT BUYS BUZZ BYES BYKE BYRE BYRL BYTE

CABA CABS CACA CADE CADI CADS CAFE CAFF CAGE CAGY CAID CAIN CAKE CAKY CALF CALK CALL CALM CALO CALP CALX CAME

CAMP CAMS CANE CANG CANN CANS CANT CANY CAPA CAPE CAPH CAPI CAPO CAPS CARB CARD CARE CARK CARL CARN CARP CARR CARS CART CASA CASE CASH CASK CAST CATE CATS CAUF CAUK CAUL CAUM CAUP CAVE CAVY CAWK CAWS CAYS CEAS CECA CEDE CEDI CEES CEIL CELL CELS CELT CENS CENT CEPE CEPS CERE CERO CERT CESS CETE CHAD CHAI CHAL CHAM CHAO CHAP CHAR CHAS CHAT CHAW CHAY CHEF CHER CHEW

CHEZ CHIA CHIC CHID CHIK CHIN CHIP CHIS CHIT CHIV CHIZ CHOC CHON CHOP CHOU CHOW CHUB CHUG CHUM CHUT CIAO CIDE CIDS CIEL CIGS CILL CINE CION CIRE CIRL CIST CITE CITO CITS CITY CIVE CLAD CLAG CLAM CLAN CLAP CLAT CLAW CLAY CLEF CLEG CLEM CLEW CLIP CLOD CLOG CLON CLOP CLOT CLOU CLOW CLOY CLUB CLUE COAL COAT COAX COBB COBS COCA COCH COCK COCO CODA CODE CODS COED COFF

COFT COGS COHO COIF COIL COIN COIR COIT COKE COKY COLA COLD COLE COLL COLS COLT COLY COMA COMB COME COMP COMS COND CONE CONF CONI CONK CONN CONS CONY COOF COOK COOL COOM COON COOP COOS COOT COPE COPS COPY CORD CORE CORF CORK CORM CORN CORS CORY COSE COSH COSS COST COSY COTE COTH COTS COTT COUP COUR COVE COWL COWP COWS COWY COXA COXY COYS COZE COZY CRAB CRAG CRAM CRAN CRAP

CRAW CRED CREE CREW CRIB CRIM CRIS CRIT CROC CROP CROW CRUD CRUE CRUS CRUX CUBE CUBS CUDS CUED CUES CUFF CUIF CUIT CUKE CULL CULM CULT CUNT CUPS CURB CURD CURE CURF CURL CURN CURR CURS CURT CUSH CUSK CUSP CUSS CUTE CUTS CWMS CYAN CYMA CYME CYST CYTE CZAR

DABS DACE DADA DADO DADS DAES DAFF DAFT DAGO DAGS DAHL DAHS DAIS DAKS DALE DALI DALS DALT DAME DAMN DAMP DAMS DANG

DANK DANS DANT DAPS DARB DARE DARG DARI DARK DARN DART DASH DATA DATE DATO DAUB DAUD DAUR DAUT DAVY DAWD DAWK DAWN DAWS DAWT DAYS DAZE DEAD DEAF DEAL DEAN DEAR DEAW DEBS DEBT DECK DECO DEED DEEK DEEM DEEN DEEP DEER DEES DEET DEEV DEFI DEFT DEFY DEID DEIL DEKE DELE DELF DELI DELL DELS DELT DEME DEMO DEMY DENE DENS DENT DENY DERE DERM DERN DERV DESK DEUS DEVA DEVS DEWS DEWY

DEXY DEYS DHAK DHAL DHOL DHOW DIAL DIBS DICE DICH DICK DICT DIDO DIDY DIEB DIED DIEL DIES DIET DIGS DIKA DIKE DILL DIME DIMS DINE DING DINK DINO DINS DINT DIOL DIPS DIPT DIRE DIRK DIRL DIRT DISA DISC DISH DISK DISS DITA DITE DITS DITT DITZ DIVA DIVE DIVI DIVS DIXI DIXY DJIN DOAB DOAT DOBS DOBY DOCK DOCS DODO DODS DOEK DOEN DOER DOES DOFF DOGE DOGS DOGY DOHS DOIT DOJO DOLE

DOLL DOLS DOLT DOME DOMS DOMY DONA DONE DONG DONS DOOB DOOK DOOL DOOM DOOR DOOS DOPA DOPE DOPS DOPY DORE DORK DORM DORP DORR DORS DORT DORY DOSE DOSH DOSS DOST DOTE DOTH DOTS DOTY DOUC DOUM DOUP DOUR DOUT DOUX DOVE DOWD DOWF DOWL DOWN DOWP DOWS DOWT DOXY DOZE DOZY DRAB DRAD DRAG DRAM DRAP DRAT DRAW DRAY DREE DREG DREK DREW DREY DRIB DRIP DROP DROW DRUB DRUG DRUM DRYS DSOS

DUAD DUAL DUAN DUAR DUBS DUCE DUCI DUCK DUCT DUDE DUDS DUED DUEL DUES DUET DUFF DUGS DUIT DUKE DULE DULL DULY DUMA DUMB DUMP DUNE DUNG DUNK DUNS DUNT DUOS DUPE DUPS DURA DURE DURN DURO DURR DUSH DUSK DUST DUTY DWAM DYAD DYED DYER DYES DYKE DYNE DZHO DZOS

EACH EALE EANS EARD EARL EARN EARS EASE EAST EASY EATH EATS EAUS EAUX EAVE EBBS EBON ECAD ECCE ECCO ECHE ECHO ECHT

ECOD ECRU ECUS EDDO EDDY EDGE EDGY EDHS EDIT EECH EELS EELY EERY EEVN EFFS EFTS EGAD EGAL EGER EGGS EGGY EGIS EGMA EGOS EHED EIDE EIKS EILD EINE EKED EKES EKKA ELAN ELDS ELFS ELHI ELKS ELLS ELMS ELMY ELSE ELTS EMES EMEU EMFS EMIC EMIR EMIT EMMA EMUS EMYD EMYS ENDS ENES ENEW ENGS ENOL ENOW ENVY EOAN EONS EORL EPEE EPHA EPIC EPOS ERAS ERED ERES ERGO ERGS ERIC ERKS ERNE ERNS

EROS ERRS ERST ESES ESKY ESNE ESPY ESSE ESTS ETAS ETAT ETCH ETEN ETHE ETHS ETIC ETNA ETUI EUGE EUGH EUKS EUOI EURO EVEN EVER EVES EVET EVIL EVOE EWER EWES EWKS EWTS EXAM EXEC EXES EXIT EXON EXPO EXUL EYAS EYED EYEN EYER EYES EYNE EYOT EYRA EYRE EYRY

FACE FACT FADE FADO FADS FADY FAFF FAGS FAHS FAIK FAIL FAIN FAIR FAIX FAKE FALL FALX FAME FAND FANE FANG FANK FANO FANS

FARD FARE FARL FARM FARO FARS FART FASH FAST FATE FATS FAUN FAUX FAVA FAVE FAWN FAWS FAYS FAZE FEAL FEAR FEAT FECK FEDS FEED FEEL FEER FEES FEET FEGS FEHM FEHS FEIS FELL FELT FEME FEMS FEND FENI FENS FENT FEOD FERE FERM FERN FESS FEST FETA FETE FETS FETT FEUD FEUS FEYS FIAR FIAT FIBS FICE FICO FIDO FIDS FIEF FIER FIFE FIGO FIGS FIKE FIKY FILA FILE FILL FILM FILO FILS FIND

FINE FINI FINK FINO FINS FIRE FIRK FIRM FIRN FIRS FISC FISH FISK FIST FITS FITT FIVE FIXT FIZZ FLAB FLAG FLAK FLAM FLAN FLAP FLAT FLAW FLAX FLAY FLEA FLED FLEE FLEG FLEW FLEX FLEY FLIC FLIP FLIT FLIX FLOC FLOE FLOG FLOP FLOR FLOW FLUB FLUE FLUS FLUX FOAL FOAM FOBS FOCI FOEN FOES FOGS FOGY FOHN FOHS FOID FOIL FOIN FOLD FOLK FOND FONE FONS FONT FOOD FOOL FOOT FOPS FORA FORB

FORD
FORE
FORK
FORM
FORT
FOSS
FOUD
FOUL
FOUR
FOUS
FOWL
FOXY
FOYS
FOZY
FRAB
FRAE
FRAG
FRAP
FRAS
FRAT
FRAU
FRAY
FREE
FRET
FRIG
FRIS
FRIT
FRIZ
FROE
FROG
FROM
FROW
FRUG
FUBS
FUCI
FUCK
FUDS
FUEL
FUFF
FUGS
FUGU
FUJI
FULL
FUME
FUMS
FUMY
FUND
FUNG
FUNK
FUNS
FURL
FURR
FURS
FURY
FUSC
FUSE
FUSS
FUST
FUTZ
FUZE
FUZZ
FYCE
FYKE
FYLE
FYRD

GABS
GABY
GADE
GADI
GADS
GAED
GAEN
GAES
GAFF
GAGA
GAGE
GAGS
GAID
GAIN
GAIR
GAIT
GAJO
GALA
GALE
GALL
GALS
GAMA
GAMB
GAME
GAMP
GAMS
GAMY
GANE
GANG
GANT
GAOL
GAPE
GAPO
GAPS
GAPY
GARB
GARE
GARS
GART
GASH
GASP
GAST
GATE
GATH
GATS
GAUD
GAUM
GAUN
GAUP
GAUR
GAUS
GAVE
GAWD
GAWK
GAWP
GAYS
GAZE
GAZY
GEAL
GEAN
GEAR
GEAT
GECK
GEDS
GEED
GEEK
GEEP
GEES
GEEZ
GEIT
GELD
GELS
GELT
GEMS
GENA
GENE
GENS
GENT
GENU
GEOS
GERE
GERM
GEST
GETA
GETS
GEUM
GHAT
GHEE
GHIS
GIBE
GIBS
GIDS
GIED
GIEN
GIES
GIFT
GIGA
GIGS
GILA
GILD
GILL
GILT
GIMP
GING
GINK
GINN
GINS
GIOS
GIPS
GIRD
GIRL
GIRN
GIRO
GIRR
GIRT
GISM
GIST
GITE
GITS
GIVE
GIZZ
GJUS
GLAD
GLAM
GLED
GLEE
GLEG
GLEI
GLEN
GLEY
GLIA
GLIB
GLID
GLIM
GLIT
GLOB
GLOM
GLOP
GLOW
GLUE
GLUG
GLUM
GLUT
GNAR
GNAT
GNAW
GNUS
GOAD
GOAF
GOAL
GOAS
GOAT
GOBO
GOBS
GOBY
GODS
GOEL
GOER
GOES
GOEY
GOFF
GOGO
GOLD
GOLE
GOLF
GOLP
GONE
GONG
GONK
GONS
GOOD
GOOF
GOOK
GOOL
GOON
GOOP
GOOR
GOOS
GORE
GORM
GORP
GORY
GOSH
GOUK
GOUT
GOVS
GOWD
GOWF
GOWK
GOWL
GOWN
GOYS
GRAB
GRAD
GRAM
GRAN
GRAT
GRAY
GREE
GREN
GREW
GREY
GRID
GRIG
GRIM
GRIN
GRIP
GRIS
GRIT
GROG
GROT
GROW
GRUB
GRUE
GRUM
GUAN
GUAR
GUBS
GUCK
GUDE
GUES
GUFF
GUGA
GUID
GULA
GULE
GULF
GULL
GULP
GULS
GULY
GUMP
GUMS
GUNK
GUNS
GUPS
GURL
GURN
GURS
GURU
GUSH
GUST
GUTS
GUVS
GUYS
GYAL
GYBE
GYMP
GYMS
GYNY
GYPS
GYRE
GYRI
GYRO
GYTE
GYVE

HAAF
HAAR
HABU
HACK
HADE
HADJ
HADS
HAED
HAEM
HAEN
HAES
HAET
HAFF
HAFT
HAGG
HAGS
HAHA
HAHS
HAIK
HAIL
HAIN
HAIR
HAJI
HAJJ
HAKA
HAKE
HALE
HALF
HALL
HALM
HALO
HALT
HAME
HAMS
HAND
HANG
HANK
HANT
HAPS
HARD
HARE
HARK
HARL
HARM
HARN
HARO
HARP
HART
HASH
HASK
HASP
HAST
HATE
HATH
HATS
HAUD
HAUL
HAUT
HAVE
HAWK
HAWM
HAWS
HAYS
HAZE
HAZY
HEAD
HEAL
HEAP
HEAR
HEAT
HEBE
HECH
HECK
HEED
HEEL
HEFT
HEHS
HEID
HEIL
HEIR
HELD
HELE
HELL
HELM
HELO
HELP
HEME
HEMP
HEMS
HEND
HENS
HENT
HEPS
HEPT
HERB
HERD
HERE
HERL
HERM
HERN
HERO
HERS
HERY
HESP
HEST
HETE
HETH
HETS
HEWN
HEWS
HEYS
HICK
HIDE
HIED
HIES
HIGH
HIKE
HILA
HILD
HILI
HILL
HILT
HIND
HING
HINS
HINT
HIPS
HIPT
HIRE
HISH
HISN
HISS
HIST
HITS
HIVE
HIYA
HIZZ
HOAR
HOAS
HOAX
HOBO
HOBS
HOCK
HODS
HOED
HOER
HOES
HOGG
HOGH
HOGS
HOHS
HOIK
HOKE
HOKI
HOLD
HOLE
HOLK
HOLM
HOLP
HOLS
HOLT
HOLY
HOME
HOMO
HOMY
HOND
HONE
HONG
HONK
HONS
HOOD
HOOF
HOOK
HOON
HOOP
HOOT
HOPE
HOPS
HORA
HORE
HORN
HORS
HOSE
HOSS
HOST
HOTE
HOTS
HOUF
HOUR
HOUT
HOVE
HOWE
HOWF
HOWK
HOWL
HOWS
HOYA
HOYS
HUBS
HUCK
HUED
HUER
HUES
HUFF
HUGE
HUGS
HUGY
HUIA
HUIC
HUIS
HULA
HULE
HULK
HULL
HUMA
HUMF
HUMP
HUMS
HUNG
HUNH
HUNK
HUNS
HUNT
HUPS
HURL
HURT
HUSH
HUSK
HUSO
HUSS
HUTS
HWAN
HWYL
HYED
HYEN
HYES
HYKE
HYLA
HYLE
HYMN
HYPE
HYPO
HYPS
HYTE

IAMB
IBEX
IBIS
ICED
ICER
ICES
ICHS
ICKY
ICON
IDEA
IDEE
IDEM
IDES
IDLE
IDLY
IDOL
IDYL
IFFY
IGAD
IGLU
IKAT
IKON
ILEA
ILEX
ILIA
ILKA
ILKS
ILLS
ILLY
IMAM
IMID
IMMY
IMPI
IMPS
INBY
INCH
INFO
INGO
INIA
INKS
INKY
INLY
INNS
INRO
INTI
INTO
IONS
IOTA
IRED
IRES
IRID
IRIS
IRKS
IRON
ISBA
ISLE
ISMS
ISOS
ITAS
ITCH
ITEM
IURE
IWIS
IXIA
IZAR

JABS
JACK
JADE
JAGG
JAGS
JAIL
JAKE
JAKS
JAMB
JAMS
JANE
JANN
JAPE
JAPS
JARK
JARL
JARS
JASP
JASS
JASY
JATO
JAUK
JAUP
JAVA
JAWS
JAYS
JAZY
JAZZ
JEAN
JEAT
JEED
JEEL
JEEP
JEER
JEES
JEEZ
JEFE
JEFF
JEHU
JELL
JEON
JERK
JESS
JEST
JETE
JETS
JEUX
JEWS
JIAO
JIBB
JIBE
JIBS
JIFF
JIGS
JILL
JILT
JIMP
JINK
JINN
JINS
JINX
JIRD
JISM
JIVE
JIZZ
JOBE
JOBS
JOCK
JOCO
JOES
JOEY
JOGS
JOHN
JOIN
JOKE
JOKY
JOLE
JOLL
JOLT
JOMO
JOOK
JORS
JOSH
JOSS
JOTA
JOTS
JOUK
JOUR
JOWL
JOWS
JOYS
JUBA
JUBE
JUDO
JUDS
JUDY
JUGA
JUGS
JUJU
JUKE
JUMP
JUNK
JUPE
JURA
JURE
JURY
JUST
JUTE
JUTS
JUVE
JYNX

KAAS
KABS
KADE
KADI

KAED KAES KAFS KAGO KAGU KAID KAIE KAIF KAIL KAIM KAIN KAIS KAKA KAKI KALE KALI KAMA KAME KAMI KANA KANE KANG KANS KANT KAON KAPA KAPH KARA KARK KARN KART KATA KATI KATS KAVA KAWS KAYO KAYS KAZI KBAR KEAS KEBS KECK KEDS KEEF KEEK KEEL KEEN KEEP KEET KEFS KEGS KEIR KEKS KELL KELP KELT KEMB KEMP KENO KENS KENT KEPI KEPS KEPT KERB KERF KERN KESH KEST KETA KETO KETS KEYS KHAF

KHAN KHAT KHET KHIS KHOR KHUD KIBE KICK KIDS KIEF KIER KIFS KIKE KILD KILL KILN KILO KILP KILT KINA KIND KINE KING KINK KINO KINS KIPE KIPP KIPS KIRK KIRN KIRS KISH KISS KIST KITE KITH KITS KIVA KIWI KNAG KNAP KNAR KNEE KNEW KNIT KNOB KNOP KNOT KNOW KNUB KNUR KNUT KOAN KOAS KOBO KOBS KOEL KOFF KOHL KOLA KOLO KOND KONK KONS KOOK KOPH KOPS KORA KORE KORS KOSS KOTO KOWS KRAB

KRIS KSAR KUDO KUDU KUES KUKU KURI KURU KUZU KVAS KYAK KYAR KYAT KYLE KYND KYNE KYTE KYUS

LABS LACE LACK LACS LACY LADE LADS LADY LAER LAGS LAHS LAIC LAID LAIK LAIN LAIR LAKE LAKH LAKY LALL LAMA LAMB LAME LAMP LAMS LANA LAND LANE LANG LANK LANT LANX LAPS LARD LARE LARI LARK LARN LARS LASE LASH LASS LAST LATE LATH LATI LATS LAUD LAUF LAVA LAVE LAVS LAWK LAWN LAWS LAYS

LAZE LAZO LAZY LEAD LEAF LEAK LEAL LEAM LEAN LEAP LEAR LEAS LEAT LECH LEED LEEK LEEP LEER LEES LEET LEFT LEGS LEHR LEIR LEIS LEKE LEKS LEKU LEME LEND LENG LENO LENS LENT LEPS LEPT LERE LERP LESS LEST LETS LEUD LEVA LEVE LEVO LEVY LEWD LEYS LEZZ LIAR LIBS LICE LICH LICK LIDO LIDS LIED LIEF LIEN LIER LIES LIEU LIFE LIFT LIGS LIKE LILL LILO LILT LILY LIMA LIMB LIME LIMN LIMO

LIMP LIMY LIND LINE LING LINK LINN LINO LINS LINT LINY LION LIPS LIRA LIRE LIRI LIRK LISK LISP LIST LITE LITH LITS LITU LIVE LOAD LOAF LOAM LOAN LOBE LOBI LOBO LOBS LOCA LOCH LOCI LOCK LOCO LODE LODS LOFT LOGE LOGO LOGS LOGY LOID LOIN LOIR LOKE LOLL LOMA LOME LONE LONG LOOF LOOK LOOM LOON LOOP LOOR LOOS LOOT LOPE LOPS LORD LORE LORN LORY LOSE LOSH LOSS LOST LOTA LOTE LOTH

LOTI LOTO LOTS LOUD LOUN LOUP LOUR LOUT LOVE LOWE LOWN LOWS LOWT LOYS LUAU LUBE LUCE LUCK LUDE LUDO LUDS LUES LUFF LUGE LUGS LUIT LUKE LULL LULU LUMP LUMS LUNA LUNE LUNG LUNK LUNT LUNY LURE LURK LURS LUSH LUSK LUST LUTE LUTZ LUVS LUXE LWEI LYAM LYES LYME LYMS LYNE LYNX LYRE LYSE LYTE

MAAR MAAS MABE MACE MACH MACK MACS MADE MADS MAES MAGE MAGG MAGI MAGS MAID MAIK MAIL

MAIM MAIN MAIR MAKE MAKO MAKS MALE MALI MALL MALM MALS MALT MAMA MAMS MANA MAND MANE MANG MANI MANO MANS MANY MAPS MARA MARC MARD MARE MARG MARK MARL MARM MARS MART MARY MASA MASE MASH MASK MASS MAST MASU MATE MATH MATS MATT MATY MAUD MAUL MAUN MAUT MAWK MAWN MAWR MAWS MAXI MAYA MAYO MAYS MAZE MAZY MEAD MEAL MEAN MEAT MEED MEEK MEER MEET MEGA MEGS MEIN MELA MELD MELL MELS

MELT MEME MEMO MEMS MEND MENE MENG MENO MENT MENU MEOU MEOW MERC MERE MERI MERK MERL MESA MESE MESH MESS META METE METH METS MEUS MEVE MEWL MEWS MEZE MHOS MIBS MICA MICE MICK MICO MIDI MIDS MIEN MIFF MIGG MIGS MIKE MILD MILE MILK MILL MILO MILS MILT MIME MINA MIND MINE MING MINI MINK MINO MINT MINX MINY MIRE MIRI MIRK MIRS MIRV MIRY MISE MISO MISS MIST MITE MITT MITY MIXT

MIXY MIZZ MNAS MOAN MOAS MOAT MOBS MOCH MOCK MOCS MODE MODI MODS MOES MOGS MOHR MOIL MOIT MOJO MOKE MOKI MOKO MOLA MOLD MOLE MOLL MOLS MOLT MOLY MOME MOMI MOMS MONA MONG MONK MONO MONS MONY MOOD MOOI MOOK MOOL MOON MOOP MOOR MOOS MOOT MOPE MOPS MOPY MORA MORE MORN MORS MORT MOSE MOSK MOSS MOST MOTE MOTH MOTS MOTT MOTU MOUE MOUP MOUS MOVE MOWA MOWN MOWS MOXA MOYA MOYL MOYS

MOZE MOZO MOZZ MUCH MUCK MUDS MUFF MUGG MUGS MUID MUIL MUIR MULE MULL MUMM MUMP MUMS MUMU MUNI MUNS MUNT MUON MURA MURE MURK MURL MURR MUSE MUSH MUSK MUSO MUSS MUST MUTE MUTI MUTS MUTT MYAL MYNA MYTH MZEE

NAAM NAAN NABE NABK NABS NACH NADA NAFF NAGA NAGS NAIF NAIK NAIL NAIN NALA NAME NAMS NANA NANS NAOI NAOS NAPA NAPE NAPS NARC NARD NARE NARK NARY NATS NAVE NAVY NAYS

NAZE
NAZI
NEAL
NEAP
NEAR
NEAT
NEBS
NECK
NEDS
NEED
NEEM
NEEP
NEFS
NEIF
NEKS
NEMA
NEMN
NENE
NEON
NEPS
NERD
NERK
NESH
NESS
NEST
NETE
NETS
NETT
NEUK
NEUM
NEVE
NEVI
NEWS
NEWT
NEXT
NIBS
NICE
NICK
NIDE
NIDI
NIDS
NIED
NIEF
NIES
NIFE
NIFF
NIGH
NILL
NILS
NIMB
NIMS
NINE
NIPA
NIPS
NIRL
NISI
NITE
NITS
NIXE
NIXY
NOBS
NOCK
NODE
NODI
NODS
NOEL
NOES
NOGG
NOGS
NOIL
NOIR
NOLE
NOLL
NOLO
NOMA
NOME
NOMS
NONA
NONE
NONG
NOOK
NOON
NOOP
NOPE
NORI
NORK
NORM
NOSE
NOSH
NOSY
NOTA
NOTE
NOTT
NOUL
NOUN
NOUP
NOUS
NOUT
NOVA
NOWL
NOWN
NOWS
NOWT
NOWY
NOYS
NUBS
NUDE
NUFF
NUKE
NULL
NUMB
NUNS
NURD
NURL
NURR
NURS
NUTS
NYAS
NYED
NYES

OAFS
OAKS
OAKY
OARS
OARY
OAST
OATH
OATS
OBAS
OBES
OBEY
OBIA
OBIS
OBIT
OBOE
OBOL
OBOS
OCAS
OCHE
OCTA
ODAL
ODAS
ODDS
ODEA
ODES
ODIC
ODOR
ODSO
ODYL
OFAY
OFFS
OGAM
OGEE
OGLE
OGRE
OHED
OHIA
OHMS
OHOS
OIKS
OILS
OILY
OINK
OINT
OKAS
OKAY
OKEH
OKES
OKRA
OKTA
OLDS
OLDY
OLEA
OLEO
OLES
OLID
OLIO
OLLA
OLMS
OLPE
OMBU
OMEN
OMER
OMIT
ONCE
ONER
ONES
ONLY
ONST
ONTO
ONUS
ONYX
OOFS
OOHS
OOMS
OONS
OONT
OOPS
OOSE
OOSY
OOTS
OOZE
OOZY
OPAH
OPAL
OPED
OPEN
OPES
OPPO
OPTS
OPUS
ORAD
ORAL
ORBS
ORBY
ORCA
ORCS
ORDO
ORDS
ORES
ORFE
ORFS
ORGY
ORLE
ORRA
ORTS
ORYX
ORZO
OSAR
OSES
OSSA
OTIC
OTTO
OUCH
OUDS
OUKS
OULD
OULK
OUPH
OUPS
OURN
OURS
OUST
OUTS
OUZO
OVAL
OVEN
OVER
OVUM
OWED
OWER
OWES
OWLS
OWLY
OWNS
OWRE
OWSE
OWTS
OXEN
OXER
OXES
OXID
OXIM
OYER
OYES
OYEZ

PACA
PACE
PACK
PACO
PACS
PACT
PACY
PADI
PADS
PAGE
PAHS
PAID
PAIK
PAIL
PAIN
PAIR
PAIS
PALE
PALL
PALM
PALP
PALS
PALY
PAMS
PAND
PANE
PANG
PANS
PANT
PAPA
PAPE
PAPS
PARA
PARD
PARE
PARK
PARP
PARR
PARS
PART
PASE
PASH
PASS
PAST
PATE
PATH
PATS
PATY
PAUA
PAUL
PAVE
PAWA
PAWK
PAWL
PAWN
PAWS
PAYS
PEAG
PEAK
PEAL
PEAN
PEAR
PEAS
PEAT
PEBA
PECH
PECK
PECS
PEDS
PEED
PEEK
PEEL
PEEN
PEEP
PEER
PEES
PEGH
PEGS
PEHS
PEIN
PEKE
PELA
PELE
PELF
PELL
PELT
PEND
PENE
PENI
PENK
PENS
PENT
PEON
PEPO
PEPS
PERE
PERI
PERK
PERM
PERN
PERT
PERV
PESO
PEST
PETS
PEWS
PFFT
PFUI
PHAT
PHEW
PHIS
PHIZ
PHOH
PHON
PHOS
PHOT
PHUT
PIAL
PIAN
PIAS
PICA
PICE
PICK
PICS
PIED
PIER
PIES
PIET
PIGS
PIKA
PIKE
PIKI
PILA
PILE
PILI
PILL
PILY
PIMA
PIMP
PINA
PINE
PING
PINK
PINS
PINT
PINY
PION
PIOY
PIPA
PIPE
PIPI
PIPS
PIPY
PIRL
PIRN
PIRS
PISE
PISH
PISO
PISS
PITA
PITH
PITS
PITY
PIUM
PIXY
PIZE
PLAN
PLAP
PLAT
PLAY
PLEA
PLEB
PLED
PLEW
PLIE
PLIM
PLOD
PLOP
PLOT
PLOW
PLOY
PLUG
PLUM
PLUS
POAS
POCK
POCO
PODS
POEM
POET
POGO
POGY
POIS
POKE
POKY
POLE
POLK
POLL
POLO
POLS
POLT
POLY
POME
POMP
POMS
POND
PONE
PONG
PONK
PONS
PONT
PONY
POOD
POOF
POOH
POOK
POOL
POON
POOP
POOR
POOS
POOT
POPE
POPS
PORE
PORK
PORN
PORT
PORY
POSE
POSH
POSS
POST
POSY
POTE
POTS
POTT
POUF
POUK
POUR
POUT
POWN
POWS
POXY
POZZ
PRAD
PRAM
PRAO
PRAT
PRAU
PRAY
PREE
PREP
PREX
PREY
PREZ
PRIG
PRIM
PROA
PROB
PROD
PROF
PROG
PROM
PROO
PROP
PROS
PROW
PRUH
PRYS
PSIS
PSST
PUBS
PUCE
PUCK
PUDS
PUDU
PUER
PUFF
PUGH
PUGS
PUIR
PUJA
PUKE
PUKU
PULA
PULE
PULI
PULK
PULL
PULP
PULS
PULU
PULY
PUMA
PUMP
PUMY
PUNA
PUNG
PUNK
PUNS
PUNT
PUNY
PUPA
PUPS
PURE
PURI
PURL
PURR
PURS
PUSH
PUSS
PUTS
PUTT
PUTZ
PUYS
PYAS
PYAT
PYES
PYET
PYIC
PYIN
PYNE
PYOT
PYRE
PYRO

QADI
QAID
QATS
QOPH
QUAD
QUAG
QUAI
QUAT
QUAY
QUEP
QUEY
QUID
QUIM
QUIN
QUIP
QUIT
QUIZ
QUOD
QUOP

RABI
RACA
RACE
RACH
RACK
RACY
RADE
RADS
RAFF
RAFT
RAGA
RAGE
RAGG
RAGI
RAGS
RAHS
RAIA
RAID
RAIK
RAIL
RAIN
RAIS
RAIT
RAJA
RAKE
RAKI
RAKU
RALE
RAMI
RAMP
RAMS
RANA
RAND
RANG
RANI
RANK
RANT
RAPE
RAPS
RAPT
RARE
RASE
RASH
RASP
RAST
RATA
RATE
RATH
RATO
RATS
RATU
RAUN
RAVE
RAWN
RAWS
RAYA
RAYS
RAZE
RAZZ
READ
REAK
REAL
REAM
REAN
REAP
REAR
REBS
RECK
RECS
REDD
REDE
REDO
REDS
REED
REEF
REEK
REEL
REEN
REES
REFS
REFT
REGO
REGS
REHS
REIF
REIK
REIN
REIS
REKE
RELY
REMS
REND
RENS
RENT
RENY
REPO
REPP
REPS
RESH
REST
RETE
RETS
REVS
REWS
RHEA
RHOS
RHUS
RIAL
RIAS
RIBS
RICE
RICH
RICK
RICY
RIDE
RIDS
RIEL
RIEM
RIFE
RIFF
RIFS
RIFT
RIGG
RIGS
RILE
RILL
RIMA
RIME
RIMS
RIMU
RIMY
RIND
RINE
RING

RINK RINS RIOT RIPE RIPP RIPS RIPT RISE RISK RISP RITE RITS RITT RITZ RIVA RIVE RIVO RIZA ROAD ROAM ROAN ROAR ROBE ROBS ROCH ROCK ROCS RODE RODS ROED ROES ROIL ROIN ROJI ROKE ROKS ROKY ROLE ROLF ROLL ROMA ROMP ROMS RONE RONG RONT ROOD ROOF ROOK ROOM ROON ROOP ROOS ROOT ROPE ROPY RORE RORT RORY ROSE ROST ROSY ROTA ROTE ROTI ROTL ROTO ROTS ROUE ROUL ROUM ROUP ROUT ROUX ROVE

ROWS ROWT RUBE RUBS RUBY RUCK RUCS RUDD RUDE RUDS RUED RUER RUES RUFF RUGA RUGS RUIN RUKH RULE RULY RUME RUMP RUMS RUND RUNE RUNG RUNS RUNT RURP RURU RUSA RUSE RUSH RUSK RUST RUTH RUTS RYAL RYAS RYES RYFE RYKE RYND RYOT RYPE

SABE SABS SACK SACS SADE SADI SAFE SAGA SAGE SAGO SAGS SAGY SAIC SAID SAIL SAIM SAIN SAIR SAIS SAKE SAKI SALE SALL SALP SALS SALT SAMA SAME SAMP

SAND SANE SANG SANK SANS SANT SAPS SARD SARI SARK SARS SASH SASS SATE SATI SAUL SAUT SAVE SAWN SAWS SAYS SCAB SCAD SCAG SCAM SCAN SCAR SCAT SCAW SCOG SCOP SCOT SCOW SCRY SCUD SCUG SCUL SCUM SCUP SCUR SCUT SCYE SEAL SEAM SEAN SEAR SEAS SEAT SECO SECS SECT SEED SEEK SEEL SEEM SEEN SEEP SEER SEES SEGO SEGS SEIF SEIK SEIL SEIR SEIS SEKT SELD SELE SELF SELL SELS SEME SEMI SENA

SEND SENE SENS SENT SEPS SEPT SERA SERE SERF SERK SERR SERS SESE SESS SETA SETS SETT SEWN SEWS SEXT SEXY SEYS SHAD SHAG SHAH SHAM SHAN SHAT SHAW SHAY SHEA SHED SHES SHET SHEW SHIM SHIN SHIP SHIR SHIT SHIV SHMO SHOD SHOE SHOG SHOO SHOP SHOT SHOW SHRI SHUL SHUN SHUT SHWA SIAL SIBB SIBS SICE SICH SICK SICS SIDA SIDE SIEN SIFT SIGH SIGN SIJO SIKA SIKE SILD SILE SILK SILL SILO

SILT SIMA SIMI SIMP SIMS SIND SINE SING SINH SINK SINS SIPE SIPS SIRE SIRI SIRS SISS SIST SITE SITH SITS SIZE SIZY SKAG SKAS SKAT SKAW SKEE SKEG SKEO SKEP SKER SKEW SKID SKIM SKIN SKIO SKIP SKIS SKIT SKOL SKRY SKUA SKUG SKYR SLAB SLAE SLAG SLAM SLAP SLAT SLAW SLAY SLED SLEE SLEW SLEY SLID SLIM SLIP SLIT SLOB SLOE SLOG SLOP SLOT SLOW SLUB SLUE SLUG SLUM SLUR SLUT SMEE SMEW

SMIR SMIT SMOG SMUG SMUR SMUT SNAB SNAG SNAP SNAR SNAW SNEB SNED SNEE SNIB SNIG SNIP SNIT SNOB SNOD SNOG SNOT SNOW SNUB SNUG SNYE SOAK SOAP SOAR SOBS SOCA SOCK SOCS SODA SODS SOFA SOFT SOGS SOHO SOHS SOIL SOJA SOKE SOLA SOLD SOLE SOLI SOLO SOLS SOMA SOME SONE SONG SONS SOOK SOOM SOON SOOP SOOT SOPH SOPS SORA SORB SORD SORE SORI SORN SORT SOSS SOTH SOTS SOUK SOUL SOUM SOUP

SOUR SOUS SOUT SOVS SOWF SOWL SOWM SOWN SOWP SOWS SOYA SOYS SPAE SPAG SPAM SPAN SPAR SPAS SPAT SPAW SPAY SPAZ SPEC SPED SPEK SPET SPEW SPIC SPIE SPIK SPIN SPIT SPIV SPOT SPRY SPUD SPUE SPUN SPUR SRIS STAB STAG STAP STAR STAT STAW STAY STED STEM STEN STEP STET STEW STEY STIE STIR STOA STOB STOP STOT STOW STUB STUD STUM STUN STYE SUBA SUBS SUCH SUCK SUDD SUDS SUED SUER SUES

SUET SUGH SUID SUIT SUKH SUKS SULK SULU SUMO SUMP SUMS SUNG SUNK SUNN SUNS SUPE SUPS SUQS SURA SURD SURE SURF SUSS SWAB SWAD SWAG SWAM SWAN SWAP SWAT SWAY SWEE SWEY SWIG SWIM SWIZ SWOB SWOP SWOT SWUM SYBO SYCE SYED SYEN SYES SYKE SYLI SYNC SYND SYNE SYPE SYPH

TABI TABS TABU TACE TACH TACK TACO TACT TADS TAED TAEL TAES TAGS TAHA TAHR TAIL TAIN TAIS TAIT TAKA TAKE TAKI

TAKS TAKY TALA TALC TALE TALI TALK TALL TAME TAMP TAMS TANA TANE TANG TANH TANK TANS TAOS TAPA TAPE TAPS TAPU TARA TARE TARN TARO TARP TARS TART TASH TASK TASS TATE TATH TATS TATT TATU TAUS TAUT TAVA TAVS TAWA TAWS TAWT TAXA TAXI TAYS TEAD TEAK TEAL TEAM TEAR TEAS TEAT TECH TEDS TEDY TEED TEEL TEEM TEEN TEER TEES TEFF TEFS TEGG TEGS TEGU TEHR TEIL TELA TELD TELE TELL TELS

TELT TEME TEMP TEMS TEND TENE TENS TENT TEPA TERF TERM TERN TEST TETE TETH TETS TEWS TEXT THAE THAN THAR THAT THAW THEE THEM THEN THEW THEY THIG THIN THIO THIR THIS THON THOU THRO THRU THUD THUG THUS TIAR TICE TICH TICK TICS TIDE TIDS TIDY TIED TIER TIES TIFF TIFT TIGE TIGS TIKA TIKE TIKI TILE TILL TILS TILT TIME TIND TINE TING TINK TINS TINT TINY TIPI TIPS TIPT TIRE TIRL

TIRO TIRR TITE TITI TITS TIVY TIZZ TOAD TOBY TOCK TOCO TOCS TODS TODY TOEA TOED TOES TOEY TOFF TOFT TOFU TOGA TOGE TOGS TOHO TOIL TOIT TOKE TOKO TOLA TOLD TOLE TOLL TOLT TOLU TOMB TOME TOMS TONE TONG TONK TONS TONY TOOK TOOL TOOM TOON TOOT TOPE TOPH TOPI TOPS TORA TORC TORE TORI TORN TORO TORR TORS TORT TORY TOSA TOSE TOSH TOSS TOST TOTE TOTS TOUK TOUN TOUR TOUT TOWN TOWS TOWT TOWY TOYO TOYS TOZE TRAD TRAM TRAP TRAT TRAY TREE TREF TREK TRES TRET TREW TREY TREZ TRIE TRIG TRIM TRIN TRIO TRIP TROD TROG TRON TROP TROT TROW TROY TRUE TRUG TRYE TRYP TSAR TSKS TUAN TUBA TUBE TUBS TUCK TUFA TUFF TUFT TUGS TUIS TULE TUMP TUMS TUNA TUND TUNE TUNG TUNS TUNY TUPS TURD TURF TURK TURM TURN TUSH TUSK TUTS TUTU TUZZ TWAE TWAL TWAS TWAT TWAY TWEE TWIG TWIN TWIT TWOS TYDE TYED TYEE TYER TYES TYGS TYKE TYMP TYND TYNE TYPE TYPO TYPP TYPY TYRE TYRO TYTE TZAR

UDAL UDOS UEYS UFOS UGHS UGLY UKES ULAN ULES ULEX ULNA ULUS ULVA UMBO UMPH UMPS UNAI UNAU UNBE UNCE UNCI UNCO UNDE UNDO UNDY UNIS UNIT UNTO UPAS UPBY UPDO UPGO UPON UPSY URAO URBS URDE URDS URDY UREA URES URGE URIC URNS URSA URUS URVA USED USER USES UTAS UTES UTIS UTUS UVAE UVAS UVEA

VACS VADE VAES VAGI VAIL VAIN VAIR VALE VALI VAMP VANE VANG VANS VANT VARA VARE VARS VARY VASA VASE VAST VATS VATU VAUS VAUT VAVS VAWS VEAL VEEP VEER VEES VEGA VEHM VEIL VEIN VELA VELD VELE VELL VENA VEND VENT VERA VERB VERS VERT VERY VEST VETO VETS VEXT VIAE VIAL VIAS VIBE VIBS VICE VIDE VIDS VIED VIER VIES VIEW VIGA VIGS VILD VILE VILL VIMS VINA VINE VINO VINS VINT VINY VIOL VIRE VIRL VISA VISE VITA VITE VIVA VIVE VIVO VIZY VLEI VOAR VOES VOID VOLA VOLE VOLK VOLS VOLT VORS VOTE VOWS VRIL VROW VUGG VUGH VUGS VULN VUMS

WABS WACK WADD WADE WADI WADS WADT WADY WAES WAFF WAFT WAGE WAGS WAID WAIF WAIL WAIN WAIR WAIT WAKA WAKE WAKF WALD WALE WALI WALK WALL WALY WAME WAND WANE WANG WANK WANS WANT WANY WAPS WAQF WARD WARE WARK WARM WARN WARP WARS WART WARY WASE WASH WASM WASP WAST WATE WATS WATT WAUK WAUL WAUR WAVE WAVY WAWE WAWL WAWS WAXY WAYS WEAK WEAL WEAN WEAR WEBS WEDS WEED WEEK WEEL WEEM WEEN WEEP WEER WEES WEET WEFT WEID WEIL WEIR WEKA WELD WELK WELL WELT WEMB WEMS WEND WENS WENT WEPT WERE WERT WEST WETA WETS WEXE WEYS WHAM WHAP WHAT WHEE WHEN WHET WHEW WHEY WHID WHIG WHIM WHIN WHIP WHIR WHIT WHIZ WHOA WHOM WHOP WHOT WHOW WHYS WICE WICH WICK WIDE WIEL WIFE WIGS WILD WILE WILI WILL WILT WILY WIMP WIND WINE WING WINK WINN WINO WINS WINY WIPE WIRE WIRY WISE WISH WISP WISS WIST WITE WITH WITS WIVE WOAD WOCK WOES WOGS WOKE WOKS WOLD WOLF WOMB WONK WONS WONT WOOD WOOF WOOL WOON WOOS WOOT WOPS WORD WORE WORK WORM WORN WORT WOST WOTS WOVE WOWF WOWS WRAP WREN WRIT WUDS WULL WUSS WYCH WYES WYLE WYND WYNN WYNS WYTE

XYST

YACK YAFF YAGI YAHS YAKS YALD YALE YAMS YANG YANK YAPP YAPS YARD YARE YARN YARR YATE YAUD YAUP YAWL YAWN YAWP YAWS YAWY YAYS YBET YEAD YEAH YEAN YEAR YEAS YECH YEDE YEED YEGG YELD YELK YELL YELM YELP YELT YENS YEPS YERD YERK YESK YEST YETI YETT YEUK YEVE YEWS YGOE YIDS YIKE YILL YINS YIPE YIPS YIRD YIRK YIRR YITE YLEM YLKE YMPE YMPT YOBS YOCK YODE YODH YODS YOGA YOGH YOGI YOKE YOKS YOLD YOLK YOMP YOND YONI YONT YOOF YOOP YORE YORK YOUK YOUR YOWE YOWL YOWS YUAN YUCA YUCH YUCK YUFT YUGA YUGS YUKE YUKO YUKS YUKY YULE YUMP YUNX YUPS YURT YWIS

ZACK ZAGS ZANY ZAPS ZARF ZATI ZEAL ZEAS ZEBU ZEDS ZEES ZEIN ZEKS ZELS ZERK ZERO ZEST ZETA ZEZE ZHOS ZIFF ZIGS ZILA ZILL ZIMB ZINC ZINE ZING ZINS ZIPS ZITE ZITI ZITS ZIZZ ZOBO ZOBU ZOEA ZOIC ZONA ZONE ZONK ZOOM ZOON ZOOS ZORI ZOUK ZULU ZUPA ZURF ZYGA ZYME

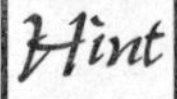

Think Big – Think Bonus

One of the reasons that some players struggle to play all seven letters for a 50-point bonus is that they don't believe they can achieve such plays and are reluctant to look very hard.

The letter distribution of the Scrabble set is such that, if you concentrate on using the higher-scoring consonants and keep the flexible letters (such as those in RETAINS), you are likely to have a bonus word sooner or later. But you must train yourself to believe there could always be a bonus word to find and constantly ask yourself with each fresh rack 'Is there a bonus word here?' before looking for alternative plays.

Your expectation should be particularly high if you have, say, seven different letters including an E and two other vowels. For example, would you bother to look for a bonus with AEFILNT or DEGILUV? The words are the common words INFLATE and DIVULGE of course!

Sometimes even the most unlikely of racks can yield a surprise bonus word. Would you be inspired to look for a bonus with the racks GHORTUW or AACCNVY for example? Check the Anagram Section for the answers to these!

So, get into the habit of *thinking big* every turn. If nothing leaps out at you then move the tiles around on your rack, or try making common endings and beginnings. You never know when a FOGHORN or a VIADUCT is going to turn up on your rack.

Also, don't forget that knowledge of the 2-letter words can be vital for finding somewhere to slot in your bonus. There's nothing more disappointing than finding a brilliant MUGWUMP and not knowing the word MI, say, to slot it in.

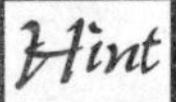

Practising with Plates

A convenient way to practise Scrabble vocabulary whilst travelling by car is to find words from car number plates. There are a number of Scrabble games playable (if you're not the driver!):

- ☆ Find the shortest word containing the three main letters of the number plate (ignoring the other letters).
- ☆ Look for 7-letter words by converting the numerals to letters thus (1=I, 2=Z, 3=E, 4=A, 5=S, 6=G, 7=T, 8=B, 9=G, 0=O) eg DGF 105H makes DOGFISH!
- ☆ Look for 7- or 8-letter words by taking the four or five letters and adding the letters A E I, or I E S, or similar, to give a good selection.

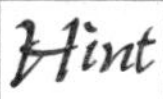

Suspicious Minds

Don't be suspicious of all your opponent's moves. It is often better to play to the strength of your own rack and think about your scoring potential than to worry too much about whether your opponent's play is a set-up for a good score next turn. Even amongst top players there are few occasions when there is a deliberate set-up play.

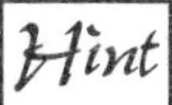

Tile Turnover

An additional consideration when deciding upon the best move is the number of tiles you use. Although other factors such as the score, the balance of the letters left on your rack and the openness of the move, are just as important, the basic philosophy that using more tiles than your opponent increases your chances of getting any of the good tiles remaining in the bag cannot be completely ignored.

When faced with a choice of moves with a poor rack, more often than not the play using most tiles is the one to favour. The exception is when the only tiles remaining are the awkward tiles that you would rather avoid (eg the Q and the V's). Keeping track of the tiles played is advantageous in judging the value of a high turnover play but ultimately you are at the mercy of your own discretion.

Spreading the Words

If you've done a little word study from *Official Scrabble® Words International* and you feel you have word-power advantage over your opponent then it can pay to keep the game fairly open in the early stages rather than play too defensively. So try to play slightly longer words if you can, and try to keep at least two areas of the board easily accessible. You will find you will then have a greater choice of opportunities which, combined with your newly acquired word-power, will enable better mid-game rack-balancing moves and scores, and maybe a bonus word or two.

Light and Heavy Words

Light words

Light words are those with many vowels, excluding Y. These words are useful for using up excessive vowels on your rack, in an attempt to return to a more balanced rack. The numbers of vowels for words of various lengths in these lists are given here:

2-letter words, 2 vowels (eg AE, OI)

3-letter words, 3 vowels (AIA, EAU)

4-letter words, 3 vowels or more (eg EUOI, IOTA)

5-letter words, 4 vowels (eg AUDIO, QUEUE)

6-letter words, 4 vowels or more (eg COOKIE, LEAGUE)

7-letter words, 5 vowels or more (eg ANAEMIA, EVACUEE)

8-letter words, 5 vowels or more (eg ALIENATE, ORATORIO)

To help you learn and recall words with many vowels, words of four or more letters are listed according to the vowel groups they contain. For example, ANEMIA and AVIATE are both listed in the group of 6-letter words having the vowels AAEI.

Heavy words

Heavy words are those with many consonants. These are useful for discarding excessive consonants from your rack, again in an attempt to return to a more balanced rack. The numbers of vowels for words of various lengths in these lists are given here:

2-letter words, no vowels except Y (eg MY, SH)

3-letter words, no vowels except Y (eg FRY, NTH)

4-letter words, no vowels except Y (eg HYMN, YMPT)

5-letter words, no vowels except Y (eg CRWTH, NYMPH)

6-letter words, 1 vowel (eg CHINTZ, RHYTHM)

To avoid the heavy word lists ballooning in size, inflections ending in -S have been omitted.

When you want to recall words with many consonants, try to home in on words with frequently-occurring clumps of letters – for example, CH, GHT, NCH, PH, SCH, SCR, TCH and TH. Of course, there are many others.

LIGHT WORDS (Many Vowels)

2-letter words – 2 vowels

AA AE AI EA EE IO OE OI OO OU

3-letter words – 3 vowels

AIA EAU

4-letter words – 3 vowels or more (by vowel content)

AAE	ALAE		AKEE		AERO		UVEA		UNAI	EIU	ETUI
	AREA		ALEE		ALOE	AII	ILIA	AOU	AUTO		IURE
	ASEA		AWEE		EOAN		INIA		URAO		LIEU
AAI	AIAS		EALE		ODEA		IXIA	AUU	LUAU	EOO	OBOE
	AMIA		EASE		OLEA	AIO	AGIO		UNAU		OLEO
	ARIA		EAVE		TOEA		CIAO	EEE	EPEE		OOSE
	RAIA	AEI	AIDE		ZOEA		IOTA	EEI	EIDE		OOZE
AAO	ANOA		AINE	AEU	AGUE		JIAO		EINE	EOU	EURO
AAU	AQUA		AMIE		AUNE		NAOI		IDEE		MEOU
	AULA		IDEA		BEAU		OBIA	EEO	EVOE		MOUE
	AURA		ILEA		EAUS		OHIA		OGEE		ROUE
	PAUA		KAIE		EAUX	AIU	AITU	EEU	EMEU	IOO	MOOI
AEE	AGEE		VIAE		UREA		HUIA		EUGE		OLIO
	AJEE	AEO	AEON		UVAE		QUAI	EIOU	EUOI	OOU	OUZO

5-letter words – 4 vowels or more (by vowel content)

AAEE	AREAE		AINEE	AIIO	AIDOI		OUIJA	EIOU	LOUIE
AAEI	AECIA	AEEO	ZOEAE		AIOLI	EEEI	EERIE		OURIE
AAEU	AQUAE	AEIU	ADIEU		OIDIA	EEOO	COOEE		
	AURAE		AUREI	AIOU	AUDIO	EEUU	QUEUE		
AAII	AALII		URAEI		AULOI	EIOO	LOOIE		
AEEI	AERIE	AEOO	ZOOEA		MIAOU		OORIE		

6-letter words – 4 vowels or more (by vowel content)

AAAE	AGAPAE		CAUSAE		BEANIE		QUAERE		ELUVIA
	AZALEA		FAUNAE		DEARIE		QUELEA		EUCAIN
AAAI	ABASIA		GATEAU		DEAWIE		RESEAU		EXUVIA
	ACACIA		LAURAE		EASIER		UNEASE		GAUCIE
	AGAPAI		NAUSEA		EASIES		UREASE		GUINEA
	ALALIA	AAII	AALIIS		EPEIRA	AEII	AIRIER		HAIQUE
	ARALIA		HAIKAI		FAERIE		BAILIE		SAIQUE
	ATAXIA		KAIKAI		FERIAE		LIAISE		SAULIE
	TAIAHA		ZAIKAI		HEARIE		SAIKEI		TAUPIE
AAAU	UJAMAA	AAIO	ADAGIO		IDEAED		TIBIAE		UNCIAE
AAEE	AERATE		AIKONA		IDEATE	AEIO	AEONIC		UREDIA
	AMEBAE		ALODIA		KEAVIE		ANOMIE		UREMIA
	EATAGE		ALOGIA		LAESIE		ARIOSE	AEOO	AMOOVE
	GALEAE		ANOPIA		MEALIE		AZIONE		ROADEO
	PALEAE		ANOXIA		MEANIE		BOATIE		ZOOEAL
	PERAEA		APORIA		MEDIAE		CODEIA		ZOOEAS
	TALEAE		ATOCIA		PEREIA		EIDOLA	AEOU	AERUGO
AAEI	ABELIA		COAITA		REDIAE		EOLIAN		AROUSE
	ACEDIA		ORARIA		SEMEIA		EONIAN		AUTOED
	AECIAL		ZOARIA		TENIAE		EPIZOA		AVOURE
	AERIAL	AAIU	ABULIA	AEEO	AEROBE		FEIJOA		COTEAU
	ALEXIA		AMUSIA		APOGEE		GOALIE		DOUANE
	AMELIA		ANURIA		AREOLE		HOAGIE		OPAQUE
	ANEMIA		AUDIAL		COATEE		IODATE		OUTAGE
	ARAISE		AUMAIL		ELODEA		LEIPOA		OUTATE
	AVAILE		GUAIAC		EVOVAE		OAKIER		OUTEAT
	AVIATE		IGUANA		FOVEAE		OARIER		ZOUAVE
	LAMIAE		QUALIA		GOATEE		OBELIA	AEUU	AUREUS
	REALIA		UAKARI		OCREAE		OPIATE		AUTEUR
	TAENIA		URANIA		OEDEMA		ROADIE		BUREAU
AAEO	AGORAE		YAUTIA		OLEATE		ROARIE		URAEUS
	AMOEBA	AAOO	MANOAO	AEEOO	ZOOEAE		SOAPIE		UVULAE
	AORTAE	AAOU	ACAJOU	AEEOUU	EUOUAE		ZOECIA	AIIO	AIKIDO
	APNOEA		AGOUTA	AEEU	AEMULE	AEIU	ACULEI		AIOLIS
	AREOLA		AMADOU		AENEUS		ADIEUS		ARIOSI
	CAEOMA		AOUDAD		AVENUE		ADIEUX		DAIMIO
	OARAGE		AURORA		BAUBEE		AECIUM		MOIRAI
	OZAENA	AAUU	AUCUBA		ELUATE		AGUISE	AIOO	ARIOSO
AAEU	ACUATE	AEEI	AEDILE		EPAULE		AGUIZE		OOIDAL
	ALULAE		AEDINE		EQUATE		AUDILE		OOMIAC
	AUBADE		AERIED		EUPNEA		AUGITE		OOMIAK
	AURATE		AERIER		EUREKA		AUNTIE		OORALI
	BATEAU		AERIES		FEAGUE		CAIQUE		OORIAL
	BAUERA		APIECE		HEAUME		CURIAE	AIOU	AGOUTI
	CADEAU		BAILEE		LEAGUE		DAUTIE		AUDIOS

	BAGUIO
	GIAOUR
	MIAOUS
	OUIJAS
	OURALI
	OURARI
	QUINOA
	SOUARI
	UTOPIA
AOOU	VAUDOO
AOUU	AUROUS
	AUSUBO
EEEE	BEEBEE
	PEEWEE
	TEEPEE
	VEEPEE
	WEEWEE
EEEI	DEEPIE
	EELIER
	EERIER
	FEERIE
	HEEZIE
	JEELIE
	KEELIE
	MEEMIE
	PEERIE
	REEKIE
	WEENIE
	WEEPIE
EEEO	EPOPEE
EEEU	EKUELE
	EMEUTE
EEII	FEIRIE
	HEINIE
	KIERIE
	MEINIE
	WIENIE
EEIO	EOSINE
	ETOILE
	OLEINE
	OREIDE
	SOIREE
	TOEIER
	VOIDEE
EEIU	ECURIE
	EPUISE
	EQUINE
	EQUIPE
	UREIDE
EEOO	BOOTEE
	COOEED
	COOEES
	DOOLEE
	SOOGEE
	TOETOE
EEOU	COULEE
	COUPEE
	EVOLUE
	MEOUED
	OEUVRE
	OUTSEE
	TOUPEE
EEUU	QUEUED
	QUEUER
	QUEUES
EIIO	IODIDE
	IODINE
	IODISE
	IODIZE
	IOLITE
	IONISE
	IONIZE
	OILIER
EIIU	EURIPI
	MILIEU
	QUINIE
EIOO	BLOOIE
	BOOBIE
	BOODIE
	BOOGIE
	BOOKIE
	BOOTIE
	COOKIE
	COOLIE
	COOTIE
	DOOLIE
	DOOZIE
	EXODOI
	FLOOIE
	FOODIE
	FOOTIE
	GOODIE
	GOOIER
	GOOLIE
	GOONIE
	HOODIE
	HOOLIE
	IONONE
	KOOKIE
	LOOIES
	LOONIE
	NOOKIE
	OOLITE
	OORIER
	OOSIER
	OOZIER
	ORIOLE
	OROIDE
	OTIOSE
	ROOKIE
	ROOMIE
	SOOGIE
	TOORIE
	WOODIE
	WOOLIE
	WOOPIE
EIOU	BOUGIE
	LOUIES
	MOUSIE
	OUGLIE
	OUREBI
	OURIER
	OUTLIE
	OUTVIE
	POURIE
	TOURIE
	TOUTIE
EIUU	UBIQUE
	UNIQUE
EOOO	HOOPOE
EOOU	QUOOKE
EOUU	UVEOUS
IIOO	OPIOID
	TOITOI
IIOU	IONIUM
	OIDIUM
IIUU	PIUPIU
IOOU	IODOUS
	KOUROI
	ODIOUS
OOOO	BOOBOO
	BOOHOO
	COOCOO
	GOOROO
	HOODOO
	HOOPOO
	HOOROO
	KOODOO
	VOODOO
	ZOOZOO
OOUU	BOUBOU
	ROUCOU
	VOUDOU
UUUU	MUUMUU

7-letter words – 5 vowels or more (by vowel content)

AAAEI	ANAEMIA
AAAIU	AQUARIA
AAEEI	TAENIAE
AAEEO	AMOEBAE
	AREOLAE
AAEEU	AUREATE
AAEII	AECIDIA
AAEIO	AEOLIAN
	AEONIAN
	AEROBIA
	OLEARIA
AAEIU	ACEQUIA
	AURELIA
	CAMAIEU
	URAEMIA
AAEOU	AUREOLA
	AURORAE
AAIOU	ABOULIA
	OUABAIN
	OUAKARI
	RAOULIA
	SAOUARI
AEEEI	ALIENEE
AEEEU	EVACUEE
AEEII	AIERIES
AEEIO	ETAERIO
AEEIU	EUCAINE
	EUGENIA
	EUTEXIA
	EXUVIAE
AEEOU	AENEOUS
	AUREOLE
	EUPNOEA
AEEOUU	EUOUAES
AEIIO	EPINAOI
AEIIU	EQUINIA
AEIOO	IPOMOEA
	ZOOECIA
AEIOU	DOULEIA
	EULOGIA
	MIAOUED
	MOINEAU
	SEQUOIA
AEOUU	AQUEOUS
	AUTOCUE
	COUTEAU
	NOUVEAU
	ROULEAU
AIOOO	OOGONIA
AIOUU	OUGUIYA
EEEIU	EPUISEE
	QUEENIE

8-letter words – 5 vowels or more (by vowel content)

AAAAE	ANABAENA
AAAAI	ARAPAIMA
	ATARAXIA
	KAMAAINA
AAAEI	ACADEMIA
	ACHAENIA
	ANAEMIAS
	ASSEGAAI
	MAZAEDIA
AAAEO	PARANOEA
AAAEU	ACAUDATE
	AGUACATE
	AQUACADE
AAAII	APIARIAN
	APIMANIA
	RADIALIA
AAAIO	PARANOIA
AAAIU	ADULARIA
	AQUARIAL
	AQUARIAN
	AULARIAN
	AVIFAUNA
	SAPUCAIA
AAAOU	AUTOMATA
AAAUU	AQUANAUT
AAEEE	AMEERATE
	DEAERATE
	HETAERAE
AAEEI	ACIERAGE
	ACIERATE
	AGACERIE
	AGENESIA
	ALIENAGE
	ALIENATE
	AWEARIED
	EMACIATE
	ENCAENIA
	EPIGAEAL
	EPIGAEAN
	ERADIATE
	FACETIAE
	HAEREMAI
	TAENIATE
AAEEO	AMOEBEAN
	ANAEROBE
	AREOLATE
	OEDEMATA
AAEEOU	AUREOLAE
AAEEU	ACULEATE
	ADEQUATE
	CAESURAE
	ECAUDATE
	EVACUATE
	EVALUATE
	LAUREATE
	NAUSEATE
	PAENULAE
	SEAQUAKE
AAEII	ACIDEMIA
	ACTINIAE
	AECIDIAL
	AKINESIA
	APIARIES
	AVIANIZE
	AVIARIES
	CAVIARIE
	FILARIAE
	HETAIRAI
	HETAIRIA
	LACINIAE
	VIRAEMIA
AAEIO	AERATION
	AGIOTAGE
	ALOPECIA
	ANOREXIA
	ANOXEMIA
	APOGAEIC
	AZOTEMIA
	CAPOEIRA
	EGOMANIA
	METANOIA
	OLEARIAS
	PAROEMIA
	TOXAEMIA
	ZABAIONE
AAEIOU	ABOIDEAU
	ABOITEAU
AAEIU	ACAULINE
	ACEQUIAS
	ACICULAE
	ALLELUIA
	AUBRETIA
	AUBRIETA
	AUMAILED
	AURELIAN
	AURELIAS
	CAMAIEUX
	DIAPAUSE
	EPIFAUNA
	INAURATE
	INFAUNAE
	MAUVAISE
	PERIAGUA
	TAQUERIA

	URAEMIAS
AAEOU	ACAULOSE
	AERONAUT
	ANALOGUE
	AQUATONE
	ARACEOUS
	ARANEOUS
	AUREOLAS
	AUROREAN
	AUTOCADE
	AUTOMATE
	MAUSOLEA
	OCEANAUT
AAEUU	QUAALUDE
	USQUABAE
AAIII	MILIARIA
	NIRAMIAI
AAIIO	APOSITIA
	AVIATION
	MAIOLICA
	ZOIATRIA
AAIIU	ACIDURIA
	AUXILIAR
	BAUHINIA
	IGUANIAN
	QUILLAIA
	UNIAXIAL
AAIOO	ANOOPSIA
	APOLOGIA
	ZOOMANIA
AAIOU	ABOULIAS
	AUTACOID
	AUTOPSIA
	AZOTURIA
	CARIACOU
	GUAIACOL
	OUABAINS
	OUAKARIS
	PAROUSIA
	RAOULIAS
	SAOUARIS
AAIUU	AQUARIUM
	AURICULA
	GUAIACUM
AAOUU	ACAULOUS
AEEEE	EMEERATE
	RELEASEE
AEEEI	ALIENEES
	DETAINEE
	EARPIECE
	EATERIES
	EMERITAE
	EXAMINEE
	SEAPIECE
AEEEU	AGUEWEED
	EMERAUDE
	EVACUEES
	SEQUELAE
AEEII	AEGIRINE
	AEGIRITE
	AERIFIED
	AERIFIES
	ASEITIES
	EPICEDIA
	GAIETIES
	IDEALISE
	IDEALIZE
	IDEATIVE
	INERTIAE
	INFERIAE
	METAIRIE
	WEIGELIA
AEEIO	ACOEMETI
	AEROLITE
	AMEIOSES

	ETAERIOS
	ETIOLATE
	FOEDARIE
	OEDIPEAN
	OEILLADE
	PAEONIES
AEEIOO	EPOPOEIA
AEEIOU	EULOGIAE
AEEIU	AGUELIKE
	AUDIENCE
	BANLIEUE
	BEAUTIED
	BEAUTIES
	BEAUXITE
	CAUSERIE
	DECIDUAE
	ELUVIATE
	EQUALISE
	EQUALIZE
	EQUIPAGE
	EQUISETA
	EUCAINES
	EUGENIAS
	EUPEPSIA
	EUTAXIES
	EUTAXITE
	EUTEXIAS
	EXEQUIAL
	EXUVIATE
	LEUCEMIA
	LEUKEMIA
	MAUVEINE
	QUEASIER
	QUEAZIER
	UNEASIER
	UNIDEAED
AEEOO	AEROTONE
	FOVEOLAE
	OOGAMETE
	OOTHECAE
	PAHOEHOE
	PEEKABOO
	ZOOGLEAE
AEEOU	AEGLOGUE
	ALEHOUSE
	ALEURONE
	AUREOLED
	AUREOLES
	COEQUATE
	EUDAEMON
	EUPNOEAS
	FEATEOUS
	JEALOUSE
	OUTEATEN
	REAROUSE
	TEAHOUSE
AEEUU	NEURULAE
	URAEUSES
	USQUEBAE
AEIII	INITIATE
	RETIARII
AEIIO	AMEIOSIS
	HEMIOLIA
	HEMIOPIA
	IBOGAINE
	IDEATION
	IODINATE
	NOTITIAE
	TAENIOID
AEIIU	ACUITIES
	AECIDIUM
	AIGUILLE
	AQUILINE
	AUDITIVE
	AURIFIED

	AURIFIES
	EQUINIAS
	INDUCIAE
	INDUVIAE
	MAIEUTIC
	MINUTIAE
	QUINIELA
	SILIQUAE
	UINTAITE
	UREDINIA
	URINEMIA
AEIOO	AEROFOIL
	AMOEBOID
	COENOBIA
	IPOMOEAS
	MOVIEOLA
	OOGAMIES
	OVARIOLE
AEIOU	AEQUORIN
	AEROBIUM
	AGOUTIES
	CAESIOUS
	DIALOGUE
	DOUANIER
	DOULEIAS
	EDACIOUS
	EQUATION
	EULOGIAS
	EUPHOBIA
	EUPHONIA
	EUPHORIA
	EXONUMIA
	JALOUSIE
	MOINEAUS
	ODALIQUE
	OUTRAISE
	POULAINE
	SAUTOIRE
	SEQUOIAS
	THIOUREA
AEIUU	AUGURIES
	AUTUNITE
	FAUTEUIL
AEOOO	ZOOGLOEA
AEOOU	APOLOGUE
	AUTOSOME
	POACEOUS
AEOUU	AUTOCUES
	BEAUCOUP
	COUTEAUX
	FEATUOUS
	HUAQUERO
	NAUSEOUS
	OUTARGUE
	OUTVALUE
	ROULEAUS
	ROULEAUX
	ROUSSEAU
AIIIO	OITICICA
AIIIU	DAIQUIRI
AIIOO	AVOISION
	IODATION
AIIOU	AUDITION
	MIAOUING
	OLIGURIA
AIOOO	OOGONIAL
	ORATORIO
	ZOONOMIA
AIOOU	AUTOCOID
	AUTOGIRO
	ORAGIOUS
	OVARIOUS
AIOUU	CAUTIOUS
	GUAIOCUM
	SUBAUDIO

AOOOU	OOGAMOUS
AOOUU	ANOUROUS
	COUMAROU
EEEEI	EYEPIECE
EEEEU	SQUEEGEE
EEEIO	EOLIENNE
	TOEPIECE
EEEIU	EUXENITE
	EXEQUIES
	MEUNIERE
	QUEENIER
	QUEENIES
	QUEENITE
EEEOU	ETOUFFEE
EEIIO	BOISERIE
	DEIONIZE
	DIOECIES
	EBIONISE
	EBIONIZE
	EGOITIES
	EOLIPILE
	EPIZOITE
	ERIONITE
	MEIONITE
	MOIETIES
	OILERIES
	OSIERIES
EEIIU	EQUITIES
	PRIEDIEU
	QUIETIVE
	UBIETIES
EEIOO	COOEEING
	EOLOPILE
	OOGENIES
	OPTIONEE
EEIOU	BOUDERIE
	EPIGEOUS
	EPILOGUE
	EQUIVOKE
	ETOURDIE
	EULOGIES
	EULOGISE
	EULOGIZE
	EUPNOEIC
	EUROKIES
	ICEHOUSE
	OBSEQUIE
	OUVRIERE
EEIUU	EUPHUISE
	EUPHUIZE
	QUEUEING
	QUIETUDE
EIIIO	IDIOCIES
EIIOO	ONIONIER
EIIOU	DIECIOUS
	EXIMIOUS
	FILIOQUE
	UNIONISE
	UNIONIZE
EIIUU	BIUNIQUE
EIOOO	FORHOOIE
	OOLOGIES
EIOOU	IDONEOUS
	ISOLOGUE
	OUTVOICE
	ZOOECIUM
EIOUU	BOUTIQUE
	EULOGIUM
	EUROPIUM
	EXIGUOUS
	OUTGUIDE
	TENUIOUS
EOOOO	BOOHOOED
	HOODOOED
	VOODOOED

EOOUU DUOLOGUE
EUROKOUS
OUTHOUSE
OUTQUOTE
VOUDOUED

IIIOU OUISTITI

IIOOU DIOICOUS
DOUPIONI

IOOOU OOGONIUM

IOOUU BOUSOUKI
BOUZOUKI
UXORIOUS

IOUUU USURIOUS

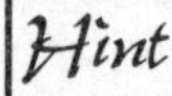

Vowel Advice

Once you have more than two of any vowel on your rack (except perhaps E's) it is all too easy to accumulate more because of the difficulty in sorting out the initial problem. Try the following exercise to become more familiar with those words that solve your multiple vowel imbalance.

Select three A's and then repeatedly pick up any four consonants and see how many A-words you can think of for the first move. Try to find the highest-scoring first move and then consult the Awkward Vowel lists for added inspiration. Do not actually play words on the board but treat each fresh rack as if it were the first move. Repeat the exercise with the O's, I's and U's.

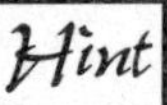

Triple Tactics

Every player recognizes the need to avoid giving the opponent easy access to the triple-word squares. However it is important not to be obsessive about giving away triple-word scores. Playing a word out to the edge of the board such that the word covers the double-letter square between two triple-word squares with a low-scoring tile, does not make it that easy for the opponent to score highly from the triple-word square. In fact, it may force the opponent to use his or her best tiles to block your use of the triple-word square next turn.

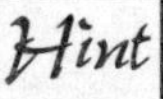

Valuing the S and Blank

The blank and the S are the most valuable tiles in the Scrabble set. Treat them as if they are worth a potential 50 points each. They are the ingredients of most 7- and 8-letter bonus plays and as such should be used wisely. It is rarely worth playing an S for just a few extra points unless the move is essential for blocking the opponent in a game where winning is all important. A blank retained on the rack, even if not utilized in a bonus play, will provide that extra degree of flexibility of choice for endgame strategy.

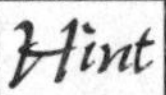

ING Addiction

Every Scrabble player has retained ING on their rack at some time or another in the hope of getting an -ING bonus word. The usefulness of this strategy is frequently overrated amongst less experienced players. Although it is a common ending, unless you have the fortune to pick up the right letter for an -ING 7-letter word you will find the G more of a hindrance. Furthermore, if you religiously cling on to the ING you are severely limiting your choice of play for each move and are effectively playing with only four tiles. The advice is to avoid any ING addiction and concentrate on just keeping any subset of the letters RETAIN that you may have. This will be more fruitful.

Bonus Hunting

Faced with a rack of seven letters in any order it is not always easy to spot even common 7-letter words. Moving the tiles around will often enable an otherwise hidden 7-letter word to come to light. But rather than frantic shuffling and reshuffling in the hope of inspiration a more organized approach is recommended. Form beginnings and endings with the letters on your rack and check the remaining tiles to see if they form a word with that beginning or ending. For example, with the rack EEFGLOR making the prefix FORE will lead you to FORELEG. With ACEORTV, the prefix OVER will inspire OVERACT. Similarly with the racks AINOORT, AGEINOS and AEFHLTU it may only be by forming the endings -TION, -ISE and -FUL that you will stumble across ORATION, AGONISE and HATEFUL respectively. Also, splitting your rack into two shorter words may enable you to spot an allowable compound word. For example, the unlikely ADEEESW yields SEA and WEED (SEAWEED) and AADORWY makes ROAD and WAY (ROADWAY).

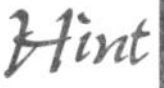

Looking at Hooks

The 2-, 3- and 4-letter hook words are probably the most important of the hook words. Try to learn a few useful ones at a time and attempt to introduce them into your game. An interesting exercise to assist is as follows:
Take each letter of the alphabet and find a 2-, 3- and 4-letter word that takes that letter before or after as a hook to make a longer word. There may be none for some of the more awkward letters. This will give you a balanced variety of some 100 hook words to study.
Note that, for ruthless blocking strategies, the 3- and 4-letter words that do not take hook letters before or after are just as important.

HEAVY WORDS (Many Consonants) except -S extensions

2-letter words – no vowels except Y

BY CH FY HM KY MM MY NY PH SH ST

3-letter words – no vowels except Y

BRR CLY CRY CWM DRY FLY FRY GYM GYP HMM HYP LYM NTH NYS PHT PLY PRY PST PYX RHY SHH SHY SKY SLY SNY SPY STY SWY SYN THY TRY TSK TWP TYG VLY WHY WRY WYN

4-letter words – no vowels except Y

BRRR BYRL CYST FYRD GYMP GYNY HWYL HYMN JYNX KYND LYNX MYTH PFFT PSST RYND SCRY SKRY SKYR SPRY SYNC SYND SYPH TRYP TYMP TYND TYPP TYPY WYCH WYND WYNN XYST YMPT

5-letter words – no vowels except Y

CHYND CRWTH CRYPT DRYLY FLYBY GHYLL GLYPH GRYPT GYNNY GYPPY GYPSY KYDST LYMPH LYNCH MYRRH MYTHY NYMPH PHPHT PSYCH PYGMY SHYLY SLYLY STYMY SYLPH SYNCH SYNTH THYMY TRYST WRYLY XYLYL

6-letter words – one vowel

BLANCH	CRANCH	GLITCH	PLIGHT	SCORCH	SHRIFT	SMUTCH	SPRONG	STRIPT	THRILL
BLENCH	CRANTS	GLUMPS	PLINTH	SCOTCH	SHRILL	SNATCH	SPRUNG	STROLL	THRIST
BLIGHT	CRATCH	GLUNCH	PLONGD	SCOWTH	SHRIMP	SNITCH	SPRUSH	STROMB	THRONG
BLINTZ	CROTCH	GRINCH	PRANCK	SCRAMB	SHRINK	SPARTH	STANCH	STROND	THROWN
BLOTCH	CRUNCH	GROWTH	PROMPT	SCRAWL	SHROFF	SPELTZ	STANCK	STRONG	THRUSH
BORSCH	CRUTCH	GRUMPH	PUTSCH	SCRAWM	SHROWD	SPERST	STARCH	STROWN	THRUST
BORSHT	CULTCH	GRUTCH	RHYTHM	SCRIMP	SHRUNK	SPETCH	STENCH	STRUCK	THWACK
BRANCH	DIRNDL	HIGHTH	SCARPH	SCRIPT	SHTCHI	SPHINX	STITCH	STRUNG	THWART
BRIGHT	DRACHM	KIRSCH	SCARTH	SCROLL	SHTETL	SPIGHT	STOWND	STRUNT	TRENCH
BROWST	DRENCH	KITSCH	SCATCH	SCROWL	SHTICK	SPILTH	STRAFF	SWARTH	TROGGS
BRUNCH	DROWND	KLATCH	SCHELM	SCRUFF	SHTUCK	SPLASH	STRAMP	SWATCH	TROWTH
CATCHT	FLANCH	KLEPHT	SCHISM	SCRUMP	SHTUMM	SPLENT	STRAND	SWITCH	TSKING
CHINCH	FLENCH	KNICKS	SCHIST	SCRUNT	SKARTH	SPLIFF	STRANG	SWOWND	TSKTSK
CHINTS	FLETCH	KNIGHT	SCHLEP	SCULPT	SKETCH	SPLINT	STRASS	TCHICK	TWIGHT
CHINTZ	FLIGHT	KNITCH	SCHNOZ	SCUTCH	SKLENT	SPLOSH	STRATH	THATCH	TWITCH
CHRISM	FLINCH	KRANTZ	SCHORL	SHLEPP	SKLIFF	SPRACK	STRAWN	THETCH	WARMTH
CHURCH	FLITCH	KVETCH	SCHRIK	SHLOCK	SKRIMP	SPRANG	STRESS	THIRST	WHILST
CLASPT	FLYSCH	LENGTH	SCHROD	SHLUMP	SKRUMP	SPRAWL	STREWN	THRALL	WHISHT
CLATCH	FRATCH	MENSCH	SCHTIK	SHMOCK	SLATCH	SPREDD	STRICH	THRANG	WRENCH
CLENCH	FRENCH	MONGST	SCHULN	SHMUCK	SLIGHT	SPRENT	STRICK	THRASH	WRETCH
CLINCH	FRICHT	PHLEGM	SCHUSS	SHNAPS	SMATCH	SPRING	STRICT	THRAWN	WRIGHT
CLUNCH	FRIGHT	PLANCH	SCLAFF	SHRANK	SMIGHT	SPRINT	STRIFT	THRESH	
CLUTCH	FROWST	PLENCH	SCLIFF	SHREWD	SMIRCH	SPRITZ	STRING	THRIFT	

Hint

Fishing

It is rarely worth holding on to a set of letters hoping to pick up that one tile that will transform your rack into a wonderful high-scoring bonus word. However, if the six letters you are holding on to are likely to yield a bonus play with *many* of the tiles that you are likely to pick up (see Bonus Word Sets section) then 'fishing' could be strategically beneficial. Always consider the chances of actually getting the tile or tiles you hope for and balance this against any alternative scoring plays. Knowledge of the letter distribution and the most fruitful 6-letter combinations is mandatory for timely 'fishing'.

Hint

Mind Your Changing

Since it is permissible to change any number of your letters instead of a turn during a game (unless there are fewer than seven tiles in the bag), it can be a wise decision to change some or all of your letters even if you can find a word to play on the board. You should consider changing when:

- ☆ You have an imbalance of vowels and consonants and the available dump words do not solve your rack problems, score very little, or provide too many scoring opportunities for your opponent.
- ☆ There are no scoring opportunities on the board and you don't wish to block your opponent with a low-scoring play.
- ☆ You have a Q with no U and none of the U-less Q words is playable. Note that the existence of QI makes the Q less of a problem, and it may be worth forgoing changing if you can score well with your other letters and there are still I's left.
- ☆ You have a promising 6-letter combination that combines well with many other letters to make a 7-letter word – but not with the seventh letter on your rack. Changing the odd letter in this situation is often not the best strategic move but the time for such a change may be ripe if you desperately need the bonus to catch up or there are no other worthwhile alternatives.

Awkward Vowel Dumps

Having two of the same vowel on your rack, except perhaps when they are two E's, is often a problem; it can be a nightmare when you are confronted with more than two, especially if they are I's or U's.

Playing just one of the multiple vowels does not always solve the problem, and you can go on being faced with the same problem on subsequent turns. This of course does not help your game. Ideally the solution needs to be found in one turn.

The following lists of words containing multiple A's, E's, I's, O's or U's will be very helpful in such situations.

The lists are summarized below:

A words:	3-letter words, 2 A's (eg ABA, BAA)
	4-letter words, 2 A's (eg AWAY, LAVA)
	5- letter words, 3 A's (eg ABACA, KAAMA)
	6-letter words, 3 A's (eg BANANA, BAZAAR)
E words:	4-letter words, 3 E's (EPEE)
	5-letter words, 3 E's (eg GEESE, MELEE)
	6-letter words, 4 E's (eg PEEWEE, TEEPEE)
I words:	4-letter words, 2 I's (eg IRIS, KIWI)
	5-letter words, 2 I's (eg ICING, RIGID)
	6-letter words, 3 I's (eg BIKINI, IRITIC)
O words:	5-letter words, 3 O's (OVOLO, POTOO)
	6-letter words, 3 O's or more (eg COCOON, VOODOO)
U words:	3-letter words, 2 U's (ULU, UTU)
	4-letter words, 2 U's (eg GURU, LUAU)
	5-letter words, 2 U's or more (eg AUGUR, UHURU)
	6-letter words, 3 U's or more (eg MUTUUM, MUUMUU)

Note that there is no list of 4-letter words with two O's – it is not too difficult to play a couple of O's in a 4-letter word. As a start, think of all the words (such as FOOD) with a double O in them.

3-letter words with two E's or two O's are also not difficult, and there are no 3-letter words with two I's.

AWKWARD VOWEL DUMPS – A's

3-letter words – 2 A's

AAH AAL AAS ABA AGA AHA AIA ALA AMA ANA AVA AWA BAA MAA

4-letter words – 2 A's

AAHS AALS ABAC ABAS ABBA ACTA ADAW AFAR AGAR AGAS AGHA
AGMA AIAS AJAR ALAE ALAN ALAP ALAR ALAS ALAY ALBA ALFA
ALGA ALMA AMAH AMAS AMIA AMLA ANAL ANAN ANAS ANGA ANNA
ANOA ANSA ANTA APAY AQUA ARAK ARAR ARBA AREA ARIA ARNA
ASAR ASEA ATAP ATMA AULA AURA AVAL AVAS AWAY AXAL AYAH
AZAN BAAL BAAS BABA CABA CACA CAPA CASA DADA DATA FAVA
GAGA GALA GAMA HAAF HAAR HAHA HAKA JAVA KAAS KAKA KAMA
KANA KAPA KARA KATA KAVA LAMA LANA LAVA MAAR MAAS MAMA
MANA MARA MASA MAYA NAAM NAAN NADA NAGA NALA NANA NAPA
PACA PAPA PARA PAUA PAWA RACA RAGA RAIA RAJA RANA RATA

RAYA SAMA TAKA TANA TARA TAWA VARA WAKA
SAGA TAHA TALA TAPA TAVA TAXA VASA

5-letter words – 3 A's

ABACA ABAYA AGAMA ALAPA ARABA KAAMA
ABAKA AFARA ALAAP ANANA ASANA

6-letter words – 3 A's

ABACAS AGAPAI ANABAS ARMADA BAHADA CABANA JATAKA KATANA PANADA TAIAHA
ABAKAS ALAAPS ANANAS ASANAS BAJADA CANADA KAAMAS LABARA PANAMA TAMARA
ABASIA ALALIA ANATTA ASRAMA BALATA CASABA KABAKA MANANA PAPAYA TARAMA
ABAYAS ALAPAS ANTARA ATABAL BANANA CASAVA KABALA MARACA PATACA UJAMAA
ACACIA ALASKA ARABAS ATAMAN BARAZA DAGABA KABAYA MASALA SALAAM ZANANA
AFARAS ALBATA ARALIA ATAXIA BATATA HALALA KAMALA NAGANA SAMAAN ZAPATA
AGAMAS ALPACA ARCANA AVATAR BAZAAR HAMADA KANAKA PAJAMA SAMARA
AGAPAE AMARNA ARGALA AZALEA CABALA JACANA KARAKA PALAMA SATARA

AWKWARD VOWEL DUMPS – E's

4-letter words – 3 E's

EPEE

5-letter words – 3 E's

BELEE EERIE EMEER EXEME GELEE LEVEE NEEZE PEWEE SEMEE WEETE
BESEE EEVEN EPEES FEESE HEEZE MELEE PEECE REEDE TEENE
DEERE ELPEE ETWEE FEEZE KEEVE NEELE PEEPE REEVE TEPEE
DEEVE EMCEE EXEEM GEESE LEESE NEESE PEEVE RESEE WEEKE

6-letter words – 4 E's

BEEBEE PEEWEE TEEPEE VEEPEE WEEWEE

AWKWARD VOWEL DUMPS – I's

4-letter words – 2 I's

DIVI IBIS INIA IWIS MIDI NISI SIMI TITI
DIXI ILIA INTI IXIA MINI PIKI SIRI WILI
FINI IMID IRID KIWI MIRI PILI TIKI ZITI
HILI IMPI IRIS LIRI NIDI PIPI TIPI

5-letter words – 2 I's

AALII CHILI FICIN IMARI INTIS KIKOI LIVID OBIIT RIGID VILLI
ACINI CILIA FINIS IMIDE INWIT KILIM MEDII OIDIA RISHI VINIC
AIDOI CIPPI FIXIT IMIDO IODIC KININ MIDIS ORIBI SIGIL VIRID
AIOLI CIRRI GENII IMIDS IODID KIRRI MILIA PIING SIMIS VISIE
ALIBI CIVIC IAMBI IMINE IODIN KIWIS MIMIC PIKIS SIRIH VISIT
AMICI CIVIE ICIER IMINO IONIC LIBRI MINIM PILEI SIRIS VIVID
ANIMI CIVIL ICILY IMMIT IRIDS LICHI MINIS PILIS TEIID VIZIR
BIALI DIDIE ICING IMMIX IRING LICIT MIRIN PIPIS TIBIA WIFIE
BIFID DIGIT ICTIC IMPIS ISSEI LIKIN MITIS PIPIT TIKIS WILIS
BIKIE DILLI IDIOM IMSHI IVIED LIMBI MODII PIRAI TIMID ZIMBI
BINDI DINIC IDIOT INDIE IVIES LIMIT NIHIL PIXIE TIPIS ZITIS
BINIT DISCI ILIAC INDRI IXIAS LININ NIMBI PRIMI TITIS ZIZIT
BIVIA DIVIS ILIAD INFIX JINNI LIPID NISEI RADII TORII
BLINI DIXIE ILIAL INION KIBBI LIPIN NITID REIKI VIGIA
CEILI DIXIT ILIUM INTIL KIBEI LITAI NIXIE RICIN VIGIL

6-letter words – 3 I's

BIKINI IMIDIC IRIDIC IRITIC IRITIS MIRITI

AWKWARD VOWEL DUMPS – O's

5-letter words – 3 O's

OVOLO POTOO

6-letter words – 3 O's or more

BOOBOO	COMODO	DOOCOT	GOOROO	HOOPOE	KOODOO	OVOLOS	ROTOLO
BOOHOO	COOCOO	FORHOO	HOLLOO	HOOPOO	OOLOGY	POTOOS	VOODOO
COCOON	COROZO	GOOGOL	HOODOO	HOOROO	OOLONG	ROCOCO	ZOOZOO

AWKWARD VOWEL DUMPS – U's

3-letter words – 2 U's

ULU UTU

4-letter words – 2 U's

FUGU	KUDU	KUZU	MUMU	PULU	TUTU	URUS
GURU	KUKU	LUAU	PUDU	RURU	ULUS	UTUS
JUJU	KURU	LULU	PUKU	SULU	UNAU	ZULU

5-letter words – 2 U's or more

AUGUR	BUTUT	GURUS	KUKUS	LUSUS	PULUS	SUNUP	UNCUT	USQUE	VOULU
AURUM	CUTUP	HUMUS	KURUS	MUCUS	QUEUE	TUQUE	UNDUE	USUAL	WUSHU
BUCHU	DURUM	JUGUM	KUZUS	MUMUS	QUIPU	TUTUS	UNDUG	USURE	ZULUS
BUCKU	FUCUS	JUJUS	LUAUS	MUNTU	RUBUS	UHURU	UNGUM	USURP	
BUNDU	FUGUE	KUDUS	LULUS	PUDUS	RURUS	UNAUS	UPRUN	USURY	
BUSSU	FUGUS	KUDZU	LUPUS	PUKUS	SULUS	UNCUS	URUBU	UVULA	

6-letter words – 3 U's or more

MUTUUM MUUMUU UHURUS URUBUS

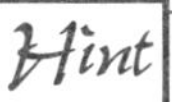

Flashcards

A popular way of testing Scrabble vocabulary is a system called flashcards. Small index cards are used which have 'questions' on one side and the 'answer words' on the reverse. For example if you were using flashcards to learn 2-letter words you may have on one card A=16, with the 16 2-letter words beginning with A on the reverse. On another card B=5, and another C=1, would reveal BA, BE, BI, BO, BYand CH on the reverse respectively. Whenever you get a moment you can quickly flick through the cards and test yourself. The system can be used for many categories such as five-vowelled 7-letter words, words containing J Q X Z, and so on. A good use of flashcards is to log every 7-letter word played against you that you didn't know, thus naturally building up your personal testing library.

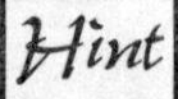

Fighting Back

Don't trade off catching up with poor rack retention. A more balanced rack will enable a greater choice of strategic plays in subsequent turns. Initially concentrate on not slipping any further behind and be wary of scoring opportunities open only to yourself. Perhaps you have the last S, or the last A for an (A)JAR hook, and so on. Try to keep the board open unless you can block and catch up in a single play. If your opponent is in front it is likely their rack is worsening whilst they are blocking. Keeping the board open and maintaining your rack balance will keep your hopes alive whereas playing too defensively will only assist your opponent to keep their lead.

Hint

Passing Thoughts

It is allowable to pass in Scrabble, that is, to not play a word or change any tiles. This is in effect what a player does at the end of the game if stuck with any unplayable tiles. However, it is rarely worth passing during the game in the hope that the opponent will give you that vital opening or letter you need.

An example of an occasion where passing may be of advantage is if you have a good rack such as TAILEND and it is your play first, or your opponent has just changed letters instead of playing first. Since TAILEND combines with each of the four vowels (A E O U) to make an 8-letter word (DENTALIA, DATELINE or ENTAILED or LINEATED, DELATION, UNTAILED), it is likely your opponent may give you a bonus play next turn.

Hint

Learn As You Play

Always have a scrap of paper with you other than the scoresheet. Jot down any promising racks you find yourself with, 7-letter words you played that might have anagrams, and any words you think of playing but are unsure of. After the game spend a few minutes with *Official Scrabble® Lists International* and check out your words and racks, noting any new discoveries. Going through this exercise after every game will gradually strengthen your vocabulary without too much effort.

Awkward Consonant Dumps

The following lists are of words of three to five letters containing one of the following consonants at least twice – B, C, F, H, V, W and Y. (Note that Y is considered here as a consonant, regardless of whether it is acting as a vowel or a consonant in any individual word.) It is usually not too difficult to dump one of these awkward consonants in an attempt to achieve a reasonable score and balance your rack. Dumping two F's, H's, and so on is more of a problem. These lists should help with your awkward consonant racks.

The lists are arranged so that all the B words come together, then the C words, and so on. The 3-letter B words come before the 4-letter B words, which come before the 5-letter B words. Similarly for the other awkward consonants.

There are no 3-letter words having two C's.

AWKWARD CONSONANT DUMPS – B's

3-letter words – 2 B's

ABB BIB BOB BUB EBB

4-letter words – 2 B's or more

ABBA BABA BABY BIBS BLOB BOBS BUBA BULB JIBB
ABBE BABE BARB BLAB BLUB BOMB BUBO COBB SIBB
ABBS BABU BIBB BLEB BOBA BOOB BUBS EBBS

5-letter words – 2 B's or more

ABBAS BABUL BIMBO BOBBY BUBBY CUBBY GOBBI KIBBE RIBBY YOBBO
ABBES BABUS BLABS BOMBE BULBS CUBEB GOBBO KIBBI SIBBS ZEBUB
ABBEY BARBE BLEBS BOMBO BUMBO DEBBY HOBBY LOBBY SLUBB
ABBOT BARBS BLOBS BOMBS BURBS DIBBS HUBBY MOBBY SUBBY
BABAS BEBOP BLUBS BOOBS BUSBY DOBBY JIBBS NABOB SYBBE
BABEL BEROB BLURB BOOBY CABBY EBBED KABAB NOBBY TABBY
BABES BIBBS BOBAC BRIBE CABOB EBBET KABOB NUBBY TUBBY
BABKA BIBLE BOBAK BUBAL COBBS FUBBY KEBAB RABBI WEBBY
BABOO BILBO BOBAS BUBAS COBBY GABBY KEBOB REBBE YABBY

AWKWARD CONSONANT DUMPS – C's

4-letter words – 2 C's

CACA CHIC COCA COCK CROC ECCO
CECA CHOC COCH COCO ECCE

5-letter words – 2 C's or more

ACCOY CABOC CERCI CHICS CIVIC COCCI CONIC CUBIC CYNIC SUCCI
ACMIC CACAO CERIC CHOCK CLACH COCCO COOCH CULCH ICTIC TICCA
ACOCK CACAS CHACE CHOCO CLACK COCKS COSEC CUMEC MECCA WICCA
BACCA CACHE CHACK CHOCS CLECK COCKY COUCH CURCH OCCAM YACCA
BACCO CACTI CHACO CHUCK CLICK COCOA CRACK CUSEC OCCUR YECCH
BACCY CAECA CHECK CINCH CLOCK COCOS CRICK CUTCH PICCY YUCCA
BICCY CASCO CHICA CINCT CLUCK CODEC CROCI CYCAD RECCE YUCCH
BOCCA CATCH CHICH CIRCA COACH COLIC CROCK CYCAS RECCO ZOCCO
BOCCE CECAL CHICK CIRCS COACT COMIC CROCS CYCLE RECCY
BOCCI CECUM CHICO CISCO COCAS CONCH CRUCK CYCLO SECCO

AWKWARD CONSONANT DUMPS – F's

3-letter words – 2 F's

AFF EFF IFF OFF

4-letter words – 2 F's or more

AFFY	CAFF	DUFF	FUFF	HUFF	LUFF	NUFF	RIFF	TUFF
BAFF	COFF	EFFS	GAFF	IFFY	MIFF	OFFS	RUFF	WAFF
BIFF	CUFF	FAFF	GOFF	JEFF	MUFF	PFFT	TEFF	YAFF
BOFF	DAFF	FIEF	GUFF	JIFF	NAFF	PUFF	TIFF	ZIFF
BUFF	DOFF	FIFE	HAFF	KOFF	NIFF	RAFF	TOFF	

5-letter words – 2 F's or more

AFFIX	BUFFO	DAFFS	FIFES	GRAFF	JIFFY	NYAFF	REFFO	SNUFF	TRIFF
BAFFS	BUFFS	DAFFY	FIFTH	GRIFF	KOFFS	OFFAL	RIFFS	SOWFF	TUFFE
BAFFY	BUFFY	DOFFS	FIFTY	GRUFF	LUFFA	OFFED	RUFFE	SPIFF	TUFFS
BIFFS	CAFFS	DRAFF	FLAFF	GUFFS	LUFFS	OFFER	RUFFS	STAFF	WAFFS
BIFFY	CHAFF	DUFFS	FLUFF	HAFFS	MIFFS	PLUFF	SCAFF	STIFF	WAUFF
BLUFF	CHUFF	EFFED	FUFFS	HOUFF	MIFFY	POUFF	SCOFF	STUFF	WHIFF
BOFFO	CLIFF	FAFFS	FUFFY	HOWFF	MUFFS	PUFFS	SCUFF	TAFFY	YAFFS
BOFFS	CLOFF	FEOFF	GAFFE	HUFFS	NAFFS	PUFFY	SKIFF	TEFFS	ZIFFS
BUFFA	COFFS	FIEFS	GAFFS	HUFFY	NIFFS	QUAFF	SKOFF	TIFFS	
BUFFE	CUFFO	FIFED	GLIFF	JEFFS	NIFFY	QUIFF	SLUFF	TOFFS	
BUFFI	CUFFS	FIFER	GOFFS	JIFFS	NUFFS	RAFFS	SNIFF	TOFFY	

AWKWARD CONSONANT DUMPS – H's

3-letter words – 2 H's

HAH HEH HOH HUH SHH

4-letter words – 2 H's

HAHA	HASH	HECH	HETH	HISH	HOHS	HUSH	SHAH
HAHS	HATH	HEHS	HIGH	HOGH	HUNH	PHOH	

5-letter words – 2 H's

AHIGH	HAITH	HAUGH	HEUCH	HILCH	HOOCH	HUMPH	HYTHE	SHAHS	WHICH
CHETH	HANCH	HEATH	HEUGH	HITCH	HOOSH	HUNCH	KHAPH	SHASH	WHISH
CHICH	HARSH	HECHT	HEWGH	HITHE	HORAH	HUSHY	KHETH	SHCHI	
EPHAH	HASHY	HEIGH	HIGHS	HOGHS	HOTCH	HUTCH	PHOHS	SHUSH	
HAHAS	HATCH	HETHS	HIGHT	HOHED	HOUGH	HYPHA	PHPHT	THIGH	

AWKWARD CONSONANT DUMPS – V's

3-letter words – 2 V's

VAV

4-letter words – 2 V's

VAVS VIVA VIVE VIVO

5-letter words – 2 V's

BEVVY	CIVVY	LUVVY	SAVVY	VARVE	VIVAS	VIVDA	VIVES	VOLVA	VULVA
BIVVY	DIVVY	NAVVY	VALVE	VERVE	VIVAT	VIVER	VIVID	VOLVE	

AWKWARD CONSONANT DUMPS – W's

3-letter words – 2 W's

WAW WOW

4-letter words – 2 W's

WAWE WAWL WAWS WHEW WHOW WOWF WOWS

5-letter words – 2 W's

EWHOW PAWAW WAWES WAWLS WHEWS WIDOW WOWED WOWEE WRAWL

AWKWARD CONSONANT DUMPS – Y's

3-letter words – 2 Y's

YAY

4-letter words – 2 Y's

EYRY GYNY TYPY YAWY YAYS YUKY

5-letter words – 2 Y's

AZYGY	DRYLY	GAYLY	MYOPY	SKYEY	TYPEY	YAPPY	YESTY	YUCKY
BYWAY	DYKEY	GYNNY	MYTHY	SLYLY	WRYLY	YAWEY	YEUKY	YUKKY
COYLY	FEYLY	GYPPY	PYGMY	STYMY	XYLYL	YAWNY	YIPPY	YUMMY
DOYLY	FLYBY	GYPSY	SHYLY	THYMY	YABBY	YECHY	YOLKY	YUPPY

Hint

Rack Balancing

Always try to keep a balanced rack of vowels and consonants. The more balanced your rack the more choice of words you will have each turn and the more chance you will have of being able to play a bonus-scoring 7-letter word. It helps to be aware that there are 42 vowels to 56 consonants (and 2 blanks) in the Scrabble set. That's three vowels for every four consonants. Counting how many vowels and consonants already played at any stage of a game will serve as a useful guide as to the vowel/consonant distribution remaining in the bag. If there is a surplus of consonants left you might wish to counteract your likely consonant pickup by retaining vowels on your rack when you play, or vice versa.
See the Awkward Vowel Dumps list and the Light and Heavy Words list for some words that will help you keep a balanced rack.

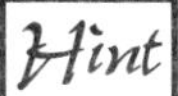

Edging the Endgame

In a tight game where the scores are close there is an advantage in being the player to be the first to play out and finish the game, thus gaining any points remaining on your opponent's rack and depriving him or her of another scoring opportunity. Playing out first is often the difference between winning and losing. A handy tip, whenever you have the opportunity or choice near the end of a game, is to ensure there is a single tile in the bag after your turn. This means that, next turn, you have the first opportunity to play with no tiles remaining in the bag, thus giving you an advantage in planning a 2-move finish. There is further advantage if you have been keeping track of the tiles since you can then have the benefit of the endgame initiative knowing your opponent's exact tiles.

Hint

Combination Management

If you have one of the promising 6-letter combinations given under the Bonus Sets section but unfortunately do not have an appropriate seventh letter to make a bonus word, or the bonus word you have does not fit on the board, then it is wiser not to be overly concerned about holding on to your useful 6-letter combination. Rather than just playing the one letter and hoping for a playable bonus word next turn, play two or three tiles. This will probably enable you to score more whilst still retaining the makings of a bonus word. The skill is in making sure you play off the right letters.

For example, with OILERS and an F on your rack there is no bonus word. Rather than just play the F, in the hope of picking a B for BOILERS or a U for LOUSIER perhaps, it is better to play IF or OF. The retention of OLERS and ILERS with a vowel pickup next turn is likely to produce another good 6-letter combination such as AILERS, OILERS or RELIES, and hopefully an obliging seventh letter to make a bonus play. If it doesn't, well at least you've scored some points meanwhile.

Hint

Unusual Clues

In browsing through the Anagram section you will find an abundance of unusual 7- and 8-letter words. Some of these are more useful than others, depending on their constituent letters. Those consisting of just the 1- and 2-point Scrabble tiles (ie A D E G I L N O R S T U) are more likely to appear on your rack and are the ones to concentrate on. A good way to remember these words is by making up a non-existent anagram that you are more likely to form on your rack and that will act as an aide-mémoire. For example, the likely rack ELNOSTU yields the bonus word LENTOUS which may best be recalled as the anagram of the non-existent OUTLENS. Similarly, SEERING makes GREISEN and LOOTIER makes TROOLIE. Both SEERING and LOOTIER are not actual words but merely the clues to GREISEN and TROOLIE. Where there is a more common anagram of an unusual word then this naturally serves as a clue, eg OUTLINE gives ELUTION and AGAINST gives GITANAS and ANTISAG.

Hint

Knowing Non-Words

Much time can be wasted in a game when you have a promising-looking set of seven letters on your rack but can't remember whether they make a 7-letter word or not. Therefore it is also beneficial to be familiar with those common sets of seven letters that *don't* make a 7-letter word. Some examples are: ENRAISE, ORALISE, and TAILEND. Note that by forming 'non-words' with these racks they can be more easily recognized during play. Having armed yourself with a selection of non-words the next task is to learn the possible 8-letter plays so that you can be aware of possible bonus plays using available letters on the board. For example, the TAILEND set makes 8-letter words with the letters A B D E F G N O P U V. These words and those of other non-words mentioned above can be readily unearthed from the 8-Letter Bonus Sets. For other non-words you might create, such as IRELAND, that don't appear in the top 8-Letter Bonus Sets, you will be able to use the 8-Letter Anagram lists to discover the relevant 8-letter words.

K and V Words

The following lists contain all the words of length two to five letters which have one or more of either a K or a V in them. Words with K or V can be particularly useful for scoring perhaps 40 or so points, helping you at the same time to offload otherwise awkward letters. If a word contains both K and V, it will appear in both the K and V lists.

K-WORDS

K – 2-letter words

KA KO KY

K – 3-letter words

AKE	EKE	IRK	KAT	KEN	KIN	KOP	MAK	SKA	YAK
ARK	ELK	JAK	KAW	KEP	KIP	KOR	NEK	SKI	YOK
ASK	ERK	KAB	KAY	KET	KIR	KOS	OAK	SKY	YUK
AUK	EUK	KAE	KEA	KEX	KIT	KOW	OIK	SUK	ZEK
BOK	EWK	KAF	KEB	KEY	KOA	KUE	OKA	TAK	
DAK	ICK	KAI	KED	KHI	KOB	KYE	OKE	TSK	
EEK	ILK	KAM	KEF	KID	KOI	KYU	OUK	UKE	
EIK	INK	KAS	KEG	KIF	KON	LEK	ROK	WOK	

K – 4-letter words

AKED	BUIK	DISK	GEEK	INKS	KAMA	KEKS	KILN	KNUT	KYND
AKEE	BUKE	DOCK	GINK	INKY	KAME	KELL	KILO	KOAN	KYNE
AKES	BULK	DOEK	GONK	IRKS	KAMI	KELP	KILP	KOAS	KYTE
AKIN	BUNK	DOOK	GOOK	JACK	KANA	KELT	KILT	KOBO	KYUS
ALKY	BURK	DORK	GOUK	JAKE	KANE	KEMB	KINA	KOBS	LACK
AMOK	BUSK	DREK	GOWK	JAKS	KANG	KEMP	KIND	KOEL	LAIK
ANKH	BYKE	DUCK	GUCK	JARK	KANS	KENO	KINE	KOFF	LAKE
ARAK	CAKE	DUKE	GUNK	JAUK	KANT	KENS	KING	KOHL	LAKH
ARKS	CAKY	DUNK	HACK	JERK	KAON	KENT	KINK	KOLA	LAKY
ASKS	CALK	DUSK	HAIK	JINK	KAPA	KEPI	KINO	KOLO	LANK
ATOK	CARK	DYKE	HAKA	JOCK	KAPH	KEPS	KINS	KOND	LARK
AUKS	CASK	EIKS	HAKE	JOKE	KARA	KEPT	KIPE	KONK	LAWK
BACK	CAUK	EKED	HANK	JOKY	KARK	KERB	KIPP	KONS	LEAK
BAKE	CAWK	EKES	HARK	JOOK	KARN	KERF	KIPS	KOOK	LEEK
BALK	CHIK	EKKA	HASK	JOUK	KART	KERN	KIRK	KOPH	LEKE
BANK	COCK	ELKS	HAWK	JUKE	KATA	KESH	KIRN	KOPS	LEKS
BARK	COKE	ERKS	HECK	JUNK	KATI	KEST	KIRS	KORA	LEKU
BASK	COKY	ESKY	HICK	KAAS	KATS	KETA	KISH	KORE	LICK
BAUK	CONK	EUKS	HIKE	KABS	KAVA	KETO	KISS	KORS	LIKE
BEAK	COOK	EWKS	HOCK	KADE	KAWS	KETS	KIST	KOSS	LINK
BECK	CORK	FAIK	HOIK	KADI	KAYO	KEYS	KITE	KOTO	LIRK
BERK	CUKE	FAKE	HOKE	KAED	KAYS	KHAF	KITH	KOWS	LISK
BIKE	CUSK	FANK	HOKI	KAES	KAZI	KHAN	KITS	KRAB	LOCK
BILK	DAKS	FECK	HOLK	KAFS	KBAR	KHAT	KIVA	KRIS	LOKE
BINK	DANK	FIKE	HONK	KAGO	KEAS	KHET	KIWI	KSAR	LOOK
BIRK	DARK	FIKY	HOOK	KAGU	KEBS	KHIS	KNAG	KUDO	LUCK
BISK	DAWK	FINK	HOWK	KAID	KECK	KHOR	KNAP	KUDU	LUKE
BOAK	DECK	FIRK	HUCK	KAIE	KEDS	KHUD	KNAR	KUES	LUNK
BOCK	DEEK	FISK	HULK	KAIF	KEEF	KIBE	KNEE	KUKU	LURK
BOKE	DEKE	FLAK	HUNK	KAIL	KEEK	KICK	KNEW	KURI	LUSK
BOKO	DESK	FOLK	HUSK	KAIM	KEEL	KIDS	KNIT	KURU	MACK
BOKS	DHAK	FORK	HYKE	KAIN	KEEN	KIEF	KNOB	KUZU	MAIK
BONK	DICK	FUCK	ICKY	KAIS	KEEP	KIER	KNOP	KVAS	MAKE
BOOK	DIKA	FUNK	IKAT	KAKA	KEET	KIFS	KNOT	KYAK	MAKO
BOSK	DIKE	FYKE	IKON	KAKI	KEFS	KIKE	KNOW	KYAR	MAKS
BOUK	DINK	GAWK	ILKA	KALE	KEGS	KILD	KNUB	KYAT	MARK
BUCK	DIRK	GECK	ILKS	KALI	KEIR	KILL	KNUR	KYLE	MASK

MAWK MEEK MERK MICK MIKE MILK MINK MIRK MOCK MOKE MOKI MOKO MONK MOOK MOSK MUCK MURK MUSK NABK NAIK NARK NECK

NEKS NERK NEUK NICK NOCK NOOK NORK NUKE OAKS OAKY OIKS OINK OKAS OKAY OKEH OKES OKRA OKTA OUKS OULK PACK PAIK

PARK PAWK PEAK PECK PEEK PEKE PENK PERK PICK PIKA PIKE PIKI PINK POCK POKE POKY POLK PONK POOK PORK POUK PUCK

PUKE PUKU PULK PUNK RACK RAIK RAKE RAKI RAKU RANK REAK RECK REEK REIK REKE RICK RINK RISK ROCK ROKE ROKS ROKY

ROOK RUCK RUKH RUSK RYKE SACK SAKE SAKI SANK SARK SEEK SEIK SEKT SERK SICK SIKA SIKE SILK SINK SKAG SKAS SKAT

SKAW SKEE SKEG SKEO SKEP SKER SKEW SKID SKIM SKIN SKIO SKIP SKIS SKIT SKOL SKRY SKUA SKUG SKYR SOAK SOCK SOKE

SOOK SOUK SPEK SPIK SUCK SUKH SUKS SULK SUNK SYKE TACK TAKA TAKE TAKI TAKS TAKY TALK TANK TASK TEAK TICK TIKA

TIKE TIKI TINK TOCK TOKE TOKO TONK TOOK TOUK TREK TSKS TUCK TURK TUSK TYKE UKES VOLK WACK WAKA WAKE WAKF WALK

WANK WARK WAUK WEAK WEEK WEKA WELK WICK WINK WOCK WOKE WOKS WONK WORK YACK YAKS YANK YELK YERK YESK YEUK YIKE

YIRK YLKE YOCK YOKE YOKS YOLK YORK YOUK YUCK YUKE YUKO YUKS YUKY ZACK ZEKS ZERK ZONK ZOUK

K – 5-letter words

ABACK ABAKA ABASK ACKEE ACOCK AKEES AKELA AKENE AKING AKKAS ALACK ALIKE ALKIE ALKYD ALKYL AMOKS AMUCK ANKER ANKHS ANKLE ANKUS APEAK APEEK ARAKS ARKED ASKED ASKER ASKEW ASKOI ASKOS ATOKE ATOKS AWAKE AWOKE AWORK BABKA BACKS BAKED BAKEN BAKER BAKES BALKS BALKY BANKS BARKS BARKY BASKS BATIK BAUKS

BAULK BEAKS BEAKY BECKE BECKS BEKAH BERKS BIKED BIKER BIKES BIKIE BILKS BINKS BIRKS BISKS BLACK BLANK BLEAK BLINK BLOCK BLOKE BLUNK BOAKS BOBAK BOCKS BOINK BOKED BOKES BOKOS BONKS BOOKS BOOKY BORAK BOSKS BOSKY BOUKS BRACK BRAKE BRAKY BRANK BREAK BRICK BRINK BRISK BROCK BROKE BROOK BRUSK BUCKO

BUCKS BUCKU BUIKS BUKES BULKS BULKY BUNKO BUNKS BURKA BURKE BURKS BUSKS BUSKY BYKED BYKES CAKED CAKES CAKEY CALKS CARKS CASKS CASKY CAUKS CAULK CAWKS CHACK CHALK CHANK CHARK CHECK CHEEK CHEKA CHICK CHIKS CHINK CHIRK CHOCK CHOKE CHOKO CHOKY CHOOK CHUCK CHUNK CLACK CLANK CLECK CLEEK CLERK CLICK

CLINK CLOAK CLOCK CLOKE CLONK CLUCK CLUNK COCKS COCKY COKED COKES CONKS CONKY COOKS COOKY CORKS CORKY CRACK CRAKE CRANK CREAK CREEK CRICK CROAK CROCK CRONK CROOK CRUCK CUKES CUSKS DAKER DANKS DARKS DARKY DAWKS DECKO DECKS DEKED DEKES DEKKO DESKS DHAKS DICKS DICKY DIKAS DIKED DIKER DIKES DIKEY

DINKS DINKY DIRKE DIRKS DISKS DOCKS DOEKS DOOKS DORKS DORKY DRAKE DRANK DRECK DREKS DRINK DROOK DROUK DRUNK DUCKS DUCKY DUKED DUKES DUMKA DUMKY DUNKS DUSKS DUSKY DYKED DYKES DYKEY EIKED EIKON EKING EKKAS ENOKI ENSKY ERICK ESKAR ESKER EUKED EVOKE EWKED FAIKS FAKED FAKER FAKES FAKEY FAKIR FANKS

FECKS FENKS FIKED FIKES FINKS FIRKS FISKS FLACK FLAKE FLAKS FLAKY FLANK FLASK FLECK FLICK FLISK FLOCK FLUKE FLUKY FLUNK FOLKS FOLKY FORKS FORKY FRACK FRANK FREAK FRISK FROCK FUCKS FUNKS FUNKY FYKED FYKES GAWKS GAWKY GECKO GECKS GEEKS GEEKY GINKS GLAIK GLEEK GLIKE GLISK GONKS GOOKS GOOKY GOPAK

GOUKS GOWKS GREEK GRIKE GRYKE GUCKS GUCKY GUNKS GUNKY HACEK HACKS HAICK HAIKA HAIKS HAIKU HAKAM HAKAS HAKES HAKIM HANKS HANKY HARKS HASKS HAWKS HECKS HICKS HIKED HIKER HIKES HOCKS HOICK HOIKS HOKED HOKES HOKEY HOKIS HOKKU HOKUM HOLKS HONKS HONKY HOOKA HOOKS HOOKY HOWKS HUCKS HULKS HULKY HUNKS

HUNKY HUSKS HUSKY HYKES ICKER IKATS IKONS INKED INKER INKLE IRKED IROKO JACKS JACKY JAKES JARKS JAUKS JERKS JERKY JINKS JOCKO JOCKS JOKED JOKER JOKES JOKEY JOKOL JOOKS JOUKS JUKED JUKES JUNKS JUNKY KAAMA KABAB KABAR KABOB KACHA KADES KADIS KAFIR KAGOS KAGUS KAHAL KAIAK KAIDS KAIES KAIFS KAILS

KAIMS KAING KAINS KAKAS KAKIS KALAM KALES KALIF KALIS KALPA KAMAS KAMES KAMIK KAMIS KAMME KANAS KANDY KANEH KANES KANGA KANGS KANJI KANTS KANZU KAONS KAPAS KAPHS KAPOK KAPPA KAPUT KARAS KARAT KARKS KARMA KARNS KAROO KARRI KARST KARSY KARTS KARZY KASHA KATAS KATIS KATTI KAUGH KAURI KAURY KAVAS

KAWED KAYAK KAYLE KAYOS KAZIS KAZOO KBARS KEBAB KEBAR KEBOB KECKS KEDGE KEDGY KEECH KEEFS KEEKS KEELS KEENS KEEPS KEETS KEEVE KEFIR KEIRS KELEP KELIM KELLS KELLY KELPS KELPY KELTS KELTY KEMBO KEMBS KEMPS KEMPT KENAF KENCH KENDO KENOS KENTS KEPIS KERBS KERFS KERNE KERNS KERRY KERVE KESAR KESTS

KETAS KETCH KETOL KEVEL KEVIL KEXES KEYED KHADI KHAFS KHAKI KHANS KHAPH KHATS KHAYA KHEDA KHETH KHETS KHOJA KHORS KHOUM KHUDS KIANG KIBBE KIBBI KIBEI KIBES KIBLA KICKS KICKY KIDDO KIDDY KIDEL KIDGE KIEFS KIERS KIEVE KIGHT KIKES KIKOI KILEY KILIM KILLS KILNS KILOS KILPS KILTS KILTY KIMBO KINAS KINDA KINDS KINDY KINES KINGS KININ KINKS KINKY KINOS KIOSK KIPES KIPPA KIPPS KIRKS KIRNS KIRRI KISAN KISSY KISTS KITED KITER KITES KITHE KITHS KITTY KIVAS

KIWIS KLANG KLONG KLOOF KLUGE KLUTZ KNACK KNAGS KNAPS KNARL KNARS KNAUR KNAVE KNEAD KNEED KNEEL KNEES KNELL KNELT KNIFE KNISH KNITS KNIVE KNOBS KNOCK KNOLL KNOPS KNOSP KNOTS KNOUT KNOWE KNOWN KNOWS KNUBS KNURL KNURR KNURS KNUTS KOALA KOANS KOBAN KOELS KOFFS KOFTA KOHLS KOINE KOKER KOKRA KOKUM KOLAS KOLOS KOMBU KONKS KOOKS KOOKY KOORI KOPEK KOPHS KOPJE KOPPA KORAI KORAS KORAT KORES KORMA KORUN KOSES KOTOS KOTOW KRAAL KRABS KRAFT KRAIT KRANG KRANS

KRANZ KRAUT KREEP KRENG KRILL KRONA KRONE KROON KRUBI KSARS KUDOS KUDUS KUDZU KUGEL KUKRI KUKUS KULAK KULAN KUMYS KURIS KURRE KURTA KURUS KUSSO KUTCH KUZUS KVASS KWELA KYACK KYAKS KYANG KYARS KYATS KYDST KYLES KYLIE KYLIN KYLIX KYLOE KYNDE KYNDS KYRIE KYTES KYTHE LACKS LAIKA LAIKS LAKED LAKER LAKES LAKHS LAKIN LANKS LANKY LARKS LARKY LATKE LAWKS LEAKS LEAKY LEEKS LICKS LIKED LIKEN LIKER LIKES LIKIN LINKS LINKY LIRKS LISKS LOCKS LOKES LOOKS LUCKS

LUCKY LUNKS LURKS LUSKS MACKS MAIKO MAIKS MAKAR MAKER MAKES MAKOS MALIK MANKY MARKS MASKS MAWKS MAWKY MELIK MERKS MICKS MICKY MIKED MIKES MIKRA MILKO MILKS MILKY MINKE MINKS MIRKS MIRKY MOCKS MOKES MOKIS MOKOS MONKS MOOKS MOSKS MUCKS MUCKY MUJIK MURKS MURKY MUSKS MUSKY NABKS NAIKS NAKED NAKER NARKS NARKY NEBEK NECKS NERKA NERKS NEUKS NICKS NIKAU NOCKS NOOKS NOOKY NORKS NUKED NUKES OAKEN OAKER OAKUM OCKER OINKS OKAPI OKAYS OKEHS OKRAS OKTAS ONKUS

OTAKU OULKS OZEKI PACKS PAIKS PAKKA PALKI PARKA PARKI PARKS PARKY PAWKS PAWKY PEAKS PEAKY PECKE PECKS PECKY PEEKS PEKAN PEKES PEKIN PEKOE PENKS PERKS PERKY PESKY PICKS PICKY PIKAS PIKED PIKER PIKES PIKIS PIKUL PINKO PINKS PINKY PISKY PLACK PLANK PLINK PLONK PLOOK PLOUK PLUCK PLUNK POAKA POAKE POCKS POCKY POKAL POKED POKER POKES POKEY POLKA POLKS PONKS POOKA POOKS PORKS PORKY POUKE POUKS PRANK PRICK PRINK PROKE PRONK PUCKA PUCKS PUKED PUKER PUKES

PUKKA PUKUS PULIK PULKA PULKS PUNKA PUNKS PUNKY QUACK QUAKE QUAKY QUARK QUICK QUIRK QUONK RACKS RAIKS RAKED RAKEE RAKER RAKES RAKIS RAKUS RANKE RANKS REAKS RECKS REEKS REEKY REIKI REIKS REINK REKED REKES REKEY RICKS RINKS RISKS RISKY ROCKS ROCKY ROKED ROKER ROKES ROOKS ROOKY RUCKS RUKHS RUSKS RYKED RYKES SACKS SAICK SAKER SAKES SAKIA SAKIS SAMEK SANKO SARKS SARKY SCULK SEEKS SEKOS SEKTS SERKS SHACK SHAKE SHAKO SHAKT SHAKY SHANK SHARK SHEIK SHIRK

SHMEK SHOCK SHOOK SHTIK SHUCK SICKO SICKS SIKAS SIKER SIKES SILKS SILKY SINKS SINKY SKAGS SKAIL SKALD SKANK SKART SKATE SKATS SKATT SKAWS SKEAN SKEAR SKEED SKEEN SKEER SKEES SKEET SKEGG SKEGS SKEIN SKELF SKELL SKELM SKELP SKENE SKEOS SKEPS SKERS SKEWS SKIDS SKIED SKIER SKIES SKIEY SKIFF SKILL SKIMO SKIMP SKIMS SKINK SKINS SKINT SKIOS SKIPS SKIRL SKIRR SKIRT SKITE SKITS SKIVE SKIVY SKLIM SKOAL SKOFF SKOSH SKRAN SKRIK SKUAS SKUGS SKULK SKULL SKUNK

SKYED SKYER SKYEY SKYRE SKYRS SKYTE SLACK SLAKE SLANK SLEEK SLICK SLINK SLUNK SMACK SMAIK SMEEK SMERK SMIRK SMOCK SMOKE SMOKO SMOKY SNACK SNAKE SNAKY SNARK SNEAK SNECK SNICK SNOEK SNOKE SNOOK SNOWK SNUCK SOAKS SOCKO SOCKS SOKAH SOKEN SOKES SOKOL SOOKS SOUKS SPAKE SPANK SPARK SPEAK SPECK SPEKS SPELK SPICK SPIKE SPIKS SPIKY SPINK SPOKE SPOOK SPUNK STACK STAKE STALK STANK STARK STEAK STEEK STICK STINK STIRK STOCK STOKE STONK STOOK STORK STUCK STUNK

SUCKS SUKHS SULKS SULKY SUNKS SWACK SWANK SWINK SYKER SYKES TACKS TACKY TAKAS TAKEN TAKER TAKES TAKHI TAKIN TAKIS TALAK TALKS TALKY TALUK TANKA TANKS TANKY TAROK TASKS TEAKS TEREK THACK THANK THEEK THICK THILK THINK THUNK TICKS TICKY TIKAS TIKES TIKIS TIKKA TILAK TINKS TOCKS TOKAY TOKED TOKEN TOKER TOKES TOKOS TONKS TOPEK TORSK TOUKS TRACK TRAIK TRANK TRECK TREKS TRICK TRIKE TROAK TROCK TROKE TRUCK TRUNK TSKED TUCKS TUPEK TUPIK TURKS TUSKS TUSKY

TWANK TWEAK TWINK TYKES UKASE UMIAK UNKED UNKET UNKID UPTAK VAKIL VODKA VOLKS WACKE WACKO WACKS WACKY WAKAS WAKED WAKEN WAKER WAKES WAKFS WALKS WANKS WANKY WARKS WAUKS WAULK WEEKE WEEKS WEKAS WELKE WELKS WELKT WHACK WHELK WHILK WHISK WICKS WICKY WINKS WOCKS WOKEN WONKS WONKY WORKS WRACK WREAK WRECK WRICK WROKE YACKS YAKKA YAKOW YANKS YAPOK YELKS YERKS YESKS YEUKS YEUKY YIKES YIRKS YLIKE YLKES YOCKS YOICK YOKED YOKEL YOKES YOKUL YOLKS YOLKY YONKS

YORKS	YUCKS	YUKED	YUKKY	ZACKS	ZERKS	ZINKY	ZOOKS
YOUKS	YUCKY	YUKES	YUKOS	ZAKAT	ZINKE	ZONKS	ZOUKS

V-WORDS

V – 3-letter words

AVA	EVE	LEV	TAV	VAR	VAW	VIA	VIN	VOR
AVE	GOV	LUV	UVA	VAS	VEE	VID	VIS	VOW
AVO	GUV	OVA	VAC	VAT	VEG	VIE	VLY	VOX
DEV	IVY	REV	VAE	VAU	VET	VIG	VOE	VUG
DIV	LAV	SOV	VAN	VAV	VEX	VIM	VOL	VUM

V – 4-letter words

ARVO	DIVI	HIVE	NAVE	TAVA	VANT	VEIN	VIBS	VIRE	VOWS
AVAL	DIVS	HOVE	NAVY	TAVS	VARA	VELA	VICE	VIRL	VRIL
AVAS	DOVE	JAVA	NEVE	TIVY	VARE	VELD	VIDE	VISA	VROW
AVER	EAVE	JIVE	NEVI	ULVA	VARS	VELE	VIDS	VISE	VUGG
AVES	EEVN	JUVE	NOVA	URVA	VARY	VELL	VIED	VITA	VUGH
AVID	ENVY	KAVA	OVAL	UVAE	VASA	VENA	VIER	VITE	VUGS
AVOS	EVEN	KIVA	OVEN	UVAS	VASE	VEND	VIES	VIVA	VULN
AVOW	EVER	KVAS	OVER	UVEA	VAST	VENT	VIEW	VIVE	VUMS
BEVY	EVES	LAVA	OVUM	VACS	VATS	VERA	VIGA	VIVO	WAVE
CAVE	EVET	LAVE	PAVE	VADE	VATU	VERB	VIGS	VIZY	WAVY
CAVY	EVIL	LAVS	PERV	VAES	VAUS	VERS	VILD	VLEI	WIVE
CHIV	EVOE	LEVA	RAVE	VAGI	VAUT	VERT	VILE	VOAR	WOVE
CIVE	FAVA	LEVE	REVS	VAIL	VAVS	VERY	VILL	VOES	YEVE
COVE	FAVE	LEVO	RIVA	VAIN	VAWS	VEST	VIMS	VOID	
DAVY	FIVE	LEVY	RIVE	VAIR	VEAL	VETO	VINA	VOLA	
DEEV	GAVE	LIVE	RIVO	VALE	VEEP	VETS	VINE	VOLE	
DERV	GIVE	LOVE	ROVE	VALI	VEER	VEXT	VINO	VOLK	
DEVA	GOVS	LUVS	SAVE	VAMP	VEES	VIAE	VINS	VOLS	
DEVS	GUVS	MEVE	SHIV	VANE	VEGA	VIAL	VINT	VOLT	
DIVA	GYVE	MIRV	SOVS	VANG	VEHM	VIAS	VINY	VORS	
DIVE	HAVE	MOVE	SPIV	VANS	VEIL	VIBE	VIOL	VOTE	

V – 5-letter words

ABOVE	BIVIA	COVED	DOVER	FAVER	HIVER	LAVES	MIEVE	OLLAV	RAVED
ADVEW	BIVVY	COVEN	DOVES	FAVES	HIVES	LAVRA	MIRVS	ORVAL	RAVEL
AGAVE	BLIVE	COVER	DOVIE	FAVOR	HOOVE	LEAVE	MOOVE	OVALS	RAVEN
AIVER	BOVID	COVES	DRAVE	FAVUS	HOVED	LEAVY	MOVED	OVARY	RAVER
AJIVA	BRAVA	COVET	DRIVE	FEVER	HOVEL	LEVEE	MOVER	OVATE	RAVES
ALIVE	BRAVE	COVEY	DROVE	FIVER	HOVEN	LEVEL	MOVES	OVENS	RAVIN
AMOVE	BRAVI	COVIN	DUVET	FIVES	HOVER	LEVER	MOVIE	OVERS	REAVE
ANVIL	BRAVO	CRAVE	EAVED	FOVEA	HOVES	LEVIN	MURVA	OVERT	REEVE
ARVAL	BREVE	CRUVE	EAVES	GANEV	INVAR	LEVIS	MVULE	OVINE	REIVE
ARVOS	CALVE	CURVE	EEVEN	GAVEL	IVIED	LIEVE	NAEVE	OVIST	REVEL
AVAIL	CARVE	CURVY	EEVNS	GAVOT	IVIES	LIVED	NAEVI	OVOID	REVET
AVALE	CARVY	CUVEE	ELVAN	GIVED	IVORY	LIVEN	NAIVE	OVOLI	REVIE
AVANT	CAVED	DAVEN	ELVER	GIVEN	JAVAS	LIVER	NAVAL	OVOLO	REVUE
AVAST	CAVEL	DAVIT	ELVES	GIVER	JAVEL	LIVES	NAVAR	OVULE	RIEVE
AVENS	CAVER	DEAVE	EMOVE	GIVES	JIVED	LIVID	NAVEL	PARVE	RIVAL
AVERS	CAVES	DEEVE	ENVOI	GLOVE	JIVER	LIVOR	NAVES	PARVO	RIVAS
AVERT	CAVIE	DEEVS	ENVOY	GRAVE	JIVES	LIVRE	NAVEW	PAVAN	RIVED
AVGAS	CAVIL	DELVE	ERVEN	GRAVY	JIVEY	LOAVE	NAVVY	PAVED	RIVEL
AVIAN	CHAVE	DERVS	ERVIL	GREVE	JUVES	LOVAT	NEIVE	PAVEN	RIVEN
AVINE	CHEVY	DEVAS	EVADE	GROVE	KAVAS	LOVED	NERVE	PAVER	RIVER
AVION	CHIVE	DEVEL	EVENS	GUAVA	KEEVE	LOVER	NERVY	PAVES	RIVES
AVISE	CHIVS	DEVIL	EVENT	GYVED	KERVE	LOVES	NEVEL	PAVID	RIVET
AVISO	CHIVY	DEVON	EVERT	GYVES	KEVEL	LOVEY	NEVER	PAVIN	RIVOS
AVIZE	CIVES	DEVOT	EVERY	HALVA	KEVIL	LURVE	NEVES	PAVIS	ROVED
AVOID	CIVET	DIVAN	EVETS	HALVE	KIEVE	LUVVY	NEVUS	PEAVY	ROVEN
AVOWS	CIVIC	DIVAS	EVHOE	HAVEN	KIVAS	MALVA	NIEVE	PEEVE	ROVER
AVYZE	CIVIE	DIVED	EVICT	HAVER	KNAVE	MARVY	NIVAL	PERVE	ROVES
AWAVE	CIVIL	DIVER	EVILS	HAVES	KNIVE	MAUVE	NOVAE	PERVS	SALVE
BAVIN	CIVVY	DIVES	EVITE	HAVOC	KVASS	MAVEN	NOVAS	PIVOT	SALVO
BEVEL	CLAVE	DIVIS	EVOHE	HEAVE	LAEVO	MAVIE	NOVEL	POOVE	SAVED
BEVER	CLAVI	DIVOT	EVOKE	HEAVY	LARVA	MAVIN	NOVUM	POOVY	SAVER
BEVOR	CLEVE	DIVVY	FAUVE	HELVE	LAVAS	MAVIS	OAVES	PREVE	SAVES
BEVUE	CLOVE	DOVED	FAVAS	HEVEA	LAVED	MEVED	OGIVE	PRIVY	SAVEY
BEVVY	CONVO	DOVEN	FAVEL	HIVED	LAVER	MEVES	OLIVE	PROVE	SAVIN

SAVOR	STIVE	VALES	VASTS	VELES	VEXES	VINCA	VISNE	VOGUE	VOXEL
SAVOY	STIVY	VALET	VASTY	VELLS	VEXIL	VINED	VISON	VOICE	VOZHD
SAVVY	STOVE	VALID	VATIC	VELUM	VEZIR	VINER	VISOR	VOIDS	VRAIC
SCHAV	SUAVE	VALIS	VATUS	VENAE	VIALS	VINES	VISTA	VOILA	VRILS
SELVA	SWIVE	VALOR	VAULT	VENAL	VIAND	VINEW	VISTO	VOILE	VROOM
SENVY	SYLVA	VALSE	VAUNT	VENDS	VIBES	VINIC	VITAE	VOLAE	VROUW
SERVE	SYVER	VALUE	VAUTE	VENEY	VIBEX	VINOS	VITAL	VOLAR	VROWS
SERVO	TAVAH	VALVE	VAUTS	VENGE	VICAR	VINTS	VITAS	VOLED	VUGGS
SEVEN	TAVAS	VAMPS	VAWTE	VENIN	VICED	VINYL	VITEX	VOLES	VUGGY
SEVER	TAVER	VANDA	VEALE	VENOM	VICES	VIOLA	VITTA	VOLET	VUGHS
SHAVE	TRAVE	VANED	VEALS	VENTS	VICHY	VIOLD	VIVAS	VOLKS	VULGO
SHEVA	TROVE	VANES	VEALY	VENUE	VIDEO	VIOLS	VIVAT	VOLTA	VULNS
SHIVA	ULVAS	VANGS	VEENA	VENUS	VIERS	VIPER	VIVDA	VOLTE	VULVA
SHIVE	URVAS	VANTS	VEEPS	VERBS	VIEWS	VIRAL	VIVER	VOLTI	VYING
SHIVS	UVEAL	VAPID	VEERS	VERGE	VIEWY	VIRED	VIVES	VOLTS	WAIVE
SHOVE	UVEAS	VAPOR	VEERY	VERRY	VIFDA	VIREO	VIVID	VOLVA	WAVED
SIEVE	UVULA	VARAN	VEGAN	VERSE	VIGAS	VIRES	VIXEN	VOLVE	WAVER
SILVA	VACUA	VARAS	VEGAS	VERSO	VIGIA	VIRGA	VIZIR	VOMER	WAVES
SIVER	VADED	VARDY	VEGES	VERST	VIGIL	VIRGE	VIZOR	VOMIT	WAVEY
SKIVE	VADES	VAREC	VEGIE	VERTS	VIGOR	VIRID	VLEIS	VOTED	WEAVE
SKIVY	VAGAL	VARES	VEHME	VERTU	VILDE	VIRLS	VLIES	VOTER	WIVED
SLAVE	VAGUE	VARIA	VEILS	VERVE	VILER	VIRTU	VOARS	VOTES	WIVER
SLIVE	VAGUS	VARIX	VEILY	VESPA	VILLA	VIRUS	VOCAB	VOUCH	WIVES
SLOVE	VAILS	VARNA	VEINS	VESTA	VILLI	VISAS	VOCAL	VOUGE	WOLVE
SOAVE	VAIRE	VARUS	VEINY	VESTS	VILLS	VISED	VOCES	VOULU	WOVEN
SOLVE	VAIRS	VARVE	VELAR	VETCH	VIMEN	VISES	VODKA	VOWED	YEVEN
SPIVS	VAIRY	VASAL	VELDS	VEXED	VINAL	VISIE	VODUN	VOWEL	YEVES
STAVE	VAKIL	VASES	VELDT	VEXER	VINAS	VISIT	VOGIE	VOWER	YRIVD

Q But No U

If you are not familiar with *Official Scrabble® Words International* you may be unaware that there are quite a few words that contain Q with no U. These are all to be found in the Q lists, but it is worth highlighting them separately. You should certainly write down and learn the shorter ones as they are so vital in situations that would otherwise necessitate a change.

QI, QAT, QADI, QAID, QOPH, WAQF, FAQIR, QANAT, QIBLA, TALAQ, TRANQ
QASIDA, QAWWAL, QIGONG, QINDAR, QINTAR, QWERTY, SHEQEL, YAQONA,
INQILAB, QABALAH, QAWWALI, TSADDIQ, TZADDIQ,
MBAQANGA, QAIMAQAM, QALAMDAN, QINDARKA, SHEQALIM,
TSADDIQIM, TZADDIQIM.

Note that -S plural forms are allowed for all the above, except for SHEQEL, which only has the plural SHEQALIM, and QINDARKA, TSADDIQIM and TZADDIQIM, which are already plural forms. QWERTY has the plural QWERTIES as well as QWERTYS.

It is also worth noting that the following Q words and their corresponding plural forms have a U, but not after the Q.

SUQ, BURQA, UMIAQ, BUQSHA, QIVIUT, MUQADDAM, QINGHAOSU.

High Scorers

All the words of length two to eight letters which contain any of the four high-scoring letters J, Q, X and Z are listed below. While most Scrabble players know the obvious words, such as JUDGE, QUEEN, EXALT and ZEROS, how many know the more obscure POOJA, SQUEG, SIXTE and NIZAM?

Knowing these words will enable you to be more adventurous when it comes to grabbing the odd triple-word-score square for 50 or so points. It could also help you to play a bonus word with six single-point letters and a high-scoring letter, such as NAARTJE, LASQUES, ANOXIAS and LAIRIZE. You might even be able to play a bonus word using a letter on the board, with words such as REJONEOS, EQUITANT, XENURINE and LAZURITE.

If a word contains two of these four high-scoring letters (as do, for example, JYNX, QUIZ, BANJAX and ZOOTAXY), then it will appear in two lists.

J-WORDS

J – 2-letter words

JO

J – 3-letter words

GJU JAK JAW JEU JIN JOG JOY JUS
HAJ JAM JAY JEW JIZ JOR JUD JUT
JAB JAP JEE JIB JOB JOT JUG RAJ
JAG JAR JET JIG JOE JOW JUN TAJ

J – 4-letter words

AJAR JACK JARK JAZZ JEON JIGS JOBS JOMO JUBE JURY
AJEE JADE JARL JEAN JERK JILL JOCK JOOK JUDO JUST
BAJU JAGG JARS JEAT JESS JILT JOCO JORS JUDS JUTE
BENJ JAGS JASP JEED JEST JIMP JOES JOSH JUDY JUTS
DJIN JAIL JASS JEEL JETE JINK JOEY JOSS JUGA JUVE
DOJO JAKE JASY JEEP JETS JINN JOGS JOTA JUGS JYNX
FUJI JAKS JATO JEER JEUX JINS JOHN JOTS JUJU MOJO
GAJO JAMB JAUK JEES JEWS JINX JOIN JOUK JUKE PUJA
GJUS JAMS JAUP JEEZ JIAO JIRD JOKE JOUR JUMP RAJA
HADJ JANE JAVA JEFE JIBB JISM JOKY JOWL JUNK ROJI
HAJI JANN JAWS JEFF JIBE JIVE JOLE JOWS JUPE SIJO
HAJJ JAPE JAYS JEHU JIBS JIZZ JOLL JOYS JURA SOJA
JABS JAPS JAZY JELL JIFF JOBE JOLT JUBA JURE

J – 5-letter words

AFLAJ DJINN HAJES JAGER JAMMY JASPS JEELY JERKS JIBBS JINNI
AJIVA DJINS HAJIS JAGGS JANES JATOS JEEPS JERKY JIBED JINNS
AJUGA DOJOS HAJJI JAGGY JANNS JAUKS JEERS JERRY JIBER JIRDS
AJWAN EJECT HEJAB JAGIR JANTY JAUNT JEFES JESSE JIBES JIRGA
BAJAN ENJOY HEJRA JAGRA JAPAN JAUPS JEFFS JESTS JIFFS JISMS
BAJRA FALAJ HIJAB JAILS JAPED JAVAS JEHAD JESUS JIFFY JIVED
BAJRI FJELD HIJRA JAKES JAPER JAVEL JEHUS JETES JIGOT JIVER
BAJUS FJORD HODJA JALAP JAPES JAWAN JELAB JETON JIHAD JIVES
BANJO FUJIS JABOT JALOP JARKS JAWED JELLO JETTY JILLS JIVEY
BIJOU GADJE JACAL JAMBE JARLS JAZZY JELLS JEUNE JILTS JNANA
BUNJE GAJOS JACKS JAMBO JARTA JEANS JELLY JEWED JIMMY JOBED
BUNJY GANJA JACKY JAMBS JARUL JEATS JEMMY JEWEL JIMPY JOBES
CAJON GAUJE JADED JAMBU JASEY JEBEL JENNY JHALA JINGO JOCKO
CAJUN HADJI JADES JAMES JASPE JEELS JERID JIAOS JINKS JOCKS

JODEL	JOLED	JORUM	JOWED	JUICE	JUNCO	JUSTS	NINJA	REJON	UPJET
JOEYS	JOLES	JOTAS	JOWLS	JUICY	JUNKS	JUTES	OBJET	RIOJA	WILJA
JOHNS	JOLLS	JOTTY	JOWLY	JUJUS	JUNKY	JUTTY	OJIME	ROJIS	YOJAN
JOINS	JOLLY	JOTUN	JOYED	JUKED	JUNTA	JUVES	OUIJA	SAJOU	ZANJA
JOINT	JOLTS	JOUAL	JUBAS	JUKES	JUNTO	KANJI	POOJA	SHOJI	
JOIST	JOLTY	JOUGS	JUBES	JULEP	JUPES	KHOJA	PUJAH	SIJOS	
JOKED	JOMOS	JOUKS	JUDAS	JUMAR	JUPON	KOPJE	PUJAS	SLOJD	
JOKER	JONES	JOULE	JUDGE	JUMBO	JURAL	LAPJE	RAJAH	SOJAS	
JOKES	JONTY	JOURS	JUDOS	JUMBY	JURAT	MAJOR	RAJAS	SUJEE	
JOKEY	JOOKS	JOUST	JUGAL	JUMPS	JUREL	MOJOS	RAJES	TAJES	
JOKOL	JORAM	JOWAR	JUGUM	JUMPY	JUROR	MUJIK	REJIG	THUJA	

J – 6-letter words

ABJECT	FAJITA	JACKAL	JAPING	JEERER	JIGGER	JOGGED	JOWARS	JUNGLE	OBJETS
ABJURE	FANJET	JACKED	JAPPED	JEFFED	JIGGLE	JOGGER	JOWING	JUNGLI	OBJURE
ACAJOU	FEIJOA	JACKER	JARFUL	JEHADS	JIGGLY	JOGGLE	JOWLED	JUNGLY	OJIMES
ADJOIN	FINJAN	JACKET	JARGON	JEJUNA	JIGJIG	JOHNNY	JOWLER	JUNIOR	OUIJAS
ADJURE	FJELDS	JACKSY	JARINA	JEJUNE	JIGOTS	JOINED	JOYFUL	JUNKED	OUTJET
ADJUST	FJORDS	JADERY	JAROOL	JELABS	JIGSAW	JOINER	JOYING	JUNKER	OUTJUT
AJIVAS	FRIJOL	JADING	JARRAH	JELLED	JIHADS	JOINTS	JOYOUS	JUNKET	PAJAMA
AJOWAN	GADJES	JADISH	JARRED	JELLOS	JILGIE	JOISTS	JOYPOP	JUNKIE	PAJOCK
AJUGAS	GAIJIN	JAEGER	JARTAS	JEMIMA	JILLET	JOJOBA	JUBATE	JUNTAS	POOJAH
AJWANS	GANJAH	JAGERS	JARULS	JENNET	JILTED	JOKERS	JUBBAH	JUNTOS	POOJAS
BAJADA	GANJAS	JAGGED	JARVEY	JERBIL	JILTER	JOKIER	JUBHAH	JUPATI	POPJOY
BAJANS	GARJAN	JAGGER	JARVIE	JERBOA	JIMINY	JOKILY	JUBILE	JUPONS	PROJET
BAJRAS	GAUJES	JAGHIR	JASEYS	JEREED	JIMJAM	JOKING	JUDDER	JURANT	PUJAHS
BAJREE	GIDJEE	JAGIRS	JASIES	JERIDS	JIMPER	JOLING	JUDGED	JURATS	RAJAHS
BAJRIS	GURJUN	JAGRAS	JASMIN	JERKED	JIMPLY	JOLLED	JUDGER	JURELS	RAMJET
BANJAX	HADJEE	JAGUAR	JASPER	JERKER	JINGAL	JOLLEY	JUDGES	JURIED	REJECT
BANJOS	HADJES	JAILED	JASPES	JERKIN	JINGKO	JOLTED	JUDIES	JURIES	REJIGS
BEJADE	HADJIS	JAILER	JASPIS	JERQUE	JINGLE	JOLTER	JUDOGI	JURIST	REJOIN
BEJANT	HAJJES	JAILOR	JASSES	JERRID	JINGLY	JOOKED	JUDOKA	JURORS	RIOJAS
BENJES	HAJJIS	JALAPS	JASSID	JERSEY	JINKED	JORAMS	JUGALS	JUSTED	SAJOUS
BHAJAN	HANJAR	JALOPS	JATAKA	JESSED	JINKER	JORDAN	JUGATE	JUSTER	SANJAK
BHAJEE	HEJABS	JALOPY	JAUKED	JESSES	JINNEE	JORUMS	JUGFUL	JUSTLE	SEJANT
BIJOUS	HEJIRA	JAMBED	JAUNCE	JESSIE	JINXED	JOSEPH	JUGGED	JUSTLY	SHOJIS
BIJOUX	HEJRAS	JAMBEE	JAUNSE	JESTED	JINXES	JOSHED	JUGGLE	JUTTED	SLOJDS
BUNJEE	HIJABS	JAMBER	JAUNTS	JESTEE	JIRBLE	JOSHER	JUGLET	JYMOLD	SOOJEY
BUNJES	HIJACK	JAMBES	JAUNTY	JESTER	JIRGAS	JOSHES	JUGULA	JYNXES	SUJEES
BUNJIE	HIJRAH	JAMBOK	JAUPED	JESUIT	JISSOM	JOSKIN	JUGUMS	KANJIS	SVARAJ
CAJOLE	HIJRAS	JAMBOS	JAVELS	JETONS	JITNEY	JOSSER	JUICED	KHODJA	SWARAJ
COJOIN	HOBJOB	JAMBUL	JAWANS	JETSAM	JITTER	JOSSES	JUICER	KHOJAS	TAJINE
CONJEE	HODJAS	JAMBUS	JAWARI	JETSOM	JIVERS	JOSTLE	JUICES	KOPJES	THUJAS
CROJIK	INJECT	JAMJAR	JAWBOX	JETSON	JIVIER	JOTTED	JUJUBE	LAPJES	TINAJA
DEEJAY	INJERA	JAMMED	JAWING	JETTED	JIVING	JOTTER	JUKING	LOGJAM	TRIJET
DEJECT	INJURE	JAMMER	JAYGEE	JETTON	JIZZES	JOTUNN	JULEPS	MAJLIS	UJAMAA
DJEBEL	INJURY	JAMPAN	JAYVEE	JEWELS	JNANAS	JOTUNS	JUMARS	MAJORS	UNJUST
DJINNI	INKJET	JAMPOT	JAZIES	JEWING	JOANNA	JOUALS	JUMART	MASJID	UPJETS
DJINNS	JABBED	JANDAL	JAZZED	JEZAIL	JOBBED	JOUKED	JUMBAL	MATJES	VEEJAY
DJINNY	JABBER	JANGLE	JAZZER	JHALAS	JOBBER	JOULED	JUMBIE	MEJLIS	WILJAS
DONJON	JABBLE	JANGLY	JAZZES	JIBBAH	JOBBIE	JOULES	JUMBLE	MOJOES	WILTJA
EJECTA	JABERS	JANKER	JEBELS	JIBBED	JOBING	JOUNCE	JUMBLY	MOUJIK	YOJANA
EJECTS	JABIRU	JANSKY	JEEING	JIBBER	JOCKEY	JOUNCY	JUMBOS	MUJIKS	YOJANS
ENJAMB	JABOTS	JANTEE	JEELED	JIBERS	JOCKOS	JOURNO	JUMPED	MUSJID	ZANJAS
ENJOIN	JACALS	JAPANS	JEELIE	JIBING	JOCOSE	JOUSTS	JUMPER	MUZJIK	
ENJOYS	JACANA	JAPERS	JEEPED	JICAMA	JOCUND	JOVIAL	JUNCOS	NINJAS	
EVEJAR	JACENT	JAPERY	JEERED	JIGGED	JODELS	JOWARI	JUNCUS	OBJECT	

J – 7-letter words

ABJECTS	ADJURER	BANJOES	BRINJAL	COJONES	DISJECT	EVEJARS	HADJEES	INJERAS
ABJOINT	ADJURES	BASENJI	BUNJEES	CONJECT	DISJOIN	FAJITAS	HANDJAR	INJOINT
ABJURED	ADJUROR	BEJADED	BUNJIES	CONJEED	DISJUNE	FANJETS	HANJARS	INJUNCT
ABJURER	ADJUSTS	BEJADES	CAJAPUT	CONJEES	DJEBELS	FEIJOAS	HARIJAN	INJURED
ABJURES	AJOWANS	BEJANTS	CAJEPUT	CONJOIN	DJIBBAH	FINJANS	HEJIRAS	INJURER
ACAJOUS	AJUTAGE	BEJESUS	CAJOLED	CONJURE	DONJONS	FRIJOLE	HIJACKS	INJURES
ADJOINS	ALFORJA	BEJEWEL	CAJOLER	CONJURY	EJECTED	GANJAHS	HIJINKS	JABBERS
ADJOINT	ANTIJAM	BHAJANS	CAJOLES	CROJIKS	EJECTOR	GARJANS	HIJRAHS	JABBING
ADJOURN	APAREJO	BHAJEES	CAJONES	DEEJAYS	ENJAMBS	GIDJEES	HOBJOBS	JABBLED
ADJUDGE	AZULEJO	BLOWJOB	CAJUPUT	DEJECTA	ENJOINS	GJETOST	IJTIHAD	JABBLES
ADJUNCT	BAJADAS	BLUEJAY	CARJACK	DEJECTS	ENJOYED	GOUJONS	INJECTS	JABIRUS
ADJURED	BAJREES	BONJOUR	COJOINS	DEJEUNE	ENJOYER	GURJUNS	INJELLY	JACALES

JACAMAR JACANAS JACCHUS JACINTH JACKALS JACKASS JACKDAW JACKEEN JACKERS JACKETS JACKIES JACKING JACKLEG JACKMAN JACKMEN JACKPOT JACKSIE JACOBIN JACOBUS JACONET JACUZZI JADEDLY JADEITE JADITIC JAEGERS JAGGARY JAGGERS JAGGERY JAGGIER JAGGING JAGHIRE JAGHIRS JAGLESS JAGUARS JAILERS JAILING JAILORS JAKESES JALAPIC JALAPIN JALOPPY JALOUSE JAMADAR JAMBEAU JAMBEES JAMBERS JAMBEUX JAMBIER JAMBING JAMBIYA JAMBOKS JAMBONE JAMBOOL JAMBULS

JAMDANI JAMESES JAMJARS JAMMERS JAMMIER JAMMIES JAMMING JAMPANI JAMPANS JAMPOTS JANDALS JANGLED JANGLER JANGLES JANITOR JANIZAR JANKERS JANNOCK JANSKYS JANTIER JANTIES JAPINGS JAPPING JARFULS JARGONS JARGOON JARHEAD JARINAS JARKMAN JARKMEN JARLDOM JAROOLS JARRAHS JARRING JARSFUL JARVEYS JARVIES JASMINE JASMINS JASPERS JASPERY JASSIDS JATAKAS JAUKING JAUNCED JAUNCES JAUNSED JAUNSES JAUNTED JAUNTEE JAUNTIE JAUPING JAVELIN JAWARIS

JAWBONE JAWFALL JAWHOLE JAWINGS JAWLIKE JAWLINE JAYBIRD JAYGEES JAYVEES JAYWALK JAZZERS JAZZIER JAZZILY JAZZING JAZZMAN JAZZMEN JEALOUS JEELIED JEELIES JEELING JEEPERS JEEPING JEEPNEY JEERERS JEERING JEFFING JEJUNAL JEJUNUM JELLABA JELLIED JELLIES JELLIFY JELLING JEMADAR JEMIDAR JEMIMAS JEMMIED JEMMIER JEMMIES JENNETS JENNIES JEOFAIL JEOPARD JERBILS JERBOAS JEREEDS JERKERS JERKIER JERKIES JERKILY JERKING JERKINS JERQUED JERQUER

JERQUES JERREED JERRIDS JERRIES JERSEYS JESSAMY JESSANT JESSIES JESSING JESTEES JESTERS JESTFUL JESTING JESUITS JETBEAD JETFOIL JETLIKE JETPORT JETSAMS JETSOMS JETSONS JETTIED JETTIER JETTIES JETTING JETTONS JEWELED JEWELER JEWELRY JEWFISH JEZAILS JEZEBEL JIBBAHS JIBBERS JIBBING JIBBOOM JICAMAS JIFFIES JIGABOO JIGAJIG JIGAJOG JIGGERS JIGGING JIGGISH JIGGLED JIGGLES JIGJIGS JIGSAWN JIGSAWS JILGIES JILLETS JILLION JILTERS JILTING

JIMJAMS JIMMIED JIMMIES JIMMINY JIMPEST JIMPIER JINGALL JINGALS JINGLED JINGLER JINGLES JINGLET JINGOES JINJILI JINKERS JINKING JINXING JIPYAPA JIRBLED JIRBLES JISSOMS JITNEYS JITTERS JITTERY JIVEASS JIVIEST JOANNAS JOANNES JOBBERS JOBBERY JOBBIES JOBBING JOBLESS JOBNAME JOCKEYS JOCKNEY JOCULAR JODHPUR JOGGERS JOGGING JOGGLED JOGGLER JOGGLES JOGTROT JOHNNIE JOINDER JOINERS JOINERY JOINING JOINTED JOINTER JOINTLY JOISTED JOJOBAS

JOKIEST JOLLEYS JOLLIED JOLLIER JOLLIES JOLLIFY JOLLILY JOLLING JOLLITY JOLLYER JOLTERS JOLTIER JOLTILY JOLTING JONESES JONQUIL JONTIES JOOKERY JOOKING JORDANS JOSEPHS JOSHERS JOSHING JOSKINS JOSSERS JOSTLED JOSTLER JOSTLES JOTTERS JOTTING JOTUNNS JOUKERY JOUKING JOULING JOUNCED JOUNCES JOURNAL JOURNEY JOURNOS JOUSTED JOUSTER JOWARIS JOWLERS JOWLIER JOWLING JOYANCE JOYLESS JOYPOPS JOYRIDE JOYRODE JUBBAHS JUBHAHS JUBILEE JUBILES

JUDASES JUDDERS JUDGERS JUDGING JUDOGIS JUDOIST JUDOKAS JUGFULS JUGGING JUGGINS JUGGLED JUGGLER JUGGLES JUGHEAD JUGLETS JUGSFUL JUGULAR JUGULUM JUICERS JUICIER JUICILY JUICING JUJITSU JUJUBES JUJUISM JUJUIST JUJUTSU JUKEBOX JUKSKEI JUMARTS JUMBALS JUMBIES JUMBLED JUMBLER JUMBLES JUMBUCK JUMELLE JUMPERS JUMPIER JUMPILY JUMPING JUMPOFF JUNCATE JUNCOES JUNGLED JUNGLES JUNGLIS JUNIORS JUNIPER JUNKERS JUNKETS JUNKIER JUNKIES JUNKING

JUNKMAN JUNKMEN JUPATIS JURALLY JURANTS JURIDIC JURISTS JURYING JURYMAN JURYMEN JUSSIVE JUSTERS JUSTEST JUSTICE JUSTIFY JUSTING JUSTLED JUSTLES JUTTIED JUTTIES JUTTING JUVENAL KAJAWAH KAJEPUT KHANJAR KHODJAS KILLJOY LOCKJAW LOGJAMS MAATJES MAHJONG MAJAGUA MAJESTY MAJORAT MAJORED MAJORLY MANJACK MASJIDS MISJOIN MOJARRA MOUJIKS MUDEJAR MUNTJAC MUNTJAK MUSJIDS MUZJIKS NAARTJE NARTJIE NONJURY OBJECTS OBJURED OBJURES OUTJEST OUTJETS

OUTJINX OUTJUMP OUTJUTS OVERJOY PAJAMAS PAJOCKE PAJOCKS PERJINK PERJURE PERJURY PIROJKI POOJAHS POPJOYS PREJINK PROJECT PROJETS PROPJET PYJAMAS RAMJETS REEJECT REENJOY REJECTS REJOICE REJOINS REJONEO REJONES REJOURN REJUDGE RESOJET SANJAKS SAPAJOU SEJEANT SJAMBOK SKYJACK SOJOURN SOOJEYS SUBJECT SUBJOIN TAJINES TINAJAS TRAJECT TRIJETS TWINJET UJAMAAS UNJADED UNJOINT VEEJAYS WILTJAS YOJANAS ZANJERO

J – 8-letter words

ABJECTED ABJECTLY ABJOINTS ABJURERS ABJURING ADJACENT ADJOINED ADJOINTS ADJOURNS ADJUDGED ADJUDGES ADJUNCTS ADJURERS ADJURING ADJURORS ADJUSTED

ADJUSTER ADJUSTOR ADJUTAGE ADJUTANT ADJUVANT AJUTAGES ALFORJAS APAREJOS AZULEJOS BANJAXED BANJAXES BANJOIST BASENJIS BEJABERS BEJADING BEJEEZUS

BEJESUIT BEJEWELS BEJUMBLE BENJAMIN BIJUGATE BIJUGOUS BIJWONER BLOWJOBS BLUEJACK BLUEJAYS BOOTJACK BRINJALS CAJAPUTS CAJEPUTS CAJOLERS CAJOLERY

CAJOLING CAJUPUTS CARCAJOU CARJACKS CARJACOU COJOINED CONJECTS CONJOINS CONJOINT CONJUGAL CONJUNCT CONJURED CONJURER CONJURES CONJUROR CRACKJAW

CUNJEVOI DEEJAYED DEJECTED DEJEUNER DEJEUNES DEMIJOHN DISJECTS DISJOINS DISJOINT DISJUNCT DISJUNES DJELLABA DJIBBAHS DOORJAMB EJECTING EJECTION

EJECTIVE EJECTORS ENJAMBED ENJOINED ENJOINER ENJOYERS ENJOYING FLAPJACK FORJUDGE FRABJOUS FRIJOLES GJETOSTS GOUJEERS HANDJARS HARIJANS HIGHJACK

HIJACKED HIJACKER IJTIHADS INJECTED INJECTOR INJOINTS INJUNCTS INJURERS INJURIES INJURING JABBERED JABBERER JABBLING JACAMARS JACINTHE JACINTHS

JACKAROO JACKBOOT JACKDAWS JACKEENS JACKEROO JACKETED JACKFISH JACKLEGS JACKPOTS JACKROLL JACKSIES JACKSTAY JACOBINS JACONETS JACQUARD JACULATE

JACUZZIS JARGONEL JERKINGS JINGLING JONGLEUR JUMPABLE MIJNHEER REJIGGER
JADEITES JARGOONS JEROBOAM JINGOISH JONQUILS JUMPIEST MISJOINS REJOICED
JADERIES JARHEADS JERQUERS JINGOISM JORDELOO JUMPOFFS MISJUDGE REJOICER
JADISHLY JARLDOMS JERQUING JINGOIST JOSTLERS JUMPSUIT MOJARRAS REJOICES
JAGGEDER JAROSITE JERREEDS JINJILIS JOSTLING JUNCATES MULTIJET REJOINED
JAGGEDLY JAROVIZE JERRICAN JIPIJAPA JOTTINGS JUNCTION MUNTJACS REJONEOS
JAGGHERY JARRINGS JERRYCAN JIPYAPAS JOUNCIER JUNCTURE MUNTJAKS REJOURNS
JAGGIEST JASMINES JERSEYED JIRBLING JOUNCING JUNCUSES NAARTJES REJUDGED
JAGHIRES JASPISES JESTBOOK JIRKINET JOURNALS JUNGLIER NARTJIES REJUDGES
JAILBAIT JAUNCING JESTINGS JITTERED JOURNEYS JUNGLIST NIGHTJAR REJUGGLE
JAILBIRD JAUNDICE JESUITIC JIUJITSU JOUSTERS JUNIPERS NINJITSU REOBJECT
JALAPENO JAUNSING JESUITRY JIUJUTSU JOUSTING JUNKANOO NINJUTSU RESOJETS
JALAPINS JAUNTIER JETBEADS JOBATION JOVIALLY JUNKETED NONJUROR SAPAJOUS
JALOPIES JAUNTIES JETFOILS JOBBINGS JOVIALTY JUNKETER NONMAJOR SCRAMJET
JALOUSED JAUNTILY JETLINER JOBNAMES JOWLIEST JUNKIEST OBJECTED SERJEANT
JALOUSES JAUNTING JETPLANE JOBSHARE JOYANCES JUNKYARD OBJECTOR SJAMBOKS
JALOUSIE JAVELINA JETPORTS JOCKETTE JOYFULLY JURATORY OBJURING SKIJORER
JAMADARS JAVELINS JETTIEST JOCKEYED JOYOUSLY JURISTIC OUTJESTS SKIPJACK
JAMBEAUX JAWBONED JETTISON JOCKNEYS JOYRIDER JURYMAST OUTJUMPS SKYJACKS
JAMBIERS JAWBONER JETTYING JOCOSELY JOYRIDES JUSSIVES OVERJOYS SLAPJACK
JAMBIYAH JAWBONES JEWELERS JOCOSITY JOYSTICK JUSTICER OVERJUMP SOJOURNS
JAMBIYAS JAWBOXES JEWELING JOCUNDLY JUBILANT JUSTICES OVERJUST STICKJAW
JAMBOLAN JAWFALLS JEWELLED JODELLED JUBILATE JUSTLING PAJAMAED SUBJECTS
JAMBONES JAWHOLES JEWELLER JODHPURS JUBILEES JUSTNESS PAJOCKES SUBJOINS
JAMBOOLS JAWLINES JEZEBELS JOGGINGS JUDDERED JUTTYING PEJORATE SUCURUJU
JAMBOREE JAYBIRDS JIBBERED JOGGLERS JUDGMENT JUVENALS PERJURED SUPERJET
JAMDANIS JAYWALKS JIBBINGS JOGGLING JUDICIAL JUVENILE PERJURER SVARAJES
JAMMIEST JAZERANT JIBBOOMS JOGPANTS JUDOISTS KABELJOU PERJURES SWARAJES
JAMPANEE JAZZIEST JIBINGLY JOGTROTS JUGGINGS KAJAWAHS POPINJAY TJANTING
JAMPANIS JAZZLIKE JICKAJOG JOHANNES JUGGLERS KAJEPUTS POPJOYED TRAJECTS
JANGLERS JEALOUSE JIGABOOS JOHNBOAT JUGGLERY KHANJARS PREJUDGE TURBOJET
JANGLIER JEALOUSY JIGAJIGS JOHNNIES JUGGLING KILLJOYS PROJECTS TWINJETS
JANGLING JEANETTE JIGAJOGS JOINABLE JUGHEADS KINKAJOU PROPJETS UNDERJAW
JANIFORM JEELYING JIGGERED JOINDERS JUGULARS KOMITAJI PULSEJET UNJOINED
JANISARY JEEPNEYS JIGGINGS JOININGS JUGULATE LOCKJAWS PULSOJET UNJOINTS
JANITORS JEERINGS JIGGLIER JOINTERS JUICIEST LOGJUICE PYJAMAED UNJOYFUL
JANITRIX JEJUNELY JIGGLING JOINTING JUJITSUS MAHARAJA QUILLAJA UNJOYOUS
JANIZARS JEJUNITY JIGSAWED JOINTURE JUJUISMS MAHJONGG RAJASHIP UNJUDGED
JANIZARY JELLABAS JILLAROO JOISTING JUJUISTS MAHJONGS READJUST UNJUSTER
JANNOCKS JELLYING JILLIONS JOKESOME JUJUTSUS MAJAGUAS REEJECTS UNJUSTLY
JANTIEST JELUTONG JIMCRACK JOKESTER JUKSKEIS MAJESTIC REENJOYS UPJETTED
JAPANIZE JEMADARS JIMMYING JOKINESS JULIENNE MAJLISES REINJECT VERJUICE
JAPANNED JEMIDARS JIMPIEST JOKINGLY JUMARRED MAJOLICA REINJURE WHIPJACK
JAPANNER JEMMIEST JIMPNESS JOLLEYER JUMBLERS MAJORATS REINJURY ZABAJONE
JAPERIES JEMMYING JINGALLS JOLLIEST JUMBLIER MAJORING REJACKET ZANJEROS
JAPINGLY JEOFAILS JINGBANG JOLLYERS JUMBLING MAJORITY REJECTED
JAPONICA JEOPARDS JINGKOES JOLLYING JUMBOISE MANJACKS REJECTEE
JARARACA JEOPARDY JINGLERS JOLTHEAD JUMBOIZE MARJORAM REJECTER
JARARAKA JEREMIAD JINGLETS JOLTIEST JUMBUCKS MARYJANE REJECTOR
JARGONED JERKIEST JINGLIER JONCANOE JUMELLES MEJLISES REJIGGED

Q-WORDS

Q – 2-letter words

QI

Q – 3-letter words

QAT QIS QUA SUQ

Q – 4-letter words

AQUA QATS QUAG QUAY QUID QUIP QUOD WAQF
QADI QOPH QUAI QUEP QUIM QUIT QUOP
QAID QUAD QUAT QUEY QUIN QUIZ SUQS

Q – 5-letter words

AQUAE EQUID MAQUI QANAT QUADS QUAIR QUALE QUARK QUASS QUAYS
AQUAS EQUIP PIQUE QIBLA QUAFF QUAIS QUALM QUART QUATE QUEAN
BURQA FAQIR QADIS QOPHS QUAGS QUAKE QUANT QUASH QUATS QUEEN
EQUAL FIQUE QAIDS QUACK QUAIL QUAKY QUARE QUASI QUAYD QUEER

QUELL	QUEUE	QUIET	QUINE	QUIRE	QUOAD	QUONK	QUYTE	SQUEG	TOQUE
QUEME	QUEYN	QUIFF	QUINS	QUIRK	QUODS	QUOPS	ROQUE	SQUIB	TRANQ
QUENA	QUEYS	QUILL	QUINT	QUIRT	QUOIF	QUOTA	SQUAB	SQUID	TUQUE
QUERN	QUICH	QUILT	QUIPO	QUIST	QUOIN	QUOTE	SQUAD	SQUIT	UMIAQ
QUERY	QUICK	QUIMS	QUIPS	QUITE	QUOIT	QUOTH	SQUAT	SQUIZ	USQUE
QUEST	QUIDS	QUINA	QUIPU	QUITS	QUOLL	QURSH	SQUAW	TALAQ	WAQFS

Q – 6-letter words

ACQUIT	EQUANT	OPAQUE	QUAILS	QUAVER	QUEUER	QUINTE	QUOLLS	SEQUIN	SQUINY
ASQUAT	EQUATE	PIQUED	QUAINT	QUEACH	QUEUES	QUINTS	QUONKS	SHEQEL	SQUIRE
BARQUE	EQUIDS	PIQUES	QUAIRS	QUEANS	QUEYNS	QUINZE	QUOOKE	SQUABS	SQUIRM
BASQUE	EQUINE	PIQUET	QUAKED	QUEASY	QUEZAL	QUIPOS	QUORUM	SQUADS	SQUIRR
BISQUE	EQUIPE	PLAQUE	QUAKER	QUEAZY	QUICHE	QUIPPU	QUOTAS	SQUAIL	SQUIRT
BOSQUE	EQUIPS	PULQUE	QUAKES	QUEENS	QUICKS	QUIPUS	QUOTED	SQUALL	SQUISH
BUQSHA	EQUITY	QANATS	QUALIA	QUEENY	QUIDAM	QUIRED	QUOTER	SQUAMA	SQUITS
BURQAS	EXEQUY	QASIDA	QUALMS	QUEERS	QUIETS	QUIRES	QUOTES	SQUAME	SQUUSH
CAIQUE	FAQIRS	QAWWAL	QUALMY	QUEEST	QUIFFS	QUIRKS	QUOTHA	SQUARE	TALAQS
CALQUE	FAQUIR	QIBLAS	QUANGO	QUEINT	QUIGHT	QUIRKY	QUOTUM	SQUASH	TOQUES
CASQUE	FIQUES	QIGONG	QUANTA	QUELCH	QUILLS	QUIRTS	QURUSH	SQUATS	TOQUET
CHEQUE	HAIQUE	QINDAR	QUANTS	QUELEA	QUILTS	QUISTS	QUYTED	SQUAWK	TORQUE
CHEQUY	JERQUE	QINTAR	QUARER	QUELLS	QUINAS	QUITCH	QUYTES	SQUAWS	TRANQS
CINQUE	LASQUE	QIVIUT	QUARKS	QUEMED	QUINCE	QUITED	QWERTY	SQUEAK	TUQUES
CIRQUE	LIQUID	QUACKS	QUARRY	QUEMES	QUINES	QUITES	REQUIN	SQUEAL	UBIQUE
CLAQUE	LIQUOR	QUAERE	QUARTE	QUENAS	QUINIC	QUIVER	REQUIT	SQUEGS	UMIAQS
CLIQUE	LOQUAT	QUAFFS	QUARTO	QUENCH	QUINIE	QUOHOG	RISQUE	SQUIBS	UNIQUE
CLIQUY	MANQUE	QUAGGA	QUARTS	QUERNS	QUININ	QUOIFS	ROQUES	SQUIDS	USQUES
CLOQUE	MAQUIS	QUAGGY	QUARTZ	QUESTS	QUINOA	QUOINS	ROQUET	SQUIER	YANQUI
COQUET	MARQUE	QUAHOG	QUASAR	QUETCH	QUINOL	QUOIST	SACQUE	SQUIFF	YAQONA
DIQUAT	MASQUE	QUAICH	QUATCH	QUETHE	QUINSY	QUOITS	SAIQUE	SQUILL	
EQUALS	MOSQUE	QUAIGH	QUATRE	QUEUED	QUINTA	QUOKKA	SEQUEL	SQUINT	

Q – 7-letter words

ACEQUIA	CHARQUI	EQUITES	OBSEQUY	QUAILED	QUEENIE	QUIETER	QUITING	REQUINS
ACQUEST	CHEQUER	ESQUIRE	OPAQUED	QUAKERS	QUEENLY	QUIETLY	QUITTAL	REQUIRE
ACQUIRE	CHEQUES	FAQUIRS	OPAQUER	QUAKIER	QUEERED	QUIETUS	QUITTED	REQUITE
ACQUIST	CINQUES	GRECQUE	OPAQUES	QUAKILY	QUEERER	QUIGHTS	QUITTER	REQUITS
ACQUITE	CIRQUES	HAIQUES	OQUASSA	QUAKING	QUEERLY	QUILLAI	QUITTOR	REQUOTE
ACQUITS	CLAQUER	INQILAB	PARQUET	QUALIFY	QUEESTS	QUILLED	QUIVERS	RISQUES
ALFAQUI	CLAQUES	INQUERE	PASQUIL	QUALITY	QUELEAS	QUILLET	QUIVERY	ROCQUET
ALIQUOT	CLIQUED	INQUEST	PERIQUE	QUAMASH	QUELLED	QUILLON	QUIXOTE	ROQUETS
ANTIQUE	CLIQUES	INQUIET	PICQUET	QUANGOS	QUELLER	QUILTED	QUIZZED	RORQUAL
AQUAFER	CLIQUEY	INQUIRE	PIQUANT	QUANNET	QUEMING	QUILTER	QUIZZER	SACQUES
AQUARIA	CLOQUES	INQUIRY	PIQUETS	QUANTAL	QUERIDA	QUINARY	QUIZZES	SAIQUES
AQUATIC	COEQUAL	JERQUED	PIQUING	QUANTED	QUERIED	QUINATE	QUODDED	SEQUELA
AQUAVIT	COMIQUE	JERQUER	PIROQUE	QUANTIC	QUERIER	QUINCES	QUODLIN	SEQUELS
AQUEOUS	CONQUER	JERQUES	PLAQUES	QUANTUM	QUERIES	QUINCHE	QUOHOGS	SEQUENT
AQUIFER	COQUETS	JONQUIL	PREQUEL	QUAREST	QUERIST	QUINELA	QUOIFED	SEQUINS
AQUILON	COQUINA	KUMQUAT	PULQUES	QUARREL	QUESTED	QUINIES	QUOINED	SEQUOIA
AQUIVER	COQUITO	LACQUER	QABALAH	QUARTAN	QUESTER	QUININA	QUOISTS	SILIQUA
ASQUINT	CROQUET	LACQUEY	QASIDAS	QUARTER	QUESTOR	QUININE	QUOITED	SILIQUE
BANQUET	CROQUIS	LASQUES	QAWWALI	QUARTES	QUETHES	QUININS	QUOITER	SQUABBY
BAROQUE	CUMQUAT	LIQUATE	QAWWALS	QUARTET	QUETSCH	QUINNAT	QUOKKAS	SQUACCO
BARQUES	DAQUIRI	LIQUEFY	QIGONGS	QUARTIC	QUETZAL	QUINOAS	QUOMODO	SQUADDY
BASQUED	DIQUATS	LIQUEUR	QINDARS	QUARTOS	QUEUERS	QUINOID	QUONDAM	SQUAILS
BASQUES	DOCQUET	LIQUIDS	QINTARS	QUARTZY	QUEUING	QUINOLS	QUONKED	SQUALID
BEQUEST	ENQUIRE	LIQUIFY	QIVIUTS	QUASARS	QUEYNIE	QUINONE	QUOPPED	SQUALLS
BEZIQUE	ENQUIRY	LIQUORS	QUACKED	QUASHED	QUEZALS	QUINTAL	QUORATE	SQUALLY
BISQUES	EQUABLE	LOQUATS	QUACKER	QUASHEE	QUIBBLE	QUINTAN	QUORUMS	SQUALOR
BOSQUES	EQUABLY	MACAQUE	QUACKLE	QUASHER	QUIBLIN	QUINTAR	QUOTERS	SQUAMAE
BOSQUET	EQUALED	MADOQUA	QUADDED	QUASHES	QUICHED	QUINTAS	QUOTING	SQUAMES
BOUQUET	EQUALLY	MARQUEE	QUADRAT	QUASHIE	QUICHES	QUINTES	QUOTUMS	SQUARED
BRIQUET	EQUANTS	MARQUES	QUADRIC	QUASSES	QUICKEN	QUINTET	QURSHES	SQUARER
BRUSQUE	EQUATED	MARQUIS	QUAERED	QUASSIA	QUICKER	QUINTIC	QUYTING	SQUARES
BUQSHAS	EQUATES	MASQUER	QUAERES	QUASSIN	QUICKIE	QUINTIN	QWERTYS	SQUASHY
CACIQUE	EQUATOR	MASQUES	QUAFFED	QUATRES	QUICKLY	QUINZES	RACQUET	SQUATLY
CAIQUES	EQUERRY	MESQUIN	QUAFFER	QUAVERS	QUIDAMS	QUIPPED	REEQUIP	SQUATTY
CALQUED	EQUINAL	MESQUIT	QUAGGAS	QUAVERY	QUIDDIT	QUIPPER	RELIQUE	SQUAWKS
CALQUES	EQUINES	MEZQUIT	QUAHAUG	QUAYAGE	QUIDDLE	QUIPPUS	REPIQUE	SQUAWKY
CASQUED	EQUINIA	MOSQUES	QUAHOGS	QUEACHY	QUIESCE	QUIRING	REQUERE	SQUEAKS
CASQUES	EQUINOX	OBLIQUE	QUAICHS	QUEECHY	QUIETED	QUIRKED	REQUEST	SQUEAKY
CAZIQUE	EQUIPES	OBLOQUY	QUAIGHS	QUEENED	QUIETEN	QUIRTED	REQUIEM	SQUEALS

SQUEEZE
SQUEEZY
SQUELCH
SQUIDGE
SQUIDGY
SQUIERS
SQUIFFY
SQUILLA
SQUILLS
SQUINCH
SQUINNY
SQUINTS
SQUINTY
SQUIRED
SQUIRES
SQUIRMS
SQUIRMY
SQUIRRS
SQUIRTS
SQUISHY
SQUITCH
SQUOOSH
SUBAQUA
TEQUILA
TOQUETS
TORQUED
TORQUER
TORQUES
TSADDIQ
TZADDIQ
UNEQUAL
UNIQUER
UNIQUES
UNQUEEN
UNQUIET
UNQUOTE
VAQUERO
YANQUIS
YAQONAS

Q – 8-letter words

ACEQUIAS
ACQUAINT
ACQUESTS
ACQUIGHT
ACQUIRAL
ACQUIRED
ACQUIRER
ACQUIRES
ACQUISTS
ACQUITES
ADEQUACY
ADEQUATE
AEQUORIN
ALFAQUIN
ALFAQUIS
ALIQUANT
ALIQUOTS
ANTIQUED
ANTIQUER
ANTIQUES
APPLIQUE
AQUACADE
AQUAFERS
AQUALUNG
AQUANAUT
AQUARIAL
AQUARIAN
AQUARIST
AQUARIUM
AQUATICS
AQUATINT
AQUATONE
AQUAVITS
AQUEDUCT
AQUIFERS
AQUILINE
AQUILONS
ARQUEBUS
BANQUETS
BARBEQUE
BAROQUES
BASQUINE
BEDQUILT
BELIQUOR
BEQUEATH
BEQUESTS
BEZIQUES
BIUNIQUE
BLANQUET
BOSQUETS
BOUQUETS
BOUTIQUE
BRELOQUE
BRIQUETS
BRUSQUER
CACIQUES
CALQUING
CAZIQUES
CHAQUETA
CHARQUID
CHARQUIS
CHEQUERS
CINQUAIN
CLAQUERS
CLAQUEUR
CLINIQUE
CLIQUIER
CLIQUING
CLIQUISH
CLIQUISM
COEQUALS
COEQUATE
COLLOQUE
COLLOQUY
COMIQUES
CONQUERS
CONQUEST
CONQUIAN
COQUETRY
COQUETTE
COQUILLA
COQUILLE
COQUINAS
COQUITOS
COTQUEAN
CRITIQUE
CROQUETS
CUMQUATS
DAIQUIRI
DAQUIRIS
DETRAQUE
DISQUIET
DOCQUETS
ELOQUENT
EMBUSQUE
ENQUIRED
ENQUIRER
ENQUIRES
EQUALING
EQUALISE
EQUALITY
EQUALIZE
EQUALLED
EQUATING
EQUATION
EQUATORS
EQUINELY
EQUINIAS
EQUINITY
EQUIPAGE
EQUIPPED
EQUIPPER
EQUISETA
EQUITANT
EQUITIES
EQUIVOKE
ESQUIRED
ESQUIRES
ESQUISSE
EXEQUIAL
EXEQUIES
FILIOQUE
FREQUENT
GRECQUES
HAQUETON
HENEQUEN
HENEQUIN
HENIQUEN
HENIQUIN
HUAQUERO
ILLIQUID
INEQUITY
INIQUITY
INQILABS
INQUERED
INQUERES
INQUESTS
INQUIETS
INQUIRED
INQUIRER
INQUIRES
JACQUARD
JERQUERS
JERQUING
JONQUILS
KUMQUATS
LACQUERS
LACQUEYS
LIQUABLE
LIQUATED
LIQUATES
LIQUESCE
LIQUEURS
LIQUIDLY
LIQUIDUS
LIQUORED
LOQUITUR
LUSTIQUE
MACAQUES
MADOQUAS
MAQUETTE
MAROQUIN
MARQUEES
MARQUESS
MARQUISE
MASQUERS
MBAQANGA
MESQUINE
MESQUITE
MESQUITS
MEZQUITE
MEZQUITS
MIQUELET
MISQUOTE
MOQUETTE
MORESQUE
MOSQUITO
MUQADDAM
MUSQUASH
MYSTIQUE
NARQUOIS
NONEQUAL
NONQUOTA
OBLIQUED
OBLIQUER
OBLIQUES
OBLIQUID
OBSEQUIE
ODALIQUE
OLDSQUAW
OPAQUELY
OPAQUEST
OPAQUING
OQUASSAS
OUTQUOTE
PARAQUAT
PARAQUET
PAROQUET
PARQUETS
PASQUILS
PERIQUES
PERRUQUE
PETANQUE
PHYSIQUE
PICQUETS
PIQUANCE
PIQUANCY
PIQUETED
PIROQUES
POSTIQUE
PRATIQUE
PREQUELS
QABALAHS
QAIMAQAM
QALAMDAN
QAWWALIS
QINDARKA
QUAALUDE
QUACKERS
QUACKERY
QUACKING
QUACKISH
QUACKISM
QUACKLED
QUACKLES
QUADDING
QUADPLEX
QUADRANS
QUADRANT
QUADRATE
QUADRATS
QUADRICS
QUADRIGA
QUADROON
QUAESTOR
QUAFFERS
QUAFFING
QUAGGIER
QUAGMIRE
QUAGMIRY
QUAHAUGS
QUAICHES
QUAILING
QUAINTER
QUAINTLY
QUAKIEST
QUAKINGS
QUALMIER
QUALMING
QUALMISH
QUANDANG
QUANDARY
QUANDONG
QUANNETS
QUANTICS
QUANTIFY
QUANTILE
QUANTING
QUANTISE
QUANTITY
QUANTIZE
QUANTONG
QUARRELS
QUARRIED
QUARRIER
QUARRIES
QUARTANS
QUARTERN
QUARTERS
QUARTETS
QUARTETT
QUARTICS
QUARTIER
QUARTILE
QUARTZES
QUASHEES
QUASHERS
QUASHIES
QUASHING
QUASSIAS
QUASSINS
QUATCHED
QUATCHES
QUATORZE
QUATRAIN
QUAVERED
QUAVERER
QUAYAGES
QUAYLIKE
QUAYSIDE
QUEACHES
QUEASIER
QUEASILY
QUEAZIER
QUEENDOM
QUEENIER
QUEENIES
QUEENING
QUEENITE
QUEENLET
QUEERDOM
QUEEREST
QUEERING
QUEERISH
QUEERITY
QUELCHED
QUELCHES
QUELLERS
QUELLING
QUENCHED
QUENCHER
QUENCHES
QUENELLE
QUERCINE
QUERIDAS
QUERIERS
QUERISTS
QUERYING
QUESTANT
QUESTERS
QUESTING
QUESTION
QUESTORS
QUETCHED
QUETCHES
QUETHING
QUETZALS
QUEUEING
QUEUINGS
QUEYNIES
QUEZALES
QUIBBLED
QUIBBLER
QUIBBLES
QUIBLINS
QUICHING
QUICKENS
QUICKEST
QUICKIES
QUICKSET
QUIDDANY
QUIDDITS
QUIDDITY
QUIDDLED
QUIDDLER
QUIDDLES
QUIDNUNC
QUIESCED
QUIESCES
QUIETENS
QUIETERS
QUIETEST
QUIETING
QUIETISM
QUIETIST
QUIETIVE
QUIETUDE
QUIGHTED
QUILLAIA
QUILLAIS
QUILLAJA
QUILLETS
QUILLING
QUILLMAN
QUILLMEN
QUILLONS
QUILTERS
QUILTING
QUINCHED
QUINCHES
QUINCUNX
QUINELAS
QUINELLA
QUINIELA
QUININAS
QUININES
QUINNATS
QUINOIDS
QUINOLIN
QUINONES
QUINSIED
QUINSIES
QUINTAIN
QUINTALS
QUINTANS
QUINTARS
QUINTETS
QUINTETT
QUINTICS
QUINTILE
QUINTINS
QUIPPERS
QUIPPING
QUIPPISH
QUIPSTER
QUIRKIER
QUIRKILY
QUIRKING
QUIRKISH
QUIRTING
QUISLING
QUITCHED
QUITCHES
QUITRENT
QUITTALS
QUITTERS
QUITTING
QUITTORS
QUIVERED
QUIVERER
QUIXOTES
QUIXOTIC
QUIXOTRY
QUIZZERS
QUIZZERY
QUIZZIFY
QUIZZING
QUODDING
QUODLINS
QUOIFING
QUOINING
QUOITERS
QUOITING
QUOMODOS
QUONKING
QUOPPING
QUOTABLE
QUOTABLY
QUOTIENT
QURUSHES
QWERTIES
RACQUETS
RAMEQUIN
REEQUIPS
RELIQUES
REMARQUE
REPIQUED
REPIQUES
REQUERED
REQUERES
REQUESTS
REQUIEMS
REQUIGHT
REQUIRED
REQUIRER
REQUIRES
REQUITAL
REQUITED
REQUITER
REQUITES
REQUOTED
REQUOTES
REQUOYLE
ROCQUETS
ROQUETED
ROQUETTE
RORQUALS
SEAQUAKE
SEQUELAE
SEQUENCE
SEQUENCY
SEQUENTS
SEQUINED
SEQUITUR
SEQUOIAS
SHEQALIM
SILIQUAE
SILIQUAS
SILIQUES
SOLIQUID
SQUABASH
SQUABBED
SQUABBER
SQUABBLE
SQUACCOS
SQUADDED
SQUADDIE
SQUADRON
SQUAILED
SQUAILER
SQUALENE
SQUALLED
SQUALLER
SQUALOID
SQUALORS
SQUAMATE
SQUAMOSE
SQUAMOUS
SQUAMULA
SQUAMULE
SQUANDER
SQUARELY
SQUARERS
SQUAREST
SQUARIAL
SQUARING
SQUARISH
SQUARSON
SQUASHED
SQUASHER
SQUASHES
SQUATTED
SQUATTER
SQUATTLE
SQUAWKED
SQUAWKER
SQUAWMAN
SQUAWMEN
SQUEAKED
SQUEAKER
SQUEALED
SQUEALER
SQUEEGEE
SQUEEZED
SQUEEZER
SQUEEZES
SQUEGGED
SQUEGGER
SQUELCHY
SQUIBBED
SQUIDDED
SQUIDGED
SQUIDGES
SQUIFFED
SQUIFFER
SQUIGGLE
SQUIGGLY
SQUILGEE

SQUILLAE	SQUIREEN	SQUIRRED	SQUOOSHY	TEQUILLA	TRUQUEUR	UNIQUELY	USQUEBAE
SQUILLAS	SQUIRELY	SQUIRREL	SQUUSHED	TOQUILLA	TSADDIQS	UNIQUEST	VANQUISH
SQUINIED	SQUIRESS	SQUIRTED	SQUUSHES	TORQUATE	TURQUOIS	UNQUEENS	VAQUEROS
SQUINIES	SQUIRING	SQUIRTER	SUBEQUAL	TORQUERS	TZADDIQS	UNQUIETS	VEHMIQUE
SQUINTED	SQUIRISH	SQUISHED	SURQUEDY	TORQUING	UBIQUITY	UNQUOTED	VERQUERE
SQUINTER	SQUIRMED	SQUISHES	TAQUERIA	TRANQUIL	UMQUHILE	UNQUOTES	VERQUIRE
SQUIRAGE	SQUIRMER	SQUIZZES	TEQUILAS	TRUQUAGE	UNEQUALS	USQUABAE	

X-WORDS

X – 2-letter words

AX	EX	OX	XI	XU

X – 3-letter words

AXE	FAX	HOX	LUX	NOX	POX	SEX	VEX	XIS
BOX	FIX	KEX	MAX	OXO	PYX	SIX	VOX	YEX
COX	FOX	LAX	MIX	OXY	RAX	SOX	WAX	ZAX
DEX	GOX	LEX	MUX	PAX	REX	TAX	WEX	ZEX
DUX	HEX	LOX	NIX	PIX	SAX	TUX	WOX	

X – 4-letter words

APEX	AXON	DIXI	EXIT	FLAX	IXIA	MINX	ORYX	PREX	VEXT
AXAL	BOXY	DIXY	EXON	FLEX	JEUX	MIXT	OXEN	ROUX	WAXY
AXED	CALX	DOUX	EXPO	FLIX	JINX	MIXY	OXER	SEXT	WEXE
AXEL	COAX	DOXY	EXUL	FLUX	JYNX	MOXA	OXES	SEXY	XYST
AXES	COXA	EAUX	FAIX	FOXY	LANX	NEXT	OXID	TAXA	YUNX
AXIL	COXY	EXAM	FALX	HOAX	LUXE	NIXE	OXIM	TAXI	
AXIS	CRUX	EXEC	FAUX	IBEX	LYNX	NIXY	PIXY	TEXT	
AXLE	DEXY	EXES	FIXT	ILEX	MAXI	ONYX	POXY	ULEX	

X – 5-letter words

ADDAX	BOXEN	DIXIT	EXTOL	HYRAX	MIXER	PHLOX	SAXES	TOXIN	XENIC
ADMIX	BOXER	DOXIE	EXTRA	IMMIX	MIXES	PIXEL	SEXED	TUXES	XENON
AFFIX	BOXES	DRUXY	EXUDE	INDEX	MIXUP	PIXES	SEXER	TWIXT	XERIC
ANNEX	BRAXY	DUXES	EXULS	INFIX	MOXAS	PIXIE	SEXES	UNBOX	XEROX
ATAXY	BUXOM	EMBOX	EXULT	IXIAS	MOXIE	PODEX	SEXTO	UNFIX	XERUS
AUXIN	CALIX	ENFIX	EXURB	IXORA	MUREX	POXED	SEXTS	UNMIX	XOANA
AXELS	CALYX	EPOXY	FAXED	IXTLE	MUXED	POXES	SILEX	UNSEX	XYLAN
AXIAL	CAREX	EXACT	FAXES	KEXES	MUXES	PREXY	SIXER	UNTAX	XYLEM
AXILE	CAXON	EXALT	FIXED	KYLIX	NEXTS	PROXY	SIXES	VARIX	XYLIC
AXILS	CHOUX	EXAMS	FIXER	LATEX	NEXUS	PYXED	SIXMO	VEXED	XYLOL
AXING	CIMEX	EXCEL	FIXES	LAXER	NIXED	PYXES	SIXTE	VEXER	XYLYL
AXIOM	CODEX	EXEAT	FIXIT	LAXES	NIXES	PYXIE	SIXTH	VEXES	XYSTI
AXION	COMIX	EXECS	FLAXY	LAXLY	NIXIE	PYXIS	SIXTY	VEXIL	XYSTS
AXITE	COXAE	EXEEM	FOXED	LEXES	NOXAL	RADIX	SOREX	VIBEX	YEXED
AXLED	COXAL	EXEME	FOXES	LEXIS	NOXES	RAXED	TAXED	VITEX	YEXES
AXLES	COXED	EXERT	GALAX	LIMAX	OXBOW	RAXES	TAXER	VIXEN	ZAXES
AXMAN	COXES	EXIES	GOXES	LOXED	OXERS	REDOX	TAXES	VOXEL	ZEXES
AXMEN	CULEX	EXILE	HAPAX	LOXES	OXEYE	REDUX	TAXIS	WAXED	
AXOID	CYLIX	EXINE	HELIX	LUXES	OXIDE	REFIX	TAXOL	WAXEN	
AXONE	DEOXY	EXIST	HEXAD	MALAX	OXIDS	RELAX	TAXON	WAXER	
AXONS	DESEX	EXITS	HEXED	MAXES	OXIME	REMEX	TAXOR	WAXES	
BEAUX	DETOX	EXODE	HEXER	MAXIM	OXIMS	REMIX	TAXUS	WEXED	
BEMIX	DEWAX	EXONS	HEXES	MAXIS	OXLIP	RETAX	TELEX	WEXES	
BOLIX	DEXES	EXPAT	HEXYL	MIREX	OXTER	REWAX	TEXAS	WOXEN	
BORAX	DEXIE	EXPEL	HOXED	MIXED	PANAX	REXES	TEXTS	XEBEC	
BOXED	DIXIE	EXPOS	HOXES	MIXEN	PAXES	SALIX	TOXIC	XENIA	

X – 6-letter words

ADIEUX	ALKOXY	ATWIXT	AXIOMS	AXONAL	BEMBIX	BOMBAX	BOXING	CERVIX	COAXES
ADMIXT	ANNEXE	AUSPEX	AXIONS	AXONES	BEMIXT	BOMBYX	BOYAUX	CHENIX	COCCYX
ADNEXA	ANOXIA	AUXINS	AXISED	AXONIC	BIAXAL	BONXIE	CALXES	CLAXON	COMMIX
AFFLUX	ANOXIC	AXEMAN	AXISES	AXSEED	BIFLEX	BOXCAR	CARFAX	CLIMAX	CONFIX
ALEXIA	APEXES	AXEMEN	AXITES	BANJAX	BIJOUX	BOXERS	CARFOX	COAXAL	CONVEX
ALEXIC	ATAXIA	AXENIC	AXLIKE	BAXTER	BOLLIX	BOXFUL	CAUDEX	COAXED	CORTEX
ALEXIN	ATAXIC	AXILLA	AXOIDS	BEMBEX	BOLLOX	BOXIER	CAXONS	COAXER	COWPOX

COXIER	EXCEPT	EXPAND	FIXIVE	HOXING	MINXES	OXTAIL	RHEXIS	TAXERS	WAXERS
COXING	EXCESS	EXPATS	FIXURE	IBEXES	MIXENS	OXTERS	SAXAUL	TAXIED	WAXIER
CRUXES	EXCIDE	EXPECT	FLAXEN	ICEBOX	MIXERS	OXYGEN	SAXONY	TAXIES	WAXILY
DEFLEX	EXCISE	EXPELS	FLAXES	ILEXES	MIXIER	OXYMEL	SCOLEX	TAXING	WAXING
DEIXES	EXCITE	EXPEND	FLEXED	IMBREX	MIXING	PAXWAX	SEXERS	TAXITE	WEXING
DEIXIS	EXCUSE	EXPERT	FLEXES	IMPLEX	MIXUPS	PEGBOX	SEXFID	TAXMAN	WRAXLE
DELUXE	EXEATS	EXPIRE	FLEXOR	INFLUX	MOXIES	PEROXY	SEXIER	TAXMEN	XEBECS
DENTEX	EXEDRA	EXPIRY	FLIXED	IXODID	MUXING	PHENIX	SEXILY	TAXOLS	XENIAL
DESOXY	EXEEMS	EXPORT	FLIXES	IXORAS	MYXOID	PICKAX	SEXING	TAXONS	XENIAS
DEXIES	EXEMED	EXPOSE	FLUXED	IXTLES	MYXOMA	PINXIT	SEXISM	TAXORS	XENIUM
DEXTER	EXEMES	EXPUGN	FLUXES	JAWBOX	NEXTLY	PIXELS	SEXIST	TEABOX	XENONS
DEXTRO	EXEMPT	EXSECT	FORFEX	JINXED	NIXIES	PIXIES	SEXPOT	TETTIX	XEROMA
DIAXON	EXEQUY	EXSERT	FORNIX	JINXES	NIXING	PLEXAL	SEXTAN	THORAX	XOANON
DIOXAN	EXERTS	EXTANT	FOXIER	JYNXES	NONTAX	PLEXOR	SEXTET	TOXICS	XYLANS
DIOXID	EXEUNT	EXTASY	FOXILY	KLAXON	ONYXES	PLEXUS	SEXTON	TOXINE	XYLEMS
DIOXIN	EXHALE	EXTEND	FOXING	LARNAX	OREXIS	POLEAX	SEXTOS	TOXINS	XYLENE
DIPLEX	EXHORT	EXTENT	FRUTEX	LARYNX	ORIFEX	POLLEX	SEXUAL	TOXOID	XYLOID
DIXIES	EXHUME	EXTERN	GALAXY	LAXEST	ORYXES	POXIER	SILVEX	TUTRIX	XYLOLS
DIXITS	EXILED	EXTINE	HALLUX	LAXISM	OUTBOX	POXING	SIXAIN	TUXEDO	XYLOMA
DOGFOX	EXILES	EXTIRP	HATBOX	LAXIST	OUTFOX	PRAXES	SIXERS	ULEXES	XYLOSE
DOXIES	EXILIC	EXTOLD	HAYBOX	LAXITY	OXALIC	PRAXIS	SIXMOS	UNFIXT	XYLYLS
DUPLEX	EXINES	EXTOLL	HEXACT	LEXEME	OXALIS	PREFIX	SIXTES	UNISEX	XYSTER
EARWAX	EXISTS	EXTOLS	HEXADE	LEXICA	OXBOWS	PREMIX	SIXTHS	UNMIXT	XYSTOI
EFFLUX	EXITED	EXTORT	HEXADS	LOXING	OXCART	PRETAX	SKYBOX	UNSEXY	XYSTOS
ELIXIR	EXODES	EXTRAS	HEXANE	LUMMOX	OXEYES	PREXES	SMILAX	UNVEXT	XYSTUS
ETHOXY	EXODIC	EXUDED	HEXENE	LUXATE	OXFORD	PROLIX	SPADIX	URTEXT	YEXING
EUTAXY	EXODOI	EXUDES	HEXERS	LUXURY	OXGANG	PTYXES	SPHINX	VERNIX	YUNXES
EXACTA	EXODOS	EXULTS	HEXING	LYNXES	OXGATE	PTYXIS	STORAX	VERTEX	
EXACTS	EXODUS	EXURBS	HEXONE	MAGNOX	OXHEAD	PYXIES	STYRAX	VEXERS	
EXALTS	EXOGEN	EXUVIA	HEXOSE	MASTIX	OXIDES	PYXING	SUBFIX	VEXILS	
EXAMEN	EXOMIS	FAXING	HEXYLS	MATRIX	OXIDIC	RAXING	SUFFIX	VEXING	
EXARCH	EXONIC	FIXATE	HOAXED	MAXIMA	OXIMES	REFLEX	SURTAX	VIXENS	
EXCAMB	EXONYM	FIXERS	HOAXER	MAXIMS	OXLAND	REFLUX	SYNTAX	VOLVOX	
EXCEED	EXOPOD	FIXING	HOAXES	MAXIXE	OXLIPS	REMIXT	SYRINX	VORTEX	
EXCELS	EXOTIC	FIXITY	HOTBOX	MENINX	OXSLIP	RHEXES	TAXEME	VOXELS	

X – 7-letter words

ABAXIAL	ATAXICS	BOXLIKE	DETOXED	EXALTER	EXEEMED	EXPANDS	EXTERNS	FLIXING
ABAXILE	ATAXIES	BOXROOM	DETOXES	EXAMENS	EXEGETE	EXPANSE	EXTINCT	FLUMMOX
ABRAXAS	AUXESES	BOXWOOD	DEWAXED	EXAMINE	EXEMING	EXPECTS	EXTINES	FLUXING
ADAXIAL	AUXESIS	BRAXIES	DEWAXES	EXAMPLE	EXEMPLA	EXPENDS	EXTIRPS	FLUXION
ADDAXES	AUXETIC	BROADAX	DEXTERS	EXARATE	EXEMPLE	EXPENSE	EXTOLLS	FLUXIVE
ADMIXED	AUXINIC	BRUXISM	DEXTRAL	EXARCHS	EXEMPTS	EXPERTS	EXTORTS	FOWLPOX
ADMIXES	AXIALLY	BUREAUX	DEXTRAN	EXARCHY	EXERGUE	EXPIATE	EXTRACT	FOXFIRE
ADNEXAL	AXILLAE	BUXOMER	DEXTRIN	EXCAMBS	EXERTED	EXPIRED	EXTRAIT	FOXFISH
AFFIXAL	AXILLAR	BUXOMLY	DIAXONS	EXCEEDS	EXHALED	EXPIRER	EXTREAT	FOXHOLE
AFFIXED	AXILLAS	CACHEXY	DIGOXIN	EXCEPTS	EXHALES	EXPIRES	EXTREMA	FOXHUNT
AFFIXER	AXINITE	CADEAUX	DIOXANE	EXCERPT	EXHAUST	EXPLAIN	EXTREME	FOXIEST
AFFIXES	AXOLOTL	CALYXES	DIOXANS	EXCHEAT	EXHEDRA	EXPLANT	EXTRUDE	FOXINGS
ALEXIAS	AXONEME	CARAPAX	DIOXIDE	EXCIDED	EXHIBIT	EXPLODE	EXUDATE	FOXLIKE
ALEXINE	AXSEEDS	CASHBOX	DIOXIDS	EXCIDES	EXHORTS	EXPLOIT	EXUDING	FOXSHIP
ALEXINS	BANDBOX	CHAMOIX	DIOXINS	EXCIMER	EXHUMED	EXPLORE	EXULTED	FOXSKIN
ALLOXAN	BATEAUX	CHOENIX	DRUXIER	EXCIPLE	EXHUMER	EXPORTS	EXURBAN	FOXTAIL
ANAXIAL	BAUXITE	CLAXONS	ELIXIRS	EXCISED	EXHUMES	EXPOSAL	EXURBIA	FOXTROT
ANNEXED	BAXTERS	COALBOX	EMBOXED	EXCISES	EXIGENT	EXPOSED	EXUVIAE	GALAXES
ANNEXES	BEESWAX	COANNEX	EMBOXES	EXCITED	EXILIAN	EXPOSER	EXUVIAL	GATEAUX
ANOREXY	BEMIXED	COAXERS	ENFIXED	EXCITER	EXILING	EXPOSES	EXUVIUM	GEARBOX
ANOXIAS	BEMIXES	COAXIAL	ENFIXES	EXCITES	EXILITY	EXPOSIT	FEEDBOX	GRAVLAX
ANTEFIX	BETAXED	COAXING	EPAXIAL	EXCITON	EXISTED	EXPOUND	FIREBOX	HAPAXES
ANTHRAX	BETWIXT	COEXERT	EPITAXY	EXCITOR	EXITING	EXPRESS	FIXABLE	HELIXES
ANTISEX	BIAXIAL	COEXIST	EPOXIDE	EXCLAIM	EXOCARP	EXPUGNS	FIXATED	HELLBOX
ANTITAX	BOLIXED	COMMIXT	EPOXIED	EXCLAVE	EXODERM	EXPULSE	FIXATES	HEXACTS
ANXIETY	BOLIXES	COMPLEX	EPOXIES	EXCLUDE	EXODIST	EXPUNCT	FIXATIF	HEXADES
ANXIOUS	BONXIES	CONFLUX	EPOXYED	EXCRETA	EXOGAMY	EXPUNGE	FIXEDLY	HEXADIC
APOPLEX	BOOMBOX	CONTEXT	EQUINOX	EXCRETE	EXOGENS	EXPURGE	FIXINGS	HEXAGON
APRAXIA	BORAXES	COTEAUX	ETHOXYL	EXCUDIT	EXOMION	EXSCIND	FIXTURE	HEXANES
APRAXIC	BOSTRYX	COXALGY	EUTEXIA	EXCURSE	EXONYMS	EXSECTS	FIXURES	HEXAPLA
APTERYX	BOXCARS	COXCOMB	EXACTAS	EXCUSAL	EXOPODS	EXSERTS	FLAXIER	HEXAPOD
ARUSPEX	BOXFISH	COXIEST	EXACTED	EXCUSED	EXORDIA	EXTATIC	FLEXILE	HEXARCH
ASEXUAL	BOXFULS	COXITIS	EXACTER	EXCUSER	EXOSMIC	EXTENDS	FLEXING	HEXENES
ASPHYXY	BOXHAUL	CURTAXE	EXACTLY	EXCUSES	EXOTICA	EXTENSE	FLEXION	HEXEREI
ATARAXY	BOXIEST	DESEXED	EXACTOR	EXECUTE	EXOTICS	EXTENTS	FLEXORS	HEXINGS
ATAXIAS	BOXINGS	DESEXES	EXALTED	EXEDRAE	EXOTISM	EXTERNE	FLEXURE	HEXONES

HEXOSAN HEXOSES HOAXERS HOAXING HOMOSEX HYDROXY HYPOXIA HYPOXIC HYRAXES IMMIXED IMMIXES INDEXAL INDEXED INDEXER INDEXES INDOXYL INEXACT INFIXED INFIXES INVEXED IXODIDS JAMBEUX JINXING JUKEBOX KLAXONS LATEXES LAXATOR LAXISMS LAXISTS LAXNESS LEXEMES LEXEMIC LEXICAL

LEXICON LEXISES LIXIVIA LOCKBOX LOXYGEN LUXATED LUXATES MAILBOX MALAXED MALAXES MARTEXT MAXILLA MAXIMAL MAXIMIN MAXIMUM MAXIXES MAXWELL METHOXY MILIEUX MINIMAX MINXISH MIREXES MIXABLE MIXEDLY MIXIBLE MIXIEST MIXTION MIXTURE MONAXON MUREXES MYXOMAS NARTHEX NEXUSES

NOXIOUS ORATRIX OUTJINX OVERLAX OVERMIX OVERTAX OXALATE OXAZINE OXBLOOD OXCARTS OXFORDS OXGANGS OXGATES OXHEADS OXHEART OXIDANT OXIDASE OXIDATE OXIDISE OXIDIZE OXLANDS OXONIUM OXSLIPS OXTAILS OXTERED OXYACID OXYGENS OXYMELS OXYMORA OXYPHIL OXYSALT OXYSOME OXYTONE

PACKWAX PANAXES PANCHAX PARADOX PAXIUBA PEMPHIX PEROXID PERPLEX PHALANX PHARYNX PHENOXY PHLOXES PHOENIX PICKAXE PILLBOX PIXYISH PLANXTY PLEXORS PLEXURE PODEXES POLEAXE POSTBOX POSTFIX POSTTAX POXIEST PREMIXT PRETEXT PREXIES PRINCOX PROXIES PROXIMO PYREXIA PYREXIC

PYXIDES PYXIDIA QUIXOTE RADIXES REAFFIX REANNEX RECTRIX REDOXES REEXPEL REFIXED REFIXES REINDEX RELAXED RELAXER RELAXES RELAXIN REMIXED REMIXES RESEAUX RETAXED RETAXES REWAXED REWAXES SALPINX SALTBOX SANDBOX SAXAULS SAXHORN SAXTUBA SEALWAX SEEDBOX SEXFOIL SEXIEST

SEXISMS SEXISTS SEXLESS SEXPERT SEXPOTS SEXTAIN SEXTANS SEXTANT SEXTETS SEXTETT SEXTILE SEXTONS SEXTUOR SHOWBOX SILEXES SIMPLEX SIXAINE SIXAINS SIXFOLD SIXTEEN SIXTHLY SIXTIES SOAPBOX SONOVOX SOREXES SPANDEX SUBTAXA SUBTEXT SYNAXES SYNAXIS TAXABLE TAXABLY TAXEMES

TAXEMIC TAXICAB TAXIING TAXIMAN TAXIMEN TAXINGS TAXITES TAXITIC TAXIWAY TAXLESS TAXPAID TAXWISE TAXYING TECTRIX TELEFAX TELETEX TELEXED TELEXES TEXASES TEXTILE TEXTUAL TEXTURE TOOLBOX TORTRIX TOXEMIA TOXEMIC TOXICAL TOXINES TOXOIDS TRIAXON TRIOXID TRIPLEX TUBIFEX

TUXEDOS ULEXITE UNBOXED UNBOXES UNFIXED UNFIXES UNMIXED UNMIXES UNSEXED UNSEXES UNTAXED UNTAXES UNVEXED UNWAXED URTEXTS UXORIAL VAUDOUX VEXEDLY VEXILLA VEXINGS VICTRIX VITEXES VITRAUX VIXENLY WAXBILL WAXIEST WAXINGS WAXLIKE WAXWEED WAXWING WAXWORK WAXWORM WOADWAX

WOODBOX WOODWAX WORKBOX WRAXLED WRAXLES XANTHAM XANTHAN XANTHIC XANTHIN XERAFIN XERARCH XERASIA XEROMAS XEROSES XEROSIS XEROTES XEROTIC XEROXED XEROXES XERUSES XIPHOID XYLENES XYLENOL XYLIDIN XYLITOL XYLOGEN XYLOMAS XYLONIC XYLOSES XYSTERS ZEUXITE ZOOTAXY

X – 8-letter words

ACETOXYL ADMIXING AFFIXERS AFFIXIAL AFFIXING AFFLUXES AFTERTAX ALEXINES ALKOXIDE ALLOXANS AMPHIOXI AMPLEXUS ANATOXIN ANNEXING ANNEXION ANNEXURE ANOREXIA ANOREXIC ANOXEMIA ANOXEMIC ANTEFIXA ANTHELIX APOMIXES APOMIXIS APOPLEXY APPENDIX APRAXIAS APYREXIA ASPHYXIA ATARAXIA ATARAXIC AUXETICS AUXILIAR AVIATRIX AXIALITY AXILLARS AXILLARY AXINITES

AXIOLOGY AXLETREE AXOLOTLS AXONEMAL AXONEMES AXOPLASM BANDEAUX BANJAXED BANJAXES BANXRING BATTEAUX BAUXITES BAUXITIC BEAUXITE BEMBEXES BEMBIXES BEMIXING BERCEAUX BICONVEX BIOTOXIN BISEXUAL BOLIXING BOLLIXED BOLLIXES BOLLOXED BOLLOXES BOMBAXES BOMBYXES BORDEAUX BOXBERRY BOXBOARD BOXHAULS BOXINESS BOXROOMS BOXTHORN BOXWOODS BRAINBOX BREADBOX

BROADAXE BRUXISMS BUXOMEST CACHEXIA CACHEXIC CACODOXY CACOMIXL CAMAIEUX CARBOXYL CARFAXES CARFOXES CARNIFEX CATHEXES CATHEXIS CAUDEXES CERVIXES CHAPEAUX CHATEAUX CHENIXES CHRONAXY CICATRIX CINEPLEX CLACKBOX CLANGBOX CLIMAXED CLIMAXES COCCYXES COEXERTS COEXISTS COEXTEND COMMIXED COMMIXES CONFIXED CONFIXES CONTEXTS CONVEXED CONVEXES CONVEXLY

CORTEXES COUTEAUX COWPOXES COXALGIA COXALGIC COXCOMBS COXINESS COXSWAIN CREATRIX CRUCIFIX CURATRIX CURTALAX CURTAXES CYBERSEX DEFLEXED DEFLEXES DEIXISES DENTEXES DESEXING DETOXIFY DETOXING DEWAXING DEXTRANS DEXTRINE DEXTRINS DEXTROSE DEXTROUS DIGOXINS DIOXANES DIOXIDES DIPLEXER DISANNEX DOGFOXES DOXOLOGY DRUXIEST DUPLEXED DUPLEXER DUPLEXES

DUXELLES DYSLEXIA DYSLEXIC DYSTAXIA EARTHWAX EARWAXES ECONOBOX ECOTOXIC EFFLUXES EKTEXINE EMBOXING ENDEIXES ENDEIXIS ENDEXINE ENFIXING EPICALYX EPITAXIC EPOXIDES EPOXYING ETHOXIES ETHOXYLS EUTAXIES EUTAXITE EUTEXIAS EUXENITE EXACTERS EXACTEST EXACTING EXACTION EXACTORS EXALTERS EXALTING EXAMINED EXAMINEE EXAMINER EXAMINES EXAMPLAR EXAMPLED

EXAMPLES EXANTHEM EXARCHAL EXCAMBED EXCAVATE EXCEEDED EXCEEDER EXCELLED EXCEPTED EXCEPTOR EXCERPTA EXCERPTS EXCESSED EXCESSES EXCHANGE EXCHEATS EXCIDING EXCIMERS EXCIPLES EXCISING EXCISION EXCITANT EXCITERS EXCITING EXCITONS EXCITORS EXCLAIMS EXCLAVES EXCLUDED EXCLUDEE EXCLUDER EXCLUDES EXCRETAL EXCRETED EXCRETER EXCRETES EXCUBANT EXCURSED

EXCURSES EXCURSUS EXCUSALS EXCUSERS EXCUSING EXCUSIVE EXECRATE EXECUTED EXECUTER EXECUTES EXECUTOR EXECUTRY EXEEMING EXEGESES EXEGESIS EXEGETES EXEGETIC EXEMPLAR EXEMPLES EXEMPLUM EXEMPTED EXEQUIAL EXEQUIES EXERCISE EXERGUAL EXERGUES EXERTING EXERTION EXERTIVE EXHALANT EXHALENT EXHALING EXHAUSTS EXHEDRAE EXHIBITS EXHORTED EXHORTER EXHUMATE

EXHUMERS EXHUMING EXIGEANT EXIGENCE EXIGENCY EXIGENTS EXIGIBLE EXIGUITY EXIGUOUS EXIMIOUS EXISTENT EXISTING EXITANCE EXITLESS EXOCARPS EXOCRINE EXODERMS EXODISTS EXODUSES EXOERGIC EXOGAMIC EXOMIONS EXOMISES EXONUMIA EXOPHAGY EXOPLASM EXORABLE EXORCISE EXORCISM EXORCIST EXORCIZE EXORDIAL EXORDIUM EXOSMOSE EXOSPORE EXOTERIC EXOTISMS EXOTOXIC

EXOTOXIN EXPANDED EXPANDER EXPANDOR EXPANSES EXPECTED EXPECTER EXPEDITE EXPELLED EXPELLEE EXPELLER EXPENDED EXPENDER EXPENSED EXPENSES EXPERTED EXPERTLY EXPIABLE EXPIATED EXPIATES EXPIATOR EXPIRANT EXPIRERS EXPIRIES EXPIRING EXPLAINS EXPLANTS EXPLICIT EXPLODED EXPLODER EXPLODES EXPLOITS EXPLORED EXPLORER EXPLORES EXPONENT EXPORTED EXPORTER EXPOSALS EXPOSERS EXPOSING EXPOSITS EXPOSURE EXPOUNDS EXPRESSO EXPUGNED EXPULSED EXPULSES EXPUNCTS EXPUNGED EXPUNGER EXPUNGES EXPURGED EXPURGES EXSCINDS EXSECANT EXSECTED EXSERTED EXTASIES EXTENDED EXTENDER EXTENSOR EXTERIOR EXTERNAL EXTERNAT EXTERNES EXTINCTS

EXTIRPED EXTOLLED EXTOLLER EXTORTED EXTORTER EXTRACTS EXTRADOS EXTRAITS EXTRANET EXTREATS EXTREMER EXTREMES EXTREMUM EXTRORSE EXTRUDED EXTRUDER EXTRUDES EXTUBATE EXUDATES EXULTANT EXULTING EXURBIAS EXUVIATE FABLIAUX FIXATIFS FIXATING FIXATION FIXATIVE FIXATURE FIXITIES FIXTURES FLAXIEST FLAXSEED FLEXAGON FLEXIBLE FLEXIBLY FLEXIONS FLEXTIME FLEXUOSE FLEXUOUS FLEXURAL FLEXURES FLUXGATE FLUXIONS FORFEXES FOURPLEX FOXBERRY FOXFIRES FOXGLOVE FOXHOLES FOXHOUND FOXHUNTS FOXINESS FOXSHARK FOXSHIPS FOXSKINS FOXTAILS FOXTROTS GALAXIES GENETRIX GENITRIX GEOTAXES GEOTAXIS GIAMBEUX GLOXINIA HARUSPEX HATBOXES

HAYBOXES HERETRIX HERITRIX HEXAFOIL HEXAGLOT HEXAGONS HEXAGRAM HEXAMINE HEXAPLAR HEXAPLAS HEXAPODS HEXAPODY HEXARCHY HEXEREIS HEXOSANS HEXYLENE HOMEOBOX HORSEPOX HOTBOXES HYDROXYL HYPOXIAS ICEBOXES IMMIXING IMPLEXES INDEXERS INDEXING INDOXYLS INEXPERT INFIXING INFIXION INFLEXED INFLUXES INTERMIX INTERREX INTERSEX JAMBEAUX JANITRIX JAWBOXES KLAXONED LARYNXES LAXATION LAXATIVE LAXATORS LAXITIES LEXICONS LEXIGRAM LIXIVIAL LIXIVIUM LOXYGENS LUMMOXES LUXATING LUXATION LUXMETER LUXURIES LUXURIST MAGNOXES MALAXAGE MALAXATE MALAXING MANTEAUX MARTEXTS MASTIXES MATCHBOX MATRIXES MAXICOAT MAXILLAE MAXILLAS

MAXIMALS MAXIMINS MAXIMISE MAXIMIST MAXIMITE MAXIMIZE MAXIMUMS MAXWELLS METHOXYL MICROLUX MILLILUX MIREPOIX MIXOLOGY MIXTIONS MIXTURES MONAXIAL MONAXONS MONOXIDE MORCEAUX MYXEDEMA MYXOCYTE MYXOMATA NALOXONE NEOTOXIN NEURAXON NEXTDOOR NEXTNESS NITROXYL NONTAXES NONTOXIC OCTUPLEX OPOPANAX OREXISES ORIFEXES ORTHODOX OTOTOXIC OUTBOXED OUTBOXES OUTFOXED OUTFOXES OXALATED OXALATES OXALISES OXAZEPAM OXAZINES OXBLOODS OXHEARTS OXIDABLE OXIDANTS OXIDASES OXIDASIC OXIDATED OXIDATES OXIDISED OXIDISER OXIDISES OXIDIZED OXIDIZER OXIDIZES OXIMETER OXONIUMS OXPECKER OXTERING OXTONGUE OXYACIDS OXYGENIC OXYMORON

OXYPHILE OXYPHILS OXYSALTS OXYSOMES OXYTOCIC OXYTOCIN OXYTONES PANMIXES PANMIXIA PANMIXIS PARADOXY PARALLAX PAROXYSM PAXIUBAS PAXWAXES PEGBOXES PEROXIDE PEROXIDS PHENIXES PHORMINX PHYLAXIS PICKAXED PICKAXES PIXIEISH PIXINESS PLATEAUX PLEXURES PLEXUSES POLEAXED POLEAXES POLYAXON PONCEAUX PONTIFEX POXVIRUS PRAXISES PREAXIAL PRECIEUX PREEXIST PREFIXAL PREFIXED PREFIXES PREMIXED PREMIXES PRETEXTS PROLIXLY PROTOXID PROXEMIC PROXIMAL PTYXISES PYREXIAL PYREXIAS PYROXENE PYROXYLE PYXIDIUM QUADPLEX QUINCUNX QUIXOTES QUIXOTIC QUIXOTRY REEXPELS REEXPORT REEXPOSE REFIXING REFLEXED REFLEXES REFLEXLY REFLUXED

REFLUXES RELAXANT RELAXERS RELAXING RELAXINS REMIXING RETAXING REWAXING RHEXISES RONDEAUX ROULEAUX SARDONYX SAUCEBOX SAXATILE SAXHORNS SAXONIES SAXONITE SAXTUBAS SCRUMPOX SEXFOILS SEXINESS SEXOLOGY SEXPERTS SEXTAINS SEXTANTS SEXTARII SEXTETTE SEXTETTS SEXTILES SEXTOLET SEXTUORS SEXTUPLE SEXTUPLY SEXUALLY SILOXANE SILVEXES SIXAINES SIXPENCE SIXPENNY SIXSCORE SIXTEENS SIXTIETH SIXTYISH SKYBOXES SMALLPOX SMILAXES SNUFFBOX SOUNDBOX SPADIXES SPARAXIS SPHINXES SPINIFEX SPINTEXT STORAXES STYRAXES SUBAXIAL SUBFIXES SUBINDEX SUBOXIDE SUBTAXON SUBTEXTS SUFFIXAL SUFFIXED SUFFIXES SUPERFIX SUPERSEX SUPERTAX

SURTAXED SURTAXES SWEATBOX SWINEPOX SYNTAXES SYNTEXIS SYRINXES TABLEAUX TAXABLES TAXATION TAXATIVE TAXIARCH TAXICABS TAXINGLY TAXIWAYS TAXONOMY TAXPAYER TEABOXES TEGUEXIN TELETEXT TELEXING TETRAXON TETROXID TETTIXES TEXTBOOK TEXTILES TEXTLESS TEXTUARY TEXTURAL TEXTURED TEXTURES THORAXES THYROXIN TOADFLAX TONNEAUX TOXAEMIA TOXAEMIC TOXEMIAS TOXICANT TOXICITY TOXOCARA TRACTRIX TRANSFIX TRIAXIAL TRIAXONS TRIOXIDE TRIOXIDS TRUMEAUX TUTRIXES TUXEDOED TUXEDOES ULEXITES UNBOXING UNDERTAX UNEXOTIC UNEXPERT UNFIXING UNFIXITY UNFLEXED UNIAXIAL UNISEXES UNMIXING UNSEXING UNSEXIST UNSEXUAL UNTAXING UXORIOUS

VERNIXES VERTEXES VEXATION VEXATORY VEXILLAR VEXILLUM VEXINGLY VIDEOTEX VIXENISH VOLVOXES VORTEXES WATCHBOX WATERPOX WAXBERRY WAXBILLS WAXCLOTH WAXINESS WAXPLANT WAXWEEDS WAXWINGS WAXWORKS WAXWORMS WRAXLING XANTHAMS XANTHANS XANTHATE XANTHEIN XANTHENE XANTHINE XANTHINS XANTHOMA XANTHONE XANTHOUS XENOGAMY XENOGENY XENOLITH XENOPHYA XENOTIME XENURINE XERAFINS XERANSES XERANSIS XERANTIC XERAPHIM XERASIAS XEROMATA XEROSERE XEROXING XIPHOIDS XYLENOLS XYLIDINE XYLIDINS XYLITOLS XYLOCARP XYLOGENS XYLOIDIN XYLOLOGY XYLOMATA XYLONITE XYLOTOMY ZELATRIX ZEUXITES ZOOTOXIN

Z-WORDS

Z – 2-letter words

ZO

Z – 3-letter words

ADZ	COZ	FIZ	MIZ	RIZ	ZAG	ZED	ZEX	ZIP	ZOO
AZO	CUZ	JIZ	MOZ	SAZ	ZAP	ZEE	ZHO	ZIT	ZOS
BEZ	DZO	LEZ	POZ	SEZ	ZAX	ZEK	ZIG	ZIZ	ZUZ
BIZ	FEZ	LUZ	REZ	WIZ	ZEA	ZEL	ZIN	ZOA	

Z – 4-letter words

ADZE	DOZE	GIZZ	LEZZ	ORZO	SIZY	ZARF	ZEZE	ZITS	ZULU
AZAN	DOZY	HAZE	LUTZ	OUZO	SPAZ	ZATI	ZHOS	ZIZZ	ZUPA
AZON	DZHO	HAZY	MAZE	OYEZ	SWIZ	ZEAL	ZIFF	ZOBO	ZURF
AZYM	DZOS	HIZZ	MAZY	PHIZ	TIZZ	ZEAS	ZIGS	ZOBU	ZYGA
BIZE	FAZE	IZAR	MEZE	PIZE	TOZE	ZEBU	ZILA	ZOEA	ZYME
BOZO	FIZZ	JAZY	MIZZ	POZZ	TREZ	ZEDS	ZILL	ZOIC	
BUZZ	FOZY	JAZZ	MOZE	PREZ	TUZZ	ZEES	ZIMB	ZONA	
CHEZ	FRIZ	JEEZ	MOZO	PUTZ	TZAR	ZEIN	ZINC	ZONE	
CHIZ	FUTZ	JIZZ	MOZZ	QUIZ	VIZY	ZEKS	ZINE	ZONK	
COZE	FUZE	KAZI	MZEE	RAZE	WHIZ	ZELS	ZING	ZOOM	
COZY	FUZZ	KUZU	NAZE	RAZZ	ZACK	ZERK	ZINS	ZOON	
CZAR	GAZE	LAZE	NAZI	RITZ	ZAGS	ZERO	ZIPS	ZOOS	
DAZE	GAZY	LAZO	OOZE	RIZA	ZANY	ZEST	ZITE	ZORI	
DITZ	GEEZ	LAZY	OOZY	SIZE	ZAPS	ZETA	ZITI	ZOUK	

Z – 5-letter words

ABUZZ	BONZE	DOZED	GLAZY	LAZZI	OUZEL	SIZES	WIZES	ZIBET	ZONAL
ADOZE	BOOZE	DOZEN	GLITZ	LAZZO	OUZOS	SMAZE	WOOTZ	ZIFFS	ZONDA
ADZES	BOOZY	DOZER	GLOZE	LEAZE	OZEKI	SOYUZ	WOOZY	ZIGAN	ZONED
AGAZE	BORTZ	DOZES	GONZO	LEZES	OZONE	SOZIN	ZABRA	ZILAS	ZONER
AIZLE	BOZOS	DZHOS	GRAZE	LEZZY	PEAZE	SPAZZ	ZACKS	ZILCH	ZONES
AMAZE	BRAZA	ENZYM	GRIZE	LOZEN	PEIZE	SPITZ	ZAIRE	ZILLS	ZONKS
AVIZE	BRAZE	FAZED	GROSZ	MAIZE	PIEZO	SQUIZ	ZAKAT	ZIMBI	ZOOEA
AVYZE	BRIZE	FAZES	HAFIZ	MATZA	PIZES	TAZZA	ZAMAN	ZIMBS	ZOOID
AZANS	BUAZE	FEAZE	HAMZA	MATZO	PIZZA	TAZZE	ZAMBO	ZINCO	ZOOKS
AZIDE	BUZZY	FEEZE	HAZAN	MAZED	PLAZA	TEAZE	ZAMIA	ZINCS	ZOOMS
AZIDO	BWAZI	FEZES	HAZED	MAZER	PLOTZ	TIZZY	ZANJA	ZINCY	ZOONS
AZINE	CAPIZ	FIZZY	HAZEL	MAZES	POZZY	TOAZE	ZANTE	ZINEB	ZOOTY
AZLON	CEAZE	FRITZ	HAZER	MAZUT	PRIZE	TOPAZ	ZANZA	ZINES	ZOPPA
AZOIC	CHIZZ	FRIZE	HAZES	MEZES	PUZEL	TOUZE	ZANZE	ZINGS	ZOPPO
AZOLE	CLOZE	FRIZZ	HEEZE	MEZZE	PZAZZ	TOUZY	ZAPPY	ZINGY	ZORIL
AZONS	COBZA	FROZE	HERTZ	MEZZO	RAZED	TOWZE	ZARFS	ZINKE	ZORIS
AZOTE	COLZA	FURZE	HIZEN	MILTZ	RAZEE	TOWZY	ZATIS	ZINKY	ZORRO
AZOTH	COZED	FURZY	HUZZA	MIRZA	RAZER	TOZED	ZAXES	ZIPPO	ZOUKS
AZURE	COZEN	FUZED	HUZZY	MIZEN	RAZES	TOZES	ZAYIN	ZIPPY	ZOWIE
AZURN	COZES	FUZEE	IZARD	MOTZA	RAZOO	TOZIE	ZAZEN	ZIRAM	ZULUS
AZURY	COZEY	FUZES	IZARS	MOZED	RAZOR	TROOZ	ZEALS	ZITIS	ZUPAN
AZYGY	COZIE	FUZIL	IZZAT	MOZES	RITZY	TZARS	ZEBEC	ZIZEL	ZUPAS
AZYME	CRAZE	FUZZY	JAZZY	MOZOS	RIZAS	ULZIE	ZEBRA	ZIZIT	ZURFS
AZYMS	CRAZY	GAUZE	KANZU	MUZZY	ROZET	UNZIP	ZEBUB	ZLOTE	ZUZIM
BAIZA	CROZE	GAUZY	KARZY	MZEES	ROZIT	VEZIR	ZEBUS	ZLOTY	ZYGAL
BAIZE	CZARS	GAZAL	KAZIS	NAZES	SADZA	VIZIR	ZEINS	ZOBOS	ZYGON
BAZAR	DARZI	GAZAR	KAZOO	NAZIR	SAZES	VIZOR	ZERDA	ZOBUS	ZYMES
BAZOO	DAZED	GAZED	KLUTZ	NAZIS	SCUZZ	VOZHD	ZERKS	ZOCCO	ZYMIC
BEZEL	DAZER	GAZER	KRANZ	NEEZE	SEAZE	WALTZ	ZEROS	ZOEAE	
BEZES	DAZES	GAZES	KUDZU	NERTZ	SEIZE	WANZE	ZESTS	ZOEAL	
BEZIL	DIAZO	GAZON	KUZUS	NIZAM	SENZA	WAZIR	ZESTY	ZOEAS	
BIZES	DITZY	GAZOO	LAZAR	NUDZH	SIZAR	WEIZE	ZETAS	ZOISM	
BLAZE	DIZEN	GHAZI	LAZED	OOZED	SIZED	WHIZZ	ZEXES	ZOIST	
BLITZ	DIZZY	GIZMO	LAZES	OOZES	SIZEL	WINZE	ZEZES	ZOMBI	
BONZA	DOOZY	GLAZE	LAZOS	ORZOS	SIZER	WIZEN	ZHOMO	ZONAE	

Z – 6-letter words

ABLAZE	ALTEZA	AVYZES	AZONIC	BAIZED	BEEZER	BEZELS	BLAZER	BOOZER	BRAZES
ABRAZO	AMAZED	AZALEA	AZOTED	BAIZES	BEGAZE	BEZILS	BLAZES	BOOZES	BRAZIL
ADZUKI	AMAZES	AZIDES	AZOTES	BANZAI	BENZAL	BEZOAR	BLAZON	BOOZEY	BREEZE
AGAZED	AMAZON	AZINES	AZOTHS	BARAZA	BENZIL	BEZZLE	BLINTZ	BORZOI	BREEZY
AGNIZE	APOZEM	AZIONE	AZOTIC	BAZAAR	BENZIN	BIZAZZ	BLOWZE	BRAIZE	BRIZES
AGRIZE	ASSIZE	AZLONS	AZURES	BAZARS	BENZOL	BIZONE	BLOWZY	BRAZAS	BRONZE
AGRYZE	AVIZED	AZOLES	AZYGOS	BAZAZZ	BENZYL	BIZZES	BONZER	BRAZED	BRONZY
AGUIZE	AVIZES	AZOLLA	AZYMES	BAZOOS	BEZANT	BLAIZE	BONZES	BRAZEN	BROUZE
AIZLES	AVYZED	AZONAL	BAIZAS	BEDAZE	BEZAZZ	BLAZED	BOOZED	BRAZER	BUAZES

BUZUKI BUZZED BUZZER BUZZES BWAZIS BYZANT CEAZED CEAZES CHAZAN CHINTZ CIZERS CLOZES COBZAS COLZAS COROZO CORYZA COZENS COZEYS COZIED COZIER COZIES COZILY COZING COZZES CRAZED CRAZES CROZER CROZES CUZZES CZAPKA DARZIS DAZERS DAZING DAZZLE DEFUZE DEZINC DIAZIN DIAZOS DITZES DIZAIN DIZENS DONZEL DOOZER DOOZIE DORIZE DOZENS DOZERS DOZIER DOZILY DOZING DRAZEL DZEREN ECZEMA ENTREZ ENZIAN ENZONE

ENZYME ENZYMS EPIZOA ERSATZ EVZONE FAZING FEAZED FEAZES FEEZED FEEZES FEZZED FEZZES FIZGIG FIZZED FIZZEN FIZZER FIZZES FIZZLE FLOOZY FOOZLE FOZIER FRANZY FRAZIL FREEZE FRENZY FRIEZE FRIZED FRIZER FRIZES FRIZZY FROUZY FROWZY FROZEN FURZES FUTZED FUTZES FUZEES FUZILS FUZING FUZZED FUZZES FUZZLE GAUZES GAZABO GAZALS GAZARS GAZEBO GAZERS GAZIER GAZING GAZONS GAZOON GAZOOS GAZUMP GEEZER GHAZAL

GHAZEL GHAZIS GIZMOS GIZZEN GIZZES GLAZED GLAZEN GLAZER GLAZES GLITZY GLOZED GLOZES GOZZAN GRAZED GRAZER GRAZES GRIZES GROSZE GROSZY GUIZER GUTZER GUZZLE HALUTZ HAMZAH HAMZAS HAZANS HAZARD HAZELS HAZERS HAZIER HAZILY HAZING HAZZAN HEEZED HEEZES HEEZIE HIZENS HIZZED HIZZES HOWZAT HUTZPA HUZOOR HUZZAH HUZZAS IODIZE IONIZE IZARDS IZZARD IZZATS JAZIES JAZZED JAZZER JAZZES JEZAIL JIZZES KAIZEN

KAMEEZ KANZUS KAZOOS KHAZEN KIBITZ KLUTZY KOLHOZ KOLKOZ KRANTZ KUDZUS KUVASZ KWANZA LAZARS LAZIED LAZIER LAZIES LAZILY LAZING LAZOED LAZOES LAZULI LEAZES LEZZES LEZZIE LIZARD LOZELL LOZENS LUTZES LUZERN LUZZES MAHZOR MAIZES MAMZER MATZAH MATZAS MATZOH MATZOS MATZOT MAZARD MAZERS MAZHBI MAZIER MAZILY MAZING MAZOUT MAZUMA MAZUTS MEAZEL MEZAIL MEZCAL MEZUZA MEZZES MEZZOS MIRZAS MIZENS MIZZEN

MIZZES MIZZLE MIZZLY MOMZER MOTZAS MOZING MOZZES MOZZIE MOZZLE MUZAKY MUZHIK MUZJIK MUZZLE MZUNGU NAZIFY NAZIRS NEEZED NEEZES NIZAMS NOZZER NOZZLE NUZZER NUZZLE NYANZA OOZIER OOZILY OOZING OUZELS OYEZES OZAENA OZEKIS OZONES OZONIC PANZER PATZER PAZAZZ PEAZED PEAZES PEIZED PEIZES PEZANT PHEEZE PHIZES PHIZOG PIAZZA PIAZZE PIZAZZ PIZZAS PIZZLE PLAZAS PODZOL POTZER PREZES PRIZED PRIZER PRIZES

PUTZED PUTZES PUZELS PUZZEL PUZZLE QUARTZ QUEAZY QUEZAL QUINZE RANZEL RAZEED RAZEES RAZERS RAZING RAZOOS RAZORS RAZURE RAZZED RAZZES RAZZIA RAZZLE REBOZO RESIZE REZONE REZZES RHIZIC RITZES RIZARD RIZZAR RIZZER RIZZOR ROZETS ROZITS ROZZER SADZAS SAZHEN SAZZES SCAZON SCHIZO SCHIZY SCHNOZ SCRUZE SCUZZY SEAZED SEAZES SEIZED SEIZER SEIZES SEIZIN SEIZOR SIZARS SIZELS SIZERS SIZIER SIZING SIZISM

SIZIST SIZZLE SLEAZE SLEAZO SLEAZY SLEEZY SMAZES SNAZZY SNEEZE SNEEZY SNOOZE SNOOZY SOZINE SOZINS SOZZLE SOZZLY SPELTZ SPRITZ STANZA STANZE STANZO SUIVEZ SYZYGY TARZAN TAZZAS TEAZED TEAZEL TEAZES TEAZLE TENZON TIZWAS TIZZES TOAZED TOAZES TOLZEY TOUZED TOUZES TOUZLE TOWZED TOWZES TOZIES TOZING TREZES TUZZES TWEEZE TZETSE TZETZE TZURIS ULZIES UNZIPS UPGAZE VEZIRS VIZARD VIZIED VIZIER VIZIES

VIZIRS VIZORS VIZSLA VIZZIE VOZHDS WANZED WANZES WAZIRS WEAZEN WEIZED WEIZES WEZAND WHEEZE WHEEZY WINZES WIZARD WIZENS WIZIER WIZZEN WURZEL WUZZLE YAKUZA ZABETA ZABRAS ZADDIK ZAFFAR ZAFFER ZAFFIR ZAFFRE ZAFTIG ZAGGED ZAIKAI ZAIRES ZAKATS ZAMANG ZAMANS ZAMBOS ZAMBUK ZAMIAS ZANANA ZANDER ZANIED ZANIER ZANIES ZANILY ZANJAS ZANTES ZANZAS ZANZES ZAPATA ZAPPED ZAPPER ZARAPE ZAREBA ZARIBA ZARNEC

ZAYINS ZAZENS ZEALOT ZEATIN ZEBECK ZEBECS ZEBRAS ZEBUBS ZECHIN ZELANT ZELOSO ZENANA ZENDIK ZENITH ZEPHYR ZERDAS ZEREBA ZERIBA ZEROED ZEROES ZEROTH ZESTED ZESTER ZEUGMA ZHOMOS ZIBETH ZIBETS ZIGANS ZIGGED ZIGZAG ZILLAH ZIMBIS ZIMMER ZINCED ZINCIC ZINCKY ZINCOS ZINEBS ZINGED ZINGEL ZINGER ZINKED ZINKES ZINNIA ZIPPED ZIPPER ZIPPOS ZIPTOP ZIRAMS ZIRCON ZITHER ZIZELS ZIZITH ZIZZED ZIZZES ZIZZLE

ZLOTYS ZOARIA ZOCCOS ZODIAC ZOECIA ZOETIC ZOFTIG ZOISMS ZOISTS ZOMBIE ZOMBIS ZONARY ZONATE ZONDAS ZONERS ZONING ZONKED ZONOID ZONULA ZONULE ZONURE ZOOEAE ZOOEAL ZOOEAS ZOOIDS ZOOMED ZOONAL ZOONIC ZOOZOO ZORILS ZORINO ZORROS ZOSTER ZOUAVE ZOUNDS ZOYSIA ZUFOLI ZUFOLO ZUPANS ZYDECO ZYGOID ZYGOMA ZYGOSE ZYGOTE ZYMASE ZYMITE ZYMOID ZYMOME ZYTHUM

Z – 7-letter words

ABRAZOS ADONIZE ADZUKIS AGATIZE AGENIZE AGNIZED AGNIZES AGONIZE AGRIZED AGRIZES AGRYZED AGRYZES AGUIZED AGUIZES ALBIZIA

ALCAZAR ALCORZA ALFEREZ ALIZARI ALTEZAS ALTEZZA AMAZING AMAZONS ANALYZE ANODIZE ANZIANI APOZEMS APPRIZE ARABIZE ASSIZED

ASSIZER ASSIZES ATHEIZE ATOMIZE AVIZING AVYZING AZALEAS AZIMUTH AZIONES AZOLLAS AZOTISE AZOTIZE AZOTOUS AZULEJO AZUREAN

AZURINE AZURITE AZYGIES AZYGOUS AZYMITE AZYMOUS BAIZING BANZAIS BAPTIZE BARAZAS BAZAARS BAZOOKA BAZOOMS BAZOUKI BEDAZED

BEDAZES BEDIZEN BEEZERS BEGAZED BEGAZES BEMAZED BENZALS BENZENE BENZILS BENZINE BENZINS BENZOIC BENZOIN BENZOLE BENZOLS

BENZOYL BENZYLS BEZANTS BEZIQUE BEZOARS BEZZANT BEZZLED BEZZLES BIZARRE BIZNAGA BIZONAL BIZONES BLAZERS BLAZING BLAZONS

BLINTZE BLITZED BLITZES BLOWZED BLOWZES BONANZA BOOZERS BOOZIER BOOZILY BOOZING BORAZON BORTZES BORZOIS BRAIZES BRAZENS

BRAZERS BRAZIER BRAZILS BRAZING BREEZED BREEZES BRITZKA BROMIZE BRONZED BRONZEN BRONZER BRONZES BROUZES BRULZIE BUMBAZE

BUZUKIA BUZUKIS BUZZARD BUZZERS BUZZIER BUZZING BUZZWIG BYZANTS CABEZON CADENZA CALZONE CALZONI CANZONA CANZONE CANZONI

CAPIZES
CAPSIZE
CAZIQUE
CEAZING
CHALAZA
CHALUTZ
CHAZANS
CHAZZAN
CHAZZEN
CHINTZY
CHIZZED
CHIZZES
CHORIZO
CHUTZPA
CITIZEN
COALIZE
COGNIZE
COROZOS
CORYZAL
CORYZAS
COZENED
COZENER
COZIERS
COZIEST
COZYING
CRAZIER
CRAZIES
CRAZILY
CRAZING
CROZERS
CROZIER
CRUZADO
CYANIZE
CYCLIZE
CZAPKAS
CZARDAS
CZARDOM
CZARINA
CZARISM
CZARIST
DAMOZEL
DAZEDLY
DAZZLED
DAZZLER
DAZZLES
DEFROZE
DEFUZED
DEFUZES
DEGLAZE
DENIZEN
DEUTZIA
DEZINCS
DIALYZE
DIARIZE
DIAZINE
DIAZINS
DIAZOES
DIAZOLE
DITZIER
DIZAINS
DIZENED
DIZZARD
DIZZIED
DIZZIER
DIZZIES
DIZZILY
DOCKIZE
DONZELS
DOOZERS
DOOZIES
DORIZED
DORIZES
DOZENED
DOZENTH
DOZIEST
DOZINGS
DRAZELS
DRIZZLE
DRIZZLY
DUALIZE
DZERENS
EBONIZE
ECHOIZE
ECTOZOA
ECZEMAS
EGOTIZE
ELEGIZE
EMBLAZE
EMPRIZE
ENDOZOA
ENFROZE
ENTOZOA
ENZIANS
ENZONED
ENZONES
ENZYMES
ENZYMIC
EPAZOTE
EPIZOAN
EPIZOIC
EPIZOON
EROTIZE
EVZONES
FAHLERZ
FANZINE
FAZENDA
FEAZING
FEEZING
FILAZER
FIZGIGS
FIZZENS
FIZZERS
FIZZGIG
FIZZIER
FIZZING
FIZZLED
FIZZLES
FLOOZIE
FOOZLED
FOOZLER
FOOZLES
FORZATI
FORZATO
FOZIEST
FRAZILS
FRAZZLE
FREEZER
FREEZES
FRIEZED
FRIEZES
FRITZES
FRIZERS
FRIZING
FRIZZED
FRIZZER
FRIZZES
FRIZZLE
FRIZZLY
FURZIER
FUTZING
FUZZIER
FUZZILY
FUZZING
FUZZLED
FUZZLES
GALLIZE
GAUZIER
GAUZILY
GAZABOS
GAZANIA
GAZEBOS
GAZEFUL
GAZELLE
GAZETTE
GAZIEST
GAZOOKA
GAZOONS
GAZUMPS
GEEZERS
GENIZAH
GHAZALS
GHAZELS
GHAZIES
GIZZARD
GIZZENS
GLAZERS
GLAZIER
GLAZING
GLITZES
GLOZING
GOZZANS
GRAZERS
GRAZIER
GRAZING
GRECIZE
GRIZZLE
GRIZZLY
GUEREZA
GUIZERS
GUTZERS
GUZZLED
GUZZLER
GUZZLES
HAMZAHS
HAZANIM
HAZARDS
HAZELLY
HAZIEST
HAZINGS
HAZZANS
HEEZIES
HEEZING
HEROIZE
HERTZES
HIZZING
HOATZIN
HORIZON
HUMBUZZ
HUTZPAH
HUTZPAS
HUZOORS
HUZZAED
HUZZAHS
HUZZIES
ICONIZE
IDOLIZE
IMBLAZE
IODIZED
IODIZER
IODIZES
IONIZED
IONIZER
IONIZES
IRIDIZE
IRONIZE
ISOZYME
ITEMIZE
IZZARDS
JACUZZI
JANIZAR
JAZZERS
JAZZIER
JAZZILY
JAZZING
JAZZMAN
JAZZMEN
JEZAILS
JEZEBEL
KAIZENS
KARZIES
KHAZENS
KIBBITZ
KIBBUTZ
KLEZMER
KLUTZES
KOLHOZY
KOLKHOZ
KOLKOZY
KRANZES
KREUZER
KUNZITE
KWANZAS
KYANIZE
LAICIZE
LAIRIZE
LAZARET
LAZIEST
LAZOING
LAZULIS
LAZYING
LAZYISH
LEZZIES
LIONIZE
LIZARDS
LOZELLS
LOZENGE
LOZENGY
LUZERNS
MACHZOR
MADZOON
MAHZORS
MAMZERS
MATZAHS
MATZOHS
MATZOON
MATZOTH
MAZARDS
MAZEDLY
MAZEFUL
MAZHBIS
MAZIEST
MAZOUTS
MAZUMAS
MAZURKA
MAZZARD
MEAZELS
MENAZON
MESTIZA
MESTIZO
METAZOA
MEZAILS
MEZCALS
MEZQUIT
MEZUZAH
MEZUZAS
MEZUZOT
MIDSIZE
MILTZES
MITZVAH
MIZMAZE
MIZZENS
MIZZLED
MIZZLES
MOMZERS
MOZETTA
MOZETTE
MOZZIES
MOZZLES
MUEZZIN
MUZHIKS
MUZJIKS
MUZZIER
MUZZILY
MUZZLED
MUZZLER
MUZZLES
MYTHIZE
MZUNGUS
NEEZING
NETIZEN
NONZERO
NOZZERS
NOZZLES
NUDZHED
NUDZHES
NUZZERS
NUZZLED
NUZZLER
NUZZLES
NYANZAS
OBELIZE
ODORIZE
ODZOOKS
OOZIEST
ORGANZA
OUTSIZE
OXAZINE
OXIDIZE
OZAENAS
OZONATE
OZONIDE
OZONISE
OZONIZE
OZONOUS
PALAZZI
PALAZZO
PANZERS
PARAZOA
PATZERS
PEAZING
PECTIZE
PEIZING
PEPTIZE
PEZANTS
PHEAZAR
PHEEZED
PHEEZES
PHIZOGS
PHIZZES
PIAZZAS
PIZAZZY
PIZZLES
PLOTZED
PLOTZES
PODZOLS
POETIZE
POLYZOA
POTZERS
POZZIES
PRENZIE
PRETZEL
PREZZIE
PRIZERS
PRIZING
PUTZING
PUZZELS
PUZZLED
PUZZLER
PUZZLES
PZAZZES
QUARTZY
QUETZAL
QUEZALS
QUINZES
QUIZZED
QUIZZER
QUIZZES
RANZELS
RAZORED
RAZURES
RAZZIAS
RAZZING
RAZZLES
REALIZE
REBOZOS
REFROZE
REGLAZE
REPRIZE
RESEIZE
RESIZED
RESIZES
REZONED
REZONES
RHIZINE
RHIZOID
RHIZOMA
RHIZOME
RHIZOPI
RIOTIZE
RITZIER
RITZILY
RIZARDS
RIZZARS
RIZZART
RIZZERS
RIZZORS
ROZELLE
ROZETED
ROZITED
ROZZERS
SAZERAC
SAZHENS
SCAZONS
SCHANZE
SCHERZI
SCHERZO
SCHIZOS
SCHIZZY
SCHMALZ
SCHMELZ
SCHMOOZ
SCHNOZZ
SCRUZED
SCRUZES
SCUZZES
SEAZING
SEIZERS
SEIZING
SEIZINS
SEIZORS
SEIZURE
SELTZER
SHEGETZ
SHIATZU
SHMALTZ
SHMOOZE
SHOWBIZ
SIAMEZE
SIZABLE
SIZABLY
SIZEISM
SIZEIST
SIZIEST
SIZINGS
SIZISMS
SIZISTS
SIZZLED
SIZZLER
SIZZLES
SLEAZES
SNEEZED
SNEEZER
SNEEZES
SNOOZED
SNOOZER
SNOOZES
SNOOZLE
SNUZZLE
SOVKHOZ
SOYUZES
SOZINES
SOZZLED
SOZZLES
SPATZLE
SPAZZED
SPAZZES
SPITZES
SPREAZE
SPREEZE
SPULZIE
SQUEEZE
SQUEEZY
STANZAS
STANZES
STANZOS
STARETZ
STYLIZE
SUBZERO
SUBZONE
SWAZZLE
SWIZZED
SWIZZES
SWIZZLE
SWOZZLE
SYZYGAL
TAILZIE
TARZANS
TEAZELS
TEAZING
TEAZLED
TEAZLES
TENDENZ
TENZONS
THIAZIN
THIAZOL
TIZZIES
TOAZING
TOLZEYS
TOPAZES
TOUZIER
TOUZING
TOUZLED
TOUZLES
TOWZIER
TOWZING
TRAPEZE
TRIAZIN
TRIZONE
TUILZIE
TWEEZED
TWEEZER
TWEEZES
TWIZZLE
TZADDIK
TZADDIQ
TZARDOM
TZARINA
TZARISM
TZARIST
TZETSES
TZETZES
TZIGANE
TZIGANY
TZIMMES
TZITZIS
TZITZIT
UNCRAZY
UNFAZED
UNFROZE
UNITIZE
UNRAZED
UNSIZED
UNZONED
UPGAZED
UPGAZES
UTILIZE
VIZARDS
VIZIERS
VIZORED
VIZSLAS
VIZYING
VIZZIED
VIZZIES
WALTZED
WALTZER
WALTZES
WANZING
WEAZAND
WEAZENS
WEIZING
WEZANDS
WHAIZLE
WHEEZED
WHEEZER
WHEEZES
WHEEZLE
WHIZZED
WHIZZER
WHIZZES
WIZARDS
WIZENED
WIZIERS
WIZZENS
WOOTZES
WOOZIER
WOOZILY
WRIZLED
WURZELS
WUZZLED
WUZZLES
ZABETAS
ZABTIEH
ZACATON
ZADDICK
ZADDIKS
ZAFFARS
ZAFFERS
ZAFFIRS
ZAFFRES
ZAGGING
ZAIKAIS
ZAITECH
ZAKUSKA
ZAKUSKI
ZAMANGS
ZAMARRA
ZAMARRO
ZAMBUCK
ZAMBUKS
ZAMOUSE
ZAMPONE
ZAMPONI
ZANANAS
ZANDERS
ZANELLA
ZANIEST
ZANJERO
ZANYING
ZANYISH
ZANYISM
ZAPATEO
ZAPPERS
ZAPPIER
ZAPPING
ZAPTIAH
ZAPTIEH
ZARAPES
ZAREBAS
ZAREEBA
ZARIBAS
ZARNECS
ZARNICH
ZEALANT
ZEALFUL
ZEALOTS
ZEALOUS
ZEATINS
ZEBECKS
ZEBRAIC
ZEBRASS
ZEBRINA
ZEBRINE
ZEBROID
ZEBRULA
ZEBRULE
ZECCHIN
ZECHINS
ZEDOARY
ZELANTS
ZELATOR
ZELKOVA
ZEMSTVA
ZEMSTVO
ZENAIDA
ZENANAS
ZENDIKS
ZENITHS
ZEOLITE
ZEPHYRS
ZEREBAS
ZERIBAS
ZEROING
ZESTERS
ZESTFUL
ZESTIER
ZESTING
ZETETIC
ZEUGMAS
ZEUXITE
ZIBETHS
ZIFFIUS
ZIGANKA
ZIGGING
ZIGZAGS
ZIKURAT
ZILCHES
ZILLAHS
ZILLION
ZIMMERS
ZIMOCCA
ZINCATE
ZINCIER
ZINCIFY
ZINCING
ZINCITE
ZINCKED
ZINCODE
ZINCOID
ZINCOUS
ZINGANI
ZINGANO
ZINGARA
ZINGARE
ZINGARI
ZINGARO

ZINGELS ZINGERS ZINGIER ZINGING ZINKIER ZINKIFY ZINKING ZINNIAS ZIPLESS ZIPLOCK
ZIPPERS ZIPPIER ZIPPING ZIRCONS ZITHERN ZITHERS ZIZANIA ZIZZING ZIZZLED ZIZZLES
ZLOTIES ZLOTYCH ZOARIAL ZOARIUM ZOCCOLO ZODIACS ZOECIUM ZOEFORM ZOISITE ZOMBIES
ZOMBIFY ZONALLY ZONATED ZONINGS ZONKING ZONULAE ZONULAR ZONULAS ZONULES ZONULET
ZONURES ZOOECIA ZOOGAMY ZOOGENY ZOOGLEA ZOOGONY ZOOIDAL ZOOLITE ZOOLITH ZOOLOGY
ZOOMING ZOONITE ZOONOMY ZOOPERY ZOOTAXY ZOOTIER ZOOTOMY ZOOTYPE ZOOZOOS ZORGITE
ZORILLA ZORILLE ZORILLO ZORINOS ZOSTERS ZOUAVES ZOYSIAS ZUFFOLI ZUFFOLO ZYDECOS
ZYGOMAS ZYGOSES ZYGOSIS ZYGOTES ZYGOTIC ZYMASES ZYMITES ZYMOGEN ZYMOMES ZYMOSAN
ZYMOSES ZYMOSIS ZYMOTIC ZYMURGY ZYTHUMS ZYZZYVA

Z – 8-letter words

ACTIVIZE ADONIZED ADONIZES AGATIZED AGATIZES AGENIZED AGENIZES AGNIZING AGONIZED AGONIZES AGRIZING AGRYZING AGUIZING ALBITIZE ALBIZIAS ALBIZZIA ALCAZARS ALCORZAS ALGUAZIL ALIZARIN ALIZARIS ALKALIZE ALTEZZAS AMAZEDLY AMORTIZE ANALYZED ANALYZER ANALYZES ANNALIZE ANODIZED ANODIZES ANTICIZE APHETIZE APHORIZE APPETIZE APPRIZED APPRIZER APPRIZES ARABIZED ARABIZES ARBORIZE ARCHAIZE ARMOZEEN ARMOZINE ARRHIZAL ASSIZERS ASSIZING ATHEIZED ATHEIZES ATHETIZE ATMOLYZE ATOMIZED ATOMIZER ATOMIZES ATRAZINE AUTOLYZE AVIANIZE AZIMUTHS AZOTEMIA AZOTEMIC AZOTISED

AZOTISES AZOTIZED AZOTIZES AZOTURIA AZULEJOS AZURINES AZURITES AZYGOSES AZYMITES BANALIZE BAPTIZED BAPTIZER BAPTIZES BAROMETZ BARTIZAN BAZAZZES BAZOOKAS BAZOUKIS BEDAZING BEDAZZLE BEDIZENS BEGAZING BEJEEZUS BEMUZZLE BENZENES BENZIDIN BENZINES BENZOATE BENZOINS BENZOLES BENZOYLS BENZYLIC BEZAZZES BEZIQUES BEZONIAN BEZZANTS BEZZLING BITESIZE BIZARRES BIZAZZES BIZCACHA BIZNAGAS BLAZERED BLAZONED BLAZONER BLAZONRY BLINTZES BLITZING BLIZZARD BLOWZIER BLOWZILY BONANZAS BOOZIEST BORAZONS BOTANIZE BOUZOUKI BOZZETTI BOZZETTO BRAZENED BRAZENLY BRAZENRY

BRAZIERS BRAZILIN BREEZIER BREEZILY BREEZING BRITZKAS BRITZSKA BROMIZED BROMIZES BRONZERS BRONZIER BRONZIFY BRONZING BRONZITE BRUILZIE BRULZIES BRUNIZEM BRYOZOAN BULLDOZE BUMBAZED BUMBAZES BUZZARDS BUZZIEST BUZZINGS BUZZWIGS BUZZWORD CABEZONE CABEZONS CADENZAS CALORIZE CALZONES CANALIZE CANONIZE CANZONAS CANZONES CANZONET CAPONIZE CAPSIZAL CAPSIZED CAPSIZES CATALYZE CAZIQUES CHALAZAE CHALAZAL CHALAZAS CHALAZIA CHAZANIM CHAZZANS CHAZZENS CHINTZES CHIZZING CHORIZOS CHROMIZE CHUTZPAH CHUTZPAS CITIZENS CIVILIZE COALIZED COALIZES COENZYME COGNIZED

COGNIZER COGNIZES COLONIZE COLORIZE COMPRIZE COZENAGE COZENERS COZENING COZINESS CRAZIEST CREDENZA CREOLIZE CREUTZER CROZIERS CRUZADOS CRUZEIRO CURARIZE CUTINIZE CYANIZED CYANIZES CYCLIZED CYCLIZES CZARDOMS CZAREVNA CZARINAS CZARISMS CZARISTS CZARITSA CZARITZA DAMOZELS DAZZLERS DAZZLING DEFREEZE DEFROZEN DEFUZING DEGLAZED DEGLAZES DEIONIZE DEMONIZE DENAZIFY DENIZENS DEPUTIZE DEUTZIAS DEZINCED DIALYZED DIALYZER DIALYZES DIARIZED DIARIZES DIAZEPAM DIAZINES DIAZINON DIAZOLES DIGITIZE DIMERIZE DIPLOZOA DISPRIZE DISSEIZE DITZIEST DIVINIZE DIZENING

DIZYGOUS DIZZARDS DIZZIEST DIZZYING DOCKIZED DOCKIZES DORIZING DOUZEPER DOWNSIZE DOZENING DOZENTHS DOZINESS DRIZZLED DRIZZLES DUALIZED DUALIZES DYNAMIZE EBENEZER EBIONIZE EBONIZED EBONIZES ECHOIZED ECHOIZES ECTOZOAN ECTOZOIC ECTOZOON EGOTIZED EGOTIZES ELEGIZED ELEGIZES EMBEZZLE EMBLAZED EMBLAZER EMBLAZES EMBLAZON EMPERIZE EMPRIZES ENDOZOIC ENDOZOON ENERGIZE ENFREEZE ENFROZEN ENTOZOAL ENTOZOAN ENTOZOIC ENTOZOON ENZONING ENZOOTIC EPAZOTES EPIZOANS EPIZOISM EPIZOITE EPIZOOTY EQUALIZE ERGOTIZE EROTIZED EROTIZES ERSATZES ETERNIZE ETHERIZE ETHICIZE

EULOGIZE EUPHUIZE EXORCIZE FABULIZE FANZINES FARADIZE FAZENDAS FEMINIZE FIBERIZE FILAZERS FINALIZE FIZZGIGS FIZZIEST FIZZINGS FIZZLING FLOOZIES FLUIDIZE FOCALIZE FOOZLERS FOOZLING FORZANDI FORZANDO FORZATOS FOZINESS FRANZIER FRAZZLED FRAZZLES FREEZERS FREEZING FRENZIED FRENZIES FRENZILY FRIEZING FRIZETTE FRIZZERS FRIZZIER FRIZZILY FRIZZING FRIZZLED FRIZZLER FRIZZLES FROUZIER FROWZIER FROWZILY FROZENLY FURZIEST FUZZIEST FUZZLING GADZOOKS GALLIZED GALLIZES GARBANZO GAUZIEST GAZABOES GAZANIAS GAZEBOES GAZELLES GAZEMENT GAZETTED GAZETTES GAZOGENE

GAZOOKAS GAZPACHO GAZUMPED GAZUMPER GAZUNDER GENIZAHS GIZZARDS GIZZENED GLAZIERS GLAZIERY GLAZIEST GLAZINGS GLITZIER GLITZILY GLOZINGS GOLDSIZE GRAECIZE GRAZABLE GRAZIERS GRAZINGS GRAZIOSO GRECIZED GRECIZES GRIZZLED GRIZZLER GRIZZLES GUEREZAS GUZZLERS GUZZLING HALAZONE HALUTZIM HAZARDED HAZARDRY HAZELHEN HAZELNUT HAZINESS HAZZANIM HEBRAIZE HEMOLYZE HEPATIZE HEROIZED HEROIZES HIZZONER HOACTZIN HOATZINS HOLOZOIC HOMINIZE HORIZONS HOWITZER HUMANIZE HUTZPAHS HUZZAHED HUZZAING HYDROZOA HYLOZOIC ICONIZED ICONIZES IDEALIZE IDOLIZED IDOLIZER IDOLIZES

IMBLAZED IMBLAZES IMMUNIZE INFAMIZE IODIZERS IODIZING IONIZERS IONIZING IRIDIZED IRIDIZES IRONIZED IRONIZES ISOZYMES ISOZYMIC ITEMIZED ITEMIZER ITEMIZES IZVESTIA JACUZZIS JANIZARS JANIZARY JAPANIZE JAROVIZE JAZERANT JAZZIEST JAZZLIKE JEZEBELS JUMBOIZE KAMEEZES KAMIKAZE KAZACHKI KAZACHOK KAZATSKI KAZATSKY KAZATZKA KHAZENIM KIBITZED KIBITZER KIBITZES KLUTZIER KOLHOZES KOLKHOZY KOLKOZES KRANTZES KREUTZER KREUZERS KUNZITES KUVASZOK KYANIZED KYANIZES LAICIZED LAICIZES LAIRIZED LAIRIZES LATERIZE LATINIZE LAZARETS LAZINESS LAZULITE LAZURITE LEGALIZE

LIONIZED
LIONIZER
LIONIZES
LOCALIZE
LOGICIZE
LOZENGED
LOZENGES
LYRICIZE
LYSOZYME
MACARIZE
MACHZORS
MADERIZE
MADZOONS
MAGAZINE
MAHZORIM
MAMZERIM
MANZELLO
MARZIPAN
MATZOONS
MAXIMIZE
MAZAEDIA
MAZARINE
MAZELIKE
MAZELTOV
MAZEMENT
MAZINESS
MAZOURKA
MAZURKAS
MAZZARDS
MELANIZE
MELODIZE
MEMORIZE
MENAZONS
MESPRIZE
MESTIZAS
MESTIZOS
METALIZE
METAZOAL
METAZOAN
METAZOIC
METAZOON
MEZEREON
MEZEREUM
MEZQUITE
MEZQUITS
MEZUZAHS
MEZUZOTH
MIDSIZED
MINIMIZE
MISPRIZE
MITZVAHS
MITZVOTH
MIZMAZES
MIZZLIER
MIZZLING
MOBILIZE
MOMZERIM
MONAZITE
MONETIZE
MORALIZE
MOTORIZE
MOZETTAS
MOZZETTA
MOZZETTE
MUEZZINS
MUZZIEST
MUZZLERS
MUZZLING
MYTHIZED
MYTHIZES
NASALIZE
NAZIFIED
NAZIFIES
NEBULIZE
NETIZENS
NIZAMATE
NODALIZE
NOMADIZE
NOTARIZE
NOVELIZE
NUDZHING
NUZZLERS
NUZZLING
OBELIZED
OBELIZES
ODORIZED
ODORIZES
OOZINESS
OPALIZED
OPSONIZE
OPTIMIZE
ORGANIZE
ORGANZAS
OUTBLAZE
OUTPRIZE
OUTSIZED
OUTSIZES
OVERSIZE
OVERZEAL
OXAZEPAM
OXAZINES
OXIDIZED
OXIDIZER
OXIDIZES
OZONATED
OZONATES
OZONIDES
OZONISED
OZONISER
OZONISES
OZONIZED
OZONIZER
OZONIZES
PAGANIZE
PALAZZOS
PAPALIZE
PARALYZE
PARAZOAN
PARAZOON
PARTIZAN
PATINIZE
PAZAZZES
PECTIZED
PECTIZES
PENALIZE
PEPTIZED
PEPTIZER
PEPTIZES
PETUNTZE
PEZIZOID
PHEAZARS
PHEEZING
PHENAZIN
PIAZZIAN
PINTSIZE
PIROZHKI
PIROZHOK
PIZAZZES
PIZZERIA
PLOTZING
PODZOLIC
POETIZED
POETIZER
POETIZES
POLARIZE
POLEMIZE
POLONIZE
POLYZOAN
POLYZOIC
POLYZOON
POZZOLAN
PREFROZE
PRETZELS
PREZZIES
PRIZABLE
PRIZEMAN
PRIZEMEN
PROTOZOA
PTYALIZE
PUZZLERS
PUZZLING
PYRITIZE
PYROLIZE
PYROLYZE
QUANTIZE
QUARTZES
QUATORZE
QUEAZIER
QUETZALS
QUEZALES
QUIZZERS
QUIZZERY
QUIZZIFY
QUIZZING
RACEMIZE
RAZEEING
RAZMATAZ
RAZORING
REALIZED
REALIZER
REALIZES
REFREEZE
REFROZEN
REGLAZED
REGLAZES
REGULIZE
RENDZINA
REPRIZED
REPRIZES
RESEIZED
RESEIZES
RESINIZE
RESIZING
REZONING
RHIZINES
RHIZOBIA
RHIZOIDS
RHIZOMES
RHIZOMIC
RHIZOPOD
RHIZOPUS
RIBOZYME
RIGIDIZE
RIOTIZES
RITZIEST
RIVALIZE
RIZZARED
RIZZARTS
RIZZERED
RIZZORED
ROBOTIZE
ROMANIZE
ROYALIZE
ROZELLES
ROZETING
ROZITING
RURALIZE
SALINIZE
SAMIZDAT
SANITIZE
SARRAZIN
SATIRIZE
SAZERACS
SCHANTZE
SCHANZES
SCHERZOS
SCHIZIER
SCHIZOID
SCHIZONT
SCHMALTZ
SCHMALZY
SCHMELZE
SCHMOOZE
SCRUZING
SCUZZIER
SEIZABLE
SEIZINGS
SEIZURES
SELTZERS
SFORZATI
SFORZATO
SHIATZUS
SHKOTZIM
SHMALTZY
SHMOOZED
SHMOOZES
SIAMEZED
SIAMEZES
SIEROZEM
SIMAZINE
SIMILIZE
SIMONIZE
SINICIZE
SIRENIZE
SITZMARK
SIZEABLE
SIZEABLY
SIZEISMS
SIZEISTS
SIZINESS
SIZZLERS
SIZZLING
SLEAZIER
SLEAZILY
SLEEZIER
SMORZATO
SNAZZIER
SNEEZERS
SNEEZIER
SNEEZING
SNOOZERS
SNOOZIER
SNOOZING
SNOOZLED
SNOOZLES
SNUZZLED
SNUZZLES
SOBERIZE
SODOMIZE
SOLARIZE
SOLECIZE
SOLONETZ
SORORIZE
SOVKHOZY
SOZZLIER
SOZZLING
SPAETZLE
SPAZZING
SPELTZES
SPETSNAZ
SPETZNAZ
SPOROZOA
SPREAZED
SPREAZES
SPREEZED
SPREEZES
SPRITZED
SPRITZER
SPRITZES
SPRITZIG
SPUILZIE
SPULZIED
SPULZIES
SQUEEZED
SQUEEZER
SQUEEZES
SQUIZZES
STANZAED
STANZAIC
STANZOES
STARGAZE
STRELITZ
STYLIZED
STYLIZER
STYLIZES
SUBERIZE
SUBITIZE
SUBSIZAR
SUBZONAL
SUBZONES
SURPRIZE
SUZERAIN
SWAZZLES
SWIZZING
SWIZZLED
SWIZZLER
SWIZZLES
SWOZZLES
SYZYGIAL
SYZYGIES
TAILZIES
TEAZELED
TEAZLING
TERRAZZO
TERZETTA
TERZETTI
TERZETTO
TETANIZE
THEORIZE
THIAZIDE
THIAZINE
THIAZINS
THIAZOLE
THIAZOLS
TIZWASES
TOPAZINE
TOTALIZE
TOUZIEST
TOUZLING
TOWZIEST
TRAPEZED
TRAPEZES
TRAPEZIA
TRAPEZII
TRIAZINE
TRIAZINS
TRIAZOLE
TRISTEZA
TRIZONAL
TRIZONES
TSARITZA
TUILZIED
TUILZIES
TUTORIZE
TWEEZERS
TWEEZING
TWIZZLED
TWIZZLES
TZADDIKS
TZADDIQS
TZARDOMS
TZAREVNA
TZARINAS
TZARISMS
TZARISTS
TZARITZA
TZATZIKI
TZIGANES
TZITZITH
UNAMAZED
UNDAZZLE
UNFREEZE
UNFROZEN
UNGLAZED
UNGRAZED
UNIONIZE
UNITIZED
UNITIZER
UNITIZES
UNMUZZLE
UNPRIZED
UNPUZZLE
UNSEIZED
UNVIZARD
UNZIPPED
UPGAZING
URBANIZE
UTILIZED
UTILIZER
UTILIZES
VALORIZE
VAPORIZE
VELARIZE
VITALIZE
VIZAMENT
VIZARDED
VIZCACHA
VIZIRATE
VIZIRIAL
VIZORING
VOCALIZE
VOLUMIZE
VOWELIZE
WALTZERS
WALTZING
WEAZANDS
WEAZENED
WHAIZLED
WHAIZLES
WHEEZERS
WHEEZIER
WHEEZILY
WHEEZING
WHEEZLED
WHEEZLES
WHIZBANG
WHIZZERS
WHIZZING
WIZARDLY
WIZARDRY
WIZENING
WOMANIZE
WOOZIEST
WURTZITE
WUZZLING
YAHRZEIT
YOKOZUNA
ZABAIONE
ZABAJONE
ZABTIEHS
ZACATONS
ZADDIKIM
ZAIBATSU
ZAITECHS
ZAMARRAS
ZAMARROS
ZAMBOMBA
ZAMBUCKS
ZAMINDAR
ZAMOUSES
ZAMPOGNA
ZANELLAS
ZANINESS
ZANJEROS
ZANYISMS
ZAPATEOS
ZAPPIEST
ZAPTIAHS
ZAPTIEHS
ZARATITE
ZAREEBAS
ZARNICHS
ZARZUELA
ZASTRUGA
ZASTRUGI
ZEALANTS
ZEALLESS
ZEALOTRY
ZEBRINAS
ZEBRINNY
ZEBRULAS
ZEBRULES
ZECCHINE
ZECCHINI
ZECCHINO
ZECCHINS
ZELATORS
ZELATRIX
ZELKOVAS
ZEMINDAR
ZEMSTVOS
ZENAIDAS
ZENITHAL
ZEOLITES
ZEOLITIC
ZEPPELIN
ZERUMBET
ZESTIEST
ZESTLESS
ZETETICS
ZEUXITES
ZIBELINE
ZIGANKAS
ZIGGURAT
ZIGZAGGY
ZIKKURAT
ZIKURATS
ZILLIONS
ZIMOCCAS
ZINCATES
ZINCIEST
ZINCITES
ZINCKIER
ZINCKIFY
ZINCKING
ZINCODES
ZINGIBER
ZINGIEST
ZINKIEST
ZIPPERED
ZIPPIEST
ZIRCALOY
ZIRCONIA
ZIRCONIC
ZITHERNS
ZIZANIAS
ZIZYPHUS
ZIZZLING
ZOCCOLOS
ZODIACAL
ZOETROPE
ZOIATRIA
ZOISITES
ZOMBIISM
ZOMBORUK
ZONATION
ZONELESS
ZONETIME
ZONULETS
ZOOBLAST
ZOOCHORE
ZOOCHORY
ZOOCYTIA
ZOOECIUM
ZOOGENIC
ZOOGLEAE
ZOOGLEAL
ZOOGLEAS
ZOOGLOEA
ZOOGRAFT
ZOOLATER
ZOOLATRY
ZOOLITES
ZOOLITHS
ZOOLITIC
ZOOLOGIC
ZOOMANCY
ZOOMANIA
ZOOMETRY
ZOOMORPH
ZOONITES
ZOONITIC
ZOONOMIA
ZOONOMIC
ZOONOSES
ZOONOSIS
ZOONOTIC
ZOOPATHY
ZOOPERAL
ZOOPHAGY
ZOOPHILE
ZOOPHILY
ZOOPHOBE
ZOOPHORI
ZOOPHYTE
ZOOSCOPY
ZOOSPERM
ZOOSPORE
ZOOTHOME
ZOOTIEST
ZOOTOMIC
ZOOTOXIN
ZOOTROPE
ZOOTYPES
ZOOTYPIC
ZOPILOTE
ZORGITES
ZORILLAS
ZORILLES
ZORILLOS
ZUCCHINI
ZUCHETTA
ZUCHETTO
ZUGZWANG
ZWIEBACK
ZYGAENID
ZYGANTRA
ZYGODONT
ZYGOMATA
ZYGOSITY
ZYGOTENE
ZYLONITE
ZYMOGENE
ZYMOGENS
ZYMOGRAM
ZYMOLOGY
ZYMOSANS
ZYMOTICS
ZYZZYVAS

Hint

Managing the Big Four

It is rarely worth holding on to the J, Q, X or Z in the hope of a very high score later in the game unless you are aware of the letters you are likely to pick up and you are not sacrificing scores in the process. Generally, keeping the high-score letters back will hinder future opportunities and rack balance. It is often wiser to score what you can rather than wait for something better. But if you are to hold on to any of the big four the X is probably the safest and most flexible simply because of the 2-letter words playable. It is also the one your opponent is most likely unwittingly to provide a scoring opportunity for.

Hint

Learning the J Q X Z Words

If you have trouble remembering those useful words containing the J, Q, X or Z then try the following solo game as a learning exercise. Take the J, X, Z, Q and one U out of the letter bag and put to one side. Take six letters at random from the letter bag and place on your rack. Then give yourself a couple of minutes with each of J, Q, X and Z to see how many different words you can make by combining them with the six letters on your rack. When playing with the Q, if you haven't also picked a U, utilize the U you've put to one side. Make a note of the highest-scoring play you found with each of J, Q, X and Z and then check with the lists in this book to see if there was anything you missed. Having completed the exercise with the first rack, play any word from your six letters on the board, keeping the J, Q, X, Z and U to one side, and return any remaining letters to the bag. Select another six letters at random for the second turn. Repeat the exercise with the fresh rack and so on.

Hint

Do-It-Yourself 6-Letter Sets

The 250 6-letter combinations (stems) in this book represent those most useful to the Scrabble player. There are many more stems that are useful to study and, as is nearly always the case, compiling lists yourself not only helps you memorize the words but is also more interesting than simply learning from those readily provided. Try deriving your own 6-letter stem lists based on names (SHEILA, DANIEL, etc) or fictitious words (INCORE, POSIER, etc) as mnemonics. The Anagram section will be your ideal hunting-ground for this exercise.

Hint

Tile-Tracking

It is acceptable in tournament Scrabble to have a note of the letter distribution and to use it during play as a checklist of what letters are still to come. Most top players use this method to enable them to work out what tiles their opponents have at the end of the game. Such a checklist, when used skilfully, can also provide mid-game information about likely pickups and enable the right combination of tiles to be kept on the rack to give the greatest possibility of playing a bonus word. If you practise tile-tracking whilst playing you will soon find you are more aware of the letter distribution which in turn will assist you to maintain a balanced rack. Even if you don't track all the tiles, keeping a note of the vowels, the S's and blanks, the J, Q, X, Z and the awkward consonants C,V and K will help improve your rack management.

Section Two

Beginnings

Introduction

Beginnings of words are what you naturally think about when you are looking for a play. Is there a word playable beginning with BE-, DIS-, OUT-, RE- or UN- ? Sometimes you may be hoping to prefix a word already on the board with letters from your rack. Is there a good score available through adding some letters to the front of an existing word?

In this section there are two categories of lists, each focusing on beginnings of words. The first is a set of lists arranged according to a variety of common prefix letters. These are the Prefix lists.

The second set, the 5 to 8's, is a little more specialist and contains useful 3-letter extensions of 5-letter words. More about this set later on.

Useful Prefixes

The following lists are of 7- and 8-letter words starting with these prefixes:

AB-	EM-	MIS-	SEA-
AD-	EN-	NON-	SUB-
AIR-	EX-	OUT-	SUN-
BE-	FOOT-	OVER-	TRI-
BI-	FOR-	PER-	UN-
COM-	IM-	PRE-	UP-
CON-	IN-	PRO-	WAR-
DE-	ISO-	RE-	
DIS-	MAN-	RED-	

These prefixes have been chosen because each provides a reasonable selection of words. Some of the prefixes, eg MAN- and SEA-, are used for forming compound words, and others are more common prefixes such as RE- and UN-. All are likely to turn up on your rack on a regular basis and if your remaining tiles form a valid word to go with the prefix then, board permitting, you'll be able to play a bonus word.

All the lists contain only those words where, if the prefix is removed, a valid word remains. This eliminates the many words that happen to begin with the prefix but which are not of interest; for example, TRICKING and TRIBUNE are not on the TRI- list because 'CKING' and 'BUNE' are not valid words. However, in the lists there will be some words that coincidentally qualify for inclusion, even though the prefix in question is not strictly used as such. For example, REACHED appears on the RE- list because RE- can be added to the front of ACHED. Similarly, as WAR- can be added at the beginning of BLED, WARBLED appears on the WAR- list. All the words, though, are of genuine interest.

WORDS PREFIXED WITH AB-

7-letter words AB-

ABACTOR ABAXILE ABJOINT ABOMASA ABREAST ABSEILS ABSURDS ABUTTER
ABALONE ABDUCES ABLATED ABOUGHT ABREGES ABSENTS ABTHANE ABVOLTS
ABASHED ABDUCTS ABLINGS ABRAIDS ABRIDGE ABSOLVE ABUSAGE ABWATTS
ABASHES ABFARAD ABLUTED ABRAYED ABROACH ABSORBS ABUSERS
ABAXIAL ABHENRY ABOLLAS ABREACT ABROADS ABSTAIN ABUSING

8-letter words AB-

ABACTORS ABEARING ABJOINTS ABOMASUM ABREACTS ABSEILED ABSOLVES ABTHANES
ABAMPERE ABERRANT ABLEGATE ABORALLY ABRIDGED ABSENTED ABSONANT ABUSABLE
ABAPICAL ABESSIVE ABNEGATE ABORIGIN ABRIDGER ABSOLUTE ABSORBED ABUSAGES
ABASHING ABFARADS ABNORMAL ABRAIDED ABRIDGES ABSOLVED ABSTAINS ABUTTERS
ABDUCTED ABHENRYS ABOMASAL ABRAYING ABROOKED ABSOLVER ABSTRICT

WORDS PREFIXED WITH AD-

7-letter words AD-

ADAGIOS ADDEEMS ADDUCES ADJUDGE ADMIRES ADOPTER ADVENTS ADVISED
ADAPTED ADDICTS ADDUCTS ADJUROR ADMIXED ADPRESS ADVERBS ADVISES
ADAPTER ADDOOMS ADHERES ADJUSTS ADMIXES ADREADS ADVERSE ADVISOR
ADAWING ADDRESS ADJOINS ADLANDS ADNOUNS ADRENAL ADVERTS ADWARDS
ADAXIAL ADDREST ADJOINT ADMIRED ADOPTED ADSORBS ADVICES

8-letter words AD-

ADAPTING ADDUCTED ADJACENT ADJURORS ADMIXING ADOPTION ADVERSER
ADDEBTED ADENOSES ADJOINED ADJUSTED ADMONISH ADSCRIPT ADVERTED
ADDEEMED ADENOSIS ADJOINTS ADJUSTER ADNATION ADSORBED ADVISING
ADDICTED ADEQUATE ADJUDGED ADMASSES ADOPTERS ADUMBRAL ADVISORS
ADDOOMED ADESSIVE ADJUDGES ADMIRING ADOPTING ADUNCATE ADWARDED

WORDS PREFIXED WITH AIR-

7-letter words AIR-

AIRBASE AIRDROP AIRGAPS AIRLESS AIRLOCK AIRPORT AIRSICK AIRTING AIRWISE
AIRBOAT AIRFARE AIRGLOW AIRLIFT AIRMAIL AIRPOST AIRSIDE AIRWARD
AIRCREW AIRFLOW AIRHEAD AIRLIKE AIRPARK AIRSHED AIRSTOP AIRWAVE
AIRDATE AIRFOIL AIRHOLE AIRLINE AIRPLAY AIRSHIP AIRTIME AIRWAYS

8-letter words AIR-

AIRBASES AIRCHECK AIRDROPS AIRGRAPH AIRMAILS AIRPROOF AIRSPACE AIRWARDS
AIRBOATS AIRCOACH AIRFARES AIRHEADS AIRPARKS AIRSCAPE AIRSPEED AIRWAVES
AIRBORNE AIRCRAFT AIRFIELD AIRHOLES AIRPLANE AIRSCREW AIRSTOPS AIRWOMAN
AIRBOUND AIRCREWS AIRFLOWS AIRLIFTS AIRPLAYS AIRSHAFT AIRSTRIP AIRWOMEN
AIRBRUSH AIRDATES AIRFOILS AIRLINER AIRPORTS AIRSHEDS AIRTHING
AIRBURST AIRDRAWN AIRFRAME AIRLINES AIRPOSTS AIRSHIPS AIRTIGHT
AIRBUSES AIRDROME AIRGLOWS AIRLOCKS AIRPOWER AIRSIDES AIRTIMES

WORDS PREFIXED WITH BE-

7-letter words BE-

BEACHED BECHARM BECURSE BEDIRTY BEDUSTS BEGAZED BEGROAN BEHOOVE BELABOR
BEACHES BECLASP BECURST BEDIZEN BEDWARF BEGAZES BEGUILE BEHOVED BELACED
BEADMAN BECLOAK BEDAMNS BEDRAIL BEECHES BEGIFTS BEGULFS BEHOVES BELACES
BEADMEN BECLOGS BEDAUBS BEDRAPE BEFALLS BEGILDS BEGUNKS BEHOWLS BELATED
BEARISH BECLOUD BEDAZED BEDROLL BEFLAGS BEGIRDS BEHAVER BEINKED BELAUDS
BEAVERS BECLOWN BEDAZES BEDROPS BEFLEAS BEGLADS BEHAVES BEJADED BELAYED
BEBLOOD BECOMES BEDECKS BEDROPT BEFLECK BEGLOOM BEHEADS BEJADES BELEAPS
BEBUNGS BECRAWL BEDELLS BEDRUGS BEFOAMS BEGNAWS BEHESTS BEJESUS BELEAPT
BECALLS BECRIME BEDEMAN BEDUCKS BEFOOLS BEGOING BEHIGHT BEJEWEL BELIEFS
BECALMS BECROWD BEDEVIL BEDUMBS BEFOULS BEGONIA BEHINDS BEKNAVE BELIERS
BECAUSE BECRUST BEDEWED BEDUNCE BEFRETS BEGORED BEHOLDS BEKNOTS BELIEVE
BECHALK BECURLS BEDIGHT BEDUNGS BEGALLS BEGRIME BEHOOFS BEKNOWN BELONGS

BELOVED BELOVES BELYING BEMADAM BEMAULS BEMAZED BEMEANS BEMEANT BEMEDAL BEMETED BEMETES BEMIRED BEMIRES BEMISTS
BEMIXED BEMIXES BEMOANS BEMOCKS BEMOILS BEMOUTH BEMUSED BEMUSES BENAMED BENAMES BENEATH BENEMPT BENIGHT BENUMBS
BEPAINT BEPEARL BEPELTS BEPROSE BEPUFFS BEQUEST BERAKED BERAKES BERATED BERATES BERAYED BEREAVE BERHYME BERIMED
BERIMES BEROBED BESAINT BESCOUR BESEEMS BESHAME BESHINE BESHONE BESHOUT BESHREW BESIDES BESIEGE BESIGHS BESINGS
BESLAVE BESLIME BESMEAR BESMILE BESMOKE BESMUTS BESNOWS BESORTS BESPAKE BESPATE BESPEAK BESPEED BESPICE BESPITS
BESPOKE BESPORT BESPOTS BESPOUT BESTAIN BESTARS BESTEAD BESTICK BESTILL BESTING BESTIRS BESTORM BESTOWS BESTREW
BESTROW BESTUCK BESTUDS BESWARM BETAKEN BETAKES BETAXED BETEEMS BETHANK BETHINK BETHORN BETHUMB BETHUMP BETIDED
BETIDES BETIGHT BETIMED BETIMES BETITLE BETOILS BETOKEN BETRAYS BETREAD BETRIMS BETROTH BETWEEN BETWIXT BEVOMIT
BEWAILS BEWARED BEWARES BEWEARY BEWEEPS BEWHORE BEWITCH BEWORMS BEWORRY BEWRAPS BEWRAPT

8-letter words BE-

BEACHIER BEACHING BEARABLE BEBLOODS BEBOPPED BEBOPPER BECALLED BECALMED BECAPPED BECARPET BECHALKS BECHANCE BECHARMS BECLAMOR BECLASPS BECLOAKS BECLOTHE BECLOUDS BECLOWNS BECOMING BECOWARD BECRAWLS BECRIMED BECRIMES BECROWDS BECRUSTS BECUDGEL BECURLED BECURSED BECURSES BEDABBLE BEDAGGLE BEDAMNED BEDARKEN BEDASHED BEDASHES BEDAUBED
BEDAZING BEDAZZLE BEDEAFEN BEDECKED BEDESMAN BEDEVILS BEDEWING BEDIAPER BEDIGHTS BEDIMMED BEDIMPLE BEDIZENS BEDOTTED BEDRAILS BEDRAPED BEDRAPES BEDRENCH BEDRIVEL BEDROLLS BEDUCKED BEDUMBED BEDUNCES BEDUNGED BEDUSTED BEDWARFS BEDYEING BEFALLEN BEFINGER BEFINNED BEFITTED BEFLECKS BEFLOWER BEFOAMED BEFOGGED BEFOOLED BEFOULED BEFOULER
BEFRIEND BEFRINGE BEFUDDLE BEGALLED BEGAZING BEGEMMED BEGETTER BEGIFTED BEGILDED BEGINNER BEGIRDED BEGIRDLE BEGLAMOR BEGLOOMS BEGNAWED BEGOTTEN BEGRIMED BEGRIMES BEGROANS BEGRUDGE BEGUILED BEGUILER BEGUILES BEGULFED BEHALVES BEHAPPEN BEHATTED BEHAVERS BEHAVING BEHAVIOR BEHEADED BEHIGHTS BEHOLDEN BEHOLDER BEHOOVED BEHOOVES BEHOVING
BEHOWLED BEJABERS BEJADING BEJESUIT BEJEWELS BEJUMBLE BEKISSED BEKISSES BEKNAVES BEKNIGHT BELABORS BELABOUR BELACING BELADIES BELAUDED BELAYING BELEAPED BELEEING BELIEVER BELIQUOR BELITTLE BELONGED BELONGER BELOVING BEMADAMS BEMADDED BEMADDEN BEMAULED BEMEANED BEMEDALS BEMETING BEMINGLE BEMIRING BEMISTED BEMIXING BEMOANED BEMOANER
BEMOCKED BEMOILED BEMOUTHS BEMUDDED BEMUDDLE BEMUFFLE BEMURMUR BEMUSING BEMUZZLE BENAMING BENETTED BENIGHTS BENUMBED BEPAINTS BEPATTED BEPEARLS BEPELTED BEPEPPER BEPESTER BEPIMPLE BEPITIED BEPITIES BEPLUMED BEPOMMEL BEPOWDER BEPRAISE BEPROSED BEPROSES BEPUFFED BEQUESTS BERAKING BERASCAL BERATING BERAYING BEREAVED BEREAVER BEREAVES
BERHYMED BERHYMES BERIMING BERINGED BEROBBED BEROUGED BESAINTS BESCORCH BESCOURS BESCRAWL BESCREEN BESEEING BESEEMED BESEEMLY BESETTER BESHADOW BESHAMED BESHAMES BESHINES BESHIVER BESHOUTS BESHREWS BESHROUD BESIEGED BESIEGER BESIEGES BESIGHED BESLAVED BESLAVER BESLAVES BESLIMED BESLIMES BESMEARS BESMILED BESMILES BESMIRCH BESMOKED
BESMOKES BESMOOTH BESMUDGE BESMUTCH BESNOWED BESOOTHE BESORTED BESOTTED BESOUGHT BESOULED BESPEAKS BESPEEDS BESPICED BESPICES BESPOKEN BESPORTS BESPOUSE BESPOUTS BESPREAD BESPRENT BESTAINS BESTEADS BESTICKS BESTILLS BESTORMS BESTOWED BESTOWER BESTREAK BESTREWN BESTREWS BESTRIDE BESTRODE BESTROWN BESTROWS BESUITED BESWARMS BETAKING
BETATTER BETEEMED BETHANKS BETHINKS BETHORNS BETHRALL BETHUMBS BETHUMPS BETHWACK BETIDING BETIMING BETITLED BETITLES BETOILED BETOKENS BETONIES BETOSSED BETOSSES BETREADS BETROTHS BEUNCLED BEVOMITS BEWAILED BEWAILER BEWARING BEWETTED BEWHORED BEWHORES BEWIGGED BEWILDER BEWINGED BEWORMED

WORDS PREFIXED WITH BI-

7-letter words BI-

BIASSES BIAXIAL BIBASIC BIBLESS BIBLIST
BICARBS BICHORD BICOLOR BICORNS BICYCLE
BIDENTS BIDINGS BIFACES BIFILAR BIFOCAL
BIKINGS BILAYER BILIMBI BILOBAR BILOBED
BIMETAL BIMODAL BIMORPH BIOLOGY BIONTIC
BIOPTIC BIPACKS BIPARTY BIPEDAL BIPLANE
BIPOLAR BISECTS BISHOPS BISTATE BITABLE
BITINGS BITONAL BIVALVE BIVINYL BIZONAL
BIZONES

8-letter words BI-

BIACETYL BIANNUAL BICAUDAL BICHROME BICOLORS
BICOLOUR BICONVEX BICUSPID BICYCLED BICYCLER
BICYCLES BICYCLIC BIDENTAL BIELDING BIFACIAL
BIFORKED BIFORMED BIGEMINY BIHOURLY BIJUGATE
BILABIAL BILANDER BILAYERS BILINEAR BILOBATE
BIMANUAL BIMENSAL BIMETALS BIMETHYL BIMORPHS
BIOBLAST BIOTITIC BIOVULAR BIPAROUS BIPARTED
BIPHASIC BIPHENYL BIPLANES BIRACIAL BIRADIAL

BIRAMOSE BISECTOR BISEXUAL BISTOURY BITINGLY BIVALVED BIVINYLS BIYEARLY
BIRAMOUS BISERIAL BISTABLE BITEWING BIUNIQUE BIVALVES BIWEEKLY

WORDS PREFIXED WITH COM-

7-letter words COM-

COMAKES COMBINE COMFORT COMMIXT COMMUTE COMPASS COMPILE COMPOSE
COMARBS COMBING COMICES COMMODE COMPACT COMPAST COMPING COMPOST
COMARTS COMBUST COMMAND COMMONS COMPAGE COMPEAR COMPLOT COMPOTE
COMATES COMETIC COMMEND COMMOTE COMPAND COMPEER COMPONE COMPOTS
COMBATS COMFIER COMMENT COMMOTS COMPARE COMPEND COMPONY COMRADE
COMBIER COMFITS COMMERE COMMOVE COMPART COMPERE COMPORT COMUSES

8-letter words COM-

COMAKING COMFIEST COMMODES COMMUTES COMPARTS COMPINGS COMPOSED COMPRISE
COMBATED COMFORTS COMMONER COMPACTS COMPEARS COMPLAIN COMPOSER COMPRIZE
COMBINES COMINGLE COMMONEY COMPADRE COMPEERS COMPLEAT COMPOSES COMPULSE
COMBINGS COMMENDS COMMOTES COMPAGES COMPENDS COMPLIED COMPOSTS
COMBLESS COMMERES COMMOVED COMPANDS COMPERES COMPLIER COMPOTES
COMBUSTS COMMERGE COMMOVES COMPARED COMPILED COMPLIES COMPOUND
COMEMBER COMMIXED COMMUTED COMPARER COMPILER COMPLOTS COMPRESS
COMETHER COMMIXES COMMUTER COMPARES COMPILES COMPORTS COMPRINT

WORDS PREFIXED WITH CON-

7-letter words CON-

CONACRE CONCREW CONDORS CONFITS CONGEST CONJURY CONSOLE CONTEXT CONVIVE
CONARIA CONCURS CONDUCE CONFLUX CONGOES CONKIER CONSOLS CONTORT
CONCAVE CONCUSS CONDUCT CONFORM CONGREE CONKING CONSORT CONTOUR
CONCEDE CONDIES CONDUIT CONFUSE CONGRUE CONNOTE CONTACT CONTRAT
CONCENT CONDOES CONFESS CONGAED CONJEED CONSEIL CONTAIN CONTUND
CONCERT CONDOLE CONFEST CONGEAL CONJEES CONSENT CONTEND CONURES
CONCHAL CONDOMS CONFINE CONGEED CONJOIN CONSIGN CONTENT CONVENT
CONCORD CONDONE CONFIRM CONGEES CONJURE CONSIST CONTEST CONVERT

8-letter words CON-

CONACRED CONCOLOR CONFINER CONFUSES CONJOINT CONSISTS CONTENDS CONTUNDS
CONACRES CONCORDS CONFINES CONGEALS CONJUGAL CONSOLED CONTENTS CONURBAN
CONCAUSE CONCOURS CONFIRMS CONGENIC CONJUROR CONSOLER CONTESTS CONURBIA
CONCAVED CONCREWS CONFIXED CONGESTS CONNOTED CONSOLES CONTEXTS CONVENTS
CONCAVES CONDENSE CONFIXES CONGLOBE CONNOTES CONSORTS CONTORTS CONVERGE
CONCEDED CONDOLED CONFOCAL CONGREED CONQUEST CONSPIRE CONTOURS CONVERSE
CONCEDER CONDOLES CONFORMS CONGREES CONSEILS CONSTATE CONTRACT CONVERTS
CONCEDES CONDUCES CONFOUND CONGREET CONSENTS CONTACTS CONTRAIL CONVEXED
CONCENTS CONDUCTS CONFRERE CONGRUED CONSERVE CONTAINS CONTRATS CONVEXES
CONCERTS CONDUITS CONFRONT CONGRUES CONSIDER CONTANGO CONTRIST CONVIVES
CONCLAVE CONFINED CONFUSED CONJOINS CONSIGNS CONTEMPT CONTRITE CONVOLVE

WORDS PREFIXED WITH DE-

7-letter words DE-

DEAIRED DEBRIEF DECLASS DECRIER DEFEATS DEFRAGS DEGLAZE DELEADS DEMARKS
DEALATE DEBUNKS DECLAWS DECRIES DEFENCE DEFRAUD DEGOUTS DELEAVE DEMASTS
DEASHED DECADES DECLINE DECROWN DEFENDS DEFRAYS DEGRADE DELIGHT DEMEANE
DEASHES DECAFFS DECODED DECRYPT DEFILED DEFROCK DEGREED DELIMED DEMEANS
DEBARKS DECAMPS DECODER DECURIA DEFILER DEFROST DEGREES DELIMES DEMERGE
DEBASED DECANAL DECODES DECURVE DEFILES DEFROZE DEGUSTS DELIMIT DEMERIT
DEBASER DECANES DECOKED DEDUCES DEFINED DEFUNDS DEHORNS DELISTS DEMERSE
DEBASES DECANTS DECOKES DEDUCTS DEFINER DEFUSED DEICERS DELIVER DEMESNE
DEBATED DECARBS DECOLOR DEFACED DEFINES DEFUSES DEICING DELOPED DEMISES
DEBATES DECARES DECOYED DEFACER DEFLEAS DEFUZED DEICTIC DELOPES DEMISTS
DEBEAKS DECEASE DECOYER DEFACES DEFOAMS DEFUZES DEJEUNE DELOUSE DEMOSES
DEBONED DECIDED DECREED DEFAMED DEFOCUS DEGAMES DELAPSE DELUDES DEMOTED
DEBONER DECIDER DECREES DEFAMES DEFORCE DEGASES DELATED DELUGED DEMOTES
DEBONES DECIDES DECREWS DEFANGS DEFORMS DEGAUSS DELAYED DELUGES DEMOUNT
DEBRIDE DECLAIM DECRIED DEFAULT DEFOULS DEGERMS DELAYER DEMAINS DEMURED

DEMURES DEPENDS DEPOSIT DERIVER DESEXES DESPOIL DETENUE DEVEINS DEWATER
DENOTED DEPERMS DEPRESS DERIVES DESIGNS DESPOTS DETESTS DEVESTS DEWAXED
DENOTES DEPLANE DERAILS DESALTS DESINED DESTAIN DETICKS DEVICES DEWAXES
DENUDER DEPLOYS DERANGE DESANDS DESINES DESTROY DETORTS DEVISED DEWOOLS
DENUDES DEPLUME DERATED DESCALE DESIRED DESUGAR DETOURS DEVISES DEWORMS
DENYING DEPONES DERATES DESCANT DESIRES DESYNED DETRACT DEVISOR DEZINCS
DEONTIC DEPORTS DERAYED DESCEND DESISTS DESYNES DETRAIN DEVOICE
DEORBIT DEPOSED DERIDER DESCENT DESKILL DETAILS DETUNED DEVOLVE
DEPAINT DEPOSER DERIDES DESERVE DESORBS DETAINS DETUNES DEVOTED
DEPARTS DEPOSES DERIVED DESEXED DESPITE DETENTS DEVALUE DEVOTES

8-letter words DE-

DEAERATE DECEASED DEFANGED DEFROZEN DELIVERS DEPARTER DESCALES DETAILED
DEAIRING DECEASES DEFATTED DEFUNDED DELIVERY DEPEINCT DESCANTS DETAILER
DEALATED DECENTER DEFAULTS DEFUSING DELOPING DEPENDED DESCENDS DETASSEL
DEALATES DECENTRE DEFEATED DEFUZING DELOUSED DEPERMED DESCENTS DETENUES
DEARLING DECERNED DEFEATER DEGASSED DELOUSES DEPLANED DESCHOOL DETESTED
DEASHING DECIDERS DEFENCED DEGASSER DELUGING DEPLANES DESCRIBE DETESTER
DEBAGGED DECIDING DEFENCES DEGASSES DELUSTER DEPLOYED DESCRIED DETHRONE
DEBARKED DECIPHER DEFENDED DEGENDER DEMANNED DEPLUMED DESCRIES DETICKED
DEBARRED DECLAIMS DEFENDER DEGERMED DEMARKED DEPLUMES DESCRIVE DETICKER
DEBASING DECLAWED DEFIANCE DEGLAZED DEMASTED DEPOLISH DESELECT DETOURED
DEBATING DECLINAL DEFILERS DEGLAZES DEMEANED DEPONENT DESERVED DETRACTS
DEBEAKED DECLINES DEFILING DEGRADED DEMEANES DEPORTED DESERVER DETRAINS
DEBELLED DECLUTCH DEFINERS DEGRADER DEMERGED DEPOSERS DESERVES DETUNING
DEBITING DECODERS DEFINING DEGRADES DEMERGER DEPOSING DESEXING DEVALUED
DEBONERS DECODING DEFINITE DEGREASE DEMERGES DEPOSITS DESIGNED DEVALUES
DEBONING DECOKING DEFLEXED DEGUMMED DEMERITS DERAILED DESIGNEE DEVEINED
DEBOSHES DECOLORS DEFLEXES DEGUSTED DEMERSES DERAILER DESIGNER DEVERBAL
DEBOSSED DECOLOUR DEFLOWER DEHORNED DEMESNES DERANGED DESILVER DEVESTED
DEBOSSES DECOUPLE DEFLUENT DEHORNER DEMISTED DERANGES DESINING DEVIATOR
DEBOUCHE DECOYING DEFOAMED DEIONIZE DEMISTER DERATING DESIRING DEVISING
DEBRIDED DECREASE DEFOAMER DELAPSED DEMOBBED DERATION DESISTED DEVISORS
DEBRIDES DECREWED DEFOGGED DELAPSES DEMONISM DERATTED DESKILLS DEVOICED
DEBRIEFS DECRIERS DEFOGGER DELAYERS DEMONIST DERAYING DESOLATE DEVOICES
DEBRUISE DECROWNS DEFORCED DELAYING DEMOTION DERELICT DESORBED DEVOLVED
DEBUGGED DECRYING DEFORCES DELEADED DEMOUNTS DERIDERS DESPIGHT DEVOLVES
DEBUGGER DECRYPTS DEFOREST DELEAVED DEMURING DERIDING DESPITED DEVOTING
DEBUNKED DECURIAS DEFORMED DELEAVES DENATURE DERIGGED DESPITES DEWATERS
DEBUNKER DECURIES DEFORMER DELEGACY DENAZIFY DERINGER DESPOILS DEWAXING
DEBUSSED DECURVED DEFOULED DELEGATE DENETTED DERIVERS DESTAINS DEWITTED
DEBUSSES DECURVES DEFRAUDS DELIBATE DENOTATE DERIVING DESTROYS DEWOOLED
DECADENT DEDUCTED DEFRAYED DELIGHTS DENOTING DESALTED DESUGARS DEWORMED
DECAMPED DEFACERS DEFREEZE DELIMING DEORBITS DESALTER DESULFUR DEWORMER
DECANTED DEFACING DEFROCKS DELIMITS DEPAINTS DESANDED DESYNING DEZINCED
DECANTER DEFAMING DEFROSTS DELISTED DEPARTED DESCALED DETACHES

WORDS PREFIXED WITH DIS-

7-letter words DIS-

DISABLE DISCANT DISEDGE DISHORN DISLOAD DISOWNS DISPOSE DISSECT DISTOME
DISALLY DISCARD DISFAME DISJOIN DISMALS DISPACE DISPOST DISSENT DISTORT
DISARMS DISCASE DISFORM DISKING DISMANS DISPARK DISPRAD DISSING DISTUNE
DISAVOW DISCIDE DISGEST DISLEAF DISMASK DISPART DISRANK DISTAIN DISUSED
DISBAND DISCOED DISGOWN DISLEAL DISMAST DISPEND DISRATE DISTEND DISUSES
DISBARK DISCORD DISGUST DISLIKE DISMAYS DISPLAY DISROBE DISTENT DISYOKE
DISBARS DISCURE DISHELM DISLIMB DISMISS DISPLED DISROOT DISTICH
DISBUDS DISCUSS DISHING DISLIMN DISNEST DISPONE DISSAVE DISTILL
DISCAGE DISEASE DISHOME DISLINK DISOBEY DISPORT DISSEAT DISTILS

8-letter words DIS-

DISABLED DISAPPLY DISBENCH DISCANTS DISCLOSE DISCURES DISFAVOR DISGRACE
DISABLES DISARMED DISBOSOM DISCARDS DISCOLOR DISEASED DISFLESH DISGRADE
DISABUSE DISARMER DISBOUND DISCASED DISCORDS DISEASES DISFORMS DISGUISE
DISADORN DISARRAY DISBOWEL DISCASES DISCOUNT DISEDGED DISFROCK DISGUSTS
DISAGREE DISASTER DISBURSE DISCIDED DISCOURE DISEDGES DISGAVEL DISHABIT
DISALLOW DISAVOWS DISCAGED DISCIDES DISCOVER DISENDOW DISGESTS DISHABLE
DISANNEX DISBANDS DISCAGES DISCINCT DISCROWN DISENROL DISGORGE DISHELMS
DISANNUL DISBARKS DISCANDY DISCLAIM DISCURED DISFAMES DISGOWNS DISHINGS

DISHOMED DISHOMES DISHONOR DISHORNS DISHORSE DISHOUSE DISINTER DISINURE DISJOINS DISJOINT DISLEAFS DISLEAVE DISLIKED
DISLIKEN DISLIKER DISLIKES DISLIMBS DISLIMNS DISLINKS DISLOADS DISLODGE DISLOYAL DISMASKS DISMASTS DISMAYED DISMOUNT
DISNESTS DISOBEYS DISORBED DISORDER DISOWNED DISOWNER DISPACED DISPACES DISPARKS DISPARTS DISPATCH DISPEACE DISPENCE
DISPENDS DISPERSE DISPLACE DISPLANT DISPLAYS DISPLING DISPLUME DISPONES DISPORTS DISPOSED DISPOSER DISPOSES DISPOSTS
DISPRIZE DISPROOF DISPROVE DISPURSE DISQUIET DISRANKS DISRATED DISRATES DISROBED DISROBES DISROOTS DISSAVED DISSAVES
DISSEATS DISSECTS DISSEISE DISSEIZE DISSENTS DISSERVE DISSEVER DISSIGHT DISSOLVE DISTAINS DISTALLY DISTASTE DISTENDS
DISTILLS DISTINCT DISTOMES DISTORTS DISTRACT DISTRAIL DISTRAIN DISTRAIT DISTRESS DISTRUST DISTUNED DISTUNES DISUNION
DISUNITE DISUNITY DISUSAGE DISUSING DISVALUE DISVOUCH DISYOKED DISYOKES

WORDS PREFIXED WITH EM-

7-letter words EM-

EMAILED EMBAILS EMBALED EMBALES EMBALLS EMBALMS EMBANKS
EMBARKS EMBASED EMBASES EMBASSY EMBASTE EMBATHE EMBAYED
EMBLAZE EMBLOOM EMBOILS EMBOLUS EMBOSKS EMBOSOM EMBOUND
EMBOWED EMBOWEL EMBOWER EMBOXED EMBOXES EMBRACE EMBRAID
EMBRAVE EMBREAD EMBROIL EMBROWN EMBRUTE EMENDED EMENDER
EMIRATE EMMEWED EMMOVED EMMOVES EMPAIRE EMPALED EMPALER
EMPALES EMPANEL EMPARED EMPARES EMPARTS EMPEACH EMPERCE
EMPIGHT EMPLACE EMPLANE EMPLOYS EMPLUME EMPOWER EMPRESS
EMPRISE EMPRIZE EMPUSES

8-letter words EM-

EMAILING EMBAILED EMBALING EMBALLED EMBALMED EMBANKED EMBANKER EMBARKED EMBARRED EMBASING EMBATHED EMBATHES
EMBATTLE EMBAYING EMBEDDED EMBEZZLE EMBITTER EMBLAZED EMBLAZER EMBLAZES EMBLAZON EMBLOOMS EMBODIED EMBODIES
EMBOGGED EMBOILED EMBOLDEN EMBORDER EMBOSOMS EMBOSSED EMBOSSER EMBOSSES EMBOUNDS EMBOWELS EMBOWERS EMBOWING
EMBOXING EMBRACED EMBRACER EMBRACES EMBRAIDS EMBRAVED EMBRAVES EMBREADS EMBREWED EMBROILS EMBROWNS EMBRUTED
EMBRUTES EMBUSIED EMBUSIES EMBUSSED EMBUSSES EMENDERS EMENDING EMMARBLE EMMESHED EMMESHES EMMEWING EMMOVING
EMPACKET EMPAIRED EMPAIRES EMPALING EMPANADA EMPANELS EMPARING EMPARLED EMPARTED EMPATHIC EMPATRON EMPEOPLE
EMPERCED EMPERCES EMPERISH EMPHASES EMPHASIS EMPHATIC EMPIERCE EMPLACED EMPLACES EMPLANED EMPLANES EMPLEACH
EMPLONGE EMPLOYED EMPLUMED EMPLUMES EMPOISON EMPOLDER EMPOWERS EMPRISES EMPRIZES EMPURPLE EMPYEMIC

WORDS PREFIXED WITH EN-

7-letter words EN-

ENABLED ENABLER ENABLES ENACTED ENACTOR ENAMINE ENAMOUR ENARMED ENCAGED ENCAGES ENCALMS ENCAMPS ENCASED ENCASES ENCAVED ENCAVES ENCHAFE ENCHAIN ENCHANT ENCHARM ENCHASE ENCHEER
ENCLASP ENCLAVE ENCLOSE ENCLOUD ENCODED ENCODER ENCODES ENCORED ENCORES ENCRUST ENCRYPT ENCYSTS ENDARTS ENDEARS ENDEMIC ENDEWED ENDINGS ENDITED ENDITES ENDIVES ENDORSE ENDOWED
ENDOWER ENDUING ENDURED ENDURES ENDUROS ENFACED ENFACES ENFELON ENFEOFF ENFEVER ENFILED ENFIRED ENFIRES ENFIXED ENFIXES ENFLAME ENFLESH ENFOLDS ENFORCE ENFORMS ENFRAME ENFREED
ENFREES ENFROZE ENGAGED ENGAGER ENGAGES ENGAOLS ENGILDS ENGIRDS ENGLOBE ENGLOOM ENGLUTS ENGORED ENGORES ENGORGE ENGRACE ENGRAFF ENGRAFT ENGRAIL ENGRAIN ENGRAMS ENGRASP ENGRAVE
ENGROSS ENGUARD ENGULFS ENGULPH ENHALOS ENHANCE ENISLED ENISLES ENJAMBS ENJOINS ENJOYED ENLACED ENLACES ENLARDS ENLARGE ENLIGHT ENLINKS ENLISTS ENLIVEN ENLOCKS ENMEWED ENMOVED
ENMOVES ENNOBLE ENOLOGY ENOUNCE ENPLANE ENPRINT ENQUIRE ENRACED ENRACES ENRAGED ENRAGES ENRANGE ENRANKS ENRHEUM ENRINGS ENRIVEN ENROBED ENROBES ENROLLS ENROOTS ENROUGH ENROUND
ENSEALS ENSEAMS ENSEARS ENSERFS ENSEWED ENSHELL ENSIGNS ENSILED ENSILES ENSKIED ENSKIES ENSKYED ENSLAVE ENSNARE ENSNARL ENSOULS ENSTAMP ENSTEEP ENSTYLE ENSUING ENSURED ENSURER
ENSURES ENSWEEP ENSWEPT ENTAILS ENTAMED ENTAMES ENTICED ENTICES ENTIRES ENTITLE ENTOILS ENTOMBS ENTOPIC ENTRAIL ENTRAIN ENTRANT ENTRAPS ENTREAT ENTREES ENTRIES ENTRIST ENTRUST
ENTWINE ENTWIST ENVAULT ENVENOM ENVIERS ENVYING ENWALLS ENWHEEL ENWINDS ENWOMBS ENWOUND ENWRAPS ENZONED ENZONES ENZYMES ENZYMIC

8-letter words EN-

ENABLING ENCIRCLE ENDOSSED ENGILDED ENHYDROS ENQUIRED ENSHRINE ENTICING
ENACTING ENCLASPS ENDOSSES ENGIRDED ENISLING ENQUIRES ENSHROUD ENTITLED
ENACTION ENCLAVES ENDOWERS ENGIRDLE ENJAMBED ENRACING ENSIGNED ENTITLES
ENACTIVE ENCLITIC ENDOWING ENGLOBED ENJOINED ENRAGING ENSILAGE ENTOILED
ENACTORS ENCLOSED ENDURING ENGLOBES ENJOINER ENRANGED ENSILING ENTOMBED
ENACTURE ENCLOSER ENFACING ENGLOOMS ENJOYING ENRANGES ENSKYING ENTRAILS
ENAMINES ENCLOSES ENFEEBLE ENGORGED ENKERNEL ENRANKED ENSLAVED ENTRAINS
ENAMOURS ENCLOTHE ENFELONS ENGORGES ENKINDLE ENRAUNGE ENSLAVER ENTRANCE
ENARCHED ENCLOUDS ENFEOFFS ENGORING ENLACING ENRAVISH ENSLAVES ENTRANTS
ENARCHES ENCODERS ENFETTER ENGRACED ENLARDED ENRHEUMS ENSNARED ENTREATS
ENARMING ENCODING ENFEVERS ENGRACES ENLARGEN ENRICHED ENSNARER ENTREATY
ENAUNTER ENCOLOUR ENFIERCE ENGRAFFS ENLARGER ENRICHER ENSNARES ENTRENCH
ENCAGING ENCOLURE ENFIRING ENGRAFTS ENLARGES ENRICHES ENSNARLS ENTROPIC
ENCALMED ENCORING ENFIXING ENGRAILS ENLIGHTS ENRIDGED ENSOULED ENTRUSTS
ENCAMPED ENCRADLE ENFLAMED ENGRAINS ENLINKED ENRINGED ENSPHERE ENTWINED
ENCARPUS ENCREASE ENFLAMES ENGRAMMA ENLISTED ENROBING ENSTAMPS ENTWINES
ENCASHED ENCRINAL ENFLOWER ENGRAMME ENLISTEE ENROLLED ENSTEEPS ENTWISTS
ENCASHES ENCRUSTS ENFOLDED ENGRASPS ENLISTER ENROLLER ENSTYLED ENURESES
ENCASING ENCRYPTS ENFOLDER ENGRAVED ENLIVENS ENROOTED ENSTYLES ENURESIS
ENCAVING ENCUMBER ENFORCED ENGRAVEN ENLOCKED ENROUGHS ENSURING ENURETIC
ENCHAFED ENCYCLIC ENFORCER ENGRAVER ENLUMINE ENROUNDS ENSWATHE ENVASSAL
ENCHAFES ENDAMAGE ENFORCES ENGRAVES ENMESHED ENSAMPLE ENSWEEPS ENVAULTS
ENCHAINS ENDANGER ENFOREST ENGRIEVE ENMESHES ENSCONCE ENTAILED ENVENOMS
ENCHANTS ENDARTED ENFORMED ENGROOVE ENMEWING ENSCROLL ENTAILER ENVIABLE
ENCHARGE ENDEARED ENFRAMED ENGUARDS ENMOSSED ENSEALED ENTAMING ENVIABLY
ENCHARMS ENDEIXES ENFRAMES ENGULFED ENMOVING ENSEAMED ENTANGLE ENVISAGE
ENCHASED ENDEIXIS ENFREEZE ENGULPHS ENNOBLER ENSEARED ENTELLUS ENVISION
ENCHASER ENDERMIC ENFROZEN ENHALOED ENNOBLES ENSEMBLE ENTENDER ENWALLED
ENCHASES ENDEWING ENGAGERS ENHALOES ENOUNCES ENSEWING ENTHETIC ENWALLOW
ENCHEERS ENDITING ENGAGING ENHANCES ENPLANED ENSHEATH ENTHRALL ENWHEELS
ENCHORIC ENDORSER ENGAOLED ENHEARSE ENPLANES ENSHELLS ENTHRONE ENWOMBED
ENCIPHER ENDORSES ENGENDER ENHUNGER ENPRINTS ENSHIELD ENTHUSES ENZONING

WORDS PREFIXED WITH EX-

7-letter words EX-

EXACTED EXCHEAT EXCLAIM EXOSMIC EXPORTS EXPRESS EXTENTS EXTORTS EXURBIA
EXACTOR EXCIDED EXCLAVE EXPANDS EXPOSED EXPULSE EXTERNE EXTRACT
EXALTER EXCIDES EXCURSE EXPENDS EXPOSER EXPURGE EXTERNS EXTRAIT
EXAMENS EXCITED EXHALED EXPERTS EXPOSES EXSECTS EXTINCT EXTREAT
EXAMINE EXCITER EXHALES EXPLAIN EXPOSIT EXTENDS EXTINES EXTREMA
EXAMPLE EXCITES EXODIST EXPLANT EXPOUND EXTENSE EXTOLLS EXURBAN

8-letter words EX-

EXACTING EXCESSED EXCLAIMS EXODISTS EXPLANTS EXPOUNDS EXTENDER EXTRACTS
EXACTION EXCESSES EXCLAVES EXOGAMIC EXPONENT EXPULSED EXTENSOR EXTRAITS
EXACTORS EXCHANGE EXCURSED EXOSMOSE EXPORTED EXPULSES EXTERNAL EXTREATS
EXALTERS EXCHEATS EXCURSES EXPANDER EXPORTER EXPURGED EXTERNES EXTUBATE
EXAMINES EXCIDING EXCURSUS EXPENDED EXPOSERS EXPURGES EXTINCTS EXURBIAS
EXANTHEM EXCITERS EXHALING EXPERTLY EXPOSING EXSECANT EXTOLLED
EXCELLED EXCITING EXHUMATE EXPLAINS EXPOSITS EXTENDED EXTOLLER

WORDS PREFIXED WITH FOOT-

7-letter words FOOT-

FOOTAGE FOOTBOY FOOTLED FOOTMAN FOOTPAD FOOTROT
FOOTBAR FOOTERS FOOTLES FOOTMEN FOOTRAS FOOTWAY

8-letter words FOOT-

FOOTAGES FOOTFALL FOOTLIKE FOOTPACE FOOTRACE FOOTSLOG FOOTWEAR
FOOTBALL FOOTGEAR FOOTLING FOOTPADS FOOTREST FOOTSORE FOOTWELL
FOOTBARS FOOTHILL FOOTMARK FOOTPAGE FOOTROPE FOOTSTEP FOOTWORK
FOOTBATH FOOTHOLD FOOTMUFF FOOTPATH FOOTROTS FOOTWALL FOOTWORN
FOOTBOYS FOOTLESS FOOTNOTE FOOTPOST FOOTRULE FOOTWAYS

WORDS PREFIXED WITH FOR-

7-letter words FOR-

FORAGED FORBODE FORESTS FORGIVE FORKING FORMATE FORRAYS FORTIES FORZATI
FORAGER FORBORE FOREVER FORGOER FORLANA FORMATS FORSAID FORTING
FORAGES FORCATS FORFAIR FORGOES FORLEND FORMING FORSAKE FORTUNE
FORAMEN FORCEPS FORFEND FORGONE FORLENT FORMOLS FORSAYS FORWARD
FORBADE FORDING FORGAVE FORHENT FORLORE FORPETS FORSLOE FORWARN
FORBEAR FORDOES FORGETS FORHOWS FORLORN FORPINE FORSLOW FORWENT
FORBIDS FORDONE FORGING FORKIER FORMALS FORPITS FORSOOK FORWORN

8-letter words FOR-

FORAGERS FORDOING FORFENDS FORHENTS FORMINGS FORSLOES FORSWEAR FORTUNES
FORAGING FOREKING FORGINGS FORJUDGE FORPINED FORSLOWS FORSWINK FORWARDS
FORAMENS FORELAIN FORGIVEN FORLANAS FORPINES FORSOOTH FORSWORE FORWARNS
FORBEARS FORELAND FORGIVER FORLENDS FORRAYED FORSPEAK FORSWORN FORWASTE
FORBODED FORESTER FORGIVES FORLESES FORSAKER FORSPEND FORTHINK FORWEARY
FORBODES FORFAIRS FORGOERS FORMATED FORSAKES FORSPENT FORTRESS
FORBORNE FORFAULT FORGOING FORMATES FORSLACK FORSPOKE FORTUNED

WORDS PREFIXED WITH IM-

7-letter words IM-

IMAGERS IMBASES IMBURSE IMMURED IMPANEL IMPEACH IMPLATE IMPOSTS IMPULSE
IMAGING IMBATHE IMMASKS IMMURES IMPARKS IMPEARL IMPLEAD IMPOUND IMPURER
IMAGISM IMBLAZE IMMENSE IMPACTS IMPARTS IMPEDES IMPLIED IMPOWER
IMAGIST IMBOSKS IMMERGE IMPAINT IMPASSE IMPENDS IMPLIES IMPRESA
IMAMATE IMBOSOM IMMERSE IMPAIRS IMPASTE IMPERIL IMPONES IMPRESE
IMARETS IMBOWER IMMEWED IMPALAS IMPAVED IMPIETY IMPORTS IMPRESS
IMBALMS IMBRAST IMMIXED IMPALED IMPAVES IMPINGS IMPOSED IMPREST
IMBARKS IMBROWN IMMIXES IMPALER IMPAVID IMPIOUS IMPOSER IMPRINT
IMBASED IMBRUTE IMMORAL IMPALES IMPAWNS IMPLANT IMPOSES IMPROVE

8-letter words IM-

IMAGINGS IMBLAZES IMMANENT IMMOBILE IMPARTED IMPLATED IMPORTED IMPROPER
IMAGISMS IMBODIED IMMANTLE IMMODEST IMPARTER IMPLATES IMPORTER IMPROVED
IMAGISTS IMBODIES IMMASKED IMMOMENT IMPASSES IMPLEACH IMPOSERS IMPROVER
IMAMATES IMBOLDEN IMMATURE IMMORTAL IMPASTED IMPLEADS IMPOSING IMPROVES
IMBALMED IMBORDER IMMERGED IMMOTILE IMPASTES IMPLEDGE IMPOSTED IMPUDENT
IMBARKED IMBOSOMS IMMERGES IMMURING IMPAVING IMPLUNGE IMPOSTER IMPULSED
IMBARRED IMBOSSED IMMERSES IMPAINTS IMPAWNED IMPLYING IMPOTENT IMPULSES
IMBASING IMBOSSES IMMESHED IMPAIRED IMPEARLS IMPOCKET IMPOUNDS IMPURELY
IMBATHED IMBOWERS IMMESHES IMPALING IMPENDED IMPOLDER IMPOWERS IMPUREST
IMBATHES IMBROWNS IMMEWING IMPANELS IMPERILS IMPOLICY IMPRESES IMPURITY
IMBEDDED IMBRUTED IMMINGLE IMPARITY IMPINGED IMPOLITE IMPRESTS IMPURPLE
IMBITTER IMBRUTES IMMINUTE IMPARKED IMPINGER IMPONENT IMPRINTS
IMBLAZED IMBURSES IMMIXING IMPARLED IMPLANTS IMPOROUS IMPRISON

WORDS PREFIXED WITH IN-

7-letter words IN-

INAPTLY INCAVES INCRUST INDRAWN INFIELD INGESTS INHERES INNERVE INSHORE
INARMED INCEDED INCURVE INDUCES INFIGHT INGLOBE INHOOPS INORBED INSIDER
INBEING INCEDES INDARTS INDUCTS INFILLS INGOING INHUMAN INPHASE INSIDES
INBOARD INCENSE INDENES INDUING INFIRMS INGRAFT INISLED INPOURS INSIGHT
INBOUND INCHASE INDENTS INDWELL INFIXED INGRAIN INISLES INQUEST INSINEW
INBREAK INCITED INDEWED INDWELT INFIXES INGRATE INJELLY INQUIET INSISTS
INBREED INCITER INDEXES INEARTH INFLAME INGROSS INJOINT INQUIRE INSNARE
INBRING INCITES INDICES INEXACT INFLOWS INGROUP INLACED INROADS INSOFAR
INBUILT INCIVIL INDICTS INFALLS INFOLDS INGROWN INLACES INSANER INSOLES
INBURST INCLASP INDITED INFAMED INFORCE INGULFS INLANDS INSCAPE INSOOTH
INCAGED INCLINE INDITES INFAMES INFORMS INGULPH INLAYER INSCULP INSOULS
INCAGES INCLIPS INDOLES INFANCY INFRACT INHABIT INLIERS INSEAMS INSPANS
INCANTS INCLOSE INDOORS INFARES INFUSED INHALED INLOCKS INSECTS INSPIRE
INCASED INCOMER INDORSE INFAUNA INFUSES INHALER INLYING INSEEMS INSTALL
INCASES INCOMES INDOWED INFEOFF INGATES INHALES INMATES INSHELL INSTARS
INCAVED INCROSS INDRAFT INFESTS INGENUS INHAULS INNARDS INSHIPS INSTATE

INSTEAD INSWEPT INTERNE INTONER INTRUST INVADED INVESTS INWARDS INWOVEN
INSTEPS INSWING INTERNS INTONES INTURNS INVADES INVEXED INWEAVE INWRAPS
INSTILL INTAKES INTINES INTORTS INTWINE INVALID INVITAL INWICKS
INSURED INTENDS INTITLE INTRANT INTWIST INVENTS INVOICE INWINDS
INSURER INTENSE INTOMBS INTREAT INURNED INVERSE INVOLVE INWORKS
INSURES INTENTS INTONED INTRONS INUTILE INVERTS INWALLS INWOUND

8-letter words IN-

INACTION INCLOSED INEARTHS INFOLDED INHUMANE INSCONCE INSTRESS INUNDATE
INACTIVE INCLOSER INEDIBLE INFOLDER INHUMATE INSCRIBE INSTROKE INURBANE
INARABLE INCLOSES INEDITED INFORCED INISLING INSCROLL INSUCKEN INURNING
INARCHED INCOMERS INEQUITY INFORCES INJOINTS INSCULPS INSURING INUSTION
INARCHES INCOMING INERRANT INFORMAL INJURIES INSCULPT INSWATHE INVADING
INARMING INCORPSE INESSIVE INFORMED INLACING INSEAMED INSWINGS INVENTED
INAURATE INCREASE INEXPERT INFORMER INLANDER INSECURE INTARSIA INVENTER
INBEINGS INCREATE INFAMING INFOUGHT INLAYERS INSEEMED INTENDED INVERITY
INBOARDS INCRUSTS INFAMOUS INFRACTS INLAYING INSETTER INTENDER INVERSES
INBOUNDS INCUMBER INFAUNAE INFRINGE INLOCKED INSHEATH INTENSER INVERTED
INBREAKS INCURRED INFAUNAL INFRUGAL INMESHED INSHELLS INTERNAL INVESTED
INBREEDS INCURVED INFAUNAS INFUSING INMESHES INSHRINE INTERNED INVIABLE
INBRINGS INCURVES INFECUND INFUSION INNATIVE INSIDERS INTERNES INVIABLY
INBURSTS INDARTED INFEOFFS INGATHER INNERVED INSIGHTS INTHRALL INVIRILE
INCAGING INDEBTED INFERIAE INGLOBED INNERVES INSINEWS INTHRONE INVISCID
INCANTED INDECENT INFESTER INGLOBES INNOCENT INSISTED INTIMIST INVOICED
INCASING INDENTED INFIELDS INGOINGS INORBING INSISTER INTITLED INVOICES
INCAVING INDEVOUT INFIGHTS INGRAFTS INORNATE INSNARED INTITLES INVOLUTE
INCEDING INDEWING INFILLED INGRAINS INPOURED INSNARER INTITULE INVOLVED
INCENSED INDICTED INFINITE INGRATES INPUTTED INSNARES INTOMBED INVOLVES
INCENSER INDIGEST INFIRMED INGROOVE INPUTTER INSOLATE INTONERS INWALLED
INCENSES INDIRECT INFIRMER INGROUPS INQUESTS INSOULED INTONING INWEAVED
INCENSOR INDITING INFIRMLY INGROWTH INQUIETS INSPHERE INTRANTS INWEAVES
INCENTER INDOCILE INFIXING INGULFED INQUIRED INSPIRED INTREATS INWICKED
INCENTRE INDOLENT INFLAMED INGULPHS INQUIRES INSPIRES INTRENCH INWORKED
INCHASED INDORSER INFLAMER INHABITS INRUSHES INSPIRIT INTREPID
INCHASES INDORSES INFLAMES INHALERS INSANELY INSTABLE INTRUSTS
INCITERS INDOWING INFLATUS INHALING INSANEST INSTALLS INTUBATE
INCITING INDRAFTS INFLEXED INHAULER INSANIES INSTANCE INTURNED
INCIVISM INDRENCH INFLIGHT INHEARSE INSANITY INSTATED INTWINED
INCLASPS INDUCTED INFLUENT INHOLDER INSCAPES INSTATES INTWINES
INCLINES INDWELLS INFLUXES INHOOPED INSCIENT INSTILLS INTWISTS

WORDS PREFIXED WITH ISO-

7-letter words ISO-

ISOBARE ISOBATH ISOGONE ISOLATE ISOLOGS ISOSPIN ISOTOPE ISOZYME
ISOBARS ISODOSE ISOGONS ISOLEAD ISOMERE ISOTACH ISOTRON
ISOBASE ISOGAMY ISOGRAM ISOLINE ISOPODS ISOTONE ISOTYPE

8-letter words ISO-

ISOBARES ISOCHIME ISOGLOSS ISOLEADS ISOSPINS ISOTONIC ISOTYPIC
ISOBARIC ISOCHORE ISOGRAFT ISOLINES ISOTACHS ISOTOPES ISOZYMES
ISOBASES ISOCLINE ISOGRAMS ISOMERES ISOTHERE ISOTOPIC ISOZYMIC
ISOBATHS ISOGAMIC ISOGRAPH ISOMORPH ISOTHERM ISOTRONS
ISOCHASM ISOGENIC ISOLATED ISONOMIC ISOTONES ISOTYPES

WORDS PREFIXED WITH MAN-

7-letter words MAN-

MANAGED MANDOMS MANGOES MANKIER MANMADE MANRENT MANTIES MANWISE
MANAGER MANGABY MANGOLD MANKIND MANNANS MANROPE MANTOES
MANAGES MANGALS MANHOLE MANLESS MANNITE MANSARD MANTRAM
MANAKIN MANGELS MANHOOD MANLIER MANNOSE MANTEEL MANTRAP
MANANAS MANGING MANHUNT MANLIKE MANPACK MANTELS MANURES
MANDATE MANGLED MANJACK MANLILY MANREDS MANTIDS MANWARD

8-letter words MAN-

MANAGERS MANAGING MANDATED MANDATES MANDRAKE MANDRILL MANFULLY MANGOLDS

MANGROVE MANHUNTS MANNITES MANPOWER MANROPES MANSWORN MANTRAPS
MANHOLES MANJACKS MANNOSES MANRENTS MANSARDS MANTEELS MANURIAL
MANHOODS MANKINDS MANPACKS MANRIDER MANSHIFT MANTRAMS MANWARDS

WORDS PREFIXED WITH MIS-

7-letter words MIS-

MISACTS MISCOOK MISDRAW MISGAVE MISKEYS MISMARK MISRULE MISSING MISTOOK
MISADDS MISCOPY MISDREW MISGIVE MISKICK MISMATE MISSAID MISSORT MISTUNE
MISAIMS MISCUED MISEASE MISGOES MISKNEW MISMEET MISSALS MISSOUT MISTYPE
MISALLY MISCUES MISEATS MISGONE MISKNOW MISMOVE MISSAYS MISSTEP MISUSED
MISAVER MISCUTS MISEDIT MISGREW MISLAID MISNAME MISSEAT MISSTOP MISUSER
MISBIAS MISDATE MISERES MISGROW MISLAIN MISPAGE MISSEEM MISSUIT MISUSES
MISBILL MISDEAL MISFALL MISHAPS MISLAYS MISPART MISSEEN MISTAKE MISWEEN
MISBIND MISDEED MISFARE MISHEAR MISLEAD MISPENS MISSEES MISTELL MISWEND
MISBORN MISDEEM MISFEED MISHITS MISLIES MISPLAN MISSELS MISTEND MISWENT
MISCALL MISDIAL MISFELL MISJOIN MISLIKE MISPLAY MISSEND MISTERM MISWORD
MISCAST MISDIET MISFILE MISKEEP MISLIVE MISPLED MISSENT MISTIER MISWRIT
MISCITE MISDOER MISFIRE MISKENS MISLUCK MISRATE MISSETS MISTIME MISYOKE
MISCODE MISDOES MISFITS MISKENT MISMADE MISREAD MISSHOD MISTING
MISCOIN MISDONE MISFORM MISKEPT MISMAKE MISRELY MISSILE MISTOLD

8-letter words MIS-

MISACTED MISCHIEF MISDRAWS MISGOING MISLIVED MISPLAYS MISSOUTS MISTINGS
MISADAPT MISCITED MISDREAD MISGRADE MISLIVES MISPLEAD MISSPACE MISTITLE
MISADDED MISCITES MISDRIVE MISGRAFF MISLODGE MISPOINT MISSPEAK MISTOUCH
MISAGENT MISCLAIM MISDROVE MISGRAFT MISLUCKS MISPOISE MISSPELL MISTRACE
MISAIMED MISCLASS MISEASES MISGROWN MISLYING MISPRICE MISSPELT MISTRAIN
MISALIGN MISCODED MISEATEN MISGROWS MISMAKES MISPRINT MISSPEND MISTREAT
MISALLOT MISCODES MISEDITS MISGUESS MISMARKS MISPRISE MISSPENT MISTRESS
MISALTER MISCOINS MISENROL MISGUIDE MISMARRY MISPRIZE MISSPOKE MISTRIAL
MISAPPLY MISCOLOR MISENTER MISHEARD MISMATCH MISPROUD MISSTART MISTRUST
MISARRAY MISCOOKS MISENTRY MISHEARS MISMATED MISQUOTE MISSTATE MISTRUTH
MISASSAY MISCOUNT MISEVENT MISINFER MISMATES MISRAISE MISSTEER MISTRYST
MISATONE MISCREED MISFAITH MISINTER MISMEETS MISRATED MISSTEPS MISTUNED
MISAVERS MISCUING MISFALLS MISJOINS MISMETRE MISRATES MISSTOPS MISTUNES
MISAWARD MISDATED MISFARED MISJUDGE MISMOVED MISREADS MISSTYLE MISTUTOR
MISBEGAN MISDATES MISFARES MISKEEPS MISMOVES MISREFER MISSUITS MISTYPED
MISBEGIN MISDEALS MISFEEDS MISKEYED MISNAMED MISROUTE MISSUSES MISTYPES
MISBEGOT MISDEALT MISFEIGN MISKICKS MISNAMES MISRULED MISTAKEN MISUNION
MISBEGUN MISDEEDS MISFIELD MISKNOWN MISOLOGY MISRULES MISTAKER MISUSAGE
MISBILLS MISDEEMS MISFILED MISKNOWS MISORDER MISSABLE MISTAKES MISUSERS
MISBINDS MISDEMPT MISFILES MISLABEL MISPAGED MISSEATS MISTEACH MISUSING
MISBIRTH MISDIALS MISFIRED MISLABOR MISPAGES MISSEEMS MISTELLS MISVALUE
MISBOUND MISDIETS MISFIRES MISLAYER MISPAINT MISSENDS MISTENDS MISWEENS
MISBRAND MISDIGHT MISFOCUS MISLEADS MISPARSE MISSENSE MISTERMS MISWENDS
MISBUILD MISDOERS MISFORMS MISLEARN MISPARTS MISSHAPE MISTHINK MISWORDS
MISBUILT MISDOING MISFRAME MISLIGHT MISPATCH MISSILES MISTHREW MISWRITE
MISCALLS MISDONNE MISGAUGE MISLIKED MISPLACE MISSISES MISTHROW MISWROTE
MISCARRY MISDOUBT MISGIVEN MISLIKER MISPLANS MISSORTS MISTIMED MISYOKED
MISCASTS MISDRAWN MISGIVES MISLIKES MISPLANT MISSOUND MISTIMES MISYOKES

WORDS PREFIXED WITH NON-

7-letter words NON-

NONACID NONBANK NONDRUG NONFUEL NONIRON NONOILY NONPOOR NONSUCH NONWORK
NONAGED NONBODY NONEGOS NONGAME NONJURY NONPAID NONPROS NONSUIT NONZERO
NONAGES NONBOOK NONFACT NONGAYS NONLIFE NONPAST NONSELF NONUSER
NONAGON NONCASH NONFANS NONHEME NONMEAT NONPEAK NONSKID NONUSES
NONANES NONCOLA NONFARM NONHERO NONNEWS NONPLAY NONSLIP NONWARS
NONARTS NONCOMS NONFOOD NONHOME NONNIES NONPLUS NONSTOP NONWORD

8-letter words NON-

NONACIDS NONBASIC NONCLASS NONDANCE NONEQUAL NONFINAL NONGUEST NONIMAGE
NONACTOR NONBEING NONCLING NONELECT NONEVENT NONFLUID NONGUILT NONIONIC
NONADULT NONBLACK NONCOLOR NONELITE NONFACTS NONFOCAL NONHARDY NONISSUE
NONAGONS NONBOOKS NONCRIME NONEMPTY NONFATAL NONGLARE NONHUMAN NONJUROR
NONBANKS NONBRAND NONDAIRY NONENTRY NONFATTY NONGREEN NONIDEAL NONLABOR

NONLEAFY NONMONEY NONPAGAN NONQUOTA NONSOLAR NONTIDAL NONUSERS NONWORDS
NONLEGAL NONMORAL NONPAPAL NONRATED NONSOLID NONTITLE NONUSING NONWOVEN
NONLIVES NONMUSIC NONPARTY NONRIGID NONSTICK NONTONAL NONVALID
NONLOCAL NONNAVAL NONPASTS NONRIVAL NONSTORY NONTOXIC NONVIRAL
NONMAJOR NONNOVEL NONPLAYS NONROYAL NONSTYLE NONTRUMP NONVOCAL
NONMETAL NONOBESE NONPOINT NONRURAL NONSUGAR NONTRUTH NONVOTER
NONMETRO NONOHMIC NONPOLAR NONSENSE NONSUITS NONUNION NONWHITE
NONMODAL NONOWNER NONPRINT NONSKIER NONTAXES NONURBAN NONWOODY

WORDS PREFIXED WITH OUT-

7-letter words OUT-

OUTACTS OUTDARE OUTFIRE OUTHIRE OUTLIED OUTPOLL OUTROOT OUTSTAY OUTWARS
OUTADDS OUTDATE OUTFISH OUTHITS OUTLIER OUTPORT OUTROPE OUTSTEP OUTWASH
OUTAGES OUTDOER OUTFITS OUTHOWL OUTLIES OUTPOST OUTROWS OUTSULK OUTWEAR
OUTASKS OUTDOES OUTFLEW OUTHUNT OUTLINE OUTPOUR OUTRUNG OUTSUMS OUTWEED
OUTBACK OUTDONE OUTFLOW OUTJEST OUTLIVE OUTPRAY OUTRUNS OUTSUNG OUTWEEP
OUTBAKE OUTDOOR OUTFOOL OUTJETS OUTLOOK OUTPULL OUTRUSH OUTSWAM OUTWELL
OUTBARK OUTDRAG OUTFOOT OUTJINX OUTLOVE OUTPUSH OUTSAIL OUTSWIM OUTWENT
OUTBARS OUTDRAW OUTGAIN OUTJUMP OUTMANS OUTPUTS OUTSANG OUTSWUM OUTWEPT
OUTBAWL OUTDREW OUTGATE OUTJUTS OUTMODE OUTRACE OUTSEEN OUTTAKE OUTWICK
OUTBEAM OUTDROP OUTGAVE OUTKEEP OUTMOST OUTRAGE OUTSEES OUTTALK OUTWILE
OUTBEGS OUTDUEL OUTGIVE OUTKEPT OUTMOVE OUTRANG OUTSELL OUTTASK OUTWILL
OUTBIDS OUTDURE OUTGLOW OUTKICK OUTNAME OUTRANK OUTSETS OUTTELL OUTWIND
OUTBRAG OUTEARN OUTGNAW OUTKILL OUTNESS OUTRATE OUTSHOT OUTTOLD OUTWING
OUTBRED OUTEATS OUTGOER OUTKISS OUTPACE OUTRAVE OUTSIDE OUTTOOK OUTWINS
OUTBULK OUTECHO OUTGOES OUTLAID OUTPART OUTREAD OUTSING OUTTOPS OUTWISH
OUTBURN OUTEDGE OUTGONE OUTLAIN OUTPASS OUTREDS OUTSINS OUTTROT OUTWITH
OUTBUYS OUTFACE OUTGREW OUTLAND OUTPEEP OUTRIDE OUTSITS OUTTURN OUTWITS
OUTCAST OUTFALL OUTGRIN OUTLASH OUTPEER OUTRING OUTSIZE OUTVIED OUTWORE
OUTCHID OUTFAST OUTGROW OUTLAST OUTPITY OUTROAR OUTSOAR OUTVIES OUTWORK
OUTCOME OUTFAWN OUTGUNS OUTLAWS OUTPLAN OUTROCK OUTSOLD OUTVOTE OUTWORN
OUTCOOK OUTFEEL OUTGUSH OUTLAYS OUTPLAY OUTRODE OUTSOLE OUTWAIT OUTWRIT
OUTCROP OUTFELT OUTHAUL OUTLEAP OUTPLOD OUTROLL OUTSPAN OUTWALK OUTYELL
OUTCROW OUTFIND OUTHEAR OUTLETS OUTPLOT OUTROOP OUTSPED OUTWARD OUTYELP

8-letter words OUT-

OUTACTED OUTBURNT OUTDRAGS OUTFLIES OUTHOMER OUTNAMES OUTRANGE OUTSHOTS
OUTADDED OUTBURST OUTDRANK OUTFLING OUTHOUSE OUTNIGHT OUTRANKS OUTSHOUT
OUTARGUE OUTCAPER OUTDRAWN OUTFLOWN OUTHOWLS OUTPACED OUTRATED OUTSIDER
OUTASKED OUTCASTE OUTDRAWS OUTFLOWS OUTHUMOR OUTPACES OUTRATES OUTSIDES
OUTBACKS OUTCASTS OUTDREAM OUTFLUSH OUTHUNTS OUTPAINT OUTRAVED OUTSIGHT
OUTBAKED OUTCATCH OUTDRESS OUTFOOLS OUTJESTS OUTPARTS OUTRAVES OUTSINGS
OUTBAKES OUTCAVIL OUTDRINK OUTFOOTS OUTJUMPS OUTPEEPS OUTREACH OUTSIZED
OUTBARKS OUTCHARM OUTDRIVE OUTFOUND OUTKEEPS OUTPEERS OUTREADS OUTSIZES
OUTBAWLS OUTCHEAT OUTDROPS OUTFOXED OUTKICKS OUTPITCH OUTREIGN OUTSKATE
OUTBEAMS OUTCHIDE OUTDROVE OUTFOXES OUTKILLS OUTPLACE OUTRIDER OUTSKIRT
OUTBITCH OUTCLASS OUTDRUNK OUTFROWN OUTLANDS OUTPLANS OUTRIDES OUTSLEEP
OUTBLAZE OUTCLIMB OUTDUELS OUTGAINS OUTLASTS OUTPLAYS OUTRIGHT OUTSLEPT
OUTBLEAT OUTCLOMB OUTDURED OUTGATES OUTLAUGH OUTPLODS OUTRINGS OUTSLICK
OUTBLESS OUTCOACH OUTDURES OUTGIVEN OUTLAWED OUTPLOTS OUTRIVAL OUTSMART
OUTBLOOM OUTCOMES OUTDWELL OUTGIVES OUTLEAPS OUTPOINT OUTROARS OUTSMILE
OUTBLUFF OUTCOOKS OUTDWELT OUTGLARE OUTLEAPT OUTPOLLS OUTROCKS OUTSMOKE
OUTBLUSH OUTCOUNT OUTEARNS OUTGLOWS OUTLEARN OUTPORTS OUTROLLS OUTSNORE
OUTBOARD OUTCRAWL OUTEATEN OUTGNAWN OUTLIERS OUTPOSTS OUTROOPS OUTSOARS
OUTBOAST OUTCRIED OUTEDGES OUTGNAWS OUTLINED OUTPOURS OUTROOTS OUTSOLES
OUTBOUND OUTCRIES OUTFABLE OUTGOERS OUTLINER OUTPOWER OUTROPER OUTSPANS
OUTBOXED OUTCROPS OUTFACED OUTGOING OUTLINES OUTPRAYS OUTROPES OUTSPEAK
OUTBOXES OUTCROSS OUTFACES OUTGRINS OUTLIVED OUTPREEN OUTROWED OUTSPEED
OUTBRAGS OUTCROWS OUTFALLS OUTGROSS OUTLIVER OUTPRESS OUTSAILS OUTSPELL
OUTBRAVE OUTCURSE OUTFASTS OUTGROUP OUTLIVES OUTPRICE OUTSAVOR OUTSPELT
OUTBRAWL OUTCURVE OUTFAWNS OUTGROWN OUTLOOKS OUTPRIZE OUTSCOLD OUTSPEND
OUTBREAK OUTDANCE OUTFEAST OUTGROWS OUTLOVED OUTPULLS OUTSCOOP OUTSPENT
OUTBREED OUTDARED OUTFEELS OUTGUARD OUTLOVES OUTPUNCH OUTSCORE OUTSPOKE
OUTBRIBE OUTDARES OUTFIELD OUTGUESS OUTLYING OUTQUOTE OUTSCORN OUTSPORT
OUTBROKE OUTDATED OUTFIGHT OUTGUIDE OUTMARCH OUTRACED OUTSELLS OUTSTAND
OUTBUILD OUTDATES OUTFINDS OUTHAULS OUTMATCH OUTRACES OUTSERVE OUTSTARE
OUTBUILT OUTDODGE OUTFIRED OUTHEARD OUTMODES OUTRAGED OUTSHAME OUTSTART
OUTBULKS OUTDOERS OUTFIRES OUTHEARS OUTMOVED OUTRAGES OUTSHINE OUTSTATE
OUTBULLY OUTDOING OUTFLANK OUTHIRED OUTMOVES OUTRAISE OUTSHONE OUTSTAYS
OUTBURNS OUTDOORS OUTFLASH OUTHIRES OUTNAMED OUTRANCE OUTSHOOT OUTSTEER

OUTSTEPS OUTSTOOD OUTSTRIP OUTSTUDY OUTSTUNT OUTSULKS OUTSWARE OUTSWEAR
OUTSWELL OUTSWIMS OUTSWING OUTSWORE OUTSWORN OUTTAKEN OUTTAKES OUTTALKS
OUTTASKS OUTTELLS OUTTHANK OUTTHINK OUTTHREW OUTTHROB OUTTHROW OUTTOWER
OUTTRADE OUTTRICK OUTTROTS OUTTRUMP OUTTURNS OUTVALUE OUTVAUNT OUTVENOM
OUTVOICE OUTVOTED OUTVOTER OUTVOTES OUTVYING OUTWAITS OUTWALKS OUTWARDS
OUTWASTE OUTWATCH OUTWEARS OUTWEARY OUTWEEDS OUTWEEPS OUTWEIGH OUTWELLS
OUTWHIRL OUTWICKS OUTWILED OUTWILES OUTWILLS OUTWINDS OUTWINGS OUTWORKS
OUTWORTH OUTWOUND OUTWREST OUTWRITE OUTWROTE OUTYELLS OUTYELPS OUTYIELD

WORDS PREFIXED WITH OVER-

7-letter words OVER-

OVERACT OVERAGE OVERALL OVERAPT OVERARM OVERATE OVERAWE
OVERBED OVERBET OVERBID OVERBIG OVERBUY OVERCOY OVERCUT
OVERDID OVERDOG OVERDRY OVERDUB OVERDUE OVERDYE OVEREAT
OVEREYE OVERFAR OVERFAT OVERFED OVERFLY OVERGET OVERGOT
OVERHIT OVERHOT OVERJOY OVERLAP OVERLAX OVERLAY OVERLET
OVERLIE OVERLIT OVERMAN OVERMEN OVERMIX OVERNET OVERNEW
OVERPAY OVERPLY OVERRAN OVERRED OVERREN OVERRUN OVERSAD
OVERSAW OVERSEA OVERSEE OVERSET OVERSEW OVERSOW OVERSUP
OVERTAX OVERTIP OVERTOP OVERUSE OVERWET

8-letter words OVER-

OVERABLE OVERACTS OVERAGED OVERAGES OVERALLS OVERARCH OVERAWED OVERAWES OVERBAKE OVERBEAR OVERBEAT OVERBETS OVERBIDS OVERBILL OVERBITE OVERBLEW OVERBLOW OVERBOIL OVERBOLD OVERBOOK OVERBORE OVERBORN OVERBRED OVERBRIM OVERBROW OVERBULK OVERBURN OVERBUSY OVERBUYS OVERCALL OVERCAME OVERCAST OVERCLAD OVERCLOY OVERCOAT
OVERCOLD OVERCOME OVERCOOK OVERCOOL OVERCRAM OVERCRAW OVERCROP OVERCROW OVERCURE OVERCUTS OVERDARE OVERDEAR OVERDECK OVERDOER OVERDOES OVERDOGS OVERDONE OVERDOSE OVERDRAW OVERDREW OVERDUBS OVERDUST OVERDYED OVERDYES OVEREASY OVEREATS OVEREDIT OVEREYED OVEREYES OVERFALL OVERFAST OVERFEAR OVERFEED OVERFELL OVERFILL
OVERFINE OVERFISH OVERFLEW OVERFLOW OVERFOLD OVERFOND OVERFOUL OVERFREE OVERFULL OVERFUND OVERGALL OVERGANG OVERGAVE OVERGETS OVERGILD OVERGILT OVERGIRD OVERGIRT OVERGIVE OVERGLAD OVERGOAD OVERGOES OVERGONE OVERGREW OVERGROW OVERHAIR OVERHALE OVERHAND OVERHANG OVERHARD OVERHATE OVERHAUL OVERHEAD OVERHEAP OVERHEAR
OVERHEAT OVERHELD OVERHENT OVERHIGH OVERHITS OVERHOLD OVERHOLY OVERHOPE OVERHUNG OVERHUNT OVERHYPE OVERIDLE OVERJOYS OVERJUMP OVERJUST OVERKEEN OVERKEEP OVERKEPT OVERKEST OVERKILL OVERKIND OVERKING OVERKNEE OVERLADE OVERLAID OVERLAIN OVERLAND OVERLAPS OVERLARD OVERLATE OVERLAYS OVERLEAF OVERLEAP OVERLEND OVERLENT
OVERLETS OVERLEWD OVERLIER OVERLIES OVERLIVE OVERLOAD OVERLOCK OVERLONG OVERLOOK OVERLORD OVERLOUD OVERLOVE OVERLUSH OVERMANS OVERMANY OVERMAST OVERMEEK OVERMELT OVERMILD OVERMILK OVERMINE OVERMUCH OVERNAME OVERNEAR OVERNEAT OVERNETS OVERNICE OVERPAGE OVERPAID OVERPART OVERPASS OVERPAST OVERPAYS OVERPEER OVERPERT
OVERPLAN OVERPLAY OVERPLOT OVERPLUS OVERPOST OVERPUMP OVERRACK OVERRAKE OVERRANK OVERRASH OVERRATE OVERREAD OVERREDS OVERRENS OVERRICH OVERRIDE OVERRIFE OVERRIPE OVERRODE OVERRUDE OVERRUFF OVERRULE OVERRUNS OVERSAIL OVERSALE OVERSALT OVERSAVE OVERSEAS OVERSEED OVERSEEN OVERSEER OVERSEES OVERSELL OVERSETS OVERSEWN
OVERSEWS OVERSHOE OVERSHOT OVERSICK OVERSIDE OVERSIZE OVERSKIP OVERSLIP OVERSLOW OVERSOAK OVERSOFT OVERSOLD OVERSOON OVERSOUL OVERSOWN OVERSOWS OVERSPIN OVERSTAY OVERSTEP OVERSTIR OVERSUDS OVERSUPS OVERSURE OVERSWAM OVERSWAY OVERSWIM OVERSWUM OVERTAKE OVERTALK OVERTAME OVERTART OVERTASK OVERTEEM OVERTHIN OVERTIME
OVERTIPS OVERTIRE OVERTOIL OVERTONE OVERTOOK OVERTOPS OVERTRIM OVERTRIP OVERTURN OVERTYPE OVERURGE OVERUSED OVERUSES OVERVEIL OVERVIEW OVERVOTE OVERWARM OVERWARY OVERWASH OVERWEAK OVERWEAR OVERWEEN OVERWENT OVERWETS OVERWIDE OVERWILY OVERWIND OVERWING OVERWISE OVERWORD OVERWORE OVERWORK OVERWORN OVERYEAR OVERZEAL

WORDS PREFIXED WITH PER-

7-letter words PER-

PERACID PERAEON PERCASE PERCENT PERCHER PERCINE
PERCUSS PERDUES PERDURE PEREGAL PERFORM PERFUME
PERFUMY PERFUSE PERHAPS PERICON PERJINK PERJURE
PERJURY PERKIER PERKING PERKINS PERKISH PERLITE
PERMING PERMUTE PERONES PERORAL PEROXID PERPEND
PERPENT PERSALT PERSANT PERSING PERSIST PERSONS
PERSUED PERSUES PERTAIN PERTAKE PERTEST PERTOOK
PERUKES PERUSED PERUSER PERUSES PERVADE PERVERT

8-letter words PER-

PERACIDS PERDURES PERFUSED PERMEANT PEROXIDE PERSAUNT PERTAINS PERVADES
PERACUTE PERFORCE PERFUSES PERMEASE PEROXIDS PERSEITY PERTAKEN PERVERSE
PERAEONS PERFORMS PERIODIC PERMUTED PERPENDS PERSISTS PERTAKES PERVERTS
PERCENTS PERFUMED PERIODID PERMUTES PERPENTS PERSPIRE PERUSERS
PERCOLIN PERFUMER PERISHES PERNANCY PERRADII PERSPIRY PERUSING
PERDURED PERFUMES PERLITES PERORATE PERSALTS PERSUING PERVADED

WORDS PREFIXED WITH PRE-

7-letter words PRE-

PREACED PREBOIL PRECUTS PREFADE PREMADE PREPAID PRESELL PRETEND PREWARN
PREACES PREBOOK PREDATE PREFARD PREMEAL PREPARE PRESENT PRETERM PREWASH
PREACHY PREBOOM PREDAWN PREFILE PREMEET PREPAYS PRESETS PRETEST PREWORK
PREACTS PREBORN PREDIAL PREFIRE PREMISE PREPILL PRESHOW PRETEXT PREWRAP
PREAGED PRECAST PREDICT PREFORM PREMISS PREPLAN PRESIDE PRETORS PREWYNS
PREAMPS PRECEDE PREDIED PREGAME PREMIXT PREPONE PRESIFT PRETRIM
PREANAL PRECENT PREDIES PREHEAT PREMOLD PREPOSE PRESOAK PRETYPE
PREARMS PRECESS PREDIVE PREHEND PREMOLT PREPUCE PRESOLD PREVAIL
PREAVER PRECODE PREDOOM PREJINK PREMOVE PRERACE PRESONG PREVENT
PREBAKE PRECOOK PREDUSK PRELACY PRENAME PRERIOT PRESORT PREVERB
PREBEND PRECOOL PREEDIT PRELATE PRENOON PREROCK PRESTED PREVIEW
PREBILL PRECOUP PREEVES PRELIFE PREORAL PRESAGE PRETAPE PREVISE
PREBIND PRECURE PREFACE PRELUDE PREPACK PRESALE PRETEEN PREWARM

8-letter words PRE-

PREACHED PREBLESS PRECURSE PREFILED PREMISES PREPLANT PRESIDED PRETRIAL
PREACHES PREBOILS PREDATED PREFILES PREMIXED PREPONES PRESIDER PRETRIMS
PREACING PREBOOKS PREDATES PREFIRED PREMIXES PREPOSED PRESIDES PRETYPED
PREACTED PREBOUND PREDAWNS PREFIRES PREMOLAR PREPOSES PRESIFTS PRETYPES
PREADAPT PRECASTS PREDIALS PREFIXED PREMOLDS PREPRICE PRESLEEP PREUNION
PREADMIT PRECEDED PREDICTS PREFIXES PREMORAL PREPRINT PRESLICE PREUNITE
PREADOPT PRECEDES PREDOOMS PREFLAME PREMORSE PREPUCES PRESOAKS PREVAILS
PREADULT PRECENTS PREDRILL PREFOCUS PREMOVED PREPUNCH PRESORTS PREVENTS
PREALLOT PRECHECK PREDUSKS PREFORMS PREMOVES PREPUPAL PRESPLIT PREVERBS
PREAMBLE PRECHILL PREDYING PREFRANK PRENAMES PRERENAL PRESTAMP PREVIEWS
PREARMED PRECINCT PREEDITS PREFROZE PRENASAL PRERINSE PRESTING PREVISED
PREASSES PRECITED PREELECT PREHEATS PRENATAL PRESAGER PRETAPED PREVISES
PREAUDIT PRECLEAN PREENACT PREHENDS PRENOMEN PRESAGES PRETAPES PREVISOR
PREAVERS PRECLEAR PREERECT PREHUMAN PREORDER PRESCORE PRETASTE PREWARMS
PREAXIAL PRECODED PREEXIST PREJUDGE PREPACKS PRESCUTA PRETEENS PREWARNS
PREBAKED PRECODES PREFACED PRELEGAL PREPARED PRESELLS PRETENDS PREWRAPS
PREBAKES PRECOOKS PREFACER PRELIMIT PREPARER PRESENTS PRETENSE
PREBASAL PRECOOLS PREFACES PRELIVES PREPARES PRESERVE PRETESTS
PREBENDS PRECRASH PREFADED PRELUDES PREPASTE PRESHAPE PRETEXTS
PREBILLS PRECURED PREFADES PRELUNCH PREPLACE PRESHOWN PRETRAIN
PREBINDS PRECURES PREFIGHT PREMEDIC PREPLANS PRESHOWS PRETREAT

WORDS PREFIXED WITH PRO-

7-letter words PRO-

PROBALL PROCESS PROFILE PROLEGS PROMOTE PROPAGE PROPOSE PROSTIE PROVEND
PROBAND PROCURE PROFITS PROLINE PRONAOI PROPALE PRORATE PROTEAS PROVERB
PROBANG PRODUCE PROFUSE PROLING PRONAOS PROPANE PROSAIC PROTEND PROVERS
PROBATE PRODUCT PROGRAM PROLOGS PRONEST PROPEND PROSECT PROTEST PROVIDE
PROBING PROFACE PROJETS PROLONG PRONOTA PROPENE PROSERS PROTONS PROVINE
PROBITS PROFANE PROKING PROMINE PRONOUN PROPINE PROSING PROTORE PROWEST
PROCARP PROFESS PROLATE PROMISE PROOTIC PROPONE PROSOMA PROVANT

8-letter words PRO-

PROBANDS PROCLAIM PROFANES PROLABOR PROMINES PRONOTAL PROPANES PROPOLIS
PROBANGS PROCURED PROFILED PROLAPSE PROMISER PRONOTUM PROPENDS PROPONES
PROBATED PROCURER PROFILER PROLATED PROMISES PRONOUNS PROPENES PROPOSED
PROBATES PROCURES PROFILES PROLINES PROMOTED PROPAGED PROPHAGE PROPOSER
PROCARPS PRODROME PROFOUND PROLONGE PROMOTES PROPAGES PROPHASE PROPOSES
PROCHAIN PRODUCES PROGRADE PROLONGS PROMOTOR PROPALED PROPINED PROPOUND
PROCINCT PRODUCTS PROGRAMS PROMETAL PRONATES PROPALES PROPINES PROPYLON

PRORATED PROSECTS PROSOMAS PROTAMIN PROTESTS PROUNION PROVINES
PRORATES PROSEMEN PROSTATE PROTEASE PROTONIC PROVENDS PROVIRAL
PROROGUE PROSINGS PROSTIES PROTENDS PROTORES PROVERBS PROVIRUS
PROSAIST PROSODIC PROSTYLE PROTENSE PROTRACT PROVINED PROVISOR

WORDS PREFIXED WITH RE-

7-letter words RE-

REACHED RECARRY REDRILL REFUSED RELIEVE REPATCH RESALES RESTAMP RETYING
REACHES RECASTS REDRIVE REFUSES RELIGHT REPAVED RESAWED RESTART RETYPED
REACTED RECATCH REDROVE REGAINS RELINED REPAVES RESCALE RESTATE RETYPES
REACTOR RECEDED REDUCES REGALES RELINES REPEALS RESCORE RESTEMS REUNIFY
READAPT RECEDES REDUITS REGALLY RELINKS REPEATS RESEALS RESTIFF REUNION
READDED RECENSE REEARNS REGAUGE RELISTS REPENTS RESEATS RESTING REUNITE
READMIT RECHART REECHED REGEARS RELIVED REPERKS RESECTS RESTIVE REURGED
READOPT RECHEAT REECHES REGENTS RELIVER REPINED RESEEDS RESTOCK REURGES
READORN RECHECK REEDIFY REGESTS RELIVES REPINES RESEEKS RESTOKE REUSING
REAFFIX RECHEWS REEDITS REGILDS RELOADS REPIQUE RESEIZE RESTORE REUTTER
REAGENT RECHOSE REEJECT REGIVEN RELOANS REPLACE RESELLS RESTUDY REVALUE
REAKING RECITAL REEKING REGIVES RELOCKS REPLANS RESENDS RESTUFF REVAMPS
REALIGN RECITED REELECT REGLAZE RELOOKS REPLANT RESENTS RESTYLE REVEALS
REALIST RECITER REELMEN REGLOSS RELYING REPLATE RESERVE RESURGE REVENGE
REALLOT RECITES REEMITS REGLOWS REMAILS REPLAYS RESEWED RETABLE REVENUE
REALTER RECLAIM REENACT REGLUED REMAINS REPLEAD RESHAPE RETACKS REVERBS
REAMEND RECLAME REENDOW REGLUES REMAKER REPLICA RESHAVE RETAILS REVERSE
REANNEX RECLASP REENJOY REGORGE REMAKES REPLIED RESHINE RETAINS REVERSO
REAPERS RECLEAN REENTER REGRADE REMANET REPLIER RESHIPS RETAKEN REVERTS
REAPING RECLIMB REENTRY REGRAFT REMARKS REPLIES RESHOES RETAKER REVESTS
REAPPLY RECLINE REEQUIP REGRANT REMARRY REPLOTS RESHONE RETAKES REVIEWS
REARGUE RECLOSE REERECT REGRATE REMATCH REPLUMB RESHOOT RETAPED REVILER
REARISE RECOALS REEVOKE REGREEN REMATED REPOINT RESHOWN RETAPES REVISED
REARMED RECOCKS REEXPEL REGREET REMATES REPOLLS RESHOWS RETASTE REVISES
REAROSE RECODED REFACED REGRIND REMEADS REPONES RESIDED RETAXED REVISIT
REAVAIL RECODES REFACES REGROOM REMEETS REPORTS RESIDER RETAXES REVISOR
REAVERS RECOILS REFALLS REGROUP REMELTS REPOSED RESIDES RETEACH REVIVER
REAVOWS RECOINS REFEEDS REGROWN REMENDS REPOSER RESIFTS RETEAMS REVIVES
REAWAKE RECOLOR REFEELS REGROWS REMERCY REPOSES RESIGHT RETEARS REVOICE
REAWOKE RECOMBS REFENCE REGULAR REMERGE REPOSIT RESIGNS RETELLS REVOLTS
REBACKS RECOOKS REFIGHT REHANGS REMINDS REPOSTS RESILED RETENES REVOLVE
REBADGE RECORDS REFILED REHEARD REMINTS REPOURS RESILES RETESTS REVOTED
REBAITS RECORKS REFILES REHEARS REMISES REPOWER RESINED RETHINK REVOTES
REBATED RECOUNT REFILLS REHEATS REMIXED REPRESS RESISTS RETILED REVYING
REBATES RECOUPE REFILMS REHEELS REMIXES REPRICE RESITED RETILES REWAKED
REBECKS RECOUPS REFINDS REHINGE REMODEL REPRIME RESITES RETIMED REWAKEN
REBEGAN RECOURE REFINED REHIRED REMOLDS REPRINT RESIZED RETIMES REWAKES
REBEGIN RECOVER REFINER REHIRES REMORAS REPRISE RESIZES RETINES REWARDS
REBEGUN RECOWER REFINES REHOUSE REMORSE REPRIZE RESKEWS RETINTS REWARMS
REBILLS RECRATE REFIRED REIMAGE REMOTES REPROBE RESKILL RETIRED REWAXED
REBINDS RECROSS REFIRES REINCUR REMOULD REPROOF RESLATE RETIRES REWAXES
REBIRTH RECROWN REFIXED REINDEX REMOUNT REPROVE RESMELT RETITLE REWEAVE
REBITES RECURED REFIXES REINKED REMOVED REPULPS RESOAKS RETOOLS REWEIGH
REBLEND RECURES REFLAGS REINTER REMOVER REPULSE RESOLED RETORTS REWELDS
REBLOOM RECURVE REFLIES REISSUE REMOVES REPUMPS RESOLES RETOUCH REWIDEN
REBOARD RECYCLE REFLOAT REJOINS RENAILS REPURED RESOLVE RETOURS REWINDS
REBOILS REDATED REFLOOD REJONES RENAMED REPURES RESORBS RETRACE REWIRED
REBOOKS REDATES REFLOWN REJUDGE RENAMES REQUEST RESORTS RETRACK REWIRES
REBOOTS REDEALS REFLOWS REKEYED RENESTS REQUINS RESOUND RETRACT REWOKEN
REBORED REDEALT REFOCUS REKNITS RENEWED REQUIRE RESOWED RETRAIN REWORDS
REBORES REDEARS REFOLDS RELABEL RENEWER REQUITE RESPACE RETRAIT REWORKS
REBOUND REDEEMS REFOOTS RELACED RENYING REQUITS RESPADE RETREAD REWOUND
REBOZOS REDIALS REFORGE RELACES REOCCUR REQUOTE RESPEAK RETREAT REWOVEN
REBRACE REDOCKS REFORMS RELAPSE REOFFER RERACKS RESPELL RETREES REWRAPS
REBREED REDOING REFOUND RELATED REOILED RERAILS RESPELT RETRIAL REWRAPT
REBUFFS REDOUBT REFRACT RELATER REOPENS RERAISE RESPIRE RETRIED REWRITE
REBUILD REDOUTS REFRAME RELAXER REORDER REREADS RESPITE RETRIES REWROTE
REBUILT REDRAFT REFRESH RELAXES REPACKS REREDOS RESPLIT RETRIMS REZONED
REBUKES REDRAWN REFRIED RELAYED REPAINT RERISEN RESPOKE RETUNDS REZONES
REBUSES REDRAWS REFRIES RELEARN REPAIRS RERISES RESPOTS RETUNED
RECALLS REDREAM REFRONT RELEASE REPANEL REROLLS RESPRAY RETUNES
RECANED REDRESS REFROZE RELENDS REPAPER REROOFS RESTACK RETURFS
RECANES REDRIED REFUELS RELIEFS REPARKS REROUTE RESTAFF RETURNS
RECANTS REDRIES REFUNDS RELIERS REPASTS RESAILS RESTAGE RETWIST

8-letter words RE-

REABSORB
REACCEDE
REACCENT
REACCEPT
REACCUSE
REACHING
REACTING
REACTION
REACTIVE
REACTORS
READAPTS
READDICT
READDING
READJUST
READMITS
READOPTS
READORNS
READVISE
REAFFIRM
REAGENCY
REAGENTS
REALIGNS
REALLIED
REALLIES
REALLOTS
REALTERS
REAMENDS
REANOINT
REANSWER
REAPPEAR
REARGUED
REARGUES
REARISEN
REARISES
REARMING
REAROUSE
REARREST
REASCEND
REASCENT
REASSAIL
REASSERT
REASSESS
REASSIGN
REASSORT
REASSUME
REASSURE
REATTACH
REATTACK
REATTAIN
REAVAILS
REAVOWED
REAWAKED
REAWAKEN
REAWAKES
REAWOKEN
REBACKED
REBADGED
REBADGES
REBAITED
REBATING
REBEGINS
REBELLED
REBELLOW
REBIDDEN
REBILLED
REBIRTHS
REBITING
REBITTEN
REBLENDS
REBLOOMS
REBOARDS
REBODIED
REBODIES
REBOILED
REBOOKED
REBOOTED
REBORING
REBORROW
REBOTTLE
REBOUGHT
REBOUNDS
REBRACED
REBRACES
REBRANCH
REBREEDS
REBUFFED
REBUILDS
REBURIAL
REBURIED
REBURIES
REBUTTED
REBUTTER
REBUTTON
REBUYING
RECALLED
RECALLER
RECANING
RECANTED
RECANTER
RECAPPED
RECAPTOR
RECAUGHT
RECEDING
RECENSED
RECENSES
RECENTER
RECENTRE
RECESSED
RECESSES
RECHANGE
RECHARGE
RECHARTS
RECHEATS
RECHECKS
RECHEWED
RECHOOSE
RECHOSEN
RECIRCLE
RECITALS
RECITERS
RECITING
RECLAIMS
RECLAMES
RECLASPS
RECLEANS
RECLIMBS
RECLINES
RECLOSED
RECLOSES
RECLOTHE
RECOALED
RECOCKED
RECODIFY
RECODING
RECOILED
RECOILER
RECOINED
RECOLLET
RECOLORS
RECOMBED
RECOMMIT
RECONVEY
RECOOKED
RECOPIED
RECOPIES
RECORDED
RECORDER
RECORKED
RECOUNTS
RECOUPED
RECOUPLE
RECOURED
RECOURES
RECOURSE
RECOVERS
RECOWERS
RECRATED
RECRATES
RECREANT
RECREATE
RECROWNS
RECURING
RECURRED
RECURVED
RECURVES
RECYCLED
RECYCLER
RECYCLES
REDAMAGE
REDATING
REDECIDE
REDEEMED
REDEFEAT
REDEFECT
REDEFIED
REDEFIES
REDEFINE
REDEMAND
REDENIED
REDENIES
REDEPLOY
REDESIGN
REDIALED
REDIGEST
REDIPPED
REDIRECT
REDISTIL
REDIVIDE
REDOCKED
REDOLENT
REDONNED
REDOUBLE
REDOUBTS
REDRAFTS
REDRAWER
REDREAMS
REDREAMT
REDRILLS
REDRIVEN
REDRIVES
REDRYING
REDUBBED
REDYEING
REEARNED
REECHING
REECHOED
REECHOES
REEDITED
REEJECTS
REELECTS
REEMBARK
REEMBODY
REEMERGE
REEMPLOY
REENACTS
REENDOWS
REENGAGE
REENJOYS
REENLIST
REENROLL
REENTERS
REEQUIPS
REERECTS
REEVOKED
REEVOKES
REEXPELS
REEXPORT
REEXPOSE
REFACING
REFALLEN
REFASTEN
REFELLED
REFENCED
REFENCES
REFIGHTS
REFIGURE
REFILING
REFILLED
REFILMED
REFILTER
REFINERS
REFINERY
REFINING
REFINISH
REFIRING
REFITTED
REFIXING
REFLEXED
REFLEXES
REFLOATS
REFLOODS
REFLOWED
REFLOWER
REFLUENT
REFLUXED
REFLUXES
REFLYING
REFOLDED
REFOOTED
REFOREST
REFORGED
REFORGES
REFORMAT
REFORMED
REFORMER
REFOUGHT
REFOUNDS
REFRACTS
REFRAMED
REFRAMES
REFREEZE
REFRINGE
REFRONTS
REFROZEN
REFRYING
REFUELED
REFUNDED
REFUNDER
REFUSING
REFUSION
REGAINED
REGAINER
REGATHER
REGAUGED
REGAUGES
REGEARED
REGELATE
REGILDED
REGIVING
REGLAZED
REGLAZES
REGLOWED
REGLUING
REGORGED
REGORGES
REGRADED
REGRADES
REGRAFTS
REGRANTS
REGRATED
REGRATER
REGRATES
REGREENS
REGREETS
REGRINDS
REGROOMS
REGROOVE
REGROUND
REGROUPS
REGROWTH
REHAMMER
REHANDLE
REHANGED
REHARDEN
REHASHED
REHASHES
REHEARSE
REHEATED
REHEATER
REHEELED
REHEMMED
REHINGED
REHINGES
REHIRING
REHOUSED
REHOUSES
REIGNITE
REILLUME
REIMAGED
REIMAGES
REIMPORT
REIMPOSE
REINCITE
REINCURS
REINDICT
REINDUCE
REINDUCT
REINFECT
REINFORM
REINFUSE
REINJECT
REINJURE
REINJURY
REINKING
REINSERT
REINSURE
REINTERS
REINVADE
REINVENT
REINVEST
REINVITE
REINVOKE
REISSUED
REISSUER
REISSUES
REJACKET
REJIGGED
REJIGGER
REJOINED
REJUDGED
REJUDGES
REJUGGLE
REKEYING
REKINDLE
RELABELS
RELACHES
RELACING
RELAPSED
RELAPSER
RELAPSES
RELAUNCH
RELAYING
RELEARNS
RELEARNT
RELEASED
RELEASER
RELEASES
RELEGATE
RELETTER
RELEVANT
RELIABLE
RELIEVER
RELIGHTS
RELINING
RELINKED
RELISTED
RELIVERS
RELIVING
RELOADED
RELOADER
RELOANED
RELOCATE
RELOCKED
RELOOKED
RELUCENT
RELUMINE
REMAILED
REMAINED
REMAKERS
REMAKING
REMANENT
REMANIES
REMANNED
REMAPPED
REMARKED
REMARKER
REMARKET
REMARQUE
REMASTER
REMATING
REMEDIAL
REMELTED
REMEMBER
REMENDED
REMERGED
REMERGES
REMINDED
REMINDER
REMINTED
REMIXING
REMODELS
REMODIFY
REMOLDED
REMORSES
REMOTION
REMOULDS
REMOUNTS
REMOVERS
REMOVING
REMURMUR
RENAILED
RENAMING
RENATURE
RENEGATE
RENESTED
RENEWING
RENOTIFY
RENUMBER
REOBJECT
REOBTAIN
REOCCUPY
REOCCURS
REOFFEND
REOFFERS
REOILING
REOPENED
REOPENER
REOPPOSE
REORDAIN
REORDERS
REORIENT
REOUTFIT
REPACIFY
REPACKED
REPAINTS
REPAIRED
REPANELS
REPAPERS
REPARKED
REPASSED
REPASSES
REPASTED
REPAVING
REPAYING
REPEALED
REPEGGED
REPEOPLE
REPERKED
REPERUSE
REPHRASE
REPINING
REPINNED
REPIQUED
REPIQUES
REPLACED
REPLACER
REPLACES
REPLANTS
REPLATED
REPLATES
REPLAYED
REPLEADS
REPLEDGE
REPLIERS
REPLUMBS
REPLUNGE
REPLYING
REPOINTS
REPOLISH
REPOLLED
REPORTED
REPORTER
REPOSERS
REPOSING
REPOSITS
REPOSTED
REPOTTED
REPOURED
REPOUSSE
REPOWERS
REPREEVE
REPRICED
REPRICES
REPRIEFE
REPRIEVE
REPRIMED
REPRIMES
REPRINTS
REPRISED
REPRISES
REPRIZED
REPRIZES
REPROBED
REPROBES
REPROOFS
REPROVED
REPROVER
REPROVES
REPUBLIC
REPULPED
REPULSED
REPULSER
REPULSES
REPUMPED
REPURIFY
REPURING
REPURSUE
REQUESTS
REQUIGHT
REQUIRED
REQUIRES
REQUITED
REQUITES
REQUOTED
REQUOTES
RERACKED
RERAILED
RERAISED
RERAISES
RERECORD
REREMIND
REREPEAT
REREVIEW
REREVISE
REREWARD
RERIGGED
RERISING
REROLLED
REROLLER
REROOFED
REROUTED
REROUTES
RESADDLE
RESAILED
RESALUTE
RESAMPLE
RESAWING
RESAYING
RESCALED
RESCALES
RESCHOOL
RESCORED
RESCORES
RESCREEN
RESCRIPT
RESCULPT
RESEALED
RESEARCH
RESEASON
RESEATED
RESECURE
RESEEDED
RESEEING
RESEIZED
RESEIZES
RESELECT
RESELLER
RESEMBLE
RESENTED
RESERVED
RESERVER
RESERVES
RESETTER
RESETTLE

RESEWING RESLATED RESPIRES RESTORES RETAKERS RETRAITS REVENGER REVOTING
RESHAPED RESLATES RESPITED RESTRAIN RETAKING RETREADS REVENGES REWAKENS
RESHAPER RESMELTS RESPITES RESTRESS RETAPING RETREATS REVENUES REWAKING
RESHAPES RESMOOTH RESPLICE RESTRICT RETARGET RETRENCH REVERIFY REWARDED
RESHAVED RESOAKED RESPLITS RESTRIKE RETASTED RETRIALS REVERIST REWARDER
RESHAVEN RESODDED RESPOKEN RESTRING RETASTES RETRYING REVERSAL REWARMED
RESHAVES RESOLDER RESPRANG RESTRIVE RETAUGHT RETUNDED REVERSED REWASHED
RESHINED RESOLING RESPRAYS RESTROVE RETAXING RETUNING REVERSER REWASHES
RESHINES RESOLUTE RESPREAD RESTRUCK RETEAMED RETURFED REVERSES REWAXING
RESHOOTS RESOLVED RESPRING RESTRUNG RETELLER RETURNED REVERSOS REWEAVED
RESHOWED RESOLVER RESPROUT RESTUFFS RETEMPER RETURNER REVERTED REWEAVES
RESIDERS RESOLVES RESPRUNG RESTYLED RETESTED RETWISTS REVESTED REWEDDED
RESIDING RESONANT RESTACKS RESTYLES RETHINKS RETYPING REVESTRY REWEIGHS
RESIFTED RESORBED RESTAFFS RESUBMIT RETHREAD REUNIONS REVETTED REWELDED
RESIGHTS RESORTED RESTAGED RESUMMON RETILING REUNITED REVIEWED REWETTED
RESIGNED RESORTER RESTAGES RESUPINE RETIMING REUNITER REVIEWER REWIDENS
RESIGNER RESOUGHT RESTAMPS RESUPPLY RETINTED REUNITES REVISING REWINDED
RESILING RESOUNDS RESTARTS RESURGED RETIRING REURGING REVISION REWINDER
RESILVER RESOURCE RESTATED RESURGES RETITLED REUSABLE REVISITS REWIRING
RESINING RESOWING RESTATES RESURVEY RETITLES REUTTERS REVISORS REWORDED
RESISTED RESPACED RESTINGS RETABLES RETOOLED REVALUED REVIVERS REWORKED
RESISTER RESPACES RESTITCH RETACKED RETOURED REVALUES REVIVIFY REWRITER
RESITING RESPADED RESTOCKS RETACKLE RETRACED REVAMPED REVOICED REWRITES
RESIZING RESPADES RESTOKED RETAGGED RETRACES REVAMPER REVOICES REZONING
RESKETCH RESPEAKS RESTOKES RETAILED RETRACKS REVEALED REVOLUTE
RESKEWED RESPELLS RESTORED RETAILER RETRACTS REVEALER REVOLVED
RESKILLS RESPIRED RESTORER RETAILOR RETRAINS REVENGED REVOLVES

WORDS PREFIXED WITH RED-

7-letter words RED-

REDACTS REDBIRD REDCOAT REDEYES REDLINE REDPOLL REDRILL REDSKIN REDWOOD
REDATES REDBONE REDDENS REDFINS REDNECK REDRAFT REDRIVE REDTAIL
REDBACK REDBUDS REDDING REDFISH REDNESS REDRAWN REDROOT REDTOPS
REDBAIT REDBUGS REDDISH REDHEAD REDOUTS REDRAWS REDROVE REDWARE
REDBAYS REDCAPS REDEARS REDLEGS REDOXES REDREAM REDSEAR REDWING

8-letter words RED-

REDACTED REDBELLY REDDINGS REDNECKS REDRAWER REDROOTS REDSHIRT REDWARES
REDACTOR REDBIRDS REDHEADS REDOLENT REDREAMS REDSHANK REDSHORT REDWATER
REDARGUE REDBONES REDHORSE REDONNED REDRILLS REDSHARE REDSKINS REDWINGS
REDBACKS REDBRICK REDLINED REDPOLLS REDRIVEN REDSHIFT REDSTART REDWOODS
REDBAITS REDCOATS REDLINES REDRAFTS REDRIVES REDSHIRE REDTAILS

WORDS PREFIXED WITH SEA-

7-letter words SEA-

SEABAGS SEACOCK SEAGIRT SEALANT SEAMING SEASICK SEATING SEAWARE SEAZING
SEABANK SEADOGS SEAGULL SEALINE SEAPORT SEASIDE SEAWALL SEAWAYS
SEABEDS SEAFOLK SEAHAWK SEALING SEARATS SEASING SEAWANS SEAWEED
SEABIRD SEAFOOD SEAHOGS SEAMAID SEAREST SEASONS SEAWANT SEAWIFE
SEABOOT SEAFOWL SEAKALE SEAMARK SEARING SEASURE SEAWARD SEAWORM

8-letter words SEA-

SEABANKS SEACOAST SEAFOODS SEAHOUND SEAMARKS SEAROBIN SEASURES SEAWATER
SEABEACH SEACOCKS SEAFOWLS SEAKALES SEAMOUNT SEASCAPE SEATINGS SEAWEEDS
SEABIRDS SEACRAFT SEAFRONT SEALANTS SEAPIECE SEASCOUT SEATRAIN SEAWIVES
SEABLITE SEADROME SEAGOING SEALINES SEAPLANE SEASHELL SEAWALLS SEAWOMAN
SEABOARD SEAFARER SEAGULLS SEALINGS SEAPORTS SEASHORE SEAWANTS SEAWOMEN
SEABOOTS SEAFLOOR SEAHAWKS SEAMAIDS SEAQUAKE SEASIDES SEAWARDS SEAWORMS
SEABORNE SEAFOLKS SEAHORSE SEAMANLY SEARINGS SEASPEAK SEAWARES

WORDS PREFIXED WITH SUB-

7-letter words SUB-

SUBACID SUBACTS SUBALAR SUBAQUA SUBAREA SUBARID SUBATOM SUBBASE SUBBASS

SUBBING SUBDEWS SUBERIC SUBITEM SUBMISS SUBRING SUBSITE SUBTEST SUBWAYS
SUBCELL SUBDUAL SUBFEUS SUBJOIN SUBNETS SUBRULE SUBSOIL SUBTEXT SUBZERO
SUBCLAN SUBDUCE SUBFILE SUBLATE SUBORAL SUBSALE SUBSONG SUBTILE SUBZONE
SUBCODE SUBDUCT SUBFUSC SUBLETS SUBOVAL SUBSECT SUBTACK SUBTONE
SUBCOOL SUBDUED SUBGOAL SUBLIME SUBPART SUBSERE SUBTASK SUBTYPE
SUBCULT SUBDUES SUBGUMS SUBLINE SUBPLOT SUBSETS SUBTAXA SUBUNIT
SUBDEAN SUBECHO SUBHEAD SUBLOTS SUBRACE SUBSIDE SUBTEEN SUBURBS
SUBDEBS SUBEDIT SUBIDEA SUBMENU SUBRENT SUBSIST SUBTEND SUBVERT

8-letter words SUB-

SUBABBOT SUBCHIEF SUBDUPLE SUBGROUP SUBNASAL SUBSCALE SUBSTAGE SUBTREND
SUBACRID SUBCHORD SUBDURAL SUBHEADS SUBNICHE SUBSECTS SUBSTATE SUBTRIBE
SUBACTED SUBCLAIM SUBEDITS SUBHUMAN SUBNODAL SUBSENSE SUBSTYLE SUBTRIST
SUBACUTE SUBCLANS SUBENTRY SUBHUMID SUBOPTIC SUBSERES SUBTACKS SUBTUNIC
SUBADULT SUBCLASS SUBEPOCH SUBIDEAS SUBORDER SUBSERVE SUBTASKS SUBTYPES
SUBAGENT SUBCLERK SUBEQUAL SUBIMAGO SUBOVATE SUBSHAFT SUBTAXON SUBUNITS
SUBAREAS SUBCODES SUBERECT SUBINDEX SUBOXIDE SUBSHELL SUBTEENS SUBURBAN
SUBATOMS SUBCOOLS SUBEROSE SUBITEMS SUBPANEL SUBSHRUB SUBTENDS SUBURBIA
SUBAUDIO SUBCOSTA SUBFEUED SUBJOINS SUBPARTS SUBSIDED SUBTENSE SUBVERSE
SUBAURAL SUBCRUST SUBFIELD SUBLATED SUBPHASE SUBSIDER SUBTESTS SUBVERST
SUBAXIAL SUBCULTS SUBFILES SUBLEASE SUBPHYLA SUBSIDES SUBTEXTS SUBVERTS
SUBBASAL SUBCUTES SUBFIXES SUBLEVEL SUBPLOTS SUBSISTS SUBTHEME SUBVICAR
SUBBASES SUBCUTIS SUBFLOOR SUBLIMED SUBPOLAR SUBSITES SUBTIDAL SUBVIRAL
SUBBASIN SUBDEANS SUBFLUID SUBLIMES SUBPRIOR SUBSIZAR SUBTILER SUBVOCAL
SUBBINGS SUBDEPOT SUBFRAME SUBLINES SUBPUBIC SUBSKILL SUBTITLE SUBWAYED
SUBBLOCK SUBDEWED SUBGENRE SUBLUNAR SUBRACES SUBSOILS SUBTONES SUBWORLD
SUBBREED SUBDUALS SUBGENUS SUBMENTA SUBRENTS SUBSOLAR SUBTONIC SUBZONAL
SUBCASTE SUBDUCES SUBGOALS SUBMENUS SUBRINGS SUBSONGS SUBTOPIC SUBZONES
SUBCAUSE SUBDUCTS SUBGRADE SUBMERGE SUBRULES SUBSONIC SUBTOTAL
SUBCELLS SUBDUING SUBGRAPH SUBMERSE SUBSALES SUBSPACE SUBTRACT

WORDS PREFIXED WITH SUN-

7-letter words SUN-

SUNBACK SUNBEDS SUNDAES SUNDOGS SUNGLOW SUNLESS SUNROOM SUNTRAP
SUNBAKE SUNBELT SUNDARI SUNDOWN SUNHATS SUNLIKE SUNSETS SUNWARD
SUNBATH SUNBIRD SUNDECK SUNFAST SUNKETS SUNRAYS SUNSPOT SUNWISE
SUNBEAM SUNBOWS SUNDEWS SUNFISH SUNLAMP SUNRISE SUNSUIT
SUNBEAT SUNBURN SUNDIAL SUNGARS SUNLAND SUNROOF SUNTANS

8-letter words SUN-

SUNBAKED SUNBELTS SUNBURNT SUNDIALS SUNGLOWS SUNRISES SUNSHINY
SUNBAKES SUNBERRY SUNBURST SUNDOWNS SUNLAMPS SUNROOFS SUNSPOTS
SUNBATHE SUNBIRDS SUNCHOKE SUNDRESS SUNLANDS SUNROOMS SUNSTONE
SUNBATHS SUNBLIND SUNDARIS SUNDRIES SUNLIGHT SUNSCALD SUNSUITS
SUNBEAMS SUNBLOCK SUNDECKS SUNDROPS SUNPORCH SUNSHADE SUNTRAPS
SUNBEAMY SUNBURNS SUNDERED SUNGLASS SUNPROOF SUNSHINE SUNWARDS

WORDS PREFIXED WITH TRI-

7-letter words TRI-

TRIABLE TRIBADE TRICORN TRIFLED TRIJETS TRIONES TRIPLED TRISOME TRIVETS
TRIACID TRIBLET TRICOTS TRIFOLD TRILITH TRIOSES TRIPODS TRITEST TRIVIAL
TRIAGED TRIBUTE TRIDARN TRIFORM TRILOBE TRIOXID TRIPSIS TRITIDE TRIZONE
TRIAGES TRICARS TRIDENT TRIGAMY TRILOGY TRIPACK TRISECT TRITONE
TRIARCH TRICEPS TRIDUAN TRIGONS TRINARY TRIPART TRISEME TRITONS
TRIAXON TRICLAD TRIENES TRIGRAM TRIODES TRIPIER TRISHAW TRIUMPH

8-letter words TRI-

TRIACIDS TRIAZOLE TRICHORD TRIETHYL TRILITHS TRIOXIDE TRIPLIED
TRIAGING TRIBALLY TRICLADS TRIFLING TRILOBED TRIOXIDS TRIPLIES
TRIALIST TRIBASIC TRICOLOR TRIFOCAL TRILOBES TRIPACKS TRIPLING
TRIANGLE TRIBLETS TRICORNS TRIGLYPH TRIMETER TRIPEDAL TRIPODAL
TRIAXIAL TRIBRACH TRICYCLE TRIGRAMS TRIMORPH TRIPHASE TRIPOLIS
TRIAXONS TRIBUTES TRIDARNS TRIGRAPH TRIMOTOR TRIPHONE TRIPOSES
TRIAZINE TRICHINA TRIDENTS TRILEMMA TRINODAL TRIPLANE TRISECTS

TRISEMES TRISTATE TRITHING TRITIDES TRIUNITY TRIZONAL
TRISHAWS TRISTICH TRITICAL TRITONES TRIVALVE TRIZONES

WORDS PREFIXED WITH UN-

7-letter words UN-

UNACTED UNCAKED UNDOCKS UNGLUES UNLEADS UNPAGED UNSAFER UNSPIDE UNTUNES
UNADULT UNCAKES UNDOERS UNGODLY UNLEARN UNPAINT UNSAINT UNSPIED UNTURFS
UNAGILE UNCANNY UNDOING UNGORED UNLEASH UNPANEL UNSATED UNSPILT UNTURNS
UNAGING UNCAPED UNDRAPE UNGOWNS UNLEVEL UNPAPER UNSAVED UNSPLIT UNTWINE
UNAIDED UNCAPES UNDRAWN UNGROWN UNLIKES UNPARED UNSAWED UNSPOKE UNTWIST
UNAIMED UNCARTS UNDRAWS UNGUARD UNLIMED UNPAVED UNSCALE UNSTACK UNTYING
UNAIRED UNCASED UNDRESS UNGULAR UNLIMES UNPERCH UNSCARY UNSTAID UNURGED
UNAKING UNCASES UNDREST UNGYVED UNLINED UNPICKS UNSCREW UNSTATE UNUSUAL
UNALIKE UNCHAIN UNDRIED UNGYVES UNLINES UNPILED UNSEALS UNSTEEL UNVAILS
UNALIST UNCHARM UNDRUNK UNHABLE UNLINKS UNPILES UNSEAMS UNSTEPS UNVEILS
UNALIVE UNCHARY UNDYING UNHAIRS UNLIVED UNPLACE UNSEATS UNSTICK UNVEXED
UNAPTLY UNCHECK UNEAGER UNHANDS UNLIVES UNPLAIT UNSEELS UNSTOCK UNVISOR
UNARMED UNCHILD UNEARED UNHANDY UNLOADS UNPLUGS UNSELFS UNSTOPS UNVITAL
UNASKED UNCHOKE UNEARTH UNHANGS UNLOBED UNPLUMB UNSELLS UNSTOWS UNVOCAL
UNAWARE UNCITED UNEASES UNHAPPY UNLOCKS UNPLUME UNSENSE UNSTRAP UNVOICE
UNBAKED UNCIVIL UNEATEN UNHARDY UNLOOSE UNPOPES UNSEWED UNSTRIP UNWAGED
UNBARED UNCLAMP UNEDGED UNHASPS UNLORDS UNPOSED UNSEXED UNSTUCK UNWAKED
UNBARES UNCLASP UNEDGES UNHASTY UNLOVED UNPRAYS UNSEXES UNSTUNG UNWARES
UNBARKS UNCLEAN UNENDED UNHEADS UNLOVES UNPROPS UNSHALE UNSUITS UNWATER
UNBASED UNCLEAR UNEQUAL UNHEALS UNLUCKY UNPURSE UNSHAPE UNSUNNY UNWAXED
UNBATED UNCLEWS UNFACTS UNHEARD UNMACHO UNQUEEN UNSHARP UNSURED UNWAYED
UNBEARS UNCLING UNFADED UNHEART UNMAKER UNQUIET UNSHELL UNSURER UNWEALS
UNBEGET UNCLIPS UNFAIRS UNHEEDY UNMAKES UNQUOTE UNSHENT UNSWEAR UNWEARY
UNBEGOT UNCLIPT UNFAITH UNHELED UNMANLY UNRACED UNSHEWN UNSWEET UNWEAVE
UNBEGUN UNCLOAK UNFAKED UNHELES UNMARRY UNRAKED UNSHIFT UNSWEPT UNWHIPT
UNBEING UNCLOGS UNFAMED UNHELMS UNMASKS UNRAKES UNSHIPS UNSWORE UNWHITE
UNBELTS UNCLOSE UNFANCY UNHINGE UNMATED UNRATED UNSHOED UNSWORN UNWILLS
UNBENDS UNCLOUD UNFAZED UNHIRED UNMEANT UNRAVEL UNSHOES UNTACKS UNWINDS
UNBINDS UNCOCKS UNFENCE UNHITCH UNMERRY UNRAZED UNSHOOT UNTAKEN UNWIPED
UNBITTS UNCODED UNFEUED UNHIVED UNMETED UNREADY UNSHORN UNTAMED UNWIRED
UNBLENT UNCOILS UNFILED UNHIVES UNMEWED UNREAVE UNSHOUT UNTAMES UNWIRES
UNBLESS UNCOLTS UNFIRED UNHOARD UNMINED UNREELS UNSHOWN UNTAXED UNWISER
UNBLEST UNCOMIC UNFITLY UNHOODS UNMITER UNREEVE UNSHOWY UNTAXES UNWITCH
UNBLIND UNCOPED UNFIXED UNHOOKS UNMITRE UNREINS UNSHUTS UNTEACH UNWITTY
UNBLOCK UNCOPES UNFIXES UNHOOPS UNMIXED UNRESTS UNSIGHT UNTEAMS UNWIVED
UNBLOWN UNCORDS UNFLESH UNHOPED UNMIXES UNRIGHT UNSINEW UNTENTS UNWIVES
UNBOLTS UNCORKS UNFLUSH UNHORSE UNMOLDS UNRIMED UNSIZED UNTENTY UNWOMAN
UNBONED UNCOUTH UNFOLDS UNHOUSE UNMOORS UNRIPER UNSLAIN UNTHAWS UNWOOED
UNBONES UNCOVER UNFOOLS UNHUMAN UNMORAL UNRISEN UNSLING UNTHINK UNWORKS
UNBOOTS UNCOWLS UNFORMS UNHUSKS UNMOULD UNRIVEN UNSLUNG UNTILED UNWORTH
UNBORNE UNCRATE UNFOUND UNIDEAL UNMOUNT UNRIVET UNSMART UNTILES UNWOUND
UNBOSOM UNCRAZY UNFREED UNJADED UNMOVED UNROBED UNSMOTE UNTIRED UNWOVEN
UNBOUND UNCROSS UNFREES UNJOINT UNNAILS UNROBES UNSNAPS UNTOMBS UNWRAPS
UNBOWED UNCROWN UNFROCK UNKEMPT UNNAMED UNROLLS UNSNARL UNTONED UNWRITE
UNBOXED UNCUFFS UNFROZE UNKINGS UNNEATH UNROOFS UNSNECK UNTRACE UNWROTE
UNBOXES UNCURBS UNFUMED UNKINKS UNNERVE UNROOST UNSOBER UNTREAD UNWRUNG
UNBRACE UNCURED UNFUNNY UNKNITS UNNESTS UNROOTS UNSOLID UNTRIDE UNYOKED
UNBRAID UNCURLS UNFURLS UNKNOTS UNNOBLE UNROPED UNSONSY UNTRIED UNYOKES
UNBRAKE UNCURSE UNFUSED UNKNOWN UNNOISY UNROPES UNSOOTE UNTRIMS UNYOUNG
UNBROKE UNDATED UNFUSSY UNLACED UNNOTED UNROUGH UNSOULS UNTRUER UNZONED
UNBUILD UNDEALT UNGEARS UNLACES UNOFTEN UNROUND UNSOUND UNTRULY
UNBUILT UNDECKS UNGILDS UNLADED UNOILED UNROVEN UNSOWED UNTRUSS
UNBULKY UNDEIFY UNGIRDS UNLADEN UNORDER UNROYAL UNSPARS UNTRUST
UNBURNT UNDERNS UNGIRTH UNLADES UNOWNED UNRUFFE UNSPEAK UNTRUTH
UNCAGED UNDIGHT UNGLOVE UNLATCH UNPACED UNRULED UNSPELL UNTUCKS
UNCAGES UNDINES UNGLUED UNLAWED UNPACKS UNRULES UNSPENT UNTUNED

8-letter words UN-

UNABATED UNALLIED UNARMING UNBAITED UNBARRED UNBEINGS UNBIASED UNBITTER
UNABUSED UNAMAZED UNARTFUL UNBANDED UNBATHED UNBELIEF UNBIASES UNBLAMED
UNACHING UNAMUSED UNATONED UNBANKED UNBEARED UNBELTED UNBIDDEN UNBLINDS
UNACTIVE UNANCHOR UNAVOWED UNBANNED UNBEATEN UNBENDED UNBILLED UNBLOCKS
UNADORED UNANELED UNAWAKED UNBARBED UNBEDDED UNBENIGN UNBISHOP UNBLOODY
UNAFRAID UNARGUED UNBACKED UNBARING UNBEGETS UNBEREFT UNBITTED UNBLOWED
UNAGEING UNARISEN UNBAGGED UNBARKED UNBEGGED UNBESEEM UNBITTEN UNBODIED

UNBODING
UNBOLTED
UNBONING
UNBONNET
UNBOOKED
UNBOOTED
UNBOSOMS
UNBOUGHT
UNBOUNCY
UNBOXING
UNBRACED
UNBRACES
UNBRAIDS
UNBRAKED
UNBRAKES
UNBREECH
UNBRIDLE
UNBRIGHT
UNBROKEN
UNBUCKLE
UNBUDDED
UNBUILDS
UNBUNDLE
UNBURDEN
UNBURIED
UNBURIES
UNBURNED
UNBURROW
UNBUSTED
UNBUTTON
UNCAGING
UNCAKING
UNCALLED
UNCANDID
UNCAPING
UNCAPPED
UNCARING
UNCARTED
UNCASHED
UNCASING
UNCASKED
UNCATCHY
UNCAUGHT
UNCAUSED
UNCHAINS
UNCHANCY
UNCHARGE
UNCHARMS
UNCHASTE
UNCHECKS
UNCHEWED
UNCHICLY
UNCHILDS
UNCHOKED
UNCHOKES
UNCHOSEN
UNCHURCH
UNCIPHER
UNCLAMPS
UNCLASPS
UNCLASSY
UNCLENCH
UNCLEWED
UNCLINCH
UNCLOAKS
UNCLOSED
UNCLOSES
UNCLOTHE
UNCLOUDS
UNCLOUDY
UNCLOVEN
UNCLOYED
UNCLUTCH
UNCOATED
UNCOCKED
UNCOFFIN
UNCOILED
UNCOINED
UNCOLTED
UNCOMBED
UNCOMELY
UNCOMMON
UNCOOKED
UNCOOLED
UNCOPING
UNCORDED
UNCORKED
UNCOSTLY
UNCOUPLE
UNCOVERS
UNCOWLED
UNCRATED
UNCRATES
UNCREATE
UNCROWNS
UNCUFFED
UNCULLED
UNCURBED
UNCURLED
UNCURSED
UNCURSES
UNCURVED
UNDAMMED
UNDAMNED
UNDAMPED
UNDARING
UNDASHED
UNDAZZLE
UNDECENT
UNDECKED
UNDEEDED
UNDEFIED
UNDENIED
UNDERATE
UNDESERT
UNDEVOUT
UNDIGHTS
UNDIMMED
UNDINTED
UNDIPPED
UNDIVINE
UNDOABLE
UNDOCILE
UNDOCKED
UNDOINGS
UNDOOMED
UNDOTTED
UNDOUBLE
UNDRAPED
UNDRAPES
UNDREAMT
UNDRIVEN
UNDROSSY
UNDUBBED
UNDULLED
UNEARNED
UNEARTHS
UNEASIER
UNEASILY
UNEDGING
UNEDIBLE
UNEDITED
UNELATED
UNENDING
UNENVIED
UNEQUALS
UNERASED
UNEROTIC
UNERRING
UNESPIED
UNEVADED
UNEVENER
UNEVENLY
UNEXOTIC
UNEXPERT
UNFABLED
UNFADING
UNFAIRED
UNFAIRER
UNFAIRLY
UNFAITHS
UNFALLEN
UNFAMOUS
UNFANNED
UNFASTEN
UNFAULTY
UNFEARED
UNFELLED
UNFENCED
UNFENCES
UNFETTER
UNFEUDAL
UNFILIAL
UNFILLED
UNFILMED
UNFISHED
UNFITTED
UNFITTER
UNFIXING
UNFIXITY
UNFLASHY
UNFLAWED
UNFLEXED
UNFOILED
UNFOLDED
UNFOLDER
UNFOOLED
UNFOOTED
UNFORBID
UNFORCED
UNFORGED
UNFORGOT
UNFORKED
UNFORMAL
UNFORMED
UNFOUGHT
UNFRAMED
UNFREEZE
UNFRIEND
UNFROCKS
UNFROZEN
UNFUNDED
UNFURLED
UNFURRED
UNGAGGED
UNGAINLY
UNGALLED
UNGAUGED
UNGEARED
UNGENIAL
UNGENTLE
UNGENTLY
UNGIFTED
UNGILDED
UNGIRDED
UNGIRTHS
UNGIVING
UNGLAZED
UNGLOVED
UNGLOVES
UNGLUING
UNGODDED
UNGORGED
UNGOTTEN
UNGOWNED
UNGRACED
UNGRADED
UNGRAZED
UNGREEDY
UNGROUND
UNGUARDS
UNGUIDED
UNGUILTY
UNGUMMED
UNGYVING
UNHACKED
UNHAILED
UNHAIRED
UNHALLOW
UNHALSED
UNHALVED
UNHANDED
UNHANGED
UNHARMED
UNHASPED
UNHATTED
UNHEADED
UNHEALED
UNHEALTH
UNHEARSE
UNHEARTS
UNHEATED
UNHEDGED
UNHEEDED
UNHELING
UNHELMED
UNHELPED
UNHEROIC
UNHIDDEN
UNHINGED
UNHINGES
UNHIVING
UNHOARDS
UNHOLIER
UNHOLILY
UNHOLPEN
UNHOMELY
UNHONEST
UNHOODED
UNHOOKED
UNHOOPED
UNHORSED
UNHORSES
UNHOUSED
UNHOUSES
UNHUNTED
UNHUSKED
UNIDEAED
UNIMBUED
UNINURED
UNIONISE
UNIONIZE
UNIRONED
UNISSUED
UNJOINED
UNJOINTS
UNJOYFUL
UNJOYOUS
UNJUDGED
UNJUSTER
UNJUSTLY
UNKENNED
UNKENNEL
UNKINDER
UNKINDLY
UNKINGED
UNKINGLY
UNKINKED
UNKISSED
UNKISSES
UNKNIGHT
UNKNOWNS
UNKOSHER
UNLACING
UNLADING
UNLASHED
UNLASHES
UNLAWFUL
UNLAWING
UNLAYING
UNLEADED
UNLEARNS
UNLEARNT
UNLEASED
UNLETHAL
UNLETTED
UNLEVELS
UNLEVIED
UNLICKED
UNLIDDED
UNLIKELY
UNLIMBER
UNLIMING
UNLINEAL
UNLINING
UNLINKED
UNLISTED
UNLIVELY
UNLIVING
UNLOADED
UNLOADER
UNLOCKED
UNLOOKED
UNLOOSED
UNLOOSEN
UNLOOSES
UNLOPPED
UNLORDED
UNLORDLY
UNLOVELY
UNLOVING
UNMAILED
UNMAIMED
UNMAKERS
UNMAKING
UNMANFUL
UNMANNED
UNMANTLE
UNMAPPED
UNMARKED
UNMARRED
UNMASKED
UNMASKER
UNMATTED
UNMEETLY
UNMELLOW
UNMELTED
UNMENDED
UNMESHED
UNMESHES
UNMEWING
UNMILKED
UNMILLED
UNMINDED
UNMINGLE
UNMISSED
UNMITERS
UNMITRED
UNMITRES
UNMIXING
UNMOANED
UNMODISH
UNMOLDED
UNMOLTEN
UNMONIED
UNMOORED
UNMOULDS
UNMOUNTS
UNMOVING
UNMUFFLE
UNMUZZLE
UNNAILED
UNNATIVE
UNNEEDED
UNNERVED
UNNERVES
UNNESTED
UNNETTED
UNNOBLES
UNOBEYED
UNOPENED
UNORDERS
UNORNATE
UNPACKED
UNPACKER
UNPAINED
UNPAINTS
UNPAIRED
UNPANELS
UNPANGED
UNPAPERS
UNPARTED
UNPATHED
UNPAYING
UNPEELED
UNPEERED
UNPEGGED
UNPENNED
UNPEOPLE
UNPERSON
UNPICKED
UNPILING
UNPINKED
UNPINNED
UNPITIED
UNPLACED
UNPLACES
UNPLAITS
UNPLAYED
UNPLIANT
UNPLOWED
UNPLUMBS
UNPLUMED
UNPLUMES
UNPOETIC
UNPOISED
UNPOISON
UNPOLISH
UNPOLITE
UNPOLLED
UNPOSTED
UNPOTTED
UNPRAISE
UNPRAYED
UNPREACH
UNPRETTY
UNPRICED
UNPRIEST
UNPRIMED
UNPRISON
UNPRIZED
UNPROBED
UNPROPER
UNPROVED
UNPROVEN
UNPRUNED
UNPUCKER
UNPULLED
UNPURGED
UNPURSED
UNPURSES
UNPUZZLE
UNQUEENS
UNQUIETS
UNQUOTED
UNQUOTES
UNRACKED
UNRAISED
UNRAKING
UNRANKED
UNRAVELS
UNREALLY
UNREAPED
UNREASON
UNREAVED
UNREAVES
UNRECKED
UNREELED
UNREELER
UNREEVED
UNREEVES
UNREINED
UNRENTED
UNREPAID
UNREPAIR
UNRESTED
UNRHYMED
UNRIBBED
UNRIDDEN
UNRIDDLE
UNRIFLED
UNRIGGED
UNRIGHTS
UNRINGED
UNRINSED
UNRIPELY
UNRIPEST
UNRIPPED
UNRIVETS
UNROBING
UNROLLED
UNROOFED
UNROOSTS
UNROOTED
UNROPING
UNROTTED
UNROTTEN
UNROUGED
UNROUNDS
UNROUSED
UNRUBBED
UNRUFFLE
UNRULIER
UNRUSHED
UNRUSTED
UNSADDLE
UNSAFELY
UNSAFEST
UNSAFETY
UNSAILED
UNSAINED
UNSAINTS
UNSALTED
UNSAPPED
UNSASHED
UNSATING
UNSAVORY
UNSAYING
UNSCALED
UNSCALES
UNSCREWS
UNSEALED
UNSEAMED
UNSEARED
UNSEASON
UNSEATED
UNSECRET
UNSEEDED
UNSEEING
UNSEELED
UNSEEMLY
UNSEIZED
UNSELDOM
UNSELFED
UNSELVES
UNSENSED
UNSENSES
UNSERVED
UNSETTLE
UNSEWING
UNSEXING
UNSEXIST
UNSEXUAL
UNSHADED
UNSHADOW
UNSHAKED
UNSHAKEN
UNSHALED
UNSHALES
UNSHAMED
UNSHAPED
UNSHAPEN
UNSHAPES
UNSHARED
UNSHAVED
UNSHAVEN
UNSHELLS
UNSHIFTS
UNSHOOTS
UNSHOUTS
UNSHROUD
UNSHRUNK
UNSICKER
UNSIFTED
UNSIGHTS
UNSIGNED
UNSILENT
UNSINEWS
UNSINFUL
UNSLAKED
UNSLICED
UNSLINGS
UNSLUICE
UNSMOKED
UNSMOOTH
UNSNARLS
UNSNECKS
UNSOAKED
UNSOAPED
UNSOCIAL
UNSOCKET
UNSODDEN
UNSOILED
UNSOLDER
UNSOLEMN
UNSOLVED
UNSONSIE
UNSORTED
UNSOUGHT
UNSOULED
UNSOURED
UNSPARED
UNSPEAKS
UNSPELLS
UNSPHERE
UNSPOILT
UNSPOKEN
UNSPRUNG
UNSTABLE
UNSTABLY

UNSTACKS	UNSUCKED	UNTAXING	UNTILTED	UNTUNING	UNVIEWED	UNWEANED	UNWISHED
UNSTARCH	UNSUITED	UNTEAMED	UNTIMELY	UNTURBID	UNVIRTUE	UNWEAPON	UNWISHES
UNSTATED	UNSUMMED	UNTEMPER	UNTINGED	UNTURFED	UNVISORS	UNWEAVES	UNWITTED
UNSTATES	UNSUNNED	UNTENANT	UNTINNED	UNTURNED	UNVIZARD	UNWEBBED	UNWIVING
UNSTAYED	UNSUPPLE	UNTENDED	UNTIPPED	UNTWINED	UNVOICED	UNWEDDED	UNWOMANS
UNSTEADY	UNSURELY	UNTENDER	UNTIRING	UNTWINES	UNVOICES	UNWEEDED	UNWONTED
UNSTEELS	UNSUREST	UNTENTED	UNTITLED	UNTWISTS	UNVULGAR	UNWEENED	UNWOODED
UNSTICKS	UNSWATHE	UNTESTED	UNTOMBED	UNUNITED	UNWALLED	UNWEIGHT	UNWORDED
UNSTITCH	UNSWAYED	UNTETHER	UNTOWARD	UNUSABLE	UNWANING	UNWELDED	UNWORKED
UNSTOCKS	UNSWEARS	UNTHATCH	UNTRACED	UNUSABLY	UNWANTED	UNWETTED	UNWORMED
UNSTONED	UNTACKED	UNTHAWED	UNTRACES	UNUSEFUL	UNWARDED	UNWIELDY	UNWORTHS
UNSTOWED	UNTACKLE	UNTHINKS	UNTRADED	UNVAILED	UNWARIER	UNWIFELY	UNWORTHY
UNSTRAPS	UNTAGGED	UNTHREAD	UNTREADS	UNVALUED	UNWARILY	UNWIGGED	UNWRITES
UNSTRESS	UNTAILED	UNTHRIFT	UNTRENDY	UNVARIED	UNWARMED	UNWILFUL	UNYEANED
UNSTRING	UNTAMING	UNTHRONE	UNTRUEST	UNVEILED	UNWARNED	UNWILLED	UNYOKING
UNSTRIPS	UNTANGLE	UNTIDIED	UNTRUISM	UNVEILER	UNWARPED	UNWINDER	UNZIPPED
UNSTRUCK	UNTANNED	UNTIDIER	UNTRUSTS	UNVEINED	UNWASHED	UNWINGED	
UNSTRUNG	UNTAPPED	UNTIDIES	UNTRUSTY	UNVENTED	UNWASHEN	UNWIRING	
UNSTUFFY	UNTARRED	UNTIDILY	UNTRUTHS	UNVERSED	UNWASTED	UNWISDOM	
UNSUBTLE	UNTASTED	UNTILING	UNTUCKED	UNVETTED	UNWATERS	UNWISELY	
UNSUBTLY	UNTAUGHT	UNTILLED	UNTUFTED	UNVIABLE	UNWATERY	UNWISEST	

WORDS PREFIXED WITH UP-

7-letter words UP-

UPBEARS	UPCATCH	UPDRAWN	UPGRADE	UPLEANT	UPRATES	UPSIDES	UPSWAYS	UPTURNS
UPBEATS	UPCHEER	UPDRAWS	UPGROWN	UPLEAPS	UPREACH	UPSOARS	UPSWEEP	UPTYING
UPBINDS	UPCHUCK	UPDRIED	UPGROWS	UPLEAPT	UPREARS	UPSPAKE	UPSWELL	UPVALUE
UPBLOWN	UPCLIMB	UPDRIES	UPHANGS	UPLIFTS	UPRESTS	UPSPEAK	UPSWEPT	UPWAFTS
UPBLOWS	UPCLOSE	UPENDED	UPHAUDS	UPLIGHT	UPRIGHT	UPSPEAR	UPSWING	UPWARDS
UPBOILS	UPCOAST	UPFIELD	UPHEAPS	UPLINKS	UPRISEN	UPSPOKE	UPSWUNG	UPWELLS
UPBORNE	UPCOILS	UPFILLS	UPHEAVE	UPLOADS	UPRISER	UPSTAGE	UPTAKEN	UPWHIRL
UPBOUND	UPCOMES	UPFLING	UPHILLS	UPLOCKS	UPRISES	UPSTAIR	UPTAKES	UPWINDS
UPBRAID	UPCURLS	UPFLOWS	UPHOARD	UPLOOKS	UPRIVER	UPSTAND	UPTEARS	UPWOUND
UPBRAST	UPCURVE	UPFLUNG	UPHOIST	UPLYING	UPROARS	UPSTARE	UPTHREW	UPWRAPS
UPBRAYS	UPDARTS	UPFOLDS	UPHOLDS	UPMAKER	UPROLLS	UPSTART	UPTHROW	
UPBREAK	UPDATED	UPFRONT	UPHOORD	UPMAKES	UPROOTS	UPSTATE	UPTICKS	
UPBRING	UPDATER	UPFURLS	UPHURLS	UPPILED	UPROUSE	UPSTAYS	UPTIGHT	
UPBROKE	UPDATES	UPGANGS	UPKEEPS	UPPILES	UPSCALE	UPSTEPS	UPTILTS	
UPBUILD	UPDIVED	UPGAZED	UPKNITS	UPPINGS	UPSENDS	UPSTIRS	UPTIMES	
UPBUILT	UPDIVES	UPGAZES	UPLANDS	UPPROPS	UPSHIFT	UPSTOOD	UPTOWNS	
UPBURST	UPDRAFT	UPGIRDS	UPLEADS	UPRAISE	UPSHOOT	UPSURGE	UPTRAIN	
UPCASTS	UPDRAGS	UPGOING	UPLEANS	UPRATED	UPSHOTS	UPSWARM	UPTREND	

8-letter words UP-

UPBEARER	UPCURLED	UPGAZING	UPHUDDEN	UPRAISED	UPSCALED	UPSTARES	UPTHRUST
UPBOILED	UPCURVED	UPGIRDED	UPHURLED	UPRAISER	UPSCALES	UPSTARTS	UPTILTED
UPBRAIDS	UPCURVES	UPGOINGS	UPJETTED	UPRAISES	UPSETTER	UPSTATER	UPTOSSED
UPBRAYED	UPDARTED	UPGRADED	UPLANDER	UPRATING	UPSHIFTS	UPSTATES	UPTOSSES
UPBREAKS	UPDATERS	UPGRADER	UPLAYING	UPREARED	UPSHOOTS	UPSTAYED	UPTRAINS
UPBRINGS	UPDATING	UPGRADES	UPLEANED	UPRIGHTS	UPSOARED	UPSTREAM	UPTRENDS
UPBROKEN	UPDIVING	UPGROWTH	UPLEAPED	UPRISERS	UPSPEAKS	UPSTROKE	UPTURNED
UPBUILDS	UPDRAFTS	UPGUSHED	UPLIFTED	UPRISING	UPSPEARS	UPSURGED	UPVALUED
UPBURSTS	UPDRYING	UPGUSHES	UPLIFTER	UPRIVERS	UPSPOKEN	UPSURGES	UPVALUES
UPCAUGHT	UPENDING	UPHEAPED	UPLIGHTS	UPROARED	UPSPRANG	UPSWARMS	UPWAFTED
UPCHEERS	UPFILLED	UPHEAVED	UPLOADED	UPROLLED	UPSPRING	UPSWAYED	UPWELLED
UPCHUCKS	UPFLINGS	UPHEAVER	UPLOCKED	UPROOTED	UPSPRUNG	UPSWEEPS	UPWHIRLS
UPCLIMBS	UPFLOWED	UPHEAVES	UPLOOKED	UPROOTER	UPSTAGED	UPSWELLS	
UPCLOSED	UPFOLDED	UPHOARDS	UPMAKERS	UPROUSED	UPSTAGES	UPSWINGS	
UPCLOSES	UPFOLLOW	UPHOISTS	UPMAKING	UPROUSES	UPSTAIRS	UPTAKING	
UPCOILED	UPFURLED	UPHOLDER	UPMARKET	UPRUSHED	UPSTANDS	UPTHROWN	
UPCOMING	UPGATHER	UPHOORDS	UPPILING	UPRUSHES	UPSTARED	UPTHROWS	

WORDS PREFIXED WITH WAR-

7-letter words WAR-

WARBIER	WARDOGS	WARKING	WARLOCK	WARPATH	WARRAYS	WARSHIP	WARWOLF
WARBLED	WARDROP	WARLESS	WARLORD	WARPING	WARRENS	WARSLED	WARWORK
WARDENS	WARFARE	WARLIKE	WARMING	WARRAND	WARRING	WARTIER	WARWORN
WARDING	WARHEAD	WARLING	WARPAGE	WARRANT	WARSAWS	WARTIME	

8-letter words WAR-

WARCRAFT WARDROPS WARHABLE WARLOCKS WARMOUTH WARPLANE WARRAYED WARTWEED
WARDERED WARFARED WARHEADS WARLORDS WARPAGES WARPOWER WARSHIPS WARWORKS
WARDINGS WARFARER WARHORSE WARMAKER WARPATHS WARRANDS WARSLING
WARDRESS WARFARES WARLINGS WARMINGS WARPINGS WARRANTS WARTIMES

5 to 8's

5 to 8's describes the addition of any three letters at the front or end of a 5-letter word to form a valid 8-letter word. Why are such additions of special interest to the Scrabble player?

Many games will start with a 5-letter play in order to cover one of the double-letter squares. Such plays will either start or end on the centre square. If such a play starts on the centre square it could have the potential to be extended by three letters to reach the triple word square to the right. Note that, as it is easier to spot extensions to the right (we read from left to right, so it is more natural to look at extending a word in this direction) we have not listed here any words formed by adding a suffix such as -ING, -FUL or -EST, though 8-letter words ending in the last two can be found in Section Three in the 'Useful Suffixes' list.

If a 5-letter play ends on the centre square then it is possible that it could be extended by three letters at the front to reach the triple word square to the left. These formations are of particular interest because they are not so easy to spot. As we have noted, it is more natural to see extensions to the right, and it takes extra effort to think about how a word might be extended to the left. Such plays can therefore surprise your opponent and rope in some great triple word scores through clever use of just three letters.

The following is a list of all the possible 8-letter words that can be formed by adding three letters to the front of an existing 5-letter word. Although quite a few of the words will be formed with recognizable prefixes (eg SUB-SOILS, OUT-RAGED) there is also an abundance of more surprising extensions to introduce into your game (eg CLU-BLAND, PEN-CHANT).

You may be amazed at how many possibilities there sometimes are. If a game starts with CABLE with the E on the centre square then there are no fewer than six possible front extensions (AMI-CABLE, CAS-CABLE, EDU-CABLE, EVO-CABLE, PEC-CABLE, PLA-CABLE). That's between 39 and 48 points for just three letters.

SAR-ABAND
DAT-ABASE
CAL-ABASH
SQU-ABASH
SUB-ABBOT
DIS-ABLED
PAR-ABLED
UNF-ABLED
CAP-ABLER
BUY-ABLES
DIS-ABLES
DUR-ABLES
EAT-ABLES
MOV-ABLES
NOT-ABLES
PAR-ABLES
PAY-ABLES
POT-ABLES
RET-ABLES
TAX-ABLES
VOC-ABLES
GAD-ABOUT
LAY-ABOUT
MAR-ABOUT
RUN-ABOUT
DIS-ABUSE
DEF-ACERS
EFF-ACERS
FIL-ACERS
MEN-ACERS
SOL-ACERS
ARE-ACHED
ATT-ACHED
BLE-ACHED
BRE-ACHED
BRO-ACHED
DET-ACHED
PLE-ACHED
PRE-ACHED
ARE-ACHES
ATT-ACHES
BLE-ACHES
BRE-ACHES
BRO-ACHES
DET-ACHES
EAR-ACHES
GAN-ACHES
GOU-ACHES
PAN-ACHES
PLE-ACHES
PRE-ACHES
QUE-ACHES
REL-ACHES
ANT-ACIDS
MON-ACIDS
NON-ACIDS
OXY-ACIDS
PER-ACIDS
TRI-ACIDS
BEL-ACING
DEF-ACING
EFF-ACING
EMB-ACING
ENF-ACING
ENL-ACING
ENR-ACING
INL-ACING
MEN-ACING
PRE-ACING
REF-ACING
REL-ACING
SOL-ACING
UNL-ACING
PAR-ACMES
CON-ACRED

CON-ACRES
POL-ACRES
SUB-ACRID
IMP-ACTED
MIS-ACTED
OLF-ACTED
OUT-ACTED
PRE-ACTED
RED-ACTED
SUB-ACTED
COF-ACTOR
IMP-ACTOR
NON-ACTOR
RED-ACTOR
VAR-ACTOR
PER-ACUTE
SUB-ACUTE
MIS-ADAPT
PRE-ADAPT
FAR-ADAYS
ILK-ADAYS
NOW-ADAYS
BEM-ADDED
MIS-ADDED
OUT-ADDED
SEP-ADDED
SQU-ADDED
RES-ADDLE
SPR-ADDLE
STR-ADDLE
UNS-ADDLE
PRE-ADMIT
PRE-ADOPT
MAT-ADORE
DIS-ADORN
NON-ADULT
PRE-ADULT
SUB-ADULT
GYN-AECIA
PER-AEONS
PIN-AFORE
DIV-AGATE
IND-AGATE
RUN-AGATE
MIS-AGENT
SUB-AGENT
ALN-AGERS
DAM-AGERS
DOW-AGERS
ENG-AGERS
FOR-AGERS
HOM-AGERS
MAN-AGERS
POT-AGERS
RAV-AGERS
SOC-AGERS
TAN-AGERS
VOY-AGERS
DAM-AGING
ENC-AGING
ENG-AGING
ENR-AGING
FOR-AGING
GAR-AGING
HOM-AGING
INC-AGING
MAN-AGING
MAR-AGING
MEN-AGING
RAV-AGING
SAV-AGING
SIL-AGING
TRI-AGING
ULL-AGING
UNC-AGING

VOY-AGING
SAV-AGISM
GAR-AGIST
VIS-AGIST
PAR-AGOGE
DEC-AGONS
HEX-AGONS
NON-AGONS
OCT-AGONS
PAR-AGONS
DIS-AGREE
FIL-AGREE
REN-AGUED
REN-AGUES
TRE-AGUES
OBE-AHING
ABR-AIDED
ALC-AIDES
ASS-AILED
AUM-AILED
BEW-AILED
CAM-AILED
DER-AILED
DET-AILED
EMB-AILED
ENT-AILED
REM-AILED
REN-AILED
RER-AILED
RES-AILED
RET-AILED
SQU-AILED
UNH-AILED
UNM-AILED
UNN-AILED
UNS-AILED
UNT-AILED
UNV-AILED
MIS-AIMED
UNM-AIMED
DET-AINEE
APP-AIRED
EMP-AIRED
IMP-AIRED
REP-AIRED
UNF-AIRED
UNH-AIRED
UNP-AIRED
IMP-AIRER
REP-AIRER
UNF-AIRER
ASL-AKING
BER-AKING
BET-AKING
BRE-AKING
CLO-AKING
COM-AKING
CRE-AKING
CRO-AKING
FRE-AKING
KAI-AKING
KAY-AKING
REM-AKING
RET-AKING
REW-AKING
SNE-AKING
SPE-AKING
TRO-AKING
TWE-AKING
UNC-AKING
UNM-AKING
UNR-AKING
UPM-AKING
UPT-AKING
WRE-AKING

EXH-ALANT
INH-ALANT
ESC-ALATE
ALF-ALFAS
UNI-ALGAL
HID-ALGAS
REG-ALIAS
ROS-ALIAS
VED-ALIAS
MIS-ALIGN
LAV-ALIKE
NOV-ALIKE
ALK-ALINE
BUB-ALINE
PET-ALINE
SEP-ALINE
ANN-ALIST
ARB-ALIST
CAB-ALIST
FAT-ALIST
FIN-ALIST
IDE-ALIST
LEG-ALIST
LOC-ALIST
LOY-ALIST
MED-ALIST
MET-ALIST
MOD-ALIST
MOR-ALIST
MUR-ALIST
PAP-ALIST
REG-ALIST
ROY-ALIST
RUR-ALIST
SOD-ALIST
TOT-ALIST
TRI-ALIST
VIT-ALIST
VOC-ALIST
PAR-ALLEL
TOM-ALLEY
MIS-ALLOT
PRE-ALLOT
DIS-ALLOW
ENW-ALLOW
UNH-ALLOW
ENH-ALOED
CAT-ALOES
ENH-ALOES
PED-ALOES
TAG-ALONG
DES-ALTER
MIS-ALTER
NIZ-AMATE
PAL-AMATE
SQU-AMATE
PRE-AMBLE
SCR-AMBLE
END-AMEBA
ENT-AMEBA
DUR-AMENS
FOR-AMENS
ARM-AMENT
ATR-AMENT
FIL-AMENT
LIG-AMENT
ORN-AMENT
PAR-AMENT
VIZ-AMENT
BON-AMIAS
SOD-AMIDE
PYR-AMIDS
BEL-AMIES
BIG-AMIES
DIG-AMIES

GOR-AMIES
INF-AMIES
OCC-AMIES
OOG-AMIES
STE-AMIES
CAL-AMINE
COR-AMINE
DOP-AMINE
HEX-AMINE
IND-AMINE
KET-AMINE
MEL-AMINE
SYC-AMINE
THI-AMINE
TYR-AMINE
VIT-AMINE
PAL-AMINO
IND-AMINS
SUR-AMINS
THI-AMINS
VIT-AMINS
CAL-AMITY
PAR-AMOUR
ENS-AMPLE
RES-AMPLE
IMM-ANENT
REM-ANENT
GAL-ANGAS
MAL-ANGAS
ARR-ANGER
END-ANGER
ETR-ANGER
STR-ANGER
ENT-ANGLE
OCT-ANGLE
SPR-ANGLE
STR-ANGLE
TRI-ANGLE
UNT-ANGLE
BOT-ANISE
HUM-ANISE
ORG-ANISE
PAG-ANISE
ROM-ANISE
TET-ANISE
URB-ANISE
WOM-ANISE
EMB-ANKER
CAR-ANNAS
HOS-ANNAS
RAB-ANNAS
SAV-ANNAS
DIS-ANNEX
DIS-ANNUL
INF-ANTAS
MAR-ANTAS
TAR-ANTAS
ASK-ANTED
DEC-ANTED
INC-ANTED
LEV-ANTED
REC-ANTED
TEN-ANTED
TRU-ANTED
TYR-ANTED
UNW-ANTED
AND-ANTES
ATL-ANTES
INF-ANTES
VOL-ANTES
GIG-ANTIC
PED-ANTIC
ROM-ANTIC
SEM-ANTIC
SON-ANTIC

XER-ANTIC
SEM-ANTRA
ZYG-ANTRA
CAR-APACE
ESC-APERS
HAN-APERS
REP-APERS
SCR-APERS
UNP-APERS
MAL-APERT
AWH-APING
ESC-APING
RET-APING
SCR-APING
SNE-APING
UNC-APING
CHE-APISH
ESC-APISM
PRI-APISM
SIN-APISM
MEG-APODE
DEC-APODS
HEX-APODS
MEG-APODS
MAY-APPLE
SCR-APPLE
THR-APPLE
DIS-APPLY
MIS-APPLY
DEL-APSES
ILL-APSES
REL-APSES
SYN-APSES
APO-APSIS
SYN-APSIS
SUB-AREAS
CAB-ARETS
CIG-ARETS
LAZ-ARETS
MIN-ARETS
TAB-ARETS
ESC-ARGOT
OUT-ARGUE
RED-ARGUE
POD-ARGUS
ANG-ARIAS
DAT-ARIAS
FIL-ARIAS
MAL-ARIAS
OLE-ARIAS
TIM-ARIOT
CUR-ARISE
MAC-ARISE
NOT-ARISE
POL-ARISE
SOL-ARISE
VEL-ARISE
SQU-ARISH
TOV-ARISH
VAG-ARISH
DEB-ARKED
DEM-ARKED
EMB-ARKED
IMB-ARKED
IMP-ARKED
REM-ARKED
REP-ARKED
UNB-ARKED
UNM-ARKED
EMP-ARLED
IMP-ARLED
DIS-ARMED
PRE-ARMED
REW-ARMED
UNH-ARMED

UNW-ARMED
DIS-ARMER
ALG-AROBA
MAL-AROMA
MOJ-ARRAS
ZAM-ARRAS
DIS-ARRAY
MIS-ARRAY
SQU-ARSON
LAB-ARUMS
BED-ASHED
ENC-ASHED
POT-ASHED
REH-ASHED
REW-ASHED
SPL-ASHED
SQU-ASHED
THR-ASHED
UNC-ASHED
UND-ASHED
UNL-ASHED
UNS-ASHED
UNW-ASHED
UNW-ASHEN
BED-ASHES
CAL-ASHES
CAM-ASHES
ENC-ASHES
FOG-ASHES
GAM-ASHES
POT-ASHES
REH-ASHES
REW-ASHES
SIW-ASHES
SPL-ASHES
SQU-ASHES
THR-ASHES
UNL-ASHES
ATT-ASKED
DAM-ASKED
IMM-ASKED
OUT-ASKED
UNC-ASKED
UNM-ASKED
UNM-ASKER
BIO-ASSAY
MIS-ASSAY
ADM-ASSES
AVG-ASSES
BAD-ASSES
BAG-ASSES
BEC-ASSES
BYP-ASSES
CAM-ASSES
CAV-ASSES
DEG-ASSES
FIL-ASSES
HAR-ASSES
IMP-ASSES
KAV-ASSES
MEG-ASSES
MOL-ASSES
MOR-ASSES
POT-ASSES
PRE-ASSES
REP-ASSES
RUB-ASSES
STR-ASSES
TIR-ASSES
VAK-ASSES
VIN-ASSES
CAD-ASTER
CAN-ASTER
CYT-ASTER
DIS-ASTER

OLE-ASTER
PIL-ASTER
PIN-ASTER
REM-ASTER
MAH-ATMAS
SUB-ATOMS
AQU-ATONE
MIS-ATONE
CAT-ATONY
GEM-ATRIA
VER-ATRIA
ZOI-ATRIA
SUB-AUDIO
PRE-AUDIT
ARR-AUGHT
REC-AUGHT
RET-AUGHT
STR-AUGHT
UNC-AUGHT
UNT-AUGHT
UPC-AUGHT
POS-AUNES
PES-AUNTS
ROM-AUNTS
TAL-AUNTS
BIN-AURAL
MON-AURAL
SUB-AURAL
PAR-AVAIL
GAL-AVANT
PAR-AVANT
BEH-AVERS
CAD-AVERS
CLE-AVERS
MIS-AVERS
PAL-AVERS
PRE-AVERS
DIS-AVOWS
MIS-AWARD
THR-AWARD
ARE-AWAYS
CAR-AWAYS
CUT-AWAYS
FAR-AWAYS
FLY-AWAYS
GET-AWAYS
LAY-AWAYS
RUN-AWAYS
TOW-AWAYS
UNL-AWFUL
PAR-AWING
PAW-AWING
PSH-AWING
RES-AWING
STR-AWING
THR-AWING
UNL-AWING
IMP-AWNED
MON-AXIAL
PRE-AXIAL
SUB-AXIAL
TRI-AXIAL
UNI-AXIAL
DEW-AXING
MAL-AXING
REL-AXING
RET-AXING
REW-AXING
UNT-AXING
EUT-AXITE
MON-AXONS
TRI-AXONS
EMP-AYRES
THI-AZIDE
ATR-AZINE

MAG-AZINE
SIM-AZINE
THI-AZINE
TOP-AZINE
TRI-AZINE
MET-AZOIC
THI-AZOLE
TRI-AZOLE
BOR-AZONS
MEN-AZONS
RUB-BABOO
BUY-BACKS
CUT-BACKS
DIE-BACKS
FAT-BACKS
FIN-BACKS
HOG-BACKS
LAY-BACKS
OUT-BACKS
PAY-BACKS
RED-BACKS
RUN-BACKS
SET-BACKS
SOW-BACKS
TIE-BACKS
TOM-BACKS
WET-BACKS
RED-BAITS
OUT-BAKED
PRE-BAKED
SUN-BAKED
OUT-BAKES
PRE-BAKES
SUN-BAKES
CAB-BALAS
FAL-BALAS
KAB-BALAS
TAM-BALAS
PIE-BALDS
PYE-BALDS
GIM-BALED
CYM-BALER
TIM-BALES
EYE-BALLS
ICE-BALLS
LOW-BALLS
NET-BALLS
ODD-BALLS
PAT-BALLS
PIN-BALLS
GLO-BALLY
TRI-BALLY
VER-BALLY
ARM-BANDS
DIS-BANDS
HAT-BANDS
HAY-BANDS
HUS-BANDS
PRO-BANDS
RIB-BANDS
SAL-BANDS
TUR-BANDS
TUR-BANED
BUG-BANES
COW-BANES
DOG-BANES
FLY-BANES
HEN-BANES
MIR-BANES
MYR-BANES
LUM-BANGS
PRO-BANGS
SHE-BANGS
CAN-BANKS
CUT-BANKS

NON-BANKS
SEA-BANKS
TUR-BANTS
RHU-BARBS
BOM-BARDS
GAB-BARDS
LIB-BARDS
LUB-BARDS
ISO-BARES
BAR-BARIC
ISO-BARIC
DIS-BARKS
OUT-BARKS
TAN-BARKS
CAR-BARNS
PRE-BASAL
SUB-BASAL
SUR-BASED
AIR-BASES
ANA-BASES
DIA-BASES
ISO-BASES
SUB-BASES
SUR-BASES
DIA-BASIC
NON-BASIC
TRI-BASIC
SUB-BASIN
ANA-BASIS
KOL-BASIS
KOL-BASSI
LAM-BASTE
BOM-BASTS
LAM-BASTS
BAR-BATED
COM-BATED
GLO-BATED
PRO-BATED
SUR-BATED
UNA-BATED
NIO-BATES
PRO-BATES
SOR-BATES
SUR-BATES
SUN-BATHE
ISO-BATHS
MUD-BATHS
SAB-BATHS
SUN-BATHS
CIA-BATTA
OUT-BAWLS
SEA-BEACH
JET-BEADS
EYE-BEAMS
OUT-BEAMS
SUN-BEAMS
SUN-BEAMY
BOG-BEANS
SHE-BEANS
SOY-BEANS
ANT-BEARS
BUG-BEARS
CUD-BEARS
FOR-BEARS
DRY-BEATS
OFF-BEATS
COR-BEAUS
JAM-BEAUX
LIM-BECKS
MIS-BEGAN
MIS-BEGIN
MIS-BEGOT
MIS-BEGUN
NON-BEING
BAR-BELLS

COW-BELLS
GOR-BELLY
POT-BELLY
RED-BELLY
SOW-BELLY
TUN-BELLY
FUR-BELOW
RUM-BELOW
FLY-BELTS
SUN-BELTS
ALE-BENCH
DIS-BENCH
PRE-BENDS
SOR-BENTS
ICE-BERGS
HAU-BERKS
BAR-BERRY
BAY-BERRY
BIL-BERRY
BOX-BERRY
COW-BERRY
DEW-BERRY
DOG-BERRY
FOX-BERRY
HAG-BERRY
INK-BERRY
MUL-BERRY
NIS-BERRY
PEA-BERRY
SUN-BERRY
TAY-BERRY
TEA-BERRY
WAX-BERRY
GIB-BETED
RAB-BETED
DIA-BETES
TUR-BETHS
GAM-BETTA
MOR-BIDER
CAR-BIDES
GAM-BIERS
JAM-BIERS
STA-BILES
VER-BILES
MIS-BILLS
PRE-BILLS
SAW-BILLS
TWI-BILLS
WAX-BILLS
WAY-BILLS
WRY-BILLS
TUR-BINAL
COW-BINDS
HOP-BINDS
MIS-BINDS
PRE-BINDS
CAR-BINES
COM-BINES
HOP-BINES
STI-BINES
TUR-BINES
BOM-BINGS
COM-BINGS
CUB-BINGS
CUR-BINGS
DAU-BINGS
DUB-BINGS
JIB-BINGS
JOB-BINGS
MOB-BINGS
RIB-BINGS
RUB-BINGS
SOB-BINGS
SUB-BINGS
TUB-BINGS

WEB-BINGS
SYM-BIONT
ANT-BIRDS
AWL-BIRDS
CAT-BIRDS
COW-BIRDS
FAT-BIRDS
JAY-BIRDS
OIL-BIRDS
RED-BIRDS
SEA-BIRDS
SUN-BIRDS
WOS-BIRDS
MIS-BIRTH
ARA-BISES
SOU-BISES
TAB-BISES
OUT-BITCH
RAB-BITER
NIO-BITES
SOR-BITES
BAB-BITTS
BOB-BITTS
ARA-BIZES
NON-BLACK
SAW-BLADE
CLU-BLAND
SCA-BLAND
SLO-BLAND
BIO-BLAST
EPI-BLAST
MYO-BLAST
NEO-BLAST
ZOO-BLAST
OUT-BLAZE
OUT-BLEAT
BAR-BLESS
COM-BLESS
CUR-BLESS
GAR-BLESS
HER-BLESS
LIM-BLESS
OUT-BLESS
PRE-BLESS
TOM-BLESS
VER-BLESS
FEE-BLEST
HUM-BLEST
NIM-BLEST
STA-BLEST
BOM-BLETS
BUL-BLETS
DOU-BLETS
DRI-BLETS
HER-BLETS
TRI-BLETS
GOR-BLIMY
PUR-BLIND
SUN-BLIND
ICE-BLINK
QUI-BLINS
SEA-BLITE
SUB-BLOCK
SUN-BLOCK
HOT-BLOOD
OUT-BLOOM
INK-BLOTS
FLY-BLOWN
FLY-BLOWS
OUT-BLUFF
OUT-BLUSH
BOX-BOARD
CUP-BOARD
DAM-BOARD
FUN-BOARD

GAR-BOARD
KEY-BOARD
LAP-BOARD
LAR-BOARD
LEE-BOARD
LOG-BOARD
MOP-BOARD
OUT-BOARD
PEG-BOARD
SEA-BOARD
TAG-BOARD
TEA-BOARD
WAY-BOARD
OUT-BOAST
AIR-BOATS
BUM-BOATS
CAT-BOATS
FLY-BOATS
GUN-BOATS
ICE-BOATS
PIG-BOATS
ROW-BOATS
TOW-BOATS
TUG-BOATS
KEB-BOCKS
FOR-BODED
FOR-BODES
GAR-BOILS
GUM-BOILS
PAR-BOILS
POT-BOILS
PRE-BOILS
KEM-BOING
KIM-BOING
MAM-BOING
BAR-BOLAS
TOM-BOLAS
SYM-BOLES
DIA-BOLOS
TOM-BOLOS
DOG-BOLTS
EYE-BOLTS
HAG-BOLTS
RAG-BOLTS
TUR-BONDS
HAM-BONED
JAW-BONED
RAW-BONED
RIB-BONED
JAW-BONER
HAM-BONES
HIP-BONES
JAM-BONES
JAW-BONES
PIN-BONES
RED-BONES
SAW-BONES
BOO-BOOKS
DAY-BOOKS
FLY-BOOKS
LAW-BOOKS
LOG-BOOKS
NON-BOOKS
PRE-BOOKS
JAM-BOOLS
JIB-BOOMS
TOL-BOOTH
GUM-BOOTS
SEA-BOOTS
SLY-BOOTS
BOM-BORAS
CAR-BORAS
RAS-BORAS
HAR-BORED
JAM-BOREE

HAR-BORER
AIR-BORNE
FOR-BORNE
SEA-BORNE
SKY-BORNE
DIS-BOSOM
CHA-BOUKS
CHI-BOUKS
AIR-BOUND
DIS-BOUND
FOG-BOUND
ICE-BOUND
MAW-BOUND
MIS-BOUND
OUT-BOUND
PRE-BOUND
FAU-BOURG
DIS-BOWEL
TEA-BOWLS
OUT-BOXED
HAT-BOXES
HAY-BOXES
HOT-BOXES
ICE-BOXES
JAW-BOXES
OUT-BOXES
PEG-BOXES
SKY-BOXES
TEA-BOXES
CAR-BOYED
VAM-BRACE
TRI-BRACH
SHA-BRACK
OUT-BRAGS
END-BRAIN
MAD-BRAIN
MID-BRAIN
MIS-BRAND
NON-BRAND
OUT-BRAVE
OUT-BRAWL
BEE-BREAD
RYE-BREAD
SOW-BREAD
WAY-BREAD
DAY-BREAK
OUT-BREAK
PAR-BREAK
OUT-BREED
SUB-BREED
OUT-BRIBE
RED-BRICK
CAT-BRIER
AUM-BRIES
DAU-BRIES
DAW-BRIES
SOM-BRING
ATA-BRINS
ATE-BRINS
DAM-BRODS
PAN-BROIL
OUT-BROKE
PEM-BROKE
CLU-BROOM
CRI-BROSE
NUT-BROWN
EYE-BROWS
LOW-BROWS
AIR-BRUSH
CLU-BRUSH
HAT-BRUSH
HAW-BUCKS
JUM-BUCKS
KEB-BUCKS
ROE-BUCKS

SAW-BUCKS
ZAM-BUCKS
KEY-BUGLE
MIS-BUILD
OUT-BUILD
MIS-BUILT
OUT-BUILT
SAM-BUKES
OUT-BULKS
OUT-BULLY
GEE-BUNGS
TAM-BURAS
CAR-BURET
HAM-BURGS
HOM-BURGS
TAM-BURIN
MOW-BURNS
OUT-BURNS
SUN-BURNS
MOW-BURNT
OUT-BURNT
SUN-BURNT
DIS-BURSE
AIR-BURST
OUT-BURST
SUN-BURST
NIM-BUSED
UNA-BUSED
AIR-BUSES
IAM-BUSES
LIM-BUSES
MOR-BUSES
NIM-BUSES
SOR-BUSES
COM-BUSTS
TRI-BUTES
AMI-CABLE
CAS-CABLE
EDU-CABLE
EVO-CABLE
PEC-CABLE
PLA-CABLE
BRO-CADES
CAS-CADES
FAL-CADES
SAC-CADES
SUC-CADES
MUS-CADET
DIS-CAGED
BOS-CAGES
BRO-CAGES
DIS-CAGES
RIB-CAGES
SOC-CAGES
TRU-CAGES
PAN-CAKED
CAR-CAKES
CUP-CAKES
HOE-CAKES
HOT-CAKES
OAT-CAKES
PAN-CAKES
TEA-CAKES
CAT-CALLS
MIS-CALLS
EPI-CALYX
OIL-CAMPS
DIS-CANDY
CHI-CANED
CHI-CANER
CHI-CANES
JON-CANOE
ALI-CANTS
DES-CANTS
DIS-CANTS

OUT-CAPER
INS-CAPES
BAC-CARAT
BRO-CARDS
DIS-CARDS
KEY-CARDS
PLA-CARDS
APO-CARPS
EPI-CARPS
EXO-CARPS
PRO-CARPS
SYN-CARPS
MIS-CARRY
DOG-CARTS
TEA-CARTS
TIP-CARTS
CAR-CASED
DIS-CASED
CAR-CASES
DIS-CASES
FRA-CASES
NUT-CASES
PIN-CASES
URI-CASES
OUT-CASTE
SUB-CASTE
MET-CASTS
MIS-CASTS
OFF-CASTS
OUT-CASTS
PRE-CASTS
OUT-CATCH
SEE-CATCH
PLA-CATER
EDU-CATES
EMI-CATES
EVO-CATES
FUR-CATES
JUN-CATES
PLA-CATES
PLI-CATES
ZIN-CATES
CON-CAUSE
SUB-CAUSE
CON-CAVED
CON-CAVES
OUT-CAVIL
SUR-CEASE
CON-CEDED
PRE-CEDED
CON-CEDER
CON-CEDES
EPI-CEDES
PRE-CEDES
BRU-CELLA
MAR-CELLA
CAN-CELLI
SUB-CELLS
DUE-CENTO
SEI-CENTO
TRE-CENTO
CON-CENTS
DES-CENTS
PER-CENTS
PRE-CENTS
PIN-CERED
GLY-CERIA
GLY-CERIC
BRA-CEROS
CON-CERTS
BIA-CETYL
DIA-CETYL
PRO-CHAIN
ARM-CHAIR
BED-CHAIR

PAS-CHALS
BRE-CHAMS
BAC-CHANT
COU-CHANT
MER-CHANT
PEN-CHANT
CLO-CHARD
MOU-CHARD
PIL-CHARD
OUT-CHARM
TRO-CHARS
PET-CHARY
PUR-CHASE
ISO-CHASM
TEU-CHATS
OUT-CHEAT
AIR-CHECK
HAT-CHECK
PAY-CHECK
PIN-CHECK
PRE-CHECK
TOR-CHERE
BUT-CHEST
GAU-CHEST
TEU-CHEST
FIT-CHEWS
CHE-CHIAS
ONY-CHIAS
COL-CHICA
BOY-CHICK
DAB-CHICK
DIP-CHICK
DOB-CHICK
PSY-CHICS
OUT-CHIDE
KER-CHIEF
MIS-CHIEF
SUB-CHIEF
BOY-CHIKS
GOD-CHILD
MER-CHILD
TWI-CHILD
TRO-CHILI
PRE-CHILL
ISO-CHIME
KAT-CHINA
TRI-CHINA
ZEC-CHINE
ZEC-CHINO
KIN-CHINS
SCU-CHINS
ZEC-CHINS
BIO-CHIPS
PUT-CHOCK
MOU-CHOIR
SUN-CHOKE
FAU-CHONS
TOR-CHONS
ULI-CHONS
SUB-CHORD
TRI-CHORD
URO-CHORD
ISO-CHORE
POE-CHORE
ZOO-CHORE
PIT-CHOUT
WAT-CHOUT
SAL-CHOWS
DIS-CIDED
SUI-CIDED
PLA-CIDER
RAN-CIDER
BIO-CIDES
DEI-CIDES
DIS-CIDES

ECO-CIDES
OVI-CIDES
SUI-CIDES
DIS-CINCT
PRE-CINCT
PRO-CINCT
SUC-CINCT
BRU-CINES
CAL-CINES
DOU-CINES
FAS-CINES
GLY-CINES
HYA-CINES
LEU-CINES
PIS-CINES
VAC-CINES
EPI-CISTS
FAS-CISTS
NAR-CISTS
ELI-CITED
MIS-CITED
PRE-CITED
CIR-CITER
BRU-CITES
CAL-CITES
DUL-CITES
LEU-CITES
MIS-CITES
ZIN-CITES
TRI-CLADS
DIS-CLAIM
MIS-CLAIM
PRO-CLAIM
SUB-CLAIM
SUB-CLANS
TIE-CLASP
MIS-CLASS
NON-CLASS
OUT-CLASS
SUB-CLASS
CON-CLAVE
CAT-CLAWS
DEW-CLAWS
BIO-CLEAN
PRE-CLEAN
PRE-CLEAR
SUB-CLERK
OUT-CLIMB
ISO-CLINE
SYN-CLINE
CIR-CLING
MUS-CLING
NON-CLING
ORA-CLING
CIR-CLIPS
TOE-CLIPS
OUT-CLOMB
DIS-CLOSE
PAR-CLOSE
OIL-CLOTH
WAX-CLOTH
AIR-COACH
OUT-COACH
SEA-COAST
PEA-COATS
RED-COATS
SUR-COATS
TOP-COATS
BAW-COCKS
BIB-COCKS
DAW-COCKS
GOR-COCKS
HAY-COCKS
MEA-COCKS
PEA-COCKS

PET-COCKS
SEA-COCKS
PEA-COCKY
MIS-CODED
PRE-CODED
MIS-CODES
PRE-CODES
SAR-CODES
SUB-CODES
ZIN-CODES
MIS-COINS
BRI-COLES
GLY-COLIC
PER-COLIN
CON-COLOR
DIS-COLOR
MIS-COLOR
NON-COLOR
TRI-COLOR
UNI-COLOR
LEU-COMAS
SAR-COMAS
BUN-COMBE
COX-COMBS
NEW-COMER
WEL-COMER
OUT-COMES
WEL-COMES
BEA-CONED
DEA-CONED
DRA-CONES
MUS-CONES
ZIR-CONIA
ANI-CONIC
DRA-CONIC
GLY-CONIC
ZIR-CONIC
CHA-CONNE
MIS-COOKS
OLY-COOKS
OUT-COOKS
PRE-COOKS
PRE-COOLS
SUB-COOLS
PUC-COONS
RAC-COONS
HEN-COOPS
SYN-COPAL
APO-COPES
SYN-COPES
CON-CORDS
DIS-CORDS
RIP-CORDS
RAN-CORED
RES-CORED
SUC-CORED
SUC-CORER
RES-CORES
PIL-CORNS
POP-CORNS
TRI-CORNS
UNI-CORNS
ARC-COSES
DUL-COSES
GLU-COSES
GLY-COSES
NAR-COSES
SAC-COSES
VIS-COSES
SUB-COSTA
ALE-COSTS
BOY-COTTS
HIC-COUGH
DIS COUNT
MIS-COUNT
OUT-COUNT
VIS-COUNT
DIS-COURE
BES-COURS
CON-COURS
RAN-COURS
SUC-COURS
SEL-COUTH
BED-COVER
DIS-COVER
GIM-CRACK
JIM-CRACK
AIR-CRAFT
PEN-CRAFT
SEA-CRAFT
WAR-CRAFT
PRE-CRASH
EXE-CRATE
FUL-CRATE
BES-CRAWL
OUT-CRAWL
MIS-CREED
AIR-CREWS
CON-CREWS
UNS-CREWS
DES-CRIED
OUT-CRIED
DES-CRIER
DES-CRIES
OUT-CRIES
NON-CRIME
APO-CRINE
CAN-CRINE
EXO-CRINE
OUT-CROPS
OUT-CROSS
TOP-CROSS
DIS-CROWN
GOR-CROWS
OUT-CROWS
PIL-CROWS
PIE-CRUST
SUB-CRUST
MIS-CUING
RES-CUING
BIS-CUITS
CIR-CUITS
MID-CULTS
SUB-CULTS
CUR-CUMIN
DIS-CURED
OBS-CURED
PRE-CURED
PRO-CURED
OBS-CURER
PRO-CURER
DIS-CURES
EPI-CURES
OBS-CURES
PRE-CURES
PRO-CURES
OUT-CURSE
PRE-CURSE
OUT-CURVE
EXE-CUTER
ELO-CUTES
EXE-CUTES
SUB-CUTES
SUB-CUTIS
BIO-CYCLE
EPI-CYCLE
TRI-CYCLE
UNI-CYCLE
OTO-CYSTS
VEN-DACES
SOL-DADOS
FRE-DAINE
MON-DAINE
NON-DAIRY
UPA-DAISY
PAR-DALES
RUN-DALES
PAR-DALIS
ANO-DALLY
BRI-DALLY
CAU-DALLY
FEU-DALLY
BEL-DAMES
MES-DAMES
GOD-DAMNS
ABI-DANCE
GUI-DANCE
NON-DANCE
OUT-DANCE
RID-DANCE
TEN-DANCE
VOI-DANCE
MRI-DANGS
SLA-DANGS
YAR-DANGS
FON-DANTS
GAR-DANTS
MOR-DANTS
OXI-DANTS
PEN-DANTS
OUT-DARED
PAN-DARED
OUT-DARES
PIN-DARIS
SUN-DARIS
GOL-DARNS
TRI-DARNS
CAU-DATED
GRA-DATED
MAN-DATED
MIS-DATED
OUT-DATED
OXI-DATED
PRE-DATED
AIR-DATES
CAU-DATES
DEO-DATES
EXU-DATES
GRA-DATES
MAN-DATES
MIS-DATES
OUT-DATES
OXI-DATES
PRE-DATES
PRE-DAWNS
MIS-DEALS
MIS-DEALT
SUB-DEANS
SUN-DECKS
MIS-DEEDS
MIS-DEEMS
GON-DELAY
URO-DELES
SON-DELIS
BRI-DEMAN
SPA-DEMAN
ACA-DEMES
ACA-DEMIC
EPI-DEMIC
PAN-DEMIC
MIS-DEMPT
CON-DENSE
ERO-DENTS
EVI-DENTS
MOR-DENTS
PEN-DENTS
STU-DENTS
TRI-DENTS
SUB-DEPOT
BOR-DERED
CIN-DERED
DAN-DERED
DID-DERED
DOD-DERED
DON-DERED
FEN-DERED
FOD-DERED
GAN-DERED
GEN-DERED
HIN-DERED
JUD-DERED
LAD-DERED
MOI-DERED
MOL-DERED
MUR-DERED
PAN-DERED
POL-DERED
PON-DERED
POW-DERED
PUD-DERED
REN-DERED
SAW-DERED
SOL-DERED
SUN-DERED
TEN-DERED
WAN-DERED
WAR-DERED
WED-DERED
WIL-DERED
WON-DERED
PYO-DERMA
EPI-DERMS
EXO-DERMS
MIL-DEWED
SUB-DEWED
CAU-DEXES
FEE-DHOLE
WOO-DHOLE
COR-DIALS
MIS-DIALS
PRE-DIALS
STA-DIALS
SUN-DIALS
CAD-DICES
CAU-DICES
SPA-DICES
PRE-DICTS
VER-DICTS
MIS-DIETS
MIS-DIGHT
COR-DINER
AMI-DINES
GRA-DINES
NAN-DINES
NUN-DINES
SAR-DINES
SOR-DINES
URE-DINES
URI-DINES
ABI-DINGS
BAN-DINGS
BEA-DINGS
BED-DINGS
BEN-DINGS
BID-DINGS
BIN-DINGS
BIR-DINGS
BON-DINGS
BUD-DINGS
CAR-DINGS
CHI-DINGS
COR-DINGS
EIL-DINGS
FAR-DINGS
FEE-DINGS
FEU-DINGS
FIN-DINGS
FOL-DINGS
FUN-DINGS
GEL-DINGS
GIL-DINGS
GIR-DINGS
GLI-DINGS
GUI-DINGS
HEA-DINGS
HIL-DINGS
HOL-DINGS
HYL-DINGS
LAN-DINGS
LEA-DINGS
LEN-DINGS
LOA-DINGS
LOR-DINGS
MEN-DINGS
MIN-DINGS
MOL-DINGS
NOD-DINGS
PAD-DINGS
PUD-DINGS
REA-DINGS
RED-DINGS
REE-DINGS
ROA-DINGS
ROD-DINGS
SAN-DINGS
SEE-DINGS
SEN-DINGS
SHA-DINGS
SIN-DINGS
SLI-DINGS
SYN-DINGS
TRA-DINGS
VOI-DINGS
WAD-DINGS
WAR-DINGS
WED-DINGS
WEE-DINGS
WEL-DINGS
WIL-DINGS
WIN-DINGS
WOR-DINGS
PUD-DINGY
RON-DINOS
TON-DINOS
COE-DITED
CRE-DITED
INE-DITED
REE-DITED
UNE-DITED
CHE-DITES
COR-DITES
CRU-DITES
ERU-DITES
LYD-DITES
VER-DITES
KHE-DIVAS
SKY-DIVED
SAN-DIVER
SKY-DIVER
KHE-DIVES
SKY-DIVES
BUR-DOCKS
CAN-DOCKS
DAD-DOCKS
HAD-DOCKS
HOR-DOCKS
MAD-DOCKS
PAD-DOCKS
PID-DOCKS
PUD-DOCKS
RUD-DOCKS
WIN-DOCKS
OUT-DODGE
MIS-DOERS
OUT-DOERS
HAN-DOFFS
LEA-DOFFS
SEN-DOFFS
FOR-DOING
MIS-DOING
OUT-DOING
CON-DOLED
CON-DOLES
MIS-DONNE
PUN-DONOR
BAN-DOOKS
BUN-DOOKS
PRE-DOOMS
OUT-DOORS
PAN-DOORS
TAN-DOORS
ACI-DOSES
APO-DOSES
LOR-DOSES
EPI-DOTES
MIS-DOUBT
FOL-DOUTS
HAN-DOUTS
HOL-DOUTS
REA-DOUTS
HAN-DOVER
HOL-DOVER
PAN-DOWDY
SHA-DOWED
WIN-DOWED
SHA-DOWER
CUT-DOWNS
HAG-DOWNS
HOE-DOWNS
LET-DOWNS
LOW-DOWNS
PIN-DOWNS
RUB-DOWNS
RUN-DOWNS
SUN-DOWNS
OUT-DRAGS
HAN-DRAIL
HEA-DRAIL
LAN-DRAIL
MAN-DRAKE
FIN-DRAMS
OUT-DRANK
QUA-DRANT
QUA-DRATS
AIR-DRAWN
MIS-DRAWN
OUT-DRAWN
MIS-DRAWS
OUT-DRAWS
MIS-DREAD
DAY-DREAM
OUT-DREAM
OUT-DRESS
SUN-DRESS
WAR-DRESS
HEA-DREST
TAW-DRIER
BAW-DRIES
FOU-DRIES
SUN-DRIES

TAW-DRIES
MAN-DRILL
PRE-DRILL
TAW-DRILY
OUT-DRINK
MIS-DRIVE
OUT-DRIVE
BEA-DROLL
AIR-DROME
PRO-DROME
SEA-DROME
SYN-DROME
AIR-DROPS
DEW-DROPS
EAR-DROPS
EYE-DROPS
GUM-DROPS
OUT-DROPS
SUN-DROPS
WAR-DROPS
MIS-DROVE
OUT-DROVE
WIN-DROWS
DOL-DRUMS
EAR-DRUMS
HUM-DRUMS
OUT-DRUNK
GRA-DUALS
SUB-DUALS
OVI-DUCAL
CON-DUCES
PRO-DUCES
SUB-DUCES
TRA-DUCES
GEO-DUCKS
GWE-DUCKS
HEY-DUCKS
CON-DUCTS
OVI-DUCTS
PRO-DUCTS
SUB-DUCTS
VIA-DUCTS
OUT-DUELS
SUB-DUING
CON-DUITS
SCE-DULES
SUB-DUPLE
EPI-DURAL
SUB-DURAL
BAN-DURAS
PAN-DURAS
OUT-DURED
PER-DURED
VER-DURED
BOR-DURES
OUT-DURES
PER-DURES
RON-DURES
VER-DURES
GOL-DURNS
COR-DUROY
PRE-DUSKS
SAW-DUSTS
SAW-DUSTY
WOO-DWALE
OUT-DWELL
OUT-DWELT
BAN-DYING
BOO-DYING
BUD-DYING
CAD-DYING
CAN-DYING
GID-DYING
HOW-DYING
KID-DYING

MAR-DYING
MOO-DYING
MUD-DYING
PAN-DYING
PRE-DYING
REA-DYING
RUD-DYING
STU-DYING
TAR-DYING
TOA-DYING
WAD-DYING
VAN-DYKED
VAN-DYKES
ANO-DYNES
INV-EAGLE
BEM-EANED
DEM-EANED
UNW-EANED
UNY-EANED
UPL-EANED
AFF-EARED
APP-EARED
DOG-EARED
END-EARED
ENS-EARED
PAS-EARED
REG-EARED
UNB-EARED
UNF-EARED
UNG-EARED
UNS-EARED
UPR-EARED
BEP-EARLS
IMP-EARLS
BIY-EARLY
LIN-EARLY
OUT-EARNS
REL-EARNS
UNL-EARNS
APP-EASED
DEC-EASED
DIS-EASED
REL-EASED
UNL-EASED
APP-EASES
CAS-EASES
DEC-EASES
DIS-EASES
MIS-EASES
REL-EASES
CIN-EASTS
MIS-EATEN
OUT-EATEN
THR-EATEN
UNB-EATEN
ANT-EATER
DEF-EATER
FIG-EATER
REH-EATER
REP-EATER
SPR-EATHE
BER-EAVED
DEL-EAVED
INW-EAVED
REW-EAVED
UNR-EAVED
UPH-EAVED
BER-EAVES
DEL-EAVES
INW-EAVES
REW-EAVES
THR-EAVES
UNR-EAVES
UNW-EAVES
UPH-EAVES

UNW-EBBED
BRE-ECHED
FLE-ECHED
SME-ECHED
SPE-ECHED
WHE-ECHED
BOB-ECHES
BRE-ECHES
CAL-ECHES
DEP-ECHES
FLE-ECHES
SLE-ECHES
SME-ECHES
SPE-ECHES
MYX-EDEMA
ALL-EDGED
DIS-EDGED
UNH-EDGED
ALL-EDGES
DIS-EDGES
OUT-EDGES
BEN-EDICT
MAL-EDICT
REA-EDIFY
MIS-EDITS
PRE-EDITS
SUB-EDITS
AQU-EDUCT
ALL-EGERS
INT-EGERS
REN-EGERS
ALL-EGGED
REP-EGGED
SQU-EGGED
UNB-EGGED
UNP-EGGED
SQU-EGGER
STR-EIGHT
UNW-EIGHT
STR-EIGNE
SHR-EIKED
CHE-EKING
CLE-EKING
FOR-EKING
GLE-EKING
GRE-EKING
SLE-EKING
SME-EKING
STE-EKING
THE-EKING
FOR-ELAIN
DUN-ELAND
FOR-ELAND
HOM-ELAND
LAK-ELAND
PIN-ELAND
TID-ELAND
CAP-ELANS
GAM-ELANS
COR-ELATE
REG-ELATE
VEG-ELATE
STE-ELBOW
SHI-ELDER
DES-ELECT
NON-ELECT
PRA-ELECT
PRE-ELECT
RES-ELECT
UNS-ELFED
NON-ELITE
NOS-ELITE
GAV-ELMEN
HOT-ELMEN
STE-ELMEN

WHE-ELMEN
ANT-ELOPE
DEV-ELOPE
ENV-ELOPE
DEV-ELOPS
ENV-ELOPS
UNS-ELVES
COM-EMBER
REM-EMBER
DIL-EMMAS
MAR-EMMAS
NON-EMPTY
PRE-ENACT
ALI-ENATE
ARS-ENATE
CAT-ENATE
SEL-ENATE
SER-ENATE
VEN-ENATE
ACC-ENDED
APP-ENDED
ASC-ENDED
ATT-ENDED
DEF-ENDED
DEP-ENDED
EXP-ENDED
EXT-ENDED
FRI-ENDED
IMP-ENDED
INT-ENDED
OBT-ENDED
OFF-ENDED
REM-ENDED
UNB-ENDED
UNM-ENDED
UNT-ENDED
ASC-ENDER
ATT-ENDER
CAL-ENDER
DEF-ENDER
DEG-ENDER
ENG-ENDER
ENT-ENDER
EXP-ENDER
EXT-ENDER
INT-ENDER
LAV-ENDER
OFF-ENDER
UNT-ENDER
DIS-ENDOW
EUG-ENOLS
XYL-ENOLS
DIS-ENROL
MIS-ENROL
ABS-ENTER
ASS-ENTER
CEM-ENTER
DEC-ENTER
FOM-ENTER
INC-ENTER
IND-ENTER
INV-ENTER
LAM-ENTER
MIS-ENTER
REC-ENTER
REP-ENTER
RES-ENTER
SCI-ENTER
SIL-ENTER
DEM-ENTIA
MIS-ENTRY
NON-ENTRY
SUB-ENTRY
CAN-EPHOR
SUB-EPOCH

NON-EQUAL
SUB-EQUAL
EST-ERASE
YTT-ERBIA
PRE-ERECT
SUB-ERECT
PAR-ERGON
LIM-ERICK
MAV-ERICK
ENT-ERICS
FLU-ERICS
GEN-ERICS
ICT-ERICS
NUM-ERICS
SPH-ERICS
ADH-ERING
ALT-ERING
ANG-ERING
BOW-ERING
BRE-ERING
CAP-ERING
CAT-ERING
CHE-ERING
COH-ERING
COP-ERING
COV-ERING
COW-ERING
DAK-ERING
DOV-ERING
DOW-ERING
EFF-ERING
ENT-ERING
FEV-ERING
FLE-ERING
HAV-ERING
HOM-ERING
HOV-ERING
INH-ERING
LAG-ERING
LAY-ERING
LEG-ERING
LEV-ERING
LOW-ERING
MET-ERING
MIT-ERING
NID-ERING
OCH-ERING
OFF-ERING
ORD-ERING
OTT-ERING
OXT-ERING
PAP-ERING
PET-ERING
POW-ERING
QUE-ERING
REV-ERING
ROG-ERING
RUL-ERING
SAB-ERING
SAL-ERING
SEV-ERING
SEW-ERING
SHE-ERING
SKE-ERING
SNE-ERING
SOB-ERING
SPE-ERING
SPH-ERING
SPI-ERING
STE-ERING
SUP-ERING
TAB-ERING
TAP-ERING
TAS-ERING
TAV-ERING

TOW-ERING
TWE-ERING
ULC-ERING
UMB-ERING
USH-ERING
UTT-ERING
WAF-ERING
WAG-ERING
WAT-ERING
WAV-ERING
CAV-ERNED
DEC-ERNED
GOV-ERNED
INT-ERNED
SEC-ERNED
ALT-ERNES
CAS-ERNES
EXT-ERNES
INT-ERNES
LUC-ERNES
LIT-EROSE
SCL-EROSE
SUB-EROSE
TUB-EROSE
DEF-ERRED
DET-ERRED
INF-ERRED
INT-ERRED
REF-ERRED
ASP-ERSES
DEM-ERSES
DIV-ERSES
IMM-ERSES
INV-ERSES
OBV-ERSES
REV-ERSES
DEM-ESNES
ABB-ESSES
ACC-ESSES
ALT-ESSES
ASS-ESSES
CAR-ESSES
CIT-ESSES
DUR-ESSES
EGR-ESSES
EXC-ESSES
FIN-ESSES
IDL-ESSES
IVR-ESSES
OBS-ESSES
OGR-ESSES
REC-ESSES
STR-ESSES
VIT-ESSES
VOW-ESSES
ARR-ESTER
ATT-ESTER
BEP-ESTER
BIM-ESTER
DET-ESTER
DIG-ESTER
DOP-ESTER
FOR-ESTER
GAM-ESTER
HON-ESTER
INF-ESTER
JOK-ESTER
MIM-ESTER
MOD-ESTER
MOL-ESTER
RIM-ESTER
SEM-ESTER
CAB-ESTRO
NAM-ETAPE
QUI-ETENS

SWE-ETENS
UNL-ETHAL
COM-ETHER
TOG-ETHER
UNT-ETHER
BIO-ETHIC
BIM-ETHYL
DIM-ETHYL
TRI-ETHYL
RES-ETTLE
UNS-ETTLE
HEB-ETUDE
QUI-ETUDE
MIS-EVENT
NON-EVENT
ANT-EVERT
THI-EVERY
BED-EVILS
REN-EWERS
SCR-EWERS
STR-EWERS
EKT-EXINE
END-EXINE
PRE-EXIST
UNS-EXIST
MON-EYERS
BOG-EYING
COO-EYING
HON-EYING
MOS-EYING
REK-EYING
REN-EYING
SAV-EYING
BUF-FABLE
OUT-FABLE
REE-FABLE
SUR-FABLE
OUT-FACED
PRE-FACED
SUR-FACED
PRE-FACER
SUR-FACER
CAT-FACES
DOG-FACES
OUT-FACES
PRE-FACES
SUR-FACES
UNI-FACES
GEO-FACTS
NON-FACTS
PRE-FADED
PRE-FADES
JEO-FAILS
FOR-FAIRS
FUN-FAIRS
FUR-FAIRS
MIS-FAITH
ASH-FALLS
CAT-FALLS
DEW-FALLS
ICE-FALLS
JAW-FALLS
MIS-FALLS
OUT-FALLS
PIT-FALLS
DIS-FAMES
PRO-FANES
GON-FANON
FAN-FARED
MIS-FARED
WAR-FARED
WAY-FARED
SEA-FARER
WAR-FARER
WAY-FARER
AIR-FARES
CAR-FARES
EEL-FARES
FAN-FARES
MIS-FARES
WAR-FARES
WAY-FARES
WEL-FARES
OUT-FASTS
SIT-FASTS
TUB-FASTS
NON-FATAL
SUL-FATED
SUL-FATES
NON-FATTY
FOR-FAULT
AVI-FAUNA
EPI-FAUNA
DIS-FAVOR
OUT-FAWNS
CAR-FAXES
OUT-FEAST
MIS-FEEDS
PIG-FEEDS
OUT-FEELS
MIS-FEIGN
MAT-FELON
FOR-FENDS
PIL-FERER
SUF-FERER
SAL-FERNS
GAB-FESTS
TAF-FETAS
BUF-FETED
SUF-FETES
SUB-FEUED
EDI-FICES
ORI-FICES
SUF-FICES
AIR-FIELD
CAN-FIELD
GAS-FIELD
HAY-FIELD
ICE-FIELD
MID-FIELD
MIS-FIELD
OIL-FIELD
OUT-FIELD
SUB-FIELD
URN-FIELD
BEE-FIEST
BUF-FIEST
COM-FIEST
DAF-FIEST
FUF-FIEST
GOO-FIEST
GUL-FIEST
HUF-FIEST
LEA-FIEST
MIF-FIEST
NIF-FIEST
POO-FIEST
PUF-FIEST
REE-FIEST
ROO-FIEST
SUR-FIEST
TOF-FIEST
TUR-FIEST
WOO-FIEST
CAT-FIGHT
DOG-FIGHT
GUN-FIGHT
OUT-FIGHT
PRE-FIGHT
UNI-FILAR
MIS-FILED
PRE-FILED
PRO-FILED
PRO-FILER
MIS-FILES
PRE-FILES
PRO-FILES
SUB-FILES
FUL-FILLS
NON-FINAL
HAW-FINCH
OUT-FINDS
COF-FINED
CON-FINED
TIF-FINED
CON-FINER
CON-FINES
OLE-FINES
RAT-FINKS
MIS-FIRED
OUT-FIRED
PRE-FIRED
BON-FIRES
FOX-FIRES
GUN-FIRES
MIS-FIRES
OUT-FIRES
PRE-FIRES
RIM-FIRES
CON-FIRMS
SEL-FISTS
CON-FIXED
PRE-FIXED
SUF-FIXED
CON-FIXES
PRE-FIXES
SUB-FIXES
SUF-FIXES
PRE-FLAME
OUT-FLANK
COW-FLAPS
EAR-FLAPS
MUD-FLAPS
OUT-FLASH
MUD-FLATS
DIS-FLESH
PAR-FLESH
CAL-FLICK
RUF-FLIER
WAF-FLIER
BAR-FLIES
BOT-FLIES
DAY-FLIES
GAD-FLIES
MAY-FLIES
MED-FLIES
OUT-FLIES
SAW-FLIES
BAF-FLING
COF-FLING
CUF-FLING
HAL-FLING
MAF-FLING
MUF-FLING
OUT-FLING
PIF-FLING
PUR-FLING
RAF-FLING
RIF-FLING
RUF-FLING
SIF-FLING
STI-FLING
TRI-FLING
WAF-FLING
WOL-FLING
GUN-FLINT
SEA-FLOOR
SUB-FLOOR
COW-FLOPS
RYE-FLOUR
OUT-FLOWN
AIR-FLOWS
MUD-FLOWS
OUT-FLOWS
NON-FLUID
SUB-FLUID
OUT-FLUSH
CON-FOCAL
EPI-FOCAL
NON-FOCAL
PAR-FOCAL
TRI-FOCAL
MIS-FOCUS
PRE-FOCUS
AIR-FOILS
JET-FOILS
MIL-FOILS
SEX-FOILS
TIN-FOILS
TRE-FOILS
FAN-FOLDS
PEN-FOLDS
PIN-FOLDS
TEN-FOLDS
TWO-FOLDS
KIN-FOLKS
MEN-FOLKS
MER-FOLKS
SEA-FOLKS
PLA-FONDS
SEA-FOODS
OUT-FOOLS
TOM-FOOLS
BIG-FOOTS
FIN-FOOTS
HOT-FOOTS
OUT-FOOTS
PER-FORCE
REN-FORCE
TEL-FORDS
HAY-FORKS
AUS-FORMS
CON-FORMS
DIS-FORMS
MIS-FORMS
PER-FORMS
PRE-FORMS
UNI-FORMS
COM-FORTS
PIE-FORTS
CON-FOUND
DUM-FOUND
NEW-FOUND
OUT-FOUND
PRO-FOUND
BAT-FOWLS
PEA-FOWLS
SEA-FOWLS
OUT-FOXED
CAR-FOXES
DOG-FOXES
OUT-FOXES
DIF-FRACT
TAF-FRAIL
AIR-FRAME
BED-FRAME
MIS-FRAME
SUB-FRAME
PRE-FRANK
ECO-FREAK
CON-FRERE
COF-FRETS
POM-FRETS
BEL-FRIED
PAN-FRIED
BEL-FRIES
PAN-FRIES
DIS-FROCK
SAF-FRONS
BOW-FRONT
CON-FRONT
SEA-FRONT
SHO-FROTH
OUT-FROWN
PRE-FROZE
FOG-FRUIT
SYN-FUELS
AIM-FULLY
ART-FULLY
FIT-FULLY
IRE-FULLY
JOY-FULLY
LAW-FULLY
MAN-FULLY
RUE-FULLY
SIN-FULLY
USE-FULLY
WIL-FULLY
WOE-FULLY
PER-FUMED
PER-FUMER
PER-FUMES
FUR-FURAL
FUR-FURAN
FUR-FUROL
CON-FUSED
DIF-FUSED
PER-FUSED
SUF-FUSED
CON-FUSES
DIF-FUSES
DOO-FUSES
PER-FUSES
SUF-FUSES
DIG-GABLE
HAN-GABLE
HUG-GABLE
LUG-GABLE
SIN-GABLE
BRI-GADES
FOU-GADES
RHA-GADES
BAG-GAGES
BUR-GAGES
FOG-GAGES
LUG-GAGES
BAR-GAINS
OUT-GAINS
GRE-GALES
CUP-GALLS
GIN-GALLS
JIN-GALLS
NUT-GALLS
FRU-GALLY
BER-GAMAS
END-GAMES
APO-GAMIC
EPI-GAMIC
EXO-GAMIC
ISO-GAMIC
PAN-GAMIC
SYN-GAMIC
SIR-GANGS
BIO-GASES
SYN-GASES
FRI-GATES
OUT-GATES
VIR-GATES
VUL-GATES
AVI-GATOR
MIS-GAUGE
ARM-GAUNT
DIS-GAVEL
CON-GEALS
BAR-GEESE
CAR-GEESE
MON-GEESE
WER-GELDS
GIN-GELLY
WER-GELTS
PAN-GENES
BIO-GENIC
CON-GENIC
DYS-GENIC
EPI-GENIC
ERO-GENIC
ISO-GENIC
MYO-GENIC
ORO-GENIC
OXY-GENIC
PYO-GENIC
ZOO-GENIC
SUB-GENRE
COA-GENTS
EXI-GENTS
MAR-GENTS
REA-GENTS
TAN-GENTS
SUB-GENUS
BER-GERES
ETA-GERES
GOU-GERES
LAR-GESSE
BAR-GESTS
CON-GESTS
DIS-GESTS
SUG-GESTS
BAR-GHEST
LAI-GHEST
ROU-GHEST
TEU-GHEST
TOU-GHEST
ZIN-GIBER
WER-GILDS
NAR-GILLY
BAG-GINGS
BAN-GINGS
BEG-GINGS
BIG-GINGS
BUG-GINGS
COG-GINGS
DAG-GINGS
DIG-GINGS
DOD-GINGS
DOG-GINGS
FAG-GINGS
FOR-GINGS
GAN-GINGS
GAU-GINGS
HAN-GINGS
HED-GINGS
HOG-GINGS
IMA-GINGS
JIG-GINGS
JOG-GINGS
JUG-GINGS
LAG-GINGS
LEG-GINGS
LIG-GINGS
LOD-GINGS

LOG-GINGS
LON-GINGS
MUG-GINGS
NOG-GINGS
PAR-GINGS
PEG-GINGS
PIG-GINGS
PUG-GINGS
PUR-GINGS
RAG-GINGS
RID-GINGS
RIG-GINGS
RIN-GINGS
RUG-GINGS
SAG-GINGS
SER-GINGS
SIN-GINGS
SOG-GINGS
STA-GINGS
SUG-GINGS
SUR-GINGS
TAG-GINGS
TUG-GINGS
WED-GINGS
WIG-GINGS
BUS-GIRLS
COW-GIRLS
IMA-GISMS
LEG-GISMS
ELE-GISTS
ELO-GISTS
IMA-GISTS
OLI-GISTS
OLO-GISTS
TER-GITES
TUR-GITES
ZOR-GITES
FOR-GIVEN
MIS-GIVEN
OUT-GIVEN
FOR-GIVER
LAW-GIVER
FOR-GIVES
MIS-GIVES
OUT-GIVES
GAN-GLAND
NON-GLARE
OUT-GLARE
BUR-GLARY
CUT-GLASS
EYE-GLASS
SPY-GLASS
SUN-GLASS
LAN-GLEYS
GAN-GLIAL
SCA-GLIAS
FAN-GLIKE
FRO-GLIKE
GON-GLIKE
KIN-GLIKE
RIN-GLIKE
SNA-GLIKE
SON-GLIKE
TWI-GLIKE
WIN-GLIKE
CON-GLOBE
ISO-GLOSS
FOX-GLOVE
AIR-GLOWS
DAY-GLOWS
OUT-GLOWS
SUN-GLOWS
ANA-GLYPH
DIA-GLYPH
TRI-GLYPH

OUT-GNAWN
OUT-GNAWS
SUB-GOALS
FOR-GOERS
OUT-GOERS
CAR-GOING
FOR-GOING
MIS-GOING
OUT-GOING
SEA-GOING
TAN-GOING
WAY-GOING
MAN-GOLDS
DOG-GONER
WAG-GONER
DRA-GOONS
JAR-GOONS
BAR-GOOSE
CAR-GOOSE
MON-GOOSE
MUN-GOOSE
WAY-GOOSE
DIS-GORGE
BUR-GOUTS
HAN-GOUTS
BED-GOWNS
DIS-GOWNS
BON-GRACE
DIS-GRACE
DIS-GRADE
MIS-GRADE
PAY-GRADE
PRO-GRADE
SUB-GRADE
MIS-GRAFF
ISO-GRAFT
MIS-GRAFT
ZOO-GRAFT
ANA-GRAMS
DIA-GRAMS
EPI-GRAMS
GRO-GRAMS
ISO-GRAMS
MYO-GRAMS
PAN-GRAMS
PRO-GRAMS
TAN-GRAMS
TRI-GRAMS
EMI-GRANT
FLA-GRANT
FRA-GRANT
AIR-GRAPH
APO-GRAPH
BIO-GRAPH
DIA-GRAPH
EPI-GRAPH
ISO-GRAPH
MYO-GRAPH
ODO-GRAPH
SUB-GRAPH
SYN-GRAPH
TRI-GRAPH
COW-GRASS
CUT-GRASS
EEL-GRASS
LOP-GRASS
MAT-GRASS
NUT-GRASS
PIN-GRASS
RAY-GRASS
RIB-GRASS
ROT-GRASS
RYE-GRASS
EMI-GRATE
BUR-GRAVE

MAR-GRAVE
CON-GREED
NON-GREEN
SEN-GREEN
SHA-GREEN
CON-GREES
PUG-GREES
CON-GREET
DIA-GRIDS
CHA-GRINS
OUT-GRINS
DRA-GROPE
OUT-GROSS
OUT-GROUP
SUB-GROUP
MAN-GROVE
MIS-GROWN
OUT-GROWN
MIS-GROWS
OUT-GROWS
CON-GRUED
CON-GRUES
HAT-GUARD
MUD-GUARD
OUT-GUARD
VAN-GUARD
COU-GUARS
MIS-GUESS
OUT-GUESS
BAR-GUEST
NON-GUEST
MIS-GUIDE
OUT-GUIDE
NON-GUILT
DIS-GUISE
LIN-GULAR
SIN-GULAR
ARU-GULAS
LIN-GULAS
TRA-GULES
VIR-GULES
SEA-GULLS
BUR-GUNDY
DIS-GUSTS
DIS-HABIT
CAS-HABLE
DIS-HABLE
FIS-HABLE
OAT-HABLE
TIT-HABLE
WAR-HABLE
WAS-HABLE
UNS-HADED
BRU-HAHAS
ENC-HAINS
UNC-HAINS
COC-HAIRS
MAC-HAIRS
UNS-HALED
UNS-HALES
OMP-HALOS
ASP-HALTS
BES-HAMED
UNS-HAMED
BES-HAMES
BEC-HANCE
COW-HANDS
BET-HANKS
ENC-HANTS
ETC-HANTS
BEG-HARDS
DIE-HARDS
ORC-HARDS
POC-HARDS
NON-HARDY

UNS-HARED
FUT-HARKS
BEC-HARMS
ENC-HARMS
UNC-HARMS
REC-HARTS
UNC-HASTE
NUT-HATCH
UNT-HATCH
LIT-HATES
REC-HATES
BOX-HAULS
OUT-HAULS
RES-HAVEN
UNS-HAVEN
RES-HAVES
HEE-HAWED
UNT-HAWED
DOR-HAWKS
GOS-HAWKS
SEA-HAWKS
SAS-HAYED
AIR-HEADS
BIG-HEADS
BOW-HEADS
CAT-HEADS
CUP-HEADS
EGG-HEADS
FAT-HEADS
GOD-HEADS
HOP-HEADS
HOT-HEADS
JAR-HEADS
JUG-HEADS
MOP-HEADS
PIN-HEADS
PIT-HEADS
POT-HEADS
RAG-HEADS
RAW-HEADS
RED-HEADS
SAP-HEADS
SUB-HEADS
TOW-HEADS
WAR-HEADS
ALL-HEALS
COW-HEARD
MIS-HEARD
OUT-HEARD
UPC-HEARD
MIS-HEARS
OUT-HEARS
ENS-HEATH
INS-HEATH
ESC-HEATS
EXC-HEATS
PRE-HEATS
REC-HEATS
REC-HECKS
UNC-HECKS
COW-HEELS
ENW-HEELS
CEP-HEIDS
DIT-HEIST
BUS-HELED
ANT-HELIX
ENS-HELLS
INS-HELLS
MOC-HELLS
MUC-HELLS
UNS-HELLS
DIS-HELMS
ALC-HEMIC
ANT-HEMIC
ISC-HEMIC

LIT-HEMIC
SAC-HEMIC
NOW-HENCE
SIT-HENCE
PRE-HENDS
FOR-HENTS
PSC-HENTS
COW-HERBS
POT-HERBS
COW-HERDS
NOW-HERES
BIO-HERMS
CIT-HERNS
LUT-HERNS
ZIT-HERNS
EST-HETES
MAC-HETES
ESC-HEWED
REC-HEWED
UNC-HEWED
ESC-HEWER
CAT-HEXES
COW-HIDED
RAW-HIDED
COW-HIDES
RAC-HIDES
RAP-HIDES
RAW-HIDES
ANT-HILLS
ARC-HINGS
BAS-HINGS
BUS-HINGS
DIS-HINGS
ETC-HINGS
FIS-HINGS
ITC-HINGS
LAS-HINGS
LAT-HINGS
MAS-HINGS
MES-HINGS
MIC-HINGS
MOS-HINGS
NIT-HINGS
NOT-HINGS
RUC-HINGS
RUS-HINGS
TIT-HINGS
WAS-HINGS
WIS-HINGS
OUT-HIRED
JAG-HIRES
OUT-HIRES
MYT-HISTS
SOP-HISTS
TAC-HISTS
ARC-HIVED
BES-HIVER
ARC-HIVES
BEE-HIVES
PAT-HOGEN
LIT-HOING
UNC-HOKED
UNC-HOKES
TOE-HOLDS
POT-HOLED
AIR-HOLES
ARM-HOLES
ASS-HOLES
BOT-HOLES
CAT-HOLES
DOG-HOLES
EYE-HOLES
FOX-HOLES
JAW-HOLES
KEY-HOLES

LUG-HOLES
MAN-HOLES
MUD-HOLES
OIL-HOLES
PIN-HOLES
POT-HOLES
RAT-HOLES
SPY-HOLES
TAP-HOLES
DIS-HOMED
FAT-HOMED
OUT-HOMER
DIS-HOMES
SIP-HONED
SYP-HONED
DIP-HONES
DIS-HONOR
APE-HOODS
BOY-HOODS
CAT-HOODS
CUB-HOODS
ELF-HOODS
GOD-HOODS
HOG-HOODS
MAN-HOODS
NUN-HOODS
SON-HOODS
EYE-HOOKS
MUD-HOOKS
POT-HOOKS
SKY-HOOKS
TYP-HOONS
RES-HOOTS
UNS-HOOTS
UPS-HOOTS
BIS-HOPED
WAN-HOPES
AMP-HORAL
AMP-HORAS
SEN-HORAS
ALP-HORNS
ALT-HORNS
BET-HORNS
BIG-HORNS
COE-HORNS
DIS-HORNS
FOG-HORNS
INK-HORNS
LEG-HORNS
SAX-HORNS
TIN-HORNS
BAT-HORSE
DIS-HORSE
PIL-HORSE
RED-HORSE
SAW-HORSE
SEA-HORSE
WAR-HORSE
REC-HOSEN
UNC-HOSEN
BAT-HOSES
KYP-HOSES
ORT-HOSES
PAT-HOSES
ALT-HOUGH
ELK-HOUND
FOX-HOUND
SEA-HOUND
ALE-HOUSE
BAG-HOUSE
BUG-HOUSE
CAT-HOUSE
COW-HOUSE
DIS-HOUSE
DOG-HOUSE

GAS-HOUSE
GIN-HOUSE
GUN-HOUSE
HEN-HOUSE
HOT-HOUSE
ICE-HOUSE
MAD-HOUSE
NUT-HOUSE
OUT-HOUSE
POT-HOUSE
TAP-HOUSE
TEA-HOUSE
BES-HOUTS
UNS-HOUTS
WAS-HOUTS
WIT-HOUTS
PUS-HOVER
OUT-HOWLS
UPC-HUCKS
NON-HUMAN
PAN-HUMAN
PRE-HUMAN
SUB-HUMAN
SUB-HUMID
OUT-HUMOR
BET-HUMPS
FOX-HUNTS
MAN-HUNTS
OUT-HUNTS
YOG-HURTS
MET-HYLIC
BOT-HYMEN
OMO-HYOID
ENT-ICERS
NOT-ICERS
OFF-ICERS
PUM-ICERS
SPL-ICERS
ENR-ICHED
AFF-ICHES
BAB-ICHES
CAL-ICHES
CEV-ICHES
ENR-ICHES
FET-ICHES
MOR-ICHES
POT-ICHES
QUA-ICHES
SEV-ICHES
STR-ICHES
SLU-ICIER
ENT-ICING
MAL-ICING
NOT-ICING
POL-ICING
PUM-ICING
SLU-ICING
SPL-ICING
DET-ICKER
MIM-ICKER
MON-ICKER
MUS-ICKER
UNS-ICKER
VRA-ICKER
HEL-ICONS
LEX-ICONS
LYR-ICONS
RUB-ICONS
SER-ICONS
SIL-ICONS
VID-ICONS
DIV-IDANT
NON-IDEAL
SUB-IDEAS
FAM-ILIAL

UNF-ILIAL
SED-ILIUM
BRA-ILLER
CAV-ILLER
SCH-ILLER
SHR-ILLER
THR-ILLER
NON-IMAGE
SUB-IMAGO
SCR-IMPED
SHR-IMPED
SKR-IMPED
SCR-IMPLY
SUB-INDEX
MIS-INFER
BEM-INGLE
COM-INGLE
IMM-INGLE
SPR-INGLE
UNM-INGLE
DOM-INION
ENL-INKED
REL-INKED
UNK-INKED
UNL-INKED
UNP-INKED
SHR-INKER
SPR-INKLE
STR-INKLE
CHA-INLET
BEF-INNED
REP-INNED
UNP-INNED
UNT-INNED
BEG-INNER
COW-INNER
ANO-INTER
DIS-INTER
MIS-INTER
QUA-INTER
SPL-INTER
SPR-INTER
SQU-INTER
RET-INULA
VAG-INULA
DIS-INURE
PER-IODIC
PER-IODID
AMN-IONIC
CAT-IONIC
NEP-IONIC
NON-IONIC
TAL-IONIC
ASP-IRATE
LEV-IRATE
VIZ-IRATE
EPE-IRIDS
ADM-IRING
ASP-IRING
ATT-IRING
BEM-IRING
CHA-IRING
CHO-IRING
DEA-IRING
DES-IRING
ENF-IRING
EXP-IRING
GLA-IRING
REF-IRING
REH-IRING
RET-IRING
REW-IRING
SPE-IRING
SQU-IRING
UMP-IRING

UNT-IRING
UNW-IRING
AND-IRONS
END-IRONS
ENV-IRONS
MID-IRONS
SAD-IRONS
ARR-ISHES
BAN-ISHES
EAD-ISHES
EDD-ISHES
FAM-ISHES
FET-ISHES
FIN-ISHES
GAR-ISHES
LAV-ISHES
LIN-ISHES
MAR-ISHES
MIN-ISHES
MON-ISHES
NEB-ISHES
PAP-ISHES
PAR-ISHES
PER-ISHES
POL-ISHES
PUN-ISHES
RAD-ISHES
RAV-ISHES
REL-ISHES
SQU-ISHES
UNW-ISHES
VAN-ISHES
WHA-ISLED
WHA-ISLES
NON-ISSUE
THR-ISTLE
SUB-ITEMS
OMN-IVORY
UNV-IZARD
JAN-IZARS
CAR-JACKS
MAN-JACKS
SKY-JACKS
GOU-JEERS
OUT-JESTS
CON-JOINS
DIS-JOINS
MIS-JOINS
SUB-JOINS
CON-JOINT
DIS-JOINT
BAN-JOIST
FRI-JOLES
MAR-JORAM
POP-JOYED
FOR-JUDGE
MIS-JUDGE
PRE-JUDGE
CON-JUGAL
LOG-JUICE
VER-JUICE
OUT-JUMPS
CON-JUROR
NON-JUROR
COC-KADES
POL-KAING
SEA-KALES
SER-KALIS
CHI-KARAS
BUC-KAROO
JAC-KAROO
FLO-KATIS
BUC-KEENS
JAC-KEENS
NAN-KEENS

BAR-KEEPS
MIS-KEEPS
OUT-KEEPS
RES-KETCH
COC-KEYED
HAW-KEYED
JOC-KEYED
LAC-KEYED
MIC-KEYED
MIS-KEYED
MON-KEYED
BAR-KHANS
SAB-KHATS
CHI-KHORS
MAR-KHORS
MIS-KICKS
OUT-KICKS
TOP-KICKS
ROC-KIERS
DES-KILLS
OUT-KILLS
RES-KILLS
MAN-KINDS
ARC-KINGS
AWA-KINGS
BAC-KINGS
BAL-KINGS
BAN-KINGS
BOO-KINGS
BRO-KINGS
BUC-KINGS
BUS-KINGS
COO-KINGS
DEC-KINGS
DOC-KINGS
DUC-KINGS
ERL-KINGS
FUC-KINGS
GAS-KINGS
HAC-KINGS
HAW-KINGS
HUS-KINGS
JER-KINGS
KIR-KINGS
LEK-KINGS
LIC-KINGS
LUR-KINGS
MAR-KINGS
MAS-KINGS
MIL-KINGS
MOC-KINGS
NEC-KINGS
PAC-KINGS
PAR-KINGS
PEC-KINGS
PIC-KINGS
PIN-KINGS
QUA-KINGS
RAC-KINGS
RAN-KINGS
ROC-KINGS
SAC-KINGS
SAR-KINGS
SHA-KINGS
SIN-KINGS
SMO-KINGS
SOA-KINGS
SUC-KINGS
TAC-KINGS
TAL-KINGS
TAN-KINGS
TAS-KINGS
TIC-KINGS
TUS-KINGS
WAL-KINGS

WIC-KINGS
WIN-KINGS
WOR-KINGS
CHE-KISTS
BUR-KITES
UNA-KITES
WEE-KLONG
NIC-KNACK
PEN-KNIFE
BOW-KNOTS
TOP-KNOTS
MIS-KNOWN
MIS-KNOWS
LOC-KNUTS
KIC-KOFFS
PIC-KOFFS
LEU-KOSES
SAK-KOSES
SHA-KUDOS
VAL-KYRIE
WAL-KYRIE
MIS-LABEL
GAL-LABIA
MIS-LABOR
NON-LABOR
PRO-LABOR
EMP-LACED
REP-LACED
UNP-LACED
REP-LACER
ANE-LACES
BUL-LACES
BYP-LACES
EMP-LACES
REP-LACES
UNP-LACES
PEL-LACKS
POL-LACKS
BAL-LADED
BAL-LADES
PHO-LADES
ROU-LADES
SCA-LADES
PIL-LAGER
SCH-LAGER
VIL-LAGER
UNS-LAKED
BYR-LAKIN
ENF-LAMED
INF-LAMED
UNB-LAMED
INF-LAMER
ENF-LAMES
INF-LAMES
REC-LAMES
BED-LAMPS
SUN-LAMPS
UNC-LAMPS
FOR-LANAS
FUR-LANAS
PAR-LANCE
BAD-LANDS
BOG-LANDS
COT-LANDS
ELF-LANDS
FEN-LANDS
GAR-LANDS
GOL-LANDS
GOW-LANDS
HOL-LANDS
LAL-LANDS
LAW-LANDS
LOW-LANDS
MID-LANDS
NOR-LANDS

OUT-LANDS
RIM-LANDS
SUN-LANDS
TRO-LANDS
WET-LANDS
BIP-LANES
DEP-LANES
EMP-LANES
ENP-LANES
BAL-LANTS
CAL-LANTS
COO-LANTS
EXP-LANTS
GAL-LANTS
GEL-LANTS
IMP-LANTS
REP-LANTS
SEA-LANTS
ZEA-LANTS
COL-LAPSE
PRO-LAPSE
PHY-LARCH
BOL-LARDS
COL-LARDS
DUL-LARDS
FOU-LARDS
MAL-LARDS
POL-LARDS
POU-LARDS
TAI-LARDS
DEC-LARES
SCA-LARES
MUD-LARKS
SKY-LARKS
TIT-LARKS
MUL-LARKY
AMY-LASES
CUT-LASES
CYC-LASES
DOW-LASES
ENO-LASES
EUC-LASES
INU-LASES
KIL-LASES
AGE-LASTS
ARB-LASTS
BAL-LASTS
OUT-LASTS
POT-LATCH
ACY-LATED
ADU-LATED
AFF-LATED
BAL-LATED
CHE-LATED
COL-LATED
DEA-LATED
DEF-LATED
EMU-LATED
EPI-LATED
FEL-LATED
IMP-LATED
INF-LATED
ISO-LATED
OCU-LATED
OVU-LATED
OXA-LATED
PRO-LATED
REF-LATED
REP-LATED
RES-LATED
SUB-LATED
ULU-LATED
UNE-LATED
VIO-LATED
DEF-LATER

IDO-LATER
INF-LATER
VIO-LATER
ZOO-LATER
APP-LAUDS
OUT-LAUGH
BAC-LAVAS
BAK-LAVAS
BES-LAVED
ENC-LAVED
ENS-LAVED
BES-LAVER
ENS-LAVER
BES-LAVES
ENC-LAVES
ENS-LAVES
EXC-LAVES
DEC-LAWED
OUT-LAWED
UNF-LAWED
SMI-LAXES
PAR-LAYED
REP-LAYED
UNP-LAYED
GUN-LAYER
MIS-LAYER
WAY-LAYER
DEG-LAZED
EMB-LAZED
IMB-LAZED
REG-LAZED
UNG-LAZED
DEG-LAZES
EMB-LAZES
IMB-LAZES
REG-LAZES
EMP-LEACH
IMP-LEACH
IMP-LEADS
ISO-LEADS
MIS-LEADS
REP-LEADS
DIS-LEAFS
NON-LEAFY
REC-LEANS
OUT-LEAPS
OUT-LEAPT
MIS-LEARN
OUT-LEARN
NUC-LEASE
SUB-LEASE
DIS-LEAVE
WAY-LEAVE
IMP-LEDGE
REP-LEDGE
BEL-LEEKS
NON-LEGAL
PRE-LEGAL
COL-LEGER
COL-LEGES
FUG-LEMAN
NOB-LEMAN
RIF-LEMAN
WHA-LEMAN
EMB-LEMED
ANA-LEMMA
TRI-LEMMA
FOR-LENDS
REB-LENDS
AMY-LENES
ANT-LERED
ASH-LERED
BUL-LERED
BUT-LERED
FUL-LERED
GOL-LERED
HOL-LERED
TEL-LERED
TIL-LERED
FOR-LESES
PHY-LESES
SUB-LEVEL
BUP-LEVER
REP-LEVIN
DEF-LEXES
DUP-LEXES
IMP-LEXES
REF-LEXES
KAO-LIANG
BIL-LIARD
GAL-LIARD
HAL-LIARD
MIL-LIARD
PAL-LIARD
EXP-LICIT
IMP-LICIT
COW-LICKS
KIL-LICKS
NIB-LICKS
ROL-LICKS
APP-LIERS
ATE-LIERS
COL-LIERS
DAL-LIERS
DOL-LIERS
HAU-LIERS
HEL-LIERS
MIL-LIERS
OUT-LIERS
RAL-LIERS
REP-LIERS
SAL-LIERS
TAB-LIERS
TAL-LIERS
PUR-LIEUS
LOW-LIFER
AIR-LIFTS
HOO-LIGAN
MUL-LIGAN
DAY-LIGHT
FAN-LIGHT
GAS-LIGHT
INF-LIGHT
LOW-LIGHT
MIS-LIGHT
PEN-LIGHT
SKY-LIGHT
SUN-LIGHT
TWI-LIGHT
DIS-LIKED
MIS-LIKED
DIS-LIKEN
DIS-LIKER
MIS-LIKER
DIS-LIKES
MIS-LIKES
SPI-LIKIN
DIS-LIMBS
REC-LIMBS
UPC-LIMBS
BES-LIMED
SUB-LIMED
BES-LIMES
MIL-LIMES
SUB-LIMES
PRE-LIMIT
DIS-LIMNS
UNC-LINCH
UNB-LINDS
BEE-LINED
DEC-LINED
INC-LINED
MUS-LINED
OUT-LINED
REC-LINED
RED-LINED
TOP-LINED
AIR-LINER
DEC-LINER
EYE-LINER
INC-LINER
JET-LINER
MIL-LINER
OUT-LINER
REC-LINER
TOP-LINER
AIR-LINES
ANI-LINES
BEE-LINES
BER-LINES
BOW-LINES
CAR-LINES
CHO-LINES
CUT-LINES
DEC-LINES
DYE-LINES
GUY-LINES
HEM-LINES
HIP-LINES
HOT-LINES
HYA-LINES
INC-LINES
ISO-LINES
JAW-LINES
KAO-LINES
KEY-LINES
LOG-LINES
MAR-LINES
MID-LINES
MIL-LINES
MYE-LINES
OPA-LINES
OUT-LINES
POT-LINES
PRA-LINES
PRO-LINES
PUR-LINES
RAT-LINES
REC-LINES
RED-LINES
SEA-LINES
SET-LINES
SKY-LINES
SUB-LINES
TOP-LINES
TOW-LINES
AIS-LINGS
AMB-LINGS
ANG-LINGS
BAL-LINGS
BAW-LINGS
BIL-LINGS
BIR-LINGS
BOI-LINGS
BOW-LINGS
BUL-LINGS
CAB-LINGS
CAL-LINGS
CAR-LINGS
CAT-LINGS
CEI-LINGS
CIE-LINGS
COD-LINGS
COL-LINGS
COW-LINGS
CUL-LINGS
CUR-LINGS
CYC-LINGS
CYM-LINGS
DAR-LINGS
DEA-LINGS
DEV-LINGS
DIA-LINGS
DIL-LINGS
EAN-LINGS
FAB-LINGS
FAI-LINGS
FAL-LINGS
FAT-LINGS
FEE-LINGS
FIL-LINGS
FOI-LINGS
FOO-LINGS
FOP-LINGS
FOU-LINGS
FOW-LINGS
GAD-LINGS
GOD-LINGS
GOS-LINGS
HAL-LINGS
HAR-LINGS
HEA-LINGS
HEE-LINGS
HER-LINGS
HID-LINGS
HIR-LINGS
HOW-LINGS
HUR-LINGS
INK-LINGS
KEE-LINGS
KEG-LINGS
KID-LINGS
KIL-LINGS
KIT-LINGS
LAL-LINGS
MAD-LINGS
MAI-LINGS
MAR-LINGS
MER-LINGS
MIL-LINGS
MOR-LINGS
MOS-LINGS
NAI-LINGS
NUL-LINGS
OAK-LINGS
PEE-LINGS
PIG-LINGS
PIL-LINGS
POL-LINGS
PUR-LINGS
RAI-LINGS
RAT-LINGS
REE-LINGS
RIF-LINGS
RIG-LINGS
ROL-LINGS
SAI-LINGS
SAP-LINGS
SCA-LINGS
SEA-LINGS
SEE-LINGS
SIB-LINGS
SMI-LINGS
SOI-LINGS
SPI-LINGS
STY-LINGS
SWA-LINGS
TAB-LINGS
TAI-LINGS
TAN-LINGS
TEL-LINGS
TIL-LINGS
TIT-LINGS
TOI-LINGS
TOL-LINGS
TOO-LINGS
UNS-LINGS
UPF-LINGS
VEI-LINGS
WAI-LINGS
WAL-LINGS
WAR-LINGS
WAU-LINGS
WAW-LINGS
WEL-LINGS
WHA-LINGS
WIT-LINGS
YEA-LINGS
YEL-LINGS
YOW-LINGS
DIS-LINKS
BIR-LINNS
ANT-LIONS
BIL-LIONS
BUL-LIONS
CUL-LIONS
GIL-LIONS
HAL-LIONS
HEL-LIONS
JIL-LIONS
MIL-LIONS
MUL-LIONS
PIL-LIONS
RUL-LIONS
ZIL-LIONS
OBE-LISKS
ODA-LISKS
ANG-LISTS
BIB-LISTS
CEL-LISTS
CYC-LISTS
DIA-LISTS
DUA-LISTS
DUE-LISTS
IDO-LISTS
IDY-LISTS
OCU-LISTS
ORA-LISTS
POL-LISTS
REA-LISTS
STY-LISTS
TIT-LISTS
UNA-LISTS
VIO-LISTS
WHO-LISTS
EGA-LITES
HAP-LITES
HOP-LITES
HYA-LITES
MAR-LITES
MEL-LITES
MUL-LITES
PEN-LITES
PER-LITES
SPI-LITES
STY-LITES
THU-LITES
TIL-LITES
URA-LITES
ZEO-LITES
ZOO-LITES
NEO-LITHS
OTO-LITHS
TAL-LITHS
TRI-LITHS
URO-LITHS
ZOO-LITHS
MIS-LIVED
OUT-LIVED
OUT-LIVER
LOW-LIVES
MID-LIVES
MIS-LIVES
NON-LIVES
OUT-LIVES
PRE-LIVES
ARM-LOADS
BUS-LOADS
CAR-LOADS
DIS-LOADS
OFF-LOADS
PAY-LOADS
UNI-LOBAR
ENG-LOBED
ING-LOBED
TRI-LOBED
UNI-LOBED
EAR-LOBES
ENG-LOBES
ING-LOBES
TRI-LOBES
NON-LOCAL
RAP-LOCHS
YEL-LOCHS
AIR-LOCKS
ARM-LOCKS
BAL-LOCKS
BOL-LOCKS
BUL-LOCKS
CAR-LOCKS
DAG-LOCKS
EAR-LOCKS
ELF-LOCKS
FET-LOCKS
GEN-LOCKS
GUN-LOCKS
HEM-LOCKS
HIL-LOCKS
HOO-LOCKS
KIL-LOCKS
LAY-LOCKS
MUL-LOCKS
OAR-LOCKS
PAD-LOCKS
PEL-LOCKS
PIL-LOCKS
POL-LOCKS
PUT-LOCKS
ROL-LOCKS
ROW-LOCKS
RUL-LOCKS
SCH-LOCKS
SHY-LOCKS
SIL-LOCKS
UNB-LOCKS
WAR-LOCKS
WED-LOCKS
EXP-LODES
IMP-LODES
DIS-LODGE
MIS-LODGE
HAY-LOFTS
TOP-LOFTY
APO-LOGIA
ANA-LOGIC
BIO-LOGIC
DIA-LOGIC
ECO-LOGIC
EPI-LOGIC
GEO-LOGIC

MYO-LOGIC
NEO-LOGIC
URO-LOGIC
ZOO-LOGIC
KIL-LOGIE
ANA-LOGON
AMY-LOIDS
CHE-LOIDS
COL-LOIDS
CYC-LOIDS
DIP-LOIDS
EUP-LOIDS
HAP-LOIDS
HYA-LOIDS
STY-LOIDS
TAB-LOIDS
ACY-LOINS
PUR-LOINS
SIR-LOINS
SUR-LOINS
COU-LOIRS
RAC-LOIRS
LOB-LOLLY
DIP-LOMAS
MYE-LOMAS
SLA-LOMED
CAU-LOMES
COE-LOMES
EMP-LONGE
PRO-LONGE
ANK-LONGS
FUR-LONGS
PRO-LONGS
HAL-LOOED
HOL-LOOED
WIT-LOOFS
OUT-LOOKS
BEG-LOOMS
EMB-LOOMS
ENG-LOOMS
REB-LOOMS
BAL-LOONS
GAL-LOONS
GAL-LOOTS
DOL-LOPED
GAL-LOPED
GOL-LOPED
LOL-LOPED
WAL-LOPED
GAL-LOPER
WAL-LOPER
CYC-LOPES
WAR-LORDS
DEP-LORES
EXP-LORES
FAH-LORES
IMP-LORES
ENC-LOSED
INC-LOSED
REC-LOSED
UNC-LOSED
UPC-LOSED
ENC-LOSER
INC-LOSER
AMY-LOSES
CAL-LOSES
CEL-LOSES
CYC-LOSES
DIP-LOSES
ENC-LOSES
HAP-LOSES
INC-LOSES
KYL-LOSES
PEP-LOSES
PSI-LOSES

PTI-LOSES
REC-LOSES
THY-LOSES
UNC-LOSES
UPC-LOSES
EPU-LOTIC
PSI-LOTIC
FUR-LOUGH
TUR-LOUGH
PAR-LOURS
JEA-LOUSE
GEA-LOUSY
JEA-LOUSY
BAI-LOUTS
FAL-LOUTS
PUL-LOUTS
ROL-LOUTS
SEL-LOUTS
OUT-LOVED
UNG-LOVED
PUL-LOVER
ROL-LOVER
OUT-LOVES
UNG-LOVES
BEL-LOWED
BIL-LOWED
FAL-LOWED
FEL-LOWED
FOL-LOWED
GAL-LOWED
HAL-LOWED
HOL-LOWED
MEL-LOWED
PIL-LOWED
REF-LOWED
REG-LOWED
SAL-LOWED
TAL-LOWED
UNB-LOWED
UNP-LOWED
UPF-LOWED
WAL-LOWED
WIL-LOWED
YEL-LOWED
BEF-LOWER
BEL-LOWER
CAL-LOWER
DEF-LOWER
ENF-LOWER
FAL-LOWER
FOL-LOWER
HAL-LOWER
HOL-LOWER
MEL-LOWER
REF-LOWER
SAL-LOWER
WAL-LOWER
WIL-LOWER
YEL-LOWER
FEL-LOWLY
HOL-LOWLY
MEL-LOWLY
SAL-LOWLY
YEL-LOWLY
BEC-LOWNS
BOL-LOXED
BOL-LOXES
DIS-LOYAL
HAL-LUCES
PEL-LUCID
MIS-LUCKS
POT-LUCKS
COL-LUDES
EXC-LUDES
INC-LUDES

OCC-LUDES
PRE-LUDES
SEC-LUDES
SCH-LUMPS
CIS-LUNAR
SUB-LUNAR
CAL-LUNAS
PRE-LUNCH
APO-LUNES
IMP-LUNGE
REP-LUNGE
ANK-LUNGS
SPE-LUNKS
FAI-LURES
GYP-LURES
SOI-LURES
MOL-LUSKS
EVO-LUTED
POL-LUTED
POL-LUTER
BAL-LUTES
EVO-LUTES
POL-LUTES
AFF-LUXES
EFF-LUXES
INF-LUXES
REF-LUXES
COA-LYARD
HAU-LYARD
KAI-LYARD
WIL-LYARD
WIL-LYART
APP-LYING
BEL-LYING
BUL-LYING
COL-LYING
CUL-LYING
DAL-LYING
DOL-LYING
DUP-LYING
FER-LYING
FOL-LYING
GAL-LYING
GIL-LYING
GUL-LYING
IMP-LYING
JEE-LYING
JEL-LYING
JOL-LYING
MIS-LYING
OUT-LYING
RAL-LYING
REF-LYING
REP-LYING
SAL-LYING
SUL-LYING
TAL-LYING
WIL-LYING
ANA-LYSED
DIA-LYSED
ANA-LYSES
BIO-LYSES
DIA-LYSES
ANA-LYSIS
BIO-LYSIS
DIA-LYSIS
ACO-LYTES
ANO-LYTES
ANA-LYTIC
BIO-LYTIC
DIA-LYTIC
GRI-MACED
GRI-MACER
GRI-MACES
STO-MACHS

CRO-MACKS
FRO-MAGES
PLU-MAGES
PRI-MAGES
REI-MAGES
RUM-MAGES
BAR-MAIDS
MER-MAIDS
SEA-MAIDS
AIR-MAILS
CRE-MAINS
GER-MAINS
PTO-MAINS
NON-MAJOR
BED-MAKER
CAP-MAKER
CAR-MAKER
DIE-MAKER
FLY-MAKER
GUN-MAKER
HAT-MAKER
HAY-MAKER
LAW-MAKER
MAP-MAKER
TEA-MAKER
TOP-MAKER
WAR-MAKER
WIG-MAKER
MIS-MAKES
ANI-MALIC
HOG-MANES
SIA-MANGS
API-MANIA
EGO-MANIA
ZOO-MANIA
GER-MANIC
SHA-MANIC
SEA-MANLY
YEO-MANLY
OUT-MARCH
DAY-MARES
DAY-MARKS
EAR-MARKS
FIN-MARKS
MIS-MARKS
OST-MARKS
PUG-MARKS
SEA-MARKS
WAY-MARKS
MIS-MARRY
FOU-MARTS
DIS-MASKS
DIS-MASTS
DUR-MASTS
TOP-MASTS
ABO-MASUS
MIS-MATCH
OUT-MATCH
ANI-MATED
BRO-MATED
CLI-MATED
CRE-MATED
FOR-MATED
GEM-MATED
MIS-MATED
PAL-MATED
SIG-MATED
SUM-MATED
ANI-MATER
ANI-MATES
BED-MATES
BRO-MATES
CLI-MATES
CRE-MATES
FOR-MATES

GEM-MATES
IMA-MATES
MIS-MATES
PRI-MATES
SIG-MATES
STO-MATES
SUM-MATES
HAE-MATIN
CLI-MAXES
DIS-MAYED
UNA-MAZED
MIZ-MAZES
NUT-MEALS
OAT-MEALS
PER-MEANT
PER-MEASE
NUT-MEATS
PIG-MEATS
PRE-MEDIC
SCH-MEERS
MIS-MEETS
DYS-MELIC
TRA-MELLS
VER-MELLS
RES-MELTS
TAG-MEMES
COM-MENDS
REA-MENDS
STA-MENED
SAR-MENTA
SUB-MENTA
TEG-MENTA
TOR-MENTA
SUB-MENUS
GEM-MEOUS
GRA-MERCY
HAM-MERED
MAM-MERED
SIM-MERED
SUM-MERED
YAM-MERED
DUM-MERER
HAM-MERER
YAM-MERER
CHI-MERES
COM-MERES
EPI-MERES
ISO-MERES
URO-MERES
COM-MERGE
REE-MERGE
SUB-MERGE
SUB-MERSE
COS-MESES
SIA-MESES
GUN-METAL
NON-METAL
PRO-METAL
HEL-METED
DIA-METER
GEO-METER
LUX-METER
ODO-METER
OHM-METER
ORO-METER
OXI-METER
TRI-METER
UDO-METER
VIA-METER
YAW-METER
AGA-METES
COS-METIC
HER-METIC
KIS-METIC
MIS-METRE

NON-METRO
SIA-MEZES
GIM-MICKS
MIM-MICKS
GIM-MICKY
BES-MILES
SOY-MILKS
SAW-MILLS
ALU-MINAS
STA-MINAS
EXA-MINED
FUL-MINED
VER-MINED
EXA-MINER
TER-MINER
ALU-MINES
BRO-MINES
CAR-MINES
DES-MINES
DIA-MINES
ENA-MINES
ETA-MINES
EXA-MINES
FLA-MINES
FUL-MINES
HAR-MINES
JAS-MINES
PRI-MINES
PRO-MINES
THY-MINES
BEA-MINGS
BOO-MINGS
BRI-MINGS
COA-MINGS
FAR-MINGS
FOA-MINGS
FOR-MINGS
FRA-MINGS
GUM-MINGS
HUM-MINGS
LAM-MINGS
LEM-MINGS
MAI-MINGS
MUM-MINGS
PRI-MINGS
RIM-MINGS
ROA-MINGS
ROU-MINGS
SEE-MINGS
SOU-MINGS
SUM-MINGS
TEA-MINGS
WAR-MINGS
TRO-MINOS
CAT-MINTS
VAR-MINTS
TER-MINUS
PIS-MIRES
ATO-MISER
PRO-MISER
SUR-MISER
ATO-MISES
CHA-MISES
CHE-MISES
DER-MISES
EXO-MISES
ITE-MISES
KER-MISES
KOU-MISES
PRE-MISES
PRO-MISES
SUR-MISES
CHA-MISOS
ANI-MISTS
ATO-MISTS

CHE-MISTS
CHY-MISTS
COS-MISTS
GNO-MISTS
PAL-MISTS
PLU-MISTS
RHY-MISTS
SUM-MISTS
SCI-MITER
AZY-MITES
ERE-MITES
GUM-MITES
MAR-MITES
TER-MITES
MAM-MITIS
COM-MIXED
PRE-MIXED
APO-MIXES
COM-MIXES
PAN-MIXES
PRE-MIXES
BUM-MOCKS
GAM-MOCKS
HAM-MOCKS
HOM-MOCKS
HUM-MOCKS
MAM-MOCKS
MUM-MOCKS
SCH-MOCKS
NON-MODAL
ALA-MODES
COM-MODES
OUT-MODES
TUR-MOILS
GRI-MOIRE
WAG-MOIRE
BES-MOKES
PRE-MOLAR
PRE-MOLDS
WAD-MOLLS
HOR-MONAL
CRE-MONAS
COM-MONER
GAM-MONER
SER-MONER
SUM-MONER
COM-MONEY
NON-MONEY
OKI-MONOS
MID-MONTH
SCH-MOOSE
BAL-MORAL
NON-MORAL
PRE-MORAL
CRE-MORNE
CRO-MORNE
OXY-MORON
BIO-MORPH
ISO-MORPH
NEO-MORPH
TRI-MORPH
ZOO-MORPH
PRE-MORSE
ANE-MOSES
COS-MOSES
GUM-MOSES
HOM-MOSES
KOS-MOSES
MAR-MOSES
PHI-MOSES
HAR-MOSTS
MID-MOSTS
PRO-MOTED
COM-MOTES
PRO-MOTES

MAM-MOTHS
PRO-MOTOR
PUL-MOTOR
TRI-MOTOR
DIS-MOUNT
SEA-MOUNT
SUR-MOUNT
DOR-MOUSE
TIT-MOUSE
BAD-MOUTH
BIG-MOUTH
DRY-MOUTH
VER-MOUTH
WAR-MOUTH
COM-MOVED
MIS-MOVED
OUT-MOVED
PRE-MOVED
COM-MOVES
MIS-MOVES
OUT-MOVES
PRE-MOVES
ATE-MOYAS
SCH-MUCKS
BES-MUDGE
EAR-MUFFS
GEM-MULES
PLU-MULES
MUL-MULLS
MUR-MURED
UNA-MUSED
ANI-MUSES
COR-MUSES
HOU-MUSES
HUM-MUSES
LAC-MUSES
LIT-MUSES
PRI-MUSES
SHA-MUSES
THY-MUSES
WAM-MUSES
NON-MUSIC
BES-MUTCH
COM-MUTED
PER-MUTED
COM-MUTER
COM-MUTES
PER-MUTES
GEO-MYOID
WAN-NABES
CAN-NABIS
COR-NACRE
BIS-NAGAS
BIZ-NAGAS
HOB-NAILS
TOE-NAILS
TRE-NAILS
SIG-NALED
MIS-NAMED
OUT-NAMED
SIR-NAMED
SUR-NAMED
SUR-NAMER
JOB-NAMES
MIS-NAMES
OUT-NAMES
PEN-NAMES
PRE-NAMES
SIR-NAMES
SUR-NAMES
ORD-NANCE
PER-NANCY
REG-NANCY
LAG-NAPPE
GUR-NARDS

REY-NARDS
ENS-NARES
INS-NARES
ORI-NASAL
PRE-NASAL
SUB-NASAL
EPI-NASTY
NEO-NATAL
PRE-NATAL
COG-NATES
CYA-NATES
EMA-NATES
KHA-NATES
MAG-NATES
NEO-NATES
ODO-NATES
OZO-NATES
PHE-NATES
PHO-NATES
PRO-NATES
RUI-NATES
TAN-NATES
URI-NATES
NON-NAVAL
BEK-NAVES
DOR-NECKS
RED-NECKS
UNS-NECKS
WRY-NECKS
KER-NELLY
BAN-NEROL
DIS-NESTS
EAR-NESTS
COR-NETTS
WHE-NEVER
COR-NICHE
SUB-NICHE
DOR-NICKS
MIN-NICKS
NUD-NICKS
PAN-NICKS
CYA-NIDED
CYA-NIDES
OZO-NIDES
URA-NIDES
ALL-NIGHT
BEK-NIGHT
MID-NIGHT
OUT-NIGHT
SEN-NIGHT
TWI-NIGHT
UNK-NIGHT
ADE-NINES
ALA-NINES
CYA-NINES
GUA-NINES
PEN-NINES
QUI-NINES
STA-NINES
REU-NITER
ACO-NITES
ALU-NITES
ARE-NITES
AXI-NITES
BAI-NITES
BOR-NITES
CRI-NITES
CYA-NITES
DUN-NITES
EBO-NITES
ERI-NITES
FAI-NITES
GAH-NITES
GRA-NITES
ICH-NITES

KAI-NITES
KER-NITES
KYA-NITES
LIG-NITES
MAN-NITES
PYC-NITES
REU-NITES
SIE-NITES
SYE-NITES
URA-NITES
ZOO-NITES
CAR-NIVAL
CHE-NIXES
PHE-NIXES
VER-NIXES
HOB-NOBBY
BAN-NOCKS
BON-NOCKS
DOR-NOCKS
DUN-NOCKS
FIN-NOCKS
JAN-NOCKS
MIN-NOCKS
PIN-NOCKS
WIN-NOCKS
CRU-NODAL
DIA-NODAL
SUB-NODAL
TRI-NODAL
CRU-NODES
SPI-NODES
TAC-NODES
REA-NOINT
ADE-NOMAS
COG-NOMEN
PRE-NOMEN
BIO-NOMIC
ECO-NOMIC
ISO-NOMIC
ZOO-NOMIC
CHI-NONES
HYP-NONES
QUI-NONES
CHI-NOOKS
SCH-NOOKS
MID-NOONS
BUR-NOOSE
SIG-NORIA
CYA-NOSED
STE-NOSED
ADE-NOSES
CYA-NOSES
ETH-NOSES
HOG-NOSES
HYP-NOSES
LIG-NOSES
MAN-NOSES
PYC-NOSES
PYK-NOSES
STE-NOSES
ZOO-NOSES
PRO-NOTAL
TOP-NOTCH
CON-NOTED
KEY-NOTED
KEY-NOTER
CON-NOTES
END-NOTES
KEY-NOTES
PRO-NOTUM
PRO-NOUNS
NON-NOVEL
BES-NOWED
WIN-NOWED
MAG-NOXES

TAN-NOYED
CAR-NYING
HIN-NYING
NAN-NYING
PHO-NYING
STO-NYING
UPR-OARED
UPS-OARED
ACC-OASTS
NON-OBESE
DIS-OBEYS
KIL-OBITS
HYP-OBOLE
BAS-OCHES
BRI-OCHES
BRO-OCHES
CAR-OCHES
GAL-OCHES
KLO-OCHES
PAN-OCHES
PEN-OCHES
SMO-OCHES
SOR-OCHES
HAV-OCKER
SYN-ODALS
MEL-ODEON
MEL-ODIST
MON-ODIST
PAR-ODIST
SAR-ODIST
ALL-ODIUM
MAL-ODORS
MAL-ODOUR
DYS-ODYLE
CAC-ODYLS
KAK-ODYLS
SHR-OFFED
TOB-OGGIN
SHO-OGLED
SHO-OGLES
NON-OHMIC
ASS-OILED
BEM-OILED
BET-OILED
EMB-OILED
ENT-OILED
REB-OILED
REC-OILED
UNC-OILED
UNF-OILED
UNS-OILED
UPB-OILED
UPC-OILED
REC-OILER
ABJ-OINTS
ADJ-OINTS
APP-OINTS
INJ-OINTS
REP-OINTS
UNJ-OINTS
BEH-OLDEN
EMB-OLDEN
IMB-OLDEN
BEH-OLDER
COH-OLDER
EMP-OLDER
ENF-OLDER
IMP-OLDER
INF-OLDER
INH-OLDER
RES-OLDER
UNF-OLDER
UNS-OLDER
UPH-OLDER
ACR-OLEIN

IND-OLENT
INS-OLENT
RED-OLENT
VIN-OLENT
LIN-OLEUM
ROS-OLIOS
COR-OLLAS
AER-OLOGY
AGR-OLOGY
ALG-OLOGY
API-OLOGY
ARC-OLOGY
ARE-OLOGY
ATM-OLOGY
AUT-OLOGY
AXI-OLOGY
BAT-OLOGY
BRY-OLOGY
CAC-OLOGY
CET-OLOGY
CHA-OLOGY
CYT-OLOGY
DEM-OLOGY
DOS-OLOGY
DOX-OLOGY
ETH-OLOGY
ETI-OLOGY
FET-OLOGY
GEM-OLOGY
HOM-OLOGY
HOR-OLOGY
IDE-OLOGY
KID-OLOGY
MEN-OLOGY
MIS-OLOGY
MIX-OLOGY
MON-OLOGY
MYC-OLOGY
NOM-OLOGY
NOS-OLOGY
OEC-OLOGY
OEN-OLOGY
OIN-OLOGY
ONC-OLOGY
ONT-OLOGY
OPT-OLOGY
ORE-OLOGY
OUR-OLOGY
PED-OLOGY
PEL-OLOGY
PEN-OLOGY
POD-OLOGY
POM-OLOGY
POS-OLOGY
PYR-OLOGY
RHE-OLOGY
SER-OLOGY
SEX-OLOGY
SIN-OLOGY
SIT-OLOGY
THE-OLOGY
TOC-OLOGY
TOK-OLOGY
TOP-OLOGY
TYP-OLOGY
VIN-OLOGY
VIR-OLOGY
XYL-OLOGY
ZYM-OLOGY
STR-OMBUS
THR-OMBUS
ABD-OMENS
AGN-OMENS
BLO-OMERS
GRO-OMERS

INC-OMERS
ION-OMERS
MON-OMERS
VEN-OMERS
BEV-OMITS
ALM-ONERS
BAC-ONERS
BYW-ONERS
COR-ONERS
CRO-ONERS
DEB-ONERS
INT-ONERS
SWO-ONERS
TEN-ONERS
WAG-ONERS
AMM-ONIUM
COR-ONIUM
MEC-ONIUM
OOG-ONIUM
OPS-ONIUM
PEP-ONIUM
POL-ONIUM
SYC-ONIUM
RED-ONNED
GER-ONTIC
STR-ONTIC
INH-OOPED
SCR-OOPED
UNH-OOPED
CAB-OOSES
PAP-OOSES
SHM-OOSES
UNL-OOSES
VAM-OOSES
SHM-OOZED
SHM-OOZES
ATR-OPINE
BLO-OPING
DEL-OPING
DRO-OPING
GAL-OPING
GLO-OPING
SCO-OPING
SNO-OPING
STO-OPING
SWO-OPING
TRO-OPING
UNC-OPING
UNP-OPING
UNR-OPING
WHO-OPING
EUR-OPIUM
IOD-OPSIN
AUT-OPTIC
ENT-OPTIC
HOL-OPTIC
PAN-OPTIC
SUB-OPTIC
SYN-OPTIC
CAP-ORALS
CHL-ORALS
COL-ORANT
IGN-ORANT
ROB-ORANT
SON-ORANT
BIF-ORATE
CHL-ORATE
DEC-ORATE
EPH-ORATE
PEJ-ORATE
PER-ORATE
PRI-ORATE
SOR-ORATE
ABS-ORBED
ADS-ORBED

DES-ORBED
DIS-ORBED
RES-ORBED
MIN-ORCAS
RES-ORCIN
ACC-ORDER
DIS-ORDER
EMB-ORDER
IMB-ORDER
MIS-ORDER
PRE-ORDER
REC-ORDER
SUB-ORDER
DEF-ORMER
DEW-ORMER
INF-ORMER
REF-ORMER
NOT-ORNIS
CHO-OSIER
SMO-OTHER
ALL-OTTER
GAR-OTTER
ARN-OTTOS
RID-OTTOS
RIS-OTTOS
BES-OUGHT
INF-OUGHT
REB-OUGHT
REF-OUGHT
RES-OUGHT
UNB-OUGHT
UNF-OUGHT
UNS-OUGHT
ANN-OUNCE
DEN-OUNCE
REN-OUNCE
REC-OUPED
CAR-OUSEL
RAG-OUTED
RER-OUTED
SPR-OUTED
STR-OUTED
ACC-OUTER
DEV-OUTER
ACC-OUTRE
REM-OVALS
INN-OVATE
REN-OVATE
ROT-OVATE
SUB-OVATE
ALL-OVERS
CUT-OVERS
EST-OVERS
FLY-OVERS
GRO-OVERS
LAY-OVERS
POP-OVERS
REC-OVERS
REM-OVERS
RUN-OVERS
UNC-OVERS
ALL-OWING
ARR-OWING
ELB-OWING
EMB-OWING
END-OWING
IND-OWING
KOT-OWING
MIA-OWING
RES-OWING
SHR-OWING
STR-OWING
THR-OWING
WID-OWING
BEH-OWLED

SCR-OWLED
UNC-OWLED
DIS-OWNED
REN-OWNED
UNG-OWNED
DIS-OWNER
NON-OWNER
REN-OWNER
UPT-OWNER
ALK-OXIDE
MON-OXIDE
PER-OXIDE
SUB-OXIDE
TRI-OXIDE
PER-OXIDS
TRI-OXIDS
ANN-OYERS
CAL-OYERS
DEC-OYERS
ENJ-OYERS
STR-OYERS
TUT-OYERS
DIS-PACED
OUT-PACED
RES-PACED
DIS-PACES
OUT-PACES
RES-PACES
CAL-PACKS
ICE-PACKS
MAN-PACKS
MUD-PACKS
PRE-PACKS
RAT-PACKS
TRI-PACKS
COM-PACTS
COM-PADRE
NEO-PAGAN
NON-PAGAN
MIS-PAGED
PRO-PAGED
RAM-PAGED
RAM-PAGER
COM-PAGES
KIP-PAGES
MIS-PAGES
PRO-PAGES
RAM-PAGES
SEE-PAGES
WAR-PAGES
MIS-PAINT
OUT-PAINT
DES-PAIRS
TAM-PALAS
PRO-PALED
PRO-PALES
PUL-PALLY
OPO-PANAX
CRE-PANCE
COM-PANDS
SUB-PANEL
PAR-PANES
PRO-PANES
TRE-PANGS
TYM-PANIC
JOG-PANTS
NON-PAPAL
END-PAPER
FLY-PAPER
GUN-PAPER
OIL-PAPER
TAR-PAPER
HIP-PARCH
JEO-PARDS
LEO-PARDS

JEO-PARDY
COM-PARED
PRE-PARED
UNS-PARED
COM-PARER
PRE-PARER
COM-PARES
PRE-PARES
AIR-PARKS
CAR-PARKS
DIS-PARKS
MIS-PARSE
CLI-PARTS
COM-PARTS
DIS-PARTS
MIS-PARTS
OUT-PARTS
RAM-PARTS
SUB-PARTS
NON-PARTY
DIA-PASES
LAM-PASES
PAM-PASES
LAM-PASSE
PRE-PASTE
FLY-PASTS
NON-PASTS
DES-PATCH
DIS-PATCH
MIS-PATCH
CUS-PATED
PAL-PATED
PAL-PATES
TOW-PATHS
WAR-PATHS
DIA-PAUSE
SUP-PAWNS
TAX-PAYER
DIS-PEACE
BES-PEAKS
RES-PEAKS
UNS-PEAKS
UPS-PEAKS
PAM-PEANS
COM-PEARS
UPS-PEARS
HEN-PECKS
RYE-PECKS
TRI-PEDAL
STA-PEDES
OUT-PEEPS
COM-PEERS
OUT-PEERS
RES-PELLS
UNS-PELLS
DIS-PENCE
FIP-PENCE
SIX-PENCE
SUS-PENCE
TEN-PENCE
TUP-PENCE
TWO-PENCE
COM-PENDS
DIS-PENDS
PAR-PENDS
PER-PENDS
PRO-PENDS
STI-PENDS
SUS-PENDS
DAM-PENED
DEE-PENED
HAP-PENED
LIP-PENED
REO-PENED
UNO-PENED

PRO-PENES
TER-PENES
SIX-PENNY
TEN-PENNY
TUP-PENNY
TWO-PENNY
PAR-PENTS
PER-PENTS
SER-PENTS
COM-PERES
OOS-PERMS
LAM-PERNS
DIS-PERSE
SEX-PERTS
ANA-PESTS
TEM-PESTS
RIS-PETTI
RIS-PETTO
PRO-PHAGE
ANA-PHASE
PRO-PHASE
SUB-PHASE
TRI-PHASE
CAM-PHENE
DIA-PHONE
EAR-PHONE
GEO-PHONE
SUL-PHONE
TRI-PHONE
GRY-PHONS
APO-PHONY
DIA-PHONY
SYM-PHONY
SUB-PHYLA
SAL-PIANS
UTO-PIANS
ABA-PICAL
ATY-PICAL
ETY-PICAL
TRO-PICAL
EAR-PICKS
NIT-PICKS
NUT-PICKS
RAM-PICKS
NIT-PICKY
COD-PIECE
EAR-PIECE
EYE-PIECE
SEA-PIECE
TOE-PIECE
DRA-PIERS
RIP-PIERS
DES-PIGHT
GAR-PIKES
MUS-PIKES
RAM-PIKES
RAN-PIKES
COM-PILED
COM-PILER
COM-PILES
HUI-PILES
FOR-PINED
PRO-PINED
ALE-PINES
CHO-PINES
FOR-PINES
PRO-PINES
TRO-PINES
BUM-PINGS
CAM-PINGS
CAP-PINGS
CAR-PINGS
COM-PINGS
CUP-PINGS
DAM-PINGS

DIP-PINGS
DOP-PINGS
DUM-PINGS
GAS-PINGS
HAR-PINGS
HEL-PINGS
HIP-PINGS
HOP-PINGS
KEE-PINGS
KEM-PINGS
LAM-PINGS
LAP-PINGS
LIM-PINGS
LIP-PINGS
LIS-PINGS
LOO-PINGS
LOP-PINGS
MAP-PINGS
RAM-PINGS
RAP-PINGS
RAS-PINGS
REP-PINGS
RIS-PINGS
SHA-PINGS
SNI-PINGS
SOO-PINGS
SOP-PINGS
STO-PINGS
TAM-PINGS
TAP-PINGS
TIP-PINGS
TOP-PINGS
VAM-PINGS
WAR-PINGS
WEE-PINGS
YAW-PINGS
YEL-PINGS
CAM-PIONS
LAM-PIONS
POM-PIONS
PUM-PIONS
RAM-PIONS
TAM-PIONS
TOM-PIONS
BAG-PIPER
BAG-PIPES
PAN-PIPES
DES-PISES
JAS-PISES
KAL-PISES
FLY-PITCH
OUT-PITCH
ANY-PLACE
DIS-PLACE
MIS-PLACE
OUT-PLACE
PRE-PLACE
CHA-PLAIN
COM-PLAIN
AIR-PLANE
JET-PLANE
SEA-PLANE
SKI-PLANE
SPY-PLANE
TRI-PLANE
VOL-PLANE
WAR-PLANE
MIS-PLANS
OUT-PLANS
PRE-PLANS
ASH-PLANT
DIS PLANT
EGG-PLANT
MIS-PLANT
PIE-PLANT

PRE-PLANT
SUP-PLANT
WAX-PLANT
SHI-PLAPS
WHI-PLASH
AXO-PLASM
BIO-PLASM
EXO-PLASM
NEO-PLASM
BIO-PLAST
SYM-PLAST
BED-PLATE
END-PLATE
OMO-PLATE
TEM-PLATE
TIN-PLATE
TOE-PLATE
VAM-PLATE
AIR-PLAYS
DIS-PLAYS
GUN-PLAYS
MIS-PLAYS
NON-PLAYS
OUT-PLAYS
MIS-PLEAD
COM-PLEAT
COM-PLIED
SUP-PLIED
TRI-PLIED
COM-PLIER
DIM-PLIER
PIM-PLIER
POP-PLIER
PUR-PLIER
RIP-PLIER
RUM-PLIER
SUP-PLIER
COM-PLIES
SUP-PLIES
TRI-PLIES
CAM-PLING
COU-PLING
DAP-PLING
DIM-PLING
DIS-PLING
DUM-PLING
HIR-PLING
HOP-PLING
NIP-PLING
PEO-PLING
POP-PLING
PUR-PLING
RIM-PLING
RIP-PLING
RUM-PLING
SAM-PLING
SAP-PLING
SIM-PLING
SIP-PLING
SOU-PLING
STA-PLING
SUP-PLING
TIP-PLING
TOP-PLING
TRI-PLING
WIM-PLING
OUT-PLODS
COW-PLOPS
COM-PLOTS
MAR-PLOTS
OUT-PLOTS
SUB-PLOTS
EAR-PLUGS
DIS-PLUME
KER-PLUNK
TRI-PODAL
URO-PODAL
SYM-PODIA
ACU-POINT
DEW-POINT
DRY-POINT
END-POINT
EYE-POINT
GUN-POINT
MID-POINT
MIS-POINT
NON-POINT
OUT-POINT
PAR-POINT
PEN-POINT
PIN-POINT
MIS-POISE
POR-POISE
COW-POKES
NON-POLAR
SUB-POLAR
UNI-POLAR
MAY-POLES
RAM-POLES
TAD-POLES
PRO-POLIS
TRI-POLIS
OUT-POLLS
RED-POLLS
DES-PONDS
RES-PONDS
DIS-PONES
PRE-PONES
PRO-PONES
ARA-PONGA
CAM-PONGS
KAM-PONGS
CAR-POOLS
VAN-POOLS
HAR-POONS
LAM-POONS
POM-POONS
COR-PORAL
TEM-PORAL
SUN-PORCH
OOS-PORES
AIR-PORTS
BES-PORTS
CAR-PORTS
COM-PORTS
DIS-PORTS
GOS-PORTS
GUN-PORTS
JET-PORTS
OUT-PORTS
PUR-PORTS
RAP-PORTS
SEA-PORTS
SUP-PORTS
COM-POSED
DIS-POSED
MAL-POSED
PRE-POSED
PRO-POSED
PUR-POSED
SUP-POSED
COM-POSER
DIS-POSER
PRO-POSER
SUP-POSER
ADI-POSES
COM-POSES
DIS-POSES
PRE-POSES
PRO-POSES
PUR-POSES
SUP-POSES
TRI-POSES
OVI-POSIT
AIR-POSTS
BED-POSTS
COM-POSTS
DIS-POSTS
OUT-POSTS
WAY-POSTS
COM-POTES
COM-POUND
GEE-POUND
LIS-POUND
PRO-POUND
OUT-POURS
BES-POUTS
DRO-POUTS
EEL-POUTS
SLI-POUTS
AIR-POWER
MAN-POWER
OUT-POWER
WAR-POWER
COW-POXES
RES-PRANG
UPS-PRANG
STU-PRATE
OUT-PRAYS
RES-PRAYS
WHI-PRAYS
OUT-PREEN
BES-PRENT
COM-PRESS
HOT-PRESS
OUT-PRESS
SUP-PRESS
KOU-PREYS
LAM-PREYS
MIS-PRICE
OUT-PRICE
PRE-PRICE
PIN-PRICK
COM-PRINT
MIS-PRINT
NON-PRINT
OFF-PRINT
PRE-PRINT
SUR-PRINT
SUB-PRIOR
COM-PRISE
MES-PRISE
MIS-PRISE
SUR-PRISE
COM-PRIZE
DIS-PRIZE
MES-PRIZE
MIS-PRIZE
OUT-PRIZE
SUR-PRIZE
GEO-PROBE
AIR-PROOF
DIS-PROOF
OIL-PROOF
RAT-PROOF
SUN-PROOF
WET-PROOF
PIT-PROPS
MIS-PROUD
DIS-PROVE
SUB-PUBIC
PRE-PUCES
SEP-PUKUS
SCA-PULAS
SCO-PULAS
STI-PULED
STI-PULES
OUT-PULLS
COM-PULSE
KEY-PUNCH
OUT-PUNCH
PRE-PUNCH
ARA-PUNGA
TRA-PUNTO
PRE-PUPAL
MUD-PUPPY
COU-PURES
GUI-PURES
PUR-PURES
PUR-PURIN
CUT-PURSE
DIS-PURSE
CAM-PUSES
GAU-PUSES
GAW-PUSES
HIP-PUSES
MAW-PUSES
PAP-PUSES
RUM-PUSES
WAM-PUSES
PRO-PYLON
SEA-QUAKE
ALI-QUANT
MUS-QUASH
ADE-QUATE
COE-QUATE
TOR-QUATE
CUM-QUATS
KUM-QUATS
COT-QUEAN
CON-QUEST
OPA-QUEST
UNI-QUEST
LAC-QUEYS
DIS-QUIET
BED-QUILT
BAS-QUINE
MES-QUINE
REE-QUIPS
VER-QUIRE
MES-QUITE
MEZ-QUITE
MES-QUITS
MEZ-QUITS
NON-QUOTA
MIS-QUOTE
OUT-QUOTE
AGG-RACED
EMB-RACED
ENG-RACED
OUT-RACED
REB-RACED
RET-RACED
TER-RACED
UNB-RACED
UNG-RACED
UNT-RACED
EMB-RACER
AGG-RACES
BAR-RACES
EMB-RACES
ENG-RACES
OUT-RACES
REB-RACES
RET-RACES
SUB-RACES
TER-RACES
THO-RACES
UNB-RACES
UNT-RACES
HUA-RACHE
AMT-RACKS
BAR-RACKS
CAR-RACKS
HAT-RACKS
HAY-RACKS
RET-RACKS
OST-RACON
PER-RADII
ENG-RAFFS
ENG-RAFTS
IND-RAFTS
ING-RAFTS
RED-RAFTS
REG-RAFTS
UPD-RAFTS
SMA-RAGDE
AVE-RAGED
BAR-RAGED
OUT-RAGED
OVE-RAGED
UMB-RAGED
AVE-RAGES
BAR-RAGES
BEE-RAGES
COU-RAGES
LAI-RAGES
MOO-RAGES
OUT-RAGES
OUV-RAGES
OVE-RAGES
PEE-RAGES
PIE-RAGES
STO-RAGES
UMB-RAGES
VIT-RAGES
HOO-RAHED
HUR-RAHED
EMB-RAIDS
UNB-RAIDS
UPB-RAIDS
BED-RAILS
ENG-RAILS
ENT-RAILS
PED-RAILS
DAR-RAINE
MIG-RAINE
CLA-RAINS
DAR-RAINS
DET-RAINS
ENG-RAINS
ENT-RAINS
ING-RAINS
MUR-RAINS
REF-RAINS
RET-RAINS
TER-RAINS
UPT-RAINS
VIT-RAINS
APP-RAISE
BEP-RAISE
MIS-RAISE
OUT-RAISE
UNP-RAISE
EXT-RAITS
RET-RAITS
SVA-RAJES
SWA-RAJES
UNB-RAKED
UNB-RAKES
BUN-RAKUS
CHO-RALES
PET-RALES
ABO-RALLY
AMO-RALLY
AST-RALLY
CHO-RALLY
FLO-RALLY
NEU-RALLY
PLU-RALLY
RET-RALLY
SPI-RALLY
GOU-RAMIS
MAC-RAMIS
OFF-RAMPS
GUA-RANAS
AMO-RANCE
ENT-RANCE
ITE-RANCE
OUT-RANCE
VIB-RANCE
REB-RANCH
OPE-RANDS
WAR-RANDS
CIT-RANGE
EST-RANGE
MID-RANGE
OUT-RANGE
SER-RANID
GUA-RANIS
DIS-RANKS
OUT-RANKS
AMA-RANTS
COU-RANTS
CUR-RANTS
ENT-RANTS
HYD-RANTS
INT-RANTS
MIG-RANTS
ODO-RANTS
OPE-RANTS
REG-RANTS
SPI-RANTS
TIT-RANTS
VAG-RANTS
VIB-RANTS
WAR-RANTS
BED-RAPED
UND-RAPED
BED-RAPES
IGA-RAPES
UND-RAPES
INF-RARED
ULT-RARED
UNE-RASED
APY-RASES
CHA-RASES
HYD-RASES
MAD-RASES
NAR-RASES
SUC-RASES
TAR-RASES
TER-RASES
ENG-RASPS
ACE-RATED
AGG-RATED
CIT-RATED
DIS-RATED
EPU-RATED
EVI-RATED
HYD-RATED
ITE-RATED
LIB-RATED
MIG-RATED
MIS-RATED
NAR-RATED
NIT-RATED
NON-RATED
OPE-RATED
OUT-RATED

PIC-RATED
PRO-RATED
REC-RATED
REG-RATED
RET-RATED
SER-RATED
SPI-RATED
TIT-RATED
UMB-RATED
UNC-RATED
VIB-RATED
BAR-RATER
NAR-RATER
REG-RATER
AGG-RATES
AMI-RATES
CAP-RATES
CED-RATES
CIT-RATES
DIS-RATES
EMI-RATES
EPU-RATES
EVI-RATES
FER-RATES
HYD-RATES
ING-RATES
ITE-RATES
LIB-RATES
MIG-RATES
MIS-RATES
NAR-RATES
NIT-RATES
OPE-RATES
OUT-RATES
PHO-RATES
PIC-RATES
PRO-RATES
REC-RATES
REG-RATES
RET-RATES
SER-RATES
TIT-RATES
UNC-RATES
VIB-RATES
VIB-RATOS
SER-RATUS
DEP-RAVED
EMB-RAVED
ENG-RAVED
OUT-RAVED
ENG-RAVEN
DEP-RAVER
ENG-RAVER
DEP-RAVES
EMB-RAVES
ENG-RAVES
OUT-RAVES
RED-RAWER
STO-RAXES
STY-RAXES
THO-RAXES
AFF-RAYED
BET-RAYED
BEW-RAYED
DEF-RAYED
EST-RAYED
FOR-RAYED
HOO-RAYED
HUR-RAYED
UNP-RAYED
UPB-RAYED
WAR-RAYED
UNG-RAZED
OUT-REACH
UNP-REACH
BET-READS
EMB-READS
MIS-READS
OUT-READS
RET-READS
UNT-READS
INB-REAKS
UPB-REAKS
RED-REAMS
COC-REATE
INC-REATE
LAU-REATE
OCH-REATE
REC-REATE
UNC-REATE
SUR-REBUT
REG-REDED
HAE-REDES
REG-REDES
SAC-REDLY
UNB-REECH
INB-REEDS
JER-REEDS
REB-REEDS
UNG-REEDY
SHE-REEFS
REG-REENS
TER-REENS
REP-REEVE
MIS-REFER
OUT-REIGN
MUR-RELET
CHO-REMAN
SHA-REMAN
SHI-REMAN
SHO-REMAN
STO-REMAN
CHO-REMEN
SHA-REMEN
SHI-REMEN
SHO-REMEN
STO-REMEN
PRE-RENAL
UPT-RENDS
YEA-RENDS
CUR-RENTS
MAN-RENTS
SUB-RENTS
TOR-RENTS
ENT-REPOT
ANU-RESES
CYP-RESES
DIE-RESES
DIU-RESES
ENU-RESES
IMP-RESES
ARM-RESTS
IMP-RESTS
ACC-RETES
EXC-RETES
SEC-RETES
AUB-RETIA
BAR-RETRY
ACC-REWED
DEC-REWED
EMB-REWED
MUR-RHINE
MYR-RHINE
DEC-RIALS
GHA-RIALS
PAI-RIALS
PAT-RIALS
RET-RIALS
HAU-RIANT
ASC-RIBES
ESC-RIBES
REP-RICED
UNP-RICED
ALT-RICES
AVA-RICES
CAP-RICES
IMB-RICES
MAT-RICES
MOR-RICES
NOU-RICES
OPO-RICES
REP-RICES
TUT-RICES
DER-RICKS
HAY-RICKS
PAT-RICKS
FLO-RIDER
HOR-RIDER
JOY-RIDER
LOW-RIDER
MAN-RIDER
OUT-RIDER
PUT-RIDER
TOR-RIDER
CYP-RIDES
DEB-RIDES
HAG-RIDES
HAY-RIDES
HYD-RIDES
JOY-RIDES
NIT-RIDES
OUT-RIDES
EST-RIDGE
PAR-RIDGE
POR-RIDGE
POR-RIDGY
AGG-RIEVE
ENG-RIEVE
REP-RIEVE
RET-RIEVE
THU-RIFER
MID-RIFFS
SHE-RIFFS
AFF-RIGHT
BED-RIGHT
OUT-RIGHT
UNB-RIGHT
NON-RIGID
FAV-RILES
NIT-RILES
MOO-RILLS
RED-RILLS
BEC-RIMED
BEG-RIMED
REP-RIMED
UNP-RIMED
BEC-RIMES
BEG-RIMES
REP-RIMES
REG-RINDS
ACA-RINES
AZU-RINES
CHO-RINES
CIT-RINES
DOU-RINES
ESE-RINES
LAT-RINES
NEU-RINES
PEB-RINES
TAU-RINES
TER-RINES
VIT-RINES
BAR-RINGS
BEA-RINGS
EAR-RINGS
FAI-RINGS
FEE-RINGS
FIR-RINGS
FUR-RINGS
GEA-RINGS
HEA-RINGS
HER-RINGS
INB-RINGS
JAR-RINGS
JEE-RINGS
LEE-RINGS
LOU-RINGS
MOO-RINGS
OUT-RINGS
PAI-RINGS
POU-RINGS
PUR-RINGS
ROA-RINGS
SAC-RINGS
SCO-RINGS
SEA-RINGS
SHA-RINGS
SHO-RINGS
SNA-RINGS
SNO-RINGS
SOA-RINGS
SOU-RINGS
STA-RINGS
SUB-RINGS
TAR-RINGS
TOU-RINGS
UPB-RINGS
VEE-RINGS
WEA-RINGS
PRE-RINSE
CHA-RIOTS
PAT-RIOTS
CIR-RIPED
REA-RISEN
UNA-RISEN
APP-RISER
APP-RISES
CER-RISES
CHO-RISES
DER-RISES
DIA-RISES
ECC-RISES
EMP-RISES
HUB-RISES
HYB-RISES
IBE-RISES
IND-RISES
LAI-RISES
MOR-RISES
NEB-RISES
REA-RISES
REP-RISES
SUN-RISES
TSU-RISES
ATT-RITES
AZU-RITES
COW-RITES
CUP-RITES
DIO-RITES
EUC-RITES
FER-RITES
GUE-RITES
NAC-RITES
NEU-RITES
NIT-RITES
PIC-RITES
REW-RITES
THO-RITES
UNW-RITES
YPE-RITES
COR-RIVAL
DEP-RIVAL
NON-RIVAL
OUT-RIVAL
DEP-RIVED
REP-RIVED
BED-RIVEL
COD-RIVEN
RED-RIVEN
UND-RIVEN
COD-RIVER
DEP-RIVER
COD-RIVES
DEP-RIVES
RED-RIVES
REP-RIVES
APP-ROACH
ENC-ROACH
REP-ROACH
BEG-ROANS
OUT-ROARS
CAP-ROATE
DIS-ROBED
REP-ROBED
UNP-ROBED
DIS-ROBES
MIC-ROBES
REP-ROBES
SAP-ROBES
SEA-ROBIN
BED-ROCKS
CAP-ROCKS
DEF-ROCKS
LAV-ROCKS
MUD-ROCKS
OUT-ROCKS
PAR-ROCKS
RIM-ROCKS
SOU-ROCKS
TAR-ROCKS
UNF-ROCKS
COR-RODED
COR-RODES
TET-RODES
PRO-ROGUE
EMB-ROILS
FIB-ROINS
LIG-ROINS
PYR-ROLES
SAF-ROLES
BED-ROLLS
ESC-ROLLS
LOG-ROLLS
OUT-ROLLS
PAY-ROLLS
FIB-ROMAS
NEU-ROMAS
PLE-ROMAS
EST-RONES
LAD-RONES
MAD-RONES
MUC-RONES
NEU-RONES
PAD-RONES
PAT-RONNE
AFF-RONTE
AFF-RONTS
REF-RONTS
APP-ROOFS
REP-ROOFS
SUN-ROOFS
BAR-ROOMS
BED-ROOMS
BOX-ROOMS
DAY-ROOMS
GUN-ROOMS
LEG-ROOMS
MUD-ROOMS
REG-ROOMS
SUN-ROOMS
TAP-ROOMS
TEA-ROOMS
GAD-ROONS
GOD-ROONS
PAT-ROONS
OUT-ROOPS
CHE-ROOTS
DIS-ROOTS
OUT-ROOTS
RED-ROOTS
SHE-ROOTS
TAP-ROOTS
IMP-ROPER
OUT-ROPER
UNP-ROPER
MAN-ROPES
OUT-ROPES
TOW-ROPES
BEP-ROSED
FIB-ROSED
NEC-ROSED
AGA-ROSES
BEP-ROSES
FIB-ROSES
HID-ROSES
NEC-ROSES
NEU-ROSES
PHA-ROSES
SUC-ROSES
CHA-ROSET
NIG-ROSIN
DEF-ROSTS
DIC-ROTAL
BIR-ROTCH
GAR-ROTED
PAR-ROTED
GAR-ROTES
GAR-ROTTE
THO-ROUGH
REG-ROUND
RUN-ROUND
SUR-ROUND
UNG-ROUND
ING-ROUPS
REG-ROUPS
REA-ROUSE
MIS-ROUTE
APP-ROVED
IMP-ROVED
REP-ROVED
UNP-ROVED
UNP-ROVEN
APP-ROVER
IMP-ROVER
REP-ROVER
APP-ROVES
IMP-ROVES
REP-ROVES
BOR-ROWED
BUR-ROWED
ESC-ROWED
FAR-ROWED
FUR-ROWED
HAR-ROWED
MAR-ROWED
NAR-ROWED
OUT-ROWED
SOR-ROWED
TAR-ROWED
BOR-ROWER

BUR-ROWER
FUR-ROWER
HAR-ROWER
NAR-ROWER
SOR-ROWER
ING-ROWTH
REG-ROWTH
UPG-ROWTH
NON-ROYAL
SUR-ROYAL
CHE-RUBIN
EXT-RUDER
INT-RUDER
OBT-RUDER
DET-RUDES
EXT-RUDES
INT-RUDES
OBT-RUDES
INF-RUGAL
ACC-RUING
EMB-RUING
IMB-RUING
FER-RULED
MIS-RULED
FER-RULES
MIS-RULES
SPO-RULES
SUB-RULES
ZEB-RULES
UNP-RUNED
MAC-RURAL
NON-RURAL
CHO-RUSES
CIT-RUSES
CYP-RUSES
EST-RUSES
MIU-RUSES
OVE-RUSES
UTE-RUSES
WAL-RUSES
BUL-RUSHY
BEC-RUSTS
ENC-RUSTS
ENT-RUSTS
INC-RUSTS
INT-RUSTS
UNT-RUSTS
UNT-RUSTY
UNT-RUTHS
ABU-SABLE
AMU-SABLE
CAU-SABLE
CLO-SABLE
ERA-SABLE
KIS-SABLE
LAP-SABLE
LEA-SABLE
MIS-SABLE
PAR-SABLE
PAS-SABLE
RAI-SABLE
REU-SABLE
RIN-SABLE
SEI-SABLE
UNU-SABLE
COS-SACKS
DAY-SACKS
HOP-SACKS
RAN-SACKS
CRU-SADES
DIP-SADES
PAS-SADES
TOR-SADES
MAS-SAGER
PRE-SAGER

ABU-SAGES
COR-SAGES
MAS-SAGES
MES-SAGES
PAS-SAGES
PAY-SAGES
PLU-SAGES
PRE-SAGES
PRI-SAGES
SAU-SAGES
SAP-SAGOS
MEM-SAHIB
LUG-SAILS
OUT-SAILS
SKY-SAILS
TOP-SAILS
TRY-SAILS
VAS-SAILS
VES-SAILS
WAS-SAILS
COR-SAIRS
PRO-SAIST
FOR-SAKER
FOR-SAKES
SUB-SALES
CAU-SALLY
DOR-SALLY
OXY-SALTS
PER-SALTS
WEA-SANDS
WES-SANDS
LAP-SANGS
LIN-SANGS
PEA-SANTS
PIS-SANTS
VER-SANTS
GUI-SARDS
MAN-SARDS
IRI-SATED
PUL-SATED
SEN-SATED
IRI-SATES
PUL-SATES
SEN-SATES
SAK-SAULS
PER-SAUNT
DIS-SAVED
DIS-SAVES
OUT-SAVOR
JIG-SAWED
SEE-SAWED
NAY-SAYER
YEA-SAYER
SUN-SCALD
SUB-SCALE
AIR-SCAPE
SEA-SCAPE
SKY-SCAPE
TWI-SCARS
REA-SCEND
ACE-SCENT
CRE-SCENT
REA-SCENT
OUT-SCOLD
OUT-SCOOP
BIO-SCOPE
DIA-SCOPE
EPI-SCOPE
IRI-SCOPE
MYO-SCOPE
OTO-SCOPE
OUT-SCORE
PRE-SCORE
SIX-SCORE
OUT-SCORN

SEA-SCOUT
MUD-SCOWS
AIR-SCREW
SET-SCREW
OFF-SCUMS
PRE-SCUTA
DEI-SEALS
DIS-SEATS
MIS-SEATS
DIS-SECTS
PRO-SECTS
SUB-SECTS
TRI-SECTS
CUR-SEDER
NUT-SEDGE
ALL-SEEDS
ANI-SEEDS
BUG-SEEDS
BUR-SEEDS
HAY-SEEDS
LIN-SEEDS
MAW-SEEDS
OIL-SEEDS
BER-SEEMS
MIS-SEEMS
MAH-SEERS
CON-SEILS
DIS-SEISE
PER-SEITY
DIS-SEIZE
BON-SELLA
TES-SELLA
VUL-SELLA
MAM-SELLE
AIN-SELLS
NOU-SELLS
OUT-SELLS
PRE-SELLS
TAS-SELLS
WOO-SELLS
HOR-SEMEN
HOU-SEMEN
PRO-SEMEN
VER-SEMEN
TRI-SEMES
GOD-SENDS
MIS-SENDS
MIS-SENSE
NON-SENSE
SUB-SENSE
CON-SENTS
DIS-SENTS
PRE-SENTS
TES-SERAL
PRI-SERES
SUB-SERES
SAN-SERIF
KAI-SERIN
BER-SERKS
CON-SERVE
DIS-SERVE
OUT-SERVE
PRE-SERVE
SUB-SERVE
BAS-SETTS
WAD-SETTS
DIS-SEVER
WHO-SEVER
PUR-SEWED
UNI-SEXES
EYE-SHADE
SUN-SHADE
AIR-SHAFT
CAM-SHAFT
SUB-SHAFT

PAD-SHAHS
MAR-SHALL
OUT-SHAME
RED-SHANK
DAR-SHANS
MIS-SHAPE
PRE-SHAPE
POT-SHARD
JOB-SHARE
POT-SHARE
RED-SHARE
FOX-SHARK
SAW-SHARK
CUM-SHAWS
RIK-SHAWS
TRI-SHAWS
DEI-SHEAL
AIR-SHEDS
COW-SHEDS
DRI-SHEEN
BED-SHEET
EGG-SHELL
NUT-SHELL
SEA-SHELL
SUB-SHELL
POT-SHERD
BLU-SHETS
FRE-SHETS
PLA-SHETS
BLA-SHIER
BOL-SHIER
BRA-SHIER
BRU-SHIER
FLA-SHIER
FLE-SHIER
FLU-SHIER
MAR-SHIER
PLA-SHIER
PLU-SHIER
SLO-SHIER
SLU-SHIER
SPO-SHIER
SWA-SHIER
SWI-SHIER
TRA-SHIER
BAN-SHIES
BOL-SHIES
QUA-SHIES
STA-SHIES
STI-SHIES
STU-SHIES
TUM-SHIES
MAN-SHIFT
RED-SHIFT
FLA-SHILY
PLU-SHILY
SLU-SHILY
TRA-SHILY
OUT-SHINE
SUN-SHINE
SUN-SHINY
AIR-SHIPS
DOG-SHIPS
DON-SHIPS
END-SHIPS
FOX-SHIPS
GOD-SHIPS
GUN-SHIPS
HER-SHIPS
KIN-SHIPS
LUD-SHIPS
MID-SHIPS
NUN-SHIPS
PAL-SHIPS
SIB-SHIPS

SON-SHIPS
WAR-SHIPS
WOR-SHIPS
RED-SHIRE
RED-SHIRT
GOB-SHITE
GUM-SHOED
GUM-SHOES
TOE-SHOES
OUT-SHONE
ATI-SHOOS
SAM-SHOOS
OFF-SHOOT
OUT-SHOOT
COP-SHOPS
GIN-SHOPS
POT-SHOPS
TEA-SHOPS
TOY-SHOPS
OFF-SHORE
SEA-SHORE
GEM-SHORN
RAM-SHORN
RED-SHORT
BOW-SHOTS
EAR-SHOTS
EYE-SHOTS
GUN-SHOTS
HOT-SHOTS
MUG-SHOTS
OUT-SHOTS
POT-SHOTS
OUT-SHOUT
PRE-SHOWN
PRE-SHOWS
SUB-SHRUB
PEI-SHWAS
FOS-SICKS
LOP-SIDED
PRE-SIDED
SUB-SIDED
CON-SIDER
OFF-SIDER
OUT-SIDER
PRE-SIDER
SUB-SIDER
TOP-SIDER
AIR-SIDES
BED-SIDES
DAY-SIDES
DEP-SIDES
FAR-SIDES
OFF-SIDES
OUT-SIDES
PRE-SIDES
SEA-SIDES
SUB-SIDES
TOP-SIDES
WAY-SIDES
MON-SIEUR
PRE-SIFTS
DIS-SIGHT
EYE-SIGHT
OUT-SIGHT
CON-SIGNS
MIS-SILES
MUD-SILLS
COO-SINED
ARC-SINES
CUI-SINES
PEP-SINES
VER-SINES
BIA-SINGS
BUS-SINGS
CEA-SINGS

CHA-SINGS
CLO-SINGS
CUR-SINGS
GAS-SINGS
GUI-SINGS
HIS-SINGS
HOR-SINGS
HOU-SINGS
LEA-SINGS
MOU-SINGS
NUR-SINGS
OUT-SINGS
PAR-SINGS
PAS-SINGS
PAU-SINGS
PRO-SINGS
RAI-SINGS
RIN-SINGS
SEI-SINGS
SEN-SINGS
SOS-SINGS
SOU-SINGS
TEA-SINGS
TOS-SINGS
TOU-SINGS
VER-SINGS
FIS-SIPED
GOS-SIPED
TAR-SIPED
CAS-SISES
ECE-SISES
ENO-SISES
MIS-SISES
NOE-SISES
TUS-SISES
WHO-SISES
BAS-SISTS
CON-SISTS
PER-SISTS
SEN-SISTS
SUB-SISTS
AMO-SITES
COE-SITES
FEL-SITES
HES-SITES
INO-SITES
SUB-SITES
WEB-SITES
ZOI-SITES
SUB-SIZAR
CAP-SIZED
MID-SIZED
OUT-SIZED
CAP-SIZES
OUT-SIZES
OUT-SKATE
FRI-SKERS
WHI-SKERS
FLI-SKIER
FRI-SKIER
NON-SKIER
DRO-SKIES
PLI-SKIES
WHI-SKIES
SUB-SKILL
CAT-SKINS
COW-SKINS
DOE-SKINS
DOG-SKINS
FOX-SKINS
GRI-SKINS
KID-SKINS
KIP-SKINS
OIL-SKINS
PIG-SKINS

RED-SKINS
OUT-SKIRT
NUM-SKULL
FOR-SLACK
PUR-SLAIN
PUR-SLANE
BOB-SLEDS
DOG-SLEDS
DOG-SLEEP
OUT-SLEEP
PRE-SLEEP
OUT-SLEPT
PAI-SLEYS
PAR-SLEYS
PUS-SLEYS
PRE-SLICE
OUT-SLICK
MUD-SLIDE
GRI-SLIER
MEA-SLIER
BIR-SLING
BRI-SLING
ENI-SLING
FIS-SLING
HAS-SLING
HIR-SLING
HOU-SLING
INI-SLING
MEA-SLING
MOU-SLING
NOU-SLING
NUR-SLING
QUI-SLING
RAS-SLING
RIE-SLING
TOU-SLING
TUS-SLING
WAR-SLING
COW-SLIPS
PAY-SLIPS
FOR-SLOES
FOR-SLOWS
OUT-SMART
MOU-SMEES
OUT-SMILE
GUN-SMITH
TIN-SMITH
OUT-SMOKE
COR-SNEDS
PIG-SNIES
PAR-SNIPS
TIN-SNIPS
OUT-SNORE
PRE-SOAKS
OUT-SOARS
BED-SOCKS
CAS-SOCKS
HAS-SOCKS
LAS-SOCKS
TUS-SOCKS
EPI-SODIC
PRO-SODIC
DEA-SOILS
SUB-SOILS
TOP-SOILS
NON-SOLAR
SUB-SOLAR
CON-SOLED
CON-SOLER
ANI-SOLES
CON-SOLES
MID-SOLES
OUT-SOLES
RIS-SOLES
NON-SOLID

DIS-SOLVE
PRO-SOMAS
CAS-SONES
DAP-SONES
SUB-SONGS
PAR-SONIC
SUB-SONIC
TEL-SONIC
RAI-SONNE
FOR-SOOTH
PAN-SOPHY
CEN-SORED
BED-SORES
CUR-SORES
EYE-SORES
TUS-SORES
ALL-SORTS
CON-SORTS
MIS-SORTS
PRE-SORTS
MIS-SOUND
MIS-SOUTS
PAS-SOUTS
LEA-SOWED
AIR-SPACE
MID-SPACE
MIS-SPACE
SUB-SPACE
OUT-SPANS
FEL-SPARS
CRI-SPATE
CAT-SPAWS
FOR-SPEAK
MIS-SPEAK
NEW-SPEAK
OUT-SPEAK
SEA-SPEAK
FLY-SPECK
KEN-SPECK
AIR-SPEED
GOD-SPEED
OUT-SPEED
BON-SPELL
MIS-SPELL
OUT-SPELL
MIS-SPELT
OUT-SPELT
FOR-SPEND
MIS-SPEND
OUT-SPEND
FOR-SPENT
MIS-SPENT
OUT-SPENT
EPI-SPERM
ZOO-SPERM
ALL-SPICE
UNE-SPIED
BON-SPIEL
CRI-SPIER
CRI-SPINS
ISO-SPINS
TOP-SPINS
CON-SPIRE
PER-SPIRE
PER-SPIRY
CES-SPITS
PRE-SPLIT
FOR-SPOKE
MIS-SPOKE
OUT-SPOKE
CES-SPOOL
SES-SPOOL
TEA-SPOON
DIA-SPORE
EPI-SPORE

EXO-SPORE
ZOO-SPORE
MAR-SPORT
OUT-SPORT
PAS-SPORT
EYE-SPOTS
FUS-SPOTS
INK-SPOTS
SUN-SPOTS
TOS-SPOTS
BOW-SPRIT
HOT-SPURS
OLD-SQUAW
HAY-STACK
PAL-STAFF
TIP-STAFF
OFF-STAGE
SUB-STAGE
EYE-STALK
BOR-STALL
LAY-STALL
PRE-STAMP
BED-STAND
CAB-STAND
HAT-STAND
INK-STAND
OUT-STAND
CAM-STANE
PRI-STANE
OUT-STARE
DAY-STARS
MIS-START
OUT-START
RED-START
APO-STATE
ARI-STATE
CON-STATE
CRI-STATE
CRU-STATE
ECO-STATE
MIS-STATE
OUT-STATE
PRO-STATE
SUB-STATE
TRI-STATE
PAL-STAVE
BOB-STAYS
OUT-STAYS
BED-STEAD
BIL-STEDS
FRO-STEDS
OER-STEDS
WOR-STEDS
TRU-STEED
MIS-STEER
OUT-STEER
EIN-STEIN
HOL-STEIN
DIA-STEMS
CHA-STENS
GLI-STENS
GUE-STENS
MOI-STENS
EXI-STENT
MIS-STEPS
OUT-STEPS
TRI-STICH
CAN-STICK
DIP-STICK
GUN-STICK
JOY-STICK
LIP-STICK
LOB-STICK
LOP-STICK
MAL-STICK

MAP-STICK
MOP-STICK
NON-STICK
PIG-STICK
BEA-STIES
BHI-STIES
BLA-STIES
CRU-STIES
PIG-STIES
PRO-STIES
TOA-STIES
TRU-STIES
ADU-STING
AGI-STING
BLA-STING
BOA-STING
BOO-STING
BRA-STING
BRU-STING
BUI-STING
BUR-STING
CHE-STING
COA-STING
CRE-STING
CRU-STING
EGE-STING
EXI-STING
FEA-STING
FOI-STING
FRI-STING
FRO-STING
GHA-STING
GHO-STING
GIU-STING
GUE-STING
HEI-STING
HOA-STING
HOI-STING
JOI-STING
JOU-STING
MOI-STING
MOU-STING
MUI-STING
PRE-STING
QUE-STING
REA-STING
REE-STING
REI-STING
ROA-STING
ROI-STING
ROO-STING
ROU-STING
ROY-STING
TOA-STING
TRU-STING
TRY-STING
TWI-STING
WAI-STING
WHI-STING
WOR-STING
WRA-STING
WRE-STING
YEA-STING
EGE-STIVE
BIT-STOCK
DIE-STOCK
FAT-STOCK
GUN-STOCK
LIN-STOCK
PEN-STOCK
TIP-STOCK
ASY-STOLE
DIA-STOLE
BLA-STOMA
BUR-STONE

CAM-STONE
CAP-STONE
DRY-STONE
EAR-STONE
EYE-STONE
FEL-STONE
GEM-STONE
GUN-STONE
ICE-STONE
INK-STONE
KEY-STONE
LAP-STONE
MUD-STONE
OIL-STONE
POT-STONE
RAG-STONE
RIB-STONE
ROE-STONE
RUB-STONE
SUN-STONE
TIN-STONE
TOP-STONE
OUT-STOOD
BAR-STOOL
AIR-STOPS
MIS-STOPS
RIP-STOPS
HER-STORY
MID-STORY
NON-STORY
BED-STRAW
AIR-STRIP
OUT-STRIP
ANE-STRUM
DIE-STRUM
HUM-STRUM
PLA-STRUM
OUT-STUDY
DYE-STUFF
FRU-STUMS
OUT-STUNT
MOI-STURE
DIA-STYLE
EPI-STYLE
MIS-STYLE
NON-STYLE
OLD-STYLE
PRO-STYLE
SUB-STYLE
URO-STYLE
TUS-SUCKS
WAE-SUCKS
PUR-SUERS
NON-SUGAR
PER-SUING
PUR-SUING
TIS-SUING
CAT-SUITS
LAW-SUITS
MIS-SUITS
NON-SUITS
PUR-SUITS
SUN-SUITS
OUT-SULKS
CAE-SURAL
MEN-SURAL
CAE-SURAS
CEN-SURED
CLO-SURED
FIS-SURED
LEI-SURED
MEA-SURED
TON-SURED
CEN-SURER
MEA-SURER

BRI-SURES
CEN-SURES
CLO-SURES
ERA-SURES
FIS-SURES
FRI-SURES
LEA-SURES
LEI-SURES
MEA-SURES
MOR-SURES
SEA-SURES
SEI-SURES
SEY-SURES
TON-SURES
BYS-SUSES
CEN-SUSES
CIS-SUSES
MIS-SUSES
PAS-SUSES
RHE-SUSES
TAS-SWAGE
COX-SWAIN
OUT-SWARE
FOR-SWEAR
MEN-SWEAR
OUT-SWEAR
PEE-SWEEP
OUT-SWELL
PIG-SWILL
OUT-SWIMS
BAT-SWING
BEE-SWING
OUT-SWING
FOR-SWINK
NEW-SWIRE
CUS-SWORD
PAS-SWORD
FOR-SWORE
OUT-SWORE
FOR-SWORN
MAN-SWORN
OUT-SWORN
ABA-TABLE
AGI-TABLE
BEA-TABLE
BIS-TABLE
BOA-TABLE
BOO-TABLE
CAR-TABLE
CAS-TABLE
CUT-TABLE
EDI-TABLE
EVI-TABLE
FIT-TABLE
GET-TABLE
GUS-TABLE
HEA-TABLE
HUN-TABLE
IMI-TABLE
INS-TABLE
LET-TABLE
LIF-TABLE
LIS-TABLE
MEL-TABLE
MOO-TABLE
NES-TABLE
NET-TABLE
PAN-TABLE
PIN-TABLE
POR-TABLE
QUO-TABLE
REN-TABLE
RUS-TABLE
SOR-TABLE
STA-TABLE

SUI-TABLE
TAS-TABLE
TES-TABLE
TIL-TABLE
UNS-TABLE
WAS-TABLE
WET-TABLE
WRI-TABLE
CAT-TABUS
COT-TABUS
MUS-TACHE
PIS-TACHE
SOU-TACHE
ISO-TACHS
RES-TACKS
SUB-TACKS
TIE-TACKS
TIN-TACKS
UNS-TACKS
CON-TACTS
PEN-TACTS
SYN-TAGMA
BOB-TAILS
CAT-TAILS
CUR-TAILS
FAN-TAILS
FOX-TAILS
PIG-TAILS
PIN-TAILS
RAT-TAILS
RED-TAILS
VEN-TAILS
WAG-TAILS
ABS-TAINS
BES-TAINS
CAP-TAINS
CON-TAINS
CUR-TAINS
DES-TAINS
DIS-TAINS
HUI-TAINS
PER-TAINS
SEX-TAINS
SUS-TAINS
MIS-TAKEN
OUT-TAKEN
PAR-TAKEN
PER-TAKEN
MIS-TAKER
PAR-TAKER
MIS-TAKES
OFF-TAKES
OUT-TAKES
PAR-TAKES
PER-TAKES
SHI-TAKES
CAN-TALAS
DAY-TALER
DAY-TALES
SCY-TALES
OUT-TALKS
BRU-TALLY
COI-TALLY
DEN-TALLY
DIS-TALLY
FES-TALLY
MEN-TALLY
MOR-TALLY
POS-TALLY
REC-TALLY
VES-TALLY
PAN-TALON
TAN-TALUS
HIS-TAMIN
PRO-TAMIN

ENS-TAMPS
RES-TAMPS
CUR-TANAS
LAN-TANAS
SUL-TANAS
TAR-TANAS
VEN-TANAS
BOS-TANGI
CON-TANGO
MUS-TANGS
PLA-TANNA
MON-TANTO
PRE-TAPED
PRE-TAPES
WAT-TAPES
HAF-TARAS
TAN-TARAS
TUA-TARAS
BAS-TARDY
CUS-TARDY
DAS-TARDY
MUS-TARDY
MOR-TARED
NEC-TARED
UPS-TARED
CEN-TARES
HEC-TARES
HEK-TARES
LAE-TARES
TAR-TARES
UPS-TARES
HAF-TAROT
RES-TARTS
UPS-TARTS
OUT-TASKS
SUB-TASKS
DIS-TASTE
PRE-TASTE
UPS-TATER
ACE-TATES
AGI-TATES
CAN-TATES
DIC-TATES
EVI-TATES
GES-TATES
GUT-TATES
IMI-TATES
INS-TATES
LAC-TATES
NIC-TATES
PEC-TATES
RES-TATES
SAL-TATES
TES-TATES
UNS-TATES
UPS-TATES
SUR-TAXED
CUR-TAXES
GEO-TAXES
NON-TAXES
SUR-TAXES
SYN-TAXES
GEO-TAXIS
SUB-TAXON
MIS-TEACH
BES-TEADS
ONS-TEADS
LAC-TEALS
PRO-TEASE
BIO-TECHS
ZAI-TECHS
MAN-TEELS
UNS-TEELS
CAN-TEENS
FIF-TEENS

POS-TEENS
POT-TEENS
PRE-TEENS
RAT-TEENS
SIX-TEENS
SUB-TEENS
DOG-TEETH
EYE-TEETH
SAW-TEETH
EUS-TELES
KAN-TELES
MIS-TELLS
OUT-TELLS
SYS-TEMED
ERO-TEMES
CON-TEMPT
BAR-TENDS
CON-TENDS
DIS-TENDS
MIS-TENDS
POR-TENDS
PRE-TENDS
PRO-TENDS
SUB-TENDS
HAP-TENES
PEN-TENES
PRE-TENSE
PRO-TENSE
SUB-TENSE
CON-TENTS
POR-TENTS
DIP-TERAS
TUA-TERAS
SES-TERCE
HAL-TERES
MID-TERMS
MIS-TERMS
SAU-TERNE
BIT-TERNS
CIS-TERNS
CIT-TERNS
GIT-TERNS
LAN-TERNS
LEC-TERNS
LET-TERNS
PAS-TERNS
PAT-TERNS
POS-TERNS
SAL-TERNS
TES-TERNS
WES-TERNS
CON-TESTS
MOS-TESTS
PRE-TESTS
PRO-TESTS
SUB-TESTS
CON-TEXTS
MAR-TEXTS
PRE-TEXTS
SUB-TEXTS
URE-THANE
OUT-THANK
URE-THANS
XAN-THANS
XAN-THEIN
ANA-THEMA
EPI-THEMA
ERY-THEMA
SUB-THEME
BUR-THENS
HEA-THENS
YOU-THENS
ISO-THERE
ISO-THERM
AES-THETE

FOO-THILL
WAN-THILL
IAN-THINE
XAN-THINE
AIR-THING
ANY-THING
BEA-THING
BER-THING
BIR-THING
CLO-THING
EAR-THING
FAI-THING
FAR-THING
FRO-THING
GIR-THING
LOA-THING
MOU-THING
NAE-THING
NOR-THING
QUE-THING
SCA-THING
SCY-THING
SEE-THING
SLO-THING
SMI-THING
SOO-THING
SOU-THING
SOW-THING
SWA-THING
TEE-THING
TOO-THING
TRI-THING
TRO-THING
WOR-THING
WRA-THING
WRE-THING
WRI-THING
FOR-THINK
MIS-THINK
OUT-THINK
XAN-THINS
ANE-THOLE
BOL-THOLE
KNO-THOLE
PES-THOLE
POR-THOLE
POS-THOLE
SHI-THOLE
SHO-THOLE
BOX-THORN
HAW-THORN
LAN-THORN
BOO-THOSE
SPA-THOSE
APH-THOUS
XAN-THOUS
URE-THRAE
MIS-THREW
OUT-THREW
OUT-THROB
MIS-THROW
OUT-THROW
BIO-TICAL
COR-TICAL
CRI-TICAL
EME-TICAL
ERO-TICAL
FIS-TICAL
GES-TICAL
HAP-TICAL
HEC-TICAL
MYS-TICAL
NAU-TICAL
POE-TICAL
RUS-TICAL

SEP-TICAL
STA-TICAL
TAC-TICAL
THE-TICAL
TRI-TICAL
VER-TICAL
VIA-TICAL
VOR-TICAL
LAT-TICED
MOR-TICED
PEN-TICED
COR-TICES
FAC-TICES
FRU-TICES
JUS-TICES
LAT-TICES
MOR-TICES
PEN-TICES
STA-TICES
VER-TICES
VOR-TICES
BED-TICKS
BES-TICKS
SCH-TICKS
UNS-TICKS
STA-TICKY
NON-TIDAL
SUB-TIDAL
BAS-TIDES
EBB-TIDES
OTI-TIDES
PEP-TIDES
RIP-TIDES
TRI-TIDES
BUS-TIERS
COT-TIERS
EMP-TIERS
FLY-TIERS
PAR-TIERS
PUT-TIERS
REN-TIERS
SAL-TIERS
CAI-TIFFS
MAS-TIFFS
PON-TIFFS
SCU-TIGER
VEN-TIGES
VES-TIGES
AIR-TIGHT
GAS-TIGHT
OIL-TIGHT
DEN-TILED
PAN-TILED
FER-TILER
SUB-TILER
BAS-TILES
CEN-TILES
GEN-TILES
HOS-TILES
PAN-TILES
PON-TILES
REP-TILES
SEX-TILES
TEX-TILES
BAT-TILLS
BES-TILLS
DIS-TILLS
INS-TILLS
MIS-TIMED
RAG-TIMER
AIR-TIMES
BED-TIMES
CEN-TIMES
DAY-TIMES
LAY-TIMES

MIS-TIMES
OFT-TIMES
PAS-TIMES
RAG-TIMES
SEP-TIMES
TEA-TIMES
WAR-TIMES
DIS-TINCT
INS-TINCT
DES-TINED
BOT-TINES
CYS-TINES
DEN-TINES
DES-TINES
DIE-TINES
EME-TINES
ISA-TINES
PAN-TINES
PEC-TINES
ROU-TINES
SAL-TINES
SES-TINES
TAR-TINES
TON-TINES
BAI-TINGS
BAN-TINGS
BAS-TINGS
BAT-TINGS
BEA-TINGS
BEL-TINGS
BET-TINGS
BIT-TINGS
BOA-TINGS
BOL-TINGS
BRU-TINGS
BUN-TINGS
BUS-TINGS
CAN-TINGS
CAS-TINGS
COA-TINGS
CUT-TINGS
DOA-TINGS
DUC-TINGS
EAS-TINGS
EMP-TINGS
FAS-TINGS
FEL-TINGS
FIT-TINGS
FLU-TINGS
FLY-TINGS
FOO-TINGS
GET-TINGS
GRA-TINGS
HAL-TINGS
HAS-TINGS
HAT-TINGS
HEA-TINGS
HOS-TINGS
HOT-TINGS
HOU-TINGS
HUN-TINGS
HUS-TINGS
HUT-TINGS
JES-TINGS
JOT-TINGS
KAR-TINGS
KIL-TINGS
LAS-TINGS
LET-TINGS
LIS-TINGS
LOO-TINGS
MAL-TINGS
MAT-TINGS
MEE-TINGS
MEL-TINGS

MIS-TINGS
MOO-TINGS
MUN-TINGS
NES-TINGS
NET-TINGS
NUT-TINGS
PAN-TINGS
PAR-TINGS
PAS-TINGS
PEL-TINGS
PET-TINGS
PIT-TINGS
PLA-TINGS
POS-TINGS
POU-TINGS
PRA-TINGS
PUT-TINGS
RAN-TINGS
RAT-TINGS
RES-TINGS
RIO-TINGS
ROO-TINGS
ROU-TINGS
RUS-TINGS
RUT-TINGS
SAL-TINGS
SEA-TINGS
SET-TINGS
SIF-TINGS
SIT-TINGS
SKA-TINGS
SLA-TINGS
SOR-TINGS
SOT-TINGS
SUI-TINGS
TAS-TINGS
TAT-TINGS
TEN-TINGS
TES-TINGS
TIL-TINGS
TIN-TINGS
TOT-TINGS
TUF-TINGS
TUT-TINGS
UNI-TINGS
VEN-TINGS
VES-TINGS
WAF-TINGS
WAI-TINGS
WAN-TINGS
WAS-TINGS
WEL-TINGS
WES-TINGS
WET-TINGS
WHI-TINGS
WIT-TINGS
WRI-TINGS
SAL-TIRES
RES-TITCH
UNS-TITCH
AOR-TITIS
CYS-TITIS
MAS-TITIS
OUS-TITIS
REC-TITIS
WIS-TITIS
MIS-TITLE
NON-TITLE
SUB-TITLE
SUR-TITLE
HOP-TOADS
BIT-TOCKS
BUT-TOCKS
CAS-TOCKS
CUS-TOCKS
FUT-TOCKS
HAT-TOCKS
MAT-TOCKS
PUT-TOCKS
RES-TOCKS
UNS-TOCKS
CAS-TOFFS
DUS-TOFFS
LIF-TOFFS
SHU-TOFFS
POR-TOISE
TOR-TOISE
RES-TOKED
RES-TOKES
POR-TOLAN
PIS-TOLED
PIS-TOLES
SCA-TOLES
SKA-TOLES
SYS-TOLES
DIS-TOMES
EPI-TOMES
LEP-TOMES
MYO-TOMES
SCO-TOMIA
CAN-TONAL
ECO-TONAL
NON-TONAL
BUT-TONED
CAN-TONED
CAR-TONED
COT-TONED
DAN-TONED
UNA-TONED
UNS-TONED
WAN-TONED
BUT-TONER
WAN-TONER
ACE-TONES
CEN-TONES
DUO-TONES
ECO-TONES
HIS-TONES
ISO-TONES
LAC-TONES
OXY-TONES
PEP-TONES
SUB-TONES
TRI-TONES
BIL-TONGS
PAK-TONGS
ACE-TONIC
CRA-TONIC
DAL-TONIC
DIA-TONIC
DYS-TONIC
EPI-TONIC
ISO-TONIC
LAC-TONIC
LEP-TONIC
MYO-TONIC
NEK-TONIC
PEP-TONIC
PHO-TONIC
PHY-TONIC
PLA-TONIC
PLU-TONIC
PRO-TONIC
SUB-TONIC
SYN-TONIC
TEC-TONIC
BOU-TONNE
CRE-TONNE
CAR-TOONS
FES-TOONS
PLA-TOONS
PON-TOONS
PUL-TOONS
RAT-TOONS
TES-TOONS
DOG-TOOTH
EYE-TOOTH
SAW-TOOTH
BIO-TOPES
EPI-TOPES
ISO-TOPES
ISO-TOPIC
PHO-TOPIC
SCO-TOPIC
SUB-TOPIC
HAF-TORAH
PRO-TORES
RES-TORES
VIA-TORES
CLI-TORIC
HIS-TORIC
RHE-TORIC
SAR-TORII
HAF-TOROT
BIS-TORTS
CON-TORTS
DIS-TORTS
AMI-TOSES
CES-TOSES
HEP-TOSES
KUR-TOSES
LAC-TOSES
MAL-TOSES
PEC-TOSES
PEN-TOSES
PHY-TOSES
SUB-TOTAL
TEE-TOTAL
CAR-TOUCH
MIS-TOUCH
ACA-TOURS
BIT-TOURS
CON-TOURS
DOR-TOURS
FAI-TOURS
SAN-TOURS
SHU-TOUTS
SUR-TOUTS
BES-TOWED
KOW-TOWED
TAT-TOWED
UNS-TOWED
BES-TOWER
KOW-TOWER
OUT-TOWER
COT-TOWNS
DOG-TOWNS
MID-TOWNS
ECO-TOXIC
EXO-TOXIC
NON-TOXIC
OTO-TOXIC
ANA-TOXIN
BIO-TOXIN
EXO-TOXIN
NEO-TOXIN
ZOO-TOXIN
FOO-TRACE
MIS-TRACE
POS-TRACE
COA-TRACK
OFF-TRACK
WHI-TRACK
ABS-TRACT
CON-TRACT
DIS-TRACT
PRO-TRACT
SUB-TRACT
OUT-TRADE
CON-TRAIL
DIS-TRAIL
DIS-TRAIN
MIS-TRAIN
PRE-TRAIN
QUA-TRAIN
RES-TRAIN
SEA-TRAIN
DIS-TRAIT
POR-TRAIT
MAN-TRAMS
DEX-TRANS
CAL-TRAPS
CAN-TRAPS
FLY-TRAPS
MAN-TRAPS
RAT-TRAPS
SUN-TRAPS
UNS-TRAPS
MAT-TRASS
CON-TRATS
ASH-TRAYS
POR-TRAYS
MAL-TREAT
MIS-TREAT
PRE-TREAT
YES-TREEN
COW-TREES
GUM-TREES
SUB-TREND
BUT-TRESS
DIS-TRESS
DOC-TRESS
EDI-TRESS
FOR-TRESS
FOS-TRESS
HUN-TRESS
INS-TRESS
LEC-TRESS
MAT-TRESS
MIS-TRESS
ORA-TRESS
POR-TRESS
REC-TRESS
RES-TRESS
SUI-TRESS
UNS-TRESS
VIC-TRESS
WAI-TRESS
FOO-TREST
WHI-TRETS
BES-TREWS
MIS-TRIAL
PRE-TRIAL
DIA-TRIBE
SUB-TRIBE
GEN-TRICE
OUT-TRICK
PAI-TRICK
BES-TRIDE
DES-TRIER
PAL-TRIER
SUL-TRIER
WIN-TRIER
CEN-TRIES
FRA-TRIES
GAN-TRIES
GEN-TRIES
HOS-TRIES
PAN-TRIES
PAS-TRIES
PEL-TRIES
POE-TRIES
RIO-TRIES
SEN-TRIES
SMY-TRIES
VES-TRIES
VIN-TRIES
WAS-TRIES
RES-TRIKE
TES-TRILL
PRE-TRIMS
DEX-TRINE
DOC-TRINE
LUS-TRINE
DEX-TRINS
GAS-TRINS
OES-TRINS
OES-TRIOL
HIS-TRIOS
CAN-TRIPS
UNS-TRIPS
CEN-TRIST
CON-TRIST
SUB-TRIST
CON-TRITE
EPI-TRITE
CAR-TROAD
BES-TRODE
CEN-TRODE
INS-TROKE
UPS-TROKE
OES-TRONE
BIO-TRONS
CIS-TRONS
DIA-TRONS
ISO-TRONS
KRY-TRONS
NEU-TRONS
BOL-TROPE
FOO-TROPE
ZOE-TROPE
ZOO-TROPE
DOG-TROTS
FOO-TROTS
FOX-TROTS
JOG-TROTS
OUT-TROTS
RES-TROVE
BES-TROWS
DES-TROYS
RES-TRUCK
UNS-TRUCK
NON-TRUMP
OUT-TRUMP
DIS-TRUST
MIS-TRUST
UNI-TRUST
MIS-TRUTH
NON-TRUTH
MIS-TRYST
TSK-TSKED
SAX-TUBAS
MYO-TUBES
SCH-TUCKS
TAR-TUFFE
RES-TUFFS
DUC-TULES
NOC-TULES
PUS-TULES
SPA-TULES
CON-TUNDS
DIS-TUNED
FOR-TUNED
MIS-TUNED
DIS-TUNES
FOR-TUNES
MIS-TUNES
SUB-TUNIC
LEC-TURNS
NOC-TURNS
OUT-TURNS
VUL-TURNS
MIS-TUTOR
BEL-TWAYS
CAR-TWAYS
FLA-TWAYS
FOO-TWAYS
GOA-TWEED
GOU-TWEED
KNO-TWEED
WAR-TWEED
PEE-TWEET
PAR-TYERS
DIR-TYING
DIT-TYING
EMP-TYING
HOG-TYING
JET-TYING
JUT-TYING
PAR-TYING
PUT-TYING
MIS-TYPED
PRE-TYPED
BIO-TYPES
ECO-TYPES
ISO-TYPES
MIS-TYPES
NEO-TYPES
PRE-TYPES
SUB-TYPES
TIN-TYPES
ZOO-TYPES
BIO-TYPIC
ECO-TYPIC
ISO-TYPIC
ZOO-TYPIC
MAR-TYRED
DEB-UGGED
SHR-UGGED
CUC-UMBER
ENC-UMBER
INC-UMBER
REN-UMBER
NEL-UMBOS
PEN-UMBRA
GAZ-UMPED
REP-UMPED
SCR-UMPED
SHL-UMPED
SKR-UMPED
LAC-UNARY
BED-UNCES
CHA-UNCES
ENO-UNCES
FLO-UNCES
FRO-UNCES
PRA-UNCES
TRO-UNCES
USA-UNCES
SEM-UNCIA
CAR-UNCLE
FUR-UNCLE
HOM-UNCLE
PED-UNCLE
FLO-UNDER
GAZ-UNDER
GRO-UNDER
REF-UNDER
ROT-UNDER
DIS-UNION

MIS-UNION
NON-UNION
PRE-UNION
PRO-UNION
AUT-UNITE
BRA-UNITE
DIS-UNITE
PRE-UNITE
REP-UNITS
SUB-UNITS
DIS-UNITY
IMM-UNITY
IMP-UNITY
JEJ-UNITY
TRI-UNITY
BEG-UNKED
DEB-UNKED
DEC-UPLED
OCT-UPLED
SCR-UPLED
SHT-UPPED
TIT-UPPED
ACC-URATE
DEP-URATE
FIG-URATE
INA-URATE
IND-URATE
MAT-URATE
OBD-URATE
OBT-URATE
SAT-URATE
CON-URBAN
NON-URBAN
SUB-URBAN
CON-URBIA
SUB-URBIA
EXP-URGED
RES-URGED
SCO-URGED
SPL-URGED
UNP-URGED
UPS-URGED
SCO-URGER
SPL-URGER
EXP-URGES
RES-URGES
SCO-URGES
SPL-URGES
UPS-URGES
MAN-URIAL
REB-URIAL
TEN-URIAL
DAT-URINE
FIG-URINE
LEM-URINE
SCI-URINE
XEN-URINE
LAZ-URITE
ROB-URITE
INT-URNED
RET-URNED
UNB-URNED
UNT-URNED
UPT-URNED
DIS-USAGE
MIS-USAGE
SPO-USAGE
ACC-USERS
ARO-USERS
CHO-USERS
EXC-USERS
FOC-USERS
GRO-USERS
INF-USERS
MIS-USERS
NON-USERS
PER-USERS
REF-USERS
SCO-USERS
SMO-USERS
TRO-USERS
AMB-USHER
ACC-USING
ARO-USING
BEM-USING
BLO-USING
CHO-USING
DEF-USING
DIS-USING
EFF-USING
EXC-USING
FLO-USING
FOC-USING
GRO-USING
HOC-USING
INC-USING
INF-USING
MIS-USING
NON-USING
PER-USING
REC-USING
REF-USING
SMO-USING
SPO-USING
EMB-USQUE
AFL-UTTER
INP-UTTER
REB-UTTER
SPL-UTTER
STR-UTTER
PER-VADED
UNE-VADED
COU-VADES
PER-VADES
PRE-VAILS
REA-VAILS
TRA-VAILS
CHE-VALET
NON-VALID
DIS-VALUE
MIS-VALUE
OUT-VALUE
TRI-VALVE
UNI-VALVE
DOG-VANES
SER-VANTS
CAL-VARIA
CAN-VASES
SIL-VATIC
SYL-VATIC
OUT-VAUNT
SUR-VEILS
MAU-VEINS
LOW-VELDS
KNE-VELLS
PRO-VENDS
SCA-VENGE
OUT-VENOM
CON-VENTS
PRE-VENTS
SOL-VENTS
PAR-VENUE
PAR-VENUS
PRE-VERBS
PRO-VERBS
CON-VERGE
CON-VERSE
PER-VERSE
REN-VERSE
SUB-VERSE
TRA-VERSE
UNI-VERSE
REN-VERST
SUB-VERST
CON-VERTS
COU-VERTS
CUL-VERTS
PER-VERTS
SIE-VERTS
SUB-VERTS
HAR-VESTS
CON-VEXED
CON-VEXES
SIL-VEXES
PLU-VIALS
SUB-VICAR
CRE-VICED
SER-VICED
CER-VICES
CRE-VICES
SER-VICES
BOU-VIERS
BRE-VIERS
CLA-VIERS
KLA-VIERS
PRE-VIEWS
PUR-VIEWS
SUR-VIEWS
PUL-VILLI
DRE-VILLS
COR-VINAS
PRO-VINED
SPA-VINED
FLA-VINES
MAU-VINES
NER-VINES
OLI-VINES
PRO-VINES
SYL-VINES
OLI-VINIC
NON-VIRAL
PRO-VIRAL
SUB-VIRAL
POX-VIRUS
PRO-VIRUS
REO-VIRUS
PRE-VISED
CLE-VISES
PAR-VISES
PEL-VISES
PRE-VISES
TRA-VISES
TRE-VISES
PRE-VISOR
PRO-VISOR
CUR-VITAL
GRA-VITAS
SUR-VIVER
CON-VIVES
SUR-VIVES
NON-VOCAL
SUB-VOCAL
UNI-VOCAL
OUT-VOICE
FRI-VOLED
COE-VOLVE
CON-VOLVE
OUT-VOTED
NON-VOTER
OUT-VOTER
OUT-VOTES
DIS-VOUCH
REA-VOWED
UNA-VOWED
BIV-VYING
CHE-VYING
CHI-VYING
DIV-VYING
NAV-VYING
OUT-VYING
SAV-VYING
ASS-WAGED
ASS-WAGES
BRE-WAGES
FLO-WAGES
STO-WAGES
OUT-WAITS
REA-WAKED
UNA-WAKED
REA-WAKEN
REA-WAKES
GUN-WALES
PIN-WALES
QAW-WALIS
CAT-WALKS
JAY-WALKS
OUT-WALKS
SKY-WALKS
DRY-WALLS
GAD-WALLS
SEA-WALLS
SET-WALLS
WIT-WALLS
ELL-WANDS
SEA-WANTS
AIR-WARDS
BED-WARDS
FOR-WARDS
FRO-WARDS
GOD-WARDS
HAY-WARDS
HOG-WARDS
LEE-WARDS
MAN-WARDS
NAY-WARDS
NOR-WARDS
OUT-WARDS
SEA-WARDS
SKY-WARDS
STE-WARDS
SUN-WARDS
BAR-WARES
RED-WARES
SEA-WARES
TEA-WARES
TIN-WARES
UNA-WARES
WET-WARES
BUL-WARKS
BES-WARMS
PRE-WARMS
UPS-WARMS
FOR-WARNS
PRE-WARNS
BLE-WARTS
TIS-WASES
TIZ-WASES
FOR-WASTE
OUT-WASTE
RAD-WASTE
DOG-WATCH
MID-WATCH
OUT-WATCH
CUT-WATER
EYE-WATER
POM-WATER
RED-WATER
SEA-WATER
AIR-WAVES
EAR-WAXES
PAX-WAXES
SUB-WAYED
UNS-WAYED
UPS-WAYED
LEG-WEARS
OUT-WEARS
UNS-WEARS
FOR-WEARY
OUT-WEARY
COB-WEBBY
BUR-WEEDS
CUD-WEEDS
DYE-WEEDS
GUM-WEEDS
HOG-WEEDS
MAT-WEEDS
MAY-WEEDS
OAR-WEEDS
ORE-WEEDS
OUT-WEEDS
PIG-WEEDS
PIN-WEEDS
RAG-WEEDS
SEA-WEEDS
TAR-WEEDS
WAX-WEEDS
MID-WEEKS
BET-WEENS
MIS-WEENS
ENS-WEEPS
OUT-WEEPS
UPS-WEEPS
OUT-WEIGH
IND-WELLS
INK-WELLS
MAX-WELLS
OUT-WELLS
UPS-WELLS
MIS-WENDS
NAR-WHALE
BOB-WHEEL
COG-WHEEL
FLY-WHEEL
PIN-WHEEL
RAG-WHEEL
WEB-WHEEL
ANY-WHERE
ERE-WHILE
TAR-WHINE
OUT-WHIRL
BOB-WHITE
NON-WHITE
BLO-WHOLE
OUT-WICKS
MID-WIFED
HUS-WIFES
MID-WIFES
EAR-WIGGY
OUT-WILED
OUT-WILES
OUT-WILLS
OUT-WINDS
ENT-WINED
INT-WINED
UNT-WINED
ENT-WINES
INT-WINES
LAU-WINES
UNT-WINES
BRE-WINGS
DRA-WINGS
GAY-WINGS
GNA-WINGS
GRO-WINGS
INS-WINGS
KNO-WINGS
LAP-WINGS
OUT-WINGS
RED-WINGS
SHO-WINGS
SLO-WINGS
STE-WINGS
STO-WINGS
THA-WINGS
UPS-WINGS
VIE-WINGS
WAX-WINGS
CHE-WINKS
EYE-WINKS
HAY-WIRES
WAY-WISER
BRE-WISES
ENT-WISTS
INT-WISTS
RET-WISTS
UNT-WISTS
MID-WIVED
ALE-WIVES
HUS-WIVES
MID-WIVES
OLD-WIVES
SEA-WIVES
REA-WOKEN
AIR-WOMAN
BAT-WOMAN
LAY-WOMAN
MAD-WOMAN
PEN-WOMAN
SEA-WOMAN
TOY-WOMAN
AIR-WOMEN
BAT-WOMEN
LAY-WOMEN
MAD-WOMEN
PEN-WOMEN
SEA-WOMEN
TOY-WOMEN
BAR-WOODS
BAY-WOODS
BOG-WOODS
BOX-WOODS
CAM-WOODS
DAG-WOODS
DOG-WOODS
DYE-WOODS
ELM-WOODS
FAT-WOODS
GUM-WOODS
INK-WOODS
LOG-WOODS
NUT-WOODS
PLY-WOODS
RED-WOODS
SAP-WOODS
NON-WOODY
KEY-WORDS
MIS-WORDS
NAY-WORDS
NON-WORDS
WAN-WORDY
ART-WORKS
CAT-WORKS
CUT-WORKS
DAY-WORKS
GAS-WORKS
LAP-WORKS
LEG-WORKS
NET-WORKS
OUT-WORKS
PIN-WORKS

RAG-WORKS
RIB-WORKS
TIN-WORKS
TOP-WORKS
TRY-WORKS
TUT-WORKS
WAR-WORKS
WAX-WORKS
WEB-WORKS
SUB-WORLD
BAG-WORMS
BUD-WORMS
CAT-WORMS
CUT-WORMS
EAR-WORMS
EEL-WORMS
LOB-WORMS
LUG-WORMS
PIN-WORMS
RAG-WORMS
SEA-WORMS
WAX-WORMS
WEB-WORMS
OUT-WORTH
TAM-WORTH
WAN-WORTH
AWL-WORTS
BLA-WORTS
BUG-WORTS
FAN-WORTS
FEL-WORTS
FIG-WORTS
MAD-WORTS
MUD-WORTS
MUG-WORTS
RAG-WORTS
RIB-WORTS
OUT-WOUND
NON-WOVEN
BOW-WOWED
POW-WOWED
EEL-WRACK
PRE-WRAPS
OUT-WREST
AVO-WRIES
CHO-WRIES
SCO-WRIES
SHO-WRING
MIS-WRITE
OUT-WRITE
SKY-WRITE
MIS-WROTE
OUT-WROTE
SKY-WROTE
BOW-YANGS
BEE-YARDS
HAL-YARDS
INN-YARDS
LAN-YARDS
TAN-YARDS
BIC-YCLED
CAL-YCLED
REC-YCLED
MID-YEARS
OUT-YELLS
OUT-YELPS
EMP-YESES
OUT-YIELD
CLA-YLIKE
LAD-YLIKE
LIL-YLIKE
PLA-YLIKE
QUA-YLIKE
RUB-YLIKE
WHE-YLIKE
DIS-YOKED
MIS-YOKED
DIS-YOKES
MIS-YOKES
BAR-YONIC
GUA-YULES
BEN-ZINES
DIA-ZINES
FAN-ZINES
OXA-ZINES
RHI-ZINES
BUZ-ZINGS
FIZ-ZINGS
GLA-ZINGS
GLO-ZINGS
GRA-ZINGS
SEI-ZINGS
EPI-ZOISM
SUB-ZONAL
TRI-ZONAL
BLA-ZONED
BLA-ZONER
HIZ-ZONER
CAL-ZONES
CAN-ZONES
SUB-ZONES
TRI-ZONES
GAD-ZOOKS
MAD-ZOONS
MAT-ZOONS
EPI-ZOOTY
ISO-ZYMES
ISO-ZYMIC

Section Three

Endings

Introduction

Although it may be easier to spot beginnings of words when looking for a play (perhaps there is a word beginning with BE- or DIS- or QU- or RE- or UN- ?) some of the common endings, such as -ED, -ER and -ING – not forgetting the humble -S – also come easily to mind. As you become more adept, however, you will start looking for other endings in the hope of discovering a bonus word.

In the following sets of lists the words are arranged according to their endings rather than their beginnings. The first set of lists covers useful suffixes, and the second set words ending in A, I, O or U.

Useful Suffixes

The following lists are of 7- and 8-letter words ending with these suffixes:

-ABLE	-FORM	-LAND	-SMEN
-AGE	-FUL	-LESS	-SOME
-ANCE	-GEN	-LET	-TIME
-ANCY	-GRAM	-LIKE	-TION
-ARCH	-HOLE	-LOGY	-URE
-BACK	-HOOD	-LY	-WARD
-BALL	-HORN	-MAN	-WARDS
-BAND	-IBLE	-MEN	-WAY
-BIRD	-IFY	-NESS	-WISE
-DOM	-INGS	-OID	-WOOD
-EAUX	-ISE	-OR	-WORK
-ENCE	-ISH	-OUS	-WORM
-ENCY	-ISM	-OUT	-WORT
-EST	-IST	-SET	-YARD
-ETTE	-ITY	-SHIP	
-EUR	-IUM	-SKIN	
-FISH	-KIN	-SMAN	

Words ending with -INGS, -LY and -EST should be especially useful, as Scrabble players often ponder questions such as:

'I know HOSTING is a word, but does it take an S?'

'I know SULTRY is all right, but what about SULTRILY?'

'I know the adjective OARY, but is the superlative OARIEST acceptable?'

Familiarity with the lists here should provide instant answers to these and similar questions.

In the case of the -EST words, where these are superlatives, it can be assumed that the corresponding comparatives ending in -ER, eg OARIER, are also acceptable.

Note that sometimes words qualify for more than one suffix list. For example, the -FISH words also appear in the -ISH list, the -SKIN words also appear in the -KIN list, and the-SMAN and -SMEN words also appear in the -MAN and -MEN lists respectively.

As it was felt that it would be helpful if all the lists were complete, words that coincidentally end in the suffix letters have been retained, even though the letters are not used as a suffix in them. Examples of such words are OUTDANCE and UNDEVOUT, which are shown in the -ANCE and -OUT lists respectively.

Chambers Back-Words, which lists all words according to alphabetical sequence of endings, can be used as a pointer to other endings, but note that it is *not* based on *Official Scrabble® Words International.*

WORDS ENDING IN -ABLE

7-letter words -ABLE

ACCABLE ACTABLE ADDABLE AFFABLE AMIABLE ASTABLE BATABLE BITABLE BUYABLE CAPABLE
CITABLE CODABLE CURABLE DATABLE DISABLE DOWABLE DRYABLE DUPABLE DURABLE DYEABLE
EATABLE EFFABLE EQUABLE ERRABLE EYEABLE FADABLE FINABLE FIXABLE FLYABLE FRIABLE
GELABLE GETABLE HATABLE HEWABLE HIDABLE HIRABLE LIKABLE LINABLE LIVABLE LOSABLE
LOVABLE MAKABLE MINABLE MIRABLE MIXABLE MOVABLE MUTABLE NAMABLE NOTABLE OWNABLE
PACABLE PAPABLE PARABLE PAYABLE PLIABLE POTABLE RATABLE RETABLE RIDABLE ROPABLE
ROWABLE RULABLE SALABLE SAVABLE SAYABLE SEEABLE SEWABLE SIZABLE SKIABLE SOWABLE
SUEABLE TAKABLE TAMABLE TAXABLE TENABLE TOTABLE TOWABLE TRIABLE TUNABLE TYPABLE
UNHABLE USEABLE VATABLE VOCABLE VOLABLE VOTABLE WADABLE WIRABLE

8-letter words -ABLE

ABATABLE ABUSABLE ADORABLE AGITABLE ALLIABLE AMENABLE AMICABLE AMUSABLE ARGUABLE ATONABLE AVOWABLE BAILABLE BANKABLE BARRABLE BEARABLE BEATABLE BEDDABLE BENDABLE BIDDABLE BILLABLE BINDABLE BISTABLE BITEABLE BLAMABLE BOATABLE BOILABLE BONDABLE BOOKABLE BOOTABLE BRIBABLE BUFFABLE BURNABLE CALLABLE CARTABLE CASCABLE CASHABLE
CASTABLE CAUSABLE CHEWABLE CITEABLE CLOSABLE CLUBABLE COINABLE COOKABLE CULPABLE CURBABLE CUTTABLE DAMNABLE DATEABLE DENIABLE DIGGABLE DIMMABLE DIPPABLE DISHABLE DRAPABLE DRAWABLE DRIVABLE DUTIABLE EDITABLE EDUCABLE ENVIABLE ERASABLE EVADABLE EVITABLE EVOCABLE EXORABLE EXPIABLE FACEABLE FARMABLE FEEDABLE FELLABLE FILEABLE
FILMABLE FINDABLE FINEABLE FIREABLE FISHABLE FITTABLE FOAMABLE FOILABLE FOLDABLE FORDABLE FORMABLE FRAMABLE FUNDABLE FURLABLE GAINABLE GETTABLE GIVEABLE GNAWABLE GRADABLE GRAZABLE GROWABLE GUIDABLE GULLABLE GUSTABLE HANGABLE HATEABLE HEALABLE HEARABLE HEATABLE HELPABLE HIREABLE HOLDABLE HUGGABLE HUMMABLE HUNTABLE IMITABLE
INARABLE INSTABLE INVIABLE ISOLABLE ISSUABLE JOINABLE JUMPABLE KEEPABLE KICKABLE KISSABLE KNOWABLE LAPSABLE LAUDABLE LEASABLE LENDABLE LETTABLE LEVIABLE LIENABLE LIFTABLE LIKEABLE LINEABLE LINKABLE LIQUABLE LISTABLE LIVEABLE LOANABLE LOCKABLE LOVEABLE LUGGABLE MAILABLE MAKEABLE MAPPABLE MASKABLE MELTABLE MENDABLE MILLABLE
MINEABLE MISSABLE MOCKABLE MOLDABLE MOOTABLE MOVEABLE NAMEABLE NESTABLE NETTABLE OATHABLE OBEYABLE OBVIABLE OPENABLE OPERABLE OPINABLE OUTFABLE OVERABLE OXIDABLE PACKABLE PALPABLE PANTABLE PARSABLE PASSABLE PAWNABLE PECCABLE PEELABLE PINTABLE PITIABLE PLACABLE PLAYABLE PLOWABLE PORTABLE POSEABLE POURABLE PRIZABLE PROBABLE
PROVABLE PRUNABLE QUOTABLE RADIABLE RAISABLE RATEABLE READABLE REAPABLE REEFABLE REELABLE RELIABLE RENTABLE REUSABLE RIDEABLE RINSABLE RIPPABLE ROLLABLE ROPEABLE RUINABLE RUNNABLE RUSTABLE SAILABLE SALEABLE SALVABLE SATIABLE SAVEABLE SCALABLE SEALABLE SEISABLE SEIZABLE SELLABLE SENDABLE SERVABLE SHAKABLE SHAMABLE SHAPABLE
SHARABLE SHAVABLE SHEDABLE SHOWABLE SINGABLE SINKABLE SIZEABLE SLAKABLE SLIDABLE SMOKABLE SOCIABLE SOLVABLE SORBABLE SORTABLE SPARABLE STATABLE STONABLE STORABLE STOWABLE SUITABLE SUMMABLE SURFABLE SWAYABLE SYLLABLE TAKEABLE TALKABLE TAMEABLE TANNABLE TAPEABLE TAPPABLE TASTABLE TEARABLE TELLABLE TESTABLE TILLABLE TILTABLE
TIPPABLE TITHABLE TITRABLE TOLLABLE TRADABLE TUBBABLE TUNEABLE TURNABLE TYPEABLE UNDOABLE UNSTABLE UNUSABLE UNVIABLE VALUABLE VARIABLE VENDABLE VIEWABLE VIOLABLE VITIABLE VOIDABLE VOTEABLE WADEABLE WALKABLE WARHABLE WASHABLE WASTABLE WEARABLE WELDABLE WETTABLE WILLABLE WINDABLE WINNABLE WORKABLE WRITABLE

WORDS ENDING IN -AGE

7-letter words -AGE

ABUSAGE ACREAGE AJUTAGE AMENAGE APANAGE ARRIAGE ASSUAGE ASSWAGE AULNAGE AVERAGE BAGGAGE BANDAGE BARRAGE BEERAGE BONDAGE BOSCAGE
BOSKAGE BREWAGE BROCAGE BROKAGE BULKAGE BUOYAGE BURGAGE CABBAGE CARNAGE CARTAGE CENTAGE COINAGE COLLAGE COMPAGE CORDAGE CORKAGE
CORNAGE CORSAGE COTTAGE COURAGE COWHAGE CRANAGE CUTTAGE DISCAGE DOCKAGE DRAYAGE DUNNAGE ESCUAGE ETALAGE FALDAGE FARDAGE FLOTAGE
FLOWAGE FOGGAGE FOLIAGE FOOTAGE FROMAGE FULLAGE GARBAGE GUIDAGE GUNNAGE HAULAGE HAYLAGE HEADAGE HERBAGE HIREAGE HOSTAGE KEELAGE
KIPPAGE LAIRAGE LASTAGE LEAFAGE LEAKAGE LIGNAGE LINEAGE LINKAGE LOCKAGE LUGGAGE MASSAGE MELTAGE MESSAGE MILEAGE MILLAGE MINTAGE
MISPAGE MOCKAGE MONTAGE MOORAGE MOULAGE ONSTAGE OUTRAGE OUVRAGE OVERAGE PACKAGE PANNAGE PASSAGE PAWNAGE PAYSAGE PEERAGE PEONAGE
PIERAGE PILLAGE PIPEAGE PLUMAGE PLUSAGE PONDAGE PONTAGE PORTAGE POSTAGE POTTAGE PRESAGE PRIMAGE PRISAGE PROPAGE QUAYAGE RAMPAGE
REIMAGE REMUAGE RESTAGE RIBCAGE ROOTAGE RUMMAGE SACKAGE SALVAGE SAUSAGE SCALAGE SCAVAGE SCUTAGE SEEPAGE SELVAGE SERFAGE SIGNAGE
SINKAGE SOAKAGE SOCCAGE SOILAGE SONDAGE SPINAGE STORAGE STOWAGE SULLAGE TALLAGE TANKAGE TANNAGE TEENAGE TENTAGE THANAGE THENAGE

TILLAGE TRUCAGE UNITAGE VENDAGE VILLAGE VOLTAGE WAINAGE WASTAGE WINDAGE
TOLLAGE TUNNAGE UPSTAGE VENTAGE VINTAGE VORLAGE WANTAGE WATTAGE WORDAGE
TONNAGE UMBRAGE VANTAGE VIDUAGE VITRAGE WAFTAGE WARPAGE WEFTAGE YARDAGE

8-letter words -AGE

ACCORAGE BREAKAGE DRAINAGE FUSELAGE METAYAGE REDAMAGE STERNAGE VAULTAGE
ACIERAGE BROCKAGE DRESSAGE GRAFTAGE METERAGE REENGAGE STILLAGE VAUNTAGE
ADJUTAGE CABOTAGE DRIFTAGE GRAINAGE MISUSAGE ROUGHAGE STOPPAGE VERBIAGE
AGIOTAGE CARRIAGE ENALLAGE GRILLAGE MORTGAGE SABOTAGE STRAVAGE VICARAGE
ALIENAGE CARUCAGE ENDAMAGE GROUPAGE MUCILAGE SEWERAGE STREWAGE VICINAGE
ALTARAGE CHANTAGE ENSILAGE GUARDAGE MULTIAGE SHORTAGE STUMPAGE WAGONAGE
AMPERAGE CHUMMAGE ENVISAGE HELOTAGE NONIMAGE SLIPPAGE SUBSTAGE WATERAGE
APPANAGE CLEARAGE EQUIPAGE HERITAGE OFFSTAGE SMALLAGE SUFFRAGE WEIGHAGE
BADINAGE CLEAVAGE FERRIAGE INTERAGE OVERPAGE SPILLAGE TASSWAGE WHARFAGE
BARONAGE CLOUDAGE FLOATAGE LANGRAGE PILOTAGE SPOILAGE THIRLAGE WRAPPAGE
BERTHAGE COMANAGE FLOORAGE LANGUAGE PLANTAGE SPOUSAGE TRACKAGE WRECKAGE
BEVERAGE COVERAGE FOOTPAGE LAYERAGE PLOTTAGE SQUIRAGE TRUCKAGE
BIRDCAGE COZENAGE FRAUTAGE LEVERAGE PLUSSAGE STAFFAGE TRUQUAGE
BLINDAGE CREEPAGE FRONDAGE MALAXAGE POUNDAGE STALLAGE TUTELAGE
BLOCKAGE CRIBBAGE FRONTAGE MARITAGE PROPHAGE STEALAGE TUTORAGE
BRAKEAGE DIALLAGE FROTTAGE MARRIAGE PUCELAGE STEARAGE UMPIRAGE
BRASSAGE DISUSAGE FRUITAGE MESSUAGE PUPILAGE STEERAGE UNDERAGE

WORDS ENDING IN -ANCE

7-letter words -ANCE

ADVANCE ASKANCE CREANCE ENHANCE JOYANCE PENANCE SONANCE VACANCE
AIDANCE BALANCE DURANCE FINANCE NOYANCE ROMANCE SURANCE VALANCE

8-letter words -ANCE

ABEYANCE AMBIANCE DEFIANCE FEASANCE NONDANCE PASTANCE RESIANCE VARIANCE
ABIDANCE AMORANCE DEVIANCE GUIDANCE NUISANCE PIQUANCE RIDDANCE VIBRANCE
ACUTANCE BECHANCE DISTANCE INSTANCE ORDNANCE PITTANCE SORTANCE VOIDANCE
ADAMANCE BRISANCE ELEGANCE ISSUANCE OUTDANCE PORTANCE TADVANCE
AFFIANCE BUOYANCE ENTRANCE ITERANCE OUTRANCE RADIANCE TENDANCE
ALLIANCE CREPANCE EXITANCE LAITANCE PARLANCE RELIANCE VALIANCE

WORDS ENDING IN -ANCY

7-letter words -ANCY

ERRANCY INFANCY PLIANCY SONANCY TENANCY TRUANCY UNFANCY VACANCY

8-letter words -ANCY

ABEYANCY CLAMANCY GEOMANCY MYOMANCY RADIANCY VAGRANCY ZOOMANCY
ADAMANCY DEVIANCY IMITANCY PECCANCY RAMPANCY VALIANCY
BLATANCY DORMANCY INSTANCY PERNANCY REGNANCY VERDANCY
BUOYANCY ELEGANCY MORDANCY PIQUANCY UNCHANCY VIBRANCY

WORDS ENDING IN -ARCH

7-letter words -ARCH

ENDARCH HEXARCH MESARCH MONARCH NAVARCH NOMARCH TOPARCH TRIARCH XERARCH

8-letter words -ARCH

ETHNARCH HIERARCH OLIGARCH OUTMARCH PENTARCH POLYARCH TAXIARCH UNSTARCH
HEPTARCH HIPPARCH OMNIARCH OVERARCH PHYLARCH RESEARCH TETRARCH

WORDS ENDING IN -BACK

7-letter words -BACK

BUYBACK CUTBACK DIEBACK FATBACK FINBACK HOGBACK LAYBACK OUTBACK PAYBACK

REDBACK RUNBACK SETBACK SOWBACK SUNBACK TIEBACK TOMBACK WETBACK

8-letter words -BACK

BAREBACK DRAWBACK FULLBACK HUMPBACK PLAYBACK SKEWBACK TAILBACK
BLOWBACK FALLBACK GIVEBACK KICKBACK PLOWBACK SLOTBACK TALKBACK
BLUEBACK FASTBACK GRAYBACK LIFTBACK PULLBACK SLOWBACK TURNBACK
CALLBACK FEEDBACK HALFBACK LOANBACK ROLLBACK SNAPBACK WINGBACK
CLAWBACK FIREBACK HARDBACK MOSSBACK ROORBACK SOFTBACK ZWIEBACK
COMEBACK FLATBACK HOLDBACK PICKBACK SCATBACK SWAYBACK

WORDS ENDING IN -BALL

7-letter words -BALL

EYEBALL ICEBALL LOWBALL NETBALL ODDBALL PATBALL PINBALL PROBALL

8-letter words -BALL

BASEBALL COALBALL FISHBALL GOOFBALL HEELBALL MEATBALL PUSHBALL SPITBALL
BEANBALL CORNBALL FOOTBALL HAIRBALL HIGHBALL MOTHBALL SNOWBALL TRAPBALL
BLOWBALL FASTBALL FORKBALL HANDBALL KICKBALL PITHBALL SOFTBALL WASHBALL
BLUEBALL FIREBALL GOALBALL HARDBALL KORFBALL PUFFBALL SOURBALL

WORDS ENDING IN -BAND

7-letter words -BAND

ARMBAND DISBAND HATBAND HAYBAND HUSBAND PROBAND RIBBAND SALBAND TURBAND

8-letter words -BAND

BACKBAND BROWBAND HAIRBAND NECKBAND PASSBAND RAINBAND SIDEBAND WIDEBAND
BASEBAND FAHLBAND HEADBAND NOSEBAND PLATBAND SARABAND WAVEBAND

WORDS ENDING IN -BIRD

7-letter words -BIRD

ANTBIRD CATBIRD FATBIRD OILBIRD SEABIRD WOSBIRD
AWLBIRD COWBIRD JAYBIRD REDBIRD SUNBIRD

8-letter words -BIRD

BELLBIRD COCKBIRD HANGBIRD LADYBIRD OVENBIRD RAINBIRD SNOWBIRD WHIPBIRD
BLUEBIRD FERNBIRD JAILBIRD LOVEBIRD PUFFBIRD REEDBIRD SONGBIRD YARDBIRD
CAGEBIRD FIREBIRD KINGBIRD LYREBIRD RAILBIRD RICEBIRD SURFBIRD

WORDS ENDING IN -DOM

7-letter words -DOM

BABUDOM CZARDOM EARLDOM FREEDOM HOBODOM RHABDOM STARDOM
BOREDOM DOGEDOM FIEFDOM GURUDOM JARLDOM SELFDOM TSARDOM
BOSSDOM DOLLDOM FILMDOM HALIDOM KINGDOM SERFDOM TZARDOM
CHEFDOM DUKEDOM FOGYDOM HEIRDOM POPEDOM SHAHDOM WIFEDOM

8-letter words -DOM

BABELDOM DEVILDOM HIPPYDOM MOVIEDOM PASHADOM SAINTDOM UNSELDOM
BIRTHDOM DUNCEDOM HOTELDOM NOVELDOM PUPPYDOM SHEIKDOM UNWISDOM
BLOKEDOM FAIRYDOM LEECHDOM PACHADOM QUEENDOM SWELLDOM VILLADOM
CHIEFDOM FOGEYDOM LIEGEDOM PAGANDOM QUEERDOM THANEDOM WHOREDOM
CLERKDOM GYPSYDOM MOTORDOM PAPPADOM REBELDOM THRALDOM

WORDS ENDING IN -EAUX

7-letter words -EAUX

BATEAUX BUREAUX CADEAUX COTEAUX GATEAUX RESEAUX

8-letter words -EAUX

BANDEAUX BORDEAUX COUTEAUX MORCEAUX RONDEAUX TONNEAUX
BATTEAUX CHAPEAUX JAMBEAUX PLATEAUX ROULEAUX TRUMEAUX
BERCEAUX CHATEAUX MANTEAUX PONCEAUX TABLEAUX

WORDS ENDING IN -ENCE

7-letter words -ENCE

ABSENCE DEFENCE FAYENCE LICENCE POTENCE SCIENCE URGENCE
CADENCE ESSENCE FLUENCE LUCENCE REFENCE SILENCE VALENCE
COGENCE FAIENCE LATENCE OFFENCE REGENCE UNFENCE

8-letter words -ENCE

AMBIENCE DISPENCE FLORENCE OPULENCE PUNGENCE SITHENCE TENPENCE
AUDIENCE EMINENCE LENIENCE PATIENCE SALIENCE SIXPENCE TUPPENCE
CLARENCE EVIDENCE MERGENCE PRESENCE SAPIENCE SUSPENCE TWOPENCE
COMMENCE EXIGENCE NASCENCE PRETENCE SENTENCE TANGENCE VERGENCE
CREDENCE FIPPENCE NOWHENCE PRUDENCE SEQUENCE TENDENCE VIOLENCE

WORDS ENDING IN -ENCY

7-letter words -ENCY

ARDENCY COGENCY FLUENCY LUCENCY PATENCY PUDENCY REGENCY VALENCY
CADENCY DECENCY LATENCY ORIENCY POTENCY RECENCY URGENCY VIVENCY

8-letter words -ENCY

CLEMENCY EMINENCY FULGENCY NASCENCY PUNGENCY SAPIENCY TANGENCY VERGENCY
COAGENCY EXIGENCY LAMBENCY OPULENCY REAGENCY SEQUENCY TENDENCY
CURRENCY FERVENCY LENIENCY PENDENCY SALIENCY SOLVENCY TURGENCY

WORDS ENDING IN -EST

7-letter words -EST

ACHIEST BLATEST COXIEST DOTIEST FALSEST GRAVEST KINDEST MAINEST NOBLEST
ACIDEST BLUIEST COZIEST DOUCEST FASTEST GRAYEST LACIEST MATIEST NOSIEST
ACQUEST BOLDEST CRUDEST DOUREST FATTEST GREYEST LAKIEST MAUVEST NUMBEST
ACUTEST BONIEST CURTEST DOVIEST FEATEST HADDEST LANGEST MAZIEST OAKIEST
ADDREST BOSSEST DAFTEST DOWIEST FELLEST HARDEST LANKEST MEANEST OARIEST
AERIEST BOXIEST DAMPEST DOZIEST FIKIEST HARVEST LARGEST MEEKEST OBESEST
AGILEST BRAVEST DANKEST DROLEST FIRMEST HAZIEST LAZIEST MEETEST OILIEST
AIRIEST BRAWEST DARKEST DUFFEST FITTEST HEPPEST LEANEST MIDDEST ONLIEST
AMPLEST BUMMEST DEADEST DULLEST FLUIEST HIGHEST LEFTEST MILDEST OORIEST
ANAPEST BUSIEST DEAFEST DUMBEST FONDEST HIPPEST LENGEST MIMMEST OOSIEST
ARCHEST CAGIEST DEAREST DUNNEST FOULEST HOKIEST LEWDEST MINIEST OOZIEST
ARIDEST CAKIEST DEEDEST DUSKEST FOXIEST HOLIEST LIEFEST MIRIEST OPENEST
ARMREST CALMEST DEEPEST DYKIEST FOZIEST HOMIEST LIEVEST MIRKEST ORBIEST
ARTIEST CAMPEST DEFFEST EARNEST FULLEST HOTTEST LIMIEST MITIEST OULDEST
ASHIEST CANIEST DEFTEST EASIEST FUMIEST ICKIEST LIMPEST MIXIEST OURIEST
AULDEST CANTEST DEIDEST EDGIEST FUNNEST IFFIEST LINIEST MOOTEST OUTJEST
AVIDEST CHICEST DENSEST EELIEST GABFEST IMPREST LITHEST MOPIEST OWLIEST
AWAREST CLOSEST DEWIEST EERIEST GAINEST INANEST LOGIEST MOSTEST OWRIEST
AWNIEST COKIEST DICIEST EGGIEST GAMIEST INKIEST LONGEST MOTIEST PACIEST
BABIEST COLDEST DIKIEST ELMIEST GASHEST INQUEST LOOSEST MURKEST PALIEST
BADDEST CONFEST DIMMEST EVENEST GAZIEST IRATEST LOTHEST NAIFEST PERTEST
BALDEST CONGEST DINKEST EVILEST GLUIEST JIMPEST LOUDEST NAIVEST PINIEST
BARGEST CONTEST DISGEST FABBEST GOLDEST JIVIEST LOWSEST NEAREST PINKEST
BASSEST COOLEST DISNEST FADIEST GOOIEST JOKIEST LUNIEST NEATEST PIPIEST
BEQUEST COSIEST DOMIEST FAINEST GORIEST JUSTEST LUSHEST NESHEST POKIEST
BIGGEST COWIEST DOPIEST FAIREST GOWDEST KEENEST MADDEST NIGHEST POOREST

PORIEST POSHEST POSIEST POXIEST PRETEST PRONEST PROTEST PROWEST PUIREST PULIEST PUNIEST PUNKEST
QUAREST RACIEST RADDEST RADGEST RANKEST RASHEST RATHEST REALEST REDDEST REQUEST RICHEST RICIEST
RILIEST RIMIEST ROKIEST ROPIEST RORIEST ROSIEST RUBIEST RULIEST RUMMEST SADDEST SAGIEST SAIDEST
SAIREST SALTEST SAMIEST SEAREST SEIKEST SEXIEST SICKEST SIZIEST SKEWEST SKYIEST SLOWEST SNIDEST
SOFTEST SOONEST SOUREST SPAREST SPRIEST SPRYEST STALEST STEYEST SUAVEST SUBTEST SUGGEST TAKIEST
TALLEST TANNEST TARTEST TAUTEST TAWIEST TEDIEST TEMPEST TENSEST TERSEST TIDIEST TINIEST TOEIEST
TONIEST TOOMEST TOWIEST TRITEST TUNIEST TYPIEST UGLIEST UNBLEST UNDREST VAGUEST VAINEST VASTEST
VERIEST VINIEST VOGIEST WALIEST WANIEST WANNEST WARIEST WARMEST WATTEST WAVIEST WAXIEST WEAKEST
WEETEST WETTEST WHITEST WILDEST WILIEST WILLEST WINIEST WIRIEST WOTTEST WOWFEST YUKIEST ZANIEST

8-letter words -EST

ACERBEST ACIDIEST ACRIDEST ADEPTEST AFFOREST ALCAHEST ALERTEST ALKAHEST ALMAGEST ANAPAEST ANGRIEST ANTSIEST ARBALEST ARBELEST ARTSIEST ASTUTEST BACKREST BAGGIEST BALDIEST BALKIEST BALMIEST BANALEST BANDIEST BARDIEST BARGHEST BARGUEST BARKIEST BARMIEST BARNIEST BASSIEST BATTIEST BAWDIEST BEADIEST BEAKIEST BEAMIEST BEEFIEST BEERIEST BENDIEST BENTIEST BILGIEST BIRKIEST BIRSIEST BITSIEST BITTIEST BLACKEST BLANDEST BLANKEST BLEAKEST BLEAREST BLINDEST BLITHEST BLOKIEST BLONDEST BLOWIEST BLUDIEST BLUFFEST BLUNTEST BODGIEST BOGGIEST
BONNIEST BOOKIEST BOOKREST BOOMIEST BOOZIEST BOSKIEST BOSSIEST BOUSIEST BRAGGEST BRAIDEST BRAKIEST BRASHEST BRENTEST BRIEFEST BRILLEST BRINIEST BRISKEST BROADEST BROWNEST BRUSKEST BUDDIEST BUFFIEST BUGGIEST BULGIEST BULKIEST BULLIEST BUMPIEST BUNTIEST BURLIEST BURRIEST BUSHIEST BUSTIEST BUTCHEST BUXOMEST BUZZIEST CADGIEST CALMIEST CAMPIEST CANNIEST CANTIEST CARNIEST CATTIEST CAULDEST CHARIEST CHASTEST CHEAPEST CHEWIEST CHIEFEST CHILLEST CHIRKEST CHOICEST CHOKIEST CHUFFEST CISSIEST CLAYIEST CLEANEST CLEAREST COALIEST COARSEST
COATTEST COBBIEST COCKIEST COMBIEST COMFIEST CONKIEST CONQUEST COOMIEST COPSIEST CORKIEST CORNIEST COULDEST COUTHEST CRANKEST CRAPIEST CRASSEST CRAZIEST CREPIEST CRISPEST CRONKEST CROOKEST CROSSEST CRUELEST CRUMPEST CUPPIEST CURDIEST CURLIEST CURNIEST CURVIEST CUSHIEST CUTTIEST DAFFIEST DAGGIEST DAMNDEST DAMPIEST DANDIEST DARNDEST DASHIEST DAUBIEST DEBBIEST DEEDIEST DEFOREST DEMUREST DICKIEST DICTIEST DIDDIEST DILLIEST DINGIEST DINKIEST DIPPIEST DIRTIEST DISHIEST DITSIEST DITZIEST DIVINEST DIZZIEST DOCILEST DODDIEST DODGIEST
DOGGIEST DOILTEST DONSIEST DOOMIEST DORKIEST DORTIEST DOTTIEST DOTTLEST DOWDIEST DOWNIEST DRABBEST DREAREST DROLLEST DRONIEST DRUNKEST DRUSIEST DRUXIEST DUCKIEST DUDDIEST DULLIEST DUMMIEST DUMPIEST DUNGIEST DUNNIEST DURGIEST DURNDEST DUSKIEST DUSTIEST DWARFEST EAGEREST EARLIEST EMONGEST EMPTIEST ENFOREST EVILLEST EXACTEST FADDIEST FAINTEST FANCIEST FARTHEST FATTIEST FAWNIEST FEEBLEST FEINTEST FELTIEST FENDIEST FENNIEST FERLIEST FERNIEST FETIDEST FICKLEST FIERCEST FIERIEST FILMIEST FINNIEST FIRRIEST FISHIEST FISTIEST FITLIEST
FIZZIEST FLAKIEST FLAMIEST FLARIEST FLASHEST FLATTEST FLAWIEST FLAXIEST FLEETEST FLIPPEST FLORIEST FLUKIEST FLUSHEST FLUTIEST FOAMIEST FOGGIEST FOOTIEST FOOTREST FORKIEST FRAILEST FRANKEST FRESHEST FROWIEST FUBBIEST FUBSIEST FUFFIEST FUGGIEST FUNKIEST FUNNIEST FURRIEST FURTHEST FURZIEST FUSSIEST FUSTIEST FUTILEST FUZZIEST GABBIEST GAMMIEST GAPPIEST GASPIEST GASSIEST GAUCHEST GAUCIEST GAUDIEST GAUMIEST GAUNTEST GAUZIEST GAWCIEST GAWKIEST GAWSIEST GEEKIEST GELIDEST GEMMIEST GENTIEST GENTLEST GERMIEST GIDDIEST GIMPIEST GINNIEST
GIRNIEST GLADDEST GLADIEST GLARIEST GLAZIEST GLEGGEST GLIBBEST GLIDDEST GLUMMEST GOATIEST GODLIEST GOLDIEST GOODIEST GOOFIEST GOOPIEST GOOSIEST GORMIEST GORSIEST GOUTIEST GRANDEST GRAPIEST GREATEST GREENEST GRIMIEST GRIMMEST GRIPIEST GRITTEST GRODIEST GROSSEST GROUSEST GRUFFEST GRUMMEST GUCKIEST GULFIEST GULPIEST GUMMIEST GUNGIEST GURLIEST GUSHIEST GUSTIEST GUTSIEST GUTTIEST HAILIEST HAIRIEST HAMMIEST HANDIEST HANGNEST HAPPIEST HARDIEST HARSHEST HASHIEST HASTIEST HEADIEST HEADREST HEAPIEST HEAVIEST HEDGIEST HEFTIEST HEMPIEST
HENNIEST HERBIEST HILLIEST HIPPIEST HOARIEST HOARSEST HOODIEST HOOKIEST HOOLIEST HOOTIEST HOPPIEST HORNIEST HORSIEST HOUSIEST HUFFIEST HULKIEST HULLIEST HUMANEST HUMBLEST HUMIDEST HUMPIEST HUNKIEST HUSHIEST HUSKIEST IMMODEST IMPUREST INDIGEST INEPTEST INERTEST INSANEST INTEREST IRONIEST ITCHIEST JAGGIEST JAMMIEST JANTIEST JAZZIEST JEMMIEST JERKIEST JETTIEST JIMPIEST JOLLIEST JOLTIEST JOWLIEST JUICIEST JUMPIEST JUNKIEST KEDGIEST KICKIEST KIDGIEST KINKIEST KITTLEST KOOKIEST LAIGHEST LAIRIEST LAMBIEST LANKIEST LARDIEST LARKIEST
LATHIEST LAWNIEST LEADIEST LEAFIEST LEAKIEST LEARIEST LEAVIEST LEDGIEST LEERIEST LEGGIEST LEISHEST LICHTEST LIGHTEST LIMBIEST LINGIEST LINTIEST LIPPIEST LITTLEST LIVIDEST LOAMIEST LOATHEST LOFTIEST LOGGIEST LOOBIEST LOONIEST LOOPIEST LOPPIEST LOSSIEST LOURIEST LOUSIEST LOWLIEST LOYALEST LUCIDEST LUCKIEST LUMMIEST LUMPIEST LURIDEST LUSHIEST LUSTIEST MALMIEST MALTIEST MANGIEST MANIFEST MANKIEST MANLIEST MARDIEST MARLIEST MASHIEST MASSIEST MASTIEST MATUREST MAWKIEST MEAGREST MEALIEST MEATIEST MELTIEST MERRIEST MESHIEST MESSIEST

MICKLEST MIFFIEST MIGHTEST MILKIEST MILTIEST MIMSIEST MINCIEST MINGIEST MINTIEST MINUTEST MIRKIEST MIRLIEST MISSIEST MISTIEST MOCHIEST MOISTEST MOLDIEST MOODIEST MOONIEST MOORIEST MOPPIEST MOROSEST MOSSIEST MOTHIEST MOTLIEST MOTTIEST MOUSIEST MUCKIEST MUDDIEST MUGGIEST MUMSIEST MURKIEST MURLIEST MUSHIEST MUSKIEST MUSSIEST MUSTIEST MUZZIEST MYTHIEST NAGGIEST NAKEDEST NAPPIEST NARKIEST NASTIEST NATTIEST NEEDIEST NERDIEST NERVIEST NETTIEST NEWSIEST NIFFIEST NIFTIEST NIMBLEST NIPPIEST NIRLIEST NITTIEST NOBBIEST NOISIEST NONGUEST NOOKIEST NOUNIEST NUBBIEST NUTSIEST NUTTIEST OBTUSEST OFTENEST ONERIEST OPAQUEST ORANGEST ORNATEST OUTWREST OVERKEST PALLIEST PALMIEST PALSIEST PAPPIEST PARKIEST PASTIEST PAWKIEST PEAKIEST PEARTEST PEATIEST PECKIEST PEERIEST PEPPIEST PERKIEST PESKIEST PESTIEST PETTIEST PHATTEST PHONIEST PICKIEST PIGGIEST PINKIEST PIPPIEST PITHIEST PLAINEST PLATIEST PLUMIEST PLUMPEST PLUSHEST POCKIEST PODDIEST PODGIEST POLITEST PONCIEST PONGIEST POOFIEST POOVIEST POPPIEST PORKIEST PORNIEST PORTIEST POSTTEST POTTIEST POUTIEST PRICIEST PRIMMEST PRIVIEST PROSIEST PROUDEST PUDGIEST PUDSIEST PUFFIEST PUGGIEST PULPIEST PUNKIEST PUNNIEST PURPLEST PURSIEST PURTIEST PUSHIEST PUSSIEST QUAKIEST QUEEREST QUICKEST QUIETEST RABIDEST RAGGIEST RAINIEST RAMMIEST RANDIEST RANGIEST RAPIDEST RASPIEST RATTIEST RAUCLEST READIEST REAMIEST REARREST REDDIEST REDIGEST REEDIEST REEFIEST REEKIEST REFOREST REINVEST REMOTEST RESTIEST RIBBIEST RICHTEST RIDGIEST RIFTIEST RIGHTEST RIGIDEST RINDIEST RISKIEST RITZIEST ROARIEST ROCKIEST ROILIEST ROOFIEST ROOKIEST ROOMIEST ROOPIEST ROOTIEST RORTIEST ROUGHEST ROUNDEST ROUPIEST ROWDIEST RUDDIEST RUGGIEST RUMMIEST RUNNIEST RUNTIEST RUSHIEST RUSTIEST RUTTIEST SAGGIEST SALTIEST SANDIEST SAPPIEST SARKIEST SASSIEST SAUCIEST SAVAGEST SAVVIEST SCALIEST SCANTEST SCARCEST SCARIEST SEAMIEST SECUREST SEDATEST SEDGIEST SEEDIEST SEELIEST SEEPIEST SEMPLEST SERENEST SEVEREST SHADIEST SHAKIEST SHALIEST SHARPEST SHEEREST SHINIEST SHOALEST SHORTEST SHOWIEST SILKIEST SILLIEST SILTIEST SIMPLEST SINKIEST SISSIEST SKIEYEST SKINTEST SKIVIEST SLACKEST SLATIEST SLEEKEST SLICKEST SLIMIEST SLIMMEST SLOPIEST SLUGFEST SMALLEST SMARTEST SMOKIEST SMUGGEST SNAKIEST SNARIEST SNELLEST SNIPIEST SNODDEST SNOWIEST SNUGGEST SOAPIEST SOBEREST SODDIEST SOGGIEST SOILIEST SOLIDEST SOMBREST SONGFEST SONSIEST SOOTHEST SOOTIEST SOPPIEST SORRIEST SOUNDEST SOUPIEST SPACIEST SPARSEST SPEWIEST SPICIEST SPICKEST SPIKIEST SPINIEST SPIRIEST SPRUCEST SPUMIEST SQUAREST STABLEST STAGIEST STAIDEST STARKEST STEEPEST STEEVEST STERNEST STEWIEST STIEVEST STIFFEST STILLEST STIVIEST STONIEST STOUTEST SUBTLEST SUDSIEST SUETIEST SULKIEST SUNNIEST SUPPLEST SURFIEST SURGIEST SURLIEST SVELTEST SWALIEST SWANKEST SWEETEST SWELLEST SWIFTEST SWIPIEST SWISHEST TACKIEST TAGGIEST TALCIEST TALKFEST TALKIEST TANGIEST TARDIEST TARRIEST TARTIEST TASTIEST TATTIEST TAWNIEST TAWTIEST TEARIEST TECHIEST TEENIEST TENTIEST TEPIDEST TESTIEST TEUCHEST TEUGHEST THAWIEST THEWIEST THICKEST THINNEST THYMIEST TICHIEST TIDDIEST TIGHTEST TILLIEST TIMIDEST TINNIEST TINTIEST TIPPIEST TIPSIEST TIREDEST TOFFIEST TOSHIEST TOSSIEST TOTTIEST TOUGHEST TOUSIEST TOUTIEST TOUZIEST TOWNIEST TOWSIEST TOWZIEST TRAPNEST TRIFFEST TRIGGEST TRIMMEST TRIPIEST TUBBIEST TUFTIEST TUMPIEST TURFIEST TUSKIEST TWINIEST UNHONEST UNIQUEST UNPRIEST UNRIPEST UNSAFEST UNSUREST UNTRUEST UNWISEST URBANEST UTTEREST VAIRIEST VALIDEST VAPIDEST VASTIEST VEALIEST VEILIEST VEINIEST VIEWIEST VIVIDEST VOGUIEST VUGGIEST WACKIEST WALLIEST WALTIEST WANKIEST WARBIEST WARTIEST WASHIEST WASPIEST WASPNEST WEARIEST WEBBIEST WEDGIEST WEEDIEST WEENIEST WEEPIEST WEIRDEST WENNIEST WERSHEST WHEYIEST WHINIEST WHITIEST WIFTIEST WIGGIEST WIMPIEST WINDIEST WINGIEST WISPIEST WITHIEST WITTIEST WOMBIEST WONKIEST WOODIEST WOOFIEST WOOLIEST WOOZIEST WORDIEST WORMIEST WOULDEST WRONGEST WUSSIEST YAPPIEST YAWNIEST YOLKIEST YOUNGEST YUCKIEST YUKKIEST YUMMIEST ZAPPIEST ZESTIEST ZINCIEST ZINGIEST ZINKIEST ZIPPIEST ZOOTIEST

WORDS ENDING IN -ETTE

7-letter words -ETTE

AILETTE ARIETTE AVIETTE BLUETTE BURETTE BUVETTE CASETTE CUNETTE CURETTE CUVETTE DINETTE FOUETTE FUMETTE GALETTE GAZETTE GENETTE LADETTE LAYETTE LORETTE LUNETTE MINETTE MOFETTE MOZETTE MUSETTE NAVETTE NONETTE OCTETTE PALETTE PIPETTE PROETTE ROSETTE STRETTE TONETTE VEDETTE VIDETTE

8-letter words -ETTE

AIGRETTE AMUSETTE ANISETTE BAGUETTE BARBETTE BARRETTE BIMBETTE BRUNETTE CASSETTE COQUETTE CORVETTE CREVETTE DANCETTE DISKETTE DRABETTE FAUVETTE FOSSETTE FRISETTE FRIZETTE GRISETTE HACKETTE JEANETTE JOCKETTE MAQUETTE MOFFETTE MOQUETTE MOZZETTE NOISETTE OMELETTE PALLETTE PALMETTE PIANETTE POCHETTE RACLETTE REINETTE ROOMETTE ROQUETTE ROULETTE SEPTETTE SESTETTE SEXTETTE SOCKETTE SPINETTE SUEDETTE TOILETTE UMBRETTE VIGNETTE

WORDS ENDING IN -EUR

7-letter words -EUR

AMATEUR DOUCEUR FLANEUR HAUTEUR MASSEUR PRIMEUR REMUEUR SIGNEUR
DANSEUR FARCEUR FRISEUR LIQUEUR MINCEUR PRONEUR SABREUR

8-letter words -EUR

BATELEUR CISELEUR ECRASEUR FROTTEUR LONGUEUR SECATEUR SIGNIEUR TRUQUEUR
BLAGUEUR CLAQUEUR FROIDEUR GRANDEUR MONSIEUR SEIGNEUR TAILLEUR VOYAGEUR
CHASSEUR COIFFEUR FRONDEUR JONGLEUR SABOTEUR SIFFLEUR TROUVEUR

WORDS ENDING IN -FISH

7-letter words -FISH

BATFISH COWFISH FOXFISH HOGFISH MUDFISH PANFISH RAFFISH SELFISH TUBFISH
BOXFISH DEAFISH GARFISH HUFFISH MUFFISH PIGFISH RATFISH SERFISH WOLFISH
CATFISH DOGFISH GEMFISH JEWFISH OARFISH PINFISH REDFISH SUNFISH
CODFISH FINFISH HAGFISH LUBFISH OUTFISH PUPFISH SAWFISH TOFFISH

8-letter words -FISH

BAITFISH COALFISH FALLFISH GRAYFISH LUMPFISH PIPEFISH SCOMFISH SUCKFISH
BILLFISH CRAWFISH FILEFISH GRUFFISH LUNGFISH ROCKFISH SCUMFISH SURFFISH
BLOWFISH CRAYFISH FLATFISH HEADFISH MILKFISH ROSEFISH SNIFFISH TILEFISH
BLUEFISH DEALFISH FOOLFISH JACKFISH MONKFISH SAILFISH SPOFFISH TOADFISH
BOARFISH DRAFFISH FROGFISH KINGFISH MOONFISH SALTFISH STARFISH WALLFISH
BONEFISH DRUMFISH GOATFISH LADYFISH NUMBFISH SANDFISH STIFFISH WEAKFISH
CAVEFISH DWARFISH GOLDFISH LIONFISH OVERFISH SCARFISH STUDFISH WOLFFISH

WORDS ENDING IN -FORM

7-letter words -FORM

ACIFORM AUSFORM CONFORM DIFFORM MISFORM PERFORM TRIFORM ZOEFORM
ALIFORM AVIFORM DEIFORM DISFORM OVIFORM PREFORM UNIFORM

8-letter words -FORM

AERIFORM ENSIFORM JANIFORM NATIFORM PILIFORM RAMIFORM SLIPFORM
ARCIFORM FILIFORM LANDFORM NUBIFORM PIRIFORM RANIFORM TUBIFORM
AURIFORM FREEFORM LAVAFORM OMNIFORM PISIFORM REINFORM UNCIFORM
COLIFORM FUSIFORM LYRIFORM PALIFORM PLANFORM RENIFORM URSIFORM
CONIFORM GASIFORM MANIFORM PARAFORM PLATFORM RETIFORM VARIFORM
CUBIFORM GRUIFORM MURIFORM PEDIFORM POSTFORM ROTIFORM VASIFORM
CUNIFORM IODOFORM NAPIFORM PICIFORM PYRIFORM SETIFORM WAVEFORM

WORDS ENDING IN -FUL

7-letter words -FUL

ARMSFUL CUPSFUL FISHFUL HARMFUL LISTFUL PAILFUL RAGEFUL SWAYFUL WAKEFUL
BAGSFUL DAREFUL FISTFUL HATEFUL LOCKFUL PAINFUL RESTFUL TACTFUL WAMEFUL
BALEFUL DEEDFUL FOODFUL HATSFUL LOOFFUL PALMFUL RISKFUL TALEFUL WILEFUL
BANEFUL DERNFUL FORKFUL HEEDFUL LUNGFUL PESTFUL ROOMFUL TANKFUL WILLFUL
BASHFUL DIREFUL FORMFUL HELPFUL LUSTFUL PIPEFUL RUTHFUL TEARFUL WISHFUL
BOATFUL DISHFUL FRETFUL HOPEFUL MASTFUL PITHFUL SACKFUL TEEMFUL WISTFUL
BODEFUL DOLEFUL GAINFUL HORNFUL MAZEFUL PITIFUL SHIPFUL TEENFUL WORKFUL
BOOKFUL DOOMFUL GASHFUL HURTFUL MINDFUL PLAYFUL SHOPFUL TENTFUL ZEALFUL
BOWLFUL DUREFUL GAZEFUL HUSHFUL MISTFUL PLOTFUL SIGHFUL TOILFUL ZESTFUL
BRIMFUL DUTIFUL GLADFUL JARSFUL MOANFUL POKEFUL SKEPFUL TRAYFUL
CAGEFUL EASEFUL GLEEFUL JESTFUL MUSEFUL POUTFUL SKILFUL TUBEFUL
CANSFUL FACTFUL GUSTFUL JUGSFUL NEEDFUL PREYFUL SKINFUL TUNEFUL
CAREFUL FATEFUL GUTSFUL KISTFUL NESTFUL PUSHFUL SONGFUL VIALFUL
CROPFUL FEARFUL HANDFUL LIFEFUL ODORFUL RACKFUL SOULFUL WAILFUL

8-letter words -FUL

APRONFUL DIRGEFUL GLASSFUL MERCIFUL PRESSFUL SNEERFUL THANKFUL UNUSEFUL
AVAILFUL DOUBTFUL GLOOMFUL MIGHTFUL PRIDEFUL SNOOTFUL TOOTHFUL UNWILFUL
BASINFUL DREADFUL GRACEFUL MIRTHFUL PROUDFUL SOOTHFUL TRADEFUL VAUNTFUL
BELLYFUL DREAMFUL GRATEFUL MOISTFUL PURSEFUL SPADEFUL TRAINFUL VENGEFUL
BLAMEFUL EVENTFUL GRIEFFUL MOURNFUL RIGHTFUL SPEEDFUL TRISTFUL VOICEFUL
BLISSFUL FAITHFUL GROANFUL MOUTHFUL SACKSFUL SPELLFUL TROTHFUL WAGONFUL
BLUSHFUL FANCIFUL GUILEFUL NIEVEFUL SCENTFUL SPITEFUL TROUTFUL WASTEFUL
BOASTFUL FAULTFUL HANDSFUL NOISEFUL SCOOPFUL SPOILFUL TRUCKFUL WATCHFUL
CHARMFUL FEASTFUL HASTEFUL ODOURFUL SCORNFUL SPOONFUL TRUNKFUL WEARIFUL
CHEEKFUL FORCEFUL HONEYFUL PAILSFUL SENSEFUL SPORTFUL TRUSTFUL WORTHFUL
CHEERFUL FORKSFUL HOUSEFUL PAUSEFUL SHAMEFUL STAGEFUL TRUTHFUL WRACKFUL
CHESTFUL FOUNTFUL HUMORFUL PEACEFUL SHEENFUL STARTFUL UDDERFUL WRATHFUL
CHOCKFUL FRAUDFUL LADLEFUL PLAINFUL SHELFFUL STICKFUL UNARTFUL WREAKFUL
COLORFUL FREAKFUL LAUGHFUL PLATEFUL SHELLFUL STORMFUL UNJOYFUL WRECKFUL
CRIMEFUL FRISKFUL LIGHTFUL POUCHFUL SKILLFUL SURGEFUL UNLAWFUL WRONGFUL
DEARNFUL FRUITFUL LOATHFUL POWERFUL SLOTHFUL TABLEFUL UNMANFUL WROTHFUL
DEATHFUL GHASTFUL MENSEFUL PRANKFUL SMILEFUL TASTEFUL UNSINFUL YOUTHFUL

WORDS ENDING IN -GEN

7-letter words -GEN

ACROGEN CRYOGEN HUMOGEN KEROGEN LYSOGEN MUTAGEN PYROGEN TRUDGEN ZYMOGEN
ANLAGEN ENDOGEN INDIGEN LOXYGEN MITOGEN ONCOGEN RONTGEN TWIGGEN
ANTIGEN HALOGEN IONOGEN LUCIGEN MUCIGEN PIROGEN SMIDGEN XYLOGEN

8-letter words -GEN

ABORIGEN AMYLOGEN CULTIGEN ENLARGEN GLYCOGEN HYDROGEN OSTEOGEN ROENTGEN
ALLERGEN ANDROGEN CYANOGEN ESTROGEN HISTOGEN MISCEGEN PATHOGEN STARAGEN
AMIDOGEN COLLAGEN DIPLOGEN FLORIGEN HYALOGEN NITROGEN PHOTOGEN

WORDS ENDING IN -GRAM

7-letter words -GRAM

ANAGRAM EPIGRAM ISOGRAM PANGRAM TANGRAM
DIAGRAM GROGRAM MYOGRAM PROGRAM TRIGRAM

8-letter words -GRAM

AEROGRAM DEKAGRAM HOLOGRAM LEXIGRAM MARIGRAM ONDOGRAM SKIAGRAM VENOGRAM
BAROGRAM ECHOGRAM IDEOGRAM LIPOGRAM MONOGRAM PARAGRAM SONOGRAM ZYMOGRAM
DECAGRAM ERGOGRAM KILOGRAM LOGOGRAM NANOGRAM PICOGRAM TELEGRAM
DECIGRAM HEXAGRAM KYMOGRAM MAILGRAM NOMOGRAM RENOGRAM TOMOGRAM

WORDS ENDING IN -HOLE

7-letter words -HOLE

AIRHOLE BOTHOLE EYEHOLE KEYHOLE MUDHOLE POTHOLE TAPHOLE
ARMHOLE CATHOLE FOXHOLE LUGHOLE OILHOLE RATHOLE
ASSHOLE DOGHOLE JAWHOLE MANHOLE PINHOLE SPYHOLE

8-letter words -HOLE

ANETHOLE BOREHOLE FEEDHOLE KNEEHOLE PEEPHOLE SHITHOLE WELLHOLE
ARSEHOLE BUNGHOLE FUNKHOLE KNOTHOLE PESTHOLE SHOTHOLE WOODHOLE
BLOWHOLE COALHOLE GUNKHOLE LAMPHOLE PORTHOLE SINKHOLE WORMHOLE
BOLTHOLE DOWNHOLE HELLHOLE LOOPHOLE POSTHOLE WEEPHOLE

WORDS ENDING IN -HOOD

7-letter words -HOOD

APEHOOD CUBHOOD HOGHOOD SONHOOD
BOYHOOD ELFHOOD MANHOOD
CATHOOD GODHOOD NUNHOOD

8-letter words -HOOD

AUNTHOOD GIRLHOOD LADYHOOD MONKHOOD PUMPHOOD WIFEHOOD
BABYHOOD IDLEHOOD MAIDHOOD PAGEHOOD SELFHOOD WIVEHOOD
DOLLHOOD KINGHOOD MISSHOOD POPEHOOD SERFHOOD

WORDS ENDING IN -HORN

7-letter words -HORN

ALPHORN BETHORN COEHORN FOGHORN LEGHORN TINHORN
ALTHORN BIGHORN DISHORN INKHORN SAXHORN UNSHORN

8-letter words -HORN

BOXTHORN BULLHORN DEERHORN HAWTHORN LANTHORN RAMSHORN SLUGHORN
BUCKHORN CRUMHORN GEMSHORN KRUMHORN LONGHORN SHOEHORN WALDHORN

WORDS ENDING IN -IBLE

7-letter words -IBLE

ADDIBLE DELIBLE FUSIBLE MIXIBLE RIBIBLE VISIBLE
AUDIBLE DOCIBLE LEGIBLE PATIBLE RISIBLE

8-letter words -IBLE

CREDIBLE ELUDIBLE EXIGIBLE FORCIBLE LAPSIBLE POSSIBLE SUASIBLE UNEDIBLE
CRUCIBLE ERODIBLE FALLIBLE FUNGIBLE MANDIBLE RENDIBLE TANGIBLE VENDIBLE
EDUCIBLE EROSIBLE FEASIBLE GULLIBLE MISCIBLE RINSIBLE TENSIBLE VINCIBLE
ELIDIBLE EVADIBLE FENCIBLE HORRIBLE PARTIBLE RUNCIBLE TERRIBLE
ELIGIBLE EVASIBLE FLEXIBLE INEDIBLE PASSIBLE SENSIBLE THURIBLE

WORDS ENDING IN -IFY

7-letter words -IFY

ACETIFY CERTIFY DIGNIFY GRATIFY MAGNIFY NIGRIFY QUALIFY SIGNIFY VERBIFY
ACIDIFY CHYLIFY DULCIFY HORRIFY MERCIFY NITRIFY RECTIFY SPECIFY VERSIFY
AMPLIFY CHYMIFY FALSIFY ICONIFY METRIFY NULLIFY REEDIFY TACKIFY VITRIFY
ANGLIFY CLARIFY FANCIFY JELLIFY MICRIFY OPACIFY REUNIFY TERRIFY YUPPIFY
BEATIFY COALIFY FARCIFY JOLLIFY MOLLIFY PETRIFY RUSSIFY TESTIFY ZINCIFY
BRUTIFY CRUCIFY FISHIFY JUSTIFY MORTIFY PLEBIFY SACRIFY THURIFY ZINKIFY
CALCIFY DAMNIFY FORTIFY LIGNIFY MUMMIFY PONTIFY SALSIFY TIPSIFY ZOMBIFY
CAPRIFY DANDIFY FRUTIFY LIQUIFY MUNDIFY PROSIFY SCARIFY TORRIFY
CARNIFY DENSIFY GLORIFY LITHIFY MYSTIFY PULPIFY SCORIFY UNDEIFY

8-letter words -IFY

ALKALIFY COPURIFY ETHERIFY HUMIDIFY PRETTIFY RENOTIFY RIGIDIFY SOLIDIFY
AMMONIFY DENAZIFY FLINTIFY IDENTIFY QUANTIFY REPACIFY SANCTIFY STELLIFY
BEAUTIFY DETOXIFY FLUIDIFY KARSTIFY QUIZZIFY REPURIFY SANGUIFY STRATIFY
BRONZIFY DIVINIFY FRUCTIFY LAPIDIFY REAEDIFY RESINIFY SAPONIFY STULTIFY
CLASSIFY EMULSIFY GENTRIFY MOISTIFY RECODIFY REVERIFY SILICIFY ZINCKIFY
COCKNIFY ESTERIFY GLASSIFY OPSONIFY REMODIFY REVIVIFY SIMPLIFY

WORDS ENDING IN -INGS

7-letter words -INGS

ABLINGS AWNINGS BORINGS COMINGS DOPINGS ENRINGS FRYINGS HEXINGS LACINGS
ACHINGS BAAINGS BOWINGS COOINGS DOTINGS ERRINGS GAMINGS HIDINGS LADINGS
ACTINGS BAKINGS BOXINGS COPINGS DOZINGS FACINGS GAPINGS HIRINGS LAKINGS
AGEINGS BESINGS BUSINGS COVINGS DRYINGS FADINGS GATINGS HOLINGS LASINGS
AIRINGS BIDINGS CAKINGS CRYINGS DYEINGS FILINGS GIVINGS HOMINGS LAWINGS
ANTINGS BIKINGS CANINGS DARINGS EARINGS FININGS GORINGS IMPINGS LAYINGS
ARCINGS BITINGS CASINGS DATINGS EATINGS FIRINGS HAVINGS INNINGS LIKINGS
ARMINGS BLUINGS CAVINGS DICINGS EDGINGS FIXINGS HAYINGS JAPINGS LIMINGS
ASKINGS BODINGS CAWINGS DIVINGS ELDINGS FLYINGS HAZINGS JAWINGS LININGS
AUDINGS BONINGS CODINGS DONINGS ENDINGS FOXINGS HEWINGS KITINGS LIVINGS

LOBINGS LORINGS LOSINGS LOVINGS LOWINGS LUGINGS LUTINGS MAKINGS MATINGS MAYINGS MININGS
MOWINGS MUSINGS NAMINGS NIDINGS NOSINGS OFFINGS OGLINGS ONDINGS OUTINGS PAGINGS PALINGS
PARINGS PAVINGS PAYINGS PILINGS PIPINGS POLINGS POSINGS PRYINGS PULINGS RACINGS RAGINGS
RAKINGS RATINGS RAVINGS RAWINGS RIDINGS RISINGS ROBINGS RODINGS ROPINGS ROVINGS ROWINGS
RUEINGS RULINGS SAVINGS SAWINGS SAYINGS SEEINGS SEWINGS SIDINGS SIZINGS SKIINGS SORINGS
SOWINGS SPAINGS SPRINGS SPYINGS STRINGS TAKINGS TAMINGS TARINGS TAWINGS TAXINGS TIDINGS
TILINGS TIMINGS TIRINGS TOLINGS TONINGS TOWINGS TOYINGS TRYINGS TUBINGS TUNINGS TYPINGS
ULLINGS UNKINGS UPPINGS URGINGS URNINGS VEXINGS VIKINGS WADINGS WAKINGS WANINGS WAVINGS
WAXINGS WIPINGS WIRINGS WONINGS WOOINGS YOKINGS ZONINGS

8-letter words -INGS

ABIDINGS AISLINGS AMBLINGS ANGLINGS ARCHINGS ARCKINGS AWAKINGS BACKINGS BAGGINGS BAITINGS BALKINGS BALLINGS BANDINGS BANGINGS BANKINGS BANTINGS BARRINGS BASHINGS BASTINGS BATTINGS BAWLINGS BEADINGS BEAMINGS BEARINGS BEATINGS BEDDINGS BEGGINGS BELTINGS BENDINGS BETTINGS BIASINGS BIDDINGS BIGGINGS BILLINGS BINDINGS BIRDINGS BIRLINGS BITTINGS BLUEINGS BOATINGS BOILINGS BOLTINGS BOMBINGS BONDINGS BOOKINGS BOOMINGS BOWLINGS BRACINGS BREWINGS BRIMINGS BROKINGS BRUTINGS BUCKINGS BUDDINGS BUFFINGS BUGGINGS BULLINGS BUMPINGS BUNTINGS BURNINGS
BUSHINGS BUSKINGS BUSSINGS BUSTINGS BUZZINGS CABLINGS CALLINGS CAMPINGS CANNINGS CANTINGS CAPPINGS CARDINGS CARLINGS CARPINGS CARVINGS CASTINGS CATLINGS CEASINGS CEILINGS CHASINGS CHIDINGS CIELINGS CLONINGS CLOSINGS COAMINGS COATINGS CODLINGS COGGINGS COININGS COLLINGS COMBINGS COMPINGS CONNINGS COOKINGS CORDINGS COWLINGS CRAVINGS CUBBINGS CULLINGS CUNNINGS CUPPINGS CURBINGS CURLINGS CURSINGS CUTTINGS CYCLINGS CYMLINGS DAFFINGS DAGGINGS DAMPINGS DANCINGS DARLINGS DARNINGS DAUBINGS DAWNINGS DEALINGS DECKINGS DEVLINGS DIALINGS DIGGINGS
DILLINGS DIPPINGS DISHINGS DOATINGS DOCKINGS DODGINGS DOGGINGS DOPPINGS DRAWINGS DRIVINGS DROVINGS DUBBINGS DUCKINGS DUCTINGS DUFFINGS DUMPINGS DUNNINGS EANLINGS EARNINGS EARRINGS EASTINGS EEVNINGS EILDINGS EMPTINGS ENVYINGS ERLKINGS ETCHINGS EVENINGS FABLINGS FAGGINGS FAILINGS FAIRINGS FALLINGS FANNINGS FARCINGS FARDINGS FARMINGS FASTINGS FATLINGS FAWNINGS FEEDINGS FEELINGS FEERINGS FELTINGS FENCINGS FERNINGS FEUDINGS FILLINGS FINDINGS FIRRINGS FISHINGS FITTINGS FIZZINGS FLUTINGS FLYTINGS FOAMINGS FOILINGS FOLDINGS FOOLINGS FOOTINGS
FOPLINGS FORGINGS FORMINGS FOULINGS FOWLINGS FRAMINGS FRAYINGS FUCKINGS FUNDINGS FURRINGS GADLINGS GAFFINGS GAININGS GANGINGS GASKINGS GASPINGS GASSINGS GAUGINGS GAYWINGS GEARINGS GELDINGS GETTINGS GILDINGS GINNINGS GIRDINGS GLAZINGS GLEYINGS GLIDINGS GLOVINGS GLOZINGS GNAWINGS GODLINGS GOLFINGS GOSLINGS GRATINGS GRAVINGS GRAZINGS GREYINGS GRICINGS GROWINGS GUIDINGS GUISINGS GUMMINGS GUNNINGS HACKINGS HAININGS HALLINGS HALTINGS HANGINGS HARLINGS HARPINGS HASTINGS HATTINGS HAWKINGS HEADINGS HEALINGS HEARINGS HEATINGS HEAVINGS HEDGINGS
HEELINGS HELPINGS HERLINGS HERRINGS HIDLINGS HILDINGS HIPPINGS HIRLINGS HISSINGS HOGGINGS HOLDINGS HOPPINGS HORNINGS HORSINGS HOSTINGS HOTTINGS HOUSINGS HOUTINGS HOWLINGS HUMMINGS HUNTINGS HURLINGS HUSKINGS HUSTINGS HUTTINGS HYLDINGS IMAGINGS INBEINGS INBRINGS INGOINGS INKLINGS INSWINGS IRONINGS ITCHINGS JARRINGS JEERINGS JERKINGS JESTINGS JIBBINGS JIGGINGS JOBBINGS JOGGINGS JOININGS JOTTINGS JUGGINGS KARTINGS KAYOINGS KEELINGS KEENINGS KEEPINGS KEGLINGS KEMPINGS KENNINGS KERNINGS KIDLINGS KILLINGS KILTINGS KIRKINGS KITLINGS KNIFINGS
KNOWINGS LAGGINGS LALLINGS LAMMINGS LAMPINGS LANDINGS LAPPINGS LAPWINGS LASHINGS LASTINGS LATHINGS LEADINGS LEANINGS LEASINGS LEAVINGS LEERINGS LEGGINGS LEKKINGS LEMMINGS LENDINGS LETTINGS LICKINGS LIGGINGS LIMPINGS LIPPINGS LISPINGS LISTINGS LOADINGS LOAFINGS LOANINGS LODGINGS LOGGINGS LONGINGS LOONINGS LOOPINGS LOOTINGS LOPPINGS LORDINGS LOURINGS LUGEINGS LURKINGS MADLINGS MAILINGS MAIMINGS MALTINGS MAPPINGS MARKINGS MARLINGS MASHINGS MASKINGS MATTINGS MEANINGS MEETINGS MELTINGS MENDINGS MERLINGS MESHINGS MICHINGS MILKINGS MILLINGS
MINCINGS MINDINGS MISTINGS MOBBINGS MOCKINGS MOLDINGS MOORINGS MOOTINGS MORLINGS MORNINGS MOSHINGS MOSLINGS MOUSINGS MUGGINGS MUMMINGS MUNTINGS NAILINGS NECKINGS NERVINGS NESTINGS NETTINGS NITHINGS NODDINGS NOGGINGS NOONINGS NOTHINGS NULLINGS NURSINGS NUTTINGS OAKLINGS ONGOINGS OPENINGS OUTRINGS OUTSINGS OUTWINGS PACKINGS PADDINGS PAIRINGS PANNINGS PANTINGS PARGINGS PARKINGS PARSINGS PARTINGS PASSINGS PASTINGS PAUSINGS PECKINGS PEELINGS PEGGINGS PELTINGS PETTINGS PICKINGS PIECINGS PIGGINGS PIGLINGS PILLINGS PINKINGS PINNINGS PIONINGS
PITTINGS PLACINGS PLATINGS POLLINGS POSTINGS POURINGS POUTINGS PRATINGS PRAYINGS PRIMINGS PROSINGS PROVINGS PRUNINGS PUDDINGS PUFFINGS PUGGINGS PUNNINGS PURGINGS PURLINGS PURRINGS PUTTINGS PYONINGS QUAKINGS QUEUINGS RACKINGS RAGGINGS RAILINGS RAISINGS RAMPINGS RANKINGS RANTINGS RAPPINGS RASPINGS RATLINGS RATTINGS READINGS REDDINGS REDWINGS REEDINGS REEFINGS REELINGS RENNINGS REPPINGS RESTINGS RIBBINGS RIDGINGS RIFLINGS RIGGINGS RIGLINGS RIMMINGS RINGINGS RINSINGS RIOTINGS RISPINGS ROADINGS ROAMINGS ROARINGS ROCKINGS RODDINGS ROLFINGS

ROLLINGS ROOFINGS ROOTINGS ROUMINGS ROUTINGS RUBBINGS RUCHINGS RUGGINGS RUININGS RUNNINGS RUSHINGS RUSTINGS RUTTINGS SACKINGS SACRINGS SAGGINGS SAILINGS SALTINGS SALVINGS SANDINGS SAPLINGS SARKINGS SCALINGS SCORINGS SCRYINGS SEALINGS SEARINGS SEATINGS SEEDINGS
SEELINGS SEEMINGS SEININGS SEISINGS SEIZINGS SELFINGS SENDINGS SENSINGS SERGINGS SERVINGS SETTINGS SHADINGS SHAKINGS SHAPINGS SHARINGS SHAVINGS SHOEINGS SHORINGS SHOWINGS SIBLINGS SIFTINGS SIGNINGS SINDINGS SINGINGS SINKINGS SITTINGS SKATINGS SKIVINGS SLATINGS
SLICINGS SLIDINGS SLOWINGS SMILINGS SMOKINGS SNARINGS SNIPINGS SNORINGS SOAKINGS SOARINGS SOBBINGS SOGGINGS SOILINGS SOOPINGS SOPPINGS SORNINGS SORTINGS SOSSINGS SOTTINGS SOUMINGS SOURINGS SOUSINGS SPACINGS SPAEINGS SPILINGS STAGINGS STARINGS STEWINGS STONINGS
STOPINGS STOVINGS STOWINGS STYLINGS SUBBINGS SUBRINGS SUCKINGS SUGGINGS SUITINGS SUMMINGS SURFINGS SURGINGS SWALINGS SWAYINGS SYNDINGS TABLINGS TACKINGS TAGGINGS TAILINGS TALKINGS TAMPINGS TANKINGS TANLINGS TANNINGS TAPPINGS TARRINGS TASKINGS TASTINGS TATTINGS
TEAMINGS TEASINGS TELLINGS TENTINGS TESTINGS THAWINGS TICKINGS TIFFINGS TILLINGS TILTINGS TINNINGS TINTINGS TIPPINGS TITHINGS TITLINGS TOILINGS TOLLINGS TOOLINGS TOPPINGS TOSSINGS TOTTINGS TOURINGS TOUSINGS TRACINGS TRADINGS TUBBINGS TUFTINGS TUGGINGS TUNNINGS
TURFINGS TURNINGS TUSKINGS TUTTINGS TWININGS UNBEINGS UNDOINGS UNITINGS UNSLINGS UNTYINGS UPBRINGS UPFLINGS UPGOINGS UPSWINGS VAMPINGS VANNINGS VARYINGS VEERINGS VEILINGS VEININGS VENTINGS VERSINGS VESTINGS VIEWINGS VOGUINGS VOICINGS VOIDINGS WADDINGS WAFTINGS
WAILINGS WAITINGS WALKINGS WALLINGS WANTINGS WARDINGS WARLINGS WARMINGS WARNINGS WARPINGS WASHINGS WASTINGS WAULINGS WAWLINGS WAXWINGS WEARINGS WEAVINGS WEBBINGS WEDDINGS WEDGINGS WEEDINGS WEEPINGS WELDINGS WELLINGS WELTINGS WESTINGS WETTINGS WHALINGS WHININGS
WHITINGS WICKINGS WIGGINGS WILDINGS WINCINGS WINDINGS WINKINGS WINNINGS WISHINGS WITLINGS WITTINGS WOLFINGS WOLVINGS WONNINGS WORDINGS WORKINGS WRITINGS YAWNINGS YAWPINGS YEALINGS YELLINGS YELPINGS YOWLINGS

WORDS ENDING IN -ISE

7-letter words -ISE

ABSCISE ADONISE AGONISE AIRWISE ANODISE ANYWISE APPRISE ARABISE ATHEISE
ATOMISE AZOTISE BAPTISE CHAMISE CHEMISE COALISE COGNISE CONCISE COTTISE
CYANISE DESPISE DIARISE DOCKISE EBONISE ECHOISE EGOTISE ELEGISE EMPRISE
ENDWISE FADAISE FANWISE GALLISE GENOISE HEROISE ICONISE IDOLISE IRIDISE
IRONISE ITEMISE KYANISE LAICISE LAIRISE LIONISE MALAISE MANWISE MAPWISE
MORTISE MYTHISE OBELISE OXIDISE OZONISE PARVISE PECTISE PENTISE PEPTISE
POETISE PRECISE PREMISE PREVISE PROMISE REALISE REARISE REPRISE RERAISE
RIOTISE SOUBISE STYLISE SUCCISE SUNRISE SUNWISE SURMISE TAXWISE TRENISE
UNITISE UPRAISE UTILISE

8-letter words -ISE

ALBITISE ALKALISE AMORTISE ANNALISE APHETISE APHORISE APPETISE APPRAISE ARCHAISE ARCHWISE ATHETISE BANALISE BENDWISE BEPRAISE BOTANISE BRANDISE CANALISE CANONISE CAPONISE CHASTISE CIVILISE COLONISE
COMBWISE COMPRISE COVETISE CRABWISE CREOLISE CURARISE CUTINISE DEBRUISE DEMONISE DEPUTISE DIGITISE DIMERISE DISGUISE DISSEISE DIVINISE DROPWISE DYNAMISE EBIONISE EDGEWISE EGLOMISE ELSEWISE EMPERISE
ENERGISE EQUALISE ERGOTISE ETERNISE ETHERISE ETHICISE EULOGISE EUPHUISE EXERCISE EXORCISE FABULISE FARADISE FEMINISE FESSWISE FINALISE FLATWISE FLUIDISE FOCALISE HEPATISE HUMANISE IDEALISE IMMUNISE
INFAMISE JUMBOISE LEGALISE LIKEWISE LOCALISE LOGICISE LONGWISE LYRICISE MACARISE MADERISE MARQUISE MAUVAISE MAXIMISE MELODISE MEMORISE MESPRISE METALISE MINIMISE MISPOISE MISPRISE MISRAISE MOBILISE
MONETISE MOONRISE MORALISE MOTORISE NASALISE NEBULISE NODALISE NOMADISE NOTARISE NOVELISE OPTIMISE ORGANISE OUTRAISE OVERWISE PAGANISE PAIRWISE PALEWISE PAPALISE PARADISE PENALISE POLARISE POLEMISE
POLONISE PORPOISE PORTOISE PRACTISE PTYALISE PYRITISE QUANTISE RACEMISE READVISE REGULISE REREVISE RESINISE RIGIDISE RINGWISE RIVALISE ROBOTISE ROMANISE ROYALISE RURALISE SANITISE SATIRISE SIDEWISE
SIMILISE SINICISE SIRENISE SOBERISE SODOMISE SOLARISE SOLECISE SOMEWISE SORORISE STEPWISE SUBERISE SUBITISE SUCHWISE SURPRISE TEAMWISE TELEVISE TENTWISE TETANISE THEORISE THUSWISE TORTOISE TOTALISE
TRAVOISE TREATISE TUTORISE UNIONISE UNPRAISE URBANISE VALORISE VAPORISE VELARISE VITALISE VOCALISE VOLUMISE VOWELISE WARPWISE WEFTWISE WOMANISE

WORDS ENDING IN -ISH

7-letter words -ISH

ABOLISH CATTISH DUNNISH GNOMISH KERNISH MUFFISH PLANISH RUTTISH TUBBISH
ALUMISH CHERISH DUSKISH GOATISH KIDDISH MUGGISH PLENISH SADDISH TUBFISH
ANGUISH CLAYISH ENGLISH GOLDISH KNAVISH MUMPISH POORISH SALTISH TUNDISH
BABYISH COCKISH EVANISH GOODISH LADDISH MURKISH POPPISH SAWFISH VAMPISH
BADDISH CODFISH FADDISH GRAYISH LADYISH NEBBISH PRUDISH SELFISH VARNISH
BALDISH COLDISH FAIRISH GREYISH LARGISH NERDISH PUBLISH SERFISH VOGUISH
BATFISH COLTISH FALSISH GUARISH LARKISH NICEISH PUCKISH SICKISH WAGGISH
BEAMISH COOLISH FASTISH GULLISH LAZYISH NOIRISH PUGGISH SLAVISH WAMPISH
BEARISH COWFISH FATTISH HAGFISH LEFTISH NOURISH PUNKISH SLOWISH WANNISH
BEAUISH CUBBISH FENNISH HAGGISH LOMPISH NUNNISH PUPFISH SNAKISH WARMISH
BIGGISH CULTISH FILMISH HARDISH LONGISH OARFISH RAFFISH SNOWISH WASPISH
BLEMISH CURRISH FINEISH HASHISH LOUDISH OGREISH RAMMISH SOFTISH WEAKISH
BLUEISH DAMPISH FINFISH HAWKISH LOUTISH OOFTISH RANKISH SOTTISH WEARISH
BOARISH DANKISH FLEMISH HEIMISH LUBFISH OUTFISH RASPISH SOURISH WENNISH
BOBBISH DARKISH FOGYISH HELLISH LUMPISH OUTWISH RATFISH STONISH WETTISH
BOGGISH DEAFISH FOLKISH HICKISH LUSKISH PANFISH RATTISH STYLISH WHEYISH
BOOBISH DERVISH FOOLISH HIGHISH MADDISH PARKISH REDDISH SUNFISH WHITISH
BOOKISH DIMMISH FOPPISH HIPPISH MAIDISH PEAKISH REDFISH SWINISH WHORISH
BOORISH DOGFISH FOXFISH HOBBISH MANNISH PECKISH RELLISH TALLISH WILDISH
BOXFISH DOGGISH FULLISH HOGFISH MAWKISH PEEVISH RIGGISH TANNISH WIMPISH
BRINISH DOLLISH FURBISH HOGGISH MINXISH PERKISH ROGUISH TARNISH WISPISH
BRUTISH DOLTISH FURNISH HORNISH MISSISH PETTISH ROINISH TARTISH WOLFISH
BUCKISH DONNISH GAMPISH HOTTISH MOBBISH PIEDISH ROMPISH TIGRISH WOLVISH
BULLISH DOVEISH GARFISH HUFFISH MONKISH PIGFISH ROOKISH TITTISH WORDISH
BURNISH DRONISH GARNISH HUNNISH MOONISH PIGGISH ROYNISH TOADISH WORMISH
CADDISH DULLISH GAWKISH JEWFISH MOORISH PINFISH RUBBISH TOFFISH YOBBISH
CARLISH DUMPISH GEMFISH JIGGISH MOREISH PINKISH RUMMISH TONNISH ZANYISH
CATFISH DUNCISH GIRLISH KADDISH MUDFISH PIXYISH RUNTISH TOWNISH

8-letter words -ISH

ACTORISH CAMELISH DREGGISH GOATFISH NUMBFISH SAILFISH SORRYISH TIGHTISH
ADMONISH CAVEFISH DROLLISH GOLDFISH NYMPHISH SAINTISH SPARKISH TILEFISH
ASTONISH CEORLISH DROOGISH GRAYFISH ORANGISH SALTFISH SPOFFISH TINGLISH
BABELISH CHEAPISH DRUMFISH GREENISH OVERFISH SANDFISH SPOOKISH TOADFISH
BAIRNISH CHILDISH DWARFISH GRUFFISH PAGANISH SCAMPISH SQUARISH TOADYISH
BAITFISH CHURLISH EMPERISH GRUMPISH PIPEFISH SCARFISH SQUIRISH TOLLDISH
BAKSHISH CLANNISH ENRAVISH GYPSYISH PIXIEISH SCOMFISH STABLISH TOUGHISH
BILLFISH CLAPDISH ESSAYISH HEADFISH PLAINISH SCUMFISH STANDISH TOVARISH
BLACKISH CLERKISH ETHERISH IDIOTISH PLUMPISH SHARPISH STARFISH TRAMPISH
BLANDISH CLIQUISH FAINTISH JACKFISH POKERISH SHEEPISH STARTISH TRICKISH
BLEAKISH CLODDISH FALLFISH JINGOISH PRANKISH SHORTISH STEEPISH UNMODISH
BLIMPISH CLOWNISH FEEBLISH KINGFISH PRIGGISH SHREWISH STIFFISH UNPOLISH
BLOCKISH CLUBBISH FEVERISH KNACKISH PROUDISH SISSYISH STILTISH VAGARISH
BLOKEISH CLUMPISH FIENDISH LADYFISH PSEUDISH SIXTYISH STOCKISH VANQUISH
BLONDISH COALFISH FIFTYISH LANGUISH PUPPYISH SKIRMISH STOUTISH VAPORISH
BLOWFISH COARSISH FILEFISH LEMONISH PURPLISH SKITTISH STUDFISH VIGORISH
BLUEFISH COMPLISH FLATFISH LIGHTISH PYGMYISH SLANGISH SUCKFISH VIPERISH
BLUNTISH CRANKISH FLATTISH LIONFISH QUACKISH SLIMMISH SUMPHISH VIXENISH
BOARFISH CRAWFISH FLIRTISH LITTLISH QUALMISH SLOBBISH SURFFISH WALLFISH
BONEFISH CRAYFISH FLOURISH LIVERISH QUEERISH SLUGGISH SWAINISH WATERISH
BOOBYISH CROSSISH FOGEYISH LUMPFISH QUIPPISH SLUTTISH SWAMPISH WEAKFISH
BRACKISH DANDYISH FOOLFISH LUNGFISH QUIRKISH SMALLISH SWEETISH WOLFFISH
BRAINISH DEALFISH FORTYISH MILKFISH REFINISH SMARTISH SWELLISH WOMANISH
BRANDISH DEMOLISH FRAILISH MONKFISH REPOLISH SNAPPISH SYLPHISH YOKELISH
BRASSISH DEPOLISH FREAKISH MOONFISH RIGHTISH SNEAKISH THICKISH YOUNGISH
BRATTISH DEVILISH FRESHISH NABOBISH ROCKFISH SNIFFISH THIEVISH
BRISKISH DIMINISH FROGFISH NANNYISH ROSEFISH SNOBBISH THINNISH
BROADISH DOWDYISH FRUMPISH NINNYISH ROUGHISH SNOUTISH THUGGISH
BROGUISH DRABBISH GHOULISH NOHOWISH ROUNDISH SNUBBISH TICKLISH
BROWNISH DRAFFISH GLUMPISH NOVELISH ROWDYISH SOLIDISH TIGERISH

WORDS ENDING IN -ISM

7-letter words -ISM

ABLEISM ASTEISM ATOMISM BAPTISM BROMISM CAMBISM CHORISM COPYISM CULTISM
AMORISM ATAVISM BAALISM BOGYISM BRUTISM CHARISM CLADISM COSMISM CZARISM
ANIMISM ATHEISM BABUISM BOSSISM BRUXISM CHEMISM CLONISM CRETISM DADAISM

DIORISM	EROTISM	FIDEISM	ITACISM	LOOKISM	ONANISM	REALISM	TOURISM	ZANYISM
DODOISM	ETACISM	FOGYISM	JUJUISM	MAIDISM	ORALISM	SELFISM	TROPISM	
DONNISM	ETATISM	FOODISM	KARAISM	MYALISM	PEONISM	SENSISM	TSARISM	
DUALISM	EXOTISM	GURUISM	LADYISM	MYTHISM	PHAEISM	SIZEISM	TYCHISM	
ECHOISM	FADDISM	HEROISM	LAICISM	NARCISM	PHOBISM	SLUMISM	TZARISM	
EGOTISM	FALSISM	HEURISM	LEFTISM	NEURISM	PHOTISM	SOPHISM	URANISM	
ELITISM	FASCISM	HOBOISM	LEGGISM	OBELISM	PIANISM	STATISM	UTOPISM	
ENTRISM	FATTISM	IDOLISM	LIONISM	ODYLISM	PIETISM	TACHISM	WHOLISM	
EPICISM	FAUVISM	IMAGISM	LOCOISM	OGREISM	PLENISM	TACTISM	YOBBISM	

8-letter words -ISM

ACOSMISM	BOYARISM	DRUIDISM	FUTURISM	METOPISM	PALUDISM	REGALISM	TERATISM
ACROTISM	BULLYISM	DWARFISM	GIANTISM	MINIMISM	PAPALISM	RIGHTISM	THUGGISM
ACTINISM	CABALISM	DYNAMISM	GYPSYISM	MODALISM	PARECISM	RIGORISM	TIGERISM
ACTIVISM	CAFFEISM	EBIONISM	HEDONISM	MONADISM	PARTYISM	ROBOTISM	TITANISM
ALARMISM	CASTEISM	EMBOLISM	HELOTISM	MORALISM	PELORISM	ROWDYISM	TOADYISM
ALBINISM	CENTRISM	ENDEMISM	HOBBYISM	MORONISM	PETALISM	ROYALISM	TOKENISM
ALGORISM	CHARTISM	ENTRYISM	HUMANISM	NABOBISM	PEYOTISM	RURALISM	TOTALISM
ALIENISM	CIVICISM	EPIZOISM	HYLICISM	NATIVISM	PHALLISM	SAINTISM	TOTEMISM
ALLELISM	CLASSISM	ERETHISM	IDEALISM	NATURISM	PHRENISM	SAPPHISM	TRIADISM
ALPINISM	CLIQUISM	ERGOTISM	IDIOTISM	NAVALISM	PLUMBISM	SATANISM	TRIALISM
ALTRUISM	CLUBBISM	ESCAPISM	INCIVISM	NEGROISM	POLONISM	SAVAGISM	TROILISM
ANEURISM	COLORISM	ETHERISM	INTIMISM	NEPHRISM	POPULISM	SCIOLISM	TUTORISM
APHORISM	CRONYISM	ETHICISM	IOTACISM	NEPOTISM	PRIAPISM	SCRIBISM	ULTRAISM
APTERISM	CULLYISM	EUGENISM	JINGOISM	NIHILISM	PRIGGISM	SEISMISM	UNDINISM
ARCHAISM	CYNICISM	EUMERISM	LACONISM	NIMBYISM	PROSAISM	SIMPLISM	UNIONISM
ASTERISM	DANDYISM	EUPHUISM	LEGALISM	NOMADISM	PSELLISM	SINAPISM	UNTRUISM
ATROPISM	DEMONISM	EXORCISM	LOBBYISM	NOVELISM	PSEPHISM	SNOBBISM	URBANISM
ATTICISM	DEVILISM	FAIRYISM	LOCALISM	OBEAHISM	PSYCHISM	SOLARISM	VEGANISM
AUTECISM	DIMERISM	FAKIRISM	LOGICISM	OCKERISM	PTYALISM	SOLECISM	VIRILISM
BABELISM	DIOECISM	FAMILISM	LOYALISM	OPIUMISM	PUGILISM	SOLIDISM	VITALISM
BATHMISM	DIRIGISM	FARADISM	LUMINISM	OPTIMISM	PUPPYISM	SOMATISM	VOCALISM
BETACISM	DITHEISM	FATALISM	LYRICISM	ORGANISM	PYGMYISM	STOICISM	VOLTAISM
BOGEYISM	DONATISM	FEMINISM	MACARISM	PACIFISM	QUACKISM	STRABISM	YAHOOISM
BOOBYISM	DOWDYISM	FINALISM	MELANISM	PAEANISM	QUIETISM	SWINGISM	ZOMBIISM
BOTULISM	DRUDGISM	FOGEYISM	MERYCISM	PAGANISM	RACEMISM	SYBOTISM	

WORDS ENDING IN -IST

7-letter words -IST

ABLEIST	CAMBIST	CYCLIST	ELOGIST	FLUTIST	IRONIST	PALMIST	RHYMIST	TROPIST
ACQUIST	CASUIST	CZARIST	ENTRIST	FUGUIST	IVORIST	PERSIST	SACRIST	TSARIST
AGONIST	CELLIST	DADAIST	ENTWIST	GAMBIST	JUDOIST	PHOBIST	SELFIST	TUBAIST
ALTOIST	CHEKIST	DENTIST	EPEEIST	GNOMIST	JUJUIST	PIANIST	SENSIST	TZARIST
AMORIST	CHEMIST	DIALIST	EPICIST	HARPIST	LEFTIST	PIARIST	SIZEIST	UNALIST
ANGLIST	CHORIST	DIARIST	ETATIST	HERBIST	MAPPIST	PIETIST	SOLOIST	UNTWIST
ANIMIST	CHUTIST	DIETIST	EXODIST	HORNIST	METRIST	PLENIST	SOPHIST	UPHOIST
ATAVIST	CHYMIST	DUALIST	FADDIST	HYGEIST	MYTHIST	PLUMIST	STATIST	UTOPIST
ATHEIST	CLADIST	DUELIST	FASCIST	HYLOIST	NAIVIST	POLLIST	STYLIST	VACUIST
ATOMIST	COEXIST	DUMAIST	FATTIST	HYMNIST	NARCIST	POLOIST	SUBSIST	VIOLIST
ATTRIST	CONSIST	EBONIST	FAUNIST	IAMBIST	OCULIST	PROTIST	SUMMIST	WHOLIST
BAPTIST	COPYIST	ECHOIST	FAUVIST	IDOLIST	OLIGIST	QUERIST	TACHIST	
BASSIST	CORNIST	EGOTIST	FEUDIST	IDYLIST	OLOGIST	REALIST	TENNIST	
BIBLIST	COSMIST	ELEGIST	FIDEIST	IMAGIST	ONANIST	RETWIST	TITLIST	
BUNDIST	CULTIST	ELITIST	FLORIST	INTWIST	ORALIST	REVUIST	TOURIST	

8-letter words -IST

ACOSMIST	ARCHAIST	CANOEIST	CREOLIST	ESSAYIST	FUTURIST	HYPOCIST	LOYALIST
ACTIVIST	ARMORIST	CANONIST	DEMONIST	ETHERIST	GARAGIST	IDEALIST	LUMINIST
ALARMIST	ARSONIST	CENTOIST	DEMOTIST	ETHICIST	GROUPIST	IDYLLIST	LUNARIST
ALIENIST	ATTICIST	CENTRIST	DIALLIST	EUGENIST	HAGADIST	INTIMIST	LUTANIST
ALPINIST	AVIARIST	CERAMIST	DIGAMIST	EULOGIST	HALAKIST	JINGOIST	LUTENIST
ALTRUIST	BACKLIST	CHARTIST	DITHEIST	EUPHUIST	HANDLIST	JUNGLIST	LUXURIST
ANNALIST	BANJOIST	CIVILIST	DRUGGIST	EXORCIST	HEDONIST	LAPIDIST	LYRICIST
APHORIST	BIGAMIST	CLASSIST	DUELLIST	FABULIST	HOBBYIST	LEGALIST	MAXIMIST
APIARIST	BONGOIST	CLUBBIST	DUETTIST	FATALIST	HOMILIST	LIBELIST	MEDALIST
AQUARIST	BOTANIST	COASSIST	DYNAMIST	FEMINIST	HUMANIST	LINGUIST	MELANIST
ARBALIST	BURINIST	COLONIST	ENTRYIST	FIGURIST	HUMORIST	LOBBYIST	MELODIST
ARBORIST	CABALIST	COLORIST	ERRORIST	FINALIST	HYGIEIST	LOCALIST	METALIST
ARCANIST	CALORIST	CONTRIST	ESCAPIST	FLAUTIST	HYLICIST	LOGICIST	MINIMIST

MODALIST NOVELIST PARODIST PUGILIST SAPPHIST SODALIST TOTALIST VITALIST
MODELIST ODONTIST PEYOTIST QUIETIST SARODIST SODOMIST TOTEMIST VOCALIST
MONODIST OGHAMIST PHALLIST RALLYIST SATANIST SOLARIST TRIADIST VOLUMIST
MORALIST OOLOGIST PLAYLIST REENLIST SATIRIST SOLECIST TRIALIST VOTARIST
MOTORIST OPTICIST POLEMIST REGALIST SCIOLIST SOLIDIST TROILIST
MURALIST OPTIMIST POPULIST REVERIST SEMITIST SOMATIST ULTRAIST
NATIVIST ORGANIST PREEXIST RIGHTIST SHOOTIST STOCKIST UNIONIST
NATURIST PACIFIST PROSAIST RIGORIST SILURIST SUBTRIST UNSEXIST
NEPOTIST PAGANIST PSALMIST ROYALIST SIMONIST TANGOIST URBANIST
NIELLIST PANELIST PSYCHIST RURALIST SIMPLIST TENORIST VEGETIST
NIHILIST PAPALIST PUCKFIST SAFARIST SITARIST THEORIST VISAGIST

WORDS ENDING IN -ITY

7-letter words -ITY

ABILITY ARIDITY CURVITY EGALITY JOLLITY OVALITY RABBITY TENUITY
ACIDITY AUREITY DABBITY EXILITY LAICITY PANEITY RAUCITY TRINITY
AGILITY AVIDITY DACOITY FALSITY NULLITY PAUCITY REALITY UNICITY
AMENITY BIGGITY DAKOITY FATUITY OBESITY PIOSITY SICCITY UTILITY
AMINITY BREVITY DENSITY FURMITY OMNEITY PRAVITY SPIRITY VACUITY
ANALITY CHARITY DIGNITY GASEITY OPACITY PRIVITY SUAVITY VARSITY
ANILITY CLARITY DUALITY GRAVITY ORALITY PROBITY SURDITY VASTITY
ANNUITY CRUDITY EDACITY INANITY OUTPITY QUALITY TENSITY VIDUITY

8-letter words -ITY

ACERBITY CHASTITY FEROCITY IMPUNITY MODALITY POLARITY SECURITY UNFIXITY
ACRIDITY CIRCUITY FIDELITY IMPURITY MOLALITY POROSITY SEDULITY URBANITY
ACTIVITY CIVILITY FINALITY INEQUITY MOLARITY PRIORITY SENILITY VAGILITY
ADUNCITY CONCEITY FLUIDITY INFINITY MORALITY PUDICITY SERENITY VALIDITY
AFFINITY CONICITY FORTUITY INIQUITY MORONITY QUANTITY SEROSITY VAPIDITY
ALACRITY CUBICITY FUGACITY INSANITY MOROSITY QUEERITY SEVERITY VELLEITY
ALGIDITY CUPIDITY FUMOSITY INTIMITY MOTILITY QUIDDITY SODALITY VELOCITY
ALTERITY DEBILITY FURACITY INVERITY MOTIVITY RABIDITY SOLICITY VENALITY
ANTICITY DICACITY FUTILITY IONICITY MUCIDITY RAMOSITY SOLIDITY VENOSITY
ASPERITY DISUNITY FUTURITY JEJUNITY MUCOSITY RAPACITY SONORITY VERACITY
ASTUCITY DIVINITY GELIDITY JOCOSITY MULTEITY RAPIDITY SORORITY VICINITY
ATROCITY DOCILITY GRATUITY LABILITY NASALITY REGALITY SPARSITY VINOSITY
AUDACITY DUMOSITY GULOSITY LANOSITY NATALITY RIGIDITY TEMERITY VIRIDITY
AXIALITY ENORMITY HELICITY LATINITY NATIVITY RIMOSITY TENACITY VIRILITY
BANALITY EQUALITY HEREDITY LEGALITY NIHILITY RIVALITY TEPIDITY VITALITY
BASICITY EQUINITY HILARITY LEGERITY NOBILITY RUGOSITY TIMIDITY VIVACITY
BIFIDITY ETERNITY HUMANITY LIVIDITY NODALITY RURALITY TONALITY VIVIDITY
BISCUITY EXIGUITY HUMIDITY LOCALITY NODOSITY SAGACITY TONICITY VOCALITY
BOVINITY FACILITY HUMILITY LUCIDITY NUBILITY SALACITY TOROSITY VORACITY
CADUCITY FATALITY IDEALITY MAJORITY OBTUSITY SALINITY TOTALITY ZYGOSITY
CALAMITY FELICITY IDENTITY MATURITY ORGANITY SANCTITY TOXICITY
CALIDITY FELINITY IDONEITY MEGACITY OTIOSITY SAPIDITY TRIALITY
CANINITY FEMALITY IMMANITY MINACITY PENALITY SATANITY TRIUNITY
CAPACITY FEMINITY IMMUNITY MINORITY PERSEITY SCANTITY TUMIDITY
CELERITY FERACITY IMPARITY MOBILITY PILOSITY SCARCITY UBIQUITY

WORDS ENDING IN -IUM

7-letter words -IUM

ALODIUM CAMBIUM FERMIUM ISCHIUM OXONIUM RHENIUM TERBIUM UREDIUM
ALUMIUM CRANIUM GALLIUM LITHIUM PALLIUM RHODIUM THORIUM YTTRIUM
BALLIUM ELOGIUM HAFNIUM MUONIUM PLAGIUM SPODIUM THULIUM ZOARIUM
CADMIUM ELUVIUM HAHNIUM NATRIUM PREMIUM STADIUM TRITIUM ZOECIUM
CAESIUM ERODIUM HOLMIUM NIOBIUM PROTIUM STIBIUM TRIVIUM
CALCIUM EXUVIUM IRIDIUM ORARIUM PYTHIUM TAEDIUM URANIUM

8-letter words -IUM

ACHENIUM ALLUVIUM ASPIDIUM BRACHIUM CONIDIUM DELIRIUM EMPORIUM EXORDIUM
ACTINIUM AMMONIUM BASIDIUM CALADIUM COREMIUM DIDYMIUM ENCOMIUM FRANCIUM
AECIDIUM APTERIUM BDELLIUM CHROMIUM CORONIUM DILUVIUM ERYNGIUM GERANIUM
AEROBIUM AQUARIUM BIENNIUM CIBORIUM CYATHIUM DOMATIUM EULOGIUM GONIDIUM
ALLODIUM ASCIDIUM BOTHRIUM CONARIUM CYMATIUM DOMINIUM EUROPIUM GRAPHIUM

GYNECIUM INGENIUM NEBULIUM PATAGIUM PYGIDIUM SCHOLIUM SOREDIUM VELARIUM
HELENIUM LIXIVIUM NOBELIUM PECULIUM PYXIDIUM SEDILIUM SPLENIUM VENIDIUM
HYMENIUM LUTECIUM ONCIDIUM PEPONIUM RANARIUM SELENIUM SUDARIUM VIVARIUM
ILLINIUM LUTETIUM ONYCHIUM PERIDIUM REFUGIUM SILICIUM SYCONIUM ZOOECIUM
ILLUVIUM MASURIUM OOGONIUM PHORMIUM ROSARIUM SILPHIUM THALLIUM
IMPERIUM MECONIUM OPSONIUM POLONIUM RUBIDIUM SIMULIUM TITANIUM
INDICIUM MOTORIUM ORDALIUM PSYLLIUM SAMARIUM SOLARIUM TRILLIUM
INDUSIUM MYCELIUM OSSARIUM PUPARIUM SCANDIUM SOLATIUM VANADIUM

WORDS ENDING IN -KIN

7-letter words -KIN

BARMKIN BUMPKIN CUTIKIN FOXSKIN KIPSKIN LUMPKIN PIGSKIN SIMPKIN
BAWDKIN CANAKIN DOESKIN GHERKIN LADYKIN MANAKIN PUMPKIN WOLFKIN
BODIKIN CANIKIN DOGSKIN GRISKIN LAMBKIN MANIKIN RAMAKIN
BOOMKIN CATSKIN DOITKIN HUFFKIN LIMPKIN MINIKIN RAMEKIN
BRODKIN COWSKIN FINIKIN KIDSKIN LORDKIN OILSKIN REDSKIN

8-letter words -KIN

BAUDEKIN BYRLAKIN COONSKIN DEVILKIN GOATSKIN MOUSEKIN SEALSKIN WINESKIN
BEARSKIN CALFSKIN COOTIKIN DUNNAKIN LAMBSKIN MUNCHKIN SPILIKIN WOLFSKIN
BOOTIKIN CANNIKIN CUITIKIN FINICKIN LARRIKIN MUTCHKIN SWANSKIN WOODSKIN
BRODEKIN CAPESKIN DAMASKIN FISHSKIN MANNIKIN PANNIKIN THUMBKIN WOOLSKIN
BUCKSKIN CIDERKIN DEERSKIN FORESKIN MOLESKIN PONYSKIN TURNSKIN

WORDS ENDING IN -LAND

7-letter words -LAND

BADLAND DRYLAND GARLAND HOLLAND LOWLAND OUTLAND TROLAND
BOGLAND ELFLAND GOLLAND LALLAND MIDLAND RIMLAND WETLAND
COTLAND FENLAND GOWLAND LAWLAND NORLAND SUNLAND

8-letter words -LAND

BACKLAND DOCKLAND FLATLAND HOMELAND OVERLAND SCABLAND TOWNLAND
BOOKLAND DOWNLAND FOLKLAND LACKLAND PARKLAND SHETLAND WASHLAND
BUSHLAND DUNELAND FORELAND LAKELAND PINELAND SLOBLAND WILDLAND
CLUBLAND EASTLAND GANGLAND MAINLAND PLAYLAND SNOWLAND WOODLAND
CORNLAND FARMLAND HEADLAND MOORLAND PLOWLAND SOAPLAND YARDLAND
CROPLAND FILMLAND HIGHLAND MOSSLAND PORTLAND TIDELAND

WORDS ENDING IN -LESS

7-letter words -LESS

AGELESS BIBLESS EGGLESS GODLESS INNLESS MANLESS RUNLESS TOELESS WINLESS
AIDLESS BITLESS EGOLESS GUMLESS IRELESS MATLESS SACLESS TOPLESS WITLESS
AIMLESS BOWLESS ENDLESS GUNLESS JAGLESS NAPLESS SAPLESS TOYLESS ZIPLESS
AIRLESS BRALESS EYELESS GUTLESS JOBLESS NETLESS SEXLESS TUGLESS
ARMLESS BUDLESS FATLESS HAPLESS JOYLESS OARLESS SINLESS UNBLESS
ARTLESS CAPLESS FEELESS HATLESS KEYLESS PEGLESS SONLESS USELESS
ASHLESS CARLESS FINLESS HIPLESS KINLESS PIPLESS SUMLESS VOWLESS
AWELESS CUBLESS FLYLESS HITLESS LAWLESS RAYLESS SUNLESS WARLESS
AWNLESS DEWLESS FOGLESS HUELESS LEGLESS RIBLESS TAXLESS WAYLESS
BARLESS EARLESS FURLESS ICELESS LIDLESS RIMLESS TIELESS WEBLESS
BEDLESS EBBLESS GASLESS INKLESS LIPLESS RODLESS TIPLESS WIGLESS

8-letter words -LESS

BACKLESS BEAMLESS BOOTLESS CHAPLESS COMBLESS CURBLESS DRIPLESS FADELESS
BARBLESS BEATLESS BRIMLESS CHINLESS COOKLESS CURELESS DUCTLESS FAMELESS
BARKLESS BEEFLESS BROWLESS CLAWLESS CORDLESS DATELESS DUSTLESS FANGLESS
BASELESS BELTLESS BUSHLESS CLOYLESS CORELESS DEBTLESS EASELESS FEARLESS
BASHLESS BLOTLESS CALFLESS CLUELESS COSTLESS DEEDLESS ECHOLESS FECKLESS
BATELESS BODILESS CARELESS COALLESS CREWLESS DEVILESS EDGELESS FEETLESS
BATHLESS BONELESS CASHLESS COATLESS CROPLESS DISKLESS EXITLESS FERNLESS
BEAKLESS BOOKLESS CHADLESS CODELESS CUFFLESS DOORLESS FACELESS FINELESS

FIRELESS HEATLESS LENSLESS NORMLESS REINLESS SIGHLESS TAPELESS VESTLESS
FIRMLESS HEEDLESS LIFELESS NOSELESS RESTLESS SIGNLESS TEARLESS VICELESS
FISHLESS HEELLESS LIMBLESS NOTELESS RIFTLESS SKILLESS TEEMLESS VIEWLESS
FLAGLESS HEIRLESS LIMELESS NOUNLESS RINDLESS SKINLESS TENTLESS VOTELESS
FLAPLESS HELMLESS LINELESS ODORLESS RINGLESS SLIPLESS TERMLESS WAGELESS
FLAWLESS HELPLESS LINTLESS OUTBLESS RISKLESS SLITLESS TEXTLESS WAKELESS
FOAMLESS HERBLESS LISTLESS PAINLESS RITELESS SMOGLESS THAWLESS WARELESS
FOODLESS HIDELESS LOAMLESS PANGLESS RIVALESS SNAPLESS THEWLESS WARTLESS
FOOTLESS HILTLESS LOFTLESS PASSLESS ROADLESS SNOWLESS THOWLESS WATTLESS
FORDLESS HIVELESS LORDLESS PASTLESS ROCKLESS SOAPLESS TIDELESS WAVELESS
FORKLESS HOLELESS LOVELESS PATHLESS ROOFLESS SOCKLESS TIMELESS WEEDLESS
FORMLESS HOMELESS LUCKLESS PEAKLESS ROOTLESS SODALESS TINTLESS WEETLESS
FRETLESS HOODLESS LUSTLESS PEERLESS ROSELESS SOILLESS TIRELESS WELDLESS
FUMELESS HOOFLESS MAIDLESS PILELESS RULELESS SOLELESS TOADLESS WIFELESS
FUNDLESS HOOKLESS MAILLESS PIPELESS RUMPLESS SONGLESS TOILLESS WINDLESS
FUSELESS HOOPLESS MAKELESS PITHLESS RUNGLESS SOOTLESS TOMBLESS WINELESS
GAINLESS HOPELESS MANELESS PITILESS RUSTLESS SOULLESS TONELESS WINGLESS
GARBLESS HORNLESS MASSLESS PLANLESS RUTHLESS SPANLESS TOOLLESS WIRELESS
GATELESS HUMPLESS MASTLESS PLAYLESS SACKLESS SPINLESS TOWNLESS WISHLESS
GAUMLESS HURTLESS MATELESS PLOTLESS SAIKLESS SPOTLESS TRAMLESS WITELESS
GEARLESS HYMNLESS MEALLESS PLUGLESS SAILLESS SPURLESS TREELESS WONTLESS
GIFTLESS IDEALESS MEATLESS POETLESS SALTLESS STARLESS TUBELESS WOODLESS
GOALLESS ISLELESS MILKLESS POLELESS SATELESS STAYLESS TUNELESS WORDLESS
GOLDLESS KEELLESS MINDLESS POPELESS SCARLESS STEMLESS TURFLESS WORKLESS
GORMLESS KINDLESS MOONLESS PORTLESS SEAMLESS STIRLESS TUSKLESS YOKELESS
GUSTLESS KINGLESS MOVELESS PREBLESS SEATLESS STOPLESS TWIGLESS ZEALLESS
HAIRLESS KNOTLESS NAILLESS PULPLESS SEEDLESS SUCKLESS TYRELESS ZESTLESS
HALTLESS LACELESS NAMELESS PUMPLESS SEEMLESS SUDSLESS VANELESS ZONELESS
HANDLESS LANDLESS NATHLESS RAILLESS SELFLESS TACKLESS VEILLESS
HARMLESS LEADLESS NECKLESS RAINLESS SHIPLESS TACTLESS VEINLESS
HATELESS LEAFLESS NEEDLESS RECKLESS SHOELESS TAILLESS VENTLESS
HEADLESS LEAKLESS NEWSLESS REDELESS SHUNLESS TAMELESS VERBLESS

WORDS ENDING IN -LET

7-letter words -LET

ANNULET CANTLET DEVILET FROGLET KINGLET NOTELET RIVULET STERLET WAVELET
ARCHLET CAPELET DOUBLET GANTLET LAKELET OSSELET ROOTLET SWALLET WINGLET
BEAMLET CHAMLET DOVELET GURGLET LEAFLET OVERLET ROYALET TARTLET ZONULET
BENDLET CHAPLET DRIBLET HACKLET LOBELET PARTLET RUNDLET TEMPLET
BOMBLET CIRCLET DROPLET HARSLET MANTLET PIKELET SCARLET TOWNLET
BOOKLET CORSLET EPAULET HERBLET MARTLET PLAYLET SINGLET TRIBLET
BOOMLET COUPLET FLATLET HOOKLET MEDALET QUILLET SKILLET TRIOLET
BULBLET COVELET FONTLET HORNLET MOONLET RINGLET STARLET TRIPLET
CACOLET DEERLET FORTLET JINGLET NECKLET RIPPLET STEMLET VEINLET

8-letter words -LET

BANDELET CHEVALET DRIBBLET GLOBULET MIQUELET PLANTLET SEXTOLET TROUTLET
BARRULET CLOUDLET DRUPELET GREENLET MURRELET PLATELET SPANGLET UMBELLET
BRACELET CORSELET FLAMELET GROUPLET NERVELET PLUMELET SPARKLET UNDERLET
BRACTLET COURTLET FOVEOLET HEARTLET NONUPLET QUEENLET SPIKELET VALVELET
BROOKLET COVERLET FRONTLET HERBELET OCTUPLET RECOLLET SWIFTLET VEINULET
CAPELLET CROSSLET FRUITLET LANCELET PAMPHLET RONDELET TERCELET VERSELET
CHAINLET CROWNLET GAUNTLET MANTELET PISTOLET ROUNDLET TRICKLET WRISTLET

WORDS ENDING IN -LIKE

7-letter words -LIKE

AIRLIKE BOXLIKE FATLIKE HOBLIKE LAWLIKE OAKLIKE RATLIKE TAGLIKE WEBLIKE
ANTLIKE BUDLIKE FINLIKE HOELIKE LEGLIKE OARLIKE RAYLIKE TEALIKE WIGLIKE
APELIKE CATLIKE FOXLIKE HOGLIKE LIPLIKE OATLIKE RIBLIKE TINLIKE
ARMLIKE CUPLIKE GEMLIKE HUTLIKE MANLIKE OWLLIKE RODLIKE TOELIKE
ASSLIKE DISLIKE GODLIKE ICELIKE MAPLIKE PEALIKE RUGLIKE TOYLIKE
BATLIKE DOGLIKE GUMLIKE INKLIKE MISLIKE PEGLIKE SACLIKE TUBLIKE
BEDLIKE EELLIKE GUTLIKE IVYLIKE NETLIKE PIGLIKE SAWLIKE UNALIKE
BEELIKE ELFLIKE HATLIKE JAWLIKE NIBLIKE PODLIKE SICLIKE URNLIKE
BIBLIKE EYELIKE HENLIKE JETLIKE NUNLIKE POTLIKE SONLIKE WARLIKE
BOWLIKE FANLIKE HIPLIKE KIDLIKE NUTLIKE PUSLIKE SUNLIKE WAXLIKE

8-letter words -LIKE

AGUELIKE DEERLIKE GLUELIKE KINGLIKE MOTHLIKE ROOTLIKE SOULLIKE VEINLIKE
AUNTLIKE DISCLIKE GNATLIKE KITELIKE NECKLIKE ROPELIKE SPARLIKE VESTLIKE
BALMLIKE DISHLIKE GOADLIKE KNOBLIKE NESTLIKE ROSELIKE STARLIKE VISELIKE
BARNLIKE DISKLIKE GOATLIKE KNOTLIKE NOOKLIKE RUBYLIKE STEMLIKE WAIFLIKE
BEADLIKE DOMELIKE GONGLIKE LACELIKE NOSELIKE RUFFLIKE STEPLIKE WARTLIKE
BEAKLIKE DOVELIKE GULFLIKE LADYLIKE NOVALIKE RUNELIKE SUCHLIKE WASPLIKE
BEAMLIKE DRUMLIKE HAIRLIKE LAKELIKE OVENLIKE RUSHLIKE SUITLIKE WAVELIKE
BEANLIKE DUNELIKE HALOLIKE LAMBLIKE PALMLIKE SACKLIKE SURFLIKE WEEDLIKE
BEARLIKE DUSTLIKE HANDLIKE LARDLIKE PARKLIKE SALTLIKE SWANLIKE WHEYLIKE
BIRDLIKE EPICLIKE HARELIKE LATHLIKE PEAKLIKE SANDLIKE TAILLIKE WHIPLIKE
BOATLIKE FANGLIKE HAWKLIKE LAVALIKE PINELIKE SCABLIKE TANKLIKE WIFELIKE
BOWLLIKE FAUNLIKE HEMPLIKE LEAFLIKE PIPELIKE SCUMLIKE TAPELIKE WINGLIKE
BUSHLIKE FAWNLIKE HERBLIKE LIFELIKE PITHLIKE SEALLIKE TENTLIKE WIRELIKE
CALFLIKE FELTLIKE HERDLIKE LILYLIKE PLAYLIKE SEAMLIKE TIDELIKE WISPLIKE
CAVELIKE FERNLIKE HIVELIKE LINELIKE PLUMLIKE SEEDLIKE TILELIKE WOLFLIKE
CLAWLIKE FISHLIKE HOMELIKE LIONLIKE POETLIKE SERFLIKE TOADLIKE WOMBLIKE
CLAYLIKE FOAMLIKE HOODLIKE LOFTLIKE POPELIKE SHEDLIKE TOMBLIKE WOOLLIKE
COCKLIKE FOLKLIKE HOOFLIKE LORDLIKE PUMPLIKE SIGHLIKE TRAPLIKE WORMLIKE
COMBLIKE FOOTLIKE HOOKLIKE MASKLIKE PUSSLIKE SILKLIKE TREELIKE
CORDLIKE FORKLIKE HOOPLIKE MASTLIKE QUAYLIKE SKINLIKE TUBELIKE
CORKLIKE FROGLIKE HORNLIKE MAZELIKE RASHLIKE SLABLIKE TURFLIKE
CORMLIKE FUMELIKE HUSKLIKE MILKLIKE REEDLIKE SNAGLIKE TUSKLIKE
CRABLIKE GAMELIKE HYMNLIKE MOATLIKE RINGLIKE SNOWLIKE TWIGLIKE
CULTLIKE GATELIKE IRONLIKE MOONLIKE ROCKLIKE SOAPLIKE VASELIKE
DAWNLIKE GLENLIKE JAZZLIKE MOSSLIKE ROOFLIKE SONGLIKE VEILLIKE

WORDS ENDING IN -LOGY

7-letter words -LOGY

ANALOGY BIOLOGY ECOLOGY GEOLOGY NEOLOGY OROLOGY TRILOGY UROLOGY
APOLOGY DYSLOGY ENOLOGY MYOLOGY NOOLOGY OTOLOGY UFOLOGY ZOOLOGY

8-letter words -LOGY

AEROLOGY AXIOLOGY DOSOLOGY IDEOLOGY OECOLOGY PEDOLOGY SEXOLOGY VIROLOGY
AGROLOGY BATOLOGY DOXOLOGY KIDOLOGY OENOLOGY PELOLOGY SINOLOGY XYLOLOGY
ALGOLOGY BRYOLOGY ETHOLOGY MENOLOGY OINOLOGY PENOLOGY SITOLOGY ZYMOLOGY
ANTILOGY CACOLOGY ETIOLOGY MISOLOGY ONCOLOGY PODOLOGY THEOLOGY
APIOLOGY CETOLOGY FETOLOGY MIXOLOGY ONTOLOGY POMOLOGY TOCOLOGY
ARCOLOGY CHAOLOGY GEMOLOGY MONOLOGY OPTOLOGY POSOLOGY TOKOLOGY
AREOLOGY CYTOLOGY HOMOLOGY MYCOLOGY OREOLOGY PYROLOGY TOPOLOGY
ATMOLOGY DEKALOGY HOROLOGY NOMOLOGY OUROLOGY RHEOLOGY TYPOLOGY
AUTOLOGY DEMOLOGY IDEALOGY NOSOLOGY PARALOGY SEROLOGY VINOLOGY

WORDS ENDING IN -LY

7-letter words -LY

ACRIDLY AWFULLY BONNILY CAVALLY CRINKLY DICYCLY ELDERLY FISHILY FUSTILY
ACUTELY AXIALLY BOOZILY CECALLY CRISPLY DINGILY EMPTILY FIXEDLY FUZZILY
ADDEDLY BAGGILY BOSSILY CHARILY CROSSLY DIRTILY EPIBOLY FLAKILY GALLFLY
ADEPTLY BAIRNLY BRAMBLY CHEAPLY CRUDELY DISALLY EQUABLY FLEETLY GASSILY
ADULTLY BALKILY BRASHLY CHEERLY CRUELLY DIZZILY EQUALLY FLESHLY GAUDILY
AFFABLY BALMILY BRAVELY CHIEFLY CRUMBLY DOOMILY ERECTLY FLUIDLY GAUNTLY
AGILELY BANALLY BRIEFLY CHILDLY CRUMPLY DOTTILY EROSELY FOAMILY GAUZILY
ALERTLY BASALLY BRISKLY CHIMBLY CRUSILY DOUCELY EXACTLY FOCALLY GAWKILY
ALIENLY BAWDILY BRISTLY CIVILLY CUBICLY DOWDILY FADEDLY FOGGILY GELIDLY
ALONELY BEADILY BRITTLY CLEANLY CURABLY DREADLY FAINTLY FRAILLY GEMMILY
ALOOFLY BEAMILY BROADLY CLEARLY CURLILY DRIBBLY FAIRILY FRANKLY GHASTLY
AMIABLY BEASTLY BRUTELY CLERKLY CUSHILY DRIZZLY FALSELY FRECKLY GHOSTLY
ANGERLY BEEFILY BUIRDLY CLOSELY DAFFILY DROPFLY FANCILY FRESHLY GIANTLY
ANGRILY BIFIDLY BULKILY COCKILY DANDILY DUCALLY FATALLY FRIARLY GIDDILY
ANOMALY BLACKLY BUMPILY CORNFLY DATEDLY DUMPILY FATTILY FRITFLY GINGELY
ANTICLY BLANDLY BURLILY CORNILY DAYLILY DUOPOLY FETIDLY FRIZZLY GLOWFLY
APETALY BLANKLY BUSHILY COURTLY DAZEDLY DURABLY FIERILY FUGALLY GODLILY
APHYLLY BLEAKLY BUXOMLY COWEDLY DEARNLY DUSKILY FIFTHLY FUGGILY GOOFILY
APISHLY BLINDLY CAMPILY CRACKLY DEATHLY DUSTILY FILMILY FUNNILY GOUTFLY
AREALLY BLOWFLY CANNILY CRANKLY DEEDILY DYINGLY FINALLY FURRILY GOUTILY
AUDIBLY BLUFFLY CAPABLY CRASSLY DEERFLY EAGERLY FIREFLY FUSIBLY GRADELY
AURALLY BLUNTLY CATTILY CRAZILY DENSELY EARTHLY FIRSTLY FUSSILY GRANDLY

GRAVELY GRAYFLY GREATLY GREENLY GREISLY GRIESLY GRIMILY GRISELY GRISTLY GRIZZLY GROSSLY GRUFFLY GRUMBLY GRYESLY GRYSELY GUSHILY GUSTILY GUTSILY GYRALLY HAMMILY HANDILY HAPPILY HARDILY HARSHLY HARTELY HASTILY HAZELLY HEADILY HEARTLY HEAVILY HEFTILY HOARILY HORNILY HORSILY HUFFILY HUMANLY HUMIDLY HUSKILY IDEALLY IGNOBLY INANELY INAPTLY INEPTLY INERTLY
INJELLY INNERLY IRATELY ITCHILY JADEDLY JAZZILY JERKILY JOINTLY JOLLILY JOLTILY JUICILY JUMPILY JURALLY KINKILY KNOBBLY KNUBBLY KNUCKLY LADYFLY LAIRDLY LAITHLY LANKILY LARGELY LEAKILY LEERILY LEGALLY LEGIBLY LEVELLY LICHTLY LICITLY LIGHTLY LITHELY LIVIDLY LOATHLY LOCALLY LOFTILY LOOBILY LOOSELY LOUSILY LOVABLY LOVERLY LOWLILY LOYALLY LUCIDLY LUCKILY
LUMPILY LURIDLY LUSTILY LYINGLY MAJORLY MANGILY MANLILY MASCULY MAZEDLY MEATILY MERRILY MESALLY MESSILY METALLY MIFFILY MILKILY MIRKILY MISALLY MISERLY MISRELY MISTILY MIXEDLY MODALLY MOISTLY MONTHLY MOODILY MOONILY MORALLY MOUSILY MOVABLY MUCKILY MUDDILY MUGGILY MURKILY MUSHILY MUSKILY MUSSILY MUSTILY MUTABLY MUTEDLY MUZZILY NAIVELY NAKEDLY NARGILY
NASALLY NASTILY NATTILY NAVALLY NEEDILY NERVILY NIFTILY NIGHTLY NINTHLY NIPPILY NOBBILY NODALLY NOISILY NONOILY NOTABLY NOTEDLY NOVELLY NUTTILY NYMPHLY OBESELY OCTUPLY ORDERLY OVATELY OVERFLY OVERPLY OVERTLY PANOPLY PAPALLY PAWKILY PAYABLY PEARTLY PENALLY PEPPILY PERKILY PESKILY PETTILY PHONILY PIOUSLY PITHILY PLAINLY PLIABLY PLUMPLY PLUSHLY POCKILY
PODGILY PRICKLY PRIMELY PRIORLY PRIVILY PRONELY PROSILY PROUDLY PUDGILY PUFFILY PULPILY PURSILY PUSHILY QUAKILY QUEENLY QUEERLY QUICKLY QUIETLY RABIDLY RAINILY RAPIDLY RATABLY RAVELLY READILY REAPPLY REEDILY REGALLY RIANTLY RIGHTLY RIGIDLY RISIBLY RISKILY RITZILY ROCKILY ROOMILY ROUGHLY ROUNDLY ROUPILY ROWDILY ROYALLY RUDDILY RUMMILY RURALLY RUSTILY
RUTTILY SAINTLY SALABLY SALTILY SANDFLY SAPPILY SASSILY SAUCILY SCANTLY SCARILY SCRAWLY SEEDILY SHADFLY SHADILY SHAKILY SHAMBLY SHAPELY SHARPLY SHEERLY SHINGLY SHINILY SHOGGLY SHOOFLY SHOOGLY SHORTLY SHOWILY SHRILLY SIGHTLY SILKILY SILLILY SIXTHLY SIZABLY SLACKLY SLANTLY SLEEKLY SLICKLY SLIMILY SMARTLY SMICKLY SMOKILY SNAKILY SNIDELY SNOWILY SNUFFLY
SOAPILY SOBERLY SOGGILY SOLIDLY SOLUBLY SOOTHLY SOOTILY SOPPILY SORRILY SOUNDLY SPANGLY SPARELY SPARKLY SPICILY SPIKILY SPINDLY SPRAWLY SQUALLY SQUATLY STAGILY STAIDLY STALELY STARKLY STARTLY STATELY STEEPLY STERNLY STIFFLY STONILY STOUTLY STUBBLY STUMBLY SUAVELY SULKILY SUNNILY SURLILY SWEETLY SWIFTLY SWITHLY TACITLY TACKILY TARDILY TASTILY TATTILY
TAWNILY TAXABLY TEARILY TECHILY TENABLY TENSELY TENTHLY TEPIDLY TERSELY TESTILY TEUGHLY THEGNLY THICKLY THIRDLY THISTLY THRILLY TIDALLY TIGERLY TIGHTLY TIMIDLY TINNILY TIPSILY TIREDLY TONALLY TOSSILY TOTALLY TOUGHLY TREACLY TREMBLY TRICKLY TRIFOLY TRITELY TUFTILY TUMIDLY TUNABLY TWADDLY TWIDDLY TWINKLY UNAPTLY UNFITLY UNGODLY UNMANLY UNTRULY USEABLY
USUALLY UTTERLY VAGALLY VAGUELY VALIDLY VAPIDLY VENALLY VERMILY VEXEDLY VICARLY VIRALLY VISIBLY VITALLY VIVIDLY VIXENLY VOCABLY VOCALLY VOLUBLY VOWELLY VYINGLY WACKILY WASPILY WEARILY WEASELY WEEDILY WEEVILY WEIRDLY WHITELY WIGHTLY WINDILY WISPILY WITTILY WOFULLY WOMANLY WOOZILY WORDILY WORLDLY WRIGGLY WRINKLY WRONGLY YOUNGLY YOUTHLY ZONALLY

8-letter words -LY

ABASEDLY ABJECTLY ABORALLY ABRUPTLY ABSENTLY ABSURDLY ACHINGLY ACTIVELY ACTUALLY ADORABLY ADROITLY AERIALLY AFFINELY AGUISHLY AIMFULLY ALDERFLY ALPINELY AMAZEDLY AMENABLY AMICABLY AMORALLY AMUSEDLY ANIMALLY ANNUALLY ANODALLY APICALLY ARCANELY
ARDENTLY ARGUABLY ARGUTELY ARRANTLY ARTFULLY ASSEMBLY ASTRALLY ASTUTELY ATONALLY AUGUSTLY AVERSELY AVOWABLY AVOWEDLY BADGERLY BANKERLY BARRENLY BEARABLY BEASTILY BEGGARLY BEHOVELY BENIGNLY BESEEMLY BIASEDLY BIDDABLY BIHOURLY BINATELY BITCHILY
BITINGLY BITTERLY BIWEEKLY BIYEARLY BLACKFLY BLAMABLY BLEARILY BLITHELY BLOODILY BLOUSILY BLOWSILY BLOWZILY BLURRILY BODINGLY BORINGLY BOTCHILY BOUNCILY BOVINELY BOWINGLY BOYISHLY BRAINILY BRASSILY BRAWNILY BRAZENLY BREEZILY BRIDALLY BRIGHTLY
BROKENLY BROODILY BRUTALLY BUCCALLY BUNCHILY CAECALLY CANDIDLY CARNALLY CASUALLY CATCHFLY CAUDALLY CAUSALLY CHANCILY CHASTELY CHATTILY CHEEKILY CHEERILY CHEESILY CHILLILY CHIRPILY CHOICELY CHOPPILY CHORALLY CHUBBILY CHUMMILY CHUNKILY CHURCHLY
CLAMMILY CLASSILY CLEVERLY CLINALLY CLONALLY CLOUDILY CLUMSILY COARSELY COEVALLY COGENTLY COITALLY COMELILY COMMONLY CONVEXLY COOINGLY COUSINLY COVERTLY COWARDLY COYISHLY CRABBILY CRAFTILY CRAGGILY CRANEFLY CRANKILY CRAVENLY CREAKILY CREAMILY
CREDIBLY CREEPILY CRISPILY CROAKILY CROUPILY CROUSELY CRUSTILY CRYINGLY CULPABLY CURSEDLY CURVEDLY CUSSEDLY CYCLICLY CYMOSELY DAINTILY DAMNABLY DAPPERLY DARINGLY DATIVELY DECENTLY DEMISSLY DEMURELY DENIABLY DENTALLY DEUCEDLY DEVOUTLY DIRECTLY
DISAPPLY DISMALLY DISTALLY DIVERSLY DIVINELY DOCILELY DOCTORLY DOGGEDLY DOOLALLY DORSALLY DOTARDLY DOTINGLY DRAFTILY DREAMILY DREARILY DRESSILY DROOPILY DROWSILY DUDISHLY DULCETLY EARTHILY EASTERLY EFFETELY EIGHTHLY ELATEDLY ELFISHLY ELIGIBLY
ELVISHLY ENTIRELY ENVIABLY EPICALLY EQUINELY ERRANTLY ERRINGLY EVANGELY EXPERTLY FACETELY FACIALLY FACILELY FALLIBLY FAMOUSLY FATHERLY FAULTILY FAUNALLY FEASIBLY FELINELY FELLOWLY FERVIDLY FESTALLY FEUDALLY FIERCELY FILIALLY FILTHILY FINITELY

FISCALLY
FITFULLY
FLABBILY
FLASHILY
FLEECILY
FLEXIBLY
FLIMSILY
FLINTILY
FLOPPILY
FLORALLY
FLORIDLY
FLOSSILY
FLUENTLY
FLUFFILY
FOLKSILY
FORCEDLY
FORCIBLY
FORKEDLY
FORMALLY
FORMERLY
FOURTHLY
FREAKILY
FRENZILY
FRIENDLY
FRIGIDLY
FRISKILY
FRIZZILY
FROSTILY
FROTHILY
FROWZILY
FROZENLY
FRUGALLY
FRUITILY
FRUMPILY
FUMINGLY
FUTILELY
GAPINGLY
GARISHLY
GAUCHELY
GENIALLY
GIBINGLY
GIFTEDLY
GINGELLY
GINGERLY
GLASSILY
GLITZILY
GLOBALLY
GLOOMILY
GLOSSILY
GLUMPILY
GOLDENLY
GORBELLY
GORGEDLY
GRAITHLY
GRASSILY
GRAVELLY
GRAVIDLY
GREASILY
GREEDILY
GREENFLY
GRITTILY
GROGGILY
GRUBBILY
GRUFFILY
GRUMPILY
GUILTILY
GULLABLY
GULLIBLY
HEARTILY
HEATEDLY
HEAVENLY
HECTICLY
HECTORLY
HEROICLY
HIDDENLY
HITCHILY
HOARSELY
HOLLOWLY
HOMELILY
HONESTLY
HOPINGLY
HORRIBLY
HORRIDLY
HORSEFLY
HOUSEFLY
HUMANELY
HUNGERLY
HUNGRILY
HUNTEDLY
HUSHEDLY
IMMANELY
IMPISHLY
IMPURELY
INDIGNLY
INFIRMLY
INNATELY
INSANELY
INTENTLY
INVIABLY
INWARDLY
IREFULLY
ISSUABLY
JADISHLY
JAGGEDLY
JAPINGLY
JAUNTILY
JEJUNELY
JIBINGLY
JOCOSELY
JOCUNDLY
JOKINGLY
JOVIALLY
JOYFULLY
JOYOUSLY
KERNELLY
KINDLILY
KISSABLY
KNIGHTLY
KNOTTILY
LABIALLY
LAICALLY
LATENTLY
LATTERLY
LAUDABLY
LAVISHLY
LAWFULLY
LAWYERLY
LEADENLY
LETHALLY
LIMBERLY
LIMPIDLY
LINEALLY
LINEARLY
LIQUIDLY
LISSOMLY
LITHERLY
LIVELILY
LIVINGLY
LOBATELY
LOBLOLLY
LONELILY
LOSINGLY
LOUCHELY
LOVEABLY
LOVELILY
LOVINGLY
LUBBERLY
LUCENTLY
LUMBERLY
LUMPENLY
LUNATELY
LYRATELY
MAIDENLY
MALIGNLY
MANFULLY
MANNERLY
MANUALLY
MARKEDLY
MARTYRLY
MASSEDLY
MASTERLY
MATRONLY
MATTEDLY
MATURELY
MEAGERLY
MEAGRELY
MEDIALLY
MEDIANLY
MELLOWLY
MENIALLY
MENTALLY
MESIALLY
MIGHTILY
MINUTELY
MISAPPLY
MODERNLY
MODESTLY
MODISHLY
MOLTENLY
MOMENTLY
MONOPOLY
MOPINGLY
MOPISHLY
MORBIDLY
MOROSELY
MORTALLY
MOTHERLY
MOUTHILY
MOVEABLY
MOVINGLY
MULISHLY
MULTIPLY
MUSINGLY
MUTUALLY
MYSTICLY
NARGHILY
NARGILLY
NARROWLY
NATANTLY
NATIVELY
NEURALLY
NEWISHLY
NOCENTLY
NORMALLY
NOUNALLY
OAFISHLY
OBLATELY
OBLONGLY
OBTUSELY
OCCULTLY
OCULARLY
ODIOUSLY
OFFISHLY
OGRISHLY
ONWARDLY
OPAQUELY
OPERABLY
ORNATELY
OTIOSELY
OUTBULLY
OVERHOLY
OVERWILY
OWLISHLY
PALLIDLY
PALPABLY
PALTRILY
PANDERLY
PASSABLY
PASSIBLY
PASTORLY
PATCHILY
PATENTLY
PATRONLY
PEDATELY
PETTEDLY
PIPINGLY
PITCHILY
PITIABLY
PLACABLY
PLACIDLY
PLAGUILY
PLIANTLY
PLUCKILY
PLUGUGLY
PLURALLY
PLUSHILY
PLYINGLY
POLITELY
POPISHLY
POROUSLY
PORTABLY
PORTERLY
POSINGLY
POSSIBLY
POSTALLY
POTBELLY
POTENTLY
PREPPILY
PRETTILY
PRIESTLY
PRIMALLY
PRINCELY
PRISSILY
PROBABLY
PROLIXLY
PROMPTLY
PROPERLY
PROVABLY
PROVENLY
PRYINGLY
PUBLICLY
PULINGLY
PULPALLY
PUNCHILY
PUTRIDLY
QUAINTLY
QUEASILY
QUIRKILY
QUOTABLY
RACIALLY
RADIALLY
RAGGEDLY
RAGINGLY
RAKISHLY
RAMOSELY
RANCIDLY
RANDOMLY
RASCALLY
RATEABLY
RAVINGLY
READABLY
READERLY
RECENTLY
RECTALLY
REDBELLY
REFLEXLY
RELIABLY
REMISSLY
REMOTELY
REPANDLY
RESUPPLY
RETRALLY
RIBALDLY
RIMOSELY
RITUALLY
ROBUSTLY
ROOTEDLY
ROTTENLY
ROTUNDLY
ROVINGLY
RUEFULLY
RUGGEDLY
RUGOSELY
RUSTICLY
SACREDLY
SAILORLY
SALEABLY
SALLOWLY
SALVABLY
SATIABLY
SAVAGELY
SAVINGLY
SAVORILY
SAVOURLY
SCABBILY
SCALABLY
SCANTILY
SCARCELY
SCRABBLY
SCRAGGLY
SCRIBBLY
SCRIGGLY
SCRIMPLY
SCURVILY
SEAMANLY
SECANTLY
SECONDLY
SECRETLY
SECUNDLY
SECURELY
SEDATELY
SELDOMLY
SELECTLY
SENILELY
SENSIBLY
SERENELY
SERIALLY
SEVERELY
SEXTUPLY
SEXUALLY
SHABBILY
SHAGGILY
SHAUCHLY
SHIFTILY
SHIRTILY
SHODDILY
SHREWDLY
SICKERLY
SICKLILY
SIGNALLY
SILENTLY
SILVERLY
SINFULLY
SISTERLY
SIZEABLY
SKIMPILY
SLANGILY
SLEAZILY
SLEEPILY
SLIGHTLY
SLINKILY
SLOPPILY
SLOVENLY
SLUSHILY
SMALMILY
SMARMILY
SMEARILY
SMOOTHLY
SMUDGILY
SMUTTILY
SNAPPILY
SNEAKILY
SNIFFILY
SNIPPILY
SNIVELLY
SNOBBILY
SNOOPILY
SNOOTILY
SNOTTILY
SNUFFILY
SOCIABLY
SOCIALLY
SODDENLY
SOLEMNLY
SOMBERLY
SOMBRELY
SORDIDLY
SORTABLY
SOUTERLY
SOVRANLY
SOWBELLY
SPARKILY
SPARSELY
SPEEDILY
SPIFFILY
SPINALLY
SPIRALLY
SPONGILY
SPOOKILY
SPOONILY
SPORTILY
SPOTTILY
SPRITELY
SPRUCELY
SPUNKILY
SQUARELY
SQUIGGLY
SQUIRELY
STALKILY
STANCHLY
STARRILY
STATEDLY
STEADILY
STEAMILY
STEEVELY
STICKILY
STIEVELY
STINGILY
STOCKILY
STODGILY
STOLIDLY
STONEFLY
STORMILY
STRAGGLY
STRAITLY
STRICTLY
STRONGLY
STUBBILY
STUFFILY
STUMPILY
STUPIDLY
STURDILY
SUDDENLY
SUITABLY
SULLENLY
SULTRILY
SUMMERLY
SUPERBLY
SUPINELY
SUPPLELY
SVELTELY
SWANKILY
SWEATILY
SWIMMILY
SYMPHILY
TAKINGLY
TANGIBLY
TARNALLY
TARTARLY
TASSELLY
TAWDRILY
TAXINGLY
TENDERLY
TENSIBLY
TERRIBLY
TETCHILY
THORNILY
THRAWNLY
THWARTLY
TIMOUSLY
TINSELLY
TONISHLY
TOOTHILY
TORPIDLY
TORRIDLY
TOUCHILY
TOWARDLY
TOYISHLY
TRASHILY
TRENDILY
TREVALLY
TRIBALLY
TRICKILY
TRUSTILY
TRYINGLY
TUNBELLY
TUNEABLY
TURBIDLY
TURGIDLY
UNCHICLY
UNCIALLY
UNCOMELY
UNCOSTLY
UNEASILY
UNEVENLY
UNFAIRLY
UNGAINLY
UNGENTLY
UNHOLILY
UNHOMELY
UNIQUELY
UNITEDLY
UNJUSTLY
UNKINDLY
UNKINGLY
UNLIKELY
UNLIVELY
UNLORDLY
UNLOVELY
UNMEETLY
UNREALLY
UNRIPELY
UNSAFELY
UNSEEMLY
UNSTABLY
UNSUBTLY
UNSURELY
UNTIDILY
UNTIMELY
UNUSABLY
UNWARELY
UNWARILY
UNWIFELY
UNWISELY
UPPISHLY
UPWARDLY
URBANELY
URGENTLY
URGINGLY
USEFULLY
UVULARLY
VACANTLY
VALUABLY
VARIABLY
VARIEDLY
VEILEDLY
VENDIBLY
VENIALLY
VENOUSLY
VERBALLY
VERNALLY
VESTALLY
VEXINGLY
VINCIBLY
VINOUSLY
VIOLABLY
VIRGINLY
VIRILELY
VISCIDLY
VISUALLY
VOTIVELY
VULGARLY
WANTONLY
WATERILY
WEASELLY
WEEVILLY
WESTERLY
WHEEZILY
WHIMSILY
WHITEFLY
WICKEDLY
WILFULLY
WINGEDLY
WINTERLY
WINTRILY
WITTOLLY
WIZARDLY
WOEFULLY
WONTEDLY
WOODENLY
WOOINGLY
WOOLLILY
WORTHILY
WOUNDILY
WRATHILY
WRITERLY
YEASTILY
YELLOWLY
YEOMANLY
YONDERLY
YONGTHLY
ZOOPHILY

WORDS ENDING IN -MAN

7-letter words -MAN

ALMSMAN ANTIMAN ARTSMAN AUTOMAN BASEMAN BATSMAN BEADMAN BEDEMAN BELLMAN BELTMAN BILLMAN BIRDMAN BOATMAN BOGYMAN BONDMAN BOOKMAN
BUSHMAN BYREMAN CASEMAN CAVEMAN CHAPMAN CLUBMAN COALMAN CREWMAN DAYSMAN DECUMAN DESKMAN DOORMAN DRAYMAN DUSTMAN FACEMAN FIREMAN
FLAGMAN FOOTMAN FOREMAN FREEMAN FROGMAN GADSMAN GATEMAN GLEEMAN GOODMAN GOWNMAN GRIPMAN GUDEMAN HACKMAN HANGMAN HANUMAN HEADMAN
HELIMAN HERDMAN HIGHMAN HOODMAN HOSEMAN INHUMAN ISLEMAN JACKMAN JARKMAN JAZZMAN JUNKMAN JURYMAN KEELMAN KINSMAN KIRKMAN LANDMAN
LEADMAN LENSMAN LIFTMAN LINEMAN LINKMAN LOCKMAN LOCOMAN MAGSMAN MAILMAN MALTMAN MARKMAN MASHMAN MEATMAN MESSMAN MILKMAN MOBSMAN
MOORMAN MOOTMAN NEWSMAN OARSMAN ODDSMAN OTTOMAN OVERMAN PACKMAN PASSMAN PEATMAN PIKEMAN PLOWMAN POLLMAN PORTMAN POSTMAN PROPMAN
PULLMAN RAFTMAN RAILMAN REEDMAN REELMAN REPOMAN RINGMAN ROADMAN RODSMAN SAGAMAN SANDMAN SEEDMAN SHIPMAN SHOPMAN SHOWMAN SIDEMAN
SNOWMAN SOCKMAN SOKEMAN SONGMAN SPAEMAN SURFMAN SWAGMAN TAPSMAN TAXIMAN TELEMAN TOLLMAN TONGMAN TOOLMAN TOPSMAN TRUEMAN TURFMAN
UNHUMAN UNWOMAN WAKEMAN WINGMAN WIREMAN WOODMAN WOOLMAN WORKMAN YARDMAN YEGGMAN

8-letter words -MAN

AIRWOMAN ALDERMAN BAILSMAN BANDSMAN BANDYMAN BANKSMAN BARGEMAN BATWOMAN BEADSMAN BEDESMAN BLUESMAN BOARDMAN BOATSMAN BOGEYMAN BONDSMAN BOOGYMAN BOTHYMAN BRAKEMAN BRIDEMAN BRINKMAN BUTTYMAN
CHAINMAN CHAIRMAN CHESSMAN CHOIRMAN CHOREMAN CLANSMAN CLASSMAN COACHMAN COLORMAN CORPSMAN CRAGSMAN DAIRYMAN DALESMAN DOOMSMAN DOORSMAN DRAGOMAN DRAGSMAN DUTCHMAN EARTHMAN EVERYMAN FERRYMAN
FOILSMAN FORGEMAN FREEDMAN FRESHMAN FRONTMAN FUGLEMAN FUNNYMAN GAMESMAN GANGSMAN GAVELMAN GLASSMAN GOADSMAN GOWNSMAN HANDYMAN HEADSMAN HELMSMAN HENCHMAN HERDSMAN HIELAMAN HOASTMAN HOISTMAN
HORSEMAN HOTELMAN HOUSEMAN HUNTSMAN ISLESMAN LANDSMAN LAYWOMAN LEADSMAN LIEGEMAN LINESMAN LINKSMAN LOCKSMAN LODESMAN MADWOMAN MARCHMAN MARKSMAN MERESMAN MERRYMAN MONEYMAN MOTORMAN NOBLEMAN
NONHUMAN OVERSMAN PANHUMAN PENWOMAN PETERMAN PILOTMAN PITCHMAN PIVOTMAN PLACEMAN PLAIDMAN PLATEMAN POINTMAN PREHUMAN PRESSMAN PRIZEMAN PROSEMAN PUNTSMAN QUILLMAN RADIOMAN RAFTSMAN RAMPSMAN
RANCHMAN REINSMAN RIFLEMAN RIVERMAN ROADSMAN ROUTEMAN SALESMAN SCENEMAN SEAWOMAN SEEDSMAN SHAREMAN SHEARMAN SHEEPMAN SHIREMAN SHOREMAN SIDESMAN SONARMAN SOUNDMAN SPACEMAN SPADEMAN SPEARMAN
SQUAWMAN STALLMAN STEELMAN STICKMAN STILLMAN STOCKMAN STOREMAN STUNTMAN SUBHUMAN SUPERMAN SWAGSMAN SWINGMAN SWORDMAN TACKSMAN TALESMAN TALISMAN TALLYMAN TIDESMAN TOWNSMAN TOYWOMAN TRACKMAN
TRAINMAN TRASHMAN TREWSMAN TRUCHMAN TRUCKMAN UNDERMAN VERSEMAN WATCHMAN WATERMAN WEALSMAN WEIGHMAN WHALEMAN WHEELMAN WIDOWMAN WINCHMAN WOODSMAN YACHTMAN YARRAMAN

WORDS ENDING IN -MEN

7-letter words -MEN

ABDOMEN AGNOMEN ALBUMEN ALMSMEN ARTSMEN AUTOMEN BASEMEN BATSMEN BEADMEN BEDEMEN BELLMEN BELTMEN BILLMEN BIRDMEN BITUMEN BOATMEN BOGYMEN
BONDMEN BOOKMEN BUSHMEN BYREMEN CACUMEN CASEMEN CAVEMEN CERUMEN CHAPMEN CLUBMEN COALMEN CREWMEN DAYSMEN DESKMEN DOORMEN DRAYMEN DURAMEN
DUSTMEN FACEMEN FIREMEN FLAGMEN FOOTMEN FORAMEN FOREMEN FREEMEN FROGMEN GADSMEN GATEMEN GLEEMEN GOODMEN GOWNMEN GRIPMEN GUDEMEN HACKMEN
HANGMEN HEADMEN HEGUMEN HELIMEN HERDMEN HIGHMEN HILLMEN HOODMEN HOSEMEN ISLEMEN JACKMEN JARKMEN JAZZMEN JUNKMEN JURYMEN KEELMEN KINSMEN
KIRKMEN LANDMEN LEADMEN LENSMEN LIFTMEN LINEMEN LINKMEN LOCKMEN LOCOMEN MAGSMEN MAILMEN MALTMEN MARKMEN MASHMEN MEATMEN MESSMEN MILKMEN
MOBSMEN MOLIMEN MOORMEN MOOTMEN NEWSMEN OARSMEN ODDSMEN OVERMEN PACKMEN PASSMEN PEATMEN PIKEMEN PLOWMEN POLLMEN PORTMEN POSTMEN PROPMEN
PUTAMEN RAFTMEN RAILMEN REEDMEN REELMEN REGIMEN REPOMEN RINGMEN ROADMEN RODSMEN SAGAMEN SANDMEN SEEDMEN SHIPMEN SHOPMEN SHOWMEN SIDEMEN
SNOWMEN SOCKMEN SOKEMEN SONGMEN SPAEMEN SUDAMEN SURFMEN SWAGMEN TAPSMEN TAXIMEN TEGUMEN TELEMEN TOLLMEN TONGMEN TOOLMEN TOPSMEN TRUEMEN
TURFMEN VELAMEN WAKEMEN WINGMEN WIREMEN WOODMEN WOOLMEN WORKMEN YARDMEN YEGGMEN

8-letter words -MEN

AIRWOMEN ALDERMEN BAILSMEN
BANDSMEN BANDYMEN BANKSMEN
BARGEMEN BATWOMEN BEADSMEN
BEDESMEN BLUESMEN BOARDMEN
BOATSMEN BOGEYMEN BONDSMEN
BOOGYMEN BOTHYMEN BRAKEMEN
BRIDEMEN BRINKMEN BUTTYMEN
CHAINMEN CHAIRMEN CHESSMEN

CHOIRMEN EARTHMEN HEADSMEN LODESMEN POINTMEN SEAWOMEN STILLMEN TRUCHMEN
CHOREMEN EVERYMEN HELMSMEN MADWOMEN PRENOMEN SEEDSMEN STOCKMEN TRUCKMEN
CLANSMEN FERRYMEN HENCHMEN MARCHMEN PRESSMEN SHAREMEN STOREMEN UNDERMEN
CLASSMEN FOILSMEN HERDSMEN MARKSMEN PRIZEMEN SHEARMEN STUNTMEN VERSEMEN
CLINAMEN FORGEMEN HOASTMEN MERESMEN PROSEMEN SHEEPMEN SUPERMEN WATCHMEN
COACHMEN FREEDMEN HOISTMEN MERRYMEN PUNTSMEN SHIREMEN SWAGSMEN WATERMEN
COGNOMEN FRESHMEN HORSEMEN MONEYMEN QUILLMEN SHOREMEN SWINGMEN WEALSMEN
COLORMEN FRONTMEN HOTELMEN MOTORMEN RADIOMEN SIDESMEN SWORDMEN WEIGHMEN
CORPSMEN FUGLEMEN HOUSEMEN NOBLEMEN RAFTSMEN SONARMEN TACKSMEN WHALEMEN
CRAGSMEN FUNNYMEN HUNTSMEN OVERSMEN RAMPSMEN SOUNDMEN TALESMEN WHEELMEN
CYCLAMEN GAMESMEN ISLESMEN PENWOMEN RANCHMEN SPACEMEN TALLYMEN WIDOWMEN
DAIRYMEN GANGSMEN LANDSMEN PETERMEN REINSMEN SPADEMEN TIDESMEN WINCHMEN
DALESMEN GAVELMEN LAYWOMEN PILOTMEN RIFLEMEN SPEARMEN TOWNSMEN WOODSMEN
DOOMSMEN GLASSMEN LEADSMEN PITCHMEN RIVERMEN SPECIMEN TOYWOMEN YACHTMEN
DOORSMEN GOADSMEN LIEGEMEN PIVOTMEN ROADSMEN SQUAWMEN TRACKMEN
DRAGOMEN GOWNSMEN LINESMEN PLACEMEN ROUTEMEN STALLMEN TRAINMEN
DRAGSMEN GRAVAMEN LINKSMEN PLAIDMEN SALESMEN STEELMEN TRASHMEN
DUTCHMEN HANDYMEN LOCKSMEN PLATEMEN SCENEMEN STICKMEN TREWSMEN

WORDS ENDING IN -NESS

7-letter words -NESS

ALLNESS DRYNESS FEWNESS HIPNESS LOWNESS ONENESS SADNESS WAENESS
APTNESS DUENESS FEYNESS HOTNESS MADNESS OUTNESS SETNESS WANNESS
BADNESS DULNESS FITNESS ICINESS NEWNESS PATNESS SHINESS WETNESS
BIGNESS DUNNESS FULNESS ILLNESS NOWNESS RAWNESS SHYNESS WITNESS
COYNESS FARNESS GAYNESS LAXNESS ODDNESS REDNESS SLYNESS WOENESS
DIMNESS FATNESS HARNESS LIONESS OLDNESS RUMNESS TWONESS WRYNESS

8-letter words -NESS

ACHINESS COOLNESS EVILNESS HALFNESS LONENESS PACKNESS SAMENESS TITANESS
ACIDNESS COSINESS EYEDNESS HARDNESS LONGNESS PALENESS SANENESS TRIGNESS
AGEDNESS COXINESS FAINNESS HAZINESS LORNNESS PASTNESS SEARNESS TRIMNESS
AIRINESS COZINESS FAIRNESS HERENESS LOSTNESS PERTNESS SEEDNESS TRUENESS
ALBINESS CURTNESS FASTNESS HIGHNESS LOUDNESS PIEDNESS SELFNESS TWEENESS
ARCHNESS CUTENESS FELLNESS HOKINESS LUSHNESS PINKNESS SEXINESS UGLINESS
ARIDNESS DAFTNESS FINENESS HOLINESS MALENESS PIPINESS SICKNESS VAINNESS
ARTINESS DAMPNESS FIRMNESS HOMINESS MATINESS PIXINESS SIZINESS VASTNESS
ASHINESS DANKNESS FLATNESS HUGENESS MAZINESS POKINESS SKEWNESS VILDNESS
AVIDNESS DARKNESS FONDNESS ICKINESS MEANNESS POORNESS SLIMNESS VILENESS
AWAYNESS DEADNESS FOULNESS IDLENESS MEEKNESS PORINESS SLOWNESS VOIDNESS
BALDNESS DEAFNESS FOXINESS IFFINESS MEETNESS POSHNESS SMUGNESS WARINESS
BARENESS DEARNESS FOZINESS INKINESS MILDNESS PRIMNESS SNUBNESS WARMNESS
BARONESS DEEPNESS FREENESS IRONNESS MIRINESS PUNINESS SNUGNESS WASTNESS
BASENESS DEFTNESS FULLNESS JIMPNESS MUCHNESS PURENESS SOFTNESS WAVINESS
BASSNESS DEMONESS GAMENESS JOKINESS MUTENESS RACINESS SOLENESS WAXINESS
BEINNESS DEWINESS GAMINESS JUSTNESS NAFFNESS RANKNESS SORENESS WEAKNESS
BIASNESS DIRENESS GAMYNESS KEENNESS NEARNESS RAPTNESS SOURNESS WELLNESS
BLUENESS DONENESS GASTNESS KINDNESS NEATNESS RARENESS SPRYNESS WHATNESS
BOLDNESS DOPINESS GLADNESS LACINESS NESHNESS RASHNESS SUCHNESS WIDENESS
BONINESS DOURNESS GLEGNESS LAMENESS NEXTNESS REALNESS SURENESS WILDNESS
BOXINESS DOWFNESS GLIBNESS LANKNESS NICENESS RICHNESS TALLNESS WILINESS
BUSINESS DOZINESS GLUMNESS LATENESS NIGHNESS RIFENESS TAMENESS WIRINESS
BUSYNESS DRABNESS GONENESS LAZINESS NOSINESS RIMINESS TARTNESS WISENESS
CAGINESS DULLNESS GOODNESS LEANNESS NUDENESS RIPENESS TAUTNESS WOODNESS
CAGYNESS DUMBNESS GORINESS LEWDNESS NULLNESS ROPINESS THATNESS WORNNESS
CALMNESS DUSKNESS GRAYNESS LIKENESS NUMBNESS ROSINESS THINNESS ZANINESS
CAMPNESS EASINESS GREYNESS LIMINESS OILINESS RUDENESS THISNESS
CANONESS EDGINESS GRIMNESS LIMPNESS OOZINESS SAFENESS THUSNESS
CHICNESS EERINESS GRUMNESS LIVENESS OPENNESS SAGENESS TIDINESS
COLDNESS EVENNESS HALENESS LOGINESS OVALNESS SALTNESS TININESS

WORDS ENDING IN -OID

7-letter words -OID

ACAROID AMBROID ANEROID BYSSOID CHOROID COLLOID CRINOID DELTOID DIPLOID
ADENOID AMEBOID ANTHOID CACTOID CIRSOID CORMOID CTENOID DENTOID DISCOID
AGAMOID AMYLOID ARCTOID CESTOID CISSOID COTTOID CYCLOID DERMOID EMEROID
AGATOID ANDROID ASTROID CHELOID COCCOID CRICOID CYSTOID DESMOID ERICOID

ETHMOID	GOBIOID	HYENOID	MATTOID	OCELOID	PLACOID	SIGMOID	TABLOID	VALGOID
EUPLOID	HAEMOID	HYPNOID	MUSCOID	OCHROID	PYGMOID	SIMIOID	TENIOID	VESPOID
FACTOID	HAPLOID	LABROID	MYELOID	OSTEOID	QUINOID	SPAROID	THEROID	VISCOID
FIBROID	HELCOID	LENTOID	NAEVOID	PERCOID	RHIZOID	SPIROID	THYROID	XIPHOID
FUNGOID	HISTOID	LIANOID	NEGROID	PHACOID	SARCOID	SPOROID	TIGROID	ZEBROID
GLENOID	HYALOID	LITHOID	NEUROID	PHYTOID	SAUROID	STEROID	TURDOID	ZINCOID
GLOBOID	HYDROID	MASTOID	OBOVOID	PIGMOID	SIALOID	STYLOID	TYPHOID	

8-letter words -OID

ACTINOID	CARDIOID	EMBRYOID	INDIGOID	NOCTUOID	POLYPOID	SESAMOID	THALLOID
ALKALOID	CATENOID	EMULSOID	ISTHMOID	NUCLEOID	PRISMOID	SILUROID	THYREOID
AMBEROID	CENTROID	ERGATOID	KERATOID	ODONTOID	PSYCHOID	SINUSOID	THYRSOID
AMMONOID	CERATOID	GABBROID	LAMBDOID	OMOHYOID	PYRANOID	SISTROID	TRICHOID
AMOEBOID	CHOREOID	GALENOID	LEMUROID	ONISCOID	PYRENOID	SOLENOID	TRIPLOID
ANCONOID	CHORIOID	GEOMYOID	LIGULOID	PARANOID	RACEMOID	SORICOID	TROCHOID
ARILLOID	CICHLOID	GROUPOID	LIMULOID	PAROTOID	RESINOID	SPHENOID	TUBEROID
ASTEROID	CLUPEOID	GYNECOID	LYMPHOID	PETALOID	RETINOID	SPHEROID	VIBRIOID
ATHETOID	CONCHOID	HELICOID	MANATOID	PEZIZOID	RHABDOID	SPONGOID	VOLUTOID
AUTACOID	CORACOID	HEMATOID	MEDUSOID	PHALLOID	RHOMBOID	SQUALOID	YPSILOID
AUTOCOID	CORONOID	HISTIOID	MELANOID	PHELLOID	SCAPHOID	STURNOID	
BLASTOID	COTYLOID	HOMALOID	MUCINOID	PHYLLOID	SCHIZOID	TAENIOID	
BOTRYOID	DENDROID	HOMINOID	MYCELOID	PINACOID	SCINCOID	TAPIROID	
CALYCOID	DORIDOID	HUMANOID	MYTILOID	PINAKOID	SCIUROID	TARSIOID	
CAMELOID	ECHINOID	HYDATOID	NEMATOID	PITYROID	SCLEROID	TERATOID	
CANCROID	ELYTROID	HYRACOID	NEPHROID	PLASMOID	SEPALOID	TETANOID	

WORDS ENDING IN -OR

7-letter words -OR

ABACTOR	AVIATOR	DECOLOR	ERECTOR	ISOCHOR	MORMAOR	PROCTOR	SEXTUOR	UNVISOR
ABETTOR	BELABOR	DELATOR	EVERTOR	JANITOR	NEGATOR	QUESTOR	SIGNIOR	VAVASOR
ABLATOR	BICOLOR	DEVISOR	EVICTOR	LANGUOR	NONPOOR	QUITTOR	SIMILOR	VENATOR
ADAPTOR	BIOPHOR	DILATOR	EXACTOR	LAXATOR	OBLIGOR	REACTOR	SPONSOR	VISITOR
ADJUROR	CAMPHOR	DILUTOR	EXCITOR	LEGATOR	OFFEROR	REALTOR	SQUALOR	WARRIOR
ADVISOR	CHADDOR	DIVISOR	FEOFFOR	LEVATOR	OUTDOOR	RECOLOR	STENTOR	ZELATOR
AERATOR	CHANTOR	DONATOR	FUNCTOR	LOCATOR	PANDOOR	RELATOR	STERTOR	
AGISTOR	CHIKHOR	EDUCTOR	GENITOR	MACHZOR	PARADOR	REVISOR	STRIDOR	
ALASTOR	CITATOR	EJECTOR	GRANTOR	MALODOR	PARITOR	REVIVOR	TANDOOR	
ALIENOR	CLANGOR	ELECTOR	GYRATOR	MAORMOR	PICADOR	ROTATOR	TEMBLOR	
ANAPHOR	COACTOR	EMPEROR	HERITOR	MARKHOR	PLEDGOR	SCISSOR	TRACTOR	
ASSUROR	CREATOR	EMULSOR	HUMIDOR	MATADOR	PLESSOR	SENATOR	TRAITOR	
ATHANOR	CURATOR	ENACTOR	IGNITOR	MIRADOR	PRAETOR	SEPTUOR	TRUSTOR	
AUDITOR	DEBITOR	EQUATOR	INCISOR	MONITOR	PRESSOR	SETTLOR	TWISTOR	

8-letter words -OR

ABDUCTOR	BARRETOR	CREMATOR	ENDORSOR	INDUCTOR	MISTUTOR	PREVISOR	RETAILOR
ACCENTOR	BECLAMOR	CURSITOR	EPILATOR	INFECTOR	NARRATOR	PRODITOR	RONCADOR
ACCEPTOR	BEGLAMOR	CUSPIDOR	EVOCATOR	INFERIOR	NEIGHBOR	PROLABOR	SCULPTOR
ACTUATOR	BEHAVIOR	DEFECTOR	EXCEPTOR	INFLATOR	NEXTDOOR	PROMISOR	SEAFLOOR
ADDUCTOR	BELIQUOR	DEFLATOR	EXECUTOR	INJECTOR	NITRATOR	PROMOTOR	SECRETOR
ADJUSTOR	BISECTOR	DEMEANOR	EXPANDOR	INTERIOR	NONACTOR	PRONATOR	SECTATOR
ADULATOR	CANEPHOR	DEPICTOR	EXPIATOR	INVENTOR	NONCOLOR	PROVEDOR	SEDUCTOR
AGITATOR	CAVEATOR	DETECTOR	EXTENSOR	INVERTOR	NONJUROR	PROVIDOR	SEIGNIOR
ANCESTOR	CHELATOR	DEVIATOR	EXTERIOR	INVESTOR	NONLABOR	PROVISOR	SELECTOR
ANIMATOR	COANCHOR	DICTATOR	FELLATOR	IODOPHOR	NONMAJOR	PULMOTOR	SERVITOR
ANTERIOR	COAUTHOR	DIFFUSOR	GILLYVOR	ISOLATOR	OBJECTOR	PULSATOR	SPLENDOR
APPELLOR	CODEBTOR	DIGESTOR	GOVERNOR	KOMONDOR	OBSESSOR	PUNDONOR	STRESSOR
ARRESTOR	COEDITOR	DIRECTOR	HELIODOR	KURVEYOR	OBVIATOR	PURVEYOR	SUBFLOOR
ASPERSOR	COENAMOR	DISCOLOR	HYDRATOR	LABRADOR	OCCLUSOR	QUAESTOR	SUBPRIOR
ASSENTOR	COFACTOR	DISFAVOR	IDOLATOR	LAUDATOR	OPERATOR	RADIATOR	SUPERIOR
ASSERTOR	COLESSOR	DISHONOR	IMITATOR	LICENSOR	OUTHUMOR	RECAPTOR	SURVEYOR
ASSESSOR	COLLATOR	EDUCATOR	IMPACTOR	MAINDOOR	OUTSAVOR	RECEPTOR	SURVIVOR
ASSIGNOR	CONCOLOR	EFFECTOR	IMPELLOR	MANDATOR	PALPATOR	REDACTOR	TESTATOR
ASSISTOR	CONJUROR	ELEVATOR	IMPOSTOR	MARKHOOR	PARACHOR	REDUCTOR	THEREFOR
ATTESTOR	CONVENOR	ELICITOR	INCENSOR	MEDIATOR	PATENTOR	REGRATOR	THRUSTOR
AVIGATOR	CONVEYOR	EMANATOR	INCEPTOR	METAPHOR	PHOSPHOR	REJECTOR	TITRATOR
BACHELOR	COPASTOR	EMBRASOR	INDENTOR	MIGRATOR	PISCATOR	RELEASOR	TOREADOR
BACKDOOR	CORRIDOR	EMULATOR	INDICTOR	MISCOLOR	PLEDGEOR	REMITTOR	TRADITOR
BARRATOR	CREDITOR	ENDEAVOR	INDORSOR	MISLABOR	PREDATOR	RESISTOR	TRAPDOOR

TRICOLOR ULTERIOR UNICOLOR UTILIDOR VARACTOR VAVASSOR VIBRATOR VITIATOR
TRIMOTOR UNANCHOR URINATOR VALUATOR VARISTOR VERDEROR VIOLATOR WHEREFOR

WORDS ENDING IN -OUS

7-letter words -OUS

ACAJOUS ACEROUS ACETOUS ACINOUS ADIPOUS AENEOUS AGAMOUS AMADOUS AMOROUS ANUROUS ANXIOUS APODOUS AQUEOUS ARDUOUS ARENOUS ATHEOUS ATOKOUS AZOTOUS AZYGOUS AZYMOUS BADIOUS BILIOUS BIVIOUS BOUBOUS BRUMOUS BULBOUS BULLOUS BURNOUS CACHOUS CALLOUS CARIOUS CASEOUS CEREOUS CHYLOUS CHYMOUS CIRROUS CITROUS COCCOUS CONGOUS COPIOUS CORIOUS CORMOUS COYPOUS CUPROUS CURIOUS DEVIOUS DUBIOUS DUTEOUS EMULOUS ENVIOUS ESTROUS FATUOUS FEATOUS FERROUS FIBROUS FOLIOUS FULVOUS FUNGOUS FURIOUS FUSCOUS GALLOUS GASEOUS GEALOUS GIBBOUS GLEBOUS GLOBOUS GRUMOUS GUMMOUS HEINOUS HERBOUS HIDEOUS HUGEOUS HYDROUS IGNEOUS IMPIOUS INVIOUS JEALOUS LENTOUS LEPROUS LIMBOUS LUTEOUS NACROUS NERVOUS NIMIOUS NIOBOUS NITROUS NIVEOUS NOCUOUS NOXIOUS OBVIOUS OCHROUS ODOROUS OMINOUS ONEROUS ONYMOUS OPACOUS OSMIOUS OSSEOUS OZONOUS PAPPOUS PARLOUS PERLOUS PETROUS PICEOUS PILEOUS PITEOUS PLUMOUS POMPOUS PORTOUS PULPOUS RAMEOUS RAUCOUS RHODOUS RIOTOUS ROUCOUS ROUTOUS RUBIOUS RUINOUS SANIOUS SARCOUS SERIOUS SIMIOUS SINUOUS SOUKOUS SPINOUS SPUMOUS SUCCOUS TALCOUS TEDIOUS TENUOUS TIMEOUS TYPHOUS UBEROUS UMBROUS URANOUS URINOUS USUROUS VACUOUS VALGOUS VARIOUS VEINOUS VICIOUS VIDUOUS VILLOUS VISCOUS VOUDOUS ZEALOUS ZINCOUS

8-letter words -OUS

ACARPOUS ACAULOUS ADUNCOUS AMBEROUS ANGINOUS ANGULOUS ANOUROUS ANSEROUS ANTICOUS APHONOUS APHTHOUS APTEROUS ARACEOUS ARANEOUS ARBOROUS ARSENOUS ARSONOUS ASPEROUS ASTOMOUS ATROPOUS BIBULOUS BIGAMOUS BIJUGOUS BIMANOUS BIPAROUS BIRAMOUS BUTYROUS CADUCOUS CAESIOUS CANOROUS CAPTIOUS CARIBOUS CARNEOUS CAUTIOUS CERNUOUS CHLOROUS CHROMOUS CITREOUS CORNEOUS COUSCOUS COVETOUS COVINOUS CRANKOUS CRIBROUS CROCEOUS CROUPOUS CUMBROUS CUMULOUS CUPREOUS DARTROUS DECOROUS DESIROUS DEXTROUS DIDYMOUS DIECIOUS DIGAMOUS DIGYNOUS DIMEROUS DIOICOUS DIPNOOUS DITOKOUS DIZYGOUS DOLOROUS EDACIOUS ELYTROUS ENGINOUS ENORMOUS EPIGEOUS EUROKOUS EXIGUOUS EXIMIOUS FABULOUS FACTIOUS FASHIOUS FASTUOUS FEATEOUS FEATUOUS FELONOUS FERREOUS FEVEROUS FIDDIOUS FLATUOUS FLEXUOUS FRABJOUS GEMINOUS GEMMEOUS GENEROUS GLABROUS GLAREOUS GLAUCOUS GLORIOUS GOITROUS GORGEOUS GRACIOUS GRIEVOUS GRISEOUS GYPSEOUS HALITOUS HAMULOUS HUMOROUS ICHOROUS IDONEOUS IMPOROUS INCUBOUS INERMOUS INFAMOUS KOUSKOUS LACTEOUS LAMINOUS LEAPROUS LIBELOUS LIGNEOUS LUMINOUS LUSCIOUS LUSTROUS MANITOUS MARABOUS MELANOUS MIASMOUS MUCINOUS MUTICOUS MUTINOUS NACREOUS NAUSEOUS NEBULOUS NEMOROUS NIDOROUS NODULOUS NUBILOUS NUMEROUS NUMINOUS OCHEROUS OCHREOUS OESTROUS OOGAMOUS ORAGIOUS ORDUROUS ORGULOUS OVARIOUS PABULOUS PALUDOUS PAPULOUS PATULOUS PERILOUS PERVIOUS PETALOUS PLUMBOUS PLUVIOUS POACEOUS POLYPOUS POPULOUS PORTEOUS PRECIOUS PREVIOUS PYRITOUS PYRRHOUS RACEMOUS RAMULOUS RAVENOUS RESINOUS RIGOROUS ROSINOUS RUCTIOUS RUMOROUS SABULOUS SAPAJOUS SAPOROUS SAVOROUS SCABIOUS SCABROUS SCARIOUS SCIOLOUS SCLEROUS SCORIOUS SEDULOUS SELENOUS SENSUOUS SEPALOUS SETULOUS SIBILOUS SOMBROUS SONOROUS SOPOROUS SPACIOUS SPECIOUS SPERMOUS SPURIOUS SQUAMOUS STANNOUS STOCIOUS STOTIOUS STRATOUS STRUMOUS STUDIOUS SUBEROUS SUDOROUS TEMEROUS TENUIOUS THALLOUS TIMOROUS TINAMOUS TITANOUS TORTIOUS TORTUOUS TRAPPOUS TUBEROUS TUBULOUS TUMOROUS TUMULOUS TURACOUS ULCEROUS UNCTUOUS UNDULOUS UNFAMOUS UNJOYOUS USURIOUS UXORIOUS VALOROUS VANADOUS VAPOROUS VENOMOUS VENTROUS VENULOUS VERTUOUS VIGOROUS VIPEROUS VIRTUOUS VITREOUS VOMITOUS WAMEFOUS WAVEROUS WONDROUS WRONGOUS XANTHOUS YTTRIOUS

WORDS ENDING IN -OUT

7-letter words -OUT

ASPROUT BACKOUT BAILOUT BESHOUT BESPOUT BLOWOUT BURGOUT BURNOUT COOKOUT DROPOUT EELPOUT FALLOUT FOLDOUT GRAYOUT HANDOUT HANGOUT HIDEOUT HOLDOUT LOCKOUT LOOKOUT MISSOUT PASSOUT PULLOUT RAINOUT READOUT ROLLOUT SELLOUT SHUTOUT SICKOUT SLIPOUT SPINOUT SURTOUT TAKEOUT TIMEOUT TURNOUT UNSHOUT WALKOUT WASHOUT WIDEOUT WIPEOUT WITHOUT WORKOUT

8-letter words -OUT

BLACKOUT BREAKOUT BROWNOUT BULLPOUT CARRYOUT CHECKOUT CLOSEOUT FLAMEOUT FREAKOUT GADABOUT HORNPOUT INDEVOUT KNOCKOUT LAYABOUT MARABOUT OUTSHOUT

PHASEOUT RACAHOUT SEASCOUT SLEEPOUT STANDOUT THEREOUT WHEREOUT
PITCHOUT RESPROUT SHAKEOUT SPEAKOUT STICKOUT UNDEVOUT WHITEOUT
PRINTOUT RUNABOUT SHOOTOUT STAKEOUT TACAHOUT WATCHOUT

WORDS ENDING IN -SET

7-letter words -SET

BACKSET BRASSET CRESSET HANDSET HAROSET KNESSET MOONSET OVERSET TWINSET
BONESET CHIPSET FILMSET HARDSET HEADSET MINDSET NAILSET SEAMSET TYPESET

8-letter words -SET

CHAROSET HEAVYSET PHOTOSET SOMERSET THORNSET
EARTHSET MARMOSET QUICKSET THICKSET UNDERSET

WORDS ENDING IN -SHIP

7-letter words -SHIP

AIRSHIP DONSHIP FOXSHIP GUNSHIP KINSHIP MIDSHIP PALSHIP SONSHIP WORSHIP
DOGSHIP ENDSHIP GODSHIP HERSHIP LUDSHIP NUNSHIP SIBSHIP WARSHIP

8-letter words -SHIP

AMIDSHIP DEANSHIP FIRESHIP HEADSHIP LONGSHIP POETSHIP TANKSHIP WARDSHIP
ANTISHIP DEMYSHIP FLAGSHIP HEIRSHIP LORDSHIP POPESHIP TOWNSHIP WINDSHIP
BARDSHIP DOGESHIP FORESHIP HEROSHIP MAGESHIP RAJASHIP TRANSHIP
CHUMSHIP DUKESHIP GURUSHIP KINGSHIP MATESHIP SERFSHIP TREESHIP
CLANSHIP EARLSHIP HARDSHIP LADYSHIP PEATSHIP STARSHIP TWINSHIP

WORDS ENDING IN -SKIN

7-letter words -SKIN

CATSKIN DOESKIN FOXSKIN KIDSKIN OILSKIN REDSKIN
COWSKIN DOGSKIN GRISKIN KIPSKIN PIGSKIN

8-letter words -SKIN

BEARSKIN CAPESKIN DEERSKIN GOATSKIN PONYSKIN TURNSKIN WOODSKIN
BUCKSKIN COONSKIN FISHSKIN LAMBSKIN SEALSKIN WINESKIN WOOLSKIN
CALFSKIN DAMASKIN FORESKIN MOLESKIN SWANSKIN WOLFSKIN

WORDS ENDING IN -SMAN

7-letter words -SMAN

ALMSMAN BATSMAN GADSMAN LENSMAN MESSMAN NEWSMAN ODDSMAN RODSMAN TOPSMAN
ARTSMAN DAYSMAN KINSMAN MAGSMAN MOBSMAN OARSMAN PASSMAN TAPSMAN

8-letter words -SMAN

BAILSMAN BONDSMAN DOOMSMAN GOADSMAN LANDSMAN MERESMAN ROADSMAN TALISMAN
BANDSMAN CHESSMAN DOORSMAN GOWNSMAN LEADSMAN OVERSMAN SALESMAN TIDESMAN
BANKSMAN CLANSMAN DRAGSMAN HEADSMAN LINESMAN PRESSMAN SEEDSMAN TOWNSMAN
BEADSMAN CLASSMAN FOILSMAN HELMSMAN LINKSMAN PUNTSMAN SIDESMAN TREWSMAN
BEDESMAN CORPSMAN GAMESMAN HERDSMAN LOCKSMAN RAFTSMAN SWAGSMAN WEALSMAN
BLUESMAN CRAGSMAN GANGSMAN HUNTSMAN LODESMAN RAMPSMAN TACKSMAN WOODSMAN
BOATSMAN DALESMAN GLASSMAN ISLESMAN MARKSMAN REINSMAN TALESMAN

WORDS ENDING IN -SMEN

7-letter words -SMEN

ALMSMEN DAYSMEN LENSMEN MOBSMEN ODDSMEN TAPSMEN
ARTSMEN GADSMEN MAGSMEN NEWSMEN PASSMEN TOPSMEN
BATSMEN KINSMEN MESSMEN OARSMEN RODSMEN

8-letter words -SMEN

BAILSMEN	BONDSMEN	DOOMSMEN	GOADSMEN	LANDSMEN	MERESMEN	ROADSMEN	TIDESMEN
BANDSMEN	CHESSMEN	DOORSMEN	GOWNSMEN	LEADSMEN	OVERSMEN	SALESMEN	TOWNSMEN
BANKSMEN	CLANSMEN	DRAGSMEN	HEADSMEN	LINESMEN	PRESSMEN	SEEDSMEN	TREWSMEN
BEADSMEN	CLASSMEN	FOILSMEN	HELMSMEN	LINKSMEN	PUNTSMEN	SIDESMEN	WEALSMEN
BEDESMEN	CORPSMEN	GAMESMEN	HERDSMEN	LOCKSMEN	RAFTSMEN	SWAGSMEN	WOODSMEN
BLUESMEN	CRAGSMEN	GANGSMEN	HUNTSMEN	LODESMEN	RAMPSMEN	TACKSMEN	
BOATSMEN	DALESMEN	GLASSMEN	ISLESMEN	MARKSMEN	REINSMEN	TALESMEN	

WORDS ENDING IN -SOME

7-letter words -SOME

AWESOME	EYESOME	IRKSOME	NOYSOME	TRISOME	UROSOME	WINSOME
BEESOME	FULSOME	LISSOME	OXYSOME	TWASOME	WAESOME	WOESOME
EPISOME	GAYSOME	NOISOME	TOYSOME	TWOSOME	WAGSOME	

8-letter words -SOME

ACROSOME	DOLESOME	FRETSOME	HANDSOME	LIPOSOME	MEROSOME	PYROSOME	TWIGSOME
AUTOSOME	DUELSOME	GAMESOME	HEALSOME	LONESOME	MESOSOME	RIBOSOME	WAILSOME
BORESOME	ENDOSOME	GLADSOME	HOLESOME	LONGSOME	MONOSOME	ROOMSOME	WORKSOME
CLOYSOME	FEARSOME	GLEESOME	JOKESOME	LOTHSOME	MURKSOME	TEDISOME	
CYTOSOME	FLEASOME	GREWSOME	LARKSOME	LOVESOME	PLAYSOME	TIRESOME	
DARKSOME	FOURSOME	GRUESOME	LIFESOME	LYSOSOME	POLYSOME	TOILSOME	

WORDS ENDING IN -TIME

7-letter words -TIME

AIRTIME	BEDTIME	DAYTIME	MISTIME	PASTIME	SEPTIME	WARTIME
ANYTIME	CENTIME	LAYTIME	ONETIME	RAGTIME	TEATIME	

8-letter words -TIME

CHOWTIME	FORETIME	LIFETIME	MEALTIME	OVERTIME	SEEDTIME	XENOTIME
DOWNTIME	GOODTIME	LONGTIME	MEANTIME	PLAYTIME	SOMETIME	ZONETIME
FLEXTIME	HALFTIME	MARITIME	NOONTIME	REALTIME	TERMTIME	

WORDS ENDING IN -TION

7-letter words -TION

ALATION	BASTION	COCTION	ELATION	ENATION	MENTION	OVATION	RUCTION	TACTION
AMATION	CANTION	COITION	ELUTION	FACTION	MICTION	PACTION	SECTION	TUITION
AMOTION	CAPTION	DICTION	EMOTION	FICTION	MIXTION	PORTION	STATION	UNCTION
AUCTION	CAUTION	EDITION	EMPTION	LECTION	ORATION	RECTION	SUCTION	UNITION

8-letter words -TION

ABLATION	COACTION	EGESTION	FRACTION	JOBATION	MUNITION	POTATION	SORPTION
ABLUTION	CONATION	EJECTION	FRICTION	JUNCTION	MUTATION	PUNITION	STICTION
ABORTION	COOPTION	ELECTION	FRUITION	LAVATION	NATATION	PUPATION	SUDATION
ADAPTION	CREATION	EMICTION	FUNCTION	LAXATION	NEGATION	QUESTION	SWAPTION
ADDITION	DELATION	ENACTION	GELATION	LEGATION	NIDATION	REACTION	TAXATION
ADNATION	DELETION	EQUATION	GUMPTION	LENITION	NODATION	RELATION	TRACTION
ADOPTION	DEMOTION	ERECTION	GYRATION	LIBATION	NOLITION	REMOTION	VACATION
AERATION	DERATION	ERUPTION	HALATION	LIGATION	NOTATION	ROGATION	VENATION
AGNATION	DEVOTION	EVECTION	HIMATION	LIMATION	NOVATION	ROTATION	VEXATION
AMBITION	DILATION	EVICTION	IDEATION	LOBATION	NUDATION	SANCTION	VOCATION
AUDITION	DILUTION	EXACTION	IGNITION	LOCATION	NUTATION	SCONTION	VOLITION
AVIATION	DONATION	EXERTION	ILLATION	LOCUTION	OBLATION	SEDATION	VOLUTION
BIBATION	DOTATION	FETATION	INACTION	LUNATION	PACATION	SEDITION	ZONATION
CIBATION	DURATION	FIXATION	INUSTION	LUXATION	PETITION	SOLATION	
CITATION	EDUCTION	FLECTION	IODATION	MONITION	POSITION	SOLUTION	

WORDS ENDING IN -URE

7-letter words -URE

ABATURE COUPURE FEATURE GYPLURE NERVURE POSTURE SEISURE VESTURE
BORDURE COUTURE FISSURE HACHURE NURTURE PRECURE SEIZURE VOITURE
BRAVURE CULTURE FIXTURE LEASURE OBSCURE PROCURE SEYSURE VULTURE
BRISURE DASYURE FLEXURE LECTURE OUTDURE PULTURE SOILURE WAFTURE
CAPTURE DENTURE FRISURE LEISURE PARTURE PURPURE STATURE
CENSURE DISCURE FRITURE MEASURE PASTURE RAPTURE TEXTURE
CLOSURE EPICURE GARBURE MIXTURE PERDURE RECOURE TONSURE
CLOTURE ERASURE GESTURE MONTURE PERJURE RONDURE TORTURE
COENURE FACTURE GRAVURE MORSURE PICTURE RUPTURE VENTURE
CONJURE FAILURE GUIPURE MULTURE PLEXURE SEASURE VERDURE

8-letter words -URE

ANNEXURE CISELURE DENATURE FIXATURE LIGATURE PEDICURE RENATURE TINCTURE
APERTURE COCKSURE DISCOURE FRACTURE LINCTURE PLEASURE REPOSURE TOURNURE
ARCATURE COENDURE DISINURE GENITURE MANICURE PRESSURE RESECURE TREASURE
ARMATURE COIFFURE DOUBLURE IMMATURE MOISTURE PUNCTURE ROUNDURE TRESSURE
AVENTURE COINSURE ENACTURE INCISURE OVERCURE REASSURE SCISSURE TUBULURE
BROCHURE CREATURE ENCOLURE INSECURE OVERSURE REFIGURE SCRIMURE
CEINTURE CUBATURE EXPOSURE JOINTURE OVERTURE REINJURE SINECURE
CINCTURE CYNOSURE FILATURE JUNCTURE PAINTURE REINSURE TAINTURE

WORDS ENDING IN -WARD

7-letter words -WARD

AIRWARD FORWARD HAYWARD MANWARD OUTWARD STEWARD WAYWARD
AWKWARD FROWARD HOGWARD NAYWARD SEAWARD SUNWARD WEYWARD
BEDWARD GODWARD LEEWARD NORWARD SKYWARD VANWARD

8-letter words -WARD

BACKWARD DOWNWARD HELLWARD KIRKWARD MOONWARD REREWARD UNTOWARD WOOLWARD
BEARWARD EASTWARD HINDWARD LANDWARD PARKWARD SELFWARD WESTWARD
BECOWARD FOREWARD HIVEWARD LEFTWARD POLEWARD SIDEWARD WINDWARD
CITYWARD GOALWARD HOMEWARD MISAWARD REARWARD THRAWARD WOODWARD

WORDS ENDING IN -WARDS

7-letter words -WARDS

ADWARDS COWARDS INWARDS ONWARDS REWARDS TOWARDS UPWARDS USWARDS VAWARDS

8-letter words -WARDS

AIRWARDS FORWARDS GODWARDS HOGWARDS MANWARDS NORWARDS SEAWARDS STEWARDS
BEDWARDS FROWARDS HAYWARDS LEEWARDS NAYWARDS OUTWARDS SKYWARDS SUNWARDS

WORDS ENDING IN -WAY

7-letter words -WAY

ARCHWAY CUTAWAY FOLKWAY HALFWAY LICHWAY RACEWAY ROPEWAY SOMEWAY TOWAWAY
AREAWAY DOORWAY FOOTWAY HALLWAY LIFEWAY RAILWAY RUNAWAY SPURWAY TRAMWAY
BELTWAY FAIRWAY FREEWAY HEADWAY PACKWAY RINGWAY SHIPWAY TAXIWAY WALKWAY
BIKEWAY FARAWAY GANGWAY HIGHWAY PARKWAY ROADWAY SIDEWAY THRUWAY WELAWAY
CARAWAY FISHWAY GATEWAY LANEWAY PARTWAY RODEWAY SKIDWAY TIDEWAY WINDWAY
CARTWAY FLYAWAY GETAWAY LAYAWAY PATHWAY ROLLWAY SLIPWAY TOLLWAY WIREWAY

8-letter words -WAY

AISLEWAY CASTAWAY CYCLEWAY FALLAWAY GUIDEWAY HORSEWAY RIDGEWAY SLIDEWAY
ALLEYWAY CAUSEWAY DRIVEWAY FLOODWAY HATCHWAY LOCKAWAY RIVERWAY SOAKAWAY
BROADWAY CLEARWAY ENTRYWAY FOLDAWAY HEREAWAY MOTORWAY ROCKAWAY SOARAWAY
CABLEWAY CRAWLWAY EVERYWAY GIVEAWAY HIDEAWAY MULLOWAY ROLLAWAY SPEEDWAY
CARRAWAY CROSSWAY FADEAWAY GREENWAY HOISTWAY OVERSWAY ROUTEWAY SPILLWAY

STAIRWAY STERNWAY TAKEAWAY THATAWAY TRAINWAY WALKAWAY WATERWAY WIDTHWAY
STAYAWAY STOWAWAY TEARAWAY TRACKWAY UNDERWAY WASTEWAY WELLAWAY

WORDS ENDING IN -WISE

7-letter words -WISE

AIRWISE ANYWISE ENDWISE FANWISE MANWISE MAPWISE SUNWISE TAXWISE

8-letter words -WISE

ARCHWISE CRABWISE ELSEWISE LIKEWISE PAIRWISE SIDEWISE SUCHWISE THUSWISE
BENDWISE DROPWISE FESSWISE LONGWISE PALEWISE SOMEWISE TEAMWISE WARPWISE
COMBWISE EDGEWISE FLATWISE OVERWISE RINGWISE STEPWISE TENTWISE WEFTWISE

WORDS ENDING IN -WOOD

7-letter words -WOOD

BARWOOD BOGWOOD CAMWOOD DOGWOOD ELMWOOD GUMWOOD LOGWOOD PLYWOOD SAPWOOD
BAYWOOD BOXWOOD DAGWOOD DYEWOOD FATWOOD INKWOOD NUTWOOD REDWOOD

8-letter words -WOOD

AGALWOOD BEEFWOOD CORDWOOD FUELWOOD IRONWOOD MILKWOOD PULPWOOD SOURWOOD
BACKWOOD BENTWOOD CORKWOOD GILTWOOD KINGWOOD OVENWOOD ROSEWOOD TEAKWOOD
BASSWOOD BLUEWOOD DEADWOOD HARDWOOD LACEWOOD PINEWOOD SASSWOOD WILDWOOD
BEARWOOD COLTWOOD FIREWOOD HAREWOOD LATEWOOD PORKWOOD SOFTWOOD WORMWOOD

WORDS ENDING IN -WORK

7-letter words -WORK

ARTWORK DAYWORK LEGWORK NONWORK PINWORK RAGWORK TINWORK TUTWORK WAXWORK
CUTWORK LAPWORK NETWORK OUTWORK PREWORK RIBWORK TOPWORK WARWORK WEBWORK

8-letter words -WORK

BACKWORK CAPEWORK FLUEWORK HEADWORK LATHWORK OVERWORK ROCKWORK TEAMWORK
BEADWORK CASEWORK FOOTWORK HOMEWORK LEADWORK PARTWORK ROPEWORK TIMEWORK
BODYWORK CRIBWORK FORMWORK HORNWORK LIFEWORK PILEWORK SALTWORK TUBEWORK
BOOKWORK DUCTWORK FRETWORK IRONWORK LINKWORK PIPEWORK SEATWORK WIREWORK
BUHLWORK FARMWORK HACKWORK KNOTWORK MESHWORK RACKWORK SLOPWORK WOODWORK
BUSYWORK FIREWORK HAIRWORK KOFTWORK MILLWORK RINGWORK STUDWORK WOOLWORK
CAGEWORK FLATWORK HANDWORK LACEWORK OPENWORK ROADWORK TASKWORK YARDWORK

WORDS ENDING IN -WORM

7-letter words -WORM

BAGWORM CATWORM EARWORM LOBWORM PINWORM SEAWORM WEBWORM
BUDWORM CUTWORM EELWORM LUGWORM RAGWORM WAXWORM

8-letter words -WORM

ARMYWORM CORNWORM GLOWWORM INCHWORM MEALWORM SHIPWORM WHIPWORM
BOLLWORM FIREWORM GRUBWORM LEAFWORM MUCKWORM SILKWORM WIREWORM
BOOKWORM FISHWORM HAIRWORM LINDWORM PILLWORM SLOWWORM WOODWORM
CASEWORM FLATWORM HOOKWORM LUNGWORM RINGWORM SPANWORM
CLAMWORM GAPEWORM HORNWORM MALTWORM SANDWORM TAPEWORM

WORDS ENDING IN -WORT

7-letter words -WORT

AWLWORT BUGWORT FELWORT MADWORT MUGWORT RIBWORT
BLAWORT FANWORT FIGWORT MUDWORT RAGWORT

8-letter words -WORT

BELLWORT DANEWORT GOUTWORT LEADWORT MODIWORT PILEWORT SALTWORT STARWORT
COLEWORT DROPWORT HONEWORT LUNGWORT MOONWORT PILLWORT SANDWORT WALLWORT
DAMEWORT FLEAWORT HORNWORT MILKWORT MOORWORT PIPEWORT SOAPWORT WARTWORT

WORDS ENDING IN -YARD

7-letter words -YARD

BEEYARD HALYARD INNYARD LANYARD TANYARD

8-letter words -YARD

BACKYARD COALYARD FARMYARD KAILYARD METEYARD SHIPYARD WHINYARD
BARNYARD DEERYARD FOREYARD KALEYARD RICKYARD SHOWYARD WILLYARD
BOATYARD DOCKYARD HAULYARD KIRKYARD SALEYARD TILTYARD WOODYARD
BONEYARD DOORYARD JUNKYARD MAINYARD SAVOYARD VINEYARD

Unusual Vowel Endings

When Scrabble players think about the endings of words, they are likely to concentrate on words with the more obvious endings, for example -ATE, -ISE, -URE and -ENT, and the common extensions -ED, -ER and -S. Such words tend to end with a fairly restricted group of letters – usually D, E, R, S and T.

Words ending with unusual letters don't spring easily to mind. It takes some effort to start thinking about words ending in A, I, O and U, yet these four letters make up 30% of the tiles in a Scrabble set and they will frequently appear on your rack. Familiarity with everyday English does not encourage you to think of these letters at the end of words, but they can be very useful for linking on to other letters on the board, making 2-letter words which begin or end with A, I, O or U.

The following lists provide ammunition for correcting that rather limiting view of word endings. They are of all valid words of length two to eight letters which end with A, I, O or U.

WORDS ENDING IN -A

2-letter words ending in -A

AA	DA	FA	KA	MA	PA	YA
BA	EA	HA	LA	NA	TA	

3-letter words ending in -A

ABA	ANA	CHA	ITA	MOA	OVA	RIA	SPA	WHA
AGA	AVA	ERA	KEA	OBA	PEA	RYA	TEA	YEA
AHA	AWA	ETA	KOA	OCA	PIA	SEA	TWA	ZEA
AIA	BAA	FRA	LEA	ODA	POA	SHA	UTA	ZOA
ALA	BOA	GOA	MAA	OKA	PYA	SKA	UVA	
AMA	BRA	HOA	MNA	ORA	QUA	SMA	VIA	

4-letter words ending in -A

ABBA	BABA	COXA	GAGA	INIA	LEVA	MURA	PACA	RAJA	SODA
ACTA	BEMA	CYMA	GALA	IOTA	LIMA	MYNA	PAPA	RANA	SOFA
AGHA	BETA	DADA	GAMA	ISBA	LIRA	NADA	PARA	RATA	SOJA
AGMA	BIGA	DATA	GENA	IXIA	LOCA	NAGA	PAUA	RAYA	SOLA
ALBA	BIMA	DEVA	GETA	JAVA	LOMA	NALA	PAWA	RHEA	SOMA
ALFA	BOBA	DIKA	GIGA	JOTA	LOTA	NANA	PEBA	RIMA	SORA
ALGA	BOLA	DISA	GILA	JUBA	LUNA	NAPA	PELA	RIVA	SOYA
ALMA	BOMA	DITA	GLIA	JUGA	MAMA	NEMA	PICA	RIZA	STOA
AMIA	BONA	DIVA	GUGA	JURA	MANA	NIPA	PIKA	ROMA	SUBA
AMLA	BORA	DONA	GULA	KAKA	MARA	NOMA	PILA	ROTA	SURA
ANGA	BOTA	DOPA	HAHA	KAMA	MASA	NONA	PIMA	RUGA	TAHA
ANNA	BUBA	DUMA	HAKA	KANA	MAYA	NOTA	PINA	RUSA	TAKA
ANOA	BUNA	DURA	HILA	KAPA	MEGA	NOVA	PIPA	SAGA	TALA
ANSA	BURA	EGMA	HIYA	KARA	MELA	OBIA	PITA	SAMA	TANA
ANTA	CABA	EKKA	HORA	KATA	MESA	OCTA	PLEA	SENA	TAPA
AQUA	CACA	EMMA	HOYA	KAVA	META	ODEA	PROA	SERA	TARA
ARBA	CAPA	EPHA	HUIA	KETA	MICA	OHIA	PUJA	SETA	TAVA
AREA	CASA	ETNA	HULA	KINA	MINA	OKRA	PULA	SHEA	TAWA
ARIA	CECA	EYRA	HUMA	KIVA	MOLA	OKTA	PUMA	SHWA	TAXA
ARNA	CHIA	FAVA	HYLA	KOLA	MONA	OLEA	PUNA	SIDA	TELA
ASEA	COCA	FETA	IDEA	KORA	MORA	OLLA	PUPA	SIKA	TEPA
ATMA	CODA	FILA	ILEA	LAMA	MOWA	ORCA	RACA	SIMA	TIKA
AULA	COLA	FLEA	ILIA	LANA	MOXA	ORRA	RAGA	SKUA	TOEA
AURA	COMA	FORA	ILKA	LAVA	MOYA	OSSA	RAIA	SOCA	TOGA

TOLA TUFA UREA VARA VENA VISA WAKA YOGA ZILA ZYGA
TORA TUNA URSA VASA VERA VITA WEKA YUCA ZOEA
TOSA ULNA URVA VEGA VIGA VIVA WETA YUGA ZONA
TUBA ULVA UVEA VELA VINA VOLA WHOA ZETA ZUPA

5-letter words ending in -A

ABACA BOYLA DIOTA GRANA KOFTA MILIA PASHA RIOJA STUPA UNCIA
ABAKA BRAVA DOBLA GROMA KOKRA MILPA PASTA ROOSA SULFA URBIA
ABAYA BRAZA DOBRA GUANA KOPPA MIRZA PELMA RUANA SUMMA URENA
ABOMA BUFFA DOGMA GUAVA KORMA MISSA PELTA RUMBA SUNNA USNEA
ABUNA BULLA DOLIA GUMMA KRONA MOCHA PENNA RUPIA SUPRA UVULA
ACETA BUNIA DOLMA GUSLA KURTA MOIRA PEPLA RUSMA SURRA VACUA
ADYTA BUNYA DONGA GUTTA KWELA MOLLA PEREA SABRA SUTRA VANDA
AECIA BURKA DONNA HAIKA LABDA MOMMA PHOCA SACRA SUTTA VARIA
AFARA BURQA DOONA HALFA LABIA MOOLA PHYLA SADZA SYLVA VARNA
AGAMA BURSA DORSA HALMA LABRA MORIA PICRA SAIGA TABLA VEENA
AGILA BWANA DOUMA HALVA LAIKA MORRA PIETA SAKIA TAFIA VESPA
AGORA CAECA DOURA HAMZA LAMIA MOTZA PILEA SALPA TAGMA VESTA
AGRIA CALLA DOWNA HANSA LARVA MOWRA PINNA SALSA TAIGA VIFDA
AJIVA CALPA DRAMA HAOMA LAURA MUDRA PINTA SAMBA TAIRA VIGIA
AJUGA CANNA DULIA HASTA LAVRA MULGA PITTA SANGA TALEA VILLA
AKELA CARTA DUMKA HEJRA LEHUA MULLA PIZZA SANSA TALMA VINCA
ALAPA CAUSA DURRA HENNA LEMMA MURRA PLAYA SAUBA TALPA VIOLA
ALDEA CEIBA EDEMA HERMA LEPRA MURVA PLAZA SAUNA TANGA VIRGA
ALIYA CELLA ENEMA HEVEA LEPTA MUSCA PLENA SCALA TANKA VISTA
ALOHA CERIA ENTIA HIJRA LIANA MUSHA PLICA SCAPA TANNA VITTA
ALPHA CESTA ERBIA HODJA LIBRA MYOMA POAKA SCENA TAPPA VIVDA
ALULA CHARA ERICA HOLLA LIMBA NABLA PODIA SCHWA TAYRA VODKA
AMEBA CHAYA ETYMA HONDA LIMMA NAIRA POLKA SCOPA TAZZA VOILA
AMIGA CHEKA EXTRA HOOKA LIMPA NALLA PONGA SCUBA TECTA VOLTA
AMNIA CHELA FACIA HOSTA LINGA NANNA POOJA SCUTA TEGUA VOLVA
ANANA CHICA FAENA HURRA LLAMA NAPPA POOKA SELLA TELIA VULVA
ANIMA CHINA FANGA HUTIA LOGIA NERKA POPPA SELVA TENIA WALLA
ANTRA CHOTA FATWA HUZZA LONGA NGANA PORTA SENNA TERGA WANNA
AORTA CHUFA FAUNA HYDRA LOOFA NINJA PRANA SENSA TERRA WICCA
APNEA CILIA FELLA HYENA LUBRA NORIA PRESA SENZA TESLA WILGA
ARABA CIRCA FERIA HYPHA LUFFA NORMA PRIMA SEPIA TESTA WILJA
ARECA CNIDA FESTA IDOLA LUTEA NUBIA PRUTA SEPTA TETRA WINNA
ARENA COALA FETTA INFRA LYCEA NUCHA PSORA SERRA THANA WIRRA
AROBA COBIA FETWA INTRA LYSSA NULLA PUCKA SESSA THECA WISHA
AROMA COBRA FLORA INULA LYTTA NYALA PUKKA SHAMA THEMA WONGA
ASANA COBZA FLOTA IXORA MAFIA NYSSA PULKA SHAYA THETA XENIA
ASYLA COCOA FOLIA JAGRA MAGMA OCREA PUNGA SHEVA THUJA XOANA
ATRIA COLZA FONDA JARTA MAHUA OIDIA PUNKA SHIVA THUYA YACCA
BABKA COMMA FOSSA JHALA MAHWA OMASA PURDA SHOLA TIARA YAKKA
BACCA CONGA FOVEA JIRGA MALVA OMEGA QIBLA SHURA TIBIA YARFA
BAIZA CONIA FRENA JNANA MAMBA OPERA QUENA SIDHA TICCA YARTA
BAJRA COPRA GALEA JUNTA MAMMA ORGIA QUINA SIGLA TIKKA YENTA
BALSA CORIA GAMBA KAAMA MANGA OSSIA QUOTA SIGMA TINEA YERBA
BANDA COSTA GAMMA KACHA MANIA OSTIA RAGGA SILVA TOMIA YUCCA
BANIA COTTA GANJA KALPA MANNA OUIJA RAITA SIRRA TONGA YURTA
BARCA CRENA GARDA KANGA MANTA PACHA RASTA SOFTA TREFA ZABRA
BASTA CRURA GEMMA KAPPA MARIA PACTA REATA SOPRA TREMA ZAMIA
BATTA CULPA GENOA KARMA MASSA PADMA RECTA SORDA TRONA ZANJA
BELGA CUPPA GENUA KASHA MATZA PAISA REDIA SORRA TRYMA ZANZA
BETTA CURIA GLEBA KHAYA MBIRA PAKKA REGMA SPICA TSUBA ZEBRA
BIGHA DACHA GOMPA KHEDA MECCA PALEA REGNA SPINA TUGRA ZERDA
BIOTA DAGGA GONIA KHOJA MEDIA PALLA RENGA SPUTA TUINA ZONDA
BIVIA DARGA GONNA KIBLA MENSA PAMPA REPLA STELA ULAMA ZOOEA
BOCCA DELTA GOTTA KINDA MENTA PANDA RETIA STIPA ULEMA ZOPPA
BOHEA DERMA GOURA KIPPA MICRA PANGA RHYTA STOMA ULTRA
BONZA DICTA GRAMA KOALA MIKRA PARKA RIATA STRIA UMBRA

6-letter words ending in -A

ABASIA AGENDA ALISMA AMELIA ANGINA APHTHA ARMADA AUCUBA BAJADA BEFANA
ABELIA AGOUTA ALODIA AMENTA ANGOLA APNOEA ARNICA AURORA BALATA BEFLEA
ABOLLA AHIMSA ALOGIA AMOEBA ANGORA APORIA AROLLA AXILLA BALBOA BELUGA
ABULIA AIKONA ALPACA AMRITA ANOPIA ARALIA ARROBA AZALEA BANANA BEMATA
ACACIA ALALIA ALTEZA AMUSIA ANOXIA ARCANA ASRAMA AZOLLA BARAZA BERTHA
ACEDIA ALASKA ALTHEA ANATTA ANTARA AREOLA ASTHMA BACKRA BARYTA BHAKTA
ADNEXA ALBATA ALUMNA ANCORA ANTLIA ARGALA ATAXIA BACULA BATATA BILBOA
AFTOSA ALEXIA AMARNA ANEMIA ANURIA ARISTA ATOCIA BAHADA BAUERA BOCCIA

BODEGA BONITA BOORKA BOSHTA BRAHMA BREGMA BROLGA BUCKRA BUDDHA BUGSHA BUNNIA BUQSHA BUSHWA CABALA CABANA CAEOMA CAFILA CALESA CALIMA CALTHA CAMBIA CAMERA CAMISA CANADA CANCHA CANOLA CANULA CAPITA CARDIA CARINA CASABA CASAVA CASITA CASSIA CATENA CEDULA CEMBRA CENTRA CESURA CHACMA CHAETA CHAKRA CHALLA CHAPKA CHARKA CHARTA CHATTA CHICHA CHIMLA CHOANA CHOKRA CHOLLA CHORDA CHOREA CHORIA CHROMA

CHUKKA CICADA CICALA CICUTA CINEMA CITOLA CLIVIA CLOACA CLUSIA COAITA CODEIA CONCHA CONIMA CONTRA COPITA COPPRA COPULA CORNEA CORNUA CORONA CORYZA COSMEA COWPEA CRANIA CRISSA CRISTA CRUSTA CUBICA CUESTA CUPOLA CUPULA CURARA CUTCHA CZAPKA DAGABA DAGOBA DAHLIA DATCHA DATURA DEFLEA DHARMA DHARNA DHOORA DHURNA DHURRA DOLINA DUENNA ECZEMA EGESTA EIDOLA EJECTA ELODEA ELUVIA ELYTRA EMPUSA ENCINA

ENIGMA ENTERA EPEIRA EPIZOA EPOCHA ERRATA ESPADA EUPNEA EUREKA EXACTA EXEDRA EXUVIA FACULA FAJITA FANEGA FARINA FASCIA FATSIA FAVELA FECULA FEDORA FEIJOA FEMORA FERULA FIBULA FIESTA FOOTRA FOUSSA FOUTRA FRAENA FRISKA FRUSTA FULCRA FUNKIA GALENA GAMBIA GARRYA GARUDA GEISHA GELADA GENERA GENEVA GITANA GLIOMA GLORIA GLOSSA GOANNA GOONDA GOPURA GORGIA GRAMMA GRAPPA GUINEA HALALA HALLOA HAMADA

HANIWA HEBONA HEGIRA HEJIRA HEMINA HERNIA HILLOA HOLLOA HOLMIA HOOPLA HULLOA HUTZPA HYAENA HYDRIA IGUANA IMPALA INDABA INDUNA INFULA INJERA INSULA INTIMA INYALA ISCHIA JACANA JARINA JATAKA JEJUNA JEMIMA JERBOA JICAMA JOANNA JOJOBA JUDOKA JUGULA KABAKA KABALA KABAYA KACCHA KAFILA KAHUNA KALMIA KAMALA KAMELA KAMILA KANAKA KANGHA KANTHA KARAKA KATANA KENTIA KERRIA KGOTLA KHANGA KHODJA KHURTA

KINEMA KISHKA KORORA KORUNA KUMARA KUTCHA KWACHA KWANZA LABARA LACUNA LAGENA LAGUNA LAMBDA LAMINA LATRIA LEIPOA LEXICA LIGULA LIKUTA LIMINA LINGUA LIPOMA LITHIA LOCHIA LOGGIA LOMATA LORCHA LORICA LUCUMA LUMINA LUNULA LUSTRA MACOYA MACULA MAFFIA MAKUTA MALTHA MANANA MANILA MANTRA MANTUA MANUKA MARACA MARINA MARKKA MASALA MASHUA MASULA MAUNNA MAXIMA MAZUMA MEDAKA MEDINA MEDUSA MEGARA MESETA

METEPA MEZUZA MGANGA MIASMA MIMOSA MINIMA MODENA MODICA MONERA MOORVA MORULA MOTUCA MUCOSA MULETA MUMMIA MURENA MURRHA MUTUCA MYOPIA MYRICA MYXOMA NAGANA NATURA NAUSEA NEBULA NEPETA NOCTUA NOMINA NOVENA NUMINA NUTRIA NYANZA NYMPHA OBELIA OCHREA OEDEMA OMENTA OMERTA ONYCHA OPTIMA ORARIA ORBITA ORGANA OSCULA OTTAVA OZAENA PAELLA PAGODA PAJAMA PAKEHA PAKORA PALAMA PALLIA PANADA PANAMA PAPAYA

PAPULA PARURA PATACA PATERA PATINA PAYOLA PELOTA PENNIA PERAEA PEREIA PESETA PESEWA PESHWA PETARA PHOBIA PIAZZA PICARA PILULA PINATA PINETA PIRANA PIRAYA PITARA PLANTA PLASMA PLEURA PNEUMA POISHA POSADA PREMIA PROTEA PRUINA PSYLLA PTERIA PULKHA PUNCTA PURANA PYEMIA PYROLA PYURIA QASIDA QUAGGA QUALIA QUANTA QUELEA QUINOA QUINTA QUOKKA QUOTHA RADULA RAFFIA RANULA RAPHIA RAZZIA REALIA REDOWA

REGINA REGULA REMORA REMUDA RESEDA RETAMA RETINA RHUMBA ROSTRA ROSULA ROTULA RUCOLA RUGOLA RUGOSA RUMINA RUSSIA SABKHA SAHIBA SALINA SALIVA SALVIA SAMARA SAMOSA SANCTA SAPOTA SATARA SATYRA SCARPA SCHEMA SCILLA SCLERA SCOLIA SCORIA SCOTIA SCROTA SEMEIA SEMINA SENECA SENEGA SENORA SEROSA SHAMBA SHARIA SHEILA SHELTA SHERIA SHERPA SHIKSA SHIRRA SIDDHA SIENNA SIERRA SIESTA SIFAKA SILICA SISTRA

SITULA SKOLIA SMEGMA SOLERA SOMATA SONATA SPIREA SQUAMA SRADHA STADDA STADIA STANZA STATUA STELLA STEMMA STERNA STIGMA STIRRA STRATA STRIGA STROMA STRUMA SUBSEA SULPHA SUNDRA SYLVIA SYNURA TABULA TAENIA TAFFIA TAHINA TAIAHA TALUKA TAMARA TANKIA TANTRA TAPETA TARAMA TARSIA TEGULA TELEGA TEPHRA TERATA TERBIA TEREFA TERTIA THANNA THORIA THULIA TINAJA TIPULA TORANA TORULA TOTARA TRAUMA TRIVIA

TROIKA TSAMBA TUGHRA TUNDRA TUNICA UJAMAA ULTIMA UNGULA URANIA UREDIA UREMIA URTICA UTOPIA VAGINA VALETA VALUTA VARROA VEDUTA VELETA VESICA VICUNA VIHARA VIMANA VIMINA VIZSLA VOMICA WHATNA WILTJA WOMERA XEROMA XYLOMA YAKUZA YANTRA YAQONA YARPHA YAUTIA YOJANA YTTRIA YUKATA ZABETA ZANANA ZAPATA ZAREBA ZARIBA ZENANA ZEREBA ZERIBA ZEUGMA ZINNIA ZOARIA ZOECIA ZONULA ZOYSIA ZYGOMA

7-letter words ending in -A

ABOMASA ABOULIA ABROSIA ACANTHA ACAPNIA ACCIDIA ACEQUIA ACEROLA ACHARYA ACHENIA ACHOLIA ACICULA ACRASIA ACROMIA ACTINIA

ACUSHLA ADDENDA ADENOMA ADHARMA AECIDIA AEROBIA AGNOSIA AGRAPHA ALAMEDA ALBIZIA ALCHERA ALCORZA ALFALFA ALFORJA ALGEBRA

ALGESIA ALLODIA ALLUVIA ALTEZZA ALTHAEA ALUMINA AMANITA AMBOINA AMBOYNA AMENTIA AMMONIA AMNESIA AMOROSA AMPHORA AMPULLA

AMREETA ANAEMIA ANALGIA ANALOGA ANCHUSA ANCILIA ANCILLA ANERGIA ANESTRA ANGARIA ANGIOMA ANHINGA ANNATTA ANONYMA ANOPSIA

ANOSMIA ANTENNA APADANA APEPSIA APHAGIA APHASIA APHELIA APHONIA APLASIA APRAXIA APTERIA AQUARIA ARABICA ARAROBA ARCADIA

ARGYRIA ARIETTA ARMILLA ARUGOLA ARUGULA ASCIDIA ASHRAMA ASPIDIA ASTASIA ASTERIA ATALAYA ATEMOYA ATHLETA ATRESIA ATROPIA

AURELIA AUREOLA BABESIA BACCARA BACLAVA BAKLAVA BAKLAWA BALISTA BANDANA BANDORA BANDURA BANKSIA BARBOLA BARILLA BASIDIA

BATTUTA BAZOOKA BEFFANA BEGONIA BEGORRA BERETTA BERGAMA BHANGRA BIDARKA BIENNIA BIODATA BIRETTA BISNAGA BIZNAGA BOFFOLA

BOHEMIA BOLIVIA BOLOGNA BOMBORA BONAMIA BONANZA BORONIA BOTHRIA BOTTEGA BOURKHA BRACCIA BRACHIA BRAVURA BRECCIA BRITSKA

BRITZKA	COQUINA	EUPNOEA	HETAERA	MAGMATA	NOVALIA	PLANULA	SAMSARA	TAMASHA
BRUHAHA	CORALLA	EUTEXIA	HETAIRA	MAHATMA	NOVELLA	PLATINA	SANGOMA	TAMBALA
BUBINGA	CORBINA	EXCRETA	HEUREKA	MAHONIA	OCARINA	PLECTRA	SANGRIA	TAMBURA
BUCCINA	CORDOBA	EXEMPLA	HEXAPLA	MAJAGUA	OCTAPLA	PLEROMA	SAPHENA	TAMPALA
BULIMIA	CORELLA	EXHEDRA	HIDALGA	MALACCA	OLEARIA	PLUGOLA	SARCOMA	TANAGRA
BURSERA	COREMIA	EXORDIA	HIMATIA	MALACIA	OMMATEA	PLUMULA	SARDANA	TANIWHA
BUZUKIA	COROLLA	EXOTICA	HOSANNA	MALANGA	OMNIANA	PODAGRA	SATSUMA	TANTARA
CABBALA	CORPORA	EXTREMA	HYMENIA	MALARIA	ONDATRA	PODESTA	SAVANNA	TAPIOCA
CABOMBA	CORRIDA	EXURBIA	HYPOGEA	MAMILLA	ONYCHIA	POGONIA	SAXTUBA	TARTANA
CADENZA	CORVINA	FALBALA	HYPONEA	MANCALA	OOGONIA	POLACCA	SCAGLIA	TAVERNA
CAESURA	COTINGA	FALCULA	HYPOXIA	MANDALA	OOTHECA	POLENTA	SCANDIA	TEDESCA
CAFFILA	CREMONA	FARINHA	IGNATIA	MANDIRA	OPHIURA	POLYNIA	SCAPULA	TEGMINA
CALDERA	CRIMINA	FARRUCA	IKEBANA	MANDOLA	OPUNTIA	POLYNYA	SCHISMA	TEMPERA
CALLUNA	CROTALA	FAVELLA	ILLUVIA	MANDORA	OQUASSA	POLYOMA	SCHOLIA	TEMPURA
CALUMBA	CURACOA	FAZENDA	IMPERIA	MANILLA	ORGANZA	POLYZOA	SCOPULA	TEQUILA
CAMELIA	CURCUMA	FELICIA	IMPRESA	MANIOCA	OROPESA	POTASSA	SCOTOMA	TEREBRA
CAMISIA	CURIOSA	FELUCCA	INDICIA	MANUMEA	OSMUNDA	PRECAVA	SCYBALA	TESSERA
CAMORRA	CURTANA	FERMATA	INDUSIA	MANYATA	OSTEOMA	PRIMULA	SECRETA	THEMATA
CAMPANA	CYATHIA	FIBROMA	INEDITA	MARANTA	OSTRACA	PRONOTA	SEDILIA	THRIMSA
CANASTA	CYMATIA	FILARIA	INERTIA	MARASCA	OSTRAKA	PROPYLA	SENHORA	THRYMSA
CANDELA	CYPSELA	FIMBRIA	INFANTA	MAREMMA	OTALGIA	PROSOMA	SENOPIA	TILAPIA
CANDIDA	CZARINA	FISTULA	INFAUNA	MARGOSA	OUGUIYA	PTERYLA	SEQUELA	TIMPANA
CANELLA	DAPHNIA	FLUTINA	INGESTA	MARIMBA	OVERSEA	PUDENDA	SEQUOIA	TITANIA
CANNULA	DATARIA	FONTINA	INOCULA	MARKKAA	OVIPARA	PUNALUA	SERIEMA	TOCCATA
CANTALA	DAVIDIA	FORLANA	INTRADA	MARSALA	OXYMORA	PUPARIA	SERINGA	TOHEROA
CANTATA	DECIDUA	FORMULA	IPOMOEA	MASCARA	PADELLA	PUPUNHA	SERPULA	TOHUNGA
CANTINA	DECURIA	FOSSULA	ISODICA	MASTABA	PAENULA	PURPURA	SESTINA	TOMBOLA
CANZONA	DEJECTA	FOVEOLA	ISODOMA	MATILDA	PAISANA	PYAEMIA	SEVRUGA	TOMENTA
CAPUERA	DELENDA	FREESIA	JAMBIYA	MAXILLA	PALABRA	PYGIDIA	SHASTRA	TORMINA
CARAMBA	DELIRIA	FRENULA	JELLABA	MAZURKA	PALMYRA	PYREXIA	SHEHITA	TOSTADA
CARANNA	DEODARA	FUCHSIA	JIPYAPA	MEDACCA	PALOOKA	PYXIDIA	SHEIKHA	TOXEMIA
CARAUNA	DEUTZIA	FURCULA	KABBALA	MEDULLA	PANACEA	QUASSIA	SHICKSA	TRACHEA
CARBORA	DHOURRA	FURLANA	KACHCHA	MELISMA	PANDORA	QUERIDA	SHORTIA	TREHALA
CARIAMA	DIGAMMA	GALABEA	KACHINA	MELODIA	PANDURA	QUINELA	SIGNORA	TRISULA
CARIOCA	DIHEDRA	GALABIA	KALIMBA	MEROPIA	PANOCHA	QUININA	SILESIA	TRITOMA
CASCARA	DILEMMA	GALANGA	KANTELA	MESHUGA	PAPILLA	RABANNA	SILIQUA	TRYMATA
CASSABA	DILUVIA	GALATEA	KATCINA	MESTIZA	PAPRICA	RADIATA	SILPHIA	TSARINA
CASSATA	DIORAMA	GALLETA	KATORGA	METAZOA	PAPRIKA	RAMENTA	SINOPIA	TUATARA
CASSAVA	DIPLOMA	GANGLIA	KEITLOA	MICELLA	PARATHA	RAOULIA	SKIMMIA	TUATERA
CATALPA	DIPTERA	GANGSTA	KERYGMA	MILITIA	PARAZOA	RASBORA	SOKAIYA	TURISTA
CATASTA	DIPTYCA	GASTREA	KHALIFA	MINEOLA	PAREIRA	RATAFIA	SOLARIA	TUTANIA
CATAWBA	DOGMATA	GAZANIA	KHEDIVA	MINORCA	PARELLA	REFUGIA	SOLATIA	TYMPANA
CAVALLA	DOMATIA	GAZOOKA	KIBITKA	MINUTIA	PARERGA	REGALIA	SOREDIA	TZARINA
CEDILLA	DONGOLA	GENISTA	KITHARA	MOCHILA	PARGANA	REGATTA	SPATULA	ULNARIA
CELESTA	DOPATTA	GERBERA	KUCHCHA	MOJARRA	PARTITA	REGMATA	SPECTRA	URAEMIA
CELOSIA	DOULEIA	GERMINA	LABELLA	MOMENTA	PASSATA	REPLICA	SPECULA	URETHRA
CEMENTA	DRACHMA	GERTCHA	LACINIA	MONARDA	PASTINA	RESIDUA	SPICULA	VACCINA
CEREBRA	DROSERA	GINGIVA	LAMBADA	MONILIA	PATAGIA	RETSINA	SPINULA	VALONEA
CHALAZA	DUODENA	GLOMERA	LAMELLA	MORPHIA	PATELLA	RHIZOMA	SPIRAEA	VALONIA
CHARKHA	DUPATTA	GLUCINA	LAMPUKA	MORRHUA	PAVLOVA	RHODORA	SPIRULA	VALVULA
CHECHIA	DVANDVA	GOBURRA	LANGAHA	MOUSAKA	PAXIUBA	RHYTINA	SPLENIA	VANESSA
CHIASMA	DYSPNEA	GODETIA	LANTANA	MOVIOLA	PECULIA	RICKSHA	SQUILLA	VANILLA
CHICANA	DYSURIA	GONDOLA	LASAGNA	MOZETTA	PEISHWA	RICOTTA	SRADDHA	VARIOLA
CHIKARA	ECHIDNA	GONIDIA	LATAKIA	MUDIRIA	PELORIA	RIKISHA	STAMINA	VASCULA
CHIMERA	ECTHYMA	GORILLA	LAVOLTA	MULATTA	PEMBINA	RIVIERA	STASIMA	VEDALIA
CHOLERA	ECTOPIA	GRANDMA	LEMMATA	MURAENA	PENTHIA	ROBINIA	STHENIA	VELARIA
CHRISMA	ECTOZOA	GRANDPA	LEMPIRA	MUTANDA	PEREIRA	ROBUSTA	STOMATA	VENTANA
CHUTZPA	EDEMATA	GRANITA	LEUCOMA	MYALGIA	PERGOLA	ROMAIKA	STRETTA	VERANDA
CIBORIA	EMBLEMA	GRANOLA	LEUKOMA	MYCELIA	PERIDIA	ROMNEYA	STRIATA	VERBENA
CIMELIA	EMERITA	GRAVIDA	LEWISIA	MYELOMA	PERILLA	ROSACEA	SUBAQUA	VERRUCA
CINEREA	EMPORIA	GUARANA	LINGULA	MYOMATA	PERINEA	ROSALIA	SUBAREA	VERRUGA
CINGULA	EMPYEMA	GUEREZA	LIXIVIA	MYRINGA	PERSONA	ROSARIA	SUBIDEA	VETTURA
CITHARA	ENCOMIA	GUMMATA	LOBELIA	NANDINA	PESSIMA	ROSELLA	SUBPENA	VEXILLA
CLARKIA	ENDOZOA	GUNNERA	LOCUSTA	NAPHTHA	PETUNIA	ROSEOLA	SUBTAXA	VIATICA
COAGULA	ENEMATA	GYNECIA	LOGANIA	NEMESIA	PHILTRA	ROTUNDA	SUCCUBA	VICUGNA
COCHLEA	ENTASIA	HAFTARA	LOMENTA	NEUROMA	PIASABA	RUBELLA	SUDARIA	VIDENDA
CODEINA	ENTOZOA	HAGGADA	LORDOMA	NEURULA	PIASAVA	RUBEOLA	SULTANA	VIHUELA
CODETTA	EPHEDRA	HALACHA	MACCHIA	NIGELLA	PIGNORA	RUELLIA	SUMATRA	VINCULA
CODILLA	EPISCIA	HALAKHA	MACUMBA	NIHONGA	PINNULA	RUFIYAA	SYCONIA	VIRANDA
COMITIA	EQUINIA	HAMMADA	MADEIRA	NIRVANA	PINTADA	RUSALKA	SYNOVIA	VIREMIA
COMMATA	EROTEMA	HARIANA	MADONNA	NONCOLA	PIRAGUA	SABELLA	SYRINGA	VISCERA
CONARIA	EROTICA	HARMALA	MADOQUA	NORTENA	PIRANHA	SABURRA	TAFFETA	VIVARIA
CONIDIA	EUGENIA	HELLOVA	MADRASA	NOTANDA	PISCINA	SACELLA	TAGMATA	VIVERRA
COPAIBA	EUGLENA	HELLUVA	MADRONA	NOTITIA	PITUITA	SAGITTA	TALARIA	VOLUSPA
COPAIVA	EULOGIA	HEMIOLA	MAGENTA	NOUMENA	PLACITA	SAMBUCA	TALOOKA	WAKANDA

WALLABA WOODSIA YAMALKA ZAMARRA ZEBRULA ZIGANKA ZOOECIA
WEIGELA WOOMERA YAMULKA ZANELLA ZELKOVA ZIMOCCA ZOOGLEA
WHOOPLA WOORARA YESHIVA ZAREEBA ZEMSTVA ZINGARA ZORILLA
WOMMERA XERASIA ZAKUSKA ZEBRINA ZENAIDA ZIZANIA ZYZZYVA

8-letter words ending in -A

ABDOMINA AUTOMATA CARAGANA DEMENTIA FORAMINA IMPLUVIA MAZAEDIA PIASSABA
ABRACHIA AUTOPSIA CARNAUBA DEMERARA FRITTATA INSIGNIA MAZOURKA PIASSAVA
ABSCISSA AVIFAUNA CARPALIA DENTALIA FUGHETTA INSOMNIA MBAQANGA PIGNOLIA
ACADEMIA AYURVEDA CASTELLA DENTARIA FURCRAEA INTARSIA MELANOMA PIZZERIA
ACELDAMA AZOTEMIA CATHEDRA DIARRHEA GALABIYA INTIFADA MELODICA PLACENTA
ACHAENIA AZOTURIA CATHISMA DIASPORA GALLABEA ISABELLA MENSTRUA PLANARIA
ACHILLEA BABIRUSA CATTLEYA DIASTEMA GALLABIA ISCHEMIA MESHUGGA PLANURIA
ACIDEMIA BABUSHKA CAVATINA DICENTRA GALLERIA ISCHURIA MESOGLEA PLATANNA
ACIDURIA BACTERIA CECROPIA DICHASIA GALTONIA IZVESTIA METANOIA PLATYSMA
ADESPOTA BAIDARKA CELOMATA DIELYTRA GAMBETTA JAPONICA MIASMATA PLETHORA
ADULARIA BALLISTA CERCARIA DIPLEGIA GAMBUSIA JARARACA MILIARIA PLUMERIA
ADYNAMIA BANDANNA CHALAZIA DIPLOPIA GAMMADIA JARARAKA MILTONIA POLLINIA
AGENESIA BAPTISIA CHAQUETA DIPLOZOA GAMMATIA JAVELINA MINNEOLA POLYGALA
AGNOMINA BARATHEA CHARISMA DJELLABA GARCINIA JIPIJAPA MONSTERA POLYPNEA
AGRAPHIA BARRANCA CHATCHKA DRACAENA GARDENIA KALYPTRA MONTARIA POLYURIA
AGRYPNIA BASILICA CHICKPEA DULCIANA GASTRAEA KAMAAINA MOUSSAKA POSTCAVA
AKINESIA BATTALIA CHILLADA DULCINEA GASTRULA KARATEKA MOVIEOLA PRAECAVA
ALBIZZIA BAUHINIA CHIMAERA DYSCHROA GELSEMIA KATAKANA MOZZETTA PREDELLA
ALGAROBA BEDSONIA CHINAMPA DYSLEXIA GEMATRIA KATCHINA MRIDANGA PRESCUTA
ALIGARTA BERGENIA CHINKARA DYSMELIA GERARDIA KAVAKAVA MYCETOMA PRESIDIA
ALLELUIA BERRETTA CHIRAGRA DYSPNOEA GEROPIGA KAZATZKA MYOTONIA PROFORMA
ALOPECIA BERYLLIA CHLOASMA DYSTAXIA GESNERIA KERATOMA MYXEDEMA PROGERIA
AMBERINA BETHESDA CHOLEMIA DYSTOCIA GLABELLA KHANSAMA MYXOMATA PROTOZOA
AMBROSIA BIGNONIA CHURINGA DYSTONIA GLADIOLA KIELBASA NAVICULA PRUNELLA
AMPHIBIA BIRRETTA CHYLURIA DYSTOPIA GLAUCOMA KINAKINA NONQUOTA PRYTANEA
AMYGDALA BISCACHA CIABATTA EARTHPEA GLIOMATA KRAMERIA NUBECULA PSORALEA
ANABAENA BIZCACHA CINCHONA ECCLESIA GLORIOSA LABRUSCA NYMPHAEA PTERYGIA
ANACONDA BLASTEMA CISTERNA EFFLUVIA GLOSSINA LAVALAVA OCCIPITA PUTAMINA
ANALECTA BLASTOMA CLAUSTRA EGOMANIA GLOXINIA LAVATERA ODONTOMA PYCNIDIA
ANALEMMA BLASTULA CLAUSULA EMPANADA GLUMELLA LECANORA OEDEMATA PYODERMA
ANAPHORA BOLTONIA CLITELLA ENCAENIA GLYCERIA LEUCEMIA OITICICA PYORRHEA
ANASARCA BONSELLA COCCIDIA ENDAMEBA GOLCONDA LEUKEMIA OLIGURIA QINDARKA
ANATHEMA BOTANICA COCINERA ENDOSTEA GOLFIANA LEVODOPA OMBRELLA QUADRIGA
ANECDOTA BRACIOLA COCOBOLA ENGRAMMA GOLGOTHA LIPOMATA OMNIVORA QUILLAIA
ANGELICA BRANCHIA COENOBIA ENIGMATA GUERILLA LISTERIA OPERCULA QUILLAJA
ANOESTRA BRASSICA COLCHICA ENTAMEBA GURDWARA LITHEMIA OPERETTA QUINELLA
ANOOPSIA BREGMATA COLLEGIA EPENDYMA GYMKHANA LODICULA OPUSCULA QUINIELA
ANOREXIA BRITZSKA COLLUVIA EPHEMERA GYMNASIA LONICERA ORCHELLA RACHILLA
ANOXEMIA BROMELIA COLLYRIA EPICEDIA GYNAECEA LYMPHOMA ORCHILLA RADIALIA
ANTEFIXA BRONCHIA COLOBOMA EPIFAUNA GYNAECIA MACAHUBA PALESTRA RAKSHASA
ANTHELIA BROUHAHA COMATULA EPIMYSIA GYNOECIA MADRASSA PALLADIA RAPHANIA
ANTHEMIA BRUCELLA CONFERVA EPITHEMA HABANERA MAGNESIA PALPEBRA REDDENDA
ANTHODIA BUDDLEIA CONSULTA EPOPOEIA HACIENDA MAGNOLIA PANATELA RENDZINA
ANTIDORA BURLETTA CONTAGIA EQUISETA HAMARTIA MAHARAJA PANCETTA RESINATA
ANTISERA CAATINGA CONTESSA ERYTHEMA HAPHTARA MAIOLICA PANDEMIA RESPONSA
APIMANIA CABRESTA CONTINUA ESTANCIA HAPLOPIA MAJOLICA PANETELA RETICULA
APOLOGIA CABRETTA CONURBIA ESTHESIA HATTERIA MALAROMA PANMIXIA RETINULA
APOSITIA CABRILLA COPREMIA ETCETERA HEARTPEA MALVASIA PANORAMA REWAREWA
APYREXIA CACHEXIA COPROSMA EUPEPSIA HEMATOMA MAMALIGA PARABEMA RHIZOBIA
ARAPAIMA CACHUCHA COQUILLA EUPHOBIA HEMIOLIA MAMMILLA PARABOLA ROSTELLA
ARAPONGA CACUMINA CORMIDIA EUPHONIA HEMIOPIA MANDIOCA PARANOEA RUTABAGA
ARAPUNGA CALATHEA COXALGIA EUPHORIA HEPATICA MANDORLA PARANOIA SACRARIA
ARBORETA CALCANEA CREDENDA EXCERPTA HEPATOMA MANTILLA PARHELIA SALICETA
ARETHUSA CALCARIA CREDENZA EXONUMIA HERBARIA MANTISSA PAROEMIA SALSILLA
ARMONICA CALCTUFA CRIBELLA FALDETTA HETAIRIA MANUBRIA PAROUSIA SAPREMIA
ARYTHMIA CALDARIA CRITERIA FANEGADA HIRAGANA MANYATTA PASHMINA SAPUCAIA
ASPHYXIA CALISAYA CROMORNA FANTASIA HORDEOLA MARCELLA PELLAGRA SARMENTA
ASPIRATA CALVARIA CTENIDIA FASCIOLA HOSPITIA MARCHESA PENUMBRA SASARARA
ASTHENIA CALYPTRA CUBICULA FASCISTA HYDREMIA MARINARA PEPONIDA SASTRUGA
ASTIGMIA CAMBOGIA CUNABULA FENESTRA HYDROZOA MARINERA PERFECTA SAYONARA
ASYNDETA CAMELLIA CUTICULA FETERITA HYPALGIA MARIPOSA PERIAGUA SCABIOSA
ATARAXIA CAMPAGNA CYMBIDIA FIBRILLA HYPHEMIA MARSUPIA PETECHIA SCHAPSKA
ATHEROMA CAPITULA CZAREVNA FISTIANA HYPOGAEA MARTYRIA PHACELIA SCHEMATA
ATROPHIA CAPOEIRA CZARITSA FLABELLA HYPONOIA MASSOOLA PHELONIA SCIATICA
AUBRETIA CAPONATA CZARITZA FLAGELLA HYPOPNEA MATADORA PHOTINIA SCLEREMA
AUBRIETA CAPYBARA DAHABIYA FLOTILLA HYSTERIA MATAMATA PHOTOPIA SCLEROMA
AURICULA CARACARA DECENNIA FOCACCIA ICEKHANA MAUSOLEA PHYSALIA SCOLIOMA

SCOTOMIA	SIGNORIA	STROMATA	SYNTAGMA	TOKONOMA	TSAREVNA	VESICULA	YERSINIA
SCOTOPIA	SILICULA	STRONTIA	SYSSITIA	TOQUILLA	TSARITSA	VESTIGIA	YOKOZUNA
SCROFULA	SIMARUBA	SUBCOSTA	TAKAMAKA	TORMENTA	TSARITZA	VIBRISSA	YTTERBIA
SCUTELLA	SINFONIA	SUBMENTA	TAMANDUA	TORTILLA	TZAREVNA	VICTORIA	ZAMBOMBA
SEMANTRA	SONATINA	SUBPHYLA	TAMBOURA	TOXAEMIA	TZARITZA	VIEWDATA	ZAMPOGNA
SEMICOMA	SORBARIA	SUBPOENA	TAPADERA	TOXOCARA	ULTIMATA	VINIFERA	ZARZUELA
SEMIGALA	SPIRILLA	SUBTOPIA	TAQUERIA	TRACHOMA	UMBRELLA	VIRAEMIA	ZASTRUGA
SEMOLINA	SPORIDIA	SUBUCULA	TEGMENTA	TRAPEZIA	UNDERSEA	VIRTUOSA	ZIRCONIA
SEMUNCIA	SPOROZOA	SUBURBIA	TEGUMINA	TRAUMATA	UNGUENTA	VISCACHA	ZOIATRIA
SENORITA	SQUAMULA	SUDAMINA	TENACULA	TRICHINA	UREDINIA	VITICETA	ZOOCYTIA
SENSILLA	STAPELIA	SVASTIKA	TENTORIA	TRIDACNA	URINEMIA	VIVIPARA	ZOOGLOEA
SENSORIA	STAROSTA	SWASTICA	TEQUILLA	TRIENNIA	UROPYGIA	VIZCACHA	ZOOMANIA
SEPARATA	STEATOMA	SWASTIKA	TERATOMA	TRIFECTA	VACCINIA	VULSELLA	ZOONOMIA
SEPTARIA	STEMMATA	SWEETPEA	TERRARIA	TRIFORIA	VAGINULA	WAHCONDA	ZUCHETTA
SEPTLEVA	STERIGMA	SYMPODIA	TERRELLA	TRIHEDRA	VALENCIA	WEIGELIA	ZYGANTRA
SERENATA	STICHERA	SYMPOSIA	TERZETTA	TRILEMMA	VALLONIA	WISTARIA	ZYGOMATA
SHAMIANA	STIGMATA	SYNANGIA	TESSELLA	TRIPTYCA	VELAMINA	WISTERIA	
SHECHITA	STOCCATA	SYNAPHEA	TETRAPLA	TRIPUDIA	VELATURA	XANTHOMA	
SHIGELLA	STOKESIA	SYNCYTIA	THERIACA	TRISTEZA	VENDETTA	XENOPHYA	
SHILLALA	STOMODEA	SYNECHIA	THIOTEPA	TRITONIA	VERATRIA	XEROMATA	
SHRADDHA	STOTINKA	SYNEDRIA	THIOUREA	TROCHLEA	VERONICA	XYLOMATA	
SIDALCEA	STROBILA	SYNERGIA	TITHONIA	TROPARIA	VERTEBRA	YARMULKA	

WORDS ENDING IN -I

2-letter words ending in -I

AI	DI	HI	MI	PI	SI	XI
BI	GI	LI	OI	QI	TI	

3-letter words ending in -I

AMI	DEI	HOI	KHI	MOI	POI	REI	SKI	TAI
ANI	DUI	HUI	KOI	OBI	PSI	SAI	SRI	TUI
CHI	GHI	KAI	LEI	PHI	RAI	SEI	SUI	UNI

4-letter words ending in -I

ABRI	DELI	GLEI	KEPI	MAXI	NEVI	PURI	SATI	TIPI	YETI
ANTI	DIVI	GYRI	KIWI	MERI	NIDI	QADI	SEMI	TITI	YOGI
ASCI	DIXI	HAJI	KURI	MIDI	NISI	QUAI	SHRI	TOPI	YONI
BANI	DUCI	HILI	LARI	MINI	NODI	RABI	SIMI	TORI	ZATI
BENI	ELHI	HOKI	LATI	MIRI	NORI	RAGI	SIRI	UNAI	ZITI
CADI	ETUI	IMPI	LIRI	MODI	PADI	RAKI	SOLI	UNCI	ZORI
CAPI	EUOI	INTI	LOBI	MOKI	PENI	RAMI	SORI	VAGI	
CEDI	FENI	KADI	LOCI	MOMI	PERI	RANI	SYLI	VALI	
CHAI	FINI	KAKI	LOTI	MOOI	PFUI	ROJI	TABI	VLEI	
CONI	FOCI	KALI	LWEI	MUNI	PIKI	ROTI	TAKI	WADI	
DALI	FUCI	KAMI	MAGI	MUTI	PILI	SADI	TALI	WALI	
DARI	FUJI	KATI	MALI	NAOI	PIPI	SAKI	TAXI	WILI	
DEFI	GADI	KAZI	MANI	NAZI	PULI	SARI	TIKI	YAGI	

5-letter words ending in -I

AALII	BAJRI	CESTI	DHUTI	GARNI	KAURI	LICHI	OCULI	PIRAI	SENTI
ABACI	BASSI	CHILI	DILLI	GENII	KHADI	LIMBI	OKAPI	POORI	SERAI
ACARI	BENNI	CHOLI	DISCI	GHAZI	KHAKI	LITAI	ORIBI	PRIMI	SHCHI
ACINI	BIALI	CIPPI	DOLCI	GOBBI	KIBBI	LOGOI	OVOLI	PSOAI	SHOGI
AGAMI	BINDI	CIRRI	DUOMI	GUSLI	KIBEI	LUNGI	OZEKI	PUTTI	SHOJI
AGGRI	BLINI	CLAVI	ELCHI	HADJI	KIKOI	LURGI	PADRI	QUASI	SOLDI
AGUTI	BOCCI	COATI	ELEMI	HAJJI	KIRRI	MAQUI	PAGRI	RABBI	SOLEI
AIDOI	BRAVI	COCCI	ENNUI	HONGI	KOORI	MEDII	PALKI	RADII	SPAHI
AIOLI	BUFFI	COMBI	ENOKI	HOURI	KORAI	MODII	PALPI	RECTI	STOAI
ALIBI	BWAZI	CORGI	ENVOI	IAMBI	KRUBI	MOOLI	PAOLI	REIKI	STYLI
AMICI	BYSSI	CORNI	FARCI	IMARI	KUKRI	MUFTI	PAPPI	RISHI	SUCCI
ANIMI	CACTI	CROCI	FASCI	IMSHI	LAARI	MYTHI	PARDI	RUBAI	SULCI
APPUI	CAMPI	CULTI	FASTI	INDRI	LANAI	NAEVI	PARKI	SALMI	SUSHI
ARDRI	CARDI	CURSI	FERMI	ISSEI	LASSI	NIMBI	PARTI	SAMPI	SWAMI
ASKOI	CARPI	DARZI	FRATI	JINNI	LATHI	NISEI	PENNI	SCAPI	TAKHI
ASSAI	CEILI	DASHI	FUNDI	KANJI	LAZZI	NOMOI	PERAI	SCUDI	TANGI
AULOI	CELLI	DHOBI	FUNGI	KARRI	LENTI	OBELI	PETTI	SEGNI	TANTI
AUREI	CERCI	DHOTI	GADDI	KATTI	LIBRI	OBOLI	PILEI	SENGI	TARSI

TELOI THAGI TONDI TORII TSADI URALI VILLI XYSTI
TEMPI THOLI TOPHI TORSI TUTTI URARI VOLTI ZIMBI
TERAI THYMI TOPOI TRAGI URAEI UTERI WONGI ZOMBI

6-letter words ending in -I

ACULEI BOLETI CUMULI FUMULI JUDOGI MEISHI OUREBI SACCOI SIMPAI TROCHI
ADZUKI BONACI CURARI GARDAI JUNGLI MILADI PALAGI SAFARI SMALTI TROPHI
AGAPAI BONSAI CYATHI GELATI JUPATI MIRITI PAPYRI SAIKEI SOLIDI TSOTSI
AGOUTI BORZOI CYTISI GEMINI KABIKI MISHMI PERITI SAKKOI SONERI TUFOLI
ALFAKI BUKSHI DALASI GHARRI KABUKI MODULI PETSAI SALAMI SOUARI TULADI
ALKALI BURITI DECANI GHIBLI KAIKAI MOIRAI PHALLI SALUKI STELAI TUMULI
ALUMNI BUZUKI DEGAMI GILGAI KIMCHI MOPANI PIROGI SAMITI STRATI UAKARI
AMBARI CALAMI DEWANI GLUTEI KOUROI MUESLI PITHOI SANCAI SUNDRI UNCINI
ANNULI CANTHI DHOOTI GOMUTI KOWHAI MUNSHI PITURI SANDHI SURIMI URACHI
ARCHEI CAROLI DJINNI GRIGRI KROONI MYTHOI PLUTEI SANSEI TABULI WAKIKI
ARGALI CASINI DROMOI GURAMI KULAKI NAGARI POLYPI SATORI TAHINI WAPITI
ARGULI CESTOI DUELLI HAIKAI KUMARI NEROLI PRIAPI SBIRRI TAMARI WASABI
ARILLI CESTUI DUETTI HAMULI LAZULI NIELLI PROTEI SCAMPI TANUKI XYSTOI
ARIOSI CHADRI ECHINI HEGARI LIMULI NILGAI PUTELI SCYPHI TAPETI YANQUI
ASKARI CHATTI ELTCHI HEISHI LITCHI NOSTOI PYLORI SENITI TATAMI YOGINI
AVANTI CHICHI EMBOLI HERMAI LOBULI NUCLEI RAGINI SESELI TENUTI ZAIKAI
BAILLI CHILLI EPHEBI HUMERI LOCULI OCELLI RAMULI SHALLI THALLI ZUFOLI
BANZAI CHOKRI EPHORI ILLUPI LUNGYI OCTOPI RAPINI SHANTI THOLOI
BHAKTI CHOWRI EURIPI INCAVI MALLEI OCTROI REGULI SHTCHI THYRSI
BHINDI CLYPEI EXODOI INCUBI MALOTI ONAGRI RENVOI SHUFTI TIFOSI
BHISTI COLOBI FAMULI ISTHMI MANATI OORALI RHOMBI SIDDHI TITOKI
BIKINI COLONI FLOCCI JAWARI MAULVI OURALI RUBATI SIGLOI TOITOI
BINGHI CONGII FRACTI JOWARI MAZHBI OURARI RUMAKI SILENI TORULI

7-letter words ending in -I

ABOMASI BROCOLI CRIMINI FUSILLI LAMPUKI OMPHALI QUILLAI SECONDI TIMPANI
ACANTHI BRONCHI DACTYLI GHILGAI LAPILLI ORIGAMI RABBONI SENARII TONDINI
ACOUCHI CADUCEI DAKOITI GINGELI LECYTHI OUAKARI RANGOLI SERKALI TORTONI
AFGHANI CALATHI DAQUIRI GINGILI LEKYTHI OUSTITI RAPPINI SERRATI TRIPOLI
ALFAQUI CALCULI DASHEKI GLUTAEI MACRAMI PACHISI RAVIOLI SHIKARI TSUNAMI
ALIZARI CALZONI DASHIKI GNOCCHI MAESTRI PADRONI REMBLAI SIGNORI TURFSKI
ALVEOLI CANNOLI DEMENTI GOURAMI MAFIOSI PAESANI REVERSI SKYPHOI TYMPANI
AMORINI CANZONI DENARII GRADINI MAMMATI PAHLAVI RHIZOPI SONDELI URCEOLI
ANESTRI CAVETTI DIDAKAI GUARANI MARCONI PALAZZI RHOMBOI SOPRANI VENTURI
ANZIANI CEMBALI DIDAKEI HALLALI MARTINI PANDANI RHONCHI SORDINI VIRELAI
APICULI CHAPATI DIDICOI HAVARTI MATSURI PARODOI RHYTHMI SPLENII VITELLI
APPALTI CHARPAI DOCHMII HELLERI MENISCI PECCAVI RIKISHI SPUMONI VOLVULI
ARCHAEI CHARQUI EFFENDI HEXEREI MINISKI PENUCHI RILIEVI STAMNOI WISTITI
ASSAGAI CHIASMI ELENCHI HIBACHI MODELLI PIEROGI RIPIENI STICHOI WOORALI
ASSEGAI CHILIOI EMERITI INTAGLI MODIOLI PIGNOLI SACCULI STIMULI WOORARI
ASTATKI CHIVARI EPHEBOI JACUZZI MOLOSSI PINDARI SAIMIRI STRETTI WOURALI
BACCHII CHONDRI EPIGONI JAMDANI NAUPLII PIROGHI SAMADHI SUCCUBI ZAKUSKI
BACILLI CHORAGI EPINAOI JAMPANI NAUTILI PIROJKI SAMURAI SUFFARI ZAMPONI
BAMBINI CHOREGI EREMURI JINJILI NEGRONI PLATYPI SANTIMI SUNDARI ZINGANI
BASENJI CHUPATI ETOURDI JUKSKEI NILGHAI POLYNYI SAOUARI SURCULI ZINGARI
BASMATI CLARINI FAGOTTI KABADDI NONETTI PORCINI SARANGI SYLLABI ZUFFOLI
BAZOUKI COENURI FIASCHI KACHERI NUCELLI PRELUDI SASHIMI TABOULI
BILIMBI COLIBRI FLOKATI KAHAWAI NURAGHI PRONAOI SCALENI TERMINI
BIRYANI COLOSSI FORZATI KAMICHI NYLGHAI PULVINI SCHERZI THALAMI
BOUILLI CORTILI FUMETTI KOLBASI OBLASTI QAWWALI SCIRRHI THROMBI

8-letter words ending in -I

ACERVULI BONAMANI CAPITANI CONFETTI DUPONDII GINGLYMI KOFTGARI MAHIMAHI
ACOEMETI BOSTANGI CAPRICCI CORNETTI DURUKULI GLADIOLI KOHLRABI MALIHINI
ALBERGHI BOUSOUKI CASTRATI COTHURNI DUUMVIRI GRAFFITI KOLBASSI MALLEOLI
AMARETTI BOUZOUKI CHAPATTI CROSTINI ESOPHAGI HAEREMAI KOLINSKI MARAVEDI
AMORETTI BOZZETTI CHAPPATI CUNJEVOI FASCISMI HALLOUMI KOMITAJI MARCHESI
AMPHIOXI BRINDISI CHIGETAI DAIQUIRI FASCISTI HETAIRAI LEKYTHOI MARIACHI
ANOESTRI BROCCOLI CHUPATTI DAISHIKI FEDELINI HYDROSKI LEMNISCI MENOMINI
ANTENATI BUMALOTI CICERONI DECUBITI FLOCCULI IGNORAMI LIBRETTI MONOKINI
ASSEGAAI CALAMARI CICISBEI DIADOCHI FORZANDI KACHAHRI LINGUINI MORBILLI
BANDITTI CALCANEI CONCEPTI DIPTEROI FRASCATI KAZACHKI LITERATI NANNYGAI
BERIBERI CALYCULI CONCERTI DIVIDIVI FUNICULI KAZATSKI LUMBRICI NARCISSI
BIMBASHI CANCELLI CONCETTI DOUPIONI GINGELLI KIELBASI MACARONI NENNIGAI
BIRIYANI CANTHARI CONDUCTI DRACHMAI GINGILLI KIRIGAMI MAHARANI NIRAMIAI

NOTTURNI	PASTROMI	POSTNATI	SANNYASI	SIGISBEI	SUKIYAKI	TERZETTI	YAKITORI
NUCLEOLI	PECORINI	PRINCIPI	SARTORII	SIGNIORI	SUMOTORI	THESAURI	ZASTRUGI
OBLIGATI	PEDICULI	PRODROMI	SASTRUGI	SOFFIONI	TAGLIONI	TRAPEZII	ZECCHINI
OUISTITI	PEPERONI	PULVILLI	SCALDINI	SOLFEGGI	TANDOORI	TROCHILI	ZOOPHORI
PACHOULI	PERFECTI	RENMINBI	SEXTARII	SOUVLAKI	TARAKIHI	TZATZIKI	ZUCCHINI
PARCHESI	PERIBOLI	RETIARII	SFORZATI	STACCATI	TEDESCHI	UMBILICI	
PARCHISI	PERRADII	RIGATONI	SHANGHAI	STAPEDII	TEOCALLI	URANISCI	
PASTICCI	PIROSHKI	RISPETTI	SHERWANI	STOTINKI	TERAKIHI	UTRICULI	
PASTRAMI	PIROZHKI	RYOTWARI	SHILINGI	STROBILI	TERIYAKI	VIRTUOSI	

WORDS ENDING IN -O

2-letter words ending in -O

BO	GO	IO	KO	MO	OO	SO	WO	ZO
DO	HO	JO	LO	NO	PO	TO	YO	

3-letter words ending in -O

ABO	BIO	DSO	GEO	ISO	OBO	PRO	TOO	WHO
ADO	BOO	DUO	GIO	LOO	OHO	RHO	TWO	WOO
AGO	BRO	DZO	GOO	MHO	OXO	ROO	UDO	YGO
AVO	COO	EGO	HAO	MOO	PHO	TAO	UFO	ZHO
AZO	DOO	FRO	HOO	NOO	POO	THO	UPO	ZOO

4-letter words ending in -O

AERO	BROO	DINO	FINO	INTO	LEVO	MISO	PESO	SHOO	TOYO
AFRO	BUBO	DODO	GAJO	JATO	LIDO	MOJO	PISO	SIJO	TRIO
AGIO	BUDO	DOJO	GAPO	JIAO	LILO	MOKO	POCO	SILO	TYPO
ALSO	BUFO	DURO	GIRO	JOCO	LIMO	MONO	POGO	SKEO	TYRO
ALTO	CALO	DZHO	GOBO	JOMO	LINO	MOZO	POLO	SKIO	UMBO
AMBO	CAPO	ECCO	GOGO	JUDO	LOBO	MUSO	PRAO	SOHO	UNCO
AMMO	CERO	ECHO	GYRO	KAGO	LOCO	NOLO	PROO	SOLO	UNDO
ANNO	CHAO	EDDO	HALO	KAYO	LOGO	ODSO	PYRO	SUMO	UNTO
ARCO	CIAO	ERGO	HARO	KENO	LOTO	OLEO	RATO	SYBO	UPDO
ARVO	CITO	EURO	HELO	KETO	LUDO	OLIO	REDO	TACO	UPGO
AUTO	COCO	EXPO	HERO	KILO	MAKO	ONTO	REGO	TARO	URAO
BEGO	COHO	FADO	HOBO	KINO	MANO	OPPO	REPO	THIO	VETO
BITO	DADO	FANO	HOMO	KOBO	MAYO	ORDO	RIVO	THRO	VINO
BOKO	DAGO	FARO	HUSO	KOLO	MEMO	ORZO	ROTO	TIRO	VIVO
BOLO	DATO	FICO	HYPO	KOTO	MENO	OTTO	SAGO	TOCO	WINO
BOYO	DECO	FIDO	INFO	KUDO	MICO	OUZO	SECO	TOHO	YUKO
BOZO	DEMO	FIGO	INGO	LAZO	MILO	PACO	SEGO	TOKO	ZERO
BRIO	DIDO	FILO	INRO	LENO	MINO	PEPO	SHMO	TORO	ZOBO

5-letter words ending in -O

ABMHO	BAZOO	CARBO	CONVO	DUMBO	GIZMO	IMAGO	LESBO	MONDO	PEDRO
ACHOO	BEANO	CARGO	CORNO	DUNNO	GOBBO	IMIDO	LIMBO	MONGO	PENGO
ADDIO	BILBO	CASCO	CORSO	DUOMO	GODSO	IMINO	LINGO	MORRO	PESTO
ADOBO	BIMBO	CELLO	CREDO	ERUGO	GOMBO	INTRO	LITHO	MOSSO	PETTO
AGGRO	BINGO	CENTO	CUFFO	ESTRO	GONZO	IROKO	LLANO	MOTTO	PHONO
ALAMO	BOFFO	CHACO	CURIO	FANGO	GREGO	JAMBO	LOTTO	MUCRO	PHOTO
ALTHO	BOMBO	CHEMO	CUSSO	FATSO	GUACO	JELLO	MACHO	MUNGO	PIANO
AMIDO	BONGO	CHIAO	CUTTO	FIBRO	GUANO	JINGO	MACRO	NACHO	PIEZO
AMIGO	BORGO	CHICO	CYANO	FILLO	GUIRO	JOCKO	MAIKO	NAPOO	PINGO
AMINO	BRAVO	CHIMO	CYCLO	FOLIO	GUMBO	JUMBO	MAMBO	NARCO	PINKO
AMNIO	BROMO	CHINO	DANIO	FORDO	GUSTO	JUNCO	MANGO	NEGRO	PINTO
AUDIO	BUCKO	CHIRO	DATTO	FORGO	GYPPO	JUNTO	MANTO	NGAIO	PISCO
AVISO	BUFFO	CHOCO	DECKO	FUERO	HALLO	KAROO	MATLO	NITRO	POLIO
AWETO	BUMBO	CHOKO	DEKKO	FUGIO	HELIO	KAZOO	MATZO	ORTHO	PONGO
AZIDO	BUNCO	CHOLO	DIAZO	FUNGO	HELLO	KEMBO	MENTO	OUTDO	PORNO
BABOO	BUNKO	CISCO	DILDO	GADSO	HILLO	KENDO	MESTO	OUTGO	POTOO
BACCO	BUROO	CLARO	DINGO	GAMBO	HIMBO	KIDDO	METRO	OVOLO	POTTO
BALOO	BURRO	COCCO	DIPSO	GARBO	HIPPO	KIMBO	MEZZO	PANTO	PRIMO
BANCO	BUTEO	COMBO	DISCO	GAZOO	HOLLO	KUSSO	MICRO	PAOLO	PROMO
BANJO	CACAO	COMMO	DITTO	GECKO	HOWSO	LAEVO	MILKO	PAREO	PROSO
BARDO	CAMEO	COMPO	DOGGO	GENRO	HULLO	LARGO	MIMEO	PARGO	PULMO
BASHO	CAMPO	CONDO	DOHYO	GESSO	HYDRO	LASSO	MISDO	PARVO	PUNTO
BASSO	CANSO	CONGO	DSOBO	GIPPO	IGAPO	LAZZO	MISGO	PASEO	PUTTO
BASTO	CANTO	CONTO	DSOMO	GISMO	IGLOO	LENTO	MOLTO	PATIO	QUIPO

RADIO REGGO RUMBO SCHMO SIXMO STENO TEMPO TYPTO WAHOO ZHOMO
RATIO REPRO SADDO SCUDO SKIMO STYLO TENNO UREDO WHAMO ZINCO
RATOO RETRO SALTO SECCO SMOKO SULFO THORO VERSO WHOSO ZIPPO
RAZOO RHINO SALVO SEGNO SOCKO TABOO TIMBO VIDEO WILCO ZOCCO
REALO RODEO SAMBO SERVO SOLDO TACHO TONDO VIREO YAHOO ZOPPO
RECCO ROMEO SANKO SEXTO SORDO TANGO TORSO VISTO YARTO ZORRO
RECTO RONDO SANTO SHAKO SORGO TANTO TRIGO VULGO YOBBO
REFFO RONEO SARGO SICKO SPADO TARDO TURBO WACKO ZAMBO

6-letter words ending in -O

ABRAZO BASUCO COLUGO FIASCO GORGIO LANUGO NYMPHO RANCHO SLEAZO TORERO
ADAGIO BAYAMO COMEDO FINSKO GRINGO LATIGO OCTAVO REBATO SMALTO TRILLO
AERUGO BISTRO COMODO FOREDO GROTTO LATINO OVERDO REBOZO SOLANO TROPPO
AHCHOO BLANCO COOCOO FOREGO GUANGO LAVABO OVERGO REECHO SOLITO TUPELO
AIKIDO BLOTTO COROZO FORHOO HAIRDO LEGATO PALOLO REGULO SORGHO TURACO
AKIMBO BOLERO CRAMBO FRANCO HALLOO LIBERO PARAMO RIALTO SPEEDO TUXEDO
ALBEDO BONITO CRYPTO FRESCO HERETO LIBIDO PEDALO RIGHTO SPINTO ULTIMO
ALBINO BOOBOO CUCKOO FUGATO HETERO LOLIGO PEPINO ROADEO STALKO VAUDOO
ALBUGO BOOHOO DAIMIO FUMADO HOLLOO LUCUMO PHYLLO ROBALO STANZO VIBRIO
ALNICO BRONCO DAIMYO GABBRO HONCHO MACACO PHYSIO ROCOCO STEREO VIGORO
AMMINO BUMALO DAYGLO GALAGO HOODOO MADURO PICARO ROMANO STINGO VIRAGO
AMMONO BURGOO DEXTRO GAUCHO HOOPOO MANITO POMATO ROTOLO STINKO VIRINO
ANATTO CALICO DINERO GAZABO HOOROO MANOAO POMELO RUBATO STUCCO VOMITO
ANGICO CALIGO DOMINO GAZEBO IGNARO MATICO PONCHO RUBIGO STUDIO VOODOO
APOLLO CAMSHO DORADO GELATO INCAVO MEDICO POTATO SAMFOO SUBITO VORAGO
ARIOSO CASHOO DRONGO GENTOO INDIGO MELANO PRESTO SANCHO TAPALO WANDOO
ARISTO CASINO DUELLO GHERAO JINGKO MERINO PRONTO SAPEGO TATTOO WEIRDO
ARROYO CATALO DUETTO GHETTO JOURNO MIKADO PSEUDO SBIRRO TECHNO WHACKO
ARSENO CHARRO DYNAMO GIGOLO KAKAPO MIOMBO PSYCHO SCHIZO TENUTO WHAMMO
ARSINO CHEAPO EMBRYO GINGKO KARROO MODULO PUEBLO SCRUTO TERCIO WHATSO
AUSUBO CHEERO ENDURO GINKGO KATIPO MORPHO PUKEKO SHACKO TEREDO WHOMSO
BABACO CHOCHO ENHALO GITANO KIMONO NANDOO PUMELO SHEEPO THICKO ZELOSO
BAGNIO CHOCKO ERINGO GIUSTO KOODOO NARDOO PUNCTO SHIPPO THUGGO ZOOZOO
BAGUIO CHROMO ERYNGO GOMBRO KORERO NIELLO QUANGO SHIVOO TIFOSO ZORINO
BAMBOO CICERO ESCUDO GOMUTO KOUSSO NONEGO QUARTO SISSOO TOLEDO ZUFOLO
BARRIO COGITO FASCIO GOOROO LADINO NUNCIO RABATO SKIDOO TOMATO ZYDECO

7-letter words ending in -O

AGITATO BRONCHO CRIOLLO IMPASTO MOROCCO PICCOLO RONDINO SUBZERO VERTIGO
AILANTO BUDGERO CRUSADO INFERNO MULATTO PIFFERO ROSOLIO SUPREMO VIBRATO
ALBERGO BUFFALO CRUZADO JIGABOO NATHEMO PIMENTO RUBABOO SYNCHRO VILIACO
ALLEGRO BUGABOO CURACAO KERCHOO NAVARHO PINTADO SAGUARO TALLYHO VILIAGO
AMORINO BUMMALO CYMBALO LENTIGO NELUMBO PINTANO SAHUARO TAMARAO VIRANDO
AMOROSO BURRITO DIABOLO LLANERO NITROSO PLACEBO SALTATO TANGELO VOLCANO
ANIMATO BUSHIDO DINITRO LUMBAGO NONETTO PLENIPO SAMSHOO TEDESCO VOLPINO
ANNATTO CABILDO EIGHTVO MADRONO NONHERO POINADO SAPSAGO TENTIGO WENDIGO
APAREJO CALANDO ELECTRO MAESTRO NONZERO POMPANO SCALADO TESTUDO WHERESO
APPALTO CALYPSO EMBARGO MAFIOSO NORTENO POMPELO SCHERZO THEORBO WHERETO
ARNATTO CANTICO ESPARTO MAGNETO OKIMONO PORCINO SCIOLTO THERETO WINDIGO
ARNOTTO CARABAO ETAERIO MALICHO OLOROSO PORRIGO SECONDO TIMPANO ZAMARRO
ARRIERO CASSINO FAGOTTO MARCATO OREGANO PORTICO SEMIPRO TOBACCO ZANJERO
ASINICO CATTALO FARRAGO MARENGO OUTECHO POTOROO SENECIO TOMBOLO ZAPATEO
ATISHOO CAVETTO FERRUGO MARRANO PACHUCO PRIMERO SENTIMO TONDINO ZEMSTVO
AVOCADO CEMBALO FINNSKO MEMENTO PAESANO PRIVADO SERPIGO TORNADO ZINGANO
AZULEJO CENTAVO FORZATO MENDIGO PAISANO PROVISO SERRANO TORPEDO ZINGARO
BACALAO CENTIMO FUMETTO MESTESO PAKAPOO PROXIMO SFUMATO TOSTADO ZOCCOLO
BAMBINO CHAMISO FURIOSO MESTINO PALAZZO PRURIGO SHAKUDO TOURACO ZORILLO
BAROCCO CHEERIO GAMBADO MESTIZO PAMPERO PUMMELO SHAMPOO TREMOLO ZUFFOLO
BARRICO CHICANO GESTAPO MISTICO PAPILIO QUOMODO SIROCCO TROMINO
BATTERO CHORIZO GIOCOSO MOCKADO PASSADO REJONEO SKIDDOO TWIGLOO
BEEFALO CLARINO GRADINO MODELLO PATRICO RELIEVO SOLDADO TYMPANO
BOTARGO COMMODO GUANACO MOMENTO PEDRERO REVERSO SOPRANO UNDERDO
BRACCIO CONCEDO HIDALGO MONTERO PEEKABO RIDOTTO SORDINO UNDERGO
BRACERO COQUITO HISTRIO MORELLO PERSICO RILIEVO SQUACCO UNMACHO
BRASERO CORANTO HORNITO MORENDO PIANINO RIPIENO STRETTO VAQUERO
BRAVADO CORNUTO HUANACO MORISCO PICACHO RISOTTO SUBECHO VERISMO

8-letter words ending in -O

ALFRESCO AMARETTO AMORETTO ANTIHERO ARMIGERO ARPEGGIO ASSIENTO ATAMASCO AUTOGIRO AUTOGYRO BALLYHOO BARBASCO BARGELLO BARRANCO BESOGNIO BOCACCIO BONAMANO BORACHIO BORDELLO BOZZETTO BUCKAROO BUCKAYRO BUCKEROO CABESTRO CABRESTO CACAFOGO CALLALOO CAMISADO CAPITANO
CAPUCCIO CASTRATO CAUDILLO CAVALERO CHARANGO CHARNECO CHECHAKO CHUBASCO CICISBEO CILANTRO CIOPPINO CLASSICO COCKAPOO COCKATOO COCOBOLO COLORADO COMMANDO CONCERTO CONCETTO CONFETTO CONTANGO CONTINUO CONTORNO CORAGGIO CORNETTO COROCORO COURANTO CRUZEIRO CURCULIO
DOLOROSO DUECENTO DUETTINO ENCIERRO ESCALADO ESCAPADO ESPRESSO ESPUMOSO EXPRESSO FALSETTO FANDANGO FASCISMO FELLATIO FINNESKO FINOCHIO FLAMENCO FLAMINGO FORZANDO FRICANDO GALAPAGO GARBANZO GARDYLOO GAZPACHO GILLAROO GRACIOSO GRAFFITO GRAZIOSO GUACHARO HALLALOO
HEREINTO HEREUNTO HITHERTO HUAQUERO HUARACHO HUBBUBOO IMPETIGO INNUENDO INTAGLIO INTONACO JACKAROO JACKEROO JALAPENO JILLAROO JORDELOO JUNKANOO KAKEMONO KANGAROO LARGANDO LEGGIERO LENTANDO LIBECCIO LIBRETTO LITERATO LOCOFOCO LOTHARIO MACHISMO MAESTOSO MAKIMONO
MALGRADO MALLECHO MAMELUCO MANCANDO MANZELLO MARTELLO MERCAPTO MICROMHO MILESIMO MILLIMHO MODERATO MONTANTO MOSQUITO MUCHACHO MUNDUNGO NEUTRINO NOCTILIO NONMETRO NOTTURNO OBLIGATO OCOTILLO ORATORIO OSTINATO OTTAVINO PACHINKO PADERERO PALAMINO PALISADO PALMETTO
PALOMINO PARLANDO PATERERO PECORINO PEDERERO PEEKABOO PEPERINO PERDENDO PERFECTO PIMIENTO PLUMBAGO POIGNADO POLITICO PRELUDIO PRESIDIO PRUNELLO PULVILIO RANCHERO REDDENDO RENEGADO RISOLUTO RISPETTO RITENUTO ROSOGLIO RUBBABOO SALTANDO SARGASSO SCALDINO SCENARIO
SCIROCCO SCORDATO SEICENTO SEMIHOBO SERAGLIO SESTETTO SFORZATO SIGISBEO SMORZATO SOLIDAGO SOMBRERO SPADILLO SPICCATO STACCATO STAMPEDO STICCADO STICCATO STILETTO STOCCADO SUBAUDIO SUBIMAGO SUPEREGO SUPERLOO SUPERPRO SUPPEAGO TAPACOLO TAPACULO TAPADERO TENEBRIO
TERRAZZO TERZETTO TORNILLO TRAPUNTO TRECENTO TUCOTUCO TUCUTUCO TWELVEMO UMBRELLO VARGUENO VARLETTO VERDELHO VIGOROSO VILLAGIO VILLIAGO VINDALOO VIRTUOSO VITILIGO WALLAROO WANDEROO WATERLOO YAKIMONO ZECCHINO ZUCHETTO

WORDS ENDING IN -U

2-letter words ending in -U

GU MU NU OU XU YU

3-letter words ending in -U

AMU AYU CRU EAU ECU EMU FEU FLU FOU GAU GJU GNU JEU KYU LEU MEU MOU PIU SAU SOU TAU ULU UTU VAU YOU

4-letter words ending in -U

AITU BABU BAJU BALU BAPU BEAU BEDU CHOU CLOU ECRU EMEU FRAU FUGU GENU GURU HABU IGLU JEHU JUJU KAGU KUDU KUKU KURU KUZU LEKU LIEU LITU LUAU LULU MASU MENU MEOU MOTU MUMU OMBU PRAU PUDU PUKU PULU RAKU RATU RIMU RURU SULU TABU TAPU TATU TEGU THOU THRU TOFU TOLU TUTU UNAU VATU ZEBU ZOBU ZULU

5-letter words ending in -U

ADIEU BANTU BATTU BAYOU BIJOU BOYAU BUCHU BUCKU BUNDU BUSSU CORNU COYPU FICHU FONDU HAIKU HOKKU JAMBU KANZU KOMBU KUDZU LASSU MIAOU MUNTU NANDU NIKAU NOYAU OTAKU PAREU PERDU PILAU POILU POYOU PRAHU QUIPU SADHU SAJOU SAMFU SHOYU SNAFU TATOU UHURU URUBU VERTU VIRTU VOULU WUSHU

6-letter words ending in -U

ABATTU ACAJOU AMADOU APERCU BATEAU BOUBOU BUREAU CACHOU CADEAU CONGOU COTEAU COYPOU DETENU EPERDU GAGAKU GATEAU GOMOKU GRUGRU HALERU INGENU JABIRU KIKUYU LANDAU MANITU MILIEU MUUMUU MZUNGU NHANDU NILGAU NOGAKU ORMOLU PILLAU PIUPIU QUIPPU RESEAU ROUCOU SADDHU SAMSHU SENRYU SUBFEU TAMANU TELEDU VOUDOU YNAMBU

7-letter words ending in -U

ANTIFLU BUNRAKU CHANOYU INCONNU MARABOU PARVENU ROULEAU TABLEAU TRUMEAU
BABASSU CAMAIEU CHAPEAU JAMBEAU MOINEAU PLATEAU SAPAJOU TAMANDU TURACOU
BANDEAU CARDECU CHATEAU JUJITSU MORCEAU PONCEAU SEPPUKU TAMARAU WAMEFOU
BATTEAU CARIBOU CORBEAU JUJUTSU NILGHAU PURLIEU SHIATSU TIMARAU
BEBEERU CATECHU COUTEAU MANITOU NOUVEAU ROKKAKU SHIATZU TINAMOU
BERCEAU CATTABU FABLIAU MANTEAU NYLGHAU RONDEAU SUBMENU TONNEAU

8-letter words ending in -U

ABOIDEAU CARJACOU FROUFROU KABELJOU NINJUTSU PYENGADU THANKYOU WILLIWAU
ABOITEAU COUMAROU HAUSFRAU KINKAJOU NUNCHAKU ROUSSEAU TIRAMISU ZAIBATSU
CARCAJOU FELDGRAU JIUJITSU MINSHUKU PIRARUCU SUCURUJU TSUTSUMU
CARIACOU FLAMBEAU JIUJUTSU NINJITSU PRIEDIEU SURUCUCU VERMOULU

Section Four

Variants

Introduction

Can't remember if the correct spelling is KEIR or KIER or both? And what about those American spellings? Can you have VIGOR as well as VIGOUR, and are PALLOR and PALLOUR both right? And then there is the confusing array of words that end with -EY, -IE and -Y? Can you remember which is which?

The lists in this section show you variant spellings, all of which – there may be two or even three variants – are valid words. Sometimes they are of completely different words which just look similar (as MEIN and MIEN); often they are just different spellings of the same word (as KEIR and KIER).

The words shown in the lists are of various lengths; only the most useful lengths, judged by practical use, are included here. Brief descriptions of the lists are:

Lists 1 and 2

Words spelled with either AE or E (such as AESTIVAL and ESTIVAL), and those spelled with either OE or E (such as OESTRAL and ESTRAL). Only genuine alternative spellings of the same word have been included. So words such as NAEVE and NEVE, SPAED and SPED, TOENAIL and TENAIL are all excluded.

List 3

Words with either EI or IE (such as MEIN and MIEN). Oddities such as SIZEIST, SIZIEST have been excluded.

Lists 4 to 6

Words spelled with either ER or RE endings (such as CENTER and CENTRE), those with either ER or OR endings (such as ADVISER and ADVISOR), and those with either OUR or OR endings (such as HARBOUR and HARBOR). Inappropriate pairs such as BARRE, BARER, OUTDOER, OUTDOOR and FLOUR, FLOR have been excluded.

Lists 7 and 8

Words spelled with either ABLE or IBLE endings (such as IGNITABLE and IGNITIBLE) and those with either SMAN or MAN endings (such as WOODSMAN and WOODMAN).

List 9

Words spelled with either EN or IN beginnings (such as ENCLOSE and INCLOSE).

Lists 10 to 13

Words spelled with various combinations of the EY, IE and Y endings (such as BLIMEY/BLIMY, SARNEY/SARNIE, BOLSHIE/BOLSHY and the 3-way DICKEY/DICKIE/DICKY).

List 1: VARIANTS AE/E (Latin roots)

5/4-letter words

AEGIS - EGIS
AEONS - EONS
CAECA - CECA
LAEVO - LEVO
NAEVI - NEVI
PAEAN - PEAN

6/5-letter words

AEDILE - EDILE
AEMULE - EMULE
AERUGO - ERUGO
AETHER - ETHER
CAECAL - CECAL
CAECUM - CECUM
DAEDAL - DEDAL
DAEMON - DEMON
FAECAL - FECAL
FAECES - FECES
FRAENA - FRENA
HAEMAL - HEMAL
HAEMIC - HEMIC
HAEMIN - HEMIN
HAERES - HERES
HYAENA - HYENA
MAENAD - MENAD
NAEVUS - NEVUS
PAEANS - PEANS
PAEONY - PEONY
PERAEA - PEREA
TAENIA - TENIA

7/6-letter words

AEDILES - EDILES
AEGISES - EGISES
AEMULED - EMULED
AEMULES - EMULES
AEOLIAN - EOLIAN
AEONIAN - EONIAN
AERUGOS - ERUGOS
AETHERS - ETHERS
ALTHAEA - ALTHEA
ANAEMIA - ANEMIA
ANAEMIC - ANEMIC
ARCHAEI - ARCHEI
CAERULE - CERULE
CAESIUM - CESIUM
CAESTUS - CESTUS
CAESURA - CESURA
COAEVAL - COEVAL
DAEMONS - DEMONS
FRAENUM - FRENUM
GLUTAEI - GLUTEI
HAEMINS - HEMINS
HAEMOID - HEMOID
HYAENAS - HYENAS
HYAENIC - HYENIC
MAENADS - MENADS
MURAENA - MURENA
NAEVOID - NEVOID
PERAEON - PEREON
PRAESES - PRESES
PRAETOR - PRETOR
PYAEMIA - PYEMIA
PYAEMIC - PYEMIC
SPHAERE - SPHERE
SPIRAEA - SPIREA
TAEDIUM - TEDIUM
TAENIAE - TENIAE
TAENIAS - TENIAS
URAEMIA - UREMIA
URAEMIC - UREMIC

8/7-letter words

ACHAENIA - ACHENIA
AEMULING - EMULING
AESTHETE - ESTHETE
AESTIVAL - ESTIVAL
AETHERIC - ETHERIC
ALTHAEAS - ALTHEAS
ANAEMIAS - ANEMIAS
ANAPAEST - ANAPEST
APOGAEIC - APOGEIC
ARCHAEUS - ARCHEUS
CAECALLY - CECALLY
CAECITIS - CECITIS
CAESIUMS - CESIUMS
CAESURAE - CESURAE
CAESURAL - CESURAL
CAESURAS - CESURAS
CHIMAERA - CHIMERA
COAEVALS - COEVALS
DAEMONIC - DEMONIC
EPIGAEAL - EPIGEAL
EPIGAEAN - EPIGEAN
EUDAEMON - EUDEMON
FRAENUMS - FRENUMS
GASTRAEA - GASTREA
GLUTAEAL - GLUTEAL
GLUTAEUS - GLUTEUS
GRAECIZE - GRECIZE
GYNAECIA - GYNECIA
HAEMATAL - HEMATAL
HAEMATIC - HEMATIC
HAEMATIN - HEMATIN
HAEREDES - HEREDES
HYPOGAEA - HYPOGEA
LERNAEAN - LERNEAN
MURAENAS - MURENAS
PAEONIES - PEONIES
PIGMAEAN - PIGMEAN
PRAECAVA - PRECAVA
PRAECIPE - PRECIPE
PRAEDIAL - PREDIAL
PRAEFECT - PREFECT
PRAELECT - PRELECT
PRAETORS - PRETORS
PYAEMIAS - PYEMIAS
PYGMAEAN - PYGMEAN
QUAESTOR - QUESTOR
REAEDIFY - REEDIFY
SAECULUM - SECULUM
SPELAEAN - SPELEAN
SPHAERES - SPHERES
SPIRAEAS - SPIREAS
TAEDIUMS - TEDIUMS
TAENIOID - TENIOID
TOXAEMIA - TOXEMIA
TOXAEMIC - TOXEMIC
URAEMIAS - UREMIAS
VIRAEMIA - VIREMIA
VIRAEMIC - VIREMIC

9/8-letter words

ACHAENIUM - ACHENIUM
AEOLIPILE - EOLIPILE
AESTHESES - ESTHESES
AESTHESIA - ESTHESIA
AESTHESIS - ESTHESIS
AESTHETES - ESTHETES
AESTHETIC - ESTHETIC
AESTIVATE - ESTIVATE
AETIOLOGY - ETIOLOGY
AMOEBAEAN - AMOEBEAN
ANAPAESTS - ANAPESTS
ATHENAEUM - ATHENEUM
CAERULEAN - CERULEAN
CAESAREAN - CESAREAN
CAESARIAN - CESARIAN
CAESTUSES - CESTUSES
CHIMAERAS - CHIMERAS
CHIMAERIC - CHIMERIC
CHOLAEMIA - CHOLEMIA
DAEDALIAN - DEDALIAN
DEFAECATE - DEFECATE
DIAERESES - DIERESES
DIAERESIS - DIERESIS
DIAERETIC - DIERETIC
EPIGAEOUS - EPIGEOUS
EUDAEMONS - EUDEMONS
GASTRAEAS - GASTREAS
GRAECIZED - GRECIZED
GRAECIZES - GRECIZES
GYNAECIUM - GYNECIUM
GYNAECOID - GYNECOID
HAEMATICS - HEMATICS
HAEMATINS - HEMATINS
HAEMATITE - HEMATITE
HAEMATOID - HEMATOID
HAEMATOMA - HEMATOMA
HAEMOCOEL - HEMOCOEL
HAEMOCYTE - HEMOCYTE
HAEMOSTAT - HEMOSTAT
HYDRAEMIA - HYDREMIA
HYMENAEAL - HYMENEAL
HYMENAEAN - HYMENEAN
HYPOGAEAL - HYPOGEAL
HYPOGAEAN - HYPOGEAN
HYPOGAEUM - HYPOGEUM
ISCHAEMIA - ISCHEMIA
ISCHAEMIC - ISCHEMIC
LAEVIGATE - LEVIGATE
LAEVULOSE - LEVULOSE
LEUCAEMIA - LEUCEMIA
LEUCAEMIC - LEUCEMIC
LEUKAEMIA - LEUKEMIA
LONGAEVAL - LONGEVAL
MEDIAEVAL - MEDIEVAL
PAEDERAST - PEDERAST
PAEDOLOGY - PEDOLOGY
PALAESTRA - PALESTRA
PERAEOPOD - PEREOPOD
PERINAEUM - PERINEUM
PHAENOGAM - PHENOGAM
PRAEAMBLE - PREAMBLE
PRAECAVAE - PRECAVAE
PRAECIPES - PRECIPES
PRAEDIALS - PREDIALS
PRAEFECTS - PREFECTS
PRAELECTS - PRELECTS
PRAENOMEN - PRENOMEN
PRAESIDIA - PRESIDIA
PRIMAEVAL - PRIMEVAL
QUAESTORS - QUESTORS
SAECULUMS - SECULUMS
SAPRAEMIA - SAPREMIA

SAPRAEMIC - SAPREMIC
STOMODAEA - STOMODEA
TAENIASES - TENIASES
TAENIASIS - TENIASIS
TOXAEMIAS - TOXEMIAS
VIRAEMIAS - VIREMIAS

List 2: VARIANTS OE/E (Latin/Greek roots)

5/4-letter words

ZOOEA - ZOEA

6/5-letter words

AMOEBA - AMEBA
APNOEA - APNEA
COELOM - CELOM
FOETAL - FETAL
FOETID - FETID
FOETOR - FETOR
FOETUS - FETUS
OEDEMA - EDEMA
ZOOEAE - ZOEAE
ZOOEAL - ZOEAL
ZOOEAS - ZOEAS

7/6-letter words

AMOEBAE - AMEBAE
AMOEBAN - AMEBAN
AMOEBAS - AMEBAS
AMOEBIC - AMEBIC
APNOEAL - APNEAL
APNOEAS - APNEAS
APNOEIC - APNEIC
CHOENIX - CHENIX
COELIAC - CELIAC
COELOMS - CELOMS
EUPNOEA - EUPNEA
FOETORS - FETORS
OEDEMAS - EDEMAS
OESTRAL - ESTRAL
OESTRIN - ESTRIN
OESTRUM - ESTRUM
OESTRUS - ESTRUS
PHOENIX - PHENIX
ZOOECIA - ZOECIA

8/7-letter words

AMOEBEAN - AMEBEAN
AMOEBOID - AMEBOID
ANOESTRA - ANESTRA
ANOESTRI - ANESTRI
COELIACS - CELIACS
DYSPNOEA - DYSPNEA
EUPNOEAS - EUPNEAS
EUPNOEIC - EUPNEIC
FOEDARIE - FEDARIE
FOETIDER - FETIDER
FOETUSES - FETUSES
GYNOECIA - GYNECIA
OECOLOGY - ECOLOGY
OEDEMATA - EDEMATA
OENOLOGY - ENOLOGY
OESTRINS - ESTRINS
OESTRIOL - ESTRIOL
OESTRONE - ESTRONE
OESTROUS - ESTROUS
OESTRUMS - ESTRUMS
SUBPOENA - SUBPENA
ZOOECIUM - ZOECIUM
ZOOGLOEA - ZOOGLEA

9/8-letter words

ANOESTRUM - ANESTRUM
ANOESTRUS - ANESTRUS
AUTOECISM - AUTECISM
CHOENIXES - CHENIXES
COELOMATA - CELOMATA
COENOBITE - CENOBITE
DIARRHOEA - DIARRHEA
DIOECIOUS - DIECIOUS
DIOESTRUS - DIESTRUS
DYSPNOEAL - DYSPNEAL
DYSPNOEAS - DYSPNEAS
DYSPNOEIC - DYSPNEIC
ENDAMOEBA - ENDAMEBA
ENTAMOEBA - ENTAMEBA
FOEDARIES - FEDARIES
FOETICIDE - FETICIDE
FOETIDEST - FETIDEST
GYNOECIUM - GYNECIUM
HOMOEOBOX - HOMEOBOX
HOMOEOSES - HOMEOSES
HOMOEOSIS - HOMEOSIS
HOMOEOTIC - HOMEOTIC
MESOGLOEA - MESOGLEA
MYXOEDEMA - MYXEDEMA
OECUMENIC - ECUMENIC
OESOPHAGI - ESOPHAGI
OESTRIOLS - ESTRIOLS
OESTROGEN - ESTROGEN
OESTRONES - ESTRONES
OESTRUSES - ESTRUSES
PHOENIXES - PHENIXES
POENOLOGY - PENOLOGY
PYORRHOEA - PYORRHEA
SUBPOENAS - SUBPENAS
ZOOGLOEAE - ZOOGLEAE
ZOOGLOEAS - ZOOGLEAS

List 3: VARIANTS EI/IE (all words)

4-letter words

BEIN - BIEN
CEIL - CIEL
DEID - DIED
DEIL - DIEL
HEID - HIED
KEIR - KIER
LEIR - LIER
LEIS - LIES
MEIN - MIEN
NEIF - NIEF
WEIL - WIEL

5-letter words

CEILS - CIELS
FEINT - FIENT
FEIST - FIEST
KEIRS - KIERS
LEIRS - LIERS
MEINS - MIENS
NEIFS - NIEFS
NEIVE - NIEVE
PREIF - PRIEF
REIVE - RIEVE
SPEIL - SPIEL
SPEIR - SPIER
VLEIS - VLIES
WEILS - WIELS

6-letter words

CEILED - CIELED
DREIGH - DRIEGH
FEINTS - FIENTS
LEIGER - LIEGER
NEIVES - NIEVES
PREIFE - PRIEFE
PREIFS - PRIEFS
REIVER - RIEVER
REIVES - RIEVES
SHREIK - SHRIEK
SPEILS - SPIELS
SPEIRS - SPIERS
WEINER - WIENER

7-letter words

CEILING - CIELING
GREISLY - GRIESLY
KEISTER - KIESTER
LEIGERS - LIEGERS
OMNEITY - OMNIETY
PREIFES - PRIEFES
REIVERS - RIEVERS
REIVING - RIEVING
SCREICH - SCRIECH
SHREIKS - SHRIEKS
SKREIGH - SKRIEGH
SPEILED - SPIELED
SPEIRED - SPIERED
WEINERS - WIENERS

8-letter words

CEILINGS - CIELINGS
KEISTERS - KIESTERS
SCREICHS - SCRIECHS
SHEILING - SHIELING
SHREIKED - SHRIEKED
SKREIGHS - SKRIEGHS
SPEILING - SPIELING
SPEIRING - SPIERING

9-letter words

OMNEITIES - OMNIETIES
SCREICHED - SCRIECHED
SHEILINGS - SHIELINGS
SHREIKING - SHRIEKING
SKREIGHED - SKRIEGHED

List 4: VARIANTS -RE/-ER endings (Similar meanings)

5-letter words

CABRE - CABER
EAGRE - EAGER
FIBRE - FIBER
LITRE - LITER
LIVRE - LIVER
METRE - METER
MITRE - MITER
NITRE - NITER
OCHRE - OCHER
OMBRE - OMBER
OUTRE - OUTER
PETRE - PETER
SABRE - SABER
TITRE - TITER
UMBRE - UMBER

6-letter words

BISTRE - BISTER
CENTRE - CENTER
DARTRE - DARTER
FOUTRE - FOUTER
GAUFRE - GAUFER
GOITRE - GOITER
LETTRE - LETTER
LOUVRE - LOUVER
LUSTRE - LUSTER
MAUGRE - MAUGER
MEAGRE - MEAGER
ONEYRE - ONEYER
POUDRE - POUDER
SEMPRE - SEMPER
SOMBRE - SOMBER
TENDRE - TENDER
TIMBRE - TIMBER
VENTRE - VENTER
ZAFFRE - ZAFFER

7-letter words

CALIBRE - CALIBER
CHAMBRE - CHAMBER
CHANCRE - CHANCER
DIOPTRE - DIOPTER
MACABRE - MACABER
PHILTRE - PHILTER
PIASTRE - PIASTER
POULDRE - POULDER
SCEPTRE - SCEPTER
SPECTRE - SPECTER
THEATRE - THEATER
UNMITRE - UNMITER

8-letter words

ACCOUTRE - ACCOUTER
CADASTRE - CADASTER
DECENTRE - DECENTER
INCENTRE - INCENTER
RECENTRE - RECENTER

9-letter words

CONCENTRE - CONCENTER
DECALITRE - DECALITER
DECAMETRE - DECAMETER
DECILITRE - DECILITER
DECIMETRE - DECIMETER
EPICENTRE - EPICENTER
KILOMETRE - KILOMETER
NANOMETRE - NANOMETER
SALTPETRE - SALTPETER
SEPULCHRE - SEPULCHER

List 5: VARIANTS -ER/-OR endings

5-letter words

ARMER - ARMOR
BEVER - BEVOR
FAVER - FAVOR
HONER - HONOR
LIVER - LIVOR
MILER - MILOR
MINER - MINOR
PAYER - PAYOR
PRIER - PRIOR
RAZER - RAZOR
SAVER - SAVOR
TABER - TABOR
TAXER - TAXOR
TRIER - TRIOR

6-letter words

ABATER - ABATOR
BAILER - BAILOR
BETTER - BETTOR
BITTER - BITTOR
CANTER - CANTOR
CASTER - CASTOR
CENSER - CENSOR
CONDER - CONDOR
CURSER - CURSOR
GIMMER - GIMMOR
JAILER - JAILOR
KRONER - KRONOR
LESSER - LESSOR
MAINER - MAINOR
NESTER - NESTOR
PASTER - PASTOR
PAWNER - PAWNOR
RIZZER - RIZZOR
SAILER - SAILOR
SALVER - SALVOR
SEISER - SEISOR
SEIZER - SEIZOR
SIGNER - SIGNOR
STATER - STATOR
SUITER - SUITOR
TAILER - TAILOR
TENSER - TENSOR
TERMER - TERMOR
TUSSER - TUSSOR
VENDER - VENDOR
WELDER - WELDOR

7-letter words

ABETTER - ABETTOR
ADAPTER - ADAPTOR
ADJURER - ADJUROR
ADVISER - ADVISOR
AGISTER - AGISTOR
ALIENER - ALIENOR
ASSURER - ASSUROR
CHANTER - CHANTOR
CLANGER - CLANGOR
DEVISER - DEVISOR
DILATER - DILATOR
DILUTER - DILUTOR
ERECTER - ERECTOR
EXACTER - EXACTOR
EXCITER - EXCITOR
FEOFFER - FEOFFOR
GRANTER - GRANTOR
HUMIDER - HUMIDOR
IGNITER - IGNITOR
LOCATER - LOCATOR
NEGATER - NEGATOR
OBLIGER - OBLIGOR
OFFERER - OFFEROR
PARADER - PARADOR
PLEDGER - PLEDGOR
PRESSER - PRESSOR
QUESTER - QUESTOR
QUITTER - QUITTOR
REALTER - REALTOR
RELATER - RELATOR
REVISER - REVISOR
REVIVER - REVIVOR
SETTLER - SETTLOR
STRIDER - STRIDOR
TRUSTER - TRUSTOR
TWISTER - TWISTOR
VISITER - VISITOR

8-letter words

ACCEPTER - ACCEPTOR
ADJUSTER - ADJUSTOR
ANIMATER - ANIMATOR
ARRESTER - ARRESTOR
ASPERSER - ASPERSOR
ASSENTER - ASSENTOR
ASSERTER - ASSERTOR
ASSIGNER - ASSIGNOR
ASSISTER - ASSISTOR
ATTESTER - ATTESTOR
BARRATER - BARRATOR
CONJURER - CONJUROR
CONVENER - CONVENOR
CONVEYER - CONVEYOR
DEFLATER - DEFLATOR
DEPICTER - DEPICTOR
DETECTER - DETECTOR
DIFFUSER - DIFFUSOR
DIGESTER - DIGESTOR
DIRECTER - DIRECTOR
EFFECTER - EFFECTOR
ENDORSER - ENDORSOR
EXECUTER - EXECUTOR
EXPANDER - EXPANDOR
IDOLATER - IDOLATOR
IMPACTER - IMPACTOR
IMPELLER - IMPELLOR
IMPOSTER - IMPOSTOR
INCENSER - INCENSOR
INDENTER - INDENTOR
INDICTER - INDICTOR
INDORSER - INDORSOR
INFECTER - INFECTOR
INFLATER - INFLATOR
INVENTER - INVENTOR
INVERTER - INVERTOR
LICENSER - LICENSOR
NARRATER - NARRATOR
PROMISER - PROMISOR
PROMOTER - PROMOTOR
PROVIDER - PROVIDOR
REGRATER - REGRATOR
REJECTER - REJECTOR
RELEASER - RELEASOR
REMITTER - REMITTOR
RESISTER - RESISTOR
RETAILER - RETAILOR
SECRETER - SECRETOR
SURVIVER - SURVIVOR
THRUSTER - THRUSTOR
VERDERER - VERDEROR
VIOLATER - VIOLATOR

9-letter words

ADDRESSER - ADDRESSOR
AUGMENTER - AUGMENTOR
COMMENTER - COMMENTOR
COMPACTER - COMPACTOR
COMPANDER - COMPANDOR
CONCOCTER - CONCOCTOR
CONDEMNER - CONDEMNOR
CONFIRMER - CONFIRMOR
CONNECTER - CONNECTOR
CONSIGNER - CONSIGNOR
CONSULTER - CONSULTOR
CONTEMNER - CONTEMNOR
CONVERTER - CONVERTOR
CORRECTER - CORRECTOR
CORRUPTER - CORRUPTOR
DESOLATER - DESOLATOR
DISRUPTER - DISRUPTOR
EXCERPTER - EXCERPTOR
EXHIBITER - EXHIBITOR
EXPEDITER - EXPEDITOR
FERMENTER - FERMENTOR
HESITATER - HESITATOR
HUNDREDER - HUNDREDOR
INFLICTER - INFLICTOR
INHABITER - INHABITOR
INHIBITER - INHIBITOR
MORTGAGER - MORTGAGOR
PERFECTER - PERFECTOR
PREDICTER - PREDICTOR
PROPELLER - PROPELLOR
PROTESTER - PROTESTOR
RECOVERER - RECOVEROR
REFLECTER - REFLECTOR
REQUESTER - REQUESTOR
RESPONSER - RESPONSOR
SUSPENSER - SUSPENSOR
TELEVISER - TELEVISOR
TORMENTER - TORMENTOR
WARRANTER - WARRANTOR

List 6: VARIANTS -OUR/-OR endings

5/4-letter words

ODOUR - ODOR

6/5-letter words

ARBOUR - ARBOR
ARDOUR - ARDOR
ARMOUR - ARMOR
COLOUR - COLOR
DOLOUR - DOLOR
FAVOUR - FAVOR
HONOUR - HONOR
HUMOUR - HUMOR
LABOUR - LABOR
RIGOUR - RIGOR
RUMOUR - RUMOR
SAPOUR - SAPOR
SAVOUR - SAVOR
TABOUR - TABOR
TENOUR - TENOR
TUMOUR - TUMOR
VALOUR - VALOR
VAPOUR - VAPOR
VIGOUR - VIGOR

7/6-letter words

BITTOUR - BITTOR
CANDOUR - CANDOR
CLAMOUR - CLAMOR
ENAMOUR - ENAMOR
FAITOUR - FAITOR
FERVOUR - FERVOR
FLAVOUR - FLAVOR
FULGOUR - FULGOR
GLAMOUR - GLAMOR
HARBOUR - HARBOR
HAVIOUR - HAVIOR
MAINOUR - MAINOR
PARLOUR - PARLOR
PAVIOUR - PAVIOR
RANCOUR - RANCOR
SAVIOUR - SAVIOR
SUCCOUR - SUCCOR

8/7-letter words

BELABOUR - BELABOR
BICOLOUR - BICOLOR
CLANGOUR - CLANGOR
DECOLOUR - DECOLOR
MALODOUR - MALODOR
STENTOUR - STENTOR
VAVASOUR - VAVASOR

9/8-letter words

BEGLAMOUR - BEGLAMOR
BEHAVIOUR - BEHAVIOR
DEMEANOUR - DEMEANOR
DISCOLOUR - DISCOLOR
DISFAVOUR - DISFAVOR
DISHONOUR - DISHONOR
ENDEAVOUR - ENDEAVOR
MISCOLOUR - MISCOLOR
NEIGHBOUR - NEIGHBOR
SPLENDOUR - SPLENDOR
TRICOLOUR - TRICOLOR
UNICOLOUR - UNICOLOR

List 7: VARIANTS -ABLE/-IBLE endings

7-letter words

ADDABLE - ADDIBLE
MIXABLE - MIXIBLE

8-letter words

EDUCABLE - EDUCIBLE
EVADABLE - EVADIBLE
GULLABLE - GULLIBLE
LAPSABLE - LAPSIBLE
PASSABLE - PASSIBLE
RINSABLE - RINSIBLE
VENDABLE - VENDIBLE

9-letter words

AVERTABLE - AVERTIBLE
CLASSABLE - CLASSIBLE
COMPTABLE - COMPTIBLE
IGNITABLE - IGNITIBLE
INTENABLE - INTENIBLE

List 8: VARIANTS -SMAN/-MAN endings

7/6-letter words

BATSMAN - BATMAN
RODSMAN - RODMAN
TOPSMAN - TOPMAN

8/7-letter words

BEADSMAN - BEADMAN
BEDESMAN - BEDEMAN
BOATSMAN - BOATMAN
BONDSMAN - BONDMAN
DOORSMAN - DOORMAN
GOWNSMAN - GOWNMAN
HEADSMAN - HEADMAN
HERDSMAN - HERDMAN
ISLESMAN - ISLEMAN
LANDSMAN - LANDMAN
LEADSMAN - LEADMAN
LINESMAN - LINEMAN
LINKSMAN - LINKMAN
LOCKSMAN - LOCKMAN
MARKSMAN - MARKMAN
OVERSMAN - OVERMAN
RAFTSMAN - RAFTMAN
ROADSMAN - ROADMAN
SEEDSMAN - SEEDMAN
SIDESMAN - SIDEMAN
SWAGSMAN - SWAGMAN
WOODSMAN - WOODMAN

9/8-letter words

BRIDESMAN - BRIDEMAN
POINTSMAN - POINTMAN
SHARESMAN - SHAREMAN
SHORESMAN - SHOREMAN
SPADESMAN - SPADEMAN
SWORDSMAN - SWORDMAN
WHEELSMAN - WHEELMAN
YACHTSMAN - YACHTMAN

List 9: VARIANTS EN-/IN- beginnings

7-letter words

ENARMED - INARMED
ENCAGED - INCAGED
ENCAGES - INCAGES
ENCASED - INCASED
ENCASES - INCASES
ENCAVED - INCAVED
ENCAVES - INCAVES
ENCHASE - INCHASE
ENCLASP - INCLASP
ENCLOSE - INCLOSE
ENCRUST - INCRUST
ENDARTS - INDARTS
ENDEWED - INDEWED
ENDITED - INDITED
ENDITES - INDITES
ENDORSE - INDORSE
ENDOWED - INDOWED
ENDUING - INDUING
ENFANTS - INFANTS
ENFEOFF - INFEOFF
ENFIXED - INFIXED
ENFIXES - INFIXES
ENFLAME - INFLAME
ENFOLDS - INFOLDS
ENFORCE - INFORCE
ENFORMS - INFORMS
ENGINES - INGINES
ENGLOBE - INGLOBE
ENGRAFT - INGRAFT
ENGRAIN - INGRAIN
ENGROSS - INGROSS
ENGULFS - INGULFS
ENGULPH - INGULPH
ENISLED - INISLED
ENISLES - INISLES
ENLACED - INLACED
ENLACES - INLACES
ENLOCKS - INLOCKS
ENQUIRE - INQUIRE
ENQUIRY - INQUIRY
ENSEAMS - INSEAMS
ENSHELL - INSHELL
ENSNARE - INSNARE
ENSOULS - INSOULS
ENSURED - INSURED
ENSURER - INSURER
ENSURES - INSURES
ENSWEPT - INSWEPT
ENTHRAL - INTHRAL
ENTITLE - INTITLE
ENTOMBS - INTOMBS
ENTRANT - INTRANT
ENTREAT - INTREAT
ENTROLD - INTROLD
ENTRUST - INTRUST
ENTWINE - INTWINE
ENTWIST - INTWIST
ENURING - INURING
ENVIOUS - INVIOUS
ENWALLS - INWALLS
ENWINDS - INWINDS
ENWOUND - INWOUND
ENWRAPS - INWRAPS

8-letter words

ENACTION - INACTION
ENACTIVE - INACTIVE
ENARCHED - INARCHED
ENARCHES - INARCHES
ENARMING - INARMING
ENCAGING - INCAGING
ENCASING - INCASING
ENCAVING - INCAVING
ENCHASED - INCHASED
ENCHASES - INCHASES
ENCLASPS - INCLASPS
ENCLOSED - INCLOSED
ENCLOSER - INCLOSER
ENCLOSES - INCLOSES
ENCREASE - INCREASE
ENCRUSTS - INCRUSTS
ENCUMBER - INCUMBER
ENDARTED - INDARTED
ENDEWING - INDEWING
ENDITING - INDITING
ENDORSED - INDORSED
ENDORSEE - INDORSEE
ENDORSER - INDORSER
ENDORSES - INDORSES
ENDORSOR - INDORSOR
ENDOWING - INDOWING
ENFEOFFS - INFEOFFS
ENFESTED - INFESTED
ENFIXING - INFIXING
ENFLAMED - INFLAMED
ENFLAMES - INFLAMES
ENFOLDED - INFOLDED
ENFOLDER - INFOLDER
ENFORCED - INFORCED
ENFORCES - INFORCES
ENFORMED - INFORMED
ENGLOBED - INGLOBED
ENGLOBES - INGLOBES
ENGRAFTS - INGRAFTS
ENGRAINS - INGRAINS
ENGROOVE - INGROOVE
ENGULFED - INGULFED
ENGULPHS - INGULPHS
ENHEARSE - INHEARSE
ENISLING - INISLING
ENLACING - INLACING
ENLOCKED - INLOCKED
ENMESHED - INMESHED
ENMESHES - INMESHES
ENQUIRED - INQUIRED
ENQUIRER - INQUIRER
ENQUIRES - INQUIRES
ENSCONCE - INSCONCE
ENSCROLL - INSCROLL
ENSEAMED - INSEAMED
ENSHEATH - INSHEATH
ENSHELLS - INSHELLS
ENSHRINE - INSHRINE
ENSNARED - INSNARED
ENSNARER - INSNARER
ENSNARES - INSNARES
ENSOULED - INSOULED
ENSPHERE - INSPHERE
ENSURERS - INSURERS
ENSURING - INSURING
ENSWATHE - INSWATHE
ENTENDER - INTENDER
ENTHRALL - INTHRALL
ENTHRALS - INTHRALS
ENTHRONE - INTHRONE
ENTITLED - INTITLED
ENTITLES - INTITLES
ENTOMBED - INTOMBED
ENTRANTS - INTRANTS
ENTREATS - INTREATS
ENTRENCH - INTRENCH
ENTRUSTS - INTRUSTS
ENTWINED - INTWINED
ENTWINES - INTWINES
ENTWISTS - INTWISTS
ENVEIGLE - INVEIGLE
ENVIABLE - INVIABLE
ENVIABLY - INVIABLY
ENWALLED - INWALLED

9-letter words

ENACTIONS - INACTIONS
ENARCHING - INARCHING
ENCHASING - INCHASING
ENCLASPED - INCLASPED
ENCLOSERS - INCLOSERS
ENCLOSING - INCLOSING
ENCLOSURE - INCLOSURE
ENCREASED - INCREASED
ENCREASES - INCREASES
ENCRUSTED - INCRUSTED
ENCUMBERS - INCUMBERS
ENDARTING - INDARTING
ENDORSEES - INDORSEES
ENDORSERS - INDORSERS
ENDORSING - INDORSING
ENDORSORS - INDORSORS
ENFEOFFED - INFEOFFED
ENFLAMING - INFLAMING
ENFOLDERS - INFOLDERS
ENFOLDING - INFOLDING
ENFORCING - INFORCING
ENFORMING - INFORMING
ENGLOBING - INGLOBING
ENGRAFTED - INGRAFTED
ENGRAINED - INGRAINED
ENGROOVED - INGROOVED
ENGROOVES - INGROOVES
ENGROSSED - INGROSSED
ENGROSSES - INGROSSES
ENGULFING - INGULFING
ENGULPHED - INGULPHED
ENHEARSED - INHEARSED
ENHEARSES - INHEARSES
ENLOCKING - INLOCKING
ENMESHING - INMESHING
ENQUIRERS - INQUIRERS
ENQUIRIES - INQUIRIES
ENQUIRING - INQUIRING
ENSCONCED - INSCONCED
ENSCONCES - INSCONCES
ENSCROLLS - INSCROLLS
ENSEAMING - INSEAMING
ENSHEATHE - INSHEATHE
ENSHEATHS - INSHEATHS
ENSHELLED - INSHELLED
ENSHELTER - INSHELTER
ENSHRINED - INSHRINED
ENSHRINES - INSHRINES
ENSNARERS - INSNARERS
ENSNARING - INSNARING
ENSOULING - INSOULING
ENSPHERED - INSPHERED
ENSPHERES - INSPHERES
ENSWATHED - INSWATHED
ENSWATHES - INSWATHES
ENTENDERS - INTENDERS
ENTHRALLS - INTHRALLS
ENTHRONED - INTHRONED
ENTHRONES - INTHRONES
ENTITLING - INTITLING
ENTOMBING - INTOMBING
ENTREATED - INTREATED
ENTRUSTED - INTRUSTED
ENTWINING - INTWINING
ENTWISTED - INTWISTED
ENUREMENT - INUREMENT
ENVEIGLED - INVEIGLED
ENVEIGLES - INVEIGLES
ENWALLING - INWALLING
ENWINDING - INWINDING
ENWRAPPED - INWRAPPED
ENWREATHE - INWREATHE

VARIANTS -EY/-IE/-Y endings

List 10: -EY/-Y endings only

5/4-letter words

AGLEY - AGLY
ALLEY - ALLY
CAGEY - CAGY
CAKEY - CAKY
COLEY - COLY
CONEY - CONY
COREY - CORY
DOPEY - DOPY
GAMEY - GAMY
HOLEY - HOLY
HOMEY - HOMY
JASEY - JASY
JOKEY - JOKY
LACEY - LACY
LIMEY - LIMY
LINEY - LINY
MATEY - MATY
MOPEY - MOPY
NOSEY - NOSY
PACEY - PACY
PINEY - PINY
POGEY - POGY
POKEY - POKY
POLEY - POLY
PONEY - PONY
POSEY - POSY
RENEY - RENY
RICEY - RICY
ROPEY - ROPY
TONEY - TONY
TYPEY - TYPY
UPSEY - UPSY
WANEY - WANY
WAVEY - WAVY
WINEY - WINY
YAWEY - YAWY

6/5-letter words

BARNEY - BARNY
BLIMEY - BLIMY
BOOGEY - BOOGY
BOOZEY - BOOZY
BUNGEY - BUNGY
BURLEY - BURLY
CARNEY - CARNY
CHOKEY - CHOKY
COOKEY - COOKY
CREPEY - CREPY
CURNEY - CURNY
CURVEY - CURVY
DARKEY - DARKY
DICKEY - DICKY
DINGEY - DINGY
DINKEY - DINKY
DOYLEY - DOYLY
FLAKEY - FLAKY
FLUKEY - FLUKY
FLUTEY - FLUTY
GALLEY - GALLY
GILPEY - GILPY
GOOLEY - GOOLY
GOONEY - GOONY
GOOSEY - GOOSY
GRAPEY - GRAPY
GRIPEY - GRIPY
GULLEY - GULLY
GYNNEY - GYNNY
HONKEY - HONKY
HOOKEY - HOOKY
HOOLEY - HOOLY
HORSEY - HORSY
HURLEY - HURLY
JOLLEY - JOLLY
KARSEY - KARSY
LINNEY - LINNY
LOONEY - LOONY
MAMMEY - MAMMY
MANGEY - MANGY
MEINEY - MEINY
MICKEY - MICKY
MIMSEY - MIMSY
MOOLEY - MOOLY
MOUSEY - MOUSY
MURREY - MURRY
OCHREY - OCHRY
PARLEY - PARLY
PEAVEY - PEAVY
PHONEY - PHONY
PINKEY - PINKY
PIONEY - PIONY
PONCEY - PONCY
POWNEY - POWNY
PRICEY - PRICY
PUDSEY - PUDSY
PUNKEY - PUNKY
SAVVEY - SAVVY
SCAREY - SCARY
SHALEY - SHALY
SLATEY - SLATY
SMOKEY - SMOKY
SNAKEY - SNAKY
SPACEY - SPACY
SPICEY - SPICY
SPIKEY - SPIKY
STAGEY - STAGY
STOGEY - STOGY
STONEY - STONY
STOREY - STORY
TACKEY - TACKY
TAWNEY - TAWNY
THYMEY - THYMY
TICKEY - TICKY
TRIPEY - TRIPY
VERREY - VERRY
WHINEY - WHINY
WHITEY - WHITY
WILLEY - WILLY

7/6-letter words

CHANCEY - CHANCY
CHANTEY - CHANTY
CHOOSEY - CHOOSY
CLIQUEY - CLIQUY
CRICKEY - CRICKY
CURTSEY - CURTSY
DIDDLEY - DIDDLY
FIDDLEY - FIDDLY
FLUNKEY - FLUNKY
LIMPSEY - LIMPSY
ORANGEY - ORANGY
PIGSNEY - PIGSNY
PLAGUEY - PLAGUY
PUSSLEY - PUSSLY
SHANTEY - SHANTY
SHEENEY - SHEENY
SHIMMEY - SHIMMY
SHINNEY - SHINNY
SPINNEY - SPINNY
SPOONEY - SPOONY
SPURREY - SPURRY
STRIPEY - STRIPY
SWANKEY - SWANKY
SWEENEY - SWEENY
TIDDLEY - TIDDLY
TROLLEY - TROLLY
WHIMSEY - WHIMSY
WHISKEY - WHISKY

8/7-letter words

CHIMBLEY - CHIMBLY
GINGELEY - GINGELY
MALARKEY - MALARKY
MANGABEY - MANGABY

List 11: -EY/-IE endings only

5-letter words

CUTEY - CUTIE
LOOEY - LOOIE
MAMEY - MAMIE

6-letter words

BAILEY - BAILIE
BLOOEY - BLOOIE
FLOOEY - FLOOIE
GARVEY - GARVIE
HAWKEY - HAWKIE
JARVEY - JARVIE
SARNEY - SARNIE

7-letter words

CHARLEY - CHARLIE
DOVEKEY - DOVEKIE
SHAWLEY - SHAWLIE

List 12: -IE/-Y endings only

5/4-letter words

AERIE - AERY
ALKIE - ALKY
CAVIE - CAVY
DEXIE - DEXY
DIDIE - DIDY
DIXIE - DIXY
DOBIE - DOBY
DOXIE - DOXY
EERIE - EERY
EYRIE - EYRY
GYNIE - GYNY
LOGIE - LOGY
NIXIE - NIXY
OLDIE - OLDY
PIXIE - PIXY
PUMIE - PUMY
RELIE - RELY
RORIE - RORY
TOWIE - TOWY

6/5-letter words

ANOMIE - ANOMY
AUNTIE - AUNTY
AWMRIE - AWMRY
BADDIE - BADDY
BAGGIE - BAGGY
BARMIE - BARMY
BAWTIE - BAWTY
BIGGIE - BIGGY
BILLIE - BILLY
BITTIE - BITTY
BLOWIE - BLOWY
BLUDIE - BLUDY
BONNIE - BONNY
BOOBIE - BOOBY
BOODIE - BOODY
BOOGIE - BOOGY
BOOKIE - BOOKY
BOOTIE - BOOTY
BOTHIE - BOTHY
BUNGIE - BUNGY
BUNJIE - BUNJY
BUPPIE - BUPPY
CABBIE - CABBY
CADDIE - CADDY
CANDIE - CANDY
CANNIE - CANNY
CARNIE - CARNY
CATTIE - CATTY
CHEWIE - CHEWY
CIGGIE - CIGGY
COLLIE - COLLY
COMMIE - COMMY
COOKIE - COOKY
COOLIE - COOLY
CORBIE - CORBY
COWRIE - COWRY
CRUSIE - CRUSY
CUDDIE - CUDDY
CURRIE - CURRY
DARKIE - DARKY
DEARIE - DEARY
DEAWIE - DEAWY
DICKIE - DICKY
DOBBIE - DOBBY
DOGGIE - DOGGY
DONSIE - DONSY
DOOLIE - DOOLY
DOOZIE - DOOZY
DORMIE - DORMY
DUCKIE - DUCKY
DUDDIE - DUDDY
FAERIE - FAERY
FARCIE - FARCY
FERLIE - FERLY
FOLKIE - FOLKY
FOODIE - FOODY
FOOTIE - FOOTY
FROWIE - FROWY
FUNDIE - FUNDY
GAUCIE - GAUCY
GAWSIE - GAWSY
GILLIE - GILLY
GIRLIE - GIRLY
GOODIE - GOODY
GOOLIE - GOOLY
GOONIE - GOONY
GUSSIE - GUSSY
GUSTIE - GUSTY
GYPPIE - GYPPY
HANKIE - HANKY
HEMPIE - HEMPY
HIPPIE - HIPPY
HOAGIE - HOAGY
HONKIE - HONKY
HOODIE - HOODY
HOOLIE - HOOLY
HOWDIE - HOWDY
JEELIE - JEELY
JUMBIE - JUMBY
JUNKIE - JUNKY
KELPIE - KELPY
KELTIE - KELTY
KIDDIE - KIDDY
KILTIE - KILTY
KOOKIE - KOOKY
LALDIE - LALDY
LAMBIE - LAMBY
LAMMIE - LAMMY
LEFTIE - LEFTY
LEZZIE - LEZZY
LINTIE - LINTY
LIPPIE - LIPPY
LOGGIE - LOGGY
LOONIE - LOONY
LUCKIE - LUCKY
LUVVIE - LUVVY
MAMMIE - MAMMY
MASHIE - MASHY
MEALIE - MEALY
MEANIE - MEANY
MEINIE - MEINY
MINNIE - MINNY
MOBBIE - MOBBY
MOCHIE - MOCHY
MOGGIE - MOGGY
MOLLIE - MOLLY
MOSSIE - MOSSY
MOUSIE - MOUSY
MUSKIE - MUSKY
NANNIE - NANNY
NAPPIE - NAPPY
NELLIE - NELLY
NEWSIE - NEWSY
NIRLIE - NIRLY
NOOKIE - NOOKY
PALMIE - PALMY
PANTIE - PANTY
PARDIE - PARDY
PARKIE - PARKY
PASTIE - PASTY
PATTIE - PATTY
PEERIE - PEERY
PERDIE - PERDY
PIGGIE - PIGGY
PINKIE - PINKY
PINNIE - PINNY
POMMIE - POMMY
PONTIE - PONTY
POPSIE - POPSY
PORGIE - PORGY
POTSIE - POTSY
POWNIE - POWNY
PRATIE - PRATY
PREMIE - PREMY
PUGGIE - PUGGY
PUNKIE - PUNKY
PURPIE - PURPY
PUTTIE - PUTTY
RANDIE - RANDY
REEKIE - REEKY
RHODIE - RHODY
ROARIE - ROARY
ROOKIE - ROOKY
ROOMIE - ROOMY
SALTIE - SALTY
SILKIE - SILKY
SKIVIE - SKIVY
SOAPIE - SOAPY
SOFTIE - SOFTY
SONSIE - SONSY
STIMIE - STIMY
STOGIE - STOGY
STYMIE - STYMY
SUBBIE - SUBBY
SURFIE - SURFY
TALKIE - TALKY
TAMMIE - TAMMY
TANGIE - TANGY
TATTIE - TATTY
TECHIE - TECHY
TEDDIE - TEDDY
TENTIE - TENTY
TINNIE - TINNY
TITTIE - TITTY
TOTTIE - TOTTY
TOWNIE - TOWNY
TUSHIE - TUSHY
WADDIE - WADDY
WALLIE - WALLY
WASPIE - WASPY
WEDGIE - WEDGY
WEENIE - WEENY
WEEPIE - WEEPY
WELLIE - WELLY
WIDDIE - WIDDY
WILLIE - WILLY
WOODIE - WOODY
WOOLIE - WOOLY
YABBIE - YABBY
YAPPIE - YAPPY
YIPPIE - YIPPY
YUPPIE - YUPPY

7/6-letter words

BLASTIE - BLASTY
BOLSHIE - BOLSHY
BOOKSIE - BOOKSY
BRASSIE - BRASSY
BRAWLIE - BRAWLY
BRICKIE - BRICKY
BROWNIE - BROWNY
CALORIE - CALORY
CHALLIE - CHALLY
CHAPPIE - CHAPPY
CHEAPIE - CHEAPY
CHINKIE - CHINKY
CHIPPIE - CHIPPY
CHUCKIE - CHUCKY
CONCHIE - CONCHY
COONTIE - COONTY
COUTHIE - COUTHY
CRAPPIE - CRAPPY
CREEPIE - CREEPY
CROPPIE - CROPPY
CROWDIE - CROWDY
CRUMMIE - CRUMMY
CUTESIE - CUTESY
DRAPPIE - DRAPPY
DRUGGIE - DRUGGY
FLOOSIE - FLOOSY
FLOOZIE - FLOOZY
FLOSSIE - FLOSSY
FOOTSIE - FOOTSY
GLASSIE - GLASSY
GRANNIE - GRANNY
GREENIE - GREENY
GREMMIE - GREMMY
GRIESIE - GRIESY
GROUPIE - GROUPY
INCONIE - INCONY
JACKSIE - JACKSY
JAUNTIE - JAUNTY
JOHNNIE - JOHNNY
NIGHTIE - NIGHTY
NITERIE - NITERY
OVERLIE - OVERLY
PLISKIE - PLISKY
PLOTTIE - PLOTTY
PLUMPIE - PLUMPY
POLONIE - POLONY
PREPPIE - PREPPY
QUEENIE - QUEENY
REALLIE - REALLY
REALTIE - REALTY
REECHIE - REECHY
REVERIE - REVERY
ROUGHIE - ROUGHY
SHARPIE - SHARPY
SHELTIE - SHELTY
SHORTIE - SHORTY
SKELLIE - SKELLY
SKOLLIE - SKOLLY
SMARTIE - SMARTY
SNOTTIE - SNOTTY
SPARKIE - SPARKY
SPUNKIE - SPUNKY
STAGGIE - STAGGY
STEAMIE - STEAMY
STEELIE - STEELY
STIFFIE - STIFFY
STOURIE - STOURY
SWABBIE - SWABBY
SWEETIE - SWEETY
TOASTIE - TOASTY
TOOTSIE - TOOTSY
TOUGHIE - TOUGHY
TRANNIE - TRANNY
TRICKIE - TRICKY
TROELIE - TROELY
UNWARIE - UNWARY
VAUNTIE - VAUNTY
WASTRIE - WASTRY
WEIRDIE - WEIRDY
WHEELIE - WHEELY

8/7-letter words

BATTERIE - BATTERY
BHEESTIE - BHEESTY
CHRISTIE - CHRISTY
FANTASIE - FANTASY
GRUMPHIE - GRUMPHY
OBSEQUIE - OBSEQUY
ORGANDIE - ORGANDY
POLLICIE - POLLICY
SCROGGIE - SCROGGY
SMOOTHIE - SMOOTHY
SQUADDIE - SQUADDY
UNSONSIE - UNSONSY
VISNOMIE - VISNOMY
WASTERIE - WASTERY

List 13: -EY/-IE/-Y endings

5/5/4-letter words

BOGEY - BOGIE - BOGY
BONEY - BONIE - BONY
COSEY - COSIE - COSY
COZEY - COZIE - COZY
DOGEY - DOGIE - DOGY
FOGEY - FOGIE - FOGY
MONEY - MONIE - MONY

6/6/5-letter words

BOOGEY - BOOGIE - BOOGY
BUNGEY - BUNGIE - BUNGY
CARNEY - CARNIE - CARNY
COOKEY - COOKIE - COOKY
DARKEY - DARKIE - DARKY
DICKEY - DICKIE - DICKY
GOOLEY - GOOLIE - GOOLY
GOONEY - GOONIE - GOONY
HONKEY - HONKIE - HONKY
HOOLEY - HOOLIE - HOOLY
LOONEY - LOONIE - LOONY
MAMMEY - MAMMIE - MAMMY
MEINEY - MEINIE - MEINY
MOUSEY - MOUSIE - MOUSY
PINKEY - PINKIE - PINKY
POWNEY - POWNIE - POWNY
PUNKEY - PUNKIE - PUNKY
STOGEY - STOGIE - STOGY
WILLEY - WILLIE - WILLY

7/7/6-letter words

CHANTEY - CHANTIE - CHANTY
PIGSNEY - PIGSNIE - PIGSNY
SHEENEY - SHEENIE - SHEENY
SWANKEY - SWANKIE - SWANKY

Section Five

Bonus Word Lists

Introduction

As there is a 50-point bonus for playing all seven tiles in one turn, 7-letter words are an essential part of the Scrabble player's vocabulary. Seven tiles can of course also be played around an existing letter on the board, so 8-letter words too are a key part of the Scrabble player's word knowledge.

Any words which use all seven of the letters on your rack are called bonus words, or just plain bonuses. Bonuses usually have seven or eight letters, but very occasionally can have more if played around several letters on the board. In the USA and some other parts of the world, words which score a 50-point bonus are called 'bingos'.

6-plus-1 sets

Some 7-letter words are more useful than others, simply because they are more likely to occur, given the distribution of letters in the Scrabble set. For this reason, it is an unnecessary task (and a painstakingly lengthy one!) to attempt to learn all of the 7-letter words. There are over 31,000 of these, and it is much more worthwhile (and a lot easier!) to concentrate on some of the 15% or so that are going to be the most useful to you.

Such 7-letter words can be arranged conveniently according to common 6-letter groups of letters (stems). Each stem yields a set of 7-letter words that can be made by the addition of a single seventh letter. These are the '6-plus-1 sets' – six letters plus another one letter to make a variety of 7-letter words. The more different letters of the alphabet that can be added to a stem, the more useful it is to the Scrabble player.

7-plus-1 sets

Perhaps your seven letters do not make a bonus word by themselves. Even if they do, perhaps the bonus word won't fit in on the board anywhere. These are the occasions when you may need to think bigger – 8-letter words! Of course, it is possible that the 7-letter word on your rack could go down on the board, but the 8-letter word might score quite a few more points. Sometimes an 8-letter word will score a lot more points, if it covers two triple-word-score squares – this is the 'nine-timer' that Scrabble players strive for.

As with the 6-plus-1 sets, some stems are more useful than others and the lists given here are based on these.

The 6-letter stems

The 250 6-letter stems used as the basis for the 6-plus-1 sets represent the 250 most likely and most fruitful stems, based on an algorithm of the probability of the six letters occurring and the probability of picking up letters that combine with the stem.

A list of these stems is shown before the 6-plus-1 sets. The letters in the stems are in alphabetical order and, in turn, the stems are listed in alphabetical order. Alongside each stem is shown its ranking in the top 250, as well as a mnemonic keyword of the stem and a suggested mnemonic phrase for the combining letters as an aide-mémoire.

The mnemonic phrase in each case contains only the combining letters for the stem and so can help you remember whether a particular stem does or does not make a bonus word with the seventh letter. For example, AEINRT has a ranking of 1 (the top ranking), mnemonic keyword RETAIN and mnemonic phrase 'keep light brown ducks from Jim'. The phrase does not contain an A, which tells you that RETAIN plus an A does not yield a 7-letter word. Similarly, AAEMNT has a ranking of 225, mnemonic keyword (MAN ATE) and mnemonic phrase 'slurped dumplings'.

Note that not all the mnemonic keywords are real words or words that are valid for Scrabble. In either of these cases the keyword is shown in brackets, as at MAN ATE above. Where possible, as with (MAN ATE) and 'slurped dumplings', keywords and mnemonics are specifically chosen so that there is some meaningful connection between them.

These 6-letter stems make learning easier and should help recollection during an actual game. If the concept is new to you, then just concentrate on two or three of the most fertile stems, such as AEINRT, AENRSTand EGINRS. You might also have fun dreaming up your own mnemonic phrases for your favourite stems.

The 7-letter stems

The 250 7-letter stems used as the basis for the 7-plus-1 sets represent the 250 most likely and most fruitful stems, based on an algorithm of the probability of the seven letters occurring and the probability of an eighth letter combining with the stem. As with the 6-letter stems, a list of the stems, their ranking, mnemonic keyword and suggested mnemonic phrase are supplied before the bonus lists. Note that in some cases the combining letters are all consonants so no mnemonic sentence is possible.

Alphabetic lists of all the words in the bonus sets

Following the 6-plus-1 sets is a straightforward alphabetical listing of all the 7-letter words appearing in the 6-plus-1 sets. Duplicates have been removed. Similarly, an alphabetic list of the 8-letter words follows the 7-plus-1 sets.

Additional bonus sets

Section Five also contains:

☆ additional high-probability bonus words

☆ AEIO bonus words

☆ 6-letter stems combining with each vowel

More about all of these later on.

SUMMARY OF 6-LETTER STEMS
in alphabetical order with ranking, keywords, combining letters and mnemonic

Stem	Rank	Keyword	Combining Letters	Mnemonic
AAEMNT	225	(MAN ATE)	DEGILMNPRSU	slurped dumplings
ABDEIR	141	(ABRIDE)	CDEGLMNRSTUW	clustered new gem
ABEILS	153	ISABEL	ADEFIKLMNORSTWYZ	zesty lady winks for more
ABELRT	210	ALBERT	AEHIMNOSTW	showiest man
ABEORS	142	(A SOBER)	BCEGIJLNPRTUVXYZ	JP vexing nice blitz jury
ABERST	130	BREAST	ABDEGHILMNORSTUVWXY	why even buxom girls date
ACDERS	244	SACRED	ABEFGHIKLNOPRTU	holier, but liar kept fibbing
ACEILR	131	ECLAIR	BDFGHMNOPRSTUVY	thumbs up for no groovy food
ACEINR	65	CANIER	ABDEFGHLMNPRST	pampas grass belted left hand
ACEINS	125	INCASE	DFGHLMNOPRSTUVY	sporty thugs found mouldy TV
ACELST	247	CASTLE	ABDEHIKLMNOPRSUY	an absurdly pink home
ACENRS	181	CRANES	CDEHIKLNOPSTUVYZ	hoisted up unlucky dozy luvvies
ACENRT	100	NECTAR	ADEFHILOSTUY	hideously fatty stuff
ACENST	156	STANCE	ACDEHIKLNOPRSTU	postured in chalk
ACEORS	102	COARSE	ABDEGHILMNRSTUX	right sand and ballast mixture
ACEOST	154	(ACTOSE)	DEILMNPRTUV	inverted lump
ACERST	147	CATERS	ADEHIKLMNOPRSTUY	desperately link mouths
ACIRST	221	ARTICS	ABCDEGIKLMNRSTUWYZ	many trucks will zigzag by danger
ADEERS	73	SEARED	BCDGHIKLMNOPRSTVW	shocking! MTV drops bowls
ADEEST	89	SEATED	BCDFHILMNRSTUWY	truly finds bum twitchy
ADEGLN	203	DANGLE	BCDEFIJMNRSTUW	if it's December it's just mid-winter
ADEGNR	138	DANGER	EILOPRSTU	too perilous
ADEGRS	194	GRADES	BCDEFGILNOPRSTU	bungled specific OU results
ADEILR	18	DERAIL	ABCDEGILOPRSTUVY	cobbles upset gravity ride
ADEILS	39	LADIES	BCDEFGHIKLMNOPRSTUVY	sickly blondes hug TV performer
ADEINR	4	RAINED	ABCDFGHIMNOPRSTUV	storm giving bad FA Cup match
ADEINS	24	(SANDIE)	ABCDEGKLMOPRSTVW	swamp track above glade
ADEIRS	15	RAISED	ABCEFGHIKLMNOPRTUVX	lifting cake box over hump
ADEIST	28	(IDATES)	BCDEFGLMNORSUVW	November wolf cudgels
ADELNR	75	LANDER	ABCDEGHKLMOSUY	ably smuggled hock
ADELNS	134	(SANDLE)	CDEGHIKORSTUY	shoes get yucky dirt
ADELRS	85	ALDERS	BCDEFGHIKLMNOPRSTUWZ	computer whizz kid gets flu bug in shop
ADELST	104	SALTED	BCDEHIKLMNOPRSTU	helped mend bloodier skin cuts
ADEMNS	242	AMENDS	ABDEGIKNOPRSTUY	redesigns your pretty art book
ADENRS	62	SANDER	BCDEFGHIKLMPRSTUWZ	club set mid-week prize-fight
ADENRU	66	UNREAD	BCDEGHIKLMOPSTYZ	cops blitzed mighty bookshop
ADENST	44	STANED	ACEGHIKLMNOPRTUVY	having mucky petrol
ADEORS	26	ADORES	CDEFGILMORSTUVW	wife's good multi-curved form
ADEPRT	232	PARTED	AEIMOPSTU	semi-utopia
ADERRS	237	DARERS	ACEGILNOPTW	go lie on cowpat
ADERST	53	STARED	BCDEFGHIKLMNOPRTVWY	women looked fetching by the privy
ADGINR	122	DARING	BCDEFGIKLMNOPRSTUWY	kids stop ferociously big women
ADINRS	111	DRAINS	ABEFGKLMNOQTUW	baulk monumental quag flow
AEELRS	67	LEASER	CDEGHIKMNOPSTUVXY	tough men pick sexy videos
AEEMRS	241	SEAMER	BCDGHIKLNPRSTU	thugs drink in public
AEEPRT	144	REPEAT	ADHIKLMOPRSUYZ	ask hourly you dozy imp
AEERRS	155	ERASER	BCDFGHIMNOPRSTUVW	chimp rubbing out VW front doors
AEERST	21	EATERS	ABCDFGHIKLMNOPRSTUWX	anxious about light pub food and warm snacks
AEGILN	59	(EALING)	CDEFGHKLMNPRSTUVY	kung fu speed, clever myth
AEGINR	12	REGAIN	ABCDEFGHKLMNOPRSTVWZ	got back vodka from frazzled posh women
AEGLNR	88	ANGLER	ABCDEFGIJLMPSTUWY	Jimmy gutted awful bass species
AEGLNS	173	GLEANS	ABCDFGIJLMOPRSTUWY	joyful impact from wordbags
AEGLNT	113	TANGLE	DEHILORSTUW	twisted her soul
AEGLRS	172	LAGERS	ABDEFGIKMNOPSTVYZ	vat stopped making fizzy booze
AEGLST	193	AGLETS	ABEHILNORTW	brother-in-law
AEGNRS	90	ANGERS	BDEGHILMOPRSTUW	grumped whilst bored
AEGNRT	32	GARNET	ADEFILMNOPRSUWY	Alf is superior wordy man
AEGNST	96	AGENTS	ADEHILMNORT	deal in theatredom
AEGRST	81	GREATS	ABDEGHILNOPRSTVY	very old thespians brag
AEHLRT	215	LATHER	ABCEFIMNOSY	foamy ambiences

AEHRST	174	HATERS	BCDEFGHILMNOPSTVW	hostile VIP's wife coming to bed
AEILMN	108	MENIAL	ABCFGHKLMNOPRSTU	mops batch of gunk on floor
AEILNT	14	ENTAIL	AEFGKMOPRSUV	Pam favours egg or pork
AEILRS	20	SAILER	ABCDEGHIJKLMNPRSTVW	jackman viewing the pirate's blade
AEILRT	13	RETAIL	BCDEHKLMNPRSTUWY	spend the weekly crumbs
AEILSS	238	LASSIE	ABCDFGHIKLMNPRSTUVW	filmstar pup having drawbacks
AEILST	25	SALTIE	BCDFGHIKLNOPRSUVWYZ	providing folks' boozy working lunch
AEIMNR	64	REMAIN	BCDEFGHKLORSTVW	fevered dog left chewed books
AEIMNS	95	MANIES	ACDEFGHJKLMORSTW	lots of jackdaws gather moss
AEIMNT	36	INMATE	ABCDEGHILNORSXY	exercising badly in hell-hole
AEIMRS	109	ARMIES	BDEFGHLMNPRSTUVW	bullets left the mugwump unnerved
AEIMST	99	MISEAT	CDEGHIKMNOPRSTZ	choking on imported zos
AEINRS	6	SARNIE	CDFGHIJKLMNOPRSTV	giving Josh mild pork flitch
AEINRT	1	RETAIN	BCDEFGHIJKLMNOPRSTUW	keep light brown ducks from Jim
AEINST	2	(SATINE)	ABCDEFGHIJKLMNOPRSTUVWXZ	jukebox whizz prevented glam-rock fest
AEIPRS	78	PRAISE	ACDEGHKLMNOPRSTUVW	acknowledge mother's veg and pud
AEIRST	3	SATIRE	ABCDEFGHIKLMNOPRSTVW	keep waking as vampires fetch blood
AEIRTT	34	ATTIRE	ABCDEFLNPRSTVWX	vest, belt, scarf and waxed cap
AEISTT	83	(TASTIE)	ABCFHKMNOPRTUVWXY	buy wok from chap but no VAT tax
AELMNT	214	LAMENT	ABDEIMOSTU	mutated bodies
AELNRS	49	LEARNS	ABCDEFGIKMNOPRSTZ	trains to make fine booze, cigs, and pot
AELNRT	33	ANTLER	BCEGHILNPSTUV	visit huge public tine
AELNST	40	LATENS	ACDEGHIKMNOPRTUVYZ	making chap tardy, overdue and dazed
AELORS	29	(ALOSER)	ABCDEFGHLMNOPST	gambled pot cash so none left
AELOST	42	SOLATE	BCDEFGHIKMNPRSVZ	Viking chief missed big prize
AELPRS	216	PEARLS	ACDEFGHIKLMNOPRSTUWY	simply delightful to wear around neck
AELPRT	209	PLATER	ACEIMNOSTY	non-systematic
AELRST	48	ALERTS	BCDEFGHIKLMNOPSTUVWY	we give botulism check on lumpy food
AEMNST	171	STAMEN	ABDEGHILOPRSUY	spoiled large shrubbery
AEMRST	136	MATERS	ABCDEHIJKLMNOPRSTUWY	plucky mothers sunbathed with joy
AENNST	150	(ANNETS)	ABCDEFGIKLRTW	wide ball cricket flag
AENPST	157	PATENS	ACDEHILMOPRSTUWYZ	the clumsy wizard drops pot
AENRRT	91	ERRANT	AEGIOPSTY	gay postie
AENRSS	228	SNARES	ACDEFGHIKLORSTWY	God catches wicker fly
AENRST	11	ASTERN	ABCDEGHIKLMNOPRSTUVWY	moved ship light back to runway
AENRTT	74	NATTER	ACDEILNPRSUY	discuss and parley
AENSTT	123	(ATTENS)	BCDEFGILNOPRTUX	flexed copper tubing
AEORST	9	ORATES	ABCDEGHILMNPRT	garbled chat in Parliament
AEPRST	140	PATERS	ACDEGHILMNOPRSTUYZ	long-standing much-prized daddy
AERRST	106	STARER	ABCDEFGIKMNOPSTVY	caveman eyeing bats picking at food
AERSST	224	ASSERT	ABCEFGHIKLMNPRSTVWY	I'm clever by fighting newspeak
AERSTT	101	TASTER	BCDEGHILMNOPRSTUVWYZ	zombie's rhyming couplets with video
AERSTW	199	WATERS	ABDEFHILMNSTY	lamented by fish
AGILNR	204	(RALING)	BCDEFGHIKMNOPTWY	mighty bone picked by bitchy wife
AGILNS	223	SIGNAL	ABCDEFGHIJKMNPSTUVWY	defying Jack waved thumbs-up
AGILNT	179	(LATING)	BCEFHIKMNOPRSY	bishop's hymnbook on fire shook choir
AGINRS	135	GRAINS	ABCDEFGHIKMNOPTVWY	feed the pack by moving wheat
AGINRT	70	RATING	ACDEFGIKLMNOPRSTWY	I get sick and tired of playing if mine is low
AGINST	115	SATING	ABCDEFGHKLMNOPRTUVWXY	why do you vengefully mock the bad expert?
AINRST	38	TRAINS	ABCDEGHLMOPQSTU	quest to help bad gut muscle
AINSTT	200	TAINTS	ADEGILMNORS	smearing gold
ANORST	63	(NO RATS)	ABCEILMNOPTUY	yet public moan
BDEIRS	246	BRIDES	ABCDEGIKLNORTUV	begun divorce talk
BEILRS	245	LIBERS	ABDEGIJKLMNORST	marked job listings
BEIRST	189	TRIBES	ADEFHIKLMOSTU	folk must all hide
BEORST	217	STROBE	ADHILMNOPSTUVWZ	zits and odd lumps will all vanish
CEINOS	118	COSINE	ABCDEGILMNRSTV	made big vertical angles
CEINRS	191	(NICERS)	ADEGHIKMOPSTVW	give vodka to the wimps
CEINST	202	INSECT	AEFHIJKLOPRSY	apish horsefly jokes
CEIORS	163	COSIER	ABCDHLNPRSTUVWZ	Tarzan vaults, a bad crash and traps walnuts

CEIRST	170	CITERS	ACDEHIKLMNOPTUW	liked to chant well on podium
CENORS	177	CENSOR	ADEFGIKLNOPRSTU	stopped speaker's effing language
CENOST	230	CENTOS	ADEFGHIKNRTUV	taking five hundred
CEORST	236	ESCORT	AHIKLNOPRSTUV	punkish violator
DEEINR	45	DENIER	BCEFGHKLMOPRSUWX	welcome leg hose for super sexbomb looks
DEEIRS	57	DESIRE	ABCDEFGLMNOPRSTUVZ	loves buzz and pace of grand metro
DEELNS	240	LENSED	ABDEFGILRSTWY	refitted glass by law
DEENRS	97	ENDERS	ABCDEFGHILMOPRSTUVZ	I gazed at Chambers for plural of LEV
DEENST	117	NESTED	ACDEILMNORSTUX	is column x-rated?
DEERST	159	RESTED	ACDEINOPSVWXY	Picasso views sine wave on X and Y axis
DEGILN	158	DINGLE	ABCEGHIJMNOPSTUVW	bungee jump victim was shot
DEGINR	84	RINGED	ABCDEFHINORSUWY	we are surrounded by fire chiefs
DEGINS	162	SIGNED	AEGILMNORSTUWY	wrote amusingly
DEGIRS	213	DIRGES	ABEFGILNRSU	big funerals
DEILNS	119	(IN SLED)	ABDEGIKMNOPTWY	pigmy went week-day tobogganing
DEILRT	76	(LITRED)	ABDEFHKLNOPUWY	pa knew he would buy fuel
DEINOS	43	ONSIDE	ACDGHIKLMNPRST	marking pitch lads
DEINRS	56	DINERS	ABCEFGHIKMNOPTUVW	weeping into a bucket of vintage champagne
DEINRU	58	RUINED	ACDEFGHIJMNOSTW	James is no good at fetching wood
DEINST	37	(SINTED)	ABDEFGIKLMNOPRSTUY	king buys platformed boots
DEIORS	31	(DI &ROSE)	ABCDEHLMNOPSTVWZ	amazed twelve blond chaps
DEIOST	41	(ODSITE)	ACDFHJMNOPRTUVWXZ	coax vacant farm cow to jump hazard
DEIPRT	220	(TRIPED)	ACEILMNOPS	a noise clamp
DEIRST	61	STRIDE	ABCEFHIKNOPRSUV	car runs over fake bishop
DEIRSU	149	RUDIES	ABCDEGHKNPQRST	eats qat and gets back near garden path
DELNOS	176	OLDENS	ABDFGHIMORSUWZ	Wizard of Oz is a humbug
DELORS	151	(OLDERS)	ABCEFGHIMNPSTWY	bigwig faces nymphet
DELORT	94	(DOLTER)	ADFILNOPSTU	so dull and pitiful
DENORU	93	UNDOER	ABCDFGHILMNPRSW	farmhand scrapping bad wall
DENOST	77	STONED	ABCEFIMNORTU	I am a fat bouncer
DENRSU	185	NURSED	ABDEFGHIKLNOPSTU	liked to help patient's flu bugs
DENSTU	219	NUDEST	ABDEHIMNORT	mention bare behind
DEORST	55	STORED	ABEFGHIKLMNOPRTUWY	rifleman put away the rogue blank
DEOSTU	187	OUSTED	CGHIJLMNOPRTUX	hint - joining or mixing lip colour
DERSTU	243	RUSTED	BCGILNOPRSTUY	ugly rust spots ruin club
DGINOR	212	RODING	ACDEFHLNRSTVW	we searched twelve fans
EEFIRS	239	(IS FREE)	ADEFHILNPRSXZ	dazed sphinx flies in air
EEGNRS	235	GREENS	ADEIMOSTVY	avoids tasty meat
EEILRS	86	RELIES	ABCDEFGHLNPRSTUV	trusts TV ads can help ban fags
EEILRV	226	RELIVE	ABDEGILMNORS	born-again models
EEILST	92	ELITES	CEFGHKLMNOPRSVX	frogs expel venom from cheeks
EEIMNS	198	(EMINES)	ADEGILMORSTWY	wild mister dayglo
EEIMRS	207	MISERE	ABCDEGHMNOPRSTX	grass expected amongst herbs
EEINRT	8	ENTIRE	ABCEFGHIKNPRSTU	backing super fight
EEIRRS	180	RERISE	ABDFHJKLMNOPSTVW	folk vow to hold jobs at bomb plant
EEIRST	30	RETIES	ABCDEHKLMNPRSTUVWZ	draws back then pumas and zebras are revealed
EEIRSV	227	REVISE	CDEGHLNOPRSTVW	prevented clog show
EELNST	167	NESTLE	ADEGILPRSTUY	guilty spread
EELRST	129	RELETS	ABCFGHIKLMNOPSTVWYZ	allows lazy fish to gawp at bikini victim again
EENRST	46	ENTERS	ACDEGHILNOPRSTUVWXY	or cleverly exits through open doorway
EEORSV	248	(OVERSE)	ABCEIKLMRTUW	writable muck
EERRST	229	RESTER	ABEFGIMNOPSTUVW	wife stops moving about
EERSTT	195	STREET	ABCEFGHILNOPRSTUVWY	police chief vows to be busy patrolling
EFIRST	182	STRIFE	ABDFHIKLMNOPSTUWZ	found ham pizza on walkabouts
EGHINT	250	HETING	ABCDEFILMNRST	bald man finds Scrabble a test
EGILNR	126	LINGER	ACEFGHIJKMPSTY	stay! - make peach jam gifts
EGILNS	124	SINGLE	ABDEFGHIJKLMNOPRSTUWZ	howzat! fumbling fielder jumps keeper
EGILNT	72	TINGLE	ABDEFHIJKLMOPRSTUW	dim halfwit jumps off kerb
EGILOS	128	LOGIES	ABELMNOPRSTU	unsupportable team
EGILRS	164	(GIRLES)	ABDEGIKLNOSTUY	studying a bloke

EGILST	186	LEGIST	ABEGHLMNOPRSUWZ	ploughman wears blazer
EGINNR	161	GINNER	ACDEFGIKMNORSTUVY	device for making your soft cotton
EGINOS	68	INGOES	ABCDEHJLMOPRUWY	jury approached marble archway
EGINRS	71	SINGER	ABCDEFGHLMNOPRSTUVWYZ	dwarf sang crazy vocals by empty house
EGINRT	51	(TINGER)	AEHILMNOSTUVY	evil human toys
EGINST	116	INGEST	ABDHIJKLMNRSTUVWZ	wizard's junk habit is valium
EGNORS	114	GONERS	ACEHILMOPSTUVY	escapees have timely coup
EHINRS	196	SHRINE	ACDEGIKMOSTVW	stage wicked movies
EHIRST	143	(HITERS)	ABCDEFGHILMNOPTUVWZ	cow fighting at medieval booze-up
EHORST	197	OTHERS	ABCDEFILMNOPRSTUWX	mixed up fan bets on World Cup
EIILST	146	(TILIES)	ACIKLMNOPRTUW	column paintwork
EIINRT	35	INTIRE	ACDEFGHLMNTVW	fame changed twelve men
EILNOS	23	LESION	ACDEFGIKLMOPRSTU	cut leg amid fork spikes
EILNRS	80	LINERS	ABEGIKMOPTV	make a boat pivot at gap
EILNST	52	SILENT	ACDEGIKLNOPRSUVW	uncle avoids speaking words
EILORS	47	OILERS	BCDGIMNOPRSTUV	doping sunburn victim
EILORT	19	LOITER	BCDEFJMNOPSTUV	convened on top of jumbo bus
EILOST	22	(ELIOTS)	ABCEGHILMNOPRTUVWZ	amazing poet wrote at the VIP club
EILRST	50	TILERS	ABCEFGHIJKLMNOPSTU	fitting junk specimen tiles on bath
EILSTU	133	(LUSTIE)	ABCDFGILNOPRT	fling can trap libido
EIMNOS	127	MONIES	ACDEGHLOPRSTW	cash word gets spelt
EIMNRS	183	MINERS	ACDEGHKLMOTUV	hated coal glove muck
EIMNST	206	(MINEST)	ADEGIKOPRSTUW	I worked upstage
EIMOST	152	SOMITE	ADFGHLMNPRSTUVXZ	mad Max vandal turns up gas - flash! zap!
EIMRST	145	MITRES	ABCEFHIKLMNOPRSTUY	scornfully mock the bishop's hat
EINNST	120	SINNET	ADEGILOPRSTUV	I upstaged lover
EINOPS	105	PONIES	ADEGHIKLMNPRSTWY	happily trekking amidst wetlands
EINORS	7	SENIOR	ACDGHIJLMOPRSTUVW	old jovial chap strums with guitar
EINOSS	169	SONSIE	ABCDEIKLMNPRSTUZ	brazen lass disrupts Mick
EINOST	10	TONIES	ABCDHIJLMNOPRSTWX	six actors plan major award bash
EINPRS	165	SNIPER	ACDEGIKLNOPSTU	picks out distant leg
EINPST	148	INSTEP	ACDEIKLMNOPRSTUW	crowd must walk in step
EINRSS	249	RESINS	ACEGHKNOPRTUV	over tough pancake
EINRST	17	INTERS	ACDEFGHKLMNOPSTUVWY	WPC dug hole to keep venom safely
EINRSV	231	VINERS	ACDEGHLMOSTW	matches glowed
EINRTT	79	TINTER	ABCDEGIKOSUW	abused wicked ego
EINRTU	27	UNITER	ABDEGMOPRSTVW	wordgames proved to be better
EINSST	222	INSETS	ACDEFGHLMNOPRSUVWY	could you add very many pages when full?
EINSTT	166	(INTEST)	ADGIKMNOPRUWY	making up a wordy pun
EINSTU	82	UNITES	ADGILMNPQRST	qanat plans and diagrams
EIOPST	103	POSTIE	ACDEHKLMNOPRSTUXY	has empty letter sack next round
EIORSS	205	(SORIES)	BCDEFHLMNPRSTUVXZ	helpful buzzer prevents next sect murder
EIORST	5	TORIES	ABCDFGHIKLMNOPRSTUVW	if voting slumps, this is a drawback
EIORSV	137	VIROSE	ACDEILMNRST	terminal disease scare
EIOSTT	98	(OTTIES)	ABCDEGHLMNOPRTUW	placed wrong thumb on button
EIPRST	132	PRIEST	ACDEFHILMNOPRSTUVXY	vicar found expletives in hymn
EIRRST	160	TRIERS	ADEKMOPRSTUVW	attempted to overwork us
EIRSTT	110	SITTER	ABCEFHJKLMNOPRSTUVW	just watch known volume pour from burette
EIRSTV	168	RIVETS	ADEGHINOPRSTU	are tapped in on tough heads
ELNSTU	218	(LETSUN)	ABEFGINOPRT	print bingo on front page
ELORST	54	OSTLER	ABCDEFHIJLMNOPSTUVW	he's a man with awful low-paid vacation job
ELOSTU	178	TOUSLE	BDFILNOPRSTUVZ	provision for doubtful zoo
ELRSTU	211	ULSTER	ABCDFGHINOPRSTY	coat for body shaping
EMNORS	233	SERMON	ADEFGILOST	sit deaf to false god
EMNOST	190	(MONETS)	ABDEFGHILMOPRSUY	buyer of gold has mishap
EMORST	188	METROS	ABDEGHILNOPRSU	Paris has le bon underground
ENOPRS	208	PERSON	ACDEGHIORSTUY	sues dog charity
ENORST	16	STONER	ABCDEFGHIKLMNOPRSTUY	sculpturing my hall from bedrock
ENOSTT	201	TESTON	ACDHIJLOPRSU	rich judo pals
ENOSTU	69	(OUTENS)	ABCDEGLMNORSTU	ousted combat general
ENRSTU	87	TUNERS	ABCDEFGHILMNOPRST	old pianofortes become all right
EOPRST	192	POSTER	ABCDFHIJLMNOPRSTUWXZ	photo shows mix of fjords and waltz clubs
EORRST	112	SORTER	ACDEGHIKMNOPRSTUVWY	dynamic worker puts vague chaos into order
EORSTT	121	OTTERS	ABCDEHIJLNOPRTUWXY	why include an expert on the job?

GIINRT	234	TIRING	ABCDEFGLMNORSTW	common words are forgettable
GILNOT	175	TOLING	ABCEFHIJLMOPSTUW	it's a whale! jump off beach towel
GINORS	139	SIGNOR	ABCDEGHILMNOPSTUVWY	he loves watching and spying bums
GINORT	107	ROTING	ADEFIKOPRSTUW	task for proud wife
GINOST	184	TOSING	ACDFHKLMNOPRSTUVWY	top hymns favour duckwalk
INORST	60	INTROS	ABCEFGHILNOPTU	hopeful beginning to act

7-LETTER SETS
from the top 250 6-letter stems

AAEMNT 225
(MAN ATE)
D MANDATE
E EMANATE
ENEMATA
MANATEE
G GATEMAN
MAGENTA
MAGNATE
NAMETAG
I AMENTIA
ANIMATE
L AMENTAL
M MEATMAN
N EMANANT
P PEATMAN
R RAMENTA
S NAMASTE
U MANTEAU

ABDEIR 141
(ABRIDE)
C CARBIDE
D BRAIDED
E BEADIER
BEARDIE
G ABRIDGE
BRIGADE
L BALDIER
BEDRAIL
BRAILED
RAILBED
RIDABLE
M EMBRAID
N BANDIER
BRAINED
R BARDIER
BRAIDER
BRIARED
RABIDER
S ABIDERS
BRAISED
DARBIES
SEABIRD
SIDEBAR
T REDBAIT
TRIBADE
U DAUBIER
W BAWDIER

ABEILS 153
ISABEL
A ABELIAS
D BALDIES
DIABLES
DISABLE
E BAILEES
F FAIBLES
I ALIBIES
BAILIES
K SKIABLE
L BALLIES
M ABLEISM
EMBAILS
LAMBIES
N LESBIAN
O OBELIAS
R BAILERS
S ABSEILS
ISABELS
LABISES
T ABLEIST
ALBITES
ASTILBE
BASTILE
BESTIAL
BLASTIE
LIBATES
STABILE
W BEWAILS
Y BAILEYS
Z SIZABLE

ABELRT 210
ALBERT
A RATABLE
E BLEATER
RETABLE
H BLATHER
HALBERT
I LIBRATE
TABLIER
TRIABLE
M LAMBERT
N BRANTLE
O BLOATER
S ALBERTS
BATLERS
BLASTER
LABRETS
STABLER
T BATTLER
BLATTER
BRATTLE
W BLEWART

ABEORS 142
(A SOBER)
B EARBOBS
C BORACES
E AEROBES
G BORAGES
I ISOBARE
J JERBOAS
L LABROSE
N BORANES
P SAPROBE
R ARBORES
BRASERO
T BOASTER
BOATERS
BORATES
REBATOS
SORBATE
U AEROBUS
V BRAVOES
X BORAXES
Y ROSEBAY
Z BEZOARS

ABERST 130
BREAST
A ABATERS
ABREAST
B BARBETS
RABBETS
STABBER
D DABSTER
TABERDS
E BEATERS
BERATES
REBATES
G BARGEST
H BATHERS
BERTHAS
BREATHS
I BAITERS
BARITES
REBAITS
TERBIAS
L ALBERTS
BATLERS
BLASTER
LABRETS
STABLER
M TAMBERS
N BANTERS
O BOASTER
BOATERS
BORATES
REBATOS
SORBATE
R BARRETS
BARTERS
S BASTERS
BESTARS
BRASSET
BREASTS
T BATTERS
TABRETS
U ARBUTES
BURSATE
SURBATE
V BRAVEST
W BRAWEST
WABSTER
X BAXTERS
Y BARYTES
BETRAYS

ACDERS 244
SACRED
A ARCADES
B DECARBS
E CREASED
DECARES
SEARCED
F SCARFED
G CADGERS
H CRASHED
ECHARDS
I CARDIES
DARCIES
RADICES
SIDECAR
K DACKERS
L CRADLES
SCALDER
N DANCERS
O SARCODE
P REDCAPS
SCARPED
SCRAPED
R CARDERS
SCARRED
T REDACTS
SCARTED
U CRUSADE
SCAURED

ACEILR 131
ECLAIR
B CALIBER
CALIBRE
D DECRIAL
RADICEL
RADICLE
F FILACER
G GLACIER
GRACILE
H CHARLIE
M CALMIER
CLAIMER
MIRACLE
RECLAIM
N CARLINE
O CALORIE
CARIOLE
COALIER
LORICAE
P CALIPER
REPLICA
R CERRIAL
S CLARIES
ECLAIRS
SCALIER
T ARTICLE
RECITAL
TALCIER
U AURICLE
V CALIVER
CAVILER
CLAVIER
VALERIC
VELARIC
Y CLAYIER

ACEINR 65
CANIER
A ACARINE
CARINAE
B CARBINE
D CAIRNED
CARNIED
E CINEREA
F FANCIER
G ANERGIC
GRECIAN
H ARCHINE
L CARLINE
M CARMINE
N CANNIER
NARCEIN
P CAPRINE
R CARNIER
S ARCSINE
ARSENIC
CARNIES
CERASIN
T CANTIER
CERATIN
CERTAIN
CREATIN
CRINATE
NACRITE

ACEINS 125
INCASE
D CANDIES
INCASED
F FANCIES
FASCINE
FIANCES
G CEASING
INCAGES
H CHAINES
INCHASE
L INLACES
SANICLE
SCALENI
M AMNESIC
CINEMAS
N CANINES
ENCINAS
NANCIES
O ACINOSE
P INSCAPE
PINCASE
R ARCSINE
ARSENIC
CARNIES
CERASIN
S CASEINS
INCASES
T ACETINS
CANIEST
CINEAST
U EUCAINS
V INCAVES
Y CYANISE

ACELST 247
CASTLE
A ACETALS
LACTASE
B CABLETS
D CASTLED
SCLATED
E CELESTA
H CHALETS
LATCHES
SATCHEL
I ASTELIC
ELASTIC
LACIEST
LATICES
SALICET
K TACKLES
L CALLETS
M CALMEST
CAMLETS
N CANTLES
CENTALS
LANCETS
SCANTLE
O ALECOST
LACTOSE
LOCATES
SCATOLE
TALCOSE
P CAPLETS
PLACETS
R CARTELS
CLARETS
CRESTAL
SCARLET
TARCELS
S CASTLES
SCLATES
U CAUTELS
SULCATE
Y ACETYLS
SCYTALE

ACENRS 181
CRANES
C CANCERS
D DANCERS
E CAREENS
CASERNE
ENRACES
RECANES
H CHENARS
RANCHES
I ARCSINE
ARSENIC
CARNIES
CERASIN
K CANKERS
L LANCERS
RANCELS
N CANNERS
SCANNER
O CARNOSE
COARSEN
CORNEAS
EARCONS
NARCOSE
P PRANCES
S ANCRESS
CASERNS
T CANTERS
CARNETS
NECTARS
RECANTS
SCANTER
TANRECS
TRANCES
U SURANCE
V CAVERNS
CRAVENS
Y CARNEYS
SCENARY
Z ZARNECS

ACENRT 100
NECTAR
A CATERAN
D CANTRED
TRANCED
E CENTARE
CRENATE
REENACT
F CANTREF
H CHANTER
TRANCHE
I CANTIER
CERATIN
CERTAIN
CREATIN
CRINATE
NACRITE
L CENTRAL
O ENACTOR

S CANTERS
CARNETS
NECTARS
RECANTS
SCANTER
TANRECS
TRANCES
T TRANECT
U CENTAUR
UNCRATE
UNTRACE
Y ENCRATY
NECTARY

ACENST 156
STANCE
A CATENAS
C ACCENTS
D DECANTS
DESCANT
SCANTED
E CETANES
TENACES
H CHASTEN
NATCHES
I ACETINS
CANIEST
CINEAST
K NACKETS
L CANTLES
CENTALS
LANCETS
SCANTLE
N NASCENT
O COSTEAN
OCTANES
P CATNEPS
R CANTERS
CARNETS
NECTARS
RECANTS
SCANTER
TANRECS
TRANCES
S ASCENTS
SECANTS
STANCES
T CANTEST
U NUTCASE

ACEORS 102
COARSE
A ROSACEA
B BORACES
D SARCODE
E ACEROSE
G CARGOES
CORSAGE
SOCAGER
H CHOREAS
ORACHES
ROACHES
I ORACIES
SCORIAE
L CLAROES
COALERS
ESCOLAR
ORACLES
RECOALS
SOLACER
M AMORCES
N CARNOSE
COARSEN
CORNEAS
EARCONS
NARCOSE
R COARSER
S ROSACES
T COASTER
COATERS
U ACEROUS
CAROUSE
X COAXERS

ACEOST 154
(ACTOSE)
D COASTED
E ACETOSE
COATEES
I SOCIATE
L ALECOST
LACTOSE
LOCATES
SCATOLE
TALCOSE
M CAMOTES
COMATES
N COSTEAN
OCTANES
P CAPOTES
SCOPATE
TOECAPS
R COASTER
COATERS
T COSTATE
U ACETOUS
V AVOCETS
OCTAVES

ACERST 147
CATERS
A ACATERS
CARATES
D REDACTS
SCARTED
E CERATES
CREATES
ECARTES
SECRETA
H ARCHEST
CHARETS
CHASTER
RACHETS
RATCHES
I CRISTAE
RACIEST
STEARIC
K RACKETS
RESTACK
RETACKS
STACKER
TACKERS
L CARTELS
CLARETS
CRESTAL
SCARLET
TARCELS
M MERCATS
N CANTERS
CARNETS
NECTARS
RECANTS
SCANTER
TANRECS
TRANCES
O COASTER
COATERS
P CARPETS
PREACTS
PRECAST
SPECTRA
R CARTERS
CRATERS
TRACERS
S ACTRESS
CASTERS
RECASTS
T SCATTER
U ACTURES
CAUTERS
CRUSTAE
CURATES
Y SECTARY

ACIRST 221
ARTICS
A CARITAS
B CABRITS
C ARCTICS
D DRASTIC
E CRISTAE
RACIEST
STEARIC
G GASTRIC
TRAGICS
I SATIRIC
K KARSTIC
L CITRALS
M MATRICS
N NARCIST
R TRICARS
S RACISTS
SACRIST
T ASTRICT
U URTICAS
W TWISCAR
Y SATYRIC
Z CZARIST

ADEERS 73
SEARED
B DEBASER
SABERED
C CREASED
DECARES
SEARCED
D DEADERS
G DRAGEES
GREASED
H ADHERES
HEADERS
HEARSED
SHEARED
I DEARIES
READIES
K DEKARES
SKEARED
L DEALERS
LEADERS
REDEALS
M REMADES
REMEADS
SMEARED
N DEANERS
ENDEARS
O OREADES
P PREASED
RESPADE
SPEARED
R DREARES
READERS
REDEARS
REDSEAR
REREADS
S RESEDAS
T DEAREST
DERATES
ESTRADE
REASTED
REDATES
SEDATER
STEARED
TASERED
V ADVERSE
EVADERS
W DRAWEES
RESAWED

ADEEST 89
SEATED
B BESTEAD
DEBATES
C TEDESCA
D DEADEST
SEDATED
STEADED
F DEAFEST
DEFASTE
DEFEATS
FEASTED
H HEADSET
I IDEATES
L DELATES
STEALED
M STEAMED
N STANDEE
STEANED
R DEAREST
DERATES
ESTRADE
REASTED
REDATES
SEDATER
STEARED
TASERED
S SEDATES
T ESTATED
U SAUTEED
W SWEATED
Y YEASTED

ADEGLN 203
DANGLE
B BANGLED
C CANGLED
CLANGED
GLANCED
D DANGLED
GLADDEN
E ANGELED
GLEANED
F FANGLED
FLANGED
I ALIGNED
DEALING
LEADING
J JANGLED
M MANGLED
N ENDLANG
R DANGLER
GNARLED
S DANGLES
GLANDES
LAGENDS
SLANGED
T TANGLED
U LANGUED
W WANGLED

ADEGNR 138
DANGER
E ANGERED
DERANGE
ENRAGED
GRANDEE
GRENADE
I AREDING
DEARING
DERAIGN
EARDING
GRADINE
GRAINED
READING
L DANGLER
GNARLED
O GROANED
P PRANGED
R GNARRED
GRANDER
S DANGERS
GANDERS
GARDENS
T DRAGNET
GRANTED
U ENGUARD
RAUNGED

ADEGRS 194
GRADES
B BADGERS
C CADGERS
D GADDERS
E DRAGEES
GREASED
F DEFRAGS
G DAGGERS
I AGRISED
L DARGLES
N DANGERS
GANDERS
GARDENS
O DOGEARS
P GRASPED
SPADGER
SPARGED
R GRADERS
REGARDS
S GRASSED
T RADGEST
U DESUGAR
SUGARED

ADEILR 18
DERAIL
A RADIALE
B BALDIER
BEDRAIL
BRAILED
RAILBED
RIDABLE
C DECRIAL
RADICEL
RADICLE
D DIEDRAL
DRAILED
E LEADIER
G GLADIER
GLAIRED
I DELIRIA
IRIDEAL
L DALLIER
DIALLER
RALLIED
O DARIOLE
P PEDRAIL
PREDIAL
R LARDIER
S DERAILS
DIALERS
REDIALS
SIDERAL
T DILATER
REDTAIL
TRAILED
U UREDIAL
V RIVALED
VALIDER
Y READILY

ADEILS 39
LADIES
B BALDIES
DIABLES
DISABLE
C SCAILED
D DAIDLES
LADDIES
E AEDILES
DEISEAL
F DISLEAF
G SILAGED
H HALIDES
I DAILIES
LIAISED
SEDILIA
K SKAILED
L DALLIES
DISLEAL
LALDIES
SALLIED
M MAELIDS
MEDIALS
MISDEAL
MISLEAD
N DENIALS
SNAILED
O DEASOIL
ISOLEAD
P ALIPEDS
ELAPIDS
LAPIDES
PAIDLES
PALSIED
PLEIADS
R DERAILS
DIALERS
REDIALS
SIDERAL
S AIDLESS
DEASILS
T DETAILS
DILATES
U AUDILES
DEASIUL
V DEVISAL
Y DIALYSE
EYLIADS

ADEINR 4
RAINED
A ARANEID
B BANDIER
BRAINED
C CAIRNED
CARNIED
D DANDIER
DRAINED
F FRIANDE
G AREDING

DEARING
DERAIGN
EARDING
GRADINE
GRAINED
READING
H HANDIER
I DENARII
M ADERMIN
INARMED
N NARDINE
O ANEROID
P PARDINE
R DRAINER
RANDIER
S RANDIES
SANDIER
SARDINE
T ANTIRED
DETRAIN
TRAINED
U UNAIRED
URANIDE
V INVADER
RAVINED

ADEINS 24
(SANDIE)
A NAIADES
B BANDIES
BASINED
C CANDIES
INCASED
D DANDIES
SDAINED
E ANISEED
G AGNISED
K KANDIES
L DENIALS
SNAILED
M DEMAINS
MAIDENS
MEDIANS
MEDINAS
SIDEMAN
O ADONISE
ANODISE
SODAINE
P PANDIES
PANSIED
SPAINED
R RANDIES
SANDIER
SARDINE
S SDAINES
T DESTAIN
DETAINS
INSTEAD
SAINTED
SATINED
STAINED
V INVADES
W DEWANIS

ADEIRS 15
RAISED
A ARAISED
B ABIDERS
BRAISED
DARBIES
SEABIRD
SIDEBAR
C CARDIES
DARCIES
RADICES

SIDECAR
E DEARIES
READIES
F FARSIDE
FRAISED
G AGRISED
H AIRSHED
DASHIER
HARDIES
SHADIER
I AIRSIDE
DAIRIES
DIARIES
DIARISE
K DAIKERS
DARKIES
L DERAILS
DIALERS
REDIALS
SIDERAL
M ADMIRES
MARDIES
MISREAD
SEDARIM
SIDEARM
N RANDIES
SANDIER
SARDINE
O ROADIES
SOREDIA
P ASPIRED
DESPAIR
DIAPERS
PRAISED
R ARRIDES
RAIDERS
T ARIDEST
ASTERID
ASTRIDE
DIASTER
DISRATE
STAIDER
STAIRED
TARDIES
TIRADES
U RESIDUA
V ADVISER
VARDIES
X RADIXES

ADEIST 28
(IDATES)
B BASTIDE
C ACIDEST
DACITES
D TADDIES
E IDEATES
F DAFTIES
FADIEST
G AGISTED
L DETAILS
DILATES
M DIASTEM
MISDATE
N DESTAIN
DETAINS
INSTEAD
SAINTED
SATINED
STAINED
O IODATES
TOADIES
R ARIDEST
ASTERID
ASTRIDE

DIASTER
DISRATE
STAIDER
STAIRED
TARDIES
TIRADES
S DISSEAT
SAIDEST
U DAUTIES
V AVIDEST
DATIVES
VISTAED
W DAWTIES
WAISTED

ADELNR 75
LANDER
A ADRENAL
B BLANDER
C CANDLER
D DANDLER
E LEARNED
G DANGLER
GNARLED
H HANDLER
K RANKLED
L LANDLER
M MANDREL
O LADRONE
S DARNELS
ENLARDS
LANDERS
SLANDER
SNARLED
U LAUNDER
LURDANE
RUNDALE
Y DEARNLY

ADELNS 134
(SANDLE)
C CALENDS
CANDLES
D DANDLES
E LEADENS
G DANGLES
GLANDES
LAGENDS
SLANGED
H HANDLES
HANDSEL
I DENIALS
SNAILED
K KALENDS
O LOADENS
R DARNELS
ENLARDS
LANDERS
SLANDER
SNARLED
S SENDALS
T DENTALS
SLANTED
U UNLADES
UNLEADS
Y ADENYLS

ADELRS 85
ALDERS
B BEDRALS
C CRADLES
SCALDER
D LADDERS
RADDLES
SADDLER

E DEALERS
LEADERS
REDEALS
F FARDELS
G DARGLES
H HARELDS
HERALDS
I DERAILS
DIALERS
REDIALS
SIDERAL
K DARKLES
L LADLERS
M MEDLARS
N DARNELS
ENLARDS
LANDERS
SLANDER
SNARLED
O LOADERS
ORDEALS
RELOADS
P PEDLARS
R LARDERS
S RASSLED
SARDELS
T DARTLES
U LAUDERS
W WARSLED
Z DRAZELS

ADELST 104
SALTED
B BALDEST
BLASTED
STABLED
C CASTLED
SCLATED
D STADDLE
E DELATES
STEALED
H DALETHS
I DETAILS
DILATES
K SKLATED
STALKED
L STALLED
M MALTEDS
N DENTALS
SLANTED
O SALTOED
SOLATED
P SPALTED
STAPLED
R DARTLES
S DESALTS
T SLATTED
U AULDEST
SALUTED

ADEMNS 242
AMENDS
A ANADEMS
MAENADS
B BEDAMNS
D DEMANDS
MADDENS
E AMENDES
DEMEANS
SEEDMAN
G GADSMEN
I DEMAINS
MAIDENS
MEDIANS
MEDINAS

SIDEMAN
K DESKMAN
N SANDMEN
O DAEMONS
MASONED
MODENAS
MONADES
NOMADES
P DAMPENS
R DAMNERS
MANREDS
RANDEMS
REMANDS
S DESMANS
MADNESS
T TANDEMS
U MEDUSAN
SUDAMEN
Y DAYSMEN

ADENRS 62
SANDER
B BANDERS
C DANCERS
D DANDERS
E DEANERS
ENDEARS
F FARDENS
G DANGERS
GANDERS
GARDENS
H HANDERS
HARDENS
I RANDIES
SANDIER
SARDINE
K DARKENS
L DARNELS
ENLARDS
LANDERS
SLANDER
SNARLED
M DAMNERS
MANREDS
RANDEMS
REMANDS
P PANDERS
R DARNERS
ERRANDS
SNARRED
S SANDERS
SARSDEN
T ENDARTS
STANDER
STARNED
U ASUNDER
DANSEUR
DAUNERS
W DAWNERS
WANDERS
WARDENS
Z ZANDERS

ADENRU 66
UNREAD
B UNBARED
C DURANCE
UNRACED
D DAUNDER
E UNEARED
G ENGUARD
RAUNGED
H UNHEARD
I UNAIRED
URANIDE

K UNRAKED
L LAUNDER
LURDANE
RUNDALE
M DURAMEN
MANURED
MAUNDER
UNARMED
O RONDEAU
P UNDRAPE
UNPARED
S ASUNDER
DANSEUR
DAUNERS
T DAUNTER
NATURED
UNRATED
UNTREAD
Y UNREADY
Z UNRAZED

ADENST 44
STANED
A ANSATED
C DECANTS
DESCANT
SCANTED
E STANDEE
STEANED
G STANGED
H HANDSET
I DESTAIN
DETAINS
INSTEAD
SAINTED
SATINED
STAINED
K DANKEST
L DENTALS
SLANTED
M TANDEMS
N STANDEN
O ASTONED
DONATES
ONSTEAD
P PEDANTS
PENTADS
R ENDARTS
STANDER
STARNED
T ATTENDS
U SAUNTED
UNSATED
V ADVENTS
Y STAYNED

ADEORS 26
ADORES
C SARCODE
D DEODARS
E OREADES
F FEDORAS
G DOGEARS
I ROADIES
SOREDIA
L LOADERS
ORDEALS
RELOADS
M RADOMES
O ROADEOS
R ADORERS
DROSERA
S SARODES
T DOATERS
ROASTED

TORSADE
TROADES
U AROUSED
V OVERSAD
SAVORED
W REDOWAS

ADEPRT 232
PARTED
A ADAPTER
READAPT
E ADEPTER
PREDATE
RETAPED
TAPERED
I DIPTERA
PARTIED
PIRATED
M TRAMPED
O ADOPTER
READOPT
P TRAPPED
S DEPARTS
DRAPETS
PETARDS
T PRATTED
U UPDATER
UPRATED

ADERRS 237
DARERS
A ARRASED
C CARDERS
SCARRED
E DREARES
READERS
REDEARS
REDSEAR
REREADS
G GRADERS
REGARDS
I ARRIDES
RAIDERS
L LARDERS
N DARNERS
ERRANDS
SNARRED
O ADORERS
DROSERA
P DRAPERS
SPARRED
T DARTERS
DARTRES
RETARDS
STARRED
TRADERS
W DRAWERS
REDRAWS
REWARDS
WARDERS

ADERST 53
STARED
B DABSTER
TABERDS
C REDACTS
SCARTED
D ADDREST
RADDEST
E DEAREST
DERATES
ESTRADE
REASTED
REDATES
SEDATER
STEARED
TASERED
F STRAFED
G RADGEST
H DEARTHS
HARDEST
HARDSET
HATREDS
THREADS
TRASHED
I ARIDEST
ASTERID
ASTRIDE
DIASTER
DISRATE
STAIDER
STAIRED
TARDIES
TIRADES
K DARKEST
STARKED
STRAKED
L DARTLES
M SMARTED
N ENDARTS
STANDER
STARNED
O DOATERS
ROASTED
TORSADE
TROADES
P DEPARTS
DRAPETS
PETARDS
R DARTERS
DARTRES
RETARDS
STARRED
TRADERS
T STARTED
TETRADS
V ADVERTS
STARVED
W STEWARD
STRAWED
WRASTED
Y STRAYED

ADGINR 122
DARING
B BARDING
BRIGAND
C CARDING
D RADDING
E AREDING
DEARING
DERAIGN
EARDING
GRADINE
GRAINED
READING
F FARDING
G GRADING
NIGGARD
I GRADINI
RAIDING
K DARKING
L DARLING
LARDING
M MRIDANG
N DARNING
NARDING
RANDING
O ADORING
GRADINO
ROADING
P DRAPING
R DARRING
S DARINGS
GRADINS
T DARTING
TRADING
U DAURING
W DRAWING
WARDING
Y DRAYING
YARDING

ADINRS 111
DRAINS
A RADIANS
B RIBANDS
E RANDIES
SANDIER
SARDINE
F FRIANDS
G DARINGS
GRADINS
K DISRANK
L ALDRINS
M MANDIRS
N INNARDS
O INROADS
ORDAINS
SADIRON
Q QINDARS
T INDARTS
U DURIANS
SUNDARI
W INWARDS

AEELRS 67
LEASER
C ALERCES
CEREALS
RELACES
RESCALE
SCLERAE
D DEALERS
LEADERS
REDEALS
E RELEASE
G GALERES
REGALES
H HEALERS
I EARLIES
REALISE
K LEAKERS
M MEALERS
N LEANERS
O AREOLES
P LEAPERS
PLEASER
PRESALE
RELAPSE
REPEALS
S EARLESS
LEASERS
RESALES
RESEALS
SEALERS
T ELATERS
REALEST
RELATES
RESLATE
STEALER
U LEASURE
V LAVEERS
LEAVERS
REVEALS
SEVERAL
VEALERS
X RELAXES
Y SEALERY

AEEMRS 241
SEAMER
B AMBEERS
BEAMERS
BESMEAR
C AMERCES
CAREMES
RACEMES
D REMADES
REMEADS
SMEARED
G MEAGRES
H HAREEMS
MAHSEER
I SEAMIER
SERIEMA
K REMAKES
L MEALERS
N MEANERS
RENAMES
P AMPERES
EMPARES
R REAMERS
SMEARER
S SEAMERS
T REMATES
RETEAMS
STEAMER
TEAMERS
U MEASURE

AEEPRT 144
REPEAT
A PATERAE
D ADEPTER
PREDATE
RETAPED
TAPERED
H PREHEAT
I PEATIER
K PERTAKE
L PETRALE
PLEATER
PRELATE
REPLATE
M TEMPERA
O OPERATE
P PRETAPE
R PEARTER
TAPERER
S REPEATS
RETAPES
U EPURATE
Y PEATERY
Z TRAPEZE

AEERRS 155
ERASER
B BEARERS
BREARES
C CAREERS
CREASER
D DREARES
READERS
REDEARS
REDSEAR
REREADS
F FEARERS
G GREASER
REGEARS
H HEARERS
REHEARS
SHEARER
I REARISE
RERAISE
M REAMERS
SMEARER
N EARNERS
REEARNS
O REAROSE
P REAPERS
SPEARER
R REARERS
S ERASERS
T RETEARS
SERRATE
TEARERS
U ERASURE
V REAVERS
W SWEARER
WEARERS

AEERST 21
EATERS
A AERATES
B BEATERS
BERATES
REBATES
C CERATES
CREATES
ECARTES
SECRETA
D DEAREST
DERATES
ESTRADE
REASTED
REDATES
SEDATER
STEARED
TASERED
F AFREETS
FEASTER
G ERGATES
RESTAGE
H AETHERS
HEATERS
REHEATS
I AERIEST
SERIATE
K RETAKES
SAKERET
L ELATERS
REALEST
RELATES
RESLATE
STEALER
M REMATES
RETEAMS
STEAMER
TEAMERS
N EARNEST
EASTERN
NEAREST
O ROSEATE
P REPEATS
RETAPES
R RETEARS
SERRATE
TEARERS
S EASTERS
RESEATS
SAETERS
SEAREST
SEATERS
STEARES
TEASERS
TESSERA
T ESTREAT
RESTATE
RETASTE
U AUSTERE
W SWEATER
X RETAXES

AEGILN 59
(EALING)
C ANGELIC
ANGLICE
GALENIC
D ALIGNED
DEALING
LEADING
E LINEAGE
F FEALING
FINAGLE
LEAFING
G GEALING
LIGNAGE
H HEALING
K LEAKING
LINKAGE
L GALLEIN
NIGELLA
M GEMINAL
LEAMING
MEALING
N ANELING
EANLING
LEANING
NEALING
P LEAPING
PEALING
PLEAING
R ALIGNER
ENGRAIL
LAERING
LEARING
NARGILE
REALIGN
REGINAL
S LEASING
LINAGES
SEALING
T ATINGLE
ELATING
GELATIN
GENITAL
U LINGUAE
UNAGILE
V LEAVING
VEALING
Y ALEYING
YEALING

AEGINR 12
REGAIN
A ANERGIA
B BEARING
C ANERGIC
GRECIAN
D AREDING
DEARING
DERAIGN
EARDING
GRADINE
GRAINED
READING
E REGINAE
F FEARING
G GEARING

NAGGIER
H HEARING
K REAKING
L ALIGNER
ENGRAIL
LAERING
LEARING
NARGILE
REALIGN
REGINAL
M GERMAIN
GERMINA
MANGIER
MEARING
REAMING
N AGINNER
EARNING
ENGRAIN
GRANNIE
NEARING
O ORIGANE
P REAPING
R ANGRIER
EARRING
GRAINER
RANGIER
REARING
S ANGRIES
EARINGS
ERASING
GAINERS
GRAINES
REAGINS
REGAINS
REGINAS
SEARING
SERINGA
T GRANITE
GRATINE
INGRATE
TANGIER
TEARING
V REAVING
VINEGAR
W WEARING
Z ZINGARE

AEGLNR 88
ANGLER
A ALNAGER
B BRANGLE
C CLANGER
GLANCER
D DANGLER
GNARLED
E ENLARGE
GENERAL
GLEANER
F FLANGER
G GANGREL
I ALIGNER
ENGRAIL
LAERING
LEARING
NARGILE
REALIGN
REGINAL
J JANGLER
L LANGREL
M MANGLER
P GRAPNEL
S ANGLERS
LARGENS
SLANGER
T TANGLER
TRANGLE
U GRANULE
W WANGLER
WRANGLE
Y ANGERLY

AEGLNS 173
GLEANS
A ALNAGES
ANLAGES
GALENAS
LAGENAS
LASAGNE
B BANGLES
C CANGLES
GLANCES
D DANGLES
GLANDES
LAGENDS
SLANGED
F FANGLES
FLANGES
G LAGGENS
I LEASING
LINAGES
SEALING
J JANGLES
L LEGLANS
M MANGELS
MANGLES
O ENGAOLS
P SPANGLE
R ANGLERS
LARGENS
SLANGER
S GLASSEN
T GELANTS
LANGEST
TANGLES
U ANGELUS
LAGUNES
LANGUES
W WANGLES
Y LYNAGES

AEGLNT 113
TANGLE
D TANGLED
E ELEGANT
H ALENGTH
I ATINGLE
ELATING
GELATIN
GENITAL
L GELLANT
O TANGELO
R TANGLER
TRANGLE
S GELANTS
LANGEST
TANGLES
T GANTLET
U LANGUET
W TWANGLE

AEGLRS 172
LAGERS
A ALEGARS
LAAGERS
B GARBLES
D DARGLES
E GALERES
REGALES
F REFLAGS
G GARGLES
LAGGERS
RAGGLES
I GLAIRES
GRAILES
K GRAKLES
M MALGRES
N ANGLERS
LARGENS
SLANGER
O GALORES
GAOLERS
P GRAPLES
S LARGESS
T LARGEST
V GRAVELS
VERGLAS
Y ARGYLES
GRAYLES
Z GLAZERS

AEGLST 193
AGLETS
A AGELAST
ALGATES
LASTAGE
B GABLETS
E EAGLETS
GELATES
LEGATES
SEGETAL
TEAGLES
TELEGAS
H HAGLETS
I AGILEST
AIGLETS
LIGATES
TAIGLES
L GALLETS
N GELANTS
LANGEST
TANGLES
O GELATOS
LEGATOS
R LARGEST
T GESTALT
W TALWEGS

AEGNRS 90
ANGERS
B BANGERS
GRABENS
D DANGERS
GANDERS
GARDENS
E ENRAGES
G GANGERS
GRANGES
NAGGERS
H GNASHER
HANGERS
REHANGS
I ANGRIES
EARINGS
ERASING
GAINERS
GRAINES
REAGINS
REGAINS
REGINAS
SEARING
SERINGA
L ANGLERS
LARGENS
SLANGER
M ENGRAMS
GERMANS
MANGERS
O ONAGERS
ORANGES
P ENGRASP
R GARNERS
RANGERS
S SANGERS
SERANGS
T ARGENTS
GARNETS
STRANGE
U RAUNGES
UNGEARS
W GNAWERS

AEGNRT 32
GARNET
A TANAGER
D DRAGNET
GRANTED
E GRANTEE
GREATEN
NEGATER
REAGENT
F ENGRAFT
I GRANITE
GRATINE
INGRATE
TANGIER
TEARING
L TANGLER
TRANGLE
M GARMENT
MARGENT
RAGMENT
N REGNANT
O NEGATOR
P TREPANG
R GRANTER
REGRANT
S ARGENTS
GARNETS
STRANGE
U GAUNTER
W TWANGER
Y AGENTRY

AEGNST 96
AGENTS
A AGNATES
D STANGED
E NEGATES
H STENGAH
I EASTING
EATINGS
GAINEST
GENISTA
INGATES
INGESTA
SEATING
TANGIES
TEASING
TSIGANE
L GELANTS
LANGEST
TANGLES
M MAGNETS
N GANNETS
O ONSTAGE
R ARGENTS
GARNETS
STRANGE
T GESTANT

AEGRST 81
GREATS
A AGRASTE
GASTREA
TEARGAS
B BARGEST
D RADGEST
E ERGATES
RESTAGE
G GAGSTER
GARGETS
STAGGER
TAGGERS
H GATHERS
I AGISTER
AIGRETS
GAITERS
SEAGIRT
STAGIER
STRIGAE
TRIAGES
L LARGEST
N ARGENTS
GARNETS
STRANGE
O GAROTES
ORGEATS
STORAGE
TOERAGS
P PARGETS
R GARRETS
GARTERS
GRATERS
S GASTERS
STAGERS
T TARGETS
V GRAVEST
Y GRAYEST
GYRATES
STAGERY

AEHLRT 215
LATHER
A TREHALA
B BLATHER
HALBERT
C ARCHLET
TRACHLE
E HALTERE
LEATHER
F FARTHEL
I LATHIER
M THERMAL
N ENTHRAL
O LOATHER
RATHOLE
S HALTERS
HARSLET
LATHERS
SLATHER
THALERS
Y EARTHLY
HARTELY
HEARTLY
LATHERY

AEHRST 174
HATERS
B BATHERS
BERTHAS
BREATHS
C ARCHEST
CHARETS
CHASTER
RACHETS
RATCHES
D DEARTHS
HARDEST
HARDSET
HATREDS
THREADS
TRASHED
E AETHERS
HEATERS
REHEATS
F FATHERS
HAFTERS
SHAFTER
G GATHERS
H HEARTHS
I HASTIER
SHERIAT
L HALTERS
HARSLET
LATHERS
SLATHER
THALERS
M HAMSTER
N ANTHERS
HARTENS
THENARS
O ASTHORE
EARSHOT
HAROSET
P SPARTHE
TEPHRAS
THREAPS
S RASHEST
SHASTER
TRASHES
T HATTERS
RATHEST
SHATTER
THREATS
V HARVEST
THRAVES
W SWATHER
THAWERS
WREATHS

AEILMN 108
MENIAL
A LAMINAE
B MINABLE
C CNEMIAL
MELANIC
F FEMINAL
INFLAME
G GEMINAL
LEAMING
MEALING
H HELIMAN
K MANLIKE
L MANILLE
M MAILMEN
N LINEMAN
MELANIN
O MINEOLA
P IMPANEL
MANIPLE
R MANLIER
MARLINE
MINERAL
RAILMEN
S ISLEMAN
MALINES
MENIALS
SEMINAL
T AILMENT
ALIMENT

U ALUMINE

AEILNT 14
ENTAIL
A ANTLIAE
E LINEATE
F INFLATE
G ATINGLE
ELATING
GELATIN
GENITAL
K ANTLIKE
M AILMENT
ALIMENT
O ELATION
TOENAIL
P PANTILE
R ENTRAIL
LATRINE
RATLINE
RELIANT
RETINAL
TRENAIL
S EASTLIN
ELASTIN
ENTAILS
NAILSET
SALIENT
SALTINE
SLAINTE
STANIEL
TENAILS
U ALUNITE
V VENTAIL

AEILRS 20
SAILER
A AERIALS
B BAILERS
C CLARIES
ECLAIRS
SCALIER
D DERAILS
DIALERS
REDIALS
SIDERAL
E EARLIES
REALISE
G GLAIRES
GRAILES
H HAILERS
SHALIER
I LAIRISE
J JAILERS
K LAIKERS
SERKALI
L RALLIES
SALLIER
M MAILERS
REALISM
REMAILS
N ALINERS
NAILERS
RENAILS
P PALSIER
PARLIES
R RAILERS
RERAILS
S AIRLESS
RESAILS
SAILERS
SERAILS
SERIALS
T REALIST
RETAILS
SALTIER
SALTIRE
SLATIER
TAILERS
V REVISAL
W SWALIER
WAILERS

AEILRT 13
RETAIL
B LIBRATE
TABLIER
TRIABLE
C ARTICLE
RECITAL
TALCIER
D DILATER
REDTAIL
TRAILED
E ATELIER
REALTIE
H LATHIER
K RATLIKE
TALKIER
L LITERAL
TALLIER
M LAMITER
MALTIER
MARLITE
N ENTRAIL
LATRINE
RATLINE
RELIANT
RETINAL
TRENAIL
P PLAITER
PLATIER
R RETIRAL
RETRIAL
TRAILER
S REALIST
RETAILS
SALTIER
SALTIRE
SLATIER
TAILERS
T TERTIAL
U URALITE
W WALTIER
Y IRATELY
REALITY
TEARILY

AEILSS 238
LASSIE
A ALIASES
B ABSEILS
ISABELS
LABISES
C SALICES
D AIDLESS
DEASILS
F FALSIES
FILASSE
G ALGESIS
GLASSIE
LIGASES
SILAGES
H SHEILAS
I LIAISES
SILESIA
K ALSIKES
ASSLIKE
L ALLISES
SALLIES
M AIMLESS
MESAILS
SAMIELS
SEISMAL
N SALINES
SILANES
P ESPIALS
LAPISES
LIPASES
PALSIES
R AIRLESS
RESAILS
SAILERS
SERAILS
SERIALS
S LAISSES
LASSIES
T SALTIES
U SAULIES
V VALISES
VESSAIL
W WALISES

AEILST 25
SALTIE
B ABLEIST
ALBITES
ASTILBE
BASTILE
BESTIAL
BLASTIE
LIBATES
STABILE
C ASTELIC
ELASTIC
LACIEST
LATICES
SALICET
D DETAILS
DILATES
F FETIALS
G AGILEST
AIGLETS
LIGATES
TAIGLES
H HALITES
HELIAST
I LAITIES
K LAKIEST
TALKIES
L TAILLES
TALLIES
N EASTLIN
ELASTIN
ENTAILS
NAILSET
SALIENT
SALTINE
SLAINTE
STANIEL
TENAILS
O ISOLATE
P APLITES
PALIEST
PLATIES
TALIPES
R REALIST
RETAILS
SALTIER
SALTIRE
SLATIER
TAILERS
S SALTIES
U SITULAE
V ESTIVAL
W WALIEST
Y TAILYES
Z LAZIEST

AEIMNR 64
REMAIN
B MIRBANE
C CARMINE
D ADERMIN
INARMED
E REMANIE
F FIREMAN
G GERMAIN
GERMINA
MANGIER
MEARING
REAMING
H HARMINE
K MANKIER
RAMEKIN
L MANLIER
MARLINE
MINERAL
RAILMEN
O MORAINE
ROMAINE
R MARINER
S MARINES
REMAINS
SEMINAR
SIRNAME
T MINARET
RAIMENT
V VERMIAN
W WIREMAN

AEIMNS 95
MANIES
A AMNESIA
ANEMIAS
C AMNESIC
CINEMAS
D DEMAINS
MAIDENS
MEDIANS
MEDINAS
SIDEMAN
E MEANIES
NEMESIA
F FAMINES
INFAMES
G ENIGMAS
GAMINES
MEASING
SEAMING
H HAEMINS
HEMINAS
J JASMINE
K KINEMAS
L ISLEMAN
MALINES
MENIALS
SEMINAL
M AMMINES
MISNAME
O ANOMIES
R MARINES
REMAINS
SEMINAR
SIRNAME
S INSEAMS
SAMISEN
T ETAMINS
INMATES
MAINEST
MANTIES
TAMEINS
TAMINES
W MANWISE

AEIMNT 36
INMATE
A AMENTIA
ANIMATE
B AMBIENT
C EMICANT
NEMATIC
D MEDIANT
E ETAMINE
MATINEE
G MINTAGE
TEAMING
TEGMINA
H HEMATIN
I INTIMAE
MINIATE
L AILMENT
ALIMENT
N MANNITE
O AMNIOTE
R MINARET
RAIMENT
S ETAMINS
INMATES
MAINEST
MANTIES
TAMEINS
TAMINES
X TAXIMEN
Y AMENITY
ANYTIME

AEIMRS 109
ARMIES
B AMBRIES
D ADMIRES
MARDIES
MISREAD
SEDARIM
SIDEARM
E SEAMIER
SERIEMA
F MISFARE
G GISARME
IMAGERS
MAIGRES
MIRAGES
H MASHIER
MISHEAR
L MAILERS
REALISM
REMAILS
M MAIMERS
RAMMIES
N MARINES
REMAINS
SEMINAR
SIRNAME
P IMPRESA
SAMPIRE
R MARRIES
SIMARRE
S MASSIER
T IMARETS
MAESTRI
MAISTER
MASTIER
MISRATE
SEMITAR
SMARTIE
U UREMIAS
V MISAVER
W AWMRIES
SEMIRAW

AEIMST 99
MISEAT
C ACMITES
ETACISM
MICATES
SEMATIC
D DIASTEM
MISDATE
E STEAMIE
G GAMIEST
SIGMATE
H ATHEISM
I AMITIES
ATIMIES
K MISTAKE
M MISMATE
SEMIMAT
TAMMIES
N ETAMINS
INMATES
MAINEST
MANTIES
TAMEINS
TAMINES
O AMOSITE
ATOMIES
ATOMISE
OSMIATE
P IMPASTE
PASTIME
R IMARETS
MAESTRI
MAISTER
MASTIER
MISRATE
SEMITAR
SMARTIE
S ASTEISM
MISEATS
MISSEAT
SAMIEST
SAMITES
TAMISES
T ETATISM
MATIEST
MATTIES
Z MAZIEST
MESTIZA

AEINRS 6
SARNIE
C ARCSINE
ARSENIC
CARNIES
CERASIN
D RANDIES
SANDIER
SARDINE
F INFARES
SERAFIN
G ANGRIES
EARINGS
ERASING
GAINERS
GRAINES
REAGINS
REGAINS
REGINAS
SEARING
SERINGA

H ARSHINE
HERNIAS
I SENARII
J INJERAS
K SNAKIER
L ALINERS
NAILERS
RENAILS
M MARINES
REMAINS
SEMINAR
SIRNAME
N INSANER
INSNARE
O ERASION
P PANIERS
RAPINES
R SIERRAN
SNARIER
S ARSINES
SARNIES
T ANESTRI
ANTSIER
NASTIER
RATINES
RESIANT
RETAINS
RETINAS
RETSINA
STAINER
STARNIE
STEARIN
V AVENIRS
RAVINES

AEINRT 1
RETAIN
B ATEBRIN
C CANTIER
CERATIN
CERTAIN
CREATIN
CRINATE
NACRITE
D ANTIRED
DETRAIN
TRAINED
E ARENITE
RETINAE
TRAINEE
F FAINTER
FENITAR
G GRANITE
GRATINE
INGRATE
TANGIER
TEARING
H HAIRNET
INEARTH
THERIAN
I INERTIA
J JANTIER
NARTJIE
K KERATIN
L ENTRAIL
LATRINE
RATLINE
RELIANT
RETINAL
TRENAIL
M MINARET
RAIMENT
N ENTRAIN
TRANNIE
O OTARINE

P PAINTER
PERTAIN
REPAINT
R RETRAIN
TERRAIN
TRAINER
S ANESTRI
ANTSIER
NASTIER
RATINES
RESIANT
RETAINS
RETINAS
RETSINA
STAINER
STARNIE
STEARIN
T INTREAT
ITERANT
NATTIER
NITRATE
TARTINE
TERTIAN
U RUINATE
TAURINE
URANITE
URINATE
W TAWNIER
TINWARE

AEINST 2
(SATINE)
A ENTASIA
TAENIAS
B BANTIES
BASINET
BESAINT
BESTAIN
C ACETINS
CANIEST
CINEAST
D DESTAIN
DETAINS
INSTEAD
SAINTED
SATINED
STAINED
E ETESIAN
F FAINEST
NAIFEST
G EASTING
EATINGS
GAINEST
GENISTA
INGATES
INGESTA
SEATING
TANGIES
TEASING
TSIGANE
H SHEITAN
STHENIA
I ISATINE
J JANTIES
TAJINES
K INTAKES
KENTIAS
TANKIES
L EASTLIN
ELASTIN
ENTAILS
NAILSET
SALIENT
SALTINE
SLAINTE

STANIEL
TENAILS
M ETAMINS
INMATES
MAINEST
MANTIES
TAMEINS
TAMINES
N INANEST
STANINE
O ATONIES
P PANTIES
PATINES
SAPIENT
SPINATE
R ANESTRI
ANTSIER
NASTIER
RATINES
RESIANT
RETAINS
RETINAS
RETSINA
STAINER
STARNIE
STEARIN
S ENTASIS
NASTIES
SESTINA
TANSIES
TISANES
T INSTATE
SATINET
U AUNTIES
SINUATE
V NAIVEST
NATIVES
VAINEST
W AWNIEST
TAWNIES
WANIEST
WANTIES
X ANTISEX
SEXTAIN
Z ZANIEST
ZEATINS

AEIPRS 78
PRAISE
A SPIRAEA
C EPACRIS
SCRAPIE
SPACIER
D ASPIRED
DESPAIR
DIAPERS
PRAISED
E APERIES
EPEIRAS
G GASPIER
PRISAGE
SPAIRGE
H HARPIES
SHARPIE
K PARKIES
SPARKIE
L PALSIER
PARLIES
M IMPRESA
SAMPIRE
N PANIERS
RAPINES
O SOAPIER
P APPRISE
SAPPIER

R ASPIRER
PARRIES
PRAISER
RAPIERS
RASPIER
REPAIRS
S ASPIRES
PARESIS
PARISES
PRAISES
SPIREAS
T PARTIES
PASTIER
PIASTER
PIASTRE
PIRATES
PRATIES
TRAIPSE
U SPURIAE
UPRAISE
V PARVISE
PAVISER
W WASPIER

AEIRST 3
SATIRE
A ARISTAE
ASTERIA
ATRESIA
B BAITERS
BARITES
REBAITS
TERBIAS
C CRISTAE
RACIEST
STEARIC
D ARIDEST
ASTERID
ASTRIDE
DIASTER
DISRATE
STAIDER
STAIRED
TARDIES
TIRADES
E AERIEST
SERIATE
F FAIREST
G AGISTER
AIGRETS
GAITERS
SEAGIRT
STAGIER
STRIGAE
TRIAGES
H HASTIER
SHERIAT
I AIRIEST
IRISATE
K ARKITES
KARITES
L REALIST
RETAILS
SALTIER
SALTIRE
SLATIER
TAILERS
M IMARETS
MAESTRI
MAISTER
MASTIER
MISRATE
SEMITAR
SMARTIE
N ANESTRI

ANTSIER
NASTIER
RATINES
RESIANT
RETAINS
RETINAS
RETSINA
STAINER
STARNIE
STEARIN
O OARIEST
OTARIES
P PARTIES
PASTIER
PIASTER
PIASTRE
PIRATES
PRATIES
TRAIPSE
R ARTSIER
SERRATI
TARRIES
TARSIER
S ARTSIES
SAIREST
SATIRES
TIRASSE
T ARTIEST
ARTISTE
ATTIRES
IRATEST
RATITES
STRIATE
TASTIER
TERTIAS
V TAIVERS
VASTIER
VERITAS
W WAISTER
WAITERS
WARIEST
WASTRIE

AEIRTT 34
ATTIRE
A ARIETTA
B BATTIER
BIRETTA
C CATTIER
CITRATE
D ATTIRED
E ARIETTE
ITERATE
F FATTIER
L TERTIAL
N INTREAT
ITERANT
NATTIER
NITRATE
TARTINE
TERTIAN
P PARTITE
R RATTIER
RETRAIT
TARTIER
S ARTIEST
ARTISTE
ATTIRES
IRATEST
RATITES
STRIATE
TASTIER
TERTIAS
T ATTRITE
TATTIER

TITRATE
V TAIVERT
W TAWTIER
X EXTRAIT

AEISTT 83
(TASTIE)
A SATIATE
B BATISTE
BISTATE
C CATTIES
STATICE
TIETACS
F FATTIES
H ATHEIST
STAITHE
K TAKIEST
M ETATISM
MATIEST
MATTIES
N INSTATE
SATINET
O OSTIATE
TOASTIE
P PATTIES
TAPETIS
R ARTIEST
ARTISTE
ATTIRES
IRATEST
RATITES
STRIATE
TASTIER
TERTIAS
T ETATIST
TATTIES
U SITUATE
V STATIVE
W TAWIEST
TWAITES
X TAXITES
Y SATIETY

AELMNT 214
LAMENT
A AMENTAL
B BELTMAN
LAMBENT
D MANTLED
E MANTEEL
TELEMAN
I AILMENT
ALIMENT
M MALTMEN
O LOMENTA
OMENTAL
TELAMON
S LAMENTS
MANTELS
MANTLES
T MANTLET
U NUTMEAL

AELNRS 49
LEARNS
A ARSENAL
B BRANLES
BRANSLE
C LANCERS
RANCELS
D DARNELS
ENLARDS
LANDERS
SLANDER
SNARLED

E LEANERS
F SALFERN
G ANGLERS
LARGENS
SLANGER
I ALINERS
NAILERS
RENAILS
K RANKLES
M ALMNERS
N ENSNARL
LANNERS
O LOANERS
ORLEANS
RELOANS
P PLANERS
REPLANS
R SNARLER
S RANSELS
T ANTLERS
RENTALS
SALTERN
STERNAL
Z RANZELS

AELNRT 33
ANTLER
B BRANTLE
C CENTRAL
E ALTERNE
ENTERAL
ETERNAL
TELERAN
G TANGLER
TRANGLE
H ENTHRAL
I ENTRAIL
LATRINE
RATLINE
RELIANT
RETINAL
TRENAIL
L ENTRALL
N LANTERN
P PANTLER
PLANTER
REPLANT
S ANTLERS
RENTALS
SALTERN
STERNAL
T TRENTAL
U NEUTRAL
V VENTRAL

AELNST 40
LATENS
A SEALANT
C CANTLES
CENTALS
LANCETS
SCANTLE
D DENTALS
SLANTED
E ELANETS
LATEENS
LEANEST
G GELANTS
LANGEST
TANGLES
H HANTLES
I EASTLIN
ELASTIN
ENTAILS
NAILSET
SALIENT
SALTINE
SLAINTE
STANIEL
TENAILS
K ANKLETS
ASKLENT
LANKEST
M LAMENTS
MANTELS
MANTLES
N STANNEL
O ETALONS
TOLANES
P PLANETS
PLATENS
R ANTLERS
RENTALS
SALTERN
STERNAL
T LATENTS
LATTENS
TALENTS
U ELUANTS
UNLASTE
V LEVANTS
Y STANYEL
Z ZELANTS

AELORS 29
(ALOSER)
A AREOLAS
B LABROSE
C CLAROES
COALERS
ESCOLAR
ORACLES
RECOALS
SOLACER
D LOADERS
ORDEALS
RELOADS
E AREOLES
F LOAFERS
SAFROLE
G GALORES
GAOLERS
H SHOALER
L ROSELLA
M MORALES
N LOANERS
ORLEANS
RELOANS
O AEROSOL
ROSEOLA
P PAROLES
REPOSAL
S LASSOER
OARLESS
SEROSAL
SOLERAS
T OESTRAL

AELOST 42
SOLATE
B BOATELS
OBLATES
C ALECOST
LACTOSE
LOCATES
SCATOLE
TALCOSE
D SALTOED
SOLATED
E OLEATES
F FOLATES
G GELATOS
LEGATOS
H LOATHES
I ISOLATE
K SKATOLE
M MALTOSE
N ETALONS
TOLANES
P APOSTLE
PELOTAS
R OESTRAL
S SOLATES
V SOLVATE
Z ZEALOTS

AELPRS 216
PEARLS
A EARLAPS
C CARPELS
CLASPER
CRAPLES
PARCELS
PLACERS
RECLASP
SCALPER
D PEDLARS
E LEAPERS
PLEASER
PRESALE
RELAPSE
REPEALS
F FELSPAR
G GRAPLES
H PLASHER
SPHERAL
I PALSIER
PARLIES
K SPARKLE
L SPALLER
M EMPARLS
LAMPERS
PALMERS
SAMPLER
N PLANERS
REPLANS
O PAROLES
REPOSAL
P LAPPERS
RAPPELS
SLAPPER
R PARRELS
S LAPSERS
T PALTERS
PERSALT
PLASTER
PLATERS
PSALTER
STAPLER
U PERUSAL
PLEURAS
SERPULA
W PRAWLES
Y PARLEYS
PARSLEY
PLAYERS
REPLAYS
SPARELY

AELPRT 209
PLATER
A APTERAL
C PLECTRA
E PETRALE
PLEATER
PRELATE
REPLATE
I PLAITER
PLATIER
M TEMPLAR
TRAMPLE
N PANTLER
PLANTER
REPLANT
O PROLATE
S PALTERS
PERSALT
PLASTER
PLATERS
PSALTER
STAPLER
T PARTLET
PLATTER
PRATTLE
Y PEARTLY
PEYTRAL
PRELATY
PTERYLA

AELRST 48
ALERTS
B ALBERTS
BATLERS
BLASTER
LABRETS
STABLER
C CARTELS
CLARETS
CRESTAL
SCARLET
TARCELS
D DARTLES
E ELATERS
REALEST
RELATES
RESLATE
STEALER
F FALTERS
G LARGEST
H HALTERS
HARSLET
LATHERS
SLATHER
THALERS
I REALIST
RETAILS
SALTIER
SALTIRE
SLATIER
TAILERS
K STALKER
TALKERS
L STELLAR
TELLARS
M ARMLETS
LAMSTER
MARTELS
TRAMELS
N ANTLERS
RENTALS
SALTERN
STERNAL
O OESTRAL
P PALTERS
PERSALT
PLASTER
PLATERS
PSALTER
STAPLER
S ARTLESS
LASTERS
SALTERS
SLATERS
TARSELS
T RATTLES
SLATTER
STARLET
STARTLE
TATLERS
U ESTRUAL
SALUTER
V TRAVELS
VARLETS
VESTRAL
W WARSTLE
WASTREL
WRASTLE
Y RAYLETS

AEMNST 171
STAMEN
A NAMASTE
B BATSMEN
D TANDEMS
E ENTAMES
MEANEST
G MAGNETS
H ANTHEMS
HETMANS
I ETAMINS
INMATES
MAINEST
MANTIES
TAMEINS
TAMINES
L LAMENTS
MANTELS
MANTLES
O MANTOES
P ENSTAMP
TAPSMEN
R ARTSMEN
MARTENS
SARMENT
SMARTEN
S STAMENS
U UNTAMES
UNTEAMS
Y AMNESTY

AEMRST 136
MATERS
A AMEARST
RETAMAS
B TAMBERS
C MERCATS
D SMARTED
E REMATES
RETEAMS
STEAMER
TEAMERS
H HAMSTER
I IMARETS
MAESTRI
MAISTER
MASTIER
MISRATE
SEMITAR
SMARTIE
J RAMJETS
K MARKETS
L ARMLETS
LAMSTER
MARTELS
TRAMELS
M STAMMER
N ARTSMEN
MARTENS
SARMENT
SMARTEN
O AMORETS
MAESTRO
OMERTAS
P EMPARTS
RESTAMP
STAMPER
TAMPERS
R ARMREST
SMARTER
S MASTERS
STREAMS
T MATTERS
SMATTER
U MATURES
STRUMAE
W WARMEST
Y MASTERY
MAYSTER
STREAMY

AENNST 150
(ANNETS)
A ANNATES
B BANNETS
C NASCENT
D STANDEN
E NEATENS
F ENFANTS
G GANNETS
I INANEST
STANINE
K KANTENS
L STANNEL
R TANNERS
T TANNEST
TENANTS
W WANNEST

AENPST 157
PATENS
A ANAPEST
PEASANT
C CATNEPS
D PEDANTS
PENTADS
E NEPETAS
PENATES
PESANTE
H HAPTENS
I PANTIES
PATINES
SAPIENT
SPINATE
L PLANETS
PLATENS
M ENSTAMP
TAPSMEN
O TEOPANS
P PETNAPS
R ARPENTS
ENTRAPS
PANTERS
PARENTS
PASTERN
PERSANT
TREPANS
S APTNESS
PATNESS
PESANTS
T PATENTS

PATTENS
U PEANUTS
PESAUNT
W STEWPAN
Y SYNAPTE
Z PEZANTS

AENRRT 91
ERRANT
A NARRATE
E TERRANE
G GRANTER
REGRANT
I RETRAIN
TERRAIN
TRAINER
O ORNATER
P PARTNER
S ERRANTS
RANTERS
T TRANTER
Y TERNARY

AENRSS 228
SNARES
A NARASES
C ANCRESS
CASERNS
D SANDERS
SARSDEN
E ENSEARS
F FARNESS
G SANGERS
SERANGS
H HARNESS
I ARSINES
SARNIES
K KRANSES
L RANSELS
O REASONS
SENORAS
R SERRANS
SNARERS
S SARSENS
T SARSNET
TRANSES
W ANSWERS
RAWNESS
Y SARNEYS

AENRST 11
ASTERN
A ANESTRA
B BANTERS
C CANTERS
CARNETS
NECTARS
RECANTS
SCANTER
TANRECS
TRANCES
D ENDARTS
STANDER
STARNED
E EARNEST
EASTERN
NEAREST
G ARGENTS
GARNETS
STRANGE
H ANTHERS
HARTENS
THENARS
I ANESTRI
ANTSIER
NASTIER
RATINES
RESIANT
RETAINS
RETINAS
RETSINA
STAINER
STARNIE
STEARIN
K RANKEST
STARKEN
TANKERS
L ANTLERS
RENTALS
SALTERN
STERNAL
M ARTSMEN
MARTENS
SARMENT
SMARTEN
N TANNERS
O ATONERS
SENATOR
TREASON
P ARPENTS
ENTRAPS
PANTERS
PARENTS
PASTERN
PERSANT
TREPANS
R ERRANTS
RANTERS
S SARSNET
TRANSES
T NATTERS
RATTENS
U AUNTERS
NATURES
SAUNTER
V SERVANT
TAVERNS
VERSANT
W STRAWEN
WANTERS
Y TRAYNES

AENRTT 74
NATTER
A TARTANE
C TRANECT
D TRANTED
E ENTREAT
RATTEEN
TERNATE
I INTREAT
ITERANT
NATTIER
NITRATE
TARTINE
TERTIAN
L TRENTAL
N ENTRANT
P PATTERN
REPTANT
R TRANTER
S NATTERS
RATTENS
U TAUNTER
Y NATTERY

AENSTT 123
(ATTENS)
B BATTENS
C CANTEST
D ATTENDS
E NEATEST
F FATTENS
G GESTANT
I INSTATE
SATINET
L LATENTS
LATTENS
TALENTS
N TANNEST
TENANTS
O ATTONES
NOTATES
P PATENTS
PATTENS
R NATTERS
RATTENS
T ATTENTS
U ATTUNES
NUTATES
TAUTENS
TETANUS
UNSTATE
X SEXTANT

AEORST 9
ORATES
A AEROSAT
B BOASTER
BOATERS
BORATES
REBATOS
SORBATE
C COASTER
COATERS
D DOATERS
ROASTED
TORSADE
TROADES
E ROSEATE
G GAROTES
ORGEATS
STORAGE
TOERAGS
H ASTHORE
EARSHOT
HAROSET
I OARIEST
OTARIES
L OESTRAL
M AMORETS
MAESTRO
OMERTAS
N ATONERS
SENATOR
TREASON
P ESPARTO
PROTEAS
SEAPORT
R ROASTER
T ROTATES
TOASTER

AEPRST 140
PATERS
A PETARAS
C CARPETS
PREACTS
PRECAST
SPECTRA
D DEPARTS
DRAPETS
PETARDS
E REPEATS
RETAPES
G PARGETS
H SPARTHE
TEPHRAS
THREAPS
I PARTIES
PASTIER
PIASTER
PIASTRE
PIRATES
PRATIES
TRAIPSE
L PALTERS
PERSALT
PLASTER
PLATERS
PSALTER
STAPLER
M EMPARTS
RESTAMP
STAMPER
TAMPERS
N ARPENTS
ENTRAPS
PANTERS
PARENTS
PASTERN
PERSANT
TREPANS
O ESPARTO
PROTEAS
SEAPORT
P TAPPERS
R PARTERS
PRATERS
S PASTERS
REPASTS
SPAREST
T PATTERS
SPATTER
TAPSTER
U PASTURE
UPRATES
UPSTARE
UPTEARS
Y YAPSTER
Z PATZERS

AERRST 106
STARER
A ERRATAS
B BARRETS
BARTERS
C CARTERS
CRATERS
TRACERS
D DARTERS
DARTRES
RETARDS
STARRED
TRADERS
E RETEARS
SERRATE
TEARERS
F FRATERS
RAFTERS
STRAFER
G GARRETS
GARTERS
GRATERS
I ARTSIER
SERRATI
TARRIES
TARSIER
K KARTERS
KRATERS
STARKER
M ARMREST
SMARTER
N ERRANTS
RANTERS
O ROASTER
P PARTERS
PRATERS
S ARRESTS
RASTERS
STARERS
T RATTERS
RESTART
STARTER
V STARVER
Y STRAYER

AERSST 224
ASSERT
A SEARATS
B BASTERS
BESTARS
BRASSET
BREASTS
C ACTRESS
CASTERS
RECASTS
E EASTERS
RESEATS
SAETERS
SEAREST
SEATERS
STEARES
TEASERS
TESSERA
F FASTERS
STRAFES
G GASTERS
STAGERS
H RASHEST
SHASTER
TRASHES
I ARTSIES
SAIREST
SATIRES
TIRASSE
K SKATERS
STRAKES
STREAKS
TASKERS
L ARTLESS
LASTERS
SALTERS
SLATERS
TARSELS
M MASTERS
STREAMS
N SARSNET
TRANSES
P PASTERS
REPASTS
SPAREST
R ARRESTS
RASTERS
STARERS
S ASSERTS
TRASSES
T ASTERTS
STARETS
STATERS
TASTERS
V STARVES
W WASTERS
Y ESTRAYS
STAYERS
STAYRES

AERSTT 101
TASTER
B BATTERS
TABRETS
C SCATTER
D STARTED
TETRADS
E ESTREAT
RESTATE
RETASTE
G TARGETS
H HATTERS
RATHEST
SHATTER
THREATS
I ARTIEST
ARTISTE
ATTIRES
IRATEST
RATITES
STRIATE
TASTIER
TERTIAS
L RATTLES
SLATTER
STARLET
STARTLE
TATLERS
M MATTERS
SMATTER
N NATTERS
RATTENS
O ROTATES
TOASTER
P PATTERS
SPATTER
TAPSTER
R RATTERS
RESTART
STARTER
S ASTERTS
STARETS
STATERS
TASTERS
T STRETTA
TARTEST
TATTERS
U ASTUTER
STATURE
V VATTERS
W SWATTER
TEWARTS
Y YATTERS
Z STARETZ

AERSTW 199
WATERS
A AWAREST
B BRAWEST
WABSTER
D STEWARD
STRAWED
WRASTED
E SWEATER
F FRETSAW
WAFTERS
H SWATHER
THAWERS
WREATHS
I WAISTER
WAITERS
WARIEST
WASTRIE

L WARSTLE
WASTREL
WRASTLE
M WARMEST
N STRAWEN
WANTERS
S WASTERS
T SWATTER
TEWARTS
Y WASTERY

AGILNR 204
(RALING)
B BLARING
C CARLING
D DARLING
LARDING
E ALIGNER
ENGRAIL
LAERING
LEARING
NARGILE
REALIGN
REGINAL
F FLARING
G ARGLING
GLARING
H HARLING
I GLAIRIN
LAIRING
RAILING
K LARKING
M MARLING
N LARNING
O RANGOLI
P GRAPLIN
PARLING
T RATLING
W WARLING
Y ANGRILY
NARGILY
RAYLING

AGILNS 223
SIGNAL
A AGNAILS
B ABLINGS
SABLING
C LACINGS
SCALING
D LADINGS
LIGANDS
E LEASING
LINAGES
SEALING
F FALSING
G GINGALS
LAGGINS
H HALSING
LASHING
SHALING
I AISLING
NILGAIS
SAILING
J JINGALS
K LAKINGS
SLAKING
M LINGAMS
MALIGNS
N LINSANG
P LAPSING
PALINGS
SAPLING
S LASINGS
SIGNALS

T ANGLIST
LASTING
SALTING
SLATING
STALING
U LINGUAS
NILGAUS
SALUING
V SALVING
SLAVING
VALSING
W LAWINGS
SWALING
Y LAYINGS
SLAYING

AGILNT 179
(LATING)
B TABLING
C CATLING
TALCING
E ATINGLE
ELATING
GELATIN
GENITAL
F FATLING
H HALTING
LATHING
I INTAGLI
TAILING
K TALKING
M MALTING
N TANLING
O ANTILOG
P PLATING
R RATLING
S ANGLIST
LASTING
SALTING
SLATING
STALING
Y GIANTLY

AGINRS 135
GRAINS
A NAGARIS
SANGRIA
SARANGI
B SABRING
C ARCINGS
RACINGS
SACRING
SCARING
D DARINGS
GRADINS
E ANGRIES
EARINGS
ERASING
GAINERS
GRAINES
REAGINS
REGAINS
REGINAS
SEARING
SERINGA
F FARSING
G RAGINGS
SIRGANG
H GARNISH
RASHING
SHARING
I AIRINGS
ARISING
RAGINIS
RAISING

SAIRING
K RAKINGS
SARKING
M ARMINGS
MARGINS
N SNARING
O IGNAROS
ORIGANS
SIGNORA
SOARING
P PARINGS
PARSING
RASPING
SPARING
T GASTRIN
GRATINS
RATINGS
STARING
TARINGS
V RAVINGS
W RAWINGS
Y SIGNARY
SYRINGA

AGINRT 70
RATING
A GRANITA
C CARTING
CRATING
TRACING
D DARTING
TRADING
E GRANITE
GRATINE
INGRATE
TANGIER
TEARING
F FARTING
INGRAFT
RAFTING
G GRATING
TARGING
I AIRTING
RAITING
K KARTING
L RATLING
M MARTING
MIGRANT
N RANTING
O ORATING
ROATING
P PARTING
PRATING
TRAPING
R TARRING
S GASTRIN
GRATINS
RATINGS
STARING
TARINGS
T RATTING
TARTING
W RINGTAW
Y GIANTRY

AGINST 115
SATING
A AGAINST
ANTISAG
GITANAS
B BASTING
C ACTINGS
CASTING
D DATINGS
E EASTING

EATINGS
GAINEST
GENISTA
INGATES
INGESTA
SEATING
TANGIES
TEASING
TSIGANE
F FASTING
G GASTING
GATINGS
STAGING
H HASTING
TASHING
K SKATING
STAKING
TAKINGS
TASKING
L ANGLIST
LASTING
SALTING
SLATING
STALING
M MASTING
MATINGS
TAMINGS
N ANTINGS
STANING
O AGONIST
GITANOS
P PASTING
R GASTRIN
GRATINS
RATINGS
STARING
TARINGS
T STATING
TASTING
U SAUTING
V STAVING
W STAWING
TAWINGS
TAWSING
WASTING
X TAXINGS
Y STAYING
STYGIAN

AINRST 38
TRAINS
A ANTIARS
ARTISAN
TSARINA
B BRISANT
C NARCIST
D INDARTS
E ANESTRI
ANTSIER
NASTIER
RATINES
RESIANT
RETAINS
RETINAS
RETSINA
STAINER
STARNIE
STEARIN
G GASTRIN
GRATINS
RATINGS
STARING
TARINGS
H TARNISH
L RATLINS

M MARTINS
O AROINTS
RATIONS
P SPIRANT
SPRAINT
Q QINTARS
S INSTARS
SANTIRS
STRAINS
T STRAINT
TRANSIT
U NUTRIAS

AINSTT 200
TAINTS
A ATTAINS
D DISTANT
E INSTATE
SATINET
G STATING
TASTING
I TITANIS
TITIANS
L LATTINS
M MATTINS
N INSTANT
O STATION
R STRAINT
TRANSIT
S TANISTS

ANORST 63
(NO RATS)
A TORANAS
B BARTONS
C CANTORS
CARTONS
CONTRAS
CRATONS
E ATONERS
SENATOR
TREASON
I AROINTS
RATIONS
L LATRONS
M MATRONS
TRANSOM
N NATRONS
NONARTS
O RATOONS
P PARTONS
PATRONS
TARPONS
T ATTORNS
RATTONS
ROTTANS
U ROUSANT
SANTOUR
Y AROYNTS

BDEIRS 246
BRIDES
A ABIDERS
BRAISED
DARBIES
SEABIRD
SIDEBAR
B DIBBERS
C SCRIBED
D BIDDERS
E DERBIES
G BEGIRDS
BRIDGES
I BIRDIES
BRIDIES

K BRISKED
L BIRSLED
BRIDLES
N BINDERS
INBREDS
REBINDS
O BORIDES
DISROBE
R BIRDERS
T BESTRID
BISTRED
U BRUISED
BURDIES
V VERBIDS

BEILRS 245
LIBERS
A BAILERS
B LIBBERS
D BIRSLED
BRIDLES
E BELIERS
G GERBILS
I RISIBLE
J JERBILS
JIRBLES
K BILKERS
L BILLERS
REBILLS
M LIMBERS
N BERLINS
O BOILERS
LIBEROS
REBOILS
R BIRLERS
S BIRSLES
RIBLESS
T BLISTER
BRISTLE
RIBLETS

BEIRST 189
TRIBES
A BAITERS
BARITES
REBAITS
TERBIAS
D BESTRID
BISTRED
E REBITES
F FIBSTER
H HERBIST
I BITSIER
K BRISKET
L BLISTER
BRISTLE
RIBLETS
M BETRIMS
TIMBERS
TIMBRES
O ORBIEST
SORBITE
S BESTIRS
BISTERS
BISTRES
T BITTERS
U BUSTIER
RUBIEST

BEORST 217
STROBE
A BOASTER
BOATERS
BORATES
REBATOS

SORBATE
D DEBTORS
STROBED
H BOSHTER
BOTHERS
I ORBIEST
SORBITE
L BOLSTER
BOLTERS
LOBSTER
M BESTORM
MOBSTER
N BRETONS
SORBENT
O BOOSTER
REBOOTS
P BESPORT
S BESORTS
SORBETS
STROBES
T BETTORS
U OBTUSER
V OBVERTS
W BESTROW
Z BORTZES

CEINOS 118
COSINE
A ACINOSE
B EBONICS
C CONCISE
D CODEINS
CONDIES
SECONDI
E SENECIO
G COGNISE
COIGNES
I EOSINIC
ICONISE
L CINEOLS
CONSEIL
INCLOSE
M INCOMES
MESONIC
N CONINES
R COINERS
CRINOSE
CRONIES
ORCEINS
ORCINES
RECOINS
SERICON
S CESSION
COSINES
OSCINES
T NOTICES
SECTION
V NOVICES

CEINRS 191
(NICERS)
A ARCSINE
ARSENIC
CARNIES
CERASIN
D CINDERS
DISCERN
RESCIND
E CERESIN
SCRIENE
SINCERE
G CRINGES
H NICHERS
RICHENS
I IRENICS
SERICIN
SIRENIC
K NICKERS
SNICKER
M CREMSIN
MINCERS
O COINERS
CRINOSE
CRONIES
ORCEINS
ORCINES
RECOINS
SERICON
P CRISPEN
PINCERS
PRINCES
S SCRINES
T CISTERN
CRETINS
V CRIVENS
W WINCERS

CEINST 202
INSECT
A ACETINS
CANIEST
CINEAST
E ENTICES
F INFECTS
H ETHNICS
STHENIC
I INCITES
J INJECTS
K SNICKET
TICKENS
L CLIENTS
LECTINS
STENCIL
O NOTICES
SECTION
P INCEPTS
INSPECT
PECTINS
PEINCTS
R CISTERN
CRETINS
S INCESTS
INSECTS
Y CYSTEIN
CYSTINE

CEIORS 163
COSIER
A ORACIES
SCORIAE
B CORBIES
C CICEROS
D DISCOER
H COHEIRS
HEROICS
L COILERS
RECOILS
N COINERS
CRINOSE
CRONIES
ORCEINS
ORCINES
RECOINS
SERICON
P COPIERS
COPSIER
PERSICO
R CIRROSE
CORRIES
CROSIER
ORRICES
S COSIERS
T EROTICS
TERCIOS
U SCOURIE
V CORSIVE
VOICERS
W COWRIES
SCOWRIE
Z COZIERS

CEIRST 170
CITERS
A CRISTAE
RACIEST
STEARIC
C CRETICS
D CREDITS
DIRECTS
E CERITES
RECITES
TIERCES
H CITHERS
ESTRICH
RICHEST
I ERISTIC
RICIEST
K RICKETS
STICKER
TICKERS
L RELICTS
M CRETISM
METRICS
N CISTERN
CRETINS
O EROTICS
TERCIOS
P TRICEPS
T TRISECT
U CUITERS
CURIETS
CURITES
ICTERUS
W TWICERS

CENORS 177
CENSOR
A CARNOSE
COARSEN
CORNEAS
EARCONS
NARCOSE
D CONDERS
CORSNED
SCORNED
E ENCORES
NECROSE
F CONFERS
G CONGERS
I COINERS
CRINOSE
CRONIES
ORCEINS
ORCINES
RECOINS
SERICON
K CONKERS
RECKONS
L CLONERS
CORNELS
N CONNERS
O CEROONS
P CREPONS
R CORNERS
SCORNER
S CENSORS
T CONSTER
CORNETS
CRESTON
CRONETS
U CONURES
ROUNCES

CENOST 230
CENTOS
A COSTEAN
OCTANES
D DOCENTS
E CENOTES
F CONFEST
G CONGEST
H NOTCHES
TECHNOS
I NOTICES
SECTION
K NOCKETS
N CONSENT
NOCENTS
R CONSTER
CORNETS
CRESTON
CRONETS
T CONTEST
U CONTUSE
ECONUTS
V COVENTS

CEORST 236
ESCORT
A COASTER
COATERS
H HECTORS
ROCHETS
ROTCHES
TOCHERS
TORCHES
TROCHES
I EROTICS
TERCIOS
K RESTOCK
ROCKETS
STOCKER
L COLTERS
CORSLET
COSTREL
LECTORS
N CONSTER
CORNETS
CRESTON
CRONETS
O COOTERS
SCOOTER
P COPTERS
PROSECT
R RECTORS
S CORSETS
COSTERS
ESCORTS
SCOTERS
SECTORS
T COTTERS
U COUTERS
CROUTES
SCOUTER
V CORVETS
COVERTS
VECTORS

DEEINR 45
DENIER
B BENDIER
INBREED
C CEDRINE
E NEEDIER
F DEFINER
ENFIRED
FENDIER
REFINED
G DREEING
ENERGID
GREINED
REEDING
REIGNED
H INHERED
K REINKED
L REDLINE
RELINED
M ERMINED
O ORDINEE
P REPINED
RIPENED
R DERNIER
NERDIER
S DENIERS
NEREIDS
RESINED
U UREDINE
W REWIDEN
WIDENER
X INDEXER
REINDEX

DEEIRS 57
DESIRE
A DEARIES
READIES
B DERBIES
C DECRIES
DEICERS
D DERIDES
DESIRED
DIEDRES
RESIDED
E SEEDIER
F DEFIERS
SERIFED
G SEDGIER
L RESILED
M REMEIDS
REMISED
N DENIERS
NEREIDS
RESINED
O OREIDES
OSIERED
P PREDIES
PRESIDE
SPEIRED
SPIERED
R DERRIES
DESIRER
REDRIES
RESIDER
SERRIED
S DESIRES
RESIDES
T DIESTER
DIETERS
REEDITS
REISTED
RESITED
U RESIDUE
UREIDES
V DERIVES
DEVISER
DIVERSE
REVISED
Z RESIZED

DEELNS 240
LENSED
A LEADENS
B BLENDES
D LEDDENS
E NEEDLES
F FLENSED
G LEGENDS
I ENISLED
ENSILED
LINSEED
L SNELLED
R LENDERS
RELENDS
SLENDER
S ENDLESS
T DENTELS
NESTLED
W WEDELNS
Y DENSELY

DEENRS 97
ENDERS
A DEANERS
ENDEARS
B BENDERS
C DECERNS
SCERNED
D REDDENS
E NEEDERS
SERENED
SNEERED
F FENDERS
G GENDERS
H HERDENS
I DENIERS
NEREIDS
RESINED
L LENDERS
RELENDS
SLENDER
M MENDERS
REMENDS
O ENDORSE
P SPENDER
R RENDERS
S REDNESS
RESENDS
SENDERS
T STERNED
TENDERS
TENDRES
U ENDURES
ENSURED
V VENDERS
Z DZERENS

DEENST 117
NESTED
A STANDEE
STEANED
C DESCENT
SCENTED
D STENDED
E STEENED
I DESTINE
ENDITES
STEINED
L DENTELS

NESTLED
M DEMENTS
N DENNETS
STENNED
O DENOTES
R STERNED
TENDERS
TENDRES
S DENSEST
T DETENTS
STENTED
U DETENUS
DETUNES
X EXTENDS

DEERST 159
RESTED
A DEAREST
DERATES
ESTRADE
REASTED
REDATES
SEDATER
STEARED
TASERED
C CRESTED
D REDDEST
TEDDERS
E REESTED
STEERED
I DIESTER
DIETERS
REEDITS
REISTED
RESITED
N STERNED
TENDERS
TENDRES
O OERSTED
ROSETED
TEREDOS
P PRESTED
S DESERTS
DESSERT
TRESSED
V STERVED
VERDETS
W STREWED
WRESTED
X DEXTERS
Y DYESTER

DEGILN 158
DINGLE
A ALIGNED
DEALING
LEADING
B BINGLED
C CLINGED
E DELEING
G GELDING
NIGGLED
H HINDLEG
I EILDING
ELIDING
J JINGLED
M MEDLING
MELDING
MINGLED
N LENDING
O GLENOID
P PINGLED
S DINGLES
ELDINGS
ENGILDS
SINGLED
T GLINTED
TINGLED
U DUELING
ELUDING
INDULGE
V DELVING
DEVLING
W WELDING

DEGINR 84
RINGED
A AREDING
DEARING
DERAIGN
EARDING
GRADINE
GRAINED
READING
B BREDING
C CRINGED
D GRINDED
REDDING
E DREEING
ENERGID
GREINED
REEDING
REIGNED
F FRINGED
H HERDING
I DINGIER
N GRINNED
RENDING
O ERODING
GROINED
IGNORED
NEGROID
REDOING
R GRINDER
REGRIND
S DINGERS
ENGIRDS
U DUNGIER
W REDWING
WRINGED
Y YERDING

DEGINS 162
SIGNED
A AGNISED
E SDEIGNE
SEEDING
G EDGINGS
SNIGGED
I DINGIES
L DINGLES
ELDINGS
ENGILDS
SINGLED
M SMIDGEN
N ENDINGS
SENDING
O DINGOES
R DINGERS
ENGIRDS
S DESIGNS
SDEIGNS
T NIDGETS
STEDING
STINGED
U GUNDIES
SUEDING
W SWINDGE
SWINGED
Y DINGEYS
DYEINGS

DEGIRS 213
DIRGES
A AGRISED
B BEGIRDS
BRIDGES
E SEDGIER
F FRIDGES
G DIGGERS
I DIRIGES
L GILDERS
GIRDLES
GLIDERS
GRISLED
LIDGERS
REGILDS
RIDGELS
N DINGERS
ENGIRDS
R GIRDERS
RIDGERS
S DIGRESS
U GUIDERS

DEILNS 119
(IN SLED)
A DENIALS
SNAILED
B BINDLES
D DINDLES
SLIDDEN
E ENISLED
ENSILED
LINSEED
G DINGLES
ELDINGS
ENGILDS
SINGLED
I INISLED
LINDIES
K KINDLES
SLINKED
M MILDENS
N DINNLES
LINDENS
O DOLINES
INDOLES
SONDELI
P SPELDIN
SPINDLE
SPLINED
T DENTILS
W SWINDLE
WINDLES
Y SNIDELY

DEILRT 76
(LITRED)
A DILATER
REDTAIL
TRAILED
B DRIBLET
D TIDDLER
E RETILED
F FLIRTED
TRIFLED
H THIRLED
K KIRTLED
L TRILLED
N TENDRIL
TRINDLE
O DOILTER
P TRIPLED
U DILUTER
W TWIRLED
Y TIREDLY

DEINOS 43
ONSIDE
A ADONISE
ANODISE
SODAINE
C CODEINS
CONDIES
SECONDI
D NODDIES
G DINGOES
H HOIDENS
I IODINES
IONISED
K DOESKIN
L DOLINES
INDOLES
SONDELI
M DOMINES
EMODINS
MISDONE
N ONDINES
P DISPONE
SPINODE
R DINEROS
DONSIER
INDORSE
ORDINES
ROSINED
SORDINE
S ONSIDES
T DITONES
STONIED

DEINRS 56
DINERS
A RANDIES
SANDIER
SARDINE
B BINDERS
INBREDS
REBINDS
C CINDERS
DISCERN
RESCIND
E DENIERS
NEREIDS
RESINED
F FINDERS
FRIENDS
REDFINS
REFINDS
G DINGERS
ENGIRDS
H HINDERS
NERDISH
SHRINED
I INSIDER
K KINDERS
KINREDS
REDSKIN
M MINDERS
REMINDS
N DINNERS
ENDRINS
O DINEROS
DONSIER
INDORSE
ORDINES
ROSINED
SORDINE
P PINDERS
T TINDERS
U INSURED
V VERDINS
W REWINDS
WINDERS

DEINRU 58
RUINED
A UNAIRED
URANIDE
C INDUCER
D UNDRIED
E UREDINE
F UNFIRED
G DUNGIER
H UNHIRED
I URIDINE
J INJURED
M UNRIMED
N DUNNIER
INURNED
O DOURINE
NEUROID
S INSURED
T INTRUDE
TURDINE
UNTIRED
UNTRIDE
UNTRIED
W UNWIRED

DEINST 37
(SINTED)
A DESTAIN
DETAINS
INSTEAD
SAINTED
SATINED
STAINED
B BIDENTS
D DISTEND
E DESTINE
ENDITES
STEINED
F SNIFTED
G NIDGETS
STEDING
STINGED
I INDITES
TINEIDS
K DINKEST
KINDEST
L DENTILS
M MINDSET
MISTEND
N DENTINS
INDENTS
INTENDS
O DITONES
STONIED
P DIPNETS
STIPEND
R TINDERS
S DISNEST
DISSENT
SNIDEST
T DENTIST
DISTENT
STINTED
U DISTUNE
DUNITES
Y DENSITY
DESTINY

DEIORS 31
(DI & ROSE)
A ROADIES
SOREDIA
B BORIDES
DISROBE
C DISCOER
D DORISED
SODDIER
E OREIDES
OSIERED
H RHODIES
L SOLDIER
SOLIDER
M MISDOER
MOIDERS
N DINEROS
DONSIER
INDORSE
ORDINES
ROSINED
SORDINE
O OROIDES
P PERIODS
S DORISES
DOSSIER
T EDITORS
ROISTED
ROSITED
SORTIED
STEROID
STORIED
TIERODS
TRIODES
V DEVISOR
DEVOIRS
VISORED
VOIDERS
W DOWRIES
ROWDIES
WEIRDOS
Z DORIZES

DEIOST 41
(ODSITE)
A IODATES
TOADIES
C CESTOID
COEDITS
COTISED
D TODDIES
F FOISTED
H HOISTED
J JOISTED
M DISTOME
DOMIEST
MODISTE
MOISTED
N DITONES
STONIED
O OSTEOID
P DEPOSIT
DOPIEST
PODITES
POSITED
SOPITED
TOPSIDE
R EDITORS
ROISTED
ROSITED
SORTIED
STEROID
STORIED
TIERODS
TRIODES

T DOTIEST
STOITED
U OUTSIDE
TEDIOUS
V DOVIEST
W DOWIEST
X EXODIST
Z DOZIEST

DEIPRT 220
(TRIPED)
A DIPTERA
PARTIED
PIRATED
C PREDICT
E PREEDIT
TEPIDER
I RIPTIDE
TIDERIP
L TRIPLED
M DIREMPT
N PRINTED
O DIOPTER
DIOPTRE
PERIDOT
PROTEID
P TRIPPED
S SPIRTED
STRIPED

DEIRST 61
STRIDE
A ARIDEST
ASTERID
ASTRIDE
DIASTER
DISRATE
STAIDER
STAIRED
TARDIES
TIRADES
B BESTRID
BISTRED
C CREDITS
DIRECTS
E DIESTER
DIETERS
REEDITS
REISTED
RESITED
F FRISTED
H DITHERS
SHIRTED
I DIRTIES
DITSIER
TIDIERS
K SKIRTED
N TINDERS
O EDITORS
ROISTED
ROSITED
SORTIED
STEROID
STORIED
TIERODS
TRIODES
P SPIRTED
STRIPED
R STIRRED
STRIDER
S DISSERT
STRIDES
U DUSTIER
REDUITS
STUDIER

V DIVERTS
STRIVED
VERDITS

DEIRSU 149
RUDIES
A RESIDUA
B BRUISED
BURDIES
C CRUISED
DISCURE
D RUDDIES
E RESIDUE
UREIDES
G GUIDERS
H HURDIES
K DUIKERS
DUSKIER
N INSURED
P PUDSIER
SIRUPED
UPDRIES
Q SQUIRED
R DRUSIER
DURRIES
S DISEURS
SUDSIER
T DUSTIER
REDUITS
STUDIER

DELNOS 176
OLDENS
A LOADENS
B BLONDES
BOLDENS
D NODDLES
F ENFOLDS
FONDLES
G DONGLES
GOLDENS
H HONDLES
I DOLINES
INDOLES
SONDELI
M DOLMENS
O NOODLES
SNOOLED
R RONDELS
S OLDNESS
U LOUDENS
NODULES
NOUSLED
W DOWLNES
Z DONZELS

DELORS 151
(OLDERS)
A LOADERS
ORDEALS
RELOADS
B BORDELS
C SCOLDER
E RESOLED
F FOLDERS
REFOLDS
G LODGERS
H HOLDERS
I SOLDIER
SOLIDER
M MOLDERS
REMOLDS
SMOLDER
N RONDELS
P POLDERS

PRESOLD
S DORSELS
RODLESS
SOLDERS
T DROLEST
OLDSTER
STRODLE
W WELDORS
Y YODLERS

DELORT 94
(DOLTER)
A DELATOR
LEOTARD
D TODDLER
F TELFORD
I DOILTER
L TROLLED
N ENTROLD
O ROOTLED
P DROPLET
S DROLEST
OLDSTER
STRODLE
T DOTTLER
DOTTREL
U TROULED

DENORU 93
UNDOER
A RONDEAU
B BOUNDER
REBOUND
UNROBED
C CRUNODE
D REDOUND
ROUNDED
UNDERDO
F FOUNDER
REFOUND
G GUERDON
UNDERGO
UNGORED
H HOUNDER
I DOURINE
NEUROID
L LOUNDER
ROUNDEL
ROUNDLE
M MOURNED
N ENROUND
P POUNDER
UNROPED
R RONDURE
ROUNDER
UNORDER
S ENDUROS
RESOUND
SOUNDER
UNDOERS
W REWOUND
WOUNDER

DENOST 77
STONED
A ASTONED
DONATES
ONSTEAD
B OBTENDS
C DOCENTS
E DENOTES
F FONDEST
I DITONES
STONIED
M ENDMOST

N STONNED
TENDONS
O SNOOTED
STOODEN
R RODENTS
SNORTED
T SNOTTED
U DEUTONS
SNOUTED

DENRSU 185
NURSED
A ASUNDER
DANSEUR
DAUNERS
B BURDENS
D DUNDERS
E ENDURES
ENSURED
F FUNDERS
REFUNDS
G GERUNDS
NUDGERS
H HURDENS
I INSURED
K DUNKERS
L LURDENS
NURDLES
NURSLED
RUNDLES
N UNDERNS
O ENDUROS
RESOUND
SOUNDER
UNDOERS
P SPURNED
S SUNDERS
UNDRESS
T RETUNDS
UNDREST
U UNSURED

DENSTU 219
NUDEST
A SAUNTED
UNSATED
B SUBTEND
D STUDDEN
E DETENUS
DETUNES
H SHUNTED
I DISTUNE
DUNITES
M DUSTMEN
N DUNNEST
STUNNED
O DEUTONS
SNOUTED
R RETUNDS
UNDREST
T STUDENT
STUNTED

DEORST 55
STORED
A DOATERS
ROASTED
TORSADE
TROADES
B DEBTORS
STROBED
E OERSTED
ROSETED
TEREDOS
F DEFROST

FROSTED
G STODGER
H DEHORTS
SHORTED
I EDITORS
ROISTED
ROSITED
SORTIED
STEROID
STORIED
TIERODS
TRIODES
K STROKED
L DROLEST
OLDSTER
STRODLE
M STORMED
N RODENTS
SNORTED
O ROOSTED
P DEPORTS
REDTOPS
SPORTED
R DORTERS
RODSTER
T DETORTS
DOTTERS
U DETOURS
DOUREST
DOUTERS
OUTREDS
REDOUTS
ROUSTED
W STROWED
WORSTED
Y DESTROY
ROYSTED
STROYED

DEOSTU 187
OUSTED
C CUSTODE
DOUCEST
DOUCETS
SCOUTED
G DEGOUTS
H SHOUTED
SOUTHED
I OUTSIDE
TEDIOUS
J JOUSTED
L LOUDEST
OULDEST
TOUSLED
M MOUSTED
SMOUTED
N DEUTONS
SNOUTED
O OUTDOES
P OUTSPED
SPOUTED
R DETOURS
DOUREST
DOUTERS
OUTREDS
REDOUTS
ROUSTED
T DUETTOS
TESTUDO
U DUTEOUS
X TUXEDOS

DERSTU 243
RUSTED
B BURSTED

C CRUDEST
CRUSTED
G TRUDGES
I DUSTIER
REDUITS
STUDIER
L LUSTRED
RUSTLED
STRUDEL
N RETUNDS
UNDREST
O DETOURS
DOUREST
DOUTERS
OUTREDS
REDOUTS
ROUSTED
P SPURTED
R RUSTRED
S DUSTERS
TRUSSED
T STURTED
TRUSTED
U SUTURED
Y RESTUDY

DGINOR 212
RODING
A ADORING
GRADINO
ROADING
C CORDING
D RODDING
E ERODING
GROINED
IGNORED
NEGROID
REDOING
F FORDING
H HORDING
L GIRLOND
LORDING
N DRONING
R DORRING
S RODINGS
T DORTING
V DROVING
W WORDING

EEFIRS 239
(IS FREE)
A AREFIES
FAERIES
FREESIA
D DEFIERS
SERIFED
E FEERIES
F EFFEIRS
H HEIFERS
I REIFIES
L FERLIES
REFILES
REFLIES
RELIEFS
N ENFIRES
FEERINS
FINEERS
REFINES
P PREIFES
PRIEFES
R FERRIES
REFIRES
REFRIES
S FRISEES
X REFIXES

Z FRIEZES

EEGNRS 235
GREENS
A ENRAGES
D GENDERS
E RENEGES
I GREISEN
M GERMENS
O ENGORES
NEGROES
S NEGRESS
T GERENTS
REGENTS
V VENGERS
Y GYRENES

EEILRS 86
RELIES
A EARLIES
REALISE
B BELIERS
C CEILERS
D RESILED
E SEELIER
F FERLIES
REFILES
REFLIES
RELIEFS
G LEIGERS
LIEGERS
H LEISHER
L LEISLER
N LIERNES
RELINES
P REPLIES
SPIELER
R RELIERS
S IRELESS
RESILES
T LEISTER
RETILES
STERILE
U LEISURE
V LEVIERS
RELIVES
REVILES
SERVILE
VEILERS

EEILRV 226
RELIVE
A LEAVIER
VEALIER
B VERBILE
D DELIVER
RELIVED
REVILED
E RELIEVE
G VELIGER
I VEILIER
L EVILLER
M VERMEIL
N LIVENER
O OVERLIE
RELIEVO
R RELIVER
REVILER
S LEVIERS
RELIVES
REVILES
SERVILE
VEILERS

EEILST 92
ELITES
C SECTILE
E EELIEST
STEELIE
F FELSITE
LEFTIES
LIEFEST
G ELEGIST
ELEGITS
H SHELTIE
K KELTIES
SLEEKIT
L TELLIES
M ELMIEST
N LISENTE
SETLINE
TENSILE
O ESTOILE
ETOILES
P EPISTLE
PELITES
R LEISTER
RETILES
STERILE
S LISTEES
TELESIS
TIELESS
V EVILEST
LEVITES
LIEVEST
VELITES
X SEXTILE

EEIMNS 198
(EMINES)
A MEANIES
NEMESIA
D DESMINE
SIDEMEN
E ENEMIES
G SEEMING
I MEINIES
L ISLEMEN
M IMMENSE
O SEMEION
R ERMINES
S INSEEMS
MISSEEN
NEMESIS
SIEMENS
T EMETINS
W MISWEEN
Y MEINEYS
MENYIES

EEIMRS 207
MISERE
A SEAMIER
SERIEMA
B BEMIRES
BERIMES
BIREMES
C MERCIES
D REMEIDS
REMISED
E EMERIES
G EMIGRES
REGIMES
REMIGES
H MESHIER
M IMMERSE
N ERMINES
O ISOMERE
P EMPIRES
EMPRISE
EPIMERS
IMPRESE
PREMIES
PREMISE
SPIREME
R MERRIES
S MERISES
MESSIER
MISERES
REMISES
T MEISTER
METIERS
REEMITS
RETIMES
TREMIES
TRISEME
X MIREXES
REMIXES

EEINRT 8
ENTIRE
A ARENITE
RETINAE
TRAINEE
B BENTIER
C ENTERIC
ENTICER
E TEENIER
F FEINTER
G GENTIER
INTEGER
TEERING
TREEING
H NEITHER
THEREIN
I ERINITE
NITERIE
K KERNITE
N INTERNE
P INEPTER
R INERTER
REINTER
RENTIER
TERRINE
S ENTIRES
ENTRIES
NERITES
RETINES
TRENISE
TRIENES
T NETTIER
TENTIER
U NEURITE
RETINUE
REUNITE
UTERINE

EEIRRS 180
RERISE
A REARISE
RERAISE
B BERRIES
D DERRIES
DESIRER
REDRIES
RESIDER
SERRIED
F FERRIES
REFIRES
REFRIES
H HERRIES
REHIRES
J JERRIES
K KERRIES
L RELIERS
M MERRIES
N RERISEN
RESINER
O ROSIERE
P PERRIES
PRISERE
REPRISE
RESPIRE
S RERISES
SERRIES
SIRREES
T ETRIERS
REITERS
RESTIER
RETIRES
RETRIES
TERRIES
V REIVERS
REVERSI
REVISER
RIEVERS
W REWIRES

EEIRST 30
RETIES
A AERIEST
SERIATE
B REBITES
C CERITES
RECITES
TIERCES
D DIESTER
DIETERS
REEDITS
REISTED
RESITED
E EERIEST
H HEISTER
K KEISTER
KIESTER
L LEISTER
RETILES
STERILE
M MEISTER
METIERS
REEMITS
RETIMES
TREMIES
TRISEME
N ENTIRES
ENTRIES
NERITES
RETINES
TRENISE
TRIENES
P PESTIER
RESPITE
R ETRIERS
REITERS
RESTIER
RETIRES
RETRIES
TERRIES
S RESITES
T TESTIER
U SUETIER
V RESTIVE
SIEVERT
STIEVER
VERIEST
VERITES
W STEWIER
Z ZESTIER

EEIRSV 227
REVISE
C SCRIEVE
SERVICE
D DERIVES
DEVISER
DIVERSE
REVISED
E VEERIES
G GRIEVES
REGIVES
H SHRIEVE
L LEVIERS
RELIVES
REVILES
SERVILE
VEILERS
N ENVIERS
INVERSE
VEINERS
VENIRES
VERSINE
O EROSIVE
P PREVISE
PRIEVES
R REIVERS
REVERSI
REVISER
RIEVERS
S IVRESSE
REVISES
T RESTIVE
SIEVERT
STIEVER
VERIEST
VERITES
V REVIVES
W REVIEWS
VIEWERS

EELNST 167
NESTLE
A ELANETS
LATEENS
LEANEST
D DENTELS
NESTLED
E STELENE
G GENTLES
LENGEST
I LISENTE
SETLINE
TENSILE
L TELLENS
P PENTELS
R NESTLER
RELENTS
SLENTER
S NESTLES
NETLESS
T NETTLES
TELNETS
U ELUENTS
UNSTEEL
Y ENSTYLE
TENSELY

EELRST 129
RELETS
A ELATERS
REALEST
RELATES
RESLATE
STEALER
B BELTERS
TREBLES
C TERCELS
F FELTERS
REFLETS
TELFERS
G REGLETS
H SHELTER
I LEISTER
RETILES
STERILE
K KELTERS
KESTREL
SKELTER
L RETELLS
TELLERS
M MELTERS
REMELTS
RESMELT
SMELTER
N NESTLER
RELENTS
SLENTER
O SOLERET
P PELTERS
PETRELS
RESPELT
SPELTER
S STREELS
TRESSEL
T LETTERS
LETTRES
SETTLER
STERLET
TRESTLE
V SVELTER
W SWELTER
WELTERS
WRESTLE
Y RESTYLE
TERSELY
Z SELTZER

EENRST 46
ENTERS
A EARNEST
EASTERN
NEAREST
C CENTERS
CENTRES
TENRECS
D STERNED
TENDERS
TENDRES
E ENTREES
RETENES
TEENERS
G GERENTS
REGENTS
H THRENES
I ENTIRES
ENTRIES
NERITES
RETINES
TRENISE
TRIENES
L NESTLER
RELENTS
SLENTER
N RENNETS
TENNERS
O ESTRONE
P PENSTER
PRESENT
REPENTS
SERPENT

R RENTERS
STERNER
S NESTERS
RENESTS
RESENTS
STRENES
T NETTERS
TENTERS
TESTERN
U NEUTERS
RETUNES
TENURES
TUREENS
V VENTERS
VENTRES
W WESTERN
X EXTERNS
Y STYRENE
YESTERN

EEORSV 248
(OVERSE)
A OVERSEA
B OBSERVE
OBVERSE
VERBOSE
C CORVEES
E OVERSEE
I EROSIVE
K EVOKERS
REVOKES
L RESOLVE
M REMOVES
R REVERSO
T ESTOVER
OVERSET
REVOTES
VETOERS
U OEUVRES
OVERUSE
W OVERSEW

EERRST 229
RESTER
A RETEARS
SERRATE
TEARERS
B BERRETS
E RETREES
STEERER
F FERRETS
G REGRETS
I ETRIERS
REITERS
RESTIER
RETIRES
RETRIES
TERRIES
M TERMERS
N RENTERS
STERNER
O RESTORE
P PRESTER
S RESTERS
T TERRETS
U URETERS
V REVERTS
W STREWER
WRESTER

EERSTT 195
STREET
A ESTREAT
RESTATE
RETASTE

B BETTERS
C TERCETS
E TEETERS
TERETES
F FETTERS
G GETTERS
H TETHERS
I TESTIER
L LETTERS
LETTRES
SETTLER
STERLET
TRESTLE
N NETTERS
TENTERS
TESTERN
O ROSETTE
P PERTEST
PETTERS
PRETEST
R TERRETS
S RETESTS
SETTERS
STREETS
TERSEST
TESTERS
T STRETTE
TETTERS
U TRUSTEE
V TREVETS
W WETTERS
Y STREETY

EFIRST 182
STRIFE
A FAIREST
B FIBSTER
D FRISTED
F RESTIFF
STIFFER
H SHIFTER
I FISTIER
K FRISKET
L FILTERS
LIFTERS
STIFLER
TRIFLES
M FIRMEST
FREMITS
N SNIFTER
O FOISTER
FORTIES
P PRESIFT
S RESIFTS
SIFTERS
STRIFES
T FITTERS
TITFERS
U FUSTIER
SURFEIT
W SWIFTER
Z FRITZES

EGHINT 250
HETING
A GAHNITE
HEATING
B BENIGHT
C ETCHING
D NIGHTED
E THEEING
F HEFTING
I NIGHTIE
L ENLIGHT
LIGHTEN

M THEMING
N HENTING
R RIGHTEN
S NIGHEST
T TIGHTEN

EGILNR 126
LINGER
A ALIGNER
ENGRAIL
LAERING
LEARING
NARGILE
REALIGN
REGINAL
C CLINGER
CRINGLE
E LEERING
REELING
F FLINGER
G NIGGLER
H HERLING
I LEIRING
LINGIER
J JINGLER
K ERLKING
M GREMLIN
MERLING
MINGLER
P PINGLER
S GIRNELS
LINGERS
SLINGER
T RINGLET
TINGLER
TRINGLE
Y RELYING

EGILNS 124
SINGLE
A LEASING
LINAGES
SEALING
B BINGLES
D DINGLES
ELDINGS
ENGILDS
SINGLED
E LEESING
SEELING
F SELFING
G GINGLES
LEGGINS
NIGGLES
SNIGGLE
H ENGLISH
SHINGLE
I SEILING
J JINGLES
K KINGLES
L LEGLINS
LINGELS
LINGLES
SELLING
M MINGLES
N GINNELS
LENSING
O ELOIGNS
LEGIONS
LIGNOSE
LINGOES
LONGIES
P PINGLES
SPIGNEL
R GIRNELS

LINGERS
SLINGER
S SINGLES
T GLISTEN
LESTING
SINGLET
TINGLES
U LUNGIES
SLUEING
W SLEWING
SWINGLE
Z ZINGELS

EGILNT 72
TINGLE
A ATINGLE
ELATING
GELATIN
GENITAL
B BELTING
D GLINTED
TINGLED
E GENTILE
F FELTING
H ENLIGHT
LIGHTEN
I LIGNITE
J JINGLET
K KINGLET
L GILLNET
TELLING
M MELTING
O LENTIGO
P PELTING
R RINGLET
TINGLER
TRINGLE
S GLISTEN
LESTING
SINGLET
TINGLES
T ETTLING
LETTING
U ELUTING
W WELTING
WINGLET

EGILOS 128
LOGIES
A GOALIES
SOILAGE
B OBLIGES
E ELOGIES
L GOLLIES
M SEMILOG
N ELOIGNS
LEGIONS
LIGNOSE
LINGOES
LONGIES
O GOOLIES
OLOGIES
P EPILOGS
R GLOIRES
GLORIES
S GLIOSES
T ELOGIST
LOGIEST
U OUGLIES

EGILRS 164
(GIRLES)
A GLAIRES
GRAILES
B GERBILS

D GILDERS
GIRDLES
GLIDERS
GRISLED
LIDGERS
REGILDS
RIDGELS
E LEIGERS
LIEGERS
G LIGGERS
I GIRLIES
K KILERGS
L GILLERS
GRILLES
N GIRNELS
LINGERS
SLINGER
O GLOIRES
GLORIES
S GRILSES
T GLISTER
GRISTLE
U GUILERS
LIGURES
LURGIES
Y GREISLY
GRIESLY
GRISELY

EGILST 186
LEGIST
A AGILEST
AIGLETS
LIGATES
TAIGLES
B GIBLETS
E ELEGIST
ELEGITS
G GIGLETS
H SLEIGHT
L GILLETS
M GIMLETS
N GLISTEN
LESTING
SINGLET
TINGLES
O ELOGIST
LOGIEST
P PIGLETS
R GLISTER
GRISTLE
S LEGISTS
U GLUIEST
UGLIEST
W WIGLETS
Z GLITZES

EGINNR 161
GINNER
A AGINNER
EARNING
ENGRAIN
GRANNIE
NEARING
C CERNING
D GRINNED
RENDING
E ENGINER
INGENER
F FERNING
G GERNING
I GINNIER
REINING
K KERNING
M RINGMEN

N RENNING
O NEGRONI
R GRINNER
S ENRINGS
GINNERS
T RENTING
RINGENT
TERNING
U ENURING
V NERVING
Y GINNERY
RENYING

EGINOS 68
INGOES
A AGONIES
AGONISE
B BIOGENS
C COGNISE
COIGNES
D DINGOES
E GENOISE
SOIGNEE
H SHOEING
J JINGOES
L ELOIGNS
LEGIONS
LIGNOSE
LINGOES
LONGIES
M MISGONE
O GOONIES
ISOGONE
P EPIGONS
PIGEONS
PINGOES
R ERINGOS
IGNORES
REGIONS
SIGNORE
U IGNEOUS
W WIGEONS
Y ISOGENY

EGINRS 71
SINGER
A ANGRIES
EARINGS
ERASING
GAINERS
GRAINES
REAGINS
REGAINS
REGINAS
SEARING
SERINGA
B BINGERS
C CRINGES
D DINGERS
ENGIRDS
E GREISEN
F FINGERS
FRINGES
G GINGERS
NIGGERS
SERGING
SNIGGER
H HINGERS
L GIRNELS
LINGERS
SLINGER
M GERMINS
N ENRINGS
GINNERS
O ERINGOS

IGNORES
REGIONS
SIGNORE
P PERSING
PINGERS
SPRINGE
R ERRINGS
GIRNERS
RINGERS
SERRING
S INGRESS
RESIGNS
SIGNERS
SINGERS
T RESTING
STINGER
U REUSING
RUEINGS
SIGNEUR
V SERVING
VERSING
W SWINGER
WINGERS
Y SYRINGE
Z ZINGERS

EGINRT 51
(TINGER)
A GRANITE
GRATINE
INGRATE
TANGIER
TEARING
E GENTIER
INTEGER
TEERING
TREEING
H RIGHTEN
I IGNITER
TIERING
TIGRINE
L RINGLET
TINGLER
TRINGLE
M METRING
TERMING
N RENTING
RINGENT
TERNING
O GENITOR
S RESTING
STINGER
T GITTERN
RETTING
U TRUEING
V VERTING
Y RETYING

EGINST 116
INGEST
A EASTING
EATINGS
GAINEST
GENISTA
INGATES
INGESTA
SEATING
TANGIES
TEASING
TSIGANE
B BESTING
D NIDGETS
STEDING
STINGED
H NIGHEST
I IGNITES
J JESTING
K KESTING
L GLISTEN
LESTING
SINGLET
TINGLES
M STEMING
TEMSING
N NESTING
SENTING
TENSING
R RESTING
STINGER
S INGESTS
SIGNETS
T SETTING
TESTING
U GUNITES
V VESTING
W STEWING
TWINGES
WESTING
Z ZESTING

EGNORS 114
GONERS
A ONAGERS
ORANGES
C CONGERS
E ENGORES
NEGROES
H GORHENS
I ERINGOS
IGNORES
REGIONS
SIGNORE
L LONGERS
M MONGERS
MORGENS
O ORGONES
OROGENS
P PRESONG
SPONGER
S ENGROSS
T TONGERS
U SURGEON
V GOVERNS
Y ERYNGOS
GROYNES

EHINRS 196
SHRINE
A ARSHINE
HERNIAS
C NICHERS
RICHENS
D HINDERS
NERDISH
SHRINED
E HENRIES
INHERES
RESHINE
G HINGERS
I SHINIER
K KERNISH
M MENHIRS
O HEROINS
INSHORE
S SHINERS
SHRINES
T HINTERS
V SHRIVEN
W WHINERS

EHIRST 143
(HITERS)
A HASTIER
SHERIAT
B HERBIST
C CITHERS
ESTRICH
RICHEST
D DITHERS
SHIRTED
E HEISTER
F SHIFTER
G RESIGHT
SIGHTER
H HITHERS
I HIRSTIE
L SLITHER
M HERMITS
MITHERS
N HINTERS
O HERIOTS
HOISTER
SHORTIE
TOSHIER
P HIPSTER
T HITTERS
TITHERS
U HIRSUTE
V THRIVES
W SWITHER
WITHERS
WRITHES
Z ZITHERS

EHORST 197
OTHERS
A ASTHORE
EARSHOT
HAROSET
B BOSHTER
BOTHERS
C HECTORS
ROCHETS
ROTCHES
TOCHERS
TORCHES
TROCHES
D DEHORTS
SHORTED
E HETEROS
F FOTHERS
I HERIOTS
HOISTER
SHORTIE
TOSHIER
L HOLSTER
HOSTLER
M MOTHERS
SMOTHER
THERMOS
N HORNETS
SHORTEN
THRENOS
THRONES
O HOOTERS
RESHOOT
SHEROOT
SHOOTER
SOOTHER
P POTHERS
STROPHE
THORPES
R RHETORS
ROTHERS
SHORTER
S HORSTES
TOSHERS
T HOTTERS
U SHOUTER
SOUTHER
W THROWES
X EXHORTS

EIILST 146
(TILIES)
A LAITIES
C ELICITS
I ILEITIS
K KILTIES
L ILLITES
M ELITISM
LIMIEST
LIMITES
N LINIEST
LINTIES
O IOLITES
OILIEST
P SPILITE
R RILIEST
SILTIER
T ELITIST
U UTILISE
W WILIEST

EIINRT 35
INTIRE
A INERTIA
C CITRINE
CRINITE
INCITER
NERITIC
D INDITER
NITRIDE
E ERINITE
NITERIE
F NIFTIER
G IGNITER
TIERING
TIGRINE
H INHERIT
L LINTIER
NITRILE
M INTERIM
MINTIER
TERMINI
N TINNIER
T NITRITE
NITTIER
TINTIER
V INVITER
VITRINE
W TWINIER

EILNOS 23
LESION
A ANISOLE
C CINEOLS
CONSEIL
INCLOSE
D DOLINES
INDOLES
SONDELI
E OLEINES
F OLEFINS
G ELOIGNS
LEGIONS
LIGNOSE
LINGOES
LONGIES
I ELISION
ISOLINE
LIONISE
K SONLIKE
L LIONELS
NIELLOS
M LOMEINS
MOLINES
O LOONIES
P EPSILON
PINOLES
R NEROLIS
S ESLOINS
INSOLES
LESIONS
LIONESS
T ENTOILS
LIONETS
ONLIEST
U ELUSION

EILNRS 80
LINERS
A ALINERS
NAILERS
RENAILS
B BERLINS
E LIERNES
RELINES
G GIRNELS
LINGERS
SLINGER
I INLIERS
K LINKERS
RELINKS
SLINKER
M LIMNERS
MERLINS
O NEROLIS
P PILSNER
T LINTERS
SLINTER
SNIRTLE
V SILVERN

EILNST 52
SILENT
A EASTLIN
ELASTIN
ENTAILS
NAILSET
SALIENT
SALTINE
SLAINTE
STANIEL
TENAILS
C CLIENTS
LECTINS
STENCIL
D DENTILS
E LISENTE
SETLINE
TENSILE
G GLISTEN
LESTING
SINGLET
TINGLES
I LINIEST
LINTIES
K LENTISK
TINKLES
L LENTILS
LINTELS
TELLINS
N LINNETS
O ENTOILS
LIONETS
ONLIEST
P PINTLES
PLENIST
R LINTERS
SLINTER
SNIRTLE
S ENLISTS
LISTENS
SILENTS
TINSELS
U LUNIEST
LUTEINS
UNTILES
UTENSIL
V VENTILS
W WESTLIN
WINTLES

EILORS 47
OILERS
B BOILERS
LIBEROS
REBOILS
C COILERS
RECOILS
D SOLDIER
SOLIDER
G GLOIRES
GLORIES
I SOILIER
M MOILERS
N NEROLIS
O ORIOLES
P SLOPIER
SPOILER
R LORRIES
S LORISES
LOSSIER
RISSOLE
T ESTRIOL
LOITERS
TOILERS
U LOUSIER
SOILURE
V OLIVERS
VIOLERS

EILORT 19
LOITER
B TRILOBE
C CORTILE
D DOILTER
E TROELIE
F LOFTIER
TREFOIL
J JOLTIER
M MOTLIER
N RETINOL
O TROOLIE
P POITREL
POLITER
S ESTRIOL
LOITERS
TOILERS
T TORTILE
TRIOLET
U OUTLIER
V OVERLIT

EILOST 22
(ELIOTS)
A ISOLATE
B BETOILS
C CITOLES

E ESTOILE
ETOILES
G ELOGIST
LOGIEST
H EOLITHS
HOLIEST
HOSTILE
I IOLITES
OILIEST
L OILLETS
M MOTILES
N ENTOILS
LIONETS
ONLIEST
O OOLITES
OSTIOLE
STOOLIE
P PIOLETS
PISTOLE
R ESTRIOL
LOITERS
TOILERS
T LITOTES
TOILETS
U OUTLIES
V OLIVETS
VIOLETS
W OWLIEST
Z ZLOTIES

EILRST 50
TILERS
A REALIST
RETAILS
SALTIER
SALTIRE
SLATIER
TAILERS
B BLISTER
BRISTLE
RIBLETS
C RELICTS
E LEISTER
RETILES
STERILE
F FILTERS
LIFTERS
STIFLER
TRIFLES
G GLISTER
GRISTLE
H SLITHER
I RILIEST
SILTIER
J JILTERS
K KILTERS
KIRTLES
KLISTER
L RILLETS
STILLER
TILLERS
TRELLIS
M MILTERS
N LINTERS
SLINTER
SNIRTLE
O ESTRIOL
LOITERS
TOILERS
P RESPLIT
SPIRTLE
TRIPLES
S LISTERS
RELISTS
T LITTERS
SLITTER
STILTER
TESTRIL
TILTERS
TITLERS
U LUSTIER
RULIEST
RUTILES

EILSTU 133
(LUSTIE)
A SITULAE
B BLUIEST
SUBTILE
C LUETICS
D DILUTES
DUELIST
F FLUIEST
SULFITE
G GLUIEST
UGLIEST
I UTILISE
L TUILLES
N LUNIEST
LUTEINS
UNTILES
UTENSIL
O OUTLIES
P PULIEST
PUTELIS
STIPULE
R LUSTIER
RULIEST
RUTILES
T TITULES

EIMNOS 127
MONIES
A ANOMIES
C INCOMES
MESONIC
D DOMINES
EMODINS
MISDONE
E SEMEION
G MISGONE
H HOMINES
L LOMEINS
MOLINES
O MOONIES
NOISOME
P IMPONES
PEONISM
R MERINOS
MERSION
S EONISMS
T MESTINO
MOISTEN
MONTIES
SENTIMO
W WINSOME

EIMNRS 183
MINERS
A MARINES
REMAINS
SEMINAR
SIRNAME
C CREMSIN
MINCERS
D MINDERS
REMINDS
E ERMINES
G GERMINS
H MENHIRS
K MERKINS
L LIMNERS
MERLINS
M NIMMERS
O MERINOS
MERSION
T ENTRISM
MINSTER
MINTERS
REMINTS
U MUREINS
MURINES
NEURISM
V VERMINS

EIMNST 206
(MINEST)
A ETAMINS
INMATES
MAINEST
MANTIES
TAMEINS
TAMINES
D MINDSET
MISTEND
E EMETINS
G STEMING
TEMSING
I MINIEST
K MISKENT
O MESTINO
MOISTEN
MONTIES
SENTIMO
P EMPTINS
PIMENTS
R ENTRISM
MINSTER
MINTERS
REMINTS
S MISSENT
T MITTENS
SMITTEN
U MINUETS
MINUTES
MISTUNE
MUNITES
MUTINES
W MISWENT

EIMOST 152
SOMITE
A AMOSITE
ATOMIES
ATOMISE
OSMIATE
D DISTOME
DOMIEST
MODISTE
MOISTED
F FOMITES
G EGOTISM
H HOMIEST
L MOTILES
M TOMMIES
N MESTINO
MOISTEN
MONTIES
SENTIMO
P MOPIEST
OPTIMES
R EROTISM
MOISTER
MORTISE
TRISOME
S MITOSES
SOMITES
T MOTIEST
TITMOSE
U TIMEOUS
V MOTIVES
X EXOTISM
Z MESTIZO

EIMRST 145
MITRES
A IMARETS
MAESTRI
MAISTER
MASTIER
MISRATE
SEMITAR
SMARTIE
B BETRIMS
TIMBERS
TIMBRES
C CRETISM
METRICS
E MEISTER
METIERS
REEMITS
RETIMES
TREMIES
TRISEME
F FIRMEST
FREMITS
H HERMITS
MITHERS
I MIRIEST
MISTIER
RIMIEST
K MIRKEST
L MILTERS
M MISTERM
N ENTRISM
MINSTER
MINTERS
REMINTS
O EROTISM
MOISTER
MORTISE
TRISOME
P IMPREST
PERMITS
R RETRIMS
TRIMERS
S MISTERS
SMITERS
T METRIST
U MUSTIER
Y MISTERY
SMYTRIE

EINNST 120
SINNET
A INANEST
STANINE
D DENTINS
INDENTS
INTENDS
E INTENSE
TENNIES
G NESTING
SENTING
TENSING
I INTINES
TINNIES
L LINNETS
O INTONES
TENSION
P PINNETS
SPINNET
TENPINS
R INTERNS
TINNERS
S SENNITS
SINNETS
T INTENTS
TENNIST
U TUNNIES
V INVENTS

EINOPS 105
PONIES
A EPINAOS
SENOPIA
D DISPONE
SPINODE
E PEONIES
G EPIGONS
PIGEONS
PINGOES
H PHONIES
I PIONIES
SINOPIE
K PINKOES
L EPSILON
PINOLES
M IMPONES
PEONISM
N PENSION
PINONES
P PEPINOS
R ORPINES
PIONERS
PROINES
S SPINOSE
T PINTOES
POINTES
PONTIES
W POWNIES
WINESOP
Y PIONEYS

EINORS 7
SENIOR
A ERASION
C COINERS
CRINOSE
CRONIES
ORCEINS
ORCINES
RECOINS
SERICON
D DINEROS
DONSIER
INDORSE
ORDINES
ROSINED
SORDINE
G ERINGOS
IGNORES
REGIONS
SIGNORE
H HEROINS
INSHORE
I IONISER
IRONIES
IRONISE
NOISIER
J JOINERS
REJOINS
L NEROLIS
M MERINOS
MERSION
O EROSION
P ORPINES
PIONERS
PROINES
R IRONERS
S ORNISES
SENIORS
SONERIS
SONSIER
T NORITES
OESTRIN
ORIENTS
STONIER
TERSION
TRIONES
U URINOSE
V RENVOIS
VERSION
W SNOWIER

EINOSS 169
SONSIE
A ANOESIS
B BESOINS
C CESSION
COSINES
OSCINES
D ONSIDES
E EOSINES
I IONISES
K KENOSIS
L ESLOINS
INSOLES
LESIONS
LIONESS
M EONISMS
N SONNIES
P SPINOSE
R ORNISES
SENIORS
SONERIS
SONSIER
S ESSOINS
OSSEINS
SESSION
T NOSIEST
SONTIES
STONIES
U SINUOSE
Z SOZINES

EINOST 10
TONIES
A ATONIES
B BONIEST
EBONIST
C NOTICES
SECTION
D DITONES
STONIED
H ETHIONS
HISTONE
I INOSITE
J JONTIES
L ENTOILS
LIONETS
ONLIEST
M MESTINO
MOISTEN
MONTIES
SENTIMO
N INTONES
TENSION
O ISOTONE
P PINTOES

POINTES
PONTIES
R NORITES
OESTRIN
ORIENTS
STONIER
TERSION
TRIONES
S NOSIEST
SONTIES
STONIES
T SNOTTIE
TONIEST
TONITES
W TOWNIES
X TOXINES

EINPRS 165
SNIPER
A PANIERS
RAPINES
C CRISPEN
PINCERS
PRINCES
D PINDERS
E EREPSIN
REPINES
G PERSING
PINGERS
SPRINGE
I INSPIRE
PIRNIES
SNIPIER
SPINIER
K PERKINS
PINKERS
L PILSNER
N PINNERS
SPINNER
O ORPINES
PIONERS
PROINES
P NIPPERS
SNIPPER
S SNIPERS
T NIPTERS
PTERINS
U PRUINES
PURINES
UPRISEN

EINPST 148
INSTEP
A PANTIES
PATINES
SAPIENT
SPINATE
C INCEPTS
INSPECT
PECTINS
PEINCTS
D DIPNETS
STIPEND
E PENTISE
I PINIEST
PINITES
TIEPINS
K PINKEST
L PINTLES
PLENIST
M EMPTINS
PIMENTS
N PINNETS
SPINNET
TENPINS
O PINTOES
POINTES
PONTIES
P SNIPPET
R NIPTERS
PTERINS
S INSTEPS
SPINETS
T SPITTEN
U PUNIEST
PUNTIES
W INSWEPT

EINRSS 249
RESINS
A ARSINES
SARNIES
C SCRINES
E SEINERS
SEREINS
SERINES
G INGRESS
RESIGNS
SIGNERS
SINGERS
H SHINERS
SHRINES
K SINKERS
N SINNERS
O ORNISES
SENIORS
SONERIS
SONSIER
P SNIPERS
R RINSERS
T ESTRINS
INSERTS
SINTERS
U INSURES
SUNRISE
V VERSINS

EINRST 17
INTERS
A ANESTRI
ANTSIER
NASTIER
RATINES
RESIANT
RETAINS
RETINAS
RETSINA
STAINER
STARNIE
STEARIN
C CISTERN
CRETINS
D TINDERS
E ENTIRES
ENTRIES
NERITES
RETINES
TRENISE
TRIENES
F SNIFTER
G RESTING
STINGER
H HINTERS
K REKNITS
SKINTER
STINKER
TINKERS
L LINTERS
SLINTER
SNIRTLE
M ENTRISM
MINSTER
MINTERS
REMINTS
N INTERNS
TINNERS
O NORITES
OESTRIN
ORIENTS
STONIER
TERSION
TRIONES
P NIPTERS
PTERINS
S ESTRINS
INSERTS
SINTERS
T ENTRIST
RETINTS
STINTER
TINTERS
U NUTSIER
TRIUNES
UNITERS
V INVERTS
STRIVEN
W TWINERS
WINTERS
Y SINTERY

EINRSV 231
VINERS
A AVENIRS
RAVINES
C CRIVENS
D VERDINS
E ENVIERS
INVERSE
VEINERS
VENIRES
VERSINE
G SERVING
VERSING
H SHRIVEN
L SILVERN
M VERMINS
O RENVOIS
VERSION
S VERSINS
T INVERTS
STRIVEN
W WIVERNS

EINRTT 79
TINTER
A INTREAT
ITERANT
NATTIER
NITRATE
TARTINE
TERTIAN
B BITTERN
C CITTERN
D TRIDENT
E NETTIER
TENTIER
G GITTERN
RETTING
I NITRITE
NITTIER
TINTIER
K KNITTER
TRINKET
O TRITONE
S ENTRIST
RETINTS
STINTER
TINTERS
U NUTTIER
W TWINTER
WRITTEN

EINRTU 27
UNITER
A RUINATE
TAURINE
URANITE
URINATE
B BUNTIER
TRIBUNE
TURBINE
D INTRUDE
TURDINE
UNTIRED
UNTRIDE
UNTRIED
E NEURITE
RETINUE
REUNITE
UTERINE
G TRUEING
M MINUTER
UNMITER
UNMITRE
O ROUTINE
P REPUNIT
R RUNTIER
S NUTSIER
TRIUNES
UNITERS
T NUTTIER
V UNRIVET
VENTURI
W UNWRITE

EINSST 222
INSETS
A ENTASIS
NASTIES
SESTINA
TANSIES
TISANES
C INCESTS
INSECTS
D DISNEST
DISSENT
SNIDEST
E SEITENS
SESTINE
F FITNESS
INFESTS
G INGESTS
SIGNETS
H SITHENS
L ENLISTS
LISTENS
SILENTS
TINSELS
M MISSENT
N SENNITS
SINNETS
O NOSIEST
SONTIES
STONIES
P INSTEPS
SPINETS
R ESTRINS
INSERTS
SINTERS
S SENSIST
U INTUSES
V INVESTS
W WISENTS
WITNESS
Y TINSEYS

EINSTT 166
(INTEST)
A INSTATE
SATINET
D DENTIST
DISTENT
STINTED
G SETTING
TESTING
I SITTINE
TINIEST
K KITTENS
M MITTENS
SMITTEN
N INTENTS
TENNIST
O SNOTTIE
TONIEST
TONITES
P SPITTEN
R ENTRIST
RETINTS
STINTER
TINTERS
U TUNIEST
W ENTWIST
TWINSET
Y TENSITY

EINSTU 82
UNITES
A AUNTIES
SINUATE
D DISTUNE
DUNITES
G GUNITES
I UNITIES
UNITISE
L LUNIEST
LUTEINS
UNTILES
UTENSIL
M MINUETS
MINUTES
MISTUNE
MUNITES
MUTINES
N TUNNIES
P PUNIEST
PUNTIES
Q INQUEST
QUINTES
R NUTSIER
TRIUNES
UNITERS
S INTUSES
T TUNIEST

EIOPST 103
POSTIE
A ATOPIES
OPIATES
C POETICS
D DEPOSIT
DOPIEST
PODITES
POSITED
SOPITED
TOPSIDE
E POETISE
H ETHIOPS
OPHITES
K POKIEST
L PIOLETS
PISTOLE
M MOPIEST
OPTIMES
N PINTOES
POINTES
PONTIES
O ISOTOPE
P POTPIES
R PERIOST
PORIEST
PROSTIE
REPOSIT
RIPOSTE
ROPIEST
S POSIEST
POSTIES
POTSIES
SEPIOST
SOPITES
T POTTIES
TIPTOES
U PITEOUS
X EXPOSIT
POXIEST
Y ISOTYPE

EIORSS 205
(SORIES)
B BOSSIER
RIBOSES
C COSIERS
D DORISES
DOSSIER
E SOIREES
F FROISES
H HOSIERS
L LORISES
LOSSIER
RISSOLE
M ISOMERS
MOISERS
MOSSIER
N ORNISES
SENIORS
SONERIS
SONSIER
P POISERS
PROSSIE
R ORRISES
ROSIERS
S SEISORS
T ROSIEST
SORITES
SORTIES
STORIES
TOSSIER
TRIOSES
U SERIOUS
V VIROSES
X XEROSIS
Z SEIZORS

EIORST 5
TORIES
A OARIEST
OTARIES
B ORBIEST
SORBITE
C EROTICS
TERCIOS

D EDITORS
ROISTED
ROSITED
SORTIED
STEROID
STORIED
TIERODS
TRIODES
F FOISTER
FORTIES
G GOITERS
GOITRES
GORIEST
H HERIOTS
HOISTER
SHORTIE
TOSHIER
I RIOTISE
K ROKIEST
L ESTRIOL
LOITERS
TOILERS
M EROTISM
MOISTER
MORTISE
TRISOME
N NORITES
OESTRIN
ORIENTS
STONIER
TERSION
TRIONES
O OORIEST
ROOTIES
SOOTIER
TOORIES
P PERIOST
PORIEST
PROSTIE
REPOSIT
RIPOSTE
ROPIEST
R RIOTERS
ROISTER
RORIEST
S ROSIEST
SORITES
SORTIES
STORIES
TOSSIER
TRIOSES
T STOITER
U OURIEST
STOURIE
TOURIES
TOUSIER
V TORSIVE
W OWRIEST
TOWSIER

EIORSV 137
VIROSE
A OVARIES
C CORSIVE
VOICERS
D DEVISOR
DEVOIRS
VISORED
VOIDERS
E EROSIVE
I IVORIES
L OLIVERS
VIOLERS
M VERISMO
N RENVOIS
VERSION
R REVISOR
S VIROSES
T TORSIVE

EIOSTT 98
(OTTIES)
A OSTIATE
TOASTIE
B BOTTIES
C COTTISE
SCOTTIE
D DOTIEST
STOITED
E TOEIEST
G EGOTIST
H HOTTIES
L LITOTES
TOILETS
M MOTIEST
TITMOSE
N SNOTTIE
TONIEST
TONITES
O TOOTSIE
P POTTIES
TIPTOES
R STOITER
T TOTTIES
U TOUSTIE
W TOWIEST

EIPRST 132
PRIEST
A PARTIES
PASTIER
PIASTER
PIASTRE
PIRATES
PRATIES
TRAIPSE
C TRICEPS
D SPIRTED
STRIPED
E PESTIER
RESPITE
F PRESIFT
H HIPSTER
I PITIERS
TIPSIER
L RESPLIT
SPIRTLE
TRIPLES
M IMPREST
PERMITS
N NIPTERS
PTERINS
O PERIOST
PORIEST
PROSTIE
REPOSIT
RIPOSTE
ROPIEST
P TIPPERS
R STRIPER
S ESPRITS
PERSIST
PRIESTS
SITREPS
SPRIEST
SPRITES
STIRPES
STRIPES
TRIPSES
T PITTERS
SPITTER
TIPSTER
U PERITUS
PUIREST
V PRIVETS
X EXTIRPS
Y PYRITES
STRIPEY

EIRRST 160
TRIERS
A ARTSIER
SERRATI
TARRIES
TARSIER
D STIRRED
STRIDER
E ETRIERS
REITERS
RESTIER
RETIRES
RETRIES
TERRIES
K SKIRRET
SKIRTER
STRIKER
M RETRIMS
TRIMERS
O RIOTERS
ROISTER
RORIEST
P STRIPER
R STIRRER
S STIRRES
T RITTERS
TERRITS
U RUSTIER
V STRIVER
W WRITERS

EIRSTT 110
SITTER
A ARTIEST
ARTISTE
ATTIRES
IRATEST
RATITES
STRIATE
TASTIER
TERTIAS
B BITTERS
C TRISECT
E TESTIER
F FITTERS
TITFERS
H HITTERS
TITHERS
J JITTERS
TRIJETS
K SKITTER
L LITTERS
SLITTER
STILTER
TESTRIL
TILTERS
TITLERS
M METRIST
N ENTRIST
RETINTS
STINTER
TINTERS
O STOITER
P PITTERS
SPITTER
TIPSTER
R RITTERS
TERRITS
S SITTERS
T STRETTI
TITTERS
TRITEST
U TERTIUS
V TRIVETS
W RETWIST
TWISTER
WITTERS

EIRSTV 168
RIVETS
A TAIVERS
VASTIER
VERITAS
D DIVERTS
STRIVED
VERDITS
E RESTIVE
SIEVERT
STIEVER
VERIEST
VERITES
G GRIVETS
H THRIVES
I REVISIT
STIVIER
VISITER
N INVERTS
STRIVEN
O TORSIVE
P PRIVETS
R STRIVER
S STIVERS
STRIVES
TREVISS
VERISTS
T TRIVETS
U REVUIST
STUIVER
VIRTUES

ELNSTU 218
(LETSUN)
A ELUANTS
UNLASTE
B SUNBELT
UNBELTS
UNBLEST
E ELUENTS
UNSTEEL
F FLUENTS
NESTFUL
NETFULS
G ENGLUTS
GLUTENS
I LUNIEST
LUTEINS
UNTILES
UTENSIL
N TUNNELS
O LENTOUS
P PENULTS
R RUNLETS
T NUTLETS

ELORST 54
OSTLER
A OESTRAL
B BOLSTER
BOLTERS
LOBSTER
C COLTERS
CORSLET
COSTREL
LECTORS
D DROLEST
OLDSTER
STRODLE
E SOLERET
F FLORETS
LOFTERS
H HOLSTER
HOSTLER
I ESTRIOL
LOITERS
TOILERS
J JOLTERS
JOSTLER
L TOLLERS
M MERLOTS
MOLTERS
N LENTORS
O LOOTERS
RETOOLS
ROOTLES
TOOLERS
P PETROLS
REPLOTS
S OSTLERS
STEROLS
TORSELS
T SETTLOR
SLOTTER
TOLTERS
U ELUTORS
OUTLERS
TROULES
V REVOLTS
W TROWELS
WORTLES

ELOSTU 178
TOUSLE
B BOLETUS
D LOUDEST
OULDEST
TOUSLED
F FOULEST
I OUTLIES
L OUTSELL
SELLOUT
N LENTOUS
O OUTSOLE
P TUPELOS
R ELUTORS
OUTLERS
TROULES
S LOTUSES
SOLUTES
TOUSLES
T OUTLETS
U LUTEOUS
V VOLUTES
Z TOUZLES

ELRSTU 211
ULSTER
A ESTRUAL
SALUTER
B BLUSTER
BUSTLER
BUTLERS
SUBTLER
C CLUSTER
CULTERS
CUSTREL
CUTLERS
RELUCTS
D LUSTRED
RUSTLED
STRUDEL
F FLUSTER
FLUTERS
RESTFUL
G GURLETS
H HURTLES
HUSTLER
I LUSTIER
RULIEST
RUTILES
N RUNLETS
O ELUTORS
OUTLERS
TROULES
P SPURTLE
R RUSTLER
S LUSTERS
LUSTRES
RESULTS
RUSTLES
SUTLERS
ULSTERS
T TURTLES
Y SUTLERY

EMNORS 233
SERMON
A ENAMORS
MOANERS
OARSMEN
D MODERNS
RODSMEN
E MOREENS
F ENFORMS
G MONGERS
MORGENS
I MERINOS
MERSION
L MERLONS
O MOONERS
S SERMONS
T MENTORS
MONSTER
MONTRES

EMNOST 190
(MONETS)
A MANTOES
B ENTOMBS
D ENDMOST
E TEMENOS
TONEMES
F FOMENTS
G EMONGST
H MONETHS
I MESTINO
MOISTEN
MONTIES
SENTIMO
L LOMENTS
MELTONS
M MOMENTS
MONTEMS
O MOONSET
P POSTMEN
TOPSMEN
R MENTORS
MONSTER
MONTRES
S STEMSON
U UNSMOTE
Y ETYMONS

EMORST 188
METROS
A AMORETS
MAESTRO
OMERTAS
B BESTORM
MOBSTER
D STORMED
E EMOTERS
METEORS
REMOTES
G GROMETS
H MOTHERS
SMOTHER
THERMOS
I EROTISM
MOISTER
MORTISE
TRISOME
L MERLOTS
MOLTERS
N MENTORS
MONSTER
MONTRES
O MOOTERS
P STOMPER
TROMPES
R TERMORS
TREMORS
S MOTSERS
U MOUTERS
OESTRUM

ENOPRS 208
PERSON
A PERSONA
C CREPONS
D PONDERS
RESPOND
E OPENERS
PERONES
REOPENS
REPONES
G PRESONG
SPONGER
H PHONERS
I ORPINES
PIONERS
PROINES
O OPERONS
SNOOPER
R PERRONS
S PERSONS
T POSTERN
PRONEST
U UNROPES
Y PROYNES
PYONERS
PYRONES

ENORST 16
STONER
A ATONERS
SENATOR
TREASON
B BRETONS
SORBENT
C CONSTER
CORNETS
CRESTON
CRONETS
D RODENTS
SNORTED
E ESTRONE
F FRONTES
G TONGERS
H HORNETS
SHORTEN
THRENOS
THRONES
I NORITES
OESTRIN
ORIENTS
STONIER
TERSION
TRIONES
K STONKER
STROKEN
TONKERS
L LENTORS
M MENTORS
MONSTER
MONTRES
N STONERN
TONNERS
O ENROOTS
P POSTERN
PRONEST
R SNORTER
S NESTORS
STONERS
TENSORS
T ROTTENS
SNOTTER
STENTOR
U TENOURS
TONSURE
Y TYRONES

ENOSTT 201
TESTON
A ATTONES
NOTATES
C CONTEST
D SNOTTED
H SHOTTEN
I SNOTTIE
TONIEST
TONITES
J JETTONS
L TONLETS
O TESTOON
P POTENTS
R ROTTENS
SNOTTER
STENTOR
S OSTENTS
TESTONS
U STOUTEN
TENUTOS

ENOSTU 69
(OUTENS)
A SOUTANE
B SUBTONE
C CONTUSE
ECONUTS
D DEUTONS
SNOUTED
E OUTSEEN
G TONGUES
L LENTOUS
M UNSMOTE
N NEUSTON
O UNSOOTE
R TENOURS
TONSURE
S OUTNESS
TONUSES
T STOUTEN
TENUTOS
U TENUOUS

ENRSTU 87
TUNERS
A AUNTERS
NATURES
SAUNTER
B BRUNETS
BUNTERS
BURNETS
BURSTEN
SUBRENT
C ENCRUST
D RETUNDS
UNDREST
E NEUTERS
RETUNES
TENURES
TUREENS
F FUNSTER
G GUNTERS
GURNETS
SURGENT
H HUNTERS
SHUNTER
UNHERST
I NUTSIER
TRIUNES
UNITERS
L RUNLETS
M MUNSTER
STERNUM
N RUNNETS
STUNNER
O TENOURS
TONSURE
P PUNSTER
PUNTERS
R RETURNS
TURNERS
S UNRESTS
T ENTRUST
NUTTERS

EOPRST 192
POSTER
A ESPARTO
PROTEAS
SEAPORT
B BESPORT
C COPTERS
PROSECT
D DEPORTS
REDTOPS
SPORTED
F FORPETS
H POTHERS
STROPHE
THORPES
I PERIOST
PORIEST
PROSTIE
REPOSIT
RIPOSTE
ROPIEST
J PROJETS
L PETROLS
REPLOTS
M STOMPER
TROMPES
N POSTERN
PRONEST
O POOREST
POOTERS
STOOPER
P STOPPER
TOPPERS
R PORTERS
PRESORT
PRETORS
REPORTS
SPORTER
S PORTESS
POSTERS
PRESTOS
REPOSTS
RESPOTS
STOPERS
T POTTERS
PROTEST
SPOTTER
U PETROUS
POSTURE
POUTERS
PROTEUS
SEPTUOR
SPOUTER
TROUPES
W POWTERS
PROWEST
X EXPORTS
Z POTZERS

EORRST 112
SORTER
A ROASTER
C RECTORS
D DORTERS
RODSTER
E RESTORE
G GROSERT
H RHETORS
ROTHERS
SHORTER
I RIOTERS
ROISTER
RORIEST
K STROKER
M TERMORS
TREMORS
N SNORTER
O ROOSTER
ROOTERS
TOREROS
P PORTERS
PRESORT
PRETORS
REPORTS
SPORTER
R RORTERS
TERRORS
S RESORTS
ROSTERS
SORTERS
STORERS
T RETORTS
ROTTERS
STERTOR
TORRETS
U RETOURS
ROUSTER
ROUTERS
TOURERS
TROUSER
V TROVERS
W STROWER
Y ROYSTER
STROYER

EORSTT 121
OTTERS
A ROTATES
TOASTER
B BETTORS
C COTTERS
D DETORTS
DOTTERS
E ROSETTE
H HOTTERS
I STOITER
J JOTTERS
L SETTLOR
SLOTTER
TOLTERS
N ROTTENS
SNOTTER
STENTOR
O TOOTERS
P POTTERS
PROTEST
SPOTTER
R RETORTS
ROTTERS
STERTOR
TORRETS
T STOTTER
STRETTO
TOTTERS
U OUTSERT
STOUTER
TOUTERS
W SWOTTER
X EXTORTS
Y ROSETTY

GIINRT 234
TIRING
A AIRTING
RAITING
B RINGBIT
C TRICING
D DIRTING
E IGNITER
TIERING
TIGRINE
F RIFTING
G GIRTING
RINGGIT
L TIRLING
M MITRING
N TRINING
O IGNITOR
RIOTING
R TIRRING
S STIRING
TIRINGS
T RITTING
W TWIRING
WRITING

GILNOT 175
TOLING
A ANTILOG
B BILTONG
BOLTING
C COLTING
E LENTIGO
F LOFTING
H THOLING
I TOILING
J JOLTING
L TOLLING
M MOLTING
O LOOTING
TOOLING
P POLTING
S LINGOTS
TIGLONS
TOLINGS
T LOTTING
U LOUTING
W LOWTING

GINORS 139
SIGNOR
A IGNAROS
ORIGANS
SIGNORA
SOARING
B BORINGS
ROBINGS
SORBING
C SCORING
D RODINGS
E ERINGOS
IGNORES
REGIONS
SIGNORE
G GORINGS
GRINGOS
H HORSING
SHORING
I ORIGINS
SIGNIOR
SIGNORI
L LORINGS
M SMORING
N SNORING
SORNING
O ROOSING
P PROIGNS
PROSING
ROPINGS
SPORING
S GRISONS
INGROSS
SIGNORS
SORINGS
T ROSTING
SORTING
STORING
TRIGONS
U ROUSING
SOURING
V ROVINGS
W ROWINGS
WORSING
Y ROSYING
SIGNORY

GINORT 107
ROTING
A ORATING
ROATING
D DORTING
E GENITOR
F FORTING
I IGNITOR
RIOTING
K TROKING
O ROOTING
P PORTING
TROPING
R RORTING
S ROSTING
SORTING
STORING
TRIGONS
T ROTTING

U OUTGRIN
OUTRING
ROUTING
TOURING
W ROWTING
TROWING

GINOST 184
TOSING
A AGONIST
GITANOS
C COSTING
GNOSTIC
D DOTINGS
F SOFTING
H HOSTING
TOSHING
K STOKING
L LINGOTS
TIGLONS
TOLINGS
M GNOMIST
N STONING
TONINGS
O SOOTING
P POSTING
STOPING
R ROSTING
SORTING
STORING
TRIGONS
S STINGOS
TOSSING
T SOTTING
U OUSTING
OUTINGS
OUTSING
TOUSING
V STOVING
W STOWING
TOWINGS
TOWSING
Y TOYINGS

INORST 60
INTROS
A AROINTS
RATIONS
B RIBSTON
C CISTRON
CITRONS
CORNIST
CORTINS
E NORITES
OESTRIN
ORIENTS
STONIER
TERSION
TRIONES
F FORINTS
G ROSTING
SORTING
STORING
TRIGONS
H HORNIST
I IRONIST
L NOSTRIL
N INTRONS
O ISOTRON
NITROSO
TORSION
P TROPINS
T INTORTS
TRITONS
U NITROUS
TURIONS

7-LETTER SETS LIST

alphabetical list of all words appearing in 7-Letter Sets

ABATERS
ABELIAS
ABIDERS
ABLEISM
ABLEIST
ABLINGS
ABREAST
ABRIDGE
ABSEILS
ACARINE
ACATERS
ACCENTS
ACEROSE
ACEROUS
ACETALS
ACETINS
ACETOSE
ACETOUS
ACETYLS
ACIDEST
ACINOSE
ACMITES
ACTINGS
ACTRESS
ACTURES
ADAPTER
ADDREST
ADENYLS
ADEPTER
ADERMIN
ADHERES
ADMIRES
ADONISE
ADOPTER
ADORERS
ADORING
ADRENAL
ADVENTS
ADVERSE
ADVERTS
ADVISER
AEDILES
AERATES
AERIALS
AERIEST
AEROBES
AEROBUS
AEROSAT
AEROSOL
AETHERS
AFREETS
AGAINST
AGELAST
AGENTRY
AGILEST
AGINNER
AGISTED
AGISTER
AGNAILS
AGNATES
AGNISED
AGONIES
AGONISE
AGONIST
AGRASTE
AGRISED
AIDLESS
AIGLETS
AIGRETS
AILMENT
AIMLESS
AIRIEST
AIRINGS
AIRLESS
AIRSHED
AIRSIDE
AIRTING
AISLING
ALBERTS
ALBITES
ALDRINS
ALECOST
ALEGARS
ALENGTH
ALERCES
ALEYING
ALGATES
ALGESIS
ALIASES
ALIBIES
ALIGNED
ALIGNER
ALIMENT
ALINERS
ALIPEDS
ALLISES
ALMNERS
ALNAGER
ALNAGES
ALSIKES
ALTERNE
ALUMINE
ALUNITE
AMBEERS
AMBIENT
AMBRIES
AMEARST
AMENDES
AMENITY
AMENTAL
AMENTIA
AMERCES
AMITIES
AMMINES
AMNESIA
AMNESIC
AMNESTY
AMNIOTE
AMORCES
AMORETS
AMOSITE
AMPERES
ANADEMS
ANAPEST
ANCRESS
ANELING
ANEMIAS
ANERGIA
ANERGIC
ANEROID
ANESTRA
ANESTRI
ANGELED
ANGELIC
ANGELUS
ANGERED
ANGERLY
ANGLERS
ANGLICE
ANGLIST
ANGRIER
ANGRIES
ANGRILY
ANIMATE
ANISEED
ANISOLE
ANKLETS
ANLAGES
ANNATES
ANODISE
ANOESIS
ANOMIES
ANSATED
ANSWERS
ANTHEMS
ANTHERS
ANTIARS
ANTILOG
ANTINGS
ANTIRED
ANTISAG
ANTISEX
ANTLERS
ANTLIAE
ANTLIKE
ANTSIER
ANYTIME
APERIES
APLITES
APOSTLE
APPRISE
APTERAL
APTNESS
ARAISED
ARANEID
ARBORES
ARBUTES
ARCADES
ARCHEST
ARCHINE
ARCHLET
ARCINGS
ARCSINE
ARCTICS
AREDING
AREFIES
ARENITE
AREOLAS
AREOLES
ARGENTS
ARGLING
ARGYLES
ARIDEST
ARIETTA
ARIETTE
ARISING
ARISTAE
ARKITES
ARMINGS
ARMLETS
ARMREST
AROINTS
AROUSED
AROYNTS
ARPENTS
ARRASED
ARRESTS
ARRIDES
ARSENAL
ARSENIC
ARSHINE
ARSINES
ARTICLE
ARTIEST
ARTISAN
ARTISTE
ARTLESS
ARTSIER
ARTSIES
ARTSMEN
ASCENTS
ASKLENT
ASPIRED
ASPIRER
ASPIRES
ASSERTS
ASSLIKE
ASTEISM
ASTELIC
ASTERIA
ASTERID
ASTERTS
ASTHORE
ASTILBE
ASTONED
ASTRICT
ASTRIDE
ASTUTER
ASUNDER
ATEBRIN
ATELIER
ATHEISM
ATHEIST
ATIMIES
ATINGLE
ATOMIES
ATOMISE
ATONERS
ATONIES
ATOPIES
ATRESIA
ATTAINS
ATTENDS
ATTENTS
ATTIRED
ATTIRES
ATTONES
ATTORNS
ATTRITE
ATTUNES
AUDILES
AULDEST
AUNTERS
AUNTIES
AURICLE
AUSTERE
AVENIRS
AVIDEST
AVOCETS
AWAREST
AWMRIES
AWNIEST
BADGERS
BAILEES
BAILERS
BAILEYS
BAILIES
BAITERS
BALDEST
BALDIER
BALDIES
BALLIES
BANDERS
BANDIER
BANDIES
BANGERS
BANGLED
BANGLES
BANNETS
BANTERS
BANTIES
BARBETS
BARDIER
BARDING
BARGEST
BARITES
BARRETS
BARTERS
BARTONS
BARYTES
BASINED
BASINET
BASTERS
BASTIDE
BASTILE
BASTING
BATHERS
BATISTE
BATLERS
BATSMEN
BATTENS
BATTERS
BATTIER
BATTLER
BAWDIER
BAXTERS
BEADIER
BEAMERS
BEARDIE
BEARERS
BEARING
BEATERS
BEDAMNS
BEDRAIL
BEDRALS
BEGIRDS
BELIERS
BELTERS
BELTING
BELTMAN
BEMIRES
BENDERS
BENDIER
BENIGHT
BENTIER
BERATES
BERIMES
BERLINS
BERRETS
BERRIES
BERTHAS
BESAINT
BESMEAR
BESOINS
BESORTS
BESPORT
BESTAIN
BESTARS
BESTEAD
BESTIAL
BESTING
BESTIRS
BESTORM
BESTRID
BESTROW
BETOILS
BETRAYS
BETRIMS
BETTERS
BETTORS
BEWAILS
BEZOARS
BIDDERS
BIDENTS
BILKERS
BILLERS
BILTONG
BINDERS
BINDLES
BINGERS
BINGLED
BINGLES
BIOGENS
BIRDERS
BIRDIES
BIREMES
BIRETTA
BIRLERS
BIRSLED
BIRSLES
BISTATE
BISTERS
BISTRED
BISTRES
BITSIER
BITTERN
BITTERS
BLANDER
BLARING
BLASTED
BLASTER
BLASTIE
BLATHER
BLATTER
BLEATER
BLENDES
BLEWART
BLISTER
BLOATER
BLONDES
BLUIEST
BLUSTER
BOASTER
BOATELS
BOATERS
BOILERS
BOLDENS
BOLETUS
BOLSTER
BOLTERS
BOLTING
BONIEST
BOOSTER
BORACES
BORAGES
BORANES
BORATES
BORAXES
BORDELS
BORIDES
BORINGS
BORTZES
BOSHTER
BOSSIER
BOTHERS
BOTTIES
BOUNDER
BRAIDED
BRAIDER
BRAILED
BRAINED
BRAISED
BRANGLE
BRANLES
BRANSLE
BRANTLE
BRASERO
BRASSET
BRATTLE
BRAVEST
BRAVOES
BRAWEST
BREARES
BREASTS
BREATHS
BREDING
BRETONS
BRIARED
BRIDGES
BRIDIES
BRIDLES
BRIGADE
BRIGAND
BRISANT
BRISKED
BRISKET
BRISTLE
BRUISED
BRUNETS
BUNTERS
BUNTIER
BURDENS
BURDIES
BURNETS
BURSATE
BURSTED
BURSTEN
BUSTIER
BUSTLER
BUTLERS
CABLETS
CABRITS
CADGERS
CAIRNED
CALENDS
CALIBER
CALIBRE
CALIPER
CALIVER
CALLETS
CALMEST
CALMIER
CALORIE
CAMLETS
CAMOTES
CANCERS
CANDIES
CANDLER
CANDLES
CANGLED
CANGLES
CANIEST
CANINES
CANKERS
CANNERS
CANNIER
CANTERS
CANTEST
CANTIER
CANTLES
CANTORS
CANTRED
CANTREF
CAPLETS
CAPOTES
CAPRINE
CARATES
CARBIDE
CARBINE
CARDERS
CARDIES
CARDING
CAREENS
CAREERS
CAREMES
CARGOES
CARINAE
CARIOLE
CARITAS
CARLINE
CARLING
CARMINE
CARNETS
CARNEYS
CARNIED
CARNIER
CARNIES
CARNOSE
CAROUSE
CARPELS
CARPETS
CARTELS
CARTERS
CARTING
CARTONS
CASEINS
CASERNE
CASERNS
CASTERS
CASTING
CASTLED
CASTLES
CATENAS
CATERAN
CATLING
CATNEPS
CATTIER
CATTIES
CAUTELS
CAUTERS
CAVERNS
CAVILER
CEASING
CEDRINE
CEILERS
CELESTA
CENOTES
CENSORS
CENTALS
CENTARE
CENTAUR
CENTERS
CENTRAL
CENTRES
CERASIN
CERATES
CERATIN
CEREALS
CERESIN
CERITES
CERNING
CEROONS
CERRIAL
CERTAIN
CESSION
CESTOID
CETANES
CHAINES
CHALETS
CHANTER
CHARETS
CHARLIE
CHASTEN
CHASTER
CHENARS
CHOREAS
CICEROS
CINDERS
CINEAST
CINEMAS
CINEOLS
CINEREA
CIRROSE
CISTERN
CISTRON
CITHERS
CITOLES
CITRALS
CITRATE
CITRINE
CITRONS
CITTERN
CLAIMER
CLANGED
CLANGER
CLARETS
CLARIES
CLAROES
CLASPER
CLAVIER
CLAYIER
CLIENTS
CLINGED
CLINGER
CLONERS
CLUSTER
CNEMIAL
COALERS
COALIER
COARSEN
COARSER

COASTED
COASTER
COATEES
COATERS
COAXERS
CODEINS
COEDITS
COGNISE
COHEIRS
COIGNES
COILERS
COINERS
COLTERS
COLTING
COMATES
CONCISE
CONDERS
CONDIES
CONFERS
CONFEST
CONGERS
CONGEST
CONINES
CONKERS
CONNERS
CONSEIL
CONSENT
CONSTER
CONTEST
CONTRAS
CONTUSE
CONURES
COOTERS
COPIERS
COPSIER
COPTERS
CORBIES
CORDING
CORNEAS
CORNELS
CORNERS
CORNETS
CORNIST
CORRIES
CORSAGE
CORSETS
CORSIVE
CORSLET
CORSNED
CORTILE
CORTINS
CORVEES
CORVETS
COSIERS
COSINES
COSTATE
COSTEAN
COSTERS
COSTING
COSTREL
COTISED
COTTERS
COTTISE
COUTERS
COVENTS
COVERTS
COWRIES
COZIERS
CRADLES
CRAPLES
CRASHED
CRATERS
CRATING
CRATONS
CRAVENS
CREASED
CREASER
CREATES
CREATIN
CREDITS
CREMSIN
CRENATE
CREPONS
CRESTAL
CRESTED
CRESTON
CRETICS
CRETINS
CRETISM
CRINATE
CRINGED
CRINGES
CRINGLE
CRINITE
CRINOSE
CRISPEN
CRISTAE
CRIVENS
CRONETS
CRONIES
CROSIER
CROUTES
CRUDEST
CRUISED
CRUNODE
CRUSADE
CRUSTAE
CRUSTED
CUITERS
CULTERS
CURATES
CURIETS
CURITES
CUSTODE
CUSTREL
CUTLERS
CYANISE
CYSTEIN
CYSTINE
CZARIST
DABSTER
DACITES
DACKERS
DAEMONS
DAFTIES
DAGGERS
DAIDLES
DAIKERS
DAILIES
DAIRIES
DALETHS
DALLIER
DALLIES
DAMNERS
DAMPENS
DANCERS
DANDERS
DANDIER
DANDIES
DANDLER
DANDLES
DANGERS
DANGLED
DANGLER
DANGLES
DANKEST
DANSEUR
DARBIES
DARCIES
DARGLES
DARINGS
DARIOLE
DARKENS
DARKEST
DARKIES
DARKING
DARKLES
DARLING
DARNELS
DARNERS
DARNING
DARRING
DARTERS
DARTING
DARTLES
DARTRES
DASHIER
DATINGS
DATIVES
DAUBIER
DAUNDER
DAUNERS
DAUNTER
DAURING
DAUTIES
DAWNERS
DAWTIES
DAYSMEN
DEADERS
DEADEST
DEAFEST
DEALERS
DEALING
DEANERS
DEAREST
DEARIES
DEARING
DEARNLY
DEARTHS
DEASILS
DEASIUL
DEASOIL
DEBASER
DEBATES
DEBTORS
DECANTS
DECARBS
DECARES
DECERNS
DECRIAL
DECRIES
DEFASTE
DEFEATS
DEFIERS
DEFINER
DEFRAGS
DEFROST
DEGOUTS
DEHORTS
DEICERS
DEISEAL
DEKARES
DELATES
DELATOR
DELEING
DELIRIA
DELIVER
DELVING
DEMAINS
DEMANDS
DEMEANS
DEMENTS
DENARII
DENTALS
DENIERS
DENNETS
DENOTES
DENSELY
DENSEST
DENSITY
DENTALS
DENTELS
DENTILS
DENTINS
DENTIST
DEODARS
DEPARTS
DEPORTS
DEPOSIT
DERAIGN
DERAILS
DERANGE
DERATES
DERBIES
DERIDES
DERIVES
DERNIER
DERRIES
DESALTS
DESCANT
DESCENT
DESERTS
DESIGNS
DESIRED
DESIRER
DESIRES
DESKMAN
DESMANS
DESMINE
DESPAIR
DESSERT
DESTAIN
DESTINE
DESTINY
DESTROY
DESUGAR
DETAILS
DETAINS
DETENTS
DETENUS
DETORTS
DETOURS
DETRAIN
DETUNES
DEUTONS
DEVISAL
DEVISER
DEVISOR
DEVLING
DEVOIRS
DEWANIS
DEXTERS
DIABLES
DIALERS
DIALLER
DIALYSE
DIAPERS
DIARIES
DIARISE
DIASTEM
DIASTER
DIBBERS
DIEDRAL
DIEDRES
DIESTER
DIETERS
DIGGERS
DIGRESS
DILATER
DILATES
DILUTER
DILUTES
DINDLES
DINEROS
DINGERS
DINGEYS
DINGIER
DINGIES
DINGLES
DINGOES
DINKEST
DINNERS
DINNLES
DIOPTER
DIOPTRE
DIPNETS
DIPTERA
DIRECTS
DIREMPT
DIRIGES
DIRTIES
DIRTING
DISABLE
DISCERN
DISCOER
DISCURE
DISEURS
DISLEAF
DISLEAL
DISNEST
DISPONE
DISRANK
DISRATE
DISROBE
DISSEAT
DISSENT
DISSERT
DISTANT
DISTEND
DISTENT
DISTOME
DISTUNE
DITHERS
DITONES
DITSIER
DIVERSE
DIVERTS
DOATERS
DOCENTS
DOESKIN
DOGEARS
DOILTER
DOLINES
DOLMENS
DOMIEST
DOMINES
DONATES
DONGLES
DONSIER
DONZELS
DOPIEST
DORISED
DORISES
DORIZES
DORRING
DORSELS
DORTERS
DORTING
DOSSIER
DOTIEST
DOTINGS
DOTTERS
DOTTLER
DOTTREL
DOUCEST
DOUCETS
DOUREST
DOURINE
DOUTERS
DOVIEST
DOWIEST
DOWLNES
DOWRIES
DOZIEST
DRAGEES
DRAGNET
DRAILED
DRAINED
DRAINER
DRAPERS
DRAPETS
DRAPING
DRASTIC
DRAWEES
DRAWERS
DRAWING
DRAYING
DRAZELS
DREARES
DREEING
DRIBLET
DROLEST
DRONING
DROPLET
DROSERA
DROVING
DRUSIER
DUELING
DUELIST
DUETTOS
DUIKERS
DUNDERS
DUNGIER
DUNITES
DUNKERS
DUNNEST
DUNNIER
DURAMEN
DURANCE
DURIANS
DURRIES
DUSKIER
DUSTERS
DUSTIER
DUSTMEN
DUTEOUS
DYEINGS
DYESTER
DZERENS
EAGLETS
EANLING
EARBOBS
EARCONS
EARDING
EARINGS
EARLAPS
EARLESS
EARLIES
EARNERS
EARNEST
EARNING
EARRING
EARSHOT
EARTHLY
EASTERN
EASTERS
EASTING
EASTLIN
EATINGS
EBONICS
EBONIST
ECARTES
ECHARDS
ECLAIRS
ECONUTS
EDGINGS
EDITORS
EELIEST
EERIEST
EFFEIRS
EGOTISM
EGOTIST
EILDING
ELANETS
ELAPIDS
ELASTIC
ELASTIN
ELATERS
ELATING
ELATION
ELDINGS
ELEGANT
ELEGIST
ELEGITS
ELICITS
ELIDING
ELISION
ELITISM
ELITIST
ELMIEST
ELOGIES
ELOGIST
ELOIGNS
ELUANTS
ELUDING
ELUENTS
ELUSION
ELUTING
ELUTORS
EMANANT
EMANATE
EMBAILS
EMBRAID
EMERIES
EMETINS
EMICANT
EMIGRES
EMODINS
EMONGST
EMOTERS
EMPARES
EMPARLS
EMPARTS
EMPIRES
EMPRISE
EMPTINS
ENACTOR
ENAMORS
ENCINAS
ENCORES
ENCRATY
ENCRUST
ENDARTS
ENDEARS
ENDINGS
ENDITES
ENDLANG
ENDLESS
ENDMOST
ENDORSE
ENDRINS
ENDURES
ENDUROS
ENEMATA
ENEMIES
ENERGID
ENFANTS
ENFIRED
ENFIRES
ENFOLDS
ENFORMS
ENGAOLS
ENGILDS
ENGINER
ENGIRDS
ENGLISH
ENGLUTS
ENGORES
ENGRAFT
ENGRAIL
ENGRAIN
ENGRAMS
ENGRASP
ENGROSS
ENGUARD
ENIGMAS
ENISLED
ENLARDS
ENLARGE
ENLIGHT
ENLISTS
ENRACES
ENRAGED
ENRAGES
ENRINGS
ENROOTS
ENROUND
ENSEARS
ENSILED
ENSNARL
ENSTAMP
ENSTYLE
ENSURED
ENTAILS
ENTAMES
ENTASIA
ENTASIS
ENTERAL
ENTERIC
ENTHRAL
ENTICER
ENTICES
ENTIRES
ENTOILS
ENTOMBS
ENTRAIL
ENTRAIN
ENTRALL
ENTRANT
ENTRAPS
ENTREAT
ENTREES
ENTRIES
ENTRISM
ENTRIST
ENTROLD
ENTRUST
ENTWIST
ENURING
ENVIERS
EOLITHS
EONISMS
EOSINES
EOSINIC
EPACRIS
EPEIRAS
EPIGONS
EPILOGS
EPIMERS
EPINAOS
EPISTLE
EPSILON
EPURATE
ERASERS
ERASING
ERASION
ERASURE
EREPSIN
ERGATES
ERINGOS
ERINITE
ERISTIC
ERLKING
ERMINED
ERMINES
ERODING
EROSION
EROSIVE
EROTICS
EROTISM
ERRANDS
ERRANTS
ERRATAS
ERRINGS
ERYNGOS
ESCOLAR
ESCORTS
ESLOINS
ESPARTO
ESPIALS
ESPRITS
ESSOINS
ESTATED
ESTIVAL
ESTOILE
ESTOVER
ESTRADE
ESTRAYS
ESTREAT
ESTRICH
ESTRINS
ESTRIOL
ESTRONE
ESTRUAL
ETACISM
ETALONS
ETAMINE
ETAMINS
ETATISM
ETATIST
ETCHING
ETERNAL
ETESIAN
ETHIONS
ETHIOPS
ETHNICS
ETOILES
ETRIERS
ETTLING
ETYMONS
EUCAINS
EVADERS
EVILEST
EVILLER
EVOKERS
EXHORTS
EXODIST
EXOTISM
EXPORTS
EXPOSIT
EXTENDS
EXTERNS
EXTIRPS
EXTORTS
EXTRAIT

EYLIADS
FADIEST
FAERIES
FAIBLES
FAINEST
FAINTER
FAIREST
FALSIES
FALSING
FALTERS
FAMINES
FANCIER
FANCIES
FANGLED
FANGLES
FARDELS
FARDENS
FARDING
FARNESS
FARSIDE
FARSING
FARTHEL
FARTING
FASCINE
FASTERS
FASTING
FATHERS
FATLING
FATTENS
FATTIER
FATTIES
FEALING
FEARERS
FEARING
FEASTED
FEASTER
FEDORAS
FEERIES
FEERINS
FEINTER
FELSITE
FELSPAR
FELTERS
FELTING
FEMINAL
FENDERS
FENDIER
FENITAR
FERLIES
FERNING
FERRETS
FERRIES
FETIALS
FETTERS
FIANCES
FIBSTER
FILACER
FILASSE
FILTERS
FINAGLE
FINDERS
FINEERS
FINGERS
FIREMAN
FIRMEST
FISTIER
FITNESS
FITTERS
FLANGED
FLANGER
FLANGES
FLARING
FLENSED
FLINGER
FLIRTED
FLORETS
FLUENTS
FLUIEST
FLUSTER
FLUTERS
FOISTED
FOISTER
FOLATES
FOLDERS
FOMENTS
FOMITES
FONDEST
FONDLES
FORDING
FORINTS
FORPETS
FORTIES
FORTING
FOTHERS
FOULEST
FOUNDER
FRAISED
FRATERS
FREESIA
FREMITS
FRETSAW
FRIANDE
FRIANDS
FRIDGES
FRIENDS
FRIEZES
FRINGED
FRINGES
FRISEES
FRISKET
FRISTED
FRITZES
FROISES
FRONTES
FROSTED
FUNDERS
FUNSTER
FUSTIER
GABLETS
GADDERS
GADSMEN
GAGSTER
GAHNITE
GAINERS
GAINEST
GAITERS
GALENAS
GALENIC
GALERES
GALLEIN
GALLETS
GALORES
GAMIEST
GAMINES
GANDERS
GANGERS
GANGREL
GANNETS
GANTLET
GAOLERS
GARBLES
GARDENS
GARGETS
GARGLES
GARMENT
GARNERS
GARNETS
GARNISH
GAROTES
GARRETS
GARTERS
GASPIER
GASTERS
GASTING
GASTREA
GASTRIC
GASTRIN
GATEMAN
GATHERS
GATINGS
GAUNTER
GEALING
GEARING
GELANTS
GELATES
GELATIN
GELATOS
GELDING
GELLANT
GEMINAL
GENDERS
GENERAL
GENISTA
GENITAL
GENITOR
GENOISE
GENTIER
GENTILE
GENTLES
GERBILS
GERENTS
GERMAIN
GERMANS
GERMENS
GERMINA
GERMINS
GERNING
GERUNDS
GESTALT
GESTANT
GETTERS
GIANTLY
GIANTRY
GIBLETS
GIGLETS
GILDERS
GILLERS
GILLETS
GILLNET
GIMLETS
GINGALS
GINGERS
GINGLES
GINNELS
GINNERS
GINNERY
GINNIER
GIRDERS
GIRDLES
GIRLIES
GIRLOND
GIRNELS
GIRNERS
GIRTING
GISARME
GITANAS
GITANOS
GITTERN
GLACIER
GLADDEN
GLADIER
GLAIRED
GLAIRES
GLAIRIN
GLANCED
GLANCER
GLANCES
GLANDES
GLARING
GLASSEN
GLASSIE
GLAZERS
GLEANED
GLEANER
GLENOID
GLIDERS
GLINTED
GLIOSES
GLISTEN
GLISTER
GLITZES
GLOIRES
GLORIES
GLUIEST
GLUTENS
GNARLED
GNARRED
GNASHER
GNAWERS
GNOMIST
GNOSTIC
GOALIES
GOITERS
GOITRES
GOLDENS
GOLLIES
GOOLIES
GOONIES
GORHENS
GORIEST
GORINGS
GOVERNS
GRABENS
GRACILE
GRADERS
GRADINE
GRADING
GRADINI
GRADINO
GRADINS
GRAILES
GRAINED
GRAINER
GRAINES
GRAKLES
GRANDEE
GRANDER
GRANGES
GRANITA
GRANITE
GRANNIE
GRANTED
GRANTEE
GRANTER
GRANULE
GRAPLES
GRAPLIN
GRAPNEL
GRASPED
GRASSED
GRATERS
GRATINE
GRATING
GRATINS
GRAVELS
GRAVEST
GRAYEST
GRAYLES
GREASED
GREASER
GREATEN
GRECIAN
GREINED
GREISEN
GREISLY
GREMLIN
GRENADE
GRIESLY
GRIEVES
GRILLES
GRILSES
GRINDED
GRINDER
GRINGOS
GRINNED
GRINNER
GRISELY
GRISLED
GRISONS
GRISTLE
GRIVETS
GROANED
GROINED
GROMETS
GROSERT
GROYNES
GUERDON
GUIDERS
GUILERS
GUNDIES
GUNITES
GUNTERS
GURLETS
GURNETS
GYRATES
GYRENES
HAEMINS
HAFTERS
HAGLETS
HAILERS
HAIRNET
HALBERT
HALIDES
HALITES
HALSING
HALTERE
HALTERS
HALTING
HAMSTER
HANDERS
HANDIER
HANDLER
HANDLES
HANDSEL
HANDSET
HANGERS
HANTLES
HAPTENS
HARDENS
HARDEST
HARDIES
HARDSET
HAREEMS
HARELDS
HARLING
HARMINE
HARNESS
HAROSET
HARPIES
HARSLET
HARTELY
HARTENS
HARVEST
HASTIER
HASTING
HATREDS
HATTERS
HEADERS
HEADSET
HEALERS
HEALING
HEARERS
HEARING
HEARSED
HEARTHS
HEARTLY
HEATERS
HEATING
HECTORS
HEFTING
HEIFERS
HEISTER
HELIAST
HELIMAN
HEMATIN
HEMINAS
HENRIES
HENTING
HERALDS
HERBIST
HERDENS
HERDING
HERIOTS
HERLING
HERMITS
HERNIAS
HEROICS
HEROINS
HERRIES
HETEROS
HETMANS
HINDERS
HINDLEG
HINGERS
HINTERS
HIPSTER
HIRSTIE
HIRSUTE
HISTONE
HITHERS
HITTERS
HOIDENS
HOISTED
HOISTER
HOLDERS
HOLIEST
HOLSTER
HOMIEST
HOMINES
HONDLES
HOOTERS
HORDING
HORNETS
HORNIST
HORSING
HORSTES
HOSIERS
HOSTILE
HOSTING
HOSTLER
HOTTERS
HOTTIES
HOUNDER
HUNTERS
HURDENS
HURDIES
HURTLES
HUSTLER
ICONISE
ICTERUS
IDEATES
IGNAROS
IGNEOUS
IGNITER
IGNITES
IGNITOR
IGNORED
IGNORES
ILEITIS
ILLITES
IMAGERS
IMARETS
IMMENSE
IMMERSE
IMPANEL
IMPASTE
IMPONES
IMPRESA
IMPRESE
IMPREST
INANEST
INARMED
INBREDS
INBREED
INCAGES
INCASED
INCASES
INCAVES
INCEPTS
INCESTS
INCHASE
INCITER
INCITES
INCLOSE
INCOMES
INDARTS
INDENTS
INDEXER
INDITER
INDITES
INDOLES
INDORSE
INDUCER
INDULGE
INEARTH
INEPTER
INERTER
INERTIA
INFAMES
INFARES
INFECTS
INFESTS
INFLAME
INFLATE
INGATES
INGENER
INGESTA
INGESTS
INGRAFT
INGRATE
INGRESS
INGROSS
INHERED
INHERES
INHERIT
INISLED
INJECTS
INJERAS
INJURED
INLACES
INLIERS
INMATES
INNARDS
INOSITE
INQUEST
INROADS
INSANER
INSCAPE
INSEAMS
INSECTS
INSEEMS
INSERTS
INSHORE
INSIDER
INSNARE
INSOLES
INSPECT
INSPIRE
INSTANT
INSTARS
INSTATE
INSTEAD
INSTEPS
INSURED
INSURES
INSWEPT
INTAGLI
INTAKES
INTEGER
INTENDS
INTENSE
INTENTS
INTERIM
INTERNE
INTERNS
INTIMAE
INTINES
INTONES
INTORTS
INTREAT
INTRONS
INTRUDE
INTUSES
INURNED
INVADER
INVADES
INVENTS
INVERSE
INVERTS
INVESTS
INVITER
INWARDS
IODATES
IODINES
IOLITES
IONISED
IONISER
IONISES
IRATELY
IRATEST
IRELESS
IRENICS
IRIDEAL
IRISATE
IRONERS
IRONIES
IRONISE
IRONIST
ISABELS
ISATINE
ISLEMAN
ISLEMEN
ISOBARE
ISOGENY
ISOGONE
ISOLATE
ISOLEAD
ISOLINE
ISOMERE
ISOMERS
ISOTONE
ISOTOPE
ISOTRON
ISOTYPE
ITERANT
ITERATE
IVORIES
IVRESSE
JAILERS
JANGLED
JANGLER
JANGLES
JANTIER
JANTIES
JASMINE
JERBILS
JERBOAS
JERRIES
JESTING
JETTONS
JILTERS
JINGALS
JINGLED
JINGLER
JINGLES
JINGLET
JINGOES
JIRBLES
JITTERS
JOINERS
JOISTED
JOLTERS
JOLTIER
JOLTING
JONTIES
JOSTLER
JOTTERS
JOUSTED
KALENDS
KANDIES
KANTENS
KARITES
KARSTIC
KARTERS
KARTING
KEISTER
KELTERS
KELTIES
KENOSIS
KENTIAS
KERATIN
KERNING
KERNISH
KERNITE
KERRIES
KESTING
KESTREL
KIESTER
KILERGS
KILTERS
KILTIES
KINDERS
KINDEST
KINDLES
KINEMAS
KINGLES
KINGLET
KINREDS
KIRTLED
KIRTLES
KITTENS
KLISTER
KNITTER
KRANSES
KRATERS

LAAGERS LABISES LABRETS LABROSE LACIEST LACINGS LACTASE LACTOSE LADDERS LADDIES LADINGS LADLERS LADRONE LAERING LAGENAS LAGENDS LAGGENS LAGGERS LAGGINS LAGUNES LAIKERS LAIRING LAIRISE LAISSES LAITIES LAKIEST LAKINGS LALDIES LAMBENT LAMBERT LAMBIES LAMENTS LAMINAE LAMITER LAMPERS LAMSTER LANCERS LANCETS LANDERS LANDLER LANGEST LANGREL LANGUED LANGUES LANGUET LANKEST LANNERS LANTERN LAPIDES LAPISES LAPPERS LAPSERS LAPSING LARDERS LARDIER LARDING LARGENS LARGESS LARGEST LARKING LARNING LASAGNE LASHING LASINGS LASSIES LASSOER LASTAGE LASTERS LASTING LATCHES LATEENS LATENTS LATHERS LATHERY LATHIER

LATHING LATICES LATRINE LATRONS LATTENS LATTINS LAUDERS LAUNDER LAVEERS LAWINGS LAYINGS LAZIEST LEADENS LEADERS LEADIER LEADING LEAFING LEAKERS LEAKING LEAMING LEANERS LEANEST LEANING LEAPERS LEAPING LEARING LEARNED LEASERS LEASING LEASURE LEATHER LEAVERS LEAVIER LEAVING LECTINS LECTORS LEDDENS LEERING LEESING LEFTIES LEGATES LEGATOS LEGENDS LEGGINS LEGIONS LEGISTS LEGLANS LEGLINS LEIGERS LEIRING LEISHER LEISLER LEISTER LEISURE LENDERS LENDING LENGEST LENSING LENTIGO LENTILS LENTISK LENTORS LENTOUS LEOTARD LESBIAN LESIONS LESTING LETTERS LETTING LETTRES LEVANTS LEVIERS LEVITES LIAISED LIAISES

LIBATES LIBBERS LIBEROS LIBRATE LIDGERS LIEFEST LIEGERS LIERNES LIEVEST LIFTERS LIGANDS LIGASES LIGATES LIGGERS LIGHTEN LIGNAGE LIGNITE LIGNOSE LIGURES LIMBERS LIMIEST LIMITES LIMNERS LINAGES LINDENS LINDIES LINEAGE LINEATE LINEMAN LINGAMS LINGELS LINGERS LINGIER LINGLES LINGOES LINGOTS LINGUAE LINGUAS LINIEST LINKAGE LINKERS LINNETS LINSANG LINSEED LINTELS LINTERS LINTIER LINTIES LIONELS LIONESS LIONETS LIONISE LIPASES LISENTE LISTEES LISTENS LISTERS LITERAL LITOTES LITTERS LIVENER LOADENS LOADERS LOAFERS LOANERS LOATHER LOATHES LOBSTER LOCATES LODGERS LOFTERS LOFTIER LOFTING LOGIEST LOITERS

LOMEINS LOMENTA LOMENTS LONGERS LONGIES LOONIES LOOTERS LOOTING LORDING LORICAE LORINGS LORISES LORRIES LOSSIER LOTTING LOTUSES LOUDENS LOUDEST LOUNDER LOUSIER LOUTING LOWTING LUETICS LUNGIES LUNIEST LURDANE LURDENS LURGIES LUSTERS LUSTIER LUSTRED LUSTRES LUTEINS LUTEOUS LYNAGES MADDENS MADNESS MAELIDS MAENADS MAESTRI MAESTRO MAGENTA MAGNATE MAGNETS MAHSEER MAIDENS MAIGRES MAILERS MAILMEN MAIMERS MAINEST MAISTER MALGRES MALIGNS MALINES MALTEDS MALTIER MALTING MALTMEN MALTOSE MANATEE MANDATE MANDIRS MANDREL MANGELS MANGERS MANGIER MANGLED MANGLER MANGLES MANILLE MANIPLE MANKIER MANLIER MANLIKE

MANNITE MANREDS MANTEAU MANTEEL MANTELS MANTIES MANTLED MANTLES MANTLET MANTOES MANURED MANWISE MARDIES MARGENT MARGINS MARINER MARINES MARKETS MARLINE MARLING MARLITE MARRIES MARTELS MARTENS MARTING MARTINS MASHIER MASONED MASSIER MASTERS MASTERY MASTIER MASTING MATIEST MATINEE MATINGS MATRICS MATRONS MATTERS MATTIES MATTINS MATURES MAUNDER MAYSTER MAZIEST MEAGRES MEALERS MEALING MEANERS MEANEST MEANIES MEARING MEASING MEASURE MEATMAN MEDIALS MEDIANS MEDIANT MEDINAS MEDLARS MEDLING MEDUSAN MEINEYS MEINIES MEISTER MELANIC MELANIN MELDING MELTERS MELTING MELTONS MENDERS MENHIRS MENIALS MENTORS

MENYIES MERCATS MERCIES MERINOS MERISES MERKINS MERLING MERLINS MERLONS MERLOTS MERRIES MERSION MESAILS MESHIER MESONIC MESSIER MESTINO MESTIZA MESTIZO METEORS METIERS METRICS METRING METRIST MICATES MIGRANT MILDENS MILTERS MINABLE MINARET MINCERS MINDERS MINDSET MINEOLA MINERAL MINGLED MINGLER MINGLES MINIATE MINIEST MINSTER MINTAGE MINTERS MINTIER MINUETS MINUTER MINUTES MIRACLE MIRAGES MIRBANE MIREXES MIRIEST MIRKEST MISAVER MISDATE MISDEAL MISDOER MISDONE MISEATS MISERES MISFARE MISGONE MISHEAR MISKENT MISLEAD MISMATE MISNAME MISRATE MISREAD MISSEAT MISSEEN MISSENT MISTAKE MISTEND MISTERM

MISTERS MISTERY MISTIER MISTUNE MISWEEN MISWENT MITHERS MITOSES MITRING MITTENS MOANERS MOBSTER MODENAS MODERNS MODISTE MOIDERS MOILERS MOISERS MOISTED MOISTEN MOISTER MOLDERS MOLINES MOLTERS MOLTING MOMENTS MONADES MONETHS MONGERS MONSTER MONTEMS MONTIES MONTRES MOONERS MOONIES MOONSET MOOTERS MOPIEST MORAINE MORALES MOREENS MORGENS MORTISE MOSSIER MOTHERS MOTIEST MOTILES MOTIVES MOTLIER MOTSERS MOURNED MOUSTED MOUTERS MRIDANG MUNITES MUNSTER MUREINS MURINES MUSTIER MUTINES NACKETS NACRITE NAGARIS NAGGERS NAGGIER NAIADES NAIFEST NAILERS NAILSET NAIVEST NAMASTE NAMETAG NANCIES NARASES NARCEIN

NARCIST NARCOSE NARDINE NARDING NARGILE NARGILY NARRATE NARTJIE NASCENT NASTIER NASTIES NATCHES NATIVES NATRONS NATTERS NATTERY NATTIER NATURED NATURES NEALING NEAREST NEARING NEATENS NEATEST NECROSE NECTARS NECTARY NEEDERS NEEDIER NEEDLES NEGATER NEGATES NEGATOR NEGRESS NEGROES NEGROID NEGRONI NEITHER NEMATIC NEMESIA NEMESIS NEPETAS NERDIER NERDISH NEREIDS NERITES NERITIC NEROLIS NERVING NESTERS NESTFUL NESTING NESTLED NESTLER NESTLES NESTORS NETFULS NETLESS NETTERS NETTIER NETTLES NEURISM NEURITE NEUROID NEUSTON NEUTERS NEUTRAL NICHERS NICKERS NIDGETS NIELLOS NIFTIER NIGELLA NIGGARD NIGGERS

NIGGLED NIGGLER NIGGLES NIGHEST NIGHTED NIGHTIE NILGAIS NILGAUS NIMMERS NIPPERS NIPTERS NITERIE NITRATE NITRIDE NITRILE NITRITE NITROSO NITROUS NITTIER NOCENTS NOCKETS NODDIES NODDLES NODULES NOISIER NOISOME NOMADES NONARTS NOODLES NORITES NOSIEST NOSTRIL NOTATES NOTCHES NOTICES NOUSLED NOVICES NUDGERS NURDLES NURSLED NUTATES NUTCASE NUTLETS NUTMEAL NUTRIAS NUTSIER NUTTERS NUTTIER OARIEST OARLESS OARSMEN OBELIAS OBLATES OBLIGES OBSERVE OBTENDS OBTUSER OBVERSE OBVERTS OCTANES OCTAVES OERSTED OESTRAL OESTRIN OESTRUM OEUVRES OILIEST OILLETS OLDNESS OLDSTER OLEATES OLEFINS OLEINES OLIVERS OLIVETS

OLOGIES OMENTAL OMERTAS ONAGERS ONDINES ONLIEST ONSIDES ONSTAGE ONSTEAD OOLITES OORIEST OPENERS OPERATE OPERONS OPHITES OPIATES OPTIMES ORACHES ORACIES ORACLES ORANGES ORATING ORBIEST ORCEINS ORCINES ORDAINS ORDEALS ORDINEE ORDINES OREADES OREIDES ORGEATS ORGONES ORIENTS ORIGANE ORIGANS ORIGINS ORIOLES ORLEANS ORNATER ORNISES OROGENS OROIDES ORPINES ORRICES ORRISES OSCINES OSIERED OSMIATE OSSEINS OSTENTS OSTEOID OSTIATE OSTIOLE OSTLERS OTARIES OTARINE OUGLIES OULDEST OURIEST OUSTING OUTDOES OUTGRIN OUTINGS OUTLERS OUTLETS OUTLIER OUTLIES OUTNESS OUTREDS OUTRING OUTSEEN OUTSELL OUTSERT OUTSIDE

OUTSING OUTSOLE OUTSPED OVARIES OVERLIE OVERLIT OVERSAD OVERSEA OVERSEE OVERSET OVERSEW OVERUSE OWLIEST OWRIEST PAIDLES PAINTER PALIEST PALINGS PALMERS PALSIED PALSIER PALSIES PALTERS PANDERS PANDIES PANIERS PANSIED PANTERS PANTIES PANTILE PANTLER PARCELS PARDINE PARENTS PARESIS PARGETS PARINGS PARISES PARKIES PARLEYS PARLIES PARLING PAROLES PARRELS PARRIES PARSING PARSLEY PARTERS PARTIED PARTIES PARTING PARTITE PARTLET PARTNER PARTONS PARVISE PASTERN PASTERS PASTIER PASTIME PASTING PASTURE PATENTS PATERAE PATINES PATNESS PATRONS PATTENS PATTERN PATTERS PATTIES PATZERS PAVISER PEALING PEANUTS

PEARTER PEARTLY PEASANT PEATERY PEATIER PEATMAN PECTINS PEDANTS PEDLARS PEDRAIL PEINCTS PELITES PELOTAS PELTERS PELTING PENATES PENSION PENSTER PENTADS PENTELS PENTISE PENULTS PEONIES PEONISM PEPINOS PERIDOT PERIODS PERIOST PERITUS PERKINS PERMITS PERONES PERRIES PERRONS PERSALT PERSANT PERSICO PERSING PERSIST PERSONA PERSONS PERTAIN PERTAKE PERTEST PERUSAL PESANTE PESANTS PESAUNT PESTIER PETARAS PETARDS PETNAPS PETRALE PETRELS PETROLS PETROUS PETTERS PEYTRAL PEZANTS PHONERS PHONIES PIASTER PIASTRE PIGEONS PIGLETS PILSNER PIMENTS PINCASE PINCERS PINDERS PINGERS PINGLED PINGLER PINGLES PINGOES

PINIEST PINITES PINKERS PINKEST PINKOES PINNERS PINNETS PINOLES PINONES PINTLES PINTOES PIOLETS PIONERS PIONEYS PIONIES PIRATED PIRATES PIRNIES PISTOLE PITEOUS PITIERS PITTERS PLACERS PLACETS PLAITER PLANERS PLANETS PLANTER PLASHER PLASTER PLATENS PLATERS PLATIER PLATIES PLATING PLATTER PLAYERS PLEAING PLEASER PLEATER PLECTRA PLEIADS PLENIST PLEURAS PODITES POETICS POETISE POINTES POISERS POITREL POKIEST POLDERS POLITER POLTING PONDERS PONTIES POOREST POOTERS PORIEST PORTERS PORTESS PORTING POSIEST POSITED POSTERN POSTERS POSTIES POSTING POSTMEN POSTURE POTENTS POTHERS POTPIES POTSIES POTTERS

POTTIES POTZERS POUNDER POUTERS POWNIES POWTERS POXIEST PRAISED PRAISER PRAISES PRANCES PRANGED PRATERS PRATIES PRATING PRATTED PRATTLE PRAWLES PREACTS PREASED PRECAST PREDATE PREDIAL PREDICT PREDIES PREEDIT PREHEAT PREIFES PRELATE PRELATY PREMIES PREMISE PRESALE PRESENT PRESIDE PRESIFT PRESOLD PRESONG PRESORT PRESTED PRESTER PRESTOS PRETAPE PRETEST PRETORS PREVISE PRIEFES PRIESTS PRIEVES PRINCES PRINTED PRISAGE PRISERE PRIVETS PROIGNS PROINES PROJETS PROLATE PRONEST PROSECT PROSING PROSSIE PROSTIE PROTEAS PROTEID PROTEST PROTEUS PROWEST PROYNES PRUINES PSALTER PTERINS PTERYLA PUDSIER PUIREST

PULIEST PUNIEST PUNSTER PUNTERS PUNTIES PURINES PUTELIS PYONERS PYRITES PYRONES QINDARS QINTARS QUINTES RABBETS RABIDER RACEMES RACHETS RACIEST RACINGS RACISTS RACKETS RADDEST RADDING RADDLES RADGEST RADIALE RADIANS RADICEL RADICES RADICLE RADIXES RADOMES RAFTERS RAFTING RAGGLES RAGINGS RAGINIS RAGMENT RAIDERS RAIDING RAILBED RAILERS RAILING RAILMEN RAIMENT RAISING RAITING RAKINGS RALLIED RALLIES RAMEKIN RAMENTA RAMJETS RAMMIES RANCELS RANCHES RANDEMS RANDIER RANDIES RANDING RANGERS RANGIER RANGOLI RANKEST RANKLED RANKLES RANSELS RANTERS RANTING RANZELS RAPIERS RAPINES RAPPELS RASHEST RASHING

RASPIER RASPING RASSLED RASTERS RATABLE RATCHES RATHEST RATHOLE RATINES RATINGS RATIONS RATITES RATLIKE RATLINE RATLING RATLINS RATOONS RATTEEN RATTENS RATTERS RATTIER RATTING RATTLES RATTONS RAUNGED RAUNGES RAVINED RAVINES RAVINGS RAWINGS RAWNESS RAYLETS RAYLING READAPT READERS READIES READILY READING READOPT REAGENT REAGINS REAKING REALEST REALIGN REALISE REALISM REALIST REALITY REALTIE REAMERS REAMING REAPERS REAPING REARERS REARING REARISE REAROSE REASONS REASTED REAVERS REAVING REBAITS REBATES REBATOS REBILLS REBINDS REBITES REBOILS REBOOTS REBOUND RECANES RECANTS RECASTS RECITAL RECITES

RECKONS RECLAIM RECLASP RECOALS RECOILS RECOINS RECTORS REDACTS REDATES REDBAIT REDCAPS REDDENS REDDEST REDDING REDEALS REDEARS REDFINS REDIALS REDLINE REDNESS REDOING REDOUND REDOUTS REDOWAS REDRAWS REDRIES REDSEAR REDSKIN REDTAIL REDTOPS REDUITS REDWING REEARNS REEDING REEDITS REELING REEMITS REENACT REESTED REFILES REFINDS REFINED REFINES REFIRES REFIXES REFLAGS REFLETS REFLIES REFOLDS REFOUND REFRIES REFUNDS REGAINS REGALES REGARDS REGEARS REGENTS REGILDS REGIMES REGINAE REGINAL REGINAS REGIONS REGIVES REGLETS REGNANT REGRANT REGRETS REGRIND REHANGS REHEARS REHEATS REHIRES REIFIES REIGNED

REINDEX REINING REINKED REINTER REISTED REITERS REIVERS REJOINS REKNITS RELACES RELAPSE RELATES RELAXES RELEASE RELENDS RELENTS RELIANT RELICTS RELIEFS RELIERS RELIEVE RELIEVO RELINED RELINES RELINKS RELISTS RELIVED RELIVER RELIVES RELOADS RELOANS RELUCTS RELYING REMADES REMAILS REMAINS REMAKES REMANDS REMANIE REMATES REMEADS REMEIDS REMELTS REMENDS REMIGES REMINDS REMINTS REMISED REMISES REMIXES REMOLDS REMOTES REMOVES RENAILS RENAMES RENDERS RENDING RENEGES RENESTS RENNETS RENNING RENTALS RENTERS RENTIER RENTING RENVOIS RENYING REOPENS REPAINT REPAIRS REPASTS REPEALS REPEATS REPENTS REPINED

REPINES
REPLANS
REPLANT
REPLATE
REPLAYS
REPLICA
REPLIES
REPLOTS
REPONES
REPORTS
REPOSAL
REPOSIT
REPOSTS
REPRISE
REPTANT
REPUNIT
RERAILS
RERAISE
REREADS
RERISEN
RERISES
RESAILS
RESALES
RESAWED
RESCALE
RESCIND
RESEALS
RESEATS
RESEDAS
RESENDS
RESENTS
RESHINE
RESHOOT
RESIANT
RESIDED
RESIDER
RESIDES
RESIDUA
RESIDUE
RESIFTS
RESIGHT
RESIGNS
RESILED
RESILES
RESINED
RESINER
RESITED
RESITES
RESIZED
RESLATE
RESMELT
RESOLED
RESOLVE
RESORTS
RESOUND
RESPADE
RESPELT
RESPIRE
RESPITE
RESPLIT
RESPOND
RESPOTS
RESTACK
RESTAGE
RESTAMP
RESTART
RESTATE
RESTERS
RESTFUL
RESTIER
RESTIFF
RESTING
RESTIVE
RESTOCK
RESTORE
RESTUDY
RESTYLE
RESULTS
RETABLE
RETACKS
RETAILS
RETAINS
RETAKES
RETAMAS
RETAPED
RETAPES
RETARDS
RETASTE
RETAXES
RETEAMS
RETEARS
RETELLS
RETENES
RETESTS
RETILED
RETILES
RETIMES
RETINAE
RETINAL
RETINAS
RETINES
RETINOL
RETINTS
RETINUE
RETIRAL
RETIRES
RETOOLS
RETORTS
RETOURS
RETRAIN
RETRAIT
RETREES
RETRIAL
RETRIES
RETRIMS
RETSINA
RETTING
RETUNDS
RETUNES
RETURNS
RETWIST
RETYING
REUNITE
REUSING
REVEALS
REVERSI
REVERSO
REVERTS
REVIEWS
REVILED
REVILER
REVILES
REVISAL
REVISED
REVISER
REVISES
REVISIT
REVISOR
REVIVES
REVOKES
REVOLTS
REVOTES
REVUIST
REWARDS
REWIDEN
REWINDS
REWIRES
REWOUND
RHETORS
RHODIES
RIBANDS
RIBLESS
RIBLETS
RIBOSES
RIBSTON
RICHENS
RICHEST
RICIEST
RICKETS
RIDABLE
RIDGELS
RIDGERS
RIEVERS
RIFTING
RIGHTEN
RILIEST
RILLETS
RIMIEST
RINGBIT
RINGENT
RINGERS
RINGGIT
RINGLET
RINGMEN
RINGTAW
RINSERS
RIOTERS
RIOTING
RIOTISE
RIPENED
RIPOSTE
RIPTIDE
RISIBLE
RISSOLE
RITTERS
RITTING
RIVALED
ROACHES
ROADEOS
ROADIES
ROADING
ROASTED
ROASTER
ROATING
ROBINGS
ROCHETS
ROCKETS
RODDING
RODENTS
RODINGS
RODLESS
RODSMEN
RODSTER
ROISTED
ROISTER
ROKIEST
ROMAINE
RONDEAU
RONDELS
RONDURE
ROOSING
ROOSTED
ROOSTER
ROOTERS
ROOTIES
ROOTING
ROOTLED
ROOTLES
ROPIEST
ROPINGS
RORIEST
RORTERS
RORTING
ROSACEA
ROSACES
ROSEATE
ROSEBAY
ROSELLA
ROSEOLA
ROSETED
ROSETTE
ROSETTY
ROSIERE
ROSIERS
ROSIEST
ROSINED
ROSITED
ROSTERS
ROSTING
ROSYING
ROTATES
ROTCHES
ROTHERS
ROTTANS
ROTTENS
ROTTERS
ROTTING
ROUNCES
ROUNDED
ROUNDEL
ROUNDER
ROUNDLE
ROUSANT
ROUSING
ROUSTED
ROUSTER
ROUTERS
ROUTINE
ROUTING
ROVINGS
ROWDIES
ROWINGS
ROWTING
ROYSTED
ROYSTER
RUBIEST
RUDDIES
RUEINGS
RUINATE
RULIEST
RUNDALE
RUNDLES
RUNLETS
RUNNETS
RUNTIER
RUSTIER
RUSTLED
RUSTLER
RUSTLES
RUSTRED
RUTILES
SABERED
SABLING
SABRING
SACRING
SACRIST
SADDLER
SADIRON
SAETERS
SAFROLE
SAIDEST
SAILERS
SAILING
SAINTED
SAIREST
SAIRING
SAKERET
SALFERN
SALICES
SALICET
SALIENT
SALINES
SALLIED
SALLIER
SALLIES
SALTERN
SALTERS
SALTIER
SALTIES
SALTINE
SALTING
SALTIRE
SALTOED
SALUING
SALUTED
SALUTER
SALVING
SAMIELS
SAMIEST
SAMISEN
SAMITES
SAMPIRE
SAMPLER
SANDERS
SANDIER
SANDMEN
SANGERS
SANGRIA
SANICLE
SANTIRS
SANTOUR
SAPIENT
SAPLING
SAPPIER
SAPROBE
SARANGI
SARCODE
SARDELS
SARDINE
SARKING
SARMENT
SARNEYS
SARNIES
SARODES
SARSDEN
SARSENS
SARSNET
SATCHEL
SATIATE
SATIETY
SATINED
SATINET
SATIRES
SATIRIC
SATYRIC
SAULIES
SAUNTED
SAUNTER
SAUTEED
SAUTING
SAVORED
SCAILED
SCALDER
SCALENI
SCALIER
SCALING
SCALPER
SCANNER
SCANTED
SCANTER
SCANTLE
SCARFED
SCARING
SCARLET
SCARPED
SCARRED
SCARTED
SCATOLE
SCATTER
SCAURED
SCENARY
SCENTED
SCERNED
SCLATED
SCLATES
SCLERAE
SCOLDER
SCOOTER
SCOPATE
SCORIAE
SCORING
SCORNED
SCORNER
SCOTERS
SCOTTIE
SCOURIE
SCOUTED
SCOUTER
SCOWRIE
SCRAPED
SCRAPIE
SCRIBED
SCRIENE
SCRIEVE
SCRINES
SCYTALE
SDAINED
SDAINES
SDEIGNE
SDEIGNS
SEABIRD
SEAGIRT
SEALANT
SEALERS
SEALERY
SEALING
SEAMERS
SEAMIER
SEAMING
SEAPORT
SEARATS
SEARCED
SEAREST
SEARING
SEATERS
SEATING
SECANTS
SECONDI
SECRETA
SECTARY
SECTILE
SECTION
SECTORS
SEDARIM
SEDATED
SEDATER
SEDATES
SEDGIER
SEDILIA
SEEDIER
SEEDING
SEEDMAN
SEELIER
SEELING
SEEMING
SEGETAL
SEILING
SEINERS
SEISMAL
SEISORS
SEITENS
SEIZORS
SELFING
SELLING
SELLOUT
SELTZER
SEMATIC
SEMEION
SEMILOG
SEMIMAT
SEMINAL
SEMINAR
SEMIRAW
SEMITAR
SENARII
SENATOR
SENDALS
SENDERS
SENDING
SENECIO
SENIORS
SENNITS
SENOPIA
SENORAS
SENSIST
SENTIMO
SENTING
SEPIOST
SEPTUOR
SERAFIN
SERAILS
SERANGS
SEREINS
SERENED
SERGING
SERIALS
SERIATE
SERICIN
SERICON
SERIEMA
SERIFED
SERINES
SERINGA
SERIOUS
SERKALI
SERMONS
SEROSAL
SERPENT
SERPULA
SERRANS
SERRATE
SERRATI
SERRIED
SERRIES
SERRING
SERVANT
SERVICE
SERVILE
SERVING
SESSION
SESTINA
SESTINE
SETLINE
SETTERS
SETTING
SETTLER
SETTLOR
SEVERAL
SEXTAIN
SEXTANT
SEXTILE
SHADIER
SHAFTER
SHALIER
SHALING
SHARING
SHARPIE
SHASTER
SHATTER
SHEARED
SHEARER
SHEILAS
SHEITAN
SHELTER
SHELTIE
SHERIAT
SHEROOT
SHIFTER
SHINERS
SHINGLE
SHINIER
SHIRTED
SHOALER
SHOEING
SHOOTER
SHORING
SHORTED
SHORTEN
SHORTER
SHORTIE
SHOTTEN
SHOUTED
SHOUTER
SHRIEVE
SHRINED
SHRINES
SHRIVEN
SHUNTED
SHUNTER
SIDEARM
SIDEBAR
SIDECAR
SIDEMAN
SIDEMEN
SIDERAL
SIEMENS
SIERRAN
SIEVERT
SIFTERS
SIGHTER
SIGMATE
SIGNALS
SIGNARY
SIGNERS
SIGNETS
SIGNEUR
SIGNIOR
SIGNORA
SIGNORE
SIGNORI
SIGNORS
SIGNORY
SILAGED
SILAGES
SILANES
SILENTS
SILESIA
SILTIER
SILVERN
SIMARRE
SINCERE
SINGERS
SINGLED
SINGLES
SINGLET
SINKERS
SINNERS
SINNETS
SINOPIE
SINTERS
SINTERY
SINUATE
SINUOSE
SIRENIC
SIRGANG
SIRNAME
SIRREES
SIRUPED
SITHENS
SITREPS
SITTERS
SITTINE
SITUATE
SITULAE
SIZABLE
SKAILED
SKATERS
SKATING
SKATOLE
SKEARED
SKELTER
SKIABLE
SKINTER
SKIRRET
SKIRTED
SKIRTER
SKITTER
SKLATED
SLAINTE
SLAKING
SLANDER
SLANGED
SLANGER
SLANTED
SLAPPER
SLATERS
SLATHER
SLATIER
SLATING
SLATTED
SLATTER
SLAVING
SLAYING
SLEEKIT
SLEIGHT
SLENDER
SLENTER
SLEWING
SLIDDEN
SLINGER
SLINKED
SLINKER
SLINTER
SLITHER
SLITTER
SLOPIER
SLOTTER
SLUEING
SMARTED
SMARTEN
SMARTER
SMARTIE
SMATTER
SMEARED
SMEARER
SMELTER
SMIDGEN
SMITERS
SMITTEN
SMOLDER
SMORING
SMOTHER
SMOUTED
SMYTRIE
SNAILED

SNAKIER
SNARERS
SNARIER
SNARING
SNARLED
SNARLER
SNARRED
SNEERED
SNELLED
SNICKER
SNICKET
SNIDELY
SNIDEST
SNIFTED
SNIFTER
SNIGGED
SNIGGER
SNIGGLE
SNIPERS
SNIPIER
SNIPPER
SNIPPET
SNIRTLE
SNOOLED
SNOOPER
SNOOTED
SNORING
SNORTED
SNORTER
SNOTTED
SNOTTER
SNOTTIE
SNOUTED
SNOWIER
SOAPIER
SOARING
SOCAGER
SOCIATE
SODAINE
SODDIER
SOFTING
SOIGNEE
SOILAGE
SOILIER
SOILURE
SOIREES
SOLACER
SOLATED
SOLATES
SOLDERS
SOLDIER
SOLERAS
SOLERET
SOLIDER
SOLUTES
SOLVATE
SOMITES
SONDELI
SONERIS
SONLIKE
SONNIES
SONSIER
SONTIES
SOOTHER
SOOTIER
SOOTING
SOPITED
SOPITES
SORBATE
SORBENT
SORBETS
SORBING
SORBITE
SORDINE
SOREDIA
SORINGS
SORITES
SORNING
SORTERS
SORTIED
SORTIES
SORTING
SOTTING
SOUNDER
SOURING
SOUTANE
SOUTHED
SOUTHER
SOZINES
SPACIER
SPADGER
SPAINED
SPAIRGE
SPALLER
SPALTED
SPANGLE
SPARELY
SPAREST
SPARGED
SPARING
SPARKIE
SPARKLE
SPARRED
SPARTHE
SPATTER
SPEARED
SPEARER
SPECTRA
SPEIRED
SPELDIN
SPELTER
SPENDER
SPHERAL
SPIELER
SPIERED
SPIGNEL
SPILITE
SPINATE
SPINDLE
SPINETS
SPINIER
SPINNER
SPINNET
SPINODE
SPINOSE
SPIRAEA
SPIRANT
SPIREAS
SPIREME
SPIRTED
SPIRTLE
SPITTEN
SPITTER
SPLINED
SPOILER
SPONGER
SPORING
SPORTED
SPORTER
SPOTTER
SPOUTED
SPOUTER
SPRAINT
SPRIEST
SPRINGE
SPRITES
SPURIAE
SPURNED
SPURTED
SPURTLE
SQUIRED
STABBER
STABILE
STABLED
STABLER
STACKER
STADDLE
STAGERS
STAGERY
STAGGER
STAGIER
STAGING
STAIDER
STAINED
STAINER
STAIRED
STAITHE
STAKING
STALING
STALKED
STALKER
STALLED
STAMENS
STAMMER
STAMPER
STANCES
STANDEE
STANDEN
STANDER
STANGED
STANIEL
STANINE
STANING
STANNEL
STANYEL
STAPLED
STAPLER
STARERS
STARETS
STARETZ
STARING
STARKED
STARKEN
STARKER
STARLET
STARNED
STARNIE
STARRED
STARTED
STARTER
STARTLE
STARVED
STARVER
STARVES
STATERS
STATICE
STATING
STATION
STATIVE
STATURE
STAVING
STAWING
STAYERS
STAYING
STAYNED
STAYRES
STEADED
STEALED
STEALER
STEAMED
STEAMER
STEAMIE
STEANED
STEARED
STEARES
STEARIC
STEARIN
STEDING
STEELIE
STEENED
STEERED
STEERER
STEINED
STELENE
STELLAR
STEMING
STEMSON
STENCIL
STENDED
STENGAH
STENNED
STENTED
STENTOR
STERILE
STERLET
STERNAL
STERNED
STERNER
STERNUM
STEROID
STEROLS
STERTOR
STERVED
STEWARD
STEWIER
STEWING
STEWPAN
STHENIA
STHENIC
STICKER
STIEVER
STIFFER
STIFLER
STILLER
STILTER
STINGED
STINGER
STINGOS
STINKER
STINTED
STINTER
STIPEND
STIPULE
STIRING
STIRPES
STIRRED
STIRRER
STIRRES
STIVERS
STIVIER
STOCKER
STODGER
STOITED
STOITER
STOKING
STOMPER
STONERN
STONERS
STONIED
STONIER
STONIES
STONING
STONKER
STONNED
STOODEN
STOOLIE
STOOPER
STOPERS
STOPING
STOPPER
STORAGE
STORERS
STORIED
STORIES
STORING
STORMED
STOTTER
STOURIE
STOUTEN
STOUTER
STOVING
STOWING
STRAFED
STRAFER
STRAFES
STRAINS
STRAINT
STRAKED
STRAKES
STRANGE
STRAWED
STRAWEN
STRAYED
STRAYER
STREAKS
STREAMS
STREAMY
STREELS
STREETS
STREETY
STRENES
STRETTA
STRETTE
STRETTI
STRETTO
STREWED
STREWER
STRIATE
STRIDER
STRIDES
STRIFES
STRIGAE
STRIKER
STRIPED
STRIPER
STRIPES
STRIPEY
STRIVED
STRIVEN
STRIVER
STRIVES
STROBED
STROBES
STRODLE
STROKED
STROKEN
STROKER
STROPHE
STROWED
STROWER
STROYED
STROYER
STRUDEL
STRUMAE
STUDDEN
STUDENT
STUDIER
STUIVER
STUNNED
STUNNER
STUNTED
STURTED
STYGIAN
STYRENE
SUBRENT
SUBTEND
SUBTILE
SUBTLER
SUBTONE
SUDAMEN
SUDSIER
SUEDING
SUETIER
SUGARED
SULCATE
SULFITE
SUNBELT
SUNDARI
SUNDERS
SUNRISE
SURANCE
SURBATE
SURFEIT
SURGENT
SURGEON
SUTLERS
SUTLERY
SUTURED
SVELTER
SWALIER
SWALING
SWATHER
SWATTER
SWEARER
SWEATED
SWEATER
SWELTER
SWIFTER
SWINDGE
SWINDLE
SWINGED
SWINGER
SWINGLE
SWITHER
SWOTTER
SYNAPTE
SYRINGA
SYRINGE
TABERDS
TABLIER
TABLING
TABRETS
TACKERS
TACKLES
TADDIES
TAENIAS
TAGGERS
TAIGLES
TAILERS
TAILING
TAILLES
TAILYES
TAIVERS
TAIVERT
TAJINES
TAKIEST
TAKINGS
TALCIER
TALCING
TALCOSE
TALENTS
TALIPES
TALKERS
TALKIER
TALKIES
TALKING
TALLIER
TALLIES
TALWEGS
TAMBERS
TAMEINS
TAMINES
TAMINGS
TAMISES
TAMMIES
TAMPERS
TANAGER
TANDEMS
TANGELO
TANGIER
TANGIES
TANGLED
TANGLER
TANGLES
TANISTS
TANKERS
TANKIES
TANLING
TANNERS
TANNEST
TANRECS
TANSIES
TAPERED
TAPERER
TAPETIS
TAPPERS
TAPSMEN
TAPSTER
TARCELS
TARDIES
TARGETS
TARGING
TARINGS
TARNISH
TARPONS
TARRIES
TARRING
TARSELS
TARSIER
TARTANE
TARTEST
TARTIER
TARTINE
TARTING
TASERED
TASHING
TASKERS
TASKING
TASTERS
TASTIER
TASTING
TATLERS
TATTERS
TATTIER
TATTIES
TAUNTER
TAURINE
TAUTENS
TAVERNS
TAWIEST
TAWINGS
TAWNIER
TAWNIES
TAWSING
TAWTIER
TAXIMEN
TAXINGS
TAXITES
TEAGLES
TEAMERS
TEAMING
TEARERS
TEARGAS
TEARILY
TEARING
TEASERS
TEASING
TECHNOS
TEDDERS
TEDESCA
TEDIOUS
TEENERS
TEENIER
TEERING
TEETERS
TEGMINA
TELAMON
TELEGAS
TELEMAN
TELERAN
TELESIS
TELFERS
TELFORD
TELLARS
TELLENS
TELLERS
TELLIES
TELLING
TELLINS
TELNETS
TEMENOS
TEMPERA
TEMPLAR
TEMSING
TENACES
TENAILS
TENANTS
TENDERS
TENDONS
TENDRES
TENDRIL
TENNERS
TENNIES
TENNIST
TENOURS
TENPINS
TENRECS
TENSELY
TENSILE
TENSING
TENSION
TENSITY
TENSORS
TENTERS
TENTIER
TENUOUS
TENURES
TENUTOS
TEOPANS
TEPHRAS
TEPIDER
TERBIAS
TERCELS
TERCETS
TERCIOS
TEREDOS
TERETES
TERMERS
TERMING
TERMINI
TERMORS
TERNARY
TERNATE
TERNING
TERRAIN
TERRANE
TERRETS
TERRIES
TERRINE
TERRITS
TERRORS
TERSELY
TERSEST
TERSION
TERTIAL
TERTIAN
TERTIAS
TERTIUS
TESSERA
TESTERN
TESTERS
TESTIER
TESTING
TESTONS
TESTOON
TESTRIL
TESTUDO
TETANUS
TETHERS
TETRADS
TETTERS
TEWARTS
THALERS
THAWERS
THEEING
THEMING
THENARS
THEREIN
THERIAN
THERMAL
THERMOS
THIRLED
THOLING
THORPES
THRAVES
THREADS
THREAPS
THREATS
THRENES
THRENOS
THRIVES
THRONES
THROWES
TICKENS
TICKERS
TIDDLER
TIDERIP
TIDIERS
TIELESS
TIEPINS
TIERCES
TIERING
TIERODS
TIETACS
TIGHTEN
TIGLONS
TIGRINE
TILLERS
TILTERS
TIMBERS
TIMBRES
TIMEOUS
TINDERS
TINEIDS
TINGLED
TINGLER
TINGLES
TINIEST
TINKERS
TINKLES
TINNERS
TINNIER
TINNIES
TINSELS
TINSEYS

TINTERS
TINTIER
TINWARE
TIPPERS
TIPSIER
TIPSTER
TIPTOES
TIRADES
TIRASSE
TIREDLY
TIRINGS
TIRLING
TIRRING
TISANES
TITANIS
TITFERS
TITHERS
TITIANS
TITLERS
TITMOSE
TITRATE
TITTERS
TITULES
TOADIES
TOASTER
TOASTIE
TOCHERS
TODDIES
TODDLER
TOECAPS
TOEIEST
TOENAIL
TOERAGS
TOILERS
TOILETS
TOILING
TOLANES
TOLINGS
TOLLERS
TOLLING
TOLTERS
TOMMIES
TONEMES
TONGERS
TONGUES
TONIEST
TONINGS
TONITES
TONKERS
TONLETS
TONNERS
TONSURE
TONUSES
TOOLERS
TOOLING
TOORIES
TOOTERS
TOOTSIE
TOPPERS
TOPSIDE
TOPSMEN
TORANAS
TORCHES
TOREROS
TORRETS
TORSADE
TORSELS
TORSION
TORSIVE
TORTILE
TOSHERS
TOSHIER
TOSHING
TOSSIER
TOSSING
TOTTERS
TOTTIES
TOURERS
TOURIES
TOURING
TOUSIER
TOUSING
TOUSLED
TOUSLES
TOUSTIE
TOUTERS
TOUZLES
TOWIEST
TOWINGS
TOWNIES
TOWSIER
TOWSING
TOXINES
TOYINGS
TRACERS
TRACHLE
TRACING
TRADERS
TRADING
TRAGICS
TRAILED
TRAILER
TRAINED
TRAINEE
TRAINER
TRAIPSE
TRAMELS
TRAMPED
TRAMPLE
TRANCED
TRANCES
TRANCHE
TRANECT
TRANGLE
TRANNIE
TRANSES
TRANSIT
TRANSOM
TRANTED
TRANTER
TRAPEZE
TRAPING
TRAPPED
TRASHED
TRASHES
TRASSES
TRAVELS
TRAYNES
TREASON
TREBLES
TREEING
TREFOIL
TREHALA
TRELLIS
TREMIES
TREMORS
TRENAIL
TRENISE
TRENTAL
TREPANG
TREPANS
TRESSED
TRESSEL
TRESTLE
TREVETS
TREVISS
TRIABLE
TRIAGES
TRIBADE
TRIBUNE
TRICARS
TRICEPS
TRICING
TRIDENT
TRIENES
TRIFLED
TRIFLES
TRIGONS
TRIJETS
TRILLED
TRILOBE
TRIMERS
TRINDLE
TRINGLE
TRINING
TRINKET
TRIODES
TRIOLET
TRIONES
TRIOSES
TRIPLED
TRIPLES
TRIPPED
TRIPSES
TRISECT
TRISEME
TRISOME
TRITEST
TRITONE
TRITONS
TRIUNES
TRIVETS
TROADES
TROCHES
TROELIE
TROKING
TROLLED
TROMPES
TROOLIE
TROPING
TROPINS
TROULED
TROULES
TROUPES
TROUSER
TROVERS
TROWELS
TROWING
TRUDGES
TRUEING
TRUSSED
TRUSTED
TRUSTEE
TSARINA
TSIGANE
TUILLES
TUNIEST
TUNNELS
TUNNIES
TUPELOS
TURBINE
TURDINE
TUREENS
TURIONS
TURNERS
TURTLES
TUXEDOS
TWAITES
TWANGER
TWANGLE
TWICERS
TWINERS
TWINGES
TWINIER
TWINSET
TWINTER
TWIRING
TWIRLED
TWISCAR
TWISTER
TYRONES
UGLIEST
ULSTERS
UNAGILE
UNAIRED
UNARMED
UNBARED
UNBELTS
UNBLEST
UNCRATE
UNDERDO
UNDERGO
UNDERNS
UNDOERS
UNDRAPE
UNDRESS
UNDREST
UNDRIED
UNEARED
UNFIRED
UNGEARS
UNGORED
UNHEARD
UNHERST
UNHIRED
UNITERS
UNITIES
UNITISE
UNLADES
UNLASTE
UNLEADS
UNMITER
UNMITRE
UNORDER
UNPARED
UNRACED
UNRAKED
UNRATED
UNRAZED
UNREADY
UNRESTS
UNRIMED
UNRIVET
UNROBED
UNROPED
UNROPES
UNSATED
UNSMOTE
UNSOOTE
UNSTATE
UNSTEEL
UNSURED
UNTAMES
UNTEAMS
UNTILES
UNTIRED
UNTRACE
UNTREAD
UNTRIDE
UNTRIED
UNWIRED
UNWRITE
UPDATER
UPDRIES
UPRAISE
UPRATED
UPRATES
UPRISEN
UPSTARE
UPTEARS
URALITE
URANIDE
URANITE
UREDIAL
UREDINE
UREIDES
UREMIAS
URETERS
URIDINE
URINATE
URINOSE
URTICAS
UTENSIL
UTERINE
UTILISE
VAINEST
VALERIC
VALIDER
VALISES
VALSING
VARDIES
VARLETS
VASTIER
VATTERS
VEALERS
VEALIER
VEALING
VECTORS
VEERIES
VEILERS
VEILIER
VEINERS
VELARIC
VELIGER
VELITES
VENDERS
VENGERS
VENIRES
VENTAIL
VENTERS
VENTILS
VENTRAL
VENTRES
VENTURI
VERBIDS
VERBILE
VERBOSE
VERDETS
VERDINS
VERDITS
VERGLAS
VERIEST
VERISMO
VERISTS
VERITAS
VERITES
VERMEIL
VERMIAN
VERMINS
VERSANT
VERSINE
VERSING
VERSINS
VERSION
VERTING
VESSAIL
VESTING
VESTRAL
VETOERS
VIEWERS
VINEGAR
VIOLERS
VIOLETS
VIROSES
VIRTUES
VISITER
VISORED
VISTAED
VITRINE
VOICERS
VOIDERS
VOLUTES
WABSTER
WAFTERS
WAILERS
WAISTED
WAISTER
WAITERS
WALIEST
WALISES
WALTIER
WANDERS
WANGLED
WANGLER
WANGLES
WANIEST
WANNEST
WANTERS
WANTIES
WARDENS
WARDERS
WARDING
WARIEST
WARLING
WARMEST
WARSLED
WARSTLE
WASPIER
WASTERS
WASTERY
WASTING
WASTREL
WASTRIE
WEARERS
WEARING
WEDELNS
WEIRDOS
WELDING
WELDORS
WELTERS
WELTING
WESTERN
WESTING
WESTLIN
WETTERS
WHINERS
WIDENER
WIGEONS
WIGLETS
WILIEST
WINCERS
WINDERS
WINDLES
WINESOP
WINGERS
WINGLET
WINSOME
WINTERS
WINTLES
WIREMAN
WISENTS
WITHERS
WITNESS
WITTERS
WIVERNS
WORDING
WORSING
WORSTED
WORTLES
WOUNDER
WRANGLE
WRASTED
WRASTLE
WREATHS
WRESTED
WRESTER
WRESTLE
WRINGED
WRITERS
WRITHES
WRITING
WRITTEN
XEROSIS
YAPSTER
YARDING
YATTERS
YEALING
YEASTED
YERDING
YESTERN
YODLERS
ZANDERS
ZANIEST
ZARNECS
ZEALOTS
ZEATINS
ZELANTS
ZESTIER
ZESTING
ZINGARE
ZINGELS
ZINGERS
ZITHERS
ZLOTIES

SUMMARY OF 7-LETTER STEMS in alphabetical order with ranking, keywords, combining letters and mnemonic

Stem	Rank	Keyword	Combining Letters	Mnemonic
AADEIRT	141	RADIATE	CDELNSV	needed seven cells
AAEGINR	247	ANERGIA	BCDFGLNST	–
AAEILNT	102	ANTLIAE	CDEGHKLMPTV	vet helped GM check
AAEINRT	30	(ARANITE)	BCDGMOPSTUWZ	bug zooms up cut dogwood
AAEINST	169	TAENIAS	BCFGHMRSTV	–
AAEINTT	225	(A NATTIE)	DELNPRST	depleted dress sense
AAEIRST	181	ASTERIA	DHMNPSTVW	–
AAENRST	112	ANESTRA	BCEGIJLMORTV	give job to girl comic
ABEINST	121	BESTAIN	ACDEGHIKLMOPRST	slight pock-marked
ABEORST	160	BOASTER	ACDEHILMNPRSTU	claimed he is superintendent
ACDEINR	240	CAIRNED	ADEHINRT	heard the rain
ACEILRT	206	RECITAL	ADKMNOPRSTUVY	man spurts out vodka story
ACEINOT	139	ACONITE	CDHMNRSTVX	–
ACEINRS	132	ARSENIC	ABEFGHIKLMNOST	something to kill off bats
ACEINRT	69	CERTAIN	ABCDEGLOSTUVX	gave club's gold to tax
ACEINST	114	CANIEST	ABDEFHIMNORSTVYZ	never store dirty bamboo in the freezer
ACENORT	124	(CORN TEA)	CDEHIOPSTUY	hideous cup oddity
ACEORST	223	COASTER	BCDEFGHLNPRSTUVX	defence vessel expunged the rebel
ACINORT	211	(CORTINA)	ACDEFHKLMRSTY	fleet car that makes my day
ADEEGNR	145	ANGERED	ACDEHILMNORSUV	made human cross and livid
ADEEILR	146	(LEADIER)	BDLMNPRSTZ	–
ADEEILS	217	AEDILES	BHIKMNPRSTVY	my brisk visit in his privy
ADEEILT	250	(DILATEE)	BCDNPRS	–
ADEEINR	101	(DEANIER)	CFGLMPSTV	–
ADEEINS	242	ANISEED	LMNRST	–
ADEEINT	62	(NITE ADE)	DELMPRSW	redeems swell sleep
ADEEIRS	125	READIES	BCFGJLMNPRTV	–
ADEEIRT	48	(DIE RATE)	ABHLMNSTV	shall blast vatman
ADEEIST	155	IDEATES	BDFHJLMNRSV	–
ADEELRT	218	RELATED	CDFHILMNPRSV	VIP's child is infirm
ADEENRS	147	ENDEARS	CEGIKMNOSUWY	micky-mouse gown
ADEENRT	137	(END TEAR)	BCDHILPTUV	pitbull bit livid child
ADEERST	123	DERATES	BCEFGHIKLMPRSTWY	pricy big milky wet fish
ADEGINR	38	READING	ABDEHIKLMNORSTY	held storybook in my hands
ADEGINT	220	(INGATED)	ABILRSV	arrivals' visa bills
ADEGNOR	205	GROANED	BEFIJMNPT	pitmen benefit jet
ADEGORT	128	GAROTED	EHINPRSTUW	punish with wire
ADEIINT	193	INEDITA	CGMORSV	cogs vroom
ADEILNS	159	DENIALS	DEGKNOPRUV	no, never puked over dung
ADEILNT	43	(LENT AID)	ABDEFGNOPUV	gave up pub and food
ADEILOR	182	DARIOLE	FGLSTVX	–
ADEILOS	148	DEASOIL	CGMNPRSTUZ	snug cuz trumps
ADEILOT	98	(ADOLITE)	FKNPRSTV	–
ADEILRS	57	DERAILS	ABCDEGILMNOPTUY	delay coming to pub
ADEILRT	54	TRAILED	ABCELOPSTY	by a telescope
ADEILST	140	DILATES	BCEGIMOPRVY	my iceberg movie epic
ADEINOR	33	ANEROID	BDGMRSTU	must bust drugs
ADEINOS	56	ANODISE	BCDGHLMRSTXZ	–
ADEINOT	9	(ON A DIET)	BCILMNPRSTV	slim in BBC TV script
ADEINRS	11	RANDIES	ABEFGILMNOPRSTUVY	film about spying perv
ADEINRT	8	TRAINED	ACDEGHIOPSTU	educated pigs to chase cats
ADEINRU	107	UNAIRED	FHIMOPSTV	mist stops VHF
ADEINST	22	INSTEAD	BCDEGHIMOPRSTUVY	Tom Thumb discovers pigmy
ADEIORS	109	ROADIES	CDFLNPTV	–
ADEIORT	17	(TOADIER)	CGKLMNRSTV	–
ADEIOST	127	TOADIES	GLMNPRXZ	–
ADEIPRS	232	DESPAIR	ACDEGHILNOPRSTU	poor English education
ADEIRST	16	TARDIES	ABCDEHIKLMNOPSTW	slowcoach kept behind men
ADEIRTT	216	ATTIRED	CELMNOST	to collect some men
ADELNOR	214	LADRONE	BCEFPSUV	Eve's beef cup
ADENORS	78	(DARES ON)	BCEHILMPRT	her implicit bet
ADENORT	37	TORNADE	CGINOPSTWY	twisting copy
ADENRST	202	STANDER	BCDGIORSUX	rigid discus box
ADENRTU	120	NATURED	BCDEHILMPRSTX	six spiders bit ill chimp

ADEORST	91	ROASTED	BCGILMNPRSUX	spring club mix
ADINORS	116	ORDAINS	BCDEGLNPRSTUV	pub reverend gets selected
ADINORT	60	(TIN ROAD)	ACELNOSU	unclean soles
ADINRST	208	INDARTS	ABEFGIKORU	broke a figure
ADIORST	152	ASTROID	CEILNPSTU	puts cusps in line
AEEGINR	74	REGINAE	BDGILMPRSTZ	prim bird's glitz
AEEGIRT	184	(AGERITE)	FHIMNTV	fifth mini vin
AEEGNRS	249	ENRAGES	ACDGHILMNTUV	living Dutchman
AEEGNRT	161	NEGATER	EILMNRSU	nurse's smile
AEEGRST	246	RESTAGE	ABDEMNRSTUW	bans water and mud
AEEILNS	118	SEALINE	BCDEGNPRSX	BP exceeds Greens' decree
AEEILNT	75	LINEATE	ADGLMPRV	damp lava rag
AEEILRS	76	REALISE	CDFGHLMNPRSTVYZ	–
AEEILRT	19	ATELIER	BDFHLMNOPRSTVZ	posh bozo from London TV
AEEILST	136	(EALIEST)	BDFGKLMPRSTV	–
AEEINRS	29	(ENRAISE)	CDGHKLMNPRSTU	hunk dug up rust clumps
AEEINRT	12	TRAINEE	CDGHIKLMPRS	dim girl licks chips
AEEINST	80	ETESIAN	BCDGMRSTV	–
AEEIRST	10	SERIATE	DEHLMNOPRSTVWY	world symphony event
AEELNRT	61	ETERNAL	BDEGHIMNRSVWX	whenever bedding six men
AEELORT	85	(ORELATE)	ACISTVW	awaits CV
AEELRST	55	STEALER	ABCDEFHIMNOPRSTUXY	thief raids bus and taxi company
AEENORS	197	ARENOSE	BDPRST	–
AEENRST	20	EASTERN	ABCEFGHIJLMORSTUV	Bush chooses flight from Java
AEENRTT	238	ENTREAT	ABDEFHRSVXY	shredded every bad fax
AEENRTV	244	VETERAN	DELMNORSTU	tremendous lot
AEEORST	105	ROSEATE	BCIKLMNPV	civil MP in bikini
AEERRST	219	TEARERS	BCDEFGIKLMNPRSTUVW	but we like fingerlicking virus dump!
AEGILNR	26	REALIGN	ABCDEFGHIJLMNOPRSTVXY	straightened box of lovely spicy jam
AEGILNS	134	LEASING	BDEFGHKLMNOPRSTVWY	bloke rented lovely gown from shop
AEGILNT	52	GENITAL	ABCDEGHKMNOPRSVXZ	Bob's sex-change even amazed sperm-bank
AEGILRS	190	GRAILES	ACDEGMNOSTYZ	stones got coated enzymes
AEGINOR	157	ORIGANE	BDLRSZ	–
AEGINOS	168	AGONIES	BCDGLNRSZ	–
AEGINRS	36	REGAINS	ABCDEGHKLMNOPRSTVWY	very happy lord gets back women
AEGINRT	32	TEARING	ABCDEHKLMPSTVWX	Dave wept at smashed back axle
AEGINST	42	TEASING	ABDEFGHLMNRSTUVWYZ	very naughty bawdy females gaze at me
AEGNRST	133	STRANGE	ABDEFGILMOPRUW	odd formidable purple wig
AEGORST	151	TOERAGS	CDFHLNOPRSTU	untruthful clodpolls
AEHIRST	131	HASTIER	ACDEINOPRSUWY	sped away in our car
AEIINRS	167	SENARII	BCDKLNSTY	–
AEIINST	138	ISATINE	BCDFKLMPRSVXZ	–
AEIIRST	108	AIRIEST	DFHLMNPRSVWXZ	–
AEILNOR	50	ALIENOR	CFGLPSTV	–
AEILNOS	49	ANISOLE	CDGKMNPRSTX	–
AEILNOT	35	ELATION	BDFGPRST	–
AEILNPT	183	PANTILE	ABCDEGOPRSTY	gets a card by post
AEILNRS	18	NAILERS	BCDEGHIMOPRSTUVXY	medic's itchy poxvirus bug
AEILNRT	7	ENTRAIL	CEFGIMNOPSTUVY	iffy veg consumption
AEILNRU	210	(UI LEARN)	ABFHMST	fab maths
AEILNST	63	ENTAILS	BFGIKMOPRSUVW	survivor of mugwump book
AEILORS	28	(ORALISE)	ACDFGHMNPSTVYZ	vast zany champ had fag
AEILORT	4	(ORALITE)	BCDEFHMNPRSTVZ	freeze prevented chef's best theme
AEILOST	40	ISOLATE	CDFGKMNPRSTV	–
AEILOTT	178	(A TOILET)	DENRSVZ	severed sneeze
AEILPRT	154	PLAITER	ABCDEIKNORSV	breakdance vision
AEILRST	14	RETAILS	BCDEFGIKLMNOPRSTU	kept selling record bumf
AEILRSU	191	(URALISE)	ACDFHLNPQRT	talaq had craft plan
AEILRTT	103	TERTIAL	BCDEFGIMNORSY	my boyfriend is misscoring
AEIMNOT	194	AMNIOTE	ACDMNPSZ	zaps sandman's cap
AEIMNRS	149	SEMINAR	BCDEGHKLNORSTUY	lecture on chunky bodgers
AEIMNRT	110	MINARET	AEGLNSTUWY	always sung late
AEIMNST	122	INMATES	ABCDEFGHIKLNORS	sharing food in cell block
AEIMRST	82	SMARTIE	ABCDEGIKLMNOPSTUVWXY	lovely sweety compound packed in long box
AEINNOT	117	ENATION	CDGMRSTV	–
AEINNRS	97	INSNARE	CDEGIMOPRSTUW	mug tripped up stupid cow
AEINORS	15	ERASION	BCDFGLMNSTV	–
AEINORT	1	OTARINE	ABCDHLNPRSTZ	hazard blasts can apart

AEINOST	21	ATONIES	BCDLMNPRSVX	–
AEINOTT	86	(ATONITE)	CDFHILNR	find chilli rind
AEINPRS	207	RAPINES	ADEFGHKLNPTUW	laughed at awful punk
AEINPRT	41	PAINTER	ADEGHILORSTUX	Dulux is a lot tougher
AEINPST	195	SPINATE	BDHILNOPRSTUY	thy truly spiny body
AEINRRT	106	TERRAIN	ENOPSTVW	snow on even steppes
AEINRSS	239	SARNIES	CDEFGHILMNOTUWX	welcome to foxhunting mud
AEINRST	2	RETAINS	ABCDEFGHIJKLMNOPRSTUW	stopped wrongful hijack mob
AEINRSU	70	UNRAISE	BDELMNPSTVZ	zz - embedded sleep event
AEINRTT	51	NITRATE	ACDGLMNOPRSU	gas cloud drops on man
AEINRTU	31	URINATE	ABCDHJLMPQSTV	lav has qat jab damp patch
AEINSTT	104	INSTATE	ABCDEFGHJNPRSTVW	Javan dwarf sheep can't beg
AEINSTU	192	AUNTIES	DGJKLPQRSV	–
AEINSTV	170	NATIVES	ACDEGIKLOTU	tackled dialogue
AEIORST	5	OTARIES	BDEHJLMNRTUV	he never jumbled the truth
AEIPRST	130	PARTIES	ACDEGHIKLMNPRSVWY	champagne and very silly awkward dancing
AEIRRST	92	ARTSIER	BCEFHILNOPRSTW	celebrities will often be posh
AEIRSST	213	SATIRES	ACDEGHIKLMNPRSTVW	watching skimpier devil
AEIRSTT	73	ATTIRES	ABCDEGLMNORSTWXZ	garments ooze cold beeswax
AEIRSTV	235	VASTIER	ABEGIMOPSY	mega-biopsy
AEIRSTW	158	WAITERS	ABDEFHIMNPRST	need fish, meat, and beer tips
AELNORS	226	ORLEANS	DFILMPUV	film-vid pupil
AELNRST	88	RENTALS	ABCEGHINPSTUV	begin chasing up TVs
AELORST	44	OESTRAL	BCDEFGHILMPRUVYZ	verify much puzzled bug
AELORSU	156	(SOUR ALE)	ABCDEFGMNPTU	defunct pub game
AELRSTU	224	SALUTER	BCEFGIMNOPSTV	inspecting mob of five
AENORST	6	SENATOR	ABCDEFGIMNPRSTUVW	big fat American VIP used newsman
AENORTT	166	(RAT NOTE)	BCDGILMPSXY	digs pixy climb
AENRSTT	221	NATTERS	ACEILNOPRSU	peculiar son
AENRSTU	77	NATURES	BCDEGHILMOPSTVW	glimpsed how wolves' victim bled
AEOPRST	228	SEAPORT	BCDEFGHLNPRSTUV	preserved the French flu bug
AEORRST	126	ROASTER	ABCDGILMNOPRST	blaming cold pot-roast
AEORSTT	185	ROTATES	ABCGHINPRSTU	puts punchbag straight
AGILNOT	175	ANTILOG	ABCEFGHIPRSTY	specify best graph
AGINORS	196	SOARING	CDEHILMRSTUV	vultures ditch mice
AGINORT	142	ORATING	BGIKLNOSTVY	lobbying to visit king
AGINRST	179	STARING	ABCDEFGHKLMNOPRSTVWY	vagrant watchmaker's body flops
AILNORT	68	(TRIONAL)	ACDEFGHLMSZ	glass amazed chef
AILNOST	153	LATINOS	AEGLNORY	are nearly orange
AILORST	164	TAILORS	BCDEMNOSUY	obscene dummy
AINORST	39	RATIONS	BCDEGHJKLOPSTUX	expected stock budget to be just hopeless
BEINOST	204	BONIEST	ABEIKNORSTU	our skinniest beatnik
CEEINRT	245	ENTICER	AFGIJNOPSTU	just patting foot
CEINORS	188	COINERS	ABCDFGHILMNPRSTU	FT brings lad cash triumph
CEINORT	94	RECTION	ACDEFGHJMPRSTUV	chef judged Spam advert
CEINOST	172	NOTICES	ACDEGKLMOPRSTUXY	spots extremely gaudy cake
DEEINRS	96	DENIERS	ABEFGHKLNOSTUWX	knew nowt about the golf sex
DEEINRT	47	(DENTIER)	ABDKMNORSTUVWX	two marks on VDU box
DEEINST	46	DESTINE	ABDEFGHILMNOPRSTUV	disproving humble fate
DEEIRST	58	DIETERS	ABCDEFGHILMNPRSTUVW	having awful vast bumps reduced
DEENORS	143	ENDORSE	ABCDEIMNRSTW	warm bed antics
DEENORT	186	ERODENT	CHILMOSU	much soil loss
DEENRTU	237	DENTURE	ADEILNORSV	island lover
DEIINRT	231	NITRIDE	ACDGMOPSU	Scamp's a pup dog
DEIIRST	248	(TIDIERS)	ACEGHLNOPT	change the plot
DEILNOS	144	INDOLES	ACEGIORSU	ice or sugar
DEILORS	200	SOLDIER	ACILNPSTUY	cast in UN play
DEINORS	25	INDORSE	ACDEGHIJLNPRSTUW	upheld rights and cut jaw
DEINORT	24	(IRODENT)	ACEIMNPST	cats snap at mice
DEINOST	79	DITONES	ACEHIMRSW	wise charm
DEINRST	87	TINDERS	ADEGILOPTUX	poll-tax guide
DEINRTU	83	INTRUDE	ABCDEILMNPRSW	clamber inside palace wall
DEINSTU	203	DUNITES	ADEFGILMNQRSU	minerals in quaggier fields
DEIORST	53	EDITORS	ABCGIKLMNPSTUW	masking public wit
DEIORTU	199	OUTRIDE	BCEFHRSV	chef serves beef
DEIRSTU	229	DUSTIER	CDEGLMNOPQRSTX	QPR expected to lose long term
DENORST	209	SNORTED	AEIMNPUY	puma in my pen
DENORTU	176	(NOT RUDE)	CDEFGLORSTW	good flowers cost lots
EEGINRS	113	GREISEN	ABCDEFGHJKLMNOPRSTUVW	hoped job takeover gamble was unsuccessful
EEGINRT	162	INTEGER	ACGIMNPSUVWX	savings mixup was manic
EEGINST	171	(SEETING)	ABCDGHKLMNOPRTUVWX	black VW on orthodox campground
EEILNST	89	TENSILE	BCDEGHIKNOPRSTV	do keep overstretching biceps

EEILORS	163	(SORE LIE)	BCFIKLNPTVW	if VIP will lick kilt, I'll bin it
EEILORT	129	TROELIE	ADHKMRS	shark mad
EEILRST	81	STERILE	ACDEFIKLMNOPST	cannot make life so adopts
EEINORS	115	EROSINE	DGHKLMPSTV	–
EEINORT	23	(TRIE ONE)	BCDHIMRSTX	six timid rich birds
EEINOST	95	(ETONIES)	BCDGLMRST	–
EEINRST	13	ENTRIES	ACDEFGIKLMNORSTUVXY	make index of curvy girls' measurements
EEINRSU	198	(INSUREE)	ACDFGNPQRSTV	qat pangs and fast caravan
EEINRTT	165	TENTIER	BCDEHILNOSY	lynched bodies
EEINSTT	187	(SITE TEN)	ABDEFGILMNOPRTWX	rainbow got exemplified
EEIORST	71	(OTERIES)	ACGHLMNPSZ	plaza chap calls gasman
EELORST	150	SOLERET	ACEHILMNSTUV	little sun has much value
EENORST	45	(NO TREES)	ADFGHILMNOPSTVX	so having to fix dogs to lampposts
EGILNOR	222	(ONE GIRL)	ABEFISW	is fab wife
EGINORS	64	IGNORES	ABCDEILMNPRSTWY	calmly pass by entwined rabbit
EGINORT	180	GENITOR	CHNSTUVWXZ	TV cuz hunts tux wus
EGINRST	111	RESTING	ACDEHILNOPRSTVW	recover in hospital ward
EGIORST	233	GORIEST	DEHMNSUVYZ	seven mushed enzymes
EGNORST	236	(STRONG E)	AEGINRSTUW	new guitar string
EHIORST	230	HOISTER	ACEGMNPRSTUVW	water games can upset vac
EIILRST	215	SILTIER	ABDEFLMNOPTU	boat fouled up on mud
EIINORT	99	(IRONITE)	DEFPRS	feed press
EIINRST	66	(TINIERS)	ABCDEFGHKLMOPSTUV	small ducks have to beg off people
EILNORS	59	NEROLIS	ACDEGIMPRT	magic carpet ride
EILNORT	72	RETINOL	APRSTUW	wart pus
EILNOST	34	ENTOILS	ACEHILMNOPRUVW	win lamp voucher
EILNRST	93	SNIRTLE	ADEGIKMOPSUY	amused podgy kid
EILORST	27	LOITERS	ABCDEFILNOPSTU	idles about at place of fun
EILRSTU	189	LUSTIER	ABCDGHIMNOQRSTV	qanat - Arabic irrigation having no dams
EIMNOST	243	MOISTEN	ACDEGHKLNOPS	chalk and sponge
EIMORST	173	MOISTER	ACDEFGHOPRSTUVWY	heavy wet dog appears at Crufts
EINOPRS	177	ORPINES	CDEFGILMOPRSTUV	most golf is productive
EINOPRT	212	POINTER	ACDHILMSU	dial music hall
EINORRT	90	(TORRINE)	ACEFHILSVW	vehicle was safe
EINORST	3	(IN STORE)	ABCDEGHIJKLNOPRSTUVYZ	sick crazy juveniles shopped by night
EINORSU	227	URINOSE	CDFMNPSTV	–
EINORTT	84	TRITONE	ACDEGKLNSU	sang and clucked
EINORTU	119	ROUTINE	CGJLNPST	–
EINOSTT	241	TONIEST	BCEFGJNPRSTW	begs perfect new jet
EINRSTT	234	TINTERS	ABCDEGIKOSUWY	causeway guidebook
EINRSTU	65	UNITERS	ABCDEILMNOPQTVW	cabmen to develop low IQ
EIOPRST	201	ROPIEST	CDEFHKLMNORSTUV	thunder struck lover for me
EIORRST	135	RIOTERS	ABFHIMNOPRSTUV	ambush pub via front
EIORSTT	174	STOITER	ACDHLMNOPRSUV	sharp vocals and drums
EIORSTU	67	TOUSIER	ACDFGHLMNPQRTV	champ had fag and tranq at lav
ENORSTU	100	(NOT SURE)	ABCDFGHILMNOSTVY	cannot fight in dim visibility

8-LETTER SETS
from the top 250 7-letter stems

AADEIRT 141
RADIATE
C RADICATE
D RADIATED
E ERADIATE
L LARIATED
N DENTARIA
RAINDATE
S AIRDATES
DATARIES
RADIATES
V VARIATED

AAEGINR 247
ANERGIA
B ABEARING
C CANAIGRE
D AREADING
DRAINAGE
GARDENIA
F AFEARING
G GRAINAGE
L GERANIAL
REGALIAN
N ANEARING
S ANERGIAS
ANGARIES
ARGINASE
T AERATING

AAEILNT 102
ANTLIAE
C ANALCITE
LAITANCE
D DENTALIA
E ALIENATE
G AGENTIAL
ALGINATE
H ANTHELIA
K ANTILEAK
L ALLANITE
M ALAIMENT
ANTIMALE
LAMINATE
P PALATINE
T ANTLIATE
V AVENTAIL

AAEINRT 30
(ARANITE)
B RABATINE
C CARINATE
CRANIATE
D DENTARIA
RAINDATE
G AERATING
M ANIMATER
MARINATE
O AERATION
P ANTIRAPE
S ANTISERA
ARTESIAN
RATANIES
RESINATA
SEATRAIN
T ATTAINER
REATTAIN
U INAURATE
W ANTIWEAR
Z ATRAZINE

AAEINST 169
TAENIAS
B BASANITE
C ESTANCIA
F FANTASIE
G SAGINATE
H ASTHENIA
M AMENTIAS
ANIMATES
R ANTISERA
ARTESIAN
RATANIES
RESINATA
SEATRAIN
S ENTASIAS
T ASTATINE
SANITATE
TANAISTE
V SANATIVE

AAEINTT 225
(A NATTIE)
D ATTAINED
E TAENIATE
L ANTLIATE
N ANTENATI
P PATINATE
R ATTAINER
REATTAIN
S ASTATINE
SANITATE
TANAISTE
T TITANATE

AAEIRST 181
ASTERIA
D AIRDATES
DATARIES
RADIATES
H HETAIRAS
M AMIRATES
N ANTISERA
ARTESIAN
RATANIES
RESINATA
SEATRAIN
P ASPIRATE
PARASITE
SEPTARIA
S ASTERIAS
ATRESIAS
T ARIETTAS
ARISTATE
V VARIATES
W AWAITERS

AAENRST 112
ANESTRA
B ANTBEARS
RATSBANE
C CANASTER
CATERANS
E ARSENATE
SERENATA
G STARAGEN
TANAGERS
I ANTISERA
ARTESIAN
RATANIES
RESINATA
SEATRAIN
J NAARTJES
L ASTERNAL
M SARMENTA
SEMANTRA
O ANOESTRA
R NARRATES
T TARTANES
V TAVERNAS
TSAREVNA

ABEINST 121
BESTAIN
A BASANITE
C CABINETS
D BANDIEST
E BETAINES
G BEATINGS
H ABSINTHE
I BAINITES
K BEATNIKS
SNAKEBIT
L INSTABLE
M AMBIENTS
O BOTANIES
BOTANISE
NIOBATES
OBEISANT
P BEPAINTS
R ATEBRINS
BANISTER
BARNIEST
S BASINETS
BASSINET
BESAINTS
BESTAINS
T TABINETS

ABEORST 160
BOASTER
A RABATOES
C CABESTRO
CABRESTO
D BROADEST
E ABORTEES
REBATOES
H BATHORSE
I SABOTIER
L BLOATERS
SORTABLE
STORABLE
M BROMATES
N BARONETS
P PROBATES
R ABORTERS
ARBORETS
TABORERS
S BOASTERS
SORBATES
T ABETTORS
BATTEROS
TABORETS
U SABOTEUR

ACDEINR 240
CAIRNED
A CANARIED
RADIANCE
D CANDIDER
RIDDANCE
E DERACINE
H INARCHED
I ACRIDINE
N CRANNIED
R RANCIDER
T CRINATED
DICENTRA

ACEILRT 206
RECITAL
A TAILRACE
D ARTICLED
LACERTID
K TALCKIER
M METRICAL
N CLARINET
O EROTICAL
LORICATE
P PARTICLE
PRELATIC
R CLARTIER
S ALTRICES
ARTICLES
RECITALS
SELICTAR
STERICAL
T TRACTILE
U RETICULA
V VERTICAL
Y LITERACY

ACEINOT 139
ACONITE
C ACETONIC
D ACTIONED
CATENOID
H INCHOATE
M COINMATE
N ENACTION
R ACTIONER
ANORETIC
CREATION
REACTION
S ACONITES
CANOEIST
SONICATE
T TACONITE
V CONATIVE
INVOCATE
X EXACTION

ACEINRS 132
ARSENIC
A ACARINES
CANARIES
CESARIAN
B BRISANCE
CARBINES
E CINEREAS
INCREASE
RESIANCE
F FANCIERS
G CREASING
GRECIANS
SEARCING
H ARCHINES
INARCHES
I RIANCIES
K SKINCARE
L CARLINES
LANCIERS
M CARMINES
CREMAINS
N CRANNIES
NARCEINS
O SCENARIO
S ARCSINES
ARSENICS
CERASINS
RACINESS
T CANISTER
CARNIEST
CERATINS
CISTERNA
CREATINS
NACRITES
SCANTIER

ACEINRT 69
CERTAIN
A CARINATE
CRANIATE
B BACTERIN
C ACENTRIC
D CRINATED
DICENTRA
E CENTIARE
CREATINE
INCREATE
ITERANCE
G ARGENTIC
CATERING
CITRANGE
CREATING
REACTING
L CLARINET
O ACTIONER
ANORETIC
CREATION
REACTION
S CANISTER
CARNIEST
CERATINS
CISTERNA
CREATINS
NACRITES
SCANTIER
T INTERACT
U ANURETIC
V NAVICERT
X XERANTIC

ACEINST 114
CANIEST
A ESTANCIA
B CABINETS
D DISTANCE
E CINEASTE
F FANCIEST
H ASTHENIC
CHANTIES
I CANITIES
M AMNESTIC
SEMANTIC
N ANCIENTS
CANNIEST
INSECTAN
INSTANCE
O ACONITES
CANOEIST
SONICATE
R CANISTER
CARNIEST
CERATINS
CISTERNA
CREATINS
NACRITES
SCANTIER
S CINEASTS
SCANTIES
T CANTIEST
ENTASTIC
NICTATES
TETANICS
V CISTVAEN
VESICANT
Y CYANITES
Z ZINCATES

ACENORT 124
(CORN TEA)
C ACCENTOR
D CARTONED
E CAROTENE
H ANCHORET
I ACTIONER
ANORETIC
CREATION
REACTION
O CORONATE
P COPARENT
PORTANCE
S ANCESTOR
ENACTORS
SARCONET
SORTANCE
T CONTRATE
U COURANTE
OUTRANCE
Y ENACTORY

ACEORST 223
COASTER
B CABESTRO
CABRESTO
C ECTOSARC
D REDCOATS
E CREASOTE
F FORECAST
G ESCARGOT
H CHAROSET
THORACES
L LOCATERS
SECTORAL
N ANCESTOR
ENACTORS
SARCONET
SORTANCE
P POSTRACE
R ACROTERS
CREATORS

REACTORS
S COARSEST
COASTERS
T SECTATOR
U OUTRACES
V OVERACTS
OVERCAST
X EXACTORS

ACINORT 211
(CORTINA)
A RAINCOAT
C CRATONIC
NARCOTIC
D TORNADIC
E ACTIONER
ANORETIC
CREATION
REACTION
F FRACTION
H ANORTHIC
K ANTIROCK
L CILANTRO
CONTRAIL
M ROMANTIC
R CARROTIN
CONTRAIR
S CANTORIS
CAROTINS
T TRACTION
Y CARYOTIN

ADEEGNR 145
ANGERED
A GADARENE
C ENGRACED
D DANGERED
DERANGED
GANDERED
GARDENED
E RENEGADE
H REHANGED
I REGAINED
L ENLARGED
LARGENED
M GENDARME
N ENDANGER
ENRANGED
O RENEGADO
R GARDENER
GARNERED
S DERANGES
GRANDEES
GRENADES
U DUNGAREE
RENAGUED
UNDERAGE
UNGEARED
V ENGRAVED

ADEEILR 146
(LEADIER)
B RIDEABLE
D DEADLIER
DERAILED
REDIALED
L REALLIED
M REMAILED
REMEDIAL
N RENAILED
P PEDALIER
R DERAILER
RERAILED
S REALISED
RESAILED

SIDEREAL
T DETAILER
ELATERID
RETAILED
Z REALIZED

ADEEILS 217
AEDILES
B ABSEILED
BELADIES
H DEISHEAL
I IDEALISE
K LAKESIDE
M LIMEADES
N DELAINES
P PLEIADES
R REALISED
RESAILED
SIDEREAL
S DEISEALS
IDEALESS
T LEADIEST
V DISLEAVE
Y EYELIADS

ADEEILT 250
(DILATEE)
B DELIBATE
EDITABLE
C DELICATE
D DETAILED
N DATELINE
ENTAILED
LINEATED
P DEPILATE
EPILATED
PILEATED
R DETAILER
ELATERID
RETAILED
S LEADIEST

ADEEINR 101
(DEANIER)
C DERACINE
F FREDAINE
G REGAINED
L RENAILED
M REMAINED
P PINDAREE
S ARSENIDE
DENARIES
DRAISENE
NEARSIDE
T DETAINER
RETAINED
V REINVADE

ADEEINS 242
ANISEED
L DELAINES
M DEMAINES
INSEAMED
N ADENINES
ANDESINE
R ARSENIDE
DENARIES
DRAISENE
NEARSIDE
S ANISEEDS
T ANDESITE

ADEEINT 62
(NITE ADE)
D DETAINED

E DETAINEE
L DATELINE
ENTAILED
LINEATED
M DEMENTIA
P DIAPENTE
R DETAINER
RETAINED
S ANDESITE
W ANTIWEED

ADEEIRS 125
READIES
B BEARDIES
C DECIARES
F FEDARIES
G DISAGREE
J JADERIES
L REALISED
RESAILED
SIDEREAL
M MADERISE
N ARSENIDE
DENARIES
DRAISENE
NEARSIDE
P AIRSPEED
R DREARIES
RERAISED
T READIEST
SERIATED
SIDERATE
STEADIER
V READVISE

ADEEIRT 48
(DIE RATE)
A ERADIATE
B EBRIATED
REBAITED
H DEATHIER
L DETAILER
ELATERID
RETAILED
M DIAMETER
REMEDIAT
N DETAINER
RETAINED
S READIEST
SERIATED
SIDERATE
STEADIER
T ITERATED
V DERIVATE
EVIRATED
TAIVERED

ADEEIST 155
IDEATES
B BEADIEST
DIABETES
D STEADIED
F SAFETIED
H ATHEISED
HEADIEST
J JADEITES
L LEADIEST
M MEDIATES
N ANDESITE
R READIEST
SERIATED
SIDERATE
STEADIER
S STEADIES
V DEVIATES

SEDATIVE

ADEELRT 218
RELATED
C CLARETED
DECRETAL
TREACLED
D TREADLED
F DEFLATER
FALTERED
REFLATED
H HALTERED
LATHERED
I DETAILER
ELATERID
RETAILED
L TELLARED
M TRAMELED
N ANTLERED
P PALTERED
REPLATED
R TREADLER
S DESALTER
RESLATED
TREADLES
V TRAVELED

ADEENRS 147
ENDEARS
C ASCENDER
REASCEND
E ENSEARED
SERENADE
G DERANGES
GRANDEES
GRENADES
I ARSENIDE
DENARIES
DRAISENE
NEARSIDE
K KNEADERS
M AMENDERS
MEANDERS
REAMENDS
N ENSNARED
O REASONED
S DEARNESS
U UNDERSEA
UNERASED
UNSEARED
W ANSWERED
Y YEARENDS

ADEENRT 137
(END TEAR)
B BANTERED
C CANTERED
CRENATED
DECANTER
NECTARED
RECANTED
D ENDARTED
H ADHERENT
HARTENED
NEATHERD
THREADEN
I DETAINER
RETAINED
L ANTLERED
P PARENTED
T ATTENDER
NATTERED
RATTENED
U DENATURE
UNDERATE

UNDEREAT
V AVENTRED

ADEERST 123
DERATES
B BETREADS
BREASTED
DEBATERS
C CEDRATES
E RESEATED
F DRAFTEES
G RESTAGED
H HEADREST
I READIEST
SERIATED
SIDERATE
STEADIER
K STREAKED
L DESALTER
RESLATED
TREADLES
M MASTERED
STREAMED
P PEDERAST
PREDATES
REPASTED
TRAPESED
R ARRESTED
DREAREST
RETREADS
SERRATED
TREADERS
S ASSERTED
ESTRADES
T ASTERTED
RESTATED
RETASTED
W DEWATERS
TARWEEDS
WASTERED
Y ESTRAYED

ADEGINR 38
READING
A AREADING
DRAINAGE
GARDENIA
B BEARDING
BREADING
D DREADING
READDING
E REGAINED
H ADHERING
HEADRING
I DEAIRING
K DAKERING
L DANGLIER
DEARLING
DRAGLINE
M DREAMING
MARGINED
MIDRANGE
N GRANNIED
O ORGANDIE
R DREARING
S DERAIGNS
GRADINES
READINGS
T DERATING
GRADIENT
REDATING
TREADING
Y DERAYING
READYING
YEARDING

ADEGINT 220
(INGATED)
A INDAGATE
B DEBATING
I IDEATING
L DELATING
R DERATING
GRADIENT
REDATING
TREADING
S SEDATING
STEADING
V VINTAGED

ADEGNOR 205
GROANED
B BONDAGER
E RENEGADO
F FRONDAGE
I ORGANDIE
J JARGONED
M DRAGOMEN
N ANDROGEN
DRAGONNE
P DOGNAPER
T DRAGONET

ADEGORT 128
GAROTED
E DEROGATE
H GOATHERD
I ERGATOID
N DRAGONET
P PORTAGED
R GARROTED
S GOADSTER
T GAROTTED
U OUTRAGED
RAGOUTED
W WATERDOG

ADEIINT 193
INEDITA
C ACTINIDE
CTENIDIA
DIACTINE
INDICATE
G IDEATING
M MINIATED
O IDEATION
IODINATE
TAENIOID
R DAINTIER
S ADENITIS
DAINTIES
V VANITIED

ADEILNS 159
DENIALS
D ISLANDED
LANDSIDE
E DELAINES
G DEALINGS
LEADINGS
SIGNALED
K SANDLIKE
N ANNELIDS
LINDANES
O NODALISE
P SANDPILE
R ISLANDER
U UNSATLED
V ANDVILES

ADEILNT 43
(LENT AID)
A DENTALIA
B BIDENTAL
D TIDELAND
E DATELINE
ENTAILED
LINEATED
F INFLATED
G DELATING
N DENTINAL
O DELATION
P PANTILED
U UNTAILED
V DIVALENT

ADEILOR 182
DARIOLE
F FORELAID
G DIALOGER
L ARILLODE
S DARIOLES
SOLIDARE
SOREDIAL
T IDOLATER
TAILORED
V OVERLAID
X EXORDIAL

ADEILOS 148
DEASOIL
C COALISED
G GOLIASED
M DAMOISEL
MELODIAS
N NODALISE
P EPISODAL
OPALISED
SEPALOID
R DARIOLES
SOLIDARE
SOREDIAL
S ASSOILED
DEASOILS
ISOLEADS
T DIASTOLE
ISOLATED
SODALITE
SOLIDATE
U DOULEIAS
Z DIAZOLES

ADEILOT 98
(ADOLITE)
F FOLIATED
K TOADLIKE
N DELATION
P PETALOID
R IDOLATER
TAILORED
S DIASTOLE
ISOLATED
SODALITE
SOLIDATE
T DATOLITE
V DOVETAIL
VIOLATED

ADEILRS 57
DERAILS
A SALARIED
B BEDRAILS
RAILBEDS
C DECRIALS
RADICELS
RADICLES
D DIEDRALS
E REALISED
RESAILED
SIDEREAL
G SLAIRGED
I LAIRISED
L DALLIERS
DIALLERS
M DISMALER
N ISLANDER
O DARIOLES
SOLIDARE
SOREDIAL
P PARSLIED
PEDRAILS
PREDIALS
SPIRALED
T DILATERS
LARDIEST
REDTAILS
U RESIDUAL
Y DIALYSER

ADEILRT 54
TRAILED
A LARIATED
B LIBRATED
C ARTICLED
LACERTID
E DETAILER
ELATERID
RETAILED
L TRIALLED
O IDOLATER
TAILORED
P DIPTERAL
TRIPEDAL
S DILATERS
LARDIEST
REDTAILS
T DETRITAL
Y DIELYTRA

ADEILST 140
DILATES
B BALDIEST
C CITADELS
DIALECTS
E LEADIEST
G GLADIEST
I IDEALIST
M MEDALIST
MISDEALT
O DIASTOLE
ISOLATED
SODALITE
SOLIDATE
P TALIPEDS
R DILATERS
LARDIEST
REDTAILS
V VALIDEST
Y DIASTYLE
STEADILY

ADEINOR 33
ANEROID
B DEBONAIR
D ORDAINED
G ORGANDIE
M RADIOMEN
R ORDAINER
REORDAIN
S ANEROIDS
DONARIES
T AROINTED
DERATION
ORDINATE
RATIONED
U DOUANIER

ADEINOS 56
ANODISE
B BEDSONIA
C CODEINAS
DIOCESAN
OCEANIDS
D ADENOIDS
ADONISED
ANODISED
G AGONISED
DIAGNOSE
H ADHESION
L NODALISE
M AMIDONES
DAIMONES
NOMADIES
NOMADISE
R ANEROIDS
DONARIES
S ADENOSIS
ADONISES
ANODISES
T ASTONIED
SEDATION
X DIOXANES
Z ADONIZES
ANODIZES

ADEINOT 9
(ON A DIET)
B OBTAINED
C ACTIONED
CATENOID
I IDEATION
IODINATE
TAENIOID
L DELATION
M DOMINATE
NEMATOID
N ANOINTED
ANTINODE
P ANTIPODE
R AROINTED
DERATION
ORDINATE
RATIONED
S ASTONIED
SEDATION
T ANTIDOTE
TETANOID
V DONATIVE

ADEINRS 11
RANDIES
A ARANEIDS
B BRANDIES
BRANDISE
E ARSENIDE
DENARIES
DRAISENE
NEARSIDE
F FRIANDES
G DERAIGNS
GRADINES
READINGS
I DRAISINE
L ISLANDER
M ADERMINS
SIRNAMED
N INSNARED
O ANEROIDS
DONARIES
P SPRAINED
R DRAINERS
SERRANID
S ARIDNESS
SARDINES
T DETRAINS
RANDIEST
STRAINED
U DENARIUS
UNRAISED
URANIDES
V INVADERS
SANDIVER
Y SYNEDRIA

ADEINRT 8
TRAINED
A DENTARIA
RAINDATE
C CRINATED
DICENTRA
D INDARTED
E DETAINER
RETAINED
G DERATING
GRADIENT
REDATING
TREADING
H ANTHERID
I DAINTIER
O AROINTED
DERATION
ORDINATE
RATIONED
P DIPTERAN
S DETRAINS
RANDIEST
STRAINED
T NITRATED
U DATURINE
INDURATE
RUINATED
URINATED

ADEINRU 107
UNAIRED
F UNFAIRED
H UNHAIRED
I UREDINIA
M MURAENID
O DOUANIER
P UNPAIRED
UNREPAID
S DENARIUS
UNRAISED
URANIDES
T DATURINE
INDURATE
RUINATED
URINATED
V UNVARIED

ADEINST 22
INSTEAD
B BANDIEST
C DISTANCE
D DANDIEST
E ANDESITE
G SEDATING
STEADING
H HANDIEST
I ADENITIS
DAINTIES
M MEDIANTS
TIDESMAN
O ASTONIED
SEDATION
P DEPAINTS
R DETRAINS
RANDIEST
STRAINED
S DESTAINS
SANDIEST
T INSTATED
U AUDIENTS
SINUATED
V DEVIANTS
Y DESYATIN

ADEIORS 109
ROADIES
C IDOCRASE
D ROADSIDE
SIDEROAD
F FORESAID
L DARIOLES
SOLIDARE
SOREDIAL
N ANEROIDS
DONARIES
P DIASPORE
PARODIES
T ASTEROID
V AVODIRES
AVOIDERS

ADEIORT 17
(TOADIER)
C CERATOID
G ERGATOID
K KERATOID
L IDOLATER
TAILORED
M MEDIATOR
N AROINTED
DERATION
ORDINATE
RATIONED
R ADROITER
S ASTEROID
T TERATOID
V DEVIATOR

ADEIOST 127
TOADIES
G GODETIAS
L DIASTOLE
ISOLATED
SODALITE
SOLIDATE
M ATOMISED
N ASTONIED
SEDATION
P DIOPTASE
R ASTEROID
X OXIDATES
Z AZOTISED

ADEIPRS 232
DESPAIR
A PARADISE
C EPACRIDS
PERACIDS
D DISPREAD
E AIRSPEED
G SPAIRGED
H RAPHIDES
I PRESIDIA
L PARSLIED
PEDRAILS
PREDIALS
SPIRALED
N SPRAINED
O DIASPORE
PARODIES
P APPRISED
DRAPPIES
R DRAPIERS
S DESPAIRS
T DIPTERAS
RAPIDEST
SPIRATED
TARSIPED
TRAIPSED
U UPRAISED

ADEIRST 16
TARDIES
A AIRDATES
DATARIES
RADIATES
B BARDIEST
BRAIDEST
RABIDEST
REDBAITS
TRIBADES
C ACRIDEST
D DISRATED
E READIEST
SERIATED
SIDERATE
STEADIER
H HAIRSTED
HARDIEST
I IRISATED
K STRAIKED
L DILATERS
LARDIEST
REDTAILS
M MARDIEST
MISRATED
READMITS
N DETRAINS
RANDIEST
STRAINED
O ASTEROID
P DIPTERAS
RAPIDEST
SPIRATED
TARSIPED
TRAIPSED
S ASTERIDS
DIASTERS
DISASTER
DISRATES
T STRAITED
STRIATED
TARDIEST
W TAWDRIES

ADEIRTT 216
ATTIRED
C CITRATED
TETRACID
TETRADIC
E ITERATED
L DETRITAL
M ADMITTER
N NITRATED
O TERATOID
S STRAITED

STRIATED
TARDIEST
T ATTRITED
TITRATED

ADELNOR 214
LADRONE
B BANDEROL
C COLANDER
CONELRAD
E OLEANDER
RELOANED
F FORELAND
P PONDERAL
S LADRONES
SOLANDER
U UNLOADER
URODELAN
V OVERLAND
RONDAVEL

ADENORS 78
(DARES ON)
B BANDORES
BROADENS
C DRACONES
ENDOSARC
E REASONED
H HARDNOSE
I ANEROIDS
DONARIES
L LADRONES
SOLANDER
M MADRONES
RANSOMED
ROADSMEN
P OPERANDS
PADRONES
PANDORES
R ADORNERS
READORNS
T TORNADES

ADENORT 37
TORNADE
C CARTONED
G DRAGONET
I AROINTED
DERATION
ORDINATE
RATIONED
N NONRATED
O RATOONED
P PRONATED
S TORNADES
T ATTORNED
W DANEWORT
TEARDOWN
Y AROYNTED

ADENRST 202
STANDER
B BANDSTER
BARTENDS
C CANTREDS
D DARNDEST
STRANDED
G DRAGNETS
GRANDEST
I DETRAINS
RANDIEST
STRAINED
O TORNADES
R STRANDER
S STANDERS

U DAUNTERS
TRANSUDE
UNTREADS
X DEXTRANS

ADENRTU 120
NATURED
B BREADNUT
TURBANED
C UNCARTED
UNCRATED
UNDERACT
UNTRACED
D DRAUNTED
UNTRADED
E DENATURE
UNDERATE
UNDEREAT
H UNTHREAD
I DATURINE
INDURATE
RUINATED
URINATED
L DENTURAL
M UNDREAMT
P DEPURANT
UNPARTED
R UNTARRED
S DAUNTERS
TRANSUDE
UNTREADS
T TRUANTED
X UNDERTAX

ADEORST 91
ROASTED
B BROADEST
C REDCOATS
G GOADSTER
I ASTEROID
L DELATORS
LEOTARDS
LODESTAR
M STROAMED
N TORNADES
P ADOPTERS
ASPORTED
PASTORED
READOPTS
R ROADSTER
S ASSORTED
TORSADES
U OUTDARES
OUTREADS
READOUTS
X EXTRADOS

ADINORS 116
ORDAINS
B INBOARDS
C SARDONIC
D ANDROIDS
DISADORN
E ANEROIDS
DONARIES
G ROADINGS
L ORDINALS
N ANDIRONS
P PONIARDS
R ORDINARS
S SADIRONS
T DIATRONS
INTRADOS
U DINOSAUR
V VIRANDOS

ADINORT 60
(TIN ROAD)
A ANTIDORA
C TORNADIC
E AROINTED
DERATION
ORDINATE
RATIONED
L TRINODAL
N ORDINANT
O TANDOORI
S DIATRONS
INTRADOS
U DURATION

ADINRST 208
INDARTS
A INTRADAS
RADIANTS
B ANTBIRDS
E DETRAINS
RANDIEST
STRAINED
F INDRAFTS
G TRADINGS
I DISTRAIN
K STINKARD
O DIATRONS
INTRADOS
R TRIDARNS
U UNITARDS

ADIORST 152
ASTROID
C CAROTIDS
E ASTEROID
I TARSIOID
L DILATORS
N DIATRONS
INTRADOS
P PARODIST
PAROTIDS
S ASTROIDS
SARODIST
T STRADIOT
U AUDITORS

AEEGINR 74
REGINAE
B BAREGINE
BERGENIA
D REGAINED
G AGREEING
I AEGIRINE
L ALGERINE
M GERMAINE
P PERIGEAN
R REGAINER
S ANERGIES
GESNERIA
T GRATINEE
INTERAGE
Z RAZEEING

AEEGIRT 184
(AGERITE)
F FIGEATER
H HERITAGE
I AEGIRITE
M EMIGRATE
REMIGATE
N GRATINEE
INTERAGE
T AIGRETTE
V ERGATIVE

AEEGNRS 249
ENRAGES
A SANGAREE
C ENGRACES
D DERANGES
GRANDEES
GRENADES
G ENGAGERS
H SHAGREEN
I ANERGIES
GESNERIA
L ENLARGES
GENERALS
GLEANERS
M AGREMENS
N ENRANGES
T ESTRANGE
GRANTEES
GREATENS
NEGATERS
REAGENTS
SEGREANT
SERGEANT
STERNAGE
U RENAGUES
V AVENGERS
ENGRAVES

AEEGNRT 161
NEGATER
E GENERATE
RENEGATE
TEENAGER
I GRATINEE
INTERAGE
L REGENTAL
M AGREMENT
N GENERANT
R ETRANGER
S ESTRANGE
GRANTEES
GREATENS
NEGATERS
REAGENTS
SEGREANT
SERGEANT
STERNAGE
U GAUNTREE

AEEGRST 246
RESTAGE
A STEARAGE
B ABSTERGE
D RESTAGED
E EAGEREST
ETAGERES
STEERAGE
M GAMESTER
MEAGREST
N ESTRANGE
GRANTEES
GREATENS
NEGATERS
REAGENTS
SEGREANT
SERGEANT
STERNAGE
R REGRATES
S RESTAGES
T GREATEST
U TREAGUES
W STREWAGE

AEEILNS 118
SEALINE
B BASELINE
C SALIENCE
D DELAINES
E ALIENEES
G ENSILAGE
LINEAGES
N SELENIAN
P ALEPINES
PENALISE
SEPALINE
R ALIENERS
S SEALINES
X ALEXINES

AEEILNT 75
LINEATE
A ALIENATE
D DATELINE
ENTAILED
LINEATED
G GALENITE
GELATINE
LEGATINE
L TENAILLE
M MELANITE
P PETALINE
TAPELINE
R ELATERIN
ENTAILER
TREENAIL
V ELVANITE
VENTAILE

AEEILRS 76
REALISE
C ESCALIER
D REALISED
RESAILED
SIDEREAL
F FILAREES
SERAFILE
G GASELIER
H SHIRALEE
L REALLIES
M ALMERIES
MEASLIER
N ALIENERS
P ESPALIER
PEARLIES
R REALISER
S REALISES
T ATELIERS
EARLIEST
LEARIEST
REALTIES
V VELARISE
Y YEARLIES
Z REALIZES
SLEAZIER

AEEILRT 19
ATELIER
B LIBERATE
D DETAILER
ELATERID
RETAILED
F FEATLIER
FRAILTEE
H ETHERIAL
L LAETRILE
M EREMITAL
MATERIEL
REALTIME

N ELATERIN
ENTAILER
TREENAIL
O AEROLITE
P PEARLITE
R RETAILER
S ATELIERS
EARLIEST
LEARIEST
REALTIES
T LATERITE
LITERATE
V LEVIRATE
RELATIVE
Z LATERIZE

AEEILST 136
(EALIEST)
B SEABLITE
D LEADIEST
F FEALTIES
FETIALES
LEAFIEST
G EGALITES
ELEGIAST
K LEAKIEST
L LEALTIES
M MEALIEST
METALISE
P EPILATES
R ATELIERS
EARLIEST
LEARIEST
REALTIES
S ASTELIES
T AILETTES
V ELATIVES
LEAVIEST
VEALIEST

AEEINRS 29
(ENRAISE)
C CINEREAS
INCREASE
RESIANCE
D ARSENIDE
DENARIES
DRAISENE
NEARSIDE
G ANERGIES
GESNERIA
H INHEARSE
K SNEAKIER
L ALIENERS
M REMANIES
N ANSERINE
P NAPERIES
R REARISEN
S SENARIES
T ARENITES
ARSENITE
RESINATE
STEARINE
TRAINEES
U UNEASIER

AEEINRT 12
TRAINEE
C CENTIARE
CREATINE
INCREATE
ITERANCE
D DETAINER
RETAINED
G GRATINEE

INTERAGE
H ATHERINE
HERNIATE
I INERTIAE
K ANKERITE
KREATINE
L ELATERIN
ENTAILER
TREENAIL
M ANTIMERE
P APERIENT
R RETAINER
S ARENITES
ARSENITE
RESINATE
STEARINE
TRAINEES

AEEINST 80
ETESIAN
B BETAINES
C CINEASTE
D ANDESITE
G SAGENITE
M ETAMINES
MATINEES
MISEATEN
SEMINATE
R ARENITES
ARSENITE
RESINATE
STEARINE
TRAINEES
S ETESIANS
TENIASES
T ANISETTE
TETANIES
TETANISE
V NAIVETES

AEEIRST 10
SERIATE
D READIEST
SERIATED
SIDERATE
STEADIER
E EATERIES
H HEARTIES
L ATELIERS
EARLIEST
LEARIEST
REALTIES
M EMIRATES
REAMIEST
STEAMIER
N ARENITES
ARSENITE
RESINATE
STEARINE
TRAINEES
O ETAERIOS
P PARIETES
PETARIES
R ARTERIES
REASTIER
S SERIATES
T ARIETTES
ITERATES
TEARIEST
TREATIES
TREATISE
V EVIRATES
W SWEATIER
TAWERIES
WASTERIE
WEARIEST
Y YEASTIER

AEELNRT 61
ETERNAL
B RENTABLE
D ANTLERED
E LATEENER
G REGENTAL
H LEATHERN
I ELATERIN
ENTAILER
TREENAIL
M LAMENTER
N LANNERET
R RELEARNT
S ALTERNES
ETERNALS
TELERANS
V LEVANTER
RELEVANT
W TREELAWN
X EXTERNAL

AEELORT 85
(ORELATE)
A AREOLATE
C CORELATE
RELOCATE
I AEROLITE
S OLEASTER
T TOLERATE
V ELEVATOR
OVERLATE
W TOLEWARE

AEELRST 55
STEALER
A LAETARES
B ARBELEST
BLEAREST
BLEATERS
RETABLES
C CLEAREST
SCELERAT
TREACLES
D DESALTER
RESLATED
TREADLES
E TEASELER
F REFLATES
H HALTERES
LEATHERS
I ATELIERS
EARLIEST
LEARIEST
REALTIES
M LAMETERS
N ALTERNES
ETERNALS
TELERANS
O OLEASTER
P PETRALES
PLEATERS
PRELATES
REPLATES
R ALTERERS
REALTERS
RELATERS
S RESLATES
STEALERS
TEARLESS
TESSERAL
T ALERTEST
U RESALUTE
X EXALTERS
Y EASTERLY

AEENORS 197
ARENOSE
B SEABORNE
D REASONED
P PERAEONS
PERSONAE
R REASONER
S RESEASON
SEASONER
T EARSTONE
RESONATE

AEENRST 20
EASTERN
A ARSENATE
SERENATA
B ABSENTER
C CENTARES
REASCENT
REENACTS
SARCENET
E SERENATE
F FASTENER
FENESTRA
REFASTEN
G ESTRANGE
GRANTEES
GREATENS
NEGATERS
REAGENTS
SEGREANT
SERGEANT
STERNAGE
H HASTENER
HEARTENS
I ARENITES
ARSENITE
RESINATE
STEARINE
TRAINEES
J SERJEANT
L ALTERNES
ETERNALS
TELERANS
M REMANETS
O EARSTONE
RESONATE
R TERRANES
S ASSENTER
EARNESTS
SARSENET
T ENTREATS
RATTEENS
U SAUTERNE
V AVENTRES
VETERANS

AEENRTT 238
ENTREAT
A ANTEATER
B BATTENER
D ATTENDER
NATTERED
RATTENED
E ENTERATE
F FATTENER
H HATERENT
THREATEN
R NATTERER
RATTENER
S ENTREATS
RATTEENS
V ANTEVERT
X EXTERNAT
EXTRANET
Y ENTREATY

AEENRTV 244
VETERAN
D AVENTRED
E ENERVATE
VENERATE
L LEVANTER
RELEVANT
M AVERMENT
N REVENANT
O OVERNEAT
RENOVATE
R TAVERNER
S AVENTRES
VETERANS
T ANTEVERT
U AVENTURE

AEEORST 105
ROSEATE
B ABORTEES
REBATOES
C CREASOTE
I ETAERIOS
K KERATOSE
KREASOTE
L OLEASTER
M EROTEMAS
N EARSTONE
RESONATE
P OPERATES
PROTEASE
V OVEREATS

AEERRST 219
TEARERS
B REBATERS
TABRERES
TEREBRAS
C CATERERS
RECRATES
RETRACES
TERRACES
D ARRESTED
DREAREST
RETREADS
SERRATED
TREADERS
E ARRESTEE
F FERRATES
G REGRATES
I ARTERIES
REASTIER
K RETAKERS
STREAKER
L ALTERERS
REALTERS
RELATERS
M REMASTER
STREAMER
N TERRANES
P TAPERERS
R ARRESTER
REARREST
S ASSERTER
REASSERT
SERRATES
TERRASES
T RETRATES
RETREATS
TREATERS
U AUSTERER
TREASURE
V TRAVERSE
W WATERERS

AEGILNR 26
REALIGN
A GERANIAL
REGALIAN
B BLEARING
C CLEARING
RELACING
D DANGLIER
DEARLING
DRAGLINE
E ALGERINE
F FINAGLER
G GANGLIER
LAGERING
REGALING
H NARGHILE
NARGILEH
I GAINLIER
J JANGLIER
L ALLERGIN
M GERMINAL
MALIGNER
MALINGER
N LEARNING
O GERANIOL
REGIONAL
P GRAPLINE
PEARLING
R GNARLIER
S ALIGNERS
ENGRAILS
NARGILES
REALIGNS
SALERING
SANGLIER
SIGNALER
SLANGIER
T ALERTING
ALTERING
INTEGRAL
RELATING
TANGLIER
TRIANGLE
V RAVELING
X RELAXING
Y LAYERING
RELAYING
YEARLING

AEGILNS 134
LEASING
B SINGABLE
D DEALINGS
LEADINGS
SIGNALED
E ENSILAGE
LINEAGES
F FINAGLES
G LIGNAGES
H HEALINGS
LEASHING
SHEALING
K LINKAGES
SNAGLIKE
L GALLEINS
NIGELLAS
M MEASLING
N EANLINGS
LEANINGS
O GASOLINE
P ELAPSING
PLEASING
R ALIGNERS
ENGRAILS
NARGILES
REALIGNS
SALERING
SANGLIER
SIGNALER
SLANGIER
S GAINLESS
GLASSINE
LEASINGS
SEALINGS
T EASTLING
GELATINS
GENITALS
STEALING
V LEAVINGS
SLEAVING
W SWEALING
Y YEALINGS

AEGILNT 52
GENITAL
A AGENTIAL
ALGINATE
B BELATING
BLEATING
TANGIBLE
C CLEATING
D DELATING
E GALENITE
GELATINE
LEGATINE
G GELATING
LEGATING
TEAGLING
H ATHELING
K GNATLIKE
M LIGAMENT
METALING
TEGMINAL
N GANTLINE
LATENING
O GELATION
LEGATION
P PLEATING
R ALERTING
ALTERING
INTEGRAL
RELATING
TANGLIER
TRIANGLE
S EASTLING
GELATINS
GENITALS
STEALING
V VALETING
X EXALTING
Z TEAZLING

AEGILRS 190
GRAILES
A GASALIER
LAIRAGES
REGALIAS
C GLACIERS
GRACILES
D SLAIRGED
E GASELIER
G SLAGGIER
M GREMIALS
LAMIGERS
REGALISM

N ALIGNERS
ENGRAILS
NARGILES
REALIGNS
SALERING
SANGLIER
SIGNALER
SLANGIER
O GASOLIER
GIRASOLE
SERAGLIO
S GLASSIER
T GLARIEST
REGALIST
Y GREASILY
Z GLAZIERS

AEGINOR 157
ORIGANE
B ABORIGEN
D ORGANDIE
L GERANIOL
REGIONAL
R ORANGIER
S IGNAROES
ORGANISE
ORIGANES
Z ORGANIZE

AEGINOS 168
AGONIES
B BEGONIAS
C COINAGES
D AGONISED
DIAGNOSE
G SEAGOING
L GASOLINE
N ANGINOSE
GANOINES
R IGNAROES
ORGANISE
ORIGANES
S AGONISES
Z AGONIZES

AEGINRS 36
REGAINS
A ANERGIAS
ANGARIES
ARGINASE
B BEARINGS
SABERING
C CREASING
GRECIANS
SEARCING
D DERAIGNS
GRADINES
READINGS
E ANERGIES
GESNERIA
G GEARINGS
GREASING
SNAGGIER
H HEARINGS
HEARSING
SHEARING
K SKEARING
L ALIGNERS
ENGRAILS
NARGILES
REALIGNS
SALERING
SANGLIER
SIGNALER
SLANGIER
M GERMAINS
SMEARING
N AGINNERS
EARNINGS
ENGRAINS
GRANNIES
O IGNAROES
ORGANISE
ORIGANES
P PREASING
SPEARING
R EARRINGS
GRAINERS
S ASSIGNER
REASSIGN
SEARINGS
SERINGAS
T ANGRIEST
ASTRINGE
GANISTER
GANTRIES
GRANITES
INGRATES
RANGIEST
REASTING
STEARING
TASERING
V VINEGARS
W RESAWING
SWEARING
WEARINGS
Y RESAYING
SYNERGIA

AEGINRT 32
TEARING
A AERATING
B BERATING
REBATING
TABERING
C ARGENTIC
CATERING
CITRANGE
CREATING
REACTING
D DERATING
GRADIENT
REDATING
TREADING
E GRATINEE
INTERAGE
H EARTHING
HEARTING
INGATHER
K RETAKING
L ALERTING
ALTERING
INTEGRAL
RELATING
TANGLIER
TRIANGLE
M EMIGRANT
REMATING
P RETAPING
TAPERING
S ANGRIEST
ASTRINGE
GANISTER
GANTRIES
GRANITES
INGRATES
RANGIEST
REASTING
STEARING
TASERING
T ARETTING
GNATTIER
TREATING
V AVERTING
GRIEVANT
TAVERING
VINTAGER
W TWANGIER
WATERING
X RETAXING

AEGINST 42
TEASING
A SAGINATE
B BEATINGS
D SEDATING
STEADING
E SAGENITE
F FEASTING
G NAGGIEST
H GAHNITES
HEATINGS
L EASTLING
GELATINS
GENITALS
STEALING
M MANGIEST
MINTAGES
MISAGENT
STEAMING
TEAMINGS
N ANTIGENS
GENTIANS
STEANING
R ANGRIEST
ASTRINGE
GANISTER
GANTRIES
GRANITES
INGRATES
RANGIEST
REASTING
STEARING
TASERING
S EASTINGS
GENISTAS
GIANTESS
SEATINGS
TEASINGS
TSIGANES
T ESTATING
TANGIEST
U SAUTEING
UNITAGES
V VINTAGES
W SWEATING
Y YEASTING
Z TZIGANES

AEGNRST 133
STRANGE
A STARAGEN
TANAGERS
B BANGSTER
D DRAGNETS
GRANDEST
E ESTRANGE
GRANTEES
GREATENS
NEGATERS
REAGENTS
SEGREANT
SERGEANT
STERNAGE
F ENGRAFTS
G GANGSTER
I ANGRIEST
ASTRINGE
GANISTER
GANTRIES
GRANITES
INGRATES
RANGIEST
REASTING
STEARING
TASERING
L STRANGLE
TANGLERS
TRANGLES
M GARMENTS
MARGENTS
RAGMENTS
O ESTRAGON
NEGATORS
ORANGEST
RAGSTONE
STONERAG
P TREPANGS
R GRANTERS
REGRANTS
STRANGER
U STRAUNGE
W TWANGERS

AEGORST 151
TOERAGS
C ESCARGOT
D GOADSTER
F FAGOTERS
H SHORTAGE
L GLOATERS
LEGATORS
N ESTRAGON
NEGATORS
ORANGEST
RAGSTONE
STONERAG
O ROOTAGES
P PORTAGES
POTAGERS
R GARROTES
S STORAGES
T GAROTTES
U OUTRAGES

AEHIRST 131
HASTIER
A HETAIRAS
C CHARIEST
STICHERA
THERIACS
D HAIRSTED
HARDIEST
E HEARTIES
I HAIRIEST
N HAIRNETS
INEARTHS
THERIANS
O HOARIEST
P TRIPHASE
R TRASHIER
S SHERIATS
U THESAURI
W SWATHIER
WATERISH
Y HYSTERIA

AEIINRS 167
SENARII
B BINARIES
C RIANCIES
D DRAISINE
K KAISERIN
L AIRLINES
SNAILIER
N SIRENIAN
S AIRINESS
T INERTIAS
RAINIEST
Y YERSINIA

AEIINST 138
ISATINE
B BAINITES
C CANITIES
D ADENITIS
DAINTIES
F FAINITES
K KAINITES
L ALIENIST
LITANIES
M MINIATES
P PIANISTE
R INERTIAS
RAINIEST
S ISATINES
SANITIES
SANITISE
TENIASIS
V VANITIES
X AXINITES
Z SANITIZE

AEIIRST 108
AIRIEST
D IRISATED
F RATIFIES
H HAIRIEST
L LAIRIEST
LISTERIA
M AIRTIMES
SERIATIM
N INERTIAS
RAINIEST
P PARITIES
R RARITIES
S IRISATES
SATIRISE
V VAIRIEST
W WISTERIA
X SEXTARII
Z SATIRIZE

AEILNOR 50
ALIENOR
C ACROLEIN
COLINEAR
CREOLIAN
LONICERA
F FORELAIN
G GERANIOL
REGIONAL
L ALLERION
P PELORIAN
S AILERONS
ALERIONS
ALIENORS
T ORIENTAL
RELATION
TAILERON
V OVERLAIN

AEILNOS 49
ANISOLE
C ALNICOES
D NODALISE
G GASOLINE
K KAOLINES
M LAMINOSE
MINEOLAS
SEMOLINA
N SOLANINE
P OPALINES
R AILERONS
ALERIONS
ALIENORS
S ANISOLES
T ELATIONS
INSOLATE
TOENAILS
X SILOXANE

AEILNOT 35
ELATION
B TAILBONE
D DELATION
F OLEFIANT
G GELATION
LEGATION
P ANTIPOLE
R ORIENTAL
RELATION
TAILERON
S ELATIONS
INSOLATE
TOENAILS
T TONALITE

AEILNPT 183
PANTILE
A PALATINE
B PINTABLE
C PECTINAL
PLANETIC
D PANTILED
E PETALINE
TAPELINE
G PLEATING
O ANTIPOLE
P PIEPLANT
R INTERLAP
TRAPLINE
TRIPLANE
S PANELIST
PANTILES
PLAINEST
T TINPLATE
Y PENALITY

AEILNRS 18
NAILERS
B RINSABLE
C CARLINES
LANCIERS
D ISLANDER
E ALIENERS
G ALIGNERS
ENGRAILS
NARGILES
REALIGNS
SALERING
SANGLIER
SIGNALER
SLANGIER
H INHALERS
I AIRLINES
SNAILIER
M MARLINES
MINERALS
MISLEARN

O AILERONS
ALERIONS
ALIENORS
P PEARLINS
PRALINES
R SNARLIER
S RAINLESS
T ENTRAILS
LATRINES
RATLINES
RETINALS
TRENAILS
U LUNARIES
V RAVELINS
X RELAXINS
Y INLAYERS
SNAILERY

AEILNRT 7
ENTRAIL
C CLARINET
E ELATERIN
ENTAILER
TREENAIL
F INFLATER
G ALERTING
ALTERING
INTEGRAL
RELATING
TANGLIER
TRIANGLE
I INERTIAL
M TERMINAL
TRAMLINE
N INTERNAL
O ORIENTAL
RELATION
TAILERON
P INTERLAP
TRAPLINE
TRIPLANE
S ENTRAILS
LATRINES
RATLINES
RETINALS
TRENAILS
T RATTLINE
U AUNTLIER
RETINULA
TENURIAL
V INTERVAL
Y INTERLAY

AEILNRU 210
(U &I LEARN)
A AURELIAN
B RUINABLE
F FRAULEIN
H INHAULER
M LEMURIAN
S LUNARIES
T AUNTLIER
RETINULA
TENURIAL

AEILNST 63
ENTAILS
B INSTABLE
F INFLATES
G EASTLING
GELATINS
GENITALS
STEALING
I ALIENIST
LITANIES
K LANKIEST
M AILMENTS
ALIMENTS
MANLIEST
MELANIST
SMALTINE
O ELATIONS
INSOLATE
TOENAILS
P PANELIST
PANTILES
PLAINEST
R ENTRAILS
LATRINES
RATLINES
RETINALS
TRENAILS
S EASTLINS
ELASTINS
NAILSETS
SALIENTS
SALTINES
STANIELS
U ALUNITES
INSULATE
V VENTAILS
W LAWNIEST

AEILORS 28
(ORALISE)
A OLEARIAS
C CALORIES
CARIOLES
D DARIOLES
SOLIDARE
SOREDIAL
F FORESAIL
G GASOLIER
GIRASOLE
SERAGLIO
H AIRHOLES
SHOALIER
M MORALISE
N AILERONS
ALERIONS
ALIENORS
P PELORIAS
POLARISE
S SOLARISE
T SOTERIAL
V OVERSAIL
VALORISE
VARIOLES
VOLARIES
Y ROYALISE
Z SOLARIZE

AEILORT 4
(ORALITE)
B LABORITE
C EROTICAL
LORICATE
D IDOLATER
TAILORED
E AEROLITE
F FLOATIER
H AEROLITH
M AMITROLE
ROLAMITE
N ORIENTAL
RELATION
TAILERON
P EPILATOR
PETIOLAR
R RETAILOR
S SOTERIAL
T LITERATO
V VIOLATER
Z TRIAZOLE

AEILOST 40
ISOLATE
C ALOETICS
COALIEST
SOCIETAL
D DIASTOLE
ISOLATED
SODALITE
SOLIDATE
F FOLIATES
G LATIGOES
OTALGIES
K KEITLOAS
M LOAMIEST
N ELATIONS
INSOLATE
TOENAILS
P SPOLIATE
R SOTERIAL
S ISOLATES
T TOTALISE
V VIOLATES

AEILOTT 178
(A TOILET)
D DATOLITE
E ETIOLATE
N TONALITE
R LITERATO
S TOTALISE
V VOLITATE
Z TOTALIZE

AEILPRT 154
PLAITER
A PARIETAL
B PARTIBLE
C PARTICLE
PRELATIC
D DIPTERAL
TRIPEDAL
E PEARLITE
I LIPARITE
K TRAPLIKE
N INTERLAP
TRAPLINE
TRIPLANE
O EPILATOR
PETIOLAR
R PALTRIER
PRETRIAL
S PILASTER
PLAISTER
PLAITERS
V LIVETRAP

AEILRST 14
RETAILS
B BLASTIER
LIBRATES
TABLIERS
C ALTRICES
ARTICLES
RECITALS
SELICTAR
STERICAL
D DILATERS
LARDIEST
REDTAILS
E ATELIERS
EARLIEST
LEARIEST
REALTIES
F FLARIEST
FRAILEST
G GLARIEST
REGALIST
I LAIRIEST
LISTERIA
K LARKIEST
STALKIER
STARLIKE
L LITERALS
TALLIERS
M LAMISTER
LAMITERS
MARLIEST
MARLITES
MISALTER
N ENTRAILS
LATRINES
RATLINES
RETINALS
TRENAILS
O SOTERIAL
P PILASTER
PLAISTER
PLAITERS
R RETIRALS
RETRIALS
TRAILERS
S REALISTS
SALTIERS
SALTIRES
SLAISTER
T TERTIALS
U URALITES

AEILRSU 191
(URALISE)
A AURELIAS
C AURICLES
D RESIDUAL
F FAILURES
H HAULIERS
L RUELLIAS
N LUNARIES
P SPIRULAE
Q SQUAILER
R RURALISE
T URALITES

AEILRTT 103
TERTIAL
B TITRABLE
C TRACTILE
D DETRITAL
E LATERITE
LITERATE
F FILTRATE
G AGLITTER
I LITERATI
M REMITTAL
N RATTLINE
O LITERATO
R RATTLIER
S TERTIALS
Y ALTERITY

AEIMNOT 194
AMNIOTE
A METANOIA
C COINMATE
D DOMINATE
NEMATOID
M AMMONITE
N NOMINATE
P PTOMAINE
S AMNIOTES
MISATONE
SOMNIATE
Z MONAZITE

AEIMNRS 149
SEMINAR
B MIRBANES
C CARMINES
CREMAINS
D ADERMINS
SIRNAMED
E REMANIES
G GERMAINS
SMEARING
H HARMINES
SHIREMAN
K RAMEKINS
L MARLINES
MINERALS
MISLEARN
N REINSMAN
O MORAINES
ROMAINES
ROMANISE
R MARINERS
S SEMINARS
SIRNAMES
T MINARETS
RAIMENTS
U ANEURISM
Y SEMINARY

AEIMNRT 110
MINARET
A ANIMATER
MARINATE
E ANTIMERE
G EMIGRANT
REMATING
L TERMINAL
TRAMLINE
N TRAINMEN
S MINARETS
RAIMENTS
T MARTINET
U RUMINATE
W WARIMENT
Y TYRAMINE

AEIMNST 122
INMATES
A AMENTIAS
ANIMATES
B AMBIENTS
C AMNESTIC
SEMANTIC
D MEDIANTS
TIDESMAN
E ETAMINES
MATINEES
MISEATEN
SEMINATE
F MANIFEST
G MANGIEST
MINTAGES
MISAGENT
STEAMING
TEAMINGS
H HEMATINS
I MINIATES
K MANKIEST
MISTAKEN
L AILMENTS
ALIMENTS
MANLIEST
MELANIST
SMALTINE
N MANNITES
O AMNIOTES
MISATONE
SOMNIATE
R MINARETS
RAIMENTS
S MANTISES
MATINESS

AEIMRST 82
SMARTIE
A AMIRATES
B BARMIEST
C CERAMIST
MATRICES
MISTRACE
SCIMETAR
D MARDIEST
MISRATED
READMITS
E EMIRATES
REAMIEST
STEAMIER
G MAGISTER
MIGRATES
RAGTIMES
STERIGMA
I AIRTIMES
SERIATIM
K MISTAKER
L LAMISTER
LAMITERS
MARLIEST
MARLITES
MISALTER
M MARMITES
RAMMIEST
N MINARETS
RAIMENTS
O AMORTISE
ATOMISER
P APTERISM
PRIMATES
S ASTERISM
MAISTERS
MISRATES
SEMITARS
SMARTIES
T MISTREAT
TERATISM
U MURIATES
SEMITAUR
V VITAMERS
W WARTIMES
X MATRIXES
Y SYMITARE

AEINNOT 117
ENATION
C ENACTION
D ANOINTED
ANTINODE
G NEGATION
M NOMINATE
R ANOINTER
INORNATE
REANOINT
S ENATIONS
SONATINE

T INTONATE
V INNOVATE
VENATION

AEINNRS 97
INSNARE
C CRANNIES
NARCEINS
D INSNARED
E ANSERINE
G AGINNERS
EARNINGS
ENGRAINS
GRANNIES
I SIRENIAN
M REINSMAN
O RAISONNE
P PANNIERS
R INSNARER
S INSNARES
T ENTRAINS
TRANNIES
U ANEURINS
UNARISEN
W SWANNIER

AEINORS 15
ERASION
B BARONIES
SEAROBIN
C SCENARIO
D ANEROIDS
DONARIES
F FARINOSE
G IGNAROES
ORGANISE
ORIGANES
L AILERONS
ALERIONS
ALIENORS
M MORAINES
ROMAINES
ROMANISE
N RAISONNE
S ERASIONS
SENSORIA
T ANOESTRI
ARSONITE
NOTARIES
NOTARISE
ROSINATE
SENORITA
V AVERSION

AEINORT 1
OTARINE
A AERATION
B BARITONE
OBTAINER
REOBTAIN
TABORINE
C ACTIONER
ANORETIC
CREATION
REACTION
D AROINTED
DERATION
ORDINATE
RATIONED
H ANTIHERO
L ORIENTAL
RELATION
TAILERON
N ANOINTER
INORNATE
REANOINT
P ATROPINE
R ANTERIOR
S ANOESTRI
ARSONITE
NOTARIES
NOTARISE
ROSINATE
SENORITA
T TENTORIA
Z NOTARIZE

AEINOST 21
ATONIES
B BOTANIES
BOTANISE
NIOBATES
OBEISANT
C ACONITES
CANOEIST
SONICATE
D ASTONIED
SEDATION
L ELATIONS
INSOLATE
TOENAILS
M AMNIOTES
MISATONE
SOMNIATE
N ENATIONS
SONATINE
P SAPONITE
R ANOESTRI
ARSONITE
NOTARIES
NOTARISE
ROSINATE
SENORITA
S ASSIENTO
ASTONIES
V STOVAINE
X SAXONITE

AEINOTT 86
(ATONITE)
C TACONITE
D ANTIDOTE
TETANOID
F FETATION
H THIONATE
I NOTITIAE
L TONALITE
N INTONATE
R TENTORIA

AEINPRS 207
RAPINES
A PANARIES
D SPRAINED
E NAPERIES
F FIREPANS
PANFRIES
G PREASING
SPEARING
H HEPARINS
PARISHEN
SERAPHIN
K RANPIKES
L PEARLINS
PRALINES
N PANNIERS
P SNAPPIER
T PAINTERS
PANTRIES
PERTAINS
PINASTER
PRISTANE
REPAINTS
U UNPRAISE
W SPAWNIER

AEINPRT 41
PAINTER
A ANTIRAPE
D DIPTERAN
E APERIENT
G RETAPING
TAPERING
H PERIANTH
I PAINTIER
L INTERLAP
TRAPLINE
TRIPLANE
O ATROPINE
R PRETRAIN
TERRAPIN
S PAINTERS
PANTRIES
PERTAINS
PINASTER
PRISTANE
REPAINTS
T TRIPTANE
U PAINTURE
X EXPIRANT

AEINPST 195
SPINATE
B BEPAINTS
D DEPAINTS
H PENTHIAS
THESPIAN
I PIANISTE
L PANELIST
PANTILES
PLAINEST
N PANTINES
O SAPONITE
P NAPPIEST
R PAINTERS
PANTRIES
PERTAINS
PINASTER
PRISTANE
REPAINTS
S STEAPSIN
T PATIENTS
U PETUNIAS
SUPINATE
Y EPINASTY

AEINRRT 106
TERRAIN
E RETAINER
N INERRANT
O ANTERIOR
P PRETRAIN
TERRAPIN
S RESTRAIN
RETRAINS
STRAINER
TERRAINS
TRAINERS
TRANSIRE
T RETIRANT
V VERATRIN
W INTERWAR

AEINRSS 239
SARNIES
C ARCSINES
ARSENICS
CERASINS
RACINESS
D ARIDNESS
SARDINES
E SENARIES
F FAIRNESS
SANSERIF
SERAFINS
G ASSIGNER
REASSIGN
SEARINGS
SERINGAS
H ARSHINES
I AIRINESS
L RAINLESS
M SEMINARS
SIRNAMES
N INSNARES
O ERASIONS
SENSORIA
T ARTINESS
RESIANTS
RETSINAS
SNARIEST
STAINERS
STARNIES
STEARINS
U ANURESIS
SENARIUS
W WARINESS
X XERANSIS

AEINRST 2
RETAINS
A ANTISERA
ARTESIAN
RATANIES
RESINATA
SEATRAIN
B ATEBRINS
BANISTER
BARNIEST
C CANISTER
CARNIEST
CERATINS
CISTERNA
CREATINS
NACRITES
SCANTIER
D DETRAINS
RANDIEST
STRAINED
E ARENITES
ARSENITE
RESINATE
STEARINE
TRAINEES
F FAINTERS
FENITARS
G ANGRIEST
ASTRINGE
GANISTER
GANTRIES
GRANITES
INGRATES
RANGIEST
REASTING
STEARING
TASERING
H HAIRNETS
INEARTHS
THERIANS
I INERTIAS
RAINIEST
J NARTJIES
K KERATINS
NARKIEST
L ENTRAILS
LATRINES
RATLINES
RETINALS
TRENAILS
M MINARETS
RAIMENTS
N ENTRAINS
TRANNIES
O ANOESTRI
ARSONITE
NOTARIES
NOTARISE
ROSINATE
SENORITA
P PAINTERS
PANTRIES
PERTAINS
PINASTER
PRISTANE
REPAINTS
R RESTRAIN
RETRAINS
STRAINER
TERRAINS
TRAINERS
TRANSIRE
S ARTINESS
RESIANTS
RETSINAS
SNARIEST
STAINERS
STARNIES
STEARINS
T INTREATS
NITRATES
STRAITEN
TARTINES
TERTIANS
U RUINATES
TAURINES
URANITES
URINATES
W TINWARES

AEINRSU 70
UNRAISE
B ANBURIES
URBANISE
D DENARIUS
UNRAISED
URANIDES
E UNEASIER
L LUNARIES
M ANEURISM
N ANEURINS
UNARISEN
P UNPRAISE
S ANURESIS
SENARIUS
T RUINATES
TAURINES
URANITES
URINATES
V VAURIENS
Z AZURINES
SUZERAIN

AEINRTT 51
NITRATE
A ATTAINER
REATTAIN
C INTERACT
D NITRATED
G ARETTING
GNATTIER
TREATING
L RATTLINE
M MARTINET
N INTRANET
O TENTORIA
P TRIPTANE
R RETIRANT
S INTREATS
NITRATES
STRAITEN
TARTINES
TERTIANS
U TAINTURE

AEINRTU 31
URINATE
A INAURATE
B BRAUNITE
URBANITE
C ANURETIC
D DATURINE
INDURATE
RUINATED
URINATED
H HAURIENT
J JAUNTIER
L AUNTLIER
RETINULA
TENURIAL
M RUMINATE
P PAINTURE
Q ANTIQUER
QUAINTER
S RUINATES
TAURINES
URANITES
URINATES
T TAINTURE
V VAUNTIER

AEINSTT 104
INSTATE
A ASTATINE
SANITATE
TANAISTE
B TABINETS
C CANTIEST
ENTASTIC
NICTATES
TETANICS
D INSTATED
E ANISETTE
TETANIES
TETANISE
F FAINTEST
G ESTATING
TANGIEST
H HESITANT
J JANTIEST
N ANTIENTS
STANNITE
P PATIENTS
R INTREATS
NITRATES
STRAITEN
TARTINES
TERTIANS

S ANTSIEST
INSTATES
NASTIEST
SATINETS
TITANESS
T NATTIEST
V TASTEVIN
W TAWNIEST

AEINSTU 192
AUNTIES
D AUDIENTS
SINUATED
G SAUTEING
UNITAGES
J JAUNTIES
K UNAKITES
L ALUNITES
INSULATE
P PETUNIAS
SUPINATE
Q ANTIQUES
QUANTISE
R RUINATES
TAURINES
URANITES
URINATES
S SINUATES
V SUIVANTE

AEINSTV 170
NATIVES
A SANATIVE
C CISTVAEN
VESICANT
D DEVIANTS
E NAIVETES
G VINTAGES
I VANITIES
K KISTVAEN
L VENTAILS
O STOVAINE
T TASTEVIN
U SUIVANTE

AEIORST 5
OTARIES
B SABOTIER
D ASTEROID
E ETAERIOS
H HOARIEST
J JAROSITE
L SOTERIAL
M AMORTISE
ATOMISER
N ANOESTRI
ARSONITE
NOTARIES
NOTARISE
ROSINATE
SENORITA
R ROARIEST
ROTARIES
T TOASTIER
U OUTRAISE
SAUTOIRE
V TRAVOISE
VIATORES
VOTARIES

AEIPRST 130
PARTIES
A ASPIRATE
PARASITE
SEPTARIA
C CRAPIEST
CRISPATE
PARETICS
PICRATES
PRACTISE
D DIPTERAS
RAPIDEST
SPIRATED
TARSIPED
TRAIPSED
E PARIETES
PETARIES
G GRAPIEST
H TRIPHASE
I PARITIES
K PARKIEST
L PILASTER
PLAISTER
PLAITERS
M APTERISM
PRIMATES
N PAINTERS
PANTRIES
PERTAINS
PINASTER
PRISTANE
REPAINTS
P PERIAPTS
R PARTIERS
S PASTRIES
PIASTERS
PIASTRES
RASPIEST
TRAIPSES
V PRIVATES
W WIRETAPS
Y ASPERITY

AEIRRST 92
ARTSIER
B ARBITERS
RAREBITS
C ERRATICS
E ARTERIES
REASTIER
F FRATRIES
H TRASHIER
I RARITIES
L RETIRALS
RETRIALS
TRAILERS
N RESTRAIN
RETRAINS
STRAINER
TERRAINS
TRAINERS
TRANSIRE
O ROARIEST
ROTARIES
P PARTIERS
R STARRIER
TARRIERS
S TARSIERS
T RETRAITS
STRAITER
TARRIEST
W STRAWIER

AEIRSST 213
SATIRES
A ASTERIAS
ATRESIAS
C SCARIEST
D ASTERIDS
DIASTERS
DISASTER
DISRATES
E SERIATES
G AGISTERS
H SHERIATS
I IRISATES
SATIRISE
K ASTERISK
SARKIEST
L REALISTS
SALTIERS
SALTIRES
SLAISTER
M ASTERISM
MAISTERS
MISRATES
SEMITARS
SMARTIES
N ARTINESS
RESIANTS
RETSINAS
SNARIEST
STAINERS
STARNIES
STEARINS
P PASTRIES
PIASTERS
PIASTRES
RASPIEST
TRAIPSES
R TARSIERS
S ASSISTER
TIRASSES
T ARTISTES
ARTSIEST
STRIATES
V TRAVISES
W WAISTERS
WAITRESS
WASTRIES

AEIRSTT 73
ATTIRES
A ARIETTAS
ARISTATE
B BIRETTAS
C CITRATES
CRISTATE
SCATTIER
D STRAITED
STRIATED
TARDIEST
E ARIETTES
ITERATES
TEARIEST
TREATIES
TREATISE
G STRIGATE
L TERTIALS
M MISTREAT
TERATISM
N INTREATS
NITRATES
STRAITEN
TARTINES
TERTIANS
O TOASTIER
R RETRAITS
STRAITER
TARRIEST
S ARTISTES
ARTSIEST
STRIATES
T ATTRITES
RATTIEST
TARTIEST
TITRATES
TRISTATE
W WARTIEST
X EXTRAITS
Z TRISTEZA

AEIRSTV 235
VASTIER
A VARIATES
B VIBRATES
E EVIRATES
G VIRGATES
VITRAGES
I VAIRIEST
M VITAMERS
O TRAVOISE
VIATORES
VOTARIES
P PRIVATES
S TRAVISES
Y VESTIARY

AEIRSTW 158
WAITERS
A AWAITERS
B WARBIEST
D TAWDRIES
E SWEATIER
TAWERIES
WASTERIE
WEARIEST
F WASTRIFE
H SWATHIER
WATERISH
I WISTERIA
M WARTIMES
N TINWARES
P WIRETAPS
R STRAWIER
S WAISTERS
WAITRESS
WASTRIES
T WARTIEST

AELNORS 226
ORLEANS
D LADRONES
SOLANDER
F FARNESOL
I AILERONS
ALERIONS
ALIENORS
L LLANEROS
M ALMONERS
P PERSONAL
PSORALEN
U ALEURONS
NEUROSAL
V VERONALS

AELNRST 88
RENTALS
A ASTERNAL
B BRANTLES
C CENTRALS
E ALTERNES
ETERNALS
TELERANS
G STRANGLE
TANGLERS
TRANGLES
H ENTHRALS
I ENTRAILS
LATRINES
RATLINES
RETINALS
TRENAILS
N LANTERNS
P PANTLERS
PLANTERS
REPLANTS
S SALTERNS
T SLATTERN
TRENTALS
U NEUTRALS
V VENTRALS

AELORST 44
OESTRAL
B BLOATERS
SORTABLE
STORABLE
C LOCATERS
SECTORAL
D DELATORS
LEOTARDS
LODESTAR
E OLEASTER
F FLOATERS
FORESTAL
REFLOATS
G GLOATERS
LEGATORS
H LOATHERS
RATHOLES
I SOTERIAL
L REALLOTS
ROSTELLA
M MOLERATS
P PETROSAL
POLESTAR
PROLATES
R REALTORS
RELATORS
RESTORAL
U ROSULATE
V LEVATORS
OVERSALT
Y ROYALETS
Z ZELATORS

AELORSU 156
(SOUR ALE)
A AUREOLAS
B RUBEOLAS
C CAROUSEL
D ROULADES
E AUREOLES
F FUSAROLE
G GLAREOUS
M RAMULOSE
N ALEURONS
NEUROSAL
P LEAPROUS
T ROSULATE
U ROULEAUS

AELRSTU 224
SALUTER
B BALUSTER
RUSTABLE
C RAUCLEST
E RESALUTE
F REFUTALS
G GAULTERS
GESTURAL
TRAGULES
I URALITES
M STAUMREL
N NEUTRALS
O ROSULATE
P APLUSTRE
S SALUTERS
T LUSTRATE
TUTELARS
V VAULTERS
VESTURAL

AENORST 6
SENATOR
A ANOESTRA
B BARONETS
C ANCESTOR
ENACTORS
SARCONET
SORTANCE
D TORNADES
E EARSTONE
RESONATE
F SEAFRONT
G ESTRAGON
NEGATORS
ORANGEST
RAGSTONE
STONERAG
I ANOESTRI
ARSONITE
NOTARIES
NOTARISE
ROSINATE
SENORITA
M MONSTERA
ONSTREAM
STOREMAN
TONEARMS
N NORTENAS
RESONANT
P OPERANTS
PRONATES
PROTEANS
R ANTRORSE
S ASSENTOR
SENATORS
STARNOSE
TREASONS
T ORNATEST
U OUTEARNS
V VENATORS
W STONERAW

AENORTT 166
(RAT NOTE)
B BETATRON
C CONTRATE
D ATTORNED
G TETRAGON
I TENTORIA
L TETRONAL
TOLERANT
M TORMENTA
P PATENTOR
S ORNATEST
X TETRAXON
Y ATTORNEY

AENRSTT 221
NATTERS
A TARTANES
C TRANECTS
TRANSECT
E ENTREATS
RATTEENS
I INTREATS
NITRATES

STRAITEN
TARTINES
TERTIANS
L SLATTERN
TRENTALS
N ENTRANTS
O ORNATEST
P PATTERNS
TRANSEPT
TRAPNEST
R TRANTERS
S TARTNESS
U TAUNTERS

AENRSTU 77
NATURES
B UNBRASTE
URBANEST
C CENTAURS
RECUSANT
UNCRATES
UNTRACES
D DAUNTERS
TRANSUDE
UNTREADS
E SAUTERNE
G STRAUNGE
H HAUNTERS
UNEARTHS
UNHEARTS
URETHANS
I RUINATES
TAURINES
URANITES
URINATES
L NEUTRALS
M ANESTRUM
MENSTRUA
TRANSUME
O OUTEARNS
P PERSAUNT
S ANESTRUS
SAUNTERS
T TAUNTERS
V VAUNTERS
W UNWATERS

AEOPRST 228
SEAPORT
B PROBATES
C POSTRACE
D ADOPTERS
ASPORTED
PASTORED
READOPTS
E OPERATES
PROTEASE
F FOREPAST
G PORTAGES
POTAGERS
H PHORATES
POTSHARE
L PETROSAL
POLESTAR
PROLATES
N OPERANTS
PRONATES
PROTEANS
P TRAPPOSE
R PRAETORS
PRORATES
S ESPARTOS
PORTASES
PROTASES
SEAPORTS

T PROSTATE
U APTEROUS
V OVERPAST

AEORRST 126
ROASTER
A AERATORS
B ABORTERS
ARBORETS
TABORERS
C ACROTERS
CREATORS
REACTORS
D ROADSTER
G GARROTES
I ROARIEST
ROTARIES
L REALTORS
RELATORS
RESTORAL
M REARMOST
N ANTRORSE
O SORORATE
P PRAETORS
PRORATES
R ARRESTOR
S ASSERTOR
ASSORTER
ORATRESS
REASSORT
ROASTERS
T ROSTRATE

AEORSTT 185
ROTATES
A AEROSTAT
B ABETTORS
BATTEROS
TABORETS
C SECTATOR
G GAROTTES
H RHEOSTAT
I TOASTIER
N ORNATEST
P PROSTATE
R ROSTRATE
S STRATOSE
TOASTERS
T ATTESTOR
TESTATOR
U OUTRATES
OUTSTARE

AGILNOT 175
ANTILOG
A GALTONIA
B BLOATING
OBLIGANT
C LOCATING
E GELATION
LEGATION
F FLOATING
G GLOATING
GOATLING
H LOATHING
I INTAGLIO
LIGATION
TAGLIONI
P PLOATING
R TRIGONAL
S ANTILOGS
SALTOING
SOLATING
T TOTALING
Y ANTILOGY

AGINORS 196
SOARING
C ORGANICS
D ROADINGS
E IGNAROES
ORGANISE
ORIGANES
H ORANGISH
I SIGNORIA
L RANGOLIS
M ORGANISM
ROAMINGS
R GARRISON
ROARINGS
S ASSIGNOR
SIGNORAS
SOARINGS
T ORGANIST
ROASTING
U AROUSING
V SAVORING

AGINORT 142
ORATING
B ABORTING
BORATING
TABORING
G GAROTING
I RIGATONI
K TROAKING
L TRIGONAL
N IGNORANT
O ROGATION
S ORGANIST
ROASTING
T ROTATING
TROATING
V GRAVITON
Y GYRATION
ORGANITY

AGINRST 179
STARING
A GRANITAS
B BRASTING
C SCARTING
TRACINGS
D TRADINGS
E ANGRIEST
ASTRINGE
GANISTER
GANTRIES
GRANITES
INGRATES
RANGIEST
REASTING
STEARING
TASERING
F INGRAFTS
STRAFING
G GRATINGS
H TRASHING
K KARTINGS
STARKING
L RATLINGS
STARLING
M MIGRANTS
SMARTING
N RANTINGS
STARNING
O ORGANIST
ROASTING
P PARTINGS
PRATINGS
R STARRING

TARRINGS
S GASTRINS
STARINGS
T RATTINGS
STARTING
V STARVING
W RINGTAWS
STRAWING
WRASTING
Y STINGRAY
STRAYING

AILNORT 68
(TRIONAL)
A NOTARIAL
RATIONAL
C CILANTRO
CONTRAIL
D TRINODAL
E ORIENTAL
RELATION
TAILERON
F FLATIRON
INFLATOR
G TRIGONAL
H HORNTAIL
L ANTIROLL
M TORMINAL
S TONSILAR
Z TRIZONAL

AILNOST 153
LATINOS
A AILANTOS
ALATIONS
E ELATIONS
INSOLATE
TOENAILS
G ANTILOGS
SALTOING
SOLATING
L STALLION
N ANTLIONS
O SOLATION
R TONSILAR
Y LANOSITY

AILORST 164
TAILORS
B ORBITALS
STROBILA
C CALORIST
D DILATORS
E SOTERIAL
M MORALIST
N TONSILAR
O ISOLATOR
OSTIOLAR
S ORALISTS
SOLARIST
U SUTORIAL
Y ROYALIST
SOLITARY

AINORST 39
RATIONS
B TABORINS
C CANTORIS
CAROTINS
D DIATRONS
INTRADOS
E ANOESTRI
ARSONITE
NOTARIES
NOTARISE

ROSINATE
SENORITA
G ORGANIST
ROASTING
H TRAHISON
J JANITORS
K SKIATRON
L TONSILAR
O ORATIONS
P ATROPINS
S ARSONIST
T STRONTIA
U RAINOUTS
SUTORIAN
X TRIAXONS

BEINOST 204
BONIEST
A BOTANIES
BOTANISE
NIOBATES
OBEISANT
B NOBBIEST
E BETONIES
EBONITES
I NIOBITES
K STEINBOK
N BONNIEST
O BONITOES
EOBIONTS
R BORNITES
RIBSTONE
S EBONISTS
T BOTTINES
U BOUNTIES

CEEINRT 245
ENTICER
A CENTIARE
CREATINE
INCREATE
ITERANCE
F FRENETIC
INFECTER
REINFECT
G ERECTING
GENTRICE
I ICTERINE
REINCITE
J REINJECT
N INCENTER
INCENTRE
O ERECTION
NEOTERIC
P PRENTICE
TERPENIC
S CENTRIES
ENTERICS
ENTICERS
SCIENTER
SECRETIN
T RETICENT
U CEINTURE
ENURETIC

CEINORS 188
COINERS
A SCENARIO
B BICORNES
C CONCISER
CORNICES
CROCEINS
D CONSIDER
F COINFERS
CONIFERS

FORENSIC
FORINSEC
FORNICES
INFORCES
G COREIGNS
COSIGNER
H CHORINES
I RECISION
SORICINE
L INCLOSER
LICENSOR
M CREMOSIN
INCOMERS
SERMONIC
N INCENSOR
P CONSPIRE
INCORPSE
R RESORCIN
S NECROSIS
SERICONS
T COINTERS
CORNIEST
NOTICERS
RECTIONS
U COINSURE
NOURICES
ROUNCIES

CEINORT 94
RECTION
A ACTIONER
ANORETIC
CREATION
REACTION
C CONCERTI
NECROTIC
D CENTROID
DOCTRINE
E ERECTION
NEOTERIC
F INFECTOR
G GERONTIC
H NOTCHIER
J INJECTOR
M INTERCOM
P ENTROPIC
INCEPTOR
R TRICORNE
S COINTERS
CORNIEST
NOTICERS
RECTIONS
T CONTRITE
CORNETTI
U NEUROTIC
UNEROTIC
V CONTRIVE

CEINOST 172
NOTICES
A ACONITES
CANOEIST
SONICATE
C CONCEITS
D DEONTICS
E ICESTONE
SEICENTO
G ESCOTING
K CONKIEST
L LECTIONS
TELSONIC
M CENTIMOS
O COONTIES
P PONCIEST
R COINTERS

CORNIEST
NOTICERS
RECTIONS
S SECTIONS
T CENTOIST
STENOTIC
TONETICS
U COUNTIES
X EXCITONS
Y CYTOSINE

DEEINRS 96
DENIERS
A ARSENIDE
DENARIES
DRAISENE
NEARSIDE
B INBREEDS
E NEREIDES
REDENIES
F DEFINERS
G DESIGNER
ENERGIDS
REDESIGN
REEDINGS
RESIGNED
H DRISHEEN
RESHINED
K DEERSKIN
L REDLINES
N SINNERED
O INDORSEE
ORDINEES
S DIRENESS
T INSERTED
NERDIEST
RESIDENT
SINTERED
TRENDIES
U UREDINES
W REWIDENS
WIDENERS
X INDEXERS

DEEINRT 47
(DENTIER)
A DETAINER
RETAINED
B INTERBED
D DENDRITE
K TINKERED
M REMINTED
N INDENTER
INTENDER
INTERNED
O ORIENTED
R INTERRED
TRENDIER
S INSERTED
NERDIEST
RESIDENT
SINTERED
TRENDIES
T RETINTED
U RETINUED
REUNITED
V INVERTED
W WINTERED
X DEXTRINE

DEEINST 46
DESTINE
A ANDESITE
B BENDIEST
D DESTINED
E NEEDIEST
F FENDIEST
INFESTED
G INGESTED
SIGNETED
STEEDING
H DISTHENE
I DIETINES
L ENLISTED
LINTSEED
LISTENED
TINSELED
M DEMENTIS
SEDIMENT
TIDESMEN
N DENTINES
DESINENT
O SIDENOTE
P PENTISED
R INSERTED
NERDIEST
RESIDENT
SINTERED
TRENDIES
S DESTINES
T DINETTES
INSETTED
U DETINUES
V EVIDENTS
INVESTED

DEEIRST 58
DIETERS
A READIEST
SERIATED
SIDERATE
STEADIER
B BESTRIDE
BISTERED
C DESERTIC
DISCREET
DISCRETE
D REDDIEST
E REEDIEST
F RESIFTED
G DIGESTER
ESTRIDGE
REDIGEST
H DIETHERS
I SIDERITE
L RELISTED
M DEMERITS
DEMISTER
DIMETERS
MISTERED
N INSERTED
NERDIEST
RESIDENT
SINTERED
TRENDIES
P PREEDITS
PRIESTED
RESPITED
R DESTRIER
S DIESTERS
EDITRESS
RESISTED
SISTERED
T TIREDEST
U ERUDITES
SURETIED
V VERDITES
W WEIRDEST

DEENORS 143
ENDORSE
A REASONED
B DEBONERS
REDBONES
C CENSORED
ENCODERS
NECROSED
SECONDER
D ENDORSED
E ENDORSEE
I INDORSEE
ORDINEES
M SERMONED
N ENDERONS
R ENDORSER
S ENDORSES
T ERODENTS
W ENDOWERS
REENDOWS
WORSENED

DEENORT 186
ERODENT
C CENTRODE
H DETHRONE
THRENODE
I ORIENTED
L REDOLENT
RONDELET
M ENTODERM
MENTORED
O ENROOTED
S ERODENTS
U DEUTERON

DEENRTU 237
DENTURE
A DENATURE
UNDERATE
UNDEREAT
D RETUNDED
E NEUTERED
I RETINUED
REUNITED
L UNDERLET
N UNRENTED
UNTENDER
O DEUTERON
R RETURNED
S DENTURES
SEDERUNT
UNDERSET
UNDESERT
UNRESTED
V VENTURED

DEIINRT 231
NITRIDE
A DAINTIER
C INDICTER
INDIRECT
REINDICT
D NITRIDED
G DIRIGENT
M DIRIMENT
O RETINOID
P INTREPID
S DISINTER
INDITERS
NITRIDES
RINDIEST
U UNTIDIER

DEIIRST 248
(TIDIERS)
A IRISATED
C ICTERIDS
E SIDERITE
G RIDGIEST
RIGIDEST
H DISHERIT
L REDISTIL
N DISINTER
INDITERS
NITRIDES
RINDIEST
O DIORITES
P RIPTIDES
SPIRITED
TIDERIPS
T DIRTIEST
TRITIDES

DEILNOS 144
INDOLES
A NODALISE
C INCLOSED
E ESLOINED
LESIONED
G GLENOIDS
SIDELONG
I LIONISED
O EIDOLONS
SOLENOID
R DISENROL
S SONDELIS
U DELUSION
INSOULED
UNSOILED

DEILORS 200
SOLDIER
A DARIOLES
SOLIDARE
SOREDIAL
C SCLEROID
I IDOLISER
L DOLLIERS
N DISENROL
P LEPORIDS
S SOLDIERS
T STOLIDER
U SOULDIER
Y SOLDIERY

DEINORS 25
INDORSE
A ANEROIDS
DONARIES
C CONSIDER
D INDORSED
E INDORSEE
ORDINEES
G NEGROIDS
H HORDEINS
I DERISION
IRONISED
IRONSIDE
RESINOID
J JOINDERS
L DISENROL
N ENDIRONS
P DISPONER
POINDERS
PRISONED
R INDORSER
S INDORSES
SORDINES
T DRONIEST
U DOURINES
SOURDINE
W DISOWNER
WINDORES
WINDROSE

DEINORT 24
(IRODENT)
A AROINTED
DERATION
ORDINATE
RATIONED
C CENTROID
DOCTRINE
E ORIENTED
I RETINOID
M DORMIENT
N INDENTOR
P DIPTERON
S DRONIEST
T INTORTED

DEINOST 79
DITONES
A ASTONIED
SEDATION
C DEONTICS
E SIDENOTE
H HEDONIST
I EDITIONS
SEDITION
M DEMONIST
R DRONIEST
S DONSIEST
W DOWNIEST

DEINRST 87
TINDERS
A DETRAINS
RANDIEST
STRAINED
D STRIDDEN
E INSERTED
NERDIEST
RESIDENT
SINTERED
TRENDIES
G STRINGED
I DISINTER
INDITERS
NITRIDES
RINDIEST
L SNIRTLED
TENDRILS
TRINDLES
O DRONIEST
P SPRINTED
T STRIDENT
TRIDENTS
U INTRUDES
X DEXTRINS

DEINRTU 83
INTRUDE
A DATURINE
INDURATE
RUINATED
URINATED
B TURBINED
UNDERBIT
C REINDUCT
D INTRUDED
E RETINUED
REUNITED
I UNTIDIER
L UNDERLIT
M RUDIMENT
UNMITRED
N INTURNED
P TURNIPED
R INTRUDER
S INTRUDES
W UNDERWIT

DEINSTU 203
DUNITES
A AUDIENTS
SINUATED
D DISTUNED
E DETINUES
F UNSIFTED
G DUNGIEST
I DISUNITE
NUDITIES
UNITISED
UNTIDIES
L DILUENTS
INSULTED
UNLISTED
M MISTUNED
N DUNNIEST
DUNNITES
Q SQUINTED
R INTRUDES
S DISTUNES
U UNSUITED

DEIORST 53
EDITORS
A ASTEROID
B DEBITORS
DEORBITS
C CORDITES
G DIGESTOR
GRODIEST
STODGIER
I DIORITES
K DORKIEST
L STOLIDER
M MORTISED
N DRONIEST
P DIOPTERS
DIOPTRES
DIPTEROS
PERIDOTS
PROTEIDS
RIPOSTED
TOPSIDER
S STEROIDS
T DORTIEST
U IODURETS
OUTRIDES
OUTSIDER
SUITORED
W ROWDIEST
WORDIEST

DEIORTU 199
OUTRIDE
B TUBEROID
C OUTCRIED
E ETOURDIE
F OUTFIRED
H OUTHIRED
R OUTRIDER
S IODURETS
OUTRIDES
OUTSIDER
SUITORED

V OUTDRIVE

DEIRSTU 229
DUSTIER
C CRUDITES
CURDIEST
CURTSIED
D RUDDIEST
STURDIED
E ERUDITES
SURETIED
G DURGIEST
L DILUTERS
LURIDEST
STUDLIER
M DIESTRUM
N INTRUDES
O IODURETS
OUTRIDES
OUTSIDER
SUITORED
P DISPUTER
STUPIDER
Q SQUIRTED
R STURDIER
S DIESTRUS
DRUSIEST
STUDIERS
STURDIES
T DETRITUS
X DRUXIEST

DENORST 209
SNORTED
A TORNADES
E ERODENTS
I DRONIEST
M MORDENTS
N TENDRONS
P PORTENDS
PROTENDS
U ROUNDEST
TONSURED
UNSORTED
Y DRYSTONE

DENORTU 176
(NOT RUDE)
C CORNUTED
TROUNCED
D ROTUNDED
E DEUTERON
F FORTUNED
G TRUDGEON
L ROUNDLET
O UNROOTED
R ROTUNDER
S ROUNDEST
TONSURED
UNSORTED
T UNROTTED
W UNDERTOW

EEGINRS 113
GREISEN
A ANERGIES
GESNERIA
B BIGENERS
REBEGINS
C CREESING
GENERICS
D DESIGNER
ENERGIDS
REDESIGN
REEDINGS
RESIGNED
E ENERGIES
ENERGISE
GREENIES
RESEEING
F FEERINGS
FEIGNERS
REEFINGS
G GREESING
H GREENISH
REHINGES
SHEERING
J JEERINGS
K KREESING
SKEERING
L LEERINGS
REELINGS
M REGIMENS
N ENGINERS
INGENERS
SERENING
SNEERING
O ERINGOES
P SPEERING
SPREEING
R RESIGNER
S GREISENS
T GENTRIES
INTEGERS
REESTING
STEERING
STREIGNE
U SEIGNEUR
V SEVERING
VEERINGS
W RESEWING
SEWERING

EEGINRT 162
INTEGER
A GRATINEE
INTERAGE
C ERECTING
GENTRICE
G GREETING
I REIGNITE
M METERING
REGIMENT
N ENTERING
P PETERING
S GENTRIES
INTEGERS
REESTING
STEERING
STREIGNE
U GENITURE
V EVERTING
W TWEERING
X EXERTING
GENETRIX

EEGINST 1[illegible]1
(SEETING)
A SAGENITE
B BEIGNETS
C GENETICS
D INGESTED
SIGNETED
STEEDING
G EGESTING
H SEETHING
SHEETING
K KITENGES
STEEKING
L GENTILES
SLEETING
STEELING
M MEETINGS
STEEMING
N STEENING
O EGESTION
P STEEPING
R GENTRIES
INTEGERS
REESTING
STEERING
STREIGNE
T GENTIEST
U EUGENIST
V STEEVING
VENTIGES
W SWEETING
X EXIGENTS

EEILNST 89
TENSILE
B STILBENE
TENSIBLE
C CENTILES
D ENLISTED
LINTSEED
LISTENED
TINSELED
E ENLISTEE
SELENITE
G GENTILES
SLEETING
STEELING
H THEELINS
I LENITIES
K NESTLIKE
N LENIENTS
SENTINEL
O NOSELITE
P PENLITES
PLENTIES
R ENLISTER
LISTENER
REENLIST
SILENTER
S SETLINES
T ENTITLES
V VEINLETS

EEILORS 163
(SORE LIE)
B EROSIBLE
C CREOLISE
F FORELIES
I OILERIES
K ROSELIKE
L ORSEILLE
N ELOINERS
P PELORIES
T LITEROSE
TROELIES
V OVERLIES
RELIEVOS
VOLERIES
W OWLERIES

EEILORT 129
TROELIE
A AEROLITE
D DOLERITE
LOITERED
H HOTELIER
K LORIKEET
M MOTELIER
R LOITERER
S LITEROSE
TROELIES

EEILRST 81
STERILE
A ATELIERS
EARLIEST
LEARIEST
REALTIES
C RETICLES
SCLERITE
TIERCELS
TRISCELE
D RELISTED
E LEERIEST
SLEETIER
STEELIER
F FERLIEST
I TILERIES
K TRISKELE
L TREILLES
M TERMLIES
N ENLISTER
LISTENER
REENLIST
SILENTER
O LITEROSE
TROELIES
P EPISTLER
PELTRIES
PERLITES
REPTILES
S LEISTERS
RITELESS
TIRELESS
T RETITLES

EEINORS 115
EROSINE
D INDORSEE
ORDINEES
G ERINGOES
H HEROINES
K KEROSINE
L ELOINERS
M EMERSION
P ISOPRENE
PIONEERS
S ESSOINER
T ONERIEST
SEROTINE
V EVERSION

EEINORT 23
(TRIE ONE)
B TENEBRIO
C ERECTION
NEOTERIC
D ORIENTED
H ETHERION
HEREINTO
I ERIONITE
M TIMONEER
R REORIENT
S ONERIEST
SEROTINE
T TENORITE
X EXERTION

EEINOST 95
(ETONIES)
B BETONIES
EBONITES
C ICESTONE
SEICENTO
D SIDENOTE
G EGESTION
L NOSELITE
M MONETISE
SEMITONE
R ONERIEST
SEROTINE
S ESSONITE
T NOISETTE
TEOSINTE

EEINRST 13
ENTRIES
A ARENITES
ARSENITE
RESINATE
STEARINE
TRAINEES
C CENTRIES
ENTERICS
ENTICERS
SCIENTER
SECRETIN
D INSERTED
NERDIEST
RESIDENT
SINTERED
TRENDIES
E ETERNISE
TEENSIER
F FERNIEST
INFESTER
G GENTRIES
INTEGERS
REESTING
STEERING
STREIGNE
I ERINITES
NITERIES
K KERNITES
L ENLISTER
LISTENER
REENLIST
SILENTER
M MISENTER
N INTENSER
INTERNES
O ONERIEST
SEROTINE
R INSERTER
REINSERT
REINTERS
RENTIERS
TERRINES
S INTERESS
SENTRIES
TRENISES
T INERTEST
INSETTER
INTEREST
STERNITE
TRIENTES
U ESURIENT
NEURITES
RETINUES
REUNITES
V NERVIEST
REINVEST
SERVIENT
SIRVENTE
X INTERSEX
Y SERENITY

EEINRSU 198
(INSUREE)
A UNEASIER
C INSECURE
SINECURE
D UREDINES
F REINFUSE
G SEIGNEUR
N NEURINES
P PENURIES
RESUPINE
Q ENQUIRES
INQUERES
SQUIREEN
R REINSURE
S ENURESIS
T ESURIENT
NEURITES
RETINUES
REUNITES
V UNIVERSE

EEINRTT 165
TENTIER
B REBITTEN
C RETICENT
D RETINTED
E REINETTE
TEENTIER
H THIRTEEN
I INTERTIE
RETINITE
L NETTLIER
N RENITENT
O TENORITE
S INERTEST
INSETTER
INTEREST
STERNITE
TRIENTES
Y ENTIRETY
ETERNITY

EEINSTT 187
(SITE TEN)
A ANISETTE
TETANIES
TETANISE
B BENTIEST
D DINETTES
INSETTED
E TEENIEST
F FEINTEST
G GENTIEST
I ENTITIES
L ENTITLES
M MINETTES
N SENTIENT
O NOISETTE
TEOSINTE
P INEPTEST
SPINETTE
R INERTEST
INSETTER
INTEREST
STERNITE
TRIENTES
T NETTIEST
TENTIEST
W TENTWISE
TWENTIES
X EXISTENT

EEIORST 71
(OTERIES)
A ETAERIOS
C COTERIES
ESOTERIC
G ERGOTISE
H ISOTHERE
THEORIES
THEORISE
L LITEROSE
TROELIES
M TIRESOME
N ONERIEST
SEROTINE
P POETISER
POETRIES
S EROTESIS
Z EROTIZES

EELORST 150
SOLERET
A OLEASTER
C CORSELET
ELECTORS
ELECTROS
SELECTOR
E SLOETREE
H HOSTELER
I LITEROSE
TROELIES
L SOLLERET
M MOLESTER
N ENTRESOL
S SOLERETS
T LORETTES
U RESOLUTE
V OVERLETS

EENORST 45
(NO TREES)
A EARSTONE
RESONATE
D ERODENTS
F ENFOREST
SOFTENER
G ESTROGEN
H HONESTER
I ONERIEST
SEROTINE
L ENTRESOL
M SERMONET
STOREMEN
N ENTERONS
TENONERS
O OESTRONE
ROESTONE
P PROTENSE
S ESTRONES
T ONSETTER
V OVERNETS
X EXTENSOR

EGILNOR 222
(ONE GIRL)
A GERANIOL
REGIONAL
B IGNOBLER
E ELOIGNER
F FLORIGEN
I LIGROINE
RELIGION
REOILING
S RESOLING
W LOWERING
ROWELING

EGINORS 64
IGNORES
A IGNAROES
ORGANISE
ORIGANES
B SOBERING
C COREIGNS
COSIGNER
D NEGROIDS
E ERINGOES
I SEIGNIOR
L RESOLING
M NEGROISM
N NEGRONIS
P PERIGONS
REPOSING
SPONGIER
R IGNORERS
S GORINESS
SIGNORES
T GENITORS
ROSETING
W RESOWING
Y SEIGNORY

EGINORT 180
GENITOR
C GERONTIC
H THROEING
N NITROGEN
S GENITORS
ROSETING
T OTTERING
U OUTREIGN
ROUTEING
V REVOTING
W TOWERING
X OXTERING
Z ROZETING

EGINRST 111
RESTING
A ANGRIEST
ASTRINGE
GANISTER
GANTRIES
GRANITES
INGRATES
RANGIEST
REASTING
STEARING
TASERING
C CRESTING
D STRINGED
E GENTRIES
INTEGERS
REESTING
STEERING
STREIGNE
H RIGHTENS
I GIRNIEST
IGNITERS
REISTING
RESITING
STINGIER
STRIGINE
L LINGSTER
RINGLETS
STERLING
TINGLERS
TRINGLES
N STERNING
O GENITORS
ROSETING
P PRESTING
R RESTRING
RINGSTER
STRINGER
S RESTINGS
STINGERS
TRESSING
TRIGNESS
T GITTERNS
V STERVING
W STREWING
WRESTING

EGIORST 233
GORIEST
D DIGESTOR
GRODIEST
STODGIER
E ERGOTISE
H GHOSTIER
M ERGOTISM
GORMIEST
N GENITORS
ROSETING
S GORSIEST
STRIGOSE
U GOUSTIER
V VERTIGOS
Y OYSTRIGE
Z ZORGITES

EGNORST 236
(STRONG E)
A ESTRAGON
NEGATORS
ORANGEST
RAGSTONE
STONERAG
E ESTROGEN
G GONGSTER
I GENITORS
ROSETING
N RONTGENS
R STRONGER
S SONGSTER
T TONGSTER
U STURGEON
W WRONGEST

EHIORST 230
HOISTER
A HOARIEST
C ROTCHIES
THEORICS
E ISOTHERE
THEORIES
THEORISE
G GHOSTIER
M ISOTHERM
MOITHERS
N HORNIEST
ORNITHES
P TROPHIES
R HERITORS
S HOISTERS
HORSIEST
HOSTRIES
SHORTIES
T THEORIST
THORITES
U OUTHIRES
V OVERHITS
W WORTHIES

EIILRST 215
SILTIER
A LAIRIEST
LISTERIA
B TRILBIES
D REDISTIL
E TILERIES
F FILISTER
L STILLIER
M LIMITERS
MIRLIEST
N NIRLIEST
NITRILES
O ROILIEST
P TRIPLIES
T STILTIER
U UTILISER

EIINORT 99
(IRONITE)
D RETINOID
E ERIONITE
F NOTIFIER
P POINTIER
R INTERIOR
S IRONIEST

EIINRST 66
(TINIERS)
A INERTIAS
RAINIEST
B BRINIEST
C CITRINES
CRINITES
INCITERS
D DISINTER
INDITERS
NITRIDES
RINDIEST
E ERINITES
NITERIES
F SNIFTIER
G GIRNIEST
IGNITERS
REISTING
RESITING
STINGIER
STRIGINE
H INHERITS
K STINKIER
L NIRLIEST
NITRILES
M INTERIMS
MINISTER
MISINTER
O IRONIEST
P PRISTINE
S INSISTER
SINISTER
T NITRITES
STINTIER
U NEURITIS
V INVITERS
VINTRIES
VITRINES

EILNORS 59
NEROLIS
A AILERONS
ALERIONS
ALIENORS
C INCLOSER
LICENSOR
D DISENROL
E ELOINERS
G RESOLING
I LIONISER
M MISENROL
P PROLINES
R LORINERS
T RETINOLS

EILNORT 72
RETINOL
A ORIENTAL
RELATION
TAILERON
P TERPINOL
TOPLINER
R RITORNEL
S RETINOLS
T TROTLINE
U OUTLINER
W TOWNLIER

EILNOST 34
ENTOILS
A ELATIONS
INSOLATE
TOENAILS
C LECTIONS
TELSONIC
E NOSELITE
H HOLSTEIN
HOTLINES
NEOLITHS
I ETIOLINS
L STELLION
M MOLINETS
N INSOLENT
O LOONIEST
OILSTONE
P POINTELS
PONTILES
POTLINES
TOPLINES
R RETINOLS
U ELUTIONS
OUTLINES
V NOVELIST
VIOLENTS
W TOWLINES

EILNRST 93
SNIRTLE
A ENTRAILS
LATRINES
RATLINES
RETINALS
TRENAILS
D SNIRTLED
TENDRILS
TRINDLES
E ENLISTER
LISTENER
REENLIST
SILENTER
G LINGSTER
RINGLETS
STERLING
TINGLERS
TRINGLES
I NIRLIEST
NITRILES
K LINKSTER
STRINKLE
TINKLERS
M MINSTREL
O RETINOLS
P SPLINTER
S SLINTERS
SNIRTLES
U INSULTER
LUSTRINE
Y TINSELRY

EILORST 27
LOITERS
A SOTERIAL
B STROBILE
TRILOBES
C CLOISTER
COISTREL
COSTLIER
CREOLIST
D STOLIDER
E LITEROSE
TROELIES
F FLORIEST
TREFOILS
I ROILIEST
L TRILLOES
TROLLIES
N RETINOLS
O OESTRIOL
TROOLIES
P POITRELS
S ESTRIOLS
T TRIOLETS
U LOURIEST
OUTLIERS

EILRSTU 189
LUSTIER
A URALITES
B BURLIEST
SUBTILER
C CURLIEST
UTRICLES
D DILUTERS
LURIDEST
STUDLIER
G GURLIEST
H LUTHIERS
I UTILISER
M MURLIEST
N INSULTER
LUSTRINE
O LOURIEST
OUTLIERS
Q QUILTERS
R SULTRIER
S SURLIEST
T SLUTTIER
SURTITLE
V RIVULETS

EIMNOST 243
MOISTEN
A AMNIOTES
MISATONE
SOMNIATE
C CENTIMOS
D DEMONIST
E MONETISE
SEMITONE
G MITOGENS
H HOISTMEN
K TOKENISM
L MOLINETS
N MENTIONS
O EMOTIONS
MOONIEST
P EMPTIONS
NEPOTISM

PIMENTOS
S MESTINOS
MOISTENS
SENTIMOS

EIMORST 173
MOISTER
A AMORTISE
ATOMISER
C MORTICES
D MORTISED
E TIRESOME
F SETIFORM
G ERGOTISM
GORMIEST
H ISOTHERM
MOITHERS
O MOORIEST
MOTORISE
ROOMIEST
P IMPOSTER
R MORTISER
STORMIER
S EROTISMS
MORTISES
TRISOMES
T OMITTERS
U MISROUTE
MOISTURE
V VOMITERS
W MISWROTE
WORMIEST
Y ISOMETRY

EINOPRS 177
ORPINES
C CONSPIRE
INCORPSE
D DISPONER
POINDERS
PRISONED
E ISOPRENE
PIONEERS
F FORPINES
G PERIGONS
REPOSING
SPONGIER
I RIPIENOS
L PROLINES
M PROMINES
O POISONER
SNOOPIER
SPOONIER
P POPERINS
PROPINES
R PRISONER
S PORINESS
PRESSION
ROPINESS
T POINTERS
PORNIEST
PROTEINS
REPOINTS
TROPINES
U PRUINOSE
V OVERSPIN
PROVINES

EINOPRT 212
POINTER
A ATROPINE
C ENTROPIC
INCEPTOR

D DIPTERON
H TRIPHONE
I POINTIER
L TERPINOL
TOPLINER
M ORPIMENT
S POINTERS
PORNIEST
PROTEINS
REPOINTS
TROPINES
U ERUPTION

EINORRT 90
(TORRINE)
A ANTERIOR
C TRICORNE
E REORIENT
F FRONTIER
H THORNIER
I INTERIOR
L RITORNEL
S INTRORSE
SNORTIER
V INVERTOR
W INTERROW

EINORST 3
(IN STORE)
A ANOESTRI
ARSONITE
NOTARIES
NOTARISE
ROSINATE
SENORITA
B BORNITES
RIBSTONE
C COINTERS
CORNIEST
NOTICERS
RECTIONS
D DRONIEST
E ONERIEST
SEROTINE
G GENITORS
ROSETING
H HORNIEST
ORNITHES
I IRONIEST
J JOINTERS
K INSTROKE
L RETINOLS
N INTONERS
TERNIONS
O SNOOTIER
P POINTERS
PORNIEST
PROTEINS
REPOINTS
TROPINES
R INTRORSE
SNORTIER
S OESTRINS
TERSIONS
T SNOTTIER
TENORIST
TRITONES
U ROUTINES
SNOUTIER
V INVESTOR
Y TYROSINE
Z TRIZONES

EINORSU 227
URINOSE
C COINSURE
NOURICES
ROUNCIES
D DOURINES
SOURDINE
F REFUSION
M INERMOUS
MONSIEUR
N REUNIONS
P PRUINOSE
S NEUROSIS
RESINOUS
T ROUTINES
SNOUTIER
V SOUVENIR

EINORTT 84
TRITONE
A TENTORIA
C CONTRITE
CORNETTI
D INTORTED
E TENORITE
G OTTERING
K KNOTTIER
L TROTLINE
N TONTINER
S SNOTTIER
TENORIST
TRITONES
U RITENUTO

EINORTU 119
ROUTINE
C NEUROTIC
UNEROTIC
G OUTREIGN
ROUTEING
J JOINTURE
L OUTLINER
N NEUTRINO
P ERUPTION
S ROUTINES
SNOUTIER
T RITENUTO

EINOSTT 241
TONIEST
B BOTTINES
C CENTOIST
STENOTIC
TONETICS
E NOISETTE
TEOSINTE
F FISTNOTE
G TENTIGOS
J JETTISON
N TINSTONE
TONTINES
P NEPOTIST
R SNOTTIER
TENORIST
TRITONES
U SNOTTIES
STONIEST
T TOTIENTS
W TOWNIEST

EINRSTT 234
TINTERS
A INTREATS
NITRATES
STRAITEN
TARTINES
TERTIANS
B BITTERNS
C CENTRIST
CITTERNS
D STRIDENT
TRIDENTS
E INERTEST
INSETTER
INTEREST
STERNITE
TRIENTES
G GITTERNS
I NITRITES
STINTIER
K KNITTERS
TRINKETS
O SNOTTIER
TENORIST
TRITONES
S ENTRISTS
STINTERS
U RUNTIEST
W TWINTERS
Y ENTRYIST

EINRSTU 65
UNITERS
A RUINATES
TAURINES
URANITES
URINATES
B TRIBUNES
TURBINES
C CURNIEST
D INTRUDES
E ESURIENT
NEURITES
RETINUES
REUNITES
I NEURITIS
L INSULTER
LUSTRINE
M TERMINUS
UNMITERS
UNMITRES
N RUNNIEST
STURNINE
O ROUTINES
SNOUTIER
P REPUNITS
UNPRIEST
UNRIPEST
Q SQUINTER
T RUNTIEST
V UNRIVETS
VENTURIS
W UNWRITES

EIOPRST 201
ROPIEST
C PERSICOT
D DIOPTERS
DIOPTRES
DIPTEROS
PERIDOTS
PROTEIDS
RIPOSTED

TOPSIDER
E POETISER
POETRIES
F FIREPOTS
PIEFORTS
POSTFIRE
H TROPHIES
K PORKIEST
L POITRELS
M IMPOSTER
N POINTERS
PORNIEST
PROTEINS
REPOINTS
TROPINES
O PORTOISE
ROOPIEST
R PIERROTS
SPORTIER
S PERIOSTS
PROSIEST
PROSTIES
REPOSITS
RIPOSTES
TRIPOSES
T PORTIEST
RISPETTO
SPOTTIER
U ROUPIEST
SPOUTIER
V OVERTIPS
PIVOTERS
SORPTIVE
SPORTIVE

EIORRST 135
RIOTERS
A ROARIEST
ROTARIES
B ORBITERS
F FROSTIER
ROTIFERS
H HERITORS
I RIOTRIES
M MORTISER
STORMIER
N INTRORSE
SNORTIER
O ROOTSIER
P PIERROTS
SPORTIER
R ERRORIST
S RESISTOR
ROISTERS
SORRIEST
T RORTIEST
U STOURIER
V OVERSTIR
SERVITOR

EIORSTT 174
STOITER
A TOASTIER
C COTTIERS
D DORTIEST
H THEORIST
THORITES
L TRIOLETS
M OMITTERS
N SNOTTIER
TENORIST
TRITONES
O ROOTIEST

TORTOISE
P PORTIEST
RISPETTO
SPOTTIER
R RORTIEST
S STOITERS
U TOUSTIER
TUTORISE
V VIRETOTS

EIORSTU 67
TOUSIER
A OUTRAISE
SAUTOIRE
C CITREOUS
OUTCRIES
D IODURETS
OUTRIDES
OUTSIDER
SUITORED
F FOUSTIER
OUTFIRES
G GOUSTIER
H OUTHIRES
L LOURIEST
OUTLIERS
M MISROUTE
MOISTURE
N ROUTINES
SNOUTIER
P ROUPIEST
SPOUTIER
Q QUOITERS
R STOURIER
T TOUSTIER
TUTORISE
V VIRTUOSE
VITREOUS
VOITURES

ENORSTU 100
(NOT SURE)
A OUTEARNS
B BURSTONE
RUBSTONE
C CONSTRUE
CORNUTOS
COUNTERS
RECOUNTS
TROUNCES
D ROUNDEST
TONSURED
UNSORTED
F FORTUNES
G STURGEON
H SOUTHERN
I ROUTINES
SNOUTIER
L TURNSOLE
M MONTURES
MOUNTERS
REMOUNTS
N NEUTRONS
O OUTSNORE
S TONSURES
T STENTOUR
V VENTROUS
Y TOURNEYS

8-LETTER SETS LIST

alphabetical list of all words appearing in 8-Letter Sets

ABEARING
ABETTORS
ABORIGEN
ABORTEES
ABORTERS
ABORTING
ABSEILED
ABSENTER
ABSINTHE
ABSTERGE
ACARINES
ACCENTOR
ACENTRIC
ACETONIC
ACONITES
ACRIDEST
ACRIDINE
ACROLEIN
ACROTERS
ACTINIDE
ACTIONED
ACTIONER
ADENINES
ADENITIS
ADENOIDS
ADENOSIS
ADERMINS
ADHERENT
ADHERING
ADHESION
ADMITTER
ADONISED
ADONISES
ADONIZES
ADOPTERS
ADORNERS
ADROITER
AEGIRINE
AEGIRITE
AERATING
AERATION
AERATORS
AEROLITE
AEROLITH
AEROSTAT
AFEARING
AGENTIAL
AGINNERS
AGISTERS
AGLITTER
AGONISED
AGONISES
AGONIZES
AGREEING
AGREMENS
AGREMENT
AIGRETTE
AILANTOS
AILERONS
AILETTES
AILMENTS
AIRDATES
AIRHOLES
AIRINESS
AIRLINES
AIRSPEED
AIRTIMES
ALAIMENT
ALATIONS
ALEPINES
ALERIONS
ALERTEST
ALERTING
ALEURONS
ALEXINES
ALGERINE
ALGINATE
ALIENATE
ALIENEES
ALIENERS
ALIENIST
ALIENORS
ALIGNERS
ALIMENTS
ALLANITE
ALLERGIN
ALLERION
ALMERIES
ALMONERS
ALNICOES
ALOETICS
ALTERERS
ALTERING
ALTERITY
ALTERNES
ALTRICES
ALUNITES
AMBIENTS
AMENDERS
AMENTIAS
AMIDONES
AMIRATES
AMITROLE
AMMONITE
AMNESTIC
AMNIOTES
AMORTISE
ANALCITE
ANBURIES
ANCESTOR
ANCHORET
ANCIENTS
ANDESINE
ANDESITE
ANDIRONS
ANDROGEN
ANDROIDS
ANDVILES
ANEARING
ANERGIAS
ANERGIES
ANEROIDS
ANESTRUM
ANESTRUS
ANEURINS
ANEURISM
ANGARIES
ANGINOSE
ANGRIEST
ANIMATER
ANIMATES
ANISEEDS
ANISETTE
ANISOLES
ANKERITE
ANNELIDS
ANODISED
ANODISES
ANODIZES
ANOESTRA
ANOESTRI
ANOINTED
ANOINTER
ANORETIC
ANORTHIC
ANSERINE
ANSWERED
ANTBEARS
ANTBIRDS
ANTEATER
ANTENATI
ANTERIOR
ANTEVERT
ANTHELIA
ANTHERID
ANTIDORA
ANTIDOTE
ANTIENTS
ANTIGENS
ANTIHERO
ANTILEAK
ANTILOGS
ANTILOGY
ANTIMALE
ANTIMERE
ANTINODE
ANTIPODE
ANTIPOLE
ANTIQUER
ANTIQUES
ANTIRAPE
ANTIROCK
ANTIROLL
ANTISERA
ANTIWEAR
ANTIWEED
ANTLERED
ANTLIATE
ANTLIONS
ANTRORSE
ANTSIEST
ANURESIS
ANURETIC
APERIENT
APLUSTRE
APPRISED
APTERISM
APTEROUS
ARANEIDS
ARBELEST
ARBITERS
ARBORETS
ARCHINES
ARCSINES
AREADING
ARENITES
AREOLATE
ARETTING
ARGENTIC
ARGINASE
ARIDNESS
ARIETTAS
ARIETTES
ARILLODE
ARISTATE
AROINTED
AROUSING
AROYNTED
ARRESTED
ARRESTEE
ARRESTER
ARRESTOR
ARSENATE
ARSENICS
ARSENIDE
ARSENITE
ARSHINES
ARSONIST
ARSONITE
ARTERIES
ARTESIAN
ARTICLED
ARTICLES
ARTINESS
ARTISTES
ARTSIEST
ASCENDER
ASPERITY
ASPIRATE
ASPORTED
ASSENTER
ASSENTOR
ASSERTED
ASSERTER
ASSERTOR
ASSIENTO
ASSIGNER
ASSIGNOR
ASSISTER
ASSOILED
ASSORTED
ASSORTER
ASTATINE
ASTELIES
ASTERIAS
ASTERIDS
ASTERISK
ASTERISM
ASTERNAL
ASTEROID
ASTERTED
ASTHENIA
ASTHENIC
ASTONIED
ASTONIES
ASTRINGE
ASTROIDS
ATEBRINS
ATELIERS
ATHEISED
ATHELING
ATHERINE
ATOMISED
ATOMISER
ATRAZINE
ATRESIAS
ATROPINE
ATROPINS
ATTAINED
ATTAINER
ATTENDER
ATTESTOR
ATTORNED
ATTORNEY
ATTRITED
ATTRITES
AUDIENTS
AUDITORS
AUNTLIER
AURELIAN
AURELIAS
AUREOLAS
AUREOLES
AURICLES
AUSTERER
AVENGERS
AVENTAIL
AVENTRED
AVENTRES
AVENTURE
AVERMENT
AVERSION
AVERTING
AVODIRES
AVOIDERS
AWAITERS
AXINITES
AZOTISED
AZURINES
BACTERIN
BAINITES
BALDIEST
BALUSTER
BANDEROL
BANDIEST
BANDORES
BANDSTER
BANGSTER
BANISTER
BANTERED
BARDIEST
BAREGINE
BARITONE
BARMIEST
BARNIEST
BARONETS
BARONIES
BARTENDS
BASANITE
BASELINE
BASINETS
BASSINET
BATHORSE
BATTENER
BATTEROS
BEADIEST
BEARDIES
BEARDING
BEARINGS
BEATINGS
BEATNIKS
BEDRAILS
BEDSONIA
BEGONIAS
BEIGNETS
BELADIES
BELATING
BENDIEST
BENTIEST
BEPAINTS
BERATING
BERGENIA
BESAINTS
BESTAINS
BESTRIDE
BETAINES
BETATRON
BETONIES
BETREADS
BICORNES
BIDENTAL
BIGENERS
BINARIES
BIRETTAS
BISTERED
BITTERNS
BLASTIER
BLEAREST
BLEARING
BLEATERS
BLEATING
BLOATERS
BLOATING
BOASTERS
BONDAGER
BONITOES
BONNIEST
BORATING
BORNITES
BOTANIES
BOTANISE
BOTTINES
BOUNTIES
BRAIDEST
BRANDIES
BRANDISE
BRANTLES
BRASTING
BRAUNITE
BREADING
BREADNUT
BREASTED
BRINIEST
BRISANCE
BROADENS
BROADEST
BROMATES
BURLIEST
BURSTONE
CABESTRO
CABINETS
CABRESTO
CALORIES
CALORIST
CANAIGRE
CANARIED
CANARIES
CANASTER
CANDIDER
CANISTER
CANITIES
CANNIEST
CANOEIST
CANTERED
CANTIEST
CANTORIS
CANTREDS
CARBINES
CARINATE
CARIOLES
CARLINES
CARMINES
CARNIEST
CAROTENE
CAROTIDS
CAROTINS
CAROUSEL
CARROTIN
CARTONED
CARYOTIN
CATENOID
CATERANS
CATERERS
CATERING
CEDRATES
CEINTURE
CENSORED
CENTARES
CENTAURS
CENTIARE
CENTILES
CENTIMOS
CENTOIST
CENTRALS
CENTRIES
CENTRIST
CENTRODE
CENTROID
CERAMIST
CERASINS
CERATINS
CERATOID
CESARIAN
CHANTIES
CHARIEST
CHAROSET
CHORINES
CILANTRO
CINEASTE
CINEASTS
CINEREAS
CISTERNA
CISTVAEN
CITADELS
CITRANGE
CITRATED
CITRATES
CITREOUS
CITRINES
CITTERNS
CLARETED
CLARINET
CLARTIER
CLEAREST
CLEARING
CLEATING
CLOISTER
COALIEST
COALISED
COARSEST
COASTERS
CODEINAS
COINAGES
COINFERS
COINMATE
COINSURE
COINTERS
COISTREL
COLANDER
COLINEAR
CONATIVE
CONCEITS
CONCERTI
CONCISER
CONELRAD
CONIFERS
CONKIEST
CONSIDER
CONSPIRE
CONSTRUE
CONTRAIL
CONTRAIR
CONTRATE
CONTRITE
CONTRIVE
COONTIES
COPARENT
CORDITES
COREIGNS
CORELATE
CORNETTI
CORNICES
CORNIEST
CORNUTED
CORNUTES
CORONATE
CORSELET
COSIGNER
COSTLIER
COTERIES
COTTIERS
COUNTERS
COUNTIES
COURANTE
CRANIATE
CRANNIED
CRANNIES
CRAPIEST
CRATONIC
CREASING
CREASOTE
CREATINE
CREATING
CREATINS
CREATION
CREATORS
CREESING
CREMAINS
CREMOSIN
CRENATED
CREOLIAN
CREOLISE
CREOLIST
CRESTING
CRINATED
CRINITES
CRISPATE
CRISTATE
CROCEINS
CRUDITES
CTENIDIA
CURDIEST
CURLIEST
CURNIEST
CURTSIED
CYANITES
CYTOSINE
DAIMONES
DAINTIER
DAINTIES
DAKERING
DALLIERS

DAMOISEL
DANDIEST
DANEWORT
DANGERED
DANGLIER
DARIOLES
DARNDEST
DATARIES
DATELINE
DATOLITE
DATURINE
DAUNTERS
DEADLIER
DEAIRING
DEALINGS
DEARLING
DEARNESS
DEASOILS
DEATHIER
DEBATERS
DEBATING
DEBITORS
DEBONAIR
DEBONERS
DECANTER
DECIARES
DECRETAL
DECRIALS
DEERSKIN
DEFINERS
DEFLATER
DEISEALS
DEISHEAL
DELAINES
DELATING
DELATION
DELATORS
DELIBATE
DELICATE
DELUSION
DEMAINES
DEMENTIA
DEMENTIS
DEMERITS
DEMISTER
DEMONIST
DENARIES
DENARIUS
DENATURE
DENDRITE
DENTALIA
DENTARIA
DENTINAL
DENTINES
DENTURAL
DENTURES
DEONTICS
DEORBITS
DEPAINTS
DEPILATE
DEPURANT
DERACINE
DERAIGNS
DERAILED
DERAILER
DERANGED
DERANGES
DERATING
DERATION
DERAYING
DERISION
DERIVATE
DEROGATE
DESALTER
DESERTIC
DESIGNER
DESINENT
DESPAIRS
DESTAINS
DESTINED
DESTINES
DESTRIER
DESYATIN
DETAILED
DETAILER
DETAINED
DETAINEE
DETAINER
DETHRONE
DETINUES
DETRAINS
DETRITAL
DETRITUS
DEUTERON
DEVIANTS
DEVIATES
DEVIATOR
DEWATERS
DEXTRANS
DEXTRINE
DEXTRINS
DIABETES
DIACTINE
DIAGNOSE
DIALECTS
DIALLERS
DIALOGER
DIALYSER
DIAMETER
DIAPENTE
DIASPORE
DIASTERS
DIASTOLE
DIASTYLE
DIATRONS
DIAZOLES
DICENTRA
DIEDRALS
DIELYTRA
DIESTERS
DIESTRUM
DIESTRUS
DIETHERS
DIETINES
DIGESTER
DIGESTOR
DILATERS
DILATORS
DILUENTS
DILUTERS
DIMETERS
DINETTES
DINOSAUR
DIOCESAN
DIOPTASE
DIOPTERS
DIOPTRES
DIORITES
DIOXANES
DIPTERAL
DIPTERAN
DIPTERAS
DIPTERON
DIPTEROS
DIRENESS
DIRIGENT
DIRIMENT
DIRTIEST
DISADORN
DISAGREE
DISASTER
DISCREET
DISCRETE
DISENROL
DISHERIT
DISINTER
DISLEAVE
DISMALER
DISOWNER
DISPONER
DISPREAD
DISPUTER
DISRATED
DISRATES
DISTANCE
DISTHENE
DISTRAIN
DISTUNED
DISTUNES
DISUNITE
DIVALENT
DOCTRINE
DOGNAPER
DOLERITE
DOLLIERS
DOMINATE
DONARIES
DONATIVE
DONSIEST
DORKIEST
DORMIENT
DORTIEST
DOUANIER
DOULEIAS
DOURINES
DOVETAIL
DOWNIEST
DRACONES
DRAFTEES
DRAGLINE
DRAGNETS
DRAGOMEN
DRAGONET
DRAGONNE
DRAINAGE
DRAINERS
DRAISENE
DRAISINE
DRAPIERS
DRAPPIES
DRAUNTED
DREADING
DREAMING
DREAREST
DREARIES
DREARING
DRISHEEN
DRONIEST
DRUSIEST
DRUXIEST
DRYSTONE
DUNGAREE
DUNGIEST
DUNNIEST
DUNNITES
DURATION
DURGIEST
EAGEREST
EANLINGS
EARLIEST
EARNESTS
EARNINGS
EARRINGS
EARSTONE
EARTHING
EASTERLY
EASTINGS
EASTLING
EASTLINS
EATERIES
EBONISTS
EBONITES
EBRIATED
ECTOSARC
EDITABLE
EDITIONS
EDITRESS
EGALITES
EGESTING
EGESTION
EIDOLONS
ELAPSING
ELASTINS
ELATERID
ELATERIN
ELATIONS
ELATIVES
ELECTORS
ELECTROS
ELEGIAST
ELEVATOR
ELOIGNER
ELOINERS
ELUTIONS
ELVANITE
EMERSION
EMIGRANT
EMIGRATE
EMIRATES
EMOTIONS
EMPTIONS
ENACTION
ENACTORS
ENACTORY
ENATIONS
ENCODERS
ENDANGER
ENDARTED
ENDERONS
ENDIRONS
ENDORSED
ENDORSEE
ENDORSER
ENDORSES
ENDOSARC
ENDOWERS
ENERGIDS
ENERGIES
ENERGISE
ENERVATE
ENFOREST
ENGAGERS
ENGINERS
ENGRACED
ENGRACES
ENGRAFTS
ENGRAILS
ENGRAINS
ENGRAVED
ENGRAVES
ENLARGED
ENLARGES
ENLISTED
ENLISTEE
ENLISTER
ENQUIRES
ENRANGED
ENRANGES
ENROOTED
ENSEARED
ENSILAGE
ENSNARED
ENTAILED
ENTAILER
ENTASIAS
ENTASTIC
ENTERATE
ENTERICS
ENTERING
ENTERONS
ENTHRALS
ENTICERS
ENTIRETY
ENTITIES
ENTITLES
ENTODERM
ENTRAILS
ENTRAINS
ENTRANTS
ENTREATS
ENTREATY
ENTRESOL
ENTRISTS
ENTROPIC
ENTRYIST
ENURESIS
ENURETIC
EOBIONTS
EPACRIDS
EPILATED
EPILATES
EPILATOR
EPINASTY
EPISODAL
EPISTLER
ERADIATE
ERASIONS
ERECTING
ERECTION
EREMITAL
ERGATIVE
ERGATOID
ERGOTISE
ERGOTISM
ERINGOES
ERINITES
ERIONITE
ERODENTS
EROSIBLE
EROTEMAS
EROTESIS
EROTICAL
EROTISMS
EROTIZES
ERRATICS
ERRORIST
ERUDITES
ERUPTION
ESCALIER
ESCARGOT
ESCOTING
ESLOINED
ESOTERIC
ESPALIER
ESPARTOS
ESSOINER
ESSONITE
ESTANCIA
ESTATING
ESTRADES
ESTRAGON
ESTRANGE
ESTRAYED
ESTRIDGE
ESTRIOLS
ESTROGEN
ESTRONES
ESURIENT
ETAERIOS
ETAGERES
ETAMINES
ETERNALS
ETERNISE
ETERNITY
ETESIANS
ETHERIAL
ETHERION
ETIOLATE
ETIOLINS
ETOURDIE
ETRANGER
EUGENIST
EVERSION
EVERTING
EVIDENTS
EVIRATED
EVIRATES
EXACTION
EXACTORS
EXALTERS
EXALTING
EXCITONS
EXERTING
EXERTION
EXIGENTS
EXISTENT
EXORDIAL
EXPIRANT
EXTENSOR
EXTERNAL
EXTERNAT
EXTRADOS
EXTRAITS
EXTRANET
EYELIADS
FAGOTERS
FAILURES
FAINITES
FAINTERS
FAINTEST
FAIRNESS
FALTERED
FANCIERS
FANCIEST
FANTASIE
FARINOSE
FARNESOL
FASTENER
FATTENER
FEALTIES
FEASTING
FEATLIER
FEDARIES
FEERINGS
FEIGNERS
FEINTEST
FENDIEST
FENESTRA
FENITARS
FERLIEST
FERNIEST
FERRATES
FETATION
FETIALES
FIGEATER
FILAREES
FILISTER
FILTRATE
FINAGLER
FINAGLES
FIREPANS
FIREPOTS
FISTNOTE
FLARIEST
FLATIRON
FLOATERS
FLOATIER
FLOATING
FLORIEST
FLORIGEN
FOLIATED
FOLIATES
FORECAST
FORELAID
FORELAIN
FORELAND
FORELIES
FORENSIC
FOREPAST
FORESAID
FORESAIL
FORESTAL
FORINSEC
FORNICES
FORPINES
FORTUNED
FORTUNES
FOUSTIER
FRACTION
FRAILEST
FRAILTEE
FRATRIES
FRAULEIN
FREDAINE
FRENETIC
FRIANDES
FRONDAGE
FRONTIER
FROSTIER
FUSAROLE
GADARENE
GAHNITES
GAINLESS
GAINLIER
GALENITE
GALLEINS
GALTONIA
GAMESTER
GANDERED
GANGLIER
GANGSTER
GANISTER
GANOINES
GANTLINE
GANTRIES
GARDENED
GARDENER
GARDENIA
GARMENTS
GARNERED
GAROTING
GAROTTED
GAROTTES
GARRISON
GARROTED
GARROTES
GASALIER
GASELIER
GASOLIER
GASOLINE
GASTRINS
GAULTERS
GAUNTREE
GEARINGS
GELATINE
GELATING
GELATINS
GELATION
GENDARME
GENERALS
GENERANT
GENERATE
GENERICS
GENETICS
GENETRIX
GENISTAS
GENITALS
GENITORS
GENITURE
GENTIANS
GENTIEST
GENTILES
GENTRICE
GENTRIES
GERANIAL
GERANIOL
GERMAINE
GERMAINS
GERMINAL
GERONTIC
GESNERIA
GESTURAL
GHOSTIER
GIANTESS
GIRASOLE
GIRNIEST
GITTERNS
GLACIERS
GLADIEST
GLAREOUS
GLARIEST
GLASSIER
GLASSINE
GLAZIERS
GLEANERS
GLENOIDS
GLOATERS
GLOATING
GNARLIER
GNATLIKE
GNATTIER
GOADSTER
GOATHERD
GOATLING
GODETIAS
GOLIASED
GONGSTER
GORINESS
GORMIEST
GORSIEST
GOUSTIER
GRACILES
GRADIENT
GRADINES
GRAINAGE
GRAINERS
GRANDEES
GRANDEST
GRANITAS
GRANITES
GRANNIED
GRANNIES
GRANTEES
GRANTERS
GRAPIEST
GRAPLINE
GRATINEE
GRATINGS
GRAVITON
GREASILY

GREASING
GREATENS
GREATEST
GRECIANS
GREENIES
GREENISH
GREESING
GREETING
GREISENS
GREMIALS
GRENADES
GRIEVANT
GRODIEST
GURLIEST
GYRATION
HAIRIEST
HAIRNETS
HAIRSTED
HALTERED
HALTERES
HANDIEST
HARDIEST
HARDNOSE
HARMINES
HARTENED
HASTENER
HATERENT
HAULIERS
HAUNTERS
HAURIENT
HEADIEST
HEADREST
HEADRING
HEALINGS
HEARINGS
HEARSING
HEARTENS
HEARTIES
HEARTING
HEATINGS
HEDONIST
HEMATINS
HEPARINS
HEREINTO
HERITAGE
HERITORS
HERNIATE
HEROINES
HESITANT
HETAIRAS
HOARIEST
HOISTERS
HOISTMEN
HOLSTEIN
HONESTER
HORDEINS
HORNIEST
HORNTAIL
HORSIEST
HOSTELER
HOSTRIES
HOTELIER
HOTLINES
HYSTERIA
ICESTONE
ICTERIDS
ICTERINE
IDEALESS
IDEALISE
IDEALIST
IDEATING
IDEATION
IDOCRASE
IDOLATER
IDOLISER

IGNAROES
IGNITERS
IGNOBLER
IGNORANT
IGNORERS
IMPOSTER
INARCHED
INARCHES
INAURATE
INBOARDS
INBREEDS
INCENSOR
INCENTER
INCENTRE
INCEPTOR
INCHOATE
INCITERS
INCLOSED
INCLOSER
INCOMERS
INCORPSE
INCREASE
INCREATE
INDAGATE
INDARTED
INDENTER
INDENTOR
INDEXERS
INDICATE
INDICTER
INDIRECT
INDITERS
INDORSED
INDORSEE
INDORSER
INDORSES
INDRAFTS
INDURATE
INEARTHS
INEPTEST
INERMOUS
INERRANT
INERTEST
INERTIAE
INERTIAL
INERTIAS
INFECTER
INFECTOR
INFESTED
INFESTER
INFLATED
INFLATER
INFLATES
INFLATOR
INFORCES
INGATHER
INGENERS
INGESTED
INGRAFTS
INGRATES
INHALERS
INHAULER
INHEARSE
INHERITS
INJECTOR
INLAYERS
INNOVATE
INORNATE
INQUERES
INSEAMED
INSECTAN
INSECURE
INSERTED
INSERTER
INSETTED

INSETTER
INSISTER
INSNARED
INSNARER
INSNARES
INSOLATE
INSOLENT
INSOULED
INSTABLE
INSTANCE
INSTATED
INSTATES
INSTROKE
INSULATE
INSULTED
INSULTER
INTAGLIO
INTEGERS
INTEGRAL
INTENDER
INTENSER
INTERACT
INTERAGE
INTERBED
INTERCOM
INTERESS
INTEREST
INTERIMS
INTERIOR
INTERLAP
INTERLAY
INTERNAL
INTERNED
INTERNES
INTERRED
INTERROW
INTERSEX
INTERTIE
INTERVAL
INTERWAR
INTONATE
INTONERS
INTORTED
INTRADAS
INTRADOS
INTRANET
INTREATS
INTREPID
INTRORSE
INTRUDED
INTRUDER
INTRUDES
INTURNED
INVADERS
INVERTED
INVERTOR
INVESTED
INVESTOR
INVITERS
INVOCATE
IODINATE
IODURETS
IRISATED
IRISATES
IRONIEST
IRONISED
IRONSIDE
ISATINES
ISLANDED
ISLANDER
ISOLATED
ISOLATES
ISOLATOR
ISOLEADS
ISOMETRY

ISOPRENE
ISOTHERE
ISOTHERM
ITERANCE
ITERATED
ITERATES
JADEITES
JADERIES
JANGLIER
JANITORS
JANTIEST
JARGONED
JAROSITE
JAUNTIER
JAUNTIES
JEERINGS
JETTISON
JOINDERS
JOINTERS
JOINTURE
KAINITES
KAISERIN
KAOLINES
KARTINGS
KEITLOAS
KERATINS
KERATOID
KERATOSE
KERNITES
KEROSINE
KISTVAEN
KITENGES
KNEADERS
KNITTERS
KNOTTIER
KREASOTE
KREATINE
KREESING
LABORITE
LACERTID
LADRONES
LAETARES
LAETRILE
LAGERING
LAIRAGES
LAIRIEST
LAIRISED
LAITANCE
LAKESIDE
LAMENTER
LAMETERS
LAMIGERS
LAMINATE
LAMINOSE
LAMISTER
LAMITERS
LANCIERS
LANDSIDE
LANKIEST
LANNERET
LANOSITY
LANTERNS
LARDIEST
LARGENED
LARIATED
LARKIEST
LATEENER
LATENING
LATERITE
LATERIZE
LATHERED
LATIGOES
LATRINES
LAWNIEST
LAYERING

LEADIEST
LEADINGS
LEAFIEST
LEAKIEST
LEALTIES
LEANINGS
LEAPROUS
LEARIEST
LEARNING
LEASHING
LEASINGS
LEATHERN
LEATHERS
LEAVIEST
LEAVINGS
LECTIONS
LEERIEST
LEERINGS
LEGATINE
LEGATING
LEGATION
LEGATORS
LEISTERS
LEMURIAN
LENIENTS
LENITIES
LEOTARDS
LEPORIDS
LESIONED
LEVANTER
LEVATORS
LEVIRATE
LIBERATE
LIBRATED
LIBRATES
LICENSOR
LIGAMENT
LIGATION
LIGNAGES
LIGROINE
LIMEADES
LIMITERS
LINDANES
LINEAGES
LINEATED
LINGSTER
LINKAGES
LINKSTER
LINTSEED
LIONISED
LIONISER
LIPARITE
LISTENED
LISTENER
LISTERIA
LITANIES
LITERACY
LITERALS
LITERATE
LITERATI
LITERATO
LITEROSE
LIVETRAP
LLANEROS
LOAMIEST
LOATHERS
LOATHING
LOCATERS
LOCATING
LODESTAR
LOITERED
LOITERER
LONICERA
LOONIEST
LORETTES

LORICATE
LORIKEET
LORINERS
LOURIEST
LOWERING
LUNARIES
LURIDEST
LUSTRATE
LUSTRINE
LUTHIERS
MADERISE
MADRONES
MAGISTER
MAISTERS
MALIGNER
MALINGER
MANGIEST
MANIFEST
MANKIEST
MANLIEST
MANNITES
MANTISES
MARDIEST
MARGENTS
MARGINED
MARINATE
MARINERS
MARLIEST
MARLINES
MARLITES
MARMITES
MARTINET
MASTERED
MATERIEL
MATINEES
MATINESS
MATRICES
MATRIXES
MEAGREST
MEALIEST
MEANDERS
MEASLIER
MEASLING
MEDALIST
MEDIANTS
MEDIATES
MEDIATOR
MEETINGS
MELANIST
MELANITE
MELODIAS
MENSTRUA
MENTIONS
MENTORED
MESTINOS
METALING
METALISE
METANOIA
METERING
METRICAL
MIDRANGE
MIGRANTS
MIGRATES
MINARETS
MINEOLAS
MINERALS
MINETTES
MINIATED
MINIATES
MINISTER
MINSTREL
MINTAGES
MIRBANES
MIRLIEST
MISAGENT

MISALTER
MISATONE
MISDEALT
MISEATEN
MISENROL
MISENTER
MISINTER
MISLEARN
MISRATED
MISRATES
MISROUTE
MISTAKEN
MISTAKER
MISTERED
MISTRACE
MISTREAT
MISTUNED
MISWROTE
MITOGENS
MOISTENS
MOISTURE
MOITHERS
MOLERATS
MOLESTER
MOLINETS
MONAZITE
MONETISE
MONSIEUR
MONSTERA
MONTURES
MOONIEST
MOORIEST
MORAINES
MORALISE
MORALIST
MORDENTS
MORTICES
MORTISED
MORTISER
MORTISES
MOTELIER
MOTORISE
MOUNTERS
MURAENID
MURIATES
MURLIEST
NAARTJES
NACRITES
NAGGIEST
NAILSETS
NAIVETES
NAPERIES
NAPPIEST
NARCEINS
NARCOTIC
NARGHILE
NARGILEH
NARGILES
NARKIEST
NARRATES
NARTJIES
NASTIEST
NATTERED
NATTERER
NATTIEST
NAVICERT
NEARSIDE
NEATHERD
NECROSED
NECROSIS
NECROTIC
NECTARED
NEEDIEST
NEGATERS
NEGATION

NEGATORS
NEGROIDS
NEGROISM
NEGRONIS
NEMATOID
NEOLITHS
NEOTERIC
NEPOTISM
NEPOTIST
NERDIEST
NEREIDES
NERVIEST
NESTLIKE
NETTIEST
NETTLIER
NEURINES
NEURITES
NEURITIS
NEUROSAL
NEUROSIS
NEUROTIC
NEUTERED
NEUTRALS
NEUTRINO
NEUTRONS
NICTATES
NIGELLAS
NIOBATES
NIOBITES
NIRLIEST
NITERIES
NITRATED
NITRATES
NITRIDED
NITRIDES
NITRILES
NITRITES
NITROGEN
NOBBIEST
NODALISE
NOISETTE
NOMADIES
NOMADISE
NOMINATE
NONRATED
NORTENAS
NOSELITE
NOTARIAL
NOTARIES
NOTARISE
NOTARIZE
NOTCHIER
NOTICERS
NOTIFIER
NOTITIAE
NOURICES
NOVELIST
NUDITIES
OBEISANT
OBLIGANT
OBTAINED
OBTAINER
OCEANIDS
OESTRINS
OESTRIOL
OESTRONE
OILERIES
OILSTONE
OLEANDER
OLEARIAS
OLEASTER
OLEFIANT
OMITTERS
ONERIEST
ONSETTER

ONSTREAM
OPALINES
OPALISED
OPERANDS
OPERANTS
OPERATES
ORALISTS
ORANGEST
ORANGIER
ORANGISH
ORATIONS
ORATRESS
ORBITALS
ORBITERS
ORDAINED
ORDAINER
ORDINALS
ORDINANT
ORDINARS
ORDINATE
ORDINEES
ORGANDIE
ORGANICS
ORGANISE
ORGANISM
ORGANIST
ORGANITY
ORGANIZE
ORIENTAL
ORIENTED
ORIGANES
ORNATEST
ORNITHES
ORPIMENT
ORSEILLE
OSTIOLAR
OTALGIES
OTTERING
OUTCRIED
OUTCRIES
OUTDARES
OUTDRIVE
OUTEARNS
OUTFIRED
OUTFIRES
OUTHIRED
OUTHIRES
OUTLIERS
OUTLINER
OUTLINES
OUTRACES
OUTRAGED
OUTRAGES
OUTRAISE
OUTRANCE
OUTRATES
OUTREADS
OUTREIGN
OUTRIDER
OUTRIDES
OUTSIDER
OUTSNORE
OUTSTARE
OVERACTS
OVERCAST
OVEREATS
OVERHITS
OVERLAID
OVERLAIN
OVERLAND
OVERLATE
OVERLETS
OVERLIES
OVERNEAT
OVERNETS
OVERPAST
OVERSAIL
OVERSALT
OVERSPIN
OVERSTIR
OVERTIPS
OWLERIES
OXIDATES
OXTERING
OYSTRIGE
PADRONES
PAINTERS
PAINTIER
PAINTURE
PALATINE
PALTERED
PALTRIER
PANARIES
PANDORES
PANELIST
PANFRIES
PANNIERS
PANTILED
PANTILES
PANTINES
PANTLERS
PANTRIES
PARADISE
PARASITE
PARENTED
PARETICS
PARIETAL
PARIETES
PARISHEN
PARITIES
PARKIEST
PARODIES
PARODIST
PAROTIDS
PARSLIED
PARTIBLE
PARTICLE
PARTIERS
PARTINGS
PASTORED
PASTRIES
PATENTOR
PATIENTS
PATINATE
PATTERNS
PEARLIES
PEARLING
PEARLINS
PEARLITE
PECTINAL
PEDALIER
PEDERAST
PEDRAILS
PELORIAN
PELORIAS
PELORIES
PELTRIES
PENALISE
PENALITY
PENLITES
PENTHIAS
PENTISED
PENURIES
PERACIDS
PERAEONS
PERIANTH
PERIAPTS
PERIDOTS
PERIGEAN
PERIGONS
PERIOSTS
PERLITES
PERSAUNT
PERSICOT
PERSONAE
PERSONAL
PERTAINS
PETALINE
PETALOID
PETARIES
PETERING
PETIOLAR
PETRALES
PETROSAL
PETUNIAS
PHORATES
PIANISTE
PIASTERS
PIASTRES
PICRATES
PIEFORTS
PIEPLANT
PIERROTS
PILASTER
PILEATED
PIMENTOS
PINASTER
PINDAREE
PINTABLE
PIONEERS
PIVOTERS
PLAINEST
PLAISTER
PLAITERS
PLANETIC
PLANTERS
PLEASING
PLEATERS
PLEATING
PLEIADES
PLENTIES
PLOATING
POETISER
POETRIES
POINDERS
POINTELS
POINTERS
POINTIER
POISONER
POITRELS
POLARISE
POLESTAR
PONCIEST
PONDERAL
PONIARDS
PONTILES
POPERINS
PORINESS
PORKIEST
PORNIEST
PORTAGED
PORTAGES
PORTANCE
PORTASES
PORTENDS
PORTIEST
PORTOISE
POSTFIRE
POSTRACE
POTAGERS
POTLINES
POTSHARE
PRACTISE
PRAETORS
PRALINES
PRATINGS
PREASING
PREDATES
PREDIALS
PREEDITS
PRELATES
PRELATIC
PRENTICE
PRESIDIA
PRESSION
PRESTING
PRETRAIN
PRETRIAL
PRIESTED
PRIMATES
PRISONED
PRISONER
PRISTANE
PRISTINE
PRIVATES
PROBATES
PROLATES
PROLINES
PROMINES
PRONATED
PRONATES
PROPINES
PRORATES
PROSIEST
PROSTATE
PROSTIES
PROTASES
PROTEANS
PROTEASE
PROTEIDS
PROTEINS
PROTENDS
PROTENSE
PROVINES
PRUINOSE
PSORALEN
PTOMAINE
QUAINTER
QUANTISE
QUILTERS
QUOITERS
RABATINE
RABATOES
RABIDEST
RACINESS
RADIANCE
RADIANTS
RADIATED
RADIATES
RADICATE
RADICELS
RADICLES
RADIOMEN
RAGMENTS
RAGOUTED
RAGSTONE
RAGTIMES
RAILBEDS
RAIMENTS
RAINCOAT
RAINDATE
RAINIEST
RAINLESS
RAINOUTS
RAISONNE
RAMEKINS
RAMMIEST
RAMULOSE
RANCIDER
RANDIEST
RANGIEST
RANGOLIS
RANPIKES
RANSOMED
RANTINGS
RAPHIDES
RAPIDEST
RAREBITS
RARITIES
RASPIEST
RATANIES
RATHOLES
RATIFIES
RATIONAL
RATIONED
RATLINES
RATLINGS
RATOONED
RATSBANE
RATTEENS
RATTENED
RATTENER
RATTIEST
RATTINGS
RATTLIER
RATTLINE
RAUCLEST
RAVELING
RAVELINS
RAZEEING
REACTING
REACTION
REACTORS
READDING
READIEST
READINGS
READMITS
READOPTS
READORNS
READOUTS
READVISE
READYING
REAGENTS
REALIGNS
REALISED
REALISER
REALISES
REALISTS
REALIZED
REALIZES
REALLIED
REALLIES
REALLOTS
REALTERS
REALTIES
REALTIME
REALTORS
REAMENDS
REAMIEST
REANOINT
REARISEN
REARMOST
REARREST
REASCEND
REASCENT
REASONED
REASONER
REASSERT
REASSIGN
REASSORT
REASTIER
REASTING
REATTAIN
REBAITED
REBATERS
REBATING
REBATOES
REBEGINS
REBITTEN
RECANTED
RECISION
RECITALS
RECOUNTS
RECRATES
RECTIONS
RECUSANT
REDATING
REDBAITS
REDBONES
REDCOATS
REDDIEST
REDENIES
REDESIGN
REDIALED
REDIGEST
REDISTIL
REDLINES
REDOLENT
REDTAILS
REEDIEST
REEDINGS
REEFINGS
REELINGS
REENACTS
REENDOWS
REENLIST
REESTING
REFASTEN
REFLATED
REFLATES
REFLOATS
REFUSION
REFUTALS
REGAINED
REGAINER
REGALIAN
REGALIAS
REGALING
REGALISM
REGALIST
REGENTAL
REGIMENS
REGIMENT
REGIONAL
REGRANTS
REGRATES
REHANGED
REHINGES
REIGNITE
REINCITE
REINDICT
REINDUCT
REINETTE
REINFECT
REINFUSE
REINJECT
REINSERT
REINSMAN
REINSURE
REINTERS
REINVADE
REINVEST
REISTING
RELACING
RELATERS
RELATING
RELATION
RELATIVE
RELATORS
RELAXING
RELAXINS
RELAYING
RELEARNT
RELEVANT
RELIEVOS
RELIGION
RELISTED
RELOANED
RELOCATE
REMAILED
REMAINED
REMANETS
REMANIES
REMASTER
REMATING
REMEDIAL
REMEDIAT
REMIGATE
REMINTED
REMITTAL
REMOUNTS
RENAGUED
RENAGUES
RENAILED
RENEGADE
RENEGADO
RENEGATE
RENITENT
RENOVATE
RENTABLE
RENTIERS
REOBTAIN
REOILING
REORDAIN
REORIENT
REPAINTS
REPASTED
REPLANTS
REPLATED
REPLATES
REPOINTS
REPOSING
REPOSITS
REPTILES
REPUNITS
RERAILED
RERAISED
RESAILED
RESALUTE
RESAWING
RESAYING
RESEASON
RESEATED
RESEEING
RESEWING
RESHINED
RESIANCE
RESIANTS
RESIDENT
RESIDUAL
RESIFTED
RESIGNED
RESIGNER
RESINATA
RESINATE
RESINOID
RESINOUS
RESISTED
RESISTOR
RESITING
RESLATED
RESLATES
RESOLING
RESOLUTE
RESONANT
RESONATE
RESORCIN
RESOWING
RESPITED
RESTAGED
RESTAGES
RESTATED
RESTINGS
RESTORAL
RESTRAIN
RESTRING
RESUPINE
RETABLES
RETAILED
RETAILER
RETAILOR
RETAINED
RETAINER
RETAKERS
RETAKING
RETAPING
RETASTED
RETAXING
RETICENT
RETICLES
RETICULA
RETINALS
RETINITE
RETINOID
RETINOLS
RETINTED
RETINUED
RETINUES
RETINULA
RETIRALS
RETIRANT
RETITLES
RETRACES
RETRAINS
RETRAITS
RETRATES
RETREADS
RETREATS
RETRIALS
RETSINAS
RETUNDED
RETURNED
REUNIONS
REUNITED
REUNITES
REVENANT
REVOTING
REWIDENS
RHEOSTAT
RIANCIES
RIBSTONE
RIDDANCE
RIDEABLE
RIDGIEST
RIGATONI
RIGHTENS
RIGIDEST
RINDIEST
RINGLETS
RINGSTER
RINGTAWS
RINSABLE
RIOTRIES
RIPIENOS
RIPOSTED
RIPOSTES
RIPTIDES
RISPETTO
RITELESS
RITENUTO

RITORNEL
RIVULETS
ROADINGS
ROADSIDE
ROADSMEN
ROADSTER
ROAMINGS
ROARIEST
ROARINGS
ROASTERS
ROASTING
ROESTONE
ROGATION
ROILIEST
ROISTERS
ROLAMITE
ROMAINES
ROMANISE
ROMANTIC
RONDAVEL
RONDELET
RONTGENS
ROOMIEST
ROOPIEST
ROOTAGES
ROOTIEST
ROOTSIER
ROPINESS
RORTIEST
ROSELIKE
ROSETING
ROSINATE
ROSTELLA
ROSTRATE
ROSULATE
ROTARIES
ROTATING
ROTCHIES
ROTIFERS
ROTUNDED
ROTUNDER
ROULADES
ROULEAUS
ROUNCIES
ROUNDEST
ROUNDLET
ROUPIEST
ROUTEING
ROUTINES
ROWDIEST
ROWELING
ROYALETS
ROYALISE
ROYALIST
ROZETING
RUBEOLAS
RUBSTONE
RUDDIEST
RUDIMENT
RUELLIAS
RUINABLE
RUINATED
RUINATES
RUMINATE
RUNNIEST
RUNTIEST
RURALISE
RUSTABLE
SABERING
SABOTEUR
SABOTIER
SADIRONS
SAFETIED
SAGENITE
SAGINATE
SALARIED
SALERING
SALIENCE
SALIENTS
SALTERNS
SALTIERS
SALTINES
SALTIRES
SALTOING
SALUTERS
SANATIVE
SANDIEST
SANDIVER
SANDLIKE
SANDPILE
SANGAREE
SANGLIER
SANITATE
SANITIES
SANITISE
SANITIZE
SANSERIF
SAPONITE
SARCENET
SARCONET
SARDINES
SARDONIC
SARKIEST
SARMENTA
SARODIST
SARSENET
SATINETS
SATIRISE
SATIRIZE
SAUNTERS
SAUTEING
SAUTERNE
SAUTOIRE
SAVORING
SAXONITE
SCANTIER
SCANTIES
SCARIEST
SCARTING
SCATTIER
SCELERAT
SCENARIO
SCIENTER
SCIMETAR
SCLERITE
SCLEROID
SEABLITE
SEABORNE
SEAFRONT
SEAGOING
SEALINES
SEALINGS
SEAPORTS
SEARCING
SEARINGS
SEAROBIN
SEASONER
SEATINGS
SEATRAIN
SECONDER
SECRETIN
SECTATOR
SECTIONS
SECTORAL
SEDATING
SEDATION
SEDATIVE
SEDERUNT
SEDIMENT
SEDITION
SEETHING
SEGREANT
SEICENTO
SEIGNEUR
SEIGNIOR
SEIGNORY
SELECTOR
SELENIAN
SELENITE
SELICTAR
SEMANTIC
SEMANTRA
SEMINARS
SEMINARY
SEMINATE
SEMITARS
SEMITAUR
SEMITONE
SEMOLINA
SENARIES
SENARIUS
SENATORS
SENORITA
SENSORIA
SENTIENT
SENTIMOS
SENTINEL
SENTRIES
SEPALINE
SEPALOID
SEPTARIA
SERAFILE
SERAFINS
SERAGLIO
SERAPHIN
SERENADE
SERENATA
SERENATE
SERENING
SERENITY
SERGEANT
SERIATED
SERIATES
SERIATIM
SERICONS
SERINGAS
SERJEANT
SERMONED
SERMONET
SERMONIC
SEROTINE
SERRANID
SERRATED
SERRATES
SERVIENT
SERVITOR
SETIFORM
SETLINES
SEVERING
SEWERING
SEXTARII
SHAGREEN
SHEALING
SHEARING
SHEERING
SHEETING
SHERIATS
SHIRALEE
SHIREMAN
SHOALIER
SHORTAGE
SHORTIES
SIDELONG
SIDENOTE
SIDERATE
SIDEREAL
SIDERITE
SIDEROAD
SIGNALED
SIGNALER
SIGNETED
SIGNORAS
SIGNORES
SIGNORIA
SILENTER
SILOXANE
SINECURE
SINGABLE
SINISTER
SINNERED
SINTERED
SINUATED
SINUATES
SIRENIAN
SIRNAMED
SIRNAMES
SIRVENTE
SISTERED
SKEARING
SKEERING
SKIATRON
SKINCARE
SLAGGIER
SLAIRGED
SLAISTER
SLANGIER
SLATTERN
SLEAVING
SLEAZIER
SLEETIER
SLEETING
SLINTERS
SLOETREE
SLUTTIER
SMALTINE
SMARTIES
SMARTING
SMEARING
SNAGGIER
SNAGLIKE
SNAILERY
SNAILIER
SNAKEBIT
SNAPPIER
SNARIEST
SNARLIER
SNEAKIER
SNEERING
SNIFTIER
SNIRTLED
SNIRTLES
SNOOPIER
SNOOTIER
SNORTIER
SNOTTIER
SNOTTIES
SNOUTIER
SOARINGS
SOBERING
SOCIETAL
SODALITE
SOFTENER
SOLANDER
SOLANINE
SOLARISE
SOLARIST
SOLARIZE
SOLATING
SOLATION
SOLDIERS
SOLDIERY
SOLENOID
SOLERETS
SOLIDARE
SOLIDATE
SOLITARY
SOLLERET
SOMNIATE
SONATINE
SONDELIS
SONGSTER
SONICATE
SORBATES
SORDINES
SOREDIAL
SORICINE
SORORATE
SORPTIVE
SORRIEST
SORTABLE
SORTANCE
SOTERIAL
SOULDIER
SOURDINE
SOUTHERN
SOUVENIR
SPAIRGED
SPAWNIER
SPEARING
SPEERING
SPINETTE
SPIRALED
SPIRATED
SPIRITED
SPIRULAE
SPLINTER
SPOLIATE
SPONGIER
SPOONIER
SPORTIER
SPORTIVE
SPOTTIER
SPOUTIER
SPRAINED
SPREEING
SPRINTED
SQUAILER
SQUINTED
SQUINTER
SQUIREEN
SQUIRTED
STAINERS
STALKIER
STALLION
STANDERS
STANIELS
STANNITE
STARAGEN
STARINGS
STARKING
STARLIKE
STARLING
STARNIES
STARNING
STARNOSE
STARRIER
STARRING
STARTING
STARVING
STAUMREL
STEADIED
STEADIER
STEADIES
STEADILY
STEADING
STEALERS
STEALING
STEAMIER
STEAMING
STEANING
STEAPSIN
STEARAGE
STEARINE
STEARING
STEARINS
STEEDING
STEEKING
STEELIER
STEELING
STEEMING
STEENING
STEEPING
STEERAGE
STEERING
STEEVING
STEINBOK
STELLION
STENOTIC
STENTOUR
STERICAL
STERIGMA
STERLING
STERNAGE
STERNING
STERNITE
STEROIDS
STERVING
STICHERA
STILBENE
STILLIER
STILTIER
STINGERS
STINGIER
STINGRAY
STINKARD
STINKIER
STINTERS
STINTIER
STODGIER
STOITERS
STOLIDER
STONERAG
STONERAW
STONIEST
STORABLE
STORAGES
STOREMAN
STOREMEN
STORMIER
STOURIER
STOVAINE
STRADIOT
STRAFING
STRAIKED
STRAINED
STRAINER
STRAITED
STRAITEN
STRAITER
STRANDED
STRANDER
STRANGER
STRANGLE
STRATOSE
STRAUNGE
STRAWIER
STRAWING
STRAYING
STREAKED
STREAKER
STREAMED
STREAMER
STREIGNE
STREWAGE
STREWING
STRIATED
STRIATES
STRIDDEN
STRIDENT
STRIGATE
STRIGINE
STRIGOSE
STRINGED
STRINGER
STRINKLE
STROAMED
STROBILA
STROBILE
STRONGER
STRONTIA
STUDIERS
STUDLIER
STUPIDER
STURDIED
STURDIER
STURDIES
STURGEON
STURNINE
SUBTILER
SUITORED
SUIVANTE
SULTRIER
SUPINATE
SURETIED
SURLIEST
SURTITLE
SUTORIAL
SUTORIAN
SUZERAIN
SWANNIER
SWATHIER
SWEALING
SWEARING
SWEATIER
SWEATING
SWEETING
SYMITARE
SYNEDRIA
SYNERGIA
TABERING
TABINETS
TABLIERS
TABORERS
TABORETS
TABORINE
TABORING
TABORINS
TABRERES
TACONITE
TAENIATE
TAENIOID
TAGLIONI
TAILBONE
TAILERON
TAILORED
TAILRACE
TAINTURE
TAIVERED
TALCKIER
TALIPEDS
TALLIERS
TANAGERS
TANAISTE
TANDOORI
TANGIBLE
TANGIEST
TANGLERS
TANGLIER
TAPELINE
TAPERERS
TAPERING
TARDIEST
TARRIERS
TARRIEST
TARRINGS
TARSIERS
TARSIOID
TARSIPED
TARTANES
TARTIEST
TARTINES
TARTNESS
TARWEEDS
TASERING
TASTEVIN
TAUNTERS
TAURINES
TAVERING
TAVERNAS
TAVERNER
TAWDRIES
TAWERIES
TAWNIEST
TEAGLING
TEAMINGS
TEARDOWN
TEARIEST
TEARLESS
TEASELER
TEASINGS
TEAZLING
TEENAGER
TEENIEST
TEENSIER
TEENTIER
TEGMINAL
TELERANS
TELLARED
TELSONIC
TENAILLE
TENDRILS
TENDRONS
TENEBRIO
TENIASES
TENIASIS
TENONERS
TENORIST
TENORITE
TENSIBLE
TENTIEST
TENTIGOS
TENTORIA
TENTWISE
TENURIAL
TEOSINTE
TERATISM
TERATOID
TEREBRAS
TERMINAL
TERMINUS
TERMLIES
TERNIONS
TERPENIC
TERPINOL
TERRACES
TERRAINS
TERRANES
TERRAPIN
TERRASES
TERRINES

TERSIONS
TERTIALS
TERTIANS
TESSERAL
TESTATOR
TETANICS
TETANIES
TETANISE
TETANOID
TETRACID
TETRADIC
TETRAGON
TETRAXON
TETRONAL
THEELINS
THEORICS
THEORIES
THEORISE
THEORIST
THERIACS
THERIANS
THESAURI
THESPIAN
THIONATE
THIRTEEN
THORACES
THORITES
THORNIER
THREADEN
THREATEN
THRENODE
THROEING
TIDELAND
TIDERIPS
TIDESMAN
TIDESMEN
TIERCELS
TILERIES
TIMONEER
TINGLERS
TINKERED
TINKLERS
TINPLATE
TINSELED
TINSELRY
TINSTONE
TINWARES
TIRASSES
TIREDEST
TIRELESS
TIRESOME
TITANATE
TITANESS
TITRABLE
TITRATED
TITRATES
TOADLIKE
TOASTERS
TOASTIER
TOENAILS
TOKENISM
TOLERANT
TOLERATE
TOLEWARE
TONALITE
TONEARMS
TONETICS
TONGSTER
TONSILAR
TONSURED
TONSURES
TONTINER
TONTINES
TOPLINER
TOPLINES
TOPSIDER
TORMENTA
TORMINAL
TORNADES
TORNADIC
TORSADES
TORTOISE
TOTALING
TOTALISE
TOTALIZE
TOTIENTS
TOURNEYS
TOUSTIER
TOWERING
TOWLINES
TOWNIEST
TOWNLIER
TRACINGS
TRACTILE
TRACTION
TRADINGS
TRAGULES
TRAHISON
TRAILERS
TRAINEES
TRAINERS
TRAINMEN
TRAIPSED
TRAIPSES
TRAMELED
TRAMLINE
TRANECTS
TRANGLES
TRANNIES
TRANSECT
TRANSEPT
TRANSIRE
TRANSUDE
TRANSUME
TRANTERS
TRAPESED
TRAPLIKE
TRAPLINE
TRAPNEST
TRAPPOSE
TRASHIER
TRASHING
TRAVELED
TRAVERSE
TRAVISES
TRAVOISE
TREACLED
TREACLES
TREADERS
TREADING
TREADLED
TREADLER
TREADLES
TREAGUES
TREASONS
TREASURE
TREATERS
TREATIES
TREATING
TREATISE
TREELAWN
TREENAIL
TREFOILS
TREILLES
TRENAILS
TRENDIER
TRENDIES
TRENISES
TRENTALS
TREPANGS
TRESSING
TRIALLED
TRIANGLE
TRIAXONS
TRIAZOLE
TRIBADES
TRIBUNES
TRICORNE
TRIDARNS
TRIDENTS
TRIENTES
TRIGNESS
TRIGONAL
TRILBIES
TRILLOES
TRILOBES
TRINDLES
TRINGLES
TRINKETS
TRINODAL
TRIOLETS
TRIPEDAL
TRIPHASE
TRIPHONE
TRIPLANE
TRIPLIES
TRIPOSES
TRIPTANE
TRISCELE
TRISKELE
TRISOMES
TRISTATE
TRISTEZA
TRITIDES
TRITONES
TRIZONAL
TRIZONES
TROAKING
TROATING
TROELIES
TROLLIES
TROOLIES
TROPHIES
TROPINES
TROTLINE
TROUNCED
TROUNCES
TRUANTED
TRUDGEON
TSAREVNA
TSIGANES
TUBEROID
TURBANED
TURBINED
TURBINES
TURNIPED
TURNSOLE
TUTELARS
TUTORISE
TWANGERS
TWANGIER
TWEERING
TWENTIES
TWINTERS
TYRAMINE
TYROSINE
TZIGANES
UNAKITES
UNARISEN
UNBRASTE
UNCARTED
UNCRATED
UNCRATES
UNDERACT
UNDERAGE
UNDERATE
UNDERBIT
UNDEREAT
UNDERLET
UNDERLIT
UNDERSEA
UNDERSET
UNDERTAX
UNDERTOW
UNDERWIT
UNDESERT
UNDREAMT
UNEARTHS
UNEASIER
UNERASED
UNEROTIC
UNFAIRED
UNGEARED
UNHAIRED
UNHEARTS
UNITAGES
UNITARDS
UNITISED
UNIVERSE
UNLISTED
UNLOADER
UNMITERS
UNMITRED
UNMITRES
UNPAIRED
UNPARTED
UNPRAISE
UNPRIEST
UNRAISED
UNRENTED
UNREPAID
UNRESTED
UNRIPEST
UNRIVETS
UNROOTED
UNROTTED
UNSAILED
UNSEARED
UNSIFTED
UNSOILED
UNSORTED
UNSUITED
UNTAILED
UNTARRED
UNTENDER
UNTHREAD
UNTIDIER
UNTIDIES
UNTRACED
UNTRACES
UNTRADED
UNTREADS
UNVARIED
UNWATERS
UNWRITES
UPRAISED
URALITES
URANIDES
URANITES
URBANEST
URBANISE
URBANITE
UREDINES
UREDINIA
URETHANS
URINATED
URINATES
URODELAN
UTILISER
UTRICLES
VAIRIEST
VALETING
VALIDEST
VALORISE
VANITIED
VANITIES
VARIATED
VARIATES
VARIOLES
VAULTERS
VAUNTERS
VAUNTIER
VAURIENS
VEALIEST
VEERINGS
VEINLETS
VELARISE
VENATION
VENATORS
VENERATE
VENTAILE
VENTAILS
VENTIGES
VENTRALS
VENTROUS
VENTURED
VENTURIS
VERATRIN
VERDITES
VERONALS
VERTICAL
VERTIGOS
VESICANT
VESTIARY
VESTURAL
VETERANS
VIATORES
VIBRATES
VINEGARS
VINTAGED
VINTAGER
VINTAGES
VINTRIES
VIOLATED
VIOLATER
VIOLATES
VIOLENTS
VIRANDOS
VIRETOTS
VIRGATES
VIRTUOSE
VITAMERS
VITRAGES
VITREOUS
VITRINES
VOITURES
VOLARIES
VOLERIES
VOLITATE
VOMITERS
VOTARIES
WAISTERS
WAITRESS
WARBIEST
WARIMENT
WARINESS
WARTIEST
WARTIMES
WASTERED
WASTERIE
WASTRIES
WASTRIFE
WATERDOG
WATERERS
WATERING
WATERISH
WEARIEST
WEARINGS
WEIRDEST
WIDENERS
WINDORES
WINDROSE
WINTERED
WIRETAPS
WISTERIA
WORDIEST
WORMIEST
WORSENED
WORTHIES
WRASTING
WRESTING
WRONGEST
XERANSIS
XERANTIC
YEALINGS
YEARDING
YEARENDS
YEARLIES
YEARLING
YEASTIER
YEASTING
YERSINIA
ZELATORS
ZINCATES
ZORGITES

Additional High-probability Words

There are many 7- and 8-letter words that use likely combinations of letters but which don't appear in the 6-plus-1 and 7-plus-1 bonus sets. These are listed under the headings shown below, along with their criteria for inclusion.

Additional words – 1- and 2-point tiles

This section contains two alphabetical listings, one of 7-letter words and one of 8-letter words. Criteria for inclusion are that the words:

☆ are not included in the 6-plus-1 and 7-plus-1 bonus sets

☆ contain only the 1- and 2-point tiles ADEGILNORSTU

☆ contain no duplicates, except for A (up to 2 allowed), E (up to 3), I (up to 2) and O (up to 2). Note that multiple duplicate letters are allowed, as in DEITIES (2 E's and 2 I's) and GAINSAID (2 A's and 2 I's).

Additional words – 3- and 4-point tiles

This section contains two alphabetical listings, one of 7-letter words and one of 8-letter words. Criteria for inclusion are that the words:

☆ are not included in the 6-plus-1 and 7-plus-1 bonus sets

☆ contain any one of the 3- and 4-point tiles BCFHMPVWY. For ease of learning, the words containing any one of the tiles BCFHMPVWY have been grouped according to the tile contained – that is, all the B words are grouped together, then the C words, and so on

☆ otherwise contain only the 1- and 2-point tiles ADEGILNORSTU

☆ contain no duplicates, except for A (up to 2 allowed), E (up to 3), I (up to 2), O (up to 2). Note that multiple duplicate letters are allowed, as in ABIGAIL (2 A's and 2 I's) and ABNEGATE (2 A's and 2 E's).

ADDITIONAL BONUS WORDS (1 and 2 point tiles only)

7-letter words (1 and 2 point tiles only)

ADAGIOS ADULATE AENEOUS AEOLIAN AERATED AEROGEL AERUGOS AGAROSE AGATOID AGENDAS AGENTED AGISTOR AGNOSIA AGOUTAS AGOUTIS AGROUND AGUISED AIERIES AILANTO AILERON AIRDATE AIRLINE ALASTOR ALATION ALERION ALERTED ALEURON ALGESIA ALIENED ALIENEE ALIENER ALIENOR ALIUNDE ALOGIAS ALONGST ALSOONE ALTERED ANALOGS ANEARED ANGORAS ANGULAR ANTIAIR ANURIAS ARENOSE ARENOUS AREOLAE ARGALIS ARGANDS AROUSAL ARUGOLA ASTOUND ASTRAND ASTROID AUDIENT AUDINGS AUDITOR AUGENDS AUGITES AULNAGE AURATED AURATES AUREATE AURELIA AUREOLA

AUREOLE AUSTRAL AUTOING DALTONS DATURAS DAUTING DEALATE DEERLET DEGREES DEITIES DELAINE DELETES DELOUSE DELUGES DENGUES DENTURE DETENUE DETERGE DETINUE DIALING DIALIST DIALOGS DIARIAL DIARIAN DIARIST DIATRON DIETINE DIETING DIGITAL DIGLOTS DIGONAL DILATOR DILUENT DILUTEE DILUTOR DINITRO DIORITE DIRLING DISROOT DISTAIN DIURNAL DIURONS DOATING DOGATES DOGEATE DOILIES DOLINAS DOLOURS DONATOR DONGOLA DOOLEES DOOLIES DOTAGES DOUANES DOULEIA DOUSING DOUTING DRAGONS DRAGOON DRAUNTS DROGUES DROGUET DRONGOS DUALINS

DUALIST DUELERS DUOLOGS DUOTONE DURANTS DURGANS DURIONS DUSTING DUSTRAG EATAGES EDENTAL EDGIEST EDITING EDITION EGALITE EGESTED EGOTISE EIDOLON ELEGIES ELEGISE ELODEAS ELOINED ELOINER ELUATES ELUDERS ELUTION ENGORED ENOLASE ENTERED ERELONG ERODENT ERUDITE ESERINE ETAERIO ETAGERE ETALAGE ETIOLIN ETOURDI EUGENIA EUGENOL EUGLENA EULOGIA EUSTELE GADROON GALEATE GALIOTS GALOOTS GANOIDS GARDANT GARIALS GARLAND GAROTED GARUDAS GASTRAL GATEAUS GAUDIER GAUDIES GAULTER GAUNTED GEALOUS GELADAS GELATED GELDERS GELIDER

GENTEEL GENTLED GENTLER GENTOOS GEOIDAL GESTURE GIAOURS GIRASOL GIROSOL GIUSTED GLADIUS GLEETED GLENTED GLIADIN GLOATED GLOATER GLORIAS GLORIED GLOUTED GLUTAEI GOATEED GOATEES GOATIER GODETIA GODLIER GOETIES GOITRED GOLDARN GOLDEST GOLDIER GOLDURN GOLIARD GONADAL GONDOLA GONIDIA GOODIER GOODIES GOOIEST GOONDAS GOORALS GOOSIER GOURDES GOUTIER GRADATE GRADUAL GRANOLA GREENED GREENIE GREETED GREETES GRIESIE GROUNDS GROUSED GROUTED GRUELED GRUNTED GRUNTLE GUANASE GUARANI GUARDEE GUERITE GUESTED GUESTEN GUIDONS

GUILDER GUINEAS GUISARD GUITARS GULDENS GUSTIER GUTSIER IDOLISE IDOLIST IGNATIA IGNITED IGUANAS IGUANID INDIGOS INDOORS INDULTS INDUSIA INEDITA INGOTED INSULAE INSULAR INTRADA INTROLD INULASE INUTILE IODURET ISODONT LADINOS LADRONS LAETARE LAGERED LAGOONS LAGUNAS LAIDING LAIRAGE LANATED LANDAUS LANGUID LANGUOR LANGURS LANIARD LANUGOS LARDONS LARDOON LARIATS LATENED LATERAD LATIGOS LATINOS LATRIAS LAUDING LEAGUED LEAGUER LEAGUES LEDGERS LEDGIER LEGATED LEGATEE LEGATOR LEIDGER LENTOID LIAISON LIANOID LIGATED

LIGROIN LISTING LOADING LOGANIA LOGIONS LOGOUTS LOIDING LONGEST LOONIER LOOSING LORIOTS LOTIONS LOUNGED LOUNGER LOUNGES LOURING LOUSING LUNATED LUNGEES LUNGERS LURDANS LUSTING LUTINGS NADIRAL NARDOOS NATURAE NATURAL NAUTILI NEEDLER NEGATED NITRIDS NITRILS NODULAR NOODGES NOUGATS NOURSLE OARAGES ODONATE ODORANT ODORATE OILNUTS OILSEED OLEARIA OLIGIST OLOGIST ONDATRA ONEROUS OODLINS OORALIS OORIALS ORALIST ORATION ORDINAL OREGANO ORGIAST OROTUND ORTOLAN OTALGIA OUGLIED OULONGS OURALIS OURANGS OUTAGES OUTDARE

OUTDOER OUTDONE OUTDRAG OUTEARN OUTEDGE OUTGAIN OUTGOER OUTGOES OUTGONE OUTLAID OUTLAIN OUTLAND OUTLIED OUTLINE OUTRAGE OUTRANG OUTREAD OUTRIDE OUTRODE OUTSAIL OUTSANG OUTSOAR OUTSOLD RADIALS RADIANT RADIATE RADULAE RADULAS RAGLANS RAGOUTS RAGULED RAINOUT RANULAS RAOULIA READOUT REDEALT REDLEGS REGALED REGALIA REGLUED REGLUES REGOSOL REGULAE REGULOS RELATED RENAGUE RENEGED RENEGUE REOILED RETUNED RIALTOS RIDGILS RIDINGS RIGLINS RIOTOUS RITUALS ROILING RONEOED ROOTAGE ROSALIA ROSINOL ROTULAS ROTUNDA ROTUNDS

ROULADE RUGOLAS RULINGS RUNDLET RUSTING SAGOUIN SAGUARO SALIGOT SANDLOT SAOUARI SAURIAN SAUROID SAUTOIR SEALINE SETUALE SIALOID SIDLING SIENITE SIGANID SILOING SILTING SILURID SINGULT SIRLOIN SLADANG SLEDGER SLEETED SLIDING SOILING SOLARIA SOLATIA SOLITON SOLOING SONDAGE SOOGEED SOOGIED SOOLING SORDINI SORDINO SOULDAN STADIAL STEELED STILING STOOGED STOOLED STRIGIL SUDARIA SUDORAL SUIDIAN SUITING SULTANA SUNDIAL SURLOIN TAENIAE TAGUANS TAIGLED TAILARD TAILORS TALIONS TALONED TANDOOR TANGOED TARANDS TAUREAN

TEAGLED TEENAGE TEGULAE TEGULAR TELEDUS TENIOID TENURED TIARAED TIDINGS TIGROID TILINGS TINDALS TOLEDOS TOLIDIN TOLUENE TOLUIDE TOLUIDS TONGUED TORDION TORNADE TORNADO TOROIDS TORULAE TORULAS TORULIN TRAGULE TREADLE TREAGUE TRIAGED TRIDUAN TRISULA TROGONS TROILUS TROLAND TRUDGEN TRUNDLE TULADIS TUNDRAS TURDION ULNARIA ULTIONS UNALIST UNDEALT UNEAGER UNEDGES UNGILDS UNGIRDS UNIDEAL UNITAGE UNITARD UNLOADS UNLOOSE UNLORDS UNOILED UNREELS UNROOST UNROOTS UNSOLID UNSTAID UNTILED URANIAS URINALS URODELE

8-letter words (1 and 2 point tiles only)

ADRENALS ADULATES ADULATOR ADUSTING

AEROGELS AERONAUT AEROTONE AGENESIA

AGOUTIES AGRESTAL ALEURONE ALIASING

ALIENAGE ALNAGERS ANALOGUE ANGULATE

ANGULOSE ANTIDRUG ARAISING ARANEOUS

ARGENTAL ARGONAUT ARUGOLAS AUDITING

AUDITION AULNAGER AULNAGES AUREOLAE

AUREOLED AUTOGIRO DANEGELT DANGLERS

DARLINGS
DARTLING
DEAERATE
DEALATES
DEERLETS
DEGREASE
DELEGATE
DELETING
DELETION
DELOUSER
DELUSTER
DESIGNEE
DESIRING
DESOLATE
DETENUES
DETERGES
DIAGONAL
DIALINGS
DIALOGUE
DIASTRAL
DIGITALS
DILATING
DILATION
DILIGENT
DILUTEES
DILUTING
DILUTION
DILUTORS
DINGIEST
DISINURE
DISLOIGN
DISTRAIL
DIURNALS
DOATINGS
DOGEATES
DONATORS
DONGOLAS
DOORNAIL
DORISING
DRAGOONS
DRAILING
DROGUETS
DROILING
DRONGOES
DROOLING
DUOTONES
EASTLAND
EGLATERE
EGOITIES
EGOTISED
EILDINGS
ELEGISED
ELOIGNED
ELONGATE
ENDOSTEA
ENGAOLED
ENGIRDLE
ENGOULED
ENGUARDS
ENSEALED
ENSOULED
ENTOILED
ETALAGES
EUGENIAS
EUGENOLS
EUGLENAS
EULOGIAE
EULOGIAS
EULOGIES
EULOGISE
EULOGIST
GADROONS
GAIETIES
GAINSAID
GALEATED
GALENOID
GARDANTS
GARLANDS
GASOLENE
GASTRULA
GAUDIEST
GELIDEST
GENERALE
GENEROUS
GESTURED
GIRLONDS
GIRTLINE
GLADIATE
GLAIRINS
GLANDERS
GLEETIER
GLIADINE
GLIADINS
GLORIOSA
GLORIOUS
GODLIEST
GOITROUS
GOLDARNS
GOLDENER
GOLDIEST
GOLDURNS
GOLIARDS
GONADIAL
GONDOLAS
GONIDIAL
GOODIEST
GOODLIER
GOODSIRE
GRADATES
GRADUALS
GRADUATE
GRANOLAS
GRANULES
GREENEST
GREENLET
GRIDELIN
GRUNTLED
GRUNTLES
GUARANIS
GUARDANT
GUARDEES
GUARDIAN
GUDESIRE
GUERDONS
GUERIDON
GUERITES
GUILDERS
GUILTIER
IDOLATOR
IDONEOUS
IGNATIAS
IGNITORS
IGUANIDS
INDIGEST
INDIGOES
INDULGER
INDULGES
INDUSIAL
INOSITOL
INTARSIA
INTRIGUE
IODATING
IODATION
ISOGONAL
ISOLOGUE
LAAGERED
LANGUETS
LANGUORS
LANIARDS
LARDOONS
LARGANDO
LAUDATOR
LAUNDERS
LAUREATE
LEAGUERS
LEDGIEST
LEGATEES
LEGIONED
LEIDGERS
LEISURED
LIGATURE
LIGNEOUS
LIGNITES
LIGROINS
LINGERED
LINGERIE
LINGIEST
LINGUIST
LOADINGS
LOADSTAR
LOGANIAS
LOOSENED
LOOSENER
LOOTINGS
LORDINGS
LOUNDERS
LOUNGERS
LOURINGS
LUNARIST
LURDANES
LUSTERED
LUSTRING
NATURALS
NAUSEATE
NEEDLERS
NEEDLIER
NIDOROUS
NODULOSE
NOURSLED
NUTSEDGE
ODONATES
ODORANTS
OLIGURIA
ONDATRAS
OOGENIES
ORAGIOUS
ORDALIAN
OREGANOS
ORIGINAL
ORINASAL
ORTOLANS
OSTEOGEN
OTALGIAS
OUTDOERS
OUTDOING
OUTDRAGS
OUTEDGES
OUTGAINS
OUTGLARE
OUTGOERS
OUTGRINS
OUTLANDS
OUTLEARN
OUTLINED
OUTRANGE
OUTRINGS
RADIOING
RADULATE
RAILINGS
RAOULIAS
REEDLING
REGELATE
REGULATE
REGULINE
REGULISE
RELEASED
RELEGATE
RELENTED
RENEGUED
RENEGUES
RENESTED
RESEALED
RESENTED
RESIDING
RESILING
RESULTED
RETILING
RETOOLED
RIESLING
RIGADOON
RIGAUDON
RINGSIDE
RINGTAIL
RIOTINGS
RISOLUTO
RODEOING
ROISTING
ROOSTING
ROOTINGS
ROOTLING
ROSITING
ROTUNDAS
ROUNDELS
ROUNDLES
ROUSTING
ROUTINGS
RUNAGATE
RUNDALES
RUNDLETS
RUSTLING
SALADING
SALTANDO
SALUTING
SEEDLING
SEGOLATE
SELADANG
SELENATE
SELENIDE
SIALIDAN
SIDELINE
SIDELING
SIGNIEUR
SILUROID
SINGULAR
SLUDGIER
SOLIDAGO
SOLITUDE
SOLUTION
STEALAGE
STEGODON
STEREOED
STOOLING
STREELED
STRIDING
STURNOID
SUDATING
SUDATION
TAILARDS
TAILINGS
TANDOORS
TANGELOS
TEASELED
TEENAGED
TINGLIER
TIRELING
TOILINGS
TOLIDINE
TOLIDINS
TOLUENES
TOLUIDES
TOLUIDIN
TOOLINGS
TORDIONS
TORNADOS
TOROIDAL
TORULINS
TORULOSE
TOURINGS
TOUSLING
TRAILING
TROLANDS
TROULING
TRUDGENS
TRUNDLES
TURDIONS
ULSTERED
UNDERLIE
UNELATED
UNLEASED
UNLOOSED
UNREELED
UNSALTED
UNSEALED
UNSEATED
UNSEELED
UNSOLDER
URIDINES
URODELES
UROSTEGE
UTILIDOR
UTILISED

ADDITIONAL BONUS WORDS (with one 3 or 4 point tile)

7-letter words with one B and six 1–2 point tiles

ABALONE
ABASING
ABATING
ABATORS
ABATURE
ABELIAN
ABIDING
ABIGAIL
ABLATED
ABLATES
ABLATOR
ABLAUTS
ABLUENT
ABLUTED
ABODING
ABORTED
ABORTEE
ABOULIA
ABOUNDS
ABRADES
ABRAIDS
ABREGES
ABROADS
ABROSIA
ABSTAIN
ABULIAS
ABUSAGE
ABUSING
ABUSION
AEROBIA
AIBLINS
AIRBASE
AIRBOAT
ALBEDOS
ALBERGO
ALBINOS
ALBUGOS
ALGEBRA
ALIBIED
ANTBEAR
ANTBIRD
ANTIBUG
ARABINS
ARABISE
ARABLES
ARBLAST
ASTABLE
ATABEGS
ATABRIN
AUBADES
AUBERGE
AUDIBLE
BAAINGS
BADIOUS
BAGNIOS
BAGUETS
BAGUIOS
BAILING
BAILORS
BAILOUT
BAINITE
BAITING
BALADIN
BALDING
BALEENS
BALISTA
BANALER
BANDAGE
BANDARS
BANDEAU
BANDITS
BANDOGS
BANDORA
BANDORE
BANDROL
BANDURA
BAREGES
BARGAIN
BARGEES
BARONET
BARONGS
BARTEND
BASIDIA
BASILAR
BASINAL
BASTARD
BASTION
BATONED
BATOONS
BAUERAS
BAUSOND
BEADING
BEADLES
BEAGLED
BEAGLER
BEAGLES
BEANIES
BEASTIE
BEATING
BEDERAL
BEDOUIN
BEDRUGS
BEDSORE
BEDUINS
BEDUNGS
BEELINE
BEERAGE
BEETING
BEETLED
BEETLER
BEETLES
BEGILDS
BEGLADS
BEGONIA
BEGORED
BEGROAN
BEGUILE
BEGUINE
BEGUINS
BEIGELS
BEIGNET
BELATED
BELATES
BELAUDS
BELGARD
BELONGS
BELUGAS
BENDEES
BENDLET
BERATED
BERLINE
BESIEGE
BETAINE
BETIDES
BETREAD
BIASING
BIDINGS
BIGENER
BIGOTED
BILGIER
BILIANS
BILIOUS
BILSTED
BINGIES
BIODATA
BIOTINS
BIOTRON
BIRDING
BIRLING
BISNAGA
BITINGS
BITONAL
BLAGUES
BLEARED
BLEATED
BLEEDER
BLENDER
BLINDER
BLOATED
BLONDER
BLOUSED
BLOUSON
BLUDGER
BLUDGES
BLUDIER
BLUEING
BLUINGS
BLUNDER
BLUNGED
BLUNGER
BLUNGES
BLUNTED
BLUNTER
BLURTED
BOASTED
BOATIES
BOATING
BODEGAS
BODGERS
BODGIER
BODGIES
BODINGS
BODRAGS
BOGLAND
BOILING
BOINGED
BOLDEST
BOLEROS
BOLETES
BOLIDES
BOLOGNA
BONDAGE
BONDERS
BONESET
BONGOES
BONITAS
BONITOS
BONSOIR
BOODIES
BOODLER
BOODLES
BOOGERS
BOOGIED
BOOGIES
BOONIES
BOORDES
BOOSING
BOOSTED
BOOTEES
BOOTIES
BOOTING
BOOTLEG
BORATED
BOREENS
BORNEOL
BORNITE
BORONIA
BORSTAL
BOTARGO
BOTONEE
BOTULIN
BOUDOIR
BOUGETS
BOUGIES
BOULDER
BOULTED
BOULTER
BOURDON
BOURNES
BOUSIER
BOUSING
BOUTADE
BOUTONS
BRADOON
BRIDALS
BRIDING
BRIDOON
BRIGUED
BRIGUES
BRINDLE
BRINIES
BRISTOL
BROADEN

BROGANS
BROGUES
BROILED
BROLGAS
BRUITED
BRULOTS
BRUNTED
BRUTING
BUDGERO
BUDGERS
BUDGETS
BUDGIES
BUGLERS
BUGLETS
BUGSEED
BUILDER
BUISTED
BULGERS
BULGIER
BULGINE
BUNDIST
BUNDLER
BUNDLES
BUNGEES
BUNGIES
BUNGLED
BUNGLER
BUNGLES
BUNTALS
BURGEES
BURGEON
BURGLED
BURGLES
BURGOOS
BURIALS
BURITIS
BURLING
BURNIES
BURSEED
BURTONS
BUSGIRL
BUSLOAD
BUSTARD
BUSTING
BUSTLED
BUTANES
BUTANOL
BUTENES
BUTLING
DAGOBAS
DATABLE
DATABUS
DAUBERS
DAUBING
DEBATER
DEBITOR
DEBONER
DEBONES
DEBTEES
DEORBIT
DIABASE
DIABOLO
DINGBAT
DIOBOLS
DIRTBAG
DISTURB
DOBLONS
DOGBANE
DOGBOLT
DORBUGS
DOUBLER
DOUBLES
DOUBLET
DOUBTER
DURABLE
DUSTBIN
EARLOBE
EATABLE
EBONIES
EBONISE
EBONITE
EBRIATE
EBRIOSE
EDIBLES
ENABLED
ENABLER
ENABLES
ENGLOBE
ENGOBES
ENROBED
ENROBES
EOBIONT
GABIONS
GABOONS
GARBLED
GARBOIL
GETABLE
GILBERT
GLEBOUS
GLOBATE
GLOBINS
GLOBOID
GLOBOSE
GLOBOUS
GOBIIDS
GOBIOID
GOBLETS
GOBLINS
GOBONEE
GOOBERS
GUNBOAT
IGNOBLE
INBOARD
INBUILT
INBURST
INDABAS
INGLOBE
INORBED
LABIATE
LABORED
LABOURS
LABRIDS
LABROID
LIBATED
LIBIDOS
LOBATED
LOBINGS
LOOBIER
LOOBIES
NEBULAE
NEBULAR
NEBULAS
NEBULES
NIOBATE
NIOBITE
NIOBOUS
NOBLEST
NOSEBAG
NOTABLE
OBDURES
OBELION
OBELISE
OBITUAL
OBLASTI
OBLIGED
OBLIGEE
OBLIGER
OBLIGOR
OBLONGS
OBTAINS
OBTRUDE
OBTUNDS
OILBIRD
ONBOARD
ORBITAL
ORBITAS
ORBITED
OUABAIN
OUREBIS
OUTBARS
OUTBEGS
OUTBIDS
OUTBRAG
OUTBRED
RABATOS
RAGBOLT
RAILBUS
RATBAGS
REBADGE
REBATED
REBEGAN
REBEGIN
REBEGUN
REBLEND
REBOANT
REBUILD
REBUILT
REDBONE
REDBUGS
REDOUBT
RIBALDS
RIBAUDS
ROBALOS
ROBANDS
ROBINIA
ROBUSTA
ROSEBUD
ROUBLES
RUBATOS
RUBEOLA
RUBIGOS
RUBINES
RUGBIES
SABATON
SABEING
SALBAND
SANDBAG
SANDBAR
SANDBUR
SEABOOT
SEEABLE
SIBLING
SLURBAN
SOBERED
SOROBAN
STIBIAL
STIBINE
STROBIL
SUBADAR
SUBALAR
SUBAREA
SUBARID
SUBDEAN
SUBEDAR
SUBEDIT
SUBERIN
SUBGOAL
SUBIDEA
SUBLATE
SUBLINE
SUBORAL
SUBRING
SUBTEEN
SUEABLE
SUNBEAT
SUNBIRD
TABANID
TABARDS
TABERED
TABLEAU
TABLOID
TABOOED
TABORED
TABORIN
TABOULI
TABOURS
TABUING
TABULAE
TABULAR
TABULIS
TENABLE
TOOLBAG
TOOLBAR
TREBLED
TROUBLE
TUBAGES
TUBINGS
TULBANS
TUNABLE
TURBAND
TURBANS
TURBOND
UNBARES
UNBASED
UNBATED
UNBEARS
UNBEGET
UNBEGOT
UNBOLTS
UNBOOTS
UNBRAID
UNLOBED
UNROBES
UNSOBER
USEABLE

7-letter words with one C and six 1–2 point tiles

ACARIDS
ACAROID
ACATOUR
ACEDIAS
ACERATE
ACEROLA
ACETONE
ACIDIER
ACINOUS
ACNODES
ACONITE
ACORNED
ACRASIN
ACREAGE
ACRIDIN
ACROGEN
ACTINAL
ACTINIA
ACTIONS
AECIDIA
AGARICS
AGNATIC
AIDANCE
ALCADES
ALCAIDE
ALGINIC
ALICANT
ALOETIC
ANCILIA
ANELACE
ANGICOS
ANICUTS
ANLACES
ANOETIC
ANTACID
ANTICAR
ARCTANS
ARCTIID
ARCTOID
ARCUATE
ARGOTIC
ARNICAS
ASCARID
ASCAUNT
ASCIDIA
ASINICO
ASOCIAL
ATOCIAS
ATONICS
AUCTION
AUGITIC
AUTOCAR
CADGIER
CADRANS
CAERULE
CAESURA
CAGIEST
CAGOULE
CAGOULS
CALANDO
CALDERA
CALDRON
CALIGOS
CANALED
CANARDS
CANDELA
CANDORS
CANDOUR
CANGUES
CANTARS
CANTDOG
CANTLED
CANULAE
CANULAS
CARDIAE
CARDIAS
CARDOON
CARGOED
CARINAL
CARINAS
CARIOUS
CARLINS
CARLOAD
CARLOTS
CARNAGE
CARNALS
CAROLED
CAROLUS
CAROTID
CAROTIN
CARTAGE
CARTOON
CASEATE
CASTRAL
CATALOG
CATALOS
CATELOG
CATENAE
CATERED
CATIONS
CATLINS
CAUDATE
CAUDLES
CAUDRON
CAULDER
CAULINE
CAUSING
CAUTION
CEDRATE
CEDULAS
CEILING
CELADON
CELESTE
CELOSIA
CENSUAL
CENSURE
CENTAGE
CENTILE
CENTRED
CERATED
CEREOUS
CESTODE
CESURAE
CESURAL
CIDARIS
CIELING
CIERGES
CIGARET
CILIATE
CINEOLE
CINGULA
CIRSOID
CITADEL
CITOLAS
CITRINS
CITROUS
CLADIST
CLANGOR
CLARAIN
CLARINI
CLARINO
CLARION
CLARTED
CLAUTED
CLEANED
CLEANER
CLEANSE
CLEARED
CLEATED
CLERIDS
CLOISON
CLOSING
CLOSURE
CLOTURE
CLOURED
CLOUTED
CLOUTER
CLUDGIE
CLUEING
COAGENT
COAGULA
COAITAS
COALING
COALISE
COALTAR
COASTAL
COATING
CODEIAS
CODEINA
CODEINE
CODGERS
CODINGS
CODLING
CODLINS
COENURE
COENURI
COESITE
COGENER
COGITOS
COGNATE
COIGNED
COILING
COINAGE
COINTER
COITION
COLDEST
COLEADS
COLITIS
COLOGNE
COLONES
COLONUS
COLORED
COLOURS
COLUGOS
COLURES
CONARIA
CONATUS
CONDOES
CONDOLE
CONDORS
CONDUIT
CONGAED
CONGEAL
CONGEED
CONGEES
CONGIUS
CONGOES
CONGOUS
CONGREE
CONGRUE
CONIDIA
CONOIDS
CONSOLE
CONSORT
CONSULT
CONTOUR
CONTROL
COOINGS
COOLANT
COOLERS
COOLEST
COOLIES
COOLING
COONTIE
COOTIES
CORANTO
CORDAGE
CORDATE
CORDIAL
CORDITE
CORDONS
COREIGN
CORIOUS
CORNAGE
CORNEAL
CORNUAL
CORNUTE
CORNUTO
CORONAE
CORONAL
CORONAS
CORONEL
CORONET
CORONIS
CORTEGE
CORTILI
COSTARD
COTERIE
COTIDAL
COTINGA
COTLAND
COUGARS
COULDST
COULEES
COULOIR
COULTER
COUNSEL
COUNTED
COUNTER
COURAGE
COURANT
COURING
COURLAN
COURSED
COURTED
COUTILS
CRAALED
CRANAGE
CRANIAL
CREATED
CREDENT
CREEDAL
CREEING
CREELED
CREESED
CRENELS
CREOLES
CREOSOL
CRINOID
CROODLE
CROONED
CROTALA
CROTALS
CROTONS
CROUTON
CRUISIE
CRUSADO
CRUSIAN
CRUSTAL
CTENOID
CUDGELS
CUISINE
CUNDIES
CUNEATE
CURATED
CURDING
CURDLES
CURIOSA
CURLING
CURSING
CURTAIL
CURTAIN
CURTALS
CURTANA
CUSTARD
CUTESIE
CUTLINE
DACOITS
DATURIC
DEACONS
DECAGON
DECALOG
DECANAL
DECANES
DECEASE
DECEITS
DECIARE
DECILES
DECLARE
DECLINE
DECOLOR
DECREES
DECREET
DECURIA
DEICING
DEISTIC
DELICES
DELICTS
DELTAIC
DEONTIC
DESCALE
DEUCING
DIALECT
DICIEST
DICINGS
DICTIER
DICTING
DICTION
DINERIC
DIOCESE
DISCAGE
DISCANT
DISCING
DOCILER
DOCTORS
DOGCART
DOUCINE
DRACONE
DUCTILE
DUCTING
DULCETS
DULCIAN
DULCITE
DULCOSE
DULOTIC
DUNITIC
ECLOGUE
ECLOSED
ECOTONE
ECURIES
EDICTAL
EDUCATE
EDUCING
EDUCTOR
EGENCES
EIDETIC
EIDOLIC
EIRENIC
ELANCED

ELANCES ELECTED ELECTOR ELECTRO ELEGIAC ELOCUTE ENACTED ENCAGED ENCAGES ENCASED ENCLOSE ENCLOUD ENCODER ENCODES ENCORED ENERGIC ENGRACE ENLACED ENLACES ENRACED ENTICED ERECTED ERGODIC ERGOTIC ERICOID EROTICA ERUCTED ESCOTED ESCUAGE EUCAINE EUCLASE

EUCRITE EUGENIC GARCONS GARLICS GAUCIER GENERIC GENETIC GIRONIC GLACEED GLUCANS GLUCINA GLUCOSE GONADIC GONIDIC GREECES GRIECED GRIECES GUAIACS GUANACO ICTERID IDENTIC ILIACUS INCAGED INCEDES INCISAL INCISED INCISOR INCITED INCLUDE INCRUST INCUDAL

INCUDES INCUSED INDICES INDICTS INDUCES INDUCTS INLACED INOCULA IRACUND ISODICA ITALICS LACINIA LACTEAN LACTONE LACUNAE LACUNAR LACUNAS LACUNES LAICISE LATENCE LAUNCED LAUNCES LECTERN LECTION LECTURE LECTURN LEUCINE LEUCINS LEUCITE LICENSE LICENTE

LICTORS LINCTUS LINECUT LINGCOD LINOCUT LOCATED LOCATER LOCATOR LOCOING LOCUSTA LUCARNE LUCERNE LUCERNS LUCIDER LUCIGEN LUNATIC NACROUS NAUTICS NEGLECT NOCTUAS NOCTUID NOCTULE NODICAL NORITIC NOTICED NOTICER NOURICE NUCLEAR NUCLIDE OCARINA OCEANID

OCELOID OCELOTS OCREATE OCTAGON OCTANOL OCTROIS OCTUORS OCULARS OCULATE OCULIST ODONTIC OILCANS ONEIRIC OOLITIC ORACLED ORCINOL ORGANIC OSCULAR OSTRACA OTALGIC OUTRACE RACOONS RADICAL REACTED RECANED RECEDES RECENSE RECITED RECLEAN RECLINE RECLOSE

RECLUSE RECODES RECOUNT RECTION RECUILE RECULED RECULES RECUSAL RECUSED REDCOAT REDUCES REELECT REGENCE RELACED RESCUED RETICLE RICINUS RUCOLAS RUCTION SACATON SALICIN SARCOID SARONIC SATANIC SAUCIER SAUCING SCAGLIA SCALADE SCALADO SCALAGE SCALARE

SCALENE SCANDAL SCANDIA SCEDULE SCIARID SCIOLTO SCIURID SCOLION SCOOGED SCOOTED SCOUGED SCOURED SCOURGE SCROOGE SCROTAL SCROUGE SCUDLER SCUNGED SCUTAGE SECEDER SECLUDE SECONDE SECONDO SECRETE SECULAR SECURED SEDUCER SELENIC SILENCE SILICON SINICAL

SLICING SLUICED SOLACED SOLICIT SORITIC SOUCING SOURCED STOICAL SUCTION SUICIDE SURCOAT TACNODE TALCOUS TEDESCO TIERCED TIERCEL TINCALS TOUCANS TOURACO TRADUCE TREACLE TRIACID TRIADIC TRICLAD TROUNCE TRUCAGE TRUCIAL TRUCING TRUNCAL TUNICAE TUNICLE

TURACIN TURACOS ULCERED ULICONS UNACTED UNCAGED UNCAGES UNCARTS UNCASED UNCIALS UNCITED UNCLEAR UNCLOGS UNCLOSE UNCOILS UNCOLTS UNCORDS UNLACED UNLACES UNSCALE URACILS URCEOLI URGENCE URICASE UTRICLE

7-letter words with one F and six 1–2 point tiles

AEFAULD AFEARED AGRAFES AIRFOIL AIRLIFT ANTIFLU ANTIFUR AREFIED DAFTARS DAREFUL DEAFENS DEFANGS DEFAULT DEFENSE DEFIANT DEFILER DEFILES DEFINES DEFLATE DEFLEAS DEFOULS DEIFIER DEIFIES DERNFUL DIREFUL DOOFERS DRAFTEE EARFULS EASEFUL EDIFIER EDIFIES EELFARE EFTSOON ENDLEAF ENFILED ENFREED ENFREES

ENGULFS FADAISE FADEURS FADINGS FAGOTED FAGOTER FAILING FAILURE FAINTED FAIRIES FAIRING FAITORS FAITOUR FALDAGE FANEGAS FANTADS FANTAIL FANTEEG FANTODS FARDAGE FARINAS FATIGUE FAULTED FAUNIST FAUTORS FEAGUED FEAGUES FEASING FEATING FEATOUS FEATURE FEDARIE FEDERAL FEEDERS FEEDING FEEDLOT FEELERS

FEELING FEERING FEESING FEIGNED FEIGNER FEINTED FELINES FELTIER FENAGLE FERLIED FERTILE FERULAE FERULAS FERULED FERULES FESTOON FETIDER FEUDING FEUDIST FEUTRED FEUTRES FIATING FIAUNTS FIDEIST FIDGETS FIELDER FIGURAL FIGURED FIGURES FILAREE FILARIA FILETED FILIATE FILINGS FINALES FINALIS FINIALS

FINITES FIORINS FIREDOG FIRELIT FIRINGS FIRLOTS FISTING FISTULA FITLIER FLAGONS FLANEUR FLAUNES FLAUNTS FLEDGES FLEEING FLEERED FLEETED FLEETER FLENSER FLEURET FLEURON FLINDER FLINTED FLITING FLOATED FLOATER FLOODER FLOORED FLOOSIE FLOREAT FLORINS FLORIST FLORUIT FLOTAGE FLOURED FLOUSED FLOUTED

FLOUTER FLUATES FLUORID FLUORIN FLUTIER FLUTINA FLUTING FOALING FOETORS FOILING FOLDING FOLDOUT FOLIAGE FOLIATE FOLIOED FOLIOSE FOLIOUS FONDLER FONDUES FOODIES FOOLING FOOTAGE FOOTERS FOOTIER FOOTIES FOOTING FOOTLED FOOTLER FOOTLES FOOTRAS FOOTSIE FORAGED FORAGES FORDOES FORDONE FOREGUT FOREIGN

FORELEG FORELIE FORESEE FORGETS FORGOES FORGONE FORLANA FORLEND FORLENT FORLESE FORSAID FORSLOE FORTUNE FOUDRIE FOUGADE FOULARD FOULDER FOULING FOURGON FOUTERS FOUTRAS FOUTRED FOUTRES FRAGILE FREEING FRENULA FRESNEL FRIGATE FRIGOTS FROGLET FRONTAL FRONTED FRUITED FUELERS FUELING FUGATOS FULGENT

FULGORS FUNDIES FUNERAL FUNGALS FUNGOES FUNGOID FURANES FURIOSO FURLANA FURLING FURLONG FUROLES FUSAROL FUSTIAN FUSTING FUTILER GAINFUL GAUFERS GAUFRES GOLFERS GOOFIER GRAFTED GRIFTED GRUFTED GULFIER GUNFIRE INDRAFT INFAUST INFIDEL INFIELD INFOLDS INFULAE INFUSED INFUSER INGULFS INSOFAR LEAFAGE

LEAFIER LIFTING LOAFING NEEDFUL NIFTIES ODORFUL OFTENER OLEFINE ONEFOLD ONESELF OURSELF OUTFEEL OUTFIND OUTFIRE RAFALES RAGEFUL RATAFEE REEFING REFEEDS REFEELS REFILED REFLATE REFLOAT REFLOOD REFOOTS REFUELS REFUGED REFUGEE REFUGES REFUGIA REFUSAL REFUSED REFUTAL REFUTED REFUTES REIFIED RIFLING

ROLFING ROOFING RUNFLAT SEAFOOD SERFAGE SIFTING SNAFUED SOLFEGE SONGFUL STIFLED SULFATE SULFIDE SULFONE SUNROOF SURFING TAILFAN TEARFUL TEENFUL TENFOLD TINFOIL TINFULS TRIFOLD TURFING UNDEAFS UNFAIRS UNFILDE UNFILED UNFOLDS UNFOOLS UNFREED UNFREES UNIFIED UNIFIER UNIFIES UNROOFS UNSAFER

7-letter words with one H and six 1–2 point tiles

AGOROTH AIRHEAD AIRHOLE AIRTHED ALIGHTS ALRIGHT ALTHEAS ALTHORN ANETHOL ANGUISH ANOTHER ANTHOID ARGHANS ARSHEEN ATHANOR ATHEISE ATHEOUS ATISHOO AUTHORS DAHLIAS DAHOONS DARSHAN DASHEEN DASHING DEHORNS DELIGHT DHARNAS DHOORAS DHOOTIE DHOOTIS DHURNAS DIETHER DISHIER DISHING DISHORN DISHRAG DITHIOL DOGHOLE DOLTISH DOURAHS
DRAUGHT DRONISH DROUGHT DROUTHS DUSHING EARTHED EARTHEN ENHALOS ENOUGHS ENROUGH ENTHUSE ETHANES ETHANOL ETHENES GALOSHE GALUTHS GASAHOL GASOHOL GHARIAL GHASTED GHERAOS GHOSTED GHOULIE GIRLISH GIRTHED GNASHED GNATHAL GOATISH GOLDISH GOLOSHE GOODISH GOULASH GRAITHS GREENTH GRUSHIE GUARISH GUNSHOT GUSHIER HADRONS HAGDENS
HAGDONS HAGRIDE HAGRODE HAILIER HAILING HAIRDOS HAIRING HALITUS HALOGEN HALOIDS HALOING HANDOUT HANGARS HANGOUT HARLOTS HARTALS HAUDING HAULAGE HAULERS HAULIER HAULING HAUNTED HAUNTER HAUSING HEADAGE HEADIER HEADING HEADRIG HEARTED HEARTEN HEDERAL HEDGERS HEDGIER HEEDERS HEEDING HEELERS HEELING HEGARIS HEGIRAS HEILING
HEINIES HEINOUS HEIRING HEISTED HEREDES HERNIAE HERNIAL HEROINE HEROISE HEROONS HETAERA HETAIRA HIDAGES HIDALGA HIDALGO HIDEOUS HIDEOUT HIDINGS HIDLING HIDLINS HILDING HILTING HINDGUT HIRAGES HIREAGE HIRINGS HIRLING HIRSLED HIRUDIN HISTING HISTOID HISTRIO HOAGIES HOARING HOARSEN HOASTED HOGNOSE HOGNUTS HOGTIED HOGTIES
HOISING HOLARDS HOLDING HOLDOUT HOLINGS HONORED HONOREE HONOURS HOODIER HOODIES HOODING HOOLIER HOOTIER HOOTING HORDEIN HORNITO HORNLET HOSTAGE HOTDOGS HOTLINE HOTRODS HOUDANS HOUSIER HOUSING HOUTING HUITAIN HUNGERS HURDLES HURLIES HURLING HURTING HURTLED HUSTLED INHALED INHALER INHALES INHAULS INHAUST INSIGHT INSOOTH
INTHRAL LAIGHER LARGISH LATHEES LAUGHED LAUGHER LEASHED LEGHORN LENGTHS LETHEAN LETHEES LETHIED LEUGHEN LIGHTED LIGHTER LITHIAS LITHING LITHOED LITHOID LOATHED LONGISH LOUDISH LOUTISH LUSHIER LUSHING LUTHERN LUTHIER NAUGHTS NEIGHED NEOLITH NILGHAI NILGHAU NOIRISH NORTHED NOUGHTS NOURISH NURAGHE NURAGHI NURHAGS OGREISH
ONSHORE OOLITHS ORTHIAN OUGHTED OUTHEAR OUTHIRE OUTLASH RAGHEAD REHEELS REHINGE REHOUSE RELIGHT RESHONE RHODOUS RIGHTED RIGHTOS ROGUISH ROINISH ROUGHED ROUGHEN ROUGHIE ROUTHIE RUNTISH RUSHING SAHUARO SANDHOG SEETHED SEETHER SENHORA SHADING SHAITAN SHARIAT SHAULED SHEALED SHEELED SHEENED SHEENIE SHEERED SHEETED SHEETER
SHIELED SHINDIG SHITING SHOALED SHOOGIE SHOOGLE SHOOING SHOOLED SHORTIA SHOTGUN SHRINAL SHULING SHUTING SIGHTED SITHING SLOTHED SOOTHED SOREHON SOUGHED TAHINAS TAHINIS TEUGHER THALIAN THANAGE THEELIN THEINES THENAGE THEOLOG THEREON THEROID THONDER THONGED THORIAS THORNED THORONS THOUING THRANGS THRONED THRONGS THULIAS
THUNDER TIGRISH TOADISH TOEHOLD TOESHOE TOHEROA TOHUNGA TOUGHED TOUGHEN TOUGHER TOUGHIE TROUGHS TUGHRAS TUNDISH TUSHING UNDIGHT UNEARTH UNGIRTH UNHAIRS UNHEADS UNHEALS UNHEART UNHELED UNHELES UNHOARD UNHOODS UNHORSE UNLEASH UNRIGHT UNSHALE UNSHOED UNSHOOT UNSIGHT URETHAN UROLITH USHERED

7-letter words with one M and six 1–2 point tiles

ADENOMA ADMIRAL AEMULED AEMULES AGAMETE AGAMIDS AGAMOID AGAMOUS AGENDUM AGNAMED AGNAMES AIRMAIL AIRTIME ALAMODE ALAMORT ALARMED ALARUMS ALMAINS ALMONDS ALMONER ALMUDES ALODIUM ALUMINA ALUMINS ALUMNAE AMADOUS AMATEUR AMATING AMATION
AMATOLS AMELIAS AMENAGE AMENDER AMIDASE AMIDINE AMIDINS AMIDOLS AMIDONE AMILDAR AMIRATE AMONGST AMORANT AMORINI AMORINO AMORIST AMOROSA AMOROUS AMOTION AMOUNTS AMREETA AMRITAS AMULETS AMUSING ANGIOMA ANIMALS ANIMATO ANIMIST ANOSMIA
ANTRUMS ARAMIDS ARMLOAD ARTSMAN ATRIUMS AUGMENT AUMAILS AUTOMAN AUTOMEN DAIMIOS DAIMONS DAMAGER DAMAGES DAMOSEL DEEMING DEGAMES DEGAMIS DEGERMS DELIMES DELIMIT DEMAINE DEMEANE DEMENTI DEMERGE DEMERIT DEMERSE DEMESNE DEMETON DEMOTES
DEMOUNT DEMURES DIAGRAM DIAMINE DIAMINS DIATOMS DIMETER DIMOUTS DIORAMA DIORISM DISLIMN DOGMATA DOLMANS DOMAINS DOMATIA DOMINEE DOMINIE DOMINOS DOOMIER DOOMING DOORMAN DOORMAT DOORMEN DORMANT DORMINS DROMONS DROOMES DRUMLIN DUALISM
DUMAIST DURMAST DUSTMAN EARLDOM EDEMATA ELEMENT ELOGIUM EMAILED EMENDER EMERALD EMERGED EMERGES EMERIED EMERITA EMERITI EMERODS EMEROID EMERSED EMETINE EMEUTES EMIRATE EMONGES EMOTING EMOTION EMULATE EMULGED EMULGES EMULING EMULSIN
EMULSOR EMUNGED EMUNGES EMURING ENAMELS ENAMOUR ENARMED ENDGAME ENGLOOM ENTAMED EREMITE ERMELIN ERODIUM EROTEMA EROTEME EUDEMON GADSMAN GAMELAN GAMETAL GAMETES GATEMEN GAUMIER GEMOTES GENOMES GEOMANT GERMANE GLAMORS GLAMOUR GLAUMED
GLEAMED GLEAMER GLEEMAN GLEEMEN GLIOMAS GLOMERA GLOOMED GOMERAL GOMEREL GOMERIL GOMUTIS GOMUTOS GOODMAN GOODMEN GORMAND GOURAMI GOURMET GRANDAM GRANDMA GREMIAL GROOMED GRUMOSE GUDEMAN GUDEMEN GUMTREE GUNROOM GURAMIS IDOLISM IMAGINE
IMAGIST IMAGOES INDIUMS INTIMAL INTIMAS IONIUMS IONOMER ISODOMA ISOGRAM ITEMING ITEMISE LADANUM LAMETER LAMIGER LAMINAR LAMINAS LEADMAN LEADMEN LEGITIM LEGROOM LEGUMES LEGUMIN LEMONED LEMURES LIGNUMS LIMEADE LIMINGS LIMITED LIMITER
LIONISM LOAMIER LOAMING LOOMING LORDOMA LUMINED LUMINES MADEIRA MADLING MADRONA MADRONE MADRONO MADUROS MAGIANS MAGNETO MAIDANS MAIDING MAILING MAINORS MAINOUR MALAISE MALATES MALEATE MALGRED MALISON MALODOR MALTASE MANAGED MANAGER

MANAGES MANATIS MANDIRA MANDOLA MANDORA MANDRIL MANEGED MANEGES MANGALS MANGOES MANGOLD MANILAS MANITOS MANITOU MANITUS MANOAOS MANSARD MANTIDS MANTRAS MANTUAS MANUALS MANURES MARAUDS MARENGO MARGOSA MARINAS MARITAL MARLINS MAROONS MARTIAL MARTIAN MARTINI MASTOID MATADOR MATILDA MATINAL MATSURI MATURED MAUDLIN MAUGRED MAUGRES

MAULERS MAULGRE MAULING MEALIER MEALIES MEANDER MEASLED MEATIER MEDALET MEDIATE MEDUSAE MEDUSAL MEERING MEETERS MEETING MEGARAD MEGARON MEGATON MELANGE MELANOS MELDERS MELODIA MELOIDS MELTAGE MELTIER MENAGED MENAGES MENDIGO MENEERS MENSUAL MENTEES MEOUING MERITED MESELED METAGES METALED METERED MEUSING MIAOUED MIAULED MIDAIRS

MIDGETS MIDGUTS MIDIRON MIDLEGS MIDLINE MIDSOLE MIGRATE MILADIS MILAGES MILDEST MILEAGE MILIEUS MILITAR MILORDS MILREIS MILTIER MILTING MINGIER MINORED MINUTED MINUTIA MISDIAL MISDIET MISEDIT MISLAID MISLAIN MISRULE MISTING MISTLED MISTOLD MISTRAL MITERED MITOGEN MOATING MODELER MODERNE MODIOLI MODULAR MODULES MOGULED MOIDORE

MOILING MOINEAU MOLDIER MOLDING MOLERAT MOLINET MONADAL MONARDA MONAULS MONDIAL MONGOES MONGOLS MONGREL MONIALS MONILIA MONITOR MONTAGE MONTERO MONTURE MOODIER MOODIES MOOLIES MOOLING MOONIER MOONLET MOONLIT MOORAGE MOORING MOOTING MORDANT MORDENT MORENDO MORGANS MORGUES MORIONS MORLING MORTALS MORULAE MORULAS MOTIONS MOTORED

MOULAGE MOULDER MOULINS MOULTED MOULTEN MOULTER MOUNTED MOUNTER MOUSIER MOUSING MOUSLED MOUTANS MOUTONS MUDGERS MUDIRIA MUISTED MULETAS MUNITED MURAENA MURAGES MURENAS MURGEON MURIATE MURLAIN MURLANS MURLING MURLINS MUSTANG MUSTARD MUSTING MUTAGEN MUTANDA MUTINED NATRIUM NEMORAL NEUROMA NIMIOUS NIMRODS NORMALS NOSTRUM NOTAEUM

NUMERAL NUTMEGS OARSMAN OATMEAL OEDEMAS OENOMEL OGREISM OINOMEL OMELETS OMINOUS ONETIME ORALISM ORGANUM ORIGAMI ORMOLUS OSMOLAR OSMUNDA OSTEOMA OUTMANS OUTMODE OUTNAME RADIUMS RAGMANS RAGTIME RAILMAN RAMEOUS RAMILIE RAMTILS RANDOMS READMIT REAMEND REDEEMS REEDMAN REEDMEN REELMAN REELMEN REGIMEN REGMATA REIMAGE RELUMED RELUMES

REMANET REMATED REMEDES REMEETS REMODEL REMOULD REMOUNT REMUAGE REMUDAS RENAMED RESUMED RETIMED RIMLAND ROADMAN ROADMEN ROAMING RODSMAN ROMAGES ROMANOS ROMAUNT ROOMIES ROOMING ROUMING RUMINAL SAGAMEN SALAMON SAMURAI SANGOMA SANTIMI SEAMAID SEEDMEN SEGMENT SERUMAL SIAMANG SIGMOID SIMILAR SIMILOR SIMITAR SIMULAR SLIMIER SLIMING

SLOOMED SMARAGD SMELTED SMIDGIN SMILING SMITING SMOILED SMOORED SMOOTED SMUDGER SOLANUM SOLIDUM SOMEONE SOMITAL SOMNIAL SOOMING SOUMING STADIUM STAMINA STAMNOI STARDOM STEEMED STIGMAL STIMIED STIMING STIMULI STROMAL SUMATRA SUNROOM SURAMIN SURNAME TAEDIUM TALMUDS TAMALES TAMANDU TAMANUS TAMARIN TAMARIS TANGRAM TEAROOM TEDIUMS

TEEMERS TEEMING TEGUMEN TELEMEN TELOMES TIMARAU TIMIDER TIMINGS TINAMOU TONEARM TOOLMAN TOOLMEN TOOMING TORMINA TOURISM TRANGAM TRAUMAS TREMOLO TROMINO TRUEMAN TRUEMEN TSARDOM TSUNAMI TUMORAL TURMOIL ULTIMAS UNAIMED UNLIMED UNLIMES UNMATED UNMETED UNMOLDS UNMOORS UNMORAL UNSMART UNTAMED UNTRIMS URAEMIA URANISM UROSOME

7-letter words with one P and six 1–2 point tiles

ADAPTOR ADIPOSE ADIPOUS ADOPTEE AIRGAPS AIRPOST AIRSTOP ALEPINE ALPEENS ALPINES ANOPIAS ANOPSIA APNOEAL APNOEAS APODOUS APOGEAL APOGEAN APOGEES APOLOGS APOLUNE APORIAS APOSTIL APRONED APSIDAL APTERIA ASPERGE ASPIDIA ASPIRIN ASPREAD ASPROUT

ATROPIA ATROPIN DALAPON DAPSONE DEEPENS DEEPEST DEEPIES DELAPSE DELOPES DEPAINT DEPLANE DEPLETE DEPLORE DEPONES DEPOSAL DEPOSER DEPUTES DESPITE DESPOIL DIAPASE DIAPIRS DIPLOES DIPLONS DIPLONT DIPOLAR DIPOLES DISPART DISPORT DISPUTE DISRUPT

DOGNAPS DOPANTS DOPINGS DROPOUT DRUPELS DUPIONS DUPLETS DUPLIES DUSTPAN EARPLUG EELPOUT ELAPINE ELAPSED ELOPERS ELOPING ENSTEEP EPAULES EPAULET EPEEIST EPEIRID EPERDUE EPERGNE EPIDOTE EPIGEAL EPIGEAN EPIGENE EPIGONE EPIGONI EPILATE EPINAOI

EPISODE EPUISEE ERUPTED ESPANOL ESTREPE EUPLOID EUPNEAS EUPNOEA GALIPOT GALOPED GALOPIN GAUPERS GESTAPO GILPIES GIPSIED GLOOPED GLUEPOT GOOPIER GOPURAS GOSPORT GRANDPA GRAUPEL GROUPED GROUPIE GULPERS GULPIER GUNPORT IGARAPE INGROUP INPOURS

LAPDOGS LAPSANG LEEPING LEIPOAS LEOPARD LEPORID LEPROSE LEPROUS LEPTONS LINEUPS LIPIDES LIPOIDS LISPING LISPUND LOOPERS LOOPIER LOOPING LOUPING LUPANAR LUPINES NAGAPIE NAPOOED NAUPLII NOTEPAD NUPTIAL OEDIPAL OPALINE OPENEST OPERAND OPERANT

OPEROSE OPIATED OPIOIDS OPTIONS OPULENT OPUNTIA OROPESA OUTDROP OUTLEAP OUTPEER OUTPLAN OUTPLOD OUTROPE OUTSPAN PADANGS PADNAGS PADRONE PADRONI PAENULA PAESANI PAESANO PAGEANT PAGINAL PAGODAS PAGURID PAIGLES PAINTED PAIRIAL PAIRING PAISANO

PALADIN PALAGIS PALATED PALATES PANDARS PANDITS PANDOOR PANDORA PANDORE PANDOUR PANDURA PANELED PARADES PARADOS PARAGES PARAGON PARANGS PARASOL PARDALE PARDALS PARDONS PARIALS PARIANS PARISON PARLOUS PARODOI PARODOS PAROLED PAROLEE PAROTID

PAROTIS PARTANS PARTIAL PARULIS PASTINA PATINAE PATINAS PATINED PATRIAL PATROLS PATROON PATULIN PAULINS PAUSING PEARLED PEARLIN PEASING PEDALOS PEDLERS PEELERS PEELING PEENGED PEENGES PEERAGE PEERIES PEERING PEISING PELAGES PELOIDS PELORIA

PELORUS PENLITE PENSILE PENTODE PENTOSE PEONAGE PERAEON PERDUES PEREGAL PEREION PERGOLA PERIDIA PERIGEE PERIGON PERILED PERINEA PERLITE PERLOUS PERSUED PERTUSE PERUSED PESTLED PETALED PETERED PETIOLE PETUNIA PIANIST PIARIST PIDGEON PIDGINS

PIERAGE PIERIDS PIEROGI PIETIES PIGNOLI PIGNORA PIGNUTS PIGOUTS PIGSNIE PIGTAIL PILEATE PILEOUS PILINGS PILOTED PILOTIS PINATAS PINDARI PINEALS PINGUID PINITOL PINTADA PINTADO PINTAIL PIONEER PIRAGUA PIRANAS PIROGEN PIROGUE PITARAS PITURIS PLAGUED PLAGUER PLAGUES PLAINED PLAINER PLAINTS PLAITED PLANATE
PLANTAR PLANTAS PLANTED PLASTID PLATANE PLATANS PLATEAU PLATINA PLATOON PLAUDIT PLEADER PLEASED PLEATED PLEDGEE PLEDGER PLEDGES PLEDGET PLEDGOR PLEURAE PLEURON PLOATED PLONGED PLONGES PLOSION PLOUTER PLUNDER PLUNGED PLUNGER PLUNGES PLUSAGE PLUSING PLUTONS PODAGRA PODESTA PODGIER POESIED POGONIA POINADO
POINDER POINTED POINTEL POINTER POISING POLARON POLENTA POLINGS POLOIST POLONIE PONDAGE PONGEES PONGIDS PONGIER PONGOES PONIARD PONTAGE PONTILE PONTILS POODLES POOLING POOTING PORGIES PORTAGE PORTALS PORTEND PORTION PORTOUS POSAUNE POSITON POSTAGE POSTEEN POTAGER POTAGES POTEENS POTGUNS POTIONS POTLINE
POUDERS POUDRES POULARD POULDER POULDRE POULTER POUNDAL POURIES POURING POUTIER POUTING PRALINE PREAGED PREANAL PREEING PREENED PRELUDE PRELUDI PRENTED PRESAGE PRETEEN PRETEND PRIDIAN PRIDING PRISING PROINED PROLANS PROLEGS PROLINE PROLING PROLOGS PROLONG PRONAOI PRONAOS PRONATE PRONGED PRONOTA PROTEAN
PROTEGE PROTEIN PROTEND PROTONS PROULED PRUDENT PRUINAS PRUNTED PTERION PUDGIER PUERILE PUERING PUGAREE PUGREES PULDRON PULINGS PULSANT PULSATE PULSING PULSION PULTANS PULTONS PULTOON PUNDITS PUNGLED PUNGLES PUNTEES PURANAS PURITAN PURLINE PURLING PURLINS PURLOIN PURSING PUSLING PUTEALS PUTLOGS RAGTOPS
REPANEL REPLEAD REPLETE REPLIED REPOINT REPONED REPOSED REPTILE REPUGNS REPULSE REPUTED REPUTES RIPIENO RISPING ROOPING ROUPING SALPIAN SALTPAN SANDPIT SEEDLIP SEEPAGE SEEPIER SEEPING SEPALED SERPIGO SINOPIA SLEEPER SLIPING SLIPOUT SLOPING SLURPED SNEAPED SNOOPED SOAPING SOLIPED SOOPING SOPRANI SOPRANO
SOUPIER SOUPING SOUPLED SPADING SPAEING SPANGED SPANIEL SPAROID SPARTAN SPATIAL SPATULA SPATULE SPEANED SPEEDER SPEELED SPEELER SPEERED SPEILED SPELDER SPELEAN SPIEGEL SPIELED SPILING SPINAGE SPINOUT SPINULA SPINULE SPIRING SPIROID SPIRULA SPITING SPLENIA SPLENII SPLODGE SPLURGE SPOILED SPONDEE SPONGED
SPOOLED SPOOLER SPOONED SPOORED SPOROID SPORULE SPUEING STANDUP STEEPED STEEPEN STEEPER STEEPLE STOOPED STUPING SUNTRAP SUPERED TADPOLE TAIPANS TALIPED TAPALOS TAPUING TARPANS TAUPIES TERPENE TILAPIA TIPULAS TONEPAD TOPLINE TOPSAIL TOPSOIL TORPEDO TORPIDS TOUPEES TRAPANS TRIPODS TRIPOLI TROOPED TROPINE
TROUPED TURNIPS UNIPEDS UNIPODS UNPAGED UNPILED UNPILES UNPLAIT UNPOSED UNSPIDE UNSPIED UNSPILT UNSPLIT UNSTRAP UNSTRIP UPDARTS UPDATES UPDRAGS UPGIRDS UPGRADE UPLANDS UPLEADS UPLEANS UPLEANT UPLOADS UPRISAL UPROOTS UPSILON UPSTAGE UPSTAIR UPSTAND UPSTOOD UPTRAIN UPTREND UROPODS UTOPIAN UTOPIAS

7-letter words with one V and six 1–2 point tiles

ADVENES ADVISEE ADVISOR ALEVINS ANDVILE ANVILED AVAILED AVAILES AVALING AVAUNTS AVENGED AVENGER AVENGES AVENTRE AVENUES AVERAGE AVERTED AVIATED AVIATES AVIATOR AVIDINS AVISING AVODIRE AVOIDER AVOURES AVULSED DATIVAL DEAVING DEEVING DELEAVE DELVERS DESERVE DEVALUE
DEVEINS DEVIANT DEVIATE DEVILET DEVIOUS DEVISEE DEVOTEE DEVOTES DEVOURS DILUVIA DIVERGE DIVINER DIVINES DIVINGS DIVISOR DIVULGE DOGVANE DOVELET DRIVELS DRIVING ELATIVE ELEVATE ELEVENS ELEVONS ELUSIVE ENDIVES ENERVED ENERVES ENGRAVE ENSLAVE ENVAULT ENVIOUS EVADING
EVANGEL EVASION EVENERS EVENEST EVENTED EVENTER EVERTED EVIDENT EVIRATE EVITING EVOLUES EVOLUTE EVULSED GARVIES GAVELED GAVIALS GENEVAS GLAIVED GLAIVES GLEAVES GLOVERS GRAVIDA GRAVIES GREAVED GREAVES GRIEVED GROOVED GROOVES GROVELS GROVETS INVALID INVIOUS INVITAL
INVITED INVITEE INVITES ISOGRIV IVORIED IVORIST LARVATE LAVAGES LEAVENS LEVATOR LEVERED LEVERET LIVENED LIVIDER LIVIERS LIVINGS LOAVING LOUVERS LOUVRED LOUVRES LOVAGES LOVERED LOVINGS NAEVOID NAIVETE NAIVIST NAVAIDS NERVATE NERVOUS NERVULE NIVEOUS NOVALIA OLIVINE
OUTGAVE OUTGIVE OUTLIVE OUTLOVE OUTRAVE OUTVIED OUTVIES OUVERTE OUVRAGE OVARIAL OVARIAN OVATING OVATION OVATORS OVERAGE OVERATE OVERDOG OVERDUE OVEREAT OVERGET OVERGOT OVERING OVERLET OVERNET OVOIDAL OVULATE RAVAGED RAVAGES RAVELED RAVELIN RAVENED RAVIOLI REAVAIL
REEVING REGIVEN REIVING RELEVES REVALUE REVELED REVENGE REVENUE REVEUSE REVOTED RIEVING RILIEVO RIVAGES RIVETED RIVLINS RIVULET SALVAGE SALVETE SALVOED SAVAGED SAVAGER SAVARIN SAVIOUR SELVAGE SEVERED SEVRUGA SIEVING SLEAVED SLEEVED SLEEVER SLIVING SOLVENT SOLVING
STEEVED STEEVER STIVING SURVEIL TARDIVE TAVERED TAVERNA TENSIVE TRAVAIL TRAVOIS TRIVIAL UNALIVE UNGLOVE UNITIVE UNLIVED UNLIVES UNLOVED UNLOVES UNRAVEL UNREAVE UNREEVE UNSAVED UNVAILE UNVAILS UNVEILS UNVISOR UNVITAL UVEITIS VAGINAE VAGINAL VAGINAS VAGITUS VAGRANT
VAGUEST VAILING VALETAS VALETED VALETES VALGOID VALGOUS VALIANT VALINES VALONEA VALONIA VALOURS VALUATE VALUERS VALUING VALUTAS VANDALS VANITAS VANTAGE VAREUSE VARIANT VARIATE VARIOLA VARIOLE VARIOUS VAUDOOS VAULTED VAULTER VAUNTED VAUNTER VAUNTIE VAURIEN VAUTING
VEDALIA VEERING VEGETAL VEILING VEINIER VEINLET VEINOUS VEINULE VELARIA VELATED VELETAS VELOURS VELOUTE VELURED VELURES VENATOR VENDAGE VENDEES VENDORS VENDUES VENEERS VENITES VENTAGE VENTIGE VENTOSE VENTRED VENTURE VENULAR VENULES VERANDA VERDANT VERDITE VERONAL

VERSUTE VERTIGO VERTUES VESTIGE VESTURE VETERAN VETOING
VIALING VIATORS VIDUAGE VIGOROS VIGOURS VILIAGO VINIEST
VINTAGE VIOLATE VIOLENT VIOLINS VIOLIST VIOLONE VIRAGOS
VIRANDA VIRANDO VIRELAI VIRGATE VIRGINS VIRGULE VIRINOS
VIRIONS VIROIDS VIRTUAL VISAGED VISAING VISEING VISITED
VISITEE VISITOR VITRAGE VITRAIL VITRAIN VITRIOL VITULAR
VODOUNS VOGIEST VOGUERS VOGUIER VOIDEES VOIDING VOITURE
VOLANTE VOLTAGE VOLUTED VOLUTIN VORLAGE VOTEENS VOULGES
VULGARS VULGATE

7-letter words with one W and six 1–2 point tiles

ADAWING AIRGLOW AIRWISE ANTIWAR AWAITED AWAITER AWARDEE AWARNED DANELAW DAWTING DEEWANS DEWATER DEWIEST DEWOOLS DISGOWN DOGTOWN DOWAGER DOWNERS DOWNIER DOWSING EARWIGS EISWEIN ENDOWER ENDWISE ENSEWED GAWSIER
GLOWERS GODOWNS GODWITS GOWANED GOWDEST GOWLAND GOWLANS GROWLED GUNWALE GWINIAD INDWELT LAUWINE LAWINES LAWNIER LAWSUIT LEASOWE LEEWARD LEGWEAR LETDOWN LEWDEST LEWISIA LOWERED LOWINGS LOWSING NARWALS NEWSIER
NUTWOOD OARWEED ONWARDS OREWEED OUTDRAW OUTDREW OUTGLOW OUTGNAW OUTGREW OUTGROW OUTLAWS OUTROWS OUTWARD OUTWARS OUTWEAR OUTWEED OUTWILE OUTWIND OUTWING OUTWINS OUTWORE OUTWORN RAGWEED REENDOW REGLOWS RENEWAL
RENEWED RESEWED RESOWED REWELDS ROWELED SEAWANT SEAWARD SEAWARE SEAWEED SEEWING SERUEWE SEWERED SINEWED SLOWING SOWLING STOWAGE SUNGLOW SUNWARD SWEALED SWEEING SWEELED SWEERED SWEETED SWEETEN SWEETER SWEETIE
SWELTED SWIRLED SWOONED SWOONER SWOUNED TARWEED TEAWARE TOWAGES TOWARDS TOWELED TOWERED TOWLINE TOWNEES TOWNIER TRAWLED TULWARS TWANGED TWEEDLE TWEELED TWEERED TWIGLOO TWINGED UNAWARE UNDRAWS UNLAWED UNSAWED
UNSEWED UNSOWED UNSWEAR UNSWEET UNSWORE UNWAGED UNWARES UNWARIE UNWATER UNWEALS UNWIRES UNWISER UNWOOED UNWROTE WADINGS WAGERED WAGONED WAGONER WAGTAIL WAILING WAINAGE WAIRING WAITING WALNUTS WANDOOS WANTAGE
WARDOGS WARISON WASTAGE WATERED WAULING WAURING WEANELS WEANERS WEARIED WEARIES WEASAND WEDGIER WEDGIES WEEDERS WEEDIER WEEDING WEENIER WEENIES WEETING WEIGELA WEINERS WEIRDIE WEIRING WEISING WELDERS WENDIGO
WERGELD WERGELT WERGILD WETLAND WIDEOUT WIDGEON WIDGETS WIDGIES WIELDER WIENERS WIENIES WILDERS WILDEST WILDING WILTING WINDAGE WINDIER WINDIGO WINDORE WINGIER WINIEST WINTLED WIRIEST WIRINGS WISTING WITLING
WONDERS WONGIED WOODIER WOODIES WOODING WOODSIA WOOINGS WOOLDER WOOLENS WOOLERS WOOLIER WOOLIES WOORALI WORDAGE WOULDST WOURALI WRONGED WROOTED WURLIES

7-letter words with one Y and six 1–2 point tiles

AGILITY ALAYING ALREADY ANALITY ANALOGY ANALYSE ANALYST ANILITY ANOLYTE ANTIGAY ANYROAD ARAYSED ARIDITY ASTYLAR AUREITY DARESAY DASYURE DAYLONG DAYSTAR DAYTALE DEANERY
DELAYER DENTARY DIETARY DIGNITY DINGILY DIRTILY DISTYLE DOYLIES DRAYAGE DRYINGS DRYLOTS DUALITY DUSTILY DYELINE DYSURIA EAGERLY EGALITY ELUSORY ELYSIAN ELYTRON ENOLOGY
ENTAYLE EROSELY ESLOYNE ESOTERY ESTUARY EUSTYLE EYALETS EYELETS EYELIAD EYELIDS EYESORE GAINSAY GASEITY GAUDERY GAUDILY GAUNTLY GAUNTRY GEODESY GOLDEYE GOOLEYS GOONEYS
GOOSERY GOUTILY GRADELY GRANDLY GRAYOUT GREATLY GREENLY GREYEST GRISTLY GUANAYS GUILDRY GURNEYS GUSTILY GUTSILY GUYLERS GUYLINE GYRATED IDYLIST INERTLY INLAYER INYALAS
ISOGONY LANIARY LANYARD LAUNDRY LAYERED LAYOUTS LITURGY LOONEYS LUNGYIS LUNYIES LYRATED LYSOGEN NAILERY NASTILY NEEDILY NEOLOGY NITRYLS NOISILY NOSEGAY NOTEDLY NOYADES
OLITORY ONEYERS ONEYRES ORALITY ORANGEY ORGANDY OROGENY OSTIARY OUTLAYS RAINILY RAISINY RAIYATS REDEYES REEDILY RELAYED RENAYED RENEYED RIANTLY RIDLEYS RIGIDLY ROUNDLY
ROYALET RUSTILY SAINTLY SATYRAL SATYRID SEEDILY SOOTILY SOUNDLY STAGILY STAIDLY STERNLY STONILY STRINGY STYLING STYLOID STYRING SURDITY SYENITE SYNODAL SYNURAE TANYARD
TARDILY TARDYON TELERGY TIDYING TIGERLY TINDERY TOURNEY TRAGEDY TRAYNED TRILOGY TRYINGS TRYSAIL TUILYIE TUYERES TYLOSIN TYRANED UNGODLY UNITARY UNROYAL URANYLS UROLOGY
YANTRAS YAOURTS YARDAGE YARDANG YAUTIAS YEADING YEALDON YEAREND YEARNED YEEDING YEELINS YIELDER YIRDING YODELER YODLING YOGINIS YOGURTS YONDERS YOUNGER

8-letter words with one B and six 1–2 point tiles

ABALONES ABATURES ABIDINGS ABIGAILS ABLATING ABLATION ABLATORS ABLEGATE ABLUENTS ABLUTION
ABNEGATE ABOIDEAU ABOITEAU ABORDING ABORIGIN ABORTION ABOULIAS ABRADING ABRASION ABRIDGES
ABROGATE ABSENTED ABSENTEE ABSOLUTE ABUTILON ADORABLE AGITABLE AIRBOATS AIRBOUND ALBEDOES
ALBITISE ALGEBRAS ANAEROBE ANTIBIAS ARABISED ARBALEST ARBALIST ARBUTEAN ARGUABLE ATABRINS
ATONABLE AUBERGES AUBRETIA AUBRIETA AUDIBLES BADINAGE BAILOUTS BAITINGS BALADINE BALADINS
BALISAUR BALISTAE BANALEST BANALISE BANDAGER BANDAGES BANDEAUS BANDELET BANDORAS BANDROLS
BANDURAS BANGTAIL BANLIEUE BARDLING BARGAINS BARGEESE BARGOOSE BARGUEST BARONAGE BARONIAL
BARSTOOL BARTISAN BASELARD BASIDIAL BATELEUR BATOONED BAUDRONS BEADINGS BEAGLERS BEAUTIED

BEAUTIES
BEDEGUAR
BEDERALS
BEDOUINS
BEELINED
BEELINES
BEERAGES
BEERIEST
BEETLERS
BEETLING
BEGIRDLE
BEGROANS
BEGUILED
BEGUILER
BEGUILES
BEGUINES
BELEEING
BELGARDS
BELONGED
BELONGER
BELTINGS
BENDLETS
BENISEED
BENITIER
BERINGED
BERLINES
BEROUGED
BESEEING
BESIEGED
BESIEGER
BESOGNIO
BESORTED
BESOULED
BESTRODE
BESUITED
BETIDING
BETOILED
BIELDIER
BIELDING
BIGARADE
BIGAROON
BILANDER
BILGIEST
BILINEAR
BILTONGS
BINAURAL
BIOTRONS
BIRADIAL
BIRDINGS
BIRDSONG
BIRLINGS
BIRSLING
BISERIAL
BLANDEST
BLASTING
BLASTOID
BLAUDING
BLEEDERS
BLEEDING
BLENDERS
BLEUATRE
BLINDAGE
BLINDERS
BLINDEST
BLONDEST
BLOODIER
BLOODIES
BLOODING
BLOUSIER
BLOUSING
BLUDGEON
BLUDGERS
BLUDIEST
BLUEINGS
BLUENOSE
BLUESIER
BLUIDIER
BLUNDERS
BLUNGERS
BLURTING
BOARDING
BOASTING
BOATINGS
BOATLOAD
BODGIEST
BOGLANDS
BOILINGS
BOISERIE
BOLOGNAS
BOLTINGS
BOLTONIA
BONDAGES
BONGOIST
BOODLERS
BOODLING
BOOSTING
BOOTLEGS
BORNEOLS
BORONIAS
BOSTANGI
BOTARGOS
BOTULINS
BOUDERIE
BOUDOIRS
BOULDERS
BOULTERS
BOULTING
BOUNDERS
BOUNTIED
BOUNTREE
BOURDONS
BOURGEON
BOUTADES
BRADOONS
BRAIDING
BRAILING
BRAISING
BRANGLED
BRANGLES
BRANTAIL
BRASILIN
BRATLING
BREEDING
BRIDLING
BRIDOONS
BRIGADES
BRIGANDS
BRINDLES
BRIONIES
BRISLING
BRISTLED
BROILING
BROODING
BRUISING
BRUITING
BRUSTING
BRUTINGS
BUDGEREE
BUDGEROS
BUDGETER
BUILDERS
BUILDING
BUISTING
BULGIEST
BULGINES
BUNDLERS
BUNGLERS
BURGANET
BURGEONS
BURGONET
BURINIST
BURNOOSE
BURNSIDE
BURSTING
BUSTLINE
BUSTLING
BUTANOLS
BUTLERED
DATEABLE
DAUBIEST
DAUBINGS
DAUBRIES
DEALBATE
DEBASING
DEBITING
DEBRUISE
DEBUTING
DENIABLE
DIABOLOS
DIATRIBE
DINGBATS
DIRTBAGS
DOBLONES
DOGBANES
DOGBOLTS
DOUBLERS
DOUBLETS
DOUBLING
DOUBTERS
DOUBTING
DRIBLETS
DURABLES
DUTIABLE
EARLOBES
EATABLES
EBENISTE
EBIONISE
EBONISED
EDGEBONE
ENABLERS
ENGLOBED
ENGLOBES
ERASABLE
ERODIBLE
GABIONED
GADABOUT
GAINABLE
GARBOILS
GILBERTS
GLABRATE
GLABROUS
GLOBATED
GLOBOIDS
GOBIOIDS
GRADABLE
GUIDABLE
GUNBOATS
GUSTABLE
IBOGAINE
INARABLE
INEDIBLE
INGLOBED
INGLOBES
ISOBRONT
LABIATED
LABIATES
LABORING
LABOURED
LABROIDS
LANDGRAB
LEEBOARD
LIBATING
LIBATION
LINEBRED
LOBATION
LOGBOARD
LONGBOAT
LOOBIEST
NEBULISE
NEBULOSE
NEOBLAST
NESTABLE
NOBODIES
NOTABLES
NUBILOSE
OBDURATE
OBDURING
OBEDIENT
OBELISED
OBLATION
OBLIGATE
OBLIGATI
OBLIGATO
OBLIGEES
OBLIGERS
OBLIGORS
OBSIDIAN
OBSIGNED
OBSOLETE
OBTRUDES
OILBIRDS
ORBITIES
ORBITING
ORIBATID
OSNABURG
OUABAINS
OUTBOARD
OUTBRAGS
OUTBREED
RADIABLE
RAGBOLTS
RAISABLE
RATEABLE
READABLE
REBADGES
REBITING
REBLENDS
REBODIES
REBOILED
REBOOTED
REBOUNDS
REBUILDS
REDOUBLE
REDOUBTS
RENDIBLE
REUSABLE
RINGBITS
RINGBOLT
RINSIBLE
ROBINIAS
ROBOTISE
SABOTAGE
SABULINE
SAIBLING
SAILBOAT
SATIABLE
SEABOARD
SENDABLE
SIBILANT
SIBILATE
SLUGABED
SONGBIRD
SORBITOL
STABLING
STONABLE
STROBILI
STROBING
SUBAGENT
SUBERATE
SUBGENRE
SUBGRADE
SUBLATED
SUBNODAL
SUBORNED
SUBTIDAL
SUBTILIN
SUBTREND
SUITABLE
SURBATED
TABANIDS
TABLEAUS
TABLINGS
TABLOIDS
TABOOING
TABOULIS
TABOURED
TABOURIN
TAGBOARD
TEABOARD
TEARABLE
TENEBRAE
TOOLBAGS
TOOLBARS
TRADABLE
TREBLING
TRIBUNAL
TRILOBED
TROUBLED
TROUBLES
TUBENOSE
TUBEROSE
TUNEABLE
TURBANDS
TURBINAL
TURBONDS
TURNABLE
UBERTIES
UBIETIES
UNABATED
UNBAITED
UNBEARED
UNBEGETS
UNBELTED
UNBIASED
UNBOLTED
UNBOOTED
UNBRAIDS
UNBRIDLE
UNDOABLE
UNEDIBLE
UNILOBAR
UNILOBED
UNSTABLE
URBANIST

8-letter words with one C and six 1–2 point tiles

ACATOURS
ACAULINE
ACAULOSE
ACERATED
ACEROLAS
ACETONES
ACIDIEST
ACIDURIA
ACIERAGE
ACIERATE
ACREAGES
ACRIDINS
ACRODONT
ACROGENS
ACTINIAE
ACTINIAS
ACTINOID
ACUITIES
ACULEATE
ADUNCATE
AECIDIAL
AERODUCT
AESCULIN
AGACERIE
AGENCIES
AGENETIC
AGNOSTIC
AGRESTIC
AIDANCES
ALCAIDES
ALCIDINE
ALGICIDE
ALICANTS
ANALECTS
ANALOGIC
ANECDOTA
ANECDOTE
ANELACES
ANGELICA
ANTACIDS
ANTALGIC
ANTECEDE
ANTICOLD
ANTICOUS
AORISTIC
ARACEOUS
ARCADING
ARCANIST
ARCTIIDS
ARCUATED
ASCIDIAN
AUCTIONS
AUDIENCE
AURICLED
AUTACOID
AUTOCADE
AUTOCARS
AUTOCOID
CADASTER
CADASTRE
CADGIEST
CAESURAE
CAESURAL
CAGOULES
CALDERAS
CALDRONS
CALENDAR
CALENDER
CALIGOES
CALUTRON
CANALISE
CANDELAS
CANDLERS
CANDOURS
CANOODLE
CANOROUS
CANTDOGS
CANULATE
CARAGEEN
CARANGID
CARDIGAN
CARDINAL
CARDINGS
CARDITIS
CARDOONS
CAREENED
CARGEESE
CARGOOSE
CARLINGS
CARLOADS
CARNAGES
CARNEOUS
CAROLING
CAROUSAL
CAROUSED
CARTAGES
CARTLOAD
CARTOONS
CASEATED
CASELOAD
CASTLING
CATALOES
CATALOGS
CATELOGS
CATLINGS
CAUDATES
CAUDLING
CAUDRONS
CAULDEST
CAULDRON
CAUSERIE
CAUTIONS
CEILINGS
CELADONS
CELERIES
CENSURED
CENTAGES
CENTERED
CERESINE
CERULEAN
CERULEIN
CERUSITE
CESAREAN
CIELINGS
CIGARETS
CILIATED
CILIATES
CINEOLES
CINEREAL
CISELEUR
CISELURE
CISLUNAR
CLANGERS
CLANGORS
CLANGOUR
CLARAINS
CLARINOS
CLARIONS
CLARTING
CLAUSTRA
CLAUTING
CLEANERS
CLEANEST
CLEANSED
CLEANSER
CLEARAGE
CLERGIES
CLINGERS
CLINGIER
CLITORIS
CLOSEOUT
CLOSETED
CLOSURED
CLOTURED
CLOTURES
CLOUDAGE
CLOUDIER
CLOUDING
CLOURING
CLOUTERS
CLOUTING
CLUDGIES
COAGENTS
COALTARS
COASTING
COATINGS
CODEINES
CODESIGN
CODLINGS
COEDITOR
COENDURE
COENURES
COGENERS
COGNATES
COGNISED
COISTRIL
COITIONS
COLEADER
COLESEED
COLISTIN
COLOGNED
COLOGNES
COLONIES
COLONISE
COLONIST
COLORANT
COLOREDS
COLORING
COLORIST
COLOURED
CONARIAL
CONDOLER
CONDOLES
CONDORES
CONDUITS
CONGEALS
CONGRATS
CONGREED
CONGREES
CONGREET
CONGRUED
CONGRUES
CONIDIAL
CONOIDAL
CONSOLED
CONSOLER
CONSULAR
CONSULTA

CONTAGIA
CONTOURS
CONTROLE
CONTROLS
CONTROUL
CONTUSED
COOEEING
COOLANTS
COOSENED
COOSINED
CORANTOS
CORDAGES
CORDIALS
CORDINGS
COREGENT
CORNAGES
CORNEOUS
CORNUTOS
CORODIES
CORONALS
CORONELS
CORONETS
CORSETED
CORTEGES
CORTISOL
COSIGNED
COTELINE
COTINGAS
COTISING
COTLANDS
COULDEST
COULOIRS
COULTERS
COUNTROL
COURAGES
COURANTO
COURANTS
COURLANS
COURSING
COURTING
CRAALING
CRADLING
CRANAGES
CREELING
CRENELED
CREODONT
CREOSOTE
CRINGLES
CRINOIDS
CROODLES
CROSTINI
CROUTONS
CRUELEST
CRUISING
CRUNODAL
CRUNODES
CRUSTING
CUDGELER
CUITERED
CULTIGEN
CUNEATED
CURATING
CURDLING
CURLINGS
CURTAILS
CURTAINS
CURTANAS
CUTESIER
CUTINISE
CUTLINES
DALTONIC
DECAGONS
DECALOGS
DECENTER
DECENTRE
DECISION
DECLARES
DECLINER
DECLINES
DECOLORS
DECOLOUR
DECORATE
DECOROUS
DECREASE
DECREETS
DECURIAS
DECURIES
DECURION
DENTICLE
DERELICT
DESELECT
DEUTERIC
DIACONAL
DIALOGIC
DIATONIC
DICROTAL
DICTIONS
DIECIOUS
DIERETIC
DIOECIES
DIOICOUS
DISCOING
DISCOLOR
DISCOUNT
DISCOURE
DISGRACE
DIURETIC
DOCILEST
DOCTORAL
DOGCARTS
DOUCINES
DUCATOON
DUCTINGS
DUECENTO
DULCIANA
DULCIANS
DULCINEA
DULCITES
DURANCES
ECAUDATE
ECLOGITE
ECLOGUES
ECLOSING
ECLOSION
ECOTONAL
ECOTONES
EDACIOUS
EDUCATES
EDUCATOR
EDUCTION
EDUCTORS
EGENCIES
EGOISTIC
EIDETICS
ELECTING
ELECTION
ELECTRON
ELEGANCE
ELEGIACS
ELICITED
ELICITOR
ELOCUTED
ELOCUTES
ENACTURE
ENCLOSED
ENCLOSER
ENCLOUDS
ENCOLOUR
ENCOLURE
ENCRADLE
ENCREASE
ENDOCAST
ENSORCEL
ERECTILE
ERGASTIC
EROGENIC
ERUCTING
ESCALADE
ESCALADO
ESCALATE
ESCAROLE
ESCORTED
ESCULENT
ESTACADE
EUCAINES
EUCRITES
EUGENICS
GARCINIA
GAUCIEST
GEARCASE
GELASTIC
GENOCIDE
GENTILIC
GEODESIC
GEODETIC
GESTICAL
GLACIATE
GLANCERS
GLUCINAS
GOLCONDA
GRACILIS
GRACIOSO
GRACIOUS
GRANITIC
GUAIACOL
GUANACOS
GUIDANCE
IATRICAL
ICONISED
IDIOLECT
INCISURE
INCLUDES
INCUDATE
INDICTEE
INDICTOR
INDOCILE
INDUCERS
INDUCIAE
INDUCTEE
INDUCTOR
IRENICAL
IRONCLAD
IRONICAL
ISOCLINE
ISODICON
ISOGENIC
ISOGONIC
ISOTONIC
LACERANT
LACERATE
LACINIAE
LACTEOUS
LACTONES
LACUNARS
LACUNATE
LACUNOSE
LAICISED
LANCETED
LANDRACE
LATENCES
LECANORA
LECTERNS
LECTURED
LECTURES
LECTURNS
LEGACIES
LEUCINES
LEUCITES
LEUCOSIN
LICENSED
LICENSEE
LICENSER
LINCTURE
LINECUTS
LINGCODS
LINOCUTS
LITURGIC
LOCATION
LOCATORS
LOCUSTAE
LOCUSTED
LOCUTION
LOGICIAN
LOGICISE
LOGICIST
LOGISTIC
LORDOTIC
LUCARNES
LUCERNES
LUCIDEST
LUCIGENS
LUNACIES
LUNATICS
NACREOUS
NAUTICAL
NEGLECTS
NEOLOGIC
NEURITIC
NICETIES
NITROLIC
NOCTILIO
NOCTUIDS
NOCTULES
NOCTUOID
NOTECASE
NUCLEASE
NUCLEATE
NUCLEIDE
NUCLEOID
NUCLIDES
OCARINAS
OCEANAUT
OCTAGONS
OCTANGLE
OCTANOLS
OCULATED
ONISCOID
ORACLING
ORCINOLS
ORGASTIC
OROGENIC
OSCULANT
OSCULATE
OSTRACOD
OSTRACON
OUTDANCE
OUTRACED
OUTSCOLD
OUTSCORE
OUTSCORN
RADICALS
RADICANT
RADICULE
RATICIDE
REAGINIC
RECEDING
RECENSED
RECITING
RECLEANS
RECLINED
RECLINES
RECLOSED
RECOALED
RECODING
RECOILED
RECOINED
RECUILED
RECUILES
RECULING
RECUSING
REDUCING
REELECTS
REGENCES
REGICIDE
REINDUCE
RELIANCE
RELUCENT
RELUCTED
RESCALED
RESCUING
RESECTED
RESELECT
RETICULE
RIDICULE
RUCTIONS
RUSTICAL
SALICETA
SALICINE
SANTALIC
SATURNIC
SCAILING
SCALDING
SCALDINI
SCALDINO
SCANTLED
SCAUDING
SCAURING
SCIAENID
SCIURINE
SCIUROID
SCLATING
SCLEREID
SCOLDING
SCOOTING
SCORDATO
SCOURGED
SCOURING
SCOUTING
SCREENED
SCROOGED
SCROUGED
SCROUNGE
SCUNGIER
SCUTIGER
SECATEUR
SECEDING
SECERNED
SECODONT
SECONDEE
SECRETED
SECTORED
SECURING
SEDUCING
SEDUCTOR
SELECTED
SERICITE
SIDALCEA
SILENCED
SILENCER
SILICATE
SILICONE
SLUICIER
SLUICING
SOLACING
SORICOID
SOURCING
STOLONIC
SUICIDAL
SULCATED
SULTANIC
SURGICAL
SURICATE
TACNODES
TALIONIC
TELECINE
TELERGIC
TENACULA
TOURACOS
TRADUCES
TRAGICAL
TRIACIDS
TRIADICS
TRICLADS
TRIDACNA
TRIGONIC
TRUCAGES
TUNICLES
TURACINS
ULCERATE
ULCERING
UNCLOSED
UNCOATED
UNCOILED
UNCOLTED
UNCOOLED
UNCREATE
UNDOCILE
UNGRACED
UNICOLOR
UNSCALED
UNSECRET
UNSLICED
UNSOCIAL
URALITIC
URANISCI
URANITIC
URGENCES
UROLOGIC

8-letter words with one F and six 1–2 point tiles

AERIFIED
AERIFIES
AEROFOIL
AIRFIELD
AIRFOILS
AIRLIFTS
ANTILIFE
ARGUFIED
ARGUFIES
AURIFIED
AURIFIES
DEARNFUL
DEFAULTS
DEFEATER
DEFERENT
DEFILERS
DEFILING
DEFINITE
DEFLATES
DEFLATOR
DEFLUENT
DEFOREST
DEFUSING
DEIFIERS
DIOLEFIN
DIRGEFUL
DRAFTING
DRIFTAGE
DRIFTING
EDIFIERS
EELFARES
ENFESTED
ENFILADE
ENFOLDER
ENGULFED
ENSERFED
FAILINGS
FAINTIER
FAIRINGS
FAIRLEAD
FAITOURS
FALDAGES
FANTAILS
FANTEEGS
FANTIGUE
FARADISE
FARDAGES
FARDINGS
FASTENED
FATIGUED
FATIGUES
FATLINGS
FAULTIER
FAULTING
FAUSTIAN
FEATEOUS
FEATURED
FEATURES
FEDELINI
FEDERALS
FEDERATE
FEEDINGS
FEEDLOTS
FEELGOOD
FEELINGS
FEGARIES
FEISTIER
FELDGRAU
FELONIES
FELONOUS
FELSTONE
FELTERED
FELTINGS
FENAGLED
FENAGLES
FERITIES
FERULING
FESTERED
FETIALIS
FEUDINGS
FEUTRING
FIDGETER
FIELDERS
FIELDING
FIERIEST
FIGULINE
FIGURANT
FIGURATE
FIGURINE
FIGURIST
FILAGREE
FILANDER
FILARIAE
FILARIAN
FILARIAS
FILATURE
FILETING
FILIATED
FILIATES
FILIGREE
FILTERED
FINAGLED
FINALISE
FINALIST
FINEERED
FINERIES
FINGERED
FINIALED
FINITUDE
FIREDOGS
FIRESIDE
FISTIANA
FISTULAE
FISTULAR
FLAGRANT
FLANERIE
FLANEURS
FLANGERS
FLAUNTED
FLAUNTER
FLEDGIER
FLEERING
FLEETING
FLEURETS
FLEURONS
FLINDERS
FLINGERS
FLINTIER
FLIRTING
FLOATAGE
FLOODERS
FLOODING
FLOORAGE
FLOORING
FLORUITS
FLOTAGES
FLOUNDER
FLOURING
FLOUSING
FLOUTERS
FLOUTING
FLUIDISE
FLUORENE
FLUORIDE

FLUORIDS FOOTRULE FOULDERS FUNGOIDS INFOLDER RATIFIED SANIFIED UNAFRAID
FLUORINE FORDOING FOULINGS FURANOSE INFRUGAL REDEFEAT SAUFGARD UNFEARED
FLUORINS FOREDATE FOUNDERS FURLANAS INGULFED REDEFIES SEAFLOOR UNFOILED
FLUORITE FOREDOES FOURGONS FURLONGS INTIFADA REDEFINE SNEERFUL UNFOLDER
FLUTINAS FOREDONE FOURTEEN FUSELAGE ISOGRAFT REEFIEST SNOOTFUL UNFOOLED
FLUTINGS FOREGOES FOUTERED FUSILEER LADIFIES REFILING SOFTENED UNFOOTED
FOEDARIE FOREGONE FOUTRING FUSILIER LEAFAGES REFLOODS SOFTLING UNFORGED
FOETIDER FOREGUTS FRAISING GADFLIES LENIFIED REFLUENT STAGEFUL UNFORGOT
FOILINGS FORELEGS FRAUTAGE GASFIELD LENIFIES REFOOTED STIFLING UNGIFTED
FOISTING FORELEND FREELOAD GASIFIED LOAFINGS REFOUNDS SULFATED UNIFIERS
FOLDINGS FORELENT FRIGATES GASIFIER NEEDFIRE REFUELED TAILFANS UNIFILAR
FOLDOUTS FORESEEN FRISTING GATEFOLD NEEDFULS REFUGEES TELFERED UNRIFLED
FOLIAGED FORESIDE FROGLETS GOLFIANA NOISEFUL REFUSING TELFORDS UNROOFED
FOLIAGES FORESTED FRONDOSE GOOFIEST NOTIFIED REFUTING TENFOLDS UNSELFED
FOLIOING FORETOLD FRONTAGE GRATEFUL NOTIFIES RIFLINGS TINFOILS URNFIELD
FONDLERS FORLANAS FRONTALS GROANFUL OLEFINES ROLFINGS TRADEFUL
FOOLINGS FORLENDS FROSTING GULFIEST OUTFEELS ROOFIEST TRAINFUL
FOOTAGES FORSLOED FRUITAGE GUNFIRES OUTFIELD ROOFINGS TRIFLING
FOOTGEAR FOSTERED FRUITING INFERIAE OUTFINDS ROOFLINE TURFINGS
FOOTINGS FOUDRIES FRUITION INFIDELS OUTFLIES SAFARIED UGLIFIED
FOOTLERS FOUGADES FUNERALS INFIELDS OUTFLING SAFRONAL UGLIFIER
FOOTLING FOULARDS FUNEREAL INFLATUS RATAFEES SALIFIED UGLIFIES

8-letter words with one H and six 1–2 point tiles

AIRHEADS ENHALOES HANDOUTS HETAIRIA HOUTINGS OUTSHONE SHOETREE THUNDERS
AIRTHING ENHEARSE HANDRAIL HIDALGAS HUITAINS RAGHEADS SHOGUNAL TIGERISH
ALEHOUSE ENLIGHTS HANGARED HIDALGOS HUNGERED RAILHEAD SHOOGIED TINGLISH
ALIGHTED ENROUGHS HANGOUTS HIDEOUTS HURDLING REGOLITH SHOOGLED TOADRUSH
ALTHORNS ENSHIELD HANSELED HIDLINGS HURLINGS REHANDLE SHOOLING TOEHOLDS
ANETHOLE ENSHROUD HARANGUE HILDINGS HURTLING REHEATED SHOOTING TOHEROAS
ANETHOLS ENTHUSED HARDLINE HINDGUTS HUSTLING REHINGED SHORTING TOHUNGAS
ANHEDRAL ETHANOLS HARIGALS HINDLEGS INHOLDER REHOUSED SHOULDER TOOLHEAD
ANTHERAL ETHEREAL HARLINGS HIREAGES INTHRALS RELIGHTS SHOUTING TOOLSHED
ANTHODIA ETHERISE HASTENED HIRELING LAIGHEST RELISHED SLEIGHED TOUGHENS
ARETHUSA GALOSHED HATGUARD HIRLINGS LANGUISH RESOUGHT SLEIGHER TOUGHIES
ARSEHOLE GARISHED HAULAGES HIRSELED LATHINGS RHAGADES SLEUTHED TREHALAS
ASHLARED GATHERED HAURIANT HIRSLING LAUGHERS RIGHTIES SLIGHTED UNDIGHTS
ASHLERED GHARIALS HEADAGES HIRUDINS LAUGHIER RINGHALS SLIGHTER UNEATHES
ATHANORS GHERAOED HEADGATE HISTOGEN LAUGHTER ROUGHENS SLOTHING UNGIRTHS
AUNTHOOD GHERAOES HEADGEAR HISTRION LEGHORNS ROUGHEST SLOUGHED UNHAILED
AUTHORED GHOULIES HEADINGS HOARDING LIGHTENS ROUGHIES SLUGHORN UNHALSED
DANELAGH GILTHEAD HEADLINE HOASTING LIGHTERS ROUNDISH SOOTHING UNHEALED
DAUGHTER GINHOUSE HEADLONG HOISTING LINISHED SEAHOUND SOREHEAD UNHEARSE
DEASHING GIRLHOOD HEADNOTE HOLDINGS LINISHER SHAGROON SOUTHING UNHEATED
DELIGHTS GOLOSHED HEADRAIL HOLDOUTS LITHARGE SHAULING SOUTHRON UNHOARDS
DHOOLIES GRAITHED HEADRIGS HONOREES LITHOING SHEADING SUNLIGHT UNHOLIER
DHOOTIES GREENTHS HEADSAIL HONOURED LONGHAIR SHEARLEG TEAHOUSE UNHORSED
DIANTHUS HAEREDES HEALDING HOODIEST LONGHEAD SHEELING THANAGES UNLASHED
DINGHIES HAGADIST HEDGIEST HOOLIEST LOTHARIO SHEENIER THENAGES UNRIGHTS
DISHONOR HAGRIDES HEELINGS HOOLIGAN LUTHERNS SHEERLEG THEOLOGS UNSHALED
DOGHOLES HAILIEST HEISTING HORDEOLA NAILHEAD SHEETIER THINGIER UNSHARED
DOGHOUSE HAIRLINE HELIODOR HORNGELD NIGHTIES SHEILING THINGIES URETHANE
DOUGHIER HALATION HELOTAGE HORNITOS NILGHAIS SHETLAND THIOUREA UROLITHS
DRAUGHTS HALIOTIS HEREUNTO HORNLETS NILGHAUS SHIELDER THIRDING USHERING
DROOGISH HALITOUS HERLINGS HOSTELED OUGHLIED SHIELING THIRLAGE
DROUGHTS HALOGENS HEROISED HOUNDERS OUGHLIES SHINGLED THIRLING
EIGHTEEN HALTINGS HETAERAE HOURLONG OUTHEARD SHINGLER THOUSAND
EIGHTIES HANDLERS HETAERAS HOUSELED OUTHEARS SHIRTING THRANGED
ENHALOED HANDLIST HETAIRAI HOUSLING OUTSHINE SHOALING THRONGED

8-letter words with one M and six 1–2 point tiles

ADAMSITE AIRMAILS ALODIUMS AMIDINES ANTISMOG DALESMEN DEMILUNE DIAMINES
ADEEMING ALAMODES ALTRUISM AMIDOGEN ARGEMONE DAMAGERS DEMISING DIASTEMA
ADENOMAS ALARMING ALUMINAS AMILDARS ARGENTUM DEEMSTER DEMIURGE DIGAMIES
ADMIRALS ALARMIST ALUMINES AMOTIONS ARGUMENT DELIMING DEMONISE DIGAMIST
ADMIRING ALARUMED ALUMROOT AMOUNTED ARMGAUNT DELIMITS DEMOTING DIGAMOUS
AEMULING ALASTRIM AMATEURS AMREETAS ARMLOADS DELIRIUM DEMOTION DIMERISE
AGAMETES ALDERMAN AMATIONS ANGIOMAS ASTIGMIA DEMEANES DEMOUNTS DIMEROUS
AGAMOIDS ALDERMEN AMEERATE ANGSTROM AUGMENTS DEMEANOR DEMUREST DIORAMAS
AGENDUMS ALGORISM AMENAGED ANIMATED AUMAILED DEMERGES DEMURING DISMOUNT
AGERATUM ALIENISM AMENAGES ANIMATOR AUTOSOME DEMERSAL DIAGRAMS DOLESOME
AGMINATE ALMAGEST AMIANTUS ANTEROOM DALESMAN DEMETONS DIAMANTE DOLOMITE

DOMAINAL
DOMANIAL
DOMINEER
DOMINEES
DOMINIES
DOMINOES
DONATISM
DOOMIEST
DOOMSTER
DOORMATS
DOORSMAN
DOORSMEN
DORMANTS
DORMOUSE
DRAGOMAN
DRAGSMAN
DRAGSMEN
DRUMLINS
DUELSOME
DUNGMERE
DURAMENS
EARLDOMS
EASEMENT
EGLOMISE
EGOMANIA
ELEMENTS
ELOGIUMS
EMAILING
EMANATED
EMANATES
EMANATOR
EMENDALS
EMENDATE
EMENDERS
EMERALDS
EMERAUDE
EMERGENT
EMERITAE
EMERITUS
EMEROIDS
EMETINES
EMONGEST
EMULATED
EMULATES
EMULATOR
EMULGENT
EMULSION
EMULSOID
ENAMELED
ENAMELER
ENAMORED
ENAMOURS
ENDAMAGE
ENDEMIAL
ENDGAMES
ENDOSOME
ENGLOOMS
ENIGMATA
ENMITIES
ENORMOUS
ENSEAMED
ENTREMES
EREMITES
ERMELINS

ERODIUMS
EROTEMES
EUDAEMON
EUDEMONS
EUGENISM
GAMELANS
GAMESIER
GAUMIEST
GELSEMIA
GEMATRIA
GEMINATE
GEMINIES
GEMINOUS
GEMSTONE
GEOMANTS
GEOMETER
GERANIUM
GERMIEST
GIANTISM
GIMLETED
GLADSOME
GLAMORED
GLAMOURS
GLEAMERS
GLEAMIER
GLEESOME
GLIOMATA
GLOOMIER
GOADSMAN
GOADSMEN
GOMERALS
GOMERELS
GOMERILS
GONIDIUM
GOODTIME
GORAMIES
GORMANDS
GOURAMIS
GOURMAND
GOURMETS
GRADATIM
GRANDAME
GRANDAMS
GRANDMAS
GREMLINS
GRIMIEST
GRUESOME
GUMTREES
GUNMETAL
GUNROOMS
IDEALISM
IDEOGRAM
IGNOMIES
IGNORAMI
ILMENITE
IMAGINAL
IMAGINED
IMAGINER
IMAGINES
INSEEMED
IONOMERS
ITEMISED
LADANUMS
LAMENTED

LAMINOUS
LEADSMAN
LEADSMEN
LEGITIMS
LEGROOMS
LEGUMINS
LEMONADE
LEMONIER
LEMURINE
LEMUROID
LIEGEDOM
LIEGEMAN
LIEGEMEN
LIMATION
LIMITEDS
LIMNAEID
LIMONITE
LODESMAN
LODESMEN
LODGMENT
LONESOME
LONGSOME
LONGTIME
LORDOMAS
LUMINIST
MADEIRAS
MADLINGS
MADRIGAL
MADRONAS
MADRONOS
MAENADES
MAGDALEN
MAGENTAS
MAGNATES
MAGNESIA
MAGNETOS
MAGNOLIA
MAILINGS
MAINDOOR
MAINOURS
MAINSAIL
MALADIES
MALANDER
MALEATES
MALGRADO
MALIGNED
MALODORS
MALODOUR
MALONATE
MALTINGS
MANAGERS
MANATEES
MANATOID
MANDATES
MANDATOR
MANDIRAS
MANDOLAS
MANDORAS
MANDORLA
MANDRELS
MANDRILS
MANGLERS
MANGOLDS
MANITOUS

MANORIAL
MANSUETE
MANTEAUS
MANTEELS
MANURIAL
MARGINAL
MARIGOLD
MARINADE
MARITAGE
MARLINGS
MAROONED
MARTAGON
MARTIANS
MARTINIS
MASTODON
MATADORE
MATADORS
MATERIAL
MATERNAL
MATILDAS
MATRONAL
MATURING
MAULGRED
MAULGRES
MAUNDERS
MAUNDIES
MAUNGIER
MAUSOLEA
MEASURED
MEDALETS
MEDALING
MEGADEAL
MEGADOSE
MEGARADS
MEGARONS
MEGASTAR
MEGATONS
MEIONITE
MELANGES
MELANOID
MELANOUS
MELINITE
MELODEON
MELODIES
MELODION
MELODISE
MELODIST
MELTAGES
MELTINGS
MENDIGOS
MENSURAL
MERENGUE
MERIDIAN
MERINGUE
MERITING
MERLINGS
MESOGLEA
MESOLITE
MESOTRON
METAIRIE
METERAGE
MEUNIERE
MIAOUING
MIAULING

MIDIRONS
MIDLINES
MIGRAINE
MIGRATED
MILADIES
MILEAGES
MILTONIA
MINGIEST
MINGLERS
MINUTIAE
MINUTIAL
MIRLITON
MISALIGN
MISDOING
MISGRADE
MISGUIDE
MISLETOE
MISLODGE
MISRULED
MISTLING
MISTRAIN
MISTRIAL
MITERING
MODALIST
MODELERS
MODELING
MODELIST
MODERATE
MODERATO
MODESTER
MODIOLAR
MODIOLUS
MODULATE
MOIDORES
MOIETIES
MOINEAUS
MOISTING
MOLDIEST
MOLDINGS
MOLESTED
MONARDAS
MONAURAL
MONGEESE
MONGERED
MONGRELS
MONILIAS
MONITORS
MONODIES
MONODIST
MONORAIL
MONTAGED
MONTAGES
MONTARIA
MONTEROS
MOODIEST
MOONDUST
MOONLETS
MOONRISE
MOONSAIL
MOONSEED
MOORAGES
MOORINGS
MOORLAND
MOOTINGS

MORAINAL
MORDANTS
MORLINGS
MORSELED
MORTLING
MOTIONAL
MOTIONED
MOTIONER
MOTORAIL
MOTORIAL
MOTORING
MOULAGES
MOULDERS
MOULDIER
MOULDING
MOULINET
MOULTERS
MOULTING
MOUNSEER
MOUSLING
MOUSTING
MOUTERED
MRIDANGA
MRIDANGS
MUDIRIAS
MUDSTONE
MUENSTER
MUISTING
MULETEER
MULTIAGE
MUNGOOSE
MURAENAS
MURALIST
MURGEONS
MURIATED
MURLAINS
MUSLINED
MUSLINET
MUSTERED
MUTAGENS
MUTINEER
MUTINIED
MUTINIES
NAMETAGS
NATRIUMS
NATURISM
NEMATODE
NEMOROUS
NEUROMAS
NOTAEUMS
NUMERALS
NUMERATE
NUTMEALS
OATMEALS
ODOMETER
OEDEMATA
OENOMELS
OINOMELS
OLIGOMER
ONDOGRAM
OOGAMETE
OOGAMIES
ORDALIUM
ORGANUMS

ORGASMED
ORIGAMIS
ORIGANUM
OUTDREAM
OUTMODES
OUTNAMED
OUTNAMES
OUTSMILE
RADIOMAN
RAMILIES
REDAMAGE
REIMAGED
REIMAGES
RELUMINE
RELUMING
REMEDIES
REMEDING
REMELTED
REMIGIAL
REMISING
REMODELS
REMOLADE
REMOTION
REMOULDS
REMUAGES
RESUMING
RETEAMED
RETIMING
RIMLANDS
ROADSMAN
ROMAUNTS
ROUMINGS
ROUTEMAN
ROUTEMEN
SAGAMORE
SAILROOM
SAINTDOM
SALEROOM
SALMONET
SALMONID
SEADROME
SEAMOUNT
SEDILIUM
SEEDTIME
SEEMLIER
SELENIUM
SEMIARID
SEMIGALA
SEMILUNE
SEMINUDE
SIGMATED
SIMOLEON
SIMULANT
SIMULATE
SLOOMIER
SLOOMING
SMARAGDE
SMELTING
SMIDGEON
SMILODON
SMOILING
SMOORING
SMOOTING
SMOULDER

SMOUTING
SMUDGIER
SODOMITE
SOLARIUM
SOLATIUM
SOLEMNER
SOMEDEAL
SOMEDELE
SOMEGATE
SONOGRAM
SOREDIUM
STAMENED
STAMINAL
STEELMAN
STEELMEN
STEREOME
STOMODEA
STORMING
SUDAMINA
SUMOTORI
SURNAMED
TAEDIUMS
TALESMAN
TALESMEN
TALISMAN
TAMANDUS
TAMANOIR
TAMARIND
TAMARINS
TANGRAMS
TEAROOMS
TEDISOME
TEGUMINA
TELEGRAM
TELOMERE
TEMEROUS
TIGERISM
TIMARAUS
TIMELIER
TIMELINE
TIMOROUS
TINAMOUS
TIRAMISU
TOILSOME
TRANGAMS
TREMOLOS
TRIADISM
TRIALISM
TROILISM
TROMINOS
TURMOILS
UDOMETER
ULTRAISM
UMANGITE
UNMAILED
UNMELTED
UNMOORED
UNSEAMED
UNSELDOM
UNTEAMED
URAEMIAS
URINEMIA

8-letter words with one P and six 1–2 point tiles

ADAPTERS
ADAPTING
ADAPTION
ADAPTORS
ADESPOTA
ADOPTEES
ADOPTING

ADOPTION
AIRPLANE
ALPINIST
ANGLEPOD
ANGUIPED
ANOOPSIA
ANTELOPE

ANTISLIP
APIARIES
APIARIST
APOLOGIA
APOLOGUE
APOLUNES
APOSITIA

ASPERATE
ASPERGED
ASPIRANT
ASPIRING
ATROPIAS
ATROPOUS
AUTOPSIA

DALAPONS
DELOPING
DEPARTEE
DEPLANES
DEPLETES
DEPLORES
DEPORTEE

DEPOSING
DEPURATE
DEPUTIES
DEPUTING
DEPUTISE
DIAPASON
DIAPAUSE

DIASPORA
DIOPTRAL
DIPLEGIA
DIPLOGEN
DIPLONTS
DIPNOOUS
DIPTEROI

DISPLANT
DISPLING
DISPONEE
DISPONGE
DISPUNGE
DOGSLEEP
DOORSTEP

DOPESTER
DOUPIONI
DROOPING
DROPLETS
DROPOUTS
DRUPELET
DUPERIES
EARPLUGS
EELPOUTS
ENDPLATE
EPANODOS
EPAULETS
EPEIRIDS
EPERGNES
EPIDOTES
EPIDURAL
EPIGAEAL
EPIGAEAN
EPIGEOUS
EPIGONES
EPIGONUS
EPILOGUE
EPISTLED
EPULIDES
EPURATED
EPURATES
ERUPTING
ESPIEGLE
ESTREPED
EUPATRID
EUPLOIDS
EUPNOEAS
GALIPOTS
GALOPADE
GALOPINS
GANTLOPE
GAPESEED
GEEPOUND
GLOOPIER
GLUEPOTS
GOALPOST
GOOPIEST
GOSPELER
GOSPODAR
GRANDPAS
GRAPLINS
GRAPNELS
GRAUPELS
GRIPIEST
GROUPIES
GROUPIST
GROUPLET
GROUPOID
GULPIEST
GUNPORTS
IGARAPES
INGROUPS
INPOURED
INSPIRED
IODOPSIN
ISOPODAN
LAPIDATE
LAPIDIST
LAPSTONE
LEOPARDS
LEPIDOTE
LEPORINE
LISPOUND
LONGSPUR
LOOPIEST
LOOPINGS
LUPANARS
NAGAPIES
NEUROPIL
NOTEPADS
NUPTIALS
OEDIPEAN
OPERATED
OPIATING
OPTIONAL
OPTIONED
OPTIONEE
OPUNTIAS
OUTDROPS
OUTLEAPS
OUTPEERS
OUTPLANS
OUTPLODS
OUTPREEN
OUTROPES
OUTSLEEP
OUTSPEED
OUTSPEND
PAENULAE
PAENULAS
PAEONIES
PAGANISE
PAGANIST
PAGEANTS
PAGINATE
PAGURIAN
PAGURIDS
PAIRIALS
PAIRINGS
PALADINS
PALATING
PALESTRA
PALINODE
PALISADE
PALISADO
PALUDINE
PALUDOSE
PANDOORS
PANDORAS
PANDOURS
PANDURAS
PANETELA
PARADING
PARAGONS
PARANETE
PARANOID
PARDALES
PARDALIS
PARENTAL
PARGETED
PARLANDO
PARLANTE
PAROLEES
PAROLING
PAROTOID
PAROUSIA
PARTIALS
PARTISAN
PASEARED
PASTORAL
PASTURAL
PASTURED
PATERNAL
PATRIALS
PATRONAL
PATROONS
PATULINS
PAULDRON
PEDALING
PEDALOES
PEDESTAL
PEDIGREE
PEELINGS
PEERAGES
PEERIEST
PEIGNOIR
PELAGIAN
PELERINE
PELTERED
PELTINGS
PENDULAR
PENTODES
PEONAGES
PEREGALS
PERGOLAS
PERIAGUA
PERIDIAL
PERIDOTE
PERIGEAL
PERIGEES
PERIGONE
PERILING
PERILOUS
PERILUNE
PERINEAL
PERONEAL
PERONEUS
PERSUADE
PERSUING
PERTUSED
PERUSING
PESTERED
PESTLING
PETALOUS
PETIOLED
PETIOLES
PETRONEL
PIDGEONS
PIERAGES
PIGEONED
PIGNOLIA
PIGNOLIS
PIGTAILS
PILOTAGE
PILOTING
PILSENER
PINDARIS
PINERIES
PINGLERS
PINITOLS
PINTADAS
PINTADOS
PINTAILS
PIRAGUAS
PIRATING
PIROGIES
PIROGUES
PISOLITE
PISTOLED
PLAGUERS
PLAGUIER
PLAIDING
PLAITING
PLANTAGE
PLANURIA
PLASTRON
PLATANES
PLATEAUS
PLATINAS
PLATINGS
PLATOONS
PLAUDITE
PLAUDITS
PLEADERS
PLEADING
PLEASANT
PLEASURE
PLEDGEES
PLEDGEOR
PLEDGERS
PLEDGETS
PLEDGORS
PLEONAST
PLEUSTON
PLIOSAUR
PLIOTRON
PLOIDIES
PLOUTERS
PLUNDERS
PLUNGERS
PLURISIE
PODAGRAL
PODAGRAS
PODARGUS
PODGIEST
POETISED
POGONIAS
POIGNADO
POISONED
POLARONS
POLENTAS
POLITIES
POLONIES
POLONISE
PONDAGES
PONGIEST
PONTAGES
POOLSIDE
PORTAGUE
PORTALED
PORTEOUS
PORTIGUE
PORTIONS
PORTLAND
PORTOLAN
PORTULAN
POSITING
POSITION
POSITRON
POSTANAL
POSTDRUG
POSTERED
POSTLUDE
POSTORAL
POSTURAL
POSTURED
POULAINE
POULARDE
POULARDS
POULDERS
POULDRES
POULDRON
POULTERS
POUNDAGE
POUNDALS
POUNDERS
POURINGS
POUTINGS
PRAEDIAL
PRAISING
PRANDIAL
PREADULT
PREAUDIT
PRELUDES
PRELUDIO
PRENASAL
PRENATAL
PRESAGED
PRESIDIO
PRESTIGE
PRETEENS
PRETENDS
PRETENSE
PREUNITE
PRIEDIEU
PRODIGAL
PRODNOSE
PROGNOSE
PROIGNED
PROLATED
PROLOGED
PROLOGUE
PROLONGE
PROLONGS
PRONOTAL
PROTEGEE
PROTEGES
PROTEIDE
PROTEOSE
PROUDEST
PROULING
PSORALEA
PUDGIEST
PUGAREES
PUGILIST
PULDRONS
PULSATED
PULSATOR
PULSIDGE
PULTOONS
PUREEING
PURITANS
PURITIES
PURLINES
PURLINGS
PURLOINS
PURSLAIN
PURSLANE
RAPESEED
READAPTS
REEDSTOP
RELAPSED
REOPENED
REPANELS
REPEALED
REPEATED
REPENTED
REPETEND
REPLEADS
REPLEDGE
REPLETED
REPLETES
REPLUNGE
REPOSTED
REPUGNED
REPULSED
REPUTING
RESPLEND
SALOPIAN
SATINPOD
SAUROPOD
SEAPLANE
SEPARATE
SERPULAE
SINOPITE
SIRUPING
SLEEPIER
SLEEPING
SLEEPOUT
SLURPING
SOAPLAND
SOLPUGID
SOPITING
SORPTION
SOUPLING
SPADROON
SPALTING
SPANDREL
SPANDRIL
SPANGLED
SPANGLER
SPANGLET
SPARLING
SPATULAR
SPEARGUN
SPEEDIER
SPEEDING
SPEELING
SPEILING
SPEIRING
SPELAEAN
SPELDING
SPELDRIN
SPERLING
SPIELING
SPIERING
SPINDLER
SPINULAE
SPIRLING
SPIRTING
SPLENDOR
SPLINTED
SPLURGED
SPOILAGE
SPOILING
SPONGOID
SPOOLING
SPOORING
SPORIDIA
SPORTING
SPOUTING
SPRANGLE
SPRINGAL
SPRINGED
SPRINGLE
SPROUTED
SPURLING
SPURTING
STAPEDII
STAPELIA
STAPLING
STEEPIER
STEEPLED
STIPULAR
STIPULED
STOOPING
STRIPING
STROUPAN
SUPERATE
SUPEREGO
SUPERING
SUPERLIE
SUPERLOO
SUPERNAL
TADPOLES
TAILSPIN
TALAPOIN
TAPADERO
TAPENADE
TAPIROID
TEASPOON
TERPENES
TILAPIAS
TONEPADS
TOPLINED
TORPEDOS
TRAGOPAN
TRIAPSAL
TRIPLIED
TRIPLING
TRIPLOID
TRIPODAL
TRIPOLIS
TRIPUDIA
TROOPIAL
TROOPING
TROUPIAL
TROUPING
UNDERLAP
UNDERLIP
UNDRAPES
UNESPIED
UNIPOLAR
UNPEELED
UNPEERED
UNPITIED
UNPLAITS
UNPOISED
UNPOLITE
UNPOSTED
UNREAPED
UNSOAPED
UNSPARED
UNSPOILT
UPDATERS
UPDATING
UPGRADES
UPLANDER
UPLEANED
UPRATING
UPRISING
UPROOTAL
UPROOTED
UPSOARED
UPSTAGED
UPSTARED
UPTRAINS
UPTRENDS
UROPODAL
UTOPIANS

8-letter words with one V and six 1–2 point tiles

AASVOGEL
ADVISING
AESTIVAL
AGENTIVE
ALVEATED
ANOVULAR
AUDITIVE
AVAILING
AVAUNTED
AVERAGED
AVERAGES
AVIARIES
AVIARIST
AVIATING
AVIATION
AVIATORS
AVIGATOR
AVOIDING
AVOISION
AVULSING
AVULSION
DELEAVES
DELETIVE
DELIVERS
DELUSIVE
DENOTIVE
DERISIVE
DERIVING
DESILVER
DEVALUES
DEVELING
DEVILETS
DEVILING
DEVISING
DEVLINGS
DEVOTEES
DEVOTING
DEVOTION
DEVOUTER
DILATIVE
DILUTIVE
DILUVIAN
DILUVION
DISGAVEL
DISVALUE
DIVAGATE
DIVERGES
DIVINERS
DIVINEST
DIVULGER
DIVULGES
DOGVANES
DOVELETS
DOVERING
DRIVINGS
DROVINGS
DURATIVE
DUVETINE
EGESTIVE
ELEVATED
ELEVATES
ELUVIATE
ENDEAVOR
ENGRIEVE
ENGROOVE
ENSLAVED
ENSLAVER
ENVAULTS
ENVEIGLE
ENVISAGE
EVALUATE
EVANGELS
EVENTERS
EVENTIDE
EVENTUAL
EVILDOER
EVOLUTED
EVOLUTES
EVULGATE
EVULSING

EVULSION GALIVANT GENITIVE GOVERNED GRAVELED GRAVIDAE GRAVIDAS GRAVITAS GRIEVOUS GROVELED IDEATIVE INDEVOUT INDUVIAE INDUVIAL INGROOVE INVALIDS INVEAGLE INVEIGLE INVITEES INVOLUTE LARVATED LAVATION LAVEERED LAVENDER LEAVENED LENITIVE LEVANTED LEVEEING LEVERAGE LEVERETS LEVERING LEVIGATE LEVITIES

LIGATIVE LIVENERS LIVERIED LIVERIES LIVIDEST LOUVERED NAVIGATE NEGATIVE NERVELET NERVULES NOSEDIVE NOVELESE NOVELISE NOVITIES OLIVINES OUTDROVE OUTGIVEN OUTGIVES OUTLIVED OUTLIVER OUTLIVES OUTLOVED OUTLOVES OUTRAVED OUTRAVES OUTRIVAL OUTSAVOR OUTSERVE OUVRAGES OVARIOLE OVARIOUS OVARITIS OVATIONS

OVERAGED OVERAGES OVERDOES OVERDOGS OVERDONE OVERDOSE OVERDUST OVEREDIT OVERGETS OVERGILD OVERGILT OVERGLAD OVERGOAD OVERGOES OVERGONE OVERIDLE OVERLADE OVERLEND OVERLENT OVERLOAD OVERLONG OVERLOUD OVERSALE OVERSEED OVERSEEN OVERSIDE OVERSOLD OVERSOUL OVERTOIL OVERTONE OVERUSED OVULATED OVULATES

RAVENOUS RAVIGOTE RAVIOLIS REAVAILS REINVITE RELIEVED RELIEVES RELIVING RESOLVED REVALUED REVALUES REVEALED REVELING REVENGED REVENGES REVENUAL REVENUED REVENUES REVESTED REVILING REVISING REVISION REVOLTED REVOLUTE REVULSED RINGDOVE RIVALING RIVALISE RIVETING RIVULOSE SALIVATE SALVAGED SALVAGEE

SALVAGER SALVOING SAVEGARD SAVOURED SELVAGED SELVAGEE SELVEDGE SILVERED SLAVERED SLEEVING SLIVERED SNIVELED SNIVELER SOLUTIVE SOLVATED STRAVAGE STRAVAIG STRIVING TELEVISE TRAVAILS TRAVELOG TRUELOVE UNGLOVED UNGLOVES UNLEVIED UNRAVELS UNREAVED UNREAVES UNREEVED UNREEVES UNSERVED UNSOLVED UNVAILED

UNVAILES UNVEILED UNVEILER UNVERSED VAGARIES VAGINATE VAGINULA VAGINULE VAGRANTS VALERATE VALERIAN VALIANTS VALIDATE VALONEAS VALONIAS VALOROUS VALUATED VALUATES VALUATOR VANADOUS VANGUARD VANTAGED VANTAGES VARGUENO VARIANTS VARIETAL VARIOLAS VAULTAGE VAULTIER VAULTING VAUNTAGE VEDALIAS VEGELATE

VEGETALS VEILIEST VEILINGS VEINIEST VEINULES VEINULET VELATURA VELIGERS VELOUTES VELURING VENDAGES VENDEUSE VENEREAL VENERIES VENTAGES VENTURES VENULOSE VERANDAS VERITIES VERLIGTE VERSELET VESTIGIA VESTURED VIDEOING VIDUAGES VIGILANT VIGOROUS VILIAGOS VINDALOO VINERIES VIOLATOR VIOLONES VIRAGOES

VIRANDAS VIRELAIS VIRGINAL VIRGINED VIRGULES VIROGENE VIRTUOSA VIRTUOSI VIRTUOSO VIRULENT VISIONAL VISIONED VISIONER VISORING VISTAING VITALISE VITRAINS VITRIOLS VITULINE VOGUIEST VOIDINGS VOLANTES VOLITION VOLTAGES VOLUTINS VOLUTION VOLUTOID VORAGOES VORLAGES VULGATES

8-letter words with one W and six 1–2 point tiles

AGALWOOD AGUEWEED AIRGLOWS AWAITING AWARDEES AWARDING AWEARIED DANELAWS DOGTOWNS DOWAGERS DOWELING DOWERIES DOWERING DRAWINGS DRAWLING DROWSING EASTWARD EDGEWISE GILTWOOD GLOWERED GOALWARD GOATWEED GOUTWEED

GOWLANDS GUNWALES GWINIADS IRONWEED LATEWOOD LAUWINES LEADWORT LEASOWED LEEWARDS LEGWEARS LETDOWNS LEWDSTER LEWISITE LOANWORD LONGWISE LUNGWORT NEWSGIRL NEWSREEL NUTWOODS OARWEEDS OREWEEDS OUTDRAWN OUTDRAWS

OUTGLOWS OUTGNAWS OUTGROWN OUTGROWS OUTLAWED OUTROWED OUTSWARE OUTSWEAR OUTSWING OUTSWORE OUTSWORN OUTWARDS OUTWEARS OUTWEEDS OUTWILED OUTWILES OUTWINDS OUTWINGS OWELTIES RADWASTE RAGWEEDS REDWINGS REGLOWED

RENEWALS RINGWISE SANDWORT SEAWATER SERUEWED SEWERAGE SINEWIER STROWING SWARDING SWEELING SWELTING SWINDLER SWINGIER SWINGLED SWIRLING SWORDING TAILWIND TEAWARES TOILWORN TOWELING TRAWLING TROWELED TWANGLED

TWANGLER TWANGLES TWEEDIER TWEEDLER TWEEDLES TWEELING TWEENIES TWIGLOOS TWIRLING UNAWARES UNSTOWED UNTOWARD UNWASTED WAGONERS WAGTAILS WAILINGS WAINAGES WAISTING WAITINGS WANDEROO WANGLERS WANTAGES WARDINGS

WARLINGS WARSLING WARSTLED WATERAGE WATERLOG WATERLOO WAULINGS WEASELED WEASELER WEDELING WEDGIEST WEEDIEST WEEDINGS WEENIEST WEENSIER WEIGELAS WEIGELIA WEIRDIES WEIRDING WEIRDOES WELDINGS WELTERED WELTINGS

WENDIGOS WEREGILD WERGELDS WERGELTS WERGILDS WESTERED WETLANDS WIDEOUTS WIDGEONS WIELDERS WIELDIER WIELDING WILDINGS WINDAGES WINDIEST WINDIGOS WINDSAIL WINERIES WINGIEST WINGLETS WISELIER WISELING WISTARIA

WITLINGS WONDROUS WOODENER WOODIEST WOODSIER WOOLDERS WOOLDING WOOLIEST WOORALIS WORDAGES WORDINGS WORSTING WOULDEST WOUNDERS WOURALIS WRANGLED WRANGLES WRASTLED WRESTLED WRITINGS WRONGOUS WROOTING

8-letter words with one Y and six 1–2 point tiles

ADROITLY ADULTERY AERODYNE AEROLOGY ALEATORY ALGIDITY ANALYSED ANALYSER ANDESYTE ANOLYTES ARAYSING ARDENTLY

AREOLOGY ARGUTELY ASYNDETA AUDITORY AUTODYNE AUTOGENY AUTOGYRO AUTOLOGY AUTOLYSE DAINTILY DAIRYING DARINGLY

DAYTALER DAYTALES DELAYERS DELAYING DELETORY DELUSORY DIGYNOUS DILATORY DIRTYING DISUNITY DONATARY DONATORY

DOTINGLY DRAYAGES DYELINES DYSTONIA ELYTROID ELYTROUS ENSTYLED ENTAYLED ENTAYLES ENTIRELY ERYNGOES ESLOYNED

ETIOLOGY EYELINER EYESTONE GARDYLOO GAYETIES GEALOUSY GELIDITY GEOLATRY GOLDEYES GOLIARDY GONDELAY GOODYEAR

GRAYOUTS GREEDILY GUARANTY GUERNSEY GULOSITY GUNLAYER GUYLINES GYROIDAL GYROLITE IDEALITY IDEALOGY IDEOLOGY

IDOLATRY IDONEITY INDUSTRY INTRADAY IODYRITE LANYARDS LARYNGES LAYERAGE LEGATARY LEGENDRY LEGERITY LIENTERY

NASALITY NEGATORY NITROSYL NODALITY NODOSITY NUGATORY ODIOUSLY ORNATELY OTIOSELY OUTLYING OUTYIELD OYSTERED

REDYEING
REGALITY
RESTYLED
ROOTEDLY
ROTUNDLY
ROYSTING
RUGOSELY
RUGOSITY
SALEYARD
SALINITY
SALUTARY
SANATORY
SANITARY
SEDATELY
SEDULITY
SENILITY
SERENELY
SEROLOGY
SIGNIORY
SINOLOGY
SITOLOGY
SNOOTILY
SODALITY
SOLIDARY
SOLIDITY
SONORITY
SOUTERLY
STINGILY
STODGILY
STOREYED
STORYING
STRONGLY
STRONGYL
STROYING
STUDYING
STURDILY
SUDATORY
SYNERGID
SYRINGED
TANYARDS
TARDYING
TARDYONS
TELEGONY
TENDERLY
TIGEREYE
TOADYING
TRENDILY
TUILYIED
TUILYIES
TURGIDLY
UNDERLAY
UNDERSAY
UNEASILY
UNGREEDY
UNITEDLY
UNSTAYED
UNSTEADY
UNTIDILY
URGENTLY
UROSTYLE
YARDAGES
YARDANGS
YEALDONS
YEARLONG
YELDRING
YESTREEN
YGLAUNST
YIELDERS
YIELDING
YODELERS
YODELING
YOLDRING
YOUNGERS
YOUNGEST
YULETIDE

AEIO Bonus Words

All 7- and 8-letter words which contain one each of the four vowels AEIO are given in the following lists. These lists may repeat words in the 6-plus-1 and 7-plus-1 bonus sets.

To make them easier to learn, the words are grouped according to the sequence of the four vowels – for example, AVOIDED, AGONISE and CALORIE all appear in the AOIE portion of the 7-letter list. The vowel groupings (such as AOIE) are listed alphabetically.

Within a vowel grouping, the words are listed in alphabetical order of the last three letters. Thus, in the AOIE portion of the 7-letter list, AVOIDED occurs before AGONISE, as the sequence -DED alphabetically precedes -ISE. This helps to keep similar word forms together for easier learning.

Where there are several words with the same last three letters, they are listed alphabetically by the first four letters. Thus, ADONISE precedes AGONISE.

AEIO bonus words containing only these vowels are listed first, followed by lists of the few that also contain a U.

AEIO BONUS WORDS

AEIO BONUS WORDS (no U)

7-letter AEIO words (no U)

AEIO ALERION
AEOI AEROBIC
PAEONIC
ADENOID
AMEBOID
ANEROID
HAEMOID
NAEVOID
ALVEOLI
AIEO ARRIERO
ALIENOR
AILERON
AIOE PAIOCKE
AZIONES
VAIVODE
WAIVODE
WAIWODE
RADIOED
AIRHOLE
ANISOLE
CARIOLE
DARIOLE
VARIOLE
AMIDONE
ACINOSE
ADIPOSE
ACHIOTE
AMNIOTE
ABIOSES
AOEI AMOEBIC
APNOEIC
APOGEIC
ANOESIS
ALOETIC
ANOETIC
AOIE AVOIDED
AVOIDER
CAMOGIE
ACCOIED
AGONIES
ANOMIES
ATOMIES
ATONIES
ATOPIES
GANOINE
KAOLINE
ARMOIRE
AVODIRE
ADONISE
AGONISE
ANODISE
ATOMISE
AZOTISE
ACONITE
AMOSITE
ADONIZE
AGONIZE
ANODIZE
ATOMIZE
AZOTIZE
CALORIE
EAIO ELATION
ENATION
ERASION
EVASION
EAOI DEASOIL
EIAO EPINAOS
EIOA KEITLOA
EPIZOAN
FEIJOAS
LEIPOAS
HEMIOLA
EOAI JEOFAIL
EOIA GEOIDAL
EXORDIA
MELODIA
EROTICA
EXOTICA
ENCOMIA
BEGONIA
ECTOPIA
MEROPIA
SENOPIA
EMPORIA
PELORIA
CELOSIA
IAOE DIAZOES
IMAGOES
ISAGOGE
DIAZOLE
MIAOWED
IEOA ICEBOAT
MINEOLA
IOAE DIOXANE
ISOBARE
ISOBASE
ISOLATE
NIOBATE
VIOLATE
IODATED
IODATES
IOEA ISOLEAD
OAIE OAKIEST
OARIEST
TOADIED
COALIER
FOAMIER
GOATIER
HOARIER
LOAMIER
ROARIER
SOAPIER
BOATIES
GOALIES
HOAGIES
ORACIES
OTARIES
OVARIES
ROADIES
SOAPIES
TOADIES
OAKLIKE
OARLIKE
OATLIKE
COCAINE
MORAINE
OPALINE
OTARINE
OXAZINE
ROMAINE
SODAINE
COALISE
COALIZE
TOASTIE
OEAI TOENAIL
OCEANIC
OCEANID
OEIA SOREDIA
COELIAC
CODEIAS
OBELIAS
CODEINA
LOBELIA
BOHEMIA
COREMIA
TOXEMIA
OEDIPAL
GODETIA
OIAE COINAGE
FOLIAGE
SOILAGE
ORIGANE
OXIDASE
FOLIATE
OBVIATE
OSMIATE
OSTIATE
OXIDATE
SOCIATE
LORICAE
VOMICAE
SCORIAE
OPIATED
OPIATES

8-letter AEIO words (no U)

AEIO ARPEGGIO
ADHESION
ALLERION
ANNEXION
APHELION
AVERSION
ANTERIOR
ALERIONS
AERIFORM
AEOI AEROBICS
PAEONICS
ADENOIDS
ANEROIDS
CAMEOING
AEROLITH
ACETONIC
DAEMONIC
ANECHOIC
AMBEROID
ASTEROID
ATHETOID
CAMELOID
CATENOID
GALENOID
RACEMOID
MALLEOLI
ADENOSIS
ANEMOSIS
AIEO ANTIHERO
ARMIGERO
KAKIEMON
ASSIENTO
AILERONS
ALIENORS
TAILERON
ARRIEROS
AIOE VAIVODES
WAIVODES
WAIWODES
AMIDOGEN
PAIOCKES
AIRHOLES
ANISOLES
CARIOLES
DARIOLES
VARIOLES
AIRWOMEN
RADIOMEN
ACTIONED
GABIONED
RATIONED
ACTIONER
AMIDONES
DAIMONES
RAISONNE
ANTINODE
ANTIPODE
ARILLODE
PALINODE
ALNICOES
CALICOES
CALIGOES
LATIGOES
AMITROLE
ANTIPOLE
ARVICOLE
BRACIOLE
CABRIOLE
CAMISOLE
CAPRIOLE
CARRIOLE
FASCIOLE
GLADIOLE
AIRDROME
HALIDOME
WAILSOME
BARITONE
TAILBONE
ANTIPOPE
CALLIOPE
ALBICORE
HALICORE
ANGINOSE
FARINOSE
LAMINOSE
SCARIOSE
VARICOSE
ANTIDOTE
HALIMOTE
RAVIGOTE
TAILORED
AIRBORNE
ACIDOSES
ADIPOSES
AMITOSES
ACHIOTES
AMNIOTES
AIRPOWER
AOEI ALOPECIC
ACROLEIN
ALOETICS
CANOEING
CANOEIST
ANOXEMIC
AZOTEMIC
ANORETIC
ANOESTRI
AMORETTI
ANOREXIC
AOIE AVOIDERS
ABORIGEN
ALKOXIDE
ASTONIED
CANOPIED
PARODIED
CAPONIER
GASOLIER
SABOTIER
SAVORIER
APHONIES
ARGOSIES
ARMORIES
ASTONIES
AVOWRIES
BARONIES
CALORIES
CAMOGIES
CANOPIES
JALOPIES
PARODIES
SAVORIES
SAXONIES
HALOLIKE
CAMOMILE
APOCRINE
ARMOZINE
ATROPINE
GASOLINE
LANOLINE
PAVONINE
SAPONINE
TABORINE
WAGMOIRE
AMORTISE
APHORISE
CANONISE
CAPONISE
TRAVOISE
VALORISE
VAPORISE
AMMONITE
APPOSITE
ARSONITE
DATOLITE
FAVORITE
JAROSITE
LABORITE
SAPONITE
SAXONITE
TACONITE

ABORTIVE
ADOPTIVE
AMORTIZE
APHORIZE
ARBORIZE
CALORIZE
CANONIZE
CAPONIZE
JAROVIZE
VALORIZE
VAPORIZE
ASSOILED
ADJOINED
GANOINES
KAOLINES
ARMOIRES
AVODIRES
ADONISED
AGONISED
ANODISED
ATOMISED
AZOTISED
DAMOISEL
ATOMISER
ADONISES
AGONISES
ANODISES
ATOMISES
AZOTISES
ANOINTED
AROINTED
ADROITER
ANOINTER
ACONITES
AMOSITES
APOMIXES
ADONIZED
AGONIZED
ANODIZED
ATOMIZED
AZOTIZED
ATOMIZER
ADONIZES
AGONIZES
ANODIZES
ATOMIZES
AZOTIZES
EAIO GERANIOL
CREATION
DELATION
DERATION
ENACTION
EXACTION
FETATION
GELATION
LEGATION
NEGATION
REACTION
RELATION
SEDATION
VENATION
VEXATION
BEHAVIOR
SERAGLIO
RETAILOR
ELATIONS
ENATIONS
ERASIONS
EVASIONS
SCENARIO
FELLATIO
EAOI SEAROBIN
EPAGOGIC
DEASOILS
SEAGOING

REANOINT
METAZOIC
CERATOID
ERGATOID
HEMATOID
KERATOID
MELANOID
NEMATOID
PETALOID
SEPALOID
SESAMOID
TERATOID
TETANOID
HEXAFOIL
EIAO DEVIATOR
EPILATOR
EXPIATOR
MEDIATOR
EIOA EPIZOANS
EPIFOCAL
EPISODAL
PETIOLAR
HEMIOLAS
EPISOMAL
REGIONAL
KEITLOAS
SEMICOMA
EOAI ESOPHAGI
REOBTAIN
REORDAIN
DEBONAIR
JEOFAILS
TEOCALLI
EXOGAMIC
GEOTAXIS
EOIA EROTICAL
HEROICAL
ECOCIDAL
KELOIDAL
DEMONIAC
EXORDIAL
MEMORIAL
BESONIAN
BEZONIAN
CREOLIAN
DEMONIAN
PELORIAN
BEGONIAS
CELOSIAS
ECTOPIAS
MELODIAS
MEROPIAS
PELORIAS
SENOPIAS
MELODICA
VERONICA
PEPONIDA
GEROPIGA
SEMOLINA
SENORITA
BEDSONIA
PHELONIA
CECROPIA
SENSORIA
TENTORIA
IAOE DIALOGED
DIALOGER
ISAGOGES
DIAZOLES
FIASCOES
IGNAROES
VIRAGOES
DIASTOLE
GIRASOLE
THIAZOLE

TRIAZOLE
DIAPHONE
MISATONE
DIASCOPE
DIASPORE
PINAFORE
BIRAMOSE
DIAGNOSE
VIATORES
IEAO LITERATO
IDEALOGY
IEOA ICEBOATS
MINEOLAS
SIDEROAD
FIREBOAT
LIFEBOAT
MINNEOLA
IDEOGRAM
IOAE HILLOAED
PILOTAGE
SILOXANE
IRONWARE
DIOPTASE
IDOCRASE
KILOBASE
BIFORATE
BILOBATE
IMMOLATE
INCHOATE
INNOVATE
INORNATE
INSOLATE
INTONATE
INVOCATE
PRIORATE
THIONATE
ISOLABLE
VIOLABLE
DIOXANES
ISOBARES
BIOGASES
ISOBASES
ISOLATED
VIOLATED
IDOLATER
VIOLATER
ISOLATES
NIOBATES
VIOLATES
IOEA ISOLEADS
BIOCLEAN
THIOTEPA
DIOCESAN
OAEI TOXAEMIC
OAIE ORGANDIE
COALIEST
FOAMIEST
GOATIEST
HOARIEST
LOAMIEST
ROARIEST
SOAPIEST
ROADSIDE
SODAMIDE
COVARIED
CROAKIER
FLOATIER
ORANGIER
POACHIER
SHOALIER
TOASTIER
BOTANIES
COACHIES
COVARIES
DONARIES

GORAMIES
NOMADIES
NOTARIES
OCCAMIES
OTALGIES
ROSARIES
ROTARIES
TOASTIES
VOLARIES
VOTARIES
BOATLIKE
FOAMLIKE
GOADLIKE
GOATLIKE
MOATLIKE
NOVALIKE
SOAPLIKE
TOADLIKE
FORHAILE
VOLATILE
COALMINE
CORAMINE
DOPAMINE
MONDAINE
PROCAINE
PTOMAINE
SOLANINE
SONATINE
STOVAINE
TOPAZINE
COADMIRE
BOTANISE
FOCALISE
LOCALISE
MORALISE
NODALISE
NOMADISE
NOTARISE
ORGANISE
POLARISE
ROMANISE
ROYALISE
SOLARISE
TOTALISE
VOCALISE
WOMANISE
BORACITE
LOCALITE
MONAZITE
ROLAMITE
SODALITE
TONALITE
COACTIVE
CONATIVE
DONATIVE
LOCATIVE
OPTATIVE
ROTATIVE
VOCATIVE
BOTANIZE
FOCALIZE
LOCALIZE
MORALIZE
NODALIZE
NOMADIZE
NOTARIZE
ORGANIZE
POLARIZE
ROMANIZE
ROYALIZE
SOLARIZE
TOTALIZE
VOCALIZE
WOMANIZE
ROCAILLE

OBTAINED
ORDAINED
OBTAINER
ORDAINER
COCAINES
MORAINES
OPALINES
OXAZINES
ROMAINES
COALISED
OPALISED
COALISES
OXALISES
COALIZED
OPALIZED
COALIZES
OEAI FORELAID
FORESAID
OVERLAID
OVERPAID
DOVETAIL
FORESAIL
OVERSAIL
FORELAIN
OVERLAIN
OVERHAIR
OCEANIDS
TOENAILS
OBEAHING
OBEAHISM
OPERATIC
POEMATIC
OEIA COELIACS
OBEISANT
OLEFIANT
POETICAL
GYNOECIA
COLLEGIA
LOESSIAL
PROEMIAL
SOREDIAL
SOTERIAL
BOHEMIAN
COMEDIAN
MONECIAN
BOHEMIAS
GODETIAS
LOBELIAS
TOXEMIAS
BROMELIA
CHOLEMIA
COPREMIA
CODEINAS
PROGERIA
STOKESIA
OIAE BONIFACE
NONIMAGE
SPOILAGE
SOLIDARE
BLOVIATE
COGITATE
COINMATE
DOMINATE
FORMIATE
LORICATE
MOTIVATE
NOMINATE
OBLIGATE
OPPILATE
OPTIMATE
ORDINATE
OSCITATE
ROSINATE
SOLIDATE
SOMNIATE

SONICATE SPOLIATE VOLITATE BOILABLE COINABLE FOILABLE JOINABLE OBVIABLE OPINABLE OXIDABLE SOCIABLE VOIDABLE FOLIAGED COINAGES FOLIAGES SOILAGES VOIDANCE ORIGANES OILPAPER GOLIASED GOLIASES OXIDASES FOLIATED OBVIATED OXIDATED FOLIATES OBVIATES OSMIATES OXIDATES SOCIATES

OIEA TOISEACH NONIDEAL HYOIDEAN COLINEAR COCINERA LONICERA ORIENTAL SOCIETAL

AEIO BONUS WORDS (with U)

7-letter AEIO words (with U)

EOIA EULOGIA SEQUOIA

IAOE MIAOUED

OEIA DOULEIA

OIEA MOINEAU

8-letter AEIO words (with U)

AEIO CAESIOUS

AEOI AEROBIUM AEQUORIN

AOIE AGOUTIES SAUTOIRE JALOUSIE

EAIO EQUATION EDACIOUS

EOIA EUPHOBIA EULOGIAS SEQUOIAS EXONUMIA EUPHONIA EUPHORIA

IAOE DIALOGUE

IOEA THIOUREA

OAIE DOUANIER POULAINE OUTRAISE ODALIQUE

OEIA DOULEIAS

OIEA MOINEAUS

Further Bonus Sets

6-letter stems that combine with each vowel

All the bonus sets shown earlier are worth knowing because the words are likely to appear on your rack and, in the case of 8-letter words, be playable through a letter already on the board. This additional category of bonus word sets focuses on those 6-letter stems that are of particular interest because they combine with each of the five vowels.

The vowels make up some 40% of the letter pool at the start of a game, with the chances of picking a vowel from the bag varying as the game progresses. Often the chance of picking any vowel may rise to 50% or more towards the end of a game and it may be a good idea to play off one awkward consonant to 'fish' for a vowel in the hope of a late winning bonus play.

Many of the 6-letter stems are memorable, forming everyday keywords such as CANDLE and PARDON, making it easier for you to spot the 7-letter bonuses whenever and however the letters arrive on your rack. When the keywords are not real words or are not allowable for Scrabble, they are shown in brackets.

Not every 6-letter stem combining with each of the vowels is listed here. We have excluded some where the 6-letter stem itself is less likely or less memorable. Also excluded from these lists are the 71 stems already shown in the top 250 6-letter bonus stems, but for convenience these have been listed at the end of this introduction.

There are four categories selected as follows:

☆ 6-letter stems that have two vowels and no S

☆ 6-letter stems that have two vowels and just one S

☆ 6-letter stems that combine with AEIOU and Y only

☆ 6-letter stems that combine with AEIOU only

There are a few stems that meet two or more criteria. In such cases the stems are included in all of the relevant categories for completeness.

The following are stems in the top 250 6-letter bonus stems that combine with each vowel and which are excluded from the Further Bonus Sets. Some of these stems have three vowels and so would not qualify for inclusion anyway.

ABERST	AELPRS	DEGINS	EGNORS	ELORST
ACDERS	AEMNST	DEINRS	EHIRST	EMNOST
ACELST	AEMRST	DEINST	EHORST	EMORST
ACENRT	AENPST	DEIRST	EILNOS	ENOPRS
ACENST	AENRST	DENOST	EILNST	ENORST
ACERST	AEPRST	DENRSU	EILOST	EORRST
ADEILR	ANORST	DEORST	EILRST	EORSTT
ADEIRS	BDEIRS	EENRST	EIMNST	GILNOT
ADEMNS	BEIRST	EERRST	EIMRST	GINORS
ADENST	CEIRST	EERSTT	EINNST	GINORT
ADEPRT	CENORS	EGILNS	EINPRS	INORST
AEGNRT	DEENRS	EGILNT	EINPST	
AEINST	DEENST	EGILRS	EINRTT	
AELMNT	DEGILN	EGINNR	EIPRST	
AELNST	DEGINR	EGINRT	EIRSTV	

FURTHER BONUS SETS – STEMS COMBINING WITH EACH VOWEL

6-LETTER STEMS – 2 VOWELS, NO S

ABDELT
TABLED
A ABLATED
DATABLE
E BELATED
BLEATED
F FLATBED
I LIBATED
O BLOATED
LOBATED
S BALDEST
BLASTED
STABLED
T BATTLED
BLATTED
U ABLUTED

ABERTT
BATTER
A RABATTE
TABARET
E ABETTER
BERETTA
I BATTIER
BIRETTA
L BATTLER
BLATTER
BRATTLE
O ABETTOR
BATTERO
TABORET
S BATTERS
TABRETS
U ABUTTER
Y BATTERY

ABGINT
BATING
A ABATING
B TABBING
D DINGBAT
E BEATING
H BATHING
I BAITING
L TABLING
N BANTING
O BOATING
S BASTING
T BATTING
U ANTIBUG
TABUING
W BATWING
Y BAYTING

ACDELN
CANDLE
A CANALED
CANDELA
DECANAL
D CANDLED
E CLEANED
ELANCED
ENLACED
G CANGLED
CLANGED
GLANCED
H LANCHED
I INLACED
K CLANKED
O CELADON
R CANDLER
S CALENDS
CANDLES
T CANTLED
U LAUNCED
UNLACED

ACDELR
CRADLE
A CALDERA
CRAALED
D CLADDER
CRADDLED
E CLEARED
CREEDAL
DECLARE
RELACED
H CHALDER
I DECRIAL
RADICEL
RADICLE
N CANDLER
O CAROLED
ORACLED
R CRADLER
S CRADLES
SCALDER
T CLARTED
U CAULDER
W CRAWLED

ADNOPR
PARDON
A PANDORA
B PROBAND
E APRONED
OPERAND
PADRONE
PANDORE
I PADRONI
PONIARD
O PANDOOR
S PARDONS
U PANDOUR
V PROVAND

ADNORT
(RODANT)
A ONDATRA
E TORNADE
I DIATRON
L TROLAND
M DORMANT
MORDANT
N DONNART
O DONATOR
ODORANT
TANDOOR
TORNADO
U ROTUNDA
Y TARDYON

AEGMNT
MAGNET
A GATEMAN
MAGENTA
MAGNATE
NAMETAG
E GATEMEN
I MINTAGE
TEAMING
TEGMINA
O GEOMANT
MAGNETO
MEGATON
MONTAGE
R GARMENT
MARGENT
RAGMENT
S MAGNETS
U AUGMENT
MUTAGEN

AEMNRT
MARTEN
A RAMENTA
E REMANET
F RAFTMEN
G GARMENT
MARGENT
RAGMENT
I MINARET
RAIMENT
N MANRENT
REMNANT
O TONEARM
S ARTSMEN
MARTENS
SARMENT
SMARTEN
U TRUEMAN
V VARMENT

AGILNV
VALING
A AVALING
VAGINAL
C CALVING
E LEAVING
VEALING
H HALVING
I VAILING
VIALING
O LOAVING
S SALVING
SLAVING
VALSING
U VALUING
V VALVING

AIMNRT
MARTIN
A MARTIAN
TAMARIN
C MANTRIC
E MINARET
RAIMENT
G MARTING
MIGRANT
I MARTINI
O TORMINA
S MARTINS
U NATRIUM
V VARMINT

BDEORR
BORDER
A ARBORED
BOARDER
BROADER
REBOARD
E REBORED
I BROIDER
O BROODER
S BORDERS
U BORDURE
BOURDER

CDDEER
(CEDDER)
A CEDARED
E DECREED
RECEDED
I DECIDER
DECRIED
O DECODER
RECODED
U REDUCED

CEEGNR
(CRENGE)
A ENGRACE
E REGENCE
I CREEING
ENERGIC
GENERIC
O COGENER
CONGREE
U URGENCE
Y REGENCY

CEELRT
TERCEL
A TREACLE
E REELECT
F REFLECT
I RETICLE
TIERCEL
N LECTERN
O ELECTOR
ELECTRO
P PLECTRE
PRELECT
S TERCELS
U LECTURE
Y ERECTLY

CEIPPR
(CIPPER)
A CRAPPIE
EPICARP
E PRECIPE
H CHIPPER
I PIPERIC
L CLIPPER
CRIPPLE
O CROPPIE
U CUPPIER

DEELRV
DELVER
A RAVELED
E LEVERED
REVELED
I DELIVER
RELIVED
REVILED
O LOVERED
S DELVERS
U VELURED

DEERRV
(VERRED)
A AVERRED
E REVERED
I DERIVER
REDRIVE
RIVERED
O OVERRED
REDROVE
U VERDURE

DEFLRU
FURLED
A DAREFUL
D FUDDLER
E FERULED
F RUFFLED
I DIREFUL
N DERNFUL
O FLOURED
FOULDER
P PURFLED
R FLURRED
U DUREFUL

DEHLLO
(HOLLED)
A HALLOED
HOLLAED
E HELLOED
I HILLOED
O HOLLOED
U HULLOED

DEMNOR
MODERN
A MADRONE
ROADMEN
E MODERNE
I MINORED
O DOORMEN
MORENDO
S MODERNS
RODSMEN
T MORDENT
U MOURNED
Y DEMONRY

EEMPRT
TEMPER
A TEMPERA
E PREMEET
I EMPTIER
O TEMPORE
P PREEMPT
R PRETERM
S TEMPERS
T TEMPTER
U PERMUTE

EENRRV
NERVER
A RAVENER
E VENERER
I NERVIER
VERNIER
O OVERREN
S NERVERS
U NERVURE

EGINNP
PENING
A NEAPING
PEANING
D PENDING
E PEENING
F PFENNIG
I PEINING
N PENNING
O OPENING
U PENGUIN

ENNORT
TONNER
A NORTENA
D DONNERT
TENDRON
E ENTERON
TENONER
F FORNENT
G RONTGEN
I INTONER
TERNION
O NORTENO
S STONERN
TONNERS
U NEUTRON

GILNOP
POLING
A GALOPIN
E ELOPING
F FOPLING
I PIGNOLI
K POLKING
L POLLING
O LOOPING
POOLING
P LOPPING
R PROLING
S POLINGS
SLOPING
T POLTING
U LOUPING
W PLOWING
Y PLOYING

6-LETTER STEMS – 2 VOWELS, ONE S

AACNST
SANCTA
A CANASTA
E CATENAS
F CAFTANS
H ACANTHS
I SATANIC
O SACATON
P CAPSTAN
CAPTANS
CATNAPS
R ARCTANS
CANTARS
U ASCAUNT

AAGLNS
LAGANS
A LASAGNA
D SLADANG
E ALNAGES
ANLAGES
GALENAS
LAGENAS
LASAGNE
I AGNAILS
L LALANGS
M MANGALS
O ANALOGS
P LAPSANG
R RAGLANS
U LAGUNAS

ABELST
TABLES
A ABLATES
ASTABLE
C CABLETS
D BALDEST
BLASTED
STABLED
E BELATES
G GABLETS
I ABLEIST
ALBITES
ASTILBE
BASTILE
BESTIAL
BLASTIE
LIBATES
STABILE
L BALLETS
O BOATELS
OBLATES
R ALBERTS
BATLERS
BLASTER
LABRETS
STABLER
S BASTLES
STABLES
T BATLETS
BATTELS
BATTLES
BLATEST
TABLETS
U SUBLATE
Y BAETYLS
BEASTLY

ABGINS
BASING
A ABASING
BAAINGS
BISNAGA
B SABBING
E SABEING
H BASHING
I BIASING
K BAKINGS
BASKING
L ABLINGS
SABLING
O BAGNIOS
GABIONS
R SABRING
S BASSING
T BASTING
U ABUSING

ABILST
(LABIST)
A BALISTA
E ABLEIST
ALBITES
ASTILBE
BASTILE
BESTIAL
BLASTIE
LIBATES
STABILE
I STIBIAL
M TIMBALS
O OBLASTI
U TABULIS

ACDELS
SCALED
A ALCADES
SCALADE
D SCALDED
E DESCALE
H CLASHED
I SCAILED
K SLACKED
L SCALLED
M MASCLED
N CALENDS
CANDLES
O COLEADS
SOLACED
P CLASPED
SCALPED
R CRADLES
SCALDER
S CLASSED
DECLASS
T CASTLED
SCLATED
U CAUDLES
CEDULAS
W DECLAWS

ACDEPS
SPACED
A SCAPAED
E ESCAPED
I DISPACE
L CLASPED
SCALPED
M DECAMPS
SCAMPED
O PEACODS
PEASCOD
R REDCAPS
SCARPED
SCRAPED
U SCAUPED

ACELRS
SCALER
A SCALARE
C CARCELS
D CRADLES
SCALDER
E ALERCES
CEREALS
RELACES
RESCALE
SCLERAE
H CLASHER
LARCHES
RASCHEL
I CLARIES
ECLAIRS
SCALIER
K CALKERS
LACKERS
SLACKER
L CALLERS
CELLARS
RECALLS
SCLERAL
M MARCELS
N LANCERS
RANCELS
O CLAROES
COALERS
ESCOLAR
ORACLES
RECOALS
SOLACER
P CARPELS
CLASPER
CRAPLES
PARCELS
PLACERS
RECLASP
SCALPER
R CARRELS
S CARLESS
CLASSER
SCALERS
SCLERAS
T CARTELS
CLARETS
CRESTAL
SCARLET
TARCELS
U CESURAL
RECUSAL
SECULAR
V CALVERS
CARVELS
CLAVERS
W CLAWERS

ACEMNS
(MANCES)
A CASEMAN
E CASEMEN
MENACES
H MANCHES
I AMNESIC
CINEMAS
L ENCALMS
O ANCOMES
P ENCAMPS
U ACUMENS

ACLMSU
LACMUS
A CALAMUS
MACULAS
E ALMUCES
MACULES
I MUSICAL
O MUCOSAL
T TALCUMS
U LUCUMAS
Y MASCULY

AEPPRS
SAPPER
A APPEARS
C CAPPERS
D DAPPERS
E RAPPEES
F FRAPPES
H PERHAPS
I APPRISE
SAPPIER
L LAPPERS
RAPPELS
SLAPPER
M MAPPERS
PAMPERS
PREAMPS
N NAPPERS
PARPENS
PARSNEP
SNAPPER
O APPOSER
R RAPPERS
S APPRESS
SAPPERS
T TAPPERS
U PAUPERS
UPSPEAR
W SWAPPER
WAPPERS
Y PREPAYS
YAPPERS
Z ZAPPERS

AGINNS
SANING
A ANGINAS
C CANINGS
D SANDING
E SEANING
F FINGANS
I SAINING
K SNAKING
L LINSANG
M NAMINGS
O GANOINS
P PINANGS
SPANING
R SNARING
T ANTINGS
STANING
U GUANINS
W AWNINGS
SNAWING
WANINGS

AHLLOS
HALLOS
A HALLOAS
C CHOLLAS
E HALLOES
I HILLOAS
M MOLLAHS
OLLAMHS
N SHALLON
O HALLOOS
HOLLOAS
P SHALLOP
T SHALLOT
U HULLOAS
W HALLOWS
SHALLOW

AIKNST
TAKINS
A TANKIAS
C ANTICKS
CATKINS
CATSKIN
E INTAKES
KENTIAS
TANKIES
G SKATING
STAKING
TAKINGS
TASKING
I KAINITS
O KATIONS
U TANUKIS

AILMNS
MASLIN
A ALMAINS
ANIMALS
LAMINAS
MANILAS
E ISLEMAN
MALINES
MENIALS
SEMINAL
G LINGAMS
MALIGNS
H MASHLIN
I MISLAIN
K MALKINS
O MALISON
MONIALS
SOMNIAL
P MISPLAN
PLASMIN
R MARLINS
S MASLINS
U ALUMINS

AIMNST
MATINS
A MANATIS
STAMINA
D MANTIDS
E ETAMINS
INMATES
MAINEST
MANTIES
TAMEINS
TAMINES
G MASTING
MATINGS
TAMINGS
I ANIMIST
INTIMAS
SANTIMI
O MANITOS
STAMNOI
P PITMANS
R MARTINS
S SANTIMS
T MATTINS
U MANITUS
TSUNAMI

AIMRST
AMRITS
A AMRITAS
TAMARIS
B IMBRAST
C MATRICS
E IMARETS
MAESTRI
MAISTER
MASTIER
MISRATE
SEMITAR
SMARTIE
F MAFTIRS
H THAIRMS
THIRAMS
THRIMSA
I SIMITAR
L MISTRAL
RAMTILS
N MARTINS
O AMORIST
P ARMPITS
IMPARTS
MISPART
S TSARISM
U ATRIUMS
MATSURI
Y MAISTRY
SYMITAR
Z TZARISM

AINPRS
SPRAIN
A PARIANS
PIRANAS
E PANIERS
RAPINES
G PARINGS
PARSING
RASPING
SPARING
H HARPINS
I ASPIRIN
K KIRPANS
PARKINS
O PARISON
SOPRANI
P PARSNIP
S SPINARS
SPRAINS
T SPIRANT
SPRAINT
U PRUINAS
W INWRAPS

AIPRST
RAPIST
A PITARAS
D DISPART
E PARTIES
PASTIER
PIASTER
PIASTRE
PIRATES
PRATIES
TRAIPSE
H HARPIST

I PIARIST
M ARMPITS
IMPARTS
MISPART
N SPIRANT
SPRAINT
O AIRPOST
AIRSTOP
PAROTIS
S RAPISTS
U UPSTAIR

ALMNSU
MANULS
A MANUALS
E MENSUAL
I ALUMINS
O MONAULS
SOLANUM
P SUNLAMP
R MURLANS
U ALUMNUS

ALMRSU
MURALS
A ALARUMS
B LABRUMS
LUMBARS
E MAULERS
SERUMAL
F ARMFULS
ARMSFUL
FULMARS
I SIMULAR
N MURLANS
O MORULAS
U RAMULUS

ALRSTU
ULTRAS
A AUSTRAL
C CRUSTAL
CURTALS
E ESTRUAL
SALUTER
I RITUALS
TRISULA
L LUSTRAL
O ROTULAS
TORULAS
U SUTURAL
W TULWARS

AMNSTU
(UNMATS)
A MANTUAS
TAMANUS
B NUMBATS
C SANCTUM
D DUSTMAN
E UNTAMES
UNTEAMS
G MUSTANG
I MANITUS
TSUNAMI
N STANNUM
O AMOUNTS
MOUTANS
OUTMANS
R ANTRUMS
UNSMART
T MUTANTS
U AUTUMNS

BDERSU
SURBED
A DAUBERS
SUBEDAR
B DUBBERS
D BUDDERS
REDBUDS
E BURSEED
G BEDRUGS
BUDGERS
REDBUGS
H BRUSHED
I BRUISED
BURDIES
N BURDENS
O OBDURES
ROSEBUD
S SURBEDS
T BURSTED
U SUBDUER
Y RUDESBY

BEISTT
(BITTES)
A BATISTE
BISTATE
E BETTIES
H THIBETS
I BITTIES
O BOTTIES
R BITTERS
U BUTTIES

CDDEES
(DESCED)
A DECADES
E SECEDED
I DECIDES
N DESCEND
SCENDED
O DECODES
U DEDUCES
SEDUCED

CDDEIS
DISCED
A CADDIES
E DECIDES
I DISCIDE
O DISCOED
U CUDDIES

CDEERS
SCREED
A CREASED
DECARES
SEARCED
E CREESED
DECREES
RECEDES
SECEDER
H CHEDERS
I DECRIES
DEICERS
K DECKERS
N DECERNS
SCERNED
O RECODES
S SCREEDS
T CRESTED
U RECUSED
REDUCES
RESCUED
SECURED
SEDUCER

W DECREWS
SCREWED

CDEINS
(DINCES)
A CANDIES
INCASED
E INCEDES
I INCISED
INDICES
K DICKENS
SNICKED
O CODEINS
CONDIES
SECONDI
R CINDERS
DISCERN
RESCIND
U CUNDIES
INCUDES
INCUSED
INDUCES
X EXSCIND
Z DEZINCS

CDEOST
COSTED
A COASTED
C DECOCTS
E CESTODE
ESCOTED
TEDESCO
I CESTOID
COEDITS
COTISED
K DOCKETS
STOCKED
L COLDEST
N DOCENTS
O SCOOTED
U CUSTODE
DOUCEST
DOUCETS
SCOUTED
Y CYTODES

CEENRS
SCREEN
A CAREENS
CASERNE
ENRACES
RECANES
D DECERNS
SCERNED
E RECENSE
F FENCERS
I CERESIN
SCRIENE
SINCERE
K NECKERS
L CRENELS
O ENCORES
NECROSE
P SPENCER
S CENSERS
SCERNES
SCREENS
SECERNS
T CENTERS
CENTRES
TENRECS
U CENSURE
Y SCENERY

CEHORS
OCHERS
A CHOREAS
ORACHES
ROACHES
B BROCHES
C CROCHES
E CHEEROS
CHOREES
COHERES
ECHOERS
RECHOSE
I COHEIRS
HEROICS
K CHOKERS
HOCKERS
SHOCKER
L CHOLERS
ORCHELS
M CHROMES
O CHOOSER
SOROCHE
P PORCHES
S COSHERS
T HECTORS
ROCHETS
ROTCHES
TOCHERS
TORCHES
TROCHES
U CHOREUS
CHOUSER
ROUCHES
Y COSHERY
Z SCHERZO

CEILST
STELIC
A ASTELIC
ELASTIC
LACIEST
LATICES
SALICET
D DELICTS
E SECTILE
H ELTCHIS
I ELICITS
K STICKLE
TICKLES
L CELLIST
N CLIENTS
LECTINS
STENCIL
O CITOLES
R RELICTS
U LUETICS

CELORS
CLOSER
A CLAROES
COALERS
ESCOLAR
ORACLES
RECOALS
SOLACER
B CORBELS
D SCOLDER
E CREOLES
RECLOSE
H CHOLERS
ORCHELS
I COILERS
RECOILS
K LOCKERS
RELOCKS

L ESCROLL
M CORMELS
N CLONERS
CORNELS
O COOLERS
CREOSOL
S CLOSERS
CRESOLS
ESCROLS
T COLTERS
CORSLET
COSTREL
LECTORS
U CLOSURE
COLURES
V CLOVERS
W SCOWLER
SCROWLE
Y SCROYLE

CILNOS
COLINS
A OILCANS
D CODLINS
E CINEOLS
CONSEIL
INCLOSE
G CLOSING
I SILICON
K INLOCKS
L COLLINS
M CLONISM
O CLOISON
SCOLION
U ULICONS
UNCOILS

CILOST
(STOLIC)
A CITOLAS
STOICAL
E CITOLES
H COLTISH
I COLITIS
SOLICIT
O SCIOLTO
R LICTORS
U COUTILS
OCULIST

DDEIMS
DESMID
A DIADEMS
E DEMISED
MISDEED
I MIDDIES
L MIDDLES
N MIDDENS
O DESMOID
S DESMIDS
T MIDDEST
U DEDIMUS
MUDDIES

DDEIST
(EDDITS)
A TADDIES
E DEIDEST
TEDDIES
I STIDDIE
TIDDIES
L TIDDLES
M MIDDEST
N DISTEND
O TODDIES

U STUDDIE
STUDIED

DEEMRS
(MERSED)
A REMADES
REMEADS
SMEARED
E DEMERSE
EMERSED
REDEEMS
REMEDES
G DEGERMS
I REMEIDS
REMISED
K SMERKED
L MELDERS
N MENDERS
REMENDS
O EMERODS
P DEPERMS
PREMEDS
U DEMURES
RESUMED

DEEPRS
SPREED
A PREASED
RESPADE
SPEARED
D PEDDERS
SPREDDE
E SPEEDER
SPEERED
H SPHERED
I PREDIES
PRESIDE
SPEIRED
SPIERED
L PEDLERS
SPELDER
M DEPERMS
PREMEDS
N SPENDER
O DEPOSER
REPOSED
R SPERRED
S DEPRESS
PRESSED
SPERSED
T PRESTED
U PERDUES
PERSUED
PERUSED
SUPERED

DEILLS
(DILLES)
A DALLIES
DISLEAL
LALDIES
SALLIED
E DELLIES
H SHILLED
I DILLIES
K DESKILL
SKILLED
O DOLLIES
P SPILLED
S LIDLESS
T STILLED
U ILLUDES
SULLIED
W SWILLED

DEILPS
DISPEL
A ALIPEDS
ELAPIDS
LAPIDES
PAIDLES
PALSIED
PLEIADS
C SPLICED
D DISPLED
PIDDLES
E SEEDLIP
SPEILED
SPIELED
I LIPIDES
L SPILLED
M DIMPLES
MISPLED
SIMPLED
N SPELDIN
SPINDLE
SPLINED
O DESPOIL
DIPLOES
DIPOLES
PELOIDS
SOLIPED
SPOILED
P SIPPLED
SLIPPED
S DISPELS
DISPLES
U DUPLIES

DEIPRS
SPIDER
A ASPIRED
DESPAIR
DIAPERS
PRAISED
C CRISPED
DISCERP
D DISPRED
E PREDIES
PRESIDE
SPEIRED
SPIERED
I PIERIDS
N PINDERS
O PERIODS
P DIPPERS
S PRISSED
SPIDERS
T SPIRTED
STRIPED
U PUDSIER
SIRUPED
UPDRIES
Y SPIDERY

DELOPS
SLOPED
A DEPOSAL
PEDALOS
E DELOPES
G SPLODGE
I DESPOIL
DIPLOES
DIPOLES
PELOIDS
SOLIPED
SPOILED
O POODLES
SPOOLED
P SLOPPED
R POLDERS
PRESOLD
U SOUPLED
Y DEPLOYS
PODLEYS

DENOPS
(SPONED)
A DAPSONE
D DESPOND
E DEPONES
SPONDEE
G SPONGED
I DISPONE
SPINODE
O SNOOPED
SPOONED
R PONDERS
RESPOND
U UNPOSED

DINORS
NIDORS
A INROADS
ORDAINS
SADIRON
E DINEROS
DONSIER
INDORSE
ORDINES
ROSINED
SORDINE
G RODINGS
H DISHORN
DRONISH
I SORDINI
M DORMINS
NIMRODS
O INDOORS
SORDINO
U DIURONS
DURIONS

EEKPRS
KREEPS
A PARKEES
RESPEAK
SPEAKER
C PECKERS
E KEEPERS
I PESKIER
L KELPERS
M KEMPERS
O RESPOKE
R REPERKS
U PERUKES

EELPRS
LEPERS
A LEAPERS
PLEASER
PRESALE
RELAPSE
REPEALS
D PEDLERS
SPELDER
E PEELERS
SLEEPER
SPEELER
H HELPERS
I REPLIES
SPIELER
K KELPERS
L PRESELL
RESPELL
SPELLER
M SEMPLER
O ELOPERS
LEPROSE
T PELTERS
PETRELS
RESPELT
SPELTER
U REPULSE
Y SLEEPRY
YELPERS

EELRSV
LEVERS
A LAVEERS
LEAVERS
REVEALS
SEVERAL
VEALERS
D DELVERS
E RELEVES
SLEEVER
H SHELVER
I LEVIERS
RELIVES
REVILES
SERVILE
VEILERS
O RESOLVE
R VERRELS
T SVELTER
U VELURES
V VERVELS

EENPST
(PESTEN)
A NEPETAS
PENATES
PESANTE
C PECTENS
E ENSTEEP
STEEPEN
I PENTISE
L PENTELS
O OPENEST
PENTOSE
POSTEEN
POTEENS
R PENSTER
PRESENT
REPENTS
SERPENT
U PUNTEES
W ENSWEPT
Y STEPNEY

EERRSV
SERVER
A REAVERS
B REVERBS
E RESERVE
REVERES
REVERSE
SEVERER
G VERGERS
I REIVERS
REVERSI
REVISER
RIEVERS
L VERRELS
N NERVERS
O REVERSO
S SERVERS
VERSERS
T REVERTS
U REVEURS
W SWERVER
Y SERVERY

EERSVW
SWERVE
A WEAVERS
D SWERVED
E SERVEWE
WEEVERS
H WHERVES
I REVIEWS
VIEWERS
O OVERSEW
R SWERVER
S SWERVES
U SURVEWE

EGILLS
(GILLES)
A GALLIES
GALLISE
E GELLIES
I GILLIES
N LEGLINS
LINGELS
LINGLES
SELLING
O GOLLIES
R GILLERS
GRILLES
T GILLETS
U GULLIES
LIGULES

EGINPS
GIPSEN
A PEASING
SPAEING
SPINAGE
E SEEPING
H HESPING
PHESING
I PEISING
PIGSNIE
L PINGLES
SPIGNEL
O EPIGONS
PIGEONS
PINGOES
P PIGPENS
R PERSING
PINGERS
SPRINGE
S GIPSENS
U SPUEING
W SPEWING
Y ESPYING
PEYSING
PIGSNEY

EGLNSU
LUNGES
A ANGELUS
LAGUNES
LANGUES
B BLUNGES
BUNGLES
D GULDENS
E LUNGEES
F ENGULFS
G SNUGGLE
I LUNGIES
SLUEING
J JUNGLES
N GUNNELS
O LOUNGES
P PLUNGES
PUNGLES
R LUNGERS
S GUNLESS
GUNSELS
T ENGLUTS
GLUTENS
U UNGLUES

EHLLOS
HELLOS
A HALLOES
E HELLOES
I HILLOES
HOLLIES
O HOLLOES
R HOLLERS
U HULLOES

EHNORS
HONERS
A HOARSEN
SENHORA
B BREHONS
D DEHORNS
E RESHONE
G GORHENS
I HEROINS
INSHORE
K HONKERS
O HEROONS
ONSHORE
SOREHON
P PHONERS
R HORNERS
S NOSHERS
SENHORS
T HORNETS
SHORTEN
THRENOS
THRONES
U UNHORSE
W RESHOWN
Y NOSHERY

EILLPS
(SPILLE)
A ILLAPSE
D SPILLED
E ELLIPSE
I ILLIPES
O POLLIES
R SPILLER
S LIPLESS
U PILULES

EILLST
ILLEST
A TAILLES
TALLIES
B BESTILL
BILLETS
C CELLIST
D STILLED
E TELLIES
F FILLETS
G GILLETS
I ILLITES
J JILLETS
K SKILLET
M MILLETS
MISTELL
N LENTILS
LINTELS
TELLINS
O OILLETS
R RILLETS
STILLER
TILLERS
TRELLIS
S LISTELS
T LITTLES
U TUILLES
W WILLEST
WILLETS

EILNPS
SPLINE
A ALPINES
PINEALS
SPANIEL
SPLENIA
C PENCILS
SPLENIC
D SPELDIN
SPINDLE
SPLINED
E PENSILE
G PINGLES
SPIGNEL
H PLENISH
I SPLENII
M PLENISM
O EPSILON
PINOLES
P LIPPENS
NIPPLES
R PILSNER
S PENSILS
SPINELS
SPLINES
T PINTLES
PLENIST
U LINEUPS
LUPINES
SPINULE
UNPILES

EILPST
STIPEL
A APLITES
PALIEST
PLATIES
TALIPES
E EPISTLE
PELITES
G PIGLETS
I SPILITE
K SKELPIT
M LIMPEST
LIMPETS
N PINTLES
PLENIST
O PIOLETS
PISTOLE
P STIPPLE
TIPPLES
R RESPLIT
SPIRTLE
TRIPLES
S STIPELS
TIPLESS
T SPITTLE
U PULIEST
PUTELIS
STIPULE

EILRSV
SILVER
A REVISAL
C CLIVERS
D DRIVELS
E LEVIERS
RELIVES
REVILES
SERVILE
VEILERS
H SHRIVEL
I LIVIERS
M VERMILS
N SILVERN
O OLIVERS
VIOLERS
S SILVERS
SLIVERS
U SURVEIL
Y LIVYERS
SILVERY

EIMMRS
SIMMER
A MAIMERS
RAMMIES
D DIMMERS
E IMMERSE
G GIMMERS
MEGRIMS
H SHIMMER
I MIMSIER
K KIMMERS
SKIMMER
L LIMMERS
SLIMMER
N NIMMERS
O MEMOIRS
R RIMMERS
S MERISMS
SIMMERS
T MISTERM
U IMMURES
MUMSIER
RUMMIES
W SWIMMER
Z ZIMMERS

EIMMST
SEMMIT
A MISMATE
SEMIMAT
TAMMIES
D DIMMEST
E MISMEET
I MISTIME
M MIMMEST
O TOMMIES
R MISTERM
S SEMMITS
TSIMMES
U TUMMIES
Z TZIMMES

EIMPRS
SIMPER
A IMPRESA
SAMPIRE
C SPERMIC
E EMPIRES
EMPRISE
EPIMERS
IMPRESE
PREMIES
PREMISE
SPIREME
I PISMIRE
PRIMSIE
L LIMPERS
PRELIMS
RIMPLES
SIMPLER
O IMPOSER
PROMISE
SEMIPRO
R PRIMERS
S IMPRESS
PREMISS
SIMPERS
SPIREMS
T IMPREST
PERMITS
U RUMPIES
SPUMIER
UMPIRES

EIMPST
(IMPEST)
A IMPASTE
PASTIME
E EMPTIES
SEPTIME
I PIETISM
J JIMPEST
K MISKEPT
L LIMPEST
LIMPETS
N EMPTINS
PIMENTS
O MOPIEST
OPTIMES
R IMPREST
PERMITS
S MISSTEP
U IMPETUS
IMPUTES
UPTIMES
Y MISTYPE

EIPRRS
PRISER
A ASPIRER
PARRIES
PRAISER
RAPIERS
RASPIER
REPAIRS
C CRISPER
PRICERS
E PERRIES
PRISERE
REPRISE
RESPIRE
G GRIPERS
I SPIRIER
M PRIMERS
O PROSIER
P RIPPERS
S PRISERS
T STRIPER
U PURSIER
UPRISER
Z PRIZERS

EIPSTT
(PITTES)
A PATTIES
TAPETIS
D SPITTED
E PETITES
PETTIES
H PETTISH
I PIETIST
L SPITTLE
N SPITTEN
O POTTIES
TIPTOES
P TIPPETS
R PITTERS
SPITTER
TIPSTER
U PUTTIES
Y TYPIEST

ELOPRS
POLERS
A PAROLES
REPOSAL
D POLDERS
PRESOLD
E ELOPERS
LEPROSE
G PROLEGS
I SLOPIER
SPOILER
L POLLERS
REPOLLS
O LOOPERS
SPOOLER
P LOPPERS
PROPELS
R PROLERS
S PLESSOR
SLOPERS
SPLORES
T PETROLS
REPLOTS
U LEPROUS
PELORUS
PERLOUS
SPORULE
V PLOVERS
W PLOWERS
X PLEXORS
Y LEPROSY

EOPPRS
(SOPPER)
A APPOSER
B BOPPERS
C COPPERS
D DOPPERS
E PREPOSE
H HOPPERS
SHOPPER
I SOPPIER
L LOPPERS
PROPELS
M MOPPERS
O OPPOSER
PROPOSE
P POPPERS
R PROPERS
PROSPER
S OPPRESS
PORPESS
T STOPPER
TOPPERS
U PURPOSE
W SWOPPER
Y PYROPES
YOPPERS

EPRRSU
PURSER
A PARURES
UPREARS
C SPRUCER
D SPURRED
E PERUSER
REPURES
G PURGERS
I PURSIER
UPRISER
L PURLERS
SLURPER
N PRUNERS
SPURNER
O POURERS
REPOURS
R SPURRER
S PURSERS
U PURSUER
USURPER
Y SPURREY

EPRSTU
UPREST
A PASTURE
UPRATES
UPSTARE
UPTEARS
C PRECUTS
D SPURTED
E PERTUSE
REPUTES
I PERITUS
PUIREST
L SPURTLE
M STUMPER
SUMPTER
N PUNSTER
PUNTERS
O PETROUS
POSTURE
POUTERS
PROTEUS
SEPTUOR
SPOUTER
TROUPES
S UPRESTS
T PUTTERS
SPUTTER
U PUTURES

GINOPS
POSING
A SOAPING
C COPINGS
COPSING
SCOPING
D DOPINGS
PONGIDS
E EPIGONS
PIGEONS
PINGOES
H GINSHOP
POSHING
I POISING
K SPOKING
L POLINGS
SLOPING
N SPONGIN
O SOOPING
P SOPPING
R PROIGNS
PROSING
ROPINGS
SPORING
S POSINGS
POSSING
T POSTING
STOPING
U SOUPING
Y POYSING

IKLNOS
(LIKONS)
A KAOLINS
C INLOCKS
E SONLIKE
I OILSKIN
O SKOLION
U ULIKONS

ILOPST
PILOTS
A APOSTIL
TOPSAIL
E PIOLETS
PISTOLE
I PILOTIS
L POLLIST
N PONTILS
O POLOIST
TOPSOIL
S PISTOLS
POSTILS
T SPOTLIT
U SLIPOUT

NORSTU
(UNROTS)
A ROUSANT
SANTOUR
B BURTONS
D ROTUNDS
E TENOURS
TONSURE
I NITROUS
TURIONS
M NOSTRUM
O UNROOST
UNROOTS
U OUTRUNS
RUNOUTS

6-LETTER STEMS THAT COMBINE WITH AEIOU AND Y ONLY

ACLRST
A CASTRAL
E CARTELS
CLARETS
CRESTAL
SCARLET
TARCELS
I CITRALS
O CARLOTS
CROTALS
SCROTAL
U CRUSTAL
CURTALS
Y CRYSTAL

ANRSTT
A RATTANS
TANTRAS
TARTANS
E NATTERS
RATTENS
I STRAINT
TRANSIT
O ATTORNS
RATTONS
ROTTANS
U TRUANTS
Y TYRANTS

BELMRT
A LAMBERT
E TREMBLE
I TIMBREL
O TEMBLOR
U TUMBLER
TUMBREL
Y TREMBLY

CEEGNR
A ENGRACE
E REGENCE
I CREEING
ENERGIC
GENERIC
O COGENER
CONGREE
U URGENCE
Y REGENCY

CEHPRS
A EPARCHS
PARCHES
E PERCHES
I CERIPHS
CIPHERS
SPHERIC
O PORCHES
U CHERUPS
Y CHYPRES
CYPHERS

CELRST
A CARTELS
CLARETS
CRESTAL
SCARLET
TARCELS
E TERCELS
I RELICTS
O COLTERS
CORSLET
COSTREL
LECTORS
U CLUSTER
CULTERS
CUSTREL
CUTLERS

RELUCTS
Y CLYSTER

CEPRSS
A ESCARPS
PARSECS
SCRAPES
SECPARS
SPACERS
E PRECESS
I SPICERS
O CORPSES
PROCESS
U PERCUSS
SPRUCES
Y CYPRESS

CEPRST
A CARPETS
PREACTS
PRECAST
SPECTRA
E RECEPTS
RESPECT
SCEPTER
SCEPTRE
SPECTER
SPECTRE
I TRICEPS
O COPTERS
PROSECT
U PRECUTS
Y SCEPTRY

DGINRS
A DARINGS
GRADINS
E DINGERS
ENGIRDS
I RIDINGS
O RODINGS
U UNGIRDS
Y DRYINGS

ELNRST
A ANTLERS
RENTALS
SALTERN
STERNAL
E NESTLER
RELENTS
SLENTER
I LINTERS
SLINTER
SNIRTLE
O LENTORS
U RUNLETS
Y STERNLY

ELRSST
A ARTLESS
LASTERS
SALTERS
SLATERS
TARSELS
E STREELS
TRESSEL
I LISTERS
RELISTS
O OSTLERS
STEROLS
TORSELS
U LUSTERS
LUSTRES
RESULTS
RUSTLES
SUTLERS
ULSTERS
Y STYLERS

ELRSTT
A RATTLES
SLATTER
STARLET
STARTLE
TATLERS
E LETTERS
LETTRES
SETTLER
STERLET
TRESTLE
I LITTERS
SLITTER
STILTER
TESTRIL
TILTERS
TITLERS
O SETTLOR
SLOTTER
TOLTERS
U TURTLES
Y TETRYLS

EPRSST
A PASTERS
REPASTS
SPAREST
E PESTERS
PRESETS
I ESPRITS
PERSIST
PRIESTS
SITREPS
SPRIEST
SPRITES
STIRPES
STRIPES
TRIPSES
O PORTESS
POSTERS
PRESTOS
REPOSTS
RESPOTS
STOPERS
U UPRESTS
Y SPRYEST

ERRSTT
A RATTERS
RESTART
STARTER
E TERRETS
I RITTERS
TERRITS
O RETORTS
ROTTERS
STERTOR
TORRETS
U RUTTERS
TRUSTER
TURRETS
Y TRYSTER

FGILNT
A FATLING
E FELTING
I FLITING
LIFTING
O LOFTING
U FLUTING
Y FLYTING

GHINTT
A HATTING
TATHING
E TIGHTEN
I HITTING
TITHING
O HOTTING
TONIGHT
U HUTTING
Y TYTHING

GILNST
A ANGLIST
LASTING
SALTING
SLATING
STALING
E GLISTEN
LESTING
SINGLET
TINGLES
I LISTING
SILTING
STILING
TILINGS
O LINGOTS
TIGLONS
TOLINGS
U LUSTING
LUTINGS
SINGULT
Y STYLING

GIMNST
A MASTING
MATINGS
TAMINGS
E STEMING
TEMSING
I MISTING
SMITING
STIMING
TIMINGS
O GNOMIST
U MUSTING
Y STYMING

GINSTT
A STATING
TASTING
E SETTING
TESTING
I SITTING
O SOTTING
U TUTSING
Y STYTING

6-LETTER STEMS THAT COMBINE WITH AEIOU ONLY

ABDNRS
A BANDARS
SANDBAR
E BANDERS
I RIBANDS
O ROBANDS
U SANDBUR

ACHKRS
A CHAKRAS
CHARKAS
E HACKERS
I RICKSHA
O CHOKRAS
U CHUKARS

ACNRST
A ARCTANS
CANTARS
E CANTERS
CARNETS
NECTARS
RECANTS
SCANTER
TANRECS
TRANCES
I NARCIST
O CANTORS
CARTONS
CONTRAS
CRATONS
U UNCARTS

ACRRST
A CARRATS
E CARTERS
CRATERS
TRACERS
I TRICARS
O CARROTS
TROCARS
U CRATURS

ADGNRS
A ARGANDS
E DANGERS
GANDERS
GARDENS
I DARINGS
GRADINS
O DRAGONS
U DURGANS

ADLNSS
A SANDALS
E SENDALS
I ISLANDS
O SOLANDS
SOLDANS
U SULDANS

AMNRST
A ARTSMAN
MANTRAS
E ARTSMEN
MARTENS
SARMENT
SMARTEN
I MARTINS
O MATRONS
TRANSOM
U ANTRUMS
UNSMART

ANPRST
A PARTANS
SPARTAN
TARPANS
TRAPANS
E ARPENTS
ENTRAPS
PANTERS
PARENTS
PASTERN
PERSANT
TREPANS
I SPIRANT
SPRAINT
O PARTONS
PATRONS
TARPONS
U SUNTRAP
UNSTRAP

BDELNR
A BLANDER
E BLENDER
REBLEND
I BLINDER
BRINDLE
O BLONDER
U BLUNDER
BUNDLER

BDENRS
A BANDERS
E BENDERS
I BINDERS
INBREDS
REBINDS
O BONDERS
U BURDENS

BDGINN
A BANDING
E BENDING
I BINDING
O BONDING
U BUNDING

BEKRRS
A BARKERS
E BERSERK
I BRISKER
O BROKERS
U BRUSKER
BURKERS

BELRST
A ALBERTS
BATLERS
BLASTER
LABRETS
STABLER
E BELTERS
TREBLES
I BLISTER
BRISTLE
RIBLETS
O BOLSTER
BOLTERS
LOBSTER
U BLUSTER
BUSTLER
BUTLERS
SUBTLER

BERSTT
A BATTERS
TABRETS
E BETTERS
I BITTERS
O BETTORS
U BUTTERS

BGGGIN
A BAGGING
E BEGGING
I BIGGING
O BOGGING
U BUGGING

BGILLN
A BALLING
E BELLING
I BILLING
O BOLLING
U BULLING

BGILNS
A ABLINGS
SABLING
E BINGLES
I SIBLING
O GLOBINS
GOBLINS
LOBINGS
U BLUINGS

BGINTT
A BATTING
E BETTING
I BITTING
O BOTTING
U BUTTING

CCDEKL
A CACKLED
CLACKED
E CLECKED
I CLICKED
O CLOCKED
COCKLED
U CLUCKED

CCEHRS
A CREACHS
E CRECHES
SCREECH
I SCREICH
SCRIECH
O CROCHES
U CURCHES

CDDEER
A CEDARED
E DECREED
RECEDED
I DECIDER
DECRIED
O DECODER
RECODED
U REDUCED

CDDEIS
A CADDIES
E DECIDES
I DISCIDE
O DISCOED
U CUDDIES

CDEKNS
A SNACKED
E SNECKED
I DICKENS
SNICKED
O DOCKENS
U SUNDECK
UNDECKS

CDEKRS
A DACKERS
E DECKERS
I DICKERS
SCRIKED
O DOCKERS
REDOCKS
U DUCKERS

CDEKRT
A TRACKED
E TRECKED
I TRICKED
O TROCKED
U TRUCKED

CENRST
A CANTERS
CARNETS
NECTARS
RECANTS
SCANTER
TANRECS
TRANCES
E CENTERS
CENTRES
TENRECS
I CISTERN
CRETINS
O CONSTER
CORNETS
CRESTON
CRONETS
U ENCRUST

CGIKNP
A PACKING
E PECKING
I PICKING
O POCKING
U KINGCUP

CGIKNR
A ARCKING
CARKING
CRAKING
RACKING
E RECKING
I RICKING
O CORKING
ROCKING
U RUCKING

CHILST
A CHITALS
E ELTCHIS
I LITCHIS
O COLTISH
U CULTISH

CINRST
A NARCIST
E CISTERN
CRETINS
I CITRINS
O CISTRON
CITRONS
CORNIST
CORTINS
U INCRUST

DDDELP
A PADDLED
E PEDDLED
I PIDDLED
O PLODDED
U PUDDLED

DDELPR
A PADDLER
E PEDDLER
I PIDDLER
O PLODDER
U PUDDLER

DDGINR
A RADDING
E GRINDED
REDDING
I RIDDING
O RODDING
U RUDDING

DEERRV
A AVERRED
E REVERED
I DERIVER
REDRIVE
RIVERED
O OVERRED
REDROVE
U VERDURE

DEGLNS
A DANGLES
GLANDES
LAGENDS
SLANGED
E LEGENDS
I DINGLES
ELDINGS
ENGILDS
SINGLED
O DONGLES
GOLDENS
U GULDENS

DEHLLO
A HALLOED
HOLLAED
E HELLOED
I HILLOED
O HOLLOED
U HULLOED

DEHNRS
A HANDERS
HARDENS
E HERDENS
I HINDERS
NERDISH
SHRINED
O DEHORNS
U HURDENS

DELSTT
A SLATTED
E SETTLED
I SLITTED
STILTED
O DOTTELS
DOTTLES
SLOTTED
U SUTTLED

DEMNST
A TANDEMS
E DEMENTS
I MINDSET
MISTEND
O ENDMOST
U DUSTMEN

DENNST
A STANDEN
E DENNETS
STENNED
I DENTINS
INDENTS
INTENDS
O STONNED
TENDONS
U DUNNEST
STUNNED

DENPRS
A PANDERS
E SPENDER
I PINDERS
O PONDERS
RESPOND
U SPURNED

DENRST
A ENDARTS
STANDER
STARNED
E STERNED
TENDERS
TENDRES
I TINDERS
O RODENTS
SNORTED
U RETUNDS
UNDREST

DENSTT
A ATTENDS
E DETENTS
STENTED
I DENTIST
DISTENT
STINTED
O SNOTTED
U STUDENT
STUNTED

DEPRST
A DEPARTS
DRAPETS
PETARDS
E PRESTED
I SPIRTED
STRIPED
O DEPORTS
REDTOPS
SPORTED
U SPURTED

DFGINN
A FANDING
E FENDING
I FINDING
O FONDING
U FUNDING

DGINNR
A DARNING
NARDING
RANDING
E GRINNED
RENDING
I RINDING
O DRONING
U DURNING

DGINNW
A DAWNING
E WENDING
I DWINING
WINDING
O DOWNING
U WINDGUN

DGINST
A DATINGS
E NIDGETS
STEDING
STINGED
I TIDINGS
O DOTINGS
U DUSTING

DILSTY
A STAIDLY
E DISTYLE
I IDYLIST
O STYLOID
U DUSTILY

EFHLSS
A FLASHES
E FLESHES
I HISSELF
SELFISH
O FLOSHES
U FLUSHES

EFLRST
A FALTERS
E FELTERS
REFLETS
TELFERS
I FILTERS
LIFTERS
STIFLER
TRIFLES
O FLORETS
LOFTERS
U FLUSTER
FLUTERS
RESTFUL

EFLRTT
A FLATTER
E FETTLER
I FLITTER
O FORTLET
U FLUTTER

EGGLRS
A GARGLES
LAGGERS
RAGGLES
E EGGLERS
LEGGERS
I LIGGERS
O LOGGERS
SLOGGER
U GURGLES
LUGGERS
SLUGGER

EGMNST
A MAGNETS
E SEGMENT
I STEMING
TEMSING
O EMONGST
U NUTMEGS

EGNRST
A ARGENTS
GARNETS
STRANGE
E GERENTS
REGENTS
I RESTING
STINGER
O TONGERS
U GUNTERS
GURNETS
SURGENT

EGRSST
A GASTERS
STAGERS
E REGESTS
I TIGRESS
O GROSETS
STORGES
U GUTSERS

EHKRSS
A KASHERS
SHAKERS
E SHREEKS
I SHREIKS
SHRIEKS
SHRIKES
O KOSHERS
U HUSKERS

EHLLRS
A HERSALL
E HELLERS
SHELLER
I HILLERS
RELLISH
O HOLLERS
U HULLERS

EHLRST
A HALTERS
HARSLET
LATHERS
SLATHER
THALERS
E SHELTER
I SLITHER
O HOLSTER
HOSTLER
U HURTLES
HUSTLER

EHNRST
A ANTHERS
HARTENS
THENARS
E THRENES
I HINTERS
O HORNETS
SHORTEN
THRENOS
THRONES
U HUNTERS
SHUNTER
UNHERST

EKLNRS
A RANKLES
E KERNELS
I LINKERS
RELINKS
SLINKER
O SNORKEL
U LUNKERS
RUNKLES

EKRSST
A SKATERS
STRAKES
STREAKS
TASKERS
E STREEKS
I STRIKES
O STOKERS
STROKES
U TUSKERS

ELLPRS
A SPALLER
E PRESELL
RESPELL
SPELLER
I SPILLER
O POLLERS
REPOLLS
U PULLERS

ELPRST
A PALTERS
PERSALT
PLASTER
PLATERS
PSALTER
STAPLER
E PELTERS
PETRELS
RESPELT
SPELTER
I RESPLIT
SPIRTLE
TRIPLES
O PETROLS
REPLOTS
U SPURTLE

EMPRST
A EMPARTS
RESTAMP
STAMPER
TAMPERS
E TEMPERS
I IMPREST
PERMITS
O STOMPER
TROMPES
U STUMPER
SUMPTER

EMRRST
A ARMREST
SMARTER

E TERMERS
I RETRIMS
TRIMERS
O TERMORS
TREMORS
U STURMER

EMRSST
A MASTERS
STREAMS
E RESTEMS
I MISTERS
SMITERS
O MOTSERS
U ESTRUMS
MUSTERS
STUMERS

ENNRST
A TANNERS
E RENNETS
TENNERS
I INTERNS
TINNERS
O STONERN
TONNERS
U RUNNETS
STUNNER

ENPRST
A ARPENTS
ENTRAPS
PANTERS
PARENTS
PASTERN
PERSANT
TREPANS
E PENSTER
PRESENT
REPENTS
SERPENT
I NIPTERS
PTERINS
O POSTERN
PRONEST
U PUNSTER
PUNTERS

ENRSST
A SARSNET
TRANSES
E NESTERS
RENESTS
RESENTS
STRENES

I ESTRINS
INSERTS
SINTERS
O NESTORS
STONERS
TENSORS
U UNRESTS

ENRSTT
A NATTERS
RATTENS
E NETTERS
TENTERS
TESTERN
I ENTRIST
RETINTS
STINTER
TINTERS
O ROTTENS
SNOTTER
STENTOR
U ENTRUST
NUTTERS

ENSSST
A ASSENTS
SNASTES
E SETNESS
I SENSIST
O SESTONS
U SUNSETS

EPRRSS
A PARSERS
RASPERS
SPARERS
SPARRES
SPARSER
E PRESSER
REPRESS
SPERRES
I PRISERS
O PRESSOR
PROSERS
U PURSERS

EPRSSS
A PASSERS
E PRESSES
SPERSES
I PISSERS
PRISSES
O POSSERS
PROSSES
U PUSSERS

EPRSTT
A PATTERS
SPATTER
TAPSTER
E PERTEST
PETTERS
PRETEST
I PITTERS
SPITTER
TIPSTER
O POTTERS
PROTEST
SPOTTER
U PUTTERS
SPUTTER

ERRSST
A ARRESTS
RASTERS
STARERS
E RESTERS
I STIRRES
O RESORTS
ROSTERS
SORTERS
STORERS
U RUSTRES
TRUSSER

ERSSST
A ASSERTS
TRASSES
E TRESSES
I RESISTS
SISTERS
O TOSSERS
U RUSSETS
TRUSSES
TUSSERS

ERSTTT
A STRETTA
TARTEST
TATTERS
E STRETTE
TETTERS
I STRETTI
TITTERS
TRITEST
O STOTTER
STRETTO
TOTTERS
U STUTTER

FGILNR
A FLARING
E FLINGER
I RIFLING
O ROLFING
U FURLING

GGGILN
A LAGGING
E LEGGING
I LIGGING
O LOGGING
U LUGGING

GGINNR
A RANGING
E GERNING
I GIRNING
RINGING
O GRONING
U GURNING

GGINRS
A RAGINGS
SIRGANG
E GINGERS
NIGGERS
SERGING
SNIGGER
I GRISING
O GORINGS
GRINGOS
U SURGING
URGINGS

GHINNT
A HANTING
TANGHIN
E HENTING
I HINTING
NITHING
O NOTHING
U HUNTING

GHINPS
A HASPING
PASHING
PHASING
SHAPING
E HESPING
PHESING
I PISHING
O GINSHOP
POSHING
U GUNSHIP

PUSHING

GHINRS
A GARNISH
RASHING
SHARING
E HINGERS
I HIRINGS
O HORSING
SHORING
U RUSHING

GILNPP
A LAPPING
PALPING
E LEPPING
I LIPPING
O LOPPING
U PULPING

GILNPS
A LAPSING
PALINGS
SAPLING
E PINGLES
SPIGNEL
I LISPING
PILINGS
SLIPING
SPILING
O POLINGS
SLOPING
U PLUSING
PULINGS
PULSING
PUSLING

GIMNPR
A GRIPMAN
RAMPING
E GRIPMEN
IMPREGN
PERMING
I PRIMING
O ROMPING
U RUMPING

GIMNSS
A MASSING
E MESSING
I MISSING
O MOSSING
U MUSINGS
MUSSING

GINNRS
A SNARING
E ENRINGS
GINNERS
I RINSING
O SNORING
SORNING
U NURSING
URNINGS

GINPPP
A PAPPING
E PEPPING
I PIPPING
O POPPING
U PUPPING

GINPPS
A SAPPING
E PIGPENS
I PIPINGS
SIPPING
O SOPPING
U SUPPING
UPPINGS

GINPTT
A PATTING
E PETTING
I PITTING
O POTTING
U PUTTING

GINRTT
A RATTING
TARTING
E GITTERN
RETTING
I RITTING
O ROTTING
U RUTTING

LNPSTU
A PULSANT
PULTANS
E PENULTS
I UNSPILT
UNSPLIT
O PLUTONS
PULTONS
U PULTUNS

Section Six

Hooks and Blockers

Introduction

Which 2-letter words can be transformed into which 3-letter words by adding a single letter at either the beginning or the end? An example is HI, which by the addition of a letter at the front becomes CHI, GHI, KHI and PHI and by the addition of a letter at the back becomes HIC, HID, HIE, HIM, HIN, HIP, HIS and HIT. Such words, which can add a letter at the front or back, are called hooks, as they provide places for other words to hook on to.

Conversely, words which cannot have a letter added at the front or back are called blockers.

Hooks

There are two parts to this section. The first, and main, part is a complete list of hooks showing words of length two to eight letters which can have a letter added, either at the front or the back, to create a longer word. The second is a selection of useful -S hooks worthy of specific note. More about these later.

In actual play, it can be useful to play a 3-letter word (BAP, say) which has an unusual extension to four letters (BAPU, in this case). If the S's and blanks have already been played, the chances are that your opponent won't know BAPU, so the BAP opening is likely to be safe until you have a U to put on to it.

It was felt that for learning purposes it would be valuable also to include in the 2- and 3-letter lists those words that *cannot* be extended (and are therefore blockers rather than hooks). These words are of course also listed in the Blockers section.

For 8-letter word -S hooks, only a specific subset of the possible hooks is shown. All 9-letter words which are -S inflections of 8-letter words have been omitted, being of little practical interest. For example, the hook AARDVARK-S is not listed. However, where 9-letter words are *non-plural* -S hooks of 8-letter words already ending in S (for example, NERVINES-S and TYRANNES-S) these have been retained.

HOOKS

2-LETTER WORD HOOKS: including all root words

B-**AA** M-AA AA-H AA-L AA-S C-**AB** D-AB F-AB G-AB J-AB K-AB L-AB N-AB S-AB T-AB W-AB AB-A AB-B AB-O AB-S AB-Y B-**AD** C-AD D-AD F-AD G-AD H-AD L-AD M-AD P-AD R-AD S-AD T-AD W-AD AD-D AD-O AD-S AD-Z D-**AE** G-AE H-AE K-AE M-AE N-AE S-AE T-AE V-AE W-AE B-**AG** D-AG F-AG G-AG H-AG J-AG L-AG M-AG N-AG R-AG S-AG T-AG W-AG Z-AG AG-A AG-E AG-O A-**AH** B-AH D-AH F-AH H-AH

L-AH N-AH P-AH R-AH Y-AH AH-A AH-S K-**AI** R-AI S-AI T-AI AI-A AI-D AI-L AI-M AI-N AI-R AI-S AI-T A-**AL** B-AL D-AL G-AL M-AL P-AL S-AL AL-A AL-B AL-E AL-L AL-P AL-S AL-T B-**AM** C-AM D-AM G-AM H-AM J-AM K-AM L-AM M-AM N-AM P-AM R-AM S-AM T-AM Y-AM AM-A AM-I AM-P AM-U B-**AN** C-AN D-AN E-AN F-AN G-AN H-AN M-AN N-AN P-AN R-AN S-AN T-AN V-AN W-AN AN-A AN-D AN-E

AN-I AN-N AN-T AN-Y B-**AR** C-AR E-AR F-AR G-AR J-AR L-AR M-AR O-AR P-AR S-AR T-AR V-AR W-AR Y-AR AR-B AR-C AR-D AR-E AR-F AR-K AR-M AR-S AR-T AR-Y A-**AS** B-AS D-AS E-AS F-AS G-AS H-AS K-AS L-AS M-AS N-AS P-AS R-AS T-AS V-AS W-AS AS-H AS-K AS-P AS-S B-**AT** C-AT E-AT F-AT G-AT H-AT K-AT L-AT M-AT N-AT O-AT P-AT Q-AT R-AT S-AT T-AT V-AT W-AT AT-E AT-T C-**AW**

D-AW F-AW H-AW J-AW K-AW L-AW M-AW N-AW P-AW R-AW S-AW T-AW V-AW W-AW Y-AW AW-A AW-E AW-L AW-N F-**AX** L-AX M-AX P-AX R-AX S-AX T-AX W-AX Z-AX AX-E B-**AY** C-AY D-AY F-AY G-AY H-AY J-AY K-AY L-AY M-AY N-AY P-AY R-AY S-AY T-AY W-AY Y-AY AY-E AY-S AY-U A-**BA** O-BA BA-A BA-C BA-D BA-G BA-H BA-L BA-M BA-N BA-P BA-R BA-S BA-T BA-Y O-**BE** BE-D BE-E BE-G BE-L BE-N

BE-T BE-Y BE-Z O-**BI** BI-B BI-D BI-G BI-N BI-O BI-S BI-T BI-Z A-**BO** O-BO BO-A BO-B BO-D BO-G BO-H BO-K BO-N BO-O BO-P BO-R BO-S BO-T BO-W BO-X BO-Y A-**BY** BY-E BY-S A-**CH** E-CH I-CH O-CH CH-A CH-E CH-I O-**DA** DA-B DA-D DA-E DA-G DA-H DA-K DA-L DA-M DA-N DA-P DA-S DA-W DA-Y I-**DE** O-DE DE-B DE-E DE-F DE-I DE-L DE-N DE-V DE-W DE-X DE-Y **DI**-B DI-D DI-E DI-G DI-M

DI-N DI-P DI-S DI-T DI-V A-**DO** U-DO DO-B DO-C DO-D DO-E DO-G DO-H DO-L DO-M DO-N DO-O DO-P DO-R DO-S DO-T DO-W K-**EA** L-EA P-EA S-EA T-EA Y-EA Z-EA EA-N EA-R EA-S EA-T EA-U B-**ED** F-ED G-ED K-ED L-ED M-ED N-ED P-ED R-ED S-ED T-ED W-ED Z-ED ED-H B-**EE** C-EE D-EE F-EE G-EE J-EE L-EE N-EE P-EE R-EE S-EE T-EE V-EE W-EE Z-EE EE-K EE-L EE-N D-**EF** K-EF N-EF R-EF

T-EF EF-F EF-S EF-T F-**EH** H-EH P-EH R-EH Y-EH EH-S B-**EL** C-EL D-EL E-EL G-EL M-EL S-EL T-EL Z-EL EL-D EL-F EL-K EL-L EL-M EL-S EL-T F-**EM** G-EM H-EM M-EM R-EM W-EM EM-E EM-F EM-S EM-U B-**EN** D-EN E-EN F-EN G-EN H-EN K-EN M-EN P-EN R-EN S-EN T-EN W-EN Y-EN EN-D EN-E EN-G EN-S F-**ER** H-ER P-ER S-ER ER-A ER-E ER-F ER-G ER-K ER-N ER-R ER-S H-**ES** L-ES M-ES O-ES

P-ES R-ES T-ES Y-ES ES-S ES-T B-**ET** F-ET G-ET H-ET J-ET K-ET L-ET M-ET N-ET P-ET R-ET S-ET T-ET V-ET W-ET Y-ET ET-A ET-H D-**EX** H-EX K-EX L-EX R-EX S-EX V-EX W-EX Y-EX Z-EX **FA**-B FA-D FA-G FA-H FA-N FA-P FA-R FA-S FA-T FA-W FA-X FA-Y **FY** **GI**-B GI-D GI-E GI-F GI-G GI-N GI-O GI-P GI-S GI-T A-**GO** E-GO Y-GO GO-A GO-B GO-D GO-E GO-N GO-O GO-R GO-S GO-T GO-V

GO-X GO-Y **GU**-B GU-E GU-L GU-M GU-N GU-P GU-R GU-S GU-T GU-V GU-Y A-**HA** C-HA S-HA W-HA HA-D HA-E HA-G HA-H HA-J HA-M HA-N HA-O HA-P HA-S HA-T HA-W HA-Y C-**HE** S-HE T-HE HE-H HE-M HE-N HE-P HE-R HE-S HE-T HE-W HE-X HE-Y C-**HI** G-HI K-HI P-HI HI-C HI-D HI-E HI-M HI-N HI-P HI-S HI-T O-**HM** HM-M M-**HO** O-HO P-HO R-HO T-HO W-HO Z-HO HO-A HO-B HO-C HO-D HO-E HO-G

HO-H HO-I HO-N HO-O HO-P HO-S HO-T HO-W HO-X HO-Y A-**ID** B-ID C-ID D-ID F-ID G-ID H-ID K-ID L-ID M-ID N-ID R-ID T-ID V-ID Y-ID ID-E ID-S G-**IF** K-IF R-IF IF-F IF-S A-**IN** B-IN D-IN F-IN G-IN H-IN J-IN K-IN L-IN P-IN R-IN S-IN T-IN V-IN W-IN Y-IN Z-IN IN-K IN-N IN-S B-**IO** G-IO IO-N IO-S A-**IS** B-IS C-IS D-IS G-IS H-IS L-IS M-IS N-IS P-IS Q-IS S-IS T-IS V-IS

W-IS
X-IS
IS-H
IS-M
IS-O
A-**IT**
B-IT
C-IT
D-IT
F-IT
G-IT
H-IT
K-IT
L-IT
N-IT
P-IT
R-IT
S-IT
T-IT
W-IT
Z-IT
IT-A
IT-S
JO-B
JO-E
JO-G
JO-R
JO-T
JO-W
JO-Y
O-**KA**
S-KA
KA-B
KA-E
KA-F
KA-I
KA-M
KA-S
KA-T
KA-W
KA-Y
KO-A
KO-B
KO-I
KO-N
KO-P
KO-R
KO-S
KO-W
S-**KY**
KY-E
KY-U
A-**LA**
LA-B
LA-C
LA-D
LA-G
LA-H
LA-M
LA-P
LA-R
LA-S
LA-T
LA-V
LA-W
LA-X
LA-Y
LI-B
LI-D
LI-E
LI-G
LI-N
LI-P
LI-S
LI-T
LO-B
LO-D
LO-G
LO-O
LO-P
LO-R
LO-S
LO-T
LO-W
LO-X
LO-Y
A-**MA**
S-MA
MA-A
MA-C
MA-D
MA-E
MA-G
MA-K
MA-L
MA-M
MA-N
MA-P
MA-R
MA-S
MA-T
MA-W
MA-X
MA-Y
E-**ME**
ME-D
ME-G
ME-L
ME-M
ME-N
ME-S
ME-T
ME-U
ME-W
A-**MI**
MI-B
MI-D
MI-G
MI-L
MI-M
MI-R
MI-S
MI-X
MI-Z
H-**MM**
U-MM
MO-A
MO-B
MO-C
MO-D
MO-E
MO-G
MO-I
MO-L
MO-M
MO-N
MO-O
MO-P
MO-R
MO-S
MO-T
MO-U
MO-W
MO-Y
MO-Z
A-**MU**
E-MU
MU-D
MU-G
MU-M
MU-N
MU-S
MU-T
MU-X
MY
A-**NA**
M-NA
NA-B
NA-E
NA-G
NA-H
NA-M
NA-N
NA-P
NA-S
NA-T
NA-W
NA-Y
A-**NE**
E-NE
O-NE
NE-B
NE-D
NE-E
NE-F
NE-K
NE-P
NE-T
NE-W
NO-B
NO-D
NO-G
NO-H
NO-M
NO-N
NO-O
NO-R
NO-S
NO-T
NO-W
NO-X
NO-Y
G-**NU**
NU-B
NU-N
NU-R
NU-S
NU-T
A-**NY**
S-NY
NY-E
NY-S
B-**OB**
C-OB
D-OB
F-OB
G-OB
H-OB
J-OB
K-OB
L-OB
M-OB
N-OB
R-OB
S-OB
Y-OB
OB-A
OB-E
OB-I
OB-O
OB-S
B-**OD**
C-OD
D-OD
G-OD
H-OD
L-OD
M-OD
N-OD
P-OD
R-OD
S-OD
T-OD
Y-OD
OD-A
OD-D
OD-E
OD-S
D-**OE**
F-OE
G-OE
H-OE
J-OE
M-OE
R-OE
T-OE
V-OE
W-OE
OE-S
O-**OF**
OF-F
OF-T
B-**OH**
D-OH
F-OH
H-OH
N-OH
O-OH
P-OH
S-OH
OH-M
OH-O
OH-S
H-**OI**
K-OI
M-OI
P-OI
OI-K
OI-L
D-**OM**
M-OM
N-OM
O-OM
P-OM
R-OM
T-OM
Y-OM
OM-S
B-**ON**
C-ON
D-ON
E-ON
F-ON
G-ON
H-ON
I-ON
K-ON
M-ON
N-ON
O-ON
S-ON
T-ON
W-ON
Y-ON
ON-E
ON-S
B-**OO**
C-OO
D-OO
G-OO
H-OO
L-OO
M-OO
N-OO
P-OO
R-OO
T-OO
W-OO
Z-OO
OO-F
OO-H
OO-M
OO-N
OO-P
OO-R
OO-S
OO-T
B-**OP**
C-OP
D-OP
F-OP
H-OP
K-OP
L-OP
M-OP
O-OP
P-OP
S-OP
T-OP
W-OP
OP-E
OP-S
OP-T
B-**OR**
C-OR
D-OR
F-OR
G-OR
J-OR
K-OR
L-OR
M-OR
N-OR
O-OR
T-OR
V-OR
OR-A
OR-B
OR-C
OR-D
OR-E
OR-F
OR-S
OR-T
B-**OS**
C-OS
D-OS
G-OS
H-OS
I-OS
K-OS
L-OS
M-OS
N-OS
O-OS
P-OS
S-OS
W-OS
Y-OS
Z-OS
OS-E
F-**OU**
M-OU
S-OU
Y-OU
OU-D
OU-K
OU-P
OU-R
OU-T
B-**OW**
C-OW
D-OW
H-OW
J-OW
K-OW
L-OW
M-OW
N-OW
P-OW
R-OW
S-OW
T-OW
V-OW
W-OW
Y-OW
OW-E
OW-L
OW-N
OW-T
B-**OX**
C-OX
F-OX
G-OX
H-OX
L-OX
N-OX
P-OX
S-OX
V-OX
W-OX
OX-O
OX-Y
B-**OY**
C-OY
F-OY
G-OY
H-OY
J-OY
L-OY
M-OY
N-OY
S-OY
T-OY
OY-E
OY-S
S-**PA**
PA-C
PA-D
PA-H
PA-L
PA-M
PA-N
PA-P
PA-R
PA-S
PA-T
PA-W
PA-X
PA-Y
A-**PE**
O-PE
PE-A
PE-C
PE-D
PE-E
PE-G
PE-H
PE-N
PE-P
PE-R
PE-S
PE-T
PE-W
PH-I
PH-O
PH-S
PH-T
PI-A
PI-C
PI-E
PI-G
PI-N
PI-P
PI-R
PI-S
PI-T
PI-U
PI-X
U-**PO**
PO-A
PO-D
PO-H
PO-I
PO-L
PO-M
PO-O
PO-P
PO-S
PO-T
PO-W
PO-X
PO-Z
QI-S
A-**RE**
E-RE
I-RE
O-RE
P-RE
U-RE
RE-B
RE-C
RE-D
RE-E
RE-F
RE-G
RE-H
RE-I
RE-M
RE-N
RE-P
RE-S
RE-T
RE-V
RE-W
RE-X
RE-Z
A-**SH**
I-SH
SH-A
SH-E
SH-H
SH-Y
P-**SI**
SI-B
SI-C
SI-M
SI-N
SI-P
SI-R
SI-S
SI-T
SI-X
D-**SO**
I-SO
SO-B
SO-C
SO-D
SO-G
SO-H
SO-L
SO-N
SO-P
SO-S
SO-T
SO-U
SO-V
SO-W
SO-X
SO-Y
E-**ST**
P-ST
ST-Y
E-**TA**
I-TA
U-TA
TA-B
TA-D
TA-E
TA-G
TA-I
TA-J
TA-K
TA-M
TA-N
TA-O
TA-P
TA-R
TA-S
TA-T
TA-U
TA-V
TA-W
TA-X
TA-Y
A-**TE**
U-TE
TE-A
TE-D
TE-E
TE-F
TE-G
TE-L
TE-N
TE-S
TE-T
TE-W
TI-C
TI-D
TI-E
TI-G
TI-L
TI-N
TI-P
TI-S
TI-T
TO-C
TO-D
TO-E
TO-G
TO-M
TO-N
TO-O
TO-P
TO-R
TO-T
TO-W
TO-Y
B-**UG**
D-UG
F-UG
H-UG
J-UG
L-UG
M-UG
P-UG
R-UG
T-UG
V-UG
Y-UG
UG-H
UG-S
H-**UH**
P-UH
B-**UM**
C-UM
F-UM
G-UM
H-UM
L-UM
M-UM
R-UM
S-UM
T-UM
V-UM
Y-UM
UM-M
UM-P
B-**UN**
D-UN
F-UN
G-UN
H-UN
J-UN
M-UN
N-UN
P-UN
R-UN
S-UN
T-UN
UN-I
UN-S
C-**UP**
D-UP
G-UP
H-UP
O-UP
P-UP
S-UP
T-UP
Y-UP
UP-O
UP-S
B-**UR**
C-UR
F-UR
G-UR
L-UR
N-UR
O-UR
P-UR
S-UR
UR-B
UR-D
UR-E
UR-N
B-**US**
G-US
J-US
M-US
N-US
P-US
S-US
W-US
Y-US
US-E
B-**UT**
C-UT
G-UT
H-UT
J-UT
M-UT
N-UT
O-UT
P-UT
R-UT
T-UT
UT-A
UT-E
UT-S
UT-U
A-**WE**
E-WE
O-WE
WE-B
WE-D
WE-E
WE-M
WE-N
WE-T
WE-X
WE-Y
T-**WO**
WO-E
WO-G
WO-K
WO-N
WO-O
WO-P
WO-S
WO-T
WO-W
WO-X
XI-S
XU
P-**YA**
R-YA
YA-H
YA-K
YA-M
YA-P
YA-R
YA-W
YA-Y
A-**YE**
B-YE
D-YE
E-YE
H-YE
K-YE
L-YE
N-YE
O-YE
P-YE
R-YE
S-YE
T-YE
W-YE
YE-A
YE-H
YE-N
YE-P
YE-S
YE-T
YE-W
YE-X
YO-B
YO-D
YO-K
YO-M

YO-N YO-S YO-U YO-W A-**YU** K-YU YU-G YU-K YU-M YU-P YU-S A-**ZO** D-ZO ZO-A ZO-O ZO-S

3-LETTER WORD HOOKS: including all root words

AAH-S B-**AAL** AAL-S B-**AAS** K-AAS M-AAS B-**ABA** C-ABA ABA-C ABA-S **ABB**-A ABB-E ABB-S **ABO**-S C-**ABS** D-ABS G-ABS J-ABS K-ABS L-ABS N-ABS S-ABS T-ABS W-ABS B-**ABY** G-ABY ABY-E ABY-S D-**ACE** F-ACE L-ACE M-ACE P-ACE R-ACE T-ACE ACE-D ACE-R ACE-S B-**ACH** E-ACH M-ACH N-ACH R-ACH T-ACH ACH-E ACH-Y F-**ACT** P-ACT T-ACT ACT-A ACT-S W-**ADD** ADD-S D-**ADO** F-ADO ADO-S B-**ADS** C-ADS D-ADS F-ADS G-ADS H-ADS L-ADS M-ADS P-ADS R-ADS T-ADS W-ADS **ADZ**-E

B-**AFF** C-AFF D-AFF F-AFF G-AFF H-AFF N-AFF R-AFF W-AFF Y-AFF AFF-Y B-**AFT** D-AFT H-AFT R-AFT W-AFT G-**AGA** N-AGA R-AGA S-AGA AGA-R AGA-S C-**AGE** G-AGE M-AGE P-AGE R-AGE S-AGE W-AGE AGE-D AGE-E AGE-N AGE-R AGE-S D-**AGO** K-AGO S-AGO AGO-G AGO-N H-**AHA** T-AHA A-**AHS** D-AHS F-AHS H-AHS L-AHS P-AHS R-AHS Y-AHS R-**AIA** AIA-S C-**AID** G-AID K-AID L-AID M-AID P-AID Q-AID R-AID S-AID W-AID AID-E AID-S B-**AIL** F-AIL H-AIL J-AIL K-AIL M-AIL

N-AIL P-AIL R-AIL S-AIL T-AIL V-AIL W-AIL AIL-S K-**AIM** M-AIM S-AIM AIM-S C-**AIN** F-AIN G-AIN H-AIN K-AIN L-AIN M-AIN N-AIN P-AIN R-AIN S-AIN T-AIN V-AIN W-AIN AIN-E AIN-S F-**AIR** G-AIR H-AIR L-AIR M-AIR P-AIR S-AIR V-AIR W-AIR AIR-N AIR-S AIR-T AIR-Y D-**AIS** K-AIS P-AIS R-AIS S-AIS T-AIS B-**AIT** G-AIT R-AIT T-AIT W-AIT AIT-S AIT-U B-**AKE** C-AKE F-AKE H-AKE J-AKE L-AKE M-AKE R-AKE S-AKE T-AKE W-AKE AKE-D AKE-E AKE-S G-**ALA**

N-ALA T-ALA ALA-E ALA-N ALA-P ALA-R ALA-S ALA-Y **ALB**-A ALB-E ALB-S B-**ALE** D-ALE E-ALE G-ALE H-ALE K-ALE M-ALE P-ALE R-ALE S-ALE T-ALE V-ALE W-ALE Y-ALE ALE-C ALE-E ALE-F ALE-S ALE-W B-**ALL** C-ALL F-ALL G-ALL H-ALL L-ALL M-ALL P-ALL S-ALL T-ALL W-ALL ALL-S ALL-Y C-**ALP** P-ALP S-ALP ALP-S A-**ALS** B-ALS D-ALS G-ALS M-ALS P-ALS S-ALS ALS-O D-**ALT** H-ALT M-ALT S-ALT ALT-O ALT-S G-**AMA** K-AMA L-AMA M-AMA S-AMA AMA-H AMA-S K-**AMI**

R-AMI AMI-A AMI-D AMI-E AMI-N AMI-R AMI-S C-**AMP** D-AMP G-AMP L-AMP R-AMP S-AMP T-AMP V-AMP AMP-S **AMU**-S K-**ANA** L-ANA M-ANA N-ANA R-ANA T-ANA ANA-L ANA-N ANA-S B-**AND** F-AND H-AND L-AND M-AND P-AND R-AND S-AND W-AND AND-S B-**ANE** C-ANE F-ANE G-ANE J-ANE K-ANE L-ANE M-ANE P-ANE S-ANE T-ANE V-ANE W-ANE ANE-S ANE-W B-**ANI** M-ANI R-ANI ANI-L ANI-S C-**ANN** J-ANN ANN-A ANN-O ANN-S B-**ANT** C-ANT D-ANT G-ANT H-ANT K-ANT L-ANT P-ANT

R-ANT S-ANT V-ANT W-ANT ANT-A ANT-E ANT-I ANT-S C-**ANY** M-ANY W-ANY Z-ANY C-**APE** G-APE J-APE N-APE P-APE R-APE T-APE APE-D APE-R APE-S APE-X R-**APT** APT-S B-**ARB** C-ARB D-ARB G-ARB ARB-A ARB-S M-**ARC** N-ARC ARC-H ARC-O ARC-S B-**ARD** C-ARD E-ARD F-ARD H-ARD L-ARD M-ARD N-ARD P-ARD S-ARD W-ARD Y-ARD ARD-S B-**ARE** C-ARE D-ARE F-ARE G-ARE H-ARE L-ARE M-ARE N-ARE P-ARE R-ARE T-ARE V-ARE W-ARE Y-ARE ARE-A ARE-D ARE-G ARE-S ARE-T

ARE-W B-**ARF** Z-ARF ARF-S B-**ARK** C-ARK D-ARK H-ARK J-ARK K-ARK L-ARK M-ARK N-ARK P-ARK S-ARK W-ARK ARK-S B-**ARM** F-ARM H-ARM M-ARM W-ARM ARM-S ARM-Y B-**ARS** C-ARS E-ARS F-ARS G-ARS J-ARS L-ARS M-ARS O-ARS P-ARS S-ARS T-ARS V-ARS W-ARS ARS-E C-**ART** D-ART F-ART G-ART H-ART K-ART M-ART P-ART T-ART W-ART ART-S ART-Y M-**ARY** N-ARY O-ARY V-ARY W-ARY ARY-L B-**ASH** C-ASH D-ASH F-ASH G-ASH H-ASH L-ASH M-ASH P-ASH R-ASH S-ASH T-ASH

W-ASH ASH-Y B-**ASK** C-ASK H-ASK M-ASK T-ASK ASK-S G-**ASP** H-ASP J-ASP R-ASP W-ASP ASP-S B-**ASS** J-ASS L-ASS M-ASS P-ASS S-ASS T-ASS B-**ATE** C-ATE D-ATE F-ATE G-ATE H-ATE L-ATE M-ATE P-ATE R-ATE S-ATE T-ATE W-ATE Y-ATE ATE-S B-**ATT** M-ATT T-ATT W-ATT C-**AUF** L-AUF AUF-S B-**AUK** C-AUK J-AUK W-AUK AUK-S F-**AVA** J-AVA K-AVA L-AVA T-AVA AVA-L AVA-S C-**AVE** E-AVE F-AVE G-AVE H-AVE L-AVE N-AVE P-AVE R-AVE S-AVE W-AVE AVE-R AVE-S **AVO**-S

AVO-W P-**AWA** T-AWA AWA-Y W-**AWE** AWE-D AWE-E AWE-S B-**AWL** P-AWL W-AWL Y-AWL AWL-S B-**AWN** D-AWN F-AWN L-AWN M-AWN P-AWN R-AWN S-AWN Y-AWN AWN-S AWN-Y **AXE**-D AXE-L AXE-S B-**AYE** AYE-S B-**AYS** C-AYS D-AYS F-AYS G-AYS H-AYS J-AYS K-AYS L-AYS M-AYS N-AYS P-AYS R-AYS S-AYS T-AYS W-AYS Y-AYS **AYU**-S L-**AZO** AZO-N **BAA**-L BAA-S A-**BAC** BAC-H BAC-K BAC-S **BAD**-E BAD-S **BAG**-S **BAH**-T **BAL**-D BAL-E BAL-K BAL-L BAL-M BAL-S BAL-U **BAM**-S **BAN**-C BAN-D

BAN-E
BAN-G
BAN-I
BAN-K
BAN-S
BAN-T
BAP-S
BAP-U
K-**BAR**
BAR-B
BAR-D
BAR-E
BAR-F
BAR-K
BAR-M
BAR-N
BAR-P
BAR-S
A-**BAS**
O-BAS
BAS-E
BAS-H
BAS-K
BAS-S
BAS-T
BAT-E
BAT-H
BAT-S
BAT-T
BAY-E
BAY-S
BAY-T
A-**BED**
BED-E
BED-S
BED-U
BEE-F
BEE-N
BEE-P
BEE-R
BEE-S
BEE-T
BEG-O
BEG-S
BEL-L
BEL-S
BEL-T
BEN-D
BEN-E
BEN-I
BEN-J
BEN-S
BEN-T
A-**BET**
Y-BET
BET-A
BET-E
BET-H
BET-S
O-**BEY**
BEY-S
BEZ
BIB-B
BIB-S
A-**BID**
BID-E
BID-S
BIG-A
BIG-G
BIG-S
BIN-D
BIN-E
BIN-G
BIN-K
BIN-S

BIN-T
BIO-G
BIO-S
I-**BIS**
O-BIS
BIS-E
BIS-H
BIS-K
O-**BIT**
BIT-E
BIT-O
BIT-S
BIT-T
BIZ-E
BOA-K
BOA-R
BOA-S
BOA-T
BOB-A
BOB-S
BOD-E
BOD-S
BOD-Y
BOG-S
BOG-Y
BOH-S
BOK-E
BOK-O
BOK-S
E-**BON**
BON-A
BON-D
BON-E
BON-G
BON-K
BON-Y
BOO-B
BOO-H
BOO-K
BOO-L
BOO-M
BOO-N
BOO-R
BOO-S
BOO-T
BOP-S
BOR-A
BOR-D
BOR-E
BOR-N
BOR-S
BOR-T
A-**BOS**
O-BOS
BOS-H
BOS-K
BOS-S
BOT-A
BOT-H
BOT-S
BOT-T
BOW-L
BOW-R
BOW-S
BOX-Y
BOY-G
BOY-O
BOY-S
BRA-D
BRA-E
BRA-G
BRA-N
BRA-S
BRA-T
BRA-W

BRA-Y
BRO-D
BRO-G
BRO-O
BRO-S
BRO-W
BRR-R
BUB-A
BUB-O
BUB-S
BUD-O
BUD-S
BUG-S
BUM-F
BUM-P
BUM-S
BUN-A
BUN-D
BUN-G
BUN-K
BUN-N
BUN-S
BUN-T
BUR-A
BUR-D
BUR-G
BUR-K
BUR-L
BUR-N
BUR-P
BUR-R
BUR-S
BUR-Y
BUS-H
BUS-K
BUS-S
BUS-T
BUS-Y
A-**BUT**
BUT-E
BUT-S
BUT-T
BUY-S
A-**BYE**
BYE-S
A-**BYS**
S-**CAB**
CAB-A
CAB-S
E-**CAD**
S-CAD
CAD-E
CAD-I
CAD-S
S-**CAM**
CAM-E
CAM-P
CAM-S
S-**CAN**
CAN-E
CAN-G
CAN-N
CAN-S
CAN-T
CAN-Y
CAP-A
CAP-E
CAP-H
CAP-I
CAP-O
CAP-S
S-**CAR**
CAR-B
CAR-D
CAR-E

CAR-K
CAR-L
CAR-N
CAR-P
CAR-R
CAR-S
CAR-T
S-**CAT**
CAT-E
CAT-S
S-**CAW**
CAW-K
CAW-S
CAY-S
CEE-S
CEL-L
CEL-S
CEL-T
CEP-E
CEP-S
CHA-D
CHA-I
CHA-L
CHA-M
CHA-O
CHA-P
CHA-R
CHA-S
CHA-T
CHA-W
CHA-Y
A-**CHE**
E-CHE
O-CHE
CHE-F
CHE-R
CHE-W
CHE-Z
CHI-A
CHI-C
CHI-D
CHI-K
CHI-N
CHI-P
CHI-S
CHI-T
CHI-V
CHI-Z
A-**CID**
CID-E
CID-S
CIG-S
CIS-T
CIT-E
CIT-O
CIT-S
CIT-Y
CLY
COB-B
COB-S
E-**COD**
COD-A
COD-E
COD-S
S-**COG**
COG-S
COL-A
COL-D
COL-E
COL-L
COL-S
COL-T
COL-Y
I-**CON**
CON-D

CON-E
CON-F
CON-I
CON-K
CON-N
CON-S
CON-Y
COO-F
COO-K
COO-L
COO-M
COO-N
COO-P
COO-S
COO-T
S-**COP**
COP-E
COP-S
COP-Y
COR-D
COR-E
COR-F
COR-K
COR-M
COR-N
COR-S
COR-Y
COS-E
COS-H
COS-S
COS-T
COS-Y
S-**COT**
COT-E
COT-H
COT-S
COT-T
S-**COW**
COW-L
COW-P
COW-S
COW-Y
COX-A
COX-Y
COY-S
COZ-E
COZ-Y
E-**CRU**
CRU-D
CRU-E
CRU-S
CRU-X
S-**CRY**
CUB-E
CUB-S
S-**CUD**
CUD-S
CUE-D
CUE-S
S-**CUM**
S-**CUP**
CUP-S
S-**CUR**
CUR-B
CUR-D
CUR-E
CUR-F
CUR-L
CUR-N
CUR-R
CUR-S
CUR-T
S-**CUT**
CUT-E
CUT-S

CUZ
CWM-S
DAB-S
DAD-A
DAD-O
DAD-S
DAE-S
DAG-O
DAG-S
DAH-L
DAH-S
DAK-S
O-**DAL**
U-DAL
DAL-E
DAL-I
DAL-S
DAL-T
DAM-E
DAM-N
DAM-P
DAM-S
DAN-G
DAN-K
DAN-S
DAN-T
DAP-S
O-**DAS**
DAS-H
A-**DAW**
DAW-D
DAW-K
DAW-N
DAW-S
DAW-T
DAY-S
DEB-S
DEB-T
I-**DEE**
DEE-D
DEE-K
DEE-M
DEE-N
DEE-P
DEE-R
DEE-S
DEE-T
DEE-V
DEF-I
DEF-T
DEF-Y
DEI-D
DEI-L
DEL-E
DEL-F
DEL-I
DEL-L
DEL-S
DEL-T
DEN-E
DEN-S
DEN-T
DEN-Y
DEV-A
DEV-S
DEW-S
DEW-Y
DEX-Y
DEY-S
DIB-S
DID-O
DID-Y
DIE-B
DIE-D
DIE-L

DIE-S
DIE-T
DIG-S
DIM-E
DIM-S
DIN-E
DIN-G
DIN-K
DIN-O
DIN-S
DIN-T
DIP-S
DIP-T
DIS-A
DIS-C
DIS-H
DIS-K
DIS-S
A-**DIT**
E-DIT
DIT-A
DIT-E
DIT-S
DIT-T
DIT-Z
DIV-A
DIV-E
DIV-I
DIV-S
DOB-S
DOB-Y
DOC-K
DOC-S
DOD-O
DOD-S
DOE-K
DOE-N
DOE-R
DOE-S
DOG-E
DOG-S
DOG-Y
DOH-S
I-**DOL**
DOL-E
DOL-L
DOL-S
DOL-T
DOM-E
DOM-S
DOM-Y
DON-A
DON-E
DON-G
DON-S
DOO-B
DOO-K
DOO-L
DOO-M
DOO-R
DOO-S
DOP-A
DOP-E
DOP-S
DOP-Y
O-**DOR**
DOR-E
DOR-K
DOR-M
DOR-P
DOR-R
DOR-S
DOR-T
DOR-Y
A-**DOS**

U-DOS
DOS-E
DOS-H
DOS-S
DOS-T
DOT-E
DOT-H
DOT-S
DOT-Y
DOW-D
DOW-F
DOW-L
DOW-N
DOW-P
DOW-S
DOW-T
A-**DRY**
DRY-S
O-**DSO**
DSO-S
DUB-S
DUD-E
DUD-S
DUE-D
DUE-L
DUE-S
DUE-T
DUG-S
DUI-T
DUN-E
DUN-G
DUN-K
DUN-S
DUN-T
DUO-S
DUP-E
DUP-S
DUX
DYE-D
DYE-R
DYE-S
DZO-S
B-**EAN**
D-EAN
G-EAN
J-EAN
L-EAN
M-EAN
P-EAN
R-EAN
S-EAN
W-EAN
Y-EAN
EAN-S
B-**EAR**
D-EAR
F-EAR
G-EAR
H-EAR
L-EAR
N-EAR
P-EAR
R-EAR
S-EAR
T-EAR
W-EAR
Y-EAR
EAR-D
EAR-L
EAR-N
EAR-S
C-**EAS**
K-EAS
L-EAS
P-EAS

S-EAS
T-EAS
Y-EAS
Z-EAS
EAS-E
EAS-T
EAS-Y
B-**EAT**
F-EAT
G-EAT
H-EAT
J-EAT
L-EAT
M-EAT
N-EAT
P-EAT
S-EAT
T-EAT
EAT-H
EAT-S
B-**EAU**
EAU-S
EAU-X
EBB-S
E-**ECH**
H-ECH
L-ECH
P-ECH
T-ECH
Y-ECH
ECH-E
ECH-O
ECH-T
ECU-S
EDH-S
D-**EEK**
G-EEK
K-EEK
L-EEK
M-EEK
P-EEK
R-EEK
S-EEK
W-EEK
F-**EEL**
H-EEL
J-EEL
K-EEL
P-EEL
R-EEL
S-EEL
T-EEL
W-EEL
EEL-S
EEL-Y
B-**EEN**
D-EEN
K-EEN
P-EEN
R-EEN
S-EEN
T-EEN
W-EEN
J-**EFF**
T-EFF
EFF-S
K-**EFS**
N-EFS
R-EFS
T-EFS
D-**EFT**
H-EFT
L-EFT
R-EFT
W-EFT

EFT-S
T-**EGG**
Y-EGG
EGG-S
EGG-Y
B-**EGO**
R-EGO
S-EGO
EGO-S
F-**EHS**
H-EHS
P-EHS
R-EHS
R-**EIK**
S-EIK
EIK-S
D-**EKE**
L-EKE
P-EKE
R-EKE
EKE-D
EKE-S
G-**ELD**
H-ELD
M-ELD
S-ELD
T-ELD
V-ELD
W-ELD
Y-ELD
ELD-S
D-**ELF**
P-ELF
S-ELF
ELF-S
W-**ELK**
Y-ELK
ELK-S
B-**ELL**
C-ELL
D-ELL
F-ELL
H-ELL
J-ELL
K-ELL
M-ELL
P-ELL
S-ELL
T-ELL
V-ELL
W-ELL
Y-ELL
ELL-S
H-**ELM**
Y-ELM
ELM-S
ELM-Y
B-**ELS**
C-ELS
D-ELS
E-ELS
G-ELS
M-ELS
S-ELS
T-ELS
Z-ELS
ELS-E
B-**ELT**
C-ELT
D-ELT
F-ELT
G-ELT
K-ELT
M-ELT
P-ELT
T-ELT
W-ELT
Y-ELT
ELT-S
D-**EME**
F-EME
H-EME
L-EME
M-EME
S-EME
T-EME
EME-S
EME-U
EMF-S
F-**EMS**
G-EMS
H-EMS
M-EMS
R-EMS
T-EMS
W-EMS
EMU-S
B-**END**
F-END
H-END
L-END
M-END
P-END
R-END
S-END
T-END
V-END
W-END
END-S
B-**ENE**
D-ENE
G-ENE
M-ENE
N-ENE
P-ENE
S-ENE
T-ENE
ENE-S
ENE-W
L-**ENG**
M-ENG
ENG-S
B-**ENS**
C-ENS
D-ENS
F-ENS
G-ENS
H-ENS
K-ENS
L-ENS
P-ENS
R-ENS
S-ENS
T-ENS
W-ENS
Y-ENS
A-**EON**
J-EON
N-EON
P-EON
EON-S
S-**ERA**
V-ERA
ERA-S
B-**ERE**
C-ERE
D-ERE
F-ERE
G-ERE
H-ERE
L-ERE
M-ERE
P-ERE
S-ERE
W-ERE
ERE-D
ERE-S
K-**ERF**
S-ERF
T-ERF
B-**ERG**
ERG-O
ERG-S
B-**ERK**
J-ERK
M-ERK
N-ERK
P-ERK
S-ERK
Y-ERK
Z-ERK
ERK-S
D-**ERN**
F-ERN
H-ERN
K-ERN
P-ERN
T-ERN
ERN-E
ERN-S
S-**ERR**
ERR-S
H-**ERS**
S-ERS
V-ERS
ERS-T
C-**ESS**
F-ESS
J-ESS
L-ESS
M-ESS
N-ESS
S-ESS
ESS-E
B-**EST**
F-EST
G-EST
H-EST
J-EST
K-EST
L-EST
N-EST
P-EST
R-EST
T-EST
V-EST
W-EST
Y-EST
Z-EST
EST-S
B-**ETA**
F-ETA
G-ETA
K-ETA
M-ETA
S-ETA
W-ETA
Z-ETA
ETA-S
ETA-T
B-**ETH**
H-ETH
M-ETH
T-ETH
ETH-E
ETH-S
N-**EUK**
Y-EUK
EUK-S
L-**EVE**
M-EVE
N-EVE
Y-EVE
EVE-N
EVE-R
EVE-S
EVE-T
EWE-R
EWE-S
EWK-S
N-**EWT**
EWT-S
EYE-D
EYE-N
EYE-R
EYE-S
FAB
FAD-E
FAD-O
FAD-S
FAD-Y
FAG-S
FAH-S
FAN-D
FAN-E
FAN-G
FAN-K
FAN-O
FAN-S
FAP
A-**FAR**
FAR-D
FAR-E
FAR-L
FAR-M
FAR-O
FAR-S
FAR-T
FAS-H
FAS-T
FAT-E
FAT-S
FAW-N
FAW-S
FAX
O-**FAY**
FAY-S
FED-S
FEE-D
FEE-L
FEE-R
FEE-S
FEE-T
FEH-M
FEH-S
FEM-E
FEM-S
FEN-D
FEN-I
FEN-S
FEN-T
FER-E
FER-M
FER-N
FET-A
FET-E
FET-S
FET-T
FEU-D
FEU-S
FEW
FEY-S
FEZ
FIB-S
FID-O
FID-S
FIE-F
FIE-R
FIG-O
FIG-S
FIL-A
FIL-E
FIL-L
FIL-M
FIL-O
FIL-S
FIN-D
FIN-E
FIN-I
FIN-K
FIN-O
FIN-S
FIR-E
FIR-K
FIR-M
FIR-N
FIR-S
FIT-S
FIT-T
FIX-T
FIZ-Z
FLU-B
FLU-E
FLU-S
FLU-X
FLY
FOB-S
FOE-N
FOE-S
FOG-S
FOG-Y
FOH-N
FOH-S
FON-D
FON-E
FON-S
FON-T
FOP-S
FOR-A
FOR-B
FOR-D
FOR-E
FOR-K
FOR-M
FOR-T
FOU-D
FOU-L
FOU-R
FOU-S
FOX-Y
FOY-S
FRA-B
FRA-E
FRA-G
FRA-P
FRA-S
FRA-T
FRA-U
FRA-Y
A-**FRO**
FRO-E
FRO-G
FRO-M
FRO-W
FRY
FUB-S
FUD-S
FUG-S
FUG-U
FUM-E
FUM-S
FUM-Y
FUN-D
FUN-G
FUN-K
FUN-S
FUR-L
FUR-R
FUR-S
FUR-Y
GAB-S
GAB-Y
E-**GAD**
I-GAD
GAD-E
GAD-I
GAD-S
GAE-D
GAE-N
GAE-S
GAG-A
GAG-E
GAG-S
E-**GAL**
GAL-A
GAL-E
GAL-L
GAL-S
O-**GAM**
GAM-A
GAM-B
GAM-E
GAM-P
GAM-S
GAM-Y
GAN-E
GAN-G
GAN-T
GAP-E
GAP-O
GAP-S
GAP-Y
A-**GAR**
GAR-B
GAR-E
GAR-S
GAR-T
A-**GAS**
GAS-H
GAS-P
GAS-T
GAT-E
GAT-H
GAT-S
GAU-D
GAU-M
GAU-N
GAU-P
GAU-R
GAU-S
GAY-S
A-**GED**
GED-S
A-**GEE**
O-GEE
GEE-D
GEE-K
GEE-P
GEE-S
GEE-Z
GEL-D
GEL-S
GEL-T
GEM-S
A-**GEN**
GEN-A
GEN-E
GEN-S
GEN-T
GEN-U
GEO-S
GET-A
GET-S
GEY
GHI-S
GIB-E
GIB-S
GID-S
GIE-D
GIE-N
GIE-S
GIF-T
GIG-A
GIG-S
A-**GIN**
GIN-G
GIN-K
GIN-N
GIN-S
A-**GIO**
GIO-S
GIP-S
E-**GIS**
GIS-M
GIS-T
GIT-E
GIT-S
GJU-S
GNU-S
GOA-D
GOA-F
GOA-L
GOA-S
GOA-T
GOB-O
GOB-S
GOB-Y
GOD-S
Y-**GOE**
GOE-L
GOE-R
GOE-S
GOE-Y
A-**GON**
GON-E
GON-G
GON-K
GON-S
GOO-D
GOO-F
GOO-K
GOO-L
GOO-N
GOO-P
GOO-R
GOO-S
GOR-E
GOR-M
GOR-P
GOR-Y
E-**GOS**
GOS-H
GOT
GOV-S
GOX
GOY-S
GUB-S
A-**GUE**
GUE-S
GUL-A
GUL-E
GUL-F
GUL-L
GUL-P
GUL-S
GUL-Y
GUM-P
GUM-S
GUN-K
GUN-S
GUP-S
GUR-L
GUR-N
GUR-S
GUR-U
GUS-H
GUS-T
GUT-S
GUV-S
GUY-S
GYM-P
GYM-S
GYP-S
C-**HAD**
S-HAD
HAD-E
HAD-J
HAD-S
T-**HAE**
HAE-D
HAE-M
HAE-N
HAE-S
HAE-T
S-**HAG**
HAG-G
HAG-S
S-**HAH**
HAH-A
HAH-S
HAJ-I
HAJ-J
C-**HAM**
S-HAM
W-HAM
HAM-E
HAM-S
K-**HAN**
S-HAN
T-HAN
HAN-D
HAN-G
HAN-K
HAN-T
C-**HAO**
C-**HAP**
W-HAP
HAP-S
C-**HAS**
HAS-H
HAS-K
HAS-P
HAS-T
C-**HAT**
G-HAT
K-HAT
P-HAT
S-HAT
T-HAT
W-HAT
HAT-E
HAT-H
HAT-S
C-**HAW**
S-HAW
T-HAW
HAW-K
HAW-M
HAW-S
C-**HAY**
S-HAY
HAY-S
HEH-S
A-**HEM**
T-HEM
HEM-E
HEM-P
HEM-S
T-**HEN**
W-HEN
HEN-D
HEN-S
HEN-T
HEP-S
HEP-T
C-**HER**
HER-B
HER-D
HER-E
HER-L
HER-M
HER-N
HER-O
HER-S
HER-Y
S-**HES**
HES-P
HES-T
K-**HET**
S-HET
W-HET
HET-E
HET-H
HET-S
C-**HEW**
P-HEW
S-HEW
T-HEW
W-HEW
HEW-N
HEW-S
HEX
T-**HEY**
W-HEY
HEY-S
C-**HIC**
HIC-K
C-**HID**
W-HID
HID-E
HIE-D
HIE-S
S-**HIM**
W-HIM
C-**HIN**
S-HIN
T-HIN
W-HIN
HIN-D
HIN-G
HIN-S
HIN-T
C-**HIP**
S-HIP
W-HIP

HIP-S
HIP-T
C-**HIS**
G-HIS
K-HIS
P-HIS
T-HIS
HIS-H
HIS-N
HIS-S
HIS-T
C-**HIT**
S-HIT
W-HIT
HIT-S
HMM
W-**HOA**
HOA-R
HOA-S
HOA-X
HOB-O
HOB-S
C-**HOC**
HOC-K
S-**HOD**
HOD-S
S-**HOE**
HOE-D
HOE-R
HOE-S
S-**HOG**
HOG-G
HOG-H
HOG-S
P-**HOH**
HOH-S
HOI-K
C-**HON**
P-HON
T-HON
HON-D
HON-E
HON-G
HON-K
HON-S
S-**HOO**
HOO-D
HOO-F
HOO-K
HOO-N
HOO-P
HOO-T
C-**HOP**
S-HOP
W-HOP
HOP-E
HOP-S
M-**HOS**
O-HOS
P-HOS
R-HOS
Z-HOS
HOS-E
HOS-S
HOS-T
P-**HOT**
S-HOT
W-HOT
HOT-E
HOT-S
C-**HOW**
D-HOW
S-HOW
W-HOW
HOW-E
HOW-F
HOW-K
HOW-L
HOW-S
HOX
A-**HOY**
HOY-A
HOY-S
C-**HUB**
HUB-S
HUE-D
HUE-R
HUE-S
C-**HUG**
T-HUG
HUG-E
HUG-S
HUG-Y
HUH
HUI-A
HUI-C
HUI-S
C-**HUM**
HUM-A
HUM-F
HUM-P
HUM-S
S-**HUN**
HUN-G
HUN-H
HUN-K
HUN-S
HUN-T
HUP-S
B-**HUT**
C-HUT
P-HUT
S-HUT
HUT-S
HYE-D
HYE-N
HYE-S
HYP-E
HYP-O
HYP-S
B-**ICE**
D-ICE
F-ICE
L-ICE
M-ICE
N-ICE
P-ICE
R-ICE
S-ICE
T-ICE
V-ICE
W-ICE
ICE-D
ICE-R
ICE-S
D-**ICH**
L-ICH
R-ICH
S-ICH
T-ICH
W-ICH
ICH-S
D-**ICK**
H-ICK
K-ICK
L-ICK
M-ICK
N-ICK
P-ICK
R-ICK
S-ICK
T-ICK
W-ICK
ICK-Y
R-**ICY**
A-**IDE**
B-IDE
C-IDE
E-IDE
H-IDE
N-IDE
R-IDE
S-IDE
T-IDE
V-IDE
W-IDE
IDE-A
IDE-E
IDE-M
IDE-S
A-**IDS**
B-IDS
C-IDS
F-IDS
G-IDS
K-IDS
L-IDS
M-IDS
N-IDS
R-IDS
T-IDS
V-IDS
Y-IDS
B-**IFF**
J-IFF
M-IFF
N-IFF
R-IFF
T-IFF
Z-IFF
IFF-Y
K-**IFS**
R-IFS
B-**ILK**
M-ILK
S-ILK
ILK-A
ILK-S
B-**ILL**
C-ILL
D-ILL
F-ILL
G-ILL
H-ILL
J-ILL
K-ILL
L-ILL
M-ILL
N-ILL
P-ILL
R-ILL
S-ILL
T-ILL
V-ILL
W-ILL
Y-ILL
Z-ILL
ILL-S
ILL-Y
G-**IMP**
J-IMP
L-IMP
P-IMP
S-IMP
W-IMP
IMP-I
IMP-S
B-**INK**
D-INK
F-INK
G-INK
J-INK
K-INK
L-INK
M-INK
O-INK
P-INK
R-INK
S-INK
T-INK
W-INK
INK-S
INK-Y
G-**INN**
J-INN
L-INN
W-INN
INN-S
A-**INS**
B-INS
D-INS
F-INS
G-INS
H-INS
J-INS
K-INS
L-INS
P-INS
R-INS
S-INS
T-INS
V-INS
W-INS
Y-INS
Z-INS
C-**ION**
L-ION
P-ION
ION-S
B-**IOS**
G-IOS
C-**IRE**
D-IRE
F-IRE
H-IRE
L-IRE
M-IRE
S-IRE
T-IRE
V-IRE
W-IRE
IRE-D
IRE-S
B-**IRK**
D-IRK
F-IRK
K-IRK
L-IRK
M-IRK
Y-IRK
IRK-S
B-**ISH**
D-ISH
F-ISH
H-ISH
K-ISH
P-ISH
W-ISH
G-**ISM**
J-ISM
ISM-S
M-**ISO**
P-ISO
ISO-S
D-**ITA**
P-ITA
V-ITA
ITA-S
A-**ITS**
B-ITS
C-ITS
D-ITS
F-ITS
G-ITS
H-ITS
K-ITS
L-ITS
N-ITS
P-ITS
R-ITS
S-ITS
T-ITS
W-ITS
Z-ITS
T-**IVY**
JAB-S
JAG-G
JAG-S
JAK-E
JAK-S
JAM-B
JAM-S
JAP-E
JAP-S
A-**JAR**
JAR-K
JAR-L
JAR-S
JAW-S
JAY-S
A-**JEE**
JEE-D
JEE-L
JEE-P
JEE-R
JEE-S
JEE-Z
JET-E
JET-S
JEU-X
JEW-S
JIB-B
JIB-E
JIB-S
JIG-S
D-**JIN**
JIN-K
JIN-N
JIN-S
JIN-X
JIZ-Z
JOB-E
JOB-S
JOE-S
JOE-Y
JOG-S
JOR-S
JOT-A
JOT-S
JOW-L
JOW-S
JOY-S
JUD-O
JUD-S
JUD-Y
JUG-A
JUG-S
JUN-K
G-**JUS**
JUS-T
JUT-E
JUT-S
KAB-S
KAE-D
KAE-S
KAF-S
KAI-D
KAI-E
KAI-F
KAI-L
KAI-M
KAI-N
KAI-S
KAM-A
KAM-E
KAM-I
O-**KAS**
S-KAS
I-**KAT**
S-KAT
KAT-A
KAT-I
KAT-S
S-**KAW**
KAW-S
O-**KAY**
KAY-O
KAY-S
KEA-S
KEB-S
A-**KED**
E-KED
KED-S
KEF-S
S-**KEG**
KEG-S
KEN-O
KEN-S
KEN-T
S-**KEP**
KEP-I
KEP-S
KEP-T
KET-A
KET-O
KET-S
KEX
KEY-S
KHI-S
S-**KID**
KID-S
KIF-S
A-**KIN**
S-KIN
KIN-A
KIN-D
KIN-E
KIN-G
KIN-K
KIN-O
KIN-S
S-**KIP**
KIP-E
KIP-P
KIP-S
KIR-K
KIR-N
KIR-S
S-**KIT**
KIT-E
KIT-H
KIT-S
KOA-N
KOA-S
KOB-O
KOB-S
KOI
I-**KON**
KON-D
KON-K
KON-S
KOP-H
KOP-S
KOR-A
KOR-E
KOR-S
KOS-S
KOW-S
KUE-S
KYE
KYU-S
B-**LAB**
F-LAB
S-LAB
LAB-S
LAC-E
LAC-K
LAC-S
LAC-Y
B-**LAD**
C-LAD
G-LAD
LAD-E
LAD-S
LAD-Y
B-**LAG**
C-LAG
F-LAG
S-LAG
LAG-S
B-**LAH**
LAH-S
B-**LAM**
C-LAM
F-LAM
G-LAM
S-LAM
LAM-A
LAM-B
LAM-E
LAM-P
LAM-S
A-**LAP**
C-LAP
F-LAP
P-LAP
S-LAP
LAP-S
A-**LAR**
LAR-D
LAR-E
LAR-I
LAR-K
LAR-N
LAR-S
A-**LAS**
LAS-E
LAS-H
LAS-S
LAS-T
B-**LAT**
C-LAT
F-LAT
P-LAT
S-LAT
LAT-E
LAT-H
LAT-I
LAT-S
LAV-A
LAV-E
LAV-S
B-**LAW**
C-LAW
F-LAW
S-LAW
LAW-K
LAW-N
LAW-S
F-**LAX**
A-**LAY**
B-LAY
C-LAY
F-LAY
P-LAY
S-LAY
LAY-S
F-**LEA**
I-LEA
O-LEA
P-LEA
LEA-D
LEA-F
LEA-K
LEA-L
LEA-M
LEA-N
LEA-P
LEA-R
LEA-S
LEA-T
B-**LED**
F-LED
G-LED
P-LED
S-LED
A-**LEE**
B-LEE
F-LEE
G-LEE
S-LEE
LEE-D
LEE-K
LEE-P
LEE-R
LEE-S
LEE-T
C-**LEG**
F-LEG
G-LEG
LEG-S
G-**LEI**
V-LEI
LEI-R
LEI-S
LEK-E
LEK-S
LEK-U
LEP-S
LEP-T
A-**LES**
O-LES
U-LES
LES-S
LES-T
B-**LET**
LET-S
LEU-D
LEV-A
LEV-E
LEV-O
LEV-Y
A-**LEW**
B-LEW
C-LEW
F-LEW
P-LEW
S-LEW
LEW-D
F-**LEX**
I-LEX
U-LEX
B-**LEY**
F-LEY
G-LEY
S-LEY
LEY-S
LEZ-Z
G-**LIB**
LIB-S
G-**LID**
O-LID
S-LID
LID-O
LID-S
P-**LIE**
LIE-D
LIE-F
LIE-N
LIE-R
LIE-S
LIE-U
LIG-S
B-**LIN**
LIN-D
LIN-E
LIN-G
LIN-K
LIN-N
LIN-O
LIN-S
LIN-T
LIN-Y
B-**LIP**
C-LIP
F-LIP
S-LIP
LIP-S
LIS-K
LIS-P
LIS-T
A-**LIT**
F-LIT
G-LIT
S-LIT
LIT-E
LIT-H
LIT-S
LIT-U
B-**LOB**
G-LOB
S-LOB
LOB-E
LOB-I
LOB-O
LOB-S
A-**LOD**
C-LOD
P-LOD
LOD-E
LOD-S
C-**LOG**
F-LOG
S-LOG
LOG-E

LOG-O
LOG-S
LOG-Y
LOO-F
LOO-K
LOO-M
LOO-N
LOO-P
LOO-R
LOO-S
LOO-T
C-**LOP**
F-LOP
G-LOP
P-LOP
S-LOP
LOP-E
LOP-S
F-**LOR**
LOR-D
LOR-E
LOR-N
LOR-Y
LOS-E
LOS-H
LOS-S
LOS-T
B-**LOT**
C-LOT
P-LOT
S-LOT
LOT-A
LOT-E
LOT-H
LOT-I
LOT-O
LOT-S
A-**LOW**
B-LOW
C-LOW
F-LOW
G-LOW
P-LOW
S-LOW
LOW-E
LOW-N
LOW-S
LOW-T
LOX
C-**LOY**
P-LOY
LOY-S
LUD-E
LUD-O
LUD-S
G-**LUG**
P-LUG
S-LUG
LUG-E
LUG-S
A-**LUM**
G-LUM
P-LUM
S-LUM
LUM-P
LUM-S
B-**LUR**
S-LUR
LUR-E
LUR-K
LUR-S
LUV-S
F-**LUX**
LUX-E
LUZ
LYE-S
LYM-E
LYM-S
MAA-R
MAA-S
MAC-E
MAC-H
MAC-K
MAC-S
MAD-E
MAD-S
MAE-S
MAG-E
MAG-G
MAG-I
MAG-S
MAK-E
MAK-O
MAK-S
MAL-E
MAL-I
MAL-L
MAL-M
MAL-S
MAL-T
I-**MAM**
MAM-A
MAM-S
MAN-A
MAN-D
MAN-E
MAN-G
MAN-I
MAN-O
MAN-S
MAN-Y
MAP-S
MAR-A
MAR-C
MAR-D
MAR-E
MAR-G
MAR-K
MAR-L
MAR-M
MAR-S
MAR-T
MAR-Y
A-**MAS**
MAS-A
MAS-E
MAS-H
MAS-K
MAS-S
MAS-T
MAS-U
MAT-E
MAT-H
MAT-S
MAT-T
MAT-Y
MAW-K
MAW-N
MAW-R
MAW-S
MAX-I
MAY-A
MAY-O
MAY-S
MED
MEG-A
MEG-S
MEL-A
MEL-D
MEL-L
MEL-S
MEL-T
MEM-E
MEM-O
MEM-S
A-**MEN**
O-MEN
MEN-D
MEN-E
MEN-G
MEN-O
MEN-T
MEN-U
E-**MES**
MES-A
MES-E
MES-H
MES-S
MET-A
MET-E
MET-H
MET-S
E-**MEU**
MEU-S
S-**MEW**
MEW-L
MEW-S
MHO-S
MIB-S
A-**MID**
I-MID
MID-I
MID-S
MIG-G
MIG-S
MIL-D
MIL-E
MIL-K
MIL-L
MIL-O
MIL-S
MIL-T
MIM-E
A-**MIR**
E-MIR
S-MIR
MIR-E
MIR-I
MIR-K
MIR-S
MIR-V
MIR-Y
A-**MIS**
MIS-E
MIS-O
MIS-S
MIS-T
MIX-T
MIX-Y
MIZ-Z
MNA-S
MOA-N
MOA-S
MOA-T
MOB-S
MOC-H
MOC-K
MOC-S
MOD-E
MOD-I
MOD-S
MOE-S
S-**MOG**
MOG-S
MOI-L
MOI-T
MOL-A
MOL-D
MOL-E
MOL-L
MOL-S
MOL-T
MOL-Y
MOM-E
MOM-I
MOM-S
MON-A
MON-G
MON-K
MON-O
MON-S
MON-Y
MOO-D
MOO-I
MOO-K
MOO-L
MOO-N
MOO-P
MOO-R
MOO-S
MOO-T
MOP-E
MOP-S
MOP-Y
MOR-A
MOR-E
MOR-N
MOR-S
MOR-T
MOS-E
MOS-K
MOS-S
MOS-T
MOT-E
MOT-H
MOT-S
MOT-T
MOT-U
MOU-E
MOU-P
MOU-S
MOW-A
MOW-N
MOW-S
MOY-A
MOY-L
MOY-S
MOZ-E
MOZ-O
MOZ-Z
MUD-S
S-**MUG**
MUG-G
MUG-S
MUM-M
MUM-P
MUM-S
MUM-U
MUN-I
MUN-S
MUN-T
A-**MUS**
E-MUS
MUS-E
MUS-H
MUS-K
MUS-O
MUS-S
MUS-T
S-**MUT**
MUT-E
MUT-I
MUT-S
MUT-T
MUX
S-**NAB**
NAB-E
NAB-K
NAB-S
NAE
K-**NAG**
S-NAG
NAG-A
NAG-S
NAH
NAM-E
NAM-S
A-**NAN**
NAN-A
NAN-S
K-**NAP**
S-NAP
NAP-A
NAP-E
NAP-S
A-**NAS**
M-NAS
G-**NAT**
NAT-S
G-**NAW**
S-NAW
NAY-S
S-**NEB**
NEB-S
S-**NED**
NED-S
K-**NEE**
S-NEE
NEE-D
NEE-M
NEE-P
NEF-S
NEK-S
NEP-S
NET-E
NET-S
NET-T
A-**NEW**
E-NEW
K-NEW
NEW-S
NEW-T
S-**NIB**
NIB-S
NID-E
NID-I
NID-S
NIE-D
NIE-F
NIE-S
A-**NIL**
NIL-L
NIL-S
NIM-B
NIM-S
S-**NIP**
NIP-A
NIP-S
A-**NIS**
U-NIS
NIS-I
K-**NIT**
S-NIT
U-NIT
NIT-E
NIT-S
NIX-E
NIX-Y
K-**NOB**
S-NOB
NOB-S
S-**NOD**
NOD-E
NOD-I
NOD-S
S-**NOG**
NOG-G
NOG-S
NOH
NOM-A
NOM-E
NOM-S
A-**NON**
NON-A
NON-E
NON-G
NOO-K
NOO-N
NOO-P
NOR-I
NOR-K
NOR-M
NOS-E
NOS-H
NOS-Y
K-**NOT**
S-NOT
NOT-A
NOT-E
NOT-T
A-**NOW**
E-NOW
K-NOW
S-NOW
NOW-L
NOW-N
NOW-S
NOW-T
NOW-Y
NOX
NOY-S
NTH
K-**NUB**
S-NUB
NUB-S
NUN-S
K-**NUR**
NUR-D
NUR-L
NUR-R
NUR-S
A-**NUS**
G-NUS
O-NUS
K-**NUT**
NUT-S
S-**NYE**
NYE-D
NYE-S
NYS
G-**OAF**
L-OAF
OAF-S
B-**OAK**
S-OAK
OAK-S
OAK-Y
B-**OAR**
H-OAR
R-OAR
S-OAR
V-OAR
OAR-S
OAR-Y
B-**OAT**
C-OAT
D-OAT
G-OAT
M-OAT
OAT-H
OAT-S
B-**OBA**
OBA-S
J-**OBE**
L-OBE
R-OBE
OBE-S
OBE-Y
L-**OBI**
OBI-A
OBI-S
OBI-T
G-**OBO**
H-OBO
K-OBO
L-OBO
Z-OBO
OBO-E
OBO-L
OBO-S
B-**OBS**
C-OBS
D-OBS
F-OBS
G-OBS
H-OBS
J-OBS
K-OBS
L-OBS
M-OBS
N-OBS
R-OBS
S-OBS
Y-OBS
C-**OCA**
L-OCA
S-OCA
OCA-S
C-**OCH**
L-OCH
M-OCH
R-OCH
OCH-E
C-**ODA**
S-ODA
ODA-L
ODA-S
ODD-S
B-**ODE**
C-ODE
L-ODE
M-ODE
N-ODE
R-ODE
Y-ODE
ODE-A
ODE-S
B-**ODS**
C-ODS
D-ODS
G-ODS
H-ODS
L-ODS
M-ODS
N-ODS
P-ODS
R-ODS
S-ODS
T-ODS
Y-ODS
ODS-O
D-**OES**
F-OES
G-OES
H-OES
J-OES
M-OES
N-OES
R-OES
T-OES
V-OES
W-OES
B-**OFF**
C-OFF
D-OFF
G-OFF
K-OFF
T-OFF
OFF-S
C-**OFT**
L-OFT
S-OFT
T-OFT
OHM-S
C-**OHO**
S-OHO
T-OHO
OHO-S
B-**OHS**
D-OHS
F-OHS
H-OHS
O-OHS
S-OHS
H-**OIK**
OIK-S
B-**OIL**
C-OIL
F-OIL
M-OIL
N-OIL
R-OIL
S-OIL
T-OIL
OIL-S
OIL-Y
OKA-S
OKA-Y
B-**OKE**
C-OKE
H-OKE
J-OKE
L-OKE
M-OKE
P-OKE
R-OKE
S-OKE
T-OKE
W-OKE
Y-OKE
OKE-H
OKE-S
B-**OLD**
C-OLD
F-OLD
G-OLD
H-OLD
M-OLD
S-OLD
T-OLD
W-OLD
Y-OLD
OLD-S
OLD-Y
B-**OLE**
C-OLE
D-OLE
G-OLE
H-OLE
J-OLE
M-OLE
N-OLE
P-OLE
R-OLE
S-OLE
T-OLE
V-OLE
OLE-A
OLE-O
OLE-S
H-**OLM**
OLM-S
C-**OMS**
D-OMS
M-OMS
N-OMS
O-OMS
P-OMS
R-OMS
T-OMS
B-**ONE**
C-ONE
D-ONE
F-ONE
G-ONE
H-ONE
L-ONE
N-ONE
P-ONE
R-ONE
S-ONE
T-ONE
Z-ONE
ONE-R
ONE-S
C-**ONS**
D-ONS
E-ONS
F-ONS
G-ONS
H-ONS
I-ONS
K-ONS
M-ONS
O-ONS
P-ONS
S-ONS
T-ONS
W-ONS
ONS-T
C-**OOF**
G-OOF
H-OOF
L-OOF
P-OOF
R-OOF
W-OOF
Y-OOF
OOF-S
B-**OOH**
P-OOH
OOH-S
B-**OOM**
C-OOM
D-OOM

L-OOM
R-OOM
S-OOM
T-OOM
Z-OOM
OOM-S
B-**OON**
C-OON
G-OON
H-OON
L-OON
M-OON
N-OON
P-OON
R-OON
S-OON
T-OON
W-OON
Z-OON
OON-S
OON-T
C-**OOP**
G-OOP
H-OOP
L-OOP
M-OOP
N-OOP
P-OOP
R-OOP
S-OOP
Y-OOP
OOP-S
B-**OOR**
D-OOR
G-OOR
L-OOR
M-OOR
P-OOR
B-**OOS**
C-OOS
D-OOS
G-OOS
L-OOS
M-OOS
P-OOS
R-OOS
W-OOS
Z-OOS
OOS-E
OOS-Y
B-**OOT**
C-OOT
F-OOT
H-OOT
L-OOT
M-OOT
P-OOT
R-OOT
S-OOT
T-OOT
W-OOT
OOT-S
C-**OPE**
D-OPE
H-OPE
L-OPE
M-OPE
N-OPE
P-OPE
R-OPE
T-OPE
OPE-D
OPE-N
OPE-S
B-**OPS**

C-OPS
D-OPS
F-OPS
H-OPS
K-OPS
L-OPS
M-OPS
O-OPS
P-OPS
S-OPS
T-OPS
W-OPS
OPT-S
B-**ORA**
F-ORA
H-ORA
K-ORA
M-ORA
S-ORA
T-ORA
ORA-D
ORA-L
F-**ORB**
S-ORB
ORB-S
ORB-Y
T-**ORC**
ORC-A
ORC-S
B-**ORD**
C-ORD
F-ORD
L-ORD
S-ORD
W-ORD
ORD-O
ORD-S
B-**ORE**
C-ORE
D-ORE
F-ORE
G-ORE
H-ORE
K-ORE
L-ORE
M-ORE
P-ORE
R-ORE
S-ORE
T-ORE
W-ORE
Y-ORE
ORE-S
C-**ORF**
ORF-E
ORF-S
B-**ORS**
C-ORS
D-ORS
H-ORS
J-ORS
K-ORS
M-ORS
T-ORS
V-ORS
B-**ORT**
D-ORT
F-ORT
M-ORT
P-ORT
R-ORT
S-ORT
T-ORT
W-ORT
ORT-S

C-**OSE**
D-OSE
H-OSE
L-OSE
M-OSE
N-OSE
O-OSE
P-OSE
R-OSE
T-OSE
OSE-S
F-**OUD**
L-OUD
OUD-S
B-**OUK**
G-OUK
J-OUK
P-OUK
S-OUK
T-OUK
Y-OUK
Z-OUK
OUK-S
C-**OUP**
D-OUP
L-OUP
M-OUP
N-OUP
R-OUP
S-OUP
OUP-H
OUP-S
C-**OUR**
D-OUR
F-OUR
H-OUR
J-OUR
L-OUR
P-OUR
S-OUR
T-OUR
Y-OUR
OUR-N
OUR-S
B-**OUT**
D-OUT
G-OUT
H-OUT
L-OUT
N-OUT
P-OUT
R-OUT
S-OUT
T-OUT
OUT-S
N-**OVA**
OVA-L
H-**OWE**
L-OWE
Y-OWE
OWE-D
OWE-R
OWE-S
B-**OWL**
C-OWL
D-OWL
F-OWL
G-OWL
H-OWL
J-OWL
N-OWL
S-OWL
Y-OWL
OWL-S
OWL-Y

D-**OWN**
G-OWN
L-OWN
M-OWN
N-OWN
P-OWN
S-OWN
T-OWN
OWN-S
D-**OWT**
L-OWT
N-OWT
R-OWT
T-OWT
OWT-S
OXO
B-**OXY**
C-OXY
D-OXY
F-OXY
P-OXY
OYE-R
OYE-S
OYE-Z
B-**OYS**
C-OYS
F-OYS
G-OYS
H-OYS
J-OYS
L-OYS
M-OYS
N-OYS
S-OYS
T-OYS
PAC-A
PAC-E
PAC-K
PAC-O
PAC-S
PAC-T
PAC-Y
PAD-I
PAD-S
O-**PAH**
PAH-S
O-**PAL**
PAL-E
PAL-L
PAL-M
PAL-P
PAL-S
PAL-Y
S-**PAM**
PAM-S
S-**PAN**
PAN-D
PAN-E
PAN-G
PAN-S
PAN-T
PAP-A
PAP-E
PAP-S
S-**PAR**
PAR-A
PAR-D
PAR-E
PAR-K
PAR-P
PAR-R
PAR-S
PAR-T
S-**PAS**
U-PAS

PAS-E
PAS-H
PAS-S
PAS-T
S-**PAT**
PAT-E
PAT-H
PAT-S
PAT-Y
S-**PAW**
PAW-A
PAW-K
PAW-L
PAW-N
PAW-S
PAX
A-**PAY**
S-PAY
PAY-S
PEA-G
PEA-K
PEA-L
PEA-N
PEA-R
PEA-S
PEA-T
S-**PEC**
PEC-H
PEC-K
PEC-S
A-**PED**
O-PED
S-PED
PED-S
E-**PEE**
PEE-D
PEE-K
PEE-L
PEE-N
PEE-P
PEE-R
PEE-S
PEG-H
PEG-S
PEH-S
O-**PEN**
PEN-D
PEN-E
PEN-I
PEN-K
PEN-S
PEN-T
PEP-O
PEP-S
A-**PER**
PER-E
PER-I
PER-K
PER-M
PER-N
PER-T
PER-V
A-**PES**
O-PES
PES-O
PES-T
S-**PET**
PET-S
S-**PEW**
PEW-S
PHI-S
PHI-Z
PHO-H
PHO-N
PHO-S

PHO-T
PHS
PHT
PIA-L
PIA-N
PIA-S
E-**PIC**
S-PIC
PIC-A
PIC-E
PIC-K
PIC-S
S-**PIE**
PIE-D
PIE-R
PIE-S
PIE-T
PIG-S
S-**PIN**
PIN-A
PIN-E
PIN-G
PIN-K
PIN-S
PIN-T
PIN-Y
PIP-A
PIP-E
PIP-I
PIP-S
PIP-Y
PIR-L
PIR-N
PIR-S
PIS-E
PIS-H
PIS-O
PIS-S
S-**PIT**
PIT-A
PIT-H
PIT-S
PIT-Y
PIU-M
PIX-Y
PLY
POA-S
A-**POD**
POD-S
POH
POI-S
POL-E
POL-K
POL-L
POL-O
POL-S
POL-T
POL-Y
POM-E
POM-P
POM-S
POO-D
POO-F
POO-H
POO-K
POO-L
POO-N
POO-P
POO-R
POO-S
POO-T
POP-E
POP-S
E-**POS**
POS-E

POS-H
POS-S
POS-T
POS-Y
S-**POT**
POT-E
POT-S
POT-T
POW-N
POW-S
POX-Y
POZ-Z
PRE-E
PRE-P
PRE-X
PRE-Y
PRE-Z
PRO-A
PRO-B
PRO-D
PRO-F
PRO-G
PRO-M
PRO-O
PRO-P
PRO-S
PRO-W
S-**PRY**
PRY-S
PSI-S
PST
PUB-S
S-**PUD**
PUD-S
PUD-U
PUG-H
PUG-S
PUH
PUL-A
PUL-E
PUL-I
PUL-K
PUL-L
PUL-P
PUL-S
PUL-U
PUL-Y
S-**PUN**
PUN-A
PUN-G
PUN-K
PUN-S
PUN-T
PUN-Y
PUP-A
PUP-S
S-**PUR**
PUR-E
PUR-I
PUR-L
PUR-R
PUR-S
O-**PUS**
PUS-H
PUS-S
PUT-S
PUT-T
PUT-Z
PUY-S
PYA-S
PYA-T
PYE-S
PYE-T
PYX
QAT-S

QIS
A-**QUA**
QUA-D
QUA-G
QUA-I
QUA-T
QUA-Y
B-**RAD**
D-RAD
G-RAD
O-RAD
P-RAD
T-RAD
RAD-E
RAD-S
B-**RAG**
C-RAG
D-RAG
F-RAG
RAG-A
RAG-E
RAG-G
RAG-I
RAG-S
RAH-S
RAI-A
RAI-D
RAI-K
RAI-L
RAI-N
RAI-S
RAI-T
RAJ-A
C-**RAM**
D-RAM
G-RAM
P-RAM
T-RAM
RAM-I
RAM-P
RAM-S
B-**RAN**
C-RAN
G-RAN
RAN-A
RAN-D
RAN-G
RAN-I
RAN-K
RAN-T
C-**RAP**
D-RAP
F-RAP
T-RAP
W-RAP
RAP-E
RAP-S
RAP-T
B-**RAS**
E-RAS
F-RAS
RAS-E
RAS-H
RAS-P
RAS-T
B-**RAT**
D-RAT
F-RAT
G-RAT
P-RAT
T-RAT
RAT-A
RAT-E
RAT-H
RAT-O

RAT-S
RAT-U
B-**RAW**
C-RAW
D-RAW
RAW-N
RAW-S
RAX
B-**RAY**
D-RAY
F-RAY
G-RAY
P-RAY
T-RAY
RAY-A
RAY-S
REB-S
REC-K
REC-S
A-**RED**
B-RED
C-RED
E-RED
I-RED
RED-D
RED-E
RED-O
RED-S
B-**REE**
C-REE
D-REE
F-REE
G-REE
P-REE
T-REE
REE-D
REE-F
REE-K
REE-L
REE-N
REE-S
T-**REF**
REF-S
REF-T
A-**REG**
D-REG
REG-O
REG-S
REH-S
REI-F
REI-K
REI-N
REI-S
REM-S
B-**REN**
G-REN
W-REN
REN-D
REN-S
REN-T
REN-Y
P-**REP**
REP-O
REP-P
REP-S
A-**RES**
E-RES
I-RES
O-RES
T-RES
U-RES
RES-H
RES-T
A-**RET**
F-RET

T-RET
RET-E
RET-S
REV-S
A-**REW**
B-REW
C-REW
D-REW
G-REW
T-REW
REW-S
P-**REX**
P-**REZ**
T-REZ
RHO-S
RHY
A-**RIA**
RIA-L
RIA-S
C-**RIB**
D-RIB
RIB-S
A-**RID**
G-RID
I-RID
RID-E
RID-S
RIF-E
RIF-F
RIF-S
RIF-T
B-**RIG**
F-RIG
G-RIG
P-RIG
T-RIG
RIG-G
RIG-S
B-**RIM**
C-RIM
G-RIM
P-RIM
T-RIM
RIM-A
RIM-E
RIM-S
RIM-U
RIM-Y
B-**RIN**
G-RIN
T-RIN
RIN-D
RIN-E
RIN-G
RIN-K
RIN-S
D-**RIP**
G-RIP
T-RIP
RIP-E
RIP-P
RIP-S
RIP-T
B-**RIT**
C-RIT
F-RIT
G-RIT
W-RIT
RIT-E
RIT-S
RIT-T
RIT-Z
F-**RIZ**
RIZ-A
P-**ROB**

ROB-E
ROB-S
C-**ROC**
ROC-H
ROC-K
ROC-S
B-**ROD**
P-ROD
T-ROD
ROD-E
ROD-S
F-**ROE**
ROE-D
ROE-S
ROK-E
ROK-S
ROK-Y
F-**ROM**
P-ROM
ROM-A
ROM-P
ROM-S
B-**ROO**
P-ROO
ROO-D
ROO-F
ROO-K
ROO-M
ROO-N
ROO-P
ROO-S
ROO-T
G-**ROT**
T-ROT
ROT-A
ROT-E
ROT-I
ROT-L
ROT-O
ROT-S
A-**ROW**
B-ROW
C-ROW
D-ROW
F-ROW
G-ROW
P-ROW
T-ROW
V-ROW
ROW-S
ROW-T
D-**RUB**
G-RUB
RUB-E
RUB-S
RUB-Y
RUC-K
RUC-S
C-**RUD**
RUD-D
RUD-E
RUD-S
C-**RUE**
G-RUE
T-RUE
RUE-D
RUE-R
RUE-S
D-**RUG**
F-RUG
T-RUG
RUG-A
RUG-S
A-**RUM**
D-RUM

G-RUM
RUM-E
RUM-P
RUM-S
RUN-D
RUN-E
RUN-G
RUN-S
RUN-T
B-**RUT**
RUT-H
RUT-S
RYA-L
RYA-S
T-**RYE**
RYE-S
SAB-E
SAB-S
SAC-K
SAC-S
SAD-E
SAD-I
SAE
SAG-A
SAG-E
SAG-O
SAG-S
SAG-Y
SAI-C
SAI-D
SAI-L
SAI-M
SAI-N
SAI-R
SAI-S
SAL-E
SAL-L
SAL-P
SAL-S
SAL-T
SAM-A
SAM-E
SAM-P
SAN-D
SAN-E
SAN-G
SAN-K
SAN-S
SAN-T
SAP-S
A-**SAR**
K-SAR
O-SAR
T-SAR
SAR-D
SAR-I
SAR-K
SAR-S
SAT-E
SAT-I
SAU-L
SAU-T
SAW-N
SAW-S
SAX
SAY-S
SAZ
A-**SEA**
SEA-L
SEA-M
SEA-N
SEA-R
SEA-S
SEA-T
SEC-O

SEC-S
SEC-T
U-**SED**
SEE-D
SEE-K
SEE-L
SEE-M
SEE-N
SEE-P
SEE-R
SEE-S
SEG-O
SEG-S
SEI-F
SEI-K
SEI-L
SEI-R
SEI-S
SEL-D
SEL-E
SEL-F
SEL-L
SEL-S
SEN-A
SEN-D
SEN-E
SEN-S
SEN-T
U-**SER**
SER-A
SER-E
SER-F
SER-K
SER-R
SER-S
SET-A
SET-S
SET-T
SEW-N
SEW-S
SEX-T
SEX-Y
SEY-S
SEZ
SHA-D
SHA-G
SHA-H
SHA-M
SHA-N
SHA-T
SHA-W
SHA-Y
SHE-A
SHE-D
SHE-S
SHE-T
SHE-W
SHH
A-**SHY**
SIB-B
SIB-S
SIC-E
SIC-H
SIC-K
SIC-S
SIM-A
SIM-I
SIM-P
SIM-S
SIN-D
SIN-E
SIN-G
SIN-H
SIN-K
SIN-S

SIP-E
SIP-S
SIR-E
SIR-I
SIR-S
P-**SIS**
SIS-S
SIS-T
SIT-E
SIT-H
SIT-S
SIX
SKA-G
SKA-S
SKA-T
SKA-W
SKI-D
SKI-M
SKI-N
SKI-O
SKI-P
SKI-S
SKI-T
E-**SKY**
SKY-R
SLY
SMA
SNY-E
SOB-S
SOC-A
SOC-K
SOC-S
SOD-A
SOD-S
SOG-S
SOH-O
SOH-S
SOL-A
SOL-D
SOL-E
SOL-I
SOL-O
SOL-S
SON-E
SON-G
SON-S
SOP-H
SOP-S
D-**SOS**
I-SOS
SOS-S
SOT-H
SOT-S
SOU-K
SOU-L
SOU-M
SOU-P
SOU-R
SOU-S
SOU-T
SOV-S
SOW-F
SOW-L
SOW-M
SOW-N
SOW-P
SOW-S
SOX
SOY-A
SOY-S
SPA-E
SPA-G
SPA-M
SPA-N
SPA-R

SPA-S
SPA-T
SPA-W
SPA-Y
SPA-Z
E-**SPY**
SRI-S
STY-E
SUB-A
SUB-S
SUD-D
SUD-S
SUE-D
SUE-R
SUE-S
SUE-T
SUI-D
SUI-T
SUK-H
SUK-S
SUM-O
SUM-P
SUM-S
SUN-G
SUN-K
SUN-N
SUN-S
SUP-E
SUP-S
SUQ-S
SUR-A
SUR-D
SUR-E
SUR-F
SUS-S
SWY
SYE-D
SYE-N
SYE-S
SYN-C
SYN-D
SYN-E
S-**TAB**
TAB-I
TAB-S
TAB-U
TAD-S
TAE-D
TAE-L
TAE-S
S-**TAG**
TAG-S
TAI-L
TAI-N
TAI-S
TAI-T
TAJ
TAK-A
TAK-E
TAK-I
TAK-S
TAK-Y
TAM-E
TAM-P
TAM-S
TAN-A
TAN-E
TAN-G
TAN-H
TAN-K
TAN-S
TAO-S
A-**TAP**
S-TAP
TAP-A

TAP-E
TAP-S
TAP-U
S-**TAR**
TAR-A
TAR-E
TAR-N
TAR-O
TAR-P
TAR-S
TAR-T
E-**TAS**
I-TAS
U-TAS
TAS-H
TAS-K
TAS-S
E-**TAT**
S-TAT
TAT-E
TAT-H
TAT-S
TAT-T
TAT-U
TAU-S
TAU-T
TAV-A
TAV-S
S-**TAW**
TAW-A
TAW-S
TAW-T
TAX-A
TAX-I
S-**TAY**
TAY-S
TEA-D
TEA-K
TEA-L
TEA-M
TEA-R
TEA-S
TEA-T
S-**TED**
TED-S
TED-Y
TEE-D
TEE-L
TEE-M
TEE-N
TEE-R
TEE-S
TEF-F
TEF-S
TEG-G
TEG-S
TEG-U
TEL-A
TEL-D
TEL-E
TEL-L
TEL-S
TEL-T
E-**TEN**
S-TEN
TEN-D
TEN-E
TEN-S
TEN-T
A-**TES**
U-TES
TES-T
S-**TET**
TET-E
TET-H

TET-S
S-**TEW**
TEW-S
E-**THE**
THE-E
THE-M
THE-N
THE-W
THE-Y
THO-N
THO-U
THY
E-**TIC**
O-TIC
TIC-E
TIC-H
TIC-K
TIC-S
TID-E
TID-S
TID-Y
S-**TIE**
TIE-D
TIE-R
TIE-S
TIG-E
TIG-S
TIL-E
TIL-L
TIL-S
TIL-T
TIN-D
TIN-E
TIN-G
TIN-K
TIN-S
TIN-T
TIN-Y
TIP-I
TIP-S
TIP-T
U-**TIS**
TIT-E
TIT-I
TIT-S
A-**TOC**
TOC-K
TOC-O
TOC-S
TOD-S
TOD-Y
TOE-A
TOE-D
TOE-S
TOE-Y
TOG-A
TOG-E
TOG-S
A-**TOM**
TOM-B
TOM-E
TOM-S
TON-E
TON-G
TON-K
TON-S
TON-Y
TOO-K
TOO-L
TOO-M
TOO-N
TOO-T
A-**TOP**
S-TOP
TOP-E

TOP-H
TOP-I
TOP-S
TOR-A
TOR-C
TOR-E
TOR-I
TOR-N
TOR-O
TOR-R
TOR-S
TOR-T
TOR-Y
S-**TOT**
TOT-E
TOT-S
S-**TOW**
TOW-N
TOW-S
TOW-T
TOW-Y
TOY-O
TOY-S
TRY-E
TRY-P
TSK-S
S-**TUB**
TUB-A
TUB-E
TUB-S
TUG-S
E-**TUI**
TUI-S
S-**TUM**
TUM-P
TUM-S
S-**TUN**
TUN-A
TUN-D
TUN-E
TUN-G
TUN-S
TUN-Y
TUP-S
TUT-S
TUT-U
TUX
TWA-E
TWA-L
TWA-S
TWA-T
TWA-Y
TWO-S
TWP
S-**TYE**
TYE-D
TYE-E
TYE-R
TYE-S
TYG-S
B-**UDO**
J-UDO
K-UDO
L-UDO
UDO-S
B-**UDS**
C-UDS
D-UDS
F-UDS
J-UDS
L-UDS
M-UDS
O-UDS
P-UDS
R-UDS

S-UDS W-UDS Q-**UEY** UEY-S B-**UFO** UFO-S E-**UGH** P-UGH S-UGH V-UGH UGH-S B-**UGS** D-UGS F-UGS H-UGS J-UGS L-UGS M-UGS P-UGS R-UGS T-UGS V-UGS Y-UGS B-**UKE** C-UKE D-UKE J-UKE L-UKE N-UKE P-UKE Y-UKE UKE-S D-**ULE** G-ULE H-ULE M-ULE P-ULE R-ULE T-ULE Y-ULE ULE-S ULE-X L-**ULU** P-ULU S-ULU Z-ULU ULU-S M-**UMM** B-**UMP** D-UMP G-UMP H-UMP

J-UMP L-UMP M-UMP P-UMP R-UMP S-UMP T-UMP Y-UMP UMP-H UMP-S M-**UNI** UNI-S UNI-T B-**UNS** D-UNS F-UNS G-UNS H-UNS M-UNS N-UNS P-UNS R-UNS S-UNS T-UNS **UPO**-N C-**UPS** D-UPS G-UPS H-UPS O-UPS P-UPS S-UPS T-UPS Y-UPS UPS-Y C-**URB** URB-S B-**URD** C-URD N-URD S-URD T-URD URD-E URD-S URD-Y C-**URE** D-URE I-URE J-URE L-URE M-URE P-URE

S-URE URE-A URE-S B-**URN** C-URN D-URN G-URN O-URN T-URN URN-S F-**USE** M-USE R-USE USE-D USE-R USE-S **UTA**-S B-**UTE** C-UTE J-UTE L-UTE M-UTE UTE-S B-**UTS** C-UTS G-UTS H-UTS J-UTS M-UTS N-UTS O-UTS P-UTS R-UTS T-UTS T-**UTU** UTU-S **UVA**-E UVA-S **VAC**-S U-**VAE** VAE-S **VAN**-E VAN-G VAN-S VAN-T **VAR**-A VAR-E VAR-S VAR-Y A-**VAS** K-VAS U-VAS

VAS-A VAS-E VAS-T **VAT**-S VAT-U **VAU**-S VAU-T **VAV**-S **VAW**-S **VEE**-P VEE-R VEE-S **VEG**-A E-**VET** VET-O VET-S **VEX**-T **VIA**-E VIA-L VIA-S A-**VID** VID-E VID-S **VIE**-D VIE-R VIE-S VIE-W **VIG**-A VIG-S **VIM**-S **VIN**-A VIN-E VIN-O VIN-S VIN-T VIN-Y **VIS**-A VIS-E **VLY** E-**VOE** VOE-S **VOL**-A VOL-E VOL-K VOL-S VOL-T **VOR**-S A-**VOW** VOW-S **VOX** **VUG**-G VUG-H

VUG-S O-**VUM** VUM-S S-**WAB** WAB-S S-**WAD** WAD-D WAD-E WAD-I WAD-S WAD-T WAD-Y T-**WAE** WAE-S S-**WAG** WAG-E WAG-S H-**WAN** S-WAN WAN-D WAN-E WAN-G WAN-K WAN-S WAN-T WAN-Y S-**WAP** WAP-S **WAR**-D WAR-E WAR-K WAR-M WAR-N WAR-P WAR-S WAR-T WAR-Y T-**WAS** WAS-E WAS-H WAS-M WAS-P WAS-T S-**WAT** T-WAT WAT-E WAT-S WAT-T **WAW**-E WAW-L WAW-S **WAX**-Y

A-**WAY** S-WAY T-WAY WAY-S **WEB**-S A-**WED** O-WED WED-S A-**WEE** S-WEE T-WEE WEE-D WEE-K WEE-L WEE-M WEE-N WEE-P WEE-R WEE-S WEE-T **WEM**-B WEM-S **WEN**-D WEN-S WEN-T **WET**-A WET-S **WEX**-E S-**WEY** WEY-S **WHA**-M WHA-P WHA-T **WHO**-A WHO-M WHO-P WHO-T WHO-W **WHY**-S S-**WIG** T-WIG WIG-S T-**WIN** WIN-D WIN-E WIN-G WIN-K WIN-N WIN-O WIN-S WIN-Y I-**WIS**

Y-WIS WIS-E WIS-H WIS-P WIS-S WIS-T T-**WIT** WIT-E WIT-H WIT-S S-**WIZ** **WOE**-S **WOG**-S **WOK**-E WOK-S **WON**-K WON-S WON-T **WOO**-D WOO-F WOO-L WOO-N WOO-S WOO-T S-**WOP** WOP-S T-**WOS** WOS-T S-**WOT** WOT-S **WOW**-F WOW-S **WOX** A-**WRY** **WUD**-S **WUS**-S **WYE**-S **WYN**-D WYN-N WYN-S A-**XIS** A-**YAH** YAH-S K-**YAK** YAK-S L-**YAM** YAM-S **YAP**-P YAP-S K-**YAR** YAR-D YAR-E

YAR-N YAR-R **YAW**-L YAW-N YAW-P YAW-S YAW-Y **YAY**-S **YEA**-D YEA-H YEA-N YEA-R YEA-S **YEH** E-**YEN** H-YEN S-YEN YEN-S **YEP**-S A-**YES** B-YES D-YES E-YES H-YES L-YES N-YES O-YES P-YES R-YES S-YES T-YES W-YES YES-K YES-T P-**YET** YET-I YET-T **YEW**-S **YEX** **YGO**-E **YID**-S A-**YIN** P-YIN YIN-S **YIP**-E YIP-S **YOB**-S **YOD**-E YOD-H YOD-S **YOK**-E YOK-S

YOM-P **YON**-D YON-I YON-T **YOS** **YOU**-K YOU-R **YOW**-E YOW-L YOW-S **YUG**-A YUG-S **YUK**-E YUK-O YUK-S YUK-Y **YUM**-P **YUP**-S A-**YUS** K-YUS **ZAG**-S **ZAP**-S **ZAX** **ZEA**-L ZEA-S **ZED**-S M-**ZEE** ZEE-S **ZEK**-S **ZEL**-S **ZEX** D-**ZHO** ZHO-S **ZIG**-S **ZIN**-C ZIN-E ZIN-G ZIN-S **ZIP**-S **ZIT**-E ZIT-I ZIT-S **ZIZ**-Z **ZOA** **ZOO**-M ZOO-N ZOO-S D-**ZOS** **ZUZ**

4-LETTER WORD HOOKS: extensible words only

B-**AALS** **ABAC**-A ABAC-I ABAC-K ABAC-S B-**ABAS** C-ABAS ABAS-E ABAS-H ABAS-K **ABBA**-S **ABBE**-S ABBE-Y S-**ABED** **ABET**-S

R-**ABID** T-ABID ABID-E C-**ABLE** F-ABLE G-ABLE H-ABLE S-ABLE T-ABLE ABLE-D ABLE-R ABLE-S ABLE-T **ABRI**-M ABRI-N

ABRI-S **ABUT**-S **ABYE**-S **ABYS**-M ABYS-S F-**ACED** L-ACED M-ACED P-ACED R-ACED F-**ACER** L-ACER M-ACER P-ACER R-ACER

ACER-B ACER-S D-**ACES** F-ACES L-ACES M-ACES P-ACES R-ACES T-ACES C-**ACHE** M-ACHE N-ACHE R-ACHE T-ACHE ACHE-D

ACHE-S **ACID**-S ACID-Y **ACME**-S **ACNE**-D ACNE-S N-**ACRE** ACRE-D ACRE-S P-**ACTA** F-**ACTS** P-ACTS T-ACTS **ACYL**-S **ADAW**-S

W-**ADDS** **ADIT**-S D-**ADOS** F-ADOS **ADZE**-S P-**AEON** AEON-S **AERO**-S F-**AERY** **AFAR**-A AFAR-S B-**AFFY** D-AFFY T-AFFY **AFRO**-S

AGAR-S N-**AGAS** R-AGAS S-AGAS AGAS-T C-**AGED** G-AGED P-AGED R-AGED W-AGED R-**AGEE** **AGEN**-E AGEN-T C-**AGER** E-AGER

G-AGER J-AGER L-AGER P-AGER R-AGER S-AGER W-AGER Y-AGER AGER-S C-**AGES** G-AGES M-AGES P-AGES R-AGES S-AGES

W-AGES
AGHA-S
F-**AGIN**
AGIN-G
AGIO-S
M-**AGMA**
T-AGMA
AGMA-S
AGOG-E
W-**AGON**
AGON-E
AGON-S
AGON-Y
V-**AGUE**
AGUE-D
AGUE-S
A-**AHED**
R-AHED
R-**AIAS**
W-**AIDE**
AIDE-D
AIDE-R
AIDE-S
C-**AIDS**
G-AIDS
K-AIDS
L-AIDS
M-AIDS
Q-AIDS
R-AIDS
S-AIDS
B-**AILS**
F-AILS
H-AILS
J-AILS
K-AILS
M-AILS
N-AILS
P-AILS
R-AILS
S-AILS
T-AILS
V-AILS
W-AILS
K-**AIMS**
M-AIMS
S-AIMS
D-**AINE**
F-AINE
R-AINE
S-AINE
AINE-E
C-**AINS**
F-AINS
G-AINS
H-AINS
K-AINS
M-AINS
P-AINS
R-AINS
S-AINS
T-AINS
W-AINS
B-**AIRN**
C-AIRN
AIRN-S
F-**AIRS**
G-AIRS
H-AIRS
L-AIRS
M-AIRS
P-AIRS
S-AIRS
V-AIRS
W-AIRS

AIRT-H
AIRT-S
D-**AIRY**
F-AIRY
H-AIRY
L-AIRY
V-AIRY
B-**AITS**
G-AITS
R-AITS
T-AITS
W-AITS
AITU-S
B-**AKED**
C-AKED
F-AKED
L-AKED
N-AKED
R-AKED
W-AKED
R-**AKEE**
AKEE-S
B-**AKES**
C-AKES
F-AKES
H-AKES
J-AKES
L-AKES
M-AKES
R-AKES
S-AKES
T-AKES
W-AKES
L-**AKIN**
T-AKIN
AKIN-G
ALAN-D
ALAN-E
ALAN-G
ALAN-S
ALAN-T
J-**ALAP**
ALAP-A
ALAP-S
M-**ALAR**
T-ALAR
ALAR-M
ALAR-Y
B-**ALAS**
G-ALAS
N-ALAS
P-ALAS
T-ALAS
P-**ALAY**
ALAY-S
ALBA-S
ALBE-E
ALEC-S
ALEF-S
ALEF-T
B-**ALES**
D-ALES
E-ALES
G-ALES
H-ALES
K-ALES
M-ALES
P-ALES
R-ALES
S-ALES
T-ALES
V-ALES
W-ALES
Y-ALES
ALEW-S

H-**ALFA**
ALFA-S
ALGA-E
ALGA-L
ALGA-S
C-**ALIF**
K-ALIF
ALIF-S
B-**ALKY**
T-ALKY
ALKY-D
ALKY-L
B-**ALLS**
C-ALLS
F-ALLS
G-ALLS
H-ALLS
L-ALLS
M-ALLS
P-ALLS
W-ALLS
B-**ALLY**
D-ALLY
G-ALLY
P-ALLY
R-ALLY
S-ALLY
T-ALLY
W-ALLY
ALLY-L
H-**ALMA**
T-ALMA
ALMA-H
ALMA-S
ALME-H
ALME-S
B-**ALMS**
C-ALMS
H-ALMS
M-ALMS
P-ALMS
ALOD-S
ALOE-D
ALOE-S
ALOW-E
C-**ALPS**
P-ALPS
S-ALPS
S-**ALTO**
ALTO-S
D-**ALTS**
H-ALTS
M-ALTS
S-ALTS
ALUM-S
AMAH-S
C-**AMAS**
G-AMAS
K-AMAS
L-AMAS
M-AMAS
S-AMAS
AMAS-S
G-**AMBO**
J-AMBO
M-AMBO
S-AMBO
Z-AMBO
AMBO-S
R-**AMEN**
S-AMEN
Y-AMEN
AMEN-D
AMEN-E
AMEN-S

AMEN-T
L-**AMIA**
Z-AMIA
AMIA-S
AMID-E
AMID-O
AMID-S
M-**AMIE**
R-AMIE
AMIE-S
G-**AMIN**
R-AMIN
T-AMIN
AMIN-E
AMIN-O
AMIN-S
AMIR-S
C-**AMIS**
K-AMIS
R-AMIS
T-AMIS
AMIS-S
AMLA-S
AMMO-N
AMMO-S
AMOK-S
C-**AMPS**
D-AMPS
G-AMPS
L-AMPS
R-AMPS
S-AMPS
T-AMPS
V-AMPS
C-**AMUS**
R-AMUS
W-AMUS
AMUS-E
AMYL-S
B-**ANAL**
C-ANAL
F-ANAL
ANAN-A
K-**ANAS**
L-ANAS
M-ANAS
N-ANAS
R-ANAS
T-ANAS
D-**ANCE**
H-ANCE
L-ANCE
N-ANCE
P-ANCE
R-ANCE
B-**ANDS**
F-ANDS
H-ANDS
L-ANDS
P-ANDS
R-ANDS
S-ANDS
W-ANDS
B-**ANES**
C-ANES
F-ANES
J-ANES
K-ANES
L-ANES
M-ANES
P-ANES
S-ANES
V-ANES
W-ANES
F-**ANGA**

K-ANGA
M-ANGA
P-ANGA
S-ANGA
T-ANGA
ANGA-S
ANIL-E
ANIL-S
M-**ANIS**
R-ANIS
ANIS-E
ANKH-S
C-**ANNA**
M-ANNA
N-ANNA
T-ANNA
W-ANNA
ANNA-L
ANNA-S
ANNA-T
ANNO-Y
B-**ANNS**
C-ANNS
J-ANNS
ANOA-S
C-**ANON**
F-ANON
H-**ANSA**
S-ANSA
ANSA-E
M-**ANTA**
ANTA-E
ANTA-R
ANTA-S
Z-**ANTE**
ANTE-D
ANTE-S
T-**ANTI**
ANTI-C
ANTI-S
B-**ANTS**
C-ANTS
D-ANTS
G-ANTS
H-ANTS
K-ANTS
L-ANTS
P-ANTS
R-ANTS
S-ANTS
V-ANTS
W-ANTS
ANTS-Y
M-**ANUS**
APAY-D
APAY-S
C-**APED**
G-APED
J-APED
R-APED
T-APED
C-**APER**
G-APER
J-APER
P-APER
R-APER
T-APER
APER-S
APER-T
APER-Y
C-**APES**
G-APES
J-APES
N-APES
P-APES

R-APES
T-APES
APOD-E
APOD-S
L-**APSE**
APSE-S
AQUA-E
AQUA-S
ARAK-S
ARAR-S
ARBA-S
B-**ARBS**
C-ARBS
D-ARBS
G-ARBS
L-**ARCH**
M-ARCH
P-ARCH
N-**ARCO**
M-**ARCS**
N-ARCS
B-**ARDS**
C-ARDS
E-ARDS
F-ARDS
H-ARDS
L-ARDS
N-ARDS
P-ARDS
S-ARDS
W-ARDS
Y-ARDS
AREA-D
AREA-E
AREA-L
AREA-R
AREA-S
B-**ARED**
C-ARED
D-ARED
E-ARED
F-ARED
H-ARED
O-ARED
P-ARED
R-ARED
S-ARED
T-ARED
W-ARED
ARED-D
ARED-E
B-**ARES**
C-ARES
D-ARES
F-ARES
H-ARES
L-ARES
M-ARES
N-ARES
P-ARES
R-ARES
T-ARES
V-ARES
W-ARES
C-**ARET**
ARET-E
ARET-S
ARET-T
B-**ARFS**
Z-ARFS
M-**ARIA**
V-ARIA
ARIA-S
M-**ARID**
ARIL-S

D-**ARIS**
L-ARIS
N-ARIS
P-ARIS
S-ARIS
ARIS-E
ARIS-H
B-**ARKS**
C-ARKS
D-ARKS
H-ARKS
J-ARKS
K-ARKS
L-ARKS
M-ARKS
N-ARKS
P-ARKS
S-ARKS
W-ARKS
C-**ARLE**
F-ARLE
M-ARLE
P-ARLE
ARLE-D
ARLE-S
B-**ARMS**
F-ARMS
H-ARMS
M-ARMS
W-ARMS
B-**ARMY**
V-**ARNA**
ARNA-S
C-**ARSE**
F-ARSE
M-ARSE
P-ARSE
ARSE-S
C-**ARTS**
D-ARTS
F-ARTS
H-ARTS
K-ARTS
M-ARTS
P-ARTS
T-ARTS
W-ARTS
ARTS-Y
P-**ARTY**
T-ARTY
W-ARTY
G-**ARUM**
L-ARUM
ARUM-S
P-**ARVO**
ARVO-S
ARYL-S
T-**ASAR**
F-**ASCI**
D-**ASHY**
H-ASHY
M-ASHY
W-ASHY
B-**ASKS**
C-ASKS
H-ASKS
M-ASKS
T-ASKS
G-**ASPS**
H-ASPS
J-ASPS
R-ASPS
W-ASPS
W-**ATAP**
ATAP-S

B-**ATES**
C-ATES
D-ATES
F-ATES
G-ATES
H-ATES
M-ATES
N-ATES
P-ATES
R-ATES
S-ATES
T-ATES
Y-ATES
ATMA-N
ATMA-S
ATOC-S
ATOK-E
ATOK-S
ATOM-S
ATOM-Y
ATOP-Y
L-**AUFS**
B-**AUKS**
C-AUKS
J-AUKS
W-AUKS
AULA-S
C-**AULD**
F-AULD
H-AULD
T-AULD
Y-AULD
AUNE-S
D-**AUNT**
G-AUNT
H-AUNT
J-AUNT
N-AUNT
S-AUNT
T-AUNT
V-AUNT
AUNT-S
AUNT-Y
L-**AURA**
AURA-E
AURA-L
AURA-R
AURA-S
AUTO-S
N-**AVAL**
AVAL-E
F-**AVAS**
J-AVAS
K-AVAS
L-AVAS
T-AVAS
AVAS-T
C-**AVER**
F-AVER
H-AVER
L-AVER
P-AVER
R-AVER
S-AVER
T-AVER
W-AVER
AVER-S
AVER-T
C-**AVES**
E-AVES
F-AVES
H-AVES
L-AVES
N-AVES
O-AVES

P-AVES
R-AVES
S-AVES
W-AVES
P-**AVID**
AVOW-S
AWAY-S
AWDL-S
C-**AWED**
D-AWED
H-AWED
J-AWED
K-AWED
L-AWED
M-AWED
P-AWED
S-AWED
T-AWED
Y-AWED
AWEE-L
W-**AWES**
B-**AWLS**
P-AWLS
W-AWLS
Y-AWLS
B-**AWNS**
D-AWNS
F-AWNS
L-AWNS
P-AWNS
R-AWNS
Y-AWNS
F-**AWNY**
L-AWNY
T-AWNY
Y-AWNY
AWOL-S
F-**AXED**
R-AXED
T-AXED
W-AXED
AXEL-S
F-**AXES**
L-AXES
M-AXES
P-AXES
R-AXES
S-AXES
T-AXES
W-AXES
Z-AXES
AXIL-E
AXIL-S
M-**AXIS**
T-AXIS
AXLE-D
AXLE-S
C-**AXON**
T-AXON
AXON-E
AXON-S
R-**AYAH**
AYAH-S
B-**AYES**
Z-**AYIN**
AYIN-S
F-**AYRE**
AYRE-S
H-**AZAN**
AZAN-S
G-**AZON**
AZON-S
AZYM-E
AZYM-S
BAAL-S

BABA-S
BABE-L
BABE-S
BABU-L
BABU-S
BACH-S
A-**BACK**
BACK-S
A-**BACS**
BAEL-S
BAFF-S
BAFF-Y
A-**BAFT**
BAFT-S
BAHT-S
BAIL-S
BAIT-H
BAIT-S
BAJU-S
BAKE-D
BAKE-N
BAKE-R
BAKE-S
BALD-S
BALD-Y
BALE-D
BALE-R
BALE-S
BALK-S
BALK-Y
BALL-S
BALL-Y
BALM-S
BALM-Y
BALS-A
BALU-S
BANC-O
BANC-S
A-**BAND**
BAND-A
BAND-S
BAND-Y
BANE-D
BANE-S
O-**BANG**
BANG-S
BANI-A
BANK-S
BANT-S
BANT-U
BANT-Y
BAPU-S
BARB-E
BARB-S
BARD-E
BARD-O
BARD-S
BARD-Y
BARE-D
BARE-R
BARE-S
BARF-S
BARK-S
BARK-Y
BARM-S
BARM-Y
BARN-S
BARN-Y
BARP-S
K-**BARS**
A-**BASE**
BASE-D
BASE-R
BASE-S
A-**BASH**

BASH-O
A-**BASK**
BASK-S
BASS-E
BASS-I
BASS-O
BASS-Y
BAST-A
BAST-E
BAST-O
BAST-S
A-**BATE**
BATE-D
BATE-S
BATH-E
BATH-S
BATT-A
BATT-S
BATT-U
BATT-Y
BAUD-S
BAUK-S
BAUR-S
BAWD-S
BAWD-Y
BAWL-S
BAWN-S
BAWR-S
BAYE-D
BAYE-S
BAYT-S
BEAD-S
BEAD-Y
BEAK-S
BEAK-Y
A-**BEAM**
BEAM-S
BEAM-Y
BEAN-O
BEAN-S
A-**BEAR**
BEAR-D
BEAR-E
BEAR-S
BEAT-H
BEAT-S
BEAU-S
BEAU-T
BEAU-X
BECK-E
BECK-S
BEDE-L
BEDE-S
BEDE-W
BEEF-S
BEEF-Y
BEEP-S
BEER-S
BEER-Y
BEET-S
BEGO-T
BEIN-G
BELL-E
BELL-S
BELL-Y
BELT-S
BEMA-D
BEMA-S
BEND-S
BEND-Y
BENE-S
BENE-T
BENI-S
BENT-S
BENT-Y

BERE-S
BERE-T
BERG-S
BERK-S
BERM-E
BERM-S
BEST-S
BETA-S
BETE-D
BETE-L
BETE-S
BETH-S
A-**BETS**
O-**BEYS**
BHEL-S
BHUT-S
O-**BIAS**
BIBB-S
BICE-S
A-**BIDE**
BIDE-D
BIDE-R
BIDE-S
BIDE-T
BIER-S
BIFF-S
BIFF-Y
BIGA-E
BIGG-S
BIGG-Y
BIKE-D
BIKE-R
BIKE-S
BILE-S
BILK-S
BILL-S
BILL-Y
BIMA-H
BIMA-S
BIND-I
BIND-S
BINE-S
BING-E
BING-O
BING-S
BING-Y
BINK-S
BINT-S
BIOG-S
BIRD-S
BIRK-S
BIRL-E
BIRL-S
BIRR-S
BISE-S
BISK-S
BITE-R
BITE-S
BITO-S
O-**BITS**
BITS-Y
BITT-E
BITT-S
BITT-Y
BIZE-S
BLAB-S
BLAD-E
BLAD-S
BLAE-R
BLAE-S
BLAG-S
BLAH-S
BLAM-E
BLAM-S
BLAT-E

BLAT-S
BLAT-T
BLAW-N
BLAW-S
BLAY-S
BLEB-S
A-**BLED**
BLEE-D
BLEE-P
BLEE-S
A-**BLET**
BLET-S
BLEY-S
BLIN-D
BLIN-I
BLIN-K
BLIN-S
BLIP-S
BLOB-S
BLOC-K
BLOC-S
BLOT-S
A-**BLOW**
BLOW-N
BLOW-S
BLOW-Y
BLUB-S
BLUE-D
BLUE-R
BLUE-S
BLUE-T
BLUE-Y
BLUR-B
BLUR-S
BLUR-T
BOAK-S
BOAR-D
BOAR-S
BOAR-T
BOAS-T
BOAT-S
BOBA-C
BOBA-K
BOBA-S
BOCK-S
A-**BODE**
BODE-D
BODE-S
BOFF-O
BOFF-S
A-**BOIL**
BOIL-S
BOKE-D
BOKE-S
BOKO-S
BOLA-R
BOLA-S
BOLD-S
O-**BOLE**
BOLE-S
BOLL-S
BOLO-S
BOLT-S
A-**BOMA**
BOMA-S
BOMB-E
BOMB-O
BOMB-S
BOND-S
BONE-D
BONE-R
BONE-S
BONE-Y
BONG-O
BONG-S

BONK-S
E-**BONY**
BOOB-S
BOOB-Y
BOOH-S
BOOK-S
BOOK-Y
BOOL-S
BOOM-S
BOOM-Y
A-**BOON**
BOON-G
BOON-S
BOOR-D
BOOR-S
BOOS-E
BOOS-T
BOOT-H
BOOT-S
BOOT-Y
BORA-K
BORA-L
BORA-S
BORA-X
A-**BORD**
BORD-E
BORD-S
A-**BORE**
Y-BORE
BORE-D
BORE-E
BORE-L
BORE-R
BORE-S
BORN-E
A-**BORT**
BORT-S
BORT-Y
BORT-Z
BOSK-S
BOSK-Y
BOSS-Y
BOTA-S
BOTH-Y
BOTT-E
BOTT-S
BOTT-Y
BOUK-S
BOUN-D
BOUN-S
A-**BOUT**
BOUT-S
BOWL-S
BOWR-S
BOWS-E
BOYG-S
BOYO-S
BOZO-S
BRAD-S
BRAE-S
BRAG-S
BRAN-D
BRAN-K
BRAN-S
BRAN-T
BRAS-H
BRAS-S
BRAS-T
BRAT-S
BRAW-L
BRAW-N
BRAW-S
A-**BRAY**
BRAY-S
BRED-E

BREE-D
BREE-M
BREE-R
BREE-S
BREN-S
BREN-T
BRER-E
BRER-S
BREW-S
BRIE-F
BRIE-R
BRIE-S
BRIG-S
A-**BRIM**
BRIM-S
A-**BRIN**
BRIN-E
BRIN-G
BRIN-K
BRIN-S
BRIN-Y
BRIO-S
A-**BRIS**
BRIS-E
BRIS-K
BRIT-S
BRIT-T
BROD-S
BROG-H
BROG-S
BROO-D
BROO-K
BROO-L
BROO-M
BROO-S
BROS-E
BROS-Y
BROW-N
BROW-S
BRUT-E
BUAT-S
BUBA-L
BUBA-S
BUCK-O
BUCK-S
BUCK-U
BUDO-S
BUFF-A
BUFF-E
BUFF-I
BUFF-O
BUFF-S
BUFF-Y
BUFO-S
BUHL-S
BUHR-S
BUIK-S
BUKE-S
BULB-S
BULK-S
BULK-Y
BULL-A
BULL-S
BULL-Y
BUMF-S
BUMP-H
BUMP-S
BUMP-Y
A-**BUNA**
BUNA-S
BUND-S
BUND-T
BUND-U
BUNG-S
BUNG-Y

BUNK-O
BUNK-S
BUNN-S
BUNN-Y
BUNT-S
BUNT-Y
BUOY-S
BURA-N
BURA-S
BURD-S
BURG-H
BURG-S
BURK-A
BURK-E
BURK-S
BURL-S
BURL-Y
BURN-S
BURN-T
BURP-S
BURR-O
BURR-S
BURR-Y
BURS-A
BURS-E
BURS-T
BUSH-Y
BUSK-S
BUSK-Y
BUSS-U
BUST-S
BUST-Y
BUTE-O
BUTE-S
A-**BUTS**
BUTT-E
BUTT-S
BUTT-Y
A-**BUZZ**
BUZZ-Y
A-**BYES**
BYKE-D
BYKE-S
BYRE-S
BYRL-S
BYTE-S
CABA-L
CABA-S
S-**CABS**
CACA-O
CACA-S
CADE-E
CADE-S
CADE-T
CADI-E
CADI-S
E-**CADS**
S-CADS
CAFE-S
S-**CAFF**
CAFF-S
CAGE-D
CAGE-R
CAGE-S
CAGE-Y
CAID-S
CAIN-S
CAKE-D
CAKE-S
CAKE-Y
CALF-S
CALK-S
S-**CALL**
CALL-A
CALL-S

CALM-S
CALM-Y
S-**CALP**
CALP-A
CALP-S
CAME-L
CAME-O
CAME-S
S-**CAMP**
CAMP-I
CAMP-O
CAMP-S
CAMP-Y
S-**CAMS**
CANE-D
CANE-H
CANE-R
CANE-S
CANG-S
CANN-A
CANN-S
CANN-Y
S-**CANS**
CANS-O
CANS-T
S-**CANT**
CANT-O
CANT-S
CANT-Y
S-**CAPA**
CAPA-S
S-**CAPE**
CAPE-D
CAPE-R
CAPE-S
CAPH-S
S-**CAPI**
CAPI-Z
CAPO-N
CAPO-S
CAPO-T
CARB-O
CARB-S
CARB-Y
CARD-I
CARD-S
CARD-Y
S-**CARE**
CARE-D
CARE-R
CARE-S
CARE-T
CARE-X
CARK-S
CARL-E
CARL-S
CARN-S
CARN-Y
S-**CARP**
CARP-I
CARP-S
CARR-S
CARR-Y
S-**CARS**
CARS-E
S-**CART**
CART-A
CART-E
CART-S
CASA-S
CASE-D
CASE-S
CASK-S
CASK-Y
CAST-E
CAST-S
CATE-R
CATE-S
S-**CATS**
CAUK-S
CAUL-D
CAUL-K
CAUL-S
CAUM-S
S-**CAUP**
CAUP-S
CAVE-D
CAVE-L
CAVE-R
CAVE-S
CAWK-S
S-**CAWS**
CEAS-E
CECA-L
CEDE-D
CEDE-R
CEDE-S
CEDI-S
CEIL-I
CEIL-S
CELL-A
CELL-I
CELL-O
CELL-S
CELT-S
CENS-E
S-**CENT**
CENT-O
CENT-S
CEPE-S
CERE-D
CERE-S
CERO-S
CERT-S
CESS-E
CETE-S
CHAD-S
CHAI-N
CHAI-R
CHAI-S
CHAL-K
CHAL-S
CHAM-P
CHAM-S
CHAO-S
CHAP-E
CHAP-S
CHAP-T
CHAR-A
CHAR-D
CHAR-E
CHAR-K
CHAR-M
CHAR-R
CHAR-S
CHAR-T
CHAR-Y
CHAS-E
CHAS-M
CHAT-S
CHAW-S
CHAY-A
CHAY-S
CHEF-S
O-**CHER**
CHER-E
CHER-T
CHEW-S
CHEW-Y
CHIA-O
CHIA-S
CHIC-A
CHIC-H
CHIC-K
CHIC-O
CHIC-S
CHID-E
CHIK-S
CHIN-A
CHIN-E
CHIN-K
CHIN-O
CHIN-S
CHIP-S
CHIT-S
CHIV-E
CHIV-S
CHIV-Y
CHIZ-Z
CHOC-K
CHOC-O
CHOC-S
CHON-S
CHOP-S
CHOU-T
CHOU-X
CHOW-S
CHUB-S
CHUG-S
CHUM-P
CHUM-S
CHUT-E
CIAO-S
CIDE-D
CIDE-R
CIDE-S
A-**CIDS**
CIEL-S
CILL-S
CINE-S
S-**CION**
CION-S
CIRE-S
CIRL-S
CIST-S
CITE-D
CITE-R
CITE-S
CIVE-S
CIVE-T
Y-**CLAD**
CLAD-E
CLAD-S
CLAG-S
CLAM-E
CLAM-P
CLAM-S
CLAN-G
CLAN-K
CLAN-S
CLAP-S
CLAP-T
E-**CLAT**
CLAT-S
CLAW-S
CLAY-S
CLEF-S
CLEF-T
CLEG-S
CLEM-S
CLEW-S
CLIP-E
CLIP-S
CLIP-T
CLOD-S
CLOG-S
CLON-E
CLON-K
CLON-S
CLOP-S
CLOT-E
CLOT-H
CLOT-S
CLOU-D
CLOU-R
CLOU-S
CLOU-T
CLOW-N
CLOW-S
CLOY-E
CLOY-S
CLUB-S
CLUE-D
CLUE-S
COAL-A
COAL-S
COAL-Y
COAT-E
COAT-I
COAT-S
COBB-S
COBB-Y
COCA-S
A-**COCK**
COCK-S
COCK-Y
COCO-A
COCO-S
CODA-S
CODE-C
CODE-D
CODE-N
CODE-R
CODE-S
CODE-X
COED-S
S-**COFF**
COFF-S
S-**COGS**
COHO-E
COHO-G
COHO-S
COIF-S
COIL-S
COIN-S
COIR-S
COIT-S
COKE-D
COKE-S
COLA-S
A-**COLD**
S-COLD
COLD-S
COLE-D
COLE-S
COLE-Y
COLL-S
COLL-Y
COLT-S
COMA-E
COMA-L
COMA-S
COMB-E
COMB-I
COMB-O
COMB-S
COMB-Y
COME-R
COME-S
COME-T
COMP-O
COMP-S
COMP-T
Y-**COND**
COND-O
S-**CONE**
CONE-D
CONE-S
CONE-Y
CONF-S
CONI-A
CONI-C
CONI-N
CONK-S
CONK-Y
CONN-E
CONN-S
I-**CONS**
COOF-S
COOK-S
COOK-Y
COOL-S
COOL-Y
COOM-B
COOM-S
COOM-Y
COON-S
S-**COOP**
COOP-S
COOP-T
COOS-T
S-**COOT**
COOT-S
S-**COPE**
COPE-D
COPE-N
COPE-R
COPE-S
S-**COPS**
COPS-E
COPS-Y
CORD-S
S-**CORE**
CORE-D
CORE-R
CORE-S
CORE-Y
CORK-S
CORK-Y
CORM-S
A-**CORN**
S-CORN
CORN-I
CORN-O
CORN-S
CORN-U
CORN-Y
CORS-E
CORS-O
COSE-C
COSE-D
COSE-S
COSE-T
COSE-Y
COST-A
COST-E
COST-S
COTE-D
COTE-S
COTH-S
S-**COTS**
COTT-A
COTT-S
S-**COUP**
COUP-E
COUP-S
S-**COUR**
COUR-B
COUR-D
COUR-E
COUR-S
COUR-T
COVE-D
COVE-N
COVE-R
COVE-S
COVE-T
COVE-Y
S-**COWL**
COWL-S
S-**COWP**
COWP-S
S-**COWS**
COXA-E
COXA-L
COZE-D
COZE-N
COZE-S
COZE-Y
S-**CRAB**
CRAB-S
S-**CRAG**
CRAG-S
S-**CRAM**
CRAM-E
CRAM-P
CRAM-S
S-**CRAN**
CRAN-E
CRAN-K
CRAN-S
S-**CRAP**
CRAP-E
CRAP-S
CRAP-Y
S-**CRAW**
CRAW-L
CRAW-S
A-**CRED**
CRED-O
CRED-S
S-**CREE**
CREE-D
CREE-K
CREE-L
CREE-P
CREE-S
S-**CREW**
CREW-E
CREW-S
CRIB-S
S-**CRIM**
CRIM-E
CRIM-P
CRIM-S
CRIS-E
CRIS-P
CRIT-H
CRIT-S
CROC-I
CROC-K
CROC-S
CROP-S
S-**CROW**
CROW-D
CROW-N
CROW-S
CRUD-E
CRUD-S
CRUD-Y
CRUE-L
CRUE-S
CRUE-T
E-**CRUS**
CRUS-E
CRUS-H
CRUS-T
CRUS-Y
CUBE-B
CUBE-D
CUBE-R
CUBE-S
S-**CUDS**
S-**CUFF**
CUFF-O
CUFF-S
CUIF-S
CUIT-S
CUKE-S
S-**CULL**
CULL-S
CULL-Y
CULM-S
CULT-I
CULT-S
CUNT-S
S-**CUPS**
CURB-S
CURD-S
CURD-Y
CURE-D
CURE-R
CURE-S
CURE-T
S-**CURF**
CURF-S
CURL-S
CURL-Y
CURN-S
CURN-Y
CURR-S
CURR-Y
S-**CURS**
CURS-E
CURS-I
CURS-T
CUSH-Y
CUSK-S
CUSP-S
CUSS-O
A-**CUTE**
S-CUTE
CUTE-R
CUTE-S
CUTE-Y
S-**CUTS**
CYAN-O
CYAN-S
CYMA-E
CYMA-R
CYMA-S
CYME-S
CYST-S
CYTE-S
CZAR-S
DACE-S
DADA-S
DADO-S
DAFF-S
DAFF-Y
DAGO-S
DAHL-S
DAIS-Y
DALE-S
DALI-S
O-**DALS**
U-DALS
DALT-S
DAME-S
DAMN-S
DAMP-S
DAMP-Y
DANG-S
DANK-S
I-**DANT**
DANT-S
DARB-S
DARE-D
DARE-R
DARE-S
DARG-A
DARG-S
DARI-C
DARI-S
DARK-S
DARK-Y
DARN-S
DART-S
DASH-I
DASH-Y
DATA-L
DATE-D
DATE-R
DATE-S
DATO-S
DAUB-E
DAUB-S
DAUB-Y
DAUD-S
DAUR-S
DAUT-S
DAWD-S
DAWK-S
DAWN-S
A-**DAWS**
DAWT-S
A-**DAYS**
DAZE-D
DAZE-R
DAZE-S
DEAD-S
I-**DEAL**
DEAL-S
DEAL-T
DEAN-S
DEAR-E
DEAR-N
DEAR-S
DEAR-Y
DEAW-S
DEAW-Y
DEBT-S
DECK-O
DECK-S
DECO-R
DECO-S
DECO-Y
DEED-S
DEED-Y
A-**DEEM**
DEEM-S
DEEN-S
DEEP-S
DEER-E
DEER-S
I-**DEES**
DEET-S
DEEV-E
DEEV-S
DEFI-S

DEID-S
DEIL-S
DEKE-D
DEKE-S
DELE-D
DELE-S
DELF-S
DELF-T
DELI-S
DELL-S
DELL-Y
DELT-A
DELT-S
DEME-S
DEMO-B
DEMO-N
DEMO-S
DENE-S
DENE-T
DENS-E
DENT-S
DERE-D
DERE-S
DERM-A
DERM-S
DERN-S
DERV-S
DESK-S
DEVA-S
DHAK-S
DHAL-S
DHOL-E
DHOL-L
DHOL-S
DHOW-S
DIAL-S
DICE-D
DICE-R
DICE-S
DICE-Y
DICH-T
DICK-S
DICK-Y
E-**DICT**
DICT-A
DICT-S
DICT-Y
DIDO-S
DIEB-S
DIET-S
DIKA-S
DIKE-D
DIKE-R
DIKE-S
DIKE-Y
DILL-I
DILL-S
DILL-Y
DIME-R
DIME-S
DINE-D
DINE-R
DINE-S
DING-E
DING-O
DING-S
DING-Y
DINK-S
DINK-Y
DINO-S
DINT-S
DIOL-S
DIPS-O
DIRE-R
DIRK-E
DIRK-S
DIRL-S
DIRT-S
DIRT-Y
DISA-S
DISC-I
DISC-O
DISC-S
DISH-Y
DISK-S
DITA-L
DITA-S
DITE-D
DITE-S
A-**DITS**
E-DITS
DITS-Y
DITT-O
DITT-S
DITT-Y
DITZ-Y
DIVA-N
DIVA-S
DIVE-D
DIVE-R
DIVE-S
DIVI-S
DIXI-E
DIXI-T
DJIN-N
DJIN-S
DOAB-S
DOAT-S
DOCK-S
DODO-S
DOEK-S
DOER-S
DOES-T
DOFF-S
DOGE-S
DOGE-Y
DOIT-S
DOJO-S
DOLE-D
DOLE-S
DOLL-S
DOLL-Y
I-**DOLS**
DOLT-S
DOME-D
DOME-S
DONA-H
DONA-S
DONE-E
DONG-A
DONG-S
DONS-Y
DOOB-S
DOOK-S
DOOL-E
DOOL-S
DOOL-Y
DOOM-S
DOOM-Y
DOOR-N
DOOR-S
DOPA-S
DOPE-D
DOPE-R
DOPE-S
DOPE-Y
A-**DORE**
DORE-E
DORK-S
DORK-Y
DORM-S
DORM-Y
DORP-S
DORR-S
O-**DORS**
DORS-A
DORS-E
DORT-S
DORT-Y
DOSE-D
DOSE-H
DOSE-R
DOSE-S
DOTE-D
DOTE-R
DOTE-S
DOUC-E
DOUC-S
DOUM-A
DOUM-S
DOUP-S
O-**DOUR**
DOUR-A
DOUT-S
DOVE-D
DOVE-N
DOVE-R
DOVE-S
DOWD-S
DOWD-Y
DOWL-E
DOWL-S
A-**DOWN**
DOWN-A
DOWN-S
DOWN-Y
DOWP-S
DOWS-E
DOWT-S
A-**DOZE**
DOZE-D
DOZE-N
DOZE-R
DOZE-S
DRAB-S
A-**DRAD**
Y-DRAD
DRAG-S
DRAM-A
DRAM-S
DRAP-E
DRAP-S
DRAT-S
DRAW-L
DRAW-N
DRAW-S
DRAY-S
DREE-D
DREE-S
DREG-S
DREK-S
DREY-S
DRIB-S
DRIP-S
DRIP-T
DROP-S
DROP-T
DROW-N
DROW-S
DRUB-S
DRUG-S
DRUM-S
O-**DSOS**
DUAD-S
DUAL-S
DUAN-S
DUAR-S
E-**DUCE**
DUCE-S
DUCK-S
DUCK-Y
E-**DUCT**
DUCT-S
DUDE-D
DUDE-S
DUEL-S
DUET-S
DUET-T
DUFF-S
DUIT-S
DUKE-D
DUKE-S
DULE-S
DULL-S
DULL-Y
DUMA-S
DUMB-O
DUMB-S
DUMP-S
DUMP-Y
DUNE-S
DUNG-S
DUNG-Y
DUNK-S
DUNS-H
DUNT-S
DUPE-D
DUPE-R
DUPE-S
DURA-L
DURA-S
DURE-D
DURE-S
DURN-S
DURO-C
DURO-S
DURO-Y
DURR-A
DURR-S
DUSK-S
DUSK-Y
A-**DUST**
DUST-S
DUST-Y
DWAM-S
DYAD-S
DYER-S
DYKE-D
DYKE-S
DYKE-Y
DYNE-L
DYNE-S
DZHO-S
B-**EACH**
L-EACH
P-EACH
R-EACH
T-EACH
V-**EALE**
EALE-S
B-**EANS**
D-EANS
G-EANS
J-EANS
L-EANS
M-EANS
P-EANS
R-EANS
S-EANS
W-EANS
Y-EANS
B-**EARD**
H-EARD
Y-EARD
EARD-S
P-**EARL**
EARL-S
EARL-Y
D-**EARN**
L-EARN
Y-EARN
EARN-S
B-**EARS**
D-EARS
F-EARS
G-EARS
H-EARS
L-EARS
N-EARS
P-EARS
R-EARS
S-EARS
T-EARS
W-EARS
Y-EARS
EARS-T
C-**EASE**
F-EASE
L-EASE
M-EASE
P-EASE
S-EASE
T-EASE
EASE-D
EASE-L
EASE-S
B-**EAST**
F-EAST
H-EAST
L-EAST
R-EAST
Y-EAST
EAST-S
B-**EATH**
D-EATH
H-EATH
M-EATH
N-EATH
EATH-E
B-**EATS**
F-EATS
G-EATS
H-EATS
J-EATS
L-EATS
M-EATS
N-EATS
P-EATS
S-EATS
T-EATS
B-**EAUS**
B-**EAUX**
D-**EAVE**
H-EAVE
L-EAVE
R-EAVE
W-EAVE
EAVE-D
EAVE-S
EBON-S
EBON-Y
D-**ECAD**
ECAD-S
R-**ECCE**
R-**ECCO**
S-ECCO
ECHE-D
ECHE-S
ECHO-S
F-**ECHT**
H-ECHT
W-ECHT
ECRU-S
N-**EDDY**
R-EDDY
T-EDDY
H-**EDGE**
K-EDGE
L-EDGE
S-EDGE
W-EDGE
EDGE-D
EDGE-R
EDGE-S
H-**EDGY**
K-EDGY
L-EDGY
S-EDGY
W-EDGY
EDIT-S
B-**EECH**
K-EECH
L-EECH
R-EECH
F-**EELS**
H-EELS
J-EELS
K-EELS
P-EELS
R-EELS
S-EELS
T-EELS
W-EELS
J-**EELY**
S-EELY
B-**EERY**
L-EERY
P-EERY
V-EERY
EEVN-S
J-**EFFS**
T-EFFS
H-**EFTS**
L-EFTS
W-EFTS
B-**EGAD**
EGAD-S
L-**EGAL**
R-EGAL
L-**EGER**
EGER-S
T-**EGGS**
Y-EGGS
L-**EGGY**
P-EGGY
A-**EGIS**
R-**EGMA**
EGMA-S
R-**EGOS**
S-EGOS
EIDE-R
R-**EIKS**
EILD-S
S-**EINE**
D-**EKED**
R-EKED
D-**EKES**
P-EKES
R-EKES
EKKA-S
ELAN-D
ELAN-S
G-**ELDS**
M-ELDS
V-ELDS
W-ELDS
D-**ELFS**
P-ELFS
S-ELFS
W-**ELKS**
Y-ELKS
B-**ELLS**
C-ELLS
D-ELLS
F-ELLS
H-ELLS
J-ELLS
K-ELLS
M-ELLS
P-ELLS
S-ELLS
T-ELLS
V-ELLS
W-ELLS
Y-ELLS
H-**ELMS**
Y-ELMS
B-**ELTS**
C-ELTS
D-ELTS
F-ELTS
G-ELTS
K-ELTS
M-ELTS
P-ELTS
W-ELTS
Y-ELTS
D-**EMES**
F-EMES
H-EMES
L-EMES
M-EMES
S-EMES
T-EMES
EMEU-S
D-**EMIC**
H-EMIC
EMIR-S
D-**EMIT**
R-EMIT
EMIT-S
G-**EMMA**
L-EMMA
EMMA-S
EMYD-E
EMYD-S
B-**ENDS**
F-ENDS
H-ENDS
L-ENDS
M-ENDS
P-ENDS
R-ENDS
S-ENDS
T-ENDS
V-ENDS
W-ENDS
B-**ENES**
D-ENES
G-ENES
L-ENES
M-ENES
N-ENES
P-ENES
T-ENES
R-**ENEW**
ENEW-S
L-**ENGS**
M-ENGS
ENOL-S
ENOW-S
S-**ENVY**
A-**EONS**
N-EONS
P-EONS
C-**EORL**
EORL-S
T-**EPEE**
EPEE-S
EPHA-H
EPHA-S
S-**EPIC**
EPIC-S
P-**EPOS**
R-EPOS
T-**ERAS**
ERAS-E
C-**ERED**
D-ERED
L-ERED
M-ERED
S-ERED
B-**ERES**
C-ERES
D-ERES
F-ERES
G-ERES
H-ERES
L-ERES
M-ERES
P-ERES
S-ERES
T-ERES
ERGO-N
ERGO-T
B-**ERGS**
C-**ERIC**
S-ERIC
X-ERIC
ERIC-A
ERIC-K
ERIC-S
B-**ERKS**
J-ERKS
M-ERKS
N-ERKS
P-ERKS
S-ERKS
Y-ERKS
Z-ERKS
C-**ERNE**
G-ERNE
K-ERNE
T-ERNE
ERNE-D
ERNE-S
D-**ERNS**
F-ERNS
H-ERNS
K-ERNS
P-ERNS
T-ERNS
A-**EROS**
C-EROS
H-EROS
Z-EROS
EROS-E
S-**ERRS**
P-**ERST**
V-ERST

L-**ESES**
M-ESES
R-ESES
Y-ESES
P-**ESKY**
M-**ESNE**
ESNE-S
C-**ESSE**
D-ESSE
F-ESSE
G-ESSE
J-ESSE
ESSE-S
B-**ESTS**
F-ESTS
G-ESTS
H-ESTS
J-ESTS
K-ESTS
L-ESTS
N-ESTS
P-ESTS
R-ESTS
T-ESTS
V-ESTS
W-ESTS
Y-ESTS
Z-ESTS
B-**ETAS**
F-ETAS
G-ETAS
K-ETAS
W-ETAS
Z-ETAS
ETAT-S
F-**ETCH**
K-ETCH
L-ETCH
R-ETCH
V-ETCH
ETEN-S
L-**ETHE**
ETHE-R
B-**ETHS**
H-ETHS
M-ETHS
T-ETHS
M-**ETIC**
ETNA-S
ETUI-S
H-**EUGH**
L-EUGH
T-EUGH
EUGH-S
N-**EUKS**
Y-EUKS
EURO-S
E-**EVEN**
S-EVEN
Y-EVEN
EVEN-S
EVEN-T
B-**EVER**
F-EVER
L-EVER
N-EVER
S-EVER
EVER-T
EVER-Y
M-**EVES**
N-EVES
Y-EVES
R-**EVET**
EVET-S
D-**EVIL**

K-EVIL
EVIL-S
F-**EWER**
H-EWER
N-EWER
S-EWER
EWER-S
EWES-T
N-**EWTS**
EXAM-S
EXEC-S
D-**EXES**
H-EXES
K-EXES
L-EXES
R-EXES
S-EXES
V-EXES
W-EXES
Y-EXES
Z-EXES
EXIT-S
EXON-S
EXPO-S
EXUL-S
EXUL-T
F-**EYED**
H-EYED
K-EYED
S-**EYEN**
F-**EYER**
G-EYER
EYER-S
EYOT-S
EYRA-S
EYRE-S
FACE-D
FACE-R
FACE-S
FACE-T
FACT-S
FADE-D
FADE-R
FADE-S
FADO-S
FAFF-S
FAIK-S
FAIL-S
FAIN-E
FAIN-S
FAIN-T
FAIR-S
FAIR-Y
FAKE-D
FAKE-R
FAKE-S
FAKE-Y
FALL-S
FAME-D
FAME-S
FAND-S
FANE-S
FANG-A
FANG-O
FANG-S
FANK-S
FANO-N
FANO-S
FARD-S
FARE-D
FARE-R
FARE-S
FARL-E
FARL-S
FARM-S

FARO-S
A-**FARS**
FARS-E
FART-S
FAST-I
FAST-S
FATE-D
FATE-S
FATS-O
FAUN-A
FAUN-S
FAVA-S
FAVE-L
FAVE-R
FAVE-S
FAWN-S
FAWN-Y
O-**FAYS**
FAZE-D
FAZE-S
FEAL-S
A-**FEAR**
FEAR-E
FEAR-S
FEAT-S
FECK-S
FEED-S
FEEL-S
FEER-S
FEES-E
FEHM-E
FEIS-T
FELL-A
FELL-S
FELL-Y
FELT-S
FELT-Y
FEME-S
FEND-S
FEND-Y
FENI-S
FENT-S
FEOD-S
Y-**FERE**
FERE-R
FERE-S
FERM-I
FERM-S
FERN-S
FERN-Y
FESS-E
FEST-A
FEST-S
FETA-L
FETA-S
FETE-D
FETE-S
FETT-A
FETT-S
FEUD-S
FIAR-S
FIAT-S
FICE-S
FICO-S
FIDO-S
FIEF-S
FIER-E
FIER-Y
FIFE-D
FIFE-R
FIFE-S
FIGO-S
FIKE-D
FIKE-S
FILA-R

FILE-D
FILE-R
FILE-S
FILE-T
FILL-E
FILL-O
FILL-S
FILL-Y
FILM-S
FILM-Y
FILO-S
FIND-S
FINE-D
FINE-R
FINE-S
FINI-S
FINK-S
FINO-S
A-**FIRE**
FIRE-D
FIRE-R
FIRE-S
FIRK-S
FIRM-S
FIRN-S
FIRS-T
FISC-S
FISH-Y
FISK-S
FIST-S
FIST-Y
FITT-E
FITT-S
FIVE-R
FIVE-S
FIZZ-Y
FLAB-S
O-**FLAG**
FLAG-S
FLAK-E
FLAK-S
FLAK-Y
FLAM-E
FLAM-M
FLAM-S
FLAM-Y
FLAN-K
FLAN-S
FLAP-S
FLAT-S
FLAW-N
FLAW-S
FLAW-Y
FLAX-Y
FLAY-S
FLEA-M
FLEA-S
FLEE-R
FLEE-S
FLEE-T
FLEG-S
FLEW-S
FLEY-S
FLIC-K
FLIC-S
FLIP-S
FLIT-E
FLIT-S
FLIT-T
FLOC-K
FLOC-S
FLOE-S
FLOG-S
FLOP-S
FLOR-A

FLOR-S
FLOR-Y
FLOW-N
FLOW-S
FLUB-S
FLUE-D
FLUE-S
FLUE-Y
FLUS-H
FOAL-S
FOAM-S
FOAM-Y
FOHN-S
FOID-S
FOIL-S
FOIN-S
FOLD-S
FOLK-S
FOLK-Y
FOND-A
FOND-S
FOND-U
FONT-S
FOOD-S
FOOD-Y
FOOL-S
A-**FOOT**
FOOT-S
FOOT-Y
FORA-M
FORA-Y
FORB-S
FORB-Y
FORD-O
FORD-S
A-**FORE**
FORE-L
FORE-S
FORK-S
FORK-Y
FORM-E
FORM-S
FORT-E
FORT-H
FORT-S
FORT-Y
FOSS-A
FOSS-E
FOUD-S
A-**FOUL**
FOUL-E
FOUL-S
FOUR-S
FOWL-S
FRAB-S
FRAG-S
FRAP-S
FRAS-S
FRAT-E
FRAT-I
FRAT-S
FRAU-D
FRAU-S
FRAY-S
FREE-D
FREE-R
FREE-S
FREE-T
FRET-S
FRIG-S
FRIS-E
FRIS-K
FRIS-T
A-**FRIT**
FRIT-H

FRIT-S
FRIT-T
FRIT-Z
FRIZ-E
FRIZ-Z
FROE-S
FROG-S
FROW-N
FROW-S
FROW-Y
FRUG-S
FUBS-Y
FUCK-S
FUEL-S
FUFF-S
FUFF-Y
FUGU-E
FUGU-S
FUJI-S
FULL-S
FULL-Y
FUME-D
FUME-R
FUME-S
FUME-T
FUND-I
FUND-S
FUND-Y
FUNG-I
FUNG-O
FUNG-S
FUNK-S
FUNK-Y
FURL-S
FURR-S
FURR-Y
FUSE-D
FUSE-E
FUSE-L
FUSE-S
FUSS-Y
FUST-S
FUST-Y
FUZE-D
FUZE-E
FUZE-S
FUZZ-Y
FYCE-S
FYKE-D
FYKE-S
FYLE-S
FYRD-S
GADE-S
GADI-D
GADI-S
E-**GADS**
GADS-O
GAFF-E
GAFF-S
GAGE-D
GAGE-R
GAGE-S
GAID-S
A-**GAIN**
GAIN-S
GAIR-S
GAIT-S
GAIT-T
GAJO-S
GALA-H
GALA-S
GALA-X
GALE-A
GALE-S
GALL-S

GALL-Y
A-**GAMA**
GAMA-S
GAMA-Y
GAMB-A
GAMB-E
GAMB-O
GAMB-S
GAME-D
GAME-R
GAME-S
GAME-Y
GAMP-S
O-**GAMS**
GANE-F
GANE-V
GANG-S
GANT-S
GAOL-S
A-**GAPE**
GAPE-D
GAPE-R
GAPE-S
I-**GAPO**
GAPO-S
GARB-E
GARB-O
GARB-S
A-**GARS**
GART-H
GASP-S
GASP-Y
A-**GAST**
GAST-S
A-**GATE**
GATE-D
GATE-S
GATH-S
GAUD-S
GAUD-Y
GAUM-S
GAUM-Y
GAUN-T
GAUP-S
GAUR-S
GAUS-S
A-**GAVE**
GAVE-L
GAWD-S
GAWK-S
GAWK-Y
GAWP-S
A-**GAZE**
GAZE-D
GAZE-R
GAZE-S
GEAL-S
GEAN-S
GEAR-E
GEAR-S
GEAT-S
GECK-O
GECK-S
GEEK-S
GEEK-Y
GEEP-S
O-**GEES**
GEES-E
GEES-T
GEIT-S
GELD-S
GELT-S
GENA-L
GENA-S
A-**GENE**

GENE-S
GENE-T
A-**GENT**
GENT-S
GENT-Y
GENU-A
GENU-S
GERE-S
GERM-S
GERM-Y
E-**GEST**
GEST-E
GEST-S
GETA-S
GEUM-S
GHAT-S
GHEE-S
GIBE-D
GIBE-L
GIBE-R
GIBE-S
GIFT-S
GIGA-S
A-**GILA**
GILA-S
GILD-S
GILL-S
GILL-Y
GILT-S
GIMP-S
GIMP-Y
A-**GING**
GING-S
GINK-S
GINN-Y
A-**GIOS**
GIPS-Y
GIRD-S
GIRL-S
GIRL-Y
GIRN-S
GIRO-N
GIRO-S
GIRR-S
GIRT-H
GIRT-S
A-**GISM**
GISM-O
GISM-S
A-**GIST**
GIST-S
GITE-S
O-**GIVE**
GIVE-D
GIVE-N
GIVE-R
GIVE-S
GLAD-E
GLAD-S
GLAD-Y
GLAM-S
O-**GLED**
GLED-E
GLED-S
A-**GLEE**
GLEE-D
GLEE-K
GLEE-S
GLEE-T
GLEI-S
GLEN-S
GLEN-T
A-**GLEY**
GLEY-S
GLIA-L

GLIA-S
GLIB-S
GLID-E
GLIM-E
GLIM-S
GLIT-S
GLIT-Z
GLOB-E
GLOB-S
GLOB-Y
GLOM-S
GLOP-S
A-**GLOW**
GLOW-S
GLUE-D
GLUE-R
GLUE-S
GLUE-Y
GLUG-S
GLUM-E
GLUT-S
GNAR-L
GNAR-R
GNAR-S
GNAT-S
GNAW-N
GNAW-S
GOAD-S
GOAF-S
GOAL-S
GOAT-S
GOAT-Y
GOBO-S
GODS-O
GOEL-S
GOER-S
GOFF-S
GOGO-S
GOLD-S
GOLD-Y
GOLE-M
GOLE-S
GOLF-S
GOLP-E
GOLP-S
A-**GONE**
GONE-F
GONE-R
GONG-S
GONK-S
A-**GONS**
A-**GOOD**
GOOD-S
GOOD-Y
GOOF-S
GOOF-Y
GOOK-S
GOOK-Y
GOOL-D
GOOL-S
GOOL-Y
GOON-S
GOON-Y
GOOP-S
GOOP-Y
GOOR-S
GOOS-E
GOOS-Y
GORE-D
GORE-S
GORM-S
GORM-Y
GORP-S
GOSH-T
GOUK-S

GOUT-S
GOUT-Y
GOWD-S
GOWF-S
GOWK-S
GOWL-S
GOWN-S
GRAB-S
GRAD-E
GRAD-S
GRAM-A
GRAM-E
GRAM-P
GRAM-S
GRAN-A
GRAN-D
GRAN-S
GRAN-T
GRAT-E
GRAY-S
A-**GREE**
GREE-D
GREE-K
GREE-N
GREE-S
GREE-T
GREN-S
GREW-S
GREY-S
GRID-E
GRID-S
GRIG-S
GRIM-E
GRIM-Y
A-**GRIN**
GRIN-D
GRIN-S
GRIP-E
GRIP-S
GRIP-T
GRIP-Y
GRIS-E
GRIS-T
GRIS-Y
GRIT-H
GRIT-S
GROG-S
GROT-S
GROW-L
GROW-N
GROW-S
GRUB-S
GRUE-D
GRUE-L
GRUE-S
GRUM-E
GRUM-P
GUAN-A
GUAN-O
GUAN-S
GUAR-D
GUAR-S
GUCK-S
GUCK-Y
GUDE-S
A-**GUES**
GUES-S
GUES-T
GUFF-S
GUGA-S
GUID-E
GUID-S
GULA-G
GULA-R
GULA-S

GULE-S
GULF-S
GULF-Y
GULL-S
GULL-Y
GULP-H
GULP-S
GULP-Y
GUMP-S
GUNK-S
GUNK-Y
GURL-S
GURL-Y
GURN-S
GURS-H
GURU-S
GUSH-Y
GUST-O
GUST-S
GUST-Y
GUTS-Y
GUYS-E
GYAL-S
GYBE-D
GYBE-S
GYMP-S
GYPS-Y
GYRE-D
GYRE-S
GYRO-N
GYRO-S
GYTE-S
GYVE-D
GYVE-S
HAAF-S
HAAR-S
HABU-S
C-**HACK**
S-HACK
T-HACK
W-HACK
HACK-S
S-**HADE**
HADE-D
HADE-S
HADJ-I
C-**HADS**
S-HADS
HADS-T
HAEM-S
HAET-S
C-**HAFF**
HAFF-S
C-**HAFT**
S-HAFT
HAFT-S
HAGG-S
S-**HAGS**
HAHA-S
S-**HAHS**
HAIK-A
HAIK-S
HAIK-U
HAIL-S
HAIL-Y
C-**HAIN**
HAIN-S
C-**HAIR**
HAIR-S
HAIR-Y
HAJI-S
HAJJ-I
HAKA-M
HAKA-S
S-**HAKE**

HAKE-S
S-**HALE**
W-HALE
HALE-D
HALE-R
HALE-S
HALF-A
HALF-S
S-**HALL**
HALL-O
HALL-S
S-**HALM**
HALM-A
HALM-S
HALO-N
HALO-S
S-**HALT**
HALT-S
S-**HAME**
HAME-D
HAME-S
C-**HAMS**
S-HAMS
W-HAMS
S-**HAND**
HAND-S
HAND-Y
B-**HANG**
C-HANG
P-HANG
W-HANG
HANG-S
C-**HANK**
S-HANK
T-HANK
HANK-S
HANK-Y
C-**HANT**
HANT-S
C-**HAPS**
S-HAPS
W-HAPS
C-**HARD**
S-HARD
HARD-S
HARD-Y
C-**HARE**
P-HARE
S-HARE
W-HARE
HARE-D
HARE-M
HARE-S
C-**HARK**
S-HARK
HARK-S
HARL-S
C-**HARM**
T-HARM
HARM-S
S-**HARN**
HARN-S
HARO-S
S-**HARP**
HARP-S
HARP-Y
C-**HART**
HART-S
S-**HASH**
HASH-Y
HASK-S
HASP-S
G-**HAST**
HAST-A
HAST-E

HAST-Y
HATE-D
HATE-R
HATE-S
C-**HATS**
G-HATS
K-HATS
W-HATS
HAUD-S
S-**HAUL**
HAUL-D
HAUL-M
HAUL-S
HAUL-T
G-**HAUT**
HAUT-E
C-**HAVE**
S-HAVE
HAVE-N
HAVE-R
HAVE-S
HAWK-S
S-**HAWM**
HAWM-S
C-**HAWS**
S-HAWS
T-HAWS
HAWS-E
C-**HAYS**
S-HAYS
HAZE-D
HAZE-L
HAZE-R
HAZE-S
A-**HEAD**
HEAD-S
HEAD-Y
S-**HEAL**
W-HEAL
HEAL-D
HEAL-S
A-**HEAP**
C-HEAP
HEAP-S
HEAP-Y
S-**HEAR**
W-HEAR
HEAR-D
HEAR-E
HEAR-S
HEAR-T
C-**HEAT**
W-HEAT
HEAT-H
HEAT-S
T-**HEBE**
HEBE-N
HEBE-S
HECH-T
C-**HECK**
HECK-S
T-**HEED**
HEED-S
HEED-Y
S-**HEEL**
W-HEEL
HEEL-S
T-**HEFT**
W-HEFT
HEFT-E
HEFT-S
HEFT-Y
HEID-S
HEIL-S
T-**HEIR**

HEIR-S
HELE-D
HELE-S
S-**HELL**
HELL-O
HELL-S
W-**HELM**
HELM-S
HELO-S
HELO-T
W-**HELP**
HELP-S
T-**HEME**
HEME-S
HEMP-S
HEMP-Y
S-**HEND**
HEND-S
T-**HENS**
W-HENS
A-**HENT**
S-HENT
HENT-S
HERB-S
HERB-Y
S-**HERD**
HERD-S
C-**HERE**
S-HERE
T-HERE
W-HERE
HERE-S
HERL-S
T-**HERM**
HERM-A
HERM-S
HERN-S
HERO-E
HERO-N
HERO-S
HERS-E
HERY-E
HESP-S
C-**HEST**
G-HEST
HEST-S
T-**HETE**
HETE-S
C-**HETH**
K-HETH
HETH-S
K-**HETS**
S-HETS
W-HETS
S-**HEWN**
C-**HEWS**
S-HEWS
T-HEWS
W-HEWS
W-**HEYS**
C-**HICK**
T-HICK
HICK-S
C-**HIDE**
HIDE-D
HIDE-R
HIDE-S
S-**HIED**
R-**HIES**
S-HIES
A-**HIGH**
T-HIGH
HIGH-S
HIGH-T
HIKE-D

HIKE-R
HIKE-S
HILA-R
C-**HILD**
C-**HILI**
C-**HILL**
S-HILL
T-HILL
HILL-O
HILL-S
HILL-Y
HILT-S
A-**HIND**
HIND-S
A-**HING**
E-HING
O-HING
T-HING
HING-E
HING-S
C-**HINS**
S-HINS
T-HINS
W-HINS
A-**HINT**
HINT-S
C-**HIPS**
S-HIPS
W-HIPS
W-**HIPT**
S-**HIRE**
HIRE-D
HIRE-R
HIRE-S
W-**HISH**
W-**HISS**
HISS-Y
S-**HIST**
W-HIST
HIST-S
C-**HITS**
S-HITS
W-HITS
C-**HIVE**
S-HIVE
HIVE-D
HIVE-R
HIVE-S
C-**HIZZ**
W-HIZZ
HOAR-D
HOAR-S
HOAR-Y
HOAS-T
HOBO-S
C-**HOCK**
S-HOCK
HOCK-S
S-**HOED**
S-**HOER**
HOER-S
S-**HOES**
HOGG-S
HOGH-S
S-**HOGS**
P-**HOHS**
HOIK-S
C-**HOKE**
HOKE-D
HOKE-S
HOKE-Y
HOKI-S
A-**HOLD**
HOLD-S
D-**HOLE**

T-HOLE
W-HOLE
HOLE-D
HOLE-S
HOLE-Y
HOLK-S
HOLM-S
D-**HOLS**
HOLT-S
HOME-D
HOME-R
HOME-S
HOME-Y
Z-**HOMO**
HOMO-S
HOND-A
HOND-S
O-**HONE**
P-HONE
R-HONE
S-HONE
HONE-D
HONE-R
HONE-S
HONE-Y
T-**HONG**
HONG-I
HONG-S
HONK-S
HONK-Y
C-**HONS**
P-HONS
HOOD-S
HOOD-Y
C-**HOOF**
W-HOOF
HOOF-S
C-**HOOK**
S-HOOK
HOOK-A
HOOK-S
HOOK-Y
S-**HOON**
HOON-S
W-**HOOP**
HOOP-S
B-**HOOT**
S-HOOT
W-HOOT
HOOT-S
HOOT-Y
S-**HOPE**
HOPE-D
HOPE-R
HOPE-S
C-**HOPS**
S-HOPS
W-HOPS
HORA-H
HORA-L
HORA-S
C-**HORE**
S-HORE
W-HORE
S-**HORN**
T-HORN
HORN-S
HORN-Y
K-**HORS**
HORS-E
HORS-T
HORS-Y
C-**HOSE**
T-HOSE
W-HOSE

HOSE-D
HOSE-L
HOSE-N
HOSE-S
G-**HOST**
HOST-A
HOST-S
S-**HOTE**
HOTE-L
HOTE-N
P-**HOTS**
S-HOTS
HOUF-F
HOUF-S
HOUR-I
HOUR-S
C-**HOUT**
S-HOUT
HOUT-S
S-**HOVE**
HOVE-D
HOVE-L
HOVE-N
HOVE-R
HOVE-S
HOWE-S
HOWF-F
HOWF-S
HOWK-S
T-**HOWL**
HOWL-S
C-**HOWS**
D-HOWS
S-HOWS
HOWS-O
HOYA-S
C-**HUBS**
C-**HUCK**
S-HUCK
HUCK-S
HUER-S
C-**HUFF**
HUFF-S
HUFF-Y
HUGE-R
C-**HUGS**
T-HUGS
HUIA-S
HULA-S
S-**HULE**
HULE-S
HULK-S
HULK-Y
A-**HULL**
HULL-O
HULL-S
HULL-Y
HUMA-N
HUMA-S
HUMF-S
C-**HUMP**
T-HUMP
W-HUMP
HUMP-H
HUMP-S
HUMP-Y
C-**HUMS**
C-**HUNK**
T-HUNK
HUNK-S
HUNK-Y
S-**HUNS**
S-**HUNT**
HUNT-S
C-**HURL**
T-HURL
HURL-S
HURL-Y
HURT-S
S-**HUSH**
HUSH-Y
HUSK-S
HUSK-Y
HUSO-S
HUSS-Y
B-**HUTS**
P-HUTS
S-HUTS
HWYL-S
HYEN-A
HYEN-S
HYKE-S
P-**HYLA**
HYLA-S
C-**HYLE**
P-HYLE
HYLE-G
HYLE-S
HYMN-S
HYPE-D
HYPE-R
HYPE-S
HYPO-S
IAMB-I
IAMB-S
V-**IBEX**
D-**ICED**
R-ICED
T-ICED
V-ICED
D-**ICER**
N-ICER
R-ICER
ICER-S
B-**ICES**
D-ICES
F-ICES
R-ICES
S-ICES
T-ICES
V-ICES
D-**ICKY**
K-ICKY
M-ICKY
P-ICKY
T-ICKY
W-ICKY
ICON-S
IDEA-L
IDEA-S
IDEE-S
A-**IDES**
B-IDES
C-IDES
H-IDES
N-IDES
R-IDES
S-IDES
T-IDES
W-IDES
S-**IDLE**
IDLE-D
IDLE-R
IDLE-S
IDOL-A
IDOL-S
IDYL-L
IDYL-S
B-**IFFY**
J-IFFY
M-IFFY
N-IFFY
IGLU-S
IKAT-S
E-**IKON**
IKON-S
P-**ILEA**
ILEA-C
ILEA-L
S-**ILEX**
C-**ILIA**
M-ILIA
ILIA-C
ILIA-D
ILIA-L
B-**ILKS**
M-ILKS
S-ILKS
B-**ILLS**
C-ILLS
D-ILLS
F-ILLS
G-ILLS
H-ILLS
J-ILLS
K-ILLS
L-ILLS
M-ILLS
N-ILLS
P-ILLS
R-ILLS
S-ILLS
T-ILLS
V-ILLS
W-ILLS
Y-ILLS
Z-ILLS
B-**ILLY**
D-ILLY
F-ILLY
G-ILLY
H-ILLY
S-ILLY
T-ILLY
W-ILLY
IMAM-S
T-**IMID**
IMID-E
IMID-O
IMID-S
J-**IMMY**
IMPI-S
G-**IMPS**
L-IMPS
P-IMPS
S-IMPS
T-IMPS
W-IMPS
INBY-E
C-**INCH**
F-INCH
L-INCH
P-INCH
W-INCH
INFO-S
B-**INGO**
D-INGO
J-INGO
L-INGO
P-INGO
INGO-T
B-**INKS**
D-INKS
F-INKS
G-INKS
J-INKS
K-INKS
L-INKS
M-INKS
O-INKS
P-INKS
R-INKS
S-INKS
T-INKS
W-INKS
D-**INKY**
K-INKY
L-INKY
P-INKY
S-INKY
Z-INKY
J-**INNS**
L-INNS
W-INNS
INTI-L
INTI-S
P-**INTO**
C-**IONS**
L-IONS
P-IONS
B-**IOTA**
D-IOTA
IOTA-S
A-**IRED**
F-IRED
H-IRED
M-IRED
S-IRED
T-IRED
V-IRED
W-IRED
C-**IRES**
F-IRES
H-IRES
M-IRES
S-IRES
T-IRES
V-IRES
W-IRES
V-**IRID**
IRID-S
S-**IRIS**
B-**IRKS**
D-IRKS
F-IRKS
K-IRKS
L-IRKS
M-IRKS
Y-IRKS
G-**IRON**
IRON-E
IRON-S
IRON-Y
ISBA-S
A-**ISLE**
L-ISLE
ISLE-D
ISLE-S
ISLE-T
G-**ISMS**
J-ISMS
M-**ISOS**
P-ISOS
D-**ITAS**
L-ITAS
P-ITAS
V-ITAS
A-**ITCH**
B-ITCH
D-ITCH
F-ITCH
H-ITCH
M-ITCH
P-ITCH
T-ITCH
W-ITCH
ITCH-Y
ITEM-S
K-**IWIS**
IXIA-S
S-**IZAR**
IZAR-D
IZAR-S
JACK-S
JACK-Y
JADE-D
JADE-S
JAGG-S
JAGG-Y
JAIL-S
JAKE-S
JAMB-E
JAMB-O
JAMB-S
JAMB-U
JANE-S
JANN-S
JAPE-D
JAPE-R
JAPE-S
JARK-S
JARL-S
JASP-E
JASP-S
JATO-S
JAUK-S
JAUP-S
JAVA-S
JAZZ-Y
JEAN-S
JEAT-S
JEEL-S
JEEL-Y
JEEP-S
JEER-S
JEFE-S
JEFF-S
JEHU-S
JELL-O
JELL-S
JELL-Y
JERK-S
JERK-Y
JESS-E
JEST-S
JETE-S
JIAO-S
JIBB-S
JIBE-D
JIBE-R
JIBE-S
JIFF-S
JIFF-Y
JILL-S
JILT-S
JIMP-Y
JINK-S
D-**JINN**
JINN-I
JINN-S
D-**JINS**
JIRD-S
JISM-S
JIVE-D
JIVE-R
JIVE-S
JIVE-Y
JOBE-D
JOBE-S
JOCK-O
JOCK-S
JOEY-S
JOHN-S
JOIN-S
JOIN-T
JOKE-D
JOKE-R
JOKE-S
JOKE-Y
JOLE-D
JOLE-S
JOLL-S
JOLL-Y
JOLT-S
JOLT-Y
JOMO-S
JOOK-S
JOTA-S
JOUK-S
JOUR-S
JOWL-S
JOWL-Y
JUBA-S
JUBE-S
JUDO-S
A-**JUGA**
JUGA-L
JUJU-S
JUKE-D
JUKE-S
JUMP-S
JUMP-Y
JUNK-S
JUNK-Y
JUPE-S
JURA-L
JURA-T
JURE-L
JUST-S
JUTE-S
JUVE-S
KADE-S
KADI-S
KAGO-S
KAGU-S
KAID-S
KAIE-S
KAIF-S
S-**KAIL**
KAIL-S
KAIM-S
KAIN-G
KAIN-S
KAKA-S
KAKI-S
KALE-S
KALI-F
KALI-S
KAMA-S
KAME-S
KAMI-K
KAMI-S
KANA-S
KANE-H
KANE-S
KANG-A
KANG-S
KANT-S
KAON-S
KAPA-S
KAPH-S
KARA-S
KARA-T
KARK-S
KARN-S
S-**KART**
KART-S
KATA-S
KATI-S
I-**KATS**
S-KATS
KAVA-S
S-**KAWS**
KAYO-S
O-**KAYS**
KAZI-S
KBAR-S
KECK-S
KEEF-S
KEEK-S
KEEL-S
S-**KEEN**
KEEN-S
KEEP-S
S-**KEET**
KEET-S
S-**KEGS**
KEIR-S
S-**KELL**
KELL-S
KELL-Y
S-**KELP**
KELP-S
KELP-Y
KELT-S
KELT-Y
KEMB-O
KEMB-S
KEMP-S
KEMP-T
KENO-S
KENT-S
KEPI-S
S-**KEPS**
KERB-S
KERF-S
KERN-E
KERN-S
KEST-S
KETA-S
KETO-L
KHAF-S
KHAN-S
KHAT-S
KHET-H
KHET-S
KHOR-S
KHUD-S
KIBE-I
KIBE-S
KICK-S
KICK-Y
S-**KIDS**
KIEF-S
S-**KIER**
KIER-S
KIKE-S
S-**KILL**
KILL-S
KILN-S
KILO-S
KILP-S
KILT-S
KILT-Y
KINA-S
KIND-A
KIND-S
KIND-Y
KINE-S
A-**KING**
E-KING
KING-S
S-**KINK**
KINK-S
KINK-Y
KINO-S
S-**KINS**
KIPE-S
KIPP-A
KIPP-S
S-**KIPS**
KIRK-S
KIRN-S
KISS-Y
KIST-S
S-**KITE**
KITE-D
KITE-R
KITE-S
KITH-E
KITH-S
S-**KITS**
KIVA-S
KIWI-S
KNAG-S
KNAP-S
KNAR-L
KNAR-S
KNEE-D
KNEE-L
KNEE-S
KNIT-S
KNOB-S
KNOP-S
KNOT-S
KNOW-E
KNOW-N
KNOW-S
KNUB-S
KNUR-L
KNUR-R
KNUR-S
KNUT-S
KOAN-S
KOEL-S
S-**KOFF**
KOFF-S
KOHL-S
KOLA-S
KOLO-S
KONK-S
I-**KONS**
KOOK-S
KOOK-Y
KOPH-S
KORA-I
KORA-S
KORA-T
KORE-S
KOTO-S
KOTO-W
KRAB-S
KSAR-S
KUDO-S
KUDU-S
KUKU-S
KURI-S
KURU-S
KUZU-S
KVAS-S

KYAK-S
KYAR-S
KYAT-S
KYLE-S
KYND-E
KYND-S
S-**KYTE**
KYTE-S
B-**LABS**
F-LABS
S-LABS
G-**LACE**
P-LACE
LACE-D
LACE-R
LACE-S
LACE-T
LACE-Y
A-**LACK**
B-LACK
C-LACK
F-LACK
P-LACK
S-LACK
LACK-S
B-**LADE**
C-LADE
G-LADE
S-LADE
LADE-D
LADE-N
LADE-R
LADE-S
B-**LADS**
C-LADS
G-LADS
G-**LADY**
B-**LAER**
LAER-S
B-**LAGS**
C-LAGS
F-LAGS
S-LAGS
B-**LAHS**
LAIC-H
LAIC-S
P-**LAID**
S-LAID
LAID-S
G-**LAIK**
LAIK-A
LAIK-S
B-**LAIN**
E-LAIN
P-LAIN
S-LAIN
F-**LAIR**
G-LAIR
LAIR-D
LAIR-S
LAIR-Y
F-**LAKE**
S-LAKE
LAKE-D
LAKE-R
LAKE-S
LAKH-S
F-**LAKY**
LALL-S
L-**LAMA**
U-LAMA
LAMA-S
LAMB-S
LAMB-Y
B-**LAME**
C-LAME
F-LAME
LAME-D
LAME-R
LAME-S
C-**LAMP**
LAMP-S
B-**LAMS**
C-LAMS
F-LAMS
G-LAMS
S-LAMS
LANA-I
LANA-S
A-**LAND**
B-LAND
E-LAND
G-LAND
LAND-E
LAND-S
A-**LANE**
P-LANE
S-LANE
LANE-S
A-**LANG**
C-LANG
K-LANG
S-LANG
B-**LANK**
C-LANK
F-LANK
P-LANK
S-LANK
LANK-S
LANK-Y
A-**LANT**
P-LANT
S-LANT
LANT-S
A-**LAPS**
C-LAPS
F-LAPS
P-LAPS
S-LAPS
LAPS-E
LARD-S
LARD-Y
B-**LARE**
F-LARE
G-LARE
LARE-E
LARE-S
LARI-S
LARK-S
LARK-Y
LARN-S
B-**LASE**
LASE-D
LASE-R
LASE-S
B-**LASH**
C-LASH
F-LASH
P-LASH
S-LASH
C-**LASS**
G-LASS
LASS-I
LASS-O
LASS-U
B-**LAST**
C-LAST
P-LAST
LAST-S
A-**LATE**
B-LATE
E-LATE
P-LATE
S-LATE
LATE-D
LATE-N
LATE-R
LATE-X
LATH-E
LATH-I
LATH-S
LATH-Y
B-**LATS**
C-LATS
F-LATS
P-LATS
S-LATS
B-**LAUD**
LAUD-S
LAUF-S
LAVA-S
C-**LAVE**
S-LAVE
LAVE-D
LAVE-R
LAVE-S
LAWK-S
B-**LAWN**
F-LAWN
LAWN-S
LAWN-Y
B-**LAWS**
C-LAWS
F-LAWS
S-LAWS
A-**LAYS**
B-LAYS
C-LAYS
F-LAYS
P-LAYS
S-LAYS
B-**LAZE**
G-LAZE
LAZE-D
LAZE-S
LAZO-S
G-**LAZY**
P-**LEAD**
LEAD-S
LEAD-Y
LEAF-S
LEAF-Y
B-**LEAK**
LEAK-S
LEAK-Y
I-**LEAL**
F-**LEAM**
G-LEAM
LEAM-S
C-**LEAN**
G-LEAN
LEAN-S
LEAN-T
LEAN-Y
LEAP-S
LEAP-T
B-**LEAR**
C-LEAR
LEAR-E
LEAR-N
LEAR-S
LEAR-Y
F-**LEAS**
P-LEAS
LEAS-E
LEAS-H
LEAS-T
B-**LEAT**
C-LEAT
P-LEAT
LEAT-S
B-**LEED**
G-LEED
C-**LEEK**
G-LEEK
S-LEEK
LEEK-S
B-**LEEP**
C-LEEP
S-LEEP
LEEP-S
F-**LEER**
S-LEER
LEER-S
LEER-Y
B-**LEES**
F-LEES
G-LEES
LEES-E
F-**LEET**
G-LEET
S-LEET
LEET-S
A-**LEFT**
C-LEFT
LEFT-E
LEFT-S
LEFT-Y
C-**LEGS**
F-LEGS
LEHR-S
LEIR-S
G-**LEIS**
V-LEIS
LEIS-H
F-**LEME**
LEME-D
LEME-L
LEME-S
B-**LEND**
LEND-S
LENG-S
LENO-S
G-**LENS**
LENS-E
B-**LENT**
G-LENT
O-LENT
LENT-I
LENT-O
C-**LEPT**
S-LEPT
LEPT-A
LERE-D
LERE-S
LERP-S
B-**LESS**
B-**LEST**
LEST-S
B-**LETS**
LEUD-S
C-**LEVE**
LEVE-E
LEVE-L
LEVE-R
B-**LEYS**
F-LEYS
G-LEYS
S-LEYS
LEZZ-Y
LIAR-D
LIAR-S
LIAR-T
G-**LIBS**
S-**LICE**
LICH-I
LICH-T
C-**LICK**
F-LICK
S-LICK
LICK-S
LIDO-S
C-**LIED**
F-LIED
P-LIED
LIEF-S
A-**LIEN**
LIEN-S
F-**LIER**
P-LIER
S-LIER
LIER-S
C-**LIES**
F-LIES
P-LIES
V-LIES
LIEU-S
LIFE-R
C-**LIFT**
G-LIFT
LIFT-S
A-**LIKE**
G-LIKE
Y-LIKE
LIKE-D
LIKE-N
LIKE-R
LIKE-S
LILL-S
LILO-S
LILT-S
S-**LILY**
LIMA-N
LIMA-S
LIMA-X
C-**LIMB**
LIMB-A
LIMB-I
LIMB-O
LIMB-S
LIMB-Y
C-**LIME**
G-LIME
S-LIME
LIME-D
LIME-N
LIME-S
LIME-Y
LIMN-S
LIMO-S
B-**LIMP**
F-LIMP
LIMP-A
LIMP-S
B-**LIMY**
S-LIMY
B-**LIND**
LIND-S
LIND-Y
A-**LINE**
C-LINE
LINE-D
LINE-N
LINE-R
LINE-S
LINE-Y
C-**LING**
F-LING
P-LING
S-LING
LING-A
LING-O
LING-S
LING-Y
B-**LINK**
C-LINK
P-LINK
S-LINK
LINK-S
LINK-Y
LINN-S
LINN-Y
LINO-S
B-**LINS**
C-**LINT**
E-LINT
F-LINT
G-LINT
LINT-S
LINT-Y
LION-S
B-**LIPS**
C-LIPS
F-LIPS
S-LIPS
LIRA-S
LIRK-S
F-**LISK**
G-LISK
LISK-S
LISP-S
A-**LIST**
B-LIST
LIST-S
B-**LITE**
E-LITE
F-LITE
LITE-D
LITE-R
LITE-S
LITH-E
LITH-O
LITH-S
F-**LITS**
G-LITS
S-LITS
A-**LIVE**
B-LIVE
O-LIVE
S-LIVE
LIVE-D
LIVE-N
LIVE-R
LIVE-S
LOAD-S
LOAF-S
C-**LOAM**
G-LOAM
LOAM-S
LOAM-Y
S-**LOAN**
LOAN-S
G-**LOBE**
LOBE-D
LOBE-S
LOBO-S
B-**LOBS**
G-LOBS
S-LOBS
LOCA-L
LOCH-S
B-**LOCK**
C-LOCK
F-LOCK
LOCK-S
LOCO-S
G-**LODE**
LODE-N
LODE-S
A-**LODS**
C-LODS
P-LODS
A-**LOFT**
LOFT-S
LOFT-Y
E-**LOGE**
LOGE-S
LOGO-I
LOGO-N
LOGO-S
C-**LOGS**
F-LOGS
S-LOGS
E-**LOGY**
O-LOGY
S-**LOID**
LOID-S
A-**LOIN**
E-LOIN
LOIN-S
LOIR-S
B-**LOKE**
C-LOKE
LOKE-S
LOLL-S
LOLL-Y
LOMA-S
LOME-D
LOME-S
A-**LONE**
C-LONE
LONE-R
A-**LONG**
F-LONG
K-LONG
P-LONG
LONG-A
LONG-E
LONG-S
A-**LOOF**
K-LOOF
LOOF-A
LOOF-S
P-**LOOK**
LOOK-S
B-**LOOM**
G-LOOM
S-LOOM
LOOM-S
LOON-S
LOON-Y
B-**LOOP**
C-LOOP
G-LOOP
S-LOOP
LOOP-S
LOOP-Y
F-**LOOR**
LOOR-D
LOOS-E
C-**LOOT**
S-LOOT
LOOT-S
E-**LOPE**
S-LOPE
LOPE-D
LOPE-R
LOPE-S
C-**LOPS**
E-LOPS
F-LOPS
G-LOPS
P-LOPS
S-LOPS
LORD-S
LORD-Y
B-**LORE**
LORE-L
LORE-S
F-**LORY**
G-LORY
C-**LOSE**
LOSE-D
LOSE-L
LOSE-N
LOSE-R
LOSE-S
F-**LOSH**
S-LOSH
F-**LOSS**
G-LOSS
LOSS-Y
G-**LOST**
F-**LOTA**
LOTA-H
LOTA-S
C-**LOTE**
F-LOTE
Z-LOTE
LOTE-S
C-**LOTH**
S-LOTH
LOTI-C
LOTO-S
B-**LOTS**
C-LOTS
P-LOTS
S-LOTS
A-**LOUD**
C-LOUD
LOUN-D
LOUN-S
LOUP-E
LOUP-S
C-**LOUR**
F-LOUR
LOUR-E
LOUR-S
LOUR-Y
C-**LOUT**
F-LOUT
G-LOUT
LOUT-S
C-**LOVE**
G-LOVE
S-LOVE
LOVE-D
LOVE-R
LOVE-S
LOVE-Y
A-**LOWE**
LOWE-D
LOWE-R
LOWE-S
B-**LOWN**
C-LOWN
F-LOWN
LOWN-D
LOWN-E
LOWN-S

B-**LOWS**
C-LOWS
F-LOWS
G-LOWS
P-LOWS
S-LOWS
LOWS-E
LOWT-S
C-**LOYS**
P-LOYS
LUAU-S
LUBE-S
LUCE-S
C-**LUCK**
P-LUCK
LUCK-S
LUCK-Y
B-**LUDE**
E-LUDE
LUDE-S
LUDO-S
B-**LUES**
C-LUES
F-LUES
G-LUES
S-LUES
B-**LUFF**
F-LUFF
P-LUFF
S-LUFF
LUFF-A
LUFF-S
K-**LUGE**
LUGE-D
LUGE-R
LUGE-S
G-**LUGS**
P-LUGS
S-LUGS
S-**LUIT**
F-**LUKE**
LULL-S
LULU-S
C-**LUMP**
F-LUMP
P-LUMP
S-LUMP
LUMP-S
LUMP-Y
A-**LUMS**
P-LUMS
S-LUMS
LUNA-R
LUNA-S
LUNE-S
LUNE-T
C-**LUNG**
F-LUNG
S-LUNG
LUNG-E
LUNG-I
LUNG-S
B-**LUNK**
C-LUNK
F-LUNK
P-LUNK
S-LUNK
LUNK-S
B-**LUNT**
LUNT-S
A-**LURE**
LURE-D
LURE-R
LURE-S
LURK-S

B-**LURS**
S-LURS
B-**LUSH**
F-LUSH
P-LUSH
S-LUSH
LUSH-Y
LUSK-S
LUST-S
LUST-Y
E-**LUTE**
F-LUTE
LUTE-A
LUTE-D
LUTE-R
LUTE-S
K-**LUTZ**
LUXE-S
LWEI-S
LYAM-S
LYME-S
LYNE-S
LYRE-S
LYSE-D
LYSE-S
F-**LYTE**
LYTE-D
LYTE-S
MAAR-S
MABE-S
MACE-D
MACE-R
MACE-S
MACH-E
MACH-O
MACH-S
S-**MACK**
MACK-S
I-**MAGE**
MAGE-S
MAGG-S
MAGI-C
MAID-S
S-**MAIK**
MAIK-O
MAIK-S
E-**MAIL**
MAIL-E
MAIL-L
MAIL-S
MAIM-S
A-**MAIN**
MAIN-S
MAIR-E
MAIR-S
MAKE-R
MAKE-S
MAKO-S
MALE-S
MALI-C
MALI-K
MALI-S
S-**MALL**
MALL-S
S-**MALM**
MALM-S
MALM-Y
S-**MALT**
MALT-S
MALT-Y
MAMA-S
I-**MAMS**
MANA-S
MANE-D
MANE-H

MANE-S
MANE-T
MANG-A
MANG-E
MANG-O
MANG-S
MANG-Y
MANI-A
MANI-C
MANI-S
MANO-R
MANO-S
MANS-E
MARA-E
MARA-H
MARA-S
MARC-H
MARC-S
MARD-Y
MARE-S
MARG-E
MARG-S
MARK-S
MARL-E
MARL-S
MARL-Y
S-**MARM**
MARM-S
MARS-E
MARS-H
S-**MART**
MART-S
O-**MASA**
MASA-S
MASE-D
MASE-R
MASE-S
S-**MASH**
MASH-Y
MASK-S
A-**MASS**
MASS-A
MASS-E
MASS-Y
MAST-S
MAST-Y
MASU-S
A-**MATE**
MATE-D
MATE-R
MATE-S
MATE-Y
MATH-S
MATT-E
MATT-S
MAUD-S
MAUL-S
MAUN-D
MAUT-S
MAWK-S
MAWK-Y
MAWR-S
MAXI-M
MAXI-S
MAYA-N
MAYA-S
MAYO-R
MAYO-S
MAYS-T
A-**MAZE**
S-MAZE
MAZE-D
MAZE-R
MAZE-S
MEAD-S

MEAL-S
MEAL-Y
MEAN-E
MEAN-S
MEAN-T
MEAN-Y
MEAT-H
MEAT-S
MEAT-Y
MEED-S
S-**MEEK**
A-**MEER**
E-MEER
MEER-S
MEET-S
O-**MEGA**
MEIN-S
MEIN-T
MEIN-Y
MELA-S
MELD-S
S-**MELL**
MELL-S
S-**MELT**
MELT-S
MELT-Y
MEME-S
MEMO-S
A-**MEND**
E-MEND
MEND-S
A-**MENE**
MENE-D
MENE-S
MENG-E
MENG-S
A-**MENT**
MENT-A
MENT-O
MENU-S
MEOU-S
MEOW-S
MERC-S
MERC-Y
MERE-D
MERE-L
MERE-R
MERE-S
MERI-L
MERI-S
MERI-T
S-**MERK**
MERK-S
MERL-E
MERL-S
MESA-L
MESA-S
MESE-L
MESE-S
MESH-Y
MESS-Y
META-L
METE-D
METE-R
METE-S
METH-S
E-**MEUS**
MEUS-E
MEVE-D
MEVE-S
MEWL-S
S-**MEWS**
MEZE-S
MICA-S
A-**MICE**

MICK-S
MICK-Y
MICO-S
MIDI-S
A-**MIDS**
I-MIDS
MIDS-T
MIEN-S
MIFF-S
MIFF-Y
MIGG-S
MIKE-D
MIKE-S
MILD-S
S-**MILE**
MILE-R
MILE-S
MILK-O
MILK-S
MILK-Y
MILL-E
MILL-S
MILO-R
MILO-S
MILT-S
MILT-Y
MILT-Z
MIME-D
MIME-O
MIME-R
MIME-S
MINA-E
MINA-R
MINA-S
MIND-S
A-**MINE**
I-MINE
MINE-D
MINE-R
MINE-S
MING-E
MING-S
MING-Y
MINI-M
MINI-S
MINK-E
MINK-S
A-**MINO**
I-MINO
MINO-R
MINO-S
MINT-S
MINT-Y
MIRE-D
MIRE-S
MIRE-X
MIRI-N
S-**MIRK**
MIRK-S
MIRK-Y
A-**MIRS**
E-MIRS
S-MIRS
MIRV-S
MISE-R
MISE-S
MISO-S
A-**MISS**
MISS-A
MISS-Y
MIST-S
MIST-Y
S-**MITE**
MITE-R
MITE-S

MITT-S
A-**MITY**
MOAN-S
MOAT-S
MOCH-A
MOCH-S
MOCH-Y
S-**MOCK**
MOCK-S
MODE-L
MODE-M
MODE-R
MODE-S
MODI-I
S-**MOGS**
MOHR-S
MOIL-S
MOIT-S
MOJO-S
S-**MOKE**
MOKE-S
MOKI-S
S-**MOKO**
MOKO-S
MOLA-L
MOLA-R
MOLA-S
MOLD-S
MOLD-Y
A-**MOLE**
MOLE-S
MOLL-A
MOLL-S
MOLL-Y
S-**MOLT**
Y-MOLT
MOLT-O
MOLT-S
MOME-S
MONA-D
MONA-L
MONA-S
A-**MONG**
E-MONG
MONG-O
MONG-S
MONK-S
MONO-S
MOOD-S
MOOD-Y
MOOK-S
MOOL-A
MOOL-I
MOOL-S
MOOL-Y
MOON-S
MOON-Y
MOOP-S
S-**MOOR**
MOOR-S
MOOR-Y
MOOS-E
S-**MOOT**
MOOT-S
MOPE-D
MOPE-R
MOPE-S
MOPE-Y
MOPS-Y
MORA-E
MORA-L
MORA-S
MORA-T
MORA-Y
S-**MORE**

MORE-L
MORE-S
MORN-E
MORN-S
MORS-E
A-**MORT**
MORT-S
MOSE-D
MOSE-S
MOSE-Y
MOSK-S
MOSS-O
MOSS-Y
MOST-E
MOST-S
E-**MOTE**
S-MOTE
MOTE-D
MOTE-L
MOTE-N
MOTE-S
MOTE-T
MOTE-Y
MOTH-S
MOTH-Y
MOTT-E
MOTT-O
MOTT-S
MOTT-Y
MOTU-S
MOUE-S
MOUP-S
MOUS-E
MOUS-T
MOUS-Y
A-**MOVE**
E-MOVE
MOVE-D
MOVE-R
MOVE-S
MOWA-S
MOXA-S
MOYA-S
MOYL-E
MOYL-S
MOZE-D
MOZE-S
MOZO-S
A-**MUCK**
MUCK-S
MUCK-Y
MUFF-S
MUGG-S
MUGG-Y
S-**MUGS**
MUID-S
MUIL-S
MUIR-S
E-**MULE**
MULE-D
MULE-S
MULE-Y
MULL-A
MULL-S
MUMM-S
MUMM-Y
MUMP-S
MUMS-Y
MUMU-S
MUNI-S
MUNT-S
MUNT-U
MUON-S
MURA-L
MURA-S

E-**MURE**
MURE-D
MURE-S
MURE-X
MURK-S
MURK-Y
MURL-S
MURL-Y
MURR-A
MURR-E
MURR-S
MURR-Y
A-**MUSE**
MUSE-D
MUSE-R
MUSE-S
MUSE-T
MUSH-A
MUSH-Y
MUSK-S
MUSK-Y
MUSO-S
MUSS-E
MUSS-Y
MUST-H
MUST-S
MUST-Y
MUTE-D
MUTE-R
MUTE-S
MUTI-S
S-**MUTS**
MUTT-S
MYAL-L
MYNA-H
MYNA-S
MYTH-I
MYTH-S
MYTH-Y
MZEE-S
NAAM-S
NAAN-S
NABE-S
NABK-S
S-**NABS**
NACH-E
NACH-O
NADA-S
NAFF-S
NAGA-S
K-**NAGS**
S-NAGS
NAIF-S
NAIK-S
S-**NAIL**
NAIL-S
NALA-S
NAME-D
NAME-R
NAME-S
A-**NANA**
J-NANA
NANA-S
NAPA-S
NAPE-S
K-**NAPS**
S-NAPS
NARC-O
NARC-S
NARD-S
S-**NARE**
NARE-S
S-**NARK**
NARK-S
NARK-Y

S-**NARY**
U-NARY
G-**NATS**
K-**NAVE**
NAVE-L
NAVE-S
NAVE-W
NAZE-S
NAZI-R
NAZI-S
NEAL-S
S-**NEAP**
NEAP-S
A-**NEAR**
NEAR-S
NEAT-H
NEAT-S
S-**NEBS**
S-**NECK**
NECK-S
S-**NEDS**
K-**NEED**
S-NEED
NEED-S
NEED-Y
NEEM-B
NEEM-S
NEEP-S
NEIF-S
E-**NEMA**
NEMA-S
NEMN-S
NENE-S
NEON-S
NERD-S
NERD-Y
NERK-A
NERK-S
NEST-S
NETE-S
NETT-S
NETT-Y
NEUK-S
NEUM-E
NEUM-S
NEVE-L
NEVE-R
NEVE-S
E-**NEWS**
NEWS-Y
NEWT-S
NEXT-S
S-**NIBS**
NICE-R
S-**NICK**
NICK-S
S-**NIDE**
NIDE-D
NIDE-S
NIEF-S
S-**NIES**
K-**NIFE**
NIFE-S
S-**NIFF**
NIFF-S
NIFF-Y
A-**NIGH**
NIGH-S
NIGH-T
NILL-S
A-**NILS**
NIMB-I
NIMB-S
NINE-S
NIPA-S

S-**NIPS**
NIRL-S
NIRL-Y
U-**NITE**
NITE-R
NITE-S
K-**NITS**
S-NITS
U-NITS
NIXE-D
NIXE-S
K-**NOBS**
S-NOBS
K-**NOCK**
NOCK-S
A-**NODE**
NODE-S
S-**NODS**
NOEL-S
NOGG-S
S-**NOGS**
NOIL-S
NOIL-Y
NOIR-S
A-**NOLE**
NOLE-S
K-**NOLL**
NOLL-S
NOLO-S
NOMA-D
NOMA-S
G-**NOME**
NOME-N
NOME-S
NONA-S
NONE-S
NONE-T
NONG-S
S-**NOOK**
NOOK-S
NOOK-Y
NOON-S
S-**NOOP**
NOOP-S
NORI-A
NORI-S
NORK-S
E-**NORM**
NORM-A
NORM-S
NOSE-D
NOSE-R
NOSE-S
NOSE-Y
NOTA-L
NOTE-D
NOTE-R
NOTE-S
NOUL-D
NOUL-E
NOUL-S
NOUN-S
NOUN-Y
NOUP-S
K-**NOUT**
S-NOUT
NOVA-E
NOVA-S
NOWL-S
K-**NOWN**
E-**NOWS**
K-NOWS
S-NOWS
NOWT-S
S-**NOWY**

K-**NUBS**
S-NUBS
NUDE-R
NUDE-S
S-**NUFF**
NUFF-S
NUKE-D
NUKE-S
NULL-A
NULL-S
NUMB-S
NURD-S
K-**NURL**
NURL-S
K-**NURR**
NURR-S
K-**NURS**
NURS-E
K-**NUTS**
NUTS-Y
S-**NYES**
G-**OAFS**
L-OAFS
B-**OAKS**
S-OAKS
B-**OARS**
H-OARS
R-OARS
S-OARS
V-OARS
G-**OARY**
H-OARY
R-OARY
B-**OAST**
C-OAST
H-OAST
L-OAST
R-OAST
T-OAST
OAST-S
L-**OATH**
OATH-S
B-**OATS**
C-OATS
D-OATS
G-OATS
M-OATS
B-**OBAS**
J-**OBES**
L-OBES
R-OBES
OBES-E
OBEY-S
C-**OBIA**
OBIA-S
O-**OBIT**
OBIT-S
OBOE-S
OBOL-E
OBOL-I
OBOL-S
G-**OBOS**
H-OBOS
L-OBOS
Z-OBOS
C-**OCAS**
S-OCAS
B-**OCHE**
OCHE-R
OCHE-S
OCTA-D
OCTA-L
OCTA-N
OCTA-S
M-**ODAL**

N-ODAL
P-ODAL
ODAL-S
C-**ODAS**
S-ODAS
B-**ODES**
C-ODES
L-ODES
M-ODES
N-ODES
R-ODES
I-**ODIC**
S-ODIC
ODOR-S
G-**ODSO**
ODSO-S
ODYL-E
ODYL-S
OFAY-S
B-**OFFS**
C-OFFS
D-OFFS
G-OFFS
K-OFFS
T-OFFS
OGAM-S
Y-**OGEE**
OGEE-S
B-**OGLE**
F-OGLE
OGLE-D
OGLE-R
OGLE-S
OGRE-S
H-**OHED**
O-OHED
OHIA-S
C-**OHOS**
T-OHOS
H-**OIKS**
B-**OILS**
C-OILS
F-OILS
M-OILS
N-OILS
R-OILS
S-OILS
T-OILS
D-**OILY**
N-OILY
R-OILY
S-OILY
B-**OINK**
OINK-S
J-**OINT**
N-OINT
P-OINT
OINT-S
T-**OKAY**
OKAY-S
OKEH-S
B-**OKES**
C-OKES
H-OKES
J-OKES
L-OKES
M-OKES
P-OKES
R-OKES
S-OKES
T-OKES
Y-OKES
K-**OKRA**
OKRA-S
OKTA-S

B-**OLDS**
C-OLDS
F-OLDS
G-OLDS
H-OLDS
M-OLDS
S-OLDS
W-OLDS
G-**OLDY**
M-OLDY
OLEO-S
B-**OLES**
C-OLES
D-OLES
G-OLES
H-OLES
J-OLES
M-OLES
N-OLES
P-OLES
R-OLES
S-OLES
T-OLES
V-OLES
S-**OLID**
F-**OLIO**
P-OLIO
OLIO-S
H-**OLLA**
M-OLLA
OLLA-S
OLLA-V
H-**OLMS**
G-**OLPE**
OLPE-S
K-**OMBU**
OMBU-S
N-**OMEN**
W-OMEN
OMEN-S
C-**OMER**
H-OMER
V-OMER
OMER-S
V-**OMIT**
OMIT-S
B-**ONCE**
N-ONCE
P-ONCE
S-ONCE
ONCE-R
ONCE-S
B-**ONER**
G-ONER
H-ONER
L-ONER
M-ONER
T-ONER
Z-ONER
ONER-S
ONER-Y
B-**ONES**
C-ONES
H-ONES
J-ONES
N-ONES
P-ONES
R-ONES
S-ONES
T-ONES
Z-ONES
F-**ONLY**
S-ONLY
C-**ONTO**
B-**ONUS**

C-ONUS
T-ONUS
C-**OOFS**
G-OOFS
H-OOFS
L-OOFS
P-OOFS
R-OOFS
W-OOFS
Y-OOFS
B-**OOHS**
P-OOHS
B-**OOMS**
C-OOMS
D-OOMS
L-OOMS
R-OOMS
S-OOMS
T-OOMS
Z-OOMS
B-**OONS**
C-OONS
G-OONS
H-OONS
L-OONS
M-OONS
N-OONS
P-OONS
R-OONS
T-OONS
W-OONS
Z-OONS
OONT-S
C-**OOPS**
G-OOPS
H-OOPS
L-OOPS
M-OOPS
N-OOPS
P-OOPS
R-OOPS
S-OOPS
W-OOPS
Y-OOPS
B-**OOSE**
G-OOSE
L-OOSE
M-OOSE
N-OOSE
R-OOSE
OOSE-S
G-**OOSY**
B-**OOTS**
C-OOTS
F-OOTS
H-OOTS
L-OOTS
M-OOTS
P-OOTS
R-OOTS
S-OOTS
T-OOTS
B-**OOZE**
OOZE-D
OOZE-S
B-**OOZY**
D-OOZY
W-OOZY
OPAH-S
C-**OPAL**
N-OPAL
OPAL-S
C-**OPED**
D-OPED
H-OPED

L-OPED
M-OPED
O-OPED
R-OPED
T-OPED
C-**OPEN**
OPEN-S
C-**OPES**
D-OPES
H-OPES
L-OPES
M-OPES
P-OPES
R-OPES
T-OPES
Z-**OPPO**
OPPO-S
M-**OPUS**
D-**ORAD**
B-**ORAL**
C-ORAL
G-ORAL
H-ORAL
L-ORAL
M-ORAL
P-ORAL
R-ORAL
S-ORAL
ORAL-S
F-**ORBS**
S-ORBS
C-**ORBY**
F-ORBY
ORCA-S
T-**ORCS**
F-**ORDO**
S-ORDO
ORDO-S
B-**ORDS**
C-ORDS
F-ORDS
L-ORDS
S-ORDS
W-ORDS
B-**ORES**
C-ORES
F-ORES
G-ORES
K-ORES
L-ORES
M-ORES
P-ORES
R-ORES
S-ORES
T-ORES
Y-ORES
ORFE-S
P-**ORGY**
ORLE-S
M-**ORRA**
S-ORRA
B-**ORTS**
D-ORTS
F-ORTS
M-ORTS
P-ORTS
R-ORTS
S-ORTS
T-ORTS
W-ORTS
ORZO-S
C-**OSES**
D-OSES
H-OSES
K-OSES

L-OSES
M-OSES
N-OSES
O-OSES
P-OSES
R-OSES
T-OSES
F-**OSSA**
L-**OTIC**
L-**OTTO**
M-OTTO
P-OTTO
OTTO-S
C-**OUCH**
M-OUCH
P-OUCH
T-OUCH
V-OUCH
OUCH-T
F-**OUDS**
B-**OUKS**
G-OUKS
J-OUKS
P-OUKS
S-OUKS
T-OUKS
Y-OUKS
Z-OUKS
C-**OULD**
M-OULD
N-OULD
W-OULD
OULK-S
OUPH-E
OUPH-S
C-**OUPS**
D-OUPS
L-OUPS
M-OUPS
N-OUPS
R-OUPS
S-OUPS
B-**OURN**
M-OURN
Y-OURN
C-**OURS**
F-OURS
H-OURS
J-OURS
L-OURS
P-OURS
S-OURS
T-OURS
Y-OURS
J-**OUST**
M-OUST
R-OUST
OUST-S
B-**OUTS**
D-OUTS
G-OUTS
H-OUTS
L-OUTS
P-OUTS
R-OUTS
S-OUTS
T-OUTS
OUZO-S
OVAL-S
C-**OVEN**
D-OVEN
H-OVEN
R-OVEN
W-OVEN
OVEN-S

C-**OVER**
D-OVER
H-OVER
L-OVER
M-OVER
R-OVER
OVER-S
OVER-T
N-**OVUM**
B-**OWED**
C-OWED
D-OWED
J-OWED
L-OWED
M-OWED
N-OWED
R-OWED
S-OWED
T-OWED
V-OWED
W-OWED
Y-OWED
B-**OWER**
C-OWER
D-OWER
L-OWER
M-OWER
P-OWER
R-OWER
S-OWER
T-OWER
V-OWER
B-**OWES**
H-OWES
L-OWES
Y-OWES
B-**OWLS**
C-OWLS
D-OWLS
F-OWLS
G-OWLS
H-OWLS
J-OWLS
N-OWLS
S-OWLS
Y-OWLS
J-**OWLY**
L-OWLY
D-**OWNS**
G-OWNS
L-OWNS
P-OWNS
T-OWNS
H-**OWRE**
P-OWRE
OWRE-S
B-**OWSE**
D-OWSE
L-OWSE
S-OWSE
T-OWSE
OWSE-N
D-**OWTS**
L-OWTS
N-OWTS
R-OWTS
T-OWTS
B-**OXEN**
W-OXEN
B-**OXER**
OXER-S
B-**OXES**
C-OXES
F-OXES
G-OXES
H-OXES
L-OXES
N-OXES
P-OXES
OXID-E
OXID-S
OXIM-E
OXIM-S
C-**OYER**
F-OYER
T-OYER
OYER-S
N-**OYES**
PACA-S
A-**PACE**
S-PACE
PACE-D
PACE-R
PACE-S
PACE-Y
PACK-S
PACO-S
E-**PACT**
PACT-A
PACT-S
S-**PACY**
PADI-S
A-**PAGE**
PAGE-D
PAGE-R
PAGE-S
O-**PAHS**
A-**PAID**
PAIK-S
S-**PAIL**
PAIL-S
S-**PAIN**
PAIN-S
PAIN-T
PAIR-E
PAIR-S
PAIS-A
PAIS-E
S-**PALE**
PALE-A
PALE-D
PALE-R
PALE-S
PALE-T
S-**PALL**
PALL-A
PALL-S
PALL-Y
PALM-S
PALM-Y
PALP-I
PALP-S
O-**PALS**
PALS-Y
S-**PAMS**
PAND-A
PAND-S
PAND-Y
S-**PANE**
PANE-D
PANE-L
PANE-S
S-**PANG**
PANG-A
PANG-S
S-**PANS**
PANS-Y
PANT-O
PANT-S
PANT-Y
PAPA-L
PAPA-S
PAPA-W
PAPE-R
PAPE-S
PARA-S
S-**PARD**
PARD-I
PARD-S
PARD-Y
S-**PARE**
PARE-D
PARE-O
PARE-R
PARE-S
PARE-U
S-**PARK**
PARK-A
PARK-I
PARK-S
PARK-Y
PARP-S
PARR-S
PARR-Y
S-**PARS**
PARS-E
A-**PART**
S-PART
PART-I
PART-S
PART-Y
PASE-O
PASE-S
PASH-A
PASH-M
PASS-E
PAST-A
PAST-E
PAST-S
PAST-Y
S-**PATE**
PATE-D
PATE-N
PATE-R
PATE-S
PATH-S
S-**PATS**
PATS-Y
PAUA-S
S-**PAUL**
PAUL-S
PAVE-D
PAVE-N
PAVE-R
PAVE-S
PAWA-S
PAWA-W
PAWK-S
PAWK-Y
S-**PAWL**
PAWL-S
S-**PAWN**
PAWN-S
S-**PAWS**
A-**PAYS**
S-PAYS
PAYS-D
PEAG-E
PEAG-S
A-**PEAK**
S-PEAK
PEAK-S
PEAK-Y
S-**PEAL**
PEAL-S
S-**PEAN**
PEAN-S
S-**PEAR**
PEAR-E
PEAR-L
PEAR-S
PEAR-T
PEAS-E
S-**PEAT**
PEAT-S
PEAT-Y
PEBA-S
PECH-S
S-**PECK**
PECK-E
PECK-S
PECK-Y
S-**PECS**
S-**PEED**
A-**PEEK**
PEEK-S
S-**PEEL**
PEEL-S
PEEN-S
PEEP-E
PEEP-S
S-**PEER**
PEER-S
PEER-Y
E-**PEES**
PEGH-S
PEIN-S
PEKE-S
PELA-S
PELE-S
PELF-S
S-**PELL**
PELL-S
S-**PELT**
PELT-A
PELT-S
S-**PEND**
U-PEND
PEND-S
PENE-D
PENE-S
PENI-E
PENI-S
PENK-S
O-**PENS**
S-**PENT**
PENT-S
PEON-S
PEON-Y
PEPO-S
PERE-A
PERE-S
PERI-L
PERI-S
PERK-S
PERK-Y
S-**PERM**
PERM-S
PERN-S
A-**PERT**
PERT-S
PERV-E
PERV-S
PESO-S
PEST-O
PEST-S
PEST-Y
S-**PETS**
S-**PEWS**
A-**PHIS**
PHOH-S
PHON-E
PHON-O
PHON-S
PHON-Y
PHOT-O
PHOT-S
PHUT-S
S-**PIAL**
A-**PIAN**
PIAN-O
PIAN-S
S-**PICA**
PICA-L
PICA-S
S-**PICE**
S-**PICK**
PICK-S
PICK-Y
E-**PICS**
S-PICS
S-**PIED**
S-**PIER**
PIER-S
PIER-T
S-**PIES**
PIET-A
PIET-S
PIET-Y
PIKA-S
S-**PIKE**
PIKE-D
PIKE-R
PIKE-S
PIKI-S
PILA-F
PILA-R
PILA-U
PILA-W
S-**PILE**
PILE-A
PILE-D
PILE-I
PILE-R
PILE-S
PILI-S
S-**PILL**
PILL-S
PIMA-S
PIMP-S
S-**PINA**
PINA-S
O-**PINE**
S-PINE
PINE-D
PINE-S
PINE-Y
A-**PING**
O-PING
PING-O
PING-S
S-**PINK**
PINK-O
PINK-S
PINK-Y
S-**PINS**
PINT-A
PINT-O
PINT-S
S-**PINY**
PION-S
PION-Y
PIOY-E
PIOY-S
PIPA-L
PIPA-S
PIPE-D
PIPE-R
PIPE-S
PIPE-T
PIPI-S
PIPI-T
PIRL-S
PIRN-S
PISE-S
A-**PISH**
PISO-S
PITA-S
PITH-S
PITH-Y
S-**PITS**
O-**PIUM**
PIUM-S
PIZE-S
PLAN-E
PLAN-K
PLAN-S
PLAN-T
PLAP-S
S-**PLAT**
PLAT-E
PLAT-S
PLAT-Y
S-**PLAY**
U-PLAY
PLAY-A
PLAY-S
PLEA-D
PLEA-S
PLEA-T
PLEB-E
PLEB-S
U-**PLED**
PLEW-S
PLIE-D
PLIE-R
PLIE-S
PLIM-S
PLOD-S
PLOP-S
PLOT-S
PLOT-Z
PLOW-S
PLOY-S
PLUG-S
PLUM-B
PLUM-E
PLUM-P
PLUM-S
PLUM-Y
PLUS-H
POCK-S
POCK-Y
A-**PODS**
POEM-S
POET-S
POGO-S
POIS-E
S-**POKE**
POKE-D
POKE-R
POKE-S
POKE-Y
POLE-D
POLE-R
POLE-S
POLE-Y
POLK-A
POLK-S
POLL-S
POLL-Y
POLO-S
POLT-S
POLY-P
POLY-S
POME-S
POMP-S
POND-S
PONE-S
PONE-Y
PONG-A
PONG-O
PONG-S
PONG-Y
PONK-S
PONT-S
PONT-Y
POOD-S
S-**POOF**
POOF-S
POOF-Y
POOH-S
S-**POOK**
POOK-A
POOK-S
S-**POOL**
POOL-S
S-**POON**
POON-S
A-**POOP**
POOP-S
S-**POOR**
POOR-I
POOR-T
S-**POOT**
POOT-S
POPE-S
POPS-Y
S-**PORE**
PORE-D
PORE-R
PORE-S
PORK-S
PORK-Y
PORN-O
PORN-S
PORN-Y
A-**PORT**
S-PORT
PORT-A
PORT-S
PORT-Y
POSE-D
POSE-R
POSE-S
POSE-Y
S-**POSH**
POSS-E
POST-S
POTE-D
POTE-S
S-**POTS**
POTS-Y
POTT-O
POTT-S
POTT-Y
POUF-F
POUF-S
POUK-E
POUK-S
POUR-S
S-**POUT**
POUT-S
POUT-Y
POWN-D
POWN-S
POWN-Y
E-**POXY**
POZZ-Y
S-**PRAD**
PRAD-S
PRAM-S
PRAO-S
S-**PRAT**
PRAT-E
PRAT-S
PRAT-T
PRAT-Y
PRAU-S
S-**PRAY**
PRAY-S
S-**PREE**
PREE-D
PREE-N
PREE-S
PREP-S
PREX-Y
PREY-S
S-**PRIG**
PRIG-S
PRIM-A
PRIM-E
PRIM-I
PRIM-O
PRIM-P
PRIM-S
PRIM-Y
PROA-S
PROB-E
PROB-S
S-**PROD**
PROD-S
PROF-S
S-**PROG**
PROG-S
E-**PROM**
PROM-O
PROM-S
PROO-F
PROP-S
PROS-E
PROS-O
PROS-S
PROS-T
PROS-Y
PROW-L
PROW-S
PRYS-E
A-**PSIS**
PUCE-R
PUCE-S
PUCK-A
PUCK-S
S-**PUDS**
PUDS-Y
PUDU-S
PUER-S
PUFF-S
PUFF-Y
PUJA-H
PUJA-S
PUKE-D
PUKE-R
PUKE-S
PUKU-S
PULA-S
S-**PULE**
PULE-D
PULE-R
PULE-S

PULI-K
PULI-S
PULK-A
PULK-S
PULL-S
PULP-S
PULP-Y
PULS-E
PULU-S
PUMA-S
PUMP-S
S-**PUMY**
PUNA-S
PUNG-A
PUNG-S
S-**PUNK**
PUNK-A
PUNK-S
PUNK-Y
PUNT-O
PUNT-S
PUNT-Y
PUPA-E
PUPA-L
PUPA-S
PURE-D
PURE-E
PURE-R
PURE-S
PURI-M
PURI-N
PURI-S
PURL-S
PURR-S
S-**PURS**
PURS-E
PURS-Y
PUSH-Y
PUSS-Y
PUTT-I
PUTT-O
PUTT-S
PUTT-Y
PYAT-S
PYET-S
PYIN-S
PYNE-D
PYNE-S
PYOT-S
S-**PYRE**
PYRE-S
PYRO-S
QADI-S
QAID-S
QOPH-S
S-**QUAD**
QUAD-S
QUAG-S
QUAI-L
QUAI-R
QUAI-S
S-**QUAT**
QUAT-E
QUAT-S
QUAY-D
QUAY-S
QUEY-N
QUEY-S
E-**QUID**
S-QUID
QUID-S
QUIM-S
QUIN-A
QUIN-E
QUIN-S

QUIN-T
E-**QUIP**
QUIP-O
QUIP-S
QUIP-U
S-**QUIT**
QUIT-E
QUIT-S
S-**QUIZ**
QUOD-S
QUOP-S
RABI-C
RABI-D
RABI-S
B-**RACE**
G-RACE
T-RACE
RACE-D
RACE-R
RACE-S
B-**RACH**
O-RACH
RACH-E
B-**RACK**
C-RACK
F-RACK
T-RACK
W-RACK
RACK-S
O-**RACY**
G-**RADE**
I-RADE
T-RADE
B-**RADS**
G-RADS
P-RADS
T-RADS
D-**RAFF**
G-RAFF
RAFF-S
C-**RAFT**
D-RAFT
G-RAFT
K-RAFT
RAFT-S
RAGA-S
RAGE-D
RAGE-E
RAGE-R
RAGE-S
RAGG-A
RAGG-S
RAGG-Y
T-**RAGI**
RAGI-S
B-**RAGS**
C-RAGS
D-RAGS
F-RAGS
RAIA-S
B-**RAID**
RAID-S
T-**RAIK**
RAIK-S
B-**RAIL**
D-RAIL
F-RAIL
G-RAIL
T-RAIL
RAIL-E
RAIL-S
B-**RAIN**
D-RAIN
G-RAIN
T-RAIN

RAIN-E
RAIN-S
RAIN-Y
RAIS-E
K-**RAIT**
T-RAIT
RAIT-A
RAIT-S
RAJA-H
RAJA-S
B-**RAKE**
C-RAKE
D-RAKE
RAKE-D
RAKE-E
RAKE-R
RAKE-S
RAKI-S
RAKU-S
RALE-S
RAMI-E
RAMI-N
RAMI-S
C-**RAMP**
G-RAMP
T-RAMP
RAMP-S
C-**RAMS**
D-RAMS
G-RAMS
P-RAMS
T-RAMS
G-**RANA**
P-RANA
RANA-S
B-**RAND**
G-RAND
RAND-S
RAND-Y
K-**RANG**
O-RANG
P-RANG
W-RANG
RANG-E
RANG-Y
RANI-D
RANI-S
B-**RANK**
C-RANK
D-RANK
F-RANK
P-RANK
T-RANK
RANK-E
RANK-S
B-**RANT**
D-RANT
G-RANT
O-RANT
T-RANT
RANT-S
C-**RAPE**
D-RAPE
G-RAPE
T-RAPE
RAPE-D
RAPE-R
RAPE-S
C-**RAPS**
D-RAPS
F-RAPS
T-RAPS
W-RAPS
T-**RAPT**
W-RAPT

Y-RAPT
C-**RARE**
U-RARE
RARE-D
RARE-R
RARE-S
E-**RASE**
P-RASE
U-RASE
RASE-D
RASE-R
RASE-S
B-**RASH**
C-RASH
T-RASH
G-**RASP**
RASP-S
RASP-Y
B-**RAST**
W-RAST
RAST-A
RATA-L
RATA-N
RATA-S
C-**RATE**
F-RATE
G-RATE
I-RATE
O-RATE
P-RATE
U-RATE
W-RATE
RATE-D
RATE-L
RATE-R
RATE-S
W-**RATH**
RATH-E
RATH-S
RATO-O
RATO-S
B-**RATS**
D-RATS
F-RATS
P-RATS
T-RATS
RATU-S
RAUN-S
B-**RAVE**
C-RAVE
D-RAVE
G-RAVE
T-RAVE
RAVE-D
RAVE-L
RAVE-N
RAVE-R
RAVE-S
B-**RAWN**
D-RAWN
P-RAWN
RAWN-S
B-**RAWS**
C-RAWS
D-RAWS
RAYA-H
RAYA-S
B-**RAYS**
D-RAYS
F-RAYS
G-RAYS
P-RAYS
T-RAYS
B-**RAZE**
C-RAZE

G-RAZE
RAZE-D
RAZE-E
RAZE-R
RAZE-S
A-**READ**
B-READ
D-READ
O-READ
T-READ
READ-D
READ-S
READ-Y
B-**REAK**
C-REAK
F-REAK
W-REAK
REAK-S
A-**REAL**
U-REAL
REAL-M
REAL-O
REAL-S
B-**REAM**
C-REAM
D-REAM
REAM-E
REAM-S
REAM-Y
REAN-S
REAP-S
A-**REAR**
D-REAR
REAR-M
REAR-S
D-**RECK**
T-RECK
W-RECK
RECK-S
A-**REDD**
REDD-S
REDD-Y
A-**REDE**
B-REDE
REDE-D
REDE-S
C-**REDO**
U-REDO
REDO-N
REDO-S
REDO-X
C-**REDS**
B-**REED**
C-REED
D-REED
F-REED
G-REED
P-REED
T-REED
REED-E
REED-S
REED-Y
REEF-S
REEF-Y
C-**REEK**
G-REEK
REEK-S
REEK-Y
C-**REEL**
REEL-S
G-**REEN**
P-REEN
T-REEN
REEN-S
B-**REES**

C-REES
D-REES
F-REES
G-REES
P-REES
T-REES
REES-T
G-**REGO**
REGO-S
D-**REGS**
P-**REIF**
T-REIF
REIF-S
REIF-Y
REIK-I
REIK-S
G-**REIN**
REIN-K
REIN-S
REIS-T
REKE-D
REKE-S
REKE-Y
T-**REND**
REND-S
B-**RENS**
G-RENS
W-RENS
B-**RENT**
D-RENT
P-RENT
U-RENT
Y-RENT
RENT-E
RENT-S
REPO-S
REPO-T
REPP-S
P-**REPS**
F-**RESH**
C-**REST**
D-REST
P-REST
T-REST
W-REST
REST-S
REST-Y
A-**RETE**
RETE-M
RETE-S
A-**RETS**
F-RETS
T-RETS
B-**REWS**
C-REWS
G-REWS
T-REWS
RHEA-S
P-**RIAL**
T-RIAL
U-RIAL
RIAL-S
A-**RIAS**
C-**RIBS**
D-RIBS
D-**RICE**
G-RICE
P-RICE
T-RICE
RICE-D
RICE-R
RICE-S
RICE-Y
RICH-T
B-**RICK**

C-RICK
E-RICK
P-RICK
T-RICK
W-RICK
RICK-S
P-**RICY**
B-**RIDE**
G-RIDE
P-RIDE
T-RIDE
RIDE-R
RIDE-S
G-**RIDS**
I-RIDS
A-**RIEL**
O-RIEL
RIEL-S
RIEM-S
RIFE-R
G-**RIFF**
T-RIFF
RIFF-S
D-**RIFT**
G-RIFT
RIFT-E
RIFT-S
RIFT-Y
RIGG-S
B-**RIGS**
F-RIGS
G-RIGS
P-RIGS
T-RIGS
RILE-D
RILE-S
RILE-Y
B-**RILL**
D-RILL
F-RILL
G-RILL
K-RILL
P-RILL
T-RILL
RILL-E
RILL-S
P-**RIMA**
RIMA-E
C-**RIME**
G-RIME
P-RIME
RIME-D
RIME-R
RIME-S
B-**RIMS**
C-RIMS
P-RIMS
T-RIMS
RIMU-S
G-**RIMY**
P-RIMY
G-**RIND**
RIND-S
RIND-Y
B-**RINE**
C-RINE
T-RINE
U-RINE
RINE-S
B-**RING**
E-RING
I-RING
W-RING
RING-S
B-**RINK**

D-RINK
P-RINK
RINK-S
B-**RINS**
G-RINS
T-RINS
RINS-E
A-**RIOT**
G-RIOT
RIOT-S
C-**RIPE**
G-RIPE
T-RIPE
RIPE-D
RIPE-N
RIPE-R
RIPE-S
RIPP-S
D-**RIPS**
G-RIPS
T-RIPS
D-**RIPT**
G-RIPT
A-**RISE**
B-RISE
C-RISE
F-RISE
G-RISE
P-RISE
RISE-N
RISE-R
RISE-S
B-**RISK**
F-RISK
RISK-S
RISK-Y
C-**RISP**
RISP-S
T-**RITE**
U-RITE
W-RITE
RITE-S
B-**RITS**
C-RITS
F-RITS
G-RITS
W-RITS
B-**RITT**
F-RITT
RITT-S
F-**RITZ**
RITZ-Y
RIVA-L
RIVA-S
D-**RIVE**
RIVE-D
RIVE-L
RIVE-N
RIVE-R
RIVE-S
RIVE-T
RIVO-S
RIZA-S
B-**ROAD**
T-ROAD
ROAD-S
ROAM-S
G-**ROAN**
ROAN-S
ROAR-S
ROAR-Y
P-**ROBE**
ROBE-D
ROBE-S
P-**ROBS**

B-**ROCH**
B-**ROCK**
C-ROCK
F-ROCK
T-ROCK
ROCK-S
ROCK-Y
C-**ROCS**
E-**RODE**
T-RODE
RODE-D
RODE-O
RODE-S
B-**RODS**
P-RODS
T-RODS
F-**ROES**
B-**ROIL**
D-ROIL
ROIL-S
ROIL-Y
G-**ROIN**
P-ROIN
ROIN-S
ROJI-S
B-**ROKE**
P-ROKE
T-ROKE
W-ROKE
ROKE-D
ROKE-R
ROKE-S
D-**ROLE**
P-ROLE
ROLE-S
ROLF-S
D-**ROLL**
P-ROLL
T-ROLL
ROLL-S
A-**ROMA**
G-ROMA
ROMA-L
ROMA-N
ROMA-S
T-**ROMP**
ROMP-S
P-**ROMS**
C-**RONE**
D-RONE
G-RONE
I-RONE
K-RONE
P-RONE
T-RONE
RONE-O
RONE-S
P-**RONG**
W-RONG
F-**RONT**
RONT-E
RONT-S
B-**ROOD**
ROOD-S
G-**ROOF**
P-ROOF
ROOF-S
ROOF-Y
B-**ROOK**
C-ROOK
D-ROOK
ROOK-S
ROOK-Y
B-**ROOM**
G-ROOM
V-ROOM
ROOM-S
ROOM-Y
C-**ROON**
K-ROON
ROON-S
D-**ROOP**
T-ROOP
ROOP-S
ROOP-Y
B-**ROOS**
ROOS-A
ROOS-E
ROOS-T
W-**ROOT**
ROOT-S
ROOT-Y
G-**ROPE**
T-ROPE
ROPE-D
ROPE-R
ROPE-S
ROPE-Y
C-**RORE**
F-RORE
P-RORE
RORE-S
RORT-S
RORT-Y
F-**RORY**
A-**ROSE**
B-ROSE
E-ROSE
P-ROSE
ROSE-D
ROSE-S
ROSE-T
C-**ROST**
F-ROST
P-ROST
ROST-S
B-**ROSY**
P-ROSY
ROTA-L
ROTA-S
W-**ROTE**
ROTE-D
ROTE-S
ROTI-S
ROTL-S
ROTO-R
ROTO-S
G-**ROTS**
T-ROTS
ROUE-N
ROUE-S
P-**ROUL**
ROUL-E
ROUL-S
ROUM-S
C-**ROUP**
G-ROUP
ROUP-S
ROUP-Y
C-**ROUT**
G-ROUT
T-ROUT
ROUT-E
ROUT-H
ROUT-S
D-**ROVE**
G-ROVE
P-ROVE
T-ROVE
ROVE-D
ROVE-N
ROVE-R
ROVE-S
B-**ROWS**
C-ROWS
D-ROWS
F-ROWS
G-ROWS
P-ROWS
T-ROWS
V-ROWS
ROWT-H
ROWT-S
RUBE-S
D-**RUBS**
G-RUBS
C-**RUCK**
T-RUCK
RUCK-S
RUDD-S
RUDD-Y
C-**RUDE**
P-RUDE
RUDE-R
RUDE-S
C-**RUDS**
G-**RUED**
T-RUED
T-**RUER**
RUER-S
C-**RUES**
G-RUES
T-RUES
G-**RUFF**
RUFF-E
RUFF-S
RUGA-E
RUGA-L
D-**RUGS**
F-RUGS
T-RUGS
B-**RUIN**
RUIN-G
RUIN-S
RUKH-S
B-**RULE**
RULE-D
RULE-R
RULE-S
T-**RULY**
B-**RUME**
G-RUME
RUME-N
RUME-S
C-**RUMP**
F-RUMP
G-RUMP
T-RUMP
RUMP-S
RUMP-Y
A-**RUMS**
D-RUMS
RUND-S
P-**RUNE**
RUNE-D
RUNE-S
W-**RUNG**
RUNG-S
B-**RUNT**
G-RUNT
P-RUNT
RUNT-S
RUNT-Y
RURP-S
RURU-S
RUSA-S
C-**RUSE**
D-RUSE
RUSE-S
B-**RUSH**
C-RUSH
F-RUSH
RUSH-Y
B-**RUSK**
RUSK-S
B-**RUST**
C-RUST
F-RUST
T-RUST
RUST-S
RUST-Y
T-**RUTH**
RUTH-S
RYAL-S
G-**RYKE**
RYKE-D
RYKE-S
RYND-S
RYOT-S
G-**RYPE**
RYPE-R
SABE-D
SABE-R
SABE-S
SACK-S
T-**SADE**
SADE-S
T-**SADI**
SADI-S
SAFE-D
SAFE-R
SAFE-S
SAGA-S
U-**SAGE**
SAGE-R
SAGE-S
SAGO-S
SAIC-E
SAIC-K
SAIC-S
SAID-S
SAIL-S
SAIM-S
SAIN-E
SAIN-S
SAIN-T
SAIR-S
SAIS-T
SAKE-R
SAKE-S
SAKI-A
SAKI-S
SALE-P
SALE-S
SALE-T
SALL-E
SALL-Y
SALP-A
SALP-S
SALS-A
SALS-E
SALT-O
SALT-S
SALT-Y
SAMA-N
SAMA-S
Y-**SAME**
SAME-K
SAME-L
SAME-N
SAME-S
SAME-Y
SAMP-I
SAMP-S
SAND-S
SAND-Y
SANE-D
SANE-R
SANE-S
SANG-A
SANG-H
SANG-S
SANK-O
SANS-A
SANT-O
SANT-S
SARD-S
SARI-N
SARI-S
SARK-S
SARK-Y
K-**SARS**
T-SARS
SASS-E
SASS-Y
SATE-D
SATE-M
SATE-S
SATI-N
SATI-S
SAUL-S
SAUL-T
SAUT-E
SAUT-S
SAVE-D
SAVE-R
SAVE-S
SAVE-Y
SAYS-T
SCAB-S
SCAD-S
SCAG-S
SCAM-P
SCAM-S
SCAN-D
SCAN-S
SCAN-T
E-**SCAR**
SCAR-E
SCAR-F
SCAR-P
SCAR-S
SCAR-T
SCAR-Y
SCAT-H
SCAT-S
SCAT-T
SCAW-S
SCOG-S
SCOP-A
SCOP-E
SCOP-S
A-**SCOT**
E-SCOT
SCOT-S
SCOW-L
SCOW-P
SCOW-S
SCUD-I
SCUD-O
SCUD-S
SCUG-S
SCUL-K
SCUL-L
SCUL-P
SCUL-S
SCUM-S
SCUP-S
SCUR-F
SCUR-S
SCUT-A
SCUT-E
SCUT-S
SCYE-S
SEAL-S
SEAM-E
SEAM-S
SEAM-Y
SEAN-S
SEAR-E
SEAR-S
SEAS-E
SEAT-S
SECT-S
SEED-S
SEED-Y
SEEK-S
SEEL-D
SEEL-S
SEEL-Y
SEEM-S
SEEP-S
SEEP-Y
SEER-S
SEGO-L
SEGO-S
SEIF-S
SEIL-S
SEIR-S
SEIS-E
SEIS-M
SEKT-S
SELE-S
SELF-S
SELL-A
SELL-E
SELL-S
SEME-E
SEME-N
SEME-S
SEMI-E
SEMI-S
SENA-S
SEND-S
SENS-A
SENS-E
SENT-E
SENT-I
SENT-S
SEPT-A
SEPT-S
SERA-C
SERA-I
SERA-L
SERE-D
SERE-R
SERE-S
SERF-S
SERK-S
SERR-A
SERR-E
SERR-S
SERR-Y
U-**SERS**
SESE-Y
SESS-A
SETA-E
SETA-L
SETT-S
SEXT-O
SEXT-S
SHAD-E
SHAD-S
SHAD-Y
SHAG-S
SHAH-S
SHAM-A
SHAM-E
SHAM-S
SHAN-D
SHAN-K
SHAN-S
P-**SHAW**
SHAW-L
SHAW-M
SHAW-N
SHAW-S
SHAY-A
SHAY-S
SHEA-F
SHEA-L
SHEA-R
SHEA-S
A-**SHED**
SHED-S
A-**SHES**
I-SHES
A-**SHET**
SHET-S
SHEW-N
SHEW-S
SHIM-S
SHIN-E
SHIN-S
SHIN-Y
SHIP-S
SHIR-E
SHIR-K
SHIR-R
SHIR-S
SHIR-T
SHIT-E
SHIT-S
SHIV-A
SHIV-E
SHIV-S
SHOE-D
SHOE-R
SHOE-S
SHOG-I
SHOG-S
SHOO-K
SHOO-L
SHOO-N
SHOO-S
SHOO-T
SHOP-E
SHOP-S
SHOT-E
SHOT-S
SHOT-T
SHOW-N
SHOW-S
SHOW-Y
SHRI-S
SHUL-E
SHUL-N
SHUL-S
SHUN-S
SHUN-T
SHUT-E
SHUT-S
SHWA-S
SIAL-S
SIBB-S
SICE-S
SICK-O
SICK-S
SIDA-S
A-**SIDE**
SIDE-D
SIDE-R
SIDE-S
SIEN-S
SIEN-T
SIFT-S
SIGH-S
SIGH-T
SIGN-S
SIJO-S
SIKA-S
SIKE-R
SIKE-S
SILD-S
E-**SILE**
SILE-D
SILE-N
SILE-R
SILE-S
SILE-X
SILK-S
SILK-Y
SILL-S
SILL-Y
SILO-S
SILT-S
SILT-Y
SIMA-R
SIMA-S
SIMI-S
SIMP-S
SIND-S
SINE-D
SINE-S
SINE-W
U-**SING**
SING-E
SING-S
SINH-S
SINK-S
SINK-Y
SIPE-D
SIPE-S
SIRE-D
SIRE-E
SIRE-N
SIRE-S
SIRI-H
SIRI-S
SISS-Y
SIST-S
SITE-D
SITE-S
SITH-E
SIZE-D
SIZE-L
SIZE-R
SIZE-S
SKAG-S
SKAT-E
SKAT-S
SKAT-T
SKAW-S
SKEE-D
SKEE-N
SKEE-R
SKEE-S
SKEE-T
SKEG-G
SKEG-S

SKEO-S
SKEP-S
A-**SKER**
E-SKER
SKER-S
A-**SKEW**
SKEW-S
SKID-S
SKIM-O
SKIM-P
SKIM-S
SKIN-K
SKIN-S
SKIN-T
SKIO-S
SKIP-S
SKIT-E
SKIT-S
SKUA-S
SKUG-S
SKYR-E
SKYR-S
SLAB-S
SLAE-S
SLAG-S
SLAM-S
SLAP-S
SLAT-E
SLAT-S
SLAT-Y
SLAW-S
SLAY-S
I-**SLED**
SLED-S
SLEE-K
SLEE-P
SLEE-R
SLEE-T
SLEW-S
SLEY-S
SLID-E
SLIM-E
SLIM-S
SLIM-Y
SLIP-E
SLIP-S
SLIP-T
SLIT-S
SLOB-S
SLOE-S
SLOG-S
SLOP-E
SLOP-S
SLOP-Y
SLOT-H
SLOT-S
SLOW-S
SLUB-B
SLUB-S
SLUE-D
SLUE-S
SLUG-S
SLUM-P
SLUM-S
SLUR-B
SLUR-P
SLUR-S
SLUT-S
SMEE-K
SMEE-S
SMEW-S
SMIR-K
SMIR-R
SMIR-S
SMIT-E
SMIT-H
SMIT-S
SMOG-S
SMUG-S
SMUR-S
SMUT-S
SNAB-S
SNAG-S
SNAP-S
SNAR-E
SNAR-K
SNAR-L
SNAR-S
SNAR-Y
SNAW-S
SNEB-S
SNED-S
SNEE-D
SNEE-R
SNEE-S
SNIB-S
SNIG-S
SNIP-E
SNIP-S
SNIP-Y
SNIT-S
SNOB-S
SNOD-S
SNOG-S
SNOT-S
SNOW-K
SNOW-S
SNOW-Y
SNUB-S
SNUG-S
SNYE-S
SOAK-S
SOAP-S
SOAP-Y
SOAR-E
SOAR-S
SOCA-S
SOCK-O
SOCK-S
SODA-S
SOFA-R
SOFA-S
SOFT-A
SOFT-S
SOFT-Y
SOIL-S
SOIL-Y
SOJA-S
SOKE-N
SOKE-S
SOLA-H
SOLA-N
SOLA-R
SOLA-S
SOLD-E
SOLD-I
SOLD-O
SOLD-S
SOLE-D
SOLE-I
SOLE-R
SOLE-S
SOLI-D
SOLO-N
SOLO-S
SOMA-N
SOMA-S
SONE-S
SONG-S
SONS-E
SONS-Y
SOOK-S
SOOM-S
SOOP-S
SOOT-E
SOOT-H
SOOT-S
SOOT-Y
SOPH-S
SOPH-Y
P-**SORA**
SORA-L
SORA-S
SORB-S
SORD-A
SORD-O
SORD-S
SORE-D
SORE-E
SORE-L
SORE-R
SORE-S
SORE-X
SORN-S
SORT-S
SOTH-S
SOUK-S
SOUL-S
SOUM-S
SOUP-S
SOUP-Y
SOUR-S
SOUS-E
SOUT-H
SOUT-S
SOWF-F
SOWF-S
SOWL-E
SOWL-S
SOWM-S
SOWN-D
SOWN-E
SOWP-S
SOWS-E
SOYA-S
SPAE-D
SPAE-R
SPAE-S
SPAG-S
SPAM-S
SPAN-E
SPAN-G
SPAN-K
SPAN-S
SPAR-D
SPAR-E
SPAR-K
SPAR-S
SPAR-T
SPAS-M
SPAT-E
SPAT-S
SPAW-L
SPAW-N
SPAW-S
SPAY-D
SPAY-S
SPAZ-Z
SPEC-K
SPEC-S
SPEK-S
SPET-S
SPEW-S
SPEW-Y
A-**SPIC**
SPIC-A
SPIC-E
SPIC-K
SPIC-S
SPIC-Y
SPIE-D
SPIE-L
SPIE-R
SPIE-S
SPIK-E
SPIK-S
SPIK-Y
SPIN-A
SPIN-E
SPIN-K
SPIN-S
SPIN-Y
SPIT-E
SPIT-S
SPIT-Z
SPIV-S
SPOT-S
SPUD-S
SPUE-D
SPUE-S
SPUN-K
SPUR-N
SPUR-S
SPUR-T
STAB-S
STAG-E
STAG-S
STAG-Y
STAP-H
STAP-S
STAR-E
STAR-K
STAR-N
STAR-R
STAR-S
STAR-T
STAT-E
STAT-S
STAW-S
STAY-S
STED-D
STED-E
STED-S
STEM-E
STEM-S
STEN-D
STEN-O
STEN-S
STEN-T
STEP-S
STEP-T
STET-S
STEW-S
STEW-Y
STIE-D
STIE-S
A-**STIR**
STIR-E
STIR-K
STIR-P
STIR-S
STOA-E
STOA-I
STOA-S
STOA-T
STOB-S
E-**STOP**
STOP-E
STOP-S
STOP-T
STOT-S
STOW-N
STOW-P
STOW-S
STUB-S
STUD-S
STUD-Y
STUM-M
STUM-P
STUM-S
A-**STUN**
STUN-G
STUN-K
STUN-S
STUN-T
STYE-D
STYE-S
T-**SUBA**
SUBA-H
SUBA-S
SUCK-S
SUDD-S
SUDS-Y
SUED-E
SUER-S
SUET-S
SUET-Y
SUGH-S
SUID-S
SUIT-E
SUIT-S
SUKH-S
SULK-S
SULK-Y
SULU-S
SUMO-S
SUMP-H
SUMP-S
SUNK-S
SUNN-A
SUNN-S
SUNN-Y
SUPE-R
SUPE-S
SURA-H
SURA-L
SURA-S
SURA-T
SURD-S
U-**SURE**
SURE-D
SURE-R
SURE-S
SURF-S
SURF-Y
SWAB-S
SWAD-S
SWAG-E
SWAG-S
SWAM-I
SWAM-P
SWAM-Y
SWAN-G
SWAN-K
SWAN-S
SWAP-S
SWAP-T
SWAT-H
SWAT-S
A-**SWAY**
SWAY-L
SWAY-S
SWEE-D
SWEE-L
SWEE-P
SWEE-R
SWEE-S
SWEE-T
SWEY-S
SWIG-S
A-**SWIM**
SWIM-S
SWOB-S
SWOP-S
SWOP-T
SWOT-S
SYBO-E
SYBO-W
SYCE-E
SYCE-S
SYEN-S
SYKE-R
SYKE-S
SYLI-S
SYNC-H
SYNC-S
SYND-S
SYNE-D
SYNE-S
SYPE-D
SYPE-S
SYPH-S
TABI-D
TABI-S
S-**TABS**
TABU-N
TABU-S
TACE-S
TACE-T
TACH-E
TACH-O
TACH-S
S-**TACK**
TACK-S
TACK-Y
TACO-S
TACT-S
TAEL-S
S-**TAGS**
TAHA-S
TAHR-S
TAIL-S
S-**TAIN**
TAIN-S
TAIN-T
TAIS-H
TAIT-S
TAKA-S
S-**TAKE**
TAKE-N
TAKE-R
TAKE-S
TAKI-N
TAKI-S
TALA-K
TALA-Q
TALA-R
TALA-S
TALC-S
TALC-Y
S-**TALE**
TALE-A
TALE-R
TALE-S
S-**TALK**
TALK-S
TALK-Y
S-**TALL**
TALL-Y
TAME-D
TAME-R
TAME-S
S-**TAMP**
TAMP-S
TANA-S
S-**TANE**
S-**TANG**
TANG-A
TANG-I
TANG-O
TANG-S
TANG-Y
TANH-S
S-**TANK**
TANK-A
TANK-S
TANK-Y
TANS-Y
TAPA-S
E-**TAPE**
TAPE-D
TAPE-N
TAPE-R
TAPE-S
TAPE-T
A-**TAPS**
S-TAPS
TAPU-S
TARA-S
S-**TARE**
TARE-D
TARE-S
S-**TARN**
TARN-S
TARO-C
TARO-K
TARO-S
TARO-T
TARP-S
S-**TARS**
TARS-I
S-**TART**
TART-S
TART-Y
S-**TASH**
TASK-S
TASS-E
S-**TATE**
TATE-R
TATE-S
TATH-S
E-**TATS**
S-TATS
TATT-S
TATT-Y
TATU-S
TAUT-S
TAVA-H
TAVA-S
TAWA-S
S-**TAWS**
TAWS-E
TAWT-S
TAXI-S
S-**TAYS**
S-**TEAD**
TEAD-E
TEAD-S
S-**TEAK**
TEAK-S
S-**TEAL**
TEAL-S
S-**TEAM**
TEAM-S
S-**TEAR**
TEAR-S
TEAR-Y
TEAS-E
TEAT-S
TECH-S
TECH-Y
S-**TEDS**
S-**TEED**
S-**TEEL**
TEEL-S
S-**TEEM**
TEEM-S
S-**TEEN**
TEEN-D
TEEN-E
TEEN-S
TEEN-Y
S-**TEER**
TEER-S
TEFF-S
TEGG-S
TEGU-A
TEGU-S
TEHR-S
S-**TEIL**
TEIL-S
S-**TELA**
TELA-E
S-**TELE**
TELE-S
TELE-X
S-**TELL**
TELL-S
TELL-Y
S-**TEME**
TEME-D
TEME-S
TEMP-I
TEMP-O
TEMP-S
TEMP-T
I-**TEMS**
S-TEMS
TEMS-E
S-**TEND**
TEND-S
C-**TENE**
TENE-S
TENE-T
E-**TENS**
S-TENS
TENS-E
S-**TENT**
TENT-H
TENT-S
TENT-Y
TEPA-L
TEPA-S
TERF-E
TERF-S
TERM-S
S-**TERN**
TERN-E
TERN-S
TEST-A
TEST-E
TEST-S
TEST-Y
TETE-S
TETH-S
S-**TETS**
S-**TEWS**
TEXT-S
THAN-A
THAN-E

THAN-K
THAN-S
THAR-M
THAR-S
THAW-S
THAW-Y
THEE-D
THEE-K
THEE-S
THEM-A
THEM-E
THEN-S
THEW-S
THEW-Y
THIG-H
THIG-S
THIN-E
THIN-G
THIN-K
THIN-S
THIO-L
THIR-D
THIR-L
THON-G
THOU-S
THRO-B
THRO-E
THRO-W
THRU-M
THUD-S
THUG-S
TIAR-A
TIAR-S
TICE-D
TICE-S
S-**TICH**
TICH-Y
S-**TICK**
TICK-S
TICK-Y
TIDE-D
TIDE-S
S-**TIED**
TIER-S
S-**TIES**
S-**TIFF**
TIFF-S
TIFT-S
TIGE-R
TIGE-S
TIKA-S
TIKE-S
TIKI-S
S-**TILE**
U-TILE
TILE-D
TILE-R
TILE-S
S-**TILL**
TILL-S
TILL-Y
A-**TILT**
S-TILT
TILT-H
TILT-S
S-**TIME**
TIME-D
TIME-R
TIME-S
TIND-S
TINE-A
TINE-D
TINE-S
S-**TING**
TING-E
TING-S
S-**TINK**
TINK-S
S-**TINT**
TINT-S
TINT-Y
TIPI-S
TIPS-Y
S-**TIRE**
TIRE-D
TIRE-S
TIRL-S
TIRO-S
TIRR-S
TITE-R
TITI-S
S-**TIVY**
TIZZ-Y
TOAD-S
TOAD-Y
S-**TOCK**
TOCK-S
TOCO-S
A-**TOCS**
TOEA-S
TOFF-S
TOFF-Y
TOFT-S
TOFU-S
TOGA-E
TOGA-S
TOGE-D
TOGE-S
TOHO-S
TOIL-E
TOIL-S
S-**TOIT**
TOIT-S
A-**TOKE**
S-TOKE
TOKE-D
TOKE-N
TOKE-R
TOKE-S
TOKO-S
TOLA-N
TOLA-S
S-**TOLE**
TOLE-D
TOLE-S
A-**TOLL**
TOLL-S
TOLT-S
TOLU-S
TOMB-S
TOME-S
A-**TOMS**
A-**TONE**
S-TONE
TONE-D
TONE-R
TONE-S
TONE-Y
S-**TONG**
TONG-A
TONG-S
S-**TONK**
TONK-S
A-**TONY**
S-TONY
S-**TOOK**
S-**TOOL**
TOOL-S
TOOM-S
TOON-S
TOOT-H
TOOT-S
S-**TOPE**
TOPE-D
TOPE-E
TOPE-K
TOPE-R
TOPE-S
TOPH-E
TOPH-I
TOPH-S
TOPI-C
TOPI-S
S-**TOPS**
TORA-H
TORA-N
TORA-S
TORC-H
TORC-S
S-**TORE**
TORE-S
TORI-C
TORI-I
TORO-S
TORO-T
TORR-S
TORS-E
TORS-I
TORS-K
TORS-O
TORT-E
TORT-S
S-**TORY**
TOSA-S
TOSE-D
TOSE-S
TOSH-Y
S-**TOSS**
TOSS-Y
Y-**TOST**
TOTE-D
TOTE-M
TOTE-R
TOTE-S
S-**TOTS**
TOUK-S
S-**TOUN**
TOUN-S
S-**TOUR**
TOUR-S
S-**TOUT**
TOUT-S
S-**TOWN**
TOWN-S
TOWN-Y
S-**TOWS**
TOWS-E
TOWS-Y
TOWT-S
TOYO-N
TOYO-S
TOZE-D
TOZE-S
S-**TRAD**
TRAD-E
TRAD-S
TRAM-P
TRAM-S
S-**TRAP**
TRAP-E
TRAP-S
TRAP-T
TRAT-S
TRAT-T
S-**TRAY**
TRAY-S
TREE-D
TREE-N
TREE-S
TREF-A
TREK-S
TRES-S
TRES-T
TRET-S
S-**TREW**
TREW-S
TREY-S
TRIE-D
TRIE-R
TRIE-S
S-**TRIG**
TRIG-O
TRIG-S
TRIM-S
TRIN-E
TRIN-S
TRIO-L
TRIO-R
TRIO-S
A-**TRIP**
S-TRIP
TRIP-E
TRIP-S
TRIP-Y
TROD-E
TROD-S
TROG-S
TRON-A
TRON-C
TRON-E
TRON-S
S-**TROP**
TROP-E
TROT-H
TROT-S
S-**TROW**
TROW-S
S-**TROY**
TROY-S
TRUE-D
TRUE-R
TRUE-S
TRUG-S
TRYE-R
TRYP-S
TSAR-S
TUAN-S
TUBA-E
TUBA-L
TUBA-R
TUBA-S
TUBE-D
TUBE-R
TUBE-S
S-**TUBS**
S-**TUCK**
TUCK-S
TUFA-S
S-**TUFF**
TUFF-E
TUFF-S
TUFT-S
TUFT-Y
E-**TUIS**
TUIS-M
TULE-S
S-**TUMP**
TUMP-S
TUMP-Y
S-**TUMS**
TUNA-S
TUND-S
TUNE-D
TUNE-R
TUNE-S
S-**TUNG**
TUNG-S
S-**TUNS**
TURD-S
TURF-S
TURF-Y
TURK-S
TURM-E
TURM-S
TURN-S
TUSH-Y
TUSK-S
TUSK-Y
TUTU-S
TWAE-S
TWAL-S
TWAT-S
TWAY-S
E-**TWEE**
TWEE-D
TWEE-L
TWEE-N
TWEE-R
TWEE-T
TWIG-S
TWIN-E
TWIN-K
TWIN-S
TWIN-Y
TWIT-E
TWIT-S
S-**TYED**
TYEE-S
TYER-S
S-**TYES**
TYKE-S
TYMP-S
TYND-E
TYNE-D
TYNE-S
TYPE-D
TYPE-S
TYPE-Y
TYPO-S
TYPP-S
S-**TYRE**
TYRE-D
TYRE-S
TYRO-S
S-**TYTE**
TZAR-S
UDAL-S
B-**UDOS**
J-UDOS
K-UDOS
L-UDOS
Q-**UEYS**
B-**UFOS**
E-**UGHS**
S-UGHS
V-UGHS
B-**UKES**
C-UKES
D-UKES
J-UKES
N-UKES
P-UKES
Y-UKES
K-**ULAN**
Y-ULAN
ULAN-S
D-**ULES**
G-ULES
H-ULES
M-ULES
P-ULES
R-ULES
T-ULES
Y-ULES
C-**ULEX**
ULNA-D
ULNA-E
ULNA-R
ULNA-S
L-**ULUS**
P-ULUS
S-ULUS
Z-ULUS
V-**ULVA**
ULVA-S
B-**UMBO**
D-UMBO
G-UMBO
J-UMBO
R-UMBO
UMBO-S
B-**UMPH**
H-UMPH
S-UMPH
B-**UMPS**
D-UMPS
G-UMPS
H-UMPS
J-UMPS
L-UMPS
M-UMPS
P-UMPS
R-UMPS
S-UMPS
T-UMPS
Y-UMPS
UNAI-S
UNAU-S
UNBE-D
B-**UNCE**
D-UNCE
O-UNCE
P-UNCE
UNCE-S
UNCI-A
B-**UNCO**
J-UNCO
UNCO-S
UNCO-Y
UNDE-E
UNDE-R
C-**UNDY**
F-UNDY
G-UNDY
O-UNDY
M-**UNIS**
UNIT-E
UNIT-S
UNIT-Y
J-**UNTO**
P-UNTO
P-**UPAS**
Z-UPAS
UPBY-E
UPDO-S
J-**UPON**
Y-UPON
URAO-S
B-**URBS**
C-URBS
URDE-E
B-**URDS**
C-URDS
H-URDS
N-URDS
S-URDS
T-URDS
C-**URDY**
UREA-L
UREA-S
A-**URES**
C-URES
D-URES
L-URES
M-URES
P-URES
S-URES
G-**URGE**
P-URGE
S-URGE
URGE-D
URGE-R
URGE-S
A-**URIC**
B-**URNS**
C-URNS
D-URNS
G-URNS
T-URNS
B-**URSA**
URSA-E
G-**URUS**
K-URUS
R-URUS
M-**URVA**
URVA-S
B-**USED**
F-USED
M-USED
M-**USER**
USER-S
B-**USES**
F-USES
M-USES
P-USES
R-USES
S-USES
W-USES
B-**UTES**
C-UTES
J-UTES
L-UTES
M-UTES
C-**UTIS**
M-UTIS
T-**UTUS**
UVEA-L
UVEA-S
E-**VADE**
VADE-D
VADE-S
A-**VAIL**
VAIL-S
VAIR-E
VAIR-S
VAIR-Y
A-**VALE**
VALE-S
VALE-T
VALI-D
VALI-S
VAMP-S
VANE-D
VANE-S
VANG-S
A-**VANT**
VANT-S
VARA-N
VARA-S
VARE-C
VARE-S
O-**VARY**
VASA-L
VASE-S
A-**VAST**
VAST-S
VAST-Y
VATU-S
VAUT-E
VAUT-S
U-**VEAL**
VEAL-E
VEAL-S
VEAL-Y
VEEP-S
VEER-S
VEER-Y
VEGA-N
VEGA-S
VEHM-E
VEIL-S
VEIL-Y
VEIN-S
VEIN-Y
VELA-R
VELD-S
VELD-T
VELE-S
VELL-S
VENA-E
VENA-L
VEND-S
E-**VENT**
VENT-S
VERB-S
A-**VERS**
O-VERS
VERS-E
VERS-O
VERS-T
A-**VERT**
E-VERT
O-VERT
VERT-S
VERT-U
E-**VERY**
VEST-A
VEST-S
E-**VETS**
VIAL-S
VIBE-S
VIBE-X
VICE-D
VICE-S
VIDE-O
I-**VIED**
VIER-S
I-**VIES**
VIEW-S
VIEW-Y
VIGA-S
VILD-E
VILE-R
VILL-A
VILL-I
VILL-S
VINA-L
VINA-S
A-**VINE**
O-VINE

VINE-D
VINE-R
VINE-S
VINE-W
VINO-S
VINT-S
VINY-L
VIOL-A
VIOL-D
VIOL-S
VIRE-D
VIRE-O
VIRE-S
VIRL-S
VISA-S
A-**VISE**
VISE-D
VISE-S
VITA-E
VITA-L
VITA-S
E-**VITE**
VITE-X
VIVA-S
VIVA-T
VIVE-R
VIVE-S
VLEI-S
VOAR-S
A-**VOID**
O-VOID
VOID-S
VOLA-E
VOLA-R
VOLE-D
VOLE-S
VOLE-T
VOLK-S
VOLT-A
VOLT-E
VOLT-I
VOLT-S
VOTE-D
VOTE-R
VOTE-S
A-**VOWS**
VRIL-S
VROW-S
VUGG-S
VUGG-Y
VUGH-S
VULN-S
S-**WABS**
S-**WACK**
WACK-E
WACK-O
WACK-S
WACK-Y
WADD-S
WADD-Y
WADE-D
WADE-R
WADE-S
WADI-S
S-**WADS**
WADT-S
T-**WAES**
WAFF-S
WAFT-S
S-**WAGE**
WAGE-D
WAGE-R
WAGE-S
S-**WAGS**
WAID-E
WAIF-S
WAIF-T
S-**WAIL**
WAIL-S
S-**WAIN**
T-WAIN
WAIN-S
WAIR-S
A-**WAIT**
WAIT-E
WAIT-S
WAKA-S
A-**WAKE**
WAKE-D
WAKE-N
WAKE-R
WAKE-S
WAKF-S
WALD-S
D-**WALE**
S-WALE
WALE-D
WALE-R
WALE-S
WALI-S
WALK-S
WALL-A
WALL-S
WALL-Y
S-**WALY**
WAME-D
WAME-S
WAND-S
WANE-D
WANE-S
WANE-Y
D-**WANG**
S-WANG
T-WANG
WANG-S
S-**WANK**
T-WANK
WANK-S
WANK-Y
S-**WANS**
WANT-S
WANT-Y
S-**WAPS**
WAQF-S
A-**WARD**
S-WARD
WARD-S
A-**WARE**
S-WARE
WARE-D
WARE-S
WARK-S
S-**WARM**
WARM-S
A-**WARN**
WARN-S
WARP-S
WARS-T
S-**WART**
WART-S
WART-Y
WASE-S
A-**WASH**
S-WASH
WASH-Y
WASM-S
WASP-S
WASP-Y
WAST-E
WAST-S
WATE-R
S-**WATS**
T-WATS
WATT-S
WAUK-S
WAUL-K
WAUL-S
WAUR-S
A-**WAVE**
WAVE-D
WAVE-R
WAVE-S
WAVE-Y
WAWE-S
WAWL-S
A-**WAYS**
S-WAYS
T-WAYS
T-**WEAK**
S-**WEAL**
WEAL-D
WEAL-S
WEAN-S
S-**WEAR**
WEAR-S
WEAR-Y
S-**WEED**
T-WEED
WEED-S
WEED-Y
WEEK-E
WEEK-S
A-**WEEL**
S-WEEL
T-WEEL
WEEL-S
WEEM-S
T-**WEEN**
WEEN-S
WEEN-Y
S-**WEEP**
WEEP-S
WEEP-Y
S-**WEER**
T-WEER
S-**WEES**
WEES-T
S-**WEET**
T-WEET
WEET-E
WEET-S
WEFT-E
WEFT-S
WEID-S
WEIL-S
S-**WEIR**
WEIR-D
WEIR-S
WEKA-S
WELD-S
WELK-E
WELK-S
WELK-T
D-**WELL**
S-WELL
WELL-S
WELL-Y
D-**WELT**
S-WELT
WELT-S
WEMB-S
WEND-S
WENT-S
S-**WEPT**
E-**WEST**
WEST-S
WETA-S
WEXE-D
WEXE-S
S-**WEYS**
WHAM-O
WHAM-S
WHAP-S
WHAT-S
WHEE-L
WHEE-N
WHEE-P
WHEN-S
WHET-S
WHEW-S
WHEY-S
WHID-S
WHIG-S
WHIM-S
WHIN-E
WHIN-S
WHIN-Y
WHIP-S
WHIP-T
WHIR-L
WHIR-R
WHIR-S
WHIT-E
WHIT-S
WHIT-Y
WHIZ-Z
WHOM-P
WHOP-S
E-**WHOW**
T-**WICE**
WICK-S
WICK-Y
WIDE-N
WIDE-R
WIDE-S
WIEL-D
WIEL-S
WIFE-D
WIFE-S
S-**WIGS**
T-WIGS
WILD-S
D-**WILE**
WILE-D
WILE-S
WILI-S
S-**WILL**
T-WILL
WILL-S
WILL-Y
T-**WILT**
WILT-S
WIMP-S
WIMP-Y
WIND-S
WIND-Y
D-**WINE**
S-WINE
T-WINE
WINE-D
WINE-S
WINE-Y
A-**WING**
O-WING
S-WING
WING-E
WING-S
WING-Y
S-**WINK**
T-WINK
WINK-S
WINN-A
WINN-S
WINO-S
T-**WINS**
T-**WINY**
S-**WIPE**
WIPE-D
WIPE-R
WIPE-S
S-**WIRE**
T-WIRE
WIRE-D
WIRE-R
WIRE-S
WISE-D
WISE-R
WISE-S
S-**WISH**
WISH-A
WISP-S
WISP-Y
S-**WISS**
T-**WIST**
WIST-S
T-**WITE**
WITE-D
WITE-S
S-**WITH**
WITH-E
WITH-S
WITH-Y
S-**WITS**
T-WITS
S-**WIVE**
WIVE-D
WIVE-R
WIVE-S
WOAD-S
WOCK-S
A-**WOKE**
WOKE-N
WOLD-S
WOLF-S
WOMB-S
WOMB-Y
WONK-S
WONK-Y
WONT-S
WOOD-S
WOOD-Y
WOOF-S
WOOF-Y
WOOL-D
WOOL-S
WOOL-Y
S-**WOON**
WOON-S
WOOS-H
WOOT-Z
S-**WOPS**
S-**WORD**
WORD-S
WORD-Y
S-**WORE**
A-**WORK**
WORK-S
WORM-S
WORM-Y
S-**WORN**
WORT-H
WORT-S
S-**WOTS**
WOVE-N
WRAP-S
WRAP-T
WREN-S
WRIT-E
WRIT-S
WULL-S
WUSS-Y
WYLE-D
WYLE-S
WYND-S
WYNN-S
WYTE-D
WYTE-S
XYST-I
XYST-S
K-**YACK**
YACK-S
N-**YAFF**
YAFF-S
YAGI-S
A-**YAHS**
K-**YAKS**
YALE-S
L-**YAMS**
K-**YANG**
YANG-S
YANK-S
YAPP-S
YAPP-Y
L-**YARD**
YARD-S
YARE-R
YARN-S
YARR-S
YATE-S
YAUD-S
YAUP-S
YAWL-S
YAWN-S
YAWN-Y
YAWP-S
YEAD-S
YEAN-S
YEAR-D
YEAR-N
YEAR-S
YEAS-T
YECH-S
YECH-Y
YEDE-S
YEED-S
YEGG-S
G-**YELD**
YELK-S
YELL-S
YELM-S
A-**YELP**
YELP-S
YELT-S
H-**YENS**
S-YENS
YERD-S
YERK-S
YESK-S
YEST-S
YEST-Y
YETI-S
YETT-S
YEUK-S
YEUK-Y
YEVE-N
YEVE-S
YIKE-S
YILL-S
A-**YINS**
P-YINS
YIPE-S
YIRD-S
YIRK-S
YIRR-S
YITE-S
X-**YLEM**
YLEM-S
YLKE-S
YMPE-S
YOCK-S
YODE-L
YODH-S
YOGA-S
YOGH-S
YOGI-C
YOGI-N
YOGI-S
YOKE-D
YOKE-L
YOKE-S
YOLK-S
YOLK-Y
YOMP-S
YONI-C
YONI-S
A-**YONT**
YOOF-S
YOOP-S
YORE-S
YORK-S
YOUK-S
YOUR-N
YOUR-S
YOUR-T
YOWE-D
YOWE-S
YOWL-S
YUAN-S
YUCA-S
YUCK-S
YUCK-Y
YUFT-S
YUGA-S
YUKE-D
YUKE-S
YUKO-S
YULE-S
YUMP-S
YURT-A
YURT-S
ZACK-S
ZARF-S
ZATI-S
ZEAL-S
ZEBU-B
ZEBU-S
M-**ZEES**
ZEIN-S
ZERK-S
ZERO-S
ZEST-S
ZEST-Y
ZETA-S
ZEZE-S
D-**ZHOS**
ZIFF-S
ZILA-S
ZILL-S
ZIMB-I
ZIMB-S
ZINC-O
ZINC-S
ZINC-Y
A-**ZINE**
ZINE-B
ZINE-S
ZING-S
ZING-Y
ZITI-S
ZOBO-S
ZOBU-S
ZOEA-E
ZOEA-L
ZOEA-S
A-**ZOIC**
ZONA-E
ZONA-L
O-**ZONE**
ZONE-D
ZONE-R
ZONE-S
ZONK-S
ZOOM-S
ZOON-S
ZORI-L
ZORI-S
ZOUK-S
ZULU-S
ZUPA-N
ZUPA-S
ZURF-S
ZYGA-L
A-**ZYME**
ZYME-S

5-LETTER WORD HOOKS: extensible words only

AALII-S
ABACA-S
K-**ABAKA**
ABAKA-S
ABAMP-S
ABAND-S
ABASE-D
ABASE-R
ABASE-S
ABATE-D
ABATE-R
ABATE-S
K-**ABAYA**
ABAYA-S
ABBES-S
ABBEY-S
ABBOT-S
ABCEE-S
ABEAR-S
K-**ABELE**
ABELE-S
ABHOR-S
ABIDE-D
ABIDE-R
ABIDE-S
B-**ABIES**
G-ABIES
R-ABIES
C-**ABLED**
F-ABLED
G-ABLED
S-ABLED
T-ABLED
F-**ABLER**
C-**ABLES**
F-ABLES
G-ABLES
S-ABLES
T-ABLES
ABLES-T
C-**ABLET**
G-ABLET
T-ABLET
ABLET-S
ABMHO-S
ABODE-D
ABODE-S
ABOHM-S
ABOMA-S
B-**ABOON**
G-ABOON
ABORD-S
ABORT-S
ABOUT-S
ABOVE-S
ABRAY-S
ABRIN-S
ABSEY-S
ABSIT-S
ABUNA-S
ABUSE-D
ABUSE-R
ABUSE-S
ABYSM-S
ACARI-D
ACCOY-S
F-**ACERS**
L-ACERS
M-ACERS
P-ACERS
R-ACERS
ACETA-L
B-**ACHED**
C-ACHED
B-**ACHES**
C-ACHES
L-ACHES
M-ACHES
N-ACHES
R-ACHES
T-ACHES
F-**ACING**
L-ACING
M-ACING
P-ACING
R-ACING
ACINI-C
H-**ACKEE**
ACKEE-S
ACORN-S
N-**ACRED**
S-ACRED
N-**ACRES**
ACTIN-G
ACTIN-S
ACTON-S
F-**ACTOR**
ACTOR-S
ACUTE-R
ACUTE-S
ADAGE-S
ADAPT-S
D-**ADDED**
G-ADDED
M-ADDED
P-ADDED
R-ADDED
W-ADDED
B-**ADDER**
G-ADDER
L-ADDER
M-ADDER
P-ADDER
R-ADDER
S-ADDER
W-ADDER
ADDER-S
ADDIO-S
D-**ADDLE**
F-ADDLE
P-ADDLE
R-ADDLE
S-ADDLE
W-ADDLE
ADDLE-D
ADDLE-S
ADEEM-S
ADEPT-S
ADIEU-S
ADIEU-X
R-**ADIOS**
B-**ADMAN**
M-ADMAN
B-**ADMEN**
M-ADMEN
ADMIN-S
ADMIT-S
ADMIX-T
ADOBE-S
ADOBO-S
ADOPT-S
ADORE-D
ADORE-R
ADORE-S
ADORN-S
ADULT-S
ADUST-S
ADVEW-S
AECIA-L
P-**AEONS**
F-**AERIE**
AERIE-D
AERIE-R
AERIE-S
AFARA-S
AFEAR-D
AFEAR-S
AFRIT-S
D-**AFTER**
H-AFTER
R-AFTER
W-AFTER
AFTER-S
AGAMA-S
AGAMI-C
AGAMI-D
AGAMI-S
AGATE-S
AGAVE-S
AGAZE-D
S-**AGENE**
AGENE-S
AGENT-S
C-**AGERS**
E-AGERS
G-AGERS
J-AGERS
L-AGERS
P-AGERS
R-AGERS
W-AGERS
Y-AGERS
B-**AGGER**
D-AGGER
G-AGGER
J-AGGER
L-AGGER
N-AGGER
S-AGGER
T-AGGER
W-AGGER
Y-AGGER
AGGER-S
B-**AGGIE**
AGGIE-S
AGGRO-S
AGHAS-T
AGILA-S
V-**AGILE**
AGILE-R
C-**AGING**
G-AGING
P-AGING
R-AGING
W-AGING
AGING-S
M-**AGISM**
AGISM-S
AGIST-S
E-**AGLET**
H-AGLET
AGLET-S
M-**AGMAS**
AGOGE-S
AGONE-S
W-**AGONS**
AGORA-E
AGORA-S
AGREE-D
AGREE-S
AGRIA-S
V-**AGUED**
V-**AGUES**
AGUTI-S
A-**AHING**
R-AHING
AHOLD-S
L-**AIDED**
M-AIDED
R-AIDED
R-**AIDER**
AIDER-S
B-**AILED**
F-AILED
H-AILED
J-AILED
M-AILED
N-AILED
R-AILED
S-AILED
T-AILED
V-AILED
W-AILED
M-**AIMED**
M-**AIMER**
AIMER-S
AIOLI-S
F-**AIRED**
H-AIRED
L-AIRED
P-AIRED
S-AIRED
W-AIRED
F-**AIRER**
S-AIRER
AIRER-S
B-**AIRNS**
C-AIRNS
AIRTH-S
AISLE-D
AISLE-S
N-**AIVER**
T-AIVER
W-AIVER
AIVER-S
AIZLE-S
AJIVA-S
AJUGA-S
AJWAN-S
R-**AKEES**
AKELA-S
AKENE-S
B-**AKING**
C-AKING
F-AKING
L-AKING
M-AKING
R-AKING
T-AKING
W-AKING
Y-**AKKAS**
ALAAP-S
ALAMO-S
ALAND-S
L-**ALANG**
ALANG-S
G-**ALANT**
T-ALANT
ALANT-S
ALAPA-S
J-**ALAPS**
ALARM-S
S-**ALARY**
M-**ALATE**
P-ALATE
ALATE-D
ALATE-S
P-**ALAYS**
ALBUM-S
ALCID-S
ALDEA-S
B-**ALDER**
ALDER-N
ALDER-S
ALDOL-S
ALEPH-S
ALERT-S
ALEYE-D
ALEYE-S
H-**ALFAS**
ALGIN-S
ALGOR-S
ALGUM-S
ALIBI-S
ALIEN-S
C-**ALIFS**
K-ALIFS
M-**ALIGN**
ALIGN-S
M-**ALINE**
S-ALINE
V-ALINE
ALINE-D
ALINE-R
ALINE-S
M-**ALIST**
ALIYA-H
ALIYA-S
T-**ALKIE**
ALKIE-S
ALKYD-S
ALKYL-S
ALLAY-S
M-**ALLEE**
S-ALLEE
ALLEE-S
H-**ALLEL**
ALLEL-E
ALLEL-S
G-**ALLEY**
V-ALLEY
ALLEY-S
T-**ALLIS**
ALLOD-S
B-**ALLOT**
H-ALLOT
T-ALLOT
ALLOT-S
B-**ALLOW**
C-ALLOW
F-ALLOW
G-ALLOW
H-ALLOW
M-ALLOW
S-ALLOW
T-ALLOW
W-ALLOW
ALLOW-S
ALLOY-S
ALLYL-S
ALMAH-S
H-**ALMAS**
T-ALMAS
ALMEH-S
T-**ALMUD**
ALMUD-E
ALMUD-S
ALMUG-S
H-**ALOED**
H-**ALOES**
ALOHA-S
ALOIN-S
K-**ALONG**
ALPHA-S
ALTAR-S
F-**ALTER**
H-ALTER
P-ALTER
S-ALTER
ALTER-N
ALTER-S
S-**ALTOS**
ALULA-E
ALULA-R
ALURE-S
ALWAY-S
C-**AMASS**
H-**AMATE**
R-AMATE
AMATE-D
AMATE-S
AMAZE-D
AMAZE-S
AMBAN-S
C-**AMBER**
J-AMBER
L-AMBER
T-AMBER
AMBER-S
AMBER-Y
G-**AMBIT**
AMBIT-S
G-**AMBLE**
H-AMBLE
R-AMBLE
W-AMBLE
AMBLE-D
AMBLE-R
AMBLE-S
G-**AMBOS**
J-AMBOS
M-AMBOS
S-AMBOS
Z-AMBOS
AMEBA-E
AMEBA-N
AMEBA-S
AMEER-S
AMEND-E
AMEND-S
AMENE-D
R-**AMENS**
Y-AMENS
L-**AMENT**
AMENT-A
AMENT-S
L-**AMIAS**
Z-AMIAS
AMICE-S
AMIDE-S
AMIDO-L
AMIDS-T
M-**AMIES**
R-AMIES
AMIGA-S
AMIGO-S
F-**AMINE**
G-AMINE
T-AMINE
AMINE-S
G-**AMINS**
R-AMINS
T-AMINS
AMMAN-S
G-**AMMON**
M-AMMON
AMMON-O
AMMON-S
AMNIO-N
AMNIO-S
AMOLE-S
AMOUR-S
AMOVE-D
AMOVE-S
C-**AMPLE**
S-AMPLE
AMPLE-R
C-**AMPLY**
D-AMPLY
AMPUL-E
AMPUL-S
AMRIT-A
AMRIT-S
AMUCK-S
AMUSE-D
AMUSE-R
AMUSE-S
B-**ANANA**
M-ANANA
Z-ANANA
ANANA-S
ANCLE-S
ANCON-E
ANEAR-S
ANELE-D
ANELE-S
M-**ANENT**
F-**ANGAS**
K-ANGAS
M-ANGAS
P-ANGAS
S-ANGAS
T-ANGAS
M-**ANGEL**
ANGEL-S
B-**ANGER**
D-ANGER
G-ANGER
H-ANGER
L-ANGER
M-ANGER
R-ANGER
S-ANGER
ANGER-S
B-**ANGLE**
C-ANGLE
D-ANGLE
F-ANGLE
J-ANGLE
M-ANGLE
T-ANGLE
W-ANGLE
ANGLE-D
ANGLE-R
ANGLE-S
ANGST-S
ANIGH-T
ANIMA-L
ANIMA-S
ANIME-S
ANIMI-S

F-**ANION**
W-ANION
ANION-S
ANISE-S
B-**ANKER**
C-ANKER
D-ANKER
H-ANKER
J-ANKER
L-ANKER
R-ANKER
T-ANKER
W-ANKER
Y-ANKER
ANKER-S
F-**ANKLE**
R-ANKLE
W-ANKLE
ANKLE-D
ANKLE-S
ANKLE-T
ANKUS-H
ANNAL-S
C-**ANNAS**
M-ANNAS
N-ANNAS
T-ANNAS
ANNAT-S
ANNEX-E
T-**ANNOY**
ANNOY-S
ANNUL-I
ANNUL-S
ANODE-S
ANOLE-S
C-**ANTAR**
K-ANTAR
ANTAR-A
ANTAR-S
M-**ANTAS**
B-**ANTED**
C-ANTED
D-ANTED
G-ANTED
H-ANTED
K-ANTED
P-ANTED
R-ANTED
W-ANTED
M-**ANTES**
Z-ANTES
C-**ANTIC**
M-ANTIC
ANTIC-K
ANTIC-S
M-**ANTIS**
M-**ANTRA**
T-ANTRA
Y-ANTRA
ANTRA-L
ANTRE-S
ANVIL-S
AORTA-E
AORTA-L
AORTA-S
C-**APERS**
G-APERS
J-APERS
P-APERS
R-APERS
T-APERS
J-**APERY**
N-APERY
P-APERY
APHID-S
R-**APHIS**
C-**APING**
G-APING
J-APING
R-APING
T-APING
APIOL-S
P-**APISH**
P-**APISM**
APISM-S
APNEA-L
APNEA-S
APODE-S
APPAL-L
APPAL-S
APPAY-D
APPAY-S
L-**APPEL**
R-APPEL
APPEL-S
D-**APPLE**
S-APPLE
APPLE-S
APPLE-T
APPUI-S
APPUY-S
N-**APRON**
APRON-S
L-**APSES**
R-**APTLY**
ARABA-S
ARAME-S
H-**ARBOR**
ARBOR-S
F-**ARCED**
ARDEB-S
ARDOR-S
ARDRI-S
AREAD-S
ARECA-S
AREDE-S
R-**AREFY**
ARENA-S
ARETE-S
C-**ARETS**
ARETT-S
ARGAL-A
ARGAL-I
ARGAL-S
ARGAN-D
ARGAN-S
ARGIL-S
D-**ARGLE**
G-ARGLE
ARGLE-D
ARGLE-S
ARGOL-S
J-**ARGON**
ARGON-S
ARGOT-S
ARGUE-D
ARGUE-R
ARGUE-S
S-**ARGUS**
ARHAT-S
ARIEL-S
ARISE-N
ARISE-S
B-**ARISH**
G-ARISH
H-ARISH
M-ARISH
P-ARISH
B-**ARKED**
C-ARKED
D-ARKED
H-ARKED
K-ARKED
L-ARKED
M-ARKED
N-ARKED
P-ARKED
W-ARKED
H-**ARLED**
M-ARLED
P-ARLED
C-**ARLES**
F-ARLES
M-ARLES
P-ARLES
F-**ARMED**
H-ARMED
W-ARMED
F-**ARMER**
H-ARMER
W-ARMER
ARMER-S
ARMET-S
ARMIL-S
ARMOR-S
ARMOR-Y
V-**ARNAS**
ARNUT-S
AROBA-S
L-**AROID**
AROID-S
AROMA-S
P-**ARPEN**
ARPEN-S
ARPEN-T
J-**ARRAH**
N-**ARRAS**
T-ARRAS
W-**ARRAY**
ARRAY-S
B-**ARRET**
G-ARRET
ARRET-S
K-**ARRIS**
ARRIS-H
B-**ARROW**
F-ARROW
H-ARROW
M-ARROW
N-ARROW
T-ARROW
Y-ARROW
ARROW-S
ARROW-Y
C-**ARSES**
F-ARSES
M-ARSES
P-ARSES
P-**ARSON**
ARSON-S
H-**ARTAL**
C-**ARTEL**
M-ARTEL
ARTEL-S
ARTIC-S
G-**ARUMS**
L-ARUMS
L-**ARVAL**
P-**ARVOS**
ASANA-S
M-**ASCOT**
ASCOT-S
ASDIC-S
B-**ASHED**
C-ASHED
D-ASHED
F-ASHED
G-ASHED
H-ASHED
L-ASHED
M-ASHED
P-ASHED
R-ASHED
S-ASHED
T-ASHED
W-ASHED
W-**ASHEN**
B-**ASHES**
C-ASHES
D-ASHES
F-ASHES
G-ASHES
H-ASHES
L-ASHES
M-ASHES
P-ASHES
R-ASHES
S-ASHES
T-ASHES
W-ASHES
ASHET-S
ASIDE-S
B-**ASKED**
C-ASKED
M-ASKED
T-ASKED
M-**ASKER**
T-ASKER
ASKER-S
ASPEN-S
G-**ASPER**
J-ASPER
R-ASPER
ASPER-S
ASPIC-K
ASPIC-S
J-**ASPIS**
ASPIS-H
ASSAI-L
ASSAI-S
ASSAY-S
B-**ASSES**
G-ASSES
J-ASSES
L-ASSES
M-ASSES
P-ASSES
R-ASSES
S-ASSES
T-ASSES
ASSES-S
B-**ASSET**
T-ASSET
ASSET-S
ASSOT-S
ASSOT-T
B-**ASTER**
C-ASTER
E-ASTER
F-ASTER
G-ASTER
L-ASTER
M-ASTER
P-ASTER
R-ASTER
T-ASTER
V-ASTER
W-ASTER
ASTER-N
ASTER-S
ASTER-T
ASTUN-S
W-**ATAPS**
B-**ATMAN**
V-ATMAN
ATMAN-S
M-**ATOKE**
ATOKE-S
ATOLL-S
ATONE-D
ATONE-R
ATONE-S
L-**ATRIA**
ATRIA-L
ATTAP-S
ATTAR-S
ATTIC-S
C-**AUDAD**
AUDAD-S
AUDIO-S
AUDIT-S
G-**AUGER**
M-AUGER
S-AUGER
AUGER-S
C-**AUGHT**
H-AUGHT
N-AUGHT
R-AUGHT
T-AUGHT
W-AUGHT
AUGHT-S
AUGUR-S
AUGUR-Y
AUMIL-S
D-**AUNTS**
G-AUNTS
H-AUNTS
J-AUNTS
N-AUNTS
S-AUNTS
T-AUNTS
V-AUNTS
J-**AUNTY**
V-AUNTY
L-**AURAE**
L-**AURAS**
T-**AURIC**
K-**AURIS**
AURIS-T
AURUM-S
AUXIN-S
AVAIL-E
AVAIL-S
AVALE-D
AVALE-S
S-**AVANT**
AVANT-I
D-**AVENS**
H-AVENS
M-AVENS
P-AVENS
R-AVENS
C-**AVERS**
H-AVERS
L-AVERS
P-AVERS
R-AVERS
S-AVERS
T-AVERS
W-AVERS
AVERS-E
T-**AVERT**
AVERT-S
AVIAN-S
R-**AVINE**
S-AVINE
AVION-S
P-**AVISE**
AVISE-D
AVISE-S
AVISO-S
AVIZE-D
AVIZE-S
AVOID-S
AVYZE-D
AVYZE-S
AWAIT-S
AWAKE-D
AWAKE-N
AWAKE-S
V-**AWARD**
AWARD-S
AWARE-R
AWARN-S
AWETO-S
L-**AWFUL**
C-**AWING**
D-AWING
H-AWING
J-AWING
K-AWING
L-AWING
M-AWING
P-AWING
R-AWING
S-AWING
T-AWING
Y-AWING
D-**AWNED**
F-AWNED
P-AWNED
Y-AWNED
D-**AWNER**
F-AWNER
P-AWNER
Y-AWNER
AWNER-S
AWOKE-N
F-**AXING**
R-AXING
T-AXING
W-AXING
AXIOM-S
AXION-S
T-**AXITE**
AXITE-S
T-**AXMAN**
T-**AXMEN**
AXOID-S
AXONE-S
C-**AXONS**
T-AXONS
R-**AYAHS**
Z-**AYINS**
F-**AYRES**
AYRIE-S
H-**AZANS**
AZIDE-S
AZINE-S
AZLON-S
AZOLE-S
G-**AZONS**
AZOTE-D
AZOTE-S
AZOTH-S
R-**AZURE**
AZURE-S
AZYME-S
BABEL-S
BABKA-S
BABOO-L
BABOO-N
BABOO-S
BABUL-S
BACCA-E
BACCA-S
BACCO-S
BACON-S
BADGE-D
BADGE-R
BADGE-S
BAGEL-S
BAHUT-S
BAIRN-S
BAIZA-S
BAIZE-D
BAIZE-S
BAJAN-S
BAJRA-S
BAJRI-S
BAKER-S
BAKER-Y
BALER-S
BALLS-Y
BALOO-S
BALSA-M
BALSA-S
BANCO-S
BANDA-R
BANDA-S
A-**BANDS**
O-**BANGS**
BANIA-N
BANIA-S
BANJO-S
BANTU-S
BARBE-D
BARBE-L
BARBE-R
BARBE-S
BARBE-T
BARCA-S
BARDE-D
BARDE-S
BARDO-S
BARES-T
BARGE-D
BARGE-E
BARGE-S
BARON-G
BARON-S
BARON-Y
BARRE-D
BARRE-L
BARRE-N
BARRE-S
BARRE-T
BARYE-S
BASAL-T
BASAN-S
A-**BASED**
A-**BASER**
A-**BASES**
BASES-T
BASIC-S
BASIL-S
BASIN-G
BASIN-S
BASON-S
BASSE-D
BASSE-R
BASSE-S
BASSE-T
BASSO-S

BASTE-D
BASTE-R
BASTE-S
BASTO-S
A-**BATED**
A-**BATES**
BATHE-D
BATHE-R
BATHE-S
BATIK-S
BATON-S
BATTA-S
A-**BATTU**
BATTU-E
BAULK-S
BAULK-Y
BAVIN-S
BAYLE-S
BAYOU-S
BAZAR-S
BAZOO-S
BEACH-Y
BEANO-S
BEARD-S
BEARE-D
BEARE-R
BEARE-S
A-**BEARS**
BEAST-S
BEATH-S
BEAUT-S
BEAUT-Y
BEBOP-S
BECAP-S
BECKE-D
BECKE-S
BECKE-T
BEDEL-L
BEDEL-S
BEDEW-S
BEDIM-S
BEDYE-D
BEDYE-S
BEECH-Y
BEFIT-S
BEFOG-S
BEGAR-S
BEGEM-S
BEGET-S
BEGIN-S
BEGUM-S
BEGUN-K
BEIGE-L
BEIGE-S
BEING-S
BEKAH-S
BELAH-S
BELAY-S
BELEE-D
BELEE-S
BELGA-S
BELIE-D
BELIE-F
BELIE-R
BELIE-S
BELLE-D
BELLE-S
BELOW-S
BEMAD-S
BEMIX-T
BEMUD-S
BENDY-S
BENET-S
BENNE-S
BENNE-T

BENNI-S
BEPAT-S
BERAY-S
BERET-S
BERME-S
BEROB-S
BERTH-A
BERTH-E
BERTH-S
BERYL-S
BESEE-M
BESEE-N
BESEE-S
BESET-S
BESIT-S
BESOM-S
BESOT-S
BETEL-S
BETID-E
BETON-S
BETON-Y
BETTA-S
BEVEL-S
BEVER-S
BEVOR-S
BEVUE-S
BEWET-S
BEWIG-S
BEZEL-S
BEZIL-S
BHANG-S
BHOOT-S
BIALI-S
BIALY-S
BIBLE-S
I-**BICES**
A-**BIDED**
A-**BIDER**
BIDER-S
A-**BIDES**
BIDET-S
BIDON-S
BIELD-S
BIELD-Y
BIGHA-S
BIGHT-S
BIGOT-S
BIJOU-S
BIJOU-X
BIKER-S
BIKIE-S
BILBO-A
BILBO-S
BILGE-D
BILGE-S
BIMAH-S
BIMBO-S
BINDI-S
BINGE-D
BINGE-R
BINGE-S
BINGO-S
BINIT-S
BIOME-S
BIONT-S
BIOTA-S
BIPED-S
BIPOD-S
BIRLE-D
BIRLE-R
BIRLE-S
BIRSE-S
BIRTH-S
I-**BISES**
BISON-S

BITCH-Y
O-**BITER**
BITER-S
BITTE-D
BITTE-N
BITTE-R
BLACK-S
BLADE-D
BLADE-S
BLAES-T
BLAIN-S
BLAME-D
BLAME-R
BLAME-S
BLAND-S
BLANK-S
BLANK-Y
BLARE-D
BLARE-S
BLASH-Y
O-**BLAST**
BLAST-S
BLAST-Y
A-**BLATE**
O-BLATE
BLATE-R
BLATT-S
BLAUD-S
A-**BLAZE**
BLAZE-D
BLAZE-R
BLAZE-S
BLEAK-S
BLEAK-Y
BLEAR-S
BLEAR-Y
BLEAT-S
BLEED-S
BLEEP-S
BLEND-E
BLEND-S
Y-**BLENT**
A-**BLEST**
A-**BLETS**
BLIMP-S
BLIND-S
BLINI-S
BLINK-S
A-**BLINS**
BLITE-S
BLOAT-S
BLOCK-S
BLOCK-Y
BLOKE-S
BLOKE-Y
BLOND-E
BLOND-S
BLOOD-S
BLOOD-Y
A-**BLOOM**
BLOOM-S
BLOOM-Y
BLOOP-S
BLORE-S
BLOWS-E
BLOWS-Y
BLUDE-S
BLUES-T
BLUES-Y
BLUET-S
BLUEY-S
BLUFF-S
BLUID-S
BLUID-Y
BLUME-D

BLUME-S
BLUNK-S
BLUNT-S
BLURB-S
BLURT-S
A-**BLUSH**
BLYPE-S
A-**BOARD**
BOARD-S
BOART-S
BOAST-S
BOBAC-S
BOBAK-S
BOCCA-S
BOCCE-S
BOCCI-A
BOCCI-E
BOCCI-S
BOCHE-S
A-**BODED**
A-**BODES**
BODGE-D
BODGE-R
BODGE-S
BODLE-S
BOFFO-S
BOGAN-S
BOGEY-S
BOGIE-S
BOGLE-S
BOHEA-S
BOING-S
BOINK-S
BOITE-S
O-**BOLES**
O-**BOLUS**
A-**BOMAS**
BOMBE-D
BOMBE-R
BOMBE-S
BOMBO-S
BONCE-S
BONER-S
BONGO-S
BONIE-R
BONNE-S
BONNE-T
BONZE-R
BONZE-S
BOOKS-Y
BOONG-S
BOORD-E
BOORD-S
BOOSE-D
BOOSE-S
BOOST-S
BOOTH-S
BOOZE-D
BOOZE-R
BOOZE-S
BOOZE-Y
BORAK-S
A-**BORAL**
BORAL-S
BORDE-L
BORDE-R
BORDE-S
A-**BORDS**
BOREE-N
BOREE-S
BORER-S
BORGO-S
A-**BORNE**
BORON-S
A-**BORTS**

BOSOM-S
BOSOM-Y
BOSON-S
BOSUN-S
BOTCH-Y
BOTEL-S
BOTTE-D
BOTTE-S
BOUGE-D
BOUGE-S
BOUGE-T
BOUGH-S
BOUGH-T
BOULE-S
BOULT-S
A-**BOUND**
Y-BOUND
BOUND-S
BOURD-S
BOURG-S
BOURN-E
BOURN-S
BOUSE-D
BOUSE-S
A-**BOUTS**
BOVID-S
BOWAT-S
BOWEL-S
BOWER-S
BOWER-Y
BOWET-S
BOWNE-D
BOWNE-S
BOWSE-D
BOWSE-R
BOWSE-S
BOXER-S
BOYAR-D
BOYAR-S
BOYAU-X
BOYLA-S
BRACE-D
BRACE-R
BRACE-S
BRACH-S
BRACK-S
BRACT-S
A-**BRAID**
BRAID-E
BRAID-S
BRAIL-S
BRAIN-S
BRAIN-Y
BRAKE-D
BRAKE-S
BRAME-S
BRAND-S
BRAND-Y
BRANK-S
BRANK-Y
BRANT-S
BRASH-Y
BRASS-Y
BRAST-S
BRAVA-S
BRAVE-D
BRAVE-R
BRAVE-S
BRAVO-S
BRAWL-S
BRAWL-Y
BRAWN-S
BRAWN-Y
A-**BRAYS**
BRAZA-S

BRAZE-D
BRAZE-N
BRAZE-R
BRAZE-S
BREAD-S
BREAD-Y
BREAK-S
BREAM-S
BREDE-D
BREDE-S
BREED-S
BREER-S
BREES-E
Y-**BRENT**
BRENT-S
BRERE-S
BREVE-S
BREVE-T
BRIAR-D
BRIAR-S
BRIAR-Y
BRIBE-D
BRIBE-E
BRIBE-R
BRIBE-S
BRICK-S
BRICK-Y
BRIDE-D
BRIDE-S
BRIEF-S
BRIER-S
BRIER-Y
BRILL-S
BRINE-D
BRINE-R
BRINE-S
BRING-S
BRINK-S
A-**BRINS**
BRISE-S
BRISK-S
BRISK-Y
BRITT-S
BRIZE-S
A-**BROAD**
BROAD-S
BROCH-E
BROCH-S
BROCK-S
BROGH-S
BROIL-S
BROKE-D
BROKE-N
BROKE-R
BROKE-S
BROME-S
BROMO-S
BRONC-O
BRONC-S
BROND-S
BROOD-S
BROOD-Y
BROOK-S
BROOL-S
BROOM-S
BROOM-Y
BROOS-E
BROSE-S
BROTH-S
BROTH-Y
BROWN-S
BROWN-Y
BROWS-E
BROWS-T
BROWS-Y

BRUGH-S
BRUIN-S
BRUIT-S
BRUME-S
BRUNT-S
BRUSH-Y
BRUST-S
BRUTE-D
BRUTE-R
BRUTE-S
BUAZE-S
BUBAL-E
BUBAL-S
BUCHU-S
BUCKU-S
BUDGE-D
BUDGE-R
BUDGE-S
BUDGE-T
BUFFE-D
BUFFE-R
BUFFE-T
BUFFO-S
BUGLE-D
BUGLE-R
BUGLE-S
BUGLE-T
BUILD-S
BUIST-S
BULGE-D
BULGE-R
BULGE-S
BULLA-E
BULSE-S
BUMBO-S
BUMPH-S
A-**BUNAS**
BUNCE-D
BUNCE-S
BUNCH-Y
BUNCO-S
BUNDT-S
BUNDU-S
BUNIA-S
BUNJE-E
BUNJE-S
BUNKO-S
BUNYA-S
BURAN-S
BURET-S
BURGH-S
BURIN-S
BURKA-S
BURKE-D
BURKE-R
BURKE-S
BUROO-S
BURQA-S
BURRO-S
BURRO-W
BURSA-E
BURSA-L
BURSA-R
BURSA-S
BURSE-S
A-**BURST**
BURST-S
A-**BUSED**
A-**BUSES**
BUSSU-S
BUTEO-S
BUTLE-D
BUTLE-R
BUTLE-S
BUTTE-D

BUTTE-R
BUTTE-S
BUTUT-S
BUTYL-S
BUYER-S
BWANA-S
BWAZI-S
BYLAW-S
BYWAY-S
CABAL-A
CABAL-S
S-**CABBY**
CABER-S
CABIN-S
CABLE-D
CABLE-S
CABLE-T
CABOB-S
CABOC-S
CACAO-S
CACHE-D
CACHE-S
CACHE-T
CADEE-S
CADET-S
CADGE-D
CADGE-R
CADGE-S
CADIE-S
CADRE-S
CAECA-L
S-**CAFFS**
CAGER-S
CAGOT-S
CAHOW-S
CAIRD-S
CAIRN-S
CAIRN-Y
CALIF-S
CALLA-N
CALLA-S
S-**CALLS**
CALPA-C
CALPA-S
S-**CALPS**
CALVE-D
CALVE-R
CALVE-S
CAMAN-S
CAMAS-H
CAMAS-S
S-**CAMEL**
CAMEL-S
CAMEO-S
CAMES-E
CAMIS-A
CAMIS-E
S-**CAMPI**
CAMPO-S
S-**CAMPS**
CANAL-S
CANEH-S
CANER-S
CANID-S
CANNA-E
CANNA-S
CANOE-D
CANOE-S
CANON-S
CANSO-S
CANTO-N
CANTO-R
CANTO-S
S-**CANTS**
S-**CANTY**

S-**CAPAS**
S-**CAPED**
CAPER-S
S-**CAPES**
CAPLE-S
CAPLE-T
CAPON-S
CAPOT-E
CAPOT-S
CAPUL-S
CARAP-S
CARAT-E
CARAT-S
CARBO-N
CARBO-S
CARBO-Y
CARDI-A
CARDI-S
S-**CARED**
S-**CARER**
CARER-S
S-**CARES**
CARES-S
CARET-S
CARGO-S
CARLE-S
CAROB-S
CAROL-I
CAROL-S
CAROM-S
S-**CARPS**
S-**CARRY**
CARSE-S
CARSE-Y
CARTA-S
E-**CARTE**
CARTE-D
CARTE-L
CARTE-R
CARTE-S
S-**CARTS**
CARVE-D
CARVE-L
CARVE-N
CARVE-R
CARVE-S
CASCO-S
CASTE-D
CASTE-R
CASTE-S
S-**CATCH**
CATCH-T
CATCH-Y
A-**CATER**
CATER-S
A-**CATES**
S-**CATTY**
CAULD-S
CAULK-S
S-**CAUPS**
CAUSA-E
CAUSA-L
CAUSE-D
CAUSE-N
CAUSE-R
CAUSE-S
CAUSE-Y
CAVEL-S
CAVER-N
CAVER-S
CAVIE-R
CAVIE-S
CAVIL-S
CAXON-S
CEASE-D

CEASE-S
CEAZE-D
CEAZE-S
CEBID-S
CEDAR-N
CEDAR-S
CEDER-S
CEIBA-S
CEILI-S
CELEB-S
CELLA-E
CELLA-R
O-**CELLI**
CELLO-S
CELOM-S
CENSE-D
CENSE-R
CENSE-S
CENTO-S
S-**CENTS**
CEORL-S
CERCI-S
CERGE-S
CERIA-S
S-**CERNE**
CERNE-D
CERNE-S
CESSE-D
CESSE-R
CESSE-S
CESTA-S
A-**CETYL**
CETYL-S
CHACE-D
CHACE-S
CHACK-S
CHACO-S
CHAFE-D
CHAFE-R
CHAFE-S
CHAFF-S
CHAFF-Y
CHAFT-S
CHAIN-E
CHAIN-S
CHAIR-S
CHAIS-E
CHALK-S
CHALK-Y
CHAMP-S
CHAMP-Y
CHANG-E
CHANG-S
CHANK-S
CHANT-S
CHANT-Y
CHAPE-L
CHAPE-S
CHARA-S
E-**CHARD**
CHARD-S
CHARE-D
CHARE-S
CHARE-T
CHARK-A
CHARK-S
CHARM-S
CHARR-O
CHARR-S
CHARR-Y
CHART-A
CHART-S
CHASE-D
CHASE-R
CHASE-S

CHASM-S
CHASM-Y
CHAYA-S
CHEAP-O
CHEAP-S
CHEAP-Y
CHEAT-S
CHECK-S
CHECK-Y
CHEEK-S
CHEEK-Y
CHEEP-S
CHEER-O
CHEER-S
CHEER-Y
CHEKA-S
CHELA-E
CHELA-S
CHEMO-S
CHERT-S
CHERT-Y
CHEST-S
CHEST-Y
CHETH-S
CHIAS-M
CHICA-S
CHICH-A
CHICH-I
T-**CHICK**
CHICK-S
CHICO-N
CHICO-S
CHIDE-D
CHIDE-R
CHIDE-S
CHIEF-S
CHIEL-D
CHIEL-S
CHILD-E
CHILD-S
CHILE-S
CHILI-S
CHILL-I
CHILL-S
CHILL-Y
CHIMB-S
CHIME-D
CHIME-R
CHIME-S
CHIMP-S
CHINA-R
CHINA-S
CHINE-D
CHINE-S
CHINK-S
CHINK-Y
CHINO-S
CHIRK-S
CHIRL-S
CHIRM-S
CHIRO-S
CHIRP-S
CHIRP-Y
CHIRR-E
CHIRR-S
CHIRT-S
CHIVE-D
CHIVE-S
CHOCK-O
CHOCK-S
CHOCO-S
CHOIR-S
CHOKE-D
CHOKE-R
CHOKE-S

CHOKE-Y
CHOKO-S
CHOLI-C
CHOLI-S
CHOLO-S
CHOMP-S
CHOOF-S
CHOOK-S
CHOOM-S
CHORD-A
CHORD-S
CHORE-A
CHORE-D
CHORE-E
CHORE-S
CHOSE-N
CHOSE-S
CHOTT-S
S-**CHOUT**
CHOUT-S
CHOWS-E
CHUCK-S
CHUCK-Y
CHUFA-S
CHUFF-S
CHUFF-Y
CHUMP-S
CHUNK-S
CHUNK-Y
CHURL-S
CHURN-S
CHURR-S
CHUSE-S
CHUTE-D
CHUTE-S
CHYLE-S
CHYME-S
CIBOL-S
A-**CIDER**
CIDER-S
CIDER-Y
CIGAR-S
CIMAR-S
S-**CIONS**
CIRCA-R
CISCO-S
CITAL-S
CITER-S
CITES-S
CIVET-S
CIVIC-S
CIVIE-S
CLACH-S
CLACK-S
CLADE-S
CLAIM-S
CLAME-S
CLAMP-S
CLANG-S
CLANK-S
CLARO-S
CLART-S
CLART-Y
CLASP-S
CLASP-T
CLASS-Y
CLAST-S
E-**CLATS**
CLAUT-S
S-**CLAVE**
CLAVE-R
CLAVE-S
CLAVI-E
CLAVI-S
CLEAN-S

CLEAR-S
CLEAT-S
CLECK-S
CLEEK-S
CLEEP-S
CLEFT-S
CLEPE-D
CLEPE-S
Y-**CLEPT**
CLERK-S
CLEVE-R
CLEVE-S
CLICK-S
S-**CLIFF**
CLIFF-S
CLIFF-Y
CLIFT-S
CLIFT-Y
CLIMB-S
CLIME-S
CLINE-S
CLING-S
CLING-Y
CLINK-S
CLINT-S
CLIPE-D
CLIPE-S
CLOAK-S
CLOAM-S
CLOCK-S
CLOFF-S
CLOKE-D
CLOKE-S
CLOMP-S
CLONE-D
CLONE-R
CLONE-S
CLONK-S
CLOOP-S
CLOOT-S
E-**CLOSE**
CLOSE-D
CLOSE-R
CLOSE-S
CLOSE-T
CLOTE-S
CLOTH-E
CLOTH-S
CLOUD-S
CLOUD-Y
CLOUR-S
CLOUT-S
CLOVE-N
CLOVE-R
CLOVE-S
CLOWN-S
CLOYE-D
CLOYE-S
CLOZE-S
CLUCK-S
CLUCK-Y
CLUMP-S
CLUMP-Y
CLUNK-S
CLUNK-Y
CLYPE-D
CLYPE-I
CLYPE-S
CNIDA-E
COACH-Y
COACT-S
COALA-S
COAPT-S
COARB-S
COAST-S

COATE-D
COATE-E
COATE-R
COATE-S
COATI-S
COBIA-S
COBLE-S
COBRA-S
COBZA-S
COCCI-C
COCCI-D
COCCO-S
COCKS-Y
COCOA-S
CODEC-S
CODEN-S
CODER-S
CODON-S
S-**COFFS**
COGIE-S
COGON-S
COGUE-S
COHAB-S
COHOE-S
COHOG-S
COHOS-H
COHOS-T
COIGN-E
COIGN-S
S-**COLDS**
COLEY-S
COLIC-S
COLIN-S
COLOG-S
COLON-E
COLON-I
COLON-S
COLON-Y
COLOR-S
COLZA-S
COMBE-D
COMBE-R
COMBE-S
COMBI-S
COMBO-S
COMER-S
COMET-H
COMET-S
COMIC-E
COMIC-S
COMMA-S
COMMO-N
COMMO-S
COMMO-T
COMPO-S
COMPO-T
COMPT-S
COMTE-S
CONCH-A
CONCH-E
CONCH-S
CONCH-Y
CONDO-M
CONDO-R
CONDO-S
I-**CONES**
S-CONES
CONEY-S
CONGA-S
CONGE-D
CONGE-E
CONGE-R
CONGE-S
CONGO-S
CONGO-U

CONIA-S
I-**CONIC**
CONIC-S
CONIN-E
CONIN-G
CONIN-S
CONNE-D
CONNE-R
CONNE-S
CONTE-S
CONTO-S
CONVO-S
CONVO-Y
COOEE-D
COOEE-S
COOER-S
COOEY-S
COOMB-E
COOMB-S
S-**COOPS**
COOPT-S
S-**COOTS**
COPAL-M
COPAL-S
S-**COPED**
COPEN-S
COPER-S
S-**COPES**
COPRA-H
COPRA-S
COPSE-D
COPSE-S
CORAL-S
CORBE-L
CORBE-S
S-**CORED**
S-**CORER**
CORER-S
S-**CORES**
COREY-S
CORGI-S
S-**CORIA**
A-**CORNS**
S-CORNS
CORNU-A
CORNU-S
CORPS-E
S-**CORSE**
CORSE-S
CORSE-T
CORSO-S
COSEC-H
COSEC-S
COSET-S
COSEY-S
COSIE-D
COSIE-R
COSIE-S
COSTA-E
COSTA-L
COSTA-R
COSTE-D
COSTE-R
COSTE-S
COTAN-S
COTTA-E
COTTA-R
COTTA-S
COUCH-E
COUGH-S
COUNT-S
COUNT-Y
COUPE-D
COUPE-E
COUPE-R
COUPE-S
S-**COUPS**
COURB-S
COURE-D
COURE-S
S-**COURS**
COURS-E
COURT-S
S-**COUTH**
COUTH-S
COUTH-Y
COVEN-S
COVEN-T
COVER-S
COVER-T
COVET-S
COVEY-S
COVIN-G
COVIN-S
COWAL-S
COWAN-S
S-**COWED**
COWER-S
S-**COWLS**
S-**COWPS**
COYPU-S
COZEN-S
COZEY-S
COZIE-D
COZIE-R
COZIE-S
CRAAL-S
S-**CRABS**
CRACK-S
CRACK-Y
CRAFT-S
CRAFT-Y
S-**CRAGS**
CRAIG-S
CRAKE-D
CRAKE-S
CRAME-S
CRAMP-S
CRAMP-Y
S-**CRAMS**
CRANE-D
CRANE-S
CRANK-S
CRANK-Y
S-**CRANS**
S-**CRAPE**
CRAPE-D
CRAPE-S
S-**CRAPS**
CRARE-S
CRATE-D
CRATE-R
CRATE-S
CRAVE-D
CRAVE-N
CRAVE-R
CRAVE-S
A-**CRAWL**
S-CRAWL
CRAWL-S
CRAWL-Y
S-**CRAWS**
CRAZE-D
CRAZE-S
S-**CREAK**
CREAK-S
CREAK-Y
S-**CREAM**
CREAM-S
CREAM-Y
CREDO-S
S-**CREED**
CREED-S
CREEK-S
CREEK-Y
CREEL-S
CREEP-S
CREEP-Y
S-**CREES**
CREES-E
CREES-H
CREME-S
CRENA-S
CREPE-D
CREPE-S
CREPE-Y
CREST-S
CREWE-D
CREWE-L
CREWE-S
S-**CREWS**
CRICK-S
CRICK-Y
S-**CRIED**
CRIER-S
S-**CRIES**
CRIME-D
CRIME-N
CRIME-S
S-**CRIMP**
CRIMP-S
CRIMP-Y
S-**CRIMS**
S-**CRINE**
CRINE-D
CRINE-S
CRIPE-S
CRISE-S
CRISP-S
CRISP-Y
CRITH-S
CROAK-S
CROAK-Y
CROCK-S
CROFT-S
CROMB-S
CROME-D
CROME-S
CRONE-S
CRONE-T
CROOK-S
CROON-S
CRORE-S
A-**CROSS**
CROSS-E
CROUP-E
CROUP-S
CROUP-Y
CROUT-E
CROUT-S
CROWD-S
CROWD-Y
CROWN-S
S-**CROWS**
CROZE-R
CROZE-S
CRUCK-S
CRUDE-R
CRUDE-S
CRUEL-S
CRUET-S
CRUMB-S
CRUMB-Y
S-**CRUMP**
CRUMP-S
CRUMP-Y
CRUOR-S
CRURA-L
CRUSE-S
CRUSE-T
CRUST-A
CRUST-S
CRUST-Y
CRUVE-S
CRWTH-S
CRYPT-O
CRYPT-S
CTENE-S
CUBEB-S
CUBER-S
CUBIC-A
CUBIC-S
CUBIT-S
S-**CUFFS**
CULET-S
S-**CULLS**
CULPA-E
CULTI-C
CUMEC-S
CUMIN-S
CUPEL-S
CUPID-S
CUPPA-S
CURAT-E
CURAT-S
CURER-S
CURET-S
S-**CURFS**
CURIA-E
CURIA-L
CURIA-S
E-**CURIE**
CURIE-S
CURIE-T
CURIO-S
S-**CURRY**
CURSE-D
CURSE-R
CURSE-S
CURVE-D
CURVE-S
CURVE-T
CURVE-Y
S-**CURVY**
CUSEC-S
CUSSO-S
S-**CUTCH**
CUTCH-A
A-**CUTER**
A-**CUTES**
S-CUTES
CUTES-T
CUTES-Y
CUTEY-S
CUTIE-S
CUTIN-S
CUTTO-E
CUTUP-S
CUVEE-S
CYCAD-S
CYCLE-D
CYCLE-R
CYCLE-S
CYCLO-S
CYDER-S
CYMAR-S
CYMOL-S
CYNIC-S
CYTON-S
DACHA-S
DAGGA-S
S-**DAINE**
DAINE-D
DAINE-S
DAINT-Y
DAKER-S
DALLE-S
DAMAN-S
DAMAR-S
DAMME-D
DAMME-R
DANCE-D
DANCE-R
DANCE-S
DANIO-S
I-**DANTS**
DARAF-S
DARCY-S
DARER-S
DARGA-S
DARIC-S
DARRE-D
DARRE-S
DARZI-S
DASHI-S
DATAL-S
DATER-S
DATTO-S
DATUM-S
DAUBE-D
DAUBE-R
DAUBE-S
DAULT-S
DAUNT-S
DAVEN-S
DAVIT-S
A-**DAWED**
DAZER-S
DEAIR-S
I-**DEALS**
DEARE-D
DEARE-R
DEARE-S
DEARN-S
DEATH-S
DEATH-Y
DEAVE-D
DEAVE-S
DEBAG-S
DEBAR-K
DEBAR-S
DEBEL-S
DEBIT-S
DEBUG-S
DEBUT-S
DEBYE-S
DECAD-E
DECAD-S
DECAF-F
DECAF-S
DECAL-S
DECAY-S
DECKO-S
DECOR-S
DECOY-S
A-**DEEMS**
DEEVE-D
DEEVE-S
DEFAT-S
DEFER-S
DEFOG-S
DEGUM-S
DEICE-D
DEICE-R
DEICE-S
S-**DEIGN**
DEIGN-S
DEISM-S
DEIST-S
DEKKO-S
DELAY-S
DELFT-S
DELIS-T
DELPH-S
DELTA-S
DELVE-D
DELVE-R
DELVE-S
DEMAN-D
DEMAN-S
DEMIT-S
DEMOB-S
DEMON-S
DEMUR-E
DEMUR-S
DENAY-S
DENET-S
DENIM-S
DENSE-R
DEPOT-S
DEPTH-S
DERAT-E
DERAT-S
DERAY-S
DERIG-S
DERMA-L
DERMA-S
DERTH-S
DESSE-S
DETER-S
DEUCE-D
DEUCE-S
DEVEL-S
DEVIL-S
DEVON-S
DEVOT-E
DEVOT-S
DEWAN-I
DEWAN-S
DEWAR-S
DEXIE-S
DHOBI-S
DHOLE-S
DHOLL-S
DHOTI-S
DHUTI-S
DIAZO-S
DICER-S
DICHT-S
DICOT-S
E-**DICTS**
DIDIE-S
DIENE-S
DIGHT-S
DIGIT-S
DIKAS-T
DIKER-S
DILDO-E
DILDO-S
DILLI-S
DIMER-S
DINAR-S
DINER-O
DINER-S
DINGE-D
DINGE-R
DINGE-S
DINGE-Y
DINIC-S
DIODE-S
DIOTA-S
DIPSO-S
DIRGE-S
DIRKE-D
DIRKE-S
DISCO-S
DISME-S
DITAL-S
E-**DITED**
DITTO-S
DIVAN-S
DIVER-S
DIVER-T
DIVES-T
DIVOT-S
DIWAN-S
DIXIE-S
DIXIT-S
DIZEN-S
DJINN-I
DJINN-S
DJINN-Y
DOBIE-S
DOBLA-S
DOBRA-S
DODGE-D
DODGE-M
DODGE-R
DODGE-S
DOGEY-S
DOGIE-S
DOGMA-S
DOHYO-S
DOING-S
DOLCE-S
DOLMA-N
DOLMA-S
DOLOR-S
DONAH-S
DONEE-S
DONGA-S
DONNA-S
DONNA-T
DONNE-D
DONNE-E
DONNE-S
DONOR-S
DONUT-S
DOOLE-E
DOOLE-S
DOONA-S
DOORN-S
A-**DOORS**
DOPER-S
DORAD-O
DORAD-S
DOREE-S
DORSA-D
DORSA-L
DORSE-L
DORSE-R
DORSE-S
DOSEH-S
DOSER-S
DOTER-S
DOUAR-S
DOUBT-S
DOUCE-R
DOUCE-T
DOUGH-S
DOUGH-T
DOUGH-Y
DOUMA-S
DOURA-H
DOURA-S

DOUSE-D
DOUSE-R
DOUSE-S
DOVEN-S
DOVER-S
DOVIE-R
DOWAR-S
DOWEL-S
DOWER-S
DOWER-Y
DOWIE-R
DOWLE-S
DOWSE-D
DOWSE-R
DOWSE-S
DOWSE-T
DOXIE-S
DOYEN-S
DOZEN-S
DOZER-S
DRAFF-S
DRAFF-Y
DRAFT-S
DRAFT-Y
DRAIL-S
DRAIN-S
DRAKE-S
DRAMA-S
DRANT-S
DRAPE-D
DRAPE-R
DRAPE-S
DRAPE-T
DRAPE-Y
DRAWL-S
DRAWL-Y
A-**DREAD**
DREAD-S
DREAM-S
DREAM-T
DREAM-Y
DREAR-E
DREAR-S
DREAR-Y
DRECK-S
DRECK-Y
DRERE-S
DRESS-Y
DRICE-S
DRIER-S
DRIES-T
A-**DRIFT**
DRIFT-S
DRIFT-Y
DRILL-S
DRINK-S
DRIVE-L
DRIVE-N
DRIVE-R
DRIVE-S
DROIL-S
A-**DROIT**
DROIT-S
DROLE-R
DROLE-S
DROLL-S
DROLL-Y
DROME-S
DRONE-D
DRONE-R
DRONE-S
DROOG-S
DROOK-S
DROOL-S
DROOP-S
DROOP-Y
DROPS-Y
DROSS-Y
DROUK-S
DROVE-D
DROVE-R
DROVE-S
DROWN-D
DROWN-S
DROWS-E
DROWS-Y
DRUID-S
DRUNK-S
DRUPE-L
DRUPE-S
DRUSE-S
DRYAD-S
DRYER-S
DSOBO-S
DSOMO-S
DUCAT-S
E-**DUCES**
E-**DUCTS**
DUETT-I
DUETT-O
DUETT-S
DULIA-S
DULSE-S
DUMBO-S
DUNAM-S
DUNCE-S
DUOMO-S
DUPER-S
DUPER-Y
DUPLE-T
DUPLE-X
DURAL-S
DURES-S
DUROC-S
DUROY-S
DURRA-S
DURUM-S
A-**DUSTS**
DUVET-S
DWALE-S
DWALM-S
DWANG-S
DWARF-S
DWAUM-S
DWEEB-S
DWELL-S
DWILE-S
DWINE-D
DWINE-S
DYING-S
DYNEL-S
M-**EAGER**
EAGER-S
B-**EAGLE**
T-EAGLE
EAGLE-S
EAGLE-T
M-**EAGRE**
EAGRE-S
R-**EALES**
V-EALES
B-**EANED**
D-EANED
L-EANED
M-EANED
P-EANED
S-EANED
W-EANED
Y-EANED
B-**EARDS**
H-EARDS
Y-EARDS
B-**EARED**
D-EARED
F-EARED
G-EARED
L-EARED
N-EARED
R-EARED
S-EARED
T-EARED
W-EARED
P-**EARLS**
D-**EARLY**
N-EARLY
P-EARLY
R-EARLY
Y-EARLY
D-**EARNS**
L-EARNS
Y-EARNS
P-**EARST**
D-**EARTH**
H-EARTH
EARTH-S
EARTH-Y
C-**EASED**
F-EASED
L-EASED
M-EASED
P-EASED
S-EASED
T-EASED
T-**EASEL**
W-EASEL
EASEL-S
C-**EASES**
F-EASES
L-EASES
M-EASES
P-EASES
S-EASES
T-EASES
M-**EASLE**
EASLE-S
B-**EASTS**
F-EASTS
H-EASTS
L-EASTS
R-EASTS
Y-EASTS
B-**EATEN**
N-EATEN
B-**EATER**
F-EATER
H-EATER
N-EATER
S-EATER
EATER-S
EATER-Y
M-**EATHE**
D-**EAVED**
H-EAVED
L-EAVED
R-EAVED
W-EAVED
D-**EAVES**
H-EAVES
L-EAVES
R-EAVES
W-EAVES
K-**EBBED**
N-EBBED
W-EBBED
EBBET-S
D-**ECADS**
E-**ECHED**
L-ECHED
P-ECHED
T-ECHED
E-**ECHES**
L-ECHES
ECLAT-S
O-**EDEMA**
EDEMA-S
H-**EDGED**
K-EDGED
S-EDGED
W-EDGED
H-**EDGER**
K-EDGER
L-EDGER
EDGER-S
H-**EDGES**
K-EDGES
L-EDGES
S-EDGES
W-EDGES
EDICT-S
A-**EDILE**
S-EDILE
EDILE-S
D-**EDUCE**
R-EDUCE
S-EDUCE
EDUCE-D
EDUCE-S
D-**EDUCT**
EDUCT-S
F-**EERIE**
P-EERIE
EERIE-R
EEVEN-S
J-**EFFED**
R-EFFED
L-**EGERS**
R-**EGEST**
EGEST-A
EGEST-S
B-**EGGAR**
S-EGGAR
EGGAR-S
B-**EGGED**
L-EGGED
P-EGGED
V-EGGED
L-**EGGER**
EGGER-S
EGGER-Y
R-**EGRET**
EGRET-S
D-**EIDER**
EIDER-S
H-**EIGHT**
K-EIGHT
W-EIGHT
EIGHT-H
EIGHT-S
EIGHT-Y
EIKON-S
EISEL-L
EISEL-S
D-**EJECT**
R-EJECT
EJECT-A
EJECT-S
D-**EKING**
R-EKING
ELAIN-S
ELAND-S
B-**ELATE**
D-ELATE
G-ELATE
R-ELATE
V-ELATE
ELATE-D
ELATE-R
ELATE-S
ELBOW-S
ELCHI-S
G-**ELDER**
M-ELDER
W-ELDER
ELDER-S
ELDIN-G
ELDIN-S
S-**ELECT**
ELECT-S
ELEMI-S
S-**ELFED**
ELFIN-G
ELFIN-S
ELIAD-S
R-**ELIDE**
ELIDE-D
ELIDE-S
ELINT-S
P-**ELITE**
ELITE-S
ELOGE-S
ELOIN-S
D-**ELOPE**
ELOPE-D
ELOPE-R
ELOPE-S
ELPEE-S
ELSIN-S
D-**ELUDE**
ELUDE-D
ELUDE-R
ELUDE-S
ELUTE-D
ELUTE-S
ELVAN-S
D-**ELVER**
ELVER-S
D-**ELVES**
H-ELVES
P-ELVES
S-ELVES
R-**EMAIL**
EMAIL-S
EMBAR-K
EMBAR-S
EMBAY-S
K-**EMBED**
EMBED-S
M-**EMBER**
EMBER-S
EMBOG-S
EMBOW-S
EMBUS-Y
EMCEE-D
EMCEE-S
EMEER-S
R-**EMEND**
EMEND-S
D-**EMITS**
R-EMITS
L-**EMMAS**
H-**EMMER**
EMMER-S
EMMET-S
EMMEW-S
D-**EMOTE**
G-EMOTE
R-EMOTE
EMOTE-D
EMOTE-R
EMOTE-S
R-**EMOVE**
EMOVE-D
EMOVE-S
A-**EMULE**
EMULE-D
EMULE-S
D-**EMURE**
EMURE-D
EMURE-S
EMYDE-S
ENACT-S
ENARM-S
S-**ENATE**
ENATE-S
B-**ENDED**
F-ENDED
H-ENDED
M-ENDED
P-ENDED
R-ENDED
S-ENDED
T-ENDED
V-ENDED
W-ENDED
B-**ENDER**
F-ENDER
G-ENDER
L-ENDER
M-ENDER
R-ENDER
S-ENDER
T-ENDER
V-ENDER
ENDER-S
ENDEW-S
ENDOW-S
V-**ENDUE**
ENDUE-D
ENDUE-S
ENEMA-S
R-**ENEWS**
ENIAC-S
ENJOY-S
ENMEW-S
ENNUI-S
ENOKI-S
ENROL-L
ENROL-S
ENSEW-S
ENSUE-D
ENSUE-S
C-**ENTER**
R-ENTER
T-ENTER
V-ENTER
ENTER-A
ENTER-S
K-**ENTIA**
C-**ENTRY**
G-ENTRY
S-ENTRY
T-**ENURE**
ENURE-D
ENURE-S
R-**ENVOI**
ENVOI-S
L-**ENVOY**
R-ENVOY
ENVOY-S
ENZYM-E
ENZYM-S
C-**EORLS**
EOSIN-E
EOSIN-S
EPACT-S
T-**EPEES**
EPHAH-S
EPHOD-S
EPHOR-I
EPHOR-S
EPOCH-A
EPOCH-S
EPODE-S
EPOPT-S
EPRIS-E
EPROM-S
EQUAL-S
EQUID-S
EQUIP-E
EQUIP-S
ERASE-D
ERASE-R
ERASE-S
T-**ERBIA**
ERBIA-S
ERECT-S
ERGON-S
ERGOT-S
ERICA-S
ERICK-S
C-**ERING**
D-ERING
L-ERING
M-ERING
S-ERING
ERING-O
C-**ERNED**
G-ERNED
K-ERNED
T-ERNED
C-**ERNES**
G-ERNES
K-ERNES
T-ERNES
ERODE-D
ERODE-S
R-**EROSE**
EROSE-S
S-**ERRED**
T-**ERROR**
ERROR-S
H-**ERSES**
M-ERSES
P-ERSES
V-ERSES
ERUCT-S
A-**ERUGO**
ERUGO-S
ERUPT-S
V-**ERVEN**
ERVIL-S
ESCAR-P
ESCAR-S
ESCOT-S
R-**ESILE**
ESILE-S
ESKAR-S
ESKER-S
M-**ESNES**
ESSAY-S
C-**ESSES**
D-ESSES
F-ESSES
G-ESSES
J-ESSES

L-ESSES
M-ESSES
N-ESSES
S-ESSES
Y-ESSES
F-**ESTER**
J-ESTER
N-ESTER
P-ESTER
R-ESTER
T-ESTER
W-ESTER
Y-ESTER
Z-ESTER
ESTER-S
ESTOC-S
ESTOP-S
ESTRO-S
M-**ETAGE**
ETAGE-S
R-**ETAPE**
ETAPE-S
L-**ETHAL**
ETHAL-S
A-**ETHER**
H-ETHER
N-ETHER
P-ETHER
T-ETHER
W-ETHER
ETHER-S
ETHIC-S
M-**ETHYL**
ETHYL-S
ETTIN-S
F-**ETTLE**
K-ETTLE
M-ETTLE
N-ETTLE
P-ETTLE
S-ETTLE
ETTLE-D
ETTLE-S
ETUDE-S
ETWEE-S
H-**EUGHS**
Y-**EUKED**
EUPAD-S
EUSOL-S
EVADE-D
EVADE-R
EVADE-S
E-**EVENS**
S-EVENS
EVENT-S
R-**EVERT**
EVERT-S
R-**EVERY**
S-EVERY
R-**EVETS**
EVICT-S
D-**EVILS**
K-EVILS
L-**EVITE**
EVITE-D
EVITE-S
R-**EVOKE**
EVOKE-D
EVOKE-R
EVOKE-S
H-**EWERS**
S-EWERS
F-**EWEST**
N-EWEST
H-**EXACT**

EXACT-A
EXACT-S
EXALT-S
EXCEL-S
EXEAT-S
EXEEM-S
L-**EXEME**
EXEME-D
EXEME-S
EXERT-S
D-**EXIES**
EXILE-D
EXILE-S
EXINE-S
S-**EXIST**
EXIST-S
EXODE-S
EXPAT-S
EXPEL-S
EXPOS-E
EXTOL-D
EXTOL-L
EXTOL-S
EXTRA-S
EXUDE-D
EXUDE-S
EXULT-S
EXURB-S
F-**EYING**
H-EYING
K-EYING
EYRIE-S
FABLE-D
FABLE-R
FABLE-S
FACER-S
FACET-E
FACET-S
FACIA-L
FACIA-S
FADER-S
FADGE-D
FADGE-S
FAENA-S
FAGIN-S
FAGOT-S
FAINE-D
FAINE-R
FAINE-S
FAINT-S
FAINT-Y
FAITH-S
FAKER-S
FAKER-Y
FAKIR-S
FALSE-D
FALSE-R
FALSE-S
FANAL-S
FANGA-S
FANGO-S
FANON-S
FANUM-S
FAQIR-S
FARAD-S
FARCE-D
FARCE-R
FARCE-S
FARCI-E
FARCI-N
FARER-S
FARLE-S
FARSE-D
FARSE-S
FASCI-A

FASCI-O
FATSO-S
FATWA-H
FATWA-S
FAULD-S
FAULT-S
FAULT-Y
FAUNA-E
FAUNA-L
FAUNA-S
FAUVE-S
FAVEL-A
FAVEL-L
FAVES-T
FAVOR-S
FAYNE-D
FAYNE-S
FAYRE-S
FEARE-D
FEARE-R
FEARE-S
A-**FEARS**
FEASE-D
FEASE-S
FEAST-S
FEAZE-D
FEAZE-S
FECHT-S
FEESE-D
FEESE-S
FEEZE-D
FEEZE-S
FEIGN-S
FEINT-S
FEIST-S
FEIST-Y
FELID-S
FELLA-H
FELLA-S
FELON-S
FELON-Y
FEMAL-E
FEMAL-S
FEMME-S
FEMUR-S
FENCE-D
FENCE-R
FENCE-S
FEOFF-S
FERES-T
FERIA-E
FERIA-L
FERIA-S
FERMI-S
FESSE-D
FESSE-S
FESTA-L
FESTA-S
FETOR-S
FETTA-S
FETWA-S
FEUAR-S
FEVER-S
FIBER-S
FIBRE-D
FIBRE-S
FIBRO-S
FICHE-S
FICHU-S
FICIN-S
FIDGE-D
FIDGE-S
FIDGE-T
A-**FIELD**
FIELD-S

FIEND-S
FIENT-S
FIERE-S
FIEST-A
FIFER-S
FIFTH-S
FIGHT-S
FILER-S
FILET-S
FILLE-D
FILLE-R
FILLE-S
FILLE-T
FILLO-S
FILOS-E
FILTH-S
FILTH-Y
FINAL-E
FINAL-S
FINER-S
FINER-Y
FINES-T
FINIS-H
FIORD-S
FIQUE-S
FIRER-S
FIRST-S
FIRTH-S
FITCH-E
FITCH-Y
FITTE-D
FITTE-R
FITTE-S
FIVER-S
FIXER-S
FIXIT-Y
FJELD-S
FJORD-S
FLACK-S
FLAFF-S
O-**FLAGS**
FLAIL-S
FLAIR-S
FLAKE-D
FLAKE-R
FLAKE-S
FLAKE-Y
A-**FLAME**
FLAME-D
FLAME-N
FLAME-R
FLAME-S
FLAMM-S
FLANK-S
FLARE-D
FLARE-S
FLASH-Y
FLASK-S
FLAWN-S
FLEAM-S
FLECK-S
FLECK-Y
FLEER-S
FLEET-S
FLEME-S
FLESH-Y
FLICK-S
FLIER-S
FLIES-T
FLIMP-S
FLING-S
FLINT-S
FLINT-Y
FLIRT-S
FLIRT-Y

FLISK-S
FLISK-Y
FLITE-D
FLITE-S
A-**FLOAT**
FLOAT-S
FLOAT-Y
FLOCK-S
FLOCK-Y
FLONG-S
FLOOD-S
FLOOR-S
FLORA-E
FLORA-L
FLORA-S
FLOSS-Y
FLOTA-S
FLOTE-L
FLOTE-S
FLOUR-S
FLOUR-Y
FLOUT-S
FLUFF-S
FLUFF-Y
FLUID-S
FLUKE-D
FLUKE-S
FLUKE-Y
FLUME-D
FLUME-S
FLUMP-S
FLUNK-S
FLUNK-Y
FLUOR-S
FLURR-S
FLURR-Y
FLUSH-Y
FLUTE-D
FLUTE-R
FLUTE-S
FLUTE-Y
FLUYT-S
FLYBY-S
FLYER-S
FLYPE-D
FLYPE-S
FLYTE-D
FLYTE-S
FOEHN-S
FOGEY-S
FOGIE-S
FOGLE-S
FOIST-S
FOLIA-R
FOLIE-S
FOLIO-S
FOLKS-Y
FONDA-S
FONDU-E
FONDU-S
FOOTS-Y
FORAM-S
FORAY-S
FORBY-E
FORCE-D
FORCE-R
FORCE-S
FOREL-S
FORES-T
FORGE-D
FORGE-R
FORGE-S
FORGE-T
FORGO-T
FORME-D

FORME-E
FORME-R
FORME-S
FORTE-D
FORTE-S
FORTH-Y
FORUM-S
FOSSA-E
FOSSA-S
FOSSE-D
FOSSE-S
FOUAT-S
FOUET-S
FOULE-D
FOULE-R
FOULE-S
FOUND-S
FOUNT-S
FOUTH-S
FOVEA-E
FOVEA-L
FOVEA-S
FOWTH-S
FOYER-S
FOYLE-D
FOYLE-S
FOYNE-D
FOYNE-S
FRACT-I
FRACT-S
FRAIL-S
FRAIM-S
FRAME-D
FRAME-R
FRAME-S
FRANC-O
FRANC-S
FRANK-S
FRATE-R
FRAUD-S
FREAK-S
FREAK-Y
FREER-S
FREES-T
A-**FREET**
FREET-S
FREET-Y
FREIT-S
FREIT-Y
FREMD-S
FREON-S
FRERE-S
A-**FRESH**
FRIAR-S
FRIAR-Y
FRIER-S
FRILL-S
FRILL-Y
FRISE-E
FRISE-S
FRISK-A
FRISK-S
FRISK-Y
FRIST-S
FRITH-S
A-**FRITS**
FRITT-S
FRIZE-D
FRIZE-R
FRIZE-S
FRIZZ-Y
FROCK-S
FROND-S
A-**FRONT**
FRONT-S

FRORE-N
FRORN-E
FROST-S
FROST-Y
FROTH-S
FROTH-Y
FROWN-S
FROWS-T
FROWS-Y
FROZE-N
FRUIT-S
FRUIT-Y
FRUMP-S
FRUMP-Y
FRUST-A
FRUST-S
FRYER-S
FUDGE-D
FUDGE-S
FUERO-S
FUGIE-S
FUGIO-S
FUGLE-D
FUGLE-S
FUGUE-D
FUGUE-S
FUMER-S
FUMET-S
FUNDI-C
FUNDI-E
FUNDI-S
FUNGI-C
FURAL-S
FURAN-E
FURAN-S
FUROL-E
FUROL-S
FUROR-E
FUROR-S
FURZE-S
FUSEE-S
FUSEL-S
FUSIL-E
FUSIL-S
FUTON-S
FUZEE-S
FUZIL-S
FYTTE-S
GABLE-D
GABLE-S
GABLE-T
GADDI-S
GADGE-S
GADGE-T
GADID-S
GADJE-S
GADSO-S
GAFFE-D
GAFFE-R
GAFFE-S
GAGER-S
GAINS-T
GAITT-S
GALAH-S
GALAX-Y
GALEA-E
GALEA-S
E-**GALLY**
GALOP-S
GALUT-H
GALUT-S
A-**GAMAS**
GAMAS-H
GAMAY-S
GAMBA-S

GAMBE-S
GAMBE-T
GAMBO-L
GAMBO-S
GAMER-S
GAMES-T
GAMES-Y
A-**GAMIC**
O-GAMIC
GAMIN-E
GAMIN-G
GAMIN-S
GAMMA-S
GAMME-D
GAMME-R
GAMME-S
GAMUT-S
GANEF-S
GANEV-S
GANJA-H
GANJA-S
GANOF-S
GAPER-S
I-**GAPOS**
GARBE-D
GARBE-S
GARBO-S
GARDA-I
GARRE-D
GARRE-S
GARRE-T
GARTH-S
GARUM-S
A-**GATES**
GATOR-S
GAUGE-D
GAUGE-R
GAUGE-S
GAUJE-S
GAULT-S
GAUNT-S
GAUZE-S
GAVEL-S
GAVOT-S
GAYAL-S
GAZAL-S
GAZAR-S
A-**GAZED**
GAZER-S
GAZON-S
GAZOO-N
GAZOO-S
GEARE-D
GEARE-S
GEBUR-S
GECKO-S
GEEST-S
A-**GEIST**
GEIST-S
GELEE-S
GEMEL-S
GEMMA-E
GEMMA-N
GEMOT-E
GEMOT-S
A-**GENES**
GENET-S
GENIE-S
GENIP-S
GENOA-S
GENOM-E
GENOM-S
GENRE-S
GENRO-S
A-**GENTS**
GEODE-S
GEOID-S
GERAH-S
GERBE-S
GERLE-S
GERNE-D
GERNE-S
GESSE-D
GESSE-S
GESTE-S
E-**GESTS**
GETUP-S
A-**GHAST**
GHAST-S
GHAUT-S
GHAZI-S
GHOST-S
GHOST-Y
GHOUL-S
GHYLL-S
GIANT-S
GIBEL-S
GIBER-S
GIGOT-S
GIGUE-S
A-**GILAS**
GILET-S
GIMEL-S
GIMME-R
GIMME-S
A-**GINGS**
GIPON-S
GIPPO-S
GIRON-S
GIRTH-S
GISMO-S
A-**GISMS**
A-**GISTS**
GIUST-O
GIUST-S
GIVEN-S
GIVER-S
O-**GIVES**
GIZMO-S
GLACE-S
GLADE-S
GLAIK-S
GLAIR-E
GLAIR-S
GLAIR-Y
GLAND-S
A-**GLARE**
GLARE-D
GLARE-S
GLASS-Y
GLAUM-S
GLAUR-S
GLAUR-Y
GLAZE-D
GLAZE-N
GLAZE-R
GLAZE-S
A-**GLEAM**
GLEAM-S
GLEAM-Y
GLEAN-S
GLEBA-E
GLEBE-S
GLEDE-S
GLEED-S
GLEEK-S
GLEET-S
GLEET-Y
GLENT-S
GLIDE-D
GLIDE-R
GLIDE-S
GLIFF-S
GLIFT-S
GLIKE-S
GLIME-D
GLIME-S
GLINT-S
GLISK-S
GLITZ-Y
GLOAM-S
GLOAT-S
GLOBE-D
GLOBE-S
GLOGG-S
GLOOM-S
GLOOM-Y
GLOOP-S
GLOOP-Y
GLOSS-A
GLOSS-Y
GLOST-S
GLOUT-S
GLOVE-D
GLOVE-R
GLOVE-S
GLOZE-D
GLOZE-S
GLUER-S
GLUME-S
GLUON-S
GLYPH-S
GNARL-S
GNARL-Y
GNARR-S
GNOME-S
GOBAN-G
GOBAN-S
GODET-S
GODSO-N
GODSO-S
GOFER-S
A-**GOING**
GOING-S
GOLEM-S
GOLPE-S
GOMBO-S
GOMPA-S
GONAD-S
GONEF-S
GONER-S
GONIF-F
GONIF-S
GONOF-S
GOOLD-S
GOOSE-D
GOOSE-S
GOOSE-Y
GOPAK-S
GORAL-S
GORGE-D
GORGE-R
GORGE-S
GORGE-T
GORSE-S
GOSHT-S
GOSSE-S
GOUGE-D
GOUGE-R
GOUGE-S
GOURA-S
GOURD-E
GOURD-S
GOURD-Y
A-**GOUTY**
GOWAN-S
GOWAN-Y
GRAAL-S
GRACE-D
GRACE-S
GRADE-D
GRADE-R
GRADE-S
GRAFF-S
GRAFT-S
GRAIL-E
GRAIL-S
GRAIN-E
GRAIN-S
GRAIN-Y
GRAIP-S
GRAMA-S
GRAME-S
GRAMP-S
GRAND-E
GRAND-S
GRANT-S
GRAPE-D
GRAPE-S
GRAPE-Y
GRAPH-S
GRASP-S
GRASS-Y
GRATE-D
GRATE-R
GRATE-S
GRAVE-D
GRAVE-L
GRAVE-N
GRAVE-R
GRAVE-S
GRAZE-D
GRAZE-R
GRAZE-S
GREAT-S
GREBE-S
GRECE-S
A-**GREED**
GREED-S
GREED-Y
GREEN-S
GREEN-Y
A-**GREES**
GREES-E
GREET-E
GREET-S
A-**GREGE**
GREGO-S
GREIN-S
GRESE-S
GREVE-S
GRICE-R
GRICE-S
GRIDE-D
GRIDE-S
GRIEF-S
GRIFF-E
GRIFF-S
GRIFT-S
GRIKE-S
GRILL-E
GRILL-S
GRIME-D
GRIME-S
GRIND-S
GRIOT-S
GRIPE-D
GRIPE-R
GRIPE-S
GRIPE-Y
A-**GRISE**
GRISE-D
GRISE-S
GRIST-S
GRITH-S
A-**GRIZE**
GRIZE-S
GROAN-S
GROAT-S
GROIN-S
GROMA-S
GRONE-D
GRONE-S
GROOF-S
GROOM-S
GROPE-D
GROPE-R
GROPE-S
GROSZ-E
GROSZ-Y
GROUF-S
GROUP-S
GROUP-Y
GROUT-S
GROUT-Y
GROVE-D
GROVE-L
GROVE-S
GROVE-T
GROWL-S
GROWL-Y
GRUEL-S
GRUFE-S
GRUFF-S
GRUFF-Y
GRUME-S
GRUMP-H
GRUMP-S
GRUMP-Y
GRUNT-S
GRYCE-S
GRYDE-D
GRYDE-S
GRYKE-S
GRYPE-S
GUACO-S
I-**GUANA**
GUANA-S
GUANA-Y
GUANO-S
GUARD-S
GUAVA-S
GUEST-S
GUIDE-D
GUIDE-R
GUIDE-S
GUILD-S
GUILE-D
GUILE-R
GUILE-S
GUILT-S
GUILT-Y
GUIMP-E
GUIMP-S
GUIRO-S
A-**GUISE**
GUISE-D
GUISE-R
GUISE-S
GULAG-S
GULPH-S
GUMBO-S
GUMMA-S
GUNGE-S
GURGE-D
GURGE-S
GUSLA-R
GUSLA-S
GUSLE-S
GUSLI-S
GUSTO-S
GUTTA-E
GUTTA-S
GUYLE-D
GUYLE-R
GUYLE-S
GUYOT-S
GUYSE-S
GYELD-S
GYNAE-S
GYNIE-S
GYPPO-S
GYRON-S
GYROS-E
HABIT-S
HACEK-S
C-**HACKS**
S-HACKS
T-HACKS
W-HACKS
S-**HADED**
S-**HADES**
HADJI-S
C-**HAFFS**
C-**HAFTS**
S-HAFTS
HAICK-S
HAIKA-I
C-**HAINS**
C-**HAIRS**
HAIRS-T
HAJJI-S
HAKAM-S
S-**HAKES**
HAKIM-S
HALAL-A
HALAL-S
S-**HALED**
W-HALED
T-**HALER**
W-HALER
HALER-S
HALER-U
S-**HALES**
W-HALES
HALES-T
HALFA-S
HALID-E
HALID-S
HALLO-A
HALLO-O
HALLO-S
HALLO-T
HALLO-W
HALMA-S
S-**HALMS**
HALON-S
HALSE-D
HALSE-R
HALSE-S
HALVA-H
HALVA-S
HALVE-D
HALVE-R
HALVE-S
HAMAL-S
S-**HAMED**
S-**HAMES**
C-**HAMMY**
S-HAMMY
W-HAMMY
HAMZA-H
HAMZA-S
HANAP-S
C-**HANCE**
HANCE-S
S-**HANDS**
S-**HANDY**
B-**HANGS**
C-HANGS
P-HANGS
W-HANGS
C-**HANKS**
S-HANKS
T-HANKS
HANSA-S
HANSE-L
HANSE-S
C-**HANTS**
HAOLE-S
HAOMA-S
C-**HAPPY**
HARAM-S
C-**HARDS**
S-HARDS
C-**HARED**
S-HARED
HAREM-S
C-**HARES**
P-HARES
S-HARES
W-HARES
HARIM-S
C-**HARKS**
S-HARKS
C-**HARMS**
T-HARMS
S-**HARNS**
P-**HAROS**
S-**HARPS**
S-**HARPY**
C-**HARRY**
G-HARRY
C-**HARTS**
C-**HASTE**
HASTE-D
HASTE-N
HASTE-S
T-**HATCH**
HATER-S
S-**HAUGH**
HAUGH-S
HAUGH-T
HAULD-S
HAULM-S
HAULM-Y
S-**HAULS**
HAULS-T
C-**HAUNT**
HAUNT-S
HAUSE-D
HAUSE-N
HAUSE-S
S-**HAVEN**
HAVEN-S
S-**HAVER**
HAVER-S
S-**HAVES**
HAVOC-S
C-**HAWED**
S-HAWED
T-HAWED
S-**HAWMS**
HAWSE-D
HAWSE-R

HAWSE-S
HAYER-S
HAYLE-S
C-**HAZAN**
HAZAN-S
G-**HAZEL**
HAZEL-S
HAZER-S
HEALD-S
S-**HEALS**
W-HEALS
C-**HEAPS**
C-**HEAPY**
HEARD-S
W-**HEARE**
HEARE-R
HEARE-S
S-**HEARS**
HEARS-E
HEARS-Y
HEART-H
HEART-S
HEART-Y
HEAST-E
HEAST-S
S-**HEATH**
HEATH-S
HEATH-Y
C-**HEATS**
W-HEATS
S-**HEAVE**
T-HEAVE
HEAVE-D
HEAVE-N
HEAVE-R
HEAVE-S
HEBEN-S
HECHT-S
C-**HECKS**
C-**HEDER**
HEDER-S
HEDGE-D
HEDGE-R
HEDGE-S
S-**HEELS**
W-HEELS
P-**HEEZE**
W-HEEZE
HEEZE-D
HEEZE-S
HEFTE-D
HEFTE-R
T-**HEFTS**
W-HEFTS
HEIGH-T
T-**HEIRS**
T-**HEIST**
HEIST-S
HEJAB-S
HEJRA-S
HELIO-S
HELLO-S
S-**HELLS**
W-**HELMS**
HELOT-S
W-**HELPS**
S-**HELVE**
HELVE-D
HELVE-S
T-**HEMES**
C-**HEMIC**
HEMIN-A
HEMIN-S
T-**HENCE**
W-HENCE
S-**HENDS**
HENGE-S
HENNA-S
HENRY-S
HEPAR-S
S-**HERDS**
T-**HERES**
W-HERES
HERES-Y
HERMA-E
HERMA-I
T-**HERMS**
HEROE-S
HERON-S
C-**HERRY**
S-HERRY
W-HERRY
HERSE-D
HERSE-S
HERYE-D
HERYE-S
C-**HESTS**
T-**HETES**
C-**HETHS**
K-HETHS
S-**HEUCH**
HEUCH-S
S-**HEUGH**
W-HEUGH
HEUGH-S
HEVEA-S
C-**HEWED**
S-HEWED
T-HEWED
W-HEWED
C-**HEWER**
S-HEWER
HEWER-S
HEXAD-E
HEXAD-S
HEXER-S
R-**HEXES**
HEXYL-S
C-**HICKS**
T-HICKS
C-**HIDED**
C-**HIDER**
HIDER-S
C-**HIDES**
T-**HIGHS**
HIGHT-H
HIGHT-S
HIJAB-S
HIJRA-H
HIJRA-S
HIKER-S
HILLO-A
HILLO-S
C-**HILLS**
S-HILLS
T-HILLS
C-**HILLY**
W-HILLY
HIMBO-S
W-**HINGE**
HINGE-D
HINGE-R
HINGE-S
T-**HINGS**
S-**HINNY**
W-HINNY
C-**HINTS**
S-**HIPPO**
HIPPO-S
C-**HIPPY**
W-HIPPY
HIRER-S
S-**HIRES**
S-**HISTS**
W-HISTS
HITCH-Y
HITHE-R
HITHE-S
C-**HIVED**
S-**HIVER**
HIVER-S
C-**HIVES**
S-HIVES
HIZEN-S
HOARD-S
HOARS-E
HOAST-S
C-**HOCKS**
S-HOCKS
HODAD-S
K-**HODJA**
HODJA-S
S-**HOERS**
HOGAN-S
HOGEN-S
HOICK-S
HOISE-D
HOISE-S
HOIST-S
C-**HOKED**
C-**HOKES**
C-**HOKEY**
HOKUM-S
A-**HOLDS**
T-**HOLED**
D-**HOLES**
T-HOLES
W-HOLES
C-**HOLLA**
HOLLA-S
HOLLO-A
HOLLO-O
HOLLO-S
HOLLO-W
W-**HOLLY**
HOMER-S
HOMME-S
Z-**HOMOS**
HONAN-S
HONDA-S
P-**HONED**
P-**HONER**
HONER-S
P-**HONES**
R-HONES
HONES-T
P-**HONEY**
HONEY-S
HONGI-S
T-**HONGS**
S-**HONKY**
HONOR-S
P-**HOOEY**
HOOEY-S
C-**HOOFS**
W-HOOFS
HOOKA-H
HOOKA-S
C-**HOOKS**
S-HOOKS
D-**HOOLY**
W-**HOOPS**
HOORD-S
W-**HOOSH**
B-**HOOTS**
S-HOOTS
W-HOOTS
HOOVE-D
HOOVE-N
HOOVE-R
HOOVE-S
HOPER-S
C-**HOPPY**
S-HOPPY
HORAH-S
C-**HORAL**
HORDE-D
HORDE-S
HORME-S
T-**HORNS**
T-**HORNY**
A-**HORSE**
HORSE-D
HORSE-S
HORSE-Y
HORST-E
HORST-S
HOSEL-S
C-**HOSEN**
C-**HOSES**
HOSTA-S
G-**HOSTS**
HOTEL-S
HOUFF-S
C-**HOUGH**
S-HOUGH
T-HOUGH
HOUGH-S
HOUND-S
HOURI-S
C-**HOUSE**
HOUSE-D
HOUSE-L
HOUSE-R
HOUSE-S
HOUSE-Y
C-**HOUTS**
S-HOUTS
S-**HOVED**
S-**HOVEL**
HOVEL-S
S-**HOVER**
HOVER-S
S-**HOVES**
HOWFF-S
T-**HOWLS**
HOWRE-S
HOYLE-S
C-**HUBBY**
C-**HUCKS**
S-HUCKS
C-**HUFFS**
C-**HUFFY**
S-**HULES**
HULLO-A
HULLO-S
HUMAN-E
HUMAN-S
HUMOR-S
HUMPH-S
C-**HUMPS**
T-HUMPS
W-HUMPS
HUMUS-Y
C-**HUNKS**
T-HUNKS
C-**HUNKY**
S-**HUNTS**
C-**HURLS**
T-HURLS
D-**HURRA**
HURRA-H
HURRA-S
HURRA-Y
HURST-S
HUTIA-S
HUZZA-H
HUZZA-S
HYDRA-E
HYDRA-S
HYDRO-S
HYENA-S
S-**HYING**
HYLEG-S
C-**HYLES**
P-**HYLIC**
HYMEN-S
HYNDE-S
HYOID-S
HYPER-S
HYPHA-E
HYPHA-L
HYSON-S
HYTHE-S
IAMBI-C
D-**ICERS**
R-ICERS
M-**ICHED**
N-ICHED
R-ICHED
F-**ICHES**
L-ICHES
M-ICHES
N-ICHES
R-ICHES
T-ICHES
W-ICHES
ICHOR-S
D-**ICIER**
R-ICIER
D-**ICING**
R-ICING
T-ICING
V-ICING
ICING-S
B-**ICKER**
D-ICKER
K-ICKER
L-ICKER
N-ICKER
P-ICKER
R-ICKER
S-ICKER
T-ICKER
W-ICKER
Y-ICKER
ICKER-S
R-**ICTAL**
R-**ICTUS**
A-**IDANT**
IDANT-S
IDEAL-S
IDIOM-S
IDIOT-S
S-**IDLED**
S-**IDLER**
IDLER-S
S-**IDLES**
IDLES-T
E-**IDOLA**
IDYLL-S
IGAPO-S
IGLOO-S
IHRAM-S
E-**IKONS**
P-**ILEUM**
P-**ILEUS**
ILIAD-S
F-**ILIAL**
C-**ILIUM**
M-ILIUM
B-**ILLER**
F-ILLER
G-ILLER
H-ILLER
K-ILLER
M-ILLER
S-ILLER
T-ILLER
W-ILLER
ILLTH-S
IMAGE-D
IMAGE-R
IMAGE-S
IMAGO-S
IMARI-S
IMAUM-S
M-**IMBAR**
IMBAR-K
IMBAR-S
L-**IMBED**
N-IMBED
IMBED-S
IMBUE-D
IMBUE-S
IMIDE-S
IMINE-S
IMMEW-S
IMMIT-S
G-**IMPED**
L-IMPED
P-IMPED
IMPED-E
IMPEL-S
IMPIS-H
D-**IMPLY**
J-IMPLY
L-IMPLY
P-IMPLY
S-IMPLY
IMPOT-S
INANE-R
INANE-S
INARM-S
INCLE-S
INCOG-S
INCUR-S
INCUS-E
INDEW-S
INDIE-S
INDOL-E
INDOL-S
W-**INDOW**
INDOW-S
INDRI-S
INDUE-D
INDUE-S
INERT-S
INFER-E
INFER-S
F-**INGAN**
INGAN-S
B-**INGLE**
D-INGLE
G-INGLE
J-INGLE
K-INGLE
L-INGLE
M-INGLE
P-INGLE
S-INGLE
T-INGLE
INGLE-S
L-**INGOT**
INGOT-S
M-**INION**
P-INION
D-**INKED**
F-INKED
J-INKED
K-INKED
L-INKED
O-INKED
P-INKED
R-INKED
T-INKED
W-INKED
Z-INKED
D-**INKER**
J-INKER
L-INKER
P-INKER
S-INKER
T-INKER
W-INKER
INKER-S
K-**INKLE**
T-INKLE
W-INKLE
INKLE-D
INKLE-S
INLAY-S
INLET-S
B-**INNED**
D-INNED
F-INNED
G-INNED
L-INNED
P-INNED
S-INNED
T-INNED
W-INNED
D-**INNER**
F-INNER
G-INNER
P-INNER
S-INNER
T-INNER
W-INNER
INNER-S
INORB-S
INPUT-S
INSET-S
H-**INTER**
L-INTER
M-INTER
S-INTER
T-INTER
W-INTER
INTER-N
INTER-S
INTRO-N
INTRO-S
INULA-S
INURE-D
INURE-S
INURN-S
INVAR-S
INWIT-H
INWIT-S
IODID-E
IODID-S
IODIN-E
IODIN-S
B-**IONIC**

P-IONIC
IONIC-S
B-**IOTAS**
D-IOTAS
IPPON-S
T-**IRADE**
IRADE-S
P-**IRATE**
IRATE-R
A-**IRING**
F-IRING
H-IRING
M-IRING
S-IRING
T-IRING
V-IRING
W-IRING
D-**IRKED**
F-IRKED
K-IRKED
L-IRKED
Y-IRKED
IROKO-S
IRONE-D
IRONE-R
IRONE-S
G-**IRONS**
B-**ISHES**
D-ISHES
F-ISHES
H-ISHES
K-ISHES
P-ISHES
W-ISHES
A-**ISLED**
M-ISLED
A-**ISLES**
L-ISLES
ISLET-S
ISSEI-S
T-**ISSUE**
ISSUE-D
ISSUE-R
ISSUE-S
M-**ISTLE**
ISTLE-S
B-**ITCHY**
F-ITCHY
H-ITCHY
P-ITCHY
T-ITCHY
W-ITCHY
C-**ITHER**
D-ITHER
E-ITHER
H-ITHER
L-ITHER
M-ITHER
T-ITHER
W-ITHER
Z-ITHER
C-**IVIES**
IXORA-S
IXTLE-S
L-**IZARD**
R-IZARD
V-IZARD
W-IZARD
IZARD-S
S-**IZARS**
IZZAT-S
JABOT-S
JACAL-S
JACKS-Y
JAGER-S

JAGIR-S
JAGRA-S
JALAP-S
JALOP-S
JALOP-Y
JAMBE-D
JAMBE-E
JAMBE-R
JAMBE-S
JAMBO-K
JAMBO-S
JAMBU-L
JAMBU-S
JAPAN-S
JAPER-S
JAPER-Y
JARTA-S
JARUL-S
JASEY-S
JASPE-R
JASPE-S
JAUNT-S
JAUNT-Y
JAVEL-S
JAWAN-S
D-**JEBEL**
JEBEL-S
JEHAD-S
JELAB-S
JELLO-S
JERID-S
JESSE-D
JESSE-S
JETON-S
JEWEL-S
JHALA-S
JIBER-S
JIGOT-S
JIHAD-S
D-**JINNI**
D-**JINNS**
JIRGA-S
JIVER-S
JNANA-S
JOCKO-S
JODEL-S
JOINT-S
JOIST-S
JOKER-S
JORAM-S
JORUM-S
JOTUN-N
JOTUN-S
JOUAL-S
JOULE-D
JOULE-S
JOUST-S
JOWAR-I
JOWAR-S
JUDGE-D
JUDGE-R
JUDGE-S
JUGAL-S
JUGUM-S
JUICE-D
JUICE-R
JUICE-S
JULEP-S
JUMAR-S
JUMAR-T
JUMBO-S
JUNCO-S
JUNTA-S
JUNTO-S
JUPON-S

JURAT-S
JUREL-S
JUROR-S
KAAMA-S
KABAB-S
KABAR-S
KABOB-S
KAFIR-S
KAHAL-S
KAIAK-S
S-**KAILS**
KALAM-S
KALIF-S
KALPA-K
KALPA-S
KAMIK-S
KANEH-S
KANGA-S
KANJI-S
KANZU-S
KAPOK-S
KAPPA-S
KAPUT-T
KARAT-E
KARAT-S
KARMA-S
KAROO-S
KARRI-S
KARST-S
S-**KARTS**
KASHA-S
KATTI-S
KAUGH-S
KAURI-S
KAVAS-S
KAYAK-S
KAYLE-S
KAZOO-S
KEBAB-S
KEBAR-S
KEBOB-S
KECKS-Y
KEDGE-D
KEDGE-R
KEDGE-S
S-**KEENS**
S-**KEETS**
KEEVE-S
KEFIR-S
KELEP-S
KELIM-S
S-**KELLS**
S-**KELLY**
S-**KELPS**
KEMBO-S
KENAF-S
KENDO-S
KERNE-D
KERNE-L
KERNE-S
S-**KERRY**
KERVE-D
KERVE-S
KESAR-S
S-**KETCH**
KETOL-S
KEVEL-S
KEVIL-S
KHADI-S
KHAKI-S
KHAPH-S
KHAYA-S
KHEDA-H
KHEDA-S
KHETH-S

KHOJA-S
KHOUM-S
KIANG-S
KIBBE-H
KIBBE-S
KIBBI-S
KIBEI-S
KIBLA-H
KIBLA-S
KIDDO-S
S-**KIDDY**
KIDEL-S
S-**KIERS**
KIEVE-S
KIGHT-S
KIKOI-S
KILEY-S
KILIM-S
S-**KILLS**
A-**KIMBO**
KIMBO-S
KINAS-E
KININ-S
S-**KINKS**
KIOSK-S
KIPPA-S
KIRRI-S
KISAN-S
S-**KITED**
KITER-S
S-**KITES**
KITHE-D
KITHE-S
KLANG-S
KLONG-S
KLOOF-S
KLUGE-S
KLUTZ-Y
KNACK-S
KNACK-Y
KNARL-S
KNAUR-S
KNAVE-S
KNEAD-S
KNEEL-S
KNELL-S
KNIFE-D
KNIFE-R
KNIFE-S
KNIVE-D
KNIVE-S
KNOCK-S
KNOLL-S
KNOLL-Y
KNOSP-S
KNOUT-S
KNOWE-R
KNOWE-S
KNOWN-S
KNURL-S
KNURL-Y
KNURR-S
KOALA-S
KOBAN-G
KOBAN-S
S-**KOFFS**
KOFTA-S
KOINE-S
KOKER-S
KOKRA-S
KOKUM-S
KOMBU-S
KOORI-S
KOPEK-S
KOPJE-S

KOPPA-S
KORAT-S
KORMA-S
KORUN-A
KORUN-Y
KOTOW-S
KRAAL-S
KRAFT-S
KRAIT-S
KRANG-S
S-**KRANS**
KRAUT-S
KREEP-S
KRENG-S
KRILL-S
KRONE-N
KRONE-R
KROON-I
KROON-S
KRUBI-S
KUDZU-S
KUGEL-S
KUKRI-S
KULAK-I
KULAK-S
KULAN-S
KURRE-S
KURTA-S
KUSSO-S
KUTCH-A
KWELA-S
KYACK-S
KYANG-S
KYLIE-S
KYLIN-S
KYLOE-S
KYNDE-D
KYNDE-S
KYRIE-S
S-**KYTES**
KYTHE-D
KYTHE-S
LABDA-S
LABEL-S
LABIA-L
LABOR-S
P-**LACED**
P-**LACER**
LACER-S
G-**LACES**
P-LACES
P-**LACET**
LACET-S
B-**LACKS**
C-LACKS
F-LACKS
P-LACKS
S-LACKS
B-**LADED**
LADEN-S
LADER-S
B-**LADES**
C-LADES
G-LADES
S-LADES
LADLE-D
LADLE-R
LADLE-S
LAGAN-S
LAGER-S
LAHAR-S
LAICH-S
P-**LAIDS**
LAIGH-S
LAIKA-S

G-**LAIKS**
LAIRD-S
F-**LAIRS**
G-LAIRS
G-**LAIRY**
F-**LAKED**
S-LAKED
F-**LAKER**
S-LAKER
LAKER-S
F-**LAKES**
S-LAKES
LAKIN-G
LAKIN-S
L-**LAMAS**
U-LAMAS
B-**LAMED**
F-LAMED
LAMED-H
LAMED-S
B-**LAMER**
F-LAMER
B-**LAMES**
C-LAMES
F-LAMES
LAMES-T
LAMIA-E
LAMIA-S
C-**LAMMY**
C-**LAMPS**
LANAI-S
E-**LANCE**
G-LANCE
LANCE-D
LANCE-R
LANCE-S
LANCE-T
B-**LANCH**
F-LANCH
P-LANCH
LANDE-D
LANDE-R
LANDE-S
A-**LANDS**
B-LANDS
E-LANDS
G-LANDS
F-**LANES**
P-LANES
S-LANES
B-**LANKS**
C-LANKS
F-LANKS
P-LANKS
B-**LANKY**
A-**LANTS**
P-LANTS
S-LANTS
LAPEL-S
LAPIN-S
LAPJE-S
E-**LAPSE**
LAPSE-D
LAPSE-R
LAPSE-S
LAREE-S
B-**LARES**
F-LARES
G-LARES
LARGE-N
LARGE-R
LARGE-S
LARGO-S
A-**LARUM**
LARUM-S

LARVA-E
LARVA-L
LARVA-S
F-**LASER**
LASER-S
LASSI-E
LASSI-S
LASSO-S
LASSU-S
B-**LASTS**
C-LASTS
C-**LATCH**
K-LATCH
S-LATCH
A-**LATED**
E-LATED
P-LATED
S-LATED
P-**LATEN**
LATEN-S
LATEN-T
B-**LATER**
E-LATER
P-LATER
S-LATER
LATHE-D
LATHE-E
LATHE-N
LATHE-R
LATHE-S
LATHI-S
LATKE-S
LATTE-N
LATTE-R
LATTE-S
LAUAN-S
LAUCH-S
B-**LAUDS**
LAUGH-S
LAUGH-Y
LAUND-S
LAURA-E
LAURA-S
S-**LAVED**
C-**LAVER**
S-LAVER
LAVER-S
C-**LAVES**
S-LAVES
LAVRA-S
B-**LAWED**
C-LAWED
F-LAWED
C-**LAWER**
LAWIN-E
LAWIN-G
LAWIN-S
F-**LAWNS**
F-**LAXES**
LAXES-T
A-**LAYED**
C-LAYED
F-LAYED
P-LAYED
S-LAYED
F-**LAYER**
P-LAYER
S-LAYER
LAYER-S
LAYUP-S
LAZAR-S
B-**LAZED**
G-LAZED
B-**LAZES**
G-LAZES

B-**LEACH**
P-LEACH
LEACH-Y
P-**LEADS**
B-**LEAKS**
B-**LEAKY**
F-**LEAMS**
G-LEAMS
C-**LEANS**
G-LEANS
LEARE-D
LEARE-S
LEARN-S
LEARN-T
B-**LEARS**
C-LEARS
B-**LEARY**
P-**LEASE**
LEASE-D
LEASE-R
LEASE-S
LEAST-S
B-**LEATS**
C-LEATS
P-LEATS
C-**LEAVE**
G-LEAVE
S-LEAVE
LEAVE-D
LEAVE-N
LEAVE-R
LEAVE-S
S-**LEAZE**
LEAZE-S
LEBEN-S
F-**LEDGE**
G-LEDGE
P-LEDGE
S-LEDGE
LEDGE-R
LEDGE-S
F-**LEDGY**
LEDUM-S
LEEAR-S
F-**LEECH**
S-LEECH
C-**LEEKS**
G-LEEKS
S-LEEKS
B-**LEEPS**
C-LEEPS
S-LEEPS
F-**LEERS**
LEESE-S
F-**LEETS**
G-LEETS
S-LEETS
LEFTE-R
C-**LEFTS**
LEGAL-S
LEGER-S
A-**LEGGE**
LEGGE-D
LEGGE-R
LEGGE-S
E-**LEGIT**
LEGIT-S
LEHUA-S
LEMAN-S
LEMEL-S
F-**LEMES**
LEMMA-S
LEMON-S
LEMON-Y
LEMUR-S

B-**LENDS**
F-**LENSE**
LENSE-D
LENSE-S
LENTI-C
LENTI-L
LENTO-R
LENTO-S
LEONE-S
LEPER-S
LEPRA-S
LESBO-S
F-**LETCH**
LETHE-E
LETHE-S
LETUP-S
C-**LEUCH**
P-LEUCH
C-**LEUGH**
P-LEUGH
LEVEE-D
LEVEE-S
LEVEL-S
C-**LEVER**
LEVER-S
A-**LEVIN**
LEVIN-S
C-**LEVIS**
F-**LEXES**
I-LEXES
U-LEXES
LIANA-S
LIANE-S
LIANG-S
LIARD-S
LIBEL-S
LIBER-O
LIBER-S
LIBRA-E
LIBRA-S
LICHI-S
LICHT-S
E-**LICIT**
C-**LICKS**
F-LICKS
S-LICKS
LIDAR-S
LIEGE-R
LIEGE-S
A-**LIENS**
F-**LIERS**
P-LIERS
LIEVE-R
LIFER-S
C-**LIFTS**
G-LIFTS
LIGAN-D
LIGAN-S
LIGER-S
LIGGE-D
LIGGE-N
LIGGE-R
LIGGE-S
A-**LIGHT**
B-LIGHT
F-LIGHT
P-LIGHT
S-LIGHT
LIGHT-S
LIGNE-S
LIKEN-S
LIKER-S
G-**LIKES**
LIKES-T
LIKIN-G

LIKIN-S
LILAC-S
LIMAN-S
C-**LIMAX**
LIMBA-S
LIMBI-C
LIMBO-S
C-**LIMBS**
G-**LIMED**
S-LIMED
LIMEN-S
C-**LIMES**
G-LIMES
S-LIMES
B-**LIMEY**
LIMEY-S
LIMIT-S
LIMMA-S
LIMPA-S
B-**LIMPS**
F-LIMPS
LIMPS-Y
LINAC-S
C-**LINCH**
F-LINCH
B-**LINDS**
A-**LINED**
LINEN-S
LINEN-Y
A-**LINER**
LINER-S
A-**LINES**
C-LINES
LINGA-M
LINGA-S
LINGO-T
C-**LINGS**
F-LINGS
P-LINGS
S-LINGS
C-**LINGY**
LININ-G
LININ-S
B-**LINKS**
C-LINKS
P-LINKS
S-LINKS
S-**LINKY**
C-**LINTS**
E-LINTS
F-LINTS
G-LINTS
F-**LINTY**
LINUM-S
LIPID-E
LIPID-S
LIPIN-S
F-**LIPPY**
S-LIPPY
LIROT-H
F-**LISKS**
G-LISKS
LISLE-S
F-**LITED**
LITER-S
B-**LITES**
E-LITES
F-LITES
B-**LITHE**
LITHE-D
LITHE-R
LITHE-S
LITHO-S
LITRE-S
S-**LIVED**

S-**LIVEN**
LIVEN-S
O-**LIVER**
S-LIVER
LIVER-S
LIVER-Y
O-**LIVES**
S-LIVES
LIVES-T
LIVOR-S
LIVRE-S
LLAMA-S
LLANO-S
C-**LOAMS**
G-LOAMS
S-**LOANS**
LOATH-E
LOATH-Y
LOAVE-D
LOAVE-S
G-**LOBBY**
S-LOBBY
G-**LOBED**
G-**LOBES**
LOBOS-E
LOCAL-E
LOCAL-S
B-**LOCKS**
C-LOCKS
F-LOCKS
LOCUM-S
LOCUS-T
LODEN-S
LODGE-D
LODGE-R
LODGE-S
S-**LOGAN**
LOGAN-S
E-**LOGES**
C-**LOGGY**
A-**LOGIA**
LOGIC-S
LOGIE-R
LOGIE-S
LOGIN-S
LOGON-S
S-**LOIDS**
A-**LOINS**
E-LOINS
LOIPE-N
B-**LOKES**
C-LOKES
LOLOG-S
C-**LONER**
LONER-S
LONGA-N
LONGA-S
P-**LONGE**
LONGE-D
LONGE-R
LONGE-S
F-**LONGS**
K-LONGS
P-LONGS
B-**LOOEY**
F-LOOEY
LOOEY-S
LOOFA-H
LOOFA-S
K-**LOOFS**
B-**LOOIE**
F-LOOIE
LOOIE-S
P-**LOOKS**
B-**LOOMS**

G-LOOMS
S-LOOMS
B-**LOOPS**
C-LOOPS
G-LOOPS
S-LOOPS
G-**LOOPY**
LOORD-S
LOOSE-D
LOOSE-N
LOOSE-R
LOOSE-S
C-**LOOTS**
S-LOOTS
E-**LOPED**
S-LOPED
E-**LOPER**
S-LOPER
LOPER-S
E-**LOPES**
S-LOPES
F-**LOPPY**
G-LOPPY
S-LOPPY
F-**LORAL**
LORAN-S
LOREL-S
B-**LORES**
LORIC-A
LORIC-S
C-**LOSED**
LOSEL-S
C-**LOSER**
LOSER-S
C-**LOSES**
U-LOSES
F-**LOSSY**
G-LOSSY
LOTAH-S
F-**LOTAS**
C-**LOTES**
F-LOTES
LOTTE-D
LOTTE-S
B-**LOTTO**
LOTTO-S
C-**LOUGH**
P-LOUGH
S-LOUGH
LOUGH-S
LOUIE-S
LOUND-S
LOUPE-D
LOUPE-N
LOUPE-S
LOURE-D
LOURE-S
C-**LOURS**
F-LOURS
F-**LOURY**
B-**LOUSE**
F-LOUSE
LOUSE-D
LOUSE-S
B-**LOUSY**
C-**LOUTS**
F-LOUTS
G-LOUTS
LOVAT-S
G-**LOVED**
C-**LOVER**
G-LOVER
P-LOVER
LOVER-S
C-**LOVES**

G-LOVES
LOVEY-S
LOWAN-S
B-**LOWED**
F-LOWED
G-LOWED
P-LOWED
S-LOWED
B-**LOWER**
F-LOWER
G-LOWER
P-LOWER
S-LOWER
LOWER-S
LOWER-Y
LOWES-T
S-**LOWLY**
LOWND-S
LOWNE-D
LOWNE-S
C-**LOWNS**
B-**LOWSE**
LOWSE-R
LOWSE-S
LOZEN-S
LUBRA-S
C-**LUCKS**
P-LUCKS
C-**LUCKY**
P-LUCKY
LUCRE-S
B-**LUDES**
E-LUDES
LUFFA-S
B-**LUFFS**
F-LUFFS
P-LUFFS
S-LUFFS
LUGER-S
K-**LUGES**
LUMEN-S
P-**LUMMY**
S-LUMMY
C-**LUMPS**
F-LUMPS
G-LUMPS
P-LUMPS
S-LUMPS
C-**LUMPY**
G-LUMPY
P-LUMPY
S-LUMPY
LUNAR-S
LUNAR-Y
C-**LUNCH**
G-LUNCH
LUNET-S
B-**LUNGE**
P-LUNGE
LUNGE-D
LUNGE-E
LUNGE-R
LUNGE-S
LUNGI-E
LUNGI-S
B-**LUNKS**
C-LUNKS
F-LUNKS
P-LUNKS
B-**LUNTS**
LUPIN-E
LUPIN-S
LURER-S
A-**LURES**
LURGI-S

B-**LURRY**
F-LURRY
S-LURRY
LURVE-S
F-**LUSHY**
P-LUSHY
S-LUSHY
LUTEA-L
E-**LUTED**
F-LUTED
F-**LUTER**
LUTER-S
E-**LUTES**
F-LUTES
F-**LUXES**
LYASE-S
LYCEE-S
C-**LYING**
F-LYING
P-LYING
LYING-S
LYMPH-S
LYRIC-S
LYSIN-E
LYSIN-G
LYSIN-S
LYSOL-S
LYSSA-S
F-**LYTED**
F-**LYTES**
LYTHE-S
LYTTA-E
LYTTA-S
MACAW-S
MACER-S
MACHE-S
MACHO-S
S-**MACKS**
MACLE-D
MACLE-S
MACON-S
MACRO-N
MACRO-S
MADAM-E
MADAM-S
MADGE-S
MADRE-S
MAFIA-S
MAFIC-S
I-**MAGES**
MAGIC-S
MAGMA-S
MAGOT-S
MAHOE-S
MAHUA-S
MAHWA-S
MAIKO-S
S-**MAIKS**
MAILE-D
MAILE-R
MAILE-S
MAILL-S
E-**MAILS**
MAIRE-S
MAISE-S
MAIST-S
MAIZE-S
MAJOR-S
MAKAR-S
MAKER-S
MALAR-S
MALIC-E
MALIK-S
MALIS-M
MALIS-T

S-**MALLS**
S-**MALMS**
S-**MALMY**
S-**MALTS**
MALVA-S
MAMBA-S
MAMBO-S
MAMEE-S
MAMEY-S
MAMIE-S
MAMMA-E
MAMMA-L
MAMMA-S
MANEH-S
MANGA-L
MANGA-S
MANGE-D
MANGE-L
MANGE-R
MANGE-S
MANGE-Y
MANGO-S
MANIA-C
MANIA-S
MANIC-S
MANNA-N
MANNA-S
MANOR-S
MANSE-S
MANTA-S
MANTO-S
MANUL-S
MAPLE-S
MAQUI-S
MARAE-S
MARAH-S
MARGE-S
MARID-S
MARLE-D
MARLE-S
S-**MARMS**
MARON-S
MAROR-S
MARSE-S
MARSH-Y
S-**MARTS**
MASER-S
MASON-S
MASSA-S
MASSE-D
MASSE-S
S-**MATCH**
A-**MATED**
MATER-S
A-**MATES**
MATEY-S
MATIN-G
MATIN-S
MATLO-S
MATLO-W
MATTE-D
MATTE-R
MATTE-S
MATZA-H
MATZA-S
MATZO-H
MATZO-S
MATZO-T
MAUND-S
MAUND-Y
MAUVE-R
MAUVE-S
MAVEN-S
MAVIE-S
MAVIN-S
MAXIM-A
MAXIM-S
MAYBE-S
MAYOR-S
A-**MAZED**
MAZER-S
A-**MAZES**
S-MAZES
MAZUT-S
MBIRA-S
MEANE-D
MEANE-R
MEANE-S
MEARE-S
MEASE-D
MEASE-S
S-**MEATH**
MEATH-E
MEATH-S
MECCA-S
MEDAL-S
MEDIA-D
MEDIA-E
MEDIA-L
MEDIA-N
MEDIA-S
MEDIC-K
MEDIC-O
MEDIC-S
MEDLE-D
MEDLE-S
MEDLE-Y
A-**MEERS**
E-MEERS
MEITH-S
MELEE-S
MELIC-S
MELIK-S
S-**MELLS**
MELON-S
S-**MELTS**
MENAD-S
A-**MENDS**
E-MENDS
A-**MENED**
O-MENED
MENGE-D
MENGE-S
MENSA-E
MENSA-L
MENSA-S
MENSE-D
MENSE-S
A-**MENTA**
O-MENTA
MENTA-L
MENTO-R
MENTO-S
MERDE-S
MEREL-L
MEREL-S
MEREL-Y
MERES-T
E-**MERGE**
MERGE-D
MERGE-R
MERGE-S
MERIL-S
MERIS-M
MERIT-S
S-**MERKS**
MERLE-S
MERSE-S
MESEL-S
E-**MESES**
T-MESES
MESNE-S
MESON-S
METAL-S
METER-S
E-**METIC**
METIC-S
METIF-S
METOL-S
METRE-D
METRE-S
METRO-S
S-**MEUSE**
MEUSE-D
MEUSE-S
MEZZE-S
MEZZO-S
MHORR-S
MIAOU-S
MIAOW-S
MIASM-A
MIASM-S
MIAUL-S
MICHE-D
MICHE-R
MICHE-S
MICRO-N
MICRO-S
S-**MIDDY**
S-**MIDGE**
MIDGE-S
MIDGE-T
A-**MIDST**
MIDST-S
MIEVE-D
MIEVE-S
S-**MIGHT**
MIGHT-S
MIGHT-Y
S-**MILER**
MILER-S
S-**MILES**
MILKO-S
MILLE-D
MILLE-R
MILLE-S
MILLE-T
MILOR-D
MILOR-S
MILPA-S
MIMEO-S
MIMER-S
MIMIC-S
MINAR-S
MINCE-D
MINCE-R
MINCE-S
MINER-S
A-**MINES**
I-MINES
MINGE-D
MINGE-S
MINIM-A
MINIM-S
MINIS-H
MINKE-S
MINOR-S
MIRIN-G
MIRIN-S
S-**MIRKS**
S-**MIRKY**
MIRTH-S
MIRZA-S
MISER-E
MISER-S
MISER-Y
A-**MISES**
MISSA-E
MISSA-L
MISSA-W
MISSA-Y
S-**MITER**
MITER-S
S-**MITES**
MITRE-D
MITRE-S
MIXEN-S
MIXER-S
MIXUP-S
MIZEN-S
MNEME-S
MOBLE-D
MOBLE-S
MOCHA-S
S-**MOCKS**
MODAL-S
MODEL-S
MODEM-S
MODER-N
MODER-S
MODES-T
S-**MOGGY**
MOGUL-S
MOHEL-S
MOHUR-S
MOIRA-I
MOIRE-S
MOIST-S
S-**MOKES**
S-**MOKOS**
MOLAR-S
A-**MOLES**
MOLES-T
MOLLA-H
MOLLA-S
S-**MOLTS**
MOMMA-S
MONAD-S
MONAL-S
MONDE-S
MONDO-S
MONER-A
MONEY-S
MONGO-E
MONGO-L
MONGO-S
MONGS-T
MONIE-D
MONIE-S
MONOS-Y
MONTE-M
MONTE-S
MONTH-S
S-**MOOCH**
MOOLA-H
MOOLA-S
MOOLI-S
S-**MOORS**
S-**MOOTS**
A-**MOOVE**
MOOVE-D
MOOVE-S
MOPED-S
MOPER-S
MOPER-Y
A-**MORAL**
MORAL-E
MORAL-L
MORAL-S
MORAS-S
MORAT-S
MORAY-S
MOREL-S
S-**MORES**
MORIA-S
MORNE-D
MORNE-S
MORON-S
MORPH-O
MORPH-S
MORRA-S
MORRO-S
MORRO-W
MORSE-L
MORSE-S
MOSEY-S
E-**MOTED**
MOTEL-S
E-**MOTES**
MOTET-S
MOTET-T
MOTIF-S
MOTOR-S
MOTOR-Y
MOTTE-S
MOTTO-S
MOTZA-S
S-**MOUCH**
MOULD-S
MOULD-Y
MOULT-S
MOUND-S
A-**MOUNT**
MOUNT-S
MOURN-S
S-**MOUSE**
MOUSE-D
MOUSE-R
MOUSE-S
MOUSE-Y
MOUST-S
MOUTH-S
MOUTH-Y
A-**MOVED**
E-MOVED
MOVER-S
A-**MOVES**
E-MOVES
MOVIE-S
MOWER-S
MOWRA-S
MOXIE-S
S-**MOYLE**
MOYLE-D
MOYLE-S
MPRET-S
MUCIN-S
A-**MUCKS**
MUCOR-S
MUCRO-S
S-**MUDGE**
MUDGE-D
MUDGE-R
MUDGE-S
MUDIR-S
MUDRA-S
MUFTI-S
MUIST-S
MUJIK-S
MULCT-S
E-**MULED**
E-**MULES**
MULEY-S
MULGA-S
MULLA-H
MULLA-S
MULSE-S
MUNGO-S
MUNTU-S
MURAL-S
E-**MURED**
E-**MURES**
MURID-S
MURRA-M
MURRA-S
MURRA-Y
MURRE-N
MURRE-S
MURRE-Y
S-**MURRY**
MURVA-S
MUSCA-E
MUSCA-T
A-**MUSED**
A-**MUSER**
MUSER-S
A-**MUSES**
MUSET-S
MUSIC-S
MUSIT-S
MUSSE-D
MUSSE-L
MUSSE-S
MUSTH-S
S-**MUTCH**
MUTES-T
MUTIS-M
MUTON-S
MVULE-S
MYALL-S
MYNAH-S
MYOMA-S
MYOPE-S
MYRRH-S
MYSID-S
MYTHI-C
NABLA-S
NABOB-S
NACHE-S
NACHO-S
NACRE-D
NACRE-S
NADIR-S
NAEVE-S
K-**NAGGY**
S-NAGGY
NAGOR-S
NAHAL-S
NAIAD-S
S-**NAILS**
NAIRA-S
NAIVE-R
NAIVE-S
S-**NAKED**
NAKER-S
NALED-S
NALLA-H
NALLA-S
NAMER-S
A-**NANAS**
J-NANAS
NANCE-S
NANDU-S
NANNA-S
NAPOO-S
NAPPA-S
NAPPE-D
NAPPE-R
NAPPE-S
S-**NAPPY**
NARCO-S
S-**NARES**
S-**NARKS**
S-**NARKY**
NASAL-S
S-**NATCH**
E-**NATES**
G-**NATTY**
NAUNT-S
NAVAR-S
NAVEL-S
K-**NAVES**
NAVEW-S
NAWAB-S
NAZIR-S
NEAFE-S
S-**NEAPS**
A-**NEARS**
A-**NEATH**
S-NEATH
U-NEATH
NEBEK-S
NEBEL-S
S-**NECKS**
NEELD-S
NEELE-S
NEEMB-S
NEESE-D
NEESE-S
S-**NEEZE**
NEEZE-D
NEEZE-S
NEIGH-S
NEIVE-S
S-**NELLY**
E-**NEMAS**
NEPER-S
NEPIT-S
NERKA-S
NEROL-I
NEROL-S
I-**NERTS**
E-**NERVE**
NERVE-D
NERVE-R
NERVE-S
NETOP-S
NEUME-S
NEVEL-S
E-**NEWED**
NEWEL-L
NEWEL-S
NEWIE-S
NGAIO-S
NGANA-S
NICAD-S
NICHE-D
NICHE-R
NICHE-S
K-**NICKS**
S-NICKS
NICOL-S
S-**NIDES**
NIDOR-S
NIECE-S
NIEVE-S
K-**NIFES**
S-**NIFFS**
S-**NIFFY**
S-**NIFTY**
NIGER-S
A-**NIGHT**
K-NIGHT
NIGHT-S
NIGHT-Y

NIHIL-S
NIKAU-S
NINJA-S
NINON-S
NINTH-S
S-**NIPPY**
NISEI-S
NISSE-S
U-**NITER**
NITER-S
NITER-Y
U-**NITES**
NITON-S
NITRE-S
NITRO-S
NITRY-L
NIXIE-S
NIZAM-S
K-**NOBBY**
S-NOBBY
NOBLE-R
NOBLE-S
K-**NOCKS**
A-**NODAL**
E-NODAL
A-**NODES**
A-**NOINT**
NOINT-S
NOISE-D
NOISE-S
A-**NOLES**
K-**NOLLS**
NOMAD-E
NOMAD-S
NOMAD-Y
G-**NOMES**
A-**NOMIC**
G-NOMIC
NONCE-S
NONET-S
NONYL-S
S-**NOOKS**
S-**NOOPS**
NOOSE-D
NOOSE-R
NOOSE-S
NOPAL-S
NORIA-S
NORMA-L
NORMA-N
NORMA-S
NORTH-S
NOSER-S
E-**NOSES**
G-NOSES
NOSEY-S
NOTCH-Y
NOTER-S
NOULD-E
NOULE-S
NOVEL-S
NOVUM-S
NOWAY-S
S-**NOWED**
U-NOWED
NOYAU-S
K-**NUBBY**
S-NUBBY
NUBIA-S
NUCHA-E
NUCHA-L
NUDES-T
S-**NUDGE**
NUDGE-D
NUDGE-R
NUDGE-S
NUDIE-S
S-**NUFFS**
NULLA-H
NULLA-S
K-**NURLS**
K-**NURRS**
NURSE-D
NURSE-R
NURSE-S
NYAFF-S
I-**NYALA**
NYALA-S
NYLON-S
NYMPH-A
NYMPH-O
NYMPH-S
NYSSA-S
S-**OAKEN**
S-**OAKER**
OAKER-S
OAKUM-S
H-**OARED**
R-OARED
S-OARED
B-**OASTS**
C-OASTS
H-OASTS
R-OASTS
T-OASTS
B-**OATER**
C-OATER
D-OATER
OATER-S
L-**OAVES**
S-OAVES
G-**OBANG**
K-OBANG
OBANG-S
OBEAH-S
OBELI-A
OBESE-R
C-**OBIAS**
O-**OBITS**
OBJET-S
G-**OBOES**
H-OBOES
S-**OBOLE**
OBOLE-S
OCCAM-S
OCCAM-Y
OCCUR-S
OCEAN-S
T-**OCHER**
OCHER-S
OCHER-Y
B-**OCHES**
C-OCHES
R-OCHES
OCHRE-A
OCHRE-D
OCHRE-S
OCHRE-Y
C-**OCKER**
D-OCKER
H-OCKER
L-OCKER
M-OCKER
R-OCKER
OCKER-S
OCREA-E
OCTAD-S
OCTAL-S
OCTAN-E
OCTAN-S
OCTAN-T
OCTET-S
OCTET-T
OCTYL-S
L-**OCULI**
M-**ODALS**
C-**ODDER**
D-ODDER
F-ODDER
N-ODDER
ODEON-S
ODEUM-S
I-**ODISM**
ODISM-S
C-**ODIST**
M-ODIST
ODIST-S
P-**ODIUM**
S-ODIUM
ODIUM-S
ODOUR-S
G-**ODSOS**
ODYLE-S
OFFAL-S
B-**OFFED**
C-OFFED
D-OFFED
G-OFFED
C-**OFFER**
D-OFFER
G-OFFER
OFFER-S
OFLAG-S
S-**OFTEN**
L-**OFTER**
S-OFTER
Y-**OGEES**
H-**OGGIN**
N-OGGIN
OGGIN-S
OGHAM-S
OGIVE-S
OGLER-S
B-**OGLES**
F-OGLES
OGRES-S
H-**OHING**
O-OHING
B-**OILED**
C-OILED
D-OILED
F-OILED
M-OILED
R-OILED
S-OILED
T-OILED
B-**OILER**
C-OILER
M-OILER
T-OILER
OILER-S
OILER-Y
B-**OINKS**
J-**OINTS**
N-OINTS
P-OINTS
OJIME-S
OKAPI-S
T-**OKAYS**
K-**OKRAS**
B-**OLDEN**
G-OLDEN
H-OLDEN
OLDEN-S
B-**OLDER**
C-OLDER
F-OLDER
G-OLDER
H-OLDER
M-OLDER
P-OLDER
S-OLDER
OLDIE-S
S-**OLEIN**
OLEIN-E
OLEIN-S
D-**OLENT**
OLEUM-S
F-**OLIOS**
P-OLIOS
S-**OLIVE**
OLIVE-R
OLIVE-S
OLIVE-T
H-**OLLAS**
M-OLLAS
OLLAV-S
O-**OLOGY**
G-**OLPES**
OMASA-L
B-**OMBER**
C-OMBER
S-OMBER
OMBER-S
H-**OMBRE**
S-OMBRE
OMBRE-S
K-**OMBUS**
OMEGA-S
C-**OMERS**
H-OMERS
V-OMERS
V-**OMITS**
OMLAH-S
OMRAH-S
ONCER-S
B-**ONCES**
N-ONCES
P-ONCES
S-ONCES
L-**ONELY**
B-**ONERS**
G-ONERS
H-ONERS
L-ONERS
T-ONERS
Z-ONERS
G-**ONION**
R-ONION
ONION-S
ONION-Y
C-**ONIUM**
G-ONIUM
I-ONIUM
C-**ONNED**
D-ONNED
F-ONNED
W-ONNED
ONSET-S
P-**ONTIC**
OOBIT-S
B-**OOHED**
P-OOHED
OOMPH-S
C-**OOPED**
H-OOPED
L-OOPED
M-OOPED
P-OOPED
R-OOPED
S-OOPED
T-**OORIE**
OORIE-R
B-**OOSES**
G-OOSES
L-OOSES
N-OOSES
R-OOSES
OOTID-S
B-**OOZED**
B-**OOZES**
C-**OPALS**
N-OPALS
C-**OPENS**
OPEPE-S
OPERA-S
OPINE-D
OPINE-S
C-**OPING**
D-OPING
H-OPING
L-OPING
M-OPING
O-OPING
R-OPING
T-OPING
OPIUM-S
OPPOS-E
OPSIN-S
C-**OPTER**
OPTER-S
OPTIC-S
ORACH-E
B-**ORALS**
C-ORALS
G-ORALS
M-ORALS
ORANG-E
ORANG-S
ORANG-Y
V-**ORANT**
ORANT-S
B-**ORATE**
L-ORATE
ORATE-D
ORATE-S
S-**ORBED**
ORBIT-A
ORBIT-S
ORBIT-Y
ORCIN-E
ORCIN-S
B-**ORDER**
C-ORDER
ORDER-S
OREAD-S
M-**ORGAN**
ORGAN-A
ORGAN-S
G-**ORGIA**
ORGIA-C
ORGIA-S
M-**ORGUE**
ORGUE-S
ORIBI-S
ORIEL-S
ORLOP-S
D-**ORMER**
F-ORMER
W-ORMER
ORMER-S
ORPIN-E
ORPIN-S
M-**ORRIS**
ORTHO-S
ORVAL-S
OSHAC-S
C-**OSIER**
H-OSIER
N-OSIER
O-OSIER
P-OSIER
R-OSIER
OSIER-S
OSIER-Y
C-**OSMIC**
OSMIC-S
OSMOL-E
OSMOL-S
OSTIA-L
N-**OTARY**
R-OTARY
V-OTARY
B-**OTHER**
F-OTHER
L-OTHER
M-OTHER
N-OTHER
P-OTHER
R-OTHER
T-OTHER
OTHER-S
C-**OTTAR**
OTTAR-S
C-**OTTER**
D-OTTER
H-OTTER
J-OTTER
P-OTTER
R-OTTER
T-OTTER
OTTER-S
L-**OTTOS**
M-OTTOS
P-OTTOS
W-**OUBIT**
OUBIT-S
OUCHT-S
B-**OUGHT**
D-OUGHT
F-OUGHT
M-OUGHT
N-OUGHT
R-OUGHT
S-OUGHT
OUGHT-S
OUIJA-S
B-**OUNCE**
J-OUNCE
P-OUNCE
R-OUNCE
OUNCE-S
W-**OUNDY**
C-**OUPED**
L-OUPED
M-OUPED
P-OUPED
R-OUPED
S-OUPED
OUPHE-S
P-**OURIE**
T-OURIE
OURIE-R
H-**OUSEL**
OUSEL-S
J-**OUSTS**
M-OUSTS
R-OUSTS
OUTBY-E
D-**OUTED**
H-OUTED
L-OUTED
P-OUTED
R-OUTED
T-OUTED
C-**OUTER**
D-OUTER
F-OUTER
M-OUTER
P-OUTER
R-OUTER
S-OUTER
T-OUTER
OUTER-S
F-**OUTRE**
OUTRE-D
OUZEL-S
C-**OVARY**
B-**OVATE**
OVATE-D
OVATE-S
C-**OVENS**
D-OVENS
W-OVENS
C-**OVERS**
D-OVERS
H-OVERS
L-OVERS
M-OVERS
R-OVERS
C-**OVERT**
B-**OVINE**
OVINE-S
OVIST-S
OVOID-S
OVOLO-S
OVULE-S
OWCHE-S
B-**OWING**
C-OWING
D-OWING
J-OWING
L-OWING
M-OWING
R-OWING
S-OWING
T-OWING
V-OWING
W-OWING
Y-OWING
B-**OWLED**
C-OWLED
F-OWLED
G-OWLED
H-OWLED
J-OWLED
S-OWLED
Y-OWLED
B-**OWLER**
F-OWLER
H-OWLER
J-OWLER
Y-OWLER
OWLER-S
OWLER-Y
H-**OWLET**
OWLET-S
B-**OWNED**
D-OWNED
G-OWNED
L-OWNED
D-**OWNER**
OWNER-S
H-**OWRES**
P-OWRES

C-**OWRIE**
OWRIE-R
OXBOW-S
B-**OXERS**
OXEYE-S
OXIDE-S
OXIME-S
OXLIP-S
OXTER-S
F-**OYERS**
T-OYERS
OZEKI-S
OZONE-S
S-**PACED**
S-**PACER**
PACER-S
S-**PACES**
S-**PACEY**
PACHA-K
PACHA-S
E-**PACTS**
PADLE-S
PADMA-S
PADRE-S
PAEAN-S
PAEON-S
PAEON-Y
PAGAN-S
PAGER-S
PAGLE-S
PAGOD-A
PAGOD-S
PAGRI-S
S-**PAILS**
S-**PAINS**
PAINT-S
PAINT-Y
PAIRE-D
PAIRE-S
PAISA-N
PAISA-S
PALAY-S
PALEA-E
PALEA-L
O-**PALED**
S-**PALES**
PALES-T
PALET-S
PALKI-S
PALLA-E
PALLA-H
S-**PALLS**
PAMPA-S
PANCE-S
PANDA-R
PANDA-S
S-**PANED**
PANEL-S
S-**PANES**
PANGA-S
S-**PANGS**
PANIC-K
PANIC-S
PANIM-S
PANNE-D
PANNE-S
PANTO-N
PANTO-S
PAPAW-S
PAPER-S
PAPER-Y
E-**PARCH**
PARDI-E
S-**PARED**
PAREO-S
S-**PARER**
PARER-S
S-**PARES**
PAREU-S
S-**PARGE**
PARGE-D
PARGE-S
PARGE-T
PARGO-S
PARIS-H
PARKA-S
PARKI-E
PARKI-N
PARKI-S
S-**PARKS**
S-**PARKY**
PARLE-D
PARLE-S
PARLE-Y
PAROL-E
PAROL-S
S-**PARRY**
S-**PARSE**
PARSE-C
PARSE-D
PARSE-R
PARSE-S
PARTI-M
PARTI-S
S-**PARTS**
PARVO-S
PASEO-S
U-**PASES**
PASHA-S
PASHM-S
PASSE-D
PASSE-E
PASSE-L
PASSE-R
PASSE-S
PASTA-S
PASTE-D
PASTE-L
PASTE-R
PASTE-S
PATCH-Y
PATEN-S
PATEN-T
PATER-A
PATER-S
S-**PATES**
PATIN-A
PATIN-E
PATIN-S
PATIO-S
PATTE-D
PATTE-E
PATTE-N
PATTE-R
PATTE-S
S-**PAULS**
PAUSE-D
PAUSE-R
PAUSE-S
PAVAN-E
PAVAN-S
PAVEN-S
PAVER-S
S-**PAVIN**
PAVIN-G
PAVIN-S
PAVIS-E
PAWAW-S
PAWER-S
S-**PAWLS**
S-**PAWNS**
S-**PAYED**
PAYEE-S
PAYER-S
PAYOR-S
PEACE-D
PEACE-S
PEACH-Y
PEAGE-S
S-**PEAKS**
S-**PEALS**
S-**PEANS**
PEARE-S
PEARL-S
PEARL-Y
S-**PEARS**
PEARS-T
PEASE-D
PEASE-N
PEASE-S
S-**PEATS**
PEAZE-D
PEAZE-S
PECAN-S
PECKE-D
PECKE-R
PECKE-S
S-**PECKS**
S-**PECKY**
PEDAL-O
PEDAL-S
PEDRO-S
PEECE-S
S-**PEELS**
PEEOY-S
PEEPE-D
PEEPE-R
PEEPE-S
S-**PEERS**
PEEVE-D
PEEVE-R
PEEVE-S
S-**PEISE**
PEISE-D
PEISE-S
PEIZE-D
PEIZE-S
PEKAN-S
PEKIN-S
PEKOE-S
S-**PELLS**
PELMA-S
PELTA-E
PELTA-S
S-**PELTS**
S-**PENCE**
PENCE-L
PENCE-S
S-**PENDS**
U-PENDS
O-**PENED**
PENGO-S
PENIE-S
PENNA-E
PENNA-L
PENNE-D
PENNE-R
PENNE-S
PENNI-A
PENNI-S
PERAI-S
PERCE-D
PERCE-N
PERCE-S
E-**PERDU**
PERDU-E
PERDU-S
PERIL-S
PERIS-H
S-**PERMS**
S-**PERSE**
PERSE-S
S-**PERST**
PERVE-D
PERVE-S
PESTO-S
PETAL-S
PETAR-A
PETAR-D
PETAR-S
PETAR-Y
PETER-S
PETIT-E
PETRE-L
PETRE-S
PEWEE-S
PEWIT-S
PEYSE-D
PEYSE-S
PHAGE-S
U-**PHANG**
PHANG-S
PHARE-S
PHASE-D
PHASE-S
PHEER-E
PHEER-S
S-**PHENE**
PHENE-S
PHEON-S
PHESE-D
PHESE-S
PHIAL-S
PHOCA-E
PHOCA-S
PHONE-D
PHONE-R
PHONE-S
PHONE-Y
PHONO-N
PHONO-S
A-**PHONY**
PHOTO-G
PHOTO-N
PHOTO-S
PHYLA-E
PHYLA-R
PIANO-S
PIBAL-S
A-**PICAL**
E-PICAL
S-**PICAS**
S-**PICKS**
PICOT-E
PICOT-S
PICRA-S
PICUL-S
A-**PIECE**
PIECE-D
PIECE-N
PIECE-R
PIECE-S
PIEND-S
S-**PIERS**
PIERS-T
PIETA-S
S-**PIGHT**
Y-PIGHT
PIGHT-S
S-**PIKED**
S-**PIKER**
PIKER-S
S-**PIKES**
PIKUL-S
PILAF-F
PILAF-S
PILAU-S
PILAW-S
S-**PILED**
PILER-S
S-**PILES**
S-**PILLS**
PILOT-S
PILOW-S
S-**PINAS**
O-**PINED**
S-PINED
O-**PINES**
S-PINES
PINGO-S
PINKO-S
S-**PINKS**
PINNA-E
PINNA-L
PINNA-S
S-**PINNY**
PINON-S
PINOT-S
PINTA-S
S-**PINTO**
PINTO-S
PINUP-S
PIOYE-S
PIPAL-S
PIPER-S
PIPET-S
PIPIT-S
PIPUL-S
PIQUE-D
PIQUE-S
PIQUE-T
PIRAI-S
PIROG-I
PISCO-S
PISTE-S
PITCH-Y
PITON-S
PITTA-S
O-**PIUMS**
PIVOT-S
PIXEL-S
PIXIE-S
PIZZA-S
PLACE-D
PLACE-R
PLACE-S
PLACE-T
PLACK-S
PLAGE-S
U-**PLAID**
PLAID-S
PLAIN-S
PLAIN-T
PLAIT-S
PLANE-D
PLANE-R
PLANE-S
PLANE-T
PLANK-S
PLANT-A
PLANT-S
S-**PLASH**
PLASH-Y
PLASM-A
PLASM-S
Y-**PLAST**
PLAST-E
PLATE-D
PLATE-N
PLATE-R
PLATE-S
S-**PLATS**
PLATY-S
PLAYA-S
S-**PLAYS**
U-PLAYS
PLAZA-S
U-**PLEAD**
PLEAD-S
PLEAS-E
PLEAT-S
PLEBE-S
PLEON-S
PLICA-E
PLICA-L
PLIER-S
PLING-S
U-**PLINK**
PLINK-S
PLOAT-S
PLONG-D
PLONG-E
PLONG-S
PLONK-S
PLONK-Y
U-**PLOOK**
PLOOK-S
PLOUK-S
PLUCK-S
PLUCK-Y
PLUFF-S
PLUFF-Y
PLUMB-S
PLUME-D
PLUME-S
PLUMP-S
PLUMP-Y
PLUNK-S
PLUSH-Y
PLYER-S
POACH-Y
POAKA-S
POAKE-S
A-**PODAL**
PODGE-S
PODIA-L
POGEY-S
POGGE-S
POILU-S
POIND-S
POINT-E
POINT-S
POINT-Y
POISE-D
POISE-R
POISE-S
POKAL-S
S-**POKED**
POKER-S
S-**POKES**
POKEY-S
POLAR-S
POLER-S
POLEY-N
POLEY-S
POLIO-S
POLIS-H
POLKA-S
POLYP-E
POLYP-I
POLYP-S
POMBE-S
PONCE-D
PONCE-S
PONCE-Y
PONEY-S
PONGA-S
PONGO-S
S-**PONGY**
S-**POOFS**
S-**POOFY**
POOJA-H
POOJA-S
POOKA-S
S-**POOKS**
S-**POOLS**
S-**POONS**
POORI-S
POORT-S
S-**POOTS**
POOVE-S
POPPA-S
S-**PORAL**
S-**PORED**
PORER-S
S-**PORES**
PORGE-D
PORGE-S
PORNO-S
PORTA-L
PORTA-S
S-**PORTS**
S-**PORTY**
POSER-S
E-**POSES**
POSIT-S
POSSE-D
POSSE-R
POSSE-S
POSSE-T
POTCH-E
POTIN-G
POTIN-S
POTOO-S
POTTO-S
S-**POTTY**
POUCH-Y
POUFF-E
POUFF-S
POUKE-S
POULE-S
POULP-E
POULP-S
POULT-S
POUND-S
POUPE-D
POUPE-S
S-**POUTS**
S-**POUTY**
POWAN-S
POWER-S
POWIN-S
POWND-S
POWRE-D
POWRE-S
POYNT-S
POYOU-S
POYSE-D
POYSE-S
PRAAM-S
PRAHU-S
PRANA-S
S-**PRANG**
PRANG-S
PRANK-S

PRANK-Y
PRASE-S
U-**PRATE**
PRATE-D
PRATE-R
PRATE-S
S-**PRATS**
PRATT-S
PRAWN-S
S-**PRAYS**
S-**PREED**
PREEN-S
S-**PREES**
PREIF-E
PREIF-S
S-**PRENT**
PRENT-S
PRESE-S
PRESE-T
U-**PREST**
PREST-O
PREST-S
PREVE-D
PREVE-S
PRIAL-S
PRICE-D
PRICE-R
PRICE-S
PRICE-Y
PRICK-S
PRICK-Y
PRIDE-D
PRIDE-S
PRIEF-E
PRIEF-S
S-**PRIER**
PRIER-S
PRIES-T
S-**PRIGS**
PRILL-S
PRIMA-L
PRIMA-S
PRIME-D
PRIME-R
PRIME-S
PRIMO-S
PRIMP-S
PRINK-S
S-**PRINT**
PRINT-S
PRION-S
PRIOR-S
PRIOR-Y
E-**PRISE**
U-PRISE
PRISE-D
PRISE-R
PRISE-S
PRISM-S
PRISM-Y
PRISS-Y
PRIZE-D
PRIZE-R
PRIZE-S
PROBE-D
PROBE-R
PROBE-S
S-**PRODS**
PROEM-S
S-**PROGS**
PROIN-E
PROIN-S
PROKE-D
PROKE-R
PROKE-S
PROLE-D
PROLE-G
PROLE-R
PROLE-S
U-**PROLL**
PROLL-S
PROMO-S
E-**PROMS**
PRONE-R
PRONE-S
S-**PRONG**
PRONG-S
PRONK-S
PROOF-S
PRORE-S
U-**PROSE**
PROSE-D
PROSE-R
PROSE-S
PROSO-S
PROUL-S
PROVE-D
PROVE-N
PROVE-R
PROVE-S
PROWL-S
PROYN-E
PROYN-S
PRUDE-S
PRUNE-D
PRUNE-R
PRUNE-S
PRUNT-S
PRUTA-H
S-**PRYER**
PRYER-S
PRYSE-D
PRYSE-S
PSALM-S
PSEUD-O
PSEUD-S
PSHAW-S
PSION-S
PSORA-S
PSYCH-E
PSYCH-O
PSYCH-S
PSYOP-S
PUCES-T
S-**PUDDY**
PUDGE-S
PUDOR-S
PUGIL-S
PUJAH-S
PUKER-S
PULER-S
S-**PULES**
E-**PULIS**
PULKA-S
PULSE-D
PULSE-R
PULSE-S
O-**PULUS**
PUMIE-S
PUNCE-D
PUNCE-S
PUNCH-Y
PUNGA-S
PUNKA-H
PUNKA-S
S-**PUNKS**
S-**PUNKY**
PUNTO-S
PUPIL-S
PURDA-H
PURDA-S
PUREE-D
PUREE-S
PURES-T
S-**PURGE**
PURGE-D
PURGE-R
PURGE-S
PURIM-S
PURIN-E
PURIN-G
PURIN-S
PURIS-M
PURIS-T
PURSE-D
PURSE-R
PURSE-S
PURSE-W
O-**PUSES**
PUSLE-D
PUSLE-S
PUSLE-Y
PUTON-S
PUTTI-E
PUZEL-S
PYGAL-S
PYLON-S
PYRAN-S
S-**PYRES**
PYXIE-S
QANAT-S
QIBLA-S
QUACK-S
S-**QUADS**
QUAFF-S
S-**QUAIL**
QUAIL-S
QUAIR-S
QUAKE-D
QUAKE-R
QUAKE-S
QUALM-S
QUALM-Y
E-**QUANT**
QUANT-A
QUANT-S
S-**QUARE**
QUARE-R
QUARK-S
QUART-E
QUART-O
QUART-S
QUART-Z
S-**QUASH**
E-**QUATE**
S-**QUATS**
QUEAN-S
QUEEN-S
QUEEN-Y
QUEER-S
QUELL-S
QUEME-D
QUEME-S
QUENA-S
QUERN-S
QUEST-S
QUEUE-D
QUEUE-R
QUEUE-S
QUEYN-S
QUICH-E
QUICK-S
E-**QUIDS**
S-QUIDS
QUIET-S
S-**QUIFF**
QUIFF-S
S-**QUILL**
QUILL-S
QUILT-S
QUINA-S
E-**QUINE**
QUINE-S
QUINS-Y
S-**QUINT**
QUINT-A
QUINT-E
QUINT-S
QUIPO-S
E-**QUIPS**
QUIPU-S
S-**QUIRE**
QUIRE-D
QUIRE-S
QUIRK-S
QUIRK-Y
S-**QUIRT**
QUIRT-S
QUIST-S
QUITE-D
QUITE-S
S-**QUITS**
QUOIF-S
QUOIN-S
QUOIT-S
QUOLL-S
QUONK-S
QUOTA-S
QUOTE-D
QUOTE-R
QUOTE-S
QUOTH-A
QUYTE-D
QUYTE-S
RABAT-O
RABAT-S
RABBI-N
RABBI-S
RABBI-T
A-**RABIC**
A-**RABIS**
B-**RACED**
G-RACED
T-RACED
B-**RACER**
T-RACER
RACER-S
B-**RACES**
G-RACES
T-RACES
O-**RACHE**
RACHE-S
RACHE-T
B-**RACKS**
C-RACKS
T-RACKS
W-RACKS
RACON-S
RADAR-S
RADGE-R
RADGE-S
RADIO-S
RADON-S
D-**RAFFS**
G-RAFFS
C-**RAFTS**
D-RAFTS
G-RAFTS
K-RAFTS
D-**RAGEE**
RAGEE-S
RAGER-S
RAGGA-S
B-**RAGGY**
C-RAGGY
D-RAGGY
B-**RAIDS**
T-**RAIKS**
G-**RAILE**
RAILE-D
RAILE-R
RAILE-S
B-**RAILS**
D-RAILS
F-RAILS
G-RAILS
T-RAILS
G-**RAINE**
RAINE-D
RAINE-S
B-**RAINS**
D-RAINS
G-RAINS
T-RAINS
B-**RAINY**
G-RAINY
B-**RAIRD**
RAIRD-S
A-**RAISE**
B-RAISE
F-RAISE
P-RAISE
RAISE-D
RAISE-R
RAISE-S
RAITA-S
K-**RAITS**
T-RAITS
RAJAH-S
B-**RAKED**
C-RAKED
RAKEE-S
RAKER-S
RAKER-Y
B-**RAKES**
C-RAKES
D-RAKES
RAKIS-H
O-**RALLY**
RALLY-E
RALPH-S
RAMEE-S
RAMEN-S
RAMET-S
RAMIE-S
RAMIN-S
C-**RAMPS**
G-RAMPS
T-RAMPS
P-**RANAS**
P-**RANCE**
T-RANCE
RANCE-D
RANCE-L
RANCE-S
B-**RANCH**
C-RANCH
RANCH-O
B-**RANDS**
G-RANDS
B-**RANDY**
RANEE-S
G-**RANGE**
O-RANGE
RANGE-D
RANGE-R
RANGE-S
O-**RANGY**
RANID-S
RANKE-D
RANKE-R
RANKE-S
B-**RANKS**
C-RANKS
F-RANKS
P-RANKS
T-RANKS
B-**RANTS**
C-RANTS
D-RANTS
G-RANTS
O-RANTS
T-RANTS
C-**RAPED**
D-RAPED
G-RAPED
T-RAPED
D-**RAPER**
RAPER-S
C-**RAPES**
D-RAPES
G-RAPES
T-RAPES
RAPHE-S
RAPID-S
C-**RARES**
U-RARES
RARES-T
E-**RASED**
E-**RASER**
RASER-S
B-**RASES**
C-RASES
E-RASES
P-RASES
U-RASES
G-**RASPS**
W-**RASSE**
RASSE-S
RATAL-S
RATAN-S
RATAN-Y
C-**RATCH**
F-RATCH
C-**RATED**
G-RATED
O-RATED
P-RATED
RATEL-S
C-**RATER**
F-RATER
G-RATER
I-RATER
K-RATER
P-RATER
RATER-S
C-**RATES**
G-RATES
O-RATES
P-RATES
U-RATES
RATHE-R
W-**RATHS**
RATIO-N
RATIO-S
RATOO-N
RATOO-S
B-**RATTY**
B-**RAVED**
C-RAVED
G-RAVED
G-**RAVEL**
T-RAVEL
RAVEL-S
C-**RAVEN**
G-RAVEN
RAVEN-S
B-**RAVER**
C-RAVER
G-RAVER
RAVER-S
B-**RAVES**
C-RAVES
G-RAVES
T-RAVES
RAVIN-E
RAVIN-G
RAVIN-S
B-**RAWER**
D-RAWER
RAWIN-G
RAWIN-S
B-**RAWLY**
C-RAWLY
D-RAWLY
B-**RAWNS**
P-RAWNS
P-**RAXES**
RAYAH-S
B-**RAYED**
D-RAYED
F-RAYED
G-RAYED
P-RAYED
G-**RAYLE**
RAYLE-D
RAYLE-S
RAYLE-T
T-**RAYNE**
RAYNE-S
C-**RAYON**
RAYON-S
B-**RAZED**
C-RAZED
G-RAZED
RAZEE-D
RAZEE-S
B-**RAZER**
G-RAZER
RAZER-S
B-**RAZES**
C-RAZES
G-RAZES
RAZOO-S
RAZOR-S
A-**REACH**
B-REACH
C-REACH
P-REACH
P-**REACT**
REACT-S
READD-S
A-**READS**
B-READS
D-READS
O-READS
T-READS
B-**READY**
B-**REAKS**
C-REAKS
F-REAKS
W-REAKS
REALM-S
REALO-S
REAME-D

REAME-R
REAME-S
B-**REAMS**
C-REAMS
D-REAMS
C-**REAMY**
D-REAMY
P-**REARM**
REARM-S
D-**REARS**
B-**REAST**
REAST-S
REAST-Y
REATA-S
C-**REATE**
REATE-S
G-**REAVE**
REAVE-D
REAVE-R
REAVE-S
REBAR-S
REBBE-S
REBEC-K
REBEC-S
REBEL-S
REBID-S
REBIT-E
REBOP-S
REBUT-S
REBUY-S
RECAL-L
RECAL-S
RECAP-S
RECCE-D
RECCE-S
RECCO-S
RECIT-E
RECIT-S
D-**RECKS**
T-RECKS
W-RECKS
RECON-S
RECTA-L
RECTO-R
RECTO-S
RECUR-E
RECUR-S
P-**RECUT**
RECUT-S
REDAN-S
B-**REDED**
A-**REDES**
B-REDES
U-**REDIA**
REDIA-E
REDIA-L
REDIA-S
REDIP-S
REDIP-T
REDON-E
REDON-S
C-**REDOS**
U-REDOS
REDUB-S
REDYE-D
REDYE-S
B-**REECH**
REECH-O
REECH-Y
REEDE-D
REEDE-N
REEDE-R
REEDE-S
B-**REEDS**
C-REEDS
G-REEDS
G-**REEDY**
B-**REEKS**
C-REEKS
C-**REEKY**
C-**REELS**
G-**REENS**
P-REENS
T-REENS
F-**REEST**
REEST-S
REEST-Y
P-**REEVE**
REEVE-D
REEVE-S
REFEL-L
REFEL-S
REFEL-T
P-**REFER**
REFER-S
REFFO-S
REFIT-S
P-**REFIX**
REGAL-E
REGAL-S
REGAR-D
REGAR-S
REGES-T
REGGO-S
REGIE-S
B-**REGMA**
REGNA-L
G-**REGOS**
REGUR-S
REHAB-S
REHEM-S
P-**REIFS**
REIGN-S
REIKI-S
REINK-S
G-**REINS**
REIRD-S
REIST-S
REIVE-D
REIVE-R
REIVE-S
REJIG-S
REKEY-S
RELAY-S
RELET-S
RELIC-S
RELIC-T
RELIE-D
RELIE-F
RELIE-R
RELIE-S
P-**REMAN**
REMAN-D
REMAN-S
REMAP-S
P-**REMEN**
REMEN-D
REMEN-S
F-**REMIT**
REMIT-S
P-**REMIX**
REMIX-T
RENAY-S
T-**RENDS**
RENEW-S
RENEY-S
RENGA-S
RENIG-S
RENIN-S
B-**RENNE**
F-RENNE
RENNE-D
RENNE-S
RENNE-T
RENTE-D
RENTE-R
RENTE-S
B-**RENTS**
P-RENTS
REOIL-S
P-**REPAY**
REPAY-S
REPEG-S
REPEL-S
REPIN-E
REPIN-S
REPLA-N
REPLA-Y
REPOS-E
REPOS-T
REPOT-S
REPRO-S
RERIG-S
RERUN-S
RESAW-N
RESAW-S
RESAY-S
RESEE-D
RESEE-K
RESEE-N
RESEE-S
G-**RESES**
P-RESES
U-RESES
P-**RESET**
RESET-S
RESEW-N
RESEW-S
RESID-E
RESID-S
RESIN-S
RESIN-Y
RESIT-E
RESIT-S
RESOD-S
RESOW-N
RESOW-S
C-**RESTS**
P-RESTS
T-RESTS
W-RESTS
RETAG-S
P-**RETAX**
W-**RETCH**
RETEM-S
A-**RETES**
RETES-T
RETIA-L
RETIE-D
RETIE-S
RETRO-D
RETRO-S
REUSE-D
REUSE-S
REVEL-S
B-**REVET**
T-REVET
REVET-S
REVIE-D
REVIE-S
REVIE-W
P-**REVUE**
REVUE-S
B-**REWED**
C-REWED
G-REWED
REWED-S
REWET-S
REWIN-D
REWIN-S
REWTH-S
P-**REXES**
RHEUM-S
RHEUM-Y
RHIME-S
RHINE-S
RHINO-S
RHOMB-I
RHOMB-S
RHONE-S
RHUMB-A
RHUMB-S
RHYME-D
RHYME-R
RHYME-S
RHYNE-S
P-**RIALS**
T-RIALS
U-RIALS
C-**RIANT**
RIATA-S
B-**RIBES**
T-RIBES
P-**RICED**
T-RICED
G-**RICER**
P-RICER
RICER-S
D-**RICES**
G-RICES
P-RICES
T-RICES
P-**RICEY**
F-**RICHT**
RICHT-S
RICIN-G
RICIN-S
B-**RICKS**
C-RICKS
E-RICKS
P-RICKS
T-RICKS
W-RICKS
A-**RIDER**
RIDER-S
B-**RIDES**
G-RIDES
I-RIDES
P-RIDES
B-**RIDGE**
F-RIDGE
RIDGE-D
RIDGE-L
RIDGE-R
RIDGE-S
A-**RIELS**
O-RIELS
G-**RIEVE**
P-RIEVE
RIEVE-R
RIEVE-S
G-**RIFFS**
T-**RIFLE**
RIFLE-D
RIFLE-R
RIFLE-S
RIFTE-D
D-**RIFTS**
G-RIFTS
D-**RIFTY**
A-**RIGHT**
B-RIGHT
F-RIGHT
W-RIGHT
RIGHT-O
RIGHT-S
RIGHT-Y
F-**RIGID**
RIGID-S
RIGOL-L
RIGOL-S
RIGOR-S
A-**RILED**
G-**RILLE**
RILLE-D
RILLE-S
RILLE-T
B-**RILLS**
D-RILLS
F-RILLS
G-RILLS
K-RILLS
P-RILLS
T-RILLS
C-**RIMED**
G-RIMED
P-RIMED
P-**RIMER**
T-RIMER
RIMER-S
C-**RIMES**
G-RIMES
P-RIMES
P-**RIMUS**
G-**RINDS**
B-**RINES**
C-RINES
T-RINES
U-RINES
B-**RINGS**
W-RINGS
B-**RINKS**
D-RINKS
P-RINKS
RINSE-D
RINSE-R
RINSE-S
RIOJA-S
G-**RIOTS**
G-**RIPED**
RIPEN-S
G-**RIPER**
RIPER-S
C-**RIPES**
G-RIPES
T-RIPES
RIPES-T
A-**RISEN**
P-**RISER**
RISER-S
A-**RISES**
B-RISES
C-RISES
F-RISES
G-RISES
I-RISES
K-RISES
P-RISES
RISHI-S
B-**RISKS**
F-RISKS
B-**RISKY**
F-RISKY
C-**RISPS**
T-**RITES**
U-RITES
W-RITES
B-**RITTS**
F-RITTS
RIVAL-S
D-**RIVEL**
RIVEL-S
D-**RIVEN**
D-**RIVER**
RIVER-S
RIVER-Y
D-**RIVES**
G-**RIVET**
P-RIVET
T-RIVET
RIVET-S
RIYAL-S
B-**ROACH**
B-**ROADS**
T-ROADS
G-**ROANS**
ROAST-S
ROATE-D
ROATE-S
P-**ROBED**
P-**ROBES**
ROBIN-G
ROBIN-S
ROBLE-S
ROBOT-S
B-**ROCKS**
C-ROCKS
F-ROCKS
T-ROCKS
E-**RODED**
RODEO-S
E-**RODES**
T-RODES
D-**ROGER**
ROGER-S
B-**ROGUE**
D-ROGUE
ROGUE-D
ROGUE-S
B-**ROILS**
D-ROILS
G-**ROINS**
P-ROINS
ROIST-S
B-**ROKED**
P-ROKED
T-ROKED
B-**ROKER**
P-ROKER
ROKER-S
B-**ROKES**
P-ROKES
T-ROKES
ROLAG-S
D-**ROLES**
P-ROLES
D-**ROLLS**
P-ROLLS
T-ROLLS
B-**ROMAL**
ROMAL-S
ROMAN-O
ROMAN-S
A-**ROMAS**
G-ROMAS
ROMEO-S
T-**ROMPS**
RONDE-L
RONDE-S
RONDO-S
RONEO-S
C-**RONES**
D-RONES
G-RONES
I-RONES
P-RONES
T-RONES
RONNE-L
RONTE-S
F-**RONTS**
B-**ROODS**
G-**ROOFS**
P-ROOFS
B-**ROOKS**
C-ROOKS
D-ROOKS
B-**ROOMS**
G-ROOMS
V-ROOMS
B-**ROOMY**
C-**ROONS**
K-ROONS
D-**ROOPS**
T-ROOPS
D-**ROOPY**
ROOSA-S
B-**ROOSE**
ROOSE-D
ROOSE-R
ROOSE-S
ROOST-S
W-**ROOTS**
ROOTS-Y
G-**ROPED**
T-ROPED
G-**ROPER**
P-ROPER
ROPER-S
ROPER-Y
G-**ROPES**
T-ROPES
ROQUE-S
ROQUE-T
C-**RORES**
P-RORES
RORIE-R
P-**ROSED**
B-**ROSES**
E-ROSES
P-ROSES
U-ROSES
G-**ROSET**
ROSET-S
ROSET-Y
ROSIN-G
ROSIN-S
ROSIN-Y
P-**ROSIT**
ROSIT-S
F-**ROSTS**
C-**ROTAL**
C-**ROTCH**
ROTCH-E
ROTOR-S
ROTTE-D
ROTTE-N
ROTTE-R
ROTTE-S
ROUEN-S
ROUGE-D
ROUGE-S
B-**ROUGH**
G-ROUGH
T-ROUGH
ROUGH-S

ROUGH-T
ROUGH-Y
T-**ROULE**
ROULE-S
P-**ROULS**
A-**ROUND**
G-ROUND
ROUND-S
C-**ROUPS**
G-ROUPS
C-**ROUPY**
G-ROUPY
A-**ROUSE**
C-ROUSE
G-ROUSE
T-ROUSE
ROUSE-D
ROUSE-R
ROUSE-S
ROUST-S
C-**ROUTE**
ROUTE-D
ROUTE-R
ROUTE-S
D-**ROUTH**
ROUTH-S
C-**ROUTS**
G-ROUTS
T-ROUTS
D-**ROVED**
G-ROVED
P-ROVED
P-**ROVEN**
D-**ROVER**
P-ROVER
T-ROVER
ROVER-S
D-**ROVES**
G-ROVES
P-ROVES
T-ROVES
ROWAN-S
C-**ROWDY**
B-**ROWED**
C-ROWED
T-ROWED
T-**ROWEL**
ROWEL-S
ROWEN-S
C-**ROWER**
G-ROWER
P-ROWER
ROWER-S
ROWME-S
D-**ROWND**
ROWND-S
G-**ROWTH**
T-ROWTH
ROWTH-S
ROYAL-S
G-**ROYNE**
P-ROYNE
ROYNE-D
ROYNE-S
ROYST-S
ROZET-S
ROZIT-S
RUANA-S
RUBIN-E
RUBIN-S
RUBLE-S
U-**RUBUS**
RUCHE-D
RUCHE-S
C-**RUCKS**

T-RUCKS
C-**RUDDY**
C-**RUDER**
RUDER-Y
C-**RUDES**
P-RUDES
RUDES-T
RUDIE-S
T-**RUFFE**
RUFFE-D
RUFFE-S
G-**RUFFS**
F-**RUGAL**
D-**RUGGY**
G-**RUING**
T-RUING
RUING-S
B-**RUINS**
RULER-S
B-**RUMAL**
RUMAL-S
RUMBA-S
RUMBO-S
C-**RUMEN**
RUMEN-S
B-**RUMES**
G-RUMES
D-**RUMLY**
G-RUMLY
C-**RUMMY**
RUMOR-S
C-**RUMPS**
F-RUMPS
G-RUMPS
T-RUMPS
C-**RUMPY**
F-RUMPY
G-RUMPY
B-**RUNCH**
C-RUNCH
P-**RUNED**
P-**RUNES**
B-**RUNTS**
G-RUNTS
P-RUNTS
RUPEE-S
RUPIA-H
RUPIA-S
C-**RURAL**
RURAL-S
C-**RUSES**
D-RUSES
U-RUSES
B-**RUSHY**
RUSMA-S
B-**RUSTS**
C-RUSTS
F-RUSTS
T-RUSTS
C-**RUSTY**
T-RUSTY
T-**RUTHS**
RUTIN-S
RYBAT-S
G-**RYKES**
RYMME-D
RYMME-S
SABER-S
SABIN-E
SABIN-S
SABIR-S
U-**SABLE**
SABLE-D
SABLE-S
SABOT-S

SABRA-S
SABRE-D
SABRE-S
SACRA-L
SADDO-S
T-**SADES**
SADHE-S
SADHU-S
T-**SADIS**
SADIS-M
SADIS-T
SADZA-S
SAFES-T
U-**SAGER**
U-**SAGES**
SAGES-T
SAHIB-A
SAHIB-S
SAICE-S
SAICK-S
SAIDS-T
SAIGA-S
SAINE-D
SAINT-S
SAITH-E
SAITH-S
SAJOU-S
SAKER-S
SAKIA-S
SALAD-E
SALAD-S
SALAL-S
SALEP-S
SALET-S
SALLE-E
SALLE-S
SALLE-T
SALMI-S
SALOL-S
SALON-S
SALOP-S
SALPA-E
SALPA-S
SALSA-S
SALSE-S
SALTO-S
SALUE-D
SALUE-S
SALVE-D
SALVE-R
SALVE-S
SALVO-R
SALVO-S
SAMAN-S
T-**SAMBA**
SAMBA-L
SAMBA-R
SAMBA-S
SAMBO-S
SAMEK-H
SAMEK-S
SAMEL-Y
SAMFU-S
SAMPI-S
SANES-T
SANGA-R
SANGA-S
SANGH-S
SANKO-S
SANSA-R
SANSA-S
SANTO-L
SANTO-N
SANTO-S
SAPAN-S

SAPOR-S
SARAN-S
SAREE-S
SARGE-S
SARGO-S
SARIN-G
SARIN-S
SAROD-E
SAROD-S
SASIN-E
SASIN-S
SASSE-D
SASSE-S
SATAY-S
I-**SATIN**
SATIN-G
SATIN-S
SATIN-Y
SATYR-A
SATYR-S
SAUBA-S
SAUCE-D
SAUCE-R
SAUCE-S
SAUCH-S
SAUGH-S
SAUGH-Y
SAULT-S
SAUNA-S
SAUNT-S
SAUTE-D
SAUTE-S
SAVER-S
SAVEY-S
SAVIN-E
SAVIN-G
SAVIN-S
SAVOR-S
SAVOR-Y
SAVOY-S
SAWAH-S
SAWER-S
SAYER-S
SAYID-S
SAYON-S
SCAFF-S
SCAIL-S
SCALA-E
SCALA-R
SCALD-S
SCALE-D
SCALE-R
SCALE-S
SCALL-S
SCALL-Y
SCALP-S
SCAMP-I
SCAMP-S
SCANT-S
SCANT-Y
SCAPA-S
E-**SCAPE**
SCAPE-D
SCAPE-S
SCARE-D
SCARE-R
SCARE-S
SCARE-Y
SCARF-S
E-**SCARP**
SCARP-A
SCARP-H
SCARP-S
E-**SCARS**
SCART-H

SCART-S
SCATH-E
SCATH-S
SCATT-S
SCATT-Y
SCAUD-S
SCAUP-S
SCAUR-S
SCAUR-Y
SCEAT-T
SCENA-S
A-**SCEND**
SCEND-S
SCENE-D
SCENE-S
A-**SCENT**
SCENT-S
SCHAV-S
SCHMO-E
SCHMO-S
SCHUL-N
SCHWA-S
SCION-S
SCLIM-S
SCOFF-S
SCOLD-S
SCONE-S
SCOOG-S
SCOOP-S
SCOOT-S
SCOPA-E
SCOPA-S
SCOPE-D
SCOPE-S
SCORE-D
SCORE-R
SCORE-S
SCORN-S
A-**SCOTS**
E-SCOTS
SCOUG-S
SCOUP-S
SCOUR-S
SCOUT-H
SCOUT-S
SCOWL-S
SCOWP-S
SCRAB-S
SCRAE-S
SCRAG-S
SCRAM-B
SCRAM-S
SCRAN-S
SCRAP-E
SCRAP-S
SCRAT-S
SCRAW-L
SCRAW-M
SCRAW-S
SCRAY-E
SCRAY-S
SCREE-D
SCREE-N
SCREE-S
SCREW-S
SCREW-Y
SCRIM-P
SCRIM-S
SCRIP-S
SCRIP-T
SCROD-S
SCROG-S
E-**SCROW**
SCROW-L
SCROW-S

SCRUB-S
SCRUM-P
SCRUM-S
SCUBA-S
E-**SCUDO**
SCUFF-S
SCUFT-S
SCULK-S
SCULL-E
SCULL-S
SCULP-S
SCULP-T
SCURF-S
SCURF-Y
SCUSE-D
SCUSE-S
SCUTA-L
SCUTE-S
SCUZZ-Y
SDAYN-S
SDEIN-S
SEAME-D
SEAME-N
SEAME-R
SEAME-S
SEARE-D
SEARE-R
SEASE-D
SEASE-S
SEAZE-D
SEAZE-S
SEBUM-S
SECCO-S
SEDAN-S
SEDER-S
SEDGE-D
SEDGE-S
SEDUM-S
SEGAR-S
SEGNO-S
SEGOL-S
SEGUE-D
SEGUE-S
SEINE-D
SEINE-R
SEINE-S
SEISE-D
SEISE-R
SEISE-S
SEISM-S
A-**SEITY**
SEIZE-D
SEIZE-R
SEIZE-S
SELAH-S
SELLA-E
SELLA-S
SELLE-R
SELLE-S
SELVA-S
SEMEE-D
SEMEN-S
SEMIE-S
SENNA-S
SENOR-A
SENOR-S
SENSE-D
SENSE-S
SENTE-D
SEPAD-S
SEPAL-S
SEPIA-S
SEPOY-S
SEPTA-L
SERAC-S

SERAI-L
SERAI-S
SERES-T
SERGE-S
SERIF-S
SERIN-E
SERIN-G
SERIN-S
SERON-S
SEROW-S
SERRA-E
SERRA-N
SERRA-S
SERRE-D
SERRE-S
SERUM-S
SERVE-D
SERVE-R
SERVE-S
SERVO-S
SETON-S
SETUP-S
SEVEN-S
SEVER-E
SEVER-S
SEVER-Y
SEWAN-S
SEWAR-S
SEWEL-S
SEWEN-S
SEWER-S
SEWIN-G
SEWIN-S
SEXER-S
SEXTO-N
SEXTO-S
SEYEN-S
SHACK-O
SHACK-S
SHADE-D
SHADE-R
SHADE-S
SHAFT-S
A-**SHAKE**
SHAKE-D
SHAKE-N
SHAKE-R
SHAKE-S
SHAKO-S
SHALE-D
SHALE-S
SHALE-Y
SHALL-I
SHALM-S
SHAMA-N
SHAMA-S
A-**SHAME**
SHAME-D
SHAME-R
SHAME-S
SHAND-S
SHAND-Y
SHANK-S
SHAPE-D
SHAPE-N
SHAPE-R
SHAPE-S
SHARD-S
SHARE-D
SHARE-R
SHARE-S
SHARK-S
SHARN-S
SHARN-Y
SHARP-S

SHARP-Y
SHAUL-S
SHAVE-D
SHAVE-N
SHAVE-R
SHAVE-S
SHAWL-S
SHAWM-S
P-**SHAWS**
SHAYA-S
SHCHI-S
SHEAF-S
SHEAF-Y
SHEAL-S
SHEAR-S
SHEEL-S
SHEEN-S
SHEEN-Y
SHEEP-O
SHEEP-Y
SHEER-S
SHEET-S
SHEET-Y
SHEIK-H
SHEIK-S
SHELF-S
SHELF-Y
SHELL-S
SHELL-Y
Y-**SHEND**
SHEND-S
Y-**SHENT**
SHEOL-S
SHERD-S
A-**SHETS**
SHEVA-S
SHIEL-D
SHIEL-S
A-**SHIER**
SHIER-S
SHIES-T
SHIFT-S
SHIFT-Y
SHILL-S
A-**SHINE**
SHINE-D
SHINE-R
SHINE-S
SHIRE-S
SHIRK-S
SHIRR-A
SHIRR-S
SHIRT-S
SHIRT-Y
SHIST-S
SHITE-D
SHITE-S
SHIVA-H
SHIVA-S
SHIVE-R
SHIVE-S
SHLEP-P
SHLEP-S
SHMEK-S
SHOAL-S
SHOAL-Y
SHOAT-S
SHOCK-S
SHOER-S
SHOGI-S
SHOJI-S
SHOLA-S
SHOOK-S
SHOOL-E
SHOOL-S
SHOOT-S
A-**SHORE**
SHORE-D
SHORE-R
SHORE-S
SHORL-S
SHORT-S
SHORT-Y
SHOTE-S
SHOTT-E
SHOTT-S
SHOUT-S
SHOVE-D
SHOVE-L
SHOVE-R
SHOVE-S
SHOYU-S
SHRED-S
SHREW-D
SHREW-S
SHROW-D
SHROW-S
SHRUB-S
SHRUG-S
SHTIK-S
SHTUM-M
SHTUP-S
SHUCK-S
SHULE-D
SHULE-S
SHUNT-S
SHURA-S
SHUTE-D
SHUTE-S
SHYER-S
SIBYL-S
SICKO-S
SIDER-S
A-**SIDES**
SIDHA-S
SIDLE-D
SIDLE-R
SIDLE-S
SIEGE-D
SIEGE-R
SIEGE-S
SIENT-S
SIETH-S
SIEUR-S
SIEVE-D
SIEVE-S
SIGHT-S
SIGIL-S
SIGMA-S
SILEN-E
SILEN-I
SILEN-S
SILEN-T
SILER-S
E-**SILES**
SILVA-E
SILVA-N
SILVA-S
SIMAR-S
SIMUL-S
SINEW-S
SINEW-Y
SINGE-D
SINGE-R
SINGE-S
SIREE-S
SIREN-S
SIRIH-S
SIROC-S
SIRRA-H
SIRRA-S
SIRUP-S
SIRUP-Y
SISAL-S
SITAR-S
SITHE-D
SITHE-N
SITHE-S
SITUP-S
SIVER-S
SIXER-S
SIXMO-S
SIXTE-S
SIXTH-S
SIZAR-S
SIZEL-S
SIZER-S
SKAIL-S
SKALD-S
SKANK-S
SKART-H
SKART-S
SKATE-D
SKATE-R
SKATE-S
SKATT-S
SKEAN-E
SKEAN-S
SKEAR-S
SKEAR-Y
SKEEN-S
SKEER-S
SKEER-Y
SKEET-S
SKEGG-S
SKEIN-S
SKELF-S
SKELL-S
SKELL-Y
SKELM-S
SKELP-S
SKENE-S
A-**SKERS**
E-SKERS
SKIER-S
E-**SKIES**
SKIFF-S
SKILL-S
SKILL-Y
SKIMO-S
SKIMP-S
SKIMP-Y
SKINK-S
SKIRL-S
SKIRR-S
SKIRT-S
SKITE-D
SKITE-S
SKIVE-D
SKIVE-R
SKIVE-S
SKLIM-S
SKOAL-S
SKOFF-S
SKRAN-S
SKRIK-S
SKULK-S
SKULL-S
SKUNK-S
SKYER-S
SKYRE-D
SKYRE-S
SKYTE-D
SKYTE-S
SLACK-S
SLADE-S
A-**SLAKE**
SLAKE-D
SLAKE-R
SLAKE-S
SLANE-S
SLANG-S
SLANG-Y
A-**SLANT**
SLANT-S
SLANT-Y
SLATE-D
SLATE-R
SLATE-S
SLATE-Y
SLAVE-D
SLAVE-R
SLAVE-S
SLAVE-Y
SLEEK-S
SLEEK-Y
A-**SLEEP**
SLEEP-S
SLEEP-Y
SLEET-S
SLEET-Y
SLICE-D
SLICE-R
SLICE-S
SLICK-S
SLIDE-D
SLIDE-R
SLIDE-S
SLIME-D
SLIME-S
SLIMS-Y
I-**SLING**
SLING-S
SLINK-S
SLINK-Y
SLIPE-D
SLIPE-S
SLIVE-D
SLIVE-N
SLIVE-R
SLIVE-S
SLOAN-S
SLOID-S
SLOJD-S
SLOOM-S
SLOOM-Y
SLOOP-S
SLOOT-S
A-**SLOPE**
SLOPE-D
SLOPE-R
SLOPE-S
SLOSH-Y
SLOTH-S
SLOVE-N
SLOYD-S
SLUBB-S
SLUBB-Y
SLUFF-S
SLUIT-S
SLUMP-S
SLUMP-Y
SLURB-S
SLURP-S
SLUSE-S
SLUSH-Y
SLYPE-S
SMACK-S
SMAIK-S
SMALL-S
SMALM-S
SMALM-Y
SMALT-I
SMALT-O
SMALT-S
SMARM-S
SMARM-Y
SMART-S
SMART-Y
SMAZE-S
A-**SMEAR**
SMEAR-S
SMEAR-Y
SMEEK-S
SMELL-S
SMELL-Y
SMELT-S
SMERK-S
SMILE-D
SMILE-R
SMILE-S
SMILE-T
SMILE-Y
SMIRK-S
SMIRK-Y
SMIRR-S
SMIRR-Y
SMITE-R
SMITE-S
SMITH-S
SMITH-Y
SMOCK-S
SMOKE-D
SMOKE-R
SMOKE-S
SMOKE-Y
SMOKO-S
SMOLT-S
SMOOR-S
SMOOT-H
SMOOT-S
SMORE-D
SMORE-S
SMOUT-S
SMOWT-S
SNACK-S
SNAFU-S
SNAIL-S
SNAIL-Y
SNAKE-D
SNAKE-S
SNAKE-Y
SNARE-D
SNARE-R
SNARE-S
SNARK-S
SNARK-Y
SNARL-S
SNARL-Y
SNATH-E
SNATH-S
SNEAD-S
SNEAK-S
SNEAK-Y
SNEAP-S
SNECK-S
SNEER-S
SNEER-Y
SNEES-H
SNELL-S
SNELL-Y
SNICK-S
SNIDE-R
SNIDE-S
SNIFF-S
SNIFF-Y
SNIFT-S
SNIFT-Y
SNIPE-D
SNIPE-R
SNIPE-S
SNIRT-S
SNOEK-S
SNOKE-D
SNOKE-S
SNOOD-S
SNOOK-S
SNOOL-S
SNOOP-S
SNOOP-Y
SNOOT-S
SNOOT-Y
SNORE-D
SNORE-R
SNORE-S
SNORT-S
SNORT-Y
SNOUT-S
SNOUT-Y
SNOWK-S
SNUFF-S
SNUFF-Y
SOARE-D
SOARE-R
SOARE-S
SOAVE-S
SOBER-S
SOCLE-S
SODOM-S
SODOM-Y
SOFAR-S
SOFTA-S
SOGER-S
SOKAH-S
SOKEN-S
SOKOL-S
SOLAH-S
SOLAN-D
SOLAN-O
SOLAN-S
SOLAR-S
SOLDE-R
SOLDE-S
SOLEI-N
SOLER-A
SOLER-S
SOLID-I
SOLID-S
SOLON-S
SOLUM-S
SOLVE-D
SOLVE-R
SOLVE-S
SOMAN-S
SONAR-S
SONCE-S
SONDE-R
SONDE-S
SONIC-S
SONNE-S
SONNE-T
SONSE-S
SOOLE-D
SOOLE-S
SOOTE-D
SOOTE-S
SOOTH-E
SOOTH-S
SOPOR-S
P-**SORAS**
SORDO-R
SOREE-S
SOREL-L
SOREL-S
SOREL-Y
T-**SORES**
SORES-T
SORGO-S
SORRA-S
SOTOL-S
SOUCE-D
SOUCE-S
SOUGH-S
SOUGH-T
SOUND-S
SOURS-E
SOUSE-D
SOUSE-S
SOUTH-S
SOWAR-S
SOWCE-D
SOWCE-S
SOWER-S
SOWFF-S
SOWLE-D
SOWLE-S
SOWND-S
SOWNE-S
SOWSE-D
SOWSE-S
SOWTH-S
SOYLE-S
SOZIN-E
SOZIN-S
SPACE-D
SPACE-R
SPACE-S
SPACE-Y
SPADE-D
SPADE-R
SPADE-S
SPADO-S
SPAER-S
SPAHI-S
SPAIL-S
SPAIN-G
SPAIN-S
SPAIT-S
SPALD-S
SPALE-S
SPALL-E
SPALL-S
SPALT-S
SPANE-D
SPANE-S
SPANG-S
SPANK-S
SPARE-D
SPARE-R
SPARE-S
SPARK-E
SPARK-S
SPARK-Y
SPARS-E
SPART-H
SPART-S
SPASM-S
SPATE-S
SPAUL-D
SPAUL-S
SPAWL-S
SPAWN-S
SPAWN-Y
SPAYD-S
SPEAK-S

SPEAL-S
SPEAN-S
SPEAR-S
SPEAR-Y
SPEAT-S
SPECK-S
SPECK-Y
SPEED-O
SPEED-S
SPEED-Y
SPEEL-S
SPEER-S
SPEIL-S
SPEIR-S
SPELD-S
SPELK-S
SPELL-S
SPELT-S
SPELT-Z
SPEND-S
SPERM-S
E-**SPIAL**
SPIAL-S
SPICA-E
SPICA-S
SPICE-D
SPICE-R
SPICE-S
SPICE-Y
A-**SPICK**
SPICK-S
A-**SPICS**
SPIDE-R
E-**SPIED**
SPIEL-S
SPIER-S
E-**SPIES**
SPIFF-S
SPIFF-Y
SPIKE-D
SPIKE-R
SPIKE-S
SPIKE-Y
SPILE-D
SPILE-S
SPILL-S
SPILT-H
SPINA-E
SPINA-L
SPINA-R
SPINA-S
A-**SPINE**
SPINE-D
SPINE-L
SPINE-S
SPINE-T
SPINK-S
A-**SPIRE**
SPIRE-A
SPIRE-D
SPIRE-M
SPIRE-S
SPIRT-S
SPITE-D
SPITE-S
SPLAT-S
SPLAY-S
SPLIT-S
SPODE-S
SPOIL-S
SPOIL-T
SPOKE-D
SPOKE-N
SPOKE-S
SPOOF-S

SPOOF-Y
SPOOK-S
SPOOK-Y
SPOOL-S
SPOOM-S
SPOON-S
SPOON-Y
SPOOR-S
SPOOT-S
SPORE-D
SPORE-S
A-**SPORT**
SPORT-S
SPORT-Y
SPOSH-Y
A-**SPOUT**
SPOUT-S
SPOUT-Y
SPRAG-S
SPRAT-S
SPRAY-S
SPRED-D
SPRED-S
SPREE-D
SPREE-S
SPREW-S
SPRIG-S
E-**SPRIT**
SPRIT-E
SPRIT-S
SPRIT-Z
SPROD-S
SPROG-S
SPRUE-S
SPRUG-S
SPULE-S
SPUME-D
SPUME-S
SPUNK-S
SPUNK-Y
SPURN-E
SPURN-S
SPURT-S
SPYAL-S
SPYRE-S
SQUAB-S
SQUAD-S
A-**SQUAT**
SQUAT-S
SQUAW-K
SQUAW-S
SQUEG-S
SQUIB-S
SQUID-S
SQUIT-S
STACK-S
STADE-S
STAFF-S
STAGE-D
STAGE-R
STAGE-S
STAGE-Y
STAIG-S
STAIN-S
STAIR-S
STAKE-D
STAKE-S
STALE-D
STALE-R
STALE-S
STALK-O
STALK-S
STALK-Y
STALL-S
STAMP-S

STAND-S
STANE-D
STANE-S
STANG-S
STANK-S
STAPH-S
A-**STARE**
STARE-D
STARE-R
STARE-S
STARK-S
STARN-S
STARR-S
STARR-Y
A-**START**
START-S
E-**STATE**
STATE-D
STATE-R
STATE-S
STAVE-D
STAVE-S
STEAD-S
STEAD-Y
STEAK-S
O-**STEAL**
STEAL-E
STEAL-S
STEAL-T
STEAM-S
STEAM-Y
STEAN-E
STEAN-S
STEAR-D
STEAR-E
STEAR-S
STEDD-E
STEDD-S
STEDD-Y
STEDE-D
STEDE-S
STEED-S
STEED-Y
STEEK-S
STEEL-D
STEEL-S
STEEL-Y
E-**STEEM**
STEEM-S
STEEN-S
STEEP-S
STEEP-Y
STEER-S
STEER-Y
STEIL-S
STEIN-S
STELA-E
STELA-I
STELA-R
STELE-S
STELL-A
STELL-S
STEME-D
STEME-S
STEND-S
STENO-S
O-**STENT**
STENT-S
STERE-O
STERE-S
A-**STERN**
STERN-A
STERN-S
STICH-S
STICK-S

STICK-Y
STIFF-S
STIFF-Y
STILB-S
STILE-D
STILE-S
STILE-T
STILL-S
STILL-Y
STILT-S
STILT-Y
STIME-D
STIME-S
STING-O
STING-S
STING-Y
STINK-O
STINK-S
STINK-Y
STINT-S
STINT-Y
STIPA-S
STIPE-D
STIPE-L
STIPE-S
STIRE-D
STIRE-S
STIRK-S
STIRP-S
STIVE-D
STIVE-R
STIVE-S
STOAT-S
STOCK-S
STOCK-Y
STOEP-S
STOIC-S
STOIT-S
STOKE-D
STOKE-R
STOKE-S
STOLE-D
STOLE-N
STOLE-S
STOMA-L
STOMA-S
STOMP-S
STOND-S
A-**STONE**
STONE-D
STONE-N
STONE-R
STONE-S
STONE-Y
STONK-S
STONN-E
STONN-S
A-**STONY**
STOOK-S
STOOL-S
A-**STOOP**
STOOP-E
STOOP-S
STOOR-S
STOPE-D
STOPE-R
STOPE-S
E-**STOPS**
STORE-D
STORE-R
STORE-S
STORE-Y
STORK-S
STORM-S
STORM-Y

STOUN-D
STOUN-S
STOUP-S
STOUR-E
STOUR-S
STOUR-Y
STOUT-H
STOUT-S
STOVE-D
STOVE-R
STOVE-S
STOWN-D
STOWP-S
STRAD-S
STRAE-S
STRAG-S
STRAP-S
STRAW-N
STRAW-S
STRAW-Y
A-**STRAY**
E-STRAY
STRAY-S
STREP-S
STREW-N
STREW-S
STRIA-E
STRIG-A
STRIG-S
STRIP-E
STRIP-S
STRIP-T
STRIP-Y
STROP-S
STROW-N
STROW-S
STROY-S
E-**STRUM**
STRUM-A
STRUM-S
A-**STRUT**
STRUT-S
STUCK-S
STUFF-S
STUFF-Y
STULL-S
STULM-S
STUMP-S
STUMP-Y
A-**STUNS**
STUNT-S
STUPA-S
STUPE-D
STUPE-S
STURT-S
STYLE-D
STYLE-R
STYLE-S
STYLE-T
STYLO-S
STYME-D
STYME-S
STYRE-D
STYRE-S
STYTE-D
STYTE-S
SUAVE-R
SUBAH-S
T-**SUBAS**
SUBER-S
SUCRE-S
SUDOR-S
SUEDE-D
SUEDE-S
SUGAR-S

SUGAR-Y
SUING-S
SUINT-S
SUITE-D
SUITE-R
SUITE-S
SUJEE-S
SULFA-S
SUMAC-H
SUMAC-S
SUMMA-E
SUMMA-R
SUMMA-S
SUMMA-T
SUMPH-S
SUNNA-H
SUNNA-S
SUNUP-S
SUPER-B
SUPER-S
SURAH-S
SURAT-S
U-**SURED**
U-**SURER**
U-**SURES**
SURES-T
SURGE-D
SURGE-R
SURGE-S
SURRA-S
SUSHI-S
SUTOR-S
SUTRA-S
SUTTA-S
SWAGE-D
SWAGE-R
SWAGE-S
SWAIL-S
SWAIN-S
SWALE-D
SWALE-S
SWAMI-S
SWAMP-S
SWAMP-Y
SWANK-S
SWANK-Y
U-**SWARD**
SWARD-S
SWARD-Y
SWARF-S
A-**SWARM**
SWARM-S
SWART-H
SWART-Y
SWASH-Y
SWATH-E
SWATH-S
SWATH-Y
SWAYL-S
SWEAL-S
SWEAR-D
SWEAR-S
SWEAT-S
SWEAT-Y
SWEDE-S
SWEEL-S
SWEEP-S
SWEEP-Y
SWEER-T
SWEET-S
SWEET-Y
SWEIR-T
SWELL-S
SWELT-S
SWERF-S

SWIFT-S
SWILL-S
A-**SWING**
SWING-E
SWING-S
SWING-Y
SWINK-S
SWIPE-D
SWIPE-R
SWIPE-S
SWIPE-Y
SWIRE-S
A-**SWIRL**
SWIRL-S
SWIRL-Y
SWISH-Y
SWITH-E
SWIVE-D
SWIVE-L
SWIVE-S
SWIVE-T
SWONE-S
A-**SWOON**
SWOON-S
SWOOP-S
SWORD-S
SWOUN-D
SWOUN-E
SWOUN-S
SYBBE-S
SYBIL-S
SYBOE-S
SYBOW-S
SYCEE-S
SYLPH-S
SYLPH-Y
SYLVA-E
SYLVA-N
SYLVA-S
SYMAR-S
SYNCH-S
SYNOD-S
SYNTH-S
SYRAH-S
SYREN-S
SYRUP-S
SYRUP-Y
SYSOP-S
SYTHE-S
SYVER-S
TABER-D
TABER-S
TABLA-S
S-**TABLE**
TABLE-D
TABLE-S
TABLE-T
TABOO-S
TABOR-S
TABUN-S
TACAN-S
TACHE-S
TACHO-S
S-**TACKS**
TAFIA-S
S-**TAGGY**
TAIGA-S
S-**TAINS**
TAINT-S
TAIRA-S
TAKER-S
S-**TAKES**
TAKHI-S
TAKIN-G
TAKIN-S

TALAK-S
TALAQ-S
TALAR-S
TALEA-E
S-**TALER**
TALER-S
S-**TALES**
S-**TALKS**
S-**TALKY**
TALMA-S
E-**TALON**
TALON-S
TALPA-E
TALPA-S
TALUK-A
TALUK-S
TAMAL-E
TAMAL-S
TAMER-S
TAMES-T
E-**TAMIN**
TAMIN-E
TAMIN-G
TAMIN-S
TAMIS-E
S-**TAMPS**
TANGA-S
TANGI-E
TANGI-S
TANGO-S
S-**TANGS**
TANKA-S
S-**TANKS**
TANNA-H
TANNA-S
TAPER-S
E-**TAPES**
S-TAPES
TAPET-A
TAPET-I
TAPET-S
TAPIR-S
TAPIS-T
TAPPA-S
S-**TARED**
S-**TARES**
TARGE-D
TARGE-S
TARGE-T
S-**TARNS**
TAROC-S
TAROK-S
TAROT-S
TARRE-D
TARRE-S
S-**TARRY**
TARSI-A
S-**TARTS**
TASAR-S
TASER-S
TASSE-L
TASSE-S
TASSE-T
TASTE-D
TASTE-R
TASTE-S
TATAR-S
S-**TATER**
TATER-S
S-**TATES**
TATIE-S
TATOU-S
S-**TATUS**
TAUBE-S
TAUNT-S
TAUPE-S
TAVAH-S
TAVER-N
TAVER-S
TAVER-T
S-**TAWED**
TAWER-S
TAWER-Y
TAWIE-R
TAWSE-D
TAWSE-S
TAXER-S
TAXOL-S
TAXON-S
TAXOR-S
TAYRA-S
TAZZA-S
TEADE-S
S-**TEADS**
S-**TEAKS**
S-**TEALS**
S-**TEAMS**
S-**TEARS**
TEASE-D
TEASE-L
TEASE-R
TEASE-S
TEAZE-D
TEAZE-L
TEAZE-S
TECTA-L
S-**TEDDY**
S-**TEELS**
S-**TEEMS**
TEEND-S
TEENE-D
TEENE-R
TEENE-S
S-**TEENS**
TEENS-Y
S-**TEERS**
TEETH-E
TEGUA-S
TEIID-S
S-**TEILS**
TEIND-S
S-**TELAE**
S-**TELES**
TELES-M
TELIA-L
A-**TELIC**
S-TELIC
S-**TELLS**
TELLY-S
I-**TEMED**
S-TEMED
S-**TEMES**
TEMPO-S
TEMPT-S
TEMSE-D
TEMSE-S
S-**TENCH**
S-**TENDS**
C-**TENES**
TENET-S
TENIA-E
TENIA-S
TENNE-R
TENNE-S
TENNO-S
TENON-S
TENOR-S
TENSE-D
TENSE-R
TENSE-S
TENTH-S
S-**TENTS**
TENUE-S
TEPAL-S
TEPEE-S
TEPOY-S
TERAI-S
TERCE-L
TERCE-S
TERCE-T
TEREK-S
S-**TERES**
TERFE-S
TERGA-L
E-**TERNE**
TERNE-D
TERNE-S
S-**TERNS**
TERRA-E
TERRA-S
TERSE-R
TESLA-S
TESTA-E
TESTE-D
TESTE-E
TESTE-R
TESTE-S
TETRA-D
TETRA-S
S-**TEWED**
TEWEL-S
TEWIT-S
THACK-S
THAGI-S
THANA-H
THANA-S
E-**THANE**
THANE-S
THANK-S
THARM-S
THECA-E
THECA-L
THEEK-S
THEFT-S
THEGN-S
THEIC-S
THEIN-E
THEIN-S
THEIR-S
THEME-D
THEME-S
THEOW-S
THERE-S
THERM-E
THERM-S
THESE-S
THETA-S
THETE-S
THICK-O
THICK-S
THICK-Y
THIGH-S
THILL-S
THING-S
THING-Y
THINK-S
THIOL-S
THIRD-S
THIRL-S
THOFT-S
THOLE-D
THOLE-S
THONG-S
THORN-S
THORN-Y
THORO-N
THORP-E
THORP-S
THOWL-S
THRAW-N
THRAW-S
THREE-P
THREE-S
THRID-S
THRIP-S
A-**THROB**
THROB-S
THROE-D
THROE-S
THROW-E
THROW-N
THROW-S
THRUM-S
THUJA-S
THUMB-S
THUMB-Y
THUMP-S
THUNK-S
THURL-S
THUYA-S
THYME-S
THYME-Y
THYMI-C
TIARA-S
TIBIA-E
TIBIA-L
TIBIA-S
TICAL-S
S-**TICKS**
S-**TICKY**
S-**TIFFS**
TIGER-S
TIGER-Y
TIGHT-S
TIGON-S
TILAK-S
TILDE-S
S-**TILED**
TILER-S
TILER-Y
S-**TILES**
S-**TILLS**
S-**TILLY**
TILTH-S
S-**TILTS**
TIMBO-S
S-**TIMED**
TIMER-S
S-**TIMES**
TIMON-S
TINCT-S
TINEA-L
TINEA-S
TINGE-D
TINGE-S
S-**TINGS**
S-**TINKS**
S-**TINTS**
S-**TINTY**
S-**TIRED**
S-**TIRES**
TITAN-S
S-**TITCH**
TITCH-Y
TITER-S
TITHE-D
TITHE-R
TITHE-S
O-**TITIS**
TITLE-D
TITLE-R
TITLE-S
TITRE-S
TITUP-S
TITUP-Y
TOAST-S
TOAST-Y
TOAZE-D
TOAZE-S
S-**TOCKS**
TODAY-S
TODDE-D
TODDE-S
TOGAE-D
TOGUE-S
E-**TOILE**
TOILE-D
TOILE-R
TOILE-S
TOILE-T
TOISE-S
S-**TOITS**
TOKAY-S
S-**TOKED**
TOKEN-S
S-**TOKER**
TOKER-S
A-**TOKES**
S-TOKES
TOLAN-E
TOLAN-S
S-**TOLED**
TOLED-O
S-**TOLES**
A-**TOLLS**
TOLYL-S
TOMAN-S
TOMIA-L
A-**TONAL**
TONDO-S
A-**TONED**
S-TONED
A-**TONER**
S-TONER
TONER-S
A-**TONES**
S-TONES
S-**TONEY**
TONGA-S
A-**TONIC**
TONIC-S
S-**TONKS**
S-**TONNE**
TONNE-R
TONNE-S
S-**TOOLS**
TOOTH-S
TOOTH-Y
TOOTS-Y
S-**TOPED**
TOPEE-S
TOPEK-S
S-**TOPER**
TOPER-S
S-**TOPES**
TOPHE-S
A-**TOPIC**
TOPIC-S
TOQUE-S
TOQUE-T
TORAH-S
TORAN-A
TORAN-S
TORCH-Y
S-**TORES**
TOROS-E
TOROT-H
TORSE-L
TORSE-S
TORSK-S
TORSO-S
TORTE-N
TORTE-S
P-**TOSES**
TOTAL-S
TOTEM-S
TOTER-S
TOUCH-E
TOUCH-Y
TOUGH-S
TOUGH-Y
S-**TOUNS**
S-**TOURS**
TOUSE-D
TOUSE-R
TOUSE-S
S-**TOUTS**
TOUZE-D
TOUZE-S
S-**TOWED**
TOWEL-S
S-**TOWER**
TOWER-S
TOWER-Y
TOWIE-R
TOWIE-S
TOWSE-D
TOWSE-R
TOWSE-S
TOWZE-D
TOWZE-S
TOXIC-S
TOXIN-E
TOXIN-S
TOYER-S
TOYON-S
TOZIE-S
TRACE-D
TRACE-R
TRACE-S
TRACK-S
TRACT-S
TRADE-D
TRADE-R
TRADE-S
S-**TRADS**
TRAGI-C
S-**TRAIK**
TRAIK-S
TRAIL-S
S-**TRAIN**
TRAIN-S
S-**TRAIT**
TRAIT-S
S-**TRAMP**
TRAMP-S
TRANK-S
TRANQ-S
TRANS-E
TRANT-S
TRAPE-D
TRAPE-S
S-**TRAPS**
TRASH-Y
S-**TRASS**
TRATT-S
TRAVE-L
TRAVE-S
TRAWL-S
S-**TRAYS**
TREAD-S
TREAT-S
TREAT-Y
TRECK-S
TREEN-S
TREFA-H
TREMA-S
TREND-S
TREND-Y
S-**TRESS**
TRESS-Y
TREST-S
S-**TREWS**
TRIAC-S
TRIAC-T
TRIAD-S
A-**TRIAL**
TRIAL-S
TRIBE-S
TRICE-D
TRICE-S
S-**TRICK**
TRICK-S
TRICK-Y
S-**TRIDE**
E-**TRIER**
TRIER-S
TRIGO-N
TRIGO-S
S-**TRIGS**
S-**TRIKE**
TRIKE-S
TRILL-O
TRILL-S
TRINE-D
TRINE-S
TRIOL-S
TRIOR-S
TRIOS-E
S-**TRIPE**
TRIPE-S
TRIPE-Y
S-**TRIPS**
S-**TRIPY**
TRIST-E
TRITE-R
TRITE-S
TROAD-E
TROAD-S
TROAK-S
TROAT-S
TROCK-S
S-**TRODE**
TRODE-S
S-**TROKE**
TROKE-D
TROKE-S
S-**TROLL**
TROLL-S
TROLL-Y
TROMP-E
TROMP-S
TRONA-S
TRONC-S
TRONE-S
TROOP-S
TROPE-D
TROPE-S
TROTH-S
S-**TROUT**
TROUT-S
TROUT-Y
S-**TROVE**
TROVE-R
TROVE-S

S-**TROWS**
S-**TROYS**
TRUCE-D
TRUCE-S
S-**TRUCK**
TRUCK-S
TRUES-T
TRULL-S
TRUMP-S
TRUNK-S
TRUST-S
TRUST-Y
TRUTH-S
TRUTH-Y
TRYER-S
TRYST-E
TRYST-S
TSADE-S
TSADI-S
TSUBA-S
TUART-S
TUATH-S
S-**TUBBY**
TUBER-S
S-**TUCKS**
TUFFE-S
TUFFE-T
S-**TUFFS**
TUGRA-S
TUINA-S
TUISM-S
TULIP-S
TULLE-S
TUMOR-S
S-**TUMPS**
S-**TUMPY**
TUNER-S
TUNIC-A
TUNIC-S
TUPEK-S
TUPIK-S
TUQUE-S
TURBO-S
TURBO-T
TURME-S
TUTEE-S
TUTOR-S
TUTTI-S
TUYER-E
TUYER-S
A-**TWAIN**
TWAIN-S
TWANG-S
TWANG-Y
TWANK-S
TWANK-Y
TWEAK-S
TWEAK-Y
TWEED-S
TWEED-Y
A-**TWEEL**
TWEEL-S
TWEEL-Y
A-**TWEEN**
TWEEN-Y
TWEER-S
TWEET-S
TWERP-S
TWICE-R
TWIER-S
TWILL-S
TWILL-Y
TWILT-S
TWINE-D
TWINE-R
TWINE-S
TWINK-S
TWIRE-D
TWIRE-S
TWIRL-S
TWIRL-Y
TWIRP-S
TWIST-S
TWIST-Y
TWITE-S
A-**TWIXT**
TWOER-S
TWYER-E
TWYER-S
S-**TYING**
S-**TYLER**
TYLER-S
A-**TYPIC**
E-TYPIC
TYPTO-S
TYRAN-S
TYRAN-T
S-**TYRED**
S-**TYRES**
TYTHE-D
TYTHE-S
B-**UDDER**
D-UDDER
J-UDDER
M-UDDER
P-UDDER
R-UDDER
S-UDDER
UDDER-S
B-**UGGED**
F-UGGED
H-UGGED
J-UGGED
L-UGGED
M-UGGED
P-UGGED
R-UGGED
T-UGGED
UHLAN-S
UHURU-S
UKASE-S
ULAMA-S
K-**ULANS**
Y-ULANS
ULCER-S
ULEMA-S
ULMIN-S
ULNAR-E
ULTRA-S
V-**ULVAS**
ULYIE-S
ULZIE-S
UMBEL-S
C-**UMBER**
D-UMBER
L-UMBER
N-UMBER
UMBER-S
UMBER-Y
B-**UMBOS**
D-UMBOS
G-UMBOS
J-UMBOS
R-UMBOS
UMBRA-E
UMBRA-L
UMBRA-S
UMBRE-L
UMBRE-S
UMIAC-K
UMIAC-S
UMIAK-S
UMIAQ-S
B-**UMPED**
D-UMPED
G-UMPED
H-UMPED
J-UMPED
L-UMPED
M-UMPED
P-UMPED
R-UMPED
T-UMPED
Y-UMPED
H-**UMPTY**
N-UMPTY
UNARM-S
L-**UNARY**
UNBAG-S
UNBAN-S
UNBAR-E
UNBAR-K
UNBAR-S
S-**UNBED**
UNBED-S
UNCAP-E
UNCAP-S
B-**UNCES**
D-UNCES
O-UNCES
P-UNCES
UNCIA-E
UNCIA-L
N-**UNCLE**
UNCLE-D
UNCLE-S
UNCLE-W
B-**UNCOS**
J-UNCOS
J-**UNCUS**
UNCUT-E
UNDAM-S
D-**UNDER**
F-UNDER
S-UNDER
UNDER-N
UNFIT-S
UNFIX-T
UNGAG-S
UNGET-S
UNGOD-S
UNGUM-S
S-**UNHAT**
UNHAT-S
M-**UNIFY**
B-**UNION**
UNION-S
D-**UNITE**
G-UNITE
M-UNITE
UNITE-D
UNITE-R
UNITE-S
B-**UNKED**
D-UNKED
F-UNKED
J-UNKED
J-**UNKET**
S-UNKET
UNLAW-S
UNLAY-S
R-**UNLET**
UNLID-S
S-**UNLIT**
G-**UNMAN**
UNMAN-S
UNMEW-S
UNMIX-T
UNPAY-S
UNPEG-S
UNPEN-S
UNPEN-T
UNPIN-S
UNRED-Y
R-**UNRIG**
UNRIG-S
UNRIP-E
UNRIP-S
UNSAY-S
S-**UNSET**
UNSET-S
UNSEW-N
UNSEW-S
UNSEX-Y
A-**UNTIE**
UNTIE-D
UNTIE-S
UNTIL-E
M-**UNTIN**
UNTIN-S
UNWIT-S
UNWON-T
UNZIP-S
UPBOW-S
UPEND-S
UPJET-S
UPLAY-S
C-**UPPED**
D-UPPED
H-UPPED
P-UPPED
S-UPPED
T-UPPED
C-**UPPER**
S-UPPER
UPPER-S
UPRUN-S
UPSEE-S
UPSET-S
UPSEY-S
UPTAK-E
UPTAK-S
UPTIE-D
UPTIE-S
O-**URALI**
URALI-S
C-**URARE**
URARE-S
C-**URARI**
O-URARI
URARI-S
URASE-S
A-**URATE**
C-URATE
URATE-S
R-**URBAN**
T-URBAN
URBAN-E
URBIA-S
UREAS-E
UREDO-S
M-**URENA**
URENA-S
G-**URGED**
P-URGED
S-URGED
B-**URGER**
P-URGER
S-URGER
URGER-S
G-**URGES**
P-URGES
S-URGES
B-**URIAL**
C-URIAL
URIAL-S
M-**URINE**
P-URINE
URINE-D
URINE-S
C-**URITE**
URITE-S
URMAN-S
B-**URNED**
D-URNED
G-URNED
T-URNED
B-**URSAE**
URSON-S
URUBU-S
M-**URVAS**
USAGE-R
USAGE-S
M-**USERS**
B-**USHER**
G-USHER
H-USHER
L-USHER
M-USHER
P-USHER
R-USHER
USHER-S
B-**USING**
F-USING
M-USING
USNEA-S
USQUE-S
USUAL-S
USURE-D
USURE-R
USURE-S
USURP-S
F-**UTILE**
R-UTILE
S-UTILE
B-**UTTER**
C-UTTER
G-UTTER
M-UTTER
N-UTTER
P-UTTER
R-UTTER
UTTER-S
UVULA-E
UVULA-R
UVULA-S
E-**VADED**
E-**VADES**
VAGUE-D
VAGUE-R
VAGUE-S
A-**VAILS**
VAKIL-S
A-**VALES**
VALET-A
VALET-E
VALET-S
VALIS-E
VALOR-S
VALSE-D
VALSE-S
VALUE-D
VALUE-R
VALUE-S
VALVE-D
VALVE-S
VANDA-L
VANDA-S
VAPOR-S
VAPOR-Y
VARAN-S
VAREC-H
VAREC-S
VARNA-S
VARVE-D
VARVE-L
VARVE-S
K-**VASES**
VAULT-S
VAULT-Y
A-**VAUNT**
VAUNT-S
VAUNT-Y
VAUTE-D
VAUTE-S
VAWTE-D
VAWTE-S
VEALE-D
VEALE-R
VEALE-S
VEENA-S
VEGAN-S
VEGIE-S
VELAR-S
VELDT-S
VENEY-S
A-**VENGE**
VENGE-D
VENGE-R
VENGE-S
VENIN-E
VENIN-S
VENOM-S
E-**VENTS**
A-**VENUE**
VENUE-S
VERGE-D
VERGE-R
VERGE-S
A-**VERSE**
VERSE-D
VERSE-R
VERSE-S
VERSE-T
VERSO-S
VERST-E
VERST-S
A-**VERTS**
E-VERTS
VERTU-E
VERTU-S
VERVE-L
VERVE-N
VERVE-S
VERVE-T
VESPA-S
VESTA-L
VESTA-S
K-**VETCH**
VETCH-Y
VEXER-S
VEXIL-S
VEZIR-S
VIAND-S
VICAR-S
VICAR-Y
VIDEO-S
VIFDA-S
VIGIA-S
VIGIL-S
VIGOR-O
VIGOR-S
E-**VILER**
VILLA-E
VILLA-N
VILLA-R
VILLA-S
VINAL-S
VINCA-S
VINER-S
VINER-Y
O-**VINES**
VINEW-S
VINYL-S
VIOLA-S
VIPER-S
VIREO-S
VIRGA-S
VIRGE-R
VIRGE-S
VIRTU-E
VIRTU-S
A-**VISED**
A-**VISES**
VISIE-D
VISIE-R
VISIE-S
VISIT-E
VISIT-S
VISNE-S
VISON-S
VISOR-S
VISTA-L
VISTA-S
VISTO-S
A-**VITAL**
VITAL-S
VITTA-E
VIVAT-S
VIVDA-S
VIVER-S
VIXEN-S
VIZIR-S
VIZOR-S
VOCAB-S
VOCAL-S
VODKA-S
VODUN-S
VOGIE-R
VOGUE-D
VOGUE-R
VOGUE-S
VOGUE-Y
VOICE-D
VOICE-R
VOICE-S
A-**VOIDS**
O-VOIDS
VOILE-S
VOLAR-Y
VOLET-S
VOLTE-S
VOLVA-S
E-**VOLVE**
VOLVE-D
VOLVE-S
VOMER-S
VOMIT-O
VOMIT-S
VOTER-S
A-**VOUCH**
VOUGE-S
A-**VOWED**
VOWEL-S
A-**VOWER**

VOWER-S
VOXEL-S
VOZHD-S
VRAIC-S
VROOM-S
VROUW-S
VULVA-E
VULVA-L
VULVA-R
VULVA-S
WACKE-R
WACKE-S
WACKO-S
S-WADDY
WADER-S
WAFER-S
WAFER-Y
S-WAGED
S-WAGER
WAGER-S
S-WAGES
WAGON-S
WAHOO-S
WAIFT-S
S-WAILS
S-WAINS
T-WAINS
WAIST-S
T-WAITE
WAITE-D
WAITE-R
WAITE-S
A-WAITS
WAIVE-D
WAIVE-R
WAIVE-S
A-WAKED
A-WAKEN
WAKEN-S
WAKER-S
A-WAKES
S-WALED
WALER-S
D-WALES
S-WALES
WALIS-E
WALLA-H
WALLA-S
D-WANGS
T-WANGS
S-WANKS
T-WANKS
S-WANKY
T-WANKY
WANZE-D
WANZE-S
A-WARDS
S-WARDS
S-WARMS
A-WARNS
WARRE-D
WARRE-N
WARRE-Y
S-WARTY
S-WASHY
WASTE-D
WASTE-L
WASTE-R
WASTE-S
WATAP-E
WATAP-S
A-WATCH
S-WATCH
WATER-S
WATER-Y
WAUFF-S
WAUGH-S
WAUGH-T
WAULK-S
WAURS-T
WAVER-S
WAVER-Y
WAVEY-S
WAXER-S
S-WAYED
WAZIR-S
WEALD-S
S-WEALS
WEAMB-S
S-WEARS
A-WEARY
WEAVE-D
WEAVE-R
WEAVE-S
WEBER-S
WECHT-S
WEDEL-N
WEDEL-S
WEDGE-D
WEDGE-S
T-WEEDS
T-WEEDY
WEEKE-S
S-WEELS
T-WEELS
WEENS-Y
S-WEENY
T-WEENY
S-WEEPS
S-WEEPY
T-WEEST
WEETE-D
WEETE-N
WEETE-R
S-WEETS
T-WEETS
WEFTE-D
WEFTE-S
A-WEIGH
WEIGH-S
WEIGH-T
WEIRD-O
WEIRD-S
WEIRD-Y
WEISE-D
WEISE-S
WEIZE-D
WEIZE-S
WELKE-D
WELKE-S
D-WELLS
S-WELLS
S-WELTS
WHACK-O
WHACK-S
WHACK-Y
WHALE-D
WHALE-R
WHALE-S
WHANG-S
WHARE-S
WHARF-S
WHATS-O
WHAUP-S
WHAUR-S
WHEAL-S
WHEAR-E
WHEAT-S
WHEAT-Y
A-WHEEL
WHEEL-S
WHEEL-Y
WHEEN-S
WHEEP-S
WHEFT-S
WHELK-S
WHELK-Y
WHELM-S
WHELP-S
WHERE-S
WHIFF-S
WHIFF-Y
WHIFT-S
A-WHILE
WHILE-D
WHILE-S
WHIMS-Y
WHINE-D
WHINE-R
WHINE-S
WHINE-Y
A-WHIRL
WHIRL-S
WHIRL-Y
WHIRR-S
WHIRR-Y
WHISH-T
WHISK-S
WHISK-Y
WHIST-S
WHITE-D
WHITE-N
WHITE-R
WHITE-S
WHITE-Y
WHOLE-S
WHOMP-S
WHOOF-S
WHOOP-S
WHOOT-S
WHORE-D
WHORE-S
WHORL-S
WHORT-S
WHUMP-S
WICCA-N
WICCA-S
WIDEN-S
WIDES-T
WIDOW-S
WIDTH-S
WIELD-S
WIELD-Y
WIFIE-S
WIGAN-S
T-WIGGY
T-WIGHT
WIGHT-S
D-WILES
WILGA-S
WILJA-S
S-WILLS
T-WILLS
T-WILLY
T-WILTS
WINCE-D
WINCE-R
WINCE-S
WINCE-Y
D-WINED
T-WINED
D-WINES
T-WINES
S-WINGE
T-WINGE
WINGE-D
WINGE-R
WINGE-S
S-WINGS
S-WINGY
S-WINKS
T-WINKS
WINZE-S
S-WIPED
S-WIPER
WIPER-S
S-WIPES
T-WIRED
WIRER-S
S-WIRES
T-WIRES
WISES-T
T-WISTS
S-WITCH
T-WITCH
WITCH-Y
T-WITES
S-WITHE
WITHE-D
WITHE-R
WITHE-S
S-WIVED
WIVER-N
WIVER-S
S-WIVES
WIZEN-S
WOALD-S
WODGE-S
A-WOKEN
WOLVE-D
WOLVE-R
WOLVE-S
WOMAN-S
WONGA-S
WONGI-S
WOODS-Y
WOOER-S
WOOLD-S
S-WOONS
S-WOOPS
S-WOOSH
S-WORDS
WORLD-S
WORSE-D
WORSE-N
WORSE-R
WORSE-S
WORSE-T
WORST-S
WORTH-S
WORTH-Y
WOULD-S
S-WOUND
WOUND-S
WOUND-Y
WOVEN-S
A-WRACK
WRACK-S
WRANG-S
WRAST-S
WRATH-S
WRATH-Y
WRAWL-S
WREAK-S
WRECK-S
WREST-S
WRICK-S
O-WRIER
WRIES-T
WRING-S
WRIST-S
WRIST-Y
WRITE-R
WRITE-S
Y-WROKE
WROKE-N
A-WRONG
WRONG-S
WROOT-S
WURST-S
WUSHU-S
XEBEC-S
XENIA-L
XENIA-S
A-XENIC
XENON-S
XYLAN-S
XYLEM-S
XYLOL-S
XYLYL-S
YACCA-S
YACHT-S
K-YACKS
N-YAFFS
YAGER-S
YAHOO-S
YAIRD-S
YAKKA-S
YAKOW-S
YAMEN-S
YAMUN-S
K-YANGS
YAPOK-S
YAPON-S
YARFA-S
YARTA-S
YARTO-S
C-YCLED
YEALM-S
YEARD-S
YEARN-S
YEAST-S
YEAST-Y
YECCH-S
YENTA-S
YENTE-S
YERBA-S
C-YESES
O-YESES
YIELD-S
YIRTH-S
X-YLEMS
YOBBO-S
YODEL-S
YODLE-D
YODLE-R
YODLE-S
YOGEE-S
YOGIN-I
YOGIN-S
YOGIS-M
YOICK-S
YOJAN-A
YOJAN-S
YOKEL-S
YOUNG-S
YOURT-S
YOUTH-S
YOUTH-Y
YOWIE-S
YRNEH-S
YUCCA-S
YULAN-S
YUPON-S
ZABRA-S
ZAIRE-S
ZAKAT-S
ZAMAN-G
ZAMAN-S
ZAMBO-S
ZAMIA-S
ZANJA-S
ZANTE-S
ZANZA-S
ZANZE-S
ZAYIN-S
ZAZEN-S
ZEBEC-K
ZEBEC-S
ZEBRA-S
ZEBUB-S
ZERDA-S
ZHOMO-S
ZIBET-H
ZIBET-S
ZIGAN-S
ZIMBI-S
ZINCO-S
ZINEB-S
A-ZINES
ZINKE-D
ZINKE-S
ZIPPO-S
ZIRAM-S
ZIZEL-S
ZIZIT-H
ZLOTY-S
ZOCCO-S
ZOISM-S
ZOIST-S
ZOMBI-E
ZOMBI-S
A-ZONAL
ZONDA-S
ZONER-S
O-ZONES
ZOOEA-E
ZOOEA-L
ZOOEA-S
ZOOID-S
ZORIL-S
ZORRO-S
ZUPAN-S
A-ZYMES

6-LETTER WORD HOOKS: extensible words only

AARRGH-H
K-ABAKAS
ABASER-S
ABASIA-S
ABATER-S
ABATOR-S
K-ABAYAS
H-ABDABS
ABDUCE-D
ABDUCE-S
ABDUCT-S
K-ABELES
ABELIA-N
ABELIA-S
R-ABIDER
ABIDER-S
ABJECT-S
ABJURE-D
ABJURE-R
ABJURE-S
ABLATE-D
ABLATE-S
ABLAUT-S
C-ABLETS
G-ABLETS
T-ABLETS
C-ABLING
F-ABLING
G-ABLING
S-ABLING
T-ABLING
ABLING-S
ABOLLA-E
ABOLLA-S
ABOMAS-A
ABOMAS-I
ABOUND-S
ABRADE-D
ABRADE-R
ABRADE-S
ABRAID-S
ABRAZO-S
ABREGE-S
ABROAD-S
ABRUPT-S
ABSEIL-S
ABSENT-S
ABSORB-S
ABSURD-S
ABULIA-S
ABUSER-S
ABVOLT-S
ABWATT-S
B-ABYING
ACACIA-S
ACAJOU-S
ACANTH-A
ACANTH-I
ACANTH-S
ACARID-S

ACATER-S
V-**ACATES**
ACCEDE-D
ACCEDE-R
ACCEDE-S
ACCEND-S
ACCENT-S
ACCEPT-S
ACCITE-D
ACCITE-S
ACCLOY-S
ACCOIL-S
ACCORD-S
ACCOST-S
ACCREW-S
ACCRUE-D
ACCRUE-S
ACCUSE-D
ACCUSE-R
ACCUSE-S
ACEDIA-S
ACETAL-S
ACETIN-S
ACETYL-S
ACHAGE-S
ACHENE-S
B-**ACHING**
C-ACHING
ACHING-S
ACHKAN-S
H-**ACKEES**
B-**ACKERS**
D-ACKERS
H-ACKERS
J-ACKERS
L-ACKERS
P-ACKERS
R-ACKERS
S-ACKERS
T-ACKERS
W-ACKERS
Y-ACKERS
ACKNOW-N
ACKNOW-S
ACMITE-S
T-**ACNODE**
ACNODE-S
ACQUIT-E
ACQUIT-S
ACTING-S
F-**ACTION**
P-ACTION
T-ACTION
ACTION-S
F-**ACTIVE**
ACTIVE-S
F-**ACTORS**
F-**ACTUAL**
T-ACTUAL
F-**ACTURE**
ACTURE-S
V-**ACUATE**
V-**ACUITY**
C-**ACUMEN**
ACUMEN-S
ACUTES-T
ADAGIO-S
ADDEEM-S
ADDEND-A
ADDEND-S
G-**ADDERS**
L-ADDERS
M-ADDERS
P-ADDERS
W-ADDERS
ADDICT-S
D-**ADDING**
G-ADDING
H-ADDING
M-ADDING
P-ADDING
R-ADDING
W-ADDING
D-**ADDLED**
F-ADDLED
P-ADDLED
R-ADDLED
S-ADDLED
W-ADDLED
D-**ADDLES**
F-ADDLES
P-ADDLES
R-ADDLES
S-ADDLES
W-ADDLES
ADDOOM-S
ADDUCE-D
ADDUCE-R
ADDUCE-S
ADDUCT-S
ADENYL-S
ADHERE-D
ADHERE-R
ADHERE-S
ADJOIN-S
ADJOIN-T
ADJURE-D
ADJURE-R
ADJURE-S
ADJUST-S
B-**ADLAND**
ADLAND-S
ADMIRE-D
ADMIRE-R
ADMIRE-S
ADNEXA-L
ADNOUN-S
ADONIS-E
ADORER-S
ADREAD-S
ADSORB-S
ADVECT-S
ADVENE-D
ADVENE-S
ADVENT-S
ADVERB-S
ADVERT-S
ADVICE-S
ADVISE-D
ADVISE-E
ADVISE-R
ADVISE-S
ADWARD-S
ADZUKI-S
AEDILE-S
AEMULE-D
AEMULE-S
P-**AEONIC**
AERATE-D
AERATE-S
AERIAL-S
F-**AERIES**
AERIES-T
AEROBE-S
AERUGO-S
AETHER-S
AFFAIR-E
AFFAIR-S
AFFEAR-D
AFFEAR-E
AFFEAR-S
AFFECT-S
AFFEER-S
B-**AFFIES**
D-AFFIES
T-AFFIES
W-AFFIES
AFFINE-D
AFFINE-S
AFFIRM-S
AFFORD-S
AFFRAP-S
AFFRAY-S
AFFRET-S
AFGHAN-I
AFGHAN-S
AFREET-S
H-**AFTERS**
R-AFTERS
W-AFTERS
AFTOSA-S
AGAMID-S
AGARIC-S
AGEING-S
AGEISM-S
AGEIST-S
AGENDA-S
S-**AGENES**
B-**AGGERS**
D-AGGERS
G-AGGERS
J-AGGERS
L-AGGERS
N-AGGERS
S-AGGERS
T-AGGERS
W-AGGERS
Y-AGGERS
B-**AGGIES**
R-AGGIES
P-**AGINGS**
R-AGINGS
M-**AGISMS**
E-**AGLETS**
H-AGLETS
AGNAIL-S
AGNAME-D
AGNAME-S
M-**AGNATE**
AGNATE-S
AGNISE-D
AGNISE-S
AGNIZE-D
AGNIZE-S
AGOGIC-S
AGOROT-H
AGOUTA-S
AGOUTI-S
AGRAFE-S
AGREGE-S
AGRISE-D
AGRISE-S
AGRIZE-D
AGRIZE-S
AGRYZE-D
AGRYZE-S
AGUISE-D
AGUISE-S
AGUIZE-D
AGUIZE-S
AHIMSA-S
R-**AIDERS**
L-**AIDING**
M-AIDING
R-AIDING
AIGLET-S
AIGRET-S
AIKIDO-S
B-**AILING**
F-AILING
H-AILING
J-AILING
M-AILING
N-AILING
R-AILING
S-AILING
T-AILING
V-AILING
W-AILING
M-**AIMERS**
M-**AIMING**
F-**AIREST**
S-AIREST
AIRGAP-S
H-**AIRIER**
L-AIRIER
V-AIRIER
F-**AIRILY**
F-**AIRING**
H-AIRING
L-AIRING
P-AIRING
S-AIRING
W-AIRING
AIRING-S
C-**AIRNED**
F-**AIRWAY**
AIRWAY-S
T-**AIVERS**
W-AIVERS
AJOWAN-S
AKEDAH-S
ALALIA-S
L-**ALANGS**
ALANIN-E
ALANIN-S
T-**ALANTS**
ALANYL-S
ALARUM-S
ALASKA-S
P-**ALATED**
M-**ALATES**
P-ALATES
ALBATA-S
ALBEDO-S
H-**ALBERT**
ALBERT-S
ALBINO-S
ALBITE-S
ALBUGO-S
F-**ALCADE**
ALCADE-S
ALCAIC-S
ALCOVE-D
ALCOVE-S
ALDOSE-S
ALDRIN-S
ALEGAR-S
ALEGGE-D
ALEGGE-S
ALERCE-S
ALEVIN-S
ALEXIA-S
ALEXIN-E
ALEXIN-S
ALFAKI-S
ALGATE-S
V-**ALGOID**
ALIDAD-E
ALIDAD-S
ALIGHT-S
M-**ALIGNS**
ALINER-S
M-**ALINES**
S-ALINES
V-ALINES
T-**ALIPED**
ALIPED-S
ALISMA-S
ALIYAH-S
ALIYOT-H
ALKALI-C
ALKALI-N
ALKALI-S
ALKANE-S
ALKANE-T
ALKENE-S
T-**ALKIES**
ALKINE-S
ALKYNE-S
M-**ALLEES**
S-ALLEES
ALLEGE-D
ALLEGE-R
ALLEGE-S
ALLELE-S
H-**ALLELS**
G-**ALLEYS**
V-ALLEYS
ALLICE-S
D-**ALLIED**
G-ALLIED
R-ALLIED
S-ALLIED
T-ALLIED
B-**ALLIES**
D-ALLIES
G-ALLIES
R-ALLIES
S-ALLIES
T-ALLIES
W-ALLIES
B-**ALLIUM**
G-ALLIUM
P-ALLIUM
ALLIUM-S
B-**ALLONS**
G-ALLONS
B-**ALLOTS**
T-ALLOTS
B-**ALLOWS**
C-ALLOWS
F-ALLOWS
G-ALLOWS
H-ALLOWS
M-ALLOWS
S-ALLOWS
T-ALLOWS
W-ALLOWS
ALLUDE-D
ALLUDE-S
ALLURE-D
ALLURE-R
ALLURE-S
ALMAIN-S
ALMNER-S
ALMOND-S
ALMUCE-S
ALMUDE-S
T-**ALMUDS**
ALNAGE-R
ALNAGE-S
ALODIA-L
ALOGIA-S
ALPACA-S
ALPEEN-S
ALPHYL-S
ALPINE-S
ALSIKE-S
ALSOON-E
S-**ALTERN**
ALTERN-E
F-**ALTERS**
H-ALTERS
P-ALTERS
S-ALTERS
ALTEZA-S
ALTHEA-S
ALUDEL-S
ALUMIN-A
ALUMIN-E
ALUMIN-S
ALUMNA-E
AMADOU-S
H-**AMATES**
AMATOL-S
AMAZON-S
AMBAGE-S
AMBARI-S
AMBEER-S
C-**AMBERS**
J-AMBERS
L-AMBERS
T-AMBERS
G-**AMBITS**
G-**AMBLED**
H-AMBLED
R-AMBLED
W-AMBLED
G-**AMBLER**
R-AMBLER
AMBLER-S
G-**AMBLES**
H-AMBLES
R-AMBLES
W-AMBLES
C-**AMELIA**
AMELIA-S
AMENDE-D
AMENDE-R
AMENDE-S
R-**AMENTA**
AMENTA-L
L-**AMENTS**
AMERCE-D
AMERCE-R
AMERCE-S
AMIDIN-E
AMIDIN-S
AMIDOL-S
F-**AMINES**
G-AMINES
T-AMINES
C-**AMISES**
K-AMISES
T-AMISES
AMMINE-S
G-**AMMONS**
M-AMMONS
AMNION-S
AMOEBA-E
AMOEBA-N
AMOEBA-S
AMOMUM-S
AMOOVE-D
AMOOVE-S
AMORCE-S
AMORET-S
AMOUNT-S
AMPERE-S

S-**AMPLER**
AMPULE-S
AMRITA-S
AMTMAN-S
AMTRAC-K
AMTRAC-S
AMULET-S
AMUSER-S
C-**AMUSES**
W-AMUSES
AMUSIA-S
AMYLUM-S
AMYTAL-S
ANADEM-S
B-**ANALLY**
ANALOG-A
ANALOG-S
ANALOG-Y
B-**ANANAS**
M-ANANAS
Z-ANANAS
ANANKE-S
ANARCH-S
ANARCH-Y
ANATTA-S
ANATTO-S
ANCHOR-S
ANCOME-S
ANCONE-S
P-**ANELED**
ANEMIA-S
M-**ANGELS**
B-**ANGERS**
D-ANGERS
G-ANGERS
H-ANGERS
M-ANGERS
R-ANGERS
S-ANGERS
ANGICO-S
ANGINA-L
ANGINA-S
B-**ANGLED**
C-ANGLED
D-ANGLED
F-ANGLED
J-ANGLED
M-ANGLED
T-ANGLED
W-ANGLED
D-**ANGLER**
J-ANGLER
M-ANGLER
T-ANGLER
W-ANGLER
ANGLER-S
B-**ANGLES**
C-ANGLES
D-ANGLES
F-ANGLES
J-ANGLES
M-ANGLES
T-ANGLES
W-ANGLES
ANGORA-S
ANICUT-S
ANILIN-E
ANILIN-S
ANIMAL-S
ANIMIS-M
ANIMIS-T
F-**ANIONS**
W-ANIONS
B-**ANKERS**
C-ANKERS
H-ANKERS
J-ANKERS
R-ANKERS
T-ANKERS
W-ANKERS
Y-ANKERS
F-**ANKLED**
R-ANKLED
F-**ANKLES**
R-ANKLES
ANKLET-S
ANLACE-S
ANLAGE-N
ANLAGE-S
ANNEAL-S
ANNEXE-D
ANNEXE-S
T-**ANNOYS**
ANNUAL-S
ANOINT-S
ANOMIE-S
ANONYM-A
ANONYM-S
ANOPIA-S
ANORAK-S
ANOXIA-S
ANSATE-D
ANSWER-S
T-**ANTARA**
ANTARA-S
C-**ANTARS**
K-ANTARS
ANTHEM-S
P-**ANTHER**
ANTHER-S
ANTIAR-S
ANTICK-E
ANTICK-S
B-**ANTING**
C-ANTING
D-ANTING
G-ANTING
H-ANTING
K-ANTING
P-ANTING
R-ANTING
W-ANTING
ANTING-S
P-**ANTLER**
ANTLER-S
ANTLIA-E
T-**ANTRUM**
ANTRUM-S
ANURAN-S
ANURIA-S
ANYONE-S
ANYWAY-S
AORIST-S
AOUDAD-S
APACHE-S
APEDOM-S
APERCU-S
N-**APHTHA**
APHTHA-E
APICAL-S
P-**APISMS**
H-**APLITE**
APLITE-S
APLOMB-S
APNOEA-L
APNOEA-S
APOGEE-S
APOLLO-S
APOLOG-S
APOLOG-Y
APORIA-S
APOZEM-S
APPAIR-S
APPALL-S
APPEAL-S
APPEAR-S
L-**APPELS**
R-APPELS
W-**APPEND**
APPEND-S
D-**APPLES**
S-APPLES
APPLET-S
R-**APPORT**
APPORT-S
P-**APPOSE**
APPOSE-D
APPOSE-R
APPOSE-S
N-**APRONS**
APTOTE-S
ARABIC-A
C-**ARABIN**
ARABIN-S
ARABIS-E
P-**ARABLE**
ARABLE-S
ARAISE-D
ARAISE-S
ARALIA-S
ARAMID-S
ARAYSE-D
ARAYSE-S
H-**ARBORS**
H-**ARBOUR**
ARBOUR-S
ARBUTE-S
ARCADE-D
ARCADE-S
M-**ARCHED**
P-ARCHED
M-**ARCHER**
ARCHER-S
ARCHER-Y
L-**ARCHES**
M-ARCHES
P-ARCHES
ARCHES-T
ARCHIL-S
ARCHON-S
F-**ARCING**
ARCING-S
ARCSIN-E
ARCSIN-S
ARCTAN-S
ARCTIC-S
ARDOUR-S
AREOLA-E
AREOLA-R
AREOLA-S
AREOLE-S
ARGALA-S
ARGALI-S
ARGAND-S
M-**ARGENT**
ARGENT-S
ARGHAN-S
G-**ARGLED**
D-**ARGLES**
G-ARGLES
J-**ARGONS**
ARGUER-S
ARGYLE-S
ARGYLL-S
ARIOSO-S
P-**ARISES**
ARISTA-E
ARISTA-S
ARISTO-S
B-**ARKING**
C-ARKING
D-ARKING
H-ARKING
K-ARKING
L-ARKING
M-ARKING
N-ARKING
P-ARKING
S-ARKING
W-ARKING
ARKITE-S
ARKOSE-S
C-**ARLING**
D-ARLING
H-ARLING
M-ARLING
P-ARLING
W-ARLING
ARMADA-S
F-**ARMERS**
H-ARMERS
W-ARMERS
H-**ARMFUL**
ARMFUL-S
F-**ARMING**
H-ARMING
W-ARMING
ARMING-S
ARMLET-S
ARMOUR-S
ARMOUR-Y
ARMPIT-S
ARMURE-S
ARNICA-S
AROINT-S
AROLLA-S
C-**AROUSE**
AROUSE-D
AROUSE-R
AROUSE-S
AROYNT-S
P-**ARPENS**
P-**ARPENT**
ARPENT-S
B-**ARRACK**
C-ARRACK
ARRACK-S
F-**ARRANT**
W-ARRANT
W-**ARRAYS**
ARREAR-S
C-**ARRECT**
ARREST-S
B-**ARRETS**
G-ARRETS
ARRIDE-D
ARRIDE-S
ARRIVE-D
ARRIVE-R
ARRIVE-S
ARROBA-S
B-**ARROWS**
F-ARROWS
H-ARROWS
M-ARROWS
N-ARROWS
T-ARROWS
Y-ARROWS
M-**ARROWY**
ARROYO-S
ARSHIN-E
ARSHIN-S
ARSINE-S
P-**ARSONS**
C-**ARTELS**
M-ARTELS
P-**ARTIER**
T-ARTIER
W-ARTIER
P-**ARTIES**
ARTIES-T
ARTIST-E
ARTIST-S
ASARUM-S
ASCEND-S
N-**ASCENT**
ASCENT-S
ASCIAN-S
M-**ASCOTS**
G-**ASEITY**
ASHAME-D
ASHAME-S
ASHCAN-S
F-**ASHERY**
W-ASHERY
C-**ASHIER**
D-ASHIER
H-ASHIER
M-ASHIER
W-ASHIER
B-**ASHING**
C-ASHING
D-ASHING
F-ASHING
G-ASHING
H-ASHING
L-ASHING
M-ASHING
P-ASHING
R-ASHING
S-ASHING
T-ASHING
W-ASHING
ASHLAR-S
ASHLER-S
M-**ASHMAN**
M-**ASHMEN**
ASHRAM-A
ASHRAM-S
ASKANT-S
ASKARI-S
M-**ASKERS**
T-ASKERS
B-**ASKING**
C-ASKING
G-ASKING
M-ASKING
T-ASKING
ASKING-S
ASLAKE-D
ASLAKE-S
ASPECT-S
G-**ASPERS**
J-ASPERS
R-ASPERS
ASPERS-E
ASPICK-S
ASPINE-S
ASPIRE-D
ASPIRE-R
ASPIRE-S
R-**ASPISH**
W-ASPISH
ASPORT-S
ASRAMA-S
V-**ASSAIL**
W-ASSAIL
ASSAIL-S
ASSART-S
ASSENT-S
ASSERT-S
B-**ASSETS**
T-ASSETS
ASSIGN-S
B-**ASSIST**
ASSIST-S
ASSIZE-D
ASSIZE-R
ASSIZE-S
ASSOIL-S
ASSORT-S
ASSUME-D
ASSUME-R
ASSUME-S
ASSURE-D
ASSURE-R
ASSURE-S
ASTART-S
E-**ASTERN**
P-ASTERN
B-**ASTERS**
C-ASTERS
E-ASTERS
F-ASTERS
G-ASTERS
L-ASTERS
M-ASTERS
P-ASTERS
R-ASTERS
T-ASTERS
W-ASTERS
ASTERT-S
ASTHMA-S
ASTONE-D
ASTONE-S
C-**ASTRAL**
G-ASTRAL
ASTRAL-S
ASTUTE-R
ASYLUM-S
ATABAL-S
ATABEG-S
ATABEK-S
ATAMAN-S
ATAXIA-S
ATAXIC-S
ATLATL-S
ATOCIA-S
M-**ATOKES**
ATOMIC-S
B-**ATONED**
ATONER-S
ATONIC-S
P-**ATRIAL**
N-**ATRIUM**
ATRIUM-S
ATTACH-E
ATTACK-S
ATTAIN-S
ATTAIN-T
ATTASK-S
ATTASK-T
ATTEND-S
ATTENT-S
F-**ATTEST**
W-ATTEST
ATTEST-S
ATTIRE-D
ATTIRE-S
ATTONE-S

ATTORN-S
R-ATTRAP
ATTRAP-S
ATTRIT-E
ATTRIT-S
ATTUNE-D
ATTUNE-S
AUBADE-S
AUBURN-S
AUCUBA-S
AUDILE-S
D-AUDING
G-AUDING
H-AUDING
L-AUDING
AUDING-S
AUGEND-S
G-AUGERS
S-AUGERS
N-AUGHTS
W-AUGHTS
AUGITE-S
AUGUST-E
AUGUST-S
AUKLET-S
C-AULDER
AUMAIL-S
D-AUNTER
G-AUNTER
H-AUNTER
S-AUNTER
T-AUNTER
V-AUNTER
AUNTER-S
J-AUNTIE
V-AUNTIE
AUNTIE-S
G-AUNTLY
AURATE-D
AURATE-S
AURIST-S
AURORA-E
AURORA-L
AURORA-S
AUSUBO-S
H-AUTEUR
AUTEUR-S
AUTHOR-S
AUTISM-S
AUTUMN-S
AUTUMN-Y
AVAILE-D
AVAILE-S
AVATAR-S
AVAUNT-S
AVENGE-D
AVENGE-R
AVENGE-S
AVENIR-S
AVENUE-S
AVIATE-D
AVIATE-S
AVIDIN-S
M-AVISES
P-AVISES
AVOCET-S
AVOSET-S
AVOURE-S
AVOWAL-S
AVOWER-S
AVOYER-S
AVULSE-D
AVULSE-S
AWAKEN-S
V-AWARDS
AWHAPE-D
AWHAPE-S
AWHEEL-S
L-AWLESS
AWMRIE-S
D-AWNERS
F-AWNERS
P-AWNERS
Y-AWNERS
F-AWNIER
L-AWNIER
T-AWNIER
Y-AWNIER
D-AWNING
F-AWNING
P-AWNING
Y-AWNING
AWNING-S
M-AXILLA
AXILLA-E
AXILLA-R
AXILLA-S
T-AXITES
W-AXLIKE
AXSEED-S
N-AYWORD
AYWORD-S
AZALEA-S
AZIONE-S
AZOLLA-S
R-AZURES
BAAING-S
BABACO-S
BABBLE-D
BABBLE-R
BABBLE-S
BABIES-T
BABLAH-S
BABOOL-S
BABOON-S
BABOOS-H
BACKER-S
BACKET-S
BACKRA-S
BACKUP-S
BADDIE-S
BADGER-S
BAETYL-S
BAFFLE-D
BAFFLE-R
BAFFLE-S
BAGASS-E
BAGFUL-S
BAGGER-S
BAGGIE-R
BAGGIE-S
BAGGIT-S
BAGNIO-S
BAGUET-S
BAGUIO-S
BAGWIG-S
BAHADA-S
BAILEE-S
BAILER-S
BAILEY-S
BAILIE-S
BAILLI-E
BAILLI-S
BAILOR-S
BAININ-S
BAITER-S
BAJADA-S
BAJREE-S
BAKING-S
BALATA-S
BALBOA-S
BALEEN-S
BALKER-S
BALLAD-E
BALLAD-S
BALLAN-S
BALLAN-T
BALLAT-S
BALLER-S
BALLET-S
BALLON-S
BALLOT-S
BALLOW-S
BALLUP-S
BALSAM-S
BALSAM-Y
BAMBOO-S
BAMMER-S
BAMPOT-S
BANANA-S
BANDAR-S
A-BANDED
BANDER-S
BANDIT-S
BANDOG-S
BANGER-S
BANGLE-D
BANGLE-S
BANIAN-S
BANKER-S
BANKET-S
BANNER-S
BANNET-S
BANTAM-S
BANTER-S
BANYAN-S
BANZAI-S
BAOBAB-S
BARAZA-S
BARBEL-L
BARBEL-S
BARBER-S
BARBET-S
BARBIE-S
BARBUT-S
BAREGE-S
BARGEE-S
BARGES-T
BARHOP-S
BARITE-S
BARIUM-S
BARKAN-S
BARKEN-S
BARKER-S
BARLEY-S
BARLOW-S
BARMIE-R
BARNEY-S
BAROCK-S
BARONG-S
BARQUE-S
BARRAT-S
BARREL-S
BARREN-S
BARRET-S
BARRIO-S
BARROW-S
BARTER-S
BARTON-S
BARYON-S
BARYTA-S
BARYTE-S
BASALT-S
BASHAW-S
A-BASHED
BASHER-S
A-BASHES
A-BASING
BASION-S
BASKET-S
BASNET-S
BASQUE-D
BASQUE-S
BASSES-T
BASSET-S
BASSET-T
BASTER-S
BASTLE-S
BASUCO-S
BATATA-S
BATBOY-S
BATEAU-X
BATHER-S
A-BATING
BATLER-S
BATLET-S
BATOON-S
BATTEL-S
BATTEN-S
BATTER-O
BATTER-S
BATTER-Y
BATTIK-S
BATTLE-D
BATTLE-R
BATTLE-S
BATTUE-S
BAUBEE-S
BAUBLE-S
BAUERA-S
BAWBEE-S
BAWBLE-S
BAWLER-S
BAWLEY-S
BAWTIE-S
BAXTER-S
BAYAMO-S
BAYARD-S
BAZAAR-S
BEACON-S
BEADLE-S
BEAGLE-D
BEAGLE-R
BEAGLE-S
BEAKER-S
BEAMER-S
BEANIE-S
BEARER-S
BEATER-S
BEAVER-S
BEAVER-Y
BEBUNG-S
BECALL-S
BECALM-S
BECKET-S
BECKON-S
BECLOG-S
BECOME-S
BECURL-S
BEDAMN-S
BEDAUB-S
BEDAZE-D
BEDAZE-S
BEDBUG-S
BEDDER-S
BEDECK-S
BEDELL-S
BEDLAM-P
BEDLAM-S
BEDPAN-S
BEDRAL-S
BEDROP-S
BEDROP-T
BEDRUG-S
BEDSIT-S
BEDUCK-S
BEDUIN-S
BEDUMB-S
BEDUNG-S
BEDUST-S
BEEBEE-S
BEEGAH-S
BEENAH-S
BEEPER-S
BEETLE-D
BEETLE-R
BEETLE-S
BEEZER-S
BEFALL-S
BEFANA-S
BEFLAG-S
BEFLEA-S
BEFLUM-S
BEFOAM-S
BEFOOL-S
BEFOUL-S
BEFRET-S
BEGALL-S
BEGAZE-D
BEGAZE-S
BEGGAR-S
BEGGAR-Y
BEGIFT-S
BEGILD-S
BEGIRD-S
BEGLAD-S
BEGNAW-S
BEGRIM-E
BEGRIM-S
BEGUIN-E
BEGUIN-S
BEGULF-S
BEGUNK-S
BEHAVE-D
BEHAVE-R
BEHAVE-S
BEHEAD-S
BEHEST-S
BEHIND-S
BEHOLD-S
BEHOOF-S
BEHOTE-S
BEHOVE-D
BEHOVE-S
BEHOWL-S
BEIGEL-S
BEJADE-D
BEJADE-S
BEJANT-S
BEKNOT-S
BELACE-D
BELACE-S
BELATE-D
BELATE-S
BELAUD-S
BELDAM-E
BELDAM-S
BELEAP-S
BELEAP-T
BELIEF-S
BELIER-S
BELLOW-S
BELONG-S
BELOVE-D
BELOVE-S
BELTER-S
BELUGA-S
BEMAUL-S
BEMEAN-S
BEMEAN-T
BEMETE-D
BEMETE-S
BEMIRE-D
BEMIRE-S
BEMIST-S
BEMOAN-S
BEMOCK-S
BEMOIL-S
BEMUSE-D
BEMUSE-S
BENAME-D
BENAME-S
BENDAY-S
BENDEE-S
BENDER-S
BENNET-S
BENUMB-S
BENZAL-S
BENZIL-S
BENZIN-E
BENZIN-S
BENZOL-E
BENZOL-S
BENZYL-S
BEPELT-S
BEPUFF-S
BERAKE-D
BERAKE-S
BERATE-D
BERATE-S
BERIME-D
BERIME-S
BERLEY-S
BERLIN-E
BERLIN-S
BERRET-S
BERTHA-S
BERTHE-D
BERTHE-S
BESEEM-S
BESIDE-S
BESIGH-S
BESING-S
BESMUT-S
BESNOW-S
BESOIN-S
BESORT-S
BESPAT-E
BESPIT-S
BESPOT-S
BESTAR-S
BESTIR-S
BESTOW-S
BESTUD-S
BETAKE-N
BETAKE-S
BETEEM-E
BETEEM-S
BETHEL-S
BETIDE-D
BETIDE-S
BETIME-D
BETIME-S
BETISE-S
BETOIL-S
BETRAY-S
BETRIM-S
A-BETTED
A-BETTER
BETTER-S

A-**BETTOR**
BETTOR-S
BEURRE-S
BEWAIL-S
BEWARE-D
BEWARE-S
BEWEEP-S
BEWORM-S
BEWRAP-S
BEWRAP-T
BEWRAY-S
BEYLIC-S
BEYLIK-S
BEYOND-S
BEZANT-S
BEZOAR-S
BEZZLE-D
BEZZLE-S
BHAGEE-S
BHAJAN-S
BHAJEE-S
BHAKTA-S
BHAKTI-S
BHARAL-S
BHINDI-S
BHISTI-E
BHISTI-S
BIBBER-S
BIBBER-Y
BIBLES-S
BICARB-S
BICKER-S
BICORN-E
BICORN-S
BICRON-S
A-**BIDDEN**
BIDDER-S
BIDENT-S
A-**BIDERS**
A-**BIDING**
BIDING-S
BIFACE-S
BIFFIN-G
BIFFIN-S
BIGEYE-S
BIGGIE-S
BIGGIN-G
BIGGIN-S
BIGWIG-S
BIKING-S
BIKINI-S
BILBOA-S
BILIAN-S
BILKER-S
BILLER-S
BILLET-S
BILLIE-S
BILLON-S
BILLOW-S
BILLOW-Y
BINDER-S
BINDER-Y
BINDLE-S
BINGER-S
BINGHI-S
BINGLE-D
BINGLE-S
BIOGEN-S
BIOGEN-Y
BIONIC-S
BIOPIC-S
A-**BIOTIC**
BIOTIC-S
BIOTIN-S
BIPACK-S

BIRDER-S
BIRDIE-D
BIRDIE-S
BIREME-S
BIRKIE-R
BIRKIE-S
BIRLER-S
BIRSLE-D
BIRSLE-S
BISECT-S
BISHOP-S
BISMAR-S
BISQUE-S
BISTER-S
BISTRE-D
BISTRE-S
BISTRO-S
BITING-S
BITMAP-S
BITTER-N
BITTER-S
BITTIE-R
BITTIE-S
BITTOR-S
BITTUR-S
BIZONE-S
BLAGUE-S
BLAMER-S
BLANCO-S
O-**BLASTS**
BLAZER-S
BLAZON-S
BLENDE-D
BLENDE-R
BLENDE-S
BLIGHT-S
BLIGHT-Y
BLINTZ-E
BLITHE-R
BLONDE-R
BLONDE-S
BLOTCH-Y
BLOUSE-D
BLOUSE-S
BLOWBY-S
BLOWER-S
BLOWIE-R
BLOWIE-S
BLOWSE-D
BLOWSE-S
BLOWUP-S
BLOWZE-D
BLOWZE-S
BLUDGE-D
BLUDGE-R
BLUDGE-S
BLUDIE-R
BLUING-S
BLUNGE-D
BLUNGE-R
BLUNGE-S
BOATEL-S
BOATER-S
BOATIE-S
BOBBER-S
BOBBER-Y
BOBBIN-G
BOBBIN-S
BOBBLE-D
BOBBLE-S
BOBCAT-S
BOBWIG-S
BOCAGE-S
BOCCIA-S
BOCCIE-S

BODACH-S
BODDLE-S
BODEGA-S
BODGER-S
BODGIE-R
BODGIE-S
BODICE-S
A-**BODING**
BODING-S
BODKIN-S
BODRAG-S
BOFFIN-G
BOFFIN-S
BOGGLE-D
BOGGLE-R
BOGGLE-S
BOGOAK-S
BOGONG-S
BOHUNK-S
BOILER-S
BOILER-Y
BOLDEN-S
BOLERO-S
BOLETE-S
BOLIDE-S
BOLSON-S
BOLTER-S
BOMBER-S
BONACI-S
BONBON-S
BONDER-S
BONDUC-S
BONING-S
BONISM-S
E-**BONIST**
BONIST-S
BONITA-S
BONITO-S
BONNET-S
BONNIE-R
BONNIE-S
BONSAI-S
BONXIE-S
BOOBIE-S
BOOBOO-K
BOOBOO-S
BOODIE-D
BOODIE-S
BOODLE-D
BOODLE-R
BOODLE-S
BOOGER-S
BOOGEY-S
BOOGIE-D
BOOGIE-S
BOOHOO-S
BOOKER-S
BOOKIE-R
BOOKIE-S
BOOMER-S
BOORDE-S
BOORKA-S
BOOTEE-S
BOOTIE-S
BOOZER-S
BOPEEP-S
BOPPER-S
BORAGE-S
BORANE-S
BORATE-D
BORATE-S
BORDAR-S
BORDEL-S
BORDER-S
BOREEN-S

BORIDE-S
BORING-S
BORREL-L
BORROW-S
BORSCH-T
BORSHT-S
BORZOI-S
BOSBOK-S
BOSCHE-S
BOSKET-S
BOSQUE-S
BOSQUE-T
BOSSES-T
BOSTON-S
BOTHAN-S
BOTHER-S
BOTHIE-S
BOTONE-E
BOTTLE-D
BOTTLE-R
BOTTLE-S
BOTTOM-S
BOUBOU-S
BOUCHE-E
BOUCHE-S
BOUCLE-S
BOUFFE-S
BOUGET-S
A-**BOUGHT**
BOUGHT-S
BOUGIE-S
BOULLE-S
BOUNCE-D
BOUNCE-R
BOUNCE-S
A-**BOUNDS**
BOURNE-S
BOURSE-S
BOUTON-S
O-**BOVATE**
BOVATE-S
BOVINE-S
BOVVER-S
BOWFIN-S
BOWGET-S
BOWING-S
BOWLEG-S
BOWLER-S
BOWPOT-S
BOWSER-S
BOWWOW-S
BOWYER-S
BOXCAR-S
BOXFUL-S
BOXING-S
BOYARD-S
BRACER-O
BRACER-S
BRAHMA-S
BRAIDE-D
BRAIDE-R
A-**BRAIDS**
BRAIRD-S
BRAISE-D
BRAISE-S
BRAIZE-S
BRANCH-Y
BRANLE-S
BRASIL-S
BRAVER-S
BRAVER-Y
BRAVES-T
A-**BRAYED**
BRAYER-S
BRAZEN-S

BRAZER-S
BRAZIL-S
BREARE-S
A-**BREAST**
BREAST-S
BREATH-E
BREATH-S
BREATH-Y
BREESE-S
BREEZE-D
BREEZE-S
BREHON-S
BRENNE-S
BRETON-S
BREVET-E
BREVET-S
BREWER-S
BREWER-Y
BRIARD-S
BRIBEE-S
BRIBER-S
BRIBER-Y
BRIDAL-S
A-**BRIDGE**
BRIDGE-D
BRIDGE-S
BRIDIE-S
BRIDLE-D
BRIDLE-R
BRIDLE-S
BRIGHT-S
BRIGUE-D
BRIGUE-S
BRINER-S
A-**BROACH**
A-**BROADS**
BROCHE-D
BROCHE-S
BROGAN-S
BROGUE-S
BROKER-S
BROKER-Y
BROLGA-S
BROMAL-S
BROMID-E
BROMID-S
BROMIN-E
BROMIN-S
BRONCO-S
BRONZE-D
BRONZE-N
BRONZE-R
BRONZE-S
BROOSE-S
BROUGH-S
BROUGH-T
BROUZE-S
BROWSE-D
BROWSE-R
BROWSE-S
BROWST-S
BRUCIN-E
BRUCIN-S
BRUISE-D
BRUISE-R
BRUISE-S
BRULOT-S
BRUNET-S
BRUTER-S
BUBALE-S
A-**BUBBLE**
BUBBLE-D
BUBBLE-R
BUBBLE-S
BUCKER-S

BUCKET-S
BUCKIE-S
BUCKLE-D
BUCKLE-R
BUCKLE-S
BUCKRA-M
BUCKRA-S
BUDDER-S
BUDDHA-S
BUDDLE-D
BUDDLE-S
BUDGER-O
BUDGER-S
BUDGET-S
BUDGIE-S
BUFFER-S
BUFFET-S
BUGEYE-S
BUGGAN-E
BUGGAN-S
BUGGER-S
BUGGER-Y
BUGGIN-G
BUGGIN-S
BUGLER-S
BUGLET-S
BUGONG-S
BUGSHA-S
BUKSHI-S
BULBEL-S
BULBIL-S
BULBUL-S
BULGER-S
BULGUR-S
BULKER-S
BULLER-S
BULLET-S
BUMBAG-S
BUMBLE-D
BUMBLE-R
BUMBLE-S
BUMKIN-S
BUMMEL-S
BUMMER-S
BUMMLE-D
BUMMLE-S
BUMPER-S
BUNDLE-D
BUNDLE-R
BUNDLE-S
BUNGEE-S
BUNGEY-S
BUNGIE-S
BUNGLE-D
BUNGLE-R
BUNGLE-S
BUNION-S
BUNJEE-S
BUNJIE-S
BUNKER-S
BUNKUM-S
BUNNIA-S
BUNSEN-S
BUNTAL-S
BUNTER-S
BUNYIP-S
BUPPIE-S
BUQSHA-S
BURBLE-D
BURBLE-R
BURBLE-S
BURBOT-S
BURDEN-S
BURDIE-S
BUREAU-S

BUREAU-X
BURGEE-S
BURGER-S
BURGLE-D
BURGLE-S
BURGOO-S
BURHEL-S
BURIAL-S
BURIER-S
BURITI-S
BURKER-S
BURLAP-S
BURLER-S
BURLEY-S
BURNER-S
BURNET-S
BURNIE-S
BURREL-L
BURREL-S
BURRER-S
BURROW-S
BURSAR-S
BURSAR-Y
BURTON-S
BUSBAR-S
BUSBOY-S
BUSHEL-S
BUSHER-S
BUSHWA-H
BUSHWA-S
BUSIES-T
A-**BUSING**
BUSING-S
BUSKER-S
BUSKET-S
BUSKIN-G
BUSKIN-S
BUSTEE-S
BUSTER-S
BUSTIC-S
BUSTLE-D
BUSTLE-R
BUSTLE-S
BUTANE-S
BUTENE-S
BUTLER-S
BUTLER-Y
A-**BUTTED**
A-**BUTTER**
BUTTER-S
BUTTER-Y
BUTTLE-D
BUTTLE-S
BUTTON-S
BUTTON-Y
BUYOUT-S
BUZUKI-A
BUZUKI-S
BUZZER-S
BYELAW-S
BYGONE-S
BYLINE-D
BYLINE-R
BYLINE-S
BYNAME-S
BYPATH-S
BYPLAY-S
BYRLAW-S
BYRNIE-S
BYROAD-S
BYROOM-S
A-**BYSSAL**
BYTALK-S
BYWORD-S
BYWORK-S
BYZANT-S
CABALA-S
CABANA-S
S-**CABBED**
CABBIE-S
CABLET-S
CABRIE-S
CABRIT-S
CACHET-S
CACHOU-S
CACKLE-D
CACKLE-R
CACKLE-S
CACOON-S
CADDIE-D
CADDIE-S
CADDIS-H
CADEAU-X
CADGER-S
CADUAC-S
CAEOMA-S
CAESAR-S
CAFARD-S
CAFILA-S
CAFTAN-S
CAGOUL-E
CAGOUL-S
CAHIER-S
CAHOOT-S
CAILLE-S
CAIMAC-S
CAIMAN-S
CAIQUE-S
CAJOLE-D
CAJOLE-R
CAJOLE-S
CAKING-S
CALCAR-S
CALESA-S
CALICO-S
CALIGO-S
CALIMA-S
CALIPH-S
CALKER-S
CALKIN-G
CALKIN-S
CALLAN-S
CALLAN-T
S-**CALLED**
CALLER-S
CALLET-S
CALLOW-S
CALPAC-K
CALPAC-S
CALQUE-D
CALQUE-S
CALTHA-S
CALVER-S
CAMAIL-S
CAMBER-S
CAMBIA-L
S-**CAMELS**
CAMERA-E
CAMERA-L
CAMERA-S
CAMESE-S
CAMION-S
CAMISA-S
CAMISE-S
CAMLET-S
S-**CAMMED**
CAMOTE-S
S-**CAMPED**
S-**CAMPER**
CAMPER-S
CAMPLE-D
CAMPLE-S
CANADA-S
CANAPE-S
CANARD-S
CANCAN-S
CANCEL-S
CANCER-S
CANCHA-S
CANDID-A
CANDID-S
CANDIE-D
CANDIE-S
CANDLE-D
CANDLE-R
CANDLE-S
CANDOR-S
CANFUL-S
CANGLE-D
CANGLE-S
CANGUE-S
CANINE-S
CANING-S
CANKER-S
CANKER-Y
S-**CANNED**
CANNEL-S
S-**CANNER**
CANNER-S
CANNER-Y
CANNIE-R
CANNON-S
CANTAR-S
S-**CANTED**
S-**CANTER**
CANTER-S
A-**CANTHI**
CANTIC-O
S-**CANTLE**
CANTLE-D
CANTLE-S
CANTLE-T
CANTON-S
CANTOR-S
CANULA-E
CANULA-S
CANVAS-S
CANYON-S
CAPFUL-S
S-**CAPING**
CAPITA-L
CAPITA-N
CAPLES-S
CAPLET-S
CAPLIN-S
CAPOTE-S
CAPPER-S
CAPRIC-E
CAPRID-S
CAPSID-S
CAPTAN-S
CAPTOR-S
CARACK-S
CARACT-S
CARAFE-S
CARATE-S
CARBON-S
CARBOY-S
CARCEL-S
CARDER-S
CARDIA-C
CARDIA-E
CARDIA-S
CAREEN-S
CAREER-S
CAREME-S
S-**CARERS**
CARFUL-S
CARHOP-S
CARIBE-S
O-**CARINA**
CARINA-E
CARINA-L
CARINA-S
S-**CARING**
CARLES-S
CARLIN-E
CARLIN-G
CARLIN-S
CARLOT-S
CARNAL-S
CARNET-S
CARNEY-S
CARNIE-D
CARNIE-R
CARNIE-S
CAROCH-E
CARPAL-E
CARPAL-S
S-**CARPED**
CARPEL-S
S-**CARPER**
CARPER-S
CARPET-S
CARRAT-S
CARREL-L
CARREL-S
CARROM-S
CARROT-S
CARROT-Y
CARSEY-S
S-**CARTED**
CARTEL-S
CARTER-S
E-**CARTES**
CARTON-S
CARVEL-S
CARVER-S
CARVER-Y
S-**CARVES**
CASABA-S
CASAVA-S
CASBAH-S
CASEIN-S
CASERN-E
CASERN-S
CASHAW-S
CASHEW-S
CASHOO-S
CASING-S
CASINO-S
CASITA-S
CASKET-S
CASQUE-D
CASQUE-S
CASSIA-S
CASTER-S
CASTLE-D
CASTLE-S
CASTOR-S
CASTOR-Y
CASUAL-S
CATALO-G
CATALO-S
CATENA-E
CATENA-S
A-**CATERS**
CATGUT-S
CATION-S
CATKIN-S
CATLIN-G
CATLIN-S
CATNAP-S
CATNEP-S
CATNIP-S
CATSUP-S
S-**CATTED**
CATTIE-R
CATTIE-S
A-**CAUDAL**
CAUDLE-D
CAUDLE-S
CAUKER-S
CAUSAL-S
CAUSER-S
CAUSEY-S
CAUTEL-S
CAUTER-S
CAUTER-Y
CAVEAT-S
CAVERN-S
CAVIAR-E
CAVIAR-S
CAVIER-S
CAVING-S
CAVORT-S
CAWING-S
CAWKER-S
CAYMAN-S
CAYUSE-S
CEBOID-S
CEDULA-S
CEILER-S
CELIAC-S
O-**CELLAR**
CELLAR-S
CELLOS-E
CEMBRA-S
CEMENT-A
CEMENT-S
CENOTE-S
CENSER-S
CENSOR-S
CENTAL-S
CENTER-S
CENTRA-L
CENTRE-D
CENTRE-S
CENTUM-S
A-**CERATE**
CERATE-D
CERATE-S
CEREAL-S
CERIPH-S
CERISE-S
CERITE-S
CERIUM-S
CERMET-S
S-**CERNED**
S-**CERNES**
CEROON-S
A-**CEROUS**
CERUSE-S
CERVID-S
CESIUM-S
CESSER-S
CESTOI-D
CESTUI-S
CESURA-E
CESURA-L
CESURA-S
CESURE-S
CETANE-S
A-**CETYLS**
CHABUK-S
CHACMA-S
CHADAR-S
CHADOR-S
CHAETA-E
CHAETA-L
CHAFER-S
CHAGAN-S
CHAINE-D
CHAINE-S
CHAISE-S
CHAKRA-S
CHALAH-S
CHALAN-S
CHALEH-S
CHALET-S
CHALLA-H
CHALLA-N
CHALLA-S
CHALOT-H
CHANCE-D
CHANCE-L
CHANCE-R
CHANCE-S
CHANCE-Y
CHANGE-D
CHANGE-R
CHANGE-S
CHAPEL-S
CHAPES-S
CHAPKA-S
E-**CHARDS**
CHARET-S
CHARGE-D
CHARGE-R
CHARGE-S
CHARKA-S
CHARRO-S
CHARTA-S
CHASER-S
CHASSE-D
CHASSE-S
CHASTE-N
CHASTE-R
CHATON-S
CHATTA-S
CHATTI-S
CHAUFE-D
CHAUFE-R
CHAUFE-S
CHAUFF-S
CHAUNT-S
CHAWER-S
CHAZAN-S
CHEAPO-S
CHEBEC-S
CHEDER-S
CHEERO-S
CHEESE-D
CHEESE-S
CHEGOE-S
CHEMIC-S
CHENAR-S
CHENET-S
CHEQUE-R
CHEQUE-S
CHERUB-S
CHERUP-S
CHESIL-S
CHETAH-S
CHEVEN-S
CHEVET-S
CHEVIN-S
CHEVRE-S
CHEWER-S
CHEWET-S

CHEWIE-R
CHEWIE-S
CHIACK-S
CHIASM-A
CHIASM-I
CHIASM-S
CHIBOL-S
CHICHA-S
CHICHI-S
T-**CHICKS**
CHICLE-S
CHICON-S
CHIDER-S
CHIELD-S
CHIGOE-S
CHIGRE-S
CHIKOR-S
CHILDE-D
CHILDE-R
CHILDE-S
CHILLI-S
CHIMAR-S
CHIMER-A
CHIMER-E
CHIMER-S
CHIMLA-S
CHINAR-S
CHINCH-Y
CHINES-E
CHINTZ-Y
CHIRRE-D
CHIRRE-S
CHISEL-S
CHITAL-S
CHITIN-S
CHITON-S
CHOANA-E
CHOCHO-S
CHOCKO-S
CHOICE-R
CHOICE-S
CHOKER-S
CHOKEY-S
CHOKRA-S
CHOKRI-S
CHOLER-A
CHOLER-S
CHOLLA-S
CHOOSE-R
CHOOSE-S
CHOOSE-Y
CHOPIN-E
CHOPIN-S
CHORAL-E
CHORAL-S
CHORDA-E
CHORDA-L
CHOREA-L
CHOREA-S
CHOREE-S
CHORIA-L
CHOUGH-S
CHOUSE-D
CHOUSE-R
CHOUSE-S
S-**CHOUTS**
CHOWRI-S
CHOWSE-D
CHOWSE-S
CHRISM-A
CHRISM-S
CHROMA-S
CHROME-D
CHROME-L
CHROME-S

CHROMO-S
CHUKAR-S
CHUKKA-R
CHUKKA-S
CHUKOR-S
CHURCH-Y
CHYACK-S
CHYMIC-S
CHYPRE-S
CICADA-E
CICADA-S
CICALA-S
CICERO-S
CICUTA-S
CIERGE-S
CIGGIE-S
CILICE-S
CIMIER-S
CINDER-S
CINDER-Y
CINEMA-S
CINEOL-E
CINEOL-S
CINQUE-S
CIPHER-S
CIRCAR-S
CIRCLE-D
CIRCLE-R
CIRCLE-S
CIRCLE-T
CIRCUS-Y
CIRQUE-S
CITHER-N
CITHER-S
CITOLA-S
CITOLE-S
CITRAL-S
CITRIN-E
CITRIN-S
CITRON-S
CITRUS-Y
CIVISM-S
CLAMBE-R
CLAMOR-S
CLAQUE-R
CLAQUE-S
CLARET-S
CLAUSE-S
CLAVER-S
S-**CLAVES**
CLAVIE-R
CLAVIE-S
CLAWER-S
CLAXON-S
CLEANS-E
CLEAVE-D
CLEAVE-R
CLEAVE-S
CLEEVE-S
CLEOME-S
Y-**CLEPED**
CLERIC-S
CLERID-S
CLEUCH-S
CLEUGH-S
CLICHE-D
CLICHE-S
CLIENT-S
S-**CLIFFS**
A-**CLINIC**
CLINIC-S
CLIQUE-D
CLIQUE-S
CLIQUE-Y
CLITIC-S

CLIVIA-S
CLOACA-E
CLOACA-L
CLOACA-S
CLOCHE-S
CLONER-S
CLOQUE-S
E-**CLOSED**
CLOSER-S
E-**CLOSES**
CLOSES-T
CLOSET-S
CLOTHE-D
CLOTHE-S
CLOUGH-S
CLOVER-S
CLOVER-Y
CLUSIA-S
CLUTCH-Y
COAITA-S
COALER-S
COARSE-N
COARSE-R
COATEE-S
COATER-S
COAXER-S
COBALT-S
COBBER-S
COBBLE-D
COBBLE-R
COBBLE-S
COBNUT-S
COBURG-S
COBWEB-S
COCAIN-E
COCAIN-S
COCCID-S
COCHIN-S
COCKER-S
COCKET-S
COCKLE-D
COCKLE-S
COCKUP-S
COCOON-S
CODDER-S
CODDLE-D
CODDLE-R
CODDLE-S
CODEIA-S
CODEIN-A
CODEIN-E
CODEIN-S
CODGER-S
CODING-S
CODIST-S
CODLIN-G
CODLIN-S
COEDIT-S
COELOM-E
COELOM-S
COEMPT-S
COERCE-D
COERCE-R
COERCE-S
COEVAL-S
S-**COFFED**
COFFEE-S
S-**COFFER**
COFFER-S
COFFIN-G
COFFIN-S
COFFLE-D
COFFLE-S
S-**COGGED**
COGGER-S

COGGIE-S
COGGLE-D
COGGLE-S
COGITO-S
COGNAC-S
COGWAY-S
COHEAD-S
COHEIR-S
COHERE-D
COHERE-R
COHERE-S
COHORN-S
COHORT-S
COHOST-S
COHUNE-S
COIFFE-D
COIFFE-S
COIGNE-D
COIGNE-S
COILER-S
COINER-S
COJOIN-S
S-**COLDER**
COLEAD-S
COLLAR-D
COLLAR-S
COLLET-S
COLLIE-D
COLLIE-R
COLLIE-S
S-**COLLOP**
COLLOP-S
COLOBI-D
COLONE-L
COLONE-S
COLONI-C
COLOUR-S
COLOUR-Y
COLTER-S
COLUGO-S
COLUMN-S
COLURE-S
COMAKE-R
COMAKE-S
COMARB-S
COMART-S
COMATE-S
COMBAT-S
COMBER-S
COMBLE-S
COMEDO-S
COMFIT-S
COMICE-S
COMING-S
COMMER-E
COMMER-S
COMMIE-S
COMMIT-S
COMMIX-T
COMMON-S
COMMOT-E
COMMOT-S
COMPEL-S
COMPER-E
COMPER-S
COMPOS-E
COMPOS-T
COMPOT-E
COMPOT-S
CONCHA-E
CONCHA-L
CONCHE-D
CONCHE-S
CONCUR-S
CONDER-S

CONDIE-S
CONDOM-S
CONDOR-S
CONFAB-S
CONFER-S
CONFIT-S
CONGEE-D
CONGEE-S
CONGER-S
CONGES-T
CONGOU-S
CONIMA-S
CONINE-S
CONIUM-S
CONJEE-D
CONJEE-S
CONKER-S
CONNER-S
CONOID-S
CONSOL-E
CONSOL-S
CONSUL-S
CONSUL-T
CONTES-T
CONTRA-S
CONTRA-T
CONURE-S
CONVEY-S
CONVOY-S
COOING-S
COOKER-S
COOKER-Y
COOKEY-S
COOKIE-S
COOLER-S
COOLIE-S
COOLTH-S
COOMBE-S
S-**COOPED**
S-**COOPER**
COOPER-S
COOPER-Y
COOSEN-S
COOSER-S
COOSIN-S
S-**COOTER**
COOTER-S
COOTIE-S
COPALM-S
COPECK-S
COPIER-S
S-**COPING**
COPING-S
COPITA-S
COPLOT-S
COPPER-S
COPPER-Y
COPPIN-G
COPPIN-S
COPPLE-S
COPPRA-S
COPRAH-S
COPTER-S
S-**COPULA**
COPULA-E
COPULA-R
COPULA-S
COQUET-S
CORBAN-S
CORBEL-S
CORBIE-S
CORDER-S
CORDON-S
S-**CORERS**
S-**CORING**

CORIUM-S
CORKER-S
CORKIR-S
CORMEL-S
CORNEA-L
CORNEA-S
A-**CORNED**
S-CORNED
CORNEL-S
S-**CORNER**
CORNER-S
CORNET-S
CORNET-T
CORNUA-L
CORONA-E
CORONA-L
CORONA-S
COROZO-S
CORPSE-D
CORPSE-S
CORRAL-S
CORRIE-S
CORSAC-S
S-**CORSES**
CORSET-S
CORTIN-S
CORVEE-S
CORVET-S
CORVID-S
CORYMB-S
CORYZA-L
CORYZA-S
COSECH-S
COSHER-S
COSHER-Y
COSIER-S
COSIES-T
COSIGN-S
COSINE-S
COSMEA-S
COSSET-S
COSSIE-S
COSTAL-S
COSTAR-D
COSTAR-S
COSTER-S
COTEAU-X
COTING-A
COTISE-D
COTISE-S
COTTAR-S
COTTER-S
COTTID-S
COTTON-S
COTTON-Y
COTWAL-S
COTYLE-S
E-**COTYPE**
COTYPE-S
COUCAL-S
COUCHE-D
COUCHE-E
COUCHE-R
COUCHE-S
COUGAR-S
COULEE-S
S-**COUPED**
COUPEE-S
COUPER-S
COUPLE-D
COUPLE-R
COUPLE-S
COUPLE-T
COUPON-S
S-**COURED**

S-**COURSE**
COURSE-D
COURSE-R
COURSE-S
COUSIN-S
S-**COUTER**
COUTER-S
S-**COUTHS**
COUTIL-S
COVENT-S
COVERT-S
COVING-S
COVYNE-S
COWAGE-S
COWARD-S
COWBOY-S
S-**COWING**
S-**COWLED**
COWPAT-S
COWPEA-S
S-**COWPED**
COWPIE-S
S-**COWRIE**
COWRIE-S
COYDOG-S
COYOTE-S
COYPOU-S
COZIER-S
COZIES-T
CRADLE-D
CRADLE-R
CRADLE-S
S-**CRAGGY**
CRAMBE-S
CRAMBO-S
CRAMES-Y
S-**CRANCH**
CRANIA-L
S-**CRANNY**
S-**CRAPED**
S-**CRAPES**
CRAPLE-S
S-**CRAPPY**
S-**CRATCH**
CRATER-S
CRATON-S
CRATUR-S
CRAVAT-S
CRAVEN-S
CRAVER-S
S-**CRAWLS**
S-**CRAWLY**
CRAYER-S
CRAYON-S
CREACH-S
CREAGH-S
S-**CREAKS**
S-**CREAKY**
S-**CREAMS**
CREASE-D
CREASE-R
CREASE-S
O-**CREATE**
CREATE-D
CREATE-S
CRECHE-S
CREDIT-S
S-**CREEDS**
CREESE-D
CREESE-S
CREESH-Y
CREMOR-S
CRENEL-S
CREOLE-S
CREPON-S
CRESOL-S
CRESYL-S
CRETIC-S
CRETIN-S
S-**CREWED**
CREWEL-S
S-**CRIMPS**
S-**CRIMPY**
S-**CRINES**
CRINGE-D
CRINGE-R
CRINGE-S
CRINUM-S
CRISSA-L
CRISTA-E
CRITIC-S
CROCHE-S
CROCHE-T
CROJIK-S
CRONET-S
CROOVE-S
CROSSE-D
CROSSE-R
CROSSE-S
S-**CROTAL**
CROTAL-A
CROTAL-S
CROTON-S
CROUPE-D
CROUPE-R
CROUPE-S
CROUTE-S
CROWER-S
CROZER-S
CRUDES-T
CRUISE-D
CRUISE-R
CRUISE-S
CRUIVE-S
CRUMEN-S
S-**CRUMMY**
S-**CRUMPS**
S-**CRUMPY**
S-**CRUNCH**
CRUNCH-Y
CRUSET-S
CRUSIE-S
CRUSTA-E
CRUSTA-L
S-**CRYING**
CRYING-S
CRYPTO-N
CRYPTO-S
CUBAGE-S
CUBICA-L
CUBICA-S
CUBISM-S
CUBIST-S
CUBOID-S
CUCKOO-S
CUDDEN-S
CUDDIE-S
CUDDIN-S
S-**CUDDLE**
CUDDLE-D
CUDDLE-R
CUDDLE-S
CUDGEL-S
CUEIST-S
CUESTA-S
S-**CUFFED**
CUFFIN-G
CUFFIN-S
S-**CUFFLE**
CUFFLE-D
CUFFLE-S
CUISSE-R
CUISSE-S
CUITER-S
CULLAY-S
S-**CULLED**
S-**CULLER**
CULLER-S
CULLET-S
CULMEN-S
CULTER-S
CULVER-S
CULVER-T
S-**CUMBER**
CUMBER-S
S-**CUMMER**
CUMMER-S
CUMMIN-S
CUNDUM-S
S-**CUNNER**
CUNNER-S
CUPFUL-S
CUPOLA-R
CUPOLA-S
S-**CUPPER**
CUPPER-S
CUPRUM-S
CUPULA-E
CUPULA-R
CUPULE-S
CURAGH-S
CURARA-S
CURARE-S
CURARI-S
CURATE-D
CURATE-S
CURBER-S
CURDLE-D
CURDLE-R
CURDLE-S
CURFEW-S
E-**CURIES**
CURIET-S
CURIOS-A
CURITE-S
CURIUM-S
CURLER-S
CURLEW-S
CURPEL-S
CURRAN-S
CURRAN-T
S-**CURRED**
CURRIE-D
CURRIE-R
CURRIE-S
CURSER-S
CURSOR-S
CURSOR-Y
CURTAL-S
CURVET-S
CUSHAT-S
CUSHAW-S
CUSPID-S
CUSSER-S
CUSTOM-S
A-**CUTELY**
A-**CUTEST**
CUTLAS-S
CUTLER-S
CUTLER-Y
CUTLET-S
CUTOFF-S
CUTOUT-S
S-**CUTTER**
CUTTER-S
S-**CUTTLE**
CUTTLE-D
CUTTLE-S
CUTTOE-S
S-**CUZZES**
CYANID-E
CYANID-S
CYANIN-E
CYANIN-S
CYATHI-A
CYBORG-S
CYBRID-S
CYCLER-S
CYCLER-Y
A-**CYCLIC**
CYGNET-S
CYMBAL-O
CYMBAL-S
CYMENE-S
CYMLIN-G
CYMLIN-S
CYPHER-S
CYPRES-S
CYPRID-S
CYSTID-S
CYTASE-S
CYTODE-S
CZAPKA-S
DABBER-S
DABBLE-D
DABBLE-R
DABBLE-S
DACITE-S
DACKER-S
DACOIT-S
DACOIT-Y
DACTYL-I
DACTYL-S
DADDLE-D
DADDLE-S
DAEMON-S
DAFTAR-S
DAFTIE-S
DAGABA-S
DAGGER-S
DAGGLE-D
DAGGLE-S
DAGOBA-S
DAHLIA-S
DAHOON-S
DAIDLE-D
DAIDLE-S
DAIKER-S
DAIKON-S
DAIMIO-S
DAIMON-S
DAIMYO-S
S-**DAINED**
S-**DAINES**
DAKOIT-I
DAKOIT-S
DAKOIT-Y
DALASI-S
DALEDH-S
DALETH-S
DALLOP-S
DALTON-S
DAMAGE-D
DAMAGE-R
DAMAGE-S
DAMASK-S
DAMMAR-S
DAMMER-S
DAMNER-S
DAMPEN-S
DAMPER-S
DAMSEL-S
DAMSON-S
DANCER-S
DANDER-S
DANDLE-D
DANDLE-R
DANDLE-S
DANGER-S
DANGLE-D
DANGLE-R
DANGLE-S
DANTON-S
DAPHNE-S
DAPPER-S
DAPPLE-D
DAPPLE-S
DARGLE-S
DARING-S
DARKEN-S
DARKEY-S
DARKIE-S
DARKLE-D
DARKLE-S
DARNEL-S
DARNER-S
DARTER-S
DARTLE-D
DARTLE-S
DARTRE-S
DASHER-S
DASSIE-S
DATCHA-S
DATING-S
DATIVE-S
DATURA-S
DAUBER-S
DAUBER-Y
DAUNER-S
DAUTIE-S
DAWDLE-D
DAWDLE-R
DAWDLE-S
A-**DAWING**
DAWNER-S
DAWTIE-S
DAYBED-S
DAYGLO-W
DAZZLE-D
DAZZLE-R
DAZZLE-S
DEACON-S
DEADEN-S
DEADER-S
DEAFEN-S
DEALER-S
DEANER-S
DEANER-Y
DEARES-T
DEARIE-S
DEARTH-S
DEASIL-S
DEBARK-S
DEBASE-D
DEBASE-R
DEBASE-S
DEBATE-D
DEBATE-R
DEBATE-S
DEBEAK-S
DEBONE-D
DEBONE-R
DEBONE-S
DEBTEE-S
DEBTOR-S
DEBUNK-S
DECADE-S
DECAFF-S
DECAMP-S
DECANE-S
DECANT-S
DECARB-S
DECARE-S
DECCIE-S
DECEIT-S
DECERN-S
DECIDE-D
DECIDE-R
DECIDE-S
DECILE-S
DECIME-S
DECKEL-S
DECKER-S
DECKLE-D
DECKLE-S
DECLAW-S
DECOCT-S
DECODE-D
DECODE-R
DECODE-S
DECOKE-D
DECOKE-S
DECREE-D
DECREE-R
DECREE-S
DECREE-T
DECREW-S
DECTET-S
DEDUCE-D
DEDUCE-S
DEDUCT-S
DEEJAY-S
A-**DEEMED**
DEEPEN-S
DEEPIE-S
DEEWAN-S
DEFACE-D
DEFACE-R
DEFACE-S
DEFAME-D
DEFAME-R
DEFAME-S
DEFANG-S
DEFAST-E
DEFEAT-S
DEFECT-S
DEFEND-S
DEFIER-S
DEFILE-D
DEFILE-R
DEFILE-S
DEFINE-D
DEFINE-R
DEFINE-S
DEFLEA-S
DEFOAM-S
DEFORM-S
DEFOUL-S
DEFRAG-S
DEFRAY-S
DEFUND-S
DEFUSE-D
DEFUSE-S
DEFUZE-D
DEFUZE-S
DEGAME-S
DEGAMI-S
DEGERM-S
DEGOUT-S
DEGREE-D

DEGREE-S
DEGUST-S
DEHORN-S
DEHORT-S
DEICER-S
S-**DEIGNS**
DEJECT-A
DEJECT-S
DEKARE-S
DELATE-D
DELATE-S
DELEAD-S
DELETE-D
DELETE-S
DELICE-S
DELICT-S
DELIME-D
DELIME-S
DELIST-S
DELOPE-D
DELOPE-S
DELUDE-D
DELUDE-R
DELUDE-S
DELUGE-D
DELUGE-S
DELVER-S
DEMAIN-E
DEMAIN-S
DEMAND-S
DEMARK-S
DEMAST-S
DEMEAN-E
DEMEAN-S
DEMENT-I
DEMENT-S
DEMISE-D
DEMISE-S
DEMIST-S
DEMODE-D
DEMOTE-D
DEMOTE-S
DEMURE-D
DEMURE-R
DEMURE-S
DENGUE-S
DENIAL-S
DENIER-S
DENNET-S
DENOTE-D
DENOTE-S
E-**DENTAL**
DENTAL-S
DENTEL-S
DENTIL-S
DENTIN-E
DENTIN-G
DENTIN-S
DENUDE-D
DENUDE-R
DENUDE-S
DEODAR-A
DEODAR-S
DEPART-S
DEPEND-S
DEPERM-S
DEPICT-S
DEPLOY-S
DEPONE-D
DEPONE-S
DEPORT-S
DEPOSE-D
DEPOSE-R
DEPOSE-S
DEPUTE-D
DEPUTE-S
DERAIL-S
DERATE-D
DERATE-S
DERHAM-S
DERIDE-D
DERIDE-R
DERIDE-S
DERIVE-D
DERIVE-R
DERIVE-S
DESALT-S
DESAND-S
DESERT-S
DESIGN-S
DESINE-D
DESINE-S
DESIRE-D
DESIRE-R
DESIRE-S
DESIST-S
DESMAN-S
DESMID-S
DESORB-S
DESPOT-S
DESYNE-D
DESYNE-S
DETAIL-S
DETAIN-S
DETECT-S
DETENT-E
DETENT-S
DETENU-E
DETENU-S
DETEST-S
DETICK-S
DETORT-S
DETOUR-S
DETUNE-D
DETUNE-S
DEUTON-S
DEVALL-S
DEVEIN-S
DEVEST-S
DEVICE-S
DEVISE-D
DEVISE-E
DEVISE-R
DEVISE-S
DEVOIR-S
DEVOTE-D
DEVOTE-E
DEVOTE-S
DEVOUR-S
DEVVEL-S
DEWANI-S
DEWITT-S
DEWLAP-S
DEWLAP-T
DEWOOL-S
DEWORM-S
DEXTER-S
DEZINC-S
A-**DHARMA**
DHARMA-S
DHARNA-S
DHOORA-S
DHOOTI-E
DHOOTI-S
DHURNA-S
DHURRA-S
DIABLE-S
DIACID-S
DIADEM-S
DIALER-S
DIALOG-S
DIAMIN-E
DIAMIN-S
DIAPER-S
DIAPIR-S
DIARCH-Y
DIATOM-S
DIAXON-S
DIAZIN-E
DIAZIN-S
DIBBER-S
DIBBLE-D
DIBBLE-R
DIBBLE-S
DIBBUK-S
DICAST-S
DICING-S
DICKER-S
DICKEY-S
DICKIE-R
DICKIE-S
DICTUM-S
DIDACT-S
DIDDER-S
DIDDLE-D
DIDDLE-R
DIDDLE-S
DIDDLE-Y
DIEDRE-S
DIESEL-S
DIETER-S
DIFFER-S
DIGEST-S
DIGGER-S
DIGLOT-S
DIKAST-S
DIKDIK-S
DIKKOP-S
DIKTAT-S
DILATE-D
DILATE-R
DILATE-S
DILDOE-S
DILUTE-D
DILUTE-E
DILUTE-R
DILUTE-S
DIMBLE-S
DIMMER-S
DIMOUT-S
DIMPLE-D
DIMPLE-S
DIMWIT-S
DINDLE-D
DINDLE-S
DINERO-S
DINGER-S
DINGEY-S
DINGLE-S
DINKEY-S
DINKUM-S
DINNER-S
DINNLE-D
DINNLE-S
DIOBOL-S
DIOXAN-E
DIOXAN-S
DIOXID-E
DIOXID-S
DIOXIN-S
DIPLOE-S
DIPLON-S
DIPLON-T
DIPNET-S
DIPOLE-S
DIPPER-S
DIQUAT-S
DIRDAM-S
DIRDUM-S
DIRECT-S
DIRHAM-S
DIRHEM-S
DIRIGE-S
DIRNDL-S
DISARM-S
DISBAR-K
DISBAR-S
DISBUD-S
DISCUS-S
DISEUR-S
DISMAL-S
DISMAN-S
DISMAY-D
DISMAY-L
DISMAY-S
DISOWN-S
DISPEL-S
DISPLE-D
DISPLE-S
DISTIL-L
DISTIL-S
DISUSE-D
DISUSE-S
DITHER-S
DITHER-Y
E-**DITING**
DITONE-S
DITTAY-S
DIURON-S
DIVERS-E
DIVERT-S
DIVEST-S
DIVIDE-D
DIVIDE-R
DIVIDE-S
DIVINE-D
DIVINE-R
DIVINE-S
DIVING-S
DIZAIN-S
DJEBEL-S
DOATER-S
DOBBER-S
DOBBIE-S
DOBBIN-G
DOBBIN-S
DOBLON-S
DOBSON-S
DOCENT-S
DOCILE-R
DOCKEN-S
DOCKER-S
DOCKET-S
DOCTOR-S
DODDER-S
DODDER-Y
DODDLE-S
DODGEM-S
DODGER-S
DODGER-Y
DODKIN-S
DODMAN-S
DOFFER-S
DOGATE-S
DOGDOM-S
DOGEAR-S
DOGGER-S
DOGGER-Y
DOGGIE-R
DOGGIE-S
DOGLEG-S
DOGNAP-S
DOLINA-S
DOLINE-S
DOLLAR-S
DOLLOP-S
DOLMAN-S
DOLMEN-S
DOLOUR-S
DOMAIN-S
DOMETT-S
DOMINE-E
DOMINE-S
DOMINO-S
O-**DONATE**
DONATE-D
DONATE-S
DONDER-S
DONGLE-S
DONING-S
DONJON-S
DONKEY-S
DONNAT-S
DONNEE-S
DONNOT-S
DONSIE-R
DONZEL-S
DOOCOT-S
DOODAD-S
DOODAH-S
DOODLE-D
DOODLE-R
DOODLE-S
DOOFER-S
DOOKET-S
DOOLEE-S
DOOLIE-S
DOOZER-S
DOOZIE-S
DOPANT-S
DOPING-S
DOPPER-S
DOPPIE-S
DORADO-S
DORBUG-S
DORISE-D
DORISE-S
O-**DORIZE**
DORIZE-D
DORIZE-S
DORMER-S
DORMIN-S
DORPER-S
DORSAL-S
DORSEL-S
DORSER-S
DORTER-S
DOSAGE-S
DOSSAL-S
DOSSEL-S
DOSSER-S
DOSSIL-S
DOTAGE-S
DOTANT-S
DOTARD-S
DOTING-S
DOTTEL-S
DOTTER-S
DOTTLE-D
DOTTLE-R
DOTTLE-S
DOUANE-S
DOUBLE-D
DOUBLE-R
DOUBLE-S
DOUBLE-T
DOUCET-S
DOUCHE-D
DOUCHE-S
DOUGHT-Y
DOURAH-S
DOUSER-S
DOUTER-S
DOWLNE-S
DOWLNE-Y
DOWNER-S
DOWSER-S
DOWSET-S
DOYLEY-S
DOZING-S
DRACHM-A
DRACHM-S
DRAGEE-S
DRAGON-S
DRAPER-S
DRAPER-Y
DRAPET-S
DRAUNT-S
DRAWEE-S
DRAWER-S
DRAZEL-S
A-**DREADS**
DREARE-R
DREARE-S
DREDGE-D
DREDGE-R
DREDGE-S
DREIDL-S
DRIVEL-S
DRIVER-S
DROGER-S
DROGUE-S
DROGUE-T
DROICH-S
DROICH-Y
DROLES-T
DROMON-D
DROMON-S
DRONER-S
DRONGO-S
DROOME-S
DROUTH-S
DROUTH-Y
DROVER-S
DROWND-S
DROWSE-D
DROWSE-S
DRUDGE-D
DRUDGE-R
DRUDGE-S
DRUPEL-S
DRYING-S
DRYLOT-S
DUALIN-S
DUBBER-S
DUBBIN-G
DUBBIN-S
DUCKER-S
DUCKIE-R
DUCKIE-S
DUDDER-S
DUDDER-Y
DUDDIE-R
DUDEEN-S
DUDISM-S
DUELER-S
DUELLO-S
DUENDE-S
DUENNA-S
DUETTO-S

DUFFEL-S
DUFFER-S
DUFFLE-S
DUGONG-S
DUGOUT-S
DUIKER-S
DULCET-S
DUMDUM-S
DUMPER-S
DUMPLE-D
DUMPLE-S
DUNDER-S
DUNITE-S
DUNKER-S
DUNLIN-S
DUOLOG-S
DUPION-S
DUPLET-S
DURANT-S
DURBAR-S
DURDUM-S
DURESS-E
DURGAN-S
DURIAN-S
DURION-S
DURRIE-S
DUSKEN-S
A-**DUSTED**
DUSTER-S
DUSTUP-S
DUYKER-S
DYADIC-S
DYBBUK-S
DYEING-S
DYNAMO-S
DYNAST-S
DYNAST-Y
DYNODE-S
DYVOUR-S
DYVOUR-Y
DZEREN-S
B-**EAGLES**
T-EAGLES
EAGLET-S
M-**EAGRES**
B-**EANING**
D-EANING
L-EANING
M-EANING
P-EANING
S-EANING
W-EANING
Y-EANING
EARBOB-S
EARCON-S
B-**EARDED**
Y-EARDED
F-**EARFUL**
T-EARFUL
EARFUL-S
B-**EARING**
D-EARING
F-EARING
G-EARING
H-EARING
L-EARING
M-EARING
N-EARING
R-EARING
S-EARING
T-EARING
W-EARING
EARING-S
EARLAP-S
L-**EARNED**
Y-EARNED
L-**EARNER**
Y-EARNER
EARNER-S
D-**EARTHS**
H-EARTHS
EARWIG-S
T-**EASELS**
W-EASELS
EASIES-T
C-**EASING**
F-EASING
L-EASING
M-EASING
P-EASING
S-EASING
T-EASING
M-**EASLES**
F-**EASTED**
R-EASTED
Y-EASTED
F-**EASTER**
EASTER-N
EASTER-S
EATAGE-S
EATCHE-S
B-**EATERS**
H-EATERS
S-EATERS
P-**EATERY**
D-**EATHLY**
B-**EATING**
F-EATING
H-EATING
S-EATING
EATING-S
K-**EBBING**
N-EBBING
W-EBBING
ECARTE-S
ECBOLE-S
ECHARD-S
E-**ECHING**
L-ECHING
P-ECHING
ECHOER-S
ECLAIR-S
R-**ECLOSE**
ECLOSE-D
ECLOSE-S
ECONUT-S
ECTYPE-S
ECURIE-S
ECZEMA-S
N-**EDDIES**
T-EDDIES
R-**EDDISH**
O-**EDEMAS**
H-**EDGERS**
K-EDGERS
L-EDGERS
H-**EDGIER**
K-EDGIER
L-EDGIER
S-EDGIER
W-EDGIER
H-**EDGING**
K-EDGING
W-EDGING
EDGING-S
EDIBLE-S
A-**EDILES**
EDITOR-S
D-**EDUCED**
R-EDUCED
S-EDUCED
D-**EDUCES**
R-EDUCES
S-EDUCES
D-**EDUCTS**
L-**EECHED**
R-EECHED
B-**EECHES**
K-EECHES
L-EECHES
R-EECHES
S-**EELIER**
B-**EERIER**
L-EERIER
P-EERIER
L-**EERILY**
EFFACE-D
EFFACE-R
EFFACE-S
EFFECT-S
EFFEIR-S
EFFERE-D
EFFERE-S
J-**EFFING**
R-EFFING
EFFORT-S
EFFRAY-S
EFFUSE-D
EFFUSE-S
D-**EFTEST**
L-EFTEST
L-**EGALLY**
R-EGALLY
R-**EGENCE**
EGENCE-S
R-**EGENCY**
R-**EGESTS**
B-**EGGARS**
S-EGGARS
EGGCUP-S
L-**EGGERS**
L-**EGGIER**
B-**EGGING**
L-EGGING
P-EGGING
V-EGGING
EGGLER-S
EGGNOG-S
A-**EGISES**
EGOISM-S
EGOIST-S
N-**EGRESS**
R-EGRESS
R-**EGRETS**
H-**EIGHTH**
EIGHTH-S
H-**EIGHTS**
W-EIGHTS
W-**EIGHTY**
EIRACK-S
EISELL-S
N-**EITHER**
D-**EJECTA**
D-**EJECTS**
R-EJECTS
ELANCE-D
ELANCE-S
ELANET-S
ELAPID-S
D-**ELAPSE**
R-ELAPSE
ELAPSE-D
ELAPSE-S
B-**ELATED**
D-ELATED
G-ELATED
R-ELATED
V-ELATED
R-**ELATER**
ELATER-S
B-**ELATES**
D-ELATES
G-ELATES
R-ELATES
ELCHEE-S
G-**ELDERS**
M-ELDERS
W-ELDERS
G-**ELDING**
M-ELDING
W-ELDING
ELDING-S
S-**ELECTS**
ELEGIT-S
ELENCH-I
ELENCH-S
ELEVEN-S
ELEVON-S
S-**ELFING**
S-**ELFISH**
ELICIT-S
P-**ELITES**
V-ELITES
ELIXIR-S
ELODEA-S
ELOIGN-S
D-**ELOPED**
ELOPER-S
D-**ELOPES**
ELSHIN-S
ELTCHI-S
ELUANT-S
ELUATE-S
D-**ELUDED**
D-**ELUDER**
ELUDER-S
D-**ELUDES**
ELUENT-S
ELUTOR-S
ELUVIA-L
D-**ELVERS**
ELYTRA-L
R-**EMAILS**
EMBACE-S
EMBAIL-S
EMBALE-D
EMBALE-S
EMBALL-S
EMBALM-S
EMBANK-S
EMBARK-S
EMBASE-D
EMBASE-S
M-**EMBERS**
EMBLEM-A
EMBLEM-S
EMBLIC-S
EMBOIL-S
EMBOLI-C
EMBOSK-S
EMBRUE-D
EMBRUE-S
EMBRYO-N
EMBRYO-S
R-**EMENDS**
D-**EMERGE**
R-EMERGE
EMERGE-D
EMERGE-S
EMEROD-S
N-**EMESES**
N-**EMESIS**
EMETIC-S
EMETIN-E
EMETIN-S
EMEUTE-S
EMIGRE-S
H-**EMMERS**
EMMOVE-D
EMMOVE-S
EMODIN-S
D-**EMOTED**
R-**EMOTER**
EMOTER-S
D-**EMOTES**
G-EMOTES
R-EMOTES
R-**EMOVED**
R-**EMOVES**
EMPALE-D
EMPALE-R
EMPALE-S
EMPARE-D
EMPARE-S
EMPARL-S
EMPART-S
EMPIRE-S
EMPLOY-E
EMPLOY-S
EMPUSA-S
EMPUSE-S
A-**EMULED**
A-**EMULES**
EMULGE-D
EMULGE-S
EMUNGE-D
EMUNGE-S
D-**EMURED**
D-**EMURES**
L-EMURES
T-**ENABLE**
ENABLE-D
ENABLE-R
ENABLE-S
ENAMEL-S
ENAMOR-S
P-**ENATES**
S-ENATES
V-**ENATIC**
ENCAGE-D
ENCAGE-S
ENCALM-S
ENCAMP-S
ENCASE-D
ENCASE-S
ENCAVE-D
ENCAVE-S
ENCINA-L
ENCINA-S
ENCODE-D
ENCODE-R
ENCODE-S
ENCORE-D
ENCORE-S
ENCYST-S
ENDART-S
ENDEAR-S
B-**ENDERS**
F-ENDERS
G-ENDERS
L-ENDERS
M-ENDERS
R-ENDERS
S-ENDERS
T-ENDERS
V-ENDERS
B-**ENDING**
F-ENDING
H-ENDING
L-ENDING
M-ENDING
P-ENDING
R-ENDING
S-ENDING
T-ENDING
V-ENDING
W-ENDING
ENDING-S
ENDITE-D
ENDITE-S
ENDIVE-S
ENDRIN-S
V-**ENDUES**
ENDURE-D
ENDURE-R
ENDURE-S
ENDURO-S
ENERVE-D
ENERVE-S
R-**ENEWED**
ENFACE-D
ENFACE-S
ENFANT-S
ENFIRE-D
ENFIRE-S
P-**ENFOLD**
T-ENFOLD
ENFOLD-S
ENFORM-S
ENFREE-D
ENFREE-S
ENGAGE-D
ENGAGE-R
ENGAGE-S
ENGAOL-S
ENGILD-S
ENGINE-D
ENGINE-R
ENGINE-S
ENGIRD-S
ENGLUT-S
ENGOBE-S
ENGORE-D
ENGORE-S
ENGRAM-S
ENGULF-S
ENHALO-S
ENIGMA-S
ENISLE-D
ENISLE-S
ENJAMB-S
ENJOIN-S
ENLACE-D
ENLACE-S
ENLARD-S
ENLINK-S
ENLIST-S
G-**ENLOCK**
ENLOCK-S
ENMOVE-D
ENMOVE-S
ENNAGE-S
ENNEAD-S
ENNUYE-D
ENNUYE-E
K-**ENOSES**
K-**ENOSIS**
ENOUGH-S
ENRACE-D
ENRACE-S

ENRAGE-D
ENRAGE-S
ENRANK-S
ENRING-S
ENROBE-D
ENROBE-R
ENROBE-S
ENROLL-S
ENROOT-S
S-**ENSATE**
ENSEAL-S
ENSEAM-S
ENSEAR-S
ENSERF-S
ENSIGN-S
P-**ENSILE**
S-ENSILE
T-ENSILE
ENSILE-D
ENSILE-S
ENSOUL-S
C-**ENSURE**
ENSURE-D
ENSURE-R
ENSURE-S
V-**ENTAIL**
ENTAIL-S
ENTAME-D
ENTAME-S
ENTERA-L
C-**ENTERS**
R-ENTERS
T-ENTERS
V-ENTERS
ENTETE-E
P-**ENTICE**
ENTICE-D
ENTICE-R
ENTICE-S
ENTIRE-S
ENTOIL-S
ENTOMB-S
ENTRAP-S
ENTREE-S
T-**ENURED**
T-**ENURES**
ENVIER-S
S-**ENVIES**
R-**ENVOIS**
L-**ENVOYS**
R-ENVOYS
ENWALL-S
ENWIND-S
ENWOMB-S
ENWRAP-S
ENZIAN-S
ENZONE-D
ENZONE-S
ENZYME-S
A-**EOLIAN**
N-**EOLITH**
EOLITH-S
A-**EONIAN**
P-**EONISM**
EONISM-S
EOSINE-S
EPARCH-S
EPARCH-Y
EPAULE-S
EPAULE-T
EPEIRA-S
EPERDU-E
EPHEBE-S
EPHEBI-C
EPIGON-E
EPIGON-I
EPIGON-S
EPILOG-S
EPIMER-E
EPIMER-S
EPIZOA-N
EPOCHA-L
EPOCHA-S
EPONYM-S
EPONYM-Y
EPOPEE-S
D-**EPOSES**
R-EPOSES
R-**EPRISE**
EPUISE-E
EQUANT-S
EQUATE-D
EQUATE-S
EQUINE-S
EQUIPE-S
ERASER-S
T-**ERBIAS**
T-**ERBIUM**
ERBIUM-S
ERGATE-S
ERIACH-S
ERINGO-S
ERMINE-D
ERMINE-S
C-**ERNING**
F-ERNING
G-ERNING
K-ERNING
T-ERNING
X-**EROSES**
C-**EROTIC**
X-EROTIC
EROTIC-A
EROTIC-S
ERRAND-S
ERRANT-S
ERRATA-S
H-**ERRING**
S-ERRING
ERRING-S
T-**ERRORS**
A-**ERUGOS**
ERYNGO-S
ESCAPE-D
ESCAPE-E
ESCAPE-R
ESCAPE-S
ESCARP-S
ESCHAR-S
ESCHEW-S
ESCORT-S
ESCROC-S
ESCROL-L
ESCROL-S
ESCROW-S
ESCUDO-S
R-**ESILES**
ESLOIN-S
ESPADA-S
ESPIAL-S
ESPRIT-S
ESSIVE-S
ESSOIN-S
G-**ESTATE**
R-ESTATE
T-ESTATE
ESTATE-D
ESTATE-S
ESTEEM-S
F-**ESTERS**
J-ESTERS
N-ESTERS
P-ESTERS
R-ESTERS
T-ESTERS
W-ESTERS
Z-ESTERS
O-**ESTRAL**
V-ESTRAL
ESTRAY-S
O-**ESTRIN**
ESTRIN-S
O-**ESTRUM**
ESTRUM-S
O-**ESTRUS**
M-**ETAGES**
ETALON-S
ETAMIN-E
ETAMIN-S
R-**ETAPES**
F-**ETCHED**
L-ETCHED
R-ETCHED
T-ETCHED
F-**ETCHER**
ETCHER-S
F-**ETCHES**
K-ETCHES
L-ETCHES
R-ETCHES
V-ETCHES
L-**ETHALS**
M-**ETHANE**
ETHANE-S
ETHENE-S
A-**ETHERS**
P-ETHERS
T-ETHERS
W-ETHERS
ETHION-S
ETHNIC-S
M-**ETHOXY**
ETHOXY-L
M-**ETHYLS**
ETHYNE-S
ETOILE-S
ETRIER-S
F-**ETTLED**
M-ETTLED
N-ETTLED
P-ETTLED
S-ETTLED
F-**ETTLES**
K-ETTLES
M-ETTLES
N-ETTLES
P-ETTLES
S-ETTLES
ETYMON-S
EUCAIN-E
EUCAIN-S
EUCHRE-D
EUCHRE-S
L-**EUGHEN**
Y-**EUKING**
EUNUCH-S
EUOUAE-S
EUPHON-S
EUPHON-Y
EUPNEA-S
H-**EUREKA**
EUREKA-S
EVADER-S
EVEJAR-S
EVENER-S
R-**EVERTS**
R-**EVILER**
EVINCE-D
EVINCE-S
L-**EVITES**
R-**EVOKED**
R-**EVOKER**
EVOKER-S
R-**EVOKES**
EVOLUE-S
D-**EVOLVE**
R-EVOLVE
EVOLVE-D
EVOLVE-R
EVOLVE-S
EVOVAE-S
EVULSE-D
EVULSE-S
EVZONE-S
EXACTA-S
H-**EXACTS**
EXAMEN-S
H-**EXARCH**
EXARCH-S
EXARCH-Y
EXCAMB-S
EXCEED-S
EXCEPT-S
EXCIDE-D
EXCIDE-S
EXCISE-D
EXCISE-S
EXCITE-D
EXCITE-R
EXCITE-S
EXCUSE-D
EXCUSE-R
EXCUSE-S
EXEDRA-E
L-**EXEMES**
EXEMPT-S
EXHALE-D
EXHALE-S
EXHORT-S
EXHUME-D
EXHUME-R
EXHUME-S
S-**EXISTS**
EXOGEN-S
EXONYM-S
EXOPOD-S
EXOTIC-A
EXOTIC-S
EXPAND-S
EXPECT-S
EXPEND-S
S-**EXPERT**
EXPERT-S
EXPIRE-D
EXPIRE-R
EXPIRE-S
EXPORT-S
EXPOSE-D
EXPOSE-R
EXPOSE-S
EXPUGN-S
EXSECT-S
EXSERT-S
S-**EXTANT**
EXTEND-S
EXTENT-S
EXTERN-E
EXTERN-S
EXTINE-S
EXTIRP-S
EXTOLL-S
EXTORT-S
EXUVIA-E
EXUVIA-L
EYALET-S
EYEBAR-S
EYECUP-S
EYEFUL-S
EYELET-S
EYELID-S
EYLIAD-S
FABLER-S
FABRIC-S
FACADE-S
FACETE-D
FACIAL-S
FACING-S
FACTOR-S
FACTOR-Y
FACTUM-S
FACULA-E
FACULA-R
FADDLE-D
FADDLE-S
FADEUR-S
FADING-S
FAERIE-S
FAGGOT-S
FAGGOT-Y
FAIBLE-S
FAILLE-S
FAINES-T
FAITOR-S
FAJITA-S
FAKEER-S
FALCON-S
FALLAL-S
FALLER-S
FALLOW-S
FALSER-S
FALSES-T
FALSIE-S
FALTER-S
FAMINE-S
FANDOM-S
FANEGA-S
FANGLE-D
FANGLE-S
FANION-S
FANJET-S
FANKLE-D
FANKLE-S
FANNEL-L
FANNEL-S
FANNER-S
FANTAD-S
FANTOD-S
FANTOM-S
FAQUIR-S
FARCER-S
FARCIE-D
FARCIE-S
FARCIN-G
FARCIN-S
FARDEL-S
FARDEN-S
FARFAL-S
FARFEL-S
FARINA-S
FARMER-S
FARMER-Y
FARREN-S
FARROW-S
FASCIA-E
FASCIA-L
FASCIA-S
FASTEN-S
FASTER-S
FATHER-S
FATHOM-S
FATSIA-S
FATTEN-S
FATWAH-S
FAUCAL-S
FAUCET-S
FAUTOR-S
FAVELA-S
FAVELL-A
FAVISM-S
FAVOUR-S
FAWNER-S
FEAGUE-D
FEAGUE-S
A-**FEARED**
FEARER-S
FECIAL-S
FECULA-E
FECULA-S
FEDORA-S
FEEBLE-D
FEEBLE-R
FEEBLE-S
FEEDER-S
FEELER-S
FEERIE-S
FEERIN-G
FEERIN-S
FEIJOA-S
FELINE-S
FELLAH-S
FELLER-S
FELLOE-S
FELLOW-S
FELTER-S
FEMALE-S
FEMORA-L
FENCER-S
FENDER-S
FENNEC-S
FENNEL-S
FERBAM-S
FERLIE-D
FERLIE-R
FERLIE-S
FERREL-S
FERRET-S
FERRET-Y
FERRUM-S
FERULA-E
FERULA-S
FERULE-D
FERULE-S
FERVOR-S
FESCUE-S
FESTAL-S
FESTER-S
FETIAL-S
FETICH-E
FETTER-S
FETTLE-D
FETTLE-R
FETTLE-S
FEUTRE-D
FEUTRE-S
FEWMET-S
FEWTER-S
FIACRE-S
FIANCE-E
FIANCE-S
FIASCO-S

FIAUNT-S
FIBBER-S
FIBBER-Y
FIBRIL-S
FIBRIN-S
FIBROS-E
FIBULA-E
FIBULA-R
FIBULA-S
FICKLE-D
FICKLE-R
FICKLE-S
FICTOR-S
FIDDLE-D
FIDDLE-R
FIDDLE-S
FIDDLE-Y
FIDGET-S
FIDGET-Y
FIERCE-R
FIESTA-S
FIGURE-D
FIGURE-R
FIGURE-S
FILFOT-S
FILING-S
FILLER-S
FILLET-S
FILLIP-S
FILMER-S
FILTER-S
FIMBLE-S
FINALE-S
FINDER-S
FINEER-S
FINGAN-S
FINGER-S
FINIAL-S
FINING-S
FINITE-S
FINJAN-S
FINNAC-K
FINNAC-S
FINNAN-S
FINNER-S
FIORIN-S
FIPPLE-S
FIRING-S
FIRKIN-G
FIRKIN-S
FIRLOT-S
FIRMAN-S
FIRMER-S
FISCAL-S
FISGIG-S
FISHER-S
FISHER-Y
FISSLE-D
FISSLE-S
FITCHE-E
FITCHE-S
FITCHE-T
FITCHE-W
FITTER-S
FITTES-T
FIXATE-D
FIXATE-S
FIXING-S
FIXURE-S
FIZGIG-S
FIZZEN-S
FIZZER-S
FIZZLE-D
FIZZLE-S
FLACON-S
FLAGON-S
FLAKER-S
FLAMBE-E
FLAMBE-S
FLAMEN-S
FLAMER-S
FLANGE-D
FLANGE-R
FLANGE-S
FLASER-S
FLAUNE-S
FLAUNT-S
FLAUNT-Y
FLAVIN-E
FLAVIN-S
FLAVOR-S
FLAVOR-Y
FLAYER-S
FLECHE-S
FLEDGE-D
FLEDGE-S
FLEECE-D
FLEECE-R
FLEECE-S
FLENSE-D
FLENSE-R
FLENSE-S
FLEXOR-S
FLIGHT-S
FLIGHT-Y
FLORAL-S
FLORET-S
FLORIN-S
FLOTEL-S
FLOUSE-D
FLOUSE-S
FLOWER-S
FLOWER-Y
FLUATE-S
FLUENT-S
FLUGEL-S
FLUTER-S
FLYBOY-S
FLYING-S
FLYOFF-S
FLYWAY-S
FOAMER-S
FODDER-S
FOETOR-S
FOGBOW-S
FOGDOG-S
FOGGER-S
FOGLES-S
FOGRAM-S
FOIBLE-S
FOISON-S
FOLATE-S
FOLDER-S
FOLIOS-E
FOLIUM-S
FOLKIE-S
FOLLOW-S
FOMENT-S
FOMITE-S
FONDLE-D
FONDLE-R
FONDLE-S
FONDUE-S
FOODIE-S
FOOTER-S
FOOTIE-R
FOOTIE-S
FOOTLE-D
FOOTLE-R
FOOTLE-S
FOOTRA-S
FOOZLE-D
FOOZLE-R
FOOZLE-S
FORAGE-D
FORAGE-R
FORAGE-S
FORBAD-E
FORBID-S
FORCAT-S
FORCER-S
FOREBY-E
FOREST-S
FORGER-S
FORGER-Y
FORGET-S
FORHOO-S
FORHOW-S
FORINT-S
FORKER-S
FORMAL-S
FORMAT-E
FORMAT-S
FORMER-S
FORMOL-S
FORMYL-S
FORPET-S
FORPIT-S
FORRAY-S
FORSAY-S
FOSSIL-S
FOSSOR-S
FOSTER-S
FOTHER-S
FOUGHT-Y
FOULES-T
FOURTH-S
FOUSSA-S
FOUTER-S
FOUTRA-S
FOUTRE-D
FOUTRE-S
FOWLER-S
FOXING-S
FRAGOR-S
FRAISE-D
FRAISE-S
FRAMER-S
FRAPPE-D
FRAPPE-E
FRAPPE-S
FRATCH-Y
FRATER-S
FRATER-Y
FRAZIL-S
A-**FREETS**
FREEZE-R
FREEZE-S
FREMIT-S
FRENUM-S
FRESCO-S
FRIAND-E
FRIAND-S
FRICHT-S
FRIDGE-D
FRIDGE-S
FRIEND-S
FRIEZE-D
FRIEZE-S
FRIGHT-S
FRIGOT-S
FRIJOL-E
FRINGE-D
FRINGE-S
FRIPON-S
FRISEE-S
FRISKA-S
FRIVOL-S
FRIZER-S
FROISE-S
FROLIC-S
FROWIE-R
FROWST-S
FROWST-Y
FRUICT-S
FRYING-S
FRYPAN-S
FUCKER-S
FUCKUP-S
FUCOID-S
FUCOSE-S
FUDDLE-D
FUDDLE-R
FUDDLE-S
FUELER-S
FUGATO-S
FUHRER-S
FULFIL-L
FULFIL-S
FULGOR-S
FULHAM-S
FULLAM-S
FULLAN-S
FULLER-S
FULLER-Y
FULMAR-S
FUMADO-S
FUMAGE-S
FUMBLE-D
FUMBLE-R
FUMBLE-S
FUNDER-S
FUNDIE-S
FUNGAL-S
FUNKER-S
FUNKIA-S
FUNNEL-S
FURANE-S
FUREUR-S
FURFUR-S
FURLER-S
FUROLE-S
FURORE-S
FURROW-S
FURROW-Y
FUSAIN-S
FUSION-S
FUSSER-S
FUSTET-S
FUSTIC-S
FUSTOC-S
FUTILE-R
FUTURE-S
FUZZLE-D
FUZZLE-S
FYLFOT-S
GABBER-S
GABBLE-D
GABBLE-R
GABBLE-S
GABBRO-S
GABION-S
GABLET-S
GABOON-S
GADDER-S
GADGET-S
GADGET-Y
GADGIE-S
GADOID-S
GAFFER-S
GAGAKU-S
GAGGER-S
GAGGLE-D
GAGGLE-S
GAINER-S
A-**GAINST**
GAITER-S
GALAGE-S
GALAGO-S
GALENA-S
GALERE-S
GALIOT-S
GALLET-A
GALLET-S
GALLEY-S
GALLON-S
GALLOP-S
GALLOW-S
GALOOT-S
GALORE-S
GALOSH-E
GALUTH-S
GALYAC-S
GALYAK-S
GAMBET-S
GAMBIA-S
GAMBIR-S
GAMBIT-S
GAMBLE-D
GAMBLE-R
GAMBLE-S
GAMBOL-S
A-**GAMETE**
GAMETE-S
GAMINE-S
GAMING-S
GAMMER-S
GAMMON-S
GANDER-S
GANGER-S
GANGUE-S
GANJAH-S
GANNET-S
GANOID-S
GANOIN-E
GANOIN-S
GANSEY-S
GAOLER-S
GAPING-S
GARAGE-D
GARAGE-S
GARBLE-D
GARBLE-R
GARBLE-S
GARCON-S
GARDEN-S
GARGET-S
GARGET-Y
GARGLE-D
GARGLE-R
GARGLE-S
GARIAL-S
GARJAN-S
GARLIC-S
GARNER-S
GARNET-S
GAROTE-D
GAROTE-S
GARRAN-S
GARRET-S
GARRON-S
GARROT-E
GARROT-S
GARRYA-S
GARTER-S
GARUDA-S
GARVEY-S
GARVIE-S
GASBAG-S
GASCON-S
GASHES-T
GASKET-S
GASKIN-G
GASKIN-S
GASPER-S
GASSER-S
GASTER-S
GATEAU-S
GATEAU-X
GATHER-S
GATING-S
GAUCHE-R
GAUCHO-S
GAUCIE-R
GAUFER-S
GAUFRE-S
GAUGER-S
GAUPER-S
GAVAGE-S
GAVIAL-S
GAWKER-S
GAWPER-S
GAWSIE-R
GAZABO-S
GAZEBO-S
GAZOON-S
GAZUMP-S
GEEGAW-S
GEEZER-S
GEISHA-S
A-**GEISTS**
GELADA-S
GELANT-S
GELATE-D
GELATE-S
GELATI-N
GELATO-S
GELDER-S
GEMOTE-S
GENDER-S
GENERA-L
GENEVA-S
GENNEL-S
GENNET-S
GENOME-S
GENTIL-E
GENTLE-D
GENTLE-R
GENTLE-S
GENTOO-S
A-**GENTRY**
GEODES-Y
GERBIL-S
GERENT-S
GERMAN-E
GERMAN-S
GERMEN-S
GERMIN-A
GERMIN-G
GERMIN-S
GERUND-S
GETTER-S
GEWGAW-S
GEYSER-S
GHARRI-S
GHAZAL-S
GHAZEL-S
GHERAO-S
GHESSE-D
GHESSE-S

GHETTO-S
GHIBLI-S
GIAOUR-S
GIBBER-S
GIBBET-S
GIBBON-S
GIBLET-S
GIBSON-S
GIDGEE-S
GIDJEE-S
GIGGIT-S
GIGGLE-D
GIGGLE-R
GIGGLE-S
GIGLET-S
GIGLOT-S
GIGOLO-S
GILCUP-S
GILDER-S
GILGAI-S
GILGIE-S
GILLER-S
GILLET-S
GILLIE-D
GILLIE-S
GILPEY-S
GIMBAL-S
GIMLET-S
GIMMAL-S
GIMMER-S
GIMMIE-S
GIMMOR-S
GINGAL-L
GINGAL-S
GINGER-S
GINGER-Y
GINGLE-S
GINKGO-S
GINNEL-S
A-**GINNER**
GINNER-S
GINNER-Y
GIPPER-S
GIPSEN-S
GIRDER-S
GIRDLE-D
GIRDLE-R
GIRDLE-S
GIRKIN-S
GIRLIE-S
GIRNEL-S
GIRNER-S
GIRNIE-R
GITANA-S
GITANO-S
GIVING-S
GIZZEN-S
GLAIRE-D
GLAIRE-S
GLAIVE-D
GLAIVE-S
GLAMOR-S
GLANCE-D
GLANCE-R
GLANCE-S
GLAZER-S
GLEAVE-S
GLEDGE-D
GLEDGE-S
GLIDER-S
GLIOMA-S
GLITCH-Y
GLOBIN-G
GLOBIN-S
GLOIRE-S
GLORIA-S
GLOSSA-E
GLOSSA-L
GLOSSA-S
GLOVER-S
GLOWER-S
GLUCAN-S
GLUTEN-S
GLYCAN-S
GLYCIN-E
GLYCIN-S
GLYCOL-S
GLYCYL-S
GNAWER-S
GNOMON-S
GOALIE-S
GOANNA-S
GOATEE-D
GOATEE-S
GOBANG-S
GOBBET-S
GOBBLE-D
GOBBLE-R
GOBBLE-S
GOBIID-S
GOBLET-S
GOBLIN-S
GODDAM-N
GODDAM-S
GODDEN-S
GODOWN-S
GODSON-S
GODWIT-S
GOFFER-S
GOGGLE-D
GOGGLE-R
GOGGLE-S
GOGLET-S
GOITER-S
GOITRE-D
GOITRE-S
GOLDEN-S
GOLFER-S
GOLLAN-D
GOLLAN-S
GOLLAR-S
GOLLER-S
GOLLOP-S
GOLOSH-E
GOMBRO-S
GOMOKU-S
GOMUTI-S
GOMUTO-S
GONIFF-S
GONOPH-S
GOOBER-S
GOODBY-E
GOODBY-S
GOODIE-R
GOODIE-S
GOOGLE-D
GOOGLE-S
GOOGOL-S
GOOLEY-S
GOOLIE-S
GOONDA-S
GOONEY-S
GOONIE-S
GOORAL-S
GOOROO-S
GOOSEY-S
GOPHER-S
GOPURA-M
GOPURA-S
GORGER-S
GORGET-S
GORGIA-S
GORGIO-S
GORGON-S
GORHEN-S
GORING-S
GOSLET-S
GOSPEL-S
GOSSAN-S
GOSSIB-S
GOSSIP-S
GOSSIP-Y
GOTHIC-S
GOUGER-E
GOUGER-S
GOURDE-S
GOUTTE-S
GOVERN-S
GOWFER-S
GOWLAN-D
GOWLAN-S
GOWPEN-S
GOZZAN-S
GRABEN-S
GRADER-S
GRADIN-E
GRADIN-G
GRADIN-I
GRADIN-O
GRADIN-S
GRAHAM-S
GRAILE-S
GRAINE-D
GRAINE-R
GRAINE-S
GRAITH-S
GRAKLE-S
GRAMAS-H
GRAMMA-R
GRAMMA-S
GRAMME-S
GRANDE-E
GRANDE-R
GRANGE-R
GRANGE-S
GRAPLE-S
GRAPPA-S
A-**GRASTE**
GRATER-S
GRATIN-E
GRATIN-G
GRATIN-S
GRAVEL-S
GRAVEL-Y
GRAVER-S
GRAVES-T
GRAVID-A
GRAYLE-S
GRAZER-S
GREASE-D
GREASE-R
GREASE-S
GREAVE-D
GREAVE-S
GREECE-S
GREESE-S
GREETE-D
GREETE-R
GREETE-S
GREIGE-S
GRICER-S
GRIECE-D
GRIECE-S
GRIEVE-D
GRIEVE-R
GRIEVE-S
GRIFFE-S
GRIGRI-S
GRILLE-D
GRILLE-R
GRILLE-S
GRILSE-S
GRINGO-S
GRIPER-S
GRIPPE-D
GRIPPE-R
GRIPPE-S
A-**GRISED**
A-**GRISES**
GRISON-S
GRIVET-S
A-**GRIZES**
GROCER-S
GROCER-Y
GROMET-S
GROOVE-D
GROOVE-R
GROOVE-S
GROPER-S
GROSER-S
GROSER-T
GROSET-S
GROTTO-S
GROUCH-Y
GROUGH-S
A-**GROUND**
GROUND-S
GROUSE-D
GROUSE-R
GROUSE-S
GROVEL-S
GROVET-S
GROWER-S
GROWTH-S
GROWTH-Y
GROYNE-S
GRUDGE-D
GRUDGE-R
GRUDGE-S
GRUGRU-S
GRUMPH-S
GRUMPH-Y
GRUNGE-S
GRYFON-S
GUAIAC-S
I-**GUANAS**
GUANAS-E
GUANAY-S
GUANGO-S
GUANIN-E
GUANIN-S
GUBBAH-S
GUDDLE-D
GUDDLE-S
GUENON-S
GUFFAW-S
GUFFIE-S
GUGGLE-D
GUGGLE-S
GUGLET-S
GUIDER-S
GUIDON-S
GUILER-S
GUIMPE-D
GUIMPE-S
GUINEA-S
A-**GUISED**
GUISER-S
A-**GUISES**
GUITAR-S
GUIZER-S
GULDEN-S
GULLER-S
GULLER-Y
GULLET-S
GULLEY-S
GULPER-S
GUMMER-S
GUMNUT-S
GUNDOG-S
GUNITE-S
GUNNEL-S
GUNNER-A
GUNNER-S
GUNNER-Y
GUNSEL-S
GUNTER-S
GUNYAH-S
GURAMI-S
GURGLE-D
GURGLE-S
GURGLE-T
GURJUN-S
GURLET-S
GURNET-S
GURNEY-S
GURRAH-S
GUSHER-S
GUSLAR-S
GUSSET-S
GUSSIE-D
GUSSIE-S
GUSTIE-R
GUTFUL-S
GUTROT-S
GUTSER-S
GUTTER-S
GUTTER-Y
GUTTLE-D
GUTTLE-R
GUTTLE-S
GUTZER-S
GUYLER-S
GUZZLE-D
GUZZLE-R
GUZZLE-S
GWEDUC-K
GWEDUC-S
GYMBAL-S
GYMMAL-S
GYNNEY-S
GYPPER-S
GYPPIE-S
GYPSUM-S
GYRASE-S
GYRATE-D
GYRATE-S
GYRENE-S
HABOOB-S
R-**HACHIS**
C-**HACKED**
T-HACKED
W-HACKED
HACKEE-S
W-**HACKER**
HACKER-S
HACKER-Y
HACKIE-S
S-**HACKLE**
HACKLE-D
HACKLE-R
HACKLE-S
HACKLE-T
HADDIE-S
S-**HADING**
HADITH-S
HADJEE-S
HADRON-S
HAEMIN-S
HAFFET-S
HAFFIT-S
S-**HAFTED**
S-**HAFTER**
HAFTER-S
HAGBUT-S
HAGDEN-S
HAGDON-S
S-**HAGGED**
HAGGIS-H
HAGGLE-D
HAGGLE-R
HAGGLE-S
HAGLET-S
HAIDUK-S
HAILER-S
C-**HAINED**
HAIQUE-S
HAIRDO-S
C-**HAIRED**
HAIRST-S
HAKEEM-S
HALALA-H
HALALA-S
T-**HALERS**
W-HALERS
HALIDE-S
S-**HALING**
W-HALING
HALITE-S
C-**HALLAH**
HALLAH-S
HALLAL-I
HALLAL-S
C-**HALLAN**
HALLAN-S
HALLEL-S
HALLOA-S
HALLOO-S
C-**HALLOT**
S-HALLOT
HALLOT-H
S-**HALLOW**
HALLOW-S
HALOID-S
HALSER-S
HALTER-E
HALTER-S
C-**HALUTZ**
HALVAH-S
HALVER-S
HAMADA-S
HAMATE-S
HAMAUL-S
S-**HAMBLE**
HAMBLE-D
HAMBLE-S
S-**HAMING**
C-**HAMLET**
HAMLET-S
HAMMAL-S
HAMMAM-S
S-**HAMMED**
W-HAMMED
S-**HAMMER**
HAMMER-S
C-**HAMPER**
HAMPER-S
HAMZAH-S
C-**HANCES**
HANDER-S

HANDLE-D
HANDLE-R
HANDLE-S
HANGAR-S
C-**HANGED**
P-HANGED
W-HANGED
C-**HANGER**
HANGER-S
HANGUP-S
K-**HANJAR**
HANJAR-S
S-**HANKED**
T-HANKED
T-**HANKER**
HANKER-S
HANKIE-S
HANSEL-S
HANSOM-S
C-**HANTED**
HANTLE-S
C-**HAPPED**
W-HAPPED
HAPPEN-S
HAPTEN-E
HAPTEN-S
HAPTIC-S
HARBOR-S
HARDEN-S
HAREEM-S
HARELD-S
C-**HARING**
S-HARING
C-**HARKED**
S-HARKED
HARKEN-S
HARLOT-S
HARMAN-S
C-**HARMED**
HARMEL-S
C-**HARMER**
HARMER-S
HARMIN-E
HARMIN-G
HARMIN-S
S-**HARPED**
S-**HARPER**
HARPER-S
HARPIN-G
HARPIN-S
HARROW-S
HARTAL-S
HARTEN-S
S-**HASHED**
S-**HASHES**
HASLET-S
HASSAR-S
HASSEL-S
HASSLE-D
HASSLE-S
G-**HASTED**
C-**HASTEN**
HASTEN-S
HATFUL-S
HATPEG-S
HATPIN-S
HATRED-S
C-**HATTED**
C-**HATTER**
P-HATTER
S-HATTER
HATTER-S
S-**HAUGHS**
HAUGHT-Y
S-**HAULED**

HAULER-S
C-**HAUNTS**
HAUSEN-S
HAUYNE-S
S-**HAVERS**
S-**HAVING**
HAVING-S
HAVIOR-S
C-**HAWING**
S-HAWING
T-HAWING
HAWKER-S
HAWKEY-S
HAWKIE-S
HAWSER-S
HAYING-S
HAYMOW-S
HAYSEL-S
C-**HAZANS**
HAZARD-S
G-**HAZELS**
HAZING-S
C-**HAZZAN**
HAZZAN-S
HEADER-S
S-**HEALED**
HEALER-S
HEALTH-S
HEALTH-Y
S-**HEARER**
HEARER-S
HEARSE-D
HEARSE-S
HEARTH-S
HEASTE-S
C-**HEATED**
C-**HEATER**
T-HEATER
HEATER-S
S-**HEATHS**
S-**HEATHY**
HEAUME-S
S-**HEAVED**
HEAVEN-S
HEAVER-S
S-**HEAVES**
T-HEAVES
HEBONA-S
HECKLE-D
HECKLE-R
HECKLE-S
HECTIC-S
HECTOR-S
HEDDLE-D
HEDDLE-S
C-**HEDERS**
HEDGER-S
HEEDER-S
HEEHAW-S
S-**HEELED**
W-HEELED
W-**HEELER**
HEELER-S
P-**HEEZED**
W-HEEZED
P-**HEEZES**
W-HEEZES
HEEZIE-S
HEFTER-S
HEGARI-S
HEGIRA-S
HEIFER-S
A-**HEIGHT**
HEIGHT-H
HEIGHT-S

HEINIE-S
T-**HEISTS**
HEJIRA-S
HELIUM-S
S-**HELLED**
S-**HELLER**
HELLER-I
HELLER-S
HELLER-Y
W-**HELMED**
HELMET-S
W-**HELPED**
HELPER-S
S-**HELVED**
S-**HELVES**
T-HELVES
HEMINA-S
HEMMER-S
HEMPIE-R
HEMPIE-S
HENBIT-S
HENNER-S
HENNER-Y
HENNIN-G
HENNIN-S
HEPCAT-S
HEPTAD-S
HERALD-S
HERBAL-S
HERBAR-S
HERBAR-Y
HERDEN-S
HERDER-S
HERDIC-S
T-**HEREAT**
W-HEREAT
T-**HEREBY**
W-HEREBY
T-**HEREIN**
W-HEREIN
T-**HEREOF**
W-HEREOF
T-**HEREON**
W-HEREON
T-**HERETO**
W-HERETO
HERIOT-S
T-**HERMAE**
HERMIT-S
HERNIA-E
HERNIA-L
HERNIA-S
HEROIC-S
HEROIN-E
HEROIN-S
HEROON-S
HETERO-S
T-**HETHER**
W-HETHER
HETMAN-S
S-**HEUCHS**
S-**HEUGHS**
W-HEUGHS
C-**HEWERS**
S-HEWERS
C-**HEWING**
S-HEWING
W-HEWING
HEWING-S
HEXACT-S
HEXADE-S
HEXANE-S
HEXENE-S
HEXING-S
HEXONE-S

HEXOSE-S
HEYDAY-S
HEYDEY-S
HICCUP-S
HICCUP-Y
HICKEY-S
HIDAGE-S
C-**HIDDEN**
S-**HIDDER**
W-HIDDER
HIDDER-S
C-**HIDERS**
C-**HIDING**
HIDING-S
HIGGLE-D
HIGGLE-R
HIGGLE-S
T-**HIGHED**
HIGHER-S
HIGHTH-S
HIJACK-S
HIJRAH-S
C-**HILLED**
S-HILLED
C-**HILLER**
T-HILLER
HILLER-S
HILLOA-S
HINDER-S
W-**HINGED**
W-**HINGER**
HINGER-S
W-**HINGES**
HINTER-S
C-**HIPPED**
S-HIPPED
W-HIPPED
S-**HIPPEN**
HIPPEN-S
C-**HIPPER**
S-HIPPER
W-HIPPER
C-**HIPPIE**
HIPPIE-R
HIPPIE-S
HIPPIN-G
HIPPIN-S
S-**HIPPOS**
HIRAGE-S
HIRING-S
HIRPLE-D
HIRPLE-S
HIRSEL-S
HIRSLE-D
HIRSLE-S
W-**HISHED**
W-**HISHES**
W-**HISSED**
HISSER-S
W-**HISSES**
W-**HISTED**
B-**HISTIE**
T-**HITHER**
W-HITHER
HITHER-S
C-**HITTER**
W-HITTER
HITTER-S
S-**HIVERS**
C-**HIVING**
C-**HIZZED**
W-HIZZED
C-**HIZZES**
P-HIZZES
W-HIZZES

HOAGIE-S
HOARSE-N
HOARSE-R
HOAXER-S
HOBBIT-S
HOBBLE-D
HOBBLE-R
HOBBLE-S
HOBDAY-S
HOBJOB-S
HOBNOB-S
C-**HOCKED**
S-HOCKED
C-**HOCKER**
S-HOCKER
HOCKER-S
HOCKEY-S
S-**HODDEN**
HODDEN-S
HODDIN-G
HODDIN-S
HODDLE-D
HODDLE-S
K-**HODJAS**
S-**HOEING**
S-**HOGGED**
HOGGER-S
HOGGER-Y
HOGGET-S
HOGGIN-G
HOGGIN-S
HOGNUT-S
HOGTIE-D
HOGTIE-S
HOIDEN-S
C-**HOKIER**
C-**HOKING**
HOLARD-S
HOLDER-S
HOLDUP-S
HOLIES-T
T-**HOLING**
HOLING-S
W-**HOLISM**
HOLISM-S
W-**HOLIST**
HOLIST-S
C-**HOLLAS**
HOLLER-S
HOLLOA-S
HOLLOO-S
HOLLOW-S
HOLMIA-S
HOMAGE-D
HOMAGE-R
HOMAGE-S
HOMBRE-S
HOMELY-N
HOMING-S
HONCHO-S
HONDLE-D
HONDLE-S
P-**HONERS**
HONEST-Y
P-**HONEYS**
P-**HONIED**
P-**HONING**
HONKER-S
HONKEY-S
HONKIE-S
HONOUR-S
HOODIE-R
HOODIE-S
HOODOO-S
C-**HOOFED**

W-HOOFED
HOOFER-S
HOOKAH-S
HOOKER-S
HOOKEY-S
HOOKUP-S
HOOLEY-S
HOOLIE-R
W-**HOOPED**
W-**HOOPER**
HOOPER-S
W-**HOOPLA**
HOOPLA-S
HOOPOE-S
HOOPOO-S
HOORAH-S
HOORAY-S
W-**HOOTED**
S-**HOOTER**
HOOTER-S
HOOVER-S
HOPDOG-S
C-**HOPPED**
S-HOPPED
W-HOPPED
C-**HOPPER**
S-HOPPER
W-HOPPER
HOPPER-S
HOPPLE-D
HOPPLE-S
C-**HORDED**
HORKEY-S
T-**HORNED**
HORNER-S
HORNET-S
HORROR-S
HORSON-S
HORSTE-S
HOSIER-S
HOSIER-Y
G-**HOSTED**
HOSTEL-S
G-**HOSTLY**
HOTBED-S
HOTDOG-S
HOTPOT-S
HOTROD-S
S-**HOTTED**
HOTTER-S
HOTTIE-S
HOUDAH-S
HOUDAN-S
C-**HOUGHS**
S-HOUGHS
C-**HOUSED**
HOUSEL-S
C-**HOUSER**
HOUSER-S
C-**HOUSES**
S-**HOUTED**
S-**HOVELS**
S-**HOVERS**
S-**HOVING**
HOWDAH-S
HOWDIE-D
HOWDIE-S
HOWKER-S
HOWLER-S
HOWLET-S
HOYDEN-S
HUBBUB-S
HUBCAP-S
C-**HUCKLE**
HUCKLE-S

HUDDLE-D
HUDDLE-R
HUDDLE-S
C-**HUFFED**
C-**HUGGED**
C-**HUGGER**
HUGGER-S
HUIPIL-S
HULLER-S
HULLOA-S
HUMANE-R
HUMATE-S
HUMBLE-D
HUMBLE-R
HUMBLE-S
HUMBUG-S
HUMECT-S
HUMHUM-S
HUMITE-S
HUMLIE-S
C-**HUMMED**
HUMMEL-S
HUMMER-S
HUMMUM-S
HUMOUR-S
C-**HUMPED**
T-HUMPED
W-HUMPED
HUMPEN-S
T-**HUMPER**
HUMPER-S
HUMVEE-S
HUNGER-S
A-**HUNGRY**
HUNKER-S
S-**HUNTED**
C-**HUNTER**
S-HUNTER
HUNTER-S
C-**HUPPAH**
HUPPAH-S
HURDEN-S
HURDLE-D
HURDLE-R
HURDLE-S
HURLER-S
HURLEY-S
HURRAH-S
D-**HURRAS**
HURRAY-S
HURTER-S
HURTLE-D
HURTLE-S
S-**HUSHED**
HUSHER-S
S-**HUSHES**
HUSKER-S
HUSSAR-S
HUSSIF-S
HUSTLE-D
HUSTLE-R
HUSTLE-S
P-**HUTTED**
C-**HUTZPA**
HUTZPA-H
HUTZPA-S
HUZOOR-S
HUZZAH-S
HYAENA-S
HYALIN-E
HYALIN-S
HYBRID-S
HYDRAS-E
HYDRIA-E
HYDRID-E
HYDRID-S
HYDYNE-S
HYLISM-S
HYLIST-S
HYMNAL-S
HYPATE-S
HYPHEN-S
HYPNIC-S
HYPNUM-S
HYSSOP-S
IAMBIC-S
V-**IBICES**
ICECAP-S
M-**ICHING**
N-ICHING
R-ICHING
ICICLE-D
ICICLE-S
D-**ICIEST**
R-ICIEST
D-**ICINGS**
B-**ICKERS**
D-ICKERS
K-ICKERS
L-ICKERS
N-ICKERS
P-ICKERS
R-ICKERS
T-ICKERS
W-ICKERS
Y-ICKERS
D-**ICKIER**
K-ICKIER
P-ICKIER
IDEATE-D
IDEATE-S
S-**IDLERS**
H-**IDLING**
K-IDLING
S-IDLING
M-**IFFIER**
N-IFFIER
IGNARO-S
D-**IGNIFY**
L-IGNIFY
S-IGNIFY
L-**IGNITE**
IGNITE-D
IGNITE-R
IGNITE-S
S-**IGNORE**
IGNORE-D
IGNORE-R
IGNORE-S
IGUANA-S
S-**ILEXES**
C-**ILICES**
W-**ILLEST**
ILLIAD-S
ILLIPE-S
T-**ILLITE**
ILLITE-S
ILLUDE-D
ILLUDE-S
ILLUME-D
ILLUME-S
ILLUPI-S
IMAGER-S
IMAGER-Y
IMARET-S
IMBALM-S
IMBARK-S
M-**IMBARS**
IMBASE-D
IMBASE-S
IMBIBE-D
IMBIBE-R
IMBIBE-S
IMBOSK-S
IMBRUE-D
IMBRUE-S
IMMASK-S
G-**IMMIES**
J-IMMIES
IMMUNE-S
IMMURE-D
IMMURE-S
IMPACT-S
IMPAIR-S
IMPALA-S
IMPALE-D
IMPALE-R
IMPALE-S
IMPARK-S
IMPARL-S
IMPART-S
IMPAVE-D
IMPAVE-S
IMPAWN-S
IMPEDE-D
IMPEDE-R
IMPEDE-S
IMPEND-S
IMPHEE-S
G-**IMPING**
L-IMPING
P-IMPING
IMPING-E
IMPING-S
W-**IMPISH**
S-**IMPLEX**
IMPONE-D
IMPONE-S
IMPORT-S
IMPOSE-D
IMPOSE-R
IMPOSE-S
IMPOST-S
IMPROV-E
IMPROV-S
IMPUGN-S
IMPURE-R
IMPUTE-D
IMPUTE-R
IMPUTE-S
INANES-T
INBRED-S
INCAGE-D
INCAGE-S
INCANT-S
P-**INCASE**
INCASE-D
INCASE-S
INCAVE-D
INCAVE-S
INCEDE-D
INCEDE-S
INCEPT-S
INCEST-S
C-**INCHED**
F-INCHED
P-INCHED
W-INCHED
C-**INCHES**
F-INCHES
L-INCHES
P-INCHES
W-INCHES
INCISE-D
INCISE-S
Z-**INCITE**
INCITE-D
INCITE-R
INCITE-S
INCLIP-S
INCOME-R
INCOME-S
INCUSE-D
INCUSE-S
INDABA-S
INDART-S
INDENE-S
INDENT-S
INDICT-S
K-**INDIES**
L-INDIES
W-**INDIGO**
INDIGO-S
INDITE-D
INDITE-R
INDITE-S
INDIUM-S
INDOLE-S
INDOOR-S
W-**INDOWS**
INDUCE-D
INDUCE-R
INDUCE-S
INDUCT-S
INDULT-S
INDUNA-S
INFALL-S
INFAME-D
INFAME-S
INFANT-A
INFANT-E
INFANT-S
INFARE-S
INFECT-S
INFEFT-S
INFEST-S
INFILL-S
INFIRM-S
INFLOW-S
P-**INFOLD**
INFOLD-S
INFORM-S
INFULA-E
INFUSE-D
INFUSE-R
INFUSE-S
F-**INGANS**
INGATE-S
INGENU-E
INGENU-S
INGEST-A
INGEST-S
INGINE-S
B-**INGLES**
D-INGLES
G-INGLES
J-INGLES
K-INGLES
L-INGLES
M-INGLES
P-INGLES
S-INGLES
T-INGLES
D-**INGOES**
J-INGOES
L-INGOES
P-INGOES
L-**INGOTS**
INGULF-S
INHALE-D
INHALE-R
INHALE-S
INHAUL-S
INHERE-D
INHERE-S
INHOOP-S
INHUME-D
INHUME-R
INHUME-S
INISLE-D
INISLE-S
INJECT-S
INJERA-S
INJURE-D
INJURE-R
INJURE-S
J-**INKERS**
L-INKERS
P-INKERS
S-INKERS
T-INKERS
W-INKERS
D-**INKIER**
K-INKIER
P-INKIER
S-INKIER
Z-INKIER
D-**INKING**
F-INKING
J-INKING
K-INKING
L-INKING
O-INKING
P-INKING
R-INKING
S-INKING
T-INKING
W-INKING
Z-INKING
T-**INKLED**
W-INKLED
K-**INKLES**
T-INKLES
W-INKLES
INKLES-S
INKPOT-S
INLACE-D
INLACE-S
INLAND-S
INLIER-S
INLOCK-S
INMATE-S
P-**INNATE**
D-**INNERS**
F-INNERS
G-INNERS
P-INNERS
S-INNERS
T-INNERS
W-INNERS
B-**INNING**
D-INNING
F-INNING
G-INNING
L-INNING
P-INNING
R-INNING
S-INNING
T-INNING
W-INNING
INNING-S
INPOUR-S
INROAD-S
INSANE-R
INSEAM-S
INSECT-S
INSEEM-S
INSERT-S
K-**INSHIP**
INSHIP-S
INSIDE-R
INSIDE-S
INSIST-S
INSOLE-S
INSOUL-S
INSPAN-S
INSTAL-L
INSTAL-S
INSTAR-S
INSTEP-S
INSTIL-L
INSTIL-S
INSULA-E
INSULA-R
INSULA-S
INSULT-S
INSURE-D
INSURE-R
INSURE-S
INTAKE-S
INTEND-S
INTENT-S
INTERN-E
INTERN-S
H-**INTERS**
L-INTERS
M-INTERS
S-INTERS
T-INTERS
W-INTERS
INTIMA-E
INTIMA-L
INTIMA-S
INTINE-S
INTOMB-S
INTONE-D
INTONE-R
INTONE-S
INTORT-S
INTRON-S
INTUIT-S
INTURN-S
INTUSE-S
INULAS-E
INULIN-S
INVADE-D
INVADE-R
INVADE-S
INVENT-S
INVERT-S
INVEST-S
INVITE-D
INVITE-E
INVITE-R
INVITE-S
INVOKE-D
INVOKE-R
INVOKE-S
INWALL-S
INWARD-S
INWICK-S
INWIND-S
P-**INWORK**
T-INWORK
INWORK-S
INWOVE-N
INWRAP-S
INYALA-S
IODATE-D
IODATE-S

IODIDE-S
IODINE-S
IODISE-D
IODISE-S
IODISM-S
IODIZE-D
IODIZE-R
IODIZE-S
IOLITE-S
B-**IONICS**
L-**IONISE**
IONISE-D
IONISE-R
IONISE-S
IONIUM-S
L-**IONIZE**
IONIZE-D
IONIZE-R
IONIZE-S
IONONE-S
IPECAC-S
T-**IRADES**
D-**IREFUL**
E-**IRENIC**
S-IRENIC
IRENIC-S
M-**IRITIS**
D-**IRKING**
F-IRKING
K-IRKING
L-IRKING
Y-IRKING
IRONER-S
G-**IRONIC**
IRRUPT-S
ISABEL-S
ISATIN-E
ISATIN-S
ISCHIA-L
ISLAND-S
A-**ISLING**
ISOBAR-E
ISOBAR-S
ISOGON-E
ISOGON-S
ISOGON-Y
ISOHEL-S
ISOLOG-S
ISOMER-E
ISOMER-S
ISOPOD-S
T-**ISSUED**
ISSUER-S
T-**ISSUES**
ISTHMI-C
M-**ISTLES**
ITALIC-S
B-**ITCHED**
D-ITCHED
H-ITCHED
M-ITCHED
P-ITCHED
W-ITCHED
A-**ITCHES**
B-ITCHES
D-ITCHES
F-ITCHES
H-ITCHES
M-ITCHES
P-ITCHES
T-ITCHES
W-ITCHES
IXODID-S
L-**IZARDS**
R-IZARDS

V-IZARDS
W-IZARDS
D-**IZZARD**
G-IZZARD
IZZARD-S
JABBER-S
JABBLE-D
JABBLE-S
JABIRU-S
JACANA-S
JACKAL-S
JACKER-S
JACKET-S
JAEGER-S
JAGGER-S
JAGGER-Y
JAGHIR-E
JAGHIR-S
JAGUAR-S
JAILER-S
JAILOR-S
JAMBEE-S
JAMBER-S
S-**JAMBOK**
JAMBOK-S
JAMBUL-S
JAMJAR-S
JAMMER-S
JAMPAN-I
JAMPAN-S
JAMPOT-S
JANDAL-S
JANGLE-D
JANGLE-R
JANGLE-S
JANKER-S
JANSKY-S
JAPING-S
JARFUL-S
JARGON-S
JARINA-S
JAROOL-S
JARRAH-S
JARVEY-S
JARVIE-S
JASMIN-E
JASMIN-S
JASPER-S
JASPER-Y
JASSID-S
JATAKA-S
JAUNCE-D
JAUNCE-S
JAUNSE-D
JAUNSE-S
JAWARI-S
JAWING-S
JAYGEE-S
JAYVEE-S
JAZZER-S
D-**JEBELS**
JEELIE-D
JEELIE-S
JEERER-S
JEJUNA-L
JEMIMA-S
JENNET-S
JERBIL-S
JERBOA-S
JEREED-S
JERKER-S
JERKIN-G
JERKIN-S
JERQUE-D
JERQUE-R

JERQUE-S
JERRID-S
JERSEY-S
JESSIE-S
JESTEE-S
JESTER-S
JESUIT-S
JETSAM-S
JETSOM-S
JETSON-S
JETTON-S
JEZAIL-S
D-**JIBBAH**
JIBBAH-S
JIBBER-S
JICAMA-S
JIGGER-S
JIGGLE-D
JIGGLE-S
JIGJIG-S
JIGSAW-N
JIGSAW-S
JILGIE-S
JILLET-S
JILTER-S
JIMJAM-S
JINGAL-L
JINGAL-S
JINGLE-D
JINGLE-R
JINGLE-S
JINGLE-T
JINKER-S
JIRBLE-D
JIRBLE-S
JISSOM-S
JITNEY-S
JITTER-S
JITTER-Y
JOANNA-S
JOBBER-S
JOBBER-Y
JOBBIE-S
JOCKEY-S
JOGGER-S
JOGGLE-D
JOGGLE-R
JOGGLE-S
JOINER-S
JOINER-Y
JOJOBA-S
JOLLEY-S
JOLTER-S
JORDAN-S
JOSEPH-S
JOSHER-S
JOSKIN-S
JOSSER-S
JOSTLE-D
JOSTLE-R
JOSTLE-S
JOTTER-S
JOTUNN-S
JOUNCE-D
JOUNCE-S
JOURNO-S
JOWARI-S
JOWLER-S
JOYPOP-S
JUBBAH-S
JUBHAH-S
JUBILE-E
JUBILE-S
JUDDER-S
JUDGER-S

JUDOGI-S
JUDOKA-S
JUGFUL-S
JUGGLE-D
JUGGLE-R
JUGGLE-S
JUGLET-S
JUGULA-R
JUICER-S
JUJUBE-S
JUMART-S
JUMBAL-S
JUMBIE-S
JUMBLE-D
JUMBLE-R
JUMBLE-S
JUMPER-S
JUNGLE-D
JUNGLE-S
JUNGLI-S
JUNIOR-S
JUNKER-S
JUNKET-S
JUNKIE-R
JUNKIE-S
JUPATI-S
JURANT-S
JURIST-S
JUSTER-S
JUSTLE-D
JUSTLE-S
KABAKA-S
KABALA-S
KABAYA-S
KABELE-S
KABIKI-S
KABUKI-S
KACCHA-S
KAFFIR-S
KAFILA-S
KAFTAN-S
KAGOOL-S
KAGOUL-E
KAGOUL-S
KAHUNA-S
KAIKAI-S
KAINIT-E
KAINIT-S
KAISER-S
KAIZEN-S
KAKAPO-S
KALIAN-S
KALIPH-S
KALIUM-S
KALMIA-S
KALONG-S
KALPAK-S
KAMALA-S
KAMELA-S
KAMILA-S
KAMSIN-S
KANAKA-S
KANBAN-S
KANGHA-S
KANTAR-S
KANTEN-S
KANTHA-S
KAOLIN-E
KAOLIN-S
KARAIT-S
KARAKA-S
KARATE-S
KARITE-S
KARROO-S
KARSEY-S

KARTER-S
KARYON-S
KASBAH-S
KASHER-S
KATANA-S
KATHAK-S
KATION-S
KATIPO-S
KEASAR-S
KEAVIE-S
KEBBIE-S
KEBELE-S
KEBLAH-S
KECKLE-D
KECKLE-S
KEDDAH-S
KEDGER-S
KEEKER-S
KEELER-S
KEELIE-S
KEENER-S
KEEPER-S
KEFFEL-S
KEGLER-S
KEKSYE-S
KELOID-S
S-**KELPED**
KELPER-S
KELPIE-S
KELSON-S
S-**KELTER**
KELTER-S
KELTIE-S
KELVIN-S
KEMPER-S
KEMPLE-S
KENNEL-S
KENNER-S
KENNET-S
KENTIA-S
KEPHIR-S
S-**KEPPED**
KERMES-S
KERNEL-S
KERRIA-S
KERSEY-S
KETENE-S
KETONE-S
KETOSE-S
KETTLE-S
KEYPAD-S
KEYSET-S
KEYWAY-S
KGOTLA-S
KHALAT-S
KHALIF-A
KHALIF-S
KHANGA-S
KHANUM-S
KHARIF-S
KHAZEN-S
KHEDAH-S
KHILAT-S
KHILIM-S
KHODJA-S
KHURTA-S
KIAUGH-S
KIBBEH-S
KIBBLE-D
KIBBLE-S
KIBLAH-S
KICKER-S
KICKUP-S
S-**KIDDED**
S-**KIDDER**

KIDDER-S
KIDDIE-D
KIDDIE-R
KIDDIE-S
KIDDLE-S
KIDGIE-R
KIDLET-S
KIDNAP-S
KIDNEY-S
KIDULT-S
KIDVID-S
KIERIE-S
KIKUYU-S
KILERG-S
S-**KILLED**
KILLER-S
KILLIE-S
KILLUT-S
KILTER-S
KILTIE-S
KIMCHI-S
S-**KIMMER**
KIMMER-S
O-**KIMONO**
KIMONO-S
KINASE-S
KINCOB-S
KINDER-S
KINDLE-D
KINDLE-R
KINDLE-S
KINEMA-S
KINGLE-S
KINGLE-T
S-**KINKED**
KINKLE-S
KINONE-S
KINRED-S
S-**KIPPED**
S-**KIPPER**
KIPPER-S
KIRBEH-S
KIRPAN-S
KIRTLE-D
KIRTLE-S
KISHKA-S
KISHKE-S
KISMAT-S
KISMET-S
KISSEL-S
KISSER-S
S-**KITING**
KITING-S
KITSCH-Y
KITTEN-S
KITTEN-Y
S-**KITTLE**
KITTLE-D
KITTLE-R
KITTLE-S
KITTUL-S
KLAXON-S
KLEPHT-S
KLUDGE-S
KNAWEL-S
KNIFER-S
KNIGHT-S
KNOWER-S
KOBANG-S
KOBOLD-S
KOLHOZ-Y
KOLKOZ-Y
KONFYT-S
KOODOO-S
KOOKIE-R

KOOLAH-S
KOPECK-S
KOPPIE-S
KORERO-S
KORKIR-S
KORORA-S
KORUNA-S
KOSHER-S
KOTWAL-S
KOULAN-S
KOUMIS-S
KOUMYS-S
KOUSSO-S
KOWHAI-S
KOWTOW-S
KRAKEN-S
KRATER-S
KREESE-D
KREESE-S
KRUBUT-S
KULTUR-S
KUMARA-S
KUMARI-S
KUMMEL-S
KUNKAR-S
KUNKUR-S
KURGAN-S
KURVEY-S
KVETCH-Y
KWACHA-S
KWANZA-S
KYOGEN-S
LAAGER-S
LABIAL-S
LABLAB-S
LABOUR-S
LABRET-S
LABRID-S
LABRUM-S
P-**LACERS**
P-**LACETS**
G-**LACIER**
P-**LACING**
LACING-S
B-**LACKED**
C-LACKED
F-LACKED
S-LACKED
B-**LACKER**
C-LACKER
F-LACKER
S-LACKER
LACKER-S
LACKEY-S
LACTAM-S
LACUNA-E
LACUNA-L
LACUNA-R
LACUNA-S
LACUNE-S
B-**LADDER**
C-LADDER
G-LADDER
LADDER-S
LADDER-Y
G-**LADDIE**
LADDIE-S
LADING-S
LADINO-S
LADLER-S
LADRON-E
LADRON-S
LAGENA-S
LAGEND-S
B-**LAGGED**
C-LAGGED
F-LAGGED
S-LAGGED
LAGGEN-S
B-**LAGGER**
F-LAGGER
LAGGER-S
LAGGIN-G
LAGGIN-S
LAGOON-S
LAGUNA-S
LAGUNE-S
P-**LAIDED**
LAIKER-S
G-**LAIRED**
LAISSE-S
F-**LAKERS**
S-LAKERS
F-**LAKIER**
F-**LAKING**
S-LAKING
LAKING-S
LALANG-S
LALDIE-S
LALLAN-D
LALLAN-S
LAMBDA-S
C-**LAMBER**
LAMBER-S
LAMBER-T
LAMBIE-R
LAMBIE-S
LAMEDH-S
LAMENT-S
LAMINA-E
LAMINA-L
LAMINA-R
LAMINA-S
B-**LAMING**
F-LAMING
C-**LAMMED**
F-LAMMED
S-LAMMED
C-**LAMMER**
S-LAMMER
LAMMER-S
LAMMIE-S
LAMPAD-S
C-**LAMPED**
P-**LANATE**
LANATE-D
E-**LANCED**
G-LANCED
G-**LANCER**
LANCER-S
E-**LANCES**
G-LANCES
LANCET-S
LANDAU-S
B-**LANDER**
S-LANDER
LANDER-S
G-**LANDES**
C-**LANGER**
F-LANGER
S-LANGER
LANGUE-D
LANGUE-S
LANGUE-T
LANGUR-S
B-**LANKED**
C-LANKED
F-LANKED
P-LANKED
B-**LANKER**
F-LANKER
B-**LANKLY**
P-**LANNER**
LANNER-S
LANUGO-S
LAPDOG-S
LAPFUL-S
C-**LAPPED**
F-LAPPED
P-LAPPED
S-LAPPED
LAPPEL-S
C-**LAPPER**
F-LAPPER
S-LAPPER
LAPPER-S
LAPPET-S
LAPPIE-S
E-**LAPSED**
LAPSER-S
E-**LAPSES**
LAPTOP-S
LARDER-S
LARDON-S
LARGEN-S
LARGES-S
LARGES-T
LARIAT-S
LARKER-S
LARRUP-S
A-**LARUMS**
LASCAR-S
F-**LASERS**
C-**LASHED**
F-LASHED
P-LASHED
S-LASHED
C-**LASHER**
F-LASHER
P-LASHER
S-LASHER
LASHER-S
B-**LASHES**
C-LASHES
F-LASHES
P-LASHES
S-LASHES
LASING-S
F-**LASKET**
LASKET-S
LASQUE-S
C-**LASSES**
G-LASSES
G-**LASSIE**
LASSIE-S
C-**LASSIS**
B-**LASTED**
B-**LASTER**
P-LASTER
LASTER-S
LATEEN-S
P-**LATENS**
LATENT-S
B-**LATEST**
LATEST-S
LATHEE-S
B-**LATHER**
S-LATHER
LATHER-S
LATHER-Y
LATIGO-S
LATINO-S
LATRIA-S
LATRON-S
F-**LATTEN**
LATTEN-S
B-**LATTER**
C-LATTER
F-LATTER
P-LATTER
S-LATTER
LATTIN-S
B-**LAUDED**
LAUDER-S
LAUNCE-D
LAUNCE-S
F-**LAUNCH**
LAUREL-S
LAVABO-S
LAVAGE-S
LAVEER-S
C-**LAVERS**
S-LAVERS
S-**LAVING**
S-**LAVISH**
LAVOLT-A
LAVOLT-S
LAWINE-S
B-**LAWING**
C-LAWING
F-LAWING
LAWING-S
LAWYER-S
LAXISM-S
LAXIST-S
F-**LAYERS**
P-LAYERS
S-LAYERS
A-**LAYING**
C-LAYING
F-LAYING
P-LAYING
S-LAYING
LAYING-S
P-**LAYOFF**
LAYOFF-S
LAYOUT-S
G-**LAZIER**
LAZIES-T
B-**LAZING**
G-LAZING
LAZULI-S
P-**LEADED**
LEADEN-S
P-**LEADER**
LEADER-S
LEAGUE-D
LEAGUE-R
LEAGUE-S
B-**LEAKER**
LEAKER-S
G-**LEAMED**
C-**LEANED**
G-LEANED
C-**LEANER**
G-LEANER
LEANER-S
C-**LEANLY**
LEAPER-S
B-**LEARED**
C-LEARED
P-**LEASED**
P-**LEASER**
LEASER-S
P-**LEASES**
LEASOW-E
LEASOW-S
C-**LEAVED**
S-LEAVED
LEAVEN-S
C-**LEAVER**
LEAVER-S
C-**LEAVES**
G-LEAVES
S-LEAVES
S-**LEAZES**
LEBBEK-S
LECHER-S
LECHER-Y
F-**LECHES**
LECHWE-S
LECTIN-S
E-**LECTOR**
LECTOR-S
LEDDEN-S
P-**LEDGER**
S-LEDGER
LEDGER-S
F-**LEDGES**
G-LEDGES
P-LEDGES
S-LEDGES
F-**LEEING**
G-LEEING
B-**LEEPED**
C-LEEPED
F-**LEERED**
LEEWAY-S
LEFTIE-S
LEGATE-D
LEGATE-E
LEGATE-S
LEGATO-R
LEGATO-S
LEGEND-S
A-**LEGGED**
F-LEGGED
G-**LEGGER**
LEGGER-S
A-**LEGGES**
LEGGIN-G
LEGGIN-S
LEGION-S
E-**LEGIST**
LEGIST-S
E-**LEGITS**
LEGLAN-S
LEGLEN-S
LEGLET-S
LEGLIN-S
LEGONG-S
LEGUME-S
LEIGER-S
LEIPOA-S
LEKVAR-S
F-**LEMING**
B-**LENDER**
S-LENDER
LENDER-S
A-**LENGTH**
LENGTH-S
LENGTH-Y
F-**LENSED**
F-**LENSES**
LENTIL-S
LENTOR-S
LENVOY-S
LEPTON-S
LESION-S
LESSEE-S
LESSEN-S
B-**LESSER**
B-**LESSES**
LESSON-S
P-**LESSOR**
LESSOR-S
LETHAL-S
LETHEE-S
B-**LETTED**
LETTER-N
LETTER-S
LETTRE-S
LEUCIN-E
LEUCIN-S
LEUKON-S
LEVANT-S
LEVIER-S
A-**LEVINS**
LEVITE-S
LEXEME-S
LEXICA-L
LEZZIE-S
P-**LIABLE**
LIAISE-D
LIAISE-S
LIBATE-D
LIBATE-S
G-**LIBBED**
G-**LIBBER**
LIBBER-S
LIBERO-S
LIBIDO-S
LIBKEN-S
LIBLAB-S
LICHEE-S
LICHEN-S
C-**LICHES**
C-**LICKED**
F-LICKED
S-LICKED
C-**LICKER**
F-LICKER
S-LICKER
LICKER-S
LICTOR-S
LIDGER-S
LIEGER-S
LIERNE-S
C-**LIFTED**
LIFTER-S
LIGAND-S
LIGASE-S
LIGATE-D
LIGATE-S
LIGGER-S
A-**LIGHTS**
B-LIGHTS
F-LIGHTS
P-LIGHTS
S-LIGHTS
LIGNIN-S
LIGNUM-S
LIGULA-E
LIGULA-R
LIGULA-S
LIGULE-S
LIGURE-S
LIKING-S
LIMAIL-S
LIMBEC-K
LIMBEC-S
C-**LIMBED**
C-**LIMBER**
LIMBER-S
S-**LIMIER**
LIMINA-L
G-**LIMING**
S-LIMING
LIMING-S
G-**LIMMER**

S-LIMMER
LIMMER-S
LIMNER-S
F-**LIMPED**
LIMPER-S
LIMPET-S
S-**LIMPSY**
LINAGE-S
LINDEN-S
A-**LINERS**
LINEUP-S
LINGAM-S
LINGEL-S
C-**LINGER**
F-LINGER
S-LINGER
LINGER-S
LINGLE-S
LINGOT-S
LINGUA-E
LINGUA-L
LINGUA-S
LINHAY-S
A-**LINING**
LINING-S
B-**LINKED**
C-LINKED
P-LINKED
S-LINKED
B-**LINKER**
C-LINKER
K-LINKER
P-LINKER
S-LINKER
LINKER-S
LINKUP-S
B-**LINNED**
LINNET-S
LINNEY-S
LINSEY-S
LINTEL-S
S-**LINTER**
LINTER-S
LINTIE-R
LINTIE-S
LINTOL-S
LIONEL-S
LIONET-S
LIPASE-S
LIPIDE-S
LIPOID-S
LIPOMA-S
B-**LIPPED**
C-LIPPED
F-LIPPED
S-LIPPED
LIPPEN-S
C-**LIPPER**
F-LIPPER
S-LIPPER
LIPPER-S
C-**LIPPIE**
LIPPIE-R
LIPPIE-S
LIQUID-S
LIQUOR-S
LISPER-S
B-**LISSES**
P-LISSES
LISSOM-E
LISTEE-S
LISTEL-S
G-**LISTEN**
LISTEN-S
B-**LISTER**

G-LISTER
K-LISTER
LISTER-S
LITCHI-S
B-**LITHER**
S-LITHER
LITHES-T
LITHIA-S
F-**LITING**
C-**LITTER**
F-LITTER
G-LITTER
S-LITTER
LITTER-S
LITTER-Y
LITTLE-R
LITTLE-S
C-**LIVERS**
O-LIVERS
S-LIVERS
LIVIER-S
S-**LIVING**
LIVING-S
LIVYER-S
LIZARD-S
LOADEN-S
LOADER-S
LOAFER-S
LOANER-S
LOATHE-D
LOATHE-R
LOATHE-S
G-**LOBATE**
LOBATE-D
B-**LOBBED**
C-**LOBBER**
S-LOBBER
LOBBER-S
G-**LOBING**
LOBING-S
G-**LOBOSE**
G-**LOBULE**
LOBULE-S
LOCALE-S
LOCATE-D
LOCATE-R
LOCATE-S
LOCHAN-S
LOCHIA-L
B-**LOCKED**
C-LOCKED
F-LOCKED
B-**LOCKER**
C-LOCKER
LOCKER-S
LOCKET-S
LOCKUP-S
LOCULE-D
LOCULE-S
LOCUST-A
LOCUST-S
LODGER-S
LOFTER-S
S-**LOGANS**
LOGGAT-S
C-**LOGGED**
F-LOGGED
S-LOGGED
C-**LOGGER**
F-LOGGER
S-LOGGER
LOGGER-S
LOGGIA-S
LOGGIE-R
E-**LOGIES**

O-LOGIES
LOGIES-T
LOGION-S
LOGJAM-S
LOGLOG-S
LOGOFF-S
LOGOUT-S
LOGWAY-S
LOITER-S
LOLIGO-S
LOLIUM-S
LOLLER-S
LOLLOP-S
LOMEIN-S
LOMENT-A
LOMENT-S
A-**LONELY**
C-**LONERS**
LONGAN-S
P-**LONGED**
LONGER-S
P-**LONGES**
LONGES-T
LOOFAH-S
LOOKER-S
LOOKUP-S
B-**LOOMED**
G-LOOMED
S-LOOMED
LOONEY-S
LOONIE-R
LOONIE-S
B-**LOOPED**
G-LOOPED
B-**LOOPER**
LOOPER-S
LOOSEN-S
LOOSES-T
LOOTER-S
E-**LOPERS**
S-LOPERS
E-**LOPING**
S-LOPING
C-**LOPPED**
F-LOPPED
G-LOPPED
P-LOPPED
S-LOPPED
F-**LOPPER**
LOPPER-S
LOQUAT-S
LORCHA-S
LORICA-E
G-**LORIES**
LORING-S
LORIOT-S
C-**LOSERS**
C-**LOSING**
LOSING-S
F-**LOSSES**
G-LOSSES
LOTION-S
B-**LOTTED**
C-LOTTED
P-LOTTED
S-LOTTED
LOUDEN-S
C-**LOUGHS**
P-LOUGHS
S-LOUGHS
LOUNGE-D
LOUNGE-R
LOUNGE-S
C-**LOURED**
F-LOURED

B-**LOUSED**
F-LOUSED
B-**LOUSES**
F-LOUSES
C-**LOUTED**
F-LOUTED
G-LOUTED
LOUVER-S
LOUVRE-D
LOUVRE-S
LOVAGE-S
C-**LOVERS**
G-LOVERS
P-LOVERS
G-**LOVING**
LOVING-S
P-**LOWBOY**
LOWBOY-S
B-**LOWERS**
F-LOWERS
G-LOWERS
P-LOWERS
F-**LOWERY**
S-**LOWEST**
B-**LOWING**
F-LOWING
G-LOWING
P-LOWING
S-LOWING
LOWING-S
S-**LOWISH**
C-**LOWNED**
LOWNES-S
B-**LOWSES**
LOWSES-T
LOZELL-S
B-**LUBBER**
C-LUBBER
F-LUBBER
S-LUBBER
LUBBER-S
LUCERN-E
LUCERN-S
C-**LUCKED**
P-LUCKED
LUCKIE-R
LUCKIE-S
LUCUMA-S
LUCUMO-S
LUETIC-S
B-**LUFFED**
F-LUFFED
P-LUFFED
S-LUFFED
G-**LUGGED**
P-LUGGED
S-LUGGED
P-**LUGGER**
S-LUGGER
LUGGER-S
LUGGIE-S
LUGING-S
LUMBAR-S
C-**LUMBER**
P-LUMBER
S-LUMBER
LUMBER-S
A-**LUMINA**
LUMINA-L
A-**LUMINE**
LUMINE-D
LUMINE-S
F-**LUMMOX**
C-**LUMPED**
F-LUMPED

P-LUMPED
S-LUMPED
P-**LUMPEN**
LUMPEN-S
C-**LUMPER**
P-LUMPER
LUMPER-S
LUNATE-D
LUNGAN-S
B-**LUNGED**
P-LUNGED
LUNGEE-S
B-**LUNGER**
P-LUNGER
LUNGER-S
B-**LUNGES**
P-LUNGES
LUNGIE-S
LUNGYI-S
LUNIES-T
B-**LUNKER**
C-LUNKER
F-LUNKER
P-LUNKER
LUNKER-S
B-**LUNTED**
LUNULA-E
LUNULA-R
LUNULE-S
LUNYIE-S
LUPINE-S
LURDAN-E
LURDAN-S
LURDEN-S
LURKER-S
B-**LUSHED**
F-LUSHED
S-LUSHED
B-**LUSHER**
F-LUSHER
P-LUSHER
LUSHER-S
B-**LUSHES**
F-LUSHES
P-LUSHES
S-LUSHES
LUSHES-T
P-**LUSHLY**
B-**LUSTER**
C-LUSTER
F-LUSTER
LUSTER-S
LUSTRA-L
LUSTRE-D
LUSTRE-S
G-**LUTEAL**
P-LUTEAL
LUTEIN-S
F-**LUTERS**
E-**LUTING**
F-LUTING
LUTING-S
F-**LUTIST**
LUTIST-S
K-**LUTZES**
LUVVIE-S
LUXATE-D
LUXATE-S
LUZERN-S
LYCEUM-S
LYCHEE-S
F-**LYINGS**
LYNAGE-S
LYRATE-D
LYRISM-S

LYRIST-S
LYSATE-S
LYSINE-S
F-**LYTING**
MACACO-S
MACHAN-S
MACKLE-D
MACKLE-S
MACOYA-S
MACRON-S
MACULA-E
MACULA-R
MACULA-S
MACULE-D
MACULE-S
MADAME-D
MADAME-S
MADCAP-S
MADDEN-S
MADDER-S
MADRAS-A
MADURO-S
MAELID-S
MAENAD-S
MAFFIA-S
MAFTIR-S
MAGGOT-S
MAGGOT-Y
MAGIAN-S
MAGILP-S
I-**MAGISM**
MAGISM-S
MAGLEV-S
MAGNET-O
MAGNET-S
MAGNON-S
MAGNUM-S
MAGPIE-S
MAGUEY-S
MAHMAL-S
MAHOUT-S
MAHSIR-S
MAHZOR-S
MAIDAN-S
MAIDEN-S
MAIGRE-S
MAIHEM-S
E-**MAILED**
MAILER-S
MAIMER-S
MAINOR-S
MAKEUP-S
MAKING-S
MALATE-S
MALGRE-D
MALGRE-S
MALICE-D
MALICE-S
MALIGN-S
MALINE-S
MALISM-S
MALKIN-S
MALLAM-S
S-**MALLED**
MALLEE-S
MALLET-S
MALLOW-S
MALMAG-S
MALTED-S
MALTHA-S
MALTOL-S
MAMLUK-S
MAMMAL-S
MAMMEE-S
MAMMER-S

MAMMET-S
MAMMEY-S
MAMMIE-S
MAMMON-S
MAMZER-S
MANAGE-D
MANAGE-R
MANAGE-S
MANANA-S
MANATI-S
MANCHE-S
MANCHE-T
MANDIR-A
MANDIR-S
MANDOM-S
MANEGE-D
MANEGE-S
MANGAL-S
MANGEL-S
MANGER-S
MANGLE-D
MANGLE-R
MANGLE-S
MANIAC-S
MANILA-S
MANIOC-A
MANIOC-S
MANITO-S
MANITO-U
MANITU-S
MANNAN-S
MANNER-S
MANOAO-S
MANRED-S
MANTEL-S
MANTID-S
MANTLE-D
MANTLE-S
MANTLE-T
MANTRA-M
MANTRA-P
MANTRA-S
MANTUA-S
MANUAL-S
MANUKA-S
MANURE-D
MANURE-R
MANURE-S
MAPPER-S
MAPPER-Y
MARACA-S
MARAUD-S
MARBLE-D
MARBLE-R
MARBLE-S
MARCEL-S
MARGAY-S
MARGIN-S
MARINA-S
MARINE-R
MARINE-S
MARKER-S
MARKET-S
MARKKA-A
MARKKA-S
MARKUP-S
MARLIN-E
MARLIN-G
MARLIN-S
MARMOT-S
MAROON-S
MARQUE-E
MARQUE-S
MARRAM-S
MARRER-S
MARRON-S
MARROW-S
MARROW-Y
MARRUM-S
S-**MARTED**
MARTEL-S
S-**MARTEN**
MARTEN-S
MARTIN-G
MARTIN-I
MARTIN-S
MARTYR-S
MARTYR-Y
MARVEL-S
MARVER-S
MASALA-S
MASCLE-D
MASCLE-S
MASCON-S
MASCOT-S
S-**MASHED**
S-**MASHER**
MASHER-S
S-**MASHES**
MASHIE-R
MASHIE-S
MASHUA-S
MASJID-S
MASKEG-S
MASKER-S
MASLIN-S
MASQUE-R
MASQUE-S
A-**MASSED**
A-**MASSES**
MASSIF-S
MASTER-S
MASTER-Y
MASTIC-H
MASTIC-S
MASULA-S
MATICO-S
A-**MATING**
MATING-S
MATLOW-S
MATOKE-S
MATRIC-E
MATRIC-S
MATRON-S
MATSAH-S
S-**MATTER**
MATTER-S
MATTER-Y
MATTIE-S
MATTIN-G
MATTIN-S
MATURE-D
MATURE-R
MATURE-S
MATZAH-S
MATZOH-S
MATZOT-H
MAUGRE-D
MAUGRE-S
MAULER-S
MAULVI-S
MAUMET-S
MAUVES-T
MAUVIN-E
MAUVIN-S
MAWKIN-S
MAWMET-S
MAXIMA-L
MAXIXE-S
MAYDAY-S
MAYHEM-S
MAYING-S
MAYPOP-S
MAYVIN-S
MAZARD-S
MAZHBI-S
A-**MAZING**
MAZOUT-S
MAZUMA-S
MEADOW-S
MEADOW-Y
MEAGRE-R
MEAGRE-S
MEALER-S
MEALIE-R
MEALIE-S
MEANER-S
MEANES-T
MEANIE-S
MEASLE-D
MEASLE-S
MEATHE-S
S-**MEATHS**
MEAZEL-S
MEDAKA-S
MEDDLE-D
MEDDLE-R
MEDDLE-S
MEDIAL-S
MEDIAN-S
MEDIAN-T
MEDICK-S
MEDICO-S
MEDINA-S
MEDIUM-S
MEDLAR-S
MEDLEY-S
MEDUSA-E
MEDUSA-L
MEDUSA-N
MEDUSA-S
MEEKEN-S
MEEMIE-S
MEETER-S
MEGARA-D
MEGASS-E
MEGILP-H
MEGILP-S
MEGOHM-S
MEGRIM-S
MEINEY-S
MEINIE-S
MEISHI-S
MELANO-S
MELDER-S
MELLAY-S
S-**MELLED**
MELLOW-S
MELLOW-Y
MELOID-S
S-**MELTED**
S-**MELTER**
MELTER-S
MELTON-S
MEMBER-S
MEMOIR-S
MENACE-D
MENACE-R
MENACE-S
A-**MENAGE**
MENAGE-D
MENAGE-S
A-**MENDED**
E-MENDED
A-**MENDER**
E-MENDER
MENDER-S
MENEER-S
MENHIR-S
MENIAL-S
A-**MENING**
O-MENING
A-**MENTAL**
O-MENTAL
MENTEE-S
MENTOR-S
A-**MENTUM**
O-MENTUM
MENYIE-S
MERCAT-S
A-**MERCER**
MERCER-S
MERCER-Y
MERELL-S
E-**MERGED**
MERGER-S
E-**MERGES**
MERINO-S
MERISM-S
MERKIN-S
MERLIN-G
MERLIN-S
MERLON-S
MERLOT-S
MEROME-S
MESAIL-S
MESCAL-S
MESETA-S
MESSAN-S
MESTEE-S
METAGE-S
METATE-S
METEOR-S
METEPA-S
METHOD-S
METHYL-S
E-**METICS**
METIER-S
METOPE-S
METRIC-S
METTLE-D
METTLE-S
METUMP-S
S-**MEUSES**
MEWLER-S
MEZAIL-S
MEZCAL-S
MEZUZA-H
MEZUZA-S
MGANGA-S
MIASMA-L
MIASMA-S
E-**MICATE**
MICATE-D
MICATE-S
MICELL-A
MICELL-E
MICELL-S
MICHER-S
MICKEY-S
MICKLE-R
MICKLE-S
O-**MICRON**
MICRON-S
MIDAIR-S
MIDDAY-S
MIDDEN-S
MIDDLE-D
MIDDLE-R
MIDDLE-S
S-**MIDGES**
MIDGET-S
MIDGUT-S
MIDLEG-S
MIDRIB-S
MIDWAY-S
MIGGLE-S
S-**MIGHTS**
MIGHTS-T
MIGNON-S
MIHRAB-S
MIKADO-S
O-**MIKRON**
MIKRON-S
MIKVAH-S
MIKVEH-S
MILADI-S
MILAGE-S
MILDEN-S
MILDEW-S
MILDEW-Y
S-**MILERS**
MILIEU-S
MILIEU-X
MILKER-S
MILLER-S
MILLET-S
MILNEB-S
MILORD-S
MILSEY-S
MILTER-S
MIMBAR-S
MIMOSA-S
MINBAR-S
MINCER-S
MINDER-S
MINGIN-G
MINGLE-D
MINGLE-R
MINGLE-S
MINIMA-L
MINIMA-X
MINING-S
MINION-S
MINIUM-S
MINNIE-S
MINNOW-S
MINTER-S
MINUET-S
MINUTE-D
MINUTE-R
MINUTE-S
MINYAN-S
MIOMBO-S
MIOTIC-S
MIRAGE-S
MIRITI-S
S-**MIRKER**
MIRROR-S
MISACT-S
MISADD-S
MISAIM-S
MISCUE-D
MISCUE-S
MISCUT-S
MISEAT-S
MISERE-S
MISFIT-S
MISHAP-S
MISHAP-T
MISHIT-S
MISHMI-S
MISKAL-S
MISKEN-S
MISKEN-T
MISKEY-S
MISLAY-S
MISLIE-S
MISPEN-S
MISSAL-S
MISSAY-S
MISSEE-M
MISSEE-N
MISSEE-S
MISSEL-S
A-**MISSES**
MISSET-S
MISSIS-H
MISTER-M
MISTER-S
MISTER-Y
MISTLE-D
MISTLE-S
MISUSE-D
MISUSE-R
MISUSE-S
S-**MITERS**
MITHER-S
S-**MITTEN**
MITTEN-S
MIZZEN-S
MIZZLE-D
MIZZLE-S
MNEMON-S
MOANER-S
MOBBER-S
MOBBIE-S
MOBBLE-D
MOBBLE-S
MOBCAP-S
MOBILE-S
MOCHIE-R
S-**MOCKED**
MOCKER-S
MOCKER-Y
MOCKUP-S
MOCOCK-S
MOCUCK-S
MODENA-S
MODERN-E
MODERN-S
MODEST-Y
MODIST-E
MODIST-S
MODULE-S
MOGGAN-S
MOGGIE-S
MOHAIR-S
MOHAWK-S
MOIDER-S
S-**MOILED**
MOILER-S
MOISER-S
S-**MOLDER**
MOLDER-S
MOLEST-S
MOLINE-S
MOLINE-T
MOLLAH-S
MOLLIE-S
MOLOCH-S
Y-**MOLTEN**
MOLTER-S
MOMENT-A
MOMENT-O
MOMENT-S
MOMISM-S
MOMMET-S
MOMSER-S
MOMZER-S

MONAUL-S
MONERA-N
MONETH-S
MONGER-S
MONGER-Y
MONGOE-S
MONGOL-S
A-**MONGST**
E-MONGST
MONIAL-S
MONISM-S
MONIST-S
MONKEY-S
MONTEM-S
MONTRE-S
MOOLAH-S
MOOLEY-S
MOONER-S
S-**MOORED**
MOORVA-S
S-**MOOTED**
MOOTER-S
A-**MOOVED**
A-**MOOVES**
MOPANE-S
MOPANI-S
MOPOKE-S
MOPPER-S
MOPPET-S
MORALE-S
MORALL-S
MORALL-Y
MORASS-Y
MOREEN-S
MORGAN-S
MORGAY-S
MORGEN-S
MORGUE-S
MORION-S
MORKIN-S
MORNAY-S
MOROSE-R
MORPHO-S
MORROW-S
MORSEL-S
MORTAL-S
MORTAR-S
MORTAR-Y
MORULA-E
MORULA-R
MORULA-S
MOSAIC-S
MOSQUE-S
MOSSER-S
MOSSIE-R
MOSSIE-S
MOTETT-S
S-**MOTHER**
MOTHER-S
MOTHER-Y
MOTILE-S
A-**MOTION**
E-MOTION
MOTION-S
E-**MOTIVE**
MOTIVE-D
MOTIVE-S
MOTLEY-S
MOTMOT-S
MOTSER-S
MOTTLE-D
MOTTLE-R
MOTTLE-S
MOTUCA-S
MOUJIK-S
MOULIN-S
A-**MOUNTS**
S-**MOUSED**
S-**MOUSER**
MOUSER-S
MOUSER-Y
S-**MOUSES**
MOUSIE-R
MOUSIE-S
MOUSLE-D
MOUSLE-S
MOUSME-E
MOUSME-S
MOUSSE-D
MOUSSE-S
MOUTAN-S
MOUTER-S
MOUTON-S
A-**MOVING**
E-MOVING
MOWING-S
S-**MOYLED**
S-**MOYLES**
MOZZIE-S
MOZZLE-S
MUCATE-S
MUCHEL-L
MUCHEL-S
MUCKER-S
MUCKLE-S
MUCLUC-S
MUCOID-S
MUCOSA-E
MUCOSA-L
MUCOSA-S
MUDCAP-S
MUDCAT-S
MUDDER-S
MUDDLE-D
MUDDLE-R
MUDDLE-S
S-**MUDGED**
S-**MUDGER**
MUDGER-S
S-**MUDGES**
MUESLI-S
MUFFIN-G
MUFFIN-S
MUFFLE-D
MUFFLE-R
MUFFLE-S
MUFLON-S
MUGFUL-S
MUGGAR-S
S-**MUGGED**
MUGGEE-S
S-**MUGGER**
MUGGER-S
MUGGUR-S
MUKLUK-S
MUKTUK-S
MULETA-S
E-**MULING**
MULLAH-S
MULLEN-S
MULLER-S
MULLET-S
MULLEY-S
MULMUL-L
MULMUL-S
MULTUM-S
MUMBLE-D
MUMBLE-R
MUMBLE-S
MUMMER-S
MUMMER-Y
MUMMIA-S
MUMPER-S
MUNDIC-S
MUNITE-D
MUNITE-S
MUNSHI-S
MUNTIN-G
MUNTIN-S
MURAGE-S
MURDER-S
MUREIN-S
MURENA-S
MURINE-S
E-**MURING**
MURLAN-S
MURLIN-G
MURLIN-S
MURMUR-S
MURRAM-S
MURRAY-S
MURREN-S
MURREY-S
MURRHA-S
MURRIN-E
MURRIN-S
MUSANG-S
MUSCAT-S
MUSCID-S
MUSCLE-D
MUSCLE-S
A-**MUSERS**
MUSEUM-S
MUSHER-S
A-**MUSING**
MUSING-S
A-**MUSIVE**
MUSJID-S
MUSKEG-S
MUSKET-S
MUSKIE-R
MUSKIE-S
MUSKIT-S
MUSKLE-S
MUSLIN-S
MUSMON-S
MUSROL-S
MUSSEL-S
MUSTEE-S
MUSTER-S
MUTANT-S
MUTASE-S
MUTATE-D
MUTATE-S
MUTINE-D
MUTINE-S
MUTISM-S
MUTTER-S
MUTTON-S
MUTTON-Y
MUTUAL-S
MUTUCA-S
MUTUEL-S
MUTULE-S
MUTUUM-S
MUUMUU-S
MUZHIK-S
MUZJIK-S
MUZZLE-D
MUZZLE-R
MUZZLE-S
MYCELE-S
MYELIN-E
MYELIN-S
MYELON-S
MYGALE-S
MYOGEN-S
MYOPIA-S
MYOPIC-S
MYOSIN-S
MYOTIC-S
MYRIAD-S
MYRICA-S
MYRTLE-S
MYSOST-S
MYSTIC-S
MYXOMA-S
MZUNGU-S
NABBER-S
NACKET-S
NAGANA-S
NAGARI-S
S-**NAGGED**
NAGGER-S
S-**NAILED**
NAILER-S
NAILER-Y
NAIVES-T
NALLAH-S
NAMING-S
NANDIN-A
NANDIN-E
NANDIN-S
NANDOO-S
O-**NANISM**
NANISM-S
NANKIN-S
NANNIE-D
NANNIE-S
NAPALM-S
NAPKIN-S
K-**NAPPED**
S-NAPPED
K-**NAPPER**
S-NAPPER
NAPPER-S
NAPPIE-R
NAPPIE-S
NAPRON-S
NARCOS-E
NARDOO-S
NARROW-S
NARWAL-S
NASARD-S
NASION-S
NASUTE-S
E-**NATION**
NATION-S
NATIVE-S
NATRON-S
NATTER-S
NATTER-Y
NATURA-E
NATURA-L
NATURE-D
NATURE-S
NAUGHT-S
NAUGHT-Y
NAUSEA-S
NAUTIC-S
NAVAID-S
NEAFFE-S
S-**NEAPED**
A-**NEARED**
U-NEARED
U-**NEATEN**
NEATEN-S
S-**NEBBED**
NEBBUK-S
NEBECK-S
NEBULA-E
NEBULA-R
NEBULA-S
NEBULE-S
S-**NECKED**
NECKER-S
NECTAR-S
NECTAR-Y
NEEDER-S
NEEDLE-D
NEEDLE-R
NEEDLE-S
S-**NEEZED**
S-**NEEZES**
NEGATE-D
NEGATE-R
NEGATE-S
NEKTON-S
NELLIE-S
NELSON-S
NEPETA-S
NEPHEW-S
NEREID-S
NERINE-S
NERITE-S
NEROLI-S
E-**NERVED**
NERVER-S
E-**NERVES**
NESTER-S
NESTLE-D
NESTLE-R
NESTLE-S
NESTOR-S
NETFUL-S
NETTER-S
NETTLE-D
NETTLE-R
NETTLE-S
NEURON-E
NEURON-S
NEUTER-S
NEWBIE-S
NEWELL-S
E-**NEWING**
NEWSIE-R
NEWSIE-S
NEWTON-S
NHANDU-S
NIACIN-S
S-**NIBBED**
NIBBLE-D
NIBBLE-R
NIBBLE-S
NICHER-S
NICKAR-S
S-**NICKED**
NICKEL-S
K-**NICKER**
S-NICKER
NICKER-S
NICKLE-D
NICKLE-S
NICKUM-S
NIDGET-S
NIDING-S
NIELLO-S
S-**NIFFED**
S-**NIFFER**
NIFFER-S
S-**NIGGER**
NIGGER-S
NIGGER-Y
S-**NIGGLE**
NIGGLE-D
NIGGLE-R
NIGGLE-S
K-**NIGHTS**
NILGAI-S
NILGAU-S
NIMBLE-R
NIMMER-S
NIMROD-S
NINCOM-S
NINCUM-S
S-**NIPPED**
S-**NIPPER**
NIPPER-S
NIPPLE-D
NIPPLE-S
NIPTER-S
NIRLIE-R
U-**NITERS**
NITRID-E
NITRID-S
NITRIL-E
NITRIL-S
NITROS-O
NITRYL-S
NITWIT-S
K-**NOBBLE**
NOBBLE-D
NOBBLE-R
NOBBLE-S
NOBLES-T
NOCAKE-S
NOCENT-S
NOCHEL-S
K-**NOCKED**
NOCKET-S
NOCTUA-S
S-**NODDED**
S-**NODDER**
NODDER-S
NODDLE-D
NODDLE-S
NODULE-D
NODULE-S
A-**NOESES**
A-**NOESIS**
A-**NOETIC**
S-**NOGGED**
NOGGIN-G
NOGGIN-S
A-**NOINTS**
NOMADE-S
NOMINA-L
NOMISM-S
NONAGE-D
NONAGE-S
NONANE-S
NONART-S
NONCOM-S
NONEGO-S
NONFAN-S
NONGAY-S
NONUSE-R
NONUSE-S
NONWAR-S
NOODGE-D
NOODGE-S
NOODLE-D
NOODLE-S
NOOKIE-R
NOOKIE-S
NOONER-S
NOOSER-S
NORITE-S
NORMAL-S
NORMAN-S

NORSEL-S
NOSEAN-S
NOSHER-S
NOSHER-Y
NOSIES-T
NOSING-S
NOSODE-S
NOSTOC-S
NOTATE-D
NOTATE-S
A-NOTHER
NOTICE-D
NOTICE-R
NOTICE-S
NOTION-S
NOUGAT-S
NOUGHT-S
NOUSLE-D
NOUSLE-S
NOVENA-E
NOVENA-S
NOVICE-S
NOYADE-S
NOZZER-S
NOZZLE-S
NUANCE-D
NUANCE-S
S-NUBBED
NUBBIN-G
NUBBIN-S
K-NUBBLE
NUBBLE-D
NUBBLE-S
K-NUBBLY
NUCHAL-S
NUCLEI-N
NUCULE-S
S-NUDGED
NUDGER-S
S-NUDGES
NUDISM-S
NUDIST-S
NUDNIK-S
NUFFIN-S
NUGGAR-S
NUGGET-S
NUGGET-Y
NULLAH-S
NUMBAT-S
NUMBER-S
NUMDAH-S
NUMNAH-S
NUNCIO-S
NUNCLE-S
NURDLE-D
NURDLE-S
NURHAG-S
K-NURLED
NURSER-S
NURSER-Y
NURSLE-D
NURSLE-S
NUTATE-D
NUTATE-S
NUTLET-S
NUTMEG-S
NUTRIA-S
NUTTER-S
NUTTER-Y
NUZZER-S
S-NUZZLE
NUZZLE-D
NUZZLE-R
NUZZLE-S
I-NYALAS

NYANZA-S
NYBBLE-S
NYMPHA-E
NYMPHA-L
NYMPHO-S
S-OAKERS
OARAGE-S
H-OARIER
R-OARIER
H-OARING
R-OARING
S-OARING
B-OATERS
C-OATERS
D-OATERS
G-OBANGS
K-OBANGS
OBDURE-D
OBDURE-S
B-OBECHE
OBECHE-S
OBEISM-S
L-OBELIA
OBELIA-S
OBEYER-S
OBIISM-S
OBJECT-S
OBJURE-D
OBJURE-S
OBLAST-I
OBLAST-S
OBLATE-S
OBLIGE-D
OBLIGE-E
OBLIGE-R
OBLIGE-S
OBLONG-S
OBOIST-S
S-OBOLES
OBSIGN-S
OBTAIN-S
OBTEND-S
OBTEST-S
OBTUND-S
OBTUSE-R
OBVERT-S
OCCULT-S
OCELOT-S
T-OCHERS
OCHREA-E
C-OCKERS
D-OCKERS
H-OCKERS
L-OCKERS
M-OCKERS
R-OCKERS
OCTANE-S
OCTANT-S
OCTAVE-S
OCTAVO-S
OCTETT-E
OCTETT-S
OCTROI-S
OCTUOR-S
J-OCULAR
L-OCULAR
V-OCULAR
OCULAR-S
L-OCULUS
I-ODISMS
C-ODISTS
M-ODISTS
P-ODIUMS
S-ODIUMS
OECIST-S

OEDEMA-S
OEUVRE-S
OFFCUT-S
OFFEND-S
C-OFFERS
D-OFFERS
G-OFFERS
OFFICE-R
OFFICE-S
B-OFFING
C-OFFING
D-OFFING
G-OFFING
OFFING-S
T-OFFISH
OFFPUT-S
OFFSET-S
S-OFTEST
OGDOAD-S
H-OGGINS
N-OGGINS
OGLING-S
OGRISM-S
OHMAGE-S
OIKIST-S
OILCAN-S
OILCUP-S
B-OILERS
C-OILERS
M-OILERS
T-OILERS
B-OILERY
R-OILIER
S-OILIER
B-OILING
C-OILING
F-OILING
M-OILING
R-OILING
S-OILING
T-OILING
OILLET-S
OILNUT-S
OILWAY-S
B-OINKED
J-OINTED
N-OINTED
P-OINTED
B-OLDENS
G-OLDENS
B-OLDEST
C-OLDEST
G-OLDEST
C-OLDISH
G-OLDISH
OLEATE-S
OLEFIN-E
OLEFIN-S
OLEINE-S
OLFACT-S
OLIVER-S
S-OLIVES
OLIVET-S
OLLAMH-S
B-OMBERS
C-OMBERS
S-OMBERS
H-OMBRES
S-OMBRES
OMELET-S
L-OMENTA
M-OMENTA
T-OMENTA
OMENTA-L
OMERTA-S

OMNIUM-S
ONAGER-S
ONCOME-S
ONCOST-S
ONDINE-S
B-ONDING
F-ONDING
P-ONDING
ONDING-S
M-ONEYER
ONEYER-S
ONEYRE-S
ONFALL-S
ONFLOW-S
R-ONIONS
C-ONNING
D-ONNING
F-ONNING
K-ONNING
R-ONNING
W-ONNING
ONSIDE-S
B-ONUSES
N-ONUSES
T-ONUSES
ONWARD-S
ONYCHA-S
OOCYST-S
OOCYTE-S
B-OODLES
D-OODLES
N-OODLES
P-OODLES
Z-OOGAMY
Z-OOGENY
B-OOHING
P-OOHING
Z-OOIDAL
Z-OOLITE
OOLITE-S
Z-OOLITH
OOLITH-S
N-OOLOGY
Z-OOLOGY
OOLONG-S
OOMIAC-K
OOMIAC-S
OOMIAK-S
OOMPAH-S
C-OOPING
H-OOPING
L-OOPING
M-OOPING
P-OOPING
R-OOPING
S-OOPING
W-OORALI
OORALI-S
OORIAL-S
M-OORIER
G-OOSIER
B-OOZIER
W-OOZIER
B-OOZILY
W-OOZILY
B-OOZING
OPAQUE-D
OPAQUE-R
OPAQUE-S
OPCODE-S
OPENER-S
OPERON-S
OPHITE-S
OPIATE-D
OPIATE-S

OPIOID-S
OPPOSE-D
OPPOSE-R
OPPOSE-S
OPPUGN-S
OPTANT-S
C-OPTERS
OPTIMA-L
OPTIME-S
OPTION-S
M-OPUSES
ORACHE-S
C-ORACLE
ORACLE-D
ORACLE-S
M-ORALLY
ORANGE-R
ORANGE-S
ORANGE-Y
ORARIA-N
B-ORATED
B-ORATES
ORATOR-S
ORATOR-Y
S-ORBING
ORBITA-L
ORBITA-S
ORCEIN-S
ORCHAT-S
ORCHEL-S
ORCHID-S
ORCHIL-S
P-ORCINE
ORCINE-S
ORDAIN-S
ORDEAL-S
B-ORDERS
C-ORDERS
B-ORDURE
ORDURE-S
OREIDE-S
ORFRAY-S
M-ORGANS
ORGASM-S
ORGEAT-S
G-ORGIAS
ORGIAS-T
P-ORGIES
F-ORGONE
ORGONE-S
M-ORGUES
ORIENT-S
ORIGAN-E
ORIGAN-S
ORIGIN-S
ORIOLE-S
ORISON-S
D-ORMERS
F-ORMERS
W-ORMERS
ORMOLU-S
ORNATE-R
OROGEN-S
OROGEN-Y
OROIDE-S
ORPHAN-S
M-ORPHIC
F-ORPINE
ORPINE-S
M-ORRICE
ORRICE-S
P-ORTHOS
OSCINE-S
OSCULA-R
OSCULE-S

C-OSIERS
H-OSIERS
R-OSIERS
H-OSIERY
OSMATE-S
OSMIUM-S
OSMOLE-S
OSMOSE-D
OSMOSE-S
OSMUND-A
OSMUND-S
OSPREY-S
OSSEIN-S
OSTENT-S
H-OSTLER
J-OSTLER
OSTLER-S
B-OTHERS
F-OTHERS
M-OTHERS
P-OTHERS
R-OTHERS
C-OTTARS
OTTAVA-S
C-OTTERS
D-OTTERS
H-OTTERS
J-OTTERS
P-OTTERS
R-OTTERS
T-OTTERS
W-OUBITS
C-OUCHED
D-OUCHED
M-OUCHED
P-OUCHED
T-OUCHED
V-OUCHED
B-OUCHES
C-OUCHES
D-OUCHES
M-OUCHES
P-OUCHES
R-OUCHES
T-OUCHES
V-OUCHES
R-OUGHLY
T-OUGHLY
B-OUGHTS
N-OUGHTS
OUGLIE-D
OUGLIE-S
B-OULDER
F-OULDER
M-OULDER
P-OULDER
OULONG-S
B-OUNCES
J-OUNCES
P-OUNCES
R-OUNCES
C-OUPING
L-OUPING
M-OUPING
P-OUPING
R-OUPING
S-OUPING
W-OURALI
OURALI-S
OURANG-S
OURARI-S
OUREBI-S
C-OURIER
L-OURIER
H-OUSELS

J-**OUSTED**
M-OUSTED
R-OUSTED
J-**OUSTER**
R-OUSTER
OUSTER-S
OUTACT-S
OUTADD-S
OUTAGE-S
OUTASK-S
OUTBAR-K
OUTBAR-S
OUTBEG-S
OUTBID-S
OUTBUY-S
OUTEAT-S
C-**OUTERS**
D-OUTERS
F-OUTERS
M-OUTERS
P-OUTERS
R-OUTERS
S-OUTERS
T-OUTERS
OUTFIT-S
G-**OUTFLY**
OUTGUN-S
C-**OUTHER**
M-OUTHER
P-OUTHER
S-OUTHER
OUTHIT-S
D-**OUTING**
H-OUTING
L-OUTING
P-OUTING
R-OUTING
T-OUTING
OUTING-S
OUTJET-S
OUTJUT-S
OUTLAW-S
OUTLAY-S
OUTLER-S
OUTLET-S
OUTLIE-D
OUTLIE-R
OUTLIE-S
OUTMAN-S
OUTPUT-S
OUTRAN-G
OUTRAN-K
F-**OUTRED**
OUTRED-S
OUTROW-S
OUTRUN-G
OUTRUN-S
OUTSEE-N
OUTSEE-S
OUTSET-S
OUTSIN-G
OUTSIN-S
OUTSIT-S
OUTSUM-S
OUTTOP-S
OUTVIE-D
OUTVIE-S
OUTWAR-D
OUTWAR-S
OUTWIN-D
OUTWIN-G
OUTWIN-S
OUTWIT-H
OUTWIT-S
C-**OUVERT**

OUVERT-E
B-**OVATES**
OVATOR-S
OVERDO-G
C-**OVERED**
D-OVERED
H-OVERED
L-OVERED
OVERGO-T
L-**OVERLY**
B-**OVINES**
OVISAC-S
OVONIC-S
OVULAR-Y
B-**OWLERS**
F-OWLERS
H-OWLERS
J-OWLERS
Y-OWLERS
H-**OWLETS**
J-**OWLIER**
L-OWLIER
B-**OWLING**
C-OWLING
F-OWLING
G-OWLING
H-OWLING
J-OWLING
S-OWLING
Y-OWLING
D-**OWNERS**
B-**OWNING**
D-OWNING
G-OWNING
L-OWNING
OXCART-S
OXFORD-S
OXGANG-S
OXGATE-S
OXHEAD-S
OXLAND-S
OXSLIP-S
F-**OXTAIL**
OXTAIL-S
L-**OXYGEN**
OXYGEN-S
OXYMEL-S
N-**OYESES**
R-**OYSTER**
OYSTER-S
OZAENA-S
PABLUM-S
S-**PACERS**
PACHAK-S
S-**PACIER**
O-**PACIFY**
S-**PACING**
PACKER-S
PACKET-S
PADANG-S
PADAUK-S
PADDER-S
PADDLE-D
PADDLE-R
PADDLE-S
PADNAG-S
PADOUK-S
PADSAW-S
PAELLA-S
PAESAN-I
PAESAN-O
PAESAN-S
PAGING-S
PAGODA-S
PAIDLE-S

PAIGLE-S
S-**PAINED**
PAINIM-S
PAIOCK-E
PAIOCK-S
PAISAN-A
PAISAN-O
PAISAN-S
PAJAMA-S
PAJOCK-E
PAJOCK-S
PAKEHA-S
PAKORA-S
PALACE-D
PALACE-S
PALAGI-S
PALAMA-E
PALATE-D
PALATE-S
PALING-S
PALKEE-S
PALLAH-S
S-**PALLED**
PALLET-S
PALLIA-L
PALLOR-S
PALMAR-Y
PALMER-S
PALMIE-R
PALMIE-S
PALMIE-T
PALOLO-S
PALTER-S
PAMPER-O
PAMPER-S
PANADA-S
PANAMA-S
PANDAR-S
PANDER-S
PANDIT-S
PANFUL-S
S-**PANGED**
PANGEN-E
PANGEN-S
PANICK-S
PANICK-Y
PANIER-S
S-**PANING**
PANISC-S
PANISK-S
S-**PANNED**
PANTER-S
PANTIE-S
PANTON-S
PANTUN-S
PANZER-S
PAPAIN-S
PAPAYA-N
PAPAYA-S
PAPISM-S
PAPIST-S
PAPULA-E
PAPULA-R
PAPULE-S
PARADE-D
PARADE-R
PARADE-S
PARAGE-S
PARAMO-S
PARANG-S
PARAPH-S
PARCEL-S
PARDAH-S
PARDAL-E
PARDAL-S

PARDON-S
PARENT-S
S-**PARERS**
S-**PARGED**
S-**PARGES**
PARGET-S
PARIAH-S
PARIAL-S
PARIAN-S
S-**PARING**
PARING-S
S-**PARKED**
PARKEE-S
S-**PARKER**
PARKER-S
S-**PARKIE**
PARKIE-R
PARKIE-S
PARKIN-G
PARKIN-S
PARKIS-H
S-**PARKLY**
PARLAY-S
PARLEY-S
PARLOR-S
PAROLE-D
PAROLE-E
PAROLE-S
PARPEN-D
PARPEN-S
PARPEN-T
PARRAL-S
S-**PARRED**
PARREL-S
PARROT-S
PARROT-Y
PARSEC-S
S-**PARSER**
PARSER-S
PARSON-S
S-**PARTAN**
PARTAN-S
PARTER-S
PARTON-S
PARURA-S
PARURE-S
PARVIS-E
PASCAL-S
PASEAR-S
PASHIM-S
PASSEL-S
PASSER-S
PASTEL-S
PASTER-N
PASTER-S
PASTIE-R
PASTIE-S
PASTIL-S
PASTOR-S
PATACA-S
PATENT-S
PATERA-E
S-**PATHED**
S-**PATHIC**
PATHIC-S
PATINA-E
PATINA-S
PATINE-D
PATINE-S
PATROL-S
PATRON-S
S-**PATTED**
S-**PATTEE**
PATTEN-S
S-**PATTER**

PATTER-N
PATTER-S
PATTIE-S
PATTLE-S
PATZER-S
PAULIN-S
PAUNCE-S
PAUNCH-Y
PAUPER-S
PAUSER-S
PAVAGE-S
PAVANE-S
PAVING-S
S-**PAVINS**
PAVIOR-S
PAVISE-R
PAVISE-S
PAVONE-S
PAWNCE-S
S-**PAWNED**
PAWNEE-S
S-**PAWNER**
PAWNER-S
PAWNOR-S
PAWPAW-S
PAYDAY-S
A-**PAYING**
S-PAYING
PAYING-S
PAYNIM-S
PAYOFF-S
PAYOLA-S
PAYOUT-S
PEACOD-S
PEAHEN-S
S-**PEANED**
PEANUT-S
PEAPOD-S
PEARCE-D
PEARCE-S
PEAVEY-S
PEBBLE-D
PEBBLE-S
PECHAN-S
S-**PECKED**
PECKER-S
PECTEN-S
PECTIN-S
PEDALO-S
PEDANT-S
PEDDER-S
PEDDLE-D
PEDDLE-R
PEDDLE-S
PEDLAR-S
PEDLAR-Y
PEDLER-S
PEDLER-Y
S-**PEELED**
S-**PEELER**
PEELER-S
PEENGE-D
PEENGE-S
PEEPER-S
PEEPUL-S
S-**PEERED**
PEERIE-R
PEERIE-S
PEEVER-S
PEEWEE-S
PEEWIT-S
PEINCT-S
S-**PEISES**
PELAGE-S
PELHAM-S

PELITE-S
PELLET-S
PELMET-S
PELOID-S
PELOTA-S
PELTAS-T
S-**PELTER**
PELTER-S
PELVIC-S
PENANG-S
PENCEL-S
S-**PENCES**
PENCIL-S
U-**PENDED**
PENFUL-S
O-**PENING**
PENNAL-S
PENNER-S
PENNON-S
PENSEE-S
PENSEL-S
PENSIL-E
PENSIL-S
PENSUM-S
PENTAD-S
PENTEL-S
PENTYL-S
PENULT-S
PEOPLE-D
PEOPLE-R
PEOPLE-S
PEPINO-S
PEPLUM-S
PEPPER-S
PEPPER-Y
PEPSIN-E
PEPSIN-S
PEPTIC-S
PEPTID-E
PEPTID-S
PERCEN-T
E-**PERDUE**
PERDUE-S
PERIOD-S
PERKIN-G
PERKIN-S
PERMIT-S
PERONE-S
PERRON-S
S-**PERSES**
PERSON-A
PERSON-S
PERSUE-D
PERSUE-S
PERUKE-D
PERUKE-S
PERUSE-D
PERUSE-R
PERUSE-S
PESADE-S
PESANT-E
PESANT-S
PESETA-S
PESEWA-S
PESHWA-S
PESTER-S
PESTLE-D
PESTLE-S
PETARA-S
PETARD-S
PETHER-S
PETITE-S
PETNAP-S
PETREL-S
PETROL-S

PETSAI-S
PETTER-S
PETTLE-D
PETTLE-S
PEWTER-S
PEYOTE-S
PEYOTL-S
PEZANT-S
PHALLI-C
PHALLI-N
U-**PHANGS**
A-**PHASIC**
PHEERE-S
PHEESE-D
PHEESE-S
PHEEZE-D
PHEEZE-S
S-**PHENES**
S-**PHENIC**
PHENOL-S
PHENOM-S
PHENYL-S
A-**PHESES**
PHIZOG-S
PHLEGM-S
PHLEGM-Y
PHLOEM-S
PHOBIA-S
PHOBIC-S
PHOEBE-S
PHONER-S
PHONEY-S
A-**PHONIC**
PHONIC-S
PHONON-S
A-**PHOTIC**
PHOTIC-S
PHOTOG-S
PHOTON-S
PHRASE-D
PHRASE-R
PHRASE-S
PHREAK-S
PHYLLO-S
PHYSED-S
PHYSIC-S
PHYSIO-S
PHYTOL-S
PHYTON-S
PIAFFE-D
PIAFFE-R
PIAFFE-S
PIAZZA-S
PICARA-S
PICARO-S
E-**PICENE**
PICENE-S
PICKAX-E
S-**PICKER**
PICKER-S
PICKER-Y
PICKET-S
PICKLE-D
PICKLE-R
PICKLE-S
PICKUP-S
PICNIC-S
PICOTE-D
PICOTE-E
PIDDLE-D
PIDDLE-R
PIDDLE-S
PIDGIN-S
PIECEN-S
PIECER-S

PIERCE-D
PIERCE-R
PIERCE-S
PIERID-S
PIFFLE-D
PIFFLE-R
PIFFLE-S
PIGEON-S
PIGGIE-R
PIGGIE-S
PIGGIN-G
PIGGIN-S
S-**PIGHTS**
PIGLET-S
PIGNUT-S
PIGOUT-S
PIGPEN-S
PIKAKE-S
S-**PIKERS**
S-**PIKING**
PILAFF-S
PILEUP-S
PILFER-S
PILFER-Y
S-**PILING**
PILING-S
PILLAR-S
PILLAU-S
S-**PILLED**
PILLOW-S
PILLOW-Y
PILULA-R
PILULA-S
PILULE-S
PIMENT-O
PIMENT-S
PIMPLE-D
PIMPLE-S
PINANG-S
PINATA-S
PINCER-S
PINDER-S
PINEAL-S
PINENE-S
PINGER-S
PINGLE-D
PINGLE-R
PINGLE-S
S-**PINIER**
PINIES-T
O-**PINING**
O-**PINION**
PINION-S
PINITE-S
PINKEN-S
PINKER-S
PINKEY-E
PINKEY-S
PINKIE-R
PINKIE-S
S-**PINNER**
PINNER-S
S-**PINNET**
PINNET-S
PINNIE-S
PINOLE-S
PINTLE-S
S-**PINTOS**
PINYON-S
PIOLET-S
PIONER-S
PIONEY-S
PIPAGE-S
PIPING-S
PIPKIN-S

PIPPIN-G
PIPPIN-S
PIQUET-S
PIRANA-S
PIRATE-D
PIRATE-S
PIRAYA-S
PIRNIE-S
PISSER-S
PISTIL-S
PISTOL-E
PISTOL-S
PISTON-S
PITARA-H
PITARA-S
PITIER-S
PITMAN-S
PITSAW-S
S-**PITTED**
S-**PITTEN**
S-**PITTER**
PITTER-S
PITURI-S
PIUPIU-S
PIZAZZ-Y
PIZZLE-S
PLACER-S
PLACET-S
PLACIT-A
PLACIT-S
PLAGUE-D
PLAGUE-R
PLAGUE-S
PLAGUE-Y
PLAICE-S
PLAINT-S
PLANCH-E
PLANER-S
PLANET-S
PLANTA-R
PLANTA-S
PLAQUE-S
S-**PLASHY**
PLASMA-S
PLASTE-R
PLATAN-E
PLATAN-S
PLATEN-S
PLATER-S
S-**PLAYED**
PLAYER-S
U-**PLEADS**
PLEASE-D
PLEASE-R
PLEASE-S
PLEDGE-D
PLEDGE-E
PLEDGE-R
PLEDGE-S
PLEDGE-T
PLEIAD-S
A-**PLENTY**
PLENUM-S
PLEUCH-S
PLEUGH-S
PLEURA-E
PLEURA-L
PLEURA-S
PLEXOR-S
U-**PLIGHT**
Y-PLIGHT
PLIGHT-S
U-**PLINKS**
PLINTH-S
PLISSE-S

PLONGE-D
PLONGE-S
U-**PLOOKS**
PLOUGH-S
PLOVER-S
PLOVER-Y
PLOWER-S
PLUNGE-D
PLUNGE-R
PLUNGE-S
PLURAL-S
PLUTON-S
U-**PLYING**
PNEUMA-S
POCHAY-S
POCKET-S
PODITE-S
S-**PODIUM**
PODIUM-S
PODLEY-S
PODSOL-S
PODZOL-S
POETIC-S
POFFLE-S
POGROM-S
POINTE-D
POINTE-L
POINTE-R
POINTE-S
POISER-S
POISON-S
POKIES-T
S-**POKING**
POLDER-S
POLEAX-E
POLEYN-S
POLICE-D
POLICE-S
POLING-S
POLITE-R
POLLAN-S
POLLEE-S
POLLEN-S
POLLEN-T
POLLER-S
POLYPE-S
POMACE-S
POMADE-D
POMADE-S
POMELO-S
POMMEL-E
POMMEL-S
POMMIE-S
POMPEY-S
POMPOM-S
POMPON-S
POMROY-S
PONCHO-S
PONDER-S
PONDOK-S
S-**PONGED**
PONGEE-S
PONGID-S
PONTIE-S
PONTIL-E
PONTIL-S
PONTON-S
POODLE-S
POOGYE-E
POOGYE-S
POOJAH-S
S-**POOLED**
POONAC-S
POONCE-S
S-**POORER**

POORIS-H
POOTER-S
POPGUN-S
POPJOY-S
POPLAR-S
POPLIN-S
POPPER-S
POPPET-S
POPPIT-S
POPPLE-D
POPPLE-S
POPRIN-S
POPSIE-S
PORGIE-S
S-**PORING**
PORISM-S
PORKER-S
POROSE-S
PORTAL-S
S-**PORTED**
S-**PORTER**
PORTER-S
POSADA-S
POSEUR-S
S-**POSHES**
POSHES-T
POSIES-T
POSING-S
POSNET-S
POSSER-S
POSSES-S
POSSET-S
POSSIE-S
O-**POSSUM**
POSSUM-S
POSTAL-S
POSTER-N
POSTER-S
POSTIE-S
A-**POSTIL**
POSTIL-S
POSTIN-G
POSTIN-S
POTAGE-R
POTAGE-S
POTASS-A
POTBOY-S
POTCHE-D
POTCHE-R
POTCHE-S
POTEEN-S
POTENT-S
POTFUL-S
POTGUN-S
POTHER-B
POTHER-S
POTHER-Y
POTION-S
POTPIE-S
POTSIE-S
S-**POTTED**
S-**POTTER**
POTTER-S
POTTER-Y
POTTLE-S
POTZER-S
POUDER-S
POUDRE-S
POUFFE-D
POUFFE-S
POULPE-S
POUNCE-D
POUNCE-R
POUNCE-S
POUNCE-T

POURER-S
POURIE-S
POUSSE-S
S-**POUTED**
S-**POUTER**
POUTER-S
POWDER-S
POWDER-Y
POWNEY-S
POWNIE-S
POWTER-S
POWWOW-S
POYSON-S
U-**PRAISE**
PRAISE-D
PRAISE-R
PRAISE-S
PRANCE-D
PRANCE-R
PRANCE-S
PRANCK-E
PRANCK-S
S-**PRANGS**
U-**PRATED**
PRATER-S
U-**PRATES**
PRATIE-S
PRAWLE-S
S-**PRAYED**
S-**PRAYER**
PRAYER-S
PREACE-D
PREACE-S
U-**PREACH**
PREACH-Y
PREACT-S
PREAMP-S
PREARM-S
PREASE-D
PREASE-S
PRECIS-E
PRECUT-S
PREEVE-D
PREEVE-S
PREFAB-S
PREFER-S
PREIFE-S
PRELIM-S
PREMED-S
PREMIE-R
PREMIE-S
PREMIX-T
PREPAY-S
PRESET-S
PRESTO-S
U-**PRESTS**
PRETOR-S
PREVUE-D
PREVUE-S
PREWAR-M
PREWAR-N
PREWYN-S
PREYER-S
PRIAPI-C
PRICER-S
PRIEFE-S
S-**PRIEST**
PRIEST-S
PRIEVE-D
PRIEVE-S
PRIMER-O
PRIMER-S
PRINCE-D
PRINCE-S
S-**PRINTS**

U-**PRISER**
PRISER-E
PRISER-S
U-**PRISES**
PRISON-S
PRIVET-S
PRIZER-S
PROBER-S
PROBIT-S
PROBIT-Y
PROFIT-S
PROIGN-S
PROINE-D
PROINE-S
PROJET-S
PROKER-S
PROLAN-S
PROLEG-S
PROLER-S
U-**PROLLS**
PROLOG-S
PROMPT-S
PRONES-T
PROPEL-S
PROPER-S
PROPYL-A
PROPYL-S
PROSER-S
PROTEA-N
PROTEA-S
PROTEI-D
PROTEI-N
PROTON-S
PROTYL-E
PROTYL-S
PROVEN-D
PROVER-B
PROVER-S
PROYNE-D
PROYNE-S
PRUINA-S
PRUINE-S
PRUNER-S
PRUSIK-S
PRUTOT-H
PRYING-S
PSEUDO-S
PSOCID-S
PSYCHE-D
PSYCHE-S
PSYCHO-S
PSYLLA-S
PSYWAR-S
A-**PTERIA**
PTERIN-S
PTISAN-S
A-**PTOTIC**
PUBLIC-S
PUCKER-S
PUCKER-Y
PUCKLE-S
PUDDEN-S
S-**PUDDER**
PUDDER-S
PUDDLE-D
PUDDLE-R
PUDDLE-S
PUEBLO-S
PUFFER-S
PUFFER-Y
PUFFIN-G
PUFFIN-S
PUGGIE-R
PUGGIE-S
PUGGLE-D
PUGGLE-S
PUGREE-S
PUISNE-S
PUKEKO-S
PULING-S
PULKHA-S
PULLER-S
PULLET-S
PULLEY-S
PULLUP-S
PULPER-S
PULPIT-S
PULQUE-S
PULSAR-S
PULSER-S
PULTAN-S
PULTON-S
PULTUN-S
PULVER-S
PULVIL-S
PULWAR-S
PUMELO-S
PUMICE-D
PUMICE-R
PUMICE-S
PUMMEL-O
PUMMEL-S
PUMPER-S
PUNCTO-S
PUNDIT-S
PUNGLE-D
PUNGLE-S
PUNKAH-S
PUNKER-S
PUNKEY-S
S-**PUNKIE**
PUNKIE-R
PUNKIE-S
PUNKIN-S
PUNNER-S
PUNNET-S
PUNTEE-S
PUNTER-S
PUPATE-D
PUPATE-S
PUPPET-S
PURANA-S
PURDAH-S
PURFLE-D
PURFLE-S
PURGER-S
S-**PURGES**
PURINE-S
PURISM-S
PURIST-S
PURLER-S
PURLIN-E
PURLIN-G
PURLIN-S
PURPIE-S
PURPLE-D
PURPLE-R
PURPLE-S
S-**PURRED**
PURSER-S
PURSEW-S
PURSUE-D
PURSUE-R
PURSUE-S
PURVEY-S
PUSHER-S
PUSHUP-S
PUSLEY-S
PUSSEL-S
PUSSER-S
PUTEAL-S
PUTELI-S
PUTLOG-S
PUTOFF-S
PUTOUT-S
PUTTEE-S
S-**PUTTER**
PUTTER-S
PUTTIE-D
PUTTIE-R
PUTTIE-S
PUTURE-S
PUZZEL-S
PUZZLE-D
PUZZLE-R
PUZZLE-S
PYCNON-S
PYEMIA-S
PYGARG-S
PYKNIC-S
PYLORI-C
PYONER-S
PYRENE-S
PYRITE-S
PYROLA-S
PYRONE-S
PYROPE-S
PYRROL-E
PYRROL-S
PYTHON-S
PYURIA-S
QASIDA-S
QAWWAL-I
QAWWAL-S
QIGONG-S
QINDAR-S
QINTAR-S
QIVIUT-S
QUAERE-D
QUAERE-S
QUAGGA-S
QUAHOG-S
QUAICH-S
QUAIGH-S
S-**QUAILS**
QUAKER-S
QUANGO-S
QUANTA-L
E-**QUANTS**
S-**QUARER**
QUARTE-R
QUARTE-S
QUARTE-T
QUARTO-S
QUARTZ-Y
QUASAR-S
QUATRE-S
QUAVER-S
QUAVER-Y
QUEACH-Y
QUEEST-S
S-**QUELCH**
QUELEA-S
QUETHE-S
QUEUER-S
QUEZAL-S
QUICHE-D
QUICHE-S
QUIDAM-S
QUIGHT-S
S-**QUILLS**
QUINCE-S
E-**QUINES**
QUINIE-S
QUININ-A
QUININ-E
QUININ-S
QUINOA-S
QUINOL-S
QUINTA-L
QUINTA-N
QUINTA-R
QUINTA-S
QUINTE-S
QUINTE-T
S-**QUINTS**
QUINZE-S
QUIPPU-S
S-**QUIRED**
S-**QUIRES**
S-**QUIRTS**
S-**QUITCH**
E-**QUITES**
A-**QUIVER**
QUIVER-S
QUIVER-Y
QUOHOG-S
QUOIST-S
QUOKKA-S
QUORUM-S
QUOTER-S
QUOTUM-S
QWERTY-S
RABATO-S
D-**RABBET**
RABBET-S
RABBIN-S
F-**RABBIT**
RABBIT-S
RABBIT-Y
B-**RABBLE**
D-RABBLE
G-RABBLE
P-RABBLE
RABBLE-D
RABBLE-R
RABBLE-S
RACEME-D
RACEME-S
B-**RACERS**
T-RACERS
B-**RACHES**
O-RACHES
B-**RACHET**
RACHET-S
A-**RACHIS**
B-**RACING**
G-RACING
T-RACING
RACING-S
RACISM-S
RACIST-S
C-**RACKED**
T-RACKED
W-RACKED
C-**RACKER**
T-RACKER
RACKER-S
B-**RACKET**
RACKET-S
RACKET-T
RACKET-Y
C-**RACKLE**
G-RACKLE
RACOON-S
B-**RADDED**
RADDLE-D
RADDLE-S
RADGES-T
RADIAL-E
RADIAL-S
RADIAN-S
RADIAN-T
RADIUM-S
RADOME-S
RADULA-E
RADULA-R
RADULA-S
RAFALE-S
RAFFIA-S
RAFFLE-D
RAFFLE-R
RAFFLE-S
C-**RAFTED**
D-RAFTED
G-RAFTED
D-**RAFTER**
G-RAFTER
RAFTER-S
RAGBAG-S
D-**RAGEES**
B-**RAGGED**
C-RAGGED
D-RAGGED
F-RAGGED
RAGGED-Y
RAGGEE-S
D-**RAGGLE**
RAGGLE-D
RAGGLE-S
RAGING-S
RAGINI-S
RAGLAN-S
RAGMAN-S
RAGMEN-T
RAGOUT-S
RAGTAG-S
RAGTOP-S
B-**RAIDED**
B-**RAIDER**
RAIDER-S
T-**RAIKED**
B-**RAILED**
D-RAILED
T-RAILED
F-**RAILER**
T-RAILER
RAILER-S
G-**RAILES**
F-**RAILLY**
B-**RAINED**
D-RAINED
G-RAINED
T-RAINED
G-**RAINES**
B-**RAIRDS**
A-**RAISED**
B-RAISED
F-RAISED
P-RAISED
P-**RAISER**
RAISER-S
A-**RAISES**
B-RAISES
F-RAISES
P-RAISES
RAISIN-G
RAISIN-S
RAISIN-Y
RAIYAT-S
B-**RAKING**
C-RAKING
RAKING-S
RALLYE-S
B-**RAMBLE**
RAMBLE-D
RAMBLE-R
RAMBLE-S
RAMCAT-S
RAMJET-S
C-**RAMMED**
D-RAMMED
T-RAMMED
C-**RAMMER**
RAMMER-S
C-**RAMPED**
T-RAMPED
T-**RAMPER**
RAMPER-S
RAMROD-S
RAMSON-S
RAMTIL-S
P-**RANCED**
T-RANCED
RANCEL-S
P-**RANCES**
T-RANCES
RANCHO-S
RANCOR-S
RANDAN-S
B-**RANDED**
RANDEM-S
RANDIE-R
RANDIE-S
RANDOM-S
RANDON-S
P-**RANGED**
G-**RANGER**
O-RANGER
RANGER-S
G-**RANGES**
O-RANGES
B-**RANKED**
C-RANKED
F-RANKED
P-RANKED
C-**RANKER**
F-RANKER
RANKER-S
RANKES-T
C-**RANKLE**
P-RANKLE
RANKLE-D
RANKLE-S
C-**RANKLY**
F-RANKLY
RANSEL-S
T-**RANSOM**
RANSOM-S
D-**RANTED**
G-RANTED
T-RANTED
G-**RANTER**
T-RANTER
RANTER-S
RANULA-S
RANZEL-S
D-**RAPERS**
RAPHIA-S
C-**RAPIER**
D-RAPIER
G-RAPIER
RAPIER-S
RAPINE-S
C-**RAPING**
D-RAPING
G-RAPING
T-RAPING
RAPIST-S
C-**RAPPED**

D-RAPPED
F-RAPPED
T-RAPPED
W-RAPPED
F-**RAPPEE**
RAPPEE-S
RAPPEL-S
C-**RAPPER**
T-RAPPER
W-RAPPER
RAPPER-S
RAPTOR-S
RASCAL-S
E-**RASERS**
B-**RASHED**
C-RASHED
T-RASHED
B-**RASHER**
C-RASHER
RASHER-S
B-**RASHES**
C-RASHES
T-RASHES
RASHES-T
B-**RASHLY**
E-**RASING**
G-**RASPED**
G-**RASPER**
RASPER-S
B-**RASSES**
F-RASSES
G-RASSES
T-RASSES
W-RASSES
W-**RASSLE**
RASSLE-D
RASSLE-S
RASTER-S
E-**RASURE**
RASURE-S
RATBAG-S
C-**RATERS**
F-RATERS
G-RATERS
K-RATERS
P-RATERS
G-**RATIFY**
G-**RATINE**
RATINE-S
C-**RATING**
G-RATING
O-RATING
P-RATING
RATING-S
O-**RATION**
RATION-S
RATITE-S
RATLIN-E
RATLIN-G
RATLIN-S
RATOON-S
RATTAN-S
D-**RATTED**
P-RATTED
RATTEN-S
RATTER-S
RATTER-Y
B-**RATTLE**
P-RATTLE
RATTLE-D
RATTLE-R
RATTLE-S
RATTON-S
RAUCLE-R
D-**RAUGHT**
F-RAUGHT
B-**RAUNCH**
C-RAUNCH
G-RAUNCH
RAUNCH-Y
RAUNGE-D
RAUNGE-S
RAVAGE-D
RAVAGE-R
RAVAGE-S
G-**RAVELS**
T-RAVELS
C-**RAVENS**
B-**RAVERS**
C-RAVERS
G-RAVERS
RAVINE-D
RAVINE-S
B-**RAVING**
C-RAVING
G-RAVING
RAVING-S
B-**RAWEST**
D-**RAWING**
RAWING-S
B-**RAYING**
D-RAYING
F-RAYING
G-RAYING
P-RAYING
G-**RAYLES**
RAYLES-S
RAYLET-S
T-**RAYNES**
C-**RAYONS**
B-**RAZERS**
G-RAZERS
B-**RAZING**
C-RAZING
G-RAZING
RAZURE-S
RAZZIA-S
F-**RAZZLE**
RAZZLE-S
P-**REACTS**
D-**READER**
T-READER
READER-S
REAGIN-S
C-**REAKED**
F-REAKED
W-REAKED
REALES-T
A-**REALLY**
B-**REAMED**
C-REAMED
D-REAMED
C-**REAMER**
D-REAMER
REAMER-S
REAPER-S
D-**REARER**
REARER-S
P-**REARMS**
T-**REASON**
REASON-S
B-**REASTS**
C-**REATES**
G-**REAVED**
P-**REAVER**
REAVER-S
G-**REAVES**
REAVOW-S
REBACK-S
REBAIT-S
REBATE-D
REBATE-R
REBATE-S
REBATO-S
REBECK-S
P-**REBILL**
REBILL-S
P-**REBIND**
REBIND-S
REBITE-S
P-**REBOIL**
REBOIL-S
P-**REBOOK**
REBOOK-S
REBOOT-S
REBORE-D
REBORE-S
P-**REBORN**
REBOZO-S
REBUFF-S
REBUKE-D
REBUKE-R
REBUKE-S
RECALL-S
RECANE-D
RECANE-S
RECANT-S
P-**RECAST**
RECAST-S
P-**RECEDE**
RECEDE-D
RECEDE-S
P-**RECENT**
P-**RECEPT**
RECEPT-S
P-**RECESS**
RECHEW-S
P-**RECIPE**
RECIPE-S
RECITE-D
RECITE-R
RECITE-S
T-**RECKED**
W-RECKED
RECKON-S
RECOAL-S
RECOCK-S
P-**RECODE**
RECODE-D
RECODE-S
RECOIL-S
RECOIN-S
RECOMB-S
P-**RECOOK**
RECOOK-S
RECORD-S
RECORK-S
P-**RECOUP**
RECOUP-E
RECOUP-S
E-**RECTOR**
RECTOR-S
RECTOR-Y
RECTUM-S
RECULE-D
RECULE-S
P-**RECURE**
RECURE-D
RECURE-S
RECUSE-D
RECUSE-S
P-**RECUTS**
REDACT-S
P-**REDATE**
REDATE-D
REDATE-S
REDBAY-S
REDBUD-S
REDBUG-S
REDCAP-S
REDDEN-S
REDDER-S
T-**REDDLE**
REDDLE-D
REDDLE-S
REDEAL-S
REDEAL-T
REDEAR-S
REDEEM-S
REDEYE-S
REDFIN-S
P-**REDIAL**
U-REDIAL
REDIAL-S
A-**REDING**
B-REDING
REDLEG-S
REDOCK-S
REDOUT-S
REDOWA-S
REDRAW-N
REDRAW-S
REDTOP-S
REDUCE-D
REDUCE-R
REDUCE-S
REDUIT-S
REEARN-S
REEBOK-S
B-**REEDER**
REEDER-S
P-**REEDIT**
REEDIT-S
REEFER-S
REEKER-S
REEKIE-R
C-**REELED**
REELER-S
REEMIT-S
P-**REEVED**
P-**REEVES**
P-**REFACE**
REFACE-D
REFACE-S
REFALL-S
P-**REFECT**
REFECT-S
REFEED-S
REFEEL-S
P-**REFERS**
P-**REFILE**
REFILE-D
REFILE-S
REFILL-S
REFILM-S
REFIND-S
REFINE-D
REFINE-R
REFINE-S
P-**REFIRE**
REFIRE-D
REFIRE-S
REFLAG-S
REFLET-S
REFLOW-N
REFLOW-S
REFOLD-S
REFOOT-S
P-**REFORM**
REFORM-S
REFUEL-S
REFUGE-D
REFUGE-E
REFUGE-S
REFUND-S
REFUSE-D
REFUSE-R
REFUSE-S
REFUTE-D
REFUTE-R
REFUTE-S
REGAIN-S
G-**REGALE**
REGALE-D
REGALE-R
REGALE-S
REGARD-S
REGEAR-S
REGENT-S
REGEST-S
REGGAE-S
REGILD-S
REGIME-N
REGIME-S
REGINA-E
REGINA-L
REGINA-S
REGION-S
REGIVE-N
REGIVE-S
REGLET-S
REGLOW-S
REGLUE-D
REGLUE-S
REGRET-S
REGROW-N
REGROW-S
REGULA-E
REGULA-R
REGULO-S
REHANG-S
REHEAR-D
REHEAR-S
P-**REHEAT**
REHEAT-S
REHEEL-S
REHIRE-D
REHIRE-S
G-**REINED**
REITER-S
REIVER-S
REJECT-S
REJOIN-S
REKNIT-S
RELACE-D
RELACE-S
P-**RELATE**
RELATE-D
RELATE-R
RELATE-S
RELEND-S
RELENT-S
RELEVE-S
RELICT-S
RELIEF-S
RELIER-S
RELINE-D
RELINE-S
RELINK-S
RELIST-S
RELIVE-D
RELIVE-R
RELIVE-S
RELOAD-S
RELOAN-S
RELOCK-S
RELOOK-S
RELUCT-S
RELUME-D
RELUME-S
P-**REMADE**
REMADE-S
REMAIL-S
REMAIN-S
REMAKE-R
REMAKE-S
REMAND-S
REMARK-S
C-**REMATE**
REMATE-D
REMATE-S
T-**REMBLE**
REMBLE-D
REMBLE-S
REMEAD-S
REMEDE-D
REMEDE-S
P-**REMEET**
REMEET-S
REMEID-S
REMELT-S
REMEND-S
REMIND-S
REMINT-S
P-**REMISE**
REMISE-D
REMISE-S
P-**REMISS**
F-**REMITS**
P-**REMIXT**
P-**REMOLD**
REMOLD-S
REMORA-S
REMOTE-R
REMOTE-S
P-**REMOVE**
REMOVE-D
REMOVE-R
REMOVE-S
REMUDA-S
T-**RENAIL**
RENAIL-S
P-**RENAME**
RENAME-D
RENAME-S
T-**RENDED**
RENDER-S
RENEGE-D
RENEGE-R
RENEGE-S
RENEST-S
G-**RENNED**
B-**RENNES**
RENNET-S
RENNIN-G
RENNIN-S
RENOWN-S
T-**RENTAL**
RENTAL-S
P-**RENTED**
B-**RENTER**
RENTER-S
RENVOI-S
RENVOY-S
REOPEN-S
P-**REPACK**
REPACK-S
P-**REPAID**
REPAIR-S
REPARK-S

REPAST-S
REPAVE-D
REPAVE-S
P-**REPAYS**
REPEAL-S
REPEAT-S
REPENT-S
REPERK-S
REPINE-D
REPINE-R
REPINE-S
P-**REPLAN**
REPLAN-S
REPLAN-T
REPLAY-S
REPLOT-S
REPLUM-B
REPOLL-S
P-**REPONE**
REPONE-D
REPONE-S
REPORT-S
P-**REPOSE**
REPOSE-D
REPOSE-R
REPOSE-S
REPOST-S
REPOUR-S
P-**REPPED**
REPUGN-S
REPULP-S
REPUMP-S
REPURE-D
REPURE-S
REPUTE-D
REPUTE-S
REQUIN-S
REQUIT-E
REQUIT-S
RERACK-S
RERAIL-S
REREAD-S
RERISE-N
RERISE-S
REROLL-S
REROOF-S
RESAIL-S
P-**RESALE**
RESALE-S
RESCUE-D
RESCUE-R
RESCUE-S
RESEAL-S
RESEAT-S
RESEAU-S
RESEAU-X
RESECT-S
RESEDA-S
RESEED-S
RESEEK-S
P-**RESELL**
RESELL-S
RESEND-S
P-**RESENT**
RESENT-S
P-**RESETS**
F-**RESHES**
RESHIP-S
RESHOE-S
P-**RESHOW**
RESHOW-N
RESHOW-S
P-**RESIDE**
RESIDE-D
RESIDE-R
RESIDE-S
P-**RESIFT**
RESIFT-S
RESIGN-S
RESILE-D
RESILE-S
RESIST-S
RESITE-D
RESITE-S
RESIZE-D
RESIZE-S
RESKEW-S
RESKUE-D
RESKUE-S
P-**RESOAK**
RESOAK-S
P-**RESOLD**
RESOLE-D
RESOLE-S
RESORB-S
P-**RESORT**
RESORT-S
RESPOT-S
C-**RESTED**
P-RESTED
W-RESTED
RESTEM-S
P-**RESTER**
W-RESTER
RESTER-S
RESULT-S
P-**RESUME**
RESUME-D
RESUME-R
RESUME-S
RETACK-S
RETAIL-S
RETAIN-S
RETAKE-N
RETAKE-R
RETAKE-S
RETAMA-S
P-**RETAPE**
RETAPE-D
RETAPE-S
RETARD-S
RETEAM-S
RETEAR-S
RETELL-S
RETENE-S
P-**RETEST**
RETEST-S
RETILE-D
RETILE-S
RETIME-D
RETIME-S
RETINA-E
RETINA-L
RETINA-S
RETINE-S
RETINT-S
RETIRE-D
RETIRE-E
RETIRE-R
RETIRE-S
RETOOL-S
RETORT-S
RETOUR-S
RETREE-S
P-**RETRIM**
RETRIM-S
A-**RETTED**
F-RETTED
RETUND-S
RETUNE-D
RETUNE-S
RETURF-S
RETURN-S
P-**RETYPE**
RETYPE-D
RETYPE-S
REURGE-D
REURGE-S
REVAMP-S
REVEAL-S
P-**REVERB**
REVERB-S
REVERE-D
REVERE-R
REVERE-S
REVERS-E
REVERS-I
REVERS-O
REVERT-S
REVEST-S
B-**REVETS**
T-REVETS
REVEUR-S
P-**REVIEW**
REVIEW-S
REVILE-D
REVILE-R
REVILE-S
P-**REVISE**
REVISE-D
REVISE-R
REVISE-S
REVIVE-D
REVIVE-R
REVIVE-S
REVOKE-D
REVOKE-R
REVOKE-S
REVOLT-S
REVOTE-D
REVOTE-S
P-**REVUES**
REWAKE-D
REWAKE-N
REWAKE-S
REWARD-S
P-**REWARM**
REWARM-S
P-**REWASH**
REWELD-S
REWIND-S
REWIRE-D
REWIRE-S
REWOKE-N
REWORD-S
P-**REWORK**
REWORK-S
REWOVE-N
P-**REWRAP**
REWRAP-S
REWRAP-T
REZONE-D
REZONE-S
RHAPHE-S
RHEBOK-S
RHETOR-S
RHODIE-S
RHOMBI-C
RHUMBA-S
RHYMER-S
RHYTHM-I
RHYTHM-S
RHYTON-S
RIALTO-S
RIBALD-S
RIBAND-S
RIBAUD-S
C-**RIBBED**
D-RIBBED
C-**RIBBER**
D-RIBBER
RIBBER-S
RIBBON-S
RIBBON-Y
RIBIBE-S
RIBIER-S
D-**RIBLET**
T-RIBLET
RIBLET-S
RIBOSE-S
G-**RICERS**
P-RICERS
RICHEN-S
RICHES-T
F-**RICHTS**
P-**RICIER**
G-**RICING**
P-RICING
T-RICING
B-**RICKED**
C-RICKED
P-RICKED
T-RICKED
W-RICKED
P-**RICKER**
T-RICKER
RICKER-S
C-**RICKEY**
RICKEY-S
B-**RICKLE**
P-RICKLE
T-RICKLE
RICKLE-S
P-**RICKLY**
T-RICKLY
RICRAC-S
G-**RIDDER**
RIDDER-S
G-**RIDDLE**
RIDDLE-D
RIDDLE-R
RIDDLE-S
T-**RIDENT**
B-**RIDGED**
F-RIDGED
RIDGEL-S
RIDGER-S
B-**RIDGES**
F-RIDGES
RIDGIL-S
B-**RIDING**
G-RIDING
P-RIDING
RIDING-S
RIDLEY-S
G-**RIEVER**
RIEVER-S
G-**RIEVES**
P-RIEVES
RIFFLE-D
RIFFLE-R
RIFFLE-S
T-**RIFLED**
T-**RIFLER**
RIFLER-S
RIFLER-Y
T-**RIFLES**
D-**RIFTED**
G-RIFTED
F-**RIGGED**
G-RIGGED
P-RIGGED
T-RIGGED
F-**RIGGER**
P-RIGGER
T-RIGGER
RIGGER-S
RIGHTO-S
B-**RIGHTS**
F-RIGHTS
W-RIGHTS
RIGLIN-G
RIGLIN-S
RIGOLL-S
RIGOUR-S
D-**RILLED**
F-RILLED
G-RILLED
P-RILLED
T-RILLED
G-**RILLES**
RILLET-S
P-**RIMERS**
T-RIMERS
G-**RIMIER**
B-**RIMING**
C-RIMING
G-RIMING
P-RIMING
B-**RIMMED**
P-RIMMED
T-RIMMED
B-**RIMMER**
C-RIMMER
G-RIMMER
K-RIMMER
P-RIMMER
T-RIMMER
RIMMER-S
C-**RIMPLE**
RIMPLE-D
RIMPLE-S
B-**RINDED**
G-RINDED
C-**RINGED**
F-RINGED
W-RINGED
B-**RINGER**
C-RINGER
W-RINGER
RINGER-S
P-**RINKED**
RINSER-S
RIOTER-S
RIPECK-S
G-**RIPERS**
G-**RIPING**
RIPOFF-S
RIPOST-E
RIPOST-S
D-**RIPPED**
G-RIPPED
T-RIPPED
D-**RIPPER**
F-RIPPER
G-RIPPER
T-RIPPER
RIPPER-S
A-**RIPPLE**
C-RIPPLE
G-RIPPLE
T-RIPPLE
RIPPLE-D
RIPPLE-R
RIPPLE-S
RIPPLE-T
RIPRAP-S
RIPSAW-S
P-**RISERS**
A-**RISING**
G-RISING
I-RISING
K-RISING
P-RISING
RISING-S
B-**RISKED**
F-RISKED
B-**RISKER**
F-RISKER
RISKER-S
C-**RISPED**
RISQUE-S
RITARD-S
F-**RITTED**
G-RITTED
C-**RITTER**
F-RITTER
G-RITTER
RITTER-S
RITUAL-S
F-**RITZES**
RIVAGE-S
D-**RIVELS**
D-**RIVERS**
G-**RIVETS**
P-RIVETS
T-RIVETS
D-**RIVING**
RIVLIN-S
RIZARD-S
RIZZAR-S
RIZZAR-T
F-**RIZZER**
RIZZER-S
RIZZOR-S
ROADEO-S
ROADIE-S
ROAMER-S
ROARER-S
ROARIE-R
T-**ROATED**
ROBALO-S
P-**ROBAND**
ROBAND-S
ROBBER-S
ROBBER-Y
ROBBIN-G
ROBBIN-S
P-**ROBING**
ROBING-S
ROBUST-A
B-**ROCHES**
C-ROCHES
T-ROCHES
C-**ROCHET**
ROCHET-S
B-**ROCKED**
C-ROCKED
F-ROCKED
T-ROCKED
ROCKER-S
ROCKER-Y
B-**ROCKET**
C-ROCKET
ROCKET-S
ROCOCO-S
B-**RODDED**
P-RODDED
E-**RODENT**
RODENT-S

E-**RODING**
RODING-S
ROEMER-S
D-**ROGERS**
B-**ROGUES**
D-ROGUES
B-**ROILED**
D-ROILED
G-**ROINED**
P-ROINED
B-**ROKERS**
P-ROKERS
B-**ROKING**
P-ROKING
T-ROKING
ROLFER-S
D-**ROLLED**
P-ROLLED
T-ROLLED
D-**ROLLER**
P-ROLLER
T-ROLLER
ROLLER-S
F-**ROMAGE**
ROMAGE-S
B-**ROMALS**
ROMANO-S
T-**ROMPED**
ROMPER-S
RONDEL-S
RONION-S
RONNEL-S
F-**RONTES**
RONYON-S
P-**ROOFED**
P-**ROOFER**
ROOFER-S
B-**ROOKED**
C-ROOKED
D-ROOKED
B-**ROOKIE**
ROOKIE-R
ROOKIE-S
B-**ROOMED**
G-ROOMED
V-ROOMED
G-**ROOMER**
ROOMER-S
ROOMIE-R
ROOMIE-S
D-**ROOPED**
T-ROOPED
ROOSER-S
B-**ROOSES**
W-**ROOTED**
ROOTER-S
ROOTLE-D
ROOTLE-S
ROOTLE-T
G-**ROPERS**
P-ROPERS
G-**ROPING**
T-ROPING
ROPING-S
C-**ROQUET**
ROQUET-S
RORTER-S
ROSACE-A
ROSACE-S
ROSCOE-S
G-**ROSETS**
C-**ROSIER**
P-ROSIER
ROSIER-E
ROSIER-S
ROSIES-T
P-**ROSILY**
P-**ROSING**
C-**ROSSER**
G-ROSSER
ROSSER-S
F-**ROSTED**
ROSTER-S
ROSTRA-L
ROSULA-S
ROTATE-D
ROTATE-S
ROTCHE-S
ROTGUT-S
B-**ROTHER**
ROTHER-S
ROTOLO-S
ROTTAN-S
T-**ROTTED**
ROTTEN-S
T-**ROTTER**
ROTTER-S
ROTULA-S
O-**ROTUND**
ROTUND-A
ROTUND-S
T-**ROUBLE**
ROUBLE-S
ROUCHE-S
ROUCOU-S
B-**ROUGHS**
G-ROUGHS
T-ROUGHS
B-**ROUGHT**
D-ROUGHT
W-ROUGHT
F-**ROUGHY**
T-**ROULES**
F-**ROUNCE**
T-ROUNCE
ROUNCE-S
G-**ROUNDS**
C-**ROUPED**
G-ROUPED
T-ROUPED
A-**ROUSED**
G-ROUSED
A-**ROUSER**
G-ROUSER
T-ROUSER
ROUSER-S
A-**ROUSES**
G-ROUSES
T-ROUSES
G-**ROUTED**
G-**ROUTER**
T-ROUTER
ROUTER-S
C-**ROUTES**
D-**ROUTHS**
D-**ROVERS**
P-ROVERS
T-ROVERS
D-**ROVING**
P-ROVING
ROVING-S
T-**ROWELS**
C-**ROWERS**
G-ROWERS
C-**ROWING**
G-ROWING
T-ROWING
ROWING-S
D-**ROWNDS**
G-**ROWTHS**
T-ROWTHS
P-**ROYNED**
G-**ROYNES**
P-ROYNES
ROZZER-S
RUBACE-S
RUBATO-S
D-**RUBBED**
G-RUBBED
D-**RUBBER**
G-RUBBER
RUBBER-S
RUBBER-Y
G-**RUBBLE**
RUBBLE-D
RUBBLE-S
RUBIES-T
RUBIGO-S
RUBINE-S
RUBOFF-S
RUBOUT-S
RUBRIC-S
T-**RUCKED**
B-**RUCKLE**
T-RUCKLE
RUCKLE-D
RUCKLE-S
RUCOLA-S
C-**RUDDED**
RUDDER-S
C-**RUDDLE**
RUDDLE-D
RUDDLE-S
C-**RUDELY**
P-**RUDERY**
C-**RUDEST**
P-**RUDISH**
G-**RUEING**
T-RUEING
RUEING-S
RUELLE-S
G-**RUFFED**
T-**RUFFES**
RUFFIN-G
RUFFIN-S
T-**RUFFLE**
RUFFLE-D
RUFFLE-R
RUFFLE-S
G-**RUFFLY**
D-**RUGGED**
F-RUGGED
D-**RUGGER**
RUGGER-S
A-**RUGOLA**
RUGOLA-S
RUGOSA-S
RUINER-S
RULING-S
RUMAKI-S
C-**RUMBLE**
D-RUMBLE
G-RUMBLE
RUMBLE-D
RUMBLE-R
RUMBLE-S
C-**RUMBLY**
G-RUMBLY
C-**RUMENS**
RUMINA-L
RUMKIN-S
B-**RUMMER**
D-RUMMER
G-RUMMER
RUMMER-S
RUMOUR-S
C-**RUMPED**
F-RUMPED
G-RUMPED
T-RUMPED
C-**RUMPLE**
F-RUMPLE
RUMPLE-D
RUMPLE-S
C-**RUMPLY**
T-**RUNDLE**
RUNDLE-D
RUNDLE-S
RUNDLE-T
C-**RUNKLE**
RUNKLE-D
RUNKLE-S
RUNLET-S
T-**RUNNEL**
RUNNEL-S
RUNNER-S
RUNNET-S
RUNOFF-S
RUNOUT-S
RUNRIG-S
B-**RUNTED**
G-RUNTED
P-RUNTED
RUNWAY-S
RUPIAH-S
B-**RUSHED**
C-RUSHED
F-RUSHED
RUSHEE-S
B-**RUSHER**
C-RUSHER
RUSHER-S
B-**RUSHES**
C-RUSHES
F-RUSHES
RUSSEL-S
RUSSET-S
RUSSET-Y
RUSSIA-S
C-**RUSTED**
T-RUSTED
RUSTIC-S
RUSTLE-D
RUSTLE-R
RUSTLE-S
RUSTRE-D
RUSTRE-S
RUTILE-S
RUTTER-S
RYOKAN-S
RYPECK-S
SABBAT-H
SABBAT-S
SABINE-S
SABKHA-H
SABKHA-S
SABKHA-T
SACBUT-S
SACHEM-S
SACHET-S
SACKER-S
SACQUE-S
SACRAL-S
SACRUM-S
SADDEN-S
SADDHU-S
SADDLE-D
SADDLE-R
SADDLE-S
SADISM-S
SADIST-S
SAETER-S
SAFARI-S
SAFROL-E
SAFROL-S
SAGBUT-S
SAGENE-S
SAGGAR-D
SAGGAR-S
SAGGER-S
SAGOIN-S
SAGUIN-S
SAHIBA-H
SAHIBA-S
SAIKEI-S
SAILER-S
SAILOR-S
SAIMIN-S
SAIQUE-S
SAITHE-S
SAIYID-S
SAKIEH-S
SALAAM-S
SALADE-S
SALAMI-S
SALINA-S
SALINE-S
SALIVA-L
SALIVA-S
SALLAD-S
SALLAL-S
SALLEE-S
SALLET-S
SALLOW-S
SALLOW-Y
SALMON-S
SALOON-S
SALOOP-S
SALPID-S
P-**SALTER**
SALTER-N
SALTER-S
SALTIE-R
SALTIE-S
SALUKI-S
SALUTE-D
SALUTE-R
SALUTE-S
SALVER-S
SALVIA-S
SALVOR-S
SAMAAN-S
SAMARA-S
SAMBAL-S
SAMBAR-S
T-**SAMBAS**
SAMBUR-S
SAMECH-S
SAMEKH-S
SAMFOO-S
SAMIEL-S
SAMITE-S
SAMITI-S
SAMLET-S
SAMLOR-S
SAMOSA-S
SAMPAN-S
SAMPLE-D
SAMPLE-R
SAMPLE-S
SAMSHU-S
SANCAI-S
SANCHO-S
SANDAL-S
SANDER-S
SANDHI-S
SANGAR-S
SANGER-S
SANJAK-S
SANNIE-S
SANNOP-S
SANNUP-S
SANPAN-S
SANSAR-S
SANSEI-S
SANTAL-S
SANTIR-S
SANTOL-S
SANTON-S
SANTUR-S
SAPELE-S
SAPOTA-S
SAPOTE-S
SAPOUR-S
SAPPAN-S
SAPPER-S
SAPPLE-D
SAPPLE-S
SARAPE-S
SARDAR-S
SARDEL-S
SARNEY-S
SARNIE-S
SARODE-S
SARONG-S
SARSAR-S
SARSEN-S
SARTOR-S
SASHAY-S
SASINE-S
SATANG-S
SATARA-S
SATEEN-S
I-**SATINS**
SATIRE-S
SATORI-S
SATRAP-S
SATRAP-Y
SATYRA-L
SATYRA-S
SAUCER-S
SAUGER-S
SAULGE-S
SAULIE-S
SAUREL-S
SAVAGE-D
SAVAGE-R
SAVAGE-S
SAVANT-S
SAVATE-S
SAVINE-S
SAVING-S
SAVIOR-S
SAVOUR-S
SAVOUR-Y
SAVVEY-S
SAWDER-S
SAWING-S
SAWLOG-S
SAWNEY-S
SAWPIT-S
SAWYER-S
SAXAUL-S
SAYING-S
SAYYID-S
SAZHEN-S
SCAITH-S
SCALAR-E
SCALAR-S
SCALER-S

SCAMEL-S
SCAMPI-S
E-**SCAPED**
E-**SCAPES**
SCARAB-S
SCARCE-R
SCARER-S
SCARPA-S
SCARPH-S
E-**SCARPS**
SCARRE-D
SCARRE-S
SCARTH-S
SCATHE-D
SCATHE-S
SCAZON-S
A-**SCENDS**
A-**SCENTS**
SCERNE-D
SCERNE-S
SCHELM-S
SCHEMA-S
SCHEME-D
SCHEME-R
SCHEME-S
SCHISM-A
SCHISM-S
SCHIST-S
SCHIZO-S
SCHLEP-P
SCHLEP-S
SCHMOE-S
SCHNOZ-Z
SCHOOL-E
SCHOOL-S
SCHORL-S
SCHOUT-S
SCHRIK-S
SCHROD-S
SCHTIK-S
SCHUIT-S
SCHUYT-S
SCILLA-S
SCIROC-S
SCLAFF-S
SCLATE-D
SCLATE-S
SCLAVE-S
SCLERA-E
SCLERA-L
SCLERA-S
SCLERE-S
SCLIFF-S
A-**SCONCE**
SCONCE-D
SCONCE-S
SCORER-S
SCORIA-C
SCORIA-E
SCORSE-D
SCORSE-R
SCORSE-S
SCOTER-S
SCOTIA-S
SCOURS-E
SCOUSE-R
SCOUSE-S
SCOUTH-S
SCOWTH-S
SCRAMB-S
SCRAPE-D
SCRAPE-R
SCRAPE-S
SCRAWL-S
SCRAWL-Y

SCRAWM-S
SCRAYE-S
SCREAK-S
SCREAK-Y
SCREAM-S
SCREED-S
SCREEN-S
A-**SCRIBE**
E-SCRIBE
SCRIBE-D
SCRIBE-R
SCRIBE-S
SCRIKE-D
SCRIKE-S
SCRIMP-S
SCRIMP-Y
SCRINE-S
SCRIPT-S
SCRIVE-D
SCRIVE-S
SCROBE-S
E-**SCROLL**
SCROLL-S
SCROOP-S
SCROTA-L
SCROWL-E
SCROWL-S
E-**SCROWS**
SCRUFF-S
SCRUFF-Y
SCRUMP-S
SCRUMP-Y
SCRUNT-S
SCRUNT-Y
SCRUTO-S
SCRUZE-D
SCRUZE-S
SCRYER-S
SCRYNE-S
SCULLE-D
SCULLE-R
SCULLE-S
SCULPT-S
SCUNGE-D
SCUNGE-S
SCYTHE-D
SCYTHE-R
SCYTHE-S
SDAINE-D
SDAINE-S
SDEIGN-E
SDEIGN-S
SEABAG-S
SEABED-S
SEADOG-S
SEAHOG-S
SEALCH-S
SEALER-S
SEALER-Y
SEALGH-S
SEAMER-S
SEANCE-S
SEARAT-S
SEARCE-D
SEARCE-S
SEASON-S
SEATER-S
SEAWAN-S
SEAWAN-T
SEAWAY-S
SEBATE-S
SECANT-S
SECEDE-D
SECEDE-R
SECEDE-S

SECERN-S
SECKEL-S
SECKLE-S
SECOND-E
SECOND-I
SECOND-O
SECOND-S
SECPAR-S
SECRET-A
SECRET-E
SECRET-S
SECTOR-S
SECURE-D
SECURE-R
SECURE-S
SEDATE-D
SEDATE-R
SEDATE-S
SEDUCE-D
SEDUCE-R
SEDUCE-S
SEEDER-S
SEEING-S
SEEKER-S
SEEMER-S
SEESAW-S
SEETHE-D
SEETHE-R
SEETHE-S
SEGGAR-S
SEGHOL-S
SEICHE-S
SEIDEL-S
SEINER-S
SEISER-S
SEISIN-G
SEISIN-S
SEISOR-S
SEITEN-S
SEIZER-S
SEIZIN-G
SEIZIN-S
SEIZOR-S
SELECT-S
SELKIE-S
SELLER-S
SELSYN-S
SEMBLE-D
SEMBLE-S
SEMEME-S
SEMINA-L
SEMINA-R
SEMMIT-S
SEMPLE-R
SEMSEM-S
SENATE-S
SENDAL-S
SENDER-S
SENDUP-S
SENECA-S
SENEGA-S
SENHOR-A
SENHOR-S
SENILE-S
SENIOR-S
SENNET-S
SENNIT-S
SENORA-S
SENSOR-S
SENSOR-Y
SEPHEN-S
SEPIUM-S
A-**SEPSES**
A-**SEPSIS**
SEPTET-S

A-**SEPTIC**
SEPTIC-S
SEPTUM-S
SEQUEL-A
SEQUEL-S
SEQUIN-S
SERAIL-S
SERANG-S
SERAPE-S
SERAPH-S
SERDAB-S
SEREIN-S
SERENE-D
SERENE-R
SERENE-S
SERIAL-S
E-**SERINE**
SERINE-S
SERING-A
SERIPH-S
SERMON-S
SEROON-S
SEROSA-E
SEROSA-L
SEROSA-S
SERRAN-O
SERRAN-S
SERVAL-S
SERVER-S
SERVER-Y
SESAME-S
SESELI-S
SESTET-S
SESTET-T
SESTON-S
SETOFF-S
SETOUT-S
SETTEE-S
SETTER-S
SETTLE-D
SETTLE-R
SETTLE-S
SETULE-S
SEVERE-D
SEVERE-R
SEWAGE-S
SEWING-S
SEXISM-S
SEXIST-S
SEXPOT-S
SEXTAN-S
SEXTAN-T
SEXTET-S
SEXTET-T
SEXTON-S
A-**SEXUAL**
SHACKO-S
SHADER-S
SHADOW-S
SHADOW-Y
SHADUF-S
SHAIKH-S
SHAIRD-S
SHAIRN-S
SHAKER-S
SHALLI-S
SHALOM-S
SHALOT-S
SHAMAN-S
SHAMBA-S
A-**SHAMED**
SHAMER-S
A-**SHAMES**
SHAMOY-S
SHANTI-H

SHANTI-S
SHAPER-S
SHARER-S
SHARIA-S
SHARIA-T
SHARIF-S
SHAUGH-S
SHAVER-S
SHAVIE-S
P-**SHAWED**
SHEATH-E
SHEATH-S
SHEATH-Y
SHEAVE-D
SHEAVE-S
SHEEPO-S
SHEEVE-S
SHEIKH-A
SHEIKH-S
SHEILA-S
SHEKEL-S
SHELTA-S
SHELVE-D
SHELVE-R
SHELVE-S
Y-**SHENDS**
SHERIA-S
SHERIA-T
SHERIF-F
SHERIF-S
SHERPA-S
SHEUCH-S
SHEUGH-S
SHEWEL-S
SHEWER-S
SHIBAH-S
SHIELD-S
A-**SHIEST**
SHIKAR-I
SHIKAR-S
SHIKSA-S
SHIKSE-S
SHINDY-S
SHINER-S
SHINES-S
SHINNE-D
SHINNE-S
SHINNE-Y
SHIPPO-N
SHIPPO-S
SHIRRA-S
SHIVAH-S
A-**SHIVER**
SHIVER-S
SHIVER-Y
SHIVOO-S
SHLEPP-S
SHLOCK-S
SHLUMP-S
SHLUMP-Y
SHMEAR-S
SHMOCK-S
SHMUCK-S
SHNOOK-S
SHODER-S
SHOFAR-S
SHOGUN-S
SHOLOM-S
SHOOLE-D
SHOOLE-S
SHOPPE-D
SHOPPE-R
SHOPPE-S
SHORAN-S
SHORER-S

SHOTTE-D
SHOTTE-N
SHOTTE-S
SHOUGH-S
SHOVEL-S
SHOVER-S
SHOWER-S
SHOWER-Y
SHREEK-S
SHREIK-S
SHRIEK-S
SHRIEK-Y
SHRIFT-S
SHRIKE-D
SHRIKE-S
SHRILL-S
SHRILL-Y
SHRIMP-S
SHRIMP-Y
SHRINE-D
SHRINE-S
SHRINK-S
SHRIVE-D
SHRIVE-L
SHRIVE-N
SHRIVE-R
SHRIVE-S
SHROFF-S
SHROUD-S
SHROUD-Y
SHROVE-D
SHROVE-S
SHTCHI-S
SHTETL-S
SHTICK-S
SHTOOK-S
SHTUCK-S
SHUFTI-S
SIALID-S
SIALON-S
SICKEE-S
SICKEN-S
SICKIE-S
SICKLE-D
SICKLE-S
SIDDHA-S
SIDDHI-S
SIDDUR-S
SIDING-S
SIDLER-S
SIEGER-S
SIENNA-S
SIERRA-N
SIERRA-S
SIESTA-S
SIFAKA-S
SIFFLE-D
SIFFLE-S
SIFTER-S
SIGHER-S
SIGNAL-S
SIGNEE-S
SIGNER-S
SIGNET-S
SIGNOR-A
SIGNOR-E
SIGNOR-I
SIGNOR-S
SIGNOR-Y
SILAGE-D
SILAGE-S
SILANE-S
SILENE-S
SILENT-S
SILICA-S

SILKEN-S
SILKIE-R
SILKIE-S
SILLER-S
SILVAN-S
SILVER-N
SILVER-S
SILVER-Y
SIMIAN-S
SIMILE-S
SIMKIN-S
SIMLIN-S
SIMMER-S
SIMNEL-S
SIMOOM-S
SIMOON-S
SIMORG-S
SIMPAI-S
SIMPER-S
SIMPLE-D
SIMPLE-R
SIMPLE-S
SIMPLE-X
SIMURG-H
SIMURG-S
SINDON-S
SINGER-S
SINGLE-D
SINGLE-S
SINGLE-T
SINKER-S
SINNER-S
SINNET-S
SINTER-S
SINTER-Y
SIPHON-S
SIPPER-S
SIPPET-S
SIPPLE-D
SIPPLE-S
SIRCAR-S
SIRDAR-S
SIRKAR-S
SIRRAH-S
SIRREE-S
SISKIN-S
SISSOO-S
SISTER-S
SITCOM-S
SITHEN-S
SITREP-S
SITTAR-S
SITTER-S
SITULA-E
SIXAIN-E
SIXAIN-S
SIZING-S
SIZISM-S
SIZIST-S
SIZZLE-D
SIZZLE-R
SIZZLE-S
SKAITH-S
SKARTH-S
SKATER-S
SKATOL-E
SKATOL-S
SKEANE-S
SKELUM-S
SKETCH-Y
SKEWER-S
SKIBOB-S
SKIDOO-S
SKIING-S
SKIVER-S
SKIVIE-R
SKLATE-D
SKLATE-S
A-**SKLENT**
SKLENT-S
SKLIFF-S
SKREEN-S
SKRIMP-S
SKRUMP-S
SKRYER-S
SKYCAP-S
SKYLAB-S
SKYWAY-S
SLAIRG-S
A-**SLAKED**
Y-SLAKED
SLAKER-S
A-**SLAKES**
SLALOM-S
SLATER-S
SLAVER-S
SLAVER-Y
SLAVEY-S
SLAYER-S
SLEAVE-D
SLEAVE-S
SLEAZE-S
SLEDGE-D
SLEDGE-R
SLEDGE-S
SLEECH-Y
SLEEVE-D
SLEEVE-R
SLEEVE-S
SLEIGH-S
SLEIGH-T
SLEUTH-S
SLICER-S
SLIDER-S
SLIGHT-S
SLIPUP-S
SLIVER-S
SLOGAN-S
SLOKEN-S
SLOPER-S
SLOUCH-Y
SLOUGH-S
SLOUGH-Y
SLOVEN-S
SLUDGE-S
SLUICE-D
SLUICE-S
SMALTO-S
SMEATH-S
SMEETH-S
SMEGMA-S
SMEUSE-S
SMIDGE-N
SMIDGE-S
SMIGHT-S
SMILER-S
SMILET-S
SMILEY-S
SMITER-S
SMOILE-D
SMOILE-S
SMOKER-S
SMOOCH-Y
SMOOTH-S
SMOOTH-Y
SMOUSE-D
SMOUSE-R
SMOUSE-S
SMOYLE-D
SMOYLE-S
SMUDGE-D
SMUDGE-R
SMUDGE-S
SMUTCH-Y
SNARER-S
SNASTE-S
SNATCH-Y
SNATHE-S
SNEATH-S
SNEBBE-D
SNEBBE-S
SNEEZE-D
SNEEZE-R
SNEEZE-S
SNIDES-T
SNIPER-S
SNIVEL-S
SNOOZE-D
SNOOZE-R
SNOOZE-S
SNORER-S
SNUBBE-D
SNUBBE-R
SNUBBE-S
SNUDGE-D
SNUDGE-S
SOAKER-S
SOAPER-S
SOAPIE-R
SOAPIE-S
SOARER-S
SOBBER-S
SOBOLE-S
SOCAGE-R
SOCAGE-S
SOCCER-S
A-**SOCIAL**
SOCIAL-S
SOCKET-S
SODAIN-E
SODDEN-S
SODGER-S
SODIUM-S
SOFFIT-S
SOFTEN-S
SOFTIE-S
SOIGNE-E
SOIREE-S
SOLACE-D
SOLACE-R
SOLACE-S
SOLAND-S
SOLANO-S
I-**SOLATE**
SOLATE-D
SOLATE-S
SOLDAN-S
SOLDER-S
SOLERA-S
SOLION-S
SOLITO-N
SOLIVE-S
SOLLAR-S
SOLLER-S
SOLUTE-S
SOLVER-S
SOMBER-S
SOMBRE-D
SOMBRE-R
SOMBRE-S
SOMITE-S
SONANT-S
SONATA-S
SONDER-S
SONERI-S
SONNET-S
SONSIE-R
SONTAG-S
SOOGEE-D
SOOGEE-S
SOOGIE-D
SOOGIE-S
SOOJEY-S
SOONER-S
SOOTHE-D
SOOTHE-R
SOOTHE-S
SOPITE-D
SOPITE-S
SORAGE-S
SORBET-S
SORDOR-S
SORELL-S
SORGHO-S
SORING-S
SORNER-S
SORREL-S
SORROW-S
SORTER-S
SORTIE-D
SORTIE-S
SOUARI-S
SOUCAR-S
SOUDAN-S
SOUPER-S
SOUPLE-D
SOUPLE-S
SOURCE-D
SOURCE-S
SOURSE-S
SOUTAR-S
SOUTER-S
SOVIET-S
SOVRAN-S
SOWCAR-S
SOWING-S
SOWSSE-D
SOWSSE-S
SOWTER-S
SOZINE-S
SOZZLE-D
SOZZLE-S
SPACER-S
SPADER-S
SPAHEE-S
SPAING-S
SPALLE-D
SPALLE-R
SPALLE-S
SPARER-S
SPARES-T
SPARGE-D
SPARGE-R
SPARGE-S
SPARID-S
SPARKE-D
SPARKE-R
SPARKE-S
SPARRE-D
SPARRE-R
SPARRE-S
SPARSE-R
SPARTH-E
SPARTH-S
SPATHE-D
SPATHE-S
SPAULD-S
SPAVIE-S
SPAVIE-T
SPAVIN-S
SPAYAD-S
SPECIE-S
SPEEDO-S
SPEISE-S
SPENCE-R
SPENCE-S
SPENSE-S
SPERRE-D
SPERRE-S
A-**SPERSE**
SPERSE-D
SPERSE-S
SPEWER-S
SPHAER-E
SPHAER-S
SPHEAR-E
SPHEAR-S
SPHENE-S
SPHERE-D
SPHERE-S
E-**SPIALS**
SPICER-S
SPICER-Y
A-**SPICKS**
SPIDER-S
SPIDER-Y
SPIGHT-S
SPIGOT-S
SPIKER-S
SPIKER-Y
SPILTH-S
SPINAL-S
SPINAR-S
SPINEL-S
A-**SPINES**
SPINET-S
SPINOR-S
SPINTO-S
SPIRAL-S
SPIREA-S
A-**SPIRED**
SPIREM-E
SPIREM-S
A-**SPIRES**
SPIRIC-S
SPIRIT-S
SPIRIT-Y
SPITAL-S
SPLAKE-S
SPLASH-Y
SPLEEN-S
SPLEEN-Y
SPLENT-S
SPLICE-D
SPLICE-R
SPLICE-S
SPLIFF-S
SPLINE-D
SPLINE-S
SPLINT-S
SPLORE-S
SPONGE-D
SPONGE-R
SPONGE-S
A-**SPORTS**
E-**SPOUSE**
SPOUSE-D
SPOUSE-S
SPRAIN-S
SPRAIN-T
SPRANG-S
A-**SPRAWL**
SPRAWL-S
SPRAWL-Y
A-**SPREAD**
SPREAD-S
SPREDD-E
SPREDD-S
SPRING-E
SPRING-S
SPRING-Y
SPRINT-S
SPRITE-S
E-**SPRITS**
A-**SPROUT**
SPROUT-S
SPRUCE-D
SPRUCE-R
SPRUCE-S
SPRUIK-S
SPRUIT-S
SPULYE-D
SPULYE-S
SPUNGE-S
SPURGE-S
SPURNE-D
SPURNE-R
SPURNE-S
E-**SPYING**
SPYING-S
SQUAIL-S
SQUALL-S
SQUALL-Y
SQUAMA-E
SQUAME-S
SQUARE-D
SQUARE-R
SQUARE-S
SQUASH-Y
SQUAWK-S
SQUAWK-Y
SQUEAK-S
SQUEAK-Y
SQUEAL-S
SQUIER-S
SQUIFF-Y
SQUILL-A
SQUILL-S
A-**SQUINT**
SQUINT-S
SQUINT-Y
E-**SQUIRE**
SQUIRE-D
SQUIRE-S
SQUIRM-S
SQUIRM-Y
SQUIRR-S
SQUIRT-S
SQUISH-Y
SRADHA-S
A-**STABLE**
STABLE-D
STABLE-R
STABLE-S
STACTE-S
STADDA-S
STADIA-L
STADIA-S
STAGER-S
STAGER-Y
STAITH-E
STAITH-S
STALAG-S
STALES-T
STAMEN-S
STANCE-S
STANZA-S
STANZE-S
STANZO-S
STAPLE-D

STAPLE-R
STAPLE-S
STARCH-Y
STARER-S
A-**STARTS**
STARTS-Y
STARVE-D
STARVE-R
STARVE-S
E-**STATED**
STATER-S
E-**STATES**
A-**STATIC**
STATIC-E
STATIC-S
STATOR-S
STATUA-S
STATUE-D
STATUE-S
STATUS-Y
STAYER-S
STAYNE-D
STAYNE-S
STAYRE-S
STEALE-D
STEALE-R
STEALE-S
STEALT-H
STEANE-D
STEANE-S
STEARE-D
STEARE-S
STEDDE-D
STEDDE-S
E-**STEEMS**
STEEVE-D
STEEVE-R
STEEVE-S
A-**STELIC**
STELLA-R
STELLA-S
STEMMA-S
STEMME-D
STEMME-R
STEMME-S
STENCH-Y
O-**STENTS**
STEPPE-D
STEPPE-R
STEPPE-S
STEREO-S
STERNA-L
STEROL-S
STERVE-D
STERVE-S
STEVEN-S
STEWER-S
STIEVE-R
STIFLE-D
STIFLE-R
STIFLE-S
STIGMA-L
STIGMA-S
STIGME-S
STILET-S
STIMIE-D
STIMIE-S
STINGO-S
STIPEL-S
STIRRA-H
STIRRA-S
STIRRE-D
STIRRE-R
STIRRE-S
STIVER-S
STODGE-D
STODGE-R
STODGE-S
STOGEY-S
STOGIE-S
STOKER-S
STOLON-S
A-**STONED**
STONER-N
STONER-S
A-**STONES**
STONNE-D
STONNE-S
STOOGE-D
STOOGE-S
STOOPE-D
STOOPE-R
STOOPE-S
STOPER-S
STORER-S
STOREY-S
STORGE-S
A-**STOUND**
STOUND-S
STOURE-S
STOUTH-S
E-**STOVER**
STOVER-S
STOWER-S
STOWND-S
STOWRE-S
STRAFE-D
STRAFE-R
STRAFE-S
STRAFF-S
STRAIK-S
STRAIN-S
STRAIN-T
STRAIT-S
STRAKE-D
STRAKE-S
STRAMP-S
A-**STRAND**
STRAND-S
STRANG-E
STRATA-L
STRATA-S
STRATH-S
E-**STRAYS**
STREAK-S
STREAK-Y
STREAM-S
STREAM-Y
STREEK-S
STREEL-S
STREET-S
STREET-Y
STRENE-S
E-**STRICH**
O-STRICH
STRICK-S
A-**STRICT**
A-**STRIDE**
STRIDE-R
STRIDE-S
STRIFE-S
STRIFT-S
STRIGA-E
STRIKE-R
STRIKE-S
STRING-S
STRING-Y
STRIPE-D
STRIPE-R
STRIPE-S
STRIPE-Y
STRIVE-D
STRIVE-N
STRIVE-R
STRIVE-S
STROAM-S
STROBE-D
STROBE-S
STROKE-D
STROKE-N
STROKE-R
STROKE-S
STROLL-S
STROMA-L
STROMB-S
STROND-S
STROOK-E
STROUD-S
STROUP-S
STROUT-S
STRUMA-E
STRUMA-S
E-**STRUMS**
STRUNT-S
STUCCO-S
STUDIO-S
STUMER-S
STUPID-S
STUPOR-S
A-**STYLAR**
STYLER-S
STYLET-S
STYMIE-D
STYMIE-S
SUBACT-S
SUBBIE-S
SUBDEB-S
SUBDEW-S
SUBDUE-D
SUBDUE-R
SUBDUE-S
SUBFEU-S
SUBGUM-S
SUBLET-S
SUBLOT-S
SUBMEN-U
SUBMIT-S
SUBNET-S
SUBORN-S
SUBPAR-T
SUBSET-S
SUBTIL-E
SUBTLE-R
SUBURB-S
SUBWAY-S
SUCCAH-S
SUCCES-S
SUCCOR-S
SUCCOR-Y
SUCCOS-E
SUCCOT-H
SUCCUS-S
SUCKEN-S
SUCKER-S
SUCKET-S
SUCKLE-D
SUCKLE-R
SUCKLE-S
SUDATE-D
SUDATE-S
A-**SUDDEN**
SUDDEN-S
SUDDER-S
SUDSER-S
SUFFER-S
SUITER-S
SUITOR-S
SUKKAH-S
SUKKOT-H
SULDAN-S
SULFID-E
SULFID-S
SULFUR-S
SULFUR-Y
SULKER-S
SULPHA-S
SULTAN-A
SULTAN-S
SUMACH-S
SUMMAR-Y
SUMMAT-E
SUMMAT-S
SUMMER-S
SUMMER-Y
SUMMIT-S
SUMMON-S
SUMPIT-S
SUNBED-S
SUNBOW-S
SUNDAE-S
A-**SUNDER**
SUNDER-S
SUNDEW-S
SUNDOG-S
SUNDRA-S
SUNDRI-S
SUNGAR-S
SUNHAT-S
SUNKET-S
SUNKIE-S
SUNNAH-S
SUNRAY-S
SUNSET-S
SUNTAN-S
SUPAWN-S
SUPINE-S
SUPPER-S
SUPPLE-D
SUPPLE-R
SUPPLE-S
SURBED-S
SURFER-S
SURFIE-R
SURFIE-S
SURGER-S
SURGER-Y
U-**SURING**
SURREY-S
SURVEW-E
SURVEW-S
SURVEY-S
SUSLIK-S
SUTLER-S
SUTLER-Y
SUTTEE-S
SUTTLE-D
SUTTLE-S
SUTURE-D
SUTURE-S
SVELTE-R
SWAGER-S
U-**SWARDS**
SWARTH-S
SWARTH-Y
SWARVE-D
SWARVE-S
SWATHE-D
SWATHE-R
SWATHE-S
SWAYER-S
SWEARD-S
SWERVE-D
SWERVE-R
SWERVE-S
SWEVEN-S
SWINGE-D
SWINGE-R
SWINGE-S
SWIPER-S
SWIPLE-S
SWITCH-Y
SWITHE-R
SWIVEL-S
SWIVET-S
SWOUND-S
SWOUNE-D
SWOUNE-S
SWOWND-S
SWOWNE-S
SYLVAN-S
SYLVIA-S
SYLVIN-E
SYLVIN-S
SYMBOL-E
SYMBOL-S
SYNCOM-S
SYNDET-S
SYNDIC-S
SYNROC-S
SYNTAN-S
SYNURA-E
SYPHER-S
SYPHON-S
SYSTEM-S
TABARD-S
S-**TABBED**
TABERD-S
S-**TABLED**
S-**TABLES**
TABLET-S
TABOUR-S
TABRET-S
TABULA-E
TABULA-R
TABULI-S
S-**TACKED**
S-**TACKER**
TACKER-S
S-**TACKET**
TACKET-S
TACKET-Y
TACKLE-D
TACKLE-R
TACKLE-S
A-**TACTIC**
TACTIC-S
TADDIE-S
TAENIA-E
TAENIA-S
TAFFIA-S
S-**TAGGED**
TAGGEE-S
S-**TAGGER**
TAGGER-S
TAGRAG-S
TAGUAN-S
TAHINA-S
TAHINI-S
TAHSIL-S
TAIAHA-S
TAIGLE-D
TAIGLE-S
TAILER-S
TAILLE-S
TAILOR-S
TAILYE-S
TAIPAN-S
TAIVER-S
TAIVER-T
TAJINE-S
TAKAHE-S
TAKEUP-S
S-**TAKING**
TAKING-S
TALANT-S
TALBOT-S
TALCUM-S
TALENT-S
TALION-S
S-**TALKED**
S-**TALKER**
TALKER-S
TALKIE-R
TALKIE-S
TALLAT-S
TALLET-S
TALLIS-H
TALLIT-H
TALLOL-S
TALLOT-S
TALLOW-S
TALLOW-Y
TALMUD-S
E-**TALONS**
TALUKA-S
TALWEG-S
TAMALE-S
TAMANU-S
TAMARA-O
TAMARA-S
TAMARA-U
TAMARI-N
TAMARI-S
TAMBAC-S
TAMBAK-S
TAMBER-S
TAMBUR-A
TAMBUR-S
TAMEIN-S
E-**TAMINE**
TAMINE-S
TAMING-S
E-**TAMINS**
TAMISE-S
TAMMAR-S
TAMMIE-S
TAMPAN-S
S-**TAMPED**
S-**TAMPER**
TAMPER-S
TAMPON-S
TANDEM-S
S-**TANGED**
TANGIE-R
TANGIE-S
TANGLE-D
TANGLE-R
TANGLE-S
TANGUN-S
TANIST-S
TANKER-S
TANKIA-S
TANNAH-S
TANNER-S
TANNER-Y
S-**TANNIC**
TANNIN-G
TANNIN-S
TANNOY-S
TANREC-S

TANTRA-S
TANUKI-S
TAPALO-S
TAPETA-L
TAPETI-S
TAPIST-S
S-**TAPPED**
TAPPER-S
TAPPET-S
TARAMA-S
TARAND-S
TARBOY-S
TARCEL-S
TARGET-S
TARIFF-S
S-**TARING**
TARING-S
TARMAC-S
TARPAN-S
TARPON-S
S-**TARRED**
TARROW-S
TARSAL-S
TARSEL-S
TARSIA-S
TARTAN-A
TARTAN-E
TARTAN-S
TARTAR-E
TARTAR-S
S-**TARTED**
S-**TARTER**
S-**TARTLY**
TARZAN-S
S-**TASHED**
S-**TASHES**
TASKER-S
TASLET-S
TASSEL-L
TASSEL-S
TASSET-S
TASSIE-S
TASTER-S
TATAMI-S
S-**TATERS**
TATLER-S
TATTER-S
TATTER-Y
TATTIE-R
TATTIE-S
TATTLE-D
TATTLE-R
TATTLE-S
TATTOO-S
TATTOW-S
S-**TATUED**
TAUPIE-S
TAUTEN-S
TAUTOG-S
TAVERN-A
TAVERN-S
S-**TAWING**
TAWING-S
TAWNEY-S
TAWPIE-S
TAWTIE-R
TAXEME-S
A-**TAXIES**
TAXING-S
TAXITE-S
TCHICK-S
TEACUP-S
TEAGLE-D
TEAGLE-S
S-**TEAMED**
S-**TEAMER**
TEAMER-S
TEAPOT-S
TEAPOY-S
S-**TEARED**
TEARER-S
TEASEL-S
TEASER-S
TEAZEL-S
TEAZLE-D
TEAZLE-S
TEBBAD-S
TECHIE-R
TECHIE-S
TECHNO-S
TECKEL-S
S-**TEDDED**
TEDDER-S
TEDDIE-S
TEDIUM-S
S-**TEEMED**
TEEMER-S
S-**TEENED**
TEENER-S
TEEPEE-S
S-**TEERED**
TEETER-S
TEETHE-D
TEETHE-R
TEETHE-S
TEGULA-E
TEGULA-R
TELEDU-S
TELEGA-S
TELESM-S
TELFER-S
S-**TELLAR**
TELLAR-S
TELLEN-S
TELLER-S
TELLIN-G
TELLIN-S
TELNET-S
TELOME-S
TELSON-S
TEMPEH-S
TEMPER-A
TEMPER-S
S-**TEMPLE**
TEMPLE-D
TEMPLE-S
TEMPLE-T
TENACE-S
TENAIL-S
TENANT-S
S-**TENDED**
TENDER-S
TENDON-S
TENDRE-S
TENNER-S
TENNIS-T
TENOUR-S
TENPIN-S
TENREC-S
TENSES-T
TENSON-S
TENSOR-S
S-**TENTED**
TENTER-S
TENTIE-R
TENURE-D
TENURE-S
TENUTO-S
TENZON-S
TEOPAN-S
TEPHRA-S
TERBIA-S
TERCEL-S
TERCET-S
TERCIO-S
TEREDO-S
TEREFA-H
TERETE-S
TERMER-S
TERMOR-S
E-**TERNAL**
S-TERNAL
S-**TERNED**
TERRET-S
TERRIT-S
TERROR-S
TERTIA-L
TERTIA-N
TERTIA-S
TESTEE-S
TESTER-N
TESTER-S
TESTON-S
TETHER-S
TETRAD-S
TETRYL-S
TETTER-S
TEWART-S
TEWHIT-S
S-**TEWING**
THAIRM-S
THALER-S
THALLI-C
THANAH-S
E-**THANES**
THANNA-H
THANNA-S
THATCH-T
THATCH-Y
THAWER-S
THEAVE-S
THEINE-S
A-**THEISM**
THEISM-S
A-**THEIST**
THEIST-S
THENAR-S
THERME-L
THERME-S
THIBET-S
THIBLE-S
THICKO-S
THIEVE-D
THIEVE-S
THIRAM-S
A-**THIRST**
THIRST-S
THIRST-Y
THIVEL-S
THORIA-S
THORON-S
THORPE-S
THOUGH-T
THOWEL-S
THRALL-S
THRANG-S
THRAVE-S
THREAD-S
THREAD-Y
THREAP-S
THREAT-S
THREEP-S
THRENE-S
THRIFT-S
THRIFT-Y
A-**THRILL**
THRILL-S
THRILL-Y
THRIST-S
THRIST-Y
THRIVE-D
THRIVE-N
THRIVE-R
THRIVE-S
THROAT-S
THROAT-Y
THRONE-D
THRONE-S
THRONG-S
THROWE-R
THROWE-S
THRUST-S
THUGGO-S
THULIA-S
THWACK-S
A-**THWART**
THWART-S
THYMOL-S
THYRSE-S
S-**TIBIAL**
S-**TICKED**
TICKEN-S
S-**TICKER**
TICKER-S
TICKET-S
TICKEY-S
S-**TICKLE**
TICKLE-D
TICKLE-R
TICKLE-S
TICTAC-S
TICTOC-S
TIDBIT-S
TIDDLE-D
TIDDLE-R
TIDDLE-S
TIDDLE-Y
TIDIER-S
TIDIES-T
TIDING-S
TIEPIN-S
TIERCE-D
TIERCE-L
TIERCE-S
TIERCE-T
TIEROD-S
TIETAC-K
TIETAC-S
S-**TIFFED**
TIFFIN-G
TIFFIN-S
TIGLON-S
S-**TILING**
TILING-S
S-**TILLED**
S-**TILLER**
TILLER-S
S-**TILTED**
S-**TILTER**
TILTER-S
TIMBAL-E
TIMBAL-S
TIMBER-S
TIMBRE-L
TIMBRE-S
S-**TIMING**
TIMING-S
TIMIST-S
TINAJA-S
TINCAL-S
TINDAL-S
TINDER-S
TINDER-Y
TINEID-S
TINFUL-S
S-**TINGED**
A-**TINGLE**
TINGLE-D
TINGLE-R
TINGLE-S
TINIES-T
S-**TINKER**
TINKER-S
TINKLE-D
TINKLE-R
TINKLE-S
TINNER-S
TINNIE-R
TINNIE-S
TINPOT-S
TINSEL-S
TINSEY-S
S-**TINTED**
S-**TINTER**
TINTER-S
TIPCAT-S
TIPOFF-S
TIPPER-S
TIPPET-S
S-**TIPPLE**
TIPPLE-D
TIPPLE-R
TIPPLE-S
TIPTOE-D
TIPTOE-S
TIPTOP-S
TIPULA-S
TIRADE-S
S-**TIRING**
TIRING-S
S-**TIRRED**
TIRRIT-S
TISANE-S
TISICK-S
TISSUE-D
TISSUE-S
TISSUE-Y
TITBIT-S
TITFER-S
TITHER-S
TITIAN-S
TITLER-S
TITOKI-S
TITTER-S
TITTIE-S
TITTLE-D
TITTLE-S
TITTUP-S
TITTUP-Y
TITULE-D
TITULE-S
TOCHER-S
S-**TOCKED**
TOCSIN-S
TODDLE-D
TODDLE-R
TODDLE-S
TOECAP-S
TOERAG-S
TOETOE-S
TOFFEE-S
TOGATE-D
TOGGLE-D
TOGGLE-R
TOGGLE-S
TOILER-S
E-**TOILES**
TOILET-S
TOISON-S
S-**TOITED**
TOITOI-S
S-**TOKERS**
S-**TOKING**
TOLANE-S
TOLEDO-S
TOLING-S
TOLLER-S
TOLSEL-S
TOLSEY-S
TOLTER-S
TOLUID-E
TOLUID-S
TOLUOL-E
TOLUOL-S
TOLUYL-S
TOLZEY-S
TOMBAC-K
TOMBAC-S
TOMBAK-S
TOMBOC-S
TOMBOY-S
TOMCAT-S
TOMCOD-S
TOMPON-S
TOMTIT-S
TONEME-S
A-**TONERS**
S-TONERS
TONGER-S
TONGUE-D
TONGUE-S
A-**TONICS**
S-**TONIER**
A-**TONIES**
S-TONIES
TONIES-T
A-**TONING**
S-TONING
TONING-S
S-**TONISH**
TONITE-S
S-**TONKER**
TONKER-S
TONLET-S
TONNAG-E
TONNAG-S
TONNER-S
S-**TONNES**
TONSIL-S
TONSOR-S
TOOART-S
S-**TOOLED**
TOOLER-S
TOORIE-S
TOOTER-S
TOOTLE-D
TOOTLE-R
TOOTLE-S
S-**TOPERS**
TOPFUL-L
S-**TOPING**
S-**TOPPED**
S-**TOPPER**
TOPPER-S
S-**TOPPLE**
TOPPLE-D
TOPPLE-S
TOQUET-S
TORANA-S
TORERO-S

S-**TORIES**
TOROID-S
TORPID-S
TORPOR-S
TORQUE-D
TORQUE-R
TORQUE-S
TORRET-S
TORSEL-S
TORULA-E
TORULA-S
TORULI-N
TOSHER-S
TOSSER-S
S-**TOSSES**
TOSSUP-S
TOTARA-S
S-**TOTTED**
S-**TOTTER**
TOTTER-S
TOTTER-Y
TOTTIE-R
TOTTIE-S
TOUCAN-S
TOUCHE-D
TOUCHE-R
TOUCHE-S
TOUPEE-S
TOUPET-S
TOURER-S
S-**TOURIE**
TOURIE-S
TOUSER-S
TOUSLE-D
TOUSLE-S
S-**TOUTER**
TOUTER-S
TOUTIE-R
TOUZLE-D
TOUZLE-S
S-**TOWAGE**
TOWAGE-S
TOWARD-S
TOWBAR-S
S-**TOWERS**
TOWHEE-S
TOWIES-T
S-**TOWING**
TOWING-S
TOWMON-D
TOWMON-S
TOWMON-T
TOWNEE-S
TOWNIE-R
TOWNIE-S
TOWSER-S
TOXINE-S
TOXOID-S
TOYING-S
TRACER-S
TRACER-Y
TRADER-S
TRAGIC-S
S-**TRAIKS**
S-**TRAINS**
S-**TRAITS**
TRAMEL-L
TRAMEL-S
S-**TRAMPS**
TRANCE-D
TRANCE-S
TRANSE-S
TRAPAN-S
S-**TRAPPY**
TRAUMA-S
TRAVEL-S
TRAYNE-D
TRAYNE-S
TREBLE-D
TREBLE-S
TREMIE-S
TREMOR-S
TREPAN-G
TREPAN-S
TREVET-S
TREVIS-S
TRIAGE-D
TRIAGE-S
TRICAR-S
S-**TRICKS**
TRICKS-Y
TRICOT-S
TRIENE-S
E-**TRIERS**
TRIFLE-D
TRIFLE-R
TRIFLE-S
TRIGON-S
TRIJET-S
S-**TRIKES**
TRILBY-S
TRIMER-S
TRIODE-S
TRIOSE-S
S-**TRIPES**
S-**TRIPEY**
TRIPLE-D
TRIPLE-S
TRIPLE-T
TRIPLE-X
TRIPOD-S
TRIPOD-Y
TRISUL-A
TRISUL-S
TRITES-T
TRITON-E
TRITON-S
TRIUNE-S
TRIVET-S
TRIVIA-L
TROADE-S
TROCAR-S
TROCHE-E
TROCHE-S
TROCHI-L
TROGON-S
TROIKA-S
S-**TROKED**
S-**TROKES**
S-**TROLLS**
TROMPE-D
TROMPE-S
TROPHI-C
A-**TROPHY**
TROPIC-S
A-**TROPIN**
TROPIN-E
TROPIN-G
TROPIN-S
TROTYL-S
TROUGH-S
TROULE-D
TROULE-S
TROUPE-D
TROUPE-R
TROUPE-S
TROUSE-R
TROUSE-S
S-**TROUTS**
TROVER-S
S-**TROWED**
TROWEL-S
TROWTH-S
TRUANT-S
TRUDGE-D
TRUDGE-N
TRUDGE-R
TRUDGE-S
TRUFFE-S
TRUISM-S
TRYING-S
TRYOUT-S
TRYSTE-D
TRYSTE-R
TRYSTE-S
TSAMBA-S
TSETSE-S
TSKTSK-S
TSOTSI-S
TUBAGE-S
S-**TUBBED**
TUBBER-S
TUBFUL-S
TUBING-S
TUBIST-S
TUBULE-S
TUCHUN-S
TUCKER-S
TUCKET-S
TUFFET-S
TUFTER-S
TUGGER-S
TUGHRA-S
TUGRIK-S
TUILLE-S
TULADI-S
TULBAN-S
TULWAR-S
S-**TUMBLE**
TUMBLE-D
TUMBLE-R
TUMBLE-S
TUMOUR-S
S-**TUMPED**
TUMULT-S
TUNDRA-S
TUNDUN-S
TUNEUP-S
TUNICA-E
TUNING-S
S-**TUNNED**
TUNNEL-S
TUPELO-S
TURACO-S
TURACO-U
TURBAN-D
TURBAN-S
TURBAN-T
TURBIT-H
TURBIT-S
TURBOT-S
TUREEN-S
TURGOR-S
TURION-S
TURKEY-S
TURNER-S
TURNER-Y
TURNIP-S
TURNUP-S
TURRET-S
TURTLE-D
TURTLE-R
TURTLE-S
TUSCHE-S
S-**TUSHIE**
TUSHIE-S
TUSKAR-S
TUSKER-S
TUSSAH-S
TUSSAR-S
TUSSEH-S
TUSSER-S
TUSSLE-D
TUSSLE-S
TUSSOR-E
TUSSOR-S
TUSSUR-S
TUTSAN-S
TUXEDO-S
TUYERE-S
TWAITE-S
TWEEZE-D
TWEEZE-R
TWEEZE-S
TWELVE-S
TWIBIL-L
TWIBIL-S
TWICER-S
TWIGHT-S
TWINER-S
TWINGE-D
TWINGE-S
TWITCH-Y
TWOFER-S
TWYERE-S
TYCOON-S
S-**TYLERS**
TYLOTE-S
TYMBAL-S
TYMPAN-A
TYMPAN-I
TYMPAN-O
TYMPAN-S
TYMPAN-Y
TYPHON-S
TYPING-S
TYPIST-S
TYRANT-S
S-**TYRING**
TYSTIE-S
TZETSE-S
TZETZE-S
O-**UAKARI**
UAKARI-S
P-**UBERTY**
D-**UBIETY**
B-**UCKERS**
D-UCKERS
F-UCKERS
M-UCKERS
P-UCKERS
S-UCKERS
T-UCKERS
Y-UCKERS
B-**UDDERS**
D-UDDERS
J-UDDERS
M-UDDERS
P-UDDERS
R-UDDERS
S-UDDERS
B-**UGGING**
F-UGGING
H-UGGING
J-UGGING
L-UGGING
M-UGGING
P-UGGING
R-UGGING
S-UGGING
T-UGGING
O-**UGLIED**
O-**UGLIES**
UGLIES-T
UJAMAA-S
ULICON-S
ULIKON-S
F-**ULLAGE**
S-ULLAGE
ULLAGE-D
ULLAGE-S
B-**ULLING**
C-ULLING
D-ULLING
F-ULLING
G-ULLING
H-ULLING
L-ULLING
M-ULLING
N-ULLING
P-ULLING
W-ULLING
ULLING-S
D-**ULOSES**
D-**ULOSIS**
ULSTER-S
ULTIMA-S
ULTION-S
C-**UMBERS**
L-UMBERS
N-UMBERS
B-**UMBLES**
F-UMBLES
H-UMBLES
J-UMBLES
M-UMBLES
N-UMBLES
R-UMBLES
T-UMBLES
T-**UMBREL**
UMBREL-S
T-**UMBRIL**
UMBRIL-S
UMIACK-S
UMLAUT-S
B-**UMPING**
D-UMPING
G-UMPING
H-UMPING
J-UMPING
L-UMPING
M-UMPING
P-UMPING
R-UMPING
T-UMPING
Y-UMPING
UMPIRE-D
UMPIRE-S
T-**UNABLE**
UNAKIN-G
UNBARE-D
UNBARE-S
UNBARK-S
UNBEAR-S
S-**UNBEDS**
S-**UNBELT**
UNBELT-S
UNBEND-S
UNBIND-S
UNBITT-S
UNBOLT-S
UNBONE-D
UNBONE-S
UNBOOT-S
UNBORN-E
UNCAGE-D
UNCAGE-S
UNCAKE-D
UNCAKE-S
UNCAPE-D
UNCAPE-S
UNCART-S
UNCASE-D
UNCASE-S
J-**UNCATE**
UNCIAL-S
N-**UNCLES**
UNCLEW-S
UNCLIP-S
UNCLIP-T
UNCLOG-S
UNCOCK-S
UNCOIL-S
UNCOLT-S
UNCOPE-D
UNCOPE-S
UNCORD-S
UNCORK-S
UNCOWL-S
UNCUFF-S
UNCURB-S
UNCURL-S
UNDATE-D
UNDEAF-S
S-**UNDECK**
UNDECK-S
UNDERN-S
C-**UNDIES**
F-UNDIES
G-UNDIES
N-**UNDINE**
UNDINE-S
UNDOCK-S
UNDOER-S
UNDRAW-N
UNDRAW-S
UNEASE-S
UNEDGE-D
UNEDGE-S
UNFACT-S
F-**UNFAIR**
UNFAIR-S
UNFOLD-S
UNFOOL-S
UNFORM-S
UNFREE-D
UNFREE-S
UNFURL-S
UNGEAR-S
UNGILD-S
UNGIRD-S
UNGIRT-H
UNGLUE-D
UNGLUE-S
UNGOWN-S
UNGULA-E
UNGULA-R
UNGYVE-D
UNGYVE-S
UNHAIR-S
UNHAND-S
UNHAND-Y
UNHANG-S
UNHASP-S
S-**UNHATS**
UNHEAD-S
UNHEAL-S
UNHELE-D
UNHELE-S
UNHELM-S

UNHIVE-D
UNHIVE-S
N-**UNHOOD**
UNHOOD-S
UNHOOK-S
UNHOOP-S
UNHUSK-S
B-**UNIONS**
UNIPED-S
UNIPOD-S
UNIQUE-R
UNIQUE-S
UNISON-S
M-**UNITED**
UNITER-S
D-**UNITES**
G-UNITES
M-UNITES
B-**UNKING**
D-UNKING
F-UNKING
J-UNKING
UNKING-S
UNKINK-S
UNKNIT-S
UNKNOT-S
UNLACE-D
UNLACE-S
UNLADE-D
UNLADE-N
UNLADE-S
UNLAST-E
UNLEAD-S
G-**UNLESS**
R-UNLESS
S-UNLESS
N-**UNLIKE**
S-UNLIKE
UNLIKE-S
UNLIME-D
UNLIME-S
UNLINE-D
UNLINE-S
UNLINK-S
UNLIVE-D
UNLIVE-S
UNLOAD-S
G-**UNLOCK**
UNLOCK-S
UNLORD-S
UNLOVE-D
UNLOVE-S
UNMAKE-R
UNMAKE-S
UNMASK-S
UNMOLD-S
UNMOOR-S
UNNAIL-S
D-**UNNEST**
F-UNNEST
UNNEST-S
UNPACK-S
UNPICK-S
UNPILE-D
UNPILE-S
UNPLUG-S
UNPOPE-D
UNPOPE-S
UNPRAY-S
UNPROP-S
UNRAKE-D
UNRAKE-S
UNREAD-Y
UNREEL-S
UNREIN-S
UNREST-S
R-**UNRIGS**
UNRIPE-R
UNROBE-D
UNROBE-S
UNROLL-S
S-**UNROOF**
UNROOF-S
UNROOT-S
UNROPE-D
UNROPE-S
UNROVE-N
UNRULE-D
UNRULE-S
UNSAFE-R
UNSEAL-S
UNSEAM-S
UNSEAT-S
UNSEEL-S
UNSEEN-S
UNSELF-S
UNSELL-S
S-**UNSETS**
D-**UNSHED**
G-**UNSHIP**
N-UNSHIP
UNSHIP-S
UNSHOE-D
UNSHOE-S
G-**UNSHOT**
UNSHUT-S
UNSNAP-S
UNSOUL-S
UNSPAR-S
UNSTEP-S
UNSTOP-S
UNSTOW-S
S-**UNSUIT**
UNSUIT-S
UNSURE-D
UNSURE-R
UNTACK-S
UNTAME-D
UNTAME-S
UNTEAM-S
UNTENT-S
UNTENT-Y
UNTHAW-S
A-**UNTIES**
P-UNTIES
UNTILE-D
UNTILE-S
M-**UNTINS**
UNTOMB-S
UNTRIM-S
UNTRUE-R
UNTUCK-S
UNTUNE-D
UNTUNE-S
UNTURF-S
UNTURN-S
UNVAIL-E
UNVAIL-S
UNVEIL-S
UNWARE-S
UNWEAL-S
UNWILL-S
UNWIND-S
UNWIRE-D
UNWIRE-S
S-**UNWISE**
UNWISE-R
UNWIVE-D
UNWIVE-S
UNWORK-S
UNWOVE-N
UNWRAP-S
UNYOKE-D
UNYOKE-S
UPBEAR-S
UPBEAT-S
UPBIND-S
UPBLOW-N
UPBLOW-S
UPBOIL-S
UPBRAY-S
UPCAST-S
UPCOIL-S
UPCOME-S
UPCURL-S
UPDART-S
UPDATE-D
UPDATE-R
UPDATE-S
UPDIVE-D
UPDIVE-S
UPDRAG-S
UPDRAW-N
UPDRAW-S
UPFILL-S
UPFLOW-S
UPFOLD-S
UPFURL-S
UPGANG-S
UPGAZE-D
UPGAZE-S
UPGIRD-S
UPGROW-N
UPGROW-S
UPHANG-S
UPHAUD-S
UPHEAP-S
UPHILL-S
UPHOLD-S
E-**UPHROE**
UPHROE-S
UPHURL-S
UPKEEP-S
UPKNIT-S
UPLAND-S
UPLEAD-S
UPLEAN-S
UPLEAN-T
UPLEAP-S
UPLEAP-T
UPLIFT-S
UPLINK-S
UPLOAD-S
UPLOCK-S
UPLOOK-S
UPMAKE-R
UPMAKE-S
C-**UPPERS**
S-UPPERS
UPPILE-D
UPPILE-S
C-**UPPING**
D-UPPING
H-UPPING
P-UPPING
S-UPPING
T-UPPING
UPPING-S
UPPROP-S
UPRATE-D
UPRATE-S
UPREAR-S
UPREST-S
UPRISE-N
UPRISE-R
UPRISE-S
UPRIST-S
UPROAR-S
UPROLL-S
UPROOT-S
UPSEND-S
UPSHOT-S
UPSIDE-S
UPSOAR-S
UPSTAY-S
UPSTEP-S
UPSTIR-S
UPSWAY-S
UPTAKE-N
UPTAKE-S
UPTEAR-S
UPTICK-S
UPTILT-S
UPTIME-S
UPTOWN-S
UPTURN-S
UPWAFT-S
UPWARD-S
UPWELL-S
UPWIND-S
UPWRAP-S
URACIL-S
O-**URALIS**
URANIA-N
URANIA-S
P-**URANIC**
URANIN-S
URANYL-S
C-**URARES**
C-**URARIS**
O-URARIS
A-**URATES**
C-URATES
URBANE-R
URCHIN-S
UREASE-S
UREDIA-L
UREIDE-S
UREMIA-S
M-**URENAS**
URETER-S
S-**URGENT**
T-URGENT
B-**URGERS**
P-URGERS
S-URGERS
G-**URGING**
P-URGING
S-URGING
URGING-S
B-**URIALS**
URINAL-S
M-**URINES**
P-URINES
C-**URITES**
URNFUL-S
B-**URNING**
D-URNING
G-URNING
T-URNING
URNING-S
UROPOD-S
URTEXT-S
URTICA-S
USAGER-S
USANCE-S
M-**USEFUL**
B-**USHERS**
G-USHERS
H-USHERS
L-USHERS
M-USHERS
P-USHERS
R-USHERS
USTION-S
USURER-S
USURES-S
USWARD-S
M-**UTASES**
C-**UTISES**
O-**UTMOST**
UTMOST-S
UTOPIA-N
UTOPIA-S
B-**UTTERS**
C-UTTERS
G-UTTERS
M-UTTERS
N-UTTERS
P-UTTERS
R-UTTERS
UVULAR-S
VACATE-D
VACATE-S
VACUUM-S
E-**VADING**
VAGINA-E
VAGINA-L
VAGINA-S
VAGUES-T
VAHINE-S
A-**VAILED**
VAKEEL-S
VALETA-S
VALETE-D
VALETE-S
VALINE-S
VALISE-S
VALKYR-S
VALLAR-Y
VALLEY-S
VALLUM-S
VALOUR-S
VALUER-S
VALUTA-S
VAMOSE-D
VAMOSE-S
VAMPER-S
VANDAL-S
E-**VANISH**
VANNER-S
VAPOUR-S
VAPOUR-Y
VARECH-S
VARIER-S
O-**VARIES**
VARLET-S
VAROOM-S
VARROA-S
VARVEL-S
VASSAL-S
VATFUL-S
VATTER-S
VAUDOO-S
VAUNCE-D
VAUNCE-S
A-**VAUNTS**
VAWARD-S
VEALER-S
VECTOR-S
VEEJAY-S
VEEPEE-S
VEGGIE-S
VEILER-S
VEINER-S
VELATE-D
VELETA-S
VELLET-S
VELLON-S
VELLUM-S
VELOUR-S
VELURE-D
VELURE-S
VELVET-S
VELVET-Y
VENDEE-S
VENDER-S
VENDIS-S
VENDOR-S
VENDUE-S
VENEER-S
VENEWE-S
A-**VENGED**
A-**VENGER**
VENGER-S
A-**VENGES**
VENINE-S
VENIRE-S
VENITE-S
VENNEL-S
E-**VENTED**
E-**VENTER**
VENTER-S
VENTIL-S
A-**VENTRE**
VENTRE-D
VENTRE-S
A-**VENUES**
VENULE-S
VERBAL-S
O-**VERBID**
VERBID-S
VERDET-S
VERDIN-S
VERDIT-E
VERDIT-S
VERGER-S
VERISM-O
VERISM-S
VERIST-S
VERITE-S
VERMIL-S
VERMIL-Y
VERMIN-S
VERMIN-Y
VERREL-S
VERSAL-S
VERSER-S
O-**VERSET**
VERSET-S
VERSIN-E
VERSIN-G
VERSIN-S
VERSTE-S
A-**VERTED**
E-VERTED
VERTUE-S
VERVEL-S
VERVEN-S
VERVET-S
VESICA-E
VESICA-L
VESPER-S
VESPID-S
VESSEL-S
VESTAL-S
VESTEE-S
K-**VETCHY**
VETOER-S
VEXING-S

VIATIC-A
A-**VIATOR**
VIATOR-S
VIBIST-S
VIBRIO-N
VIBRIO-S
VICTIM-S
E-**VICTOR**
VICTOR-S
VICTOR-Y
VICUNA-S
VIDAME-S
VIELLE-S
VIEWER-S
VIGORO-S
VIGOUR-S
VIHARA-S
VIKING-S
E-**VILEST**
VILLAN-S
VILLAN-Y
VIMANA-S
VIMINA-L
VIOLER-S
VIOLET-S
VIOLIN-S
VIRAGO-S
VIRGER-S
VIRGIN-S
VIRINO-S
VIRION-S
VIROID-S
VIROSE-S
VIRTUE-S
VISAGE-D
VISAGE-S
VISARD-S
VISCIN-S
VISCUM-S
VISIER-S
VISILE-S
A-**VISING**
VISION-S
VISITE-D
VISITE-E
VISITE-R
VISITE-S
VISUAL-S
VITRIC-S
VITTLE-D
VITTLE-S
VIVACE-S
VIZARD-S
VIZIER-S
VIZSLA-S
VIZZIE-D
VIZZIE-S
VOCULE-S
VODOUN-S
VOGUER-S
VOICER-S
A-**VOIDED**
VOIDEE-S
A-**VOIDER**
VOIDER-S
VOLANT-E
VOLLEY-S
VOLOST-S
VOLUME-D
VOLUME-S
E-**VOLUTE**
VOLUTE-D
VOLUTE-S
E-**VOLVED**
E-**VOLVES**

VOMICA-E
VOMICA-S
VOMITO-S
VOODOO-S
VOTEEN-S
VOUDOU-S
VOULGE-S
A-**VOWERS**
A-**VOWING**
VOYAGE-D
VOYAGE-R
VOYAGE-S
VOYEUR-S
VULCAN-S
VULGAR-S
WABAIN-S
WABBLE-D
WABBLE-R
WABBLE-S
WABOOM-S
WACKER-S
WADDER-S
WADDIE-D
WADDIE-S
S-**WADDLE**
T-WADDLE
WADDLE-D
WADDLE-R
WADDLE-S
T-**WADDLY**
WADING-S
WADMAL-S
WADMEL-S
WADMOL-L
WADMOL-S
WADSET-S
WADSET-T
WAFFIE-S
WAFFLE-D
WAFFLE-R
WAFFLE-S
WAFTER-S
S-**WAGERS**
S-**WAGGED**
S-**WAGGER**
WAGGER-S
WAGGER-Y
WAGGLE-D
WAGGLE-S
WAGGON-S
S-**WAGING**
WAHINE-S
WAILER-S
A-**WAITED**
A-**WAITER**
WAITER-S
T-**WAITES**
WAIVER-S
WAKANE-S
A-**WAKENS**
WAKIKI-S
A-**WAKING**
WAKING-S
S-**WALIER**
WALIES-T
S-**WALING**
WALISE-S
WALKER-S
WALKUP-S
WALLAH-S
WALLER-S
S-**WALLET**
WALLET-S
WALLIE-R
WALLIE-S

WALLOP-S
S-**WALLOW**
WALLOW-S
WALNUT-S
WAMBLE-D
WAMBLE-S
WAMPEE-S
WAMPUM-S
WANDER-S
WANDOO-S
WANGAN-S
T-**WANGLE**
WANGLE-D
WANGLE-R
WANGLE-S
WANGUN-S
WANING-S
WANION-S
S-**WANKED**
S-**WANKER**
WANKER-S
S-**WANNED**
WANTER-S
WANTON-S
WAPITI-S
S-**WAPPED**
S-**WAPPER**
WAPPER-S
WARBLE-D
WARBLE-R
WARBLE-S
A-**WARDED**
S-WARDED
WARDEN-S
A-**WARDER**
WARDER-S
WARDOG-S
S-**WARMED**
S-**WARMER**
WARMER-S
WARMTH-S
WARMUP-S
A-**WARNED**
WARNER-S
WARPER-S
WARRAN-D
WARRAN-S
WARRAN-T
WARRAY-S
WARREN-S
WARREY-S
WARSAW-S
WARSLE-D
WARSLE-R
WARSLE-S
WASABI-S
S-**WASHED**
S-**WASHER**
WASHER-S
WASHER-Y
S-**WASHES**
WASHUP-S
WASPIE-R
WASPIE-S
WASTEL-S
WASTER-S
WASTER-Y
WATAPE-S
S-**WATTER**
T-**WATTLE**
WATTLE-D
WATTLE-S
WAUCHT-S
WAUGHT-S
WAUKER-S

WAVIES-T
WAVING-S
WAXING-S
S-**WAYING**
WAYLAY-S
WEAKEN-S
WEALTH-S
WEALTH-Y
WEANEL-S
WEANER-S
WEAPON-S
S-**WEARER**
WEARER-S
WEASEL-S
WEASEL-Y
WEASON-S
WEAVER-S
WEAZEN-S
WEDDER-S
WEDELN-S
WEDGIE-R
WEDGIE-S
WEEDER-S
WEEDER-Y
S-**WEEING**
WEENIE-R
WEENIE-S
S-**WEEPER**
WEEPER-S
WEEPIE-R
WEEPIE-S
S-**WEETED**
T-WEETED
S-**WEETEN**
S-**WEETER**
T-WEETER
WEEVER-S
WEEVIL-S
WEEVIL-Y
WEEWEE-D
WEEWEE-S
WEIGHT-S
WEIGHT-Y
WEINER-S
WEIRDO-S
WELDER-S
WELDOR-S
WELKIN-G
WELKIN-S
D-**WELLED**
S-WELLED
WELLIE-S
S-**WELTED**
S-**WELTER**
WELTER-S
WESAND-S
WESKIT-S
WESTER-N
WESTER-S
WETHER-S
WETTER-S
WEZAND-S
WHACKO-S
WHALER-S
WHALER-Y
WHAMMO-S
WHARVE-S
WHEECH-S
A-**WHEELS**
WHEESH-T
WHEEZE-D
WHEEZE-R
WHEEZE-S
WHENCE-S
WHERES-O

WHERVE-S
WHEUGH-S
WHIDAH-S
WHINER-S
WHINGE-D
WHINGE-R
WHINGE-S
WHISHT-S
WHITEN-S
WHITES-T
WHITEY-S
WHYDAH-S
WICCAN-S
WICKED-S
WICKEN-S
WICKER-S
WICKET-S
WIDDER-S
WIDDIE-S
T-**WIDDLE**
WIDDLE-D
WIDDLE-S
WIDGET-S
WIDGIE-S
WIENER-S
WIENIE-S
WIGEON-S
S-**WIGGED**
T-WIGGED
WIGGLE-D
WIGGLE-R
WIGGLE-S
T-**WIGHTS**
WIGLET-S
WIGWAG-S
WIGWAM-S
WIKIUP-S
WILDER-S
S-**WILLED**
T-WILLED
S-**WILLER**
WILLER-S
WILLET-S
WILLEY-S
WILLIE-D
WILLIE-S
WILLOW-S
WILLOW-Y
T-**WILTED**
WILTJA-S
WIMBLE-D
WIMBLE-S
WIMPLE-D
WIMPLE-S
WINCER-S
WINCEY-S
WINDAC-S
WINDER-S
D-**WINDLE**
S-WINDLE
WINDLE-D
WINDLE-S
WINDOW-S
WINDUP-S
S-**WINERY**
S-**WINGED**
T-WINGED
S-**WINGER**
WINGER-S
S-**WINGES**
T-WINGES
T-**WINIER**
D-**WINING**
T-WINING
S-**WINISH**

S-**WINKED**
T-WINKED
WINKER-S
T-**WINKLE**
WINKLE-D
WINKLE-R
WINKLE-S
T-**WINNED**
WINNER-S
WINNLE-S
WINNOW-S
WINSEY-S
T-**WINTER**
WINTER-S
WINTER-Y
WINTLE-D
WINTLE-S
S-**WIPERS**
S-**WIPING**
WIPING-S
WIPPEN-S
T-**WIRING**
WIRING-S
WISARD-S
WISDOM-S
WISENT-S
S-**WISHED**
S-**WISHER**
WISHER-S
S-**WISHES**
WISKET-S
S-**WISSES**
T-**WISTED**
S-**WITCHY**
T-WITCHY
WITGAT-S
S-**WITHER**
WITHER-S
WITHIN-G
WITHIN-S
WITNEY-S
T-**WITTED**
T-**WITTER**
WITTER-S
WITTOL-S
WIVERN-S
S-**WIVING**
WIZARD-S
WIZIER-S
WIZZEN-S
WOBBLE-D
WOBBLE-R
WOBBLE-S
WOGGLE-S
WOLFER-S
WOLVER-S
WOMBAT-S
WOMERA-S
WONDER-S
WONING-S
WONNER-S
WONTON-S
WOOBUT-S
WOODIE-R
WOODIE-S
WOOFER-S
WOOING-S
WOOLEN-S
WOOLER-S
WOOLIE-R
WOOLIE-S
S-**WOONED**
WOOPIE-S
WOOSEL-L
WOOSEL-S

S-**WOPPED**
S-**WORDED**
WORKER-S
WORKUP-S
WORMER-S
WORMER-Y
WORMIL-S
WORRAL-S
WORREL-S
WORRIT-S
WORSEN-S
WORSET-S
WORTLE-S
S-**WOTTED**
WOUBIT-S
WOULDS-T
S-**WOUNDS**
WOWSER-S
WRAITH-S
WRASSE-S
WRAXLE-D
WRAXLE-S
WREATH-E
WREATH-S
WREATH-Y
WRETHE-D
WRETHE-S
O-**WRIEST**
WRIGHT-S
WRITER-S
WRITHE-D
WRITHE-N
WRITHE-R
WRITHE-S
WROATH-S
WUNNER-S
WURLEY-S
WURZEL-S
WUTHER-S
WUZZLE-D
WUZZLE-S
WYVERN-S
XEROMA-S
XYLENE-S
XYLOMA-S
XYLOSE-S
XYSTER-S
YABBER-S
YABBIE-S
YACKER-S
N-**YAFFED**
YAFFLE-S
YAGGER-S
YAKKER-S
YAMMER-S
YANKER-S
YANKIE-S
YANQUI-S
YANTRA-S
YAOURT-S
YAPOCK-S
YAPPER-S
YAPPIE-R
YAPPIE-S
YAQONA-S
YARNER-S
YARPHA-S
YARROW-S
YASMAK-S
YATTER-S
YAUPER-S
YAUPON-S
YAUTIA-S
YAWNER-S
YAWPER-S
YEELIN-S
YELLER-S
YELLOW-S
YELLOW-Y
YELPER-S
O-**YESSES**
D-**YESTER**
YESTER-N
YICKER-S
YIKKER-S
YIPPER-S
YIPPIE-S
G-**YMPING**
YNAMBU-S
YODLER-S
YOGINI-S
YOGISM-S
YOGURT-S
YOJANA-S
YOKING-S
YONDER-S
YONKER-S
YOPPER-S
YORKER-S
YORKIE-S
YOUPON-S
YOWLER-S
YOWLEY-S
YSHEND-S
YTTRIA-S
YUCKER-S
YUKATA-S
YUMPIE-S
YUPPIE-S
ZABETA-S
T-**ZADDIK**
ZADDIK-S
ZAFFAR-S
ZAFFER-S
ZAFFIR-S
ZAFFRE-S
ZAIKAI-S
ZAMANG-S
ZAMBUK-S
ZANANA-S
ZANDER-S
ZANIES-T
ZAPPER-S
ZARAPE-S
ZAREBA-S
ZARIBA-S
ZARNEC-S
ZEALOT-S
ZEATIN-S
ZEBECK-S
ZEBRAS-S
ZECHIN-S
ZELANT-S
ZENANA-S
ZENDIK-S
ZENITH-S
ZEPHYR-S
ZEREBA-S
ZERIBA-S
ZESTER-S
ZEUGMA-S
ZIBETH-S
ZIGZAG-S
ZILLAH-S
ZIMMER-S
ZINGEL-S
ZINGER-S
ZINNIA-S
ZIPPER-S
ZIRCON-S
ZITHER-N
ZITHER-S
ZIZZLE-D
ZIZZLE-S
ZOARIA-L
ZODIAC-S
ZOMBIE-S
O-**ZONATE**
ZONATE-D
ZONING-S
ZONULA-E
ZONULA-R
ZONULA-S
ZONULE-S
ZONULE-T
ZONURE-S
ZOOZOO-S
ZORINO-S
ZOSTER-S
ZOUAVE-S
ZOYSIA-S
ZYDECO-S
ZYGOMA-S
ZYGOSE-S
ZYGOTE-S
ZYMASE-S
A-**ZYMITE**
ZYMITE-S
ZYMOME-S
ZYTHUM-S

7-LETTER WORD HOOKS: extensible words only

ABACTOR-S
ABALONE-S
ABANDON-S
ABATURE-S
ABDOMEN-S
ABETTAL-S
ABETTER-S
ABETTOR-S
ABFARAD-S
ABHENRY-S
ABIDING-S
ABIGAIL-S
L-**ABILITY**
ABJOINT-S
ABJURER-S
ABLATOR-S
ABLEISM-S
C-**ABLINGS**
F-ABLINGS
T-ABLINGS
ABLUENT-S
ABOMASA-L
ABORTEE-S
ABORTER-S
ABOULIA-S
ABRADER-S
ABREACT-S
ABRIDGE-D
ABRIDGE-R
ABRIDGE-S
ABROOKE-D
ABROOKE-S
ABROSIA-S
ABSCIND-S
ABSCISE-D
ABSCISE-S
ABSCISS-A
ABSCISS-E
ABSCOND-S
ABSENCE-S
ABSINTH-E
ABSINTH-S
ABSOLVE-D
ABSOLVE-R
ABSOLVE-S
ABSTAIN-S
ABTHANE-S
ABUSAGE-S
ABUSION-S
ABUTTAL-S
ABUTTER-S
ACADEME-S
ACALEPH-E
ACALEPH-S
ACANTHA-S
ACANTHI-N
ACAPNIA-S
ACARINE-S
ACATOUR-S
ACCEDER-S
ACCIDIA-S
ACCIDIE-S
ACCINGE-D
ACCINGE-S
ACCLAIM-S
ACCOAST-S
ACCOMPT-S
ACCOUNT-S
ACCOURT-S
ACCRETE-D
ACCRETE-S
ACCRUAL-S
ACCURSE-D
ACCURSE-S
ACCUSAL-S
ACCUSER-S
ACEQUIA-S
L-**ACERATE**
M-ACERATE
ACERATE-D
ACEROLA-S
ACETATE-D
ACETATE-S
ACETONE-S
ACHARYA-S
ACHENIA-L
ACHIEVE-D
ACHIEVE-R
ACHIEVE-S
ACHIOTE-S
ACHOLIA-S
ACICULA-E
ACICULA-R
ACICULA-S
ACKNOWN-E
T-**ACNODES**
ACOLYTE-S
ACOLYTH-S
T-**ACONITE**
ACONITE-S
ACOUCHI-S
ACQUEST-S
ACQUIRE-D
ACQUIRE-R
ACQUIRE-S
ACQUIST-S
ACQUITE-S
ACRASIA-S
ACRASIN-S
ACREAGE-S
ACRIDIN-E
ACRIDIN-S
ACROBAT-S
ACROGEN-S
ACROMIA-L
ACRONYM-S
ACROTER-S
ACRYLIC-S
ACTINIA-E
ACTINIA-N
ACTINIA-S
ACTINON-S
F-**ACTIONS**
P-ACTIONS
T-ACTIONS
ACTRESS-Y
ACTUATE-D
ACTUATE-S
F-**ACTURES**
ACUSHLA-S
ACYLATE-D
ACYLATE-S
ACYLOIN-S
ADAMANT-S
ADAPTER-S
ADAPTOR-S
D-**ADDLING**
F-ADDLING
P-ADDLING
R-ADDLING
S-ADDLING
W-ADDLING
ADDUCER-S
ADENINE-S
ADENOID-S
ADENOMA-S
ADERMIN-S
ADHARMA-S
ADHERER-S
ADHIBIT-S
ADIPOSE-S
ADJOINT-S
ADJOURN-S
ADJUDGE-D
ADJUDGE-S
ADJUNCT-S
ADJURER-S
ADJUROR-S
B-**ADLANDS**
ADMIRAL-S
ADMIRER-S
ADONISE-D
ADONISE-S
ADONIZE-D
ADONIZE-S
ADOPTEE-S
ADOPTER-S
ADORNER-S
ADRENAL-S
R-**ADULATE**
ADULATE-D
ADULATE-S
T-**ADVANCE**
ADVANCE-D
ADVANCE-R
ADVANCE-S
ADVERSE-R
ADVISEE-S
ADVISER-S
ADVISOR-S
ADVISOR-Y
AECIDIA-L
AERATOR-S
AEROBIC-S
AEROGEL-S
AEROSAT-S
AEROSOL-S
AFFAIRE-S
AFFEARE-D
AFFEARE-S
AFFIANT-S
AFFICHE-S
AFFIXER-S
AFFLICT-S
AFFOORD-S
AFFORCE-D
AFFORCE-S
AFFRONT-E
AFFRONT-S
AFGHANI-S
AGACANT-E
AGAMETE-S
AGAMOID-S
AGAROSE-S
AGATIZE-D
AGATIZE-S
AGELAST-S
W-**AGELESS**
AGENDUM-S
AGENIZE-D
AGENIZE-S
H-**AGGADIC**
AGGRACE-D
AGGRACE-S
AGGRADE-D
AGGRADE-S
AGGRATE-D
AGGRATE-S
V-**AGILITY**
AGINNER-S
M-**AGISTER**
AGISTER-S
AGISTOR-S
AGITATE-D
AGITATE-S
AGITATO-R
AGLYCON-E
AGLYCON-S
M-**AGNATES**
AGNOMEN-S
AGNOSIA-S
AGONISE-D
AGONISE-S
AGONIST-S
AGONIZE-D
AGONIZE-S
AGRAFFE-S
AIDANCE-S
M-**AIDLESS**
AILANTO-S
T-**AILERON**
AILERON-S
AILETTE-S
B-**AILMENT**
AILMENT-S
N-**AINSELL**

AINSELL-S
AIRBASE-S
AIRBOAT-S
AIRCREW-S
AIRDATE-S
AIRDROP-S
AIRFARE-S
AIRFLOW-S
AIRFOIL-S
AIRGLOW-S
AIRHEAD-S
AIRHOLE-S
H-AIRIEST
L-AIRIEST
V-AIRIEST
F-AIRINGS
P-AIRINGS
H-AIRLESS
AIRLIFT-S
H-AIRLIKE
H-AIRLINE
AIRLINE-R
AIRLINE-S
H-AIRLOCK
AIRLOCK-S
AIRMAIL-S
AIRPARK-S
AIRPLAY-S
AIRPORT-S
AIRPOST-S
AIRSHED-S
AIRSHIP-S
AIRSIDE-S
AIRSTOP-S
AIRTIME-S
AIRWARD-S
AIRWAVE-S
F-AIRWAYS
P-AIRWISE
AISLING-S
AJUTAGE-S
AKVAVIT-S
ALAMEDA-S
ALAMODE-S
ALANINE-S
ALANNAH-S
ALASTOR-S
H-ALATION
ALATION-S
H-ALBERTS
ALBIZIA-S
ALBUMEN-S
ALBUMIN-S
F-ALCADES
ALCAIDE-S
ALCALDE-S
ALCAYDE-S
ALCAZAR-S
ALCHERA-S
ALCOHOL-S
ALCOPOP-S
ALCORZA-S
ALECOST-S
ALEMBIC-S
ALENCON-S
ALEPINE-S
ALERION-S
ALEURON-E
ALEURON-S
K-ALEWIFE
ALEXINE-S
ALFALFA-S
ALFAQUI-N
ALFAQUI-S
ALFORJA-S

ALGEBRA-S
ALGESIA-S
ALICANT-S
ALIDADE-S
ALIENEE-S
ALIENER-S
ALIENOR-S
P-ALIFORM
M-ALIGNED
M-ALIGNER
ALIGNER-S
ALIMENT-S
P-ALIMONY
T-ALIPEDS
ALIQUOT-S
ALIZARI-N
ALIZARI-S
ALKALIN-E
ALKALIS-E
ALKANET-S
ALLAYER-S
ALLEDGE-D
ALLEDGE-S
ALLEGER-S
ALLEGGE-D
ALLEGGE-S
ALLEGRO-S
W-ALLEYED
ALLHEAL-S
ALLICIN-S
G-ALLISES
B-ALLIUMS
G-ALLIUMS
P-ALLIUMS
T-ALLNESS
ALLOBAR-S
ALLODIA-L
ALLONGE-S
ALLONYM-S
ALLOVER-S
F-ALLOWED
G-ALLOWED
H-ALLOWED
S-ALLOWED
T-ALLOWED
W-ALLOWED
ALLOXAN-S
ALLSEED-S
ALLURER-S
ALLUVIA-L
D-ALLYING
G-ALLYING
R-ALLYING
S-ALLYING
T-ALLYING
ALMANAC-S
ALMEMAR-S
ALMIRAH-S
ALMONER-S
ALNAGER-S
ALODIUM-S
ALOETIC-S
ALPHORN-S
F-ALTERED
H-ALTERED
P-ALTERED
F-ALTERER
P-ALTERER
ALTERER-S
ALTERNE-S
ALTESSE-S
ALTEZZA-S
ALTHAEA-S
ALTHORN-S
ALTOIST-S

ALUMINA-S
ALUMINE-S
ALUMIUM-S
ALUNITE-S
ALVEOLE-S
ALYSSUM-S
AMALGAM-S
AMANITA-S
AMARANT-H
AMARANT-S
AMASSER-S
C-AMASSES
AMATEUR-S
AMATION-S
C-AMBERED
AMBIENT-S
G-AMBLERS
R-AMBLERS
G-AMBLING
H-AMBLING
L-AMBLING
R-AMBLING
W-AMBLING
AMBLING-S
AMBOINA-S
H-AMBONES
J-AMBONES
AMBOYNA-S
AMBROID-S
AMBSACE-S
C-AMELIAS
AMENAGE-D
AMENAGE-S
AMENDER-S
AMENTIA-S
R-AMENTUM
AMERCER-S
AMESACE-S
AMIDASE-S
AMIDINE-S
AMIDONE-S
AMILDAR-S
AMIRATE-S
AMMETER-S
AMMIRAL-S
AMMONAL-S
AMMONIA-C
AMMONIA-S
AMNESIA-C
AMNESIA-S
AMNESIC-S
AMNIOTE-S
AMORISM-S
AMORIST-S
AMOROSA-S
AMOROSO-S
AMOSITE-S
AMOTION-S
AMPHORA-E
AMPHORA-L
AMPHORA-S
AMPOULE-S
AMPULLA-E
AMPULLA-R
AMPUTEE-S
AMREETA-S
AMTRACK-S
AMYGDAL-A
AMYGDAL-E
AMYGDAL-S
AMYLASE-S
AMYLENE-S
AMYLOID-S
AMYLOSE-S
ANAEMIA-S

ANAGOGE-S
ANAGRAM-S
ANALGIA-S
B-ANALITY
ANALYSE-D
ANALYSE-R
ANALYSE-S
ANALYST-S
ANALYZE-D
ANALYZE-R
ANALYZE-S
ANAPEST-S
ANAPHOR-A
ANAPHOR-S
ANATASE-S
ANCHUSA-S
ANCIENT-S
ANCILLA-E
ANCILLA-S
ANDANTE-S
ANDIRON-S
ANDROID-S
ANDVILE-S
ANELACE-S
P-ANELING
ANEMONE-S
ANERGIA-S
ANEROID-S
ANETHOL-E
ANETHOL-S
ANEURIN-S
ANGAKOK-S
ANGARIA-S
ANGEKOK-S
ANGELIC-A
D-ANGERED
ANGIOMA-S
D-ANGLERS
J-ANGLERS
M-ANGLERS
T-ANGLERS
W-ANGLERS
C-ANGLING
D-ANGLING
F-ANGLING
G-ANGLING
J-ANGLING
M-ANGLING
T-ANGLING
W-ANGLING
ANGLING-S
ANGLIST-S
ANGRIES-T
S-ANGUINE
L-ANGUISH
ANHINGA-S
ANILINE-S
ANIMATE-D
ANIMATE-R
ANIMATE-S
ANIMATO-R
ANIMISM-S
ANIMIST-S
ANISEED-S
ANISOLE-S
F-ANKLING
R-ANKLING
ANKLONG-S
ANKLUNG-S
T-ANNATES
ANNATTA-S
ANNATTO-S
ANNELID-S
ANNICUT-S
T-ANNOYED

ANNOYER-S
C-ANNULAR
ANNULAR-S
ANNULET-S
ANODISE-D
ANODISE-S
ANODIZE-D
ANODIZE-S
ANODYNE-S
ANOLYTE-S
ANONYMA-S
ANOPSIA-S
ANOSMIA-S
ANTACID-S
T-ANTARAS
ANTBEAR-S
ANTBIRD-S
ANTEFIX-A
ANTENNA-E
ANTENNA-L
ANTENNA-S
P-ANTHERS
W-ANTHILL
ANTHILL-S
ANTICKE-D
ANTIENT-S
ANTIGEN-E
ANTIGEN-S
ANTILOG-S
ANTILOG-Y
B-ANTINGS
C-ANTINGS
P-ANTINGS
R-ANTINGS
W-ANTINGS
ANTIQUE-D
ANTIQUE-R
ANTIQUE-S
P-ANTLERS
ANTLION-S
ANTONYM-S
ANTONYM-Y
T-ANTRUMS
APADANA-S
APAGOGE-S
APANAGE-D
APANAGE-S
APAREJO-S
APATITE-S
APEHOOD-S
T-APELIKE
APEPSIA-S
J-APERIES
N-APERIES
APHAGIA-S
APHASIA-C
APHASIA-S
APHASIC-S
APHELIA-N
R-APHIDES
APHONIA-S
APHONIC-S
APLANAT-S
APLASIA-S
H-APLITES
APOCARP-S
APOCARP-Y
APOCOPE-S
APOLUNE-S
APOMICT-S
APOPLEX-Y
APOSTIL-S
APOSTLE-S
APOTHEM-S
APPARAT-S

APPAREL-S
APPEASE-D
APPEASE-R
APPEASE-S
APPERIL-L
APPERIL-S
APPLAUD-S
APPLIER-S
APPOINT-S
R-APPORTS
APPOSER-S
APPRISE-D
APPRISE-R
APPRISE-S
APPRIZE-D
APPRIZE-R
APPRIZE-S
APPROOF-S
APPROVE-D
APPROVE-R
APPROVE-S
APPULSE-S
APRAXIA-S
APRICOT-S
C-APSIDAL
R-APTNESS
APYRASE-S
AQUAFER-S
AQUARIA-L
AQUARIA-N
AQUATIC-S
AQUAVIT-S
AQUIFER-S
AQUILON-S
ARABESK-S
ARABICA-S
C-ARABINS
ARABISE-D
ARABISE-S
ARABIZE-D
ARABIZE-S
P-ARABLES
ARANEID-S
ARAROBA-S
ARBITER-S
ARBLAST-S
H-ARBORED
ARBORET-A
ARBORET-S
H-ARBOURS
ARCADIA-N
ARCADIA-S
ARCANUM-S
M-ARCHERS
ARCHINE-S
M-ARCHING
P-ARCHING
ARCHING-S
ARCHIVE-D
ARCHIVE-S
ARCHLET-S
ARCHWAY-S
F-ARCINGS
ARCKING-S
ARCSINE-S
ARCTIID-S
ARCUATE-D
ARDRIGH-S
AREAWAY-S
R-AREFIED
R-AREFIES
ARENITE-S
M-ARGENTS
G-ARGLING
S-ARGUSES

ARGYRIA-S
ARIETTA-S
ARIETTE-S
G-**ARISHES**
M-ARISHES
P-ARISHES
ARMBAND-S
ARMHOLE-S
ARMIGER-O
ARMIGER-S
ARMILLA-E
ARMILLA-S
F-**ARMINGS**
W-ARMINGS
H-**ARMLESS**
ARMLOAD-S
ARMLOCK-S
ARMOIRE-S
ARMORER-S
ARMREST-S
ARNATTO-S
ARNOTTO-S
C-**AROUSAL**
AROUSAL-S
C-**AROUSED**
C-**AROUSER**
AROUSER-S
C-**AROUSES**
P-**ARPENTS**
B-**ARRACKS**
C-ARRACKS
D-**ARRAIGN**
ARRAIGN-S
ARRANGE-D
ARRANGE-R
ARRANGE-S
N-**ARRASES**
T-ARRASES
ARRAYAL-S
W-**ARRAYED**
ARRAYER-S
ARREEDE-S
C-**ARRIAGE**
M-ARRIAGE
ARRIAGE-S
ARRIERO-S
ARRIVAL-S
ARRIVER-S
F-**ARROWED**
H-ARROWED
M-ARROWED
N-ARROWED
T-ARROWED
ARSENAL-S
ARSENIC-S
ARSHEEN-S
ARSHINE-S
P-**ARTICLE**
ARTICLE-D
ARTICLE-S
T-**ARTIEST**
W-ARTIEST
B-**ARTISAN**
P-ARTISAN
ARTISAN-S
ARTISTE-S
W-**ARTLESS**
ARTSIES-T
P-**ARTWORK**
ARTWORK-S
ARUGOLA-S
ARUGULA-S
H-**ARUSPEX**
ASCARID-S
ASCETIC-S
ASCIDIA-N
ASCRIBE-D
ASCRIBE-S
ASEPTIC-S
ASHFALL-S
D-**ASHIEST**
H-ASHIEST
M-ASHIEST
W-ASHIEST
B-**ASHLESS**
C-ASHLESS
ASHRAMA-S
ASHTRAY-S
ASINICO-S
ASKANCE-D
ASKANCE-S
G-**ASKINGS**
M-ASKINGS
T-ASKINGS
ASPERGE-D
ASPERGE-R
ASPERGE-S
ASPERSE-D
ASPERSE-R
ASPERSE-S
ASPHALT-S
ASPIRER-S
ASPIRIN-G
ASPIRIN-S
J-**ASPISES**
ASSAGAI-S
V-**ASSAILS**
W-ASSAILS
ASSAULT-S
ASSAYER-S
ASSEGAI-S
ASSEVER-S
ASSHOLE-S
ASSIEGE-D
ASSIEGE-S
B-**ASSISTS**
ASSIZER-S
ASSUAGE-D
ASSUAGE-S
ASSUMER-S
ASSURED-S
ASSURER-S
ASSUROR-S
T-**ASSWAGE**
ASSWAGE-D
ASSWAGE-S
C-**ASTABLE**
T-ASTABLE
W-ASTABLE
ASTASIA-S
ASTATKI-S
C-**ASTEISM**
ASTEISM-S
ASTERIA-S
ASTERID-S
ASTHORE-S
ASTILBE-S
ASTOUND-S
ASTRICT-S
ASTROID-S
ATABRIN-S
Y-**ATAGHAN**
ATAGHAN-S
ATALAYA-S
ATAVISM-S
ATAVIST-S
ATEBRIN-S
ATELIER-S
ATEMOYA-S
ATHANOR-S
ATHEISE-D
ATHEISE-S
ATHEISM-S
ATHEIST-S
ATHEIZE-D
ATHEIZE-S
ATHLETA-S
ATHLETE-S
ATHODYD-S
ATISHOO-S
ATOMISE-D
ATOMISE-R
ATOMISE-S
ATOMISM-S
ATOMIST-S
ATOMIZE-D
ATOMIZE-R
ATOMIZE-S
B-**ATONING**
ATRESIA-S
N-**ATRIUMS**
ATROPIA-S
ATROPIN-E
ATROPIN-S
ATTACHE-D
ATTACHE-R
ATTACHE-S
ATTAINT-S
ATTEMPT-S
ATTRACT-S
R-**ATTRAPS**
ATTRIST-S
ATTRITE-D
ATTRITE-S
ATTUITE-D
ATTUITE-S
AUBERGE-S
AUCTION-S
AUDIBLE-S
AUDIENT-S
AUDITOR-S
AUDITOR-Y
AUFGABE-S
AUGMENT-S
AUGURER-S
AUGUSTE-R
AUGUSTE-S
C-**AULDEST**
AULNAGE-R
AULNAGE-S
D-**AUNTERS**
H-AUNTERS
S-AUNTERS
T-AUNTERS
V-AUNTERS
J-**AUNTIES**
L-**AUREATE**
AURELIA-N
AURELIA-S
AUREOLA-E
AUREOLA-S
AUREOLE-D
AUREOLE-S
AURICLE-D
AURICLE-S
AUSFORM-S
AUSPICE-S
AUSTERE-R
AUSTRAL-S
H-**AUTEURS**
AUTOCAR-P
AUTOCAR-S
AUTOCUE-S
AUTOMAT-A
AUTOMAT-E
AUTOMAT-S
T-**AUTONYM**
AUTONYM-S
AUTOVAC-S
AUXETIC-S
AVARICE-S
AVELLAN-E
AVENGER-S
AVENTRE-D
AVENTRE-S
AVERAGE-D
AVERAGE-S
AVIATOR-S
AVIETTE-S
AVIONIC-S
AVOCADO-S
AVODIRE-S
AVOIDER-S
AWAITER-S
AWAKING-S
AWARDEE-S
AWARDER-S
L-**AWFULLY**
AWLBIRD-S
AWLWORT-S
F-**AWNIEST**
L-AWNIEST
T-AWNIEST
Y-AWNIEST
D-**AWNINGS**
F-AWNINGS
Y-AWNINGS
M-**AXILLAE**
AXILLAR-S
AXILLAR-Y
M-**AXILLAS**
AXINITE-S
AXOLOTL-S
AXONEME-S
N-**AYWORDS**
AZIMUTH-S
AZOTISE-D
AZOTISE-S
AZOTIZE-D
AZOTIZE-S
AZULEJO-S
AZURINE-S
L-**AZURITE**
AZURITE-S
AZYMITE-S
BAALISM-S
BABASSU-S
BABBITT-S
BABBLER-S
BABESIA-S
BABICHE-S
BABUCHE-S
BABUDOM-S
BABUISM-S
BACALAO-S
BACCARA-S
BACCARA-T
BACCATE-D
BACKBIT-E
BACKFIT-S
BACKHOE-S
BACKING-S
BACKLOG-S
BACKLOT-S
BACKOUT-S
BACKPAY-S
BACKSAW-S
BACKSET-S
BACKSEY-S
BACLAVA-S
BACONER-S
BACULUM-S
BADLAND-S
BAFFLER-S
BAGARRE-S
BAGASSE-S
BAGGAGE-S
BAGGIES-T
BAGGING-S
BAGPIPE-R
BAGPIPE-S
BAGWORM-S
BAHADUR-S
BAILIFF-S
BAILLIE-S
BAILOUT-S
BAINITE-S
BAITING-S
BAKLAVA-S
BAKLAWA-S
BALADIN-E
BALADIN-S
BALANCE-D
BALANCE-R
BALANCE-S
BALDIES-T
BALDRIC-K
BALDRIC-S
BALISTA-E
BALISTA-S
BALKING-S
BALLADE-D
BALLADE-S
BALLANT-S
BALLAST-S
BALLING-S
BALLIUM-S
BALLOON-S
BALLUTE-S
BALONEY-S
BAMBINO-S
BANDAGE-D
BANDAGE-R
BANDAGE-S
BANDANA-S
BANDEAU-S
BANDEAU-X
BANDIES-T
A-**BANDING**
BANDING-S
BANDOOK-S
BANDORA-S
BANDORE-S
BANDROL-S
BANDURA-S
BANGING-S
BANGKOK-S
BANKING-S
BANKSIA-S
BANNOCK-S
BANQUET-S
BANSHEE-S
BANSHIE-S
BANTENG-S
BANTING-S
BAPTISE-D
BAPTISE-S
BAPTISM-S
BAPTIST-S
BAPTIZE-D
BAPTIZE-R
BAPTIZE-S
BARACAN-S
BARBATE-D
BARBELL-S
BARBOLA-S
BARBULE-S
BARCHAN-E
BARCHAN-S
BARGAIN-S
BARGEES-E
BARGEST-S
BARILLA-S
BARKEEP-S
BARKHAN-S
BARMAID-S
BARMKIN-S
BAROCCO-S
BARONET-S
BARONNE-S
BAROQUE-S
BARRACE-S
BARRACK-S
BARRAGE-D
BARRAGE-S
BARRICO-S
BARRIER-S
BARRING-S
BARROOM-S
BARTEND-S
BARWARE-S
BARWOOD-S
BARYTON-E
BARYTON-S
BASCULE-S
BASEMEN-T
BASENJI-S
A-**BASHING**
BASHING-S
BASHLIK-S
BASHLYK-S
BASIDIA-L
BASILAR-Y
BASILIC-A
BASINET-S
BASMATI-S
BASOCHE-S
BASSETT-S
BASSIST-S
BASSOON-S
BASTARD-S
BASTARD-Y
BASTIDE-S
BASTILE-S
BASTING-S
BASTION-S
A-**BATABLE**
BATCHER-S
BATFOWL-S
BATHMAT-S
BATHTUB-S
BATISTE-S
BATTEAU-X
BATTERO-S
BATTILL-S
BATTING-S
BATTLER-S
BATTUTA-S
BAUCHLE-D
BAUCHLE-S
BAUDRIC-K
BAUDRIC-S
BAUXITE-S
BAWCOCK-S
BAWDIES-T
BAWDKIN-S
BAWDRIC-S
BAWLING-S
BAYONET-S
BAYWOOD-S

BAZOOKA-S
BAZOUKI-S
BEADING-S
BEAGLER-S
BEAMING-S
BEAMLET-S
BEANBAG-S
BEARCAT-S
BEARDIE-S
BEARHUG-S
A-**BEARING**
BEARING-S
BEASTIE-S
BEATING-S
BEATNIK-S
BEAUFET-S
BEAUFIN-S
BEBEERU-S
BEBLOOD-S
BECASSE-S
BECHALK-S
BECHARM-S
BECLASP-S
BECLOAK-S
BECLOUD-S
BECLOWN-S
BECRAWL-S
BECRIME-D
BECRIME-S
BECROWD-S
BECRUST-S
BECURSE-D
BECURSE-S
BEDAWIN-S
BEDDING-S
BEDERAL-S
BEDEVIL-S
BEDGOWN-S
BEDIGHT-S
BEDIZEN-S
BEDLAMP-S
BEDMATE-S
BEDOUIN-S
BEDPOST-S
BEDRAIL-S
BEDRAPE-D
BEDRAPE-S
BEDROCK-S
BEDROLL-S
BEDROOM-S
BEDSIDE-S
BEDSORE-S
BEDTICK-S
BEDTIME-S
BEDUNCE-D
BEDUNCE-S
BEDWARD-S
BEDWARF-S
BEEFALO-S
BEEHIVE-S
BEELINE-D
BEELINE-S
BEERAGE-S
BEETLER-S
BEEYARD-S
BEFFANA-S
BEFLECK-S
BEGGING-S
BEGHARD-S
BEGINNE-R
BEGINNE-S
BEGLOOM-S
BEGONIA-S
BEGORRA-H
BEGRIME-D
BEGRIME-S
BEGROAN-S
BEGUILE-D
BEGUILE-R
BEGUILE-S
BEGUINE-S
BEHAVER-S
BEHIGHT-S
BEHOOVE-D
BEHOOVE-S
BEIGNET-S
BEJEWEL-S
BEKNAVE-D
BEKNAVE-S
BELABOR-S
BELCHER-S
BELDAME-S
BELGARD-S
BELIEVE-D
BELIEVE-R
BELIEVE-S
BELLBOY-S
BELLEEK-S
BELLHOP-S
BELOVED-S
BELTING-S
BELTWAY-S
BEMADAM-S
BEMEDAL-S
BEMOUTH-S
BENCHER-S
BENDING-S
BENDLET-S
BENEFIC-E
BENEFIT-S
BENIGHT-S
BENISON-S
BENOMYL-S
BENZENE-S
BENZINE-S
BENZOIN-S
BENZOLE-S
BENZOYL-S
BEPAINT-S
BEPEARL-S
BEPROSE-D
BEPROSE-S
BEQUEST-S
BERCEAU-X
BEREAVE-D
BEREAVE-N
BEREAVE-R
BEREAVE-S
BERETTA-S
BERGAMA-S
BERGERE-S
BERGYLT-S
BERHYME-D
BERHYME-S
BERLINE-S
BERSEEM-S
BERSERK-S
BESAINT-S
BESCOUR-S
BESEEKE-S
BESHAME-D
BESHAME-S
BESHINE-S
BESHOUT-S
BESHREW-S
BESIEGE-D
BESIEGE-R
BESIEGE-S
BESLAVE-D
BESLAVE-R
BESLAVE-S
BESLIME-D
BESLIME-S
BESMEAR-S
BESMILE-D
BESMILE-S
BESMOKE-D
BESMOKE-S
BESPEAK-S
BESPEED-S
BESPICE-D
BESPICE-S
BESPOKE-N
BESPORT-S
BESPOUT-S
BESTAIN-S
BESTEAD-S
BESTIAL-S
BESTICK-S
BESTILL-S
BESTORM-S
BESTREW-N
BESTREW-S
BESTRID-E
BESTROW-N
BESTROW-S
BESWARM-S
BETAINE-S
BETEEME-D
BETEEME-S
BETHANK-S
BETHINK-S
BETHORN-S
BETHUMB-S
BETHUMP-S
BETITLE-D
BETITLE-S
BETOKEN-S
BETREAD-S
BETROTH-S
A-**BETTERS**
A-**BETTING**
BETTING-S
A-**BETTORS**
BETWEEN-S
BEVELER-S
BEVOMIT-S
BEWHORE-D
BEWHORE-S
BEZIQUE-S
BEZZANT-S
BHANGRA-S
BHISTEE-S
BHISTIE-S
BIASING-S
BIBCOCK-S
BIBELOT-S
BIBLIST-S
BICOLOR-S
BICORNE-S
BICYCLE-D
BICYCLE-R
BICYCLE-S
BIDARKA-S
BIDDING-S
A-**BIDINGS**
BIENNIA-L
BIFOCAL-S
BIGENER-S
BIGFOOT-S
BIGGING-S
BIGHEAD-S
BIGHORN-S
BIKEWAY-S
BILAYER-S
BILIMBI-S
BILLBUG-S
BILLING-S
BILLION-S
BILSTED-S
BILTONG-S
BIMETAL-S
BIMORPH-S
BINDING-S
BINOCLE-S
BIOCHIP-S
BIOCIDE-S
BIOHERM-S
BIOPHOR-E
BIOPHOR-S
BIOTECH-S
BIOTITE-S
BIOTOPE-S
BIOTRON-S
BIOTYPE-S
BIPLANE-S
BIRDING-S
BIRETTA-S
BIRKIES-T
BIRLING-S
BIRLINN-S
BIRYANI-S
BISCUIT-S
BISCUIT-Y
BISMUTH-S
BISNAGA-S
BISTORT-S
BITTERN-S
BITTIES-T
BITTING-S
BITTOCK-S
BITTOUR-S
BITUMEN-S
BIVALVE-D
BIVALVE-S
BIVINYL-S
BIVOUAC-S
BIZARRE-S
BIZNAGA-S
BLABBER-S
BLACKEN-S
BLADDER-S
BLADDER-Y
BLAGGER-S
BLANKET-S
BLANKET-Y
BLARNEY-S
BLASTER-S
BLASTIE-R
BLASTIE-S
BLATHER-S
BLATTER-S
BLAUBOK-S
BLAWORT-S
BLEATER-S
BLEEDER-S
BLEEPER-S
BLELLUM-S
BLENDER-S
BLESBOK-S
BLESSER-S
BLETHER-S
BLEWART-S
BLINDER-S
BLINKER-S
BLINTZE-S
BLISTER-S
BLISTER-Y
BLITHER-S
BLOATER-S
BLOCKER-S
BLONDES-T
BLOOMER-S
BLOOMER-Y
BLOOPER-S
BLOOSME-D
BLOOSME-S
BLOSSOM-S
BLOSSOM-Y
BLOTTER-S
BLOUBOK-S
BLOUSON-S
BLOWGUN-S
BLOWIES-T
BLOWJOB-S
BLOWOFF-S
BLOWOUT-S
BLUBBER-S
BLUBBER-Y
BLUCHER-S
BLUDGER-S
BLUECAP-S
BLUEFIN-S
BLUEGUM-S
BLUEING-S
BLUEJAY-S
BLUETTE-S
BLUFFER-S
BLUNDER-S
BLUNGER-S
BLUNKER-S
BLURTER-S
BLUSHER-S
BLUSHET-S
BLUSTER-S
BLUSTER-Y
BOARDER-S
BOASTER-S
BOATFUL-S
BOATING-S
BOBBITT-S
BOBECHE-S
BOBSLED-S
BOBSTAY-S
BOBTAIL-S
BODGIES-T
BODHRAN-S
BODIKIN-S
BOFFOLA-S
BOGBEAN-S
BOGGARD-S
BOGGART-S
BOGGLER-S
BOGLAND-S
BOGWOOD-S
BOGYISM-S
BOHEMIA-N
BOHEMIA-S
BOILING-S
BOILOFF-S
BOLIVAR-S
BOLIVIA-S
BOLLARD-S
BOLLOCK-S
BOLOGNA-S
BOLONEY-S
BOLSHIE-R
BOLSHIE-S
BOLSTER-S
BOLTING-S
BOMBARD-S
BOMBAST-S
BOMBING-S
BOMBLET-S
BOMBORA-S
BONAMIA-S
BONANZA-S
BONDAGE-R
BONDAGE-S
BONDING-S
BONESET-S
BONFIRE-S
E-**BONISTS**
BONNIES-T
BONNOCK-S
BOOBOOK-S
BOODLER-S
BOOKEND-S
BOOKFUL-S
BOOKIES-T
BOOKING-S
BOOKLET-S
BOOKSIE-R
BOOMING-S
BOOMKIN-S
BOOMLET-S
BOOSTER-S
BOOTLEG-S
BORAZON-S
BORDURE-S
BOREDOM-S
BORNEOL-S
BORNITE-S
BORONIA-S
BOROUGH-S
BORSCHT-S
BORSTAL-L
BORSTAL-S
BOSCAGE-S
BOSHBOK-S
BOSKAGE-S
BOSQUET-S
BOSSDOM-S
BOSSIES-T
BOSSISM-S
BOTANIC-A
BOTARGO-S
BOTCHER-S
BOTCHER-Y
BOTHOLE-S
BOTTEGA-S
BOTTINE-S
BOTTLER-S
BOTULIN-S
BOUCHEE-S
BOUDOIR-S
BOUILLI-S
BOULDER-S
BOULDER-Y
BOULTER-S
BOUNCER-S
A-**BOUNDED**
Y-**BOUNDEN**
BOUNDER-S
BOUQUET-S
BOURBON-S
BOURDER-S
BOURDON-S
BOURKHA-S
BOURLAW-S
BOURREE-S
BOUTADE-S
BOUVIER-S
BOWHEAD-S
BOWKNOT-S
BOWLDER-S
BOWLFUL-S
BOWLINE-S
BOWLING-S
BOWSHOT-S

BOWYANG-S
BOXHAUL-S
BOXROOM-S
BOXWOOD-S
BOYCHIK-S
BOYCOTT-S
BOYHOOD-S
BRABBLE-D
BRABBLE-R
BRABBLE-S
BRACERO-S
BRACHET-S
A-**BRACHIA**
BRACHIA-L
BRACING-S
BRACKEN-S
BRACKET-S
BRADAWL-S
BRADOON-S
BRAGGER-S
A-**BRAIDED**
BRAIDER-S
BRAILLE-D
BRAILLE-R
BRAILLE-S
BRAMBLE-D
BRAMBLE-S
BRANDER-S
BRANGLE-D
BRANGLE-S
BRANNER-S
BRANSLE-S
BRANTLE-S
BRASERO-S
BRASHES-T
BRASIER-S
BRASSET-S
BRASSIE-R
BRASSIE-S
BRATTLE-D
BRATTLE-S
BRAVADO-S
BRAVURA-S
BRAWLER-S
BRAWLIE-R
A-**BRAYING**
BRAZIER-S
BREADTH-S
BREAKER-S
BREAKUP-S
BREATHE-D
BREATHE-R
BREATHE-S
BRECCIA-L
BRECCIA-S
BRECHAM-S
BRECHAN-S
BREEDER-S
BREVETE-D
BREVIER-S
BREWAGE-S
BREWING-S
BREWPUB-S
BRICKIE-R
BRICKIE-S
BRICKLE-S
BRICOLE-S
A-**BRIDGED**
A-**BRIDGES**
BRIDLER-S
BRIDOON-S
BRIEFER-S
BRIGADE-D
BRIGADE-S
BRIGAND-S

BRIMFUL-L
BRIMING-S
BRIMMER-S
BRINDLE-D
BRINDLE-S
BRINGER-S
BRINIES-T
BRINJAL-S
BRIOCHE-S
BRIQUET-S
BRISKEN-S
BRISKET-S
BRISTLE-D
BRISTLE-S
BRISTOL-S
BRISURE-S
BRITSKA-S
BRITTLE-D
BRITTLE-R
BRITTLE-S
BRITZKA-S
BROADAX-E
BROADEN-S
BROCADE-D
BROCADE-S
BROCAGE-S
BROCARD-S
BROCHAN-S
BROCKET-S
BROCOLI-S
BRODKIN-S
BROIDER-S
BROIDER-Y
BROILER-S
BROKAGE-S
BROKING-S
BROMATE-D
BROMATE-S
BROMIDE-S
BROMINE-S
BROMISM-S
BROMIZE-D
BROMIZE-S
BROMMER-S
BRONCHI-A
BRONCHO-S
BRONZER-S
BROODER-S
A-**BROOKED**
BROOKIE-S
BROTHEL-S
BROTHER-S
BROWNIE-R
BROWNIE-S
BROWSER-S
BRUCHID-S
BRUCINE-S
BRUCITE-S
BRUHAHA-S
BRUISER-S
BRUITER-S
BRULYIE-S
BRULZIE-S
BRUMMER-S
BRUSHER-S
BRUSHUP-S
BRUSQUE-R
BRUTING-S
BRUTISM-S
BRUXISM-S
BUBBLER-S
BUBINGA-S
BUBUKLE-S
BUCCINA-S
BUCKEEN-S

BUCKEYE-S
BUCKING-S
BUCKLER-S
BUCKRAM-S
BUCKSAW-S
BUCOLIC-S
BUDDIES-T
BUDDING-S
BUDGERO-S
BUDGERO-W
BUDWORM-S
BUFFALO-S
BUFFING-S
BUFFOON-S
BUGABOO-S
BUGBANE-S
BUGBEAR-S
BUGGANE-S
BUGGIES-T
BUGGING-S
BUGSEED-S
BUGWORT-S
BUILDER-S
BUILDUP-S
BUKSHEE-S
BULBLET-S
BULGHUR-S
BULGINE-S
BULIMIA-C
BULIMIA-S
BULIMIC-S
BULKAGE-S
BULLACE-S
BULLBAR-S
BULLBAT-S
BULLDOG-S
BULLIES-T
BULLING-S
BULLION-S
BULLOCK-S
BULLOCK-Y
BULLPEN-S
BULRUSH-Y
BULWARK-S
BUMBAZE-D
BUMBAZE-S
BUMBLER-S
BUMBOAT-S
BUMMOCK-S
BUMPING-S
BUMPKIN-S
BUNDIST-S
BUNDLER-S
BUNDOOK-S
BUNGLER-S
BUNRAKU-S
BUNTING-S
BUOYAGE-S
BURBLER-S
BURDOCK-S
BURETTE-S
BURGAGE-S
BURGEON-S
BURGHER-S
BURGHUL-S
BURGLAR-S
BURGLAR-Y
BURGOUT-S
BURKITE-S
BURLESK-S
BURNING-S
BURNOUS-E
BURNOUT-S
BURRELL-S
BURRHEL-S

BURRITO-S
BURSEED-S
BURSTER-S
BURTHEN-S
BURWEED-S
BUSGIRL-S
BUSHIDO-S
BUSHIES-T
BUSHING-S
BUSHPIG-S
BUSHTIT-S
BUSHWAH-S
BUSKING-S
BUSLOAD-S
BUSSING-S
BUSTARD-S
BUSTIER-S
BUSTING-S
BUSTLER-S
BUTANOL-S
BUTCHER-S
BUTCHER-Y
BUTCHES-T
A-**BUTMENT**
BUTMENT-S
A-**BUTTALS**
A-**BUTTERS**
A-**BUTTING**
BUTTOCK-S
BUTYRAL-S
BUTYRIN-S
BUTYRYL-S
BUVETTE-S
BUYABLE-S
BUYBACK-S
BUZZARD-S
BUZZING-S
BUZZWIG-S
BYCOKET-S
BYLINER-S
BYPLACE-S
BYWONER-S
CABARET-S
CABBAGE-D
CABBAGE-S
CABBALA-H
CABBALA-S
S-**CABBING**
CABEZON-E
CABEZON-S
CABILDO-S
CABINET-S
CABLING-S
CABOMBA-S
CABOOSE-S
CACIQUE-S
CACKLER-S
CACODYL-S
CACOLET-S
CADAVER-S
CADDICE-S
CADELLE-S
CADENCE-D
CADENCE-S
CADENZA-S
CADMIUM-S
CAESIUM-S
CAESURA-E
CAESURA-L
CAESURA-S
CAFFEIN-E
CAFFEIN-S
CAFFILA-S
CAGEFUL-S
CAGOULE-S

CAISSON-S
CAITIFF-S
CAITIVE-S
CAJAPUT-S
CAJEPUT-S
CAJOLER-S
CAJOLER-Y
CAJUPUT-S
CALAMAR-I
CALAMAR-S
CALAMAR-Y
CALCINE-D
CALCINE-S
CALCITE-S
CALCIUM-S
CALDERA-S
CALDRON-S
CALECHE-S
CALIBER-S
CALIBRE-D
CALIBRE-S
CALICHE-S
CALICLE-S
CALIPEE-S
CALIPER-S
CALIVER-S
CALLANT-S
CALLBOY-S
CALLING-S
CALLOSE-S
CALLUNA-S
CALMANT-S
CALOMEL-S
CALORIC-S
CALORIE-S
CALOTTE-S
CALOYER-S
CALPACK-S
CALTRAP-S
CALTROP-S
CALUMBA-S
CALUMET-S
CALYCLE-D
CALYCLE-S
CALYPSO-S
CALZONE-S
CAMAIEU-X
CAMARON-S
CAMBISM-S
CAMBIST-S
CAMBIUM-S
CAMBOGE-S
CAMBREL-S
CAMBRIC-S
CAMELIA-S
CAMELID-S
CAMELOT-S
CAMISIA-S
S-**CAMMING**
CAMOGIE-S
CAMORRA-S
CAMPANA-S
S-**CAMPERS**
CAMPHOL-S
CAMPHOR-S
S-**CAMPING**
CAMPING-S
CAMPION-S
CAMPONG-S
CAMWOOD-S
CANAKIN-S
CANASTA-S
CANBANK-S
CANDELA-S
S-**CANDENT**

CANDIDA-L
CANDIDA-S
CANDLER-S
CANDOCK-S
CANDOUR-S
CANELLA-S
CANIKIN-S
CANNACH-S
S-**CANNERS**
S-**CANNING**
CANNING-S
CANNULA-E
CANNULA-R
CANNULA-S
CANTALA-S
CANTATA-S
CANTATE-S
CANTDOG-S
CANTEEN-S
S-**CANTEST**
A-**CANTHUS**
CANTICO-S
CANTICO-Y
S-**CANTIER**
CANTINA-S
S-**CANTING**
CANTING-S
CANTION-S
S-**CANTLED**
S-**CANTLES**
CANTLET-S
CANTRAP-S
CANTRED-S
CANTREF-S
CANTRIP-S
CANZONA-S
CANZONE-S
CANZONE-T
CAPABLE-R
CAPELAN-S
CAPELET-S
CAPELIN-E
CAPELIN-S
CAPERER-S
CAPITAL-S
CAPITAN-I
CAPITAN-O
CAPITAN-S
CAPITOL-S
CAPORAL-S
CAPPING-S
CAPRATE-S
CAPRICE-S
CAPROCK-S
CAPSIZE-D
CAPSIZE-S
CAPSTAN-S
CAPSULE-D
CAPSULE-S
CAPTAIN-S
CAPTION-S
CAPTIVE-D
CAPTIVE-S
CAPTURE-D
CAPTURE-R
CAPTURE-S
CAPUCHE-D
CAPUCHE-S
CAPUERA-S
CARABAO-S
CARABID-S
CARABIN-E
CARABIN-S
CARACAL-S
CARACOL-E

CARACOL-S
CARACUL-S
CARAMEL-S
CARANNA-S
CARAUNA-S
CARAVAN-S
CARAVEL-S
CARAWAY-S
CARBARN-S
CARBIDE-S
CARBINE-S
CARBORA-S
CARCAKE-S
CARCASE-D
CARCASE-S
CARDECU-E
CARDECU-S
CARDIAC-S
CARDING-S
CARDOON-S
CARFARE-S
CARIAMA-S
CARIBOU-S
CARIERE-S
O-**CARINAS**
CARIOCA-S
CARIOLE-S
S-**CARIOUS**
CARJACK-S
S-**CARLESS**
CARLINE-S
CARLING-S
CARLOAD-S
CARLOCK-S
CARMINE-S
CARNAGE-S
CARNIES-T
CAROCHE-S
CAROLER-S
CAROMEL-S
CAROTID-S
CAROTIN-S
CAROUSE-D
CAROUSE-L
CAROUSE-R
CAROUSE-S
CARPARK-S
S-**CARPERS**
S-**CARPING**
CARPING-S
CARPOOL-S
CARPORT-S
CARRACK-S
CARRACT-S
CARRECT-S
CARRELL-S
S-**CARRIER**
CARRIER-S
CARRION-S
CARRYON-S
CARTAGE-S
S-**CARTING**
CARTOON-S
CARTOON-Y
CARTWAY-S
CARVING-S
CASCADE-D
CASCADE-S
CASCARA-S
CASEASE-S
CASEATE-D
CASEATE-S
CASEMEN-T
CASEOSE-S
CASERNE-S

CASETTE-S
CASHIER-S
CASSABA-S
CASSATA-S
CASSAVA-S
CASSINO-S
CASSOCK-S
CASSONE-S
CASTING-S
CASTOCK-S
CASTOFF-S
CASUIST-S
CATALOG-S
CATALPA-S
CATAPAN-S
CATARRH-S
CATASTA-S
CATAWBA-S
CATBIRD-S
CATBOAT-S
CATCALL-S
CATCHER-S
S-**CATCHES**
CATCHUP-S
CATCLAW-S
CATECHU-S
CATELOG-S
CATERAN-S
CATERER-S
CATFACE-S
CATFALL-S
CATHEAD-S
CATHECT-S
CATHODE-S
CATHOLE-S
CATHOOD-S
CATLING-S
CATMINT-S
CATSKIN-S
CATSPAW-S
CATSUIT-S
CATTABU-S
CATTAIL-S
CATTALO-S
S-**CATTERY**
S-**CATTIER**
CATTIES-T
S-**CATTING**
CATWALK-S
CATWORM-S
A-**CAUDATE**
E-CAUDATE
CAUDATE-D
CAUDATE-S
CAUDRON-S
A-**CAULINE**
CAULKER-S
CAULOME-S
CAUSTIC-S
CAUTION-S
CAVALLA-S
CAVETTO-S
CAVIARE-S
CAVILER-S
CAYENNE-D
CAYENNE-S
CAZIQUE-S
CEASING-S
CEDILLA-S
CEDRATE-S
CEILIDH-S
CEILING-S
CELADON-S
CELESTA-S
CELESTE-S

CELLIST-S
CELLOSE-S
CELLULE-S
CELOSIA-S
CEMBALO-S
CENACLE-S
CENSURE-D
CENSURE-R
CENSURE-S
CENTAGE-S
CENTARE-S
CENTAUR-S
CENTAUR-Y
CENTAVO-S
CENTILE-S
CENTIME-S
CENTIMO-S
CENTNER-S
CENTRAL-S
A-**CENTRIC**
CENTRUM-S
CEPHEID-S
CERAMAL-S
CERAMIC-S
CERASIN-S
A-**CERATED**
CERATIN-S
CEREBRA-L
CERESIN-E
CERESIN-S
S-**CERNING**
CERUMEN-S
CESSION-S
CESSPIT-S
CESTODE-S
CESTOID-S
CEVICHE-S
CHABOUK-S
CHADDAR-S
CHADDOR-S
CHAFFER-S
CHAFFER-Y
CHAGRIN-S
CHALAZA-E
CHALAZA-L
CHALAZA-S
CHALCID-S
CHALDER-S
CHALICE-D
CHALICE-S
CHALLAH-S
CHALLAN-S
CHALLIE-S
CHALLOT-H
CHALONE-S
CHAMADE-S
CHAMBER-S
CHAMFER-S
CHAMISE-S
CHAMISO-S
CHAMLET-S
CHAMPAC-S
CHAMPAK-S
CHAMPER-S
CHANCEL-S
CHANCER-S
CHANCER-Y
CHANCRE-S
CHANGER-S
CHANNEL-S
CHANNER-S
CHANOYU-S
CHANSON-S
CHANTER-S
CHANTEY-S

CHANTIE-S
CHANTOR-S
CHAPATI-S
CHAPEAU-S
CHAPEAU-X
CHAPLET-S
CHAPPAL-S
S-**CHAPPED**
CHAPPIE-R
CHAPPIE-S
CHAPTER-S
CHARACT-S
CHARADE-S
CHARGER-S
CHARIOT-S
CHARISM-A
CHARISM-S
CHARKHA-S
CHARLEY-S
CHARLIE-S
CHARMER-S
CHARNEL-S
CHARPAI-S
CHARPIE-S
CHARPOY-S
CHARQUI-D
CHARQUI-S
CHARTER-S
CHASING-S
CHASTEN-S
CHATEAU-S
CHATEAU-X
CHATTEL-S
CHATTER-S
CHATTER-Y
CHAUFER-S
CHAUMER-S
CHAUNCE-D
CHAUNCE-S
CHAUNGE-D
CHAUNGE-S
CHAUVIN-S
CHAYOTE-S
CHAZZAN-S
CHAZZEN-S
CHEAPEN-S
CHEAPIE-S
CHEATER-S
CHEATER-Y
CHECHIA-S
CHECKER-S
CHECKUP-S
CHEDDAR-S
CHEDITE-S
CHEEPER-S
CHEERER-S
CHEERIO-S
CHEETAH-S
CHEFDOM-S
CHEKIST-S
CHELATE-D
CHELATE-S
CHELOID-S
CHELONE-S
CHEMISE-S
CHEMISM-S
CHEMIST-S
CHEQUER-S
CHEROOT-S
CHERVIL-S
CHESNUT-S
CHESSEL-S
CHETNIK-S
CHETRUM-S
CHEVIOT-S

CHEVRON-S
CHEVRON-Y
CHEWIES-T
CHEWINK-S
CHIASMA-L
CHIASMA-S
CHIASMI-C
CHIBOUK-S
CHICANA-S
CHICANE-D
CHICANE-R
CHICANE-S
CHICANO-S
CHICKEE-S
CHICKEN-S
CHIDING-S
CHIEFER-Y
CHIFFON-S
CHIGGER-S
CHIGNON-S
CHIKARA-S
CHIKHOR-S
CHILIAD-S
CHILIOI-S
S-**CHILLER**
CHILLER-S
CHILLUM-S
CHIMERA-S
CHIMERE-S
CHIMLEY-S
CHIMNEY-S
CHINDIT-S
CHINKIE-R
CHINKIE-S
CHINONE-S
CHINOOK-S
CHINWAG-S
CHIPPER-S
CHIPPIE-R
CHIPPIE-S
CHIPSET-S
CHIRPER-S
CHIRRUP-S
CHIRRUP-Y
CHITLIN-G
CHITLIN-S
CHITTER-S
CHLORAL-S
CHLORID-E
CHLORID-S
CHLORIN-E
CHLORIN-S
CHOBDAR-S
CHOCTAW-S
CHOICES-T
CHOKIES-T
CHOLATE-S
CHOLENT-S
CHOLERA-S
CHOLINE-S
CHOMPER-S
CHONDRE-S
CHONDRI-N
CHOOKIE-S
CHOOSER-S
CHOPINE-S
CHOPPER-S
CHORAGI-C
CHORALE-S
CHORDEE-S
CHOREGI-C
CHORINE-S
CHORION-S
CHORISM-S
CHORIST-S

CHORIZO-S
CHOROID-S
CHORTLE-D
CHORTLE-R
CHORTLE-S
CHOUSER-S
CHOWDER-S
CHRISMA-L
CHRISOM-S
CHROMEL-S
A-**CHROMIC**
CHROMYL-S
CHRONIC-S
CHRONON-S
CHUCKIE-S
CHUCKLE-D
CHUCKLE-R
CHUCKLE-S
CHUDDAH-S
CHUDDAR-S
CHUDDER-S
CHUGGER-S
CHUKKAR-S
CHUKKER-S
CHUMLEY-S
CHUNDER-S
CHUNNEL-S
CHUNNER-S
CHUNTER-S
CHUPATI-S
CHUPPAH-S
CHURNER-S
CHUTIST-S
CHUTNEE-S
CHUTNEY-S
CHUTZPA-H
CHUTZPA-S
CHYMIST-S
CIBOULE-S
CICHLID-S
CICOREE-S
CIELING-S
CIGARET-S
CILIATE-D
CILIATE-S
CINEAST-E
CINEAST-S
CINEOLE-S
CINEREA-L
CINEREA-S
CINERIN-S
CIPOLIN-S
CIRCLER-S
CIRCLET-S
CIRCLIP-S
CIRCUIT-S
CIRCUIT-Y
CISSIES-T
CISSOID-S
CISTERN-A
CISTERN-S
CISTRON-S
CITADEL-S
CITATOR-S
CITATOR-Y
CITHARA-S
CITHERN-S
CITHREN-S
CITIZEN-S
CITRATE-D
CITRATE-S
CITRINE-S
CITTERN-S
CLABBER-S
CLACHAN-S

CLACKER-S
CLADDER-S
CLADISM-S
CLADIST-S
CLADODE-S
CLAIMER-S
CLAMBER-S
CLAMMER-S
CLAMOUR-S
CLAMPER-S
CLANGER-S
CLANGOR-S
CLAPNET-S
CLAPPER-S
CLAQUER-S
CLARAIN-S
CLARINO-S
CLARION-S
CLARKIA-S
CLASHER-S
CLASPER-S
CLASSER-S
CLASSIC-O
CLASSIC-S
CLASSIS-M
CLASSIS-T
CLASTIC-S
CLATTER-S
CLATTER-Y
CLAUCHT-S
CLAUGHT-S
CLAVATE-D
CLAVIER-S
CLAYPAN-S
CLEANER-S
CLEANSE-D
CLEANSE-R
CLEANSE-S
CLEANUP-S
CLEARER-S
CLEAVER-S
Y-**CLEEPED**
CLERUCH-S
CLERUCH-Y
CLICKER-S
CLICKET-S
CLIMATE-D
CLIMATE-S
CLIMBER-S
CLINGER-S
CLINKER-S
CLIPART-S
CLIPPER-S
CLIPPIE-S
CLITTER-S
CLOBBER-S
CLOCKER-S
CLOGGER-S
CLOISON-S
CLONING-S
CLONISM-S
E-**CLOSING**
CLOSING-S
CLOSURE-D
CLOSURE-S
CLOTBUR-S
CLOTTER-S
CLOTURE-D
CLOTURE-S
CLOUTER-S
CLOWDER-S
CLUBBER-S
CLUDGIE-S
CLUMBER-S
CLUMPER-S
CLUNKER-S
CLUPEID-S
CLUSTER-S
CLUSTER-Y
CLUTTER-S
CLUTTER-Y
CLYSTER-S
COACHEE-S
COACHER-S
COACTOR-S
COADMIT-S
COAEVAL-S
COAGENT-S
COALBIN-S
COALISE-D
COALISE-S
COALIZE-D
COALIZE-S
COALPIT-S
COALTAR-S
COAMING-S
COARSEN-S
COASTER-S
COATING-S
COBBLER-S
COBBLER-Y
COCAINE-S
COCCOID-S
COCHAIR-S
COCHLEA-E
COCHLEA-R
COCHLEA-S
COCKADE-D
COCKADE-S
COCKEYE-D
COCKEYE-S
COCKIES-T
COCKNEY-S
COCKPIT-S
COCOMAT-S
COCONUT-S
COCOPAN-S
COCOTTE-S
COCOYAM-S
COCTION-S
CODDLER-S
CODEINA-S
CODEINE-S
CODETTA-S
CODICIL-S
CODILLA-S
CODILLE-S
CODLING-S
CODRIVE-N
CODRIVE-R
CODRIVE-S
COEHORN-S
COELIAC-S
COELOME-S
COENACT-S
COENURE-S
COEQUAL-S
COERCER-S
COERECT-S
COESITE-S
COEXERT-S
COEXIST-S
S-**COFFERS**
S-**COFFING**
COFFRET-S
COFOUND-S
COGENCE-S
COGENER-S
S-**COGGING**
COGGING-S
COGNATE-S
COGNISE-D
COGNISE-S
COGNIZE-D
COGNIZE-R
COGNIZE-S
COHABIT-S
COHERER-S
COHIBIT-S
COINAGE-S
COINFER-S
COINING-S
COINTER-S
COITION-S
COLIBRI-S
COLICIN-E
COLICIN-S
COLLAGE-D
COLLAGE-N
COLLAGE-S
COLLARD-S
COLLATE-D
COLLATE-S
COLLECT-S
COLLEEN-S
COLLEGE-R
COLLEGE-S
COLLIDE-D
COLLIDE-R
COLLIDE-S
COLLIER-S
COLLIER-Y
COLLING-S
COLLOID-S
S-**COLLOPS**
COLLUDE-D
COLLUDE-R
COLLUDE-S
COLOGNE-D
COLOGNE-S
COLONEL-S
COLONIC-S
COLORED-S
COLORER-S
COLUMEL-S
COMAKER-S
COMATIK-S
COMBIES-T
COMBINE-D
COMBINE-R
COMBINE-S
COMBING-S
COMBLES-S
COMBUST-S
COMFORT-S
COMFREY-S
COMIQUE-S
COMITIA-L
COMMAND-O
COMMAND-S
COMMEND-S
COMMENT-S
COMMERE-S
COMMODE-S
COMMOTE-S
COMMOVE-D
COMMOVE-S
COMMUNE-D
COMMUNE-S
COMMUTE-D
COMMUTE-R
COMMUTE-S
COMPACT-S
COMPAGE-S
COMPAND-S
COMPARE-D
COMPARE-R
COMPARE-S
COMPART-S
COMPEAR-S
COMPEER-S
COMPEND-S
COMPERE-D
COMPERE-S
COMPETE-D
COMPETE-S
COMPILE-D
COMPILE-R
COMPILE-S
COMPING-S
COMPLIN-E
COMPLIN-S
COMPLOT-S
COMPORT-S
COMPOSE-D
COMPOSE-R
COMPOSE-S
COMPOST-S
COMPOTE-S
COMPTER-S
COMPUTE-D
COMPUTE-R
COMPUTE-S
COMRADE-S
COMSYMP-S
CONACRE-D
CONACRE-S
CONARIA-L
CONCAVE-D
CONCAVE-S
CONCEAL-S
CONCEDE-D
CONCEDE-R
CONCEDE-S
CONCEIT-S
CONCEIT-Y
CONCENT-S
CONCEPT-I
CONCEPT-S
CONCERN-S
CONCERT-I
CONCERT-O
CONCERT-S
CONCHIE-S
CONCISE-D
CONCISE-R
CONCISE-S
CONCOCT-S
CONCORD-S
CONCREW-S
CONDEMN-S
CONDOLE-D
CONDOLE-R
CONDOLE-S
CONDONE-D
CONDONE-R
CONDONE-S
CONDUCE-D
CONDUCE-R
CONDUCE-S
CONDUCT-I
CONDUCT-S
CONDUIT-S
CONDYLE-S
CONFECT-S
CONFIDE-D
CONFIDE-R
CONFIDE-S
CONFINE-D
CONFINE-R
CONFINE-S
CONFIRM-S
CONFORM-S
CONFUSE-D
CONFUSE-S
CONFUTE-D
CONFUTE-R
CONFUTE-S
CONGEAL-S
CONGEST-S
CONGREE-D
CONGREE-S
CONGREE-T
CONGRUE-D
CONGRUE-S
I-**CONICAL**
CONIDIA-L
CONIDIA-N
CONIFER-S
CONIINE-S
CONJECT-S
CONJOIN-S
CONJOIN-T
CONJURE-D
CONJURE-R
CONJURE-S
CONNECT-S
CONNING-S
CONNIVE-D
CONNIVE-R
CONNIVE-S
CONNOTE-D
CONNOTE-S
CONQUER-S
CONSEIL-S
CONSENT-S
CONSIGN-S
CONSIST-S
CONSOLE-D
CONSOLE-R
CONSOLE-S
CONSORT-S
CONSTER-S
CONSULT-A
CONSULT-S
CONSUME-D
CONSUME-R
CONSUME-S
CONTACT-S
CONTAIN-S
CONTECK-S
CONTEMN-S
CONTEND-S
CONTENT-S
CONTEST-S
CONTEXT-S
CONTORT-S
CONTOUR-S
CONTRAS-T
CONTRAT-E
CONTRAT-S
CONTROL-E
CONTROL-S
CONTUND-S
CONTUSE-D
CONTUSE-S
CONVECT-S
CONVENE-D
CONVENE-R
CONVENE-S
CONVENT-S
CONVERT-S
CONVICT-S
CONVIVE-D
CONVIVE-S
CONVOKE-D
CONVOKE-R
CONVOKE-S
COOKING-S
COOKOUT-S
COOKTOP-S
COOLANT-S
COONCAN-S
COONDOG-S
COONTIE-S
S-**COOPERS**
S-**COOPING**
S-**COOTERS**
COPAIBA-S
COPAIVA-S
COPEPOD-S
COPIHUE-S
COPILOT-S
COPPICE-D
COPPICE-S
COPSHOP-S
S-**COPULAE**
S-**COPULAS**
COPYBOY-S
COPYCAT-S
COPYISM-S
COPYIST-S
COQUINA-S
COQUITO-S
CORACLE-S
CORANTO-S
CORBEAU-S
CORBEIL-S
CORBINA-S
CORDAGE-S
CORDIAL-S
CORDING-S
CORDITE-S
CORDOBA-S
COREIGN-S
CORELLA-S
S-**CORIOUS**
CORIVAL-S
CORKAGE-S
CORNAGE-S
CORNCOB-S
S-**CORNERS**
CORNETT-I
CORNETT-O
CORNETT-S
CORNICE-D
CORNICE-S
S-**CORNING**
CORNIST-S
CORNROW-S
CORNUTE-D
CORNUTE-S
CORNUTO-S
COROLLA-S
CORONAL-S
CORONEL-S
CORONER-S
CORONET-S
CORPORA-L
CORPORA-S
CORRADE-D
CORRADE-S
CORRECT-S
CORRIDA-S
CORRODE-D
CORRODE-S
CORRUPT-S
CORSAGE-S
CORSAIR-S
CORSIVE-S

CORSLET-S
CORSNED-S
CORTEGE-S
CORULER-S
CORVINA-S
CORYPHE-E
CORYPHE-S
COSINES-S
A-COSMISM
COSMISM-S
A-COSMIST
COSMIST-S
COSSACK-S
COSTARD-S
E-COSTATE
COSTATE-D
COSTEAN-S
COSTREL-S
COSTUME-D
COSTUME-R
COSTUME-S
COSTUME-Y
COTERIE-S
COTHURN-I
COTHURN-S
COTINGA-S
COTLAND-S
COTTAGE-D
COTTAGE-R
COTTAGE-S
COTTAGE-Y
COTTIER-S
COTTISE-D
COTTISE-S
COTTOWN-S
E-COTYPES
COUCHEE-S
COUCHER-S
COUGHER-S
COUGUAR-S
COULOIR-S
COULOMB-S
COULTER-S
COUNCIL-S
COUNSEL-S
COUNTER-S
S-COUPING
COUPLER-S
COUPLET-S
COUPURE-S
COURAGE-S
COURANT-E
COURANT-O
COURANT-S
COURIER-S
S-COURING
COURLAN-S
S-COURSED
COURSER-S
S-COURSES
COURTER-S
COUTEAU-X
S-COUTERS
S-COUTHER
COUTHIE-R
COUTURE-S
COUVADE-S
COUVERT-S
COVELET-S
COVERER-S
COVERUP-S
COVETER-S
COWBANE-S
COWBELL-S
COWBIND-S
COWBIRD-S
COWFLAP-S
COWFLOP-S
COWGIRL-S
COWHAGE-S
COWHAND-S
COWHEEL-S
COWHERB-S
COWHERD-S
COWHIDE-D
COWHIDE-S
COWLICK-S
S-COWLING
COWLING-S
S-COWPING
COWPLOP-S
COWPOKE-S
S-COWRIES
COWRITE-S
COWSHED-S
COWSKIN-S
COWSLIP-S
COWTREE-S
COXCOMB-S
COZENER-S
S-CRABBED
CRABBER-S
CRACKER-S
CRACKLE-D
CRACKLE-S
CRACKUP-S
CRACOWE-S
CRADLER-S
S-CRAGGED
S-CRAMMED
CRAMMER-S
CRAMPET-S
CRAMPIT-S
CRAMPON-S
CRANAGE-S
CRANIUM-S
CRANKLE-D
CRANKLE-S
CRANNOG-E
CRANNOG-S
S-CRAPING
S-CRAPPED
S-CRAPPER
CRAPPER-S
CRAPPIE-R
CRAPPIE-S
CRASHER-S
CRAVING-S
CRAWDAD-S
S-CRAWLED
S-CRAWLER
CRAWLER-S
CRAZIES-T
S-CREAKED
S-CREAMED
S-CREAMER
CREAMER-S
CREAMER-Y
CREANCE-S
CREASER-S
CREATIN-E
CREATIN-G
CREATIN-S
CREATOR-S
CREEPER-S
CREEPIE-R
CREEPIE-S
CREMATE-D
CREMATE-S
CREMONA-S
CRENATE-D
CREOSOL-S
CRESSET-S
CRESTON-S
CRETISM-S
CREVICE-D
CREVICE-S
S-CREWING
CRIBBER-S
S-CRIBBLE
CRIBBLE-D
CRIBBLE-S
CRICKET-S
CRICOID-S
CRIMINA-L
CRIMMER-S
S-CRIMPED
S-CRIMPER
CRIMPER-S
CRIMPLE-D
CRIMPLE-S
CRIMSON-S
CRINATE-D
CRINGER-S
CRINGLE-S
CRINITE-S
CRINKLE-D
CRINKLE-S
CRINOID-S
CRIOLLO-S
CRIPPLE-D
CRIPPLE-R
CRIPPLE-S
CRISPEN-S
CRISPER-S
CRISPIN-G
CRISPIN-S
CRITTER-S
CRITTUR-S
CROAKER-S
CROCEIN-E
CROCEIN-S
CROCHET-S
CROCKET-S
CROFTER-S
CROMACK-S
CROODLE-D
CROODLE-S
CROOKER-Y
CROONER-S
CROPFUL-L
CROPFUL-S
CROPPER-S
CROPPIE-S
CROQUET-S
CROSIER-S
CROSSER-S
CROSSES-T
CROTTLE-S
CROUPER-S
CROUPON-S
CROUTON-S
CROWBAR-S
CROWDER-S
CROWDIE-S
CROWNER-S
CROWNET-S
CROZIER-S
CRUBEEN-S
CRUCIAN-S
CRUDDLE-D
CRUDDLE-S
CRUISER-S
CRUISIE-S
CRULLER-S
CRUMBER-S
CRUMBLE-D
CRUMBLE-S
CRUMBUM-S
CRUMMIE-R
CRUMMIE-S
S-CRUMPED
CRUMPET-S
CRUMPLE-D
CRUMPLE-S
S-CRUNCHY
CRUNKLE-D
CRUNKLE-S
CRUNODE-S
CRUPPER-S
CRUSADE-D
CRUSADE-R
CRUSADE-S
CRUSADO-S
CRUSHER-S
CRUSIAN-S
CRUZADO-S
S-CRYINGS
CRYOGEN-S
CRYOGEN-Y
CRYONIC-S
CRYPTON-S
CRYSTAL-S
CUBBING-S
CUBHOOD-S
CUBICLE-S
CUCKOLD-S
CUDBEAR-S
S-CUDDLED
CUDDLER-S
S-CUDDLES
CUDWEED-S
S-CUFFING
S-CUFFLED
S-CUFFLES
CUFFLES-S
CUISINE-S
CUISSER-S
CUITTLE-D
CUITTLE-S
CULCHIE-S
CULICID-S
S-CULLERS
S-CULLING
CULLING-S
S-CULLION
CULLION-S
CULOTTE-S
CULPRIT-S
CULTISM-S
CULTIST-S
CULTURE-D
CULTURE-S
CULVERT-S
CUMARIN-S
S-CUMBERS
S-CUMMERS
CUMQUAT-S
CUMSHAW-S
CUNEATE-D
CUNETTE-S
S-CUNNERS
CUNNING-S
CUPCAKE-S
CUPELER-S
CUPGALL-S
CUPHEAD-S
S-CUPPERS
CUPPING-S
CUPRITE-S
CURACAO-S
CURACOA-S
CURARIS-E
CURATOR-S
CURATOR-Y
CURBING-S
CURCUMA-S
CURDLER-S
CURETTE-D
CURETTE-S
CURLING-S
CURRACH-S
CURRAGH-S
CURRANT-S
CURRANT-Y
CURRENT-S
S-CURRIED
S-CURRIER
CURRIER-S
CURRIER-Y
S-CURRIES
S-CURRING
CURSING-S
CURSIVE-S
CURTAIL-S
CURTAIN-S
CURTANA-S
CURTAXE-S
CURTSEY-S
CURVATE-D
S-CURVIER
CUSHION-S
CUSHION-Y
CUSPATE-D
CUSTARD-S
CUSTARD-Y
CUSTOCK-S
CUSTODE-S
CUSTREL-S
CUTAWAY-S
CUTBACK-S
CUTBANK-S
S-CUTCHES
CUTDOWN-S
CUTESIE-R
CUTICLE-S
CUTIKIN-S
CUTLINE-S
CUTOVER-S
CUTTAGE-S
S-CUTTERS
CUTTIES-T
CUTTING-S
S-CUTTLED
S-CUTTLES
CUTWORK-S
CUTWORM-S
CUVETTE-S
CYANATE-S
CYANIDE-D
CYANIDE-S
CYANINE-S
CYANISE-D
CYANISE-S
CYANITE-S
CYANIZE-D
CYANIZE-S
CYCASIN-S
CYCLASE-S
CYCLING-S
CYCLIST-S
CYCLIZE-D
CYCLIZE-S
CYCLOID-S
CYCLONE-S
CYMBALO-M
CYMBALO-S
CYMLING-S
CYPRIAN-S
CYPSELA-E
CYSTEIN-E
CYSTEIN-S
CYSTINE-S
CYSTOID-S
CYTOSOL-S
CZARDOM-S
CZARINA-S
CZARISM-S
CZARIST-S
DABBLER-S
DABSTER-S
DACTYLI-C
DADAISM-S
DADAIST-S
DADDOCK-S
DAFFIES-T
DAFFING-S
DAGGING-S
DAGLOCK-S
DAGWOOD-S
S-DAINING
DAKOITI-S
DALAPON-S
DALLIER-S
DAMAGER-S
DAMBROD-S
DAMOSEL-S
DAMOZEL-S
DAMPING-S
DANCING-S
DANDIES-T
DANDLER-S
DANELAW-S
DANGLER-S
DANSEUR-S
DAPHNIA-S
DAPHNID-S
DAPSONE-S
DAQUIRI-S
DARIOLE-S
DARLING-S
DARNING-S
DARRAIN-E
DARRAIN-S
DARRAYN-S
DARSHAN-S
DASHEEN-S
DASHEKI-S
DASHIKI-S
DASHPOT-S
DASTARD-S
DASTARD-Y
DASYPOD-S
DASYURE-S
DATARIA-S
DAUBING-S
DAUNDER-S
DAUNTER-S
DAUNTON-S
DAUPHIN-E
DAUPHIN-S
DAVIDIA-S
DAWCOCK-S
DAWDLER-S
DAWNING-S
DAYBOOK-S
DAYGLOW-S
DAYMARE-S
DAYMARK-S
DAYROOM-S

DAYSACK-S
DAYSIDE-S
DAYSTAR-S
DAYTALE-R
DAYTALE-S
DAYTIME-S
DAYWORK-S
DAZZLER-S
DEADEYE-S
DEADPAN-S
DEALATE-D
DEALATE-S
DEALING-S
DEASIUL-S
DEASOIL-S
DEBACLE-S
DEBASER-S
DEBATER-S
DEBBIES-T
DEBITOR-S
DEBONER-S
DEBOUCH-E
DEBRIDE-D
DEBRIDE-S
DEBRIEF-S
DECAGON-S
DECALOG-S
DECAPOD-S
DECAYER-S
DECEASE-D
DECEASE-S
DECEIVE-D
DECEIVE-R
DECEIVE-S
DECIARE-S
DECIBEL-S
DECIDER-S
DECIDUA-E
DECIDUA-L
DECIDUA-S
DECIMAL-S
DECKING-S
DECLAIM-S
DECLARE-D
DECLARE-R
DECLARE-S
DECLASS-E
DECLINE-D
DECLINE-R
DECLINE-S
DECODER-S
DECOLOR-S
DECORUM-S
DECOYER-S
DECREER-S
DECREET-S
DECRIAL-S
DECRIER-S
DECROWN-S
DECRYPT-S
DECUMAN-S
DECUPLE-D
DECUPLE-S
DECURIA-S
DECURVE-D
DECURVE-S
A-**DEEMING**
DEERLET-S
DEFACER-S
DEFAMER-S
DEFAULT-S
DEFENCE-D
DEFENCE-S
DEFENSE-D
DEFENSE-S
DEFICIT-S
DEFILER-S
DEFINER-S
DEFLATE-D
DEFLATE-R
DEFLATE-S
DEFLECT-S
DEFORCE-D
DEFORCE-S
DEFRAUD-S
DEFROCK-S
DEFROST-S
DEFROZE-N
DEFUNCT-S
DEGLAZE-D
DEGLAZE-S
DEGRADE-D
DEGRADE-R
DEGRADE-S
DEHISCE-D
DEHISCE-S
DEICIDE-S
DEICTIC-S
DEIFIER-S
S-**DEIGNED**
DEISEAL-S
DEJEUNE-R
DEJEUNE-S
DELAINE-S
DELAPSE-D
DELAPSE-S
DELATOR-S
DELAYER-S
DELEAVE-D
DELEAVE-S
DELIGHT-S
DELIMIT-S
DELIVER-S
DELIVER-Y
DELOUSE-D
DELOUSE-R
DELOUSE-S
DELTOID-S
DELUDER-S
DEMAGOG-S
DEMAGOG-Y
DEMAINE-S
DEMAYNE-S
DEMEANE-D
DEMEANE-S
DEMENTI-A
DEMENTI-S
DEMERGE-D
DEMERGE-R
DEMERGE-S
DEMERIT-S
DEMERSE-D
DEMERSE-S
DEMESNE-S
DEMETON-S
DEMIGOD-S
DEMIREP-S
DEMOTIC-S
DEMOUNT-S
DEMURES-T
DENDRON-S
DENIZEN-S
E-**DENTATE**
DENTATE-D
DENTINE-S
DENTIST-S
DENTURE-S
DENUDER-S
DEODAND-S
DEODARA-S
DEODATE-S
DEONTIC-S
DEORBIT-S
DEPAINT-S
DEPECHE-S
DEPLANE-D
DEPLANE-S
DEPLETE-D
DEPLETE-S
DEPLORE-D
DEPLORE-R
DEPLORE-S
DEPLUME-D
DEPLUME-S
DEPOSAL-S
DEPOSER-S
DEPOSIT-S
DEPRAVE-D
DEPRAVE-R
DEPRAVE-S
DEPRIVE-D
DEPRIVE-R
DEPRIVE-S
DEPSIDE-S
DERAIGN-S
DERANGE-D
DERANGE-S
DERIDER-S
DERIVER-S
DERMOID-S
DERRICK-S
DESCALE-D
DESCALE-S
DESCANT-S
DESCEND-S
DESCENT-S
DESERVE-D
DESERVE-R
DESERVE-S
DESIRER-S
DESKILL-S
DESKTOP-S
DESMINE-S
DESMOID-S
DESPAIR-S
DESPISE-D
DESPISE-R
DESPISE-S
DESPITE-D
DESPITE-S
DESPOIL-S
DESPOND-S
DESSERT-S
DESTAIN-S
DESTINE-D
DESTINE-S
DESTROY-S
DESUGAR-S
DETENTE-S
DETENUE-S
DETERGE-D
DETERGE-R
DETERGE-S
DETINUE-S
DETRACT-S
DETRAIN-S
DETRUDE-D
DETRUDE-S
DEUTZIA-S
DEVALUE-D
DEVALUE-S
DEVELOP-E
DEVELOP-S
DEVIANT-S
DEVIATE-D
DEVIATE-S
DEVILET-S
DEVISAL-S
DEVISEE-S
DEVISER-S
DEVISOR-S
DEVLING-S
DEVOICE-D
DEVOICE-S
DEVOLVE-D
DEVOLVE-S
DEVOTEE-S
DEWATER-S
DEWCLAW-S
DEWDROP-S
DEWFALL-S
DEXTRAN-S
DEXTRIN-E
DEXTRIN-S
A-**DHARMAS**
DHOOTIE-S
DHOURRA-S
DHURRIE-S
DIABASE-S
DIABOLO-S
DIADROM-S
DIAGRAM-S
DIAGRID-S
DIALECT-S
DIALING-S
DIALIST-S
DIALLER-S
DIALYSE-D
DIALYSE-R
DIALYSE-S
DIALYZE-D
DIALYZE-R
DIALYZE-S
DIAMIDE-S
DIAMINE-S
DIAMOND-S
DIAPASE-S
DIARISE-D
DIARISE-S
DIARIST-S
DIARIZE-D
DIARIZE-S
DIASTEM-A
DIASTEM-S
DIASTER-S
DIATRON-S
DIAZINE-S
DIAZOLE-S
DIBBLER-S
DICHORD-S
DICKIES-T
DICOTYL-S
DICTATE-D
DICTATE-S
DICTION-S
DIDAKAI-S
DIDAKEI-S
DIDDIES-T
DIDDLER-S
DIDDLEY-S
DIDICOI-S
DIDICOY-S
DIEBACK-S
DIEDRAL-S
DIEHARD-S
DIESTER-S
DIETHER-S
DIETINE-S
DIETIST-S
DIFFUSE-D
DIFFUSE-R
DIFFUSE-S
DIGAMMA-S
DIGGING-S
DIGITAL-S
DIGLYPH-S
DIGOXIN-S
DIGRAPH-S
DIHEDRA-L
DILATER-S
DILATOR-S
DILATOR-Y
DILEMMA-S
DILLIES-T
DILLING-S
DILUENT-S
DILUTEE-S
DILUTER-S
DILUTOR-S
DILUVIA-L
DILUVIA-N
DIMETER-S
DIMORPH-S
DINETTE-S
DINGBAT-S
DINGIES-T
DINKIES-T
DINMONT-S
DIOCESE-S
DIOPTER-S
DIOPTRE-S
DIORAMA-S
DIORISM-S
DIORITE-S
DIOXANE-S
DIOXIDE-S
DIPHONE-S
DIPLOID-S
DIPLOID-Y
DIPLOMA-S
DIPLOMA-T
DIPLONT-S
DIPNOAN-S
DIPPING-S
DIPTERA-L
DIPTERA-N
DIPTERA-S
DIPTYCA-S
DIPTYCH-S
DIREMPT-S
DIRTBAG-S
DIRTIES-T
DISABLE-D
DISABLE-S
DISAVOW-S
DISBAND-S
DISBARK-S
DISCAGE-D
DISCAGE-S
DISCANT-S
DISCARD-S
DISCASE-D
DISCASE-S
DISCEPT-S
DISCERN-S
DISCERP-S
DISCIDE-D
DISCIDE-S
DISCOER-S
DISCOID-S
DISCORD-S
DISCURE-D
DISCURE-S
DISDAIN-S
DISEASE-D
DISEASE-S
DISEDGE-D
DISEDGE-S
DISEUSE-S
DISFAME-S
DISFORM-S
DISGEST-S
DISGOWN-S
DISGUST-S
DISHELM-S
DISHFUL-S
DISHING-S
DISHOME-D
DISHOME-S
DISHORN-S
DISHPAN-S
DISHRAG-S
DISJECT-S
DISJOIN-S
DISJOIN-T
DISJUNE-S
DISLEAF-S
DISLIKE-D
DISLIKE-N
DISLIKE-R
DISLIKE-S
DISLIMB-S
DISLIMN-S
DISLINK-S
DISLOAD-S
DISMASK-S
DISMAST-S
DISMAYL-S
DISNEST-S
DISOBEY-S
DISPACE-D
DISPACE-S
DISPARK-S
DISPART-S
DISPEND-S
DISPLAY-S
DISPONE-D
DISPONE-E
DISPONE-R
DISPONE-S
DISPORT-S
DISPOSE-D
DISPOSE-R
DISPOSE-S
DISPOST-S
DISPRED-S
DISPUTE-D
DISPUTE-R
DISPUTE-S
DISRANK-S
DISRATE-D
DISRATE-S
DISROBE-D
DISROBE-R
DISROBE-S
DISROOT-S
DISRUPT-S
DISSAVE-D
DISSAVE-S
DISSEAT-S
DISSECT-S
DISSENT-S
DISSERT-S
DISTAFF-S
DISTAIN-S
DISTEND-S
DISTICH-S
DISTILL-S
DISTOME-S
DISTORT-S

DISTUNE-D
DISTUNE-S
DISTURB-S
DISTYLE-S
DISYOKE-D
DISYOKE-S
DITCHER-S
DIURNAL-S
DIVERGE-D
DIVERGE-S
DIVERSE-D
DIVERSE-S
DIVIDER-S
DIVINER-S
DIVINES-T
DIVISOR-S
DIVORCE-D
DIVORCE-E
DIVORCE-R
DIVORCE-S
DIVULGE-D
DIVULGE-R
DIVULGE-S
DIZZARD-S
DIZZIES-T
DJIBBAH-S
DOATING-S
DOCKAGE-S
DOCKING-S
DOCKISE-D
DOCKISE-S
DOCKIZE-D
DOCKIZE-S
DOCQUET-S
DODDIES-T
DODGING-S
DODOISM-S
DOESKIN-S
DOGBANE-S
DOGBOLT-S
DOGCART-S
DOGEATE-S
DOGEDOM-S
DOGFACE-S
DOGGIES-T
DOGGING-S
DOGGONE-D
DOGGONE-R
DOGGONE-S
DOGGREL-S
DOGHOLE-S
DOGSHIP-S
DOGSKIN-S
DOGSLED-S
DOGTOWN-S
DOGTROT-S
DOGVANE-S
DOGWOOD-S
DOITKIN-S
DOLLDOM-S
DOLLIER-S
DOLPHIN-S
DOMICIL-E
DOMICIL-S
DOMINEE-R
DOMINEE-S
DOMINIE-S
O-**DONATES**
DONATOR-S
DONATOR-Y
DONGOLA-S
DONNISM-S
DONSHIP-S
DOODLER-S
DOORMAT-S
DOORWAY-S
DOPATTA-S
DOPPING-S
DORHAWK-S
O-**DORIZED**
O-**DORIZES**
DORLACH-S
DORMANT-S
DORNECK-S
DORNICK-S
DORNOCK-S
DORTOUR-S
DOSSIER-S
DOTTLES-T
DOTTREL-S
DOUBLER-S
DOUBLET-S
DOUBTER-S
DOUCEUR-S
DOUCINE-S
DOULEIA-S
DOURINE-S
DOVECOT-E
DOVECOT-S
DOVEKEY-S
DOVEKIE-S
DOVELET-S
DOWAGER-S
DOWDIES-T
DOWNBOW-S
DOYENNE-S
DOZENTH-S
DRABBER-S
DRABBET-S
DRABBLE-D
DRABBLE-R
DRABBLE-S
DRABLER-S
DRACHMA-E
DRACHMA-I
DRACHMA-S
DRACONE-S
DRAFTEE-S
DRAFTER-S
DRAGGER-S
DRAGGLE-D
DRAGGLE-S
DRAGNET-S
DRAGOON-S
DRAINER-S
DRAPIER-S
DRAPPIE-S
DRASTIC-S
DRAUGHT-S
DRAUGHT-Y
DRAWBAR-S
DRAWING-S
DRAWLER-S
DRAYAGE-S
A-**DREADED**
DREADER-S
DREAMER-S
DREAMER-Y
DREARES-T
DREDGER-S
DREIDEL-S
DRESSER-S
DREVILL-S
DRIBBER-S
DRIBBLE-D
DRIBBLE-R
DRIBBLE-S
DRIBBLE-T
DRIBLET-S
DRIFTER-S
DRILLER-S
DRINKER-S
DRIPPER-S
DRIVING-S
DRIZZLE-D
DRIZZLE-S
DROGHER-S
DROGUET-S
DROLLER-Y
DROMOND-S
DROPLET-S
DROPOUT-S
DROPPER-S
DROPPLE-S
DROSERA-S
DROSTDY-S
DROUGHT-S
DROUGHT-Y
DROVING-S
DROWNER-S
DRUBBER-S
DRUDGER-S
DRUDGER-Y
DRUGGER-S
DRUGGET-S
DRUGGIE-R
DRUGGIE-S
DRUMBLE-D
DRUMBLE-S
DRUMLIN-S
DRUMMER-S
DRYBEAT-S
DRYWALL-S
DUALISM-S
DUALIST-S
DUALIZE-D
DUALIZE-S
DUBBING-S
DUCHESS-E
DUCKIES-T
DUCKING-S
DUCKPIN-S
DUCTING-S
DUCTULE-S
DUDGEON-S
DUDHEEN-S
DUELIST-S
DUELLER-S
DUFFING-S
DUKEDOM-S
DULCIAN-A
DULCIAN-S
DULCITE-S
DULCOSE-S
DULLARD-S
DUMAIST-S
DUMMIES-T
DUMPBIN-S
DUMPIES-T
DUMPING-S
DUNGEON-S
DUNNAGE-S
DUNNART-S
DUNNIES-T
DUNNING-S
DUNNITE-S
DUNNOCK-S
DUODENA-L
DUOTONE-S
DUPATTA-S
DURABLE-S
DURAMEN-S
DURANCE-S
DURESSE-S
DURMAST-S
DUSTBIN-S
A-**DUSTING**
DUSTOFF-S
DUSTPAN-S
DUSTRAG-S
DUUMVIR-I
DUUMVIR-S
DUVETYN-E
DUVETYN-S
DVANDVA-S
DVORNIK-S
DWELLER-S
DWINDLE-D
DWINDLE-S
DYELINE-S
DYESTER-S
DYEWEED-S
DYEWOOD-S
A-**DYNAMIC**
DYNAMIC-S
DYSODIL-E
DYSODIL-S
DYSPNEA-L
DYSPNEA-S
DYSURIA-S
M-**EAGERLY**
W-**EANLING**
Y-EANLING
EANLING-S
EARACHE-S
B-**EARDING**
Y-EARDING
T-**EARDROP**
EARDROP-S
EARDRUM-S
EARFLAP-S
B-**EARINGS**
G-EARINGS
H-EARINGS
S-EARINGS
W-EARINGS
EARLDOM-S
F-**EARLESS**
G-EARLESS
T-EARLESS
N-**EARLIER**
P-EARLIER
P-**EARLIES**
Y-EARLIES
EARLIES-T
EARLOBE-S
EARLOCK-S
EARMARK-S
EARMUFF-S
L-**EARNERS**
Y-EARNERS
EARNEST-S
L-**EARNING**
Y-EARNING
EARNING-S
EARPICK-S
EARPLUG-S
EARRING-S
EARSHOT-S
EARWORM-S
F-**EASTERS**
F-**EASTING**
R-EASTING
Y-EASTING
EASTING-S
EASTLIN-G
EASTLIN-S
B-**EATABLE**
H-EATABLE
EATABLE-S
B-**EATINGS**
H-EATINGS
S-EATINGS
EBAUCHE-S
EBBTIDE-S
EBONISE-D
EBONISE-S
EBONIST-S
EBONITE-S
EBONIZE-D
EBONIZE-S
EBRIATE-D
ECBOLIC-S
ECDYSON-E
ECDYSON-S
ECHAPPE-S
ECHELLE-S
ECHELON-S
ECHIDNA-E
ECHIDNA-S
ECHOISE-D
ECHOISE-S
ECHOISM-S
ECHOIST-S
ECHOIZE-D
ECHOIZE-S
ECLIPSE-D
ECLIPSE-S
ECLOGUE-S
R-**ECLOSED**
R-**ECLOSES**
ECOCIDE-S
O-**ECOLOGY**
ECORCHE-S
ECOTONE-S
ECOTYPE-S
P-**ECTASES**
ECTHYMA-S
ECTOPIA-S
ECTOZOA-N
ECUELLE-S
D-**ECURIES**
O-**EDEMATA**
H-**EDGIEST**
K-EDGIEST
L-EDGIEST
S-EDGIEST
W-EDGIEST
H-**EDGINGS**
W-EDGINGS
EDIFICE-S
EDIFIER-S
S-**EDITION**
EDITION-S
EDUCATE-D
EDUCATE-S
D-**EDUCING**
R-EDUCING
S-EDUCING
R-**EDUCTOR**
S-EDUCTOR
EDUCTOR-S
L-**EECHING**
R-EECHING
EELFARE-S
S-**EELIEST**
EELPOUT-S
EELWORM-S
B-**EERIEST**
L-EERIEST
P-EERIEST
EEVNING-S
EFFACER-S
EFFENDI-S
EFFORCE-D
EFFORCE-S
EFFULGE-D
EFFULGE-S
EFTSOON-S
EGALITE-S
L-**EGALITY**
R-EGALITY
R-**EGENCES**
EGGHEAD-S
L-**EGGIEST**
EGOTISE-D
EGOTISE-S
EGOTISM-S
EGOTIST-S
EGOTIZE-D
EGOTIZE-S
EIDETIC-S
EIDOLON-S
H-**EIGHTHS**
EIGHTVO-S
EILDING-S
EINKORN-S
EISWEIN-S
D-**EJECTED**
R-EJECTED
R-**EJECTOR**
EJECTOR-S
EKISTIC-S
EKPWELE-S
D-**ELAPSED**
R-ELAPSED
D-**ELAPSES**
R-ELAPSES
G-**ELASTIC**
ELASTIC-S
ELASTIN-S
R-**ELATERS**
B-**ELATING**
D-ELATING
G-ELATING
R-ELATING
D-**ELATION**
G-ELATION
R-ELATION
ELATION-S
R-**ELATIVE**
ELATIVE-S
G-**ELDINGS**
W-ELDINGS
S-**ELECTED**
S-**ELECTEE**
ELECTEE-S
S-**ELECTOR**
ELECTOR-S
ELECTRO-N
ELECTRO-S
ELEGIAC-S
ELEGISE-D
ELEGISE-S
ELEGIST-S
ELEGIZE-D
ELEGIZE-S
ELEMENT-S
ELENCHI-C
ELEVATE-D
ELEVATE-S
S-**ELFHOOD**
ELFHOOD-S
ELFLAND-S
ELFLOCK-S
ELISION-S
ELITISM-S
ELITIST-S
ELLIPSE-S
ELLWAND-S

ELMWOOD-S
ELOCUTE-D
ELOCUTE-S
ELOGIST-S
ELOGIUM-S
ELOINER-S
D-**ELOPING**
D-**ELUDERS**
D-**ELUDING**
D-**ELUSION**
ELUSION-S
D-**ELUSIVE**
D-**ELUSORY**
ELUTION-S
ELUVIUM-S
R-**EMAILED**
EMANATE-D
EMANATE-S
EMBATHE-D
EMBATHE-S
EMBLAZE-D
EMBLAZE-R
EMBLAZE-S
EMBLOOM-S
EMBOGUE-D
EMBOGUE-S
EMBOSOM-S
EMBOUND-S
EMBOWEL-S
EMBOWER-S
EMBRACE-D
EMBRACE-R
EMBRACE-S
EMBRAID-S
EMBRAVE-D
EMBRAVE-S
EMBREAD-S
EMBREWE-D
EMBREWE-S
EMBROIL-S
EMBROWN-S
EMBRUTE-D
EMBRUTE-S
EMBRYON-S
R-**EMENDED**
EMENDER-S
EMERALD-S
D-**EMERGED**
R-EMERGED
D-**EMERGES**
R-EMERGES
EMERITA-E
EMEROID-S
D-**EMERSED**
EMETINE-S
EMICATE-D
EMICATE-S
EMIRATE-S
D-**EMITTED**
R-EMITTED
R-**EMITTER**
EMITTER-S
EMONGES-T
D-**EMOTING**
D-**EMOTION**
R-EMOTION
EMOTION-S
R-**EMOVING**
EMPAIRE-D
EMPAIRE-S
EMPALER-S
EMPANEL-S
EMPAYRE-D
EMPAYRE-S
EMPERCE-D
EMPERCE-S
EMPEROR-S
EMPIRIC-S
EMPLACE-D
EMPLACE-S
EMPLANE-D
EMPLANE-S
EMPLOYE-D
EMPLOYE-E
EMPLOYE-R
EMPLOYE-S
EMPLUME-D
EMPLUME-S
EMPOWER-S
EMPRESS-E
EMPRISE-S
EMPRIZE-S
EMPTIER-S
EMPTIES-T
EMPTION-S
EMPYEMA-S
EMULATE-D
EMULATE-S
A-**EMULING**
EMULSIN-S
EMULSOR-S
D-**EMURING**
ENABLER-S
ENACTOR-S
ENACTOR-Y
ENAMINE-S
ENAMOUR-S
V-**ENATION**
ENATION-S
ENCHAFE-D
ENCHAFE-S
ENCHAIN-S
P-**ENCHANT**
ENCHANT-S
ENCHARM-S
ENCHASE-D
ENCHASE-R
ENCHASE-S
ENCHEER-S
ENCLASP-S
ENCLAVE-D
ENCLAVE-S
ENCLOSE-D
ENCLOSE-R
ENCLOSE-S
ENCLOUD-S
ENCODER-S
ENCRUST-S
ENCRYPT-S
ENDARCH-Y
ENDEMIC-S
ENDERON-S
ENDGAME-S
B-**ENDINGS**
L-ENDINGS
M-ENDINGS
S-ENDINGS
ENDIRON-S
ENDNOTE-S
ENDOGEN-S
ENDOGEN-Y
ENDOPOD-S
ENDORSE-D
ENDORSE-E
ENDORSE-R
ENDORSE-S
ENDOWER-S
ENDSHIP-S
ENDURER-S
B-**ENDWAYS**
B-**ENDWISE**
ENERGID-S
R-**ENEWING**
ENFELON-S
ENFEOFF-S
ENFEVER-S
ENFLAME-D
ENFLAME-S
P-**ENFOLDS**
T-ENFOLDS
R-**ENFORCE**
ENFORCE-D
ENFORCE-R
ENFORCE-S
ENFRAME-D
ENFRAME-S
ENFROZE-N
ENGAGER-S
ENGINER-S
ENGINER-Y
ENGLOBE-D
ENGLOBE-S
ENGLOOM-S
ENGORGE-D
ENGORGE-S
ENGRACE-D
ENGRACE-S
ENGRAFF-S
ENGRAFT-S
ENGRAIL-S
ENGRAIN-S
ENGRASP-S
ENGRAVE-D
ENGRAVE-N
ENGRAVE-R
ENGRAVE-S
ENGUARD-S
ENGULPH-S
ENHANCE-D
ENHANCE-R
ENHANCE-S
ENJOYER-S
ENLARGE-D
ENLARGE-N
ENLARGE-R
ENLARGE-S
P-**ENLIGHT**
ENLIGHT-S
ENLIVEN-S
G-**ENLOCKS**
ENNOBLE-D
ENNOBLE-R
ENNOBLE-S
ENOLASE-S
M-**ENOLOGY**
O-ENOLOGY
P-ENOLOGY
D-**ENOUNCE**
R-ENOUNCE
ENOUNCE-D
ENOUNCE-S
ENPLANE-D
ENPLANE-S
ENPRINT-S
ENQUIRE-D
ENQUIRE-R
ENQUIRE-S
ENRANGE-D
ENRANGE-S
ENRHEUM-S
ENROBER-S
ENROUGH-S
ENROUND-S
ENSHELL-S
ENSLAVE-D
ENSLAVE-R
ENSLAVE-S
ENSNARE-D
ENSNARE-R
ENSNARE-S
ENSNARL-S
ENSTAMP-S
ENSTEEP-S
ENSTYLE-D
ENSTYLE-S
C-**ENSURED**
C-**ENSURER**
ENSURER-S
C-**ENSURES**
ENSWEEP-S
V-**ENTAILS**
ENTASIA-S
V-**ENTAYLE**
ENTAYLE-D
ENTAYLE-S
ENTENTE-S
C-**ENTERED**
T-ENTERED
ENTERER-S
ENTERIC-S
ENTERON-S
ENTHRAL-L
ENTHRAL-S
ENTHUSE-D
ENTHUSE-S
P-**ENTICED**
ENTICER-S
P-**ENTICES**
ENTITLE-D
ENTITLE-S
P-**ENTOMIC**
ENTOZOA-L
ENTOZOA-N
ENTRAIL-S
ENTRAIN-S
ENTRANT-S
ENTREAT-S
ENTREAT-Y
C-**ENTRIES**
G-ENTRIES
S-ENTRIES
C-**ENTRISM**
ENTRISM-S
C-**ENTRIST**
ENTRIST-S
ENTRUST-S
ENTWINE-D
ENTWINE-S
ENTWIST-S
ENVAULT-S
ENVELOP-E
ENVELOP-S
ENVENOM-S
ENVIRON-S
ENVYING-S
ENWHEEL-S
EOBIONT-S
N-**EOLITHS**
P-**EONISMS**
EPACRID-S
EPAGOGE-S
EPAULET-S
EPAZOTE-S
EPEEIST-S
EPEIRID-S
EPERGNE-S
EPHEDRA-S
EPICARP-S
EPICEDE-S
EPICENE-S
EPICIER-S
EPICISM-S
EPICIST-S
EPICURE-S
EPIDERM-S
L-**EPIDOTE**
EPIDOTE-S
EPIGONE-S
EPIGONI-C
EPIGRAM-S
D-**EPILATE**
EPILATE-D
EPILATE-S
EPIMERE-S
EPISCIA-S
EPISODE-S
EPISOME-S
EPISTLE-D
EPISTLE-R
EPISTLE-S
EPITAPH-S
EPITHEM-A
EPITHEM-S
EPITHET-S
EPITOME-S
EPITOPE-S
EPIZOAN-S
EPOXIDE-S
EPSILON-S
D-**EPURATE**
EPURATE-D
EPURATE-S
EQUATOR-S
EQUINIA-S
R-**EQUITES**
ERASION-S
ERASURE-S
ERATHEM-S
T-**ERBIUMS**
ERECTER-S
ERECTOR-S
EREMITE-S
EREPSIN-S
ERINITE-S
M-**ERISTIC**
V-ERISTIC
ERISTIC-S
ERLKING-S
ERMELIN-S
V-**ERMINED**
ERODENT-S
ERODIUM-S
EROSION-S
EROTEMA-S
EROTEME-S
EROTICA-L
EROTISM-S
EROTIZE-D
EROTIZE-S
ERRATIC-S
ERRHINE-S
H-**ERRINGS**
ERUDITE-S
ESCALOP-E
ESCALOP-S
ESCAPEE-S
ESCAPER-S
ESCHEAT-S
ESCOLAR-S
D-**ESCRIBE**
ESCRIBE-D
ESCRIBE-S
ESCROLL-S
ESCUAGE-S
ESERINE-S
ESLOYNE-D
ESLOYNE-S
ESPARTO-S
B-**ESPOUSE**
ESPOUSE-D
ESPOUSE-R
ESPOUSE-S
ESQUIRE-D
ESQUIRE-S
ESSAYER-S
ESSENCE-S
ESSOYNE-S
G-**ESTATED**
R-ESTATED
G-**ESTATES**
R-ESTATES
T-ESTATES
A-**ESTHETE**
ESTHETE-S
A-**ESTIVAL**
F-ESTIVAL
ESTOILE-S
ESTOVER-S
ESTRADE-S
ESTREAT-S
ESTREPE-D
ESTREPE-S
O-**ESTRINS**
O-**ESTRIOL**
ESTRIOL-S
O-**ESTRONE**
ESTRONE-S
O-**ESTROUS**
O-**ESTRUMS**
B-**ETACISM**
ETACISM-S
ETAERIO-S
ETAGERE-S
ETALAGE-S
K-**ETAMINE**
ETAMINE-S
ETATISM-E
ETATISM-S
ETATIST-E
ETCHANT-S
F-**ETCHERS**
F-**ETCHING**
K-ETCHING
L-ETCHING
R-ETCHING
ETCHING-S
ETERNAL-S
ETESIAN-S
M-**ETHANES**
M-**ETHANOL**
ETHANOL-S
A-**ETHERIC**
ETHICAL-S
ETHINYL-S
ETHMOID-S
M-**ETHOXYL**
ETHOXYL-S
M-**ETHYLIC**
ETHYNYL-S
ETIOLIN-S
ETOURDI-E
ETRENNE-S
F-**ETTLING**
N-ETTLING
P-ETTLING
S-ETTLING
EUCAINE-S
EUCLASE-S
EUCRITE-S
EUDEMON-S

EUGENIA-S
EUGENIC-S
EUGENOL-S
EUGLENA-S
EULOGIA-E
EULOGIA-S
EUPHROE-S
EUPLOID-S
EUPLOID-Y
EUPNOEA-S
H-**EUREKAS**
EUSTELE-S
EUSTYLE-S
EUTEXIA-S
EVACUEE-S
EVANGEL-S
EVANGEL-Y
EVASION-S
EVENING-S
EVENTER-S
R-**EVERTED**
EVERTOR-S
EVICTEE-S
EVICTOR-S
EVIDENT-S
L-**EVIRATE**
EVIRATE-D
EVIRATE-S
L-**EVITATE**
EVITATE-D
EVITATE-S
EVOCATE-D
EVOCATE-S
R-**EVOKERS**
R-**EVOKING**
R-**EVOLUTE**
EVOLUTE-D
EVOLUTE-S
D-**EVOLVED**
R-EVOLVED
R-**EVOLVER**
EVOLVER-S
D-**EVOLVES**
R-EVOLVES
R-**EVULSED**
EXACTER-S
EXACTOR-S
EXALTER-S
H-**EXAMINE**
EXAMINE-D
EXAMINE-E
EXAMINE-R
EXAMINE-S
EXAMPLE-D
EXAMPLE-S
H-**EXARCHY**
EXCERPT-A
EXCERPT-S
EXCHEAT-S
EXCIMER-S
EXCIPLE-S
EXCITER-S
EXCITON-S
EXCITOR-S
EXCLAIM-S
EXCLAVE-S
EXCLUDE-D
EXCLUDE-E
EXCLUDE-R
EXCLUDE-S
EXCRETA-L
EXCRETE-D
EXCRETE-R
EXCRETE-S
EXCURSE-D
EXCURSE-S
EXCUSAL-S
EXCUSER-S
EXECUTE-D
EXECUTE-R
EXECUTE-S
EXEGETE-S
EXEMPLA-R
EXEMPLE-S
EXERGUE-S
EXHAUST-S
EXHEDRA-E
EXHIBIT-S
EXHUMER-S
EXIGENT-S
EXOCARP-S
EXODERM-S
EXODIST-S
EXOMION-S
EXORDIA-L
EXOTISM-S
EXPANSE-S
EXPENSE-D
EXPENSE-S
S-**EXPERTS**
EXPIATE-D
EXPIATE-S
EXPIRER-S
EXPLAIN-S
EXPLANT-S
EXPLODE-D
EXPLODE-R
EXPLODE-S
EXPLOIT-S
EXPLORE-D
EXPLORE-R
EXPLORE-S
EXPOSAL-S
EXPOSER-S
EXPOSIT-S
EXPOUND-S
EXPRESS-O
EXPULSE-D
EXPULSE-S
EXPUNCT-S
EXPUNGE-D
EXPUNGE-R
EXPUNGE-S
EXPURGE-D
EXPURGE-S
EXSCIND-S
EXTERNE-S
EXTINCT-S
EXTRACT-S
EXTRAIT-S
EXTREAT-S
EXTREME-R
EXTREME-S
EXTRUDE-D
EXTRUDE-R
EXTRUDE-S
EXUDATE-S
EXURBIA-S
EYEBALL-S
EYEBEAM-S
EYEBOLT-S
EYEBROW-S
EYEHOLE-S
EYEHOOK-S
EYELIAD-S
EYESHOT-S
EYESORE-S
EYESPOT-S
EYEWINK-S
FABLIAU-X
FABLING-S
FACIEND-S
FACONNE-S
FACTICE-S
FACTION-S
FACTOID-S
FACTURE-S
FADAISE-S
FADDISM-S
FADDIST-S
FAGGING-S
FAGOTER-S
FAHLORE-S
FAIENCE-S
FAILING-S
FAILURE-S
FAINTER-S
FAIRING-S
FAIRWAY-S
FAITOUR-S
FALAFEL-S
FALBALA-S
FALCADE-S
FALCATE-D
FALCULA-S
FALDAGE-S
FALLING-S
FALLOFF-S
FALLOUT-S
FALSISM-S
FANATIC-S
FANCIER-S
FANCIES-T
FANFARE-D
FANFARE-S
FANFOLD-S
FANGLES-S
FANNELL-S
FANNING-S
FANTAIL-S
FANTASM-S
FANTAST-S
FANTEEG-S
FANWORT-S
FANZINE-S
FARADAY-S
FARAWAY-S
FARCEUR-S
FARCING-S
FARDAGE-S
FARDING-S
FARINHA-S
FARMING-S
FARRAGO-S
FARRIER-S
FARRIER-Y
FARRUCA-S
FARSIDE-S
FARTHEL-S
FARTLEK-S
FASCINE-S
FASCISM-I
FASCISM-O
FASCISM-S
FASCIST-A
FASCIST-I
FASCIST-S
FASHION-S
FASTING-S
FATBACK-S
FATBIRD-S
FATHEAD-S
FATIGUE-D
FATIGUE-S
FATLING-S
FATTIES-T
FATTISM-S
FATTIST-S
FATWOOD-S
FAUCHON-S
FAUNIST-S
FAUVISM-S
FAUVIST-S
FAVELLA-S
FAVORER-S
FAVRILE-S
FAWNING-S
FAYENCE-S
FAZENDA-S
A-**FEARING**
FEASTER-S
FEATHER-S
FEATHER-Y
FEATURE-D
FEATURE-S
A-**FEBRILE**
FECHTER-S
FEDARIE-S
FEDAYEE-N
FEDERAL-S
FEEBLES-T
FEEDBAG-S
FEEDING-S
FEEDLOT-S
FEELBAD-S
FEELING-S
FEERING-S
FEIGNER-S
FELAFEL-S
FELICIA-S
FELLATE-D
FELLATE-S
FELSITE-S
FELSPAR-S
FELTING-S
FELUCCA-S
FELWORT-S
FEMITER-S
FENAGLE-D
FENAGLE-S
FENCING-S
FENITAR-S
FENLAND-S
FENNIES-T
FENURON-S
FEOFFEE-S
FEOFFER-S
FEOFFOR-S
FERLIES-T
FERMATA-S
FERMENT-S
FERMION-S
FERMIUM-S
FERNING-S
FERRATE-S
FERRITE-S
FERRUGO-S
FERRULE-D
FERRULE-S
FERTILE-R
FERVOUR-S
FESTOON-S
FETCHER-S
FETICHE-S
FETLOCK-S
FETTLER-S
FEUDING-S
FEUDIST-S
FIANCEE-S
FIBROID-S
FIBROIN-S
FIBROMA-S
FIBROSE-D
FIBROSE-S
FIBSTER-S
FICKLES-T
FICTION-S
FIDDLER-S
FIDDLEY-S
FIDEISM-S
FIDEIST-S
FIEFDOM-S
FIELDER-S
FIFTEEN-S
FIGHTER-S
FIGMENT-S
FIGURER-S
FIGWORT-S
FILABEG-S
FILACER-S
FILAREE-S
FILARIA-E
FILARIA-L
FILARIA-N
FILARIA-S
FILASSE-S
FILAZER-S
FILBERD-S
FILBERT-S
FILCHER-S
FILEMOT-S
FILIATE-D
FILIATE-S
FILIBEG-S
FILLING-S
FILMDOM-S
FILMSET-S
FIMBRIA-E
FIMBRIA-L
FINAGLE-D
FINAGLE-R
FINAGLE-S
FINALIS-E
FINALIS-M
FINALIS-T
FINANCE-D
FINANCE-S
FINBACK-S
FINDING-S
FINDRAM-S
FINESSE-D
FINESSE-R
FINESSE-S
FINFOOT-S
FINIKIN-G
FINMARK-S
FINNACK-S
FINNOCK-S
FIREARM-S
FIREBUG-S
FIREDOG-S
FIREPAN-S
FIREPOT-S
FIRRING-S
FISHEYE-S
FISHGIG-S
FISHING-S
FISHNET-S
FISHWAY-S
FISSION-S
FISSURE-D
FISSURE-S
FISTFUL-S
FISTULA-E
FISTULA-R
FISTULA-S
FITCHET-S
FITCHEW-S
FITMENT-S
FITTING-S
FIVEPIN-S
FIXATIF-S
FIXTURE-S
FIZZGIG-S
FIZZING-S
FLACKER-S
FLACKER-Y
FLACKET-S
FLAFFER-S
FLAGGER-S
FLAKIES-T
FLAMBEE-D
FLAMFEW-S
FLAMING-O
FLANEUR-S
FLANGER-S
FLANKER-S
FLANNEL-S
FLANNEN-S
FLAPPER-S
FLASHER-S
FLASHES-T
FLASKET-S
FLATBED-S
FLATCAP-S
FLATCAR-S
FLATLET-S
FLATTEN-S
FLATTER-S
FLATTER-Y
FLATTOP-S
FLAUGHT-S
FLAVINE-S
FLAVONE-S
FLAVOUR-S
FLAVOUR-Y
FLEABAG-S
FLEAPIT-S
FLECKER-S
FLEECER-S
FLEERER-S
FLENSER-S
FLESHER-S
FLETTON-S
FLEURET-S
FLEURON-S
FLEXION-S
FLEXURE-S
FLICKER-S
FLICKER-Y
FLINDER-S
FLINGER-S
FLIPPER-S
FLIRTER-S
FLITTER-N
FLITTER-S
FLIVVER-S
FLOATEL-S
FLOATER-S
FLOGGER-S
FLOKATI-S
FLOODER-S
FLOORER-S
FLOOSIE-S
FLOOZIE-S
FLOPPER-S
FLORIST-S
FLORUIT-S
FLOSSIE-R
FLOSSIE-S

FLOTAGE-S
FLOTSAM-S
FLOUNCE-D
FLOUNCE-S
FLOUTER-S
FLOWAGE-S
FLUBBER-S
FLUBDUB-S
FLUENCE-S
FLUERIC-S
FLUIDIC-S
FLUNKER-S
FLUNKEY-S
FLUORID-E
FLUORID-S
FLUORIN-E
FLUORIN-S
FLUSHER-S
FLUSHES-T
FLUSTER-S
FLUSTER-Y
FLUTINA-S
FLUTING-S
FLUTIST-S
A-**FLUTTER**
FLUTTER-S
FLUTTER-Y
FLUXION-S
FLYAWAY-S
FLYBANE-S
FLYBELT-S
FLYBLOW-N
FLYBLOW-S
FLYBOAT-S
FLYBOOK-S
FLYOVER-S
FLYPAST-S
FLYTIER-S
FLYTING-S
FLYTRAP-S
FOAMING-S
FOCUSER-S
FOGGAGE-S
FOGHORN-S
FOGYDOM-S
FOGYISM-S
FOILING-S
FOISTER-S
FOLACIN-S
FOLDING-S
FOLDOUT-S
FOLIAGE-D
FOLIAGE-S
FOLIATE-D
FOLIATE-S
FOLIOLE-S
FOLKMOT-E
FOLKMOT-S
FOLKWAY-S
FONDANT-S
FONDLER-S
FONTINA-S
FONTLET-S
FOODISM-S
FOOLING-S
FOOTAGE-S
FOOTBAR-S
FOOTBOY-S
FOOTIES-T
FOOTING-S
FOOTLER-S
FOOTLES-S
FOOTPAD-S
FOOTROT-S
FOOTSIE-S

FOOTWAY-S
FOOZLER-S
FOPLING-S
FORAGER-S
FORAMEN-S
FORAYER-S
FORBEAR-S
FORBODE-D
FORBODE-S
FOREARM-S
FOREBAY-S
FORECAR-S
FOREGUT-S
FORELAY-S
FORELEG-S
FORELIE-S
FOREPAW-S
FORERAN-K
FORERUN-S
FORESAY-S
FORESEE-N
FORESEE-R
FORESEE-S
FORETOP-S
FOREVER-S
FORFAIR-N
FORFAIR-S
FORFEIT-S
FORFEND-S
FORGING-S
FORGIVE-N
FORGIVE-R
FORGIVE-S
FORGOER-S
FORHENT-S
FORKFUL-S
FORLANA-S
FORLEND-S
FORLESE-S
FORLORN-S
FORMANT-S
FORMATE-D
FORMATE-S
FORMING-S
FORMULA-E
FORMULA-R
FORMULA-S
FORPINE-D
FORPINE-S
FORSAKE-N
FORSAKE-R
FORSAKE-S
FORSLOE-D
FORSLOE-S
FORSLOW-S
FORTLET-S
FORTUNE-D
FORTUNE-S
FORWARD-S
FORWARN-S
S-**FORZATI**
S-**FORZATO**
FORZATO-S
FOSSICK-S
FOSSULA-E
FOUDRIE-S
FOUETTE-S
FOUGADE-S
FOULARD-S
FOULDER-S
FOULING-S
FOUMART-S
FOUNDER-S
FOURGON-S
FOVEATE-D

FOVEOLA-E
FOVEOLA-R
FOVEOLA-S
FOVEOLE-S
FOVEOLE-T
FOWLING-S
FOXFIRE-S
FOXHOLE-S
FOXHUNT-S
FOXSHIP-S
FOXSKIN-S
FOXTAIL-S
FOXTROT-S
FRACTAL-S
FRACTUR-E
FRACTUR-S
FRAENUM-S
FRAGILE-R
FRAKTUR-S
FRAMING-S
FRANION-S
FRANKER-S
FRAUGHT-S
FRAYING-S
FRAZZLE-D
FRAZZLE-S
FRECKLE-D
FRECKLE-S
FREEBEE-S
FREEBIE-S
FREEDOM-S
FREESIA-S
FREEWAY-S
FREEZER-S
FREIGHT-S
FRESHEN-S
FRESHER-S
FRESHES-T
FRESHET-S
FRESNEL-S
FRETSAW-S
FRETTER-S
FRIANDE-S
FRIBBLE-D
FRIBBLE-R
FRIBBLE-S
FRIGATE-S
FRIGGER-S
FRIJOLE-S
FRILLER-S
FRIPPER-S
FRIPPER-Y
FRISEUR-S
FRISKER-S
FRISKET-S
FRISSON-S
FRISURE-S
FRITTER-S
FRITURE-S
FRIZZER-S
FRIZZLE-D
FRIZZLE-R
FRIZZLE-S
FROGBIT-S
FROGEYE-D
FROGEYE-S
FROGLET-S
FROMAGE-S
FRONTAL-S
FRONTON-S
FROSTED-S
FROUNCE-D
FROUNCE-S
FROWARD-S
FROWNER-S

FRUITER-S
FRUITER-Y
FRUMPLE-D
FRUMPLE-S
FRUSTUM-S
FUCHSIA-S
FUCHSIN-E
FUCHSIN-S
FUCKING-S
FUDDLER-S
FUEHRER-S
FUELLER-S
FUGUIST-S
FULCRUM-S
FULFILL-S
FULGOUR-S
FULLAGE-S
FULMINE-D
FULMINE-S
FULSOME-R
FUMBLER-S
FUMETTE-S
FUNCTOR-S
FUNDING-S
FUNERAL-S
FUNFAIR-S
FUNGOID-S
FUNICLE-S
FUNNIES-T
FUNSTER-S
FURCATE-D
FURCATE-S
FURCULA-E
FURCULA-R
FURFAIR-S
FURIOSO-S
FURLANA-S
FURLONG-S
FURNACE-D
FURNACE-S
FURRIER-S
FURRIER-Y
FURRIES-T
FURRING-S
FURTHER-S
FUSAROL-E
FUSAROL-S
FUSHION-S
FUSILLI-S
FUSSPOT-S
FUSTIAN-S
FUTCHEL-S
FUTHARC-S
FUTHARK-S
FUTHORC-S
FUTHORK-S
FUTTOCK-S
GABBARD-S
GABBART-S
GABBLER-S
GABELLE-D
GABELLE-R
GABELLE-S
GABFEST-S
GADLING-S
GADROON-S
GADWALL-S
GAFFING-S
GAGSTER-S
GAHNITE-S
GAINING-S
GAINSAY-S
GALABEA-H
GALABEA-S
GALABIA-H

GALABIA-S
GALANGA-L
GALANGA-S
GALATEA-S
GALEATE-D
GALETTE-S
GALILEE-S
GALIPOT-S
GALLANT-S
GALLATE-S
GALLEIN-S
GALLEON-S
GALLETA-S
GALLIOT-S
GALLISE-D
GALLISE-S
GALLIUM-S
GALLIZE-D
GALLIZE-S
GALLNUT-S
GALLOON-S
GALLOOT-S
GALOCHE-D
GALOCHE-S
GALOPIN-G
GALOPIN-S
GALOSHE-D
GALOSHE-S
GALUMPH-S
GAMBADE-S
GAMBADO-S
GAMBIER-S
GAMBIST-S
GAMBLER-S
GAMBOGE-S
GAMBREL-S
GAMELAN-S
A-**GAMETES**
GAMINES-S
GAMMOCK-S
GANACHE-S
GANGING-S
GANGLIA-L
GANGLIA-R
GANGREL-S
GANGSTA-S
GANGWAY-S
GANOINE-S
GANTLET-S
GARBAGE-S
GARBLER-S
GARBLES-S
GARBOIL-S
GARBURE-S
GARDANT-S
GARGLER-S
GARIGUE-S
GARLAND-S
GARMENT-S
GAROTTE-D
GAROTTE-R
GAROTTE-S
GARPIKE-S
GARROTE-D
GARROTE-R
GARROTE-S
GARVOCK-S
GASAHOL-S
GASKING-S
GASOHOL-S
GASPING-S
GASSING-S
GASTREA-S
GASTRIN-S
GATEWAY-S

GAUDGIE-S
GAUDIES-T
GAUFFER-S
GAUGING-S
GAULTER-S
GAVOTTE-D
GAVOTTE-S
GAWKIES-T
GAZANIA-S
GAZELLE-S
GAZETTE-D
GAZETTE-S
GAZOOKA-S
GEALOUS-Y
GEARING-S
GEEBUNG-S
GEECHEE-S
GELATIN-E
GELATIN-G
GELATIN-S
GELDING-S
GELLANT-S
GEMMATE-D
GEMMATE-S
GEMMULE-S
GEMSBOK-S
GENAPPE-S
GENERAL-E
GENERAL-S
GENERIC-S
A-**GENESES**
A-**GENESIS**
A-**GENETIC**
GENETIC-S
GENETTE-S
GENIPAP-S
GENISTA-S
GENITAL-S
GENITOR-S
GENIZAH-S
GENLOCK-S
GENOISE-S
GENSENG-S
GENTIAN-S
GENTILE-S
GENTLES-T
GEODUCK-S
GEOFACT-S
GEOMANT-S
GEORGIC-S
GERBERA-S
GERENUK-S
GERMAIN-E
GERMAIN-S
GERMINA-L
GESTALT-S
GESTAPO-S
GESTATE-D
GESTATE-S
GESTURE-D
GESTURE-R
GESTURE-S
GETAWAY-S
GETTING-S
GHARIAL-S
GHERKIN-S
GHILGAI-S
GHILLIE-D
GHILLIE-S
GHOULIE-S
GIDDIES-T
GIGABIT-S
GIGATON-S
GIGGLER-S
GILBERT-S

GILDING-S
GILLION-S
GILLNET-S
GILTCUP-S
GIMMICK-S
GIMMICK-Y
GINGALL-S
GINGELI-S
GINGHAM-S
GINGILI-S
GINGIVA-E
GINGIVA-L
A-**GINNERS**
GINNING-S
GINSENG-S
GINSHOP-S
GIRAFFE-S
GIRASOL-E
GIRASOL-S
GIRDING-S
GIRDLER-S
GIRLOND-S
GIROSOL-S
GISARME-S
GITTERN-S
GIZZARD-S
GJETOST-S
GLACIAL-S
GLACIER-S
GLADDEN-S
GLADDIE-S
GLADDON-S
GLAIRIN-G
GLAIRIN-S
GLAMOUR-S
GLANCER-S
GLASSIE-R
GLASSIE-S
GLAZIER-S
GLAZIER-Y
GLAZING-S
GLEAMER-S
GLEANER-S
GLENOID-S
GLEYING-S
GLIADIN-E
GLIADIN-S
GLIBBER-Y
GLIDDER-Y
GLIDING-S
A-**GLIMMER**
GLIMMER-S
GLIMMER-Y
GLIMPSE-D
GLIMPSE-R
GLIMPSE-S
GLISTEN-S
GLISTER-S
A-**GLITTER**
GLITTER-S
GLITTER-Y
GLOATER-S
GLOBATE-D
GLOBOID-S
GLOBOSE-S
GLOBULE-S
GLOBULE-T
GLOCHID-S
GLONOIN-S
GLOSSER-S
GLOVING-S
GLOZING-S
GLUCINA-S
GLUCOSE-S
GLUEPOT-S
GLUTTON-S
GLUTTON-Y
GLYCINE-S
GLYCOSE-S
GLYPTIC-S
GNASHER-S
GNAWING-S
GNOCCHI-S
GNOMIST-S
A-**GNOSTIC**
GOBBLER-S
GOBIOID-S
GOBURRA-S
GODDAMN-S
GODETIA-S
GODHEAD-S
GODHOOD-S
GODLING-S
GODROON-S
GODSEND-S
GODSHIP-S
GODWARD-S
GOGGLER-S
GOLDARN-S
GOLDBUG-S
GOLDEYE-S
GOLDURN-S
GOLFING-S
GOLIARD-S
GOLIARD-Y
GOLLAND-S
GOLOSHE-D
GOLOSHE-S
GOMBEEN-S
GOMERAL-S
GOMEREL-S
GOMERIL-S
GONDOLA-S
GONIDIA-L
GOODBYE-S
GOODIES-T
GOOMBAH-S
GOOMBAY-S
GOOSIES-T
GOPURAM-S
GORCOCK-S
GORCROW-S
GORILLA-S
GORMAND-S
GORSEDD-S
GORSOON-S
GOSHAWK-S
GOSLING-S
GOSPORT-S
GOSSOON-S
GOTHITE-S
GOUACHE-S
GOUGERE-S
GOURAMI-S
GOURMET-S
GOWLAND-S
GOWNBOY-S
GRABBER-S
GRABBLE-D
GRABBLE-R
GRABBLE-S
GRACILE-S
GRACKLE-S
GRADATE-D
GRADATE-S
GRADDAN-S
GRADINE-S
GRADUAL-S
GRAFTER-S
GRAINER-S
GRAMARY-E
GRAMMAR-S
GRANDAD-S
GRANDAM-E
GRANDAM-S
GRANDEE-S
GRANDMA-S
GRANDPA-S
GRANFER-S
GRANGER-S
GRANITA-S
GRANITE-S
GRANNAM-S
GRANNIE-D
GRANNIE-S
GRANOLA-S
GRANTEE-S
GRANTER-S
GRANTOR-S
GRANULE-S
A-**GRAPHIC**
GRAPHIC-S
GRAPLIN-E
GRAPLIN-S
GRAPNEL-S
GRAPPLE-D
GRAPPLE-R
GRAPPLE-S
GRASPER-S
GRASSER-S
GRASSUM-S
GRATINE-E
GRATING-S
GRAUPEL-S
GRAVIDA-E
GRAVIDA-S
GRAVING-S
GRAVURE-S
GRAYLAG-S
GRAYOUT-S
GRAZIER-S
GRAZING-S
GREASER-S
GREATEN-S
GRECIAN-S
GRECIZE-D
GRECIZE-S
GRECQUE-S
A-**GREEING**
GREENER-S
GREENER-Y
GREENIE-R
GREENIE-S
GREENTH-S
GREETER-S
GREGALE-S
GREISEN-S
GREMIAL-S
GREMLIN-S
GREMMIE-S
GRENADE-S
GREYHEN-S
GREYING-S
GREYLAG-S
GRIBBLE-S
GRICING-S
GRIDDER-S
GRIDDLE-D
GRIDDLE-S
GRIEVER-S
GRIFFIN-S
GRIFFON-S
GRIFTER-S
GRILLER-S
GRIMACE-D
GRIMACE-R
GRIMACE-S
GRINDER-S
GRINDER-Y
GRINNER-S
GRIPPER-S
GRIPPLE-S
A-**GRISING**
GRISKIN-S
GRISTLE-S
GRITTER-S
GRIZZLE-D
GRIZZLE-R
GRIZZLE-S
GROANER-S
GROCKLE-S
GROGRAM-S
GROMMET-S
GROOMER-S
GROOVER-S
GROSERT-S
GROSSER-S
GROSSES-T
GROUPER-S
GROUPIE-S
GROUSER-S
GROUSES-T
GROUTER-S
GROWING-S
GROWLER-S
GROWLER-Y
GROWNUP-S
GRUBBER-S
GRUBBLE-D
GRUBBLE-S
GRUDGER-S
GRUELER-S
GRUMBLE-D
GRUMBLE-R
GRUMBLE-S
GRUMMET-S
GRUNION-S
GRUNTER-S
GRUNTLE-D
GRUNTLE-S
GRUYERE-S
GRYPHON-S
GRYSBOK-S
GUANACO-S
GUANASE-S
GUANINE-S
GUARANA-S
GUARANI-S
GUARDEE-S
GUARDER-S
GUAYULE-S
GUDGEON-S
GUERDON-S
GUEREZA-S
GUERITE-S
GUESSER-S
GUESTEN-S
GUICHET-S
GUIDAGE-S
GUIDING-S
GUILDER-S
GUIPURE-S
GUISARD-S
A-**GUISING**
GUISING-S
GUMBOIL-S
GUMBOOT-S
GUMDROP-S
GUMMING-S
GUMMITE-S
GUMMOSE-S
GUMSHOE-D
GUMSHOE-S
GUMTREE-S
GUMWEED-S
GUMWOOD-S
GUNBOAT-S
GUNFIRE-S
GUNLOCK-S
GUNNAGE-S
GUNNERA-S
GUNNING-S
GUNPLAY-S
GUNPORT-S
GUNROOM-S
GUNSHIP-S
GUNSHOT-S
GUNWALE-S
GURGLET-S
GURNARD-S
GURUDOM-S
GURUISM-S
GUTCHER-S
GUTSFUL-S
GUTTATE-D
GUTTATE-S
GUTTIES-T
GUTTLER-S
GUYLINE-S
GUZZLER-S
GWEDUCK-S
GWINIAD-S
GWYNIAD-S
GYMNAST-S
GYPLURE-S
GYPSTER-S
GYRATOR-S
GYRATOR-Y
GYROCAR-S
HABITAN-S
HABITAN-T
HABITAT-S
HABITUE-S
HACHURE-D
HACHURE-S
HACKBUT-S
W-**HACKERS**
C-**HACKING**
T-HACKING
W-HACKING
HACKING-S
S-**HACKLED**
S-**HACKLER**
HACKLER-S
S-**HACKLES**
HACKLET-S
HACKNEY-S
HACKSAW-S
C-**HADARIM**
S-**HADDOCK**
HADDOCK-S
HADROME-S
HAFFLIN-S
HAFNIUM-S
HAFTARA-H
HAFTARA-S
S-**HAFTERS**
S-**HAFTING**
HAGBOLT-S
HAGDOWN-S
HAGGADA-H
HAGGADA-S
HAGGARD-S
S-**HAGGING**
HAGGLER-S
HAGRIDE-S
HAHNIUM-S
C-**HAINING**
HAINING-S
HAIRCAP-S
HAIRCUT-S
C-**HAIRING**
HAIRNET-S
HAIRPIN-S
HALACHA-S
HALAKAH-S
HALAKHA-S
HALALAH-S
HALAVAH-S
HALBERD-S
HALBERT-S
HALCYON-S
HALFLIN-G
HALFLIN-S
HALFWIT-S
HALIBUT-S
HALIDOM-E
HALIDOM-S
HALIMOT-E
HALIMOT-S
C-**HALLAHS**
HALLALI-S
C-**HALLANS**
HALLIAN-S
HALLING-S
HALLION-S
C-**HALLOTH**
S-**HALLOWS**
HALLWAY-S
HALLYON-S
HALOGEN-S
HALTERE-D
HALTERE-S
HALTING-S
HALYARD-S
S-**HAMBLED**
S-**HAMBLES**
HAMBONE-D
HAMBONE-S
HAMBURG-S
C-**HAMLETS**
HAMMADA-S
S-**HAMMERS**
S-**HAMMING**
W-HAMMING
HAMMOCK-S
C-**HAMPERS**
HAMSTER-S
HANAPER-S
HANDBAG-S
HANDCAR-S
HANDCAR-T
HANDFUL-S
HANDGUN-S
HANDJAR-S
C-**HANDLER**
HANDLER-S
HANDLES-S
HANDOFF-S
HANDOUT-S
HANDSAW-S
HANDSEL-S
HANDSET-S
HANGDOG-S
C-**HANGERS**
C-**HANGING**
P-HANGING
W-HANGING
HANGING-S
HANGOUT-S

HANGTAG-S
K-**HANJARS**
T-**HANKERS**
S-**HANKING**
T-HANKING
C-**HANTING**
HANUMAN-S
C-**HAPLESS**
HAPLITE-S
HAPLOID-S
HAPLOID-Y
HAPLONT-S
C-**HAPPIER**
C-**HAPPIES**
HAPPIES-T
C-**HAPPING**
W-HAPPING
HAPTENE-S
HARBOUR-S
HARDBAG-S
HARDHAT-S
HARDIES-T
HARDOKE-S
HARDPAN-S
HARDTOP-S
HARELIP-S
HARIANA-S
HARICOT-S
HARIJAN-S
C-**HARKING**
S-HARKING
HARLING-S
HARMALA-S
C-**HARMERS**
C-**HARMFUL**
HARMINE-S
C-**HARMING**
HARMOST-S
HARMOST-Y
C-**HAROSET**
HAROSET-H
HAROSET-S
S-**HARPERS**
C-**HARPIES**
S-HARPIES
S-**HARPING**
HARPING-S
HARPIST-S
HARPOON-S
C-**HARRIER**
HARRIER-S
G-**HARRIES**
HARSHEN-S
HARSLET-S
HARUMPH-S
HARVEST-S
S-**HASHING**
HASSOCK-S
HASSOCK-Y
HASTATE-D
C-**HASTENS**
G-**HASTING**
HASTING-S
HATBAND-S
T-**HATCHED**
HATCHEL-S
T-**HATCHER**
HATCHER-S
HATCHER-Y
T-**HATCHES**
HATCHET-S
HATCHET-Y
HATRACK-S
C-**HATTERS**
S-HATTERS

C-**HATTING**
HATTING-S
HATTOCK-S
HAUBERK-S
HAULAGE-S
HAULIER-S
S-**HAULING**
C-**HAUNTED**
C-**HAUNTER**
HAUNTER-S
HAUTBOY-S
HAUTEUR-S
HAVARTI-S
HAVEOUR-S
HAVEREL-S
S-**HAVINGS**
HAVIOUR-S
HAWBUCK-S
HAWKBIT-S
HAWKING-S
HAYBAND-S
HAYCOCK-S
HAYFORK-S
HAYLAGE-S
HAYLOFT-S
HAYRACK-S
HAYRICK-S
HAYRIDE-S
HAYSEED-S
HAYWARD-S
HAYWIRE-S
C-**HAZANIM**
C-**HAZZANS**
HEADAGE-S
S-**HEADING**
HEADING-S
HEADPIN-S
HEADRIG-S
HEADSET-S
HEADWAY-S
S-**HEALING**
HEALING-S
S-**HEARERS**
S-**HEARING**
HEARING-S
HEARKEN-S
HEARSAY-S
HEARTEN-S
C-**HEATERS**
T-HEATERS
HEATHEN-S
S-**HEATHER**
HEATHER-S
HEATHER-Y
C-**HEATING**
HEATING-S
HEAVIES-T
S-**HEAVING**
HEAVING-S
HEBENON-S
HECKLER-S
HECTARE-S
HEDGING-S
HEDONIC-S
W-**HEELERS**
S-**HEELING**
W-HEELING
HEELING-S
HEELTAP-S
P-**HEEZING**
W-HEEZING
HEGUMEN-E
HEGUMEN-S
HEGUMEN-Y
HEIGHTH-S

S-**HEILING**
HEIRDOM-S
HEISTER-S
HEKTARE-S
HELIAST-S
HELICON-S
HELIPAD-S
HELLCAT-S
S-**HELLERS**
S-**HELLIER**
HELLIER-S
S-**HELLING**
HELLION-S
W-**HELMING**
W-**HELPING**
HELPING-S
S-**HELVING**
HEMAGOG-S
R-**HEMATIC**
T-HEMATIC
HEMATIC-S
HEMATIN-E
HEMATIN-S
HEMIOLA-S
HEMIONE-S
HEMLINE-S
HEMLOCK-S
HEMPIES-T
HENBANE-S
HENCOOP-S
S-**HENDING**
HENNIES-T
HENPECK-S
HEPARIN-S
HEPATIC-A
HEPATIC-S
HEPSTER-S
HEPTANE-S
HEPTOSE-S
HERBAGE-D
HERBAGE-S
HERBIST-S
HERBLET-S
HERDBOY-S
HERETIC-S
HERITOR-S
HERLING-S
HEROINE-S
HEROISE-D
HEROISE-S
HEROISM-S
HEROIZE-D
HEROIZE-S
C-**HERRIED**
W-HERRIED
C-**HERRIES**
S-HERRIES
W-HERRIES
HERRING-S
HERSALL-S
HERSHIP-S
HESSIAN-S
HESSITE-S
HETAERA-E
HETAERA-S
HETAIRA-I
HETAIRA-S
HEUREKA-S
HEURISM-S
C-**HEWABLE**
HEXAGON-S
HEXAPLA-R
HEXAPLA-S
HEXAPOD-S
HEXAPOD-Y

HEXARCH-Y
HEXEREI-S
HEXOSAN-S
HEYDUCK-S
HIBACHI-S
HICATEE-S
T-**HICKISH**
C-**HICKORY**
HIDALGA-S
HIDALGO-S
S-**HIDDERS**
W-HIDDERS
HIDEOUT-S
C-**HIDINGS**
HIDLING-S
HIGGLER-S
HIGHBOY-S
HIGHWAY-S
C-**HILDING**
HILDING-S
C-**HILLERS**
T-HILLERS
C-**HILLIER**
C-**HILLING**
S-HILLING
HILLOCK-S
HILLOCK-Y
HILLTOP-S
HINDGUT-S
HINDLEG-S
W-**HINGERS**
W-**HINGING**
S-**HINNIED**
W-HINNIED
S-**HINNIES**
W-HINNIES
HIPBONE-S
S-**HIPLESS**
W-**HIPLIKE**
HIPLINE-S
S-**HIPPENS**
C-**HIPPIER**
W-HIPPIER
C-**HIPPIES**
HIPPIES-T
C-**HIPPING**
S-HIPPING
W-HIPPING
HIPPING-S
W-**HIPSTER**
HIPSTER-S
HIREAGE-S
C-**HIRLING**
T-HIRLING
W-HIRLING
HIRLING-S
HIRUDIN-S
W-**HISHING**
W-**HISSING**
HISSING-S
W-**HISTING**
HISTONE-S
HISTRIO-N
HISTRIO-S
HITCHER-S
W-**HITHERS**
C-**HITTERS**
W-HITTERS
C-**HITTING**
S-HITTING
C-**HIZZING**
W-HIZZING
HOARDER-S
HOARSEN-S
HOATZIN-S

HOBBLER-S
HOBNAIL-S
HOBODOM-S
HOBOISM-S
S-**HOCKERS**
C-**HOCKING**
S-HOCKING
HOECAKE-S
HOEDOWN-S
HOGBACK-S
S-**HOGGING**
HOGGING-S
HOGHOOD-S
HOGMANE-S
HOGNOSE-S
HOGWARD-S
HOGWEED-S
HOISTER-S
C-**HOKIEST**
HOLDALL-S
HOLDING-S
HOLDOUT-S
HOLESOM-E
HOLIBUT-S
HOLIDAY-S
W-**HOLISMS**
W-**HOLISTS**
HOLLAND-S
HOLMIUM-S
HOLSTER-S
HOLYDAM-E
HOLYDAM-S
HOLYDAY-S
HOMAGER-S
HOMBURG-S
HOMEBOY-S
HOMELYN-S
HOMINES-S
HOMINID-S
HOMMOCK-S
HOMOLOG-S
HOMOLOG-Y
HOMONYM-S
HOMONYM-Y
P-**HONEYED**
HONOREE-S
HONORER-S
HOODIES-T
HOODLUM-S
C-**HOOFING**
W-HOOFING
HOOFROT-S
C-**HOOKIES**
HOOKIES-T
HOOKLET-S
HOOLOCK-S
W-**HOOPERS**
W-**HOOPING**
W-**HOOPLAS**
HOOSGOW-S
W-**HOOSHED**
W-**HOOSHES**
S-**HOOTERS**
S-**HOOTING**
W-HOOTING
HOPBIND-S
HOPBINE-S
HOPEFUL-S
HOPHEAD-S
HOPLITE-S
C-**HOPPERS**
S-HOPPERS
W-HOPPERS
C-**HOPPIER**
S-HOPPIER

C-**HOPPING**
S-HOPPING
W-HOPPING
HOPPING-S
HOPSACK-S
HOPTOAD-S
HORDEIN-S
C-**HORDING**
HORDOCK-S
HORIZON-S
HORMONE-S
HORNBUG-S
HORNFUL-S
T-**HORNIER**
T-**HORNILY**
T-**HORNING**
HORNING-S
HORNIST-S
HORNITO-S
HORNLET-S
HORSING-S
HOSANNA-H
HOSANNA-S
HOSPICE-S
HOSTAGE-S
HOSTILE-S
G-**HOSTING**
HOSTING-S
HOSTLER-S
HOTCAKE-S
HOTFOOT-S
HOTHEAD-S
HOTLINE-S
HOTSHOT-S
HOTSPUR-S
S-**HOTTING**
HOTTING-S
HOUNDER-S
C-**HOUSERS**
C-**HOUSING**
HOUSING-S
S-**HOUTING**
HOUTING-S
S-**HOVELED**
HOVERER-S
HOWLING-S
HUANACO-S
C-**HUCKLES**
HUDDLER-S
C-**HUFFIER**
C-**HUFFING**
HUFFKIN-S
C-**HUGGERS**
C-**HUGGING**
HUITAIN-S
HUMBLER-S
HUMBLES-T
HUMDRUM-S
HUMERAL-S
HUMIDOR-S
HUMMAUM-S
C-**HUMMING**
HUMMING-S
HUMMOCK-S
HUMMOCK-Y
HUMOGEN-S
T-**HUMPERS**
HUMPIES-T
C-**HUMPING**
T-HUMPING
W-HUMPING
HUNDRED-S
C-**HUNKIER**
HUNKIES-T
C-**HUNTERS**

S-HUNTERS
S-**HUNTING**
HUNTING-S
C-**HUPPAHS**
HURDLER-S
HURLBAT-S
HURLING-S
HURRIER-S
D-**HURRIES**
HURTLES-S
HUSBAND-S
S-**HUSHING**
HUSKIES-T
HUSKING-S
HUSTLER-S
HUSWIFE-S
HUTMENT-S
P-**HUTTING**
S-HUTTING
HUTTING-S
C-**HUTZPAH**
HUTZPAH-S
C-**HUTZPAS**
HYACINE-S
HYALINE-S
HYALITE-S
HYALOID-S
HYDATID-S
HYDRANT-H
HYDRANT-S
HYDRASE-S
HYDRATE-D
HYDRATE-S
HYDRIDE-S
HYDROID-S
HYDROPS-Y
HYDROXY-L
HYGEIST-S
HYGIENE-S
HYLDING-S
HYLOIST-S
HYMENIA-L
HYMNIST-S
HYPERON-S
HYPNONE-S
HYPOGEA-L
HYPOGEA-N
HYPONEA-S
HYPONYM-S
HYPONYM-Y
HYPOXIA-S
IAMBIST-S
ICEBALL-S
ICEBERG-S
ICEBOAT-S
ICEFALL-S
V-**ICELESS**
ICEPACK-S
ICHNITE-S
D-**ICKIEST**
K-ICKIEST
P-ICKIEST
ICONISE-D
ICONISE-S
ICONIZE-D
ICONIZE-S
ICTERIC-S
ICTERID-S
R-**ICTUSES**
IDLESSE-S
IDOLISE-D
IDOLISE-R
IDOLISE-S
IDOLISM-S
IDOLIST-S
IDOLIZE-D
IDOLIZE-R
IDOLIZE-S
IDYLIST-S
M-**IFFIEST**
N-IFFIEST
IGARAPE-S
IGNATIA-S
L-**IGNEOUS**
IGNITER-S
L-**IGNITES**
IGNITOR-S
IGNOBLE-R
IGNORER-S
S-**IGNORES**
IGUANID-S
IJTIHAD-S
IKEBANA-S
ILKADAY-S
ILLAPSE-D
ILLAPSE-S
ILLEGAL-S
T-**ILLITES**
ILLOGIC-S
ILLUVIA-L
IMAGINE-D
IMAGINE-R
IMAGINE-S
IMAGING-S
IMAGISM-S
IMAGIST-S
IMAMATE-S
IMBATHE-D
IMBATHE-S
IMBIBER-S
IMBLAZE-D
IMBLAZE-S
IMBOSOM-S
IMBOWER-S
IMBROWN-S
IMBRUTE-D
IMBRUTE-S
IMBURSE-D
IMBURSE-S
IMITANT-S
IMITATE-D
IMITATE-S
IMMENSE-R
IMMERGE-D
IMMERGE-S
IMMERSE-D
IMMERSE-S
IMPAINT-S
IMPALER-S
IMPANEL-S
IMPASSE-S
IMPASTE-D
IMPASTE-S
IMPASTO-S
IMPEARL-S
IMPEDER-S
IMPERIA-L
IMPERIL-S
IMPINGE-D
IMPINGE-R
IMPINGE-S
L-**IMPINGS**
IMPLANT-S
IMPLATE-D
IMPLATE-S
IMPLEAD-S
IMPLETE-D
IMPLETE-S
IMPLODE-D
IMPLODE-S
IMPLORE-D
IMPLORE-R
IMPLORE-S
IMPOSER-S
IMPOUND-S
IMPOWER-S
IMPREGN-S
IMPRESA-S
IMPRESE-S
IMPRESS-E
IMPREST-S
IMPRINT-S
IMPROVE-D
IMPROVE-R
IMPROVE-S
IMPULSE-D
IMPULSE-S
IMPUTER-S
INBEING-S
INBOARD-S
INBOUND-S
INBREAK-S
INBREED-S
INBRING-S
INBURST-S
P-**INCASES**
INCENSE-D
INCENSE-R
INCENSE-S
INCHASE-D
INCHASE-S
C-**INCHING**
P-INCHING
W-INCHING
L-**INCHPIN**
INCHPIN-S
INCIPIT-S
INCISOR-S
INCISOR-Y
INCITER-S
Z-**INCITES**
INCLASP-S
INCLINE-D
INCLINE-R
INCLINE-S
INCLOSE-D
INCLOSE-R
INCLOSE-S
INCLUDE-D
INCLUDE-S
INCOMER-S
INCONNU-E
INCONNU-S
INCRUST-S
INCURVE-D
INCURVE-S
INDAMIN-E
INDAMIN-S
INDEXER-S
INDICAN-S
INDICAN-T
INDICIA-L
INDICIA-S
INDIGEN-E
INDIGEN-S
INDIGEN-T
W-**INDIGOS**
INDITER-S
INDORSE-D
INDORSE-E
INDORSE-R
INDORSE-S
W-**INDOWED**
INDOXYL-S
INDRAFT-S
INDUCER-S
INDULGE-D
INDULGE-R
INDULGE-S
INDULIN-E
INDULIN-S
INDUSIA-L
INDWELL-S
INEARTH-S
INERTIA-E
INERTIA-L
INERTIA-S
INFANTA-S
INFANTE-S
INFARCT-S
INFAUNA-E
INFAUNA-L
INFAUNA-S
INFEOFF-S
INFERNO-S
INFIDEL-S
INFIELD-S
INFIGHT-S
INFIMUM-S
INFLAME-D
INFLAME-R
INFLAME-S
INFLATE-D
INFLATE-R
INFLATE-S
INFLECT-S
INFLICT-S
P-**INFOLDS**
INFORCE-D
INFORCE-S
INFRACT-S
INFUSER-S
INGENER-S
INGENUE-S
INGLOBE-D
INGLOBE-S
INGOING-S
INGRAFT-S
INGRAIN-S
INGRATE-S
INGROUP-S
INGULPH-S
INHABIT-S
INHALER-S
INHAUST-S
INHERCE-D
INHERCE-S
INHERIT-S
INHIBIN-S
INHIBIT-S
INHUMAN-E
INHUMER-S
INITIAL-S
INJOINT-S
INJUNCT-S
INJURER-S
INKBLOT-S
INKHORN-S
D-**INKIEST**
K-INKIEST
P-INKIEST
S-INKIEST
Z-INKIEST
T-**INKLING**
W-INKLING
INKLING-S
INKSPOT-S
INKWELL-S
INKWOOD-S
INLAYER-S
INNERVE-D
INNERVE-S
G-**INNINGS**
P-INNINGS
T-INNINGS
W-INNINGS
INNYARD-S
INOSITE-S
INQILAB-S
INQUERE-D
INQUERE-S
INQUEST-S
INQUIET-S
INQUIRE-D
INQUIRE-R
INQUIRE-S
INSANIE-S
INSCAPE-S
INSCULP-S
INSCULP-T
INSHELL-S
K-**INSHIPS**
INSIDER-S
INSIGHT-S
INSINEW-S
INSNARE-D
INSNARE-R
INSNARE-S
INSPECT-S
INSPIRE-D
INSPIRE-R
INSPIRE-S
INSTALL-S
INSTANT-S
INSTATE-D
INSTATE-S
INSTILL-S
INSULAR-S
INSULIN-S
INSURED-S
INSURER-S
INSWING-S
INTAGLI-O
INTEGER-S
INTENSE-R
INTERIM-S
INTERNE-D
INTERNE-E
INTERNE-S
INTHRAL-L
INTHRAL-S
INTITLE-D
INTITLE-S
INTONER-S
INTRADA-S
INTRADA-Y
INTRANT-S
INTREAT-S
INTROIT-S
INTRUDE-D
INTRUDE-R
INTRUDE-S
INTRUST-S
INTWINE-D
INTWINE-S
INTWIST-S
INULASE-S
INVADER-S
INVALID-S
INVEIGH-S
INVERSE-S
INVITEE-S
INVITER-S
INVOICE-D
INVOICE-S
INVOKER-S
INVOLVE-D
INVOLVE-R
INVOLVE-S
INWEAVE-D
INWEAVE-S
P-**INWORKS**
T-INWORKS
IODIZER-S
IODURET-S
L-**IONISED**
L-**IONISER**
IONISER-S
L-**IONISES**
L-**IONIZED**
L-**IONIZER**
IONIZER-S
L-**IONIZES**
IONOGEN-S
IONOMER-S
IPOMOEA-S
F-**IRELESS**
T-IRELESS
W-IRELESS
V-**IRIDIAN**
IRIDISE-D
IRIDISE-S
IRIDIUM-S
IRIDIZE-D
IRIDIZE-S
IRISATE-D
IRISATE-S
IRONIES-T
IRONING-S
IRONISE-D
IRONISE-S
IRONIST-S
IRONIZE-D
IRONIZE-S
ISAGOGE-S
ISATINE-S
ISOBARE-S
ISOBASE-S
ISOBATH-S
ISOCHOR-E
ISOCHOR-S
ISODONT-S
M-**ISOGAMY**
ISOGONE-S
ISOGRAM-S
ISOGRIV-S
ISOHYET-S
ISOKONT-S
ISOLATE-D
ISOLATE-S
ISOLEAD-S
ISOLINE-S
ISOMERE-S
ISOPACH-S
ISOSPIN-S
ISOTACH-S
ISOTONE-S
ISOTOPE-S
ISOTRON-S
ISOTYPE-S
ISOZYME-S
T-**ISSUING**
ITACISM-S
B-**ITCHIER**
H-ITCHIER
P-ITCHIER
T-ITCHIER
W-ITCHIER
B-**ITCHILY**
H-ITCHILY

P-ITCHILY
B-**ITCHING**
D-ITCHING
H-ITCHING
M-ITCHING
P-ITCHING
W-ITCHING
ITCHING-S
ITEMISE-D
ITEMISE-S
ITEMIZE-D
ITEMIZE-R
ITEMIZE-S
L-**ITERATE**
ITERATE-D
ITERATE-S
IVORIST-S
IVRESSE-S
D-**IZZARDS**
G-IZZARDS
JACAMAR-S
JACINTH-E
JACINTH-S
JACKDAW-S
JACKEEN-S
JACKLEG-S
JACKPOT-S
JACKSIE-S
JACOBIN-S
JACONET-S
JACUZZI-S
JADEITE-S
JAGHIRE-S
JALAPIN-S
JALOUSE-D
JALOUSE-S
JAMADAR-S
JAMBEAU-X
JAMBIER-S
JAMBIYA-H
JAMBIYA-S
S-**JAMBOKS**
JAMBONE-S
JAMBOOL-S
JAMDANI-S
JAMMIES-T
JAMPANI-S
JANGLER-S
JANITOR-S
JANIZAR-S
JANIZAR-Y
JANNOCK-S
JANTIES-T
JARGOON-S
JARHEAD-S
JARLDOM-S
JARRING-S
JASMINE-S
JAUNTIE-R
JAUNTIE-S
JAVELIN-A
JAVELIN-S
JAWBONE-D
JAWBONE-R
JAWBONE-S
JAWFALL-S
JAWHOLE-S
JAWLINE-S
JAYBIRD-S
JAYWALK-S
JEALOUS-E
JEALOUS-Y
JEEPNEY-S
JEERING-S
D-**JELLABA**
JELLABA-S
JEMADAR-S
JEMIDAR-S
JEMMIES-T
JEOFAIL-S
JEOPARD-S
JEOPARD-Y
JERKIES-T
JERKING-S
JERQUER-S
JERREED-S
JESTING-S
JETBEAD-S
JETFOIL-S
JETPORT-S
JETTIES-T
JEWELER-S
JEZEBEL-S
D-**JIBBAHS**
JIBBING-S
JIBBOOM-S
JIGABOO-S
JIGAJIG-S
JIGAJOG-S
JIGGING-S
JILLION-S
JINGALL-S
JINGLER-S
JINGLET-S
JINJILI-S
JIPYAPA-S
JOBBING-S
JOBNAME-S
JOCKNEY-S
JODHPUR-S
JOGGING-S
JOGGLER-S
JOGTROT-S
JOHNNIE-S
JOINDER-S
JOINING-S
JOINTER-S
JOLLIES-T
JOLLYER-S
JONQUIL-S
JOSTLER-S
JOTTING-S
JOURNAL-S
JOURNEY-S
JOUSTER-S
JOYANCE-S
JOYRIDE-R
JOYRIDE-S
JUBILEE-S
JUDOIST-S
JUGGING-S
JUGGLER-S
JUGGLER-Y
JUGHEAD-S
JUGULAR-S
JUJITSU-S
JUJUISM-S
JUJUIST-S
JUJUTSU-S
JUKSKEI-S
JUMBLER-S
JUMBUCK-S
JUMELLE-S
JUMPOFF-S
JUNCATE-S
JUNGLIS-T
JUNIPER-S
JUNKIES-T
JUSSIVE-S
JUSTICE-R
JUSTICE-S
JUVENAL-S
KABADDI-S
KABBALA-H
KABBALA-S
KACHERI-S
KACHINA-S
KAGOULE-S
KAHAWAI-S
KAINITE-S
KAJAWAH-S
KAJEPUT-S
KAKODYL-S
KALIMBA-S
KAMERAD-S
KAMICHI-S
KAMPONG-S
KAMSEEN-S
KANTELA-S
KANTELE-S
KAOLINE-S
KARAISM-S
KARAKUL-S
KARAOKE-S
KARTING-S
KASHMIR-S
KASHRUT-H
KASHRUT-S
KATCINA-S
KATHODE-S
KATORGA-S
KATYDID-S
KAYAKER-S
KAYOING-S
KEBBOCK-S
KEBBUCK-S
KEELAGE-S
KEELING-S
KEELSON-S
KEENING-S
KEEPING-S
KEEPNET-S
KEESTER-S
KEGELER-S
KEGLING-S
KEISTER-S
KEITLOA-S
KELLAUT-S
S-**KELLIES**
S-**KELPING**
S-**KELTERS**
KEMPING-S
KENNING-S
S-**KEPPING**
KERAMIC-S
KERATIN-S
KERMESS-E
KERNING-S
KERNITE-S
KEROGEN-S
S-**KERRIES**
KERYGMA-S
KESTREL-S
S-**KETCHES**
KETCHUP-S
KEYCARD-S
KEYHOLE-S
KEYLINE-S
KEYNOTE-D
KEYNOTE-R
KEYNOTE-S
KEYSTER-S
KEYWORD-S
KHADDAR-S
KHALIFA-H
KHALIFA-S
KHALIFA-T
KHAMSIN-S
KHANATE-S
KHANJAR-S
KHEDIVA-L
KHEDIVA-S
KHEDIVE-S
KHIRKAH-S
KHOTBAH-S
KHOTBEH-S
KHUTBAH-S
KIBITKA-S
KICKOFF-S
S-**KIDDERS**
S-**KIDDIER**
KIDDIER-S
S-**KIDDING**
KIDLING-S
KIDSKIN-S
KIESTER-S
KIKUMON-S
KILLCOW-S
KILLDEE-R
KILLDEE-S
KILLICK-S
S-**KILLIES**
S-**KILLING**
KILLING-S
KILLJOY-S
KILLOCK-S
KILOBAR-S
KILOBIT-S
KILORAD-S
KILOTON-S
KILTING-S
KIMCHEE-S
S-**KIMMERS**
O-**KIMONOS**
KINCHIN-S
KINDLER-S
KINDLES-S
KINDRED-S
A-**KINESES**
KINESIC-S
A-**KINESIS**
KINETIC-S
KINETIN-S
KINFOLK-S
KINGCUP-S
KINGDOM-S
KINGLES-S
KINGLET-S
KINGPIN-S
S-**KINKING**
S-**KINLESS**
KINSHIP-S
KIPPAGE-S
S-**KIPPERS**
S-**KIPPING**
KIPSKIN-S
KIRIMON-S
KIRKING-S
KIRKTON-S
KISTFUL-S
KITCHEN-S
KITENGE-S
KITHARA-S
KITLING-S
S-**KITTLED**
S-**KITTLES**
KITTLES-T
KLAVERN-S
KLAVIER-S
KLEAGLE-S
KLINKER-S
KLISTER-S
KNACKER-S
KNACKER-Y
KNAPPER-S
KNAPPLE-D
KNAPPLE-S
KNEADER-S
KNEECAP-S
KNEELER-S
KNEEPAD-S
KNEEPAN-S
KNESSET-S
KNEVELL-S
KNICKER-S
KNIFING-S
KNITTER-S
KNITTLE-S
KNOBBER-S
KNOBBLE-D
KNOBBLE-S
KNOCKER-S
KNOLLER-S
KNOTTER-S
KNOWHOW-S
KNOWING-S
KNUBBLE-D
KNUBBLE-S
KNUCKLE-D
KNUCKLE-R
KNUCKLE-S
KOFTGAR-I
KOFTGAR-S
KOKANEE-S
KOLBASI-S
KOLKHOS-Y
KOLKHOZ-Y
KOMATIK-S
KOTOWER-S
KOUPREY-S
KREMLIN-S
KREUZER-S
KRIMMER-S
KRULLER-S
KRYPTON-S
KRYTRON-S
KUFIYAH-S
KUMQUAT-S
KUNZITE-S
KURSAAL-S
KYANISE-D
KYANISE-S
KYANITE-S
KYANIZE-D
KYANIZE-S
LABARUM-S
LABELER-S
F-**LABELLA**
G-LABELLA
LABIATE-D
LABIATE-S
LABORER-S
LABROID-S
P-**LACINGS**
LACINIA-E
C-**LACKERS**
F-LACKERS
S-LACKERS
B-**LACKING**
C-LACKING
F-LACKING
S-LACKING
LACQUER-S
LACQUEY-S
LACTASE-S
LACTATE-D
LACTATE-S
LACTEAL-S
LACTONE-S
LACTOSE-S
LACUNAR-S
LACUNAR-Y
LADANUM-S
B-**LADDERS**
C-LADDERS
B-**LADDERY**
G-**LADDIES**
LADETTE-S
LADRONE-S
LADYBUG-S
LADYCOW-S
LADYISM-S
LADYKIN-S
LAETARE-S
LAGGARD-S
B-**LAGGERS**
F-LAGGERS
B-**LAGGING**
C-LAGGING
F-LAGGING
S-LAGGING
LAGGING-S
LAICISE-D
LAICISE-S
LAICISM-S
LAICIZE-D
LAICIZE-S
P-**LAIDING**
LAIRAGE-S
G-**LAIRIER**
G-**LAIRING**
LAIRISE-D
LAIRISE-S
LAIRIZE-D
LAIRIZE-S
LAKELET-S
F-**LAKIEST**
LALLAND-S
LALLING-S
LAMBADA-S
LAMBAST-E
LAMBAST-S
C-**LAMBERS**
LAMBERT-S
LAMBIES-T
LAMBKIN-S
LAMELLA-E
LAMELLA-R
LAMELLA-S
LAMETER-S
LAMIGER-S
LAMINAR-Y
LAMITER-S
C-**LAMMERS**
S-LAMMERS
C-**LAMMING**
F-LAMMING
S-LAMMING
LAMMING-S
LAMPERN-S
C-**LAMPERS**
C-**LAMPING**
LAMPING-S
LAMPION-S
LAMPOON-S
LAMPREY-S
LAMPUKA-S
LAMPUKI-S
LAMSTER-S
G-**LANCERS**

B-**LANCHED**
F-LANCHED
P-LANCHED
B-**LANCHES**
F-LANCHES
P-LANCHES
E-**LANCING**
G-LANCING
G-**LANDERS**
S-LANDERS
LANDING-S
LANDLER-S
LANEWAY-S
LANGAHA-S
LANGLEY-S
LANGREL-S
LANGUET-S
LANGUOR-S
LANIARD-S
LANITAL-S
B-**LANKEST**
B-**LANKING**
C-LANKING
F-LANKING
P-LANKING
P-**LANNERS**
LANOLIN-E
LANOLIN-S
LANTANA-S
LANTERN-S
LANYARD-S
C-**LAPPERS**
F-LAPPERS
S-LAPPERS
C-**LAPPING**
F-LAPPING
P-LAPPING
S-LAPPING
LAPPING-S
LAPSANG-S
E-**LAPSING**
LAPWING-S
LAPWORK-S
LARDOON-S
LARGESS-E
LARMIER-S
LARVATE-D
LASAGNA-S
LASAGNE-S
C-**LASHERS**
F-LASHERS
P-LASHERS
S-LASHERS
C-**LASHING**
F-LASHING
P-LASHING
S-LASHING
LASHING-S
LASHKAR-S
F-**LASKETS**
G-**LASSIES**
LASSOCK-S
LASSOER-S
LASTAGE-S
B-**LASTERS**
P-LASTERS
B-**LASTING**
LASTING-S
LATAKIA-S
C-**LATCHED**
C-**LATCHES**
K-LATCHES
S-LATCHES
LATCHET-S
LATENCE-S
LATERAL-S
B-**LATHERS**
S-LATHERS
LATHING-S
LATITAT-S
LATOSOL-S
LATRINE-S
F-**LATTENS**
LATTICE-D
LATTICE-S
B-**LAUDING**
LAUGHER-S
LAUNDER-S
LAUWINE-S
LAVOLTA-S
LAVROCK-S
LAWBOOK-S
LAWLAND-S
C-**LAWLESS**
F-LAWLESS
C-**LAWLIKE**
LAWSUIT-S
LAXATOR-S
LAYAWAY-S
P-**LAYBACK**
LAYBACK-S
LAYETTE-S
LAYLOCK-S
P-**LAYOFFS**
LAYOVER-S
P-**LAYTIME**
LAYTIME-S
LAZARET-S
G-**LAZIEST**
B-**LEACHED**
P-LEACHED
B-**LEACHER**
LEACHER-S
B-**LEACHES**
P-LEACHES
P-**LEADERS**
P-**LEADING**
LEADING-S
LEADOFF-S
LEAFAGE-S
LEAFBUD-S
LEAFLET-S
LEAGUER-S
LEAKAGE-S
G-**LEAMING**
C-**LEANERS**
G-LEANERS
C-**LEANEST**
C-**LEANING**
G-LEANING
LEANING-S
B-**LEARIER**
B-**LEARING**
C-LEARING
LEARNER-S
P-**LEASERS**
P-**LEASING**
LEASING-S
LEASOWE-D
LEASOWE-S
P-**LEASURE**
LEASURE-S
LEATHER-N
LEATHER-S
LEATHER-Y
C-**LEAVERS**
C-**LEAVING**
S-LEAVING
LEAVING-S
LECTERN-S
E-**LECTION**
F-LECTION
LECTION-S
E-**LECTORS**
LECTURE-D
LECTURE-R
LECTURE-S
LECTURN-S
LECYTHI-S
P-**LEDGERS**
S-LEDGERS
F-**LEDGIER**
F-**LEECHED**
LEECHEE-S
F-**LEECHES**
S-LEECHES
B-**LEEPING**
C-LEEPING
S-LEEPING
F-**LEERING**
LEERING-S
LEEWARD-S
LEFTISM-S
LEFTIST-S
LEGATEE-S
LEGATOR-S
LEGGIER-O
A-**LEGGING**
F-LEGGING
LEGGING-S
LEGGISM-S
LEGHORN-S
E-**LEGISTS**
LEGITIM-S
LEGROOM-S
LEGUMIN-S
LEGWEAR-S
LEGWORK-S
LEHAYIM-S
LEIDGER-S
LEISLER-S
LEISTER-S
LEISURE-D
LEISURE-S
LEKKING-S
C-**LEMMING**
LEMMING-S
LEMPIRA-S
B-**LENDERS**
B-**LENDING**
LENDING-S
LENIENT-S
F-**LENSING**
LENTISK-S
LEOPARD-S
LEOTARD-S
LEPORID-S
LEPTOME-S
LESBIAN-S
P-**LESSORS**
F-**LETCHED**
F-**LETCHES**
LETDOWN-S
LETTERN-S
B-**LETTING**
LETTING-S
LETTUCE-S
LEUCINE-S
LEUCITE-S
LEUCOMA-S
LEUKOMA-S
E-**LEVATOR**
LEVATOR-S
LEVELER-S
LEVERET-S
LEVULIN-S
LEWISIA-S
LEXICON-S
LIAISON-S
LIBBARD-S
G-**LIBBING**
LIBELEE-S
LIBELER-S
LIBERAL-S
LIBRATE-D
LIBRATE-S
LICENCE-D
LICENCE-E
LICENCE-R
LICENCE-S
LICENSE-D
LICENSE-E
LICENSE-R
LICENSE-S
F-**LICHTER**
LICHWAY-S
C-**LICKERS**
F-LICKERS
S-LICKERS
C-**LICKING**
F-LICKING
S-LICKING
LICKING-S
LIFEWAY-S
LIFTOFF-S
LIGGING-S
A-**LIGHTED**
B-LIGHTED
F-LIGHTED
P-LIGHTED
S-LIGHTED
LIGHTEN-S
B-**LIGHTER**
P-LIGHTER
S-LIGHTER
LIGHTER-S
S-**LIGHTLY**
LIGNAGE-S
LIGNITE-S
LIGNOSE-S
LIGROIN-E
LIGROIN-S
LIMACEL-S
LIMACON-S
LIMBECK-S
C-**LIMBERS**
B-**LIMBING**
C-LIMBING
LIMEADE-S
LIMEPIT-S
S-**LIMIEST**
LIMITED-S
LIMITER-S
G-**LIMMERS**
S-LIMMERS
F-**LIMPING**
LIMPING-S
LIMPKIN-S
LINALOL-S
C-**LINCHES**
F-LINCHES
LINCHET-S
LINDANE-S
LINEAGE-S
LINEATE-D
LINECUT-S
LINGCOD-S
C-**LINGERS**
F-LINGERS
S-LINGERS
C-**LINGIER**
LINGUAL-S
LINGULA-E
LINGULA-R
LINGULA-S
LINKAGE-S
LINKBOY-S
B-**LINKERS**
C-LINKERS
K-LINKERS
P-LINKERS
S-LINKERS
B-**LINKING**
C-LINKING
P-LINKING
S-LINKING
B-**LINNING**
LINOCUT-S
LINSANG-S
LINSEED-S
S-**LINTERS**
F-**LINTIER**
LINTIES-T
LINURON-S
LIONCEL-S
LIONISE-D
LIONISE-R
LIONISE-S
LIONISM-S
LIONIZE-D
LIONIZE-R
LIONIZE-S
S-**LIPLESS**
C-**LIPPERS**
F-LIPPERS
S-LIPPERS
S-**LIPPIER**
C-**LIPPIES**
LIPPIES-T
B-**LIPPING**
C-LIPPING
F-LIPPING
S-LIPPING
LIPPING-S
LIQUATE-D
LIQUATE-S
LIQUEUR-S
LISPING-S
LISPUND-S
G-**LISTENS**
B-**LISTERS**
G-LISTERS
K-LISTERS
LISTING-S
LITERAL-S
LITHATE-S
B-**LITHELY**
B-**LITHEST**
LITHITE-S
LITHIUM-S
C-**LITORAL**
C-**LITTERS**
F-LITTERS
G-LITTERS
S-LITTERS
G-**LITTERY**
LITTLES-T
LITTLIN-G
LITTLIN-S
LIVELOD-S
LIVENER-S
LIXIVIA-L
LLANERO-S
LOADING-S
LOAFING-S
G-**LOAMING**
LOANING-S
LOATHER-S
LOATHES-T
G-**LOBATED**
C-**LOBBERS**
S-LOBBERS
B-**LOBBING**
LOBBYER-S
LOBEFIN-S
LOBELET-S
LOBELIA-S
LOBSTER-S
G-**LOBULAR**
G-**LOBULES**
LOBWORM-S
LOCATER-S
LOCATOR-S
B-**LOCKAGE**
LOCKAGE-S
B-**LOCKERS**
C-LOCKERS
LOCKFUL-S
B-**LOCKING**
C-LOCKING
F-LOCKING
LOCKJAW-S
LOCKNUT-S
LOCKOUT-S
LOCKRAM-S
LOCOISM-S
LOCUSTA-E
LOCUSTA-L
LODGING-S
LOGANIA-S
LOGBOOK-S
C-**LOGGERS**
F-LOGGERS
S-LOGGERS
C-**LOGGIER**
C-**LOGGING**
F-LOGGING
S-LOGGING
LOGGING-S
A-**LOGICAL**
LOGLINE-S
LOGROLL-S
LOGWOOD-S
LONGBOW-S
P-**LONGING**
LONGING-S
LOOBIES-T
LOOFFUL-S
LOOKISM-S
LOOKOUT-S
B-**LOOMING**
G-LOOMING
S-LOOMING
LOONIES-T
LOONING-S
B-**LOOPERS**
G-**LOOPIER**
B-**LOOPING**
G-LOOPING
LOOPING-S
LOOTING-S
F-**LOPPERS**
F-**LOPPIER**
S-LOPPIER
C-**LOPPING**
F-LOPPING
G-LOPPING
P-LOPPING
S-LOPPING
LOPPING-S

LORDING-S
LORDKIN-S
LORDOMA-S
LORETTE-S
LORGNON-S
LORIMER-S
LORINER-S
LORRELL-S
C-**LOSABLE**
C-**LOSINGS**
F-**LOSSIER**
G-LOSSIER
B-**LOTTING**
C-LOTTING
P-LOTTING
S-LOTTING
F-**LOUNDER**
LOUNDER-S
LOUNGER-S
F-**LOURIER**
C-**LOURING**
F-LOURING
LOURING-S
B-**LOUSIER**
B-**LOUSILY**
B-**LOUSING**
F-LOUSING
C-**LOUTING**
F-LOUTING
G-LOUTING
LOVEBUG-S
C-**LOVERED**
G-**LOVINGS**
B-**LOWBALL**
LOWBALL-S
P-**LOWBOYS**
LOWBROW-S
B-**LOWDOWN**
S-LOWDOWN
LOWDOWN-S
F-**LOWERED**
G-LOWERED
S-**LOWINGS**
P-**LOWLAND**
LOWLAND-S
LOWLIFE-R
LOWLIFE-S
S-**LOWNESS**
C-**LOWNING**
LOWVELD-S
LOXYGEN-S
LOZENGE-D
LOZENGE-S
LUBBARD-S
B-**LUBBERS**
C-LUBBERS
F-LUBBERS
S-LUBBERS
LUCARNE-S
LUCENCE-S
LUCERNE-S
LUCIFER-S
LUCIGEN-S
C-**LUCKIER**
P-LUCKIER
LUCKIES-T
P-**LUCKILY**
C-**LUCKING**
P-LUCKING
LUDSHIP-S
B-**LUFFING**
F-LUFFING
P-LUFFING
S-LUFFING
LUGEING-S

LUGGAGE-S
P-**LUGGERS**
S-LUGGERS
G-**LUGGING**
P-LUGGING
S-LUGGING
LUGHOLE-S
LUGSAIL-S
LUGWORM-S
LULIBUB-S
P-**LUMBAGO**
LUMBAGO-S
LUMBANG-S
C-**LUMBERS**
P-LUMBERS
S-LUMBERS
A-**LUMINES**
P-**LUMMIER**
S-LUMMIER
P-**LUMPENS**
C-**LUMPERS**
P-LUMPERS
C-**LUMPIER**
G-LUMPIER
P-LUMPIER
S-LUMPIER
G-**LUMPILY**
C-**LUMPING**
F-LUMPING
P-LUMPING
S-LUMPING
C-**LUMPISH**
G-LUMPISH
P-LUMPISH
LUMPKIN-S
LUNATIC-S
G-**LUNCHED**
LUNCHER-S
C-**LUNCHES**
G-LUNCHES
LUNETTE-S
B-**LUNGERS**
P-LUNGERS
LUNGFUL-S
B-**LUNGING**
P-LUNGING
B-**LUNKERS**
C-LUNKERS
F-LUNKERS
P-LUNKERS
B-**LUNTING**
LUPANAR-S
LUPULIN-E
LUPULIN-S
LURCHER-S
LURDANE-S
LURKING-S
F-**LURRIES**
S-LURRIES
B-**LUSHERS**
F-LUSHERS
F-**LUSHEST**
P-LUSHEST
F-**LUSHIER**
P-LUSHIER
S-LUSHIER
B-**LUSHING**
F-LUSHING
S-LUSHING
B-**LUSTERS**
C-LUSTERS
F-LUSTERS
LUSTRUM-S
LUTHERN-S
LUTHIER-S

F-**LUTINGS**
F-**LUTISTS**
LYCOPOD-S
LYDDITE-S
P-**LYINGLY**
LYMITER-S
LYMPHAD-S
LYNCHER-S
LYNCHET-S
LYOPHIL-E
LYRICON-S
LYSOGEN-S
LYSOGEN-Y
MACADAM-S
MACAQUE-S
MACHAIR-S
MACHETE-S
MACHINE-D
MACHINE-S
MACHREE-S
MACHZOR-S
MACRAME-S
MACRAMI-S
MACUMBA-S
MADDOCK-S
MADEIRA-S
MADLING-S
MADONNA-S
MADOQUA-S
MADRASA-H
MADRASA-S
MADRONA-S
MADRONE-S
MADRONO-S
MADWORT-S
MADZOON-S
MAESTRO-S
MAFFICK-S
MAFFLIN-G
MAFFLIN-S
MAGALOG-S
MAGENTA-S
I-**MAGISMS**
MAGNATE-S
MAGNETO-N
MAGNETO-S
MAHATMA-S
MAHJONG-G
MAHJONG-S
MAHONIA-S
MAHSEER-S
MAHUANG-S
MAIDISM-S
MAILBAG-S
E-**MAILING**
MAILING-S
MAILLOT-S
MAILVAN-S
MAIMING-S
MAINOUR-S
MAINTOP-S
MAISTER-S
MAJAGUA-S
MAJORAT-S
MALACCA-S
MALACIA-S
MALAISE-S
MALANGA-S
MALARIA-L
MALARIA-N
MALARIA-S
MALEATE-S
MALEFIC-E
MALICHO-S
MALISON-S

MALLARD-S
S-**MALLING**
MALMSEY-S
MALODOR-S
MALTASE-S
MALTING-S
MALTOSE-S
MAMELON-S
MAMILLA-E
MAMILLA-R
MAMMOCK-S
MAMMOTH-S
MANACLE-D
MANACLE-S
MANAGER-S
MANAKIN-S
MANATEE-S
MANCALA-S
MANCHET-S
MANDALA-S
MANDATE-D
MANDATE-S
MANDIOC-A
MANDIOC-S
MANDIRA-S
MANDOLA-S
MANDORA-S
MANDREL-S
MANDRIL-L
MANDRIL-S
MANGLER-S
MANGOLD-S
MANHOLE-S
MANHOOD-S
MANHUNT-S
MANIHOC-S
MANIHOT-S
MANIKIN-S
MANILLA-S
MANILLE-S
MANIOCA-S
MANIPLE-S
MANITOU-S
MANJACK-S
MANKIND-S
MANNITE-S
MANNOSE-S
MANPACK-S
MANRENT-S
MANROPE-S
MANSARD-S
MANSION-S
MANTEAU-S
MANTEAU-X
MANTEEL-S
MANTLET-S
MANTRAM-S
MANTRAP-S
MANUMEA-S
MANUMIT-S
MANURER-S
MANWARD-S
MANYATA-S
MAORMOR-S
MAPPING-S
MAPPIST-S
MARABOU-S
MARABOU-T
MARANTA-S
MARASCA-S
MARBLER-S
MARCHER-S
MARCHES-A
MARCHES-E
MARCHES-I

MARCONI-S
MARDIES-T
MAREMMA-S
MARGENT-S
MARGOSA-S
MARIMBA-S
MARINER-A
MARINER-S
MARKHOR-S
MARKING-S
MARLINE-S
MARLING-S
MARLITE-S
MARMITE-S
MARMOSE-S
MARMOSE-T
MARPLOT-S
MARQUEE-S
MARQUES-S
MARQUIS-E
MARRANO-S
MARRIED-S
MARRIER-S
MARSALA-S
MARSHAL-L
MARSHAL-S
S-**MARTENS**
MARTEXT-S
MARTIAN-S
S-**MARTING**
MARTINI-S
MARTLET-S
MARYBUD-S
MASCARA-S
S-**MASHERS**
MASHIES-T
S-**MASHING**
MASHING-S
MASHLAM-S
MASHLIM-S
MASHLIN-S
MASHLUM-S
MASKING-S
MASQUER-S
MASSAGE-D
MASSAGE-R
MASSAGE-S
MASSEUR-S
A-**MASSING**
MASTABA-H
MASTABA-S
MASTICH-E
MASTICH-S
MASTIFF-S
MASTOID-S
MATADOR-A
MATADOR-E
MATADOR-S
S-**MATCHED**
MATCHER-S
S-**MATCHES**
MATCHUP-S
MATELOT-E
MATELOT-S
MATILDA-S
MATINEE-S
MATOOKE-S
MATRICE-S
MATSURI-S
S-**MATTERS**
MATTING-S
MATTOCK-S
MATTOID-S
MATURES-T
MATWEED-S

MATZOON-S
MAULGRE-D
MAULGRE-S
MAUNDER-S
MAUTHER-S
MAUVAIS-E
MAUVEIN-E
MAUVEIN-S
MAUVINE-S
MAWSEED-S
MAWTHER-S
MAXILLA-E
MAXILLA-S
MAXIMAL-S
MAXIMIN-S
MAXIMUM-S
MAXWELL-S
MAYPOLE-S
MAYSTER-S
MAYWEED-S
A-**MAZEDLY**
MAZURKA-S
MAZZARD-S
MEACOCK-S
MEAGRES-T
MEALIES-T
MEANDER-S
MEANING-S
S-**MEARING**
MEASURE-D
MEASURE-R
MEASURE-S
MECONIN-S
MEDACCA-S
MEDALET-S
MEDDLER-S
MEDEVAC-S
MEDIANT-S
MEDIATE-D
MEDIATE-S
MEDICAL-S
MEDULLA-E
MEDULLA-R
MEDULLA-S
MEDUSAN-S
MEERCAT-S
MEERKAT-S
MEETING-S
MEGABAR-S
MEGABIT-S
MEGAFOG-S
MEGAHIT-S
MEGAPOD-E
MEGAPOD-S
MEGARAD-S
MEGARON-S
MEGASSE-S
MEGATON-S
MEGILPH-S
A-**MEIOSES**
A-**MEIOSIS**
MEISTER-S
MELANGE-S
MELANIC-S
MELANIN-S
MELILOT-S
MELISMA-S
S-**MELLING**
MELLITE-S
MELODIA-S
MELODIC-A
MELODIC-S
MELTAGE-S
S-**MELTERS**
S-**MELTING**

MELTING-S
MELTITH-S
MEMENTO-S
MENACER-S
A-**MENAGED**
A-**MENAGES**
MENAZON-S
A-**MENDERS**
E-MENDERS
MENDIGO-S
A-**MENDING**
E-MENDING
MENDING-S
MENFOLK-S
MENORAH-S
MENTHOL-S
MENTION-S
A-**MERCERS**
MERCHET-S
MERFOLK-S
E-**MERGING**
MERLING-S
MERMAID-S
MERONYM-S
MERONYM-Y
MEROPIA-S
MERRIES-T
E-**MERSION**
MERSION-S
MESCLUM-S
MESCLUN-S
MESHING-S
MESHUGA-H
MESQUIN-E
MESQUIT-E
MESQUIT-S
MESSAGE-D
MESSAGE-S
MESSIAH-S
MESTESO-S
MESTINO-S
MESTIZA-S
MESTIZO-S
METAMER-E
METAMER-S
METAYER-S
METAZOA-L
METAZOA-N
METCAST-S
METHANE-S
METHINK-S
METHOXY-L
E-**METICAL**
METICAL-S
METISSE-S
METONYM-S
METONYM-Y
METOPON-S
METRIST-S
MEZQUIT-E
MEZQUIT-S
MEZUZAH-S
MEZUZOT-H
E-**MICATED**
E-**MICATES**
MICELLA-E
MICELLA-R
MICELLE-S
MICHING-S
MICKLES-T
MICROBE-S
MICROHM-S
O-**MICRONS**
E-**MICTION**
MICTION-S
MIDCULT-S
S-**MIDDIES**
MIDDLER-S
MIDIRON-S
MIDLAND-S
MIDLINE-S
A-**MIDMOST**
MIDMOST-S
MIDNOON-S
MIDRIFF-S
A-**MIDSHIP**
MIDSHIP-S
MIDSIZE-D
MIDSOLE-S
MIDTERM-S
MIDTOWN-S
MIDWEEK-S
MIDWIFE-D
MIDWIFE-S
MIDWIVE-D
MIDWIVE-S
MIDYEAR-S
E-**MIGRANT**
MIGRANT-S
E-**MIGRATE**
MIGRATE-D
MIGRATE-S
O-**MIKRONS**
MILEAGE-S
MILFOIL-S
MILITAR-Y
MILITIA-S
MILKING-S
MILKSOP-S
MILLAGE-S
MILLDAM-S
MILLIER-S
MILLIME-S
MILLINE-R
MILLINE-S
MILLING-S
MILLION-S
MILLRUN-S
MIMMICK-S
MINARET-S
MINCING-S
MINDING-S
MINDSET-S
MINEOLA-S
MINERAL-S
MINETTE-S
MINEVER-S
MINGLER-S
MINIATE-D
MINIATE-S
MINIBAR-S
MINICAB-S
MINICAM-P
MINICAM-S
MINICAR-S
MINIKIN-S
MINILAB-S
MINIMAL-S
MINIMUM-S
MINISKI-S
MINIVAN-S
MINIVER-S
MINIVET-S
MINNICK-S
MINNOCK-S
MINORCA-S
MINSTER-S
MINTAGE-S
MINUEND-S
MINUTES-T
MINUTIA-E
MINUTIA-L
MIRACLE-S
MIRADOR-S
MIRBANE-S
S-**MIRKIER**
MISAVER-S
MISBILL-S
MISBIND-S
MISCALL-S
MISCAST-S
MISCITE-D
MISCITE-S
MISCODE-D
MISCODE-S
MISCOIN-S
MISCOOK-S
MISDATE-D
MISDATE-S
MISDEAL-S
MISDEAL-T
MISDEED-S
MISDEEM-S
MISDIAL-S
MISDIET-S
MISDOER-S
MISDRAW-N
MISDRAW-S
MISEASE-S
MISEDIT-S
MISFALL-S
MISFARE-D
MISFARE-S
MISFEED-S
MISFILE-D
MISFILE-S
MISFIRE-D
MISFIRE-S
MISFORM-S
MISGIVE-N
MISGIVE-S
MISGROW-N
MISGROW-S
MISHEAR-D
MISHEAR-S
MISHMEE-S
MISJOIN-S
MISKEEP-S
MISKICK-S
MISKNOW-N
MISKNOW-S
MISLEAD-S
MISLIKE-D
MISLIKE-R
MISLIKE-S
MISLIVE-D
MISLIVE-S
MISLUCK-S
MISMAKE-S
MISMARK-S
MISMATE-D
MISMATE-S
MISMEET-S
MISMOVE-D
MISMOVE-S
MISNAME-D
MISNAME-S
MISPAGE-D
MISPAGE-S
MISPART-S
MISPLAN-S
MISPLAN-T
MISPLAY-S
MISRATE-D
MISRATE-S
MISREAD-S
MISRULE-D
MISRULE-S
MISSEAT-S
MISSEEM-S
MISSEND-S
MISSIES-T
E-**MISSILE**
MISSILE-S
A-**MISSING**
E-**MISSION**
O-MISSION
MISSION-S
E-**MISSIVE**
O-MISSIVE
MISSIVE-S
MISSORT-S
MISSOUT-S
MISSTEP-S
MISSTOP-S
MISSUIT-S
MISTAKE-N
MISTAKE-R
MISTAKE-S
MISTBOW-S
MISTELL-S
MISTEND-S
MISTERM-S
MISTICO-S
MISTIME-D
MISTIME-S
MISTING-S
MISTRAL-S
MISTUNE-D
MISTUNE-S
MISTYPE-D
MISTYPE-S
MISUSER-S
MISWEEN-S
MISWEND-S
MISWORD-S
MISWRIT-E
MISYOKE-D
MISYOKE-S
MITERER-S
S-**MITHERS**
MITOGEN-S
A-**MITOSES**
A-**MITOSIS**
A-**MITOTIC**
MITSVAH-S
MITZVAH-S
MIXTION-S
MIXTURE-S
MIZMAZE-S
MOBBING-S
MOBSTER-S
MOCHELL-S
MOCHILA-S
MOCKAGE-S
S-**MOCKING**
MOCKING-S
MODELER-S
MODELLO-S
MODERNE-R
MODICUM-S
MODISTE-S
MOELLON-S
MOFETTE-S
MOIDORE-S
S-**MOILING**
MOINEAU-S
MOISTEN-S
MOITHER-S
MOJARRA-S
S-**MOLDERS**
MOLDING-S
MOLERAT-S
MOLIMEN-S
MOLINET-S
MOLLUSC-S
MOLLUSK-S
MOMENTO-S
MONACID-S
MONARCH-S
MONARCH-Y
MONARDA-S
MONAXON-S
MONDAIN-E
MONDAIN-S
MONERAN-S
MONEYER-S
MONGREL-S
MONIKER-S
MONILIA-S
MONITOR-S
MONITOR-Y
MONOCLE-D
MONOCLE-S
MONOCOT-S
MONOFIL-S
MONOLOG-S
MONOLOG-Y
MONOMER-S
MONOPOD-E
MONOPOD-S
MONOPOD-Y
MONSOON-S
MONSTER-A
MONSTER-S
MONTAGE-D
MONTAGE-S
MONTANE-S
MONTANT-O
MONTANT-S
MONTERO-S
MONTURE-S
MONURON-S
S-**MOOCHED**
MOOCHER-S
S-**MOOCHES**
MOODIES-T
MOOKTAR-S
MOONBOW-S
MOONEYE-S
MOONIES-T
MOONLET-S
MOONSET-S
MOORAGE-S
MOORHEN-S
MOORILL-S
S-**MOORING**
MOORING-S
MOORLOG-S
S-**MOOTING**
MOOTING-S
A-**MOOVING**
MOPHEAD-S
MORAINE-S
A-**MORALLY**
MORCEAU-X
MORDANT-S
MORDENT-S
MORELLE-S
MORELLO-S
MORICHE-S
MORISCO-S
MORLING-S
MORMAOR-S
MORNING-S
MOROCCO-S
MORPHEW-S
MORPHIA-S
MORPHIN-E
MORPHIN-G
MORPHIN-S
MORRHUA-S
MORRICE-S
MORRION-S
MORSURE-S
MORTICE-D
MORTICE-R
MORTICE-S
A-**MORTISE**
MORTISE-D
MORTISE-R
MORTISE-S
MORWONG-S
MOSHING-S
MOSSIES-T
MOSTEST-S
S-**MOTHERS**
S-**MOTHERY**
A-**MOTIONS**
E-MOTIONS
MOTTLER-S
S-**MOUCHED**
MOUCHER-S
S-**MOUCHES**
MOUFLON-S
MOULAGE-S
S-**MOULDER**
MOULDER-S
MOULTER-S
A-**MOUNTED**
MOUNTER-S
MOURNER-S
MOUSAKA-S
S-**MOUSERS**
MOUSIES-T
S-**MOUSING**
MOUSING-S
MOUSMEE-S
MOUTHER-S
MOVABLE-S
MOVIOLA-S
MOWBURN-S
MOWBURN-T
S-**MOYLING**
MOZETTA-S
MRIDANG-A
MRIDANG-S
MUCHELL-S
MUCIGEN-S
MUDBATH-S
MUDDIES-T
MUDDLER-S
MUDFLAP-S
MUDFLAT-S
MUDFLOW-S
S-**MUDGERS**
S-**MUDGING**
MUDHOLE-S
MUDHOOK-S
MUDIRIA-S
MUDLARK-S
MUDPACK-S
MUDROCK-S
MUDROOM-S
MUDSCOW-S
MUDSILL-S
MUDWORT-S
MUEDDIN-S
MUEZZIN-S
MUFFLER-S

S-MUGGING
MUGGING-S
MUGSHOT-S
MUGWORT-S
MUGWUMP-S
MUKHTAR-S
MULATTA-S
MULATTO-S
MULLEIN-S
MULLION-S
MULLITE-S
MULLOCK-S
MULLOCK-Y
MULMULL-S
MULTURE-D
MULTURE-R
MULTURE-S
MUMBLER-S
MUMMING-S
MUMMOCK-S
MUNCHER-S
MUNDANE-R
MUNNION-S
MUNSTER-S
MUNTING-S
MUNTJAC-S
MUNTJAK-S
MUONIUM-S
MURAENA-S
MURGEON-S
MURIATE-D
MURIATE-S
MURLAIN-S
MURRAIN-S
MURRION-S
MURTHER-S
MUSCONE-S
A-MUSETTE
MUSETTE-S
MUSICAL-E
MUSICAL-S
MUSIMON-S
MUSKIES-T
MUSKONE-S
MUSKRAT-S
MUSPIKE-S
MUSTANG-S
MUSTARD-S
MUSTARD-Y
MUTAGEN-S
S-MUTCHES
MUZZLER-S
MYALGIA-S
MYALISM-S
MYCELIA-L
MYCELIA-N
MYELINE-S
MYELOMA-S
MYLODON-S
MYLODON-T
MYNHEER-S
MYOGRAM-S
MYOSOTE-S
MYOTOME-S
MYOTUBE-S
MYRBANE-S
MYRINGA-S
MYRRHOL-S
MYTHISE-D
MYTHISE-S
MYTHISM-S
MYTHIST-S
MYTHIZE-D
MYTHIZE-S
NAARTJE-S

NACARAT-S
NACELLE-S
NACRITE-S
NAGAPIE-S
K-NAGGIER
S-NAGGIER
S-NAGGING
NAGMAAL-S
S-NAILERY
S-NAILING
NAILING-S
NAILSET-S
NAIVETE-S
NAMASTE-S
NAMETAG-S
NANDINA-S
NANDINE-S
O-NANISMS
NANKEEN-S
NAPHTHA-S
NAPHTOL-S
S-NAPLESS
K-NAPPERS
S-NAPPERS
S-NAPPIER
NAPPIES-T
K-NAPPING
S-NAPPING
NARCEEN-S
NARCEIN-E
NARCEIN-S
NARCISM-S
NARCIST-S
NARCOSE-S
NARGILE-H
NARGILE-S
S-NARKIER
NARRATE-D
NARRATE-R
NARRATE-S
NARTJIE-S
NARWHAL-E
NARWHAL-S
NASHGAB-S
NASTIES-T
S-NATCHES
E-NATIONS
NATRIUM-S
G-NATTIER
NATURAL-S
NAVARCH-S
NAVARCH-Y
NAVARHO-S
NAVARIN-S
NAVETTE-S
NAYWARD-S
NAYWORD-S
S-NEAPING
A-NEARING
NEBBICH-S
S-NEBBING
NEBBISH-E
NEBBISH-Y
S-NECKING
NECKING-S
NECKLET-S
NECKTIE-S
NECROSE-D
NECROSE-S
NEEDFUL-S
NEEDLER-S
NEEDLES-S
S-NEEZING
NEGATER-S
NEGATON-S

NEGATOR-S
NEGATOR-Y
NEGLECT-S
NEGLIGE-E
NEGLIGE-S
NEGROID-S
NEGRONI-S
NELUMBO-S
NEMESIA-S
NEOLITH-S
NEONATE-S
NEOTYPE-S
NEPHRON-S
E-NERVATE
NERVINE-S
E-NERVING
NERVING-S
NERVULE-S
NERVURE-S
NESTFUL-S
NESTING-S
NESTLER-S
NETBALL-S
NETIZEN-S
NETSUKE-S
NETTING-S
NETTLER-S
NETWORK-S
NEURINE-S
A-NEURISM
NEURISM-S
NEURITE-S
NEUROMA-S
NEURONE-S
NEURULA-E
NEURULA-S
NEUSTON-S
NEUTRAL-S
NEUTRON-S
NEWBORN-S
NEWCOME-R
NEWSBOY-S
NEWSIES-T
S-NIBBING
NIBBLER-S
NIBLICK-S
K-NICKERS
S-NICKERS
S-NICKING
NICOTIN-E
NICOTIN-S
NICTATE-D
NICTATE-S
S-NIFFERS
S-NIFFIER
S-NIFFING
S-NIFTIER
NIFTIES-T
NIGELLA-S
NIGGARD-S
S-NIGGERS
S-NIGGLED
S-NIGGLER
NIGGLER-S
S-NIGGLES
K-NIGHTED
NIGHTIE-S
K-NIGHTLY
NIHONGA-S
NILGHAI-S
NILGHAU-S
NINEPIN-S
NIOBATE-S
NIOBITE-S
NIOBIUM-S

S-NIPPERS
S-NIPPIER
S-NIPPILY
S-NIPPING
NIRVANA-S
NITCHIE-S
NITERIE-S
NITHING-S
NITINOL-S
NITPICK-S
NITPICK-Y
NITRATE-D
NITRATE-S
NITRIDE-D
NITRIDE-S
NITRILE-S
NITRITE-S
K-NOBBIER
S-NOBBIER
S-NOBBILY
K-NOBBLED
NOBBLER-S
K-NOBBLES
K-NOCKING
NOCTUID-S
NOCTULE-S
NOCTURN-E
NOCTURN-S
A-NODALLY
S-NODDING
NODDING-S
S-NOGGING
NOGGING-S
A-NOINTED
NOMARCH-S
NOMARCH-Y
NOMBRIL-S
NOMINAL-S
NOMINEE-S
NONACID-S
NONAGON-S
NONBANK-S
NONBOOK-S
NONETTE-S
NONETTO-S
NONFACT-S
NONPAST-S
NONPLAY-S
NONSKED-S
NONSUIT-S
NONUPLE-S
NONUPLE-T
NONUSER-S
NONWORD-S
NOOKIES-T
NOONDAY-S
NOONING-S
NORIMON-S
NORLAND-S
NORTENA-S
NORTENO-S
NORTHER-N
NORTHER-S
NORWARD-S
NOSEBAG-S
NOSEGAY-S
NOSTRIL-S
NOSTRUM-S
NOTABLE-S
NOTAEUM-S
NOTCHEL-S
NOTCHER-S
NOTELET-S
NOTEPAD-S
NOTHING-S

NOTICER-S
NOTITIA-E
NOTITIA-S
NOUMENA-L
NOURICE-S
NOURSLE-D
NOURSLE-S
NOUSELL-S
NOVELLA-E
NOVELLA-S
NOWHERE-S
NOYANCE-S
K-NUBBIER
S-NUBBIER
S-NUBBING
K-NUBBLED
K-NUBBLES
NUCLEIN-S
NUCLEON-S
NUCLIDE-S
S-NUDGING
NUDNICK-S
NULLING-S
NUMERAL-S
NUMERIC-S
NUNATAK-S
NUNDINE-S
NUNHOOD-S
NUNSHIP-S
NUPTIAL-S
NURAGHI-C
K-NURLING
NURSING-S
NURTURE-D
NURTURE-R
NURTURE-S
NUTCASE-S
NUTGALL-S
NUTMEAL-S
NUTMEAT-S
NUTPICK-S
NUTTING-S
NUTWOOD-S
S-NUZZLED
NUZZLER-S
S-NUZZLES
NYLGHAI-S
NYLGHAU-S
NYMPHAE-A
NYMPHET-S
OAKLING-S
B-OARFISH
H-OARIEST
R-OARIEST
OARLOCK-S
OARWEED-S
OATCAKE-S
B-OATLIKE
G-OATLIKE
M-OATLIKE
OATMEAL-S
B-OBECHES
L-OBELIAS
OBELISE-D
OBELISE-S
OBELISK-S
OBELISM-S
OBELIZE-D
OBELIZE-S
OBLIGEE-S
OBLIGER-S
OBLIGOR-S
OBLIQUE-D
OBLIQUE-R
OBLIQUE-S

OBSCENE-R
OBSCURE-D
OBSCURE-R
OBSCURE-S
OBSERVE-D
OBSERVE-R
OBSERVE-S
OBTRUDE-D
OBTRUDE-R
OBTRUDE-S
OBVERSE-S
OBVIATE-D
OBVIATE-S
OCARINA-S
OCCIPUT-S
OCCLUDE-D
OCCLUDE-R
OCCLUDE-S
OCEANID-S
T-OCHERED
C-OCREATE
OCTAGON-S
OCTANOL-S
OCTAPLA-S
OCTETTE-S
OCTOPOD-S
OCTOPUS-H
OCTUPLE-D
OCTUPLE-S
OCTUPLE-T
OCTUPLE-X
L-OCULATE
OCULATE-D
OCULIST-S
ODALISK-S
ODALLER-S
ODDBALL-S
ODDMENT-S
ODONATE-S
ODORANT-S
ODORIZE-D
ODORIZE-S
ODYLISM-S
ODYSSEY-S
OENOMEL-S
OERSTED-S
OESTRIN-S
OESTRUM-S
OFFBEAT-S
OFFCAST-S
OFFENCE-S
OFFENSE-S
C-OFFERED
G-OFFERED
OFFEREE-S
OFFERER-S
OFFEROR-S
OFFICER-S
OFFLOAD-S
OFFRAMP-S
OFFSCUM-S
OFFSIDE-R
OFFSIDE-S
OFFTAKE-S
S-OFTENER
OGREISM-S
OILBIRD-S
OILCAMP-S
OILHOLE-S
R-OILIEST
S-OILIEST
OILSEED-S
OILSKIN-S
B-OINKING
OINOMEL-S

J-**OINTING**
N-OINTING
P-OINTING
OKIMONO-S
B-**OLDENED**
G-OLDENED
B-**OLDNESS**
C-OLDNESS
OLDSTER-S
OLEARIA-S
OLEFINE-S
OLIGIST-S
OLIVINE-S
O-**OLOGIES**
O-**OLOGIST**
OLOGIST-S
D-**OLOROSO**
OLOROSO-S
OLYCOOK-S
OLYKOEK-S
L-**OMENTUM**
M-OMENTUM
T-OMENTUM
OMENTUM-S
OMICRON-S
OMIKRON-S
OMITTER-S
S-**OMNIFIC**
OMPHALI-C
ONANISM-S
ONANIST-S
ONCOGEN-E
ONCOGEN-S
ONDATRA-S
B-**ONDINGS**
D-**ONENESS**
G-ONENESS
L-ONENESS
Z-**ONETIME**
M-**ONEYERS**
ONGOING-S
ONSTEAD-S
ONYCHIA-S
OOGONIA-L
OOLAKAN-S
Z-**OOLITES**
Z-**OOLITHS**
Z-**OOLITIC**
Z-**OOLOGIC**
OOMIACK-S
Z-**OOPHYTE**
OOPHYTE-S
W-**OORALIS**
M-**OORIEST**
G-**OOSIEST**
Z-**OOSPERM**
OOSPERM-S
Z-**OOSPORE**
OOSPORE-S
OOTHECA-E
OOTHECA-L
B-**OOZIEST**
W-OOZIEST
OPALINE-S
OPAQUES-T
OPENING-S
OPERAND-S
OPERANT-S
OPERATE-D
OPERATE-S
OPHIURA-N
OPHIURA-S
OPINION-S
OPORICE-S
OPOSSUM-S
OPPIDAN-S
OPPOSER-S
OPSONIN-S
OPTIMUM-S
OPUNTIA-S
OPUSCLE-S
OQUASSA-S
C-**ORACLES**
M-**ORALISM**
ORALISM-S
M-**ORALIST**
ORALIST-S
M-**ORALITY**
ORANGER-Y
ORANGES-T
ORARIAN-S
ORARION-S
ORARIUM-S
B-**ORATING**
ORATION-S
M-**ORATORY**
ORBITAL-S
ORBITER-S
ORCHARD-S
ORCINOL-S
B-**ORDERED**
B-**ORDERER**
ORDERER-S
ORDINAL-S
ORDINAR-S
ORDINAR-Y
ORDINEE-S
S-**ORDINES**
B-**ORDURES**
OREGANO-S
OREWEED-S
ORGANIC-S
ORGANON-S
ORGANUM-S
ORGANZA-S
ORGIAST-S
ORIFICE-S
ORIGAMI-S
ORIGANE-S
H-**OROLOGY**
OROPESA-S
ORPHREY-S
F-**ORPINES**
M-**ORRICES**
M-**ORRISES**
P-**ORTOLAN**
ORTOLAN-S
OSMIATE-S
C-**OSMOSES**
K-OSMOSES
OSMUNDA-S
OSSELET-S
OSSETER-S
OSSICLE-S
OSTEOID-S
OSTEOMA-S
OSTIOLE-S
H-**OSTLERS**
J-OSTLERS
P-**OSTMARK**
OSTMARK-S
OTALGIA-S
N-**OTARIES**
R-OTARIES
V-OTARIES
OTOCYST-S
OTOLITH-S
C-**OTTERED**
H-OTTERED
P-OTTERED
T-OTTERED
OTTOMAN-S
OUABAIN-S
OUAKARI-S
C-**OUCHING**
D-OUCHING
M-OUCHING
P-OUCHING
T-OUCHING
V-OUCHING
OULAKAN-S
C-**OULDEST**
W-OULDEST
W-**OURALIS**
L-**OURIEST**
Y-**OURSELF**
J-**OUSTERS**
R-OUSTERS
J-**OUSTING**
M-OUSTING
R-OUSTING
OUSTITI-S
OUTBACK-S
OUTBAKE-D
OUTBAKE-S
OUTBARK-S
OUTBAWL-S
OUTBEAM-S
OUTBRAG-S
OUTBULK-S
OUTBURN-S
OUTBURN-T
OUTCAST-E
OUTCAST-S
OUTCHID-E
OUTCOME-S
OUTCOOK-S
OUTCROP-S
OUTCROW-S
OUTDARE-D
OUTDARE-S
OUTDATE-D
OUTDATE-S
OUTDOER-S
OUTDOOR-S
OUTDRAG-S
OUTDRAW-N
OUTDRAW-S
OUTDROP-S
OUTDUEL-S
OUTDURE-D
OUTDURE-S
OUTEARN-S
OUTEDGE-S
OUTFACE-D
OUTFACE-S
OUTFALL-S
OUTFAST-S
OUTFAWN-S
OUTFEEL-S
OUTFIND-S
OUTFIRE-D
OUTFIRE-S
OUTFLOW-N
OUTFLOW-S
OUTFOOL-S
OUTFOOT-S
OUTGAIN-S
OUTGATE-S
OUTGIVE-N
OUTGIVE-S
OUTGLOW-S
OUTGNAW-N
OUTGNAW-S
OUTGOER-S
OUTGRIN-S
OUTGROW-N
OUTGROW-S
OUTHAUL-S
OUTHEAR-D
OUTHEAR-S
OUTHIRE-D
OUTHIRE-S
OUTHOWL-S
OUTHUNT-S
OUTHYRE-D
OUTHYRE-S
H-**OUTINGS**
P-OUTINGS
R-OUTINGS
OUTJEST-S
OUTJUMP-S
OUTKEEP-S
OUTKICK-S
OUTKILL-S
OUTLAND-S
OUTLAST-S
OUTLEAP-S
OUTLEAP-T
OUTLIER-S
OUTLINE-D
OUTLINE-R
OUTLINE-S
OUTLIVE-D
OUTLIVE-R
OUTLIVE-S
OUTLOOK-S
OUTLOVE-D
OUTLOVE-S
OUTMODE-D
OUTMODE-S
OUTMOVE-D
OUTMOVE-S
OUTNAME-D
OUTNAME-S
OUTPACE-D
OUTPACE-S
OUTPART-S
OUTPEEP-S
OUTPEER-S
OUTPLAN-S
OUTPLAY-S
OUTPLOD-S
OUTPLOT-S
OUTPOLL-S
OUTPORT-S
OUTPOST-S
OUTPOUR-S
OUTPRAY-S
OUTPULL-S
OUTRACE-D
OUTRACE-S
OUTRAGE-D
OUTRAGE-S
OUTRANG-E
OUTRANK-S
OUTRATE-D
OUTRATE-S
OUTRAVE-D
OUTRAVE-S
OUTREAD-S
OUTRIDE-R
OUTRIDE-S
F-**OUTRING**
OUTRING-S
OUTROAR-S
OUTROCK-S
OUTROLL-S
OUTROOP-S
OUTROOT-S
OUTROPE-R
OUTROPE-S
OUTSAIL-S
OUTSELL-S
OUTSERT-S
OUTSHOT-S
OUTSIDE-R
OUTSIDE-S
OUTSING-S
OUTSIZE-D
OUTSIZE-S
OUTSOAR-S
OUTSOLE-S
OUTSPAN-S
OUTSTAY-S
OUTSTEP-S
OUTSULK-S
OUTSWIM-S
OUTTAKE-N
OUTTAKE-S
OUTTALK-S
OUTTASK-S
OUTTELL-S
OUTTROT-S
OUTTURN-S
OUTVOTE-D
OUTVOTE-R
OUTVOTE-S
OUTWAIT-S
OUTWALK-S
OUTWARD-S
OUTWEAR-S
OUTWEAR-Y
G-**OUTWEED**
OUTWEED-S
OUTWEEP-S
OUTWELL-S
OUTWICK-S
OUTWILE-D
OUTWILE-S
OUTWILL-S
OUTWIND-S
OUTWING-S
OUTWORK-S
OUTWRIT-E
OUTYELL-S
OUTYELP-S
OUVRAGE-S
OUVRIER-E
OUVRIER-S
C-**OVARIES**
N-**OVATION**
OVATION-S
OVERACT-S
C-**OVERAGE**
OVERAGE-D
OVERAGE-S
C-**OVERALL**
OVERALL-S
OVERAWE-D
OVERAWE-S
OVERBET-S
OVERBID-S
OVERBUY-S
OVERCUT-S
OVERDOG-S
OVERDUB-S
OVERDYE-D
OVERDYE-S
OVEREAT-S
OVEREYE-D
OVEREYE-S
OVERGET-S
OVERHIT-S
C-**OVERING**
D-OVERING
H-OVERING
OVERJOY-S
OVERLAP-S
OVERLAY-S
C-**OVERLET**
OVERLET-S
OVERLIE-R
OVERLIE-S
OVERMAN-S
OVERMAN-Y
OVERNET-S
OVERPAY-S
OVERRAN-K
OVERRED-S
OVERREN-S
OVERRUN-S
OVERSEA-S
OVERSEE-D
OVERSEE-N
OVERSEE-R
OVERSEE-S
OVERSET-S
OVERSEW-N
OVERSEW-S
OVERSOW-N
OVERSOW-S
OVERSUP-S
OVERTIP-S
C-**OVERTLY**
OVERTOP-S
OVERUSE-D
OVERUSE-S
OVERWET-S
OVICIDE-S
OVIDUCT-S
OVULATE-D
OVULATE-S
J-**OWLIEST**
L-OWLIEST
B-**OWLLIKE**
OWRELAY-S
OXALATE-D
OXALATE-S
OXAZINE-S
OXBLOOD-S
OXHEART-S
OXIDANT-S
OXIDASE-S
OXIDATE-D
OXIDATE-S
OXIDISE-D
OXIDISE-R
OXIDISE-S
OXIDIZE-D
OXIDIZE-R
OXIDIZE-S
OXONIUM-S
F-**OXTAILS**
OXYACID-S
L-**OXYGENS**
OXYPHIL-E
OXYPHIL-S
OXYSALT-S
OXYSOME-S
OXYTONE-S
R-**OYSTERS**
OZONATE-D
OZONATE-S
OZONIDE-S
OZONISE-D
OZONISE-R
OZONISE-S
OZONIZE-D
OZONIZE-R

OZONIZE-S
PABULUM-S
PACHISI-S
PACHUCO-S
S-**PACIEST**
PACKAGE-D
PACKAGE-R
PACKAGE-S
PACKING-S
PACKWAY-S
PACTION-S
PADDING-S
PADDLER-S
PADDOCK-S
PADELLA-S
PADLOCK-S
PADRONE-S
PADSHAH-S
PAENULA-E
PAENULA-S
PAEONIC-S
PAESANO-S
PAGEANT-S
PAGEBOY-S
PAGURID-S
PAHLAVI-S
PAILFUL-S
PAILLON-S
S-**PAINING**
PAINTER-S
PAIOCKE-S
PAIRIAL-S
PAIRING-S
PAISANA-S
PAISANO-S
PAISLEY-S
PAJOCKE-S
PAKAPOO-S
PAKFONG-S
PAKTONG-S
PALABRA-S
PALADIN-S
PALATAL-S
PALAVER-S
PALAZZO-S
PALETOT-S
PALETTE-S
PALFREY-S
PALIKAR-S
S-**PALLING**
PALLIUM-S
PALLONE-S
PALMATE-D
PALMFUL-S
PALMIES-T
PALMIET-S
PALMIST-S
PALMTOP-S
PALMYRA-S
PALOOKA-S
PALPATE-D
PALPATE-S
PALSHIP-S
PALSIES-T
PAMPEAN-S
PAMPERO-S
PANACEA-N
PANACEA-S
PANACHE-S
PANCAKE-D
PANCAKE-S
PANDECT-S
PANDOOR-S
PANDORA-S
PANDORE-S
PANDOUR-S
PANDURA-S
PANGENE-S
S-**PANGING**
PANGRAM-S
PANICLE-D
PANICLE-S
PANICUM-S
PANNAGE-S
PANNICK-S
PANNIER-S
S-**PANNING**
PANNING-S
PANOCHA-S
PANOCHE-S
PANPIPE-S
PANTHER-S
PANTILE-D
PANTILE-S
PANTINE-S
PANTING-S
PANTLER-S
PANTOUM-S
PAPERER-S
PAPHIAN-S
PAPILIO-S
PAPILLA-E
PAPILLA-R
PAPOOSE-S
PAPPIES-T
PAPRICA-S
PAPRIKA-S
S-**PARABLE**
PARABLE-D
PARABLE-S
PARACME-S
PARADER-S
PARADOR-S
PARADOX-Y
PARAFLE-S
PARAGON-S
PARANYM-S
PARAPET-S
PARASOL-S
PARATHA-S
PARAZOA-N
PARBOIL-S
PARCHES-I
PARDALE-S
PARDNER-S
PAREIRA-S
PARELLA-S
PARELLE-S
PARETIC-S
PARFAIT-S
PARGANA-S
S-**PARGING**
PARGING-S
PARISON-S
PARITOR-S
S-**PARKERS**
S-**PARKIER**
S-**PARKIES**
PARKIES-T
S-**PARKING**
PARKING-S
S-**PARKISH**
PARKWAY-S
S-**PARLING**
PARLOUR-S
PAROLEE-S
PARONYM-S
PARONYM-Y
PAROTID-S
PARPANE-S
PARPEND-S
PARPENT-S
PARQUET-S
S-**PARRING**
PARROCK-S
PARSING-S
PARSLEY-S
PARSNEP-S
PARSNIP-S
PARTAKE-N
PARTAKE-R
PARTAKE-S
S-**PARTANS**
PARTIAL-S
PARTIER-S
PARTING-S
PARTITA-S
PARTLET-S
PARTNER-S
PARTURE-S
PARTYER-S
PARVENU-E
PARVENU-S
PARVISE-S
PASCHAL-S
PASQUIL-S
PASSADE-S
PASSADO-S
PASSAGE-D
PASSAGE-S
PASSATA-S
PASSING-S
PASSION-S
PASSIVE-S
PASSKEY-S
PASSMEN-T
PASSOUT-S
PASTERN-S
PASTEUP-S
PASTIES-T
PASTIME-S
PASTINA-S
PASTING-S
PASTURE-D
PASTURE-R
PASTURE-S
PATAGIA-L
PATAMAR-S
PATBALL-S
PATCHER-S
PATCHER-Y
PATELLA-E
PATELLA-R
PATELLA-S
PATHWAY-S
PATIENT-S
PATRIAL-S
PATRICK-S
PATRIOT-S
PATROON-S
PATTERN-S
S-**PATTERS**
S-**PATTING**
PATULIN-S
PAUSING-S
PAVIOUR-S
PAVISER-S
PAVLOVA-S
PAWNAGE-S
S-**PAWNERS**
S-**PAWNING**
PAXIUBA-S
PAYABLE-S
PAYBACK-S
PAYFONE-S
PAYLOAD-S
PAYMENT-S
PAYROLL-S
PAYSAGE-S
PAYSLIP-S
PEACHER-S
PEACOAT-S
PEACOCK-S
PEACOCK-Y
PEAFOWL-S
S-**PEAKING**
S-**PEANING**
PEARLER-S
PEARLIN-G
PEARLIN-S
PEASANT-S
PEASANT-Y
PEASCOD-S
PEBRINE-S
PECCAVI-S
S-**PECKIER**
S-**PECKING**
PECKING-S
PECTASE-S
S-**PECTATE**
PECTATE-S
PECTISE-D
PECTISE-S
PECTIZE-D
PECTIZE-S
PECTOSE-S
PECULIA-R
PEDAGOG-S
PEDAGOG-Y
PEDDLER-S
PEDDLER-Y
PEDICAB-S
PEDICEL-S
PEDICLE-D
PEDICLE-S
PEDOCAL-S
PEDRAIL-S
PEDRERO-S
PEEBEEN-S
PEEKABO-O
PEEKABO-S
S-**PEELERS**
S-**PEELING**
PEELING-S
PEERAGE-S
PEERIES-T
S-**PEERING**
PEGGING-S
PEISHWA-H
PEISHWA-S
PELICAN-S
PELISSE-S
PELLACH-S
PELLACK-S
PELLOCK-S
PELORIA-N
PELORIA-S
PELTAST-S
S-**PELTERS**
PELTING-S
PEMBINA-S
PEMICAN-S
PENANCE-D
PENANCE-S
PENDANT-S
PENDENT-S
S-**PENDING**
U-PENDING
PENFOLD-S
PENGUIN-S
PENICIL-S
PENLITE-S
PENNAME-S
PENNANT-S
PENNATE-D
PENNINE-S
PENOCHE-S
PENSION-E
PENSION-S
PENSTER-S
PENTACT-S
PENTANE-S
PENTENE-S
PENTHIA-S
PENTICE-D
PENTICE-S
PENTISE-D
PENTISE-S
PENTODE-S
PENTOSE-S
PENUCHE-S
PENUCHI-S
PEONAGE-S
PEONISM-S
PEOPLER-S
PEPSINE-S
PEPTIDE-S
PEPTISE-D
PEPTISE-S
PEPTIZE-D
PEPTIZE-R
PEPTIZE-S
PEPTONE-S
PERACID-S
PERAEON-S
PERCALE-S
PERCENT-S
PERCEPT-S
PERCHER-S
PERCHER-Y
PERCOID-S
PERDURE-D
PERDURE-S
PEREGAL-S
PEREIRA-S
PERFECT-A
PERFECT-I
PERFECT-O
PERFECT-S
PERFORM-S
PERFUME-D
PERFUME-R
PERFUME-S
PERFUSE-D
PERFUSE-S
PERGOLA-S
PERIAPT-S
PERIDIA-L
PERIDOT-E
PERIDOT-S
PERIGEE-S
PERIGON-E
PERIGON-S
PERILLA-S
PERINEA-L
PERIOST-S
PERIQUE-S
PERIWIG-S
PERJURE-D
PERJURE-R
PERJURE-S
PERLITE-S
PERMUTE-D
PERMUTE-S
PEROXID-E
PEROXID-S
PERPEND-S
PERPENT-S
PERRIER-S
PERSALT-S
PERSICO-S
PERSICO-T
S-**PERSING**
PERSIST-S
PERSONA-E
PERSONA-L
PERSONA-S
PERTAIN-S
PERTAKE-N
PERTAKE-S
PERTURB-S
PERTUSE-D
PERUSAL-S
PERUSER-S
PERVADE-D
PERVADE-R
PERVADE-S
PERVERT-S
PESAUNT-S
PESSIMA-L
PETCOCK-S
PETIOLE-D
PETIOLE-S
PETRALE-S
PETTIES-T
S-**PETTING**
PETTING-S
PETUNIA-S
PEYTRAL-S
PEYTREL-S
PFENNIG-E
PFENNIG-S
PHAEISM-S
PHAETON-S
PHALLIN-S
PHANTOM-S
PHANTOM-Y
PHARAOH-S
PHASMID-S
PHEAZAR-S
PHELLEM-S
PHENATE-S
PHILTER-S
PHILTRE-D
PHILTRE-S
PHOBISM-S
PHOBIST-S
PHONATE-D
PHONATE-S
PHONEME-S
A-**PHONICS**
A-**PHONIES**
PHONIES-T
E-**PHORATE**
PHORATE-S
PHOTISM-S
PHRASER-S
PHYTANE-S
PIAFFER-S
PIANINO-S
PIANISM-S
PIANIST-E
PIANIST-S
A-**PIARIST**
PIARIST-S
PIASABA-S
PIASAVA-S
PIASTER-S
PIASTRE-S
PIBROCH-S

PICACHO-S
PICADOR-S
PICAMAR-S
PICCOLO-S
E-**PICENES**
PICKAXE-D
PICKAXE-S
PICKEER-S
PICKING-S
PICKLER-S
PICKMAW-S
PICKOFF-S
PICOLIN-E
PICOLIN-S
PICOTEE-S
PICQUET-S
PICRATE-D
PICRATE-S
PICRITE-S
PICTURE-D
PICTURE-S
PIDDLER-S
PIDDOCK-S
PIDGEON-S
PIEBALD-S
PIECING-S
PIEFORT-S
PIERAGE-S
PIERCER-S
PIERROT-S
PIETISM-S
PIETIST-S
PIFFERO-S
PIFFLER-S
PIGBOAT-S
PIGFEED-S
PIGGIES-T
PIGGING-S
S-**PIGHTED**
PIGHTLE-S
PIGLING-S
PIGMEAT-S
PIGMENT-S
PIGNOLI-A
PIGNOLI-S
PIGSKIN-S
PIGSNEY-S
PIGSNIE-S
PIGTAIL-S
PIGWEED-S
S-**PIKELET**
PIKELET-S
PILCHER-S
PILCORN-S
PILCROW-S
PILEATE-D
PILGRIM-S
S-**PILINGS**
S-**PILLAGE**
PILLAGE-D
PILLAGE-R
PILLAGE-S
S-**PILLING**
PILLING-S
PILLION-S
PILLOCK-S
PILSNER-S
PIMENTO-S
PINBALL-S
PINBONE-S
PINCASE-S
PINCHER-S
PINDARI-S
PINDOWN-S
PINESAP-S
PINFOLD-S
PINGLER-S
PINGUIN-S
PINHEAD-S
PINHOLE-S
S-**PINIEST**
O-**PINIONS**
PINITOL-S
PINKEYE-S
PINKIES-T
PINKING-S
PINNACE-S
PINNATE-D
S-**PINNERS**
S-**PINNETS**
S-**PINNIES**
S-**PINNING**
PINNING-S
PINNOCK-S
PINNULA-E
PINNULA-R
PINNULA-S
PINNULE-S
PINOCLE-S
PINTADA-S
PINTADO-S
PINTAIL-S
PINTANO-S
PINWALE-S
PINWEED-S
PINWORK-S
PINWORM-S
PIONEER-S
PIONING-S
PIPEAGE-S
PIPEFUL-S
PIPETTE-D
PIPETTE-S
PIRAGUA-S
PIRANHA-S
S-**PIRATED**
PIROGUE-S
PIROQUE-S
PISCINA-E
PISCINA-L
PISCINA-S
PISCINE-S
PISHOGE-S
PISMIRE-S
PISSANT-S
PISSOIR-S
PISTOLE-D
PISTOLE-S
PISTOLE-T
PITAPAT-S
PITARAH-S
S-**PITCHER**
PITCHER-S
PITFALL-S
PITHEAD-S
PITPROP-S
S-**PITTERS**
S-**PITTING**
PITTING-S
PITTITE-S
PITUITA-S
PITUITE-S
PIVOTER-S
PLACARD-S
PLACATE-D
PLACATE-R
PLACATE-S
PLACCAT-E
PLACCAT-S
PLACEBO-S
PLACING-S
PLACKET-S
PLACOID-S
PLAFOND-S
PLAGIUM-S
PLAGUER-S
PLAITER-S
PLANCHE-D
PLANCHE-S
PLANCHE-T
PLANNER-S
PLANTER-S
PLANULA-E
PLANULA-R
S-**PLASHED**
S-**PLASHER**
PLASHER-S
S-**PLASHES**
PLASHET-S
PLASMID-S
PLASMIN-S
PLASMON-S
PLASTER-S
PLASTER-Y
A-**PLASTIC**
PLASTIC-S
PLASTID-S
PLATANE-S
PLATEAU-S
PLATEAU-X
PLATIES-T
PLATINA-S
PLATING-S
PLATOON-S
S-**PLATTED**
S-**PLATTER**
PLATTER-S
PLAUDIT-E
PLAUDIT-S
PLAYACT-S
PLAYBOY-S
PLAYDAY-S
S-**PLAYING**
U-PLAYING
PLAYLET-S
PLAYOFF-S
PLAYPEN-S
PLEADER-S
PLEASER-S
PLEATER-S
PLECTRE-S
PLEDGEE-S
PLEDGER-S
PLEDGET-S
PLEDGOR-S
PLENIPO-S
PLENISM-S
PLENIST-S
PLEOPOD-S
PLEROMA-S
PLEROME-S
PLESSOR-S
PLEXURE-S
PLICATE-D
PLICATE-S
U-**PLIGHTS**
PLIMSOL-E
PLIMSOL-L
PLIMSOL-S
PLINKER-S
PLISKIE-S
PLODDER-S
PLONKER-S
PLOOKIE-R
PLOSION-S
PLOSIVE-S
PLOTTER-S
PLOTTIE-R
PLOTTIE-S
PLOUKIE-R
PLOUTER-S
PLOWBOY-S
PLOWTER-S
PLUCKER-S
PLUGGER-S
PLUGOLA-S
PLUMAGE-D
PLUMAGE-S
PLUMBER-S
PLUMBER-Y
PLUMBUM-S
PLUMCOT-S
PLUMIST-S
PLUMMET-S
PLUMPEN-S
PLUMPER-S
PLUMPIE-R
PLUMULA-E
PLUMULA-R
PLUMULE-S
PLUNDER-S
PLUNGER-S
PLUNKER-S
PLUSAGE-S
PLUSHES-T
PLUVIAL-S
PLYWOOD-S
POACHER-S
POCHARD-S
POCHOIR-S
POCKARD-S
POCKPIT-S
POCOSIN-S
PODAGRA-L
PODAGRA-S
PODDIES-T
PODESTA-S
S-**PODIUMS**
POETISE-D
POETISE-R
POETISE-S
POETIZE-D
POETIZE-R
POETIZE-S
POGONIA-S
POGONIP-S
POINDER-S
POINTEL-S
POINTER-S
POISSON-S
POITREL-S
POKEFUL-S
POLACCA-S
POLACRE-S
POLARON-S
POLEAXE-D
POLEAXE-S
POLECAT-S
POLEMIC-S
POLENTA-S
POLITIC-K
POLITIC-O
POLITIC-S
POLLACK-S
POLLARD-S
POLLING-S
POLLIST-S
POLLOCK-S
POLLUTE-D
POLLUTE-R
POLLUTE-S
POLOIST-S
POLONIE-S
POLYCOT-S
POLYENE-S
POLYGAM-S
POLYGAM-Y
POLYGON-S
POLYGON-Y
POLYMER-S
POLYMER-Y
POLYNIA-S
POLYNYA-S
POLYOMA-S
POLYPOD-S
POLYPOD-Y
POLYZOA-N
POMATUM-S
POMEROY-S
POMFRET-S
POMMELE-D
POMPANO-S
POMPELO-S
POMPION-S
POMPOON-S
PONCEAU-S
PONCEAU-X
PONDAGE-S
S-**PONGIER**
S-**PONGING**
PONIARD-S
PONTAGE-S
PONTIFF-S
PONTILE-S
S-**PONTOON**
PONTOON-S
POOFTAH-S
POOFTER-S
POOGYEE-S
S-**POOKING**
S-**POOLING**
POPADUM-S
POPCORN-S
POPEDOM-S
POPERIN-S
POPOVER-S
POPPIES-T
POPULAR-S
PORIFER-S
PORKIES-T
PORKPIE-S
PORPESS-E
PORRECT-S
PORRIGO-S
PORTAGE-D
PORTAGE-S
PORTEND-S
PORTENT-S
S-**PORTERS**
PORTESS-E
PORTICO-S
S-**PORTIER**
PORTIER-E
S-**PORTING**
PORTION-S
PORTRAY-S
POSAUNE-S
POSEUSE-S
POSITON-S
O-**POSSUMS**
POSTAGE-S
POSTBAG-S
POSTBOY-S
POSTDOC-S
POSTEEN-S
POSTERN-S
A-**POSTILS**
POSTING-S
POSTURE-D
POSTURE-R
POSTURE-S
POTABLE-S
POTAGER-S
POTASSA-S
POTBOIL-S
POTCHER-S
POTENCE-S
POTHEAD-S
POTHEEN-S
POTHERB-S
POTHOLE-D
POTHOLE-R
POTHOLE-S
POTHOOK-S
POTICHE-S
POTLACH-E
POTLINE-S
POTLUCK-S
POTOROO-S
POTSHOP-S
POTSHOT-S
POTTAGE-S
POTTEEN-S
S-**POTTERS**
S-**POTTIER**
POTTIES-T
S-**POTTING**
POUFTAH-S
POUFTER-S
POULARD-E
POULARD-S
POULDER-S
POULDRE-S
POULTER-S
POUNCER-S
POUNCET-S
POUNDAL-S
POUNDER-S
POURING-S
POURSEW-S
POURSUE-D
POURSUE-S
POUSSIE-S
POUSSIN-S
S-**POUTERS**
POUTHER-S
S-**POUTIER**
S-**POUTING**
POUTING-S
PRABBLE-S
A-**PRACTIC**
PRACTIC-E
PRACTIC-K
PRACTIC-S
PRAETOR-S
PRAIRIE-D
PRAIRIE-S
U-**PRAISED**
U-**PRAISER**
PRAISER-S
U-**PRAISES**
PRALINE-S
PRANCER-S
PRANCKE-D
PRANCKE-S
PRANKLE-D
PRANKLE-S
U-**PRATING**
PRATING-S
S-**PRATTLE**

PRATTLE-D
PRATTLE-R
PRATTLE-S
PRAUNCE-D
PRAUNCE-S
PRAWLIN-S
PRAWNER-S
S-**PRAYERS**
S-**PRAYING**
PRAYING-S
PREASSE-D
PREASSE-S
PREAVER-S
PREBAKE-D
PREBAKE-S
PREBEND-S
PREBILL-S
PREBIND-S
PREBOIL-S
PREBOOK-S
PRECAST-S
PRECAVA-E
PRECAVA-L
PRECEDE-D
PRECEDE-S
PRECENT-S
PRECEPT-S
PRECIPE-S
PRECISE-D
PRECISE-R
PRECISE-S
PRECODE-D
PRECODE-S
PRECOOK-S
PRECOOL-S
PRECURE-D
PRECURE-S
PREDATE-D
PREDATE-S
PREDAWN-S
PREDIAL-S
PREDICT-S
PREDOOM-S
PREDUSK-S
PREEDIT-S
S-**PREEING**
PREEMIE-S
PREEMPT-S
PREENER-S
PREFACE-D
PREFACE-R
PREFACE-S
PREFADE-D
PREFADE-S
PREFECT-S
PREFILE-D
PREFILE-S
PREFIRE-D
PREFIRE-S
PREFORM-S
PREHEAT-S
PREHEND-S
PRELATE-S
PRELECT-S
PRELUDE-D
PRELUDE-R
PRELUDE-S
PRELUDI-O
PREMIER-E
PREMIER-S
PREMISE-D
PREMISE-S
PREMIUM-S
PREMOLD-S
PREMOVE-D
PREMOVE-S
PRENAME-S
PREPACK-S
PREPARE-D
PREPARE-R
PREPARE-S
PREPLAN-S
PREPLAN-T
PREPONE-D
PREPONE-S
PREPOSE-D
PREPOSE-S
PREPPIE-R
PREPPIE-S
PREPREG-S
PREPUCE-S
PREQUEL-S
PRESAGE-D
PRESAGE-R
PRESAGE-S
PRESELL-S
PRESENT-S
PRESHOW-N
PRESHOW-S
PRESIDE-D
PRESIDE-R
PRESIDE-S
PRESIFT-S
PRESOAK-S
PRESORT-S
PRESSER-S
PRESSIE-S
PRESSOR-S
PRESTER-S
PRESUME-D
PRESUME-R
PRESUME-S
PRETAPE-D
PRETAPE-S
PRETEEN-S
PRETEND-S
PRETEST-S
PRETEXT-S
PRETRIM-S
PRETYPE-D
PRETYPE-S
PRETZEL-S
PREVAIL-S
PREVENE-D
PREVENE-S
PREVENT-S
PREVERB-S
PREVIEW-S
PREVISE-D
PREVISE-S
PREWARM-S
PREWARN-S
PREWRAP-S
PREZZIE-S
PRIBBLE-S
PRICKER-S
PRICKET-S
PRICKLE-D
PRICKLE-S
S-**PRIGGED**
S-**PRIGGER**
PRIGGER-S
PRIGGER-Y
PRIMAGE-S
PRIMATE-S
PRIMERO-S
PRIMEUR-S
PRIMINE-S
PRIMING-S
PRIMMER-S
PRIMSIE-R
PRIMULA-S
PRINCES-S
PRINKER-S
S-**PRINTED**
S-**PRINTER**
PRINTER-S
PRINTER-Y
PRISAGE-S
PRISERE-S
U-**PRISERS**
U-**PRISING**
PRIVADO-S
PRIVATE-R
PRIVATE-S
PRIVIES-T
PROBAND-S
PROBANG-S
PROBATE-D
PROBATE-S
PROBLEM-S
PROCARP-S
PROCEED-S
PROCTOR-S
PROCURE-D
PROCURE-R
PROCURE-S
PRODDER-S
PRODUCE-D
PRODUCE-R
PRODUCE-S
PRODUCT-S
PROETTE-S
PROFANE-D
PROFANE-R
PROFANE-S
PROFFER-S
PROFILE-D
PROFILE-R
PROFILE-S
PROFUSE-R
PROGGER-S
PROGRAM-S
PROJECT-S
PROLATE-D
PROLATE-S
PROLINE-S
U-**PROLLED**
PROLLER-S
PROLONG-E
PROLONG-S
PROMINE-S
PROMISE-D
PROMISE-E
PROMISE-R
PROMISE-S
PROMMER-S
PROMOTE-D
PROMOTE-R
PROMOTE-S
PRONATE-D
PRONATE-S
PRONEUR-S
PRONOTA-L
PRONOUN-S
PROOFER-S
PROOTIC-S
PROPAGE-D
PROPAGE-S
PROPALE-D
PROPALE-S
PROPANE-S
PROPEND-S
PROPENE-S
PROPHET-S
PROPINE-D
PROPINE-S
PROPJET-S
PROPONE-D
PROPONE-S
PROPOSE-D
PROPOSE-R
PROPOSE-S
PRORATE-D
PRORATE-S
PROSECT-S
PROSING-S
PROSOMA-L
PROSOMA-S
PROSPER-S
PROSSIE-S
PROSTIE-S
PROTEAN-S
PROTEAS-E
PROTECT-S
PROTEGE-E
PROTEGE-S
PROTEID-E
PROTEID-S
PROTEIN-S
PROTEND-S
PROTEST-S
PROTHYL-E
PROTHYL-S
PROTIST-S
PROTIUM-S
PROTORE-S
PROTYLE-S
PROULER-S
PROVAND-S
PROVEND-S
PROVERB-S
PROVIDE-D
PROVIDE-R
PROVIDE-S
PROVINE-D
PROVINE-S
PROVING-S
PROVISO-R
PROVISO-S
PROVOKE-D
PROVOKE-R
PROVOKE-S
PROVOST-S
PROWLER-S
PRUNING-S
PRURIGO-S
PSALTER-S
PSALTER-Y
PSAMMON-S
PSCHENT-S
PSIONIC-S
PSYCHIC-S
PSYLLID-S
PTARMIC-S
PTERYLA-E
PTOMAIN-E
PTOMAIN-S
PTYALIN-S
PUCCOON-S
PUCELLE-S
S-**PUDDERS**
S-**PUDDING**
PUDDING-S
PUDDING-Y
PUDDLER-S
PUDDOCK-S
PUDENDA-L
PUFFING-S
PUGAREE-S
PUGGIES-T
PUGGING-S
PUGGREE-S
PUGMARK-S
PULDRON-S
PULLMAN-S
PULLOUT-S
PULSATE-D
PULSATE-S
PULSION-S
PULTOON-S
PULTURE-S
PUMICER-S
PUMMELO-S
PUMPION-S
PUMPKIN-S
PUNALUA-N
PUNALUA-S
PUNCHER-S
S-**PUNKIER**
S-**PUNKIES**
PUNKIES-T
PUNNING-S
PUNSTER-S
PUPARIA-L
PUPILAR-Y
PUPUNHA-S
PURGING-S
PURITAN-S
PURLIEU-S
PURLINE-S
S-**PURLING**
PURLING-S
PURLOIN-S
PURPLES-T
PURPORT-S
PURPOSE-D
PURPOSE-S
PURPURA-S
PURPURE-S
S-**PURRING**
PURRING-S
PURSUAL-S
PURSUER-S
PURSUIT-S
PURVIEW-S
PUSHPIN-S
PUSHROD-S
PUSSIES-T
PUSSLEY-S
PUSTULE-D
PUSTULE-S
PUTCHER-S
PUTCHUK-S
PUTLOCK-S
S-**PUTTERS**
PUTTIER-S
PUTTING-S
PUTTOCK-S
PUZZLER-S
PYAEMIA-S
PYCNITE-S
PYEBALD-S
PYGIDIA-L
PYRALID-S
PYRAMID-S
A-**PYRETIC**
A-**PYREXIA**
PYREXIA-L
PYREXIA-S
PYROGEN-S
PYRRHIC-S
PYRROLE-S
PYTHIUM-S
QABALAH-S
QAWWALI-S
QUACKER-S
QUACKER-Y
QUACKLE-D
QUACKLE-S
S-**QUADDED**
QUADRAT-E
QUADRAT-S
QUADRIC-S
QUAFFER-S
QUAHAUG-S
S-**QUAILED**
QUAKING-S
E-**QUALITY**
QUANNET-S
QUANTIC-S
S-**QUAREST**
QUARREL-S
QUARTAN-S
QUARTER-N
QUARTER-S
QUARTET-S
QUARTET-T
QUARTIC-S
S-**QUASHED**
QUASHEE-S
S-**QUASHER**
QUASHER-S
S-**QUASHES**
QUASHIE-S
QUASSIA-S
QUASSIN-S
QUAYAGE-S
QUEENIE-R
QUEENIE-S
QUELLER-S
QUERIDA-S
QUERIER-S
QUERIST-S
QUESTER-S
QUESTOR-S
QUETZAL-S
QUEUING-S
QUEYNIE-S
QUIBBLE-D
QUIBBLE-R
QUIBBLE-S
QUIBLIN-S
QUICKEN-S
QUICKIE-S
QUIDDIT-S
QUIDDIT-Y
QUIDDLE-D
QUIDDLE-R
QUIDDLE-S
QUIESCE-D
QUIESCE-S
QUIETEN-S
QUIETER-S
QUILLAI-A
QUILLAI-S
QUILLET-S
QUILLON-S
QUILTER-S
QUINCHE-D
QUINCHE-S
QUINELA-S
S-**QUINIES**
QUININA-S
QUININE-S
QUINNAT-S
QUINOID-S
QUINONE-S
QUINTAL-S
QUINTAN-S

QUINTAR-S
QUINTET-S
QUINTET-T
QUINTIC-S
QUINTIN-S
E-**QUIPPED**
E-**QUIPPER**
QUIPPER-S
S-**QUIRING**
S-**QUIRTED**
QUITTAL-S
QUITTER-S
QUITTOR-S
QUIXOTE-S
QUIZZER-S
QUIZZER-Y
S-**QUIZZES**
QUODLIN-S
QUOITER-S
QUOMODO-S
RABANNA-S
RABATTE-D
RABATTE-S
D-**RABBETS**
B-**RABBLED**
D-RABBLED
G-RABBLED
B-**RABBLER**
D-RABBLER
G-RABBLER
RABBLER-S
B-**RABBLES**
D-RABBLES
G-RABBLES
P-RABBLES
RABBONI-S
RACCOON-S
RACEWAY-S
B-**RACHETS**
B-**RACHIAL**
B-**RACINGS**
T-RACINGS
C-**RACKERS**
T-RACKERS
B-**RACKETS**
RACKETT-S
W-**RACKFUL**
RACKFUL-S
C-**RACKING**
F-RACKING
T-RACKING
W-RACKING
RACKING-S
RACLOIR-S
RACQUET-S
B-**RADDING**
RADIANT-S
RADIATA-S
E-**RADIATE**
RADIATE-D
RADIATE-S
RADICAL-S
RADICEL-S
RADICLE-S
D-**RAFFISH**
RAFFLER-S
D-**RAFTERS**
G-RAFTERS
C-**RAFTING**
D-RAFTING
G-RAFTING
RAGBOLT-S
B-**RAGGIER**
C-RAGGIER
D-RAGGIER
RAGGIES-T
B-**RAGGING**
D-RAGGING
F-RAGGING
RAGGING-S
D-**RAGGLED**
D-**RAGGLES**
RAGHEAD-S
F-**RAGMENT**
RAGMENT-S
RAGTIME-R
RAGTIME-S
RAGWEED-S
RAGWORK-S
RAGWORM-S
RAGWORT-S
B-**RAIDERS**
B-**RAIDING**
T-**RAIKING**
RAILBED-S
RAILCAR-D
RAILCAR-S
T-**RAILERS**
B-**RAILING**
D-RAILING
T-RAILING
RAILING-S
RAILWAY-S
RAIMENT-S
RAINBOW-S
RAINBOW-Y
B-**RAINIER**
G-RAINIER
B-**RAINILY**
B-**RAINING**
D-RAINING
G-RAINING
T-RAINING
RAINOUT-S
P-**RAISERS**
A-**RAISING**
B-RAISING
F-RAISING
P-RAISING
RAISING-S
RAKEOFF-S
RAKSHAS-A
RALLIER-S
RAMAKIN-S
B-**RAMBLED**
RAMBLER-S
B-**RAMBLES**
RAMEKIN-S
RAMILIE-S
C-**RAMMERS**
RAMMIES-T
C-**RAMMING**
D-RAMMING
T-RAMMING
RAMPAGE-D
RAMPAGE-R
RAMPAGE-S
RAMPART-S
T-**RAMPERS**
RAMPICK-S
RAMPIKE-S
C-**RAMPING**
T-RAMPING
RAMPING-S
RAMPION-S
RAMPIRE-D
RAMPIRE-S
RAMPOLE-S
B-**RANCHED**
C-RANCHED
B-**RANCHER**
RANCHER-O
RANCHER-S
B-**RANCHES**
C-RANCHES
T-RANCHES
P-**RANCING**
T-RANCING
RANCOUR-S
B-**RANDIES**
RANDIES-T
B-**RANDING**
G-**RANGERS**
O-**RANGIER**
P-**RANGING**
RANGOLI-S
F-**RANKERS**
C-**RANKEST**
F-RANKEST
B-**RANKING**
C-RANKING
F-RANKING
P-RANKING
RANKING-S
C-**RANKISH**
P-RANKISH
C-**RANKLED**
P-RANKLED
C-**RANKLES**
P-RANKLES
RANPIKE-S
RANSACK-S
T-**RANSOMS**
G-**RANTERS**
T-RANTERS
D-**RANTING**
G-RANTING
T-RANTING
RANTING-S
RAOULIA-S
RAPHIDE-S
D-**RAPIERS**
RAPLOCH-S
C-**RAPPERS**
T-RAPPERS
W-RAPPERS
C-**RAPPING**
D-RAPPING
F-RAPPING
T-RAPPING
W-RAPPING
RAPPING-S
RAPPORT-S
RAPTURE-D
RAPTURE-S
RAREBIT-S
RASBORA-S
RASCHEL-S
C-**RASHERS**
B-**RASHEST**
B-**RASHING**
C-RASHING
T-RASHING
G-**RASPERS**
G-**RASPING**
RASPING-S
W-**RASSLED**
W-**RASSLES**
RASTRUM-S
E-**RASURES**
RATAFEE-S
RATAFIA-S
RATATAT-S
C-**RATCHES**
F-RATCHES
B-**RATCHET**
RATCHET-S
RATFINK-S
RATHOLE-S
G-**RATINGS**
P-RATINGS
O-**RATIONS**
RATLINE-S
B-**RATLING**
RATLING-S
B-**RATPACK**
RATPACK-S
RATTAIL-S
RATTEEN-S
B-**RATTIER**
D-**RATTING**
P-RATTING
RATTING-S
B-**RATTISH**
B-**RATTLED**
P-RATTLED
P-**RATTLER**
RATTLER-S
B-**RATTLES**
P-RATTLES
RATTLIN-E
RATTLIN-G
RATTLIN-S
RATTOON-S
RATTRAP-S
RAVAGER-S
G-**RAVELED**
T-RAVELED
T-**RAVELER**
RAVELER-S
RAVELIN-G
RAVELIN-S
G-**RAVELLY**
C-**RAVENED**
RAVENER-S
C-**RAVINGS**
G-RAVINGS
RAVIOLI-S
RAWBONE-D
RAWHEAD-S
RAWHIDE-D
RAWHIDE-S
D-**RAWINGS**
G-**RAYLING**
F-**RAZZLES**
A-**REACHED**
B-REACHED
P-REACHED
B-**REACHER**
P-REACHER
T-REACHER
REACHER-S
A-**REACHES**
B-REACHES
P-REACHES
P-**REACTED**
REACTOR-S
P-**READAPT**
READAPT-S
D-**READERS**
T-READERS
READIES-T
A-**READING**
B-READING
D-READING
T-READING
READING-S
P-**READMIT**
READMIT-S
P-**READOPT**
READOPT-S
READORN-S
READOUT-S
REAGENT-S
B-**REAKING**
C-REAKING
F-REAKING
W-REAKING
REALGAR-S
REALIGN-S
REALISE-D
REALISE-R
REALISE-S
REALISM-S
REALIST-S
REALIZE-D
REALIZE-R
REALIZE-S
REALLIE-D
REALLIE-S
P-**REALLOT**
REALLOT-S
REALTER-S
REALTIE-S
REALTOR-S
REAMEND-S
C-**REAMERS**
D-REAMERS
C-**REAMIER**
D-REAMIER
B-**REAMING**
C-REAMING
D-REAMING
REARGUE-D
REARGUE-S
D-**REARING**
REARISE-N
REARISE-S
P-**REARMED**
T-**REASONS**
B-**REASTED**
REAVAIL-S
P-**REAVERS**
G-**REAVING**
REAWAKE-D
REAWAKE-N
REAWAKE-S
REAWOKE-N
REBADGE-D
REBADGE-S
REBATER-S
REBEGIN-S
P-**REBILLS**
P-**REBINDS**
REBIRTH-S
REBLEND-S
REBLOOM-S
REBOARD-S
P-**REBOILS**
P-**REBOOKS**
P-**REBOUND**
REBOUND-S
REBRACE-D
REBRACE-S
REBREED-S
REBUILD-S
REBUKER-S
P-**RECASTS**
P-**RECEDED**
P-**RECEDES**
RECEIPT-S
RECEIVE-D
RECEIVE-R
RECEIVE-S
RECENSE-D
RECENSE-S
P-**RECEPTS**
RECHART-S
RECHATE-S
RECHEAT-S
P-**RECHECK**
RECHECK-S
RECHOSE-N
P-**RECIPES**
RECITAL-S
P-**RECITED**
RECITER-S
T-**RECKING**
W-RECKING
RECLAIM-S
RECLAME-S
RECLASP-S
P-**RECLEAN**
RECLEAN-S
RECLIMB-S
RECLINE-D
RECLINE-R
RECLINE-S
RECLOSE-D
RECLOSE-S
RECLUSE-S
P-**RECODED**
P-**RECODES**
RECOLOR-S
P-**RECOOKS**
RECOUNT-S
RECOUPE-D
RECOURE-D
RECOURE-S
RECOVER-S
RECOVER-Y
RECOWER-S
RECOYLE-D
RECOYLE-S
RECRATE-D
RECRATE-S
RECROWN-S
RECRUIT-S
E-**RECTION**
RECTION-S
E-**RECTORS**
RECUILE-D
RECUILE-S
P-**RECURED**
P-**RECURES**
RECURVE-D
RECURVE-S
RECUSAL-S
RECYCLE-D
RECYCLE-R
RECYCLE-S
P-**REDATED**
P-**REDATES**
REDBACK-S
REDBAIT-S
REDBIRD-S
REDBONE-S
REDCOAT-S
REDDING-S
T-**REDDLED**
T-**REDDLES**
REDHEAD-S
P-**REDIALS**
REDLINE-D
REDLINE-S
REDNECK-S
REDOUBT-S
REDOUND-S
REDPOLL-S
REDRAFT-S

REDREAM-S
REDREAM-T
P-**REDRILL**
REDRILL-S
REDRIVE-N
REDRIVE-S
REDROOT-S
REDSKIN-S
REDTAIL-S
REDUCER-S
REDWARE-S
REDWING-S
REDWOOD-S
B-**REECHED**
B-**REECHES**
REECHIE-R
REEDBED-S
B-**REEDERS**
G-**REEDIER**
G-**REEDILY**
B-**REEDING**
REEDING-S
P-**REEDITS**
F-**REEDMAN**
F-**REEDMEN**
REEFING-S
REEJECT-S
C-**REEKIER**
G-**REEKING**
P-**REELECT**
REELECT-S
C-**REELING**
REELING-S
P-**REENACT**
REENACT-S
REENDOW-S
REENJOY-S
REENTER-S
REEQUIP-S
P-**REERECT**
REERECT-S
P-**REEVING**
REEVOKE-D
REEVOKE-S
REEXPEL-S
P-**REFACED**
P-**REFACES**
P-**REFECTS**
REFENCE-D
REFENCE-S
REFEREE-D
REFEREE-S
P-**REFIGHT**
REFIGHT-S
P-**REFILED**
P-**REFILES**
REFINER-S
REFINER-Y
P-**REFIRED**
P-**REFIRES**
P-**REFIXED**
P-**REFIXES**
REFLATE-D
REFLATE-S
REFLECT-S
REFLOAT-S
REFLOOD-S
P-**REFOCUS**
REFORGE-D
REFORGE-S
P-**REFORMS**
REFOUND-S
REFRACT-S
REFRAIN-S
REFRAME-D
REFRAME-S
REFRONT-S
P-**REFROZE**
REFROZE-N
REFUGEE-S
REFUSAL-S
REFUSER-S
REFUTAL-S
REFUTER-S
REGALER-S
G-**REGALES**
REGALIA-N
REGALIA-S
REGATTA-S
REGAUGE-D
REGAUGE-S
REGENCE-S
REGIMEN-S
REGIMEN-T
REGLAZE-D
REGLAZE-S
B-**REGMATA**
P-**REGNANT**
REGORGE-D
REGORGE-S
REGOSOL-S
REGRADE-D
REGRADE-S
REGRAFT-S
REGRANT-S
REGRATE-D
REGRATE-R
REGRATE-S
REGREDE-D
REGREDE-S
REGREEN-S
REGREET-S
REGRIND-S
REGROOM-S
REGROUP-S
REGULAR-S
REHEARS-E
P-**REHEATS**
REHINGE-D
REHINGE-S
REHOUSE-D
REHOUSE-S
REIFIER-S
REIMAGE-D
REIMAGE-S
REINCUR-S
G-**REINING**
REINTER-S
REISSUE-D
REISSUE-R
REISSUE-S
REITBOK-S
REJOICE-D
REJOICE-R
REJOICE-S
REJONEO-S
REJOURN-S
P-**REJUDGE**
REJUDGE-D
REJUDGE-S
RELABEL-S
RELACHE-S
RELAPSE-D
RELAPSE-R
RELAPSE-S
RELATER-S
P-**RELATES**
RELATOR-S
RELAXER-S
RELAXIN-G
RELAXIN-S
RELEARN-S
RELEARN-T
RELEASE-D
RELEASE-E
RELEASE-R
RELEASE-S
RELIEVE-D
RELIEVE-R
RELIEVE-S
RELIEVO-S
RELIGHT-S
RELIQUE-S
RELIVER-S
P-**RELIVES**
C-**REMAINS**
REMAKER-S
REMANET-S
REMANIE-S
C-**REMATED**
C-**REMATES**
REMBLAI-S
T-**REMBLED**
T-**REMBLES**
REMERGE-D
REMERGE-S
P-**REMISED**
P-**REMISES**
P-**REMIXED**
P-**REMIXES**
REMNANT-S
REMODEL-S
P-**REMOLDS**
P-**REMORSE**
REMORSE-S
REMOTES-T
REMOULD-S
REMOUNT-S
REMOVAL-S
P-**REMOVED**
REMOVER-S
P-**REMOVES**
REMUAGE-S
REMUEUR-S
RENAGUE-D
RENAGUE-S
T-**RENAILS**
P-**RENAMES**
T-**RENDING**
RENEGER-S
RENEGUE-D
RENEGUE-R
RENEGUE-S
RENEWAL-S
RENEWER-S
RENNASE-S
B-**RENNING**
G-RENNING
RENNING-S
T-**RENTALS**
RENTIER-S
P-**RENTING**
REOCCUR-S
REOFFER-S
P-**REORDER**
REORDER-S
P-**REPACKS**
REPAINT-S
REPANEL-S
REPAPER-S
REPINER-S
REPIQUE-D
REPIQUE-S
P-**REPLACE**
REPLACE-D
REPLACE-R
REPLACE-S
P-**REPLANS**
P-**REPLANT**
REPLANT-S
REPLATE-D
REPLATE-S
REPLEAD-S
REPLETE-D
REPLETE-S
REPLICA-S
REPLIER-S
REPLUMB-S
REPOINT-S
P-**REPONED**
P-**REPONES**
REPOSAL-L
REPOSAL-S
P-**REPOSED**
REPOSER-S
P-**REPOSES**
REPOSIT-S
REPOWER-S
P-**REPPING**
REPPING-S
P-**REPRICE**
REPRICE-D
REPRICE-S
REPRIME-D
REPRIME-S
P-**REPRINT**
REPRINT-S
REPRISE-D
REPRISE-S
REPRIVE-D
REPRIVE-S
REPRIZE-D
REPRIZE-S
REPROBE-D
REPROBE-S
REPROOF-S
REPROVE-D
REPROVE-R
REPROVE-S
REPRYVE-D
REPRYVE-S
REPTILE-S
REPULSE-D
REPULSE-R
REPULSE-S
REPUNIT-S
REQUERE-D
REQUERE-S
REQUEST-S
REQUIEM-S
REQUIRE-D
REQUIRE-R
REQUIRE-S
REQUITE-D
REQUITE-R
REQUITE-S
REQUOTE-D
REQUOTE-S
RERAISE-D
RERAISE-S
REROUTE-D
REROUTE-S
RESCALE-D
RESCALE-S
P-**RESCIND**
RESCIND-S
P-**RESCORE**
RESCORE-D
RESCORE-S
RESCUER-S
RESEIZE-D
RESEIZE-S
P-**RESELLS**
P-**RESENTS**
P-**RESERVE**
RESERVE-D
RESERVE-R
RESERVE-S
P-**RESHAPE**
RESHAPE-D
RESHAPE-R
RESHAPE-S
RESHAVE-D
RESHAVE-N
RESHAVE-S
RESHINE-D
RESHINE-S
RESHOOT-S
P-**RESHOWN**
P-**RESHOWS**
RESIANT-S
P-**RESIDED**
P-**RESIDER**
RESIDER-S
P-**RESIDES**
RESIDUA-L
RESIDUE-S
P-**RESIFTS**
RESIGHT-S
RESINER-S
RESKILL-S
RESLATE-D
RESLATE-S
RESMELT-S
P-**RESOAKS**
RESOJET-S
RESOLVE-D
RESOLVE-R
RESOLVE-S
P-**RESORTS**
RESOUND-S
RESPACE-D
RESPACE-S
RESPADE-D
RESPADE-S
RESPEAK-S
RESPECT-S
RESPELL-S
RESPIRE-D
RESPIRE-S
RESPITE-D
RESPITE-S
P-**RESPLIT**
RESPLIT-S
RESPOKE-N
RESPOND-S
RESPRAY-S
RESTACK-S
RESTAFF-S
RESTAGE-D
RESTAGE-S
P-**RESTAMP**
RESTAMP-S
RESTART-S
RESTATE-D
RESTATE-S
P-**RESTERS**
W-RESTERS
C-**RESTING**
P-RESTING
W-RESTING
RESTING-S
RESTOCK-S
RESTOKE-D
RESTOKE-S
RESTORE-D
RESTORE-R
RESTORE-S
RESTUFF-S
RESTYLE-D
RESTYLE-S
P-**RESUMED**
P-**RESUMER**
RESUMER-S
P-**RESUMES**
RESURGE-D
RESURGE-S
RETABLE-S
RETAKER-S
P-**RETAPED**
P-**RETAPES**
P-**RETASTE**
RETASTE-D
RETASTE-S
W-**RETCHED**
W-**RETCHES**
P-**RETESTS**
RETHINK-S
RETICLE-S
RETINAL-S
RETINOL-S
RETINUE-D
RETINUE-S
RETIRAL-S
RETIREE-S
RETIRER-S
RETITLE-D
RETITLE-S
RETRACE-D
RETRACE-S
RETRACK-S
RETRACT-S
P-**RETRAIN**
RETRAIN-S
RETRAIT-E
RETRAIT-S
RETRAIT-T
RETRATE-D
RETRATE-S
RETREAD-S
P-**RETREAT**
RETREAT-S
P-**RETRIAL**
RETRIAL-S
P-**RETRIMS**
RETSINA-S
A-**RETTING**
F-RETTING
RETWIST-S
P-**RETYPED**
P-**RETYPES**
P-**REUNION**
REUNION-S
P-**REUNITE**
REUNITE-D
REUNITE-R
REUNITE-S
REUTTER-S
REVALUE-D
REVALUE-S
REVELER-S
REVENGE-D
REVENGE-R
REVENGE-S
REVENUE-D
REVENUE-R
REVENUE-S
P-**REVERBS**
REVERER-S
REVERTE-S

REVERSE-D
REVERSE-R
REVERSE-S
REVERSI-S
REVERSO-S
REVEUSE-S
P-**REVIEWS**
REVILER-S
REVISAL-S
P-**REVISED**
REVISER-S
P-**REVISES**
T-REVISES
REVISIT-S
P-**REVISOR**
REVISOR-S
REVISOR-Y
REVIVAL-S
REVIVER-S
REVIVOR-S
REVOICE-D
REVOICE-S
REVOKER-S
REVOLVE-D
REVOLVE-R
REVOLVE-S
REVUIST-S
REWAKEN-S
P-**REWARMS**
REWEAVE-D
REWEAVE-S
REWEIGH-S
REWIDEN-S
P-**REWRAPS**
REWRITE-R
REWRITE-S
REYNARD-S
RHABDOM-E
RHABDOM-S
RHENIUM-S
RHIZINE-S
RHIZOID-S
RHIZOME-S
RHODIUM-S
RHODORA-S
RHOMBOI-D
RHUBARB-S
RHUBARB-Y
RHYMIST-S
RHYTHMI-C
RHYTINA-S
RIBBAND-S
C-**RIBBERS**
D-RIBBERS
C-**RIBBING**
D-RIBBING
RIBBING-S
RIBCAGE-S
RIBIBLE-S
D-**RIBLETS**
T-RIBLETS
RIBSTON-E
RIBSTON-S
C-**RIBWORK**
RIBWORK-S
RIBWORT-S
F-**RICHTED**
P-**RICIEST**
P-**RICKERS**
T-RICKERS
C-**RICKETS**
P-RICKETS
B-**RICKING**
C-RICKING
P-RICKING
T-RICKING
W-RICKING
B-**RICKLES**
P-RICKLES
T-RICKLES
RICKSHA-S
RICKSHA-W
RICOTTA-S
G-**RIDDERS**
G-**RIDDLED**
RIDDLER-S
G-**RIDDLES**
B-**RIDGING**
F-RIDGING
RIDGING-S
RIDOTTO-S
RIEMPIE-S
G-**RIEVERS**
G-**RIEVING**
P-RIEVING
RIFFLER-S
T-**RIFLERS**
T-**RIFLING**
RIFLING-S
D-**RIFTIER**
D-**RIFTING**
G-RIFTING
RIGGALD-S
F-**RIGGERS**
P-RIGGERS
T-RIGGERS
F-**RIGGING**
G-RIGGING
P-RIGGING
T-RIGGING
RIGGING-S
P-**RIGGISH**
F-**RIGHTED**
B-**RIGHTEN**
F-RIGHTEN
RIGHTEN-S
B-**RIGHTER**
RIGHTER-S
B-**RIGHTLY**
F-**RIGIDER**
F-**RIGIDLY**
RIGLING-S
RIKISHA-S
RIKSHAW-S
D-**RILLING**
F-RILLING
G-RILLING
P-RILLING
T-RILLING
RIMFIRE-S
G-**RIMIEST**
RIMLAND-S
B-**RIMLESS**
B-**RIMMERS**
C-RIMMERS
K-RIMMERS
P-RIMMERS
T-RIMMERS
B-**RIMMING**
P-RIMMING
T-RIMMING
RIMMING-S
C-**RIMPLED**
C-**RIMPLES**
RIMROCK-S
G-**RINDING**
RINGBIT-S
B-**RINGERS**
C-RINGERS
W-RINGERS
RINGGIT-S
B-**RINGING**
C-RINGING
F-RINGING
W-RINGING
RINGING-S
RINGLET-S
RINGTAW-S
RINGWAY-S
D-**RINKING**
P-RINKING
G-**RINNING**
RINSING-S
RIOTING-S
RIOTISE-S
RIOTIZE-S
RIPCORD-S
RIPENER-S
RIPIENO-S
RIPOSTE-D
RIPOSTE-S
D-**RIPPERS**
F-RIPPERS
G-RIPPERS
T-RIPPERS
D-**RIPPIER**
G-RIPPIER
T-RIPPIER
RIPPIER-S
D-**RIPPING**
G-RIPPING
T-RIPPING
C-**RIPPLED**
T-RIPPLED
C-**RIPPLER**
T-RIPPLER
RIPPLER-S
C-**RIPPLES**
G-RIPPLES
T-RIPPLES
RIPPLET-S
RIPSTOP-S
RIPTIDE-S
RISIBLE-S
F-**RISKERS**
F-**RISKFUL**
F-**RISKIER**
F-**RISKILY**
B-**RISKING**
F-RISKING
RISOTTO-S
C-**RISPING**
RISPING-S
RISSOLE-S
C-**RITTERS**
F-RITTERS
G-RITTERS
F-**RITTING**
G-RITTING
RIVERET-S
RIVETER-S
RIVIERA-S
RIVIERE-S
RIVULET-S
RIZZART-S
F-**RIZZERS**
B-**ROACHED**
B-**ROACHES**
ROADBED-S
ROADING-S
B-**ROADWAY**
ROADWAY-S
ROAMING-S
ROARING-S
ROASTER-S
T-**ROATING**
P-**ROBANDS**
ROBINIA-S
ROBOTIC-S
ROBUSTA-S
C-**ROCHETS**
ROCKABY-E
C-**ROCKERY**
B-**ROCKETS**
C-ROCKETS
ROCKIER-S
C-**ROCKING**
F-ROCKING
T-ROCKING
ROCKING-S
ROCKLAY-S
ROCKOON-S
ROCQUET-S
B-**RODDING**
P-RODDING
RODDING-S
E-**RODENTS**
RODEWAY-S
RODSTER-S
ROEBUCK-S
B-**ROGUERY**
B-**ROGUISH**
B-**ROILING**
D-ROILING
G-**ROINING**
P-ROINING
ROISTER-S
ROKELAY-S
ROLFING-S
P-**ROLLERS**
T-ROLLERS
ROLLICK-S
ROLLICK-Y
D-**ROLLING**
P-ROLLING
T-ROLLING
ROLLING-S
ROLLMOP-S
ROLLOCK-S
ROLLOUT-S
ROLLWAY-S
F-**ROMAGES**
ROMAIKA-S
ROMAINE-S
ROMANCE-D
ROMANCE-R
ROMANCE-S
ROMAUNT-S
ROMNEYA-S
T-**ROMPING**
RONDEAU-X
RONDINO-S
RONDURE-S
RONTGEN-S
P-**ROOFERS**
P-**ROOFING**
ROOFING-S
ROOFTOP-S
ROOINEK-S
C-**ROOKERY**
B-**ROOKIES**
ROOKIES-T
B-**ROOKING**
C-ROOKING
D-ROOKING
G-**ROOMERS**
ROOMFUL-S
B-**ROOMIER**
ROOMIES-T
B-**ROOMING**
G-ROOMING
V-ROOMING
D-**ROOPIER**
D-**ROOPING**
T-ROOPING
ROOSTER-S
ROOTAGE-S
ROOTIES-T
W-**ROOTING**
ROOTING-S
ROOTLES-S
ROOTLET-S
ROPEWAY-S
C-**ROQUETS**
RORQUAL-S
ROSACEA-S
ROSAKER-S
ROSALIA-S
ROSARIA-N
ROSEBAY-S
ROSEBUD-S
ROSEHIP-S
ROSELLA-S
ROSELLE-S
ROSEOLA-R
ROSEOLA-S
ROSETTE-D
ROSETTE-S
ROSIERE-S
C-**ROSIERS**
P-**ROSIEST**
ROSINOL-S
ROSOLIO-S
C-**ROSSERS**
G-ROSSERS
T-ROSSERS
F-**ROSTING**
ROSTRUM-S
ROTATOR-S
ROTATOR-Y
C-**ROTCHES**
ROTCHIE-S
B-**ROTHERS**
ROTIFER-S
T-**ROTTERS**
T-**ROTTING**
ROTUNDA-S
T-**ROUBLES**
C-**ROUCHES**
G-ROUCHES
ROUGHEN-S
ROUGHER-S
ROUGHIE-S
ROUILLE-S
ROULADE-S
ROULEAU-S
ROULEAU-X
ROUMING-S
F-**ROUNCES**
T-ROUNCES
G-**ROUNDED**
ROUNDEL-S
G-**ROUNDER**
ROUNDER-S
ROUNDLE-S
ROUNDLE-T
ROUNDUP-S
C-**ROUPIER**
C-**ROUPILY**
C-**ROUPING**
G-ROUPING
T-ROUPING
A-**ROUSERS**
G-ROUSERS
T-ROUSERS
A-**ROUSING**
G-ROUSING
ROUSTER-S
G-**ROUTERS**
T-ROUTERS
ROUTHIE-R
ROUTINE-S
G-**ROUTING**
T-ROUTING
ROUTING-S
D-**ROVINGS**
P-ROVINGS
G-**ROWABLE**
ROWBOAT-S
C-**ROWDIES**
ROWDIES-T
T-**ROWELED**
G-**ROWINGS**
ROWLOCK-S
D-**ROWNDED**
ROYALET-S
P-**ROYNING**
ROYSTER-S
ROZELLE-S
RUBABOO-S
RUBASSE-S
D-**RUBBERS**
G-RUBBERS
D-**RUBBING**
G-RUBBING
RUBBING-S
RUBBISH-Y
G-**RUBBLED**
G-**RUBBLES**
RUBDOWN-S
RUBELLA-N
RUBELLA-S
RUBEOLA-R
RUBEOLA-S
RUBICON-S
RUCHING-S
T-**RUCKING**
T-**RUCKLED**
T-**RUCKLES**
RUCTION-S
C-**RUDDIER**
RUDDIES-T
C-**RUDDING**
C-**RUDDLED**
C-**RUDDLES**
RUDDOCK-S
RUDERAL-S
RUELLIA-S
RUFFIAN-S
G-**RUFFING**
T-**RUFFLED**
RUFFLER-S
T-**RUFFLES**
RUFIYAA-S
D-**RUGGERS**
D-**RUGGIER**
D-**RUGGING**
F-RUGGING
RUGGING-S
A-**RUGOLAS**
RUINATE-D
RUINATE-S
RUINING-S
RULLION-S
RULLOCK-S
C-**RUMBLED**
D-RUMBLED
G-RUMBLED
G-**RUMBLER**
RUMBLER-S

C-**RUMBLES**
D-RUMBLES
G-RUMBLES
RUMMAGE-D
RUMMAGE-R
RUMMAGE-S
B-**RUMMERS**
D-RUMMERS
G-**RUMMEST**
C-**RUMMIER**
C-**RUMMIES**
RUMMIES-T
G-**RUMNESS**
C-**RUMPING**
F-RUMPING
G-RUMPING
T-RUMPING
C-**RUMPLED**
F-RUMPLED
C-**RUMPLES**
F-RUMPLES
RUMPLES-S
RUNAWAY-S
RUNBACK-S
B-**RUNCHES**
C-RUNCHES
RUNDALE-S
T-**RUNDLED**
T-**RUNDLES**
RUNDLET-S
RUNDOWN-S
C-**RUNKLED**
C-**RUNKLES**
T-**RUNNELS**
RUNNING-S
T-**RUNNION**
RUNNION-S
RUNOVER-S
RUPTURE-D
RUPTURE-S
RUSALKA-S
B-**RUSHERS**
C-RUSHERS
B-**RUSHIER**
B-**RUSHING**
C-RUSHING
F-RUSHING
RUSHING-S
C-**RUSTIER**
T-RUSTIER
C-**RUSTILY**
T-RUSTILY
B-**RUSTING**
C-RUSTING
T-RUSTING
RUSTING-S
RUSTLER-S
RUSTLES-S
T-**RUTHFUL**
RUTTING-S
RYBAULD-S
RYEPECK-S
SABATON-S
SABAYON-S
SABBATH-S
I-**SABELLA**
SABELLA-S
SABKHAH-S
SABKHAT-S
SABREUR-S
SABURRA-L
SABURRA-S
SACATON-S
SACCADE-S
SACCULE-S

SACKAGE-S
SACKBUT-S
SACKFUL-S
SACKING-S
SACRING-S
SACRIST-S
SACRIST-Y
SADDLER-S
SADDLER-Y
SADIRON-S
SAFARIS-T
SAFFIAN-S
SAFFRON-S
SAFFRON-Y
SAFROLE-S
SAGENES-S
SAGGARD-S
SAGGING-S
SAGITTA-L
SAGITTA-S
SAGOUIN-S
SAGUARO-S
SAHIBAH-S
SAHIWAL-S
SAHUARO-S
SAILING-S
SAIMIRI-S
SAKERET-S
SAKIYEH-S
SAKSAUL-S
SALAMON-S
SALBAND-S
SALCHOW-S
SALFERN-S
SALICET-A
SALICET-S
SALICIN-E
SALICIN-S
SALIENT-S
SALIGOT-S
SALLIER-S
SALPIAN-S
SALTANT-S
SALTATE-D
SALTATE-S
SALTCAT-S
SALTERN-S
P-**SALTERS**
SALTIER-S
SALTIES-T
SALTINE-S
SALTING-S
SALTIRE-S
SALTPAN-S
SALUTER-S
SALVAGE-D
SALVAGE-E
SALVAGE-R
SALVAGE-S
SALVETE-S
SALVING-S
SAMADHI-S
SAMBHAR-S
SAMBHUR-S
SAMBUCA-S
SAMBUKE-S
SAMISEN-S
SAMOVAR-S
SAMPIRE-S
SAMPLER-S
SAMPLER-Y
SAMSARA-S
SAMSHOO-S
SAMURAI-S
SANCTUM-S

SANDBAG-S
SANDBAR-S
SANDBOY-S
SANDBUR-R
SANDBUR-S
SANDDAB-S
SANDHOG-S
SANDING-S
SANDLOT-S
SANDPIT-S
SANGOMA-S
SANGRIA-S
SANICLE-S
SANTOUR-S
SAOUARI-S
SAPAJOU-S
SAPHEAD-S
SAPHENA-E
SAPHENA-S
SAPLING-S
SAPONIN-E
SAPONIN-S
SAPPHIC-S
SAPROBE-S
SAPSAGO-S
SAPWOOD-S
SARAFAN-S
SARANGI-S
SARCASM-S
SARCODE-S
SARCOID-S
SARCOMA-S
SARDANA-S
SARDINE-S
SARKING-S
SARMENT-A
SARMENT-S
SARSDEN-S
SARSNET-S
SASHIMI-S
SASSIES-T
SATCHEL-S
SATIATE-D
SATIATE-S
SATINET-S
SATSUMA-S
SATYRAL-S
SATYRID-S
SAUNTER-S
SAURIAN-S
SAUSAGE-S
SAUTOIR-E
SAUTOIR-S
SAVAGER-Y
SAVAGES-T
SAVANNA-H
SAVANNA-S
SAVARIN-S
SAVELOY-S
SAVIOUR-S
SAVORER-S
SAVVIES-T
SAWBILL-S
SAWBUCK-S
SAWDUST-S
SAWDUST-Y
SAWMILL-S
SAXHORN-S
SAXTUBA-S
SAZERAC-S
SCABBLE-D
SCABBLE-S
SCAFFIE-S
SCAGLIA-S
E-**SCALADE**

SCALADE-S
E-**SCALADO**
SCALADO-S
SCALAGE-S
SCALARE-S
SCALDER-S
SCALEUP-S
E-**SCALIER**
SCALING-S
E-**SCALLOP**
SCALLOP-S
SCALPEL-S
SCALPER-S
SCAMBLE-D
SCAMBLE-R
SCAMBLE-S
SCAMPER-S
SCAMPIS-H
SCANDAL-S
SCANDIA-S
SCANNER-S
SCANTLE-D
SCANTLE-S
E-**SCAPING**
SCAPPLE-D
SCAPPLE-S
SCAPULA-E
SCAPULA-R
SCAPULA-S
SCARLET-S
E-**SCARPED**
SCARPER-S
SCATOLE-S
SCATTER-S
SCATTER-Y
SCAUPER-S
SCAVAGE-R
SCAVAGE-S
SCEDULE-D
SCEDULE-S
A-**SCENDED**
SCEPTER-S
SCEPTIC-S
SCEPTRE-D
SCEPTRE-S
SCHANSE-S
SCHANZE-S
SCHAPPE-D
SCHAPPE-S
SCHEMER-S
SCHERZO-S
SCHISMA-S
SCHLEPP-S
SCHLEPP-Y
SCHLICH-S
SCHLOCK-S
SCHLOCK-Y
SCHLUMP-S
SCHMALZ-Y
SCHMEAR-S
SCHMECK-S
SCHMEER-S
SCHMELZ-E
SCHMOCK-S
SCHMOOS-E
SCHMOOZ-E
SCHMUCK-S
SCHNOOK-S
SCHNORR-S
SCHOLAR-S
SCHOOLE-D
SCHOOLE-S
SCHTICK-S
SCHTOOK-S
SCHTUCK-S

SCIARID-S
SCIATIC-A
SCIATIC-S
SCIENCE-D
SCIENCE-S
SCISSEL-S
SCISSIL-E
SCISSIL-S
SCISSOR-S
SCIURID-S
SCOFFER-S
SCOLDER-S
SCOLLOP-S
SCOOPER-S
SCOOTER-S
SCOPULA-E
SCOPULA-S
SCORING-S
SCORNER-S
SCORPER-S
SCORSER-S
SCOTOMA-S
SCOTTIE-S
SCOURER-S
SCOURGE-D
SCOURGE-R
SCOURGE-S
SCOURIE-S
SCOURSE-D
SCOURSE-S
SCOUSER-S
SCOUTER-S
SCOWDER-S
SCOWLER-S
SCOWRER-S
SCOWRIE-S
SCRAICH-S
SCRAIGH-S
SCRAPER-S
SCRAPIE-S
SCRATCH-Y
SCRAUCH-S
SCRAUGH-S
SCREECH-Y
SCREEVE-D
SCREEVE-R
SCREEVE-S
SCREICH-S
SCREIGH-S
SCREWER-S
SCREWUP-S
A-**SCRIBED**
E-SCRIBED
SCRIBER-S
A-**SCRIBES**
E-SCRIBES
SCRIECH-S
SCRIENE-S
SCRIEVE-D
SCRIEVE-S
E-**SCROLLS**
SCROOGE-D
SCROOGE-S
SCROTUM-S
SCROUGE-D
SCROUGE-R
SCROUGE-S
SCROWLE-D
SCROWLE-S
SCROYLE-S
SCRUNCH-Y
SCRUPLE-D
SCRUPLE-R
SCRUPLE-S
SCRYING-S

SCUCHIN-S
SCUDDER-S
SCUDDLE-D
SCUDDLE-S
SCUDLER-S
SCUFFLE-D
SCUFFLE-R
SCUFFLE-S
SCULKER-S
SCULLER-S
SCULLER-Y
SCULPIN-G
SCULPIN-S
SCUMBAG-S
SCUMBER-S
SCUMBLE-D
SCUMBLE-S
SCUMMER-S
SCUNNER-S
SCUPPER-S
SCURRIL-E
SCUTAGE-S
SCUTTER-S
SCUTTLE-D
SCUTTLE-R
SCUTTLE-S
SCYTALE-S
SCYTHER-S
SDEIGNE-D
SDEIGNE-S
SEABANK-S
SEABIRD-S
SEABOOT-S
SEACOCK-S
SEAFOLK-S
SEAFOOD-S
SEAFOWL-S
SEAGULL-S
SEAHAWK-S
SEAKALE-S
SEALANT-S
SEALINE-S
SEALING-S
SEAMAID-S
SEAMARK-S
SEAMSET-S
SEAPORT-S
SEARING-S
SEASIDE-S
SEASURE-S
SEATING-S
SEAWALL-S
SEAWANT-S
SEAWARD-S
SEAWARE-S
SEAWEED-S
SEAWORM-S
SECEDER-S
SECLUDE-D
SECLUDE-S
SECONDE-D
SECONDE-E
SECONDE-R
SECONDE-S
SECRETE-D
SECRETE-R
SECRETE-S
SECTION-S
SECULAR-S
SECULUM-S
SECURER-S
SECURES-T
SEDATES-T
SEDUCER-S
SEEDBED-S

SEEDING-S
SEEDLIP-S
SEEDPOD-S
SEELING-S
SEEMING-S
SEEPAGE-S
SEETHER-S
SEGMENT-S
SEINING-S
SEISING-S
A-**SEISMIC**
SEISURE-S
A-**SEITIES**
SEIZING-S
SEIZURE-S
SELFDOM-S
SELFING-S
SELFISM-S
SELFIST-S
SELLOUT-S
SELTZER-S
SELVAGE-D
SELVAGE-E
SELVAGE-S
SEMIMAT-T
SEMINAR-S
SEMINAR-Y
SEMIPED-S
SEMIPRO-S
SEMITAR-S
SENATOR-S
SENDING-S
SENDOFF-S
SENECIO-S
SENHORA-S
SENOPIA-S
SENSATE-D
SENSATE-S
SENSING-S
SENSISM-S
SENSIST-S
SENTIMO-S
SEPIOST-S
SEPPUKU-S
A-**SEPTATE**
A-**SEPTICS**
SEPTIME-S
SEPTUOR-S
SEQUELA-E
SEQUENT-S
SEQUOIA-S
SERAFIN-S
SERENES-T
SERFAGE-S
SERFDOM-S
SERGING-S
SERIATE-D
SERIATE-S
SERICIN-S
SERICON-S
SERIEMA-S
E-**SERINES**
SERINGA-S
SERKALI-S
SERPENT-S
SERPULA-E
SERRANO-S
SERRATE-D
SERRATE-S
SERUEWE-D
SERUEWE-S
SERVANT-S
SERVEWE-D
SERVEWE-S
SERVICE-D
SERVICE-R
SERVICE-S
SERVILE-S
SERVING-S
SESSION-S
SESTETT-E
SESTETT-O
SESTETT-S
SESTINA-S
SESTINE-S
SETBACK-S
SETLINE-S
SETTING-S
SETTLER-S
SETTLOR-S
SETUALE-S
SETWALL-S
SEVENTH-S
SEVERAL-S
SEVICHE-S
SEVRUGA-S
SEXFOIL-S
SEXPERT-S
SEXTAIN-S
SEXTANT-S
SEXTETT-E
SEXTETT-S
SEXTILE-S
SEXTUOR-S
SEYSURE-S
SFUMATO-S
SHABBLE-S
SHACKLE-D
SHACKLE-R
SHACKLE-S
SHADING-S
SHADOOF-S
SHAFTER-S
SHAHDOM-S
SHAITAN-S
SHAKEUP-S
SHAKING-S
SHAKUDO-S
SHALLON-S
SHALLOP-S
SHALLOT-S
SHALLOW-S
SHALWAR-S
SHAMBLE-D
SHAMBLE-S
A-**SHAMING**
SHAMMAS-H
SHAMMER-S
SHAMPOO-S
SHANTEY-S
SHANTIH-S
SHAPEUP-S
SHAPING-S
SHARIAT-S
SHARING-S
SHARKER-S
SHARPEN-S
SHARPER-S
SHARPIE-S
SHASLIK-S
SHASTER-S
SHASTRA-S
SHATTER-S
SHATTER-Y
SHAVING-S
P-**SHAWING**
SHAWLEY-S
SHAWLIE-S
SHEARER-S
SHEATHE-D
SHEATHE-R
SHEATHE-S
SHEBANG-S
SHEBEAN-S
SHEBEEN-S
SHEDDER-S
SHEENEY-S
SHEENIE-R
SHEENIE-S
SHEETER-S
SHEHITA-H
SHEHITA-S
SHEIKHA-S
SHEITAN-S
SHELLAC-K
SHELLAC-S
SHELLER-S
SHELTER-S
SHELTER-Y
SHELTIE-S
SHELVER-S
SHERBET-S
SHEREEF-S
SHERIAT-S
SHERIFF-S
SHEROOT-S
SHIATSU-S
SHIATZU-S
SHICKER-S
SHICKSA-S
SHIDDER-S
SHIFTER-S
SHIKARI-S
SHIKKER-S
SHIMAAL-S
SHIMMER-S
SHIMMER-Y
SHIMMEY-S
SHINDIG-S
A-**SHINESS**
SHINGLE-D
SHINGLE-R
SHINGLE-S
SHINIES-T
SHINNEY-S
SHIPFUL-S
SHIPLAP-S
SHIPMEN-T
SHIPPEN-S
SHIPPER-S
SHIPPON-S
SHIPWAY-S
SHIRKER-S
SHITAKE-S
SHITTAH-S
SHITTIM-S
SHMALTZ-Y
SHMOOSE-D
SHMOOSE-S
SHMOOZE-D
SHMOOZE-S
SHOCKER-S
SHOEING-S
SHOEPAC-K
SHOEPAC-S
SHOGGLE-D
SHOGGLE-S
SHONEEN-S
SHOOGIE-D
SHOOGIE-S
SHOOGLE-D
SHOOGLE-S
SHOOTER-S
SHOPBOY-S
SHOPFUL-S
SHOPHAR-S
SHOPPER-S
SHORING-S
SHORTEN-S
SHORTIA-S
SHORTIE-S
SHOTGUN-S
SHOTPUT-S
SHOTTLE-S
SHOUTER-S
SHOWGHE-S
SHOWING-S
SHOWOFF-S
SHRIEVE-D
SHRIEVE-S
SHRIGHT-S
SHRIVEL-S
SHRIVER-S
SHTETEL-S
SHUCKER-S
SHUDDER-S
SHUDDER-Y
SHUFFLE-D
SHUFFLE-R
SHUFFLE-S
SHUNNER-S
SHUNTER-S
SHUTEYE-S
SHUTOFF-S
SHUTOUT-S
SHUTTER-S
SHUTTLE-D
SHUTTLE-S
SHYLOCK-S
SHYSTER-S
SIAMANG-S
SIAMESE-D
SIAMESE-S
SIAMEZE-D
SIAMEZE-S
SIBLING-S
SIBSHIP-S
SICKBAY-S
SICKBED-S
SICKOUT-S
SIDEARM-S
SIDEBAR-S
SIDECAR-S
SIDEWAY-S
SIENITE-S
SIEVERT-S
SIFTING-S
SIGANID-S
SIGHTER-S
SIGMATE-D
SIGMATE-S
SIGMOID-S
SIGNAGE-S
SIGNING-S
SIGNIOR-I
SIGNIOR-S
SIGNIOR-Y
SIGNORA-S
SIGNORE-S
SIGNORI-A
SILENCE-D
SILENCE-R
SILENCE-S
SILESIA-S
SILICLE-S
SILICON-E
SILICON-S
SILIQUA-E
SILIQUA-S
SILIQUE-S
SILKIES-T
SILLIES-T
SILLOCK-S
SILURID-S
SIMARRE-S
SIMILOR-S
SIMITAR-S
SIMPKIN-S
SIMPLER-S
SIMPLES-T
SIMULAR-S
SIMURGH-S
SINCERE-R
SINDING-S
SINGING-S
SINGLET-S
SINGULT-S
SINKAGE-S
SINKING-S
SINOPIA-S
SINUATE-D
SINUATE-S
SIRGANG-S
SIRLOIN-S
SIRNAME-D
SIRNAME-S
SIROCCO-S
SISSIES-T
SISTRUM-S
SITFAST-S
SITTING-S
SITUATE-D
SITUATE-S
SIXAINE-S
SIXTEEN-S
SIZEISM-S
SIZEIST-S
SIZZLER-S
SJAMBOK-S
SKATING-S
SKATOLE-S
SKEETER-S
SKEGGER-S
SKELDER-S
SKELLIE-D
SKELLIE-R
SKELLIE-S
SKELLUM-S
SKELTER-S
SKEPFUL-S
SKEPTIC-S
SKIDDER-S
SKIDDOO-S
SKIDPAN-S
SKIDWAY-S
SKIFFLE-D
SKIFFLE-S
SKILLET-S
SKIMMER-S
SKIMMIA-S
SKINFUL-S
SKINKER-S
SKINNER-S
SKIPPER-S
SKIPPET-S
SKIRRET-S
SKIRTER-S
SKITTER-S
SKITTER-Y
SKITTLE-D
SKITTLE-S
SKIVING-S
SKOLLIE-S
SKREEGH-S
SKREIGH-S
SKRIECH-S
SKRIEGH-S
SKUDLER-S
SKULKER-S
SKULPIN-S
SKUMMER-S
SKUTTLE-D
SKUTTLE-S
SKYBORN-E
SKYDIVE-D
SKYDIVE-R
SKYDIVE-S
SKYHOOK-S
SKYJACK-S
SKYLARK-S
SKYLINE-S
SKYSAIL-S
SKYWALK-S
SKYWARD-S
SLABBER-S
SLABBER-Y
SLACKEN-S
SLACKER-S
SLADANG-S
A-**SLAKING**
SLAMMER-S
I-**SLANDER**
SLANDER-S
SLANGER-S
SLAPPER-S
SLASHER-S
SLATHER-S
SLATING-S
SLATTER-N
SLATTER-S
SLATTER-Y
SLEDDER-S
SLEDGER-S
SLEEKEN-S
SLEEKER-S
SLEEPER-S
SLEEPER-Y
SLEEVER-S
SLEIGHT-S
SLENTER-S
SLICING-S
SLICKEN-S
SLICKER-S
SLIDDER-S
SLIDDER-Y
SLIDING-S
SLIMMER-S
SLINGER-S
SLINKER-S
SLINTER-S
SLIPOUT-S
SLIPPER-S
SLIPPER-Y
SLIPWAY-S
SLITHER-S
SLITHER-Y
SLITTER-S
SLOBBER-S
SLOBBER-Y
SLOCKEN-S
SLOGGER-S
SLOTTER-S
SLOWING-S
SLUBBER-S
SLUGGER-S
SLUMBER-S
SLUMBER-Y
SLUMGUM-S
SLUMISM-S
SLUMMER-S

SLURPER-S
SMACKER-S
SMARAGD-E
SMARAGD-S
SMARTEN-S
SMARTIE-S
SMASHER-S
SMASHUP-S
SMATTER-S
SMEARER-S
SMEDDUM-S
SMELLER-S
SMELTER-S
SMELTER-Y
SMICKER-S
SMICKET-S
SMIDGEN-S
SMIDGIN-S
SMILING-S
SMIRKER-S
SMOKIES-T
SMOKING-S
SMOLDER-S
SMOTHER-S
SMOTHER-Y
SMOUSER-S
SMUDGER-S
SMUGGLE-D
SMUGGLE-R
SMUGGLE-S
SMYTRIE-S
SNABBLE-D
SNABBLE-S
SNAFFLE-D
SNAFFLE-S
SNAPPER-S
SNARING-S
SNARLER-S
SNEAKER-S
SNEERER-S
SNEEZER-S
SNICKER-S
SNICKER-Y
SNICKET-S
SNIFFER-S
SNIFFLE-D
SNIFFLE-R
SNIFFLE-S
SNIFTER-S
SNIGGER-S
SNIGGLE-D
SNIGGLE-R
SNIGGLE-S
SNIPING-S
SNIPPER-S
SNIPPET-S
SNIPPET-Y
SNIRTLE-D
SNIRTLE-S
SNOOKER-S
SNOOPER-S
SNOOZER-S
SNOOZLE-D
SNOOZLE-S
SNORING-S
SNORKEL-S
SNORTER-S
SNOTTER-S
SNOTTER-Y
SNOTTIE-R
SNOTTIE-S
SNOWCAP-S
SNUBBER-S
SNUFFER-S
SNUFFLE-D

SNUFFLE-R
SNUFFLE-S
SNUGGER-Y
SNUGGLE-D
SNUGGLE-S
SNUZZLE-D
SNUZZLE-S
SOAKAGE-S
SOAKING-S
SOAPIES-T
SOARING-S
SOBBING-S
SOCAGER-S
SOCCAGE-S
SOCIATE-S
SOCKEYE-S
SODDIES-T
SOGGING-S
SOILAGE-S
SOILING-S
SOILURE-S
SOJOURN-S
SOLACER-S
SOLANIN-E
SOLANIN-S
SOLANUM-S
I-**SOLATED**
I-**SOLATES**
SOLDADO-S
SOLDIER-S
SOLDIER-Y
SOLERET-S
SOLFEGE-S
SOLICIT-S
SOLICIT-Y
SOLIDUM-S
SOLIPED-S
SOLITON-S
SOLOIST-S
SOLUBLE-S
SOLVATE-D
SOLVATE-S
SOLVENT-S
SOMBRER-O
SOMBRES-T
SOMEONE-S
SOMEWAY-S
SONANCE-S
SONDAGE-S
SONDELI-S
SONHOOD-S
SONSHIP-S
SOOPING-S
SOOTHER-S
SOOTHES-T
SOPHISM-S
SOPHIST-S
SOPPING-S
SOPRANO-S
SORBATE-S
SORBENT-S
SORBITE-S
SORBOSE-S
SORDINE-S
SOREDIA-L
SOREHON-S
SORGHUM-S
SORNING-S
SOROBAN-S
SOROCHE-S
SORTING-S
SOSSING-S
SOTTING-S
SOUBISE-S
SOUFFLE-D

SOUFFLE-S
SOULDAN-S
SOUMING-S
SOUNDER-S
SOUPCON-S
SOURING-S
SOUROCK-S
SOURSOP-S
SOUSING-S
SOUSLIK-S
SOUTANE-S
SOUTHER-N
SOUTHER-S
SOVKHOZ-Y
SOWBACK-S
SOYBEAN-S
SOYMILK-S
SPACING-S
SPACKLE-D
SPACKLE-S
SPADGER-S
SPAEING-S
SPAIRGE-D
SPAIRGE-S
SPALLER-S
SPAMMER-S
SPANCEL-S
SPANGLE-D
SPANGLE-R
SPANGLE-S
SPANGLE-T
SPANIEL-S
SPANKER-S
SPANNER-S
SPARGER-S
SPARKER-S
SPARKIE-R
SPARKIE-S
A-**SPARKLE**
SPARKLE-D
SPARKLE-R
SPARKLE-S
SPARKLE-T
SPAROID-S
SPARRER-S
SPARROW-S
SPARTAN-S
SPARTHE-S
SPASTIC-S
SPATTEE-S
SPATTER-S
SPATULA-R
SPATULA-S
SPATULE-S
SPAWNER-S
SPEAKER-S
SPEARER-S
E-**SPECIAL**
SPECIAL-S
SPECKLE-D
SPECKLE-S
SPECTER-S
SPECTRA-L
SPECTRE-S
SPECULA-R
SPEEDER-S
SPEEDUP-S
SPEELER-S
SPELDER-S
SPELDIN-G
SPELDIN-S
SPELLER-S
SPELTER-S
SPELUNK-S
SPENCER-S

SPENDER-S
A-**SPERSED**
A-**SPERSES**
SPERTHE-S
SPHAERE-S
SPHEARE-S
A-**SPHERIC**
SPHERIC-S
SPICATE-D
SPICULA-E
SPICULA-R
SPICULE-S
SPIEGEL-S
SPIELER-S
SPIGNEL-S
SPILING-S
SPILITE-S
SPILLER-S
SPINACH-Y
SPINAGE-S
SPINDLE-D
SPINDLE-R
SPINDLE-S
SPINNER-S
SPINNER-Y
SPINNET-S
SPINNEY-S
SPINODE-S
SPINOFF-S
SPINOUT-S
SPINULA-E
SPINULE-S
SPIRAEA-S
A-**SPIRANT**
SPIRANT-S
SPIREME-S
A-**SPIRING**
SPIRTLE-S
SPIRULA-E
SPIRULA-S
SPITTER-S
SPITTLE-S
SPLENIA-L
SPLICER-S
SPLODGE-D
SPLODGE-S
SPLOTCH-Y
SPLURGE-D
SPLURGE-R
SPLURGE-S
SPODIUM-S
SPOILER-S
SPONDEE-S
SPONDYL-S
SPONGER-S
SPONGIN-G
SPONGIN-S
SPONSON-S
SPONSOR-S
SPOOFER-S
SPOOFER-Y
SPOOLER-S
SPOONEY-S
SPOORER-S
SPORRAN-S
A-**SPORTED**
SPORTER-S
SPORULE-S
SPOTTER-S
E-**SPOUSAL**
SPOUSAL-S
E-**SPOUSED**
E-**SPOUSES**
SPOUTER-S
SPRAINT-S

SPRAYER-S
SPREAGH-S
SPREAZE-D
SPREAZE-S
SPREDDE-N
SPREDDE-S
SPREEZE-D
SPREEZE-S
SPRIGHT-S
SPRINGE-D
SPRINGE-R
SPRINGE-S
SPRUCES-T
SPUDDER-S
SPULYIE-D
SPULYIE-S
SPULZIE-D
SPULZIE-S
SPUMONE-S
SPUMONI-S
SPUNKIE-R
SPUNKIE-S
SPURNER-S
SPURRER-S
SPURREY-S
SPURTLE-S
SPURWAY-S
SPUTNIK-S
SPUTTER-S
SPUTTER-Y
SPYHOLE-S
SQUACCO-S
SQUALOR-S
SQUARER-S
SQUARES-T
SQUEEZE-D
SQUEEZE-R
SQUEEZE-S
SQUELCH-Y
SQUIDGE-D
SQUIDGE-S
SQUILLA-E
SQUILLA-S
E-**SQUIRED**
E-**SQUIRES**
SQUIRES-S
SQUOOSH-Y
SRADDHA-S
STABBER-S
STABILE-S
STABLER-S
STABLES-T
STACKER-S
STACKET-S
STACKUP-S
STADDLE-S
STADIAL-S
STADIUM-S
STAFFER-S
STAGGER-S
STAGGER-Y
STAGGIE-R
STAGGIE-S
STAGING-S
STAINER-S
STAITHE-S
STALKER-S
STAMINA-L
STAMINA-S
STAMMEL-S
STAMMER-S
STAMPED-E
STAMPED-O
STAMPER-S
STANDBY-S

STANDEE-S
STANDER-S
STANIEL-S
STANINE-S
STANNEL-S
STANNUM-S
STANYEL-S
STAPLER-S
STAPPLE-S
STARDOM-S
STARING-S
STARKEN-S
STARKER-S
STARLET-S
STARNIE-S
A-**STARTED**
STARTER-S
STARTLE-D
STARTLE-R
STARTLE-S
STARTUP-S
STARVER-S
STASHIE-S
STATICE-S
E-**STATING**
STATION-S
STATISM-S
STATIST-S
STATIVE-S
STATURE-D
STATURE-S
STATUTE-S
STEALER-S
STEALTH-S
STEALTH-Y
STEAMER-S
STEAMIE-R
STEAMIE-S
STEARIN-E
STEARIN-G
STEARIN-S
STEELIE-R
STEELIE-S
E-**STEEMED**
STEEPEN-S
STEEPER-S
STEEPLE-D
STEEPLE-S
STEERER-S
STEEVES-T
STEMBOK-S
STEMLET-S
STEMMER-S
STEMMER-Y
STEMPEL-S
STEMPLE-S
STEMSON-S
STENCIL-S
STENGAH-S
STENTOR-S
STEPNEY-S
STEPPER-S
STEPSON-S
STERLET-S
A-**STERNAL**
STERNUM-S
A-**STEROID**
STEROID-S
STERTOR-S
STEWARD-S
STEWBUM-S
STEWING-S
STEWPAN-S
STEWPOT-S
A-**STHENIA**

STHENIA-S
A-**STHENIC**
STIBBLE-R
STIBBLE-S
STIBINE-S
STIBIUM-S
STICKER-S
STICKLE-D
STICKLE-R
STICKLE-S
STICKUM-S
STICKUP-S
STIDDIE-D
STIDDIE-S
STIFFEN-S
STIFFIE-S
STIFLER-S
STILLER-S
STILTER-S
STINGER-S
STINKER-S
STINTER-S
STIPEND-S
STIPPLE-D
STIPPLE-R
STIPPLE-S
STIPULE-D
STIPULE-S
STIRRAH-S
STIRRER-S
STIRRUP-S
STISHIE-S
STOCKER-S
STODGER-S
STOITER-S
STOLLEN-S
STOMACH-S
STOMACH-Y
STOMATA-L
STOMATE-S
STOMPER-S
A-**STONIED**
A-**STONIES**
STONIES-T
A-**STONING**
STONING-S
A-**STONISH**
STONKER-S
STOOKER-S
STOOLIE-S
STOOPER-S
STOPGAP-S
STOPING-S
STOPOFF-S
E-**STOPPED**
STOPPER-S
STOPPLE-D
STOPPLE-S
STORAGE-S
STOTTER-S
A-**STOUNDS**
STOURIE-R
STOUTEN-S
E-**STOVERS**
STOVING-S
STOWAGE-S
STOWING-S
STRAFER-S
STRAINT-S
E-**STRANGE**
STRANGE-R
STRATUM-S
E-**STRAYED**
STRAYER-S
STRETCH-Y
STRETTA-S
STRETTO-S
STREWER-S
STRIATE-D
STRIATE-S
STRIDER-S
STRIDOR-S
STRIGIL-S
STRIKER-S
STRIPER-S
STRIVER-S
STROBIL-A
STROBIL-E
STROBIL-I
STROBIL-S
STRODLE-D
STRODLE-S
STROKER-S
STROOKE-N
STROOKE-S
STROPHE-S
STROWER-S
STROYER-S
STRUDEL-S
STUBBLE-D
STUBBLE-S
STUDDIE-S
STUDDLE-S
STUDENT-S
STUDIER-S
STUFFER-S
STUIVER-S
STUMBLE-D
STUMBLE-R
STUMBLE-S
STUMMEL-S
STUMPER-S
A-**STUNNED**
STUNNER-S
STURMER-S
STUSHIE-S
STUTTER-S
STYLING-S
STYLISE-D
STYLISE-R
STYLISE-S
STYLIST-S
STYLITE-S
STYLIZE-D
STYLIZE-R
STYLIZE-S
STYLOID-S
STYPTIC-S
STYRENE-S
SUASION-S
SUBADAR-S
SUBAREA-S
SUBATOM-S
SUBBASE-S
SUBBING-S
SUBCELL-S
SUBCLAN-S
SUBCODE-S
SUBCOOL-S
SUBCULT-S
SUBDEAN-S
SUBDUAL-S
SUBDUCE-D
SUBDUCE-S
SUBDUCT-S
SUBDUER-S
SUBEDAR-S
SUBEDIT-S
SUBERIN-S
SUBFILE-S
SUBFUSC-S
SUBFUSK-S
SUBGOAL-S
SUBHEAD-S
SUBIDEA-S
SUBITEM-S
SUBJECT-S
SUBJOIN-S
SUBLATE-D
SUBLATE-S
SUBLIME-D
SUBLIME-R
SUBLIME-S
SUBLINE-S
SUBMENU-S
SUBPART-S
SUBPENA-S
SUBPLOT-S
SUBRACE-S
SUBRENT-S
SUBRING-S
SUBRULE-S
SUBSALE-S
SUBSECT-S
SUBSERE-S
SUBSIDE-D
SUBSIDE-R
SUBSIDE-S
SUBSIST-S
SUBSITE-S
SUBSOIL-S
SUBSONG-S
SUBSUME-D
SUBSUME-S
SUBTACK-S
SUBTASK-S
SUBTEEN-S
SUBTEND-S
SUBTEST-S
SUBTEXT-S
SUBTILE-R
SUBTONE-S
SUBTYPE-S
SUBUNIT-S
SUBVENE-D
SUBVENE-S
SUBVERT-S
SUBZONE-S
SUCCADE-S
SUCCEED-S
SUCCOUR-S
SUCCUBA-E
SUCCUBA-S
SUCCUMB-S
SUCKING-S
SUCKLER-S
SUCKLES-S
SUCRASE-S
SUCRIER-S
SUCROSE-S
SUCTION-S
SUFFARI-S
SUFFETE-S
SUFFICE-D
SUFFICE-R
SUFFICE-S
SUFFUSE-D
SUFFUSE-S
SUGGEST-S
SUGGING-S
SUICIDE-D
SUICIDE-S
SUIDIAN-S
SUITING-S
SULCATE-D
SULFATE-D
SULFATE-S
SULFIDE-S
SULFITE-S
SULFONE-S
SULFURY-L
SULKIES-T
SULLAGE-S
SULPHID-E
SULPHID-S
SULPHUR-S
SULPHUR-Y
SULTANA-S
SUMATRA-S
SUMMAND-S
SUMMATE-D
SUMMATE-S
SUMMING-S
SUMMIST-S
SUMPTER-S
SUNBAKE-D
SUNBAKE-S
SUNBATH-E
SUNBATH-S
SUNBEAM-S
SUNBEAM-Y
SUNBELT-S
SUNBIRD-S
SUNBURN-S
SUNBURN-T
SUNDARI-S
SUNDECK-S
SUNDIAL-S
SUNDOWN-S
SUNGLOW-S
SUNLAMP-S
SUNLAND-S
SUNRISE-S
SUNROOF-S
SUNROOM-S
SUNSPOT-S
SUNSUIT-S
SUNTRAP-S
SUNWARD-S
SUPPAWN-S
SUPPLES-T
SUPPORT-S
SUPPOSE-D
SUPPOSE-R
SUPPOSE-S
SUPREME-R
SUPREME-S
SUPREMO-S
SURAMIN-S
SURANCE-S
SURBASE-D
SURBASE-S
SURBATE-D
SURBATE-S
SURCOAT-S
SURFACE-D
SURFACE-R
SURFACE-S
SURFEIT-S
SURFIES-T
SURFING-S
SURGEON-S
SURGING-S
SURLOIN-S
SURMISE-D
SURMISE-R
SURMISE-S
SURNAME-D
SURNAME-R
SURNAME-S
SURTOUT-S
SURVEIL-S
SURVEWE-D
SURVEWE-S
SURVIEW-S
SURVIVE-D
SURVIVE-R
SURVIVE-S
SUSPECT-S
SUSPEND-S
SUSPENS-E
SUSPIRE-D
SUSPIRE-S
SUSTAIN-S
SWABBER-S
SWABBIE-S
SWADDLE-D
SWADDLE-R
SWADDLE-S
SWAGGER-S
SWAGGIE-S
SWALING-S
SWALLET-S
SWALLOW-S
SWAMPER-S
SWANKER-S
SWANKEY-S
SWANKIE-R
SWANKIE-S
SWANPAN-S
SWAPPER-S
SWARMER-S
SWASHER-S
SWATHER-S
SWATTER-S
SWAYING-S
SWAZZLE-S
SWEARER-S
SWEATER-S
SWEENEY-S
SWEEPER-S
SWEETEN-S
SWEETIE-S
SWELLER-S
SWELTER-S
SWERVER-S
SWIDDEN-S
SWIFTER-S
SWIGGER-S
SWILLER-S
SWIMMER-S
SWINDGE-D
SWINDGE-S
SWINDLE-D
SWINDLE-R
SWINDLE-S
SWINGBY-S
SWINGER-S
SWINGLE-D
SWINGLE-S
SWINNEY-S
SWIPPLE-S
SWISHER-S
SWISHES-T
SWITHER-S
SWIZZLE-D
SWIZZLE-R
SWIZZLE-S
SWOBBER-S
SWOONER-S
SWOOPER-S
SWOPPER-S
SWORDER-S
SWOTTER-S
SWOZZLE-S
SYENITE-S
SYLLABI-C
SYLPHID-E
SYLPHID-S
SYLVINE-S
SYLVITE-S
SYMBION-S
SYMBION-T
SYMBIOT-E
SYMBIOT-S
SYMBOLE-D
SYMBOLE-S
SYMITAR-E
SYMITAR-S
SYMPTOM-S
SYNAGOG-S
SYNANON-S
SYNAPSE-D
SYNAPSE-S
SYNAPTE-S
SYNCARP-S
SYNCARP-Y
SYNCHRO-S
SYNCOPE-S
SYNDING-S
A-**SYNERGY**
SYNFUEL-S
SYNODAL-S
SYNONYM-E
SYNONYM-S
SYNONYM-Y
SYNOVIA-L
SYNOVIA-S
SYNTAGM-A
SYNTAGM-S
SYNTHON-S
SYRINGA-S
SYRINGE-D
SYRINGE-S
SYRPHID-S
A-**SYSTOLE**
SYSTOLE-S
SYSTYLE-S
TABANID-S
TABARET-S
S-**TABBING**
TABETIC-S
TABINET-S
TABLEAU-S
TABLEAU-X
TABLIER-S
S-**TABLING**
TABLING-S
TABLOID-S
TABLOID-Y
TABORER-S
TABORET-S
TABORIN-E
TABORIN-G
TABORIN-S
TABOULI-S
TABRERE-S
TACHISM-E
TACHISM-S
TACHIST-E
TACHIST-S
TACHYON-S
S-**TACKERS**
S-**TACKETS**
TACKIES-T
S-**TACKING**
TACKING-S
TACKLER-S
TACKLES-S
TACNODE-S

TACTION-S
TACTISM-S
TADPOLE-S
TAEDIUM-S
TAFFETA-S
S-TAGGERS
S-TAGGIER
S-TAGGING
TAGGING-S
TAGMEME-S
TAILARD-S
TAILFAN-S
TAILING-S
TAILLES-S
TAILLIE-S
TAILZIE-S
TAKEOFF-S
S-TAKEOUT
TAKEOUT-S
TALAUNT-S
TALAYOT-S
TALIPAT-S
TALIPED-S
TALIPOT-S
S-TALKERS
S-TALKIER
TALKIES-T
S-TALKING
TALKING-S
S-TALLAGE
TALLAGE-D
TALLAGE-S
TALLBOY-S
TALLENT-S
TALLIER-S
TALLITH-S
TALLYHO-S
TALOOKA-S
TAMANDU-A
TAMANDU-S
TAMARAO-S
TAMARAU-S
TAMARIN-D
TAMARIN-S
TAMARIS-K
TAMASHA-S
TAMBALA-S
TAMBOUR-A
TAMBOUR-S
TAMBURA-S
E-TAMINES
TAMPALA-S
S-TAMPERS
S-TAMPING
TAMPING-S
TAMPION-S
TANADAR-S
TANAGER-S
TANAGRA-S
TANBARK-S
TANDOOR-I
TANDOOR-S
TANGELO-S
TANGENT-S
TANGHIN-S
TANGIES-T
S-TANGING
TANGLER-S
TANGRAM-S
TANIWHA-S
TANKAGE-S
TANKARD-S
TANKFUL-S
TANKING-S
TANLING-S
TANNAGE-S
S-TANNATE
TANNATE-S
TANNING-S
TANTARA-S
TANTRUM-S
TANYARD-S
TAPERER-S
TAPHOLE-S
TAPIOCA-S
TAPPICE-D
TAPPICE-S
S-TAPPING
TAPPING-S
TAPROOM-S
TAPROOT-S
TAPSTER-S
TARDIES-T
TARDYON-S
S-TARINGS
S-TARRIER
TARRIER-S
TARRIES-T
S-TARRING
TARRING-S
TARROCK-S
TARSIER-S
TARTANA-S
TARTANE-D
TARTANE-S
TARTARE-S
TARTINE-S
S-TARTING
S-TARTISH
TARTLET-S
TARTUFE-S
TARWEED-S
S-TASHING
TASKING-S
TASSELL-S
TASSELL-Y
TASTING-S
TATOUAY-S
TATTIES-T
TATTING-S
TATTLER-S
TAUNTER-S
TAURINE-S
TAUTAUG-S
TAVERNA-S
TAWNIES-T
TAXABLE-S
TAXICAB-S
TAXIWAY-S
TEABOWL-S
TEACAKE-S
TEACART-S
TEACHER-S
S-TEAMERS
S-TEAMING
TEAMING-S
S-TEARING
TEAROOM-S
TEASHOP-S
TEASING-S
TEATIME-S
TEAWARE-S
TECHIES-T
A-TECHNIC
TECHNIC-S
TECTITE-S
S-TEDDIES
S-TEDDING
S-TEEMING
TEENAGE-D
TEENAGE-R
S-TEENING
S-TEERING
TEETHER-S
TEGMINA-L
TEGUMEN-T
TEKTITE-S
TELECOM-S
TELEOST-S
TELERAN-S
TELETEX-T
TELFORD-S
S-TELLING
TELLING-S
TELPHER-S
TEMBLOR-S
TEMPERA-S
TEMPEST-S
TEMPLAR-S
S-TEMPLES
TEMPLET-S
TEMPTER-S
TEMPURA-S
S-TENCHES
S-TENDING
TENDRIL-S
TENDRON-S
TENFOLD-S
TENNIST-S
TENONER-S
TENSION-S
TENTAGE-S
TENTFUL-S
TENTIGO-S
S-TENTING
TENTING-S
TEQUILA-S
TERAOHM-S
TERBIUM-S
TEREBRA-E
TEREBRA-S
TERGITE-S
TERMITE-S
S-TERNING
TERNION-S
TERPENE-S
TERRACE-D
TERRACE-S
TERRAIN-S
TERRANE-S
TERREEN-S
TERRENE-S
TERRIER-S
TERRINE-S
TERSION-S
TERTIAL-S
TERTIAN-S
TESSERA-E
TESSERA-L
TESTATE-S
TESTERN-S
TESTING-S
TESTOON-S
TESTRIL-L
TESTRIL-S
TESTUDO-S
TETANIC-S
TETOTUM-S
TETRACT-S
TETRODE-S
TEUCHAT-S
TEXTILE-S
TEXTURE-D
TEXTURE-S
THALAMI-C
THALWEG-S
THANAGE-S
THANKER-S
THANNAH-S
THAWING-S
THEATER-S
THEATRE-S
THEELIN-S
THEELOL-S
A-THEISMS
A-THEISTS
THENAGE-S
THEOLOG-S
THEOLOG-Y
THEORBO-S
THEOREM-S
THEORIC-S
THERIAC-A
THERIAC-S
THERIAN-S
THERMAL-S
THERMEL-S
THIAMIN-E
THIAMIN-S
THIAZIN-E
THIAZIN-S
THIAZOL-E
THIAZOL-S
THICKEN-S
THICKET-S
THICKET-Y
THIGGER-S
THILLER-S
THIMBLE-D
THIMBLE-S
THINKER-S
THINNER-S
THIONIN-E
THIONIN-S
THIONYL-S
THISTLE-S
THORITE-S
THORIUM-S
THOUGHT-S
THREAVE-S
THRIMSA-S
THRIVER-S
THROMBI-N
THROWER-S
THRUPUT-S
THRUWAY-S
THRYMSA-S
THUGGEE-S
THULITE-S
THULIUM-S
THUMPER-S
THUNDER-S
THUNDER-Y
THWAITE-S
THYLOSE-S
THYMINE-S
THYROID-S
S-TICKERS
S-TICKIES
S-TICKING
TICKING-S
S-TICKLED
S-TICKLER
TICKLER-S
S-TICKLES
S-TIDDIES
TIDDIES-T
TIDDLER-S
TIDDLEY-S
TIDERIP-S
TIDEWAY-S
TIEBACK-S
TIERCEL-S
TIERCET-S
TIETACK-S
S-TIFFING
TIFFING-S
TIGHTEN-S
TILAPIA-S
S-TILLAGE
TILLAGE-S
S-TILLERS
S-TILLIER
S-TILLING
TILLING-S
TILLITE-S
S-TILTERS
S-TILTING
TILTING-S
TIMARAU-S
TIMBALE-S
TIMBREL-S
TIMEOUT-S
TIMOLOL-S
TINAMOU-S
TINCHEL-S
TINFOIL-S
S-TINGING
TINGLER-S
TINHORN-S
S-TINKERS
S-TINKING
TINKLER-S
TINNIES-T
TINNING-S
TINTACK-S
S-TINTERS
S-TINTIER
S-TINTING
TINTING-S
TINTYPE-S
TINWARE-S
TINWORK-S
TIPCART-S
TIPPING-S
S-TIPPLED
S-TIPPLER
TIPPLER-S
S-TIPPLES
TIPSTER-S
TIRASSE-S
S-TIRRING
TITANIA-S
TITANIS-M
S-TITCHES
TITHING-S
TITLARK-S
TITLING-S
TITLIST-S
TITRANT-S
TITRATE-D
TITRATE-S
TITULAR-S
TITULAR-Y
TOASTER-S
TOASTIE-R
TOASTIE-S
TOBACCO-S
S-TOCCATA
TOCCATA-S
S-TOCKING
TODDLER-S
TOECLIP-S
TOEHOLD-S
TOENAIL-S
TOESHOE-S
TOFFIES-T
TOGGLER-S
TOHEROA-S
TOHUNGA-S
TOILING-S
TOISECH-S
S-TOITING
TOKAMAK-S
TOKOMAK-S
TOLIDIN-E
TOLIDIN-S
TOLLAGE-S
TOLLBAR-S
TOLLING-S
TOLLWAY-S
TOLUATE-S
TOLUENE-S
TOLUIDE-S
TOLUOLE-S
TOMBACK-S
TOMBOLA-S
TOMBOLO-S
TOMFOOL-S
TOMPION-S
A-TONALLY
TONDINO-S
TONEARM-S
TONEPAD-S
TONETIC-S
TONETTE-S
S-TONIEST
TONIGHT-S
S-TONINGS
S-TONKERS
S-TONKING
TONNAGE-S
TONNEAU-S
TONNEAU-X
TONNELL-S
TONSURE-D
TONSURE-S
TONTINE-R
TONTINE-S
TOOLBAG-S
TOOLBAR-S
S-TOOLING
TOOLING-S
TOOLKIT-S
TOOTLER-S
TOOTSIE-S
TOPARCH-S
TOPARCH-Y
TOPCOAT-S
TOPKICK-S
TOPKNOT-S
S-TOPLESS
TOPLINE-D
TOPLINE-R
TOPLINE-S
TOPMAST-S
TOPONYM-S
TOPONYM-Y
S-TOPPERS
S-TOPPING
TOPPING-S
S-TOPPLED
S-TOPPLES
TOPSAIL-S
TOPSIDE-R
TOPSIDE-S
TOPSOIL-S
TOPSPIN-S
TOPWORK-S
TORCHER-E

TORCHER-S
TORCHON-S
TORDION-S
TORGOCH-S
TORMENT-A
TORMENT-S
TORMINA-L
TORNADE-S
TORNADO-S
TORPEDO-S
TORQUER-S
TORRENT-S
TORSADE-S
TORSION-S
TORTONI-S
TORTURE-D
TORTURE-R
TORTURE-S
TORULIN-S
TOSHACH-S
TOSSING-S
TOSSPOT-S
TOSTADA-S
TOSTADO-S
TOTIENT-S
S-**TOTTERS**
TOTTIES-T
S-**TOTTING**
TOTTING-S
TOUCHER-S
TOUCHUP-S
TOUGHEN-S
TOUGHIE-S
TOURACO-S
TOURING-S
TOURISM-S
TOURIST-S
TOURIST-Y
TOURNEY-S
TOUSING-S
TOUSTIE-R
S-**TOWABLE**
S-**TOWAGES**
S-**TOWAWAY**
TOWAWAY-S
TOWBOAT-S
TOWHEAD-S
S-**TOWINGS**
TOWLINE-S
TOWMOND-S
TOWMONT-S
TOWNIES-T
TOWNLET-S
TOWPATH-S
TOWROPE-S
TOXEMIA-S
TOYSHOP-S
TRACHEA-E
TRACHEA-L
TRACHEA-S
TRACHLE-D
TRACHLE-S
TRACING-S
TRACKER-S
TRACTOR-S
TRADING-S
TRADUCE-D
TRADUCE-R
TRADUCE-S
TRAFFIC-S
TRAGULE-S
S-**TRAIKED**
TRAILER-S
S-**TRAINED**
TRAINEE-S
S-**TRAINER**
TRAINER-S
TRAIPSE-D
TRAIPSE-S
TRAITOR-S
TRAJECT-S
TRAMCAR-S
TRAMELL-S
S-**TRAMMEL**
TRAMMEL-S
S-**TRAMPED**
TRAMPER-S
TRAMPET-S
TRAMPLE-D
TRAMPLE-R
TRAMPLE-S
TRAMWAY-S
TRANCHE-S
TRANCHE-T
TRANECT-S
TRANGAM-S
S-**TRANGLE**
TRANGLE-S
TRANKUM-S
TRANNIE-S
TRANSIT-S
TRANSOM-S
TRANTER-S
TRAPEZE-D
TRAPEZE-S
S-**TRAPPED**
S-**TRAPPER**
TRAPPER-S
S-**TRASSES**
TRAVAIL-S
TRAVOIS-E
TRAWLER-S
TRAWLEY-S
TRAYBIT-S
TRAYFUL-S
TREACLE-D
TREACLE-S
TREADER-S
TREADLE-D
TREADLE-R
TREADLE-S
TREAGUE-S
TREASON-S
TREATER-S
TREDDLE-D
TREDDLE-S
TREETOP-S
TREFOIL-S
TREHALA-S
TREILLE-S
TREKKER-S
A-**TREMBLE**
TREMBLE-D
TREMBLE-R
TREMBLE-S
TREMOLO-S
TRENAIL-S
TRENISE-S
TRENTAL-S
TREPANG-S
S-**TRESSED**
TRESSEL-S
S-**TRESSES**
TRESTLE-S
TREYBIT-S
TRIACID-S
TRIADIC-S
TRIARCH-S
TRIARCH-Y
TRIATIC-S
TRIAXON-S
TRIAZIN-E
TRIAZIN-S
TRIBADE-S
TRIBBLE-S
TRIBLET-S
TRIBUNE-S
TRIBUTE-R
TRIBUTE-S
TRICKER-S
TRICKER-Y
TRICKIE-R
S-**TRICKLE**
TRICKLE-D
TRICKLE-S
TRICKLE-T
TRICLAD-S
TRICORN-E
TRICORN-S
TRIDARN-S
S-**TRIDENT**
TRIDENT-S
TRIDUUM-S
TRIFFID-S
TRIFFID-Y
TRIFLER-S
S-**TRIGGED**
TRIGGER-S
TRIGLOT-S
TRIGRAM-S
TRILITH-S
TRILLER-S
TRILOBE-D
TRILOBE-S
TRIMMER-S
TRIMTAB-S
TRINDLE-D
TRINDLE-S
TRINGLE-S
TRINKET-S
TRINKUM-S
TRIOLET-S
TRIONYM-S
TRIOXID-E
TRIOXID-S
TRIPACK-S
S-**TRIPIER**
TRIPLET-S
TRIPOLI-S
S-**TRIPPED**
S-**TRIPPER**
TRIPPER-S
TRIPPER-Y
TRIPPET-S
TRIPPLE-D
TRIPPLE-R
TRIPPLE-S
TRIREME-S
TRISECT-S
TRISEME-S
TRISHAW-S
TRISOME-S
TRISULA-S
TRITIDE-S
TRITIUM-S
TRITOMA-S
TRITONE-S
TRIUMPH-S
TRIVIUM-S
TRIZONE-S
TROCHAR-S
TROCHEE-S
TROCHIL-I
TROCHIL-S
TROELIE-S
TROFFER-S
S-**TROKING**
TROLAND-S
S-**TROLLED**
S-**TROLLER**
TROLLER-S
TROLLEY-S
TROLLOP-S
TROLLOP-Y
TROMINO-S
TROMMEL-S
TROOLIE-S
TROOPER-S
A-**TROPHIC**
S-TROPHIC
A-**TROPINE**
TROPINE-S
A-**TROPINS**
A-**TROPISM**
TROPISM-S
TROPIST-S
TROTTER-S
TROUBLE-D
TROUBLE-R
TROUBLE-S
TROUNCE-D
TROUNCE-R
TROUNCE-S
TROUPER-S
TROUSER-S
TROUTER-S
S-**TROWING**
TRUCAGE-S
TRUCKER-S
TRUCKIE-S
TRUCKLE-D
TRUCKLE-R
TRUCKLE-S
TRUDGEN-S
TRUDGER-S
TRUFFLE-D
TRUFFLE-S
TRUMEAU-X
S-**TRUMPET**
TRUMPET-S
TRUNDLE-D
TRUNDLE-R
TRUNDLE-S
TRUNNEL-S
TRUSSER-S
TRUSTEE-D
TRUSTEE-S
TRUSTER-S
TRUSTOR-S
TRYPSIN-S
TRYSAIL-S
TRYSTER-S
TSADDIK-S
TSADDIQ-S
TSARDOM-S
TSARINA-S
TSARISM-S
TSARIST-S
TSIGANE-S
TSUNAMI-C
TSUNAMI-S
TUATARA-S
TUATERA-S
TUBAIST-S
S-**TUBBIER**
S-**TUBBING**
TUBBING-S
TUBEFUL-S
TUBFAST-S
TUBULIN-S
TUFTING-S
TUGBOAT-S
TUGGING-S
TUGHRIK-S
TUILYIE-D
TUILYIE-S
TUILZIE-D
TUILZIE-S
TUITION-S
TULCHAN-S
S-**TUMBLED**
S-**TUMBLER**
TUMBLER-S
S-**TUMBLES**
TUMBREL-S
TUMBRIL-S
TUMESCE-D
TUMESCE-S
TUMMLER-S
S-**TUMPIER**
S-**TUMPING**
TUMSHIE-S
TUMULAR-Y
TUNICIN-S
TUNICLE-S
TUNNAGE-S
S-**TUNNING**
TUNNING-S
TURACIN-S
TURACOU-S
TURBAND-S
TURBANT-S
TURBETH-S
TURBINE-D
TURBINE-S
TURBITH-S
TURBOND-S
TURDION-S
TURFING-S
TURFITE-S
TURFSKI-S
TURGITE-S
TURISTA-S
TURMOIL-S
TURNDUN-S
TURNING-S
TURNKEY-S
TURNOFF-S
TURNOUT-S
TURPETH-S
TURTLER-S
S-**TUSHIES**
TUSHKAR-S
TUSHKER-S
TUSKING-S
TUSSOCK-S
TUSSOCK-Y
TUSSORE-S
TUSSUCK-S
TUTANIA-S
TUTELAR-S
TUTELAR-Y
TUTENAG-S
TUTOYER-S
TUTTING-S
TUTWORK-S
TWADDLE-D
TWADDLE-R
TWADDLE-S
TWANGER-S
TWANGLE-D
TWANGLE-R
TWANGLE-S
TWANKAY-S
TWASOME-S
TWATTLE-D
TWATTLE-R
TWATTLE-S
TWEEDLE-D
TWEEDLE-R
TWEEDLE-S
TWEETER-S
TWEEZER-S
TWELFTH-S
TWIBILL-S
TWIDDLE-D
TWIDDLE-R
TWIDDLE-S
TWIGGER-S
TWIGLOO-S
TWINING-S
TWINJET-S
TWINKLE-D
TWINKLE-R
TWINKLE-S
TWINSET-S
TWINTER-S
TWIRLER-S
TWISCAR-S
TWISTER-S
TWISTOR-S
TWITTEN-S
A-**TWITTER**
TWITTER-S
TWITTER-Y
TWIZZLE-D
TWIZZLE-S
TWOCCER-S
TWOFOLD-S
TWOSOME-S
TYCHISM-S
TYLOPOD-S
TYLOSIN-S
TYMPANA-L
TYMPANI-C
TYPEBAR-S
TYPESET-S
TYPHOID-S
TYPHOON-S
A-**TYPICAL**
E-TYPICAL
TYRANNE-D
TYRANNE-S
TZADDIK-S
TZADDIQ-S
TZARDOM-S
TZARINA-S
TZARISM-S
TZARIST-S
TZIGANE-S
TZITZIT-H
O-**UAKARIS**
S-**UBEROUS**
T-UBEROUS
UDALLER-S
J-**UDDERED**
P-UDDERED
UKELELE-S
UKULELE-S
ULEXITE-S
ULICHON-S
F-**ULLAGES**
S-ULLAGES
B-**ULLINGS**
C-ULLINGS
N-ULLINGS
ULULATE-D
ULULATE-S
C-**UMBERED**
L-UMBERED

N-UMBERED
UMBRAGE-D
UMBRAGE-S
T-**UMBRELS**
UMBRERE-S
T-**UMBRILS**
C-**UMBROUS**
UNAKITE-S
UNALIST-S
UNAWARE-S
S-**UNBAKED**
UNBEGET-S
UNBEING-S
S-**UNBELTS**
S-**UNBLIND**
UNBLIND-S
S-**UNBLOCK**
UNBLOCK-S
UNBOSOM-S
UNBRACE-D
UNBRACE-S
UNBRAID-S
UNBRAKE-D
UNBRAKE-S
UNBROKE-N
UNBUILD-S
S-**UNBURNT**
UNCHAIN-S
UNCHARM-S
UNCHECK-S
UNCHILD-S
S-**UNCHOKE**
UNCHOKE-D
UNCHOKE-S
UNCLAMP-S
UNCLASP-S
UNCLOAK-S
UNCLOSE-D
UNCLOSE-S
UNCLOUD-S
UNCLOUD-Y
UNCOVER-S
UNCRATE-D
UNCRATE-S
UNCROWN-S
F-**UNCTION**
J-UNCTION
UNCTION-S
UNCURSE-D
UNCURSE-S
S-**UNDECKS**
UNDERDO-G
UNDERGO-D
UNDIGHT-S
N-**UNDINES**
UNDOING-S
UNDRAPE-D
UNDRAPE-S
S-**UNDRESS**
UNEARTH-S
UNEQUAL-S
F-**UNFAIRS**
UNFAITH-S
UNFENCE-D
UNFENCE-S
UNFROCK-S
UNFROZE-N
UNGIRTH-S
UNGLOVE-D
UNGLOVE-S
UNGUARD-S
UNGUENT-A
UNGUENT-S
UNHEART-S
UNHINGE-D
UNHINGE-S
UNHOARD-S
N-**UNHOODS**
UNHORSE-D
UNHORSE-S
G-**UNHOUSE**
UNHOUSE-D
UNHOUSE-S
UNICORN-S
UNIFACE-S
M-**UNIFIED**
UNIFIER-S
M-**UNIFIES**
C-**UNIFORM**
UNIFORM-S
UNIQUES-T
UNITAGE-S
UNITARD-S
M-**UNITING**
UNITING-S
M-**UNITION**
P-UNITION
UNITION-S
UNITISE-D
UNITISE-S
P-**UNITIVE**
UNITIZE-D
UNITIZE-R
UNITIZE-S
UNJOINT-S
UNKNOWN-S
UNLEARN-S
UNLEARN-T
UNLEVEL-S
G-**UNLOCKS**
UNLOOSE-D
UNLOOSE-N
UNLOOSE-S
G-**UNMAKER**
UNMAKER-S
UNMITER-S
UNMITRE-D
UNMITRE-S
UNMOULD-S
UNMOUNT-S
UNNERVE-D
UNNERVE-S
UNNOBLE-D
UNNOBLE-S
UNORDER-S
UNPAINT-S
UNPANEL-S
G-**UNPAPER**
UNPAPER-S
UNPLACE-D
UNPLACE-S
UNPLAIT-S
UNPLUMB-S
UNPLUME-D
UNPLUME-S
UNPURSE-D
UNPURSE-S
UNQUEEN-S
UNQUIET-S
UNQUOTE-D
UNQUOTE-S
UNRAVEL-S
UNREAVE-D
UNREAVE-S
UNREEVE-D
UNREEVE-S
UNRIGHT-S
UNRIVET-S
S-**UNROOFS**
UNROOST-S
R-**UNROUND**
UNROUND-S
UNSAINT-S
UNSCALE-D
UNSCALE-S
UNSCREW-S
UNSENSE-D
UNSENSE-S
UNSHALE-D
UNSHALE-S
UNSHAPE-D
UNSHAPE-N
UNSHAPE-S
UNSHELL-S
UNSHIFT-S
G-**UNSHIPS**
N-UNSHIPS
UNSHOOT-S
UNSHOUT-S
UNSIGHT-S
UNSINEW-S
UNSLING-S
UNSNARL-S
UNSNECK-S
UNSPEAK-S
UNSPELL-S
UNSPOKE-N
UNSTACK-S
UNSTATE-D
UNSTATE-S
UNSTEEL-S
G-**UNSTICK**
UNSTICK-S
G-**UNSTOCK**
UNSTOCK-S
UNSTRAP-S
UNSTRIP-S
S-**UNSUITS**
UNSWEAR-S
UNTHINK-S
UNTRACE-D
UNTRACE-S
UNTREAD-S
UNTRUST-S
UNTRUST-Y
UNTRUTH-S
UNTWINE-D
UNTWINE-S
UNTWIST-S
UNTYING-S
UNVAILE-D
UNVAILE-S
UNVISOR-S
UNVOICE-D
UNVOICE-S
UNWARIE-R
UNWATER-S
UNWATER-Y
UNWEAVE-S
UNWOMAN-S
UNWORTH-S
UNWORTH-Y
UNWRITE-S
UPBRAID-S
UPBREAK-S
UPBRING-S
UPBROKE-N
UPBUILD-S
UPBURST-S
UPCHEER-S
UPCHUCK-S
UPCLIMB-S
UPCLOSE-D
UPCLOSE-S
UPCURVE-D
UPCURVE-S
UPDATER-S
UPDRAFT-S
UPFLING-S
UPGOING-S
UPGRADE-D
UPGRADE-R
UPGRADE-S
UPHEAVE-D
UPHEAVE-R
UPHEAVE-S
UPHOARD-S
UPHOIST-S
UPHOORD-S
E-**UPHROES**
UPLIGHT-S
D-**UPLYING**
UPMAKER-S
C-**UPPINGS**
UPRAISE-D
UPRAISE-R
UPRAISE-S
UPRIGHT-S
UPRISAL-S
UPRISER-S
UPRIVER-S
UPROUSE-D
UPROUSE-S
UPSCALE-D
UPSCALE-S
UPSHIFT-S
UPSHOOT-S
UPSILON-S
UPSPEAK-S
UPSPEAR-S
UPSPOKE-N
UPSTAGE-D
UPSTAGE-S
UPSTAIR-S
UPSTAND-S
UPSTARE-D
UPSTARE-S
UPSTART-S
UPSTATE-R
UPSTATE-S
UPSURGE-D
UPSURGE-S
UPSWARM-S
UPSWEEP-S
UPSWELL-S
UPSWING-S
UPTHROW-N
UPTHROW-S
UPTRAIN-S
UPTREND-S
UPVALUE-D
UPVALUE-S
UPWHIRL-S
URAEMIA-S
R-**URALITE**
URALITE-S
URANIDE-S
URANISM-S
URANITE-S
URANIUM-S
UREDINE-S
URETHAN-E
URETHAN-S
URETHRA-E
URETHRA-L
URETHRA-S
URGENCE-S
T-**URGENCY**
P-**URGINGS**
S-URGINGS
URICASE-S
URIDINE-S
URINATE-D
URINATE-S
B-**URNINGS**
T-URNINGS
URODELE-S
UROLITH-S
O-**UROLOGY**
UROMERE-S
UROSOME-S
USAUNCE-S
F-**USELESS**
H-**USHERED**
USUCAPT-S
USURPER-S
UTENSIL-S
UTILISE-D
UTILISE-R
UTILISE-S
F-**UTILITY**
UTILIZE-D
UTILIZE-R
UTILIZE-S
UTOPIAN-S
UTOPIAS-T
UTOPISM-S
UTOPIST-S
UTRICLE-S
B-**UTTERED**
G-UTTERED
M-UTTERED
P-UTTERED
M-**UTTERER**
P-UTTERER
UTTERER-S
VACANCE-S
VACATUR-S
VACCINA-L
VACCINA-S
VACCINE-E
VACCINE-S
E-**VACUATE**
VACUATE-D
VACUATE-S
VACUIST-S
VACUOLE-S
VAGRANT-S
A-**VAILING**
VAIVODE-S
VALANCE-D
VALANCE-S
VALENCE-S
VALIANT-S
VALONEA-S
VALONIA-S
E-**VALUATE**
VALUATE-D
VALUATE-S
VALVULA-E
VALVULA-R
VALVULE-S
VAMOOSE-D
VAMOOSE-S
VAMPING-S
VAMPIRE-D
VAMPIRE-S
VANDYKE-D
VANDYKE-S
VANESSA-S
VANILLA-S
VANNING-S
VANPOOL-S
VANTAGE-D
VANTAGE-S
VAPORER-S
VAQUERO-S
VAREUSE-S
VARIANT-S
VARIATE-D
VARIATE-S
A-**VARICES**
VARIOLA-R
VARIOLA-S
O-**VARIOLE**
VARIOLE-S
O-**VARIOUS**
VARMENT-S
VARMINT-S
VARNISH-Y
VARYING-S
VASCULA-R
VASSAIL-S
VAULTER-S
A-**VAUNTED**
VAUNTER-S
VAUNTER-Y
VAUNTIE-R
VAURIEN-S
VAVASOR-S
VAVASOR-Y
VEDALIA-S
VEDETTE-S
VEERING-S
VEGETAL-S
VEHICLE-S
VEILING-S
VEINING-S
VEINLET-S
VEINULE-S
VEINULE-T
VELIGER-S
VELOUTE-S
VENATOR-S
VENDACE-S
VENDAGE-S
VENERER-S
A-**VENGERS**
A-**VENGING**
VENISON-S
VENOMER-S
VENTAGE-S
A-**VENTAIL**
VENTAIL-E
VENTAIL-S
VENTANA-S
E-**VENTERS**
VENTIGE-S
E-**VENTING**
VENTING-S
VENTRAL-S
A-**VENTRED**
A-**VENTRES**
A-**VENTURE**
VENTURE-D
VENTURE-R
VENTURE-S
VENTURI-S
VERANDA-H
VERANDA-S
VERBENA-S
O-**VERBIDS**
VERBILE-S
VERBOSE-R
VERDICT-S
VERDITE-R
VERDITE-S
VERDURE-D
VERDURE-S
VERISMO-S

VERMEIL-S
VERMELL-S
VERMUTH-S
VERNIER-S
VERONAL-S
VERRUCA-E
VERRUCA-S
VERRUGA-S
VERSANT-S
O-VERSETS
VERSINE-S
VERSING-S
A-VERSION
E-VERSION
VERSION-S
VERTIGO-S
A-VERTING
E-VERTING
VERVAIN-S
VESICLE-S
VESSAIL-S
VESTIGE-S
VESTING-S
VESTURE-D
VESTURE-R
VESTURE-S
K-VETCHES
VETERAN-S
VETIVER-S
VETIVER-T
VETKOEK-S
VETTURA-S
VEXILLA-R
VIADUCT-S
VIALFUL-S
VIATICA-L
A-VIATORS
VIBRANT-S
VIBRATE-D
VIBRATE-S
VIBRATO-R
VIBRATO-S
VIBRION-S
VICEROY-S
VICIATE-D
VICIATE-S
VICOMTE-S
E-VICTORS
VICTUAL-S
VICUGNA-S
VIDETTE-S
VIDICON-S
VIDUAGE-S
VIEWING-S
VIGOROS-O
VIHUELA-S
VILAYET-S
VILIACO-S
VILIAGO-S
VILLAGE-R
VILLAGE-S
VILLAIN-S
VILLAIN-Y
VILLEIN-S
VINASSE-S
VINEGAR-S
VINEGAR-Y
VINTAGE-D
VINTAGE-R
VINTAGE-S
VINTNER-S
VIOLATE-D
VIOLATE-R
VIOLATE-S
VIOLENT-S

VIOLIST-S
VIOLONE-S
VIRANDA-S
VIRANDO-S
VIRELAI-S
VIRELAY-S
VIREMIA-S
VIRETOT-S
VIRGATE-S
VIRGULE-S
VISCERA-L
VISCOSE-S
VISIBLE-S
VISITEE-S
VISITER-S
VISITOR-S
VITAMER-S
VITAMIN-E
VITAMIN-S
VITELLI-N
VITESSE-S
VITIATE-D
VITIATE-S
VITRAGE-S
VITRAIN-S
VITREUM-S
VITRINE-S
VITRIOL-S
VIVERRA-S
E-VOCABLE
VOCABLE-S
VOCALIC-S
VOCODER-S
VOGUING-S
VOICING-S
A-VOIDERS
A-VOIDING
VOIDING-S
VOITURE-S
VOIVODE-S
VOLANTE-S
VOLCANO-S
VOLPINO-S
VOLTAGE-S
VOLUSPA-S
E-VOLUTED
E-VOLUTES
VOLUTIN-S
E-VOLVING
VOMITER-S
VORLAGE-S
A-VOUCHED
VOUCHEE-S
A-VOUCHER
VOUCHER-S
A-VOUCHES
VOUVRAY-S
VOYAGER-S
E-VULGATE
VULGATE-S
VULTURE-S
VULTURN-S
WABBLER-S
WABSTER-S
S-WADDIES
WADDING-S
S-WADDLED
T-WADDLED
S-WADDLER
T-WADDLER
WADDLER-S
S-WADDLES
T-WADDLES
WADMAAL-S
WADMOLL-S

WADSETT-S
WAESUCK-S
WAFFLER-S
WAFTAGE-S
WAFTING-S
WAFTURE-S
WAGERER-S
S-WAGGERS
S-WAGGING
WAGONER-S
WAGTAIL-S
WAILING-S
WAINAGE-S
S-WAINING
WAISTER-S
A-WAITERS
A-WAITING
WAITING-S
WAIVODE-S
WAIWODE-S
WAKANDA-S
A-WAKENED
A-WAKENER
WAKENER-S
A-WAKINGS
S-WALIEST
WALKING-S
WALKOUT-S
WALKWAY-S
WALLABA-S
S-WALLETS
WALLEYE-D
WALLEYE-S
WALLIES-T
WALLING-S
S-WALLOWS
WALTZER-S
WAMEFOU-S
WAMEFUL-S
S-WAMPISH
T-WANGLED
T-WANGLER
WANGLER-S
T-WANGLES
WANHOPE-S
WANIGAN-S
S-WANKERS
S-WANKIER
S-WANKING
WANNABE-E
WANNABE-S
S-WANNING
WANTAGE-S
A-WANTING
WANTING-S
S-WAPPERS
S-WAPPING
WARATAH-S
WARBLER-S
A-WARDERS
A-WARDING
S-WARDING
WARDING-S
WARDROP-S
WARFARE-D
WARFARE-R
WARFARE-S
WARHEAD-S
WARISON-S
WARLING-S
WARLOCK-S
WARLORD-S
S-WARMERS
S-WARMING
WARMING-S

A-WARNING
WARNING-S
WARPAGE-S
WARPATH-S
WARPING-S
WARRAND-S
WARRANT-S
WARRANT-Y
WARRIOR-S
WARSHIP-S
WARSLER-S
WARSTLE-D
WARSTLE-R
WARSTLE-S
WARTHOG-S
WARTIME-S
WARWORK-S
WASHDAY-S
S-WASHERS
S-WASHIER
S-WASHING
WASHING-S
WASHOUT-S
WASHPOT-S
WASHRAG-S
WASHTUB-S
WASPIES-T
WASSAIL-S
WASTAGE-S
WASTING-S
WASTREL-S
WASTRIE-S
WATCHER-S
S-WATCHES
WATCHET-S
WATERER-S
WATTAGE-S
WATTAPE-S
T-WATTLED
T-WATTLES
WATTLES-S
WAULING-S
WAULKER-S
WAVELET-S
WAVEOFF-S
WAVERER-S
WAVESON-S
WAWLING-S
WAXBILL-S
WAXWEED-S
WAXWING-S
WAXWORK-S
WAXWORM-S
WAYBILL-S
WAYFARE-D
WAYFARE-R
WAYFARE-S
WAYMARK-S
WAYMENT-S
WAYPOST-S
WAYSIDE-S
WAYWODE-S
S-WEARERS
A-WEARIED
WEARIES-T
S-WEARING
WEARING-S
WEASAND-S
A-WEATHER
WEATHER-S
WEAVING-S
WEAZAND-S
WEBBING-S
WEBSITE-S
WEBSTER-S

WEBWORK-S
WEBWORM-S
WEDDING-S
WEDGIES-T
WEDGING-S
WEDLOCK-S
T-WEEDIER
WEEDING-S
WEEKDAY-S
WEEKEND-S
S-WEENIES
T-WEENIES
WEENIES-T
S-WEEPERS
S-WEEPIER
WEEPIES-T
S-WEEPING
WEEPING-S
S-WEETEST
S-WEETING
T-WEETING
WEFTAGE-S
WEIGELA-S
WEIGHER-S
WEIRDIE-S
WELCHER-S
WELCOME-D
WELCOME-R
WELCOME-S
WELDING-S
WELFARE-S
D-WELLING
S-WELLING
WELLING-S
WELSHER-S
S-WELTERS
S-WELTING
WELTING-S
WENCHER-S
WENDIGO-S
WERGELD-S
WERGELT-S
WERGILD-S
WESSAND-S
WESTERN-S
WESTING-S
WESTLIN-S
WETBACK-S
WETLAND-S
WETTING-S
WETWARE-S
WHACKER-S
WHAISLE-D
WHAISLE-S
WHAIZLE-D
WHAIZLE-S
WHALING-S
WHAMPLE-S
WHANGAM-S
WHANGEE-S
WHAPPER-S
WHATNOT-S
WHATSIT-S
WHEATEN-S
WHEEDLE-D
WHEEDLE-R
WHEEDLE-S
WHEELER-S
WHEELIE-R
WHEELIE-S
WHEENGE-D
WHEENGE-S
WHEEPLE-D
WHEEPLE-S
WHEESHT-S

WHEEZER-S
WHEEZLE-D
WHEEZLE-S
WHEMMLE-D
WHEMMLE-S
WHERRET-S
WHETTER-S
WHICKER-S
WHIDDER-S
WHIFFER-S
WHIFFET-S
WHIFFLE-D
WHIFFLE-R
WHIFFLE-S
WHIMPER-S
WHIMPLE-D
WHIMPLE-S
WHIMSEY-S
WHINGER-S
WHINING-S
WHIPCAT-S
WHIPPER-S
WHIPPET-S
WHIPRAY-S
WHIPSAW-N
WHIPSAW-S
WHIRLER-S
WHIRRET-S
WHIRTLE-S
WHISKER-S
WHISKER-Y
WHISKET-S
WHISKEY-S
WHISPER-S
WHISPER-Y
WHISTLE-D
WHISTLE-R
WHISTLE-S
WHITHER-S
WHITIES-T
WHITING-S
WHITLOW-S
WHITRET-S
WHITTAW-S
WHITTER-S
WHITTLE-D
WHITTLE-R
WHITTLE-S
WHIZZER-S
WHOLISM-S
WHOLIST-S
WHOMBLE-D
WHOMBLE-S
WHOMMLE-D
WHOMMLE-S
WHOOBUB-S
WHOOPEE-S
WHOOPER-S
WHOOPLA-S
WHOPPER-S
WHORTLE-S
WHUMMLE-D
WHUMMLE-S
WICKAPE-S
WICKING-S
WICKIUP-S
WICKYUP-S
T-WIDDLED
T-WIDDLES
WIDENER-S
WIDEOUT-S
WIDGEON-S
WIDOWER-S
WIELDER-S
WIFEDOM-S

T-**WIGGIER**
S-**WIGGING**
T-WIGGING
WIGGING-S
WIGGLER-S
T-**WIGHTED**
T-**WIGLESS**
T-**WIGLIKE**
WILDCAT-S
WILDING-S
S-**WILLERS**
T-**WILLIES**
S-**WILLING**
T-WILLING
T-**WILTING**
WIMBREL-S
WINCHER-S
WINCING-S
WINDAGE-S
WINDBAG-S
WINDGUN-S
WINDIGO-S
WINDING-S
D-**WINDLED**
S-WINDLED
D-**WINDLES**
S-WINDLES
WINDLES-S
WINDOCK-S
WINDORE-S
WINDROW-S
WINDWAY-S
WINESOP-S
WINGBOW-S
S-**WINGERS**
S-**WINGIER**
S-**WINGING**
T-WINGING
WINGLET-S
S-**WINGMAN**
S-**WINGMEN**
WINGTIP-S
T-**WINIEST**
S-**WINKING**
T-WINKING
WINKING-S
T-**WINKLED**
T-**WINKLER**
WINKLER-S
T-**WINKLES**
T-**WINNING**
WINNING-S
WINNOCK-S
WINSOME-R
T-**WINTERS**
WIPEOUT-S
WIRETAP-S
WIREWAY-S
S-**WISHERS**
S-**WISHING**
WISHING-S
S-**WISSING**
T-**WISTING**
WISTITI-S
S-**WITCHED**
T-WITCHED
WITCHEN-S
S-**WITCHES**
T-WITCHES
S-**WITHERS**
WITHIES-T
WITHOUT-S
WITLING-S
WITLOOF-S
T-**WITTERS**
T-**WITTING**
WITTING-S
WITWALL-S
WOBBLER-S
WOIWODE-S
WOLFING-S
WOLFKIN-S
WOLFRAM-S
WOLVING-S
WOMMERA-S
WONNING-S
WOODBIN-D
WOODBIN-E
WOODBIN-S
WOODCUT-S
WOODHEN-S
WOODIES-T
WOODLOT-S
WOODSIA-S
WOOFTER-S
WOOLDER-S
WOOLFAT-S
WOOLHAT-S
WOOLIES-T
WOOLLEN-S
WOOLSEY-S
WOOMERA-S
S-**WOONING**
WOORALI-S
WOORARA-S
WOORARI-S
WOOSELL-S
S-**WOOSHED**
S-**WOOSHES**
S-**WOPPING**
WORDAGE-S
S-**WORDING**
WORDING-S
WORKBAG-S
WORKDAY-S
WORKING-S
WORKOUT-S
WORKTOP-S
WORRIER-S
WORSHIP-S
WORSTED-S
WOSBIRD-S
S-**WOTTING**
S-**WOUNDED**
WOUNDER-S
WOURALI-S
WRANGLE-D
WRANGLE-R
WRANGLE-S
WRAPPER-S
WRASSLE-D
WRASSLE-S
WRASTLE-D
WRASTLE-S
WREAKER-S
WREATHE-D
WREATHE-N
WREATHE-R
WREATHE-S
WRECKER-S
WRESTER-S
WRESTLE-D
WRESTLE-R
WRESTLE-S
WRIGGLE-D
WRIGGLE-R
WRIGGLE-S
WRINGER-S
WRINKLE-D
WRINKLE-S
WRITHER-S
WRITING-S
WRONGER-S
WRYBILL-S
WRYNECK-S
WUSSIES-T
XANTHAM-S
XANTHAN-S
XANTHIN-E
XANTHIN-S
XERAFIN-S
XERASIA-S
XIPHOID-S
XYLENOL-S
XYLIDIN-E
XYLIDIN-S
XYLITOL-S
XYLOGEN-S
YACHTER-S
YACHTIE-S
N-**YAFFING**
YAKHDAN-S
YAMALKA-S
YAMULKA-S
YAPPIES-T
YAPSTER-S
YARDAGE-S
YARDANG-S
YARDARM-S
YASHMAC-S
YASHMAK-S
YATAGAN-S
YAWNING-S
YAWPING-S
YCLEEPE-D
YCLEEPE-S
YEALDON-S
YEALING-S
YEAREND-S
YEARNER-S
YELLING-S
YELLOCH-S
YELPING-S
YESHIVA-H
YESHIVA-S
YIELDER-S
YOBBISM-S
YODELER-S
YOGHURT-S
YOUNGER-S
YOUNGTH-S
YOUNKER-S
YOUTHEN-S
YOWLING-S
YPERITE-S
YPSILON-S
YTTRIUM-S
YUMMIES-T
ZABTIEH-S
ZACATON-S
T-**ZADDIKS**
ZAITECH-S
ZAMARRA-S
ZAMARRO-S
ZAMBUCK-S
ZAMOUSE-S
ZANELLA-S
ZANJERO-S
ZANYISM-S
ZAPATEO-S
ZAPTIAH-S
ZAPTIEH-S
ZAREEBA-S
ZARNICH-S
ZEALANT-S
ZEBRINA-S
ZEBRULA-S
ZEBRULE-S
ZECCHIN-E
ZECCHIN-I
ZECCHIN-O
ZECCHIN-S
ZELATOR-S
ZELKOVA-S
ZEMSTVO-S
ZENAIDA-S
ZEOLITE-S
ZETETIC-S
ZEUXITE-S
ZIGANKA-S
ZIKURAT-S
ZILLION-S
ZIMOCCA-S
ZINCATE-S
ZINCITE-S
ZINCODE-S
ZITHERN-S
ZIZANIA-S
ZOCCOLO-S
ZOISITE-S
O-**ZONATED**
ZONULET-S
ZOOGLEA-E
ZOOGLEA-L
ZOOGLEA-S
ZOOLITE-S
ZOOLITH-S
ZOONITE-S
ZOOTYPE-S
ZORGITE-S
ZORILLA-S
ZORILLE-S
ZORILLO-S
A-**ZYGOSES**
A-**ZYMITES**
ZYMOGEN-E
ZYMOGEN-S
ZYMOSAN-S
ZYMOTIC-S
ZYZZYVA-S

8-LETTER WORD HOOKS: extensible words only, except most -S inflections (see p244)

ABDICATE-D
ABDOMINA-L
ABERRATE-D
ABNEGATE-D
ABOIDEAU-X
ABOITEAU-X
ABORIGIN-E
ABROGATE-D
ABSCISIN-G
ABSCISSA-E
ABSOLUTE-R
ABSTERGE-D
ABSTRUSE-R
ACANTHIN-E
ACCORAGE-D
ACCOUTRE-D
L-**ACERATED**
M-ACERATED
ACERBATE-D
ACETAMID-E
ACIERATE-D
T-**ACONITES**
P-**ACTIONED**
ACTIVATE-D
ACTIVIZE D
F-**ACTUALLY**
T-ACTUALLY
V-**ACUITIES**
ACULEATE-D
ADULATOR-Y
ADUNCATE-D
ADVOCATE-D
AFFIANCE-D
AFFRONTE-D
AFFRONTE-E
AFTEREYE-D
AGGRIEVE-D
M-**AGISTERS**
AGNOMINA-L
T-**AILERONS**
B-**AILMENTS**
N-**AINSELLS**
H-**AIRBRUSH**
H-**AIRINESS**
H-**AIRLINES**
H-**AIRLOCKS**
H-**ALATIONS**
ALBITISE-D
ALBITIZE-D
K-**ALEWIVES**
ALIENATE-D
M-**ALIGNERS**
M-**ALIGNING**
ALIZARIN-E
ALKALISE-D
ALKALIZE-D
ALKYLATE-D
ALLELUIA-H
T-**ALLIABLE**
D-**ALLIANCE**
ALLIGATE-D
ALLOCATE-D
ALLOPATH-Y
ALLOTTER-Y
F-**ALLOWING**
G-ALLOWING
H-ALLOWING
S-ALLOWING
T-ALLOWING
W-ALLOWING
F-**ALTERERS**
P-ALTERERS
F-**ALTERING**
H-ALTERING
P-ALTERING
ALTERNAT-E
G-**AMBLINGS**
L-AMBLINGS
R-AMBLINGS
W-AMBLINGS
AMBROSIA-L
AMBROSIA-N
AMBULATE-D
M-**AMMONITE**
AMORTISE-D
AMORTIZE-D
AMPHIBIA-N
C-**AMPHORIC**
AMPULLAR-Y
AMPUTATE-D
AMYGDALA-E
ANECDOTA-L
ANGELICA-L
D-**ANGERING**
D-**ANGLINGS**
J-ANGLINGS
T-ANGLINGS
W-ANGLINGS
ANGUIPED-E
ANGULATE-D
ANKYLOSE-D
ANNALISE-D
ANNALIZE-D
ANNOTATE-D
ANNOUNCE-D
ANNOUNCE-R
T-**ANNOYING**
C-**ANNULATE**
ANNULATE-D
ANTECEDE-D
ANTEDATE-D
ANTEFIXA-E
ANTEFIXA-L
G-**ANTELOPE**
W-**ANTHILLS**
ANTICIZE-D
ANTIDOTE-D
ANTIPHON-Y
R-**ANTIPOLE**
ANTISTAT-E
APHETISE-D
APHETIZE-D
APHORISE-D
APHORISE-R
APHORIZE-D
APHORIZE-R
APOLOGIA-E
APPANAGE-D
APPETISE-D
APPETISE-R

APPETIZE-D
APPETIZE-R
APPLIQUE-D
APPRAISE-D
APPRAISE-E
APPRAISE-R
APRICATE-D
AQUATINT-A
ARBORIZE-D
H-**ARBOURED**
ARCHAISE-D
ARCHAISE-R
ARCHAIZE-D
ARCHAIZE-R
S-**ARCOLOGY**
R-**AREFYING**
AREOLATE-D
ARGUMENT-A
ARILLATE-D
ARMATURE-D
H-**ARMONICA**
C-**AROUSALS**
C-**AROUSERS**
C-**AROUSING**
H-**ARQUEBUS**
D-**ARRAIGNS**
W-**ARRAYING**
C-**ARRIAGES**
M-ARRIAGES
ARROGATE-D
F-**ARROWING**
H-ARROWING
M-ARROWING
N-ARROWING
T-ARROWING
P-**ARTICLES**
ARTIFICE-R
T-**ARTINESS**
B-**ARTISANS**
P-ARTISANS
P-**ARTWORKS**
G-**ASEITIES**
F-**ASHERIES**
W-ASHERIES
W-**ASHINESS**
ASPERATE-D
J-**ASPEROUS**
ASPERSOR-Y
ASPHYXIA-L
ASPIRATA-E
ASPIRATE-D
W-**ASSAILED**
W-**ASSAILER**
ASSEMBLE-D
ASSEMBLE-R
ASSERTOR-Y
ASSONATE-D
C-**ASTEISMS**
ASTRAGAL-I
ASTRINGE-D
ASTRINGE-R
Y-**ATAGHANS**
ATCHIEVE-D
ATHETISE-D
ATHETIZE-D
ATMOLYSE-D
ATMOLYZE-D
AUGUSTES-T
AURICULA-E
AURICULA-R
T-**AURIFORM**
T-**AUTOLOGY**
AUTOLYSE-D
AUTOLYZE-D
AUTOMATE-D

T-**AUTONYMS**
AUTOTYPE-D
AUXILIAR-Y
AVENTAIL-E
AVIANIZE-D
C-**AVIARIES**
N-**AVICULAR**
AVIFAUNA-E
AVIFAUNA-L
N-**AVIGATOR**
M-**AXILLARY**
L-**AZURITES**
BACCHANT-E
BACILLAR-Y
BACKBITE-R
BACKBONE-D
BACKDATE-D
BACKDROP-T
BACKFIRE-D
BACKSLID-E
BACTERIA-L
BACTERIA-N
BADINAGE-D
BALDPATE-D
BALLADIN-E
BALLADIN-G
BALLISTA-E
BANALISE-D
BANALIZE-D
BANDEROL-E
BARBECUE-D
BARBECUE-R
BARBEQUE-D
BARNACLE-D
BARRETTE-R
BASELINE-R
A-**BASEMENT**
A-**BASHLESS**
BASILICA-E
BASILICA-L
BASILICA-N
BASOPHIL-E
A-**BATEMENT**
BAUDRICK-E
BECHANCE-D
BECLOTHE-D
BEDABBLE-D
BEDAGGLE-D
BEDAZZLE-D
BEDIMPLE-D
BEFRINGE-D
BEFUDDLE-D
BEGIRDLE-D
BEGRUDGE-D
BEJUMBLE-D
BELITTLE-D
BELITTLE-R
BEMINGLE-D
BEMUDDLE-D
BEMUFFLE-D
BEMUZZLE-D
BENEFICE-D
BENZIDIN-E
BEPIMPLE-D
BEPRAISE-D
BERBERIN-E
BERGAMAS-K
BESMUDGE-D
BESOOTHE-D
BESPOUSE-D
A-**BIOGENIC**
BIOGRAPH-Y
BIRDLIME-D
BLASTEMA-L
BLASTIES-T

BLASTULA-E
BLASTULA-R
BLEACHER-Y
BLIZZARD-Y
BLOCKADE-D
BLOCKADE-R
BLOODIES-T
BLOVIATE-D
A-**BODEMENT**
BOLDFACE-D
BOLSHIES-T
BOTANICA-L
BOTANISE-D
BOTANIZE-D
A-**BOUNDING**
BOUSOUKI-A
BOUTONNE-E
BOUZOUKI-A
A-**BRAIDING**
BRANCHER-Y
BRANCHIA-E
BRANCHIA-L
BRASSIER-E
BRASSIES-T
BRATTICE-D
BRETTICE-D
BRICKIES-T
A-**BRIDGING**
BRITTLES-T
BROMELIA-D
BRONCHIA-L
A-**BROOKING**
BROWNIES-T
BRUCELLA-E
BUBBLIES-T
A-**BUILDING**
BULGINES-S
BULLDOZE-D
BULLDOZE-R
BULLETIN-G
BURNOOSE-D
A-**BUTMENTS**
BUTYLATE-D
CABALLER-O
CABRIOLE-T
CACUMINA-L
CALAMINE-D
CALCANEA-L
CALCANEA-N
CALCEATE-D
CALCULAR-Y
CALORIZE-D
CALYPTER-A
S-**CAMPINGS**
CANALISE-D
CANALIZE-D
CANEPHOR-A
CANEPHOR-E
S-**CANNINGS**
CANONISE-D
CANONIZE-D
CANOODLE-D
CANTHARI-D
S-**CANTIEST**
S-**CANTLING**
CANULATE-D
CAPITULA-R
CAPONIER-E
CAPONISE-D
CAPONIZE-D
CAPRICCI-O
CAPRIOLE-D
CAPSULAR-Y
CARABINE-R
CARACOLE-D

CARETAKE-N
CARETAKE-R
CARINATE-D
S-**CARPINGS**
CARTOUCH-E
CASEMATE-D
CASTELLA-N
CASTRATE-D
CASTRATO-R
CATALYSE-D
CATALYSE-R
CATALYZE-D
CATALYZE-R
CATENATE-D
CATHEDRA-E
CATHEDRA-L
S-**CATTIEST**
CAVITATE-D
A-**CELLULAR**
CENTINEL-L
CENTONEL-L
CENTUPLE-D
CERCARIA-E
CERCARIA-L
CERCARIA-N
CHANDLER-Y
CHAPERON-E
CHAPPIES-T
CHAROSET-H
CHASTISE-D
CHASTISE-R
CHATTIES-T
CHERRIES-T
CHICANER-Y
S-**CHILLERS**
CHILLIES-T
S-**CHILLING**
CHINKIES-T
CHIPPIES-T
CHITTIES-T
CHIVAREE-D
CHLORDAN-E
CHOCCIES-T
CHORIAMB-I
CHROMIZE-D
CHUMMIES-T
CICERONE-D
CINCTURE-D
CIRRIPED-E
CISTERNA-E
CISTERNA-L
CIVILISE-D
CIVILISE-R
CIVILIZE-D
CIVILIZE-R
CLAUSTRA-L
CLAUSULA-E
CLAUSULA-R
Y-**CLEEPING**
CLITELLA-R
CLODPATE-D
COADMIRE-D
COALESCE-D
COALMINE-R
COASSUME-D
COCHLEAR-E
COCREATE-D
CODERIVE-D
COENDURE-D
COEQUATE-D
COEVOLVE-D
COGITATE-D
COGNOSCE-D
COHOBATE-D
COIFFURE-D

COINCIDE-D
COINHERE-D
COINSURE-D
COINSURE-R
COLLAPSE-D
COLLEGIA-L
COLLEGIA-N
COLLOGUE-D
COLLOQUE-D
COLLUVIA-L
COLOCATE-D
COLONISE-D
COLONIZE-D
COLONIZE-R
COLOPHON-Y
COLORIZE-D
COMANAGE-D
COMANAGE-R
COMATULA-E
COMEDDLE-D
COMINGLE-D
COMMENCE-D
COMMENCE-R
COMMERCE-D
COMMERGE-D
COMPESCE-D
COMPLAIN-T
COMPLETE-D
COMPLETE-R
COMPRISE-D
COMPRIZE-D
COMPULSE-D
CONCEIVE-D
CONCEIVE-R
CONCISES-T
CONCLUDE-D
CONCLUDE-R
CONCOURS-E
CONCRETE-D
CONDENSE-D
CONDENSE-R
CONFERVA-E
CONFLATE-D
CONFRONT-E
CONGLOBE-D
I-**CONICITY**
CONSERVE-D
CONSERVE-R
CONSPIRE-D
CONSPIRE-R
CONSTATE-D
CONSTRUE-D
CONSTRUE-R
CONTINUA-L
CONTINUE-D
CONTINUE-R
CONTRAST-Y
CONTRIVE-D
CONTRIVE-R
CONVERGE-D
CONVERSE-D
CONVERSE-R
CONVINCE-D
CONVINCE-R
CONVOLVE-D
CONVULSE-D
S-**COPULATE**
COPULATE-D
COQUETTE-D
CORDELLE-D
CORELATE-D
S-**CORELESS**
CORONATE-D
COROTATE-D
CORVETTE-D

A-**COSMISMS**
A-**COSMISTS**
COSTUMER-Y
S-**COURSING**
S-**CRABBING**
S-**CRAGGIER**
S-**CRAGGILY**
S-**CRAMMING**
S-**CRANCHED**
S-**CRANCHES**
S-**CRAPPERS**
S-**CRAPPIER**
CRAPPIES-T
S-**CRAPPING**
S-**CRATCHES**
S-**CRAWLERS**
S-**CRAWLIER**
S-**CRAWLING**
S-**CREAKIER**
S-**CREAKING**
S-**CREAMERS**
S-**CREAMING**
CREASOTE-D
CREEPIES-T
CREMATOR-Y
CRENELLE-D
CREOLISE-D
CREOLIZE-D
CREOSOTE-D
CREVASSE-D
S-**CRIBBLED**
S-**CRIBBLES**
CRIBELLA-R
S-**CRIMPERS**
S-**CRIMPIER**
S-**CRIMPING**
CRITIQUE-D
CROSSBIT-E
CROTCHET-Y
S-**CRUMMIER**
CRUMMIES-T
S-**CRUMPING**
S-**CRUNCHED**
S-**CRUNCHES**
CRUSTATE-D
CRUSTIES-T
S-**CUDDLING**
S-**CUFFLING**
S-**CULLINGS**
S-**CULLIONS**
CULTRATE-D
S-**CUMBERED**
CUMULATE-D
CURARISE-D
CURARIZE-D
CURCUMIN-E
CURLICUE-D
S-**CURRIERS**
S-**CURRYING**
CURSITOR-Y
CURTALAX-E
S-**CURVIEST**
CUSPIDOR-E
A-**CUTENESS**
CUTICULA-E
CUTICULA-R
CUTINISE-D
CUTINIZE-D
S-**CUTTLING**
CYANAMID-E
DAHABIYA-H
DAINTIES-T
DAMASKIN-G
DANCETTE-E
DANDRUFF-Y

DARRAIGN-E
DARRAINE-D
DATELINE-D
DAYDREAM-T
DEAERATE-D
DEBOUCHE-D
DEBRUISE-D
DEBUTANT-E
DECEMVIR-I
DECENNIA-L
DECENTRE-D
DECIMATE-D
DECLASSE-D
DECLASSE-E
DECORATE-D
DECOUPLE-D
DECREASE-D
DEDICATE-D
DEDICATE-E
DEFECATE-D
DEFILADE-D
DEGREASE-D
DEGREASE-R
S-**DEIGNING**
DEIONIZE-D
DEIONIZE-R
DELEGATE-D
DELEGATE-E
DELIBATE-D
DEMENTIA-L
DEMOCRAT-Y
DEMONISE-D
DEMONIZE-D
DENATURE-D
DENOTATE-D
DENOUNCE-D
DENOUNCE-R
DENUDATE-D
DEPILATE-D
DEPURATE-D
DEPUTISE-D
DEPUTIZE-D
DEROGATE-D
DESCRIBE-D
DESCRIBE-R
DESCRIVE-D
DESOLATE-D
DESOLATE-R
DESPOTAT-E
DETHRONE-D
DETHRONE-R
DETONATE-D
DETRAQUE-E
DEVELOPE-D
DEVELOPE-R
DEVIATOR-Y
DIAGNOSE-D
DIALOGUE-D
DIAPAUSE-D
DIARRHEA-L
DICHASIA-L
DICTATOR-Y
DIDRACHM-A
DIGITATE-D
DIGITISE-D
DIGITISE-R
DIGITIZE-D
DIGITIZE-R
DIMERISE-D
DIMERIZE-D
DIPLOMAT-A
DIPLOMAT-E
DIRECTOR-Y
DIRIGISM-E
DISABUSE-D

DISAGREE-D
DISBURSE-D
DISBURSE-R
DISCIPLE-D
DISCLOSE-D
DISCLOSE-R
DISCOURE-D
DISCOVER-T
DISCOVER-Y
DISCRETE-R
DISGORGE-D
DISGRACE-D
DISGRACE-R
DISGRADE-D
DISGUISE-D
DISGUISE-R
DISHABLE-D
DISHORSE-D
DISHOUSE-D
DISINURE-D
DISLEAVE-D
DISLODGE-D
DISPENCE-D
DISPENSE-D
DISPENSE-R
DISPERSE-D
DISPERSE-R
DISPLACE-D
DISPLODE-D
DISPLUME-D
DISPONGE-D
DISPRIZE-D
DISPROVE-D
DISPROVE-N
DISPUNGE-D
DISPURSE-D
DISSEISE-D
DISSEIZE-D
DISSERVE-D
DISSOLVE-D
DISSOLVE-R
DISSUADE-D
DISSUADE-R
DISTANCE-D
DISTASTE-D
DISTRAIN-T
DISTRAIT-E
DISULFID-E
DISUNITE-D
DISVALUE-D
DIVAGATE-D
DIVINISE-D
DIVINIZE-D
DJELLABA-H
DOGGONES-T
DOMICILE-D
DOMINATE-D
O-**DORIZING**
DOWNSIZE-D
A-**DREADING**
DREARIES-T
DRICKSIE-R
DRUGGIES-T
DUBITATE-D
DYNAMISE-D
DYNAMITE-D
DYNAMITE-R
DYNAMIZE-D
DYSPNOEA-L
DYSTOPIA-N
W-**EANLINGS**
Y-EANLINGS
T-**EARDROPS**
N-**EARLIEST**
P-EARLIEST

L-**EARNINGS**
Y-EARNINGS
C-**EASELESS**
B-**EASTINGS**
F-EASTINGS
P-**EATERIES**
D-**EBAUCHES**
EBIONISE-D
EBIONIZE-D
D-**ECAUDATE**
ECCLESIA-E
ECCLESIA-L
ECHINATE-D
R-**ECLOSING**
ECSTASIS-E
O-**ECUMENIC**
W-**EDGEWISE**
S-**EDITIONS**
EDUCATOR-Y
D-**EDUCIBLE**
R-EDUCIBLE
D-**EDUCTION**
R-EDUCTION
S-EDUCTION
D-**EDUCTIVE**
R-EDUCTIVE
S-EDUCTIVE
R-**EDUCTORS**
S-EDUCTORS
B-**EERINESS**
EFFIERCE-D
EFFLUVIA-L
R-**EGENCIES**
EGOMANIA-C
R-**EGRESSED**
N-**EGRESSES**
R-EGRESSES
D-**EJECTING**
R-EJECTING
D-**EJECTION**
R-EJECTION
R-**EJECTIVE**
R-**EJECTORS**
D-**ELAPSING**
R-ELAPSING
B-**ELATEDLY**
R-ELATEDLY
D-**ELATIONS**
G-ELATIONS
R-ELATIONS
R-**ELATIVES**
S-**ELECTEES**
S-**ELECTING**
S-**ELECTION**
S-**ELECTIVE**
S-**ELECTORS**
ELEVATOR-Y
S-**ELFHOODS**
S-**ELFISHLY**
ELONGATE-D
D-**ELUSIONS**
ELUVIATE-D
EMACIATE-D
R-**EMAILING**
EMANATOR-Y
EMBATTLE-D
EMBEZZLE-D
EMBEZZLE-R
EMBRACER-Y
EMENDATE-D
R-**EMENDING**
D-**EMERGING**
R-EMERGING
D-**EMERSION**
R-**EMIGRATE**

EMIGRATE-D
D-**EMISSION**
R-EMISSION
D-**EMISSIVE**
R-EMISSIVE
R-**EMITTERS**
D-**EMITTING**
R-EMITTING
EMMARBLE-D
D-**EMOTIONS**
R-EMOTIONS
EMPEOPLE-D
EMPERISE-D
EMPERIZE-D
EMPHASIS-E
EMPIERCE-D
EMPLONGE-D
T-**EMPTINGS**
EMPURPLE-D
D-**EMULSIFY**
M-**ENARCHES**
V-**ENATIONS**
P-**ENCHANTS**
ENCHARGE-D
ENCIRCLE-D
ENCLOTHE-D
ENCRADLE-D
ENCREASE-D
ENDAMAGE-D
ENDAMEBA-E
ENDOSMOS-E
ENDOSTEA-L
ENERGISE-D
ENERGISE-R
ENERGIZE-D
ENERGIZE-R
D-**ENERVATE**
ENERVATE-D
ENFEEBLE-D
ENFIERCE-D
ENFILADE-D
R-**ENFORCED**
R-**ENFORCES**
ENGIRDLE-D
ENGRAVER-Y
ENGRIEVE-D
ENGROOVE-D
ENHEARSE-D
ENKINDLE-D
P-**ENLIGHTS**
ENLUMINE-D
K-**ENOSISES**
D-**ENOUNCED**
R-ENOUNCED
D-**ENOUNCES**
R-ENOUNCES
ENRAUNGE-D
ENSAMPLE-D
ENSCONCE-D
ENSHEATH-E
ENSHRINE-D
ENSHRINE-E
ENSILAGE-D
ENSORCEL-L
ENSPHERE-D
C-**ENSURERS**
C-**ENSURING**
ENSWATHE-D
ENTAMEBA-E
P-**ENTANGLE**
ENTANGLE-D
ENTANGLE-R
V-**ENTAYLES**
C-**ENTERING**
T-ENTERING

ENTHRONE-D
P-**ENTICING**
ENTRANCE-D
C-**ENTRISMS**
C-**ENTRISTS**
ENVEIGLE-D
ENVELOPE-D
ENVISAGE-D
A-**EOLIPILE**
N-**EOLITHIC**
EPHEDRIN-E
EPHEMERA-E
EPHEMERA-L
EPICEDIA-L
EPICEDIA-N
L-**EPIDOTES**
EPIFAUNA-E
EPIFAUNA-L
EPIGRAPH-Y
D-**EPILATED**
D-**EPILATES**
D-**EPILATOR**
EPILOGUE-D
D-**EPURATED**
D-**EPURATES**
EQUALISE-D
EQUALISE-R
EQUALIZE-D
EQUALIZE-R
EQUIPAGE-D
R-**ERADIATE**
ERADIATE-D
ERGOTISE-D
ERGOTIZE-D
T-**ERRORIST**
ERUCTATE-D
ERYTHEMA-L
ESCALADE-D
ESCALADE-R
ESCALATE-D
ESCALOPE-D
D-**ESCRIBED**
D-**ESCRIBES**
O-**ESOPHAGI**
ESOTERIC-A
B-**ESPOUSED**
B-**ESPOUSES**
ESQUIRES-S
H-**ESSONITE**
G-**ESTATING**
R-ESTATING
A-**ESTHESES**
A-**ESTHESIA**
A-**ESTHESIS**
A-**ESTHETES**
A-**ESTHETIC**
ESTIMATE-D
A-**ESTIVATE**
ESTIVATE-D
ESTRANGE-D
ESTRANGE-R
O-**ESTRIOLS**
O-**ESTROGEN**
O-**ESTRONES**
O-**ESTRUSES**
B-**ETACISMS**
K-**ETAMINES**
L-**ETCHINGS**
ETERNISE-D
ETERNIZE-D
M-**ETHANOLS**
ETHERISE-D
ETHERIZE-D
ETHERIZE-R
ETHICISE-D
ETHICIZE-D
ETHNARCH-Y
M-**ETHYLATE**
ETHYLATE-D
M-**ETHYLENE**
P-**ETIOLATE**
ETIOLATE-D
A-**ETIOLOGY**
ETRANGER-E
EUCALYPT-I
EUCARYOT-E
EUDAEMON-Y
EUKARYOT-E
EULOGISE-D
EULOGIZE-D
EULOGIZE-R
EUPHUISE-D
EUPHUIZE-D
EVACUATE-D
D-**EVALUATE**
R-EVALUATE
EVALUATE-D
EVANESCE-D
N-**EVERMORE**
R-**EVERSION**
R-**EVERTING**
EVIDENCE-D
L-**EVIRATES**
L-**EVITATED**
L-**EVITATES**
R-**EVOCABLE**
EVOCATOR-Y
R-**EVOLVERS**
D-**EVOLVING**
R-EVOLVING
EVULGATE-D
R-**EVULSION**
H-**EXAMINES**
EXANTHEM-A
EXCAVATE-D
EXCHANGE-D
EXCHANGE-R
EXECRATE-D
EXECUTOR-Y
EXEMPLAR-Y
EXERCISE-D
EXERCISE-R
EXHUMATE-D
EXIGEANT-E
EXORCISE-D
EXORCISE-R
EXORCIZE-D
EXORCIZE-R
EXPEDITE-D
EXPEDITE-R
EXPIATOR-Y
EXTREMES-T
D-**EXTRORSE**
EXTUBATE-D
EXUVIATE-D
FABULISE-D
FABULIZE-D
FANFARON-A
FANTASIE-D
FARADISE-D
FARADIZE-D
FASCIATE-D
FASCICLE-D
FASCISTI-C
FATIGATE-D
FEDERATE-D
FELLATIO-N
FEMINISE-D
FEMINIZE-D
FENESTRA-E
FENESTRA-L
FIBERIZE-D
FIBRILLA-E
FIBRILLA-R
FIGURANT-E
FILAGREE-D
FILIGREE-D
FILTRATE-D
FINALISE-D
FINALIZE-D
FINICKIN-G
FISSIPED-E
FLAGELLA-R
FLAMBEAU-X
FLIMSIES-T
FLOPPIES-T
FLOSSIES-T
FLOURISH-Y
FLUIDISE-D
FLUIDIZE-D
FLUIDIZE-R
FOCALISE-D
FOCALIZE-D
FOOTNOTE-D
FORAMINA-L
FOREBODE-D
FOREBODE-R
FOREDATE-D
A-**FOREHAND**
FOREKNOW-N
FOREMEAN-T
FORENAME-D
A-**FORESAID**
FORESHEW-N
FORESHOW-N
FORESTAL-L
A-**FORETIME**
FORHAILE-D
FORHOOIE-D
FORJUDGE-D
FORMULAR-Y
FORSPOKE-N
FORWASTE-D
S-**FORZANDI**
S-**FORZANDO**
S-**FORZATOS**
FRACTURE-D
FREEBASE-D
FREEBASE-R
FREEBOOT-Y
FRILLIES-T
FRONTAGE-R
FROSTBIT-E
FUMIGATE-D
FURFUROL-E
GAILLARD-E
GALLABEA-H
GALLABIA-H
GANGRENE-D
GARAGIST-E
GARGOYLE-D
GARROTTE-D
GARROTTE-R
GASTNESS-E
GASTRULA-E
GASTRULA-R
GEFUFFLE-D
A-**GELASTIC**
GEMINATE-D
GENERATE-D
A-**GENTRIES**
GESNERIA-D
GHASTFUL-L
GLABELLA-E
GLABELLA-R
GLACIATE-D
GLADSOME-R
GLASSIES-T
GLISSADE-D
GLISSADE-R
GLOSSIES-T
GLYCERIN-E
GOLLIWOG-G
GOSSAMER-Y
GRADUATE-D
GRAECIZE-D
S-**GRAFFITI**
S-**GRAFFITO**
GRANDSIR-E
GRANULAR-Y
GRATINEE-D
GREASIES-T
GREENIES-T
E-**GRESSING**
GREWSOME-R
GRUESOME-R
GUANIDIN-E
GUNKHOLE-D
GYMNASIA-L
W-**HACKINGS**
S-**HACKLERS**
S-**HACKLING**
S-**HADDOCKS**
HAFTAROT-H
HAFTOROT-H
HAGGADOT-H
S-**HALLOWED**
S-**HALLOWER**
C-**HALUTZIM**
S-**HAMBLING**
C-**HANDLERS**
HANDSOME-R
HANDWRIT-E
C-**HAPPIEST**
HARANGUE-D
HARANGUE-R
HARDLINE-R
HARDNOSE-D
HARDWIRE-D
HARMALIN-E
C-**HARMLESS**
HARMONIC-A
C-**HAROSETH**
C-**HAROSETS**
S-**HARPINGS**
C-**HASTENED**
C-**HASTENER**
T-**HATCHERS**
T-**HATCHING**
C-**HATTERED**
S-HATTERED
C-**HAUNTERS**
C-**HAUNTING**
C-**HAZZANIM**
S-**HEADINGS**
HEADLINE-D
HEADLINE-R
S-**HEALINGS**
S-**HEARINGS**
HEARTIES-T
S-**HEATHERS**
S-**HEATHIER**
C-**HEATINGS**
HEBETATE-D
HEBRAIZE-D
W-**HEELINGS**
W-**HEELLESS**
S-**HELLFIRE**
T-**HEMATICS**
HEMOLYZE-D
C-**HEMOSTAT**
HEPATICA-E
HEPATICA-L
HEPATISE-D
HEPATIZE-D
HEPTARCH-Y
HERBARIA-N
T-**HEREAWAY**
T-**HEREFROM**
W-HEREFROM
T-**HEREINTO**
W-HEREINTO
T-**HERENESS**
W-HERENESS
T-**HEREUNTO**
W-HEREUNTO
T-**HEREUPON**
W-HEREUPON
T-**HEREWITH**
W-HEREWITH
HERNIATE-D
C-**HERRYING**
W-HERRYING
HESITATE-D
HESITATE-R
C-**HIDLINGS**
HIERARCH-Y
HIERATIC-A
C-**HILLIEST**
S-**HINNYING**
W-HINNYING
C-**HIPPIEST**
W-HIPPIEST
C-**HIPPINGS**
S-HIPPINGS
W-HIPPINGS
W-**HIPSTERS**
W-**HIRLINGS**
HISTAMIN-E
HISTIDIN-E
HISTOGEN-Y
A-**HISTORIC**
W-**HITHERED**
T-**HITHERTO**
W-**HOLESOME**
W-**HOLISTIC**
HOMINIZE-D
P-**HONEYING**
W-**HOOSHING**
C-**HOPPIEST**
S-HOPPIEST
C-**HOPPINGS**
S-HOPPINGS
W-HOPPINGS
T-**HORNBILL**
T-**HORNIEST**
T-**HORNLESS**
T-**HORNLIKE**
HOROLOGE-R
C-**HOROLOGY**
HOSPITAL-E
G-**HOSTINGS**
S-**HOUTINGS**
S-**HOVELING**
S-**HOVELLED**
S-**HOVELLER**
HUCKSTER-Y
C-**HUFFIEST**
HUMANISE-D
HUMANIZE-D
HUMANIZE-R
T-**HUMBLING**
A-**HUNGERED**
C-**HUNKIEST**
S-**HUNTINGS**

C-**HUTZPAHS**
HYDROZOA-N
HYPERNYM-Y
HYPODERM-A
HYPOGAEA-L
HYPOGAEA-N
IDEALISE-D
IDEALISE-R
IDEALIZE-D
IDEALIZE-R
V-**IDEOGRAM**
M-**IFFINESS**
D-**IGNIFIED**
L-IGNIFIED
S-IGNIFIED
D-**IGNIFIES**
L-IGNIFIES
S-IGNIFIES
ILLUMINE-D
ILLUMINE-R
L-**IMITABLE**
IMMANTLE-D
IMMINGLE-D
IMMODEST-Y
IMMOLATE-D
IMMUNISE-D
IMMUNIZE-D
W-**IMPISHLY**
IMPLEDGE-D
S-**IMPLEXES**
IMPLUNGE-D
IMPOLITE-R
IMPRESSE-D
IMPURPLE-D
INCENSOR-Y
INCHOATE-D
L-**INCHPINS**
INCORPSE-D
INCREASE-D
INCREASE-R
INCUBATE-D
INDAGATE-D
V-**INDICATE**
INDICATE-D
W-**INDOWING**
INDURATE-D
INFAMISE-D
INFAMIZE-D
P-**INFOLDED**
INFRINGE-D
INFRINGE-R
INGROOVE-D
INHEARSE-D
INHUMATE-D
INITIATE-D
K-**INKINESS**
P-INKINESS
T-**INKLINGS**
P-**INNATELY**
INNOVATE-D
INSCONCE-D
INSCRIBE-D
INSCRIBE-R
P-**INSETTER**
INSHEATH-E
INSHRINE-D
INSOLATE-D
INSOMNIA-C
INSPHERE-D
INSTANCE-D
INSULATE-D
INSWATHE-D
INTERESS-E
INTERVAL-E
INTHRONE-D
INTIMATE-D
INTIMATE-R
INTIMIST-E
INTITULE-D
INTONATE-D
INTRIGUE-D
INTRIGUE-R
INTUBATE-D
INUNDATE-D
INVEAGLE-D
INVEIGLE-D
INVEIGLE-R
INVENTOR-Y
INVERTIN-G
INVOCATE-D
INVOLUTE-D
IODINATE-D
L-**IONISERS**
L-**IONISING**
L-**IONIZERS**
L-**IONIZING**
D-**IREFULLY**
E-**IRENICON**
IRRIGATE-D
IRRITATE-D
ISOCHRON-E
B-**ITCHIEST**
H-ITCHIEST
P-ITCHIEST
T-ITCHIEST
W-ITCHIEST
P-**ITCHINGS**
W-ITCHINGS
W-**ITCHWEED**
L-**ITERATES**
E-**JACULATE**
JACULATE-D
JALOUSIE-D
JAMBOLAN-A
JAPANIZE-D
JAROVIZE-D
JAUNDICE-D
JAUNTIES-T
JEALOUSE-D
D-**JELLABAS**
JEWELLER-Y
JOINTURE-D
JUBILATE-D
JUGULATE-D
JULIENNE-D
JUMBOISE-D
JUMBOIZE-D
KABELJOU-W
KEELHALE-D
KEFUFFLE-D
S-**KETCHING**
KEYSTONE-D
KHALIFAT-E
KHANSAMA-H
S-**KILLINGS**
S-**KIPPERED**
S-**KITTLING**
KLONDIKE-D
KLONDIKE-R
KLONDYKE-D
KLONDYKE-R
KREASOTE-D
KREOSOTE-D
F-**LABELLUM**
P-**LACELESS**
LACERATE-D
F-**LACKERED**
B-**LACKLAND**
B-**LADDERED**
F-**LAGGINGS**
G-**LAIRIEST**
LAMBASTE-D
LAMINATE-D
S-**LAMMINGS**
B-**LANCHING**
F-LANCHING
P-LANCHING
LANDDROS-T
G-**LANDLESS**
LANDSLID-E
S-**LANGUAGE**
LANGUAGE-D
B-**LANKNESS**
C-**LAPBOARD**
LAPIDATE-D
C-**LAPPERED**
C-**LAPPINGS**
F-LAPPINGS
C-**LASHINGS**
F-LASHINGS
P-LASHINGS
S-LASHINGS
B-**LASTINGS**
C-**LATCHING**
E-**LATERITE**
LATERIZE-D
B-**LATHERED**
S-LATHERED
B-**LATHERER**
P-**LATINIZE**
LATINIZE-D
P-**LATITUDE**
LAUDATOR-Y
F-**LAUGHTER**
S-LAUGHTER
F-**LAUNCHED**
F-**LAUNCHES**
LAUREATE-D
LAVALIER-E
C-**LAVATION**
LAVISHES-T
S-**LAVISHLY**
P-**LAYBACKS**
P-**LAYTIMES**
B-**LEACHERS**
B-**LEACHING**
P-LEACHING
P-**LEADINGS**
C-**LEANINGS**
G-LEANINGS
C-**LEANNESS**
B-**LEARIEST**
P-**LEASINGS**
P-**LEASURES**
C-**LEAVINGS**
E-**LECTIONS**
F-LECTIONS
E-**LECTRESS**
F-**LEDGIEST**
F-**LEECHING**
F-**LEERINGS**
LEGALISE-D
LEGALIZE-D
LEGALIZE-R
B-**LENDINGS**
F-**LETCHING**
E-**LEVATORS**
LEVERAGE-D
LEVIGATE-D
LEVITATE-D
LIBERATE-D
LICHENIN-G
C-**LICKINGS**
S-LICKINGS
A-**LIENABLE**
LIGATURE-D
B-**LIGHTERS**
P-LIGHTERS
S-**LIGHTEST**
P-**LIGHTFUL**
A-**LIGHTING**
B-LIGHTING
F-LIGHTING
P-LIGHTING
S-LIGHTING
S-**LIGHTISH**
A-**LIKENESS**
S-**LIMINESS**
S-**LIMPSIER**
B-**LINDWORM**
C-**LINGIEST**
F-**LINTIEST**
S-**LIPPERED**
S-**LIPPIEST**
C-**LIPPINGS**
LIQUESCE-D
G-**LISTENED**
A-**LITERACY**
A-**LITERATE**
LITERATI-M
LITERATO-R
LITIGATE-D
C-**LITTERED**
F-LITTERED
G-LITTERED
A-**LIVENESS**
LOBULATE-D
LOCALISE-D
LOCALISE-R
LOCALIZE-D
LOCALIZE-R
B-**LOCKAGES**
LOCOMOTE-D
E-**LOCUTION**
E-**LOCUTORY**
LODICULA-E
C-**LOGGIEST**
F-**LOGGINGS**
LOGICISE-D
LOGICIZE-D
LOGOMACH-Y
A-**LONENESS**
LOOPHOLE-D
G-**LOOPIEST**
F-**LOPPIEST**
S-LOPPIEST
LORICATE-D
F-**LOSSIEST**
G-LOSSIEST
F-**LOUNDERS**
F-**LOURIEST**
B-**LOUSIEST**
LOVELIES-T
B-**LOWBALLS**
B-**LOWDOWNS**
S-LOWDOWNS
F-**LOWERIER**
F-**LOWERING**
G-LOWERING
P-**LOWLANDS**
C-**LUCKIEST**
P-LUCKIEST
P-**LUMBAGOS**
S-**LUMBERED**
S-**LUMBERER**
A-**LUMINOUS**
P-**LUMMIEST**
S-LUMMIEST
F-**LUMMOXES**
C-**LUMPIEST**
G-LUMPIEST
P-LUMPIEST
S-LUMPIEST
G-**LUNCHING**
LUNULATE-D
F-**LUSHIEST**
P-LUSHIEST
S-LUSHIEST
F-**LUSHNESS**
P-LUSHNESS
B-**LUSTERED**
C-LUSTERED
F-LUSTERED
F-**LUSTRATE**
LUSTRATE-D
B-**LUSTROUS**
LYOPHILE-D
LYRICISE-D
LYRICIZE-D
MACARISE-D
MACARIZE-D
MACARONI-C
MACERATE-D
MACULATE-D
MADERISE-D
MADERIZE-D
MADRASSA-H
MAGDALEN-E
MAGISTER-Y
MAGNESIA-N
MAGNIFIC-O
MAHARAJA-H
MAINLINE-D
MAINLINE-R
MALAXATE-D
MALINGER-Y
MALLEATE-D
MAMILLAR-Y
MAMMILLA-E
MANDARIN-E
MANDATOR-Y
MANDOLIN-E
MANICURE-D
MANIFEST-O
MANUBRIA-L
MARGARIN-E
MARINADE-D
MARINATE-D
MARSUPIA-L
S-**MASHINGS**
MASSACRE-D
MASSACRE-R
MASTODON-T
MATACHIN-A
MATACHIN-I
S-**MATCHING**
S-**MATTERED**
MATURATE-D
MAUSOLEA-N
MAXIMISE-D
MAXIMIZE-D
MAXIMIZE-R
A-**MAZEMENT**
MEDIATOR-Y
MEDICATE-D
MEDICINE-D
MEDICINE-R
MEDITATE-D
MEDULLAR-Y
MELANIZE-D
G-**MELINITE**
MELODISE-D
MELODIZE-D
MELODIZE-R
S-**MELTINGS**

MEMBRANE-D
MEMORISE-D
MEMORIZE-D
MEMORIZE-R
A-**MENAGING**
A-**MENDABLE**
E-MENDABLE
MENSTRUA-L
MEPHITIS-M
E-**MERGENCE**
E-**MERSIONS**
MESCALIN-E
MESHUGGA-H
MESOPHYL-L
METALISE-D
METALIZE-D
METHADON-E
E-**MICATING**
MICROCAR-D
E-**MICTIONS**
A-**MIDSHIPS**
E-**MIGRANTS**
E-**MIGRATED**
E-**MIGRATES**
MIGRATOR-Y
MILIARIA-L
MILITATE-D
MILLEPED-E
MILLINER-Y
MILLIPED-E
MINIBIKE-R
MINIMISE-D
MINIMIZE-D
MINIMIZE-R
S-**MIRKIEST**
MISATONE-D
MISCEGEN-E
MISDRIVE-N
MISENROL-L
MISFRAME-D
MISGAUGE-D
MISGRADE-D
MISGUIDE-D
MISGUIDE-R
MISJUDGE-D
MISLEARN-T
MISLEEKE-D
MISLODGE-D
MISMETRE-D
MISPARSE-D
MISPLACE-D
MISPOISE-D
MISPRICE-D
MISPRISE-D
MISPRIZE-D
MISQUOTE-D
MISRAISE-D
MISROUTE-D
MISSHAPE-D
MISSHAPE-N
E-**MISSIONS**
O-MISSIONS
MISSPACE-D
MISSPOKE-N
MISSTATE-D
MISSTYLE-D
MISTHROW-N
MISTITLE-D
MISTRACE-D
MISVALUE-D
MITIGATE-D
MOBILISE-D
MOBILISE-R
MOBILIZE-D
MOBILIZE-R

S-**MOCKINGS**
MODERATE-D
MODERATO-R
MODULATE-D
S-**MOLDERED**
MONETISE-D
MONETIZE-D
MONOTONE-D
S-**MOOCHING**
MOONFACE-D
MORALISE-D
MORALISE-R
A-**MORALISM**
A-**MORALIST**
A-**MORALITY**
MORALIZE-D
MORALIZE-R
A-**MORNINGS**
A-**MOROSITY**
MORTGAGE-D
MORTGAGE-E
MORTGAGE-R
A-**MORTISED**
A-**MORTISES**
MOSCHATE-L
S-**MOTHERED**
E-**MOTIONAL**
MOTIVATE-D
E-**MOTIVITY**
MOTORISE-D
MOTORIZE-D
S-**MOUCHING**
S-**MOULDERS**
MOUNTAIN-Y
A-**MOUNTING**
MRIDANGA-M
MUCKRAKE-D
MUCKRAKE-R
MULTIPED-E
MULTIPLE-T
MULTIPLE-X
MULTITON-E
MULTIUSE-R
MURICATE-D
MUSCADIN-E
A-**MUSETTES**
A-**MUSINGLY**
MUSTACHE-D
MUTILATE-D
MYOGRAPH-Y
A-**MYOTONIA**
MYSTAGOG-Y
K-**NAGGIEST**
S-NAGGIEST
S-**NAPPIEST**
S-**NARKIEST**
NARRATOR-Y
NASALISE-D
NASALIZE-D
G-**NATTIEST**
NAUSEATE-D
NAVICULA-R
NAVIGATE-D
NEBBISHE-R
NEBULISE-D
NEBULISE-R
NEBULIZE-D
NEBULIZE-R
NECKLACE-D
NEGATIVE-D
NERVINES-S
P-**NEUMATIC**
A-**NEURISMS**
K-**NEVELLED**
K-**NICKERED**

S-NICKERED
NICKNAME-D
NICKNAME-R
NICOTIAN-A
NICOTINE-D
S-**NIFFIEST**
S-**NIFTIEST**
S-**NIGGERED**
S-**NIGGLERS**
S-**NIGGLING**
NIGROSIN-E
S-**NIPPIEST**
K-**NOBBIEST**
S-NOBBIEST
K-**NOBBLING**
NODALISE-D
NODALIZE-D
A-**NOINTING**
NOMADISE-D
NOMADIZE-D
NOMINATE-D
NONDANCE-R
NOSEDIVE-D
NOTARISE-D
NOTARIZE-D
NOVELISE-D
NOVELISE-R
NOVELIZE-D
NOVELIZE-R
K-**NUBBIEST**
S-NUBBIEST
K-**NUBBLIER**
K-**NUBBLING**
NUBECULA-E
A-**NUCLEATE**
E-NUCLEATE
NUCLEATE-D
NUISANCE-R
E-**NUMERATE**
NUMERATE-D
NUMMULAR-Y
S-**NUZZLING**
OBDURATE-D
OBLIGATE-D
OBLIQUES-T
OBSCURES-T
OBSOLETE-D
OBTURATE-D
OBVOLUTE-D
OCCIPITA-L
OCCUPATE-D
L-**OCELLATE**
OCELLATE-D
T-**OCHERING**
J-**OCULARLY**
H-**ODOGRAPH**
H-**ODOMETER**
H-**ODOMETRY**
P-**OENOLOGY**
OENOPHIL-E
OENOPHIL-Y
C-**OFFERING**
G-OFFERING
B-**OILERIES**
S-**OILINESS**
OKEYDOKE-Y
B-**OLDENING**
G-OLDENING
OLIGARCH-Y
O-**OLOGISTS**
L-**OMENTUMS**
M-OMENTUMS
Z-**OOGAMETE**
Z-**OOGAMIES**
Z-**OOGAMOUS**

Z-**OOGENIES**
H-**OOLACHAN**
N-**OOLOGIES**
Z-OOLOGIES
Z-**OOLOGIST**
Z-**OOPHYTES**
Z-**OOPHYTIC**
Z-**OOSPERMS**
N-**OOSPHERE**
Z-**OOSPORES**
Z-**OOSPORIC**
B-**OOZINESS**
W-OOZINESS
OPALESCE-D
OPERCULA-R
OPPILATE-D
OPSIMATH-Y
OPSONIZE-D
OPTIMISE-D
OPTIMIZE-D
OPTIMIZE-R
M-**ORALISMS**
M-**ORALISTS**
B-**ORDERERS**
B-**ORDERING**
ORDINATE-D
ORECROWE-D
ORGANISE-D
ORGANISE-R
ORGANIZE-D
ORGANIZE-R
ORTHODOX-Y
P-**ORTHOSES**
P-**ORTOLANS**
OSCITATE-D
OSCULATE-D
H-**OSIERIES**
OSTEOGEN-Y
P-**OSTMARKS**
OSTRACOD-E
H-**OTTERING**
P-OTTERING
T-OTTERING
OUTARGUE-D
OUTBLAZE-D
OUTBRAVE-D
OUTBRIBE-D
OUTBROKE-N
OUTCASTE-D
OUTCHIDE-D
OUTCURSE-D
OUTDANCE-D
OUTDODGE-D
OUTDOORS-Y
OUTDREAM-T
OUTDRIVE-N
OUTFABLE-D
G-**OUTFLIES**
OUTGLARE-D
OUTGUIDE-D
OUTLEARN-T
OUTPLACE-D
OUTPLACE-R
OUTPRICE-D
OUTPRIZE-D
OUTQUOTE-D
OUTRAISE-D
OUTRANGE-D
OUTSCORE-D
OUTSERVE-D
OUTSHAME-D
OUTSHINE-D
OUTSKATE-D
OUTSMILE-D
OUTSMOKE-D

OUTSNORE-D
OUTSPOKE-N
OUTSTARE-D
OUTSTATE-D
OUTTHROW-N
OUTTRADE-D
OUTVALUE-D
OUTVOICE-D
OUTWASTE-D
G-**OUTWEEDS**
N-**OVATIONS**
C-**OVERABLE**
C-**OVERAGES**
C-**OVERALLS**
OVERBAKE-D
OVERBLOW-N
OVERBORN-E
OVERBURN-T
OVERCOME-R
OVERCROW-D
OVERCURE-D
OVERDARE-D
OVERDOSE-D
OVERDRAW-N
OVERFLOW-N
OVERGIVE-N
OVERGROW-N
OVERHALE-D
OVERHATE-D
OVERHEAR-D
OVERHOPE-D
OVERHYPE-D
OVERLADE-D
OVERLADE-N
OVERLEAP-T
C-**OVERLETS**
OVERLIVE-D
OVERLOVE-D
OVERMINE-D
OVERNAME-D
OVERPLAN-T
OVERRAKE-D
OVERRATE-D
OVERRIDE-R
OVERRIPE-N
OVERRULE-D
OVERRULE-R
OVERSAVE-D
OVERSIZE-D
C-**OVERSLIP**
OVERSLIP-T
OVERTAKE-N
OVERTHIN-K
OVERTIME-D
OVERTIME-R
OVERTIRE-D
C-**OVERTURE**
OVERTURE-D
OVERTYPE-D
OVERURGE-D
OVERVOTE-D
OVERWEAR-Y
R-**OYSTERED**
R-**OYSTERER**
O-**PACIFIED**
O-**PACIFIES**
PAGANISE-D
PAGANIZE-D
PAGANIZE-R
PAGINATE-D
PALESTRA-E
PALISADE-D
PALLIATE-D
PALMIPED-E
PALPEBRA-E

PALPEBRA-L
PANDEMIA-N
PANNIKEL-L
PANTALON-E
PAPALISE-D
PAPALIZE-D
PAPILLAR-Y
S-**PARABLES**
PARAFFIN-E
PARAFFIN-Y
PARALYSE-D
PARALYSE-R
PARALYZE-D
PARALYZE-R
PARAMENT-A
PARANOIA-C
S-**PARKIEST**
PAROCHIN-E
PAROEMIA-C
PAROEMIA-L
PASTICCI-O
PASTORAL-E
PASTORAL-I
A-**PATHETIC**
PATHOGEN-Y
PATINATE-D
PATINIZE-D
PATRIATE-D
S-**PATTERED**
PEARLIES-T
S-**PECKIEST**
S-**PECTATES**
S-**PECULATE**
PECULATE-D
PEDERAST-Y
PEDICURE-D
PEDIGREE-D
PEDIPALP-I
PEDUNCLE-D
PEJORATE-D
PENALISE-D
PENALIZE-D
PENDICLE-R
PENSIONE-D
PENSIONE-R
PENTARCH-Y
PENTOSAN-E
PENUMBRA-E
PENUMBRA-L
PERCEIVE-D
PERCEIVE-R
PEREGRIN-E
PERFECTO-R
PERFUMER-Y
A-**PERIODIC**
PERIPTER-Y
PERMEATE-D
PERORATE-D
PEROXIDE-D
PERSPIRE-D
PERSUADE-D
PERSUADE-R
PERSWADE-D
A-**PERTNESS**
PERVERSE-R
PERVIATE-D
A-**PETALOUS**
PETECHIA-E
PETECHIA-L
PHALANGE-R
U-**PHANGING**
PHANTASM-A
PHENAZIN-E
E-**PHORATES**
PHOSPHID-E
PHOSPHIN-E
PHOSPHOR-E
PHOTOGEN-E
PHOTOGEN-Y
PHYLARCH-Y
A-**PIARISTS**
PICKADIL-L
E-**PICRITIC**
S-**PIGHTING**
S-**PIKELETS**
S-**PILLAGES**
S-**PILLINGS**
PINAFORE-D
S-**PINDLING**
S-**PINELIKE**
O-**PINIONED**
PINNACLE-D
S-**PINNINGS**
PINNIPED-E
PIPELINE-D
PIRLICUE-D
PISCATOR-Y
E-**PISTOLET**
S-**PITTINGS**
PLACEMEN-T
PLACENTA-E
PLACENTA-L
PLANARIA-N
S-**PLASHERS**
S-**PLASHIER**
S-**PLASHING**
S-**PLATTERS**
S-**PLATTING**
U-**PLEADING**
PLEASURE-D
PLEASURE-R
PLEONAST-E
U-**PLIGHTED**
U-**PLIGHTER**
U-**PLINKING**
PLOTTIES-T
POLARISE-D
POLARISE-R
POLARIZE-D
POLARIZE-R
POLEMISE-D
POLEMIZE-D
POLONISE-D
POLONIZE-D
POLYARCH-Y
POLYGLOT-T
POLYMATH-Y
POLYONYM-Y
POLYPHON-E
POLYPHON-Y
S-**PONGIEST**
PONTIFIC-E
S-**PONTOONS**
POPULATE-D
PORPOISE-D
S-**PORTABLE**
S-**PORTANCE**
S-**PORTIEST**
S-**PORTLESS**
PORTOLAN-I
PORTOLAN-O
POSITIVE-R
POSSIBLE-R
POSTCAVA-E
POSTCAVA-L
POSTCODE-D
POSTDATE-D
POSTPONE-D
POSTPONE-R
POSTPOSE-D
S-**POTTIEST**
POULTICE-D
POURSUIT-T
POURTRAY-D
S-**POUTIEST**
S-**POUTINGS**
POZZOLAN-A
PRACTICE-D
PRACTICE-R
PRACTISE-D
PRACTISE-R
PRAECAVA-E
U-**PRAISERS**
U-**PRAISING**
S-**PRATTLED**
S-**PRATTLES**
U-**PREACHED**
U-**PREACHES**
PREAMBLE-D
PRECISES-T
PRECLUDE-D
PREDATOR-Y
PREFROZE-N
PREJUDGE-D
PREJUDGE-R
PRELATES-S
PREMIERE-D
PRENTICE-D
PREPASTE-D
PREPENSE-D
PREPLACE-D
PREPPIES-T
PREPRICE-D
PRESBYTE-R
PRESCORE-D
PRESERVE-D
PRESERVE-R
PRESHAPE-D
PRESIDIA-L
PRESLICE-D
PRESSURE-D
PRETASTE-D
PRETERIT-E
PRETTIES-T
PREUNITE-D
PRIEDIEU-X
S-**PRIGGERS**
S-**PRIGGING**
PRIMROSE-D
PRINCESS-E
PRINCIPI-A
S-**PRINTERS**
S-**PRINTING**
A-**PRIORITY**
PRISSIES-T
PRIVATES-T
PROCURES-S
PRODITOR-Y
PRODNOSE-D
PRODROMI-C
PROGNOSE-D
PROGRADE-D
PROLAMIN-E
PROLAPSE-D
U-**PROLLING**
PROLOGUE-D
PROLONGE-D
PROLONGE-R
PROMULGE-D
PROROGUE-D
PROTAMIN-E
PROTOXID-E
PROTOZOA-L
PROTOZOA-N
PROTRUDE-D
PROVEDOR-E
PROVISOR-Y
PTERYGIA-L
PTYALISE-D
PTYALIZE-D
S-**PUDDINGS**
PULSATOR-Y
PULVILLE-D
PULVILLI-O
PUMICATE-D
PUNCTATE-D
PUNCTURE-D
PUNCTURE-R
S-**PUNKIEST**
PUPILLAR-Y
PURCHASE-D
PURCHASE-R
PURLICUE-D
S-**PURLINGS**
S-**PURRINGS**
S-**PUTTERED**
S-**PUTTERER**
PYCNIDIA-L
A-**PYREXIAS**
PYRITISE-D
PYRITIZE-D
PYROLIZE-D
PYROLYSE-D
PYROLYZE-D
PYROLYZE-R
S-**QUADDING**
QUADRATE-D
QUADRIGA-E
QUAGMIRE-D
S-**QUAILING**
QUANTISE-D
QUANTIZE-D
QUANTIZE-R
QUARTETT-E
QUARTETT-I
QUARTETT-O
S-**QUASHERS**
S-**QUASHING**
QUEENIES-T
S-**QUELCHED**
S-**QUELCHES**
S-**QUINCHED**
S-**QUINCHES**
QUINOLIN-E
QUINTETT-E
QUINTETT-I
QUINTETT-O
E-**QUIPPERS**
E-**QUIPPING**
S-**QUIRTING**
S-**QUITCHES**
B-**RABBLERS**
D-RABBLERS
G-RABBLERS
B-**RABBLING**
D-RABBLING
G-RABBLING
RACEMISE-D
RACEMIZE-D
RACHILLA-E
A-**RACHISES**
T-**RACHITIS**
B-**RACKETED**
C-**RACKINGS**
F-RACKINGS
T-RACKINGS
E-**RADIATED**
E-**RADIATES**
RADIATOR-Y
E-**RADICATE**
RADICATE-D
C-**RAFTSMAN**
D-RAFTSMAN
C-**RAFTSMEN**
D-RAFTSMEN
B-**RAGGIEST**
C-RAGGIEST
D-RAGGIEST
F-**RAGGINGS**
D-**RAGGLING**
F-**RAGMENTS**
T-**RAILHEAD**
T-**RAILLESS**
T-**RAINBAND**
B-**RAINIEST**
G-RAINIEST
B-**RAINLESS**
T-RAINLESS
B-**RAINWASH**
P-**RAISINGS**
RAKEHELL-Y
B-**RAMBLING**
RAMPAUGE-D
T-**RAMPINGS**
B-**RANCHERS**
B-**RANCHING**
C-RANCHING
O-**RANGIEST**
P-**RANKINGS**
C-**RANKLING**
P-RANKLING
C-**RANKNESS**
F-RANKNESS
G-**RAPESEED**
T-**RAPPINGS**
W-RAPPINGS
B-**RASHNESS**
W-**RASSLING**
B-**RATCHETS**
F-**RATCHING**
G-**RATIFIED**
G-**RATIFIER**
G-**RATIFIES**
RATIONAL-E
B-**RATLINGS**
B-**RATTIEST**
P-**RATTLERS**
B-**RATTLING**
P-RATTLING
B-**RAUNCHED**
C-RAUNCHED
G-RAUNCHED
B-**RAUNCHES**
C-RAUNCHES
G-RAUNCHES
T-**RAVELERS**
G-**RAVELING**
T-RAVELING
G-**RAVELLED**
T-RAVELLED
T-**RAVELLER**
C-**RAVENING**
Y-**RAVISHED**
REACCEDE-D
REACCUSE-D
B-**REACHERS**
P-REACHERS
T-REACHERS
A-**REACHING**
B-REACHING
P-REACHING
P-**REACTING**
P-**READAPTS**
T-**READINGS**
P-**READMITS**

P-**READOPTS**
READVISE-D
REAEDIFY-E
P-**REALLOTS**
C-**REAMIEST**
D-REAMIEST
P-**REARMING**
REAROUSE-D
P-**REASSIGN**
REASSUME-D
REASSURE-D
REASSURE-R
B-**REASTING**
P-**REBILLED**
P-**REBOILED**
P-**REBOOKED**
REBOTTLE-D
P-**RECEDING**
RECENTRE-D
P-**RECEPTOR**
P-**RECESSED**
P-**RECESSES**
RECHANGE-D
RECHARGE-D
RECHARGE-R
P-**RECHECKS**
RECIRCLE-D
P-**RECISION**
F-**RECKLING**
P-**RECLEANS**
RECLOTHE-D
P-**RECODING**
P-**RECOOKED**
RECOUPLE-D
RECOURSE-D
RECREATE-D
E-**RECTIONS**
P-**RECURING**
REDAMAGE-D
REDARGUE-D
P-**REDATING**
T-**REDDLING**
REDECIDE-D
P-**REDEFINE**
REDEFINE-D
P-**REDESIGN**
P-**REDIGEST**
REDISTIL-L
REDIVIDE-D
REDOUBLE-D
P-**REDRILLS**
B-**REECHING**
G-**REEDIEST**
B-**REEDINGS**
P-**REEDITED**
C-**REEKIEST**
P-**REELECTS**
REEMERGE-D
P-**REENACTS**
G-**REENGAGE**
REENGAGE-D
P-**REERECTS**
REEXPOSE-D
P-**REFACING**
P-**REFERRED**
P-**REFERRER**
P-**REFIGURE**
REFIGURE-D
P-**REFILING**
P-**REFILLED**
P-**REFIRING**
P-**REFIXING**
P-**REFORMAT**
REFORMAT-E
P-**REFORMED**

P-**REFREEZE**
REFRINGE-D
P-**REFROZEN**
REGELATE-D
P-**REGNANCY**
REGROOVE-D
REGULATE-D
REGULISE-D
REGULIZE-D
REHANDLE-D
REHEARSE-D
REHEARSE-R
P-**REHEATED**
P-**REHEATER**
P-**REHIRING**
REIGNITE-D
REILLUME-D
REIMPOSE-D
REINCITE-D
REINDUCE-D
REINFUSE-D
REINJURE-D
REINSURE-D
REINSURE-R
REINVADE-D
REINVITE-D
REINVOKE-D
P-**REJUDGED**
P-**REJUDGES**
REJUGGLE-D
REKINDLE-D
P-**RELATION**
P-**RELAUNCH**
RELEGATE-D
RELOCATE-D
RELOCATE-E
RELUMINE-D
P-**REMARKET**
REMARQUE-D
C-**REMASTER**
C-**REMATING**
T-**REMBLING**
REMEDIAT-E
REMIGATE-D
P-**REMISING**
P-**REMIXING**
P-**REMODIFY**
P-**REMOLDED**
P-**REMOTION**
P-**REMOVING**
C-**RENATURE**
RENATURE-D
RENEGADE-D
RENFORCE-D
P-**RENOTIFY**
RENOUNCE-D
RENOUNCE-R
RENOVATE-D
P-**RENUMBER**
RENVERSE-D
P-**REOCCUPY**
REOPPOSE-D
P-**REORDAIN**
P-**REORDERS**
P-**REPACKED**
REPARTEE-D
P-**REPASTED**
P-**REPAYING**
REPEOPLE-D
REPERUSE-D
REPHRASE-D
P-**REPLACED**
P-**REPLACES**
REPLEDGE-D
REPLICAS-E

REPLUNGE-D
P-**REPONING**
P-**REPOSING**
REPREEVE-D
P-**REPRICED**
P-**REPRICES**
REPRIEVE-D
P-**REPRINTS**
REPURSUE-D
REQUOYLE-D
P-**RERECORD**
P-**REREVIEW**
REREVISE-D
RESADDLE-D
RESALUTE-D
RESAMPLE-D
P-**RESCHOOL**
P-**RESCINDS**
P-**RESCORED**
P-**RESCORES**
P-**RESCREEN**
P-**RESCRIPT**
P-**RESEASON**
RESECURE-D
P-**RESELECT**
RESEMBLE-D
RESEMBLE-R
P-**RESENTED**
P-**RESENTER**
P-**RESERVED**
P-**RESERVER**
P-**RESERVES**
RESETTLE-D
P-**RESHAPED**
P-**RESHAPES**
P-**RESHOWED**
P-**RESIDENT**
P-**RESIDERS**
P-**RESIDING**
P-**RESIFTED**
RESINATE-D
RESINISE-D
RESINIZE-D
P-**RESOAKED**
RESOLUTE-R
RESONATE-D
P-**RESORTED**
RESOURCE-D
RESPLICE-D
RESPONSE-R
P-**RESTAMPS**
C-**RESTINGS**
C-**RESTLESS**
RESTRAIN-T
P-**RESTRESS**
P-**RESTRIKE**
RESTRING-E
RESTRIVE-N
P-**RESUMERS**
P-**RESUMING**
RETACKLE-D
P-**RETAPING**
P-**RETASTED**
P-**RETASTES**
P-**RETESTED**
RETICULA-R
C-**RETINOID**
RETINULA-E
RETINULA-R
P-**RETRAINS**
P-**RETREATS**
P-**RETRIALS**
RETRIEVE-D
RETRIEVE-R
P-**RETYPING**

P-**REUNIONS**
P-**REUNITED**
P-**REUNITES**
B-**REVETTED**
P-**REVIEWED**
P-**REVIEWER**
P-**REVISING**
P-**REVISION**
P-**REVISORS**
P-**REWARMED**
P-**REWASHED**
P-**REWASHES**
RHIZOBIA-L
RHODAMIN-E
A-**RHYTHMIC**
C-**RIBBINGS**
C-**RIBWORKS**
RICERCAR-E
RICERCAR-I
F-**RICHTING**
B-**RICKYARD**
G-**RIDDLING**
B-**RIDGINGS**
RIDICULE-D
RIDICULE-R
T-**RIFLINGS**
D-**RIFTIEST**
D-**RIFTLESS**
F-**RIGGINGS**
P-RIGGINGS
B-**RIGHTENS**
F-RIGHTENS
B-**RIGHTEST**
F-**RIGHTFUL**
F-**RIGHTING**
F-**RIGIDEST**
RIGIDISE-D
F-**RIGIDITY**
RIGIDIZE-D
T-**RIMESTER**
G-**RIMINESS**
T-**RIMMINGS**
C-**RIMPLING**
B-**RINGINGS**
C-RINGINGS
W-RINGINGS
RINGSIDE-R
C-**RIPPLERS**
T-RIPPLERS
C-**RIPPLING**
T-RIPPLING
F-**RISKIEST**
RITORNEL-L
RIVALISE-D
RIVALIZE-D
D-**RIVELLED**
B-**ROACHING**
B-**ROADSIDE**
B-**ROADWAYS**
ROBOTISE-D
ROBOTIZE-D
C-**ROCKETED**
F-**ROCKINGS**
F-**ROCKLESS**
D-**ROLLINGS**
T-ROLLINGS
ROMANISE-D
ROMANIZE-D
P-**ROOFINGS**
P-**ROOFLESS**
B-**ROOMIEST**
D-**ROOPIEST**
C-**ROQUETED**
C-**ROQUETTE**
P-**ROSINESS**

ROSTELLA-R
E-**ROSTRATE**
P-ROSTRATE
ROSTRATE-D
ROTAVATE-D
ROTOVATE-D
ROUGHHEW-N
ROULETTE-D
G-**ROUNDERS**
G-**ROUNDING**
C-**ROUPIEST**
T-**ROUSSEAU**
D-**ROUTHIER**
G-**ROUTINGS**
T-ROUTINGS
T-**ROWELING**
T-**ROWELLED**
D-**ROWNDING**
ROYALISE-D
ROYALIZE-D
D-**RUBBINGS**
G-**RUBBLING**
T-**RUCKLING**
C-**RUDDIEST**
C-**RUDDLING**
C-**RUDENESS**
P-**RUDERIES**
T-**RUFFLING**
D-**RUGGIEST**
G-**RUMBLERS**
C-**RUMBLIER**
G-RUMBLIER
C-**RUMBLING**
D-RUMBLING
G-RUMBLING
RUMINATE-D
C-**RUMMIEST**
C-**RUMPLIER**
C-**RUMPLING**
F-RUMPLING
C-**RUNKLING**
T-**RUNNIONS**
RURALISE-D
RURALIZE-D
B-**RUSHIEST**
B-**RUSHINGS**
T-**RUSTABLE**
C-**RUSTIEST**
T-RUSTIEST
C-**RUSTLESS**
T-RUSTLESS
T-**RUTHLESS**
I-**SABELLAS**
SABOTAGE-D
SAFRANIN-E
SAGINATE-D
SALINIZE-D
SALIVATE-D
SALTINES-S
SANDARAC-H
SANGUINE-D
SANITATE-D
SANITISE-D
SANITIZE-D
SANNYASI-N
SAPPHIRE-D
SARABAND-E
SATIRISE-D
SATIRIZE-D
SATURATE-D
SAVORIES-T
E-**SCALADES**
E-**SCALLOPS**
SCANTIES-T
SCAPULAR-Y

E-**SCARPING**
SCAVENGE-D
SCAVENGE-R
SCELERAT-E
A-**SCENDING**
SCHEDULE-D
SCHEDULE-R
SCHLIERE-N
SCHMALTZ-Y
SCHMOOSE-D
SCHMOOZE-D
SCHNECKE-N
SCIATICA-L
SCLEREID-E
SCLEROSE-D
SCOUTHER-Y
SCRABBLE-D
SCRABBLE-R
SCRAMBLE-D
SCRAMBLE-R
SCRATTLE-D
SCRIBBLE-D
SCRIBBLE-R
A-**SCRIBING**
E-SCRIBING
SCRIGGLE-D
SCROGGIE-R
SCROUNGE-D
SCROUNGE-R
SCROWDGE-D
SCURVIES-T
SCUTELLA-R
SECRETES-T
SECRETIN-G
SECRETOR-Y
SEIGNEUR-Y
SEIGNIOR-Y
SELVEDGE-D
SEMIDOME-D
SEMIMATT-E
SEMINATE-D
SEMUNCIA-E
SEMUNCIA-L
SENSIBLE-R
SENSILLA-E
SENSORIA-L
SENTENCE-D
SENTENCE-R
A-**SEPALOUS**
SEPARATE-D
SEPTARIA-N
SEPTUPLE-D
SEPTUPLE-T
SEQUENCE-D
SEQUENCE-R
SERAPHIN-E
SERENADE-D
SERENADE-R
SERGEANT-Y
SERJEANT-Y
SEROTYPE-D
SEXTUPLE-D
SEXTUPLE-T
A-**SEXUALLY**
SHAMIANA-H
SHAUCHLE-D
SHECHITA-H
SHEENIES-T
SHEEPCOT-E
Y-**SHENDING**
SHIGELLA-E
SHILLALA-H
SHIVAREE-D
SHODDIES-T
SHOWCASE-D

SHUNPIKE-D
SHUNPIKE-R
SIBILATE-D
SICKLIES-T
SIDELINE-D
SIDELINE-R
SIDERATE-D
SIGHTSEE-N
SIGHTSEE-R
SIGNORIA-L
SILICATE-D
SILICULA-E
SIMILISE-D
SIMILIZE-D
SIMONIZE-D
SIMPLIST-E
SIMULATE-D
SINGSONG-Y
SINICISE-D
SINICIZE-D
SIRENISE-D
SIRENIZE-D
SKELLIES-T
A-**SKEWNESS**
SKILLIES-T
SKYWRITE-R
SLAISTER-Y
I-**SLANDERS**
SLIPCASE-D
SLIVOVIC-A
SLUGHORN-E
SMOOTHES-T
A-**SMOULDER**
SNAKEBIT-E
SNEESHIN-G
SNOTTIES-T
SNOWSHOE-D
SNOWSHOE-R
SOBERISE-D
SOBERIZE-D
SODOMISE-D
SODOMIZE-D
SOLARISE-D
SOLARIZE-D
I-**SOLATING**
I-**SOLATION**
SOLECISE-D
SOLECIZE-D
SOLFEGGI-O
SOLIDATE-D
SOMNIATE-D
SONICATE-D
SORORISE-D
SORORIZE-D
SOUVLAKI-A
SPARKIES-T
SPARKLES-S
SPATLESE-N
SPECIATE-D
SPECKLES-S
SPECTATE-D
SPELDRIN-G
A-**SPERSING**
A-**SPIRANTS**
A-**SPIRATED**
SPIRILLA-R
A-**SPLENIUM**
SPLINTER-Y
SPLUTTER-Y
SPOLIATE-D
SPOONIES-T
SPORIDIA-L
SPOROZOA-N
A-**SPORTING**
E-**SPOUSALS**

E-**SPOUSING**
SPRACKLE-D
SPRADDLE-D
SPRANGLE-D
SPRATTLE-D
SPREATHE-D
SPREETHE-D
SPRINGAL-D
SPRINGLE-T
SPRINKLE-D
SPRINKLE-R
SPUILZIE-D
SPUNKIES-T
SPURRIES-T
SQUABBLE-D
SQUABBLE-R
SQUADRON-E
SQUATTLE-D
SQUEAKER-Y
SQUEEGEE-D
SQUIGGLE-D
SQUILGEE-D
E-**SQUIRESS**
E-**SQUIRING**
SQUIRREL-Y
E-**STABLISH**
STAGGIES-T
STAGNATE-D
STAMPEDE-D
STAMPEDE-R
STANCHES-T
STARGAZE-D
STARGAZE-R
A-**STARTING**
STEADIES-T
STEAMIES-T
STEELIES-T
E-**STEEMING**
STEGODON-T
STELLATE-D
A-**STEROIDS**
A-**STHENIAS**
STICKIES-T
STIPULAR-Y
STITCHER-Y
STOCKADE-D
STOMODEA-L
A-**STONYING**
E-**STOPPAGE**
E-**STOPPING**
A-**STOUNDED**
A-**STRADDLE**
STRADDLE-D
STRADDLE-R
STRAGGLE-D
STRAGGLE-R
E-**STRANGER**
STRANGLE-D
STRANGLE-R
STRAVAGE-D
E-**STRAYING**
STREIGNE-D
STRELITZ-I
E-**STRICHES**
O-STRICHES
STRICKLE-D
STRIDDLE-D
A-**STRINGED**
A-**STRINGER**
STRINKLE-D
STROBILA-E
STRODDLE-D
STRONGYL-E
STRONTIA-N
STRUGGLE-D

STRUGGLE-R
STUBBIES-T
STUMPIES-T
A-**STUNNING**
STUPRATE-D
STURDIES-T
SUBAHDAR-Y
SUBCOSTA-E
SUBCOSTA-L
SUBERISE-D
SUBERIZE-D
SUBITISE-D
SUBITIZE-D
SUBLEASE-D
SUBLIMES-T
SUBLUNAR-Y
SUBMENTA-L
SUBMERGE-D
SUBMERSE-D
SUBSERVE-D
SUBTITLE-D
SUBTOPIA-N
SUBTRUDE-D
SUBVERSE-D
SUDAMINA-L
SUFFLATE-D
SULPHATE-D
SUNBATHE-D
SUNBATHE-R
SUPERATE-D
SUPINATE-D
SUPREMES-T
SURCEASE-D
SURPLICE-D
SURPRISE-D
SURPRISE-R
SURPRIZE-D
SUSPENSE-R
SWANKIES-T
SYLLABLE-D
A-**SYMMETRY**
SYMPODIA-L
SYMPOSIA-C
SYMPOSIA-L
A-**SYNAPSES**
A-**SYNAPSIS**
SYNCYTIA-L
A-**SYNDETIC**
SYNEDRIA-L
A-**SYNERGIA**
SYNOPSIS-E
SYPHILIS-E
A-**SYSTOLES**
S-**TABLINGS**
TABOURIN-G
TABULATE-D
S-**TACKINGS**
S-**TAGGIEST**
TAILGATE-D
TAILGATE-R
TAILPIPE-D
S-**TAKEOUTS**
S-**TALKIEST**
S-**TALKINGS**
S-**TALLAGES**
TALLIATE-D
S-**TAMPINGS**
S-**TANNATES**
TARANTAS-S
S-**TARRIEST**
S-**TARRINGS**
TARTINES-S
TAUTONYM-Y
TAWDRIES-T
S-**TEAMINGS**

TEGMENTA-L
TELEPATH-Y
TELESTIC-H
TELEVISE-D
TELEVISE-R
A-**TEMPORAL**
TENTACLE-D
TENTORIA-L
TESSELLA-E
TESSELLA-R
TETANISE-D
TETANIZE-D
TETRAPOD-Y
TETRARCH-Y
TETROXID-E
A-**THEISTIC**
A-**THEMATIC**
A-**THEOLOGY**
THEORISE-D
THEORISE-R
THEORIZE-D
THEORIZE-R
THEOSOPH-Y
THEREFOR-E
THERIACA-L
THINGIES-T
E-**THIONINE**
THIOPHEN-E
THRAPPLE-D
THROPPLE-D
THROTTLE-D
THROTTLE-R
THYROXIN-E
S-**TICKINGS**
S-**TICKLERS**
S-**TICKLING**
S-**TICKSEED**
TIDDLIES-T
TIDIVATE-D
S-**TILLAGES**
S-**TILLIEST**
S-**TILLINGS**
S-**TILTINGS**
TINCTURE-D
TINPLATE-D
S-**TINTIEST**
S-**TINTINGS**
S-**TINTLESS**
S-**TIPPLERS**
S-**TIPPLING**
TIPPYTOE-D
TITIVATE-D
TITUBATE-D
TOASTIES-T
S-**TOCCATAS**
TOLERATE-D
TOLUIDIN-E
A-**TONALITY**
S-**TONELESS**
A-**TONICITY**
S-**TOPPINGS**
S-**TOPPLING**
TORCHIER-E
TORQUATE-D
TOTALISE-D
TOTALISE-R
TOTALIZE-D
TOTALIZE-R
S-**TOWAWAYS**
TRABEATE-D
TRACHEID-E
S-**TRAIKING**
S-**TRAINERS**
S-**TRAINING**
TRAMLINE-D

S-**TRAMMELS**
S-**TRAMPING**
S-**TRANGLES**
TRANSFIX-T
TRANSUDE-D
TRANSUME-D
TRAPEZIA-L
S-**TRAPLINE**
S-**TRAPPERS**
S-**TRAPPIER**
S-**TRAPPING**
TRAUCHLE-D
TRAVERSE-D
TRAVERSE-R
TREACHER-Y
TREADLES-S
TREASURE-D
TREASURE-R
TRENDIES-T
TREPHINE-D
TREPHINE-R
S-**TRESSING**
TRESSURE-D
TRIANGLE-D
TRICHINA-E
TRICHINA-L
S-**TRICKLED**
S-**TRICKLES**
TRICKLES-S
TRICYCLE-D
TRICYCLE-R
TRIENNIA-L
S-**TRIGGING**
TRIHEDRA-L
S-**TRIPIEST**
S-**TRIPLING**
TRIPLOID-Y
S-**TRIPPERS**
S-**TRIPPING**
TRITIATE-D
TRITICAL-E
TRIUMVIR-I
TRIUMVIR-Y
TRIVALVE-D
TROCHILI-C
TROCHLEA-E
TROCHLEA-R
S-**TROLLERS**
S-**TROLLING**
A-**TROPHIED**
A-**TROPHIES**
A-**TROPINES**
A-**TROPISMS**
S-**TROSSERS**
S-**TROUTING**
S-**TRUMPETS**
TRUNCATE-D
TRUSTIES-T
S-**TUBBIEST**
TUBERCLE-D
TUBULATE-D
S-**TUMBLERS**
S-**TUMBLING**
S-**TUMPIEST**
TUNICATE-D
S-**TUNNINGS**
TURQUOIS-E
TUTORISE-D
TUTORIZE-D
TYRANNES-S
TYRANNIS-E
P-**UBERTIES**
D-**UBIETIES**
ULCERATE-D
ULTIMATE-D
C-**UMBERING**
L-UMBERING
N-UMBERING
S-**UNBATHED**
S-**UNBEATEN**
S-**UNBLINDS**
S-**UNBLOCKS**
S-**UNBONNET**
UNBRIDLE-D
S-**UNBRIGHT**
UNBUCKLE-D
UNBUNDLE-D
UNBUNDLE-R
S-**UNBURNED**
UNCHARGE-D
S-**UNCHOKES**
R-**UNCINATE**
UNCINATE-D
UNCLOTHE-D
UNCOUPLE-D
UNCOUPLE-R
UNCREATE-D
F-**UNCTIONS**
J-UNCTIONS
UNDAZZLE-D
UNDERBIT-E
UNDERSAY-E
UNDERSEA-L
UNDERUSE-D
UNDOUBLE-D
UNDULATE-D
G-**UNFOUGHT**
P-**UNGENTLY**
UNHEALTH-Y
UNHEARSE-D
G-**UNHOUSES**
C-**UNIFORMS**
M-**UNIFYING**
UNIONISE-D
UNIONIZE-D
M-**UNITIONS**
P-UNITIONS
G-**UNMAKERS**
UNMANTLE-D
UNMINGLE-D
UNMUFFLE-D
UNMUZZLE-D
G-**UNPAPERS**
UNPEOPLE-D
UNPRAISE-D
UNPUZZLE-D
UNRIDDLE-D
UNRIDDLE-R
R-**UNROUNDS**
UNRUFFLE-D
UNSADDLE-D
UNSETTLE-D
UNSLUICE-D
UNSPHERE-D
UNSTABLE-R
G-**UNSTICKS**
G-**UNSTOCKS**
S-**UNSTRUCK**
UNSWATHE-D
UNTACKLE-D
UNTANGLE-D
S-**UNTANNED**
UNTHRIFT-Y
UNTHRONE-D
UNTIDIES-T
C-**UPBEARER**
R-**URALITES**
URBANISE-D
URBANIZE-D
UREDINIA-L
T-**URGENTLY**
UROPYGIA-L
O-**UROSCOPY**
B-**URSIFORM**
URTICATE-D
M-**USEFULLY**
H-**USHERING**
P-**USTULATE**
M-**UTTERERS**
P-UTTERERS
B-**UTTERING**
G-UTTERING
M-UTTERING
P-UTTERING
VACCINIA-L
E-**VACUATED**
E-**VACUATES**
E-**VAGINATE**
VAGINATE-D
VAGINULA-E
VALIDATE-D
VALORISE-D
VALORIZE-D
E-**VALUATED**
E-**VALUATES**
E-**VALUATOR**
VAMBRACE-D
E-**VANISHED**
E-**VANISHES**
VAPORISE-D
VAPORISE-R
VAPORIZE-D
VAPORIZE-R
VAPULATE-D
VARICOSE-D
O-**VARIOLES**
A-**VASCULAR**
A-**VAUNTING**
VEGETATE-D
VELARISE-D
VELARIZE-D
VENENATE-D
VENERATE-D
A-**VENGEFUL**
A-**VENTAILE**
A-**VENTAILS**
E-**VENTINGS**
E-**VENTLESS**
A-**VENTRING**
A-**VENTURES**
VERATRIN-E
VERJUICE-D
O-**VERMINED**
A-**VERSIONS**
E-VERSIONS
VERTEBRA-E
VERTEBRA-L
VESICATE-D
VESICULA-E
VESICULA-R
VESTIGIA-L
K-**VETCHIER**
VEXILLAR-Y
VIBRATOR-Y
VIBRISSA-E
VIDEOTEX-T
VIGILANT-E
VIGNETTE-D
VIGNETTE-R
VILLAGER-Y
E-**VINCIBLE**
E-**VINCIBLY**
VIRTUOSI-C
A-**VIRULENT**
VISAGIST-E
VISCOUNT-Y
VITALISE-D
VITALISE-R
VITALIZE-D
VITALIZE-R
VITELLIN-E
VOCALISE-D
VOCALISE-R
VOCALIZE-D
VOCALIZE-R
A-**VOCATION**
E-VOCATION
E-**VOCATIVE**
A-**VOIDABLE**
A-**VOIDANCE**
VOLITATE-D
VOLPLANE-D
VOLUMISE-D
VOLUMIZE-D
E-**VOLUTION**
A-**VOUCHERS**
A-**VOUCHING**
VOUTSAFE-D
VOWELISE-D
VOWELIZE-D
E-**VULGATES**
VULSELLA-E
S-**WADDLERS**
T-WADDLERS
S-**WADDLING**
T-WADDLING
A-**WAKENERS**
A-**WAKENING**
S-**WALLOWED**
S-**WALLOWER**
T-**WANGLERS**
T-**WANGLING**
S-**WANKIEST**
WARDROBE-R
WARFARIN-G
S-**WARMINGS**
S-**WASHIEST**
S-**WASHINGS**
T-**WATTLING**
S-**WEARINGS**
T-**WEEDIEST**
S-**WEEPIEST**
S-**WEEPINGS**
S-**WELLHEAD**
D-**WELLINGS**
S-WELLINGS
S-**WELTERED**
WHEELIES-T
WHEREFOR-E
WHIFFLER-Y
WHIMSIES-T
WHINNIES-T
WHIPCORD-Y
WHIRLIES-T
T-**WIDDLING**
T-**WIGGIEST**
T-**WIGHTING**
WINDBLOW-N
WINDBURN-T
D-**WINDLING**
S-WINDLING
S-**WINERIES**
S-**WINGBEAT**
S-**WINGEING**
T-WINGEING
S-**WINGIEST**
T-**WINKLERS**
T-**WINKLING**
T-**WINNINGS**
WIREDRAW-N
S-**WISHINGS**
S-**WITCHIER**
T-WITCHIER
S-**WITCHING**
T-WITCHING
WITHDRAW-N
S-**WITHERED**
T-**WITTERED**
T-**WITTINGS**
WOBBLIES-T
WOMANISE-D
WOMANISE-R
WOMANIZE-D
WOMANIZE-R
WOOLLIES-T
S-**WOOSHING**
S-**WORDLESS**
S-**WORDPLAY**
WORMHOLE-D
WORTHIES-T
S-**WOUNDING**
XYLOIDIN-E
YERSINIA-E
YESHIVOT-H
T-**ZADDIKIM**
ZAMINDAR-I
ZAMINDAR-Y
ZEMINDAR-I
ZEMINDAR-Y
O-**ZONATION**
ZOOGLOEA-E
ZOOMORPH-Y
ZOOPHORI-C

Useful -S Hooks

Here are some additional lists of useful and interesting -S hooks. These words will all appear in the main hook lists as well but have been extracted here because they are all worthy of specific note. The lists consist of:

- ☆ Words that are adjectival in formation but which can also be treated as a noun and therefore take an -S hook, ie words ending in -ABLE, -IBLE, -IC, -OID. There are some words that happen to end in -ABLE or -IBLE which are not also adjectives and so have been excluded (eg PARABLE, PINTABLE, FOIBLE, MANDIBLE).
- ☆ Words that are past tenses of verbs ending in -ED but which can also be treated as nouns. There are a good many -ED words which are not past tenses of verbs and so have been excluded (eg HATRED, PHYSED, MATWEED, OVERRED).
- ☆ Words that are -ING verbal forms which can also be treated as nouns. There are a few -ING words which are not verbal forms and so have been exluded (eg BESING, NIDING, DARLING, NOTHING).
- ☆ Words that end in consonant -Y. All such words are listed.
- ☆ Words that already end in -S. All such words are listed.

USEFUL -S HOOKS: NOUNAL ADJECTIVES ENDING IN -ABLE

6-letter nounal adjectives ending in -ABLE

ARABLE-S

7-letter nounal adjectives ending in -ABLE

BUYABLE-S EATABLE-S NOTABLE-S POTABLE-S VOCABLE-S
DURABLE-S MOVABLE-S PAYABLE-S TAXABLE-S

8-letter nounal adjectives ending in -ABLE

BURNABLE-S LUGGABLE-S RELIABLE-S VALUABLE-S
EDUCABLE-S MOVEABLE-S SOCIABLE-S VARIABLE-S
GRADABLE-S PORTABLE-S SPARABLE-S WASHABLE-S
GUSTABLE-S PROBABLE-S STORABLE-S WEARABLE-S

USEFUL -S HOOKS: NOUNAL PAST TENSES ENDING IN -ED

6-letter nounal past tenses ending in -ED

INBRED-S MALTED-S WICKED-S

7-letter nounal past tenses ending in -ED

ASSURED-S COLORED-S INSURED-S MARRIED-S
BELOVED-S FROSTED-S LIMITED-S

8-letter nounal past tenses ending in -ED

COLOURED-S HOMEBRED-S NEWLYWED-S UNWASHED-S
ELEVATED-S INTENDED-S PUREBRED-S

USEFUL -S HOOKS: NOUNAL ADJECTIVES ENDING IN -IBLE

6-letter nounal adjectives ending in -IBLE

EDIBLE-S

7-letter nounal adjectives ending in -IBLE

AUDIBLE-S RISIBLE-S VISIBLE-S

8-letter nounal adjectives ending in -IBLE

ELIGIBLE-S FUNGIBLE-S POSSIBLE-S TANGIBLE-S VENDIBLE-S
FENCIBLE-S HORRIBLE-S SENSIBLE-S TERRIBLE-S

USEFUL -S HOOKS: WORDS ENDING IN -IC

6-letter words ending in -IC

AGARIC-S CHEMIC-S EXOTIC-S IRENIC-S NAUTIC-S PYKNIC-S
AGOGIC-S CHYMIC-S FABRIC-S ITALIC-S OVONIC-S RUBRIC-S
ALCAIC-S CLERIC-S FROLIC-S LUETIC-S PATHIC-S RUSTIC-S
ARCTIC-S CLINIC-S FUSTIC-S MASTIC-S PELVIC-S SEPTIC-S
ATAXIC-S CLITIC-S GARLIC-S MATRIC-S PEPTIC-S SPIRIC-S
ATOMIC-S CRETIC-S GOTHIC-S METRIC-S PHOBIC-S STATIC-S
ATONIC-S CRITIC-S HAPTIC-S MIOTIC-S PHONIC-S SYNDIC-S
BEYLIC-S DYADIC-S HECTIC-S MOSAIC-S PHOTIC-S TACTIC-S
BIONIC-S EMBLIC-S HERDIC-S MUNDIC-S PHYSIC-S TRAGIC-S
BIOPIC-S EMETIC-S HEROIC-S MYOPIC-S PICNIC-S TROPIC-S
BIOTIC-S EROTIC-S HYPNIC-S MYOTIC-S POETIC-S VITRIC-S
BUSTIC-S ETHNIC-S IAMBIC-S MYSTIC-S PUBLIC-S

7-letter words ending in -IC

ACRYLIC-S BULIMIC-S EKISTIC-S HEMATIC-S POLITIC-S SPHERIC-S
AEROBIC-S CALORIC-S ELASTIC-S HEPATIC-S PRACTIC-S STYPTIC-S
ALEMBIC-S CAMBRIC-S EMPIRIC-S HERETIC-S PROOTIC-S TABETIC-S
ALOETIC-S CAUSTIC-S ENDEMIC-S ICTERIC-S PSIONIC-S TECHNIC-S
AMNESIC-S CERAMIC-S ENTERIC-S ILLOGIC-S PSYCHIC-S TETANIC-S
APHASIC-S CHRONIC-S ERISTIC-S KERAMIC-S PTARMIC-S THEORIC-S
APHONIC-S CLASSIC-S ERRATIC-S KINESIC-S PYRRHIC-S TONETIC-S
AQUATIC-S CLASTIC-S EUGENIC-S KINETIC-S QUADRIC-S TRAFFIC-S
ARSENIC-S COLONIC-S FANATIC-S LUNATIC-S QUANTIC-S TRIADIC-S
ASCETIC-S CRYONIC-S FLUERIC-S MELANIC-S QUARTIC-S TRIATIC-S
ASEPTIC-S DEICTIC-S FLUIDIC-S MELODIC-S QUINTIC-S VOCALIC-S
AUXETIC-S DEMOTIC-S GENERIC-S NUMERIC-S ROBOTIC-S ZETETIC-S
AVIONIC-S DEONTIC-S GENETIC-S ORGANIC-S SAPPHIC-S ZYMOTIC-S
BALDRIC-S DRASTIC-S GEORGIC-S PAEONIC-S SCEPTIC-S
BAUDRIC-S DYNAMIC-S GLYPTIC-S PARETIC-S SCIATIC-S
BAWDRIC-S ECBOLIC-S GRAPHIC-S PLASTIC-S SKEPTIC-S
BUCOLIC-S EIDETIC-S HEDONIC-S POLEMIC-S SPASTIC-S

8-letter words ending in -IC

ACADEMIC-S CARBOLIC-S ECONOMIC-S GEOPONIC-S MECHANIC-S PHENOLIC-S
ACOUSTIC-S CATHOLIC-S ECSTATIC-S GLYCONIC-S METALLIC-S PHONEMIC-S
ACROSTIC-S CEPHALIC-S ECUMENIC-S GNOMONIC-S MNEMONIC-S PHONETIC-S
AGNOSTIC-S COSMETIC-S ELECTRIC-S HAEMATIC-S MONASTIC-S PHOTONIC-S
ALLERGIC-S DACTYLIC-S ENCLITIC-S HARMONIC-S NARCOTIC-S PHTHISIC-S
ANALYTIC-S DALMATIC-S ENCYCLIC-S HERMETIC-S NEOTERIC-S PLATONIC-S
ANIMATIC-S DIABETIC-S ENTOPTIC-S HEURETIC-S NEURITIC-S PREMEDIC-S
ANORETIC-S DIDACTIC-S ENURETIC-S HIDROTIC-S NEUROTIC-S PROXEMIC-S
ANOREXIC-S DIETETIC-S ENZOOTIC-S HYGIENIC-S NONMUSIC-S PULMONIC-S
ANTALGIC-S DIOPTRIC-S EPIDEMIC-S HYPNOTIC-S OPERATIC-S REPUBLIC-S
ANTIPYIC-S DIURETIC-S EPULOTIC-S HYSTERIC-S ORTHOTIC-S RHETORIC-S
AROMATIC-S DOGMATIC-S ESTHETIC-S ISAGOGIC-S OXYTOCIC-S RHYTHMIC-S
ASTHENIC-S DOMESTIC-S EUPHENIC-S ISOGONIC-S PACHALIC-S ROMANTIC-S
ATARAXIC-S DRAMATIC-S EUTECTIC-S KEPHALIC-S PANDEMIC-S SABBATIC-S
ATHLETIC-S DYSGENIC-S EXEGETIC-S LEUKEMIC-S PARANOIC-S SEMANTIC-S
AUTISTIC-S DYSLEXIC-S FORENSIC-S LITURGIC-S PASHALIC-S SEMIOTIC-S
BIOETHIC-S ECCRITIC-S FRENETIC-S LOGISTIC-S PATHETIC-S SILASTIC-S
BIOLOGIC-S ECLECTIC-S GEODESIC-S MAGNETIC-S PERIOTIC-S SPAGERIC-S
BIONOMIC-S ECLIPTIC-S GEODETIC-S MAIEUTIC-S PHENETIC-S SPAGIRIC-S

SPAGYRIC-S
SPECIFIC-S
SPONDAIC-S
SUBTONIC-S
SUBTOPIC-S
SUBTUNIC-S
SYLLABIC-S
SYMBOLIC-S
SYNECTIC-S
SYSTEMIC-S
TAGMEMIC-S
TECTONIC-S
TELESTIC-S
THEATRIC-S
THEMATIC-S
TOREUTIC-S
TRISOMIC-S
TROCHAIC-S
TURMERIC-S
TYMPANIC-S
VOLCANIC-S

USEFUL -S HOOKS: VERBAL NOUNS ENDING IN -ING

6-letter verbal nouns ending in -ING

ABLING-S
ACHING-S
ACTING-S
AGEING-S
AIRING-S
ANTING-S
ARCING-S
ARMING-S
ASKING-S
AWNING-S
BAAING-S
BAKING-S
BIDING-S
BIKING-S
BITING-S
BLUING-S
BODING-S
BONING-S
BORING-S
BOWING-S
BOXING-S
BUSING-S
CAKING-S
CANING-S
CASING-S
CAVING-S
CAWING-S
CODING-S
COMING-S
COOING-S
COPING-S
COVING-S
CRYING-S
DARING-S
DATING-S
DICING-S
DIVING-S
DONING-S
DOPING-S
DOTING-S
DOZING-S
DRYING-S
DYEING-S
EARING-S
EATING-S
EDGING-S
ELDING-S
ENDING-S
ERRING-S
FACING-S
FADING-S
FILING-S
FINING-S
FIRING-S
FIXING-S
FLYING-S
FOXING-S
FRYING-S
GAMING-S
GAPING-S
GATING-S
GIVING-S
GORING-S
HAVING-S
HAYING-S
HAZING-S
HEWING-S
HEXING-S
HIDING-S
HIRING-S
HOLING-S
HOMING-S
IMPING-S
INNING-S
JAPING-S
JAWING-S
KITING-S
LACING-S
LADING-S
LAKING-S
LASING-S
LAWING-S
LAYING-S
LIKING-S
LIMING-S
LINING-S
LIVING-S
LOBING-S
LORING-S
LOSING-S
LOVING-S
LOWING-S
LUGING-S
LUTING-S
MAKING-S
MATING-S
MAYING-S
MINING-S
MOWING-S
MUSING-S
NAMING-S
NOSING-S
OFFING-S
OGLING-S
OUTING-S
PAGING-S
PALING-S
PARING-S
PAVING-S
PAYING-S
PILING-S
PIPING-S
POLING-S
POSING-S
PRYING-S
PULING-S
RACING-S
RAGING-S
RAKING-S
RATING-S
RAVING-S
RAWING-S
RIDING-S
RISING-S
ROBING-S
RODING-S
ROPING-S
ROVING-S
ROWING-S
RUEING-S
RULING-S
SAVING-S
SAWING-S
SAYING-S
SEEING-S
SEWING-S
SIDING-S
SIZING-S
SKIING-S
SORING-S
SOWING-S
SPAING-S
SPYING-S
TAKING-S
TAMING-S
TARING-S
TAWING-S
TAXING-S
TIDING-S
TILING-S
TIMING-S
TIRING-S
TOLING-S
TONING-S
TOWING-S
TOYING-S
TRYING-S
TUBING-S
TUNING-S
TYPING-S
UPPING-S
URGING-S
URNING-S
VEXING-S
WADING-S
WAKING-S
WANING-S
WAVING-S
WAXING-S
WIPING-S
WIRING-S
WONING-S
WOOING-S
YOKING-S
ZONING-S

7-letter verbal nouns ending in -ING

ABIDING-S
AISLING-S
AMBLING-S
ANGLING-S
ARCHING-S
ARCKING-S
AWAKING-S
BACKING-S
BAGGING-S
BAITING-S
BALKING-S
BALLING-S
BANDING-S
BANGING-S
BANKING-S
BANTING-S
BARRING-S
BASHING-S
BASTING-S
BATTING-S
BAWLING-S
BEADING-S
BEAMING-S
BEARING-S
BEATING-S
BEDDING-S
BEGGING-S
BELTING-S
BENDING-S
BETTING-S
BIASING-S
BIDDING-S
BIGGING-S
BILLING-S
BINDING-S
BIRDING-S
BIRLING-S
BITTING-S
BLUEING-S
BOATING-S
BOILING-S
BOLTING-S
BOMBING-S
BONDING-S
BOOKING-S
BOOMING-S
BOWLING-S
BRACING-S
BREWING-S
BRIMING-S
BROKING-S
BRUTING-S
BUCKING-S
BUDDING-S
BUFFING-S
BUGGING-S
BULLING-S
BUMPING-S
BUNTING-S
BURNING-S
BUSHING-S
BUSKING-S
BUSSING-S
BUSTING-S
BUZZING-S
CABLING-S
CALLING-S
CAMPING-S
CANNING-S
CANTING-S
CAPPING-S
CARDING-S
CARPING-S
CARVING-S
CASTING-S
CEASING-S
CEILING-S
CHASING-S
CHIDING-S
CIELING-S
CLONING-S
CLOSING-S
COATING-S
COGGING-S
COINING-S
COLLING-S
COMBING-S
CONNING-S
COOKING-S
CORDING-S
COWLING-S
CRAVING-S
CUBBING-S
CULLING-S
CUNNING-S
CUPPING-S
CURBING-S
CURLING-S
CURSING-S
CUTTING-S
CYCLING-S
DAFFING-S
DAGGING-S
DAMPING-S
DANCING-S
DARNING-S
DAUBING-S
DAWNING-S
DEALING-S
DECKING-S
DIALING-S
DIGGING-S
DILLING-S
DIPPING-S
DISHING-S
DOATING-S
DOCKING-S
DODGING-S
DOGGING-S
DOPPING-S
DRAWING-S
DRIVING-S
DROVING-S
DUBBING-S
DUCKING-S
DUCTING-S
DUFFING-S
DUMPING-S
DUNNING-S
EARNING-S
EASTING-S
ENVYING-S
ETCHING-S
FABLING-S
FAGGING-S
FAILING-S
FAIRING-S
FALLING-S
FANNING-S
FARCING-S
FARMING-S
FASTING-S
FAWNING-S
FEEDING-S
FEELING-S
FEERING-S
FELTING-S
FENCING-S
FERNING-S
FEUDING-S
FILLING-S
FINDING-S
FIRRING-S
FISHING-S
FITTING-S
FIZZING-S
FLUTING-S
FLYTING-S
FOAMING-S
FOILING-S
FOLDING-S
FOOLING-S
FOOTING-S
FORGING-S
FORMING-S
FOULING-S
FOWLING-S
FRAMING-S
FRAYING-S
FUCKING-S
FUNDING-S
FURRING-S
GAFFING-S
GAINING-S
GANGING-S
GASPING-S
GASSING-S
GAUGING-S
GEARING-S
GELDING-S
GETTING-S
GILDING-S
GINNING-S
GIRDING-S
GLAZING-S
GLEYING-S
GLIDING-S
GLOVING-S
GLOZING-S
GNAWING-S
GOLFING-S
GRATING-S

GRAVING-S
GRAZING-S
GREYING-S
GROWING-S
GUIDING-S
GUISING-S
GUMMING-S
GUNNING-S
HACKING-S
HAINING-S
HALLING-S
HALTING-S
HANGING-S
HARLING-S
HARPING-S
HASTING-S
HATTING-S
HAWKING-S
HEADING-S
HEALING-S
HEARING-S
HEATING-S
HEAVING-S
HEDGING-S
HEELING-S
HELPING-S
HIPPING-S
HISSING-S
HOGGING-S
HOLDING-S
HOPPING-S
HORNING-S
HORSING-S
HOSTING-S
HOTTING-S
HOUSING-S
HOWLING-S
HUMMING-S
HUNTING-S
HURLING-S
HUSKING-S
HUTTING-S
IMAGING-S
INGOING-S
INKLING-S
IRONING-S
ITCHING-S
JARRING-S
JEERING-S
JERKING-S
JESTING-S
JIBBING-S
JIGGING-S
JOBBING-S
JOGGING-S
JOINING-S
JOTTING-S
JUGGING-S
KARTING-S
KAYOING-S
KEELING-S
KEENING-S
KEEPING-S
KEMPING-S
KENNING-S
KERNING-S
KILLING-S
KILTING-S
KIRKING-S
KNIFING-S
KNOWING-S
LAGGING-S
LAMMING-S
LAMPING-S
LANDING-S
LAPPING-S
LASHING-S
LASTING-S
LATHING-S
LEADING-S
LEANING-S
LEASING-S
LEAVING-S
LEERING-S
LEGGING-S
LEKKING-S
LENDING-S
LETTING-S
LICKING-S
LIGGING-S
LIMPING-S
LIPPING-S
LISPING-S
LISTING-S
LOADING-S
LOAFING-S
LOANING-S
LODGING-S
LOGGING-S
LONGING-S
LOONING-S
LOOPING-S
LOOTING-S
LOPPING-S
LORDING-S
LOURING-S
LUGEING-S
LURKING-S
MAILING-S
MAIMING-S
MALTING-S
MAPPING-S
MARKING-S
MARLING-S
MASHING-S
MASKING-S
MATTING-S
MEANING-S
MEETING-S
MELTING-S
MENDING-S
MESHING-S
MICHING-S
MILKING-S
MILLING-S
MINCING-S
MINDING-S
MISTING-S
MOBBING-S
MOCKING-S
MOLDING-S
MOORING-S
MOOTING-S
MORNING-S
MOUSING-S
MUGGING-S
MUMMING-S
NAILING-S
NECKING-S
NERVING-S
NESTING-S
NETTING-S
NODDING-S
NOGGING-S
NOONING-S
NULLING-S
NURSING-S
NUTTING-S
OPENING-S
PACKING-S
PADDING-S
PAIRING-S
PANNING-S
PANTING-S
PARGING-S
PARKING-S
PARSING-S
PARTING-S
PASSING-S
PASTING-S
PAUSING-S
PECKING-S
PEELING-S
PEGGING-S
PELTING-S
PETTING-S
PICKING-S
PIECING-S
PIGGING-S
PILLING-S
PINKING-S
PINNING-S
PITTING-S
PLACING-S
PLATING-S
POLLING-S
POSTING-S
POURING-S
POUTING-S
PRATING-S
PRAYING-S
PRIMING-S
PROSING-S
PROVING-S
PRUNING-S
PUDDING-S
PUFFING-S
PUGGING-S
PUNNING-S
PURGING-S
PURLING-S
PURRING-S
PUTTING-S
QUAKING-S
QUEUING-S
RACKING-S
RAGGING-S
RAILING-S
RAISING-S
RAMPING-S
RANKING-S
RANTING-S
RAPPING-S
RASPING-S
RATTING-S
READING-S
REDDING-S
REEDING-S
REEFING-S
REELING-S
RENNING-S
REPPING-S
RESTING-S
RIBBING-S
RIDGING-S
RIFLING-S
RIGGING-S
RIMMING-S
RINGING-S
RINSING-S
RIOTING-S
RISPING-S
ROADING-S
ROAMING-S
ROARING-S
ROCKING-S
RODDING-S
ROLFING-S
ROLLING-S
ROOFING-S
ROOTING-S
ROUMING-S
ROUTING-S
RUBBING-S
RUCHING-S
RUGGING-S
RUINING-S
RUNNING-S
RUSHING-S
RUSTING-S
RUTTING-S
SACKING-S
SAGGING-S
SAILING-S
SALTING-S
SALVING-S
SANDING-S
SARKING-S
SCALING-S
SCORING-S
SCRYING-S
SEALING-S
SEARING-S
SEATING-S
SEEDING-S
SEELING-S
SEEMING-S
SEINING-S
SEISING-S
SEIZING-S
SELFING-S
SENDING-S
SENSING-S
SERGING-S
SERVING-S
SETTING-S
SHADING-S
SHAKING-S
SHAPING-S
SHARING-S
SHAVING-S
SHOEING-S
SHORING-S
SHOWING-S
SIFTING-S
SIGNING-S
SINDING-S
SINGING-S
SINKING-S
SITTING-S
SKATING-S
SKIVING-S
SLATING-S
SLICING-S
SLIDING-S
SLOWING-S
SMILING-S
SMOKING-S
SNARING-S
SNIPING-S
SNORING-S
SOAKING-S
SOARING-S
SOBBING-S
SOGGING-S
SOILING-S
SOOPING-S
SOPPING-S
SORNING-S
SORTING-S
SOSSING-S
SOTTING-S
SOUMING-S
SOURING-S
SOUSING-S
SPACING-S
SPAEING-S
SPILING-S
STAGING-S
STARING-S
STEWING-S
STONING-S
STOPING-S
STOVING-S
STOWING-S
STYLING-S
SUBBING-S
SUCKING-S
SUGGING-S
SUITING-S
SUMMING-S
SURFING-S
SURGING-S
SWALING-S
SWAYING-S
SYNDING-S
TABLING-S
TACKING-S
TAGGING-S
TAILING-S
TALKING-S
TAMPING-S
TANKING-S
TANNING-S
TAPPING-S
TARRING-S
TASKING-S
TASTING-S
TATTING-S
TEAMING-S
TEASING-S
TELLING-S
TENTING-S
TESTING-S
THAWING-S
TICKING-S
TIFFING-S
TILLING-S
TILTING-S
TINNING-S
TINTING-S
TIPPING-S
TITHING-S
TITLING-S
TOILING-S
TOLLING-S
TOOLING-S
TOPPING-S
TOSSING-S
TOTTING-S
TOURING-S
TOUSING-S
TRACING-S
TRADING-S
TUBBING-S
TUFTING-S
TUGGING-S
TUNNING-S
TURFING-S
TURNING-S
TUSKING-S
TUTTING-S
TWINING-S
UNBEING-S
UNDOING-S
UNITING-S
UNTYING-S
UPGOING-S
VAMPING-S
VANNING-S
VARYING-S
VEERING-S
VEILING-S
VEINING-S
VENTING-S
VERSING-S
VESTING-S
VIEWING-S
VOGUING-S
VOICING-S
VOIDING-S
WADDING-S
WAFTING-S
WAILING-S
WAITING-S
WALKING-S
WALLING-S
WANTING-S
WARDING-S
WARMING-S
WARNING-S
WARPING-S
WASHING-S
WASTING-S
WAULING-S
WAWLING-S
WEARING-S
WEAVING-S
WEBBING-S
WEDDING-S
WEDGING-S
WEEDING-S
WEEPING-S
WELDING-S
WELLING-S
WELTING-S
WESTING-S
WETTING-S
WHALING-S
WHINING-S
WHITING-S
WICKING-S
WIGGING-S
WILDING-S
WINCING-S
WINDING-S
WINKING-S
WINNING-S
WISHING-S
WITTING-S
WOLFING-S
WOLVING-S
WONNING-S
WORDING-S
WORKING-S
WRITING-S
YAWNING-S
YAWPING-S
YELLING-S
YELPING-S
YOWLING-S

8-letter verbal nouns ending in -ING

ADVISING-S
AGENTING-S
ALIASING-S
ALLAYING-S
ANTIKING-S
ARCADING-S
ASSAYING-S
ASSUMING-S
ATTIRING-S
BABBLING-S
BANDYING-S
BATCHING-S
BEAGLING-S
BECOMING-S
BELLYING-S
BERRYING-S
BIRTHING-S
BLABBING-S
BLACKING-S
BLANKING-S
BLASTING-S
BLEATING-S
BLEEDING-S
BLENDING-S
BLESSING-S
BLINDING-S
BLOATING-S
BLOCKING-S
BLOODING-S
BLOTTING-S
BLURTING-S
BLUSHING-S
BOARDING-S
BOASTING-S
BOTCHING-S
BOTTLING-S
BOULTING-S
BRAIDING-S
BRAWLING-S
BREAKING-S
BREEDING-S
BRICKING-S
BRIDGING-S
BRIEFING-S
BRIGUING-S
BRINGING-S
BRONZING-S
BROWNING-S
BROWSING-S
BRUISING-S
BRUSHING-S
BUCKLING-S
BUILDING-S
BUMBLING-S
BUNCHING-S
BUNDLING-S
BUNGLING-S
BURBLING-S
BUTCHING-S
CANOEING-S
CATCHING-S
CATERING-S
CAULKING-S
CENTRING-S
CHAFFING-S
CHEATING-S
CHILLING-S
CHIPPING-S
CHOPPING-S
CHORDING-S
CHROMING-S
CHUMPING-S
CHUNKING-S
CHURNING-S
CINCHING-S
CIRCLING-S
CLADDING-S
CLANGING-S
CLANKING-S
CLAPPING-S
CLASHING-S
CLASPING-S
CLEANING-S
CLEARING-S
CLEAVING-S
CLECKING-S
CLICKING-S
CLIMBING-S
CLIPPING-S
CLOCKING-S
CLOTHING-S
CLOTTING-S
CLOUDING-S
CLOWNING-S
CLUBBING-S
COACHING-S
COASTING-S
COBBLING-S
COLORING-S
COUCHING-S
COUGHING-S
COUPLING-S
COURSING-S
COURTING-S
COVERING-S
CRACKING-S
CRADLING-S
CRAWLING-S
CRESTING-S
CRIBBING-S
CRINGING-S
CROAKING-S
CROFTING-S
CROONING-S
CROPPING-S
CROSSING-S
CROWNING-S
CRUISING-S
CURRYING-S
DABBLING-S
DAIRYING-S
DANGLING-S
DARKLING-S
DAZZLING-S
DEFAMING-S
DERATING-S
DEVILING-S
DIALLING-S
DIVIDING-S
DOUBLING-S
DOUBTING-S
DRAFTING-S
DREAMING-S
DREARING-S
DREDGING-S
DRESSING-S
DRILLING-S
DRINKING-S
DRIPPING-S
DROLLING-S
DROOKING-S
DROPPING-S
DROUKING-S
DROWNING-S
DRUBBING-S
DUELLING-S
DWELLING-S
EMPTYING-S
ENTERING-S
ENTICING-S
EVENTING-S
FAGOTING-S
FAINTING-S
FEASTING-S
FEIGNING-S
FETTLING-S
FIELDING-S
FIGHTING-S
FILCHING-S
FLAGGING-S
FLAPPING-S
FLASHING-S
FLATTING-S
FLEERING-S
FLESHING-S
FLIRTING-S
FLITTING-S
FLOATING-S
FLOCKING-S
FLOGGING-S
FLOODING-S
FLOORING-S
FLOSSING-S
FLUSHING-S
FOCUSING-S
FONDLING-S
FOOTLING-S
FOOZLING-S
FOUNDING-S
FRAGGING-S
FREEZING-S
FRETTING-S
FRIGGING-S
FRILLING-S
FRISKING-S
FROCKING-S
FROGGING-S
FROSTING-S
FRUITING-S
FUDDLING-S
GABBLING-S
GAGGLING-S
GAMBLING-S
GARAGING-S
GARBLING-S
GHOSTING-S
GIGGLING-S
GLANCING-S
GLEAMING-S
GLEANING-S
GLIFFING-S
GLOOMING-S
GOGGLING-S
GRAFTING-S
GRAINING-S
GRASSING-S
GREENING-S
GREETING-S
GRILLING-S
GRINDING-S
GROANING-S
GROINING-S
GROUPING-S
GROUTING-S
GROWLING-S
GRUDGING-S
GRUELING-S
GRUNTING-S
GUESSING-S
HANDLING-S
HATCHING-S
HAUNTING-S
HAVERING-S
HECKLING-S
HIGGLING-S
HOARDING-S
HOBBLING-S
HOISTING-S
HUMBLING-S
HURDLING-S
HURRYING-S
HUSTLING-S
INCOMING-S
INDEXING-S
INLAYING-S
INTONING-S
INVITING-S
JANGLING-S
JERQUING-S
JOLLYING-S
JOSTLING-S
JUGGLING-S
KAYAKING-S
KECKLING-S
KINDLING-S
KNITTING-S
KNOCKING-S
KNOTTING-S
KNURLING-S
LAUGHING-S
LAYERING-S
LEACHING-S
LEARNING-S
LEGERING-S
LETCHING-S
LIBELING-S
LIGHTING-S
LIMITING-S
LITTLING-S
LOATHING-S
LOBBYING-S
LOUNGING-S
LOWERING-S
LUSTRING-S
LYNCHING-S
MANTLING-S
MANURING-S
MARBLING-S
MARRYING-S
MEDDLING-S
MIDDLING-S
MINGLING-S
MISDOING-S
MIZZLING-S
MODELING-S
MORPHING-S
MOTORING-S
MOTTLING-S
MOULDING-S
MOULTING-S
MOUNTING-S
MOURNING-S
MUMBLING-S
MUSCLING-S
NEEDLING-S
NESTLING-S
NIBBLING-S
NIGGLING-S
NORTHING-S
NOTCHING-S
NURSLING-S
OFFERING-S
ORDERING-S
OUTGOING-S
PADDLING-S
PAINTING-S
PANELING-S
PAPERING-S
PATCHING-S
PEARLING-S
PEBBLING-S
PEDDLING-S
PERCHING-S
PHRASING-S
PIERCING-S
PILOTING-S
PINCHING-S
PITCHING-S
PIVOTING-S
PLAIDING-S
PLAINING-S
PLAITING-S
PLANKING-S
PLANNING-S
PLANTING-S
PLASHING-S
PLATTING-S
PLEADING-S
PLEASING-S
PLODDING-S
PLONKING-S
PLOTTING-S
PLUGGING-S
PLUMBING-S
PLUNGING-S
POACHING-S
POINDING-S
POINTING-S
PRAISING-S
PRANCING-S
PRANKING-S
PRESSING-S
PRICKING-S
PRIGGING-S
PRINTING-S
PROOFING-S
PROWLING-S
PUDDLING-S
PURFLING-S
PURSUING-S
QUAILING-S
QUEENING-S
QUERYING-S
QUESTING-S
QUEUEING-S
QUIETING-S
QUILLING-S
QUILTING-S
QUIZZING-S
RABBLING-S
RALLYING-S
RAMBLING-S
RANCHING-S
RATTLING-S
RAVELING-S
RAVENING-S
REEDLING-S
REFINING-S
RENEWING-S
REPINING-S
REPUTING-S
RETAKING-S
REVILING-S
REVIVING-S
RIDDLING-S
RIGHTING-S
RIPPLING-S
RIVETING-S
ROASTING-S
ROGERING-S
ROUNDING-S
RUFFLING-S
RUMBLING-S
RUSTLING-S
SALADING-S
SAMPLING-S
SCALDING-S
SCALPING-S
SCAMPING-S
SCANNING-S
SCARFING-S
SCARPING-S
SCARRING-S
SCATTING-S
SCENTING-S
SCHEMING-S
SCOFFING-S
SCOLDING-S
SCOOPING-S
SCORNING-S
SCOURING-S
SCOUTING-S
SCRAPING-S
SCREWING-S
SCRIBING-S
SCULLING-S
SCUMMING-S
SEDUCING-S
SEETHING-S
SETTLING-S
SEWERING-S
SHAFTING-S
SHARKING-S
SHARPING-S
SHAWLING-S
SHEALING-S
SHEARING-S
SHEDDING-S
SHEETING-S
SHEILING-S
SHELLING-S
SHELVING-S
SHIELING-S
SHIFTING-S
SHIPPING-S
SHIRRING-S
SHIRTING-S
SHOALING-S
SHOOTING-S
SHOPPING-S
SHOUTING-S
SHRIVING-S
SHUCKING-S
SHUNTING-S
SIGHTING-S
SIMPLING-S
SINGLING-S
SIZZLING-S
SKANKING-S
SKELPING-S
SKILLING-S
SKIMMING-S
SKIPPING-S
SKIRLING-S
SKIRTING-S
SKULKING-S
SLAMMING-S
SLANGING-S

SLASHING-S
SLATTING-S
SLEDDING-S
SLEDGING-S
SLEEKING-S
SLEEPING-S
SLEEVING-S
SLICKING-S
SLIMMING-S
SLOSHING-S
SLUBBING-S
SLUMMING-S
SMACKING-S
SMASHING-S
SMELLING-S
SMELTING-S
SMOCKING-S
SNAPPING-S
SNARLING-S
SNEERING-S
SNEEZING-S
SNIFFING-S
SNIPPING-S
SNORTING-S
SNUBBING-S
SNUFFING-S
SOOTHING-S
SOUNDING-S
SOURCING-S
SOUTHING-S
SPALLING-S
SPAMMING-S
SPANKING-S
SPARRING-S
SPAWNING-S
SPEAKING-S
SPEEDING-S
SPEERING-S
SPEIRING-S
SPELDING-S
SPELLING-S
SPENDING-S
SPILLING-S
SPINNING-S
SPITTING-S
SPOOLING-S
SPOTTING-S
SPOUTING-S
SPUDDING-S
SPURNING-S
SPURRING-S
SQUARING-S
STABBING-S
STABLING-S
STACKING-S
STAINING-S
STALKING-S
STALLING-S
STAMPING-S
STANDING-S
STARRING-S
STARTING-S
STARVING-S
STEADING-S
STEALING-S
STEAMING-S
STEANING-S
STEELING-S
STEENING-S
STEERING-S
STEEVING-S
STEINING-S
STEMMING-S
STICKING-S
STIFLING-S
STILLING-S
STILTING-S
STINGING-S
STINKING-S
STINTING-S
STIRRING-S
STOCKING-S
STOPPING-S
STORMING-S
STORYING-S
STRAYING-S
STREWING-S
STRIKING-S
STRIPING-S
STRIVING-S
STROBING-S
STROKING-S
STROWING-S
STUDDING-S
STUFFING-S
STUNNING-S
SUCKLING-S
SUGARING-S
SWAINING-S
SWANNING-S
SWAPPING-S
SWARMING-S
SWASHING-S
SWATTING-S
SWAYLING-S
SWEALING-S
SWEARING-S
SWEATING-S
SWEEPING-S
SWEETING-S
SWELLING-S
SWERVING-S
SWILLING-S
SWIMMING-S
SWINGING-S
SWISHING-S
SWISSING-S
SWOONING-S
SWOPPING-S
SWOTTING-S
TACKLING-S
TANGLING-S
TAPERING-S
TATTLING-S
TAUNTING-S
TEACHING-S
TEETHING-S
TEMPTING-S
THANKING-S
THIEVING-S
THIGGING-S
THINKING-S
THINNING-S
THIRDING-S
THRIVING-S
THROWING-S
TICKLING-S
TINGLING-S
TINKLING-S
TOASTING-S
TONGUING-S
TORCHING-S
TOUCHING-S
TOWELING-S
TRACKING-S
TRAINING-S
TRAMPING-S
TRAPPING-S
TRAWLING-S
TREADING-S
TREATING-S
TRICKING-S
TRIFLING-S
TRILLING-S
TRIMMING-S
TRIPLING-S
TRIPPING-S
TROLLING-S
TROTTING-S
TROUTING-S
TRUCKING-S
TRUDGING-S
TRUMPING-S
TRUNKING-S
TRUSSING-S
TUMBLING-S
TURTLING-S
TUTORING-S
TWANGING-S
TWEAKING-S
TWILLING-S
TWINNING-S
TWISTING-S
TWITTING-S
TWOCCING-S
UNIFYING-S
UNLADING-S
UNMAKING-S
UPMAKING-S
UPRISING-S
USHERING-S
USURPING-S
UTTERING-S
VALETING-S
VAPORING-S
VAULTING-S
VAUNTING-S
VENTRING-S
VISITING-S
VOGUEING-S
VOMITING-S
WAFFLING-S
WAISTING-S
WAKENING-S
WALTZING-S
WAMBLING-S
WANGLING-S
WARBLING-S
WATERING-S
WATTLING-S
WAVERING-S
WEIGHING-S
WHACKING-S
WHARFING-S
WHEELING-S
WHEEZING-S
WHIFFING-S
WHIPPING-S
WHIRLING-S
WHIRRING-S
WHIZZING-S
WHOOPING-S
WHOPPING-S
WITCHING-S
WOBBLING-S
WOOLDING-S
WORRYING-S
WOUNDING-S
WRAPPING-S
WRAXLING-S
WRECKING-S
WRINGING-S
WRITHING-S
YACHTING-S
YEARNING-S
YIELDING-S

USEFUL -S HOOKS: WORDS ENDING IN -OID

6-letter words ending in -OID

CEBOID-S
CONOID-S
CUBOID-S
FUCOID-S
GADOID-S
GANOID-S
HALOID-S
KELOID-S
LIPOID-S
MELOID-S
MUCOID-S
OPIOID-S
PELOID-S
TOROID-S
TOXOID-S
VIROID-S

7-letter words ending in -OID

ADENOID-S
AGAMOID-S
AMBROID-S
AMYLOID-S
ANDROID-S
ANEROID-S
ASTROID-S
CESTOID-S
CHELOID-S
CHOROID-S
CISSOID-S
COCCOID-S
COLLOID-S
CRICOID-S
CRINOID-S
CYCLOID-S
CYSTOID-S
DELTOID-S
DERMOID-S
DESMOID-S
DIPLOID-S
DISCOID-S
EMEROID-S
ETHMOID-S
EUPLOID-S
FACTOID-S
FIBROID-S
FUNGOID-S
GLENOID-S
GLOBOID-S
GOBIOID-S
HAPLOID-S
HYALOID-S
HYDROID-S
LABROID-S
MASTOID-S
MATTOID-S
NEGROID-S
OSTEOID-S
PERCOID-S
PLACOID-S
QUINOID-S
RHIZOID-S
SARCOID-S
SIGMOID-S
SPAROID-S
STEROID-S
STYLOID-S
TABLOID-S
THYROID-S
TYPHOID-S
XIPHOID-S

8-letter words ending in -OID

ACTINOID-S
ALKALOID-S
AMBEROID-S
AMMONOID-S
ASTEROID-S
AUTACOID-S
AUTOCOID-S
BLASTOID-S
CAMELOID-S
CANCROID-S
CARDIOID-S
CATENOID-S
CENTROID-S
CHORIOID-S
CLUPEOID-S
CONCHOID-S
CORACOID-S
DORIDOID-S
ECHINOID-S
EMBRYOID-S
EMULSOID-S
GROUPOID-S
HELICOID-S
HOMALOID-S
HOMINOID-S
HUMANOID-S
HYRACOID-S
INDIGOID-S
LEMUROID-S
LIMULOID-S
MEDUSOID-S
MELANOID-S
NUCLEOID-S
ODONTOID-S
OMOHYOID-S
PARANOID-S
PAROTOID-S
PHYLLOID-S
PINACOID-S
PINAKOID-S
PLASMOID-S
PRISMOID-S
PSYCHOID-S
PYRENOID-S
RESINOID-S
RETINOID-S
RHABDOID-S
RHOMBOID-S
SCAPHOID-S
SCHIZOID-S
SCINCOID-S
SESAMOID-S
SILUROID-S
SINUSOID-S
SOLENOID-S
SPHENOID-S
SPHEROID-S
THYREOID-S
TRIPLOID-S
TROCHOID-S

USEFUL -S HOOKS: WORDS ENDING IN -(consonant)Y

2-letter words ending in -(consonant)Y

BY-S NY-S

3-letter words ending in -(consonant)Y

ABY-S DRY-S PRY-S WHY-S

4-letter words ending in -(consonant)Y

POLY-S

5-letter words ending in -(consonant)Y

BENDY-S DARCY-S HENRY-S TELLY-S
BIALY-S FLYBY-S PLATY-S ZLOTY-S

6-letter words ending in -(consonant)Y

BLOWBY-S GOODBY-S JANSKY-S QWERTY-S SHINDY-S TRILBY-S

7-letter words ending in -(consonant)Y

ABHENRY-S DROSTDY-S STANDBY-S SWINGBY-S

USEFUL -S HOOKS: WORDS ENDING IN -S

2-letter words ending in -S

AS-S ES-S

3-letter words ending in -S

BAS-S DOS-S LES-S MOS-S PUS-S WIS-S
BOS-S HIS-S LOS-S MUS-S SIS-S WUS-S
BUS-S HOS-S MAS-S PAS-S SOS-S
COS-S KOS-S MES-S PIS-S SUS-S
DIS-S LAS-S MIS-S POS-S TAS-S

4-letter words ending in -S

ABYS-S AMIS-S FRAS-S GUES-S PROS-S
AMAS-S BRAS-S GAUS-S KVAS-S TRES-S

5-letter words ending in -S

ABBES-S CAMAS-S CITES-S KAVAS-S OGRES-S
ASSES-S CARES-S DURES-S MORAS-S

6-letter words ending in -S

BIBLES-S CHAPES-S FOGLES-S KOUMYS-S RAYLES-S TREVIS-S
CANVAS-S CUTLAS-S INKLES-S LARGES-S SHINES-S USURES-S
CAPLES-S CYPRES-S KERMES-S LOWNES-S SUCCES-S VENDIS-S
CARLES-S DISCUS-S KOUMIS-S POSSES-S SUCCUS-S ZEBRAS-S

7-letter words ending in -S

COMBLES-S GAMINES-S KINDLES-S ROOTLES-S SUCKLES-S
COSINES-S GARBLES-S KINGLES-S RUMPLES-S TACKLES-S
CUFFLES-S HANDLES-S MARQUES-S RUSTLES-S TAILLES-S
FANGLES-S HOMINES-S NEEDLES-S SAGENES-S WATTLES-S
FOOTLES-S HURTLES-S PRINCES-S SQUIRES-S WINDLES-S

8-letter words ending in -S

BULGINES-S	PRELATES-S	SPARKLES-S	TARTINES-S	TYRANNES-S
ESQUIRES-S	PROCURES-S	SPECKLES-S	TREADLES-S	
NERVINES-S	SALTINES-S	TARANTAS-S	TRICKLES-S	

Blockers

Blockers are the opposites of hooks – they can't have a letter added either at the front or the end of the word.

Blockers of length two to six letters are given in the lists here. To 'unclutter' the 5- and 6-letter lists, so that you can focus on the more relevant blockers, we have excluded all 5- and 6-letter words ending in -ED, -J, -S, -X, -Y and -Z. It hardly seems necessary to show that words like BAKED, FALAJ, CHIPS, HELIX, DUMMY and TOPAZ are blockers!

2-LETTER WORD BLOCKERS

FY	MY	XU

3-LETTER WORD BLOCKERS

BEZ	FEZ	HOX	MUX	PAX	QIS	SIX	TWP	ZEX
CLY	FLY	HUH	NAE	PHS	RAX	SLY	VLY	ZOA
CUZ	FRY	KEX	NAH	PHT	RHY	SMA	VOX	ZUZ
DUX	GEY	KOI	NOH	PLY	SAE	SOX	WOX	
FAB	GOT	KYE	NOX	POH	SAX	SWY	YEH	
FAP	GOX	LOX	NTH	PST	SAZ	TAJ	YEX	
FAX	HEX	LUZ	NYS	PUH	SEZ	THY	YOS	
FEW	HMM	MED	OXO	PYX	SHH	TUX	ZAX	

4-LETTER WORD BLOCKERS

AAHS	BAGS	BOSH	COAX	DAMS	DODS	DUTY	FANS	FONS
ABBS	BAMS	BOTS	COBS	DANS	DOEN	DYED	FASH	FOPS
ABLY	BANS	BOXY	COCH	DAPS	DOGS	DYES	FAUX	FOUS
ABOS	BAPS	BOYS	CODS	DAVY	DOGY	DZOS	FAWS	FOXY
ACHY	BATS	BRRR	COFT	DEAF	DOHS	EASY	FEDS	FOYS
ADRY	BAYS	BUBO	COKY	DEBS	DOMS	EBBS	FEET	FOZY
AESC	BEDS	BUBS	COLS	DEEK	DOMY	ECOD	FEGS	FRAE
AGLY	BEDU	BUDS	COLY	DEFT	DOOS	ECUS	FEHS	FROM
AHEM	BEEN	BUGS	COMS	DEFY	DOPS	EDDO	FEMS	FUCI
AHOY	BEES	BUMS	CONY	DELS	DOPY	EDHS	FENS	FUDS
AJAR	BEGS	BUNS	COPY	DEMY	DORY	EHED	FETS	FUGS
AJEE	BELS	BURY	CORF	DENY	DOSH	ELHI	FEUS	FUMS
ALAE	BENJ	BUSY	CORY	DEUS	DOSS	ELMY	FEYS	FUMY
ALBS	BENS	BUYS	COSH	DEVS	DOST	ELSE	FIBS	FUNS
ALEE	BEVY	CAGY	COSS	DEWS	DOTH	EMFS	FIDS	FURS
ALIT	BIBS	CAKY	COSY	DEWY	DOTS	EMUS	FIGS	FURY
ALSO	BIDS	CALO	COWY	DEXY	DOTY	EMYS	FIKY	FUSC
ANEW	BIEN	CALX	COXY	DEYS	DOUX	EOAN	FILS	FUTZ
ANOW	BIGS	CANY	COYS	DIBS	DOWF	ESPY	FINS	GABS
APEX	BINS	CAPS	COZY	DIDY	DOXY	EUGE	FITS	GABY
APTS	BIOS	CASH	CRUX	DIED	DOZY	EUOI	FIXT	GAED
AREG	BISH	CAUF	CUBS	DIEL	DREW	EVOE	FLED	GAEN
AREW	BLEW	CAVY	CUED	DIES	DRYS	EWKS	FLEX	GAES
AROW	BOBS	CAYS	CUES	DIGS	DUBS	EYAS	FLIX	GAGA
ASEA	BODS	CEES	CURT	DIMS	DUCI	EYES	FLUX	GAGS
AVOS	BODY	CELS	CWMS	DINS	DUDS	EYNE	FOBS	GALS
AWRY	BOGS	CEPS	DABS	DIPT	DUED	EYRY	FOCI	GAMY
AXAL	BOGY	CHEZ	DADS	DISS	DUES	FADS	FOEN	GAPS
AYUS	BOHS	CHIS	DAES	DIVS	DUGS	FADY	FOES	GAPY
BAAS	BOKS	CIGS	DAFT	DIXY	DULY	FAGS	FOGS	GARE
BABY	BONA	CITO	DAGS	DOBS	DUOS	FAHS	FOGY	GASH
BADE	BOPS	CITS	DAHS	DOBY	DUPS	FAIX	FOHS	GATS
BADS	BORS	CITY	DAKS	DOCS	DUSH	FALX	FONE	GAYS

GAZY GEDS GEED GEEZ GELS GEMS GENS GEOS GETS GHIS GIBS GIDS GIED GIEN GIES GIGS GINS GITS GIZZ GJUS GLEG GNUS GOAS GOBS GOBY GOES GOEY GORY GOVS GOYS GUBS GULS GULY GUMS GUNS GUPS GUVS GYMS GYNY GYRI HAED HAEN HAES HATH HAZY HEHS HELD HEMS HEPS HEPT HISN HIYA HOAX HOBS HODS HOLP HOLY HOMY HOSS HOYS HUED HUES HUGY HUIC HUIS HUNG HUNH

HUPS HWAN HYED HYES HYPS HYTE IBIS ICHS IDEM IDLY IGAD ILKA INIA INLY INRO IURE JABS JAGS JAKS JAMS JAPS JARS JASS JASY JAWS JAYS JAZY JEED JEES JEEZ JEON JETS JEUX JEWS JIBS JIGS JINX JIZZ JOBS JOCO JOES JOGS JOKY JORS JOSH JOSS JOTS JOWS JOYS JUDS JUDY JUGS JURY JUTS JYNX KAAS KABS KAED KAES KAFS KAIS KANS KEAS KEBS KEDS KEFS KEKS

KENS KEPT KESH KETS KEYS KHIS KIFS KILD KIRS KISH KNEW KOAS KOBO KOBS KOND KOPS KORS KOSS KOWS KRIS KUES KYNE KYUS LACS LACY LANX LARS LATI LAVS LECH LEKE LEKS LEKU LEPS LEVA LEVO LEVY LEWD LIDS LIGS LINY LIRE LIRI LITU LOBI LOCI LORN LUDS LUNY LUVS LYES LYMS LYNX MAAS MACS MADE MADS MAES MAGS MAKS MALS MAND MANY MAPS MARY MATS MATY

MAWN MAWS MAZY MEGS MELS MEMS MENO METS MHOS MIBS MIGS MILS MINX MINY MIRY MIXT MIXY MIZZ MNAS MOAS MOBS MOCS MODS MOES MOLS MOLY MOMI MOMS MONS MONY MOOI MOPY MOTS MOWN MOWS MOYS MOZZ MUCH MUDS MUNS NAIN NAMS NANS NAOI NAOS NAVY NAYS NEFS NEKS NEPS NESH NESS NETS NEVI NIDI NIDS NIED NIMS NISI NIXY NODI NOES NOMS NOPE NOSH NOSY NOTT

NOUS NOYS NUNS NYAS NYED OAKY OBIS ODDS ODEA OHMS OKAS OLEA ONST ONYX OPTS ORFS ORYX OSAR OYEZ PACS PADS PALY PAPS PATY PEDS PEGS PEHS PEPS PFFT PFUI PHAT PHEW PHIZ PHOS PIAS PIGS PILY PIPS PIPY PIRS PISS PITY PIXY POAS POCO POGY POKY POLS POMS PONS PONY POOS PORY POSY POWS PREZ PRUH PSST PUBS PUGH PUGS PUIR PULY PUNS PUNY PUPS PUTS

PUTZ PUYS PYAS PYES PYIC QATS QUEP RACA RAHS RAZZ REBS RECS REFS REFT REHS RELY REMS RENY REVS RHOS RHUS RIFS ROED ROKS ROKY ROPY ROUX RUBY RUCS RUNS RUTS RYAS RYES RYFE SABS SACS SAGS SAGY SAPS SASH SAWN SAWS SCRY SECO SECS SEEN SEES SEGS SEIK SELD SELS SENE SEPS SETS SEWN SEWS SEXY SEYS SHAT SHMO SHOD SIBS SICH SICS SIMS SINS SIPS

SIRS SITS SIZY SKAS SKIS SKOL SKRY SOBS SOCS SODS SOGS SOHO SOHS SOLS SOME SOON SOPS SORI SOSS SOTS SOVS SOYS SPED SPRY SRIS STEY SUBS SUCH SUES SUKS SUMS SUNG SUNS SUPS SUQS SUSS SWIZ SWUM SYED SYES TADS TAED TAES TAKS TAKY TALI TAMS TAOS TAUS TAVS TAXA TEDY TEES TEFS TEGS TELD TELS TELT THAE THAT THEY THIS THUS TICS TIDS TIDY TIGS

TILS TINS TINY TIPT TITS TOBY TODS TODY TOED TOES TOEY TOGS TOLD TONS TORN TOWY TOYS TREZ TSKS TUGS TUNY TUPS TUTS TUZZ TWAS TWOS TYDE TYGS TYPY UGLY UNDO UPGO UPSY UTAS UVAE UVAS VACS VAES VAGI VAIN VANS VARS VATS VAUS VAVS VAWS VEES VERA VETO VEXT VIAE VIAS VIBS VIDS VIGS VIMS VINS VIVO VIZY VOES VOLS VORS VUGS VUMS WADY WANY WARY

WAVY WAWS WAXY WEBS WEDS WEMS WENS WERE WERT WETS WHOA WHOT WHYS WICH WILY WIRY WOES WOGS WOKS WONS WOST WOWF WOWS WUDS WYCH WYES WYNS YALD YAPS YAWS YAWY YAYS YBET YEAH YEPS YEWS YGOE YIDS YIPS YMPT YOBS YODS YOKS YOLD YOND YOWS YUCH YUGS YUKS YUKY YUNX YUPS YWIS ZAGS ZANY ZAPS ZEAS ZEDS ZEKS ZELS ZIGS ZINS ZIPS ZITE ZITS ZIZZ ZOOS

5-LETTER WORD BLOCKERS

(except words ending in -ED, -J, -S, -X, -Y, -Z)

AARGH ABACI ABACK ABAFT ABASH ABASK ABEAM ABLOW ABOIL ABORE ABRAM ABRIM ABUNE ACERB ACHOO ACMIC ACOCK ACOLD

ACRID
ADOWN
ADOZE
ADRAD
ADSUM
ADUNC
ADYTA
AESIR
AFALD
AFIRE
AFOOT
AFORE
AFOUL
AGAIN
AGAPE
AGAST
AGGRI
AGLEE
AGLOW
AGOOD
AGRIN
AHEAD
AHEAP
AHENT
AHIGH
AHIND
AHINT
AHULL
AIDOI
AINEE
AITCH
ALACK
ALANE
ALBEE
ALEFT
ALGAE
ALGAL
ALGID
ALIKE
ALIVE
ALOFT
ALONE
ALOOF
ALOUD
ALOWE
ALTHO
AMAIN
AMICI
AMINO
AMNIA
AMNIC
AMONG
AMORT
ANILE
ANSAE
ANTAE
APACE
APAGE
APAID
APART
APAYD
APEAK
APEEK
APERT
APIAN
APOOP
APORT
APTER
AQUAE
AREAE
AREAL
AREAR
AREDD
AREIC
ARERE

ARIOT
AROSE
ASKEW
ASKOI
ASTIR
ASWIM
ASYLA
ATILT
ATRIP
AULIC
AULOI
AURAL
AURAR
AUREI
AVAST
AWASH
AWAVE
AWEEL
AWORK
AXIAL
AXILE
AYELP
AYGRE
AYONT
AZIDO
AZOIC
AZURN
BAITH
BAKEN
BANAL
BARER
BARIC
BASHO
BASSI
BASTA
BATCH
BEDAD
BEGAD
BEGAN
BEGAT
BEGOT
BELCH
BENCH
BESAT
BESAW
BIFID
BIGAE
BINAL
BIRCH
BIVIA
BLAER
BLASE
BLAWN
BLIST
BLIVE
BLOWN
BLUER
BOLAR
BONZA
BOREL
BORIC
BOXEN
BRAVI
BREEM
BREME
BRULE
BRUSK
BUCKO
BUFFA
BUFFI
BUILT
BURNT
BUTCH
BUXOM
BYSSI

CABRE
CACTI
CAESE
CAJON
CAJUN
CALID
CANST
CAPUT
CARPI
CECAL
CECUM
CERIC
CESTI
CHAPT
CHAVE
CHERE
CHIAO
CHIMO
CHODE
CHOTA
CHYND
CILIA
CINCH
CINCT
CIPPI
CIRRI
CIVIL
CLAPT
CLASH
CLIPT
CLOMB
CLUNG
COMAE
COMAL
COOCH
COOST
CORAM
CORNI
CORNO
COUDE
COULD
COURD
COXAE
COXAL
COYER
CRASH
CREPT
CROCI
CRONK
CROST
CRUSH
CUFFO
CUING
CUISH
CULCH
CURCH
CURSI
CURST
CYANO
CYMAE
DAWEN
DAYNT
DEALT
DEASH
DEDAL
DEERE
DEMIC
DEMPT
DIACT
DICTA
DIDST
DINGO
DIRER
DISCI
DITCH

DOCHT
DOEST
DOETH
DOGGO
DOILT
DOLCI
DOLIA
DOMAL
DOMIC
DOTAL
DOWNA
DRANK
DRAVE
DRAWN
DRENT
DREST
DRIPT
DROPT
DUCAL
DUING
DUMKA
DUNCH
DUNNO
DUNSH
DUOMI
DURST
DUTCH
DWELT
EHING
EIGNE
ELMEN
EMONG
ENLIT
ENORM
ETYMA
EVHOE
EVOHE
EWHOW
EYRIR
FASTI
FATAL
FAUGH
FAURD
FAVER
FAYER
FECAL
FECIT
FEHME
FERAL
FERER
FETAL
FETCH
FETID
FEWER
FEYER
FILAR
FILCH
FILUM
FINCH
FLITT
FLOSH
FLOWN
FLUNG
FOCAL
FORDO
FOUER
FRACK
FRATI
FRENA
FROSH
FRUSH
FUGAL
FUNGO
FURTH
GANCH

GARNI
GAYER
GEESE
GELID
GENAL
GENIC
GENII
GENUA
GESSO
GEYAN
GEYER
GHEST
GIGHE
GIRSH
GLIAL
GLODE
GNASH
GNAWN
GOBBI
GOBBO
GOIER
GONIA
GONNA
GONZO
GOTTA
GOYIM
GRANA
GREEK
GRIPT
GROWN
GRYPT
GULAR
GULCH
GURSH
GYRAL
HABLE
HADAL
HADST
HAIKU
HAITH
HANCH
HARSH
HASTA
HAULT
HAUTE
HEAME
HEMAL
HEWGH
HIANT
HILAR
HILCH
HILUM
HOING
HOKKU
HOOCH
HOTCH
HOTEN
HOVEN
HOWBE
HOWSO
HUGER
HUMIC
HUMID
HUNCH
HUTCH
ICTIC
ILEAC
ILEAL
ILIAC
IMIDO
IMINO
IMSHI
INAPT
INBYE
INCUT

INEPT
INERM
INFRA
INTIL
INTRA
INUST
IODIC
JEUNE
JINGO
JOKOL
JURAL
KACHA
KAING
KAMME
KEECH
KEMPT
KENCH
KIDGE
KINDA
KNELT
KNISH
KORAI
KRONA
KYDST
LAARI
LABRA
LAEVO
LAITH
LARCH
LAXER
LAZZI
LAZZO
LEANT
LEAPT
LEASH
LEISH
LEPID
LEPTA
LIART
LIBRI
LITAI
LIVID
LOACH
LOAST
LOBAR
LOGOI
LOSEN
LOTIC
LOYAL
LUCID
LUDIC
LUMME
LURCH
LURID
LYARD
LYART
LYCEA
LYNCH
LYTIC
MADID
MANET
MARCH
MARIA
MAYAN
MAYST
MEANT
MEDII
MEINT
MENSH
MERER
MESAL
MESIC
MESTO
MEYNT
MICRA

MIKRA
MILCH
MILIA
MINAE
MISDO
MISGO
MITCH
MODII
MOLAL
MOLTO
MOOSE
MORAE
MOSSO
MOSTE
MOTEN
MUCID
MULCH
MULSH
MUNCH
MUSHA
MUTER
MYOID
NAEVI
NARIC
NARRE
NATAL
NAVAL
NEGRO
NEIST
NEMPT
NEVER
NEWER
NGWEE
NICER
NIDAL
NIMBI
NITID
NIVAL
NOHOW
NOMEN
NOMOI
NOTAL
NOTUM
NOVAE
NOXAL
NUDER
NUDZH
NUGAE
NUMEN
NYING
OATEN
OBIIT
OBOLI
OGMIC
OHMIC
OHONE
OIDIA
OLEIC
OLPAE
ORGIC
OSSIA
OTAKU
OUTDO
OUTGO
OVOLI
OWSEN
PACTA
PADRI
PAISE
PAKKA
PALER
PALPI
PAOLI
PAOLO
PAPAL

PAPPI
PARVE
PAVID
PAYSD
PEART
PELON
PENAL
PEPLA
PERCH
PEREA
PETTI
PETTO
PHPHT
PHYLE
PIERT
PIEZO
PIING
PILAR
PILCH
PILEA
PILEI
PILUM
PINCH
PLENA
PLESH
POOCH
PORCH
POUPT
PRESA
PRIMI
PROST
PROUD
PSOAE
PSOAI
PUBIC
PUCER
PUCKA
PUDIC
PUKKA
PULIK
PULMO
PUPAE
PUPAL
PURER
PUTID
PUTTO
PYOID
PYRAL
PYRIC
QUALE
QUASI
QUAYD
QUOAD
QURSH
RABID
RADII
RAGDE
RAMAL
RARER
RASTA
RECTI
REDID
REJON
RELIT
REMET
RENAL
RERAN
RESAT
REWAN
REWON
RHYTA
RIFER
RIMAE
RORAL
RORIC

RORID
RUBAI
RUGAE
RUNIC
RYPER
SAFER
SAGUM
SAIST
SALIC
SAMEN
SANER
SAPID
SATEM
SAYNE
SAYST
SCAND
SCAPI
SCUDI
SEELD
SEGNI
SENGI
SENSA
SENTI
SENZA
SEPIC
SERAL
SERER
SERIC
SESSA
SETAE
SETAL
SHAKT
SHALT
SHASH
SHAWN
SHERE
SHEWN
SHONE
SHOON
SHOPE
SHORN
SHOWN
SHULN
SHUSH
SIELD
SIGLA
SIKER
SINCE
SKINT
SKOSH
SLAID
SLAIN
SLANK
SLASH
SLEER
SLEPT
SLIER
SLIPT
SLISH
SLUNG
SLUNK
SLYER
SMASH
SMOTE
SNASH
SNUCK
SNUSH
SOCKO
SODIC
SOLDI
SOLDO
SOPRA
SORAL
SORDA
SORER

SOUCT SPAKE SPARD SPENT SPRAD SPUTA STAID STASH STEPT STOAE STOAI STOLN STONG STOOD STOPT STUMM STUNG STUNK STURE STYLI SUCCI SULCI SULFO SUPRA SURAL

SWACK SWANG SWAPT SWARE SWEPT SWINE SWOLN SWOPT SWORE SWORN SWUNG SYKER TABID TACET TACIT TAGMA TAISH TAKEN TANTI TANTO TAPEN TARDO TAULD TAZZE TEACH

TELOI TEMPI TEPID TEUCH TEUGH THAIM THEBE THELF THEMA THIEF THILK THINE THOLI THOSE THRAE THREW TICCA TIDAL TIKKA TIMID TONDI TOPHI TOPOI TORIC TORII

TORSI TRAPT TREIF TRIFF TRILD TRUER TRYMA TUBAE TUBAL TUBAR TUMID TYNDE TYPAL ULNAD ULNAE ULPAN UNAPT UNBID UNDEE UNDID UNDUE UNDUG UNETH UNGOT UNHIP

UNKID UNMET UNRID UNSOD UNWET UPBYE UPLIT UPRAN URAEI URDEE UREAL UREIC URENT URNAL UTERI UVEAL VACUA VAGAL VAIRE VALID VAPID VARIA VASAL VATIC VEHME

VELUM VENAE VENAL VILDE VILLI VIMEN VINIC VIOLD VIRAL VIRID VITAE VIVID VOILA VOLAE VOLTA VOLTI VOULU VULGO VYING WAIDE WANLE WANNA WARST WAXEN WELCH

WELKT WELSH WENCH WERSH WHAMO WHICH WHILK WHIPT WHOSE WHOSO WIDER WILCO WINCH WINNA WIRRA WISER WISHA WITAN WOFUL WOMEN WOWEE WOXEN WRAPT WRATE WROTE

WROTH WRUNG WRYER XERIC XOANA XYLIC XYSTI YARER YAULD YBORE YCLAD YCOND YDRAD YEVEN YEWEN YFERE YINCE YLIKE YMOLT YOGIC YOKUL YOMIM YONIC YOURN YOUSE

YRAPT YRENT YRIVD YSAME YTOST YUCCH YURTA ZILCH ZLOTE ZOEAE ZOEAL ZONAE ZOPPA ZOPPO ZOWIE ZUZIM ZYGAL ZYGON ZYMIC

6-LETTER WORD BLOCKERS

(except words ending in -ED, -J, -S, -X, -Y, -Z)

AAHING ABATTU ABEIGH ABLAZE ABLEST ABLOOM ABLUSH ABOARD ABORAL ABORNE ABULIC ABURST ACETIC ACETUM ACHIER ACIDER ACIDIC ACINAR ACINIC ACKNEW ACRAWL ACULEI ACUTER ADIPIC ADMIXT ADNATE ADRIFT ADROIT ADYTUM AECIAL AECIUM AEDINE AEFALD AERIER AFAWLD AFEARD AFFYDE AFIELD AFLAME AFLOAT AFRAID AFRESH AFRONT AGAMIC

AGAPAE AGAPAI AGHAST AGILER AGLARE AGLEAM AGOING AGONAL AGONIC AGORAE AGUISH AHCHOO AHORSE AIDANT AIDFUL AIDMAN AIDMEN AIKONA AIMFUL AIRMAN AIRMEN AKIMBO ALBEIT ALDERN ALEXIC ALIBLE ALMOST ALNICO ALULAE ALULAR ALUMNI ALVINE AMARNA AMBUSH AMEBAE AMEBAN AMEBIC AMIDIC AMIDST AMINIC AMMINO AMMONO AMORAL AMYLIC

ANCILE ANCORA ANEATH ANEMIC ANENST ANETIC ANGOLA ANIGHT ANISIC ANKUSH ANNULI ANODAL ANODIC ANOMIC ANOUGH ANOXIC ANTRAL ANURAL ANURIC ANYHOW AORTAE AORTAL AORTIC APEMAN APEMEN APIECE APNEAL APNEIC APODAL APPAID APPAYD APTEST APTING ARCANA ARCANE ARCHEI ARDENT AREACH ARGULI ARGUTE ARIDER ARIGHT ARILLI ARIOSE

ARIOSI ARISEN AROUND ARRISH ARSENO ARSINO ARTFUL ASHAKE ASHINE ASHORE ASLANT ASLEEP ASLOPE ASMEAR ASPOUT ASQUAT ASSOTT ASTARE ASTOOP ASTRUT ASWARM ASWING ASWIRL ASWOON ATAVIC ATELIC ATHROB ATOKAL ATONAL ATOPIC ATWAIN ATWEEL ATWEEN ATWIXT ATYPIC AUDIAL AVANTI AVERSE AVIDER AVITAL AVOUCH AWARER AWATCH AWEIGH

AWEING AWHILE AWHIRL AWOKEN AWRACK AWRONG AWSOME AXEMAN AXEMEN AXENIC AXONAL AXONIC AZONAL AZONIC AZOTIC BAALIM BABIER BACCAE BACULA BADDER BADMAN BADMEN BAGMAN BAGMEN BALDER BALING BANING BANISH BARBAL BARDIC BAREST BARFUL BARING BARISH BARMAN BARMEN BASEST BASSER BATMAN BATMEN BAYING BAYMAN BAYMEN BEATEN

BECAME BEDASH BEDIDE BEDRID BEDYDE BEFELD BEFELL BEFORE BEGILT BEGIRT BEGONE BEHALF BEHELD BELIKE BELIVE BEMATA BEMIXT BENIGN BEREFT BESANG BESEEN BESTAD BESUNG BETING BETOOK BETROD BEWENT BEWEPT BIAXAL BIFOLD BIFORM BIGGER BINATE BINMAN BINMEN BIRKEN BISSON BITTEN BIVIUM BLAEST BLAISE BLAIZE BLANCH BLATER

BLEACH BLENCH BLOOIE BLOTTO BLUEST BLUIER BLUISH BOKING BOLDER BOLETI BOLLEN BONIER BONZER BOOING BOREAL BOSHTA BOSKER BOSSER BOWMAN BOWMEN BOXIER BOYING BOYISH BRAWER BREACH BREECH BREGMA BROKEN BROMIC BROOCH BRUMAL BRUNCH BRUTAL BUCCAL BULBAR BULLAE BUMALO BURSAE BURSAL BUSIER BUSMAN BUSMEN BUYING BYKING

BYLIVE BYPAST CABMAN CABMEN CADENT CADMIC CAECAL CAECUM CAGIER CAGING CAKIER CALAMI CALASH CALCIC CALLID CALMER CAMASH CAMSHO CANIER CANNAE CANNOT CANOLA CARMAN CARMEN CAROLI CARTOP CARVEN CASEIC CASINI CATCHT CATTLE CAUDAD CAUGHT CAUSAE CAUSEN CEDARN CEDING CELLAE CENDRE CERCAL CERING CERULE CHADRI CHELAE

CHICER CHIRAL CHOLIC CHORIC CHOSEN CHOUSH CHYLDE CICALE CIDING CILIUM CISTIC CITING CITRIC CLASPT CLATCH CLECHE CLENCH CLEVER CLINAL CLINCH CLONAL CLONIC CLOVEN CLUING CLUNCH CLYING CLYPEI CNIDAE COAXAL COBRIC COCCAL COCCIC COGENT COHOSH COITAL COKIER COKING COMADE COMETH COMODO COMOSE CONGII CONING COOCOO

COSING
COSMIC
COSTAE
COTTAE
COWIER
COWISH
COWMAN
COWMEN
COXIER
COXING
COYEST
COYING
COYISH
COZING
CREANT
CREDAL
CRIANT
CRIBLE
CRIMEN
CRINAL
CRISIC
CROTCH
CROUCH
CROUSE
CRUDER
CRURAL
CRUTCH
CUBING
CUEING
CULPAE
CULTCH
CULTIC
CUMULI
CUNEAL
CUPMAN
CUPMEN
CUPRIC
CURIAE
CURIAL
CURING
CURSAL
CURTER
CURULE
CUTCHA
CYANIC
CYMOID
CYMOSE
CYSTIC
CYTISI
CYTOID
DAEDAL
DAEING
DAFTER
DAIMEN
DAMMIT
DANISH
DANKER
DARKER
DAWISH
DAYLIT
DAZING
DEAFER
DEARER
DEAWIE
DEBILE
DEBOSH
DECANI
DECENT
DEEDER
DEEING
DEEPER
DEFFER
DEFTER
DEGAGE
DEIDER
DEIFIC
DEKING
DELTIC
DELUXE
DENSER
DERING
DERMAL
DERMIC
DETACH
DEVOID
DEVORE
DEVOUT
DEWIER
DEWING
DEXTRO
DIAMYL
DICIER
DIEING
DIKIER
DIKING
DINFUL
DINING
DINKER
DIREST
DISCAL
DISTAL
DITTIT
DJINNI
DOABLE
DOITIT
DOLENT
DOLING
DOLIUM
DOMIER
DOMING
DOPIER
DORMIE
DORSAD
DORSUM
DOSING
DOTIER
DOTISH
DOUCER
DOURER
DOVIER
DOVING
DOVISH
DOWIER
DOWING
DOZIER
DREAMT
DREICH
DREIGH
DRENCH
DRIEGH
DRIEST
DRIVEN
DROLER
DROMIC
DROMOI
DRYEST
DRYISH
DUCTAL
DUDING
DUDISH
DUEFUL
DUELLI
DUETTI
DUKING
DULLER
DUMBER
DUMOSE
DUNNER
DUPING
DURING
DUSKER
DYABLE
DYKIER
DYKING
DYNEIN
EADISH
EASIER
EASSEL
EASSIL
ECHINI
ECHOIC
EDENIC
EFFETE
EGESTA
EIDENT
EIDOLA
EIKING
EKUELE
ELDEST
ELMIER
ELVISH
EMBOST
EMMESH
ENARCH
ENCASH
ENGILT
ENGIRT
ENLEVE
ENMESH
ENODAL
ENOLIC
ENRAPT
ENRICH
EOTHEN
EPHORI
EPICAL
EPODIC
EREMIC
ERENOW
ETERNE
ETYMIC
ETYPIC
EURIPI
EWGHEN
EWKING
EXEUNT
EXILIC
EXODIC
EXODOI
EXONIC
EXTOLD
EYEING
FABBER
FACEUP
FACILE
FADIER
FAECAL
FAINER
FAIRER
FAKING
FALLEN
FAMING
FAMISH
FAMULI
FARAND
FARFET
FARING
FASCIO
FATING
FATTER
FAUNAE
FAUNAL
FAVEST
FAVOSE
FAXING
FAYEST
FAYING
FAZING
FEATER
FECUND
FEEING
FEHMIC
FEIRIE
FELSIC
FENMAN
FENMEN
FEODAL
FEREST
FERIAE
FERIAL
FERINE
FERRIC
FERVID
FETING
FETISH
FEUDAL
FEUING
FEWEST
FEYEST
FEYING
FIFING
FIKIER
FIKING
FIKISH
FILIAL
FILMIC
FILOSE
FINEST
FINISH
FINSKO
FISTIC
FITFUL
FIXIVE
FLANCH
FLAXEN
FLEECH
FLEMIT
FLENCH
FLETCH
FLIEST
FLINCH
FLITCH
FLOCCI
FLOOIE
FLORAE
FLORID
FLOUSH
FLUIER
FLYEST
FLYMAN
FLYMEN
FLYSCH
FODGEL
FOEMAN
FOEMEN
FOETAL
FOETID
FOGASH
FOGMAN
FOGMEN
FOLIAR
FONDER
FONTAL
FORANE
FORBYE
FORDID
FOREDO
FOREGO
FORGAT
FORGOT
FORMEE
FORMIC
FORRAD
FORREN
FORRIT
FOSSAE
FOUEST
FOULER
FOVEAE
FOVEAL
FOXIER
FOZIER
FRACTI
FRAENA
FRANCO
FREEST
FRENCH
FRENNE
FRIGID
FROREN
FRORNE
FROZEN
FRUGAL
FRUSTA
FULCRA
FULGID
FULVID
FUMIER
FUMING
FUMULI
FUNDIC
FUNEST
FUNGIC
FUNNER
FURCAL
FURDER
FUSILE
FUSING
FUZING
FYKING
GAEING
GAGING
GAGMAN
GAGMEN
GAIJIN
GALANT
GALEAE
GALLIC
GAMASH
GAMEST
GAMIER
GARDAI
GARISH
GASHER
GASLIT
GASMAN
GASMEN
GAUNCH
GAYEST
GAZIER
GAZING
GEASON
GEDDIT
GEEING
GEMINI
GEMMAE
GEMMAN
GEMMEN
GENIAL
GEODIC
GESTIC
GEYEST
GIBING
GIDDAP
GIDDUP
GIEING
GIGMAN
GIGMEN
GILDEN
GINGKO
GITTIN
GIUSTO
GLAZEN
GLEBAE
GLOBAL
GLUIER
GLUING
GLUISH
GLUNCH
GLUTEI
GNOMAE
GNOMIC
GOETIC
GOIEST
GOLDER
GONION
GONIUM
GOOIER
GORIER
GOTTEN
GOWDER
GOYISH
GRANUM
GRAVEN
GRAYER
GREYER
GRINCH
GRIPLE
GROSZE
GRUING
GRUTCH
GRYSIE
GUNMAN
GUNMEN
GUNNEN
GUTTAE
GUYING
GYBING
GYLDEN
GYMNIC
GYRANT
GYRING
GYROSE
GYVING
HABILE
HADDEN
HAEING
HAEMAL
HAEMIC
HAIKAI
HAINCH
HALERU
HALEST
HALFEN
HAMOSE
HAMULI
HANGUL
HANIWA
HARDER
HARISH
HATING
HAULST
HAUNCH
HAWKIT
HAZIER
HEARIE
HEISHI
HELIAC
HELING
HEMOID
HEMPEN
HEPPER
HERMAI
HETING
HEYING
HIATAL
HIEING
HIEMAL
HIKING
HIPPIC
HISPID
HOAING
HODMAN
HODMEN
HOHING
HOLDEN
HOLIER
HOLMIC
HOLPEN
HOMIER
HOOROO
HOOTCH
HOOVEN
HOPING
HORRID
HOSING
HOWZAT
HOXING
HOYING
HUDDEN
HUDDUP
HUGEST
HUMERI
HYDRAE
HYDRIC
HYEING
HYENIC
HYETAL
HYMNIC
HYPHAE
HYPHAL
HYPING
HYPOID
IATRIC
IBIDEM
ICEMAN
ICEMEN
ICONIC
IDLEST
IDOLUM
IMIDIC
IMMANE
IMMESH
INANER
INARCH
INBENT
INBORN
INCAVI
INCAVO
INCUBI
INCULT
INDIGN
INFELT
INFERE
INGRAM
INGRUM
INKJET
INLAID
INMESH
INMOST
INRUSH
INTACT
INTIME
INTIRE
INTOWN
INWITH
INWORN
IRATER
IRIDAL
IRIDIC
IRITIC
IRREAL
ITERUM
ITSELF
JACENT
JADING
JADISH
JANTEE
JEEING
JEJUNE
JEWING
JIBING
JIMPER
JINGKO
JINNEE
JIVIER
JIVING
JOBING
JOCOSE
JOCUND
JOKIER
JOKING
JOLING
JOVIAL
JOWING
JOYFUL
JOYING
JUBATE
JUGATE
JUKING
JYMOLD
KAEING
KAPUTT
KARMIC
KAWING
KEIGHT
KEPPEN
KEPPIT
KEYING
KIBOSH
KIPPEN
KIRSCH
KITTEL
KLATCH
KLOOCH
KNITCH
KOUROI
KRONEN
KRONER
KRONOR
KRONUR
KROONI
KUCHEN
KULAKI
KUTCHA
KYBOSH
LABARA
LABILE
LABIUM
LACTIC
LAESIE
LAICAL
LAKISH
LAMEST
LAMIAE
LAMISH
LANOSE
LARGER
LARINE
LAROID
LARVAE
LARVAL
LATHEN
LATISH
LAURAE
LAWEST
LAWFUL
LAWMAN
LAWMEN
LAXEST
LAYMAN
LAYMEN
LEARNT
LEETLE
LEFTER
LEGMAN
LEGMEN
LENGER
LENTEN
LENTIC
LERING
LESBIC
LEWDER
LIBANT
LIBRAE
LIEDER
LIEFER
LIENAL
LIEVER
LIFULL
LIGGEN
LIKEST
LIKUTA
LIMBIC
LIMNIC
LIMPID
LIMULI
LINEAL
LINEAR
LINIER
LINISH
LIROTH
LITHIC
LITTEN
LIVEST
LOBULI
LOCULI
LOGIER
LOIPEN
LOMATA
LOMING
LOOING
LOOSER
LOOTEN
LORATE
LOREAL
LOTHER
LOUCHE
LOUDER
LOUPEN
LOUPIT
LOWSER
LOWSIT
LOXING
LUBRIC
LUCENT
LUCKEN
LUITEN
LUNIER
LUPPEN
LURING
LUTEUM
LUTTEN
LYFULL
LYSING

LYTTAE
MAAING
MACING
MADMAN
MADMEN
MAGYAR
MAINER
MAKUTA
MALEIC
MALIST
MALLEI
MALOTI
MAMMAE
MANENT
MANFUL
MANQUE
MANTIC
MARISH
MASING
MATIER
MAUGER
MAUNNA
MAUVER
MAWING
MAYEST
MAYHAP
MAZIER
MEAGER
MEATAL
MEDIAD
MEDIAE
MEEKER
MEIKLE
MENSAE
MENSAL
MENSCH
MEREST
MERING
MERMAN
MERMEN
MESIAL
MESIAN
METING
MEVING
MEWING
MIKING
MILDER
MILIUM
MILKEN
MIMING
MIMMER
MINIER
MINISH
MIRIER
MIRING
MISATE
MISDID
MISLIT
MISMET
MISSAE
MISSAW
MISUST
MITIER
MITRAL
MIXIER
MIXING
MNEMIC
MODICA
MODISH
MODULI
MODULO
MOIRAI
MONACT
MONISH
MOOING
MOPIER
MOPING
MOPISH
MORBID
MORISH
MORSAL
MOSHAV
MOSING
MOTIER
MOUGHT
MOZING
MUCOSE
MULISH
MUONIC
MURKER
MUSCAE
MUTEST
MUTING
MUXING
MYSELF
MYTHIC
MYTHOI
MYXOID
NAIANT
NAIFER
NAIVER
NARIAL
NARINE
NASIAL
NASTIC
NATANT
NAUTCH
NEANIC
NEARER
NEATER
NEBISH
NEFAST
NERVAL
NESHER
NETHER
NEUMIC
NEURAL
NEVOID
NEWEST
NEWISH
NICEST
NICISH
NIELLI
NIGHER
NIOBIC
NIRLIT
NITRIC
NIXING
NOBBUT
NOBLER
NODOSE
NOGAKU
NONFAT
NONMAN
NONMEN
NONPAR
NORDIC
NOSIER
NOSTOI
NOTING
NOTOUR
NOULDE
NOUNAL
NOWISE
NOYING
NUBILE
NUCHAE
NUDEST
NUKING
NUMINA
NUTANT
OAFISH
OAKIER
OBESER
OBIING
OBITAL
OBITER
OBTECT
OCELLI
OCHONE
OCREAE
OCTOPI
ODDEST
ODDISH
OGAMIC
OGIVAL
OGRISH
OIDIUM
OILMAN
OILMEN
OMASAL
OMASUM
ONAGRI
ONIRIC
ONLINE
ONRUSH
OPTING
ORBIER
ORGANA
ORGIAC
OSTEAL
OSTIAL
OSTIUM
OTIOSE
OTITIC
OUTATE
OUTBYE
OUTDID
OUTSAT
OUTSAW
OUTWON
OWLISH
OWRIER
OXALIC
OXIDIC
OZONIC
PACTUM
PAINCH
PALEAE
PALEAL
PALEST
PALIER
PALISH
PALLAE
PALLID
PALPAL
PAPISH
PAPYRI
PARDEE
PARDIE
PAREVE
PARISH
PARTIM
PASSEE
PASSIM
PAUSAL
PAWING
PEARST
PEASEN
PEASON
PECTIC
PEDATE
PEEING
PELTAE
PENTAL
PENILE
PENMAN
PENMEN
PENNAE
PENNIA
PEPFUL
PERAEA
PERDIE
PEREIA
PEREON
PERFET
PERISH
PERITI
PERTER
PHAEIC
PHATIC
PHOCAE
PHONAL
PHYLAE
PHYLAR
PHYLIC
PHYLON
PHYLUM
PIANIC
PIAZZE
PICINE
PICRIC
PIEING
PIEMAN
PIEMEN
PIERST
PILEUM
PILOSE
PINETA
PINNAE
PINNAL
PINXIT
PINYIN
PIONIC
PIPIER
PIRNIT
PIROGI
PITHOI
PITMEN
PLACID
PLAGAL
PLANAR
PLEACH
PLENCH
PLEXAL
PLIANT
PLICAE
PLICAL
PLONGD
PLUTEI
PODIAL
POISHA
POKIER
POLISH
POLYPI
POMATO
POMMEE
PONENT
PONTAL
PONTIC
POOING
POOKIT
POPISH
PORIER
POSHER
POSIER
POTASH
POTATO
POTING
POTMAN
POTMEN
POUKIT
POWWAW
POXIER
POXING
PREMAN
PREMEN
PREMIA
PRIMAL
PRONER
PRONTO
PROSIT
PROWAR
PROWER
PRUTAH
PSORIC
PUCEST
PUDENT
PUIRER
PUKING
PULIER
PULPAL
PUNCTA
PUNIER
PUNISH
PUREST
PURING
PUTRID
PUTSCH
PUTTEN
PYCNIC
PYEING
PYEMIC
PYNING
PYXING
QUAINT
QUALIA
QUATCH
QUEINT
QUENCH
QUETCH
QUINIC
QUOOKE
QUOTHA
QURUSH
RACIAL
RACIER
RADDER
RADGER
RADISH
RAHING
RAKISH
RAMATE
RAMEAL
RAMOSE
RAMULI
RANCID
RANINE
RAPHAE
RAPINI
RAPPEN
RAREST
RARING
RATHER
RAUCID
RAVISH
RAWISH
RAXING
REALER
REALIA
RECHIE
RECKAN
RECLAD
RECTAL
REDIAE
REDIPT
REDONE
REDREW
REECHO
REEDEN
REFELL
REFELT
REFLEW
REGAVE
REGILT
REGNAL
REGNUM
REGREW
REGULI
REHASH
REHUNG
REKING
RELAID
RELIDE
RELISH
REMOUD
REPAND
REROSE
RESAID
RESAWN
RESEEN
RESEWN
RESHOD
RESHOT
RESOWN
RETIAL
RETOLD
RETOOK
RETORE
RETORN
RETRAL
RETROD
RETUSE
RHINAL
RHIZIC
RHODIC
RHOTIC
RICHER
RICTAL
RIDDEN
RIFEST
RILIER
RILING
RIMOSE
RIPEST
RODMAN
RODMEN
ROKIER
ROOPIT
ROPIER
RORIER
ROSCID
ROSEAL
ROTING
ROUPET
ROUPIT
RUBATI
RUBBET
RUBBIT
RUBIER
RUEFUL
RUGATE
RUGOSE
RULIER
RURBAN
RUSHEN
RUSINE
RYKING
SACCOI
SADDER
SAFEST
SAFING
SAGEST
SAGIER
SAIDST
SAIRER
SAKKOI
SALEWD
SALPAE
SAMIER
SANCTA
SANEST
SANING
SAPEGO
SAPFUL
SARING
SATING
SATIVE
SAYEST
SBIRRI
SBIRRO
SCALAE
SCATCH
SCEATT
SCENIC
SCHULN
SCIENT
SCOLIA
SCOPAE
SCORCH
SCOTCH
SCRYDE
SCUTAL
SCUTCH
SCUTUM
SCYPHI
SEAMAN
SEAMEN
SEARCH
SEARER
SECESH
SECUND
SEDENT
SEDILE
SEIKER
SEJANT
SELDOM
SELLAE
SEMEIA
SEMPER
SEMPRE
SENITI
SENRYU
SENSUM
SEPMAG
SEPTAL
SEREST
SERRAE
SETOSE
SEXFID
SEXIER
SEXING
SHAKEN
SHAPEN
SHAVEN
SHEQEL
SHOULD
SHRANK
SHREWD
SHROWD
SHRUNK
SHTOOM
SHTUMM
SHYEST
SHYING
SHYISH
SIALIC
SICCAN
SICCAR
SICKER
SIGLOI
SILENI
SILING
SILVAE
SIMIAL
SINFUL
SINING
SIPING
SIRING
SISTRA
SITING
SITTEN
SIWASH
SIZIER
SKEIGH
SKOLIA
SKOOSH
SKYIER
SKYING
SKYISH
SKYLIT
SKYMAN
SKYMEN
SLATCH
SLEAZO
SLEEST
SLIEST
SLIVEN
SLOOSH
SLOWER
SLUING
SLYEST
SLYISH
SMALTI
SMATCH
SMEECH
SMIRCH
SMOUCH
SNEESH
SNIDER
SNITCH
SOAKEN
SOBEIT
SOBFUL
SOCMAN
SOCMEN
SODAIC
SOEVER
SOFTER
SOLEIN
SOLEMN
SOLGEL
SOLIDI
SOLING
SOMATA
SORBIC
SORDID
SOREST
SOUGHT
SOURER
SPEECH
SPERST
SPETCH
SPICAE
SPINAE
SPLOSH
SPOILT
SPOKEN
SPORAL
SPRACK
SPRAID
SPRENT
SPRIER
SPRONG
SPRUNG
SPRUSH
SPRYER
SPUING
SPUTUM
SQUUSH
STALER
STALKO
STANCH
STANCK
STATAL
STATIM
STEARD
STEELD
STELAE
STELAI
STELAR
STERIC
STEYER
STINKO
STITCH
STOLEN
STOLID
STOMAL
STONEN
STOUSH
STRATI
STRAWN
STREWN
STRIAE
STRIPT
STRODE
STRONG
STROVE
STROWN
STRUCK
STRUNG
STYING
SUABLE
SUAVER
SUBITO
SUBMAN
SUBSEA
SULCAL
SULLEN
SUMMAE
SUNKEN
SUNLIT
SUPERB
SURBET
SUREST
SURIMI
SUTILE
SWATCH
SWEERT
SWEIRT
SWOOSH
SYEING
SYLVAE
SYNING
SYPING
SYRLYE
TAEING
TAISCH
TAKIER
TALEAE
TALLER
TALPAE
TAMEST
TAPING
TAPPIT

TARNAL
TAUGHT
TAURIC
TAUTER
TAUTIT
TAVERT
TAWIER
TAXMAN
TAXMEN
TEAING
TECTAL
TECTUM
TEDIER
TEEING
TEGMEN
TELIAL
TELIUM
TEMENE
TENIAE
TENSER
TENUTI
TERAPH
TERATA
TERBIC
TERGAL
TERGUM
TERRAE
TERSER
TESTAE
THECAE
THECAL
THENAL
THENCE
THETCH
THETIC
THOLOI
THORIC
THRASH
THRAWN
THRESH
THRICE
THROVE
THROWN
THRUSH
THYINE
THYMIC
THYRSI
TIBIAE
TICING
TIEING
TIFOSI
TIFOSO
TINEAL
TINIER
TINING
TINMAN
TINMEN
TITMAN
TITMEN
TOEIER
TOEING
TOFORE
TOLUIC
TOMATO
TOMBAL
TOMBIC
TOMIAL
TOMIUM
TONANT
TOOMER
TOPMAN
TOPMEN
TOROSE
TOROTH
TORRID
TORTEN
TOSING
TOSSEN
TOTHER
TOTING
TOWIER
TOYISH
TOYMAN
TOYMEN
TOZING
TREFAH
TRENCH
TREPID
TRIACT
TRIBAL
TRIFID
TRILLO
TRINAL
TRISTE
TRITER
TROPPO
TRUEST
TRUING
TSKING
TUBATE
TUFOLI
TUMULI
TUNIER
TURBID
TURFEN
TURGID
TUSSAL
TUTMAN
TUTMEN
TWEEST
TWILIT
TYEING
TYKISH
TYNING
TYPIER
UBIQUE
UGLIER
UGSOME
ULNARE
ULTIMO
UMBRAE
UMBRAL
UNBEEN
UNBENT
UNBORE
UNCHIC
UNCIAE
UNCINI
UNCLAD
UNCOOL
UNCUTE
UNDEAD
UNDEAR
UNDONE
UNDREW
UNEATH
UNEVEN
UNFELT
UNFINE
UNFIRM
UNFIXT
UNFOND
UNGAIN
UNGILT
UNGLAD
UNGORD
UNGUAL
UNHEWN
UNHUNG
UNHURT
UNIFIC
UNITAL
UNJUST
UNKEND
UNKENT
UNKEPT
UNKIND
UNLAID
UNLASH
UNLEAL
UNLICH
UNLOST
UNMADE
UNMARD
UNMEEK
UNMEET
UNMESH
UNMIXT
UNMOWN
UNOPEN
UNPAID
UNPENT
UNPURE
UNREAL
UNRENT
UNRUDE
UNSAID
UNSAWN
UNSENT
UNSEWN
UNSHOD
UNSOFT
UNSOLD
UNSOWN
UNSPUN
UNSUNG
UNSUNK
UNTOLD
UNTORN
UNTROD
UNVEXT
UNWELL
UNWEPT
UNWISH
UNWIST
UNWONT
UNWORN
UPBLEW
UPBORE
UPDOVE
UPDREW
UPGIRT
UPGONE
UPGREW
UPGUSH
UPHAND
UPHELD
UPHILD
UPHOVE
UPHUNG
UPLAID
UPMOST
UPPISH
UPROSE
UPRUSH
UPRYST
UPSENT
UPTOOK
UPTORE
UPTORN
UPWENT
URACHI
URATIC
UREMIC
URETIC
URSINE
USABLE
UVULAE
VACANT
VADOSE
VAGILE
VAGROM
VAGUER
VAINER
VALVAL
VALVAR
VANMAN
VANMEN
VARSAL
VASTER
VATMAN
VATMEN
VEDUTA
VEDUTE
VEGETE
VEHMIC
VEINAL
VELOCE
VENIAL
VENOSE
VERIER
VERLIG
VERMAL
VERNAL
VIABLE
VICING
VIDUAL
VILLAE
VILLAR
VINEAL
VINIER
VINING
VIRENT
VIRILE
VIRING
VISCID
VISIVE
VISTAL
VITTAE
VOGIER
VOLAGE
VOLING
VORAGO
VORANT
VORPAL
VOTING
VOTIVE
VULVAE
VULVAL
VULVAR
WABBIT
WAEFUL
WANDLE
WANIER
WANKLE
WANNEL
WANNER
WARIER
WARING
WARMAN
WARMEN
WASHEN
WAURST
WAVIER
WAXIER
WEAKER
WEXING
WEYARD
WHATEN
WHATNA
WHATSO
WHEARE
WHILOM
WHILST
WHITER
WHOMSO
WHOOSH
WIDEST
WIDISH
WIFING
WILFUL
WILIER
WILING
WIRIER
WISEST
WISING
WITHAL
WITING
WOEFUL
WOODEN
WORSER
WOWFER
WOWING
WRENCH
WRETCH
WROKEN
WRYEST
WRYING
WYLING
WYTING
XENIAL
XENIUM
XOANON
XYLOID
XYSTOI
YAKUZA
YAREST
YAWING
YBLENT
YBOUND
YBRENT
YCLEPT
YEDING
YEOMAN
YEOMEN
YEVING
YEXING
YIPPEE
YOWING
YPIGHT
YPLAST
YSHENT
YTTRIC
YUKIER
YUKING
YWROKE
ZAFTIG
ZANIER
ZAPATA
ZELOSO
ZEROTH
ZINCIC
ZIPTOP
ZIZITH
ZOECIA
ZOETIC
ZOFTIG
ZONOID
ZOOEAE
ZOOEAL
ZOONAL
ZOONIC
ZUFOLI
ZUFOLO
ZYGOID
ZYMOID

Section Seven

Anagrams

Introduction

The final section is substantial, containing all valid 7-letter and 8-letter words arranged in alphabetical order of their constituent letters.

Suppose you have the seven letters THORCES on your rack. You are sure that there must be a valid 7-letter word there. Just arrange the letters in alphabetical order (CEHORST), then look for CEHORST in the following 7-letter lists; it appears alphabetically ordered between CEHORSS and CEHORSU. You will find that there are six valid anagrams of your seven letters!

Perhaps you have the seven letters CORLINE, and you cannot see a valid 7-letter word. Arrange the letters into alphabetical order (CEILNOR) and check the list here. Lo and behold! The list goes from CEILNOP to CEILNOS, confirming that there is no anagram of those seven letters.

The same method can be used for 8-letter words. All valid 8-letter words have been put into their alphabetically-ordered forms, which themselves have been arranged alphabetically. What anagrams, if any, are there for the eight letters THROUCES? Easy! Put the letters into alphabetical order, check CEHORSTU in the 8-letter list, and you will find that there are two valid words, SCOUTHER and TOUCHERS.

The 7-letter Anagrams list contains over 31,000 words, and the 8-letter list has over 38,000 words. Happy anagram searching!

7-LETTER ANAGRAMS

AAAADNP	APADANA
AAAALTY	ATALAYA
AAABBCL	CABBALA
AAABBKL	KABBALA
AAABCCR	BACCARA
AAABCIR	ARABICA
AAABCLO	BACALAO
AAABCLS	CABALAS
AAABCLV	BACLAVA
AAABCMR	CARAMBA
AAABCNR	BARACAN
AAABCNS	CABANAS
AAABCOR	CARABAO
AAABCSS	CASABAS
	CASSABA
AAABCTW	CATAWBA
AAABDFR	ABFARAD
AAABDGS	DAGABAS
AAABDHS	BAHADAS
AAABDJS	BAJADAS
AAABDLM	LAMBADA
AAABDNN	BANDANA
AAABEGL	GALABEA
AAABFLL	FALBALA
AAABGIL	GALABIA
AAABHLQ	QABALAH
AAABILX	ABAXIAL
AAABIPS	PIASABA
AAABISS	ABASIAS
AAABKKS	KABAKAS
AAABKLS	KABALAS
AAABKLV	BAKLAVA
AAABKLW	BAKLAWA
AAABKSY	KABAYAS
AAABLLW	WALLABA
AAABLMT	TAMBALA
AAABLPR	PALABRA
AAABLST	ALBATAS
	ATABALS
	BALATAS
AAABMOS	ABOMASA
AAABMST	MASTABA
AAABNNR	RABANNA
AAABNNS	BANANAS
AAABORR	ARAROBA
AAABRSX	ABRAXAS
AAABRSZ	BARAZAS
	BAZAARS
AAABSTT	BATATAS
AAACCIS	ACACIAS
AAACCLM	MALACCA
AAACCLR	CARACAL
AAACCRS	CASCARA
AAACDIR	ARCADIA
AAACDLU	ACAUDAL
AAACDMM	MACADAM
AAACDNS	CANADAS
AAACENP	PANACEA
AAACGNT	AGACANT
AAACHHL	HALACHA
AAACHLZ	CHALAZA
AAACHNT	ACANTHA
AAACHRY	ACHARYA
AAACILM	MALACIA
AAACIMR	CARIAMA
AAACINP	ACAPNIA
AAACINR	ACARIAN
AAACIRS	ACRASIA
AAACJMR	JACAMAR
AAACJNS	JACANAS
AAACLLV	CAVALLA
AAACLMN	ALMANAC
	MANCALA
AAACLMR	CALAMAR
AAACLNT	CANTALA
AAACLPS	ALPACAS
AAACLPT	CATALPA
AAACLRZ	ALCAZAR
AAACMNP	CAMPANA
AAACMRS	MARACAS
	MARASCA
	MASCARA
AAACNNR	CARANNA
AAACNPT	CATAPAN
AAACNRT	NACARAT
AAACNRU	CARAUNA
AAACNRV	CARAVAN
AAACNST	CANASTA
AAACNTT	CANTATA
AAACPRX	CARAPAX
AAACPST	PATACAS
AAACRWY	CARAWAY
AAACSST	CASSATA
AAACSSV	CASAVAS
	CASSAVA
AAACSTT	CATASTA
AAADELM	ALAMEDA
AAADFRY	FARADAY
AAADGGH	HAGGADA
AAADGIL	ADAGIAL
AAADHMM	HAMMADA
AAADHMR	ADHARMA
AAADHMS	HAMADAS
AAADILX	ADAXIAL
AAADIRT	DATARIA
	RADIATA
AAADJMR	JAMADAR
AAADKNW	WAKANDA
AAADLMN	MANDALA
AAADLMW	WADMAAL
AAADMNT	ADAMANT
AAADMRS	ARMADAS
	MADRASA
AAADNPS	PANADAS
AAADNRS	SARDANA
AAADNRT	TANADAR
AAAEGLT	GALATEA
AAAEGNP	APANAGE
AAAEHLT	ALTHAEA
AAAEIMN	ANAEMIA
AAAELMP	PALAMAE
AAAELSZ	AZALEAS
AAAENST	ANATASE
AAAERWY	AREAWAY
AAAFFLL	ALFALFA
AAAFHRT	HAFTARA
AAAFIRT	RATAFIA
AAAFNRS	SARAFAN
AAAFRWY	FARAWAY
AAAGGLN	GALANGA
AAAGHIP	APHAGIA
AAAGHLN	LANGAHA
AAAGHNT	ATAGHAN
AAAGHPR	AGRAPHA
AAAGILN	ANALGIA
AAAGINR	ANGARIA
AAAGINZ	GAZANIA
AAAGIPT	PATAGIA
AAAGISS	ASSAGAI
AAAGJMU	MAJAGUA
AAAGLMM	AMALGAM
AAAGLMN	MALANGA
	NAGMAAL
AAAGLNO	ANALOGA
AAAGLNS	LASAGNA
AAAGLRS	ARGALAS
AAAGMMT	MAGMATA
AAAGMNR	ANAGRAM
AAAGMNS	SAGAMAN
AAAGMTT	TAGMATA
AAAGNNS	NAGANAS
AAAGNPR	PARGANA
AAAGNRT	TANAGRA
AAAGNRU	GUARANA
AAAGNTY	YATAGAN
AAAHHKL	HALAKAH
	HALAKHA
AAAHHLL	HALALAH
AAAHHLV	HALAVAH
AAAHIKW	KAHAWAI
AAAHINR	HARIANA
AAAHIPS	APHASIA
AAAHIST	TAIAHAS
AAAHJKW	KAJAWAH
AAAHLLS	HALALAS
AAAHLMR	HARMALA
AAAHLNN	ALANNAH
AAAHMMT	MAHATMA
AAAHMRS	ASHRAMA
AAAHMST	TAMASHA
AAAHPRT	PARATHA
AAAHRTW	WARATAH
AAAIKLT	LATAKIA
AAAILLS	ALALIAS
AAAILMR	MALARIA
AAAILNX	ANAXIAL
AAAILPS	APLASIA
AAAILRS	ARALIAS
AAAILRT	TALARIA
AAAIMNT	AMANITA
AAAINPS	PAISANA
AAAIPRX	APRAXIA
AAAIPSV	PIASAVA
AAAIQRU	AQUARIA
AAAISST	ASTASIA
AAAISTX	ATAXIAS
AAAJKST	JATAKAS
AAAJMPS	PAJAMAS
AAAJMSU	UJAMAAS
AAAKKMR	MARKKAA
AAAKKNS	KANAKAS
AAAKKRS	KARAKAS
AAAKLMS	KAMALAS
AAAKLMY	YAMALKA
AAAKLSS	ALASKAS
AAAKNST	KATANAS
AAALLPT	PALATAL
AAALMPT	TAMPALA
AAALMRS	MARSALA
AAALMSS	MASALAS
	SALAAMS
AAALNNT	LANTANA
AAALNPT	APLANAT
AAALRRY	ARRAYAL
AAALWYY	LAYAWAY
AAAMNNS	MANANAS
AAAMNPS	PANAMAS
AAAMNRT	AMARANT
	MARANTA
AAAMNSS	SAMAANS
AAAMNST	ATAMANS
AAAMNTY	MANYATA
AAAMORT	TAMARAO
AAAMPRT	PATAMAR
AAAMRRZ	ZAMARRA
AAAMRSS	ASRAMAS
	SAMARAS
	SAMSARA
AAAMRST	TAMARAS
	TARAMAS
AAAMRTU	TAMARAU
AAANNSV	SAVANNA
AAANNSZ	ZANANAS
AAANNTT	ANNATTA
AAANPPY	PAPAYAN
AAANRST	ANTARAS
AAANRTT	TANTARA
	TARTANA
AAANSTT	ANATTAS
AAAOPRZ	PARAZOA
AAAPPRT	APPARAT
AAAPPSY	PAPAYAS
AAAPRSS	APSARAS
AAAPSST	PASSATA
AAARSST	SATARAS
AAARSTV	AVATARS
AAARTTT	RATATAT
AAARTTU	TUATARA
AAARTXY	ATARAXY
AABBBOS	BAOBABS
AABBCEG	CABBAGE
AABBCGY	CABBAGY
AABBCMO	CABOMBA
AABBCOS	BABACOS
AABBDGR	GABBARD
AABBDHS	HABDABS
AABBEGN	BEANBAG
AABBEIS	BABESIA
AABBELT	BATABLE
AABBERT	BARBATE
AABBGRT	GABBART
AABBHLS	BABLAHS
AABBHST	SABBATH
AABBLLS	LABLABS
AABBLOR	BARBOLA
AABBLOS	BALBOAS
AABBSST	SABBATS
AABBSSU	BABASSU
AABCCEL	ACCABLE
AABCCER	BACCARE
AABCCET	BACCATE
AABCCIR	BRACCIA
AABCDIR	CARABID
AABCEKR	BACKARE
AABCELN	BALANCE
AABCELP	CAPABLE
	PACABLE
AABCELT	ACTABLE
AABCEMR	MACABER
	MACABRE
AABCEMS	AMBSACE
AABCERR	BARRACE
AABCERT	ABREACT
	BEARCAT
	CABARET
AABCFKT	FATBACK
AABCHIR	BRACHIA
AABCHMT	AMBATCH
AABCHNR	BARCHAN
AABCHOR	ABROACH
AABCHSS	CASBAHS
AABCILM	CAMBIAL
AABCINR	CARABIN
AABCIOP	COPAIBA

AABCITX	TAXICAB
AABCKLY	LAYBACK
AABCKNN	CANBANK
AABCKPY	BACKPAY
	PAYBACK
AABCKRR	BARRACK
AABCKRS	BACKRAS
AABCKSW	BACKSAW
AABCLMU	CALUMBA
AABCLPY	CAPABLY
AABCLSY	SCYBALA
AABCMMU	MACUMBA
AABCMST	TAMBACS
AABCMSU	SAMBUCA
AABCNRR	CARBARN
AABCORR	CARBORA
AABCORT	ABACTOR
	ACROBAT
AABCOTT	CATBOAT
AABCRSS	SCARABS
AABCSUU	AUCUBAS
AABCTTU	CATTABU
AABDDEL	ADDABLE
AABDDEN	ABANDED
AABDDER	ABRADED
AABDDIK	KABADDI
AABDDLN	BADLAND
AABDDNS	SANDDAB
AABDEFL	FADABLE
AABDEGM	GAMBADE
AABDEGN	BANDAGE
AABDEHS	ABASHED
AABDEIS	DIABASE
AABDELL	BALLADE
AABDELT	ABLATED
	DATABLE
AABDELW	WADABLE
AABDEMM	BEMADAM
AABDEMN	BEADMAN
AABDEMS	SAMBAED
AABDENU	BANDEAU
AABDERR	ABRADER
AABDERS	ABRADES
AABDERY	ABRAYED
AABDESU	AUBADES
AABDGHN	HANDBAG
AABDGHR	HARDBAG
AABDGMO	GAMBADO
AABDGNS	SANDBAG
AABDGOS	DAGOBAS
AABDHMS	BADMASH
AABDHNT	HATBAND
AABDHNY	HAYBAND
AABDHRS	BARDASH
AABDHRU	BAHADUR
AABDIIS	BASIDIA
AABDIKR	BIDARKA
AABDILN	BALADIN
AABDIMR	BARMAID
AABDINS	INDABAS
AABDINT	TABANID
AABDIOT	BIODATA
AABDIRS	ABRAIDS
AABDLLS	BALLADS
AABDLMS	LAMBDAS
AABDLNS	SALBAND
AABDLRW	BRADAWL
AABDMNR	ARMBAND
AABDNNO	ABANDON
AABDNOR	BANDORA
AABDNRS	BANDARS
	SANDBAR
AABDNRU	BANDURA
AABDORS	ABROADS
AABDORV	BRAVADO
AABDORX	BROADAX
AABDRRW	DRAWBAR
AABDRST	BASTARD
	TABARDS
AABDRSU	SUBADAR
AABDRSY	BAYARDS
AABDSTU	DATABUS
AABEELT	EATABLE
AABEEMN	AMEBEAN
AABEEMO	AMOEBAE
AABEERZ	ZAREEBA
AABEFFL	AFFABLE
AABEFFN	BEFFANA
AABEFGL	FLEABAG
AABEFGU	AUFGABE
AABEFNS	BEFANAS
AABEGGG	BAGGAGE
AABEGGR	GARBAGE
AABEGLR	ALGEBRA
AABEGMR	BERGAMA
	MEGABAR
AABEGMS	AMBAGES
AABEGRR	BAGARRE
	BARRAGE
AABEGSS	BAGASSE
	SEABAGS
AABEGST	ATABEGS
AABEGSU	ABUSAGE
AABEHLT	HATABLE
AABEHNT	ABTHANE
AABEHRS	EARBASH
AABEHSS	ABASHES
AABEIKN	IKEBANA
AABEILM	AMABILE
	AMIABLE
AABEILN	ABELIAN
AABEILS	ABELIAS
AABEILT	LABIATE
AABEILX	ABAXILE
AABEIOR	AEROBIA
AABEIRS	AIRBASE
	ARABISE
AABEIRZ	ARABIZE
AABEJLL	JELLABA
AABEJMU	JAMBEAU
AABEKLM	MAKABLE
AABEKLT	TAKABLE
AABEKNS	SEABANK
AABEKRS	ARABESK
AABEKST	ATABEKS
AABELLL	LABELLA
AABELLN	BALNEAL
AABELLO	ABOLLAE
AABELLS	SABELLA
	SALABLE
AABELMN	NAMABLE
AABELMT	TAMABLE
AABELNO	ABALONE
AABELNR	BANALER
AABELPP	PAPABLE
AABELPR	PARABLE
AABELPY	PAYABLE
AABELRS	ARABLES
AABELRT	RATABLE
AABELSS	BALASES
AABELST	ABLATES
	ASTABLE
AABELSV	SAVABLE
AABELSY	SAYABLE
AABELTT	ABETTAL
AABELTU	TABLEAU
	TABULAE
AABELTV	VATABLE
AABELTX	TAXABLE
AABEMNO	AMOEBAN
AABEMNS	BASEMAN
AABEMOS	AMOEBAS
AABENNW	WANNABE
AABENRT	ANTBEAR
AABENTY	ABEYANT
AABERRW	BARWARE
AABERSS	ABASERS
AABERST	ABATERS
	ABREAST
AABERSU	BAUERAS
	SUBAREA
AABERSZ	ZAREBAS
AABERTT	RABATTE
	TABARET
AABERTU	ABATURE
AABESTZ	ZABETAS
AABETTU	BATTEAU
AABETUX	BATEAUX
AABFFLY	AFFABLY
AABFILU	FABLIAU
AABFLRU	FABULAR
AABGGRS	RAGBAGS
AABGGSS	GASBAGS
AABGHNR	BHANGRA
AABGHNS	GABNASH
	NASHGAB
AABGHSW	BAGWASH
AABGIIL	ABIGAIL
AABGILM	MAILBAG
AABGIMS	GAMBIAS
AABGINR	BARGAIN
AABGINS	ABASING
	BAAINGS
	BISNAGA
AABGINT	ABATING
AABGINZ	BIZNAGA
AABGMNY	MANGABY
AABGOSZ	GAZABOS
AABGRST	RATBAGS
AABHHIS	SAHIBAH
AABHHKS	SABKHAH
AABHHRU	BRUHAHA
AABHINT	HABITAN
AABHISS	SAHIBAS
AABHITT	HABITAT
AABHJNS	BHAJANS
AABHKNR	BARKHAN
AABHKSS	KASBAHS
	SABKHAS
AABHKST	BHAKTAS
	SABKHAT
AABHLRS	BHARALS
AABHLTY	BATHYAL
AABHMRS	BRAHMAS
	SAMBHAR
AABHMSS	SHAMBAS
AABHMTT	BATHMAT
AABHSSW	BASHAWS
AABIILX	BIAXIAL
AABIILZ	ALBIZIA
AABIJMY	JAMBIYA
AABIKLM	KALIMBA
AABIKNS	BANKSIA
AABILLN	ALBINAL
AABILLR	BARILLA
AABILLS	LABIALS
AABILMN	BIMANAL
AABILMS	BAALISM
AABILMY	AMIABLY
AABILNS	BASINAL
AABILOU	ABOULIA
AABILRS	BASILAR
AABILST	BALISTA
AABILSU	ABULIAS
AABIMMR	MARIMBA
AABIMNO	AMBOINA
	BONAMIA
AABIMOS	ABOMASI
AABIMRS	AMBARIS
AABIMST	BASMATI
AABINNS	BANIANS
AABINOU	OUABAIN
AABINRS	ARABINS
AABINRT	ATABRIN
AABINST	ABSTAIN
AABINSW	WABAINS
AABINSZ	BANZAIS
AABIORS	ABROSIA
AABIORT	AIRBOAT
AABIPUX	PAXIUBA
AABIRSZ	ZARIBAS
AABISSW	WASABIS
AABISTT	ABATTIS
AABKMST	TAMBAKS
AABKNNS	KANBANS
AABKNRS	BARKANS
AABKNRT	TANBARK
AABKOOZ	BAZOOKA
AABLLNS	BALLANS
AABLLNT	BALLANT
AABLLNY	BANALLY
AABLLOR	ALLOBAR
AABLLOS	ABOLLAS
AABLLPT	PATBALL
AABLLST	BALLAST
	BALLATS
AABLLSY	BASALLY
	SALABLY
AABLLWY	WALLABY
AABLMRU	LABARUM
AABLMSS	BALSAMS
	SAMBALS
AABLMST	LAMBAST
AABLMSY	ABYSMAL
	BALSAMY
AABLNTT	BLATANT
AABLORT	ABLATOR
AABLOSV	LAVABOS
AABLPRU	PABULAR
AABLPYY	PAYABLY
AABLRST	ARBLAST
AABLRSU	SUBALAR
AABLRTU	TABULAR
AABLRTY	RATABLY
AABLSST	BASALTS
AABLSSY	ABYSSAL
AABLSTU	ABLAUTS
AABLTTU	ABUTTAL
AABLTXY	TAXABLY
AABMNOT	BOATMAN
AABMNOY	AMBOYNA
AABMNST	BANTAMS
	BATSMAN
AABMORU	MARABOU
AABMOSY	BAYAMOS
AABMRSS	SAMBARS
AABMRTU	TAMBURA
AABMSST	TSAMBAS
AABMSSY	AMBASSY
AABNNOZ	BONANZA
AABNNSY	BANYANS
AABNOST	SABATON
AABNOSY	SABAYON
AABORRS	ARROBAS
	RASBORA
AABORST	ABATORS
	RABATOS
AABORSZ	ABRAZOS
AABOTTY	ATTABOY
AABQSUU	SUBAQUA

AABRRST	BARRATS
AABRRSU	SABURRA
AABRRUV	BRAVURA
AABRSTY	BARYTAS
AABSSSY	SASSABY
AABSTTW	ABWATTS
AABSTUX	SAXTUBA
	SUBTAXA
AABTTTU	BATTUTA
AACCDEI	CICADAE
AACCDEM	MEDACCA
AACCDES	CASCADE
	SACCADE
AACCDII	ACCIDIA
AACCDIR	CARDIAC
AACCDIS	CICADAS
AACCDSU	CADUACS
AACCEFT	CATFACE
AACCEKR	CARCAKE
AACCELO	CLOACAE
AACCENV	VACANCE
AACCERS	CARCASE
AACCEST	SACCATE
AACCHHK	KACHCHA
AACCHIM	MACCHIA
AACCHIN	CHICANA
AACCHIR	ARCHAIC
AACCHKS	KACCHAS
AACCHLN	CLACHAN
AACCHMP	CHAMPAC
AACCHMS	CHACMAS
AACCHNN	CANNACH
AACCHNS	CANCHAS
AACCHOR	CAROACH
AACCHRT	CHARACT
AACCILM	ACCLAIM
AACCILS	ALCAICS
	CICALAS
AACCILU	ACICULA
AACCIMS	CAIMACS
AACCIMT	ACMATIC
AACCINV	VACCINA
AACCIOR	CARIOCA
AACCIRT	ACRATIC
AACCITT	ATACTIC
AACCJKR	CARJACK
AACCKLP	CALPACK
AACCKRR	CARRACK
AACCKRS	CARACKS
AACCLLO	CLOACAL
AACCLLT	CATCALL
AACCLOP	POLACCA
AACCLOR	CARACOL
AACCLOS	CLOACAS
AACCLPS	CALPACS
AACCLPT	PLACCAT
AACCLRS	CALCARS
AACCLRU	ACCRUAL
	CARACUL
AACCLSU	ACCUSAL
AACCLTW	CATCLAW
AACCMOS	MACACOS
AACCNNS	CANCANS
AACCNVY	VACANCY
AACCORU	CURACAO
	CURACOA
AACCOST	ACCOAST
AACCOTT	TOCCATA
AACCRRT	CARRACT
AACCRSS	CARCASS
AACCRST	CARACTS
AACDDEL	DECADAL
AACDDER	ARCADED
AACDDHR	CHADDAR
AACDDIN	CANDIDA
AACDDRW	CRAWDAD
AACDEEM	ACADEME
AACDEFL	FALCADE
AACDEFS	FACADES
AACDEHM	CHAMADE
AACDEHR	CHARADE
AACDEHT	CATHEAD
AACDEII	AECIDIA
AACDEIL	ALCAIDE
AACDEIN	AIDANCE
AACDEIR	CARDIAE
AACDEIS	ACEDIAS
AACDELL	ALCALDE
AACDELN	CANALED
	CANDELA
	DECANAL
AACDELP	PALACED
AACDELR	CALDERA
	CRAALED
AACDELS	ALCADES
	SCALADE
AACDELY	ALCAYDE
AACDEMY	ACADEMY
AACDENV	ADVANCE
AACDENZ	CADENZA
AACDEPS	SCAPAED
AACDERS	ARCADES
AACDERV	CADAVER
AACDETU	CAUDATE
AACDETV	VACATED
AACDEUX	CADEAUX
AACDFIR	FARADIC
AACDFRS	CAFARDS
AACDGGI	AGGADIC
AACDGHI	HAGADIC
AACDHMR	DRACHMA
AACDHNR	HANDCAR
AACDHRS	CHADARS
AACDHST	DATCHAS
AACDIIS	ASCIDIA
AACDILR	RADICAL
AACDINS	SCANDIA
AACDINT	ANTACID
AACDINV	VANADIC
AACDIOR	ACAROID
AACDIRS	ACARIDS
	ASCARID
	CARDIAS
AACDJKW	JACKDAW
AACDKSY	DAYSACK
AACDLNO	CALANDO
AACDLNS	SCANDAL
AACDLOR	CARLOAD
AACDLOS	SCALADO
AACDLPR	PLACARD
AACDMPS	MADCAPS
AACDNRS	CADRANS
	CANARDS
AACDOOV	AVOCADO
AACDRSS	CSARDAS
AACDRSZ	CZARDAS
AACEEGR	ACREAGE
AACEEHR	EARACHE
AACEEHT	CHAETAE
AACEEKT	TEACAKE
AACEELN	ANELACE
AACEEMR	CAMERAE
AACEEMS	AMESACE
AACEENT	CATENAE
AACEERT	ACERATE
AACEESS	CASEASE
AACEEST	CASEATE
AACEETT	ACETATE
AACEFIS	FASCIAE
AACEFLT	FALCATE
AACEFLU	FACULAE
AACEFMN	FACEMAN
AACEFRR	CARFARE
AACEFRS	CARAFES
AACEGGR	AGGRACE
AACEGHN	GANACHE
AACEGHS	ACHAGES
AACEGIP	AGAPEIC
AACEGKP	PACKAGE
AACEGKS	SACKAGE
AACEGLS	SCALAGE
AACEGNR	CARNAGE
	CRANAGE
AACEGRT	CARTAGE
AACEGSV	SCAVAGE
AACEHIN	ACHENIA
AACEHIR	ARCHAEI
AACEHLP	ACALEPH
AACEHLR	ALCHERA
AACEHLT	CHAETAL
AACEHNO	CHOANAE
AACEHNP	PANACHE
AACEHNR	ACHARNE
AACEHPP	APPEACH
AACEHPS	APACHES
AACEHPU	CHAPEAU
AACEHRT	TRACHEA
AACEHST	ACHATES
AACEHTT	ATTACHE
AACEHTU	CHATEAU
AACEILM	CAMELIA
AACEIMN	ANAEMIC
AACEIMU	CAMAIEU
AACEINR	ACARINE
	CARINAE
AACEIQU	ACEQUIA
AACEIRV	AVARICE
	CAVIARE
AACEJLS	JACALES
AACEKNP	PANCAKE
AACEKNS	ASKANCE
AACEKOT	OATCAKE
AACELLN	CANELLA
AACELLS	SACELLA
AACELLT	LACTEAL
AACELMN	MANACLE
AACELMR	CAMERAL
	CARAMEL
	CERAMAL
AACELMU	MACULAE
AACELNP	CAPELAN
AACELNS	ANLACES
AACELNT	LACTEAN
AACELNU	CANULAE
	LACUNAE
AACELNV	VALANCE
AACELOR	ACEROLA
AACELOV	COAEVAL
AACELPR	CARPALE
AACELPS	PALACES
AACELPT	PLACATE
AACELRS	SCALARE
AACELRV	CARAVEL
AACELSS	CALESAS
AACELST	ACETALS
	LACTASE
AACELTT	LACTATE
AACELTV	CLAVATE
AACELTY	ACYLATE
AACEMMR	MACRAME
AACEMNS	CASEMAN
AACEMNV	CAVEMAN
AACEMOS	CAEOMAS
AACEMPR	PARACME
AACEMQU	MACAQUE
AACEMRS	CAMERAS
AACEMSS	CAMASES
AACENPS	CANAPES
AACENRT	CATERAN
AACENST	CATENAS
AACENTT	CANTATE
AACENTY	CYANATE
AACEOPT	PEACOAT
AACEORS	ROSACEA
AACEPRT	CAPRATE
AACEPRU	CAPUERA
AACEPRV	PRECAVA
AACERSS	CAESARS
AACERST	ACATERS
	CARATES
AACERSU	CAESURA
AACERSZ	SAZERAC
AACERTT	TEACART
AACERTU	ARCUATE
AACERWY	RACEWAY
AACESTV	CAVEATS
	VACATES
AACESTX	EXACTAS
AACETTU	ACTUATE
AACETUV	VACUATE
AACFFIL	CAFFILA
AACFILS	CAFILAS
	FACIALS
	FASCIAL
AACFILU	FAUCIAL
AACFINT	FANATIC
AACFISS	FASCIAS
AACFLLT	CATFALL
AACFLLU	FALCULA
AACFLLY	FALLACY
AACFLPT	FLATCAP
AACFLRT	FLATCAR
	FRACTAL
AACFLRU	FACULAR
AACFLSU	FAUCALS
AACFLTU	FACTUAL
AACFNST	CAFTANS
AACFRRU	FARRUCA
AACGHNS	CHAGANS
AACGILL	GLACIAL
AACGILM	MAGICAL
AACGILS	SCAGLIA
AACGINT	AGNATIC
AACGIRS	AGARICS
AACGIRV	AGRAVIC
AACGISU	GUAIACS
AACGLOT	CATALOG
AACGLOU	COAGULA
AACGLSY	GALYACS
AACGNOU	GUANACO
AACHHKR	CHARKHA
AACHHLL	CHALLAH
AACHHLS	CHALAHS
AACHIKL	HALAKIC
AACHIKN	KACHINA
AACHIKR	CHIKARA
AACHILO	ACHOLIA
AACHILR	RACHIAL
AACHILT	CALATHI
AACHIMR	MACHAIR
AACHIMS	CHIASMA
AACHINT	ACANTHI
AACHIPR	CHARPAI
	HAIRCAP
AACHIPS	APHASIC
AACHIPT	CHAPATI
AACHIRS	ARACHIS
AACHIRT	CITHARA
AACHITY	CYATHIA
AACHKMN	HACKMAN

AACHKMP	CHAMPAK
AACHKNS	ACHKANS
AACHKPS	CHAPKAS
	PACHAKS
AACHKRS	CHAKRAS
	CHARKAS
AACHKRT	HATRACK
AACHKRY	HAYRACK
AACHKSW	HACKSAW
	KWACHAS
AACHLLN	CHALLAN
AACHLLS	CHALLAS
AACHLMS	CHASMAL
AACHLNS	CHALANS
AACHLNT	CANTHAL
AACHLPP	CHAPPAL
AACHLPS	PASCHAL
AACHLST	CALTHAS
AACHLSU	ACUSHLA
AACHMNP	CHAPMAN
AACHMNS	MACHANS
AACHMSY	YASHMAC
AACHNOP	PANOCHA
AACHNOU	HUANACO
AACHNPX	PANCHAX
AACHNRS	ANARCHS
AACHNRV	NAVARCH
AACHNRY	ANARCHY
AACHNSS	ASHCANS
AACHNST	ACANTHS
AACHNSU	ANCHUSA
AACHNSZ	CHAZANS
AACHNZZ	CHAZZAN
AACHRRT	CATARRH
AACHRST	CHARTAS
AACHRSW	CARWASH
AACHRWY	ARCHWAY
AACHSSW	CASHAWS
AACHSTT	CHATTAS
AACIILN	ANCILIA
	LACINIA
AACIIMS	CAMISIA
AACIINP	APICIAN
AACIINT	ACTINIA
AACIITV	VIATICA
AACIJLP	JALAPIC
AACIJMS	JICAMAS
AACIKLL	ALKALIC
AACIKLR	CLARKIA
AACIKNN	CANAKIN
AACIKNT	KATCINA
AACILLN	ANCILLA
AACILMS	CALIMAS
	CAMAILS
AACILNR	CARINAL
	CLARAIN
	CRANIAL
AACILNT	ACTINAL
	ALICANT
AACILOS	ASOCIAL
AACILOX	COAXIAL
AACILPS	APICALS
	SPACIAL
AACILPT	CAPITAL
	PLACITA
AACILRR	RAILCAR
AACILTT	CATTAIL
AACILTV	VATICAL
AACIMMR	MACRAMI
AACIMNO	MANIOCA
AACIMNS	CAIMANS
	MANIACS
AACIMOR	ACROMIA
AACIMPR	PICAMAR
AACIMSS	CAMISAS
AACIMTY	CYMATIA
AACINNT	CANTINA
AACINOR	CONARIA
	OCARINA
AACINPT	CAPITAN
	CAPTAIN
AACINRS	ACRASIN
	ARNICAS
	CARINAS
AACINRT	ANTICAR
AACINRZ	CZARINA
AACINSS	ASCIANS
	SANCAIS
AACINST	SATANIC
AACIOPT	TAPIOCA
AACIOPV	COPAIVA
AACIOST	ATOCIAS
	COAITAS
AACIPPR	PAPRICA
AACIPRS	PICARAS
AACIPRX	APRAXIC
AACIQTU	AQUATIC
AACIRSS	ASCARIS
AACIRST	CARITAS
AACIRSV	CAVIARS
AACISSS	CASSIAS
AACISST	CASITAS
AACISTT	ASTATIC
AACISTX	ATAXICS
AACJKLS	JACKALS
AACJKMN	JACKMAN
	MANJACK
AACJKSS	JACKASS
AACJOSU	ACAJOUS
AACJPTU	CAJAPUT
AACKLTW	CATWALK
AACKMNP	MANPACK
	PACKMAN
AACKMRT	AMTRACK
AACKNRS	RANSACK
AACKPRR	CARPARK
AACKPRT	RATPACK
AACKPSZ	CZAPKAS
AACKPWX	PACKWAX
AACKPWY	PACKWAY
AACKRRS	ARRACKS
AACKSTT	ATTACKS
AACLLNS	CALLANS
AACLLNT	CALLANT
AACLLNU	CALLUNA
	LACUNAL
AACLLOR	CORALLA
AACLLSU	CLAUSAL
AACLLVY	CAVALLY
AACLMNO	COALMAN
AACLMNT	CALMANT
	CLAMANT
AACLMRU	MACULAR
AACLMST	LACTAMS
AACLMSU	CALAMUS
	MACULAS
AACLNNO	ANCONAL
AACLNNU	CANNULA
AACLNPY	CLAYPAN
AACLNRS	CARNALS
AACLNRU	LACUNAR
AACLNSU	CANULAS
	LACUNAS
AACLOPR	CAPORAL
AACLOPT	OCTAPLA
AACLORT	COALTAR
	CROTALA
AACLORZ	ALCORZA
AACLOST	CATALOS
	COASTAL
AACLOTT	CATTALO
AACLOTV	OCTAVAL
AACLPRS	CARPALS
AACLPRT	CALTRAP
AACLPSS	PASCALS
AACLPSU	PASCUAL
	SCAPULA
AACLPTY	PLAYACT
AACLRSS	LASCARS
	RASCALS
	SACRALS
	SCALARS
AACLRST	CASTRAL
AACLRTY	LACTARY
AACLRVY	CALVARY
	CAVALRY
AACLSSU	CASUALS
	CAUSALS
AACLSTT	SALTCAT
AACLSUV	VASCULA
AACLTTU	TACTUAL
AACMMOT	COMMATA
AACMNOR	CAMARON
AACMNRU	ARCANUM
AACMNSY	CAYMANS
AACMORR	CAMORRA
AACMORS	SARCOMA
AACMORT	MARCATO
AACMOSY	MACOYAS
AACMRRT	TRAMCAR
AACMRSS	SARCASM
AACMRST	AMTRACS
	RAMCATS
	TARMACS
AACNNOZ	CANZONA
AACNOST	SACATON
AACNOTZ	ZACATON
AACNPRT	CANTRAP
AACNPST	CAPSTAN
	CAPTANS
	CATNAPS
AACNRST	ARCTANS
	CANTARS
AACNRTU	CURTANA
AACNSSV	CANVASS
AACNSTU	ASCAUNT
AACOPPR	APOCARP
AACORST	OSTRACA
AACORTU	ACATOUR
	AUTOCAR
AACOTUV	AUTOVAC
AACPRSS	SCARPAS
AACPSTW	CATSPAW
AACRRST	CARRATS
AACRRSU	CURARAS
AACRSTV	CRAVATS
AACRTTT	ATTRACT
AACRTUV	VACATUR
AACRTUY	ACTUARY
AACRTWY	CARTWAY
AACTUWY	CUTAWAY
AADDDEN	ADDENDA
AADDEGM	DAMAGED
AADDEIL	ALIDADE
AADDEMM	MADAMED
AADDENP	DEADPAN
AADDEOR	DEODARA
AADDEPR	PARADED
AADDEPT	ADAPTED
AADDERS	ADREADS
AADDERW	AWARDED
AADDESX	ADDAXES
AADDGNR	GRADDAN
	GRANDAD
AADDHKR	KHADDAR
AADDHRS	SRADDHA
AADDIIK	DIDAKAI
AADDIIV	DAVIDIA
AADDILS	ALIDADS
AADDIMS	DADAISM
AADDIST	DADAIST
AADDLNS	ADLANDS
AADDNVV	DVANDVA
AADDOSU	AOUDADS
AADDRST	DASTARD
AADDRSW	ADWARDS
AADDSST	STADDAS
AADEEFR	AFEARED
AADEEGH	HEADAGE
AADEELT	DEALATE
AADEEMT	EDEMATA
AADEENR	ANEARED
AADEERT	AERATED
AADEERW	AWARDEE
AADEFFR	AFFEARD
AADEFGL	FALDAGE
AADEFGR	FARDAGE
AADEFHT	FATHEAD
AADEFIS	FADAISE
AADEFLU	AEFAULD
AADEFNZ	FAZENDA
AADEFTW	FATWAED
AADEGGR	AGGRADE
	GARAGED
AADEGHR	RAGHEAD
AADEGLS	GELADAS
AADEGMN	AGNAMED
	MANAGED
AADEGMR	DAMAGER
	MEGARAD
AADEGMS	DAMAGES
AADEGNS	AGENDAS
AADEGRT	GRADATE
AADEGRV	RAVAGED
AADEGRY	DRAYAGE
	YARDAGE
AADEGSV	SAVAGED
AADEHIR	AIRHEAD
AADEHJR	JARHEAD
AADEHKS	AKEDAHS
AADEHMN	HEADMAN
AADEHMS	ASHAMED
AADEHPS	SAPHEAD
AADEHPW	AWHAPED
AADEHRW	RAWHEAD
	WARHEAD
AADEHWY	HEADWAY
AADEIKK	KAIAKED
AADEILR	RADIALE
AADEILV	AVAILED
	VEDALIA
AADEIMR	MADEIRA
AADEIMS	AMIDASE
	SEAMAID
AADEINR	ARANEID
AADEINS	NAIADES
AADEINZ	ZENAIDA
AADEIPS	DIAPASE
AADEIRS	ARAISED
AADEIRT	AIRDATE
	RADIATE
	TIARAED
AADEITV	AVIATED
AADEITW	AWAITED
AADEJMR	JEMADAR
AADEKKY	KAYAKED
AADEKLR	KRAALED
AADEKLS	ASLAKED
AADEKMR	KAMERAD
AADEKMS	MEDAKAS

AADELLP	PADELLA
AADELLY	ALLAYED
AADELMN	LEADMAN
AADELMO	ALAMODE
AADELMR	ALARMED
AADELMX	MALAXED
AADELNR	ADRENAL
AADELNT	LANATED
AADELNW	DANELAW
AADELNX	ADNEXAL
AADELPR	PARDALE
AADELPT	PALATED
AADELRT	LATERAD
AADELRU	RADULAE
AADELRY	ALREADY
AADELSS	SALADES
	SALSAED
AADELTU	ADULATE
AADELTY	DAYTALE
AADEMMN	MANMADE
AADEMMS	MADAMES
AADEMNO	ADENOMA
AADEMNS	ANADEMS
	MAENADS
AADEMNT	MANDATE
AADEMRY	DAYMARE
AADEMSS	AMASSED
AADENNT	ANDANTE
AADENRV	VERANDA
AADENRW	AWARNED
AADENST	ANSATED
AADENSW	WEASAND
AADENWZ	WEAZAND
AADEPRR	PARADER
AADEPRS	ASPREAD
	PARADES
AADEPRT	ADAPTER
	READAPT
AADEPSS	ESPADAS
	PASSADE
AADEPWW	PAWAWED
AADERRS	ARRASED
AADERRW	AWARDER
AADERRY	ARRAYED
AADERSW	SEAWARD
AADERSY	ARAYSED
	DARESAY
AADERTU	AURATED
AADESSY	ASSAYED
AADFLTW	TWAFALD
AADFNRR	FARRAND
AADFNST	FANTADS
AADFRST	DAFTARS
AADGGHR	HAGGARD
AADGGLR	LAGGARD
AADGGRS	SAGGARD
AADGHIL	HIDALGA
AADGIMM	DIGAMMA
AADGIMO	AGAMOID
AADGIMR	DIAGRAM
AADGIMS	AGAMIDS
AADGINW	ADAWING
AADGIOS	ADAGIOS
AADGIOT	AGATOID
AADGIRV	GRAVIDA
AADGLLW	GADWALL
AADGLMY	AMYGDAL
AADGLNO	GONADAL
AADGLNR	GARLAND
AADGLNS	SLADANG
AADGLRU	GRADUAL
AADGMNR	GRANDAM
	GRANDMA
AADGMNS	GADSMAN
AADGMOT	DOGMATA
AADGMRS	SMARAGD
AADGNPR	GRANDPA
AADGNPS	PADANGS
	PADNAGS
AADGNRS	ARGANDS
AADGNRT	GARDANT
AADGNRY	YARDANG
AADGOPR	PODAGRA
AADGOPS	PAGODAS
AADGRSU	GARUDAS
AADHHPS	PADSHAH
AADHHRT	HARDHAT
AADHILS	DAHLIAS
AADHIMR	HADARIM
AADHIMS	SAMADHI
AADHINP	DAPHNIA
AADHJNR	HANDJAR
AADHKNY	YAKHDAN
AADHLRY	HALYARD
AADHMRS	DHARMAS
AADHNPR	HARDPAN
AADHNRS	DARSHAN
	DHARNAS
AADHNSW	HANDSAW
AADHPRS	PARDAHS
AADHRSS	SRADHAS
AADHRSZ	HAZARDS
AADHRWY	HAYWARD
AADHSWY	WASHDAY
AADIILR	DIARIAL
AADIINR	DIARIAN
AADIIPS	ASPIDIA
AADIJMN	JAMDANI
AADIKLY	ILKADAY
AADILLO	ALLODIA
	ALODIAL
AADILMR	ADMIRAL
	AMILDAR
AADILMT	MATILDA
AADILNP	PALADIN
AADILNR	LANIARD
	NADIRAL
AADILPS	APSIDAL
AADILRS	RADIALS
AADILRT	TAILARD
AADILSS	DALASIS
AADILST	STADIAL
AADILTV	DATIVAL
AADILWY	WAYLAID
AADIMNR	MANDIRA
AADIMNS	MAIDANS
AADIMOR	DIORAMA
AADIMOT	DOMATIA
AADIMRS	ARAMIDS
AADINNN	NANDINA
AADINNP	PANDANI
AADINPT	PINTADA
AADINRR	DARRAIN
AADINRS	RADIANS
AADINRT	INTRADA
	RADIANT
AADINRV	VIRANDA
AADINSV	NAVAIDS
AADIPTX	TAXPAID
AADIQSS	QASIDAS
AADIRRW	AIRWARD
AADIRSU	SUDARIA
AADISST	STADIAS
AADJLNS	JANDALS
AADKMRY	DAYMARK
AADKMSS	DAMASKS
AADKNRT	TANKARD
AADKPSU	PADAUKS
AADKRWW	AWKWARD
AADLLLN	LALLAND
AADLLMR	MALLARD
AADLLNW	LAWLAND
AADLLPU	PALUDAL
AADLLSS	SALLADS
AADLMNN	LANDMAN
AADLMNO	MANDOLA
	MONADAL
AADLMNU	LADANUM
AADLMOR	ARMLOAD
AADLMPS	LAMPADS
AADLMSW	WADMALS
AADLNOP	DALAPON
AADLNRY	LANYARD
AADLNSS	SANDALS
AADLNSU	LANDAUS
AADLNSV	VANDALS
AADLOPY	PAYLOAD
AADLPPU	APPLAUD
AADLPRS	PARDALS
AADLPYY	PLAYDAY
AADLRRU	RADULAR
AADLRSU	RADULAS
AADMMRS	DAMMARS
AADMNNO	MADONNA
AADMNNS	SANDMAN
AADMNOR	MADRONA
	MANDORA
	MONARDA
	ROADMAN
AADMNRS	MANSARD
AADMNRW	MANWARD
AADMNRY	DRAYMAN
	YARDMAN
AADMNSY	DAYSMAN
AADMNTU	MUTANDA
	TAMANDU
AADMOQU	MADOQUA
AADMORT	MATADOR
AADMOSU	AMADOUS
AADMRRY	YARDARM
AADMRSU	MARAUDS
AADMRSZ	MAZARDS
AADMRZZ	MAZZARD
AADMSYY	MAYDAYS
AADNNOT	NOTANDA
AADNNRS	RANDANS
AADNOPR	PANDORA
AADNORT	ONDATRA
AADNORY	ANYROAD
AADNPRS	PANDARS
AADNPRU	PANDURA
AADNRRW	WARRAND
AADNRRY	DARRAYN
AADNRSS	NASARDS
AADNRST	ASTRAND
	TARANDS
AADNRTY	TANYARD
AADNRVW	VANWARD
AADNRWY	NAYWARD
AADOPRR	PARADOR
AADOPRS	PARADOS
AADOPRT	ADAPTOR
AADOPRX	PARADOX
AADOPSS	PASSADO
	POSADAS
AADOPTT	DOPATTA
AADORWY	ROADWAY
AADOSTT	TOSTADA
AADOWWX	WOADWAX
AADPSSW	PADSAWS
AADPSSY	SPAYADS
AADPSYY	PAYDAYS
AADPTTU	DUPATTA
AADQRTU	QUADRAT
AADRRSS	SARDARS
AADRSTU	DATURAS
AADRSTY	DAYSTAR
AADRSVW	VAWARDS
AADRWWY	WAYWARD
AAEEFFR	AFFEARE
AAEEFGL	LEAFAGE
AAEEFRT	RATAFEE
AAEEGKL	LEAKAGE
AAEEGLT	ETALAGE
	GALEATE
AAEEGMN	AMENAGE
AAEEGMT	AGAMETE
AAEEGRV	AVERAGE
AAEEGST	EATAGES
AAEEHRT	HETAERA
AAEEINT	TAENIAE
AAEEKLS	SEAKALE
AAEEKRW	REAWAKE
AAEELMT	MALEATE
AAEELOR	AREOLAE
AAEELRT	LAETARE
AAEEMNT	EMANATE
	ENEMATA
	MANATEE
AAEEMRT	AMREETA
AAEEPPS	APPEASE
AAEEPRT	PATERAE
AAEERST	AERATES
AAEERSW	SEAWARE
AAEERTU	AUREATE
AAEERTW	TEAWARE
AAEERTX	EXARATE
AAEFFGR	AGRAFFE
AAEFFIR	AFFAIRE
AAEFFLL	FALAFEL
AAEFFNR	FANFARE
AAEFFRS	AFFEARS
AAEFFTT	TAFFETA
AAEFGNS	FANEGAS
AAEFGRS	AGRAFES
AAEFGTW	WAFTAGE
AAEFIRR	AIRFARE
AAEFKLO	OAKLEAF
AAEFLLV	FAVELLA
AAEFLPR	EARFLAP
	PARAFLE
AAEFLRS	RAFALES
AAEFLSV	FAVELAS
AAEFMRT	FERMATA
AAEFQRU	AQUAFER
AAEFRRW	WARFARE
AAEFRWY	WAYFARE
AAEGGLS	GALAGES
AAEGGNO	ANAGOGE
AAEGGOP	APAGOGE
AAEGGRS	GARAGES
AAEGGRT	AGGRATE
AAEGGSV	GAVAGES
AAEGHLU	HAULAGE
AAEGHLY	HAYLAGE
AAEGHNT	THANAGE
AAEGILR	LAIRAGE
	REGALIA
AAEGILS	ALGESIA
AAEGINP	NAGAPIE
AAEGINR	ANERGIA
AAEGINV	VAGINAE
AAEGINW	WAINAGE
AAEGIPR	IGARAPE
AAEGIRR	ARRIAGE
AAEGISS	ASSEGAI
AAEGITT	AGITATE
AAEGITZ	AGATIZE
AAEGJTU	AJUTAGE
AAEGKNT	TANKAGE

AAEGKOS	SOAKAGE
AAEGLLR	GLAREAL
AAEGLLT	GALLATE
	GALLETA
	TALLAGE
AAEGLMN	GAMELAN
AAEGLMT	GAMETAL
AAEGLNN	ANLAGEN
AAEGLNR	ALNAGER
AAEGLNS	ALNAGES
	ANLAGES
	GALENAS
	LAGENAS
	LASAGNE
AAEGLNU	AULNAGE
AAEGLOP	APOGEAL
AAEGLRR	REALGAR
AAEGLRS	ALEGARS
	LAAGERS
AAEGLST	AGELAST
	ALGATES
	LASTAGE
AAEGLSV	LAVAGES
	SALVAGE
AAEGLSX	GALAXES
AAEGMNR	MANAGER
AAEGMNS	AGNAMES
	MANAGES
	SAGAMEN
AAEGMNT	GATEMAN
	MAGENTA
	MAGNATE
	NAMETAG
AAEGMPR	RAMPAGE
AAEGMRT	REGMATA
AAEGMSS	MASSAGE
AAEGNNP	PANNAGE
AAEGNNT	TANNAGE
AAEGNOP	APOGEAN
AAEGNPT	PAGEANT
AAEGNPW	PAWNAGE
AAEGNRR	ARRANGE
AAEGNRT	TANAGER
AAEGNST	AGNATES
AAEGNSU	GUANASE
AAEGNTV	VANTAGE
AAEGNTW	WANTAGE
AAEGORS	AGAROSE
	OARAGES
AAEGPRR	PARERGA
AAEGPRS	PARAGES
AAEGPRW	WARPAGE
AAEGPSS	PASSAGE
AAEGPSV	PAVAGES
AAEGPSY	PAYSAGE
AAEGQUY	QUAYAGE
AAEGRRV	RAVAGER
AAEGRST	AGRASTE
	GASTREA
	TEARGAS
AAEGRSV	RAVAGES
	SAVAGER
AAEGRTT	REGATTA
AAEGSSU	ASSUAGE
	SAUSAGE
AAEGSSV	AVGASES
	SAVAGES
AAEGSSW	ASSWAGE
AAEGSTU	GATEAUS
AAEGSTW	WASTAGE
AAEGTTW	WATTAGE
AAEGTUX	GATEAUX
AAEGTWY	GATEWAY
	GETAWAY
AAEHHPR	RHAPHAE
AAEHHPT	APHTHAE
AAEHILP	APHELIA
AAEHIRT	HETAIRA
AAEHKNT	KHANATE
AAEHKPS	PAKEHAS
AAEHKST	TAKAHES
AAEHKSW	SEAHAWK
AAEHLLL	ALLHEAL
AAEHLMT	HEMATAL
AAEHLPS	PHASEAL
AAEHLPX	HEXAPLA
AAEHLRT	TREHALA
AAEHLST	ALTHEAS
AAEHLTT	ATHLETA
AAEHMSS	ASHAMES
AAEHMST	HAMATES
AAEHMTT	THEMATA
AAEHNPR	HANAPER
AAEHNPS	SAPHENA
AAEHNSY	HYAENAS
AAEHPRZ	PHEAZAR
AAEHPSW	AWHAPES
AAEHPSX	HAPAXES
AAEHRSY	HEARSAY
AAEHSTT	HASTATE
AAEILLX	AXILLAE
AAEILMN	LAMINAE
AAEILMS	AMELIAS
	MALAISE
AAEILNN	ALANINE
AAEILNO	AEOLIAN
AAEILNT	ANTLIAE
AAEILOR	OLEARIA
AAEILPX	EPAXIAL
AAEILRS	AERIALS
AAEILRU	AURELIA
AAEILRV	REAVAIL
	VELARIA
AAEILSS	ALIASES
AAEILSV	AVAILES
AAEILSX	ALEXIAS
AAEIMMT	IMAMATE
AAEIMNS	AMNESIA
	ANEMIAS
AAEIMNT	AMENTIA
	ANIMATE
AAEIMPY	PYAEMIA
AAEIMRT	AMIRATE
AAEIMRU	URAEMIA
AAEIMTV	AMATIVE
AAEINNO	AEONIAN
AAEINPS	PAESANI
AAEINPT	PATINAE
AAEINST	ENTASIA
	TAENIAS
AAEIPPS	APEPSIA
AAEIPRR	PAREIRA
AAEIPRS	SPIRAEA
AAEIPRT	APTERIA
AAEIPTT	APATITE
AAEIRSS	ARAISES
AAEIRST	ARISTAE
	ASTERIA
	ATRESIA
AAEIRSX	XERASIA
AAEIRTT	ARIETTA
AAEIRTV	VARIATE
AAEIRTW	AWAITER
AAEIRVW	AIRWAVE
AAEISTT	SATIATE
AAEISTV	AVIATES
AAEISTX	ATAXIES
AAEJMST	MAATJES
AAEJNRT	NAARTJE
AAEJOPR	APAREJO
AAEKKOR	KARAOKE
AAEKKRY	KAYAKER
AAEKLMS	KAMELAS
AAEKLNS	ALKANES
AAEKLNT	ALKANET
	KANTELA
AAEKLSS	ASLAKES
AAEKMNW	WAKEMAN
AAEKMRR	EARMARK
AAEKMRS	SEAMARK
AAEKNNS	ANANKES
AAEKNSW	AWAKENS
	WAKANES
AAEKPRT	PARTAKE
AAEKRSS	KEASARS
AAEKRST	KARATES
AAELLLM	LAMELLA
AAELLNV	AVELLAN
AAELLNZ	ZANELLA
AAELLPR	PARELLA
AAELLPS	PAELLAS
AAELLPT	PATELLA
AAELLRT	LATERAL
AAELLRY	ALLAYER
	AREALLY
AAELLSW	SEAWALL
AAELLTV	VALLATE
AAELMMR	ALMEMAR
AAELMMT	LEMMATA
AAELMNT	AMENTAL
AAELMNU	ALUMNAE
AAELMOT	OATMEAL
AAELMPT	PALMATE
AAELMST	MALATES
	MALTASE
	TAMALES
AAELMSX	MALAXES
AAELMSY	AMYLASE
AAELNNS	ANNEALS
AAELNOP	APNOEAL
AAELNOV	VALONEA
AAELNPR	PREANAL
AAELNPT	PLANATE
	PLATANE
AAELNPU	PAENULA
AAELNRS	ARSENAL
AAELNSS	ANLASES
AAELNST	SEALANT
AAELNSY	ANALYSE
AAELNTT	TETANAL
AAELNTZ	ZEALANT
AAELNWY	LANEWAY
AAELNYZ	ANALYZE
AAELORR	AREOLAR
AAELORS	AREOLAS
AAELORU	AUREOLA
AAELOTX	OXALATE
AAELPPR	APPAREL
AAELPPS	APPEALS
AAELPPT	PALPATE
AAELPPU	PAPULAE
AAELPRS	EARLAPS
AAELPRT	APTERAL
AAELPRV	PALAVER
AAELPSS	PALASES
AAELPST	PALATES
AAELPTT	TAPETAL
AAELPTU	PLATEAU
AAELPTY	APETALY
AAELRTV	LARVATE
AAELRTZ	LAZARET
AAELRVY	ALVEARY
AAELSST	ATLASES
AAELSTT	SALTATE
AAELSTV	VALETAS
AAELSTZ	ALTEZAS
AAELSUX	ASEXUAL
AAELSWX	SEALWAX
AAELTUV	VALUATE
AAELTVV	VALVATE
AAELTZZ	ALTEZZA
AAELWWY	WELAWAY
AAEMMMR	MAREMMA
AAEMMMT	MAMMATE
AAEMMNT	MEATMAN
AAEMMNU	MANUMEA
AAEMMOT	OMMATEA
AAEMNNT	EMANANT
AAEMNPP	PAMPEAN
AAEMNPS	SPAEMAN
AAEMNPT	PEATMAN
AAEMNRT	RAMENTA
AAEMNRU	MURAENA
AAEMNST	NAMASTE
AAEMNTU	MANTEAU
AAEMOTY	ATEMOYA
AAEMOTZ	METAZOA
AAEMQSU	SQUAMAE
AAEMRSS	AMASSER
AAEMRST	AMEARST
	RETAMAS
AAEMRTU	AMATEUR
AAEMSSS	AMASSES
AAENNNT	ANTENNA
AAENNST	ANNATES
AAENNSZ	ZENANAS
AAENNTT	TANNATE
AAENNTV	VENTANA
AAENOPS	APNOEAS
	PAESANO
AAENOSZ	OZAENAS
AAENPPR	PARPANE
AAENPSS	PAESANS
AAENPST	ANAPEST
	PEASANT
AAENPSV	PAVANES
AAENPSX	PANAXES
AAENPTT	EPATANT
AAENRRT	NARRATE
AAENRSS	NARASES
AAENRST	ANESTRA
AAENRTT	TARTANE
AAENRTU	NATURAE
	TAUREAN
AAENRTV	TAVERNA
AAENRUW	UNAWARE
AAENRUZ	AZUREAN
AAENSSU	NAUSEAS
AAENSSV	VANESSA
AAENSSW	SEAWANS
AAENSTW	SEAWANT
AAEOPTZ	ZAPATEO
AAEORRT	AERATOR
AAEORRU	AURORAE
AAEORST	AEROSAT
AAEPPRS	APPEARS
AAEPPRT	PARAPET
AAEPRSS	PASEARS
	SARAPES
AAEPRST	PETARAS
AAEPRSY	APYRASE
AAEPRSZ	ZARAPES
AAEPRTY	PEATARY
AAEPSTW	WATAPES
AAEPTTW	WATTAPE
AAERRRS	ARREARS
AAERRRY	ARRAYER
AAERRSS	ARRASES
AAERRST	ERRATAS
AAERRTT	TARTARE

AAERSST	SEARATS
AAERSSY	ARAYSES
	ASSAYER
AAERSTU	AURATES
AAERSTW	AWAREST
AAERTTU	TUATERA
AAESSTV	SAVATES
AAESSWY	SEAWAYS
AAFFILN	AFFINAL
AAFFILX	AFFIXAL
AAFFIMS	MAFFIAS
AAFFINS	SAFFIAN
AAFFINT	AFFIANT
AAFFIRS	AFFAIRS
	RAFFIAS
AAFFIST	TAFFIAS
AAFFLRS	FARFALS
AAFFPRS	AFFRAPS
AAFFRSY	AFFRAYS
AAFFRSZ	ZAFFARS
AAFGHIN	AFGHANI
AAFGHNS	AFGHANS
AAFGLMN	FLAGMAN
AAFGORR	FARRAGO
AAFHIKL	KHALIFA
AAFHINR	FARINHA
AAFHLLS	ASHFALL
AAFHLWY	HALFWAY
AAFHSTW	FATWAHS
AAFIILR	FILARIA
AAFIJST	FAJITAS
AAFIKLS	ALFAKIS
	KAFILAS
AAFIKSS	SIFAKAS
AAFILNT	FANTAIL
	TAILFAN
AAFILQU	ALFAQUI
AAFINNT	INFANTA
AAFINNU	INFAUNA
AAFINRS	FARINAS
AAFINTT	ANTIFAT
AAFIPRT	PARFAIT
AAFIRSS	SAFARIS
AAFIRUY	RUFIYAA
AAFIRWY	FAIRWAY
AAFISST	FATSIAS
AAFJLLW	JAWFALL
AAFJLOR	ALFORJA
AAFKNST	KAFTANS
AAFLLLS	FALLALS
AAFLLTY	FATALLY
AAFLMPR	FRAMPAL
AAFLNOR	FORLANA
AAFLNRU	FURLANA
AAFLWYY	FLYAWAY
AAFMNRT	RAFTMAN
AAFMNST	FANTASM
AAFNRRT	FARRANT
AAFNSTT	FANTAST
AAFNSTY	FANTASY
AAFOSST	AFTOSAS
AAGGHNT	HANGTAG
AAGGILN	GANGLIA
AAGGJRY	JAGGARY
AAGGKSU	GAGAKUS
AAGGLMO	MAGALOG
AAGGLOS	GALAGOS
AAGGLRY	GRAYLAG
AAGGMNS	MGANGAS
AAGGNOY	ANAGOGY
AAGGNST	GANGSTA
AAGGNWY	GANGWAY
AAGGQSU	QUAGGAS
AAGGRSS	SAGGARS
AAGGRST	RAGTAGS
	TAGRAGS
AAGHHRR	AARRGHH
AAGHILR	GHARIAL
AAGHINN	ANHINGA
AAGHJNS	GANJAHS
AAGHKNS	KANGHAS
	KHANGAS
AAGHLNT	GNATHAL
AAGHLOS	GASAHOL
AAGHLSZ	GHAZALS
AAGHMNN	HANGMAN
AAGHMNU	MAHUANG
AAGHMNW	WHANGAM
AAGHMRS	GRAHAMS
	GRAMASH
AAGHNRS	ARGHANS
	HANGARS
AAGHQUU	QUAHAUG
AAGHRSW	WASHRAG
AAGHSTY	SAGATHY
AAGIINT	IGNATIA
AAGIKNW	AWAKING
AAGIKNZ	ZIGANKA
AAGILMY	MYALGIA
AAGILNN	ANGINAL
AAGILNO	LOGANIA
AAGILNP	PAGINAL
AAGILNS	AGNAILS
AAGILNV	AVALING
	VAGINAL
AAGILNY	ALAYING
AAGILOS	ALOGIAS
AAGILOT	OTALGIA
AAGILPS	PALAGIS
AAGILRS	ARGALIS
	GARIALS
AAGILSV	GAVIALS
AAGILTW	WAGTAIL
AAGIMNO	ANGIOMA
AAGIMNS	MAGIANS
	SIAMANG
AAGIMNT	AMATING
AAGIMNZ	AMAZING
AAGINNS	ANGINAS
AAGINNW	WANIGAN
AAGINOS	AGNOSIA
AAGINPY	APAYING
AAGINRR	ARRAIGN
AAGINRS	NAGARIS
	SANGRIA
	SARANGI
AAGINRT	GRANITA
AAGINRU	GUARANI
AAGINRZ	ZINGARA
AAGINST	AGAINST
	ANTISAG
	GITANAS
AAGINSU	IGUANAS
AAGINSV	VAGINAS
AAGINSY	GAINSAY
AAGINTY	ANTIGAY
AAGIOTT	AGITATO
AAGIPRS	AIRGAPS
AAGIPRU	PIRAGUA
AAGIRRY	ARGYRIA
AAGISTT	SAGITTA
AAGJNRS	GARJANS
AAGJRSU	JAGUARS
AAGKKNO	ANGAKOK
AAGKLSY	GALYAKS
AAGKOOZ	GAZOOKA
AAGKORT	KATORGA
AAGLLNS	LALANGS
AAGLLNT	GALLANT
AAGLLVY	VAGALLY
AAGLMMS	MALMAGS
AAGLMNS	MANGALS
AAGLNOR	GRANOLA
AAGLNOS	ANALOGS
AAGLNOY	ANALOGY
AAGLNPS	LAPSANG
AAGLNRS	RAGLANS
AAGLNRU	ANGULAR
AAGLNSU	LAGUNAS
AAGLORU	ARUGOLA
AAGLRST	GASTRAL
AAGLRUU	ARUGULA
	AUGURAL
AAGLRVX	GRAVLAX
AAGLSST	STALAGS
AAGMMNS	MAGSMAN
AAGMMRR	GRAMMAR
AAGMMRS	GRAMMAS
AAGMMTU	GUMMATA
AAGMNNR	GRANNAM
AAGMNOS	SANGOMA
AAGMNPR	PANGRAM
AAGMNPY	PANGAMY
AAGMNRS	RAGMANS
AAGMNRT	TANGRAM
	TRANGAM
AAGMNSW	SWAGMAN
AAGMNSZ	ZAMANGS
AAGMOPY	APOGAMY
AAGMORS	MARGOSA
AAGMOSU	AGAMOUS
AAGMRRY	GRAMARY
AAGMRSY	MARGAYS
AAGNNOS	GOANNAS
AAGNNSW	WANGANS
AAGNOPR	PARAGON
AAGNORS	ANGORAS
AAGNORZ	ORGANZA
AAGNPRS	PARANGS
AAGNRRS	GARRANS
AAGNRRY	GRANARY
AAGNRSS	SANGARS
AAGNRTV	VAGRANT
AAGNSST	SATANGS
AAGNSTU	TAGUANS
AAGNSUY	GUANAYS
AAGOPSS	SAPSAGO
AAGORSU	SAGUARO
AAGOSTU	AGOUTAS
AAGPPRS	GRAPPAS
AAGRRSY	GARRYAS
AAGTTUU	TAUTAUG
AAHHLLS	HALLAHS
AAHHLSV	HALVAHS
AAHHMSZ	HAMZAHS
AAHHNNT	THANNAH
AAHHNPT	NAPHTHA
AAHHNST	THANAHS
AAHHOPR	PHARAOH
AAHIIMT	HIMATIA
AAHIJNR	HARIJAN
AAHIKRT	KITHARA
AAHILLL	HALLALI
AAHILLN	HALLIAN
AAHILMR	ALMIRAH
AAHILMS	SHIMAAL
AAHILMT	THALAMI
AAHILNT	THALIAN
AAHILPV	PAHLAVI
AAHILSW	SAHIWAL
AAHILSY	ALIYAHS
AAHIMNO	MAHONIA
AAHIMNZ	HAZANIM
AAHIMSS	AHIMSAS
AAHINOP	APHONIA
AAHINPP	PAPHIAN
AAHINPR	PIRANHA
AAHINST	SHAITAN
	TAHINAS
AAHINTW	TANIWHA
AAHIPRS	PARIAHS
	RAPHIAS
AAHIPRT	PITARAH
AAHIPTZ	ZAPTIAH
AAHIRSS	SHARIAS
AAHIRST	SHARIAT
AAHIRSV	VIHARAS
AAHIRTV	HAVARTI
AAHJKNR	KHANJAR
AAHJNRS	HANJARS
AAHJRRS	JARRAHS
AAHKKST	KATHAKS
AAHKLRS	LASHKAR
AAHKLST	KHALATS
AAHKMSY	YASHMAK
AAHKNST	KANTHAS
AAHKNSU	KAHUNAS
AAHKRSS	RAKSHAS
AAHLLLS	HALLALS
AAHLLNS	HALLANS
	NALLAHS
AAHLLOS	HALLOAS
AAHLLPS	PALLAHS
AAHLLSW	WALLAHS
AAHLLWY	HALLWAY
AAHLMMS	HAMMALS
	MAHMALS
	MASHLAM
AAHLMRS	MARSHAL
AAHLMRU	HAMULAR
AAHLMST	MALTHAS
AAHLMSU	HAMAULS
AAHLNPX	PHALANX
AAHLNRW	NARWHAL
AAHLPRS	PHRASAL
AAHLPST	ASPHALT
	SPATHAL
	TAPLASH
AAHLRSS	ASHLARS
AAHLRST	HARTALS
AAHLRSW	SHALWAR
AAHMMMS	HAMMAMS
AAHMMNS	MASHMAN
AAHMMSS	SHAMMAS
AAHMNNU	HANUMAN
AAHMNRS	HARMANS
AAHMNSS	SHAMANS
AAHMNTX	XANTHAM
AAHMOPR	AMPHORA
AAHMQSU	QUAMASH
AAHMRSS	ASHRAMS
AAHMSST	ASTHMAS
	MATSAHS
AAHMSSU	MASHUAS
AAHMSTZ	MATZAHS
AAHNNOS	HOSANNA
AAHNNST	TANNAHS
	THANNAS
AAHNNTX	XANTHAN
AAHNOPR	ANAPHOR
AAHNORT	ATHANOR
AAHNORV	NAVARHO
AAHNRTX	ANTHRAX
AAHNRTY	RHATANY
AAHNSZZ	HAZZANS
AAHORSU	SAHUARO
AAHPPRS	PARAPHS
AAHPRSY	YARPHAS
AAHPRTW	WARPATH
AAHPTWY	PATHWAY

AAHRSSS	HASSARS
AAHRSST	SHASTRA
AAHRSTY	ASHTRAY
AAHRTTW	ATHWART
AAHSSSY	SASHAYS
AAIIKKS	KAIKAIS
AAIIKSZ	ZAIKAIS
AAIILMR	AIRMAIL
AAIILPR	PAIRIAL
AAIILPT	TILAPIA
AAIILRZ	ALIZARI
AAIINNZ	ANZIANI
AAIINRT	ANTIAIR
AAIINTT	TITANIA
AAIINZZ	ZIZANIA
AAIIRVV	VIVARIA
AAIJLNP	JALAPIN
AAIJMNP	JAMPANI
AAIJMNT	ANTIJAM
AAIJNRS	JARINAS
AAIJNRZ	JANIZAR
AAIJNST	TINAJAS
AAIJPPY	JIPYAPA
AAIJRSW	JAWARIS
AAIKLLN	ALKALIN
AAIKLLS	ALKALIS
AAIKLMS	KALMIAS
	KAMILAS
AAIKLNS	KALIANS
AAIKLPR	PALIKAR
AAIKMNN	MANAKIN
AAIKMNR	RAMAKIN
AAIKMOR	ROMAIKA
AAIKMRS	KARAISM
AAIKNST	TANKIAS
AAIKORU	OUAKARI
AAIKOSY	SOKAIYA
AAIKPPR	PAPRIKA
AAIKPRR	AIRPARK
AAIKRSS	ASKARIS
AAIKRST	KARAITS
AAIKRSU	UAKARIS
AAIKSTT	ASTATKI
AAIKTVV	AKVAVIT
AAILLLP	PALLIAL
AAILLMM	MAMILLA
AAILLMN	LAMINAL
	MANILLA
AAILLMR	ARMILLA
AAILLMX	MAXILLA
AAILLNT	LANITAL
AAILLNV	VANILLA
AAILLPP	PAPILLA
AAILLRX	AXILLAR
AAILLSV	SALIVAL
AAILLSX	AXILLAS
AAILLUV	ALLUVIA
AAILLXY	AXIALLY
AAILMMN	MAILMAN
AAILMMR	AMMIRAL
AAILMMS	MIASMAL
AAILMMX	MAXIMAL
AAILMNR	LAMINAR
	RAILMAN
AAILMNS	ALMAINS
	ANIMALS
	LAMINAS
	MANILAS
AAILMNT	MATINAL
AAILMNU	ALUMINA
AAILMNV	MAILVAN
AAILMPS	IMPALAS
AAILMRT	MARITAL
	MARTIAL
AAILMSS	ALISMAS
	SALAMIS
AAILMSU	AUMAILS
AAILNNS	ALANINS
AAILNOT	AILANTO
	ALATION
AAILNOV	NOVALIA
	VALONIA
AAILNPS	SALPIAN
AAILNPT	PLATINA
AAILNRU	ULNARIA
AAILNRY	LANIARY
AAILNSS	SALINAS
AAILNSY	INYALAS
AAILNTV	VALIANT
AAILNTY	ANALITY
AAILORS	ROSALIA
	SOLARIA
AAILORU	RAOULIA
AAILORV	OVARIAL
	VARIOLA
AAILORZ	ZOARIAL
AAILOST	SOLATIA
AAILPPT	APPALTI
AAILPRS	PARIALS
AAILPRT	PARTIAL
	PATRIAL
AAILPRY	AIRPLAY
AAILPST	SPATIAL
AAILPTT	TALIPAT
AAILPZZ	PALAZZI
AAILQWW	QAWWALI
AAILRRV	ARRIVAL
AAILRST	LARIATS
	LATRIAS
AAILRTT	RATTAIL
AAILRTV	TRAVAIL
AAILRWY	RAILWAY
AAILSSS	ASSAILS
AAILSSV	SALIVAS
	SALVIAS
	VASSAIL
AAILSSW	WASSAIL
AAILTTT	LATITAT
AAIMMMT	MAMMATI
AAIMMNO	AMMONIA
AAIMMSS	MIASMAS
AAIMNNO	OMNIANA
AAIMNNT	ANTIMAN
AAIMNOS	ANOSMIA
AAIMNOT	AMATION
	ANIMATO
AAIMNPT	TIMPANA
AAIMNRS	MARINAS
AAIMNRT	MARTIAN
	TAMARIN
AAIMNST	MANATIS
	STAMINA
AAIMNSV	VIMANAS
AAIMNTX	TAXIMAN
AAIMRST	AMRITAS
	TAMARIS
AAIMRSU	SAMURAI
AAIMRTU	TIMARAU
AAIMSST	STASIMA
AAIMSSU	AMUSIAS
AAIMSTT	TATAMIS
AAIMSTV	ATAVISM
AAIMSUV	MAUVAIS
AAINNRU	URANIAN
AAINNRV	NAVARIN
	NIRVANA
AAINOPS	ANOPIAS
	ANOPSIA
	PAISANO
AAINORR	ORARIAN
AAINORV	OVARIAN
AAINOSX	ANOXIAS
AAINPPS	PAPAINS
AAINPRS	PARIANS
	PIRANAS
AAINPSS	PAISANS
AAINPST	PASTINA
	PATINAS
	PINATAS
	TAIPANS
AAINRST	ANTIARS
	ARTISAN
	TSARINA
AAINRSU	ANURIAS
	SAURIAN
	URANIAS
AAINRSV	SAVARIN
AAINRTV	VARIANT
AAINRTW	ANTIWAR
AAINRTZ	TZARINA
AAINSTT	ATTAINS
AAINSTV	VANITAS
AAINTTT	ATTAINT
AAINTTU	TUTANIA
AAINTTX	ANTITAX
AAIOPRS	APORIAS
AAIOPRT	ATROPIA
AAIOPRV	OVIPARA
AAIORRS	ROSARIA
AAIORSU	SAOUARI
AAIORTV	AVIATOR
AAIPPRS	APPAIRS
AAIPPRU	PUPARIA
AAIPPTT	PITAPAT
AAIPRST	PITARAS
AAIPRSY	PIRAYAS
AAIPRTT	PARTITA
AAIPSZZ	PIAZZAS
AAIQSSU	QUASSIA
AAIQTUV	AQUAVIT
AAIRSST	ARISTAS
	TARSIAS
AAIRSTT	STRIATA
AAIRSTY	RAIYATS
AAIRSWY	AIRWAYS
AAIRSZZ	RAZZIAS
AAISTTV	ATAVIST
AAISTUY	YAUTIAS
AAITWXY	TAXIWAY
AAJJMRS	JAMJARS
AAJKLWY	JAYWALK
AAJKMNR	JARKMAN
AAJKNSS	SANJAKS
AAJMNPS	JAMPANS
AAJMNZZ	JAZZMAN
AAJMORR	MOJARRA
AAJMORT	MAJORAT
AAJMPSY	PYJAMAS
AAJNNOS	JOANNAS
AAJNOSW	AJOWANS
AAJNOSY	YOJANAS
AAJOPSU	SAPAJOU
AAKKLPS	KALPAKS
AAKKLRU	KARAKUL
AAKKMOT	TOKAMAK
AAKKMRS	MARKKAS
AAKKOPS	KAKAPOS
AAKKSUZ	ZAKUSKA
AAKLMPU	LAMPUKA
AAKLMRY	MALARKY
AAKLMUY	YAMULKA
AAKLNOO	OOLAKAN
AAKLNOU	OULAKAN
AAKLOOP	PALOOKA
AAKLOOT	TALOOKA
AAKLRSU	KURSAAL
	RUSALKA
AAKLSSU	SAKSAUL
AAKLSTU	TALUKAS
AAKLWWY	WALKWAY
AAKMMNR	MARKMAN
AAKMNSU	MANUKAS
AAKMOSU	MOUSAKA
AAKMRSU	KUMARAS
AAKMRUZ	MAZURKA
AAKMRWY	WAYMARK
AAKMSSY	YASMAKS
AAKNNTU	NUNATAK
AAKNORS	ANORAKS
AAKNRST	KANTARS
AAKNSST	ASKANTS
AAKNSWZ	KWANZAS
AAKNTWY	TWANKAY
AAKOOPP	PAKAPOO
AAKOPRS	PAKORAS
AAKORST	OSTRAKA
AAKPRWY	PARKWAY
AAKRTUY	AUTARKY
AAKSSTT	ATTASKS
AAKSTTT	ATTASKT
AAKSTUY	YUKATAS
AALLLNS	LALLANS
AALLLSS	SALLALS
AALLMMS	MALLAMS
AALLMPU	AMPULLA
AALLNOX	ALLOXAN
AALLNPU	PLANULA
AALLNSY	ALANYLS
	NASALLY
AALLNVY	NAVALLY
AALLORS	AROLLAS
AALLOSZ	AZOLLAS
AALLOTV	LAVOLTA
AALLPPS	APPALLS
AALLPPY	PAPALLY
AALLRUY	AURALLY
AALLRVY	VALLARY
AALLSTT	ATLATLS
	TALLATS
AALLUVV	VALVULA
AALMMMS	MAMMALS
AALMMNO	AMMONAL
AALMMNS	ALMSMAN
AALMMNT	MALTMAN
AALMNOS	SALAMON
AALMNOY	ANOMALY
AALMNPS	NAPALMS
AALMNSU	MANUALS
AALMORT	ALAMORT
AALMORY	MAYORAL
AALMOST	AMATOLS
AALMPRY	PALMARY
	PALMYRA
AALMPSS	PLASMAS
AALMRRU	RAMULAR
AALMRSU	ALARUMS
AALMSSU	MASULAS
AALMSTY	AMYTALS
AALMTTU	MULATTA
AALNNRU	ANNULAR
AALNNSU	ANNUALS
AALNPRT	PLANTAR
AALNPRU	LUPANAR
AALNPST	PLANTAS
	PLATANS
	SALTPAN
AALNPUU	PUNALUA
AALNQTU	QUANTAL
AALNRSU	RANULAS
AALNRSW	NARWALS

AALNRTT LATRANT
AALNRTU NATURAL
AALNSST SANTALS
AALNSTT SALTANT
        TALANTS
AALNSTU SULTANA
AALNSTY ANALYST
AALNTTU TALAUNT
AALOPPT APPALTO
AALOPRS PARASOL
AALOPST TAPALOS
AALOPSY PAYOLAS
AALOPVV PAVLOVA
AALOPZZ PALAZZO
AALORRU AURORAL
AALORST ALASTOR
AALORSU AROUSAL
AALORTX LAXATOR
AALOSTT SALTATO
AALOSVW AVOWALS
AALOTTY TALAYOT
AALPPRU PAPULAR
AALPPRY PAPYRAL
AALPRRS PARRALS
AALPRSW ASPRAWL
AALPRSY PARLAYS
AALPSTU SPATULA
AALQSWW QAWWALS
AALRSST ASTRALS
        TARSALS
AALRSTT STRATAL
AALRSTU AUSTRAL
AALRSTY ASTYLAR
        SATYRAL
AALSSSV VASSALS
AALSSTU ASSAULT
AALSSUX SAXAULS
AALSTUV VALUTAS
AALSWYY WAYLAYS
AAMMMRY MAMMARY
AAMMNRT MANTRAM
AAMMNST AMTMANS
AAMMOTY MYOMATA
AAMMRRS MARRAMS
AAMMRST RAMSTAM
        TAMMARS
AAMMSUZ MAZUMAS
AAMNNNS MANNANS
AAMNNOY ANONYMA
AAMNOOS MANOAOS
AAMNORR MARRANO
AAMNORS OARSMAN
AAMNORT AMORANT
AAMNOSZ AMAZONS
AAMNOTU AUTOMAN
AAMNOTY ANATOMY
AAMNPRT MANTRAP
        RAMPANT
AAMNPRY PARANYM
AAMNPSS PASSMAN
        SAMPANS
AAMNPST TAMPANS
        TAPSMAN
AAMNPTY TYMPANA
AAMNRST ARTSMAN
        MANTRAS
AAMNRUY MANUARY
AAMNSTU MANTUAS
        TAMANUS
AAMOORS AMOROSA
AAMOPRS PARAMOS
AAMORRZ ZAMARRO
AAMORSV SAMOVAR
AAMORTY AMATORY
AAMOSSS SAMOSAS
AAMOSTT STOMATA
AAMOTTU AUTOMAT
AAMPRRT RAMPART
AAMPSSY AMPASSY
AAMRSST MATRASS
AAMRSSU ASARUMS
AAMRSTU SUMATRA
        TRAUMAS
AAMRTTY TRYMATA
AAMRTWY TRAMWAY
AAMSSTU SATSUMA
AANNOTT ANNATTO
AANNPSS SANPANS
AANNPSW SWANPAN
AANNRSU ANURANS
AANNSYZ NYANZAS
AANOQSY YAQONAS
AANORST TORANAS
AANORTT ARNATTO
AANOSST SONATAS
AANOSTT ANATTOS
AANPPSS SAPPANS
AANPRST PARTANS
        SPARTAN
        TARPANS
        TRAPANS
AANPRSU PURANAS
AANPSST PASSANT
AANQRTU QUARTAN
AANRRSW WARRANS
AANRRTW WARRANT
AANRSSS SANSARS
AANRSTT RATTANS
        TANTRAS
        TARTANS
AANRSTY YANTRAS
AANRSTZ TARZANS
AANRUWY RUNAWAY
AANSSTV SAVANTS
AANSSTZ STANZAS
AANSTTT STATANT
AANSTUV AVAUNTS
AANSWYY ANYWAYS
AAOORRW WOORARA
AAOPSST POTASSA
        SAPOTAS
AAOQSSU OQUASSA
AAORRSU AURORAS
AAORRSV VARROAS
AAORSTT TOTARAS
AAORSVV VAVASOR
AAOSTTV OTTAVAS
AAOTTUY TATOUAY
AAOTWWY TOWAWAY
AAPPSWW PAWPAWS
AAPRRSU PARURAS
AAPRRTT RATTRAP
AAPRSST SATRAPS
AAPRSTT ATTRAPS
AAPRSTY SATRAPY
AAPRTWY PARTWAY
AAQRSSU QUASARS
AARRSSS SARSARS
AARRSTT TARTARS
AARRSWY WARRAYS
AARSSST ASSARTS
AARSSTT ASTARTS
        STRATAS
AARSSTY SATYRAS
AARSSWW WARSAWS
AASSTTU STATUAS
ABBBDEL BABBLED
        BLABBED
ABBBELR BABBLER
        BLABBER
        BRABBLE
ABBBELS BABBLES
ABBBELU ABUBBLE
ABBBITT BABBITT
ABBCDER CRABBED
ABBCDES SCABBED
ABBCEHI BABICHE
ABBCEHU BABUCHE
ABBCEIS CABBIES
ABBCELR CLABBER
ABBCELS SCABBLE
ABBCERR CRABBER
ABBCGIN CABBING
ABBCIIS BIBASIC
ABBCIKT BACKBIT
ABBCIRS BICARBS
ABBCKUY BUYBACK
ABBCOST BOBCATS
ABBCOTY ABBOTCY
ABBCRYY CRYBABY
ABBDDEL DABBLED
ABBDDER DRABBED
ABBDEFR FRABBED
ABBDEGL GABBLED
ABBDEGR GRABBED
ABBDEIT TABBIED
ABBDEJL JABBLED
ABBDELR DABBLER
        DRABBLE
        RABBLED
ABBDELS DABBLES
        SLABBED
ABBDELW WABBLED
ABBDERR DRABBER
ABBDERS DABBERS
ABBDERT DRABBET
ABBDEST STABBED
        TEBBADS
ABBDESU BEDAUBS
ABBDESW SWABBED
ABBDGIN DABBING
ABBDHIJ DJIBBAH
ABBDILR LIBBARD
ABBDINR RIBBAND
ABBDITY DABBITY
ABBDLRU LUBBARD
ABBDMOR BOMBARD
ABBDMOU BABUDOM
ABBDNOX BANDBOX
ABBEESU BAUBEES
ABBEESW BAWBEES
ABBEFST FABBEST
ABBEGIR GABBIER
ABBEGLR GABBLER
        GRABBLE
ABBEGLS GABBLES
ABBEGNO BOGBEAN
ABBEGNU BUGBANE
ABBEGRR GRABBER
ABBEGRS GABBERS
ABBEGRU BUGBEAR
ABBEHLS SHABBLE
ABBEILT BITABLE
ABBEIRS BARBIES
        RABBIES
ABBEIST BABIEST
        TABBIES
ABBEISW SWABBIE
ABBEISY YABBIES
ABBEJLS JABBLES
ABBEJRS JABBERS
ABBELLR BARBELL
ABBELMR BRAMBLE
ABBELNS SNABBLE
ABBELOR BELABOR
ABBELPR PRABBLE
ABBELRR RABBLER
ABBELRS BARBELS
        RABBLES
        SLABBER
ABBELRU BARBULE
ABBELRW WABBLER
ABBELSU BAUBLES
        BUBALES
ABBELSW BAWBLES
        WABBLES
ABBELUY BUYABLE
ABBEMUZ BUMBAZE
ABBENRS NABBERS
ABBEORS EARBOBS
ABBERRS BARBERS
ABBERST BARBETS
        RABBETS
        STABBER
ABBERSW SWABBER
ABBERSY YABBERS
ABBESSU SUBBASE
ABBFIRT FRABBIT
ABBGGIN GABBING
ABBGHSU GUBBAHS
ABBGIJN JABBING
ABBGINN NABBING
ABBGINR BARBING
ABBGINS SABBING
ABBGINT TABBING
ABBGINU BUBINGA
ABBGINY BABYING
ABBGMSU BUMBAGS
ABBGOOU BUGABOO
ABBGORS GABBROS
ABBHIJS JIBBAHS
ABBHISY BABYISH
ABBHJSU JUBBAHS
ABBHOOS BABOOSH
        HABOOBS
ABBHRRU RHUBARB
ABBHTTU BATHTUB
ABBIIMN BAMBINI
ABBILLS LIBLABS
ABBILOR BILOBAR
ABBILOS BILBOAS
ABBILOT BOBTAIL
ABBILSU BUBALIS
ABBIMNO BAMBINO
ABBIMSU BABUISM
ABBINOR RABBONI
ABBINRS RABBINS
ABBIRST RABBITS
ABBIRTY RABBITY
ABBKLOU BLAUBOK
ABBLLRU BULLBAR
ABBLLTU BULLBAT
ABBLMRY BRAMBLY
ABBLOOS BABOOLS
ABBMOOR BOMBORA
ABBMOOS BAMBOOS
ABBMOST BOMBAST
ABBMOTU BUMBOAT
ABBNOOS BABOONS
ABBOORU RUBABOO
ABBORSS ABSORBS
ABBOSTY BATBOYS
        BOBSTAY
ABBQSUY SQUABBY
ABBRSSU BUSBARS
ABBRSTU BARBUTS
ABBSSSU SUBBASS
ABCCCHI BACCHIC
ABCCEIR ACERBIC
        BRECCIA

ABCCEIS	BACCIES
	SEBACIC
ABCCEOS	BACCOES
ABCCHII	BACCHII
ABCCHTY	BYCATCH
ABCCILU	CUBICAL
ABCCIMR	CAMBRIC
ABCCINU	BUCCINA
ABCCIOR	BORACIC
	BRACCIO
ABCCIOS	BOCCIAS
ABCCISU	CUBICAS
ABCCKOW	BAWCOCK
ABCCKTU	CUTBACK
ABCCOOR	BAROCCO
ABCCOOT	TOBACCO
ABCCSUU	SUCCUBA
ABCDDEU	ABDUCED
ABCDEEH	BEACHED
ABCDEEL	BELACED
	DEBACLE
ABCDEHT	BATCHED
ABCDEHU	DEBAUCH
ABCDEIK	DIEBACK
ABCDEIN	CABINED
ABCDEIP	PEDICAB
ABCDEIR	CARBIDE
ABCDEKL	BLACKED
ABCDEKR	REDBACK
ABCDELO	CODABLE
ABCDEOR	BROCADE
ABCDERS	DECARBS
ABCDERT	BRACTED
ABCDERU	CUDBEAR
ABCDESU	ABDUCES
ABCDHIO	ICHABOD
ABCDHOR	CHOBDAR
ABCDHOS	BODACHS
ABCDIIS	DIBASIC
ABCDILO	CABILDO
ABCDILR	BALDRIC
ABCDINS	ABSCIND
ABCDIRS	SCABRID
ABCDIRT	CATBIRD
ABCDIRU	BAUDRIC
ABCDIRW	BAWDRIC
ABCDISU	SUBACID
ABCDNOS	ABSCOND
ABCDOOR	CORDOBA
ABCDORR	BROCARD
ABCDSTU	ABDUCTS
ABCEEHS	BEACHES
ABCEEHU	EBAUCHE
ABCEELS	BELACES
ABCEEMR	EMBRACE
ABCEEMS	EMBACES
ABCEENS	ABSENCE
ABCEERR	ACERBER
	CEREBRA
	REBRACE
ABCEERU	BERCEAU
ABCEESS	BECASSE
ABCEESU	BECAUSE
ABCEFIS	BIFACES
ABCEGIR	RIBCAGE
ABCEGMO	CAMBOGE
ABCEGOR	BROCAGE
ABCEGOS	BOCAGES
	BOSCAGE
ABCEGSU	CUBAGES
ABCEHKL	BECHALK
ABCEHKO	BACKHOE
ABCEHLU	BAUCHLE
ABCEHMR	BECHARM
	BRECHAM
	CHAMBER
	CHAMBRE
ABCEHNR	BRECHAN
ABCEHOS	BASOCHE
ABCEHRS	BRACHES
ABCEHRT	BATCHER
	BRACHET
ABCEHST	BATCHES
ABCEIKT	TIEBACK
ABCEILL	ICEBALL
ABCEILM	ALEMBIC
	CEMBALI
ABCEILR	CALIBER
	CALIBRE
ABCEILT	CITABLE
ABCEIMO	AMOEBIC
ABCEINR	CARBINE
ABCEINT	CABINET
ABCEIOR	AEROBIC
ABCEIOT	ICEBOAT
ABCEIRS	ASCRIBE
	CABRIES
	CARBIES
	CARIBES
ABCEIRZ	ZEBRAIC
ABCEISS	ABSCISE
	SCABIES
	SEBASIC
ABCEITT	TABETIC
ABCEJST	ABJECTS
ABCEKLN	BLACKEN
ABCEKLO	BECLOAK
ABCEKLR	BLACKER
ABCEKNR	BRACKEN
ABCEKRS	BACKERS
	REBACKS
ABCEKRT	BRACKET
ABCEKST	BACKETS
	BACKSET
	SETBACK
ABCEKSY	BACKSEY
ABCEKTW	WETBACK
ABCELLS	BECALLS
ABCELLU	BULLACE
ABCELMO	CEMBALO
ABCELMR	CAMBREL
	CLAMBER
ABCELMS	BECALMS
	SCAMBLE
ABCELOP	PLACEBO
ABCELOV	VOCABLE
ABCELPS	BECLASP
ABCELPU	BLUECAP
ABCELPY	BYPLACE
ABCELRU	CURABLE
ABCELRW	BECRAWL
ABCELST	CABLETS
ABCELSU	BASCULE
ABCEMRS	CAMBERS
	CEMBRAS
	CRAMBES
ABCEMSX	EXCAMBS
ABCENOR	BACONER
ABCENOS	BEACONS
ABCENOW	COWBANE
ABCENOZ	CABEZON
ABCENRU	UNBRACE
ABCEOOS	CABOOSE
ABCEORR	BRACERO
ABCEORS	BORACES
ABCEORU	CORBEAU
ABCERRS	BRACERS
ABCERSU	RUBACES
	SUBRACE
ABCESSS	ABSCESS
ABCFIKN	FINBACK
ABCFIKT	BACKFIT
ABCFILO	BIFOCAL
ABCFIRS	FABRICS
ABCFLOO	COBLOAF
ABCFNOS	CONFABS
ABCGHIN	BACHING
ABCGHKO	HOGBACK
ABCGIKN	BACKING
ABCGILN	CABLING
ABCGINR	BRACING
ABCGKLO	BACKLOG
ABCGMSU	SCUMBAG
ABCHHII	HIBACHI
ABCHILS	CHABLIS
ABCHIMT	BATHMIC
ABCHIOT	COHABIT
ABCHKOU	CHABOUK
ABCHKSU	CHABUKS
ABCHKTU	HACKBUT
ABCHKUW	HAWBUCK
ABCHNOR	BROCHAN
ABCHNRU	BRAUNCH
ABCHNRY	BRANCHY
ABCHOSX	CASHBOX
ABCHPSU	HUBCAPS
ABCIILL	BACILLI
ABCIILN	ALBINIC
ABCIILS	BASILIC
ABCIILT	ALBITIC
ABCIIMN	MINICAB
ABCIIMS	IAMBICS
ABCIIOR	CIBORIA
ABCIIOT	ABIOTIC
ABCIJNO	JACOBIN
ABCIKLT	BACKLIT
ABCIKPS	BIPACKS
ABCIKSY	SICKBAY
ABCILNO	COALBIN
ABCILOU	ABOULIC
ABCILRS	SCRIBAL
ABCILTU	CUBITAL
ABCIMMS	CAMBISM
ABCIMMU	CAMBIUM
ABCIMST	CAMBIST
ABCINOR	CORBINA
ABCINOS	BONACIS
ABCINOT	BOTANIC
ABCIORR	BARRICO
ABCIORU	CARIBOU
ABCIOUV	BIVOUAC
ABCIRST	CABRITS
ABCIRTY	BARYTIC
ABCISSS	ABSCISS
ABCJOSU	JACOBUS
ABCKLLY	BLACKLY
ABCKLOT	BACKLOT
ABCKMOT	TOMBACK
ABCKMRU	BUCKRAM
ABCKMUZ	ZAMBUCK
ABCKNNO	BANNOCK
ABCKNRU	RUNBACK
ABCKNSU	SUNBACK
ABCKNTU	CUTBANK
ABCKORS	BAROCKS
ABCKORY	ROCKABY
ABCKOSW	SOWBACK
ABCKOTU	BACKOUT
	OUTBACK
ABCKPSU	BACKUPS
ABCKRSU	BUCKRAS
ABCKSTU	SACKBUT
	SUBTACK
ABCKSUW	BUCKSAW
	SAWBUCK
ABCLLOY	CALLBOY
ABCLMNU	CLUBMAN
ABCLMOY	CYMBALO
ABCLMSY	CYMBALS
ABCLMUU	BACULUM
ABCLNOS	BLANCOS
ABCLNOY	BALCONY
ABCLNSU	SUBCLAN
ABCLOOX	COALBOX
ABCLOST	COBALTS
ABCLOVY	VOCABLY
ABCLRUY	CURABLY
ABCMOPS	MOBCAPS
ABCMORS	COMARBS
	CRAMBOS
ABCMOST	COMBATS
	TOMBACS
ABCMRSS	SCRAMBS
ABCNORS	CARBONS
	CORBANS
ABCORRW	CROWBAR
ABCORSX	BOXCARS
ABCORSY	CARBOYS
ABCOSSU	BASUCOS
ABCSSTU	SACBUTS
	SUBACTS
ABDDDEL	BLADDED
ABDDDER	BRADDED
ABDDEEJ	BEJADED
ABDDEER	BEARDED
	BREADED
ABDDEES	DEBASED
ABDDEET	DEBATED
ABDDEEZ	BEDAZED
ABDDEIL	ADDIBLE
ABDDEIN	ABIDDEN
	BANDIED
ABDDEIR	BRAIDED
ABDDEIS	BADDIES
ABDDELR	BLADDER
ABDDELU	BLAUDED
ABDDENR	BRANDED
ABDDEOR	ABORDED
	BOARDED
	ROADBED
ABDDERW	BEDWARD
ABDDEST	BADDEST
ABDDESY	DAYBEDS
ABDDHIS	BADDISH
ABDDHSU	BUDDHAS
ABDDINS	DISBAND
ABDDLLO	ODDBALL
ABDDMOR	DAMBROD
ABDEEFG	FEEDBAG
ABDEEFL	FEELBAD
ABDEEGL	BEAGLED
ABDEEGR	REBADGE
ABDEEGZ	BEGAZED
ABDEEHO	OBEAHED
ABDEEHS	BEHEADS
ABDEEHT	BEATHED
ABDEEHV	BEHAVED
ABDEEIR	BEADIER
	BEARDIE
ABDEEJS	BEJADES
ABDEEJT	JETBEAD
ABDEEKR	BERAKED
ABDEEKS	DEBEAKS
ABDEELL	LABELED
ABDEELM	BELDAME
	BEMEDAL
	EMBALED
ABDEELN	ENABLED
ABDEELR	BEDERAL
	BLEARED

ABDEELS	BEADLES
ABDEELT	BELATED
	BLEATED
ABDEELY	BELAYED
	DYEABLE
ABDEEMN	BEADMEN
	BEDEMAN
	BENAMED
ABDEEMR	AMBERED
	BREAMED
	EMBREAD
ABDEEMS	EMBASED
ABDEEMT	BEDMATE
ABDEEMY	EMBAYED
ABDEEMZ	BEMAZED
ABDEEPR	BEDRAPE
ABDEERS	DEBASER
	SABERED
ABDEERT	BERATED
	BETREAD
	DEBATER
	REBATED
	TABERED
ABDEERW	BEWARED
ABDEERY	BEEYARD
	BERAYED
ABDEESS	DEBASES
	SEABEDS
ABDEEST	BESTEAD
	DEBATES
ABDEESZ	BEDAZES
ABDEETT	ABETTED
ABDEETX	BETAXED
ABDEFFL	BAFFLED
ABDEFLT	FLATBED
ABDEFLU	LEAFBUD
ABDEFOR	FORBADE
ABDEFRW	BEDWARF
ABDEFST	BEDFAST
ABDEGGL	BLAGGED
ABDEGGR	BRAGGED
ABDEGHI	BIGHEAD
ABDEGHR	BEGHARD
ABDEGIN	BEADING
ABDEGIR	ABRIDGE
	BRIGADE
ABDEGLM	GAMBLED
ABDEGLN	BANGLED
ABDEGLR	BELGARD
	GARBLED
ABDEGLS	BEGLADS
ABDEGNO	BONDAGE
	DOGBANE
ABDEGOS	BODEGAS
ABDEGRS	BADGERS
ABDEHIL	HIDABLE
ABDEHIT	HABITED
ABDEHLM	HAMBLED
ABDEHLR	HALBERD
ABDEHOW	BOWHEAD
ABDEHRS	BERDASH
	BRASHED
ABDEHRT	BREADTH
ABDEHSU	SUBHEAD
ABDEIIL	ALIBIED
ABDEILP	BIPEDAL
	PIEBALD
ABDEILR	BALDIER
	BEDRAIL
	BRAILED
	RAILBED
	RIDABLE
ABDEILS	BALDIES
	DIABLES
	DISABLE
ABDEILT	LIBATED
ABDEILU	AUDIBLE
ABDEILY	BEADILY
ABDEIMO	AMEBOID
ABDEIMR	EMBRAID
ABDEIMS	IMBASED
ABDEINR	BANDIER
	BRAINED
ABDEINS	BANDIES
	BASINED
ABDEINW	BEDAWIN
ABDEIRR	BARDIER
	BRAIDER
	BRIARED
	RABIDER
ABDEIRS	ABIDERS
	BRAISED
	DARBIES
	SEABIRD
	SIDEBAR
ABDEIRT	REDBAIT
	TRIBADE
ABDEIRU	DAUBIER
ABDEIRW	BAWDIER
ABDEISS	BIASSED
ABDEIST	BASTIDE
ABDEISU	SUBIDEA
ABDEISW	BAWDIES
ABDEJRU	ABJURED
ABDEKLN	BLANKED
ABDEKLU	BAULKED
ABDEKNR	BRANKED
ABDEKNU	UNBAKED
ABDEKRS	DEBARKS
ABDELMP	BEDLAMP
ABDELMR	MARBLED
	RAMBLED
ABDELMS	BEDLAMS
	BELDAMS
ABDELMW	WAMBLED
ABDELMY	EMBAYLD
ABDELNR	BLANDER
ABDELOR	LABORED
ABDELOS	ALBEDOS
ABDELOT	BLOATED
	LOBATED
ABDELOW	DOWABLE
ABDELPU	DUPABLE
ABDELPY	PYEBALD
ABDELRR	DRABLER
ABDELRS	BEDRALS
ABDELRU	DURABLE
ABDELRW	BRAWLED
	WARBLED
ABDELRY	DRYABLE
ABDELST	BALDEST
	BLASTED
	STABLED
ABDELSU	BELAUDS
ABDELTT	BATTLED
	BLATTED
ABDELTU	ABLUTED
ABDEMMO	MAMBOED
ABDEMNO	ABDOMEN
ABDEMNS	BEDAMNS
ABDEMRU	RUMBAED
ABDENNR	BRANNED
ABDENOR	BANDORE
	BROADEN
ABDENOT	BATONED
ABDENOY	NAEBODY
ABDENPS	BEDPANS
ABDENRR	BRANDER
ABDENRS	BANDERS
ABDENRT	BARTEND
ABDENRU	UNBARED
ABDENRW	BRAWNED
ABDENSS	BADNESS
ABDENSU	SUBDEAN
	UNBASED
ABDENSY	BENDAYS
ABDENTU	UNBATED
ABDEOOT	TABOOED
ABDEORR	ARBORED
	BOARDER
	BROADER
	REBOARD
ABDEORT	ABORTED
	BORATED
	TABORED
ABDEORV	BRAVOED
ABDEOST	BOASTED
ABDEOTU	BOUTADE
ABDEQSU	BASQUED
ABDERSS	BRASSED
	SERDABS
ABDERST	DABSTER
	TABERDS
ABDERSU	DAUBERS
	SUBEDAR
ABDERSV	ADVERBS
ABDERSY	REDBAYS
ABDERTY	DRYBEAT
ABDERUY	DAUBERY
ABDETTU	ABUTTED
ABDFIRT	FATBIRD
ABDGGIN	BADGING
ABDGGOR	BOGGARD
ABDGIIN	ABIDING
ABDGILN	BALDING
ABDGINN	BANDING
ABDGINO	ABODING
ABDGINR	BARDING
	BRIGAND
ABDGINT	DINGBAT
ABDGINU	DAUBING
ABDGINW	WINDBAG
ABDGIRT	DIRTBAG
ABDGLNO	BOGLAND
ABDGLUY	LADYBUG
ABDGNOS	BANDOGS
ABDGORS	BODRAGS
ABDHHOS	DOBHASH
ABDHIIT	ADHIBIT
ABDHILS	BALDISH
ABDHMOR	RHABDOM
ABDHMSU	BUDMASH
ABDHMTU	MUDBATH
ABDHNOR	BODHRAN
ABDHNSU	HUSBAND
ABDHOSY	HOBDAYS
ABDHRSU	BURDASH
	RHABDUS
ABDIJRY	JAYBIRD
ABDIKNW	BAWDKIN
ABDIKRS	DISBARK
ABDILMO	BIMODAL
ABDILOO	DIABOLO
ABDILOR	LABROID
ABDILOT	TABLOID
ABDILRS	BRIDALS
	LABRIDS
	RIBALDS
ABDILRW	AWLBIRD
ABDILRY	RABIDLY
ABDILUY	AUDIBLY
ABDILWY	BAWDILY
ABDIMNR	BIRDMAN
ABDIMOR	AMBROID
ABDINOR	INBOARD
ABDINRS	RIBANDS
ABDINRT	ANTBIRD
ABDINRU	UNBRAID
ABDINST	BANDITS
ABDIOSU	BADIOUS
ABDIPRU	UPBRAID
ABDIRRS	BRAIRDS
	BRIARDS
ABDIRSS	DISBARS
ABDIRSU	RIBAUDS
	SUBARID
ABDIRTY	TRIBADY
ABDKNOO	BANDOOK
ABDKOOY	DAYBOOK
ABDLLNY	BLANDLY
ABDLLOR	BOLLARD
ABDLNOR	BANDROL
ABDLORY	BROADLY
ABDLOSU	BUSLOAD
ABDLRUY	DURABLY
	RYBAULD
ABDLRYY	BYRLADY
ABDLSUU	SUBDUAL
ABDMNNO	BONDMAN
ABDMRUY	MARYBUD
ABDNOOR	BRADOON
	ONBOARD
ABDNOPR	PROBAND
ABDNORS	ROBANDS
ABDNOSU	ABOUNDS
	BAUSOND
ABDNOSX	SANDBOX
ABDNOSY	SANDBOY
ABDNOYY	ANYBODY
ABDNRSU	SANDBUR
ABDNRTU	TURBAND
ABDNSTY	STANDBY
ABDOORW	BARWOOD
ABDOOWY	BAYWOOD
ABDORRS	BORDARS
ABDORSS	ADSORBS
ABDORSY	BOYARDS
	BYROADS
ABDRRSU	DURBARS
ABDRSSU	ABSURDS
ABDRSTU	BUSTARD
ABDRUZZ	BUZZARD
ABEEEGR	BEERAGE
ABEEELS	SEEABLE
ABEEELY	EYEABLE
ABEEEMY	EYEBEAM
ABEEERV	BEREAVE
ABEEFFL	EFFABLE
ABEEFLM	FLAMBEE
ABEEFLO	BEEFALO
ABEEFLS	BEFLEAS
ABEEFTU	BEAUFET
ABEEGHR	HERBAGE
ABEEGHS	BEEGAHS
	BHAGEES
ABEEGLL	GABELLE
	GELABLE
ABEEGLR	BEAGLER
ABEEGLS	BEAGLES
ABEEGLT	GETABLE
ABEEGNR	REBEGAN
ABEEGRR	GERBERA
ABEEGRS	ABREGES
	BAREGES
	BARGEES
ABEEGRU	AUBERGE
ABEEGRW	BREWAGE
ABEEGSZ	BEGAZES
ABEEHJS	BHAJEES
ABEEHLW	HEWABLE

ABEEHMS	BESHAME
ABEEHMT	EMBATHE
ABEEHNN	HENBANE
ABEEHNS	BANSHEE
	BEENAHS
	SHEBEAN
ABEEHNT	BENEATH
ABEEHRT	BREATHE
ABEEHRV	BEHAVER
ABEEHSV	BEHAVES
ABEEIKR	BEAKIER
ABEEILS	BAILEES
ABEEIMR	BEAMIER
ABEEINS	BEANIES
ABEEINT	BETAINE
ABEEIRT	EBRIATE
ABEEIST	BEASTIE
ABEEJMS	JAMBEES
ABEEJRS	BAJREES
ABEEKLR	BLEAKER
ABEEKLS	KABELES
ABEEKNT	BETAKEN
ABEEKNV	BEKNAVE
ABEEKOP	PEEKABO
ABEEKPR	BARKEEP
	PREBAKE
ABEEKPS	BESPAKE
	BESPEAK
ABEEKRR	BREAKER
ABEEKRS	BEAKERS
	BERAKES
ABEEKST	BETAKES
ABEELLR	LABELER
	RELABEL
ABEELLY	EYEBALL
ABEELMM	EMBLEMA
ABEELMS	EMBALES
ABEELMT	BEAMLET
ABEELMZ	EMBLAZE
ABEELNP	PLEBEAN
ABEELNR	ENABLER
ABEELNS	BALEENS
	ENABLES
ABEELNT	TENABLE
ABEELNU	NEBULAE
ABEELOR	EARLOBE
ABEELPR	BEPEARL
ABEELPS	BELEAPS
ABEELPT	BELEAPT
ABEELQU	EQUABLE
ABEELRR	BLEARER
	ERRABLE
ABEELRT	BLEATER
	RETABLE
ABEELST	BELATES
ABEELSU	SUEABLE
	USEABLE
ABEELSV	BESLAVE
ABEELSW	SEWABLE
ABEEMNS	BASEMEN
	BEMEANS
	BENAMES
ABEEMNT	BEMEANT
ABEEMRS	AMBEERS
	BEAMERS
	BESMEAR
ABEEMRV	EMBRAVE
ABEEMSS	EMBASES
ABEEMST	EMBASTE
ABEENRV	VERBENA
ABEENRY	BEANERY
ABEEORS	AEROBES
ABEEORT	ABORTEE
ABEEPST	BESPATE
ABEERRS	BEARERS
	BREARES
ABEERRT	REBATER
	TABRERE
	TEREBRA
ABEERST	BEATERS
	BERATES
	REBATES
ABEERSV	BEAVERS
ABEERSW	BEWARES
ABEERSY	EYEBARS
ABEERSZ	ZEREBAS
ABEERTT	ABETTER
	BERETTA
ABEERVY	BEAVERY
ABEERWY	BEWEARY
ABEESST	SEBATES
ABEESWX	BEESWAX
ABEFFIS	BAFFIES
ABEFFLR	BAFFLER
ABEFFLS	BAFFLES
ABEFFOT	OFFBEAT
ABEFGIL	FILABEG
ABEFGLS	BEFLAGS
ABEFGST	GABFEST
ABEFILN	FINABLE
ABEFILR	FRIABLE
ABEFILS	FAIBLES
ABEFILU	FIBULAE
ABEFILX	FIXABLE
ABEFINU	BEAUFIN
ABEFIRT	BAREFIT
ABEFITY	BEATIFY
ABEFLLS	BEFALLS
ABEFLLU	BALEFUL
ABEFLLY	FLYABLE
ABEFLMS	FLAMBES
ABEFLNU	BANEFUL
ABEFLNY	FLYBANE
ABEFLRS	FABLERS
ABEFMOS	BEFOAMS
ABEFMRS	FERBAMS
ABEFORR	FORBEAR
ABEFORY	FOREBAY
ABEFPRS	PREFABS
ABEGGIR	BAGGIER
ABEGGIS	BAGGIES
ABEGGLR	BLAGGER
ABEGGMO	GAMBOGE
ABEGGNU	BUGGANE
ABEGGRR	BRAGGER
ABEGGRS	BAGGERS
	BEGGARS
ABEGGRU	BURGAGE
ABEGGRY	BEGGARY
ABEGHNS	SHEBANG
ABEGHOR	BEGORAH
ABEGHRU	BEARHUG
ABEGIMN	BEAMING
ABEGIMR	GAMBIER
ABEGIMT	MEGABIT
ABEGINN	BEANING
ABEGINO	BEGONIA
ABEGINR	BEARING
ABEGINS	SABEING
ABEGINT	BEATING
ABEGINY	ABYEING
ABEGIPP	BAGPIPE
ABEGKLU	BULKAGE
ABEGKOR	BROKAGE
ABEGKOS	BOSKAGE
ABEGLLS	BEGALLS
ABEGLMR	GAMBLER
	GAMBREL
ABEGLMS	GAMBLES
ABEGLNR	BRANGLE
ABEGLNS	BANGLES
ABEGLOR	ALBERGO
ABEGLOT	GLOBATE
ABEGLRR	GARBLER
ABEGLRS	GARBLES
ABEGLST	GABLETS
ABEGLSU	BELUGAS
	BLAGUES
ABEGMOR	EMBARGO
ABEGMRU	UMBRAGE
ABEGMST	GAMBETS
ABEGNNT	BANTENG
ABEGNOR	BEGROAN
ABEGNOS	NOSEBAG
ABEGNRS	BANGERS
	GRABENS
ABEGNSW	BEGNAWS
ABEGOPY	PAGEBOY
ABEGORR	BEGORRA
ABEGORS	BORAGES
ABEGORX	GEARBOX
ABEGOSZ	GAZEBOS
ABEGOTT	BOTTEGA
ABEGOUY	BUOYAGE
ABEGRRU	GARBURE
ABEGRST	BARGEST
ABEGSTU	BAGUETS
	TUBAGES
ABEHILR	HIRABLE
ABEHIMO	BOHEMIA
ABEHIMS	BEAMISH
ABEHIMT	IMBATHE
ABEHINS	BANSHIE
ABEHIRS	BEARISH
ABEHISU	BEAUISH
ABEHITU	HABITUE
ABEHITZ	ZABTIEH
ABEHKLS	KEBLAHS
ABEHKNT	BETHANK
ABEHKRU	HAUBERK
ABEHLMS	HAMBLES
	SHAMBLE
ABEHLNT	BENTHAL
ABEHLNU	UNHABLE
ABEHLRS	HERBALS
ABEHLRT	BLATHER
	HALBERT
ABEHLSS	BLASHES
ABEHMNO	HAMBONE
ABEHNOS	HEBONAS
ABEHNRY	ABHENRY
ABEHRRS	BRASHER
	HERBARS
ABEHRRY	HERBARY
ABEHRSS	BASHERS
	BRASHES
ABEHRST	BATHERS
	BERTHAS
	BREATHS
ABEHRTY	BREATHY
ABEIILL	BAILLIE
ABEIILS	ALIBIES
	BAILIES
ABEIINN	BIENNIA
ABEIINT	BAINITE
ABEIJMR	JAMBIER
ABEIJNS	BASENJI
ABEIKLL	LIKABLE
ABEIKLR	BALKIER
ABEIKLS	SKIABLE
ABEIKLT	BATLIKE
ABEIKNR	INBREAK
ABEIKNT	BEATNIK
ABEIKRR	BARKIER
	BRAKIER
ABEIKWY	BIKEWAY
ABEILLN	LINABLE
ABEILLO	LOBELIA
ABEILLP	PLIABLE
ABEILLR	BRAILLE
	LIBERAL
ABEILLS	BALLIES
ABEILLV	LIVABLE
ABEILMN	MINABLE
ABEILMR	BALMIER
	LAMBIER
	MIRABLE
	REMBLAI
ABEILMS	ABLEISM
	EMBAILS
	LAMBIES
ABEILMT	BIMETAL
	LIMBATE
	TIMBALE
ABEILMX	MIXABLE
ABEILMY	BEAMILY
ABEILMZ	IMBLAZE
ABEILNP	BIPLANE
ABEILNS	LESBIAN
ABEILOS	OBELIAS
ABEILPT	PATIBLE
ABEILRS	BAILERS
ABEILRT	LIBRATE
	TABLIER
	TRIABLE
ABEILRW	BRAWLIE
	WIRABLE
ABEILRY	BILAYER
ABEILSS	ABSEILS
	ISABELS
	LABISES
ABEILST	ABLEIST
	ALBITES
	ASTILBE
	BASTILE
	BESTIAL
	BLASTIE
	LIBATES
	STABILE
ABEILSW	BEWAILS
ABEILSY	BAILEYS
ABEILSZ	SIZABLE
ABEILVV	BIVALVE
ABEIMNP	PEMBINA
ABEIMNR	MIRBANE
ABEIMNT	AMBIENT
ABEIMRR	BARMIER
ABEIMRS	AMBRIES
ABEIMSS	IMBASES
ABEINOT	NIOBATE
ABEINPT	BEPAINT
ABEINRR	BARNIER
ABEINRT	ATEBRIN
ABEINRZ	ZEBRINA
ABEINSS	SABINES
ABEINST	BANTIES
	BASINET
	BESAINT
	BESTAIN
ABEINTT	TABINET
ABEIORS	ISOBARE
ABEIOSS	ABIOSES
	ISOBASE
ABEIOST	BOATIES
ABEIOTV	OBVIATE
ABEIPST	BAPTISE
ABEIPTZ	BAPTIZE
ABEIRRR	BARRIER
ABEIRRS	BRASIER
ABEIRRT	ARBITER

	RAREBIT
ABEIRRW	WARBIER
ABEIRRZ	BIZARRE
	BRAZIER
ABEIRSS	BASSIER
	BRAISES
	BRASSIE
ABEIRST	BAITERS
	BARITES
	REBAITS
	TERBIAS
ABEIRSX	BRAXIES
ABEIRSZ	BRAIZES
	ZERIBAS
ABEIRTT	BATTIER
	BIRETTA
ABEIRTV	VIBRATE
ABEIRUX	EXURBIA
ABEISSS	BIASSES
ABEISTT	BATISTE
	BISTATE
ABEISTW	BAWTIES
ABEISUV	ABUSIVE
ABEITUX	BAUXITE
ABEJLUY	BLUEJAY
ABEJMNO	JAMBONE
	JOBNAME
ABEJMNS	ENJAMBS
ABEJMRS	JAMBERS
ABEJMUX	JAMBEUX
ABEJNOS	BANJOES
ABEJNOW	JAWBONE
ABEJNST	BEJANTS
ABEJORS	JERBOAS
ABEJRRU	ABJURER
ABEJRSU	ABJURES
ABEKLLY	BLEAKLY
ABEKLNR	BLANKER
ABEKLNT	BLANKET
ABEKLRS	BALKERS
ABEKMNS	EMBANKS
ABEKMRS	EMBARKS
ABEKMSU	SAMBUKE
ABEKNRS	BANKERS
	BARKENS
ABEKNRU	UNBRAKE
ABEKNST	BANKETS
ABEKNSU	SUNBAKE
ABEKOOR	ABROOKE
ABEKOTU	OUTBAKE
ABEKPRU	BREAKUP
	UPBREAK
ABEKRRS	BARKERS
ABEKSST	BASKETS
ABELLMN	BELLMAN
ABELLMS	EMBALLS
ABELLNT	NETBALL
ABELLOS	LOSABLE
ABELLOV	LOVABLE
	VOLABLE
ABELLRS	BALLERS
ABELLRU	RUBELLA
	RULABLE
ABELLST	BALLETS
ABELLTU	BALLUTE
	BULLATE
ABELMMR	MEMBRAL
ABELMMS	EMBALMS
ABELMNT	BELTMAN
	LAMBENT
ABELMNU	ALBUMEN
ABELMOV	MOVABLE
ABELMRR	MARBLER
	RAMBLER
ABELMRS	AMBLERS
	BLAMERS
	LAMBERS
	MARBLES
	RAMBLES
ABELMRT	LAMBERT
ABELMSU	BEMAULS
ABELMSW	WAMBLES
ABELMTU	MUTABLE
ABELNOT	NOTABLE
ABELNOW	OWNABLE
ABELNOY	BALONEY
ABELNRS	BRANLES
	BRANSLE
ABELNRT	BRANTLE
ABELNRU	NEBULAR
ABELNRY	BLARNEY
ABELNSU	NEBULAS
ABELNSZ	BENZALS
ABELNTU	ABLUENT
	TUNABLE
ABELNTY	TENABLY
ABELOPR	ROPABLE
ABELOPT	POTABLE
ABELORR	LABORER
ABELORS	LABROSE
ABELORT	BLOATER
ABELORU	RUBEOLA
ABELORW	ROWABLE
ABELOSS	BOLASES
ABELOST	BOATELS
	OBLATES
ABELOSV	ABSOLVE
ABELOSW	SOWABLE
ABELOTT	TOTABLE
ABELOTV	VOTABLE
ABELOTW	TEABOWL
	TOWABLE
ABELPRU	PUBERAL
ABELPTY	TYPABLE
ABELQUY	EQUABLY
ABELRRS	BARRELS
ABELRRW	BRAWLER
	WARBLER
ABELRSS	BARLESS
	BRALESS
ABELRST	ALBERTS
	BATLERS
	BLASTER
	LABRETS
	STABLER
ABELRSV	VERBALS
ABELRSW	BAWLERS
	WARBLES
ABELRSY	BARLEYS
ABELRSZ	BLAZERS
ABELRTT	BATTLER
	BLATTER
	BRATTLE
ABELRTW	BLEWART
ABELRUZ	ZEBRULA
ABELRVY	BRAVELY
ABELSST	BASTLES
	STABLES
ABELSSU	SUBSALE
ABELSTT	BATLETS
	BATTELS
	BATTLES
	BLATEST
	TABLETS
ABELSTU	SUBLATE
ABELSTY	BAETYLS
	BEASTLY
ABELSUY	USEABLY
ABELSWY	BAWLEYS
	BYELAWS
ABELTWY	BELTWAY
ABEMMOS	MAMBOES
ABEMMRS	BAMMERS
ABEMNOS	AMBONES
	BEMOANS
ABEMNOT	BOATMEN
ABEMNRY	BYREMAN
	MYRBANE
ABEMNST	BATSMEN
ABEMNSU	SUNBEAM
ABEMNSY	BYNAMES
ABEMORT	BROMATE
ABEMOTU	OUTBEAM
ABEMRST	TAMBERS
ABEMRSW	BESWARM
ABEMSSY	EMBASSY
ABENNOR	BARONNE
ABENNRR	BRANNER
ABENNRS	BANNERS
ABENNST	BANNETS
ABENORS	BORANES
ABENORT	BARONET
	REBOANT
ABENORW	RAWBONE
ABENOSY	SOYBEAN
ABENOTY	BAYONET
ABENPSU	SUBPENA
ABENQTU	BANQUET
ABENRRS	BARRENS
ABENRRU	URBANER
ABENRST	BANTERS
ABENRSU	UNBARES
	UNBEARS
ABENRSY	BARNEYS
ABENRSZ	BRAZENS
ABENRUX	EXURBAN
ABENSST	ABSENTS
	BASNETS
ABENSTT	BATTENS
ABENSTU	BUTANES
	SUNBEAT
ABENSTZ	BEZANTS
ABENTZZ	BEZZANT
ABEOOST	SEABOOT
ABEOOTV	OBOVATE
ABEOPRS	SAPROBE
ABEOPRT	PROBATE
ABEOQRU	BAROQUE
ABEORRS	ARBORES
	BRASERO
ABEORRT	ABORTER
	ARBORET
	TABORER
ABEORST	BOASTER
	BOATERS
	BORATES
	REBATOS
	SORBATE
ABEORSU	AEROBUS
ABEORSV	BRAVOES
ABEORSX	BORAXES
ABEORSY	ROSEBAY
ABEORSZ	BEZOARS
ABEORTT	ABETTOR
	BATTERO
	TABORET
ABEOSTV	BOVATES
ABEPRSU	UPBEARS
ABEPRSW	BEWRAPS
ABEPRTW	BEWRAPT
ABEPRTY	TYPEBAR
ABEPSTU	UPBEATS
ABEQRSU	BARQUES
ABEQSSU	BASQUES
ABERRST	BARRETS
	BARTERS
ABERRSU	BURSERA
	SABREUR
ABERRSV	BRAVERS
ABERRSY	BRAYERS
ABERRSZ	BRAZERS
ABERRUV	BRAVURE
ABERRVY	BRAVERY
ABERSSS	BRASSES
ABERSST	BASTERS
	BESTARS
	BRASSET
	BREASTS
ABERSSU	ABUSERS
	RUBASSE
	SURBASE
ABERSSZ	ZEBRASS
ABERSTT	BATTERS
	TABRETS
ABERSTU	ARBUTES
	BURSATE
	SURBATE
ABERSTV	BRAVEST
ABERSTW	BRAWEST
	WABSTER
ABERSTX	BAXTERS
ABERSTY	BARYTES
	BETRAYS
ABERSUU	BUREAUS
ABERSWY	BEWRAYS
ABERTTU	ABUTTER
ABERTTY	BATTERY
ABERUUX	BUREAUX
ABESSST	BASSEST
	BASSETS
ABESSSY	ABYSSES
ABESSTT	BASSETT
ABESTTU	BATTUES
ABFFGIN	BAFFING
ABFFIIL	BAILIFF
ABFFLOO	BOFFOLA
ABFFLOU	BUFFALO
ABFGILN	FABLING
ABFGINR	BARFING
ABFGLSU	BAGFULS
	BAGSFUL
ABFHIST	BATFISH
ABFHLSU	BASHFUL
ABFIILR	BIFILAR
ABFIIMR	FIMBRIA
ABFILRU	FIBULAR
ABFILSU	FIBULAS
ABFIMOR	FIBROMA
ABFLOTU	BOATFUL
ABFLOTW	BATFOWL
ABFLOTY	FLYBOAT
ABFOORT	FOOTBAR
ABFSTTU	TUBFAST
ABGGGIN	BAGGING
ABGGIIT	GIGABIT
ABGGILN	GABLING
ABGGILY	BAGGILY
ABGGINN	BANGING
ABGGINR	BARGING
	GARBING
ABGGIST	BAGGITS
ABGGISW	BAGWIGS
ABGGNOS	GOBANGS
ABGGNSU	BUGGANS
ABGGORT	BOGGART
ABGHHSU	HAGBUSH
ABGHILN	BLAHING
ABGHINS	BASHING
ABGHINT	BATHING
ABGHLOT	HAGBOLT

ABGHLRU	BURGHAL
ABGHMOO	GOOMBAH
ABGHMRU	HAMBURG
ABGHNOR	HAGBORN
ABGHOTU	ABOUGHT
ABGHSSU	BUGSHAS
ABGHSTU	HAGBUTS
ABGIILN	BAILING
ABGIINS	BIASING
ABGIINT	BAITING
ABGIINZ	BAIZING
ABGIJMN	JAMBING
ABGIJOO	JIGABOO
ABGIKLN	BALKING
ABGIKNN	BANKING
ABGIKNO	BOAKING
ABGIKNR	BARKING
	BRAKING
ABGIKNS	BAKINGS
	BASKING
ABGIKNU	BAUKING
ABGILLN	BALLING
ABGILMN	AMBLING
	BALMING
	BLAMING
	LAMBING
ABGILMS	GIMBALS
ABGILNR	BLARING
ABGILNS	ABLINGS
	SABLING
ABGILNT	TABLING
ABGILNW	BAWLING
	BLAWING
ABGILNZ	BLAZING
ABGILOR	GARBOIL
ABGIMMN	BAMMING
ABGIMRS	GAMBIRS
ABGIMST	GAMBIST
	GAMBITS
ABGINNN	BANNING
ABGINNR	BARNING
ABGINNT	BANTING
ABGINOS	BAGNIOS
	GABIONS
ABGINOT	BOATING
ABGINRR	BARRING
ABGINRS	SABRING
ABGINRV	BRAVING
ABGINRY	BRAYING
ABGINRZ	BRAZING
ABGINSS	BASSING
ABGINST	BASTING
ABGINSU	ABUSING
ABGINTT	BATTING
ABGINTU	ANTIBUG
	TABUING
ABGINTW	BATWING
ABGINTY	BAYTING
ABGIOPT	PIGBOAT
ABGIOSU	BAGUIOS
ABGKKNO	BANGKOK
ABGKNOS	KOBANGS
ABGKOOS	BOGOAKS
ABGKORW	WORKBAG
ABGLMNU	LUMBANG
ABGLMOS	GAMBOLS
ABGLMOU	LUMBAGO
ABGLMSY	GYMBALS
ABGLNOO	BOLOGNA
ABGLOOT	TOOLBAG
ABGLORS	BROLGAS
ABGLORT	RAGBOLT
ABGLOSU	ALBUGOS
	SUBGOAL
ABGLRRU	BURGLAR
ABGMNOY	BOGYMAN
ABGMOOY	GOOMBAY
ABGMORW	BAGWORM
ABGNOOS	GABOONS
ABGNOPR	PROBANG
ABGNORS	BARONGS
	BROGANS
ABGNOTU	GUNBOAT
ABGNOWY	BOWYANG
ABGOORT	BOTARGO
ABGOPST	POSTBAG
ABGORRU	GOBURRA
ABGORTU	OUTBRAG
ABGOTTU	TUGBOAT
ABGSSTU	SAGBUTS
ABHHISS	SHIBAHS
ABHHJSU	JUBHAHS
ABHHKOT	KHOTBAH
ABHHKTU	KHUTBAH
ABHHSUW	BUSHWAH
ABHHSUY	HUSHABY
ABHIINT	INHABIT
ABHIKLS	BASHLIK
	KIBLAHS
ABHIKST	BHAKTIS
ABHIKTW	HAWKBIT
ABHILNO	HOBNAIL
ABHILOS	ABOLISH
ABHILTU	HALIBUT
ABHIMRS	MIHRABS
ABHIMSZ	MAZHBIS
ABHINST	ABSINTH
ABHIOPS	PHOBIAS
ABHIORS	BOARISH
ABHIORT	BOTHRIA
ABHIOST	ISOBATH
ABHISTU	HABITUS
ABHKLSY	BASHLYK
ABHKORU	BOURKHA
ABHKRSU	KURBASH
ABHLMSY	SHAMBLY
ABHLOUX	BOXHAUL
ABHLRSY	BRASHLY
ABHLRTU	HURLBAT
ABHMNSU	BUSHMAN
ABHMRSU	RHUMBAS
	SAMBHUR
ABHMSUY	MAYBUSH
ABHNOST	BOTHANS
ABHNSTU	SUNBATH
ABHOPRS	BARHOPS
ABHORRS	HARBORS
ABHORRU	HARBOUR
ABHOTUY	HAUTBOY
ABHPSTY	BYPATHS
ABHQSSU	BUQSHAS
ABHRSTU	TARBUSH
ABHSSUW	BUSHWAS
ABHSTUW	WASHTUB
ABIIKKS	KABIKIS
ABIIKKT	KIBITKA
ABIILLS	BAILLIS
ABIILMN	MINILAB
ABIILMU	BULIMIA
ABIILNQ	INQILAB
ABIILNS	AIBLINS
	BILIANS
ABIILOV	BOLIVIA
ABIILRY	BILIARY
ABIILST	STIBIAL
ABIILTY	ABILITY
ABIIMNR	MINIBAR
ABIIMSS	MISBIAS
ABIIMST	IAMBIST
ABIINNS	BAININS
ABIINOR	ROBINIA
ABIINRY	BIRYANI
ABIIOSS	ABIOSIS
ABIJLNR	BRINJAL
ABIJNOT	ABJOINT
ABIJRSU	JABIRUS
ABIKKSU	KABUKIS
ABIKLLY	BALKILY
ABIKLMN	LAMBKIN
ABIKLOR	KILOBAR
ABIKLOS	KOLBASI
ABIKMNR	BARMKIN
ABIKMRS	IMBARKS
ABIKOUZ	BAZOUKI
ABIKRST	BRITSKA
ABIKRTZ	BRITZKA
ABIKSTT	BATTIKS
ABIKUUZ	BUZUKIA
ABILLMN	BILLMAN
ABILLMU	BALLIUM
ABILLMY	BALMILY
ABILLNP	PINBALL
ABILLPY	PLIABLY
ABILLSW	SAWBILL
ABILLSY	SYLLABI
ABILLTT	BATTILL
ABILLWX	WAXBILL
ABILLWY	WAYBILL
ABILMMS	IMBALMS
ABILMNU	ALBUMIN
ABILMOX	MAILBOX
ABILMRT	TIMBRAL
ABILMST	TIMBALS
ABILNOS	ALBINOS
ABILNOT	BITONAL
ABILNOZ	BIZONAL
ABILNRY	BAIRNLY
ABILOPR	BIPOLAR
	PARBOIL
ABILORS	BAILORS
ABILORT	ORBITAL
ABILORV	BOLIVAR
ABILOST	OBLASTI
ABILOTU	BAILOUT
	OBITUAL
	TABOULI
ABILRRY	LIBRARY
ABILRSS	BRASILS
ABILRSU	BURIALS
	RAILBUS
ABILRSZ	BRAZILS
ABILSTU	TABULIS
ABILSYZ	SIZABLY
ABIMMRS	MIMBARS
ABIMNRS	MINBARS
ABIMOSS	BIOMASS
ABIMPST	BAPTISM
	BITMAPS
ABIMRSS	BISMARS
ABIMRST	IMBRAST
ABIMRSU	BARIUMS
ABIMRTT	TRIMTAB
ABIMTTY	AMBITTY
ABINNSU	BUNNIAS
ABINOOR	BORONIA
ABINORT	TABORIN
ABINORW	RAINBOW
ABINOSS	BASIONS
	BONSAIS
ABINOST	BASTION
	BONITAS
	OBTAINS
ABINOSU	ABUSION
ABINRST	BRISANT
ABINRTV	VIBRANT
ABIORRS	BARRIOS
ABIORSS	ISOBARS
ABIORST	ORBITAS
ABIORTV	VIBRATO
ABIPRTY	BIPARTY
ABIPSTT	BAPTIST
ABIRTTY	TRAYBIT
ABISSST	BASSIST
ABISTTU	TUBAIST
ABJJOOS	JOJOBAS
ABJKMOS	JAMBOKS
	SJAMBOK
ABJLMOO	JAMBOOL
ABJLMSU	JAMBULS
	JUMBALS
ABKLLNY	BLANKLY
ABKLOOW	LAWBOOK
ABKLRUW	BULWARK
ABKLSSY	SKYLABS
ABKLSTY	BYTALKS
ABKMNOO	BOOKMAN
ABKMOST	TOMBAKS
ABKMSUZ	ZAMBUKS
ABKNNNO	NONBANK
ABKNRSU	UNBARKS
ABKNRUU	BUNRAKU
ABKOORS	BOORKAS
ABKORTU	OUTBARK
ABKSSTU	SUBTASK
ABLLLOW	LOWBALL
ABLLLUY	LULLABY
ABLLNOO	BALLOON
ABLLNOS	BALLONS
ABLLOPR	PROBALL
ABLLORT	TOLLBAR
ABLLORU	LOBULAR
ABLLOST	BALLOTS
ABLLOSW	BALLOWS
ABLLOTY	TALLBOY
ABLLOVY	LOVABLY
ABLLPSU	BALLUPS
ABLLRUY	BULLARY
ABLMMOU	BUMMALO
ABLMNOU	UMBONAL
ABLMOOT	TOMBOLA
ABLMOPS	APLOMBS
ABLMORS	BROMALS
ABLMOSY	LAMBOYS
ABLMOVY	MOVABLY
ABLMPSU	PABLUMS
ABLMPUU	PABULUM
ABLMRSU	LABRUMS
	LUMBARS
ABLMSTY	TYMBALS
ABLMTUY	MUTABLY
ABLNOSZ	BLAZONS
ABLNOTU	BUTANOL
ABLNOTY	NOTABLY
ABLNRSU	SLURBAN
ABLNSTU	BUNTALS
	TULBANS
ABLNTUY	TUNABLY
ABLOORS	ROBALOS
ABLOORT	TOOLBAR
ABLOORY	OBOLARY
ABLOPYY	PLAYBOY
ABLORST	BORSTAL
ABLORSU	LABOURS
	SUBORAL
ABLORSW	BARLOWS
ABLORTW	BLAWORT
ABLORUW	BOURLAW
ABLOSST	OBLASTS
ABLOSTT	TALBOTS
ABLOSTV	ABVOLTS

ABLOSTX	SALTBOX
ABLOSUV	SUBOVAL
ABLOTUW	OUTBAWL
ABLPRSU	BURLAPS
ABLPSUY	PLAYBUS
ABLPSYY	BYPLAYS
ABLRSWY	BYRLAWS
ABLRTUU	TUBULAR
ABLRTUY	BUTYRAL
ABLSTTU	BUTTALS
ABMMNOS	MOBSMAN
ABMNSTU	NUMBATS
ABMNSUY	YNAMBUS
ABMOORR	BARROOM
ABMOOSW	WABOOMS
ABMOOSZ	BAZOOMS
ABMOPST	BAMPOTS
ABMORTU	TAMBOUR
ABMOSTU	SUBATOM
ABMOSTW	WOMBATS
ABMRSSU	SAMBURS
ABMRSTU	TAMBURS
ABNOORS	SOROBAN
ABNOORZ	BORAZON
ABNOOSS	BASSOON
ABNOOST	BATOONS
ABNORST	BARTONS
ABNORSY	BARYONS
ABNORTY	BARYTON
ABNOSSU	BONASUS
ABNOTUY	BUOYANT
ABNRSTU	TURBANS
ABNRSUU	AUBURNS
ABNRTTU	TURBANT
ABNSTUW	BAWSUNT
ABNSTYZ	BYZANTS
ABOOPSX	SOAPBOX
ABOORTW	ROWBOAT
ABOOTTW	TOWBOAT
ABORRSU	ARBOURS
ABORRSW	BARROWS
ABORSTU	OUTBARS
	ROBUSTA
	RUBATOS
	TABOURS
ABORSTW	TOWBARS
ABORSTY	TARBOYS
ABOSSUU	AUSUBOS
ABOSTUU	AUTOBUS
ABPRSTU	ABRUPTS
	SUBPART
	UPBRAST
ABPRSUY	UPBRAYS
ABRRSSU	BURSARS
ABRRSUY	BURSARY
ABRRTUY	TURBARY
ABRSTUU	ARBUTUS
ABSSUWY	SUBWAYS
ACCCILY	ACYCLIC
ACCDDEE	ACCEDED
ACCDDEI	CADDICE
ACCDEEN	CADENCE
ACCDEER	ACCEDER
ACCDEES	ACCEDES
ACCDEHK	CHACKED
ACCDEHN	CHANCED
ACCDEHO	COACHED
ACCDEHT	CATCHED
ACCDEII	ACCIDIE
ACCDEIO	ACCOIED
ACCDEIT	ACCITED
ACCDEIU	CADUCEI
ACCDEKL	CACKLED
	CLACKED
ACCDEKO	COCKADE
ACCDEKR	CRACKED
ACCDENS	ACCENDS
ACCDENY	CADENCY
ACCDEOT	COACTED
ACCDEOY	ACCOYED
ACCDERU	ACCRUED
	CARDECU
ACCDESU	ACCUSED
	SUCCADE
ACCDFIL	FLACCID
ACCDHIL	CHALCID
ACCDILS	SCALDIC
ACCDINS	SCANDIC
ACCDIOT	CACTOID
	OCTADIC
ACCDKNO	CANDOCK
ACCDKOW	DAWCOCK
ACCDLOY	ACCOYLD
	CACODYL
ACCDORS	ACCORDS
ACCEEHL	CALECHE
ACCEEHO	COACHEE
ACCEELN	CENACLE
ACCEENR	CREANCE
ACCEERT	ACCRETE
ACCEFIT	FACTICE
ACCEFLU	FELUCCA
ACCEGIN	ACCINGE
ACCEGOS	SOCCAGE
ACCEHHI	CHECHIA
ACCEHIL	CALICHE
	CHALICE
ACCEHIM	MACCHIE
ACCEHIN	CHICANE
ACCEHLN	CHANCEL
ACCEHLO	COCHLEA
ACCEHNO	CONCHAE
ACCEHNR	CHANCER
	CHANCRE
ACCEHNS	CHANCES
ACCEHNT	CATCHEN
ACCEHNU	CHAUNCE
ACCEHNY	CHANCEY
ACCEHOR	CAROCHE
	COACHER
ACCEHOS	CHACOES
	COACHES
ACCEHPU	CAPUCHE
ACCEHRS	CREACHS
ACCEHRT	CATCHER
	RECATCH
ACCEHST	CACHETS
	CATCHES
ACCEHTT	CATHECT
ACCEHTU	CATECHU
ACCEHXY	CACHEXY
ACCEIKP	ICEPACK
ACCEILL	CALICLE
ACCEILN	CALCINE
ACCEILO	COELIAC
ACCEILS	CALICES
	CELIACS
ACCEILT	CALCITE
ACCEIMR	CERAMIC
	RACEMIC
ACCEINO	COCAINE
	OCEANIC
ACCEINV	VACCINE
ACCEIPR	CAPRICE
ACCEIPS	ICECAPS
	IPECACS
ACCEIPV	PECCAVI
ACCEIQU	CACIQUE
ACCEIRS	CARICES
ACCEIRT	CREATIC
ACCEIST	ACCITES
	ASCETIC
ACCEITT	ECTATIC
ACCEKLR	CACKLER
	CLACKER
	CRACKLE
ACCEKLS	CACKLES
ACCEKMO	MEACOCK
ACCEKOP	PEACOCK
ACCEKOS	SEACOCK
ACCEKPU	CUPCAKE
ACCEKRR	CRACKER
ACCELLY	CALYCLE
	CECALLY
ACCELNO	CONCEAL
ACCELNS	CANCELS
ACCELOR	CORACLE
ACCELOT	CACOLET
ACCELRS	CARCELS
ACCELSU	SACCULE
ACCELSY	CALYCES
	CYCLASE
ACCEMNU	CACUMEN
ACCENOR	CONACRE
ACCENOS	ASCONCE
ACCENOT	COENACT
ACCENOV	CONCAVE
ACCENPT	PECCANT
ACCENRS	CANCERS
ACCENST	ACCENTS
ACCEOPY	CACOEPY
ACCEORW	CRACOWE
ACCEOTT	TOCCATE
ACCEPRY	PECCARY
ACCEPST	ACCEPTS
ACCERRS	SCARCER
ACCERRT	CARRECT
ACCERSU	ACCRUES
	ACCURSE
	ACCUSER
ACCERSW	ACCREWS
ACCESSU	ACCUSES
ACCESSY	CYCASES
ACCFIIP	PACIFIC
ACCFILY	CALCIFY
ACCGHIN	CACHING
	CHACING
ACCGNOS	COGNACS
ACCHHIS	CHICHAS
ACCHHKU	KUCHCHA
ACCHIKS	CHIACKS
ACCHIMS	CHASMIC
ACCHINO	CHICANO
ACCHIOP	PICACHO
ACCHIOR	COCHAIR
ACCHIOT	CHAOTIC
ACCHIOU	ACOUCHI
ACCHIRS	SCRAICH
ACCHJSU	JACCHUS
ACCHKOY	HAYCOCK
ACCHKSY	CHYACKS
ACCHLNO	CONCHAL
ACCHLTU	CLAUCHT
ACCHNRS	SCRANCH
ACCHNRU	CRAUNCH
ACCHOPU	CAPOUCH
	PACHUCO
ACCHORR	CARROCH
ACCHOSU	CACHOUS
ACCHOTW	CHOCTAW
ACCHOUY	ACOUCHY
ACCHPTU	CATCHUP
	UPCATCH
ACCHRRU	CURRACH
ACCHRST	SCRATCH
ACCHRSU	SCRAUCH
ACCHSSU	SUCCAHS
ACCIILN	ACLINIC
ACCIINT	ACTINIC
ACCIIST	ASCITIC
	SCIATIC
ACCIKRS	CARSICK
ACCILLU	CALCULI
ACCILMO	COMICAL
ACCILMU	CALCIUM
ACCILNO	CONICAL
	LACONIC
ACCILNY	CYNICAL
ACCILOR	CALORIC
ACCILOS	ACCOILS
	CALICOS
ACCILOV	VOCALIC
ACCILRU	CRUCIAL
ACCILRY	ACRYLIC
ACCILSS	CLASSIC
ACCILST	CLASTIC
ACCILSU	SACCULI
ACCIMOT	COMATIC
ACCIMOZ	ZIMOCCA
ACCINNO	CANONIC
ACCINOR	ACRONIC
ACCINOS	COCAINS
ACCINOT	CANTICO
ACCINRU	CRUCIAN
ACCINSW	WICCANS
ACCINSY	CYCASIN
ACCIOPR	CAPROIC
ACCIORS	SCORIAC
ACCIORT	ACROTIC
ACCIPRT	PRACTIC
ACCIRRS	CIRCARS
	RICRACS
ACCIRST	ARCTICS
ACCISTT	TACTICS
	TICTACS
ACCISTU	CAUSTIC
	CICUTAS
ACCKLOR	CARLOCK
ACCKLRY	CRACKLY
ACCKMOR	CROMACK
ACCKOPR	CAPROCK
ACCKOSS	CASSOCK
	COSSACK
ACCKOST	CASTOCK
ACCKPRU	CRACKUP
ACCLOSU	COUCALS
ACCLOSY	ACCLOYS
ACCMOOT	COCOMAT
ACCMOOY	COCOYAM
ACCMOPT	ACCOMPT
	COMPACT
ACCMRUU	CURCUMA
ACCNNOO	COONCAN
ACCNOOP	COCOPAN
ACCNOOR	RACCOON
ACCNOOS	CACOONS
ACCNOTT	CONTACT
ACCNOTU	ACCOUNT
ACCOORT	COACTOR
ACCOPTY	COPYCAT
ACCOQSU	SQUACCO
ACCORSS	CORCASS
	CORSACS
ACCORTU	ACCOURT
ACCOSST	ACCOSTS
ACCRSTU	ACCURST
ACDDDEI	CADDIED
ACDDDEL	CLADDED
ACDDDEU	ADDUCED
ACDDDKO	DADDOCK

ACDDEEF	DEFACED
ACDDEER	CEDARED
ACDDEES	DECADES
ACDDEEY	DECAYED
ACDDEHR	CHEDDAR
ACDDEIN	CANDIED
ACDDEIS	CADDIES
ACDDEIU	DECIDUA
ACDDELN	CANDLED
ACDDELO	CLADODE
ACDDELR	CLADDER
	CRADLED
ACDDELS	SCALDED
ACDDELU	CAUDLED
ACDDEMU	DUCDAME
ACDDEOP	DECAPOD
ACDDERU	ADDUCER
ACDDESU	ADDUCES
	SCAUDED
ACDDHHU	CHUDDAH
ACDDHIS	CADDISH
ACDDHKO	HADDOCK
ACDDHOR	CHADDOR
ACDDHRU	CHUDDAR
ACDDIIS	DIACIDS
ACDDIKZ	ZADDICK
ACDDINS	CANDIDS
ACDDIRS	DISCARD
ACDDIRY	DRYADIC
ACDDIST	ADDICTS
	DIDACTS
ACDDISY	DYADICS
ACDDKMO	MADDOCK
ACDDKOP	PADDOCK
ACDDSSY	CADDYSS
ACDDSTU	ADDUCTS
ACDEEES	DECEASE
ACDEEFF	EFFACED
ACDEEFN	ENFACED
ACDEEFR	DEFACER
	REFACED
ACDEEFS	DEFACES
ACDEEFT	FACETED
ACDEEGL	GLACEED
ACDEEGN	ENCAGED
ACDEEHL	LEACHED
ACDEEHP	PEACHED
ACDEEHR	REACHED
ACDEEHT	CHEATED
ACDEEIR	DECIARE
ACDEEJT	DEJECTA
ACDEEKR	CREAKED
ACDEELL	CADELLE
ACDEELN	CLEANED
	ELANCED
	ENLACED
ACDEELR	CLEARED
	CREEDAL
	DECLARE
	RELACED
ACDEELS	DESCALE
ACDEELT	CLEATED
ACDEELV	CLEAVED
ACDEEMN	MENACED
ACDEEMO	CAMEOED
ACDEEMR	AMERCED
	CREAMED
	RACEMED
ACDEEMV	MEDEVAC
ACDEENR	ENRACED
	RECANED
ACDEENS	DECANES
	ENCASED
ACDEENT	ENACTED
ACDEENV	ENCAVED
	VENDACE
ACDEEPR	CAPERED
	PEARCED
	PREACED
ACDEEPS	ESCAPED
ACDEERS	CREASED
	DECARES
	SEARCED
ACDEERT	CATERED
	CEDRATE
	CERATED
	CREATED
	REACTED
ACDEERY	DECAYER
ACDEEST	TEDESCA
ACDEETU	EDUCATE
ACDEETX	EXACTED
ACDEFFH	CHAFFED
ACDEFFS	DECAFFS
ACDEFGO	DOGFACE
ACDEFHU	CHAUFED
ACDEFIN	FACIEND
	FANCIED
ACDEFIR	FARCIED
ACDEFKL	FLACKED
ACDEFRS	SCARFED
ACDEFRT	CRAFTED
	FRACTED
ACDEGGL	CLAGGED
ACDEGGR	CRAGGED
ACDEGHN	CHANGED
	GANCHED
ACDEGHR	CHARGED
ACDEGIN	INCAGED
ACDEGIR	CADGIER
ACDEGIS	DISCAGE
ACDEGKO	DOCKAGE
ACDEGLN	CANGLED
	CLANGED
	GLANCED
ACDEGLO	DECALOG
ACDEGNO	CONGAED
	DECAGON
ACDEGNU	UNCAGED
ACDEGOR	CARGOED
	CORDAGE
ACDEGRS	CADGERS
ACDEHHN	HANCHED
ACDEHHT	HATCHED
ACDEHIN	CHAINED
	ECHIDNA
ACDEHIP	EDAPHIC
ACDEHIR	CHAIRED
ACDEHIX	HEXADIC
ACDEHKL	CHALKED
	HACKLED
ACDEHKR	CHARKED
ACDEHKT	THACKED
ACDEHKW	WHACKED
ACDEHLN	LANCHED
ACDEHLR	CHALDER
ACDEHLS	CLASHED
ACDEHLT	LATCHED
ACDEHMP	CHAMPED
ACDEHMR	CHARMED
	MARCHED
ACDEHMS	CHASMED
ACDEHMT	MATCHED
ACDEHNR	ENDARCH
	RANCHED
ACDEHNT	CHANTED
ACDEHOP	POACHED
ACDEHOR	CHORDAE
	ROACHED
ACDEHOS	COHEADS
ACDEHOT	CATHODE
ACDEHPP	CHAPPED
ACDEHPR	PARCHED
ACDEHPT	PATCHED
ACDEHPU	CUPHEAD
ACDEHRR	CHARRED
ACDEHRS	CRASHED
	ECHARDS
ACDEHRT	CHARTED
	RATCHED
ACDEHSS	CHASSED
ACDEHST	SCATHED
ACDEHTT	CHATTED
ACDEHTW	WATCHED
ACDEHTY	YACHTED
ACDEIIR	ACIDIER
ACDEILL	CEDILLA
ACDEILM	CAMELID
	CLAIMED
	DECIMAL
	DECLAIM
	MALICED
	MEDICAL
ACDEILN	INLACED
ACDEILR	DECRIAL
	RADICEL
	RADICLE
ACDEILS	SCAILED
ACDEILT	CITADEL
	DELTAIC
	DIALECT
	EDICTAL
ACDEILV	CAVILED
ACDEIMT	MICATED
ACDEIMY	MEDIACY
ACDEINO	CODEINA
	OCEANID
ACDEINR	CAIRNED
	CARNIED
ACDEINS	CANDIES
	INCASED
ACDEINV	INCAVED
ACDEINY	CYANIDE
ACDEIOS	CODEIAS
ACDEIPR	EPACRID
	PERACID
ACDEIPS	DISPACE
ACDEIRR	ACRIDER
	CARRIED
ACDEIRS	CARDIES
	DARCIES
	RADICES
	SIDECAR
ACDEIRU	DECURIA
ACDEISS	DISCASE
ACDEIST	ACIDEST
	DACITES
ACDEISV	ADVICES
ACDEITT	DICTATE
ACDEITY	EDACITY
ACDEJLO	CAJOLED
ACDEJNU	JAUNCED
ACDEKKN	KNACKED
ACDEKLM	MACKLED
ACDEKLN	CLANKED
ACDEKLO	CLOAKED
ACDEKLS	SLACKED
ACDEKLT	TACKLED
	TALCKED
ACDEKLU	CAULKED
ACDEKMS	SMACKED
ACDEKNR	CRANKED
ACDEKNS	SNACKED
ACDEKNU	UNCAKED
ACDEKOR	CROAKED
ACDEKQU	QUACKED
ACDEKRS	DACKERS
ACDEKRT	TRACKED
ACDEKRW	WRACKED
ACDEKRY	KEYCARD
ACDEKST	STACKED
ACDEKSW	SWACKED
ACDELLS	SCALLED
ACDELMM	CLAMMED
ACDELMP	CAMPLED
	CLAMPED
ACDELMS	MASCLED
ACDELMU	MACULED
ACDELNO	CELADON
ACDELNR	CANDLER
ACDELNS	CALENDS
	CANDLES
ACDELNT	CANTLED
ACDELNU	LAUNCED
	UNLACED
ACDELOP	PEDOCAL
ACDELOR	CAROLED
	ORACLED
ACDELOS	COLEADS
	SOLACED
ACDELOT	LOCATED
ACDELOV	ALCOVED
ACDELPP	CLAPPED
ACDELPS	CLASPED
	SCALPED
ACDELQU	CALQUED
ACDELRR	CRADLER
ACDELRS	CRADLES
	SCALDER
ACDELRT	CLARTED
ACDELRU	CAULDER
ACDELRW	CRAWLED
ACDELSS	CLASSED
	DECLASS
ACDELST	CASTLED
	SCLATED
ACDELSU	CAUDLES
	CEDULAS
ACDELSW	DECLAWS
ACDELTT	CLATTED
ACDELTU	CLAUTED
ACDELWW	DEWCLAW
ACDEMMR	CRAMMED
ACDEMMS	SCAMMED
ACDEMNU	DECUMAN
ACDEMOR	CAROMED
	COMRADE
ACDEMPR	CRAMPED
ACDEMPS	DECAMPS
	SCAMPED
ACDENNS	SCANNED
ACDENNT	CANDENT
ACDENNU	NUANCED
ACDENOR	ACORNED
	DRACONE
ACDENOS	ACNODES
	DEACONS
ACDENOT	TACNODE
ACDENPR	PRANCED
ACDENPT	PANDECT
ACDENPU	UNCAPED
	UNPACED
ACDENRS	DANCERS
ACDENRT	CANTRED
	TRANCED
ACDENRU	DURANCE
	UNRACED
ACDENRY	ARDENCY
ACDENSS	ASCENDS
ACDENST	DECANTS

	DESCANT
	SCANTED
ACDENSU	UNCASED
ACDENTU	UNACTED
ACDENUV	VAUNCED
ACDEOPS	PEACODS
	PEASCOD
ACDEOPT	COAPTED
ACDEORR	CORRADE
ACDEORS	SARCODE
ACDEORT	CORDATE
	REDCOAT
ACDEOST	COASTED
ACDEOTT	CODETTA
ACDEOUV	COUVADE
ACDEPPR	CRAPPED
ACDEPRS	REDCAPS
	SCARPED
	SCRAPED
ACDEPSU	SCAUPED
ACDEQSU	CASQUED
ACDERRS	CARDERS
	SCARRED
ACDERST	REDACTS
	SCARTED
ACDERSU	CRUSADE
	SCAURED
ACDERTT	DETRACT
	TRACTED
ACDERTU	CURATED
	TRADUCE
ACDESTT	SCATTED
ACDESTV	ADVECTS
ACDFIIT	FATIDIC
ACDFIIY	ACIDIFY
ACDFIOT	FACTOID
ACDGGIN	CADGING
ACDGINN	DANCING
ACDGINO	GONADIC
ACDGINR	CARDING
ACDGKLO	DAGLOCK
ACDGNOT	CANTDOG
ACDGORT	DOGCART
ACDHIIL	CHILIAD
ACDHIMR	DHARMIC
ACDHIOP	PHACOID
ACDHIRY	DIARCHY
ACDHLOR	CHORDAL
	DORLACH
ACDHMRS	DRACHMS
ACDHNOW	COWHAND
ACDHOOT	CATHOOD
ACDHOPR	POCHARD
ACDHORR	ORCHARD
ACDHORS	CHADORS
ACDHRUY	DUARCHY
ACDHRYY	DYARCHY
ACDIIIN	INDICIA
ACDIIJT	JADITIC
ACDIINN	INDICAN
ACDIINO	CONIDIA
ACDIINR	ACRIDIN
ACDIIOS	ISODICA
ACDIIRS	CIDARIS
	SCIARID
ACDIIRT	ARCTIID
	TRIACID
	TRIADIC
ACDIITY	ACIDITY
ACDIKLS	SKALDIC
ACDILLO	CODILLA
ACDILMO	DOMICAL
ACDILMS	CLADISM
ACDILNO	NODICAL
ACDILNU	DULCIAN

	INCUDAL
ACDILOP	PLACOID
	PODALIC
ACDILOR	CORDIAL
ACDILOT	COTIDAL
ACDILPU	PALUDIC
ACDILRT	TRICLAD
ACDILRY	ACRIDLY
ACDILST	CLADIST
ACDILTW	WILDCAT
ACDILTY	DACTYLI
ACDIMMU	CADMIUM
ACDIMNO	MANDIOC
	MONACID
	MONADIC
	NOMADIC
ACDIMNY	DYNAMIC
ACDIMOT	COADMIT
ACDINNO	NONACID
ACDINRU	IRACUND
ACDINST	DISCANT
ACDINSW	WINDACS
ACDINSY	CYANIDS
ACDIOPR	PARODIC
	PICADOR
ACDIORR	CORRIDA
ACDIORS	SARCOID
ACDIORT	ARCTOID
	CAROTID
ACDIOST	DACOITS
ACDIOSZ	ZODIACS
ACDIOTY	DACOITY
ACDIOXY	OXYACID
ACDIPRS	CAPRIDS
ACDIPSS	CAPSIDS
ACDIPTY	DIPTYCA
ACDIQRU	QUADRIC
ACDIRST	DRASTIC
ACDIRTU	DATURIC
ACDISST	DICASTS
ACDITUV	VIADUCT
ACDJNTU	ADJUNCT
ACDKLOP	PADLOCK
ACDKLSY	SKYCLAD
ACDKMOO	MOCKADO
ACDKMPU	MUDPACK
ACDKOPR	POCKARD
ACDLLOR	COLLARD
ACDLLUY	DUCALLY
ACDLNOR	CALDRON
ACDLNOT	COTLAND
ACDLOWY	LADYCOW
ACDLSTY	DACTYLS
ACDMMNO	COMMAND
ACDMNOP	COMPAND
ACDMOOW	CAMWOOD
ACDMORZ	CZARDOM
ACDMPSU	MUDCAPS
ACDMSTU	MUDCATS
ACDNOOR	CARDOON
ACDNORS	CANDORS
ACDNORU	CANDOUR
	CAUDRON
ACDORST	COSTARD
ACDORSU	CRUSADO
ACDORSW	COWARDS
ACDORUZ	CRUZADO
ACDRSTU	CUSTARD
ACDRSUU	CARDUUS
ACEEEPS	ESCAPEE
ACEEEUV	EVACUEE
ACEEFFR	EFFACER
ACEEFFS	EFFACES
ACEEFHN	ENCHAFE
ACEEFIN	FAIENCE

	FIANCEE
ACEEFLU	FECULAE
ACEEFMN	FACEMEN
ACEEFNS	ENFACES
ACEEFNY	FAYENCE
ACEEFPR	PREFACE
ACEEFRS	REFACES
ACEEGIL	ELEGIAC
ACEEGNR	ENGRACE
ACEEGNS	ENCAGES
ACEEGNT	CENTAGE
ACEEGSU	ESCUAGE
ACEEHHT	CHEETAH
ACEEHIP	CHEAPIE
ACEEHIT	HICATEE
	TEACHIE
ACEEHIV	ACHIEVE
ACEEHKO	HOECAKE
ACEEHKS	HACKEES
ACEEHLR	LEACHER
	RELACHE
ACEEHLS	LEACHES
ACEEHLT	CHELATE
ACEEHMP	EMPEACH
ACEEHMR	MACHREE
ACEEHMT	MACHETE
ACEEHNN	ENHANCE
ACEEHNP	CHEAPEN
ACEEHNS	ACHENES
	ENCHASE
ACEEHOR	OCHREAE
ACEEHPP	ECHAPPE
ACEEHPR	CHEAPER
	PEACHER
ACEEHPS	PEACHES
ACEEHRR	REACHER
ACEEHRS	REACHES
ACEEHRT	CHEATER
	HECTARE
	RECHATE
	RECHEAT
	RETEACH
	TEACHER
ACEEHST	EATCHES
	ESCHEAT
	TEACHES
ACEEHTT	THECATE
ACEEHTX	EXCHEAT
ACEEILP	CALIPEE
ACEEIMT	EMICATE
ACEEINR	CINEREA
ACEEINU	EUCAINE
ACEEIRR	CARIERE
ACEEISV	VESICAE
ACEEJKN	JACKEEN
ACEEKNP	KNEECAP
ACEELLN	NACELLE
ACEELMP	EMPLACE
ACEELMR	RECLAME
ACEELNR	CLEANER
	RECLEAN
ACEELNS	CLEANSE
	ELANCES
	ENLACES
	SCALENE
ACEELNT	LATENCE
ACEELNV	ENCLAVE
	VALENCE
ACEELPR	PERCALE
	REPLACE
ACEELPT	CAPELET
ACEELRR	CLEARER
ACEELRS	ALERCES
	CEREALS
	RELACES

	RESCALE
	SCLERAE
ACEELRT	TREACLE
ACEELRU	CAERULE
ACEELRV	CLEAVER
ACEELST	CELESTA
ACEELSU	EUCLASE
ACEELSV	CLEAVES
ACEELVX	EXCLAVE
ACEEMNR	MENACER
ACEEMNS	CASEMEN
	MENACES
ACEEMNT	CEMENTA
ACEEMNV	CAVEMEN
ACEEMRR	AMERCER
	CREAMER
ACEEMRS	AMERCES
	CAREMES
	RACEMES
ACEEMRT	CREMATE
	MEERCAT
ACEEMSS	CAMESES
ACEEMSZ	ECZEMAS
ACEENNP	PENANCE
ACEENNR	NARCEEN
ACEENNT	CANTEEN
ACEENNY	CAYENNE
ACEENOT	ACETONE
ACEENRS	CAREENS
	CASERNE
	ENRACES
	RECANES
ACEENRT	CENTARE
	CRENATE
	REENACT
ACEENSS	ENCASES
	SEANCES
	SENECAS
ACEENST	CETANES
	TENACES
ACEENSV	ENCAVES
ACEENTU	CUNEATE
ACEEORS	ACEROSE
ACEEORT	OCREATE
ACEEOSS	CASEOSE
ACEEOST	ACETOSE
	COATEES
ACEEOTV	EVOCATE
ACEEPRR	CAPERER
	PRERACE
ACEEPRS	ESCAPER
	PEARCES
	PERCASE
	PREACES
	RESPACE
ACEEPSS	ESCAPES
ACEEPST	PECTASE
ACEEPTT	PECTATE
ACEERRS	CAREERS
	CREASER
ACEERRT	CATERER
	RECRATE
	RETRACE
	TERRACE
ACEERSS	CREASES
	SEARCES
ACEERST	CERATES
	CREATES
	ECARTES
	SECRETA
ACEERSU	CESURAE
ACEERTX	EXACTER
	EXCRETA
ACEESSS	ASCESES
ACEESST	ECTASES

ACEESTT	CASETTE
ACEFFHI	AFFICHE
ACEFFHR	CHAFFER
ACEFFIN	CAFFEIN
ACEFFIS	SCAFFIE
ACEFFOR	AFFORCE
ACEFFST	AFFECTS
ACEFGLU	CAGEFUL
ACEFGOT	GEOFACT
ACEFHMR	CHAMFER
ACEFHRS	CHAFERS
ACEFHRU	CHAUFER
ACEFHSU	CHAUFES
ACEFIIL	FELICIA
ACEFILL	ICEFALL
ACEFILM	MALEFIC
ACEFILR	FILACER
ACEFILS	FECIALS
ACEFINN	FINANCE
ACEFINR	FANCIER
ACEFINS	FANCIES
	FASCINE
	FIANCES
ACEFINU	UNIFACE
ACEFIRS	FARCIES
	FIACRES
ACEFITV	FACTIVE
ACEFITY	ACETIFY
ACEFKLR	FLACKER
ACEFKLT	FLACKET
ACEFLRU	CAREFUL
ACEFLSU	FECULAS
ACEFNNO	FACONNE
ACEFNRT	CANTREF
ACEFNRU	FURNACE
ACEFOPR	PROFACE
ACEFORR	FORECAR
ACEFOTU	OUTFACE
ACEFRRS	FARCERS
ACEFRRT	REFRACT
ACEFRRU	FARCEUR
ACEFRSU	SURFACE
ACEFRTU	FACTURE
	FURCATE
ACEFSTU	FAUCETS
ACEGHLO	GALOCHE
ACEGHNR	CHANGER
ACEGHNS	CHANGES
	GANCHES
ACEGHNU	CHAUNGE
ACEGHOU	GOUACHE
ACEGHOW	COWHAGE
ACEGHRR	CHARGER
ACEGHRS	CHARGES
	CREAGHS
ACEGHRT	GERTCHA
ACEGHRU	GAUCHER
ACEGILL	ELLAGIC
ACEGILN	ANGELIC
	ANGLICE
	GALENIC
ACEGILP	PELAGIC
ACEGILR	GLACIER
	GRACILE
ACEGIMO	CAMOGIE
ACEGIMR	GRIMACE
ACEGIMT	GAMETIC
ACEGINO	COINAGE
ACEGINP	PEACING
ACEGINR	ANERGIC
	GRECIAN
ACEGINS	CEASING
	INCAGES
ACEGINV	VEGANIC
ACEGINY	GYNECIA
ACEGINZ	CEAZING
ACEGIOP	APOGEIC
ACEGIRT	CIGARET
ACEGIRU	GAUCIER
ACEGIRW	GAWCIER
ACEGIST	CAGIEST
ACEGJKL	JACKLEG
ACEGKLO	LOCKAGE
ACEGKLR	GRACKLE
ACEGKMO	MOCKAGE
ACEGKOR	CORKAGE
ACEGLLO	COLLAGE
ACEGLNO	CONGEAL
ACEGLNR	CLANGER
	GLANCER
ACEGLNS	CANGLES
	GLANCES
ACEGLOT	CATELOG
ACEGLOU	CAGOULE
ACEGMOP	COMPAGE
ACEGNOR	ACROGEN
	CORNAGE
ACEGNOT	COAGENT
	COGNATE
ACEGNSU	CANGUES
	UNCAGES
ACEGORS	CARGOES
	CORSAGE
	SOCAGER
ACEGORU	COURAGE
ACEGOSS	SOCAGES
ACEGOSW	COWAGES
ACEGOTT	COTTAGE
ACEGRTU	TRUCAGE
ACEGSTU	SCUTAGE
ACEGTTU	CUTTAGE
ACEHHLS	CHALEHS
ACEHHLT	HATCHEL
ACEHHNS	HANCHES
ACEHHRT	HATCHER
ACEHHRU	HACHURE
ACEHHRX	HEXARCH
ACEHHST	CHETAHS
	HATCHES
ACEHHTT	HATCHET
ACEHIKR	KACHERI
ACEHIKS	HACKIES
ACEHILL	CHALLIE
	HELICAL
ACEHILR	CHARLIE
ACEHILT	ALETHIC
	ETHICAL
ACEHIMN	MACHINE
ACEHIMP	IMPEACH
ACEHIMR	CHIMERA
ACEHIMS	CHAMISE
ACEHIMT	HEMATIC
ACEHINN	ENCHAIN
ACEHINR	ARCHINE
ACEHINS	CHAINES
	INCHASE
ACEHINT	CHANTIE
ACEHINY	HYACINE
	HYAENIC
ACEHIOT	ACHIOTE
ACEHIPP	CHAPPIE
ACEHIPR	CHARPIE
ACEHIPT	APHETIC
	HEPATIC
ACEHIRR	CHARIER
ACEHIRS	CAHIERS
	CASHIER
	ERIACHS
ACEHIRT	THERIAC
ACEHIRV	ARCHIVE
ACEHISS	CHAISES
ACEHIST	ACHIEST
	AITCHES
ACEHITY	YACHTIE
ACEHITZ	ZAITECH
ACEHKLR	HACKLER
ACEHKLS	HACKLES
	SHACKLE
ACEHKLT	HACKLET
ACEHKMN	HACKMEN
ACEHKNY	HACKNEY
ACEHKOT	HOTCAKE
ACEHKRS	HACKERS
ACEHKRW	WHACKER
ACEHKRY	HACKERY
ACEHLLP	PELLACH
ACEHLLS	SHELLAC
ACEHLLT	HELLCAT
ACEHLMT	CHAMLET
ACEHLMY	ALCHEMY
ACEHLNN	CHANNEL
ACEHLNO	CHALONE
ACEHLNP	PLANCHE
ACEHLNR	CHARNEL
	LARCHEN
ACEHLNS	LANCHES
ACEHLOP	EPOCHAL
ACEHLOR	CHOLERA
	CHORALE
	CHOREAL
ACEHLOS	LOACHES
	OSCHEAL
ACEHLOT	CATHOLE
	CHOLATE
ACEHLPS	CHAPELS
ACEHLPT	CHAPLET
ACEHLPY	CHEAPLY
ACEHLRS	CLASHER
	LARCHES
	RASCHEL
ACEHLRT	ARCHLET
	TRACHLE
ACEHLRY	CHARLEY
ACEHLSS	CLASHES
	SEALCHS
ACEHLST	CHALETS
	LATCHES
	SATCHEL
ACEHLTT	CHATTEL
	LATCHET
ACEHMNP	CHAPMEN
ACEHMNR	ENCHARM
	MARCHEN
ACEHMNS	MANCHES
ACEHMNT	MANCHET
ACEHMPR	CHAMPER
ACEHMRR	CHARMER
	MARCHER
ACEHMRS	MARCHES
	MESARCH
	SCHMEAR
ACEHMRT	MATCHER
	REMATCH
ACEHMRU	CHAUMER
ACEHMSS	SACHEMS
	SAMECHS
	SCHEMAS
ACEHMST	MATCHES
ACEHMTY	ECTHYMA
ACEHNNR	CHANNER
ACEHNNT	ENCHANT
ACEHNOP	PANOCHE
ACEHNPS	PECHANS
ACEHNRR	RANCHER
ACEHNRS	CHENARS
	RANCHES
ACEHNRT	CHANTER
	TRANCHE
ACEHNSS	SCHANSE
ACEHNST	CHASTEN
	NATCHES
ACEHNSZ	SCHANZE
ACEHNTT	ETCHANT
ACEHNTU	UNTEACH
ACEHNTY	CHANTEY
ACEHNZZ	CHAZZEN
ACEHOOT	OOTHECA
ACEHOPR	POACHER
ACEHOPS	CHEAPOS
	EPOCHAS
	POACHES
	SHOEPAC
ACEHORS	CHOREAS
	ORACHES
	ROACHES
ACEHOSS	CHAOSES
ACEHOTY	CHAYOTE
ACEHPPS	SCHAPPE
ACEHPRS	EPARCHS
	PARCHES
ACEHPRT	CHAPTER
	PATCHER
	REPATCH
ACEHPRU	UPREACH
ACEHPRY	EPARCHY
	PREACHY
ACEHPSS	CHAPESS
ACEHPST	HEPCATS
	PATCHES
ACEHQUY	QUEACHY
ACEHRRS	ARCHERS
	CRASHER
ACEHRRT	CHARTER
	RECHART
ACEHRRX	XERARCH
ACEHRRY	ARCHERY
ACEHRSS	CHASERS
	CRASHES
	ESCHARS
ACEHRST	ARCHEST
	CHARETS
	CHASTER
	RACHETS
	RATCHES
ACEHRSU	ARCHEUS
ACEHRSV	VARECHS
ACEHRSW	CHAWERS
ACEHRSX	EXARCHS
ACEHRSY	HYRACES
ACEHRTT	CHATTER
	RATCHET
ACEHRTW	WATCHER
ACEHRTY	YACHTER
ACEHRXY	EXARCHY
ACEHSSS	CHASSES
ACEHSST	SACHETS
	SCATHES
ACEHSSW	CASHEWS
ACEHSTW	WATCHES
ACEHSTX	HEXACTS
ACEHTTU	TEUCHAT
ACEHTTW	WATCHET
ACEIILM	CIMELIA
ACEIILS	LAICISE
ACEIILT	CILIATE
ACEIILZ	LAICIZE
ACEIIPS	EPISCIA
ACEIITV	CAITIVE
	VICIATE
ACEIJKS	JACKIES

	JACKSIE
ACEIKLS	SACLIKE
ACEIKLT	CATLIKE
ACEIKMR	KERAMIC
ACEIKNT	ANTICKE
ACEIKOP	PAIOCKE
ACEIKPR	EARPICK
ACEIKPW	WICKAPE
ACEIKPX	PICKAXE
ACEIKRS	EIRACKS
ACEIKRT	TACKIER
ACEIKRW	WACKIER
ACEIKSS	SEASICK
ACEIKST	CAKIEST
	TACKIES
ACEIKTT	TIETACK
ACEILLL	ALLELIC
ACEILLM	LIMACEL
	MICELLA
ACEILLS	ALLICES
	CAILLES
ACEILLX	LEXICAL
ACEILMN	CNEMIAL
	MELANIC
ACEILMR	CALMIER
	CLAIMER
	MIRACLE
	RECLAIM
ACEILMS	LIMACES
	MALICES
ACEILMT	CLIMATE
	METICAL
ACEILMX	EXCLAIM
ACEILMY	MYCELIA
ACEILNN	ENCINAL
ACEILNP	CAPELIN
	PANICLE
	PELICAN
ACEILNR	CARLINE
ACEILNS	INLACES
	SANICLE
	SCALENI
ACEILNU	CAULINE
ACEILOR	CALORIE
	CARIOLE
	COALIER
	LORICAE
ACEILOS	CELOSIA
	COALISE
ACEILOT	ALOETIC
ACEILOZ	COALIZE
ACEILPR	CALIPER
	REPLICA
ACEILPS	PLAICES
	SPECIAL
ACEILPT	PLICATE
ACEILPU	PECULIA
ACEILRR	CERRIAL
ACEILRS	CLARIES
	ECLAIRS
	SCALIER
ACEILRT	ARTICLE
	RECITAL
	TALCIER
ACEILRU	AURICLE
ACEILRV	CALIVER
	CAVILER
	CLAVIER
	VALERIC
	VELARIC
ACEILRY	CLAYIER
ACEILSS	SALICES
ACEILST	ASTELIC
	ELASTIC
	LACIEST
	LATICES
	SALICET
ACEILSV	CLAVIES
	VESICAL
ACEILTT	LATTICE
	TACTILE
ACEIMNO	ENCOMIA
ACEIMNP	PEMICAN
ACEIMNR	CARMINE
ACEIMNS	AMNESIC
	CINEMAS
ACEIMNT	EMICANT
	NEMATIC
ACEIMOR	COREMIA
ACEIMOV	VOMICAE
ACEIMPR	CAMPIER
ACEIMPY	PYAEMIC
ACEIMRT	MATRICE
ACEIMRU	URAEMIC
ACEIMSS	CAMISES
ACEIMST	ACMITES
	ETACISM
	MICATES
	SEMATIC
ACEIMSU	CAESIUM
ACEIMTX	TAXEMIC
ACEINNP	PINNACE
ACEINNR	CANNIER
	NARCEIN
ACEINNS	CANINES
	ENCINAS
	NANCIES
ACEINNT	ANCIENT
ACEINNY	CYANINE
ACEINOP	APNOEIC
	PAEONIC
ACEINOS	ACINOSE
ACEINOT	ACONITE
	ANOETIC
ACEINPR	CAPRINE
ACEINPS	INSCAPE
	PINCASE
ACEINRR	CARNIER
ACEINRS	ARCSINE
	ARSENIC
	CARNIES
	CERASIN
ACEINRT	CANTIER
	CERATIN
	CERTAIN
	CREATIN
	CRINATE
	NACRITE
ACEINSS	CASEINS
	INCASES
ACEINST	ACETINS
	CANIEST
	CINEAST
ACEINSU	EUCAINS
ACEINSV	INCAVES
ACEINSY	CYANISE
ACEINTT	NICTATE
	TETANIC
ACEINTU	TUNICAE
ACEINTV	VENATIC
ACEINTX	INEXACT
ACEINTY	CYANITE
ACEINTZ	ZINCATE
ACEINYZ	CYANIZE
ACEIOOZ	ZOOECIA
ACEIOPT	ECTOPIA
ACEIORS	ORACIES
	SCORIAE
ACEIORT	EROTICA
ACEIOST	SOCIATE
ACEIOTX	EXOTICA
ACEIPPR	CRAPPIE
	EPICARP
ACEIPPT	TAPPICE
ACEIPRR	CRAPIER
ACEIPRS	EPACRIS
	SCRAPIE
	SPACIER
ACEIPRT	PARETIC
	PICRATE
ACEIPST	ASEPTIC
	PACIEST
	SPICATE
ACEIPSU	AUSPICE
ACEIPSZ	CAPIZES
	CAPSIZE
ACEIPTV	CAPTIVE
ACEIQRU	ACQUIRE
ACEIQSU	CAIQUES
ACEIQTU	ACQUITE
ACEIQUZ	CAZIQUE
ACEIRRR	CARRIER
ACEIRRS	CARRIES
	SCARIER
ACEIRRT	CIRRATE
	ERRATIC
ACEIRRW	AIRCREW
ACEIRRZ	CRAZIER
ACEIRST	CRISTAE
	RACIEST
	STEARIC
ACEIRSU	SAUCIER
	URICASE
ACEIRSV	CARVIES
	CAVIERS
	VARICES
	VISCERA
ACEIRSZ	CRAZIES
ACEIRTT	CATTIER
	CITRATE
ACEISSS	ASCESIS
ACEISST	ASCITES
	ECTASIS
ACEISTT	CATTIES
	STATICE
	TIETACS
ACEISTV	ACTIVES
ACEISVV	VIVACES
ACEITTV	CAVETTI
ACEITTX	EXTATIC
ACEITUX	AUXETIC
ACEJKMN	JACKMEN
ACEJKOP	PAJOCKE
ACEJKRS	JACKERS
ACEJKST	JACKETS
ACEJLOR	CAJOLER
ACEJLOS	CAJOLES
ACEJNOS	CAJONES
ACEJNOT	JACONET
ACEJNOY	JOYANCE
ACEJNSU	JAUNCES
ACEJNTU	JUNCATE
ACEJPTU	CAJEPUT
ACEJRTT	TRAJECT
ACEKKNR	KNACKER
ACEKLLP	PELLACK
ACEKLMS	MACKLES
ACEKLNR	CRANKLE
ACEKLNS	SLACKEN
ACEKLOR	EARLOCK
ACEKLPS	SPACKLE
ACEKLPT	PLACKET
ACEKLQU	QUACKLE
ACEKLRS	CALKERS
	LACKERS
	SLACKER
ACEKLRT	TACKLER
ACEKLRU	CAULKER
ACEKLST	TACKLES
ACEKLSY	LACKEYS
ACEKMNP	PACKMEN
ACEKMOR	COMAKER
ACEKMOS	COMAKES
ACEKMRS	SMACKER
ACEKNOS	NOCAKES
ACEKNPR	PRANCKE
ACEKNRR	CRANKER
ACEKNRS	CANKERS
ACEKNRY	CANKERY
ACEKNST	NACKETS
ACEKNSU	UNCAKES
ACEKORR	CROAKER
ACEKPPR	PREPACK
ACEKPRS	PACKERS
	REPACKS
ACEKPST	PACKETS
ACEKQRU	QUACKER
ACEKRRS	RACKERS
	RERACKS
ACEKRRT	RETRACK
	TRACKER
ACEKRSS	SACKERS
	SCREAKS
ACEKRST	RACKETS
	RESTACK
	RETACKS
	STACKER
	TACKERS
ACEKRSU	CAUKERS
ACEKRSW	CAWKERS
	WACKERS
ACEKRSY	SCREAKY
	YACKERS
ACEKRTT	RACKETT
ACEKRTY	RACKETY
ACEKSST	CASKETS
ACEKSTT	STACKET
	TACKETS
ACEKSUW	WAESUCK
ACEKTTY	TACKETY
ACELLMO	CALOMEL
ACELLNU	NUCLEAL
ACELLNY	CLEANLY
ACELLOR	CORELLA
	OCELLAR
ACELLOS	CALLOSE
	LOCALES
ACELLOT	COLLATE
ACELLPS	SCALPEL
ACELLPY	CLYPEAL
ACELLRR	CARRELL
ACELLRS	CALLERS
	CELLARS
	RECALLS
	SCLERAL
ACELLRY	CLEARLY
ACELLST	CALLETS
ACELMMR	CLAMMER
ACELMNO	COALMEN
ACELMNS	ENCALMS
ACELMOR	CAROMEL
ACELMOT	CAMELOT
ACELMOU	CAULOME
	LEUCOMA
ACELMPR	CLAMPER
ACELMPS	CAMPLES
ACELMRS	MARCELS
ACELMRY	CAMELRY
ACELMSS	MASCLES
	MESCALS

	SCAMELS
ACELMST	CALMEST
	CAMLETS
ACELMSU	ALMUCES
	MACULES
ACELMSZ	MEZCALS
ACELMTU	CALUMET
ACELNNO	ALENCON
ACELNNS	CANNELS
ACELNNU	UNCLEAN
ACELNNY	LYNCEAN
ACELNOR	CORNEAL
ACELNOT	LACTONE
ACELNOZ	CALZONE
ACELNPS	ENCLASP
	SPANCEL
ACELNPT	CLAPNET
ACELNPU	CLEANUP
	UNPLACE
ACELNRS	LANCERS
	RANCELS
ACELNRT	CENTRAL
ACELNRU	LUCARNE
	NUCLEAR
	UNCLEAR
ACELNRY	LARCENY
ACELNST	CANTLES
	CENTALS
	LANCETS
	SCANTLE
ACELNSU	CENSUAL
	LACUNES
	LAUNCES
	UNLACES
	UNSCALE
ACELNTT	CANTLET
ACELNTY	LATENCY
ACELNVY	VALENCY
ACELOPR	POLACRE
ACELOPS	ESCALOP
ACELOPT	POLECAT
ACELOPU	COPULAE
ACELOQU	COEQUAL
ACELORR	CAROLER
ACELORS	CLAROES
	COALERS
	ESCOLAR
	ORACLES
	RECOALS
	SOLACER
ACELORT	LOCATER
ACELORY	CALOYER
ACELOSS	SOLACES
ACELOST	ALECOST
	LACTOSE
	LOCATES
	SCATOLE
	TALCOSE
ACELOSV	ALCOVES
	COEVALS
ACELOTT	CALOTTE
ACELOTU	OCULATE
ACELOTY	ACOLYTE
	COTYLAE
ACELOUV	VACUOLE
ACELPPR	CLAPPER
ACELPPS	SCAPPLE
ACELPRS	CARPELS
	CLASPER
	CRAPLES
	PARCELS
	PLACERS
	RECLASP
	SCALPER
ACELPRT	PLECTRA
ACELPRY	PRELACY
ACELPSS	CAPLESS
ACELPST	CAPLETS
	PLACETS
ACELPSU	CAPSULE
	SCALEUP
	SPECULA
	UPSCALE
ACELPSY	CYPSELA
ACELPTY	ECTYPAL
ACELPUU	CUPULAE
ACELQRU	CLAQUER
	LACQUER
ACELQSU	CALQUES
	CLAQUES
ACELQUY	LACQUEY
ACELRRS	CARRELS
ACELRRU	RAUCLER
ACELRRW	CRAWLER
ACELRSS	CARLESS
	CLASSER
	SCALERS
	SCLERAS
ACELRST	CARTELS
	CLARETS
	CRESTAL
	SCARLET
	TARCELS
ACELRSU	CESURAL
	RECUSAL
	SECULAR
ACELRSV	CALVERS
	CARVELS
	CLAVERS
ACELRSW	CLAWERS
ACELRTT	CLATTER
ACELRTY	TREACLY
ACELSSS	CLASSES
	SACLESS
ACELSST	CASTLES
	SCLATES
ACELSSU	CLAUSES
ACELSSV	SCLAVES
ACELSTU	CAUTELS
	SULCATE
ACELSTY	ACETYLS
	SCYTALE
ACELSUU	ACULEUS
ACELSUX	EXCUSAL
ACELSXY	CALYXES
ACELTUY	ACUTELY
ACELTXY	EXACTLY
ACEMMRR	CRAMMER
ACEMNOR	CREMONA
	ROMANCE
ACEMNOS	ANCOMES
ACEMNPS	ENCAMPS
ACEMNRW	CREWMAN
ACEMNSU	ACUMENS
ACEMOPR	COMPARE
	COMPEAR
ACEMOPS	POMACES
ACEMORS	AMORCES
ACEMORU	MORCEAU
ACEMOSS	COSMEAS
ACEMOST	CAMOTES
	COMATES
ACEMOSU	MUCOSAE
ACEMPRS	CAMPERS
	SCAMPER
ACEMPRT	CRAMPET
ACEMPST	CAMPEST
ACEMRSS	SCREAMS
ACEMRST	MERCATS
ACEMRSY	CRAMESY
ACEMSSU	CAMUSES
ACEMSTT	METCAST
ACEMSTU	MUCATES
ACENNOS	ANCONES
	SONANCE
ACENNOT	CONNATE
ACENNOX	COANNEX
ACENNOY	NOYANCE
ACENNOZ	CANZONE
ACENNRS	CANNERS
	SCANNER
ACENNRY	CANNERY
ACENNST	NASCENT
ACENNSU	NUANCES
ACENNTY	TENANCY
ACENOOR	CORONAE
ACENOPT	PATONCE
ACENOPU	PONCEAU
ACENORS	CARNOSE
	COARSEN
	CORNEAS
	EARCONS
	NARCOSE
ACENORT	ENACTOR
ACENOSS	CASSONE
ACENOST	COSTEAN
	OCTANES
ACENOTT	ATTONCE
ACENOTV	CENTAVO
ACENPRR	PRANCER
ACENPRS	PRANCES
ACENPRU	PRAUNCE
ACENPST	CATNEPS
ACENPSU	PAUNCES
	UNCAPES
ACENPSW	PAWNCES
ACENPTT	PENTACT
ACENPTY	PATENCY
ACENRRY	ERRANCY
ACENRSS	ANCRESS
	CASERNS
ACENRST	CANTERS
	CARNETS
	NECTARS
	RECANTS
	SCANTER
	TANRECS
	TRANCES
ACENRSU	SURANCE
ACENRSV	CAVERNS
	CRAVENS
ACENRSY	CARNEYS
	SCENARY
ACENRSZ	ZARNECS
ACENRTT	TRANECT
ACENRTU	CENTAUR
	UNCRATE
	UNTRACE
ACENRTY	ENCRATY
	NECTARY
ACENSST	ASCENTS
	SECANTS
	STANCES
ACENSSU	UNCASES
	USANCES
ACENSTT	CANTEST
ACENSTU	NUTCASE
ACENSUU	USAUNCE
ACENSUV	VAUNCES
ACEOOPP	APOCOPE
ACEOOTZ	ECTOZOA
ACEOPRX	EXOCARP
ACEOPSS	SCAPOSE
ACEOPST	CAPOTES
	SCOPATE
	TOECAPS
ACEOPSW	COWPEAS
ACEOPTU	OUTPACE
ACEORRS	COARSER
ACEORRT	ACROTER
	CREATOR
	REACTOR
ACEORSS	ROSACES
ACEORST	COASTER
	COATERS
ACEORSU	ACEROUS
	CAROUSE
ACEORSX	COAXERS
ACEORTU	OUTRACE
ACEORTV	OVERACT
ACEORTX	EXACTOR
ACEOSSU	CASEOUS
ACEOSTT	COSTATE
ACEOSTU	ACETOUS
ACEOSTV	AVOCETS
	OCTAVES
ACEOTTV	CAVETTO
ACEOTUU	AUTOCUE
	COUTEAU
ACEOTUX	COTEAUX
ACEPPRR	CRAPPER
ACEPPRS	CAPPERS
ACEPRRS	CARPERS
	SCARPER
	SCRAPER
ACEPRSS	ESCARPS
	PARSECS
	SCRAPES
	SECPARS
	SPACERS
ACEPRST	CARPETS
	PREACTS
	PRECAST
	SPECTRA
ACEPRSU	APERCUS
	SCAUPER
ACEPRTU	CAPTURE
ACEPSST	ASPECTS
ACEPSTU	CUSPATE
	TEACUPS
ACEQRTU	RACQUET
ACEQSSU	CASQUES
	SACQUES
ACEQSTU	ACQUEST
ACERRRY	RECARRY
ACERRSS	CRASSER
	SCARERS
	SCARRES
ACERRST	CARTERS
	CRATERS
	TRACERS
ACERRSU	CURARES
ACERRSV	CARVERS
	CRAVERS
ACERRSY	CRAYERS
ACERRTT	RETRACT
ACERRTY	TRACERY
ACERRUV	VERRUCA
ACERRVY	CARVERY
ACERSST	ACTRESS
	CASTERS
	RECASTS
ACERSSU	ARCUSES
	CAUSERS
	CESURAS
	SAUCERS
	SUCRASE
ACERSSV	SCARVES
ACERSSY	CARSEYS
	SCRAYES

ACERSTT	SCATTER
ACERSTU	ACTURES
	CAUTERS
	CRUSTAE
	CURATES
ACERSTY	SECTARY
ACERTTT	TETRACT
ACERTTU	CURTATE
ACERTTX	EXTRACT
ACERTTY	CATTERY
ACERTUV	CURVATE
ACERTUX	CURTAXE
ACERTUY	CAUTERY
ACESSTT	STACTES
ACESSTU	CAESTUS
	CUESTAS
ACESSTY	CYTASES
	ECSTASY
ACESSUY	CAUSEYS
	CAYUSES
ACESTTU	ACUTEST
	SCUTATE
ACESTTY	TESTACY
ACESTUY	EUSTACY
ACFFHSU	CHAUFFS
ACFFIIT	CAITIFF
ACFFIKM	MAFFICK
ACFFILT	AFFLICT
ACFFINY	FANCIFY
ACFFIRT	TRAFFIC
ACFFIRY	FARCIFY
ACFFLSS	SCLAFFS
ACFFLTU	FACTFUL
ACFFOST	CASTOFF
	OFFCAST
ACFGHIN	CHAFING
ACFGINR	FARCING
ACFGINS	FACINGS
ACFHIIS	FIASCHI
ACFHIST	CATFISH
ACFHISU	FUCHSIA
ACFHLNU	FLAUNCH
ACFHNOU	FAUCHON
ACFHRTU	FUTHARC
ACFHRTY	FRATCHY
ACFIILN	FINICAL
ACFIKNN	FINNACK
ACFIKTY	TACKIFY
ACFILNO	FOLACIN
ACFILNY	FANCILY
ACFILOY	COALIFY
ACFILRY	CLARIFY
ACFILSS	FISCALS
ACFIMOR	ACIFORM
ACFIMRU	FUMARIC
ACFIMSS	FASCISM
ACFINNS	FINNACS
ACFINNY	INFANCY
ACFINOT	FACTION
ACFINRS	FARCINS
ACFINRT	FRANTIC
	INFARCT
	INFRACT
ACFINRY	CARNIFY
ACFIOPY	OPACIFY
ACFIOSS	FIASCOS
ACFIPRY	CAPRIFY
ACFIRSY	SACRIFY
	SCARIFY
ACFISST	FASCIST
ACFKLRU	RACKFUL
ACFKLSU	SACKFUL
ACFLLOY	FOCALLY
ACFLNOS	FALCONS
	FLACONS

ACFLNSU	CANFULS
	CANSFUL
ACFLOPW	COWFLAP
ACFLOST	OLFACTS
ACFLPSU	CAPFULS
ACFLRSU	CARFULS
ACFLRUU	FURCULA
ACFLTTU	TACTFUL
ACFLTUY	FACULTY
ACFMSTU	FACTUMS
ACFNNOT	NONFACT
ACFNNUY	UNFANCY
ACFNSTU	UNFACTS
ACFORST	FACTORS
	FORCATS
ACFORTY	FACTORY
ACFRRTU	FRACTUR
ACFRSTU	FRACTUS
ACGGINR	GRACING
ACGGIOS	AGOGICS
ACGGRSY	SCRAGGY
ACGHIKN	HACKING
ACGHIMO	OGHAMIC
ACGHINR	ARCHING
	CHAGRIN
	CHARING
ACGHINS	ACHINGS
	CASHING
	CHASING
ACGHINT	GNATHIC
ACGHINW	CHAWING
	CHINWAG
ACGHIOR	CHORAGI
ACGHIPR	GRAPHIC
ACGHIRS	SCRAIGH
ACGHLTU	CLAUGHT
ACGHNRU	GRAUNCH
ACGHOSU	GAUCHOS
ACGHRRU	CURRAGH
ACGHRSU	CURAGHS
	SCRAUGH
ACGIILN	ALGINIC
ACGIITU	AUGITIC
ACGIJKN	JACKING
ACGIKLN	CALKING
	LACKING
ACGIKNP	PACKING
ACGIKNR	ARCKING
	CARKING
	CRAKING
	RACKING
ACGIKNS	CAKINGS
	CASKING
	SACKING
ACGIKNT	TACKING
ACGIKNV	VACKING
ACGIKNY	YACKING
ACGILLN	CALLING
ACGILLO	LOGICAL
ACGILMN	CALMING
ACGILMY	MYALGIC
ACGILNN	LANCING
ACGILNO	COALING
ACGILNP	PLACING
ACGILNR	CARLING
ACGILNS	LACINGS
	SCALING
ACGILNT	CATLING
	TALCING
ACGILNU	CINGULA
	GLUCINA
ACGILNV	CALVING
ACGILNW	CLAWING
ACGILNY	CLAYING
ACGILOS	CALIGOS

ACGILOT	OTALGIC
ACGILRS	GARLICS
ACGIMMN	CAMMING
ACGIMNO	COAMING
ACGIMNP	CAMPING
ACGIMNU	CAUMING
ACGINNN	CANNING
ACGINNR	CRANING
	RANCING
ACGINNS	CANINGS
ACGINNT	CANTING
ACGINOR	ORGANIC
ACGINOS	ANGICOS
ACGINOT	COATING
	COTINGA
ACGINOX	COAXING
ACGINPP	CAPPING
ACGINPR	CARPING
	CRAPING
ACGINPS	SCAPING
	SPACING
ACGINRS	ARCINGS
	RACINGS
	SACRING
	SCARING
ACGINRT	CARTING
	CRATING
	TRACING
ACGINRV	CARVING
	CRAVING
ACGINRZ	CRAZING
ACGINSS	CASINGS
ACGINST	ACTINGS
	CASTING
ACGINSU	CAUSING
	SAUCING
ACGINSV	CAVINGS
ACGINSW	CAWINGS
ACGINTT	CATTING
ACGINUV	VICUGNA
ACGIORT	ARGOTIC
ACGIRST	GASTRIC
	TRAGICS
ACGKMMO	GAMMOCK
ACGKORV	GARVOCK
ACGLLPU	CUPGALL
ACGLNOR	CLANGOR
ACGLNOY	AGLYCON
ACGLNSU	GLUCANS
ACGLNSY	GLYCANS
ACGLOSU	CAGOULS
ACGLOXY	COXALGY
ACGMNOP	CAMPONG
ACGNNOR	CRANNOG
ACGNOOT	OCTAGON
ACGNORS	GARCONS
ACGNOSS	GASCONS
ACGORRY	GYROCAR
ACGORSU	COUGARS
ACGORUU	COUGUAR
ACGOSWY	COGWAYS
ACGSTTU	CATGUTS
ACHHIRS	RHACHIS
ACHHLOT	CHALOTH
ACHHOST	TOSHACH
ACHHPPU	CHUPPAH
ACHHTTT	THATCHT
ACHHTTY	THATCHY
ACHIIKM	KAMICHI
ACHIILS	ISCHIAL
ACHIIMS	CHIASMI
ACHIIPS	PACHISI
ACHIIRV	CHIVARI
ACHIJKS	HIJACKS
ACHIJNT	JACINTH

ACHIKRS	RICKSHA
ACHIKRY	HAYRICK
ACHIKSS	SHICKSA
ACHILLO	LOCHIAL
ACHILLP	PHALLIC
ACHILLS	CHALLIS
ACHILLT	THALLIC
ACHILMO	MALICHO
	MOCHILA
ACHILMS	CHIMLAS
ACHILOR	CHORIAL
ACHILOS	SCHOLIA
ACHILPS	CALIPHS
ACHILRS	ARCHILS
	CARLISH
ACHILRY	CHARILY
ACHILST	CHITALS
ACHILSY	CLAYISH
ACHILWY	LICHWAY
ACHIMNO	MANIHOC
ACHIMOS	CHAMISO
	CHAMOIS
ACHIMOX	CHAMOIX
ACHIMRS	CHARISM
	CHIMARS
	CHRISMA
ACHIMSS	CHIASMS
	SCHISMA
ACHIMST	MASTICH
	TACHISM
ACHINNU	UNCHAIN
ACHINOP	APHONIC
ACHINOY	ONYCHIA
ACHINPS	SPINACH
ACHINRS	CHINARS
ACHINRZ	ZARNICH
ACHINTX	XANTHIC
ACHINUV	CHAUVIN
ACHIOPS	ISOPACH
ACHIOPT	APHOTIC
ACHIORT	CHARIOT
	HARICOT
ACHIOST	ISOTACH
ACHIPPS	SAPPHIC
ACHIPST	HAPTICS
	PATHICS
	SPATHIC
ACHIPTU	CHUPATI
ACHIPTW	WHIPCAT
ACHIQRU	CHARQUI
ACHIQSU	QUAICHS
ACHIRRT	TRIARCH
ACHIRTU	HAIRCUT
ACHIRTY	CHARITY
ACHISSS	CHASSIS
ACHISST	SCAITHS
ACHISTT	CATTISH
	CHATTIS
	TACHIST
ACHKKRU	CHUKKAR
ACHKKSU	CHUKKAS
ACHKLST	KLATSCH
ACHKMMO	HAMMOCK
ACHKOPS	HOPSACK
ACHKORS	CHOKRAS
ACHKOSS	HASSOCK
	SHACKOS
ACHKOSW	WHACKOS
ACHKOTT	HATTOCK
ACHKRSU	CHUKARS
ACHKSTW	THWACKS
ACHLLOO	ALCOHOL
ACHLLOR	CHLORAL
ACHLLOS	CHOLLAS
ACHLLOT	CHALLOT

ACHLMOP	CAMPHOL
ACHLMSY	CHLAMYS
ACHLMSZ	SCHMALZ
ACHLMYY	ALCHYMY
ACHLNOS	LOCHANS
ACHLNOY	HALCYON
ACHLNSU	NUCHALS
ACHLNTU	TULCHAN
	UNLATCH
ACHLOPR	RAPLOCH
ACHLOPT	POTLACH
ACHLORS	CHORALS
	LORCHAS
	SCHOLAR
ACHLORT	TROCHAL
ACHLOSW	SALCHOW
ACHLOTY	ACOLYTH
ACHLPST	SPLATCH
ACHLTUZ	CHALUTZ
ACHMNOR	MONARCH
	NOMARCH
ACHMNOU	UNMACHO
ACHMNRU	UNCHARM
ACHMOPR	CAMPHOR
ACHMORS	CHROMAS
ACHMORZ	MACHZOR
ACHMOST	STOMACH
ACHMPTU	MATCHUP
ACHMSSU	SUMACHS
ACHMSUW	CUMSHAW
ACHNNOS	CHANSON
	NONCASH
ACHNORS	ANCHORS
	ARCHONS
	RANCHOS
ACHNORT	CHANTOR
ACHNOSS	SANCHOS
ACHNOST	CHATONS
ACHNOSY	ONYCHAS
ACHNOTY	TACHYON
ACHNOUY	CHANOYU
ACHNOVY	ANCHOVY
ACHNPSS	SCHNAPS
ACHNPUY	PAUNCHY
ACHNRTY	CHANTRY
ACHNRUY	RAUNCHY
	UNCHARY
ACHNSTU	CANTHUS
	CHAUNTS
	STAUNCH
ACHNSTY	SNATCHY
ACHOOSS	CASHOOS
ACHOOST	CAHOOTS
ACHOPRS	CARHOPS
	COPRAHS
ACHOPRT	TOPARCH
ACHOPRY	CHARPOY
ACHOPSY	POCHAYS
ACHORRS	CHARROS
ACHORRT	TROCHAR
ACHORST	ORCHATS
ACHORSU	AUROCHS
ACHPRSS	SCARPHS
ACHPTUZ	CHUTZPA
ACHRSST	SCARTHS
ACHRSTY	STARCHY
ACHRSUU	URACHUS
ACHSSTU	CUSHATS
ACHSSTY	STACHYS
ACHSSUW	CUSHAWS
ACHSTUW	WAUCHTS
ACHSTUY	CYATHUS
ACIIKNN	CANIKIN
ACIIKRS	AIRSICK
ACIILLN	ALLICIN
ACIILMM	MIMICAL
ACIILMS	LAICISM
ACIILNR	CLARINI
ACIILNS	INCISAL
	SALICIN
	SINICAL
ACIILNV	VICINAL
ACIILOV	VILIACO
ACIILPT	APLITIC
ACIILPU	APICULI
ACIILRY	CILIARY
ACIILSS	SILICAS
ACIILST	ITALICS
ACIILSU	ILIACUS
ACIILSV	CLIVIAS
ACIILTY	LAICITY
ACIIMMN	MINICAM
ACIIMMS	MIASMIC
ACIIMNR	CRIMINA
	MINICAR
ACIIMOT	COMITIA
ACIIMST	ISMATIC
	ITACISM
ACIINNO	ANIONIC
ACIINNS	NIACINS
ACIINOS	ASINICO
ACIINOV	AVIONIC
ACIINPS	PISCINA
ACIINTT	TITANIC
ACIINUX	AUXINIC
ACIIPPR	PRIAPIC
ACIIPRT	PIRATIC
ACIIRST	SATIRIC
ACIIRTT	TRIATIC
ACIITTX	TAXITIC
ACIJUZZ	JACUZZI
ACIKLLY	ALKYLIC
ACIKLNS	CALKINS
ACIKLOR	AIRLOCK
ACIKLTY	TACKILY
ACIKLWY	WACKILY
ACIKMOO	OOMIACK
ACIKMOT	COMATIK
ACIKMPR	RAMPICK
ACIKMPW	PICKMAW
ACIKMSU	UMIACKS
ACIKNNP	PANNICK
ACIKNPS	PANICKS
ACIKNPY	PANICKY
ACIKNRS	NICKARS
ACIKNST	ANTICKS
	CATKINS
	CATSKIN
ACIKNTT	TINTACK
ACIKOPS	PAIOCKS
ACIKORS	ARKOSIC
ACIKPRT	PATRICK
	TRIPACK
ACIKPSS	ASPICKS
ACIKRST	KARSTIC
ACILLLY	ALLYLIC
ACILLMS	MISCALL
ACILLRY	LYRICAL
ACILLSS	SCILLAS
ACILMNO	LIMACON
ACILMOP	OILCAMP
ACILMOT	COMITAL
ACILMPS	PLASMIC
	PSALMIC
ACILMPY	CAMPILY
ACILMSU	MUSICAL
ACILNNO	CANNOLI
ACILNNU	UNCINAL
ACILNNY	CANNILY
ACILNOR	CLARINO
	CLARION
ACILNOS	OILCANS
ACILNOU	INOCULA
ACILNOY	ACYLOIN
ACILNOZ	CALZONI
ACILNPS	CAPLINS
	INCLASP
ACILNPY	PLIANCY
ACILNRS	CARLINS
ACILNST	CATLINS
	TINCALS
ACILNSU	UNCIALS
ACILNTU	LUNATIC
ACILNTY	ANTICLY
ACILNUV	VINCULA
ACILOPT	CAPITOL
	COALPIT
	OPTICAL
	TOPICAL
ACILORR	RACLOIR
ACILORV	CORIVAL
ACILOSS	SOCIALS
ACILOST	CITOLAS
	STOICAL
ACILOTV	VOLATIC
	VOLTAIC
ACILOTX	TOXICAL
ACILPRT	CLIPART
ACILPST	PLACITS
	PLASTIC
ACILPSU	SPICULA
ACILPTY	TYPICAL
ACILRSS	CRISSAL
ACILRST	CITRALS
ACILRSU	URACILS
ACILRSY	SCARILY
ACILRTU	CURTAIL
	TRUCIAL
ACILRTY	CLARITY
ACILRVY	VICARLY
ACILRYZ	CRAZILY
ACILSSS	CLASSIS
ACILSSU	CLUSIAS
ACILSUY	SAUCILY
ACILTTY	CATTILY
	TACITLY
ACILTUV	VICTUAL
ACIMMNO	AMMONIC
ACIMNOP	CAMPION
ACIMNOR	MARCONI
	MINORCA
ACIMNOS	ANOSMIC
	CAMIONS
	CONIMAS
	MANIOCS
	MASONIC
ACIMNPU	PANICUM
ACIMNRS	NARCISM
ACIMNRT	MANTRIC
ACIMNRU	CRANIUM
	CUMARIN
ACIMNTT	CATMINT
ACIMOOS	OOMIACS
ACIMOPT	APOMICT
	POTAMIC
ACIMOSS	MOSAICS
ACIMOST	ATOMICS
	MATICOS
	OSMATIC
	SOMATIC
ACIMOSV	VOMICAS
ACIMPRT	CRAMPIT
	PTARMIC
ACIMPRY	PRIMACY
ACIMPSS	SCAMPIS
	SPASMIC
ACIMPST	IMPACTS
ACIMRSS	RACISMS
ACIMRST	MATRICS
ACIMRSY	MYRICAS
ACIMRSZ	CZARISM
ACIMSST	MASTICS
	MISACTS
	MISCAST
ACIMSTT	TACTISM
ACINNOT	ACTINON
	CANTION
	CONTAIN
ACINNOZ	CANZONI
ACINNST	INCANTS
	STANNIC
ACINNSY	CYANINS
ACINNTU	ANNICUT
ACINOPT	CAPTION
	PACTION
ACINOQU	COQUINA
ACINORR	CARRION
ACINORS	SARONIC
ACINORT	CAROTIN
ACINORV	CORVINA
ACINOSS	CAISSON
	CASINOS
	CASSINO
ACINOST	ACTIONS
	ATONICS
	CATIONS
ACINOSU	ACINOUS
ACINOSY	SYCONIA
ACINOTT	TACTION
ACINOTU	AUCTION
	CAUTION
ACINPRT	CANTRIP
ACINPRU	PURANIC
ACINPRY	CYPRIAN
ACINPSS	PANISCS
ACINPST	CATNIPS
ACINQTU	QUANTIC
ACINRSS	ARCSINS
ACINRST	NARCIST
ACINRSU	CRUSIAN
ACINRTT	TANTRIC
ACINRTU	CURTAIN
	TURACIN
ACINSTU	ANICUTS
	NAUTICS
ACINSUV	VICUNAS
ACIOPRS	PICAROS
	PROSAIC
ACIOPRT	APRICOT
	APROTIC
	PAROTIC
	PATRICO
ACIOPST	COPITAS
	PSOATIC
ACIOPTT	APTOTIC
ACIOPTY	OPACITY
ACIORRS	CORSAIR
ACIORSU	CARIOUS
	CURIOSA
ACIORTT	CITATOR
	RICOTTA
ACIOSST	SCOTIAS
ACIOSSV	OVISACS
ACIPRSY	PISCARY
ACIPRTT	TIPCART
ACIPRVY	PRIVACY
ACIPSST	SPASTIC
ACIPSTT	TIPCATS
ACIPTUY	PAUCITY
ACIQRTU	QUARTIC

ACIQSTU	ACQUIST
	ACQUITS
ACIRRSS	SIRCARS
ACIRRST	TRICARS
ACIRRSU	CURARIS
ACIRSST	RACISTS
	SACRIST
ACIRSSU	CUIRASS
ACIRSTT	ASTRICT
ACIRSTU	URTICAS
ACIRSTW	TWISCAR
ACIRSTY	SATYRIC
ACIRSTZ	CZARIST
ACIRTUY	RAUCITY
ACISSTT	STATICS
ACISSTU	CASUIST
ACISTTU	CATSUIT
ACISTUV	VACUIST
ACITUVY	VACUITY
ACJKKSY	SKYJACK
ACJKLOW	LOCKJAW
ACJKNNO	JANNOCK
ACJKOPS	PAJOCKS
ACJKOPT	JACKPOT
ACJLORU	JOCULAR
ACJMNTU	MUNTJAC
ACJPTUU	CAJUPUT
ACKKLOY	KOLACKY
ACKLLOP	POLLACK
ACKLLOY	LAYLOCK
ACKLLSY	SLACKLY
ACKLMNO	LOCKMAN
ACKLMOR	ARMLOCK
	LOCKRAM
ACKLNOU	UNCLOAK
ACKLNRY	CRANKLY
ACKLOOR	OARLOCK
ACKLORV	LAVROCK
ACKLORW	WARLOCK
ACKLORY	ROCKLAY
ACKLOSS	LASSOCK
ACKMMMO	MAMMOCK
ACKMNOS	SOCKMAN
ACKMOTT	MATTOCK
ACKNNOW	ACKNOWN
ACKNOSW	ACKNOWS
ACKNPRS	PRANCKS
ACKNPSU	UNPACKS
ACKNSTU	UNSTACK
	UNTACKS
ACKOPRR	PARROCK
ACKOPSY	YAPOCKS
ACKORRT	TARROCK
ACKPSSY	SKYCAPS
ACKPSTU	STACKUP
ACLLLOY	LOCALLY
ACLLOOR	COROLLA
ACLLOPS	SCALLOP
ACLLORS	COLLARS
ACLLORU	LOCULAR
ACLLOSU	CALLOUS
ACLLOSW	CALLOWS
ACLLOVY	VOCALLY
ACLLSUY	CULLAYS
ACLMNOO	LOCOMAN
ACLMNPU	UNCLAMP
ACLMNUY	CALUMNY
ACLMOPS	COPALMS
ACLMORS	CLAMORS
ACLMORU	CLAMOUR
ACLMOSU	MUCOSAL
ACLMSTU	TALCUMS
ACLMSUU	LUCUMAS
ACLMSUY	MASCULY
ACLNNOO	NONCOLA
ACLNOOR	CORONAL
ACLNOOT	COOLANT
	OCTANOL
ACLNOOV	VOLCANO
ACLNORU	CORNUAL
	COURLAN
ACLNOSX	CLAXONS
ACLNOUV	UNVOCAL
ACLNPSU	UNCLASP
ACLNRTU	TRUNCAL
ACLNSTY	SCANTLY
ACLNSUV	VULCANS
ACLOOPP	ALCOPOP
ACLOOPR	CARPOOL
ACLOORT	LOCATOR
ACLOPRT	CALTROP
	PROCTAL
ACLOPRU	COPULAR
	CUPOLAR
ACLOPSU	COPULAS
	CUPOLAS
	SCOPULA
ACLOPSY	CALYPSO
ACLOPTY	POLYACT
ACLORRS	CORRALS
ACLORST	CARLOTS
	CROTALS
	SCROTAL
ACLORSU	CAROLUS
	OCULARS
	OSCULAR
	RUCOLAS
ACLORUV	VOCULAR
ACLORYZ	CORYZAL
ACLOSST	COSTALS
ACLOSTU	LOCUSTA
	TALCOUS
ACLOSTW	COTWALS
ACLPRTY	CRYPTAL
ACLPRUU	CUPULAR
ACLRSSW	SCRAWLS
ACLRSSY	CRASSLY
ACLRSTU	CRUSTAL
	CURTALS
ACLRSTY	CRYSTAL
ACLRSWY	SCRAWLY
ACLSSTU	CUTLASS
ACMNOPR	CRAMPON
ACMNOPY	COMPANY
ACMNORS	MACRONS
ACMNORY	ACRONYM
ACMNOSS	MASCONS
ACMNSTU	SANCTUM
ACMOOST	SCOTOMA
ACMOPRT	COMPART
ACMOPSS	COMPASS
ACMOPST	COMPAST
ACMORRS	CARROMS
ACMORST	COMARTS
ACMORTW	CATWORM
ACMOSST	MASCOTS
ACMOSSU	MUCOSAS
ACMOSTT	TOMCATS
ACMOSTU	MOTUCAS
ACMQTUU	CUMQUAT
ACMRSSU	SACRUMS
ACMRSSW	SCRAWMS
ACMSSTU	MUSCATS
ACMSTUU	MUTUCAS
ACMSUUV	VACUUMS
ACNNNOS	CANNONS
ACNNNUY	UNCANNY
ACNNORY	CANONRY
ACNNOST	CANTONS
ACNNOSY	CANYONS
	SONANCY
ACNNRSY	SCRANNY
ACNOOPS	POONACS
ACNOORS	CORONAS
	RACOONS
ACNOORT	CARTOON
	CORANTO
ACNOPSW	SNOWCAP
ACNORRS	RANCORS
ACNORRU	RANCOUR
ACNORRY	CARRYON
ACNORST	CANTORS
	CARTONS
	CONTRAS
	CRATONS
ACNORSU	NACROUS
ACNORSY	CRAYONS
ACNORTT	CONTRAT
ACNORTU	COURANT
ACNOSSZ	SCAZONS
ACNOSTT	OCTANTS
ACNOSTU	CONATUS
	NOCTUAS
	TOUCANS
ACNPRSY	SYNCARP
ACNRRSU	CURRANS
ACNRRTU	CURRANT
ACNRSTU	UNCARTS
ACNRSUY	UNSCARY
ACNRSWY	SCRAWNY
ACNRTUY	TRUANCY
ACNRUYZ	UNCRAZY
ACOOPRR	CORPORA
ACOOPSU	OPACOUS
ACOOPTT	TOPCOAT
ACOORTU	TOURACO
ACOOSTV	OCTAVOS
ACOPPRR	PROCARP
ACOPPRS	COPPRAS
ACOPRRT	CARPORT
ACOPRST	CAPTORS
ACOPSTU	UPCOAST
ACOPSTW	COWPATS
ACORRST	CARROTS
	TROCARS
ACORRTT	TRACTOR
ACORRTU	CURATOR
ACORRTY	CARROTY
ACORSST	CASTORS
	COSTARS
ACORSSU	SARCOUS
	SOUCARS
ACORSSW	SOWCARS
ACORSTT	COTTARS
ACORSTU	SURCOAT
	TURACOS
ACORSTV	CAVORTS
ACORSTX	OXCARTS
ACORSTY	CASTORY
ACORSUU	RAUCOUS
ACORSYZ	CORYZAS
ACORTUU	TURACOU
ACOSTTU	OUTACTS
	OUTCAST
ACOSUUV	VACUOUS
ACPPRSY	SCRAPPY
ACPSSTU	CATSUPS
	UPCASTS
ACPSTUU	USUCAPT
ACRRSTU	CRATURS
ACRSTTU	TRACTUS
ADDDDEL	DADDLED
ADDDDOR	DODDARD
ADDDEER	DREADED
	READDED
ADDDEFL	FADDLED
ADDDEGL	GLADDED
ADDDEIL	DAIDLED
ADDDEIS	DADDIES
ADDDEIW	WADDIED
ADDDELN	DANDLED
ADDDELP	PADDLED
ADDDELR	RADDLED
ADDDELS	DADDLES
	SADDLED
ADDDELW	DAWDLED
	WADDLED
ADDDELY	ADDEDLY
ADDDENO	DEODAND
ADDDENS	ADDENDS
ADDDEQU	QUADDED
ADDDGIN	DADDING
ADDDHOY	HODADDY
ADDDOOS	DOODADS
ADDEEEM	ADEEMED
ADDEEEY	DEADEYE
ADDEEFM	DEFAMED
ADDEEGR	DEGRADE
ADDEEHL	HEALDED
ADDEEHR	ADHERED
	REDHEAD
ADDEEHS	DEASHED
ADDEEIR	DEAIRED
	READIED
ADDEEIT	IDEATED
ADDEEKN	KNEADED
ADDEEKR	DAKERED
ADDEELM	MEDALED
ADDEELN	DELENDA
	LADENED
ADDEELP	PEDALED
	PLEADED
ADDEELS	DELEADS
ADDEELT	DELATED
ADDEELY	DELAYED
ADDEEMN	AMENDED
ADDEEMR	DREAMED
ADDEEMS	ADDEEMS
ADDEENS	DEADENS
ADDEENV	ADVENED
	DAVENED
ADDEENY	DENAYED
ADDEEOT	DEODATE
ADDEERR	DREADER
ADDEERS	DEADERS
ADDEERT	DERATED
	REDATED
	TREADED
ADDEERY	DERAYED
	YEARDED
ADDEEST	DEADEST
	SEDATED
	STEADED
ADDEEVW	ADVEWED
ADDEEWX	DEWAXED
ADDEFIR	FADDIER
ADDEFLS	FADDLES
ADDEFLY	FADEDLY
ADDEFNU	UNFADED
ADDEFRT	DRAFTED
ADDEFRU	DEFRAUD
ADDEFRW	DWARFED
ADDEGGL	DAGGLED
ADDEGGR	DRAGGED
ADDEGHO	GODHEAD
ADDEGIL	GLADDIE
ADDEGIN	DEADING
ADDEGJU	ADJUDGE
ADDEGLN	DANGLED
	GLADDEN

ADDEGLR	GLADDER
ADDEGRS	GADDERS
ADDEGRU	GUARDED
ADDEHIR	DIEHARD
	DIHEDRA
ADDEHIS	HADDIES
ADDEHKS	KEDDAHS
ADDEHLN	HANDLED
ADDEHLS	DALEDHS
ADDEHOR	HOARDED
ADDEHRS	SHARDED
ADDEHST	HADDEST
ADDEIIK	DIDAKEI
ADDEIIM	DIAMIDE
ADDEIIS	DAISIED
ADDEILL	DALLIED
	DIALLED
ADDEILP	PLAIDED
ADDEILR	DIEDRAL
	DRAILED
ADDEILS	DAIDLES
	LADDIES
ADDEILT	DILATED
ADDEIMR	ADMIRED
	MARDIED
ADDEIMS	DIADEMS
ADDEIMX	ADMIXED
ADDEINO	ADENOID
ADDEINP	PANDIED
ADDEINR	DANDIER
	DRAINED
ADDEINS	DANDIES
	SDAINED
ADDEINU	UNAIDED
ADDEINV	INVADED
	VIDENDA
ADDEIOR	RADIOED
ADDEIOT	IODATED
	TOADIED
ADDEIOV	AVOIDED
ADDEIPS	PADDIES
ADDEIRR	ARRIDED
ADDEIRT	TARDIED
ADDEIST	TADDIES
ADDEISV	ADVISED
ADDEISW	WADDIES
ADDEISY	DAYSIDE
ADDEITU	AUDITED
ADDEJLY	JADEDLY
ADDEJNU	UNJADED
ADDEJRU	ADJURED
ADDEKLR	DARKLED
ADDELLU	ALLUDED
	DUALLED
ADDELMW	DWALMED
ADDELNR	DANDLER
ADDELNS	DANDLES
ADDELNU	UNLADED
ADDELPP	DAPPLED
ADDELPR	PADDLER
ADDELPS	PADDLES
ADDELRS	LADDERS
	RADDLES
	SADDLER
ADDELRT	DARTLED
ADDELRW	DAWDLER
	DRAWLED
	WADDLER
ADDELRY	DREADLY
	LADDERY
ADDELSS	SADDLES
ADDELST	STADDLE
ADDELSW	DAWDLES
	SWADDLE
	WADDLES
ADDELTW	TWADDLE
ADDELTY	DATEDLY
ADDELYZ	DAZEDLY
ADDELZZ	DAZZLED
ADDEMMR	DRAMMED
ADDEMMW	DWAMMED
ADDEMNS	DEMANDS
	MADDENS
ADDEMNU	MAUNDED
ADDEMOP	POMADED
ADDEMRS	MADDERS
ADDEMRY	DRAMEDY
ADDEMST	MADDEST
ADDEMUW	DWAUMED
ADDENOR	ADORNED
ADDENOT	DONATED
	NODATED
ADDENOU	DUODENA
ADDENPU	PUDENDA
ADDENRS	DANDERS
ADDENRT	DRANTED
ADDENRU	DAUNDER
ADDENSS	DESANDS
	SADDENS
ADDENSU	ASUDDEN
ADDENSY	SDAYNED
ADDENTU	DAUNTED
	UNDATED
ADDEOPT	ADOPTED
ADDEORS	DEODARS
ADDEPPR	DRAPPED
ADDEPRS	PADDERS
ADDEPTU	UPDATED
ADDERSS	ADDRESS
ADDERST	ADDREST
	RADDEST
ADDERSW	SWARDED
	WADDERS
ADDERSY	DRYADES
ADDERTT	DRATTED
ADDESST	SADDEST
ADDESTU	ADUSTED
	SUDATED
ADDFHIS	FADDISH
ADDFIMS	FADDISM
ADDFINY	DANDIFY
ADDFIST	FADDIST
ADDGGIN	GADDING
ADDGHIN	HADDING
ADDGIIR	DIAGRID
ADDGILN	ADDLING
ADDGIMN	MADDING
ADDGINO	DADOING
ADDGINP	PADDING
ADDGINR	RADDING
ADDGINU	DAUDING
ADDGINW	DAWDING
	WADDING
ADDGIOS	GADOIDS
ADDGIPY	GIDDYAP
ADDGLNO	GLADDON
ADDGMNO	GODDAMN
ADDGMOS	GODDAMS
ADDGOOS	OGDOADS
ADDGOOW	DAGWOOD
ADDGORW	GODWARD
ADDGOSY	DOGDAYS
ADDHIKS	KADDISH
ADDHILS	LADDISH
ADDHIMS	MADDISH
ADDHINP	DAPHNID
ADDHISS	SADDISH
	SIDDHAS
ADDHITY	HYDATID
ADDHOOS	DOODAHS
ADDHOTY	ATHODYD
ADDHSSU	SADDHUS
ADDIINS	DISDAIN
ADDIIPS	DIAPSID
ADDIKST	TSADDIK
ADDIKSZ	ZADDIKS
ADDIKTY	KATYDID
ADDIKTZ	TZADDIK
ADDILMN	MIDLAND
ADDILNY	DANDILY
ADDILOS	DISLOAD
ADDIMNO	DIAMOND
ADDIMOR	DIADROM
ADDIMRS	DIRDAMS
ADDIMSS	MISADDS
ADDIMSY	DISMAYD
	MIDDAYS
ADDINOR	ANDROID
ADDINRY	DIANDRY
ADDIPRS	DISPRAD
ADDIQST	TSADDIQ
ADDIQTZ	TZADDIQ
ADDIRZZ	DIZZARD
ADDLLRU	DULLARD
ADDLNRY	DRYLAND
ADDLOOS	SOLDADO
ADDLTWY	TWADDLY
ADDMNOS	DODMANS
	ODDSMAN
ADDMOOS	ADDOOMS
ADDNNOR	DONNARD
ADDOORS	DORADOS
ADDOPSY	DASYPOD
ADDORST	DOTARDS
ADDOSTU	OUTADDS
ADDQSUY	SQUADDY
ADEEEFY	FEDAYEE
ADEEELV	DELEAVE
ADEEEMN	DEMEANE
ADEEERR	ARREEDE
ADEEERX	EXEDRAE
ADEEESW	SEAWEED
ADEEFGU	FEAGUED
ADEEFHS	SHEAFED
ADEEFIR	AREFIED
	FEDARIE
ADEEFKR	FREAKED
ADEEFLN	ENDLEAF
ADEEFLR	FEDERAL
ADEEFLS	DEFLEAS
ADEEFLT	DEFLATE
ADEEFMR	DEFAMER
ADEEFMS	DEFAMES
ADEEFNS	DEAFENS
ADEEFPR	PREFADE
ADEEFRT	DRAFTEE
ADEEFRW	WAFERED
ADEEFST	DEAFEST
	DEFASTE
	DEFEATS
	FEASTED
ADEEGGH	EGGHEAD
ADEEGGL	ALEGGED
ADEEGGN	ENGAGED
ADEEGLL	ALLEDGE
	ALLEGED
ADEEGLM	GLEAMED
ADEEGLN	ANGELED
	GLEANED
ADEEGLR	LAGERED
	REGALED
ADEEGLT	GELATED
	LEGATED
	TEAGLED
ADEEGLU	LEAGUED
ADEEGLV	GAVELED
ADEEGLZ	DEGLAZE
ADEEGMN	ENDGAME
	MANEGED
	MENAGED
ADEEGMS	DEGAMES
ADEEGNR	ANGERED
	DERANGE
	ENRAGED
	GRANDEE
	GRENADE
ADEEGNT	AGENTED
	NEGATED
ADEEGNV	AVENGED
	VENDAGE
ADEEGOT	DOGEATE
	GOATEED
ADEEGPR	PREAGED
ADEEGRR	REGRADE
ADEEGRS	DRAGEES
	GREASED
ADEEGRU	GUARDEE
ADEEGRV	GREAVED
ADEEGRW	RAGWEED
	WAGERED
ADEEGSS	DEGASES
ADEEHIR	HEADIER
ADEEHJS	HADJEES
ADEEHLR	HEDERAL
ADEEHLS	LEASHED
	SHEALED
ADEEHLX	EXHALED
ADEEHMN	HEADMEN
ADEEHNN	HENNAED
ADEEHNS	DASHEEN
ADEEHNV	HAVENED
ADEEHPR	EPHEDRA
ADEEHRR	ADHERER
	REHEARD
ADEEHRS	ADHERES
	HEADERS
	HEARSED
	SHEARED
ADEEHRT	EARTHED
	HEARTED
ADEEHRV	HAVERED
ADEEHRX	EXHEDRA
ADEEHSS	DEASHES
ADEEHST	HEADSET
ADEEHSV	SHEAVED
ADEEHSX	HEXADES
ADEEHSY	HAYSEED
ADEEIJT	JADEITE
ADEEILM	EMAILED
	LIMEADE
ADEEILN	ALIENED
	DELAINE
ADEEILR	LEADIER
ADEEILS	AEDILES
	DEISEAL
ADEEILY	EYELIAD
ADEEIMN	DEMAINE
ADEEIMT	MEDIATE
ADEEINN	ADENINE
ADEEINS	ANISEED
ADEEIRR	READIER
ADEEIRS	DEARIES
	READIES
ADEEIRW	WEARIED
ADEEISS	DISEASE
	SEASIDE
ADEEIST	IDEATES
ADEEISV	ADVISEE
ADEEITV	DEVIATE
ADEEJSY	DEEJAYS

ADEEKNP	KNEEPAD
ADEEKNR	KNEADER
	NAKEDER
ADEEKNS	SNEAKED
ADEEKNW	WAKENED
ADEEKRS	DEKARES
	SKEARED
ADEEKRW	REWAKED
	WREAKED
ADEEKTW	TWEAKED
ADEEKWY	WEEKDAY
ADEELLP	LAPELED
ADEELLS	ALLSEED
ADEELLY	ALLEYED
ADEELMM	MELAMED
ADEELMN	LEADMEN
ADEELMP	EMPALED
ADEELMR	EMERALD
ADEELMS	MEASLED
ADEELMT	MEDALET
	METALED
ADEELMU	AEMULED
ADEELMY	YEALMED
ADEELNP	DEPLANE
	PANELED
ADEELNR	LEARNED
ADEELNS	LEADENS
ADEELNT	EDENTAL
	LATENED
ADEELOS	ELODEAS
ADEELPR	PEARLED
	PLEADER
	REPLEAD
ADEELPS	DELAPSE
	ELAPSED
	PLEASED
	SEPALED
ADEELPT	PETALED
	PLEATED
ADEELQU	EQUALED
ADEELRS	DEALERS
	LEADERS
	REDEALS
ADEELRT	ALERTED
	ALTERED
	REDEALT
	RELATED
	TREADLE
ADEELRV	RAVELED
ADEELRW	LEEWARD
ADEELRX	RELAXED
ADEELRY	DELAYER
	LAYERED
	RELAYED
ADEELST	DELATES
	STEALED
ADEELSV	SLEAVED
ADEELSW	SWEALED
ADEELTT	LADETTE
ADEELTV	VALETED
	VELATED
ADEELTX	EXALTED
ADEELTZ	TEAZLED
ADEELUV	DEVALUE
ADEEMNR	AMENDER
	ENARMED
	MEANDER
	REAMEND
	REEDMAN
	RENAMED
ADEEMNS	AMENDES
	DEMEANS
	SEEDMAN
ADEEMNT	ENTAMED
ADEEMNY	DEMAYNE
ADEEMOS	OEDEMAS
ADEEMPR	EMPARED
	PREMADE
ADEEMRR	DREAMER
	REARMED
	REDREAM
ADEEMRS	REMADES
	REMEADS
	SMEARED
ADEEMRT	REMATED
ADEEMST	STEAMED
ADEEMSU	MEDUSAE
ADEEMSW	MAWSEED
ADEEMTW	MATWEED
ADEEMWY	MAYWEED
ADEENNS	ENNEADS
ADEENNX	ANNEXED
ADEENPS	SNEAPED
	SPEANED
ADEENRS	DEANERS
	ENDEARS
ADEENRU	UNEARED
ADEENRV	RAVENED
ADEENRY	DEANERY
	RENAYED
	YEAREND
	YEARNED
ADEENST	STANDEE
	STEANED
ADEENSV	ADVENES
ADEENSW	DEEWANS
ADEENTT	DENTATE
ADEEOPT	ADOPTEE
ADEEORS	OREADES
ADEEORW	OARWEED
ADEEPPR	PAPERED
ADEEPRS	PREASED
	RESPADE
	SPEARED
ADEEPRT	ADEPTER
	PREDATE
	RETAPED
	TAPERED
ADEEPRV	DEPRAVE
	PERVADE
	REPAVED
ADEEPSS	PESADES
ADEEQRU	QUAERED
ADEEQTU	EQUATED
ADEERRR	DREARER
ADEERRS	DREARES
	READERS
	REDEARS
	REDSEAR
	REREADS
ADEERRT	RETREAD
	TREADER
ADEERRV	AVERRED
ADEERRW	REDWARE
ADEERSS	RESEDAS
ADEERST	DEAREST
	DERATES
	ESTRADE
	REASTED
	REDATES
	SEDATER
	STEARED
	TASERED
ADEERSV	ADVERSE
	EVADERS
ADEERSW	DRAWEES
	RESAWED
ADEERTT	ARETTED
	TREATED
ADEERTV	AVERTED
	TAVERED
ADEERTW	DEWATER
	TARWEED
	WATERED
ADEERTX	RETAXED
ADEERVW	WAVERED
ADEERWX	REWAXED
ADEESST	SEDATES
ADEESSX	AXSEEDS
ADEESSY	ESSAYED
ADEESTT	ESTATED
ADEESTU	SAUTEED
ADEESTW	SWEATED
ADEESTY	YEASTED
ADEESVY	SAVEYED
ADEESWX	DEWAXES
ADEETUX	EXUDATE
ADEEWWX	WAXWEED
ADEFFFL	FLAFFED
ADEFFGR	GRAFFED
ADEFFIN	AFFINED
ADEFFIP	PIAFFED
ADEFFIR	DAFFIER
ADEFFIS	DAFFIES
ADEFFIX	AFFIXED
ADEFFLM	MAFFLED
ADEFFLO	LEADOFF
ADEFFLR	RAFFLED
ADEFFLW	WAFFLED
ADEFFNY	NYAFFED
ADEFFQU	QUAFFED
ADEFFST	STAFFED
ADEFFUW	WAUFFED
ADEFGGL	FLAGGED
ADEFGGR	FRAGGED
ADEFGLN	FANGLED
	FLANGED
ADEFGNS	DEFANGS
ADEFGOR	FORAGED
ADEFGOT	FAGOTED
ADEFGOU	FOUGADE
ADEFGRS	DEFRAGS
ADEFGRT	GRAFTED
ADEFHIS	DEAFISH
ADEFHIT	FAITHED
ADEFHLS	FLASHED
ADEFHRW	WHARFED
ADEFHST	SHAFTED
ADEFILL	FLAILED
ADEFILS	DISLEAF
ADEFIMN	INFAMED
ADEFIMS	DISFAME
ADEFINR	FRIANDE
ADEFINT	DEFIANT
	FAINTED
ADEFIRS	FARSIDE
	FRAISED
ADEFIST	DAFTIES
	FADIEST
ADEFITX	FIXATED
ADEFKLN	FANKLED
	FLANKED
ADEFKNR	FRANKED
ADEFKNU	UNFAKED
ADEFLLN	ELFLAND
ADEFLLW	DEWFALL
ADEFLMM	FLAMMED
ADEFLNN	FENLAND
ADEFLOT	FLOATED
ADEFLPP	FLAPPED
ADEFLRS	FARDELS
ADEFLRU	DAREFUL
ADEFLTT	FLATTED
ADEFLTU	DEFAULT
	FAULTED
ADEFMNU	UNFAMED
ADEFMOS	DEFOAMS
ADEFNRS	FARDENS
ADEFNSU	SNAFUED
	UNDEAFS
ADEFNUZ	UNFAZED
ADEFOOS	SEAFOOD
ADEFORS	FEDORAS
ADEFORV	FAVORED
ADEFORY	FEODARY
	FORAYED
ADEFPPR	FRAPPED
ADEFPRR	PREFARD
ADEFRRT	DRAFTER
	REDRAFT
ADEFRRW	DWARFER
ADEFRST	STRAFED
ADEFRSU	FADEURS
ADEFRSW	SWARFED
ADEFRSY	DEFRAYS
ADEFRUY	FEUDARY
ADEFSTT	DAFTEST
ADEGGGL	GAGGLED
ADEGGHL	HAGGLED
ADEGGHS	SHAGGED
ADEGGIR	DAGGIER
ADEGGIS	GADGIES
ADEGGIU	GAUDGIE
	GUIDAGE
ADEGGLR	DRAGGLE
	GARGLED
	RAGGLED
ADEGGLS	DAGGLES
	SLAGGED
ADEGGLW	WAGGLED
ADEGGMO	DEMAGOG
ADEGGNS	SNAGGED
ADEGGOP	PEDAGOG
ADEGGRR	DRAGGER
ADEGGRS	DAGGERS
ADEGGRY	RAGGEDY
ADEGGST	GADGETS
	STAGGED
ADEGGSW	SWAGGED
ADEGGTY	GADGETY
ADEGHIN	HEADING
ADEGHIR	HAGRIDE
	HEADRIG
ADEGHIS	HIDAGES
ADEGHJU	JUGHEAD
ADEGHLU	LAUGHED
ADEGHMO	HOMAGED
ADEGHNP	PHANGED
ADEGHNS	GNASHED
	HAGDENS
ADEGHNW	WHANGED
ADEGHOR	HAGRODE
ADEGHPR	GRAPHED
ADEGHST	GHASTED
ADEGHUW	WAUGHED
ADEGILL	GALLIED
ADEGILN	ALIGNED
	DEALING
	LEADING
ADEGILO	GEOIDAL
ADEGILR	GLADIER
	GLAIRED
ADEGILS	SILAGED
ADEGILT	LIGATED
	TAIGLED
ADEGILV	GLAIVED
ADEGIMS	DEGAMIS
ADEGINN	DEANING
ADEGINR	AREDING
	DEARING

	DERAIGN
	EARDING
	GRADINE
	GRAINED
	READING
ADEGINS	AGNISED
ADEGINV	DEAVING
	EVADING
ADEGINW	WINDAGE
ADEGINY	YEADING
ADEGINZ	AGNIZED
ADEGIOT	GODETIA
ADEGIRS	AGRISED
ADEGIRT	TRIAGED
ADEGIRU	GAUDIER
ADEGIRZ	AGRIZED
ADEGIST	AGISTED
ADEGISU	AGUISED
	GAUDIES
ADEGISV	VISAGED
ADEGIUV	VIDUAGE
ADEGIUZ	AGUIZED
ADEGJLN	JANGLED
ADEGLLU	ULLAGED
ADEGLMN	MANGLED
ADEGLMR	MALGRED
ADEGLMU	GLAUMED
ADEGLNN	ENDLANG
ADEGLNR	DANGLER
	GNARLED
ADEGLNS	DANGLES
	GLANDES
	LAGENDS
	SLANGED
ADEGLNT	TANGLED
ADEGLNU	LANGUED
ADEGLNW	WANGLED
ADEGLOP	GALOPED
ADEGLOT	GLOATED
ADEGLPU	PLAGUED
ADEGLRS	DARGLES
ADEGLRU	RAGULED
ADEGLRY	GRADELY
ADEGLSS	GLASSED
ADEGMNS	GADSMEN
ADEGMNU	AGENDUM
	GUDEMAN
ADEGMOP	MEGAPOD
ADEGMRU	MAUGRED
ADEGNNO	NONAGED
ADEGNNU	DUNNAGE
ADEGNOP	PONDAGE
ADEGNOR	GROANED
ADEGNOS	SONDAGE
ADEGNOT	TANGOED
ADEGNOV	DOGVANE
ADEGNOW	GOWANED
	WAGONED
ADEGNPR	PRANGED
ADEGNPS	SPANGED
ADEGNPU	UNPAGED
ADEGNRR	GNARRED
	GRANDER
ADEGNRS	DANGERS
	GANDERS
	GARDENS
ADEGNRT	DRAGNET
	GRANTED
ADEGNRU	ENGUARD
	RAUNGED
ADEGNST	STANGED
ADEGNSU	AUGENDS
ADEGNTU	GAUNTED
ADEGNTW	TWANGED
ADEGNUW	UNWAGED
ADEGORS	DOGEARS
ADEGORT	GAROTED
ADEGORW	DOWAGER
	WORDAGE
ADEGOSS	DOSAGES
	SEADOGS
ADEGOST	DOGATES
	DOTAGES
ADEGOTT	TOGATED
ADEGOVY	VOYAGED
ADEGPRS	GRASPED
	SPADGER
	SPARGED
ADEGPRU	UPGRADE
ADEGPUZ	UPGAZED
ADEGRRS	GRADERS
	REGARDS
ADEGRRU	GUARDER
ADEGRSS	GRASSED
ADEGRST	RADGEST
ADEGRSU	DESUGAR
	SUGARED
ADEGRTY	GYRATED
	TRAGEDY
ADEGRUU	AUGURED
ADEGRUY	GAUDERY
ADEGRYZ	AGRYZED
ADEGSSU	DEGAUSS
ADEHHKS	KHEDAHS
ADEHHOP	HOPHEAD
ADEHHOT	HOTHEAD
ADEHHSS	SHASHED
ADEHIKS	DASHEKI
ADEHIKV	KHEDIVA
ADEHILN	INHALED
ADEHILP	HELIPAD
ADEHILS	HALIDES
ADEHILY	HEADILY
ADEHIMO	HAEMOID
ADEHINP	HEADPIN
	PINHEAD
ADEHINR	HANDIER
ADEHIPP	HAPPIED
ADEHIPR	RAPHIDE
ADEHIPS	APHIDES
	DIPHASE
ADEHIPT	PITHEAD
ADEHIRR	HARDIER
	HARRIED
ADEHIRS	AIRSHED
	DASHIER
	HARDIES
	SHADIER
ADEHIRT	AIRTHED
ADEHIRW	RAWHIDE
ADEHIRY	HAYRIDE
	HYDRIAE
ADEHKNS	SHANKED
ADEHKNT	THANKED
ADEHKOR	HARDOKE
ADEHKOT	KATHODE
ADEHKRS	SHARKED
ADEHLLO	HALLOED
	HOLLAED
ADEHLLP	LAPHELD
ADEHLMS	LAMEDHS
ADEHLNR	HANDLER
ADEHLNS	HANDLES
	HANDSEL
ADEHLOS	SHOALED
ADEHLOT	LOATHED
ADEHLPR	RALPHED
ADEHLPS	PLASHED
ADEHLRS	HARELDS
	HERALDS
ADEHLSS	HASSLED
	SLASHED
ADEHLST	DALETHS
ADEHLSU	SHAULED
ADEHLSW	SHAWLED
ADEHLTY	DEATHLY
ADEHMMS	SHAMMED
ADEHMMW	WHAMMED
ADEHMNR	HERDMAN
ADEHMOP	MOPHEAD
ADEHMOR	HADROME
ADEHMRS	DERHAMS
ADEHMSS	SMASHED
ADEHNPS	DAPHNES
ADEHNRS	HANDERS
	HARDENS
ADEHNRU	UNHEARD
ADEHNSS	SNASHED
ADEHNST	HANDSET
ADEHNSU	UNHEADS
ADEHNTU	HAUNTED
ADEHOOP	APEHOOD
ADEHOPT	POTHEAD
ADEHOPX	HEXAPOD
ADEHORR	HOARDER
ADEHOST	HOASTED
ADEHOSX	OXHEADS
ADEHOTW	TOWHEAD
ADEHPPW	WHAPPED
ADEHPRS	PHRASED
	SHARPED
ADEHPST	HEPTADS
	SPATHED
ADEHPSW	PSHAWED
ADEHQSU	QUASHED
ADEHRRU	HURRAED
ADEHRSS	DASHERS
	SHADERS
ADEHRST	DEARTHS
	HARDEST
	HARDSET
	HATREDS
	THREADS
	TRASHED
ADEHRSY	HYDRASE
ADEHRTW	THRAWED
	WRATHED
ADEHRTY	HYDRATE
	THREADY
ADEHSST	STASHED
ADEHSSW	SWASHED
ADEHSTW	SWATHED
ADEHSYY	HEYDAYS
ADEHUZZ	HUZZAED
ADEIILR	DELIRIA
	IRIDEAL
ADEIILS	DAILIES
	LIAISED
	SEDILIA
ADEIIMN	AMIDINE
	DIAMINE
ADEIINR	DENARII
ADEIINT	INEDITA
ADEIINZ	DIAZINE
ADEIIPR	PERIDIA
ADEIIRS	AIRSIDE
	DAIRIES
	DIARIES
	DIARISE
ADEIIRZ	DIARIZE
ADEIISS	DAISIES
ADEIJMR	JEMIDAR
ADEIKLN	KNAIDEL
ADEIKLS	SKAILED
ADEIKNS	KANDIES
ADEIKRS	DAIKERS
	DARKIES
ADEIKRT	TRAIKED
ADEILLL	DIALLEL
ADEILLR	DALLIER
	DIALLER
	RALLIED
ADEILLS	DALLIES
	DISLEAL
	LALDIES
	SALLIED
ADEILLT	TALLIED
ADEILLV	VIALLED
ADEILLY	IDEALLY
ADEILMM	DILEMMA
ADEILMO	MELODIA
ADEILMP	IMPALED
	IMPLEAD
ADEILMS	MAELIDS
	MEDIALS
	MISDEAL
	MISLEAD
ADEILMU	MIAULED
ADEILNN	ANNELID
	LINDANE
ADEILNP	PLAINED
ADEILNS	DENIALS
	SNAILED
ADEILNU	ALIUNDE
	UNIDEAL
ADEILNV	ANDVILE
	ANVILED
ADEILNX	INDEXAL
ADEILOP	OEDIPAL
ADEILOR	DARIOLE
ADEILOS	DEASOIL
	ISOLEAD
ADEILOU	DOULEIA
ADEILOZ	DIAZOLE
ADEILPP	APPLIED
ADEILPR	PEDRAIL
	PREDIAL
ADEILPS	ALIPEDS
	ELAPIDS
	LAPIDES
	PAIDLES
	PALSIED
	PLEIADS
ADEILPT	PLAITED
	TALIPED
ADEILQU	QUAILED
ADEILRR	LARDIER
ADEILRS	DERAILS
	DIALERS
	REDIALS
	SIDERAL
ADEILRT	DILATER
	REDTAIL
	TRAILED
ADEILRU	UREDIAL
ADEILRV	RIVALED
	VALIDER
ADEILRY	READILY
ADEILSS	AIDLESS
	DEASILS
ADEILST	DETAILS
	DILATES
ADEILSU	AUDILES
	DEASIUL
ADEILSV	DEVISAL
ADEILSY	DIALYSE
	EYLIADS
ADEILUZ	DUALIZE
ADEILYZ	DIALYZE
ADEIMMR	MERMAID

ADEIMMS MISMADE
ADEIMNO AMIDONE
ADEIMNR ADERMIN
INARMED
ADEIMNS DEMAINS
MAIDENS
MEDIANS
MEDINAS
SIDEMAN
ADEIMNT MEDIANT
ADEIMNU UNAIMED
ADEIMOU MIAOUED
ADEIMOW MIAOWED
ADEIMPR DAMPIER
ADEIMPV IMPAVED
ADEIMRR ADMIRER
MARDIER
MARRIED
ADEIMRS ADMIRES
MARDIES
MISREAD
SEDARIM
SIDEARM
ADEIMRT READMIT
ADEIMRY MIDYEAR
ADEIMST DIASTEM
MISDATE
ADEIMSV VIDAMES
ADEIMSX ADMIXES
ADEIMTU TAEDIUM
ADEIMTY DAYTIME
ADEINNN NANDINE
NANNIED
ADEINNR NARDINE
ADEINOR ANEROID
ADEINOS ADONISE
ANODISE
SODAINE
ADEINOV NAEVOID
ADEINOX DIOXANE
ADEINOZ ADONIZE
ANODIZE
ADEINPR PARDINE
ADEINPS PANDIES
PANSIED
SPAINED
ADEINPT DEPAINT
PAINTED
PATINED
ADEINRR DRAINER
RANDIER
ADEINRS RANDIES
SANDIER
SARDINE
ADEINRT ANTIRED
DETRAIN
TRAINED
ADEINRU UNAIRED
URANIDE
ADEINRV INVADER
RAVINED
ADEINSS SDAINES
ADEINST DESTAIN
DETAINS
INSTEAD
SAINTED
SATINED
STAINED
ADEINSV INVADES
ADEINSW DEWANIS
ADEINTT TAINTED
ADEINTU AUDIENT
ADEINTV DEVIANT
ADEINVV NAVVIED
ADEIOPS ADIPOSE
ADEIOPT OPIATED
ADEIORS ROADIES
SOREDIA
ADEIORV AVODIRE
AVOIDER
ADEIORX EXORDIA
ADEIOST IODATES
TOADIES
ADEIOSX OXIDASE
ADEIOSZ DIAZOES
ADEIOTX OXIDATE
ADEIOVV VAIVODE
ADEIOVW WAIVODE
ADEIOWW WAIWODE
ADEIPPR DRAPPIE
PREPAID
ADEIPPU APPUIED
ADEIPRR DRAPIER
PARRIED
RAPIDER
ADEIPRS ASPIRED
DESPAIR
DIAPERS
PRAISED
ADEIPRT DIPTERA
PARTIED
PIRATED
ADEIPRV VAPIDER
ADEIPSS APSIDES
ADEIQRU QUERIDA
ADEIRRS ARRIDES
RAIDERS
ADEIRRT TARDIER
TARRIED
ADEIRRV ARRIVED
ADEIRST ARIDEST
ASTERID
ASTRIDE
DIASTER
DISRATE
STAIDER
STAIRED
TARDIES
TIRADES
ADEIRSU RESIDUA
ADEIRSV ADVISER
VARDIES
ADEIRSX RADIXES
ADEIRTT ATTIRED
ADEIRTV TARDIVE
ADEIRTY DIETARY
ADEISSS DASSIES
ADEISST DISSEAT
SAIDEST
ADEISSV ADVISES
DISSAVE
ADEISSZ ASSIZED
ADEISTU DAUTIES
ADEISTV AVIDEST
DATIVES
VISTAED
ADEISTW DAWTIES
WAISTED
ADEISVV SAVVIED
ADEISWY SIDEWAY
WAYSIDE
ADEITUZ DEUTZIA
ADEITWY TIDEWAY
ADEJMOR MAJORED
ADEJMRU MUDEJAR
ADEJNSU JAUNSED
ADEJNTU JAUNTED
ADEJOPR JEOPARD
ADEJRRU ADJURER
ADEJRSU ADJURES
ADEJSSU JUDASES
ADEKKNS SKANKED
ADEKLNP PLANKED
ADEKLNR RANKLED
ADEKLNS KALENDS
ADEKLNY NAKEDLY
ADEKLOP POLKAED
ADEKLOS SKOALED
ADEKLRS DARKLES
ADEKLST SKLATED
STALKED
ADEKLSY YSLAKED
ADEKLUW WAULKED
ADEKMNS DESKMAN
ADEKMRS DEMARKS
ADEKNPP KNAPPED
ADEKNPR PRANKED
ADEKNPS SPANKED
ADEKNRR KNARRED
ADEKNRS DARKENS
ADEKNRU UNRAKED
ADEKNST DANKEST
ADEKNSU UNASKED
ADEKNSW SWANKED
ADEKNUW UNWAKED
ADEKNVY VANDYKE
ADEKORT TROAKED
ADEKPRS SPARKED
ADEKPSY KEYPADS
ADEKRST DARKEST
STARKED
STRAKED
ADEKRSY DARKEYS
ADELLMS SMALLED
ADELLMU MEDULLA
ADELLNR LANDLER
ADELLNW ELLWAND
ADELLOR ODALLER
ADELLOW ALLOWED
ADELLOY ALLOYED
ADELLPS SPALLED
ADELLRS LADLERS
ADELLRU ALLURED
UDALLER
ADELLST STALLED
ADELLSU ALLUDES
ALUDELS
ADELLSV DEVALLS
ADELMMS SLAMMED
SMALMED
ADELMNN LANDMEN
ADELMNR MANDREL
ADELMNT MANTLED
ADELMOR EARLDOM
ADELMOS DAMOSEL
ADELMOZ DAMOZEL
ADELMPS PSALMED
SAMPLED
ADELMRS MEDLARS
ADELMSS DAMSELS
ADELMST MALTEDS
ADELMSU ALMUDES
MEDUSAL
ADELMSW WADMELS
ADELMYZ MAZEDLY
ADELNNP PLANNED
ADELNNU UNLADEN
ADELNOR LADRONE
ADELNOS LOADENS
ADELNOT TALONED
ADELNOY YEALDON
ADELNPT PLANTED
ADELNRS DARNELS
ENLARDS
LANDERS
SLANDER
SNARLED
ADELNRU LAUNDER
LURDANE
RUNDALE
ADELNRY DEARNLY
ADELNSS SENDALS
ADELNST DENTALS
SLANTED
ADELNSU UNLADES
UNLEADS
ADELNSY ADENYLS
ADELNTU LUNATED
UNDEALT
ADELNTW WETLAND
ADELNUW UNLAWED
ADELOPR LEOPARD
PAROLED
ADELOPS DEPOSAL
PEDALOS
ADELOPT PLOATED
TADPOLE
ADELORS LOADERS
ORDEALS
RELOADS
ADELORT DELATOR
LEOTARD
ADELORU ROULADE
ADELOSS ALDOSES
LASSOED
ADELOST SALTOED
SOLATED
ADELOSV SALVOED
ADELOTT TOTALED
ADELPPP PLAPPED
ADELPPS DAPPLES
SAPPLED
SLAPPED
ADELPRS PEDLARS
ADELPRY PEDLARY
ADELPST SPALTED
STAPLED
ADELPSU UPLEADS
ADELPSW DEWLAPS
SPAWLED
ADELPSY SPLAYED
ADELPTT PLATTED
ADELPTW DEWLAPT
ADELPTY ADEPTLY
ADELRRS LARDERS
ADELRRU RUDERAL
ADELRRW DRAWLER
ADELRSS RASSLED
SARDELS
ADELRST DARTLES
ADELRSU LAUDERS
ADELRSW WARSLED
ADELRSZ DRAZELS
ADELRTT RATTLED
ADELRTW TRAWLED
ADELRTX DEXTRAL
ADELRTY LYRATED
ADELRWW WRAWLED
ADELRWX WRAXLED
ADELRZZ DAZZLER
ADELSST DESALTS
ADELSTT SLATTED
ADELSTU AULDEST
SALUTED
ADELSUV AVULSED
ADELSWY SWAYLED
ADELSZZ DAZZLES
ADELTTT TATTLED
ADELTTW WATTLED
ADELTUV VAULTED

ADELTUX	LUXATED
ADELTWZ	WALTZED
ADEMMPS	SPAMMED
ADEMMRS	DAMMERS
	SMARMED
ADEMMRT	TRAMMED
ADEMNNS	SANDMEN
ADEMNNU	MUNDANE
	UNNAMED
ADEMNOR	MADRONE
	ROADMEN
ADEMNOS	DAEMONS
	MASONED
	MODENAS
	MONADES
	NOMADES
ADEMNOW	WOMANED
ADEMNPS	DAMPENS
ADEMNRS	DAMNERS
	MANREDS
	RANDEMS
	REMANDS
ADEMNRU	DURAMEN
	MANURED
	MAUNDER
	UNARMED
ADEMNRY	DRAYMEN
	YARDMEN
ADEMNSS	DESMANS
	MADNESS
ADEMNST	TANDEMS
ADEMNSU	MEDUSAN
	SUDAMEN
ADEMNSY	DAYSMEN
ADEMNTU	UNMATED
	UNTAMED
ADEMOOV	AMOOVED
ADEMOPS	APEDOMS
	POMADES
ADEMORR	ARMORED
ADEMORS	RADOMES
ADEMOSV	VAMOSED
ADEMOSW	MEADOWS
ADEMOSY	SOMEDAY
ADEMOWY	MEADOWY
ADEMPRS	DAMPERS
ADEMPRT	TRAMPED
ADEMPSS	SPASMED
ADEMPST	DAMPEST
	STAMPED
ADEMPSW	SWAMPED
ADEMRRU	EARDRUM
ADEMRST	SMARTED
ADEMRSU	REMUDAS
ADEMRSW	SWARMED
ADEMRTU	MATURED
ADEMSST	DEMASTS
ADEMSSU	ASSUMED
	MEDUSAS
ADEMTTU	MUTATED
ADENNOY	ANNOYED
	ANODYNE
ADENNPS	SPANNED
ADENNPT	PENDANT
ADENNST	STANDEN
ADENNSU	DUENNAS
ADENNSW	SWANNED
ADENNWY	DEWANNY
ADENOOP	NAPOOED
ADENOOT	ODONATE
ADENOOZ	ENDOZOA
ADENOPR	APRONED
	OPERAND
	PADRONE
	PANDORE
ADENOPS	DAPSONE
ADENOPT	NOTEPAD
	TONEPAD
ADENORR	ADORNER
	READORN
ADENORT	TORNADE
ADENORU	RONDEAU
ADENOST	ASTONED
	DONATES
	ONSTEAD
ADENOSU	DOUANES
ADENOSY	NOYADES
ADENOTT	NOTATED
ADENOTZ	ZONATED
ADENPPR	PARPEND
ADENPPS	APPENDS
	SNAPPED
ADENPPW	WAPPEND
ADENPRR	PARDNER
ADENPRS	PANDERS
ADENPRU	UNDRAPE
	UNPARED
ADENPRW	PRAWNED
	PREDAWN
ADENPST	PEDANTS
	PENTADS
ADENPSW	SPAWNED
ADENPSX	EXPANDS
	SPANDEX
ADENPSY	DYSPNEA
ADENPUV	UNPAVED
ADENQTU	QUANTED
ADENRRS	DARNERS
	ERRANDS
	SNARRED
ADENRRW	REDRAWN
ADENRRY	REYNARD
ADENRSS	SANDERS
	SARSDEN
ADENRST	ENDARTS
	STANDER
	STARNED
ADENRSU	ASUNDER
	DANSEUR
	DAUNERS
ADENRSW	DAWNERS
	WANDERS
	WARDENS
ADENRSZ	ZANDERS
ADENRTT	TRANTED
ADENRTU	DAUNTER
	NATURED
	UNRATED
	UNTREAD
ADENRTV	VERDANT
ADENRTX	DEXTRAN
ADENRTY	DENTARY
	TRAYNED
	TYRANED
ADENRUY	UNREADY
ADENRUZ	UNRAZED
ADENSSS	SADNESS
ADENSSU	SUNDAES
ADENSSW	WESANDS
	WESSAND
ADENSTT	ATTENDS
ADENSTU	SAUNTED
	UNSATED
ADENSTV	ADVENTS
ADENSTY	STAYNED
ADENSUV	UNSAVED
ADENSUW	UNSAWED
ADENSWY	ENDWAYS
ADENSWZ	WEZANDS
ADENTTU	ATTUNED
	NUTATED
	TAUNTED
ADENTUV	VAUNTED
ADENTUX	UNTAXED
ADENUWX	UNWAXED
ADENUWY	UNWAYED
ADEOORS	ROADEOS
ADEOORT	ODORATE
ADEOPPS	APPOSED
	PEAPODS
ADEOPQU	OPAQUED
ADEOPRR	EARDROP
ADEOPRT	ADOPTER
	READOPT
ADEOPRV	VAPORED
ADEOPSS	SPADOES
ADEOPST	PODESTA
ADEORRS	ADORERS
	DROSERA
ADEORRW	ARROWED
ADEORRZ	RAZORED
ADEORSS	SARODES
ADEORST	DOATERS
	ROASTED
	TORSADE
	TROADES
ADEORSU	AROUSED
ADEORSV	OVERSAD
	SAVORED
ADEORSW	REDOWAS
ADEORTT	ROTATED
	TROATED
ADEORTU	OUTDARE
	OUTREAD
	READOUT
ADEORWY	RODEWAY
ADEORYZ	ZEDOARY
ADEOSTT	TOASTED
ADEOTTU	OUTDATE
ADEOWWY	WAYWODE
ADEPPRS	DAPPERS
ADEPPRT	TRAPPED
ADEPPRW	WRAPPED
ADEPPST	STAPPED
ADEPPSW	SWAPPED
ADEPPTU	PUPATED
ADEPPUY	APPUYED
ADEPRRS	DRAPERS
	SPARRED
ADEPRRY	DRAPERY
ADEPRSS	ADPRESS
	SPADERS
	SPREADS
ADEPRST	DEPARTS
	DRAPETS
	PETARDS
ADEPRSY	SPRAYED
ADEPRTT	PRATTED
ADEPRTU	UPDATER
	UPRATED
ADEPSTT	SPATTED
ADEPSTU	UPDATES
ADEPSZZ	SPAZZED
ADEQRSU	SQUARED
ADERRST	DARTERS
	DARTRES
	RETARDS
	STARRED
	TRADERS
ADERRSW	DRAWERS
	REDRAWS
	REWARDS
	WARDERS
ADERSSU	ASSURED
	RUDASES
ADERSSW	SAWDERS
	SWEARDS
ADERSTT	STARTED
	TETRADS
ADERSTV	ADVERTS
	STARVED
ADERSTW	STEWARD
	STRAWED
	WRASTED
ADERSTY	STRAYED
ADERSUY	DASYURE
ADERSVW	DWARVES
	SWARVED
ADERWWY	WEYWARD
ADESSTU	SUDATES
ADESSTW	WADSETS
ADESTTU	STATUED
ADESTTW	SWATTED
	WADSETT
ADFFGIN	DAFFING
ADFFHNO	HANDOFF
	OFFHAND
ADFFILY	DAFFILY
ADFFIST	DISTAFF
ADFFLNO	FANFOLD
ADFFLOO	OFFLOAD
ADFFOOR	AFFOORD
ADFFORS	AFFORDS
ADFGGIN	FADGING
ADFGINN	FANDING
ADFGINR	FARDING
ADFGINS	FADINGS
ADFGLLU	GLADFUL
ADFHLNU	HANDFUL
ADFHLSY	SHADFLY
ADFHOOS	SHADOOF
ADFHSSU	SHADUFS
ADFILLU	FLUIDAL
ADFIMNR	FINDRAM
ADFIMNY	DAMNIFY
ADFINRS	FRIANDS
ADFINRT	INDRAFT
ADFIORS	FORSAID
ADFLLYY	LADYFLY
ADFLMOO	DAMFOOL
ADFLMPU	MUDFLAP
ADFLMTU	MUDFLAT
ADFLNOP	PLAFOND
ADFLNSY	SANDFLY
ADFLORU	FOULARD
ADFMNOS	FANDOMS
ADFMOSU	FUMADOS
ADFNNOT	FONDANT
ADFNOST	FANTODS
ADFOOPT	FOOTPAD
ADFOOTW	FATWOOD
ADFORRW	FORWARD
	FROWARD
ADFPRTU	UPDRAFT
ADGGGIN	DAGGING
ADGGHNO	HANGDOG
ADGGILN	GADLING
ADGGILR	RIGGALD
ADGGINN	DANGING
ADGGINO	GOADING
ADGGINR	GRADING
	NIGGARD
ADGGINU	GAUDING
ADGHILO	HIDALGO
ADGHINN	HANDING
ADGHINS	DASHING
	SHADING
ADGHINU	HAUDING
ADGHIPR	DIGRAPH
ADGHIRR	ARDRIGH

ADGHIRS	DISHRAG
ADGHNNU	HANDGUN
ADGHNOS	HAGDONS
	SANDHOG
ADGHNOW	HAGDOWN
ADGHORW	HOGWARD
ADGHRTU	DRAUGHT
ADGIILN	DIALING
	GLIADIN
	LAIDING
ADGIILT	DIGITAL
ADGIIMN	MAIDING
ADGIINN	DAINING
ADGIINO	GONIDIA
ADGIINR	GRADINI
	RAIDING
ADGIINS	SIGANID
ADGIINU	IGUANID
ADGIINW	GWINIAD
ADGIIPY	PYGIDIA
ADGIKNR	DARKING
ADGILLN	LADLING
ADGILMN	MADLING
ADGILNN	LANDING
ADGILNO	DIGONAL
	LOADING
ADGILNR	DARLING
	LARDING
ADGILNS	LADINGS
	LIGANDS
ADGILNU	LANGUID
	LAUDING
ADGILOR	GOLIARD
ADGILOS	DIALOGS
ADGILOV	VALGOID
ADGILSU	GLADIUS
ADGILUY	GAUDILY
ADGIMMN	DAMMING
ADGIMNN	DAMNING
ADGIMNP	DAMPING
ADGIMNR	MRIDANG
ADGINNR	DARNING
	NARDING
	RANDING
ADGINNS	SANDING
ADGINNT	DANTING
ADGINNW	DAWNING
ADGINOR	ADORING
	GRADINO
	ROADING
ADGINOS	GANOIDS
ADGINOT	DOATING
ADGINPP	DAPPING
ADGINPR	DRAPING
ADGINPS	SPADING
ADGINRR	DARRING
ADGINRS	DARINGS
	GRADINS
ADGINRT	DARTING
	TRADING
ADGINRU	DAURING
ADGINRW	DRAWING
	WARDING
ADGINRY	DRAYING
	YARDING
ADGINST	DATINGS
ADGINSU	AUDINGS
ADGINSW	WADINGS
ADGINTU	DAUTING
ADGINTW	DAWTING
ADGINWY	GWYNIAD
ADGIPRU	PAGURID
ADGIRSU	GUISARD
ADGIRZZ	GIZZARD
ADGLLNO	GOLLAND
ADGLMNO	MANGOLD
ADGLNOO	DONGOLA
	GONDOLA
ADGLNOR	GOLDARN
ADGLNOW	GOWLAND
ADGLNOY	DAYLONG
ADGLNRY	GRANDLY
ADGLOPS	LAPDOGS
ADGLOWY	DAYGLOW
ADGMNOO	GOODMAN
ADGMNOR	GORMAND
ADGNOOR	DRAGOON
	GADROON
ADGNOOS	GOONDAS
ADGNOPS	DOGNAPS
ADGNORS	DRAGONS
ADGNORU	AGROUND
ADGNORY	ORGANDY
ADGNRRU	GURNARD
ADGNRSU	DURGANS
ADGNRUU	UNGUARD
ADGORSW	WARDOGS
ADGORTU	OUTDRAG
ADGPRSU	UPDRAGS
ADGRSTU	DUSTRAG
ADHHIRS	HARDISH
ADHHIST	HADITHS
ADHHISW	WHIDAHS
ADHHMOS	SHAHDOM
ADHHOSU	HOUDAHS
ADHHOSW	HOWDAHS
ADHHSWY	WHYDAHS
ADHIIJT	IJTIHAD
ADHIIKS	DASHIKI
ADHIIMS	MAIDISH
ADHIKNS	DANKISH
ADHIKRS	DARKISH
ADHIKSU	HAIDUKS
ADHILMO	HALIDOM
ADHILNY	HANDILY
ADHILOP	HAPLOID
ADHILOS	HALOIDS
ADHILOY	HOLIDAY
	HYALOID
	HYOIDAL
ADHILRY	HARDILY
ADHILSY	LADYISH
	SHADILY
ADHIMPS	DAMPISH
	PHASMID
ADHIMRS	DIRHAMS
	MIDRASH
ADHINOT	ANTHOID
ADHINPS	DISHPAN
ADHINPU	DAUPHIN
ADHINSS	SANDHIS
ADHIORS	HAIRDOS
ADHIOST	TOADISH
ADHIRSS	SHAIRDS
ADHJKOS	KHODJAS
ADHKORW	DORHAWK
ADHKOSU	SHAKUDO
ADHLLLO	HOLDALL
ADHLLNO	HOLLAND
ADHLMOY	HOLYDAM
ADHLMPY	LYMPHAD
ADHLORS	HOLARDS
ADHLOYY	HOLYDAY
ADHMNOO	HOODMAN
	MANHOOD
ADHMNSU	NUMDAHS
ADHNNSU	NHANDUS
	UNHANDS
ADHNNUY	UNHANDY
ADHNOOS	DAHOONS
ADHNORS	HADRONS
ADHNORU	UNHOARD
ADHNOSU	HOUDANS
ADHNOTU	HANDOUT
ADHNRSU	DHURNAS
ADHNRSY	SHANDRY
ADHNRTY	HYDRANT
ADHNRUY	UNHARDY
ADHOOPT	HOPTOAD
ADHOORR	RHODORA
ADHOORS	DHOORAS
ADHOPRT	HARDTOP
ADHOPRU	UPHOARD
ADHOPST	DASHPOT
ADHORRU	DHOURRA
ADHORSU	DOURAHS
ADHOSSW	SHADOWS
ADHOSWY	SHADOWY
ADHPRSU	PURDAHS
ADHPSUU	UPHAUDS
ADHRRSU	DHURRAS
ADIIILR	IRIDIAL
ADIIINR	IRIDIAN
ADIIKOS	AIKIDOS
ADIIKOT	DAKOITI
ADIILLS	ILLIADS
ADIILMS	MILADIS
	MISDIAL
	MISLAID
ADIILNO	LIANOID
ADIILNV	INVALID
ADIILOS	SIALOID
ADIILSS	SIALIDS
ADIILST	DIALIST
ADIILUV	DILUVIA
ADIIMMS	MAIDISM
ADIIMNN	INDAMIN
ADIIMNS	AMIDINS
	DIAMINS
ADIIMOS	DAIMIOS
ADIIMPV	IMPAVID
ADIIMRS	MIDAIRS
ADIIMRU	MUDIRIA
ADIIMSS	MISSAID
ADIINPR	PINDARI
	PRIDIAN
ADIINST	DISTAIN
ADIINSU	INDUSIA
	SUIDIAN
ADIINSV	AVIDINS
ADIINSZ	DIAZINS
	DIZAINS
ADIIPRS	DIAPIRS
ADIIPXY	PYXIDIA
ADIIQRU	DAQUIRI
ADIIRST	DIARIST
ADIIRTY	ARIDITY
ADIISSY	SAIYIDS
ADIITVY	AVIDITY
ADIJMSS	MASJIDS
ADIJNOS	ADJOINS
ADIJNOT	ADJOINT
ADIJSSS	JASSIDS
ADIKLNY	LADYKIN
ADIKLOR	KILORAD
ADIKLOS	ODALISK
ADIKLPS	KLIPDAS
ADIKMNN	MANKIND
ADIKMOS	MIKADOS
ADIKMSS	DISMASK
ADIKNOS	DAIKONS
ADIKNPS	KIDNAPS
	SKIDPAN
ADIKNRS	DISRANK
ADIKOST	DAKOITS
ADIKOTY	DAKOITY
ADIKPRS	DISPARK
ADIKSST	DIKASTS
ADIKSTT	DIKTATS
ADIKSUZ	ADZUKIS
ADIKSWY	SKIDWAY
ADILLMM	MILLDAM
ADILLRY	LAIRDLY
ADILLSY	DISALLY
ADILLTY	TIDALLY
ADILLVY	VALIDLY
ADILLYY	DAYLILY
ADILMNO	MONDIAL
ADILMNR	MANDRIL
	RIMLAND
ADILMNU	MAUDLIN
ADILMOP	DIPLOMA
ADILMOS	AMIDOLS
ADILMOU	ALODIUM
ADILMOY	AMYLOID
ADILMPS	PLASMID
ADILMSS	DISMALS
ADILMSU	DUALISM
ADILMSY	DISMAYL
	LADYISM
ADILNNS	INLANDS
ADILNOR	ORDINAL
ADILNOS	DOLINAS
	LADINOS
ADILNRS	ALDRINS
ADILNRU	DIURNAL
ADILNSS	ISLANDS
ADILNST	TINDALS
ADILNSU	DUALINS
	SUNDIAL
ADILOOV	OVOIDAL
ADILOOZ	ZOOIDAL
ADILOPR	DIPOLAR
ADILORT	DILATOR
ADILOTU	OUTLAID
ADILPRY	PYRALID
	RAPIDLY
ADILPSS	SALPIDS
ADILPST	PLASTID
ADILPSY	DISPLAY
ADILPTU	PLAUDIT
ADILPVY	VAPIDLY
ADILQSU	SQUALID
ADILRSZ	LIZARDS
ADILRTY	TARDILY
ADILSTU	DUALIST
	TULADIS
ADILSTY	STAIDLY
ADILTUY	DUALITY
ADIMNNO	MONDAIN
ADIMNOS	DAIMONS
	DOMAINS
ADIMNRS	MANDIRS
ADIMNSS	DISMANS
ADIMNST	MANTIDS
ADIMOOS	ISODOMA
ADIMORR	MIRADOR
ADIMOST	DIATOMS
	MASTOID
ADIMOSY	DAIMYOS
ADIMOTT	MATTOID
ADIMPRY	PYRAMID
ADIMQSU	QUIDAMS
ADIMRSS	DISARMS
ADIMRSU	RADIUMS
ADIMRSW	MISDRAW
ADIMRSY	MYRIADS
ADIMSSS	SADISMS
ADIMSST	DISMAST
ADIMSSY	DISMAYS

ADIMSTU	DUMAIST
	STADIUM
ADIMSWY	MIDWAYS
ADINNNS	NANDINS
ADINNOP	DIPNOAN
	NONPAID
ADINNOR	ANDIRON
ADINNRS	INNARDS
ADINNRW	INDRAWN
ADINNRY	INNYARD
ADINNSU	INDUNAS
ADINOOP	POINADO
ADINOPP	OPPIDAN
ADINOPR	PADRONI
	PONIARD
ADINOPT	PINTADO
ADINORR	ORDINAR
ADINORS	INROADS
	ORDAINS
	SADIRON
ADINORT	DIATRON
ADINORV	VIRANDO
ADINOSX	DIAXONS
	DIOXANS
ADINOTX	OXIDANT
ADINPST	PANDITS
	SANDPIT
ADINQRS	QINDARS
ADINRRT	TRIDARN
ADINRST	INDARTS
ADINRSU	DURIANS
	SUNDARI
ADINRSW	INWARDS
ADINRTU	TRIDUAN
	UNITARD
ADINSTT	DISTANT
ADINSTU	UNSTAID
ADINTTY	DITTANY
ADINWWY	WINDWAY
ADIOOPR	PARODOI
ADIOOSW	WOODSIA
ADIOPRR	AIRDROP
ADIOPRS	SPAROID
ADIOPRT	PAROTID
ADIOPRV	PRIVADO
ADIOPSU	ADIPOUS
ADIORST	ASTROID
ADIORSU	SAUROID
ADIORSV	ADVISOR
ADIORTU	AUDITOR
ADIOSVW	DISAVOW
ADIPRSS	SPARIDS
ADIPRST	DISPART
ADIQSTU	DIQUATS
ADIRRSS	SIRDARS
ADIRRST	RITARDS
ADIRRSZ	RIZARDS
ADIRSSU	SARDIUS
ADIRSSV	VISARDS
ADIRSSW	WISARDS
ADIRSTY	SATYRID
ADIRSUY	DYSURIA
ADIRSVZ	VIZARDS
ADIRSWZ	WIZARDS
ADIRSZZ	IZZARDS
ADISSST	SADISTS
ADISSYY	SAYYIDS
ADISTTY	DITTAYS
ADJKOSU	JUDOKAS
ADJLMOR	JARLDOM
ADJNORS	JORDANS
ADJNORU	ADJOURN
ADJORRU	ADJUROR
ADJSSTU	ADJUSTS
ADKKLOY	KAKODYL
ADKLMRU	MUDLARK
ADKOPSU	PADOUKS
ADKORWY	DAYWORK
	WORKDAY
ADKRSWY	SKYWARD
ADLLMOW	WADMOLL
ADLLMOY	MODALLY
ADLLNOW	LOWLAND
ADLLNOY	NODALLY
ADLLOPR	POLLARD
ADLLOPS	DALLOPS
ADLLORS	DOLLARS
ADLLRWY	DRYWALL
ADLLTUY	ADULTLY
ADLMNOS	ALMONDS
	DOLMANS
ADLMOOR	LORDOMA
	MALODOR
ADLMORU	MODULAR
ADLMOSW	WADMOLS
ADLMSTU	TALMUDS
ADLNNOR	NORLAND
ADLNNSU	SUNLAND
ADLNOOR	LARDOON
ADLNOPU	POUNDAL
ADLNORS	LADRONS
	LARDONS
ADLNORT	TROLAND
ADLNORU	NODULAR
ADLNOSS	SOLANDS
	SOLDANS
ADLNOST	DALTONS
	SANDLOT
ADLNOSU	SOULDAN
	UNLOADS
ADLNOSX	OXLANDS
ADLNOSY	SYNODAL
ADLNOTU	OUTLAND
ADLNPSU	UPLANDS
ADLNRSU	LURDANS
ADLNRUU	UNDULAR
ADLNRUY	LAUNDRY
ADLNSSU	SULDANS
ADLNTUU	UNADULT
ADLOPRU	POULARD
ADLOPSU	UPLOADS
ADLORRW	WARLORD
ADLORSS	DORSALS
ADLORSU	SUDORAL
ADLOSSS	DOSSALS
ADLPSSU	SPAULDS
ADMMNOS	MANDOMS
ADMMNSU	SUMMAND
ADMNOOR	DOORMAN
	MADRONO
ADMNOOW	WOODMAN
ADMNOOZ	MADZOON
ADMNOQU	QUONDAM
ADMNORS	RANDOMS
	RODSMAN
ADMNORT	DORMANT
	MORDANT
ADMNOSS	DAMSONS
ADMNOSU	OSMUNDA
ADMNOSY	DYNAMOS
ADMNSTU	DUSTMAN
ADMOORT	DOORMAT
ADMOORY	DAYROOM
ADMOPPU	POPADUM
ADMORRS	RAMRODS
ADMORST	STARDOM
	TSARDOM
ADMORSU	MADUROS
ADMORTW	MADWORT
ADMORTZ	TZARDOM
ADMRSTU	DURMAST
	MUSTARD
ADNNOOS	NANDOOS
ADNNOOY	NOONDAY
ADNNORS	RANDONS
ADNNORT	DONNART
ADNNOST	DANTONS
	DONNATS
ADNNOSU	ADNOUNS
ADNNOTU	DAUNTON
ADNNRTU	DUNNART
ADNNRUW	UNDRAWN
ADNOOPR	PANDOOR
ADNOORS	NARDOOS
ADNOORT	DONATOR
	ODORANT
	TANDOOR
	TORNADO
ADNOOSW	WANDOOS
ADNOPRS	PARDONS
ADNOPRU	PANDOUR
ADNOPRV	PROVAND
ADNOPST	DOPANTS
ADNORRW	NORWARD
ADNORSW	ONWARDS
ADNORTU	ROTUNDA
ADNORTY	TARDYON
ADNORWY	NAYWORD
ADNOSSU	SOUDANS
ADNOSTT	DOTANTS
ADNOSTU	ASTOUND
ADNPRUW	UPDRAWN
ADNPSTU	DUSTPAN
	STANDUP
	UPSTAND
ADNRSST	STRANDS
ADNRSSU	SUNDRAS
ADNRSTU	DRAUNTS
	DURANTS
	TUNDRAS
ADNRSUW	SUNWARD
	UNDRAWS
ADNSSTY	DYNASTS
ADNSTYY	DYNASTY
ADOOPRS	PARODOS
ADOOPSU	APODOUS
ADOOPSW	SAPWOOD
ADOORWY	DOORWAY
ADOOSTT	TOSTADO
ADOOSUV	VAUDOOS
ADOOWWX	WOODWAX
ADOPRRW	WARDROP
ADORRSU	ARDOURS
ADORSTW	TOWARDS
ADORSUU	ARDUOUS
ADORSWY	AYWORDS
ADORTUW	OUTDRAW
	OUTWARD
ADOUUVX	VAUDOUX
ADPRSTU	UPDARTS
ADPRSUW	UPDRAWS
	UPWARDS
ADRSSUW	USWARDS
ADSSTUW	SAWDUST
AEEEFLR	EELFARE
AEEEGKL	KEELAGE
AEEEGLT	LEGATEE
AEEEGNT	TEENAGE
AEEEGPR	PEERAGE
AEEEGPS	SEEPAGE
AEEEGRR	EAGERER
AEEEGRT	ETAGERE
AEEEILN	ALIENEE
AEEELRS	RELEASE
AEEELTV	ELEVATE
AEEERVW	REWEAVE
AEEERWY	EYEWEAR
AEEFFLL	FELAFEL
AEEFFNS	NEAFFES
AEEFFRS	AFFEERS
AEEFGLN	FENAGLE
AEEFGNT	FANTEEG
AEEFGRS	SERFAGE
AEEFGSU	FEAGUES
AEEFGTW	WEFTAGE
AEEFHRT	FEATHER
	TEREFAH
AEEFILR	FILAREE
	LEAFIER
AEEFILW	ALEWIFE
AEEFIRS	AREFIES
	FAERIES
	FREESIA
AEEFISW	SEAWIFE
AEEFKRS	FAKEERS
AEEFLLT	FELLATE
	LEAFLET
AEEFLMN	ENFLAME
AEEFLMS	FEMALES
AEEFLRT	REFLATE
AEEFLRU	FERULAE
AEEFLRW	WELFARE
AEEFLRY	LEAFERY
AEEFLRZ	ALFEREZ
AEEFLSU	EASEFUL
AEEFLTX	TELEFAX
AEEFMNR	ENFRAME
	FREEMAN
AEEFMRR	REFRAME
AEEFMRT	FERMATE
AEEFOTV	FOVEATE
AEEFPPR	FRAPPEE
AEEFRRS	FEARERS
AEEFRRT	FERRATE
AEEFRST	AFREETS
	FEASTER
AEEFRTU	FEATURE
AEEFRWY	FREEWAY
AEEFSTT	FEATEST
AEEGGLL	ALLEGGE
AEEGGLR	GREGALE
AEEGGLS	ALEGGES
AEEGGLT	GATELEG
AEEGGNR	ENGAGER
AEEGGNS	ENGAGES
AEEGGOP	EPAGOGE
AEEGGRS	AGREGES
	RAGGEES
	REGGAES
AEEGGRU	REGAUGE
AEEGGST	TAGGEES
AEEGGSW	GEEGAWS
AEEGHIR	HIREAGE
AEEGHNT	THENAGE
AEEGHNW	WHANGEE
AEEGILL	GALILEE
AEEGILM	MILEAGE
AEEGILN	LINEAGE
AEEGILP	EPIGEAL
AEEGILT	EGALITE
AEEGILW	WEIGELA
AEEGIMR	REIMAGE
AEEGINP	EPIGEAN
AEEGINR	REGINAE
AEEGINU	EUGENIA
AEEGINZ	AGENIZE
AEEGIPP	PIPEAGE
AEEGIPR	PIERAGE
AEEGISS	AEGISES
	ASSIEGE

AEEGJRS	JAEGERS
AEEGJSY	JAYGEES
AEEGKLL	KLEAGLE
AEEGLLR	ALLEGER
AEEGLLS	ALLEGES
AEEGLLZ	GAZELLE
AEEGLMN	GLEEMAN
	MELANGE
AEEGLMR	GLEAMER
AEEGLMT	MELTAGE
AEEGLNR	ENLARGE
	GENERAL
	GLEANER
AEEGLNT	ELEGANT
AEEGLNU	EUGLENA
AEEGLNV	EVANGEL
AEEGLOR	AEROGEL
AEEGLPR	PEREGAL
AEEGLPS	PELAGES
AEEGLRR	REGALER
AEEGLRS	GALERES
	REGALES
AEEGLRU	LEAGUER
	REGULAE
AEEGLRW	LEGWEAR
AEEGLRY	EAGERLY
AEEGLRZ	REGLAZE
AEEGLSS	AGELESS
	ALGESES
AEEGLST	EAGLETS
	GELATES
	LEGATES
	SEGETAL
	TEAGLES
	TELEGAS
AEEGLSU	LEAGUES
AEEGLSV	GLEAVES
	SELVAGE
AEEGLTT	GALETTE
AEEGLTU	TEGULAE
AEEGLTV	VEGETAL
AEEGMMT	GEMMATE
	TAGMEME
AEEGMNR	GERMANE
AEEGMNS	MANEGES
	MENAGES
AEEGMNT	GATEMEN
AEEGMPR	PREGAME
AEEGMRR	MEAGRER
AEEGMRS	MEAGRES
AEEGMRU	REMUAGE
AEEGMSS	MEGASSE
	MESSAGE
AEEGMST	GAMETES
	METAGES
AEEGNNP	PANGENE
AEEGNNR	ENRANGE
AEEGNNS	ENNAGES
AEEGNOP	PEONAGE
AEEGNPP	GENAPPE
AEEGNRS	ENRAGES
AEEGNRT	GRANTEE
	GREATEN
	NEGATER
	REAGENT
AEEGNRU	RENAGUE
	UNEAGER
AEEGNRV	AVENGER
	ENGRAVE
AEEGNSS	SAGENES
	SENEGAS
AEEGNST	NEGATES
AEEGNSV	AVENGES
	GENEVAS
AEEGNTT	TENTAGE
AEEGNTV	VENTAGE
AEEGOPS	APOGEES
AEEGORV	OVERAGE
AEEGOST	GOATEES
AEEGPRS	ASPERGE
	PRESAGE
AEEGPRU	PUGAREE
AEEGRRS	GREASER
	REGEARS
AEEGRRT	GREATER
	REGRATE
AEEGRRU	REARGUE
AEEGRRW	WAGERER
AEEGRSS	GREASES
AEEGRST	ERGATES
	RESTAGE
AEEGRSV	GREAVES
AEEGRTU	TREAGUE
AEEGRUZ	GUEREZA
AEEGSSW	SEWAGES
AEEGSTT	GESTATE
	TAGETES
AEEGTTZ	GAZETTE
AEEHHNT	HEATHEN
AEEHHRT	HEATHER
AEEHHST	SHEATHE
AEEHHSW	HEEHAWS
AEEHINR	HERNIAE
AEEHIPR	HEAPIER
AEEHIRV	HEAVIER
AEEHIST	ATHEISE
AEEHISV	HEAVIES
AEEHITZ	ATHEIZE
AEEHKMS	HAKEEMS
AEEHKNR	HEARKEN
AEEHKNT	THANKEE
AEEHKRT	HEKTARE
AEEHKRU	HEUREKA
AEEHLNT	LETHEAN
AEEHLPT	HEELTAP
AEEHLRS	HEALERS
AEEHLRT	HALTERE
	LEATHER
AEEHLRV	HAVEREL
AEEHLSS	LEASHES
AEEHLST	LATHEES
AEEHLSW	AWHEELS
AEEHLSX	EXHALES
AEEHLSY	EYELASH
AEEHLTT	ATHLETE
AEEHMNT	METHANE
AEEHMRS	HAREEMS
	MAHSEER
AEEHMRT	ERATHEM
	THERMAE
AEEHMST	MEATHES
AEEHMSU	HEAUMES
AEEHNPS	PEAHENS
AEEHNPT	HAPTENE
	HEPTANE
	PHENATE
AEEHNRS	ARSHEEN
AEEHNRT	EARTHEN
	HEARTEN
AEEHNST	ETHANES
AEEHNSV	HEAVENS
AEEHNSX	HEXANES
AEEHNTW	WHEATEN
AEEHPRS	RESHAPE
	SPHAERE
	SPHEARE
AEEHPRT	PREHEAT
AEEHPSS	APHESES
	SPAHEES
AEEHPUV	UPHEAVE
AEEHQSU	QUASHEE
AEEHRRS	HEARERS
	REHEARS
	SHEARER
AEEHRSS	HEARSES
AEEHRST	AETHERS
	HEATERS
	REHEATS
AEEHRSV	HEAVERS
	RESHAVE
AEEHRSW	WHEREAS
AEEHRTT	THEATER
	THEATRE
	THEREAT
AEEHRTV	THREAVE
AEEHRTW	WEATHER
	WHEREAT
	WREATHE
AEEHSST	HEASTES
AEEHSSV	SHEAVES
AEEHSTV	THEAVES
AEEHSWY	EYEWASH
AEEIIRS	AIERIES
AEEIKLP	APELIKE
	PEALIKE
AEEIKLR	LEAKIER
AEEIKLT	TEALIKE
AEEIKPR	PEAKIER
AEEIKSV	KEAVIES
AEEILLR	REALLIE
AEEILMR	MEALIER
AEEILMS	MEALIES
AEEILNP	ALEPINE
	ELAPINE
AEEILNR	ALIENER
AEEILNS	SEALINE
AEEILNT	LINEATE
AEEILNX	ALEXINE
AEEILPT	EPILATE
	PILEATE
AEEILRR	EARLIER
	LEARIER
AEEILRS	EARLIES
	REALISE
AEEILRT	ATELIER
	REALTIE
AEEILRV	LEAVIER
	VEALIER
AEEILRZ	REALIZE
AEEILTT	AILETTE
AEEILTV	ELATIVE
AEEIMNN	ENAMINE
AEEIMNR	REMANIE
AEEIMNS	MEANIES
	NEMESIA
AEEIMNT	ETAMINE
	MATINEE
AEEIMNX	EXAMINE
AEEIMPR	EMPAIRE
AEEIMRR	REAMIER
AEEIMRS	SEAMIER
	SERIEMA
AEEIMRT	EMERITA
	EMIRATE
	MEATIER
AEEIMSS	MISEASE
	SIAMESE
AEEIMST	STEAMIE
AEEIMSZ	SIAMEZE
AEEIMTT	TEATIME
AEEINPR	PERINEA
AEEINRT	ARENITE
	RETINAE
	TRAINEE
AEEINST	ETESIAN
AEEINTV	NAIVETE
AEEINVW	INWEAVE
AEEIORT	ETAERIO
AEEIPRR	PEREIRA
AEEIPRS	APERIES
	EPEIRAS
AEEIPRT	PEATIER
AEEIPSV	PEAVIES
AEEIPTX	EXPIATE
AEEIRRR	ARRIERE
AEEIRRS	REARISE
	RERAISE
AEEIRRT	TEARIER
AEEIRRW	WEARIER
AEEIRST	AERIEST
	SERIATE
AEEIRSW	WEARIES
AEEIRTT	ARIETTE
	ITERATE
AEEIRTV	EVIRATE
AEEISST	EASIEST
AEEISVV	EVASIVE
AEEITTV	AVIETTE
	EVITATE
AEEITUX	EUTEXIA
AEEIUVX	EXUVIAE
AEEJKSS	JAKESES
AEEJMSS	JAMESES
AEEJNST	SEJEANT
AEEJNTU	JAUNTEE
AEEJRSV	EVEJARS
AEEJSVY	JAYVEES
	VEEJAYS
AEEKKNO	KOKANEE
AEEKLLT	LAKELET
AEEKLMN	KEELMAN
AEEKLNS	ALKENES
AEEKLNT	KANTELE
AEEKLPS	PALKEES
AEEKLRS	LEAKERS
AEEKLSV	VAKEELS
AEEKMNS	KAMSEEN
AEEKMNW	WAKEMEN
AEEKMRR	REMAKER
AEEKMRS	REMAKES
AEEKMRT	MEERKAT
AEEKNNN	NANKEEN
AEEKNNP	KNEEPAN
AEEKNRS	SNEAKER
AEEKNRT	RETAKEN
AEEKNRW	REWAKEN
	WAKENER
AEEKNSS	SKEANES
AEEKNSW	WEAKENS
AEEKORW	REAWOKE
AEEKPRS	PARKEES
	RESPEAK
	SPEAKER
AEEKPRT	PERTAKE
AEEKRRT	RETAKER
AEEKRRW	WREAKER
AEEKRST	RETAKES
	SAKERET
AEEKRSU	EUREKAS
AEEKRSW	REWAKES
AEEKSSS	ASKESES
AEEKSTW	WEAKEST
AEELLLS	ALLELES
AEELLMS	MALLEES
AEELLOV	ALVEOLE
AEELLPR	PARELLE
AEELLSS	SALLEES
AEELLWY	WALLEYE
AEELMNP	EMPANEL
	EMPLANE

AEELMNR	REELMAN
AEELMNS	ENAMELS
AEELMNT	MANTEEL
	TELEMAN
AEELMNV	VELAMEN
AEELMNY	AMYLENE
AEELMPR	EMPALER
	PREMEAL
AEELMPS	EMPALES
AEELMPX	EXAMPLE
	EXEMPLA
AEELMRS	MEALERS
AEELMRT	LAMETER
AEELMSS	MEASLES
AEELMSU	AEMULES
AEELMSZ	MEAZELS
AEELMTU	EMULATE
AEELNNP	ENPLANE
AEELNNR	LERNEAN
AEELNOS	ENOLASE
AEELNPR	REPANEL
AEELNPS	ALPEENS
	SPELEAN
AEELNRR	LEARNER
	RELEARN
AEELNRS	LEANERS
AEELNRT	ALTERNE
	ENTERAL
	ETERNAL
	TELERAN
AEELNRW	RENEWAL
AEELNSS	ENSEALS
AEELNST	ELANETS
	LATEENS
	LEANEST
AEELNSV	ENSLAVE
	LEAVENS
AEELNSW	WEANELS
AEELNTY	ENTAYLE
AEELOPR	PAROLEE
AEELOPX	POLEAXE
AEELORS	AREOLES
AEELORU	AUREOLE
AEELOST	OLEATES
AEELOSW	LEASOWE
AEELPRR	PEARLER
AEELPRS	LEAPERS
	PLEASER
	PRESALE
	RELAPSE
	REPEALS
AEELPRT	PETRALE
	PLEATER
	PRELATE
	REPLATE
AEELPRU	PLEURAE
AEELPSS	ELAPSES
	PLEASES
	SAPELES
AEELPSU	EPAULES
AEELPTT	PALETTE
	PELTATE
AEELPTU	EPAULET
AEELQSU	QUELEAS
	SEQUELA
AEELRRT	ALERTER
	ALTERER
	REALTER
	RELATER
AEELRRV	RAVELER
AEELRRX	RELAXER
AEELRSS	EARLESS
	LEASERS
	RESALES
	RESEALS
	SEALERS
AEELRST	ELATERS
	REALEST
	RELATES
	RESLATE
	STEALER
AEELRSU	LEASURE
AEELRSV	LAVEERS
	LEAVERS
	REVEALS
	SEVERAL
	VEALERS
AEELRSX	RELAXES
AEELRSY	SEALERY
AEELRTX	EXALTER
AEELRUV	REVALUE
AEELSST	ALTESSE
	STEALES
	TEASELS
AEELSSV	SLEAVES
AEELSSW	AWELESS
	WEASELS
AEELSSZ	SLEAZES
AEELSTU	ELUATES
	SETUALE
AEELSTV	SALVETE
	VALETES
	VELETAS
AEELSTX	LATEXES
AEELSTY	EYALETS
AEELSTZ	TEAZELS
	TEAZLES
AEELSWY	LEEWAYS
	WEASELY
AEELTTY	LAYETTE
AEELTVW	WAVELET
AEEMMMR	MAREMME
AEEMMMS	MAMMEES
AEEMMNT	MEATMEN
AEEMMPY	EMPYEMA
AEEMMRT	AMMETER
	METAMER
AEEMMSY	MAMEYES
AEEMNNO	ANEMONE
AEEMNNP	PENNAME
AEEMNOX	AXONEME
AEEMNPR	PRENAME
AEEMNPS	SPAEMEN
AEEMNPT	PEATMEN
AEEMNRS	MEANERS
	RENAMES
AEEMNRT	REMANET
AEEMNSS	ENSEAMS
AEEMNST	ENTAMES
	MEANEST
AEEMNSX	EXAMENS
AEEMOPT	METOPAE
AEEMORT	EROTEMA
AEEMOSW	AWESOME
	WAESOME
AEEMPRS	AMPERES
	EMPARES
AEEMPRT	TEMPERA
AEEMPRY	EMPAYRE
AEEMPST	METEPAS
AEEMPSW	WAMPEES
AEEMPTU	AMPUTEE
AEEMQRU	MARQUEE
AEEMRRS	REAMERS
	SMEARER
AEEMRSS	SEAMERS
AEEMRST	REMATES
	RETEAMS
	STEAMER
	TEAMERS
AEEMRSU	MEASURE
AEEMRTX	EXTREMA
AEEMRTY	METAYER
AEEMSSS	SESAMES
AEEMSST	MESETAS
	SEAMSET
AEEMSTT	METATES
AEEMSTX	TAXEMES
AEENNOT	NEONATE
AEENNOV	NOVENAE
AEENNPT	PENNATE
	PENTANE
AEENNRS	ENSNARE
	RENNASE
AEENNRX	REANNEX
AEENNST	NEATENS
AEENNSX	ANNEXES
AEENNTU	UNEATEN
AEENOPR	PERAEON
AEENOPU	EUPNOEA
AEENORS	ARENOSE
AEENOSS	ANOESES
AEENOSU	AENEOUS
AEENPST	NEPETAS
	PENATES
	PESANTE
AEENPSU	EUPNEAS
AEENPSW	PAWNEES
AEENPSX	EXPANSE
AEENRRS	EARNERS
	REEARNS
AEENRRT	TERRANE
AEENRRV	RAVENER
AEENRRY	YEARNER
AEENRSS	ENSEARS
AEENRST	EARNEST
	EASTERN
	NEAREST
AEENRSW	WEANERS
AEENRTT	ENTREAT
	RATTEEN
	TERNATE
AEENRTV	AVENTRE
	NERVATE
	VETERAN
AEENRUV	UNREAVE
AEENSST	ENTASES
	SATEENS
	SENATES
	SENSATE
	STEANES
AEENSSU	UNEASES
AEENSSV	AVENSES
AEENSSW	WAENESS
AEENSTT	NEATEST
AEENSUV	AVENUES
AEENSWZ	WEAZENS
AEENTTV	NAVETTE
AEENUVW	UNWEAVE
AEEOPRT	OPERATE
AEEOPTZ	EPAZOTE
AEEORRS	REAROSE
AEEORSS	SEROSAE
AEEORST	ROSEATE
AEEORSV	OVERSEA
AEEORTV	OVERATE
	OVEREAT
AEEORVW	OVERAWE
AEEOSUU	EUOUAES
AEEOSVV	EVOVAES
AEEPPRR	PAPERER
	PREPARE
	REPAPER
AEEPPRS	RAPPEES
AEEPPRT	PRETAPE
AEEPRRS	REAPERS
	SPEARER
AEEPRRT	PEARTER
	TAPERER
AEEPRRV	PREAVER
AEEPRSS	ASPERSE
	PARESES
	PRAESES
	PREASES
	PREASSE
	SERAPES
AEEPRST	REPEATS
	RETAPES
AEEPRSV	REPAVES
AEEPRSZ	SPREAZE
AEEPRTU	EPURATE
AEEPRTY	PEATERY
AEEPRTZ	TRAPEZE
AEEPSSS	ASEPSES
AEEPSST	PESETAS
AEEPSSW	PESEWAS
AEEPSTT	SEPTATE
	SPATTEE
AEEPSVY	PEAVEYS
AEEQRSU	QUAERES
AEEQSTU	EQUATES
AEERRRS	REARERS
AEERRSS	ERASERS
AEERRST	RETEARS
	SERRATE
	TEARERS
AEERRSU	ERASURE
AEERRSV	REAVERS
AEERRSW	SWEARER
	WEARERS
AEERRTT	RETRATE
	RETREAT
	TREATER
AEERRTW	WATERER
AEERRVW	WAVERER
AEERSST	EASTERS
	RESEATS
	SAETERS
	SEAREST
	SEATERS
	STEARES
	TEASERS
	TESSERA
AEERSSU	RESEAUS
	SEASURE
	UREASES
AEERSSV	ASSEVER
AEERSSY	ESSAYER
AEERSTT	ESTREAT
	RESTATE
	RETASTE
AEERSTU	AUSTERE
AEERSTW	SWEATER
AEERSTX	RETAXES
AEERSUV	VAREUSE
AEERSUX	RESEAUX
AEERSVW	WEAVERS
AEERSWX	REWAXES
AEERTTX	EXTREAT
AEERTWW	WETWARE
AEESSSW	SEESAWS
AEESSTT	ESTATES
AEESSTU	SAUTEES
AEESSTX	TEXASES
AEESSUX	AUXESES
AEESTTT	TESTATE
AEFFFLR	FLAFFER
AEFFGIR	GIRAFFE
AEFFGNR	ENGRAFF
AEFFGRS	GAFFERS

AEFFGRU	GAUFFER
AEFFHST	HAFFETS
AEFFINS	AFFINES
AEFFIPR	PIAFFER
AEFFIPS	PIAFFES
AEFFIRX	AFFIXER
	REAFFIX
AEFFIST	TAFFIES
AEFFISW	WAFFIES
AEFFISX	AFFIXES
AEFFKOP	OFFPEAK
AEFFKOR	RAKEOFF
AEFFKOT	OFFTAKE
	TAKEOFF
AEFFLLY	FLYLEAF
AEFFLMW	FLAMFEW
AEFFLNS	SNAFFLE
AEFFLRR	RAFFLER
AEFFLRS	FARFELS
	RAFFLES
AEFFLRU	FEARFUL
AEFFLRW	WAFFLER
AEFFLSW	WAFFLES
AEFFLSY	YAFFLES
AEFFLTU	FATEFUL
AEFFMRU	EARMUFF
AEFFOVW	WAVEOFF
AEFFQRU	QUAFFER
AEFFRST	AFFRETS
	RESTAFF
	STAFFER
AEFFRSY	EFFRAYS
AEFFRSZ	ZAFFERS
	ZAFFRES
AEFFTTY	TAFFETY
AEFGGGO	FOGGAGE
AEFGGLR	FLAGGER
AEFGGMO	MEGAFOG
AEFGGRY	FAGGERY
AEFGILN	FEALING
	FINAGLE
	LEAFING
AEFGILO	FOLIAGE
AEFGILR	FRAGILE
AEFGINR	FEARING
AEFGINS	FEASING
AEFGINT	FEATING
AEFGINZ	FEAZING
AEFGIRT	FRIGATE
AEFGIRU	REFUGIA
AEFGITU	FATIGUE
AEFGLLU	FULLAGE
AEFGLMN	FLAGMEN
AEFGLNR	FLANGER
AEFGLNS	FANGLES
	FLANGES
AEFGLOT	FLOTAGE
AEFGLOW	FLOWAGE
AEFGLRS	REFLAGS
AEFGLRU	RAGEFUL
AEFGLUZ	GAZEFUL
AEFGMOR	FROMAGE
AEFGMSU	FUMAGES
AEFGNRR	GRANFER
AEFGNRT	ENGRAFT
AEFGOOT	FOOTAGE
AEFGORR	FORAGER
AEFGORS	FORAGES
AEFGORT	FAGOTER
AEFGORV	FORGAVE
AEFGRRT	GRAFTER
	REGRAFT
AEFGRSU	GAUFERS
	GAUFRES
AEFHLLS	FELLAHS
AEFHLOR	FAHLORE
AEFHLRS	FLASHER
AEFHLRT	FARTHEL
AEFHLRZ	FAHLERZ
AEFHLSS	FLASHES
AEFHLTU	HATEFUL
AEFHRRT	FARTHER
AEFHRST	FATHERS
	HAFTERS
	SHAFTER
AEFHRSY	FASHERY
AEFIILT	FILIATE
AEFIIRS	FAIRIES
AEFIJLO	JEOFAIL
AEFIJOS	FEIJOAS
AEFIKLN	FANLIKE
AEFIKLR	FLAKIER
AEFIKLS	FLAKIES
AEFIKLT	FATLIKE
AEFILLS	FAILLES
AEFILMN	FEMINAL
	INFLAME
AEFILMR	FLAMIER
AEFILNS	FINALES
AEFILNT	INFLATE
AEFILNU	INFULAE
AEFILNV	FLAVINE
AEFILOT	FOLIATE
AEFILPT	FLEAPIT
AEFILRR	FLARIER
	FRAILER
AEFILRU	FAILURE
AEFILRV	FAVRILE
AEFILRW	FLAWIER
AEFILRX	FLAXIER
AEFILRZ	FILAZER
AEFILSS	FALSIES
	FILASSE
AEFILST	FETIALS
AEFILWY	LIFEWAY
AEFIMNR	FIREMAN
AEFIMNS	FAMINES
	INFAMES
AEFIMOR	FOAMIER
AEFIMRR	FIREARM
AEFIMRS	MISFARE
AEFINNS	FANNIES
AEFINNT	INFANTE
AEFINNZ	FANZINE
AEFINPR	FIREPAN
AEFINRR	REFRAIN
AEFINRS	INFARES
	SERAFIN
AEFINRT	FAINTER
	FENITAR
AEFINRW	FAWNIER
AEFINRX	XERAFIN
AEFINST	FAINEST
	NAIFEST
AEFINSW	FANWISE
AEFINTX	ANTEFIX
AEFIQRU	AQUIFER
AEFIRRR	FARRIER
AEFIRSS	FRAISES
AEFIRST	FAIREST
AEFIRTT	FATTIER
AEFISST	FIESTAS
	FISSATE
AEFISTT	FATTIES
AEFISTX	FIXATES
AEFJNST	FANJETS
AEFKLNN	FLANKEN
AEFKLNR	FLANKER
AEFKLNS	FANKLES
AEFKLOS	SEAFOLK
AEFKLRS	FLAKERS
AEFKLRT	FARTLEK
AEFKLST	FLASKET
AEFKLUW	WAKEFUL
AEFKNRR	FRANKER
AEFKORS	FORSAKE
AEFLLNN	FANNELL
	FLANNEL
AEFLLOT	FLOATEL
AEFLLRS	FALLERS
	REFALLS
AEFLLSY	FALSELY
AEFLLTT	FLATLET
AEFLLTU	TALEFUL
AEFLLUZ	ZEALFUL
AEFLMNS	FLAMENS
AEFLMOR	FEMORAL
AEFLMRS	FLAMERS
AEFLMUW	WAMEFUL
AEFLMUZ	MAZEFUL
AEFLNNN	FLANNEN
AEFLNNS	FANNELS
AEFLNOV	FLAVONE
AEFLNRS	SALFERN
AEFLNRU	FLANEUR
	FRENULA
	FUNERAL
AEFLNSU	FLAUNES
AEFLNTT	FLATTEN
AEFLOOV	FOVEOLA
AEFLOPW	PEAFOWL
AEFLORS	LOAFERS
	SAFROLE
AEFLORT	FLOATER
	FLOREAT
	REFLOAT
AEFLORY	FORELAY
AEFLOST	FOLATES
AEFLOSW	SEAFOWL
AEFLPPR	FLAPPER
AEFLPRS	FELSPAR
AEFLPRY	PALFREY
AEFLRSS	FALSERS
	FLASERS
AEFLRST	FALTERS
AEFLRSU	EARFULS
	FERULAS
	REFUSAL
AEFLRSY	FLAYERS
AEFLRTT	FLATTER
AEFLRTU	REFUTAL
	TEARFUL
AEFLRZZ	FRAZZLE
AEFLSST	FALSEST
	FATLESS
	FESTALS
AEFLSTU	FLUATES
	SULFATE
AEFMNOR	FORAMEN
	FOREMAN
AEFMNRT	RAFTMEN
AEFMNRU	FRAENUM
AEFMORR	FOREARM
AEFMORS	FOAMERS
AEFMORT	FORMATE
AEFMOUW	WAMEFOU
AEFMRRS	FARMERS
	FRAMERS
AEFMRRY	FARMERY
AEFNNRS	FANNERS
AEFNNST	ENFANTS
AEFNOPR	PROFANE
AEFNOPY	PAYFONE
AEFNORR	FORERAN
AEFNRRS	FARRENS
AEFNRSS	FARNESS
AEFNRSU	FURANES
	UNSAFER
AEFNRSW	FAWNERS
AEFNSST	FASTENS
	FATNESS
AEFNSTT	FATTENS
AEFOPRW	FOREPAW
AEFORRV	FAVORER
	OVERFAR
AEFORRY	FORAYER
AEFORSW	FORESAW
AEFORSY	FORESAY
AEFORTV	OVERFAT
AEFOSST	FATSOES
	FOSSATE
AEFOSTU	FEATOUS
AEFPPRS	FRAPPES
AEFRRST	FRATERS
	RAFTERS
	STRAFER
AEFRRTY	FRATERY
AEFRSSS	FRASSES
AEFRSST	FASTERS
	STRAFES
AEFRSTW	FRETSAW
	WAFTERS
AEFRTTU	TARTUFE
AEFRTUW	WAFTURE
AEFSSTT	FASTEST
AEFSSUV	FAVUSES
AEFSTTT	FATTEST
AEGGGLS	GAGGLES
AEGGGLU	LUGGAGE
AEGGGRS	GAGGERS
AEGGHLR	HAGGLER
AEGGHLS	HAGGLES
AEGGHMO	HEMAGOG
AEGGHSW	EGGWASH
AEGGIJR	JAGGIER
AEGGILN	GEALING
	LIGNAGE
AEGGINR	GEARING
	NAGGIER
AEGGINS	AGEINGS
	SIGNAGE
AEGGIOS	ISAGOGE
AEGGIRR	RAGGIER
AEGGIRS	RAGGIES
	SAGGIER
AEGGIRT	TAGGIER
AEGGIRU	GARIGUE
AEGGIST	STAGGIE
AEGGISW	SWAGGIE
AEGGJRS	JAGGERS
AEGGJRY	JAGGERY
AEGGLNO	AGELONG
AEGGLNR	GANGREL
AEGGLNS	LAGGENS
AEGGLRR	GARGLER
AEGGLRS	GARGLES
	LAGGERS
	RAGGLES
AEGGLRY	GREYLAG
AEGGLSW	WAGGLES
AEGGMNY	YEGGMAN
AEGGMSS	EGGMASS
AEGGNNU	GUNNAGE
AEGGNRR	GRANGER
AEGGNRS	GANGERS
	GRANGES
	NAGGERS
AEGGNSU	GANGUES
AEGGRRY	RAGGERY
AEGGRSS	AGGRESS

	SAGGERS
	SEGGARS
AEGGRST	GAGSTER
	GARGETS
	STAGGER
	TAGGERS
AEGGRSU	GAUGERS
AEGGRSW	SWAGGER
	WAGGERS
AEGGRSY	YAGGERS
AEGGRTY	GARGETY
AEGGRWY	WAGGERY
AEGGSWW	GEWGAWS
AEGHHIT	AHEIGHT
AEGHIJR	JAGHIRE
AEGHILN	HEALING
AEGHILR	LAIGHER
AEGHIMT	MEGAHIT
AEGHINP	HEAPING
AEGHINR	HEARING
AEGHINT	GAHNITE
	HEATING
AEGHINV	HEAVING
AEGHINZ	GENIZAH
AEGHIOS	HOAGIES
AEGHIRS	HEGARIS
	HEGIRAS
	HIRAGES
AEGHISS	GEISHAS
AEGHISZ	GHAZIES
AEGHLNO	HALOGEN
AEGHLNT	ALENGTH
AEGHLOS	GALOSHE
AEGHLRU	LAUGHER
AEGHLSS	SEALGHS
AEGHLST	HAGLETS
AEGHLSZ	GHAZELS
AEGHLTW	THALWEG
AEGHMNN	HANGMEN
AEGHMNO	HOGMANE
AEGHMOR	HOMAGER
AEGHMOS	HOMAGES
	OHMAGES
AEGHMSU	MESHUGA
AEGHNOX	HEXAGON
AEGHNRS	GNASHER
	HANGERS
	REHANGS
AEGHNRU	NURAGHE
AEGHNSS	GNASHES
AEGHNST	STENGAH
AEGHOPY	HYPOGEA
AEGHORS	GHERAOS
AEGHOSS	SEAHOGS
AEGHOST	HOSTAGE
AEGHPRS	SPREAGH
AEGHPST	HATPEGS
AEGHRST	GATHERS
AEGHSST	GASHEST
AEGIIMN	IMAGINE
AEGIKLN	LEAKING
	LINKAGE
AEGIKLT	GLAIKET
	TAGLIKE
AEGIKNP	PEAKING
AEGIKNR	REAKING
AEGIKNS	SINKAGE
AEGIKPP	KIPPAGE
AEGIKPR	GARPIKE
AEGIKRW	GAWKIER
AEGIKSW	GAWKIES
AEGILLL	ILLEGAL
AEGILLM	MILLAGE
AEGILLN	GALLEIN
	NIGELLA
AEGILLP	PILLAGE
AEGILLS	GALLIES
	GALLISE
AEGILLT	TILLAGE
AEGILLU	LIGULAE
AEGILLV	VILLAGE
AEGILLY	AGILELY
AEGILLZ	GALLIZE
AEGILMN	GEMINAL
	LEAMING
	MEALING
AEGILMR	GREMIAL
	LAMIGER
AEGILMS	MILAGES
AEGILNN	ANELING
	EANLING
	LEANING
	NEALING
AEGILNP	LEAPING
	PEALING
	PLEAING
AEGILNR	ALIGNER
	ENGRAIL
	LAERING
	LEARING
	NARGILE
	REALIGN
	REGINAL
AEGILNS	LEASING
	LINAGES
	SEALING
AEGILNT	ATINGLE
	ELATING
	GELATIN
	GENITAL
AEGILNU	LINGUAE
	UNAGILE
AEGILNV	LEAVING
	VEALING
AEGILNY	ALEYING
	YEALING
AEGILOS	GOALIES
	SOILAGE
AEGILOU	EULOGIA
AEGILPS	PAIGLES
AEGILRR	GLARIER
AEGILRS	GLAIRES
	GRAILES
AEGILRZ	GLAZIER
AEGILSS	ALGESIS
	GLASSIE
	LIGASES
	SILAGES
AEGILST	AGILEST
	AIGLETS
	LIGATES
	TAIGLES
AEGILSV	GLAIVES
AEGILTU	GLUTAEI
AEGILTY	EGALITY
AEGIMMR	GAMMIER
AEGIMNN	AMENING
	MEANING
AEGIMNP	PIGMEAN
AEGIMNR	GERMAIN
	GERMINA
	MANGIER
	MEARING
	REAMING
AEGIMNS	ENIGMAS
	GAMINES
	MEASING
	SEAMING
AEGIMNT	MINTAGE
	TEAMING
	TEGMINA
AEGIMOS	IMAGOES
AEGIMPR	EPIGRAM
	PRIMAGE
AEGIMPS	MAGPIES
	MISPAGE
AEGIMPT	PIGMEAT
AEGIMRR	ARMIGER
AEGIMRS	GISARME
	IMAGERS
	MAIGRES
	MIRAGES
AEGIMRT	MIGRATE
	RAGTIME
AEGIMRU	GAUMIER
AEGIMRY	IMAGERY
AEGIMSS	AGEISMS
AEGIMST	GAMIEST
	SIGMATE
AEGIMSV	MISGAVE
AEGINNO	GANOINE
AEGINNP	NEAPING
	PEANING
AEGINNR	AGINNER
	EARNING
	ENGRAIN
	GRANNIE
	NEARING
AEGINNS	SEANING
AEGINNT	ANTEING
	ANTIGEN
	GENTIAN
AEGINNU	ANGUINE
	GUANINE
AEGINNW	WEANING
AEGINNY	YEANING
AEGINOR	ORIGANE
AEGINOS	AGONIES
	AGONISE
AEGINOZ	AGONIZE
AEGINPP	GENIPAP
AEGINPR	REAPING
AEGINPS	PEASING
	SPAEING
	SPINAGE
AEGINPZ	PEAZING
AEGINRR	ANGRIER
	EARRING
	GRAINER
	RANGIER
	REARING
AEGINRS	ANGRIES
	EARINGS
	ERASING
	GAINERS
	GRAINES
	REAGINS
	REGAINS
	REGINAS
	SEARING
	SERINGA
AEGINRT	GRANITE
	GRATINE
	INGRATE
	TANGIER
	TEARING
AEGINRV	REAVING
	VINEGAR
AEGINRW	WEARING
AEGINRZ	ZINGARE
AEGINSS	AGNISES
	SEASING
AEGINST	EASTING
	EATINGS
	GAINEST
	GENISTA
	INGATES
	INGESTA
	SEATING
	TANGIES
	TEASING
	TSIGANE
AEGINSU	GUINEAS
AEGINSZ	AGNIZES
	SEAZING
AEGINTU	UNITAGE
AEGINTV	VINTAGE
AEGINTZ	TEAZING
	TZIGANE
AEGINVW	WEAVING
AEGIORT	GOATIER
AEGIPPR	GAPPIER
AEGIPPS	PIPAGES
AEGIPRR	GRAPIER
AEGIPRS	GASPIER
	PRISAGE
	SPAIRGE
AEGIRRZ	GRAZIER
AEGIRSS	AGRISES
	GASSIER
AEGIRST	AGISTER
	AIGRETS
	GAITERS
	SEAGIRT
	STAGIER
	STRIGAE
	TRIAGES
AEGIRSV	GARVIES
	GRAVIES
	RIVAGES
AEGIRSW	EARWIGS
	GAWSIER
AEGIRSZ	AGRIZES
AEGIRTV	VIRGATE
	VITRAGE
AEGIRUZ	GAUZIER
AEGISST	AGEISTS
	SAGIEST
AEGISSU	AGUISES
AEGISSV	VISAGES
AEGISTU	AUGITES
AEGISTY	GASEITY
AEGISTZ	GAZIEST
AEGISUZ	AGUIZES
AEGISYZ	AZYGIES
AEGJLNR	JANGLER
AEGJLNS	JANGLES
AEGJLSS	JAGLESS
AEGKKNO	ANGEKOK
AEGKLOU	KAGOULE
AEGKLRS	GRAKLES
AEGKMRY	KERYGMA
AEGKMSS	MASKEGS
AEGKRSW	GAWKERS
AEGKSST	GASKETS
AEGLLLY	LEGALLY
AEGLLNO	ALLONGE
	GALLEON
AEGLLNR	LANGREL
AEGLLNS	LEGLANS
AEGLLNT	GELLANT
AEGLLNY	LANGLEY
AEGLLOR	ALLEGRO
AEGLLOT	TOLLAGE
AEGLLRY	ALLERGY
	GALLERY
	LARGELY
	REGALLY
AEGLLST	GALLETS
AEGLLSU	SEAGULL

SULLAGE
ULLAGES
AEGLLSY GALLEYS
AEGLLTU GLUTEAL
AEGLMNR MANGLER
AEGLMNS MANGELS
MANGLES
AEGLMOR GLOMERA
GOMERAL
AEGLMOU MOULAGE
AEGLMPU PLUMAGE
AEGLMRS MALGRES
AEGLMRU MAULGRE
AEGLMSV MAGLEVS
AEGLMSY MYGALES
AEGLNOS ENGAOLS
AEGLNOT TANGELO
AEGLNPR GRAPNEL
AEGLNPS SPANGLE
AEGLNRS ANGLERS
LARGENS
SLANGER
AEGLNRT TANGLER
TRANGLE
AEGLNRU GRANULE
AEGLNRW WANGLER
WRANGLE
AEGLNRY ANGERLY
AEGLNSS GLASSEN
AEGLNST GELANTS
LANGEST
TANGLES
AEGLNSU ANGELUS
LAGUNES
LANGUES
AEGLNSW WANGLES
AEGLNSY LYNAGES
AEGLNTT GANTLET
AEGLNTU LANGUET
AEGLNTW TWANGLE
AEGLNUU UNGULAE
AEGLNUW GUNWALE
AEGLOOZ ZOOGLEA
AEGLOPR PERGOLA
AEGLORS GALORES
GAOLERS
AEGLORT GLOATER
LEGATOR
AEGLORV VORLAGE
AEGLOSS GLOSSAE
AEGLOST GELATOS
LEGATOS
AEGLOSU GEALOUS
AEGLOSV LOVAGES
AEGLOTV VOLTAGE
AEGLPPR GRAPPLE
AEGLPRS GRAPLES
AEGLPRU EARPLUG
GRAUPEL
PLAGUER
AEGLPSU PLAGUES
PLUSAGE
AEGLPUY PLAGUEY
AEGLRRU REGULAR
AEGLRSS LARGESS
AEGLRST LARGEST
AEGLRSV GRAVELS
VERGLAS
AEGLRSY ARGYLES
GRAYLES
AEGLRSZ GLAZERS
AEGLRTU GAULTER
TEGULAR
TRAGULE
AEGLRTY GREATLY
AEGLRVY GRAVELY
AEGLSSS GASLESS
GLASSES
AEGLSSU SAULGES
AEGLSTT GESTALT
AEGLSTW TALWEGS
AEGLTUV VULGATE
AEGLUUY GUAYULE
AEGLUVY VAGUELY
AEGMMNS MAGSMEN
AEGMMRS GAMMERS
GRAMMES
AEGMMRU RUMMAGE
AEGMMSS SMEGMAS
AEGMNNO AGNOMEN
NONGAME
AEGMNOR MARENGO
MEGARON
AEGMNOS MANGOES
AEGMNOT GEOMANT
MAGNETO
MEGATON
MONTAGE
AEGMNPY PYGMEAN
AEGMNRS ENGRAMS
GERMANS
MANGERS
AEGMNRT GARMENT
MARGENT
RAGMENT
AEGMNST MAGNETS
AEGMNSW SWAGMEN
AEGMNTU AUGMENT
MUTAGEN
AEGMOOR MOORAGE
AEGMORS ROMAGES
AEGMOSW WAGSOME
AEGMOSY GAYSOME
AEGMOXY EXOGAMY
AEGMRSU MAUGRES
MURAGES
AEGMSUY MAGUEYS
AEGMSUZ ZEUGMAS
AEGNNOS NONAGES
AEGNNOT NEGATON
TONNAGE
AEGNNPS PANGENS
PENANGS
AEGNNRT REGNANT
AEGNNRU GUNNERA
AEGNNST GANNETS
AEGNNTT TANGENT
AEGNNTU TUNNAGE
AEGNOOR OREGANO
AEGNOPT PONTAGE
AEGNORR GROANER
ORANGER
AEGNORS ONAGERS
ORANGES
AEGNORT NEGATOR
AEGNORW WAGONER
AEGNORY ORANGEY
AEGNOST ONSTAGE
AEGNOSY NOSEGAY
AEGNOWY WAYGONE
AEGNPRS ENGRASP
AEGNPRT TREPANG
AEGNRRS GARNERS
RANGERS
AEGNRRT GRANTER
REGRANT
AEGNRSS SANGERS
SERANGS
AEGNRST ARGENTS
GARNETS
STRANGE
AEGNRSU RAUNGES
UNGEARS
AEGNRSW GNAWERS
AEGNRTU GAUNTER
AEGNRTW TWANGER
AEGNRTY AGENTRY
AEGNSSY GANSEYS
GAYNESS
AEGNSTT GESTANT
AEGNTTU TUTENAG
AEGOORT ROOTAGE
AEGOPPR PROPAGE
AEGOPRT PORTAGE
POTAGER
AEGOPST GESTAPO
POSTAGE
POTAGES
AEGOPTT POTTAGE
AEGORRT GARROTE
AEGORSS SORAGES
AEGORST GAROTES
ORGEATS
STORAGE
TOERAGS
AEGORSU AERUGOS
AEGORTT GAROTTE
AEGORTU OUTRAGE
AEGORUV OUVRAGE
AEGORVY VOYAGER
AEGOSSU GASEOUS
AEGOSTU OUTAGES
AEGOSTW STOWAGE
TOWAGES
AEGOSTX OXGATES
AEGOSVY VOYAGES
AEGOTTU OUTGATE
AEGOTTV GAVOTTE
AEGOTUV OUTGAVE
AEGPRRS GRASPER
SPARGER
AEGPRRY GRAPERY
AEGPRSS GASPERS
SPARGES
AEGPRST PARGETS
AEGPRSU GAUPERS
AEGPRSW GAWPERS
AEGPSSU PEGASUS
AEGPSTU UPSTAGE
AEGPSUZ UPGAZES
AEGRRSS GRASSER
AEGRRST GARRETS
GARTERS
GRATERS
AEGRRSU ARGUERS
AEGRRSV GRAVERS
AEGRRSZ GRAZERS
AEGRRUU AUGURER
AEGRRUV GRAVURE
VERRUGA
AEGRSSS GASSERS
GRASSES
AEGRSST GASTERS
STAGERS
AEGRSSU ARGUSES
SAUGERS
USAGERS
AEGRSSW SWAGERS
AEGRSSY GYRASES
AEGRSTT TARGETS
AEGRSTV GRAVEST
AEGRSTY GRAYEST
GYRATES
STAGERY
AEGRSUV SEVRUGA
AEGRSVY GARVEYS
AEGRSYZ AGRYZES
AEGSSSU GAUSSES
AEGSTUU AUGUSTE
AEGSTUV VAGUEST
AEGTTTU GUTTATE
AEHHIKS SHEIKHA
AEHHIRS HASHIER
AEHHIST SHEHITA
AEHHLST HEALTHS
AEHHLTY HEALTHY
AEHHNRS HARSHEN
AEHHPRS RHAPHES
AEHHRRS HARSHER
AEHHRST HEARTHS
AEHHSSS SHASHES
AEHHSST SHEATHS
AEHHSTY SHEATHY
AEHIILR HAILIER
AEHIIRR HAIRIER
AEHIJRS HEJIRAS
AEHIKLT HATLIKE
AEHIKNS HANKIES
AEHIKPS PEAKISH
AEHIKRS SHAKIER
AEHIKSS SAKIEHS
AEHIKST SHITAKE
AEHIKSW HAWKIES
WEAKISH
AEHIKSY SAKIYEH
AEHILMN HELIMAN
AEHILMO HEMIOLA
AEHILMY LEHAYIM
AEHILNR HERNIAL
INHALER
AEHILNS INHALES
AEHILNY HYALINE
AEHILOR AIRHOLE
AEHILPR HARELIP
AEHILPT HAPLITE
AEHILRS HAILERS
SHALIER
AEHILRT LATHIER
AEHILRU HAULIER
AEHILSS SHEILAS
AEHILST HALITES
HELIAST
AEHILSW SHAWLIE
WHAISLE
AEHILTT LITHATE
AEHILTY HYALITE
AEHILUV VIHUELA
AEHILVY HEAVILY
AEHILWZ WHAIZLE
AEHIMMR HAMMIER
AEHIMMS MAIHEMS
AEHIMNR HARMINE
AEHIMNS HAEMINS
HEMINAS
AEHIMNT HEMATIN
AEHIMNY HYMENIA
AEHIMPS PHAEISM
AEHIMRS MASHIER
MISHEAR
AEHIMSS MASHIES
MESSIAH
AEHIMST ATHEISM
AEHINPR HEPARIN
AEHINPS INPHASE
AEHINPT PENTHIA
AEHINRS ARSHINE
HERNIAS
AEHINRT HAIRNET
INEARTH
THERIAN

AEHINSS	HESSIAN
AEHINST	SHEITAN
	STHENIA
AEHINSV	EVANISH
	VAHINES
AEHINSW	WAHINES
AEHIORR	HOARIER
AEHIPPR	HAPPIER
AEHIPPS	HAPPIES
AEHIPPT	EPITAPH
AEHIPRS	HARPIES
	SHARPIE
AEHIPSS	APHESIS
AEHIPSW	PEISHWA
AEHIPTZ	ZAPTIEH
AEHIQSU	HAIQUES
	QUASHIE
AEHIRRR	HARRIER
AEHIRRS	HARRIES
AEHIRSS	ARISHES
	SHERIAS
AEHIRST	HASTIER
	SHERIAT
AEHIRSV	ASHIVER
AEHIRSW	WASHIER
	WEARISH
AEHIRTW	THAWIER
AEHIRWY	HAYWIRE
AEHISST	ASHIEST
	SAITHES
	STASHIE
	TAISHES
AEHISSV	SHAVIES
AEHISTT	ATHEIST
	STAITHE
AEHISTZ	HAZIEST
AEHISVY	YESHIVA
AEHITTW	THWAITE
AEHJLOW	JAWHOLE
AEHKMSS	SAMEKHS
AEHKNRS	HANKERS
	HARKENS
AEHKNRT	THANKER
AEHKNSZ	KHAZENS
AEHKOSS	SHAKOES
AEHKPRS	PHREAKS
AEHKPSU	SHAKEUP
AEHKRRS	SHARKER
AEHKRSS	KASHERS
	SHAKERS
AEHKRSW	HAWKERS
AEHKSWY	HAWKEYS
AEHLLLS	HALLELS
AEHLLOS	HALLOES
AEHLLOV	HELLOVA
AEHLLRS	HERSALL
AEHLLST	LETHALS
AEHLLUV	HELLUVA
AEHLLYZ	HAZELLY
AEHLMNO	MANHOLE
AEHLMNY	HYMENAL
AEHLMOR	ARMHOLE
AEHLMPS	PELHAMS
AEHLMPW	WHAMPLE
AEHLMRS	HARMELS
AEHLMRT	THERMAL
AEHLMRU	HUMERAL
AEHLMST	HAMLETS
AEHLNOS	ENHALOS
AEHLNOT	ANETHOL
	ETHANOL
AEHLNRT	ENTHRAL
AEHLNSS	HANSELS
AEHLNST	HANTLES
AEHLNSU	UNHEALS
	UNLEASH
	UNSHALE
AEHLOPR	EPHORAL
AEHLOPT	TAPHOLE
AEHLORS	SHOALER
AEHLORT	LOATHER
	RATHOLE
AEHLOSS	ASSHOLE
AEHLOST	LOATHES
AEHLPRS	PLASHER
	SPHERAL
AEHLPSS	HAPLESS
	PLASHES
AEHLPST	PLASHET
AEHLPSY	SHAPELY
AEHLRSS	ASHLERS
	HALSERS
	LASHERS
	SLASHER
AEHLRST	HALTERS
	HARSLET
	LATHERS
	SLATHER
	THALERS
AEHLRSU	HAULERS
AEHLRSV	HALVERS
AEHLRSW	WHALERS
AEHLRTY	EARTHLY
	HARTELY
	HEARTLY
	LATHERY
AEHLRWY	WHALERY
AEHLSSS	ASHLESS
	HASSELS
	HASSLES
	SLASHES
AEHLSST	HASLETS
	HATLESS
	SHELTAS
AEHLSSY	HAYSELS
AEHLSTT	STEALTH
AEHLSTW	WEALTHS
AEHLSWY	SHAWLEY
AEHLTWY	WEALTHY
AEHMMNS	MASHMEN
AEHMMRS	HAMMERS
	SHAMMER
AEHMMSS	SHAMMES
AEHMMSY	MAYHEMS
AEHMNOR	MENORAH
AEHMNOS	HOSEMAN
AEHMNOT	NATHEMO
AEHMNOY	HAEMONY
AEHMNPY	NYMPHAE
AEHMNRU	HUMANER
AEHMNST	ANTHEMS
	HETMANS
AEHMOPT	APOTHEM
AEHMORT	TERAOHM
AEHMPRS	HAMPERS
AEHMPTY	EMPATHY
AEHMRRS	HARMERS
AEHMRSS	MARSHES
	MASHERS
	SHAMERS
	SHMEARS
	SMASHER
AEHMRST	HAMSTER
AEHMRTU	MAUTHER
AEHMRTW	MAWTHER
AEHMSSS	SMASHES
AEHMSST	SMEATHS
AEHMSTU	HUMATES
AEHMUZZ	MEZUZAH
AEHNNTU	UNNEATH
AEHNNWY	ANYWHEN
AEHNOPT	PHAETON
	PHONATE
AEHNOPW	WANHOPE
AEHNOPY	HYPONEA
AEHNORS	HOARSEN
	SENHORA
AEHNORT	ANOTHER
AEHNOSX	HEXOSAN
AEHNPPS	HAPPENS
AEHNPRS	SHARPEN
AEHNPRT	PANTHER
AEHNPST	HAPTENS
AEHNPSU	UNSHAPE
AEHNPTY	PHYTANE
AEHNRSS	HARNESS
AEHNRST	ANTHERS
	HARTENS
	THENARS
AEHNRTU	HAUNTER
	UNEARTH
	UNHEART
	URETHAN
AEHNRTX	NARTHEX
AEHNSSS	SNASHES
AEHNSST	HASTENS
	SNATHES
	SNEATHS
AEHNSSU	HAUSENS
AEHNSSZ	SAZHENS
AEHNSTY	ASTHENY
	SHANTEY
AEHNSUY	HAUYNES
AEHNTTW	WHATTEN
AEHOORT	TOHEROA
AEHOPRT	PHORATE
AEHOPST	TEASHOP
AEHORRS	HOARSER
AEHORST	ASTHORE
	EARSHOT
	HAROSET
AEHORSX	HOAXERS
AEHORTU	OUTHEAR
AEHORTX	OXHEART
AEHORUV	HAVEOUR
AEHOSTU	ATHEOUS
AEHPPRS	PERHAPS
AEHPPRW	WHAPPER
AEHPPSU	SHAPEUP
	UPHEAPS
AEHPRRS	HARPERS
	PHRASER
	SHARPER
AEHPRSS	PHRASES
	SERAPHS
	SHAPERS
	SHERPAS
	SPHAERS
	SPHEARS
AEHPRST	SPARTHE
	TEPHRAS
	THREAPS
AEHPRSW	PREWASH
AEHPRTT	PHATTER
AEHPRTY	THERAPY
AEHPSST	SPATHES
AEHPSSW	PESHWAS
AEHPSTY	HYPATES
AEHQRSU	QUASHER
AEHQSSU	QUASHES
AEHRRSS	RASHERS
	SHARERS
AEHRRTU	URETHRA
AEHRSST	RASHEST
	SHASTER
	TRASHES
AEHRSSV	SHAVERS
AEHRSSW	HAWSERS
	SWASHER
	WASHERS
AEHRSTT	HATTERS
	RATHEST
	SHATTER
	THREATS
AEHRSTV	HARVEST
	THRAVES
AEHRSTW	SWATHER
	THAWERS
	WREATHS
AEHRSVW	WHARVES
AEHRSWY	WASHERY
AEHRSXY	HYRAXES
AEHRTUU	HAUTEUR
AEHRTWY	WREATHY
AEHSSST	STASHES
AEHSSSW	SWASHES
AEHSSTW	SWATHES
AEHSTUX	EXHAUST
AEIIKLR	AIRLIKE
AEIIKNT	KAINITE
AEIIKSS	SAIKEIS
AEIILLT	TAILLIE
AEIILMR	RAMILIE
AEIILNN	ANILINE
AEIILNR	AIRLINE
AEIILNX	EXILIAN
AEIILRR	LAIRIER
AEIILRS	LAIRISE
AEIILRV	VIRELAI
AEIILRZ	LAIRIZE
AEIILSS	LIAISES
	SILESIA
AEIILST	LAITIES
AEIILSW	LEWISIA
AEIILTZ	TAILZIE
AEIIMNT	INTIMAE
	MINIATE
AEIIMPR	IMPERIA
AEIIMRT	AIRTIME
AEIIMRV	VIREMIA
AEIIMST	AMITIES
	ATIMIES
AEIIMTT	IMITATE
AEIINNS	ASININE
	INSANIE
AEIINOP	EPINAOI
AEIINQU	EQUINIA
AEIINRR	RAINIER
AEIINRS	SENARII
AEIINRT	INERTIA
AEIINST	ISATINE
AEIINSX	SIXAINE
AEIINTX	AXINITE
AEIIPRR	PRAIRIE
AEIIRRV	RIVIERA
	VAIRIER
AEIIRST	AIRIEST
	IRISATE
AEIIRSW	AIRWISE
AEIITTV	VITIATE
AEIJKLW	JAWLIKE
AEIJLNV	JAVELIN
AEIJLNW	JAWLINE
AEIJLRS	JAILERS
AEIJLSZ	JEZAILS
AEIJMMR	JAMMIER
AEIJMMS	JAMMIES
	JEMIMAS
AEIJMNS	JASMINE
AEIJNRS	INJERAS

AEIJNRT	JANTIER
	NARTJIE
AEIJNST	JANTIES
	TAJINES
AEIJNTU	JAUNTIE
AEIJRSV	JARVIES
AEIJRZZ	JAZZIER
AEIJSSV	JIVEASS
AEIKKLO	OAKLIKE
AEIKKPS	PIKAKES
AEIKLLW	LAWLIKE
AEIKLLY	LEAKILY
AEIKLMN	MANLIKE
AEIKLMP	MAPLIKE
AEIKLMR	ARMLIKE
AEIKLNO	KAOLINE
AEIKLNR	LANKIER
AEIKLNS	ALKINES
AEIKLNT	ANTLIKE
AEIKLNU	UNALIKE
AEIKLOR	OARLIKE
AEIKLOT	KEITLOA
	OATLIKE
AEIKLRR	LARKIER
AEIKLRS	LAIKERS
	SERKALI
AEIKLRT	RATLIKE
	TALKIER
AEIKLRV	KLAVIER
AEIKLRW	WARLIKE
AEIKLRY	RAYLIKE
AEIKLSS	ALSIKES
	ASSLIKE
AEIKLST	LAKIEST
	TALKIES
AEIKLSW	SAWLIKE
AEIKLWX	WAXLIKE
AEIKMMS	MISMAKE
AEIKMNP	PIKEMAN
AEIKMNR	MANKIER
	RAMEKIN
AEIKMNS	KINEMAS
AEIKMPR	RAMPIKE
AEIKMRW	MAWKIER
AEIKMSS	KAMISES
AEIKMST	MISTAKE
AEIKNPR	RANPIKE
AEIKNRR	NARKIER
AEIKNRS	SNAKIER
AEIKNRT	KERATIN
AEIKNRW	WANKIER
AEIKNSS	KINASES
AEIKNST	INTAKES
	KENTIAS
	TANKIES
AEIKNSW	SWANKIE
AEIKNSY	KYANISE
	YANKIES
AEIKNSZ	KAIZENS
AEIKNTU	UNAKITE
AEIKNTY	KYANITE
AEIKNYZ	KYANIZE
AEIKOST	OAKIEST
AEIKPRR	PARKIER
AEIKPRS	PARKIES
	SPARKIE
AEIKPRW	PAWKIER
AEIKQRU	QUAKIER
AEIKRRS	KERRIAS
	SARKIER
AEIKRSS	KAISERS
	KARSIES
AEIKRST	ARKITES
	KARITES
AEIKRSU	KAURIES
AEIKRSW	SKIWEAR
AEIKRSZ	KARZIES
AEIKSSS	ASKESIS
AEIKSTT	TAKIEST
AEILLMN	MANILLE
AEILLNR	RALLINE
AEILLNS	AINSELL
AEILLNY	ALIENLY
AEILLOV	ALVEOLI
AEILLPR	PALLIER
	PERILLA
AEILLPS	ILLAPSE
AEILLRR	RALLIER
AEILLRS	RALLIES
	SALLIER
AEILLRT	LITERAL
	TALLIER
AEILLRU	RUELLIA
AEILLRW	WALLIER
AEILLSS	ALLISES
	SALLIES
AEILLST	TAILLES
	TALLIES
AEILLSW	WALLIES
AEILLUV	ELUVIAL
AEILLVX	VEXILLA
AEILMMN	MAILMEN
AEILMMR	MALMIER
AEILMMS	LAMMIES
	MELISMA
AEILMNN	LINEMAN
	MELANIN
AEILMNO	MINEOLA
AEILMNP	IMPANEL
	MANIPLE
AEILMNR	MANLIER
	MARLINE
	MINERAL
	RAILMEN
AEILMNS	ISLEMAN
	MALINES
	MENIALS
	SEMINAL
AEILMNT	AILMENT
	ALIMENT
AEILMNU	ALUMINE
AEILMOR	LOAMIER
AEILMPR	IMPALER
	IMPEARL
	LEMPIRA
	PALMIER
AEILMPS	IMPALES
	PALMIES
AEILMPT	IMPLATE
	PALMIET
AEILMRR	LARMIER
	MARLIER
AEILMRS	MAILERS
	REALISM
	REMAILS
AEILMRT	LAMITER
	MALTIER
	MARLITE
AEILMSS	AIMLESS
	MESAILS
	SAMIELS
	SEISMAL
AEILMSZ	MEZAILS
AEILMTY	LAYTIME
	MEATILY
AEILNNY	INANELY
AEILNOP	OPALINE
AEILNOR	AILERON
	ALERION
	ALIENOR
AEILNOS	ANISOLE
AEILNOT	ELATION
	TOENAIL
AEILNPR	PEARLIN
	PLAINER
	PRALINE
AEILNPS	ALPINES
	PINEALS
	SPANIEL
	SPLENIA
AEILNPT	PANTILE
AEILNPW	PINWALE
AEILNPX	EXPLAIN
AEILNQU	EQUINAL
	QUINELA
AEILNRS	ALINERS
	NAILERS
	RENAILS
AEILNRT	ENTRAIL
	LATRINE
	RATLINE
	RELIANT
	RETINAL
	TRENAIL
AEILNRV	RAVELIN
AEILNRW	LAWNIER
AEILNRX	RELAXIN
AEILNRY	INLAYER
	NAILERY
AEILNSS	SALINES
	SILANES
AEILNST	EASTLIN
	ELASTIN
	ENTAILS
	NAILSET
	SALIENT
	SALTINE
	SLAINTE
	STANIEL
	TENAILS
AEILNSU	INSULAE
	INULASE
AEILNSV	ALEVINS
	VALINES
AEILNSW	LAWINES
AEILNSX	ALEXINS
AEILNSY	ELYSIAN
AEILNTU	ALUNITE
AEILNTV	VENTAIL
AEILNUV	UNALIVE
	UNVAILE
AEILNUW	LAUWINE
AEILNVY	NAIVELY
AEILOPR	PELORIA
AEILOPS	LEIPOAS
AEILORV	VARIOLE
AEILOST	ISOLATE
AEILOTV	VIOLATE
AEILPPR	APPERIL
	APPLIER
	ARIPPLE
AEILPPS	APPLIES
	LAPPIES
AEILPRS	PALSIER
	PARLIES
AEILPRT	PLAITER
	PLATIER
AEILPRV	PREVAIL
AEILPSS	ESPIALS
	LAPISES
	LIPASES
	PALSIES
AEILPST	APLITES
	PALIEST
	PLATIES
	TALIPES
AEILPSY	PAISLEY
AEILQTU	LIQUATE
	TEQUILA
AEILRRS	RAILERS
	RERAILS
AEILRRT	RETIRAL
	RETRIAL
	TRAILER
AEILRSS	AIRLESS
	RESAILS
	SAILERS
	SERAILS
	SERIALS
AEILRST	REALIST
	RETAILS
	SALTIER
	SALTIRE
	SLATIER
	TAILERS
AEILRSV	REVISAL
AEILRSW	SWALIER
	WAILERS
AEILRTT	TERTIAL
AEILRTU	URALITE
AEILRTW	WALTIER
AEILRTY	IRATELY
	REALITY
	TEARILY
AEILRVV	REVIVAL
AEILRVY	VIRELAY
AEILRWY	WEARILY
AEILSSS	LAISSES
	LASSIES
AEILSST	SALTIES
AEILSSU	SAULIES
AEILSSV	VALISES
	VESSAIL
AEILSSW	WALISES
AEILSTU	SITULAE
AEILSTV	ESTIVAL
AEILSTW	WALIEST
AEILSTY	TAILYES
AEILSTZ	LAZIEST
AEILTVY	VILAYET
AEILUVX	EXUVIAL
AEIMMMS	MAMMIES
AEIMMNS	AMMINES
	MISNAME
AEIMMRR	RAMMIER
AEIMMRS	MAIMERS
	RAMMIES
AEIMMRT	MARMITE
AEIMMST	MISMATE
	SEMIMAT
	TAMMIES
AEIMMZZ	MIZMAZE
AEIMNNT	MANNITE
AEIMNOR	MORAINE
	ROMAINE
AEIMNOS	ANOMIES
AEIMNOT	AMNIOTE
AEIMNOU	MOINEAU
AEIMNRR	MARINER
AEIMNRS	MARINES
	REMAINS
	SEMINAR
	SIRNAME
AEIMNRT	MINARET
	RAIMENT
AEIMNRV	VERMIAN
AEIMNRW	WIREMAN
AEIMNSS	INSEAMS
	SAMISEN
AEIMNST	ETAMINS

	INMATES
	MAINEST
	MANTIES
	TAMEINS
	TAMINES
AEIMNSW	MANWISE
AEIMNTX	TAXIMEN
AEIMNTY	AMENITY
	ANYTIME
AEIMNUV	MAUVEIN
	MAUVINE
AEIMOOP	IPOMOEA
AEIMOPR	EMPORIA
	MEROPIA
AEIMORR	ARMOIRE
AEIMOST	AMOSITE
	ATOMIES
	ATOMISE
	OSMIATE
AEIMOTX	TOXEMIA
AEIMOTZ	ATOMIZE
AEIMPRR	RAMPIRE
AEIMPRS	IMPRESA
	SAMPIRE
AEIMPRT	PRIMATE
AEIMPRV	VAMPIRE
AEIMPSS	IMPASSE
	PESSIMA
AEIMPST	IMPASTE
	PASTIME
AEIMPSV	IMPAVES
AEIMPSW	MAPWISE
AEIMPSY	PYEMIAS
AEIMRRR	MARRIER
AEIMRRS	MARRIES
	SIMARRE
AEIMRSS	MASSIER
AEIMRST	IMARETS
	MAESTRI
	MAISTER
	MASTIER
	MISRATE
	SEMITAR
	SMARTIE
AEIMRSU	UREMIAS
AEIMRSV	MISAVER
AEIMRSW	AWMRIES
	SEMIRAW
AEIMRTU	MURIATE
AEIMRTV	VITAMER
AEIMRTW	WARTIME
AEIMSSS	AMISSES
	MESSIAS
AEIMSST	ASTEISM
	MISEATS
	MISSEAT
	SAMIEST
	SAMITES
	TAMISES
AEIMSSV	MASSIVE
	MAVISES
AEIMSSW	SWAMIES
AEIMSSY	MYIASES
AEIMSTT	ETATISM
	MATIEST
	MATTIES
AEIMSTZ	MAZIEST
	MESTIZA
AEIMSUV	AMUSIVE
AEIMSXX	MAXIXES
AEIMTYZ	AZYMITE
AEINNNS	NANNIES
AEINNOT	ENATION
AEINNPR	PANNIER
AEINNPT	PANTINE
	PINNATE
AEINNRS	INSANER
	INSNARE
AEINNRT	ENTRAIN
	TRANNIE
AEINNRU	ANEURIN
AEINNSS	SANNIES
	SIENNAS
AEINNST	INANEST
	STANINE
AEINNSZ	ENZIANS
AEINNTT	ANTIENT
AEINOPS	EPINAOS
	SENOPIA
AEINOPZ	EPIZOAN
AEINORS	ERASION
AEINORT	OTARINE
AEINOSS	ANOESIS
AEINOST	ATONIES
AEINOSV	EVASION
AEINOSZ	AZIONES
AEINOXZ	OXAZINE
AEINPPP	PANPIPE
AEINPPR	NAPPIER
AEINPPS	NAPPIES
	PINESAP
AEINPRS	PANIERS
	RAPINES
AEINPRT	PAINTER
	PERTAIN
	REPAINT
AEINPSS	ASPINES
	PANSIES
	SAPIENS
AEINPST	PANTIES
	PATINES
	SAPIENT
	SPINATE
AEINPTT	PATIENT
AEINPTU	PETUNIA
AEINPTY	PANEITY
AEINQTU	ANTIQUE
	QUINATE
AEINRRS	SIERRAN
	SNARIER
AEINRRT	RETRAIN
	TERRAIN
	TRAINER
AEINRSS	ARSINES
	SARNIES
AEINRST	ANESTRI
	ANTSIER
	NASTIER
	RATINES
	RESIANT
	RETAINS
	RETINAS
	RETSINA
	STAINER
	STARNIE
	STEARIN
AEINRSV	AVENIRS
	RAVINES
AEINRTT	INTREAT
	ITERANT
	NATTIER
	NITRATE
	TARTINE
	TERTIAN
AEINRTU	RUINATE
	TAURINE
	URANITE
	URINATE
AEINRTW	TAWNIER
	TINWARE
AEINRUV	VAURIEN
AEINRUW	UNWARIE
AEINRUZ	AZURINE
AEINRVV	VERVAIN
AEINRWY	YAWNIER
AEINSSS	SANSEIS
	SASINES
AEINSST	ENTASIS
	NASTIES
	SESTINA
	TANSIES
	TISANES
AEINSSV	SAVINES
	VINASSE
AEINSTT	INSTATE
	SATINET
AEINSTU	AUNTIES
	SINUATE
AEINSTV	NAIVEST
	NATIVES
	VAINEST
AEINSTW	AWNIEST
	TAWNIES
	WANIEST
	WANTIES
AEINSTX	ANTISEX
	SEXTAIN
AEINSTZ	ZANIEST
	ZEATINS
AEINSVV	NAVVIES
AEINSWY	ANYWISE
AEINTUV	VAUNTIE
AEINTVW	VAWNTIE
AEINTVY	NAIVETY
AEINTXY	ANXIETY
AEIOPRS	SOAPIER
AEIOPSS	SOAPIES
AEIOPST	ATOPIES
	OPIATES
AEIOQSU	SEQUOIA
AEIORRR	ARRIERO
	ROARIER
AEIORST	OARIEST
	OTARIES
AEIORSV	OVARIES
AEIOSTT	OSTIATE
	TOASTIE
AEIOSTZ	AZOTISE
AEIOTZZ	AZOTIZE
AEIPPPR	PAPPIER
AEIPPPS	PAPPIES
AEIPPRS	APPRISE
	SAPPIER
AEIPPRT	PERIAPT
AEIPPRY	YAPPIER
AEIPPRZ	APPRIZE
	ZAPPIER
AEIPPSS	PASPIES
AEIPPSY	YAPPIES
AEIPRRS	ASPIRER
	PARRIES
	PRAISER
	RAPIERS
	RASPIER
	REPAIRS
AEIPRRT	PARTIER
AEIPRSS	ASPIRES
	PARESIS
	PARISES
	PRAISES
	SPIREAS
AEIPRST	PARTIES
	PASTIER
	PIASTER
	PIASTRE
	PIRATES
	PRATIES
	TRAIPSE
AEIPRSU	SPURIAE
	UPRAISE
AEIPRSV	PARVISE
	PAVISER
AEIPRSW	WASPIER
AEIPRTT	PARTITE
AEIPRTV	PRIVATE
AEIPRTW	WIRETAP
AEIPRXY	PYREXIA
AEIPSSS	ASEPSIS
	ASPISES
AEIPSST	PASTIES
	PATSIES
	PETSAIS
	TAPISES
AEIPSSV	PASSIVE
	PAVISES
	SPAVIES
AEIPSSW	WASPIES
AEIPSTT	PATTIES
	TAPETIS
AEIPSTU	TAUPIES
AEIPSTV	SPAVIET
AEIPSTW	TAWPIES
AEIPTXY	EPITAXY
AEIQRUV	AQUIVER
AEIQSSU	SAIQUES
AEIRRRT	TARRIER
AEIRRRV	ARRIVER
AEIRRSS	ARRISES
	RAISERS
	SIERRAS
AEIRRST	ARTSIER
	SERRATI
	TARRIES
	TARSIER
AEIRRSV	ARRIVES
	VARIERS
AEIRRTT	RATTIER
	RETRAIT
	TARTIER
AEIRRTW	WARTIER
AEIRRTY	RETIARY
AEIRRVV	VIVERRA
AEIRSSS	SASSIER
AEIRSST	ARTSIES
	SAIREST
	SATIRES
	TIRASSE
AEIRSSU	SAURIES
AEIRSSZ	ASSIZER
AEIRSTT	ARTIEST
	ARTISTE
	ATTIRES
	IRATEST
	RATITES
	STRIATE
	TASTIER
	TERTIAS
AEIRSTV	TAIVERS
	VASTIER
	VERITAS
AEIRSTW	WAISTER
	WAITERS
	WARIEST
	WASTRIE
AEIRSVV	SAVVIER
AEIRSVW	WAIVERS
AEIRTTT	ATTRITE
	TATTIER
	TITRATE
AEIRTTV	TAIVERT

AEIRTTW	TAWTIER
AEIRTTX	EXTRAIT
AEIRTUY	AUREITY
AEIRTUZ	AZURITE
AEIRTVY	VARIETY
AEIRWWY	WIREWAY
AEISSSS	SASSIES
AEISSST	SIESTAS
	TASSIES
AEISSSW	WISEASS
AEISSSZ	ASSIZES
AEISSUV	SUASIVE
AEISSUX	AUXESIS
AEISSVV	SAVVIES
AEISTTT	ETATIST
	TATTIES
AEISTTU	SITUATE
AEISTTV	STATIVE
AEISTTW	TAWIEST
	TWAITES
AEISTTX	TAXITES
AEISTTY	SATIETY
AEISTVW	WAVIEST
AEISTWX	TAXWISE
	WAXIEST
AEITTTU	ATTUITE
AEITTTV	VITTATE
AEJJLNU	JEJUNAL
AEJKMNR	JARKMEN
AEJKNRS	JANKERS
AEJKPTU	KAJEPUT
AEJLNUV	JUVENAL
AEJLOSU	JALOUSE
	JEALOUS
AEJLOUZ	AZULEJO
AEJMMRS	JAMMERS
AEJMNZZ	JAZZMEN
AEJMRST	RAMJETS
AEJMSST	JETSAMS
AEJMSSY	JESSAMY
AEJMSTY	MAJESTY
AEJNNOS	JOANNES
AEJNORZ	ZANJERO
AEJNSST	JESSANT
AEJNSSU	JAUNSES
AEJPRSS	JASPERS
AEJPRSY	JASPERY
AEJRSVY	JARVEYS
AEJRSZZ	JAZZERS
AEKKNRS	KRAKENS
AEKKRSY	YAKKERS
AEKLLTU	KELLAUT
AEKLMOU	LEUKOMA
AEKLNPP	KNAPPLE
AEKLNPR	PRANKLE
AEKLNRS	RANKLES
AEKLNRV	KLAVERN
AEKLNST	ANKLETS
	ASKLENT
	LANKEST
AEKLNSW	KNAWELS
AEKLNSY	ALKYNES
AEKLORY	ROKELAY
AEKLOST	SKATOLE
AEKLOVZ	ZELKOVA
AEKLPRS	SPARKLE
AEKLPSS	SPLAKES
AEKLRRS	LARKERS
AEKLRSS	SLAKERS
AEKLRST	STALKER
	TALKERS
AEKLRSV	LEKVARS
AEKLRSW	WALKERS
AEKLRUW	WAULKER
AEKLSST	LASKETS
	SKLATES
AEKLSTU	AUKLETS
AEKMMNR	MARKMEN
AEKMNOS	SOKEMAN
AEKMNRU	UNMAKER
AEKMNSU	UNMAKES
AEKMOOT	MATOOKE
AEKMOST	MATOKES
AEKMPRU	UPMAKER
AEKMPSU	MAKEUPS
	UPMAKES
AEKMRRS	MARKERS
	REMARKS
AEKMRSS	MASKERS
AEKMRST	MARKETS
AEKNNOP	NONPEAK
AEKNNRS	ENRANKS
AEKNNST	KANTENS
AEKNNTU	UNTAKEN
AEKNPPR	KNAPPER
AEKNPRS	SPANKER
AEKNPSU	UNSPEAK
AEKNPTU	UPTAKEN
AEKNRRS	RANKERS
AEKNRSS	KRANSES
AEKNRST	RANKEST
	STARKEN
	TANKERS
AEKNRSU	UNRAKES
AEKNRSW	SWANKER
	WANKERS
AEKNRSY	YANKERS
AEKNRSZ	KRANZES
AEKNRVY	KNAVERY
AEKNSSU	ANKUSES
AEKNSWY	SWANKEY
AEKOPRS	PRESOAK
AEKORRS	ROSAKER
AEKORSS	ARKOSES
	RESOAKS
	SOAKERS
AEKOTTU	OUTTAKE
	TAKEOUT
AEKPPSU	UPSPAKE
	UPSPEAK
AEKPRRS	PARKERS
	REPARKS
	SPARKER
AEKPRSS	SPARKES
AEKPSSY	PASSKEY
AEKPSTU	TAKEUPS
	UPTAKES
AEKQRSU	QUAKERS
AEKQSSU	SQUEAKS
AEKQSUY	SQUEAKY
AEKRRST	KARTERS
	KRATERS
	STARKER
AEKRSST	SKATERS
	STRAKES
	STREAKS
	TASKERS
AEKRSSY	KARSEYS
AEKRSTY	STREAKY
AEKRSUW	WAUKERS
AEKSSSV	KVASSES
AEKSWYY	KEYWAYS
AELLMNU	LUMENAL
AELLMRS	SMALLER
AELLMRT	TRAMELL
AELLMST	MALLETS
AELLMSU	MALLEUS
AELLMSY	MELLAYS
	MESALLY
AELLMTY	METALLY
AELLMWX	MAXWELL
AELLNOP	PALLONE
AELLNOR	LLANERO
AELLNOV	NOVELLA
AELLNOY	ALONELY
AELLNPY	PENALLY
AELLNRT	ENTRALL
AELLNSS	ALLNESS
AELLNSW	ENWALLS
AELLNTT	TALLENT
AELLNUU	LUNULAE
AELLNVY	VENALLY
AELLORS	ROSELLA
AELLORT	REALLOT
AELLORV	ALLOVER
	OVERALL
AELLORY	LOYALER
AELLOSS	LOESSAL
AELLPPS	LAPPELS
AELLPRS	SPALLER
AELLPRU	PLEURAL
AELLPSS	SPALLES
AELLPST	PALLETS
AELLPTU	PLUTEAL
AELLPTY	PLAYLET
AELLQUY	EQUALLY
AELLRRU	ALLURER
AELLRST	STELLAR
	TELLARS
AELLRSU	ALLURES
	LAURELS
AELLRSW	WALLERS
AELLRSY	RALLYES
AELLRTY	ALERTLY
	ELYTRAL
AELLRVY	RAVELLY
AELLSST	SALLETS
	STELLAS
	TASSELL
AELLSSW	LAWLESS
AELLSTT	TALLEST
	TALLETS
AELLSTW	SETWALL
	SWALLET
	WALLETS
AELLSTY	STALELY
AELLSVY	VALLEYS
AELLTUU	ULULATE
AELLUVV	VALVULE
AELMMNO	MAMELON
AELMMNS	ALMSMEN
AELMMNT	MALTMEN
AELMMOY	MYELOMA
AELMMRS	LAMMERS
	SLAMMER
AELMMRT	TRAMMEL
AELMMST	STAMMEL
AELMMSY	MALMSEY
AELMNNS	LENSMAN
AELMNOR	ALMONER
	NEMORAL
AELMNOS	MELANOS
AELMNOT	LOMENTA
	OMENTAL
	TELAMON
AELMNPR	LAMPERN
AELMNRS	ALMNERS
AELMNRU	NUMERAL
AELMNSS	MANLESS
AELMNST	LAMENTS
	MANTELS
	MANTLES
AELMNSU	MENSUAL
AELMNTT	MANTLET
AELMNTU	NUTMEAL
AELMOPR	PLEROMA
	RAMPOLE
AELMOPU	AMPOULE
AELMOPY	MAYPOLE
AELMORS	MORALES
AELMORT	MOLERAT
AELMORU	MORULAE
AELMORV	REMOVAL
AELMOST	MALTOSE
AELMOSY	AMYLOSE
AELMOTT	MATELOT
AELMPRS	EMPARLS
	LAMPERS
	PALMERS
	SAMPLER
AELMPRT	TEMPLAR
	TRAMPLE
AELMPRY	LAMPREY
AELMPSS	SAMPLES
AELMPST	AMPLEST
AELMPSU	AMPULES
AELMPTU	PLUMATE
AELMRRS	MARRELS
AELMRSS	ARMLESS
AELMRST	ARMLETS
	LAMSTER
	MARTELS
	TRAMELS
AELMRSU	MAULERS
	SERUMAL
AELMRSV	MARVELS
AELMRTT	MARTLET
AELMSST	MATLESS
	SAMLETS
AELMSTU	AMULETS
	MULETAS
AELNNPR	PLANNER
AELNNPS	PENNALS
AELNNPU	UNPANEL
AELNNRS	ENSNARL
	LANNERS
AELNNRT	LANTERN
AELNNRU	UNLEARN
AELNNST	STANNEL
AELNNTU	ANNULET
AELNOOS	ALSOONE
AELNOPS	ESPANOL
AELNOPT	POLENTA
AELNOPU	APOLUNE
AELNORS	LOANERS
	ORLEANS
	RELOANS
AELNORU	ALEURON
AELNORV	VERONAL
AELNOST	ETALONS
	TOLANES
AELNOTV	VOLANTE
AELNOTY	ANOLYTE
AELNOUZ	ZONULAE
AELNPPR	PREPLAN
AELNPPY	PLAYPEN
AELNPRS	PLANERS
	REPLANS
AELNPRT	PANTLER
	PLANTER
	REPLANT
AELNPRY	PLENARY
AELNPSS	NAPLESS
AELNPST	PLANETS
	PLATENS
AELNPSU	UPLEANS
AELNPTU	UPLEANT
AELNPTX	EXPLANT
AELNPTY	APLENTY
	PENALTY

AELNQUU	UNEQUAL
AELNRRS	SNARLER
AELNRSS	RANSELS
AELNRST	ANTLERS
	RENTALS
	SALTERN
	STERNAL
AELNRSZ	RANZELS
AELNRTT	TRENTAL
AELNRTU	NEUTRAL
AELNRTV	VENTRAL
AELNRUU	NEURULA
AELNRUV	UNRAVEL
	VENULAR
AELNSSU	SENSUAL
	UNSEALS
AELNSSW	AWNLESS
AELNSSX	LAXNESS
AELNSTT	LATENTS
	LATTENS
	TALENTS
AELNSTU	ELUANTS
	UNLASTE
AELNSTV	LEVANTS
AELNSTY	STANYEL
AELNSTZ	ZELANTS
AELNSUW	UNWEALS
AELNTUV	ENVAULT
AELOORS	AEROSOL
	ROSEOLA
AELOPPR	PROPALE
AELOPPX	APOPLEX
AELOPRR	PERORAL
	PREORAL
AELOPRS	PAROLES
	REPOSAL
AELOPRT	PROLATE
AELOPRV	OVERLAP
AELOPST	APOSTLE
	PELOTAS
AELOPSX	EXPOSAL
AELOPTT	PALETOT
AELOPTU	OUTLEAP
AELORRT	REALTOR
	RELATOR
AELORSS	LASSOER
	OARLESS
	SEROSAL
	SOLERAS
AELORST	OESTRAL
AELORTU	TORULAE
AELORTV	LEVATOR
AELORTY	ROYALET
AELORTZ	ZELATOR
AELORUU	ROULEAU
AELORVX	OVERLAX
AELORVY	LAYOVER
	OVERLAY
AELORWY	OWRELAY
AELOSSS	LASSOES
AELOSST	SOLATES
AELOSSV	SALVOES
AELOSSW	LEASOWS
AELOSTV	SOLVATE
AELOSTZ	ZEALOTS
AELOSUZ	ZEALOUS
AELOSVY	SAVELOY
AELOTTU	TOLUATE
AELOTUV	OVULATE
AELOTVV	VOLVATE
AELOTVY	OVATELY
AELPPRS	LAPPERS
	RAPPELS
	SLAPPER
AELPPRY	REAPPLY
AELPPSS	SAPPLES
AELPPST	APPLETS
	LAPPETS
	STAPPLE
AELPPSU	APPULSE
	PAPULES
	UPLEAPS
AELPPTU	UPLEAPT
AELPQSU	PLAQUES
AELPRRS	PARRELS
AELPRSS	LAPSERS
AELPRST	PALTERS
	PERSALT
	PLASTER
	PLATERS
	PSALTER
	STAPLER
AELPRSU	PERUSAL
	PLEURAS
	SERPULA
AELPRSW	PRAWLES
AELPRSY	PARLEYS
	PARSLEY
	PLAYERS
	REPLAYS
	SPARELY
AELPRTT	PARTLET
	PLATTER
	PRATTLE
AELPRTY	PEARTLY
	PEYTRAL
	PRELATY
	PTERYLA
AELPRUY	EPULARY
AELPSSS	PASSELS
	SAPLESS
AELPSST	PASTELS
	STAPLES
AELPSTT	PATTLES
	PELTAST
AELPSTU	PULSATE
	PUTEALS
	SPATULE
AELPSTZ	SPATZLE
AELPUUV	UPVALUE
AELQRRU	QUARREL
AELQSSU	LASQUES
	SQUEALS
AELQSUZ	QUEZALS
AELQTUZ	QUETZAL
AELRRSU	SURREAL
AELRRSW	WARSLER
AELRRTT	RATTLER
AELRRTW	TRAWLER
AELRSSS	RASSLES
AELRSST	ARTLESS
	LASTERS
	SALTERS
	SLATERS
	TARSELS
AELRSSU	SAURELS
AELRSSV	SALVERS
	SERVALS
	SLAVERS
	VERSALS
AELRSSW	WARLESS
	WARSLES
	WRASSLE
AELRSSY	RAYLESS
	SLAYERS
AELRSTT	RATTLES
	SLATTER
	STARLET
	STARTLE
	TATLERS
AELRSTU	ESTRUAL
	SALUTER
AELRSTV	TRAVELS
	VARLETS
	VESTRAL
AELRSTW	WARSTLE
	WASTREL
	WRASTLE
AELRSTY	RAYLETS
AELRSUV	VALUERS
AELRSVV	VARVELS
AELRSVY	SLAVERY
AELRSWX	WRAXLES
AELRSWY	LAWYERS
AELRSZZ	RAZZLES
AELRTTT	TARTLET
	TATTLER
AELRTTU	TUTELAR
AELRTUV	VAULTER
AELRTWY	TRAWLEY
AELRTWZ	WALTZER
AELSSST	TASSELS
AELSSTT	LATESTS
	SALTEST
	STALEST
	TASLETS
AELSSTU	SALUTES
	TALUSES
AELSSTV	VESTALS
AELSSTW	WASTELS
AELSSTX	TAXLESS
AELSSTY	LYSATES
AELSSUV	AVULSES
AELSSVY	SLAVEYS
AELSSWY	WAYLESS
AELSTTT	TATTLES
AELSTTW	WATTLES
AELSTTY	STATELY
	STYLATE
AELSTUX	LUXATES
AELSTWZ	WALTZES
AELSUVY	SUAVELY
AELSWZZ	SWAZZLE
AELTTTW	TWATTLE
AELTTUX	TEXTUAL
AELTUVV	VULVATE
AEMMMRS	MAMMERS
AEMMMST	MAMMETS
AEMMMSY	MAMMEYS
AEMMNOT	MOMENTA
AEMMNSS	MESSMAN
AEMMNTU	AMENTUM
AEMMORS	MARMOSE
AEMMORW	WOMMERA
AEMMPRS	SPAMMER
AEMMRRS	RAMMERS
AEMMRST	STAMMER
AEMMRSY	YAMMERS
AEMMRSZ	MAMZERS
AEMMSST	STEMMAS
AEMMSTU	MAUMETS
	SUMMATE
AEMMSTW	MAWMETS
AEMNNOR	MONERAN
AEMNNOS	MANNOSE
AEMNNOT	MONTANE
	NONMEAT
AEMNNOU	NOUMENA
AEMNNOZ	MENAZON
AEMNNRS	MANNERS
AEMNNRT	MANRENT
	REMNANT
AEMNNSW	NEWSMAN
AEMNNTU	UNMEANT
AEMNOPR	MANROPE
	REPOMAN
AEMNOPS	MOPANES
AEMNOPZ	ZAMPONE
AEMNORS	ENAMORS
	MOANERS
	OARSMEN
AEMNORT	TONEARM
AEMNORU	ENAMOUR
	NEUROMA
AEMNORV	OVERMAN
AEMNORY	ANYMORE
	ROMNEYA
AEMNOSS	MONASES
AEMNOST	MANTOES
AEMNOTT	TOMENTA
AEMNOTU	AUTOMEN
	NOTAEUM
	OUTNAME
AEMNPSS	PASSMEN
AEMNPST	ENSTAMP
	TAPSMEN
AEMNPSU	PNEUMAS
AEMNPTU	PUTAMEN
AEMNPTY	PAYMENT
AEMNRRU	MANURER
AEMNRST	ARTSMEN
	MARTENS
	SARMENT
	SMARTEN
AEMNRSU	MANURES
	MURENAS
	SURNAME
AEMNRTU	TRUEMAN
AEMNRTV	VARMENT
AEMNSSS	MESSANS
AEMNSST	STAMENS
AEMNSSU	UNSEAMS
AEMNSTU	UNTAMES
	UNTEAMS
AEMNSTY	AMNESTY
AEMNTTU	NUTMEAT
AEMNTWY	WAYMENT
AEMOORT	TEAROOM
AEMOORW	WOOMERA
AEMOOST	OSTEOMA
AEMOOSV	AMOOVES
	VAMOOSE
AEMOPPR	PAMPERO
AEMOPSZ	APOZEMS
AEMORRR	ARMORER
AEMORRS	REMORAS
	ROAMERS
AEMORRV	OVERARM
AEMORRW	EARWORM
AEMORST	AMORETS
	MAESTRO
	OMERTAS
AEMORSU	RAMEOUS
AEMORSW	SEAWORM
	WOMERAS
AEMORSX	XEROMAS
AEMOSST	OSMATES
AEMOSSV	VAMOSES
AEMOSTT	STOMATE
AEMOSTW	TWASOME
AEMOSUZ	ZAMOUSE
AEMOSWY	SOMEWAY
AEMOTTZ	MOZETTA
AEMPPRS	MAPPERS
	PAMPERS
	PREAMPS
AEMPPRY	MAPPERY
AEMPRRS	PREARMS
	RAMPERS
AEMPRRT	TRAMPER

AEMPRRW	PREWARM
AEMPRST	EMPARTS
	RESTAMP
	STAMPER
	TAMPERS
AEMPRSV	REVAMPS
	VAMPERS
AEMPRSW	SWAMPER
AEMPRTT	TRAMPET
AEMPRTU	TEMPURA
AEMPSSU	EMPUSAS
AEMPTTT	ATTEMPT
AEMPTTU	TAPETUM
AEMQRSU	MARQUES
	MASQUER
AEMQSSU	MASQUES
	SQUAMES
AEMRRRS	MARRERS
AEMRRRY	REMARRY
AEMRRST	ARMREST
	SMARTER
AEMRRSU	ARMURES
AEMRRSV	MARVERS
AEMRRSW	REWARMS
	SWARMER
	WARMERS
AEMRRTU	ERRATUM
	MATURER
AEMRSST	MASTERS
	STREAMS
AEMRSSU	AMUSERS
	ASSUMER
	MASSEUR
AEMRSTT	MATTERS
	SMATTER
AEMRSTU	MATURES
	STRUMAE
AEMRSTW	WARMEST
AEMRSTY	MASTERY
	MAYSTER
	STREAMY
AEMRTTX	MARTEXT
AEMRTTY	MATTERY
AEMRTUU	TRUMEAU
AEMSSSU	ASSUMES
AEMSSTU	MUTASES
AEMSSUW	WAMUSES
AEMSSYZ	ZYMASES
AEMSTTU	MUTATES
AEMSTUV	MAUVEST
AEMSTVZ	ZEMSTVA
AEMSUZZ	MEZUZAS
AENNNOS	NONANES
AENNNPT	PENNANT
AENNOPS	PANNOSE
AENNORT	NORTENA
AENNORY	ANNOYER
AENNOSS	NOSEANS
AENNOSV	NOVENAS
AENNOSY	ANYONES
AENNOTU	TONNEAU
AENNPRS	SPANNER
AENNQTU	QUANNET
AENNRST	TANNERS
AENNRSV	VANNERS
AENNRTT	ENTRANT
AENNRTV	VERNANT
AENNRTY	TANNERY
	TYRANNE
AENNSSW	WANNESS
AENNSTT	TANNEST
	TENANTS
AENNSTW	WANNEST
AENOOTZ	ENTOZOA
	OZONATE
AENOPPR	PROPANE
AENOPRS	PERSONA
AENOPRT	OPERANT
	PRONATE
	PROTEAN
AENOPST	TEOPANS
AENOPSU	POSAUNE
AENOPSV	PAVONES
AENOPSW	WEAPONS
AENORRS	SERRANO
AENORRT	ORNATER
AENORRV	OVERRAN
AENORSS	REASONS
	SENORAS
AENORST	ATONERS
	SENATOR
	TREASON
AENORSU	ARENOUS
AENORTU	OUTEARN
AENORTV	VENATOR
AENORXY	ANOREXY
AENOSSS	SEASONS
AENOSST	ASTONES
AENOSSW	WEASONS
AENOSTT	ATTONES
	NOTATES
AENOSTU	SOUTANE
AENOSVW	WAVESON
AENOUUV	NOUVEAU
AENPPRS	NAPPERS
	PARPENS
	PARSNEP
	SNAPPER
AENPPRT	PARPENT
AENPPRU	UNPAPER
AENPPST	PETNAPS
AENPRRT	PARTNER
AENPRRW	PRAWNER
	PREWARN
AENPRST	ARPENTS
	ENTRAPS
	PANTERS
	PARENTS
	PASTERN
	PERSANT
	TREPANS
AENPRSW	ENWRAPS
	PAWNERS
	SPAWNER
AENPRSZ	PANZERS
AENPRTT	PATTERN
	REPTANT
AENPRUV	PARVENU
AENPSST	APTNESS
	PATNESS
	PESANTS
AENPSSY	SYNAPSE
AENPSTT	PATENTS
	PATTENS
AENPSTU	PEANUTS
	PESAUNT
AENPSTW	STEWPAN
AENPSTY	SYNAPTE
AENPSTZ	PEZANTS
AENQSTU	EQUANTS
AENRRSS	SERRANS
	SNARERS
AENRRST	ERRANTS
	RANTERS
AENRRSW	WARNERS
	WARRENS
AENRRSY	YARNERS
AENRRTT	TRANTER
AENRRTY	TERNARY
AENRSSS	SARSENS
AENRSST	SARSNET
	TRANSES
AENRSSW	ANSWERS
	RAWNESS
AENRSSY	SARNEYS
AENRSTT	NATTERS
	RATTENS
AENRSTU	AUNTERS
	NATURES
	SAUNTER
AENRSTV	SERVANT
	TAVERNS
	VERSANT
AENRSTW	STRAWEN
	WANTERS
AENRSTY	TRAYNES
AENRSUW	UNSWEAR
	UNWARES
AENRSUY	SYNURAE
AENRSWY	YAWNERS
AENRTTU	TAUNTER
AENRTTY	NATTERY
AENRTUV	VAUNTER
AENRTUW	UNWATER
AENRUWY	UNWEARY
AENSSST	ASSENTS
	SNASTES
AENSSTU	NASUTES
	UNSEATS
AENSSTX	SEXTANS
AENSSTY	STAYNES
AENSSTZ	STANZES
AENSSWY	SAWNEYS
AENSSXY	SYNAXES
AENSTTT	ATTENTS
AENSTTU	ATTUNES
	NUTATES
	TAUTENS
	TETANUS
	UNSTATE
AENSTTX	SEXTANT
AENSTUX	UNTAXES
AENSTWY	TAWNEYS
AENTTTU	ATTUENT
AEOOPPS	PAPOOSE
AEOOPRS	OROPESA
AEOPPPS	PAPPOSE
AEOPPRS	APPOSER
AEOPPRV	APPROVE
AEOPPSS	APPOSES
AEOPQRU	OPAQUER
AEOPQSU	OPAQUES
AEOPRRT	PRAETOR
	PRORATE
AEOPRRV	VAPORER
AEOPRSS	SOAPERS
AEOPRST	ESPARTO
	PROTEAS
	SEAPORT
AEOPRTT	PORTATE
AEOPRTV	OVERAPT
AEOPRVY	OVERPAY
AEOPRWY	ROPEWAY
AEOPSSS	PSOASES
AEOPSST	PETASOS
	SAPOTES
AEOPSTT	APTOTES
	TEAPOTS
AEOPSTY	TEAPOYS
AEOPSTZ	TOPAZES
AEOQRTU	EQUATOR
	QUORATE
AEOQRUV	VAQUERO
AEOQSUU	AQUEOUS
AEORRRS	ROARERS
AEORRSS	SOARERS
AEORRST	ROASTER
AEORRSU	AROUSER
AEORRSV	SAVORER
AEORSSS	SAROSES
	SEROSAS
AEORSSU	AROUSES
AEORSTT	ROTATES
	TOASTER
AEORSUV	AVOURES
AEORSVW	AVOWERS
	OVERSAW
	REAVOWS
AEORSVY	AVOYERS
AEORTTU	OUTRATE
AEORTUV	OUTRAVE
AEORTUW	OUTWEAR
AEORTVX	OVERTAX
AEOSSTV	AVOSETS
AEOSTTU	OUTEATS
AEOSUVZ	ZOUAVES
AEPPRRS	RAPPERS
AEPPRRT	TRAPPER
AEPPRRW	PREWRAP
	WRAPPER
AEPPRSS	APPRESS
	SAPPERS
AEPPRST	TAPPERS
AEPPRSU	PAUPERS
	UPSPEAR
AEPPRSW	SWAPPER
	WAPPERS
AEPPRSY	PREPAYS
	YAPPERS
AEPPRSZ	ZAPPERS
AEPPSTT	TAPPETS
AEPPSTU	PASTEUP
	PUPATES
AEPQRTU	PARQUET
AEPRRRS	SPARRER
AEPRRSS	PARSERS
	RASPERS
	SPARERS
	SPARRES
	SPARSER
AEPRRST	PARTERS
	PRATERS
AEPRRSU	PARURES
	UPREARS
AEPRRSW	REWRAPS
	WARPERS
AEPRRSY	PRAYERS
	RESPRAY
	SPRAYER
AEPRRTU	PARTURE
	RAPTURE
AEPRRTW	REWRAPT
AEPRRTY	PARTYER
	PETRARY
AEPRSSS	PASSERS
AEPRSST	PASTERS
	REPASTS
	SPAREST
AEPRSSU	PAUSERS
AEPRSSY	PESSARY
AEPRSTT	PATTERS
	SPATTER
	TAPSTER
AEPRSTU	PASTURE
	UPRATES
	UPSTARE
	UPTEARS
AEPRSTY	YAPSTER
AEPRSTZ	PATZERS
AEPRSUX	ARUSPEX

AEPRSUY	YAUPERS
AEPRSWY	YAWPERS
AEPRSYY	SPRAYEY
AEPRTXY	APTERYX
AEPSSTU	PETASUS
AEPSSZZ	SPAZZES
AEPSTTU	UPSTATE
AEPSZZZ	PZAZZES
AEQRRSU	SQUARER
AEQRRTU	QUARTER
AEQRSSU	SQUARES
AEQRSTU	QUAREST
	QUARTES
	QUATRES
AEQRSUV	QUAVERS
AEQRTTU	QUARTET
AEQRUVY	QUAVERY
AEQSSSU	QUASSES
AERRSST	ARRESTS
	RASTERS
	STARERS
AERRSSU	ASSURER
	RASURES
AERRSTT	RATTERS
	RESTART
	STARTER
AERRSTV	STARVER
AERRSTY	STRAYER
AERRSUZ	RAZURES
AERRSWY	WARREYS
AERRTTY	RATTERY
AERSSST	ASSERTS
	TRASSES
AERSSSU	ASSURES
	SARUSES
AERSSSW	WRASSES
AERSSTT	ASTERTS
	STARETS
	STATERS
	TASTERS
AERSSTV	STARVES
AERSSTW	WASTERS
AERSSTY	ESTRAYS
	STAYERS
	STAYRES
AERSSUV	VARUSES
AERSSVW	SWARVES
AERSSWY	SAWYERS
	SWAYERS
AERSTTT	STRETTA
	TARTEST
	TATTERS
AERSTTU	ASTUTER
	STATURE
AERSTTV	VATTERS
AERSTTW	SWATTER
	TEWARTS
AERSTTY	YATTERS
AERSTTZ	STARETZ
AERSTUU	AUTEURS
AERSTUY	ESTUARY
AERSTWY	WASTERY
AERTTTY	TATTERY
AERTTUV	VETTURA
AESSSTT	TASSETS
AESSTTT	ATTESTS
AESSTTU	STATUES
AESSTTV	VASTEST
AESSTUV	SUAVEST
AESSTUY	EUSTASY
AESSVVY	SAVVEYS
AESTTTU	STATUTE
	TAUTEST
AESTTTW	WATTEST
AFFFGIN	FAFFING
AFFFLLO	FALLOFF
AFFGGIN	GAFFING
AFFGINN	NAFFING
AFFGINW	WAFFING
AFFGINY	AFFYING
	YAFFING
AFFGSUW	GUFFAWS
AFFHILN	HAFFLIN
AFFHIRS	RAFFISH
AFFHIST	HAFFITS
AFFIITX	FIXATIF
AFFIKRS	KAFFIRS
AFFILMN	MAFFLIN
AFFILPS	PILAFFS
AFFILSY	FALSIFY
AFFIMRS	AFFIRMS
AFFIMST	MASTIFF
AFFINRU	FUNFAIR
	RUFFIAN
AFFINTY	TIFFANY
AFFIORR	FORFAIR
AFFIRRU	FURFAIR
AFFIRST	TARIFFS
AFFIRSU	SUFFARI
AFFIRSZ	ZAFFIRS
AFFLOPY	PLAYOFF
AFFLOSY	LAYOFFS
AFFMOPR	OFFRAMP
AFFNORS	SAFFRON
AFFNORT	AFFRONT
AFFOPSY	PAYOFFS
AFFRSST	STRAFFS
AFGGGIN	FAGGING
AFGGINN	FANGING
AFGGOST	FAGGOTS
AFGGOTY	FAGGOTY
AFGHHIS	HAGFISH
AFGHINS	FASHING
AFGHINT	HAFTING
AFGHIRS	GARFISH
AFGHLSU	GASHFUL
AFGHLTU	FLAUGHT
AFGHRTU	FRAUGHT
AFGIIKN	FAIKING
AFGIILN	FAILING
AFGIINN	FAINING
AFGIINR	FAIRING
AFGIINT	FIATING
AFGIINW	WAIFING
AFGIKLN	FLAKING
AFGILLN	FALLING
AFGILMN	FLAMING
AFGILNO	FOALING
	LOAFING
AFGILNR	FLARING
AFGILNS	FALSING
AFGILNT	FATLING
AFGILNU	GAINFUL
AFGILNW	FLAWING
AFGILNY	ANGLIFY
	FLAYING
AFGILRU	FIGURAL
AFGIMNO	FOAMING
AFGIMNR	FARMING
	FRAMING
AFGIMNY	MAGNIFY
AFGINNN	FANNING
AFGINNS	FINGANS
AFGINNW	FAWNING
AFGINNY	FAYNING
AFGINRR	FARRING
AFGINRS	FARSING
AFGINRT	FARTING
	INGRAFT
	RAFTING
AFGINRY	FRAYING
AFGINST	FASTING
AFGINTT	FATTING
AFGINTW	WAFTING
AFGIOTT	FAGOTTI
AFGIRTY	GRATIFY
AFGKNOP	PAKFONG
AFGKORT	KOFTGAR
AFGLLLY	GALLFLY
AFGLLUY	FUGALLY
AFGLNOS	FLAGONS
AFGLNSU	FUNGALS
AFGLRYY	GRAYFLY
AFGMNOR	FROGMAN
AFGMORS	FOGRAMS
AFGOOTT	FAGOTTO
AFGORRS	FRAGORS
AFGOSTU	FUGATOS
AFHIIRS	FAIRISH
AFHIKLS	KHALIFS
AFHIKRS	KHARIFS
AFHIKUY	KUFIYAH
AFHILLN	HALFLIN
AFHILSS	FALSISH
AFHILTW	HALFWIT
AFHIMNU	HAFNIUM
AFHINOS	FASHION
AFHINPS	PANFISH
AFHINTU	UNFAITH
AFHIORS	OARFISH
AFHIRSS	SHARIFS
AFHIRST	RATFISH
AFHISST	FASTISH
AFHISSW	SAWFISH
AFHISTT	FATTISH
AFHISWY	FISHWAY
AFHKORY	HAYFORK
AFHKRTU	FUTHARK
AFHLMRU	HARMFUL
AFHLMSU	FULHAMS
AFHLOOS	LOOFAHS
AFHLOTY	HAYLOFT
AFHLSTU	HATFULS
	HATSFUL
AFHMOST	FATHOMS
AFHOOPT	POOFTAH
AFHOPTU	POUFTAH
AFHORSS	SHOFARS
AFIILNS	FINALIS
	FINIALS
AFIILOR	AIRFOIL
AFIILRT	AIRLIFT
AFIILRY	FAIRILY
AFIIMOS	MAFIOSI
AFIJNNS	FINJANS
AFIKLLY	FLAKILY
AFIKLOT	FLOKATI
AFIKMNR	FINMARK
AFIKNRT	RATFINK
AFIKNSU	FUNKIAS
AFIKRSS	FRISKAS
AFILLMS	MISFALL
AFILLNS	INFALLS
AFILLNY	FINALLY
AFILLPT	PITFALL
AFILLPU	PAILFUL
AFILLRY	FRAILLY
AFILLUV	FLUVIAL
	VIALFUL
AFILLUW	WAILFUL
AFILMNT	LIFTMAN
AFILMOR	ALIFORM
AFILMOY	FOAMILY
AFILMPY	AMPLIFY
AFILMSS	FALSISM
AFILNPU	PAINFUL
AFILNSV	FLAVINS
AFILNTU	ANTIFLU
	FLUTINA
AFILNTY	FAINTLY
AFILORW	AIRFLOW
AFILOTX	FOXTAIL
AFILQUY	QUALIFY
AFILRRY	FRIARLY
AFILRSZ	FRAZILS
AFILRTY	FRAILTY
AFILSSY	SALSIFY
AFILSTU	FISTULA
AFILSTY	FALSITY
AFILTTY	FATTILY
AFIMNRS	FIRMANS
AFIMOOS	MAFIOSO
AFIMORV	AVIFORM
AFIMRST	MAFTIRS
AFIMSSS	MASSIFS
AFIMSSV	FAVISMS
AFIMSTT	FATTISM
AFIMSUV	FAUVISM
AFINNNS	FINNANS
AFINNOR	FRANION
AFINNOS	FANIONS
AFINNOT	FONTINA
AFINNST	INFANTS
AFINORS	INSOFAR
AFINRSU	UNFAIRS
AFINRTU	ANTIFUR
AFINSSU	FUSAINS
AFINSTU	FAUNIST
	FIAUNTS
	FUSTIAN
	INFAUST
AFIORST	FAITORS
AFIORTU	FAITOUR
AFIORTZ	FORZATI
AFIQRSU	FAQUIRS
AFISSTT	SITFAST
AFISSTY	SATISFY
AFISTTT	FATTIST
AFISTUV	FAUVIST
AFITTUY	FATUITY
AFJLRSU	JARFULS
	JARSFUL
AFKLNRY	FRANKLY
AFKLNTU	TANKFUL
AFKLOWY	FOLKWAY
AFKRRTU	FRAKTUR
AFLLMPU	PALMFUL
AFLLMSU	FULLAMS
AFLLNOS	ONFALLS
AFLLNSU	FULLANS
AFLLOOY	ALOOFLY
AFLLORS	FLORALS
AFLLOSW	FALLOWS
AFLLOTU	FALLOUT
	OUTFALL
AFLLPSU	LAPFULS
AFLLPUY	PLAYFUL
AFLLUWY	AWFULLY
AFLMNOU	MOANFUL
AFLMORS	FORMALS
AFLMORU	FORMULA
AFLMORW	WOLFRAM
AFLMOST	FLOTSAM
AFLMRSU	ARMFULS
	ARMSFUL
	FULMARS
AFLMSTU	MASTFUL
AFLMSUU	FAMULUS
AFLNORT	FRONTAL
AFLNOTT	FLOTANT

AFLNPSU PANFULS
AFLNRTU RUNFLAT
AFLNSTU FLAUNTS
AFLNTUY FLAUNTY
AFLOOTW WOOLFAT
AFLOPTT FLATTOP
AFLORSS SAFROLS
AFLORSU FUSAROL
AFLORSV FLAVORS
AFLORUV FLAVOUR
AFLORVY FLAVORY
AFLORWW WARWOLF
AFLOSSU FOSSULA
AFLPRTY FLYTRAP
AFLPSTY FLYPAST
AFLRTUU FUTURAL
AFLRTUY TRAYFUL
AFLSTUV VATFULS
AFLSUWY SWAYFUL
AFLSWYY FLYWAYS
AFMNNOR NONFARM
AFMNOOT FOOTMAN
AFMNORT FORMANT
AFMNOST FANTOMS
AFMNRSU SURFMAN
AFMNRTU TURFMAN
AFMOOSS SAMFOOS
AFMORST FARMOST
FORMATS
AFMORSU AUSFORM
AFMORTU FOUMART
AFMOSTT AFTMOST
AFMOSTU SFUMATO
AFNNNOS NONFANS
AFNORRW FORWARN
AFNORTW FANWORT
AFNOTUW OUTFAWN
AFNPRSY FRYPANS
AFNSSTU SUNFAST
AFOOPPR APPROOF
AFOORST FOOTRAS
AFOORTZ FORZATO
AFOOTWY FOOTWAY
AFORRSW FARROWS
AFORRSY FORRAYS
ORFRAYS
AFORSSY FORSAYS
AFORSTU FAUTORS
FOUTRAS
AFORSUV FAVOURS
AFOSSSU FOUSSAS
AFOSTTU OUTFAST
AFOSTUU FATUOUS
AFPSTUW UPWAFTS
AGGGGIN GAGGING
AGGGHIN HAGGING
AGGGIJN JAGGING
AGGGILN LAGGING
AGGGIMN MAGGING
AGGGINN GANGING
NAGGING
AGGGINR RAGGING
AGGGINS SAGGING
AGGGINT TAGGING
AGGGINU GAUGING
AGGGINW WAGGING
AGGGINZ ZAGGING
AGGHHIS HAGGISH
AGGHIIL GHILGAI
AGGHIMN GINGHAM
AGGHINN HANGING
AGGHINS GASHING
AGGHISW WAGGISH
AGGIIJJ JIGAJIG
AGGIILS GILGAIS

AGGIIMN IMAGING
AGGIINN GAINING
AGGIINT GAITING
AGGIINV GINGIVA
AGGIJJO JIGAJOG
AGGIKNS GASKING
AGGIKNW GAWKING
AGGILLN GALLING
GINGALL
AGGILNN ANGLING
AGGILNO GAOLING
GOALING
AGGILNR ARGLING
GLARING
AGGILNS GINGALS
LAGGINS
AGGILNZ GLAZING
AGGILOS LOGGIAS
AGGIMMN GAMMING
AGGIMNN MANGING
AGGIMNS GAMINGS
AGGIMNU GAUMING
AGGINNP PANGING
AGGINNR RANGING
AGGINNT GANTING
TANGING
AGGINNU UNAGING
AGGINNW GNAWING
AGGINOT GIGATON
AGGINPP GAPPING
AGGINPR GRAPING
PARGING
AGGINPS GAPINGS
GASPING
PAGINGS
AGGINPU GAUPING
AGGINPW GAWPING
AGGINRR GARRING
AGGINRS RAGINGS
SIRGANG
AGGINRT GRATING
TARGING
AGGINRU ARGUING
AGGINRV GRAVING
AGGINRY GRAYING
AGGINRZ GRAZING
AGGINSS GASSING
AGGINST GASTING
GATINGS
STAGING
AGGINSW SWAGING
AGGINUV VAGUING
AGGIORS GORGIAS
AGGISWW WIGWAGS
AGGISZZ ZIGZAGS
AGGLOST LOGGATS
AGGMNOS MOGGANS
AGGMORR GROGRAM
AGGMOST MAGGOTS
AGGMOTY MAGGOTY
AGGMRSU MUGGARS
AGGNOSU GUANGOS
AGGNOSW WAGGONS
AGGNOSX OXGANGS
AGGNOSY SYNAGOG
AGGNPSU UPGANGS
AGGNRSU NUGGARS
AGGPRSY PYGARGS
AGHHIMN HIGHMAN
AGHHINS HASHING
AGHHIWY HIGHWAY
AGHHOSW HOGWASH
AGHHSSU SHAUGHS
AGHHTUY HAUGHTY
AGHIILN HAILING

NILGHAI
AGHIINN HAINING
AGHIINR HAIRING
AGHIJRS JAGHIRS
AGHIKNN HANKING
AGHIKNR HARKING
AGHIKNS SHAKING
AGHIKNW HAWKING
AGHIKSU KIAUGHS
AGHIKSW GAWKISH
AGHILLN HALLING
AGHILNO HALOING
AGHILNR HARLING
AGHILNS HALSING
LASHING
SHALING
AGHILNT HALTING
LATHING
AGHILNU HAULING
NILGHAU
AGHILNV HALVING
AGHILNW WHALING
AGHILNY NYLGHAI
AGHILRS LARGISH
AGHILRT ALRIGHT
AGHILST ALIGHTS
AGHIMMN HAMMING
AGHIMNR HARMING
AGHIMNS MASHING
SHAMING
AGHIMNW HAWMING
AGHIMPS GAMPISH
AGHINNO NIHONGA
AGHINNT HANTING
TANGHIN
AGHINOR HOARING
AGHINOX HOAXING
AGHINPP HAPPING
AGHINPR HARPING
AGHINPS HASPING
PASHING
PHASING
SHAPING
AGHINPT PATHING
AGHINRS GARNISH
RASHING
SHARING
AGHINRU NURAGHI
AGHINSS SASHING
AGHINST HASTING
TASHING
AGHINSU ANGUISH
HAUSING
AGHINSV HAVINGS
SHAVING
AGHINSW HAWSING
SHAWING
WASHING
AGHINSY HAYINGS
AGHINSZ HAZINGS
AGHINTT HATTING
TATHING
AGHINTW THAWING
AGHIOST GOATISH
AGHIPSW PIGWASH
AGHIQSU QUAIGHS
AGHIRRS GHARRIS
AGHIRST GRAITHS
AGHIRSU GUARISH
AGHIRSY GRAYISH
AGHJMNO MAHJONG
AGHKOSW GOSHAWK
AGHLMPU GALUMPH
AGHLNUY NYLGHAU
AGHLOOS GASOHOL

AGHLOSU GOULASH
AGHLSTU GALUTHS
AGHLSTY GHASTLY
AGHNNSU UNHANGS
AGHNOTU HANGOUT
TOHUNGA
AGHNPSU HANGUPS
UPHANGS
AGHNRST THRANGS
AGHNRSU NURHAGS
AGHNRUY AHUNGRY
AGHNSTU NAUGHTS
AGHNSUY GUNYAHS
AGHNTUY NAUGHTY
AGHOORT AGOROTH
AGHOQSU QUAHOGS
AGHORTW WARTHOG
AGHPTUY PAUGHTY
AGHRRSU GURRAHS
AGHRSTU TUGHRAS
AGHRSTY GYTRASH
AGHSTUW WAUGHTS
AGIIJLN JAILING
AGIIKLN LAIKING
AGIIKLT GLAIKIT
AGIIKNP PAIKING
AGIIKNR RAIKING
AGIILMN MAILING
AGIILNN ALINING
NAILING
AGIILNR GLAIRIN
LAIRING
RAILING
AGIILNS AISLING
NILGAIS
SAILING
AGIILNT INTAGLI
TAILING
AGIILNV VAILING
VIALING
AGIILNW WAILING
AGIILOV VILIAGO
AGIILPT PIGTAIL
AGIILTY AGILITY
AGIIMMN MAIMING
AGIIMMS IMAGISM
AGIIMNN MAINING
AGIIMOR ORIGAMI
AGIIMST IMAGIST
AGIINNP PAINING
AGIINNR AIRNING
INGRAIN
RAINING
AGIINNS SAINING
AGIINNW WAINING
AGIINNZ ZINGANI
AGIINPR PAIRING
AGIINRS AIRINGS
ARISING
RAGINIS
RAISING
SAIRING
AGIINRT AIRTING
RAITING
AGIINRW WAIRING
AGIINRZ ZINGARI
AGIINSV AVISING
VISAING
AGIINTW WAITING
AGIINTX TAXIING
AGIINVV VIVAING
AGIINVW WAIVING
AGIINVZ AVIZING
AGIJKNU JAUKING
AGIJLLN JINGALL

AGIJLNS	JINGALS
AGIJMMN	JAMMING
AGIJNPP	JAPPING
AGIJNPS	JAPINGS
AGIJNPU	JAUPING
AGIJNRR	JARRING
AGIJNSW	JAWINGS
	JIGSAWN
AGIJNZZ	JAZZING
AGIJSSW	JIGSAWS
AGIKKNR	KARKING
AGIKKNY	YAKKING
AGIKLNN	ANKLING
	LANKING
AGIKLNO	OAKLING
AGIKLNR	LARKING
AGIKLNS	LAKINGS
	SLAKING
AGIKLNT	TALKING
AGIKLNW	WALKING
AGIKLWY	GAWKILY
AGIKMNR	MARKING
AGIKMNS	MAKINGS
	MASKING
AGIKNNR	NARKING
	RANKING
AGIKNNS	SNAKING
AGIKNNT	KANTING
	TANKING
AGIKNNU	UNAKING
AGIKNNW	WANKING
AGIKNNY	YANKING
AGIKNOS	SOAKING
AGIKNOY	KAYOING
	OKAYING
AGIKNPR	PARKING
AGIKNQU	QUAKING
AGIKNRS	RAKINGS
	SARKING
AGIKNRT	KARTING
AGIKNRW	WARKING
AGIKNSS	ASKINGS
	GASKINS
AGIKNST	SKATING
	STAKING
	TAKINGS
	TASKING
AGIKNSW	WAKINGS
AGIKNUW	WAUKING
AGILLLN	LALLING
AGILLMN	MALLING
AGILLMU	GALLIUM
AGILLNP	PALLING
AGILLNU	LINGUAL
	LINGULA
AGILLNW	WALLING
AGILLNY	ALLYING
AGILLOR	GORILLA
AGILLOT	GALLIOT
AGILLRU	LIGULAR
AGILLSU	LIGULAS
	LUGSAIL
AGILMMN	LAMMING
AGILMMS	GIMMALS
AGILMNO	LOAMING
AGILMNP	LAMPING
	PALMING
AGILMNR	MARLING
AGILMNS	LINGAMS
	MALIGNS
AGILMNT	MALTING
AGILMNU	MAULING
AGILMNY	MANGILY
AGILMOS	GLIOMAS
AGILMPS	MAGILPS
AGILMPU	PLAGIUM
AGILMST	STIGMAL
AGILNNO	LOANING
AGILNNP	PLANING
AGILNNR	LARNING
AGILNNS	LINSANG
AGILNNT	TANLING
AGILNOP	GALOPIN
AGILNOR	RANGOLI
AGILNOT	ANTILOG
AGILNOV	LOAVING
AGILNOZ	LAZOING
AGILNPP	LAPPING
	PALPING
AGILNPR	GRAPLIN
	PARLING
AGILNPS	LAPSING
	PALINGS
	SAPLING
AGILNPT	PLATING
AGILNPW	LAPWING
AGILNPY	PLAYING
AGILNRT	RATLING
AGILNRW	WARLING
AGILNRY	ANGRILY
	NARGILY
	RAYLING
AGILNSS	LASINGS
	SIGNALS
AGILNST	ANGLIST
	LASTING
	SALTING
	SLATING
	STALING
AGILNSU	LINGUAS
	NILGAUS
	SALUING
AGILNSV	SALVING
	SLAVING
	VALSING
AGILNSW	LAWINGS
	SWALING
AGILNSY	LAYINGS
	SLAYING
AGILNTY	GIANTLY
AGILNUV	VALUING
AGILNUW	WAULING
AGILNVV	VALVING
AGILNWW	WAWLING
AGILNWY	YAWLING
AGILNYZ	LAZYING
AGILOPT	GALIPOT
AGILORS	GIRASOL
	GLORIAS
AGILORW	AIRGLOW
AGILOST	GALIOTS
	LATIGOS
	SALIGOT
AGILRSS	SLAIRGS
AGILSSY	GASSILY
AGILSTY	STAGILY
AGILUYZ	GAUZILY
AGIMMNR	RAMMING
AGIMMSS	MAGISMS
AGIMNNN	MANNING
AGIMNNO	MOANING
AGIMNNR	RINGMAN
AGIMNNS	NAMINGS
AGIMNNW	WINGMAN
AGIMNOR	ROAMING
AGIMNOT	MOATING
AGIMNOV	AMOVING
AGIMNPP	MAPPING
AGIMNPR	GRIPMAN
	RAMPING
AGIMNPT	TAMPING
AGIMNPV	VAMPING
AGIMNRR	MARRING
AGIMNRS	ARMINGS
	MARGINS
AGIMNRT	MARTING
	MIGRANT
AGIMNRW	WARMING
AGIMNRY	MYRINGA
AGIMNSS	MASSING
AGIMNST	MASTING
	MATINGS
	TAMINGS
AGIMNSU	AMUSING
AGIMNSY	MAYINGS
AGIMNTT	MATTING
AGIMORS	ISOGRAM
AGIMORU	GOURAMI
AGIMOSY	ISOGAMY
AGIMRRT	TRIGRAM
AGIMRSU	GURAMIS
AGIMRTY	TRIGAMY
AGIMSST	STIGMAS
AGIMSWW	WIGWAMS
AGINNNP	PANNING
AGINNNT	TANNING
AGINNNV	VANNING
AGINNNW	WANNING
AGINNOS	GANOINS
AGINNOT	ATONING
AGINNOZ	ZINGANO
AGINNPP	NAPPING
AGINNPS	PINANGS
	SPANING
AGINNPT	PANTING
AGINNPW	PAWNING
AGINNRS	SNARING
AGINNRT	RANTING
AGINNRW	WARNING
AGINNRY	YARNING
AGINNST	ANTINGS
	STANING
AGINNSU	GUANINS
AGINNSW	AWNINGS
	SNAWING
	WANINGS
AGINNTU	ANTIGUN
AGINNTW	WANTING
AGINNWY	YAWNING
AGINNWZ	WANZING
AGINNYZ	ZANYING
AGINOOO	OOGONIA
AGINOOP	POGONIA
AGINOPR	PIGNORA
AGINOPS	SOAPING
AGINORR	ROARING
AGINORS	IGNAROS
	ORIGANS
	SIGNORA
	SOARING
AGINORT	ORATING
	ROATING
AGINORZ	ZINGARO
AGINOSS	SAGOINS
AGINOST	AGONIST
	GITANOS
AGINOSU	SAGOUIN
AGINOTU	AUTOING
	OUTGAIN
AGINOTV	OVATING
AGINOTZ	TOAZING
AGINOVW	AVOWING
AGINPPP	PAPPING
AGINPPR	PARPING
	RAPPING
AGINPPS	SAPPING
AGINPPT	TAPPING
AGINPPW	WAPPING
AGINPPY	YAPPING
AGINPPZ	ZAPPING
AGINPRR	PARRING
AGINPRS	PARINGS
	PARSING
	RASPING
	SPARING
AGINPRT	PARTING
	PRATING
	TRAPING
AGINPRW	WARPING
AGINPRY	PRAYING
AGINPSS	PASSING
	SPAINGS
AGINPST	PASTING
AGINPSU	PAUSING
AGINPSV	PAVINGS
AGINPSY	PAYINGS
	SPAYING
AGINPTT	PATTING
AGINPTU	TAPUING
AGINPUY	YAUPING
AGINPWY	YAWPING
AGINRRT	TARRING
AGINRRW	WARRING
AGINRST	GASTRIN
	GRATINS
	RATINGS
	STARING
	TARINGS
AGINRSV	RAVINGS
AGINRSW	RAWINGS
AGINRSY	SIGNARY
	SYRINGA
AGINRTT	RATTING
	TARTING
AGINRTW	RINGTAW
AGINRTY	GIANTRY
AGINRUW	WAURING
AGINRVY	VARYING
AGINRWY	RINGWAY
AGINRZZ	RAZZING
AGINSSS	ASSIGNS
	SASSING
AGINSSU	SAGUINS
AGINSSV	SAVINGS
AGINSSW	SAWINGS
AGINSSY	SAYINGS
AGINSTT	STATING
	TASTING
AGINSTU	SAUTING
AGINSTV	STAVING
AGINSTW	STAWING
	TAWINGS
	TAWSING
	WASTING
AGINSTX	TAXINGS
AGINSTY	STAYING
	STYGIAN
AGINSVW	WAVINGS
AGINSWX	WAXINGS
AGINSWY	SWAYING
AGINTTT	TATTING
AGINTTU	TATUING
	TAUTING
AGINTTV	VATTING
AGINTTW	TAWTING
AGINTUV	VAUTING
AGINTVW	VAWTING
AGINTXY	TAXYING
AGINTYZ	TZIGANY
AGINVYZ	AVYZING

AGINWWX	WAXWING
AGIOPSS	GAPOSIS
AGIORST	AGISTOR
	ORGIAST
AGIORSU	GIAOURS
AGIORSV	VIRAGOS
AGIOSTU	AGOUTIS
AGIOUUY	OUGUIYA
AGIRSTU	GUITARS
AGIRTVY	GRAVITY
AGISTTW	WITGATS
AGISTUV	VAGITUS
AGJLMOS	LOGJAMS
AGJLRUU	JUGULAR
AGJNOOR	JARGOON
AGJNORS	JARGONS
AGKLNNO	ANKLONG
AGKLNNU	ANKLUNG
AGKLNOS	KALONGS
AGKLOOS	KAGOOLS
AGKLOST	KGOTLAS
AGKLOSU	KAGOULS
AGKMNOP	KAMPONG
AGKMPRU	PUGMARK
AGKNOPT	PAKTONG
AGKNRSU	KURGANS
AGKORRW	RAGWORK
AGLLNOO	GALLOON
AGLLNOS	GALLONS
	GOLLANS
AGLLNTU	GALLNUT
	NUTGALL
AGLLOOT	GALLOOT
AGLLOPS	GALLOPS
AGLLOPU	PLUGOLA
AGLLORS	GOLLARS
AGLLOSS	GLOSSAL
AGLLOSU	GALLOUS
AGLLOSW	GALLOWS
AGLLOTT	GLOTTAL
AGLLRSY	ARGYLLS
AGLLRYY	GYRALLY
AGLMMSY	GYMMALS
AGLMOPY	POLYGAM
AGLMORS	GLAMORS
AGLMORU	GLAMOUR
AGLNNOS	LONGANS
AGLNNSU	LUNGANS
AGLNOOS	LAGOONS
AGLNORU	LANGUOR
AGLNOSS	SLOGANS
AGLNOST	ALONGST
AGLNOSU	LANUGOS
AGLNOSW	GOWLANS
AGLNPSY	SPANGLY
AGLNPUY	GUNPLAY
AGLNRSU	LANGURS
AGLNRUU	UNGULAR
AGLNTUY	GAUNTLY
AGLOOPS	APOLOGS
AGLOOPY	APOLOGY
AGLOORS	GOORALS
AGLOOST	GALOOTS
AGLORSU	RUGOLAS
AGLOSSS	GLOSSAS
AGLOSSW	SAWLOGS
AGLOSUV	VALGOUS
AGLOSWY	LOGWAYS
AGLRSSU	GUSLARS
AGLRSUU	ARGULUS
AGLRSUV	VULGARS
AGLSYYZ	SYZYGAL
AGMMNOS	GAMMONS
AGMMNSU	MAGNUMS
AGMMORY	MYOGRAM
AGMNNOS	MAGNONS
	SONGMAN
AGMNNOT	TONGMAN
AGMNNOW	GOWNMAN
AGMNORS	MORGANS
AGMNORU	ORGANUM
AGMNOST	AMONGST
AGMNSSU	MUSANGS
AGMNSTU	MUSTANG
AGMNSTY	GYMNAST
	SYNTAGM
AGMNSYY	SYNGAMY
AGMOOYZ	ZOOGAMY
AGMOPRR	PROGRAM
AGMOPRU	GOPURAM
AGMORRW	RAGWORM
AGMORSS	ORGASMS
AGMORSY	MORGAYS
AGMOSYZ	ZYGOMAS
AGMPRSU	GRAMPUS
AGMPSUZ	GAZUMPS
AGMRSSU	GRASSUM
AGNNNOO	NONAGON
AGNNOOR	ORGANON
AGNNOST	TONNAGS
AGNNOSY	NONGAYS
AGNNSTU	TANGUNS
AGNNSUW	WANGUNS
AGNOOSZ	GAZOONS
AGNOQSU	QUANGOS
AGNORRS	GARRONS
AGNORRT	GRANTOR
AGNORSS	SARONGS
AGNORSU	OURANGS
AGNORTU	OUTRANG
AGNOSSS	GOSSANS
AGNOSST	SONTAGS
AGNOSTU	NOUGATS
	OUTSANG
AGNOSZZ	GOZZANS
AGNOTUW	OUTGNAW
AGNPRSS	SPRANGS
AGNRSSU	SUNGARS
AGNRTUY	GAUNTRY
AGOPPST	STOPGAP
AGOPRST	RAGTOPS
AGOPRSU	GOPURAS
AGORRST	GARROTS
AGORRTW	RAGWORT
AGORRTY	GYRATOR
AGORSSU	RUGOSAS
AGORSTU	RAGOUTS
AGORTUY	GRAYOUT
AGOSTTU	TAUTOGS
AGOSUYZ	AZYGOUS
AGSSTUU	AUGUSTS
AHHHISS	HASHISH
AHHIJRS	HIJRAHS
AHHIKKR	KHIRKAH
AHHIKSS	SHAIKHS
AHHIKSW	HAWKISH
AHHIMNU	HAHNIUM
AHHINST	SHANTIH
AHHIPRS	RHAPHIS
AHHISSV	SHIVAHS
AHHISTT	SHITTAH
AHHKOOS	HOOKAHS
AHHLLOT	HALLOTH
AHHLRSY	HARSHLY
AHHMPRU	HARUMPH
AHHOORS	HOORAHS
AHHOPRS	SHOPHAR
AHHPPSU	HUPPAHS
AHHPTUZ	HUTZPAH
AHHRRSU	HURRAHS
AHHSUZZ	HUZZAHS
AHIIKRS	RIKISHA
	SHIKARI
AHIILPS	SILPHIA
AHIILST	LITHIAS
AHIIMNT	THIAMIN
AHIIMSS	SASHIMI
AHIINPR	HAIRPIN
AHIINST	TAHINIS
AHIINTU	HUITAIN
AHIINTZ	THIAZIN
AHIIPRS	AIRSHIP
AHIKKSS	KISHKAS
AHIKLPS	KALIPHS
AHIKLRS	LARKISH
AHIKLSS	SHASLIK
AHIKLST	KHILATS
AHIKLSY	SHAKILY
AHIKMNS	KHAMSIN
AHIKMRS	KASHMIR
AHIKMSV	MIKVAHS
AHIKMSW	MAWKISH
AHIKNRS	RANKISH
AHIKNSS	SNAKISH
AHIKNSV	KNAVISH
AHIKOSW	KOWHAIS
AHIKPRS	PARKISH
AHIKRSS	SHIKARS
AHIKRSW	RIKSHAW
AHIKSSS	SHIKSAS
AHIKSST	SKAITHS
AHILLNO	HALLION
AHILLNP	PHALLIN
AHILLNT	ANTHILL
AHILLOS	HILLOAS
AHILLRT	ATHRILL
AHILLSS	SHALLIS
AHILLST	TALLISH
AHILLSZ	ZILLAHS
AHILLTT	TALLITH
AHILLTY	LAITHLY
AHILMMO	MOHALIM
AHILMMS	MASHLIM
AHILMMY	HAMMILY
AHILMNS	MASHLIN
AHILMOP	OMPHALI
AHILMOS	HOLMIAS
AHILMOT	HALIMOT
AHILMSU	ALUMISH
AHILNPS	PLANISH
AHILNRS	SHRINAL
AHILNRT	INTHRAL
AHILNSS	LASHINS
AHILNSU	INHAULS
AHILNSY	HYALINS
	LINHAYS
AHILORY	HOARILY
AHILOTY	ALIYOTH
AHILOTZ	THIAZOL
AHILPPS	PALSHIP
	SHIPLAP
AHILPPY	HAPPILY
AHILPRT	PHILTRA
AHILPSY	APISHLY
AHILSST	SALTISH
	TAHSILS
AHILSSV	SLAVISH
AHILSTU	HALITUS
	THULIAS
AHILSTY	HASTILY
AHILSYZ	LAZYISH
AHIMMRS	RAMMISH
AHIMNNS	MANNISH
AHIMNNU	INHUMAN
AHIMNOT	MANIHOT
AHIMNPS	SHIPMAN
AHIMNRS	HARMINS
AHIMOPR	MORPHIA
AHIMORS	MOHAIRS
AHIMORZ	RHIZOMA
AHIMOSS	SHAMOIS
AHIMPSS	MISHAPS
	PASHIMS
AHIMPST	MISHAPT
AHIMPSV	VAMPISH
AHIMPSW	WAMPISH
AHIMRSS	MAHSIRS
AHIMRST	THAIRMS
	THIRAMS
	THRIMSA
AHIMRSW	WARMISH
AHIMSTV	MITSVAH
AHIMTUZ	AZIMUTH
AHIMTVZ	MITZVAH
AHINNST	TANNISH
AHINNSW	WANNISH
AHINNTX	XANTHIN
AHINORT	ORTHIAN
AHINOTZ	HOATZIN
AHINPRS	HARPINS
AHINPST	HATPINS
AHINRSS	ARSHINS
	SHAIRNS
AHINRST	TARNISH
AHINRSU	UNHAIRS
AHINRSV	VARNISH
AHINRTY	RHYTINA
AHINSST	SHANTIS
AHINSTU	INHAUST
AHINSYZ	ZANYISH
AHIOOST	ATISHOO
AHIOPRU	OPHIURA
AHIOPXY	HYPOXIA
AHIORST	SHORTIA
	THORIAS
AHIORSV	HAVIORS
AHIORUV	HAVIOUR
AHIPRSS	RASPISH
AHIPRST	HARPIST
AHIPRSU	RUPIAHS
AHIPRSW	WARSHIP
AHIPRWY	WHIPRAY
AHIPSSW	WASPISH
AHIPSWW	WHIPSAW
AHIPSWY	SHIPWAY
AHIRRSS	SHIRRAS
	SIRRAHS
AHIRRST	STIRRAH
AHIRSST	HAIRSTS
AHIRSTT	ATHIRST
	RATTISH
	TARTISH
AHIRSTW	TRISHAW
	WRAITHS
AHISSTT	STAITHS
AHISSTU	SHIATSU
	THIASUS
AHISSTW	WHATSIS
AHISTTW	WHATSIT
AHISTUZ	SHIATZU
AHITTWW	WHITTAW
AHJOOPS	POOJAHS
AHKKSSU	SUKKAHS
AHKLOOS	KOOLAHS
AHKLPSU	PULKHAS
AHKMNSU	KHANUMS
AHKMORR	MARKHOR
AHKMOSW	MOHAWKS
AHKMRTU	MUKHTAR
AHKNPSU	PUNKAHS

AHKRSST	SKARTHS
AHKRSSU	KASHRUS
AHKRSTU	KASHRUT
	KHURTAS
	TUSHKAR
AHLLMOS	MOLLAHS
	OLLAMHS
AHLLMSU	MULLAHS
AHLLNOS	SHALLON
AHLLNOY	HALLYON
AHLLNSU	NULLAHS
AHLLOOS	HALLOOS
	HOLLOAS
AHLLOPS	SHALLOP
AHLLOST	SHALLOT
AHLLOSU	HULLOAS
AHLLOSW	HALLOWS
	SHALLOW
AHLLOTY	LOATHLY
	TALLYHO
AHLLPSU	PHALLUS
AHLLPSY	ALPHYLS
AHLLPYY	APHYLLY
AHLLRST	THRALLS
AHLLSTU	THALLUS
AHLMMSU	MASHLUM
AHLMNPY	NYMPHAL
AHLMNSY	HYMNALS
AHLMNUY	HUMANLY
AHLMOOS	MOOLAHS
AHLMORU	HUMORAL
AHLMOSS	SHALOMS
AHLMSTZ	SHMALTZ
AHLMSUU	HAMULUS
AHLNOPR	ALPHORN
AHLNOPT	HAPLONT
	NAPHTOL
AHLNORT	ALTHORN
AHLOOPS	HOOPLAS
AHLOOPW	WHOOPLA
AHLOOTW	WOOLHAT
AHLORST	HARLOTS
AHLOSST	SHALOTS
AHLOSTU	OUTLASH
AHLOTUU	OUTHAUL
AHLPRSY	SHARPLY
AHLPRUY	HYPURAL
AHLPSSU	SULPHAS
AHLPSSY	SPLASHY
AHMMMOT	MAMMOTH
AHMMMUU	HUMMAUM
AHMMOSS	SHAMMOS
AHMMOSW	WHAMMOS
AHMNNSU	NUMNAHS
AHMNNTU	MANHUNT
AHMNNUU	UNHUMAN
AHMNOPS	SHOPMAN
AHMNOPT	PHANTOM
AHMNORY	HARMONY
AHMNOSS	HANSOMS
AHMNOSW	SHOWMAN
AHMNRSU	RHAMNUS
AHMNRYY	HYMNARY
AHMOOPS	OOMPAHS
	SHAMPOO
AHMOOSS	SAMSHOO
AHMORRU	MORRHUA
AHMORST	HARMOST
AHMORSZ	MAHZORS
AHMOSSY	SHAMOYS
AHMOSTU	MAHOUTS
AHMOSTZ	MATZOHS
AHMOSWY	HAYMOWS
AHMOTTZ	MATZOTH
AHMPSSU	SMASHUP
AHMRRSU	MURRHAS
AHMRSTW	WARMTHS
AHMRSTY	THRYMSA
AHMSSSU	SAMSHUS
AHNNSSU	SUNNAHS
AHNOOPR	HARPOON
AHNOPRS	ORPHANS
AHNORSS	SHORANS
AHNORSX	SAXHORN
AHNOTTW	WHATNOT
AHNPPUU	PUPUNHA
AHNPPUY	UNHAPPY
AHNPRSU	UNSHARP
AHNPRXY	PHARYNX
AHNPSSU	UNHASPS
AHNSSTU	SUNHATS
AHNSTUW	UNTHAWS
AHNSTUY	UNHASTY
AHOORSY	HOORAYS
AHOPRTY	ATROPHY
AHOPSTW	WASHPOT
AHOPTTW	TOWPATH
AHORRSW	HARROWS
AHORSTT	THROATS
AHORSTU	AUTHORS
AHORSTW	WROATHS
AHORTTY	THROATY
AHOSTUW	OUTWASH
	WASHOUT
AHPRRTY	PHRATRY
AHPRSST	SPARTHS
AHPSSUW	WASHUPS
AHPSTUZ	HUTZPAS
AHPSXYY	ASPHYXY
AHQSSUY	SQUASHY
AHRRSUY	HURRAYS
AHRSSSU	HUSSARS
AHRSSTT	STRATHS
AHRSSTW	SWARTHS
AHRSTTW	THWARTS
AHRSTWY	SWARTHY
AHRTUWY	THRUWAY
AHSSSTU	TUSSAHS
AIIILMT	MILITIA
AIIILNT	INITIAL
AIIILVX	LIXIVIA
AIIIMRS	SAIMIRI
AIIKKSW	WAKIKIS
AIIKMMS	SKIMMIA
AIIKMNN	MANIKIN
AIIKNST	KAINITS
AIIKRTT	TRAIKIT
AIILLLP	LAPILLI
AIILLMN	LIMINAL
AIILLMS	LIMAILS
AIILLNV	VILLAIN
AIILLQU	QUILLAI
AIILLUV	ILLUVIA
AIILMMN	MINIMAL
AIILMNO	MONILIA
AIILMNS	MISLAIN
AIILMNT	INTIMAL
AIILMNV	VIMINAL
AIILMRS	SIMILAR
AIILMRT	MILITAR
AIILMRY	MILIARY
AIILNNS	ANILINS
AIILNOS	LIAISON
AIILNPT	PINTAIL
AIILNPU	NAUPLII
AIILNRY	RAINILY
AIILNTU	NAUTILI
AIILNTV	INVITAL
AIILNTY	ANILITY
AIILOPP	PAPILIO
AIILORV	RAVIOLI
AIILQSU	SILIQUA
AIILRTV	TRIVIAL
	VITRAIL
AIIMMNS	ANIMISM
AIIMMNX	MAXIMIN
	MINIMAX
AIIMMSS	MISAIMS
AIIMNNV	MINIVAN
AIIMNOR	AMORINI
AIIMNPS	PAINIMS
	PIANISM
AIIMNPT	IMPAINT
	TIMPANI
AIIMNRT	MARTINI
AIIMNSS	SAIMINS
	SIMIANS
AIIMNST	ANIMIST
	INTIMAS
	SANTIMI
AIIMNTT	IMITANT
AIIMNTU	MINUTIA
AIIMNTV	VITAMIN
AIIMNTY	AMINITY
AIIMPRS	IMPAIRS
AIIMPSS	SIMPAIS
AIIMRST	SIMITAR
AIIMSST	SAMITIS
AIIMSSY	MYIASIS
AIINNOP	PIANINO
AIINNQU	QUININA
AIINNSZ	ZINNIAS
AIINNTY	INANITY
AIINOPS	SINOPIA
AIINOTT	NOTITIA
AIINPPR	RAPPINI
AIINPRS	ASPIRIN
AIINPST	PIANIST
AIINRSS	RAISINS
AIINRSY	RAISINY
AIINRTV	VITRAIN
AIINRTZ	TRIAZIN
AIINSST	ISATINS
AIINSSX	SIXAINS
AIINSTT	TITANIS
	TITIANS
AIINSTV	NAIVIST
AIIPRST	PIARIST
AIIPSTW	WAPITIS
AIIPTTU	PITUITA
AIJJMMS	JIMJAMS
AIJLORS	JAILORS
AIJLSTW	WILTJAS
AIJLYZZ	JAZZILY
AIJMNSS	JASMINS
AIJNORT	JANITOR
AIJORSW	JOWARIS
AIJPSTU	JUPATIS
AIKKMNR	KIRKMAN
AIKKMOT	KOMATIK
AIKKSUZ	ZAKUSKI
AIKLLNY	LANKILY
AIKLMMN	MILKMAN
AIKLMNN	LINKMAN
AIKLMNS	MALKINS
AIKLMPU	LAMPUKI
AIKLMSS	MISKALS
AIKLMSU	KALIUMS
AIKLNOS	KAOLINS
AIKLNSY	SNAKILY
AIKLPWY	PAWKILY
AIKLQUY	QUAKILY
AIKLRTT	TITLARK
AIKLSSU	SALUKIS
AIKLSSY	SKYSAIL
AIKMMRS	MISMARK
AIKMMSS	IMMASKS
AIKMNNS	KINSMAN
AIKMNSS	KAMSINS
AIKMNSW	MAWKINS
AIKMOOS	OOMIAKS
AIKMPRS	IMPARKS
AIKMRSU	KUMARIS
	RUMAKIS
AIKMSST	KISMATS
AIKNNNS	NANKINS
AIKNNPS	NAPKINS
AIKNOST	KATIONS
AIKNPRS	KIRPANS
	PARKINS
AIKNPSS	PANISKS
AIKNSTU	TANUKIS
AIKOPST	KATIPOS
AIKORST	TROIKAS
AIKRRSS	SIRKARS
AIKRSST	STRAIKS
AIKRTUZ	ZIKURAT
AILLLNO	LINALOL
AILLMNU	LUMINAL
AILLMNY	MANLILY
AILLMOT	MAILLOT
AILLMPU	PALLIUM
AILLMSU	ALLIUMS
AILLMSW	SAWMILL
AILLMSY	MISALLY
AILLNNO	LANOLIN
AILLNOP	PAILLON
AILLNPY	PLAINLY
AILLNST	INSTALL
AILLNSV	VILLANS
AILLNSW	INWALLS
AILLNVY	VILLANY
AILLORT	LITORAL
AILLORZ	ZORILLA
AILLPRS	PILLARS
AILLPRU	PILULAR
AILLPSU	PILLAUS
	PILULAS
AILLPUV	PLUVIAL
AILLQSU	SQUILLA
AILLRSU	ARILLUS
AILLRVY	VIRALLY
AILLSTY	SALTILY
AILLSUZ	LAZULIS
AILLTVY	VITALLY
AILLTWW	WITWALL
AILMMOR	IMMORAL
AILMMSS	MALISMS
AILMMSY	MYALISM
AILMMUU	ALUMIUM
AILMNNO	NOMINAL
AILMNOP	LAMPION
AILMNOS	MALISON
	MONIALS
	SOMNIAL
AILMNOY	ALIMONY
AILMNPS	MISPLAN
	PLASMIN
AILMNPT	IMPLANT
AILMNPU	ULPANIM
AILMNRS	MARLINS
AILMNRU	MURLAIN
	RUMINAL
AILMNSS	MASLINS
AILMNSU	ALUMINS
AILMOOV	MOVIOLA
AILMOPS	LIPOMAS
AILMOPT	OPTIMAL
AILMORS	ORALISM
AILMOST	SOMITAL

AILMPRS	IMPARLS
AILMPRU	PRIMULA
AILMPST	PALMIST
AILMPSY	MISPLAY
AILMRST	MISTRAL
	RAMTILS
AILMRSU	SIMULAR
AILMSSS	MISSALS
AILMSSX	LAXISMS
AILMSSY	MISLAYS
AILMSTU	ULTIMAS
AILMSUV	MAULVIS
AILNNOS	SOLANIN
AILNNOT	ANTLION
AILNNPU	PINNULA
AILNNSU	UNNAILS
	UNSLAIN
AILNOPY	POLYNIA
AILNOQU	AQUILON
AILNOSS	SIALONS
AILNOST	LATINOS
	TALIONS
AILNOTU	OUTLAIN
AILNPRW	PRAWLIN
AILNPSS	SPINALS
AILNPST	PLAINTS
AILNPSU	PAULINS
	SPINULA
AILNPSX	SALPINX
AILNPTU	NUPTIAL
	PATULIN
	UNPLAIT
AILNPTY	INAPTLY
	PTYALIN
AILNPUV	PLUVIAN
AILNQTU	QUINTAL
AILNRST	RATLINS
AILNRSU	INSULAR
	URINALS
AILNRTT	RATTLIN
AILNRTY	RIANTLY
AILNSST	INSTALS
AILNSSU	INSULAS
AILNSSV	SILVANS
AILNSTT	LATTINS
AILNSTU	UNALIST
AILNSTY	NASTILY
	SAINTLY
AILNSUV	UNVAILS
AILNTTY	NATTILY
AILNTUV	UNVITAL
AILNTWY	TAWNILY
AILOORS	OORALIS
	OORIALS
AILOORW	WOORALI
AILOPST	APOSTIL
	TOPSAIL
AILOPSY	SOAPILY
AILOPTT	TALIPOT
AILOPTV	PIVOTAL
AILOQTU	ALIQUOT
AILORSS	SAILORS
AILORST	ORALIST
	RIALTOS
	TAILORS
AILORSU	OURALIS
AILORTY	ORALITY
AILORUW	WOURALI
AILORUX	UXORIAL
AILORVY	OLIVARY
AILOSSS	ASSOILS
AILOSTT	ALTOIST
AILOSTU	OUTSAIL
AILOSTX	OXTAILS
AILOSWY	OILWAYS
AILOTVY	OVALITY
AILPPRU	PUPILAR
AILPPSY	PAYSLIP
	SAPPILY
AILPPTY	PLATYPI
AILPQSU	PASQUIL
AILPRSS	SPIRALS
AILPRSU	PARULIS
	SPIRULA
	UPRISAL
AILPRSY	PYRALIS
AILPSST	PASTILS
	SPITALS
AILPSTU	TIPULAS
AILPSWY	SLIPWAY
	WASPILY
AILQSSU	SQUAILS
AILQTTU	QUITTAL
AILQTUY	QUALITY
AILRRVY	RIVALRY
AILRSTT	STARLIT
AILRSTU	RITUALS
	TRISULA
AILRSTY	TRYSAIL
AILRTTU	TITULAR
AILRTUV	VIRTUAL
	VITULAR
AILSSSY	SASSILY
AILSSTU	TISSUAL
AILSSTX	LAXISTS
AILSSUV	VISUALS
AILSSVY	SYLVIAS
AILSSVZ	VIZSLAS
AILSTTY	TASTILY
AILSTUW	LAWSUIT
AILTTTY	TATTILY
AIMMMSU	MUMMIAS
AIMMMUX	MAXIMUM
AIMMNTU	MANUMIT
AIMMORS	AMORISM
AIMMOSS	MIMOSAS
AIMMOST	ATOMISM
AIMNNOS	AMNIONS
	MANSION
	ONANISM
AIMNNSS	NANISMS
AIMNNSY	MINYANS
AIMNOOR	AMORINO
AIMNOOT	AMOTION
AIMNOPR	RAMPION
AIMNOPS	MOPANIS
AIMNOPT	MAINTOP
	PTOMAIN
	TAMPION
	TIMPANO
AIMNOPZ	ZAMPONI
AIMNORS	MAINORS
AIMNORT	TORMINA
AIMNORU	MAINOUR
AIMNOST	MANITOS
	STAMNOI
AIMNOTU	MANITOU
	TINAMOU
AIMNPST	PITMANS
AIMNPSW	IMPAWNS
AIMNPSY	PAYNIMS
AIMNPTY	TYMPANI
AIMNRRU	MURRAIN
AIMNRST	MARTINS
AIMNRSU	SURAMIN
	URANISM
AIMNRTU	NATRIUM
AIMNRTV	VARMINT
AIMNRUU	URANIUM
AIMNSST	SANTIMS
AIMNSTT	MATTINS
AIMNSTU	MANITUS
	TSUNAMI
AIMNSUV	MAUVINS
AIMNSVY	MAYVINS
AIMNSYZ	ZANYISM
AIMOPST	IMPASTO
AIMOPSY	MYOPIAS
AIMORRU	ORARIUM
AIMORST	AMORIST
AIMORTT	TRITOMA
AIMORUZ	ZOARIUM
AIMOSTT	ATOMIST
AIMPPSS	PAPISMS
AIMPPST	MAPPIST
AIMPRRY	PRIMARY
AIMPRST	ARMPITS
	IMPARTS
	MISPART
AIMPRSY	PYRAMIS
AIMQRSU	MARQUIS
AIMRSST	TSARISM
AIMRSTU	ATRIUMS
	MATSURI
AIMRSTY	MAISTRY
	SYMITAR
AIMRSTZ	TZARISM
AIMSSSY	MISSAYS
AIMSSTT	STATISM
AIMSSTU	AUTISMS
AINNNST	TANNINS
AINNOPS	SAPONIN
AINNOPT	PINTANO
AINNOSS	NASIONS
AINNOST	ANOINTS
	NATIONS
	ONANIST
AINNOSW	WANIONS
AINNPSS	INSPANS
AINNPTU	UNPAINT
AINNQTU	QUINNAT
	QUINTAN
AINNRSU	URANINS
AINNRTT	INTRANT
AINNRTU	URINANT
AINNSTT	INSTANT
AINNSTU	UNSAINT
AINNTUY	ANNUITY
AINOOPR	PRONAOI
AINOORR	ORARION
AINOORT	ORATION
AINOOTV	OVATION
AINOPPT	APPOINT
AINOPRS	PARISON
	SOPRANI
AINOPRT	ATROPIN
AINOPSS	PASSION
AINOPTT	ANTIPOT
AINOPTU	OPUNTIA
	UTOPIAN
AINOQSU	QUINOAS
AINORST	AROINTS
	RATIONS
AINORSW	WARISON
AINORTU	RAINOUT
AINORTX	TRIAXON
AINOSSU	SANIOUS
	SUASION
AINOSTT	STATION
AINOSUX	ANXIOUS
AINOSVY	SYNOVIA
AINPPRS	PARSNIP
AINPQTU	PIQUANT
AINPRSS	SPINARS
	SPRAINS
AINPRST	SPIRANT
	SPRAINT
AINPRSU	PRUINAS
AINPRSW	INWRAPS
AINPRTU	PURITAN
	UPTRAIN
AINPSST	PISSANT
	PTISANS
AINPSSV	SPAVINS
AINQRST	QINTARS
AINQRTU	QUINTAR
AINQRUY	QUINARY
AINQSSU	QUASSIN
AINQSTU	ASQUINT
	QUINTAS
AINQSUY	YANQUIS
AINRRTY	TRINARY
AINRRUY	URINARY
AINRSST	INSTARS
	SANTIRS
	STRAINS
AINRSTT	STRAINT
	TRANSIT
AINRSTU	NUTRIAS
AINRTTT	TITRANT
AINRTUY	UNITARY
AINSSTT	TANISTS
AINSSTU	ISSUANT
	SUSTAIN
AINSSXY	SYNAXIS
AINTTVY	TANTIVY
AIOORRW	WOORARI
AIOORSS	ARIOSOS
AIOPRRT	AIRPORT
	PARITOR
AIOPRST	AIRPOST
	AIRSTOP
	PAROTIS
AIOPRSV	PAVIORS
AIOPRTT	PATRIOT
AIOPRTY	TOPIARY
AIOPRUV	PAVIOUR
AIOPSTU	UTOPIAS
AIORRRW	WARRIOR
AIORRSU	OURARIS
AIORRTT	TRAITOR
AIORRTX	ORATRIX
AIORSST	AORISTS
	ARISTOS
	SATORIS
AIORSSU	SOUARIS
AIORSSV	SAVIORS
AIORSTU	SAUTOIR
AIORSTV	TRAVOIS
	VIATORS
AIORSTY	OSTIARY
AIORSUV	SAVIOUR
	VARIOUS
AIOSSYZ	ZOYSIAS
AIOTTUW	OUTWAIT
AIPPRRS	RIPRAPS
AIPPRSU	PRIAPUS
AIPPSST	PAPISTS
AIPRRTT	TRIPART
AIPRSST	RAPISTS
AIPRSSW	RIPSAWS
AIPRSTU	UPSTAIR
AIPRSUY	PYURIAS
AIPRTVY	PRAVITY
AIPSSTT	TAPISTS
AIPSSTW	PITSAWS
	SAWPITS
AIPYZZZ	PIZAZZY
AIRRSST	STIRRAS
AIRRSZZ	RIZZARS

AIRRTZZ	RIZZART
AIRSSSU	RUSSIAS
AIRSSTT	ARTISTS
	SITTARS
	STRAITS
	TSARIST
AIRSSTU	AURISTS
AIRSTTT	ATTRIST
	ATTRITS
AIRSTTU	TURISTA
AIRSTTY	YTTRIAS
AIRSTTZ	TZARIST
AIRSTVY	VARSITY
AIRTUVX	VITRAUX
AISSSST	ASSISTS
AISSTTT	STATIST
AISTTVY	VASTITY
AISTUVY	SUAVITY
AJKMNNU	JUNKMAN
AJKMNTU	MUNTJAK
AJKNSSY	JANSKYS
AJLLRUY	JURALLY
AJLMORY	MAJORLY
AJLNORU	JOURNAL
AJLOORS	JAROOLS
AJLOPPY	JALOPPY
AJMNRUY	JURYMAN
AJMOPST	JAMPOTS
AJMRSTU	JUMARTS
AJNRSTU	JURANTS
AKKKORU	ROKKAKU
AKKLRSY	SKYLARK
AKKLSWY	SKYWALK
AKKMOOT	TOKOMAK
AKKNRSU	KUNKARS
AKKOQSU	QUOKKAS
AKLMMSU	MAMLUKS
AKLNOSU	KOULANS
AKLNOSX	KLAXONS
AKLOPRW	LAPWORK
AKLOSST	SKATOLS
AKLOSTW	KOTWALS
AKLOTTU	OUTTALK
AKLOTUW	OUTWALK
	WALKOUT
AKLPRSY	SPARKLY
AKLPSUW	WALKUPS
AKLRSTY	STARKLY
AKLRSVY	VALKYRS
AKMNORW	WORKMAN
AKMNRTU	TRANKUM
AKMNSSU	UNMASKS
AKMOORT	MOOKTAR
AKMOOSS	OAKMOSS
AKMORST	OSTMARK
AKMPRSU	MARKUPS
AKMQTUU	KUMQUAT
AKMRSTU	MUSKRAT
AKNORSU	KORUNAS
AKNORSY	KARYONS
	RYOKANS
AKNORTU	OUTRANK
AKOOPRT	PARTOOK
AKOORRS	KARROOS
	KORORAS
AKOOSTU	ATOKOUS
AKORRTW	ARTWORK
AKORRWW	WARWORK
AKORWWX	WAXWORK
AKOSSTU	OUTASKS
AKOSTTU	OUTTASK
AKQSSUW	SQUAWKS
AKQSUWY	SQUAWKY
AKRSSTU	TUSKARS
AKSSWYY	SKYWAYS
ALLLOST	TALLOLS
ALLLOYY	LOYALLY
ALLMNOP	POLLMAN
ALLMNOT	TOLLMAN
ALLMNOY	ALLONYM
ALLMNPU	PULLMAN
ALLMOOS	OSMOLAL
ALLMORS	MORALLS
ALLMORY	MORALLY
ALLMOSS	SLALOMS
ALLMOST	MALTOLS
ALLMOSW	MALLOWS
ALLMPUU	PLUMULA
ALLMSUV	VALLUMS
ALLNOPS	POLLANS
ALLNOTY	TONALLY
ALLNOYZ	ZONALLY
ALLNRUU	LUNULAR
ALLNSTY	SLANTLY
ALLNTUU	ULULANT
ALLOOPS	APOLLOS
	PALOLOS
ALLOOST	LATOSOL
ALLOOTX	AXOLOTL
ALLOPRS	PALLORS
ALLOPRY	PAYROLL
ALLOPSW	WALLOPS
ALLORSS	SOLLARS
ALLORWY	ROLLWAY
ALLORYY	ROYALLY
ALLOSSW	SALLOWS
ALLOSTT	TALLOTS
ALLOSTV	LAVOLTS
ALLOSTW	TALLOWS
ALLOSWW	SWALLOW
	WALLOWS
ALLOSWY	SALLOWY
ALLOTTY	TOTALLY
ALLOTWY	TALLOWY
	TOLLWAY
ALLOTYY	LOYALTY
ALLPRSU	PLURALS
ALLPSSY	PSYLLAS
ALLQSSU	SQUALLS
ALLQSUY	SQUALLY
ALLRRUY	RURALLY
ALLRSTU	LUSTRAL
ALLSUUY	USUALLY
ALMMSUY	AMYLUMS
ALMNNUY	UNMANLY
ALMNOOP	LAMPOON
ALMNOOT	TOOLMAN
ALMNOOW	WOOLMAN
ALMNOPS	PLASMON
ALMNOPW	PLOWMAN
ALMNORS	NORMALS
ALMNORU	UNMORAL
ALMNORY	ALMONRY
ALMNOSS	SALMONS
ALMNOSU	MONAULS
	SOLANUM
ALMNOWY	WOMANLY
ALMNPSU	SUNLAMP
ALMNRSU	MURLANS
ALMNSUU	ALUMNUS
ALMOOPY	POLYOMA
ALMOORS	OSMOLAR
ALMOPPT	PALMTOP
ALMOPRT	MARPLOT
ALMORRU	MORULAR
ALMORSS	SAMLORS
ALMORST	MORTALS
	STROMAL
ALMORSU	MORULAS
ALMORTU	TUMORAL
ALMOSST	SMALTOS
ALMOSTW	MATLOWS
ALMOSXY	XYLOMAS
ALMOTTU	MULATTO
ALMRSTY	SMARTLY
ALMRSUU	RAMULUS
ALMRTUU	MUTULAR
	TUMULAR
ALMSSUY	ALYSSUM
	ASYLUMS
ALMSTUU	MUTUALS
	UMLAUTS
ALNNOPY	NONPLAY
ALNNRSU	UNSNARL
ALNNSUU	ANNULUS
ALNOOPR	POLARON
ALNOOPT	PLATOON
ALNOOPV	VANPOOL
ALNOORT	ORTOLAN
ALNOOSS	SALOONS
	SOLANOS
ALNOPPY	PANOPLY
ALNOPRS	PROLANS
ALNOPSS	SPONSAL
ALNOPTU	OUTPLAN
ALNOPYY	POLYNYA
ALNORST	LATRONS
ALNORUY	UNROYAL
ALNORUZ	ZONULAR
ALNOSST	SANTOLS
ALNOSUZ	ZONULAS
ALNPRUY	PLANURY
ALNPSTU	PULSANT
	PULTANS
ALNPTUY	UNAPTLY
ALNPTXY	PLANXTY
ALNRSUY	URANYLS
ALNSSTU	SULTANS
ALNSSVY	SYLVANS
ALNSTUW	WALNUTS
ALNSUUU	UNUSUAL
ALOOPSS	SALOOPS
ALOOPYZ	POLYZOA
ALOORRS	SORORAL
ALOPPRS	POPLARS
ALOPPRU	POPULAR
ALOPPRY	PROPYLA
ALOPPST	LAPTOPS
ALOPRRS	PARLORS
ALOPRRU	PARLOUR
ALOPRST	PATROLS
	PORTALS
ALOPRSU	PARLOUS
ALOPRSY	PYROLAS
ALOPSST	POSTALS
ALOPSSU	SPOUSAL
ALOPSUV	VOLUSPA
ALOPTUY	OUTPLAY
ALOQRRU	RORQUAL
ALOQRSU	SQUALOR
ALOQSTU	LOQUATS
ALORRST	ROSTRAL
ALORRSW	WORRALS
ALORSSU	ROSULAS
ALORSSV	SALVORS
ALORSTU	ROTULAS
	TORULAS
ALORSUV	VALOURS
ALORTWW	AWLWORT
ALORTYY	ROYALTY
ALORUVY	OVULARY
ALOSTTU	OUTLAST
ALOSTUW	OUTLAWS
ALOSTUY	LAYOUTS
	OUTLAYS
ALOSTXY	OXYSALT
ALPRRSU	LARRUPS
ALPRSSU	PULSARS
ALPRSSW	SPRAWLS
ALPRSTY	PSALTRY
ALPRSUU	PURSUAL
ALPRSUW	PULWARS
ALPRSWY	SPRAWLY
ALQSTUY	SQUATLY
ALRSTTY	STARTLY
ALRSTUU	SUTURAL
ALRSTUW	TULWARS
ALRSUUV	UVULARS
AMMMNOS	MAMMONS
AMMMOSU	AMOMUMS
AMMNOOR	MOORMAN
AMMNOOT	MOOTMAN
AMMNOPS	PSAMMON
AMMNRUY	NUMMARY
AMMOORR	MAORMOR
	MORMAOR
AMMOPTU	POMATUM
AMMORST	MARMOTS
AMMOSXY	MYXOMAS
AMMPSUW	WAMPUMS
AMMRRSU	MARRUMS
	MURRAMS
AMMRSUY	SUMMARY
AMMSSTU	SUMMATS
AMNNOOX	MONAXON
AMNNORS	NORMANS
AMNNOSW	SNOWMAN
AMNNOSY	ANONYMS
AMNNOTT	MONTANT
AMNNOTY	ANTONYM
AMNNOUW	UNWOMAN
AMNNSTU	STANNUM
AMNOOPP	POMPANO
AMNOORS	MAROONS
	ROMANOS
AMNOOTT	OTTOMAN
AMNOOTZ	MATZOON
AMNOPPR	PROPMAN
AMNOPRT	PORTMAN
AMNOPRY	PARONYM
AMNOPST	POSTMAN
	TAMPONS
	TOPSMAN
AMNOPTU	PANTOUM
AMNOPTY	TYMPANO
AMNORRS	MARRONS
AMNORSS	RAMSONS
	RANSOMS
AMNORST	MATRONS
	TRANSOM
AMNORSY	MASONRY
	MORNAYS
AMNORTU	ROMAUNT
AMNOSST	STAMNOS
AMNOSTU	AMOUNTS
	MOUTANS
	OUTMANS
AMNOSYZ	ZYMOSAN
AMNOTUY	AUTONYM
AMNPSTY	TYMPANS
AMNPTYY	TYMPANY
AMNQTUU	QUANTUM
AMNRRUY	UNMARRY
AMNRSTU	ANTRUMS
	UNSMART
AMNRTTU	TANTRUM
AMNSTTU	MUTANTS
AMNSTUU	AUTUMNS
AMNTUUY	AUTUMNY
AMOOORS	AMOROSO

AMOOPRS	PROSOMA
AMOOPRT	TAPROOM
AMOORSU	AMOROUS
AMOORSV	MOORVAS
	VAROOMS
AMOORXY	OXYMORA
AMOPPSY	MAYPOPS
AMOPSTT	TOPMAST
AMORRST	MORTARS
AMORRSU	ARMOURS
AMORRSW	MARROWS
AMORRTY	MORTARY
AMORRUY	ARMOURY
AMORRWY	MARROWY
AMORSST	MATROSS
	STROAMS
AMORSSY	MORASSY
AMORWWX	WAXWORM
AMOSTUW	OUTSWAM
AMOSTUZ	MAZOUTS
AMOSUYZ	AZYMOUS
AMPRSST	STRAMPS
AMPRSUW	UPSWARM
	WARMUPS
AMRRSTU	RASTRUM
AMRRSTY	MARTYRS
AMRRSUY	MURRAYS
AMRRTYY	MARTYRY
AMRSSTU	STRUMAS
AMRSTTU	STRATUM
ANNNOSY	SYNANON
ANNOPRS	NAPRONS
ANNOPSS	SANNOPS
ANNOPST	NONPAST
	PANTONS
ANNOPTY	POYNANT
ANNORST	NATRONS
	NONARTS
ANNORSW	NONWARS
ANNOSST	SANTONS
	SONANTS
ANNOSTW	WANTONS
ANNOSTY	TANNOYS
ANNOTTY	TANTONY
ANNPSSU	SANNUPS
	UNSNAPS
ANNPSTU	PANTUNS
ANNRTYY	TYRANNY
ANNSSTU	SUNTANS
ANNSSTY	SYNTANS
ANOOPRS	PRONAOS
	SOPRANO
ANOOPRT	PATROON
	PRONOTA
ANOORST	RATOONS
ANOORTT	ARNOTTO
	RATTOON
ANOPRRS	SPORRAN
ANOPRSS	PARSONS
ANOPRST	PARTONS
	PATRONS
	TARPONS
ANOPRSW	PAWNORS
ANOPRTV	PROVANT
ANOPSTT	OPTANTS
ANOPSTU	OUTSPAN
ANOPSUY	YAUPONS
ANORRSW	NARROWS
ANORRWW	WARWORN
ANORSSV	SOVRANS
ANORSTT	ATTORNS
	RATTONS
	ROTTANS
ANORSTU	ROUSANT
	SANTOUR
ANORSTY	AROYNTS
ANORSUU	ANUROUS
	URANOUS
ANORWWY	WAYWORN
ANOSSTZ	STANZOS
ANOSTTU	TOTANUS
ANPPSUW	SUPPAWN
ANPRSSU	UNSPARS
ANPRSTU	SUNTRAP
	UNSTRAP
ANPRSUW	UNWRAPS
ANPRSUY	UNPRAYS
ANPSSUW	SUPAWNS
ANRSSTU	SANTURS
ANRSSUY	SUNRAYS
ANRSTTU	TRUANTS
ANRSTTY	TYRANTS
ANRSUWY	RUNWAYS
ANSSTTU	TUTSANS
AOOPPRS	APROPOS
AOOPRTT	TAPROOT
AOORRST	ORATORS
AOORRSY	ARROYOS
AOORRTT	ROTATOR
AOORRTU	OUTROAR
AOORRTY	ORATORY
AOORSTT	TOOARTS
AOORSTU	OUTSOAR
AOORSTV	OVATORS
AOOSTTT	TATTOOS
AOOSTUZ	AZOTOUS
AOOTXYZ	ZOOTAXY
AOPPPSU	PAPPOUS
AOPPRRT	RAPPORT
AOPPRST	APPORTS
AOPRRST	PARROTS
	RAPTORS
AOPRRSU	UPROARS
AOPRRSW	SPARROW
AOPRRTY	PARROTY
	PORTRAY
AOPRSST	ASPORTS
	PASTORS
AOPRSSU	SAPOURS
	UPSOARS
AOPRSTU	ASPROUT
AOPRSTW	POSTWAR
AOPRSUV	VAPOURS
AOPRTTU	OUTPART
AOPRTUY	OUTPRAY
AOPRUVY	VAPOURY
AOPSSTU	OUTPASS
	PASSOUT
AOPSTTX	POSTTAX
AOPSTUY	AUTOPSY
	PAYOUTS
AOPSTWY	WAYPOST
AOQRSTU	QUARTOS
AORRSST	SARTORS
AORRSSU	ASSUROR
AORRSTW	TARROWS
AORRSWY	SOWARRY
	YARROWS
AORSSST	ASSORTS
AORSSTT	STATORS
AORSSTU	SOUTARS
AORSSUV	SAVOURS
AORSSUY	OSSUARY
	SUASORY
AORSTUW	OUTWARS
AORSTUY	YAOURTS
AORSUVY	SAVOURY
AORTUVY	AVOUTRY
AORUVVY	VOUVRAY
AOSTTTW	TATTOWS
AOSTTUY	OUTSTAY
APPRRUU	PURPURA
APPRSTY	STRAPPY
APPRSUW	UPWRAPS
APPRSUY	PAPYRUS
APRSSSU	SURPASS
APRSSWY	PSYWARS
APRSTTU	STARTUP
	UPSTART
APRSTTY	TAPSTRY
APRSUWY	SPURWAY
APSSTUY	UPSTAYS
APSSUWY	UPSWAYS
AQRTUYZ	QUARTZY
AQSTTUY	SQUATTY
ARSSSTU	TUSSARS
ARSSTTU	STRATUS
ARSSTTY	STARTSY
ASSTTUY	STATUSY
AVYYZZZ	ZYZZYVA
BBBDELO	BLOBBED
	BOBBLED
BBBDELU	BLUBBED
	BUBBLED
BBBEIOS	BOBBIES
BBBEIRS	BIBBERS
BBBEIRY	BIBBERY
BBBEISU	BUBBIES
BBBELOS	BOBBLES
BBBELRU	BLUBBER
	BUBBLER
BBBELSU	BUBBLES
BBBEORS	BOBBERS
BBBEORY	BOBBERY
BBBGIIN	BIBBING
BBBGINO	BOBBING
BBBHIOS	BOBBISH
BBBHSUU	HUBBUBS
BBBINOS	BOBBINS
BBBIOTT	BOBBITT
BBCCIKO	BIBCOCK
BBCDEIR	CRIBBED
BBCDELO	COBBLED
BBCDELU	CLUBBED
BBCEEHO	BOBECHE
BBCEHIN	NEBBICH
BBCEILR	CRIBBLE
BBCEIOR	COBBIER
BBCEIRR	CRIBBER
BBCEISU	CUBBIES
BBCEKKO	KEBBOCK
BBCEKKU	KEBBUCK
BBCELOR	CLOBBER
	COBBLER
BBCELOS	COBBLES
BBCELRU	CLUBBER
BBCEORS	COBBERS
BBCEOSW	COBWEBS
BBCGINO	COBBING
BBCGINU	CUBBING
BBCHISU	CUBBISH
BBCINOU	BUBONIC
BBCRSUY	SCRUBBY
BBDDEIL	DIBBLED
BBDDEIR	DRIBBED
BBDDERU	DRUBBED
BBDEEIR	DEBBIER
BBDEEIS	DEBBIES
BBDEEIT	EBBTIDE
BBDEELP	PEBBLED
BBDEENS	SNEBBED
BBDEEOR	BEROBED
BBDEFLU	FLUBBED
BBDEGIL	GLIBBED
BBDEGLO	GOBBLED
BBDEGRU	GRUBBED
BBDEGSU	BEDBUGS
BBDEHLO	HOBBLED
BBDEIIM	IMBIBED
BBDEIKL	KIBBLED
BBDEILN	NIBBLED
BBDEILO	BILOBED
	LOBBIED
BBDEILR	DIBBLER
	DRIBBLE
BBDEILS	DIBBLES
BBDEINS	SNIBBED
BBDEIOS	DOBBIES
BBDEIRR	DRIBBER
BBDEIRS	DIBBERS
BBDEKNO	KNOBBED
BBDELMO	MOBBLED
BBDELMU	BUMBLED
BBDELNO	NOBBLED
BBDELNU	NUBBLED
BBDELOO	BEBLOOD
BBDELOS	BOBSLED
BBDELOW	WOBBLED
BBDELRU	BLURBED
	BURBLED
	RUBBLED
BBDELSU	SLUBBED
BBDEMSU	BEDUMBS
BBDENSU	SNUBBED
BBDEORS	DOBBERS
BBDEOST	STOBBED
BBDEOSW	SWOBBED
BBDERRU	DRUBBER
BBDERSU	DUBBERS
BBDESSU	SUBDEBS
BBDESTU	STUBBED
BBDFLUU	FLUBDUB
BBDGIIN	DIBBING
BBDGINO	DOBBING
BBDGINU	DUBBING
BBDIKSU	DIBBUKS
BBDILRY	DRIBBLY
BBDINOS	DOBBINS
BBDINSU	DUBBINS
BBDKSUY	DYBBUKS
BBEEEES	BEEBEES
BBEEERU	BEBEERU
BBEEIKS	KEBBIES
BBEEIRS	BRIBEES
BBEEIRW	WEBBIER
BBEEKLS	LEBBEKS
BBEELPS	PEBBLES
BBEELSS	EBBLESS
BBEENSS	SNEBBES
BBEFILR	FRIBBLE
BBEFIRS	FIBBERS
BBEFIRU	FUBBIER
BBEFIRY	FIBBERY
BBEFLRU	FLUBBER
BBEFRUY	FUBBERY
BBEGIKN	KEBBING
BBEGILR	GLIBBER
	GRIBBLE
BBEGINN	NEBBING
BBEGINW	WEBBING
BBEGIOS	GIBBOSE
BBEGIRS	GIBBERS
BBEGIST	GIBBETS
BBEGLOR	GOBBLER
BBEGLOS	GOBBLES
BBEGLRU	GRUBBLE
BBEGNSU	BEBUNGS
BBEGOST	GOBBETS
BBEGRRU	GRUBBER
BBEHIKS	KIBBEHS

BBEHINS	NEBBISH
BBEHIOS	HOBBIES
BBEHISU	HUBBIES
BBEHLOR	HOBBLER
BBEHLOS	HOBBLES
BBEHMTU	BETHUMB
BBEIIKL	BIBLIKE
BBEIILR	RIBIBLE
BBEIIMR	IMBIBER
BBEIIMS	IMBIBES
BBEIIRR	RIBBIER
BBEIIRS	RIBIBES
BBEIJOS	JOBBIES
BBEIJRS	JIBBERS
BBEIKLS	KIBBLES
BBEILNR	NIBBLER
BBEILNS	NIBBLES
BBEILOS	BILBOES
	LOBBIES
BBEILOT	BIBELOT
BBEILPR	PRIBBLE
BBEILQU	QUIBBLE
BBEILRS	LIBBERS
BBEILRT	TRIBBLE
BBEILSS	BIBLESS
BBEILST	STIBBLE
BBEILSY	YIBBLES
BBEIMOS	BIMBOES
	MOBBIES
BBEINOR	NOBBIER
BBEINRU	NUBBIER
BBEIOOS	BOOBIES
BBEIRRS	BRIBERS
	RIBBERS
BBEIRRY	BRIBERY
BBEIRTU	TUBBIER
BBEISSU	BUSBIES
	SUBBIES
BBEJORS	JOBBERS
BBEJORY	JOBBERY
BBEKLNO	KNOBBLE
BBEKLNU	KNUBBLE
BBEKLOS	BLESBOK
BBEKLUU	BUBUKLE
BBEKNOR	KNOBBER
BBEKNSU	NEBBUKS
BBELLOY	BELLBOY
BBELLSU	BULBELS
BBELLTU	BULBLET
BBELMOS	MOBBLES
BBELMOT	BOMBLET
BBELMRU	BUMBLER
BBELMSU	BUMBLES
BBELNOR	NOBBLER
BBELNOS	NOBBLES
BBELNSU	NUBBLES
BBELNSY	NYBBLES
BBELORS	LOBBERS
	SLOBBER
BBELORW	WOBBLER
BBELORY	LOBBYER
BBELOSW	WOBBLES
BBELRRU	BURBLER
BBELRSU	BURBLES
	LUBBERS
	RUBBLES
	SLUBBER
BBELSTU	STUBBLE
BBEMNSU	BENUMBS
BBEMORS	BOMBERS
	MOBBERS
BBENOTW	BOWBENT
BBENRSU	SNUBBER
BBENSSU	SNUBBES
BBEOOSY	YOBBOES
BBEORRS	ROBBERS
BBEORRY	ROBBERY
BBEORSS	SOBBERS
BBEORSW	SWOBBER
BBEORYY	YOBBERY
BBEPRUW	BREWPUB
BBERRSU	RUBBERS
BBERRUY	RUBBERY
BBERSTU	TUBBERS
BBFGIIN	FIBBING
BBFGINO	FOBBING
BBFGINU	FUBBING
BBGGIIN	GIBBING
BBGGINO	GOBBING
BBGHINO	HOBBING
BBGIIJN	JIBBING
BBGIILN	LIBBING
BBGIINN	NIBBING
BBGIINR	BRIBING
	RIBBING
BBGIJNO	JOBBING
BBGILLU	BILLBUG
BBGILNO	LOBBING
BBGILNU	BULBING
BBGIMNO	BOMBING
	MOBBING
BBGINNU	NUBBING
BBGINOO	BOOBING
BBGINOR	ROBBING
BBGINOS	GIBBONS
	SOBBING
BBGINRU	RUBBING
BBGINSU	GUBBINS
	SUBBING
BBGINTU	TUBBING
BBGIOSU	GIBBOUS
BBGIOSW	BOBWIGS
BBHHIOS	HOBBISH
BBHIMOS	MOBBISH
BBHIOOS	BOOBISH
BBHIOST	HOBBITS
BBHIOSY	YOBBISH
BBHIRSU	RUBBISH
BBHISTU	TUBBISH
BBHJOOS	HOBJOBS
BBHKOOS	BOSHBOK
BBHNOOS	HOBNOBS
BBHOOUW	WHOOBUB
BBHRSUY	SHRUBBY
BBIIILM	BILIMBI
BBIIKTZ	KIBBITZ
BBIILST	BIBLIST
BBIJMOO	JIBBOOM
BBIKOSS	SKIBOBS
BBIKTUZ	KIBBUTZ
BBILLSU	BULBILS
BBILLUU	LULIBUB
BBILNOY	NOBBILY
BBIMOSY	YOBBISM
BBINNSU	NUBBINS
BBINORS	RIBBONS
	ROBBINS
BBINORY	RIBBONY
BBJLOOW	BLOWJOB
BBKLNOY	KNOBBLY
BBKLNUY	KNUBBLY
BBKLOOU	BLOUBOK
BBKOOOO	BOOBOOK
BBKOOSS	BOSBOKS
BBLLSUU	BULBULS
BBLOSUU	BULBOUS
BBLOSWY	BLOWBYS
BBLSTUY	STUBBLY
BBMOOOX	BOOMBOX
BBNNOOS	BONBONS
BBNOORU	BOURBON
BBOOOOS	BOOBOOS
BBOOSUU	BOUBOUS
BBORSTU	BURBOTS
BBOSSUY	BUSBOYS
BBRSSUU	SUBURBS
BCCEEHS	CHEBECS
BCCEIIS	BICCIES
BCCEILO	ECBOLIC
BCCEILU	CUBICLE
BCCEILY	BICYCLE
BCCEIOS	BOCCIES
BCCILOU	BUCOLIC
BCCILUY	CUBICLY
BCCINOO	OBCONIC
BCCISUU	SUCCUBI
BCCMOOX	COXCOMB
BCCMSUU	SUCCUMB
BCCNOOR	CORNCOB
BCDEEHL	BELCHED
BCDEEHN	BENCHED
BCDEEIL	DECIBEL
BCDEEKS	BEDECKS
BCDEENU	BEDUNCE
BCDEHIR	BIRCHED
BCDEHIT	BITCHED
BCDEHNU	BUNCHED
BCDEHOR	BROCHED
BCDEHOT	BOTCHED
BCDEHOU	DEBOUCH
BCDEIIO	BIOCIDE
BCDEIKR	BRICKED
BCDEIKS	SICKBED
BCDEIKT	BEDTICK
BCDEILM	CLIMBED
BCDEILO	DOCIBLE
BCDEIOS	BODICES
	CEBOIDS
BCDEIRS	SCRIBED
BCDEKLO	BLOCKED
BCDEKLU	BUCKLED
BCDEKOR	BEDROCK
	BROCKED
BCDEKSU	BEDUCKS
BCDELOU	BECLOUD
BCDEMOR	CROMBED
BCDEMRU	CRUMBED
BCDENOU	BOUNCED
	BUNCOED
BCDEORU	COURBED
BCDEORW	BECROWD
BCDEOSU	SUBCODE
BCDESUU	SUBDUCE
BCDHIOR	BICHORD
BCDHIRU	BRUCHID
BCDHOOU	CUBHOOD
BCDIIRU	RUBIDIC
BCDILOO	COLOBID
BCDINOW	COWBIND
BCDIORW	COWBIRD
BCDIOSU	CUBOIDS
BCDIRSY	CYBRIDS
BCDKORU	BURDOCK
BCDNOSU	BONDUCS
BCDSTUU	SUBDUCT
BCEEEHN	BEECHEN
BCEEEHS	BEECHES
	BESEECH
BCEEFIN	BENEFIC
BCEEFKL	BEFLECK
BCEEGIR	ICEBERG
BCEEHIP	EPHEBIC
BCEEHIT	HEBETIC
BCEEHLR	BELCHER
BCEEHLS	BELCHES
BCEEHNR	BENCHER
BCEEHNS	BENCHES
BCEEHOS	OBECHES
BCEEHOU	BOUCHEE
BCEEIMR	BECRIME
BCEEIPS	BESPICE
BCEEIRS	ESCRIBE
BCEEIRT	TEREBIC
BCEEKNS	NEBECKS
BCEEKNU	BUCKEEN
BCEEKRS	REBECKS
BCEEKST	BECKETS
BCEEKSZ	ZEBECKS
BCEEKUY	BUCKEYE
BCEELOS	ECBOLES
BCEEMOS	BECOMES
BCEENOS	OBSCENE
BCEENRU	CRUBEEN
BCEERSU	BECURSE
BCEFIIS	SEBIFIC
BCEGIKN	BECKING
BCEGLOS	BECLOGS
BCEHINR	BIRCHEN
BCEHINT	BENTHIC
BCEHIOR	BRIOCHE
BCEHIOT	BIOTECH
BCEHIRS	BIRCHES
BCEHIST	BITCHES
BCEHITW	BEWITCH
BCEHLRU	BLUCHER
BCEHNSU	BUNCHES
BCEHORS	BROCHES
BCEHORT	BOTCHER
BCEHORW	COWHERB
BCEHOSS	BOSCHES
BCEHOST	BOTCHES
BCEHOSU	BOUCHES
	SUBECHO
BCEHRSU	CHERUBS
BCEHRTU	BUTCHER
BCEHSTU	BUTCHES
BCEIIKR	BRICKIE
BCEIISV	VIBICES
BCEIKLM	LIMBECK
BCEIKLR	BRICKLE
BCEIKNR	BRICKEN
BCEIKRS	BICKERS
BCEIKST	BESTICK
BCEIKSU	BUCKIES
BCEILMO	EMBOLIC
BCEILMR	CLIMBER
	RECLIMB
BCEILMS	EMBLICS
	LIMBECS
BCEILNO	BINOCLE
BCEILOR	BRICOLE
	CORBEIL
BCEILOU	CIBOULE
BCEILSY	BEYLICS
BCEIMNO	COMBINE
BCEIMOR	COMBIER
	MICROBE
BCEIMOS	COMBIES
BCEINOR	BICORNE
BCEINOS	EBONICS
BCEINOZ	BENZOIC
BCEINRU	BRUCINE
BCEIORS	CORBIES
BCEIRRS	SCRIBER
BCEIRSS	SCRIBES
BCEIRSU	SUBERIC
BCEIRTU	BRUCITE
BCEISST	BISECTS
BCEJOST	OBJECTS
BCEJSTU	SUBJECT

BCEKLOR	BLOCKER
BCEKLRU	BRUCKLE
	BUCKLER
BCEKLSU	BUCKLES
BCEKMOS	BEMOCKS
BCEKNOS	BECKONS
BCEKORT	BROCKET
BCEKORU	ROEBUCK
BCEKOSU	BUCKOES
BCEKOTY	BYCOKET
BCEKRSU	BUCKERS
BCEKSTU	BESTUCK
	BUCKETS
BCELLOW	COWBELL
BCELLSU	SUBCELL
BCELMNU	CLUBMEN
BCELMOS	COMBLES
BCELMRU	CLUMBER
	CRUMBLE
BCELMSU	SCUMBLE
BCELNOW	BECLOWN
BCELORS	CORBELS
BCELOSU	BOUCLES
BCELRSU	BECURLS
BCELSSU	CUBLESS
BCEMNTU	CUMBENT
BCEMOOS	COOMBES
BCEMORS	COMBERS
	RECOMBS
BCEMRRU	CRUMBER
BCEMRSU	CUMBERS
	SCUMBER
BCENORU	BOUNCER
BCENOSU	BOUNCES
BCEORSS	SCROBES
BCEORSU	BESCOUR
	OBSCURE
BCERRSU	CURBERS
BCERSTU	BECRUST
	BECURST
BCESSTU	SUBSECT
BCFSSUU	SUBFUSC
BCGIKNO	BOCKING
BCGIKNU	BUCKING
BCGIMNO	COMBING
BCGINNU	BUNCING
BCGINRU	CURBING
BCGORSU	COBURGS
BCGORSY	CYBORGS
BCHIIOP	BIOCHIP
BCHIIOT	COHIBIT
BCHIKOU	CHIBOUK
BCHIKOY	BOYCHIK
BCHIKSU	BUCKISH
BCHILMY	CHIMBLY
BCHILOS	CHIBOLS
BCHIMOR	RHOMBIC
BCHINOR	BRONCHI
BCHIOPR	PIBROCH
BCHIOPS	PHOBICS
BCHLOTY	BLOTCHY
BCHNOOR	BRONCHO
BCHORST	BORSCHT
	BORTSCH
BCIIKLN	NIBLICK
BCIILMU	BULIMIC
BCIILOR	COLIBRI
BCIILSY	SIBYLIC
BCIINOS	BIONICS
BCIINOT	BIONTIC
BCIIOPS	BIOPICS
	BIOPSIC
BCIIOPT	BIOPTIC
BCIIOST	BIOTICS
BCIISTU	BISCUIT

BCIKNOS	KINCOBS
BCIKORT	BROCKIT
BCIKOTT	BITTOCK
BCILMPU	PLUMBIC
	UPCLIMB
BCILOOR	BICOLOR
	BROCOLI
BCILPSU	PUBLICS
BCIMNOU	UMBONIC
BCIMSSU	CUBISMS
BCINOOR	BORONIC
BCINORS	BICORNS
	BICRONS
BCINORU	RUBICON
BCINRSU	BRUCINS
BCINSUU	INCUBUS
BCIOORT	ROBOTIC
BCIORST	STROBIC
BCIOSTY	SYBOTIC
BCIRRSU	RUBRICS
BCIRTUY	BUTYRIC
BCISSTU	BUSTICS
	CUBISTS
BCISTUU	CUBITUS
BCJKMUU	JUMBUCK
BCKLLOO	BOLLOCK
BCKLLOU	BULLOCK
BCKLNOU	UNBLOCK
BCKLOOX	LOCKBOX
BCKMMOU	BUMMOCK
BCKMOSU	BUCKSOM
BCKNNOO	BONNOCK
BCKOTTU	BUTTOCK
BCLMOOU	COULOMB
BCLMRUY	CRUMBLY
BCLOOSU	COLOBUS
	SUBCOOL
BCLORTU	CLOTBUR
BCLSTUU	SUBCULT
BCMMRUU	CRUMBUM
BCMOOST	TOMBOCS
BCMORSY	CORYMBS
BCMOSTU	COMBUST
BCNOORS	BRONCOS
BCNOSTU	COBNUTS
BCNRSUU	UNCURBS
BCOOPYY	COPYBOY
BCOOSWY	COWBOYS
BCOOTTY	BOYCOTT
BDDDEIU	BUDDIED
BDDDELU	BUDDLED
BDDDEOR	BRODDED
BDDEEER	REEDBED
BDDEEES	SEEDBED
BDDEEEW	BEDEWED
BDDEEIL	BIELDED
BDDEEIR	DEBRIDE
BDDEEIS	BEDSIDE
BDDEEIT	BETIDED
	DEBITED
BDDEELN	BLENDED
BDDEENO	DEBONED
BDDEERS	BEDDERS
BDDEETU	DEBUTED
BDDEGIN	BEDDING
BDDEGIR	BRIDGED
BDDEGLU	BLUDGED
BDDEIIR	BIRDIED
BDDEIIS	BIDDIES
BDDEILN	BLINDED
BDDEILR	BRIDLED
BDDEILU	BUILDED
BDDEINR	BRINDED
BDDEIOO	BOODIED
BDDEIRR	REDBIRD

BDDEIRS	BIDDERS
BDDEIRU	BUDDIER
BDDEISU	BUDDIES
BDDELNU	BUNDLED
BDDELOO	BLOODED
	BOODLED
BDDELOS	BODDLES
BDDELOU	DOUBLED
BDDELSU	BUDDLES
BDDENOU	BOUNDED
BDDEOOR	BROODED
BDDEORU	OBDURED
BDDEOTU	DOUBTED
BDDERSU	BUDDERS
	REDBUDS
BDDESUU	SUBDUED
BDDGIIN	BIDDING
BDDGINU	BUDDING
BDDISSU	DISBUDS
BDEEEFL	FEEBLED
BDEEELL	DELEBLE
BDEEELP	BLEEPED
BDEEELR	BLEEDER
BDEEELT	BEETLED
BDEEELV	BEVELED
BDEEEMN	BEDEMEN
BDEEEMT	BEMETED
BDEEENS	BENDEES
BDEEEPS	BESPEED
BDEEERR	BREEDER
	BREERED
	REBREED
BDEEERZ	BREEZED
BDEEEST	DEBTEES
BDEEFIR	BRIEFED
	DEBRIEF
	FIBERED
BDEEFOX	FEEDBOX
BDEEGOR	BEGORED
BDEEGOY	BOGEYED
BDEEGSU	BUGSEED
BDEEHOV	BEHOVED
BDEEHRT	BERTHED
BDEEIKL	BEDLIKE
BDEEIKN	BEINKED
BDEEILL	BELLIED
	DELIBLE
	LIBELED
BDEEILS	EDIBLES
BDEEILV	BEDEVIL
BDEEIMR	BEMIRED
	BERIMED
BDEEIMT	BEDTIME
	BETIMED
BDEEIMX	BEMIXED
BDEEINR	BENDIER
	INBREED
BDEEINZ	BEDIZEN
BDEEIRR	BERRIED
	BRIERED
BDEEIRS	DERBIES
BDEEISS	BESIDES
BDEEIST	BETIDES
BDEEIVV	BEVVIED
BDEEJLS	DJEBELS
BDEEKMO	KEMBOED
BDEEKRU	REBUKED
BDEELLS	BEDELLS
BDEELMR	REMBLED
BDEELMS	SEMBLED
BDEELMU	UMBELED
BDEELNR	BLENDER
	REBLEND
BDEELNS	BLENDES
BDEELNT	BENDLET

BDEELOV	BELOVED
BDEELOW	BOWELED
	ELBOWED
BDEELRT	TREBLED
BDEELSS	BEDLESS
	BLESSED
BDEELTT	BLETTED
BDEELZZ	BEZZLED
BDEEMOS	BESOMED
BDEEMOW	EMBOWED
BDEEMOX	EMBOXED
BDEEMRU	EMBRUED
	UMBERED
BDEEMSU	BEMUSED
BDEENOR	DEBONER
	ENROBED
	REDBONE
BDEENOS	DEBONES
BDEENPR	PREBEND
BDEENRS	BENDERS
BDEEORR	REBORED
BDEEORS	BEDSORE
	SOBERED
BDEEORV	OVERBED
BDEEORW	BOWERED
BDEEOSX	SEEDBOX
BDEERSU	BURSEED
BDEERUW	BURWEED
BDEFFLU	BLUFFED
BDEFILR	FILBERD
BDEFLMU	FUMBLED
BDEFLOU	BODEFUL
BDEFOOR	FORBODE
BDEGGLO	BOGGLED
BDEGGOR	BROGGED
BDEGHIT	BEDIGHT
	BIGHTED
BDEGHOU	BOUGHED
BDEGILN	BINGLED
BDEGILO	OBLIGED
BDEGILS	BEGILDS
BDEGINN	BENDING
BDEGINO	BOINGED
BDEGINR	BREDING
BDEGIOO	BOOGIED
BDEGIOR	BODGIER
BDEGIOS	BODGIES
BDEGIOT	BIGOTED
BDEGIRS	BEGIRDS
	BRIDGES
BDEGIRU	BRIGUED
BDEGISU	BUDGIES
BDEGLNU	BLUNGED
	BUNGLED
BDEGLRU	BLUDGER
	BURGLED
BDEGLSU	BLUDGES
BDEGNOW	BEDGOWN
BDEGNSU	BEDUNGS
BDEGOOY	GOODBYE
BDEGORS	BODGERS
BDEGORU	BUDGERO
BDEGRSU	BEDRUGS
	BUDGERS
	REDBUGS
BDEGSTU	BUDGETS
BDEHINS	BEHINDS
BDEHIRT	BIRTHED
BDEHLMU	HUMBLED
BDEHLOS	BEHOLDS
BDEHLSU	BLUSHED
BDEHMTU	THUMBED
BDEHORY	HERDBOY
BDEHOST	HOTBEDS
BDEHRSU	BRUSHED

BDEIIRS	BIRDIES
	BRIDIES
BDEIIVV	BIVVIED
BDEIJLR	JIRBLED
BDEIKLN	BLINKED
BDEIKLU	BUDLIKE
BDEIKMO	KIMBOED
BDEIKNO	BOINKED
BDEIKRS	BRISKED
BDEILLU	BULLIED
BDEILMS	DIMBLES
BDEILMW	WIMBLED
BDEILNN	BLINNED
BDEILNR	BLINDER
	BRINDLE
BDEILNS	BINDLES
BDEILNY	BYLINED
BDEILOP	LOBIPED
BDEILOR	BROILED
BDEILOS	BOLIDES
BDEILOX	BOLIXED
BDEILPP	BLIPPED
BDEILRR	BRIDLER
BDEILRS	BIRSLED
	BRIDLES
BDEILRT	DRIBLET
BDEILRU	BLUDIER
	BUILDER
	REBUILD
BDEILSS	BLISSED
BDEILST	BILSTED
BDEILTZ	BLITZED
BDEIMMR	BRIMMED
BDEIMNR	BIRDMEN
BDEIMOR	BROMIDE
BDEIMRU	IMBRUED
BDEIMTU	BITUMED
BDEINOR	INORBED
BDEINOU	BEDOUIN
BDEINPR	PREBIND
BDEINRS	BINDERS
	INBREDS
	REBINDS
BDEINRY	BINDERY
BDEINST	BIDENTS
BDEINSU	BEDUINS
BDEIOOS	BOODIES
BDEIORR	BROIDER
BDEIORS	BORIDES
	DISROBE
BDEIORT	DEBITOR
	DEORBIT
	ORBITED
BDEIORV	OVERBID
BDEIORZ	ZEBROID
BDEIOSY	DISOBEY
BDEIRRS	BIRDERS
BDEIRST	BESTRID
	BISTRED
BDEIRSU	BRUISED
	BURDIES
BDEIRSV	VERBIDS
BDEIRTU	BRUITED
BDEIRTY	BEDIRTY
BDEISST	BEDSITS
BDEISSU	SUBSIDE
BDEISTU	BUISTED
	SUBEDIT
BDEITUY	DUBIETY
BDEJLMU	JUMBLED
BDEJORU	OBJURED
BDEKLNU	BLUNKED
BDEKNOO	BOOKEND
BDEKNOU	BUNKOED
BDEKNSU	DEBUNKS
BDEKOOR	BROOKED
BDELLOR	BEDROLL
BDELMMU	BUMMLED
	MUMBLED
BDELMOO	BLOOMED
BDELMPU	PLUMBED
BDELMRU	DRUMBLE
	RUMBLED
BDELMTU	TUMBLED
BDELNOR	BLONDER
BDELNOS	BLONDES
	BOLDENS
BDELNOU	UNLOBED
BDELNRU	BLUNDER
	BUNDLER
BDELNSU	BUNDLES
BDELNTU	BLUNTED
BDELOOP	BLOOPED
BDELOOR	BOODLER
BDELOOS	BOODLES
BDELORS	BORDELS
BDELORU	BOULDER
	DOUBLER
BDELORW	BOWLDER
	LOWBRED
BDELOST	BOLDEST
BDELOSU	BLOUSED
	DOUBLES
BDELOSW	BLOWSED
BDELOTT	BLOTTED
	BOTTLED
BDELOTU	BOULTED
	DOUBLET
BDELOWZ	BLOWZED
BDELRRU	BLURRED
BDELRTU	BLURTED
BDELSSU	BUDLESS
BDELSTU	BUSTLED
BDELSWY	LEWDSBY
BDELTTU	BUTTLED
BDEMNNO	BONDMEN
BDEMNOU	EMBOUND
BDEMOOR	BEDROOM
	BOREDOM
	BROOMED
BDEMOOS	BOSOMED
BDEMORS	SOMBRED
BDEMSTU	DUMBEST
BDENNOU	BOUNDEN
	UNBONED
BDENNSU	UNBENDS
BDENORS	BONDERS
BDENORU	BOUNDER
	REBOUND
	UNROBED
BDENORW	BROWNED
BDENORZ	BRONZED
BDENOST	OBTENDS
BDENOSY	BEYONDS
BDENOUW	UNBOWED
BDENOUX	UNBOXED
BDENRSU	BURDENS
BDENRTU	BRUNTED
BDENSSU	SUNBEDS
BDENSTU	SUBTEND
BDENSUY	SEBUNDY
BDEOORR	BROODER
BDEOORS	BOORDES
BDEOOST	BOOSTED
BDEOPRS	BEDROPS
BDEOPRT	BEDROPT
BDEOPST	BEDPOST
BDEORRS	BORDERS
BDEORRU	BORDURE
	BOURDER
BDEORSS	DESORBS
BDEORST	DEBTORS
	STROBED
BDEORSU	OBDURES
	ROSEBUD
BDEORSW	BROWSED
BDEORTU	DOUBTER
	OBTRUDE
	OUTBRED
	REDOUBT
BDEORUV	OVERDUB
BDERSSU	SURBEDS
BDERSTU	BURSTED
BDERSUU	SUBDUER
BDERSUY	RUDESBY
BDESSTU	BEDUSTS
	BESTUDS
BDESSUU	SUBDUES
BDESSUW	SUBDEWS
BDFIILY	BIFIDLY
BDFIIOR	FIBROID
BDFIISU	FIDIBUS
BDFIORS	FORBIDS
BDGGINO	BODGING
BDGGINU	BUDGING
BDGGLOU	GOLDBUG
BDGIINN	BINDING
BDGIINR	BIRDING
	BRIDING
BDGIINS	BIDINGS
BDGIIOO	GOBIOID
BDGIIOS	GOBIIDS
BDGILOO	GLOBOID
BDGIMNU	DUMBING
BDGINNO	BONDING
BDGINNU	BUNDING
BDGINOS	BODINGS
BDGINOY	BODYING
BDGLLOU	BULLDOG
BDGLOOT	DOGBOLT
BDGOOOW	BOGWOOD
BDGOOSY	GOODBYS
BDGORSU	DORBUGS
BDHIINS	BHINDIS
BDHINOP	HOPBIND
BDHIOSU	BUSHIDO
BDHIRSY	HYBRIDS
BDHMOOO	HOBODOM
BDHOOOY	BOYHOOD
BDIIKNO	BODIKIN
BDIILMS	DISLIMB
BDIILOR	OILBIRD
BDIILOS	LIBIDOS
BDIIMNS	MISBIND
BDIIMRS	MIDRIBS
BDIISTT	TIDBITS
BDIKNOR	BRODKIN
BDIKNOS	BODKINS
BDILLNY	BLINDLY
BDILNNU	UNBLIND
BDILNUU	UNBUILD
BDILOOS	DIOBOLS
BDILPUU	BUILDUP
	UPBUILD
BDILRUY	BUIRDLY
BDILTUY	DIBUTYL
BDIMNPU	DUMPBIN
BDIMORS	BROMIDS
BDINNOU	INBOUND
BDINNSU	UNBINDS
BDINOOR	BRIDOON
BDINOOW	WOODBIN
BDINPSU	UPBINDS
BDINRSU	SUNBIRD
BDINSTU	BUNDIST
	DUSTBIN
BDIOOOV	OBOVOID
BDIOORU	BOUDOIR
BDIORSW	WOSBIRD
BDIOSSY	BYSSOID
BDIOSTU	OUTBIDS
BDIOSUU	DUBIOUS
BDIRSTU	DISTURB
BDISSUY	SUBSIDY
BDKLOOS	KOBOLDS
BDKNOOU	BUNDOOK
BDLNOOS	DOBLONS
BDLOOOX	OXBLOOD
BDMOOSS	BOSSDOM
BDMORUW	BUDWORM
BDNNOOY	NONBODY
BDNNOUU	UNBOUND
BDNOORU	BOURDON
BDNOOSS	DOBSONS
BDNOOWW	DOWNBOW
BDNOPUU	UPBOUND
BDNORTU	TURBOND
BDNORUW	RUBDOWN
BDNOSTU	OBTUNDS
BDOOOWX	BOXWOOD
	WOODBOX
BDORSWY	BYWORDS
BEEEEFR	FREEBEE
BEEEEKS	BESEEKE
BEEEEMT	BETEEME
BEEEENP	PEEBEEN
BEEEFIR	BEEFIER
	FREEBIE
BEEEFLR	FEEBLER
BEEEFLS	FEEBLES
BEEEFTW	WEBFEET
BEEEGIS	BESIEGE
BEEEGRR	BERGERE
BEEEHIV	BEEHIVE
BEEEHNS	SHEBEEN
BEEEHPS	EPHEBES
BEEEIKL	BEELIKE
BEEEILL	LIBELEE
BEEEILN	BEELINE
BEEEILV	BELIEVE
BEEEIRR	BEERIER
BEEEJLW	BEJEWEL
BEEEJLZ	JEZEBEL
BEEEKLL	BELLEEK
BEEEKLS	KEBELES
BEEELPR	BLEEPER
BEEELRT	BEETLER
BEEELRV	BEVELER
BEEELST	BEETLES
BEEEMOS	BEESOME
BEEEMRS	BERSEEM
BEEEMRW	EMBREWE
BEEEMSS	BESEEMS
BEEEMST	BEMETES
	BETEEMS
BEEENNZ	BENZENE
BEEENTW	BETWEEN
BEEEPRS	BEEPERS
BEEEPSW	BEWEEPS
BEEERSS	BREESES
BEEERSZ	BEEZERS
	BREEZES
BEEERTV	BREVETE
BEEFGIN	BEEFING
BEEFGIT	BIGFEET
BEEFILR	FEBRILE
BEEFILS	BELIEFS
BEEFILY	BEEFILY
BEEFINT	BENEFIT
BEEFIRR	BRIEFER

BEEFNRU	FUNEBRE
BEEFORY	FOREBYE
BEEFRST	BEFRETS
BEEGGNU	GEEBUNG
BEEGILL	LEGIBLE
BEEGILO	OBLIGEE
BEEGILS	BEIGELS
BEEGILU	BEGUILE
BEEGIMR	BEGRIME
BEEGINN	BEGINNE
BEEGINP	BEEPING
BEEGINR	BIGENER
	REBEGIN
BEEGINT	BEETING
	BEIGNET
BEEGINU	BEGUINE
BEEGISY	BIGEYES
BEEGLNO	ENGLOBE
BEEGMNO	GOMBEEN
BEEGMOU	EMBOGUE
BEEGNOO	GOBONEE
BEEGNOS	ENGOBES
BEEGNRU	REBEGUN
BEEGNSU	BUNGEES
BEEGNTU	UNBEGET
BEEGRSU	BURGEES
BEEGSUY	BUGEYES
BEEHINS	BESHINE
BEEHIOP	EPHEBOI
BEEHIRR	HERBIER
BEEHIST	BHISTEE
BEEHKSU	BUKSHEE
BEEHLRT	BLETHER
	HERBLET
BEEHLST	BETHELS
BEEHMRY	BERHYME
BEEHNNO	HEBENON
BEEHNOS	BESHONE
BEEHOOV	BEHOOVE
BEEHOPS	EPHEBOS
	PHOEBES
BEEHORS	HERBOSE
BEEHORW	BEWHORE
BEEHOST	BEHOTES
BEEHOSV	BEHOVES
BEEHPSU	EPHEBUS
BEEHRST	BERTHES
	SHERBET
BEEHRSW	BESHREW
BEEHRTY	THEREBY
BEEHRWY	WHEREBY
BEEHSST	BEHESTS
BEEHSTY	BHEESTY
BEEIJLU	JUBILEE
BEEIKLW	WEBLIKE
BEEILLR	LIBELER
BEEILLS	BELLIES
BEEILMS	BESLIME
	BESMILE
BEEILNR	BERLINE
BEEILOS	OBELISE
BEEILOZ	OBELIZE
BEEILRS	BELIERS
BEEILRV	VERBILE
BEEILTT	BETITLE
BEEIMRS	BEMIRES
	BERIMES
	BIREMES
BEEIMST	BETIMES
BEEIMSX	BEMIXES
BEEINNS	BENNIES
BEEINNZ	BENZINE
BEEINOS	EBONIES
	EBONISE
BEEINOT	EBONITE
BEEINOZ	EBONIZE
BEEINPR	PEBRINE
BEEINRT	BENTIER
BEEINRZ	ZEBRINE
BEEINSW	NEWBIES
BEEIORS	EBRIOSE
BEEIQUZ	BEZIQUE
BEEIRRS	BERRIES
BEEIRRV	BREVIER
BEEIRST	REBITES
BEEIRTY	EBRIETY
BEEISST	BETISES
BEEISTT	BETTIES
BEEISTW	WEBSITE
BEEISVV	BEVVIES
BEEJNSU	BUNJEES
BEEJSSU	BEJESUS
BEEKMOS	BESMOKE
BEEKNOT	BETOKEN
BEEKOPS	BESPOKE
BEEKORS	REEBOKS
BEEKRRS	BERSERK
BEEKRRU	REBUKER
BEEKRSU	REBUKES
BEELLMN	BELLMEN
BEELLOT	LOBELET
BEELMMS	EMBLEMS
BEELMNT	BELTMEN
BEELMOW	EMBOWEL
BEELMRS	REMBLES
BEELMRT	TREMBLE
BEELMSS	SEMBLES
BEELNNO	ENNOBLE
BEELNOZ	BENZOLE
BEELNSU	NEBULES
BEELOST	BOLETES
BEELOSV	BELOVES
BEELOSY	OBESELY
BEELOTY	EYEBOLT
BEELPST	BEPELTS
BEELRSS	BLESSER
BEELRST	BELTERS
	TREBLES
BEELRSY	BERLEYS
BEELRUZ	ZEBRULE
BEELSSS	BLESSES
BEELSSW	WEBLESS
BEELSZZ	BEZZLES
BEELTTU	BLUETTE
BEEMMRS	MEMBERS
BEEMNPT	BENEMPT
BEEMNRY	BYREMEN
BEEMORW	EMBOWER
BEEMOSS	MEBOSES
BEEMOSX	EMBOXES
BEEMRRU	UMBRERE
BEEMRSU	EMBRUES
BEEMRTU	EMBRUTE
BEEMSSU	BEMUSES
BEENNRS	BRENNES
BEENNST	BENNETS
BEENOOT	BOTONEE
BEENORR	ENROBER
BEENORS	BOREENS
	ENROBES
BEENOST	BONESET
BEENRRT	BRENTER
BEENSTU	BUTENES
	SUBTEEN
BEENSUV	SUBVENE
BEEOOST	BOOTEES
BEEOPPS	BOPEEPS
BEEOPRR	REPROBE
BEEOPRS	BEPROSE
BEEORRS	REBORES
	SOBERER
BEEORRU	BOURREE
BEEORSV	OBSERVE
	OBVERSE
	VERBOSE
BEEORSY	OBEYERS
BEEORTV	OVERBET
BEEORWY	EYEBROW
BEEOSST	OBESEST
BEEPRRV	PREVERB
BEEQSTU	BEQUEST
BEERRST	BERRETS
BEERRSU	BEURRES
BEERRSV	REVERBS
BEERRSW	BREWERS
BEERRWY	BREWERY
BEERSSU	REBUSES
	SUBSERE
BEERSTT	BETTERS
BEERSTV	BREVETS
BEERSTW	BESTREW
	WEBSTER
BEERTTU	BURETTE
BEESSTU	BUSTEES
BEETTUV	BUVETTE
BEFFIIS	BIFFIES
BEFFIRU	BUFFIER
BEFFLRU	BLUFFER
BEFFOSU	BOUFFES
BEFFPSU	BEPUFFS
BEFFRSU	BUFFERS
	REBUFFS
BEFFSTU	BUFFETS
BEFGIIL	FILIBEG
BEFGIRU	FIREBUG
BEFGIST	BEGIFTS
BEFGLSU	BEGULFS
BEFHOOS	BEHOOFS
BEFILMS	FIMBLES
BEFILNO	LOBEFIN
BEFILNU	BLUEFIN
BEFILOS	FOIBLES
BEFILPY	PLEBIFY
BEFILRT	FILBERT
BEFILRY	BRIEFLY
BEFILSU	FUSIBLE
	SUBFILE
BEFINOR	BONFIRE
BEFIORS	FIBROSE
BEFIORX	FIREBOX
BEFIRST	FIBSTER
BEFIRSU	FUBSIER
BEFIRVY	VERBIFY
BEFITUX	TUBIFEX
BEFLLTY	FLYBELT
BEFLLWY	FLYBLEW
BEFLMRU	FUMBLER
BEFLMSU	BEFLUMS
	FUMBLES
BEFLOOS	BEFOOLS
BEFLOSU	BEFOULS
BEFLTUU	TUBEFUL
BEFOORR	FORBORE
BEFOOTW	WEBFOOT
BEFSSUU	SUBFEUS
BEGGGIN	BEGGING
BEGGIIS	BIGGIES
BEGGINO	BEGOING
BEGGIOR	BOGGIER
BEGGIRU	BUGGIER
BEGGIST	BIGGEST
BEGGISU	BUGGIES
BEGGITY	BIGGETY
BEGGLOR	BOGGLER
BEGGLOS	BOGGLES
BEGGRSU	BUGGERS
BEGGRUY	BUGGERY
BEGHHIT	BEHIGHT
BEGHINT	BENIGHT
BEGHISS	BESIGHS
BEGHITT	BETIGHT
BEGHRRU	BURGHER
BEGIILR	BILGIER
BEGIINN	INBEING
BEGIINS	BINGIES
BEGIKMN	KEMBING
BEGIKNR	KERBING
BEGILLN	BELLING
BEGILLY	LEGIBLY
BEGILNO	IGNOBLE
	INGLOBE
BEGILNS	BINGLES
BEGILNT	BELTING
BEGILNU	BLUEING
	BULGINE
BEGILNY	BELYING
BEGILOR	OBLIGER
BEGILOS	OBLIGES
BEGILRS	GERBILS
BEGILRT	GILBERT
BEGILRU	BULGIER
BEGILST	GIBLETS
BEGIMRS	BEGRIMS
BEGINNU	UNBEING
BEGINOS	BIOGENS
BEGINOY	BIOGENY
	OBEYING
BEGINRR	BRINGER
BEGINRS	BINGERS
BEGINRW	BREWING
BEGINSS	BESINGS
	BIGNESS
BEGINST	BESTING
BEGINSU	BEGUINS
	BUNGIES
BEGINTT	BETTING
BEGIOOS	BOOGIES
BEGIORV	OVERBIG
BEGIOSU	BOUGIES
BEGIRSU	BRIGUES
	RUGBIES
BEGISSU	GIBUSES
BEGKMOS	GEMSBOK
BEGKNSU	BEGUNKS
BEGLLOU	GLOBULE
BEGLMOO	BEGLOOM
BEGLMRU	GRUMBLE
BEGLMUU	BLUEGUM
BEGLNOS	BELONGS
BEGLNRU	BLUNGER
	BUNGLER
BEGLNSU	BLUNGES
	BUNGLES
BEGLOOS	GLOBOSE
BEGLOOT	BOOTLEG
BEGLOST	GOBLETS
BEGLOSU	GLEBOUS
BEGLOSW	BOWLEGS
BEGLOUV	LOVEBUG
BEGLRSU	BUGLERS
	BULGERS
	BURGLES
BEGLRTY	BERGYLT
BEGLSTU	BUGLETS
BEGMNOY	BOGYMEN
BEGNNUU	UNBEGUN
BEGNOOS	BONGOES
BEGNORU	BURGEON
BEGNOSY	BYGONES
BEGNOTU	UNBEGOT

BEGNSUY	BUNGEYS
BEGOORS	BOOGERS
	GOOBERS
BEGOOSY	BOOGEYS
BEGORSU	BROGUES
BEGOSTU	BOUGETS
	OUTBEGS
BEGOSTW	BOWGETS
BEGRRSU	BURGERS
BEGRSSU	BURGESS
BEHHKOT	KHOTBEH
BEHIIST	BHISTIE
BEHIITX	EXHIBIT
BEHIKLO	HOBLIKE
BEHIKNT	BETHINK
BEHIKRS	KIRBEHS
BEHILMS	BLEMISH
BEHILMT	THIMBLE
BEHILOS	BOLSHIE
BEHILRT	BLITHER
BEHILST	THIBLES
BEHILSU	BLUEISH
	HELIBUS
BEHIMOR	BIOHERM
BEHINOP	HIPBONE
	HOPBINE
BEHINST	HENBITS
BEHIOST	BOTHIES
BEHIOTW	HOWBEIT
BEHIRRT	REBIRTH
BEHIRST	HERBIST
BEHIRSU	BUSHIER
BEHISSU	BUSHIES
BEHISTT	THIBETS
BEHISTZ	ZIBETHS
BEHKORS	RHEBOKS
BEHLLOP	BELLHOP
BEHLLOX	HELLBOX
BEHLMOW	WHOMBLE
BEHLMRU	HUMBLER
BEHLMSU	HUMBLES
BEHLOOT	BOTHOLE
BEHLORT	BROTHEL
BEHLOSW	BEHOWLS
BEHLRRU	BURRHEL
BEHLRSU	BLUSHER
	BURHELS
BEHLSSU	BLUSHES
	BUSHELS
BEHLSTU	BLUSHET
BEHMNSU	BUSHMEN
BEHMOOY	HOMEBOY
BEHMORS	HOMBRES
BEHMOTU	BEMOUTH
BEHMPTU	BETHUMP
BEHNORS	BREHONS
BEHNORT	BETHORN
BEHNOST	BENTHOS
BEHNRTU	BURTHEN
BEHOORT	THEORBO
BEHOPRT	POTHERB
BEHOPSU	PHOEBUS
BEHORRT	BROTHER
BEHORST	BOSHTER
	BOTHERS
BEHORSU	HERBOUS
BEHORTT	BETROTH
BEHOSTU	BESHOUT
BEHRRSU	BRUSHER
BEHRSSU	BRUSHES
	BUSHERS
BEHRTTU	TURBETH
BEIIKLN	NIBLIKE
BEIIKLR	RIBLIKE
BEIIKRR	BIRKIER
BEIIKRS	BIRKIES
BEIILLS	BILLIES
BEIILMR	LIMBIER
BEIILMX	MIXIBLE
BEIILRS	RISIBLE
BEIILSV	VISIBLE
BEIINOT	NIOBITE
BEIINRR	BRINIER
BEIINRS	BRINIES
BEIINST	STIBINE
BEIIOTT	BIOTITE
BEIIRRS	BIRSIER
	RIBIERS
BEIIRST	BITSIER
BEIIRTT	BITTIER
BEIISTT	BITTIES
BEIISVV	BIVVIES
BEIJLRS	JERBILS
	JIRBLES
BEIJLSU	JUBILES
BEIJMSU	JUMBIES
BEIJNSU	BUNJIES
BEIKLNR	BLINKER
BEIKLNS	LIBKENS
BEIKLOR	BLOKIER
BEIKLOS	OBELISK
BEIKLOW	BOWLIKE
BEIKLOX	BOXLIKE
BEIKLRS	BILKERS
BEIKLRU	BULKIER
BEIKLSY	BEYLIKS
BEIKLTU	TUBLIKE
BEIKNRS	BRISKEN
BEIKOOR	BOOKIER
	BROOKIE
BEIKOOS	BOOKIES
	BOOKSIE
BEIKORS	BOSKIER
BEIKORT	REITBOK
BEIKRRS	BRISKER
BEIKRST	BRISKET
BEIKRTU	BURKITE
BEILLMN	BILLMEN
BEILLPR	PREBILL
BEILLRR	BRILLER
BEILLRS	BILLERS
	REBILLS
BEILLRU	BULLIER
BEILLST	BESTILL
	BILLETS
BEILLSU	BULLIES
BEILMNR	NIMBLER
BEILMNS	MILNEBS
BEILMOR	EMBROIL
BEILMOS	BEMOILS
	EMBOILS
	MOBILES
	OBELISM
BEILMRS	LIMBERS
BEILMRT	TIMBREL
BEILMRW	WIMBREL
BEILMSU	SUBLIME
BEILMSW	WIMBLES
BEILNOO	OBELION
BEILNOW	BOWLINE
BEILNRS	BERLINS
BEILNRY	BYLINER
BEILNSU	SUBLINE
BEILNSY	BYLINES
BEILNSZ	BENZILS
BEILNTZ	BLINTZE
BEILOOR	LOOBIER
BEILOOS	LOOBIES
BEILOPR	PREBOIL
BEILOPY	EPIBOLY
BEILOQU	OBLIQUE
BEILORR	BROILER
BEILORS	BOILERS
	LIBEROS
	REBOILS
BEILORT	TRILOBE
BEILORW	BLOWIER
BEILORY	BOILERY
BEILOST	BETOILS
BEILOSW	BLOWIES
BEILOSX	BOLIXES
BEILRRS	BIRLERS
BEILRRU	BURLIER
BEILRSS	BIRSLES
	RIBLESS
BEILRST	BLISTER
	BRISTLE
	RIBLETS
BEILRTT	BRITTLE
	TRIBLET
BEILRTU	REBUILT
BEILRTY	LIBERTY
BEILRUY	BRULYIE
BEILRUZ	BRULZIE
BEILSSS	BLISSES
BEILSST	BITLESS
BEILSTU	BLUIEST
	SUBTILE
BEILSTW	BLEWITS
BEILSTZ	BLITZES
BEIMMRR	BRIMMER
BEIMNOR	BROMINE
BEIMNTU	BITUMEN
BEIMOOR	BOOMIER
BEIMORW	IMBOWER
	WOMBIER
BEIMORZ	BROMIZE
BEIMOSS	OBEISMS
BEIMOSZ	ZOMBIES
BEIMOTV	BEVOMIT
BEIMPRU	BUMPIER
BEIMRST	BETRIMS
	TIMBERS
	TIMBRES
BEIMRSU	ERBIUMS
	IMBRUES
	IMBURSE
BEIMRTU	IMBRUTE
	TERBIUM
BEIMSST	BEMISTS
BEIMSTU	SUBITEM
BEINNOP	PINBONE
BEINNOR	BONNIER
BEINNOS	BENISON
	BONNIES
BEINNOZ	BENZOIN
BEINNSU	BUNNIES
BEINNSZ	BENZINS
BEINOOS	BOONIES
BEINOOT	EOBIONT
BEINORT	BORNITE
BEINORW	BROWNIE
BEINOSS	BESOINS
BEINOST	BONIEST
	EBONIST
BEINOSV	BOVINES
BEINOSX	BONXIES
BEINOSZ	BIZONES
BEINOTT	BOTTINE
BEINRRS	BRINERS
BEINRSU	BURNIES
	RUBINES
	SUBERIN
BEINRSY	BYRNIES
BEINRTT	BITTERN
BEINRTU	BUNTIER
	TRIBUNE
	TURBINE
BEINSSY	BYSSINE
BEIOOPT	BIOTOPE
BEIOORZ	BOOZIER
BEIOOST	BOOTIES
BEIOPTY	BIOTYPE
BEIORRT	ORBITER
BEIORSS	BOSSIER
	RIBOSES
BEIORST	ORBIEST
	SORBITE
BEIORSU	BOUSIER
	OUREBIS
BEIORUV	BOUVIER
BEIOSSS	BOSSIES
BEIOSSU	SOUBISE
BEIOSTT	BOTTIES
BEIOSTX	BOXIEST
BEIOSTY	OBESITY
BEIPPSU	BUPPIES
BEIPSST	BESPITS
BEIPSSU	PUBISES
BEIQRTU	BRIQUET
BEIQSSU	BISQUES
BEIRRRU	BURRIER
BEIRRSU	BRISURE
	BRUISER
	BURIERS
BEIRRTU	BRUITER
BEIRSSS	BRISSES
BEIRSST	BESTIRS
	BISTERS
	BISTRES
BEIRSSU	BRUISES
BEIRSTT	BITTERS
BEIRSTU	BUSTIER
	RUBIEST
BEIRTTU	TRIBUTE
BEIRTTY	TREYBIT
BEIRTVY	BREVITY
BEIRUZZ	BUZZIER
BEISSTU	BUSIEST
	SUBSITE
BEISTTU	BUTTIES
BEITTWX	BETWIXT
BEJJSUU	JUJUBES
BEJKOUX	JUKEBOX
BEJLMRU	JUMBLER
BEJLMSU	JUMBLES
BEJLOSS	JOBLESS
BEJORSU	OBJURES
BEKLNRU	BLUNKER
BEKLOOT	BOOKLET
BEKLRSU	BULKERS
	BURLESK
BEKMNOO	BOOKMEN
BEKMOSS	EMBOSKS
BEKMOST	STEMBOK
BEKNNOW	BEKNOWN
BEKNORS	BONKERS
BEKNORU	UNBROKE
BEKNOST	BEKNOTS
BEKNRSU	BUNKERS
BEKOOPR	PREBOOK
BEKOORS	BOOKERS
	REBOOKS
BEKOPRU	UPBROKE
BEKORRS	BROKERS
BEKORRY	BROKERY
BEKORWW	WEBWORK
BEKOSST	BOSKETS
BEKRRSU	BRUSKER
	BURKERS

BEKRSSU	BUSKERS
BEKSSTU	BUSKETS
BELLLMU	BLELLUM
BELLNPU	BULLPEN
BELLORR	BORRELL
BELLOSU	BOULLES
	LOBULES
	SOLUBLE
BELLOSW	BELLOWS
BELLOUV	VOLUBLE
BELLRRU	BURRELL
BELLRSU	BULLERS
BELLSTU	BULLETS
BELMMOO	EMBLOOM
BELMMRU	MUMBLER
BELMMSU	BUMMELS
	BUMMLES
	MUMBLES
BELMNOS	NOMBLES
BELMNOU	NELUMBO
BELMNOY	BENOMYL
BELMNSU	NUMBLES
BELMOOR	BLOOMER
	REBLOOM
BELMOOS	BLOOSME
BELMOOT	BOOMLET
BELMOPR	PROBLEM
BELMORT	TEMBLOR
BELMOSU	EMBOLUS
BELMOSY	SYMBOLE
BELMPRU	PLUMBER
	REPLUMB
BELMRRU	RUMBLER
BELMRSU	LUMBERS
	RUMBLES
	SLUMBER
	UMBRELS
BELMRTU	TUMBLER
	TUMBREL
BELMRTY	TREMBLY
BELMSTU	STUMBLE
	TUMBLES
BELNNOU	UNNOBLE
BELNNTU	UNBLENT
BELNOOR	BORNEOL
BELNOOY	BOLONEY
BELNOST	NOBLEST
BELNOSZ	BENZOLS
BELNOYZ	BENZOYL
BELNRTU	BLUNTER
BELNSSU	UNBLESS
BELNSTU	SUNBELT
	UNBELTS
	UNBLEST
BELNSYZ	BENZYLS
BELOOPR	BLOOPER
BELOORS	BOLEROS
BELOOSS	SOBOLES
BELOPSU	PUEBLOS
BELORST	BOLSTER
	BOLTERS
	LOBSTER
BELORSU	ROUBLES
BELORSW	BLOWERS
	BOWLERS
BELORSY	SOBERLY
BELORTT	BLOTTER
	BOTTLER
BELORTU	BOULTER
	TROUBLE
BELOSSU	BLOUSES
	BOLUSES
BELOSSW	BLOWSES
	BOWLESS
BELOSTT	BOTTLES

BELOSTU	BOLETUS
BELOSWZ	BLOWZES
BELRRSU	BURLERS
	BURRELS
BELRRTU	BLURTER
BELRSTU	BLUSTER
	BUSTLER
	BUTLERS
	SUBTLER
BELRSUU	SUBRULE
BELRSUY	BURLEYS
BELRTUY	BRUTELY
	BUTLERY
BELSSTU	BUSTLES
	SUBLETS
BELSTTU	BUTTLES
BELSTUU	TUBULES
BEMMNOS	MOBSMEN
BEMMOOS	EMBOSOM
BEMMORR	BROMMER
BEMMRRU	BRUMMER
BEMMRSU	BUMMERS
BEMMSTU	BUMMEST
BEMNORW	EMBROWN
BEMNORY	EMBRYON
BEMNOST	ENTOMBS
BEMNOSU	UMBONES
BEMNOSW	ENWOMBS
BEMNPTY	BYNEMPT
BEMNRSU	NUMBERS
BEMNSTU	NUMBEST
BEMNSUU	SUBMENU
BEMNTTU	BUTMENT
BEMOOPR	PREBOOM
BEMOORS	BOOMERS
BEMORRS	SOMBRER
BEMORSS	SOMBERS
	SOMBRES
BEMORST	BESTORM
	MOBSTER
BEMORSU	UMBROSE
BEMORSW	BEWORMS
BEMORSY	EMBRYOS
BEMORUX	BUXOMER
BEMORWW	WEBWORM
BEMOTUY	MYOTUBE
BEMPRSU	BUMPERS
BEMSSTU	BESMUTS
BEMSSUU	SUBSUME
BEMSTUW	STEWBUM
BENNORU	UNBORNE
BENNORW	NEWBORN
BENNORZ	BRONZEN
BENNOST	BONNETS
BENNOSU	UNBONES
BENNSSU	BUNSENS
BENOPRR	PREBORN
BENOPRU	UPBORNE
BENORRW	BROWNER
BENORRZ	BRONZER
BENORST	BRETONS
	SORBENT
BENORSU	BOURNES
	UNROBES
	UNSOBER
BENORSZ	BRONZES
BENORWY	BYWONER
BENOSSU	BONUSES
BENOSSW	BESNOWS
BENOSTU	SUBTONE
BENOSUX	UNBOXES
BENOSUZ	SUBZONE
BENOSWY	NEWSBOY
BENRRSU	BURNERS
BENRSTU	BRUNETS

	BUNTERS
	BURNETS
	BURSTEN
	SUBRENT
BENSSTU	SUBNETS
BEOORSS	BROOSES
	SORBOSE
BEOORST	BOOSTER
	REBOOTS
BEOORSZ	BOOZERS
	REBOZOS
BEOORTY	BOOTERY
BEOPPRS	BOPPERS
BEOPRRS	PROBERS
BEOPRRV	PROVERB
BEOPRST	BESPORT
BEOPSST	BESPOTS
BEOPSTU	BESPOUT
BEOQSSU	BOSQUES
BEOQSTU	BOSQUET
BEOQSUY	OBSEQUY
BEOQTUU	BOUQUET
BEORRSS	RESORBS
BEORRSW	BROWSER
BEORRWY	BEWORRY
BEORSST	BESORTS
	SORBETS
	STROBES
BEORSSU	BOURSES
BEORSSW	BOWSERS
	BROWSES
BEORSTT	BETTORS
BEORSTU	OBTUSER
BEORSTV	OBVERTS
BEORSTW	BESTROW
BEORSTZ	BORTZES
BEORSUU	UBEROUS
BEORSUZ	BROUZES
	SUBZERO
BEORSVV	BOVVERS
BEORSWY	BOWYERS
BEORUVY	OVERBUY
BEOSSST	BOSSEST
BEOSSTT	OBTESTS
BEOSSTW	BESTOWS
BEPRRTU	PERTURB
BEPRTUY	PUBERTY
BEPSTUY	SUBTYPE
BEQRSUU	BRUSQUE
BERRRSU	BURRERS
BERRSTU	BRUTERS
	BURSTER
BERSSTU	BUSTERS
BERSTTU	BUTTERS
BERSTUV	SUBVERT
BERSUZZ	BUZZERS
BERTTUY	BUTTERY
BESSSTU	SUBSETS
BESSTTU	SUBTEST
BESTTUX	SUBTEXT
BFFGIIN	BIFFING
BFFGINO	BOFFING
BFFGINU	BUFFING
BFFIINS	BIFFINS
BFFILOO	BOILOFF
BFFINOS	BOFFINS
BFFLLUY	BLUFFLY
BFFLOOW	BLOWOFF
BFFNOOU	BUFFOON
BFFORSU	RUBOFFS
BFGIOOT	BIGFOOT
BFGIORT	FROGBIT
BFGOOSW	FOGBOWS
BFHILSU	LUBFISH
BFHIOSX	BOXFISH

BFHIRSU	FURBISH
BFHISTU	TUBFISH
BFIILRS	FIBRILS
BFIINOR	FIBROIN
BFIINRS	FIBRINS
BFILMRU	BRIMFUL
BFILSUY	FUSIBLY
BFIMOYZ	ZOMBIFY
BFINOSW	BOWFINS
BFIORSU	FIBROUS
BFIRTUY	BRUTIFY
BFKLOOU	BOOKFUL
BFKLOOY	FLYBOOK
BFKSSUU	SUBFUSK
BFLLOUW	BOWLFUL
BFLLOWY	BLOWFLY
	FLYBLOW
BFLOSUX	BOXFULS
BFLOSYY	FLYBOYS
BFLSTUU	TUBFULS
BFOOOTY	FOOTBOY
BGGGIIN	BIGGING
BGGGINO	BOGGING
BGGGINU	BUGGING
BGGHIIS	BIGGISH
BGGHIOS	BOGGISH
BGGIILN	BILGING
BGGIINN	BINGING
BGGIINS	BIGGINS
BGGIISW	BIGWIGS
BGGIITY	BIGGITY
BGGILNO	GLOBING
BGGILNU	BUGLING
	BULGING
BGGINNO	BONGING
BGGINNU	BUNGING
BGGINOU	BOUGING
BGGINSU	BUGGINS
BGGNOOS	BOGONGS
BGGNOSU	BUGONGS
BGHHIOY	HIGHBOY
BGHIILS	GHIBLIS
BGHIINS	BINGHIS
BGHILST	BLIGHTS
BGHILTY	BLIGHTY
BGHINOO	BOOHING
	HOBOING
BGHINOR	BIGHORN
BGHINSU	BUSHING
BGHIPSU	BUSHPIG
BGHIRST	BRIGHTS
BGHLRUU	BULGHUR
	BURGHUL
BGHMORU	HOMBURG
BGHMSUU	HUMBUGS
BGHNORU	HORNBUG
BGHOORU	BOROUGH
BGHORSU	BROUGHS
BGHORTU	BROUGHT
BGHOSTU	BOUGHTS
BGIIKLN	BILKING
BGIIKNS	BIKINGS
BGIILLN	BILLING
BGIILMN	LIMBING
BGIILNO	BOILING
BGIILNR	BIRLING
BGIILNS	SIBLING
BGIIMNR	BRIMING
BGIIMNU	IMBUING
BGIINNN	BINNING
BGIINNR	BRINING
	INBRING
BGIINRR	BIRRING
BGIINRT	RINGBIT
BGIINST	BITINGS

BGIINTT	BITTING
BGIKLNU	BULKING
BGIKNNO	BONKING
BGIKNNU	BUNKING
BGIKNOO	BOOKING
BGIKNOR	BROKING
BGIKNRU	BURKING
BGIKNSU	BUSKING
BGILLNO	BOLLING
BGILLNU	BULLING
BGILMNO	MOBLING
BGILMNU	BLUMING
BGILMOU	GUMBOIL
BGILNOS	GLOBINS
	GOBLINS
	LOBINGS
BGILNOT	BILTONG
	BOLTING
BGILNOW	BLOWING
	BOWLING
BGILNOY	IGNOBLY
BGILNRU	BURLING
BGILNRY	BYRLING
BGILNSU	BLUINGS
BGILNTU	BUTLING
BGILOOR	OBLIGOR
BGILOOY	BIOLOGY
BGILRSU	BUSGIRL
BGIMMNU	BUMMING
BGIMNNU	NUMBING
BGIMNOO	BOOMING
BGIMNOT	TOMBING
BGIMNOW	WOMBING
BGIMNPU	BUMPING
BGIMOSY	BOGYISM
BGINNOS	BONINGS
BGINNOU	BOUNING
BGINNOW	BOWNING
BGINNRU	BURNING
BGINNTU	BUNTING
BGINOOS	BOOSING
BGINOOT	BOOTING
BGINOOZ	BOOZING
BGINOPP	BOPPING
BGINOPR	PROBING
BGINORS	BORINGS
	ROBINGS
	SORBING
BGINOSS	BOSSING
	GIBSONS
	OBSIGNS
BGINOSU	BOUSING
BGINOSW	BOWINGS
	BOWSING
BGINOSX	BOXINGS
BGINOTT	BOTTING
BGINOUY	BUOYING
BGINOWW	WINGBOW
BGINPRU	BURPING
	UPBRING
BGINRRU	BURRING
BGINRSU	SUBRING
BGINRTU	BRUTING
BGINRUY	BURYING
	RUBYING
BGINSSU	BUSINGS
	BUSSING
BGINSTU	BUSTING
	TUBINGS
BGINSUY	BUSYING
BGINSWY	SWINGBY
BGINTTU	BUTTING
BGINUZZ	BUZZING
BGIORSU	RUBIGOS
BGIORTY	BIGOTRY
BGIOSSS	GOSSIBS
BGIUWZZ	BUZZWIG
BGKLOOO	LOGBOOK
BGKORSY	GRYSBOK
BGLMRUY	GRUMBLY
BGLNOOS	OBLONGS
BGLNOOW	LONGBOW
BGLNOUW	BLOWGUN
BGLOOSU	GLOBOUS
BGLOSSU	BUGLOSS
BGLRSUU	BULGURS
BGMOORS	GOMBROS
BGMOOTU	GUMBOOT
BGMSSUU	SUBGUMS
BGNOOWY	GOWNBOY
BGNOSSU	SUBSONG
BGOORSU	BURGOOS
BGORTUU	BURGOUT
BGORTUW	BUGWORT
BHIIINN	INHIBIN
BHIIINT	INHIBIT
BHIINRS	BRINISH
BHIIPSS	SIBSHIP
BHIISST	BHISTIS
BHIKOOS	BOOKISH
BHIKSSU	BUKSHIS
BHILLSU	BULLISH
BHILOTU	HOLIBUT
BHILPSU	PUBLISH
BHILSUY	BUSHILY
BHIMOOR	RHOMBOI
BHIMOOS	HOBOISM
BHIMOPR	BIMORPH
BHIMOPS	PHOBISM
BHIMORT	THROMBI
BHIMSTU	BISMUTH
BHINRSU	BURNISH
BHIOOPR	BIOPHOR
BHIOORS	BOORISH
BHIOPSS	BISHOPS
BHIOPST	PHOBIST
BHIOSWZ	SHOWBIZ
BHIRSTU	BRUTISH
BHIRTTU	TURBITH
BHISTTU	BUSHTIT
BHKNOSU	BOHUNKS
BHLRSUU	BULRUSH
BHMOORS	RHOMBOS
BHMORSU	RHOMBUS
BHMUUZZ	HUMBUZZ
BHOOOOS	BOOHOOS
BHOOPSY	SHOPBOY
BHOOSTW	BOWSHOT
BHOOSWX	SHOWBOX
BHORSST	BORSHTS
BHPRSUU	BRUSHUP
BIIIKNS	BIKINIS
BIIKLOT	KILOBIT
BIILLMS	MISBILL
BIILLNO	BILLION
BIILLOU	BOUILLI
BIILLTW	TWIBILL
BIILNNR	BIRLINN
BIILNQU	QUIBLIN
BIILNTU	INBUILT
BIILNVY	BIVINYL
BIILOSU	BILIOUS
BIILRSY	RISIBLY
BIILSTW	TWIBILS
BIILSVY	VISIBLY
BIIMNOU	NIOBIUM
BIIMNSU	MINIBUS
BIIMOSS	OBIISMS
BIIMSTU	STIBIUM
BIINORV	VIBRION
BIINOST	BIOTINS
BIIORSV	VIBRIOS
BIIOSUV	BIVIOUS
BIIRSTU	BURITIS
BIISSTV	VIBISTS
BIISTTT	TITBITS
BIJNOSU	SUBJOIN
BIKLLUY	BULKILY
BIKLNOT	INKBLOT
BIKLNOY	LINKBOY
BIKLRSY	BRISKLY
BIKMNOO	BOOMKIN
BIKMNPU	BUMPKIN
BIKMNSU	BUMKINS
BIKMOSS	IMBOSKS
BIKNSSU	BUSKINS
BIKORRW	RIBWORK
BIKSUUZ	BUZUKIS
BILLNOS	BILLONS
BILLNOU	BULLION
BILLOOY	LOOBILY
BILLOPX	PILLBOX
BILLOSW	BILLOWS
BILLOUV	VOLUBIL
BILLOWY	BILLOWY
BILLRUY	BURLILY
BILLRWY	WRYBILL
BILMNOR	NOMBRIL
BILMOSU	LIMBOUS
BILMPUY	BUMPILY
BILMRSU	UMBRILS
BILMRTU	TUMBRIL
BILMSUU	BULIMUS
BILNNOY	BONNILY
BILNOTU	BOTULIN
BILNTUU	TUBULIN
	UNBUILT
BILOOPT	POTBOIL
BILOOYZ	BOOZILY
BILOPSU	UPBOILS
BILORST	BRISTOL
	STROBIL
BILOSSU	SUBSOIL
BILOSSY	BOSSILY
BILPTUU	UPBUILT
BILRSTY	BRISTLY
	TRILBYS
BILRTTY	BRITTLY
BILRTUY	TILBURY
BIMMOOS	IMBOSOM
	MIOMBOS
BIMMORS	BROMISM
BIMNOOY	BIONOMY
BIMNORS	BROMINS
	MISBORN
BIMNORW	IMBROWN
BIMNOSS	BONISMS
BIMNOST	INTOMBS
BIMNOSU	OMNIBUS
BIMNOSY	SYMBION
BIMOSSS	BOSSISM
BIMOSTW	MISTBOW
BIMOSTY	SYMBIOT
BIMRSTU	BRUTISM
BIMRSUX	BRUXISM
BIMSSSU	SUBMISS
BIMSSTU	SUBMITS
BINNOSU	BUNIONS
BINOORS	BONSOIR
BINOORT	BIOTRON
BINOOST	BONITOS
BINOOSU	NIOBOUS
BINORST	RIBSTON
BINOSST	BONISTS
BINPSUY	BUNYIPS
BINRSTU	INBURST
BINRTUY	BUTYRIN
BINSTTU	UNBITTS
BINSTUU	SUBUNIT
BIOORSZ	BORZOIS
BIOOSST	OBOISTS
BIOOSUV	OBVIOUS
BIOPRST	PROBITS
BIOPRTY	PROBITY
BIORRTU	BURRITO
BIORRTW	RIBWORT
BIORSST	BISTROS
BIORSTT	BISTORT
	BITTORS
BIORSUU	RUBIOUS
BIORTTU	BITTOUR
BIOSTUW	WOUBITS
BIRSTTU	BITTURS
	TURBITS
BISSSTU	SUBSIST
BISSTTU	TUBISTS
BJNOORU	BONJOUR
BKLNUUY	UNBULKY
BKLOTUU	OUTBULK
BKMNSUU	BUNKUMS
BKNNOOO	NONBOOK
BKNOOTW	BOWKNOT
BKNORSY	SKYBORN
BKOORWX	WORKBOX
BKORSWY	BYWORKS
BKRSTUU	KRUBUTS
BLLNTUY	BLUNTLY
BLLOSUU	BULLOUS
	LOBULUS
BLLOSUY	SOLUBLY
BLLOUVY	VOLUBLY
BLMMPUU	PLUMBUM
BLMNPUU	UNPLUMB
BLMOOOT	TOMBOLO
BLMOORW	LOBWORM
BLMOOSS	BLOSSOM
BLMOSSY	SYMBOLS
BLMOUXY	BUXOMLY
BLMRSUY	SLUMBRY
BLMSTUY	STUMBLY
BLNNOUW	UNBLOWN
BLNOORW	LOWBORN
BLNOOSS	BOLSONS
BLNOOSU	BLOUSON
BLNOPUW	UPBLOWN
BLNOSTU	UNBOLTS
BLOOOTX	TOOLBOX
BLOOPWY	PLOWBOY
BLOOQUY	OBLOQUY
BLOORWW	LOWBROW
BLOOSWY	LOWBOYS
BLOOTUW	BLOWOUT
BLOPSTU	SUBPLOT
BLOPSUW	BLOWUPS
	UPBLOWS
BLORSTU	BRULOTS
BLOSSTU	SUBLOTS
BLRTUYY	BUTYRYL
BMNOOOW	MOONBOW
BMNOOSU	UNBOSOM
BMNORUW	MOWBURN
BMNOSTU	UNTOMBS
BMOOORX	BOXROOM
BMOORSY	BYROOMS
BMOOSTT	BOTTOMS
BMOOSTY	TOMBOYS
BMORSST	STROMBS
BMORSUU	BRUMOUS
	UMBROUS
BNNRSUU	SUNBURN

BNNRTUU UNBURNT
BNOOSST BOSTONS
BNOOSTU BOUTONS
UNBOOTS
BNOOTTY BOTTONY
BNORSSU SUBORNS
BNORSTU BURTONS
BNORSUU BURNOUS
BNORTUU BURNOUT
OUTBURN
BNOSSUW SUNBOWS
BNOSTTU BUTTONS
BNOTTUY BUTTONY
BOOPSTW BOWPOTS
BOOPSTX POSTBOX
BOOPSTY POSTBOY
POTBOYS
BOORRSW BORROWS
BOORRTY ROBOTRY
BOOSTUW WOOBUTS
BOOSWWW BOWWOWS
BOPSSTU POSTBUS
BORRSUW BURROWS
BORSSTW BROWSTS
BORSTTU TURBOTS
BORSTUU RUBOUTS
BORSTXY BOSTRYX
BOSTUUY BUYOUTS
OUTBUYS
BPRSTUU UPBURST
CCCDIOO COCCOID
CCCDIOS COCCIDS
CCCNOOT CONCOCT
CCCOOSU COCCOUS
CCDEEER RECCEED
CCDEEHK CHECKED
CCDEEIO ECOCIDE
CCDEEIR RECCIED
CCDEEIS DECCIES
CCDEEKL CLECKED
CCDEENO CONCEDE
CCDEENY DECENCY
CCDEEOR COERCED
CCDEEPS SPECCED
CCDEESU SUCCEED
CCDEFLO FLOCCED
CCDEHIL CLICHED
CCDEHIN CINCHED
CCDEHKO CHOCKED
CCDEHKU CHUCKED
CCDEHNO CONCHED
CCDEHOU COUCHED
CCDEIIL ICICLED
CCDEIIT DEICTIC
CCDEIKL CLICKED
CCDEIKR CRICKED
CCDEILR CIRCLED
CCDEIMO COMEDIC
CCDEIOS CODICES
CCDEIOT DOCETIC
CCDEKLO CLOCKED
COCKLED
CCDEKLU CLUCKED
CCDEKOR CROCKED
CCDELOU OCCLUDE
CCDENOO CONCEDO
CCDENOS SCONCED
CCDENOU CONDUCE
CCDEOST DECOCTS
CCDHIIL CICHLID
CCDIILO CODICIL
CCDIILU CULICID
CCDIIOR CRICOID
CCDILOY CYCLOID
CCDILYY DICYCLY

CCDKLOU CUCKOLD
CCDNOOR CONCORD
CCDNOTU CONDUCT
CCEEGNO COGENCE
CCEEHIK CHICKEE
CCEEHIV CEVICHE
CCEEHKR CHECKER
RECHECK
CCEEHOR ECORCHE
CCEEHOU COUCHEE
CCEEHRS CRECHES
SCREECH
CCEEILN LICENCE
CCEEINR ECCRINE
CCEEINS SCIENCE
CCEEIOR CICOREE
CCEEIRS RECCIES
CCEEIRV CREVICE
CCEEKOY COCKEYE
CCEELNU LUCENCE
CCEELRY RECYCLE
CCEENRY RECENCY
CCEEORR COERCER
CCEEORS COERCES
CCEEORT COERECT
CCEERSY SECRECY
CCEFNOT CONFECT
CCEGINY GYNECIC
CCEGNOY COGENCY
CCEHHIS CHICHES
CCEHIKN CHICKEN
CCEHIKU CHUCKIE
CCEHILS CHICLES
CLICHES
CCEHILU CULCHIE
CCEHIMS CHEMICS
CCEHINO CONCHIE
CCEHINS CINCHES
CCEHINT TECHNIC
CCEHINZ ZECCHIN
CCEHIOR CHOICER
CHOREIC
CCEHIOS CHOICES
CCEHIRS SCREICH
SCRIECH
CCEHIST CHICEST
HECTICS
CCEHKLU CHUCKLE
CCEHKMS SCHMECK
CCEHKNU UNCHECK
CCEHKOR CHOCKER
CCEHKPU CHECKUP
CCEHLOS CLOCHES
CCEHLRU CLERUCH
CCEHLSU CLEUCHS
CULCHES
CCEHNOS CONCHES
CCEHOOS COOCHES
CCEHORS CROCHES
CCEHORT CROCHET
CCEHORU COUCHER
CCEHOSS COSECHS
CCEHOSU COUCHES
CCEHRSU CURCHES
CCEHSTU CUTCHES
CCEIILS CILICES
ICICLES
CCEIIMS CIMICES
CCEIIPS PICCIES
CCEIIRT ICTERIC
CCEIIST CECITIS
CCEIKLR CLICKER
CCEIKLT CLICKET
CCEIKOR COCKIER
CCEIKOS COCKIES

CCEIKRT CRICKET
CCEIKRY CRICKEY
CCEILOT COCTILE
CCEILRR CIRCLER
CCEILRS CIRCLES
CLERICS
CCEILRT CIRCLET
CCEILSU CULICES
CCEILSY CYLICES
CCEILTU CUTICLE
CCEILYZ CYCLIZE
CCEIMNO MECONIC
CCEIMOS COMICES
CCEIMOT COMETIC
CCEIMST SMECTIC
CCEINOR CORNICE
CROCEIN
CROCINE
CCEINOS CONCISE
CCEINOT CONCEIT
CCEINRT CENTRIC
CCEIOPP COPPICE
CCEIOPT ECTOPIC
CCEIORS CICEROS
CCEIORT CEROTIC
ORECTIC
CCEIOSS CISCOES
CCEIPST SCEPTIC
CCEIRST CRETICS
CCEISSU SUCCISE
CCEJNOT CONJECT
CCEKLOR CLOCKER
CCEKLOS COCKLES
CCEKNOT CONTECK
CCEKNOY COCKNEY
CCEKOPS COPECKS
CCEKOPT PETCOCK
CCEKORS COCKERS
RECOCKS
CCEKORT CROCKET
CCEKOST COCKETS
CCELLOT COLLECT
CCELNOY CYCLONE
CCELNUY LUCENCY
CCELRSY CYCLERS
CCELRYY CYCLERY
CCENNOR CONCERN
CCENNOT CONCENT
CONNECT
CCENOPT CONCEPT
CCENORT CONCERT
CCENORW CONCREW
CCENOSS SCONCES
CCENOTV CONVECT
CCEOOTT COCOTTE
CCEOPRT PERCOCT
CCEORRT CORRECT
CCEORRU REOCCUR
CCEORSS ESCROCS
SOCCERS
CCEORTW TWOCCER
CCEOSSU SUCCOSE
CCESSSU SUCCESS
CCFIRUY CRUCIFY
CCFLOSU FLOCCUS
CCGHINO GNOCCHI
CCGIINS SICCING
CCGIKNO COCKING
CCGILNY CYCLING
CCGKOOR GORCOCK
CCHHIIS CHICHIS
CCHHIIT ICHTHIC
CCHHILS SCHLICH
CCHHINY CHINCHY
CCHHOOS CHOCHOS

CCHHRUY CHURCHY
CCHIIST STICHIC
CCHIKOS COCKISH
CCHIKST SCHTICK
TCHICKS
CCHILOR CHLORIC
CCHIMOR CHROMIC
CCHIMSY CHYMICS
CCHINOR CHRONIC
CCHINOS CHICONS
COCHINS
CCHINSU SCUCHIN
CCHIORY CHICORY
CCHIOTW COWITCH
CCHIPSU HICCUPS
CCHIPSY PSYCHIC
CCHIPUY HICCUPY
CCHIRST SCRITCH
CCHKLOS SCHLOCK
CCHKMOS SCHMOCK
CCHKMSU SCHMUCK
CCHKOOS CHOCKOS
CCHKOSY COCKSHY
CCHKPUU UPCHUCK
CCHKSTU SCHTUCK
CCHLTUY CLUTCHY
CCHNRSU SCRUNCH
CCHNRUY CRUNCHY
CCHOORS SCROOCH
CCHOSTU SUCCOTH
CCIIILS SILICIC
CCIILNO COLICIN
CCIILNS CLINICS
CCIILOT COLITIC
CCIILPR CIRCLIP
CCIILST CLITICS
CCIINPS PICNICS
CCIIRST CRITICS
CCIIRTU CIRCUIT
CCIISTY SICCITY
CCIKLOW COWLICK
CCIKLOY COCKILY
COLICKY
CCIKOPT COCKPIT
CCILNOO COLONIC
CCILNOU COUNCIL
CCILOOP PICCOLO
CCILSTY CYCLIST
CCIMNOU UNCOMIC
CCIMOTY MYCOTIC
CCINOOT COCTION
CCINORY CRYONIC
CCINOTV CONVICT
CCIOORS SIROCCO
CCIOPTU OCCIPUT
CCIORSS SCIROCS
CCIOSTT TICTOCS
CCIPRTY CRYPTIC
CCIRSUY CIRCUSY
CCKMOOS MOCOCKS
CCKMOSU MOCUCKS
CCKNOSU UNCOCKS
CCKOOSU CUCKOOS
CCKOPSU COCKUPS
CCKOSTU CUSTOCK
CCLMSUU MUCLUCS
CCLOOOZ ZOCCOLO
CCLOPSY CYCLOPS
CCLOSTU OCCULTS
CCMOOOR MOROCCO
CCNOOOS COCOONS
CCNOOPU PUCCOON
CCNOOTU COCONUT
CCNOPUY CONCUPY
CCNORSU CONCURS

CCNOSSU CONCUSS
CCOOORS ROCOCOS
CCORSSU SUCCORS
CCORSUU SUCCOUR
CCORSUY SUCCORY
CCOSSTU STUCCOS
CCOSSUU SUCCOUS
CCSSSUU SUCCUSS
CDDDEEI DECIDED
CDDDEEO DECODED
CDDDEEU DEDUCED
CDDDELO CLODDED
CODDLED
CDDDELU CUDDLED
CDDDERU CRUDDED
CDDDESU SCUDDED
CDDEEER DECREED
RECEDED
CDDEEES SECEDED
CDDEEII DEICIDE
CDDEEIN INCEDED
CDDEEIR DECIDER
DECRIED
CDDEEIS DECIDES
CDDEEIX EXCIDED
CDDEEKL DECKLED
CDDEEKO DECKOED
DECOKED
CDDEENO ENCODED
CDDEENS DESCEND
SCENDED
CDDEEOR DECODER
RECODED
CDDEEOS DECODES
CDDEEOY DECOYED
CDDEERU REDUCED
CDDEESU DEDUCES
SEDUCED
CDDEEUW CUDWEED
CDDEHIL CHILDED
CDDEHIN CHIDDEN
CDDEHIT DICHTED
DITCHED
CDDEHNU DUNCHED
CDDEHOR CHORDED
CDDEHOU DOUCHED
CDDEHRU CHUDDER
CDDEIIS DISCIDE
CDDEINU INDUCED
CDDEIOS DISCOED
CDDEISU CUDDIES
CDDELOR CODDLER
CDDELOS CODDLES
SCOLDED
CDDELOU CLOUDED
CDDELRU CRUDDLE
CUDDLER
CURDLED
CDDELSU CUDDLES
SCUDDLE
CDDENOU UNCODED
CDDENSU CUDDENS
CDDEORS CODDERS
CDDEORW CROWDED
CDDERSU SCUDDER
CDDESTU DEDUCTS
CDDGINO CODDING
CDDHIOR DICHORD
CDDIIIO DIDICOI
CDDIIOP DIPODIC
CDDIIOS DISCOID
CDDIIOY DIDICOY
CDDIIRU DRUIDIC
CDDIKOP PIDDOCK
CDDINSU CUDDINS

CDDIORS DISCORD
CDDKOPU PUDDOCK
CDDKORU RUDDOCK
CDEEEFL FLEECED
CDEEEFN DEFENCE
CDEEEHK CHEEKED
CDEEEHL LEECHED
CDEEEHP CHEEPED
DEPECHE
CDEEEHR CHEERED
REECHED
CDEEEHS CHEESED
CDEEEIP EPICEDE
CDEEEIV DECEIVE
CDEEEJT EJECTED
CDEEEKL CLEEKED
CDEEELP CLEEPED
CDEEELR CREELED
CDEEELT ELECTED
CDEEEPR PRECEDE
CDEEERR DECREER
CDEEERS CREESED
DECREES
RECEDES
SECEDER
CDEEERT DECREET
ERECTED
CDEEESS SECEDES
CDEEESX EXCEEDS
CDEEFFH CHEFFED
CDEEFHT FETCHED
CDEEFII EDIFICE
CDEEFKL FLECKED
CDEEFLT CLEFTED
DEFLECT
CDEEFOR DEFORCE
CDEEFST DEFECTS
CDEEGIR GRIECED
CDEEGNO CONGEED
CDEEHIP CEPHEID
CDEEHIS DEHISCE
CDEEHIT CHEDITE
CDEEHIV CHEVIED
CDEEHKL HECKLED
CDEEHLT LETCHED
CDEEHLW WELCHED
CDEEHMS SCHEMED
CDEEHNW WENCHED
CDEEHOR CHORDEE
COHERED
OCHERED
CDEEHPR PERCHED
CDEEHRS CHEDERS
CDEEHRT RETCHED
CDEEHRU EUCHRED
CDEEHST CHESTED
CDEEHTT TETCHED
CDEEIIT EIDETIC
CDEEILN DECLINE
CDEEILP PEDICEL
PEDICLE
CDEEILS DECILES
DELICES
CDEEIMN ENDEMIC
CDEEIMS DECIMES
CDEEINO CODEINE
CDEEINR CEDRINE
CDEEINS INCEDES
CDEEINT ENTICED
CDEEINV EVINCED
CDEEIOS DIOCESE
CDEEIOV DEVOICE
CDEEIPR PIERCED
CDEEIPT PEDETIC
CDEEIRR DECRIER

CDEEIRS DECRIES
DEICERS
CDEEIRT RECITED
TIERCED
CDEEIST DECEITS
CDEEISV DEVICES
CDEEISX EXCIDES
EXCISED
CDEEITV EVICTED
CDEEITX EXCITED
CDEEJNO CONJEED
CDEEJST DEJECTS
CDEEKKL KECKLED
CDEEKLR CLERKED
CDEEKLS DECKELS
DECKLES
CDEEKNR REDNECK
CDEEKNS SNECKED
CDEEKOS DECOKES
CDEEKPS SPECKED
CDEEKRS DECKERS
CDEEKRT TRECKED
CDEEKRW WRECKED
CDEELMM CLEMMED
CDEELOS ECLOSED
CDEELPU CUPELED
DECUPLE
CDEELPY YCLEPED
CDEELRU RECULED
ULCERED
CDEELSU SCEDULE
SECLUDE
CDEELUX EXCLUDE
CDEENOR ENCODER
ENCORED
CDEENOS ENCODES
SECONDE
CDEENOZ COZENED
CDEENRS DECERNS
SCERNED
CDEENRT CENTRED
CREDENT
CDEENST DESCENT
SCENTED
CDEEOOY COOEYED
CDEEOPR COPERED
PRECODE
PROCEED
CDEEORS RECODES
CDEEORV COVERED
CDEEORW COWERED
CDEEORY DECOYER
CDEEOST CESTODE
ESCOTED
TEDESCO
CDEEOTV COVETED
CDEERRU RECURED
REDUCER
CDEERSS SCREEDS
CDEERST CRESTED
CDEERSU RECUSED
REDUCES
RESCUED
SECURED
SEDUCER
CDEERSW DECREWS
SCREWED
CDEERTU ERUCTED
CDEERUV DECURVE
CDEESSU SEDUCES
CDEESSY ECDYSES
CDEESTT DECTETS
DETECTS
CDEESUX EXCUSED
CDEFFHU CHUFFED

CDEFFIL CLIFFED
CDEFFIO COIFFED
CDEFFLO COFFLED
CDEFFLU CUFFLED
CDEFFOS SCOFFED
CDEFFSU SCUFFED
CDEFHIL FILCHED
CDEFHIN FINCHED
CDEFHMO CHEFDOM
CDEFHOO CHOOFED
CDEFIIT DEFICIT
CDEFIKL FICKLED
FLICKED
CDEFILT CLIFTED
CDEFINO CONFIDE
CDEFKLO FLOCKED
CDEFKOR DEFROCK
FROCKED
CDEFNOR CORNFED
CDEFNTU DEFUNCT
CDEFOSU DEFOCUS
FOCUSED
CDEFRTU FRUCTED
CDEFSUU FUCUSED
CDEGGHU CHUGGED
CDEGGLO CLOGGED
COGGLED
CDEGGOS SCOGGED
CDEGGSU SCUGGED
CDEGHLU GULCHED
CDEGHOU COUGHED
CDEGIIN DEICING
CDEGIKN DECKING
CDEGILN CLINGED
CDEGILU CLUDGIE
CDEGINO COIGNED
CDEGINR CRINGED
CDEGINU DEUCING
EDUCING
CDEGIOR ERGODIC
CDEGKOU GEODUCK
CDEGKUW GWEDUCK
CDEGLSU CUDGELS
CDEGNSU SCUNGED
CDEGOOS SCOOGED
CDEGORS CODGERS
CDEGOSU SCOUGED
CDEGSUW GWEDUCS
CDEHHIL HILCHED
CDEHHIT HITCHED
CDEHHNU HUNCHED
CDEHHOT HOTCHED
CDEHHTU HUTCHED
CDEHIIL CEILIDH
CDEHIIV CHIVIED
CDEHIKN CHINKED
CDEHIKO HOICKED
CDEHIKR CHIRKED
CDEHIKT THICKED
CDEHILL CHILLED
CDEHILO CHELOID
HELCOID
CDEHILP DELPHIC
CDEHILR CHILDER
CHIRLED
ELDRICH
CDEHILS CHIELDS
CHILDES
CDEHILT LICHTED
CDEHIMR CHIRMED
CDEHIMT MITCHED
CDEHINN CHINNED
CDEHINO HEDONIC
CDEHINP PINCHED
CDEHINW WINCHED

CDEHIOR	CHOIRED
CDEHIOW	COWHIDE
CDEHIPP	CHIPPED
CDEHIPR	CHIRPED
CDEHIPT	PITCHED
CDEHIQU	QUICHED
CDEHIRR	CHIRRED
CDEHIRS	CHIDERS
	HERDICS
CDEHIRT	CHIRTED
	DITCHER
	RICHTED
CDEHIST	DITCHES
CDEHISU	DUCHIES
CDEHITT	CHITTED
CDEHITW	WITCHED
CDEHIVV	CHIVVED
CDEHIZZ	CHIZZED
CDEHKNU	CHUNKED
CDEHKOS	SHOCKED
CDEHKSU	SHUCKED
CDEHKUY	HEYDUCK
CDEHLMU	MULCHED
CDEHLNU	LUNCHED
CDEHLNY	LYNCHED
CDEHLOT	CLOTHED
CDEHLRU	LURCHED
CDEHMMU	CHUMMED
CDEHMNU	MUNCHED
CDEHMOO	MOOCHED
CDEHMOP	CHOMPED
CDEHMOR	CHROMED
CDEHMOU	MOUCHED
CDEHMPU	CHUMPED
CDEHNOR	CHONDRE
CDEHNOT	NOTCHED
CDEHNPU	PUNCHED
CDEHNRU	CHUNDER
	CHURNED
CDEHNSU	DUNCHES
CDEHNSY	SYNCHED
CDEHOOP	POOCHED
CDEHOPP	CHOPPED
CDEHOPT	POTCHED
CDEHOPU	POUCHED
CDEHORT	TORCHED
CDEHORW	CHOWDER
	COWHERD
CDEHOSU	CHOUSED
	DOUCHES
	HOCUSED
CDEHOSW	CHOWSED
	COWSHED
CDEHOTU	TOUCHED
CDEHOUV	VOUCHED
CDEHPSY	PSYCHED
CDEHRRU	CHURRED
CDEHRSU	CRUSHED
CDEHSSU	DUCHESS
CDEHSTU	DUTCHES
CDEHSTY	SCYTHED
CDEIIKR	DICKIER
CDEIIKS	DICKIES
CDEIILO	EIDOLIC
CDEIIMR	DIMERIC
CDEIINR	DINERIC
CDEIINS	INCISED
	INDICES
CDEIINT	IDENTIC
	INCITED
CDEIIOR	ERICOID
CDEIIOV	OVICIDE
CDEIIRT	DICTIER
	ICTERID
CDEIIRV	VERIDIC
CDEIIST	DEISTIC
	DICIEST
CDEIISU	SUICIDE
CDEIJST	DISJECT
CDEIKLN	CLINKED
	NICKLED
CDEIKLP	PICKLED
CDEIKLS	SICKLED
	SLICKED
CDEIKLT	TICKLED
CDEIKMS	MEDICKS
CDEIKNS	DICKENS
	SNICKED
CDEIKNZ	ZINCKED
CDEIKOS	DOCKISE
CDEIKOY	YOICKED
CDEIKOZ	DOCKIZE
CDEIKPR	PRICKED
CDEIKRR	DERRICK
CDEIKRS	DICKERS
	SCRIKED
CDEIKRT	TRICKED
CDEIKRU	DUCKIER
CDEIKRW	WRICKED
CDEIKST	DETICKS
	STICKED
CDEIKSU	DUCKIES
CDEIKSW	WICKEDS
CDEIKSY	DICKEYS
CDEILLO	CODILLE
	COLLIDE
	COLLIED
CDEILLU	CULLIED
CDEILMO	MELODIC
CDEILNU	INCLUDE
	NUCLIDE
CDEILOO	OCELOID
CDEILOP	POLICED
CDEILOR	DOCILER
CDEILPP	CLIPPED
CDEILPS	SPLICED
CDEILPU	CLUPEID
CDEILQU	CLIQUED
CDEILRS	CLERIDS
CDEILRU	LUCIDER
CDEILST	DELICTS
CDEILSU	SLUICED
CDEILTU	DUCTILE
	DULCITE
CDEIMNO	DEMONIC
CDEIMOR	DORMICE
CDEIMOS	MEDICOS
	MISCODE
CDEIMOT	DEMOTIC
CDEIMPR	CRIMPED
CDEIMPU	PUMICED
CDEIMSU	MISCUED
CDEINOS	CODEINS
	CONDIES
	SECONDI
CDEINOT	CTENOID
	DEONTIC
	NOTICED
CDEINOU	DOUCINE
CDEINOZ	ZINCODE
CDEINPR	PRINCED
CDEINRS	CINDERS
	DISCERN
	RESCIND
CDEINRU	INDUCER
CDEINRY	CINDERY
CDEINSU	CUNDIES
	INCUDES
	INCUSED
	INDUCES
CDEINSX	EXSCIND
CDEINSZ	DEZINCS
CDEINTT	TINCTED
CDEINTU	UNCITED
CDEIOPR	PERCOID
CDEIOPT	PICOTED
CDEIORS	DISCOER
CDEIORT	CORDITE
CDEIORV	CODRIVE
	DIVORCE
CDEIORW	CROWDIE
CDEIOST	CESTOID
	COEDITS
	COTISED
CDEIPRS	CRISPED
	DISCERP
CDEIPRT	PREDICT
CDEIPST	DEPICTS
	DISCEPT
CDEIRRU	CURDIER
	CURRIED
CDEIRST	CREDITS
	DIRECTS
CDEIRSU	CRUISED
	DISCURE
CDEIRSV	CERVIDS
	SCRIVED
CDEIRTV	VERDICT
CDEISST	DISSECT
CDEISSY	ECDYSIS
CDEITUX	EXCUDIT
CDEJNOU	JOUNCED
CDEKKNO	KNOCKED
CDEKLNO	CLONKED
CDEKLNU	CLUNKED
CDEKLOW	WEDLOCK
CDEKLPU	PLUCKED
CDEKLRU	RUCKLED
CDEKLSU	SCULKED
	SUCKLED
CDEKMOS	SMOCKED
CDEKNOR	DORNECK
CDEKNOS	DOCKENS
CDEKNRU	DRUCKEN
CDEKNSU	SUNDECK
	UNDECKS
CDEKOOR	CROOKED
CDEKORS	DOCKERS
	REDOCKS
CDEKORT	TROCKED
CDEKOST	DOCKETS
	STOCKED
CDEKRSU	DUCKERS
CDEKRTU	TRUCKED
CDELLOU	COLLUDE
	LOCULED
CDELLSU	SCULLED
CDELMOP	CLOMPED
CDELMPU	CLUMPED
CDELMSU	MUSCLED
CDELMTU	MULCTED
CDELNOO	CONDOLE
CDELNOU	ENCLOUD
CDELNOW	CLOWNED
CDELNOY	CONDYLE
CDELOOR	COLORED
	CROODLE
	DECOLOR
CDELOPP	CLOPPED
CDELOPU	COUPLED
CDELORS	SCOLDER
CDELORU	CLOURED
CDELORW	CLOWDER
CDELOST	COLDEST
CDELOSU	DULCOSE
CDELOSW	SCOWLED
CDELOTT	CLOTTED
CDELOTU	CLOUTED
CDELOUY	DOUCELY
CDELOWY	COWEDLY
CDELPSU	SCULPED
CDELRRU	CURDLER
CDELRSU	CURDLES
	SCUDLER
CDELRUY	CRUDELY
CDELSTU	DULCETS
CDELTTU	CUTTLED
CDELTUU	DUCTULE
CDEMMNO	COMMEND
CDEMMOO	COMMODE
CDEMMSU	SCUMMED
CDEMNNO	CONDEMN
CDEMNOP	COMPEND
CDEMOOS	COMEDOS
CDEMOPT	COMPTED
CDEMORU	DECORUM
CDEMPRU	CRUMPED
CDENNOO	CONDONE
CDENNOT	CONTEND
CDENOOR	CROONED
CDENOOS	CONDOES
	SECONDO
CDENOPU	POUNCED
	UNCOPED
CDENORS	CONDERS
	CORSNED
	SCORNED
CDENORU	CRUNODE
CDENORW	CROWNED
	DECROWN
CDENOSS	SECONDS
CDENOST	DOCENTS
CDENOSY	ECDYSON
CDENOTU	COUNTED
CDENPUY	PUDENCY
CDENRUU	UNCURED
CDENRUY	DUNCERY
CDEOOPP	COPEPOD
CDEOOPS	OPCODES
	SCOOPED
CDEOOPT	COOPTED
CDEOORR	CORRODE
CDEOORV	CODROVE
	VOCODER
CDEOOST	SCOOTED
CDEOOTV	DOVECOT
CDEOPPR	CROPPED
CDEOPRS	CORPSED
CDEOPRU	CROUPED
	PRODUCE
CDEOPSU	SCOUPED
CDEOPSW	SCOWPED
CDEOQTU	DOCQUET
CDEORRS	CORDERS
	RECORDS
CDEORRW	CROWDER
CDEORSS	CROSSED
	SCORSED
CDEORSU	COURSED
	SCOURED
	SOURCED
CDEORSW	SCOWDER
CDEORTU	COURTED
	EDUCTOR
CDEORUU	DOUCEUR
CDEOSSU	ESCUDOS
CDEOSTU	CUSTODE
	DOUCEST
	DOUCETS
	SCOUTED

CDEOSTY CYTODES
CDEOSYZ ZYDECOS
CDEPRSU SPRUCED
CDEPRTY DECRYPT
CDERRSU SCURRED
CDERSTU CRUDEST
CRUSTED
CDERSUZ SCRUZED
CDFHIOS CODFISH
CDFIILU FLUIDIC
CDFILUY DULCIFY
CDFIOOT OCTOFID
CDFIOSU FUCOIDS
CDFNOOU COFOUND
CDGHIIN CHIDING
CDGHILO GLOCHID
CDGIIKN DICKING
CDGIINO GONIDIC
CDGIINS DICINGS
DISCING
CDGIINT DICTING
CDGIKNO DOCKING
CDGIKNU DUCKING
CDGILNO CODLING
LINGCOD
CDGINNO CONDIGN
CDGINOR CORDING
CDGINOS CODINGS
CDGINRU CURDING
CDGINTU DUCTING
CDGNOOO COONDOG
CDGOOSY COYDOGS
CDHIIMO DOCHMII
CDHIINT CHINDIT
CDHIIST DISTICH
CDHILLY CHILDLY
CDHILNU UNCHILD
CDHILOR CHLORID
CDHILOS COLDISH
CDHINOR CHONDRI
CDHINSU DUNCISH
CDHIOOR CHOROID
OCHROID
CDHIORS DROICHS
ORCHIDS
CDHIORY DROICHY
CDHIOTU OUTCHID
CDHIPTY DIPTYCH
CDHKOOR HORDOCK
CDHORSS SCHRODS
CDIIILP LIPIDIC
CDIIIOT IDIOTIC
CDIIJRU JURIDIC
CDIILLY IDYLLIC
CDIILMO DOMICIL
CDIILNY DICLINY
CDIILOP DIPLOIC
CDIIMOS DISOMIC
CDIINOR CRINOID
CDIINOT DICTION
CDIINOV VIDICON
CDIINOZ ZINCOID
CDIINST INDICTS
CDIINTU DUNITIC
CDIIOPT PODITIC
CDIIORS CIRSOID
CDIIOSS CISSOID
CDIIOSV VISCOID
CDIIOTY IDIOTCY
CDIIPRY PYRIDIC
CDIIRSU SCIURID
CDIKNNU NUDNICK
CDIKNOR DORNICK
CDIKNOW WINDOCK
CDIKNPU DUCKPIN
CDILLOO COLLOID
CDILLUY LUCIDLY
CDILMTU MIDCULT
CDILNOS CODLINS
CDILOTU DULOTIC
CDILOTY DICOTYL
CDIMMOU MODICUM
CDIMNOO MONODIC
CDIMNSU MUNDICS
CDIMOOR CORMOID
CDIMOSU MUCOIDS
MUSCOID
CDIMSSU MUSCIDS
CDIMSTU DICTUMS
CDINOOS CONOIDS
CDINOOT ODONTIC
CDINOSY SYNODIC
CDINOTU CONDUIT
NOCTUID
CDINSSY SYNDICS
CDINSTU INDUCTS
CDIOOTT COTTOID
CDIOPRR RIPCORD
CDIOPSS PSOCIDS
CDIORSV CORVIDS
CDIOSST CODISTS
CDIOSTT COTTIDS
CDIOSTY CYSTOID
CDIOTUV OVIDUCT
CDIPRSY CYPRIDS
CDIPSSU CUSPIDS
CDIRSUY DYSURIC
CDIRTUY CRUDITY
CDISSSU DISCUSS
CDISSTY CYSTIDS
CDKMORU MUDROCK
CDKNNOU DUNNOCK
CDKNOOR DORNOCK
CDKNOSU UNDOCKS
CDLNOUU UNCLOUD
CDLOOPY LYCOPOD
CDLOSTU COULDST
CDMMOOO COMMODO
CDMNOOS CONDOMS
CDMNSUU CUNDUMS
CDMOOST TOMCODS
CDMOSUW MUDSCOW
CDNNOTU CONTUND
CDNOORS CONDORS
CORDONS
CDNORSU UNCORDS
CDNOTUW CUTDOWN
CDOOOPT OCTOPOD
CDOOOST DOOCOTS
CDOOPST POSTDOC
CDOORRY CORRODY
CDOORST DOCTORS
CDOOTUW WOODCUT
CDOPRTU PRODUCT
CDOSTUY CUSTODY
CEEEEGH GEECHEE
CEEEEHL LEECHEE
CEEEELT ELECTEE
CEEEFLR FLEECER
CEEEFLS FLEECES
CEEEFNR REFENCE
CEEEGNR REGENCE
CEEEGNS EGENCES
CEEEGRS GREECES
CEEEHIR REECHIE
CEEEHKS KEECHES
CEEEHLL ECHELLE
CEEEHLS ELCHEES
LEECHES
CEEEHNR ENCHEER
CEEEHPR CHEEPER
CEEEHRR CHEERER
CEEEHRS REECHES
CEEEHSS CHEESES
CEEEINP EPICENE
CEEEIPR CREEPIE
CEEEIRV RECEIVE
CEEEITV EVICTEE
CEEEJRT REEJECT
CEEELLU ECUELLE
CEEELPY YCLEEPE
CEEELRT REELECT
CEEELST CELESTE
CEEELSV CLEEVES
CEEEMPR EMPERCE
CEEENRS RECENSE
CEEENSS ESSENCE
CEEEPRR CREEPER
CEEERRT ERECTER
REERECT
CEEERSS CREESES
CEEERST SECRETE
CEEERSV SCREEVE
CEEERTX EXCRETE
CEEETUX EXECUTE
CEEFFNO OFFENCE
CEEFFOR EFFORCE
CEEFFOS COFFEES
CEEFFST EFFECTS
CEEFHIR CHIEFER
CEEFHIT FETICHE
FITCHEE
CEEFHLS FLECHES
CEEFHRT FECHTER
FETCHER
CEEFHST FETCHES
CEEFINV VENEFIC
CEEFIRR FIERCER
CEEFKLR FLECKER
FRECKLE
CEEFLNU FLUENCE
CEEFLRT REFLECT
CEEFNNS FENNECS
CEEFNNU UNFENCE
CEEFNOR ENFORCE
CEEFNRS FENCERS
CEEFPRT PERFECT
PREFECT
CEEFRST REFECTS
CEEFSSU FESCUES
CEEGHIN EECHING
CEEGHOS CHEGOES
CEEGIIP EPIGEIC
CEEGINR CREEING
ENERGIC
GENERIC
CEEGINT GENETIC
CEEGINU EUGENIC
CEEGIRS CIERGES
GRIECES
CEEGIRZ GRECIZE
CEEGKOS GECKOES
CEEGLLO COLLEGE
CEEGLNT NEGLECT
CEEGLOU ECLOGUE
CEEGNOR COGENER
CONGREE
CEEGNOS CONGEES
CEEGNRU URGENCE
CEEGNRY REGENCY
CEEGORT CORTEGE
CEEGQRU GRECQUE
CEEHHSW WHEECHS
CEEHIKM KIMCHEE
CEEHILN ELENCHI
CEEHILS HELICES
LICHEES
CEEHILV VEHICLE
CEEHIMR CHIMERE
CEEHIMS CHEMISE
CEEHINR INHERCE
CEEHINS CHINESE
CEEHIOR CHEERIO
CEEHIOS ECHOISE
CEEHIOZ ECHOIZE
CEEHIRT ERETHIC
ETHERIC
HERETIC
TECHIER
CEEHIRW CHEWIER
CEEHISS SEICHES
CEEHIST TECHIES
CEEHISV CHEVIES
SEVICHE
CEEHISW CHEWIES
CEEHKLR HECKLER
CEEHKLS HECKLES
CEEHKNP HENPECK
CEEHKNS KENCHES
CEEHKST KETCHES
CEEHLNO CHELONE
ECHELON
CEEHLNS ELENCHS
CEEHLNU LEUCHEN
CEEHLOW COWHEEL
CEEHLRS LECHERS
CEEHLRW WELCHER
CEEHLRY CHEERLY
LECHERY
CEEHLSS CHESSEL
CEEHLST LETCHES
CEEHLSW LECHWES
WELCHES
CEEHLSY LYCHEES
SLEECHY
CEEHMRS SCHEMER
SCHMEER
CEEHMRT MERCHET
CEEHMSS SCHEMES
CEEHNOP PENOCHE
CEEHNPU PENUCHE
CEEHNRW WENCHER
CEEHNST CHENETS
TENCHES
CEEHNSV CHEVENS
CEEHNSW WENCHES
WHENCES
CEEHNTU CHUTNEE
CEEHORR COHERER
CEEHORS CHEEROS
CHOREES
COHERES
ECHOERS
RECHOSE
CEEHORT TROCHEE
CEEHOUV VOUCHEE
CEEHPRR PERCHER
CEEHPRS PERCHES
CEEHPRU UPCHEER
CEEHQRU CHEQUER
CEEHQSU CHEQUES
CEEHQUY QUEECHY
CEEHRST ETCHERS
RETCHES
CEEHRSU EUCHRES
CEEHRSV CHEVRES
CEEHRSW CHEWERS
RECHEWS
CEEHRSY CREESHY
CEEHRTU TEUCHER

CEEHSSS	CHESSES
CEEHSSW	ESCHEWS
CEEHSTV	CHEVETS
	VETCHES
CEEHSTW	CHEWETS
CEEIIKL	ICELIKE
CEEIINR	EIRENIC
CEEIIPR	EPEIRIC
	EPICIER
CEEIJOR	REJOICE
CEEIKLT	CLEEKIT
CEEIKNT	NECKTIE
CEEIKPR	PECKIER
	PICKEER
CEEIKSS	SICKEES
CEEILLM	MICELLE
CEEILMX	LEXEMIC
CEEILNO	CINEOLE
CEEILNR	RECLINE
CEEILNS	LICENSE
	SELENIC
	SILENCE
CEEILNT	CENTILE
	LICENTE
CEEILNU	LEUCINE
CEEILPS	ECLIPSE
CEEILPX	EXCIPLE
CEEILRS	CEILERS
CEEILRT	RETICLE
	TIERCEL
CEEILRU	RECUILE
CEEILSS	ICELESS
CEEILST	SECTILE
CEEILSV	VESICLE
CEEILTU	LEUCITE
CEEIMMS	SEMEMIC
CEEIMNT	CENTIME
CEEIMRS	MERCIES
CEEIMRX	EXCIMER
CEEIMST	EMETICS
CEEINNS	INCENSE
CEEINOS	SENECIO
CEEINPR	PERCINE
CEEINPS	PICENES
	PIECENS
CEEINPT	PENTICE
CEEINPU	EUPNEIC
CEEINRS	CERESIN
	SCRIENE
	SINCERE
CEEINRT	ENTERIC
	ENTICER
CEEINRV	CERVINE
CEEINST	ENTICES
CEEINSV	EVINCES
CEEIOPT	PICOTEE
CEEIORT	COTERIE
CEEIORV	REVOICE
CEEIOST	COESITE
CEEIPPR	PRECIPE
CEEIPRR	CREPIER
	PIERCER
	REPRICE
CEEIPRS	PIECERS
	PIERCES
	PRECISE
	RECIPES
CEEIPRT	RECEIPT
CEEIPRU	EPICURE
CEEIPSS	SPECIES
CEEIPST	PECTISE
CEEIPTZ	PECTIZE
CEEIQSU	QUIESCE
CEEIRRT	RECITER
CEEIRSS	CERISES
CEEIRST	CERITES
	RECITES
	TIERCES
CEEIRSU	ECURIES
CEEIRSV	SCRIEVE
	SERVICE
CEEIRTT	TIERCET
CEEIRTU	EUCRITE
CEEIRTX	EXCITER
CEEISSX	EXCISES
CEEISTU	CUTESIE
CEEISTX	EXCITES
CEEITTT	TECTITE
CEEITTZ	ZETETIC
CEEJNOS	CONJEES
CEEJORT	EJECTOR
CEEJRST	REJECTS
CEEKKLS	KECKLES
CEEKKSS	KECKSES
CEEKLNT	NECKLET
CEEKLPS	SPECKLE
CEEKLSS	SECKELS
	SECKLES
CEEKLST	TECKELS
CEEKNRS	NECKERS
CEEKOSS	COKESES
CEEKOSY	SOCKEYE
CEEKPRS	PECKERS
CEEKPRY	RYEPECK
CEEKRRW	WRECKER
CEELLLU	CELLULE
CEELLNO	COLLEEN
CEELLOS	CELLOSE
CEELLPU	PUCELLE
CEELMNT	CLEMENT
CEELMOO	COELOME
CEELMOS	CLEOMES
CEELMOT	TELECOM
CEELMOW	WELCOME
CEELMSY	MYCELES
CEELNOS	ENCLOSE
CEELNPS	PENCELS
CEELNRS	CRENELS
CEELNRT	LECTERN
CEELNRU	LUCERNE
CEELORS	CREOLES
	RECLOSE
CEELORT	ELECTOR
	ELECTRO
CEELORY	RECOYLE
CEELOSS	ECLOSES
CEELOSU	COULEES
CEELOTU	ELOCUTE
CEELOTV	COVELET
CEELPRT	PLECTRE
	PRELECT
CEELPRU	CUPELER
CEELRRU	CRUELER
CEELRSS	SCLERES
CEELRST	TERCELS
CEELRSU	RECLUSE
	RECULES
CEELRSW	CREWELS
CEELRTU	LECTURE
CEELRTY	ERECTLY
CEELSST	SELECTS
CEELTTU	LETTUCE
CEEMMOR	COMMERE
CEEMNOW	NEWCOME
CEEMNRU	CERUMEN
CEEMNRW	CREWMEN
CEEMNST	CEMENTS
CEEMNSY	CYMENES
CEEMOPR	COMPEER
	COMPERE
CEEMOPT	COMPETE
CEEMRRS	MERCERS
CEEMRRY	MERCERY
	REMERCY
CEEMRST	CERMETS
CEEMSTU	TUMESCE
CEEMSTY	MYCETES
CEENNOU	ENOUNCE
CEENNOV	CONVENE
CEENNRT	CENTNER
CEENOOT	ECOTONE
CEENOPT	POTENCE
CEENORS	ENCORES
	NECROSE
CEENORU	COENURE
CEENORZ	COZENER
CEENOST	CENOTES
CEENPRS	SPENCER
CEENPRT	PERCENT
	PRECENT
CEENPSS	SPENCES
CEENPST	PECTENS
CEENRSS	CENSERS
	SCERNES
	SCREENS
	SECERNS
CEENRST	CENTERS
	CENTRES
	TENRECS
CEENRSU	CENSURE
CEENRSY	SCENERY
CEENTTU	CUNETTE
CEEOPRU	RECOUPE
CEEOPST	PECTOSE
CEEOPSU	COUPEES
CEEOPTY	ECOTYPE
CEEORRS	RESCORE
CEEORRT	ERECTOR
CEEORRU	RECOURE
CEEORRV	COVERER
	RECOVER
CEEORRW	RECOWER
CEEORSU	CEREOUS
CEEORSV	CORVEES
CEEORTV	COVETER
CEEORTW	COWTREE
CEEORTX	COEXERT
CEEOTTT	OCTETTE
CEEPPRT	PERCEPT
	PRECEPT
CEEPPRU	PREPUCE
CEEPRRU	PRECURE
CEEPRSS	PRECESS
CEEPRST	RECEPTS
	RESPECT
	SCEPTER
	SCEPTRE
	SPECTER
	SPECTRE
CEEPRTX	EXCERPT
CEEPSTX	EXCEPTS
	EXPECTS
CEEPSTY	ECTYPES
CEEPSUY	EYECUPS
CEERRSU	RECURES
	RESCUER
	SECURER
CEERRSW	SCREWER
CEERRUV	RECURVE
CEERSSS	CESSERS
	CRESSES
CEERSST	CRESSET
	RESECTS
	SECRETS
CEERSSU	CERUSES
	CESURES
	RECUSES
	RESCUES
	SECURES
CEERSTT	TERCETS
CEERSUX	EXCURSE
	EXCUSER
CEERTTU	CURETTE
CEESSTX	EXSECTS
CEESSUX	EXCUSES
CEETTUV	CUVETTE
CEFFHRU	CHUFFER
CEFFIOR	OFFICER
CEFFIOS	COIFFES
	OFFICES
CEFFISU	SUFFICE
CEFFLOS	COFFLES
CEFFLSU	CUFFLES
	SCUFFLE
CEFFORS	COFFERS
	SCOFFER
CEFFORT	COFFRET
CEFFSTU	SUFFECT
CEFGINN	FENCING
CEFHILR	FILCHER
CEFHILS	FILCHES
CEFHILY	CHIEFLY
CEFHINS	FINCHES
CEFHIRY	CHIEFRY
CEFHIST	FITCHES
CEFHITT	FITCHET
CEFHITW	FITCHEW
CEFHLTU	FUTCHEL
CEFIILT	FICTILE
CEFIIOR	ORIFICE
CEFIITV	FICTIVE
CEFIKLR	FICKLER
	FLICKER
CEFIKLS	FICKLES
CEFILNT	INFLECT
CEFILNU	FUNICLE
CEFILRU	FLUERIC
	LUCIFER
CEFIMOR	COMFIER
CEFIMRY	MERCIFY
CEFINNO	CONFINE
CEFINOR	COINFER
	CONIFER
	INFORCE
CEFINST	INFECTS
CEFIPSY	SPECIFY
CEFIRSS	SFERICS
CEFIRTY	CERTIFY
	RECTIFY
CEFISSU	FICUSES
CEFKLLO	ELFLOCK
CEFKLOT	FETLOCK
CEFKLRY	FRECKLY
CEFKRSU	FUCKERS
CEFLNOU	FLOUNCE
CEFLNUY	FLUENCY
CEFMORY	COMFREY
CEFNORS	CONFERS
CEFNORU	FROUNCE
CEFNOSS	CONFESS
CEFNOST	CONFEST
CEFNOSU	CONFUSE
CEFNOTU	CONFUTE
CEFOPRS	FORCEPS
CEFORRS	FORCERS
CEFORRT	CROFTER
CEFORSS	FRESCOS
CEFORSU	FOCUSER
	REFOCUS
CEFOSSU	FOCUSES

	FUCOSES
CEFRSUW	CURFEWS
CEFSSUU	FUCUSES
CEGGHIR	CHIGGER
CEGGHRU	CHUGGER
CEGGIIS	CIGGIES
CEGGIKN	GECKING
CEGGIOR	GEORGIC
CEGGIOS	COGGIES
CEGGLOR	CLOGGER
CEGGLOS	COGGLES
CEGGORS	COGGERS
CEGGPSU	EGGCUPS
CEGHILN	LECHING
CEGHINO	ECHOING
CEGHINP	PECHING
CEGHINT	ETCHING
CEGHINW	CHEWING
CEGHIOR	CHOREGI
CEGHIOS	CHIGOES
CEGHIRS	CHIGRES
	SCREIGH
CEGHITU	GUICHET
CEGHLSU	CLEUGHS
	GULCHES
CEGHORU	COUGHER
CEGHRTU	GUTCHER
CEGIILN	CEILING
	CIELING
CEGIINP	PIECING
CEGIKKN	KECKING
CEGIKNN	NECKING
CEGIKNP	PECKING
CEGIKNR	RECKING
CEGIKRU	GUCKIER
CEGILLN	CELLING
CEGILNP	CLEPING
CEGILNR	CLINGER
	CRINGLE
CEGILNU	CLUEING
	LUCIGEN
CEGILNW	CLEWING
CEGILNY	GLYCINE
CEGIMNO	GENOMIC
CEGIMNU	MUCIGEN
CEGINNR	CERNING
CEGINNS	CENSING
	SCENING
CEGINOR	COREIGN
CEGINOS	COGNISE
	COIGNES
CEGINOZ	COGNIZE
CEGINPR	CREPING
	PERCING
CEGINRR	CRINGER
CEGINRS	CRINGES
CEGINRW	CREWING
CEGINSS	CESSING
CEGIORT	ERGOTIC
CEGIRRS	GRICERS
CEGKLNO	GENLOCK
CEGKLOR	GROCKLE
CEGLNOO	COLOGNE
CEGLOOY	ECOLOGY
CEGLOSU	GLUCOSE
CEGLOSY	GLYCOSE
CEGNNOO	ONCOGEN
CEGNOOS	CONGOES
CEGNORS	CONGERS
CEGNORU	CONGRUE
CEGNORY	CRYOGEN
CEGNOST	CONGEST
CEGNRUY	URGENCY
CEGNSSU	SCUNGES
CEGNSTY	CYGNETS
CEGOORS	SCROOGE
CEGORRS	GROCERS
CEGORRY	GROCERY
CEGORSU	SCOURGE
	SCROUGE
CEHHILS	HILCHES
CEHHIRS	CHERISH
	SHRIECH
CEHHIRT	HITCHER
CEHHIST	HITCHES
CEHHNSU	HUNCHES
CEHHOOS	HOOCHES
CEHHOST	HOTCHES
	SHOCHET
CEHHSSU	SHEUCHS
CEHHSTU	HUTCHES
CEHIIKN	CHINKIE
CEHIIKS	HICKIES
CEHIILS	CHILIES
CEHIINR	HIRCINE
CEHIINS	NICEISH
CEHIINT	ICHNITE
	NITCHIE
CEHIIPP	CHIPPIE
CEHIIRT	ITCHIER
	TICHIER
CEHIISV	CHIVIES
	VICHIES
CEHIKNT	CHETNIK
	KITCHEN
	THICKEN
CEHIKNW	CHEWINK
CEHIKOO	CHOOKIE
CEHIKOR	CHOKIER
CEHIKOS	CHOKIES
CEHIKPS	PECKISH
CEHIKRR	CHIRKER
CEHIKRS	SHICKER
	SKRIECH
CEHIKRT	THICKER
CEHIKRW	WHICKER
CEHIKST	CHEKIST
CEHIKSY	HICKEYS
CEHIKTT	THICKET
CEHILLR	CHILLER
CEHILMY	CHIMLEY
CEHILNO	CHOLINE
	HELICON
CEHILNS	LICHENS
	LINCHES
CEHILNT	LINCHET
	TINCHEL
CEHILPR	PILCHER
CEHILPS	PILCHES
CEHILRT	LICHTER
CEHILRV	CHERVIL
CEHILSS	CHESILS
	CHISELS
CEHILST	ELTCHIS
CEHILSZ	ZILCHES
CEHILTY	ETHYLIC
	LECYTHI
	TECHILY
CEHIMMS	CHEMISM
CEHIMNY	CHIMNEY
CEHIMOR	MOCHIER
	MORICHE
CEHIMOS	ECHOISM
CEHIMRS	CHIMERS
	MICHERS
CEHIMRT	THERMIC
CEHIMRU	RHEUMIC
CEHIMST	CHEMIST
	MITCHES
CEHINNO	CHINONE
CEHINOP	CHOPINE
	PHOCINE
CEHINOR	CHORINE
CEHINOT	HENOTIC
CEHINOX	CHOENIX
CEHINPR	NEPHRIC
	PHRENIC
	PINCHER
CEHINPS	PINCHES
	SPHENIC
CEHINPU	PENUCHI
CEHINQU	QUINCHE
CEHINRS	NICHERS
	RICHENS
CEHINRT	CITHERN
	CITHREN
CEHINRW	WINCHER
CEHINST	ETHNICS
	STHENIC
CEHINSU	ECHINUS
CEHINSV	CHEVINS
CEHINSW	WINCHES
CEHINSZ	ZECHINS
CEHINTW	WITCHEN
CEHIOPS	HOSPICE
CEHIOPT	POTICHE
CEHIOPU	COPIHUE
CEHIORS	COHEIRS
	HEROICS
CEHIORT	ROTCHIE
	THEORIC
CEHIOST	ECHOIST
	TOISECH
CEHIOTU	COUTHIE
CEHIOTV	CHEVIOT
CEHIPPR	CHIPPER
CEHIPRR	CHIRPER
CEHIPRS	CERIPHS
	CIPHERS
	SPHERIC
CEHIPRT	PITCHER
CEHIPST	CHIPSET
	PITCHES
CEHIQSU	QUICHES
CEHIRRS	CHIRRES
CEHIRRT	RICHTER
CEHIRST	CITHERS
	ESTRICH
	RICHEST
CEHIRSU	CUSHIER
CEHIRSZ	SCHERZI
CEHIRTT	CHITTER
CEHISSU	CUISHES
CEHISTT	TITCHES
CEHISTW	WITCHES
CEHISZZ	CHIZZES
CEHKKRU	CHUKKER
CEHKLMO	HEMLOCK
CEHKLSU	HUCKLES
CEHKNOU	UNCHOKE
CEHKOOR	KERCHOO
CEHKORS	CHOKERS
	HOCKERS
	SHOCKER
CEHKOSY	CHOKEYS
	HOCKEYS
CEHKPTU	KETCHUP
CEHKRSU	SHUCKER
CEHKSTU	KUTCHES
CEHKSTY	SKETCHY
CEHKTVY	KVETCHY
CEHLLMO	MOCHELL
CEHLLMU	MUCHELL
CEHLLNS	SCHNELL
CEHLLOY	YELLOCH
CEHLMOR	CHROMEL
CEHLMSS	SCHELMS
CEHLMSU	MUCHELS
	MULCHES
CEHLMSZ	SCHMELZ
CEHLMUY	CHUMLEY
CEHLNNU	CHUNNEL
CEHLNOS	NOCHELS
CEHLNOT	CHOLENT
	NOTCHEL
CEHLNRU	LUNCHER
CEHLNRY	LYNCHER
CEHLNSU	LUNCHES
CEHLNSY	LYNCHES
CEHLNTY	LYNCHET
CEHLOOS	SCHOOLE
CEHLORS	CHOLERS
	ORCHELS
CEHLORT	CHORTLE
CEHLOST	CLOTHES
CEHLPPS	SCHLEPP
CEHLPSS	SCHLEPS
CEHLPSU	PLEUCHS
CEHLQSU	SQUELCH
CEHLRRU	LURCHER
CEHLRSU	LURCHES
CEHMNRU	MUNCHER
CEHMNSU	MUNCHES
CEHMOOR	MOOCHER
CEHMOOS	MOOCHES
CEHMOPR	CHOMPER
CEHMORS	CHROMES
CEHMORU	MOUCHER
CEHMOSS	SCHMOES
CEHMOSU	MOUCHES
CEHMRTU	CHETRUM
CEHMSTU	HUMECTS
	MUTCHES
CEHNNRU	CHUNNER
CEHNOOP	HENCOOP
CEHNOOR	COEHORN
CEHNORT	NOTCHER
CEHNORV	CHEVRON
CEHNOST	NOTCHES
	TECHNOS
CEHNOSU	COHUNES
CEHNPRU	PUNCHER
	UNPERCH
CEHNPST	PSCHENT
CEHNPSU	PUNCHES
CEHNRRU	CHURNER
CEHNRSU	RUNCHES
CEHNRTU	CHUNTER
CEHNSTU	CHESNUT
CEHNSTY	STENCHY
CEHNSUU	EUNUCHS
CEHNTUY	CHUTNEY
CEHOOPS	POOCHES
CEHOORS	CHOOSER
	SOROCHE
CEHOORT	CHEROOT
CEHOOSS	CHOOSES
CEHOOSY	CHOOSEY
CEHOOTU	OUTECHO
CEHOPPR	CHOPPER
CEHOPRS	PORCHES
CEHOPRT	POTCHER
CEHOPRY	CORYPHE
CEHOPST	POTCHES
CEHOPSU	POUCHES
CEHORRT	TORCHER
CEHORSS	COSHERS
CEHORST	HECTORS
	ROCHETS
	ROTCHES

	TOCHERS
	TORCHES
	TROCHES
CEHORSU	CHOREUS
	CHOUSER
	ROUCHES
CEHORSY	COSHERY
CEHORSZ	SCHERZO
CEHORTU	COUTHER
	RETOUCH
	TOUCHER
CEHORTW	WOTCHER
CEHORUV	VOUCHER
CEHOSSU	CHOUSES
	HOCUSES
CEHOSSW	CHOWSES
CEHOSTU	TOUCHES
CEHOSUV	VOUCHES
CEHPRSU	CHERUPS
CEHPRSY	CHYPRES
	CYPHERS
CEHPRTU	PUTCHER
CEHPSSY	PSYCHES
CEHQSTU	QUETSCH
CEHRRSU	CRUSHER
CEHRSSU	CRUSHES
CEHRSTT	STRETCH
CEHRSTY	SCYTHER
CEHSSTU	TUSCHES
CEHSSTY	SCYTHES
CEIIJRU	JUICIER
CEIIKKR	KICKIER
CEIIKLS	SICLIKE
CEIIKMS	MICKIES
CEIIKNS	KINESIC
CEIIKNT	KINETIC
CEIIKPR	PICKIER
CEIIKQU	QUICKIE
CEIIKRT	TRICKIE
CEIIKSS	SICKIES
CEIIKST	EKISTIC
	ICKIEST
	TICKIES
CEIIKSW	WICKIES
CEIILLS	SILICLE
CEIILNN	INCLINE
CEIILNP	PENICIL
CEIILPP	CLIPPIE
CEIILPT	PELITIC
CEIILST	ELICITS
CEIILTV	LEVITIC
CEIIMMT	MIMETIC
CEIIMNR	CRIMINE
	MINCIER
CEIIMNS	MENISCI
CEIIMOT	MEIOTIC
CEIIMPR	EMPIRIC
CEIIMPS	EPICISM
CEIIMRS	CIMIERS
CEIIMRV	VIREMIC
CEIIMSS	SEISMIC
CEIIMST	MISCITE
CEIIMTT	TITMICE
CEIINNO	CONIINE
	INCONIE
CEIINNR	CINERIN
CEIINOR	ONEIRIC
CEIINOS	EOSINIC
	ICONISE
CEIINOV	INVOICE
CEIINOZ	ICONIZE
CEIINPS	PISCINE
CEIINRS	IRENICS
	SERICIN
	SIRENIC
CEIINRT	CITRINE
	CRINITE
	INCITER
	NERITIC
CEIINRZ	ZINCIER
CEIINSS	ICINESS
	INCISES
CEIINST	INCITES
CEIINSU	CUISINE
CEIINTZ	CITIZEN
	ZINCITE
CEIIOPZ	EPIZOIC
CEIIPPR	PIPERIC
CEIIPRR	PRICIER
CEIIPRS	SPICIER
CEIIPRT	PICRITE
CEIIPST	EPICIST
CEIIRSS	CISSIER
CEIIRST	ERISTIC
	RICIEST
CEIIRSU	CRUISIE
CEIISSS	CISSIES
CEIISVV	CIVVIES
CEIITUV	UVEITIC
CEIJNST	INJECTS
CEIJRSU	JUICERS
CEIJSTU	JUSTICE
CEIKKNR	KNICKER
CEIKKRS	KICKERS
CEIKLMR	MICKLER
CEIKLMS	MICKLES
CEIKLNR	CLINKER
	CRINKLE
CEIKLNS	NICKELS
	NICKLES
	SLICKEN
CEIKLPR	PICKLER
	PRICKLE
CEIKLPS	PICKLES
CEIKLPU	CUPLIKE
CEIKLRS	LICKERS
	RICKLES
	SLICKER
CEIKLRT	TICKLER
	TRICKLE
CEIKLRU	LUCKIER
CEIKLSS	SICKLES
CEIKLST	STICKLE
	TICKLES
CEIKLSU	LUCKIES
CEIKLSY	KYLICES
CEIKMRS	SMICKER
CEIKMRU	MUCKIER
CEIKMST	SMICKET
CEIKMSY	MICKEYS
CEIKNOR	CONKIER
CEIKNOT	KENOTIC
	KETONIC
CEIKNQU	QUICKEN
CEIKNRS	NICKERS
	SNICKER
CEIKNSS	SICKENS
CEIKNST	SNICKET
	TICKENS
CEIKNSW	WICKENS
CEIKOOS	COOKIES
CEIKOPR	POCKIER
CEIKORR	CORKIER
	ROCKIER
CEIKOST	COKIEST
CEIKOTT	KETOTIC
CEIKPRR	PRICKER
CEIKPRS	PICKERS
	RIPECKS
	SPICKER
CEIKPRT	PRICKET
CEIKPRY	PICKERY
CEIKPST	PICKETS
	SKEPTIC
CEIKQRU	QUICKER
CEIKRRS	RICKERS
CEIKRRT	TRICKER
CEIKRSS	SCRIKES
CEIKRST	RICKETS
	STICKER
	TICKERS
CEIKRSW	WICKERS
CEIKRSY	RICKEYS
	YICKERS
CEIKRTU	TRUCKIE
CEIKRTY	RICKETY
CEIKRUY	YUCKIER
CEIKSST	SICKEST
CEIKSTT	TICKETS
CEIKSTW	WICKETS
CEIKSTY	TICKEYS
CEILLMS	MICELLS
CEILLNO	LIONCEL
CEILLNU	NUCELLI
CEILLOR	COLLIER
CEILLOS	COLLIES
CEILLST	CELLIST
CEILLSU	CULLIES
CEILMOP	COMPILE
	POLEMIC
CEILMOT	TELOMIC
CEILMPR	CRIMPLE
CEILNNU	NUCLEIN
CEILNOP	PINOCLE
CEILNOS	CINEOLS
	CONSEIL
	INCLOSE
CEILNOT	LECTION
CEILNOX	LEXICON
CEILNPS	PENCILS
	SPLENIC
CEILNST	CLIENTS
	LECTINS
	STENCIL
CEILNSU	LEUCINS
CEILNTU	CUTLINE
	LINECUT
	TUNICLE
CEILOOS	COOLIES
CEILOPR	PELORIC
CEILOPS	POLICES
CEILOPT	TOECLIP
CEILORS	COILERS
	RECOILS
CEILORT	CORTILE
CEILORU	URCEOLI
CEILOSS	OSSICLE
CEILOST	CITOLES
CEILPPR	CLIPPER
	CRIPPLE
CEILPRS	SPLICER
CEILPSS	SPLICES
CEILPSU	SPICULE
CEILPSV	PELVICS
CEILQSU	CLIQUES
CEILQUY	CLIQUEY
CEILRRU	CURLIER
CEILRSS	SLICERS
CEILRST	RELICTS
CEILRSV	CLIVERS
CEILRSY	CLERISY
CEILRTT	CLITTER
CEILRTU	UTRICLE
CEILSSS	SCISSEL
CEILSSU	SLUICES
CEILSTU	LUETICS
CEILTTU	CUITTLE
CEIMMOS	COMMIES
CEIMMRR	CRIMMER
CEIMMRU	CRUMMIE
CEIMNNO	MECONIN
CEIMNOR	INCOMER
CEIMNOS	INCOMES
	MESONIC
CEIMNOT	CENTIMO
	ENTOMIC
	TONEMIC
CEIMNRS	CREMSIN
	MINCERS
CEIMNRU	MINCEUR
	NUMERIC
CEIMNYZ	ENZYMIC
CEIMOOR	COOMIER
CEIMOPR	MEROPIC
CEIMOPT	METOPIC
CEIMOQU	COMIQUE
CEIMORR	MORRICE
CEIMORT	MORTICE
CEIMOSX	EXOSMIC
CEIMOTT	TOTEMIC
CEIMOTV	VICOMTE
CEIMOTX	TOXEMIC
CEIMOUZ	ZOECIUM
CEIMPRR	CRIMPER
CEIMPRS	SPERMIC
CEIMPRU	PUMICER
CEIMPSU	PUMICES
CEIMRST	CRETISM
	METRICS
CEIMRSU	CERIUMS
	MURICES
CEIMSSU	CESIUMS
	MISCUES
CEINNOS	CONINES
CEINNOV	CONNIVE
CEINOOT	COONTIE
CEINOPR	PERICON
	PONCIER
	PORCINE
CEINOPT	ENTOPIC
	NEPOTIC
CEINORR	CORNIER
CEINORS	COINERS
	CRINOSE
	CRONIES
	ORCEINS
	ORCINES
	RECOINS
	SERICON
CEINORT	COINTER
	NOTICER
	RECTION
CEINORU	COENURI
	NOURICE
CEINORV	CORVINE
CEINORY	ORIENCY
CEINOSS	CESSION
	COSINES
	OSCINES
CEINOST	NOTICES
	SECTION
CEINOSV	NOVICES
CEINOTT	ENTOTIC
	TONETIC
CEINOTX	EXCITON
CEINOUV	UNVOICE
CEINOVV	CONVIVE
CEINPRS	CRISPEN
	PINCERS
	PRINCES

CEINPRY	CYPRINE
CEINPST	INCEPTS
	INSPECT
	PECTINS
	PEINCTS
CEINPTY	PYCNITE
CEINQSU	CINQUES
	QUINCES
CEINRRU	CURNIER
	REINCUR
CEINRSS	SCRINES
CEINRST	CISTERN
	CRETINS
CEINRSV	CRIVENS
CEINRSW	WINCERS
CEINRTT	CITTERN
CEINRUV	INCURVE
CEINSST	INCESTS
	INSECTS
CEINSSU	INCUSES
CEINSTY	CYSTEIN
	CYSTINE
CEINSWY	WINCEYS
CEINTTX	EXTINCT
CEINVVY	VIVENCY
CEIOOPR	OPORICE
CEIOOST	COOTIES
CEIOPPR	CROPPIE
CEIOPPS	COPPIES
CEIOPRS	COPIERS
	COPSIER
	PERSICO
CEIOPST	POETICS
CEIOPSU	PICEOUS
CEIOPSW	COWPIES
CEIORRS	CIRROSE
	CORRIES
	CROSIER
	ORRICES
CEIORRU	COURIER
CEIORRZ	CROZIER
CEIORSS	COSIERS
CEIORST	EROTICS
	TERCIOS
CEIORSU	SCOURIE
CEIORSV	CORSIVE
	VOICERS
CEIORSW	COWRIES
	SCOWRIE
CEIORSZ	COZIERS
CEIORTT	COTTIER
CEIORTV	EVICTOR
CEIORTW	COWRITE
CEIORTX	EXCITOR
	XEROTIC
CEIORVY	VICEROY
CEIOSSS	COSSIES
CEIOSST	COSIEST
	COTISES
	OECISTS
CEIOSSV	VISCOSE
CEIOSTT	COTTISE
	SCOTTIE
CEIOSTV	COSTIVE
CEIOSTW	COWIEST
CEIOSTX	COEXIST
	COXIEST
	EXOTICS
CEIOSTY	SOCIETY
CEIOSTZ	COZIEST
CEIPPRU	CUPPIER
CEIPPST	PEPTICS
CEIPQTU	PICQUET
CEIPRRS	CRISPER
	PRICERS
CEIPRSS	SPICERS
CEIPRST	TRICEPS
CEIPRSY	SPICERY
CEIPRTU	CUPRITE
	PICTURE
CEIPRTY	PYRETIC
CEIPRXY	PYREXIC
CEIPSSS	SCEPSIS
CEIPSST	CESSPIT
	SEPTICS
CEIQRSU	CIRQUES
CEIRRRU	CURRIER
CEIRRSU	CRUISER
	CURRIES
	SUCRIER
CEIRRTT	CRITTER
CEIRRTU	RECRUIT
CEIRRTX	RECTRIX
CEIRRUV	CURVIER
CEIRSSU	CRUISES
	CRUSIES
	CUISSER
CEIRSSV	SCRIVES
CEIRSTT	TRISECT
CEIRSTU	CUITERS
	CURIETS
	CURITES
	ICTERUS
CEIRSTW	TWICERS
CEIRSUV	CRUIVES
	CURSIVE
CEIRTTU	CUTTIER
CEIRTTX	TECTRIX
CEISSSU	CUISSES
CEISSTU	CESTUIS
	CUEISTS
	CUTISES
	ICTUSES
CEISTTU	CUTTIES
CEJKNOY	JOCKNEY
CEJKOSY	JOCKEYS
CEJNOOS	COJONES
CEJNORU	CONJURE
CEJNOSU	JOUNCES
	JUNCOES
CEJOPRT	PROJECT
CEKKLNU	KNUCKLE
CEKKNOR	KNOCKER
CEKKOPS	KOPECKS
CEKLLOP	PELLOCK
CEKLLRY	CLERKLY
CEKLMNO	LOCKMEN
CEKLMSU	MUCKLES
CEKLNOS	ENLOCKS
	SLOCKEN
CEKLNRU	CLUNKER
	CRUNKLE
CEKLORS	LOCKERS
	RELOCKS
CEKLOST	LOCKETS
CEKLPRU	PLUCKER
CEKLPSU	PUCKLES
CEKLRSU	RUCKLES
	SCULKER
	SUCKLER
CEKLRTU	TRUCKLE
CEKLSSU	SUCKLES
CEKMNOS	SOCKMEN
CEKMORS	MOCKERS
CEKMORY	MOCKERY
CEKMRSU	MUCKERS
CEKNNSU	UNSNECK
CEKNOOV	CONVOKE
CEKNORR	CRONKER
CEKNORS	CONKERS
	RECKONS
CEKNORT	TROCKEN
CEKNOST	NOCKETS
CEKNRWY	WRYNECK
CEKNSSU	SUCKENS
CEKOOPR	PRECOOK
CEKOOPW	COWPOKE
CEKOORR	CROOKER
CEKOORS	COOKERS
	RECOOKS
CEKOORY	COOKERY
CEKOOSY	COOKEYS
CEKOPRR	PREROCK
CEKOPST	POCKETS
CEKORRS	CORKERS
	RECORKS
	ROCKERS
CEKORRY	ROCKERY
CEKORST	RESTOCK
	ROCKETS
	STOCKER
CEKOSST	SOCKETS
CEKPRSU	PUCKERS
CEKPRSY	RYPECKS
CEKPRUY	PUCKERY
CEKRRTU	TRUCKER
CEKRSSU	SUCKERS
CEKRSTU	TUCKERS
CEKRSUY	YUCKERS
CEKSSTU	SUCKETS
CEKSTTU	TUCKETS
CELLMOU	COLUMEL
CELLNOO	COLONEL
CELLORS	ESCROLL
CELLOST	COLLETS
CELLOSU	LOCULES
	OCELLUS
CELLOSY	CLOSELY
CELLRRU	CRULLER
CELLRSU	CRUELLS
	CULLERS
	SCULLER
CELLRUY	CRUELLY
CELLSSU	SCULLES
CELLSTU	CULLETS
CELMMSU	MESCLUM
CELMNOO	LOCOMEN
	MONOCLE
CELMNSU	CULMENS
	MESCLUN
CELMOOS	COELOMS
CELMOPS	COMPELS
CELMOPX	COMPLEX
CELMORS	CORMELS
CELMPRU	CLUMPER
	CRUMPLE
CELMSSU	MUSCLES
CELMSUU	SECULUM
CELMSUY	LYCEUMS
CELNNOU	NUCLEON
CELNNSU	NUNCLES
CELNOOR	CORONEL
CELNOOS	COLONES
	CONSOLE
CELNORS	CLONERS
	CORNELS
CELNOSU	COUNSEL
	UNCLOSE
CELNOTU	NOCTULE
CELNRSU	LUCERNS
CELNRTU	LECTURN
CELNSUU	NUCLEUS
	NUCULES
CELNSUW	UNCLEWS
CELOOPR	PRECOOL
CELOORR	COLORER
	RECOLOR
CELOORS	COOLERS
	CREOSOL
CELOOST	COOLEST
	OCELOTS
CELOPPS	COPPLES
CELOPRU	COUPLER
CELOPSU	COUPLES
	OPUSCLE
	UPCLOSE
CELOPTU	COUPLET
	OCTUPLE
CELOQSU	CLOQUES
CELORRU	CORULER
CELORSS	CLOSERS
	CRESOLS
	ESCROLS
CELORST	COLTERS
	CORSLET
	COSTREL
	LECTORS
CELORSU	CLOSURE
	COLURES
CELORSV	CLOVERS
CELORSW	SCOWLER
	SCROWLE
CELORSY	SCROYLE
CELORTT	CLOTTER
	CROTTLE
CELORTU	CLOTURE
	CLOUTER
	COULTER
CELORVY	CLOVERY
CELOSST	CLOSEST
	CLOSETS
CELOSSU	OSCULES
CELOSTY	COTYLES
CELOSUV	VOCULES
CELOTTU	CULOTTE
CELPRSU	CURPELS
	SCRUPLE
CELPSUU	CUPULES
CELPSUY	CLYPEUS
CELRRSU	CURLERS
CELRSSY	CRESYLS
CELRSTU	CLUSTER
	CULTERS
	CUSTREL
	CUTLERS
	RELUCTS
CELRSTY	CLYSTER
CELRSUV	CULVERS
CELRSUW	CURLEWS
CELRTTU	CLUTTER
CELRTUU	CULTURE
CELRTUV	CULVERT
CELRTUY	CRUELTY
	CUTLERY
CELSTTU	CUTLETS
	CUTTLES
	SCUTTLE
CEMMNOT	COMMENT
CEMMNOU	COMMUNE
CEMMOOT	COMMOTE
CEMMOOV	COMMOVE
CEMMORS	COMMERS
CEMMOTU	COMMUTE
CEMMRSU	CUMMERS
	SCUMMER
CEMNNOT	CONTEMN
CEMNOOP	COMPONE
CEMNOOS	ONCOMES
CEMNOOY	ECONOMY
	MONOECY

CEMNOSU	CONSUME
	MUSCONE
CEMNRSU	CRUMENS
CEMNRTU	CENTRUM
CEMNSTU	CENTUMS
CEMOOPS	COMPOSE
CEMOOPT	COMPOTE
CEMOOTU	OUTCOME
CEMOPRS	COMPERS
CEMOPRT	COMPTER
CEMOPST	COEMPTS
CEMOPSU	UPCOMES
CEMOPTU	COMPUTE
CEMORRS	CREMORS
CEMOSSU	COMUSES
	MUSCOSE
CEMOSSY	MYCOSES
CEMOSTU	COSTUME
CEMPRRU	CRUMPER
CEMPRTU	CRUMPET
CEMRRUY	MERCURY
CEMRSTU	RECTUMS
CEMSSUU	MUCUSES
CENNOOT	CONNOTE
CENNORS	CONNERS
CENNOST	CONSENT
	NOCENTS
CENNOTT	CONTENT
CENNOTV	CONVENT
CENNRSU	CUNNERS
	SCUNNER
CENOOPS	POONCES
CENOORR	CORONER
	CROONER
CENOORS	CEROONS
CENOORT	CORONET
CENOOSS	COOSENS
CENOPRS	CREPONS
CENOPRU	POUNCER
CENOPSU	POUNCES
	UNCOPES
CENOPSY	SYNCOPE
CENOPTU	POUNCET
CENOPTY	POTENCY
CENOQRU	CONQUER
CENORRS	CORNERS
	SCORNER
CENORRW	CROWNER
	RECROWN
CENORSS	CENSORS
CENORST	CONSTER
	CORNETS
	CRESTON
	CRONETS
CENORSU	CONURES
	ROUNCES
CENORTT	CORNETT
CENORTU	CORNUTE
	COUNTER
	RECOUNT
	TROUNCE
CENORTV	CONVERT
CENORTW	CROWNET
CENORUV	UNCOVER
CENOSSY	COYNESS
CENOSTT	CONTEST
CENOSTU	CONTUSE
	ECONUTS
CENOSTV	COVENTS
CENOSVY	CONVEYS
	COVYNES
CENOTTX	CONTEXT
CENPRTY	ENCRYPT
CENPTUX	EXPUNCT
CENRRTU	CURRENT
CENRSSY	SCRYNES
CENRSTU	ENCRUST
CENRSUU	UNCURSE
CENRSUW	UNSCREW
CENRTUY	CENTURY
CENSSTY	ENCYSTS
CEOOPRS	COOPERS
	SCOOPER
CEOOPRY	COOPERY
CEOORSS	COOSERS
	ROSCOES
CEOORST	COOTERS
	SCOOTER
CEOORSV	CROOVES
CEOORTW	COWROTE
CEOORVY	OVERCOY
CEOOSTY	COYOTES
	OOCYTES
CEOPPRR	CROPPER
CEOPPRS	COPPERS
CEOPPRU	PRECOUP
CEOPPRY	COPPERY
CEOPRRS	SCORPER
CEOPRRT	PORRECT
CEOPRRU	CROUPER
	PROCURE
CEOPRSS	CORPSES
	PROCESS
CEOPRST	COPTERS
	PROSECT
CEOPRSU	COUPERS
	CROUPES
	RECOUPS
CEOPRTT	PROTECT
CEOPRUU	COUPURE
CEOPRUV	COVERUP
CEOPSTY	COTYPES
CEOQRTU	CROQUET
	ROCQUET
CEOQSTU	COQUETS
CEORRSS	CROSSER
	RECROSS
	SCORERS
	SCORSER
CEORRST	RECTORS
CEORRSU	COURSER
	CRUORES
	SCOURER
CEORRSW	CROWERS
	SCOWRER
CEORRSY	SORCERY
CEORRSZ	CROZERS
CEORRTU	COURTER
CEORRTY	RECTORY
CEORSSS	CROSSES
	SCORSES
CEORSST	CORSETS
	COSTERS
	ESCORTS
	SCOTERS
	SECTORS
CEORSSU	COURSES
	SCOURSE
	SCOUSER
	SOURCES
	SUCROSE
CEORSSW	ESCROWS
CEORSTT	COTTERS
CEORSTU	COUTERS
	CROUTES
	SCOUTER
CEORSTV	CORVETS
	COVERTS
	VECTORS
CEORTUU	COUTURE
CEORTUV	COUVERT
	CUTOVER
	OVERCUT
CEOSSST	COSSETS
CEOSSSU	SCOUSES
CEOSSSY	SYCOSES
CEOSTTT	OCTETTS
CEOSTTU	CUTTOES
CEPPRRU	CRUPPER
CEPPRSU	CUPPERS
	SCUPPER
CEPRRSU	SPRUCER
CEPRSSU	PERCUSS
	SPRUCES
CEPRSSY	CYPRESS
CEPRSTU	PRECUTS
CEPRSTY	SCEPTRY
CEPRSUW	SCREWUP
CEPRUUV	UPCURVE
CEPSSTU	SUSPECT
CERRSSU	CURSERS
CERRSSY	SCRYERS
CERSSSU	CUSSERS
CERSSTU	CRUSETS
CERSSUZ	SCRUZES
CERSTTU	CURTEST
	CUTTERS
	SCUTTER
CERSTUV	CURVETS
CERSTUY	CURTESY
	CURTSEY
CESSUZZ	SCUZZES
CFFGINO	COFFING
CFFGINU	CUFFING
CFFHINO	CHIFFON
CFFIIRT	TRIFFIC
CFFIKKO	KICKOFF
CFFIKOP	PICKOFF
CFFILSS	SCLIFFS
CFFINOS	COFFINS
CFFINSU	CUFFINS
CFFMOSU	OFFSCUM
CFFNSUU	UNCUFFS
CFFOSTU	CUTOFFS
	OFFCUTS
CFFRSSU	SCRUFFS
CFFRSUY	SCRUFFY
CFGIINO	COIFING
CFGIKNU	FUCKING
CFGINOR	FORCING
CFHILYY	CHYLIFY
CFHIMYY	CHYMIFY
CFHINSU	FUCHSIN
CFHIOSW	COWFISH
CFHIRST	FRICHTS
CFHORTU	FUTHORC
CFIIIMR	MIRIFIC
CFIIIVV	VIVIFIC
CFIIKNY	FINICKY
CFIILNT	INFLICT
CFIIMNO	OMNIFIC
CFIIMOT	MOTIFIC
CFIIMRY	MICRIFY
CFIINOT	FICTION
CFIINOY	ICONIFY
CFIINYZ	ZINCIFY
CFIIOSS	OSSIFIC
CFIKNNO	FINNOCK
CFIKOSS	FOSSICK
CFILORS	FROLICS
CFILORU	FLUORIC
CFIMNOR	CONFIRM
CFIMOST	COMFITS
CFINOST	CONFITS
CFIORST	FICTORS
CFIORSY	SCORIFY
CFIRSTU	FRUICTS
CFISSTU	FUSTICS
CFKLLOU	LOCKFUL
CFKNORU	UNFROCK
CFKOTTU	FUTTOCK
CFKPSUU	FUCKUPS
CFLMRUU	FULCRUM
CFLNORY	CORNFLY
CFLNOUX	CONFLUX
CFLNOUY	FLOUNCY
CFLOOPW	COWFLOP
CFLOPRU	CROPFUL
CFLPSUU	CUPFULS
	CUPSFUL
CFMNOOR	CONFORM
CFMOORT	COMFORT
CFNORTU	FUNCTOR
CFOSSTU	FUSTOCS
CFOSSUU	FUSCOUS
CGGGINO	COGGING
CGGIINR	GRICING
CGGORSY	SCROGGY
CGHHOSU	CHOUGHS
CGHIILM	MILCHIG
CGHIIMN	CHIMING
	MICHING
CGHIINN	CHINING
	INCHING
	NICHING
CGHIINR	RICHING
CGHIINT	ITCHING
CGHIINV	CHIVING
CGHIKNO	CHOKING
	HOCKING
CGHILPY	GLYPHIC
CGHILTY	GLITCHY
CGHINNO	CHIGNON
CGHINOR	CHORING
	OCHRING
CGHINOS	COSHING
CGHINOU	OUCHING
CGHINOW	CHOWING
CGHINRU	RUCHING
CGHINSU	CHUSING
CGHINTU	CHUTING
CGHIOST	GOTHICS
CGHIOSY	GOYISCH
CGHLOSU	CLOUGHS
CGHOORT	TORGOCH
CGHORUY	GROUCHY
CGIIJNU	JUICING
CGIIKKN	KICKING
CGIIKLN	LICKING
CGIIKMM	GIMMICK
CGIIKNN	NICKING
CGIIKNP	PICKING
CGIIKNR	RICKING
CGIIKNS	SICKING
CGIIKNT	TICKING
CGIIKNW	WICKING
CGIILLO	ILLOGIC
CGIILNO	COILING
CGIILNP	CLIPING
CGIILNS	SLICING
CGIIMNN	MINCING
CGIIMNR	CRIMING
CGIINNO	COINING
CGIINNR	CRINING
CGIINNW	WINCING
CGIINNZ	ZINCING
CGIINOR	GIRONIC
CGIINOV	VOICING
CGIINPR	PRICING
CGIINPS	SPICING

CGIINRT	TRICING
CGIKLNO	CLOKING
	LOCKING
CGIKLNU	LUCKING
CGIKMNO	MOCKING
CGIKMNU	MUCKING
CGIKNNO	CONKING
	NOCKING
CGIKNOO	COOKING
CGIKNOP	POCKING
CGIKNOR	CORKING
	ROCKING
CGIKNOS	SOCKING
CGIKNOT	TOCKING
CGIKNOY	YOCKING
CGIKNPU	KINGCUP
CGIKNRU	RUCKING
CGIKNSU	SUCKING
CGIKNTU	TUCKING
CGIKNUY	YUCKING
CGILLNO	COLLING
CGILLNU	CULLING
CGILMNU	CULMING
CGILMNY	CYMLING
CGILNNO	CLONING
CGILNNU	UNCLING
CGILNOO	COOLING
	LOCOING
CGILNOS	CLOSING
CGILNOT	COLTING
CGILNOW	COWLING
CGILNOY	CLOYING
CGILNPY	CLYPING
CGILNRU	CURLING
CGILNSY	GLYCINS
CGILOOO	OOLOGIC
CGILORW	COWGIRL
CGILOTT	GLOTTIC
CGILPSU	GILCUPS
CGILPTU	GILTCUP
CGILPTY	GLYPTIC
CGIMNOO	COOMING
CGIMNOP	COMPING
CGIMNOR	CROMING
CGIMNOS	COMINGS
CGINNNO	CONNING
CGINNNU	CUNNING
CGINNOP	PONCING
CGINNOR	CORNING
CGINNOS	CONSIGN
CGINNPU	PUNCING
CGINNSY	SYNCING
CGINOOP	COOPING
CGINOOS	COOINGS
CGINOPP	COPPING
CGINOPS	COPINGS
	COPSING
	SCOPING
CGINOPU	COUPING
CGINOPW	COWPING
CGINOPY	COPYING
CGINORS	SCORING
CGINORU	COURING
CGINORW	CROWING
CGINORY	GYRONIC
CGINOSS	COSIGNS
CGINOST	COSTING
	GNOSTIC
CGINOSU	CONGIUS
	SOUCING
CGINOSV	COVINGS
CGINOSW	SCOWING
	SOWCING
CGINOSY	COSYING
CGINOYZ	COZYING

CGINPPU	CUPPING
CGINRRU	CURRING
CGINRSU	CURSING
CGINRSY	CRYINGS
	SCRYING
CGINRTU	TRUCING
CGINRUV	CURVING
CGINSSU	CUSSING
	SCUSING
CGINTTU	CUTTING
CGIOOOS	GIOCOSO
CGIOOST	COGITOS
CGIOTYZ	ZYGOTIC
CGKLNOU	GUNLOCK
CGLLOSY	GLYCOLS
CGLLSYY	GLYCYLS
CGLNOSU	UNCLOGS
CGLOOSU	COLUGOS
CGNOOSU	CONGOUS
CGOORRW	GORCROW
CHHIIKS	HICKISH
CHHIKOR	CHIKHOR
CHHINOR	RHONCHI
CHHINTU	UNHITCH
CHHIRST	SHRITCH
CHHISST	SHTCHIS
CHHISTY	ICHTHYS
CHHNOOS	HONCHOS
CHHRTTU	THRUTCH
CHIIILO	CHILIOI
CHIIKMS	KIMCHIS
CHIIKNN	KINCHIN
CHIIKSS	SICKISH
CHIILLS	CHILLIS
CHIILNT	CHITLIN
CHIILOT	THIOLIC
CHIILST	LITCHIS
CHIILTY	ITCHILY
CHIIMST	ISTHMIC
CHIIMSU	ISCHIUM
CHIINNP	INCHPIN
CHIINOT	THIONIC
CHIINST	CHITINS
CHIIOPT	OPHITIC
CHIIOST	STICHOI
CHIIRRS	SCIRRHI
CHIKLLO	HILLOCK
CHIKLTY	THICKLY
CHIKNOO	CHINOOK
CHIKORS	CHIKORS
	CHOKRIS
CHIKORY	HICKORY
CHIKOST	THICKOS
CHIKPSU	PUCKISH
CHIKRSS	SCHRIKS
CHIKSST	SCHTIKS
	SHTICKS
CHIKSTY	KITSCHY
CHILLMU	CHILLUM
CHILLTY	LICHTLY
CHILNOR	CHLORIN
CHILNOU	ULICHON
CHILNSY	LYCHNIS
CHILOOS	COOLISH
CHILORS	ORCHILS
CHILORT	TROCHIL
CHILOST	COLTISH
CHILPSY	SYLPHIC
CHILSTU	CULTISH
CHILSUY	CUSHILY
CHIMMOR	MICROHM
CHIMNPY	NYMPHIC
CHIMOPR	MORPHIC
CHIMORS	CHORISM
	CHRISOM

CHIMRRY	MYRRHIC
CHIMRSS	CHRISMS
CHIMSSS	SCHISMS
CHIMSTY	CHYMIST
	TYCHISM
CHINOOR	CHORION
CHINOPS	CHOPINS
	PHONICS
CHINOPY	CIPHONY
CHINOST	CHITONS
CHINOSU	CUSHION
CHINPSY	HYPNICS
CHINQSU	SQUINCH
CHINRSU	URCHINS
CHINTUW	UNWITCH
CHINTYZ	CHINTZY
CHIOOPR	POCHOIR
CHIOORS	ISOCHOR
CHIOORZ	CHORIZO
CHIOPRT	TROPHIC
CHIOPST	PHOTICS
CHIOPXY	HYPOXIC
CHIORST	CHORIST
	OSTRICH
CHIORSW	CHOWRIS
CHIOSST	STICHOS
CHIOSSZ	SCHIZOS
CHIPRRU	CHIRRUP
CHIPRRY	PYRRHIC
CHIPSSY	PHYSICS
CHIQSTU	SQUITCH
CHIRRSU	CURRISH
CHIRSTY	CHRISTY
CHISSST	SCHISTS
CHISSTU	SCHUITS
CHISTTU	CHUTIST
CHISTWY	SWITCHY
CHISYZZ	SCHIZZY
CHITTWY	TWITCHY
CHKLOOO	HOOLOCK
CHKLOOT	KLOOTCH
CHKLOSS	SHLOCKS
CHKLOSY	SHYLOCK
CHKMMOO	HOMMOCK
CHKMMOU	HUMMOCK
CHKMOSS	SHMOCKS
CHKMSSU	SHMUCKS
CHKNOOS	SCHNOOK
CHKOOST	SCHTOOK
CHKORSU	CHUKORS
CHKPTUU	PUTCHUK
CHKSSTU	SHTUCKS
CHLMOOS	MOLOCHS
CHLMORY	CHROMYL
CHLMPSU	SCHLUMP
CHLOOSS	SCHOOLS
CHLOOST	COOLTHS
CHLOPST	SPLOTCH
CHLORSS	SCHORLS
CHLORTY	CHOLTRY
CHLOSSS	SCHLOSS
CHLOSUY	CHYLOUS
	SLOUCHY
CHLOTYZ	ZLOTYCH
CHMOORS	CHROMOS
CHMOOSS	SCHMOOS
CHMOOST	SCHTOOM
CHMOOSY	SMOOCHY
CHMOOSZ	SCHMOOZ
CHMOSUY	CHYMOUS
CHMSTUY	SMUTCHY
CHNNOOR	CHRONON
CHNNOSU	NONSUCH
CHNOOPS	PONCHOS
CHNOORS	COHORNS

CHNOORT	TORCHON
CHNORRS	SCHNORR
CHNORSY	SYNCHRO
CHNORTU	COTHURN
CHNOSZZ	SCHNOZZ
CHNOTUU	UNCOUTH
CHNSTUU	TUCHUNS
CHOOPPS	COPSHOP
CHOORST	COHORTS
CHOORSU	OCHROUS
CHOOSST	COHOSTS
CHOPSSY	PSYCHOS
CHOPTUU	TOUCHUP
CHORSTU	TROCHUS
CHOSSTU	SCHOUTS
	SCOUTHS
CHOSSTW	SCOWTHS
CHPSSUY	SCYPHUS
CHRRSUU	CHURRUS
CHSSTUY	SCHUYTS
CIIILLT	ILLICIT
	ILLITIC
CIIILNV	INCIVIL
CIIIMNR	CRIMINI
CIIINPT	INCIPIT
CIIJLUY	JUICILY
CIIKKLL	KILLICK
CIIKKMS	MISKICK
CIIKMMM	MIMMICK
CIIKMNN	MINNICK
CIIKNPT	NITPICK
CIIKNSW	INWICKS
CIIKNTU	CUTIKIN
CIIKPUW	WICKIUP
CIIKSST	TISICKS
CIIKSTT	STICKIT
CIILLTY	LICITLY
CIILLVY	CIVILLY
CIILNOP	CIPOLIN
	PICOLIN
CIILNOS	SILICON
CIILNPS	INCLIPS
CIILNUV	UNCIVIL
CIILNVY	VINYLIC
CIILOOT	OOLITIC
CIILOPT	POLITIC
CIILORT	CORTILI
CIILOST	COLITIS
	SOLICIT
CIILOTT	LITOTIC
CIILPSY	SPICILY
CIILSSS	SCISSIL
CIILSSV	SILVICS
CIIMMRY	MIMICRY
CIIMNNO	NIMONIC
CIIMNOS	MISCOIN
CIIMNOT	MICTION
CIIMOST	MIOTICS
	MISTICO
	SOMITIC
CIIMOTT	MITOTIC
CIIMOTV	MOTIVIC
CIIMRST	TRISMIC
CIIMSSV	CIVISMS
CIIMSTV	VICTIMS
CIINNOT	NICOTIN
CIINNTU	TUNICIN
CIINOOT	COITION
CIINOPR	PORCINI
CIINOPS	PSIONIC
CIINORS	INCISOR
CIINORT	NORITIC
CIINPRS	CRISPIN
CIINQTU	QUINTIC
CIINRST	CITRINS

CIINRSU	RICINUS
CIINSSV	VISCINS
CIINTUY	UNICITY
CIIORST	SORITIC
CIIOSTX	COXITIS
CIIOSUV	VICIOUS
CIIPRSS	SPIRICS
CIIPRTY	PYRITIC
CIIRSTV	VITRICS
CIIRTVX	VICTRIX
CIJKORS	CROJIKS
CIJNNOO	CONJOIN
CIJNNTU	INJUNCT
CIJNOOS	COJOINS
CIKKLLO	KILLOCK
CIKKOPT	TOPKICK
CIKKOTU	OUTKICK
CIKKPSU	KICKUPS
CIKLLOP	PILLOCK
CIKLLOR	ROLLICK
CIKLLOS	SILLOCK
CIKLLOW	KILLCOW
CIKLLSY	SLICKLY
CIKLLUY	LUCKILY
CIKLMSU	MISLUCK
CIKLMSY	SMICKLY
CIKLMUY	MUCKILY
CIKLNOS	INLOCKS
CIKLNRY	CRINKLY
CIKLOPY	POCKILY
CIKLOPZ	ZIPLOCK
CIKLORY	ROCKILY
CIKLPRY	PRICKLY
CIKLQUY	QUICKLY
CIKLRTY	TRICKLY
CIKLSTU	LUSTICK
CIKMNNO	MINNOCK
CIKMNSU	NICKUMS
CIKMOOS	MISCOOK
CIKMORR	RIMROCK
CIKMSTU	STICKUM
CIKNNOP	PINNOCK
CIKNNOW	WINNOCK
CIKNOSW	COWSKIN
CIKNPSU	UNPICKS
CIKNPSY	PYKNICS
CIKNPTU	NUTPICK
CIKNSTU	UNSTICK
CIKOPPT	POCKPIT
CIKORRS	CORKIRS
CIKOSTU	SICKOUT
CIKOTUW	OUTWICK
CIKPPSU	PICKUPS
CIKPSTU	STICKUP
	UPTICKS
CIKPUWY	WICKYUP
CIKRSST	STRICKS
CIKRSTY	TRICKSY
CILLNOS	COLLINS
CILLNOU	CULLION
CILLOOR	CRIOLLO
CILLOPY	POLLICY
CILLRUY	CURLILY
CILMNOP	COMPLIN
CILMNOS	CLONISM
CILMNSY	CYMLINS
CILMOOS	LOCOISM
CILMSTU	CULTISM
CILNOOR	ORCINOL
CILNOOS	CLOISON
	SCOLION
CILNOPR	PILCORN
CILNORY	CORNILY
	LYRICON
CILNOSU	ULICONS
	UNCOILS
CILNOTU	LINOCUT
CILNOXY	XYLONIC
CILNPSU	INSCULP
	SCULPIN
	UNCLIPS
CILNPTU	UNCLIPT
CILNSTU	LINCTUS
CILOOPT	COPILOT
CILOORU	COULOIR
CILOOSS	COLOSSI
CILOOST	SCIOLTO
CILOPRW	PILCROW
CILOPRY	PYLORIC
CILOPSU	OILCUPS
	UPCOILS
CILOPSW	COWSLIP
CILORST	LICTORS
CILOSTU	COUTILS
	OCULIST
CILPRSY	CRISPLY
CILPRTU	CULPRIT
CILRRSU	SCURRIL
CILRSUU	SURCULI
CILRSUY	CRUSILY
CILSTTU	CULTIST
CIMMNSU	CUMMINS
CIMMOSS	COSMISM
CIMMOST	COMMITS
CIMMOTX	COMMIXT
CIMNNOS	NINCOMS
CIMNNSU	NINCUMS
CIMNOOR	MORONIC
	OMICRON
CIMNORS	CRIMSON
	MICRONS
CIMNOSU	CONIUMS
CIMNRSU	CRINUMS
CIMOORS	MORISCO
CIMOORT	MOTORIC
CIMOOST	OSMOTIC
CIMOPSY	COPYISM
	MISCOPY
	MYOPICS
CIMORSU	CORIUMS
CIMOSST	COSMIST
	SITCOMS
CIMOSSY	MYCOSIS
CIMOSTY	MYOTICS
CIMOTYZ	ZYMOTIC
CIMPRSS	SCRIMPS
CIMPRSY	SCRIMPY
CIMRSSU	CRISSUM
CIMRSUU	CURIUMS
CIMSSTU	MISCUTS
CIMSSTY	MYSTICS
CIMSSUV	VISCUMS
CINNNOU	INCONNU
CINNORU	UNICORN
CINNOSU	NUNCIOS
CINNOTU	UNCTION
CINNSUU	UNCINUS
CINOOPR	PORCINO
CINOOPS	OPSONIC
	POCOSIN
CINOORS	CORONIS
CINOOSS	COOSINS
CINOOSV	OVONICS
CINOPPS	COPPINS
CINOPRX	PRINCOX
CINORRT	TRICORN
CINORSS	INCROSS
CINORST	CISTRON
	CITRONS
	CORNIST
	CORTINS
CINORSZ	ZIRCONS
CINORTU	RUCTION
CINORTY	TYRONIC
CINOSST	CONSIST
	TOCSINS
CINOSSU	COUSINS
CINOSTU	SUCTION
CINOSUZ	ZINCOUS
CINRSTU	INCRUST
CIOOPRT	PORTICO
	PROOTIC
CIOOPSU	COPIOUS
CIOOQTU	COQUITO
CIOORST	OCTROIS
CIOORSU	CORIOUS
CIOPRST	TROPICS
CIOPSTY	COPYIST
CIOQRSU	CROQUIS
CIORRSU	CIRROUS
CIORSSS	SCISSOR
CIORSTT	TRICOTS
CIORSTU	CITROUS
CIORSTV	VICTORS
CIORSUU	CURIOUS
CIORTVY	VICTORY
CIOSSSY	SYCOSIS
CIOSSUV	VISCOUS
CIPRSST	SCRIPTS
CIPRSSU	PRUSSIC
CIPRTTY	TRYPTIC
CIPSTTY	STYPTIC
CIRRTTU	CRITTUR
CIRSSTU	RUSTICS
CIRSTUY	CITRUSY
CIRTUVY	CURVITY
CISSTUY	CYTISUS
CJNORUY	CONJURY
CKKLNUY	KNUCKLY
CKLLMOU	MULLOCK
CKLLOOP	POLLOCK
CKLLOOR	ROLLOCK
CKLLORU	RULLOCK
CKLNOSU	UNLOCKS
CKLNOTU	LOCKNUT
CKLNUUY	UNLUCKY
CKLOOOY	OLYCOOK
CKLOORW	ROWLOCK
CKLOOTU	LOCKOUT
CKLOPSU	LOCKUPS
	UPLOCKS
CKLOPTU	POTLUCK
	PUTLOCK
CKMMMOU	MUMMOCK
CKMOPSU	MOCKUPS
CKNOOOR	ROCKOON
CKNORSU	UNCORKS
CKNOSTU	UNSTOCK
CKNSTUU	UNSTUCK
	UNTUCKS
CKOOOPT	COOKTOP
CKOOOTU	COOKOUT
	OUTCOOK
CKOORSU	SOUROCK
CKOORTU	OUTROCK
CKOPTTU	PUTTOCK
CKORTUW	CUTWORK
CKOSSTU	TUSSOCK
CKSSTUU	TUSSUCK
CLLMOSU	MOLLUSC
CLLOOPS	COLLOPS
	SCOLLOP
CLLORSS	SCROLLS
CLLOSUU	LOCULUS
CLMNOSU	COLUMNS
CLMOOPT	COMPLOT
CLMOPTU	PLUMCOT
CLMOSUU	LUCUMOS
	OSCULUM
CLMPRUY	CRUMPLY
CLMSUUU	CUMULUS
CLNOORT	CONTROL
CLNOOSS	CONSOLS
CLNOOSU	COLONUS
CLNOSSU	CONSULS
CLNOSTU	CONSULT
	UNCOLTS
CLNOSUW	UNCOWLS
CLNRSUU	UNCURLS
CLOOPPW	COWPLOP
CLOOPST	COPLOTS
CLOOPTY	POLYCOT
CLOORSU	COLOURS
CLOORUY	COLOURY
CLOOSTY	CYTOSOL
CLOPTUY	OCTUPLY
CLORSSW	SCROWLS
CLORSSY	CROSSLY
CLORSUY	CORYLUS
CLORTUY	COURTLY
CLOSSTU	LOCUSTS
CLPRSUU	UPCURLS
CLPSSTU	SCULPTS
CMMNOOS	COMMONS
CMMOOST	COMMOTS
CMMOPSY	COMSYMP
CMMRSUY	SCRUMMY
CMNNOOS	NONCOMS
CMNOOOT	MONOCOT
CMNOOPY	COMPONY
CMNOSSY	SYNCOMS
CMNPTUU	PUNCTUM
CMOOPRT	COMPORT
CMOOPST	COMPOST
	COMPOTS
CMOORSU	CORMOUS
CMOOSTY	SCOTOMY
CMORSTU	SCROTUM
CMORTUW	CUTWORM
CMOSSTU	CUSTOMS
CMPRSSU	SCRUMPS
CMPRSUU	CUPRUMS
CMPRSUY	SCRUMPY
CNNOPSY	PYCNONS
CNNORTU	NOCTURN
CNNORUW	UNCROWN
CNNOSUY	UNSONCY
CNOOPPR	POPCORN
CNOOPRU	CROUPON
CNOOPSU	COUPONS
	SOUPCON
CNOORRW	CORNROW
CNOORST	CONSORT
	CROTONS
CNOORTT	CONTORT
CNOORTU	CONTOUR
	CORNUTO
	CROUTON
CNOOSST	NOSTOCS
	ONCOSTS
CNOOSTT	COTTONS
CNOOSTY	TYCOONS
CNOOSUU	NOCUOUS
CNOOSVY	CONVOYS
CNOOTTW	COTTOWN
CNOOTTY	COTTONY
CNOPRTY	CRYPTON
CNOPSTU	PUNCTOS
CNORSSU	UNCROSS
CNORSSY	SYNROCS

CNORTUY	COUNTRY
CNRSSTU	SCRUNTS
CNRSTUY	SCRUNTY
COOORSZ	COROZOS
COOPRRT	PROCTOR
COOPRSS	SCROOPS
COOPRTU	OUTCROP
COOPSTU	OCTOPUS
COOPSUY	COYPOUS
COORSTU	OCTUORS
COORSUU	ROUCOUS
COORTUW	OUTCROW
COOSSTY	OOCYSTS
COOSTTY	OTOCYST
COPRRTU	CORRUPT
COPRSTY	CRYPTOS
COPRSUU	CUPROUS
CORRSSU	CURSORS
CORRSUY	CURSORY
CORSSTU	SCRUTOS
COSTTUU	CUTOUTS
DDDDEIL	DIDDLED
DDDEEGR	DREDGED
DDDEEHL	HEDDLED
DDDEEHS	SHEDDED
DDDEEIR	DERIDED
DDDEELM	MEDDLED
DDDEELP	PEDDLED
DDDEELR	REDDLED
DDDEELS	SLEDDED
DDDEELU	DELUDED
DDDEEMO	DEMODED
DDDEENS	SNEDDED
DDDEENU	DENUDED
DDDEERU	UDDERED
DDDEEST	STEDDED
DDDEFIL	FIDDLED
DDDEFLU	FUDDLED
DDDEGII	GIDDIED
DDDEGLU	GUDDLED
DDDEGRU	DRUDGED
DDDEHIW	WHIDDED
DDDEHLO	HODDLED
DDDEHLU	HUDDLED
DDDEHTU	THUDDED
DDDEIIK	KIDDIED
DDDEIIR	DIDDIER
DDDEIIS	DIDDIES
DDDEIIV	DIVIDED
DDDEIKS	SKIDDED
DDDEILM	MIDDLED
DDDEILN	DINDLED
DDDEILP	PIDDLED
DDDEILR	DIDDLER
	RIDDLED
DDDEILS	DIDDLES
DDDEILT	TIDDLED
DDDEILW	WIDDLED
DDDEILY	DIDDLEY
DDDEIMU	MUDDIED
DDDEIOR	DODDIER
DDDEIOS	DODDIES
DDDEIRS	DIDDERS
DDDEIRU	DUDDIER
	RUDDIED
DDDELMU	MUDDLED
DDDELNO	NODDLED
DDDELOO	DOODLED
DDDELOP	PLODDED
DDDELOS	DODDLES
DDDELOT	TODDLED
DDDELPU	PUDDLED
DDDELRU	RUDDLED
DDDENOS	SNODDED
DDDEOPR	PRODDED
DDDEOQU	QUODDED
DDDEORS	DODDERS
DDDEORY	DODDERY
DDDEPSU	SPUDDED
DDDERSU	DUDDERS
DDDERUY	DUDDERY
DDDESTU	STUDDED
DDDGINO	DODDING
DDEEEGR	DEGREED
DDEEEIR	DEEDIER
DDEEELN	NEEDLED
DDEEELT	DELETED
DDEEELV	DEVELED
DDEEELW	WEDELED
DDEEEMN	EMENDED
DDEEEMR	REMEDED
DDEEENT	TEENDED
DDEEENW	ENDEWED
DDEEEPS	SPEEDED
DDEEEST	DEEDEST
	STEEDED
DDEEESX	DESEXED
DDEEEWY	DYEWEED
DDEEFGL	FLEDGED
DDEEFII	DEIFIED
	EDIFIED
DDEEFIL	DEFILED
	FIELDED
DDEEFIN	DEFINED
DDEEFLU	DEEDFUL
DDEEFNS	DEFENDS
DDEEFSU	DEFUSED
DDEEFUZ	DEFUZED
DDEEGGL	GLEDGED
DDEEGIN	DEEDING
	DEIGNED
DDEEGIS	DISEDGE
DDEEGLP	PLEDGED
DDEEGLS	SLEDGED
DDEEGLU	DELUGED
DDEEGNU	UNEDGED
DDEEGRR	DREDGER
DDEEGRS	DREDGES
DDEEHLS	HEDDLES
DDEEHNU	DUDHEEN
DDEEHRS	SHEDDER
DDEEILM	DELIMED
DDEEILR	DREIDEL
DDEEILS	SLEIDED
DDEEILV	DEVILED
DDEEILW	WIELDED
DDEEILY	DEEDILY
	YIELDED
DDEEIMP	IMPEDED
DDEEIMS	DEMISED
	MISDEED
DDEEINS	DESINED
	NEDDIES
	SDEINED
DDEEINT	ENDITED
	TEINDED
DDEEINW	INDEWED
	WIDENED
DDEEINX	INDEXED
DDEEINZ	DIZENED
DDEEIOV	VIDEOED
DDEEIPR	PREDIED
DDEEIPS	DEPSIDE
DDEEIRR	DERIDER
	REDDIER
	REDRIED
	RIDERED
DDEEIRS	DERIDES
	DESIRED
	DIEDRES
	RESIDED
DDEEIRV	DERIVED
DDEEIRW	WEIRDED
DDEEIST	DEIDEST
	TEDDIES
DDEEISV	DEVISED
DDEEKKO	DEKKOED
DDEELLU	DUELLED
DDEELLW	DWELLED
DDEELMO	MODELED
DDEELMR	MEDDLER
DDEELMS	MEDDLES
DDEELNO	OLDENED
DDEELNS	LEDDENS
DDEELOP	DELOPED
DDEELOW	DOWELED
DDEELOY	YODELED
DDEELPR	PEDDLER
DDEELPS	PEDDLES
	SPELDED
DDEELRS	REDDLES
	SLEDDER
DDEELRT	TREDDLE
DDEELRU	DELUDER
DDEELSU	DELUDES
DDEEMMO	MODEMED
DDEEMOT	DEMOTED
DDEEMRU	DEMURED
DDEENNU	UNENDED
DDEENOP	DEPONED
DDEENOT	DENOTED
DDEENOV	DOVENED
DDEENOW	ENDOWED
DDEENOZ	DOZENED
DDEENPS	DEPENDS
DDEENPU	UPENDED
DDEENRS	REDDENS
DDEENRT	TRENDED
DDEENRU	DENUDER
	ENDURED
DDEENST	STENDED
DDEENSU	DENUDES
	DUDEENS
	DUENDES
DDEENSY	DESYNED
DDEENTU	DETUNED
DDEEOOR	RODEOED
DDEEOPS	DEPOSED
	SEEDPOD
DDEEORR	ORDERED
DDEEORV	DOVERED
DDEEORW	DOWERED
DDEEOTV	DEVOTED
DDEEOTX	DETOXED
DDEEPRS	PEDDERS
	SPREDDE
DDEEPTU	DEPUTED
DDEERRS	REDDERS
DDEERSS	DRESSED
DDEERST	REDDEST
	TEDDERS
DDEERSW	WEDDERS
DDEERTU	DETRUDE
DDEESST	STEDDES
DDEETTU	DUETTED
DDEFGIR	FRIDGED
DDEFILR	FIDDLER
DDEFILS	FIDDLES
DDEFILY	FIDDLEY
DDEFIOR	FOREDID
DDEFIRT	DRIFTED
DDEFLNO	FONDLED
DDEFLOO	FLOODED
DDEFLRU	FUDDLER
DDEFLSU	FUDDLES
DDEFNOR	FRONDED
DDEFNOU	FOUNDED
DDEFNSU	DEFUNDS
DDEFORS	FODDERS
DDEGGRU	DRUGGED
	GRUDGED
DDEGHIT	DIGHTED
DDEGIIR	GIDDIER
DDEGIIS	GIDDIES
DDEGILR	GIRDLED
	GLIDDER
	GRIDDLE
DDEGIMO	DEMIGOD
DDEGINR	GRINDED
	REDDING
DDEGINT	TEDDING
DDEGINW	WEDDING
DDEGINY	EDDYING
DDEGIOR	DODGIER
DDEGIRR	GRIDDER
DDEGLOS	DOGSLED
DDEGLSU	GUDDLES
DDEGMOO	DOGEDOM
DDEGMOS	DODGEMS
DDEGMSU	SMUDGED
DDEGNOO	NOODGED
DDEGNOS	GODDENS
	GODSEND
DDEGNOU	DUDGEON
DDEGNSU	SNUDGED
DDEGORS	DODGERS
	GORSEDD
DDEGORY	DODGERY
DDEGOSS	GODDESS
DDEGOST	STODGED
DDEGRRU	DRUDGER
DDEGRSU	DRUDGES
DDEGRTU	TRUDGED
DDEHIOW	HOWDIED
DDEHIRS	HIDDERS
	REDDISH
	SHIDDER
DDEHIRT	THIRDED
DDEHIRW	WHIDDER
DDEHIRY	HYDRIDE
DDEHLNO	HONDLED
DDEHLOS	HODDLES
DDEHLRU	HUDDLER
	HURDLED
DDEHLSU	HUDDLES
DDEHNOS	HODDENS
	SHODDEN
DDEHNOU	HOUNDED
DDEHNRU	HUNDRED
DDEHNSU	DUNSHED
DDEHNUZ	NUDZHED
DDEHRSU	SHUDDER
DDEHRSY	SHREDDY
DDEIIKR	KIDDIER
DDEIIKS	KIDDIES
DDEIIMS	MIDDIES
DDEIINT	INDITED
DDEIINV	DIVINED
DDEIIOS	IODIDES
	IODISED
DDEIIOX	DIOXIDE
DDEIIOZ	IODIZED
DDEIIRT	DIRTIED
	TIDDIER
DDEIIRV	DIVIDER
DDEIIST	STIDDIE
	TIDDIES
DDEIISV	DIVIDES
DDEIISW	WIDDIES
DDEIITT	DITTIED

DDEIIVV	DIVVIED
DDEIIZZ	DIZZIED
DDEIKLN	KINDLED
DDEIKLS	KIDDLES
DDEIKNR	KINDRED
DDEIKOS	KIDDOES
DDEIKRS	KIDDERS
	SKIDDER
DDEILLO	DOLLIED
DDEILLR	DRILLED
DDEILLU	ILLUDED
DDEILMP	DIMPLED
DDEILMR	MIDDLER
DDEILMS	MIDDLES
DDEILNN	DINNLED
DDEILNS	DINDLES
	SLIDDEN
DDEILNW	DWINDLE
	WINDLED
DDEILOR	DROILED
DDEILOS	DILDOES
DDEILOT	DELTOID
DDEILPR	PIDDLER
DDEILPS	DISPLED
	PIDDLES
DDEILPU	DUPLIED
DDEILQU	QUIDDLE
DDEILRR	RIDDLER
DDEILRS	DREIDLS
	RIDDLES
	SLIDDER
DDEILRT	TIDDLER
DDEILST	TIDDLES
DDEILSW	WIDDLES
DDEILTU	DILUTED
DDEILTW	TWIDDLE
DDEILTY	LYDDITE
	TIDDLEY
DDEIMMU	DUMMIED
DDEIMNS	MIDDENS
DDEIMNU	MUEDDIN
DDEIMOO	MOODIED
DDEIMOR	DERMOID
DDEIMOS	DESMOID
DDEIMRU	MUDDIER
DDEIMSS	DESMIDS
DDEIMST	MIDDEST
DDEIMSU	DEDIMUS
	MUDDIES
DDEINOP	POINDED
DDEINOS	NODDIES
DDEINOT	DENTOID
DDEINOW	INDOWED
DDEINPS	DISPEND
DDEINRU	UNDRIED
DDEINST	DISTEND
DDEINSW	SWIDDEN
DDEIOPR	PODDIER
DDEIOPS	PODDIES
DDEIORS	DORISED
	SODDIER
DDEIORV	OVERDID
DDEIORW	DOWDIER
DDEIORZ	DORIZED
DDEIOSS	SODDIES
DDEIOST	TODDIES
DDEIOSW	DOWDIES
DDEIOTT	DITTOED
DDEIOWW	WIDOWED
DDEIPPR	DRIPPED
DDEIPRS	DISPRED
DDEIPRU	UPDRIED
DDEIPSU	PUDDIES
DDEIPUV	UPDIVED
DDEIRRS	RIDDERS
DDEIRRU	RUDDIER
DDEIRSU	RUDDIES
DDEIRSW	WIDDERS
DDEISSU	DISUSED
DDEISTU	STUDDIE
	STUDIED
DDEJRSU	JUDDERS
DDEKMOU	DUKEDOM
DDEKOOR	DROOKED
DDEKORU	DROUKED
DDELLOR	DROLLED
DDELMOU	MOULDED
DDELMPU	DUMPLED
DDELMRU	MUDDLER
DDELMSU	MUDDLES
DDELNOO	NOODLED
DDELNOS	NODDLES
DDELNOU	LOUNDED
	NODULED
DDELNOW	LOWNDED
DDELNRU	NURDLED
	RUNDLED
DDELOOR	DOODLER
	DROOLED
DDELOOS	DOODLES
DDELOOW	WOOLDED
DDELOPR	PLODDER
DDELORT	TODDLER
DDELORW	WORLDED
DDELOST	TODDLES
DDELOTT	DOTTLED
DDELPRU	PUDDLER
DDELPSU	PUDDLES
DDELRSU	RUDDLES
DDELSTU	STUDDLE
DDEMMRU	DRUMMED
DDEMMSU	SMEDDUM
DDEMNOS	ODDSMEN
DDEMNOT	ODDMENT
DDEMNOU	MOUNDED
DDEMRSU	MUDDERS
DDENNOR	DENDRON
	DONNERD
DDENOOP	ENDOPOD
DDENOOS	SNOODED
DDENOPS	DESPOND
DDENOPU	POUNDED
DDENOPW	POWNDED
DDENORS	DONDERS
	NODDERS
	SNODDER
DDENORT	TRODDEN
DDENORU	REDOUND
	ROUNDED
	UNDERDO
DDENORW	DROWNED
	ROWNDED
	WONDRED
DDENOSS	ODDNESS
	SODDENS
DDENOSU	SOUNDED
DDENOSW	SOWNDED
DDENOSY	DYNODES
DDENOUW	WOUNDED
DDENPSU	PUDDENS
DDENRSU	DUNDERS
DDENSSU	SUDDENS
DDENSTU	STUDDEN
DDEOOPR	DROOPED
DDEOORU	ODOURED
DDEOORW	REDWOOD
DDEOOWY	DYEWOOD
DDEOPPR	DROPPED
DDEOPRR	PRODDER
DDEOPRW	DEWDROP
DDEORSW	DROWSED
	SWORDED
DDEPRSS	SPREDDS
DDEPRSU	PUDDERS
	SPUDDER
DDERRSU	RUDDERS
DDERSSU	SUDDERS
DDGGINO	DODGING
	GODDING
DDGHINO	HODDING
DDGHOOO	GODHOOD
DDGIIKN	KIDDING
DDGIILN	LIDDING
DDGIILY	GIDDILY
DDGIINR	RIDDING
DDGIMNU	MUDDING
DDGINNO	NODDING
DDGINOP	PODDING
DDGINOR	RODDING
DDGINOS	SODDING
DDGINOT	TODDING
DDGINPU	PUDDING
DDGINRU	RUDDING
DDGINUW	WUDDING
DDGIPUY	GIDDYUP
DDGMOOS	DOGDOMS
DDGOOOW	DOGWOOD
DDHIIKS	KIDDISH
DDHIISS	SIDDHIS
DDHIKSU	KIDDUSH
DDHINOS	HODDINS
DDHIORY	HYDROID
DDHIRSY	HYDRIDS
DDIIKKS	DIKDIKS
DDIIKSV	KIDVIDS
DDIILOP	DIPLOID
DDIIOSX	DIOXIDS
	IXODIDS
DDIIQTU	QUIDDIT
DDIKNOS	DODKINS
DDIKOOS	SKIDDOO
DDILMUY	MUDDILY
DDILNRS	DIRNDLS
DDILOSY	DYSODIL
DDILOWY	DOWDILY
DDILRUY	RUDDILY
DDILTWY	TWIDDLY
DDIMOOS	DODOISM
DDIMRSU	DIRDUMS
DDIMSSU	DUDISMS
DDINOST	SNODDIT
DDIORTU	TURDOID
DDIRSSU	SIDDURS
DDLLMOO	DOLLDOM
DDMMSUU	DUMDUMS
DDMNOOR	DROMOND
DDMRSUU	DURDUMS
DDNORSW	DROWNDS
DDORSTY	DROSTDY
DEEEEMX	EXEEMED
DEEEEWW	WEEWEED
DEEEFFR	EFFERED
DEEEFLR	FLEERED
DEEEFLT	FLEETED
DEEEFNR	ENFREED
DEEEFNS	DEFENSE
DEEEFRS	FEEDERS
	REFEEDS
DEEEFRV	FEVERED
DEEEGKL	GLEEKED
DEEEGLP	PLEDGEE
DEEEGLT	GLEETED
DEEEGMR	DEMERGE
	EMERGED
DEEEGNP	PEENGED
DEEEGNR	GREENED
	RENEGED
DEEEGRR	REGREDE
DEEEGRS	DEGREES
DEEEGRT	DETERGE
	GREETED
DEEEGST	EGESTED
DEEEHKT	THEEKED
DEEEHLS	SHEELED
DEEEHLW	WHEEDLE
	WHEELED
DEEEHNS	SHEENED
DEEEHPS	PHEESED
DEEEHPW	WHEEPED
DEEEHPZ	PHEEZED
DEEEHRS	HEEDERS
	HEREDES
	SHEERED
DEEEHST	SEETHED
	SHEETED
DEEEHTT	TEETHED
DEEEHWZ	WHEEZED
DEEEIJL	JEELIED
DEEEIMR	EMERIED
DEEEINR	NEEDIER
DEEEIPS	DEEPIES
DEEEIRR	REEDIER
DEEEIRS	SEEDIER
DEEEIRW	WEEDIER
DEEEISV	DEVISEE
DEEEJLW	JEWELED
DEEEJNU	DEJEUNE
DEEEJRR	JERREED
DEEEJRS	JEREEDS
DEEEKLN	KNEELED
DEEEKLS	SLEEKED
DEEEKMS	SMEEKED
DEEEKNW	WEEKEND
DEEEKRS	KREESED
	SKEERED
DEEEKRY	REKEYED
DEEEKST	STEEKED
DEEELLV	LEVELED
DEEELMS	MESELED
DEEELNR	NEEDLER
DEEELNS	NEEDLES
DEEELPS	SPEELED
DEEELPT	DEPLETE
DEEELRT	DEERLET
DEEELRV	LEVERED
	REVELED
DEEELST	DELETES
	SLEETED
	STEELED
DEEELSV	SLEEVED
DEEELSW	SWEELED
DEEELTW	TWEEDLE
	TWEELED
DEEELTX	TELEXED
DEEEMMW	EMMEWED
DEEEMNR	EMENDER
	REEDMEN
DEEEMNS	DEMESNE
	SEEDMEN
DEEEMNW	ENMEWED
DEEEMRS	DEMERSE
	EMERSED
	REDEEMS
	REMEDES
DEEEMRT	METERED
DEEEMST	STEEMED
DEEENPR	PREENED
DEEENPS	DEEPENS
DEEENQU	QUEENED
DEEENRS	NEEDERS

	SERENED
	SNEERED
DEEENRT	ENTERED
DEEENRV	ENERVED
DEEENRW	RENEWED
DEEENRY	RENEYED
DEEENST	STEENED
DEEENSV	VENDEES
DEEENSW	ENSEWED
DEEENSZ	SNEEZED
DEEENTT	DETENTE
DEEENTU	DETENUE
DEEENTV	EVENTED
DEEEORW	OREWEED
DEEEOTV	DEVOTEE
DEEEPRS	SPEEDER
	SPEERED
DEEEPRT	PETERED
DEEEPRU	EPERDUE
DEEEPRV	PREEVED
DEEEPSS	PEDESES
DEEEPST	DEEPEST
	STEEPED
DEEEQRU	QUEERED
DEEERRS	REEDERS
DEEERRV	REVERED
DEEERSS	RESEEDS
	SEEDERS
DEEERST	REESTED
	STEERED
DEEERSV	DESERVE
	SEVERED
DEEERSW	RESEWED
	SEWERED
	SWEERED
	WEEDERS
DEEERSY	REDEYES
DEEERTV	EVERTED
DEEERTW	TWEERED
DEEERTX	EXERTED
DEEERWY	WEEDERY
DEEESSX	DESEXES
DEEESTV	STEEVED
DEEESTW	SWEETED
DEEETTV	VEDETTE
DEEETTW	TWEETED
DEEETWZ	TWEEZED
DEEFFFO	FEOFFED
DEEFFIN	EFFENDI
DEEFFOR	OFFERED
DEEFFST	DEFFEST
DEEFFSU	EFFUSED
DEEFGGL	FLEGGED
DEEFGIN	FEEDING
	FEIGNED
DEEFGIP	PIGFEED
DEEFGLS	FLEDGES
DEEFGRU	REFUGED
DEEFHLS	FLESHED
	SHELFED
DEEFHLU	HEEDFUL
DEEFHRS	FRESHED
DEEFIIR	DEIFIER
	EDIFIER
	REIFIED
DEEFIIS	DEIFIES
	EDIFIES
DEEFILN	ENFILED
DEEFILR	DEFILER
	FERLIED
	FIELDER
	REFILED
DEEFILS	DEFILES
DEEFILT	FILETED
DEEFIMS	MISFEED
DEEFINR	DEFINER
	ENFIRED
	FENDIER
	REFINED
DEEFINS	DEFINES
DEEFINT	FEINTED
DEEFINX	ENFIXED
DEEFIRR	FERRIED
	REFIRED
	REFRIED
DEEFIRS	DEFIERS
	SERIFED
DEEFIRT	FETIDER
DEEFIRX	REFIXED
DEEFIRY	REEDIFY
DEEFIRZ	FRIEZED
DEEFLLU	FUELLED
DEEFLNS	FLENSED
DEEFLNU	NEEDFUL
DEEFLOT	FEEDLOT
DEEFLRU	FERULED
DEEFLRY	DEERFLY
DEEFLTT	FETTLED
DEEFMOR	FREEDOM
DEEFNRS	FENDERS
DEEFNRU	UNFREED
DEEFNUU	UNFEUED
DEEFORV	OVERFED
DEEFORZ	DEFROZE
DEEFRSU	REFUSED
DEEFRSW	SWERFED
DEEFRTT	FRETTED
DEEFRTU	FEUTRED
	REFUTED
DEEFSSU	DEFUSES
DEEFSTT	DEFTEST
DEEFSUZ	DEFUZES
DEEGGIS	GIDGEES
DEEGGLS	GLEDGES
DEEGHIN	HEEDING
	NEIGHED
DEEGHIR	HEDGIER
DEEGHIW	WEIGHED
DEEGHOW	HOGWEED
DEEGHRS	HEDGERS
DEEGHSS	GHESSED
DEEGIJS	GIDJEES
DEEGIKR	KEDGIER
DEEGILN	DELEING
DEEGILR	GELIDER
	LEDGIER
	LEIDGER
DEEGIMN	DEEMING
DEEGINN	ENGINED
	NEEDING
DEEGINR	DREEING
	ENERGID
	GREINED
	REEDING
	REIGNED
DEEGINS	SDEIGNE
	SEEDING
DEEGINV	DEEVING
DEEGINW	WEEDING
DEEGINY	YEEDING
DEEGIPW	PIGWEED
DEEGIRS	SEDGIER
DEEGIRV	DIVERGE
	GRIEVED
DEEGIRW	WEDGIER
DEEGIST	EDGIEST
DEEGISW	WEDGIES
DEEGJRU	REJUDGE
DEEGKRS	KEDGERS
DEEGLMU	EMULGED
DEEGLNS	LEGENDS
DEEGLNT	GENTLED
	GLENTED
DEEGLOY	GOLDEYE
DEEGLPR	PLEDGER
DEEGLPS	PLEDGES
DEEGLPT	PLEDGET
DEEGLRS	GELDERS
	LEDGERS
	REDLEGS
	SLEDGER
DEEGLRU	GRUELED
	REGLUED
DEEGLRW	WERGELD
DEEGLSS	SLEDGES
DEEGLSU	DELUGES
DEEGMNU	EMUNGED
	GUDEMEN
DEEGMRS	DEGERMS
DEEGMUW	GUMWEED
DEEGNNO	ENDOGEN
DEEGNNR	GRENNED
DEEGNOR	ENGORED
DEEGNRS	GENDERS
DEEGNSU	DENGUES
	UNEDGES
DEEGOOS	SOOGEED
DEEGORR	ROGERED
DEEGOSS	GESSOED
DEEGOSY	GEODESY
DEEGOTU	OUTEDGE
DEEGRRU	REURGED
DEEGSSU	GUESSED
DEEGSTU	GUESTED
DEEHIKV	KHEDIVE
DEEHILS	SHIELED
DEEHILT	LETHIED
DEEHINR	INHERED
DEEHIRR	HERRIED
	REHIRED
DEEHIRT	DIETHER
DEEHIST	HEISTED
DEEHITV	THIEVED
DEEHKLW	WHELKED
DEEHLLO	HELLOED
DEEHLLS	SHELLED
DEEHLMW	WHELMED
DEEHLNU	UNHELED
DEEHLOV	HOVELED
DEEHLPW	WHELPED
DEEHLSV	SHELVED
DEEHLSW	WELSHED
DEEHMNR	HERDMEN
DEEHMNS	MENSHED
DEEHMOR	HOMERED
DEEHMRU	RHEUMED
DEEHMUX	EXHUMED
DEEHNOY	HONEYED
DEEHNPR	PREHEND
DEEHNRS	HERDENS
DEEHNUY	UNHEEDY
DEEHORV	HOVERED
DEEHPRS	SPHERED
DEEHRRS	HERDERS
DEEHRSS	HERDESS
DEEHRSU	USHERED
DEEHRSW	SHREWED
DEEHRTW	WRETHED
DEEHSYY	HEYDEYS
DEEHTTW	WHETTED
DEEIINT	DIETINE
DEEIIPR	EPEIRID
DEEIIRW	WEIRDIE
DEEIIST	DEITIES
DEEIJLL	JELLIED
DEEIJMM	JEMMIED
DEEIJTT	JETTIED
DEEIKLL	KILLDEE
DEEIKLN	LIKENED
DEEIKMW	MIDWEEK
DEEIKNR	REINKED
DEEIKNS	ENSKIED
	SKEINED
DEEIKOV	DOVEKIE
DEEILLS	DELLIES
DEEILMS	DELIMES
DEEILNO	ELOINED
DEEILNR	REDLINE
	RELINED
DEEILNS	ENISLED
	ENSILED
	LINSEED
DEEILNV	LIVENED
DEEILNY	DYELINE
	NEEDILY
DEEILOR	REOILED
DEEILOS	OILSEED
DEEILPR	PERILED
	REPLIED
DEEILPS	SEEDLIP
	SPEILED
	SPIELED
DEEILRS	RESILED
DEEILRT	RETILED
DEEILRV	DELIVER
	RELIVED
	REVILED
DEEILRW	WIELDER
DEEILRY	REEDILY
	YIELDER
DEEILSS	DIESELS
	IDLESSE
	SEIDELS
DEEILSY	EYELIDS
	SEEDILY
DEEILTU	DILUTEE
DEEILTV	DEVILET
DEEILWY	WEEDILY
DEEIMMO	MIMEOED
DEEIMMS	MISDEEM
DEEIMMW	IMMEWED
DEEIMNO	DOMINEE
DEEIMNR	ERMINED
DEEIMNS	DESMINE
	SIDEMEN
DEEIMNT	DEMENTI
DEEIMOR	EMEROID
DEEIMPR	DEMIREP
	EPIDERM
	IMPEDER
DEEIMPS	IMPEDES
	SEMIPED
DEEIMPT	EMPTIED
DEEIMRS	REMEIDS
	REMISED
DEEIMRT	DEMERIT
	DIMETER
	MERITED
	MITERED
	RETIMED
DEEIMRX	REMIXED
DEEIMSS	DEMISES
DEEIMTT	EMITTED
DEEINNP	PENNIED
DEEINNS	INDENES
DEEINNT	DENTINE
DEEINNU	ENNUIED
DEEINNZ	DENIZEN
DEEINOR	ORDINEE
DEEINPR	REPINED

	RIPENED
DEEINPW	PINWEED
DEEINRR	DERNIER
	NERDIER
DEEINRS	DENIERS
	NEREIDS
	RESINED
DEEINRU	UREDINE
DEEINRW	REWIDEN
	WIDENER
DEEINRX	INDEXER
	REINDEX
DEEINSS	DESINES
DEEINST	DESTINE
	ENDITES
	STEINED
DEEINSV	DEVEINS
	ENDIVES
DEEINSW	ENDWISE
	SINEWED
DEEINSX	INDEXES
DEEINTT	DINETTE
DEEINTU	DETINUE
DEEINTV	EVIDENT
DEEINVW	VINEWED
DEEINVX	INVEXED
DEEINWZ	WIZENED
DEEIOPS	EPISODE
	POESIED
DEEIOPT	EPIDOTE
DEEIOPX	EPOXIDE
	EPOXIED
DEEIORS	OREIDES
	OSIERED
DEEIOSV	VOIDEES
DEEIPPT	PEPTIDE
DEEIPRS	PREDIES
	PRESIDE
	SPEIRED
	SPIERED
DEEIPRT	PREEDIT
	TEPIDER
DEEIPRV	DEPRIVE
	PREDIVE
	PRIEVED
DEEIPRX	EXPIRED
DEEIPSS	DESPISE
	PEDESIS
DEEIPST	DESPITE
DEEIQRU	QUERIED
DEEIQTU	QUIETED
DEEIRRS	DERRIES
	DESIRER
	REDRIES
	RESIDER
	SERRIED
DEEIRRT	RETIRED
	RETRIED
	TIREDER
DEEIRRV	DERIVER
	REDRIVE
	RIVERED
DEEIRRW	REWIRED
	WEIRDER
DEEIRSS	DESIRES
	RESIDES
DEEIRST	DIESTER
	DIETERS
	REEDITS
	REISTED
	RESITED
DEEIRSU	RESIDUE
	UREIDES
DEEIRSV	DERIVES
	DEVISER
	DIVERSE
	REVISED
DEEIRSZ	RESIZED
DEEIRTU	ERUDITE
DEEIRTV	RIVETED
	VERDITE
DEEIRVV	REVIVED
DEEISSU	DISEUSE
DEEISSV	DEVISES
DEEISTT	TEDIEST
DEEISTW	DEWIEST
DEEISTX	EXISTED
DEEITTV	VIDETTE
DEEJNOY	ENJOYED
DEEJQRU	JERQUED
DEEKKRT	TREKKED
DEEKLLN	KNELLED
DEEKLPS	SKELPED
DEEKLRS	SKELDER
DEEKMNS	DESKMEN
DEEKMRS	SMERKED
DEEKNOT	TOKENED
DEEKNSY	ENSKYED
DEEKORV	REVOKED
DEEKOVY	DOVEKEY
DEEKPPS	SKEPPED
DEEKPRU	PERUKED
DEEKRRS	SKERRED
DEEKRSU	RESKUED
DEELLMS	SMELLED
DEELLNS	SNELLED
DEELLPS	SPELLED
DEELLQU	QUELLED
DEELLRU	DUELLER
DEELLRW	DWELLER
DEELLRY	ELDERLY
DEELLST	STELLED
DEELLSW	SWELLED
DEELMNO	LEMONED
DEELMOR	MODELER
	REMODEL
DEELMPT	TEMPLED
DEELMPU	DEPLUME
DEELMRS	MELDERS
DEELMRU	RELUMED
DEELMST	SMELTED
DEELMSY	MEDLEYS
DEELMTT	METTLED
DEELNRS	LENDERS
	RELENDS
	SLENDER
DEELNSS	ENDLESS
DEELNST	DENTELS
	NESTLED
DEELNSW	WEDELNS
DEELNSY	DENSELY
DEELNTT	NETTLED
DEELOOS	DOOLEES
DEELOPP	PEOPLED
DEELOPR	DEPLORE
DEELOPS	DELOPES
DEELOPV	DEVELOP
DEELOPX	EXPLODE
DEELORS	RESOLED
DEELORU	URODELE
DEELORV	LOVERED
DEELORW	LOWERED
	ROWELED
DEELORY	YODELER
DEELOSU	DELOUSE
DEELOTV	DOVELET
DEELOTW	TOWELED
DEELOVV	DEVOLVE
	EVOLVED
DEELPRS	PEDLERS
	SPELDER
DEELPRU	PRELUDE
DEELPRY	PEDLERY
DEELPST	PESTLED
DEELPTT	PETTLED
DEELRRU	RULERED
DEELRSS	ELDRESS
DEELRSU	DUELERS
	ELUDERS
DEELRSV	DELVERS
DEELRSW	REWELDS
	WELDERS
DEELRUV	VELURED
DEELSSW	DEWLESS
DEELSTT	SETTLED
DEELSTU	TELEDUS
DEELSTW	LEWDEST
	SWELTED
DEELSUV	EVULSED
DEELSVV	DEVVELS
DEELTUX	EXULTED
DEELVXY	VEXEDLY
DEEMMOV	EMMOVED
DEEMMST	STEMMED
DEEMNOR	MODERNE
DEEMNOT	DEMETON
DEEMNOU	EUDEMON
DEEMNOV	ENMOVED
	VENOMED
DEEMNOY	MONEYED
DEEMNRS	MENDERS
	REMENDS
DEEMNST	DEMENTS
DEEMNTU	UNMETED
DEEMNUW	UNMEWED
DEEMORS	EMERODS
DEEMORV	REMOVED
DEEMORX	EXODERM
DEEMOSS	DEMOSES
DEEMOST	DEMOTES
DEEMOSY	MOSEYED
DEEMPRS	DEPERMS
	PREMEDS
DEEMPTT	TEMPTED
DEEMRRU	DEMURER
DEEMRSU	DEMURES
	RESUMED
DEENNOR	ENDERON
DEENNOS	DONNEES
DEENNOT	ENDNOTE
	TENONED
DEENNOY	DOYENNE
DEENNOZ	ENZONED
DEENNPT	PENDENT
DEENNST	DENNETS
	STENNED
DEENNTZ	TENDENZ
DEENNUY	ENNUYED
DEENOOR	RONEOED
DEENOPR	REPONED
DEENOPS	DEPONES
	SPONDEE
DEENOPT	PENTODE
DEENORS	ENDORSE
DEENORT	ERODENT
DEENORW	ENDOWER
	REENDOW
DEENORZ	REZONED
DEENOST	DENOTES
DEENPPR	PERPEND
DEENPRS	SPENDER
DEENPRT	PRENTED
	PRETEND
DEENPSX	EXPENDS
DEENRRS	RENDERS
DEENRRU	ENDURER
DEENRSS	REDNESS
	RESENDS
	SENDERS
DEENRST	STERNED
	TENDERS
	TENDRES
DEENRSU	ENDURES
	ENSURED
DEENRSV	VENDERS
DEENRSZ	DZERENS
DEENRTU	DENTURE
	RETUNED
	TENURED
DEENRTV	VENTRED
DEENSST	DENSEST
DEENSSU	DUENESS
DEENSSY	DESYNES
DEENSTT	DETENTS
	STENTED
DEENSTU	DETENUS
	DETUNES
DEENSTX	EXTENDS
DEENSUV	VENDUES
DEENSUW	UNSEWED
DEENSUX	UNSEXED
DEENUVX	UNVEXED
DEEOPPY	POPEYED
DEEOPRR	PEDRERO
DEEOPRS	DEPOSER
	REPOSED
DEEOPRW	POWERED
DEEOPSS	DEPOSES
	SPEEDOS
DEEOPSX	EXPOSED
	PODEXES
DEEOPXY	EPOXYED
DEEORRR	ORDERER
	REORDER
DEEORRS	REREDOS
DEEORRV	OVERRED
	REDROVE
DEEORST	OERSTED
	ROSETED
	TEREDOS
DEEORSW	RESOWED
DEEORSX	REDOXES
DEEORTT	OTTERED
	TETRODE
DEEORTV	REVOTED
DEEORTW	TOWERED
DEEORTX	OXTERED
DEEORTZ	ROZETED
DEEORUV	OVERDUE
DEEORVY	OVERDYE
DEEORXX	XEROXED
DEEOSTV	DEVOTES
DEEOSTX	DETOXES
DEEOTUW	OUTWEED
DEEPPPR	PREPPED
DEEPPST	STEPPED
DEEPPSU	SPEEDUP
DEEPRRS	SPERRED
DEEPRRU	PERDURE
	REPURED
DEEPRSS	DEPRESS
	PRESSED
	SPERSED
DEEPRST	PRESTED
DEEPRSU	PERDUES
	PERSUED
	PERUSED
	SUPERED
DEEPRTU	ERUPTED
	REPUTED

DEEPRTY	RETYPED
DEEPRUV	PREVUED
DEEPSTU	DEPUTES
DEEQSTU	QUESTED
DEERRSS	DRESSER
	REDRESS
DEERRUV	VERDURE
DEERSSS	DRESSES
DEERSST	DESERTS
	DESSERT
	TRESSED
DEERSSU	DURESSE
DEERSTV	STERVED
	VERDETS
DEERSTW	STREWED
	WRESTED
DEERSTX	DEXTERS
DEERSTY	DYESTER
DEERSVW	SWERVED
DEERTTU	UTTERED
DEERTUX	EXTRUDE
DEESSTT	DETESTS
DEESSTV	DEVESTS
DEESTTT	STETTED
DEFFFLU	FLUFFED
DEFFGRU	GRUFFED
DEFFHIW	WHIFFED
DEFFHOU	HOUFFED
DEFFHOW	HOWFFED
DEFFIKS	SKIFFED
DEFFILP	PIFFLED
DEFFILR	RIFFLED
DEFFILS	SIFFLED
DEFFIMO	FIEFDOM
DEFFINS	SNIFFED
DEFFIOS	OFFSIDE
DEFFIPS	SPIFFED
DEFFIRS	DIFFERS
DEFFIST	STIFFED
DEFFISU	DIFFUSE
DEFFKOS	SKOFFED
DEFFLMU	MUFFLED
DEFFLPU	PLUFFED
DEFFLRU	RUFFLED
DEFFLSU	DUFFELS
	DUFFLES
	SLUFFED
DEFFNOR	FORFEND
DEFFNOS	OFFENDS
	SENDOFF
DEFFNSU	SNUFFED
DEFFOPU	POUFFED
DEFFORS	DOFFERS
DEFFOSW	SOWFFED
DEFFRSU	DUFFERS
DEFFSTU	DUFFEST
	STUFFED
DEFGGIR	FRIGGED
DEFGGLO	FLOGGED
DEFGGOR	FROGGED
DEFGGRU	FRUGGED
DEFGINN	FENDING
DEFGINR	FRINGED
DEFGINU	FEUDING
DEFGINY	DEFYING
DEFGIOR	FIREDOG
DEFGIRS	FRIDGES
DEFGIRT	GRIFTED
DEFGIRU	FIGURED
DEFGIST	FIDGETS
DEFGITY	FIDGETY
DEFGRTU	GRUFTED
DEFHIRS	REDFISH
DEFHIST	SHIFTED
DEFHLOO	ELFHOOD
DEFHLSU	FLUSHED
DEFHOOW	WHOOFED
DEFHORT	FROTHED
DEFHRSU	FRUSHED
DEFIILM	MIDLIFE
DEFIILN	INFIDEL
	INFIELD
DEFIIMS	FIDEISM
DEFIIMW	MIDWIFE
DEFIINU	UNIFIED
DEFIINX	INFIXED
DEFIIST	FIDEIST
DEFIKLS	FLISKED
DEFIKRS	FRISKED
DEFILLO	FOLLIED
DEFILLR	FRILLED
DEFILMP	FLIMPED
DEFILNR	FLINDER
DEFILNT	FLINTED
DEFILNU	UNFILDE
	UNFILED
DEFILOO	FOLIOED
DEFILOW	OLDWIFE
DEFILPP	FLIPPED
DEFILPU	UPFIELD
DEFILRT	FLIRTED
	TRIFLED
DEFILRU	DIREFUL
DEFILSS	FISSLED
DEFILST	STIFLED
DEFILSU	SULFIDE
DEFILTT	FLITTED
DEFILTY	FETIDLY
DEFILXY	FIXEDLY
DEFILZZ	FIZZLED
DEFIMOR	DEIFORM
DEFIMOW	WIFEDOM
DEFINRS	FINDERS
	FRIENDS
	REDFINS
	REFINDS
DEFINRU	UNFIRED
DEFINST	SNIFTED
DEFINSU	FUNDIES
	INFUSED
DEFINSY	DENSIFY
DEFINUX	UNFIXED
DEFINUY	UNDEIFY
DEFIOOS	FOODIES
DEFIOQU	QUOIFED
DEFIORU	FOUDRIE
DEFIOST	FOISTED
DEFIPRY	PERFIDY
DEFIRRT	DRIFTER
DEFIRST	FRISTED
DEFIRTT	FRITTED
DEFIRTU	FRUITED
DEFIRZZ	FRIZZED
DEFISTU	FEUDIST
DEFISTW	SWIFTED
DEFKLNU	FLUNKED
DEFLLOU	DOLEFUL
DEFLLUW	DEWFULL
DEFLMOS	SELFDOM
DEFLMPU	FLUMPED
DEFLNOO	ONEFOLD
DEFLNOP	PENFOLD
DEFLNOR	FONDLER
	FORLEND
DEFLNOS	ENFOLDS
	FONDLES
DEFLNOT	TENFOLD
DEFLNRU	DERNFUL
DEFLOOR	FLOODER
	FLOORED
	REFLOOD
DEFLOOT	FOOTLED
DEFLOOZ	FOOZLED
DEFLOPP	FLOPPED
DEFLORS	FOLDERS
	REFOLDS
DEFLORT	TELFORD
DEFLORU	FLOURED
	FOULDER
DEFLOSS	FLOSSED
DEFLOSU	DEFOULS
	FLOUSED
DEFLOTU	FLOUTED
DEFLPRU	PURFLED
DEFLRRU	FLURRED
DEFLRUU	DUREFUL
DEFLUZZ	FUZZLED
DEFMNUU	UNFUMED
DEFMORS	DEFORMS
	SERFDOM
DEFMPRU	FRUMPED
DEFNOOR	FORDONE
DEFNORT	FRONTED
DEFNORU	FOUNDER
	REFOUND
DEFNORW	FROWNED
DEFNOST	FONDEST
DEFNOSU	FONDUES
DEFNRSU	FUNDERS
	REFUNDS
DEFNSUU	UNFUSED
DEFOOPR	PROOFED
DEFOOPS	SPOOFED
DEFOORS	DOOFERS
	FORDOES
DEFORST	DEFROST
	FROSTED
DEFORTU	FOUTRED
DEGGGIL	GIGGLED
DEGGGIR	GRIGGED
DEGGGLO	GOGGLED
DEGGGLU	GLUGGED
	GUGGLED
DEGGGOR	GROGGED
DEGGHIL	HIGGLED
DEGGHIN	HEDGING
DEGGHIW	WHIGGED
DEGGHOS	SHOGGED
DEGGIJL	JIGGLED
DEGGIKN	KEDGING
DEGGILN	GELDING
	NIGGLED
DEGGILW	WIGGLED
DEGGINS	EDGINGS
	SNIGGED
DEGGINW	WEDGING
DEGGIOR	DOGGIER
DEGGIOS	DOGGIES
DEGGIPR	PRIGGED
DEGGIRS	DIGGERS
DEGGIRT	TRIGGED
DEGGIRU	DRUGGIE
DEGGISW	SWIGGED
DEGGITW	TWIGGED
DEGGJLO	JOGGLED
DEGGJLU	JUGGLED
DEGGKSU	SKUGGED
DEGGLOO	GOOGLED
DEGGLOR	DOGGREL
DEGGLOS	DOGLEGS
	SLOGGED
DEGGLOT	TOGGLED
DEGGLPU	PLUGGED
	PUGGLED
DEGGLRU	GURGLED
DEGGLSU	SLUGGED
DEGGMSU	SMUGGED
DEGGNOO	DOGGONE
DEGGNOS	SNOGGED
DEGGNOU	GUDGEON
DEGGNSU	SNUGGED
DEGGOPR	PROGGED
DEGGORS	DOGGERS
DEGGORT	TROGGED
DEGGORY	DOGGERY
DEGGOSS	DOGGESS
DEGGRRU	DRUGGER
	GRUDGER
DEGGRSU	GRUDGES
DEGGRTU	DRUGGET
DEGHHIT	HIGHTED
	THIGHED
DEGHHOU	HOUGHED
DEGHILN	HINDLEG
DEGHILT	DELIGHT
	LIGHTED
DEGHINN	HENDING
DEGHINR	HERDING
DEGHINT	NIGHTED
DEGHINW	WHINGED
DEGHIOT	HOGTIED
DEGHIPT	PIGHTED
DEGHIRT	GIRTHED
	RIGHTED
DEGHIST	SIGHTED
DEGHITW	WIGHTED
DEGHLOO	DOGHOLE
DEGHNOT	THONGED
DEGHORR	DROGHER
DEGHORU	ROUGHED
DEGHOST	GHOSTED
DEGHOSU	SOUGHED
DEGHOTU	OUGHTED
	TOUGHED
DEGIIKR	KIDGIER
DEGIILL	GILLIED
DEGIILN	EILDING
	ELIDING
DEGIINN	INDIGEN
DEGIINR	DINGIER
DEGIINS	DINGIES
DEGIINT	DIETING
	EDITING
	IGNITED
DEGIIPS	GIPSIED
DEGIIRR	RIDGIER
	RIGIDER
DEGIIRS	DIRIGES
DEGIISW	WIDGIES
DEGIJLN	JINGLED
DEGIKLO	DOGLIKE
	GODLIKE
DEGILLR	GRILLED
DEGILLU	GULLIED
DEGILLY	GELIDLY
DEGILMN	MEDLING
	MELDING
	MINGLED
DEGILMS	MIDLEGS
DEGILNN	LENDING
DEGILNO	GLENOID
DEGILNP	PINGLED
DEGILNS	DINGLES
	ELDINGS
	ENGILDS
	SINGLED
DEGILNT	GLINTED
	TINGLED
DEGILNU	DUELING
	ELUDING

	INDULGE
DEGILNV	DELVING
	DEVLING
DEGILNW	WELDING
DEGILOR	GLORIED
	GODLIER
	GOLDIER
DEGILOU	OUGLIED
DEGILRR	GIRDLER
DEGILRS	GILDERS
	GIRDLES
	GLIDERS
	GRISLED
	LIDGERS
	REGILDS
	RIDGELS
DEGILRU	GUILDER
DEGILRW	WERGILD
DEGILUV	DIVULGE
DEGIMNN	MENDING
DEGIMNO	MENDIGO
DEGIMNS	SMIDGEN
DEGIMPU	GUIMPED
DEGIMSS	SMIDGES
DEGIMST	MIDGETS
DEGINNN	DENNING
DEGINNP	PENDING
DEGINNR	GRINNED
	RENDING
DEGINNS	ENDINGS
	SENDING
DEGINNT	DENTING
	TENDING
DEGINNU	ENDUING
DEGINNV	VENDING
DEGINNW	WENDING
DEGINNY	DENYING
DEGINOP	PIDGEON
DEGINOR	ERODING
	GROINED
	IGNORED
	NEGROID
	REDOING
DEGINOS	DINGOES
DEGINOT	INGOTED
DEGINOW	WENDIGO
	WIDGEON
	WONGIED
DEGINRR	GRINDER
	REGRIND
DEGINRS	DINGERS
	ENGIRDS
DEGINRU	DUNGIER
DEGINRW	REDWING
	WRINGED
DEGINRY	YERDING
DEGINSS	DESIGNS
	SDEIGNS
DEGINST	NIDGETS
	STEDING
	STINGED
DEGINSU	GUNDIES
	SUEDING
DEGINSW	SWINDGE
	SWINGED
DEGINSY	DINGEYS
	DYEINGS
DEGINTW	TWINGED
DEGINUX	EXUDING
DEGIOOR	GOODIER
DEGIOOS	GOODIES
	SOOGIED
DEGIOPR	PODGIER
DEGIORR	GRODIER
DEGIORT	GOITRED
DEGIPPR	GRIPPED
DEGIPRU	PUDGIER
DEGIPSY	GYPSIED
DEGIQSU	SQUIDGE
DEGIRRS	GIRDERS
	RIDGERS
DEGIRRU	DURGIER
DEGIRSS	DIGRESS
DEGIRSU	GUIDERS
DEGIRTT	GRITTED
DEGISST	DIGESTS
	DISGEST
DEGISSU	GUSSIED
DEGISTU	GIUSTED
DEGISTW	WIDGETS
DEGJLNU	JUNGLED
DEGJRSU	JUDGERS
DEGKLSU	KLUDGES
DEGLMMO	GLOMMED
DEGLMOO	GLOOMED
DEGLMOU	MOGULED
DEGLNNO	ENDLONG
DEGLNOP	PLONGED
DEGLNOS	DONGLES
	GOLDENS
DEGLNOU	LOUNGED
DEGLNPU	PLUNGED
	PUNGLED
DEGLNSU	GULDENS
DEGLNUU	UNGLUED
	UNGULED
DEGLOOP	GLOOPED
DEGLOPP	GLOPPED
DEGLOPR	PLEDGOR
DEGLOPS	SPLODGE
DEGLORS	LODGERS
DEGLORW	GROWLED
DEGLOSS	GLOSSED
	GODLESS
DEGLOST	GOLDEST
DEGLOTU	GLOUTED
DEGLSSU	SLUDGES
DEGLTTU	GLUTTED
	GUTTLED
DEGLUZZ	GUZZLED
DEGMNOO	GOODMEN
DEGMOOR	GROOMED
DEGMPRU	GRUMPED
DEGMRSU	MUDGERS
	SMUDGER
DEGMSSU	SMUDGES
DEGNNOU	DUNGEON
DEGNOOS	NOODGES
DEGNOPR	PRONGED
DEGNOPS	SPONGED
DEGNORU	GUERDON
	UNDERGO
	UNGORED
DEGNORW	WRONGED
DEGNOTU	TONGUED
DEGNRSU	GERUNDS
	NUDGERS
DEGNRTU	GRUNTED
	TRUDGEN
DEGNRUU	UNURGED
DEGNSSU	SNUDGES
DEGNUVY	UNGYVED
DEGOORV	GROOVED
	OVERDOG
DEGOOST	STOOGED
DEGOPRU	GROUPED
DEGORRS	DROGERS
DEGORSS	GROSSED
	SODGERS
DEGORST	STODGER
DEGORSU	DROGUES
	GOURDES
	GROUSED
DEGORTU	DROGUET
	GROUTED
DEGOSST	STODGES
DEGOSTU	DEGOUTS
DEGOSTW	GOWDEST
DEGRRTU	TRUDGER
DEGRSTU	TRUDGES
DEGSSTU	DEGUSTS
DEHHISW	WHISHED
DEHHMPU	HUMPHED
DEHHOOS	HOOSHED
DEHHSSU	SHUSHED
DEHIINN	HINNIED
DEHIIPS	PIEDISH
DEHIIRS	DISHIER
DEHIKRS	SHIRKED
	SHRIKED
DEHIKSW	WHISKED
DEHILLO	HILLOED
DEHILLS	SHILLED
DEHILMS	DISHELM
DEHILNP	DELPHIN
DEHILOT	LITHOED
DEHILPR	HIRPLED
DEHILRS	HIRSLED
DEHILRT	THIRLED
DEHILRW	WHIRLED
DEHILSS	SHIELDS
DEHILTY	DIETHYL
DEHIMMS	SHIMMED
DEHIMMW	WHIMMED
DEHIMNU	INHUMED
DEHIMOR	HEIRDOM
DEHIMOS	DISHOME
DEHIMOT	ETHMOID
DEHIMRS	DIRHEMS
DEHIMRU	HUMIDER
DEHIMST	SMITHED
DEHINNS	SHINNED
DEHINNT	THINNED
DEHINOP	DIPHONE
	PHONIED
DEHINOR	HORDEIN
DEHINOS	HOIDENS
DEHINOY	HYENOID
DEHINPS	ENDSHIP
DEHINRS	HINDERS
	NERDISH
	SHRINED
DEHINRU	UNHIRED
DEHINUV	UNHIVED
DEHIOOR	HOODIER
DEHIOOS	HOODIES
DEHIOOT	DHOOTIE
DEHIORS	RHODIES
DEHIORT	THEROID
DEHIOST	HOISTED
DEHIOSU	HIDEOUS
DEHIOSV	DOVEISH
DEHIOSW	HOWDIES
DEHIOTU	HIDEOUT
DEHIPPS	SHIPPED
DEHIPPW	WHIPPED
DEHIRRS	SHIRRED
DEHIRRU	DHURRIE
	HURRIED
DEHIRRW	WHIRRED
DEHIRST	DITHERS
	SHIRTED
DEHIRSU	HURDIES
DEHIRSV	DERVISH
	SHRIVED
DEHIRTV	THRIVED
DEHIRTW	WRITHED
DEHIRTY	DITHERY
DEHISSW	SWISHED
	WHISSED
DEHISTT	SHITTED
DEHISTW	WHISTED
DEHISVV	SHIVVED
DEHIWZZ	WHIZZED
DEHKNTU	THUNKED
DEHLLOO	HOLLOED
DEHLLOU	HULLOED
DEHLMOU	MUDHOLE
DEHLMSU	MULSHED
DEHLNOS	HONDLES
DEHLOOS	SHOOLED
DEHLOOT	TOEHOLD
DEHLOPP	HOPPLED
DEHLORS	HOLDERS
DEHLORW	WHORLED
DEHLOSS	SLOSHED
DEHLOST	SLOTHED
DEHLRRU	HURDLER
DEHLRSU	HURDLES
DEHLRTU	HURTLED
DEHLSSU	SLUSHED
DEHLSTU	HUSTLED
DEHMNOO	HOODMEN
DEHMOPR	MORPHED
DEHMOPW	WHOMPED
DEHMORU	HUMORED
DEHMOST	METHODS
DEHMOTU	MOUTHED
DEHMPTU	THUMPED
DEHMPUW	WHUMPED
DEHNNSU	SHUNNED
DEHNOOR	HONORED
DEHNOOW	HOEDOWN
	WOODHEN
DEHNOPU	UNHOPED
DEHNORS	DEHORNS
DEHNORT	NORTHED
	THONDER
	THORNED
	THRONED
DEHNORU	HOUNDER
DEHNOSU	UNSHOED
DEHNOSY	HOYDENS
DEHNOTZ	DOZENTH
DEHNRSU	HURDENS
DEHNRTU	THUNDER
DEHNSSU	DUNSHES
	SNUSHED
DEHNSSY	YSHENDS
DEHNSTU	SHUNTED
DEHNSUZ	NUDZHES
DEHNSYY	HYDYNES
DEHOOPT	PHOTOED
DEHOOPW	WHOOPED
DEHOOST	SOOTHED
DEHOOSW	WOOSHED
DEHOOTT	TOOTHED
DEHOOTW	WHOOTED
DEHOPPS	SHOPPED
DEHOPPW	WHOPPED
DEHORSS	SHODERS
DEHORST	DEHORTS
	SHORTED
DEHORSV	SHROVED
DEHORSW	SHROWED
DEHORTT	TROTHED
DEHORTW	WORTHED
DEHOSTT	SHOTTED
DEHOSTU	SHOUTED
	SOUTHED

DEHOSTW	SOWTHED
DEHPSSY	PHYSEDS
DEHPTTU	PHUTTED
DEIIIRS	IRIDISE
DEIIIRZ	IRIDIZE
DEIIJMM	JIMMIED
DEIIKKL	KIDLIKE
DEIIKLS	DISLIKE
DEIIKNR	DINKIER
DEIIKNS	DINKIES
	KINDIES
DEIIKST	DIKIEST
DEIILLR	DILLIER
DEIILLS	DILLIES
DEIILLW	WILLIED
DEIILMN	MIDLINE
DEIILMP	IMPLIED
DEIILMT	DELIMIT
	LIMITED
DEIILNS	INISLED
	LINDIES
DEIILOS	DOILIES
	IDOLISE
DEIILOZ	IDOLIZE
DEIILPS	LIPIDES
DEIILRV	LIVIDER
DEIIMMX	IMMIXED
DEIIMNO	DOMINIE
DEIIMRT	TIMIDER
DEIIMST	MISDIET
	MISEDIT
	STIMIED
DEIIMSZ	MIDSIZE
DEIIMVW	MIDWIVE
DEIINOS	IODINES
	IONISED
DEIINOT	EDITION
	TENIOID
DEIINOZ	IONIZED
DEIINRR	RINDIER
DEIINRS	INSIDER
DEIINRT	INDITER
	NITRIDE
DEIINRU	URIDINE
DEIINRV	DIVINER
DEIINRW	WINDIER
DEIINSS	INSIDES
DEIINST	INDITES
	TINEIDS
DEIINSV	DIVINES
DEIINTV	INVITED
DEIIORT	DIORITE
DEIIORV	IVORIED
DEIIORZ	IODIZER
DEIIOSS	IODISES
DEIIOSX	OXIDISE
DEIIOSZ	IODIZES
DEIIOXZ	OXIDIZE
DEIIPPR	DIPPIER
DEIIPRS	PIERIDS
DEIIPRT	RIPTIDE
	TIDERIP
DEIIRRT	DIRTIER
DEIIRST	DIRTIES
	DITSIER
	TIDIERS
DEIIRTT	TRITIDE
DEIIRTZ	DITZIER
DEIIRVV	VIVIDER
DEIIRZZ	DIZZIER
DEIISTT	DIETIST
	DITTIES
	TIDIEST
DEIISTV	VISITED
DEIISVV	DIVVIES
DEIISZZ	DIZZIES
DEIIVZZ	VIZZIED
DEIJLLO	JOLLIED
DEIJNOR	JOINDER
DEIJNOT	JOINTED
DEIJNRU	INJURED
DEIJNSU	DISJUNE
DEIJORY	JOYRIDE
DEIJOST	JOISTED
DEIJRRS	JERRIDS
DEIJTTU	JUTTIED
DEIKKNS	SKINKED
DEIKLLS	DESKILL
	SKILLED
DEIKLNP	PLINKED
DEIKLNR	KINDLER
DEIKLNS	KINDLES
	SLINKED
DEIKLNT	TINKLED
DEIKLNW	WINKLED
DEIKLOP	PODLIKE
DEIKLOR	RODLIKE
DEIKLOS	KELOIDS
DEIKLRS	SKIRLED
DEIKLRT	KIRTLED
DEIKLST	KIDLETS
DEIKLTT	KITTLED
DEIKMMS	SKIMMED
DEIKMPS	SKIMPED
DEIKMRS	SMIRKED
DEIKNNS	SKINNED
DEIKNOS	DOESKIN
DEIKNOV	INVOKED
DEIKNPR	PRINKED
DEIKNRR	DRINKER
DEIKNRS	KINDERS
	KINREDS
	REDSKIN
DEIKNST	DINKEST
	KINDEST
DEIKNSW	SWINKED
DEIKNSY	DINKEYS
	KIDNEYS
DEIKNSZ	ZENDIKS
DEIKNTT	KNITTED
DEIKNTW	TWINKED
DEIKORR	DORKIER
DEIKOSY	DISYOKE
DEIKPPS	SKIPPED
DEIKQRU	QUIRKED
DEIKRRS	SKIRRED
DEIKRST	SKIRTED
DEIKRSU	DUIKERS
	DUSKIER
DEIKSTY	DYKIEST
DEIKSVY	SKYDIVE
DEILLMO	MODELLI
DEILLMU	ILLUMED
DEILLNW	INDWELL
DEILLOR	DOLLIER
DEILLOS	DOLLIES
DEILLOV	LIVELOD
DEILLPR	PRILLED
DEILLPS	SPILLED
DEILLQU	QUILLED
DEILLRR	DRILLER
	REDRILL
DEILLRT	TRILLED
DEILLRU	DULLIER
DEILLRV	DREVILL
DEILLSS	LIDLESS
DEILLST	STILLED
DEILLSU	ILLUDES
	SULLIED
DEILLSW	SWILLED
DEILLTW	TWILLED
DEILMMP	PLIMMED
DEILMMS	SLIMMED
DEILMNS	MILDENS
DEILMNU	LUMINED
	UNLIMED
DEILMOP	IMPLODE
DEILMOR	MOLDIER
DEILMOS	MELOIDS
	MIDSOLE
	SMOILED
DEILMOY	MYELOID
DEILMPP	PIMPLED
DEILMPR	RIMPLED
DEILMPS	DIMPLES
	MISPLED
	SIMPLED
DEILMPW	WIMPLED
DEILMST	MILDEST
	MISTLED
DEILMSW	MILDEWS
DEILMWY	MILDEWY
DEILMXY	MIXEDLY
DEILMZZ	MIZZLED
DEILNNS	DINNLES
	LINDENS
DEILNNU	UNLINED
DEILNOO	EIDOLON
DEILNOS	DOLINES
	INDOLES
	SONDELI
DEILNOT	LENTOID
DEILNOU	UNOILED
DEILNPP	NIPPLED
DEILNPS	SPELDIN
	SPINDLE
	SPLINED
DEILNPU	UNPILED
DEILNRT	TENDRIL
	TRINDLE
DEILNST	DENTILS
DEILNSW	SWINDLE
	WINDLES
DEILNSY	SNIDELY
DEILNTU	DILUENT
	UNTILED
DEILNTW	INDWELT
	WINTLED
DEILNUV	UNLIVED
DEILOOS	DOOLIES
DEILOPR	LEPORID
DEILOPS	DESPOIL
	DIPLOES
	DIPOLES
	PELOIDS
	SOLIPED
	SPOILED
DEILOPT	PILOTED
DEILOPU	EUPLOID
DEILORS	SOLDIER
	SOLIDER
DEILORT	DOILTER
DEILOSY	DOYLIES
DEILOTU	OUTLIED
	TOLUIDE
DEILPPR	RIPPLED
DEILPPS	SIPPLED
	SLIPPED
DEILPPT	TIPPLED
DEILPPU	UPPILED
DEILPRT	TRIPLED
DEILPRU	PRELUDI
DEILPSS	DISPELS
	DISPLES
DEILPSU	DUPLIES
DEILPTY	TEPIDLY
DEILQTU	QUILTED
DEILRRU	LURIDER
DEILRSS	SIDLERS
	SLIDERS
DEILRSV	DRIVELS
DEILRSW	SWIRLED
	WILDERS
DEILRSY	RIDLEYS
DEILRTU	DILUTER
DEILRTW	TWIRLED
DEILRTY	TIREDLY
DEILRVY	DEVILRY
DEILRWY	WEIRDLY
DEILRWZ	WRIZLED
DEILRZZ	DRIZZLE
DEILSST	DELISTS
DEILSTT	SLITTED
	STILTED
DEILSTU	DILUTES
	DUELIST
DEILSTW	WILDEST
DEILSTY	DISTYLE
DEILSZZ	SIZZLED
DEILTTT	TITTLED
DEILTTU	TITULED
DEILTTV	VITTLED
DEILTTW	TWILTED
DEILZZZ	ZIZZLED
DEIMMMU	MUMMIED
DEIMMOT	TOMMIED
DEIMMPR	PRIMMED
DEIMMRS	DIMMERS
DEIMMRT	MIDTERM
	TRIMMED
DEIMMRU	DUMMIER
	IMMURED
DEIMMST	DIMMEST
DEIMMSU	DUMMIES
	MEDIUMS
DEIMNNU	MINUEND
	UNMINED
DEIMNOP	IMPONED
DEIMNOR	MINORED
DEIMNOS	DOMINES
	EMODINS
	MISDONE
DEIMNPS	IMPENDS
DEIMNRS	MINDERS
	REMINDS
DEIMNRU	UNRIMED
DEIMNSS	DIMNESS
	MISSEND
DEIMNST	MINDSET
	MISTEND
DEIMNSW	MISWEND
DEIMNTU	MINUTED
	MUNITED
	MUTINED
DEIMNUX	UNMIXED
DEIMOOR	DOOMIER
	MOIDORE
	MOODIER
DEIMOOS	MOODIES
DEIMOPS	IMPOSED
DEIMORR	REMORID
DEIMORS	MISDOER
	MOIDERS
DEIMORU	ERODIUM
DEIMOSS	MISDOES
DEIMOST	DISTOME
	DOMIEST
	MODISTE
	MOISTED
DEIMOTT	OMITTED

DEIMOTV MOTIVED
VOMITED
DEIMPPR PRIMPED
DEIMPRT DIREMPT
DEIMPRU DUMPIER
UMPIRED
DEIMPSU DUMPIES
DEIMPTU IMPUTED
DEIMRRS SMIRRED
DEIMRSW MISDREW
DEIMRSY SEMIDRY
DEIMRUU UREDIUM
DEIMSST DEMISTS
DEIMSSU MISUSED
DEIMSTT SMITTED
DEIMSTU MUISTED
TEDIUMS
DEIMSTY STYMIED
DEINNNU NUNDINE
DEINNOO ONIONED
DEINNOP PINNOED
DEINNOR ENDIRON
DEINNOS ONDINES
DEINNOT INTONED
NOINTED
DEINNRS DINNERS
ENDRINS
DEINNRU DUNNIER
INURNED
DEINNST DENTINS
INDENTS
INTENDS
DEINNSU DUNNIES
UNDINES
DEINNSW ENWINDS
DEINNTU DUNNITE
DEINNTW TWINNED
DEINOOZ OZONIDE
DEINOPR POINDER
PROINED
DEINOPS DISPONE
SPINODE
DEINOPT POINTED
DEINOQU QUOINED
DEINORR DRONIER
DEINORS DINEROS
DONSIER
INDORSE
ORDINES
ROSINED
SORDINE
DEINORU DOURINE
NEUROID
DEINORW DOWNIER
WINDORE
DEINOSS ONSIDES
DEINOST DITONES
STONIED
DEINPPS SNIPPED
DEINPRS PINDERS
DEINPRT PRINTED
DEINPST DIPNETS
STIPEND
DEINPSU UNIPEDS
UNSPIDE
UNSPIED
DEINPUW UNWIPED
DEINRST TINDERS
DEINRSU INSURED
DEINRSV VERDINS
DEINRSW REWINDS
WINDERS
DEINRTT TRIDENT
DEINRTU INTRUDE
TURDINE
UNTIRED
UNTRIDE
UNTRIED
DEINRTX DEXTRIN
DEINRTY TINDERY
DEINRUW UNWIRED
DEINSST DISNEST
DISSENT
SNIDEST
DEINSSU NIDUSES
DEINSSV VENDISS
DEINSSW WINDSES
DEINSTT DENTIST
DISTENT
STINTED
DEINSTU DISTUNE
DUNITES
DEINSTY DENSITY
DESTINY
DEINSUZ UNSIZED
DEINUVW UNWIVED
DEIOORS OROIDES
DEIOORW WOODIER
DEIOORZ ODORIZE
DEIOOSS ISODOSE
DEIOOST OSTEOID
DEIOOSW WOODIES
DEIOOSZ DOOZIES
DEIOOVV VOIVODE
DEIOOWW WOIWODE
DEIOPPP POPPIED
DEIOPPS DOPPIES
DEIOPRS PERIODS
DEIOPRT DIOPTER
DIOPTRE
PERIDOT
PROTEID
DEIOPRV PROVIDE
DEIOPRX PEROXID
DEIOPSS DISPOSE
DEIOPST DEPOSIT
DOPIEST
PODITES
POSITED
SOPITED
TOPSIDE
DEIOPSV VESPOID
DEIOPTT TIPTOED
DEIOPTV PIVOTED
DEIOQTU QUOITED
DEIORRT DORTIER
DEIORRW ROWDIER
WORDIER
WORRIED
DEIORSS DORISES
DOSSIER
DEIORST EDITORS
ROISTED
ROSITED
SORTIED
STEROID
STORIED
TIERODS
TRIODES
DEIORSV DEVISOR
DEVOIRS
VISORED
VOIDERS
DEIORSW DOWRIES
ROWDIES
WEIRDOS
DEIORSZ DORIZES
DEIORTT DOTTIER
DEIORTU ETOURDI
IODURET
OUTRIDE
DEIORTZ ROZITED
DEIORVZ VIZORED
DEIORWW WIDOWER
DEIOSTT DOTIEST
STOITED
DEIOSTU OUTSIDE
TEDIOUS
DEIOSTV DOVIEST
DEIOSTW DOWIEST
DEIOSTX EXODIST
DEIOSTZ DOZIEST
DEIOSUV DEVIOUS
DEIOTUV OUTVIED
DEIOTUW WIDEOUT
DEIPPPU PUPPIED
DEIPPQU QUIPPED
DEIPPRR DRIPPER
DEIPPRS DIPPERS
DEIPPRT TRIPPED
DEIPPST PEPTIDS
DEIPPSU DUPPIES
DEIPRSS PRISSED
SPIDERS
DEIPRST SPIRTED
STRIPED
DEIPRSU PUDSIER
SIRUPED
UPDRIES
DEIPRSY SPIDERY
DEIPSSU UPSIDES
DEIPSSV VESPIDS
DEIPSTT SPITTED
DEIPSTU DISPUTE
DEIPSUV UPDIVES
DEIPSXY PYXIDES
DEIPTTU PUTTIED
TITUPED
DEIQRSU SQUIRED
DEIQRTU QUIRTED
DEIQTTU QUITTED
DEIQUZZ QUIZZED
DEIRRST STIRRED
STRIDER
DEIRRSU DRUSIER
DURRIES
DEIRRSV DRIVERS
DEIRRUX DRUXIER
DEIRSST DISSERT
STRIDES
DEIRSSU DISEURS
SUDSIER
DEIRSTU DUSTIER
REDUITS
STUDIER
DEIRSTV DIVERTS
STRIVED
VERDITS
DEISSST DESISTS
DEISSSU DISUSES
DEISSTU STUDIES
TISSUED
DEISSTV DIVESTS
DEISTTW DEWITTS
TWISTED
DEISWZZ SWIZZED
DEITTTW TWITTED
DEJLOST JOSTLED
DEJLSTU JUSTLED
DEJOORY JOYRODE
DEJOSTU JOUSTED
DEKKLSU SKULKED
DEKKNSU SKUNKED
DEKLLNO KNOLLED
DEKLLSU SKULLED
DEKLNOP PLONKED
DEKLNPU PLUNKED
DEKLNRU KNURLED
RUNKLED
DEKLRSU SKUDLER
DEKNNOS NONSKED
DEKNNRU DRUNKEN
DEKNOOS SNOOKED
DEKNOPP KNOPPED
DEKNOPR PRONKED
DEKNOQU QUONKED
DEKNOSW SNOWKED
DEKNOSY DONKEYS
DEKNOTT KNOTTED
DEKNOTU KNOUTED
DEKNOUY UNYOKED
DEKNPSU SPUNKED
DEKNRRU DRUNKER
DEKNRSU DUNKERS
DEKNRTU TRUNKED
DEKNSSU DUSKENS
DEKOOPS SPOOKED
DEKOOST DOOKETS
STOOKED
DEKOOTW KOTOWED
DEKOPST DESKTOP
DEKORST STROKED
DEKORWY KEYWORD
DEKOSSU KUDOSES
DEKOSVY SKYDOVE
DEKPRSU PREDUSK
DEKRSUY DUYKERS
DEKSSTU DUSKEST
DELLMOO MODELLO
DELLOOW WOOLLED
DELLOPR PROLLED
REDPOLL
DELLORR DROLLER
DELLORT TROLLED
DELLOSU DUELLOS
DELLOVW LOWVELD
DELLSTU DULLEST
DELMMSU SLUMMED
DELMNOS DOLMENS
DELMOOS SLOOMED
DELMOOW ELMWOOD
DELMOPR PREMOLD
DELMORS MOLDERS
REMOLDS
SMOLDER
DELMORU MOULDER
REMOULD
DELMOSU MODULES
MOUSLED
DELMOSY SMOYLED
DELMOTT MOTTLED
DELMOTU MOULTED
DELMOUV VOLUMED
DELMPPU PLUMPED
DELMPRU RUMPLED
DELMPSU DUMPLES
SLUMPED
DELMTUY MUTEDLY
DELMUZZ MUZZLED
DELNOOS NOODLES
SNOOLED
DELNORS RONDELS
DELNORT ENTROLD
DELNORU LOUNDER
ROUNDEL
ROUNDLE
DELNOSS OLDNESS
DELNOSU LOUDENS
NODULES
NOUSLED

DELNOSW	DOWLNES
DELNOSZ	DONZELS
DELNOTW	LETDOWN
DELNOTY	NOTEDLY
DELNOUV	UNLOVED
DELNOWY	DOWLNEY
DELNPRU	PLUNDER
DELNRSU	LURDENS
	NURDLES
	NURSLED
	RUNDLES
DELNRTU	RUNDLET
	TRUNDLE
DELNRUU	UNRULED
DELNSSU	DULNESS
DELNUWY	UNWELDY
DELNUZZ	NUZZLED
DELOOPP	PLEOPOD
DELOOPS	POODLES
	SPOOLED
DELOORT	ROOTLED
DELOORW	WOOLDER
DELOOST	STOOLED
	TOLEDOS
DELOOSW	DEWOOLS
DELOOTT	TOOTLED
DELOPPP	PLOPPED
	POPPLED
DELOPPR	DROPPLE
DELOPPS	SLOPPED
DELOPPT	TOPPLED
DELOPRS	POLDERS
	PRESOLD
DELOPRT	DROPLET
DELOPRU	POULDER
	POULDRE
	PROULED
DELOPRW	PROWLED
DELOPSU	SOUPLED
DELOPSY	DEPLOYS
	PODLEYS
DELOPTT	PLOTTED
DELOPTZ	PLOTZED
DELORRY	ORDERLY
DELORSS	DORSELS
	RODLESS
	SOLDERS
DELORST	DROLEST
	OLDSTER
	STRODLE
DELORSW	WELDORS
DELORSY	YODLERS
DELORTT	DOTTLER
	DOTTREL
DELORTU	TROULED
DELORUV	LOUVRED
DELOSSS	DOSSELS
DELOSSU	DULOSES
DELOSTT	DOTTELS
	DOTTLES
	SLOTTED
DELOSTU	LOUDEST
	OULDEST
	TOUSLED
DELOSYY	DOYLEYS
DELOSZZ	SOZZLED
DELOTUU	OUTDUEL
DELOTUV	VOLUTED
DELOTUZ	TOUZLED
DELPPRU	PURPLED
DELPPSU	SUPPLED
DELPRSU	DRUPELS
	SLURPED
DELPSSU	PLUSSED
DELPSTU	DUPLETS

DELPSUY	SPULYED
DELPUZZ	PUZZLED
DELRRSU	SLURRED
DELRSTU	LUSTRED
	RUSTLED
	STRUDEL
DELRTTU	TURTLED
DELSSTU	TUSSLED
DELSTTU	SUTTLED
DELUWZZ	WUZZLED
DEMMRRU	DRUMMER
DEMMSTU	STUMMED
DEMNOOR	DOORMEN
	MORENDO
DEMNOOW	WOODMEN
DEMNORS	MODERNS
	RODSMEN
DEMNORT	MORDENT
DEMNORU	MOURNED
DEMNORY	DEMONRY
DEMNOST	ENDMOST
DEMNOTU	DEMOUNT
	MOUNTED
DEMNOUV	UNMOVED
DEMNSTU	DUSTMEN
DEMOOPP	POPEDOM
DEMOOPR	PREDOOM
DEMOOPS	SPOOMED
DEMOORS	DROOMES
	SMOORED
DEMOORT	MOTORED
DEMOORV	VROOMED
DEMOOSS	OSMOSED
DEMOOST	SMOOTED
DEMOOTT	MOTTOED
DEMOOTU	OUTMODE
DEMOPRT	TROMPED
DEMOPST	STOMPED
DEMORRS	DORMERS
DEMORRU	RUMORED
DEMORST	STORMED
DEMORSW	DEWORMS
DEMOSSU	MOUSSED
	SMOUSED
DEMOSTT	DOMETTS
DEMOSTU	MOUSTED
	SMOUTED
DEMOSTY	MODESTY
DEMPRSU	DUMPERS
DEMPRTU	TRUMPED
DEMPSTU	STUMPED
DEMRRSU	MURDERS
	SMURRED
DEMSTTU	SMUTTED
DENNORT	DONNERT
	TENDRON
DENNORU	ENROUND
DENNOST	STONNED
	TENDONS
DENNOTU	UNNOTED
	UNTONED
DENNOUW	ENWOUND
	UNOWNED
DENNOUZ	UNZONED
DENNRSU	UNDERNS
DENNSSU	DUNNESS
DENNSTU	DUNNEST
	STUNNED
DENNTUU	UNTUNED
DENOOPS	SNOOPED
	SPOONED
DENOOSS	NOSODES
DENOOST	SNOOTED
	STOODEN
DENOOSW	SWOONED

DENOOSZ	SNOOZED
DENOOTU	DUOTONE
	OUTDONE
DENOOUW	UNWOOED
DENOPPR	PROPEND
DENOPPU	UNPOPED
DENOPRS	PONDERS
	RESPOND
DENOPRT	PORTEND
	PROTEND
DENOPRU	POUNDER
	UNROPED
DENOPRV	PROVEND
DENOPRY	PROYNED
DENOPSU	UNPOSED
DENOPTY	POYNTED
DENOPUX	EXPOUND
DENORRS	DRONERS
DENORRU	RONDURE
	ROUNDER
	UNORDER
DENORRW	DROWNER
DENORSS	SONDERS
DENORST	RODENTS
	SNORTED
DENORSU	ENDUROS
	RESOUND
	SOUNDER
	UNDOERS
DENORSV	VENDORS
DENORSW	DOWNERS
	WONDERS
DENORSY	YONDERS
DENORUW	REWOUND
	WOUNDER
DENOSTT	SNOTTED
DENOSTU	DEUTONS
	SNOUTED
DENOSUW	SWOUNED
	UNSOWED
DENPRSU	SPURNED
DENPRTU	PRUDENT
	PRUNTED
	UPTREND
DENPSSU	SENDUPS
	SUSPEND
	UPSENDS
DENRSSU	SUNDERS
	UNDRESS
DENRSSY	DRYNESS
DENRSTU	RETUNDS
	UNDREST
DENRSUU	UNSURED
DENSSTY	SYNDETS
DENSSUW	SUNDEWS
DENSTTU	STUDENT
	STUNTED
DENTUVY	DUVETYN
DEOOPPS	OPPOSED
DEOOPRS	SPOORED
DEOOPRT	TORPEDO
	TROOPED
DEOOPST	STOOPED
DEOOPSW	SWOOPED
	WOOPSED
DEOOPSX	EXOPODS
DEOORRT	REDROOT
DEOORST	ROOSTED
DEOORSZ	DOOZERS
DEOORTU	OUTDOER
	OUTRODE
DEOORTW	WROOTED
DEOOSTT	TOOTSED
DEOOSTU	OUTDOES
DEOPPPR	PROPPED

DEOPPQU	QUOPPED
DEOPPRR	DROPPER
DEOPPRS	DOPPERS
DEOPPST	STOPPED
DEOPPSW	SWOPPED
DEOPRRS	DORPERS
DEOPRRU	PROUDER
DEOPRST	DEPORTS
	REDTOPS
	SPORTED
DEOPRSU	POUDERS
	POUDRES
DEOPRSW	POWDERS
DEOPRTU	TROUPED
DEOPRWY	POWDERY
DEOPSST	DESPOTS
DEOPSSU	PSEUDOS
	SPOUSED
DEOPSTT	SPOTTED
DEOPSTU	OUTSPED
	SPOUTED
DEOPTTY	TYPTOED
DEOQRTU	TORQUED
DEORRSS	DORSERS
DEORRST	DORTERS
	RODSTER
DEORRSU	ORDURES
DEORRSV	DROVERS
DEORRSW	REWORDS
	SWORDER
DEORRVY	OVERDRY
DEORSSS	DOSSERS
	DROSSES
DEORSSU	DOUSERS
DEORSSW	DOWSERS
	DROWSES
DEORSTT	DETORTS
	DOTTERS
DEORSTU	DETOURS
	DOUREST
	DOUTERS
	OUTREDS
	REDOUTS
	ROUSTED
DEORSTW	STROWED
	WORSTED
DEORSTY	DESTROY
	ROYSTED
	STROYED
DEORSUV	DEVOURS
DEORTTT	TROTTED
DEORTTU	TUTORED
DEORTUU	OUTDURE
DEORTUW	OUTDREW
DEOSSSW	SOWSSED
DEOSSTW	DOWSETS
DEOSSYY	ODYSSEY
DEOSTTT	STOTTED
DEOSTTU	DUETTOS
	TESTUDO
DEOSTTW	SWOTTED
DEOSTUU	DUTEOUS
DEOSTUX	TUXEDOS
DEOTTUY	TUTOYED
DEPRRSU	SPURRED
DEPRRUY	PRUDERY
DEPRSTU	SPURTED
DEPRSUU	PURSUED
	USURPED
DEPRSUY	SYRUPED
DERRSTU	RUSTRED
DERSSSU	SUDSERS
DERSSTU	DUSTERS
	TRUSSED
DERSTTU	STURTED

	TRUSTED
DERSTTY	TRYSTED
DERSTUU	SUTURED
DERSTUY	RESTUDY
DFFGINO	DOFFING
DFFGINU	DUFFING
DFFIIMR	MIDRIFF
DFFIIRT	TRIFFID
DFFIMOR	DIFFORM
DFFLOOU	FOODFUL
DFFOSTU	DUSTOFF
DFGGIIN	FIDGING
DFGGINU	FUDGING
DFGGOOS	FOGDOGS
DFGHIOS	DOGFISH
DFGIINN	FINDING
DFGIINY	DIGNIFY
DFGILNO	FOLDING
DFGINNO	FONDING
DFGINNU	FUNDING
DFGINOR	FORDING
DFGINOU	FUNGOID
DFGMOOY	FOGYDOM
DFHILSU	DISHFUL
DFHIMSU	MUDFISH
DFILLUY	FLUIDLY
DFILMMO	FILMDOM
DFILMNU	MINDFUL
DFILNOP	PINFOLD
DFILNOS	INFOLDS
DFILORT	TRIFOLD
DFILORU	FLUORID
DFILOSX	SIXFOLD
DFILOTW	TWIFOLD
DFILSSU	SULFIDS
DFILTUU	DUTIFUL
DFIMNUY	MUNDIFY
DFIMOOS	FOODISM
DFIMORS	DISFORM
DFINOTU	OUTFIND
DFLMOOU	DOOMFUL
DFLMOUW	MUDFLOW
DFLNOSU	UNFOLDS
DFLOORU	ODORFUL
DFLOOTU	FOLDOUT
DFLOOTW	TWOFOLD
DFLOPRY	DROPFLY
DFLOPSU	UPFOLDS
DFLOTWY	TWYFOLD
DFNNOOO	NONFOOD
DFNNOUU	UNFOUND
DFNORUY	FOUNDRY
DFOORSX	OXFORDS
DGGGIIN	DIGGING
DGGGINO	DOGGING
DGGHIOS	DOGGISH
DGGIILN	GILDING
	GLIDING
DGGIINN	DINGING
DGGIINR	GIRDING
	GRIDING
	RIDGING
DGGIINU	GUIDING
DGGIJNU	JUDGING
DGGILNO	GODLING
	LODGING
DGGIMNU	MUDGING
DGGINNO	DONGING
DGGINNU	DUNGING
	NUDGING
DGGINRY	GRYDING
DGGNOSU	DUGONGS
	GUNDOGS
DGHHOOO	HOGHOOD
DGHIILN	HIDLING
	HILDING
DGHIINS	DISHING
	HIDINGS
	SHINDIG
DGHILNO	HOLDING
DGHILNY	HYLDING
DGHILOS	GOLDISH
DGHILPY	DIGLYPH
DGHINOO	HOODING
DGHINOR	HORDING
DGHINSU	DUSHING
DGHINTU	HINDGUT
	UNDIGHT
DGHIOOS	GOODISH
DGHIOPS	DOGSHIP
	GODSHIP
DGHOOPS	HOPDOGS
DGHOOST	HOTDOGS
DGHORTU	DROUGHT
DGHOTUY	DOUGHTY
DGIIKLN	KIDLING
DGIIKNN	DINKING
	KINDING
DGIIKNR	DIRKING
DGIIKNS	DISKING
DGIILLN	DILLING
DGIILNO	LOIDING
DGIILNR	DIRLING
DGIILNS	SIDLING
	SLIDING
DGIILNW	WILDING
DGIILNY	DINGILY
DGIILRS	RIDGILS
DGIILRY	RIGIDLY
DGIIMMN	DIMMING
DGIIMNN	MINDING
DGIIMNS	SMIDGIN
DGIIMOP	PIGMOID
DGIIMOS	SIGMOID
DGIINNN	DINNING
DGIINNR	RINDING
DGIINNS	NIDINGS
	SINDING
DGIINNT	DINTING
	TINDING
DGIINNU	INDUING
DGIINNW	DWINING
	WINDING
DGIINOS	INDIGOS
DGIINOV	VOIDING
DGIINOW	WINDIGO
DGIINOX	DIGOXIN
DGIINPP	DIPPING
DGIINPR	PRIDING
DGIINPS	PIDGINS
DGIINPU	PINGUID
DGIINRS	RIDINGS
DGIINRT	DIRTING
DGIINRV	DRIVING
DGIINRY	YIRDING
DGIINSS	DISSING
	SIDINGS
DGIINST	TIDINGS
DGIINSV	DIVINGS
DGIINTT	DITTING
DGIINTY	DIGNITY
	TIDYING
DGIIORT	TIGROID
DGIJOSU	JUDOGIS
DGIKMNO	KINGDOM
DGIKNNU	DUNKING
DGIKNNY	KYNDING
DGIKNOO	DOOKING
DGIKNOS	DOGSKIN
DGIKNSU	DUSKING
DGILLNO	DOLLING
DGILLNU	DULLING
DGILLOY	GODLILY
DGILMNO	MOLDING
DGILNOR	GIRLOND
	LORDING
DGILNOY	YODLING
DGILNSU	UNGILDS
DGILNYY	DYINGLY
DGILOPY	PODGILY
DGILOST	DIGLOTS
DGILPUY	PUDGILY
DGILRUY	GUILDRY
DGIMNOO	DOOMING
DGIMNPU	DUMPING
DGIMOPY	PYGMOID
DGIMSTU	MIDGUTS
DGINNNO	DONNING
DGINNNU	DUNNING
DGINNOP	PONDING
DGINNOR	DRONING
DGINNOS	DONINGS
	ONDINGS
DGINNOU	UNDOING
DGINNOW	DOWNING
DGINNRU	DURNING
DGINNSY	SYNDING
DGINNTU	DUNTING
	TUNDING
DGINNUW	WINDGUN
DGINNUY	UNDYING
DGINOOW	WOODING
DGINOPP	DOPPING
DGINOPS	DOPINGS
	PONGIDS
DGINORR	DORRING
DGINORS	RODINGS
DGINORT	DORTING
DGINORV	DROVING
DGINORW	WORDING
DGINOSS	DOSSING
DGINOST	DOTINGS
DGINOSU	DOUSING
	GUIDONS
DGINOSW	DISGOWN
	DOWSING
DGINOSZ	DOZINGS
DGINOTT	DOTTING
DGINOTU	DOUTING
DGINPPU	DUPPING
DGINRSU	UNGIRDS
DGINRSY	DRYINGS
DGINSSU	SUDSING
DGINSTU	DUSTING
DGIOPRY	PRODIGY
DGIOSTW	GODWITS
DGIPRSU	UPGIRDS
DGIQSUY	SQUIDGY
DGISSTU	DISGUST
DGLNORU	GOLDURN
DGLNOUY	UNGODLY
DGLOOOW	LOGWOOD
DGLOOSU	DUOLOGS
DGLOPSY	SPLODGY
DGLOSYY	DYSLOGY
DGMOOUW	GUMWOOD
DGMOPRU	GUMDROP
DGMORUU	GURUDOM
DGNNORU	NONDRUG
DGNOOOR	GODROON
DGNOORS	DRONGOS
DGNOOSS	GODSONS
DGNOOSW	GODOWNS
DGNOOTW	DOGTOWN
DGNORSU	GROUNDS
DGNOSSU	SUNDOGS
DGOORTT	DOGTROT
DGOSTUU	DUGOUTS
DHIILNS	HIDLINS
DHIILOT	DITHIOL
	LITHOID
DHIILSW	WILDISH
DHIIMMS	DIMMISH
DHIIMNO	HOMINID
DHIIMPS	MIDSHIP
DHIINRU	HIRUDIN
DHIIOPX	XIPHOID
DHIIORZ	RHIZOID
DHIIOST	HISTOID
DHIKSSU	DUSKISH
DHILLOS	DOLLISH
DHILLSU	DULLISH
DHILMUY	HUMIDLY
DHILNOP	DOLPHIN
DHILOST	DOLTISH
DHILOSU	LOUDISH
DHILPSU	LUDSHIP
	SULPHID
DHILPSY	SYLPHID
DHILRTY	THIRDLY
DHIMOPR	DIMORPH
DHIMORU	HUMIDOR
	RHODIUM
DHIMOSS	MISSHOD
DHIMPSU	DUMPISH
DHINNOS	DONNISH
DHINNSU	DUNNISH
DHINOPS	DONSHIP
DHINOPY	HYPNOID
DHINORS	DISHORN
	DRONISH
DHINSSY	SHINDYS
DHINSTU	TUNDISH
DHIOOST	DHOOTIS
DHIOPTY	PHYTOID
	TYPHOID
DHIORSW	WORDISH
DHIORTY	THYROID
DHIPRSU	PRUDISH
DHIPRSY	SYRPHID
DHJOPRU	JODHPUR
DHKMOOU	MUDHOOK
DHKORSY	DROSHKY
DHLMOOU	HOODLUM
DHLOOTU	HOLDOUT
DHLOPSU	HOLDUPS
	UPHOLDS
DHMMRUU	HUMDRUM
DHMNOYY	HYMNODY
DHNNOOU	NUNHOOD
DHNOOOS	SONHOOD
DHNOOSU	UNHOODS
DHOOOOS	HOODOOS
DHOOPRU	UPHOORD
DHOORST	HOTRODS
DHOORSU	RHODOUS
DHOPRSU	PUSHROD
DHOPRSY	HYDROPS
DHORSSU	SHROUDS
DHORSTU	DROUTHS
DHORSUY	HYDROUS
	SHROUDY
DHORTUY	DROUTHY
DHORXYY	HYDROXY
DIIIMOS	SIMIOID
DIIIMRU	IRIDIUM
DIIIMSV	DIVISIM
DIIINPS	INSIPID
DIIJNOS	DISJOIN
DIIKKNS	KIDSKIN

DIIKLNS	DISLINK
DIIKNOT	DOITKIN
DIILLST	DISTILL
DIILLVY	LIVIDLY
DIILMNS	DISLIMN
DIILMOO	MODIOLI
DIILMOS	IDOLISM
DIILMTY	TIMIDLY
DIILNNU	INDULIN
DIILNOT	TOLIDIN
DIILNWY	WINDILY
DIILNXY	XYLIDIN
DIILOPS	LIPOIDS
DIILOST	IDOLIST
DIILQSU	LIQUIDS
DIILRSU	SILURID
DIILRTY	DIRTILY
DIILSST	DISTILS
DIILSTY	IDYLIST
DIILVVY	VIVIDLY
DIILYZZ	DIZZILY
DIIMNOR	MIDIRON
DIIMNSU	INDIUMS
DIIMORS	DIORISM
DIIMOSS	IODISMS
DIIMSSS	DISMISS
DIIMSTW	DIMWITS
DIIMSUV	VIDIMUS
DIINNOT	TONDINI
DIINNSW	INWINDS
DIINOQU	QUINOID
DIINORS	SORDINI
DIINORT	DINITRO
DIINOSX	DIOXINS
DIINRST	NITRIDS
DIIOOPS	OPIOIDS
DIIOPRS	SPIROID
DIIORSV	DIVISOR
	VIROIDS
DIIORTX	TRIOXID
DIITUVY	VIDUITY
DIJMSSU	MUSJIDS
DIJOSTU	JUDOIST
DIKKOPS	DIKKOPS
DIKLNOR	LORDKIN
DIKLSTU	KIDULTS
DIKLSUY	DUSKILY
DIKMNSU	DINKUMS
DIKNNOS	NONSKID
DIKNNSU	NUDNIKS
DIKNOOW	INKWOOD
DIKNORV	DVORNIK
DIKOORT	DROOKIT
DIKOOSS	SKIDOOS
DIKORTU	DROUKIT
DILLMSU	MUDSILL
DILLOSY	SOLIDLY
DILLPSY	PSYLLID
DILLRUY	LURIDLY
DILMNRU	DRUMLIN
DILMOOY	DOOMILY
	MOODILY
DILMORS	MILORDS
DILMOST	MISTOLD
DILMOSU	SOLIDUM
DILMOSY	ODYLISM
DILMPUY	DUMPILY
DILMTUY	TUMIDLY
DILNNSU	DUNLINS
DILNOOS	OODLINS
DILNOPS	DIPLONS
DILNOPT	DIPLONT
DILNOQU	QUODLIN
DILNORT	INTROLD
DILNOSU	UNSOLID
DILNOXY	INDOXYL
DILNPSU	LISPUND
DILNPSY	SPINDLY
DILNSTU	INDULTS
DILORTU	DILUTOR
DILORWY	ROWDILY
	WORDILY
DILOSSS	DOSSILS
DILOSSU	DULOSIS
	SOLIDUS
DILOSTU	TOLUIDS
DILOSTY	STYLOID
DILOTTY	DOTTILY
DILRYZZ	DRIZZLY
DILSTUY	DUSTILY
DIMMOST	MIDMOST
DIMNNOO	MIDNOON
DIMNNOS	DONNISM
DIMNNOT	DINMONT
DIMNOOS	DOMINOS
DIMNOPU	IMPOUND
DIMNORS	DORMINS
	NIMRODS
DIMNOTW	MIDTOWN
DIMNSSU	NUDISMS
DIMOPSU	PODIUMS
	SPODIUM
DIMORSW	MISWORD
DIMOSST	MODISTS
DIMOSSU	SODIUMS
DIMOSSW	WISDOMS
DIMOSTU	DIMOUTS
DIMRTUU	TRIDUUM
DIMRUUV	DUUMVIR
DINNOOR	RONDINO
DINNOOT	TONDINO
DINNOPW	PINDOWN
DINNOSS	SINDONS
DINNOUW	INWOUND
DINNSUW	UNWINDS
DINOORS	INDOORS
	SORDINO
DINOORT	TORDION
DINOOST	ISODONT
DINOPSU	DUPIONS
	UNIPODS
DINORSU	DIURONS
	DURIONS
DINORTU	TURDION
DINORWW	WINDROW
DINOSSW	DISOWNS
DINOSWW	WINDOWS
DINOTUW	OUTWIND
DINPSTU	PUNDITS
DINPSUW	UPWINDS
	WINDUPS
DINRSSU	SUNDRIS
DINSSTU	NUDISTS
DIOOPRS	SPOROID
DIOOPSS	ISOPODS
DIOORST	DISROOT
	TOROIDS
DIOORTT	RIDOTTO
DIOOSTX	TOXOIDS
DIOPRST	DISPORT
	TORPIDS
	TRIPODS
DIOPRTY	TRIPODY
DIOPSST	DISPOST
DIORRST	STRIDOR
DIORSTT	DISTORT
DIOSSTU	STUDIOS
DIOSUUV	VIDUOUS
DIPRSTU	DISRUPT
DIPSSTU	STUPIDS
DIRSTUY	SURDITY
DJNNOOS	DONJONS
DKNNRUU	UNDRUNK
DKNOOPS	PONDOKS
DKOOOOS	KOODOOS
DKOOOSZ	ODZOOKS
DLLOOPS	DOLLOPS
DLLORWY	WORLDLY
DLMNOOY	MYLODON
DLMNOSU	UNMOLDS
DLMNOUU	UNMOULD
DLMOSUU	MODULUS
DLNOOWW	LOWDOWN
DLNOPRU	PULDRON
DLNOPSY	SPONDYL
DLNORSU	UNLORDS
DLNORUY	ROUNDLY
DLNOSUY	SOUNDLY
DLOOOTW	WOODLOT
DLOOPPY	POLYPOD
DLOOPSS	PODSOLS
DLOOPSZ	PODZOLS
DLOOPTU	OUTPLOD
DLOOPTY	TYLOPOD
DLOOPUY	DUOPOLY
DLOOPWY	PLYWOOD
DLOORSU	DOLOURS
DLOOSTU	OUTSOLD
DLOOTTU	OUTTOLD
DLOPRUY	PROUDLY
DLORSTY	DRYLOTS
DLOSTUW	WOULDST
DMMOORU	MUDROOM
DMNOOOP	MONOPOD
DMNOORS	DROMONS
DMNOOTW	TOWMOND
DMNOSSU	OSMUNDS
DMOOOQU	QUOMODO
DMORTUW	MUDWORT
DNNOORW	NONWORD
DNNOOST	DONNOTS
DNNORUU	UNROUND
DNNORUW	RUNDOWN
DNNOSUU	UNSOUND
DNNOSUW	SUNDOWN
DNNOUUW	UNWOUND
DNNRTUU	TURNDUN
DNNSTUU	TUNDUNS
DNOORTU	OROTUND
DNOOSUV	VODOUNS
DNOOTUW	NUTWOOD
DNOPRUU	ROUNDUP
DNOPUUW	UPWOUND
DNORSST	STRONDS
DNORSTU	ROTUNDS
DNOSSTU	STOUNDS
DNOSSTW	STOWNDS
DNOSSUW	SWOUNDS
DNOSSWW	SWOWNDS
DOOOOSV	VOODOOS
DOOORSU	ODOROUS
DOOORTU	OUTDOOR
DOOPRSU	UROPODS
DOOPRSY	PROSODY
DOOPRTU	DROPOUT
	OUTDROP
DOOPSTU	UPSTOOD
DOORRSS	SORDORS
DOORRTU	DORTOUR
DOOSUUV	VOUDOUS
DORSSTU	STROUDS
DORSUVY	DYVOURS
DORUVYY	DYVOURY
DPSSTUU	DUSTUPS
EEEEFRR	REFEREE
EEEEGTX	EXEGETE
EEEENTT	ENTETEE
EEEEPST	TEEPEES
EEEEPSV	VEEPEES
EEEEPSW	PEEWEES
EEEESWW	WEEWEES
EEEFFFO	FEOFFEE
EEEFFOR	OFFEREE
EEEFFRS	EFFERES
EEEFGRU	REFUGEE
EEEFHRS	SHEREEF
EEEFIRR	REEFIER
EEEFIRS	FEERIES
EEEFLRR	FLEERER
EEEFLRS	FEELERS
	REFEELS
EEEFLRT	FLEETER
EEEFLSS	FEELESS
EEEFMNR	FREEMEN
EEEFNRS	ENFREES
EEEFNRV	ENFEVER
EEEFORS	FORESEE
EEEFRRS	REEFERS
EEEFRRZ	FREEZER
EEEFRSZ	FREEZES
EEEGHNW	WHEENGE
EEEGIKR	GEEKIER
EEEGILS	ELEGIES
	ELEGISE
EEEGILZ	ELEGIZE
EEEGINP	EPIGENE
EEEGINR	GREENIE
EEEGIPR	PERIGEE
EEEGKLR	KEGELER
EEEGLMN	GLEEMEN
EEEGLNT	GENTEEL
EEEGMRR	REMERGE
EEEGMRS	EMERGES
EEEGNPR	EPERGNE
EEEGNPS	PEENGES
EEEGNRR	GREENER
	REGREEN
	RENEGER
EEEGNRS	RENEGES
EEEGNRU	RENEGUE
EEEGNRV	REVENGE
EEEGNSS	GENESES
EEEGNTT	GENETTE
EEEGRRT	GREETER
	REGREET
EEEGRSS	GREESES
EEEGRST	GREETES
EEEGRSZ	GEEZERS
EEEGRUX	EXERGUE
EEEHILW	WHEELIE
EEEHINS	SHEENIE
EEEHIRX	HEXEREI
EEEHISZ	HEEZIES
EEEHLNW	ENWHEEL
EEEHLOY	EYEHOLE
EEEHLPW	WHEEPLE
EEEHLRS	HEELERS
	REHEELS
EEEHLRW	WHEELER
EEEHLST	LETHEES
EEEHLWZ	WHEEZLE
EEEHNST	ETHENES
EEEHNSX	HEXENES
EEEHNSY	SHEENEY
EEEHPRS	PHEERES
EEEHPSS	PHEESES
EEEHPSZ	PHEEZES
EEEHRRS	SHEERER
EEEHRST	SEETHER
	SHEETER

EEEHRTT	TEETHER
EEEHRWZ	WHEEZER
EEEHSST	SEETHES
EEEHSSV	SHEEVES
EEEHSTT	ESTHETE
	TEETHES
EEEHSWZ	WHEEZES
EEEIJLS	JEELIES
EEEIKLL	EELLIKE
EEEIKLS	KEELIES
EEEIKLY	EYELIKE
EEEIKRR	REEKIER
EEEILRR	LEERIER
EEEILRS	SEELIER
EEEILRV	RELIEVE
EEEILST	EELIEST
	STEELIE
EEEIMMS	MEEMIES
EEEIMNS	ENEMIES
EEEIMNT	EMETINE
EEEIMPR	EPIMERE
	PREEMIE
EEEIMRS	EMERIES
EEEIMRT	EREMITE
EEEINQU	QUEENIE
EEEINRS	ESERINE
EEEINRT	TEENIER
EEEINRW	WEENIER
EEEINSW	WEENIES
EEEIPRR	PEERIER
EEEIPRS	PEERIES
	SEEPIER
EEEIPRW	WEEPIER
EEEIPST	EPEEIST
EEEIPSU	EPUISEE
EEEIPSW	WEEPIES
EEEIRRT	RETIREE
EEEIRRV	REVERIE
EEEIRST	EERIEST
EEEIRSV	VEERIES
EEEIRSZ	RESEIZE
EEEISTW	SWEETIE
EEEJLRW	JEWELER
EEEJNPY	JEEPNEY
EEEJPRS	JEEPERS
EEEJRRS	JEERERS
EEEJSST	JESTEES
EEEKKRS	KEEKERS
EEEKLLU	UKELELE
EEEKLMN	KEELMEN
EEEKLNR	KNEELER
EEEKLNS	SLEEKEN
EEEKLPW	EKPWELE
EEEKLRS	KEELERS
	SLEEKER
EEEKMNS	MEEKENS
EEEKMST	MEEKEST
EEEKNPT	KEEPNET
EEEKNRS	KEENERS
EEEKNST	KEENEST
	KETENES
EEEKORV	REEVOKE
EEEKPRS	KEEPERS
EEEKRRS	REEKERS
EEEKRSS	KREESES
	RESEEKS
	SEEKERS
EEEKRST	KEESTER
	SKEETER
EEELLRV	LEVELER
EEELMNR	REELMEN
EEELMNT	ELEMENT
	TELEMEN
EEELMPX	EXEMPLE
EEELMSX	LEXEMES
EEELNST	STELENE
EEELNSV	ELEVENS
EEELPRS	PEELERS
	SLEEPER
	SPEELER
EEELPRT	REPLETE
EEELPRX	REEXPEL
EEELPST	STEEPLE
EEELRRS	REELERS
EEELRRV	REVELER
EEELRSV	RELEVES
	SLEEVER
EEELRTV	LEVERET
EEELSSS	LESSEES
EEELSST	TELESES
EEELSSV	SLEEVES
EEELSSY	EYELESS
EEELSTU	EUSTELE
EEELSTX	TELEXES
EEELSTY	EYELETS
EEELTTX	TELETEX
EEEMMSS	MESEEMS
	SEMEMES
EEEMNRS	MENEERS
EEEMNSS	NEMESES
EEEMNST	MENTEES
EEEMORT	EROTEME
EEEMOSY	EYESOME
EEEMPRT	PREMEET
EEEMRSS	SEEMERS
EEEMRST	MEETERS
	REMEETS
	TEEMERS
EEEMRTX	EXTREME
EEEMSST	ESTEEMS
	MESTEES
EEEMSTT	MEETEST
EEEMSTU	EMEUTES
EEENNPT	PENTENE
EEENNRT	ETRENNE
EEENNTT	ENTENTE
EEENNUY	ENNUYEE
EEENPRR	PREENER
EEENPRT	PRETEEN
	TERPENE
EEENPRV	PREVENE
EEENPSS	PENSEES
EEENPST	ENSTEEP
	STEEPEN
EEENPSW	ENSWEEP
EEENPSX	EXPENSE
EEENRRS	SERENER
	SNEERER
EEENRRT	ENTERER
	REENTER
	TERREEN
	TERRENE
EEENRRV	VENERER
EEENRRW	RENEWER
EEENRSS	SERENES
EEENRST	ENTREES
	RETENES
	TEENERS
EEENRSV	ENERVES
	EVENERS
	VENEERS
EEENRSZ	SNEEZER
EEENRTV	EVENTER
EEENRTX	EXTERNE
EEENRUV	REVENUE
	UNREEVE
EEENSSZ	SNEEZES
EEENSTV	EVENEST
EEENSTW	SWEETEN
EEENSTX	EXTENSE
EEENSVW	VENEWES
EEENSWY	SWEENEY
EEEOPPS	EPOPEES
EEEORSV	OVERSEE
EEEORSY	EYESORE
EEEORVY	OVEREYE
EEEPPRS	PEEPERS
EEEPRSS	PEERESS
EEEPRST	ESTREPE
	STEEPER
EEEPRSV	PEEVERS
	PREEVES
EEEPRSW	SWEEPER
	WEEPERS
EEEPRSZ	SPREEZE
EEEQRRU	QUEERER
	REQUERE
EEEQSUZ	SQUEEZE
EEERRRV	REVERER
EEERRST	RETREES
	STEERER
EEERRSV	RESERVE
	REVERES
	REVERSE
	SEVERER
EEERSSS	SEERESS
EEERSTT	TEETERS
	TERETES
EEERSTV	STEEVER
EEERSTW	SWEETER
EEERSUV	REVEUSE
EEERSUW	SERUEWE
EEERSVW	SERVEWE
	WEEVERS
EEERTTW	TWEETER
EEERTWZ	TWEEZER
EEESSTT	SETTEES
	TESTEES
EEESSTV	STEEVES
	VESTEES
EEESTTW	WEETEST
EEESTWZ	TWEEZES
EEFFFNO	ENFEOFF
EEFFFOR	FEOFFER
EEFFGLU	EFFULGE
EEFFINT	FIFTEEN
EEFFIRS	EFFEIRS
EEFFKLS	KEFFELS
EEFFNOS	OFFENSE
EEFFORR	OFFERER
	REOFFER
EEFFOST	TOFFEES
EEFFSSU	EFFUSES
EEFFSTU	SUFFETE
EEFGILN	FEELING
	FLEEING
EEFGINR	FEERING
	FEIGNER
	FREEING
	REEFING
EEFGINS	FEESING
EEFGINZ	FEEZING
EEFGLLU	GLEEFUL
EEFGLOR	FORELEG
EEFGLOS	SOLFEGE
EEFGORR	REFORGE
EEFGORY	FROGEYE
EEFGRSU	REFUGES
EEFHIRS	HEIFERS
EEFHIRT	HEFTIER
EEFHISY	FISHEYE
EEFHLNS	ENFLESH
EEFHLRS	FLESHER
	HERSELF
EEFHLSS	FLESHES
EEFHNRS	FRESHEN
EEFHORT	THEREOF
EEFHORW	WHEREOF
EEFHRRS	FRESHER
	REFRESH
EEFHRRU	FUEHRER
EEFHRSS	FRESHES
EEFHRST	FRESHET
	HEFTERS
EEFIIMN	FEMINIE
EEFIIRR	FIERIER
	REIFIER
EEFIIRS	REIFIES
EEFIKLL	ELFLIKE
EEFILLS	FELLIES
EEFILLX	FLEXILE
EEFILNO	OLEFINE
EEFILNS	FELINES
EEFILOR	FORELIE
EEFILPR	PREFILE
	PRELIFE
EEFILRR	FERLIER
EEFILRS	FERLIES
	REFILES
	REFLIES
	RELIEFS
EEFILRT	FELTIER
	FERTILE
EEFILST	FELSITE
	LEFTIES
	LIEFEST
EEFIMNR	FIREMEN
EEFIMRT	FEMITER
EEFINNR	FENNIER
EEFINNS	FENNIES
EEFINRR	FERNIER
	REFINER
EEFINRS	ENFIRES
	FEERINS
	FINEERS
	REFINES
EEFINRT	FEINTER
EEFINSS	FINESSE
EEFINSX	ENFIXES
EEFIPRR	PREFIRE
EEFIPRS	PREIFES
	PRIEFES
EEFIRRS	FERRIES
	REFIRES
	REFRIES
EEFIRRT	FERRITE
EEFIRSS	FRISEES
EEFIRSX	REFIXES
EEFIRSZ	FRIEZES
EEFISTV	FESTIVE
EEFLLOS	FELLOES
EEFLLRS	FELLERS
EEFLLRU	FUELLER
EEFLLST	FELLEST
EEFLLTY	FLEETLY
EEFLMTU	TEEMFUL
EEFLNNO	ENFELON
EEFLNNS	FENNELS
EEFLNOS	ONESELF
EEFLNRS	FLENSER
	FRESNEL
EEFLNSS	FLENSES
EEFLNTU	TEENFUL
EEFLOOV	FOVEOLE
EEFLORS	FORLESE
EEFLOTU	OUTFEEL
EEFLRRS	FERRELS
EEFLRRU	FERRULE
EEFLRST	FELTERS
	REFLETS

TELFERS
EEFLRSU FERULES
FUELERS
REFUELS
EEFLRTT FETTLER
EEFLRTU FLEURET
EEFLRUX FLEXURE
EEFLSTT FETTLES
LEFTEST
EEFLSUY EYEFULS
EEFMNOR FOREMEN
EEFMNRT FERMENT
EEFMOTT MOFETTE
EEFMPRU PERFUME
EEFMSTW FEWMETS
EEFMTTU FUMETTE
EEFNORT OFTENER
EEFNORZ ENFROZE
EEFNRRY FERNERY
EEFNRSS ENSERFS
EEFNRSU UNFREES
EEFNRTV FERVENT
EEFNSSW FEWNESS
EEFNSSY FEYNESS
EEFORRV FOREVER
EEFORRZ REFROZE
EEFOTTU FOUETTE
EEFPRRS PREFERS
EEFPRSU PERFUSE
EEFRRST FERRETS
EEFRRSU REFUSER
EEFRRTT FRETTER
EEFRRTU REFUTER
EEFRRTY FERRETY
EEFRSST FESTERS
EEFRSSU REFUSES
EEFRSTT FETTERS
EEFRSTU FEUTRES
REFUTES
EEFRSTW FEWTERS
EEFSSTU FETUSES
EEGGGLR GLEGGER
EEGGHTU THUGGEE
EEGGILN GLEEING
NEGLIGE
EEGGILR LEGGIER
EEGGINR GREEING
EEGGIPS PEGGIES
EEGGIRS GREIGES
EEGGIST EGGIEST
EEGGISV VEGGIES
EEGGKRS SKEGGER
EEGGLRS EGGLERS
LEGGERS
EEGGLSS EGGLESS
EEGGMNY YEGGMEN
EEGGMSU MUGGEES
EEGGNNS GENSENG
EEGGNOR ENGORGE
EEGGNOY GEOGENY
EEGGORR REGORGE
EEGGORU GOUGERE
EEGGPRU PUGGREE
EEGHILN HEELING
EEGHINR REHINGE
EEGHINT THEEING
EEGHINY HYGIENE
EEGHINZ HEEZING
EEGHIRW REWEIGH
WEIGHER
EEGHKRS SKREEGH
EEGHLNU LEUGHEN
EEGHMNU HEGUMEN
EEGHNRT GREENTH
EEGHNRY GREYHEN
EEGHRTU TEUGHER
EEGHSSS GHESSES
EEGHSTZ SHEGETZ
EEGIIRS GRIESIE
EEGIJLN JEELING
EEGIJNP JEEPING
EEGIJNR JEERING
EEGIKKN KEEKING
EEGIKLL LEGLIKE
EEGIKLM GEMLIKE
EEGIKLN KEELING
EEGIKLP PEGLIKE
EEGIKNN KEENING
KNEEING
EEGIKNP KEEPING
PEEKING
EEGIKNR REEKING
EEGIKNS SEEKING
SKEEING
EEGIKNT KITENGE
EEGILLS GELLIES
EEGILNP LEEPING
PEELING
EEGILNR LEERING
REELING
EEGILNS LEESING
SEELING
EEGILNT GENTILE
EEGILOS ELOGIES
EEGILPS SPIEGEL
EEGILRS LEIGERS
LIEGERS
EEGILRV VELIGER
EEGILST ELEGIST
ELEGITS
EEGIMMR GEMMIER
GREMMIE
IMMERGE
EEGIMNR MEERING
REGIMEN
EEGIMNS SEEMING
EEGIMNT MEETING
TEEMING
EEGIMNX EXEMING
EEGIMRR GERMIER
EEGIMRS EMIGRES
REGIMES
REMIGES
EEGINNP PEENING
EEGINNR ENGINER
INGENER
EEGINNS ENGINES
NEESING
SNEEING
EEGINNT TEENING
EEGINNU GENUINE
INGENUE
EEGINNV EEVNING
EVENING
EEGINNW ENEWING
WEENING
EEGINNZ NEEZING
EEGINOP EPIGONE
EEGINOS GENOISE
SOIGNEE
EEGINPP PEEPING
EEGINPR PEERING
PREEING
EEGINPS SEEPING
EEGINPV PEEVING
EEGINPW WEEPING
EEGINRS GREISEN
EEGINRT GENTIER
INTEGER
TEERING
TREEING
EEGINRV REEVING
REGIVEN
VEERING
EEGINSS GENESIS
SEEINGS
SIGNEES
EEGINSW SEEWING
SWEEING
EEGINTV VENTIGE
EEGINTW WEETING
EEGINTX EXIGENT
EEGIOST EGOTISE
GOETIES
EEGIOTZ EGOTIZE
EEGIRRV GRIEVER
EEGIRSS SIEGERS
EEGIRSV GRIEVES
REGIVES
EEGIRTT TERGITE
EEGIRTU GUERITE
EEGISTV VESTIGE
EEGKLRS KEGLERS
EEGKNOR KEROGEN
EEGKNRU GERENUK
EEGLLNS LEGLENS
EEGLLSS LEGLESS
EEGLLST LEGLETS
EEGLMMU GEMMULE
EEGLMOR GOMEREL
EEGLMSU EMULGES
LEGUMES
EEGLNNS GENNELS
EEGLNOR ERELONG
EEGLNOU EUGENOL
EEGLNOZ LOZENGE
EEGLNRT GENTLER
EEGLNRY GREENLY
EEGLNST GENTLES
LENGEST
EEGLNSU LUNGEES
EEGLOSS EGOLESS
EEGLPSS PEGLESS
EEGLRRU GRUELER
EEGLRST REGLETS
EEGLRSU REGLUES
EEGLRTW WERGELT
EEGLRTY TELERGY
EEGMMRY GEMMERY
EEGMNOS EMONGES
GENOMES
EEGMNRS GERMENS
EEGMNST SEGMENT
EEGMNSU EMUNGES
EEGMNTU TEGUMEN
EEGMOST GEMOTES
EEGMRRS MERGERS
EEGMRTU GUMTREE
EEGNNST GENNETS
EEGNOPS PONGEES
EEGNORS ENGORES
NEGROES
EEGNOSX EXOGENS
EEGNPUX EXPUNGE
EEGNRSS NEGRESS
EEGNRST GERENTS
REGENTS
EEGNRSV VENGERS
EEGNRSY GYRENES
EEGNSSU GENUSES
NEGUSES
EEGNSTU GUESTEN
EEGOOPY POOGYEE
EEGOOSS SOOGEES
EEGOPRT PROTEGE
EEGORTV OVERGET
EEGOSSS GESSOES
EEGPPRR PREPREG
EEGPRSU PUGREES
EEGPRUX EXPURGE
EEGRRSS REGRESS
EEGRRST REGRETS
EEGRRSU RESURGE
REURGES
EEGRRSV VERGERS
EEGRRUY GRUYERE
EEGRSST REGESTS
EEGRSSU GUESSER
EEGRSSY GEYSERS
EEGRSTT GETTERS
EEGRSTU GESTURE
EEGRSTY GREYEST
EEGSSSU GUESSES
EEHHRTT THETHER
EEHHRTW WHETHER
EEHHSTW WHEESHT
EEHIINS HEINIES
EEHIKLN HENLIKE
EEHIKLO HOELIKE
EEHILLR HELLERI
HELLIER
EEHILMN HELIMEN
HEMLINE
EEHILNT THEELIN
EEHILPS EPHELIS
EEHILRS LEISHER
EEHILRW WHILERE
EEHILST SHELTIE
EEHILSX HELIXES
EEHIMMS MISHMEE
EEHIMNO HEMIONE
EEHIMPR HEMPIER
EEHIMPS HEMPIES
IMPHEES
EEHIMPT EPITHEM
EEHIMRS MESHIER
EEHINNR HENNIER
EEHINNS HENNIES
EEHINNY HYENINE
EEHINOR HEROINE
EEHINRR ERRHINE
EEHINRS HENRIES
INHERES
RESHINE
EEHINRT NEITHER
THEREIN
EEHINRW WHEREIN
EEHINST THEINES
EEHIORS HEROISE
EEHIORZ HEROIZE
EEHIPRT PRITHEE
EEHIPSV PEEVISH
EEHIPTT EPITHET
EEHIRRS HERRIES
REHIRES
EEHIRSS HEIRESS
HERISSE
EEHIRST HEISTER
EEHIRSV SHRIEVE
EEHIRTW THEWIER
EEHIRWY WHEYIER
EEHISST HESSITE
EEHISTV THIEVES
EEHKLOY KEYHOLE
EEHKLSS SHEKELS
EEHKOOY EYEHOOK
EEHKRSS SHREEKS
EEHLLMP PHELLEM
EEHLLNS ENSHELL
EEHLLOS HELLOES

EEHLLOT	THEELOL
EEHLLRS	HELLERS
	SHELLER
EEHLLRY	HELLERY
EEHLMMW	WHEMMLE
EEHLMRT	THERMEL
EEHLMST	HELMETS
EEHLNSU	UNHELES
EEHLPRS	HELPERS
EEHLPRT	TELPHER
EEHLPSS	PLESHES
EEHLRST	SHELTER
EEHLRSV	SHELVER
EEHLRSW	WELSHER
EEHLRSY	SHEERLY
EEHLSSU	HUELESS
EEHLSSV	SHELVES
EEHLSSW	SHEWELS
	WELSHES
EEHLSTT	SHTETEL
EEHLSTV	THELVES
EEHMMRS	HEMMERS
EEHMNNO	NONHEME
EEHMNOP	PHONEME
EEHMNOS	HOSEMEN
EEHMNRU	ENRHEUM
EEHMNRY	MYNHEER
EEHMNSS	MENSHES
EEHMORT	THEOREM
EEHMPST	TEMPEHS
EEHMRST	THERMES
EEHMRUX	EXHUMER
EEHMSST	SMEETHS
EEHMSUV	HUMVEES
EEHMSUX	EXHUMES
EEHNNOS	SHONEEN
EEHNNRS	HENNERS
EEHNNRY	HENNERY
EEHNOOR	HONOREE
EEHNOPT	POTHEEN
EEHNORS	RESHONE
EEHNORT	THEREON
EEHNORW	NOWHERE
	WHEREON
EEHNOSX	HEXONES
EEHNPSS	SEPHENS
	SPHENES
EEHNPSW	NEPHEWS
EEHNRST	THRENES
EEHNSST	NESHEST
EEHNSTU	ENTHUSE
EEHNSTV	SEVENTH
EEHNSTY	ETHYNES
EEHOOPW	WHOOPEE
EEHOOST	TOESHOE
EEHOPRU	EUPHROE
EEHOPSS	SHEEPOS
EEHOPST	HEPTOSE
EEHORRV	HOVERER
EEHORSS	RESHOES
EEHORST	HETEROS
EEHORSU	REHOUSE
EEHORSW	WHERESO
EEHORTT	THERETO
EEHORTW	WHERETO
EEHORVW	HOWEVER
	WHOEVER
EEHOSST	ETHOSES
EEHOSSX	HEXOSES
EEHOSTW	TOWHEES
EEHOSTY	EYESHOT
EEHPPST	HEPPEST
EEHPRSS	SPHERES
EEHPRST	HEPSTER
	PETHERS
	SPERTHE
	THREEPS
EEHPRTY	PRYTHEE
EEHQSTU	QUETHES
EEHRRSW	WERSHER
EEHRRTW	WHERRET
EEHRSSU	RUSHEES
EEHRSSW	SHEWERS
EEHRSTT	TETHERS
EEHRSTW	WETHERS
	WRETHES
EEHRSTZ	HERTZES
EEHRSVW	WHERVES
EEHRTTW	WHETTER
EEHRVWY	WHYEVER
EEHSTUY	SHUTEYE
EEIIKRS	KIERIES
EEIILRV	VEILIER
EEIIMNS	MEINIES
EEIIMPR	RIEMPIE
EEIIMRT	EMERITI
EEIIMST	ITEMISE
EEIIMTZ	ITEMIZE
EEIINRT	ERINITE
	NITERIE
EEIINRV	VEINIER
EEIINST	SIENITE
EEIINSW	EISWEIN
	WIENIES
EEIINTV	INVITEE
EEIIPST	PIETIES
EEIIRRV	RIVIERE
EEIIRVW	VIEWIER
EEIISST	SEITIES
EEIISTV	VISITEE
EEIJKLT	JETLIKE
EEIJKRR	JERKIER
EEIJKRS	JERKIES
EEIJLLS	JELLIES
EEIJMMR	JEMMIER
EEIJMMS	JEMMIES
EEIJNNS	JENNIES
EEIJRRS	JERRIES
EEIJRTT	JETTIER
EEIJSSS	JESSIES
EEIJSTT	JETTIES
EEIKLLS	KELLIES
	SKELLIE
EEIKLNT	NETLIKE
EEIKLNY	KEYLINE
EEIKLOT	TOELIKE
EEIKLPS	KELPIES
EEIKLPT	PIKELET
EEIKLSS	SELKIES
EEIKLST	KELTIES
	SLEEKIT
EEIKMNP	PIKEMEN
EEIKMPS	MISKEEP
EEIKNOS	EIKONES
EEIKNPY	PINKEYE
EEIKNRT	KERNITE
EEIKNSS	ENSKIES
	KINESES
EEIKNWY	EYEWINK
EEIKPRR	PERKIER
EEIKPRS	PESKIER
EEIKRRS	KERRIES
EEIKRST	KEISTER
	KIESTER
EEIKRSY	SKIEYER
EEIKSST	SEIKEST
EEIKSTT	STEEKIT
EEIKTTT	TEKTITE
EEILLMT	MELLITE
EEILLNS	NELLIES
EEILLPS	ELLIPSE
EEILLRS	LEISLER
EEILLRT	TREILLE
EEILLRV	EVILLER
EEILLRY	LEERILY
EEILLSS	EISELLS
EEILLST	TELLIES
EEILLSV	VIELLES
EEILLSW	WELLIES
EEILMNN	LINEMEN
EEILMNR	ERMELIN
EEILMNS	ISLEMEN
EEILMNY	MYELINE
EEILMPT	IMPLETE
EEILMRT	MELTIER
EEILMRV	VERMEIL
EEILMST	ELMIEST
EEILNNO	LEONINE
EEILNNT	LENIENT
EEILNNV	ENLIVEN
EEILNOR	ELOINER
EEILNOS	OLEINES
EEILNPS	PENSILE
EEILNPT	PENLITE
EEILNRS	LIERNES
	RELINES
EEILNRV	LIVENER
EEILNSS	ENISLES
	ENSILES
	SENILES
	SENSILE
	SILENES
EEILNST	LISENTE
	SETLINE
	TENSILE
EEILNSY	YEELINS
EEILNTT	ENTITLE
EEILNTV	VEINLET
EEILNUV	VEINULE
EEILOPT	PETIOLE
EEILORT	TROELIE
EEILORV	OVERLIE
	RELIEVO
EEILOST	ESTOILE
	ETOILES
EEILOTZ	ZEOLITE
EEILPRR	REPLIER
EEILPRS	REPLIES
	SPIELER
EEILPRT	PERLITE
	REPTILE
EEILPRU	PUERILE
EEILPSS	PELISSE
EEILPST	EPISTLE
	PELITES
EEILQRU	RELIQUE
EEILRRS	RELIERS
EEILRRV	RELIVER
	REVILER
EEILRSS	IRELESS
	RESILES
EEILRST	LEISTER
	RETILES
	STERILE
EEILRSU	LEISURE
EEILRSV	LEVIERS
	RELIVES
	REVILES
	SERVILE
	VEILERS
EEILRTT	RETITLE
EEILSSS	SESELIS
	SESSILE
EEILSST	LISTEES
	TELESIS
	TIELESS
EEILSSU	ILEUSES
EEILSSW	LEWISES
EEILSSX	LEXISES
	SILEXES
EEILSTV	EVILEST
	LEVITES
	LIEVEST
	VELITES
EEILSTX	SEXTILE
EEILSUV	ELUSIVE
EEILSVW	WEEVILS
EEILSZZ	LEZZIES
EEILTTX	TEXTILE
EEILTUX	ULEXITE
EEILVWY	WEEVILY
EEIMMNS	IMMENSE
EEIMMRS	IMMERSE
EEIMMSS	MIMESES
	MISSEEM
EEIMMST	MISMEET
EEIMNNO	NOMINEE
EEIMNNT	EMINENT
EEIMNOS	SEMEION
EEIMNOT	ONETIME
EEIMNRS	ERMINES
EEIMNRV	MINEVER
EEIMNRW	WIREMEN
EEIMNSS	INSEEMS
	MISSEEN
	NEMESIS
	SIEMENS
EEIMNST	EMETINS
EEIMNSW	MISWEEN
EEIMNSY	MEINEYS
	MENYIES
EEIMNTT	MINETTE
EEIMOPS	EPISOME
EEIMOPT	EPITOME
EEIMORS	ISOMERE
EEIMOSS	MEIOSES
EEIMOTV	EMOTIVE
EEIMPRR	PREMIER
	REPRIME
EEIMPRS	EMPIRES
	EMPRISE
	EPIMERS
	IMPRESE
	PREMIES
	PREMISE
	SPIREME
EEIMPRT	EMPTIER
EEIMPRZ	EMPRIZE
EEIMPST	EMPTIES
	SEPTIME
EEIMQRU	REQUIEM
EEIMRRR	MERRIER
EEIMRRS	MERRIES
EEIMRRT	MITERER
	TRIREME
EEIMRRU	EREMURI
EEIMRSS	MERISES
	MESSIER
	MISERES
	REMISES
EEIMRST	MEISTER
	METIERS
	REEMITS
	RETIMES
	TREMIES
	TRISEME
EEIMRSX	MIREXES
	REMIXES
EEIMRTT	EMITTER
	TERMITE

EEIMSSS	MISSEES
	SEMISES
EEIMSST	METISSE
EEINNNP	PENNINE
EEINNPS	PENNIES
	PINENES
EEINNRS	NERINES
EEINNRT	INTERNE
EEINNRU	NEURINE
EEINNRV	ENRIVEN
	INNERVE
	NERVINE
EEINNRW	WENNIER
EEINNST	INTENSE
	TENNIES
EEINNSV	VENINES
EEINNTW	ENTWINE
EEINNTZ	NETIZEN
EEINOPR	PEREION
	PIONEER
EEINOPS	PEONIES
EEINORR	ONERIER
EEINOSS	EOSINES
EEINPPS	PEPSINE
EEINPRR	REPINER
	RIPENER
EEINPRS	EREPSIN
	REPINES
EEINPRT	INEPTER
EEINPRZ	PRENZIE
EEINPSS	PENISES
EEINPST	PENTISE
EEINPSV	PENSIVE
	VESPINE
EEINQRU	ENQUIRE
	INQUERE
EEINQSU	EQUINES
EEINQTU	QUIETEN
EEINQUY	QUEYNIE
EEINRRS	RERISEN
	RESINER
EEINRRT	INERTER
	REINTER
	RENTIER
	TERRINE
EEINRRV	NERVIER
	VERNIER
EEINRSS	SEINERS
	SEREINS
	SERINES
EEINRST	ENTIRES
	ENTRIES
	NERITES
	RETINES
	TRENISE
	TRIENES
EEINRSV	ENVIERS
	INVERSE
	VEINERS
	VENIRES
	VERSINE
EEINRSW	NEWSIER
	WEINERS
	WIENERS
EEINRTT	NETTIER
	TENTIER
EEINRTU	NEURITE
	RETINUE
	REUNITE
	UTERINE
EEINSST	SEITENS
	SESTINE
EEINSSV	SENVIES
EEINSSW	NEWSIES
EEINSTV	TENSIVE
	VENITES
EEINSTX	EXTINES
	SIXTEEN
EEINSTY	SYENITE
EEIOPPT	EPITOPE
EEIOPSS	POESIES
EEIOPST	POETISE
EEIOPSX	EPOXIES
EEIOPTZ	POETIZE
EEIORRS	ROSIERE
EEIORSS	SOIREES
EEIORSV	EROSIVE
EEIORTZ	EROTIZE
EEIOSST	ISOETES
EEIOSTT	TOEIEST
EEIPPPR	PEPPIER
	PREPPIE
EEIPPST	PEPTISE
EEIPPTT	PIPETTE
EEIPPTZ	PEPTIZE
EEIPQRU	PERIQUE
	REEQUIP
	REPIQUE
EEIPQSU	EQUIPES
EEIPRRR	PERRIER
EEIPRRS	PERRIES
	PRISERE
	REPRISE
	RESPIRE
EEIPRRV	REPRIVE
EEIPRRX	EXPIRER
EEIPRRZ	REPRIZE
EEIPRSS	PRESSIE
EEIPRST	PESTIER
	RESPITE
EEIPRSV	PREVISE
	PRIEVES
EEIPRSW	SPEWIER
EEIPRSX	EXPIRES
	PREXIES
EEIPRTT	PETTIER
EEIPRTY	YPERITE
EEIPRVW	PREVIEW
EEIPRZZ	PREZZIE
EEIPSSS	SPEISES
EEIPSTT	PETITES
	PETTIES
EEIPSTW	PEEWITS
EEIQRRU	QUERIER
	REQUIRE
EEIQRSU	ESQUIRE
	QUERIES
EEIQRTU	QUIETER
	REQUITE
EEIQSTU	EQUITES
EEIRRRT	RETIRER
	TERRIER
EEIRRSS	RERISES
	SERRIES
	SIRREES
EEIRRST	ETRIERS
	REITERS
	RESTIER
	RETIRES
	RETRIES
	TERRIES
EEIRRSV	REIVERS
	REVERSI
	REVISER
	RIEVERS
EEIRRSW	REWIRES
EEIRRTV	RIVERET
	RIVETER
EEIRRTW	REWRITE
EEIRRVV	REVIVER
EEIRSSS	SEISERS
EEIRSST	RESITES
EEIRSSU	REISSUE
	SEISURE
EEIRSSV	IVRESSE
	REVISES
EEIRSSZ	RESIZES
	SEIZERS
EEIRSTT	TESTIER
EEIRSTU	SUETIER
EEIRSTV	RESTIVE
	SIEVERT
	STIEVER
	VERIEST
	VERITES
EEIRSTW	STEWIER
EEIRSTZ	ZESTIER
EEIRSUZ	SEIZURE
EEIRSVV	REVIVES
EEIRSVW	REVIEWS
	VIEWERS
EEIRTVV	VETIVER
EEISSSV	ESSIVES
EEISSTV	VITESSE
EEISSTX	SEXIEST
EEISTVX	VITEXES
EEITUXZ	ZEUXITE
EEJKRRS	JERKERS
EEJLLMU	JUMELLE
EEJLRWY	JEWELRY
EEJNNST	JENNETS
EEJNOOR	REJONEO
EEJNORS	REJONES
EEJNORY	ENJOYER
	REENJOY
EEJNOSS	JONESES
EEJORST	RESOJET
EEJPRRU	PERJURE
EEJQRRU	JERQUER
EEJQRSU	JERQUES
EEJRSST	JESTERS
EEJRSSY	JERSEYS
EEKKOTV	VETKOEK
EEKKRRT	TREKKER
EEKKSSY	KEKSYES
EEKLLNV	KNEVELL
EEKLLSY	SLEEKLY
EEKLLUU	UKULELE
EEKLMPS	KEMPLES
EEKLMRZ	KLEZMER
EEKLNNS	KENNELS
EEKLNOS	KEELSON
EEKLNRS	KERNELS
EEKLPRS	KELPERS
EEKLRST	KELTERS
	KESTREL
	SKELTER
EEKLSSY	KEYLESS
EEKLSTT	KETTLES
EEKMNOS	SOKEMEN
EEKMPRS	KEMPERS
EEKMRSS	KERMESS
EEKNNRS	KENNERS
EEKNNST	KENNETS
EEKNORW	REWOKEN
EEKNOSS	KENOSES
EEKNOST	KETONES
EEKNOTY	KEYNOTE
EEKNRSS	SKREENS
EEKNSST	KNESSET
EEKNSTU	NETSUKE
EEKOPRS	RESPOKE
EEKOPTU	OUTKEEP
EEKORRV	REVOKER
EEKORST	RESTOKE
EEKORSV	EVOKERS
	REVOKES
EEKOSSS	SEKOSES
EEKOSST	KETOSES
EEKPPSU	UPKEEPS
EEKPRRS	REPERKS
EEKPRSU	PERUKES
EEKRRUZ	KREUZER
EEKRSST	STREEKS
EEKRSSU	RESKUES
EEKRSSW	RESKEWS
	SKEWERS
EEKRSSY	KERSEYS
EEKRSTY	KEYSTER
EEKSSTW	SKEWEST
EEKSSTY	KEYSETS
EELLLVY	LEVELLY
EELLMOR	MORELLE
EELLMRS	MERELLS
	SMELLER
EELLMRV	VERMELL
EELLNOV	NOVELLE
EELLNRS	SNELLER
EELLNST	TELLENS
EELLNSW	NEWELLS
EELLNUV	UNLEVEL
EELLOPS	POLLEES
EELLORS	ROSELLE
EELLORZ	ROZELLE
EELLPRS	PRESELL
	RESPELL
	SPELLER
EELLPST	PELLETS
EELLQRU	QUELLER
EELLRSS	RESELLS
	SELLERS
EELLRST	RETELLS
	TELLERS
EELLRSU	RUELLES
EELLRSW	SWELLER
EELLRSY	YELLERS
EELLSTV	VELLETS
EELMMOP	POMMELE
EELMMPU	EMPLUME
EELMNNS	LENSMEN
EELMNOO	OENOMEL
EELMOPR	PLEROME
EELMOPT	LEPTOME
EELMOPY	EMPLOYE
EELMORW	EELWORM
EELMOST	OMELETS
	TELOMES
EELMPRS	SEMPLER
EELMPST	PELMETS
	STEMPEL
	STEMPLE
	TEMPLES
EELMPTT	TEMPLET
EELMRST	MELTERS
	REMELTS
	RESMELT
	SMELTER
EELMRSU	LEMURES
	RELUMES
EELMRSW	MEWLERS
EELMSST	TELESMS
EELMSTT	METTLES
	STEMLET
EELNNSV	VENNELS
EELNOPV	ENVELOP
EELNOPY	POLYENE
EELNOSV	ELEVONS
EELNOSY	ESLOYNE
EELNOTT	NOTELET
EELNOTU	TOLUENE

EELNPSS	PENSELS
	SPLEENS
EELNPST	PENTELS
EELNPSY	SPLEENY
EELNQUY	QUEENLY
EELNRST	NESTLER
	RELENTS
	SLENTER
EELNRSU	UNREELS
EELNRTT	LETTERN
	NETTLER
EELNRUV	NERVULE
EELNSSS	LESSENS
EELNSST	NESTLES
	NETLESS
EELNSSU	UNSEELS
EELNSTT	NETTLES
	TELNETS
EELNSTU	ELUENTS
	UNSTEEL
EELNSTY	ENSTYLE
	TENSELY
EELNSUV	VENULES
EELNSXY	XYLENES
EELNTTU	LUNETTE
EELOPPR	PEOPLER
EELOPPS	PEOPLES
EELOPRS	ELOPERS
	LEPROSE
EELOPRX	EXPLORE
EELOPSS	ELOPSES
EELOPTU	EELPOUT
EELORSS	RESOLES
EELORST	SOLERET
EELORSV	RESOLVE
EELORSY	EROSELY
EELORTT	LORETTE
EELORTV	OVERLET
EELORVV	EVOLVER
	REVOLVE
EELOSSS	LOESSES
EELOSST	OSSELET
	TELOSES
	TOELESS
EELOSTT	TELEOST
EELOSUV	EVOLUES
EELOSVV	EVOLVES
EELOTUV	EVOLUTE
	VELOUTE
EELPPRX	PERPLEX
EELPPSU	PEEPULS
EELPQRU	PREQUEL
EELPRST	PELTERS
	PETRELS
	RESPELT
	SPELTER
EELPRSU	REPULSE
EELPRSY	SLEEPRY
	YELPERS
EELPRTY	PEYTREL
EELPRTZ	PRETZEL
EELPRUX	PLEXURE
EELPRVY	REPLEVY
EELPSST	PESTLES
EELPSTT	PETTLES
EELPSTY	STEEPLY
EELPSUX	EXPULSE
EELQRUY	QUEERLY
EELQSSU	SEQUELS
EELRRSV	VERRELS
EELRRVY	REVELRY
EELRSST	STREELS
	TRESSEL
EELRSSU	RULESSE
EELRSTT	LETTERS
	LETTRES
	SETTLER
	STERLET
	TRESTLE
EELRSTV	SVELTER
EELRSTW	SWELTER
	WELTERS
	WRESTLE
EELRSTY	RESTYLE
	TERSELY
EELRSTZ	SELTZER
EELRSUV	VELURES
EELRSVV	VERVELS
EELSSSU	USELESS
EELSSSV	VESSELS
EELSSSX	SEXLESS
EELSSTT	SETTLES
EELSSTU	SETULES
EELSSUV	EVULSES
EELSTUY	EUSTYLE
EELSTVV	VELVETS
EELSTVW	TWELVES
EELSTWY	SWEETLY
EELTVVY	VELVETY
EEMMNOT	MEMENTO
EEMMNSS	MESSMEN
EEMMORS	MEROMES
EEMMOSU	MOUSMEE
EEMMOSV	EMMOVES
EEMMRST	STEMMER
EEMMSSS	SEMSEMS
EEMMSST	STEMMES
EEMNNOV	ENVENOM
EEMNNSW	NEWSMEN
EEMNOOS	SOMEONE
EEMNOOY	MOONEYE
EEMNOPR	REPOMEN
EEMNORS	MOREENS
EEMNORV	OVERMEN
	VENOMER
EEMNORY	MONEYER
EEMNOST	TEMENOS
	TONEMES
EEMNOSV	ENMOVES
EEMNPRU	PREMUNE
EEMNPTU	UMPTEEN
EEMNRTU	TRUEMEN
EEMNSYZ	ENZYMES
EEMOOSW	WOESOME
EEMOPRR	EMPEROR
EEMOPRT	TEMPORE
EEMOPRV	PREMOVE
EEMOPRW	EMPOWER
EEMOPST	METOPES
EEMORRS	REMORSE
	ROEMERS
EEMORRT	REMOTER
EEMORRU	UROMERE
EEMORRV	REMOVER
EEMORST	EMOTERS
	METEORS
	REMOTES
EEMORSV	REMOVES
EEMOSST	MESTESO
EEMOTTZ	MOZETTE
EEMPPRT	PREEMPT
EEMPRRT	PRETERM
EEMPRSS	EMPRESS
EEMPRST	TEMPERS
EEMPRSU	PRESUME
	SUPREME
EEMPRTT	TEMPTER
EEMPRTU	PERMUTE
EEMPSSU	EMPUSES
EEMPSTT	TEMPEST
EEMPSTX	EXEMPTS
EEMRRST	TERMERS
EEMRRSU	RESUMER
EEMRRUU	REMUEUR
EEMRSST	RESTEMS
EEMRSSU	RESUMES
EEMRSUX	MUREXES
EEMSSSU	SMEUSES
EEMSSTU	MUSTEES
EEMSTTU	MUSETTE
EENNORT	ENTERON
	TENONER
EENNORU	NEURONE
EENNOSS	ONENESS
EENNOSZ	ENZONES
EENNOTT	NONETTE
EENNOTY	NEOTENY
EENNPRS	PENNERS
EENNQUU	UNQUEEN
EENNRST	RENNETS
	TENNERS
EENNRUV	UNNERVE
EENNSST	SENNETS
EENNSSU	UNSEENS
	UNSENSE
EENNSSW	NEWNESS
EENOPPR	PREPONE
	PROPENE
EENOPPT	PEPTONE
EENOPRS	OPENERS
	PERONES
	REOPENS
	REPONES
EENOPST	OPENEST
	PENTOSE
	POSTEEN
	POTEENS
EENOPTT	POTTEEN
EENOPTY	NEOTYPE
EENORRV	OVERREN
EENORSS	SENORES
EENORST	ESTRONE
EENORSY	ONEYERS
	ONEYRES
EENORSZ	REZONES
EENORTV	OVERNET
EENORVW	OVERNEW
	REWOVEN
EENOSSW	WOENESS
EENOSSY	ESSOYNE
	NOYESES
EENOSTU	OUTSEEN
EENOSTV	VENTOSE
	VOTEENS
EENOSTW	TOWNEES
EENOSVZ	EVZONES
EENOTTT	TONETTE
EENPPRT	PERPENT
EENPRST	PENSTER
	PRESENT
	REPENTS
	SERPENT
EENPRSY	PYRENES
EENPRTV	PREVENT
EENPSSS	SPENSES
EENPSTU	PUNTEES
EENPSTW	ENSWEPT
EENPSTY	STEPNEY
EENQSTU	SEQUENT
EENRRST	RENTERS
	STERNER
EENRRSU	ENSURER
EENRRSV	NERVERS
EENRRTY	REENTRY
EENRRUV	NERVURE
EENRSST	NESTERS
	RENESTS
	RESENTS
	STRENES
EENRSSU	ENSURES
EENRSTT	NETTERS
	TENTERS
	TESTERN
EENRSTU	NEUTERS
	RETUNES
	TENURES
	TUREENS
EENRSTV	VENTERS
	VENTRES
EENRSTW	WESTERN
EENRSTX	EXTERNS
EENRSTY	STYRENE
	YESTERN
EENRSVV	VERVENS
EENRTUV	VENTURE
EENSSST	SETNESS
EENSSSY	SYNESES
EENSSTT	TENSEST
EENSSTV	STEVENS
EENSSTW	WETNESS
EENSSUV	VENUSES
EENSSUX	NEXUSES
	UNSEXES
EENSSVW	SWEVENS
EENSTTX	EXTENTS
EENSTTY	TEENTSY
EENSTUW	UNSWEET
EENSTVY	SEVENTY
EEOOPRS	OPEROSE
EEOOSTT	TOETOES
EEOPPRS	PREPOSE
EEOPPTU	OUTPEEP
EEOPRRS	REPOSER
EEOPRRV	REPROVE
EEOPRRW	REPOWER
EEOPRSS	REPOSES
EEOPRSX	EXPOSER
EEOPRTT	PROETTE
	TREETOP
EEOPRTU	OUTPEER
EEOPSSS	SPEOSES
EEOPSST	POETESS
EEOPSSU	ESPOUSE
	POSEUSE
EEOPSSX	EXPOSES
EEOPSTU	TOUPEES
EEOPSTY	EYESPOT
	PEYOTES
EEOPTUW	OUTWEEP
EEOQRTU	REQUOTE
EEORRST	RESTORE
EEORRSV	REVERSO
EEORRTU	REROUTE
EEORRTV	EVERTOR
EEORRTW	REWROTE
EEORSST	OSSETER
	STEREOS
EEORSSX	SOREXES
	XEROSES
EEORSTT	ROSETTE
EEORSTV	ESTOVER
	OVERSET
	REVOTES
	VETOERS
EEORSTX	XEROTES
EEORSTY	ESOTERY
EEORSUV	OEUVRES
	OVERUSE
EEORSVW	OVERSEW
EEORSXX	XEROXES

EEORTUV	OUVERTE
EEORTVW	OVERWET
EEOSSSY	OYESSES
EEOSSTU	OUTSEES
EEPPPRS	PEPPERS
EEPPPRY	PEPPERY
EEPPRST	STEPPER
EEPPRTY	PRETYPE
EEPPSST	STEPPES
EEPPSTU	STEEPUP
EEPPSUW	UPSWEEP
EEPPSUY	EUPEPSY
EEPRRSS	PRESSER
	REPRESS
	SPERRES
EEPRRST	PRESTER
EEPRRSU	PERUSER
	REPURES
EEPRRSY	PREYERS
EEPRRTV	PERVERT
EEPRRVY	REPRYVE
EEPRSSS	PRESSES
	SPERSES
EEPRSST	PESTERS
	PRESETS
EEPRSSU	PERSUES
	PERUSES
EEPRSSV	VESPERS
EEPRSSW	SPEWERS
EEPRSSX	EXPRESS
EEPRSTT	PERTEST
	PETTERS
	PRETEST
EEPRSTU	PERTUSE
	REPUTES
EEPRSTW	PEWTERS
EEPRSTX	EXPERTS
	SEXPERT
EEPRSTY	RETYPES
EEPRSUV	PREVUES
EEPRTTX	PRETEXT
EEPSSTT	SEPTETS
EEPSTTU	PUTTEES
EEPSTTY	TYPESET
EEQRRUY	EQUERRY
EEQRSTU	QUESTER
	REQUEST
EEQRSUU	QUEUERS
EEQSSTU	QUEESTS
EEQSUYZ	SQUEEZY
EERRSST	RESTERS
EERRSSV	SERVERS
	VERSERS
EERRSTT	TERRETS
EERRSTU	URETERS
EERRSTV	REVERTS
EERRSTW	STREWER
	WRESTER
EERRSUV	REVEURS
EERRSVW	SWERVER
EERRSVY	SERVERY
EERRTTU	REUTTER
	UTTERER
EERRTTY	RETTERY
EERSSST	TRESSES
EERSSTT	RETESTS
	SETTERS
	STREETS
	TERSEST
	TESTERS
EERSSTV	REVESTS
	STERVES
	VERSETS
	VERSTES
EERSSTW	STEWERS
	WESTERS
EERSSTX	EXSERTS
EERSSTZ	ZESTERS
EERSSUX	XERUSES
EERSSUY	SEYSURE
EERSSVW	SWERVES
EERSTTT	STRETTE
	TETTERS
EERSTTU	TRUSTEE
EERSTTV	TREVETS
EERSTTW	WETTERS
EERSTTY	STREETY
EERSTUV	VERSUTE
	VERTUES
	VESTURE
EERSTUY	TUYERES
EERSTVV	VERVETS
EERSTWY	TWYERES
EERSUVW	SURVEWE
EERTTUX	TEXTURE
EESSSTT	SESTETS
	TSETSES
EESSTTT	SESTETT
EESSTTU	SUTTEES
EESSTTX	SEXTETS
EESSTTY	STEYEST
EESSTTZ	TZETSES
EESTTTW	WETTEST
EESTTTX	SEXTETT
EESTTZZ	TZETZES
EFFFINO	INFEOFF
EFFFIRU	FUFFIER
EFFFOOR	FEOFFOR
EFFGIJN	JEFFING
EFFGINR	REFFING
EFFGIRS	GRIFFES
EFFGISU	GUFFIES
EFFGORS	GOFFERS
EFFGRRU	GRUFFER
EFFHILW	WHIFFLE
EFFHIRS	SHERIFF
EFFHIRU	HUFFIER
EFFHIRW	WHIFFER
EFFHITW	WHIFFET
EFFHLSU	SHUFFLE
EFFIIJS	JIFFIES
EFFIIMR	MIFFIER
EFFIINR	NIFFIER
EFFIIST	FIFTIES
	IFFIEST
	STIFFIE
EFFIKLS	SKIFFLE
EFFILLU	LIFEFUL
EFFILNO	OFFLINE
EFFILNS	SNIFFLE
EFFILPR	PIFFLER
EFFILPS	PIFFLES
EFFILRR	RIFFLER
EFFILRS	RIFFLES
EFFILRY	FIREFLY
EFFILSS	SIFFLES
EFFINRS	NIFFERS
	SNIFFER
EFFINST	INFEFTS
	STIFFEN
EFFIOPR	PIFFERO
EFFIORT	FORFEIT
	TOFFIER
EFFIORX	FOXFIRE
EFFIOST	TOFFIES
EFFIPRU	PUFFIER
EFFIRRT	TRIFFER
EFFIRST	RESTIFF
	STIFFER
EFFLMRU	MUFFLER
EFFLMSU	MUFFLES
EFFLNSU	SNUFFLE
EFFLOPS	POFFLES
EFFLOSU	SOUFFLE
EFFLRRU	RUFFLER
EFFLRSU	RUFFLES
EFFLRTU	FRETFUL
	TRUFFLE
EFFNRSU	SNUFFER
EFFNRUU	UNRUFFE
EFFOORR	OFFEROR
EFFOPRR	PROFFER
EFFOPSU	POUFFES
EFFORRT	TROFFER
EFFORST	EFFORTS
EFFOSST	OFFSETS
	SETOFFS
EFFPRSU	PUFFERS
EFFPRUY	PUFFERY
EFFRSSU	SUFFERS
EFFRSTU	RESTUFF
	STUFFER
	TRUFFES
EFFSSUU	SUFFUSE
EFFSTTU	TUFFETS
EFGGIOR	FOGGIER
EFGGIRR	FRIGGER
EFGGIRU	FUGGIER
EFGGIRY	FIGGERY
EFGGLOR	FLOGGER
EFGGORS	FOGGERS
EFGHIMS	GEMFISH
EFGHINT	HEFTING
EFGHIRT	FIGHTER
	FREIGHT
	REFIGHT
EFGIKNR	KERFING
EFGILLN	FELLING
EFGILMN	FLEMING
EFGILNR	FLINGER
EFGILNS	SELFING
EFGILNT	FELTING
EFGILNU	FUELING
EFGILNX	FLEXING
EFGILNY	FLEYING
EFGILRU	GULFIER
EFGIMNT	FIGMENT
EFGINNP	PFENNIG
EFGINNR	FERNING
EFGINOR	FOREIGN
EFGINRS	FINGERS
	FRINGES
EFGINRU	GUNFIRE
EFGINSS	FESSING
EFGINTT	FETTING
EFGINTW	WEFTING
EFGIOOR	GOOFIER
EFGIORV	FORGIVE
EFGIRRT	GRIFTER
EFGIRRU	FIGURER
EFGIRSU	FIGURES
EFGLLSU	FLUGELS
EFGLNSU	ENGULFS
EFGLNTU	FULGENT
EFGLORS	GOLFERS
EFGLORT	FROGLET
EFGLOSS	FOGLESS
EFGMNOR	FROGMEN
EFGNOOR	FORGONE
EFGNOSU	FUNGOES
EFGOORR	FORGOER
EFGOORS	FORGOES
EFGORRS	FORGERS
EFGORRU	FERRUGO
EFGORRY	FORGERY
EFGORST	FORGETS
EFGORSW	GOWFERS
EFGORTU	FOREGUT
EFHIINS	FINEISH
EFHIIRS	FISHIER
EFHIJSW	JEWFISH
EFHILMS	FLEMISH
	HIMSELF
EFHILSS	HISSELF
	SELFISH
EFHILST	LEFTISH
EFHILTY	HEFTILY
EFHINNS	FENNISH
EFHINST	FISHNET
EFHIRSS	FISHERS
	SERFISH
	SHERIFS
EFHIRST	SHIFTER
EFHIRSY	FISHERY
EFHISUW	HUSWIFE
EFHLLPU	HELPFUL
EFHLLSY	FLESHLY
EFHLNSU	UNFLESH
EFHLOOX	FOXHOLE
EFHLOPU	HOPEFUL
EFHLOSS	FLOSHES
EFHLRSU	FLUSHER
EFHLRSY	FRESHLY
EFHLSSU	FLUSHES
EFHLSTY	THYSELF
EFHLTTW	TWELFTH
EFHNORT	FORHENT
EFHOORS	HOOFERS
EFHORST	FOTHERS
EFHRRSU	FUHRERS
EFHRRTU	FURTHER
EFHRSSU	FRUSHES
EFIIKLN	FINLIKE
EFIIKST	FIKIEST
EFIILLS	FILLIES
EFIILMR	FILMIER
EFIILMS	MISFILE
EFIILRT	FIRELIT
	FITLIER
EFIILRY	FIERILY
EFIILSS	FISSILE
EFIIMRR	RIMFIRE
EFIIMRS	MISFIRE
EFIIMST	SEMIFIT
EFIINNR	FINNIER
EFIINPV	FIVEPIN
EFIINRT	NIFTIER
EFIINRU	UNIFIER
EFIINSS	FINISES
EFIINST	FINITES
	NIFTIES
EFIINSU	UNIFIES
EFIINSX	INFIXES
EFIIRRR	FIRRIER
EFIIRRT	RIFTIER
EFIIRST	FISTIER
EFIIRTW	WIFTIER
EFIIRZZ	FIZZIER
EFIISSV	FISSIVE
EFIJLLY	JELLIFY
EFIJLOR	FRIJOLE
EFIJLOT	JETFOIL
EFIKLOS	FOLKIES
EFIKLOX	FOXLIKE
EFIKLRU	FLUKIER
EFIKNRS	KNIFERS
EFIKNRU	FUNKIER
EFIKORR	FORKIER
EFIKRRS	FRISKER
EFIKRST	FRISKET

EFILLMS	MISFELL
EFILLOO	FOLIOLE
EFILLOS	FOLLIES
EFILLOW	LOWLIFE
EFILLRR	FRILLER
EFILLRS	FILLERS
	REFILLS
EFILLST	FILLETS
EFILLUW	WILEFUL
EFILMNT	LIFTMEN
EFILMNU	FULMINE
EFILMOT	FILEMOT
EFILMRS	FILMERS
	REFILMS
EFILMSS	SELFISM
EFILMST	FILMSET
	LEFTISM
EFILNNO	NONLIFE
EFILNOS	OLEFINS
EFILNOX	FLEXION
EFILNSS	FINLESS
EFILOOS	FLOOSIE
	FOLIOSE
EFILOOZ	FLOOZIE
EFILOPR	PROFILE
EFILORR	FLORIER
EFILORT	LOFTIER
	TREFOIL
EFILOSS	FLOSSIE
EFILOSX	SEXFOIL
EFILPPR	FLIPPER
EFILPPS	FIPPLES
EFILPPU	PIPEFUL
EFILPRS	PILFERS
EFILPRY	PILFERY
EFILQUY	LIQUEFY
EFILRRS	RIFLERS
EFILRRT	FLIRTER
	TRIFLER
EFILRRY	RIFLERY
EFILRST	FILTERS
	LIFTERS
	STIFLER
	TRIFLES
EFILRTT	FLITTER
EFILRTU	FLUTIER
	FUTILER
EFILRTY	FLYTIER
EFILRVV	FLIVVER
EFILRZZ	FRIZZLE
EFILSSS	FISSLES
EFILSST	SELFIST
	STIFLES
EFILSTT	LEFTIST
EFILSTU	FLUIEST
	SULFITE
EFILSZZ	FIZZLES
EFILUVX	FLUXIVE
EFIMMRU	FERMIUM
EFIMNOR	FERMION
EFIMNTT	FITMENT
EFIMOST	FOMITES
EFIMRRS	FIRMERS
EFIMRST	FIRMEST
	FREMITS
EFIMRTY	METRIFY
EFIMSTU	FUMIEST
EFIMTTU	FUMETTI
EFINNOR	INFERNO
EFINNRS	FINNERS
EFINNRU	FUNNIER
EFINNSU	FUNNIES
EFINOPR	FORPINE
EFINRST	SNIFTER
EFINRSU	INFUSER
EFINRUY	REUNIFY
EFINSST	FITNESS
	INFESTS
EFINSSU	INFUSES
EFINSUX	UNFIXES
EFINSZZ	FIZZENS
EFIOOPR	POOFIER
EFIOORR	ROOFIER
EFIOORT	FOOTIER
EFIOORW	WOOFIER
EFIOOST	FOOTIES
	FOOTSIE
EFIOPRR	PORIFER
EFIOPRT	FIREPOT
	PIEFORT
EFIORRT	ROTIFER
EFIORRW	FROWIER
EFIORSS	FROISES
EFIORST	FOISTER
	FORTIES
EFIORTU	OUTFIRE
EFIOSST	SOFTIES
EFIOSTX	FOXIEST
EFIOSTZ	FOZIEST
EFIPPRR	FRIPPER
EFIPRST	PRESIFT
EFIPRTY	PETRIFY
EFIRRRU	FURRIER
EFIRRSU	FRISEUR
	FRISURE
	FURRIES
	SURFIER
EFIRRSZ	FRIZERS
EFIRRTT	FRITTER
EFIRRTU	FRITURE
	FRUITER
	TURFIER
EFIRRTY	TERRIFY
EFIRRUZ	FURZIER
EFIRRZZ	FRIZZER
EFIRSST	RESIFTS
	SIFTERS
	STRIFES
EFIRSSU	FISSURE
	FUSSIER
	SURFIES
EFIRSTT	FITTERS
	TITFERS
EFIRSTU	FUSTIER
	SURFEIT
EFIRSTW	SWIFTER
EFIRSTZ	FRITZES
EFIRSUX	FIXURES
EFIRSVY	VERSIFY
EFIRSZZ	FIZZERS
	FRIZZES
EFIRTTU	TUFTIER
	TURFITE
EFIRTUV	FURTIVE
EFIRTUX	FIXTURE
EFIRUZZ	FUZZIER
EFISTTT	FITTEST
EFISTTY	TESTIFY
EFJLSTU	JESTFUL
EFKLMNO	MENFOLK
EFKLMOR	MERFOLK
EFKLNRU	FLUNKER
EFKLNUY	FLUNKEY
EFKLOPU	POKEFUL
EFKLPSU	SKEPFUL
EFKNRSU	FUNKERS
EFKORRS	FORKERS
EFLLOST	FLOTELS
EFLLOSW	FELLOWS
EFLLRSU	FULLERS
EFLLRUY	FULLERY
EFLLSSY	FLYLESS
EFLLSTU	FULLEST
EFLMOSU	FULSOME
EFLMPRU	FRUMPLE
EFLMSUU	MUSEFUL
EFLNNOS	NONSELF
EFLNNOU	NONFUEL
EFLNNSU	FUNNELS
EFLNORT	FORLENT
EFLNORU	FLEURON
EFLNORW	REFLOWN
EFLNORY	FELONRY
EFLNOSU	SULFONE
EFLNOTT	FLETTON
	FONTLET
EFLNPSU	PENFULS
EFLNSSU	FULNESS
	UNSELFS
EFLNSTU	FLUENTS
	NESTFUL
	NETFULS
EFLNSUY	SYNFUEL
EFLNTTU	TENTFUL
EFLNTUU	TUNEFUL
EFLOORR	FLOORER
	FORLORE
EFLOORS	FORSLOE
EFLOORT	FOOTLER
EFLOORY	FOOLERY
EFLOORZ	FOOZLER
EFLOOST	FOOTLES
EFLOOSZ	FOOZLES
EFLOPPR	FLOPPER
EFLORRS	ROLFERS
EFLORST	FLORETS
	LOFTERS
EFLORSU	FUROLES
	OURSELF
EFLORSW	FLOWERS
	FOWLERS
	REFLOWS
	WOLFERS
EFLORSX	FLEXORS
EFLORTT	FORTLET
EFLORTU	FLOUTER
EFLORTW	FELWORT
EFLORVY	FLYOVER
	OVERFLY
EFLORWW	WERWOLF
EFLORWY	FLOWERY
EFLOSSS	FLOSSES
EFLOSSU	FLOUSES
EFLOSTU	FOULEST
EFLOTTU	OUTFELT
EFLOTUW	OUTFLEW
EFLPRSU	PURFLES
EFLPRUY	PREYFUL
EFLPSTU	PESTFUL
EFLRRSU	FURLERS
EFLRSSU	FURLESS
EFLRSTU	FLUSTER
	FLUTERS
	RESTFUL
EFLRTTU	FLUTTER
EFLSTUZ	ZESTFUL
EFLSUZZ	FUZZLES
EFMNOOT	FOOTMEN
EFMNORS	ENFORMS
EFMNOST	FOMENTS
EFMNRSU	FRENUMS
	SURFMEN
EFMNRTU	TURFMEN
EFMOORZ	ZOEFORM
EFMOPRR	PERFORM
	PREFORM
EFMOPRT	POMFRET
EFMORRS	FORMERS
	REFORMS
EFMOTTU	FUMETTO
EFMPRUY	PERFUMY
EFMRRSU	FERRUMS
EFMRTUY	FURMETY
EFNNORT	FORNENT
EFNNORU	FENURON
EFNNOTU	UNOFTEN
EFNNSTU	FUNNEST
EFNOOST	EFTSOON
	FESTOON
EFNORRT	FRONTER
	REFRONT
EFNORRU	FORERUN
EFNORRW	FROWNER
EFNORST	FRONTES
EFNORTU	FORTUNE
EFNORTW	FORWENT
EFNORUZ	UNFROZE
EFNOSST	SOFTENS
EFNRSTU	FUNSTER
EFOOPRR	PROOFER
	REPROOF
EFOOPRS	SPOOFER
EFOOPRT	FORETOP
	POOFTER
EFOORRS	REROOFS
	ROOFERS
EFOORST	FOETORS
	FOOTERS
	REFOOTS
EFOORSW	WOOFERS
EFOORTW	WOOFTER
EFOPPRY	FOPPERY
EFOPRSS	PROFESS
EFOPRST	FORPETS
EFOPRSU	PROFUSE
EFOPRTU	POUFTER
EFOPRTY	TORPEFY
EFORRSU	FERROUS
	FURORES
EFORRSV	FERVORS
EFORRTY	TORREFY
EFORRUV	FERVOUR
EFORSST	FORESTS
	FOSTERS
EFORSSU	FOURSES
EFORSTU	FOUTERS
	FOUTRES
EFORSTW	TWOFERS
EFOSSTT	SOFTEST
EFOSTWW	WOWFEST
EFPRTUY	PUTREFY
EFPSTUY	STUPEFY
EFRRSSU	SURFERS
EFRRSTU	RETURFS
EFRRSUU	FUREURS
EFRSSSU	FUSSERS
EFRSTTU	TUFTERS
EFRSTUU	FUTURES
EFSSTTU	FUSTETS
EGGGILN	LEGGING
EGGGILR	GIGGLER
EGGGILS	GIGGLES
EGGGINP	PEGGING
EGGGINV	VEGGING
EGGGLOR	GOGGLER
EGGGLOS	GOGGLES
EGGGLSU	GUGGLES
EGGGNOS	EGGNOGS
EGGHILR	HIGGLER
EGGHILS	HIGGLES

EGGHINP	PEGHING
EGGHIRT	THIGGER
EGGHLOS	SHOGGLE
EGGHORS	HOGGERS
EGGHORY	HOGGERY
EGGHOST	HOGGETS
EGGHRSU	HUGGERS
EGGIILN	GINGELI
EGGIILS	GILGIES
EGGIINS	SIEGING
EGGIIPR	PIGGIER
EGGIIPS	PIGGIES
EGGIIRW	WIGGIER
EGGIJLS	JIGGLES
EGGIJRS	JIGGERS
EGGIKLN	KEGLING
EGGILLN	GELLING
EGGILMS	LEGGISM
	MIGGLES
EGGILNN	LENGING
EGGILNR	NIGGLER
EGGILNS	GINGLES
	LEGGINS
	NIGGLES
	SNIGGLE
EGGILNU	GLUEING
	LUGEING
EGGILNY	GINGELY
	GLEYING
EGGILOR	LOGGIER
EGGILRS	LIGGERS
EGGILRW	WIGGLER
	WRIGGLE
EGGILST	GIGLETS
EGGILSU	LUGGIES
EGGILSW	WIGGLES
EGGIMMN	GEMMING
EGGIMNN	MENGING
EGGIMNR	GERMING
	MERGING
EGGIMOS	MOGGIES
EGGIMRU	MUGGIER
EGGINNR	GERNING
EGGINNS	GINSENG
EGGINNV	VENGING
EGGINRS	GINGERS
	NIGGERS
	SERGING
	SNIGGER
EGGINRU	GRUEING
	GUNGIER
EGGINRV	VERGING
EGGINRW	GREWING
EGGINRY	GINGERY
	GREYING
	NIGGERY
EGGINSS	GESSING
EGGINTT	GETTING
EGGINTW	TWIGGEN
EGGIORS	SOGGIER
EGGIPRR	PRIGGER
EGGIPRU	PUGGIER
EGGIPRY	PIGGERY
EGGIPSU	PUGGIES
EGGIRRS	RIGGERS
EGGIRRT	TRIGGER
EGGIRRU	RUGGIER
EGGIRSW	SWIGGER
EGGIRTW	TWIGGER
EGGIRUV	VUGGIER
EGGIRWY	WIGGERY
EGGJLOR	JOGGLER
EGGJLOS	JOGGLES
EGGJLRU	JUGGLER
EGGJLSU	JUGGLES
EGGJORS	JOGGERS
EGGLMSU	SMUGGLE
EGGLNOS	LEGONGS
EGGLNSU	SNUGGLE
EGGLOOS	GOOGLES
EGGLOOY	GEOLOGY
EGGLORS	LOGGERS
	SLOGGER
EGGLORT	TOGGLER
EGGLOST	GOGLETS
	LOGGETS
	TOGGLES
EGGLOSW	WOGGLES
EGGLPRU	PLUGGER
EGGLPSU	PUGGLES
EGGLRSU	GURGLES
	LUGGERS
	SLUGGER
EGGLRTU	GURGLET
EGGLSTU	GUGLETS
EGGMRSU	MUGGERS
	SMUGGER
EGGNOOY	GEOGONY
EGGNRSU	GRUNGES
	SNUGGER
EGGNSTU	NUGGETS
EGGNTUY	NUGGETY
EGGOPRR	PROGGER
EGGORRS	GORGERS
EGGORST	GORGETS
EGGORSU	GOUGERS
EGGORTY	TOGGERY
EGGPRUY	PUGGERY
EGGRRSU	RUGGERS
EGGRSTU	TUGGERS
EGGSSTU	SUGGEST
EGHHHIT	HEIGHTH
EGHHIMN	HIGHMEN
EGHHIRS	HIGHERS
EGHHIST	EIGHTHS
	HEIGHTS
	HIGHEST
EGHHOSW	SHOWGHE
EGHHSSU	SHEUGHS
EGHHSUW	WHEUGHS
EGHIILL	GHILLIE
EGHIILN	HEILING
EGHIINR	HEIRING
EGHIINT	NIGHTIE
EGHIINV	INVEIGH
EGHIKLO	HOGLIKE
EGHIKNR	GHERKIN
EGHIKRS	SKREIGH
	SKRIEGH
EGHILLN	HELLING
EGHILMN	HELMING
EGHILMP	MEGILPH
EGHILNP	HELPING
EGHILNR	HERLING
EGHILNS	ENGLISH
	SHINGLE
EGHILNT	ENLIGHT
	LIGHTEN
EGHILNV	HELVING
EGHILOU	GHOULIE
EGHILPT	PIGHTLE
EGHILRT	LIGHTER
	RELIGHT
EGHILSS	SLEIGHS
EGHILST	SLEIGHT
EGHIMMN	HEMMING
EGHIMNS	MESHING
EGHIMNT	THEMING
EGHIMPT	EMPIGHT
EGHINNN	HENNING
EGHINNT	HENTING
EGHINNU	UNHINGE
EGHINOS	SHOEING
EGHINPS	HESPING
	PHESING
EGHINRR	HERRING
EGHINRS	HINGERS
EGHINRT	RIGHTEN
EGHINRW	WHINGER
EGHINRY	HERYING
EGHINST	NIGHEST
EGHINSW	HEWINGS
	SHEWING
	WHINGES
EGHINSX	HEXINGS
EGHINTT	TIGHTEN
EGHINWW	WHEWING
EGHIOOS	SHOOGIE
EGHIOPS	PISHOGE
EGHIORS	OGREISH
EGHIORU	ROUGHIE
EGHIOST	HOGTIES
EGHIOTT	GOTHITE
EGHIOTU	TOUGHIE
EGHIOTV	EIGHTVO
EGHIRRT	RIGHTER
EGHIRSS	GIRSHES
	SIGHERS
EGHIRST	RESIGHT
	SIGHTER
EGHIRSU	GRUSHIE
	GUSHIER
EGHIRSY	GREYISH
EGHIRTT	TIGHTER
EGHISTW	WEIGHTS
EGHISTY	HYGEIST
EGHITWY	WEIGHTY
EGHLLOU	LUGHOLE
EGHLMPS	PHLEGMS
EGHLMPY	PHLEGMY
EGHLNOR	LEGHORN
EGHLNPU	ENGULPH
EGHLNST	LENGTHS
EGHLNTY	LENGTHY
	THEGNLY
EGHLOOS	GOLOSHE
	SHOOGLE
EGHLOOT	THEOLOG
EGHLOSS	SEGHOLS
EGHLPSU	PLEUGHS
EGHLTUY	TEUGHLY
EGHMMOS	MEGOHMS
EGHMNOU	HUMOGEN
EGHMOSU	GUMSHOE
EGHNOOS	HOGNOSE
EGHNORS	GORHENS
EGHNORU	ENROUGH
	ROUGHEN
EGHNOSU	ENOUGHS
EGHNOTU	TOUGHEN
EGHNRSU	HUNGERS
EGHOPRS	GOPHERS
EGHORRU	ROUGHER
EGHORTU	TOUGHER
EGHOSTT	GHETTOS
EGHOSUU	HUGEOUS
EGHRSSU	GURSHES
	GUSHERS
EGHRTUY	THEURGY
EGIIJLS	JILGIES
EGIIKLP	PIGLIKE
EGIIKLW	WIGLIKE
EGIILLS	GILLIES
EGIILMT	LEGITIM
EGIILNR	LEIRING
	LINGIER
EGIILNS	SEILING
EGIILNT	LIGNITE
EGIILNV	VEILING
EGIILNX	EXILING
EGIILPS	GILPIES
EGIILRS	GIRLIES
EGIIMMS	GIMMIES
EGIIMNN	MEINING
EGIIMNP	IMPINGE
EGIIMNR	MINGIER
EGIIMNT	ITEMING
EGIIMNV	MIEVING
EGIIMPR	GIMPIER
EGIIMPS	PIGMIES
EGIIMRR	GRIMIER
EGIIMSV	MISGIVE
EGIINNP	PEINING
EGIINNR	GINNIER
	REINING
EGIINNS	INGINES
	INSIGNE
	SEINING
EGIINNV	VEINING
EGIINOP	EPIGONI
EGIINPS	PEISING
	PIGSNIE
EGIINPZ	PEIZING
EGIINRR	GIRNIER
EGIINRT	IGNITER
	TIERING
	TIGRINE
EGIINRV	REIVING
	RIEVING
EGIINRW	WEIRING
	WINGIER
EGIINRZ	ZINGIER
EGIINSS	SEISING
EGIINST	IGNITES
EGIINSV	SIEVING
	VISEING
EGIINSW	WEISING
EGIINSZ	SEIZING
EGIINTV	EVITING
EGIINTX	EXITING
EGIINVW	VIEWING
EGIINWZ	WEIZING
EGIIOPR	PIEROGI
EGIIPPS	GIPPIES
EGIIPRR	GRIPIER
EGIIPRW	PERIWIG
EGIIPSS	GIPSIES
EGIJKNR	JERKING
EGIJLLN	JELLING
EGIJLNR	JINGLER
EGIJLNS	JINGLES
EGIJLNT	JINGLET
EGIJNOS	JINGOES
EGIJNSS	JESSING
EGIJNST	JESTING
EGIJNTT	JETTING
EGIKKLN	LEKKING
EGIKLMU	GUMLIKE
EGIKLNP	KELPING
EGIKLNR	ERLKING
EGIKLNS	KINGLES
EGIKLNT	KINGLET
EGIKLNW	WELKING
EGIKLRS	KILERGS
EGIKLRU	RUGLIKE
EGIKLTU	GUTLIKE
EGIKMNP	KEMPING
EGIKNNN	KENNING
EGIKNNR	KERNING
EGIKNNT	KENTING

EGIKNOV	EVOKING
EGIKNPP	KEPPING
EGIKNPR	PERKING
EGIKNRV	KERVING
EGIKNRY	YERKING
EGIKNST	KESTING
EGIKNSW	SKEWING
EGIKNSY	YESKING
EGIKNUY	YEUKING
EGILLMN	MELLING
EGILLNO	LOGLINE
EGILLNS	LEGLINS
	LINGELS
	LINGLES
	SELLING
EGILLNT	GILLNET
	TELLING
EGILLNW	WELLING
EGILLNY	YELLING
EGILLOS	GOLLIES
EGILLRR	GRILLER
EGILLRS	GILLERS
	GRILLES
EGILLST	GILLETS
EGILLSU	GULLIES
	LIGULES
EGILMMN	LEMMING
EGILMMR	GLIMMER
EGILMMY	GEMMILY
EGILMNR	GREMLIN
	MERLING
	MINGLER
EGILMNS	MINGLES
EGILMNT	MELTING
EGILMNU	EMULING
	LEGUMIN
EGILMNW	MEWLING
EGILMNY	YELMING
EGILMOR	GOMERIL
EGILMOS	SEMILOG
EGILMOU	ELOGIUM
EGILMPS	GLIMPSE
	MEGILPS
EGILMST	GIMLETS
EGILNNS	GINNELS
	LENSING
EGILNOP	ELOPING
EGILNOS	ELOIGNS
	LEGIONS
	LIGNOSE
	LINGOES
	LONGIES
EGILNOT	LENTIGO
EGILNPP	LEPPING
EGILNPR	PINGLER
EGILNPS	PINGLES
	SPIGNEL
EGILNPT	PELTING
EGILNPY	YELPING
EGILNRS	GIRNELS
	LINGERS
	SLINGER
EGILNRT	RINGLET
	TINGLER
	TRINGLE
EGILNRY	RELYING
EGILNSS	SINGLES
EGILNST	GLISTEN
	LESTING
	SINGLET
	TINGLES
EGILNSU	LUNGIES
	SLUEING
EGILNSW	SLEWING
	SWINGLE
EGILNSZ	ZINGELS
EGILNTT	ETTLING
	LETTING
EGILNTU	ELUTING
EGILNTW	WELTING
	WINGLET
EGILNUY	GUYLINE
EGILNVY	LEVYING
EGILOOS	GOOLIES
	OLOGIES
EGILOPS	EPILOGS
EGILORS	GLOIRES
	GLORIES
EGILOSS	GLIOSES
EGILOST	ELOGIST
	LOGIEST
EGILOSU	OUGLIES
EGILPPR	GRIPPLE
EGILPRU	GULPIER
EGILPST	PIGLETS
EGILPSY	GILPEYS
EGILRRU	GURLIER
EGILRSS	GRILSES
EGILRST	GLISTER
	GRISTLE
EGILRSU	GUILERS
	LIGURES
	LURGIES
EGILRSY	GREISLY
	GRIESLY
	GRISELY
EGILRTT	GLITTER
EGILRTY	TIGERLY
EGILRUV	VIRGULE
EGILRZZ	GRIZZLE
EGILSST	LEGISTS
EGILSSW	WIGLESS
EGILSTU	GLUIEST
	UGLIEST
EGILSTW	WIGLETS
EGILSTZ	GLITZES
EGIMMRR	GRIMMER
EGIMMRS	GIMMERS
	MEGRIMS
EGIMMRU	GUMMIER
EGIMMTU	GUMMITE
EGIMNNN	NEMNING
EGIMNNO	OMENING
EGIMNNR	RINGMEN
EGIMNNS	MENSING
EGIMNNW	WINGMEN
EGIMNOS	MISGONE
EGIMNOT	EMOTING
	MITOGEN
EGIMNOU	MEOUING
EGIMNOV	EMOVING
EGIMNOW	MEOWING
EGIMNPR	GRIPMEN
	IMPREGN
	PERMING
EGIMNPT	PIGMENT
	TEMPING
EGIMNQU	QUEMING
EGIMNRS	GERMINS
EGIMNRT	METRING
	TERMING
EGIMNRU	EMURING
EGIMNSS	MESSING
EGIMNST	STEMING
	TEMSING
EGIMNSU	MEUSING
EGIMNSW	MEWSING
EGIMORR	GORMIER
EGIMORS	OGREISM
EGIMOSS	EGOISMS
	MISGOES
EGIMOST	EGOTISM
EGIMPSU	GUIMPES
EGIMPSY	PYGMIES
EGIMRSW	MISGREW
EGIMSST	STIGMES
EGINNNP	PENNING
EGINNNR	RENNING
EGINNNY	YENNING
EGINNOO	IONOGEN
EGINNOP	OPENING
EGINNOR	NEGRONI
EGINNPU	PENGUIN
EGINNRR	GRINNER
EGINNRS	ENRINGS
	GINNERS
EGINNRT	RENTING
	RINGENT
	TERNING
EGINNRU	ENURING
EGINNRV	NERVING
EGINNRY	GINNERY
	RENYING
EGINNSS	ENSIGNS
	SENSING
EGINNST	NESTING
	SENTING
	TENSING
EGINNSU	ENSUING
	GUNNIES
	INGENUS
EGINNSW	NEWSING
EGINNSY	GYNNIES
EGINNTT	NETTING
	TENTING
EGINNTV	VENTING
EGINNVY	ENVYING
EGINOOS	GOONIES
	ISOGONE
EGINOPR	PERIGON
	PIROGEN
	PONGIER
EGINOPS	EPIGONS
	PIGEONS
	PINGOES
EGINORR	IGNORER
EGINORS	ERINGOS
	IGNORES
	REGIONS
	SIGNORE
EGINORT	GENITOR
EGINORV	OVERING
EGINORZ	ZEROING
EGINOSU	IGNEOUS
EGINOSW	WIGEONS
EGINOSY	ISOGENY
EGINOTT	TENTIGO
EGINOTV	VETOING
EGINPPP	PEPPING
EGINPPR	REPPING
EGINPPS	PIGPENS
EGINPRS	PERSING
	PINGERS
	SPRINGE
EGINPRU	PUERING
EGINPRV	PERVING
	PREVING
EGINPRY	PREYING
EGINPSS	GIPSENS
EGINPSU	SPUEING
EGINPSW	SPEWING
EGINPSY	ESPYING
	PEYSING
	PIGSNEY
EGINPTT	PETTING
EGINPYY	EPIGYNY
EGINQUU	QUEUING
EGINRRS	ERRINGS
	GIRNERS
	RINGERS
	SERRING
EGINRRW	WRINGER
EGINRSS	INGRESS
	RESIGNS
	SIGNERS
	SINGERS
EGINRST	RESTING
	STINGER
EGINRSU	REUSING
	RUEINGS
	SIGNEUR
EGINRSV	SERVING
	VERSING
EGINRSW	SWINGER
	WINGERS
EGINRSY	SYRINGE
EGINRSZ	ZINGERS
EGINRTT	GITTERN
	RETTING
EGINRTU	TRUEING
EGINRTV	VERTING
EGINRTY	RETYING
EGINRVV	REVVING
EGINRVY	REVYING
EGINSST	INGESTS
	SIGNETS
EGINSSW	SEWINGS
	SWINGES
EGINSSY	YESSING
EGINSTT	SETTING
	TESTING
EGINSTU	GUNITES
EGINSTV	VESTING
EGINSTW	STEWING
	TWINGES
	WESTING
EGINSTZ	ZESTING
EGINSVX	VEXINGS
EGINSWY	SWEYING
EGINSZZ	GIZZENS
EGINTTV	VETTING
EGINTTW	WETTING
EGIOOPR	GOOPIER
EGIOORS	GOOSIER
EGIOOSS	GOOSIES
	SOOGIES
EGIOOST	GOOIEST
EGIOPRS	PORGIES
	SERPIGO
EGIOPRU	GROUPIE
	PIROGUE
EGIORRS	GORSIER
EGIORST	GOITERS
	GOITRES
	GORIEST
EGIORTU	GOUTIER
EGIORTV	VERTIGO
EGIORTZ	ZORGITE
EGIORUV	VOGUIER
EGIOSST	EGOISTS
	STOGIES
EGIOSTT	EGOTIST
EGIOSTV	VOGIEST
EGIOTUV	OUTGIVE
EGIPPRR	GRIPPER
EGIPPRS	GIPPERS
	GRIPPES
EGIPPSU	GUPPIES
EGIPPSY	GYPPIES
EGIPRRS	GRIPERS

EGIPRUU	GUIPURE
EGIPSSY	GYPSIES
EGIRRSU	GURRIES
	SURGIER
EGIRRSV	VIRGERS
EGIRRTT	GRITTER
EGIRSST	TIGRESS
EGIRSSU	GUISERS
EGIRSTU	GUSTIER
	GUTSIER
EGIRSTV	GRIVETS
EGIRSUZ	GUIZERS
EGIRTTU	GUTTIER
	TURGITE
EGISSSU	GUSSIES
EGISTTU	GUTTIES
EGJLNSU	JUNGLES
EGJLSTU	JUGLETS
EGJOSTT	GJETOST
EGKLORW	LEGWORK
EGKMSSU	MUSKEGS
EGKNOSY	KYOGENS
EGLLORS	GOLLERS
EGLLRSU	GULLERS
EGLLRUY	GULLERY
EGLLSTU	GULLETS
EGLLSUY	GULLEYS
EGLMMRU	GLUMMER
EGLMNOO	ENGLOOM
EGLMNOR	MONGREL
EGLMOOR	LEGROOM
EGLMSSU	GUMLESS
EGLNNSU	GUNNELS
EGLNOOY	ENOLOGY
	NEOLOGY
EGLNOPS	PLONGES
EGLNORS	LONGERS
EGLNORU	LOUNGER
EGLNOST	LONGEST
EGLNOSU	LOUNGES
EGLNOSY	LYSOGEN
EGLNOUV	UNGLOVE
EGLNOXY	LOXYGEN
	XYLOGEN
EGLNOYZ	LOZENGY
EGLNPRU	PLUNGER
EGLNPSU	PLUNGES
	PUNGLES
EGLNRSU	LUNGERS
EGLNRTU	GRUNTLE
EGLNSSU	GUNLESS
	GUNSELS
EGLNSTU	ENGLUTS
	GLUTENS
EGLNSUU	UNGLUES
EGLOORS	REGOSOL
EGLOOSY	GOOLEYS
EGLOPRS	PROLEGS
EGLOPSS	GOSPELS
EGLOPTU	GLUEPOT
EGLORRW	GROWLER
EGLORSS	GLOSSER
	REGLOSS
EGLORSU	REGULOS
EGLORSV	GLOVERS
	GROVELS
EGLORSW	GLOWERS
	REGLOWS
EGLOSSS	GLOSSES
EGLOSST	GOSLETS
EGLOSUV	VOULGES
EGLPRSU	GULPERS
	SPLURGE
EGLPRUY	GYPLURE
EGLRSTU	GURLETS
EGLRSUU	REGULUS
EGLRSUY	GUYLERS
EGLRSYY	GRYESLY
	GRYSELY
EGLRTTU	GUTTLER
EGLRUZZ	GUZZLER
EGLSSTU	GUTLESS
	TUGLESS
EGLSTTU	GUTTLES
EGLSTUU	GLUTEUS
EGLSUZZ	GUZZLES
EGMMORT	GROMMET
EGMMOSU	GUMMOSE
EGMMRRU	GRUMMER
EGMMRSU	GUMMERS
EGMMRTU	GRUMMET
EGMNNOS	SONGMEN
EGMNNOT	TONGMEN
EGMNNOW	GOWNMEN
EGMNOOS	MONGOES
EGMNORS	MONGERS
	MORGENS
EGMNORU	MURGEON
EGMNORY	MONGERY
EGMNOST	EMONGST
EGMNOSY	MYOGENS
EGMNOYZ	ZYMOGEN
EGMNSTU	NUTMEGS
EGMOORR	GROOMER
	REGROOM
EGMORST	GROMETS
EGMORSU	GRUMOSE
	MORGUES
EGMORTU	GOURMET
EGNNOOS	NONEGOS
EGNNORT	RONTGEN
EGNNOSU	GUENONS
EGNNPTU	PUNGENT
EGNNRSU	GUNNERS
EGNNRUY	GUNNERY
EGNNSYY	GYNNEYS
EGNNTUU	UNGUENT
EGNOOPS	PONGOES
EGNOORS	ORGONES
	OROGENS
EGNOORY	OROGENY
EGNOOST	GENTOOS
EGNOOSY	GOONEYS
EGNOOTU	OUTGONE
EGNOOYZ	ZOOGENY
EGNOPRS	PRESONG
	SPONGER
EGNOPRY	PROGENY
	PYROGEN
EGNOPSS	SPONGES
EGNOPSW	GOWPENS
EGNORRW	REGROWN
	WRONGER
EGNORSS	ENGROSS
EGNORST	TONGERS
EGNORSU	SURGEON
EGNORSV	GOVERNS
EGNORSY	ERYNGOS
	GROYNES
EGNORUY	YOUNGER
EGNOSSY	GONYSES
EGNOSTU	TONGUES
EGNOSXY	OXYGENS
EGNPRSU	REPUGNS
EGNPSSU	SPUNGES
EGNPSUX	EXPUGNS
EGNRRTU	GRUNTER
EGNRSTU	GUNTERS
	GURNETS
	SURGENT
EGNRSUY	GURNEYS
EGNRSYY	SYNERGY
EGNRTTU	GRUTTEN
	TURGENT
EGNSUVY	UNGYVES
EGOOPSY	POOGYES
EGOORRV	GROOVER
EGOORSV	GROOVES
EGOORSY	GOOSERY
EGOORTU	OUTGOER
EGOORTV	OVERGOT
EGOOSST	STOOGES
EGOOSSY	GOOSEYS
EGOOSTU	OUTGOES
EGOPRRS	GROPERS
EGOPRRU	GROUPER
	REGROUP
EGORRSS	GROSERS
	GROSSER
EGORRST	GROSERT
EGORRSU	GROUSER
EGORRSW	GROWERS
	REGROWS
EGORRTU	GROUTER
EGORRUY	ROGUERY
EGORSSS	GROSSES
EGORSST	GROSETS
	STORGES
EGORSSU	GROUSES
EGORSTV	GROVETS
EGORSUV	VOGUERS
EGORTUW	OUTGREW
EGOSSTU	GUSTOES
EGOSSTY	STOGEYS
EGOSSYZ	ZYGOSES
EGOSTTU	GOUTTES
EGOSTYZ	ZYGOTES
EGPPRSY	GYPPERS
EGPRRSU	PURGERS
EGPRSSU	SPURGES
EGPRSTY	GYPSTER
EGPRSUU	UPSURGE
EGRRSSU	SURGERS
EGRRSUY	SURGERY
EGRSSTU	GUTSERS
EGRSSUY	GYRUSES
EGRSTTU	GUTTERS
EGRSTUZ	GUTZERS
EGRTTUY	GUTTERY
EGSSSTU	GUSSETS
EHHIIMS	HEIMISH
EHHIKSS	SHEIKHS
EHHILLS	HELLISH
EHHIPRS	HERSHIP
EHHIRST	HITHERS
EHHIRSU	HUSHIER
EHHIRTT	THITHER
EHHIRTW	WHITHER
EHHISSW	WHISHES
EHHISWY	WHEYISH
EHHNPSY	HYPHENS
EHHOOSS	HOOSHES
EHHORTT	THOTHER
EHHRSSU	HUSHERS
EHHSSSU	SHUSHES
EHIIKLP	HIPLIKE
EHIILLR	HILLIER
EHIILNP	HIPLINE
EHIILTT	LITHITE
EHIIMSS	MEISHIS
EHIINNS	HINNIES
EHIINRS	SHINIER
EHIINRT	INHERIT
EHIINRW	WHINIER
EHIINRZ	RHIZINE
EHIINSS	SHINIES
EHIIPPR	HIPPIER
EHIIPPS	HIPPIES
EHIIPRT	PITHIER
EHIIRST	HIRSTIE
EHIIRTW	WHITIER
	WITHIER
EHIISSS	HISSIES
EHIISST	STISHIE
EHIISTW	WHITIES
	WITHIES
EHIJNNO	JOHNNIE
EHIKKRS	SHIKKER
EHIKKSS	KISHKES
EHIKLRU	HULKIER
EHIKLTU	HUTLIKE
EHIKLTY	LEKYTHI
EHIKMNT	METHINK
EHIKMSV	MIKVEHS
EHIKNOS	HONKIES
EHIKNRS	KERNISH
EHIKNRT	RETHINK
	THINKER
EHIKNRU	HUNKIER
EHIKNSS	KNISHES
EHIKNSU	HUNKIES
EHIKOOR	HOOKIER
EHIKOOS	HOOKIES
EHIKOST	HOKIEST
EHIKPRS	KEPHIRS
	PERKISH
EHIKRRS	SHIRKER
EHIKRSS	SHREIKS
	SHRIEKS
	SHRIKES
EHIKRSU	HUSKIER
EHIKRSW	WHISKER
EHIKRSY	SHRIEKY
EHIKSSS	SHIKSES
EHIKSSU	HUSKIES
EHIKSTW	WHISKET
EHIKSWY	WHISKEY
EHILLMN	HILLMEN
EHILLNO	HELLION
EHILLNS	INSHELL
EHILLOO	OILHOLE
EHILLOS	HILLOES
	HOLLIES
EHILLRS	HILLERS
	RELLISH
EHILLRT	THILLER
EHILLRU	HULLIER
EHILLTY	LITHELY
EHILMMO	MOHELIM
EHILMPW	WHIMPLE
EHILMSU	HELIUMS
	HUMLIES
	MUHLIES
EHILMTT	MELTITH
EHILMUW	UMWHILE
EHILNOP	PINHOLE
EHILNOT	HOTLINE
	NEOLITH
EHILNPS	PLENISH
EHILNSS	ELSHINS
EHILNTY	ETHINYL
EHILOOR	HOOLIER
EHILOPT	HOPLITE
EHILOSS	ISOHELS
EHILOST	EOLITHS
	HOLIEST
	HOSTILE
EHILPRS	HIRPLES
EHILPRT	PHILTER
	PHILTRE

EHILPSS	HIPLESS
EHILRRW	WHIRLER
EHILRSS	HIRSELS
	HIRSLES
EHILRST	SLITHER
EHILRSU	HURLIES
	LUSHIER
EHILRSV	SHRIVEL
EHILRTU	LUTHIER
EHILRTW	WHIRTLE
EHILSSS	SLISHES
EHILSST	HITLESS
EHILSTT	LISTETH
	LITHEST
	THISTLE
EHILSTV	THIVELS
EHILSTW	WHISTLE
EHILTTU	THULITE
EHILTTW	WHITTLE
EHILTWY	WHITELY
EHIMMRS	SHIMMER
EHIMMSY	SHIMMEY
EHIMNOS	HOMINES
EHIMNPS	SHIPMEN
EHIMNRS	MENHIRS
EHIMNRU	INHUMER
	RHENIUM
EHIMNSU	INHUMES
EHIMNTY	THYMINE
EHIMORS	HEROISM
	MOREISH
EHIMORT	MOITHER
	MOTHIER
EHIMORZ	RHIZOME
EHIMOST	HOMIEST
EHIMPPX	PEMPHIX
EHIMPRU	HUMPIER
EHIMPRW	WHIMPER
EHIMPSU	HUMPIES
EHIMRST	HERMITS
	MITHERS
EHIMRSU	HEURISM
	MUSHIER
EHIMRTY	MYTHIER
	THYMIER
EHIMSST	THEISMS
EHIMSTU	HUMITES
	TUMSHIE
EHIMSTY	MYTHISE
EHIMSWY	WHIMSEY
EHIMTYZ	MYTHIZE
EHINNNS	HENNINS
EHINNRT	THINNER
EHINNSS	SHINNES
EHINNSW	WENNISH
EHINNSY	SHINNEY
EHINOPR	PHONIER
EHINOPS	PHONIES
EHINOPX	PHOENIX
EHINORR	HORNIER
EHINORS	HEROINS
	INSHORE
EHINOST	ETHIONS
	HISTONE
EHINOSU	HEINOUS
EHINPPS	HIPPENS
	SHIPPEN
EHINPSS	HIPNESS
EHINRSS	SHINERS
	SHRINES
EHINRST	HINTERS
EHINRSV	SHRIVEN
EHINRSW	WHINERS
EHINRTV	THRIVEN
EHINRTW	WRITHEN
EHINRTZ	ZITHERN
EHINSSS	SHINESS
EHINSST	SITHENS
EHINSTW	WHITENS
EHINSTZ	ZENITHS
EHINSUV	UNHIVES
EHINTUW	UNWHITE
EHIOORT	HOOTIER
EHIOPPR	HOPPIER
EHIOPRS	ROSEHIP
EHIOPSS	SOPHIES
EHIOPST	ETHIOPS
	OPHITES
EHIORRS	HORSIER
EHIORRT	HERITOR
EHIORSS	HOSIERS
EHIORST	HERIOTS
	HOISTER
	SHORTIE
	TOSHIER
EHIORSU	HOUSIER
EHIORSW	SHOWIER
EHIORSY	HOSIERY
EHIORTT	THORITE
EHIORTU	OUTHIRE
	ROUTHIE
EHIORTV	OVERHIT
EHIOSTT	HOTTIES
EHIOSTY	ISOHYET
EHIPPRS	SHIPPER
EHIPPRW	WHIPPER
EHIPPST	HIPPEST
EHIPPTW	WHIPPET
EHIPRSS	RESHIPS
	SERIPHS
EHIPRST	HIPSTER
EHIPRSU	PUSHIER
EHIPRSW	WHISPER
EHIPSTT	PETTISH
EHIPSZZ	PHIZZES
EHIRRRU	HURRIER
EHIRRSS	SHERRIS
EHIRRSU	HURRIES
	RUSHIER
EHIRRSV	SHRIVER
EHIRRTV	THRIVER
EHIRRTW	WHIRRET
	WRITHER
EHIRSSS	HISSERS
EHIRSSV	SHIVERS
	SHRIVES
EHIRSSW	SWISHER
	WISHERS
EHIRSTT	HITTERS
	TITHERS
EHIRSTU	HIRSUTE
EHIRSTV	THRIVES
EHIRSTW	SWITHER
	WITHERS
	WRITHES
EHIRSTZ	ZITHERS
EHIRSVY	SHIVERY
EHIRTTW	WHITRET
	WHITTER
EHIRWZZ	WHIZZER
EHISSSU	HUSSIES
EHISSSW	SWISHES
	WHISSES
EHISSTT	THEISTS
EHISSTU	STUSHIE
	TUSHIES
EHISTTW	TEWHITS
	WETTISH
	WHITEST
EHISTWY	WHITEYS
EHISUZZ	HUZZIES
EHISWZZ	WHIZZES
EHJOPSS	JOSEPHS
EHJORSS	JOSHERS
EHKLNOS	LOKSHEN
EHKLOOT	HOOKLET
EHKLPST	KLEPHTS
EHKNORS	HONKERS
EHKNOSY	HONKEYS
EHKNRSU	HUNKERS
EHKNSSU	HUNKSES
EHKOORS	HOOKERS
EHKOOSY	HOOKEYS
EHKORSS	KOSHERS
EHKORSW	HOWKERS
EHKORSY	HORKEYS
EHKOSSS	SKOSHES
EHKRSSU	HUSKERS
EHKRSTU	TUSHKER
EHLLNSU	UNSHELL
EHLLOOS	HOLLOES
EHLLORS	HOLLERS
EHLLOSU	HULLOES
EHLLRSU	HULLERS
EHLMMOW	WHOMMLE
EHLMMSU	HUMMELS
EHLMMUW	WHUMMLE
EHLMNOT	MENTHOL
EHLMNOY	HOMELYN
EHLMNSU	UNHELMS
EHLMOOS	HOLESOM
EHLMOPS	PHLOEMS
EHLMSSU	MULSHES
EHLMSTY	METHYLS
EHLNOPS	PHENOLS
EHLNORT	HORNLET
EHLNPSY	PHENYLS
EHLNRTU	LUTHERN
EHLNTTY	TENTHLY
EHLNTYY	ETHYNYL
EHLOOPT	POTHOLE
EHLOOSS	SHOOLES
EHLOOSY	HOOLEYS
EHLOPPS	HOPPLES
EHLOPSX	PHLOXES
EHLOPSY	SPYHOLE
EHLORST	HOLSTER
	HOSTLER
EHLORSW	HOWLERS
EHLORTW	WHORTLE
EHLORTY	HELOTRY
EHLOSSS	SLOSHES
EHLOSST	HOSTELS
EHLOSSU	HOUSELS
EHLOSSV	SHOVELS
EHLOSTT	LOTHEST
	SHOTTLE
EHLOSTW	HOWLETS
	THOWELS
EHLOSTY	THYLOSE
EHLOTXY	ETHOXYL
EHLPPSS	SHLEPPS
EHLPRSU	PLUSHER
EHLPSSU	PLUSHES
EHLRRSU	HURLERS
EHLRSSU	LUSHERS
EHLRSTU	HURTLES
	HUSTLER
EHLRSUY	HURLEYS
EHLSSSU	SLUSHES
EHLSSTT	SHTETLS
EHLSSTU	HUSTLES
	LUSHEST
	SLEUTHS
EHLSTTU	SHUTTLE
EHMMRSU	HUMMERS
EHMNNOO	NONHOME
EHMNOOR	HORMONE
	MOORHEN
EHMNOPS	PHENOMS
	SHOPMEN
EHMNOST	MONETHS
EHMNOSW	SHOWMEN
EHMNPSU	HUMPENS
EHMNPTY	NYMPHET
EHMNTTU	HUTMENT
EHMOOSS	SHMOOSE
EHMOOSW	SOMEHOW
EHMOOSX	HOMOSEX
EHMOOSZ	SHMOOZE
EHMOPRW	MORPHEW
EHMORST	MOTHERS
	SMOTHER
	THERMOS
EHMORTU	MOUTHER
EHMORTY	MOTHERY
EHMOSWY	SOMEWHY
EHMOTXY	METHOXY
EHMPRSU	HUMPERS
EHMPRTU	THUMPER
EHMRRSY	RHYMERS
EHMRRTU	MURTHER
EHMRSSU	MUSHERS
EHMRSUU	HUMERUS
EHMRTUV	VERMUTH
EHMSSUU	HUMUSES
EHNNOOR	NONHERO
EHNNOPR	NEPHRON
EHNNOPY	HYPNONE
EHNNRSU	SHUNNER
EHNNSTU	UNSHENT
EHNNSUW	UNSHEWN
EHNOORR	HONORER
EHNOORS	HEROONS
	ONSHORE
	SOREHON
EHNOPRS	PHONERS
EHNOPRY	HYPERON
EHNOPSU	EUPHONS
EHNOPSY	PHONEYS
EHNOPUY	EUPHONY
EHNOPXY	PHENOXY
EHNORRS	HORNERS
EHNORRT	HORRENT
	NORTHER
EHNORRY	HERONRY
EHNORSS	NOSHERS
	SENHORS
EHNORST	HORNETS
	SHORTEN
	THRENOS
	THRONES
EHNORSU	UNHORSE
EHNORSW	RESHOWN
EHNORSY	NOSHERY
EHNOSST	HOTNESS
EHNOSSU	UNSHOES
EHNOSTT	SHOTTEN
EHNOSTY	HONESTY
EHNOSUU	UNHOUSE
EHNOTUY	YOUTHEN
EHNPRSY	PHRENSY
EHNRSTU	HUNTERS
	SHUNTER
	UNHERST
EHNRTWY	WRYTHEN
EHNSSSU	SNUSHES
EHNSSSY	SHYNESS
EHOOOPS	HOOPOES
EHOOPRS	HOOPERS

EHOOPRW	WHOOPER
EHOOPTY	OOPHYTE
EHOORST	HOOTERS
	RESHOOT
	SHEROOT
	SHOOTER
	SOOTHER
EHOORSV	HOOVERS
EHOORTV	OVERHOT
EHOOSST	SOOTHES
EHOOSSW	WOOSHES
EHOPPRS	HOPPERS
	SHOPPER
EHOPPRT	PROPHET
EHOPPRW	WHOPPER
EHOPPSS	SHOPPES
EHOPRRY	ORPHREY
EHOPRST	POTHERS
	STROPHE
	THORPES
EHOPRSU	UPHROES
EHOPRSW	PRESHOW
EHOPRTU	POUTHER
EHOPRTY	POTHERY
EHOPRUY	EUPHORY
EHOPSSS	SPOSHES
EHOPSST	POSHEST
EHOPSTY	TYPHOSE
EHORRSS	SHORERS
EHORRST	RHETORS
	ROTHERS
	SHORTER
EHORRTW	THROWER
EHORSST	HORSTES
	TOSHERS
EHORSSU	HOUSERS
EHORSSV	SHOVERS
	SHROVES
EHORSSW	RESHOWS
	SHOWERS
EHORSTT	HOTTERS
EHORSTU	SHOUTER
	SOUTHER
EHORSTW	THROWES
EHORSTX	EXHORTS
EHORSWY	SHOWERY
EHORTUY	OUTHYRE
EHOSSST	HOSTESS
EHOSSTT	SHOTTES
EHOSTTT	HOTTEST
EHOTTTW	WOTTETH
EHPRSSU	PUSHERS
EHPRSSY	SYPHERS
EHPRSYZ	ZEPHYRS
EHPRTTU	TURPETH
EHPRTUW	UPTHREW
EHQRSSU	QURSHES
EHRRSSU	RUSHERS
EHRRSTU	HURTERS
EHRSSTY	SHYSTER
	THYRSES
EHRSTTU	SHUTTER
EHRSTTW	STREWTH
EHRSTUW	WUTHERS
EHRSTUY	TUSHERY
EHRTTTY	THRETTY
EHSSSTU	TUSSEHS
EIIILRV	RILIEVI
EIIILST	ILEITIS
EIIINPR	RIPIENI
EIIJMMS	JIMMIES
EIIJMPR	JIMPIER
EIIJSTV	JIVIEST
EIIKKLN	INKLIKE
EIIKKNR	KINKIER
EIIKLLP	LIPLIKE
EIIKLLS	KILLIES
EIIKLMR	MILKIER
EIIKLMS	MISLIKE
EIIKLNT	TINLIKE
EIIKLPS	PLISKIE
EIIKLRS	SILKIER
EIIKLSS	SILKIES
EIIKLST	KILTIES
EIIKLVY	IVYLIKE
EIIKMRR	MIRKIER
EIIKNNT	KINETIN
EIIKNPR	PINKIER
EIIKNPS	PINKIES
EIIKNRS	SINKIER
EIIKNRZ	ZINKIER
EIIKNSS	KINESIS
EIIKNST	INKIEST
EIIKPRS	SPIKIER
EIIKPSS	PISKIES
EIIKRRS	RISKIER
EIIKRSV	SKIVIER
EIIKSTT	KITTIES
EIILLMM	MILLIME
EIILLMN	MILLINE
EIILLMR	MILLIER
EIILLMT	LIMELIT
EIILLNV	VILLEIN
EIILLPS	ILLIPES
EIILLRS	SILLIER
EIILLRT	TILLIER
EIILLSS	SILLIES
EIILLST	ILLITES
EIILLSW	WILLIES
EIILLTT	TILLITE
EIILLTV	VITELLI
EIILMNV	MILVINE
EIILMPR	IMPERIL
EIILMPS	IMPLIES
EIILMPT	LIMEPIT
EIILMRR	MIRLIER
EIILMRS	MILREIS
	SLIMIER
EIILMRT	LIMITER
	MILTIER
EIILMSS	MISLIES
	MISSILE
	SIMILES
EIILMST	ELITISM
	LIMIEST
	LIMITES
EIILMSU	MILIEUS
EIILMSV	MISLIVE
EIILMUX	MILIEUX
EIILNNS	LINNIES
EIILNOS	ELISION
	ISOLINE
	LIONISE
EIILNOT	ETIOLIN
EIILNOV	OLIVINE
EIILNOZ	LIONIZE
EIILNPS	SPLENII
EIILNRR	NIRLIER
EIILNRS	INLIERS
EIILNRT	LINTIER
	NITRILE
EIILNSS	INISLES
EIILNST	LINIEST
	LINTIES
EIILNTT	INTITLE
EIILNTU	INUTILE
EIILORR	ROILIER
EIILORS	SOILIER
EIILORV	RILIEVO
EIILOST	IOLITES
	OILIEST
EIILPPR	LIPPIER
EIILPPS	LIPPIES
EIILPST	SPILITE
EIILQSU	SILIQUE
EIILRST	RILIEST
	SILTIER
EIILRSV	LIVIERS
EIILRSX	ELIXIRS
EIILSSV	VISILES
EIILSTT	ELITIST
EIILSTU	UTILISE
EIILSTW	WILIEST
EIILTUY	TUILYIE
EIILTUZ	TUILZIE
	UTILIZE
EIILTXY	EXILITY
EIIMMRS	MIMSIER
EIIMMSS	MIMESIS
EIIMMST	MISTIME
EIIMMSX	IMMIXES
EIIMNNS	MINNIES
EIIMNPR	PRIMINE
EIIMNRT	INTERIM
	MINTIER
	TERMINI
EIIMNRV	MINIVER
EIIMNST	MINIEST
EIIMNTV	MINIVET
EIIMNTY	NIMIETY
EIIMOSS	MEIOSIS
EIIMPRS	PISMIRE
	PRIMSIE
EIIMPRW	WIMPIER
EIIMPST	PIETISM
EIIMPTY	IMPIETY
EIIMRSS	MERISIS
	MISSIER
EIIMRST	MIRIEST
	MISTIER
	RIMIEST
EIIMSSS	MISSIES
EIIMSST	MITISES
	STIMIES
EIIMSSV	MISSIVE
EIIMSSZ	SIZEISM
EIIMSTT	MITIEST
EIIMSTX	MIXIEST
EIINNNP	NINEPIN
EIINNNS	NINNIES
EIINNPS	PINNIES
EIINNQU	QUININE
EIINNRT	TINNIER
EIINNST	INTINES
	TINNIES
EIINNSW	INSINEW
EIINNTV	INVENIT
EIINNTW	INTWINE
EIINOPR	RIPIENO
EIINOPS	PIONIES
	SINOPIE
EIINORR	IRONIER
EIINORS	IONISER
	IRONIES
	IRONISE
	NOISIER
EIINORZ	IONIZER
	IRONIZE
EIINOSS	IONISES
EIINOST	INOSITE
EIINOSZ	IONIZES
EIINPPR	NIPPIER
EIINPRS	INSPIRE
	PIRNIES
	SNIPIER
	SPINIER
EIINPST	PINIEST
	PINITES
	TIEPINS
EIINQRU	INQUIRE
EIINQSU	QUINIES
EIINQTU	INQUIET
EIINRTT	NITRITE
	NITTIER
	TINTIER
EIINRTV	INVITER
	VITRINE
EIINRTW	TWINIER
EIINSSS	SEISINS
EIINSSZ	SEIZINS
EIINSTT	SITTINE
	TINIEST
EIINSTU	UNITIES
	UNITISE
EIINSTV	INVITES
	VINIEST
EIINSTW	WINIEST
EIINTUV	UNITIVE
EIINTUZ	UNITIZE
EIIORST	RIOTISE
EIIORSV	IVORIES
EIIORTZ	RIOTIZE
EIIOSTZ	ZOISITE
EIIPPPR	PIPPIER
EIIPPRR	RIPPIER
EIIPPRT	TIPPIER
EIIPPRZ	ZIPPIER
EIIPPST	PIPIEST
EIIPPSY	YIPPIES
EIIPRRS	SPIRIER
EIIPRRT	TRIPIER
EIIPRRV	PRIVIER
EIIPRST	PITIERS
	TIPSIER
EIIPRSV	PRIVIES
EIIPRSW	SWIPIER
	WISPIER
EIIPSTT	PIETIST
EIIPTTT	PITTITE
EIIPTTU	PITUITE
EIIRRTZ	RITZIER
EIIRSSS	SISSIER
EIIRSSV	VISIERS
EIIRSTV	REVISIT
	STIVIER
	VISITER
EIIRSTW	WIRIEST
EIIRSVZ	VIZIERS
EIIRSWZ	WIZIERS
EIIRTTW	WITTIER
EIISSSS	SISSIES
EIISSTV	VISITES
EIISSTX	SIXTIES
EIISSTZ	SIZEIST
	SIZIEST
EIISTTT	TITTIES
EIISTUV	UVEITIS
EIISTZZ	TIZZIES
EIISVZZ	VIZZIES
EIJKKSU	JUKSKEI
EIJKLRY	JERKILY
EIJKNPR	PERJINK
	PREJINK
EIJKNRS	JERKINS
	JINKERS
EIJKNRU	JUNKIER
EIJKNSU	JUNKIES
EIJKOST	JOKIEST
EIJLLNY	INJELLY
EIJLLOR	JOLLIER

EIJLLOS	JOLLIES
EIJLLST	JILLETS
EIJLORT	JOLTIER
EIJLORW	JOWLIER
EIJLRST	JILTERS
EIJMPRU	JUMPIER
EIJMPST	JIMPEST
EIJNNOS	ENJOINS
EIJNORS	JOINERS
	REJOINS
EIJNORT	JOINTER
EIJNORY	JOINERY
EIJNOST	JONTIES
EIJNPRU	JUNIPER
EIJNRRU	INJURER
EIJNRSU	INJURES
EIJNSTY	JITNEYS
EIJNTTW	TWINJET
EIJRSTT	JITTERS
	TRIJETS
EIJRTTY	JITTERY
EIJSSTU	JESUITS
EIJSSUV	JUSSIVE
EIJSTTU	JUTTIES
EIKKLNR	KLINKER
EIKKLNS	KINKLES
EIKKLSY	KYLIKES
EIKKMNR	KIRKMEN
EIKKNRS	SKINKER
EIKKOOR	KOOKIER
EIKKRSY	YIKKERS
EIKKRUY	YUKKIER
EIKLLNW	INKWELL
EIKLLOS	SKOLLIE
EIKLLOW	OWLLIKE
EIKLLRS	KILLERS
	RESKILL
EIKLLST	SKILLET
EIKLMMN	MILKMEN
EIKLMNN	LINKMEN
EIKLMNR	KREMLIN
EIKLMRS	MILKERS
EIKLNNS	ENLINKS
EIKLNNU	NUNLIKE
EIKLNOS	SONLIKE
EIKLNPR	PLINKER
EIKLNRS	LINKERS
	RELINKS
	SLINKER
EIKLNRT	TINKLER
EIKLNRU	URNLIKE
EIKLNRW	WINKLER
	WRINKLE
EIKLNSS	INKLESS
	KINLESS
	SILKENS
EIKLNST	LENTISK
	TINKLES
EIKLNSU	SUNLIKE
	UNLIKES
EIKLNSV	KELVINS
EIKLNSW	WELKINS
	WINKLES
EIKLNSY	SKYLINE
EIKLNTT	KNITTLE
EIKLNTU	NUTLIKE
EIKLNTW	TWINKLE
EIKLOOP	PLOOKIE
EIKLOPT	POTLIKE
EIKLOPU	PLOUKIE
EIKLORY	YOLKIER
EIKLOTY	TOYLIKE
EIKLPRY	PERKILY
EIKLPST	SKELPIT
EIKLPSU	PUSLIKE
EIKLPSY	PESKILY
EIKLRST	KILTERS
	KIRTLES
	KLISTER
EIKLRSU	SULKIER
EIKLRTT	KITTLER
EIKLSSS	KISSELS
EIKLSSU	SULKIES
EIKLSTT	KITTLES
	SKITTLE
EIKMMRR	KRIMMER
EIKMMRS	KIMMERS
	SKIMMER
EIKMNNS	KINSMEN
EIKMNOR	MONIKER
EIKMNRS	MERKINS
EIKMNSS	MISKENS
EIKMNST	MISKENT
EIKMNSW	MISKNEW
EIKMORS	IRKSOME
	SMOKIER
EIKMOSS	SMOKIES
EIKMOSY	MISYOKE
EIKMPST	MISKEPT
EIKMPSU	MUSPIKE
EIKMRRS	SMIRKER
EIKMRRU	MURKIER
EIKMRSS	KIRMESS
EIKMRST	MIRKEST
EIKMRSU	MUSKIER
EIKMSST	KISMETS
EIKMSSU	MUSKIES
EIKMSSY	MISKEYS
EIKMSTU	MISTEUK
EIKNNOR	EINKORN
EIKNNOS	KINONES
EIKNNPS	PINKENS
EIKNNRS	SKINNER
EIKNOOR	NOOKIER
	ROOINEK
EIKNOOS	NOOKIES
EIKNOPS	PINKOES
EIKNORV	INVOKER
EIKNORW	WONKIER
EIKNOSS	KENOSIS
EIKNOSV	INVOKES
EIKNPRR	PRINKER
EIKNPRS	PERKINS
	PINKERS
EIKNPRU	PUNKIER
EIKNPST	PINKEST
EIKNPSU	PUNKIES
	SPUNKIE
EIKNPSY	PINKEYS
EIKNRSS	SINKERS
EIKNRST	REKNITS
	SKINTER
	STINKER
	TINKERS
EIKNRSW	WINKERS
EIKNRTT	KNITTER
	TRINKET
EIKNSSU	SUNKIES
EIKNSTT	KITTENS
EIKNTTY	KITTENY
EIKNTUZ	KUNZITE
EIKOORR	ROOKIER
EIKOORS	ROOKIES
EIKOPPR	PORKPIE
EIKOPPS	KOPPIES
EIKOPRR	PORKIER
EIKOPRS	PORKIES
EIKOPST	POKIEST
EIKORST	ROKIEST
EIKORSY	YORKIES
EIKOSST	KETOSIS
EIKPPRS	KIPPERS
	SKIPPER
EIKPPST	SKIPPET
EIKPRSS	SPIKERS
EIKPRSY	SPIKERY
EIKPSSS	SKEPSIS
EIKRRSS	RISKERS
EIKRRST	SKIRRET
	SKIRTER
	STRIKER
EIKRSSS	KISSERS
EIKRSST	STRIKES
EIKRSSV	SKIVERS
EIKRSTT	SKITTER
EIKRSTU	TURKIES
	TUSKIER
EIKSSTW	WESKITS
	WISKETS
EIKSSTY	SKYIEST
EIKSTUY	YUKIEST
EILLLOS	LOLLIES
EILLMNU	MULLEIN
EILLMOS	MOLLIES
EILLMOT	MELILOT
EILLMOU	MOUILLE
EILLMRS	MILLERS
EILLMST	MILLETS
	MISTELL
EILLMSU	ILLUMES
EILLMTU	MULLITE
EILLNNP	PENNILL
EILLNOS	LIONELS
	NIELLOS
EILLNSS	ILLNESS
EILLNST	LENTILS
	LINTELS
	TELLINS
EILLNUV	LEVULIN
EILLOPS	POLLIES
EILLORU	ROUILLE
EILLORW	LOWLIER
EILLORZ	ZORILLE
EILLOST	OILLETS
EILLOSV	VILLOSE
EILLOSW	WOLLIES
EILLPPR	PREPILL
EILLPRS	SPILLER
EILLPSS	LIPLESS
EILLPSU	PILULES
EILLQTU	QUILLET
EILLRRT	TRILLER
EILLRSS	SILLERS
EILLRST	RILLETS
	STILLER
	TILLERS
	TRELLIS
EILLRSW	SWILLER
	WILLERS
EILLRTT	LITTLER
EILLSST	LISTELS
EILLSSU	SULLIES
EILLSTT	LITTLES
EILLSTU	TUILLES
EILLSTW	WILLEST
	WILLETS
EILLSWY	WILLEYS
EILMMNO	MOLIMEN
EILMMRS	LIMMERS
	SLIMMER
EILMMRU	LUMMIER
EILMNOO	OINOMEL
EILMNOS	LOMEINS
	MOLINES
EILMNOT	MOLINET
EILMNPS	PLENISM
EILMNRS	LIMNERS
	MERLINS
EILMNSS	SIMNELS
EILMNSU	EMULSIN
	LUMINES
	UNLIMES
EILMNSY	MYELINS
EILMOOS	MOOLIES
EILMOPR	IMPLORE
EILMORR	LORIMER
EILMORS	MOILERS
EILMORT	MOTLIER
EILMOSS	LIMOSES
	LISSOME
	SMOILES
EILMOST	MOTILES
EILMPPS	PIMPLES
EILMPPU	PLUMPIE
EILMPRS	LIMPERS
	PRELIMS
	RIMPLES
	SIMPLER
EILMPRU	LUMPIER
	PLUMIER
EILMPRY	PRIMELY
EILMPSS	SIMPLES
EILMPST	LIMPEST
	LIMPETS
EILMPSU	IMPULSE
EILMPSW	WIMPLES
EILMPSX	SIMPLEX
EILMPSY	LIMPSEY
EILMPTY	EMPTILY
EILMRRU	MURLIER
EILMRRY	MERRILY
EILMRSS	RIMLESS
	SMILERS
EILMRST	MILTERS
EILMRSU	MISRULE
EILMRSV	VERMILS
EILMRSY	MISERLY
	MISRELY
EILMRTY	LYMITER
EILMRVY	VERMILY
EILMSSS	MISSELS
EILMSST	MISTLES
	SMILETS
EILMSSU	MUESLIS
EILMSSY	MESSILY
	MILSEYS
	SMILEYS
EILMSTT	SMITTLE
EILMSTZ	MILTZES
EILMSZZ	MIZZLES
EILMUUV	ELUVIUM
EILNNPU	PINNULE
EILNNRY	INNERLY
EILNNSS	INNLESS
EILNNST	LINNETS
EILNNSU	UNLINES
EILNNSW	WINNLES
EILNNSY	LINNEYS
EILNOOP	POLONIE
EILNOOR	LOONIER
EILNOOS	LOONIES
EILNOOV	VIOLONE
EILNOPP	PLENIPO
EILNOPR	PROLINE
EILNOPS	EPSILON
	PINOLES
EILNOPT	POINTEL
	PONTILE
	POTLINE
	TOPLINE

EILNORR	LORINER
EILNORS	NEROLIS
EILNORT	RETINOL
EILNOSS	ESLOINS
	INSOLES
	LESIONS
	LIONESS
EILNOST	ENTOILS
	LIONETS
	ONLIEST
EILNOSU	ELUSION
EILNOTU	ELUTION
	OUTLINE
EILNOTV	VIOLENT
EILNOTW	TOWLINE
EILNOVV	INVOLVE
EILNPPS	LIPPENS
	NIPPLES
EILNPRS	PILSNER
EILNPRU	PURLINE
EILNPSS	PENSILS
	SPINELS
	SPLINES
EILNPST	PINTLES
	PLENIST
EILNPSU	LINEUPS
	LUPINES
	SPINULE
	UNPILES
EILNPTY	INEPTLY
EILNPUV	VULPINE
EILNRST	LINTERS
	SLINTER
	SNIRTLE
EILNRSV	SILVERN
EILNRTY	INERTLY
EILNRVY	NERVILY
EILNSSS	SINLESS
EILNSST	ENLISTS
	LISTENS
	SILENTS
	TINSELS
EILNSSU	INSULSE
	SILENUS
EILNSSV	SNIVELS
EILNSSW	WINLESS
EILNSSY	LINSEYS
	LYSINES
EILNSTU	LUNIEST
	LUTEINS
	UNTILES
	UTENSIL
EILNSTV	VENTILS
EILNSTW	WESTLIN
	WINTLES
EILNSUV	UNLIVES
	UNVEILS
EILNSUY	LUNYIES
EILNSVY	SYLVINE
EILNVXY	VIXENLY
EILOOPR	LOOPIER
EILOORS	ORIOLES
EILOORT	TROOLIE
EILOORW	WOOLIER
EILOOST	OOLITES
	OSTIOLE
	STOOLIE
EILOOSW	WOOLIES
EILOOTZ	ZOOLITE
EILOPPR	LOPPIER
EILOPRS	SLOPIER
	SPOILER
EILOPRT	POITREL
	POLITER
EILOPST	PIOLETS
	PISTOLE
EILOPSU	PILEOUS
EILOPSV	PLOSIVE
EILOPTT	PLOTTIE
EILOPTX	EXPLOIT
EILORRS	LORRIES
EILORRU	LOURIER
EILORSS	LORISES
	LOSSIER
	RISSOLE
EILORST	ESTRIOL
	LOITERS
	TOILERS
EILORSU	LOUSIER
	SOILURE
EILORSV	OLIVERS
	VIOLERS
EILORTT	TORTILE
	TRIOLET
EILORTU	OUTLIER
EILORTV	OVERLIT
EILOSSV	SOLIVES
EILOSTT	LITOTES
	TOILETS
EILOSTU	OUTLIES
EILOSTV	OLIVETS
	VIOLETS
EILOSTW	OWLIEST
EILOSTZ	ZLOTIES
EILOTUV	OUTLIVE
EILOTUW	OUTWILE
EILPPPY	PEPPILY
EILPPRR	RIPPLER
EILPPRS	LIPPERS
	RIPPLES
	SLIPPER
EILPPRT	RIPPLET
	TIPPLER
	TRIPPLE
EILPPRU	PULPIER
EILPPSS	PIPLESS
	SIPPLES
EILPPST	STIPPLE
	TIPPLES
EILPPSU	PILEUPS
	UPPILES
EILPPSW	SWIPPLE
EILPRSS	LISPERS
EILPRST	RESPLIT
	SPIRTLE
	TRIPLES
EILPRTT	TRIPLET
EILPRTX	TRIPLEX
EILPRUU	PURLIEU
EILPSSS	PLISSES
EILPSST	STIPELS
	TIPLESS
EILPSSW	SWIPLES
EILPSSZ	ZIPLESS
EILPSTT	SPITTLE
EILPSTU	PULIEST
	PUTELIS
	STIPULE
EILPSUY	SPULYIE
EILPSUZ	SPULZIE
EILPSZZ	PIZZLES
EILPTTY	PETTILY
EILQRTU	QUILTER
EILQRUU	LIQUEUR
EILQTUY	QUIETLY
EILRRSU	LURRIES
	SURLIER
EILRRTW	TWIRLER
EILRSST	LISTERS
	RELISTS
EILRSSV	SILVERS
	SLIVERS
EILRSTT	LITTERS
	SLITTER
	STILTER
	TESTRIL
	TILTERS
	TITLERS
EILRSTU	LUSTIER
	RULIEST
	RUTILES
EILRSUV	SURVEIL
EILRSUW	WURLIES
EILRSVY	LIVYERS
	SILVERY
EILRSZZ	SIZZLER
EILRTTY	LITTERY
	TRITELY
EILRTUV	RIVULET
EILSSTT	STILETS
EILSSTW	WITLESS
EILSSTY	STYLISE
EILSSVW	SWIVELS
EILSSZZ	SIZZLES
EILSTTT	TITTLES
EILSTTU	TITULES
EILSTTV	VITTLES
EILSTTY	STYLITE
	TESTILY
EILSTVY	SYLVITE
EILSTYZ	STYLIZE
EILSUVV	LUVVIES
EILSWZZ	SWIZZLE
EILSZZZ	ZIZZLES
EILTWZZ	TWIZZLE
EIMMMOS	MOMMIES
EIMMMST	MIMMEST
EIMMMSU	MUMMIES
EIMMNRS	NIMMERS
EIMMNSU	IMMUNES
EIMMOPS	POMMIES
EIMMORS	MEMOIRS
EIMMOST	TOMMIES
EIMMOSV	MISMOVE
EIMMPRR	PRIMMER
EIMMPRU	PREMIUM
EIMMRRS	RIMMERS
EIMMRRT	TRIMMER
EIMMRRU	RUMMIER
EIMMRSS	MERISMS
	SIMMERS
EIMMRST	MISTERM
EIMMRSU	IMMURES
	MUMSIER
	RUMMIES
EIMMRSW	SWIMMER
EIMMRSZ	ZIMMERS
EIMMRUY	YUMMIER
EIMMSST	SEMMITS
	TSIMMES
EIMMSTU	TUMMIES
EIMMSTZ	TZIMMES
EIMMSUY	YUMMIES
EIMNNOT	MENTION
EIMNOOR	IONOMER
	MOONIER
EIMNOOS	MOONIES
	NOISOME
EIMNOOT	EMOTION
EIMNOOX	EXOMION
EIMNOPR	PROMINE
EIMNOPS	IMPONES
	PEONISM
EIMNOPT	EMPTION
	PIMENTO
EIMNORS	MERINOS
	MERSION
EIMNOSS	EONISMS
EIMNOST	MESTINO
	MOISTEN
	MONTIES
	SENTIMO
EIMNOSW	WINSOME
EIMNOTY	OMNEITY
	OMNIETY
EIMNPSS	MISPENS
EIMNPST	EMPTINS
	PIMENTS
EIMNPTU	PINETUM
EIMNQSU	MESQUIN
EIMNRRU	MURRINE
EIMNRST	ENTRISM
	MINSTER
	MINTERS
	REMINTS
EIMNRSU	MUREINS
	MURINES
	NEURISM
EIMNRSV	VERMINS
EIMNRTU	MINUTER
	UNMITER
	UNMITRE
EIMNRVY	VERMINY
EIMNSSS	SENSISM
EIMNSST	MISSENT
EIMNSSU	MINUSES
EIMNSTT	MITTENS
	SMITTEN
EIMNSTU	MINUETS
	MINUTES
	MISTUNE
	MUNITES
	MUTINES
EIMNSTW	MISWENT
EIMNSUX	UNMIXES
EIMNSZZ	MIZZENS
EIMNUZZ	MUEZZIN
EIMOORR	MOORIER
	ROOMIER
EIMOORS	ROOMIES
EIMOPPR	MOPPIER
	POMPIER
EIMOPRR	PRIMERO
EIMOPRS	IMPOSER
	PROMISE
	SEMIPRO
EIMOPRV	IMPROVE
EIMOPRW	IMPOWER
EIMOPSS	IMPOSES
	MOPSIES
EIMOPST	MOPIEST
	OPTIMES
EIMOPSY	MYOPIES
EIMORRW	WORMIER
EIMORSS	ISOMERS
	MOISERS
	MOSSIER
EIMORST	EROTISM
	MOISTER
	MORTISE
	TRISOME
EIMORSU	MOUSIER
EIMORSV	VERISMO
EIMORTT	MOTTIER
	OMITTER
EIMORTV	VOMITER
EIMORVX	OVERMIX
EIMOSSS	MOSSIES
EIMOSST	MITOSES
	SOMITES

EIMOSSU	MOUSIES
EIMOSTT	MOTIEST
	TITMOSE
EIMOSTU	TIMEOUS
EIMOSTV	MOTIVES
EIMOSTX	EXOTISM
EIMOSTZ	MESTIZO
EIMOSYZ	ISOZYME
EIMOSZZ	MOZZIES
EIMOTTU	TIMEOUT
EIMPRRS	PRIMERS
EIMPRRT	PRETRIM
EIMPRRU	IMPURER
	PRIMEUR
EIMPRSS	IMPRESS
	PREMISS
	SIMPERS
	SPIREMS
EIMPRST	IMPREST
	PERMITS
EIMPRSU	RUMPIES
	SPUMIER
	UMPIRES
EIMPRTU	IMPUTER
	TUMPIER
EIMPRTX	PREMIXT
EIMPSST	MISSTEP
EIMPSSU	SEPIUMS
EIMPSTU	IMPETUS
	IMPUTES
	UPTIMES
EIMPSTY	MISTYPE
EIMPSUY	YUMPIES
EIMQSTU	MESQUIT
EIMQTUZ	MEZQUIT
EIMRRST	RETRIMS
	TRIMERS
EIMRRSU	MURRIES
EIMRSST	MISTERS
	SMITERS
EIMRSSU	MISUSER
	MUSSIER
	SURMISE
EIMRSSV	VERISMS
EIMRSTT	METRIST
EIMRSTU	MUSTIER
EIMRSTY	MISTERY
	SMYTRIE
EIMRTUV	VITREUM
EIMRTUX	MIXTURE
EIMRUZZ	MUZZIER
EIMSSST	MISSETS
EIMSSSU	MISUSES
EIMSSSX	SEXISMS
EIMSSTY	STYMIES
EIMSTYZ	ZYMITES
EIMUUVX	EXUVIUM
EINNNOS	NONNIES
EINNNRS	RENNINS
EINNOOS	IONONES
EINNOPS	PENSION
	PINONES
EINNOPT	PONTINE
EINNOQU	QUINONE
EINNORT	INTONER
	TERNION
EINNORU	NOUNIER
	REUNION
EINNORV	ENVIRON
EINNOSS	SONNIES
EINNOST	INTONES
	TENSION
EINNOSV	VENISON
EINNOTT	NONETTI
	TONTINE
EINNOVW	INWOVEN
EINNPRS	PINNERS
	SPINNER
EINNPRT	ENPRINT
EINNPRU	PUNNIER
EINNPST	PINNETS
	SPINNET
	TENPINS
EINNPSY	SPINNEY
EINNRRU	RUNNIER
EINNRSS	SINNERS
EINNRST	INTERNS
	TINNERS
EINNRSU	SUNNIER
	UNREINS
	UNRISEN
EINNRSW	WINNERS
EINNRTV	VINTNER
EINNRUV	UNRIVEN
EINNSST	SENNITS
	SINNETS
EINNSSY	SINSYNE
EINNSTT	INTENTS
	TENNIST
EINNSTU	TUNNIES
EINNSTV	INVENTS
EINNSUW	UNSINEW
EINNSWY	SWINNEY
EINNTUW	UNTWINE
EINOOPZ	EPIZOON
EINOORS	EROSION
EINOOST	ISOTONE
EINOOSZ	OZONISE
EINOOTZ	ZOONITE
EINOOZZ	OZONIZE
EINOPPR	POPERIN
	PROPINE
EINOPPS	PEPINOS
EINOPRR	PORNIER
EINOPRS	ORPINES
	PIONERS
	PROINES
EINOPRT	POINTER
	PROTEIN
	PTERION
	REPOINT
	TROPINE
EINOPRV	PROVINE
EINOPSS	SPINOSE
EINOPST	PINTOES
	POINTES
	PONTIES
EINOPSW	POWNIES
	WINESOP
EINOPSY	PIONEYS
EINOQUX	EQUINOX
EINORRS	IRONERS
EINORSS	ORNISES
	SENIORS
	SONERIS
	SONSIER
EINORST	NORITES
	OESTRIN
	ORIENTS
	STONIER
	TERSION
	TRIONES
EINORSU	URINOSE
EINORSV	RENVOIS
	VERSION
EINORSW	SNOWIER
EINORTT	TRITONE
EINORTU	ROUTINE
EINORTW	TOWNIER
EINORTZ	TRIZONE
EINOSSS	ESSOINS
	OSSEINS
	SESSION
EINOSST	NOSIEST
	SONTIES
	STONIES
EINOSSU	SINUOSE
EINOSSZ	SOZINES
EINOSTT	SNOTTIE
	TONIEST
	TONITES
EINOSTW	TOWNIES
EINOSTX	TOXINES
EINOSUV	ENVIOUS
	NIVEOUS
	VEINOUS
EINOTTT	TOTIENT
EINPPRS	NIPPERS
	SNIPPER
EINPPSS	PEPSINS
EINPPST	SNIPPET
EINPPSW	WIPPENS
EINPRRT	PRINTER
	REPRINT
EINPRRU	UNRIPER
EINPRSS	SNIPERS
EINPRST	NIPTERS
	PTERINS
EINPRSU	PRUINES
	PURINES
	UPRISEN
EINPRTU	REPUNIT
EINPSST	INSTEPS
	SPINETS
EINPSSU	PUISNES
	SUPINES
EINPSTT	SPITTEN
EINPSTU	PUNIEST
	PUNTIES
EINPSTW	INSWEPT
EINPTTY	TINTYPE
EINQRSU	REQUINS
EINQRUU	UNIQUER
EINQRUY	ENQUIRY
EINQSSU	SEQUINS
EINQSTU	INQUEST
	QUINTES
EINQSUU	UNIQUES
EINQSUZ	QUINZES
EINQTTU	QUINTET
EINQTUU	UNQUIET
EINRRSS	RINSERS
EINRRSU	INSURER
	RUINERS
EINRRTU	RUNTIER
EINRSST	ESTRINS
	INSERTS
	SINTERS
EINRSSU	INSURES
	SUNRISE
EINRSSV	VERSINS
EINRSTT	ENTRIST
	RETINTS
	STINTER
	TINTERS
EINRSTU	NUTSIER
	TRIUNES
	UNITERS
EINRSTV	INVERTS
	STRIVEN
EINRSTW	TWINERS
	WINTERS
EINRSTY	SINTERY
EINRSUW	UNWIRES
	UNWISER
EINRSVW	WIVERNS
EINRSWY	SWINERY
EINRTTU	NUTTIER
EINRTTW	TWINTER
	WRITTEN
EINRTUV	UNRIVET
	VENTURI
EINRTUW	UNWRITE
EINRTWY	WINTERY
EINSSST	SENSIST
EINSSSU	SINUSES
EINSSSY	SYNESIS
EINSSTU	INTUSES
EINSSTV	INVESTS
EINSSTW	WISENTS
	WITNESS
EINSSTY	TINSEYS
EINSSUW	SUNWISE
EINSSWY	WINSEYS
EINSTTU	TUNIEST
EINSTTW	ENTWIST
	TWINSET
EINSTTY	TENSITY
EINSTWY	WITNEYS
EINSUVW	UNWIVES
EINSWZZ	WIZZENS
EINTTTW	TWITTEN
EINTTUY	TENUITY
EIOOPRR	ROOPIER
EIOOPRV	POOVIER
EIOOPST	ISOTOPE
EIOOPSW	WOOPIES
EIOORRT	ROOTIER
EIOORST	OORIEST
	ROOTIES
	SOOTIER
	TOORIES
EIOORTZ	ZOOTIER
EIOORWZ	WOOZIER
EIOOSST	OOSIEST
EIOOSTT	TOOTSIE
EIOOSTZ	OOZIEST
EIOPPPR	POPPIER
EIOPPPS	POPPIES
EIOPPRS	SOPPIER
EIOPPSS	POPSIES
EIOPPST	POTPIES
EIOPQRU	PIROQUE
EIOPRRS	PROSIER
EIOPRRT	PIERROT
	PORTIER
	PRERIOT
EIOPRRU	ROUPIER
EIOPRSS	POISERS
	PROSSIE
EIOPRST	PERIOST
	PORIEST
	PROSTIE
	REPOSIT
	RIPOSTE
	ROPIEST
EIOPRSU	POURIES
	SOUPIER
EIOPRSX	PROXIES
EIOPRTT	POTTIER
EIOPRTU	POUTIER
EIOPRTV	OVERTIP
	PIVOTER
EIOPSSS	POSSIES
EIOPSST	POSIEST
	POSTIES
	POTSIES
	SEPIOST
	SOPITES
EIOPSSU	POUSSIE

EIOPSTT	POTTIES
	TIPTOES
EIOPSTU	PITEOUS
EIOPSTX	EXPOSIT
	POXIEST
EIOPSTY	ISOTYPE
EIOPSZZ	POZZIES
EIOPTUW	WIPEOUT
EIOQRTU	QUOITER
EIOQTUX	QUIXOTE
EIORRRS	SORRIER
EIORRRT	RORTIER
EIORRRW	WORRIER
EIORRSS	ORRISES
	ROSIERS
EIORRST	RIOTERS
	ROISTER
	RORIEST
EIORRSV	REVISOR
EIORRSW	WORRIES
EIORRUV	OUVRIER
EIORRVV	REVIVOR
EIORSSS	SEISORS
EIORSST	ROSIEST
	SORITES
	SORTIES
	STORIES
	TOSSIER
	TRIOSES
EIORSSU	SERIOUS
EIORSSV	VIROSES
EIORSSX	XEROSIS
EIORSSZ	SEIZORS
EIORSTT	STOITER
EIORSTU	OURIEST
	STOURIE
	TOURIES
	TOUSIER
EIORSTV	TORSIVE
EIORSTW	OWRIEST
	TOWSIER
EIORTTT	TOTTIER
EIORTTU	TOUTIER
EIORTTV	TORTIVE
	VIRETOT
EIORTUV	VOITURE
EIORTUZ	TOUZIER
EIORTWZ	TOWZIER
EIOSSTV	SOVIETS
	STOVIES
EIOSTTT	TOTTIES
EIOSTTU	TOUSTIE
EIOSTTW	TOWIEST
EIOSTUV	OUTVIES
EIOSTUZ	OUTSIZE
EIPPPSU	PUPPIES
EIPPQRU	QUIPPER
EIPPRRS	RIPPERS
EIPPRRT	TRIPPER
EIPPRSS	SIPPERS
EIPPRST	TIPPERS
EIPPRSU	PURPIES
EIPPRSY	YIPPERS
EIPPRSZ	ZIPPERS
EIPPRTT	TRIPPET
EIPPSST	SIPPETS
EIPPSTT	TIPPETS
EIPPSUY	YUPPIES
EIPQSTU	PIQUETS
EIPRRSS	PRISERS
EIPRRST	STRIPER
EIPRRSU	PURSIER
	UPRISER
EIPRRSZ	PRIZERS
EIPRRTU	PURTIER
EIPRRTY	TRIPERY
EIPRRUV	UPRIVER
EIPRSSS	PISSERS
	PRISSES
EIPRSST	ESPRITS
	PERSIST
	PRIESTS
	SITREPS
	SPRIEST
	SPRITES
	STIRPES
	STRIPES
	TRIPSES
EIPRSSU	PUSSIER
	SUSPIRE
	UPRISES
EIPRSSW	SWIPERS
EIPRSTT	PITTERS
	SPITTER
	TIPSTER
EIPRSTU	PERITUS
	PUIREST
EIPRSTV	PRIVETS
EIPRSTX	EXTIRPS
EIPRSTY	PYRITES
	STRIPEY
EIPRSUU	EURIPUS
EIPRTTU	PUTTIER
EIPRUVW	PURVIEW
EIPSSSU	PUSSIES
EIPSSTZ	SPITZES
EIPSTTU	PUTTIES
EIPSTTY	TYPIEST
EIQRSSU	RISQUES
	SQUIERS
	SQUIRES
EIQRSTU	QUERIST
	REQUITS
EIQRSUV	QUIVERS
EIQRTTU	QUITTER
EIQRUVY	QUIVERY
EIQRUZZ	QUIZZER
EIQSTUU	QUIETUS
EIQSUZZ	QUIZZES
EIRRRST	STIRRER
EIRRSST	STIRRES
EIRRSTT	RITTERS
	TERRITS
EIRRSTU	RUSTIER
EIRRSTV	STRIVER
EIRRSTW	WRITERS
EIRRSZZ	RIZZERS
EIRRTTU	RUTTIER
EIRSSST	RESISTS
	SISTERS
EIRSSSU	ISSUERS
	RISUSES
EIRSSTT	SITTERS
EIRSSTU	SUITERS
EIRSSTV	STIVERS
	STRIVES
	TREVISS
	VERISTS
EIRSSUU	USURIES
EIRSSUV	VIRUSES
EIRSSUW	WUSSIER
EIRSTTT	STRETTI
	TITTERS
	TRITEST
EIRSTTU	TERTIUS
EIRSTTV	TRIVETS
EIRSTTW	RETWIST
	TWISTER
	WITTERS
EIRSTUV	REVUIST
	STUIVER
	VIRTUES
EIRSUVV	SURVIVE
EIRSUVW	SURVIEW
EIRTTTW	TWITTER
EISSSSW	SWISSES
EISSSTU	SITUSES
	TISSUES
EISSSTW	SWITSES
EISSSTX	SEXISTS
EISSSUW	WUSSIES
EISSTTY	TYSTIES
EISSTUV	TUSSIVE
EISSTUY	TISSUEY
EISSTVW	SWIVETS
EISSWZZ	SWIZZES
EISTTTU	TUTTIES
EJJMNUU	JEJUNUM
EJKMNNU	JUNKMEN
EJKNRSU	JUNKERS
EJKNSTU	JUNKETS
EJKOORY	JOOKERY
EJKORUY	JOUKERY
EJLLORY	JOLLYER
EJLLOSY	JOLLEYS
EJLORST	JOLTERS
	JOSTLER
EJLORSW	JOWLERS
EJLOSST	JOSTLES
EJLOSSY	JOYLESS
EJLSSTU	JUSTLES
EJMNRUY	JURYMEN
EJMOSST	JETSOMS
EJMPRSU	JUMPERS
EJNORRU	REJOURN
EJNORUY	JOURNEY
EJNOSST	JETSONS
EJNOSTT	JETTONS
EJOORVY	OVERJOY
EJOOSSY	SOOJEYS
EJOPPRT	PROPJET
EJOPRST	PROJETS
EJOPRTT	JETPORT
EJORSSS	JOSSERS
EJORSTT	JOTTERS
EJORSTU	JOUSTER
EJOSTTU	OUTJEST
	OUTJETS
EJPRRUY	PERJURY
EJRSSTU	JUSTERS
EJSSTTU	JUSTEST
EKKLOOY	OLYKOEK
EKKLRSU	SKULKER
EKKOPSU	PUKEKOS
EKLLMSU	SKELLUM
EKLLNOR	KNOLLER
EKLLRRU	KRULLER
EKLMMSU	KUMMELS
EKLMSSU	MUSKLES
	SKELUMS
EKLNOPR	PLONKER
EKLNORS	SNORKEL
EKLNOSS	KELSONS
	SLOKENS
EKLNOSU	LEUKONS
EKLNPRU	PLUNKER
EKLNPSU	SPELUNK
EKLNRSU	LUNKERS
	RUNKLES
EKLNSST	SKLENTS
EKLOORS	LOOKERS
	RELOOKS
EKLRRSU	LURKERS
EKLRSSU	SULKERS
EKLSTTU	SKUTTLE
EKLSTUZ	KLUTZES
EKMMRSU	SKUMMER
EKMNORW	WORKMEN
EKMNORY	MONKERY
EKMNOSU	MUSKONE
EKMNOSY	MONKEYS
EKMNPTU	UNKEMPT
EKMOOPS	MOPOKES
EKMORSS	SMOKERS
EKMRSTU	MURKEST
EKMSSTU	MUSKETS
EKMSSUY	KUMYSES
EKNNOST	NEKTONS
EKNOORS	SNOOKER
EKNOPSU	UNSPOKE
EKNORST	STONKER
	STROKEN
	TONKERS
EKNORSW	KNOWERS
EKNORSY	YONKERS
EKNORTT	KNOTTER
EKNORTW	NETWORK
EKNORUY	YOUNKER
EKNOSTY	STENOKY
EKNOSUY	UNYOKES
EKNPRSU	PUNKERS
EKNPSTU	PUNKEST
EKNPSUY	PUNKEYS
EKNRTUY	TURNKEY
EKNSSTU	SUNKETS
EKOOPRT	PERTOOK
EKOOPRV	PROVOKE
EKOORRS	KOREROS
EKOORRY	ROOKERY
EKOORST	STOOKER
	STROOKE
EKOORTW	KOTOWER
EKOPPSU	UPSPOKE
EKOPRRS	PORKERS
	PROKERS
EKOPRRW	PREWORK
EKOPRUY	KOUPREY
EKOPTTU	OUTKEPT
EKORRST	STROKER
EKORRSW	REWORKS
	WORKERS
EKORRSY	YORKERS
EKORSST	STOKERS
	STROKES
EKORUYY	EURYOKY
EKPPSUU	SEPPUKU
EKPRSSY	KRYPSES
EKRRSSY	SKRYERS
EKRSSTU	TUSKERS
EKRSTUY	TURKEYS
EKRSUVY	KURVEYS
ELLLORR	LORRELL
ELLLORS	LOLLERS
ELLLOSZ	LOZELLS
ELLMNOO	MOELLON
ELLMNOP	POLLMEN
ELLMNOT	TOLLMEN
ELLMNSU	MULLENS
ELLMOOR	MORELLO
ELLMOSW	MELLOWS
ELLMOWY	MELLOWY
ELLMPUU	PLUMULE
ELLMRSU	MULLERS
ELLMSTU	MULLETS
ELLMSUV	VELLUMS
ELLMSUY	MULLEYS
ELLNNOT	TONNELL
ELLNOOW	WOOLLEN
ELLNOPS	POLLENS
ELLNOPT	POLLENT

ELLNORS	ENROLLS
ELLNOST	STOLLEN
ELLNOSU	NOUSELL
ELLNOSV	VELLONS
ELLNOSW	SWOLLEN
ELLNOVY	NOVELLY
ELLNOXY	XYLENOL
ELLNPSU	UNSPELL
ELLNSSU	UNSELLS
ELLNSUU	LUNULES
ELLOOSW	WOOSELL
ELLOOSY	LOOSELY
ELLOOTU	TOLUOLE
ELLOPRR	PROLLER
ELLOPRS	POLLERS
	REPOLLS
ELLOPTU	POLLUTE
ELLORRS	REROLLS
	ROLLERS
ELLORRT	TROLLER
ELLORSS	SOLLERS
	SORELLS
ELLORST	TOLLERS
ELLORTY	TROLLEY
ELLORVY	LOVERLY
ELLOSST	TOLSELS
ELLOSTU	OUTSELL
	SELLOUT
ELLOSTX	EXTOLLS
ELLOSVY	VOLLEYS
ELLOSWY	YELLOWS
ELLOTTU	OUTTELL
ELLOTUW	OUTWELL
ELLOTUY	OUTYELL
ELLOVWY	VOWELLY
ELLOWYY	YELLOWY
ELLPRSU	PULLERS
ELLPSTU	PULLETS
ELLPSUW	UPSWELL
	UPWELLS
ELLPSUY	PULLEYS
ELMMOPS	POMMELS
ELMMOPU	PUMMELO
ELMMORT	TROMMEL
ELMMPSU	PUMMELS
ELMMPTU	PLUMMET
ELMMRSU	SLUMMER
ELMMRTU	TUMMLER
ELMMSTU	STUMMEL
ELMNOOT	MOONLET
	TOOLMEN
ELMNOOW	WOOLMEN
ELMNOPW	PLOWMEN
ELMNORS	MERLONS
ELMNOST	LOMENTS
	MELTONS
ELMNOSY	MYELONS
ELMNOTU	MOULTEN
ELMNOTY	YMOLTEN
ELMNPPU	PLUMPEN
ELMNPSU	LUMPENS
	PLENUMS
ELMNPUU	UNPLUME
ELMOOPP	POMPELO
ELMOOPS	POMELOS
ELMOORT	TREMOLO
ELMOOSS	OSMOLES
ELMOOSY	MOOLEYS
ELMOPRT	PREMOLT
ELMOPRY	POLYMER
ELMOPSU	PLUMOSE
	PUMELOS
ELMOPSY	EMPLOYS
ELMORSS	MORSELS
ELMORST	MERLOTS
	MOLTERS
ELMORSU	EMULSOR
ELMORTT	MOTTLER
ELMORTU	MOULTER
ELMOSST	MOLESTS
ELMOSSU	MOUSLES
ELMOSSY	SMOYLES
ELMOSTT	MOTTLES
ELMOSTY	MOTLEYS
ELMOSUU	EMULOUS
ELMOSUV	VOLUMES
ELMOSXY	OXYMELS
ELMOSZZ	MOZZLES
ELMPPRU	PLUMPER
ELMPPSU	PEPLUMS
ELMPRSU	LUMPERS
	RUMPLES
ELMPRUY	PLUMERY
ELMRSTY	MYRTLES
ELMRTUU	MULTURE
ELMRTUY	ELYTRUM
ELMRUZZ	MUZZLER
ELMSSSU	MUSSELS
	SUMLESS
ELMSTUU	MUTUELS
	MUTULES
ELMSUZZ	MUZZLES
ELNNOPU	NONUPLE
ELNNORS	RONNELS
ELNNOSS	NELSONS
ELNNRSU	RUNNELS
ELNNRTU	TRUNNEL
ELNNSTU	TUNNELS
ELNOOSS	LOOSENS
ELNOOSU	UNLOOSE
ELNOOSW	WOOLENS
ELNOOSY	LOONEYS
ELNOOSZ	SNOOZLE
ELNOPRU	PLEURON
ELNOPRY	PRONELY
ELNOPST	LEPTONS
ELNOPSY	POLEYNS
ELNOPTU	OPULENT
ELNORSS	NORSELS
ELNORST	LENTORS
ELNORSU	NOURSLE
ELNORTY	ELYTRON
ELNOSSS	LESSONS
	SONLESS
ELNOSST	TELSONS
ELNOSSU	ENSOULS
	NOUSLES
ELNOSSV	SLOVENS
ELNOSSW	LOWNESS
ELNOSTT	TONLETS
ELNOSTU	LENTOUS
ELNOSTV	SOLVENT
ELNOSUV	UNLOVES
ELNOSUZ	ZONULES
ELNOSVY	LENVOYS
ELNOSZZ	NOZZLES
ELNOTTW	TOWNLET
ELNOTUZ	ZONULET
ELNOTVY	NOVELTY
ELNPSST	SPLENTS
ELNPSTU	PENULTS
ELNPSTY	PENTYLS
ELNRSSU	NURSLES
	RUNLESS
ELNRSTU	RUNLETS
ELNRSTY	STERNLY
ELNRSUU	UNRULES
ELNRSUZ	LUZERNS
ELNRUZZ	NUZZLER
ELNSSSU	SUNLESS
ELNSSSY	SELSYNS
	SLYNESS
ELNSTTU	NUTLETS
ELNSUZZ	NUZZLES
	SNUZZLE
ELOOPRS	LOOPERS
	SPOOLER
ELOORST	LOOTERS
	RETOOLS
	ROOTLES
	TOOLERS
ELOORSW	WOOLERS
ELOORTT	ROOTLET
	TOOTLER
ELOOSST	LOOSEST
	LOTOSES
ELOOSSW	WOOSELS
ELOOSTT	TOOTLES
ELOOSTU	OUTSOLE
ELOOSWY	WOOLSEY
ELOOTUV	OUTLOVE
ELOPPPS	POPPLES
ELOPPRS	LOPPERS
	PROPELS
ELOPPST	STOPPLE
	TOPPLES
ELOPPSU	POULPES
ELOPPSY	POLYPES
ELOPRRS	PROLERS
ELOPRRU	PROULER
ELOPRRW	PROWLER
ELOPRRY	PYRROLE
ELOPRSS	PLESSOR
	SLOPERS
	SPLORES
ELOPRST	PETROLS
	REPLOTS
ELOPRSU	LEPROUS
	PELORUS
	PERLOUS
	SPORULE
ELOPRSV	PLOVERS
ELOPRSW	PLOWERS
ELOPRSX	PLEXORS
ELOPRSY	LEPROSY
ELOPRTT	PLOTTER
ELOPRTU	PLOUTER
	POULTER
ELOPRTW	PLOWTER
ELOPRTY	PROTYLE
ELOPRVY	OVERPLY
	PLOVERY
ELOPSST	TOPLESS
ELOPSSU	SOUPLES
ELOPSTT	POTTLES
ELOPSTU	TUPELOS
ELOPSTY	PEYOTLS
ELOPSTZ	PLOTZES
ELOPTUY	OUTYELP
ELORRSS	SORRELS
ELORRSW	WORRELS
ELORSSS	LESSORS
ELORSST	OSTLERS
	STEROLS
	TORSELS
ELORSSV	SOLVERS
ELORSTT	SETTLOR
	SLOTTER
	TOLTERS
ELORSTU	ELUTORS
	OUTLERS
	TROULES
ELORSTV	REVOLTS
ELORSTW	TROWELS
	WORTLES
ELORSUV	LOUVERS
	LOUVRES
	VELOURS
ELORSUY	ELUSORY
ELORSVW	WOLVERS
ELORSWY	YOWLERS
ELORTTY	LOTTERY
ELORTVY	OVERTLY
ELOSSTU	LOTUSES
	SOLUTES
	TOUSLES
ELOSSTW	LOWSEST
	SLOWEST
ELOSSTY	SYSTOLE
	TOLSEYS
	TOYLESS
	TYLOSES
ELOSSVW	VOWLESS
ELOSSXY	XYLOSES
ELOSSZZ	SOZZLES
ELOSTTU	OUTLETS
ELOSTTY	TYLOTES
ELOSTUU	LUTEOUS
ELOSTUV	VOLUTES
ELOSTUZ	TOUZLES
ELOSTYZ	TOLZEYS
ELOSWYY	YOWLEYS
ELOSWZZ	SWOZZLE
ELPPRRU	PURPLER
ELPPRSU	PULPERS
	PURPLES
	REPULPS
	SUPPLER
ELPPSSU	SUPPLES
ELPQSUU	PULQUES
ELPRRSU	PURLERS
	SLURPER
ELPRSSU	PULSERS
ELPRSTU	SPURTLE
ELPRSUV	PULVERS
ELPRTUU	PULTURE
ELPRUZZ	PUZZLER
ELPSSSU	PLUSSES
	PUSSELS
ELPSSUU	LUPUSES
ELPSSUY	PUSLEYS
	PUSSLEY
	SPULYES
ELPSTUU	PLUTEUS
	PUSTULE
ELPSUZZ	PUZZELS
	PUZZLES
ELRRSTU	RUSTLER
ELRRTTU	TURTLER
ELRSSSU	RUSSELS
ELRSSTU	LUSTERS
	LUSTRES
	RESULTS
	RUSTLES
	SUTLERS
	ULSTERS
ELRSSTY	STYLERS
ELRSTTU	TURTLES
ELRSTTY	TETRYLS
ELRSTUY	SUTLERY
ELRSTWY	SWELTRY
ELRSUWY	WURLEYS
ELRSUWZ	WURZELS
ELRTTUY	UTTERLY
ELRTUUV	VULTURE
ELSSSTU	TUSSLES
ELSSSUU	LUSUSES
ELSSTTU	SUTTLES
ELSSTTY	STYLETS
ELSSTYY	SYSTYLE

ELSUWZZ WUZZLES
EMMMOST MOMMETS
EMMMRSU MUMMERS
EMMMRUY MUMMERY
EMMNNOS MNEMONS
EMMNOOR MONOMER
MOORMEN
EMMNOOT MOMENTO
MOOTMEN
EMMNORY MERONYM
EMMNOST MOMENTS
MONTEMS
EMMNOTU OMENTUM
EMMNOTY METONYM
EMMOOTY MYOTOME
EMMOPRR PROMMER
EMMORSS MOMSERS
EMMORSZ MOMZERS
EMMOSSU MOMUSES
MOUSMES
EMMOSYZ ZYMOMES
EMMPRSU MUMPERS
EMMPSTU METUMPS
EMMRRSU RUMMERS
EMMRSSU SUMMERS
EMMRSTU RUMMEST
EMMRSUY SUMMERY
EMMSSUU MUSEUMS
EMNNOOR MONERON
EMNNOSW SNOWMEN
EMNNOWW NEWMOWN
EMNOOPT METOPON
EMNOORS MOONERS
EMNOORT MONTERO
EMNOOSS MONOSES
EMNOOST MOONSET
EMNOOSY NOYSOME
EMNOOTY ENOMOTY
EMNOPPR PROPMEN
EMNOPRT PORTMEN
EMNOPST POSTMEN
TOPSMEN
EMNOPSU SPUMONE
EMNOPSY EPONYMS
EMNOPYY EPONYMY
EMNORRU MOURNER
EMNORSS SERMONS
EMNORST MENTORS
MONSTER
MONTRES
EMNORTT TORMENT
EMNORTU MONTURE
MOUNTER
REMOUNT
EMNOSST STEMSON
EMNOSTU UNSMOTE
EMNOSTY ETYMONS
EMNOSXY EXONYMS
EMNPSSU PENSUMS
EMNRRSU MURRENS
EMNRRUY UNMERRY
EMNRSSU RUMNESS
EMNRSTU MUNSTER
STERNUM
EMOOPRS OOSPERM
EMOOPRT PROMOTE
EMOOPRY POMEROY
EMOORRS MOROSER
ROOMERS
EMOORST MOOTERS
EMOORSU UROSOME
EMOOSSS OSMOSES
EMOOSTT MOOTEST
MOTTOES
TOOMEST

EMOOSTW TWOSOME
EMOOSTY MYOSOTE
TOYSOME
EMOOSXY OXYSOME
EMOOTUV OUTMOVE
EMOPPRS MOPPERS
EMOPPST MOPPETS
EMOPPSY POMPEYS
EMOPRRS ROMPERS
EMOPRST STOMPER
TROMPES
EMOPRSU SUPREMO
EMOPSSU MOPUSES
EMOPSSY MYOPSES
EMOQSSU MOSQUES
EMORRST TERMORS
TREMORS
EMORRSU MORSURE
EMORRSW WORMERS
EMORRWY WORMERY
EMORSSS MOSSERS
EMORSST MOTSERS
EMORSSU MOUSERS
SMOUSER
EMORSTU MOUTERS
OESTRUM
EMORSUY MOUSERY
EMOSSSU MOUSSES
SMOUSES
EMOSSTT MOSTEST
EMOSSYZ ZYMOSES
EMOSTTT MOTETTS
EMOSTVZ ZEMSTVO
EMOTTTU TETOTUM
EMOTUZZ MEZUZOT
EMPPRSU PUMPERS
REPUMPS
EMPRSTU STUMPER
SUMPTER
EMPRTTU TRUMPET
EMPSSTU SEPTUMS
EMRRSTU STURMER
EMRRSUY MURREYS
EMRSSTU ESTRUMS
MUSTERS
STUMERS
EMRSTTU MUTTERS
EMRSTYY MYSTERY
EMSSSTY SYSTEMS
ENNNOPS PENNONS
ENNNOSW NONNEWS
ENNNRUY NUNNERY
ENNOOPR PRENOON
ENNOORS NOONERS
ENNOORT NORTENO
ENNOORZ NONZERO
ENNOOTT NONETTO
ENNORST STONERN
TONNERS
ENNORSU NEURONS
NONUSER
ENNORSW RENOWNS
WONNERS
ENNORTU NEUTRON
ENNORUV UNROVEN
ENNOSST SONNETS
STONNES
TENSONS
ENNOSSU NONUSES
ENNOSSW NOWNESS
ENNOSTU NEUSTON
ENNOSTW NEWTONS
ENNOSTZ TENZONS
ENNOUVW UNWOVEN
ENNPRSU PUNNERS

ENNPSTU PUNNETS
UNSPENT
ENNRRSU RUNNERS
ENNRSTU RUNNETS
STUNNER
ENNRSUW WUNNERS
ENNSSTU UNNESTS
ENNSTTU UNTENTS
ENNSTUU UNTUNES
ENNTTUY UNTENTY
ENOOPPR PROPONE
ENOOPRS OPERONS
SNOOPER
ENOOPSY SPOONEY
ENOORSS NOOSERS
SEROONS
SOONERS
ENOORST ENROOTS
ENOORSU ONEROUS
ENOORSW SWOONER
ENOORSZ SNOOZER
ENOOSST SOONEST
ENOOSSZ SNOOZES
ENOOSTT TESTOON
ENOOSTU UNSOOTE
ENOOTXY OXYTONE
ENOPPSU UNPOPES
ENOPRRS PERRONS
ENOPRRU PRONEUR
ENOPRSS PERSONS
ENOPRST POSTERN
PRONEST
ENOPRSU UNROPES
ENOPRSY PROYNES
PYONERS
PYRONES
ENOPRTT PORTENT
ENOPRTY ENTROPY
ENOPSST POSNETS
STEPSON
ENOPSTT POTENTS
ENOPSWY POWNEYS
ENOQTUU UNQUOTE
ENORRSS SNORERS
SORNERS
ENORRST SNORTER
ENORRTT TORRENT
ENORRUV OVERRUN
RUNOVER
ENORSSS SENSORS
ENORSST NESTORS
STONERS
TENSORS
ENORSSW WORSENS
ENORSSY SENSORY
ENORSTT ROTTENS
SNOTTER
STENTOR
ENORSTU TENOURS
TONSURE
ENORSTY TYRONES
ENORSUV NERVOUS
ENORSUW UNSWORE
ENORSUZ ZONURES
ENORSVY RENVOYS
ENORSZZ NOZZERS
ENORTUW UNWROTE
ENORTUY TOURNEY
ENOSSST SESTONS
ENOSSTT OSTENTS
TESTONS
ENOSSTU OUTNESS
TONUSES
ENOSSTW TWONESS
ENOSSTX SEXTONS

ENOSSUW SWOUNES
ENOSSWW SWOWNES
ENOSTTU STOUTEN
TENUTOS
ENOSTUU TENUOUS
ENOTTUW OUTWENT
ENPRRSU PRUNERS
SPURNER
ENPRSSU SPURNES
ENPRSTU PUNSTER
PUNTERS
ENPRSUU UNPURSE
ENPRSWY PREWYNS
ENPSSSU SUSPENS
ENPSSTU UNSTEPS
ENPSTTU STUPENT
ENPSTUU TUNEUPS
ENPSTUW UNSWEPT
ENRRSSU NURSERS
ENRRSTU RETURNS
TURNERS
ENRRSUU UNSURER
ENRRSUY NURSERY
ENRRTUU NURTURE
UNTRUER
ENRRTUY TURNERY
ENRSSTU UNRESTS
ENRSSWY WRYNESS
ENRSTTU ENTRUST
NUTTERS
ENRSUZZ NUZZERS
ENRSVWY WYVERNS
ENRTTUY NUTTERY
ENSSSTU SUNSETS
EOOOPRS OOSPORE
EOOPPRS OPPOSER
PROPOSE
EOOPPRV POPOVER
EOOPPSS OPPOSES
EOOPRRS SPOORER
EOOPRRT PROTORE
TROOPER
EOOPRSS POROSES
EOOPRST POOREST
POOTERS
STOOPER
EOOPRSW SWOOPER
EOOPRTU OUTROPE
EOOPRTV OVERTOP
EOOPRTW TOWROPE
EOOPRVY POOVERY
EOOPRYZ ZOOPERY
EOOPSST STOOPES
EOOPSSW WOOPSES
EOOPTYZ ZOOTYPE
EOORRSS ROOSERS
EOORRST ROOSTER
ROOTERS
TOREROS
EOORSSS SOROSES
EOORSTT TOOTERS
EOORSVW OVERSOW
EOORTUW OUTWORE
EOOSSST OSTOSES
EOOSSSU OSSEOUS
EOOSSTT TOOTSES
EOOSTWZ WOOTZES
EOOTTUV OUTVOTE
EOPPPRS POPPERS
EOPPPST POPPETS
EOPPRRS PROPERS
PROSPER
EOPPRSS OPPRESS
PORPESS
EOPPRST STOPPER

	TOPPERS
EOPPRSU	PURPOSE
EOPPRSW	SWOPPER
EOPPRSY	PYROPES
	YOPPERS
EOPPSSU	SUPPOSE
EOPRRSS	PRESSOR
	PROSERS
EOPRRST	PORTERS
	PRESORT
	PRETORS
	REPORTS
	SPORTER
EOPRRSU	POURERS
	REPOURS
EOPRRSV	PROVERS
EOPRRTU	TROUPER
EOPRSSS	POSSERS
	PROSSES
EOPRSST	PORTESS
	POSTERS
	PRESTOS
	REPOSTS
	RESPOTS
	STOPERS
EOPRSSU	POSEURS
	SEROPUS
	SOUPERS
EOPRSSW	PROWESS
EOPRSSY	OSPREYS
	PYROSES
EOPRSTT	POTTERS
	PROTEST
	SPOTTER
EOPRSTU	PETROUS
	POSTURE
	POUTERS
	PROTEUS
	SEPTUOR
	SPOUTER
	TROUPES
EOPRSTW	POWTERS
	PROWEST
EOPRSTX	EXPORTS
EOPRSTZ	POTZERS
EOPRSUU	POURSUE
	UPROUSE
EOPRSUV	OVERSUP
EOPRSUW	POURSEW
EOPRTTY	POTTERY
EOPRTUY	EUTROPY
EOPRTVY	POVERTY
EOPSSSS	POSSESS
EOPSSST	POSSETS
EOPSSSU	POUSSES
	SPOUSES
EOPSSTX	SEXPOTS
EOPSTTU	OUTSTEP
	TOUPETS
EOPSTTW	STEWPOT
EOPTTUW	OUTWEPT
EOQRRTU	TORQUER
EOQRSTU	QUESTOR
	QUOTERS
	ROQUETS
	TORQUES
EOQSTTU	TOQUETS
EORRRST	RORTERS
	TERRORS
EORRSSS	ROSSERS
EORRSST	RESORTS
	ROSTERS
	SORTERS
	STORERS
EORRSSU	ROUSERS
EORRSTT	RETORTS
	ROTTERS
	STERTOR
	TORRETS
EORRSTU	RETOURS
	ROUSTER
	ROUTERS
	TOURERS
	TROUSER
EORRSTV	TROVERS
EORRSTW	STROWER
EORRSTY	ROYSTER
	STROYER
EORRSZZ	ROZZERS
EORRTTT	TROTTER
EORRTTU	TORTURE
	TROUTER
EORSSST	TOSSERS
EORSSSU	SOURSES
EORSSTU	ESTROUS
	OESTRUS
	OUSTERS
	SOUREST
	SOUTERS
	STOURES
	TOUSERS
	TROUSES
	TUSSORE
EORSSTV	STOVERS
	VOTRESS
EORSSTW	SOWTERS
	STOWERS
	STOWRES
	TOWSERS
	WORSETS
EORSSTY	OYSTERS
	STOREYS
EORSSTZ	ZOSTERS
EORSSWW	WOWSERS
EORSTTT	STOTTER
	STRETTO
	TOTTERS
EORSTTU	OUTSERT
	STOUTER
	TOUTERS
EORSTTW	SWOTTER
EORSTTX	EXTORTS
EORSTTY	ROSETTY
EORSTUX	SEXTUOR
EORSUVY	VOYEURS
EORTTTY	TOTTERY
EORTTUY	TUTOYER
EOSSSST	STOSSES
EOSSSSW	SOWSSES
EOSSTTU	OUTSETS
	SETOUTS
EOSSUYZ	SOYUZES
EOSTTTW	WOTTEST
EPPPSTU	PUPPETS
EPPRRTU	PRERUPT
EPPRRUU	PURPURE
EPPRSSU	SUPPERS
EPPSSTU	UPSTEPS
EPPSTUW	UPSWEPT
EPRRRSU	SPURRER
EPRRSSU	PURSERS
EPRRSUU	PURSUER
	USURPER
EPRRSUY	SPURREY
EPRRTUU	RUPTURE
EPRSSSU	PUSSERS
EPRSSTU	UPRESTS
EPRSSTY	SPRYEST
EPRSSUU	PURSUES
EPRSSUW	PURSEWS
EPRSTTU	PUTTERS
	SPUTTER
EPRSTUU	PUTURES
EPRSUVY	PURVEYS
EQRSTWY	QWERTYS
ERRSSTU	RUSTRES
	TRUSSER
ERRSSUU	USURERS
ERRSSUY	SURREYS
ERRSTTU	RUTTERS
	TRUSTER
	TURRETS
ERRSTTY	TRYSTER
ERSSSTU	RUSSETS
	TRUSSES
	TUSSERS
ERSSSUU	USURESS
ERSSTTU	TUTRESS
ERSSTTY	TRYSTES
ERSSTUU	SUTURES
ERSSTUY	RUSSETY
ERSSTXY	XYSTERS
ERSSUVW	SURVEWS
ERSSUVY	SURVEYS
ERSTTTU	STUTTER
ERSTTUX	URTEXTS
FFFGINU	FUFFING
FFFILOT	LIFTOFF
FFFLOSY	FLYOFFS
FFGGINO	GOFFING
FFGHINU	HUFFING
FFGIIMN	MIFFING
FFGIINN	NIFFING
FFGIINR	GRIFFIN
	RIFFING
FFGIINT	TIFFING
FFGILNU	LUFFING
FFGIMNU	MUFFING
FFGINOR	GRIFFON
FFGINOS	GONIFFS
	OFFINGS
FFGINPU	PUFFING
FFGINRU	RUFFING
FFGLOOS	LOGOFFS
FFGLRUY	GRUFFLY
FFHHISU	HUFFISH
FFHIINS	FINFISH
FFHIISY	FISHIFY
FFHIKNU	HUFFKIN
FFHILSU	FISHFUL
FFHILTY	FIFTHLY
FFHILUY	HUFFILY
FFHIMSU	MUFFISH
FFHIOST	TOFFISH
FFHIOSX	FOXFISH
FFHOOSW	SHOWOFF
FFHORSS	SHROFFS
FFHOSTU	SHUTOFF
FFIILMY	MIFFILY
FFIINST	TIFFINS
FFIISUZ	ZIFFIUS
FFIKLSS	SKLIFFS
FFILLLU	FULFILL
FFILLSU	FULFILS
FFILOST	FILFOTS
FFILOUZ	ZUFFOLI
FFILPSS	SPLIFFS
FFILPUY	PUFFILY
FFILRTY	FRITFLY
FFILSTU	FISTFUL
FFILSTY	STIFFLY
FFIMNSU	MUFFINS
FFINNSU	NUFFINS
FFINOOT	FINFOOT
FFINOPS	SPINOFF
FFINOPT	PONTIFF
FFINPSU	PUFFINS
FFINRSU	RUFFINS
FFIOPRS	RIPOFFS
FFIOPST	TIPOFFS
FFIORTY	FORTIFY
FFIOSST	SOFFITS
FFIQSUY	SQUIFFY
FFIRTUY	FRUTIFY
FFJMOPU	JUMPOFF
FFKLORU	FORKFUL
FFLLOOU	LOOFFUL
FFLMORU	FORMFUL
FFLNSUY	SNUFFLY
FFLOOUZ	ZUFFOLO
FFLOSTY	FYLFOTS
FFNORSU	RUNOFFS
FFNORTU	TURNOFF
FFOOPST	STOPOFF
FFOPSTU	OFFPUTS
	PUTOFFS
FFRRSUU	FURFURS
FGGGIIN	FIGGING
FGGGINO	FOGGING
FGGGINU	FUGGING
FGGHIIS	FISHGIG
FGGIINT	GIFTING
FGGIISS	FISGIGS
FGGIISZ	FIZGIGS
FGGIIZZ	FIZZGIG
FGGILNO	GOLFING
FGGILNU	FUGLING
	GULFING
FGGILOY	FOGGILY
FGGILUY	FUGGILY
FGGINOO	GOOFING
FGGINOR	FORGING
FGGINOW	GOWFING
FGGINUU	FUGUING
FGHHIOS	HOGFISH
FGHIINS	FISHING
FGHIINT	INFIGHT
FGHIIPS	PIGFISH
FGHILST	FLIGHTS
FGHILSU	SIGHFUL
FGHILTY	FLIGHTY
FGHIMNU	HUMFING
FGHINOO	HOOFING
FGHINOU	HOUFING
FGHINOW	HOWFING
FGHIOSY	FOGYISH
FGHIRST	FRIGHTS
FGHNOOR	FOGHORN
FGHORUY	FROUGHY
FGHOTUY	FOUGHTY
FGIIKNN	FINKING
	KNIFING
FGIIKNR	FIRKING
FGIIKNS	FISKING
FGIILLN	FILLING
FGIILMN	FILMING
FGIILNO	FOILING
FGIILNR	RIFLING
FGIILNS	FILINGS
FGIILNT	FLITING
	LIFTING
FGIILNX	FLIXING
FGIILNY	LIGNIFY
FGIIMNR	FIRMING
FGIINNN	FINNING
FGIINNO	FOINING
FGIINNS	FININGS
FGIINRR	FIRRING
FGIINRS	FIRINGS
FGIINRT	RIFTING

FGIINRY	NIGRIFY
FGIINRZ	FRIZING
FGIINST	FISTING
	SIFTING
FGIINSX	FIXINGS
FGIINSY	SIGNIFY
FGIINTT	FITTING
	TIFTING
FGIINZZ	FIZZING
FGIKLNU	FLUKING
FGIKNNU	FUNKING
FGIKNOR	FORKING
FGILLNU	FULLING
FGILMNU	FLUMING
FGILNOO	FOOLING
FGILNOP	FOPLING
FGILNOR	ROLFING
FGILNOT	LOFTING
FGILNOU	FOULING
FGILNOW	FLOWING
	FOWLING
	WOLFING
FGILNOY	FOYLING
FGILNPU	UPFLING
FGILNPY	FLYPING
FGILNRU	FURLING
FGILNSU	INGULFS
FGILNSY	FLYINGS
FGILNTU	FLUTING
FGILNTY	FLYTING
FGILNUX	FLUXING
FGILOOY	GOOFILY
FGILORY	GLORIFY
FGIMNOR	FORMING
FGIMOSY	FOGYISM
FGINNNO	FONNING
FGINNNU	FUNNING
FGINNOY	FOYNING
FGINOOR	ROOFING
FGINOOT	FOOTING
FGINOOW	WOOFING
FGINOPP	FOPPING
FGINOPU	POUFING
FGINORT	FORTING
FGINOST	SOFTING
FGINOSW	SOWFING
FGINOSX	FOXINGS
FGINRRU	FURRING
FGINRSU	SURFING
FGINRSY	FRYINGS
FGINRTU	TURFING
FGINSSU	FUSSING
FGINSTU	FUSTING
FGINTTU	TUFTING
FGINTUZ	FUTZING
FGINUZZ	FUZZING
FGIORST	FRIGOTS
FGIORTW	FIGWORT
FGISTUU	FUGUIST
FGJLSUU	JUGFULS
	JUGSFUL
FGLLNUU	LUNGFUL
FGLLOWY	GLOWFLY
FGLMSUU	MUGFULS
FGLNORU	FURLONG
FGLNOSU	SONGFUL
FGLNPUU	UPFLUNG
FGLOOUY	UFOLOGY
FGLORSU	FULGORS
FGLORUU	FULGOUR
FGLOTUY	GOUTFLY
FGLSTUU	GUSTFUL
	GUTFULS
	GUTSFUL
FGNOORU	FOURGON
FGNORSY	GRYFONS
FGNOSUU	FUNGOUS
FHHLSUU	HUSHFUL
FHIILMS	FILMISH
FHIILSY	FISHILY
FHIILTY	LITHIFY
FHIINPS	PINFISH
FHIKLOS	FOLKISH
FHILLSU	FULLISH
FHILOOS	FOOLISH
FHILOSW	WOLFISH
FHILPSU	SHIPFUL
FHILPTU	PITHFUL
FHILSUW	WISHFUL
FHINOSU	FUSHION
FHINRSU	FURNISH
FHINSSU	SUNFISH
FHINSTU	UNSHIFT
FHIOOST	OOFTISH
FHIOPPS	FOPPISH
FHIOPSX	FOXSHIP
FHIORRY	HORRIFY
FHIOSST	SOFTISH
FHIOSTU	OUTFISH
FHIPPSU	PUPFISH
FHIPSTU	UPSHIFT
FHIRSST	SHRIFTS
FHIRSTT	THRIFTS
FHIRTTY	THRIFTY
FHIRTUY	THURIFY
FHISSSU	HUSSIFS
FHISSTU	SHUFTIS
FHKORTU	FUTHORK
FHLNORU	HORNFUL
FHLNSUU	UNFLUSH
FHLOOSY	SHOOFLY
FHLOPSU	SHOPFUL
FHLPSUU	PUSHFUL
FHLRTUU	HURTFUL
	RUTHFUL
FHNOTUX	FOXHUNT
FHOOORS	FORHOOS
FHOOORT	HOOFROT
FHOOOTT	HOTFOOT
FHOORSW	FORHOWS
FHORSTU	FOURTHS
FIIIKNN	FINIKIN
FIIKNRS	FIRKINS
FIIKNYZ	ZINKIFY
FIILLMO	MILFOIL
FIILLMY	FILMILY
FIILLNS	INFILLS
FIILLPS	FILLIPS
FIILLSU	FUSILLI
FIILNOT	TINFOIL
FIILNTY	NIFTILY
FIILPTU	PITIFUL
FIILQUY	LIQUIFY
FIIMMNU	INFIMUM
FIIMNRS	INFIRMS
FIIMSST	MISFITS
FIINORS	FIORINS
FIINOSS	FISSION
FIINRTY	NITRIFY
FIIPSTY	TIPSIFY
FIIRTVY	VITRIFY
FIJLLOY	JOLLIFY
FIJSTUY	JUSTIFY
FIKKLNO	KINFOLK
FIKLLSU	SKILFUL
FIKLNOW	WOLFKIN
FIKLNSU	SKINFUL
FIKLRSU	RISKFUL
FIKLSTU	KISTFUL
FIKNNOS	FINNSKO
FIKNOSX	FOXSKIN
FIKRSTU	TURFSKI
FILLLUW	WILLFUL
FILLMOY	MOLLIFY
FILLNUY	NULLIFY
FILLOTU	TOILFUL
FILLOTY	LOFTILY
FILLPSU	UPFILLS
FILLSTU	LISTFUL
FILMNOO	MONOFIL
FILMOSU	FOLIUMS
FILMSTU	MISTFUL
FILNNUY	FUNNILY
FILNORS	FLORINS
FILNORU	FLUORIN
FILNOSW	INFLOWS
FILNOUX	FLUXION
FILNSTU	TINFULS
FILNTUY	UNFITLY
FILOOSU	FOLIOUS
FILOOTW	WITLOOF
FILORST	FIRLOTS
	FLORIST
FILORSV	FRIVOLS
FILORTU	FLORUIT
FILORTY	TRIFOLY
FILOSSS	FOSSILS
FILPPUY	PULPIFY
FILPSTU	UPLIFTS
FILRRUY	FURRILY
FILRSTY	FIRSTLY
FILRYZZ	FRIZZLY
FILSSUY	FUSSILY
FILSTTU	FLUTIST
FILSTUW	WISTFUL
FILSTUY	FUSTILY
FILSTWY	SWIFTLY
FILTTUY	TUFTILY
FILUYZZ	FUZZILY
FIMMMUY	MUMMIFY
FIMMORS	MISFORM
FIMNORS	INFORMS
FIMNORU	UNIFORM
FIMOORV	OVIFORM
FIMORRT	TRIFORM
FIMORTY	MORTIFY
FIMRTUY	FURMITY
FIMSTYY	MYSTIFY
FINOOSS	FOISONS
FINOPRS	FRIPONS
FINOPTY	PONTIFY
FINORSS	FRISSON
FINORST	FORINTS
FINORTY	INTROFY
FINOSSU	FUSIONS
FIOORSU	FURIOSO
FIOPRST	FORPITS
	PROFITS
	SPORTIF
FIOPRSY	PROSIFY
FIOPSTX	POSTFIX
FIORRTY	TORRIFY
FIORSUU	FURIOUS
FIOSTTU	OUTFITS
FIPPUYY	YUPPIFY
FIRSSTT	STRIFTS
FIRSSUY	RUSSIFY
FKLMOOT	FOLKMOT
FKLORUW	WORKFUL
FKNOSTY	KONFYTS
FKOOORS	FORSOOK
FLLOOSW	FOLLOWS
FLLOPTU	PLOTFUL
	TOPFULL
FLLOSUU	SOULFUL
FLLOUWY	WOFULLY
FLLSTUU	LUSTFUL
FLMMOUX	FLUMMOX
FLMNOOU	MOUFLON
FLMNOSU	MUFLONS
FLMOOOT	TOMFOOL
FLMOORS	FORMOLS
FLMOORU	ROOMFUL
FLMORSY	FORMYLS
FLMSUUU	FUMULUS
FLNOORR	FORLORN
FLNOOSU	UNFOOLS
FLNOOSW	ONFLOWS
FLNRSUU	UNFURLS
	URNFULS
FLOOOTU	OUTFOOL
FLOOPWX	FOWLPOX
FLOORSW	FORSLOW
FLOOTUW	OUTFLOW
FLOPSTU	POTFULS
FLOPSUW	UPFLOWS
FLOPTUU	POUTFUL
FLOSUUV	FULVOUS
FLPRSUU	UPFURLS
FLRSSUU	SULFURS
FLRSUUY	SULFURY
FMNORSU	UNFORMS
FMRSTUU	FRUSTUM
FNNNUUY	UNFUNNY
FNNOORT	FRONTON
FNOORRW	FORWORN
FNOORSU	SUNROOF
	UNROOFS
FNOPRTU	UPFRONT
FNRSTUU	UNTURFS
FNSSUUY	UNFUSSY
FNSTTUU	UNSTUFT
FOOOPRT	ROOFTOP
FOOORTT	FOOTROT
FOOOTTU	OUTFOOT
FOORSSS	FOSSORS
FOORTTX	FOXTROT
FOPSSTU	FUSSPOT
FORRSUW	FURROWS
FORRUWY	FURROWY
FORSSTW	FROWSTS
FORSTWY	FROWSTY
GGGGIIN	GIGGING
GGGHINO	HOGGING
GGGHINU	HUGGING
GGGIIJN	JIGGING
GGGIILN	LIGGING
GGGIINP	PIGGING
GGGIINR	RIGGING
GGGIINT	TIGGING
GGGIINW	WIGGING
GGGIINZ	ZIGGING
GGGIIST	GIGGITS
GGGIJNO	JOGGING
GGGIJNU	JUGGING
GGGILNO	LOGGING
GGGILNU	LUGGING
GGGIMNO	MOGGING
GGGIMNU	MUGGING
GGGINNO	GONGING
	NOGGING
GGGINOR	GORGING
GGGINOS	SOGGING
GGGINOT	TOGGING
GGGINOU	GOUGING
GGGINPU	PUGGING
GGGINRU	GURGING
	RUGGING
GGGINSU	SUGGING
GGGINTU	TUGGING

GGHHIIN	HIGHING
GGHHIOS	HOGGISH
GGHIIJS	JIGGISH
GGHIINN	HINGING
	NIGHING
GGHIINS	SIGHING
GGHIIPS	PIGGISH
GGHIIRS	RIGGISH
GGHIITT	THIGGIT
GGHIMSU	MUGGISH
GGHINNO	HONGING
GGHINOS	HOGGINS
GGHINSU	GUSHING
	SUGHING
GGHIPSU	PUGGISH
GGHLOSY	SHOGGLY
GGHORSU	GROUGHS
GGHOSTU	THUGGOS
GGIIILN	GINGILI
GGIIJJS	JIGJIGS
GGIIKNN	KINGING
GGIILLN	GILLING
GGIILMN	GLIMING
GGIILNP	PIGLING
GGIILNR	RIGLING
GGIILNU	GUILING
GGIIMNN	MINGING
GGIIMNP	GIMPING
GGIIMNR	GRIMING
GGIINNN	GINNING
GGIINNO	INGOING
GGIINNP	PINGING
GGIINNR	GIRNING
	RINGING
GGIINNS	SIGNING
	SINGING
GGIINNT	TINGING
GGIINNW	WINGING
GGIINNZ	ZINGING
GGIINPP	GIPPING
GGIINPR	GRIPING
GGIINPS	PIGGINS
GGIINRS	GRISING
GGIINRT	GIRTING
	RINGGIT
GGIINSU	GUISING
GGIINSV	GIVINGS
GGIIRRS	GRIGRIS
GGIJNSU	JUGGINS
GGIKNOS	GINKGOS
GGILLNU	GULLING
GGILMUY	MUGGILY
GGILNNO	LONGING
GGILNNU	LUNGING
GGILNOS	GOSLING
	OGLINGS
GGILNOV	GLOVING
GGILNOW	GLOWING
	GOWLING
GGILNOZ	GLOZING
GGILNPU	GULPING
GGILNRU	GURLING
GGILNSU	LUGINGS
GGILNUY	GUYLING
	UGLYING
GGILOOS	GIGOLOS
GGILOST	GIGLOTS
GGILOSY	SOGGILY
GGILRWY	WRIGGLY
GGIMMNU	GUMMING
GGIMNOR	GORMING
GGIMNPU	GUMPING
GGIMNPY	GYMPING
GGIMNSU	MUGGINS
GGINNNU	GUNNING
GGINNOO	ONGOING
GGINNOP	PONGING
GGINNOR	GRONING
GGINNOS	NOGGINS
GGINNOT	TONGING
GGINNOW	GOWNING
GGINNRU	GURNING
GGINOOP	POGOING
GGINOOS	GOOSING
GGINOPR	GORPING
	GROPING
	PORGING
GGINOPU	UPGOING
GGINOQS	QIGONGS
GGINORS	GORINGS
	GRINGOS
GGINORU	ROGUING
	ROUGING
GGINORW	GROWING
GGINOUV	VOGUING
GGINPPY	GYPPING
GGINPRU	PURGING
GGINRSU	SURGING
	URGINGS
GGINSTU	GUSTING
	GUTSING
GGINTTU	GUTTING
GGIOORS	GORGIOS
GGIPRSY	SPRIGGY
GGLLOOS	LOGLOGS
GGLOOOS	GOOGOLS
GGMRSUU	MUGGURS
GGNOORS	GORGONS
GGRRSUU	GRUGRUS
GHHHIIS	HIGHISH
GHHHIST	HIGHTHS
GHHIINS	HISHING
GHHINSU	HUSHING
GHHIRST	SHRIGHT
GHHORTU	THROUGH
GHHOSSU	SHOUGHS
GHHOTTU	THOUGHT
GHIIKNO	HOIKING
GHIIKNT	KITHING
GHIILLN	HILLING
GHIILNR	HIRLING
GHIILNT	HILTING
	LITHING
GHIILNW	WHILING
GHIILRS	GIRLISH
GHIINNS	SHINING
GHIINNT	HINTING
	NITHING
GHIINNW	WHINING
GHIINOS	HOISING
GHIINPP	HIPPING
GHIINPS	PISHING
GHIINPT	PITHING
GHIINRS	HIRINGS
GHIINSS	HISSING
GHIINST	HISTING
	INSIGHT
	SHITING
	SITHING
GHIINSW	WISHING
GHIINTT	HITTING
	TITHING
GHIINTW	WHITING
	WITHING
GHIINZZ	HIZZING
GHIIOPR	PIROGHI
GHIIRST	TIGRISH
GHIJNOS	JOSHING
GHIKLNO	HOLKING
GHIKLNU	HULKING
GHIKNNO	HONKING
GHIKNOO	HOOKING
GHIKNOW	HOWKING
GHIKNST	KNIGHTS
GHIKNSU	HUSKING
GHIKNTY	KYTHING
GHIKRTU	TUGHRIK
GHILLNU	HULLING
GHILLSU	GULLISH
GHILLTY	LIGHTLY
GHILNOS	HOLINGS
	LONGISH
GHILNOT	THOLING
GHILNOW	HOWLING
GHILNPU	INGULPH
GHILNRU	HURLING
GHILNSU	LUSHING
	SHULING
GHILNSY	SHINGLY
GHILNTY	NIGHTLY
GHILPST	PLIGHTS
GHILPTU	UPLIGHT
GHILPTY	YPLIGHT
GHILRTY	RIGHTLY
GHILSST	SLIGHTS
GHILSTY	SIGHTLY
GHILSUY	GUSHILY
GHILTTY	TIGHTLY
GHILTWY	WIGHTLY
GHIMMNU	HUMMING
GHIMNNY	HYMNING
GHIMNOS	GNOMISH
	HOMINGS
	MOSHING
GHIMNPU	HUMPING
GHIMNRY	RHYMING
GHIMNSU	MUSHING
GHIMRSU	SIMURGH
GHIMSST	SMIGHTS
GHIMSTT	MIGHTST
GHINNOP	PHONING
GHINNOR	HORNING
GHINNOS	NOSHING
GHINNOT	NOTHING
GHINNTU	HUNTING
GHINOOP	HOOPING
	POOHING
GHINOOS	SHOOING
GHINOOT	HOOTING
GHINOOV	HOOVING
GHINOPP	HOPPING
GHINOPS	GINSHOP
	POSHING
GHINOPY	HYPOING
GHINORS	HORSING
	SHORING
GHINORW	WHORING
GHINOST	HOSTING
	TOSHING
GHINOSU	HOUSING
GHINOSV	SHOVING
GHINOSW	SHOWING
GHINOTT	HOTTING
	TONIGHT
GHINOTU	HOUTING
	THOUING
GHINPPU	HUPPING
GHINPPY	HYPPING
GHINPSU	GUNSHIP
	PUSHING
GHINRSU	RUSHING
GHINRTU	HURTING
	UNGIRTH
	UNRIGHT
GHINSTU	SHUTING
	TUSHING
	UNSIGHT
GHINTTU	HUTTING
GHINTTY	TYTHING
GHIOPSZ	PHIZOGS
GHIORST	RIGHTOS
GHIORSU	ROGUISH
GHIOSUV	VOGUISH
GHIPRST	SPRIGHT
GHIPRTU	UPRIGHT
GHIPSST	SPIGHTS
GHIPTTU	UPTIGHT
GHIQSTU	QUIGHTS
GHIRSTW	WRIGHTS
GHISTTW	TWIGHTS
GHLMOOO	HOMOLOG
GHLOOSY	SHOOGLY
GHLOPSU	PLOUGHS
GHLORUY	ROUGHLY
GHLOSSU	SLOUGHS
GHLOSTY	GHOSTLY
GHLOSUY	SLOUGHY
GHLOTUY	TOUGHLY
GHMORSU	SORGHUM
GHMOSTU	MUGSHOT
GHMPRSU	GRUMPHS
GHMPRUY	GRUMPHY
GHNOOPS	GONOPHS
GHNOPRY	GRYPHON
GHNORST	THRONGS
GHNORUU	UNROUGH
GHNOSSU	SHOGUNS
GHNOSTU	GUNSHOT
	HOGNUTS
	NOUGHTS
	SHOTGUN
GHNOTUY	YOUNGTH
GHOOOSW	HOOSGOW
GHOOPST	PHOTOGS
GHOOQSU	QUOHOGS
GHOORSS	SORGHOS
GHORSTU	TROUGHS
GHORSTW	GROWTHS
GHORTUW	WROUGHT
GHORTUY	YOGHURT
GHORTWY	GROWTHY
GHOSTUU	OUTGUSH
GIIINRS	IRISING
GIIJKNN	JINKING
GIIJLNT	JILTING
GIIJNNO	JOINING
GIIJNNX	JINXING
GIIKKNN	KINKING
GIIKKNR	KIRKING
GIIKLLN	KILLING
GIIKLMN	MILKING
GIIKLNN	INKLING
	KILNING
	LINKING
GIIKLNR	LIRKING
GIIKLNS	LIKINGS
	SILKING
GIIKLNT	KILTING
	KITLING
GIIKNNO	OINKING
GIIKNNP	KINGPIN
	PINKING
GIIKNNR	KIRNING
	RINKING
GIIKNNS	SINKING
GIIKNNT	TINKING
GIIKNNV	KNIVING
GIIKNNW	WINKING
GIIKNNZ	ZINKING
GIIKNPP	KIPPING

GIIKNPS	PIGSKIN
	SPIKING
GIIKNRS	GIRKINS
	GRISKIN
	KRISING
	RISKING
GIIKNRY	YIRKING
GIIKNSS	KISSING
	SKIINGS
GIIKNST	KISTING
	KITINGS
	SKITING
GIIKNSV	SKIVING
	VIKINGS
GIIKNTT	KITTING
GIILLLN	LILLING
GIILLMN	MILLING
GIILLNN	NILLING
GIILLNO	GILLION
GIILLNP	PILLING
GIILLNR	RILLING
GIILLNT	LILTING
	TILLING
GIILLNW	WILLING
GIILMNN	LIMNING
GIILMNO	MOILING
GIILMNP	LIMPING
GIILMNS	LIMINGS
	SLIMING
	SMILING
GIILMNT	MILTING
GIILMPR	PILGRIM
GIILMRY	GRIMILY
GIILNNN	LINNING
GIILNNR	NIRLING
GIILNNS	LIGNINS
	LININGS
GIILNNY	INLYING
GIILNOP	PIGNOLI
GIILNOR	LIGROIN
	ROILING
GIILNOS	SILOING
	SOILING
GIILNOT	TOILING
GIILNPP	LIPPING
GIILNPS	LISPING
	PILINGS
	SLIPING
	SPILING
GIILNRS	RIGLINS
GIILNRT	TIRLING
GIILNST	LISTING
	SILTING
	STILING
	TILINGS
GIILNSV	LIVINGS
	SLIVING
GIILNTT	TILTING
	TITLING
GIILNTW	WILTING
	WITLING
GIILOSS	GLIOSIS
GIILOST	OLIGIST
GIILRST	STRIGIL
GIIMMNN	NIMMING
GIIMMNR	RIMMING
GIIMNNS	MININGS
GIIMNNT	MINTING
GIIMNPP	PIMPING
GIIMNPR	PRIMING
GIIMNPS	IMPINGS
GIIMNRT	MITRING
GIIMNRV	MIRVING
GIIMNSS	MISSING
GIIMNST	MISTING
	SMITING
	STIMING
	TIMINGS
GIINNNP	PINNING
GIINNNR	RINNING
GIINNNS	INNINGS
	SINNING
GIINNNT	TINNING
GIINNNW	WINNING
GIINNOP	OPINING
	PIONING
GIINNOR	IRONING
	ROINING
GIINNOS	NOISING
GIINNOT	OINTING
GIINNPP	NIPPING
GIINNPS	SNIPING
GIINNPU	PINGUIN
GIINNRS	RINSING
GIINNRT	TRINING
GIINNRU	INURING
	RUINING
	URINING
GIINNSW	INSWING
GIINNTT	TINTING
GIINNTU	UNITING
GIINNTV	VINTING
GIINNTW	TWINING
GIINOPS	POISING
GIINORS	ORIGINS
	SIGNIOR
	SIGNORI
GIINORT	IGNITOR
	RIOTING
GIINOSY	YOGINIS
GIINOTT	TOITING
GIINPPP	PIPPING
GIINPPR	RIPPING
GIINPPS	PIPINGS
	SIPPING
GIINPPT	TIPPING
GIINPPY	YIPPING
GIINPPZ	ZIPPING
GIINPQU	PIQUING
GIINPRS	PRISING
	RISPING
	SPIRING
GIINPRZ	PRIZING
GIINPSS	PISSING
GIINPST	SPITING
GIINPSW	SWIPING
	WIPINGS
	WISPING
GIINPTT	PITTING
GIINPTW	WINGTIP
GIINPTY	PITYING
GIINQRU	QUIRING
GIINQTU	QUITING
GIINRRS	SIRRING
GIINRRT	TIRRING
GIINRRY	YIRRING
GIINRSS	RISINGS
GIINRST	STIRING
	TIRINGS
GIINRSV	VIRGINS
GIINRSW	WIRINGS
GIINRTT	RITTING
GIINRTW	TWIRING
	WRITING
GIINSST	SISTING
GIINSSU	ISSUING
GIINSSW	WISSING
GIINSSZ	SIZINGS
GIINSTT	SITTING
GIINSTU	SUITING
GIINSTV	STIVING
GIINSTW	WISTING
GIINSVW	SWIVING
GIINTTT	TITTING
GIINTTW	WITTING
GIINVYZ	VIZYING
GIINZZZ	ZIZZING
GIIORSV	ISOGRIV
GIJKNNU	JUNKING
GIJKNOO	JOOKING
GIJKNOU	JOUKING
GIJLLNO	JOLLING
GIJLNOT	JOLTING
GIJLNOU	JOULING
GIJLNOW	JOWLING
GIJLNSU	JUNGLIS
GIJMNPU	JUMPING
GIJNOTT	JOTTING
GIJNRUY	JURYING
GIJNSTU	JUSTING
GIJNTTU	JUTTING
GIKKNNO	KONKING
GIKKNOO	KOOKING
GIKKNOY	YOKKING
GIKKNUY	YUKKING
GIKLNOO	LOOKING
GIKLNOP	POLKING
GIKLNRU	LURKING
GIKLNSU	LUSKING
	SULKING
GIKMNOS	SMOKING
GIKMNSU	MUSKING
GIKNNNO	KONNING
GIKNNOP	PONKING
GIKNNOS	SNOKING
GIKNNOT	TONKING
GIKNNOW	KNOWING
GIKNNOZ	ZONKING
GIKNNSU	UNKINGS
GIKNOOP	POOKING
GIKNOOR	ROOKING
GIKNOPR	PROKING
GIKNOPS	SPOKING
GIKNOPU	POUKING
GIKNORT	TROKING
GIKNORW	WORKING
GIKNORY	YORKING
GIKNOST	STOKING
GIKNOSY	YOKINGS
GIKNOTU	TOUKING
GIKNOUY	YOUKING
GIKNRSY	SKRYING
	SKYRING
GIKNSTU	TUSKING
GIKNSTY	SKYTING
GIKRSTU	TUGRIKS
GILLLNO	LOLLING
GILLLNU	LULLING
GILLMNU	MULLING
GILLNNU	NULLING
GILLNOP	POLLING
GILLNOR	ROLLING
GILLNOT	TOLLING
GILLNPU	PULLING
GILLNSU	ULLINGS
GILLNUW	WULLING
GILLNYY	LYINGLY
GILLOOS	LOLIGOS
GILLORS	RIGOLLS
GILMNOO	LOOMING
	MOOLING
GILMNOR	MORLING
GILMNOT	MOLTING
GILMNOY	MOYLING
GILMNPU	LUMPING
	PLUMING
GILMNRU	MURLING
GILMNSU	LIGNUMS
GILNNOO	GLONOIN
	LOONING
GILNNOU	LOUNING
GILNNOW	LOWNING
GILNNRU	NURLING
GILNNSU	UNSLING
GILNNTU	LUNTING
GILNNUV	VULNING
GILNOOP	LOOPING
	POOLING
GILNOOS	LOGIONS
	LOOSING
	SOLOING
	SOOLING
GILNOOT	LOOTING
	TOOLING
GILNOPP	LOPPING
GILNOPR	PROLING
GILNOPS	POLINGS
	SLOPING
GILNOPT	POLTING
GILNOPU	LOUPING
GILNOPW	PLOWING
GILNOPY	PLOYING
GILNORS	LORINGS
GILNORU	LOURING
GILNOSS	LOSINGS
GILNOST	LINGOTS
	TIGLONS
	TOLINGS
GILNOSU	LOUSING
GILNOSV	LOVINGS
	SOLVING
GILNOSW	LOWINGS
	LOWSING
	SLOWING
	SOWLING
GILNOTT	LOTTING
GILNOTU	LOUTING
GILNOTW	LOWTING
GILNOVV	VOLVING
GILNOVW	WOLVING
GILNOWY	YOWLING
GILNPPU	PULPING
GILNPRU	PURLING
GILNPSU	PLUSING
	PULINGS
	PULSING
	PUSLING
GILNPUY	UPLYING
GILNRSU	RULINGS
GILNSTU	LUSTING
	LUTINGS
	SINGULT
GILNSTY	STYLING
GILNSUY	LUNGYIS
GILNVYY	VYINGLY
GILOORS	GIROSOL
GILOOSS	ISOLOGS
GILOOST	OLOGIST
GILOOTW	TWIGLOO
GILORTT	TRIGLOT
GILORTY	TRILOGY
GILOSTT	GLOTTIS
GILOTUY	GOUTILY
GILRSTY	GRISTLY
GILRTUY	LITURGY
GILRYZZ	GRIZZLY
GILSTUY	GUSTILY
	GUTSILY
GIMMMNU	MUMMING
GIMMNOT	TOMMING

GIMMNPU	MUMPING
GIMMNRY	RYMMING
GIMMNSU	SUMMING
GIMMNUV	VUMMING
GIMMORS	GIMMORS
GIMNNOO	MOONING
GIMNNOR	MORNING
GIMNNOS	MIGNONS
GIMNNTU	MUNTING
GIMNOOP	MOOPING
GIMNOOR	MOORING
	ROOMING
GIMNOOS	SOOMING
GIMNOOT	MOOTING
	TOOMING
GIMNOOV	MOOVING
GIMNOOZ	ZOOMING
GIMNOPP	MOPPING
GIMNOPR	ROMPING
GIMNOPU	MOUPING
GIMNOPY	YOMPING
GIMNORS	SMORING
GIMNORU	ROUMING
GIMNORW	WORMING
GIMNOSS	MOSSING
GIMNOST	GNOMIST
GIMNOSU	MOUSING
	SOUMING
GIMNOSW	MOWINGS
	SOWMING
GIMNPPU	PUMPING
GIMNPRU	RUMPING
GIMNPSU	IMPUGNS
	SPUMING
GIMNPTU	TUMPING
GIMNPUY	YUMPING
GIMNSSU	MUSINGS
	MUSSING
GIMNSTU	MUSTING
GIMNSTY	STYMING
GIMORSS	OGRISMS
	SIMORGS
GIMORSW	MISGROW
GIMOSSY	YOGISMS
GIMOSTU	GOMUTIS
GIMRSSU	SIMURGS
GIMRSUU	GURUISM
GINNNOO	NOONING
GINNNOR	RONNING
GINNNOW	WONNING
GINNNPU	PUNNING
GINNNRU	RUNNING
GINNNSU	SUNNING
GINNNTU	TUNNING
GINNOOS	NOOSING
GINNOOW	WOONING
GINNOPS	SPONGIN
GINNOPY	PONYING
GINNORS	SNORING
	SORNING
GINNORU	GRUNION
GINNORW	INGROWN
GINNORY	ROYNING
GINNOSS	NOSINGS
GINNOST	STONING
	TONINGS
GINNOSW	SNOWING
	WONINGS
GINNOSZ	ZONINGS
GINNOTW	WONTING
GINNPRU	PRUNING
GINNPTU	PUNTING
GINNRSU	NURSING
	URNINGS
GINNRTU	TURNING
GINNSTU	TUNINGS
GINNTTU	NUTTING
GINNTUY	UNTYING
GINOOPP	POGONIP
	POOPING
GINOOPR	ROOPING
GINOOPS	SOOPING
GINOOPT	POOTING
GINOORS	ROOSING
GINOORT	ROOTING
GINOOSS	ISOGONS
GINOOST	SOOTING
GINOOSW	WOOINGS
GINOOSY	ISOGONY
GINOOTT	TOOTING
GINOPPP	POPPING
GINOPPS	SOPPING
GINOPPT	TOPPING
GINOPPU	POUPING
GINOPPW	WOPPING
GINOPRS	PROIGNS
	PROSING
	ROPINGS
	SPORING
GINOPRT	PORTING
	TROPING
GINOPRU	INGROUP
	POURING
	ROUPING
GINOPRV	PROVING
GINOPRW	POWRING
GINOPSS	POSINGS
	POSSING
GINOPST	POSTING
	STOPING
GINOPSU	SOUPING
GINOPSY	POYSING
GINOPTT	POTTING
GINOPTU	POUTING
GINOQTU	QUOTING
GINORRT	RORTING
GINORRV	VORRING
GINORSS	GRISONS
	INGROSS
	SIGNORS
	SORINGS
GINORST	ROSTING
	SORTING
	STORING
	TRIGONS
GINORSU	ROUSING
	SOURING
GINORSV	ROVINGS
GINORSW	ROWINGS
	WORSING
GINORSY	ROSYING
	SIGNORY
GINORTT	ROTTING
GINORTU	OUTGRIN
	OUTRING
	ROUTING
	TOURING
GINORTW	ROWTING
	TROWING
GINOSSS	SOSSING
GINOSST	STINGOS
	TOSSING
GINOSSU	SOUSING
GINOSSW	SOWINGS
	SOWSING
GINOSTT	SOTTING
GINOSTU	OUSTING
	OUTINGS
	OUTSING
	TOUSING
GINOSTV	STOVING
GINOSTW	STOWING
	TOWINGS
	TOWSING
GINOSTY	TOYINGS
GINOTTT	TOTTING
GINOTTU	TOUTING
GINOTTW	TOWTING
	WOTTING
GINOTUW	OUTWING
GINOTUZ	TOUZING
GINOTWZ	TOWZING
GINPPPU	PUPPING
GINPPSU	SUPPING
	UPPINGS
GINPPTU	TUPPING
GINPRRU	PURRING
GINPRSS	SPRINGS
GINPRSU	PURSING
GINPRSY	PRYINGS
	PRYSING
	SPRINGY
GINPSSY	SPYINGS
GINPSTU	PIGNUTS
	STUPING
GINPSTY	TYPINGS
GINPSUW	UPSWING
GINPTTU	PUTTING
GINPTUY	UPTYING
GINPTUZ	PUTZING
GINQTUY	QUYTING
GINRRSU	RUNRIGS
GINRSST	STRINGS
GINRSTU	RUSTING
GINRSTY	STRINGY
	STYRING
	TRYINGS
GINRSUU	USURING
GINRTTU	RUTTING
GINSSSU	SUSSING
GINSTTU	TUTSING
GINSTTY	STYTING
GINTTTU	TUTTING
GIOOPRR	PORRIGO
GIOORSV	VIGOROS
GIOPRRU	PRURIGO
GIOPSSS	GOSSIPS
GIOPSST	SPIGOTS
GIOPSSY	GOSSIPY
GIOPSTU	PIGOUTS
GIORRSU	RIGOURS
GIORSUV	VIGOURS
GIOSSYZ	ZYGOSIS
GISWWYY	WYSIWYG
GJLMUUU	JUGULUM
GJNOOSU	GOUJONS
GJNRSUU	GURJUNS
GJOORTT	JOGTROT
GKMOOSU	GOMOKUS
GLLLOOR	LOGROLL
GLLOOPS	GOLLOPS
GLMMSUU	SLUMGUM
GLMNOOO	MONOLOG
GLMNOOS	MONGOLS
GLMOOOR	MOORLOG
GLMOOYY	MYOLOGY
GLMORUW	LUGWORM
GLNNOOR	LORGNON
GLNNSUU	UNSLUNG
GLNOOOS	OOLONGS
GLNOOOY	NOOLOGY
GLNOOPR	PROLONG
GLNOOPY	POLYGON
GLNOOSU	OULONGS
GLNORWY	WRONGLY
GLNOSUW	SUNGLOW
GLNOTTU	GLUTTON
GLNOUYY	YOUNGLY
GLNPSUU	UNPLUGS
GLOOORY	OROLOGY
GLOOOTY	OTOLOGY
GLOOOYZ	ZOOLOGY
GLOOPRS	PROLOGS
GLOORUY	UROLOGY
GLOOSTU	LOGOUTS
GLOOTUW	OUTGLOW
GLOPSTU	PUTLOGS
GLORSSY	GROSSLY
GLPRSUY	SPLURGY
GMMOSUU	GUMMOUS
GMMPUUW	MUGWUMP
GMNNOOS	GNOMONS
GMNOORU	GUNROOM
GMNOORW	MORWONG
GMNSTUU	GUMNUTS
GMNSUUZ	MZUNGUS
GMOOPRS	POGROMS
GMOOSTU	GOMUTOS
GMORSUU	GRUMOUS
GMORTUW	MUGWORT
GMPSSUY	GYPSUMS
GMRUYYZ	ZYMURGY
GNNORUW	UNGROWN
GNNORYY	GYRONNY
GNNOSUW	UNGOWNS
GNNOUUY	UNYOUNG
GNNRUUW	UNWRUNG
GNNSTUU	UNSTUNG
GNOOORS	GORSOON
GNOOOSS	GOSSOON
GNOOOYZ	ZOOGONY
GNOORST	TROGONS
GNOPPSU	OPPUGNS
	POPGUNS
GNOPRTU	GUNPORT
GNOPRUW	GROWNUP
	UPGROWN
GNOPSTU	POTGUNS
GNORTUU	OUTRUNG
GNOSTUU	OUTGUNS
	OUTSUNG
GNPSUUW	UPSWUNG
GOOOORS	GOOROOS
GOOPRST	GOSPORT
GOORSTT	GROTTOS
GOORTUW	OUTGROW
GOPRSUW	UPGROWS
GORRSTU	TURGORS
GORSTTU	GUTROTS
	ROTGUTS
GORSTUY	YOGURTS
HHIIPPS	HIPPISH
HHIISTW	WHITISH
HHIMRTY	RHYTHMI
HHINNSU	HUNNISH
HHINORS	HORNISH
HHIOPST	HIPSHOT
HHIORSW	WHORISH
HHIOSTT	HOTTISH
HHISSTW	WHISHTS
HHMMSUU	HUMHUMS
HHMRSTY	RHYTHMS
HHOOSTT	HOTSHOT
HIIIKRS	RIKISHI
HIIJKNS	HIJINKS
HIIKLMS	KHILIMS
HIIKNPS	KINSHIP
	PINKISH
HIILMTU	LITHIUM
HIILNSY	SHINILY

HIILPST	SHILPIT
HIILPSU	HUIPILS
HIILPTY	PITHILY
HIILRTT	TRILITH
HIIMMSS	MISHMIS
HIIMNSX	MINXISH
HIIMPSW	WIMPISH
HIIMSSS	MISSISH
HIIMSST	MISHITS
HIIMSTT	SHITTIM
HIINNOT	THIONIN
HIINORS	NOIRISH
	ROINISH
HIINPPS	HIPPINS
HIINPSS	INSHIPS
HIINSSW	SWINISH
HIINSTW	WITHINS
HIIOPRZ	RHIZOPI
HIIORST	HISTRIO
HIIPSSW	WISPISH
HIIPSXY	PIXYISH
HIISTTT	TITTISH
HIKLSSU	LUSKISH
HIKLSUY	HUSKILY
HIKMNOS	MONKISH
HIKMOTV	MIKVOTH
HIKMRSU	MURKISH
HIKMSUZ	MUZHIKS
HIKNNOR	INKHORN
HIKNNTU	UNTHINK
HIKNPSU	PUNKISH
HIKNRSS	SHRINKS
HIKOORS	ROOKISH
HIKOPSY	SKYPHOI
HILLOPT	HILLTOP
HILLOPY	LYOPHIL
HILLPSU	UPHILLS
HILLRSS	SHRILLS
HILLRST	THRILLS
HILLRSY	SHRILLY
HILLRTY	THRILLY
HILMMOU	HOLMIUM
HILMOPS	LOMPISH
	PHLOMIS
HILMOSS	HOLISMS
HILMOSW	WHOLISM
HILMPSU	LUMPISH
HILMSSY	HYLISMS
HILMSUY	MUSHILY
HILMTUU	THULIUM
HILNNTY	NINTHLY
HILNOPY	PHONILY
HILNORY	HORNILY
HILNOTY	THIONYL
HILNPST	PLINTHS
HILOOST	OOLITHS
HILOOTT	OTOLITH
HILOOTZ	ZOOLITH
HILOPXY	OXYPHIL
HILORSY	HORSILY
HILORTU	UROLITH
HILOSST	HOLISTS
HILOSSW	SLOWISH
HILOSTU	LOUTISH
HILOSTW	WHOLIST
HILOSTY	HYLOIST
HILOSVW	WOLVISH
HILOSWY	SHOWILY
HILOTWW	WHITLOW
HILPRUW	UPWHIRL
HILPSST	SPILTHS
HILPSUY	PUSHILY
HILSSTY	HYLISTS
	STYLISH
HILSTTY	THISTLY
HILSTWY	SWITHLY
HILSTXY	SIXTHLY
HIMMPSU	MUMPISH
HIMMRSU	RUMMISH
HIMMSTY	MYTHISM
HIMNOOS	MOONISH
HIMNOPR	MORPHIN
HIMNSSU	MUNSHIS
HIMNSTY	HYMNIST
HIMOORS	MOORISH
HIMOPRS	ROMPISH
HIMOPSS	SOPHISM
HIMOPST	PHOTISM
HIMORSW	WORMISH
HIMORTU	THORIUM
HIMOTTY	TIMOTHY
HIMPRSS	SHRIMPS
HIMPRSY	SHRIMPY
HIMPRTU	TRIUMPH
HIMPTUY	PYTHIUM
HIMRSTY	RHYMIST
HIMSSTU	ISTHMUS
HIMSTTY	MYTHIST
HINNNSU	NUNNISH
HINNORT	TINHORN
HINNOST	TONNISH
HINNPSU	NUNSHIP
HINOOPS	INHOOPS
HINOORT	HORNITO
HINOORZ	HORIZON
HINOOST	INSOOTH
HINOPPS	SHIPPON
HINOPSS	SIPHONS
	SONSHIP
HINORST	HORNIST
HINORSU	NOURISH
HINORSY	ROYNISH
HINOSST	STONISH
HINOSSW	SNOWISH
HINOSTW	TOWNISH
HINPPSU	PUSHPIN
HINPSSU	UNSHIPS
HINPTUW	UNWHIPT
HINRSTU	RUNTISH
HIOOPRS	POORISH
HIOOSSV	SHIVOOS
HIOOSSW	WHOOSIS
HIOPPPS	POPPISH
HIOPPSS	SHIPPOS
HIOPRSW	WORSHIP
HIOPSST	SOPHIST
HIOPSSY	PHYSIOS
HIOPSTU	UPHOIST
HIORSSU	SOURISH
HIORSTY	HISTORY
HIOSSTT	SOTTISH
HIOSTTU	OUTHITS
HIOSTUW	OUTWISH
HIOTTUW	OUTWITH
	WITHOUT
HIQSSUY	SQUISHY
HIRSSTT	THIRSTS
	THRISTS
HIRSTTU	RUTTISH
HIRSTTY	THIRSTY
	THRISTY
HKKLOOS	KOLKHOS
HKKLOOZ	KOLKHOZ
HKKOOSY	SKYHOOK
HKKOSTU	SUKKOTH
HKLOOYZ	KOLHOZY
HKNOOSS	SHNOOKS
HKNOOSU	UNHOOKS
HKNOOWW	KNOWHOW
HKNSSUU	UNHUSKS
HKOOOPT	POTHOOK
HKOOPSU	HOOKUPS
HKOOSST	SHTOOKS
HKOOSVZ	SOVKHOZ
HKOPSSY	SKYPHOS
HKORSWY	WORKSHY
HLLOOOS	HOLLOOS
HLLOOSW	HOLLOWS
HLLOPSY	PHYLLOS
HLLPSUY	PLUSHLY
HLMNOTY	MONTHLY
HLMNPYY	NYMPHLY
HLMOOSS	SHOLOMS
HLMORRY	MYRRHOL
HLMOSTY	THYMOLS
HLMPSSU	SHLUMPS
HLMPSUY	SHLUMPY
HLOOSTY	SOOTHLY
HLOOTUW	OUTHOWL
HLOPRTY	PROTHYL
HLOPSTY	PHYTOLS
HLORSTY	SHORTLY
HLOTUYY	YOUTHLY
HLPRSUU	SULPHUR
	UPHURLS
HMMMSUU	HUMMUMS
HMMNOOY	HOMONYM
HMMOOSU	HOUMMOS
HMMRTUY	THRUMMY
HMNOPSY	NYMPHOS
HMNOPYY	HYPONYM
HMNPSUY	HYPNUMS
HMOOPRS	MORPHOS
HMOOSST	SMOOTHS
HMOOSTY	SMOOTHY
HMORSUU	HUMOURS
HMSTUYZ	ZYTHUMS
HNNOOPS	PHONONS
HNNORSU	UNSHORN
HNNOSTY	SYNTHON
HNNOSUW	UNSHOWN
HNOOPST	PHOTONS
HNOOPSU	UNHOOPS
HNOOPTY	TYPHOON
HNOORSS	HORSONS
HNOORST	THORONS
HNOORSU	HONOURS
HNOOSTU	UNSHOOT
HNOPSSY	SYPHONS
HNOPSTY	PHYTONS
	PYTHONS
	TYPHONS
HNORSTY	RHYTONS
HNORTUW	UNWORTH
HNOSTUU	UNSHOUT
HNOSUWY	UNSHOWY
HNOTTUU	OUTHUNT
HNRTTUU	UNTRUTH
HNSSTUU	UNSHUTS
HOOOOPS	HOOPOOS
HOOPPST	POTSHOP
HOOPRST	PORTHOS
HOOPSTT	HOTPOTS
	POTSHOT
HOOPSTU	UPSHOOT
HOOPSTY	TOYSHOP
HOOQSSU	SQUOOSH
HOORRRS	HORRORS
HOORRST	ORTHROS
HOORSUZ	HUZOORS
HOOSTTU	OUTSHOT
HOPRSTU	HOTSPUR
HOPRTTU	PRUTOTH
HOPRTUW	UPTHROW
HOPSSSY	HYSSOPS
HOPSSTU	UPSHOTS
HOPSTTU	SHOTPUT
HOPSTUU	OUTPUSH
HOPSTUY	TYPHOUS
HORSTTW	TROWTHS
HORSTUU	OUTRUSH
HOSSTTU	STOUTHS
HOSTTUU	SHUTOUT
HPPSSUU	PUSHUPS
HPRTTUU	THRUPUT
HRSSTTU	THRUSTS
HRSSTUY	THYRSUS
IIIJJLN	JINJILI
IIIKMNN	MINIKIN
IIIKMNS	MINISKI
IIIMRST	MIRITIS
IIISTTW	WISTITI
IIJKOPR	PIROJKI
IIJLLNO	JILLION
IIJMMNY	JIMMINY
IIJMNOS	MISJOIN
IIJNNOT	INJOINT
IIKKLNY	KINKILY
IIKKNPS	KIPSKIN
IIKLLMY	MILKILY
IIKLLSY	SILKILY
IIKLMNP	LIMPKIN
IIKLMRY	MIRKILY
IIKLNOS	OILSKIN
IIKLPSY	SPIKILY
IIKLRSY	RISKILY
IIKMNOR	KIRIMON
IIKMNPS	SIMPKIN
IIKMNSS	SIMKINS
IIKNPPS	PIPKINS
IIKNSSS	SISKINS
IIKOSST	OIKISTS
IIKOSTT	TITOKIS
IIKPSUW	WIKIUPS
IILLLSY	SILLILY
IILLMNO	MILLION
IILLMSY	SLIMILY
IILLNOP	PILLION
IILLNOZ	ZILLION
IILLNST	INSTILL
IILLNTT	LITTLIN
IILLPSU	ILLUPIS
IILMNOS	LIONISM
IILMNSS	SIMLINS
IILMORS	SIMILOR
IILMOSS	LIMOSIS
IILMSTU	STIMULI
IILMSTY	MISTILY
IILNNOT	NITINOL
IILNNSU	INSULIN
	INULINS
IILNNTY	TINNILY
IILNOPT	PINITOL
IILNORS	SIRLOIN
IILNOSV	VIOLINS
IILNOSY	NOISILY
IILNPPY	NIPPILY
IILNPUV	PULVINI
IILNRST	NITRILS
IILNRSV	RIVLINS
IILNSST	INSTILS
IILOPRT	TRIPOLI
IILOPST	PILOTIS
IILORTV	VITRIOL
IILOSTV	VIOLIST
IILPRVY	PRIVILY
IILPSST	PISTILS
IILPSTY	TIPSILY
IILPSWY	WISPILY
IILRTYZ	RITZILY

IILSTTT	TITLIST
IILTTUY	UTILITY
IILTTWY	WITTILY
IIMMMNU	MINIMUM
IIMMNSU	MINIMUS
	MINIUMS
IIMNNOS	MINIONS
IIMNOSS	MISSION
IIMNOSU	IONIUMS
	NIMIOUS
IIMNOTX	MIXTION
IIMNPRT	IMPRINT
IIMOPSU	IMPIOUS
IIMOSST	MITOSIS
IIMOSSU	SIMIOUS
IIMRSTW	MISWRIT
IIMRTTU	TRITIUM
IIMRTUV	TRIVIUM
IIMSSSZ	SIZISMS
IIMSSTT	TIMISTS
IIMSSTU	MISSUIT
IINNOOP	OPINION
IINNOPS	PINIONS
IINNOTU	UNITION
IINNQSU	QUININS
IINNQTU	QUINTIN
IINOPSS	ISOSPIN
	SINOPIS
IINORST	IRONIST
IINORSV	VIRINOS
	VIRIONS
IINORTT	INTROIT
IINOSSV	VISIONS
IINOSUV	INVIOUS
IINOTTU	TUITION
IINPPPS	PIPPINS
IINQRUY	INQUIRY
IINRTTY	TRINITY
IINSSST	INSISTS
IINSTTU	INTUITS
IINSTTW	INTWIST
	NITWITS
IIOOSTT	TOITOIS
IIOPRSS	PISSOIR
IIOPSTY	PIOSITY
IIORSSV	VIROSIS
IIORSTV	IVORIST
	VISITOR
IIOSTTU	OUSTITI
IIPPSUU	PIUPIUS
IIPRSST	SPIRITS
	TRIPSIS
IIPRSTU	PITURIS
IIPRSTY	SPIRITY
IIPRTVY	PRIVITY
IIQSTUV	QIVIUTS
IIRRSTT	TIRRITS
IISSSTZ	SIZISTS
IISTTZZ	TZITZIS
IITTTZZ	TZITZIT
IJJMSUU	JUJUISM
IJJSTUU	JUJITSU
	JUJUIST
IJKLLOY	KILLJOY
IJKMOSU	MOUJIKS
IJKMSUZ	MUZJIKS
IJKNOSS	JOSKINS
IJLLLOY	JOLLILY
IJLLOTY	JOLLITY
	JOLTILY
IJLMPUY	JUMPILY
IJLNOQU	JONQUIL
IJLNOTY	JOINTLY
IJMOSSS	JISSOMS
IJNNOTU	UNJOINT
IJNORSU	JUNIORS
IJNOTUX	OUTJINX
IJRSSTU	JURISTS
IKKMNOU	KIKUMON
IKKNNSU	UNKINKS
IKKNORT	KIRKTON
IKKORRS	KORKIRS
IKKSUUY	KIKUYUS
IKLLOTU	OUTKILL
IKLLSTU	KILLUTS
IKLLSUY	SULKILY
IKLMNPU	LUMPKIN
IKLMOOS	LOOKISM
IKLMOPS	MILKSOP
IKLMOSY	SMOKILY
	SOYMILK
IKLMRUY	MURKILY
IKLMSUY	MUSKILY
IKLNNSU	UNLINKS
IKLNOOS	SKOLION
IKLNOOT	KILOTON
IKLNOSU	ULIKONS
IKLNPSU	LINKUPS
	SKULPIN
	UPLINKS
IKLNRWY	WRINKLY
IKLNTWY	TWINKLY
IKLOOTT	TOOLKIT
IKLOSSU	SOUSLIK
IKLSSSU	SUSLIKS
IKLSTTU	KITTULS
IKMNOOO	OKIMONO
IKMNOOR	OMIKRON
IKMNOOS	KIMONOS
IKMNORS	MIKRONS
	MORKINS
IKMNOSW	MISKNOW
IKMNPPU	PUMPKIN
IKMNRSU	RUMKINS
IKMNRTU	TRINKUM
IKMOOST	MISTOOK
IKMOSSU	KOUMISS
IKMPRSS	SKRIMPS
IKMSSTU	MUSKITS
IKNNPSU	PUNKINS
IKNNPTU	UNPINKT
IKNNSTU	UNKNITS
IKNOOST	ISOKONT
IKNOPRW	PINWORK
IKNOPST	INKPOTS
	INKSPOT
IKNORSW	INWORKS
IKNORTW	TINWORK
IKNPSTU	SPUTNIK
	UPKNITS
IKORSTU	TURKOIS
IKOSSTU	OUTKISS
IKPRSSU	PRUSIKS
	SPRUIKS
IKPRSSY	KRYPSIS
ILLLOWY	LOWLILY
ILLMNOU	MULLION
ILLMNRU	MILLRUN
ILLMOOR	MOORILL
ILLMOOT	TIMOLOL
ILLMOPS	PLIMSOL
ILLMOSU	LOLIUMS
ILLMPUY	LUMPILY
ILLMSUU	LIMULUS
ILLNOQU	QUILLON
ILLNORU	RULLION
ILLNOST	LINTOLS
ILLNPUU	LUPULIN
ILLNSUW	UNWILLS
ILLNTUY	NULLITY
ILLOORZ	ZORILLO
ILLOPRY	PILLORY
ILLOPST	POLLIST
ILLOPSW	PILLOWS
ILLOPWY	PILLOWY
ILLOSUV	VILLOUS
ILLOSUY	LOUSILY
ILLOSWW	WILLOWS
ILLOTUW	OUTWILL
ILLOTXY	XYLITOL
ILLOUVV	VOLVULI
ILLOWWY	WILLOWY
ILLPPUY	PULPILY
ILLPSUV	PULVILS
ILLQSSU	SQUILLS
ILLRSUY	SURLILY
ILLSTUY	LUSTILY
ILMMRUY	RUMMILY
ILMMSSU	SLUMISM
ILMMSUU	MIMULUS
ILMNOOT	MOONLIT
ILMNOOY	MOONILY
ILMNOSU	MOULINS
ILMNRSU	MURLINS
ILMNSSU	MUSLINS
ILMOORY	ROOMILY
ILMOOSS	MOLOSSI
ILMORSW	WORMILS
ILMORTU	TURMOIL
ILMOSTY	MOISTLY
ILMOSUY	MOUSILY
ILMPSSY	SLIMPSY
ILMPSTU	PLUMIST
ILMRSSY	LYRISMS
ILMSSUY	MUSSILY
ILMSTUY	MUSTILY
ILMUYZZ	MUZZILY
ILNNOOY	NONOILY
ILNNOPS	NONSLIP
ILNNORU	LINURON
ILNNSUY	SUNNILY
ILNOOPS	PLOSION
ILNOOPV	VOLPINO
ILNOORS	ROSINOL
ILNOOSS	SOLIONS
ILNOOST	LOTIONS
	SOLITON
ILNOPPS	POPLINS
ILNOPRU	PURLOIN
ILNOPST	PONTILS
ILNOPSU	PULSION
	UPSILON
ILNOPSY	YPSILON
ILNOPYY	POLYNYI
ILNOQSU	QUINOLS
ILNORST	NOSTRIL
ILNORSU	SURLOIN
ILNORTU	TORULIN
ILNOSST	TONSILS
ILNOSSU	INSOULS
ILNOSTU	OILNUTS
	ULTIONS
ILNOSTY	STONILY
	TYLOSIN
ILNOSWY	SNOWILY
ILNOTUV	VOLUTIN
ILNPRSU	PURLINS
ILNPSST	SPLINTS
ILNPSTU	UNSPILT
	UNSPLIT
ILNRSTY	NITRYLS
ILNSSTU	INSULTS
ILNSSVY	SYLVINS
ILNTTUY	NUTTILY
ILOOORS	ROSOLIO
ILOOPST	POLOIST
	TOPSOIL
ILOORST	LORIOTS
ILOORTY	OLITORY
ILOOSST	SOLOIST
ILOOSTY	SOOTILY
ILOOWYZ	WOOZILY
ILOPPSY	SOPPILY
ILOPRRY	PRIORLY
ILOPRSY	PROSILY
ILOPRUY	ROUPILY
ILOPSST	PISTOLS
	POSTILS
ILOPSSX	OXSLIPS
ILOPSTT	SPOTLIT
ILOPSTU	SLIPOUT
ILOPSUY	PIOUSLY
ILOQRSU	LIQUORS
ILORRSY	SORRILY
ILORSTU	TROILUS
ILOSSTY	TOSSILY
	TYLOSIS
ILOSTTW	WITTOLS
ILPPSSU	SLIPUPS
ILPPSTU	PULPITS
ILPRSUY	PURSILY
ILPSTTU	UPTILTS
ILRSSTU	TRISULS
ILRSSTY	LYRISTS
ILRSTUY	RUSTILY
ILRTTUY	RUTTILY
ILSSTTU	LUTISTS
ILSSTTY	STYLIST
IMMMOSS	MOMISMS
IMMNOSS	MONISMS
	NOMISMS
IMMNOSU	MUSIMON
	OMNIUMS
IMMNOUU	MUONIUM
IMMOOSS	SIMOOMS
IMMOPTU	OPTIMUM
IMMOSSU	OSMIUMS
IMMSSTU	MUTISMS
	SUMMIST
	SUMMITS
IMNNNOU	MUNNION
IMNNOOR	NORIMON
IMNNOSW	MINNOWS
IMNNSTU	MUNTINS
IMNOOPP	POMPION
IMNOOPT	TOMPION
IMNOORR	MORRION
IMNOORS	MORIONS
IMNOORT	MONITOR
	TROMINO
IMNOOSS	MONOSIS
	SIMOONS
IMNOOST	MOTIONS
IMNOOSU	OMINOUS
IMNOOSY	ISONOMY
IMNOOUX	OXONIUM
IMNOPPU	PUMPION
IMNOPRW	PINWORM
IMNOPSU	SPUMONI
IMNORRU	MURRION
IMNORTY	TRIONYM
IMNOSST	MONISTS
IMNOSSY	MYOSINS
IMNOSVY	VISNOMY
IMNRRSU	MURRINS
IMNRSTU	UNTRIMS
IMOOPRX	PROXIMO
IMOOSSS	OSMOSIS
IMOOSSU	OSMIOUS
IMOOSTV	VOMITOS

IMOPRSS	PORISMS
IMOPRST	IMPORTS
	TROPISM
IMOPRSV	IMPROVS
IMOPRTU	PROTIUM
IMOPSST	IMPOSTS
	MISSTOP
IMOPSTU	UTOPISM
IMORRRS	MIRRORS
IMORSST	MISSORT
IMORSTU	TOURISM
IMORSTY	TRISOMY
IMOSSTU	MISSOUT
IMOSSYZ	ZYMOSIS
IMOSTTT	TOMTITS
IMOSTUV	VOMITUS
IMOSTUW	OUTSWIM
IMPRSSU	PURISMS
IMPSSTU	SUMPITS
IMQRSSU	SQUIRMS
IMQRSUY	SQUIRMY
IMRSSTU	SISTRUM
	TRISMUS
	TRUISMS
IMRTTUY	YTTRIUM
INNNOOR	NONIRON
INNNORU	RUNNION
INNOOPS	OPSONIN
INNOORS	RONIONS
INNOOST	NOTIONS
INNOPSY	PINYONS
INNORST	INTRONS
INNOSSU	UNISONS
INNOSTU	NONSUIT
INNOSUY	UNNOISY
INNOSWW	WINNOWS
INNQSUY	SQUINNY
INNRSTU	INTURNS
INOOPRT	PORTION
INOOPSS	POISONS
	POISSON
INOOPST	OPTIONS
	POSITON
	POTIONS
INOORSS	ORISONS
INOORST	ISOTRON
	NITROSO
	TORSION
INOORSZ	ZORINOS
INOORTT	TORTONI
INOOSST	TOISONS
INOOSUX	NOXIOUS
INOPPRS	POPRINS
INOPPST	TOPSPIN
INOPRSS	PRISONS
	SPINORS
INOPRST	TROPINS
INOPRSU	INPOURS
INOPSST	PISTONS
	POSTINS
	SPINTOS
INOPSSU	POUSSIN
	SPINOUS
INOPSTT	TINPOTS
INOPSTU	SPINOUT
INORSTT	INTORTS
	TRITONS
INORSTU	NITROUS
	TURIONS
INORSUU	RUINOUS
	URINOUS
INORSUV	UNVISOR
INOSSTU	OUTSINS
	USTIONS
INOSSUU	SINUOUS
INOSTUW	OUTWINS
INPRSST	SPRINTS
INPRSTU	TURNIPS
	UNSTRIP
INPRSTY	TRYPSIN
INQSSTU	SQUINTS
INQSTUY	SQUINTY
INRSTTU	INTRUST
INSSTUU	SUNSUIT
	UNSUITS
INSTTUW	UNTWIST
INTTUWY	UNWITTY
IOOPRSS	POROSIS
IOOPRSV	PROVISO
IOOPSTY	ISOTOPY
IOORSSS	SOROSIS
IOORSST	TSOORIS
IOORSTT	RISOTTO
IOORSTU	RIOTOUS
IOOSSSS	SISSOOS
IOOSSST	OSTOSIS
IOPPPRT	PITPROP
IOPPPST	POPPITS
IOPPRST	RIPSTOP
IOPPSTT	TIPTOPS
IOPRSST	RIPOSTS
IOPRSSY	PYROSIS
IOPRSTT	PROTIST
	TROPIST
IOPSTTU	UTOPIST
IOPTTUY	OUTPITY
IOQRTTU	QUITTOR
IOQSSTU	QUOISTS
IORRSTW	WORRITS
IORRSZZ	RIZZORS
IORRTTX	TORTRIX
IORSSTU	SUITORS
	TSOURIS
IORSTTU	TOURIST
IORSTTW	TWISTOR
IORTTUW	OUTWRIT
IOSSSTT	TSOTSIS
IOSSTTU	OUTSITS
IOSTTUW	OUTWITS
IPPQSUU	QUIPPUS
IPRRSTU	IRRUPTS
	STIRRUP
IPRSSTU	PURISTS
	SPRUITS
	UPRISTS
	UPSTIRS
IPRSTUU	PURSUIT
IPSSSTY	STYPSIS
IPSSTTY	TYPISTS
IPSTTTU	TITTUPS
IPTTTUY	TITTUPY
IQRRSSU	SQUIRRS
IQRSSTU	SQUIRTS
JJSTUUU	JUJUTSU
JMOPTUU	OUTJUMP
JNNORUY	NONJURY
JNNOSTU	JOTUNNS
JNOORSU	JOURNOS
	SOJOURN
JOOPPSY	JOYPOPS
	POPJOYS
JOSTTUU	OUTJUTS
KKLMSUU	MUKLUKS
KKLOOYZ	KOLKOZY
KKMOOSU	SKOOKUM
KKMSTUU	MUKTUKS
KKNRSUU	KUNKURS
KKSSSTT	TSKTSKS
KLLMOSU	MOLLUSK
KLOOOTU	LOOKOUT
	OUTLOOK
KLOOPSU	LOOKUPS
	UPLOOKS
KLOSTUU	OUTSULK
KLRSTUU	KULTURS
KMOSSUY	KOUMYSS
KMPRSSU	SKRUMPS
KNNNOUW	UNKNOWN
KNNOORW	NONWORK
KNNOSTU	UNKNOTS
KNOOPTT	TOPKNOT
KNOPRTY	KRYPTON
KNORRTY	KRYTRON
KNORSUW	UNWORKS
KOOOTTU	OUTTOOK
KOOPRTW	TOPWORK
	WORKTOP
KOORTUW	OUTWORK
	WORKOUT
KOOSSSU	KOUSSOS
KOOSSUU	SOUKOUS
KOOSTWW	KOWTOWS
KOPRSUW	WORKUPS
KORTTUW	TUTWORK
LLLMMUU	MULMULL
LLLOOPS	LOLLOPS
LLMMSUU	MULMULS
LLMOOPR	ROLLMOP
LLMPPUY	PLUMPLY
LLNORSU	UNROLLS
LLOOPRT	ROLLTOP
	TROLLOP
LLOOPTU	OUTPOLL
LLOORTU	OUTROLL
	ROLLOUT
LLOOSTU	TOLUOLS
LLOPRSU	UPROLLS
LLOPTUU	OUTPULL
	PULLOUT
LLORSST	STROLLS
LLOSTUY	TOLUYLS
LLPPSUU	PULLUPS
LMMSTUU	MULTUMS
LMOORSU	ORMOLUS
LMOOSTY	TOYLSOM
LMOPSUU	PLUMOUS
LMORSSU	MUSROLS
LMRSTUU	LUSTRUM
LMSTTUU	TUMULTS
LMSTUUU	TUMULUS
LNNOPSU	NONPLUS
LNOOPTU	PULTOON
LNOOSST	STOLONS
LNOPSTU	PLUTONS
	PULTONS
LNOSSUU	UNSOULS
LNPSTUU	PULTUNS
LNRTUUV	VULTURN
LNRTUUY	UNTRULY
LOOOORS	OLOROSO
LOOORST	ROTOLOS
LOOPTTU	OUTPLOT
LOOSSTV	VOLOSTS
LOPPRSY	PROPYLS
LOPPSUU	PULPOUS
LOPPSUY	POLYPUS
LOPRRSY	PYRROLS
LOPRSTY	PROTYLS
LOPRSUY	PYLORUS
LOPRTUY	POULTRY
LORSTTY	TROTYLS
LORSTUU	TORULUS
LOSTTUY	STOUTLY
LPRSSUU	SURPLUS
MMNOSSU	MUSMONS
	SUMMONS
MMOOPPS	POMPOMS
MMOOSTT	MOTMOTS
MMOPSTY	SYMPTOM
MMRRSUU	MURMURS
MMSTUUU	MUTUUMS
MMSUUUU	MUUMUUS
MNNOOOS	MONSOON
MNNOORU	MONURON
MNNOSYY	SYNONYM
MNNOTUU	UNMOUNT
MNOOOPP	POMPOON
MNOOOYZ	ZOONOMY
MNOOPPS	POMPONS
MNOOPST	TOMPONS
MNOOPTY	TOPONYM
MNOORSU	SUNROOM
	UNMOORS
MNOOSTU	MOUTONS
MNOOSTW	TOWMONS
MNOOSUY	ONYMOUS
MNOOTTW	TOWMONT
MNORSTU	NOSTRUM
MNOSTTU	MUTTONS
MNOTTUY	MUTTONY
MOOOTYZ	ZOOTOMY
MOOPPSU	POMPOUS
MOOPRSY	POMROYS
MOOPSSU	OPOSSUM
MOOPSTT	TOPMOST
MOORRSW	MORROWS
MOOSTTU	OUTMOST
MOPPRST	PROMPTS
MOPSSSU	POSSUMS
MOPSSUU	SPUMOUS
MOQRSUU	QUORUMS
MOQSTUU	QUOTUMS
MORRSTU	ROSTRUM
MORRSUU	RUMOURS
MORSTUU	TUMOURS
MOSSSTY	MYSOSTS
MOSSTTU	UTMOSTS
MOSSTUU	OUTSUMS
MOSTUUW	OUTSWUM
NNNSUUY	UNSUNNY
NNOOOPR	NONPOOR
NNOOOPT	PONTOON
NNOOPRS	NONPROS
NNOOPRU	PRONOUN
NNOOPSS	SPONSON
NNOOPST	NONSTOP
	PONTONS
NNOORSY	RONYONS
NNOOSTW	WONTONS
NNORSUW	UNSWORN
NNOSSUY	UNSONSY
NNOSTYY	SYNTONY
NNRSTUU	UNTURNS
NOOOSUZ	OZONOUS
NOOOSVX	SONOVOX
NOOPRSS	SPONSOR
NOOPRST	PROTONS
NOOPSSY	POYSONS
NOOPSUY	YOUPONS
NOORSST	TONSORS
NOORSTU	UNROOST
	UNROOTS
NOORTUW	OUTWORN
NOPPRSU	UNPROPS
NOPSSTU	SUNSPOT
	UNSTOPS
NOPSTUW	UPTOWNS
NORSTUU	OUTRUNS
	RUNOUTS
NORTTUU	OUTTURN

TURNOUT
NOSSTUW UNSTOWS
NPRSTUU TURNUPS
UPTURNS
NRSSTTU STRUNTS
NRSSTUU STURNUS
UNTRUSS
NRSTTUU UNTRUST
OOOOPRT POTOROO
OOOOSZZ ZOOZOOS
OOOPRTU OUTROOP
OOORTTU OUTROOT
OOPRRST TORPORS
OOPRSSU SOURSOP
OOPRSTU PORTOUS
UPROOTS
OOPRSTV PROVOST
OOPRTTU OUTPORT
OOPRTUU OUTPOUR
OOPSSTT TOSSPOT
OOPSTTU OUTPOST
OUTTOPS
OOPSWWW POWWOWS
OORRSSW SORROWS
OORSTUU ROUTOUS
OORSTUW OUTROWS
OORTTTU OUTTROT
OPPPRSU UPPROPS
OPPRRTU PURPORT
OPPRSTU SUPPORT
OPPRSTY STROPPY
OPPRSUY PYROPUS
OPRSSTU SPROUTS
STROUPS
STUPORS
OPSSSTU TOSSUPS
OPSTTUU OUTPUTS
PUTOUTS
ORRSTTU TRUSTOR
ORSSSTU TUSSORS
ORSSTTU STROUTS
ORSSUUU USUROUS
ORSTTUU SURTOUT
ORSTTUY TRYOUTS
RSSSTUU TUSSURS

8-LETTER ANAGRAMS

AAAABENN ANABAENA
AAAABKPS BAASKAAP
AAAACCRR CARACARA
AAAACGNR CARAGANA
AAAACJRR JARARACA
AAAACNRS ANASARCA
AAAADMTV AMADAVAT
AAAADNPS APADANAS
AAAADTVV AVADAVAT
AAAAHJMR MAHARAJA
AAAAIKMN KAMAAINA
AAAAIMPR ARAPAIMA
AAAAIRTX ATARAXIA
AAAAJKRR JARARAKA
AAAAKKMT TAKAMAKA
AAAAKKNT KATAKANA
AAAAKKVV KAVAKAVA
AAAALLVV LAVALAVA
AAAALSTY ATALAYAS
AAAAMMTT MATAMATA
AAAARRSS SASARARA
AAABBCHL CABBALAH
AAABBCLS CABBALAS
AAABBELT ABATABLE
AAABBHKL KABBALAH
AAABBILT ABBATIAL
AAABBKLS KABBALAS
AAABCCMW MACCABAW
AAABCCRS BACCARAS
AAABCCRT BACCARAT
AAABCHIR ABRACHIA
AAABCHLS CALABASH
AAABCHMU MACAHUBA
AAABCILP ABAPICAL
AAABCINT ANABATIC
AAABCIRS ARABICAS
AAABCITT CIABATTA
AAABCLOS BACALAOS
AAABCLSV BACLAVAS
AAABCNRR BARRACAN
BARRANCA
AAABCNRS BARACANS
AAABCNRU CARNAUBA
AAABCORS CARABAOS
AAABCPRY CAPYBARA
AAABCSSS CASSABAS
AAABCSTW CATAWBAS
AAABDEHH DAHABEAH
AAABDEST DATABASE
AAABDFRS ABFARADS
AAABDHHI DAHABIAH
AAABDHHL HABDALAH
AAABDHIY DAHABIYA
AAABDIKR BAIDARKA
AAABDKNT DATABANK
AAABDLMS LAMBADAS
AAABDNNN BANDANNA
AAABDNNS BANDANAS
AAABDNRS SARABAND
AAABDNRT ABRADANT
AAABEGHL GALABEAH
AAABEGLL GALLABEA
AAABEGLS GALABEAS
AAABEHNR HABANERA
AAABEHRT BARATHEA
AAABEMPR PARABEMA
AAABENSS ANABASES
AAABFLLS FALBALAS
AAABGHIL GALABIAH
AAABGILL GALLABIA
AAABGILS GALABIAS
AAABGILY GALABIYA
AAABGLOR ALGAROBA
AAABGMNQ MBAQANGA
AAABGRTU RUTABAGA
AAABHLQS QABALAHS
AAABHMST MASTABAH
AAABILTT BATTALIA
AAABINSS ANABASIS
AAABIPSS PIASABAS
PIASSABA
AAABKLSV BAKLAVAS
AAABKLSW BAKLAWAS
AAABKPSS BAASSKAP
AAABLLSW WALLABAS
AAABLMOS ABOMASAL
AAABLMST TAMBALAS
AAABLOPR PARABOLA
AAABLPRS PALABRAS
AAABMSST MASTABAS
AAABNNRS RABANNAS
AAABORRS ARAROBAS
AAACCELN CALCANEA
AAACCEPR CARAPACE
AAACCILR CALCARIA
AAACCIMM CAIMACAM
AAACCLMS MALACCAS
AAACCLRS CARACALS
AAACCRSS CASCARAS
AAACCRTT CATARACT
AAACDEIM ACADEMIA
AAACDELM ACELDAMA
AAACDEMN ADAMANCE
AAACDENR DRACAENA
AAACDEQU AQUACADE
AAACDETU ACAUDATE
AAACDFIR FARADAIC
AAACDILR CALDARIA
AAACDINR ACARIDAN
ARCADIAN
AAACDIRS ARCADIAS
AAACDKLY LACKADAY
AAACDMMS MACADAMS
AAACDMNY ADAMANCY
AAACDNNO ANACONDA
AAACDNRS SANDARAC
AAACDOTV ADVOCAAT
AAACEGNT AGACANTE
AAACEGTU AGUACATE
AAACEHIN ACHAENIA
AAACEHLT CALATHEA
AAACEHLZ CHALAZAE
AAACELNT ANALECTA
AAACELST CATALASE
AAACENNP PANACEAN
AAACENPS PANACEAS
AAACEPRV PRAECAVA
AAACGINT CAATINGA
AAACGLSW SCALAWAG
AAACGMNP CAMPAGNA
AAACGMNR ARMAGNAC
AAACHHLS HALACHAS
AAACHILZ CHALAZIA
AAACHIPS APHASIAC
AAACHLLZ CHALAZAL
AAACHLNR ANARCHAL
AAACHLSZ CHALAZAS
AAACHNST ACANTHAS
AAACHRSY ACHARYAS
AAACILMN MANIACAL
AAACILMR CALAMARI
AAACILMS MALACIAS
AAACILPR CARPALIA
AAACILRV CALVARIA
AAACILSY CALISAYA
AAACIMRS CARIAMAS
AAACINPS ACAPNIAS
AAACINTV CAVATINA
AAACIPSU SAPUCAIA
AAACIRRS SACRARIA
AAACIRSS ACRASIAS
AAACIRTX ATARAXIC
AAACJMRS JACAMARS
AAACKMRT TAMARACK
AAACLLSV CAVALLAS
AAACLMNS ALMANACS
MANCALAS
AAACLMRS CALAMARS
AAACLMRY CALAMARY
AAACLNST CANTALAS
AAACLPST CATALPAS
AAACLRST ALCATRAS
AAACLRSZ ALCAZARS
AAACMNPS CAMPANAS
AAACMOST ATAMASCO
AAACMRSS MACASSAR
MARASCAS
MASCARAS
AAACMRSU AMARACUS
AAACNNRS CARANNAS
AAACNOPT CAPONATA
AAACNPST CATAPANS
AAACNRST NACARATS
AAACNRSU CARAUNAS
AAACNRSV CARAVANS
AAACNSST CANASTAS
AAACNSTT CANTATAS
AAACRRWY CARRAWAY
AAACRSWY CARAWAYS
AAACSSST CASSATAS
AAACSSSV CASSAVAS
AAACSSTT CATASTAS
AAACSTWY CASTAWAY
AAADEFGN FANEGADA
AAADEFWY FADEAWAY
AAADEGNP APANAGED
AAADEIMZ MAZAEDIA
AAADEJMP PAJAMAED
AAADELMS ALAMEDAS
SALAAMED
AAADEMNP EMPANADA
AAADENTV VANADATE
AAADEPRT TAPADERA
AAADFRSY FARADAYS
AAADGGHH HAGGADAH
AAADGGHS HAGGADAS
AAADGIMM GAMMADIA
AAADGLMY AMYGDALA
AAADGLNS SALADANG
AAADHHLV HAVDALAH
AAADHMMS HAMMADAS
AAADHMRS ADHARMAS
MADRASAH
AAADHNRT THANADAR
AAADIILR RADIALIA
AAADILLP PALLADIA
AAADILRU ADULARIA
AAADIMNY ADYNAMIA
AAADIRST DATARIAS
RADIATAS
AAADJMRS JAMADARS
AAADKLMN KALAMDAN
AAADKNSW WAKANDAS
AAADKRRV AARDVARK
AAADLMNQ QALAMDAN
AAADLMNS MANDALAS
AAADLMSW WADMAALS
AAADMNST ADAMANTS
AAADMNTU TAMANDUA
AAADMORT MATADORA
AAADMRSS MADRASAS
MADRASSA
AAADNRSS SARDANAS
AAADNRST TANADARS
AAAEGISS ASSEGAAI
AAAEGLMX MALAXAGE
AAAEGLRT ALTARAGE
AAAEGLST GALATEAS

AAAEGNPP	APPANAGE
AAAEGNPS	APANAGES
AAAEGRST	GASTRAEA
AAAEHLMT	HAEMATAL
AAAEHLST	ALTHAEAS
AAAEHMNT	ANATHEMA
AAAEHNPS	ANAPHASE
AAAEIMNS	ANAEMIAS
AAAEKKRT	KARATEKA
AAAEKTWY	TAKEAWAY
AAAELMMN	ANALEMMA
AAAELMPT	PALAMATE
AAAELMTX	MALAXATE
AAAELNPT	PANATELA
AAAELRTV	LAVATERA
AAAENNSS	ANANASES
AAAENOPR	PARANOEA
AAAENPRV	PARAVANE
AAAENPST	ANAPAEST
AAAENSST	ANATASES
AAAEPRST	SEPARATA
AAAERSWY	AREAWAYS
AAAERTWY	TEARAWAY
AAAFFLLS	ALFALFAS
AAAFHHRT	HAFTARAH
AAAFHRST	HAFTARAS
AAAFINST	FANTASIA
AAAFINUV	AVIFAUNA
AAAFIRST	RATAFIAS
AAAFLLWY	FALLAWAY
AAAFNRSS	SARAFANS
AAAFRSWY	FARAWAYS
AAAGGLLN	GALANGAL
AAAGGLNS	GALANGAS
AAAGGLOP	GALAPAGO
AAAGHINR	HIRAGANA
AAAGHIPR	AGRAPHIA
AAAGHIPS	APHAGIAS
AAAGHLNS	LANGAHAS
AAAGHNSS	SAGANASH
AAAGHNST	ATAGHANS
AAAGHNTY	YATAGHAN
AAAGILMM	MAMALIGA
AAAGILNS	ANALGIAS
AAAGILPT	PATAGIAL
AAAGILRT	ALIGARTA
AAAGIMMT	GAMMATIA
AAAGINRR	AGRARIAN
AAAGINRS	ANGARIAS
AAAGINSZ	GAZANIAS
AAAGISSS	ASSAGAIS
AAAGJMSU	MAJAGUAS
AAAGLMMS	AMALGAMS
AAAGLMNS	MALANGAS
	NAGMAALS
AAAGLNSS	LASAGNAS
AAAGLNTV	GALAVANT
AAAGLRRW	WARRAGAL
AAAGLRST	ASTRAGAL
AAAGMNRS	ANAGRAMS
AAAGMPRR	PARAGRAM
AAAGNOPR	ARAPONGA
AAAGNPRS	PARASANG
	PARGANAS
AAAGNPRU	ARAPUNGA
AAAGNRST	TANAGRAS
AAAGNRSU	GUARANAS
AAAGNSTY	YATAGANS
AAAHHKLS	HALAKAHS
	HALAKHAS
AAAHHLLS	HALALAHS
AAAHHLSV	HALAVAHS
AAAHHPRS	PARASHAH
AAAHHPRT	HAPHTARA
AAAHIKSW	KAHAWAIS
AAAHIMNR	MAHARANI
AAAHIMNS	SHAMIANA
AAAHIMRT	HAMARTIA
AAAHINPR	RAPHANIA
AAAHINRS	HARIANAS
AAAHIPSS	APHASIAS
AAAHJKSW	KAJAWAHS
AAAHKMNS	KHANSAMA
AAAHKRSS	RAKSHASA
AAAHLMRS	HARMALAS
AAAHLNNS	ALANNAHS
AAAHMMST	MAHATMAS
AAAHMNRT	AMARANTH
AAAHMRSS	ASHRAMAS
AAAHMSST	TAMASHAS
AAAHNNSV	SAVANNAH
AAAHNOPR	ANAPHORA
AAAHNSTY	ATHANASY
AAAHPRST	PARATHAS
AAAHRSTW	WARATAHS
AAAHTTWY	THATAWAY
AAAIIMNP	APIMANIA
AAAIINPR	APIARIAN
AAAIKKMM	KAIMAKAM
AAAIKLST	LATAKIAS
AAAILLMR	MALARIAL
AAAILLPT	PALATIAL
AAAILMNR	MALARIAN
AAAILMRS	MALARIAS
AAAILMSV	MALVASIA
AAAILNPR	PLANARIA
AAAILNRU	AULARIAN
AAAILPRV	PARAVAIL
AAAILPSS	APLASIAS
AAAILQRU	AQUARIAL
AAAILRST	SALARIAT
AAAIMMQQ	QAIMAQAM
AAAIMMST	MIASMATA
AAAIMNRR	MARINARA
AAAIMNST	AMANITAS
AAAINNRR	RANARIAN
AAAINOPR	PARANOIA
AAAINPSS	PAISANAS
AAAINQRU	AQUARIAN
AAAIPRST	ASPIRATA
AAAIPRSX	APRAXIAS
AAAIPSSV	PIASAVAS
	PIASSAVA
AAAISSST	ASTASIAS
AAAKKTZZ	KAZATZKA
AAAKLMSY	YAMALKAS
AAAKLWWY	WALKAWAY
AAAKMNRS	NAMASKAR
AAAKOSWY	SOAKAWAY
AAALLPRX	PARALLAX
AAALLPST	PALATALS
AAALMMOR	MALAROMA
AAALMPST	TAMPALAS
AAALMRSS	MARSALAS
AAALNNPT	PLATANNA
AAALNNST	LANTANAS
AAALNPRT	RATAPLAN
AAALNPST	APLANATS
AAALNRTT	TARLATAN
AAALPRST	SATRAPAL
AAALRRSY	ARRAYALS
AAALSWYY	LAYAWAYS
AAAMNOPR	PANORAMA
AAAMNRRY	YARRAMAN
AAAMNRST	AMARANTS
	MARANTAS
AAAMNSTY	MANYATAS
AAAMNTTY	MANYATTA
AAAMORST	TAMARAOS
AAAMOTTU	AUTOMATA
AAAMPRST	PATAMARS
AAAMPRTT	PATTAMAR
AAAMRRSZ	ZAMARRAS
AAAMRSSS	SAMSARAS
AAAMRSTU	TAMARAUS
AAAMRTTU	TRAUMATA
AAAMRTZZ	RAZMATAZ
AAANNSSV	SAVANNAS
AAANNSTT	ANNATTAS
AAANOPRZ	PARAZOAN
AAANORSY	SAYONARA
AAANPRTV	PARAVANT
AAANQTUU	AQUANAUT
AAANRSTT	TANTARAS
	TARANTAS
	TARTANAS
AAAORSWY	SOARAWAY
AAAPPRST	APPARATS
AAAPQRTU	PARAQUAT
AAAPSSST	PASSATAS
AAARSTTT	RATATATS
AAARSTTU	TUATARAS
AAASTWYY	STAYAWAY
AABBBDEK	KABABBED
AABBCDEG	CABBAGED
AABBCDKN	BACKBAND
AABBCDRS	SCABBARD
AABBCEGS	CABBAGES
AABBCEIS	ABBACIES
AABBCEKR	BAREBACK
AABBCEKT	BACKBEAT
AABBCINR	BARBICAN
AABBCIRR	BARBARIC
AABBCIST	SABBATIC
AABBCKST	BACKSTAB
AABBCMOS	CABOMBAS
AABBCORS	BARBASCO
AABBDENS	BASEBAND
AABBDERT	BARBATED
AABBDGRS	GABBARDS
AABBEELR	BEARABLE
AABBEELT	BEATABLE
AABBEGNS	BEANBAGS
AABBEILL	BAILABLE
AABBEISS	BABESIAS
AABBEKLN	BANKABLE
AABBELLM	BLAMABLE
AABBELLN	BEANBALL
AABBELLS	BASEBALL
AABBELOT	BOATABLE
AABBELRR	BARRABLE
AABBELRY	BEARABLY
AABBELSU	ABUSABLE
AABBEORT	BAREBOAT
AABBGRST	GABBARTS
AABBHKSU	BABUSHKA
AABBHSST	SABBATHS
AABBIILL	BILABIAL
AABBILRT	BARBITAL
AABBIRSU	BABIRUSA
AABBLLMY	BLAMABLY
AABBLORS	BARBOLAS
AABBLSSU	SUBBASAL
AABBMMOZ	ZAMBOMBA
AABBSSSU	BABASSUS
AABCCCHI	BACCHIAC
AABCCDET	BACCATED
AABCCEHK	BACKACHE
AABCCELS	CASCABEL
	CASCABLE
AABCCERT	BRACCATE
AABCCHIN	BACCHIAN
AABCCHIS	BISCACHA
AABCCHIZ	BIZCACHA
AABCCHKT	BACKCHAT
AABCCHNT	BACCHANT
AABCCIMR	CARBAMIC
AABCCINN	CANNABIC
AABCCKKP	BACKPACK
AABCCKLL	CALLBACK
AABCCKLP	BLACKCAP
AABCCKLW	CLAWBACK
AABCCKST	BACKCAST
	SCATBACK
AABCCMOT	CATACOMB
AABCCMOY	MACCABOY
AABCDEIN	ABIDANCE
AABCDEIT	ABDICATE
AABCDEKT	BACKDATE
AABCDELL	CABALLED
AABCDELN	BALANCED
AABCDHKN	BACKHAND
AABCDHKR	HARDBACK
AABCDIIS	DIABASIC
AABCDILL	BALLADIC
AABCDILU	BICAUDAL
AABCDINT	ABDICANT
AABCDIRS	CARABIDS
AABCDKLN	BACKLAND
AABCDKNR	BANKCARD
AABCDKRW	BACKWARD
	DRAWBACK
AABCDKRY	BACKYARD
AABCDLNS	SCABLAND
AABCDNRR	BRANCARD
AABCDNST	CABSTAND
AABCEEFL	FACEABLE
AABCEEHS	SEABEACH
AABCEENY	ABEYANCE
AABCEERS	SCARABEE
AABCEERT	ACERBATE
AABCEGOT	CABOTAGE
AABCEHLS	CASHABLE
AABCEHNR	BARCHANE
AABCEILM	AMICABLE
AABCEIMN	AMBIANCE
AABCEINR	CARABINE
AABCEIRT	BACTERIA
AABCEITT	CIABATTE
AABCEKLM	CLAMBAKE
AABCEKLP	PACKABLE
AABCEKLR	LACEBARK
AABCEKST	BACKSEAT
AABCELLL	CALLABLE
AABCELLP	PLACABLE
AABCELLR	CABALLER
AABCELLS	SCALABLE
AABCELNR	BALANCER
	BARNACLE
AABCELNS	BALANCES
AABCELOR	ALBACORE
AABCELPR	CAPABLER
AABCELRS	BERASCAL
AABCELRT	BRACTEAL
	CARTABLE
AABCELST	CASTABLE
AABCELSU	CAUSABLE
AABCELWY	CABLEWAY
AABCEMRT	CRABMEAT
AABCEMRV	VAMBRACE
AABCEMSS	AMBSACES
AABCENYY	ABEYANCY
AABCERRS	BARRACES
AABCERST	ABREACTS
	BEARCATS
	CABARETS
	CABRESTA
AABCERTT	CABRETTA
AABCESSU	ABACUSES
AABCFHKL	HALFBACK

AABCFIIL	BIFACIAL
AABCFKLL	BACKFALL
	FALLBACK
AABCFKLT	FLATBACK
AABCFKST	FASTBACK
	FATBACKS
AABCGIMO	CAMBOGIA
AABCGKRY	GRAYBACK
AABCHILR	BRACHIAL
AABCHINR	BRANCHIA
AABCHKLS	BACKLASH
AABCHKLU	BACKHAUL
AABCHKRS	SHABRACK
AABCHKSW	BACKWASH
AABCHLOO	COOLABAH
AABCHMRY	CHAMBRAY
AABCHNRS	BARCHANS
AABCIILR	BIRACIAL
AABCIILS	BASILICA
AABCIKLT	TAILBACK
AABCILLR	BACILLAR
	CABRILLA
AABCILMS	BALSAMIC
	CABALISM
AABCILMY	AMICABLY
AABCILNN	CANNIBAL
AABCILNO	ANABOLIC
AABCILOR	BRACIOLA
AABCILST	BASALTIC
	CABALIST
AABCINNN	CANNABIN
AABCINNR	CINNABAR
AABCINNS	CANNABIS
AABCINOT	BOTANICA
AABCINRS	CARABINS
AABCINSU	BANAUSIC
AABCIOPS	COPAIBAS
AABCIOSS	SCABIOSA
AABCIRSS	BRASSICA
AABCISSS	ABSCISSA
AABCISTX	TAXICABS
AABCKKLT	TALKBACK
AABCKLNO	LOANBACK
AABCKLNY	CLAYBANK
AABCKLPS	BACKSLAP
AABCKLPY	PLAYBACK
AABCKLSY	LAYBACKS
AABCKNNS	CANBANKS
AABCKNPS	SNAPBACK
AABCKPRT	BRATPACK
AABCKPRW	BACKWRAP
AABCKPSY	BACKPAYS
	PAYBACKS
AABCKRRS	BARRACKS
AABCKSSW	BACKSAWS
AABCKSTY	BACKSTAY
AABCKSWY	SWAYBACK
AABCLLLO	COALBALL
AABCLLLY	BALLCLAY
AABCLLPY	PLACABLY
AABCLLSY	SCALABLY
AABCLMRY	CARBAMYL
AABCLMSU	CALUMBAS
AABCLNTY	BLATANCY
AABCLNUU	CUNABULA
AABCLRRY	CARBARYL
AABCLRSU	LABRUSCA
AABCMMSU	MACUMBAS
AABCMSSU	SAMBUCAS
AABCNORR	BARRANCO
AABCNRRS	CARBARNS
AABCORRS	CARBORAS
AABCORST	ABACTORS
	ACROBATS
AABCOSTT	CATBOATS
AABCRSTT	ABSTRACT
AABCSTTU	CATTABUS
AABDDEET	DEADBEAT
AABDDEGN	BANDAGED
AABDDEHL	BALDHEAD
AABDDEHN	HEADBAND
AABDDEIR	ABRAIDED
AABDDELL	BALLADED
AABDDENR	BRANDADE
AABDDERT	TABARDED
AABDDESS	BADASSED
AABDDIKS	KABADDIS
AABDDLNS	BADLANDS
AABDDMOR	DAMBOARD
AABDDNSS	SANDDABS
AABDEEHL	BEHEADAL
AABDEEHR	BAREHEAD
AABDEELR	READABLE
AABDEELT	DATEABLE
	DEALBATE
AABDEELV	EVADABLE
AABDEELW	WADEABLE
AABDEEMN	ENDAMEBA
AABDEERY	BAYADEER
	BAYADERE
AABDEGIN	BADINAGE
AABDEGIR	BIGARADE
AABDEGLR	GRADABLE
AABDEGMS	GAMBADES
AABDEGNR	BANDAGER
AABDEGNS	BANDAGES
AABDEGRR	BARRAGED
AABDEHHI	DAHABIEH
AABDEHKR	HARDBAKE
AABDEHMR	HARDBEAM
AABDEILN	BALADINE
AABDEILR	RADIABLE
AABDEILT	LABIATED
AABDEIOU	ABOIDEAU
AABDEIRS	ARABISED
AABDEIRZ	ARABIZED
AABDEISS	DIABASES
AABDEJLL	DJELLABA
AABDEJNX	BANJAXED
AABDEKRY	DAYBREAK
AABDELLS	BALLADES
AABDELLT	BALLATED
AABDELLU	LAUDABLE
AABDELMN	DAMNABLE
AABDELMS	BALSAMED
AABDELOR	ADORABLE
AABDELPR	DRAPABLE
	PARABLED
AABDELPT	BALDPATE
AABDELRS	BASELARD
AABDELRT	TRADABLE
AABDELRW	DRAWABLE
AABDELRY	READABLY
AABDELSW	SAWBLADE
AABDELSY	ABASEDLY
AABDEMMS	BEMADAMS
AABDEMNS	BEADSMAN
AABDENSU	BANDEAUS
AABDENTU	UNABATED
AABDENUX	BANDEAUX
AABDENVW	WAVEBAND
AABDEORS	SEABOARD
AABDEORT	TEABOARD
AABDEORX	BROADAXE
AABDERRS	ABRADERS
AABDERRT	TABERDAR
AABDERRW	BEARWARD
AABDERTT	RABATTED
AABDERTV	VARTABED
AABDERWY	WAYBREAD
AABDESSS	BADASSES
AABDFHLN	FAHLBAND
AABDGHNS	HANDBAGS
AABDGHRS	HARDBAGS
AABDGINN	ABANDING
AABDGINR	ABRADING
AABDGLNR	LANDGRAB
AABDGMOS	GAMBADOS
AABDGNOV	VAGABOND
AABDGNSS	SANDBAGS
AABDGORR	GARBOARD
AABDGORT	TAGBOARD
AABDGOTU	GADABOUT
AABDHINR	HAIRBAND
AABDHLLN	HANDBALL
AABDHLLR	HARDBALL
AABDHNST	HATBANDS
AABDHNSY	HAYBANDS
AABDHRSU	BAHADURS
	SUBAHDAR
AABDIILR	BIRADIAL
AABDIILS	BASIDIAL
AABDIKRS	BIDARKAS
AABDILLN	BALLADIN
AABDILNS	BALADINS
AABDIMNO	ABDOMINA
AABDIMNR	MADBRAIN
AABDIMRS	BARMAIDS
AABDINNR	RAINBAND
AABDINST	TABANIDS
AABDKNNS	SANDBANK
AABDLLRY	BALLADRY
AABDLLUY	LAUDABLY
AABDLMNU	LABDANUM
AABDLMNY	DAMNABLY
AABDLMRU	ADUMBRAL
AABDLNPT	PLATBAND
AABDLNSS	SALBANDS
AABDLOOT	BOATLOAD
AABDLOPR	LAPBOARD
AABDLORR	LABRADOR
	LARBOARD
AABDLORY	ADORABLY
AABDLRSW	BRADAWLS
AABDMNNS	BANDSMAN
AABDMNNY	BANDYMAN
AABDMNOR	BOARDMAN
AABDMNRS	ARMBANDS
AABDNNOS	ABANDONS
AABDNNTU	ABUNDANT
AABDNORS	BANDORAS
AABDNPSS	PASSBAND
AABDNRRY	BARNYARD
AABDNRSS	SANDBARS
AABDNRSU	BANDURAS
AABDORSV	BRAVADOS
AABDORTY	BOATYARD
AABDORWY	BROADWAY
	WAYBOARD
AABDRRSS	BRASSARD
AABDRRSW	DRAWBARS
AABDRSST	BASTARDS
AABDRSSU	SUBADARS
AABDRSTY	BASTARDY
AABEEFLN	FLEABANE
AABEEGKR	BRAKEAGE
	BREAKAGE
AABEEGLT	ABLEGATE
AABEEGNT	ABNEGATE
AABEEHLL	HEALABLE
AABEEHLR	HEARABLE
AABEEHLT	HATEABLE
	HEATABLE
AABEEHMR	HARAMBEE
AABEEKLM	MAKEABLE
AABEEKLT	TAKEABLE
AABEEKMT	BAKEMEAT
	MAKEBATE
AABEEKRW	BAKEWARE
AABEELLS	LEASABLE
	SALEABLE
	SEALABLE
AABEELMN	AMENABLE
	NAMEABLE
AABEELMT	TAMEABLE
AABEELPR	REAPABLE
AABEELPT	TAPEABLE
AABEELRS	ERASABLE
AABEELRT	RATEABLE
	TEARABLE
AABEELRW	WEARABLE
AABEELST	EATABLES
AABEELSV	SAVEABLE
AABEEMNO	AMOEBEAN
AABEEMNT	ENTAMEBA
AABEEMPR	ABAMPERE
AABEENNW	WANNABEE
AABEENOR	ANAEROBE
AABEERRT	ABERRATE
AABEERSZ	ZAREEBAS
AABEERTT	TRABEATE
AABEFFNS	BEFFANAS
AABEFGLS	FLEABAGS
AABEFGSU	AUFGABES
AABEFHKL	HALFBEAK
AABEFLLL	FLABELLA
AABEFLMO	FOAMABLE
AABEFLMR	FARMABLE
	FRAMABLE
AABEFLMU	FLAMBEAU
AABEGGGS	BAGGAGES
AABEGGRS	GARBAGES
AABEGHIL	GALABIEH
AABEGHLN	HANGABLE
AABEGHNR	BERGHAAN
AABEGILN	GAINABLE
AABEGILT	AGITABLE
AABEGINR	ABEARING
AABEGLLL	GLABELLA
AABEGLLM	BALLGAME
AABEGLNW	GNAWABLE
AABEGLRS	ALGEBRAS
AABEGLRT	GLABRATE
AABEGLRU	ARGUABLE
AABEGLRZ	GRAZABLE
AABEGMNR	BARGEMAN
AABEGMNY	MANGABEY
AABEGMRS	BERGAMAS
	MEGABARS
AABEGMRT	BREGMATA
AABEGMTT	GAMBETTA
AABEGNOR	BARONAGE
AABEGORT	ABROGATE
AABEGOST	SABOTAGE
AABEGOSZ	GAZABOES
AABEGRRS	BAGARRES
	BARRAGES
AABEGRSS	BRASSAGE
AABEGSSS	BAGASSES
AABEGSSU	ABUSAGES
AABEHIRR	HERBARIA
AABEHKLS	SHAKABLE
AABEHLMS	SHAMABLE
AABEHLOT	OATHABLE
AABEHLPS	SHAPABLE
AABEHLPT	ALPHABET
AABEHLRS	SHARABLE
AABEHLRW	WARHABLE
AABEHLSV	SHAVABLE
AABEHLSW	WASHABLE

AABEHNST	ABTHANES
AABEIKLS	KIELBASA
AABEIKNS	IKEBANAS
AABEILLL	ALLIABLE
AABEILLM	MAILABLE
AABEILLS	ISABELLA
	SAILABLE
AABEILNR	INARABLE
AABEILNS	BANALISE
AABEILNZ	BANALIZE
AABEILRS	RAISABLE
AABEILRV	VARIABLE
AABEILST	BALISTAE
	LABIATES
	SATIABLE
AABEILTV	ABLATIVE
AABEIMNR	AMBERINA
AABEIMRS	AMBARIES
AABEINOZ	ZABAIONE
AABEINRT	RABATINE
AABEINST	BASANITE
AABEIOTU	ABOITEAU
AABEIRSS	AIRBASES
	ARABISES
AABEIRSV	ABRASIVE
AABEIRSZ	ARABIZES
AABEIRTU	AUBRETIA
	AUBRIETA
AABEISST	ABATISES
AABEJLLS	JELLABAS
AABEJMUX	JAMBEAUX
AABEJNOZ	ZABAJONE
AABEJNSX	BANJAXES
AABEKLLS	SLAKABLE
AABEKLLT	TALKABLE
AABEKLLW	WALKABLE
AABEKLMS	MASKABLE
AABEKMNR	BRAKEMAN
AABEKNSS	SEABANKS
AABEKPRR	PARBREAK
AABEKRRS	BARESARK
AABEKRSS	ARABESKS
AABELLMT	MEATBALL
AABELLNO	LOANABLE
AABELLPP	PALPABLE
AABELLPS	LAPSABLE
AABELLPY	PLAYABLE
AABELLSS	SABELLAS
AABELLSV	SALVABLE
AABELLSY	SALEABLY
AABELLUV	VALUABLE
AABELMNY	AMENABLY
AABELMPP	MAPPABLE
AABELMST	BLASTEMA
	LAMBASTE
AABELMSU	AMUSABLE
AABELMTU	AMBULATE
AABELNNT	TANNABLE
AABELNOS	ABALONES
AABELNOT	ATONABLE
AABELNPS	ANABLEPS
AABELNPT	PANTABLE
AABELNPW	PAWNABLE
AABELNRY	BALNEARY
AABELNST	BANALEST
AABELOPR	PARABOLE
AABELORR	ARBOREAL
AABELOSV	LAVABOES
AABELOVW	AVOWABLE
AABELPPR	PALPEBRA
AABELPPT	TAPPABLE
AABELPRS	PARABLES
	PARSABLE
	PREBASAL
	SPARABLE
AABELPSS	PASSABLE
AABELPSY	PAYABLES
AABELRST	ARBALEST
AABELRTY	BETRAYAL
	RATEABLY
AABELSST	BASALTES
AABELSTT	ABETTALS
	STATABLE
	TASTABLE
AABELSTU	TABLEAUS
AABELSTW	WASTABLE
AABELSTX	TAXABLES
AABELSWY	SWAYABLE
AABELTTU	TABULATE
AABELTUX	TABLEAUX
AABENNSW	WANNABES
AABENRRT	ABERRANT
AABENRST	ANTBEARS
	RATSBANE
AABENRTU	ARBUTEAN
AABEORRT	ARBORETA
AABEORST	RABATOES
AABEQSUU	USQUABAE
AABERRRT	BARRATER
AABERRSW	BARWARES
AABERSSU	SUBAREAS
AABERSTT	RABATTES
	TABARETS
AABERSTU	ABATURES
AABESZZZ	BAZAZZES
AABETTUX	BATTEAUX
AABFILUX	FABLIAUX
AABFLLST	FASTBALL
AABFLOTT	FALTBOAT
	FLATBOAT
AABGGGNN	GANGBANG
AABGGNOT	TABOGGAN
AABGGRRT	BRAGGART
AABGHINS	ABASHING
AABGHKRS	SHAGBARK
AABGHNRS	BHANGRAS
AABGHNSS	NASHGABS
AABGIILS	ABIGAILS
AABGILMS	MAILBAGS
AABGILNT	ABLATING
	BANGTAIL
AABGIMNS	SAMBAING
AABGIMSU	GAMBUSIA
AABGINRS	BARGAINS
AABGINRY	ABRAYING
AABGINSS	BISNAGAS
AABGINSZ	BIZNAGAS
AABGLLLO	GOALBALL
AABGLLRY	BALLYRAG
AABGLMNU	GALBANUM
AABGLRUY	ARGUABLY
AABGMORR	BAROGRAM
AABGNORZ	GARBANZO
AABHHISS	SAHIBAHS
AABHHKSS	SABKHAHS
AABHHORU	BROUHAHA
AABHHRSU	BRUHAHAS
AABHIIMP	AMPHIBIA
AABHIINU	BAUHINIA
AABHIJMY	JAMBIYAH
AABHILLR	HAIRBALL
AABHILTU	HABITUAL
AABHINST	HABITANS
AABHINTT	HABITANT
AABHIRST	TABASHIR
AABHISTT	HABITATS
AABHKLLW	BALLHAWK
AABHKNRS	BARKHANS
AABHKSST	SABKHATS
AABHLLSW	WASHBALL
AABHMRSS	SAMBHARS
AABHMSTT	BATHMATS
AABHNOTU	AUTOBAHN
AABHQSSU	SQUABASH
AABHRRSU	SURBAHAR
AABIIJLT	JAILBAIT
AABIILSZ	ALBIZIAS
AABIILZZ	ALBIZZIA
AABIINST	ANTIBIAS
AABIIPST	BAPTISIA
AABIJMSY	JAMBIYAS
AABIKLMS	KALIMBAS
AABIKNSS	BANKSIAS
AABILLLY	LABIALLY
AABILLRS	BARILLAS
AABILLST	BALLISTA
AABILMNS	BAILSMAN
AABILMNU	BIMANUAL
AABILMSS	BAALISMS
AABILNNU	BIANNUAL
AABILNOR	BARONIAL
AABILNOT	ABLATION
AABILNRT	BRANTAIL
AABILNRU	BINAURAL
AABILNTY	BANALITY
AABILOST	SAILBOAT
AABILOSU	ABOULIAS
AABILOTT	BOATTAIL
AABILRRT	ARBITRAL
AABILRST	ARBALIST
AABILRSU	BALISAUR
AABILRSY	BASILARY
AABILRVY	VARIABLY
AABILSST	BALISTAS
AABILSTY	SATIABLY
AABILSUX	SUBAXIAL
AABIMMRS	MARIMBAS
AABIMNNO	BONAMANI
AABIMNOS	AMBOINAS
	BONAMIAS
AABIMNRU	MANUBRIA
AABIMORS	AMBROSIA
AABIMRSU	SIMARUBA
AABIMSST	BASMATIS
AABINNPR	BRAINPAN
AABINORS	ABRASION
AABINOSU	OUABAINS
AABINRST	ATABRINS
	BARTISAN
AABINRTZ	BARTIZAN
AABINSST	ABSTAINS
AABIORRS	SORBARIA
AABIORSS	ABROSIAS
AABIORST	AIRBOATS
AABIORTT	ABATTOIR
AABIOSSY	BIOASSAY
AABIPSUX	PAXIUBAS
AABIRTUY	RUBAIYAT
AABISTUZ	ZAIBATSU
AABJLMNO	JAMBOLAN
AABKLLPR	BALLPARK
AABKMNNS	BANKSMAN
AABKNRST	TANBARKS
AABKOOSZ	BAZOOKAS
AABKOPRS	SOAPBARK
AABLLMOR	BALMORAL
AABLLNST	BALLANTS
AABLLORS	ALLOBARS
AABLLORY	ABORALLY
AABLLPPY	PALPABLY
AABLLPRT	TRAPBALL
AABLLPST	PATBALLS
AABLLSST	BALLASTS
AABLLSTU	BLASTULA
AABLLSVY	SALVABLY
AABLLUVY	VALUABLY
AABLMNOR	ABNORMAL
AABLMNTU	AMBULANT
AABLMOST	BLASTOMA
AABLMRSU	LABARUMS
AABLMSST	LAMBASTS
AABLNSSU	SUBNASAL
AABLNTTT	BLATTANT
AABLORST	ABLATORS
AABLOTUY	LAYABOUT
AABLOVWY	AVOWABLY
AABLPSSY	PASSABLY
AABLRRSU	SABURRAL
AABLRSST	ARBLASTS
AABLRSUU	SUBAURAL
AABLSTTU	ABUTTALS
AABMMOSU	ABOMASUM
AABMNNOO	BONAMANO
AABMNOST	BOATSMAN
AABMNOSY	AMBOYNAS
AABMNOTW	BATWOMAN
AABMNRTU	RAMBUTAN
AABMORSU	MARABOUS
AABMORTU	MARABOUT
	TAMBOURA
AABMOSSU	ABOMASUS
AABMRSTU	TAMBURAS
AABNNOST	ABSONANT
AABNNOSZ	BONANZAS
AABNOSST	SABATONS
AABNOSSY	SABAYONS
AABORRRT	BARRATOR
AABORRSS	RASBORAS
AABORSTT	BAROSTAT
AABRRRTY	BARRATRY
AABRRSST	BRASSART
AABRRSSU	SABURRAS
AABRRSUV	BRAVURAS
AABSSTUX	SAXTUBAS
AABSTTTU	BATTUTAS
AACCCDIS	SACCADIC
AACCCFIO	FOCACCIA
AACCCHHU	CACHUCHA
AACCCRUY	ACCURACY
AACCDDES	CASCADED
AACCDEIM	ACADEMIC
AACCDELO	ACCOLADE
AACCDEMS	MEDACCAS
AACCDENU	CADUCEAN
AACCDERR	RACECARD
AACCDERS	CARCASED
	CARDCASE
AACCDESS	CASCADES
	SACCADES
AACCDHIR	CHARACID
AACCDIIS	ACCIDIAS
AACCDIRS	CARDIACS
AACCDOVY	ADVOCACY
AACCEELT	CALCEATE
AACCEENT	CETACEAN
AACCEFLO	COALFACE
AACCEFST	CATFACES
AACCEGOR	ACCORAGE
AACCEGRU	CARUCAGE
AACCEHIX	CACHEXIA
AACCEILN	CALCANEI
AACCEILU	ACICULAE
AACCEIRR	CERCARIA
AACCEKRS	CARCAKES
AACCELLY	CAECALLY
	CALYCEAL
AACCELOR	CARACOLE
AACCELPT	PLACCATE
AACCELRR	CARCERAL
AACCELTY	CALYCATE

AACCENRT	CARCANET
AACCENSV	VACANCES
AACCENTU	ACUTANCE
AACCERSS	CARCASES
AACCERTU	ACCURATE
	CARUCATE
AACCFGOO	CACAFOGO
AACCFILR	FARCICAL
AACCFLTU	CALCTUFA
AACCGILT	GALACTIC
AACCHHKT	CHATCHKA
AACCHILL	CAILLACH
AACCHILP	PACHALIC
AACCHINR	ANARCHIC
	CHARACIN
AACCHINS	CHICANAS
AACCHIOR	AIRCOACH
AACCHISV	VISCACHA
AACCHIVZ	VIZCACHA
AACCHLLT	CATCHALL
AACCHLNS	CLACHANS
AACCHLOR	CHARCOAL
AACCHLOT	CACHALOT
AACCHLRS	CLARSACH
AACCHMNO	COACHMAN
AACCHMPS	CHAMPACS
AACCHNNS	CANNACHS
AACCHNOR	CORANACH
AACCHRST	CHARACTS
AACCIINV	VACCINIA
AACCIIST	SCIATICA
AACCILMS	ACCLAIMS
AACCILNV	VACCINAL
AACCILRU	ACICULAR
AACCILSU	ACICULAS
AACCILTT	TACTICAL
AACCIMNU	CACUMINA
AACCINSV	VACCINAS
AACCIORS	CARIOCAS
AACCIORU	CARIACOU
AACCIPRT	APRACTIC
AACCIPTY	CAPACITY
AACCIRTY	CARYATIC
AACCISTT	STACCATI
AACCJKRS	CARJACKS
AACCJKRW	CRACKJAW
AACCJORU	CARCAJOU
	CARJACOU
AACCKKPS	PACKSACK
AACCKLOS	COALSACK
AACCKLPS	CALPACKS
AACCKORT	COATRACK
AACCKRRS	CARRACKS
AACCLLRU	CALCULAR
AACCLLST	CATCALLS
AACCLMNY	CLAMANCY
AACCLOPS	POLACCAS
AACCLORS	CARACOLS
AACCLPRS	CALCSPAR
AACCLPST	PLACCATS
AACCLRSU	ACCRUALS
	CARACULS
	SACCULAR
AACCLSSU	ACCUSALS
AACCLSTW	CATCLAWS
AACCNSTU	ACCUSANT
AACCOPRS	ASCOCARP
AACCORSU	CURACAOS
	CURACOAS
AACCOSST	ACCOASTS
AACCOSTT	STACCATO
	STOCCATA
	TOCCATAS
AACCRRST	CARRACTS
AACDDEHI	ACIDHEAD

AACDDEIL	DAEDALIC
AACDDENV	ADVANCED
AACDDETU	CAUDATED
AACDDHRS	CHADDARS
AACDDILN	CANDIDAL
AACDDINR	RADICAND
AACDDINS	CANDIDAS
AACDDRSW	CRAWDADS
AACDEEHH	HEADACHE
AACDEEHR	AREACHED
	HEADRACE
AACDEEHS	HEADCASE
AACDEELS	ESCALADE
AACDEEMS	ACADEMES
AACDEEPS	ESCAPADE
AACDEERT	ACERATED
AACDEEST	CASEATED
	ESTACADE
AACDEETT	ACETATED
AACDEETU	ECAUDATE
AACDEETV	CAVEATED
AACDEFHR	HARDFACE
AACDEFLS	FALCADES
AACDEFLT	FALCATED
AACDEGGR	AGGRACED
AACDEGKP	PACKAGED
AACDEGMR	DECAGRAM
AACDEHHY	HEADACHY
AACDEHIN	HACIENDA
AACDEHLN	CHALANED
AACDEHLP	CEPHALAD
AACDEHMR	DRACHMAE
AACDEHMS	CHAMADES
AACDEHRS	CHARADES
	HARDCASE
AACDEHRT	CATHEDRA
AACDEHST	CATHEADS
AACDEHTT	ATTACHED
AACDEIIL	AECIDIAL
AACDEIIM	ACIDEMIA
AACDEILM	CAMAILED
AACDEILS	ALCAIDES
	SIDALCEA
AACDEIMN	MAENADIC
AACDEIMS	CAMISADE
AACDEIMT	ACETAMID
AACDEINR	CANARIED
	RADIANCE
AACDEINS	AIDANCES
AACDEIRT	RADICATE
AACDEJNT	ADJACENT
AACDEKNP	PANCAKED
AACDEKNS	ASKANCED
AACDEKTT	ATTACKED
AACDELLN	CALENDAL
	CANALLED
AACDELLS	ALCALDES
AACDELMN	MANACLED
AACDELNR	CALENDAR
	LANDRACE
AACDELNS	CANDELAS
AACDELNV	VALANCED
AACDELOS	CASELOAD
	ESCALADO
AACDELPT	PLACATED
AACDELRS	CALDERAS
AACDELSS	SCALADES
AACDELSY	ALCAYDES
AACDELTT	LACTATED
AACDELTV	CLAVATED
AACDELTY	ACYLATED
AACDENOT	ANECDOTA
AACDENRV	ADVANCER
AACDENSV	ADVANCES
	CANVASED

AACDENSZ	CADENZAS
AACDENTU	ADUNCATE
AACDENTV	TADVANCE
AACDEOPS	ESCAPADO
AACDEOTU	AUTOCADE
AACDEOTV	ADVOCATE
AACDEPRS	SCARPAED
AACDEQUY	ADEQUACY
AACDERST	CADASTER
	CADASTRE
AACDERSV	CADAVERS
AACDERTU	ARCUATED
AACDESTU	CAUDATES
AACDETTU	ACTUATED
AACDETUV	VACUATED
AACDFLNR	FLANCARD
AACDGGHI	HAGGADIC
AACDGINR	ARCADING
	CARANGID
	CARDIGAN
AACDHHKR	HARDHACK
AACDHHNS	SHADCHAN
AACDHHRS	SHADRACH
AACDHIIS	DICHASIA
AACDHILL	CHILLADA
AACDHILR	DIARCHAL
AACDHIMR	CHADARIM
	DRACHMAI
AACDHINP	HANDICAP
AACDHINR	ARACHNID
AACDHKRT	HARDTACK
AACDHLNP	HANDCLAP
AACDHLOT	CATHODAL
AACDHLRY	CHARLADY
AACDHMMR	DRAMMACH
AACDHMOP	PACHADOM
AACDHMRS	DRACHMAS
AACDHNOW	WAHCONDA
AACDHNRS	HANDCARS
AACDHNRT	HANDCART
AACDHPRS	CRASHPAD
AACDIINS	ASCIDIAN
AACDIIRU	ACIDURIA
AACDILLP	PALLADIC
AACDILMN	MANDALIC
AACDILMT	DALMATIC
AACDILMU	CALADIUM
AACDILNO	DIACONAL
AACDILNR	CARDINAL
AACDILNU	DULCIANA
AACDILNV	VANDALIC
AACDILOZ	ZODIACAL
AACDILPS	CAPSIDAL
AACDILRR	RAILCARD
AACDILRS	RADICALS
AACDIMNO	MANDIOCA
AACDIMNY	ADYNAMIC
	CYANAMID
AACDIMOS	CAMISADO
AACDIMRT	DRAMATIC
AACDINRT	RADICANT
	TRIDACNA
AACDINRY	RADIANCY
AACDINSS	SCANDIAS
AACDINST	ANTACIDS
AACDIOTU	AUTACOID
AACDIRSS	ASCARIDS
AACDIRTY	CARYATID
AACDITUY	AUDACITY
AACDJKSW	JACKDAWS
AACDJQRU	JACQUARD
AACDKLLN	LACKLAND
AACDKSSY	DAYSACKS
AACDLLUY	CAUDALLY
AACDLNSS	SCANDALS

AACDLORS	CARLOADS
AACDLORT	CARTLOAD
AACDLORY	COALYARD
AACDLOSS	SCALADOS
AACDLOSV	CALVADOS
AACDLPRS	PLACARDS
AACDLRTY	DACTYLAR
AACDMMOR	CARDAMOM
AACDMMRU	CARDAMUM
AACDMNNO	MANCANDO
AACDMNOR	CARDAMON
AACDOOSV	AVOCADOS
AACDORRT	CARTROAD
AACEEFIT	FACETIAE
AACEEFLP	PALEFACE
AACEEFNS	FEASANCE
AACEEGIR	ACIERAGE
	AGACERIE
AACEEGLR	CLEARAGE
AACEEGLV	CLEAVAGE
AACEEGNR	CARAGEEN
AACEEGNY	GYNAECEA
AACEEGRS	ACREAGES
	GEARCASE
AACEEHLP	ACALEPHE
AACEEHLT	LEACHATE
AACEEHRS	AREACHES
	EARACHES
AACEEHRT	TRACHEAE
AACEEIMT	EMACIATE
AACEEINN	ENCAENIA
AACEEIRT	ACIERATE
AACEEKRT	CARETAKE
AACEEKST	TEACAKES
AACEELNS	ANELACES
AACEELRT	LACERATE
AACEELST	ESCALATE
AACEELTU	ACULEATE
AACEEMRT	MACERATE
	RACEMATE
AACEEMSS	AMESACES
AACEEMST	CASEMATE
AACEENNT	CATENANE
AACEENRS	CESAREAN
AACEENRW	CANEWARE
AACEENTT	CATENATE
AACEEPRV	PRECAVAE
AACEEPSS	SEASCAPE
AACEERSU	CAESURAE
AACEERTV	ACERVATE
AACEESSS	CASEASES
AACEESST	CASEATES
AACEESTT	ACETATES
AACEETUV	EVACUATE
AACEETVX	EXCAVATE
AACEFFIN	AFFIANCE
AACEFHLP	HALFPACE
AACEFILT	CALIFATE
AACEFIST	FASCIATE
AACEFRRS	CARFARES
AACEFRRU	FURCRAEA
AACEFRSS	FRACASES
AACEFRST	SEACRAFT
AACEFRSX	CARFAXES
AACEFRTT	ARTEFACT
AACEGGRS	AGGRACES
AACEGHNS	GANACHES
AACEGHNT	CHANTAGE
AACEGILN	ANGELICA
AACEGILT	GLACIATE
AACEGINR	CANAIGRE
AACEGINY	GYNAECIA
AACEGIOP	APOGAEIC
AACEGIRR	CARRIAGE
AACEGIRV	VICARAGE

AACEGKPR	PACKAGER
AACEGKPS	PACKAGES
AACEGKRT	TRACKAGE
AACEGKSS	SACKAGES
AACEGLNY	LANCEGAY
AACEGLSS	SCALAGES
AACEGMNO	COMANAGE
AACEGMNP	CAMPAGNE
AACEGNRS	CARNAGES
	CRANAGES
AACEGRST	CARTAGES
AACEGRSV	SCAVAGER
AACEGSSV	SCAVAGES
AACEHHRU	HUARACHE
AACEHIKN	ICEKHANA
AACEHILL	ACHILLEA
	HELIACAL
AACEHILN	ACHENIAL
AACEHILP	PHACELIA
AACEHIMR	CHIMAERA
AACEHIMT	HAEMATIC
AACEHIPT	HEPATICA
AACEHIRS	ARCHAISE
AACEHIRT	THERIACA
AACEHIRZ	ARCHAIZE
AACEHLNT	CALANTHE
AACEHLNU	EULACHAN
AACEHLPS	ACALEPHS
AACEHLRS	ALCHERAS
AACEHLRT	TRACHEAL
AACEHLRX	EXARCHAL
AACEHLSS	CALASHES
AACEHLST	ALCAHEST
AACEHMNP	CAMPHANE
AACEHMRS	MARCHESA
AACEHMSS	CAMASHES
AACEHMST	SCHEMATA
AACEHNPS	PANACHES
AACEHPRT	RACEPATH
AACEHPSU	CHAPEAUS
AACEHPUX	CHAPEAUX
AACEHQTU	CHAQUETA
AACEHRSS	CHARASES
AACEHRST	TRACHEAS
AACEHRSU	ARCHAEUS
AACEHRTT	ATTACHER
	REATTACH
AACEHSTT	ATTACHES
AACEHSTU	CHATEAUS
AACEHTUX	CHATEAUX
AACEIILN	LACINIAE
AACEIINT	ACTINIAE
AACEIIRV	CAVIARIE
AACEIKMT	KAMACITE
AACEILLM	CAMELLIA
AACEILLN	ALLIANCE
	ANCILLAE
	CANAILLE
AACEILMN	ANALCIME
	CALAMINE
AACEILMS	CAMELIAS
AACEILMT	CALAMITE
AACEILNS	CANALISE
AACEILNT	ANALCITE
	LAITANCE
AACEILNU	ACAULINE
AACEILNV	VALENCIA
	VALIANCE
AACEILNZ	CANALIZE
AACEILOP	ALOPECIA
AACEILRT	TAILRACE
AACEILRV	CAVALIER
AACEILST	SALICETA
AACEIMNS	AMNESIAC
AACEIMRS	MACARISE
	MESARAIC
AACEIMRZ	MACARIZE
AACEIMTT	CATAMITE
AACEIMUX	CAMAIEUX
AACEINRS	ACARINES
	CANARIES
	CESARIAN
AACEINRT	CARINATE
	CRANIATE
AACEINRV	VARIANCE
AACEINST	ESTANCIA
AACEINTV	CAVATINE
AACEIOPR	CAPOEIRA
AACEIPPS	PAPACIES
AACEIPRS	AIRSCAPE
	AIRSPACE
AACEIPRT	APRICATE
AACEIPSS	CAPIASES
AACEIPTT	APATETIC
	CAPITATE
AACEIQSU	ACEQUIAS
AACEIRSV	AVARICES
	CAVIARES
AACEIRTV	VICARATE
AACEITTV	ACTIVATE
	CAVITATE
AACEJLTU	JACULATE
AACEKKLW	CAKEWALK
AACEKMPR	CAPMAKER
AACEKMRR	CARMAKER
AACEKNPS	PANCAKES
AACEKNSS	ASKANCES
AACEKOST	OATCAKES
AACEKRTT	ATTACKER
	REATTACK
AACELLMR	MARCELLA
AACELLNR	CANALLER
AACELLNS	CANELLAS
AACELLOT	ALLOCATE
AACELLST	CASTELLA
	LACTEALS
AACELLTY	ALLEYCAT
AACELMNP	PLACEMAN
AACELMNS	MANACLES
AACELMOT	CELOMATA
AACELMRS	CARAMELS
	CERAMALS
AACELMTU	MACULATE
AACELNNO	ANCONEAL
AACELNNU	CANNULAE
AACELNOR	LECANORA
AACELNPR	PARLANCE
AACELNPS	CAPELANS
	SCALEPAN
AACELNPT	PLACENTA
AACELNPY	ANYPLACE
AACELNRT	LACERANT
AACELNRY	ARCANELY
AACELNST	ANALECTS
AACELNSV	VALANCES
AACELNTU	CANULATE
	LACUNATE
	TENACULA
AACELORS	ACEROLAS
AACELORV	CAVALERO
AACELOST	CATALOES
AACELOSU	ACAULOSE
AACELOSV	COAEVALS
AACELPRT	PLACATER
AACELPRV	PRECAVAL
AACELPST	PLACATES
AACELPSU	SCAPULAE
AACELRSS	SCALARES
AACELRSU	CAESURAL
AACELRSV	CARAVELS
AACELRTY	ACRYLATE
AACELRWY	CLAYWARE
	CLEARWAY
AACELSST	LACTASES
AACELSTT	LACTATES
AACELSTY	ACYLATES
	CATALYSE
AACELTTY	CATTLEYA
AACELTYZ	CATALYZE
AACEMMRS	MACRAMES
AACEMNOR	AMORANCE
AACEMNPS	SPACEMAN
AACEMNST	CAMSTANE
AACEMPRS	PARACMES
AACEMQSU	MACAQUES
AACEMRSS	MASSACRE
AACEMSSS	CAMASSES
AACENOTU	OCEANAUT
AACENPRS	PANCREAS
AACENPRT	CATNAPER
AACENPST	PASTANCE
AACENPSU	SAUCEPAN
AACENPTT	PANCETTA
AACENRST	CANASTER
	CATERANS
AACENRSV	CANVASER
AACENRTT	REACTANT
AACENRTY	CATENARY
AACENRVZ	CZAREVNA
AACENSSV	CANVASES
AACENSTT	CANTATES
	CASTANET
AACENSTY	CYANATES
AACENTUV	EVACUANT
AACEOPPR	COAPPEAR
AACEOPRT	CAPROATE
AACEOPST	PEACOATS
AACEORSS	ROSACEAS
AACEORSU	ARACEOUS
AACEORTV	CAVEATOR
AACEOSST	SEACOAST
AACEPRST	CAPRATES
AACEPRSU	CAPUERAS
AACERRTU	ARCATURE
AACERSSS	RASCASSE
AACERSSU	CAESURAS
AACERSSZ	SAZERACS
AACERSTT	CASTRATE
	TEACARTS
AACERSWY	RACEWAYS
AACERTTT	TRACTATE
AACESSSV	CAVASSES
AACESSTT	SCEATTAS
AACESTTU	ACTUATES
AACESTUV	VACUATES
AACESUWY	CAUSEWAY
AACFFILS	CAFFILAS
AACFGRST	CRAGFAST
AACFHMST	CAMSHAFT
AACFILLY	FACIALLY
AACFILOS	FASCIOLA
AACFINST	FANATICS
AACFIRRT	AIRCRAFT
AACFIRST	FRASCATI
AACFIRTT	ARTIFACT
AACFISST	FASCISTA
AACFJKLP	FLAPJACK
AACFKLPT	FLATPACK
AACFLLST	CATFALLS
AACFLLSU	FALCULAS
AACFLOPR	PARFOCAL
AACFLPST	FLATCAPS
AACFLRST	FLATCARS
	FRACTALS
AACFRRSU	FARRUCAS
AACFRRTW	WARCRAFT
AACGGINO	ANAGOGIC
AACGGIOP	APAGOGIC
AACGHILT	TAIGLACH
AACGHIPR	AGRAPHIC
AACGHIRR	CHIRAGRA
AACGHLLO	AGALLOCH
AACGHNOR	CHARANGO
AACGHOPZ	GAZPACHO
AACGHORU	GUACHARO
AACGIIMN	MAGICIAN
AACGIINR	GARCINIA
AACGILLN	GALLICAN
AACGILLO	ALOGICAL
AACGILLS	GLACIALS
AACGILLU	ALGUACIL
AACGILNN	CANALING
AACGILNO	ANALOGIC
AACGILNR	CRAALING
AACGILNT	ANTALGIC
AACGILNV	GALVANIC
AACGILOU	GUAIACOL
AACGILOX	COXALGIA
AACGILRT	TRAGICAL
AACGILSS	SCAGLIAS
AACGIMMT	MAGMATIC
AACGIMNN	MANGANIC
AACGIMNP	CAMPAIGN
	PANGAMIC
AACGIMOP	APOGAMIC
AACGIMRR	MARGARIC
AACGIMUU	GUAIACUM
AACGINOT	CONTAGIA
AACGINPS	SCAPAING
AACGINTV	VACATING
AACGISTY	SAGACITY
AACGLMOU	GLAUCOMA
AACGLOST	CATALOGS
AACGMNRS	CRAGSMAN
AACGNOSU	GUANACOS
AACGNRVY	VAGRANCY
AACHHIKR	KACHAHRI
AACHHKRS	CHARKHAS
AACHHLLS	CHALLAHS
AACHHLOT	HALACHOT
AACHHORU	HUARACHO
AACHHTWY	HATCHWAY
AACHIIMR	MARIACHI
AACHIKKZ	KAZACHKI
AACHIKNR	CHINKARA
AACHIKNS	KACHINAS
AACHIKNT	KATCHINA
AACHIKRS	CHIKARAS
AACHILLP	CALIPHAL
AACHILLR	RACHILLA
AACHILMS	CHAMISAL
	CHIASMAL
AACHILMT	THALAMIC
AACHILNP	CHAPLAIN
AACHILOS	ACHOLIAS
AACHILPS	CALIPASH
	PASHALIC
AACHILPT	HAPTICAL
AACHILRV	ARCHIVAL
AACHIMNN	CHAINMAN
AACHIMNP	CHINAMPA
AACHIMNR	CHAIRMAN
AACHIMNS	SHAMANIC
AACHIMNT	MATACHIN
AACHIMNZ	CHAZANIM
AACHIMRR	ARMCHAIR
AACHIMRS	ARCHAISM
	CHARISMA
	MACHAIRS
AACHIMSS	CHIASMAS

AACHIMST	CATHISMA
AACHINNT	ACANTHIN
AACHINRT	CANTHARI
AACHINSW	CHAINSAW
AACHIPPT	CHAPPATI
AACHIPRS	CHARPAIS
	HAIRCAPS
AACHIPSS	APHASICS
AACHIPST	CHAPATIS
AACHIPTT	CHAPATTI
AACHIRST	ARCHAIST
	CITHARAS
AACHIRTX	TAXIARCH
AACHKKOZ	KAZACHOK
AACHKMPS	CHAMPAKS
AACHKPSS	SCHAPSKA
AACHKRST	HATRACKS
AACHKRSY	HAYRACKS
AACHKSSW	HACKSAWS
AACHKSTY	HAYSTACK
AACHLLNS	CHALLANS
AACHLMNO	MONACHAL
AACHLMOS	CHLOASMA
AACHLNOO	OOLACHAN
AACHLORT	THORACAL
AACHLOST	CALATHOS
AACHLPPS	CHAPPALS
AACHLPSS	PASCHALS
AACHLSSU	ACUSHLAS
AACHLSTU	CALATHUS
AACHMMNR	MARCHMAN
AACHMNNR	RANCHMAN
AACHMNTW	WATCHMAN
AACHMNTY	YACHTMAN
AACHMNUY	NAUMACHY
AACHMORT	ACHROMAT
	TRACHOMA
AACHMPRT	CHAMPART
AACHMPRY	PHARMACY
AACHMSSY	YASHMACS
AACHNOPS	PANOCHAS
AACHNOSU	HUANACOS
AACHNPRS	SARPANCH
AACHNRST	TRASHCAN
AACHNRSV	NAVARCHS
AACHNRVY	NAVARCHY
AACHNSSU	ANCHUSAS
AACHNSTU	ACANTHUS
AACHNSZZ	CHAZZANS
AACHOPPR	APPROACH
AACHOPRR	PARACHOR
AACHORTU	RACAHOUT
AACHOTTU	TACAHOUT
AACHRRST	CATARRHS
AACHRSWY	ARCHWAYS
AACHRTUY	AUTARCHY
AACIILMN	ANIMALIC
AACIILMO	MAIOLICA
AACIILRT	IATRICAL
AACIILRV	VICARIAL
AACIILTV	VIATICAL
AACIIMNT	ANIMATIC
AACIIMSS	CAMISIAS
AACIINNT	ACTINIAN
AACIINPR	PICARIAN
AACIINPT	CAPITANI
AACIINST	ACTINIAS
AACIJLMO	MAJOLICA
AACIJNOP	JAPONICA
AACIKLMS	MAILSACK
AACIKLRS	CLARKIAS
AACIKMNW	MACKINAW
AACIKNNS	CANAKINS
AACIKNST	KATCINAS
AACIKRTU	AUTARKIC
AACILLLY	LAICALLY
AACILLMR	LACRIMAL
AACILLMT	CLIMATAL
AACILLNS	ANCILLAS
AACILLPY	APICALLY
AACILLRY	RACIALLY
AACILMNT	CALAMINT
	CLAIMANT
AACILMOR	ACROMIAL
AACILMOT	ATOMICAL
AACILMTY	CALAMITY
AACILNOR	CONARIAL
AACILNRS	CLARAINS
AACILNRV	CARNIVAL
AACILNST	ALICANTS
	SANTALIC
AACILNTT	TANTALIC
AACILNTU	NAUTICAL
AACILNTY	ANALYTIC
AACILNUV	NAVICULA
AACILNVY	VALIANCY
AACILOTT	COATTAIL
	TAILCOAT
AACILPRU	PIACULAR
AACILPST	APLASTIC
	CAPITALS
AACILPSZ	CAPSIZAL
AACILPTU	CAPITULA
AACILPTY	ATYPICAL
AACILQRU	ACQUIRAL
AACILRRS	RAILCARS
AACILRTY	ALACRITY
AACILRUU	AURICULA
AACILRUV	AVICULAR
AACILSTT	CATTAILS
	STATICAL
AACILSTY	SALACITY
AACIMMNO	AMMONIAC
AACIMMRS	MACARISM
	MACRAMIS
	MARASMIC
AACIMNOR	ARMONICA
	MACARONI
	MAROCAIN
AACIMNOS	MANIOCAS
AACIMNOT	ANATOMIC
AACIMORT	AROMATIC
AACIMOTX	MAXICOAT
AACIMPRS	PICAMARS
AACINNST	CANTINAS
AACINOPR	PARANOIC
AACINOPT	CAPITANO
	PACATION
AACINORS	OCARINAS
AACINORT	RAINCOAT
AACINOTV	VACATION
AACINPRT	CANTRAIP
AACINPST	CAPITANS
	CAPTAINS
AACINPTY	CAPITAYN
AACINQTU	ACQUAINT
AACINRSS	ACRASINS
AACINRST	ARCANIST
AACINRSZ	CZARINAS
AACINSTZ	STANZAIC
AACIOPST	TAPIOCAS
AACIOPSV	COPAIVAS
AACIPPRS	PAPRICAS
AACIPRTY	RAPACITY
AACIQSTU	AQUATICS
AACIRRTT	TARTARIC
AACIRSTT	CASTRATI
AACIRSTZ	CZARITSA
AACIRTVY	CAVITARY
AACIRTZZ	CZARITZA
AACISSTW	SWASTICA
AACJKLPS	SLAPJACK
AACJKMNS	MANJACKS
AACJKOOR	JACKAROO
AACJKSTY	JACKSTAY
AACJPSTU	CAJAPUTS
AACKKNPS	KNAPSACK
AACKLNPS	KNAPSCAL
AACKLOWY	LOCKAWAY
AACKLSTW	CATWALKS
AACKMNPS	MANPACKS
AACKMNRT	TRACKMAN
AACKMNST	TACKSMAN
AACKMRST	AMTRACKS
AACKNRSS	RANSACKS
AACKORWY	ROCKAWAY
AACKPRRS	CARPARKS
AACKPRST	RATPACKS
AACKPSWY	PACKWAYS
AACKRTWY	TRACKWAY
AACLLLOO	CALLALOO
AACLLMMU	MACALLUM
AACLLMRY	LACRYMAL
AACLLNRY	CARNALLY
AACLLNST	CALLANTS
AACLLNSU	CALLUNAS
AACLLRRY	CARRYALL
AACLLRSY	RASCALLY
AACLLSUU	CLAUSULA
AACLLSUY	CASUALLY
	CAUSALLY
AACLLTUY	ACTUALLY
AACLMNNS	CLANSMAN
AACLMNSS	CLASSMAN
AACLMNST	CALMANTS
AACLMOTU	COMATULA
AACLMRRU	MACRURAL
AACLNNOT	CANTONAL
AACLNNRU	CANNULAR
AACLNNSU	CANNULAS
AACLNOPR	COPLANAR
AACLNOTT	OCTANTAL
AACLNPSY	CLAYPANS
AACLNRSU	LACUNARS
AACLNRUY	LACUNARY
AACLNTVY	VACANTLY
AACLOOPT	TAPACOLO
AACLOPRS	CAPORALS
AACLOPST	OCTAPLAS
AACLOPTU	TAPACULO
AACLORRU	ORACULAR
AACLORST	COALTARS
AACLORSU	CAROUSAL
AACLORSZ	ALCORZAS
AACLORUV	VACUOLAR
AACLOSTT	CATTALOS
AACLOSUU	ACAULOUS
AACLPPRT	CLAPTRAP
AACLPRST	CALTRAPS
AACLPRSU	CAPSULAR
	SCAPULAR
AACLPRTY	CALYPTRA
AACLPSSU	SCAPULAS
AACLPSTY	PLAYACTS
AACLPTTU	CATAPULT
AACLRSTU	CLAUSTRA
AACLRSUV	VASCULAR
AACLRTUX	CURTALAX
AACLRWWY	CRAWLWAY
AACLSSTT	SALTCATS
AACLSTTY	CATALYST
AACLSTUY	CASUALTY
AACMNOOR	MACAROON
AACMNORS	CAMARONS
	MASCARON
AACMNPRY	RAMPANCY
AACMNRRU	MACRURAN
AACMNRSU	ARCANUMS
AACMORRS	CAMORRAS
AACMORSS	SARCOMAS
AACMRRST	TRAMCARS
AACMRSSS	SARCASMS
AACNNOSZ	CANZONAS
AACNOSST	SACATONS
AACNOSTZ	ZACATONS
AACNOTTY	CATATONY
AACNPRST	CANTRAPS
AACNPSST	CAPSTANS
AACNRSTT	TRANSACT
AACNRSTU	CURTANAS
AACOORTX	TOXOCARA
AACOPPRS	APOCARPS
AACOPPRY	APOCARPY
AACOPRSU	ACARPOUS
AACOPRTU	AUTOCARP
AACOPSTV	POSTCAVA
AACOPSTY	APOSTACY
AACORRTV	VARACTOR
AACORSSW	CARASSOW
AACORSTT	CASTRATO
AACORSTU	ACATOURS
	AUTOCARS
AACORTTU	ACTUATOR
	AUTOCRAT
AACOSTUV	AUTOVACS
AACPSSTW	CATSPAWS
AACRSTTT	ATTRACTS
AACRSTUV	VACATURS
AACRSTWY	CARTWAYS
AACSTUWY	CUTAWAYS
AADDDEEH	DEADHEAD
AADDDEER	ADREADED
AADDDERW	ADWARDED
AADDDGNR	GRANDDAD
AADDEELT	DEALATED
AADDEFLL	DEADFALL
AADDEGGR	AGGRADED
AADDEGRT	GRADATED
AADDEHHR	HARDHEAD
AADDEHLN	HEADLAND
AADDEHMN	HANDMADE
AADDEHRZ	HAZARDED
AADDEILN	DEDALIAN
AADDEILS	ALIDADES
AADDEIRT	RADIATED
AADDEKMS	DAMASKED
AADDELNS	SANDALED
AADDELTU	ADULATED
AADDEMNT	MANDATED
AADDEMRU	MARAUDED
AADDEMRY	DAYDREAM
AADDENPR	PANDARED
AADDENPS	DEADPANS
AADDEORS	DEODARAS
AADDGMNR	GRANDDAM
AADDGNRS	GRADDANS
	GRANDADS
AADDGNRU	GRADUAND
AADDHHRS	SHRADDHA
AADDHIMN	HANDMAID
AADDHKRS	KHADDARS
AADDHRSS	SRADDHAS
AADDIIKS	DIDAKAIS
AADDIISV	DAVIDIAS
AADDILNO	DIANODAL
AADDIMSS	DADAISMS
AADDISST	DADAISTS
AADDKMMO	MOKADDAM
AADDLLNY	LANDLADY
AADDLNRW	LANDWARD

AADDLNRY YARDLAND
AADDMMQU MUQADDAM
AADDNRST STANDARD
AADDNRWY YARDWAND
AADDNSVV DVANDVAS
AADDRSST DASTARDS
AADDRSTY DASTARDY
AADEEERT DEAERATE
AADEEFFR AFFEARED
AADEEGHR HEADGEAR
AADEEGHS HEADAGES
AADEEGHT HEADGATE
AADEEGLM MEGADEAL
AADEEGLR LAAGERED
AADEEGLT GALEATED
AADEEGMN AMENAGED
ENDAMAGE
AADEEGMR REDAMAGE
AADEEGNR GADARENE
AADEEGRV AVERAGED
AADEEHMT MEATHEAD
AADEEIRT ERADIATE
AADEEIRW AWEARIED
AADEEKNW AWAKENED
AADEEKRW REAWAKED
AADEELNN ANNEALED
AADEELPP APPEALED
AADEELST DEALATES
AADEELTV ALVEATED
AADEEMNS MAENADES
AADEEMNT EMANATED
AADEEMOT OEDEMATA
AADEEMRR DEMERARA
AADEENPT TAPENADE
AADEENTT ANTEDATE
AADEEPPR APPEARED
AADEEPPS APPEASED
AADEEPRS PASEARED
AADEEQTU ADEQUATE
AADEERSW AWARDEES
AADEFFLT AFFLATED
AADEFFNR FANFARED
AADEFFRY AFFRAYED
AADEFGLS FALDAGES
AADEFGRS FARDAGES
AADEFHLT FLATHEAD
AADEFHST FATHEADS
HEADFAST
AADEFHTW FATWAHED
AADEFILR FAIRLEAD
AADEFIRS FARADISE
SAFARIED
AADEFIRZ FARADIZE
AADEFISS FADAISES
AADEFLLR FALDERAL
AADEFLRY DEFRAYAL
AADEFLTT FALDETTA
AADEFNSZ FAZENDAS
AADEFRRW WARFARED
AADEFRWY WAYFARED
AADEGGRS AGGRADES
SAGGARED
AADEGGRT AGGRATED
AADEGGRU GUARDAGE
AADEGHLN DANELAGH
AADEGHNR HANGARED
AADEGHRS RAGHEADS
RHAGADES
AADEGILL DIALLAGE
AADEGILT GLADIATE
AADEGINR AREADING
DRAINAGE
GARDENIA
AADEGINT INDAGATE
AADEGIRR GERARDIA

AADEGIRV GRAVIDAE
AADEGITT AGITATED
AADEGITV DIVAGATE
AADEGITZ AGATIZED
AADEGJTU ADJUTAGE
AADEGKMR DEKAGRAM
AADEGLLT TALLAGED
AADEGLMN MAGDALEN
AADEGLMY AMYGDALE
AADEGLNS SELADANG
AADEGLOP GALOPADE
AADEGLSV SALVAGED
AADEGMNR GRANDAME
AADEGMPR RAMPAGED
AADEGMRS DAMAGERS
MEGARADS
SMARAGDE
AADEGMSS MASSAGED
AADEGNRR ARRANGED
AADEGNTV VANTAGED
AADEGPRY PAYGRADE
AADEGPSS PASSAGED
AADEGRST GRADATES
AADEGRSV SAVEGARD
AADEGRSY DRAYAGES
YARDAGES
AADEGRTU GRADUATE
AADEGSSU ASSUAGED
AADEGSSW ASSWAGED
AADEHHHS HASHHEAD
AADEHHOR HOARHEAD
AADEHILN NAILHEAD
AADEHILR HEADRAIL
RAILHEAD
AADEHILS HEADSAIL
AADEHIRR DIARRHEA
AADEHIRS AIRHEADS
AADEHIWY HIDEAWAY
AADEHJRS JARHEADS
AADEHKMR HEADMARK
AADEHLLL HALALLED
AADEHLLO HALLOAED
AADEHLMP HEADLAMP
AADEHLNR ANHEDRAL
AADEHLPS SLAPHEAD
AADEHLRS ASHLARED
AADEHMNS HEADSMAN
AADEHMST MASTHEAD
AADEHNPS SANDHEAP
AADEHNRV VERANDAH
AADEHPPR PARAPHED
AADEHPSS SAPHEADS
AADEHRRW HARDWARE
AADEHRSS HARASSED
AADEHRSW RAWHEADS
WARHEADS
AADEHSSY SASHAYED
AADEHSTT HASTATED
AADEHSTY HEADSTAY
AADEHSWY HEADWAYS
AADEILMS MALADIES
AADEILMU AUMAILED
AADEILNT DENTALIA
AADEILPR PRAEDIAL
AADEILPS PALISADE
AADEILPT LAPIDATE
AADEILRS SALARIED
AADEILRT LARIATED
AADEILSS ASSAILED
AADEILSV VEDALIAS
AADEILTT DILATATE
AADEILTV VALIDATE
AADEIMNN AMANDINE
AADEIMNP PANDEMIA
AADEIMNR MARINADE

AADEIMNT ANIMATED
DIAMANTE
AADEIMPZ DIAZEPAM
AADEIMRS MADEIRAS
AADEIMRV MARAVEDI
AADEIMSS AMIDASES
SEAMAIDS
AADEIMST ADAMSITE
DIASTEMA
AADEINRR DARRAINE
AADEINRS ARANEIDS
AADEINRT DENTARIA
RAINDATE
AADEINSZ ZENAIDAS
AADEINTT ATTAINED
AADEIPPR APPAIRED
AADEIPRS PARADISE
AADEIPSS DIAPASES
AADEIPSU DIAPAUSE
AADEIPTV ADAPTIVE
AADEIRST AIRDATES
DATARIES
RADIATES
AADEIRTV VARIATED
AADEISST DIASTASE
AADEISTT SATIATED
AADEITVW VIEWDATA
AADEJMPY PYJAMAED
AADEJMRS JEMADARS
AADEJNNP JAPANNED
AADEKLLN LAKELAND
AADEKLNR KALENDAR
AADEKLRY KALEYARD
AADEKMNR MANDRAKE
AADEKMRS KAMERADS
AADEKNST ASKANTED
AADEKNUW UNAWAKED
AADEKSTT ATTASKED
AADELLOS ALDOLASE
AADELLPP APPALLED
AADELLPS PADELLAS
AADELLRT DATALLER
AADELLWY WELLADAY
AADELMNP NAPALMED
AADELMNR ALDERMAN
MALANDER
AADELMNS DALESMAN
LEADSMAN
AADELMOS ALAMODES
AADELMPT PALMATED
AADELMRU ALARUMED
AADELMYZ AMAZEDLY
AADELNRS ADRENALS
AADELNST EASTLAND
AADELNSW DANELAWS
AADELNSY ANALYSED
AADELNYZ ANALYZED
AADELOTX OXALATED
AADELPPT PALPATED
AADELPRS PARDALES
AADELPRY PARLAYED
AADELPTY PLAYDATE
AADELQUU QUAALUDE
AADELRSY SALEYARD
AADELRTU RADULATE
AADELRTV LARVATED
AADELRTY DAYTALER
AADELSTT SALTATED
AADELSTU ADULATES
AADELSTY DAYTALES
AADELTUV VALUATED
AADEMNOS ADENOMAS
AADEMNPS SPADEMAN
AADEMNST MANDATES
AADEMNUZ UNAMAZED

AADEMORT MATADORE
AADEMRRU MARAUDER
AADEMRSS MADRASES
AADEMRSY DAYMARES
AADEMSSS ADMASSES
AADENNST ANDANTES
AADENRRT NARRATED
AADENRRW WARRANED
AADENRSV VERANDAS
AADENRTT TARTANED
AADENSSW WEASANDS
AADENSTY ASYNDETA
AADENSTZ STANZAED
AADENSWZ WEAZANDS
AADENTUV AVAUNTED
AADEOPRT TAPADERO
AADEOPST ADESPOTA
AADEORRT AERODART
AADEPPRT PREADAPT
AADEPRRS PARADERS
AADEPRST ADAPTERS
READAPTS
AADEPSSS PASSADES
AADEQRTU QUADRATE
AADERRRW REARWARD
AADERRSW AWARDERS
AADERRWY WARRAYED
AADERSST ASSARTED
AADERSSW SEAWARDS
AADERSTT ASTARTED
AADERSTW EASTWARD
RADWASTE
AADERUVY AYURVEDA
AADFGNNO FANDANGO
AADFGRSU SAUFGARD
AADFHMNR FARMHAND
AADFHNST HANDFAST
AADFIINT INTIFADA
AADFIMRS FARADISM
AADFINRU UNAFRAID
AADFLLLN LANDFALL
AADFLLNT FLATLAND
AADFLMNR FARMLAND
AADFLORW AARDWOLF
AADFLOTX TOADFLAX
AADFLOWY FOLDAWAY
AADFMRRY FARMYARD
AADGGHOT HAGGADOT
AADGGHRS HAGGARDS
AADGGIMN DAMAGING
AADGGLNN GANGLAND
AADGGLRS LAGGARDS
AADGGRSS SAGGARDS
AADGGRST STAGGARD
AADGHILS HIDALGAS
AADGHIPR DIAGRAPH
AADGHIST HAGADIST
AADGHRTU HATGUARD
AADGIINS GAINSAID
AADGILLO GLADIOLA
AADGILLR GAILLARD
GALLIARD
AADGILMR MADRIGAL
AADGILNO DIAGONAL
GONADIAL
AADGILNS SALADING
AADGIMMN MADAMING
AADGIMMS DIGAMMAS
AADGIMNR MRIDANGA
AADGIMOS AGAMOIDS
AADGIMPR PARADIGM
AADGIMRS DIAGRAMS
AADGIMRT GRADATIM
AADGINPR PARADING
AADGINPT ADAPTING

AADGINRR	DARRAIGN
AADGINRU	GUARDIAN
AADGINRW	AWARDING
AADGIQRU	QUADRIGA
AADGIRSV	GRAVIDAS
AADGLLSW	GADWALLS
AADGLMOR	MALGRADO
AADGLMSY	AMYGDALS
AADGLNOR	LARGANDO
AADGLNRS	GARLANDS
AADGLNSS	SLADANGS
AADGLOOW	AGALWOOD
AADGLOPR	PODAGRAL
AADGLORW	GOALWARD
AADGLRSU	GRADUALS
AADGMNOP	PAGANDOM
AADGMNOR	DRAGOMAN
AADGMNOS	GOADSMAN
AADGMNRS	DRAGSMAN
	GRANDAMS
	GRANDMAS
AADGMRSS	SMARAGDS
AADGNNQU	QUANDANG
AADGNPRS	GRANDPAS
AADGNRST	GARDANTS
AADGNRSY	YARDANGS
AADGNRTU	GUARDANT
AADGNRUV	VANGUARD
AADGOPRS	PODAGRAS
AADGRRUW	GURDWARA
AADHHIPS	PADISHAH
AADHHPSS	PADSHAHS
AADHHRST	HARDHATS
AADHIINP	APHIDIAN
AADHILLR	HALLIARD
AADHILNR	HANDRAIL
AADHILRV	HAVILDAR
AADHIMSS	SAMADHIS
AADHINOT	ANTHODIA
AADHINPS	DAPHNIAS
AADHINRR	HARRIDAN
AADHJNRS	HANDJARS
AADHKLOT	KATHODAL
AADHKNSY	YAKHDANS
AADHLMOY	DALMAHOY
AADHLNPY	HANDPLAY
AADHLNSW	WASHLAND
AADHLPSS	SLAPDASH
AADHLRSY	HALYARDS
AADHLRUY	HAULYARD
AADHMNNY	HANDYMAN
AADHMNOU	OMADHAUN
AADHMOPS	PASHADOM
AADHNPRS	HARDPANS
AADHNRSS	DARSHANS
AADHNSSW	HANDSAWS
AADHNSTT	HATSTAND
AADHRRTW	THRAWARD
AADHRRYZ	HAZARDRY
AADHRSWY	HAYWARDS
AADHSSWY	WASHDAYS
AADIILNS	SIALIDAN
AADIJMNS	JAMDANIS
AADIKLLO	ALKALOID
AADIKLLR	KILLADAR
AADIKLRY	KAILYARD
AADIKLSY	ILKADAYS
AADIKMNS	DAMASKIN
AADIKNQR	QINDARKA
AADILLLO	ALLODIAL
AADILLNR	LANDRAIL
AADILLPR	PAILLARD
	PALLIARD
AADILLRS	SILLADAR
AADILLRY	RADIALLY

AADILMNN	MAINLAND
AADILMNO	DOMAINAL
	DOMANIAL
AADILMNP	PLAIDMAN
AADILMRS	ADMIRALS
	AMILDARS
AADILMST	MATILDAS
AADILNOR	ORDALIAN
AADILNPR	PRANDIAL
AADILNPS	PALADINS
AADILNRS	LANIARDS
AADILNTT	DILATANT
AADILOPS	PALISADO
AADILORR	RAILROAD
AADILPRS	PARDALIS
AADILPRY	LAPIDARY
AADILRRS	RISALDAR
AADILRST	DIASTRAL
	TAILARDS
AADILSST	STADIALS
AADIMNNR	MANDARIN
AADIMNOR	RADIOMAN
AADIMNOT	MANATOID
AADIMNRS	MANDIRAS
AADIMNRT	TAMARIND
AADIMNRY	DAIRYMAN
	MAINYARD
AADIMNRZ	ZAMINDAR
AADIMNSS	DAMASSIN
AADIMNSU	SUDAMINA
AADIMNUV	VANADIUM
AADIMORS	DIORAMAS
AADIMPST	MISADAPT
AADIMRSW	MISAWARD
AADIMSTZ	SAMIZDAT
AADINNNS	NANDINAS
AADINNOT	ADNATION
AADINOPR	PARANOID
AADINOPS	DIAPASON
AADINOPT	ADAPTION
AADINORT	ANTIDORA
AADINPST	PINTADAS
AADINRRS	DARRAINS
AADINRRW	AIRDRAWN
AADINRST	INTRADAS
	RADIANTS
AADINRSV	VIRANDAS
AADINRTY	INTRADAY
AADIOPRS	DIASPORA
AADIORRT	RADIATOR
AADIPSUY	UPADAISY
AADIRRSW	AIRWARDS
AADIRRSY	DISARRAY
AADISTXY	DYSTAXIA
AADJNTTU	ADJUTANT
AADJNTUV	ADJUVANT
AADKLMNR	LANDMARK
AADKLNPR	PARKLAND
AADKLRTU	TALUKDAR
AADKMNRS	DARKMANS
AADKMRSY	DAYMARKS
AADKNRST	TANKARDS
AADKORWY	WORKADAY
AADKPRRW	PARKWARD
AADLLLNS	LALLANDS
AADLLMPY	LADYPALM
AADLLMRS	MALLARDS
AADLLNOY	ANODALLY
AADLLNPY	PLAYLAND
AADLLNSW	LAWLANDS
AADLMNNS	LANDSMAN
AADLMNOR	MANDORLA
AADLMNOS	MANDOLAS
AADLMNSS	LANDMASS
AADLMNSU	LADANUMS

AADLMNUU	LAUDANUM
AADLMORS	ARMLOADS
AADLNOPR	PARLANDO
AADLNOPS	DALAPONS
	SOAPLAND
AADLNOST	SALTANDO
AADLNRSY	LANYARDS
AADLOPSY	PAYLOADS
AADLORST	LOADSTAR
AADLORTU	ADULATOR
	LAUDATOR
AADLPPRW	WALDRAPP
AADLPPSU	APPLAUDS
AADLPSYY	PLAYDAYS
AADMMNOW	MADWOMAN
AADMMNSU	MANDAMUS
AADMNNOS	MADONNAS
AADMNORS	MADRONAS
	MANDORAS
	MONARDAS
	ROADSMAN
AADMNORT	MANDATOR
AADMNRSS	MANSARDS
AADMNRSW	MANWARDS
AADMNSTU	TAMANDUS
AADMOPPP	PAPPADOM
AADMOQSU	MADOQUAS
AADMORRT	TRAMROAD
AADMORST	MATADORS
AADMRRSY	YARDARMS
AADMRSZZ	MAZZARDS
AADNNPSU	PANDANUS
AADNOPRS	PANDORAS
AADNOPSS	SANDSOAP
AADNORST	ONDATRAS
AADNORTY	DONATARY
AADNOSUV	VANADOUS
AADNOSWY	NOWADAYS
AADNPRSU	PANDURAS
AADNPSTT	STANDPAT
AADNQRSU	QUADRANS
AADNQRTU	QUADRANT
AADNQRUY	QUANDARY
AADNRRSW	WARRANDS
AADNRRSY	DARRAYNS
AADNRSTY	TANYARDS
AADNRSWY	NAYWARDS
AADOPPRR	PARADROP
AADOPRRS	PARADORS
AADOPRST	ADAPTORS
AADOPRXY	PARADOXY
AADOPSSS	PASSADOS
AADOPSTT	DOPATTAS
AADOPSUY	PADUASOY
AADORSVY	SAVOYARD
AADORSWY	ROADWAYS
AADOSSTT	TOSTADAS
AADPSTTU	DUPATTAS
AADQRSTU	QUADRATS
AADRSSTY	DAYSTARS
AAEEEHRT	HETAERAE
AAEEEMRT	AMEERATE
AAEEFFRS	AFFEARES
AAEEFGLS	LEAFAGES
AAEEFRRS	SEAFARER
AAEEFRST	RATAFEES
AAEEGILN	ALIENAGE
AAEEGILP	EPIGAEAL
AAEEGINP	EPIGAEAN
AAEEGINS	AGENESIA
AAEEGKLS	LEAKAGES
AAEEGLLN	ENALLAGE
AAEEGLRY	LAYERAGE
AAEEGLST	ETALAGES
	STEALAGE

AAEEGLSV	SALVAGEE
AAEEGMNS	AMENAGES
AAEEGMPR	AMPERAGE
AAEEGMST	AGAMETES
AAEEGMTY	METAYAGE
AAEEGNRS	SANGAREE
AAEEGRST	STEARAGE
AAEEGRSV	AVERAGES
AAEEGRTW	WATERAGE
AAEEHIMR	HAEREMAI
AAEEHMNR	HERMAEAN
AAEEHNPS	SAPHENAE
AAEEHPRT	EARTHPEA
	HEARTPEA
AAEEHRST	HETAERAS
AAEEHRTW	AWEATHER
	WHEATEAR
AAEEHRWY	HEREAWAY
AAEEILNT	ALIENATE
AAEEINTT	TAENIATE
AAEEJMNP	JAMPANEE
AAEEKLSS	SEAKALES
AAEEKLTW	LATEWAKE
AAEEKMNS	NAMESAKE
AAEEKMRT	TEAMAKER
AAEEKNRW	AWAKENER
	REAWAKEN
AAEEKPRT	PARAKEET
AAEEKPSS	SEASPEAK
AAEEKQSU	SEAQUAKE
AAEEKRSW	REAWAKES
AAEELLLM	LAMELLAE
AAEELLMR	AMARELLE
AAEELLMT	MALLEATE
AAEELLNV	AVELLANE
AAEELLPT	PATELLAE
AAEELMST	MALEATES
AAEELNNR	ANNEALER
	LERNAEAN
AAEELNPS	SEAPLANE
	SPELAEAN
AAEELNPT	PANETELA
AAEELNPU	PAENULAE
AAEELORT	AREOLATE
AAEELORU	AUREOLAE
AAEELPPR	APPEALER
AAEELRST	LAETARES
AAEELRTU	LAUREATE
AAEELRTV	VALERATE
AAEELSST	ELASTASE
AAEELTUV	EVALUATE
AAEELVWY	WAYLEAVE
AAEEMMTT	TEAMMATE
AAEEMNPT	NAMETAPE
AAEEMNST	EMANATES
	MANATEES
AAEEMPRS	PARAMESE
AAEEMRST	AMREETAS
AAEEMSTT	SEATMATE
AAEENNNT	ANTENNAE
AAEENPRT	PARANETE
AAEENRRS	ARRASENE
AAEENRST	ARSENATE
	SERENATA
AAEENRTT	ANTEATER
AAEENSTU	NAUSEATE
AAEEPPRR	APPEARER
	RAPPAREE
	REAPPEAR
AAEEPPRS	APPEASER
AAEEPPSS	APPEASES
AAEEPRST	ASPERATE
	SEPARATE
AAEEPSTT	ASEPTATE
AAEERRWW	REWAREWA

AAEERSSW	SEAWARES
AAEERSTT	STEARATE
AAEERSTW	SEAWATER
	TEAWARES
AAEERSWX	EARWAXES
AAEERSYY	YEASAYER
AAEFFGRS	AGRAFFES
AAEFFGST	STAFFAGE
AAEFFIRS	AFFAIRES
AAEFFLLS	FALAFELS
AAEFFLPR	PARAFFLE
AAEFFLRT	TAFFAREL
AAEFFNRS	FANFARES
AAEFFRRY	AFFRAYER
AAEFFSTT	TAFFETAS
AAEFGGRT	GRAFTAGE
AAEFGHRW	WHARFAGE
AAEFGINR	AFEARING
AAEFGITT	FATIGATE
AAEFGLLL	FLAGELLA
AAEFGLOT	FLOATAGE
AAEFGRTU	FRAUTAGE
AAEFGSTW	WAFTAGES
AAEFIILR	FILARIAE
AAEFIKLT	KALIFATE
AAEFILTY	FAYALITE
AAEFIMRR	AIRFRAME
AAEFINNT	FAINEANT
AAEFINNU	INFAUNAE
AAEFINPU	EPIFAUNA
AAEFINST	FANTASIE
AAEFINTX	ANTEFIXA
AAEFIRRS	AIRFARES
AAEFKMST	MAKEFAST
AAEFLLSV	FAVELLAS
AAEFLMOT	MEATLOAF
AAEFLMTT	FLATMATE
AAEFLPRS	EARFLAPS
	PARAFLES
AAEFLRTW	FLATWARE
AAEFMRST	FERMATAS
AAEFMRSU	FUMARASE
AAEFMRTU	FUMARATE
AAEFQRSU	AQUAFERS
AAEFRRRW	WARFARER
AAEFRRSW	WARFARES
AAEFRRWY	WAYFARER
AAEFRSWY	WAYFARES
AAEFRTTX	AFTERTAX
AAEGGINR	GRAINAGE
AAEGGIOT	AGIOTAGE
AAEGGLNR	LANGRAGE
AAEGGLNU	LANGUAGE
AAEGGNOS	ANAGOGES
AAEGGNOW	WAGONAGE
AAEGGNRY	GARGANEY
AAEGGOPR	PARAGOGE
AAEGGOPS	APAGOGES
AAEGGRST	AGGRATES
AAEGHLNP	PHALANGE
AAEGHLSU	HAULAGES
AAEGHLSY	HAYLAGES
AAEGHMRX	HEXAGRAM
AAEGHMSS	GAMASHES
AAEGHNRU	HARANGUE
AAEGHNST	THANAGES
AAEGHOPY	HYPOGAEA
AAEGILLP	PELAGIAL
AAEGILLR	GALLERIA
AAEGILLT	ALLIGATE
AAEGILMS	SEMIGALA
AAEGILNP	PELAGIAN
AAEGILNR	GERANIAL
	REGALIAN
AAEGILNT	AGENTIAL
	ALGINATE
AAEGILRS	GASALIER
	LAIRAGES
	REGALIAS
AAEGILSS	ALGESIAS
AAEGILSX	GALAXIES
AAEGILTT	TAILGATE
AAEGIMNO	EGOMANIA
AAEGIMNP	PIGMAEAN
AAEGIMNS	MAGNESIA
AAEGIMNT	AGMINATE
	ENIGMATA
AAEGIMNZ	MAGAZINE
AAEGIMRR	MARRIAGE
AAEGIMRT	GEMATRIA
	MARITAGE
AAEGINNR	ANEARING
AAEGINPS	NAGAPIES
	PAGANISE
AAEGINPT	PAGINATE
AAEGINPZ	PAGANIZE
AAEGINRS	ANERGIAS
	ANGARIES
	ARGINASE
AAEGINRT	AERATING
AAEGINST	SAGINATE
AAEGINSW	WAINAGES
AAEGINTV	NAVIGATE
	VAGINATE
AAEGIPRS	IGARAPES
AAEGIPRU	PERIAGUA
AAEGIRRS	ARRIAGES
AAEGIRSV	VAGARIES
AAEGISSS	ASSEGAIS
AAEGISTT	AGITATES
AAEGISTZ	AGATIZES
AAEGIVWY	GIVEAWAY
AAEGJSTU	AJUTAGES
AAEGKNST	TANKAGES
AAEGKOSS	SOAKAGES
AAEGLLMS	SMALLAGE
AAEGLLPR	PELLAGRA
AAEGLLSS	GALLEASS
AAEGLLST	GALLATES
	GALLETAS
	STALLAGE
	TALLAGES
AAEGLLTU	GLUTAEAL
AAEGLMNS	GAMELANS
AAEGLMNV	GAVELMAN
AAEGLMST	ALMAGEST
AAEGLNOU	ANALOGUE
AAEGLNPP	LAGNAPPE
AAEGLNPT	PLANTAGE
AAEGLNRS	ALNAGERS
AAEGLNRT	ARGENTAL
AAEGLNRU	AULNAGER
AAEGLNSS	LASAGNES
AAEGLNSU	AULNAGES
AAEGLNTU	ANGULATE
AAEGLOSV	AASVOGEL
AAEGLRRS	REALGARS
	RESALGAR
AAEGLRRW	WARRAGLE
AAEGLRST	AGRESTAL
AAEGLRSV	SALVAGER
AAEGLRTY	LEGATARY
AAEGLSST	AGELASTS
	LASTAGES
AAEGLSSV	SALVAGES
AAEGLSVY	SAVAGELY
AAEGLTUV	VAULTAGE
AAEGMMNR	ENGRAMMA
AAEGMMNS	GAMESMAN
AAEGMNPY	PYGMAEAN
AAEGMNRS	MANAGERS
AAEGMNRV	GRAVAMEN
AAEGMNST	MAGENTAS
	MAGNATES
	NAMETAGS
AAEGMORR	AEROGRAM
AAEGMORS	SAGAMORE
AAEGMPRR	RAMPAGER
AAEGMPRS	RAMPAGES
AAEGMPRU	RAMPAUGE
AAEGMRRV	MARGRAVE
AAEGMRRY	GRAMARYE
AAEGMRSS	MASSAGER
AAEGMRST	MEGASTAR
AAEGMRTU	AGERATUM
AAEGMSSS	MASSAGES
AAEGMTTW	MEGAWATT
AAEGNNOP	NEOPAGAN
AAEGNNPS	PANNAGES
AAEGNNST	TANNAGES
AAEGNPST	PAGEANTS
AAEGNPSW	PAWNAGES
AAEGNRRR	ARRANGER
AAEGNRRS	ARRANGES
AAEGNRST	STARAGEN
	TANAGERS
AAEGNRTU	RUNAGATE
AAEGNSSU	GUANASES
AAEGNSTT	STAGNATE
AAEGNSTV	VANTAGES
AAEGNSTW	WANTAGES
AAEGNTUV	VAUNTAGE
AAEGORRT	ARROGATE
AAEGORSS	AGAROSES
AAEGORTT	AEGROTAT
AAEGPPRW	WRAPPAGE
AAEGPRSW	WARPAGES
AAEGPSSS	PASSAGES
AAEGPSSY	PAYSAGES
AAEGQSUY	QUAYAGES
AAEGRRSV	RAVAGERS
AAEGRSST	GASTREAS
AAEGRSTT	REGATTAS
AAEGRSTV	STRAVAGE
AAEGRSTZ	STARGAZE
AAEGRSVY	SAVAGERY
AAEGSSSU	ASSUAGES
	SAUSAGES
AAEGSSSV	AVGASSES
AAEGSSSW	ASSWAGES
AAEGSSTV	SAVAGEST
AAEGSSTW	TASSWAGE
	WASTAGES
AAEGSTTW	WATTAGES
AAEGSTWY	GATEWAYS
	GETAWAYS
AAEHIIRT	HETAIRAI
	HETAIRIA
AAEHILMN	HIELAMAN
AAEHILNP	APHELIAN
AAEHILNT	ANTHELIA
AAEHILPR	PARHELIA
AAEHIMNT	ANTHEMIA
	HAEMATIN
AAEHINPT	APHANITE
AAEHINST	ASTHENIA
AAEHIPST	APATHIES
AAEHIRST	HETAIRAS
AAEHIRTT	HATTERIA
AAEHKLST	ALKAHEST
AAEHKMRT	HATMAKER
AAEHKMRY	HAYMAKER
AAEHKNST	KHANATES
AAEHKSSW	SEAHAWKS
AAEHLLLS	ALLHEALS
AAEHLMNT	METHANAL
AAEHLMNW	WHALEMAN
AAEHLMSY	SEALYHAM
AAEHLMTU	HAMULATE
AAEHLNOZ	HALAZONE
AAEHLNRT	ANTHERAL
AAEHLNRW	NARWHALE
AAEHLNTX	EXHALANT
AAEHLOPT	APHOLATE
AAEHLPRS	PEARLASH
AAEHLPRX	HEXAPLAR
AAEHLPSX	HEXAPLAS
AAEHLPUV	UPHEAVAL
AAEHLRST	TREHALAS
AAEHLRTT	THEATRAL
AAEHLSTT	ATHLETAS
AAEHMMOT	HEMATOMA
AAEHMNPY	NYMPHAEA
AAEHMNRS	SHAREMAN
	SHEARMAN
AAEHMNRT	EARTHMAN
AAEHMOPR	AMPHORAE
AAEHMOPT	HEPATOMA
AAEHMORT	ATHEROMA
AAEHNPRS	HANAPERS
AAEHNPSS	SAPHENAS
AAEHNPST	PHEASANT
AAEHNPSY	SYNAPHEA
AAEHNTTX	XANTHATE
AAEHPRSZ	PHEAZARS
AAEHRRSS	HARASSER
AAEHRSSS	HARASSES
AAEHRSSY	HEARSAYS
AAEHRSTU	ARETHUSA
AAEHRTWX	EARTHWAX
AAEIIKNS	AKINESIA
AAEIIMRV	VIRAEMIA
AAEIINVZ	AVIANIZE
AAEIIPRS	APIARIES
AAEIIRSV	AVIARIES
AAEIJLNV	JAVELINA
AAEIJNPZ	JAPANIZE
AAEIKKMZ	KAMIKAZE
AAEIKLLN	ALKALINE
AAEIKLLS	ALKALIES
	ALKALISE
AAEIKLLV	LAVALIKE
AAEIKLLZ	ALKALIZE
AAEIKLNT	ANTILEAK
AAEIKMRR	KRAMERIA
AAEIKPRT	PARAKITE
AAEILLLU	ALLELUIA
AAEILLMM	MAMILLAE
AAEILLMR	ARMILLAE
AAEILLMX	MAXILLAE
AAEILLNT	ALLANITE
AAEILLPP	PAPILLAE
AAEILLPT	PALLIATE
AAEILLRT	ARILLATE
AAEILLRV	LAVALIER
AAEILLRY	AERIALLY
AAEILLTT	TALLIATE
AAEILLTV	ALLATIVE
AAEILMNN	MELANIAN
AAEILMNT	ALAIMENT
	ANTIMALE
	LAMINATE
AAEILMNV	VELAMINA
AAEILMRT	MATERIAL
AAEILMSS	MALAISES
AAEILNNS	ALANINES
	ANNALISE
AAEILNNZ	ANNALIZE
AAEILNPR	AIRPLANE
AAEILNPT	PALATINE

AAEILNRU AURELIAN
AAEILNRV VALERIAN
AAEILNSS NASALISE
AAEILNSZ NASALIZE
AAEILNTT ANTLIATE
AAEILNTV AVENTAIL
AAEILORS OLEARIAS
AAEILPPS PAPALISE
AAEILPPZ PAPALIZE
AAEILPRT PARIETAL
AAEILPRX PREAXIAL
AAEILPST STAPELIA
AAEILRRT ARTERIAL
AAEILRSS ASSAILER
REASSAIL
SALARIES
AAEILRSU AURELIAS
AAEILRSV REAVAILS
AAEILRTV VARIETAL
AAEILSTV AESTIVAL
SALIVATE
AAEILSTX SAXATILE
AAEILSWY AISLEWAY
AAEILTVX LAXATIVE
AAEIMMST IMAMATES
AAEIMNOT METANOIA
AAEIMNOX ANOXEMIA
AAEIMNPR PEARMAIN
AAEIMNPS PAEANISM
AAEIMNPT IMPANATE
AAEIMNRR MARINERA
AAEIMNRT ANIMATER
MARINATE
AAEIMNRZ MAZARINE
AAEIMNSS AMNESIAS
AAEIMNST AMENTIAS
ANIMATES
AAEIMNTZ NIZAMATE
AAEIMOPR PAROEMIA
AAEIMOTX TOXAEMIA
AAEIMOTZ AZOTEMIA
AAEIMPRS SAPREMIA
AAEIMPSY PYAEMIAS
AAEIMRST AMIRATES
AAEIMRSU URAEMIAS
AAEIMRTT AMARETTI
AAEIMSUV MAUVAISE
AAEINNTT ANTENATI
AAEINORT AERATION
AAEINORX ANOREXIA
AAEINPPR PRIAPEAN
AAEINPRS PANARIES
AAEINPRT ANTIRAPE
AAEINPTT PATINATE
AAEINRRW RAINWEAR
AAEINRST ANTISERA
ARTESIAN
RATANIES
RESINATA
SEATRAIN
AAEINRTT ATTAINER
REATTAIN
AAEINRTU INAURATE
AAEINRTW ANTIWEAR
AAEINRTZ ATRAZINE
AAEINSST ENTASIAS
AAEINSTT ASTATINE
SANITATE
TANAISTE
AAEINSTV SANATIVE
AAEINTTT TITANATE
AAEIPPRS APPRAISE
AAEIPPSS APEPSIAS
AAEIPRRS PAREIRAS
AAEIPRSS SPIRAEAS
AAEIPRST ASPIRATE
PARASITE
SEPTARIA
AAEIPRTT PATRIATE
AAEIPRTZ TRAPEZIA
AAEIPRXY APYREXIA
AAEIPSTT APATITES
AAEIQRTU TAQUERIA
AAEIRRRT TERRARIA
AAEIRRTV VERATRIA
AAEIRSST ASTERIAS
ATRESIAS
AAEIRSSX XERASIAS
AAEIRSTT ARIETTAS
ARISTATE
AAEIRSTV VARIATES
AAEIRSTW AWAITERS
AAEIRSVW AIRWAVES
AAEIRTTZ ZARATITE
AAEISSTT SATIATES
AAEITTVX TAXATIVE
AAEJLNOP JALAPENO
AAEJMNRY MARYJANE
AAEJNNPR JAPANNER
AAEJNRST NAARTJES
AAEJNRTZ JAZERANT
AAEJOPRS APAREJOS
AAEJRSSV SVARAJES
AAEJRSSW SWARAJES
AAEKKORS KARAOKES
AAEKKRSY KAYAKERS
AAEKLLTY ALKYLATE
AAEKLMRW LAWMAKER
AAEKLMRY MALARKEY
AAEKLNRS LARNAKES
AAEKLNST ALKANETS
KANTELAS
AAEKLPRS ASPARKLE
AAEKMMPR MAPMAKER
AAEKMORT KERATOMA
AAEKMRRS EARMARKS
AAEKMRRW WARMAKER
AAEKMRSS SEAMARKS
AAEKNPRT PARTAKEN
AAEKORTY AKARYOTE
AAEKPRRT PARTAKER
AAEKPRST PARTAKES
AAEKSSSV KAVASSES
VAKASSES
AAELLLMR LAMELLAR
AAELLLMS LAMELLAS
AAELLLPR PARALLEL
AAELLMPU AMPULLAE
AAELLNPU PLANULAE
AAELLNSZ ZANELLAS
AAELLORV ALVEOLAR
AAELLPRS PARELLAS
AAELLPRT PATELLAR
AAELLPST PATELLAS
AAELLRST LATERALS
AAELLRSY ALLAYERS
AAELLSSW SEAWALLS
AAELLUVV VALVULAE
AAELLWWY WELLAWAY
AAELLWYY ALLEYWAY
AAELMMNO MELANOMA
AAELMMRS ALMEMARS
AAELMMTU MALAMUTE
AAELMNOT MALONATE
AAELMNOX AXONEMAL
AAELMNPT PLATEMAN
AAELMNRT MATERNAL
AAELMNSS SALESMAN
AAELMNST TALESMAN
AAELMNSW WEALSMAN
AAELMNSY SEAMANLY
AAELMOST OATMEALS
AAELMOSU MAUSOLEA
AAELMOTZ METAZOAL
AAELMPPY MAYAPPLE
AAELMPRT MALAPERT
AAELMPRX EXAMPLAR
AAELMPSS LAMPASES
LAMPASSE
AAELMPST PLATEASM
AAELMPTV VAMPLATE
AAELMPTY PLAYMATE
AAELMRSY LAMASERY
AAELMRTT MALTREAT
AAELMSST MALTASES
AAELMSSY AMYLASES
AAELNNNT ANTENNAL
AAELNNOT NEONATAL
AAELNNTU ANNULATE
AAELNOSS SEASONAL
AAELNOSV VALONEAS
AAELNPRS PRENASAL
AAELNPRT PARENTAL
PARLANTE
PATERNAL
PRENATAL
AAELNPRW WARPLANE
AAELNPST PLATANES
PLEASANT
AAELNPSU PAENULAS
AAELNRSS ARSENALS
AAELNRST ASTERNAL
AAELNRSY ANALYSER
AAELNRTT ALTERANT
ALTERNAT
TARLETAN
AAELNRTX RELAXANT
AAELNRYZ ANALYZER
AAELNSST SEALANTS
AAELNSSV ENVASSAL
AAELNSSY ANALYSES
AAELNSTT ATLANTES
AAELNSTZ ZEALANTS
AAELNSWY LANEWAYS
AAELNSYZ ANALYZES
AAELOPRS PSORALEA
AAELORSU AUREOLAS
AAELORTY ALEATORY
AAELOSTX OXALATES
AAELPPRS APPARELS
AAELPPST PALPATES
AAELPPSU APPLAUSE
AAELPRST PALESTRA
AAELPRSV PALAVERS
AAELPRSY PARALYSE
AAELPRTT TETRAPLA
AAELPRWY PLAYWEAR
AAELPRYZ PARALYZE
AAELPSTU PLATEAUS
AAELPSTV PALSTAVE
AAELPSWY PALEWAYS
AAELPTUV VAPULATE
AAELPTUX PLATEAUX
AAELRSTZ LAZARETS
AAELRTUV VELATURA
AAELRUZZ ZARZUELA
AAELRWYY WAYLAYER
AAELSSTT SALTATES
AAELSTUV VALUATES
AAELSTZZ ALTEZZAS
AAEMMMRS MAREMMAS
AAEMMNRT ARMAMENT
AAEMMNSU MANUMEAS
AAEMMSTT STEMMATA
AAEMNORT EMANATOR
AAEMNOSW SEAWOMAN
AAEMNOTZ METAZOAN
AAEMNPPS PAMPEANS
AAEMNPRS SPEARMAN
AAEMNPRT PARAMENT
AAEMNRST SARMENTA
SEMANTRA
AAEMNRSU MURAENAS
AAEMNRTT ATRAMENT
AAEMNRTW WATERMAN
AAEMNSST NAMASTES
AAEMNSTU MANTEAUS
AAEMNTUX MANTEAUX
AAEMOPXZ OXAZEPAM
AAEMORTT AMARETTO
TERATOMA
AAEMORTX XEROMATA
AAEMOSTT STEATOMA
AAEMOSTY ATEMOYAS
AAEMOTTU AUTOMATE
AAEMPPSS PAMPASES
AAEMPTTU AMPUTATE
AAEMQSTU SQUAMATE
AAEMRRTU ARMATURE
AAEMRSSS AMASSERS
AAEMRSTU AMATEURS
AAEMRTTU MATURATE
AAENNNST ANTENNAS
AAENNOTT ANNOTATE
AAENNSTT STANNATE
TANNATES
AAENNSTU NAUSEANT
AAENNSTV VENTANAS
AAENOPSS PAESANOS
AAENOQTU AQUATONE
AAENORRU AUROREAN
AAENORST ANOESTRA
AAENORSU ARANEOUS
AAENORTU AERONAUT
AAENOSST ASSONATE
AAENPPRS PARPANES
AAENPPRT APPARENT
TRAPPEAN
AAENPRTY PRYTANEA
AAENPSST ANAPESTS
PEASANTS
AAENPSTT ANTEPAST
AAENPSTY PEASANTY
AAENRRRT NARRATER
AAENRRSS NARRASES
AAENRRST NARRATES
AAENRSTT TARTANES
AAENRSTV TAVERNAS
TSAREVNA
AAENRSUW UNAWARES
AAENRSYY NAYSAYER
AAENRTVZ TZAREVNA
AAENSSSV VANESSAS
AAENSSTW SEAWANTS
AAENSSWY AWAYNESS
AAENTTTT ATTENTAT
AAEOPSTT APOSTATE
AAEOPSTZ ZAPATEOS
AAEORRST AERATORS
AAEORSST AEROSATS
AAEORSTT AEROSTAT
AAEORTTV ROTAVATE
AAEPPRRT TARPAPER
AAEPPRST PARAPETS
AAEPPSTT APPESTAT
AAEPQRTU PARAQUET
AAEPRSSY APYRASES
AAEPRTXY TAXPAYER
AAEPSTTW WATTAPES
AAEPSWXX PAXWAXES

AAEPSZZZ	PAZAZZES
AAERRRSY	ARRAYERS
AAERRSST	TARRASES
AAERRSTT	TARTARES
AAERRTTT	TARTRATE
AAERSSSY	ASSAYERS
AAERSTTU	SATURATE
	TUATERAS
AAERTTTW	TERAWATT
AAERTWWY	WATERWAY
AAESTWWY	WASTEWAY
AAFFIILX	AFFIXIAL
AAFFILRT	TAFFRAIL
AAFFINPR	PARAFFIN
AAFFINSS	SAFFIANS
AAFFINST	AFFIANTS
AAFFLPST	PALSTAFF
AAFFLSTU	AFFLATUS
AAFFNNOR	FANFARON
AAFFOORW	FOOFARAW
AAFGHINS	AFGHANIS
AAFGILNO	GOLFIANA
AAFGINTW	FATWAING
AAFGLLNU	LANGLAUF
AAFGLNRT	FLAGRANT
AAFGNRRT	FRAGRANT
AAFGORRS	FARRAGOS
AAFHHIKL	KHALIFAH
AAFHHORT	HAFTORAH
AAFHIKLS	KHALIFAS
AAFHIKLT	KHALIFAT
	KHILAFAT
AAFHINRS	FARINHAS
AAFHIRST	AIRSHAFT
AAFHLLSS	ASHFALLS
AAFHLSTW	FLATWASH
AAFHORTT	HAFTAROT
AAFHRSUU	HAUSFRAU
AAFIILLM	FAMILIAL
AAFIILLR	FILARIAL
AAFIILMR	FAMILIAR
AAFIILNR	FILARIAN
AAFIILRS	FILARIAS
AAFIINST	FISTIANA
AAFIKLLY	ALKALIFY
AAFILLNR	RAINFALL
AAFILLUV	AVAILFUL
AAFILMST	FATALISM
AAFILNNU	INFAUNAL
AAFILNQU	ALFAQUIN
AAFILNST	FANTAILS
	TAILFANS
AAFILOPR	PARAFOIL
AAFILQSU	ALFAQUIS
AAFILSTT	FATALIST
AAFILTTY	FATALITY
AAFIMNOR	FORAMINA
AAFIMNOT	ANTIFOAM
AAFINNOV	FAVONIAN
AAFINNRS	SAFRANIN
AAFINNST	INFANTAS
AAFINNSU	INFAUNAS
AAFINRRW	WARFARIN
AAFINSTU	FAUSTIAN
AAFIPRST	PARFAITS
AAFIRSST	SAFARIST
AAFIRSUY	RUFIYAAS
AAFIRSWY	FAIRWAYS
AAFIRTTT	FRITTATA
AAFJLLSW	JAWFALLS
AAFJLORS	ALFORJAS
AAFLLNOV	FLAVANOL
AAFLLNUY	FAUNALLY
AAFLLPRT	PRATFALL
AAFLLPST	SPATFALL

AAFLMORV	LAVAFORM
AAFLNNOT	NONFATAL
AAFLNORS	FORLANAS
	SAFRONAL
AAFLNOTT	FLOATANT
AAFLNRSU	FURLANAS
AAFLSTWY	FLATWAYS
AAFLSWYY	FLYAWAYS
AAFMNRST	RAFTSMAN
AAFMNSST	FANTASMS
AAFMOPRR	PARAFORM
AAFNPPRT	FRAPPANT
AAFNSSTT	FANTASTS
AAGGGINR	GARAGING
AAGGHNST	HANGTAGS
AAGGILLN	GANGLIAL
AAGGILNR	GANGLIAR
AAGGIMNN	MANAGING
AAGGIMNR	MARAGING
AAGGINRV	RAVAGING
AAGGINSV	SAVAGING
AAGGIRST	GARAGIST
AAGGITTW	GIGAWATT
AAGGLLLY	LALLYGAG
AAGGLMOS	MAGALOGS
AAGGLNOT	TAGALONG
AAGGLRSY	GRAYLAGS
AAGGMNNS	GANGSMAN
AAGGNSST	GANGSTAS
AAGGNSWY	GANGWAYS
AAGGRSTT	STAGGART
AAGHHINS	SHANGHAI
AAGHILNN	HANGNAIL
AAGHILPY	HYPALGIA
AAGHILRS	GHARIALS
	HARIGALS
AAGHIMNS	ASHAMING
AAGHIMRT	TAGHAIRM
AAGHINNS	ANHINGAS
AAGHINPS	PAGANISH
AAGHINPW	AWHAPING
AAGHIPRR	AIRGRAPH
AAGHIRSV	VAGARISH
AAGHKMNY	GYMKHANA
AAGHLNNS	LANGSHAN
AAGHLNPY	ANAGLYPH
AAGHLOSS	GASAHOLS
AAGHMNOY	HOGMANAY
	MAHOGANY
AAGHMNSU	MAHUANGS
AAGHMNSW	WHANGAMS
AAGHNOPR	AGRAPHON
AAGHOPPR	APOGRAPH
AAGHQSUU	QUAHAUGS
AAGHRRTU	ARRAUGHT
AAGHRSSW	WASHRAGS
AAGIIKKN	KAIAKING
AAGIILMN	IMAGINAL
AAGIILNS	ALIASING
AAGIILNV	AVAILING
AAGIIMST	ASTIGMIA
AAGIINNU	IGUANIAN
AAGIINRS	ARAISING
AAGIINST	IGNATIAS
AAGIINTV	AVIATING
AAGIINTW	AWAITING
AAGIKKNY	KAYAKING
AAGIKLNO	KAOLIANG
AAGIKLNR	KRAALING
AAGIKLNS	ASLAKING
AAGIKMRS	SKIAGRAM
AAGIKNSW	AWAKINGS
AAGIKNSZ	ZIGANKAS
AAGILLNU	UNIALGAL
AAGILLNY	ALLAYING

AAGILLSS	GALLIASS
AAGILLTV	GALLIVAT
AAGILLUZ	ALGUAZIL
AAGILMMR	MAILGRAM
AAGILMNO	MAGNOLIA
AAGILMNR	ALARMING
	MARGINAL
AAGILMNX	MALAXING
AAGILMOT	GLIOMATA
AAGILMRY	GRAYMAIL
AAGILMSY	MYALGIAS
AAGILNOS	LOGANIAS
AAGILNOT	GALTONIA
AAGILNPT	PALATING
AAGILNRR	LARRIGAN
AAGILNSS	SALSAING
AAGILNTV	GALIVANT
AAGILNUV	VAGINULA
AAGILOOP	APOLOGIA
AAGILOST	OTALGIAS
AAGILPRY	PLAGIARY
AAGILRRW	WARRIGAL
AAGILSTT	SAGITTAL
AAGILSTW	WAGTAILS
AAGIMMRR	MARIGRAM
AAGIMNNO	AGNOMINA
AAGIMNOS	ANGIOMAS
AAGIMNPS	PAGANISM
AAGIMNRR	MARGARIN
AAGIMNSS	AMASSING
	SIAMANGS
AAGIMNSY	GYMNASIA
AAGIMPTU	PATAGIUM
AAGIMSSV	SAVAGISM
AAGIMSTT	STIGMATA
AAGINNNW	WANNIGAN
AAGINNNY	NANNYGAI
AAGINNOT	AGNATION
AAGINNRW	AWARNING
AAGINNSW	WANIGANS
AAGINNSY	SYNANGIA
AAGINNTV	VAGINANT
AAGINNTW	AWANTING
AAGINOSS	AGNOSIAS
AAGINPPY	APPAYING
AAGINPRU	PAGURIAN
AAGINPRW	PARAWING
AAGINPRY	AGRYPNIA
AAGINPST	PAGANIST
AAGINPWW	PAWAWING
AAGINRRS	ARRAIGNS
AAGINRRY	ARRAYING
AAGINRSS	SANGRIAS
	SARANGIS
AAGINRST	GRANITAS
AAGINRSU	GUARANIS
AAGINRSY	ARAYSING
AAGINSST	ASSIGNAT
AAGINSSU	GAUSSIAN
AAGINSSY	ASSAYING
	GAINSAYS
AAGIORTT	AGITATOR
AAGIORTV	AVIGATOR
AAGIPRSU	PIRAGUAS
AAGIRRSY	ARGYRIAS
AAGIRSTV	GRAVITAS
	STRAVAIG
AAGISSTT	SAGITTAS
AAGKKNOS	ANGAKOKS
AAGKLRSV	GRAVLAKS
AAGKNOOR	KANGAROO
AAGKOOSZ	GAZOOKAS
AAGKORST	KATORGAS
AAGLLMOY	ALLOGAMY
AAGLLNOO	LAGOONAL

AAGLLNRY	LARYNGAL
AAGLLNST	GALLANTS
AAGLLOOP	APOLOGAL
AAGLLOPY	POLYGALA
AAGLMNSS	GLASSMAN
AAGLNNOO	ANALOGON
AAGLNORS	GRANOLAS
AAGLNPSS	LAPSANGS
AAGLNQUU	AQUALUNG
AAGLNRRU	GRANULAR
AAGLOPRY	PARALOGY
AAGLORSU	ARUGOLAS
AAGLRRUW	WARRAGUL
AAGLRSTU	GASTRULA
AAGLRSUU	ARUGULAS
AAGMMRRS	GRAMMARS
AAGMNNOR	NANOGRAM
AAGMNNRS	GRANNAMS
AAGMNOPZ	ZAMPOGNA
AAGMNORT	MARTAGON
AAGMNOSS	SANGOMAS
AAGMNPRS	PANGRAMS
AAGMNRST	TANGRAMS
	TRANGAMS
AAGMNRTU	ARMGAUNT
AAGMNSSW	SWAGSMAN
AAGMNSTY	SYNTAGMA
AAGMORSS	MARGOSAS
AAGMOTUY	AUTOGAMY
AAGMOTYZ	ZYGOMATA
AAGMRSST	MATGRASS
AAGNNNOP	NONPAGAN
AAGNNSTT	STAGNANT
AAGNOPRS	PARAGONS
AAGNOPRT	TRAGOPAN
AAGNORRT	ARROGANT
	TARRAGON
AAGNORSZ	ORGANZAS
AAGNORTU	ARGONAUT
AAGNRSTV	VAGRANTS
AAGNRTUY	GUARANTY
AAGNRTYZ	ZYGANTRA
AAGOPSSS	SAPSAGOS
AAGORSSS	SARGASSO
AAGORSSU	SAGUAROS
AAGRRSSY	RAYGRASS
AAGRSSTU	SASTRUGA
AAGRSTUZ	ZASTRUGA
AAGSTTUU	TAUTAUGS
AAHHIIMM	MAHIMAHI
AAHHKLOT	HALAKHOT
	HALAKOTH
AAHHKMRS	HASHMARK
AAHHKSWW	HAWKSHAW
AAHHMMSS	SHAMMASH
AAHHNNOS	HOSANNAH
AAHHNNST	THANNAHS
AAHHNPST	NAPHTHAS
AAHHOPRS	PHARAOHS
AAHIIKRT	TARAKIHI
AAHIJNRS	HARIJANS
AAHIJPRS	RAJASHIP
AAHIKLPS	PASHALIK
AAHIKLST	HALAKIST
AAHIKRST	KITHARAS
AAHILLLS	HALLALIS
	SHILLALA
AAHILLNS	HALLIANS
AAHILMNR	HARMALIN
AAHILMRS	ALMIRAHS
AAHILMSS	SHIMAALS
AAHILNNT	INHALANT
AAHILNOT	HALATION
AAHILOPP	HAPLOPIA
AAHILPSV	PAHLAVIS

AAHILPSY	PHYSALIA
AAHILRRZ	ARRHIZAL
AAHILSSW	SAHIWALS
AAHIMNOS	MAHONIAS
AAHIMNPS	PASHMINA
AAHIMNZZ	HAZZANIM
AAHIMRTY	ARYTHMIA
AAHINOPS	APHONIAS
AAHINPPS	PAPHIANS
AAHINPRS	PIRANHAS
AAHINRSW	RAINWASH
AAHINRTU	HAURIANT
AAHINSST	SHAITANS
AAHINSTW	TANIWHAS
AAHIOPRT	ATROPHIA
AAHIPRST	PITARAHS
AAHIPSTZ	ZAPTIAHS
AAHIPSXY	ASPHYXIA
AAHIRSST	SHARIATS
AAHIRSTV	HAVARTIS
AAHJKNRS	KHANJARS
AAHKLLMR	HALLMARK
AAHKLRSS	LASHKARS
AAHKMOTW	TOMAHAWK
AAHKMSSY	YASHMAKS
AAHKRSSW	SAWSHARK
AAHLLLOO	HALLALOO
AAHLLMRS	MARSHALL
AAHLLOPT	ALLOPATH
AAHLLSWY	HALLWAYS
AAHLMMSS	MASHLAMS
AAHLMOOS	MASOOLAH
AAHLMOPR	AMPHORAL
AAHLMRSS	MARSHALS
AAHLMSTU	THALAMUS
AAHLNPST	ASHPLANT
AAHLNRSW	NARWHALS
AAHLPRRT	PHRATRAL
AAHLPSST	ASPHALTS
AAHLRSSW	SHALWARS
AAHMNNPU	PANHUMAN
AAHMNNSU	HANUMANS
AAHMNORT	MARATHON
AAHMNOST	HOASTMAN
AAHMNOTX	XANTHOMA
AAHMNPST	PHANTASM
AAHMNRST	TRASHMAN
AAHMNSTX	XANTHAMS
AAHMOPRS	AMPHORAS
AAHMRSST	STRAMASH
AAHNNOSS	HOSANNAS
AAHNNPSW	SHWANPAN
AAHNNSTX	XANTHANS
AAHNOPRS	ANAPHORS
AAHNORST	ATHANORS
AAHNORSV	NAVARHOS
AAHNOSTT	THANATOS
AAHNPSTT	PHANTAST
AAHNPSTY	PHANTASY
AAHOPRTU	AUTOHARP
AAHORSSU	SAHUAROS
AAHPRSTW	WARPATHS
AAHPSTWY	PATHWAYS
AAHRRTTW	THRAWART
AAHRSSST	SHASTRAS
AAHRSSTY	ASHTRAYS
AAHRSTTW	STRAWHAT
AAIIILMR	MILIARIA
AAIIIMNR	NIRAMIAI
AAIIJJPP	JIPIJAPA
AAIIKKNN	KINAKINA
AAIILLQU	QUILLAIA
AAIILMNS	MAINSAIL
AAIILMRS	AIRMAILS
AAIILNRZ	ALIZARIN
AAIILNUX	UNIAXIAL
AAIILPRR	RIPARIAL
AAIILPRS	PAIRIALS
AAIILPST	TILAPIAS
AAIILRSZ	ALIZARIS
AAIILRTX	TRIAXIAL
AAIILRUX	AUXILIAR
AAIILTXY	AXIALITY
AAIIMNNT	AMANITIN
	MAINTAIN
AAIIMNPX	PANMIXIA
AAIINNRT	ANTIARIN
AAIINOTV	AVIATION
AAIINPRR	RIPARIAN
AAIINPZZ	PIAZZIAN
AAIINRST	INTARSIA
AAIINSTT	TITANIAS
AAIINSZZ	ZIZANIAS
AAIIOPST	APOSITIA
AAIIORTZ	ZOIATRIA
AAIIPRST	APIARIST
AAIIPRVV	VIVIPARA
AAIIRSTV	AVIARIST
AAIIRSTW	WISTARIA
AAIIRTVX	AVIATRIX
AAIJLLQU	QUILLAJA
AAIJLNPS	JALAPINS
AAIJMNPS	JAMPANIS
AAIJNRSY	JANISARY
AAIJNRSZ	JANIZARS
AAIJNRYZ	JANIZARY
AAIJPPSY	JIPYAPAS
AAIKKNOS	SKOKIAAN
AAIKKSTZ	KAZATSKI
AAIKLNST	NASTALIK
AAIKLPRS	PALIKARS
AAIKMNNS	MANAKINS
AAIKMNRS	RAMAKINS
AAIKMNST	ANTIMASK
AAIKMORS	ROMAIKAS
AAIKMRSS	KARAISMS
AAIKMRST	TAMARISK
AAIKNNTT	ANTITANK
AAIKORSU	OUAKARIS
AAIKPPRS	PAPRIKAS
AAIKPRRS	AIRPARKS
AAIKSSTT	ASTATKIS
AAIKSSTV	SVASTIKA
AAIKSSTW	SWASTIKA
AAIKSTVV	AKVAVITS
AAILLLSS	SALSILLA
AAILLLUV	ALLUVIAL
AAILLMMM	MAMMILLA
AAILLMMR	MAMILLAR
AAILLMNS	MANILLAS
AAILLMNT	MANTILLA
AAILLMNY	ANIMALLY
AAILLMPT	TAILLAMP
AAILLMRS	ARMILLAS
AAILLMSX	MAXILLAS
AAILLNOV	VALLONIA
AAILLNPU	NAUPLIAL
AAILLNST	LANITALS
AAILLNSV	VANILLAS
AAILLPPR	PAPILLAR
AAILLRRY	ARILLARY
AAILLRSX	AXILLARS
AAILLRXY	AXILLARY
AAILMMRS	ALARMISM
	AMMIRALS
AAILMMSX	MAXIMALS
AAILMNNT	LAMANTIN
AAILMNOP	PALAMINO
AAILMNOR	MANORIAL
	MORAINAL
AAILMNOX	MONAXIAL
AAILMNPS	PANISLAM
AAILMNRU	MANURIAL
AAILMNRY	LAMINARY
AAILMNST	STAMINAL
	TALISMAN
AAILMNSU	ALUMINAS
AAILMNSV	MAILVANS
	NAVALISM
AAILMOPT	LIPOMATA
AAILMORR	ARMORIAL
AAILMPPS	PAPALISM
AAILMPRT	PRIMATAL
AAILMRST	ALARMIST
	ALASTRIM
AAILMTTU	ULTIMATA
AAILNNOT	NATIONAL
AAILNNPT	PLAINANT
	PLANTAIN
AAILNNRU	LUNARIAN
AAILNNST	ANNALIST
	SANTALIN
AAILNOPS	SALOPIAN
AAILNOPT	TALAPOIN
AAILNORS	ORINASAL
AAILNORT	NOTARIAL
	RATIONAL
AAILNOST	AILANTOS
	ALATIONS
AAILNOSV	VALONIAS
AAILNOTV	LAVATION
AAILNOTX	LAXATION
AAILNPRU	PLANURIA
AAILNPSS	SALPIANS
AAILNPST	PLATINAS
AAILNQTU	ALIQUANT
AAILNSSY	ANALYSIS
AAILNSTV	VALIANTS
AAILNSTY	NASALITY
AAILNTTT	LATITANT
AAILNTTY	NATALITY
AAILORRS	RASORIAL
AAILORRV	VARIOLAR
AAILORSS	ROSALIAS
AAILORSU	RAOULIAS
AAILORSV	VARIOLAS
AAILPPRU	PUPARIAL
AAILPPST	PAPALIST
AAILPRST	PARTIALS
	PATRIALS
	TRIAPSAL
AAILPRSY	AIRPLAYS
AAILPSTT	TALIPATS
AAILQRSU	SQUARIAL
AAILQSWW	QAWWALIS
AAILRRSV	ARRIVALS
AAILRSTT	RATTAILS
AAILRSTV	TRAVAILS
AAILRSVY	SALIVARY
AAILRSWY	RAILWAYS
AAILSSSV	VASSAILS
AAILSSSW	WASSAILS
AAILSSTY	STAYSAIL
AAILSTTT	LATITATS
AAIMMNOS	AMMONIAS
AAIMMNST	MAINMAST
AAIMMRSU	SAMARIUM
AAIMNNRT	TRAINMAN
AAIMNOOZ	ZOOMANIA
AAIMNORT	ANIMATOR
	MONTARIA
	TAMANOIR
AAIMNORW	AIRWOMAN
AAIMNOSS	ANOSMIAS
AAIMNOST	AMATIONS
AAIMNOTT	ANTIATOM
AAIMNPRZ	MARZIPAN
AAIMNPTU	PUTAMINA
AAIMNRRT	TRIMARAN
AAIMNRRU	RANARIUM
AAIMNRST	MARTIANS
	TAMARINS
AAIMNSST	MANTISSA
	SATANISM
	STAMINAS
AAIMNSTU	AMIANTUS
AAIMNSTY	MAINSTAY
AAIMOPRS	MARIPOSA
AAIMPRST	PASTRAMI
AAIMPRSU	MARSUPIA
AAIMQRUU	AQUARIUM
AAIMRRSY	MISARRAY
AAIMRRTY	MARTYRIA
AAIMRSSU	SAMURAIS
AAIMRSTU	TIMARAUS
AAIMSSSY	MISASSAY
AAIMSSTV	ATAVISMS
AAINNOPV	PAVONIAN
AAINNOST	SONATINA
AAINNOTT	NATATION
AAINNOTX	ANATOXIN
AAINNRSV	NAVARINS
	NIRVANAS
AAINNRTU	NUTARIAN
AAINNSST	NAISSANT
AAINNSSY	SANNYASI
AAINOOPS	ANOOPSIA
AAINOPSS	ANOPSIAS
	PAISANOS
AAINORRS	ORARIANS
	ROSARIAN
AAINOTTX	TAXATION
AAINPPRY	PAPYRIAN
AAINPRST	ASPIRANT
	PARTISAN
AAINPRTZ	PARTIZAN
AAINPSST	PASTINAS
AAINQRTU	QUATRAIN
AAINQTTU	AQUATINT
AAINRRSS	SARRASIN
AAINRRSZ	SARRAZIN
AAINRSST	ARTISANS
	TSARINAS
AAINRSSU	SAURIANS
AAINRSSV	SAVARINS
AAINRSTV	VARIANTS
AAINRSTY	SANITARY
AAINRSTZ	TZARINAS
AAINRTWY	TRAINWAY
AAINSSSS	ASSASSIN
AAINSSTT	SATANIST
AAINSTTT	ANTISTAT
	ATTAINTS
AAINSTTU	TUTANIAS
AAINSTTY	SATANITY
AAIOPPSS	APOAPSIS
AAIOPRRT	TROPARIA
AAIOPRST	ATROPIAS
AAIOPRSU	PAROUSIA
AAIOPSTU	AUTOPSIA
AAIORSSU	SAOUARIS
AAIORSTV	AVIATORS
AAIORTUZ	AZOTURIA
AAIPPSTT	PITAPATS
AAIPRSSX	SPARAXIS
AAIPRSTT	PARTITAS
AAIQRSTU	AQUARIST
AAIQSSSU	QUASSIAS
AAIQSTUV	AQUAVITS
AAIRSSTT	TSARITSA

AAIRSTTZ	TSARITZA
AAIRSTWY	STAIRWAY
AAIRTTZZ	TZARITZA
AAISSTTV	ATAVISTS
AAISTWXY	TAXIWAYS
AAJKLSWY	JAYWALKS
AAJMMORR	MARJORAM
AAJMORRS	MOJARRAS
AAJMORST	MAJORATS
AAJOPSSU	SAPAJOUS
AAKKLRSU	KARAKULS
AAKKMOST	TOKAMAKS
AAKKSTYZ	KAZATSKY
AAKLMPSU	LAMPUKAS
AAKLMRUY	YARMULKA
AAKLMSUY	YAMULKAS
AAKLNOOS	OOLAKANS
AAKLNOSU	OULAKANS
AAKLOOPS	PALOOKAS
AAKLOOST	TALOOKAS
AAKLPRTY	KALYPTRA
AAKLRSSU	KURSAALS
	RUSALKAS
AAKLSSSU	SAKSAULS
AAKLSWWY	WALKWAYS
AAKMMNRS	MARKSMAN
AAKMORUZ	MAZOURKA
AAKMOSSU	MOUSAKAS
	MOUSSAKA
AAKMRSUZ	MAZURKAS
AAKMRSWY	WAYMARKS
AAKNNSTU	NUNATAKS
AAKNSTWY	TWANKAYS
AAKOOPPS	PAKAPOOS
AAKOPPRT	PORTAPAK
AAKPRSWY	PARKWAYS
AALLLSTY	LAYSTALL
AALLMNST	STALLMAN
AALLMNTY	TALLYMAN
AALLMNUY	MANUALLY
AALLMORY	AMORALLY
AALLMPRU	AMPULLAR
AALLMSST	SMALLSAT
AALLNNUY	ANNUALLY
AALLNOST	SANTALOL
AALLNOSX	ALLOXANS
AALLNOTY	ATONALLY
AALLNPRU	PLANULAR
AALLNRTY	TARNALLY
AALLOORW	WALLAROO
AALLORSU	ALLOSAUR
AALLORWY	ROLLAWAY
AALLOSTV	LAVOLTAS
AALLPRST	PLASTRAL
AALLRSTY	ASTRALLY
AALLRUVV	VALVULAR
AALMMNOS	AMMONALS
AALMNORT	MATRONAL
AALMNORU	MONAURAL
AALMNOSS	SALAMONS
AALMNOWY	LAYWOMAN
AALMNPTY	TYMPANAL
AALMNTTU	TANTALUM
AALMNTUU	AUTUMNAL
AALMOOSS	MASSOOLA
AALMOPPR	MALAPROP
AALMOPSX	AXOPLASM
AALMOSTT	STOMATAL
AALMOTXY	XYLOMATA
AALMPPSU	PASPALUM
AALMPRSY	PALMYRAS
AALMPSTY	PLATYSMA
AALMQSUU	SQUAMULA
AALMSTTU	MULATTAS
AALNNNOV	NONNAVAL
AALNNOPP	NONPAPAL
AALNNOPT	PANTALON
AALNNOST	SONANTAL
AALNNPUU	PUNALUAN
AALNNRSU	ANNULARS
AALNNTTY	NATANTLY
AALNNTUU	LUNANAUT
AALNOPRT	PATRONAL
AALNOPST	POSTANAL
AALNORUV	ANOVULAR
AALNPRSU	LUPANARS
AALNPSST	SALTPANS
AALNPSUU	PUNALUAS
AALNPTWX	WAXPLANT
AALNRRTY	ARRANTLY
AALNRSTU	NATURALS
AALNSSTT	SALTANTS
AALNSSTU	SULTANAS
AALNSSTY	ANALYSTS
AALNSTTU	TALAUNTS
	TANTALUS
AALOPPRT	PALPATOR
AALOPPRV	APPROVAL
AALOPRSS	PARASOLS
AALOPRST	PASTORAL
AALOPSVV	PAVLOVAS
AALOPSZZ	PALAZZOS
AALORSST	ALASTORS
AALORSSU	AROUSALS
AALORSTX	LAXATORS
AALORTUV	VALUATOR
AALORTVY	LAVATORY
AALOSTTY	TALAYOTS
AALPRSTU	PASTURAL
	SPATULAR
AALPSSTU	SPATULAS
AALRRTTY	TARTARLY
AALRSSTU	AUSTRALS
AALRSSTY	SATYRALS
AALRSSVY	VASSALRY
AALRSTTW	STALWART
AALRSTUY	SALUTARY
AALSSSTU	ASSAULTS
AAMMMSTU	MAMMATUS
AAMMNPRS	RAMPSMAN
AAMMNRST	MANTRAMS
AAMMOTXY	MYXOMATA
AAMMRSSU	MARASMUS
AAMNNORS	SONARMAN
AAMNNOSY	ANONYMAS
AAMNORRS	MARRANOS
AAMNPRST	MANTRAPS
AAMNPRSY	PARANYMS
AAMNQSUW	SQUAWMAN
AAMOORSS	AMOROSAS
AAMOPRRU	PARAMOUR
AAMORRSZ	ZAMARROS
AAMORSSU	MOSASAUR
AAMORSSV	SAMOVARS
AAMORSTT	STROMATA
AAMOSTTU	AUTOMATS
AAMPRRST	RAMPARTS
AAMRSSST	SMARTASS
AAMRSSTT	MATTRASS
AAMRSSTU	SUMATRAS
AAMRSTWY	TRAMWAYS
AAMSSSTU	SATSUMAS
AANNOSST	ASSONANT
AANNOSTT	ANNATTOS
AANNOTTW	NANOWATT
AANNPSSW	SWANPANS
AANNRSTY	STANNARY
AANOOPPX	OPOPANAX
AANOOPRZ	PARAZOON
AANOPRTY	ANATROPY
AANORRRT	NARRATOR
AANORSTT	ARNATTOS
AANORSTY	SANATORY
AANORTTY	NATATORY
AANPPTTY	PATTYPAN
AANPRSST	SPARTANS
AANQRSTU	QUARTANS
AANRRSTW	WARRANTS
AANRRTTY	TARTANRY
AANRRTWY	WARRANTY
AANRSTTU	SATURANT
AANRSUWY	RUNAWAYS
AAOORRSW	WOORARAS
AAOPSSST	POTASSAS
AAOPSSTY	APOSTASY
AAOQSSSU	OQUASSAS
AAORSSTT	STAROSTA
AAORSSVV	VAVASORS
	VAVASSOR
AAORSUVV	VAVASOUR
AAORSVVY	VAVASORY
AAOSTTUY	TATOUAYS
AAOSTWWY	STOWAWAY
	TOWAWAYS
AAPRRSTT	RATTRAPS
AARSTTUY	STATUARY
ABBBCDEO	CABOBBED
ABBBDEEK	KEBABBED
ABBBDEEL	BEDABBLE
ABBBDEKO	KABOBBED
ABBBDELR	BRABBLED
ABBBEILR	BABBLIER
	BRIBABLE
ABBBELRR	BRABBLER
ABBBELRS	BABBLERS
	BLABBERS
	BRABBLES
ABBBELTU	TUBBABLE
ABBBGILN	BABBLING
	BLABBING
ABBBISTT	BABBITTS
ABBBOORU	RUBBABOO
ABBBOSTU	SUBABBOT
ABBCDEKN	BACKBEND
ABBCDELS	SCABBLED
ABBCDERS	SCRABBED
ABBCDKNO	BACKBOND
ABBCEERU	BARBECUE
ABBCEGIR	CRIBBAGE
ABBCEHIS	BABICHES
ABBCEHOU	BABOUCHE
ABBCEHOY	BEACHBOY
ABBCEHSU	BABUCHES
ABBCEHTU	BATHCUBE
ABBCEIKT	BACKBITE
ABBCEILR	BARBICEL
ABBCEIRR	CRABBIER
ABBCEIRS	SCABBIER
ABBCEKLU	BLUEBACK
ABBCEKNO	BACKBONE
ABBCEKNU	BUCKBEAN
ABBCELLU	CLUBABLE
ABBCELRS	CLABBERS
	SCRABBLE
ABBCELRU	CURBABLE
ABBCELSS	SCABBLES
ABBCERRS	CRABBERS
ABBCGINR	CRABBING
ABBCGINS	SCABBING
ABBCGIOR	GABBROIC
ABBCIILL	BIBLICAL
ABBCIINR	RABBINIC
ABBCIKRT	BRICKBAT
ABBCILRY	CRABBILY
ABBCILSY	SCABBILY
ABBCKLOW	BLOWBACK
ABBCKLOY	BLACKBOY
ABBCKSUY	BUYBACKS
ABBCLRSY	SCRABBLY
ABBDDEEL	BEDDABLE
ABBDDEEU	BEDAUBED
ABBDDEIL	BIDDABLE
ABBDDELR	DRABBLED
ABBDDILY	BIDDABLY
ABBDEEER	BEEBREAD
ABBDEEHR	REHABBED
ABBDEEJR	JABBERED
ABBDEELN	BENDABLE
ABBDEERR	BARBERED
ABBDEERT	RABBETED
ABBDEERY	YABBERED
ABBDEGLR	GRABBLED
ABBDEILN	BINDABLE
ABBDEIRR	DRABBIER
ABBDEIRT	RABBITED
ABBDELMO	BABELDOM
ABBDELMR	BRAMBLED
ABBDELNO	BONDABLE
ABBDELNS	SNABBLED
ABBDELRR	DRABBLER
ABBDELRS	DABBLERS
	DRABBLES
ABBDEMUZ	BUMBAZED
ABBDENRU	UNBARBED
ABBDEORS	ABSORBED
ABBDEORX	BREADBOX
ABBDEQSU	SQUABBED
ABBDERRS	DRABBERS
ABBDERST	DRABBEST
	DRABBETS
ABBDFOOY	BABYFOOD
ABBDGILN	DABBLING
ABBDGINR	DRABBING
ABBDGIOR	GABBROID
ABBDHIJS	DJIBBAHS
ABBDHIRS	DRABBISH
ABBDHIRT	BIRDBATH
ABBDHOOY	BABYHOOD
ABBDILNO	BAILBOND
ABBDILRS	LIBBARDS
ABBDINRS	RIBBANDS
ABBDLMOO	BOMBLOAD
ABBDLRSU	LUBBARDS
ABBDMORS	BOMBARDS
ABBDMOSU	BABUDOMS
ABBDNORW	BROWBAND
ABBDOORX	BOXBOARD
ABBEEHRR	REHABBER
ABBEEILT	BITEABLE
ABBEEINR	BEARBINE
ABBEEJRR	JABBERER
ABBEEJRS	BEJABERS
ABBEELOY	OBEYABLE
ABBEENOR	BAREBONE
ABBEEQRU	BARBEQUE
ABBEERTT	BARBETTE
ABBEESSS	ABBESSES
ABBEFFLU	BUFFABLE
ABBEFILR	FLABBIER
ABBEGIRR	GRABBIER
ABBEGIST	GABBIEST
ABBEGLRR	GRABBLER
ABBEGLRS	GABBLERS
	GRABBLES
ABBEGNOS	BOGBEANS
ABBEGNSU	BUGBANES
ABBEGRRS	GRABBERS
ABBEGRSU	BUGBEARS
ABBEHILS	BABELISH
ABBEHIRS	SHABBIER

ABBEHLSS	SHABBLES
ABBEHORT	BATHROBE
ABBEILLL	BILLABLE
ABBEILLO	BOILABLE
ABBEILMS	BABELISM
ABBEILNU	BUBALINE
ABBEILOT	BILOBATE
ABBEILOV	OBVIABLE
ABBEILRS	SLABBIER
ABBEILRW	WABBLIER
ABBEILST	BISTABLE
ABBEINTT	TABBINET
ABBEIRRT	RABBITER
ABBEIRRW	BARBWIRE
ABBEISST	TABBISES
ABBEISSW	SWABBIES
ABBEKLOO	BOOKABLE
ABBELLLU	BLUEBALL
ABBELLRS	BARBELLS
ABBELMRS	BRAMBLES
ABBELNRU	BURNABLE
ABBELNSS	SNABBLES
ABBELOOT	BOOTABLE
ABBELOPR	PROBABLE
ABBELORS	BELABORS
	SORBABLE
ABBELORU	BELABOUR
ABBELPRS	PRABBLES
ABBELQSU	SQUABBLE
ABBELRRS	RABBLERS
ABBELRSS	BARBLESS
	SLABBERS
ABBELRSU	BARBULES
ABBELRSW	WABBLERS
ABBELRSY	SLABBERY
ABBELSUY	BUYABLES
ABBEMOOR	AEROBOMB
ABBEMOSX	BOMBAXES
ABBEMSUZ	BUMBAZES
ABBENORS	BASEBORN
ABBENORY	NABOBERY
ABBENOSS	NABOBESS
ABBEORRS	ABSORBER
	REABSORB
ABBEORTW	BROWBEAT
ABBEQRSU	SQUABBER
ABBERRRY	BARBERRY
ABBERRYY	BAYBERRY
ABBERSST	STABBERS
ABBERSSW	SWABBERS
ABBESSSU	SUBBASES
ABBFGINR	FRABBING
ABBFILLY	FLABBILY
ABBGGILN	GABBLING
ABBGGINR	GRABBING
ABBGIJLN	JABBLING
ABBGILNR	RABBLING
ABBGILNS	SLABBING
ABBGILNU	BAUBLING
ABBGILNW	WABBLING
ABBGINST	STABBING
ABBGINSU	BUBINGAS
ABBGINSW	SWABBING
ABBGINTY	TABBYING
ABBGOOSU	BUGABOOS
ABBHIIMS	BIMBASHI
ABBHILSY	SHABBILY
ABBHINOS	NABOBISH
ABBHRRSU	RHUBARBS
ABBHRRUY	RHUBARBY
ABBHSTTU	BATHTUBS
ABBIINOT	BIBATION
ABBILLOT	BOATBILL
ABBILLSU	SILLABUB
ABBILOST	BIOBLAST
	BOBTAILS
ABBIMNOS	BAMBINOS
	NABOBISM
ABBIMSSU	BABUISMS
ABBINORS	RABBONIS
ABBINORX	BRAINBOX
ABBINSSU	SUBBASIN
ABBIRRTY	RABBITRY
ABBIRSUU	SUBURBIA
ABBKKNOO	BANKBOOK
ABBKLOSU	BLAUBOKS
ABBLLLOW	BLOWBALL
ABBLLRSU	BULLBARS
ABBLLSTU	BULLBATS
ABBLLSUY	SYLLABUB
ABBLOPRY	PROBABLY
ABBMOORS	BOMBORAS
ABBMOSST	BOMBASTS
ABBMOSTU	BUMBOATS
ABBNRSUU	SUBURBAN
ABBOORSU	RUBABOOS
ABBOSSTY	BOBSTAYS
ABCCCIOO	BOCACCIO
ABCCDEHO	CABOCHED
ABCCDHIK	DABCHICK
ABCCEEHN	BECHANCE
ABCCEELP	PECCABLE
ABCCEEOR	CABOCEER
ABCCEILR	BRECCIAL
ABCCEILY	CELIBACY
ABCCEIRS	BRECCIAS
ABCCEIRT	BACTERIC
ABCCEKMO	COMEBACK
ABCCESUU	SUCCUBAE
ABCCHISU	BACCHIUS
ABCCHNOO	CABOCHON
ABCCHOSU	CHUBASCO
ABCCIKKK	KICKBACK
ABCCIKKP	PICKBACK
ABCCIKOR	ABRICOCK
ABCCILOR	CARBOLIC
ABCCILOT	COBALTIC
ABCCILUU	CUBICULA
ABCCIMRS	CAMBRICS
ABCCINOR	CARBONIC
ABCCINSU	BUCCINAS
ABCCIORS	ASCORBIC
ABCCKLLO	BALLCOCK
ABCCKLOX	CLACKBOX
ABCCKOOT	COCKBOAT
ABCCKOSW	BAWCOCKS
ABCCKSTU	CUTBACKS
ABCCLLUY	BUCCALLY
ABCCLOOO	COCOBOLA
ABCCMOOY	MACCOBOY
ABCCOORS	BAROCCOS
ABCCOOST	TOBACCOS
ABCCSSUU	SUCCUBAS
ABCDDEER	DECARBED
ABCDDEOR	BROCADED
ABCDDETU	ABDUCTED
ABCDEEFK	FEEDBACK
ABCDEEHL	BLEACHED
ABCDEEHR	BERDACHE
	BREACHED
ABCDEEJT	ABJECTED
ABCDEEKR	REBACKED
ABCDEELL	BECALLED
ABCDEELM	BECALMED
ABCDEELS	DEBACLES
ABCDEELU	EDUCABLE
ABCDEEMR	CAMBERED
	EMBRACED
ABCDEEMX	EXCAMBED
ABCDEENO	BEACONED
ABCDEEPP	BECAPPED
ABCDEERR	REBRACED
ABCDEETU	ABDUCTEE
ABCDEFLO	BOLDFACE
ABCDEGIR	BIRDCAGE
	CAGEBIRD
ABCDEHIR	BEDCHAIR
ABCDEHLN	BLANCHED
ABCDEHLU	BAUCHLED
ABCDEHNR	BRANCHED
ABCDEHOR	BROACHED
ABCDEHOS	CABOSHED
ABCDEIIT	DIABETIC
ABCDEIKS	BACKSIDE
	DIEBACKS
ABCDEILR	CALIBRED
ABCDEIPS	PEDICABS
ABCDEIRS	ASCRIBED
	CARBIDES
ABCDEISS	ABSCISED
ABCDEKLO	BLOCKADE
ABCDEKLV	BACKVELD
ABCDEKNN	NECKBAND
ABCDEKNU	UNBACKED
ABCDEKRS	REDBACKS
ABCDELMS	SCAMBLED
ABCDELNO	BLANCOED
ABCDELOO	CABOODLE
ABCDELRU	BARLEDUC
ABCDEMNU	DUMBCANE
ABCDEMOT	COMBATED
ABCDEMRS	SCRAMBED
ABCDENRU	UNBRACED
ABCDENSU	ABDUCENS
ABCDENTU	ABDUCENT
ABCDEORS	BROCADES
ABCDEORW	BECOWARD
ABCDEORY	CARBOYED
ABCDERSU	CUDBEARS
ABCDESTU	SUBACTED
ABCDGINU	ABDUCING
ABCDHKLO	HOLDBACK
ABCDHLNU	CLUBHAND
ABCDHORS	CHOBDARS
ABCDIILO	BIOCIDAL
	DIABOLIC
ABCDIIMY	CYMBIDIA
ABCDIIRT	TRIBADIC
ABCDIKLR	BALDRICK
ABCDIKLS	BACKSLID
ABCDIKRU	BAUDRICK
ABCDILLR	BIRDCALL
ABCDILOS	CABILDOS
ABCDILOU	CUBOIDAL
ABCDILRS	BALDRICS
ABCDINOR	BRACONID
ABCDINSS	ABSCINDS
ABCDIRST	CATBIRDS
ABCDIRSU	BAUDRICS
	SUBACRID
ABCDIRSW	BAWDRICS
ABCDKNOW	BACKDOWN
ABCDKOOR	BACKDOOR
ABCDKOOW	BACKWOOD
ABCDKOPR	BACKDROP
ABCDKORW	BACKWORD
ABCDLLNU	CLUBLAND
ABCDNOSS	ABSCONDS
ABCDOORS	CORDOBAS
ABCDOPRU	CUPBOARD
ABCDORRS	BROCARDS
ABCDORTU	ABDUCTOR
ABCDORUY	OBDURACY
ABCEEEFK	BEEFCAKE
ABCEEFNT	BENEFACT
ABCEEHIR	BEACHIER
ABCEEHLM	BECHAMEL
ABCEEHLN	ALEBENCH
ABCEEHLR	BLEACHER
ABCEEHLS	BLEACHES
ABCEEHLW	CHEWABLE
ABCEEHRR	BREACHER
ABCEEHRS	BREACHES
ABCEEHSU	EBAUCHES
ABCEEILT	CELIBATE
	CITEABLE
ABCEEIMN	AMBIENCE
ABCEELOV	EVOCABLE
ABCEELRR	CEREBRAL
ABCEELRT	BRACELET
ABCEEMRR	EMBRACER
ABCEEMRS	EMBRACES
ABCEENOZ	CABEZONE
ABCEENRT	CABERNET
ABCEENSS	ABSENCES
ABCEEPRT	BECARPET
ABCEERRS	REBRACES
ABCEERST	ACERBEST
ABCEERUX	BERCEAUX
ABCEESSS	BECASSES
ABCEFIIT	BEATIFIC
ABCEFIKL	BACKFILE
ABCEFIKR	BACKFIRE
	FIREBACK
ABCEFINO	BONIFACE
ABCEGHIN	BEACHING
ABCEGIKV	GIVEBACK
ABCEGILN	BELACING
ABCEGIMN	EMBACING
ABCEGIRS	RIBCAGES
ABCEGKLL	BLACKLEG
ABCEGKLO	BLOCKAGE
ABCEGKMU	MEGABUCK
ABCEGKOR	BROCKAGE
ABCEGMOS	CAMBOGES
ABCEGNOR	BONGRACE
ABCEGORS	BROCAGES
ABCEGOSS	BOSCAGES
ABCEHITT	BATHETIC
ABCEHKLS	BECHALKS
ABCEHKOS	BACKHOES
ABCEHKTW	BETHWACK
ABCEHLNR	BLANCHER
ABCEHLNS	BLANCHES
ABCEHLOR	BACHELOR
ABCEHLSU	BAUCHLES
	CHASUBLE
ABCEHLTU	LEACHTUB
ABCEHMOT	HECATOMB
ABCEHMRS	BECHARMS
	BRECHAMS
	CHAMBERS
ABCEHNRR	BRANCHER
	REBRANCH
ABCEHNRS	BRANCHES
	BRECHANS
ABCEHOOT	COHOBATE
ABCEHOPU	PABOUCHE
ABCEHORR	BROACHER
ABCEHORS	BROACHES
ABCEHORU	BAROUCHE
ABCEHOSS	BASOCHES
ABCEHRST	BATCHERS
	BRACHETS
ABCEHRTT	BRATCHET
ABCEIIRT	RABIETIC
ABCEIKKL	KICKABLE
ABCEIKLR	CRABLIKE
ABCEIKLS	SCABLIKE
ABCEIKST	TIEBACKS

ABCEIKWZ	ZWIEBACK
ABCEILLR	CRIBELLA
ABCEILLS	ICEBALLS
ABCEILLT	BALLETIC
ABCEILMS	ALEMBICS
ABCEILNN	BINNACLE
ABCEILNO	BIOCLEAN
	COINABLE
ABCEILNU	BACULINE
ABCEILOR	ALBICORE
	BRACIOLE
	CABRIOLE
ABCEILOS	SOCIABLE
ABCEILRS	CALIBERS
	CALIBRES
ABCEILTT	BITTACLE
ABCEILTU	BACULITE
ABCEILTY	BIACETYL
ABCEIMRW	MICAWBER
ABCEIMST	BETACISM
ABCEINOO	COENOBIA
ABCEINRS	BRISANCE
	CARBINES
ABCEINRT	BACTERIN
ABCEINRV	VIBRANCE
ABCEINST	CABINETS
ABCEINTU	INCUBATE
ABCEIORS	AEROBICS
ABCEIORT	BORACITE
ABCEIOST	ICEBOATS
ABCEIRRT	CATBRIER
	CRIBRATE
ABCEIRSS	ASCRIBES
ABCEIRSW	CRABWISE
ABCEIRTT	BRATTICE
ABCEIRTY	ACERBITY
ABCEISSS	ABSCISES
	ABSCISSE
ABCEISST	ASBESTIC
ABCEISTT	TABETICS
ABCEJKLU	BLUEJACK
ABCEJLTY	ABJECTLY
ABCEKKRU	BUCKRAKE
ABCEKKSW	SKEWBACK
ABCEKLLO	LOCKABLE
ABCEKLMO	MOCKABLE
ABCEKLNS	BLACKENS
ABCEKLOO	COOKABLE
ABCEKLOS	BECLOAKS
ABCEKLPU	PALEBUCK
ABCEKLSS	BACKLESS
ABCEKLST	BLACKEST
ABCEKNRS	BRACKENS
ABCEKOOS	BOOKCASE
	CASEBOOK
ABCEKORY	ROCKABYE
ABCEKRST	BACKREST
	BRACKETS
ABCEKSST	BACKSETS
	SETBACKS
ABCEKSSY	BACKSEYS
ABCEKSTW	WETBACKS
ABCELLOS	CLOSABLE
ABCELLPU	CULPABLE
ABCELLRU	BRUCELLA
ABCELLSU	BUCELLAS
	BULLACES
ABCELMNY	LAMBENCY
ABCELMOR	BECLAMOR
ABCELMOS	CEMBALOS
ABCELMRS	CAMBRELS
	CLAMBERS
	SCAMBLER
	SCRAMBLE
ABCELMRY	CYMBALER
ABCELMSS	SCAMBLES
ABCELNOT	BALCONET
ABCELNUU	NUBECULA
ABCELOOT	BOOTLACE
ABCELOPS	PLACEBOS
ABCELORT	BROCATEL
ABCELOST	OBSTACLE
ABCELOSV	VOCABLES
ABCELOTU	BLUECOAT
ABCELPSS	BECLASPS
ABCELPSU	BLUECAPS
ABCELPSY	BYPLACES
ABCELRSU	ARBUSCLE
ABCELRSW	BECRAWLS
	BESCRAWL
ABCELRTT	BRACTLET
ABCELSSU	BASCULES
	SUBSCALE
ABCELTTU	CUTTABLE
ABCEMORS	CRAMBOES
ABCEMORT	COMBATER
ABCENORS	BACONERS
ABCENOSW	COWBANES
ABCENOSZ	CABEZONS
ABCENOUY	BUOYANCE
ABCENRSU	UNBRACES
ABCENTUX	EXCUBANT
ABCEOOSS	CABOOSES
ABCEOPUU	BEAUCOUP
ABCEORRS	BRACEROS
ABCEORST	CABESTRO
	CABRESTO
ABCEORSU	CORBEAUS
ABCEOSUX	SAUCEBOX
ABCEPSSU	SUBSPACE
ABCERRTU	CARBURET
ABCERSSU	SUBRACES
ABCERTUU	CUBATURE
ABCESSTU	SUBCASTE
ABCESSUU	SUBCAUSE
ABCESTUU	SUBACUTE
ABCFIKLL	BACKFILL
ABCFIKLN	BLACKFIN
ABCFIKLT	BACKLIFT
	LIFTBACK
ABCFIKNS	FINBACKS
ABCFIKST	BACKFITS
ABCFILOS	BIFOCALS
ABCFKLLU	FULLBACK
ABCFKLLY	BLACKFLY
ABCFKLOW	BACKFLOW
ABCFKOST	SOFTBACK
ABCGGIMO	GAMBOGIC
ABCGHINT	BATCHING
ABCGHKOS	HOGBACKS
ABCGIINN	CABINING
ABCGIKLN	BLACKING
ABCGIKNS	BACKINGS
ABCGIKNW	WINGBACK
ABCGILNS	CABLINGS
ABCGINRS	BRACINGS
ABCGKLMU	BLACKGUM
ABCGKLOS	BACKLOGS
ABCGLNOX	CLANGBOX
ABCGMSSU	SCUMBAGS
ABCHHIIS	HIBACHIS
ABCHIIPS	BIPHASIC
ABCHIKLS	BLACKISH
ABCHIKRS	BRACKISH
ABCHILMO	CHOLIAMB
ABCHILOO	COOLIBAH
ABCHIMOR	CHORIAMB
ABCHIMRU	BRACHIUM
ABCHINOR	BRONCHIA
ABCHIOOR	BORACHIO
ABCHIOST	COHABITS
ABCHIRRT	TRIBRACH
ABCHKLOT	HACKBOLT
ABCHKMPU	HUMPBACK
ABCHKOOP	CHAPBOOK
ABCHKOOS	CASHBOOK
ABCHKOSU	CHABOUKS
ABCHKRSU	BACKRUSH
ABCHKSTU	HACKBUTS
ABCHKSUW	HAWBUCKS
ABCHLLUU	CLUBHAUL
ABCHMOTX	MATCHBOX
ABCHNORS	BROCHANS
ABCHOORR	ROORBACH
ABCHOTWX	WATCHBOX
ABCIILMU	BULIMIAC
ABCIILOT	BIOTICAL
ABCIIMNS	MINICABS
ABCIINOT	CIBATION
ABCIINSS	ABSCISIN
ABCIIORS	ISOBARIC
ABCIIRST	TRIBASIC
ABCIISTY	BASICITY
ABCIITUX	BAUXITIC
ABCIJNOS	JACOBINS
ABCIKKLL	KICKBALL
ABCIKLST	BACKLIST
ABCIKLTU	BUCKTAIL
ABCIKNPS	BACKSPIN
ABCIKSSY	SICKBAYS
ABCILLNY	BILLYCAN
ABCILLRU	LUBRICAL
ABCILLSU	BACILLUS
ABCILLSY	SYLLABIC
ABCILMMO	CIMBALOM
ABCILMSU	SUBCLAIM
ABCILNOR	CARBINOL
ABCILNOS	COALBINS
ABCILNPU	PUBLICAN
ABCILOOR	COOLIBAR
ABCILOSY	SOCIABLY
ABCILRRU	RUBRICAL
ABCIMMSS	CAMBISMS
ABCIMMSU	CAMBIUMS
ABCIMORR	MICROBAR
ABCIMRTU	UMBRATIC
ABCIMSST	CAMBISTS
ABCINNOS	NONBASIC
ABCINORS	CORBINAS
ABCINORU	CONURBIA
ABCINORY	BARYONIC
ABCINRVY	VIBRANCY
ABCIOPRS	SAPROBIC
ABCIORRS	BARRICOS
ABCIORSU	CARIBOUS
ABCIOSSU	SCABIOUS
ABCIOSUV	BIVOUACS
ABCIRSTT	ABSTRICT
ABCIRSUV	SUBVICAR
ABCJKOOT	BOOTJACK
	JACKBOOT
ABCKKOOR	BOOKRACK
ABCKKORW	BACKWORK
ABCKLLOR	ROLLBACK
ABCKLLOS	BALLOCKS
ABCKLLPU	PULLBACK
ABCKLNNO	NONBLACK
ABCKLOPT	BLACKTOP
ABCKLOPW	PLOWBACK
ABCKLOST	BACKLOTS
	SLOTBACK
ABCKLOSW	SLOWBACK
ABCKLOTU	BLACKOUT
ABCKMOOR	BACKROOM
ABCKMORR	BROCKRAM
ABCKMOSS	MOSSBACK
ABCKMOST	BACKMOST
	TOMBACKS
ABCKMRSU	BUCKRAMS
ABCKMSUZ	ZAMBUCKS
ABCKNNOS	BANNOCKS
ABCKNRSU	RUNBACKS
ABCKNRTU	TURNBACK
ABCKNSTU	CUTBANKS
ABCKOORR	ROORBACK
ABCKOORU	BUCKAROO
ABCKOPST	BACKSTOP
ABCKORUY	BUCKAYRO
ABCKOSSW	SOWBACKS
ABCKOSTU	BACKOUTS
	OUTBACKS
ABCKSSTU	SACKBUTS
	SUBTACKS
ABCKSSUW	BUCKSAWS
	SAWBUCKS
ABCLLNOR	CORNBALL
ABCLLOSY	CALLBOYS
ABCLLPUY	CULPABLY
ABCLMMOY	CYMBALOM
ABCLMOOO	COLOBOMA
ABCLMOSY	CYMBALOS
ABCLMSUU	BACULUMS
ABCLMSUY	SCYBALUM
ABCLNORY	CARBONYL
ABCLNSSU	SUBCLANS
ABCLORXY	CARBOXYL
ABCLOSUV	SUBVOCAL
ABCLSSSU	SUBCLASS
ABCLSUUU	SUBUCULA
ABCMOORT	MOBOCRAT
ABCNNORU	CONURBAN
ABCNORTY	CORYBANT
ABCNOUYY	BUOYANCY
ABCORRSS	CROSSBAR
ABCORRSW	CROWBARS
ABCORRTU	TURBOCAR
ABCORSSU	SCABROUS
ABCOSSTU	SUBCOSTA
ABCOSTTU	COTTABUS
ABCRSTTU	SUBTRACT
ABDDDEEM	BEMADDED
ABDDDEET	ADDEBTED
ABDDEEEH	BEHEADED
ABDDEEEK	DEBEAKED
ABDDEEGG	DEBAGGED
ABDDEEGR	BADGERED
	REBADGED
ABDDEEHS	BEDASHED
ABDDEEHT	DEATHBED
ABDDEEIL	BELADIED
ABDDEEKR	DEBARKED
ABDDEELU	BELAUDED
ABDDEEMN	BEDAMNED
	BEMADDEN
ABDDEENY	BENDAYED
ABDDEEPR	BEDRAPED
ABDDEERR	DEBARRED
ABDDEEST	BEDSTEAD
	BESTADDE
ABDDEGIR	ABRIDGED
	BRIGADED
ABDDEHMO	HEBDOMAD
ABDDEHMU	DUMBHEAD
ABDDEHOY	HOBDAYED
ABDDEILS	DISABLED
ABDDEILU	BUDDLEIA
ABDDEINR	BRANDIED
ABDDEINS	SIDEBAND
ABDDEINW	WIDEBAND
ABDDEIRR	BRAIRDED

ABDDELOT	DEADBOLT
ABDDELRS	BLADDERS
ABDDELRY	BLADDERY
ABDDENNU	UNBANDED
ABDDENOU	ABOUNDED
ABDDENST	BEDSTAND
ABDDEORS	ADSORBED
	ROADBEDS
ABDDERSW	BEDWARDS
ABDDGILN	BLADDING
ABDDGINR	BRADDING
ABDDHIOR	RHABDOID
ABDDILMO	LAMBDOID
ABDDILRY	LADYBIRD
ABDDIMNO	BONDMAID
ABDDINSS	DISBANDS
ABDDIRRY	YARDBIRD
ABDDLLOS	ODDBALLS
ABDDMORS	DAMBRODS
ABDEEEFL	BEFLEAED
	FEEDABLE
ABDEEEFN	BEDEAFEN
ABDEEELP	BELEAPED
ABDEEEMN	BEMEANED
ABDEEERV	BEAVERED
	BEREAVED
ABDEEFGS	FEEDBAGS
ABDEEFIT	TABEFIED
ABDEEFLM	FLAMBEED
ABDEEFLS	FEELBADS
ABDEEFMO	BEFOAMED
ABDEEFMR	BEDFRAME
ABDEEGGL	BEDAGGLE
ABDEEGGR	BEGGARED
ABDEEGHR	HERBAGED
ABDEEGLL	BEGALLED
	GABELLED
ABDEEGNW	BEGNAWED
ABDEEGRS	REBADGES
ABDEEGRU	BEDEGUAR
ABDEEHLS	SHEDABLE
ABDEEHLU	BLUEHEAD
ABDEEHMS	BESHAMED
ABDEEHMT	EMBATHED
ABDEEHNO	BONEHEAD
ABDEEHRT	BREATHED
ABDEEHSS	BEDASHES
ABDEEHST	BETHESDA
ABDEEHTT	BEHATTED
ABDEEIKL	BEADLIKE
ABDEEIKR	BIDARKEE
ABDEEILM	EMBAILED
ABDEEILN	DENIABLE
ABDEEILR	RIDEABLE
ABDEEILS	ABSEILED
	BELADIES
ABDEEILT	DELIBATE
	EDITABLE
ABDEEILV	EVADIBLE
ABDEEILW	BEWAILED
ABDEEIPR	BEDIAPER
ABDEEIRS	BEARDIES
ABDEEIRT	EBRIATED
	REBAITED
ABDEEIST	BEADIEST
	DIABETES
ABDEEITU	BEAUTIED
ABDEEJMN	ENJAMBED
ABDEEJST	JETBEADS
ABDEEKMN	EMBANKED
ABDEEKMR	BEDMAKER
	EMBARKED
ABDEEKNR	BARKENED
	BEDARKEN
ABDEEKNV	BEKNAVED
ABDEEKPR	PREBAKED
ABDEELLL	LABELLED
ABDEELLM	EMBALLED
ABDEELLN	LENDABLE
ABDEELLT	BALLETED
ABDEELLW	WELDABLE
ABDEELMM	EMBALMED
ABDEELMN	MENDABLE
ABDEELMS	BELDAMES
	BEMEDALS
ABDEELMU	BEMAULED
ABDEELMZ	EMBLAZED
ABDEELNS	SENDABLE
ABDEELNT	BANDELET
ABDEELNV	VENDABLE
ABDEELOR	LEEBOARD
ABDEELOS	ALBEDOES
ABDEELPT	BEDPLATE
ABDEELRR	BARRELED
ABDEELRS	BEDERALS
ABDEELRV	DEVERBAL
ABDEELRZ	BLAZERED
ABDEELSV	BESLAVED
ABDEELTT	BATTELED
	TABLETED
ABDEELZZ	BEDAZZLE
ABDEEMNO	BEMOANED
ABDEEMNS	BEADSMEN
	BEDESMAN
ABDEEMRR	EMBARRED
ABDEEMRS	EMBREADS
ABDEEMRV	EMBRAVED
ABDEEMST	BEDMATES
ABDEENNR	BANNERED
ABDEENRT	BANTERED
ABDEENRU	UNBEARED
ABDEENRZ	BRAZENED
ABDEENST	ABSENTED
ABDEENTT	BATTENED
ABDEEPRS	BEDRAPES
	BESPREAD
ABDEEPTT	BEPATTED
ABDEERRT	BARTERED
ABDEERRY	RYEBREAD
ABDEERSS	DEBASERS
ABDEERST	BETREADS
	BREASTED
	DEBATERS
ABDEERSY	BEEYARDS
ABDEERTT	BATTERED
	DRABETTE
ABDEERTW	WATERBED
ABDEERTY	BETRAYED
ABDEERWY	BEWRAYED
ABDEESST	BASSETED
	BESTEADS
ABDEFIIS	BASIFIED
ABDEFILN	FINDABLE
ABDEFLLO	FOLDABLE
ABDEFLNU	FUNDABLE
	UNFABLED
ABDEFLOR	FORDABLE
ABDEFLST	FLATBEDS
ABDEFLSU	LEAFBUDS
ABDEFNRU	FABURDEN
ABDEFRSW	BEDWARFS
ABDEGGIL	DIGGABLE
ABDEGGNU	UNBAGGED
ABDEGHIS	BIGHEADS
ABDEGHRS	BEGHARDS
ABDEGIJN	BEJADING
ABDEGILM	GIMBALED
ABDEGILN	BLINDAGE
ABDEGILU	GUIDABLE
ABDEGIMT	GAMBITED
ABDEGINO	GABIONED
ABDEGINR	BEARDING
	BREADING
ABDEGINS	BEADINGS
	DEBASING
ABDEGINT	DEBATING
ABDEGINZ	BEDAZING
ABDEGIRR	ABRIDGER
ABDEGIRS	ABRIDGES
	BRIGADES
ABDEGLMO	GAMBOLED
ABDEGLNR	BRANGLED
ABDEGLOT	GLOBATED
ABDEGLRS	BELGARDS
ABDEGLRY	BADGERLY
ABDEGLSU	SLUGABED
ABDEGMRU	UMBRAGED
ABDEGNOR	BONDAGER
ABDEGNOS	BONDAGES
	DOGBANES
ABDEGOPR	PEGBOARD
ABDEGRSU	SUBGRADE
ABDEHILL	BILLHEAD
ABDEHILS	DISHABLE
ABDEHIMT	IMBATHED
ABDEHINS	BANISHED
ABDEHITU	HABITUDE
ABDEHKLU	BULKHEAD
ABDEHLLN	HANDBELL
ABDEHLLO	HOLDABLE
ABDEHLLU	BULLHEAD
ABDEHLMS	SHAMBLED
ABDEHLOT	BOLTHEAD
ABDEHLRS	HALBERDS
ABDEHMNO	HAMBONED
ABDEHMOR	RHABDOME
ABDEHMRU	RHUMBAED
ABDEHMSU	AMBUSHED
ABDEHNTU	UNBATHED
ABDEHORR	ABHORRED
	HARBORED
ABDEHOSW	BESHADOW
	BOWHEADS
ABDEHRST	BREADTHS
ABDEHSSU	SUBHEADS
ABDEIIRT	DIATRIBE
ABDEIKMR	IMBARKED
ABDEIKNS	BANKSIDE
ABDEIKNU	BAUDEKIN
ABDEILLR	BRAILLED
ABDEILLS	SLIDABLE
ABDEILMM	DIMMABLE
	IMBALMED
ABDEILMN	MANDIBLE
ABDEILMS	SEMIBALD
ABDEILMZ	IMBLAZED
ABDEILNR	BILANDER
ABDEILNT	BIDENTAL
ABDEILNW	WINDABLE
ABDEILNY	DENIABLY
ABDEILOV	VOIDABLE
ABDEILOX	OXIDABLE
ABDEILPP	DIPPABLE
ABDEILPS	PIEBALDS
ABDEILRS	BEDRAILS
	RAILBEDS
ABDEILRT	LIBRATED
ABDEILRV	DRIVABLE
ABDEILRY	DIABLERY
ABDEILSS	DISABLES
ABDEILST	BALDIEST
ABDEILSU	AUDIBLES
ABDEILSY	BIASEDLY
ABDEILTU	DUTIABLE
ABDEILVV	BIVALVED
ABDEIMNR	BRIDEMAN
ABDEIMOO	AMOEBOID
ABDEIMOR	AMBEROID
ABDEIMRR	IMBARRED
ABDEIMRS	EMBRAIDS
ABDEINNR	ENDBRAIN
ABDEINOR	DEBONAIR
ABDEINOS	BEDSONIA
ABDEINOT	OBTAINED
ABDEINRS	BRANDIES
	BRANDISE
ABDEINST	BANDIEST
ABDEINSU	UNBIASED
ABDEINSW	BEDAWINS
ABDEINTU	UNBAITED
ABDEIOTV	OBVIATED
ABDEIPRT	BIPARTED
ABDEIPST	BAPTISED
ABDEIPTZ	BAPTIZED
ABDEIRRS	BRAIDERS
ABDEIRSS	SEABIRDS
	SIDEBARS
ABDEIRST	BARDIEST
	BRAIDEST
	RABIDEST
	REDBAITS
	TRIBADES
ABDEIRSU	DAUBRIES
ABDEIRSW	BAWDRIES
	DAWBRIES
ABDEIRTV	VIBRATED
ABDEISST	BASTIDES
ABDEISSU	DISABUSE
	SUBIDEAS
ABDEISTU	DAUBIEST
ABDEISTW	BAWDIEST
ABDEITTU	DUBITATE
ABDEJNOW	JAWBONED
ABDEKLSW	SKEWBALD
ABDEKNNU	UNBANKED
ABDEKNRU	UNBARKED
	UNBRAKED
ABDEKNSU	SUNBAKED
ABDEKOOR	ABROOKED
ABDEKORW	BEADWORK
ABDEKORY	KEYBOARD
ABDEKOTU	OUTBAKED
ABDELLMO	MOLDABLE
ABDELLOR	BEADROLL
ABDELLOT	BALLOTED
ABDELMNU	UNBLAMED
ABDELMPS	BEDLAMPS
ABDELNOR	BANDEROL
ABDELNOU	UNDOABLE
ABDELNOZ	BLAZONED
ABDELNRY	BYLANDER
ABDELNSS	BALDNESS
ABDELNST	BLANDEST
ABDELORU	LABOURED
ABDELOSV	ABSOLVED
ABDELOSW	DOWSABEL
ABDELPSY	PYEBALDS
ABDELRRS	DRABLERS
ABDELRSU	DURABLES
ABDELRTT	BRATTLED
ABDELSTU	SUBLATED
ABDEMNNS	BANDSMEN
ABDEMNNY	BANDYMEN
ABDEMNOR	BOARDMEN
ABDEMNOS	ABDOMENS
ABDEMORT	BROMATED
ABDEMRSU	BERMUDAS
ABDEMRTU	DRUMBEAT
	UMBRATED
ABDENNNU	UNBANNED

ABDENNOS	NOSEBAND
ABDENOOT	BATOONED
ABDENORS	BANDORES
	BROADENS
ABDENORW	RAWBONED
ABDENORY	BONEYARD
ABDENOTW	DOWNBEAT
ABDENRRS	BRANDERS
ABDENRRU	UNBARRED
ABDENRSS	DRABNESS
ABDENRST	BANDSTER
	BARTENDS
ABDENRTU	BREADNUT
	TURBANED
ABDENSSU	SUBDEANS
ABDENSUU	UNABUSED
ABDENSWY	BENDWAYS
ABDENTTU	DEBUTANT
ABDEOORW	BEARWOOD
ABDEOPRT	PROBATED
ABDEORRS	ADSORBER
	BOARDERS
	REBOARDS
ABDEORRU	ARBOURED
ABDEORRW	DRAWBORE
	WARDROBE
ABDEORST	BROADEST
ABDEORSW	SOWBREAD
ABDEORTU	OBDURATE
	TABOURED
ABDEORUX	BORDEAUX
ABDEOSTU	BOUTADES
ABDEPRSU	SUPERBAD
ABDEPRUY	UPBRAYED
ABDEPSSY	BYPASSED
ABDERRSU	ABSURDER
ABDERSST	DABSTERS
ABDERSSU	SUBEDARS
	SURBASED
ABDERSTU	SURBATED
ABDERSTW	BEDSTRAW
ABDERSTY	DRYBEATS
ABDERTUW	DRAWTUBE
ABDESUWY	SUBWAYED
ABDFILOR	FORBIDAL
ABDFIMRR	BIRDFARM
ABDFIRST	FATBIRDS
ABDFLOOT	FOLDBOAT
ABDFNORU	FUNBOARD
ABDGGORS	BOGGARDS
ABDGHINR	HANGBIRD
ABDGIINR	BRAIDING
ABDGIINS	ABIDINGS
ABDGILNR	BARDLING
ABDGILNU	BLAUDING
ABDGIMRU	GUIMBARD
ABDGINNR	BRANDING
ABDGINNS	BANDINGS
ABDGINNY	BANDYING
ABDGINOR	ABORDING
	BOARDING
ABDGINRS	BRIGANDS
ABDGINST	DINGBATS
ABDGINSU	DAUBINGS
ABDGINSW	WINDBAGS
ABDGIRST	DIRTBAGS
ABDGLNOS	BOGLANDS
ABDGLOOR	LOGBOARD
ABDGLSUY	LADYBUGS
ABDHHSSU	SHADBUSH
ABDHIIST	ADHIBITS
	DISHABIT
ABDHILLN	HANDBILL
ABDHILNS	BLANDISH
ABDHINRS	BRANDISH
ABDHIORS	BROADISH
ABDHIPRS	BARDSHIP
ABDHIRTY	BIRTHDAY
ABDHKNOO	HANDBOOK
ABDHLNSU	BUSHLAND
ABDHLORW	BLOWHARD
ABDHLOSW	SHADBLOW
ABDHMORS	RHABDOMS
ABDHMOTU	BADMOUTH
ABDHMSTU	MUDBATHS
ABDHNORS	BODHRANS
ABDHNSSU	HUSBANDS
ABDHOORT	HARDBOOT
ABDIIJLR	JAILBIRD
ABDIILLR	BILLIARD
ABDIILRR	RAILBIRD
ABDIIMNR	MIDBRAIN
ABDIIMSU	BASIDIUM
ABDIINOS	OBSIDIAN
ABDIINRR	RAINBIRD
ABDIINTT	BANDITTI
ABDIIORT	ORIBATID
ABDIIRTY	RABIDITY
ABDIJRSY	JAYBIRDS
ABDIKLNR	BLINKARD
ABDIKLOU	KILOBAUD
ABDIKNSW	BAWDKINS
ABDIKRSS	DISBARKS
ABDILLRY	BRIDALLY
	RIBALDLY
ABDILOOS	DIABOLOS
ABDILORS	LABROIDS
ABDILOST	BLASTOID
	TABLOIDS
ABDILOTY	TABLOIDY
ABDILRRY	RIBALDRY
ABDILRSW	AWLBIRDS
ABDILRZZ	BLIZZARD
ABDILSTU	SUBTIDAL
ABDIMNRS	MISBRAND
ABDIMORS	AMBROIDS
ABDINORS	INBOARDS
ABDINORU	AIRBOUND
ABDINOTY	ANTIBODY
ABDINRST	ANTBIRDS
ABDINRSU	UNBRAIDS
ABDINRTY	BANDITRY
ABDIOSUU	SUBAUDIO
ABDIPRSU	UPBRAIDS
ABDIRRUY	RIBAUDRY
ABDJMOOR	DOORJAMB
ABDKLNOO	BOOKLAND
ABDKNOOS	BANDOOKS
ABDKOOSY	DAYBOOKS
ABDLLNOS	SLOBLAND
ABDLLORS	BOLLARDS
ABDLNORS	BANDROLS
ABDLNOSU	SUBNODAL
ABDLOSSU	BUSLOADS
ABDLRSUU	SUBDURAL
ABDLRSUY	ABSURDLY
	RYBAULDS
ABDLSSUU	SUBDUALS
ABDLSTUU	SUBADULT
ABDMNNOS	BONDSMAN
ABDMNOUW	MAWBOUND
ABDMOOPR	MOPBOARD
ABDMRSUY	MARYBUDS
ABDNNNOR	NONBRAND
ABDNOORS	BRADOONS
ABDNOPRS	PROBANDS
ABDNORSU	BAUDRONS
ABDNORUY	BOUNDARY
ABDNOSSY	SANDBOYS
ABDNRRSU	SANDBURR
ABDNRSSU	SANDBURS
ABDNRSTU	TURBANDS
ABDNSSTY	STANDBYS
ABDOORSW	BARWOODS
ABDOORTU	OUTBOARD
ABDOOSSW	BASSWOOD
ABDOOSWY	BAYWOODS
ABDRSSTU	BUSTARDS
ABDRSUZZ	BUZZARDS
ABEEEFLR	REEFABLE
ABEEEFRS	FREEBASE
ABEEEGRS	BARGEESE
	BEERAGES
ABEEEGRV	BEVERAGE
ABEEEHTT	HEBETATE
ABEEEKLP	KEEPABLE
ABEEELLP	PEELABLE
ABEEELLR	REELABLE
ABEEEMSY	EYEBEAMS
ABEEENRT	TENEBRAE
ABEEENRV	BEREAVEN
ABEEENST	ABSENTEE
ABEEERRT	TEREBRAE
ABEEERRV	BEREAVER
ABEEERSV	BEREAVES
ABEEFFTU	BEAUFFET
ABEEFILL	FILEABLE
ABEEFILN	FINEABLE
ABEEFILR	AFEBRILE
	BALEFIRE
	FIREABLE
ABEEFILS	FEASIBLE
ABEEFILT	FLEABITE
ABEEFIRS	FIREBASE
ABEEFIST	TABEFIES
ABEEFLLL	FELLABLE
ABEEFLLN	BEFALLEN
ABEEFLOS	BEEFALOS
ABEEFORR	FOREBEAR
ABEEFSTU	BEAUFETS
ABEEGHRS	HERBAGES
ABEEGHRT	BERTHAGE
ABEEGILV	GIVEABLE
ABEEGINR	BAREGINE
	BERGENIA
ABEEGIRV	VERBIAGE
ABEEGLLR	GABELLER
ABEEGLLS	GABELLES
ABEEGLRS	BEAGLERS
ABEEGLTT	GETTABLE
ABEEGMNR	BARGEMEN
ABEEGMRT	BREGMATE
ABEEGMTY	MEGABYTE
ABEEGOSZ	GAZEBOES
ABEEGRRS	GERBERAS
ABEEGRST	ABSTERGE
ABEEGRSU	AUBERGES
ABEEGRSW	BREWAGES
ABEEGTTU	BAGUETTE
ABEEHILR	HIREABLE
ABEEHINT	THEBAINE
ABEEHIRZ	HEBRAIZE
ABEEHLLL	HEELBALL
ABEEHLLP	HELPABLE
ABEEHLLR	BEERHALL
	HAREBELL
ABEEHLSV	BEHALVES
ABEEHMSS	BESHAMES
ABEEHMST	EMBATHES
ABEEHNNS	HENBANES
ABEEHNPP	BEHAPPEN
ABEEHNSS	BANSHEES
	SHEBEANS
ABEEHNTT	HEBETANT
ABEEHORS	RHEOBASE
ABEEHQTU	BEQUEATH
ABEEHRRT	BREATHER
ABEEHRST	BREATHES
	HARTBEES
ABEEHRSV	BEHAVERS
ABEEIKKL	BEAKLIKE
ABEEIKLL	LIKEABLE
ABEEIKLM	BEAMLIKE
ABEEIKLN	BEANLIKE
ABEEIKLR	BEARLIKE
ABEEIKRS	BAKERIES
ABEEIKST	BEAKIEST
ABEEILLN	LIENABLE
	LINEABLE
ABEEILLR	RELIABLE
ABEEILLV	LEVIABLE
	LIVEABLE
ABEEILMN	MINEABLE
ABEEILMS	BELAMIES
ABEEILNN	BIENNALE
ABEEILNP	PLEBEIAN
ABEEILNS	BASELINE
ABEEILNU	BANLIEUE
ABEEILNV	ENVIABLE
ABEEILPX	EXPIABLE
ABEEILRR	BLEARIER
ABEEILRT	LIBERATE
ABEEILRW	BEWAILER
ABEEILSS	SEISABLE
ABEEILST	SEABLITE
ABEEILSV	EVASIBLE
ABEEILSZ	SEIZABLE
	SIZEABLE
ABEEILTV	EVITABLE
ABEEILVW	VIEWABLE
ABEEIMRS	AMBERIES
ABEEIMRT	AMBERITE
ABEEIMST	BEAMIEST
ABEEINST	BETAINES
ABEEINTY	AYENBITE
ABEEIPRS	BEPRAISE
ABEEIRTT	BATTERIE
ABEEIRTV	BREVIATE
ABEEISST	BEASTIES
ABEEISSV	ABESSIVE
ABEEISTU	BEAUTIES
ABEEITUX	BEAUXITE
ABEEJMOR	JAMBOREE
ABEEKLOT	KEELBOAT
ABEEKLSS	BEAKLESS
ABEEKLST	BLEAKEST
ABEEKMNR	BRAKEMEN
	EMBANKER
ABEEKMRR	REEMBARK
ABEEKNSV	BEKNAVES
ABEEKOOP	PEEKABOO
ABEEKOPS	PEEKABOS
ABEEKORV	OVERBAKE
ABEEKPRS	BARKEEPS
	PREBAKES
ABEEKPSS	BESPEAKS
ABEEKRRS	BREAKERS
ABEEKRST	BESTREAK
ABEELLLR	LABELLER
ABEELLLS	SELLABLE
ABEELLLT	TELLABLE
ABEELLMT	MELTABLE
ABEELLOT	BALLOTEE
ABEELLOV	LOVEABLE
ABEELLRS	LABELERS
	RELABELS
ABEELLSY	EYEBALLS
ABEELLTT	LETTABLE
ABEELMMR	EMBALMER
	EMMARBLE

ABEELMNO	BONEMEAL
ABEELMOV	MOVEABLE
ABEELMPR	PREAMBLE
ABEELMRT	ATREMBLE
ABEELMRZ	EMBLAZER
ABEELMSS	ASSEMBLE
	BEAMLESS
ABEELMST	BEAMLETS
ABEELMSZ	EMBLAZES
ABEELMTT	EMBATTLE
ABEELNOP	BEANPOLE
	OPENABLE
ABEELNRS	ENABLERS
ABEELNRT	RENTABLE
ABEELNST	NESTABLE
ABEELNTT	NETTABLE
ABEELNTU	TUNEABLE
ABEELOPR	OPERABLE
	ROPEABLE
ABEELOPS	POSEABLE
ABEELORS	EARLOBES
ABEELORV	OVERABLE
ABEELORX	EXORABLE
ABEELOTV	VOTEABLE
ABEELPRS	BEPEARLS
ABEELPTY	TYPEABLE
ABEELRST	ARBELEST
	BLEAREST
	BLEATERS
	RETABLES
ABEELRSU	REUSABLE
ABEELRSV	BESLAVER
	SERVABLE
ABEELRTT	BATTELER
ABEELRTU	BATELEUR
	BLEUATRE
ABEELSSS	BASELESS
ABEELSST	BATELESS
	BEATLESS
ABEELSSU	SUBLEASE
ABEELSSV	BESLAVES
ABEELSTT	TESTABLE
ABEELTTW	WETTABLE
ABEEMMNR	MEMBRANE
ABEEMMRU	BUMMAREE
ABEEMNOR	BEMOANER
ABEEMNST	BASEMENT
ABEEMNTT	ABETMENT
	BATEMENT
ABEEMRSS	BESMEARS
ABEEMRSV	EMBRAVES
ABEENNRT	BANNERET
ABEENNRU	EBURNEAN
ABEENNTU	UNBEATEN
ABEENORS	SEABORNE
ABEENOTZ	BENZOATE
ABEENRRR	BARRENER
ABEENRRT	BANTERER
ABEENRSS	BARENESS
ABEENRST	ABSENTER
ABEENRSV	VERBENAS
ABEENRTT	BATTENER
ABEENSSS	BASENESS
ABEEORRV	OVERBEAR
ABEEORST	ABORTEES
	REBATOES
ABEEORTV	OVERBEAT
ABEEOSTX	TEABOXES
ABEEPRRU	UPBEARER
ABEEPRRY	PEABERRY
ABEEQSUU	USQUEBAE
ABEERRRT	BARTERER
ABEERRST	REBATERS
	TABRERES
	TEREBRAS
ABEERRTT	BARRETTE
	BATTERER
	BERRETTA
ABEERRTV	VERTEBRA
ABEERRTY	BETRAYER
	TEABERRY
ABEERRWY	BEWRAYER
ABEERSTT	ABETTERS
	BERETTAS
ABEERSTU	SUBERATE
ABEERTTT	BETATTER
ABEESZZZ	BEZAZZES
ABEETTUX	EXTUBATE
ABEFFLRS	BAFFLERS
ABEFFOST	OFFBEATS
ABEFGILS	FILABEGS
ABEFGLLR	BERGFALL
ABEFGSST	GABFESTS
ABEFHILS	FISHABLE
ABEFHOOT	HOOFBEAT
ABEFIIMR	FIMBRIAE
ABEFIIRS	BASIFIER
ABEFIISS	BASIFIES
ABEFILLL	FALLIBLE
ABEFILLM	FILMABLE
ABEFILLO	FOILABLE
ABEFILLR	FIREBALL
ABEFILLT	LIFTABLE
ABEFILOT	LIFEBOAT
ABEFILRS	BARFLIES
ABEFILSU	FABULISE
ABEFILSY	FEASIBLY
ABEFILTT	FITTABLE
ABEFILUZ	FABULIZE
ABEFINNR	FIBRANNE
ABEFINSU	BEAUFINS
ABEFIORT	BIFORATE
	FIREBOAT
ABEFIRRT	FIREBRAT
ABEFITUY	BEAUTIFY
ABEFLLMU	BLAMEFUL
ABEFLLRU	FURLABLE
ABEFLLTU	TABLEFUL
ABEFLMOR	FORMABLE
ABEFLNRU	FUNEBRAL
ABEFLNSY	FLYBANES
ABEFLOTU	OUTFABLE
ABEFLRSU	SURFABLE
ABEFMRSU	SUBFRAME
ABEFOORT	BAREFOOT
ABEFORRS	FORBEARS
ABEFORSY	FOREBAYS
ABEGGHLU	HUGGABLE
ABEGGILN	BEAGLING
ABEGGINZ	BEGAZING
ABEGGIRR	BRAGGIER
ABEGGIST	BAGGIEST
ABEGGITY	GIGABYTE
ABEGGLLU	LUGGABLE
ABEGGLRS	BLAGGERS
ABEGGLRY	BEGGARLY
ABEGGMOS	GAMBOGES
ABEGGNSU	BUGGANES
ABEGGRRS	BRAGGERS
ABEGGRST	BRAGGEST
ABEGGRSU	BURGAGES
ABEGHILP	PHILABEG
ABEGHILR	ALBERGHI
ABEGHINO	OBEAHING
ABEGHINT	BEATHING
ABEGHINV	BEHAVING
ABEGHNSS	SHEBANGS
ABEGHORR	BEGORRAH
ABEGHOSU	BAGHOUSE
ABEGHRRY	HAGBERRY
ABEGHRST	BARGHEST
ABEGHRSU	BEARHUGS
ABEGIIMS	BIGAMIES
ABEGIINO	IBOGAINE
ABEGIJTU	BIJUGATE
ABEGIKNR	BERAKING
	BREAKING
ABEGIKNT	BETAKING
ABEGILLN	LABELING
ABEGILMN	EMBALING
ABEGILNN	ENABLING
ABEGILNR	BLEARING
ABEGILNS	SINGABLE
ABEGILNT	BELATING
	BLEATING
	TANGIBLE
ABEGILNY	BELAYING
ABEGILOT	OBLIGATE
ABEGIMNN	BENAMING
ABEGIMNR	BREAMING
ABEGIMNS	BEAMINGS
	EMBASING
	MISBEGAN
ABEGIMNY	EMBAYING
ABEGIMRS	GAMBIERS
ABEGIMST	MEGABITS
ABEGIMUX	GIAMBEUX
ABEGINOR	ABORIGEN
ABEGINOS	BEGONIAS
ABEGINRS	BEARINGS
	SABERING
ABEGINRT	BERATING
	REBATING
	TABERING
ABEGINRW	BEWARING
ABEGINRY	BERAYING
ABEGINST	BEATINGS
ABEGINTT	ABETTING
ABEGINTW	WINGBEAT
ABEGIOSS	BIOGASES
ABEGIPPR	BAGPIPER
ABEGIPPS	BAGPIPES
ABEGKLSU	BULKAGES
ABEGKORS	BROKAGES
	GROSBEAK
ABEGKOSS	BOSKAGES
ABEGLLLU	GULLABLE
ABEGLLOR	BARGELLO
ABEGLMOR	BEGLAMOR
ABEGLMRS	GAMBLERS
	GAMBRELS
ABEGLMUY	MEALYBUG
ABEGLNRS	BRANGLES
ABEGLORW	GROWABLE
ABEGLRRS	GARBLERS
ABEGLRSS	GARBLESS
ABEGLRUU	BLAGUEUR
ABEGLSTU	GUSTABLE
ABEGMNOS	GAMBESON
ABEGMNOY	BOGEYMAN
	MONEYBAG
ABEGMORT	BERGAMOT
ABEGMRSU	UMBRAGES
ABEGNNST	BANTENGS
ABEGNORS	BEGROANS
ABEGNOSS	NOSEBAGS
ABEGNRST	BANGSTER
ABEGNRTU	BURGANET
ABEGNSTU	SUBAGENT
ABEGOORS	BARGOOSE
ABEGOPSY	PAGEBOYS
ABEGOSTT	BOTTEGAS
ABEGOSUY	BUOYAGES
ABEGRRSU	GARBURES
ABEGRRUV	BURGRAVE
ABEGRSST	BARGESTS
ABEGRSTU	BARGUEST
ABEGSSTU	SUBSTAGE
ABEHIKLS	BLEAKISH
ABEHILLR	HAIRBELL
ABEHILNR	HIBERNAL
ABEHILRS	BLASHIER
ABEHILTT	TITHABLE
ABEHIMMS	MEMSAHIB
ABEHIMNO	BOHEMIAN
ABEHIMOS	BOHEMIAS
	OBEAHISM
ABEHIMST	IMBATHES
ABEHINRS	BANISHER
ABEHINSS	BANISHES
	BANSHIES
ABEHINST	ABSINTHE
ABEHIOPU	EUPHOBIA
ABEHIORV	BEHAVIOR
ABEHIRRS	BRASHIER
ABEHISTU	HABITUES
ABEHISTZ	ZABTIEHS
ABEHJORS	JOBSHARE
ABEHKLLW	HAWKBELL
ABEHKNOR	HORNBEAK
ABEHKNST	BETHANKS
ABEHKOPS	BAKESHOP
ABEHKRSU	HAUBERKS
ABEHLLRT	BETHRALL
ABEHLMMU	HUMMABLE
ABEHLMSS	SHAMBLES
ABEHLNOT	BENTHOAL
ABEHLNTU	HUNTABLE
ABEHLOSW	SHOWABLE
ABEHLOTY	HYLOBATE
ABEHLRST	BLATHERS
	HALBERTS
ABEHLSSS	BASHLESS
ABEHLSST	BATHLESS
ABEHMNOR	HORNBEAM
ABEHMNOS	HAMBONES
ABEHMOOR	REHOBOAM
ABEHMRSU	AMBUSHER
ABEHMSSU	AMBUSHES
ABEHNRSY	ABHENRYS
ABEHNSTU	SUNBATHE
ABEHORRR	ABHORRER
	HARBORER
ABEHORST	BATHORSE
ABEHOSST	BATHOSES
ABEHOSTX	HATBOXES
ABEHOSXY	HAYBOXES
ABEHPSSU	SUBPHASE
ABEHRSST	BRASHEST
ABEHRTUY	EURYBATH
ABEIIKLS	KIELBASI
ABEIILLS	BAILLIES
ABEIILMT	IMITABLE
ABEIILNN	BIENNIAL
ABEIILNR	BILINEAR
ABEIILNV	INVIABLE
ABEIILPT	PITIABLE
ABEIILRR	LIBRAIRE
ABEIILRS	BISERIAL
ABEIILST	ALBITISE
	SIBILATE
ABEIILTV	VITIABLE
ABEIILTZ	ALBITIZE
ABEIINRR	BRAINIER
ABEIINRS	BINARIES
ABEIINST	BAINITES
ABEIJLNO	JOINABLE
ABEIJLTU	JUBILATE
ABEIJMNN	BENJAMIN
ABEIJMRS	JAMBIERS

ABEIJNSS	BASENJIS
ABEIKLLM	BALMLIKE
	LAMBLIKE
ABEIKLLN	BALKLINE
	LINKABLE
ABEIKLLS	SLABLIKE
ABEIKLNR	BARNLIKE
ABEIKLNS	BLANKIES
	SINKABLE
ABEIKLOS	KILOBASE
ABEIKLOT	BOATLIKE
ABEIKLRU	BAULKIER
ABEIKLSS	KISSABLE
ABEIKLST	BALKIEST
ABEIKLSY	KIELBASY
ABEIKNNR	NINEBARK
ABEIKNRR	BRANKIER
ABEIKNRS	BEARSKIN
	INBREAKS
ABEIKNST	BEATNIKS
	SNAKEBIT
ABEIKRST	BARKIEST
	BRAKIEST
	BREASKIT
ABEIKSWY	BIKEWAYS
ABEILLLM	MILLABLE
ABEILLLT	TILLABLE
ABEILLLW	WILLABLE
ABEILLMM	LIMBMEAL
ABEILLMS	MISLABEL
ABEILLNT	LIBELANT
ABEILLOS	ISOLABLE
	LOBELIAS
ABEILLOV	VIOLABLE
ABEILLPS	LAPSIBLE
ABEILLQU	LIQUABLE
ABEILLRR	BRAILLER
ABEILLRS	BALLSIER
	BRAILLES
	LIBERALS
ABEILLRY	BERYLLIA
	BLEARILY
	RELIABLY
ABEILLST	BASTILLE
	LISTABLE
ABEILLTT	TILTABLE
ABEILMMR	IMBALMER
ABEILMNS	BAILSMEN
	BIMENSAL
ABEILMNT	BAILMENT
ABEILMOR	BROMELIA
ABEILMRR	MARBLIER
ABEILMRS	REMBLAIS
ABEILMRW	WAMBLIER
ABEILMSS	ABLEISMS
	MISSABLE
ABEILMST	BALMIEST
	BIMETALS
	LAMBIEST
	TIMBALES
ABEILMSZ	IMBLAZES
ABEILNNW	WINNABLE
ABEILNOP	OPINABLE
ABEILNOT	TAILBONE
ABEILNPS	BIPLANES
ABEILNPT	PINTABLE
ABEILNRS	RINSABLE
ABEILNRU	RUINABLE
ABEILNSS	ALBINESS
	LESBIANS
ABEILNST	INSTABLE
ABEILNSU	SABULINE
ABEILNTV	BIVALENT
ABEILNTY	BINATELY
ABEILNUV	UNVIABLE
ABEILNVY	ENVIABLY
ABEILORT	LABORITE
ABEILOTV	BLOVIATE
ABEILPPR	RIPPABLE
ABEILPPT	TIPPABLE
ABEILPRT	PARTIBLE
ABEILPRZ	PRIZABLE
ABEILPSS	PASSIBLE
ABEILPST	EPIBLAST
ABEILRRU	REBURIAL
ABEILRRW	BRAWLIER
ABEILRST	BLASTIER
	LIBRATES
	TABLIERS
ABEILRSY	BILAYERS
ABEILRTT	TITRABLE
ABEILRTW	WRITABLE
ABEILRYY	BIYEARLY
ABEILSST	ASTILBES
	BASTILES
	BESTIALS
	BLASTIES
	STABILES
ABEILSSU	ISSUABLE
	SUASIBLE
ABEILSTU	SUITABLE
ABEILSTY	BEASTILY
ABEILSUX	BISEXUAL
ABEILSVV	BIVALVES
ABEILSYZ	SIZEABLY
ABEIMNPS	PEMBINAS
ABEIMNRS	MIRBANES
ABEIMNST	AMBIENTS
ABEIMORS	BIRAMOSE
ABEIMORU	AEROBIUM
ABEIMRST	BARMIEST
ABEIMRSU	AUMBRIES
ABEIMRTV	AMBIVERT
	VERBATIM
ABEIMSSU	IAMBUSES
ABEINNOS	BESONIAN
ABEINNOZ	BEZONIAN
ABEINNRR	BRANNIER
ABEINNRU	INURBANE
ABEINORR	AIRBORNE
ABEINORS	BARONIES
	SEAROBIN
ABEINORT	BARITONE
	OBTAINER
	REOBTAIN
	TABORINE
ABEINOST	BOTANIES
	BOTANISE
	NIOBATES
	OBEISANT
ABEINOTZ	BOTANIZE
ABEINPST	BEPAINTS
ABEINQSU	BASQUINE
ABEINRRW	BRAWNIER
ABEINRST	ATEBRINS
	BANISTER
	BARNIEST
ABEINRSU	ANBURIES
	URBANISE
ABEINRSZ	ZEBRINAS
ABEINRTU	BRAUNITE
	URBANITE
ABEINRUZ	URBANIZE
ABEINSSS	BIASNESS
ABEINSST	BASINETS
	BASSINET
	BESAINTS
	BESTAINS
ABEINSSU	UNBIASES
ABEINSTT	TABINETS
ABEINTTU	INTUBATE
ABEIORRZ	ARBORIZE
ABEIORSS	ISOBARES
ABEIORST	SABOTIER
ABEIORTV	ABORTIVE
ABEIOSSS	ISOBASES
ABEIOSTV	OBVIATES
ABEIPRRS	SPARERIB
ABEIPRTZ	BAPTIZER
ABEIPSST	BAPTISES
ABEIPSTZ	BAPTIZES
ABEIRRRS	BARRIERS
ABEIRRSS	BRASIERS
	BRASSIER
ABEIRRST	ARBITERS
	RAREBITS
ABEIRRSZ	BIZARRES
	BRAZIERS
ABEIRRTT	BIRRETTA
	BRATTIER
ABEIRRVY	BREVIARY
ABEIRSSS	BRASSIES
ABEIRSSU	AIRBUSES
ABEIRSTT	BIRETTAS
ABEIRSTV	VIBRATES
ABEIRSTW	WARBIEST
ABEIRSTY	BESTIARY
	SYBARITE
ABEIRSUX	EXURBIAS
ABEIRTTY	YTTERBIA
ABEISSST	BASSIEST
ABEISSTT	BATISTES
ABEISTTT	BATTIEST
ABEISTUX	BAUXITES
ABEISZZZ	BIZAZZES
ABEITTTU	TITUBATE
ABEJKLOU	KABELJOU
ABEJLMPU	JUMPABLE
ABEJLSUY	BLUEJAYS
ABEJMNOS	JAMBONES
	JOBNAMES
ABEJMOOR	JEROBOAM
ABEJNORW	JAWBONER
ABEJNOSW	JAWBONES
ABEJOSWX	JAWBOXES
ABEJRRSU	ABJURERS
ABEKLMOS	ABELMOSK
	SMOKABLE
ABEKLNOW	KNOWABLE
ABEKLNRY	BANKERLY
ABEKLNST	BLANKEST
	BLANKETS
ABEKLNTY	BLANKETY
ABEKLORW	WORKABLE
ABEKLRSS	BARKLESS
ABEKMNNS	BANKSMEN
ABEKMNTU	BUNKMATE
ABEKMSSU	SAMBUKES
ABEKNNOT	BANKNOTE
ABEKNRSU	UNBRAKES
ABEKNSSU	SUNBAKES
ABEKNSSY	SNEAKSBY
ABEKOORS	ABROOKES
ABEKOORY	YEARBOOK
ABEKORTU	BREAKOUT
	OUTBREAK
ABEKOSTU	OUTBAKES
ABEKPRSU	BREAKUPS
	UPBREAKS
ABEKRSTY	BASKETRY
ABELLLMU	LABELLUM
ABELLLOR	ROLLABLE
ABELLLOT	TOLLABLE
ABELLLSY	SYLLABLE
ABELLMOR	OMBRELLA
ABELLMRU	UMBELLAR
	UMBRELLA
ABELLNNO	BALLONNE
ABELLNOS	BONSELLA
ABELLNOT	BALLONET
ABELLNRU	RUBELLAN
ABELLNST	NETBALLS
ABELLOPW	PLOWABLE
ABELLORT	BALLOTER
ABELLOSV	SOLVABLE
ABELLOTU	LOBULATE
ABELLOTY	LOBATELY
	OBLATELY
ABELLOVY	LOVEABLY
ABELLRSU	RUBELLAS
ABELLRVY	VERBALLY
ABELLSTU	BALLUTES
ABELMMSU	SUMMABLE
ABELMNNO	NOBLEMAN
ABELMNOZ	EMBLAZON
ABELMNST	SEMBLANT
ABELMNSU	ALBUMENS
	BLUESMAN
ABELMOOT	MOOTABLE
ABELMOSU	ALBUMOSE
ABELMOSV	MOVABLES
ABELMOVY	MOVEABLY
ABELMPTU	PLUMBATE
ABELMRRS	MARBLERS
	RAMBLERS
ABELMRST	LAMBERTS
ABELMSSY	ASSEMBLY
ABELNNOR	BANNEROL
ABELNNRU	RUNNABLE
ABELNORZ	BLAZONER
ABELNOST	NEOBLAST
	NOTABLES
	STONABLE
ABELNOSY	BALONEYS
ABELNPRU	PRUNABLE
ABELNPSU	SUBPANEL
ABELNQTU	BLANQUET
ABELNRRY	BARRENLY
ABELNRSS	BRANSLES
ABELNRST	BRANTLES
ABELNRSY	BLARNEYS
ABELNRTU	TURNABLE
ABELNRUY	URBANELY
ABELNRYZ	BRAZENLY
ABELNSTU	ABLUENTS
	UNSTABLE
ABELNSTY	ABSENTLY
ABELNSUU	UNUSABLE
ABELNTUY	TUNEABLY
ABELOOTY	TABOOLEY
ABELOPRT	PORTABLE
ABELOPRU	POURABLE
ABELOPRV	PROVABLE
ABELOPRY	OPERABLY
ABELOPST	POTABLES
ABELOPTT	TABLETOP
ABELOQTU	QUOTABLE
ABELORRS	LABORERS
ABELORRU	LABOURER
	RUBEOLAR
ABELORST	BLOATERS
	SORTABLE
	STORABLE
ABELORSU	RUBEOLAS
ABELORSV	ABSOLVER
ABELOSSU	SABULOSE
ABELOSSV	ABSOLVES
ABELOSTU	ABSOLUTE
ABELOSTW	BESTOWAL
	STOWABLE

	TEABOWLS
ABELOTTU	OUTBLEAT
ABELOTUZ	OUTBLAZE
ABELPRTU	PUBERTAL
ABELQSUU	SUBEQUAL
ABELRRSW	BRAWLERS
	WARBLERS
ABELRRTU	BARRULET
ABELRSST	BLASTERS
	STABLERS
ABELRSSY	LABRYSES
ABELRSTT	BATTLERS
	BLATTERS
	BRATTLES
ABELRSTU	BALUSTER
	RUSTABLE
ABELRSTW	BLEWARTS
ABELRSUZ	ZEBRULAS
ABELRTTU	BURLETTA
	REBUTTAL
ABELSSSU	SUBSALES
ABELSSTT	STABLEST
ABELSSTU	SUBLATES
ABELSTUU	SUBULATE
ABELSTWY	BELTWAYS
ABELTTUU	TUBULATE
ABELTTUY	BUTYLATE
ABEMMNOO	MOONBEAM
ABEMNOST	BOATSMEN
ABEMNOTU	UMBONATE
ABEMNOTW	BATWOMEN
ABEMNPRU	PENUMBRA
ABEMNRSY	MYRBANES
ABEMNSSU	SUNBEAMS
ABEMNSTU	SUBMENTA
ABEMNSUY	SUNBEAMY
ABEMNTTU	ABUTMENT
ABEMORRS	EMBRASOR
ABEMORST	BROMATES
ABEMORSU	AMBEROUS
ABEMORTZ	BAROMETZ
ABEMOSTU	OUTBEAMS
ABEMRSSW	BESWARMS
ABENNORS	BARONNES
ABENNOTU	BUTANONE
ABENNRRS	BRANNERS
ABENOPSU	SUBPOENA
ABENORSS	BARONESS
ABENORST	BARONETS
ABENORTT	BETATRON
ABENORTV	BEVATRON
ABENORTY	BARYTONE
ABENOSSW	SAWBONES
ABENOSSY	SOYBEANS
ABENOSTY	BAYONETS
ABENPSSU	SUBPENAS
ABENQSTU	BANQUETS
ABENRRYZ	BRAZENRY
ABENRSTU	UNBRASTE
	URBANEST
ABENSSSS	BASSNESS
ABENSTZZ	BEZZANTS
ABEOOSST	SEABOOTS
ABEOPPRY	PAPERBOY
ABEOPRSS	SAPROBES
ABEOPRST	PROBATES
ABEOPSST	POSTBASE
ABEOQRSU	BAROQUES
ABEORRRT	BARRETOR
ABEORRSS	BRASEROS
ABEORRST	ABORTERS
	ARBORETS
	TABORERS
ABEORRTU	TABOURER
ABEORSST	BOASTERS
	SORBATES
ABEORSSY	ROSEBAYS
ABEORSTT	ABETTORS
	BATTEROS
	TABORETS
ABEORSTU	SABOTEUR
ABEORTTU	OBTURATE
	TABOURET
ABEORTUV	OUTBRAVE
ABEOSSST	ASBESTOS
ABEOSTUV	SUBOVATE
ABEOSTWX	SWEATBOX
ABEPRRTU	ABRUPTER
ABEPRSSY	PASSERBY
ABEPRSTY	TYPEBARS
ABEPSSSY	BYPASSES
ABEQRSUU	ARQUEBUS
ABERRRTY	BARRETRY
ABERRSSU	SABREURS
ABERRTYY	TAYBERRY
ABERRWXY	WAXBERRY
ABERSSST	BRASSETS
ABERSSSU	RUBASSES
	SURBASES
ABERSSTU	ABSTRUSE
	SURBATES
ABERSSTW	WABSTERS
ABERSTTU	ABUTTERS
ABERTTUY	BUTYRATE
ABESSSTT	BASSETTS
ABESSSTU	ASBESTUS
ABESSTTU	SUBSTATE
ABFFGILN	BAFFLING
ABFFIILS	BAILIFFS
ABFFLLPU	PUFFBALL
ABFFLOOS	BOFFOLAS
ABFFLOST	BLASTOFF
ABFFLOSU	BUFFALOS
ABFFNOTU	BOUFFANT
ABFGILNS	FABLINGS
ABFGLLOO	GOOFBALL
ABFGORUU	FAUBOURG
ABFHIIST	BAITFISH
ABFHILLS	FISHBALL
ABFHINNO	INFOBAHN
ABFHIORS	BOARFISH
ABFHOOTT	FOOTBATH
ABFHSSTU	SUBSHAFT
ABFIILLR	FIBRILLA
ABFIILMR	FIMBRIAL
ABFILLLY	FALLIBLY
ABFILNSU	BASINFUL
ABFILSTU	FABULIST
ABFIMORS	FIBROMAS
ABFJORSU	FRABJOUS
ABFKLLOR	FORKBALL
	KORFBALL
ABFLLOOT	FOOTBALL
ABFLLOST	SOFTBALL
ABFLNSUU	BUSULFAN
ABFLOSTU	BOASTFUL
	BOATFULS
ABFLOSTW	BATFOWLS
ABFLOSTY	FLYBOATS
ABFLOSUU	FABULOUS
ABFNORTU	TURBOFAN
ABFOORST	FOOTBARS
ABFORSTU	SURFBOAT
ABFSSTTU	TUBFASTS
ABGGGILN	BLAGGING
ABGGGINR	BRAGGING
ABGGGINS	BAGGINGS
ABGGIIST	GIGABITS
ABGGIJNN	JINGBANG
ABGGILMN	GAMBLING
ABGGILNR	GARBLING
ABGGINNS	BANGINGS
ABGGNNUY	GUNNYBAG
ABGGNOOT	TOBOGGAN
ABGGORST	BOGGARTS
ABGHHILL	HIGHBALL
ABGHIINT	HABITING
ABGHILMN	HAMBLING
ABGHINRS	BRASHING
ABGHINSS	BASHINGS
ABGHINWZ	WHIZBANG
ABGHIOPR	BIOGRAPH
ABGHLOST	HAGBOLTS
ABGHMOOS	GOOMBAHS
ABGHMORU	BROUGHAM
ABGHMRSU	HAMBURGS
ABGHOSTU	BUSHGOAT
ABGHPRSU	SUBGRAPH
ABGIIILN	ALIBIING
ABGIILNR	BRAILING
ABGIILNS	SAIBLING
ABGIILNT	LIBATING
ABGIILOT	OBLIGATI
ABGIIMNS	IMBASING
ABGIIMST	BIGAMIST
ABGIINNO	BIGNONIA
ABGIINNR	BRAINING
ABGIINOR	ABORIGIN
ABGIINRS	BRAISING
ABGIINSS	BIASINGS
	BIASSING
ABGIINST	BAITINGS
ABGIJNRU	ABJURING
ABGIJOOS	JIGABOOS
ABGIKLNN	BLANKING
ABGIKLNS	BALKINGS
ABGIKLNU	BAULKING
ABGIKNNR	BRANKING
ABGIKNNS	BANKINGS
ABGIKNRR	RINGBARK
ABGILLMN	LAMBLING
ABGILLNS	BALLINGS
ABGILMNR	MARBLING
	RAMBLING
ABGILMNS	AMBLINGS
ABGILMNW	WAMBLING
ABGILNNT	BANTLING
ABGILNOR	LABORING
ABGILNOT	BLOATING
	OBLIGANT
ABGILNRT	BRATLING
ABGILNRW	BRAWLING
	WARBLING
ABGILNST	BLASTING
	STABLING
	TABLINGS
ABGILNSW	BAWLINGS
ABGILNTT	BATTLING
	BLATTING
ABGILNTY	TANGIBLY
ABGILOOT	OBLIGATO
ABGILORS	GARBOILS
ABGILORW	BRIGALOW
ABGIMMNO	MAMBOING
ABGIMNRU	RUMBAING
ABGIMOSU	BIGAMOUS
	SUBIMAGO
ABGIMSST	GAMBISTS
ABGINNNR	BRANNING
ABGINNOR	ABORNING
ABGINNOT	BATONING
ABGINNRU	UNBARING
ABGINNRX	BANXRING
ABGINNST	BANTINGS
ABGINOOR	BIGAROON
ABGINOOT	TABOOING
ABGINORT	ABORTING
	BORATING
	TABORING
ABGINORV	BRAVOING
ABGINOST	BOASTING
	BOATINGS
	BOSTANGI
ABGINRRS	BARRINGS
ABGINRSS	BRASSING
ABGINRST	BRASTING
ABGINSST	BASTINGS
ABGINSTT	BATTINGS
ABGINSTW	BATSWING
ABGINTTU	ABUTTING
ABGIOPST	PIGBOATS
ABGIRRSS	RIBGRASS
ABGKKNOS	BANGKOKS
ABGKORSW	WORKBAGS
ABGLLLOY	GLOBALLY
ABGLLLUY	GULLABLY
ABGLLORU	GLOBULAR
ABGLLRUY	BULLYRAG
ABGLMNSU	LUMBANGS
ABGLMOPU	PLUMBAGO
ABGLMOSU	LUMBAGOS
ABGLNOOS	BOLOGNAS
ABGLNOOT	LONGBOAT
ABGLNOUW	BUNGALOW
ABGLOOST	TOOLBAGS
ABGLOOTY	BATOLOGY
ABGLORST	RAGBOLTS
ABGLORSU	GLABROUS
ABGLOSSU	SUBGOALS
ABGLRRSU	BURGLARS
ABGLRRUY	BURGLARY
ABGMNOOR	GAMBROON
ABGMNOOY	BOOGYMAN
ABGMOOSY	GOOMBAYS
ABGMORSW	BAGWORMS
ABGNOPRS	PROBANGS
ABGNORSU	OSNABURG
ABGNOSTU	GUNBOATS
ABGNOSWY	BOWYANGS
ABGOORST	BOTARGOS
ABGOPSST	POSTBAGS
ABGORRSU	GOBURRAS
ABGORSTU	OUTBRAGS
ABGOSTTU	TUGBOATS
ABHHIKSS	BAKSHISH
ABHHKOST	KHOTBAHS
ABHHKSTU	KHUTBAHS
ABHHRSTU	HATBRUSH
ABHHSSUW	BUSHWAHS
ABHIINRS	BAIRNISH
	BRAINISH
ABHIINST	INHABITS
ABHIIORZ	RHIZOBIA
ABHIKLLW	HAWKBILL
ABHIKLOR	KOHLRABI
ABHIKLSS	BASHLIKS
ABHIKSTW	HAWKBITS
ABHILLPT	PITHBALL
ABHILNOS	HOBNAILS
ABHILNOT	BIATHLON
ABHILOPS	BASOPHIL
ABHILRTW	WHIRLBAT
ABHILSST	STABLISH
ABHILSTU	HALIBUTS
ABHIMMST	BATHMISM
ABHINSST	ABSINTHS
ABHIOSST	ISOBATHS
ABHIOSTU	HAUTBOIS
ABHIRRSU	AIRBRUSH
ABHIRSSS	BRASSISH

ABHIRSTT	BRATTISH
ABHJNOOT	JOHNBOAT
ABHKLSSY	BASHLYKS
ABHKLSUW	BUSHWALK
ABHKOOOT	BOATHOOK
ABHKORSU	BOURKHAS
	KOURBASH
ABHKORSV	BOSHVARK
ABHLLMOT	MOTHBALL
ABHLLOOY	BALLYHOO
ABHLLPSU	PUSHBALL
ABHLORTW	WHORLBAT
ABHLOSUX	BOXHAULS
ABHLOSWW	WASHBOWL
ABHLPSUY	SUBPHYLA
ABHLRSTU	HURLBATS
ABHLSSTU	SALTBUSH
ABHMNOTY	BOTHYMAN
ABHMNSUU	SUBHUMAN
ABHMOORT	BATHROOM
ABHMRSSU	SAMBHURS
ABHNSSTU	SUNBATHS
ABHOORST	TARBOOSH
ABHOOSTW	SHOWBOAT
ABHORRSU	HARBOURS
ABHORSTU	TARBOUSH
ABHOSTUY	HAUTBOYS
ABHSSTUW	WASHTUBS
ABIIINRY	BIRIYANI
ABIIKKST	KIBITKAS
ABIIKLSS	BASILISK
ABIILLMR	MILLIBAR
ABIILLTY	LABILITY
ABIILMNO	BINOMIAL
ABIILMNS	ALBINISM
	MINILABS
ABIILMSU	BULIMIAS
ABIILNOT	LIBATION
ABIILNQS	INQILABS
ABIILNRS	BRASILIN
ABIILNRY	BRAINILY
ABIILNRZ	BRAZILIN
ABIILNST	SIBILANT
ABIILNVY	INVIABLY
ABIILOSV	BOLIVIAS
ABIILPTY	PITIABLY
ABIIMNOT	AMBITION
ABIIMNRS	MINIBARS
ABIIMSST	IAMBISTS
ABIINORS	ROBINIAS
ABIINRSY	BIRYANIS
ABIIRSSV	VIBRISSA
ABIJLNRS	BRINJALS
ABIJLNTU	JUBILANT
ABIJNOOT	JOBATION
ABIJNOST	ABJOINTS
	BANJOIST
ABIKLLLM	LAMBKILL
ABIKLMNS	LAMBKINS
	LAMBSKIN
ABIKLNRY	BYRLAKIN
ABIKLORS	KILOBARS
ABIKLOSS	KOLBASIS
	KOLBASSI
ABIKLSSY	KISSABLY
ABIKMNNR	BRINKMAN
ABIKMNRS	BARMKINS
ABIKNORR	IRONBARK
ABIKOSUZ	BAZOUKIS
ABIKRSST	BRITSKAS
ABIKRSTZ	BRITZKAS
	BRITZSKA
ABILLLPY	PLAYBILL
ABILLMSU	BALLIUMS
ABILLNPS	PINBALLS
ABILLORT	TRILOBAL
ABILLOVY	VIOLABLY
ABILLPST	SPITBALL
ABILLRTY	TRIBALLY
ABILLSSW	SAWBILLS
ABILLSTT	BATTILLS
ABILLSWX	WAXBILLS
ABILLSWY	WAYBILLS
ABILMNOU	OLIBANUM
ABILMNSU	ALBUMINS
ABILMOPS	BIOPLASM
ABILMORS	MISLABOR
ABILMOTU	BUMALOTI
ABILNOOT	BOLTONIA
	LOBATION
	OBLATION
ABILNOPR	PANBROIL
ABILNORU	UNILOBAR
ABILNOTU	ABLUTION
	ABUTILON
ABILNRTU	TRIBUNAL
	TURBINAL
ABILNRWY	BRAWNILY
ABILOPRS	PARBOILS
ABILOPST	BIOPLAST
ABILORST	ORBITALS
	STROBILA
ABILORSV	BOLIVARS
ABILORTY	LIBATORY
ABILORUV	BIOVULAR
ABILOSTU	BAILOUTS
	TABOULIS
ABILPSSY	PASSIBLY
ABILRSSY	BRASSILY
ABILRSUV	SUBVIRAL
ABILSSUY	ISSUABLY
ABILSTUY	SUITABLY
ABIMMNOO	MAINBOOM
ABIMNOSU	BIMANOUS
ABIMNRSU	URBANISM
ABIMNRTU	TAMBURIN
ABIMORSU	BIRAMOUS
ABIMORSY	BOYARISM
ABIMPSST	BAPTISMS
ABIMRSST	STRABISM
ABIMRSTT	TRIMTABS
ABINNOST	ANTISNOB
ABINOORS	BORONIAS
ABINOORT	ABORTION
ABINORST	TABORINS
ABINORSW	RAINBOWS
ABINORTU	TABOURIN
ABINORWY	RAINBOWY
ABINOSST	ANTIBOSS
	BASTIONS
ABINOSSU	ABUSIONS
ABINOSTT	BOTANIST
ABINRSTU	URBANIST
ABINRSTV	VIBRANTS
ABINRTUY	URBANITY
ABINTTTU	TITUBANT
ABIOORTV	OBVIATOR
ABIOPRSU	BIPAROUS
ABIOPSTU	SUBTOPIA
ABIORRST	ARBORIST
ABIORRTV	VIBRATOR
ABIORSTV	VIBRATOS
ABIORTUY	OBITUARY
ABIPSSTT	BAPTISTS
ABIRRSTU	AIRBURST
ABIRSSUZ	SUBSIZAR
ABIRSTTY	TRAYBITS
ABISSSST	BASSISTS
ABISSTTU	TUBAISTS
ABJKMOSS	SJAMBOKS
ABJLMOOS	JAMBOOLS
ABKKMOOR	BOOKMARK
ABKLLNOR	BANKROLL
ABKLOOPY	PLAYBOOK
ABKLOOSW	LAWBOOKS
ABKLRSUW	BULWARKS
ABKNNNOS	NONBANKS
ABKNNOSW	SNOWBANK
ABKNOPST	STOPBANK
ABKNPRTU	BANKRUPT
ABKNRSUU	BUNRAKUS
ABKOOPSS	PASSBOOK
ABKOORTW	WORKBOAT
ABKOOSTT	KOTTABOS
ABKORSTU	OUTBARKS
ABKSSSTU	SUBTASKS
ABLLLOSW	LOWBALLS
ABLLMOOR	BALLROOM
ABLLMOPW	BLOWLAMP
ABLLNOOS	BALLOONS
ABLLNOSW	SNOWBALL
ABLLORST	BORSTALL
	TOLLBARS
ABLLORSU	SOURBALL
ABLLOSTY	TALLBOYS
ABLLRTUY	BRUTALLY
ABLLSSUY	SYLLABUS
ABLMNRUU	ALBURNUM
	LABURNUM
ABLMOOST	TOMBOLAS
ABLMOSTY	MYOBLAST
ABLMPSUU	PABULUMS
ABLNNOOR	NONLABOR
ABLNORYZ	BLAZONRY
ABLNOSTU	BUTANOLS
ABLNOSUZ	SUBZONAL
ABLNRSUU	SUBLUNAR
ABLNSTUY	UNSTABLY
ABLNSUUY	UNUSABLY
ABLOOPRR	PROLABOR
ABLOORST	BARSTOOL
	TOOLBARS
ABLOORTY	OBLATORY
ABLOOSTT	BOOTLAST
ABLOOSTZ	ZOOBLAST
ABLOPRSU	SUBPOLAR
ABLOPRTY	PORTABLY
ABLOPRVY	PROVABLY
ABLOPSUU	PABULOUS
ABLOPSYY	PLAYBOYS
ABLOQTUY	QUOTABLY
ABLORSST	BORSTALS
ABLORSSU	SUBSOLAR
ABLORSTW	BLAWORTS
ABLORSTY	SORTABLY
ABLORSUW	BOURLAWS
ABLORTUW	OUTBRAWL
ABLOSSUU	SABULOUS
ABLOSTTU	SUBTOTAL
ABLOSTUW	OUTBAWLS
ABLPRTUY	ABRUPTLY
ABLRSTUY	BUTYRALS
ABMNTTUY	BUTTYMAN
ABMOORRS	BARROOMS
ABMORSTU	TAMBOURS
ABMOSSTU	SUBATOMS
ABNNNORU	NONURBAN
ABNOORRT	ROBORANT
ABNOORSS	SOROBANS
ABNOORSZ	BORAZONS
ABNOORYZ	BRYOZOAN
ABNOOSSS	BASSOONS
ABNORSTY	BARYTONS
ABNORTUU	RUNABOUT
ABNOSSSU	BONASSUS
ABNOSTUX	SUBTAXON
ABNRSTTU	TURBANTS
ABOORRSU	ARBOROUS
ABOORSTW	ROWBOATS
ABOOSTTU	OUTBOAST
ABOOSTTW	TOWBOATS
ABORSSTU	ROBUSTAS
ABPRSSTU	SUBPARTS
ACCCDIIO	COCCIDIA
ACCCEHIX	CACHEXIC
ACCCELRY	CYCLECAR
ACCCENPY	PECCANCY
ACCCFIIL	CALCIFIC
ACCCHILO	COLCHICA
ACCCIILT	CALCITIC
ACCCIIPR	CAPRICCI
ACCCILLY	CYCLICAL
ACCCIOPU	CAPUCCIO
ACCDDEEN	ACCENDED
	CADENCED
ACCDDEIS	CADDICES
ACCDDEKO	COCKADED
ACCDDEOR	ACCORDED
ACCDDIII	DIACIDIC
ACCDDIIT	DIDACTIC
ACCDEEER	REACCEDE
ACCDEEHT	CACHETED
ACCDEELN	CANCELED
ACCDEENS	CADENCES
ACCDEENT	ACCENTED
ACCDEEPT	ACCEPTED
ACCDEERS	ACCEDERS
ACCDEERT	ACCRETED
ACCDEERU	CARDECUE
ACCDEERW	ACCREWED
ACCDEESS	ACCESSED
ACCDEGIN	ACCEDING
	ACCINGED
ACCDEHIK	CHIACKED
ACCDEHIL	CHALICED
ACCDEHIN	CHICANED
ACCDEHKY	CHYACKED
ACCDEHLT	CLATCHED
ACCDEHNR	CRANCHED
ACCDEHNU	CHAUNCED
ACCDEHPU	CAPUCHED
ACCDEIIS	ACCIDIES
ACCDEILN	CALCINED
ACCDEILO	ECOCIDAL
ACCDEILU	CAUDICLE
ACCDEILY	DELICACY
ACCDEINT	ACCIDENT
ACCDEIRT	ACCREDIT
ACCDEISU	CAUDICES
ACCDEKLR	CRACKLED
ACCDEKOS	COCKADES
ACCDELLY	CALYCLED
ACCDELOY	ACCLOYED
ACCDENOR	CONACRED
ACCDENOV	CONCAVED
ACCDEORR	ACCORDER
ACCDEOST	ACCOSTED
ACCDERSU	ACCURSED
	CARDECUS
ACCDESSU	SUCCADES
ACCDESUU	CADUCEUS
	CAUCUSED
ACCDGHOO	COACHDOG
ACCDHIIR	DIARCHIC
ACCDHILS	CHALCIDS
ACCDHIMO	DOCHMIAC
ACCDHIOT	CATHODIC
ACCDHIRY	DYARCHIC
ACCDHLOR	CLOCHARD
ACCDIIOT	ACIDOTIC

ACCDIIRT	CARDITIC
ACCDIIST	DICASTIC
ACCDIITY	DICACITY
ACCDILNU	DUNCICAL
ACCDILOY	CALYCOID
ACCDILTY	DACTYLIC
ACCDINOR	CANCROID
	DRACONIC
ACCDIOOR	CORACOID
ACCDIORS	SARCODIC
ACCDIOST	STICCADO
ACCDITUY	CADUCITY
ACCDKNOS	CANDOCKS
ACCDKOSW	DAWCOCKS
ACCDLOSY	CACODYLS
ACCDOOST	STOCCADO
ACCDOOXY	CACODOXY
ACCDOSUU	CADUCOUS
ACCEEEPT	ACCEPTEE
ACCEEHIT	HICCATEE
ACCEEHLO	COCHLEAE
ACCEEHLS	CALECHES
ACCEEHOS	COACHEES
ACCEEHRT	CETERACH
ACCEEHST	SEECATCH
ACCEEILR	CELERIAC
ACCEEILS	ECCLESIA
ACCEEINV	VACCINEE
ACCEEKLN	NECKLACE
ACCEELNR	CANCELER
	CLARENCE
ACCEELNS	CENACLES
ACCEELOS	COALESCE
ACCEELRT	CALCRETE
ACCEENNS	NASCENCE
ACCEENPR	CREPANCE
ACCEENRS	CREANCES
ACCEENRT	REACCENT
ACCEENST	ACESCENT
ACCEEORT	COCREATE
	CROCEATE
ACCEEPRT	ACCEPTER
	REACCEPT
ACCEERST	ACCRETES
ACCEERSU	REACCUSE
ACCEESSS	ACCESSES
ACCEFFIY	EFFICACY
ACCEFILS	FASCICLE
ACCEFIST	FACTICES
ACCEFLSU	FELUCCAS
ACCEGINS	ACCINGES
ACCEGKMO	GAMECOCK
ACCEGNOY	COAGENCY
ACCEGOSS	SOCCAGES
ACCEHHIS	CHECHIAS
ACCEHHKO	CHECHAKO
ACCEHHKT	CHATCHKE
	HATCHECK
ACCEHIKP	CHICKPEA
ACCEHIKR	AIRCHECK
ACCEHILM	ALCHEMIC
	CHEMICAL
ACCEHILP	CEPHALIC
ACCEHILS	CALICHES
	CHALICES
ACCEHILT	HECTICAL
ACCEHIMN	MECHANIC
ACCEHIMS	SACHEMIC
ACCEHINO	ANECHOIC
ACCEHINR	CHANCIER
	CHICANER
ACCEHINS	CHICANES
ACCEHINT	ATECHNIC
	CATECHIN
ACCEHIOS	COACHIES
ACCEHIRT	CATCHIER
ACCEHKPY	PAYCHECK
ACCEHLNS	CHANCELS
ACCEHLOR	COCHLEAR
ACCEHLOS	COCHLEAS
ACCEHLOT	CATECHOL
ACCEHLST	CLATCHES
ACCEHMNO	COACHMEN
ACCEHNNO	CHACONNE
ACCEHNNY	CYNANCHE
ACCEHNOR	CHARNECO
	ENCROACH
ACCEHNOT	CONCHATE
ACCEHNRS	CHANCERS
	CHANCRES
	CRANCHES
ACCEHNRY	CHANCERY
ACCEHNSU	CHAUNCES
ACCEHOPT	CACHEPOT
ACCEHORS	CAROCHES
	COACHERS
ACCEHPSU	CAPUCHES
ACCEHRST	CATCHERS
	CRATCHES
ACCEHSST	SCATCHES
ACCEHSTT	CATHECTS
ACCEHSTU	CATECHUS
ACCEIIST	CAECITIS
ACCEIKPS	ICEPACKS
ACCEILLN	CANCELLI
ACCEILLR	CLERICAL
ACCEILLS	CALICLES
ACCEILLU	CAULICLE
ACCEILLV	CLAVICLE
ACCEILNS	CALCINES
	SCENICAL
ACCEILNT	CANTICLE
ACCEILNV	CLAVECIN
ACCEILNY	CALYCINE
ACCEILOP	ALOPECIC
ACCEILOS	CALICOES
	COELIACS
ACCEILRV	CERVICAL
ACCEILST	CALCITES
ACCEILTY	ACETYLIC
ACCEIMOS	OCCAMIES
ACCEIMRS	CERAMICS
ACCEINNR	CANCRINE
ACCEINOR	COCINERA
ACCEINOS	COCAINES
ACCEINOT	ACETONIC
ACCEINRT	ACENTRIC
ACCEINSV	VACCINES
ACCEINTU	CUNEATIC
ACCEIOPR	CECROPIA
ACCEIOTV	COACTIVE
ACCEIPRS	CAPRICES
ACCEIPRT	PRACTICE
ACCEIPSV	PECCAVIS
ACCEIQSU	CACIQUES
ACCEIRRR	RICERCAR
ACCEIRSU	CAESURIC
	CURACIES
ACCEIRTU	CRUCIATE
ACCEISST	ASCETICS
ACCEISTT	ECSTATIC
ACCEKLNR	CRACKNEL
ACCEKLRS	CACKLERS
	CLACKERS
	CRACKLES
ACCEKMOS	MEACOCKS
ACCEKNOR	CORNCAKE
ACCEKOPS	PEACOCKS
ACCEKOPY	PEACOCKY
ACCEKOSS	SEACOCKS
ACCEKPSU	CUPCAKES
ACCEKRRS	CRACKERS
ACCELLSY	CALYCLES
ACCELLUY	CALYCULE
ACCELMNY	CYCLAMEN
ACCELNOS	CONCEALS
ACCELNOV	CONCLAVE
ACCELNRU	CARUNCLE
ACCELOOT	COLOCATE
ACCELORS	CORACLES
ACCELORT	ACROLECT
ACCELOST	CACOLETS
ACCELRSY	SCARCELY
ACCELSSU	SACCULES
ACCELSSY	CYCLASES
ACCELWYY	CYCLEWAY
ACCENNSY	NASCENCY
ACCENORR	CORNACRE
ACCENORS	CONACRES
ACCENORT	ACCENTOR
ACCENOST	COENACTS
	COSECANT
ACCENOSU	CONCAUSE
ACCENOSV	CONCAVES
ACCEOPRT	ACCEPTOR
ACCEOPTU	OCCUPATE
ACCEORSS	ARCCOSES
ACCEORST	ECTOSARC
ACCEORSW	CRACOWES
ACCEORTU	ACCOUTER
	ACCOUTRE
ACCEOSSS	SACCOSES
ACCERRST	CARRECTS
ACCERSST	SCARCEST
ACCERSSU	ACCURSES
	ACCUSERS
ACCESSTU	CACTUSES
ACCESSUU	CAUCUSES
ACCFFLTU	CALCTUFF
ACCFHLTY	CATCHFLY
ACCFIILT	LACTIFIC
ACCFIKLL	CALFLICK
ACCFLNOO	CONFOCAL
ACCFOORT	COFACTOR
ACCGHIKN	CHACKING
ACCGHINN	CHANCING
ACCGHINO	COACHING
ACCGHINT	CATCHING
ACCGHIOR	CHORAGIC
ACCGIINT	ACCITING
ACCGIKLN	CACKLING
	CLACKING
ACCGIKMR	GIMCRACK
ACCGIKNR	CRACKING
ACCGILOX	COXALGIC
ACCGINOT	COACTING
ACCGINOY	ACCOYING
ACCGINRU	ACCRUING
ACCGINSU	ACCUSING
ACCGLOOY	CACOLOGY
ACCHHITT	CHITCHAT
ACCHHMOS	CAMSHOCH
ACCHHMOU	MUCHACHO
ACCHIIMS	CHIASMIC
ACCHIIRT	RACHITIC
ACCHIIST	CHIASTIC
ACCHILNO	CHALONIC
ACCHILNY	CHANCILY
ACCHILOR	ORICHALC
ACCHILOT	CATHOLIC
ACCHIMOR	ACHROMIC
ACCHINNO	CINCHONA
ACCHINOS	CHICANOS
ACCHINPU	CAPUCHIN
ACCHIOPS	PICACHOS
ACCHIORS	COCHAIRS
ACCHIORT	THORACIC
	TROCHAIC
ACCHIOSU	ACOUCHIS
ACCHIRRT	CARRITCH
ACCHIRSS	SCRAICHS
ACCHKLOR	CHARLOCK
ACCHKOSY	HAYCOCKS
ACCHLOOT	CACHOLOT
ACCHLSTU	CLAUCHTS
ACCHMORS	CASCHROM
ACCHNNUY	UNCHANCY
ACCHNOOR	COANCHOR
	CORONACH
ACCHNOTU	COUCHANT
ACCHNTUY	UNCATCHY
ACCHOOTU	OUTCOACH
ACCHOPSU	PACHUCOS
ACCHORTU	CARTOUCH
ACCHORTY	OCTARCHY
ACCHOSTW	CHOCTAWS
ACCHOTTU	OUTCATCH
ACCHPSTU	CATCHUPS
ACCHRRSU	CURRACHS
ACCHRSSU	SCRAUCHS
ACCHRSTY	SCRATCHY
ACCHRTWY	WATCHCRY
ACCIIIOT	OITICICA
ACCIILLN	CLINICAL
ACCIILMT	CLIMATIC
ACCIILNO	ICONICAL
ACCIILRT	CRITICAL
ACCIIMNN	CINNAMIC
ACCIINNO	ANICONIC
ACCIINNP	PICCANIN
ACCIINOT	ACONITIC
	CATIONIC
ACCIINPS	CAPSICIN
ACCIINTY	CYANITIC
ACCIIOPT	OCCIPITA
ACCIIPST	PASTICCI
ACCIIRTX	CICATRIX
ACCIISST	SCIATICS
ACCIJKMR	JIMCRACK
ACCIKKNN	NICKNACK
ACCIKKRR	RICKRACK
ACCIKKTT	TICKTACK
ACCIKLOT	COCKTAIL
ACCIKNST	CANSTICK
ACCIKOPR	APRICOCK
ACCIKPRT	PRACTICK
ACCILLUY	CALYCULI
ACCILMOS	COSMICAL
ACCILMOX	CACOMIXL
ACCILMSU	CALCIUMS
ACCILMUU	ACICULUM
ACCILNOT	CICLATON
	LACTONIC
ACCILNOV	VOLCANIC
ACCILNUV	VULCANIC
ACCILORS	CALORICS
ACCILORT	CORTICAL
ACCILOSS	CLASSICO
ACCILOSV	VOCALICS
ACCILPRY	CAPRYLIC
ACCILRRU	CIRCULAR
ACCILRSY	ACRYLICS
ACCILSSS	CLASSICS
ACCILSST	CLASTICS
ACCILTUU	CUTICULA
ACCIMNOS	MOCCASIN
ACCIMNTU	CANTICUM
ACCIMORR	MICROCAR
ACCIMORU	COUMARIC
ACCIMOSZ	ZIMOCCAS

ACCIMPSU	CAPSICUM
ACCIMSTY	CYMATICS
ACCINOOS	OCCASION
ACCINOOT	COACTION
ACCINORT	CRATONIC
	NARCOTIC
ACCINORV	CAVICORN
ACCINOST	CANTICOS
ACCINOTY	CANTICOY
	CYANOTIC
ACCINRSU	CRUCIANS
ACCINSSY	CYCASINS
ACCIOOPP	APOCOPIC
ACCIOPST	SPICCATO
ACCIORST	ACROSTIC
ACCIORSY	ISOCRACY
ACCIOSTT	STICCATO
ACCIOSTU	ACOUSTIC
ACCIPRST	PRACTICS
ACCIRRTT	TRICTRAC
ACCIRSTY	SCARCITY
ACCISSTU	CAUSTICS
ACCKKRSU	RUCKSACK
ACCKLORS	CARLOCKS
ACCKMMRU	CRUMMACK
ACCKMORS	CROMACKS
ACCKOOOP	COCKAPOO
ACCKOOOT	COCKATOO
ACCKOPRS	CAPROCKS
ACCKOPRT	CRACKPOT
ACCKORST	STOCKCAR
ACCKOSSS	CASSOCKS
	COSSACKS
ACCKOSST	CASTOCKS
ACCKPRSU	CRACKUPS
ACCLLNOY	CYCLONAL
ACCLLOSU	OCCLUSAL
ACCLLSUU	CALCULUS
ACCLSSUU	SACCULUS
ACCMOOST	COCOMATS
ACCMOOSY	COCOYAMS
ACCMOPST	ACCOMPTS
	COMPACTS
ACCMOSTU	ACCUSTOM
ACCMRSUU	CURCUMAS
ACCNNOOS	COONCANS
ACCNOOPS	COCOPANS
ACCNOORS	RACCOONS
ACCNOOTU	COCOANUT
ACCNOPTU	OCCUPANT
ACCNORTT	CONTRACT
ACCNOSTT	CONTACTS
ACCNOSTU	ACCOUNTS
ACCOORST	COACTORS
ACCOPSTY	COPYCATS
ACCOQSSU	SQUACCOS
ACCORRTY	CARRYCOT
ACCORSTU	ACCOURTS
ACDDDEIT	ADDICTED
ACDDDETU	ADDUCTED
ACDDDKOS	DADDOCKS
ACDDEEES	DECEASED
ACDDEEHO	COHEADED
ACDDEEHT	DETACHED
ACDDEEIT	DEDICATE
ACDDEEIU	DECIDUAE
ACDDEEKR	DACKERED
ACDDEELR	DECLARED
ACDDEELS	DESCALED
ACDDEELW	DECLAWED
ACDDEEMP	DECAMPED
ACDDEENO	DEACONED
ACDDEENR	CREDENDA
ACDDEENS	ASCENDED
ACDDEENT	DECADENT
	DECANTED
ACDDEERT	REDACTED
ACDDEETU	EDUCATED
ACDDEETV	ADVECTED
ACDDEGIS	DISCAGED
ACDDEHIK	DICKHEAD
ACDDEHKN	DECKHAND
ACDDEHRS	CHEDDARS
ACDDEIIL	DEICIDAL
ACDDEIIM	MEDICAID
ACDDEILU	DECIDUAL
ACDDEINR	CANDIDER
	RIDDANCE
ACDDEINT	DEDICANT
ACDDEINY	CYANIDED
ACDDEIPS	DISPACED
ACDDEIRT	READDICT
ACDDEISS	CADDISES
	DISCASED
ACDDEISU	DECIDUAS
ACDDEITT	DICTATED
ACDDEKLO	DEADLOCK
ACDDEKOR	RADDOCKE
ACDDELOS	CLADODES
ACDDELRS	CLADDERS
ACDDENTU	ADDUCENT
ACDDEOPS	DECAPODS
ACDDEORR	CORRADED
ACDDEORW	COWARDED
ACDDERSU	ADDUCERS
	CRUSADED
ACDDERTU	TRADUCED
ACDDGILN	CLADDING
ACDDGINU	ADDUCING
ACDDGINY	CADDYING
ACDDHHSU	CHUDDAHS
ACDDHIIO	DIADOCHI
ACDDHIMR	DIDRACHM
ACDDHIRY	HYDRACID
ACDDHKNO	DOCKHAND
ACDDHKOS	HADDOCKS
	SHADDOCK
ACDDHORS	CHADDORS
ACDDHRSU	CHUDDARS
ACDDIIOR	CARDIOID
ACDDILNY	CANDIDLY
ACDDILTY	DIDACTYL
ACDDINNU	UNCANDID
ACDDINSY	DISCANDY
ACDDIRSS	DISCARDS
ACDDKLNO	DOCKLAND
ACDDKMOS	MADDOCKS
ACDDKOPS	PADDOCKS
ACDDKORY	DOCKYARD
ACDDORTU	ADDUCTOR
ACDEEEFT	DEFECATE
ACDEEEKS	SEEDCAKE
ACDEEEMR	REEDMACE
ACDEEENR	CAREENED
ACDEEENT	ANTECEDE
ACDEEERR	CAREERED
ACDEEERS	DECREASE
ACDEEESS	DECEASES
	SEEDCASE
ACDEEFFT	AFFECTED
ACDEEFHN	ENCHAFED
ACDEEFIL	CALEFIED
ACDEEFIN	DEFIANCE
ACDEEFIS	CASEFIED
ACDEEFPR	PREFACED
ACDEEFRS	DEFACERS
	FRESCADE
ACDEEFRY	FEDERACY
ACDEEFTT	FACETTED
ACDEEGLY	DELEGACY
ACDEEGNR	ENGRACED
ACDEEHIN	ECHIDNAE
ACDEEHIV	ACHIEVED
ACDEEHKO	COKEHEAD
ACDEEHLP	PLEACHED
ACDEEHLT	CHELATED
ACDEEHMR	DEMARCHE
ACDEEHNN	ENHANCED
ACDEEHNR	ENARCHED
ACDEEHNS	ENCASHED
	ENCHASED
ACDEEHPR	PREACHED
ACDEEHRS	SEARCHED
ACDEEHRT	DETACHER
ACDEEHSS	CHASSEED
ACDEEHST	DETACHES
	SACHETED
ACDEEIIP	EPICEDIA
ACDEEILT	DELICATE
ACDEEIMR	MEDICARE
ACDEEIMT	DECIMATE
	EMICATED
	MEDICATE
ACDEEINN	DECENNIA
	ENNEADIC
ACDEEINR	DERACINE
ACDEEINU	AUDIENCE
ACDEEINV	DEVIANCE
ACDEEIPS	DISPEACE
ACDEEIRS	DECIARES
ACDEEJKT	JACKETED
ACDEEKLR	LACKERED
ACDEEKLY	LACKEYED
ACDEEKNR	CANKERED
ACDEEKPR	REPACKED
ACDEEKPT	PACKETED
ACDEEKRR	RERACKED
ACDEEKRS	SCREAKED
ACDEEKRT	RACKETED
	RETACKED
ACDEEKST	CASKETED
ACDEELLR	CELLARED
	RECALLED
ACDEELLS	CADELLES
ACDEELMN	ENCALMED
ACDEELMP	EMPLACED
ACDEELNR	CALENDER
	ENCRADLE
ACDEELNS	CLEANSED
ACDEELNT	LANCETED
ACDEELNV	ENCLAVED
ACDEELOR	COLEADER
	RECOALED
ACDEELPR	PARCELED
	REPLACED
ACDEELRR	DECLARER
ACDEELRS	DECLARES
	RESCALED
ACDEELRT	CLARETED
	DECRETAL
	TREACLED
ACDEELRV	CALVERED
	CLAVERED
ACDEELSS	DECLASSE
	DESCALES
ACDEEMNP	ENCAMPED
ACDEEMRS	SCREAMED
ACDEEMRT	CREMATED
ACDEEMSV	MEDEVACS
ACDEENNP	PENANCED
ACDEENNT	TENDANCE
ACDEENNY	CAYENNED
ACDEENOT	ANECDOTE
ACDEENRS	ASCENDER
	REASCEND
ACDEENRT	CANTERED
	CRENATED
	DECANTER
	NECTARED
	RECANTED
ACDEENRV	CAVERNED
	CRAVENED
ACDEENRY	CARNEYED
	DECENARY
ACDEENRZ	CREDENZA
ACDEENSV	VENDACES
ACDEENTT	DANCETTE
ACDEENTU	CUNEATED
ACDEEOPS	PEASECOD
ACDEEORT	DECORATE
ACDEEOTV	EVOCATED
ACDEEPPR	RECAPPED
ACDEEPRS	ESCARPED
	RESPACED
ACDEEPRT	CARPETED
	PREACTED
ACDEEPST	ASPECTED
ACDEERRS	SCAREDER
ACDEERRT	CRATERED
	RECRATED
	RETRACED
	TERRACED
ACDEERSS	CARESSED
ACDEERST	CEDRATES
ACDEERSY	DECAYERS
ACDEESTU	EDUCATES
ACDEESUX	CAUDEXES
ACDEESUY	CAUSEYED
ACDEFFHU	CHAUFFED
ACDEFFLS	SCLAFFED
ACDEFFOR	AFFORCED
ACDEFGIN	DEFACING
ACDEFGOS	DOGFACES
ACDEFHLN	FLANCHED
ACDEFIIL	DEIFICAL
ACDEFIIP	PACIFIED
ACDEFILN	CANFIELD
ACDEFILR	FRICADEL
ACDEFINN	FINANCED
ACDEFINS	FACIENDS
ACDEFLOT	OLFACTED
ACDEFNOW	FACEDOWN
ACDEFNRU	FURNACED
ACDEFORT	FACTORED
ACDEFOTU	OUTFACED
ACDEFRSU	SURFACED
ACDEFRTU	FURCATED
ACDEGGRS	SCRAGGED
ACDEGHLO	GALOCHED
ACDEGHNU	CHAUNGED
	GAUNCHED
ACDEGIIL	ALGICIDE
ACDEGIKM	MAGICKED
ACDEGIMR	DECIGRAM
	GRIMACED
ACDEGINU	GUIDANCE
ACDEGINY	DECAYING
ACDEGIRS	DISGRACE
ACDEGISS	DISCAGES
ACDEGIST	CADGIEST
ACDEGKOS	DOCKAGES
ACDEGLLO	COLLAGED
ACDEGLOS	DECALOGS
ACDEGLOU	CLOUDAGE
ACDEGNOS	DECAGONS
ACDEGNRU	UNGRACED
ACDEGORS	CORDAGES
ACDEGOTT	COTTAGED
ACDEHHIN	HAINCHED
ACDEHHNU	HAUNCHED

ACDEHHRU	HACHURED
ACDEHHTT	THATCHED
ACDEHIIP	APHICIDE
ACDEHIJK	HIJACKED
ACDEHILR	HERALDIC
ACDEHILT	DITHECAL
ACDEHIMM	CHAMMIED
ACDEHIMN	MACHINED
ACDEHIMS	SCHIEDAM
ACDEHINR	INARCHED
ACDEHINS	ECHIDNAS
	INCHASED
ACDEHIRS	RACHIDES
ACDEHIRT	THRIDACE
	TRACHEID
ACDEHIRV	ARCHIVED
ACDEHIST	SCAITHED
ACDEHISU	CHIAUSED
ACDEHKLO	HEADLOCK
ACDEHKLS	SHACKLED
ACDEHKNU	UNHACKED
ACDEHKOV	HAVOCKED
ACDEHKRU	ARCHDUKE
ACDEHKTW	THWACKED
ACDEHLNP	PLANCHED
ACDEHLNR	CHANDLER
ACDEHLNU	LAUNCHED
ACDEHLOS	COALSHED
ACDEHLRS	CHALDERS
ACDEHLRT	TRACHLED
ACDEHLSS	CHADLESS
ACDEHMST	SMATCHED
ACDEHNOR	ANCHORED
	RONDACHE
ACDEHNPU	PAUNCHED
ACDEHNRU	RAUNCHED
ACDEHNRY	ENDARCHY
ACDEHNST	SNATCHED
	STANCHED
ACDEHNSU	UNCASHED
ACDEHNTU	CHAUNTED
ACDEHORR	HARDCORE
ACDEHORT	CHORDATE
ACDEHORW	COWHEARD
ACDEHOST	CATHODES
ACDEHOUV	AVOUCHED
ACDEHPPS	SCHAPPED
ACDEHPRS	SCARPHED
ACDEHPRU	UPCHEARD
ACDEHPST	DESPATCH
ACDEHPSU	CUPHEADS
ACDEHPTU	DEATHCUP
ACDEHQTU	QUATCHED
ACDEHRRS	CHRESARD
ACDEHRST	STARCHED
ACDEHTUW	WAUCHTED
ACDEIILN	ALCIDINE
ACDEIILS	LAICISED
ACDEIILT	CILIATED
ACDEIILZ	LAICIZED
ACDEIIMU	AECIDIUM
ACDEIINR	ACRIDINE
ACDEIINS	SCIAENID
ACDEIINT	ACTINIDE
	CTENIDIA
	DIACTINE
	INDICATE
ACDEIINU	INDUCIAE
ACDEIIRT	RATICIDE
ACDEIIST	ACIDIEST
ACDEIITV	CAVITIED
	VATICIDE
	VICIATED
ACDEIJNU	JAUNDICE
ACDEIKNP	PANICKED
ACDEIKNT	ANTICKED
ACDEIKPX	PICKAXED
ACDEILLM	MEDALLIC
ACDEILLN	DECLINAL
ACDEILLS	CEDILLAS
ACDEILLV	CAVILLED
ACDEILMN	MEDCINAL
ACDEILMO	CAMELOID
	MELODICA
ACDEILMS	CAMELIDS
	DECIMALS
	DECLAIMS
	MEDICALS
ACDEILMT	CLIMATED
	MALEDICT
ACDEILMX	CLIMAXED
ACDEILNP	PANICLED
ACDEILNU	DULCINEA
ACDEILOS	COALISED
ACDEILOZ	COALIZED
ACDEILPR	PLACIDER
ACDEILPS	DISPLACE
ACDEILPT	PLICATED
ACDEILRS	DECRIALS
	RADICELS
	RADICLES
ACDEILRT	ARTICLED
	LACERTID
ACDEILRU	AURICLED
	RADICULE
ACDEILST	CITADELS
	DIALECTS
ACDEILSY	ECDYSIAL
ACDEILTT	LATTICED
ACDEILTY	DIACETYL
ACDEIMNO	COMEDIAN
	DAEMONIC
	DEMONIAC
ACDEIMNP	PANDEMIC
ACDEIMOR	COADMIRE
	RACEMOID
ACDEIMPS	MIDSPACE
ACDEIMPT	IMPACTED
ACDEIMRT	DERMATIC
	TIMECARD
ACDEIMST	MISACTED
ACDEINNR	CRANNIED
ACDEINNT	INCANTED
ACDEINOP	CANOPIED
ACDEINOS	CODEINAS
	DIOCESAN
	OCEANIDS
ACDEINOT	ACTIONED
	CATENOID
ACDEINOV	VOIDANCE
ACDEINPT	PEDANTIC
	PENTADIC
ACDEINRR	RANCIDER
ACDEINRT	CRINATED
	DICENTRA
ACDEINSS	ACIDNESS
ACDEINST	DISTANCE
ACDEINSY	CYANIDES
	CYANISED
ACDEINTT	NICTATED
ACDEINTU	INCUDATE
ACDEINVY	DEVIANCY
ACDEINYZ	CYANIZED
ACDEIOPS	DIASCOPE
ACDEIORS	IDOCRASE
ACDEIORT	CERATOID
ACDEIORV	COVARIED
ACDEIOSS	ACIDOSES
ACDEIOSU	EDACIOUS
ACDEIPPT	TAPPICED
ACDEIPRS	EPACRIDS
	PERACIDS
ACDEIPRT	PICRATED
ACDEIPSS	DISPACES
	SPADICES
ACDEIPST	SPICATED
ACDEIPSZ	CAPSIZED
ACDEIPTV	CAPTIVED
ACDEIQRU	ACQUIRED
ACDEIRSS	SIDECARS
ACDEIRST	ACRIDEST
ACDEIRSU	DECURIAS
ACDEIRTT	CITRATED
	TETRACID
	TETRADIC
ACDEISSS	DISCASES
ACDEISTT	DICTATES
ACDEKLNR	CRANKLED
ACDEKLPS	SPACKLED
ACDEKLQU	QUACKLED
ACDEKNPR	PRANCKED
ACDEKNPU	UNPACKED
ACDEKNRU	UNRACKED
ACDEKNSU	UNCASKED
ACDEKNTU	UNTACKED
ACDEKOST	STOCKADE
ACDEKRSY	KEYCARDS
ACDELLNU	UNCALLED
ACDELLOR	CAROLLED
	COLLARED
ACDELLOT	COLLATED
ACDELLSU	CALLUSED
ACDELMOR	CLAMORED
ACDELMSU	MUSCADEL
ACDELNOO	CANOODLE
ACDELNOR	COLANDER
	CONELRAD
ACDELNOS	CELADONS
ACDELNPU	UNPLACED
ACDELNRS	CANDLERS
ACDELNRY	CALENDRY
ACDELNST	SCANTLED
ACDELNSU	UNSCALED
ACDELOOW	LACEWOOD
ACDELOPS	PEDOCALS
ACDELOPT	CLODPATE
ACDELOPU	CUPOLAED
ACDELORV	OVERCLAD
ACDELOTU	OCULATED
ACDELPPS	SCAPPLED
ACDELPSU	CAPSULED
	UPSCALED
ACDELRRS	CRADLERS
ACDELRSS	SCALDERS
ACDELRSW	SCRAWLED
ACDELRSY	SACREDLY
ACDELSTU	CAULDEST
	SULCATED
ACDELSWW	DEWCLAWS
ACDEMMRS	SCRAMMED
ACDEMNOR	ROMANCED
ACDEMNSU	DECUMANS
ACDEMOPR	COMPADRE
	COMPARED
ACDEMORR	CARROMED
ACDEMORS	COMRADES
ACDEMORT	DEMOCRAT
ACDEMPSU	CAMPUSED
ACDEMRSW	SCRAWMED
ACDEMSTU	MUSCADET
ACDEMUUV	VACUUMED
ACDENNNO	CANNONED
	NONDANCE
ACDENNOR	ORDNANCE
ACDENNOT	CANTONED
ACDENNST	SCANDENT
ACDENOPR	ENDOCARP
ACDENORR	RANCORED
ACDENORS	DRACONES
	ENDOSARC
ACDENORT	CARTONED
ACDENORY	CRAYONED
	DEACONRY
ACDENOST	ENDOCAST
	TACNODES
ACDENOSY	CYANOSED
ACDENOTT	COATTEND
ACDENOTU	OUTDANCE
	UNCOATED
ACDENPPU	UNCAPPED
ACDENPRU	PRAUNCED
ACDENPST	PANDECTS
ACDENRST	CANTREDS
ACDENRSU	DURANCES
ACDENRTU	UNCARTED
	UNCRATED
	UNDERACT
	UNTRACED
ACDENRVY	VERDANCY
ACDENSST	DESCANTS
ACDENSUU	UNCAUSED
ACDENTTY	DANCETTY
ACDEOPRS	SCOREPAD
ACDEOPRU	CROUPADE
ACDEOPRY	COPYREAD
ACDEOPSS	PEASCODS
ACDEOPTT	CAPOTTED
ACDEOPTU	OUTPACED
ACDEORRS	CORRADES
ACDEORRT	REDACTOR
ACDEORSS	SARCODES
ACDEORST	REDCOATS
ACDEORSU	CAROUSED
ACDEORTU	AERODUCT
	EDUCATOR
	OUTRACED
ACDEORTV	CAVORTED
ACDEOSTT	CODETTAS
	COSTATED
ACDEOSUV	COUVADES
ACDEOTTU	OUTACTED
ACDEPPRS	SCRAPPED
ACDEPRTU	CAPTURED
ACDEPSTU	CUSPATED
ACDEQTUU	AQUEDUCT
ACDERRSU	CRUSADER
ACDERRTU	TRADUCER
ACDERSSU	CRUSADES
ACDERSTT	DETRACTS
	SCRATTED
ACDERSTU	TRADUCES
ACDERTUV	CURVATED
ACDFFHNU	HANDCUFF
ACDFFIRT	DIFFRACT
ACDFFLOS	SCAFFOLD
ACDFIILU	FIDUCIAL
ACDFILMR	FILMCARD
ACDFILOU	FUCOIDAL
ACDFINOR	FRICANDO
ACDFIOST	FACTOIDS
ACDGHOTW	DOGWATCH
	WATCHDOG
ACDGIILO	DIALOGIC
ACDGILNN	CANDLING
ACDGILNR	CRADLING
ACDGILNS	SCALDING
ACDGILNU	CAUDLING
ACDGIMOT	DOGMATIC
ACDGINNS	DANCINGS
ACDGINNY	CANDYING

ACDGINRS	CARDINGS
ACDGINSU	SCAUDING
ACDGIOPR	PODAGRIC
ACDGKLOS	DAGLOCKS
ACDGLNOO	GOLCONDA
ACDGNOST	CANTDOGS
ACDGORST	DOGCARTS
ACDHIILS	CHILIADS
ACDHIINT	TACHINID
ACDHIIPS	DIPHASIC
ACDHIKNP	HANDPICK
ACDHIKOR	CHOKIDAR
ACDHIKOT	KATHODIC
ACDHILNT	THINCLAD
ACDHILPR	PILCHARD
ACDHILPS	CLAPDISH
ACDHIMTW	MIDWATCH
ACDHINOR	HADRONIC
	RHODANIC
ACDHINRY	DINARCHY
ACDHINSW	SANDWICH
ACDHIOPS	SCAPHOID
ACDHIOPY	HYPOACID
ACDHIORY	HYRACOID
ACDHIPST	DISPATCH
ACDHIQRU	CHARQUID
ACDHLNOR	CHALDRON
	CHLORDAN
	CHONDRAL
ACDHLORS	DORLACHS
ACDHMNTU	DUTCHMAN
ACDHMORU	MOUCHARD
ACDHNORW	CHAWDRON
ACDHNOSW	COWHANDS
ACDHOOST	CATHOODS
ACDHOOTW	WOODCHAT
ACDHOPRS	POCHARDS
ACDHORRS	ORCHARDS
ACDHORSY	DYSCHROA
ACDIIILN	INDICIAL
ACDIIINS	INDICIAS
ACDIIIPR	DIAPIRIC
ACDIIJLU	JUDICIAL
ACDIIKLP	PICKADIL
ACDIILMS	DISCLAIM
ACDIILNO	CONIDIAL
ACDIILNS	SCALDINI
ACDIILOV	OVICIDAL
ACDIILSU	SUICIDAL
ACDIILTY	CALIDITY
	DIALYTIC
ACDIIMNO	DAIMONIC
ACDIIMOR	CORMIDIA
	DIORAMIC
ACDIIMOT	DIATOMIC
ACDIIMSU	ASCIDIUM
ACDIINNO	CONIDIAN
ACDIINNS	INDICANS
ACDIINNT	INDICANT
ACDIINOP	PINACOID
ACDIINOT	ACTINOID
	DIATONIC
ACDIINPY	PYCNIDIA
ACDIINRS	ACRIDINS
ACDIIOSS	ACIDOSIS
ACDIIOSX	OXIDASIC
ACDIIRSS	SCIARIDS
ACDIIRST	ARCTIIDS
	CARDITIS
	TRIACIDS
	TRIADICS
ACDIIRTY	ACRIDITY
ACDIISST	SADISTIC
ACDIKLTU	DUCKTAIL
ACDIKMOO	COOKMAID

ACDIKRRY	RICKYARD
ACDILLOS	CODILLAS
ACDILLOU	CAUDILLO
	LODICULA
ACDILLPY	PLACIDLY
ACDILMOR	DROMICAL
ACDILMOU	MUCOIDAL
ACDILMSS	CLADISMS
ACDILMTU	TALMUDIC
ACDILNOO	CONOIDAL
ACDILNOR	IRONCLAD
ACDILNOS	SCALDINO
ACDILNOT	ANTICOLD
	DALTONIC
ACDILNRY	RANCIDLY
ACDILNSU	DULCIANS
ACDILNSY	SYNDICAL
ACDILNUU	NUDICAUL
ACDILOPS	PLACOIDS
ACDILOPY	POLYACID
ACDILORS	CORDIALS
ACDILORT	DICROTAL
ACDILOUV	OVIDUCAL
ACDILPSU	CUSPIDAL
ACDILRST	TRICLADS
ACDILSST	CLADISTS
ACDILSTW	WILDCATS
ACDIMMSU	CADMIUMS
ACDIMNOO	MONOACID
ACDIMNOS	MANDIOCS
	MONACIDS
ACDIMNSU	MUSCADIN
	SCANDIUM
ACDIMNSY	DYNAMICS
ACDIMOST	COADMITS
ACDIMOSY	DOCIMASY
ACDINNOO	ANCONOID
ACDINNOS	NONACIDS
ACDINNOY	ANODYNIC
ACDINOPS	SPONDAIC
ACDINORS	SARDONIC
ACDINORT	TORNADIC
ACDINORW	CORDWAIN
ACDINSST	DISCANTS
ACDINSTY	DYNASTIC
ACDINTUY	ADUNCITY
ACDIOOTU	AUTOCOID
ACDIOPRS	PICADORS
	SPORADIC
ACDIORRS	CORRIDAS
ACDIORSS	SARCOIDS
ACDIORST	CAROTIDS
ACDIORTT	DICTATOR
ACDIOSTY	DYSTOCIA
ACDIOSXY	OXYACIDS
ACDIPRST	ADSCRIPT
ACDIPSTY	DIPTYCAS
ACDIQRSU	QUADRICS
ACDIRSST	DRASTICS
ACDIRSTT	DISTRACT
ACDIRTWY	CITYWARD
ACDISTUV	VIADUCTS
ACDJNSTU	ADJUNCTS
ACDKKLUW	DUCKWALK
ACDKLOPS	PADLOCKS
ACDKMMOR	DRAMMOCK
ACDKMPSU	MUDPACKS
ACDKOPRS	POCKARDS
ACDLLORS	COLLARDS
ACDLNNOR	CORNLAND
ACDLNOPR	CROPLAND
ACDLNORS	CALDRONS
ACDLNORU	CAULDRON
	CRUNODAL
ACDLNORY	CONDYLAR

ACDLNOST	COTLANDS
ACDLNSSU	SUNSCALD
ACDLOOOR	COLORADO
ACDLOORT	DOCTORAL
ACDLORWY	COWARDLY
ACDLOSWY	LADYCOWS
ACDLSTUY	DACTYLUS
ACDMMNOO	COMMANDO
ACDMMNOS	COMMANDS
ACDMNOPS	COMPANDS
ACDMNORY	DORMANCY
	MORDANCY
ACDMOOPR	MACROPOD
ACDMOOSW	CAMWOODS
ACDMORSZ	CZARDOMS
ACDMPRTU	DUMPCART
ACDNOORR	RONCADOR
ACDNOORS	CARDOONS
ACDNOORT	ACRODONT
ACDNOORV	CORDOVAN
ACDNOOTU	DUCATOON
ACDNORRW	WARDCORN
ACDNORSU	CANDOURS
	CAUDRONS
ACDNOSTW	DOWNCAST
ACDNOSUU	ADUNCOUS
ACDOOPPR	PODOCARP
ACDOOPTY	OCTAPODY
ACDOORST	OSTRACOD
	SCORDATO
ACDOPRST	POSTCARD
ACDORRWY	COWARDRY
ACDORSST	COSTARDS
ACDORSSU	CRUSADOS
ACDORSUZ	CRUZADOS
ACDRSSTU	CUSTARDS
ACDRSTTU	DUSTCART
ACDRSTUY	CUSTARDY
ACEEEFRR	CAREFREE
ACEEEGLN	ELEGANCE
ACEEEGPR	CREEPAGE
ACEEEGRS	CARGEESE
ACEEEIPR	EARPIECE
ACEEEIPS	SEAPIECE
ACEEEKNT	NECKATEE
ACEEELMR	CAMELEER
ACEEENRR	CAREENER
ACEEENRS	ENCREASE
ACEEENSV	EVANESCE
ACEEEPSS	ESCAPEES
ACEEERRR	CAREERER
ACEEERRT	RECREATE
ACEEERTT	ETCETERA
ACEEERTX	EXECRATE
ACEEESUV	EVACUEES
ACEEFFIN	CAFFEINE
ACEEFFOR	FOREFACE
ACEEFFRS	EFFACERS
ACEEFFRT	AFFECTER
ACEEFHNS	ENCHAFES
ACEEFHWY	WHEYFACE
ACEEFILM	MALEFICE
ACEEFILS	CALEFIES
ACEEFINS	FAIENCES
	FIANCEES
ACEEFISS	CASEFIES
ACEEFKOR	ECOFREAK
ACEEFLPU	PEACEFUL
ACEEFLSS	FACELESS
ACEEFLTY	FACETELY
ACEEFNSY	FAYENCES
ACEEFPRR	PREFACER
ACEEFPRS	PREFACES
ACEEFPRT	PERFECTA
	PRAEFECT

ACEEFPTY	TYPEFACE
ACEEFRSU	FARCEUSE
ACEEGHNR	ENCHARGE
	RECHANGE
ACEEGHNX	EXCHANGE
ACEEGHRR	RECHARGE
ACEEGILS	ELEGIACS
	LEGACIES
ACEEGINS	AGENCIES
ACEEGINT	AGENETIC
ACEEGIRZ	GRAECIZE
ACEEGKNR	NECKGEAR
ACEEGKRW	WRECKAGE
ACEEGLNY	ELEGANCY
ACEEGLPU	PUCELAGE
ACEEGNNT	TANGENCE
ACEEGNOZ	COZENAGE
ACEEGNRS	ENGRACES
ACEEGNRY	REAGENCY
ACEEGNST	CENTAGES
ACEEGNSV	SCAVENGE
ACEEGORR	RACEGOER
ACEEGORV	COVERAGE
ACEEGSSU	ESCUAGES
ACEEHHST	CHEETAHS
ACEEHILR	LEACHIER
ACEEHINT	ECHINATE
ACEEHIPR	PEACHIER
ACEEHIPS	CHEAPIES
ACEEHIPT	PETECHIA
ACEEHIRT	AETHERIC
	HETAERIC
ACEEHIRV	ACHIEVER
	CHIVAREE
ACEEHIST	HICATEES
ACEEHISV	ACHIEVES
ACEEHITV	ATCHIEVE
ACEEHKNS	SKEECHAN
ACEEHKOS	HOECAKES
ACEEHKTT	HACKETTE
ACEEHLMP	EMPLEACH
ACEEHLOS	SHOELACE
ACEEHLPS	PLEACHES
ACEEHLRS	LEACHERS
	RELACHES
ACEEHLSS	LACHESES
ACEEHLST	CHELATES
ACEEHLSW	ESCHEWAL
ACEEHLTV	CHEVALET
ACEEHMNP	CAMPHENE
ACEEHMNR	MENARCHE
ACEEHMRS	CASHMERE
	MACHREES
	MARCHESE
ACEEHMST	MACHETES
ACEEHNNR	ENHANCER
ACEEHNNS	ENHANCES
ACEEHNPS	CHEAPENS
ACEEHNRS	ENARCHES
	ENCHASER
ACEEHNRV	REVANCHE
ACEEHNSS	ENCASHES
	ENCHASES
ACEEHOOT	OOTHECAE
ACEEHOPT	APOTHECE
ACEEHORT	OCHREATE
ACEEHPPS	ECHAPPES
ACEEHPRR	PREACHER
ACEEHPRS	PEACHERS
	PREACHES
ACEEHPRT	ETHERCAP
ACEEHPST	CHEAPEST
ACEEHQSU	QUEACHES
ACEEHRRS	REACHERS
	RESEARCH

	SEARCHER
ACEEHRRT	TREACHER
ACEEHRSS	SEARCHES
ACEEHRST	CHEATERS
	HECTARES
	RECHATES
	RECHEATS
	TEACHERS
ACEEHRTT	CATHETER
ACEEHRTY	CHEATERY
ACEEHSST	ESCHEATS
ACEEHSTX	CATHEXES
	EXCHEATS
ACEEHTWY	WATCHEYE
ACEEIKLL	LACELIKE
ACEEIKLV	CAVELIKE
ACEEIKNP	PEACENIK
ACEEIKRR	CREAKIER
ACEEILLM	MICELLAE
ACEEILLP	CALLIPEE
ACEEILMN	CAMELINE
ACEEILMT	EMETICAL
ACEEILMU	LEUCEMIA
ACEEILNP	CAPELINE
ACEEILNR	CINEREAL
	RELIANCE
ACEEILNS	SALIENCE
ACEEILPS	CALIPEES
	ESPECIAL
ACEEILRS	ESCALIER
ACEEILRV	RECEIVAL
ACEEIMOT	ACOEMETI
ACEEIMRR	CREAMIER
	REARMICE
	RECAMIER
ACEEIMRS	CASIMERE
	RACEMISE
ACEEIMRT	CEMITARE
ACEEIMRZ	RACEMIZE
ACEEIMST	EMICATES
ACEEINNR	NARCEINE
ACEEINPS	SAPIENCE
ACEEINPT	PATIENCE
ACEEINRS	CINEREAS
	INCREASE
	RESIANCE
ACEEINRT	CENTIARE
	CREATINE
	INCREATE
	ITERANCE
ACEEINST	CINEASTE
ACEEINSU	EUCAINES
ACEEINTV	ENACTIVE
ACEEINTX	EXITANCE
ACEEIPPR	PRAECIPE
ACEEIPST	SPECIATE
ACEEIRRS	CARIERES
	CREASIER
ACEEIRSU	CAUSERIE
ACEEIRSW	WISEACRE
ACEEIRTV	CREATIVE
	REACTIVE
ACEEISTV	VESICATE
ACEEJKNS	JACKEENS
ACEEJKRT	REJACKET
ACEEKLMR	MACKEREL
ACEEKLRT	RETACKLE
ACEEKLRW	EELWRACK
ACEEKMPT	EMPACKET
ACEEKNPS	KNEECAPS
ACEEKNRW	NECKWEAR
ACEEKRRT	RACKETER
ACEELLMT	CELLMATE
ACEELLNS	NACELLES
ACEELLNT	LANCELET
ACEELLOT	OCELLATE
ACEELLPT	CAPELLET
ACEELLRR	CELLARER
	RECALLER
ACEELLRT	CELLARET
ACEELLRV	CREVALLE
ACEELLSS	LACELESS
ACEELMNO	CAMELEON
ACEELMNP	PLACEMEN
ACEELMPS	EMPLACES
ACEELMRS	RECLAMES
	SCLEREMA
ACEELNPR	PRECLEAN
ACEELNPT	PENTACLE
ACEELNRR	LARCENER
ACEELNRS	CLEANERS
	CLEANSER
	RECLEANS
ACEELNRU	CERULEAN
ACEELNRV	VERNACLE
ACEELNSS	CLEANSES
ACEELNST	CLEANEST
	LATENCES
ACEELNSU	NUCLEASE
ACEELNSV	ENCLAVES
	VALENCES
ACEELNTT	TENTACLE
ACEELNTU	NUCLEATE
ACEELOPS	ESCALOPE
	OPALESCE
ACEELORS	ESCAROLE
ACEELORT	CORELATE
	RELOCATE
ACEELOSS	SECALOSE
ACEELOSV	VOCALESE
ACEELPPR	PREPLACE
ACEELPRR	PRECLEAR
	REPLACER
ACEELPRS	PERCALES
	REPLACES
ACEELPRT	PRAELECT
ACEELPST	CAPELETS
ACEELPSY	CYPSELAE
ACEELPTU	PECULATE
ACEELPTY	CLYPEATE
ACEELRRS	CLEARERS
ACEELRSS	CARELESS
	RESCALES
ACEELRST	CLEAREST
	SCELERAT
	TREACLES
ACEELRSV	CERVELAS
	CLEAVERS
ACEELRTT	RACLETTE
ACEELRTU	ULCERATE
ACEELRTV	CERVELAT
ACEELRTX	EXCRETAL
ACEELSST	CELESTAS
ACEELSSU	EUCLASES
ACEELSTT	TELECAST
ACEELSVX	EXCLAVES
ACEEMMOT	AMMOCETE
ACEEMNNS	SCENEMAN
ACEEMNOT	MECONATE
ACEEMNPS	SPACEMEN
ACEEMNRS	MENACERS
ACEEMNST	CASEMENT
ACEEMOPR	CAMPOREE
ACEEMOPT	COPEMATE
ACEEMORS	RACEMOSE
ACEEMORV	OVERCAME
ACEEMRRS	AMERCERS
	CREAMERS
	SCREAMER
ACEEMRRY	CREAMERY
ACEEMRST	CREMATES
	MEERCATS
ACEEMRTW	CREWMATE
ACEENNPS	PENANCES
ACEENNRS	NARCEENS
ACEENNRT	ENTRANCE
ACEENNST	CANTEENS
ACEENNSY	CAYENNES
ACEENOPT	CONEPATE
ACEENORT	CAROTENE
ACEENOST	ACETONES
	NOTECASE
ACEENPRR	PARCENER
ACEENPRT	PERCEANT
	PREENACT
ACEENRRT	RECANTER
	RECREANT
ACEENRSS	CASERNES
ACEENRST	CENTARES
	REASCENT
	REENACTS
	SARCENET
ACEENRTU	ENACTURE
	UNCREATE
ACEENSTX	EXSECANT
ACEEOQTU	COEQUATE
ACEEORST	CREASOTE
ACEEOSSS	CASEOSES
ACEEOSTT	ECOSTATE
ACEEOSTV	EVOCATES
ACEEPRRS	CAPERERS
ACEEPRSS	ESCAPERS
	RESPACES
ACEEPRTT	ETTERCAP
ACEEPRTU	PERACUTE
ACEEPRTX	EXCERPTA
ACEEPSST	PECTASES
ACEEPSSU	AUCEPSES
ACEEPSTT	PECTATES
	SPECTATE
ACEEPSTY	TYPECASE
ACEERRSS	CARESSER
	CREASERS
ACEERRST	CATERERS
	RECRATES
	RETRACES
	TERRACES
ACEERRSU	ECRASEUR
ACEERRTU	CREATURE
ACEERRUV	VERRUCAE
ACEERSSS	CARESSES
ACEERSST	CATERESS
	CERASTES
ACEERSSU	SURCEASE
ACEERSSV	CREVASSE
ACEERSTU	SECATEUR
ACEERSTX	EXACTERS
ACEERTTU	ERUCTATE
ACEESSST	ECSTASES
ACEESSTT	CASETTES
	CASSETTE
ACEESTTX	EXACTEST
ACEFFGIN	EFFACING
ACEFFHIR	CHAFFIER
ACEFFHIS	AFFICHES
ACEFFHRS	CHAFFERS
ACEFFHRU	CHAUFFER
ACEFFHRY	CHAFFERY
ACEFFIMS	CAFFEISM
ACEFFINS	CAFFEINS
ACEFFISS	SCAFFIES
ACEFFLLU	FULLFACE
ACEFFLRS	SCLAFFER
ACEFFORS	AFFORCES
ACEFGINN	ENFACING
ACEFGINR	REFACING
ACEFGINT	FACETING
ACEFGLRU	GRACEFUL
ACEFGLSU	CAGEFULS
ACEFGOST	GEOFACTS
ACEFHISV	CAVEFISH
ACEFHLNS	FLANCHES
ACEFHMRS	CHAMFERS
ACEFHORU	FAROUCHE
ACEFHRST	FRATCHES
ACEFHRSU	CHAUFERS
ACEFIILS	FELICIAS
ACEFIIPR	PACIFIER
ACEFIIPS	PACIFIES
ACEFIIRT	ARTIFICE
ACEFIKLL	CALFLIKE
ACEFILLS	ICEFALLS
ACEFILLY	FACILELY
ACEFILOP	EPIFOCAL
ACEFILOS	FASCIOLE
	FOCALISE
ACEFILOZ	FOCALIZE
ACEFILRS	FILACERS
ACEFILRY	FIRECLAY
ACEFIMNY	FEMINACY
ACEFIMPR	CAMPFIRE
ACEFINNS	FINANCES
ACEFINRS	FANCIERS
ACEFINRX	CARNIFEX
ACEFINSS	FASCINES
ACEFINST	FANCIEST
ACEFINSU	UNIFACES
ACEFIOSS	FIASCOES
ACEFIPRY	REPACIFY
ACEFIRRT	CRAFTIER
ACEFIRTT	TRIFECTA
ACEFIRTY	FERACITY
ACEFISST	FACTISES
ACEFKLRS	FLACKERS
ACEFKLRY	FLACKERY
ACEFKLST	FLACKETS
ACEFLLSS	CALFLESS
ACEFLMNO	FLAMENCO
ACEFLNOR	FALCONER
ACEFLNOT	CONFLATE
	FALCONET
ACEFLNRY	CRANEFLY
ACEFLORS	ALFRESCO
ACEFLRTU	FULCRATE
ACEFLRUU	FURCULAE
ACEFMNOO	MOONFACE
ACEFNNOS	FACONNES
ACEFNORV	CONFERVA
ACEFNPRT	PENCRAFT
ACEFNRST	CANTREFS
ACEFNRSU	FURNACES
ACEFOOPT	FOOTPACE
ACEFOORT	FOOTRACE
ACEFOPST	POSTFACE
ACEFORRS	FORECARS
ACEFORST	FORECAST
ACEFORSX	CARFOXES
ACEFOSTU	OUTFACES
ACEFRRST	REFRACTS
ACEFRRSU	FARCEURS
	SURFACER
ACEFRRTU	FRACTURE
ACEFRSSU	SURFACES
ACEFRSTU	FACTURES
	FURCATES
ACEGGILN	CAGELING
	GLACEING
ACEGGILR	CLAGGIER
ACEGGINN	ENCAGING
ACEGGIOP	EPAGOGIC

ACEGGIRR	CRAGGIER
ACEGHIIT	CHIGETAI
ACEGHILN	LEACHING
ACEGHILT	LICHGATE
	TEIGLACH
ACEGHINP	PEACHING
ACEGHINR	REACHING
ACEGHINT	CHEATING
	TEACHING
ACEGHLOS	GALOCHES
ACEGHLRS	SCHLAGER
ACEGHLRU	RUGELACH
ACEGHLTY	LYCHGATE
ACEGHLUY	GAUCHELY
ACEGHMMU	CHUMMAGE
ACEGHMOR	ECHOGRAM
	GRAMOCHE
ACEGHNRS	CHANGERS
ACEGHNRU	UNCHARGE
ACEGHNSU	CHAUNGES
	GAUNCHES
ACEGHOSU	GOUACHES
ACEGHOSW	COWHAGES
ACEGHRRS	CHARGERS
ACEGHRTU	RECAUGHT
ACEGHSTU	GAUCHEST
ACEGIIMP	EPIGAMIC
ACEGIINR	REAGINIC
ACEGIINV	VICINAGE
ACEGIKNR	CREAKING
ACEGILLO	COLLEGIA
ACEGILLR	ALLERGIC
ACEGILMU	MUCILAGE
ACEGILNN	CLEANING
	ELANCING
	ENLACING
ACEGILNR	CLEARING
	RELACING
ACEGILNT	CLEATING
ACEGILNV	CLEAVING
ACEGILNW	LACEWING
ACEGILOS	CALIGOES
ACEGILRS	GLACIERS
	GRACILES
ACEGILRV	CLAVIGER
ACEGILRY	GLYCERIA
ACEGILSS	GLACISES
ACEGILST	GELASTIC
	GESTICAL
ACEGIMMT	TAGMEMIC
ACEGIMNN	MENACING
ACEGIMNO	CAMEOING
ACEGIMNR	AMERCING
	CREAMING
	GERMANIC
ACEGIMNS	MAGNESIC
ACEGIMNT	MAGNETIC
ACEGIMOS	CAMOGIES
ACEGIMOX	EXOGAMIC
ACEGIMRR	GRIMACER
ACEGIMRS	GRIMACES
ACEGIMTY	MEGACITY
ACEGINNO	CANOEING
ACEGINNR	ENRACING
	RECANING
ACEGINNS	ENCASING
ACEGINNT	ENACTING
ACEGINNV	ENCAVING
ACEGINOS	COINAGES
ACEGINOY	GYNOECIA
ACEGINPR	CAPERING
	PEARCING
	PREACING
ACEGINPS	ESCAPING
ACEGINRS	CREASING
	GRECIANS
	SEARCING
ACEGINRT	ARGENTIC
	CATERING
	CITRANGE
	CREATING
	REACTING
ACEGINSS	CAGINESS
	CEASINGS
ACEGINTX	EXACTING
ACEGIOTT	COGITATE
ACEGIPRS	SPAGERIC
ACEGIRST	AGRESTIC
	CIGARETS
	ERGASTIC
ACEGISTU	GAUCIEST
ACEGISTW	GAWCIEST
ACEGJKLS	JACKLEGS
ACEGKLOS	LOCKAGES
ACEGKLOV	GAVELOCK
ACEGKLRS	GRACKLES
ACEGKMOS	MOCKAGES
ACEGKORS	CORKAGES
ACEGKORW	CAGEWORK
ACEGKRTU	TRUCKAGE
ACEGLLNO	COLLAGEN
ACEGLLOS	COLLAGES
ACEGLNOS	CONGEALS
ACEGLNOT	OCTANGLE
ACEGLNOY	AGLYCONE
ACEGLNRS	CLANGERS
	GLANCERS
ACEGLOST	CATELOGS
ACEGLOSU	CAGOULES
ACEGMNOY	GEOMANCY
ACEGMNRS	CRAGSMEN
ACEGMOPS	COMPAGES
ACEGMORS	SCARMOGE
ACEGMRRY	GRAMERCY
ACEGNNOR	CRANNOGE
ACEGNNOY	CYANOGEN
ACEGNNRY	REGNANCY
ACEGNNTY	TANGENCY
ACEGNORS	ACROGENS
	CORNAGES
ACEGNOST	COAGENTS
	COGNATES
ACEGNSSY	CAGYNESS
ACEGOORS	CARGOOSE
ACEGOPRY	GEOCARPY
ACEGORSS	CORSAGES
	SOCAGERS
ACEGORST	ESCARGOT
ACEGORSU	COURAGES
ACEGORTT	COTTAGER
ACEGORTY	CATEGORY
ACEGOSTT	COTTAGES
ACEGOTTY	COTTAGEY
ACEGRSTU	TRUCAGES
ACEGSSTU	SCUTAGES
ACEGSTTU	CUTTAGES
ACEHHINS	HAINCHES
ACEHHIPS	CHEAPISH
ACEHHIRR	HIERARCH
ACEHHIST	SHECHITA
ACEHHISU	HUISACHE
ACEHHLST	HATCHELS
ACEHHLSU	SHAUCHLE
ACEHHMNN	HENCHMAN
ACEHHNRT	ETHNARCH
ACEHHNSU	HAUNCHES
ACEHHPRT	HEPTARCH
ACEHHRST	HATCHERS
ACEHHRSU	HACHURES
ACEHHRTT	THATCHER
ACEHHRTY	HATCHERY
	THEARCHY
ACEHHRXY	HEXARCHY
ACEHHSTT	HATCHETS
	THATCHES
ACEHHTTY	HATCHETY
ACEHIIMS	ISCHEMIA
ACEHIINT	ETHICIAN
ACEHIIRT	HIERATIC
ACEHIJKR	HIJACKER
ACEHIJNT	JACINTHE
ACEHIKLP	KEPHALIC
ACEHIKLR	CHALKIER
	HACKLIER
ACEHIKLW	LICHWAKE
ACEHIKRS	KACHERIS
ACEHIKRW	WHACKIER
ACEHILLS	CHALLIES
ACEHILLT	HELLICAT
ACEHILMN	INCHMEAL
ACEHILMO	CHOLEMIA
ACEHILMP	IMPLEACH
ACEHILMS	CAMELISH
ACEHILMY	LECHAYIM
ACEHILNP	CEPHALIN
ACEHILNT	CHAINLET
	CHATLINE
	ETHNICAL
ACEHILOR	HALICORE
	HEROICAL
ACEHILPR	PARHELIC
ACEHILRS	CHARLIES
ACEHILST	ETHICALS
ACEHILTT	ATHLETIC
	THETICAL
ACEHIMMS	CHAMMIES
ACEHIMNN	CHAINMEN
ACEHIMNP	CAMPHINE
ACEHIMNR	CHAIRMEN
ACEHIMNS	MACHINES
ACEHIMNT	ANTHEMIC
ACEHIMNU	ACHENIUM
ACEHIMPR	CAMPHIRE
ACEHIMPT	EMPATHIC
	EMPHATIC
ACEHIMRS	CHASMIER
	CHIMERAS
	MARCHESI
ACEHIMRT	RHEMATIC
ACEHIMSS	CHAMISES
ACEHIMST	HEMATICS
	MASTICHE
	MISTEACH
	TACHISME
ACEHIMTT	THEMATIC
ACEHINNS	ENCHAINS
ACEHINOT	INCHOATE
ACEHINPS	PAINCHES
ACEHINPT	HAPTENIC
ACEHINRS	ARCHINES
	INARCHES
ACEHINRV	VACHERIN
ACEHINSS	ACHINESS
	INCHASES
ACEHINST	ASTHENIC
	CHANTIES
ACEHINSY	HYACINES
	SYNECHIA
ACEHIOPR	POACHIER
ACEHIOST	ACHIOTES
	TOISEACH
ACEHIPPR	CHAPPIER
ACEHIPPS	CHAPPIES
ACEHIPRS	ASPHERIC
	CHARPIES
	PARCHESI
	SERAPHIC
ACEHIPRT	CHAPITER
	PATCHIER
	PHREATIC
ACEHIPST	HEPATICS
	PASTICHE
	PISTACHE
ACEHIPTT	PATHETIC
ACEHIPTW	WHITECAP
ACEHIQSU	QUAICHES
ACEHIRRR	CHARRIER
ACEHIRSS	CASHIERS
	RACHISES
ACEHIRST	CHARIEST
	STICHERA
	THERIACS
ACEHIRSU	EUCHARIS
ACEHIRSV	ARCHIVES
ACEHIRSW	ARCHWISE
ACEHIRTT	CHATTIER
	THEATRIC
ACEHISST	CHASTISE
	TAISCHES
ACEHISSU	CHIAUSES
ACEHISTT	CHATTIES
	TACHISTE
ACEHISTX	CATHEXIS
ACEHISTY	YACHTIES
ACEHISTZ	ZAITECHS
ACEHKLLS	SHELLACK
ACEHKLOV	HAVELOCK
ACEHKLPR	KREPLACH
ACEHKLRS	HACKLERS
	SHACKLER
ACEHKLSS	SHACKLES
ACEHKLST	HACKLETS
	KLATCHES
ACEHKLTY	LATCHKEY
ACEHKMPU	MUCKHEAP
ACEHKNSY	HACKNEYS
ACEHKOPS	SHOEPACK
ACEHKORV	HAVOCKER
ACEHKOSS	SHACKOES
ACEHKOST	HOTCAKES
ACEHKOSW	WHACKOES
ACEHKOTU	TUCKAHOE
ACEHKRSW	WHACKERS
ACEHKRTW	THWACKER
ACEHLLMO	MALLECHO
ACEHLLOO	COALHOLE
ACEHLLOR	ORCHELLA
ACEHLLPS	PELLACHS
ACEHLLSS	SHELLACS
ACEHLLST	HELLCATS
ACEHLLSU	HALLUCES
ACEHLMOT	CHAMELOT
ACEHLMST	CHAMLETS
ACEHLNNS	CHANNELS
ACEHLNOS	CHALONES
ACEHLNOU	EULACHON
ACEHLNPS	PLANCHES
ACEHLNPT	PLANCHET
ACEHLNRS	CHARNELS
ACEHLNRU	LAUNCHER
	RELAUNCH
ACEHLNST	STANCHEL
ACEHLNSU	LAUNCHES
ACEHLOOT	OOTHECAL
ACEHLOPT	POTLACHE
ACEHLORS	CHOLERAS
	CHORALES
ACEHLORT	CHELATOR
	CHLORATE
	TROCHLEA

ACEHLORU	LEACHOUR
ACEHLOST	CATHOLES
	CHOLATES
	ESCHALOT
ACEHLPRT	CHAPTREL
ACEHLPRY	CHAPELRY
ACEHLPSS	CHAPLESS
ACEHLPST	CHAPLETS
ACEHLRSS	CLASHERS
	RASCHELS
ACEHLRST	ARCHLETS
	TRACHLES
ACEHLRSY	CHARLEYS
ACEHLRTU	ARCHLUTE
	TRAUCHLE
ACEHLSSS	CASHLESS
ACEHLSST	SATCHELS
	SLATCHES
ACEHLSTT	CHATTELS
	LATCHETS
ACEHLSTY	CHASTELY
ACEHMMNR	MARCHMEN
ACEHMNNR	RANCHMEN
ACEHMNOR	CHOREMAN
ACEHMNRS	ENCHARMS
ACEHMNRT	MERCHANT
ACEHMNSS	CHESSMAN
ACEHMNST	MANCHETS
ACEHMNTW	WATCHMEN
ACEHMNTY	YACHTMEN
ACEHMORT	CHROMATE
ACEHMOST	MOSCHATE
ACEHMPRS	CHAMPERS
ACEHMRRS	CHARMERS
	MARCHERS
ACEHMRSS	SCHMEARS
ACEHMRST	MATCHERS
ACEHMRSU	CHAUMERS
ACEHMSST	SMATCHES
ACEHMSTU	MUSTACHE
ACEHMSTY	ECTHYMAS
ACEHNNOP	PANCHEON
ACEHNNPT	PENCHANT
ACEHNNRS	CHANNERS
ACEHNNST	ENCHANTS
ACEHNOPR	CANEPHOR
	CHAPERON
ACEHNOPS	PANOCHES
ACEHNOPT	CENOTAPH
ACEHNORR	RANCHERO
ACEHNORT	ANCHORET
ACEHNPRT	PENTARCH
ACEHNPRU	UNPREACH
ACEHNPSU	PAUNCHES
ACEHNRRS	RANCHERS
ACEHNRSS	ARCHNESS
ACEHNRST	CHANTERS
	SNATCHER
	STANCHER
	TRANCHES
ACEHNRSU	RAUNCHES
ACEHNRTT	TRANCHET
ACEHNRTU	CHAUNTER
ACEHNSSS	SCHANSES
ACEHNSST	CHASTENS
	SNATCHES
	STANCHES
ACEHNSSZ	SCHANZES
ACEHNSTT	ETCHANTS
ACEHNSTU	NAUTCHES
	UNCHASTE
ACEHNSTY	CHANTEYS
ACEHNSTZ	SCHANTZE
ACEHNSZZ	CHAZZENS
ACEHOPPR	COPPERAH
ACEHOPRR	REPROACH
ACEHOPRS	POACHERS
ACEHOPSS	SHOEPACS
ACEHORRS	HORSECAR
ACEHORRV	OVERARCH
ACEHORST	CHAROSET
	THORACES
ACEHORTT	THEOCRAT
ACEHORTU	OUTREACH
ACEHORUV	AVOUCHER
ACEHOSSW	SHOWCASE
ACEHOSTU	CATHOUSE
	SOUTACHE
ACEHOSTY	CHAYOTES
ACEHOSUV	AVOUCHES
ACEHOTTU	OUTCHEAT
ACEHPPSS	CHAPPESS
	SCHAPPES
ACEHPRRS	PRECRASH
ACEHPRST	CHAPTERS
	PATCHERS
ACEHPRSU	PURCHASE
ACEHPRTY	PATCHERY
	PETCHARY
ACEHPSTY	SCYPHATE
ACEHQSTU	QUATCHES
ACEHRRSS	CRASHERS
ACEHRRST	CHARTERS
	RECHARTS
	STARCHER
ACEHRRTT	TETRARCH
ACEHRSST	STARCHES
ACEHRSSU	CHASSEUR
ACEHRSTT	CHATTERS
	RATCHETS
ACEHRSTW	WATCHERS
ACEHRSTY	YACHTERS
ACEHRTTY	CHATTERY
	TRACHYTE
ACEHSSSU	CHAUSSES
ACEHSSTT	CHASTEST
ACEHSSTW	SWATCHES
ACEHSTTU	CATHETUS
	TEUCHATS
ACEHSTTW	WATCHETS
ACEHTTUZ	ZUCHETTA
ACEIILMN	LIMACINE
ACEIILNR	IRENICAL
ACEIILNS	SALICINE
ACEIILSS	LAICISES
ACEIILST	CILIATES
	SILICATE
ACEIILSZ	LAICIZES
ACEIIMRS	CASIMIRE
ACEIIMRV	VIRAEMIC
ACEIIMSS	ASEISMIC
ACEIIMST	METICAIS
ACEIIMTU	MAIEUTIC
ACEIINPS	PISCINAE
ACEIINRS	RIANCIES
ACEIINST	CANITIES
ACEIINTV	INACTIVE
ACEIINTZ	ANTICIZE
ACEIIPRS	PIRACIES
ACEIIPSS	EPISCIAS
ACEIIPTX	EPITAXIC
ACEIIRRT	CRITERIA
ACEIIRSV	VICARIES
ACEIISTU	ACUITIES
ACEIISTV	CAITIVES
	CAVITIES
	VICIATES
ACEIITTV	VITICETA
ACEIITVZ	ACTIVIZE
ACEIJKSS	JACKSIES
ACEIJMST	MAJESTIC
ACEIJNRR	JERRICAN
ACEIKKLS	SACKLIKE
ACEIKKNR	KNACKIER
ACEIKLLM	MILLCAKE
ACEIKLLW	CLAWLIKE
ACEIKLLY	CLAYLIKE
ACEIKLRT	TALCKIER
ACEIKLRY	CREAKILY
ACEIKMNN	NICKNAME
ACEIKMRS	KERAMICS
ACEIKMRV	MAVERICK
ACEIKNPS	CAPESKIN
ACEIKNRR	CRANKIER
ACEIKNRS	SKINCARE
ACEIKOPS	PAIOCKES
ACEIKORR	CROAKIER
ACEIKPRS	EARPICKS
ACEIKPSW	WICKAPES
ACEIKPSX	PICKAXES
ACEIKRRV	VRAICKER
ACEIKSTT	TACKIEST
	TIETACKS
ACEIKSTW	WACKIEST
ACEILLLT	CLITELLA
ACEILLMR	MICELLAR
	MILLRACE
ACEILLMS	LIMACELS
ACEILLMT	METALLIC
ACEILLMY	MYCELIAL
ACEILLNT	CLIENTAL
ACEILLOP	CALLIOPE
ACEILLOR	ROCAILLE
ACEILLOS	LOCALISE
ACEILLOT	LOCALITE
	TEOCALLI
ACEILLOZ	LOCALIZE
ACEILLPR	CALLIPER
ACEILLPS	ALLSPICE
ACEILLPY	EPICALLY
ACEILLRV	CAVILLER
ACEILLSS	SCALLIES
ACEILMMO	CAMOMILE
ACEILMMR	CLAMMIER
ACEILMNN	CLINAMEN
ACEILMNO	COALMINE
ACEILMNP	MANCIPLE
ACEILMNS	MELANICS
	MENISCAL
	MESCALIN
ACEILMNY	MYCELIAN
ACEILMOS	CAMISOLE
ACEILMPS	MISPLACE
ACEILMPT	PELMATIC
ACEILMRS	CLAIMERS
	MIRACLES
	RECLAIMS
ACEILMRT	METRICAL
ACEILMRY	CREAMILY
ACEILMST	CALMIEST
	CLEMATIS
	CLIMATES
	METICALS
ACEILMSU	MUSICALE
ACEILMSX	CLIMAXES
	EXCLAIMS
ACEILMTU	AMULETIC
ACEILNNP	PANNICLE
	PINNACLE
ACEILNNR	ENCRINAL
ACEILNOR	ACROLEIN
	COLINEAR
	CREOLIAN
	LONICERA
ACEILNOS	ALNICOES
ACEILNPS	CAPELINS
	PANICLES
	PELICANS
ACEILNPT	PECTINAL
	PLANETIC
ACEILNRS	CARLINES
	LANCIERS
ACEILNRT	CLARINET
ACEILNSS	LACINESS
	SANICLES
ACEILNSU	AESCULIN
	LUNACIES
ACEILNSY	SALIENCY
ACEILOPR	CAPRIOLE
ACEILOPT	POETICAL
ACEILORR	CARRIOLE
ACEILORS	CALORIES
	CARIOLES
ACEILORT	EROTICAL
	LORICATE
ACEILORV	ARVICOLE
ACEILORZ	CALORIZE
ACEILOSS	CELOSIAS
	COALISES
ACEILOST	ALOETICS
	COALIEST
	SOCIETAL
ACEILOSV	VOCALISE
ACEILOSZ	COALIZES
ACEILOTV	LOCATIVE
ACEILOVZ	VOCALIZE
ACEILPPY	PIPECLAY
ACEILPRS	CALIPERS
	REPLICAS
	SPIRACLE
ACEILPRT	PARTICLE
	PRELATIC
ACEILPRU	PECULIAR
ACEILPSS	SLIPCASE
	SPECIALS
ACEILPST	PLICATES
	SEPTICAL
	TIECLASP
ACEILPSU	SPICULAE
ACEILPTY	ETYPICAL
ACEILPXY	EPICALYX
ACEILRRT	CLARTIER
ACEILRRW	CRAWLIER
ACEILRSS	CLASSIER
ACEILRST	ALTRICES
	ARTICLES
	RECITALS
	SELICTAR
	STERICAL
ACEILRSU	AURICLES
ACEILRSV	CALIVERS
	CAVILERS
	CLAVIERS
	VISCERAL
ACEILRTT	TRACTILE
ACEILRTU	RETICULA
ACEILRTV	VERTICAL
ACEILRTY	LITERACY
ACEILRUV	ACERVULI
ACEILSST	ELASTICS
	SALICETS
	SCALIEST
ACEILSTT	LATTICES
	TALCIEST
ACEILSTY	CLAYIEST
ACEILSUV	VESICULA
ACEILTVY	ACTIVELY
ACEIMMNP	PEMMICAN
ACEIMMOS	SEMICOMA
ACEIMMRS	RACEMISM

ACEIMNNO	MONECIAN
ACEIMNOR	CORAMINE
ACEIMNOT	COINMATE
ACEIMNOX	ANOXEMIC
ACEIMNPS	PEMICANS
ACEIMNRS	CARMINES
	CREMAINS
ACEIMNRU	MANICURE
ACEIMNSS	AMNESICS
ACEIMNST	AMNESTIC
	SEMANTIC
ACEIMNSU	SEMUNCIA
ACEIMNSY	SYCAMINE
ACEIMNTU	NEUMATIC
ACEIMOPR	COPREMIA
ACEIMOPT	POEMATIC
ACEIMOTX	TOXAEMIC
ACEIMOTZ	AZOTEMIC
	METAZOIC
ACEIMPRR	CRAMPIER
	MERICARP
ACEIMPRS	PARECISM
	SAPREMIC
ACEIMPRT	IMPACTER
ACEIMPSS	ESCAPISM
	MISSPACE
	SCAMPIES
ACEIMPST	CAMPIEST
	CAMPSITE
ACEIMPTU	PUMICATE
ACEIMRST	CERAMIST
	MATRICES
	MISTRACE
	SCIMETAR
ACEIMRTT	TREMATIC
ACEIMRTU	MURICATE
ACEIMSST	CASTEISM
	ETACISMS
ACEIMSSU	CAESIUMS
ACEIMSTU	AUTECISM
ACEINNOS	CANONISE
ACEINNOT	ENACTION
ACEINNOZ	CANONIZE
ACEINNPS	PINNACES
ACEINNRS	CRANNIES
	NARCEINS
ACEINNST	ANCIENTS
	CANNIEST
	INSECTAN
	INSTANCE
ACEINNSU	NUISANCE
ACEINNSY	CYANINES
ACEINNTU	UNCINATE
ACEINOPR	APOCRINE
	CAPONIER
	PROCAINE
ACEINOPS	CANOPIES
	CAPONISE
	PAEONICS
ACEINOPZ	CAPONIZE
ACEINORS	SCENARIO
ACEINORT	ACTIONER
	ANORETIC
	CREATION
	REACTION
ACEINORV	VERONICA
ACEINORX	ANOREXIC
ACEINOST	ACONITES
	CANOEIST
	SONICATE
ACEINOTT	TACONITE
ACEINOTV	CONATIVE
	INVOCATE
ACEINOTX	EXACTION
ACEINPQU	PIQUANCE
ACEINPSS	INSCAPES
	PINCASES
ACEINPSY	SAPIENCY
ACEINPTT	PITTANCE
ACEINPUY	PICAYUNE
ACEINRRU	CURARINE
ACEINRRY	CINERARY
ACEINRSS	ARCSINES
	ARSENICS
	CERASINS
	RACINESS
ACEINRST	CANISTER
	CARNIEST
	CERATINS
	CISTERNA
	CREATINS
	NACRITES
	SCANTIER
ACEINRTT	INTERACT
ACEINRTU	ANURETIC
ACEINRTV	NAVICERT
ACEINRTX	XERANTIC
ACEINRVY	VICENARY
ACEINSST	CINEASTS
	SCANTIES
ACEINSSU	ISSUANCE
ACEINSSY	CYANISES
ACEINSTT	CANTIEST
	ENTASTIC
	NICTATES
	TETANICS
ACEINSTV	CISTVAEN
	VESICANT
ACEINSTY	CYANITES
ACEINSTZ	ZINCATES
ACEINSYZ	CYANIZES
ACEINTTU	TUNICATE
ACEINTTX	EXCITANT
ACEINTTY	TENACITY
ACEINTUV	UNACTIVE
ACEIOPRT	OPERATIC
ACEIOPST	ECTOPIAS
ACEIORSS	SCARIOSE
ACEIORSV	COVARIES
	VARICOSE
ACEIOSST	SOCIATES
ACEIOSSU	CAESIOUS
ACEIOSTT	OSCITATE
ACEIOTVV	VOCATIVE
ACEIPPRR	CRAPPIER
	PERICARP
ACEIPPRS	CRAPPIES
	EPICARPS
ACEIPPST	TAPPICES
ACEIPRRS	PERISARC
ACEIPRSS	SCRAPIES
ACEIPRST	CRAPIEST
	CRISPATE
	PARETICS
	PICRATES
	PRACTISE
ACEIPRTV	PRACTIVE
ACEIPRTY	APYRETIC
ACEIPSST	ASEPTICS
	ESCAPIST
	SPACIEST
ACEIPSSU	AUSPICES
ACEIPSSZ	CAPSIZES
ACEIPSTV	CAPTIVES
ACEIQRRU	ACQUIRER
ACEIQRSU	ACQUIRES
ACEIQSTU	ACQUITES
ACEIQSUZ	CAZIQUES
ACEIRRRS	CARRIERS
	SCARRIER
ACEIRRST	ERRATICS
ACEIRRSU	CURARISE
ACEIRRSW	AIRCREWS
	AIRSCREW
ACEIRRTT	RETRAICT
ACEIRRTX	CREATRIX
ACEIRRTY	RETIRACY
ACEIRRUZ	CURARIZE
ACEIRSST	SCARIEST
ACEIRSSU	SCAURIES
	URICASES
ACEIRSSV	VICARESS
ACEIRSTT	CITRATES
	CRISTATE
	SCATTIER
ACEIRSTU	SURICATE
ACEIRSTZ	CRAZIEST
ACEIRTTU	URTICATE
ACEIRTTV	TRACTIVE
ACEIRTUV	CURATIVE
ACEIRTVY	VERACITY
ACEISSSS	CASSISES
ACEISSST	ECSTASIS
ACEISSSU	SAUCISSE
ACEISSTT	STATICES
ACEISSTU	SAUCIEST
	SUITCASE
ACEISTTT	CATTIEST
ACEISTTU	EUSTATIC
ACEISTTW	SCAWTITE
ACEISTUX	AUXETICS
ACEJKOOR	JACKEROO
ACEJKOPS	PAJOCKES
ACEJLORS	CAJOLERS
ACEJLORY	CAJOLERY
ACEJMRST	SCRAMJET
ACEJNNOO	JONCANOE
ACEJNOST	JACONETS
ACEJNOSY	JOYANCES
ACEJNRRY	JERRYCAN
ACEJNSTU	JUNCATES
ACEJPSTU	CAJEPUTS
ACEJRSTT	TRAJECTS
ACEKKMRU	MUCKRAKE
ACEKKNRS	KNACKERS
ACEKKNRY	KNACKERY
ACEKLLPS	PELLACKS
ACEKLNRS	CRANKLES
ACEKLNSS	SLACKENS
ACEKLNTU	UNTACKLE
ACEKLORS	EARLOCKS
ACEKLORV	LAVEROCK
ACEKLORW	LACEWORK
ACEKLPRS	SPRACKLE
ACEKLPSS	SPACKLES
ACEKLPST	PLACKETS
ACEKLQSU	QUACKLES
ACEKLRSS	SLACKERS
ACEKLRST	TACKLERS
ACEKLRSU	CAULKERS
ACEKLSSS	SACKLESS
ACEKLSST	SLACKEST
	TACKLESS
ACEKMNRT	TRACKMEN
ACEKMNST	TACKSMEN
ACEKMORS	COMAKERS
ACEKMRSS	SMACKERS
ACEKNNOW	ACKNOWNE
ACEKNPRS	PRANCKES
ACEKNPRU	UNPACKER
ACEKNPSS	PACKNESS
ACEKNRST	CRANKEST
ACEKOORT	CARETOOK
ACEKOORW	COOKWARE
ACEKOPRW	CAPEWORK
ACEKORRS	CROAKERS
ACEKORRV	OVERRACK
ACEKORSW	CASEWORK
ACEKPPRS	PREPACKS
ACEKPSSY	SKYSCAPE
ACEKQRSU	QUACKERS
ACEKQRUY	QUACKERY
ACEKRRST	RETRACKS
	TRACKERS
ACEKRRTY	RACKETRY
ACEKRSST	RESTACKS
	STACKERS
ACEKRSTT	RACKETTS
ACEKRSTU	RUCKSEAT
ACEKSSTT	STACKETS
ACEKSSUW	WAESUCKS
ACELLLRU	CELLULAR
ACELLMOS	CALOMELS
ACELLMSU	SACELLUM
ACELLNRU	NUCELLAR
ACELLOPS	COLLAPSE
	ESCALLOP
ACELLORR	CAROLLER
ACELLORS	CORELLAS
ACELLORT	COLLARET
ACELLORV	COVERALL
	OVERCALL
ACELLORW	CALLOWER
ACELLOSS	CALLOSES
	COALLESS
ACELLOST	COLLATES
ACELLOSW	COLESLAW
ACELLOTU	LOCULATE
ACELLOVY	COEVALLY
ACELLPSS	SCALPELS
ACELLRRS	CARRELLS
ACELLRTY	RECTALLY
ACELLSSU	CALLUSES
ACELLSSW	CLAWLESS
ACELLSTU	SCUTELLA
ACELLTWY	CETYWALL
ACELMMOU	MAMELUCO
ACELMMRS	CLAMMERS
ACELMNNS	CLANSMEN
ACELMNOR	AMELCORN
	CORNMEAL
ACELMNRU	CRUMENAL
ACELMNSS	CALMNESS
	CLASSMEN
ACELMOPT	COMPLEAT
ACELMORR	CLAMORER
ACELMORS	CAROMELS
	SCLEROMA
ACELMORY	CLAYMORE
ACELMOST	CAMELOTS
	MOLECAST
ACELMOSU	CAULOMES
	LEUCOMAS
	MACULOSE
ACELMPRS	CLAMPERS
ACELMPSY	ECLAMPSY
ACELMSSU	LACMUSES
ACELMSTU	CALUMETS
	MUSCATEL
ACELMSUU	SAECULUM
ACELMTUU	CUMULATE
ACELNNNO	CANNELON
ACELNNOS	ALENCONS
ACELNNRS	SCRANNEL
ACELNOOT	ECOTONAL
ACELNOPT	CONEPATL
ACELNORV	NOVERCAL
ACELNOST	LACTONES
ACELNOSU	LACUNOSE
ACELNOSZ	CALZONES

ACELNOTV	COVALENT
ACELNOVY	CONVEYAL
ACELNPSS	ENCLASPS
	SPANCELS
ACELNPST	CLAPNETS
ACELNPSU	CLEANUPS
	UNPLACES
ACELNRST	CENTRALS
ACELNRSU	LUCARNES
ACELNRVY	CRAVENLY
ACELNSST	SCANTLES
ACELNSSU	SCALENUS
	UNSCALES
ACELNSTT	CANTLETS
ACELNSTY	SECANTLY
ACELOPPU	POPULACE
ACELOPRS	PARCLOSE
	POLACRES
ACELOPRT	PECTORAL
ACELOPRU	OPERCULA
ACELOPSS	ESCALOPS
ACELOPST	POLECATS
ACELOPSU	SCOPULAE
ACELOPTU	COPULATE
	OUTPLACE
ACELOPTY	CALOTYPE
ACELOQSU	COEQUALS
ACELORRS	CAROLERS
ACELORRT	RECTORAL
ACELORSS	ESCOLARS
	LACROSSE
	SOLACERS
ACELORST	LOCATERS
	SECTORAL
ACELORSU	CAROUSEL
ACELORSY	CALOYERS
	COARSELY
ACELOSST	ALECOSTS
	COATLESS
	LACTOSES
	SCATOLES
ACELOSTT	CALOTTES
ACELOSTU	LACTEOUS
	LOCUSTAE
	OSCULATE
ACELOSTY	ACOLYTES
ACELOSUV	VACUOLES
ACELOTXY	ACETOXYL
ACELPPRS	CLAPPERS
	SCRAPPLE
ACELPPSS	SCAPPLES
ACELPRSS	CLASPERS
	RECLASPS
	SCALPERS
ACELPRST	SCEPTRAL
	SPECTRAL
ACELPRSU	SPECULAR
ACELPRTY	CALYPTER
ACELPSSU	CAPSULES
	SCALEUPS
	UPSCALES
ACELPTUU	CUPULATE
ACELPTUY	EUCALYPT
ACELQRSU	CLAQUERS
	LACQUERS
ACELQRUU	CLAQUEUR
ACELQSUY	LACQUEYS
ACELRRSW	CRAWLERS
	SCRAWLER
ACELRSSS	CLASSERS
	SCARLESS
ACELRSST	SCARLETS
ACELRSSU	RECUSALS
	SECULARS
ACELRSTT	CLATTERS
	SCRATTLE
ACELRSTU	RAUCLEST
ACELRTTU	CULTRATE
ACELRTTY	CLATTERY
ACELSSTT	TACTLESS
ACELSSTU	CUTLASES
ACELSSTY	SCYTALES
ACELSSUX	EXCUSALS
ACEMMOTY	MYCETOMA
ACEMMRRS	CRAMMERS
ACEMNOOR	COENAMOR
ACEMNORR	ROMANCER
ACEMNORS	CREMONAS
	ROMANCES
ACEMNOST	CAMSTONE
ACEMNPSS	CAMPNESS
ACEMNRUY	NUMERACY
ACEMNSSU	MANCUSES
ACEMOORS	ACROSOME
ACEMOOST	COMATOSE
ACEMOPRR	COMPARER
ACEMOPRS	CAPSOMER
	COMPARES
	COMPEARS
	MESOCARP
ACEMOPRT	MERCAPTO
ACEMORRT	CREMATOR
ACEMORRV	OVERCRAM
ACEMORSU	RACEMOUS
ACEMORSW	CASEWORM
ACEMORSY	SYCAMORE
ACEMORTY	COMETARY
ACEMORUX	MORCEAUX
ACEMOSSU	COASSUME
ACEMPRSS	SCAMPERS
ACEMPRST	CRAMPETS
ACEMPSSU	CAMPUSES
ACEMSSTT	METCASTS
ACENNNOU	ANNOUNCE
ACENNOSS	CANONESS
	SONANCES
ACENNOSY	NOYANCES
ACENNOSZ	CANZONES
ACENNOTT	COTENANT
ACENNOTV	COVENANT
ACENNOTZ	CANZONET
ACENNPRY	PERNANCY
ACENNRSS	SCANNERS
ACENNSUY	SEACUNNY
ACENOORT	CORONATE
ACENOOTZ	ECTOZOAN
ACENOPRT	COPARENT
	PORTANCE
ACENOPST	CAPSTONE
	OPENCAST
ACENOPSU	PONCEAUS
ACENOPUX	PONCEAUX
ACENOQTU	COTQUEAN
ACENORRW	CAREWORN
ACENORSS	COARSENS
	NARCOSES
ACENORST	ANCESTOR
	ENACTORS
	SARCONET
	SORTANCE
ACENORSU	CARNEOUS
	NACREOUS
ACENORTT	CONTRATE
ACENORTU	COURANTE
	OUTRANCE
ACENORTY	ENACTORY
ACENORUY	EUCARYON
ACENOSSS	CASSONES
ACENOSST	CONTESSA
	COSTEANS
ACENOSSV	CAVESSON
ACENOSSY	CYANOSES
ACENOSTT	CONSTATE
ACENOSTV	CENTAVOS
ACENOTTU	TOUCANET
ACENPRRS	PRANCERS
ACENPRSU	ENCARPUS
	PRAUNCES
ACENPSTT	PENTACTS
ACENPTTU	PUNCTATE
ACENRSST	CRANTSES
ACENRSSU	SURANCES
ACENRSTT	TRANECTS
	TRANSECT
ACENRSTU	CENTAURS
	RECUSANT
	UNCRATES
	UNTRACES
ACENRSTY	ANCESTRY
ACENRTTU	TRUNCATE
ACENRTUY	CENTAURY
	CYANURET
ACENSSTT	SCANTEST
ACENSSTU	NUTCASES
ACENSSTW	NEWSCAST
ACENSSUU	USAUNCES
ACEOOPPS	APOCOPES
ACEOOPSU	POACEOUS
ACEOORTT	COROTATE
ACEOORTV	EVOCATOR
	OVERCOAT
ACEOPPRS	COPPERAS
ACEOPRRT	RECAPTOR
ACEOPRST	POSTRACE
ACEOPRSX	EXOCARPS
ACEOPRTT	ATTERCOP
ACEOPRTU	OUTCAPER
ACEOPSTU	OUTPACES
ACEORRST	ACROTERS
	CREATORS
	REACTORS
ACEORRSU	CAROUSER
ACEORRTT	RETROACT
ACEORRTV	CAVORTER
ACEORRVW	OVERCRAW
ACEORSST	COARSEST
	COASTERS
ACEORSSU	CAROUSES
ACEORSTT	SECTATOR
ACEORSTU	OUTRACES
ACEORSTV	OVERACTS
	OVERCAST
ACEORSTX	EXACTORS
ACEORTUY	EUCARYOT
ACEOSSTU	SEASCOUT
ACEOSTTT	COATTEST
ACEOSTTU	OUTCASTE
ACEOSTTV	CAVETTOS
ACEOSTUU	AUTOCUES
ACEOTUUX	COUTEAUX
ACEPPRRS	CRAPPERS
	SCRAPPER
ACEPRRSS	SCARPERS
	SCRAPERS
ACEPRRSU	SUPERCAR
ACEPRRTU	CAPTURER
ACEPRSST	PRECASTS
ACEPRSSU	SCAUPERS
ACEPRSTU	CAPTURES
	PRESCUTA
ACEPSTTY	TYPECAST
ACEQRSTU	RACQUETS
ACEQSSTU	ACQUESTS
ACERRSTT	RETRACTS
ACERRSUV	VERRUCAS
ACERSSST	CRASSEST
ACERSSSU	SUCRASES
ACERSSTT	SCATTERS
ACERSSTY	ACTRESSY
ACERSTTT	TETRACTS
ACERSTTU	CRUSTATE
ACERSTTX	EXTRACTS
ACERSTTY	CYTASTER
	SCATTERY
ACERSTUX	CURTAXES
ACERTTUW	CUTWATER
ACFFGHIN	CHAFFING
ACFFHNOR	CHAFFRON
ACFFIILO	OFFICIAL
ACFFIIST	CAITIFFS
ACFFIKMS	MAFFICKS
ACFFILNU	FANCIFUL
ACFFILST	AFFLICTS
ACFFIRST	TRAFFICS
ACFFKORT	OFFTRACK
ACFFLOSW	SCOFFLAW
ACFFOSST	CASTOFFS
	OFFCASTS
ACFGHINU	CHAUFING
ACFGHITT	CATFIGHT
ACFGIIMN	MAGNIFIC
ACFGIIPR	CAPRIFIG
ACFGIKLN	FLACKING
ACFGIKNR	FRACKING
ACFGINNY	FANCYING
ACFGINRS	FARCINGS
	SCARFING
ACFGINRT	CRAFTING
	FRACTING
ACFGITUY	FUGACITY
ACFGKNOP	PACKFONG
ACFGLNOR	CORNFLAG
ACFHHINW	HAWFINCH
ACFHIJKS	JACKFISH
ACFHILNO	FALCHION
ACFHILNU	FAULCHIN
ACFHILOS	COALFISH
ACFHINOU	FAUCHION
ACFHIRSS	SCARFISH
ACFHIRSW	CRAWFISH
ACFHIRSY	CRAYFISH
ACFHISSU	FUCHSIAS
ACFHLMRU	CHARMFUL
ACFHLTUW	WATCHFUL
ACFHMNOR	CHAMFRON
ACFHNNOR	CHANFRON
ACFHNOSU	FAUCHONS
ACFHRSTU	FUTHARCS
ACFIILST	FISTICAL
ACFIILSV	SALVIFIC
ACFIILTY	FACILITY
ACFIIMPS	PACIFISM
ACFIIMSS	FASCISMI
ACFIIPST	PACIFIST
ACFIISST	FASCISTI
ACFIKLNS	CALFSKIN
ACFIKNNS	FINNACKS
ACFILLSY	FISCALLY
ACFILNOR	FORNICAL
ACFILNOS	FOLACINS
ACFILORT	TRIFOCAL
ACFILRTY	CRAFTILY
ACFILSSY	CLASSIFY
ACFILSTU	SULFATIC
ACFIMNRU	FRANCIUM
ACFIMORR	ARCIFORM
ACFIMOSS	FASCISMO
ACFIMSSS	FASCISMS
ACFINORT	FRACTION
ACFINOST	FACTIONS

ACFINPRS	SCARFPIN
ACFINRST	INFARCTS
	INFRACTS
ACFINSTY	SANCTIFY
ACFIOSTU	FACTIOUS
ACFIRTUY	FURACITY
ACFISSST	FASCISTS
ACFKLLOR	ROCKFALL
ACFKLORS	FORSLACK
ACFKLOST	LOCKFAST
ACFKLRSU	RACKFULS
ACFKLRUW	WRACKFUL
ACFKLSSU	SACKFULS
	SACKSFUL
ACFKOSTT	FATSTOCK
ACFLMNOO	MOONCALF
ACFLNNOO	NONFOCAL
ACFLNORY	FALCONRY
ACFLOOPS	FOOLSCAP
ACFLOPSW	COWFLAPS
ACFLORSU	SCROFULA
ACFLRRUU	FURCULAR
ACFMOTTU	FACTOTUM
ACFNNOST	NONFACTS
ACFNRSTU	FRUCTANS
ACFRRSTU	FRACTURS
ACGGGILN	CLAGGING
ACGGHINN	CHANGING
	GANCHING
ACGGHINR	CHARGING
ACGGHLUU	CHUGALUG
ACGGIINN	INCAGING
ACGGIINT	GIGANTIC
ACGGIIOS	ISAGOGIC
ACGGILNN	CANGLING
	CLANGING
	GLANCING
ACGGILRY	CRAGGILY
ACGGINNO	CONGAING
ACGGINNU	UNCAGING
ACGGINOR	CARGOING
ACGGIOOR	CORAGGIO
ACGGLNOU	GLUCAGON
ACGGLRSY	SCRAGGLY
ACGHHIJK	HIGHJACK
ACGHHINN	HANCHING
ACGHHINT	HATCHING
ACGHIINN	CHAINING
ACGHIINR	CHAIRING
ACGHIKLN	CHALKING
	HACKLING
ACGHIKNR	CHARKING
ACGHIKNS	HACKINGS
ACGHIKNT	THACKING
ACGHIKNW	WHACKING
ACGHILNN	LANCHING
ACGHILNS	CLASHING
ACGHILNT	LATCHING
ACGHILNU	LAUCHING
ACGHILNY	ACHINGLY
ACGHILOR	OLIGARCH
ACGHIMNP	CHAMPING
ACGHIMNR	CHARMING
	MARCHING
ACGHIMNT	MATCHING
ACGHINNR	RANCHING
ACGHINNT	CHANTING
ACGHINNU	UNACHING
ACGHINOP	POACHING
ACGHINOR	ROACHING
ACGHINPP	CHAPPING
ACGHINPR	PARCHING
ACGHINPT	NIGHTCAP
	PATCHING
ACGHINRR	CHARRING
ACGHINRS	ARCHINGS
	CHAGRINS
	CRASHING
ACGHINRT	CHARTING
	RATCHING
ACGHINRU	CHURINGA
	NURAGHIC
ACGHINSS	CHASINGS
ACGHINST	SCATHING
ACGHINSW	CHINWAGS
ACGHINTT	CHATTING
ACGHINTW	WATCHING
ACGHINTY	YACHTING
ACGHIPRS	GRAPHICS
ACGHIQTU	ACQUIGHT
ACGHIRSS	SCRAIGHS
ACGHLLOR	GRALLOCH
ACGHLMOO	LOGOMACH
ACGHLOOY	CHAOLOGY
ACGHLSTU	CLAUGHTS
ACGHNRYY	GYNARCHY
ACGHNTUU	UNCAUGHT
ACGHORSU	CHORAGUS
ACGHPTUU	UPCAUGHT
ACGHRRSU	CURRAGHS
ACGHRSSU	SCRAUGHS
ACGIILMN	CLAIMING
	MALICING
ACGIILNN	INLACING
ACGIILNO	LOGICIAN
ACGIILNS	SCAILING
ACGIILNV	CAVILING
ACGIILRS	GRACILIS
ACGIIMNT	MICATING
ACGIIMOS	ISOGAMIC
ACGIIMST	SIGMATIC
ACGIINNS	INCASING
ACGIINNV	INCAVING
ACGIINRT	GRANITIC
ACGIIPRS	SPAGIRIC
ACGIJJKO	JICKAJOG
ACGIJLNO	CAJOLING
ACGIJNNU	JAUNCING
ACGIKKNN	KNACKING
ACGIKLMN	MACKLING
ACGIKLNN	CLANKING
ACGIKLNO	CLOAKING
ACGIKLNS	SLACKING
ACGIKLNT	TACKLING
	TALCKING
ACGIKLNU	CAULKING
ACGIKLRY	GARLICKY
ACGIKMNO	COMAKING
ACGIKMNS	SMACKING
ACGIKNNR	CRANKING
ACGIKNNS	SNACKING
ACGIKNNU	UNCAKING
ACGIKNOR	CROAKING
ACGIKNPS	PACKINGS
ACGIKNQU	QUACKING
ACGIKNRS	ARCKINGS
	RACKINGS
ACGIKNRT	TRACKING
ACGIKNRW	WRACKING
ACGIKNSS	SACKINGS
ACGIKNST	STACKING
	TACKINGS
ACGIKPRS	GRIPSACK
ACGILLNS	CALLINGS
ACGILMMN	CLAMMING
ACGILMNO	GNOMICAL
ACGILMNP	CAMPLING
	CLAMPING
ACGILMNU	MACULING
ACGILNNT	CANTLING
ACGILNNU	LAUNCING
	UNLACING
ACGILNOR	CAROLING
	ORACLING
ACGILNOS	SOLACING
ACGILNOT	LOCATING
ACGILNPP	CLAPPING
ACGILNPS	CLASPING
	PLACINGS
	SCALPING
ACGILNQU	CALQUING
ACGILNRS	CARLINGS
ACGILNRT	CLARTING
ACGILNRW	CRAWLING
ACGILNSS	CLASSING
	SCALINGS
ACGILNST	CASTLING
	CATLINGS
	SCLATING
ACGILNSU	GLUCINAS
ACGILNTT	CLATTING
ACGILNTU	CLAUTING
ACGILRSU	SURGICAL
ACGIMMNR	CRAMMING
ACGIMMNS	SCAMMING
ACGIMNOR	CAROMING
ACGIMNOS	COAMINGS
ACGIMNPR	CRAMPING
ACGIMNPS	CAMPINGS
	SCAMPING
ACGIMNSY	GYMNASIC
	SYNGAMIC
ACGIMOPR	PICOGRAM
ACGIMORS	ORGASMIC
ACGIMOUU	GUAIOCUM
ACGINNNS	CANNINGS
	SCANNING
ACGINNNU	NUANCING
ACGINNPR	PRANCING
ACGINNPU	UNCAPING
ACGINNRT	TRANCING
ACGINNRU	UNCARING
ACGINNRY	CARNYING
ACGINNST	CANTINGS
	SCANTING
ACGINNSU	UNCASING
ACGINNUV	VAUNCING
ACGINOPT	COAPTING
ACGINORS	ORGANICS
ACGINORY	CONGIARY
ACGINOST	AGNOSTIC
	COASTING
	COATINGS
	COTINGAS
ACGINPPR	CRAPPING
ACGINPPS	CAPPINGS
ACGINPRS	CARPINGS
	SCARPING
	SCRAPING
ACGINPSS	SPACINGS
ACGINPSU	SCAUPING
ACGINRRS	SCARRING
ACGINRRY	CARRYING
ACGINRSS	SACRINGS
ACGINRST	SCARTING
	TRACINGS
ACGINRSU	SCAURING
ACGINRSV	CARVINGS
	CRAVINGS
ACGINRTT	TRACTING
ACGINRTU	CURATING
ACGINSST	CASTINGS
ACGINSTT	SCATTING
ACGINSUV	VICUGNAS
ACGIOORS	GRACIOSO
ACGIORST	ORGASTIC
ACGIORSU	GRACIOUS
ACGIPRSY	SPAGYRIC
ACGJLNOU	CONJUGAL
ACGKMMOS	GAMMOCKS
ACGKORSV	GARVOCKS
ACGLLPSU	CUPGALLS
ACGLMOUU	COAGULUM
ACGLNORS	CLANGORS
ACGLNORU	CLANGOUR
ACGLNOSY	AGLYCONS
ACGLOORY	ARCOLOGY
ACGLOSUU	GLAUCOUS
ACGLSSTU	CUTGLASS
ACGMNOPS	CAMPONGS
ACGNNOOT	CONTANGO
ACGNNORS	CRANNOGS
ACGNOOST	OCTAGONS
ACGNORST	CONGRATS
ACGORRSY	GYROCARS
ACGORSSW	COWGRASS
ACGORSUU	COUGUARS
ACGPPSUU	SCUPPAUG
ACGRSSTU	CUTGRASS
ACHHILPT	PHTHALIC
ACHHINTW	WHINCHAT
ACHHINTY	HYACINTH
ACHHIPPR	HIPPARCH
ACHHLLOT	CHALLOTH
ACHHLMOS	MASHLOCH
ACHHLNOR	RHONCHAL
ACHHLPRY	PHYLARCH
ACHHLSUY	SHAUCHLY
ACHHNTTU	NUTHATCH
	UNTHATCH
ACHHOSST	TOSHACHS
ACHHPPSU	CHUPPAHS
ACHHPTUZ	CHUTZPAH
ACHIIKMS	KAMICHIS
ACHIILMS	CHILIASM
ACHIILST	CHILIAST
ACHIINRT	TRICHINA
ACHIIPRS	PARCHISI
ACHIIPSS	PACHISIS
ACHIIRST	RACHITIS
ACHIIRSU	ISCHURIA
ACHIJKPW	WHIPJACK
ACHIJNST	JACINTHS
ACHIKKNS	KNACKISH
ACHIKKSW	KICKSHAW
ACHIKLLW	HICKWALL
ACHIKLOR	HAIRLOCK
ACHIKLPT	CHALKPIT
ACHIKNOP	PACHINKO
ACHIKNRS	CRANKISH
ACHIKQSU	QUACKISH
ACHIKRSS	RICKSHAS
ACHIKRSW	RICKSHAW
ACHIKRSY	HAYRICKS
ACHIKRTW	WHITRACK
ACHIKSSS	SHICKSAS
ACHILLOR	ORCHILLA
ACHILLRT	CLITHRAL
ACHILMOP	OMPHALIC
ACHILMOS	MALICHOS
	MOCHILAS
ACHILMRS	CHRISMAL
ACHILMTY	MYTHICAL
ACHILNNS	CLANNISH
ACHILNOO	HOOLICAN
ACHILNOS	LICHANOS
ACHILNPS	CLANSHIP
ACHILOPR	ORPHICAL
	RHOPALIC
ACHILOPU	PACHOULI

ACHILORT	ACROLITH
ACHILPSY	PHYSICAL
ACHILPTY	PATCHILY
ACHILRUY	CHYLURIA
ACHILRVY	CHIVALRY
ACHILSWY	LICHWAYS
ACHILTTY	CHATTILY
ACHIMMOS	MACHISMO
ACHIMMST	MISMATCH
ACHIMNNW	WINCHMAN
ACHIMNOP	CHAMPION
ACHIMNOR	CHOIRMAN
	HARMONIC
	OMNIARCH
ACHIMNOS	MANIHOCS
ACHIMNPT	PITCHMAN
ACHIMOPR	AMPHORIC
ACHIMOSS	CHAMISOS
	ISOCHASM
ACHIMPSS	SCAMPISH
ACHIMPST	MISPATCH
ACHIMRSS	CHARISMS
ACHIMRST	CHARTISM
ACHIMRTY	ARYTHMIC
ACHIMSSS	SCHISMAS
ACHIMSST	MASTICHS
	TACHISMS
ACHIMSSU	CHIASMUS
ACHIMTUY	CYATHIUM
ACHINNOP	PANCHION
ACHINNSU	ANCHUSIN
	UNCHAINS
ACHINOPR	PAROCHIN
	PROCHAIN
ACHINOPS	APHONICS
ACHINORT	ANORTHIC
ACHINOST	CHITOSAN
ACHINOSY	ONYCHIAS
ACHINOTZ	HOACTZIN
ACHINPSY	SPINACHY
ACHINRSZ	ZARNICHS
ACHINSUV	CHAUVINS
ACHIOPRT	ATROPHIC
ACHIOPSS	ISOPACHS
ACHIORSS	COARSISH
ACHIORST	ACTORISH
	CHARIOTS
	HARICOTS
ACHIORTV	TOVARICH
ACHIOSST	ISOTACHS
ACHIPPSS	SAPPHICS
ACHIPRRT	PARRITCH
	PHRATRIC
ACHIPSTU	CHUPATIS
ACHIPSTW	WHIPCATS
ACHIPTTU	CHUPATTI
ACHIQRSU	CHARQUIS
ACHIRRST	TRIARCHS
ACHIRRTY	TRIARCHY
ACHIRSTT	CHARTIST
	STRAICHT
ACHIRSTU	HAIRCUTS
ACHISSTT	TACHISTS
ACHISTTY	CHASTITY
ACHKKORW	HACKWORK
ACHKKRSU	CHUKKARS
ACHKMMOS	HAMMOCKS
ACHKMORS	SHAMROCK
ACHKNNUU	NUNCHAKU
ACHKNOOT	CANTHOOK
ACHKOPSS	HOPSACKS
ACHKOSSS	HASSOCKS
ACHKOSSY	HASSOCKY
ACHKOSTT	HATTOCKS
ACHLLOOS	ALCOHOLS
ACHLLORS	CHLORALS
ACHLLORY	CHORALLY
ACHLMOPS	CAMPHOLS
ACHLMSTZ	SCHMALTZ
ACHLMSYZ	SCHMALZY
ACHLNOOU	OULACHON
ACHLNOSY	HALCYONS
ACHLNSTU	TULCHANS
ACHLNSTY	STANCHLY
ACHLOPRS	RAPLOCHS
ACHLOPRT	CALTHROP
ACHLOPRY	POLYARCH
ACHLOPTT	POTLATCH
ACHLORSS	SCHOLARS
ACHLOSSW	SALCHOWS
ACHLOSTY	ACOLYTHS
ACHLOTWX	WAXCLOTH
ACHMNORS	MONARCHS
	NOMARCHS
ACHMNORY	MONARCHY
	NOMARCHY
ACHMNRSU	UNCHARMS
ACHMNRTU	TRUCHMAN
ACHMOPRS	CAMPHORS
ACHMORSZ	MACHZORS
ACHMORTU	OUTCHARM
	OUTMARCH
ACHMOSST	STOMACHS
ACHMOSTY	STOMACHY
ACHMOTTU	OUTMATCH
ACHMPSTU	MATCHUPS
ACHMSSUW	CUMSHAWS
ACHNNORU	UNANCHOR
ACHNNOSS	CHANSONS
ACHNORST	CHANTORS
ACHNORXY	CHRONAXY
ACHNOSTY	TACHYONS
ACHNOSUY	CHANOYUS
ACHNPPSS	SCHNAPPS
ACHNRSTU	UNSTARCH
ACHNRSYY	SYNARCHY
ACHNRTUY	CHAUNTRY
ACHOORTU	COAUTHOR
ACHOORTY	CHAYROOT
ACHOPRST	TOPARCHS
ACHOPRSY	CHARPOYS
ACHOPRTY	TOPARCHY
ACHORRST	TROCHARS
ACHOTTUW	OUTWATCH
	WATCHOUT
ACHPRSTU	PUSHCART
ACHPSTUZ	CHUTZPAS
ACHRSTTU	STRAUCHT
ACIIILMN	INIMICAL
ACIIILNV	CIVILIAN
ACIIINST	ISATINIC
ACIIKLNO	KAOLINIC
ACIIKNNN	CANNIKIN
ACIIKNNS	CANIKINS
ACIIKPRT	PAITRICK
ACIILLNS	ALLICINS
ACIILLNV	VANILLIC
ACIILLSU	SILICULA
ACIILLSV	SILVICAL
ACIILLTV	VILLATIC
ACIILMMS	MISCLAIM
ACIILMNR	CRIMINAL
ACIILMNU	ALUMINIC
ACIILMOT	COMITIAL
ACIILMRT	MARLITIC
ACIILMSS	LAICISMS
ACIILNOR	IRONICAL
ACIILNOT	TALIONIC
ACIILNPS	PISCINAL
ACIILNPT	PLATINIC
ACIILNSS	SALICINS
ACIILOSV	VILIACOS
ACIILRTT	TRITICAL
ACIILRTU	URALITIC
ACIILSST	SILASTIC
ACIILSTV	SILVATIC
ACIIMMNP	MINICAMP
ACIIMMNS	MINICAMS
ACIIMNNO	AMNIONIC
ACIIMNNT	MANNITIC
ACIIMNOR	MORAINIC
ACIIMNOS	SIMONIAC
ACIIMNOT	AMNIOTIC
ACIIMNRS	MINICARS
ACIIMNST	ACTINISM
ACIIMNSU	MUSICIAN
ACIIMNTU	ACTINIUM
ACIIMNTY	IMITANCY
	INTIMACY
	MINACITY
ACIIMOST	IOTACISM
ACIIMOTT	AMITOTIC
ACIIMPRT	PRIMATIC
ACIIMPRV	VAMPIRIC
ACIIMRST	SCIMITAR
ACIIMRTU	MURIATIC
ACIIMSST	ITACISMS
ACIIMSTT	ATTICISM
	MASTITIC
ACIIMSTV	ACTIVISM
ACIIMTUV	VIATICUM
ACIINNOT	INACTION
	NICOTIAN
ACIINNQU	CINQUAIN
ACIINNRV	NIRVANIC
ACIINNTT	INCITANT
ACIINNTY	CANINITY
ACIINOPT	OPTICIAN
ACIINORZ	ZIRCONIA
ACIINOSS	ASINICOS
ACIINOSV	AVIONICS
ACIINOTT	CITATION
ACIINPSS	PISCINAS
ACIINPTY	ANTIPYIC
ACIINRSS	NARCISSI
ACIINRSU	URANISCI
ACIINRTU	URANITIC
ACIINTTY	ANTICITY
ACIIOPST	APOSITIC
ACIIORST	AORISTIC
ACIIORTV	VICTORIA
ACIIPPST	PAPISTIC
ACIIRSTT	ARTISTIC
	TRIATICS
ACIISTTT	ATTICIST
ACIISTTU	AUTISTIC
ACIISTTV	ACTIVIST
ACIITTVY	ACTIVITY
ACIITVVY	VIVACITY
ACIJKKPS	SKIPJACK
ACIJKSTW	STICKJAW
ACIJSUZZ	JACUZZIS
ACIKLMST	MALSTICK
ACIKLNOT	ANTILOCK
ACIKLNRY	CRANKILY
ACIKLORS	AIRLOCKS
ACIKLORY	CROAKILY
ACIKMNST	STICKMAN
ACIKMOOS	OOMIACKS
ACIKMOST	COMATIKS
ACIKMPRS	RAMPICKS
ACIKMPST	MAPSTICK
ACIKMPSW	PICKMAWS
ACIKMQSU	QUACKISM
ACIKNNPR	CRANKPIN
ACIKNNPS	PANNICKS
ACIKNORT	ANTIROCK
ACIKNSST	CATSKINS
ACIKNSTT	TINTACKS
ACIKPRST	PATRICKS
	TRIPACKS
ACIKSTTY	STATICKY
ACILLLNY	CLINALLY
ACILLLOP	POLLICAL
ACILLMMY	CLAMMILY
ACILLMOS	LOCALISM
ACILLMSS	MISCALLS
ACILLNOO	COLONIAL
ACILLNOR	CARILLON
ACILLNOS	SCALLION
ACILLNUY	UNCIALLY
ACILLOQU	COQUILLA
ACILLORT	CLITORAL
ACILLORY	COLLYRIA
ACILLOST	LOCALIST
ACILLOSY	SOCIALLY
ACILLOTY	COITALLY
	LOCALITY
ACILLOUV	COLLUVIA
ACILLSSY	CLASSILY
ACILMNNY	CINNAMYL
ACILMNOP	COMPLAIN
ACILMNOS	LACONISM
	LIMACONS
ACILMOOS	SCOLIOMA
ACILMOPR	PICLORAM
	PROCLAIM
ACILMOPS	OILCAMPS
ACILMOPT	COMPITAL
ACILMOSV	VOCALISM
ACILMPTU	PLACITUM
ACILMRTU	MULTICAR
ACILMSSS	CLASSISM
	MISCLASS
ACILMSSU	MUSICALS
ACILMSTY	MYSTICAL
ACILMTUY	ULTIMACY
ACILNOOT	LOCATION
ACILNOOV	VOCALION
ACILNOPS	SALPICON
ACILNOPT	PLATONIC
ACILNORS	CLARINOS
	CLARIONS
ACILNORT	CILANTRO
	CONTRAIL
ACILNOSU	UNSOCIAL
ACILNOSY	ACYLOINS
ACILNOUV	UNIVOCAL
ACILNPSS	INCLASPS
	SCALPINS
ACILNRSU	CISLUNAR
ACILNRUY	CULINARY
	URANYLIC
ACILNSTU	LUNATICS
	SULTANIC
ACILNSTY	SCANTILY
ACILNTTU	ANTICULT
ACILOPRT	TROPICAL
ACILOPST	CAPITOLS
	COALPITS
ACILORRS	RACLOIRS
ACILORRV	CORRIVAL
ACILORST	CALORIST
ACILORSV	CORIVALS
ACILORTV	VORTICAL
ACILORYZ	ZIRCALOY
ACILOSTV	VOCALIST
ACILOTUV	OUTCAVIL
ACILOTVY	VOCALITY
ACILPRST	CLIPARTS

ACILPRSU	SPICULAR
ACILPRTU	PICTURAL
ACILPSST	PLASTICS
ACILPSUU	APICULUS
ACILRRTU	TURRICAL
ACILRSTU	CURTAILS
	RUSTICAL
ACILRTUV	CULTIVAR
	CURVITAL
ACILSSST	CLASSIST
ACILSTUV	VICTUALS
ACILSTVY	SYLVATIC
ACIMMOSS	ACOSMISM
ACIMMTUY	CYMATIUM
ACIMNNNO	CINNAMON
ACIMNOOR	ACROMION
ACIMNOPS	CAMPIONS
ACIMNORS	MARCONIS
	MINORCAS
ACIMNORT	ROMANTIC
ACIMNORU	CONARIUM
	COUMARIN
ACIMNORY	ACRIMONY
ACIMNOSS	MOCASSIN
ACIMNOST	MONASTIC
ACIMNOTU	ACONITUM
ACIMNPSU	PANICUMS
ACIMNPTY	TYMPANIC
ACIMNRSS	NARCISMS
ACIMNRSU	CRANIUMS
	CUMARINS
ACIMNSTT	CATMINTS
ACIMNSTU	TSUNAMIC
ACIMOOST	SCOTOMIA
ACIMOPRT	IMPACTOR
ACIMOPST	APOMICTS
ACIMORST	ACROTISM
ACIMORSY	CRAMOISY
ACIMOSST	ACOSMIST
	MASSICOT
ACIMOSTT	MASTICOT
	STOMATIC
ACIMPRST	CRAMPITS
	PTARMICS
ACIMRRSY	MISCARRY
ACIMRSSZ	CZARISMS
ACIMSSST	MISCASTS
ACIMSSTT	TACTISMS
ACINNOOT	CONATION
	INTONACO
ACINNOQU	CONQUIAN
ACINNORR	NARICORN
ACINNOSS	SCANSION
ACINNOST	ACTINONS
	CANONIST
	CANTIONS
	CONTAINS
	SANCTION
	SONANTIC
ACINNOTU	CONTINUA
	COUNTIAN
ACINNRTY	TYRANNIC
ACINNSTU	ANNICUTS
ACINNSTY	INSTANCY
ACINOOPR	PICAROON
ACINOOTV	VOCATION
ACINOPPT	PANOPTIC
ACINOPRS	PARSONIC
ACINOPST	CAPTIONS
	PACTIONS
ACINOPTU	ACUPOINT
ACINOQSU	COQUINAS
ACINORRS	CARRIONS
ACINORRT	CARROTIN
	CONTRAIR
ACINORSS	NARCOSIS
ACINORST	CANTORIS
	CAROTINS
ACINORSV	CORVINAS
ACINORTT	TRACTION
ACINORTY	CARYOTIN
ACINOSSS	CAISSONS
	CASSINOS
ACINOSSY	CYANOSIS
ACINOSTT	OSCITANT
	TACTIONS
ACINOSTU	ANTICOUS
	AUCTIONS
	CAUTIONS
ACINOSTW	WAINSCOT
ACINOSWX	COXSWAIN
ACINOTTX	TOXICANT
ACINPQUY	PIQUANCY
ACINPRST	CANTRIPS
ACINPRSY	CYPRIANS
ACINPSTY	SYNAPTIC
ACINQSTU	QUANTICS
ACINRSST	NARCISTS
ACINRSSU	CRUSIANS
ACINRSTU	CURTAINS
	SATURNIC
	TURACINS
ACINRTTU	TACITURN
	URTICANT
ACINSTTY	SANCTITY
	SCANTITY
ACINSTYY	SYNCYTIA
ACIOOPST	SCOTOPIA
ACIOOTYZ	ZOOCYTIA
ACIOPRST	APRICOTS
	PISCATOR
ACIOPRTT	PROTATIC
ACIOPRTY	POTICARY
ACIOPSST	POTASSIC
ACIOPSSU	SPACIOUS
ACIOPSTU	AUTOPSIC
	CAPTIOUS
ACIOPTTU	AUTOPTIC
ACIORRSS	CORSAIRS
ACIORSSU	SCARIOUS
ACIORSTT	CITATORS
	RICOTTAS
ACIORTTY	ATROCITY
	CITATORY
ACIORTVY	VORACITY
ACIOSSST	COASSIST
ACIOSTUU	CAUTIOUS
ACIPRRUU	PIRARUCU
ACIPRSTT	TIPCARTS
ACIPRTTY	TRIPTYCA
ACIPSSST	SPASTICS
ACIQRSTU	QUARTICS
ACIQSSTU	ACQUISTS
ACIRRTTX	TRACTRIX
ACIRRTUX	CURATRIX
ACIRSSST	SACRISTS
ACIRSSTT	ASTRICTS
ACIRSSTW	TWISCARS
ACIRSSTY	SACRISTY
ACIRSSTZ	CZARISTS
ACISSSTU	CASUISTS
ACISSTTU	CATSUITS
ACISSTUV	VACUISTS
ACISTTUY	ASTUCITY
ACJKKSSY	SKYJACKS
ACJKLLOR	JACKROLL
ACJKLOSW	LOCKJAWS
ACJKNNOS	JANNOCKS
ACJKOPST	JACKPOTS
ACJMNSTU	MUNTJACS
ACJPSTUU	CAJUPUTS
ACKKMOPR	POCKMARK
ACKKORRW	RACKWORK
ACKLLOPS	POLLACKS
ACKLLOSY	LAYLOCKS
ACKLLPSU	SKULLCAP
ACKLMNOS	LOCKSMAN
ACKLMORS	ARMLOCKS
	LOCKRAMS
ACKLNOSU	UNCLOAKS
ACKLOOPW	WOOLPACK
ACKLOORS	OARLOCKS
ACKLOOSW	WOOLSACK
ACKLORSV	LAVROCKS
ACKLORSW	WARLOCKS
ACKLORSY	ROCKLAYS
ACKLOSSS	LASSOCKS
ACKMMMOS	MAMMOCKS
ACKMNOST	STOCKMAN
ACKMNRTU	TRUCKMAN
ACKMOSTT	MATTOCKS
ACKNOPSW	SNOWPACK
ACKNORSU	CRANKOUS
ACKNSSTU	UNSTACKS
ACKOPRRS	PARROCKS
ACKOPRRT	TRAPROCK
ACKORRST	TARROCKS
ACKORSTW	CATWORKS
ACKPSSTU	STACKUPS
ACLLLNOY	CLONALLY
ACLLMNOU	COLUMNAL
ACLLMORU	CORALLUM
ACLLNNOO	NONLOCAL
ACLLOORS	COROLLAS
ACLLOORT	COLLATOR
ACLLOOSS	COLOSSAL
ACLLOPSS	SCALLOPS
ACLLORUY	OCULARLY
ACLLOSTU	LOCUSTAL
ACLLRTUU	CULTURAL
ACLMMNOU	COMMUNAL
ACLMMORW	CLAMWORM
ACLMNOOO	COOLAMON
ACLMNOOR	COLORMAN
ACLMNORU	COLUMNAR
ACLMNORY	NORMALCY
ACLMNPSU	UNCLAMPS
ACLMORSU	CLAMOURS
ACLMORTU	CROTALUM
ACLMPRSU	SCALPRUM
ACLMRSUU	MUSCULAR
ACLMSSTU	MASSCULT
ACLMSTUU	CUSTUMAL
ACLMSUUV	VASCULUM
ACLNNOOV	NONVOCAL
ACLNNOSS	NONCLASS
ACLNOORS	CORONALS
ACLNOORT	COLORANT
ACLNOOST	COOLANTS
	OCTANOLS
ACLNOOSV	VOLCANOS
ACLNOPSY	SYNCOPAL
ACLNORSU	CONSULAR
	COURLANS
ACLNORTU	CALUTRON
ACLNOSTU	CONSULTA
	OSCULANT
ACLNPSSU	UNCLASPS
ACLNPTUU	PUNCTUAL
ACLNSSUY	UNCLASSY
ACLOOPPS	ALCOPOPS
ACLOOPRR	CORPORAL
ACLOOPRS	CARPOOLS
ACLOORST	LOCATORS
ACLOPRRU	PROCURAL
ACLOPRST	CALTROPS
ACLOPRXY	XYLOCARP
ACLOPSSU	SCOPULAS
ACLOPSSY	CALYPSOS
ACLOPSUU	OPUSCULA
ACLORRTU	TORCULAR
ACLORTUW	OUTCRAWL
ACLOSSTU	OUTCLASS
ACLRSSTY	CRYSTALS
ACMMNOSY	SCAMMONY
ACMMNOYY	MYOMANCY
ACMNOOPR	CRAMPOON
	MONOCARP
ACMNOORR	CROMORNA
ACMNOORT	MONOCRAT
ACMNOOYZ	ZOOMANCY
ACMNOPRS	CORPSMAN
	CRAMPONS
ACMNORSY	ACRONYMS
ACMNSSTU	SANCTUMS
ACMOOORT	COATROOM
ACMOOPRS	COPROSMA
ACMOORRT	MOTORCAR
ACMOORUU	COUMAROU
ACMOOSST	SCOTOMAS
ACMOPRST	COMPARTS
ACMORRSS	CROSSARM
ACMORSTW	CATWORMS
	WORMCAST
ACMORSTY	COSTMARY
ACMQSTUU	CUMQUATS
ACNNNORY	CANNONRY
ACNNOORT	NONACTOR
ACNNOSTT	CONSTANT
ACNOOORT	OCTAROON
ACNOOPRT	COPATRON
ACNOORRY	CORONARY
ACNOORST	CARTOONS
	CORANTOS
	OSTRACON
ACNOORSU	CANOROUS
ACNOORTU	COURANTO
ACNOORTY	CARTOONY
	OCTONARY
ACNOPSSW	SNOWCAPS
ACNORRSU	RANCOURS
ACNORRSY	CARRYONS
ACNORRTY	CONTRARY
ACNORSTT	CONTRAST
	CONTRATS
ACNORSTU	COURANTS
ACNORTTU	TURNCOAT
ACNORTUY	NOCTUARY
ACNPRSSY	SYNCARPS
ACNPRSUY	SPRAUNCY
ACNPRSYY	SYNCARPY
ACNRRSTU	CURRANTS
ACNRRTUY	CURRANTY
ACOOPRRS	CORPORAS
ACOOPRST	COPASTOR
ACOOPSTT	TOPCOATS
ACOORSTU	TOURACOS
ACOPPRRS	PROCARPS
ACOPRRST	CARPORTS
ACOPRRTT	PROTRACT
ACORRSTT	TRACTORS
ACORRSTU	CURATORS
ACORRTUY	CARRYOUT
	CURATORY
ACORSSTU	SURCOATS
ACORSSUW	CURASSOW
ACORSSWY	CROSSWAY
ACORSTTY	CRYOSTAT
ACORSTUU	TURACOUS
ACOSSTTU	OUTCASTS

ACPSSTUU	USUCAPTS
ACPSSTUY	PUSSYCAT
ADDDEEEL	DELEADED
ADDDEEEM	ADDEEMED
ADDDEEEN	DEADENED
ADDDEEGR	DEGRADED
ADDDEEIM	DIADEMED
ADDDEELR	LADDERED
ADDDEEMN	DEMANDED
	MADDENED
ADDDEENR	DANDERED
	REDDENDA
ADDDEENS	DESANDED
	SADDENED
ADDDEEPS	SEPADDED
ADDDEGJU	ADJUDGED
ADDDEIMS	MISADDED
ADDDELSW	SWADDLED
ADDDELTW	TWADDLED
ADDDEMNU	ADDENDUM
ADDDEMOO	ADDOOMED
ADDDENOS	DEODANDS
ADDDENRU	DEUDDARN
ADDDEOOW	DEADWOOD
ADDDEORS	ADDORSED
ADDDEOTU	OUTADDED
ADDDEQSU	SQUADDED
ADDDGILN	DADDLING
ADDEEEFL	DEFLEAED
ADDEEEFN	DEAFENED
ADDEEEFT	DEFEATED
ADDEEEJY	DEEJAYED
ADDEEELN	LEADENED
ADDEEELV	DELEAVED
ADDEEEMN	DEMEANED
ADDEEEMR	REMEADED
ADDEEENR	DEADENER
	ENDEARED
ADDEEENW	DANEWEED
ADDEEESY	DEADEYES
ADDEEFGN	DEFANGED
ADDEEFIL	DEFILADE
ADDEEFIM	MADEFIED
ADDEEFLT	DEFLATED
ADDEEFMO	DEFOAMED
ADDEEFNU	UNDEAFED
ADDEEFPR	PREFADED
ADDEEFRY	DEFRAYED
ADDEEFTT	DEFATTED
ADDEEGGR	DAGGERED
ADDEEGHR	HARDEDGE
ADDEEGLL	ALLEDGED
ADDEEGLN	DANEGELD
ADDEEGLZ	DEGLAZED
ADDEEGNR	DANGERED
	DERANGED
	GANDERED
	GARDENED
ADDEEGOR	DOGEARED
ADDEEGRR	DEGRADER
	REGARDED
	REGRADED
ADDEEGRS	DEGRADES
ADDEEGSS	DEGASSED
ADDEEHLR	HERALDED
ADDEEHLY	ALDEHYDE
ADDEEHNR	ADHEREND
	HARDENED
ADDEEHNU	UNHEADED
ADDEEHOP	DOPEHEAD
ADDEEHRS	REDHEADS
ADDEEHRT	THREADED
ADDEEIKR	DAIKERED
ADDEEILN	DEADLINE
ADDEEILR	DEADLIER
	DERAILED
	REDIALED
ADDEEILT	DETAILED
ADDEEIMT	MEDIATED
ADDEEINT	DETAINED
ADDEEINU	UNIDEAED
ADDEEIPR	DIAPERED
ADDEEISS	DISEASED
ADDEEIST	STEADIED
ADDEEITV	DEVIATED
ADDEEKMR	DEMARKED
ADDEEKNR	DARKENED
ADDEELLM	MEDALLED
ADDEELLP	PEDALLED
ADDEELLV	DEVALLED
ADDEELNO	LOADENED
ADDEELNP	DEPLANED
ADDEELNR	ENLARDED
ADDEELNU	UNLEADED
ADDEELOR	RELOADED
ADDEELPS	DELAPSED
ADDEELRS	RESADDLE
ADDEELRT	TREADLED
ADDEELST	DESALTED
ADDEELUV	DEVALUED
ADDEEMNN	DEMANNED
ADDEEMNP	DAMPENED
ADDEEMNR	DAMNEDER
	DEMANDER
	REDEMAND
	REMANDED
ADDEEMST	DEMASTED
ADDEENPP	APPENDED
ADDEENPR	PANDERED
ADDEENPX	EXPANDED
ADDEENRR	DARNEDER
ADDEENRT	ENDARTED
ADDEENRU	DAUNERED
ADDEENRW	DAWNERED
	WANDERED
	WARDENED
ADDEENSS	DEADNESS
ADDEENTT	ATTENDED
	DENTATED
ADDEENTU	DENUDATE
ADDEENUV	UNEVADED
ADDEEOST	DEODATES
ADDEEPRS	RESPADED
ADDEEPRT	DEPARTED
	PREDATED
ADDEEPRV	DEPRAVED
	PERVADED
ADDEERRS	DREADERS
ADDEERRT	RETARDED
ADDEERRW	REWARDED
	WARDERED
ADDEERRY	DEERYARD
ADDEERSW	SAWDERED
ADDEERTT	DERATTED
ADDEERTV	ADVERTED
ADDEFFOR	AFFORDED
ADDEFIIL	LADIFIED
ADDEFILT	DEADLIFT
ADDEFILY	LADYFIED
ADDEFIST	FADDIEST
ADDEFLRU	DREADFUL
ADDEFRSU	DEFRAUDS
ADDEGGLR	DRAGGLED
ADDEGHOS	GODHEADS
ADDEGILO	DIALOGED
ADDEGILS	GLADDIES
ADDEGINR	DREADING
	READDING
ADDEGIRS	DISGRADE
ADDEGJSU	ADJUDGES
ADDEGLNS	GLADDENS
ADDEGLST	GLADDEST
ADDEGNOP	DOGNAPED
ADDEGNRU	UNGRADED
ADDEGPRU	UPGRADED
ADDEHHIN	HINDHEAD
ADDEHHLN	HANDHELD
ADDEHILR	DIHEDRAL
ADDEHINW	HEADWIND
ADDEHIRS	DIEHARDS
ADDEHIRW	RAWHIDED
ADDEHMRU	DRUMHEAD
ADDEHNNU	UNHANDED
ADDEHNSU	UNDASHED
	UNSHADED
ADDEHOPR	DROPHEAD
ADDEHORW	HEADWORD
ADDEHOSW	SHADOWED
ADDEHPRU	PURDAHED
ADDEHRTY	HYDRATED
ADDEIIKS	DIDAKEIS
ADDEIIMS	DIAMIDES
ADDEIIRS	DIARISED
ADDEIIRZ	DIARIZED
ADDEIITV	ADDITIVE
ADDEIJNO	ADJOINED
ADDEIKNP	KIDNAPED
ADDEILNS	ISLANDED
	LANDSIDE
ADDEILNT	TIDELAND
ADDEILRS	DIEDRALS
ADDEILSY	DIALYSED
ADDEILUZ	DUALIZED
ADDEILYZ	DIALYZED
ADDEIMOS	SODAMIDE
ADDEIMRS	DISARMED
	MISDREAD
ADDEIMST	MISDATED
ADDEIMSY	DISMAYED
ADDEIMTT	ADMITTED
ADDEINOR	ORDAINED
ADDEINOS	ADENOIDS
	ADONISED
	ANODISED
ADDEINOZ	ADONIZED
	ANODIZED
ADDEINRT	INDARTED
ADDEINST	DANDIEST
ADDEIOPR	PARODIED
ADDEIORS	ROADSIDE
	SIDEROAD
ADDEIOTX	OXIDATED
ADDEIPPR	DIDAPPER
ADDEIPRS	DISPREAD
ADDEIPSS	DIPSADES
ADDEIQSU	SQUADDIE
ADDEIRST	DISRATED
ADDEIRSW	SIDEWARD
ADDEIRVZ	VIZARDED
ADDEISSU	DISSUADE
ADDEISSV	DISSAVED
ADDEISSW	SWADDIES
ADDEISSY	DAYSIDES
ADDEJSTU	ADJUSTED
ADDEKNVY	VANDYKED
ADDELLOR	DOLLARED
ADDELMOS	DOLMADES
ADDELNNU	DUNELAND
ADDELNOU	DUODENAL
	UNLOADED
ADDELNPU	PUDENDAL
ADDELNRS	DANDLERS
ADDELNSU	UNSADDLE
ADDELOPU	UPLOADED
ADDELPRS	PADDLERS
	SPRADDLE
ADDELRSS	SADDLERS
ADDELRST	STRADDLE
ADDELRSW	DAWDLERS
	SWADDLER
	WADDLERS
ADDELRSY	SADDLERY
ADDELRTW	TWADDLER
ADDELSST	STADDLES
ADDELSSW	SWADDLES
ADDELSTW	TWADDLES
ADDEMMNU	UNDAMMED
ADDEMNNU	UNDAMNED
ADDEMNPU	UNDAMPED
ADDEMNST	DAMNDEST
ADDEMOSY	DOMESDAY
ADDENNOT	DANTONED
ADDENOPR	PARDONED
ADDENORU	UNADORED
ADDENPRU	UNDRAPED
ADDENRST	DARNDEST
	STRANDED
ADDENRSU	DAUNDERS
ADDENRTU	DRAUNTED
	UNTRADED
ADDENRUW	UNWARDED
ADDEORTU	OUTDARED
ADDEOTTU	OUTDATED
ADDEPRSU	SUPERADD
ADDEPRTU	UPDARTED
ADDFFILO	DAFFODIL
ADDFFINR	DANDRIFF
ADDFFNRU	DANDRUFF
ADDFGILN	FADDLING
ADDFIMSS	FADDISMS
ADDFISST	FADDISTS
ADDGGILN	GLADDING
ADDGIILN	DAIDLING
ADDGIIRS	DIAGRIDS
ADDGIKNR	GRANDKID
ADDGILNN	DANDLING
ADDGILNP	PADDLING
ADDGILNR	RADDLING
ADDGILNS	SADDLING
ADDGILNW	DAWDLING
	WADDLING
ADDGINPS	PADDINGS
ADDGINQU	QUADDING
ADDGINSW	WADDINGS
ADDGINWY	WADDYING
ADDGLNOS	GLADDONS
ADDGMNOS	GODDAMNS
ADDGMRUU	MUDGUARD
ADDGOOSW	DAGWOODS
ADDGORSW	GODWARDS
ADDHHLNO	HANDHOLD
ADDHIMOO	MAIDHOOD
ADDHINPS	DAPHNIDS
ADDHINRW	HINDWARD
ADDHINSY	DANDYISH
ADDHIOTY	HYDATOID
ADDHISTY	HYDATIDS
ADDHLOOY	LADYHOOD
ADDHOORW	HARDWOOD
ADDHOSTY	ATHODYDS
ADDIIKMZ	ZADDIKIM
ADDIILUV	DIVIDUAL
ADDIINOT	ADDITION
ADDIINSS	DISDAINS
ADDIINTV	DIVIDANT
ADDIKSST	TSADDIKS
ADDIKSTY	KATYDIDS
ADDIKSTZ	TZADDIKS
ADDILLNS	LANDSLID
ADDILLNW	WILDLAND

ADDILMNS	MIDLANDS
ADDILNNW	LANDWIND
ADDILOSS	DISLOADS
ADDIMNOS	DIAMONDS
ADDIMNSY	DANDYISM
ADDIMNYY	DIDYNAMY
ADDIMORS	DIADROMS
ADDINNOR	ORDINAND
ADDINORS	ANDROIDS
	DISADORN
ADDINQUY	QUIDDANY
ADDINRWW	WINDWARD
ADDIORTY	ADDITORY
ADDIQSST	TSADDIQS
ADDIQSTZ	TZADDIQS
ADDIRSZZ	DIZZARDS
ADDKNRRU	DRUNKARD
ADDLLNOR	LANDLORD
ADDLLRSU	DULLARDS
ADDLNNOW	DOWNLAND
ADDLNOOW	DOWNLOAD
	WOODLAND
ADDLNORS	LANDDROS
ADDLOOSS	SOLDADOS
ADDLORTY	DOTARDLY
ADDMOOSY	DOOMSDAY
ADDNOPWY	PANDOWDY
ADDNORWW	DOWNWARD
	DRAWDOWN
ADDOORRY	DOORYARD
ADDOORWW	WOODWARD
ADDOORWY	WOODYARD
ADDOPSSY	DASYPODS
ADEEEFFR	AFFEERED
ADEEEFNY	FEDAYEEN
ADEEEFRT	DEFEATER
	FEDERATE
	REDEFEAT
ADEEEGLT	DELEGATE
ADEEEGNR	RENEGADE
ADEEEGNT	TEENAGED
ADEEEGPS	GAPESEED
ADEEEGRR	REGEARED
ADEEEGRS	DEGREASE
ADEEEGUW	AGUEWEED
ADEEEHHW	HEEHAWED
ADEEEHRS	HAEREDES
ADEEEHRT	REHEATED
ADEEEHRX	EXHEDRAE
ADEEEHSY	EYESHADE
ADEEEINT	DETAINEE
ADEEEKNW	WEAKENED
ADEEELMN	ENAMELED
ADEEELNS	ENSEALED
ADEEELNV	LEAVENED
ADEEELPR	REPEALED
ADEEELRS	RELEASED
	RESEALED
ADEEELRV	LAVEERED
	REVEALED
ADEEELST	TEASELED
ADEEELSV	DELEAVES
ADEEELSW	WEASELED
ADEEELTV	ELEVATED
ADEEELTZ	TEAZELED
ADEEEMNS	DEMEANES
	ENSEAMED
ADEEEMNT	EMENDATE
ADEEEMRT	RETEAMED
ADEEEMRU	EMERAUDE
ADEEENNT	NEATENED
ADEEENRR	REEARNED
ADEEENRS	ENSEARED
	SERENADE
ADEEENTT	ATTENDEE
	EDENTATE
ADEEENWZ	WEAZENED
ADEEEPRS	RAPESEED
ADEEEPRT	DEPARTEE
	REPEATED
ADEEERRS	ARREEDES
ADEEERST	RESEATED
ADEEERVW	REWEAVED
ADEEESSW	SEAWEEDS
	SEESAWED
ADEEFFIR	EFFRAIDE
ADEEFGLN	FENAGLED
ADEEFHNR	FREEHAND
ADEEFHOR	FOREHEAD
ADEEFHRT	FATHERED
ADEEFIIR	AERIFIED
ADEEFILN	ENFILADE
ADEEFIMS	MADEFIES
	SEMIDEAF
ADEEFINR	FREDAINE
ADEEFIOR	FOEDARIE
ADEEFIRR	RAREFIED
ADEEFIRS	FEDARIES
ADEEFIRY	REAEDIFY
ADEEFIST	SAFETIED
ADEEFLLT	FELLATED
ADEEFLMN	ENFLAMED
ADEEFLOR	FREELOAD
ADEEFLPR	PEDALFER
ADEEFLRR	DEFERRAL
ADEEFLRS	FEDERALS
ADEEFLRT	DEFLATER
	FALTERED
	REFLATED
ADEEFLSS	FADELESS
ADEEFLST	DEFLATES
ADEEFLSX	FLAXSEED
ADEEFMNR	ENFRAMED
	FREEDMAN
ADEEFMOR	DEFOAMER
ADEEFMRR	REFRAMED
ADEEFMRS	DEFAMERS
ADEEFNRU	UNFEARED
ADEEFNSS	DEAFNESS
ADEEFNST	FASTENED
ADEEFNTT	FATTENED
ADEEFORR	FOREREAD
ADEEFORT	FOREDATE
ADEEFOTV	FOVEATED
ADEEFPRS	PREFADES
ADEEFRRT	RAFTERED
ADEEFRRY	DEFRAYER
	FEDERARY
ADEEFRST	DRAFTEES
ADEEFRTU	FEATURED
ADEEGGHS	EGGHEADS
ADEEGGJR	JAGGEDER
ADEEGGLL	ALLEGGED
ADEEGGRR	RAGGEDER
ADEEGGRS	SAGGERED
ADEEGGRT	RETAGGED
ADEEGGRU	REGAUGED
ADEEGHNR	REHANGED
ADEEGHOR	GHERAOED
ADEEGHRT	GATHERED
ADEEGIMN	ADEEMING
ADEEGIMR	REIMAGED
ADEEGINR	REGAINED
ADEEGINZ	AGENIZED
ADEEGIRS	DISAGREE
ADEEGISS	ASSIEGED
ADEEGLLS	ALLEDGES
ADEEGLLT	GALLETED
ADEEGLLV	GAVELLED
ADEEGLNO	ENGAOLED
ADEEGLNR	ENLARGED
	LARGENED
ADEEGLNT	DANEGELT
ADEEGLRV	GRAVELED
ADEEGLRZ	REGLAZED
ADEEGLSV	SELVAGED
ADEEGLSZ	DEGLAZES
ADEEGMMO	GAMODEME
ADEEGMMT	GEMMATED
ADEEGMNR	GENDARME
ADEEGMNS	ENDGAMES
ADEEGMNY	GANYMEDE
	MEGADYNE
ADEEGMOP	MEGAPODE
ADEEGMOS	MEGADOSE
ADEEGMSS	MESSAGED
ADEEGNNR	ENDANGER
	ENRANGED
ADEEGNNV	VENDANGE
ADEEGNOR	RENEGADO
ADEEGNRR	GARDENER
	GARNERED
ADEEGNRS	DERANGES
	GRANDEES
	GRENADES
ADEEGNRU	DUNGAREE
	RENAGUED
	UNDERAGE
	UNGEARED
ADEEGNRV	ENGRAVED
ADEEGNSS	AGEDNESS
ADEEGNSV	VENDAGES
ADEEGORT	DEROGATE
ADEEGORV	OVERAGED
ADEEGOST	DOGEATES
ADEEGOTW	GOATWEED
ADEEGPRS	ASPERGED
	PRESAGED
ADEEGPRT	PARGETED
ADEEGRRR	REGARDER
ADEEGRRS	REGRADES
ADEEGRRT	GARRETED
	GARTERED
	REGRATED
ADEEGRRU	REARGUED
	REDARGUE
ADEEGRSS	DEGASSER
	DRESSAGE
ADEEGRST	RESTAGED
ADEEGRSU	GUARDEES
ADEEGRSW	RAGWEEDS
ADEEGRTT	TARGETED
ADEEGSSS	DEGASSES
ADEEGSTT	GESTATED
ADEEGSWY	EDGEWAYS
ADEEGTTZ	GAZETTED
ADEEHHRS	REHASHED
ADEEHHST	SHEATHED
ADEEHILN	HEADLINE
ADEEHILS	DEISHEAL
ADEEHIRT	DEATHIER
ADEEHISS	EADISHES
ADEEHIST	ATHEISED
	HEADIEST
ADEEHISV	ADHESIVE
ADEEHITZ	ATHEIZED
ADEEHKNR	DAKERHEN
	HANKERED
	HARKENED
ADEEHKRS	KASHERED
ADEEHKWW	HAWKWEED
ADEEHKWY	HAWKEYED
ADEEHLLW	WELLHEAD
ADEEHLNO	ENHALOED
ADEEHLNR	REHANDLE
ADEEHLNS	HANSELED
ADEEHLNU	UNHEALED
ADEEHLRS	ASHLERED
ADEEHLRT	HALTERED
	LATHERED
ADEEHLSS	HEADLESS
ADEEHLTY	HEATEDLY
ADEEHMMO	HOMEMADE
ADEEHMMR	HAMMERED
ADEEHMNN	MENHADEN
ADEEHMNS	HEADSMEN
ADEEHMNT	ANTHEMED
ADEEHMPR	HAMPERED
ADEEHNOT	HEADNOTE
ADEEHNPP	HAPPENED
ADEEHNRR	HARDENER
	REHARDEN
ADEEHNRT	ADHERENT
	HARTENED
	NEATHERD
	THREADEN
ADEEHNSS	DASHEENS
ADEEHNST	HASTENED
ADEEHNTU	UNHEATED
ADEEHOPR	HEADROPE
ADEEHORS	SOREHEAD
ADEEHORV	OVERHEAD
ADEEHPPU	UPHEAPED
ADEEHPRS	EPHEDRAS
	RESHAPED
ADEEHPRT	THREAPED
ADEEHPUV	UPHEAVED
ADEEHRRS	ADHERERS
	REDSHARE
ADEEHRRT	RETHREAD
	THREADER
ADEEHRST	HEADREST
ADEEHRSV	RESHAVED
ADEEHRSW	REWASHED
	WASHERED
ADEEHRTT	HATTERED
	THREATED
ADEEHRTW	WREATHED
ADEEHSST	HEADSETS
ADEEHSSY	HAYSEEDS
ADEEIILS	IDEALISE
ADEEIILZ	IDEALIZE
ADEEIITV	IDEATIVE
ADEEIJMR	JEREMIAD
ADEEIJRS	JADERIES
ADEEIJST	JADEITES
ADEEIKLS	LAKESIDE
ADEEIKMR	DIEMAKER
ADEEIKNP	KIDNAPEE
ADEEIKSW	WEAKSIDE
ADEEILLO	OEILLADE
ADEEILLR	REALLIED
ADEEILMN	ENDEMIAL
ADEEILMR	REMAILED
	REMEDIAL
ADEEILMS	LIMEADES
ADEEILMV	MEDIEVAL
ADEEILNR	RENAILED
ADEEILNS	DELAINES
ADEEILNT	DATELINE
	ENTAILED
	LINEATED
ADEEILPR	PEDALIER
ADEEILPS	PLEIADES
ADEEILPT	DEPILATE
	EPILATED
	PILEATED
ADEEILRR	DERAILER
	RERAILED
ADEEILRS	REALISED

	RESAILED
	SIDEREAL
ADEEILRT	DETAILER
	ELATERID
	RETAILED
ADEEILRZ	REALIZED
ADEEILSS	DEISEALS
	IDEALESS
ADEEILST	LEADIEST
ADEEILSV	DISLEAVE
ADEEILSY	EYELIADS
ADEEIMNR	REMAINED
ADEEIMNS	DEMAINES
	INSEAMED
ADEEIMNT	DEMENTIA
ADEEIMNX	EXAMINED
ADEEIMPR	EMPAIRED
ADEEIMRR	DREAMIER
ADEEIMRS	MADERISE
ADEEIMRT	DIAMETER
	REMEDIAT
ADEEIMRZ	MADERIZE
ADEEIMSS	SIAMESED
ADEEIMST	MEDIATES
ADEEIMSZ	SIAMEZED
ADEEIMTT	MEDITATE
ADEEINNS	ADENINES
	ANDESINE
ADEEINOP	OEDIPEAN
ADEEINPR	PINDAREE
ADEEINPT	DIAPENTE
ADEEINRS	ARSENIDE
	DENARIES
	DRAISENE
	NEARSIDE
ADEEINRT	DETAINER
	RETAINED
ADEEINRV	REINVADE
ADEEINSS	ANISEEDS
ADEEINST	ANDESITE
ADEEINTW	ANTIWEED
ADEEINVW	INWEAVED
ADEEIPRR	RAPIERED
	REPAIRED
ADEEIPRS	AIRSPEED
ADEEIPTX	EXPIATED
ADEEIRRR	DREARIER
ADEEIRRS	DREARIES
	RERAISED
ADEEIRST	READIEST
	SERIATED
	SIDERATE
	STEADIER
ADEEIRSV	READVISE
ADEEIRTT	ITERATED
ADEEIRTV	DERIVATE
	EVIRATED
	TAIVERED
ADEEISSS	DISEASES
	SEASIDES
ADEEISST	STEADIES
ADEEISSV	ADESSIVE
	ADVISEES
ADEEISTV	DEVIATES
	SEDATIVE
ADEEITTV	EVITATED
ADEEITVW	TIDEWAVE
ADEEKMRR	REMARKED
ADEEKMRT	MARKETED
ADEEKNNR	ENRANKED
ADEEKNPS	KNEEPADS
ADEEKNPW	KNAPWEED
ADEEKNRR	DARKENER
ADEEKNRS	KNEADERS
ADEEKNST	NAKEDEST
ADEEKORS	RESOAKED
ADEEKPRR	REPARKED
ADEEKQSU	SQUEAKED
ADEEKRST	STREAKED
ADEEKSWY	WEEKDAYS
ADEELLLP	LAPELLED
ADEELLMT	METALLED
ADEELLMU	MEDULLAE
ADEELLNP	PANELLED
ADEELLNW	ENWALLED
ADEELLNY	LEADENLY
ADEELLPR	PEDALLER
	PREDELLA
ADEELLPS	SEPALLED
ADEELLPT	PALLETED
	PETALLED
ADEELLQU	EQUALLED
ADEELLRS	SARDELLE
ADEELLRT	TELLARED
ADEELLRU	LAURELED
ADEELLRV	RAVELLED
ADEELLSS	ALLSEEDS
	LEADLESS
ADEELLTY	ELATEDLY
ADEELLWY	WALLEYED
ADEELMNO	LEMONADE
ADEELMNP	EMPLANED
ADEELMNR	ALDERMEN
ADEELMNS	DALESMEN
	EMENDALS
	LEADSMEN
ADEELMNT	LAMENTED
ADEELMOR	REMOLADE
ADEELMOS	SOMEDEAL
ADEELMPR	EMPARLED
ADEELMPX	EXAMPLED
ADEELMRS	DEMERSAL
	EMERALDS
ADEELMRT	TRAMELED
ADEELMRV	MARVELED
ADEELMST	MEDALETS
ADEELMTU	EMULATED
ADEELNNP	ENPLANED
ADEELNNU	UNANELED
ADEELNOR	OLEANDER
	RELOANED
ADEELNPS	DEPLANES
ADEELNPT	ENDPLATE
ADEELNPU	UPLEANED
ADEELNRT	ANTLERED
ADEELNRV	LAVENDER
ADEELNSU	UNLEASED
	UNSEALED
ADEELNSV	ENSLAVED
ADEELNTT	TALENTED
ADEELNTU	UNELATED
ADEELNTV	LEVANTED
ADEELNTY	ENTAYLED
ADEELOPS	PEDALOES
ADEELOPX	POLEAXED
ADEELORR	RELOADER
ADEELORU	AUREOLED
ADEELORV	OVERLADE
ADEELOST	DESOLATE
ADEELOSW	LEASOWED
ADEELPPR	LAPPERED
	RAPPELED
ADEELPPT	LAPPETED
ADEELPPU	UPLEAPED
ADEELPRS	PLEADERS
	RELAPSED
	REPLEADS
ADEELPRT	PALTERED
	REPLATED
ADEELPRY	PARLEYED
	REPLAYED
ADEELPSS	DELAPSES
ADEELPST	PEDESTAL
ADEELPTY	PEDATELY
ADEELQSU	SQUEALED
ADEELRRR	LARDERER
ADEELRRT	TREADLER
ADEELRRY	READERLY
ADEELRST	DESALTER
	RESLATED
	TREADLES
ADEELRSV	SLAVERED
ADEELRSW	LEEWARDS
ADEELRSY	DELAYERS
ADEELRTV	TRAVELED
ADEELRUV	REVALUED
ADEELRWY	LAWYERED
ADEELSST	DATELESS
	DETASSEL
	TASSELED
ADEELSTT	LADETTES
ADEELSTY	SEDATELY
ADEELSUV	DEVALUES
ADEEMMMR	MAMMERED
ADEEMMRY	YAMMERED
ADEEMMSS	MESDAMES
ADEEMMXY	MYXEDEMA
ADEEMNNR	MANNERED
	REMANNED
ADEEMNOR	DEMEANOR
	ENAMORED
ADEEMNOT	NEMATODE
ADEEMNOU	EUDAEMON
ADEEMNPR	DAMPENER
ADEEMNPS	SPADEMEN
ADEEMNPY	EPENDYMA
ADEEMNRS	AMENDERS
	MEANDERS
	REAMENDS
ADEEMNSS	SEEDSMAN
ADEEMNST	STAMENED
ADEEMNSU	UNSEAMED
ADEEMNSY	DEMAYNES
ADEEMNTU	UNTEAMED
ADEEMNTW	METEWAND
ADEEMORS	SEADROME
ADEEMORT	MODERATE
ADEEMPPR	PAMPERED
	REMAPPED
ADEEMPRR	PREARMED
ADEEMPRT	EMPARTED
	TAMPERED
ADEEMPRV	REVAMPED
ADEEMPRY	EMPAYRED
ADEEMPST	STAMPEDE
	STEPDAME
ADEEMRRS	DREAMERS
	REDREAMS
ADEEMRRT	REDREAMT
ADEEMRRV	MARVERED
ADEEMRRW	REWARMED
ADEEMRRY	DREAMERY
ADEEMRST	MASTERED
	STREAMED
ADEEMRSU	MEASURED
ADEEMRTT	MATTERED
ADEEMRTY	METEYARD
ADEEMSSW	MAWSEEDS
ADEEMSTW	MATWEEDS
ADEEMSWY	MAYWEEDS
ADEENNPT	PENNATED
ADEENNRS	ENSNARED
ADEENNRU	UNEARNED
ADEENNTT	TENANTED
ADEENNUW	UNWEANED
ADEENNUY	UNYEANED
ADEENOPW	WEAPONED
ADEENORS	REASONED
ADEENORV	ENDEAVOR
ADEENORY	AERODYNE
ADEENOSS	ADENOSES
	SEASONED
ADEENOST	ENDOSTEA
ADEENOTT	DENOTATE
	DETONATE
ADEENPPR	ENDPAPER
ADEENPPS	SANDPEEP
ADEENPRR	PANDERER
ADEENPRT	PARENTED
ADEENPRU	UNREAPED
ADEENPRX	EXPANDER
ADEENPSW	SNAPWEED
ADEENPTT	PATENTED
	PATTENED
ADEENRRW	WANDERER
ADEENRSS	DEARNESS
ADEENRSU	UNDERSEA
	UNERASED
	UNSEARED
ADEENRSW	ANSWERED
ADEENRSY	YEARENDS
ADEENRTT	ATTENDER
	NATTERED
	RATTENED
ADEENRTU	DENATURE
	UNDERATE
	UNDEREAT
ADEENRTV	AVENTRED
ADEENRUV	UNREAVED
ADEENSST	ASSENTED
	SENSATED
	STANDEES
ADEENSSU	DANSEUSE
ADEENSTU	UNSEATED
ADEENSTY	ANDESYTE
ADEENTTU	TAUTENED
ADEENTTV	VENDETTA
ADEEOPRR	PADERERO
ADEEOPRT	OPERATED
ADEEOPST	ADOPTEES
ADEEORRV	OVERDARE
	OVERDEAR
	OVERREAD
ADEEORSW	OARWEEDS
ADEEORVW	OVERAWED
	REAVOWED
ADEEPPRR	DAPPERER
	PREPARED
ADEEPPRT	PRETAPED
ADEEPPRU	PAUPERED
ADEEPPRW	WAPPERED
ADEEPRRS	RESPREAD
	SPREADER
ADEEPRRT	DEPARTER
ADEEPRRU	UPREARED
ADEEPRRV	DEPRAVER
	PERVADER
ADEEPRSS	ASPERSED
	PREASSED
	REPASSED
	RESPADES
ADEEPRST	PEDERAST
	PREDATES
	REPASTED
	TRAPESED
ADEEPRSU	PERSUADE
ADEEPRSV	DEPRAVES
	PERVADES
ADEEPRSW	PERSWADE
ADEEPRSZ	SPREAZED

ADEEPRTT PATTERED
ADEEPRTU DEPURATE
EPURATED
ADEEPRTZ TRAPEZED
ADEEPSST STAPEDES
ADEEPSTT ADEPTEST
ADEEPSWY SPEEDWAY
ADEEQRTU DETRAQUE
ADEEQRUV QUAVERED
ADEERRRT RETARDER
ADEERRRW REDRAWER
REREWARD
REWARDER
ADEERRST ARRESTED
DREAREST
RETREADS
SERRATED
TREADERS
ADEERRSV ADVERSER
ADEERRSW REDWARES
ADEERRTT RETRATED
ADEERRTW REDWATER
ADEERRWY WARREYED
ADEERSST ASSERTED
ESTRADES
ADEERSTT ASTERTED
RESTATED
RETASTED
ADEERSTW DEWATERS
TARWEEDS
WASTERED
ADEERSTY ESTRAYED
ADEERTTT TATTERED
ADEERTTY YATTERED
ADEERTWW WARTWEED
ADEERVYY EVERYDAY
ADEESSSS ASSESSED
ADEESSTT SEDATEST
ADEESTTT ATTESTED
ADEESTUX EXUDATES
ADEESVVY SAVVEYED
ADEESWWX WAXWEEDS
ADEFFGUW GUFFAWED
ADEFFIMR AFFIRMED
ADEFFIRR DRAFFIER
ADEFFIRT TARIFFED
ADEFFIST DAFFIEST
ADEFFLNS SNAFFLED
ADEFFLOS LEADOFFS
ADEFFORT TRADEOFF
ADEFFRST STRAFFED
ADEFGGOT FAGGOTED
ADEFGIIS GASIFIED
ADEFGILN FINAGLED
ADEFGILO FOLIAGED
ADEFGILS GADFLIES
GASFIELD
ADEFGIMN DEFAMING
ADEFGIRT DRIFTAGE
ADEFGIRU ARGUFIED
ADEFGITU FATIGUED
ADEFGLOT GATEFOLD
ADEFGLRU FELDGRAU
ADEFGNOR FRONDAGE
ADEFGOSU FOUGADES
ADEFHHIS HEADFISH
ADEFHILS DEALFISH
ADEFHILY HAYFIELD
ADEFHIMS FAMISHED
ADEFHKOR FORKHEAD
ADEFHLTU DEATHFUL
ADEFHMOT FATHOMED
ADEFHNOR FOREHAND
ADEFHOST SOFTHEAD
ADEFIILN FINIALED

ADEFIILR AIRFIELD
ADEFIILS LADIFIES
SALIFIED
ADEFIILT FILIATED
ADEFIIMR RAMIFIED
ADEFIINS SANIFIED
ADEFIINZ NAZIFIED
ADEFIIRR RARIFIED
ADEFIIRT RATIFIED
ADEFIIRU AURIFIED
ADEFILMN INFLAMED
ADEFILNR FILANDER
ADEFILNT INFLATED
ADEFILOR FORELAID
ADEFILOT FOLIATED
ADEFILSS DISLEAFS
ADEFILSY DAYFLIES
LADYFIES
ADEFIMPR FIREDAMP
ADEFIMRS MISFARED
ADEFIMSS DISFAMES
ADEFINPR PANFRIED
ADEFINRR INFRARED
ADEFINRS FRIANDES
ADEFINRU UNFAIRED
ADEFINYZ DENAZIFY
ADEFIORS FORESAID
ADEFIRRT DRAFTIER
ADEFIRSS FARSIDES
ADEFLLLU LADLEFUL
ADEFLLNS ELFLANDS
ADEFLLOR FALDEROL
ADEFLLOW FALLOWED
ADEFLLRY ALDERFLY
ADEFLLSW DEWFALLS
ADEFLLUY FEUDALLY
ADEFLMRU DREAMFUL
ADEFLNNS FENLANDS
ADEFLNOR FORELAND
ADEFLNRU DEARNFUL
ADEFLNTU FLAUNTED
ADEFLNUU UNFEUDAL
ADEFLNUW UNFLAWED
ADEFLORT DEFLATOR
ADEFLORV FLAVORED
ADEFLORY FORELADY
ADEFLPRS FELDSPAR
ADEFLPSU SPADEFUL
ADEFLRSW SELFWARD
ADEFLRTU TRADEFUL
ADEFLRTW LEFTWARD
ADEFLRZZ FRAZZLED
ADEFLSTU DEFAULTS
SULFATED
ADEFMNRU UNFRAMED
ADEFMORT FORMATED
ADEFMOSU FAMOUSED
FUMADOES
ADEFNNNU UNFANNED
ADEFNOPR PROFANED
ADEFNSST DAFTNESS
ADEFOOSS SEAFOODS
ADEFORRR FORRADER
ADEFORRW FARROWED
FOREWARD
ADEFORRY FOREYARD
FORRAYED
ADEFORUV FAVOURED
ADEFPTUW UPWAFTED
ADEFRRST DRAFTERS
REDRAFTS
ADEFRSTW DWARFEST
ADEFSSTT STEDFAST
ADEGGGNU UNGAGGED
ADEGGIRR DRAGGIER

ADEGGIST DAGGIEST
ADEGGISU GAUDGIES
GUIDAGES
ADEGGJLY JAGGEDLY
ADEGGLRS DRAGGLES
ADEGGLRY RAGGEDLY
ADEGGMOS DEMAGOGS
ADEGGMOY DEMAGOGY
ADEGGNOW WAGGONED
ADEGGNTU UNTAGGED
ADEGGNUU UNGAUGED
ADEGGOPS PEDAGOGS
ADEGGOPY PEDAGOGY
ADEGGPRS SPRAGGED
ADEGGRRS DRAGGERS
ADEGGRTY GADGETRY
ADEGHHOS HOGSHEAD
ADEGHILN HEALDING
ADEGHILT ALIGHTED
GILTHEAD
ADEGHINR ADHERING
HEADRING
ADEGHINS DEASHING
HEADINGS
SHEADING
ADEGHIRS GARISHED
HAGRIDES
HEADRIGS
ADEGHIRT GRAITHED
ADEGHJSU JUGHEADS
ADEGHLNO HEADLONG
LONGHEAD
ADEGHLOS GALOSHED
ADEGHNNU UNHANGED
ADEGHNRT THRANGED
ADEGHOOP PAGEHOOD
ADEGHORT GOATHERD
ADEGHRTU DAUGHTER
ADEGHTUW WAUGHTED
ADEGIILN GLIADINE
ADEGIILP DIPLEGIA
ADEGIIMN IMAGINED
ADEGIIMS DIGAMIES
ADEGIINR DEAIRING
ADEGIINT IDEATING
ADEGIITT DIGITATE
ADEGIJSW JIGSAWED
ADEGIKLO GOADLIKE
ADEGIKNN KNEADING
ADEGIKNR DAKERING
ADEGILLO GLADIOLE
ADEGILLP PILLAGED
ADEGILLR GLADLIER
GRILLADE
ADEGILLS GALLISED
ADEGILLZ GALLIZED
ADEGILMN MALIGNED
MEDALING
ADEGILNN LADENING
ADEGILNO GALENOID
ADEGILNP PEDALING
PLEADING
ADEGILNR DANGLIER
DEARLING
DRAGLINE
ADEGILNS DEALINGS
LEADINGS
SIGNALED
ADEGILNT DELATING
ADEGILNY DELAYING
ADEGILOR DIALOGER
ADEGILOS GOLIASED
ADEGILOU DIALOGUE
ADEGILOY IDEALOGY
ADEGILRS SLAIRGED

ADEGILSS GLISSADE
ADEGILST GLADIEST
ADEGILSV DISGAVEL
ADEGIMNN AMENDING
ADEGIMNO AMIDOGEN
ADEGIMNR DREAMING
MARGINED
MIDRANGE
ADEGIMOR IDEOGRAM
ADEGIMPS MISPAGED
ADEGIMRS MISGRADE
ADEGIMRT MIGRATED
ADEGIMST SIGMATED
ADEGINNR GRANNIED
ADEGINNV ADVENING
DAVENING
ADEGINNW AWNINGED
ADEGINNY DENAYING
ADEGINOR ORGANDIE
ADEGINOS AGONISED
DIAGNOSE
ADEGINOZ AGONIZED
ADEGINPU ANGUIPED
ADEGINRR DREARING
ADEGINRS DERAIGNS
GRADINES
READINGS
ADEGINRT DERATING
GRADIENT
REDATING
TREADING
ADEGINRY DERAYING
READYING
YEARDING
ADEGINSS ASSIGNED
ADEGINST SEDATING
STEADING
ADEGINSW WINDAGES
ADEGINTV VINTAGED
ADEGINVW ADVEWING
ADEGINWX DEWAXING
ADEGINYZ ZYGAENID
ADEGIORT ERGATOID
ADEGIOST GODETIAS
ADEGIPRR PARRIDGE
ADEGIPRS SPAIRGED
ADEGIRWY RIDGEWAY
ADEGISSU DISUSAGE
ADEGISTU GAUDIEST
ADEGISUV VIDUAGES
ADEGIUWY GUIDEWAY
ADEGJNOR JARGONED
ADEGKLOY DEKALOGY
ADEGLLNU GLANDULE
UNGALLED
ADEGLLOP GALLOPED
ADEGLLOR GOLLARED
ADEGLLOW GALLOWED
ADEGLLSU GALLUSED
ADEGLMOR GLAMORED
ADEGLMOS GLADSOME
ADEGLMPU PLUMAGED
ADEGLMRU MAULGRED
ADEGLMUY AMYGDULE
ADEGLNOP ANGLEPOD
ADEGLNOY GONDELAY
ADEGLNPS SPANGLED
ADEGLNRS DANGLERS
GLANDERS
ADEGLNRW WRANGLED
ADEGLNSS GLADNESS
ADEGLNTW TWANGLED
ADEGLNUZ UNGLAZED
ADEGLOPP GALOPPED
ADEGLORV OVERGLAD

ADEGLPPR	GRAPPLED
ADEGMMNO	GAMMONED
ADEGMMRU	RUMMAGED
ADEGMNOR	DRAGOMEN
ADEGMNOS	GOADSMEN
ADEGMNOT	MONTAGED
ADEGMNOY	ENDOGAMY
ADEGMNRS	DRAGSMEN
ADEGMNSU	AGENDUMS
ADEGMOPS	MEGAPODS
ADEGMORS	ORGASMED
ADEGMORW	WORDGAME
ADEGMPUZ	GAZUMPED
ADEGNNOR	ANDROGEN
	DRAGONNE
ADEGNNPU	UNPANGED
ADEGNNSU	DUNNAGES
ADEGNOPR	DOGNAPER
ADEGNOPS	PONDAGES
ADEGNOPU	POUNDAGE
ADEGNORT	DRAGONET
ADEGNOSS	SONDAGES
ADEGNOSV	DOGVANES
ADEGNPUY	PYENGADU
ADEGNRRU	GRANDEUR
ADEGNRST	DRAGNETS
	GRANDEST
ADEGNRSU	ENGUARDS
ADEGNRUU	UNARGUED
ADEGNRUZ	GAZUNDER
	UNGRAZED
ADEGOORV	OVERGOAD
ADEGOORY	GOODYEAR
ADEGOPPR	PROPAGED
ADEGOPRR	DRAGROPE
	PROGRADE
ADEGOPRT	PORTAGED
ADEGORRT	GARROTED
ADEGORST	GOADSTER
ADEGORSW	DOWAGERS
	WORDAGES
ADEGORTT	GAROTTED
ADEGORTU	OUTRAGED
	RAGOUTED
ADEGORTW	WATERDOG
ADEGOTTV	GAVOTTED
ADEGPRRU	UPGRADER
ADEGPRSS	SPADGERS
ADEGPRSU	UPGRADES
ADEGPSTU	UPSTAGED
ADEGRRST	DRAGSTER
ADEGRRSU	GUARDERS
ADEGRSSU	DESUGARS
	GRADUSES
ADEGTTTU	GUTTATED
ADEHHIPR	RHAPHIDE
ADEHHIPS	HEADSHIP
ADEHHIST	SHITHEAD
ADEHHNTU	HEADHUNT
ADEHHOOR	HOORAHED
ADEHHOPS	HOPHEADS
ADEHHOST	HEADSHOT
	HOTHEADS
ADEHHRRU	HURRAHED
ADEHHRST	THRASHED
ADEHHUZZ	HUZZAHED
ADEHIITZ	THIAZIDE
ADEHIKLN	HANDLIKE
ADEHIKLV	KHEDIVAL
ADEHIKNS	SKINHEAD
ADEHIKSS	DASHEKIS
ADEHIKST	SKAITHED
ADEHIKSV	KHEDIVAS
ADEHILLO	HILLOAED
ADEHILLP	PHIALLED
	PILLHEAD
ADEHILMO	HALIDOME
ADEHILNR	HARDLINE
ADEHILNU	UNHAILED
ADEHILPS	HELIPADS
ADEHILSV	LAVISHED
ADEHILSW	WHAISLED
ADEHILWZ	WHAIZLED
ADEHIMMS	SHAMMIED
ADEHIMOT	HEMATOID
ADEHIMRS	MISHEARD
	SEMIHARD
ADEHIMRY	HYDREMIA
ADEHINOP	DIAPHONE
ADEHINOS	ADHESION
ADEHINOY	HYOIDEAN
ADEHINPS	DEANSHIP
	HEADPINS
	PINHEADS
ADEHINPU	DAUPHINE
ADEHINRT	ANTHERID
ADEHINRU	UNHAIRED
ADEHINSS	SHANDIES
ADEHINST	HANDIEST
ADEHINSV	VANISHED
ADEHIOTT	ATHETOID
ADEHIPRS	RAPHIDES
ADEHIPSS	PISSHEAD
ADEHIPST	PITHEADS
	SIDEPATH
ADEHIRRT	TRIHEDRA
ADEHIRRW	HARDWIRE
ADEHIRSS	AIRSHEDS
	RADISHES
ADEHIRST	HAIRSTED
	HARDIEST
ADEHIRSV	RAVISHED
ADEHIRSW	DISHWARE
	RAWHIDES
ADEHIRSY	HAYRIDES
ADEHIRVW	HIVEWARD
ADEHISST	DASHIEST
	SHADIEST
ADEHJLOT	JOLTHEAD
ADEHKLNU	LUNKHEAD
ADEHKNRS	REDSHANK
ADEHKNSU	UNSHAKED
ADEHKORS	HARDOKES
ADEHKORW	HEADWORK
ADEHKOST	KATHODES
ADEHLLOO	HALLOOED
	HOLLOAED
ADEHLLOU	HULLOAED
ADEHLLOW	HALLOWED
ADEHLLRT	THRALLED
ADEHLLRW	HELLWARD
ADEHLMNO	HOMELAND
ADEHLMOY	HOLYDAME
ADEHLNRS	HANDLERS
ADEHLNSS	HANDLESS
	HANDSELS
ADEHLNST	SHETLAND
ADEHLNSU	UNHALSED
	UNLASHED
	UNSHALED
ADEHLNUV	UNHALVED
ADEHLOOR	HORDEOLA
ADEHLOOT	TOOLHEAD
ADEHLOPS	ASPHODEL
	PHOLADES
ADEHLOPW	PLOWHEAD
ADEHLPSS	SPLASHED
ADEHLRRY	HERALDRY
ADEHMNNY	HANDYMEN
ADEHMNOS	HANDSOME
ADEHMNOT	METHADON
	THANEDOM
ADEHMNRS	HERDSMAN
ADEHMNRU	UNHARMED
ADEHMNSU	UNSHAMED
ADEHMOOP	OOMPAHED
ADEHMOOR	HEADROOM
ADEHMOPS	MOPHEADS
ADEHMORS	HADROMES
ADEHMORW	HOMEWARD
ADEHMOST	HEADMOST
ADEHMOSU	MADHOUSE
ADEHMOSY	SHAMOYED
ADEHNNSW	HANDSEWN
ADEHNOPR	ORPHANED
ADEHNOPT	PHONATED
ADEHNORS	HARDNOSE
ADEHNORV	HANDOVER
	OVERHAND
ADEHNOSS	SANDSHOE
ADEHNOSU	SEAHOUND
ADEHNPSU	UNHASPED
	UNSHAPED
ADEHNPTU	UNPATHED
ADEHNRSS	HARDNESS
ADEHNRSU	UNSHARED
ADEHNRSW	SWANHERD
ADEHNRTU	UNTHREAD
ADEHNSST	HANDSETS
ADEHNSSU	SUNSHADE
	UNSASHED
ADEHNSUV	UNSHAVED
ADEHNSUW	UNWASHED
ADEHNTTU	UNHATTED
ADEHNTUW	UNTHAWED
ADEHOOPS	APEHOODS
ADEHOORW	HAREWOOD
ADEHOORY	HOORAYED
ADEHOPRS	RHAPSODE
ADEHOPST	POTASHED
	POTHEADS
ADEHOPSX	HEXAPODS
ADEHOPXY	HEXAPODY
ADEHORRS	HOARDERS
ADEHORRV	OVERHARD
ADEHORRW	HARROWED
ADEHORSW	SHADOWER
ADEHORTT	THROATED
ADEHORTU	AUTHORED
	OUTHEARD
ADEHOSTW	TOWHEADS
ADEHPSTU	DUSTHEAP
ADEHQSSU	SQUASHED
ADEHRRUY	HURRAYED
ADEHRSSY	HYDRASES
ADEHRSTY	HYDRATES
ADEHRTTW	THWARTED
ADEIILMN	LIMNAEID
ADEIILMS	IDEALISM
	MILADIES
ADEIILPR	PERIDIAL
ADEIILRS	LAIRISED
ADEIILRZ	LAIRIZED
ADEIILST	IDEALIST
ADEIILTV	DILATIVE
ADEIILTY	IDEALITY
ADEIIMMS	MISAIMED
ADEIIMNN	INDAMINE
ADEIIMNR	MERIDIAN
ADEIIMNS	AMIDINES
	DIAMINES
ADEIIMNT	MINIATED
ADEIIMPR	IMPAIRED
ADEIIMRS	SEMIARID
ADEIIMTT	IMITATED
ADEIINNS	SANIDINE
ADEIINOT	IDEATION
	IODINATE
	TAENIOID
ADEIINRS	DRAISINE
ADEIINRT	DAINTIER
ADEIINRU	UREDINIA
ADEIINST	ADENITIS
	DAINTIES
ADEIINSZ	DIAZINES
ADEIINTV	VANITIED
ADEIINUV	INDUVIAE
ADEIIPRR	PERRADII
	PRAIRIED
ADEIIPRS	PRESIDIA
ADEIIPST	STAPEDII
ADEIIRSS	AIRSIDES
	DIARISES
ADEIIRST	IRISATED
ADEIIRSZ	DIARIZES
ADEIITTV	TIDIVATE
	VITIATED
ADEIITUV	AUDITIVE
ADEIJMRS	JEMIDARS
ADEIKLLO	KELOIDAL
ADEIKLLR	LARDLIKE
ADEIKLLY	LADYLIKE
ADEIKLNS	SANDLIKE
ADEIKLNW	DAWNLIKE
ADEIKLOT	TOADLIKE
ADEIKLOX	ALKOXIDE
ADEIKLRR	DARKLIER
ADEIKLSW	SIDEWALK
ADEIKMMS	IMMASKED
ADEIKMPR	IMPARKED
ADEIKMRT	TIDEMARK
ADEIKNPR	KIDNAPER
ADEIKNSY	KYANISED
ADEIKNYZ	KYANIZED
ADEIKORT	KERATOID
ADEIKRST	STRAIKED
ADEILLMY	MEDIALLY
ADEILLNN	LANDLINE
ADEILLNU	UNALLIED
ADEILLNV	ANVILLED
ADEILLNW	INWALLED
ADEILLOR	ARILLODE
ADEILLPR	PALLIDER
	PILLARED
ADEILLPS	ILLAPSED
	SPADILLE
ADEILLRS	DALLIERS
	DIALLERS
ADEILLRT	TRIALLED
ADEILLRV	RIVALLED
ADEILLSW	SIDEWALL
ADEILMMM	MELAMDIM
ADEILMMS	DILEMMAS
ADEILMNO	MELANOID
ADEILMNP	PLAIDMEN
ADEILMNU	UNMAILED
ADEILMNY	MAIDENLY
	MEDIANLY
ADEILMOS	DAMOISEL
	MELODIAS
ADEILMPP	PALMIPED
ADEILMPR	IMPARLED
ADEILMPS	IMPLEADS
	MISPLEAD
ADEILMPT	IMPLATED
ADEILMRS	DISMALER
ADEILMRY	DREAMILY
ADEILMSS	MAIDLESS
	MISDEALS
	MISLEADS

ADEILMST	MEDALIST
	MISDEALT
ADEILMSY	DYSMELIA
ADEILNNO	NONIDEAL
ADEILNNP	PINELAND
ADEILNNR	INLANDER
ADEILNNS	ANNELIDS
	LINDANES
ADEILNNT	DENTINAL
ADEILNNU	UNNAILED
ADEILNOP	PALINODE
ADEILNOS	NODALISE
ADEILNOT	DELATION
ADEILNOZ	NODALIZE
ADEILNPS	SANDPILE
ADEILNPT	PANTILED
ADEILNPU	PALUDINE
ADEILNRS	ISLANDER
ADEILNSU	UNSAILED
ADEILNSV	ANDVILES
ADEILNTU	UNTAILED
ADEILNTV	DIVALENT
ADEILNUV	UNVAILED
ADEILOPS	EPISODAL
	OPALISED
	SEPALOID
ADEILOPT	PETALOID
ADEILOPZ	OPALIZED
ADEILOQU	ODALIQUE
ADEILORS	DARIOLES
	SOLIDARE
	SOREDIAL
ADEILORT	IDOLATER
	TAILORED
ADEILORV	OVERLAID
ADEILORX	EXORDIAL
ADEILOSS	ASSOILED
	DEASOILS
	ISOLEADS
ADEILOST	DIASTOLE
	ISOLATED
	SODALITE
	SOLIDATE
ADEILOSU	DOULEIAS
ADEILOSZ	DIAZOLES
ADEILOTT	DATOLITE
ADEILOTV	DOVETAIL
	VIOLATED
ADEILPPP	PEDIPALP
ADEILPRS	PARSLIED
	PEDRAILS
	PREDIALS
	SPIRALED
ADEILPRT	DIPTERAL
	TRIPEDAL
ADEILPRU	EPIDURAL
ADEILPRV	DEPRIVAL
ADEILPSS	DESPISAL
ADEILPST	TALIPEDS
ADEILPTU	PLAUDITE
ADEILQSU	SQUAILED
ADEILQTU	LIQUATED
ADEILRRW	DRAWLIER
ADEILRRY	DREARILY
ADEILRST	DILATERS
	LARDIEST
	REDTAILS
ADEILRSU	RESIDUAL
ADEILRSY	DIALYSER
ADEILRTT	DETRITAL
ADEILRTY	DIELYTRA
ADEILRVY	VARIEDLY
ADEILRYZ	DIALYZER
ADEILSSU	DEASIULS
ADEILSSV	DEVISALS
ADEILSSY	DIALYSES
ADEILSTV	VALIDEST
ADEILSTY	DIASTYLE
	STEADILY
ADEILSUV	DISVALUE
ADEILSUZ	DUALIZES
ADEILSWY	SLIDEWAY
ADEILSXY	DYSLEXIA
ADEILSYZ	DIALYZES
ADEILTTU	ALTITUDE
	LATITUDE
ADEILTVY	DATIVELY
ADEIMMNS	MISNAMED
ADEIMMNU	UNMAIMED
ADEIMMRS	MERMAIDS
ADEIMMST	MISMATED
ADEIMNNO	DEMONIAN
	MONDAINE
ADEIMNOP	DOPAMINE
ADEIMNOR	RADIOMEN
ADEIMNOS	AMIDONES
	DAIMONES
	NOMADIES
	NOMADISE
ADEIMNOT	DOMINATE
	NEMATOID
ADEIMNOZ	NOMADIZE
ADEIMNPW	IMPAWNED
ADEIMNRR	MANRIDER
ADEIMNRS	ADERMINS
	SIRNAMED
ADEIMNRU	MURAENID
ADEIMNRY	DAIRYMEN
ADEIMNRZ	ZEMINDAR
ADEIMNSS	SIDESMAN
ADEIMNST	MEDIANTS
	TIDESMAN
ADEIMNSU	MAUNDIES
ADEIMNSY	DYNAMISE
ADEIMNTY	DYNAMITE
ADEIMNYZ	DYNAMIZE
ADEIMORR	AIRDROME
ADEIMORT	MEDIATOR
ADEIMOSS	SESAMOID
ADEIMOST	ATOMISED
ADEIMOTZ	ATOMIZED
ADEIMPRR	RAMPIRED
ADEIMPRT	IMPARTED
	PREADMIT
ADEIMPRV	VAMPIRED
ADEIMPST	DAMPIEST
	IMPASTED
ADEIMRRS	ADMIRERS
	DISARMER
	MARRIEDS
ADEIMRSS	MISREADS
	SIDEARMS
ADEIMRST	MARDIEST
	MISRATED
	READMITS
ADEIMRSY	MIDYEARS
ADEIMRTT	ADMITTER
ADEIMRTU	MURIATED
ADEIMSST	DIASTEMS
	MISDATES
ADEIMSTU	TAEDIUMS
ADEIMSTY	DAYTIMES
ADEINNNS	NANDINES
ADEINNOT	ANOINTED
	ANTINODE
ADEINNPT	PINNATED
ADEINNPU	UNPAINED
ADEINNRS	INSNARED
ADEINNRZ	RENDZINA
ADEINNSU	UNSAINED
ADEINNSX	DISANNEX
ADEINNTU	INUNDATE
ADEINOPP	PEPONIDA
ADEINOPT	ANTIPODE
ADEINORR	ORDAINER
	REORDAIN
ADEINORS	ANEROIDS
	DONARIES
ADEINORT	AROINTED
	DERATION
	ORDINATE
	RATIONED
ADEINORU	DOUANIER
ADEINOSS	ADENOSIS
	ADONISES
	ANODISES
ADEINOST	ASTONIED
	SEDATION
ADEINOSX	DIOXANES
ADEINOSZ	ADONIZES
	ANODIZES
ADEINOTT	ANTIDOTE
	TETANOID
ADEINOTV	DONATIVE
ADEINPPX	APPENDIX
ADEINPRS	SPRAINED
ADEINPRT	DIPTERAN
ADEINPRU	UNPAIRED
	UNREPAID
ADEINPST	DEPAINTS
ADEINPSV	SPAVINED
ADEINQTU	ANTIQUED
ADEINRRS	DRAINERS
	SERRANID
ADEINRSS	ARIDNESS
	SARDINES
ADEINRST	DETRAINS
	RANDIEST
	STRAINED
ADEINRSU	DENARIUS
	UNRAISED
	URANIDES
ADEINRSV	INVADERS
	SANDIVER
ADEINRSY	SYNEDRIA
ADEINRTT	NITRATED
ADEINRTU	DATURINE
	INDURATE
	RUINATED
	URINATED
ADEINRUV	UNVARIED
ADEINRVY	VINEYARD
ADEINSST	DESTAINS
	SANDIEST
ADEINSSV	AVIDNESS
ADEINSSW	WINDASES
ADEINSTT	INSTATED
ADEINSTU	AUDIENTS
	SINUATED
ADEINSTV	DEVIANTS
ADEINSTY	DESYATIN
ADEIOPRS	DIASPORE
	PARODIES
ADEIOPRV	OVERPAID
ADEIOPSS	ADIPOSES
ADEIOPST	DIOPTASE
ADEIOPTV	ADOPTIVE
ADEIORRT	ADROITER
ADEIORST	ASTEROID
ADEIORSV	AVODIRES
	AVOIDERS
ADEIORTT	TERATOID
ADEIORTV	DEVIATOR
ADEIOSSX	OXIDASES
ADEIOSTX	OXIDATES
ADEIOSTZ	AZOTISED
ADEIOSVV	VAIVODES
ADEIOSVW	WAIVODES
ADEIOSWW	WAIWODES
ADEIOTZZ	AZOTIZED
ADEIPPRS	APPRISED
	DRAPPIES
ADEIPPRZ	APPRIZED
ADEIPRRS	DRAPIERS
ADEIPRSS	DESPAIRS
ADEIPRST	DIPTERAS
	RAPIDEST
	SPIRATED
	TARSIPED
	TRAIPSED
ADEIPRSU	UPRAISED
ADEIPRTU	EUPATRID
	PREAUDIT
ADEIPSSX	SPADIXES
ADEIPSTV	VAPIDEST
ADEIPTTU	APTITUDE
ADEIQRRU	QUARRIED
ADEIQRSU	QUERIDAS
ADEIQSUY	QUAYSIDE
ADEIRRSW	SWARDIER
ADEIRRTW	TAWDRIER
ADEIRRWW	WIREDRAW
ADEIRRZZ	RIZZARED
ADEIRSST	ASTERIDS
	DIASTERS
	DISASTER
	DISRATES
ADEIRSSU	RADIUSES
	SUDARIES
ADEIRSSV	ADVISERS
ADEIRSTT	STRAITED
	STRIATED
	TARDIEST
ADEIRSTW	TAWDRIES
ADEIRTTT	ATTRITED
	TITRATED
ADEIRTUV	DURATIVE
ADEIRVWY	DRIVEWAY
ADEISSST	ASSISTED
	DISSEATS
ADEISSSV	DISSAVES
ADEISSTT	DISTASTE
	STAIDEST
ADEISSTV	DISTAVES
ADEISSWY	SIDEWAYS
	WAYSIDES
ADEISTTU	SITUATED
ADEISTUZ	DEUTZIAS
ADEISTWY	TIDEWAYS
ADEITTTU	ATTITUDE
	ATTUITED
ADEJLOSU	JALOUSED
ADEJMRRU	JUMARRED
ADEJNRUW	UNDERJAW
ADEJOPRS	JEOPARDS
ADEJOPRY	JEOPARDY
ADEJRRSU	ADJURERS
ADEJRSTU	ADJUSTER
	READJUST
ADEKLMRY	MARKEDLY
ADEKLNOX	KLAXONED
ADEKLNPP	KNAPPLED
ADEKLNPR	PRANKLED
ADEKLNSU	UNSLAKED
ADEKLORW	LEADWORK
ADEKLPRS	SPARKLED
ADEKMNRU	UNMARKED
ADEKMNSU	UNMASKED
ADEKMORS	DARKSOME
ADEKNNRU	UNRANKED

ADEKNNSS	DANKNESS
ADEKNOSU	UNSOAKED
ADEKNOTW	TAKEDOWN
ADEKNRSS	DARKNESS
ADEKNSVY	VANDYKES
ADEKOOTW	TEAKWOOD
ADEKOSTU	OUTASKED
ADEKQSUW	SQUAWKED
ADELLMOR	MORALLED
ADELLMOS	SLALOMED
ADELLMRU	MEDULLAR
ADELLMSU	MEDULLAS
ADELLNNU	ANNULLED
ADELLNPS	SPENDALL
ADELLNRS	LANDLERS
ADELLNSS	LANDLESS
ADELLNSW	ELLWANDS
	WALLSEND
ADELLNTY	DENTALLY
ADELLNUW	UNWALLED
ADELLOPW	WALLOPED
ADELLORS	ODALLERS
ADELLOSW	SALLOWED
ADELLOTT	ALLOTTED
	TOTALLED
ADELLOTV	LAVOLTED
ADELLOTW	TALLOWED
ADELLOVY	LADYLOVE
ADELLOWW	WALLOWED
ADELLQSU	SQUALLED
ADELLRSU	UDALLERS
ADELLTUU	ULULATED
ADELMNNS	LANDSMEN
ADELMNOS	LODESMAN
ADELMNRS	MANDRELS
ADELMOOW	WOODMEAL
ADELMOPS	MALPOSED
ADELMORS	EARLDOMS
ADELMOSS	DAMOSELS
ADELMOSZ	DAMOZELS
ADELMOTU	MODULATE
ADELMPRT	TRAMPLED
ADELMRRU	DEMURRAL
ADELMSSY	MASSEDLY
ADELMSUY	AMUSEDLY
ADELMTTY	MATTEDLY
ADELMTUU	UMLAUTED
ADELNNNU	UNNANELD
ADELNNOT	LENTANDO
ADELNOPR	PONDERAL
ADELNORS	LADRONES
	SOLANDER
ADELNORU	UNLOADER
	URODELAN
ADELNORV	OVERLAND
	RONDAVEL
ADELNOSY	YEALDONS
ADELNPRS	SPANDREL
ADELNPRU	PENDULAR
	UNDERLAP
	UPLANDER
ADELNPRY	PANDERLY
	REPANDLY
ADELNPSY	DYSPNEAL
ADELNPUY	UNPLAYED
ADELNRSS	SLANDERS
ADELNRSU	LAUNDERS
	LURDANES
	RUNDALES
ADELNRTU	DENTURAL
ADELNRTY	ARDENTLY
ADELNRUY	UNDERLAY
ADELNSTU	UNSALTED
ADELNSTW	WETLANDS
ADELNTUU	UNDULATE
ADELNUUV	UNVALUED
ADELNUZZ	UNDAZZLE
ADELOOPV	LEVODOPA
ADELOORV	OVERLOAD
ADELOOTW	LATEWOOD
ADELOOWW	WOODWALE
ADELOPPR	PROPALED
ADELOPRS	LEOPARDS
ADELOPRT	PORTALED
	PROLATED
ADELOPRU	POULARDE
ADELOPRW	POLEWARD
ADELOPSS	DEPOSALS
ADELOPST	TADPOLES
ADELOPSU	PALUDOSE
ADELOPSY	SEPALODY
ADELOPTY	PETALODY
ADELORRV	OVERLARD
ADELORSS	ROADLESS
ADELORST	DELATORS
	LEOTARDS
	LODESTAR
ADELORSU	ROULADES
ADELORTW	LEADWORT
ADELOSSS	SODALESS
ADELOSST	TOADLESS
ADELOSSW	DOWLASES
ADELOSTV	SOLVATED
ADELOTUV	OVULATED
ADELOTUW	OUTLAWED
ADELOVWY	AVOWEDLY
ADELPPRY	DAPPERLY
ADELPQUX	QUADPLEX
ADELPRRU	LARRUPED
ADELPRSW	SPRAWLED
ADELPRTT	PRATTLED
ADELPRTU	PREADULT
ADELPSTT	SPLATTED
ADELPSTU	PULSATED
ADELPUUV	UPVALUED
ADELRRSU	RUDERALS
ADELRRSW	DRAWLERS
ADELRRTU	ULTRARED
ADELRSSW	WRASSLED
ADELRSTT	STARTLED
ADELRSTW	WARSTLED
	WRASTLED
ADELRSZZ	DAZZLERS
ADELRTUY	ADULTERY
ADELSTTY	STATEDLY
ADELTTTW	TWATTLED
ADEMMNOW	MADWOMEN
ADEMMSTU	SUMMATED
ADEMNNNU	UNMANNED
ADEMNNOR	NORMANDE
ADEMNNOU	UNMOANED
ADEMNNRU	MUNDANER
	UNDERMAN
ADEMNOOR	MAROONED
ADEMNOPR	POMANDER
ADEMNOPT	TAMPONED
ADEMNORS	MADRONES
	RANSOMED
	ROADSMEN
ADEMNOTU	AMOUNTED
	OUTNAMED
ADEMNPPU	UNMAPPED
ADEMNPSS	DAMPNESS
ADEMNRRU	UNDERARM
	UNMARRED
ADEMNRSU	DURAMENS
	MAUNDERS
	SURNAMED
ADEMNRTU	UNDREAMT
ADEMNRUW	UNWARMED
ADEMNSSU	MEDUSANS
ADEMNSUU	UNAMUSED
ADEMNTTU	UNMATTED
ADEMOORT	MODERATO
ADEMOORV	VAROOMED
ADEMOOST	STOMODEA
ADEMOOSV	VAMOOSED
ADEMOPRY	PYODERMA
ADEMOPST	STAMPEDO
ADEMORRT	MORTARED
ADEMORRU	ARMOURED
ADEMORRW	MARROWED
ADEMORST	STROAMED
ADEMORTU	OUTDREAM
ADEMORTW	DAMEWORT
	WARDMOTE
ADEMPRST	STRAMPED
ADEMRRSU	EARDRUMS
ADEMRRTY	MARTYRED
ADENNNTU	UNTANNED
ADENNORT	NONRATED
ADENNOSY	ANODYNES
ADENNOTU	UNATONED
ADENNOTW	WANTONED
ADENNOTY	TANNOYED
ADENNPST	PENDANTS
ADENNRRU	UNDERRAN
ADENNRTY	TYRANNED
ADENNRUW	UNWARNED
ADENNSTU	ASTUNNED
ADENNTUW	UNWANTED
ADENOOPS	EPANODOS
ADENOORT	RATOONED
ADENOORW	WANDEROO
ADENOOST	ODONATES
ADENOOTZ	OZONATED
ADENOPRR	PARDONER
ADENOPRS	OPERANDS
	PADRONES
	PANDORES
ADENOPRT	PRONATED
ADENOPRX	EXPANDOR
ADENOPSS	DAPSONES
	SPADONES
ADENOPST	NOTEPADS
	TONEPADS
ADENOPSU	UNSOAPED
ADENOPSY	DYSPNOEA
ADENORRS	ADORNERS
	READORNS
ADENORRW	NARROWED
ADENORST	TORNADES
ADENORTT	ATTORNED
ADENORTW	DANEWORT
	TEARDOWN
ADENORTY	AROYNTED
ADENORUX	RONDEAUX
ADENOSST	ONSTEADS
ADENOTUY	AUTODYNE
ADENOUVW	UNAVOWED
ADENPPRS	PARPENDS
ADENPPSU	UNSAPPED
ADENPPTU	UNTAPPED
ADENPRRS	PARDNERS
ADENPRSU	UNDRAPES
	UNSPARED
ADENPRSW	PREDAWNS
ADENPRTU	DEPURANT
	UNPARTED
ADENPRTY	PEDANTRY
ADENPRUW	UNWARPED
ADENPRUY	UNDERPAY
	UNPRAYED
ADENPSSY	DYSPNEAS
	SYNAPSED
ADENQRSU	SQUANDER
ADENRRST	STRANDER
ADENRRSY	REYNARDS
ADENRRTU	UNTARRED
ADENRRWY	WARDENRY
ADENRSSS	SARSDENS
ADENRSST	STANDERS
ADENRSSU	DANSEURS
ADENRSTU	DAUNTERS
	TRANSUDE
	UNTREADS
ADENRSTX	DEXTRANS
ADENRSUY	UNDERSAY
ADENRTTU	TRUANTED
ADENRTTY	TYRANTED
ADENRTUX	UNDERTAX
ADENRUWY	UNDERWAY
ADENSSSW	WESSANDS
ADENSTTU	UNSTATED
	UNTASTED
ADENSTUW	UNWASTED
ADENSTUY	UNSTAYED
	UNSTEADY
ADENSUWY	UNSWAYED
ADEOOPSS	APODOSES
ADEOORRT	TOREADOR
ADEOOTTT	TATTOOED
ADEOPPRT	PREADOPT
ADEOPPRV	APPROVED
ADEOPRRS	EARDROPS
ADEOPRRT	PARROTED
	PREDATOR
	PRORATED
	TEARDROP
ADEOPRRU	UPROARED
ADEOPRST	ADOPTERS
	ASPORTED
	PASTORED
	READOPTS
ADEOPRSU	UPSOARED
ADEOPRTT	TETRAPOD
ADEOPRUV	VAPOURED
ADEOPSST	PODESTAS
ADEOPSTT	DESPOTAT
	POSTDATE
ADEORRSS	DROSERAS
ADEORRST	ROADSTER
ADEORRTW	TARROWED
ADEORRVW	OVERDRAW
ADEORSST	ASSORTED
	TORSADES
ADEORSTU	OUTDARES
	OUTREADS
	READOUTS
ADEORSTX	EXTRADOS
ADEORSUV	SAVOURED
ADEORSWY	RODEWAYS
ADEORTTU	OUTRATED
	OUTTRADE
ADEORTUV	OUTRAVED
ADEOSSTT	ASSOTTED
ADEOSTTU	OUTDATES
ADEOSWWY	WAYWODES
ADEOTTTW	TATTOWED
ADEPPRST	STRAPPED
ADEPRRTU	RAPTURED
ADEPRSTU	PASTURED
	UPDATERS
	UPSTARED
ADEPSTUY	UPSTAYED
ADEPSUWY	UPSWAYED
ADEQSTTU	SQUATTED
ADERRSSW	WARDRESS
ADERRSTT	REDSTART
ADERSSSU	ASSUREDS

ADERSSTW	STEWARDS
ADERSSUY	DASYURES
ADERSTTU	STATURED
ADERSTUX	SURTAXED
ADERSTWW	WESTWARD
ADESSTTW	WADSETTS
ADFFGIIR	GIRAFFID
ADFFGINS	DAFFINGS
ADFFHIRS	DRAFFISH
ADFFHNOS	HANDOFFS
ADFFISST	DISTAFFS
ADFFLNOS	FANFOLDS
ADFFLOOS	OFFLOADS
ADFFLRUU	FRAUDFUL
ADFFNOST	STANDOFF
ADFFOORS	AFFOORDS
ADFGINNU	UNFADING
ADFGINRS	FARDINGS
ADFGINRT	DRAFTING
ADFGINRW	DWARFING
ADFHILSY	LADYFISH
ADFHINSS	SANDFISH
ADFHIOST	TOADFISH
ADFHIRSW	DWARFISH
ADFHLNSU	HANDFULS
	HANDSFUL
ADFHLOST	HOLDFAST
ADFHOOSS	SHADOOFS
ADFIIILR	FILARIID
ADFIILPY	LAPIDIFY
ADFILLLN	LANDFILL
ADFILLMN	FILMLAND
ADFILLNO	NAILFOLD
ADFILLNW	WINDFALL
ADFILMNO	MANIFOLD
ADFILMRU	FLUIDRAM
ADFILNWW	WINDFLAW
ADFILRTY	DRAFTILY
ADFIMNRS	FINDRAMS
ADFIMORY	FAIRYDOM
ADFIMRSW	DWARFISM
ADFINORZ	FORZANDI
ADFINRST	INDRAFTS
ADFIORSV	DISFAVOR
ADFKLLNO	FOLKLAND
ADFLLNOW	DOWNFALL
ADFLMNOR	LANDFORM
ADFLMNOY	MANYFOLD
ADFLMOPR	FRAMPOLD
ADFLMPSU	MUDFLAPS
ADFLMSTU	MUDFLATS
ADFLNOPS	PLAFONDS
ADFLOOWY	FLOODWAY
ADFLORSU	FOULARDS
ADFMRSTU	STUDFARM
ADFNNOST	FONDANTS
ADFNOORZ	FORZANDO
ADFOOPST	FOOTPADS
ADFOOSTW	FATWOODS
ADFOOSWY	FOODWAYS
ADFORRSW	FORWARDS
	FROWARDS
ADFPRSTU	UPDRAFTS
ADGGGILN	DAGGLING
ADGGGINR	DRAGGING
ADGGGINS	DAGGINGS
ADGGHNOS	HANGDOGS
ADGGHORY	HYDRAGOG
ADGGILNN	DANGLING
ADGGILNS	GADLINGS
ADGGILRS	RIGGALDS
ADGGINRS	NIGGARDS
ADGGINRU	GUARDING
ADGGLRSU	SLUGGARD
ADGHHILN	HIGHLAND
ADGHHIOR	HIGHROAD
ADGHILLL	GILDHALL
ADGHILNN	HANDLING
ADGHILOS	HIDALGOS
ADGHILPY	DIAGLYPH
ADGHILTY	DAYLIGHT
ADGHINOR	HOARDING
ADGHINPR	HANDGRIP
ADGHINSS	SHADINGS
ADGHIPRS	DIGRAPHS
ADGHIRRS	ARDRIGHS
ADGHIRSS	DISHRAGS
ADGHITTW	TIGHTWAD
ADGHLNNO	LONGHAND
ADGHNNSU	HANDGUNS
ADGHNOSS	SANDHOGS
ADGHNOSW	HAGDOWNS
ADGHOOPR	ODOGRAPH
ADGHORSW	HOGWARDS
ADGHPSYY	DYSPHAGY
ADGHRSTU	DRAUGHTS
ADGHRTUY	DRAUGHTY
ADGIILLN	DIALLING
ADGIILLO	GLADIOLI
ADGIILNO	GONIDIAL
ADGIILNP	PLAIDING
ADGIILNR	DRAILING
ADGIILNS	DIALINGS
	GLIADINS
ADGIILNT	DILATING
ADGIILPY	PYGIDIAL
ADGIILST	DIGITALS
ADGIILTY	ALGIDITY
ADGIIMNR	ADMIRING
ADGIIMNX	ADMIXING
ADGIIMST	DIGAMIST
ADGIINNR	DRAINING
ADGIINNS	SDAINING
ADGIINNU	GUANIDIN
ADGIINNV	INVADING
ADGIINNY	DIGYNIAN
ADGIINOR	RADIOING
ADGIINOT	IODATING
ADGIINOV	AVOIDING
ADGIINRR	ARRIDING
ADGIINRY	DAIRYING
ADGIINSS	SIGANIDS
ADGIINSU	IGUANIDS
ADGIINSV	ADVISING
ADGIINSW	GWINIADS
ADGIINTU	AUDITING
ADGIJNRU	ADJURING
ADGIKLNR	DARKLING
ADGILLNU	ALLUDING
	DUALLING
ADGILLNW	WINDGALL
ADGILLNY	DALLYING
ADGILMNS	MADLINGS
ADGILMNW	DWALMING
ADGILMOR	MARIGOLD
ADGILNNS	LANDINGS
	SANDLING
ADGILNNU	UNLADING
ADGILNOS	LOADINGS
ADGILNPP	DAPPLING
ADGILNRS	DARLINGS
ADGILNRT	DARTLING
ADGILNRW	DRAWLING
ADGILNRY	DARINGLY
ADGILNZZ	DAZZLING
ADGILOOS	SOLIDAGO
ADGILOPR	PRODIGAL
ADGILORS	GOLIARDS
ADGILORY	GOLIARDY
	GYROIDAL
ADGILRVY	GRAVIDLY
ADGIMMNR	DRAMMING
ADGIMMNW	DWAMMING
ADGIMNNU	MAUNDING
ADGIMNOP	POMADING
ADGIMNPS	DAMPINGS
ADGIMNRS	MRIDANGS
ADGIMNRY	MARDYING
ADGIMNUW	DWAUMING
ADGIMOSU	DIGAMOUS
ADGINNOR	ADORNING
ADGINNOT	DONATING
ADGINNPY	PANDYING
ADGINNRS	DARNINGS
ADGINNRT	DRANTING
ADGINNRU	UNDARING
ADGINNSS	SANDINGS
ADGINNST	STANDING
ADGINNSW	DAWNINGS
ADGINNSY	SDAYNING
ADGINNTU	DAUNTING
ADGINOOP	POIGNADO
ADGINOOR	RIGADOON
ADGINOPT	ADOPTING
ADGINORS	ROADINGS
ADGINORU	RIGAUDON
ADGINOST	DOATINGS
ADGINOTY	TOADYING
ADGINPPR	DRAPPING
ADGINPTU	UPDATING
ADGINRRS	GRANDSIR
ADGINRST	TRADINGS
ADGINRSW	DRAWINGS
	SWARDING
	WARDINGS
ADGINRTT	DRATTING
ADGINRTU	ANTIDRUG
ADGINRTY	TARDYING
ADGINSTU	ADUSTING
	SUDATING
ADGINSWY	GWYNIADS
ADGIPRSU	PAGURIDS
ADGIRSSU	GUISARDS
ADGIRSZZ	GIZZARDS
ADGKOOSZ	GADZOOKS
ADGLLNOS	GOLLANDS
ADGLMNOS	MANGOLDS
ADGLNOOS	DONGOLAS
	GONDOLAS
ADGLNORS	GOLDARNS
ADGLNOSW	GOWLANDS
ADGLOORY	GARDYLOO
ADGLOSWY	DAYGLOWS
ADGMNOOR	ONDOGRAM
ADGMNORS	GORMANDS
ADGMNORU	GOURMAND
ADGNNOQU	QUANDONG
ADGNNORS	GRANDSON
ADGNNRYY	GYNANDRY
ADGNOORS	DRAGOONS
	GADROONS
ADGNRRSU	GURNARDS
ADGNRSUU	UNGUARDS
ADGOOPRS	GOSPODAR
ADGOPRSU	PODARGUS
ADGORSTU	OUTDRAGS
ADGORTUU	OUTGUARD
ADGRSSTU	DUSTRAGS
ADHHIPRS	HARDSHIP
ADHHMOSS	SHAHDOMS
ADHHNRTY	HYDRANTH
ADHIIIKS	DAISHIKI
ADHIIJST	IJTIHADS
ADHIIKSS	DASHIKIS
ADHIIMPS	AMIDSHIP
ADHIINOP	OPHIDIAN
ADHIINRW	WHINIARD
ADHIJLSY	JADISHLY
ADHILLMO	HOLLIDAM
ADHILLNS	SANDHILL
ADHILLOP	PHALLOID
ADHILLOT	THALLOID
ADHILMOO	HOMALOID
ADHILMOS	HALIDOMS
ADHILNST	HANDLIST
ADHILOPS	HAPLOIDS
	SHIPLOAD
ADHILOPY	HAPLOIDY
ADHILOSY	HOLIDAYS
	HYALOIDS
ADHILPSY	LADYSHIP
ADHIMNOR	RHODAMIN
ADHIMNOS	ADMONISH
ADHIMNOU	HUMANOID
ADHIMOPP	AMPHIPOD
ADHIMPSS	PHASMIDS
ADHIMRTY	MYRIADTH
ADHINOPY	DIAPHONY
ADHINPSS	DISHPANS
ADHINPSU	DAUPHINS
ADHINRTW	HANDWRIT
ADHINRWY	WHINYARD
ADHINSST	STANDISH
ADHINSTU	DIANTHUS
ADHIOSTY	TOADYISH
ADHIPRSW	WARDSHIP
ADHIPRSY	SHIPYARD
ADHIPSTY	DISPATHY
ADHIRTWW	WITHDRAW
ADHITWWY	WIDTHWAY
ADHKNORW	HANDWORK
ADHKORSW	DORHAWKS
ADHKOSSU	SHAKUDOS
ADHLLLOS	HOLDALLS
ADHLLNOS	HOLLANDS
ADHLMNOO	HANDLOOM
ADHLMORT	THRALDOM
ADHLMOSY	HOLYDAMS
ADHLMPSY	LYMPHADS
ADHLNORW	WALDHORN
ADHLNOUW	DOWNHAUL
ADHLOSYY	HOLYDAYS
ADHMNOOS	MANHOODS
ADHMOPRS	DRAMSHOP
ADHNNOOR	HONORAND
ADHNNORY	NONHARDY
ADHNOOTU	AUNTHOOD
ADHNORSU	UNHOARDS
ADHNOSTU	HANDOUTS
	THOUSAND
ADHNOSUW	UNSHADOW
ADHNOSWW	DOWNWASH
ADHNRSTY	HYDRANTS
ADHOOPRS	HOSPODAR
ADHOOPST	HOPTOADS
ADHOORRS	RHODORAS
ADHOORSW	ROADSHOW
ADHOORYZ	HYDROZOA
ADHOPRST	HARDTOPS
	POTSHARD
ADHOPRSU	UPHOARDS
ADHOPRSY	RHAPSODY
ADHOPSST	DASHPOTS
ADHORRSU	DHOURRAS
ADHORRTY	HYDRATOR
ADHORSTU	TOADRUSH
ADHORSWY	SHOWYARD
ADHPSTYY	DYSPATHY
ADIIINRV	VIRIDIAN
ADIIIQRU	DAIQUIRI

ADIIKLLN KALLIDIN
ADIIKLMM MILKMAID
ADIIKLST TAILSKID
ADIIKNOP PINAKOID
ADIIKNST ANTISKID
ADIIKOST DAKOITIS
ADIILLMR MILLIARD
ADIILLNY IDYLLIAN
ADIILLOP LIPOIDAL
ADIILLOR ARILLOID
ADIILLST DIALLIST
ADIILLUV DILUVIAL
ADIILMSS MISDIALS
ADIILNOT DILATION
ADIILNSU INDUSIAL
ADIILNSV INVALIDS
ADIILNSW WINDSAIL
ADIILNTW TAILWIND
ADIILNTY DAINTILY
ADIILNUV DILUVIAN
INDUVIAL
ADIILOPP DIPLOPIA
ADIILPST LAPIDIST
ADIILRST DISTRAIL
ADIILSST DIALISTS
ADIILSSY DIALYSIS
ADIILTVY VALIDITY
ADIIMMSS MAIDISMS
ADIIMNNS INDAMINS
ADIIMPSU ASPIDIUM
ADIIMRST TRIADISM
ADIIMRSU MUDIRIAS
ADIINNOT NIDATION
ADIINNOZ DIAZINON
ADIINOOT IODATION
ADIINOTU AUDITION
ADIINPRS PINDARIS
ADIINRST DISTRAIN
ADIINSST DISTAINS
ADIINSSU SUIDIANS
ADIIOPRS SPORIDIA
ADIIOPRT TAPIROID
ADIIOPSS ADIPOSIS
ADIIORST TARSIOID
ADIIPRTU TRIPUDIA
ADIIPRTY RAPIDITY
ADIIPSTY SAPIDITY
ADIIPTVY VAPIDITY
ADIIQRSU DAQUIRIS
ADIIRSST DIARISTS
ADIIRSTT DISTRAIT
TRIADIST
ADIJNOST ADJOINTS
ADIKKRRW KIRKWARD
ADIKKRRY KIRKYARD
ADIKLLOR ROADKILL
ADIKLNPS LANDSKIP
ADIKLNSY LADYKINS
ADIKLORS KILORADS
ADIKLOSS ODALISKS
ADIKMNNS MANKINDS
ADIKMSSS DISMASKS
ADIKNNNU DUNNAKIN
ADIKNNST INKSTAND
ADIKNPSS SKIDPANS
ADIKNRSS DISRANKS
ADIKNRST STINKARD
ADIKPRSS DISPARKS
ADIKSSWY SKIDWAYS
ADILLLPY PALLIDLY
ADILLMMS MILLDAMS
ADILLMNR MANDRILL
ADILLMOU ALLODIUM
ADILLMOV VILLADOM
ADILLMSY DISMALLY

ADILLNPS LANDSLIP
ADILLOOP POLOIDAL
ADILLOPS SPADILLO
ADILLOSW DISALLOW
ADILLOSY DISLOYAL
ADILLRWY WILLYARD
ADILLSTY DISTALLY
ADILMMOS MODALISM
ADILMNNO MANDOLIN
ADILMNOS SALMONID
ADILMNRS MANDRILS
RIMLANDS
ADILMOOR MODIOLAR
ADILMOPS DIPLOMAS
PLASMOID
ADILMOPT DIPLOMAT
ADILMOPY OLYMPIAD
ADILMORU ORDALIUM
ADILMOST MODALIST
ADILMOSU ALODIUMS
ADILMOSY AMYLOIDS
ADILMOTY MODALITY
ADILMPRY LAMPYRID
ADILMPSS PLASMIDS
ADILMPSU PALUDISM
ADILMSSU DUALISMS
ADILMSSY DISMAYLS
LADYISMS
ADILNNNU NUNDINAL
ADILNNOT NONTIDAL
ADILNNOV NONVALID
ADILNNSU DISANNUL
ADILNOOR DOORNAIL
ADILNOOV VINDALOO
ADILNOPY PALINODY
ADILNORS ORDINALS
ADILNORT TRINODAL
ADILNOTY NODALITY
ADILNPRS SPANDRIL
ADILNPST DISPLANT
ADILNRSU DIURNALS
ADILNRWY INWARDLY
ADILNSSU SUNDIALS
ADILNSSW WINDLASS
ADILOOPZ DIPLOZOA
ADILOORT IDOLATOR
TOROIDAL
ADILOPRT DIOPTRAL
TRIPODAL
ADILOPSS DISPOSAL
ADILOQSU SQUALOID
ADILORST DILATORS
ADILORSY SOLIDARY
ADILORTY ADROITLY
DILATORY
IDOLATRY
ADILOSST SODALIST
ADILOSTY SODALITY
ADILPPSY DISAPPLY
ADILPRSY PYRALIDS
ADILPSST PLASTIDS
ADILPSSY DISPLAYS
ADILPSTU PLAUDITS
ADILRTTY TILTYARD
ADILRTWY TAWDRILY
ADILRWYZ WIZARDLY
ADILSSTU DUALISTS
ADIMMNOO AMMONOID
ADIMMNOS MONADISM
NOMADISM
ADIMMNSY DYNAMISM
ADIMMOST AMIDMOST
ADIMMOTU DOMATIUM
ADIMNNOS MONDAINS
ADIMNNOT DOMINANT

ADIMNOOR MAINDOOR
ADIMNOST DONATISM
SAINTDOM
ADIMNOWW WIDOWMAN
ADIMNRSW MISDRAWN
ADIMNRSY MISANDRY
ADIMNSTY DYNAMIST
ADIMOPRY MYRIAPOD
ADIMOPSY SYMPODIA
ADIMORRS MIRADORS
ADIMOSST MASTOIDS
ADIMOSTT MATTOIDS
ADIMOSTY TOADYISM
ADIMPRSY PYRAMIDS
ADIMRSSW MISDRAWS
ADIMRSUU SUDARIUM
ADIMSSST DISMASTS
ADIMSSTU DUMAISTS
STADIUMS
ADINNNTU INUNDANT
ADINNOOT DONATION
NODATION
ADINNOPS DIPNOANS
ADINNORS ANDIRONS
ADINNORT ORDINANT
ADINNORY NONDAIRY
ADINNOTU NUDATION
ADINNRSY INNYARDS
ADINOOPS ISOPODAN
ADINOOPT ADOPTION
ADINOORT TANDOORI
ADINOOTT DOTATION
ADINOPPS OPPIDANS
ADINOPRR RAINDROP
ADINOPRS PONIARDS
ADINOPRY PYRANOID
ADINOPST PINTADOS
SATINPOD
ADINORRS ORDINARS
ADINORRY ORDINARY
ADINORSS SADIRONS
ADINORST DIATRONS
INTRADOS
ADINORSU DINOSAUR
ADINORSV VIRANDOS
ADINORTU DURATION
ADINOSTU SUDATION
ADINOSTX OXIDANTS
ADINOSTY DYSTONIA
ADINPSST SANDPITS
ADINPSSY SYNAPSID
ADINRRST TRIDARNS
ADINRSSU SUNDARIS
ADINRSTU UNITARDS
ADINRUVZ UNVIZARD
ADINSWWY WINDWAYS
ADIOOPRT PAROTOID
ADIOOPSS APODOSIS
ADIOOSSW WOODSIAS
ADIOPPST POSTPAID
ADIOPRRS AIRDROPS
ADIOPRSS SPAROIDS
ADIOPRST PARODIST
PAROTIDS
ADIOPRSV PRIVADOS
ADIOPRTY PODIATRY
ADIOPSTY DYSTOPIA
ADIORRTT TRADITOR
ADIORSST ASTROIDS
SARODIST
ADIORSSV ADVISORS
ADIORSTT STRADIOT
ADIORSTU AUDITORS
ADIORSVY ADVISORY
ADIORTUY AUDITORY

ADIOSSVW DISAVOWS
ADIPRRTU PURTRAID
ADIPRSST DISPARTS
ADIRRWYZ WIZARDRY
ADIRSSTY SATYRIDS
ADIRSSUY DYSURIAS
ADJKNRUY JUNKYARD
ADJLMORS JARLDOMS
ADJNORSU ADJOURNS
ADJORRSU ADJURORS
ADJORSTU ADJUSTOR
ADKKLOSY KAKODYLS
ADKLMRSU MUDLARKS
ADKLOORW WOODLARK
WORKLOAD
ADKMNORW MARKDOWN
ADKMOORR DARKROOM
ADKNORTU OUTDRANK
ADKNRSTU STUNKARD
ADKOORRW ROADWORK
ADKORRWY YARDWORK
ADKORSWY DAYWORKS
WORKDAYS
ADKRSSWY SKYWARDS
ADLLLOOY DOOLALLY
ADLLMOSW WADMOLLS
ADLLNOPW PLOWLAND
ADLLNOSW LOWLANDS
ADLLOPRS POLLARDS
ADLLORSY DORSALLY
ADLLRSWY DRYWALLS
ADLMNNOO NONMODAL
ADLMNOOR MOORLAND
ADLMNORY RANDOMLY
ADLMNOSS MOSSLAND
ADLMOORS LORDOMAS
MALODORS
ADLMOORU MALODOUR
ADLMOPRW MOLDWARP
ADLMOPSY PSALMODY
ADLNNORS NORLANDS
ADLNNOSW SNOWLAND
ADLNNOTU NONADULT
ADLNNOTW TOWNLAND
ADLNNSSU SUNLANDS
ADLNNTUU UNDULANT
ADLNOORS LARDOONS
ADLNOORW LOANWORD
ADLNOPRT PORTLAND
ADLNOPRU PAULDRON
ADLNOPSU POUNDALS
ADLNOPWY DOWNPLAY
PLAYDOWN
ADLNORST TROLANDS
ADLNORWY ONWARDLY
ADLNOSST SANDLOTS
ADLNOSSU SOULDANS
ADLNOSSY SYNODALS
ADLNOSTU OUTLANDS
ADLOOPRU UROPODAL
ADLOORWW WOOLWARD
ADLOPRSU POULARDS
ADLOPRWY WORDPLAY
ADLOPSUU PALUDOUS
ADLOQSUW OLDSQUAW
ADLORRSW WARLORDS
ADLORTWY TOWARDLY
ADLPRUWY UPWARDLY
ADLRRTUY ULTRADRY
ADMMNOOS DOOMSMAN
ADMMNSSU SUMMANDS
ADMMNTUU MUTANDUM
ADMNNORY MONANDRY
ADMNNOSU SOUNDMAN
ADMNNOTU NOTANDUM

ADMNOOOT	ODONTOMA
ADMNOORS	DOORSMAN
	MADRONOS
ADMNOORW	MOONWARD
ADMNOOST	MASTODON
ADMNOOSW	WOODSMAN
ADMNOOSZ	MADZOONS
ADMNORST	DORMANTS
	MORDANTS
ADMNORSW	SANDWORM
	SWORDMAN
ADMNOSSU	OSMUNDAS
ADMNPPSU	SANDPUMP
ADMOORRW	WARDROOM
ADMOORST	DOORMATS
ADMOORSY	DAYROOMS
ADMOPPPU	POPPADUM
ADMOPPSU	POPADUMS
ADMORSST	STARDOMS
	TSARDOMS
ADMORSTW	MADWORTS
ADMORSTZ	TZARDOMS
ADMRSSTU	DURMASTS
	MUSTARDS
ADMRSTUY	MUSTARDY
ADNNOOSY	NOONDAYS
ADNNORTY	DYNATRON
ADNNOSTU	DAUNTONS
ADNNRSTU	DUNNARTS
ADNOOPRS	PANDOORS
	SPADROON
ADNOOQRU	QUADROON
ADNOORST	DONATORS
	ODORANTS
	TANDOORS
	TORNADOS
ADNOORTY	DONATORY
ADNOOSVW	ADVOWSON
ADNOPRSU	PANDOURS
ADNOPRSV	PROVANDS
ADNOQRSU	SQUADRON
ADNORRSW	NORWARDS
ADNORSTU	ROTUNDAS
ADNORSTW	SANDWORT
ADNORSTY	TARDYONS
ADNORSWY	NAYWORDS
ADNORSXY	SARDONYX
ADNORTUW	OUTDRAWN
	UNTOWARD
ADNORWWY	WANWORDY
ADNOSSTU	ASTOUNDS
ADNOSTTU	OUTSTAND
	STANDOUT
ADNPRSSU	SANDSPUR
ADNPSSTU	DUSTPANS
	UPSTANDS
ADNRSSUW	SUNWARDS
ADOOPRRT	TRAPDOOR
ADOOPRSU	SAUROPOD
ADOOPSSW	SAPWOODS
ADOORSWY	DOORWAYS
ADOOSSSW	SASSWOOD
ADOOSSTT	TOSTADOS
ADOPRRSW	WARDROPS
ADOPRSSW	PASSWORD
ADOPSSSU	SOAPSUDS
ADORRSTU	DARTROUS
ADORSTUW	OUTDRAWS
	OUTWARDS
ADORSTUY	SUDATORY
ADORTUVY	ADVOUTRY
ADPRRTUY	PURTRAYD
ADRSSTTU	STARDUST
ADSSSTUW	SAWDUSTS
ADSSTUWY	SAWDUSTY

AEEEELRS	RELEASEE
AEEEEMRT	EMEERATE
AEEEFLRS	EELFARES
AEEEFRRW	FREEWARE
AEEEFRTY	AFTEREYE
AEEEGGNR	REENGAGE
AEEEGKLS	KEELAGES
AEEEGLLS	LEGALESE
AEEEGLNR	GENERALE
AEEEGLRT	EGLATERE
	REGELATE
	RELEGATE
AEEEGLRV	LEVERAGE
AEEEGLST	LEGATEES
AEEEGLSV	SELVAGEE
AEEEGLTV	VEGELATE
AEEEGMRT	METERAGE
AEEEGNRT	GENERATE
	RENEGATE
	TEENAGER
AEEEGNSS	AGENESES
AEEEGPRS	PEERAGES
AEEEGPSS	SEEPAGES
AEEEGRST	EAGEREST
	ETAGERES
	STEERAGE
AEEEGRSW	SEWERAGE
AEEEGTTV	VEGETATE
AEEEHKLL	KEELHALE
AEEEHLRT	ETHEREAL
AEEEHMPR	EPHEMERA
AEEEHNRS	ENHEARSE
AEEEHRRS	REHEARSE
AEEEHRRT	REHEATER
AEEEHSTT	AESTHETE
AEEEILNS	ALIENEES
AEEEIMNX	EXAMINEE
AEEEIMRT	EMERITAE
AEEEIRST	EATERIES
AEEEJNTT	JEANETTE
AEEEKKPS	KEEPSAKE
AEEEKMSS	KAMEESES
AEEEKMSZ	KAMEEZES
AEEEKNRW	WEAKENER
AEEELLPP	APPELLEE
AEEELLST	TELESALE
AEEELMNR	ENAMELER
AEEELNRT	LATEENER
AEEELNRV	VENEREAL
AEEELNST	SELENATE
AEEELPRR	REPEALER
AEEELQSU	SEQUELAE
AEEELRRS	RELEASER
AEEELRRV	REVEALER
AEEELRSS	RELEASES
AEEELRST	TEASELER
AEEELRSW	WEASELER
AEEELRTX	AXLETREE
AEEELSSS	EASELESS
AEEELSTV	ELEVATES
AEEEMMRT	METAMERE
AEEEMNST	EASEMENT
AEEEMPRS	PERMEASE
AEEEMPRT	PERMEATE
AEEENNRV	VENEREAN
AEEENNTV	VENENATE
AEEENPTT	PATENTEE
AEEENRST	SERENATE
AEEENRTT	ENTERATE
AEEENRTV	ENERVATE
	VENERATE
AEEEPRRT	REPARTEE
	REPEATER
	REREPEAT
AEEEPSTW	SWEETPEA

AEEERRST	ARRESTEE
AEEERSST	ESTERASE
	TESSERAE
AEEERSVW	REWEAVES
AEEERTWY	EYEWATER
AEEFFLLS	FELAFELS
AEEFFLRT	TAFFEREL
AEEFFLTT	FLATFEET
AEEFFNRT	AFFERENT
AEEFGILR	FILAGREE
AEEFGIRR	FERRIAGE
AEEFGIRS	FEGARIES
AEEFGIRT	FIGEATER
AEEFGLNS	FENAGLES
AEEFGLSU	FUSELAGE
AEEFGNST	FANTEEGS
AEEFGRSS	SERFAGES
AEEFGSTW	WEFTAGES
AEEFHIRS	SHEAFIER
AEEFHLLS	SELFHEAL
AEEFHRST	FEATHERS
AEEFHRTY	FEATHERY
AEEFIINR	INFERIAE
AEEFIIRS	AERIFIES
AEEFIKLL	LEAFLIKE
AEEFIKLW	KALEWIFE
AEEFIKRR	FREAKIER
AEEFIKRS	FAKERIES
AEEFIKRW	WAKERIFE
AEEFILMN	FILENAME
AEEFILNR	FLANERIE
AEEFILRS	FILAREES
	SERAFILE
AEEFILRT	FEATLIER
	FRAILTEE
AEEFILST	FEALTIES
	FETIALES
	LEAFIEST
AEEFIPSW	SPAEWIFE
AEEFIRRR	RAREFIER
AEEFIRRS	RAREFIES
AEEFIRSS	FREESIAS
AEEFIRTT	FETERITA
AEEFISST	SAFETIES
AEEFKMNT	FAKEMENT
AEEFKOPR	FOREPEAK
AEEFLLMR	FEMERALL
AEEFLLMT	FLAMELET
AEEFLLNR	REFALLEN
AEEFLLNV	EVENFALL
AEEFLLRW	FAREWELL
AEEFLLSS	LEAFLESS
AEEFLLST	FELLATES
	LEAFLETS
AEEFLMNS	ENFLAMES
AEEFLMOS	FLEASOME
AEEFLMPR	PREFLAME
AEEFLMSS	FAMELESS
	SELFSAME
AEEFLNRU	FUNEREAL
AEEFLOOV	FOVEOLAE
AEEFLORV	OVERLEAF
AEEFLRRR	REFERRAL
AEEFLRRT	FALTERER
AEEFLRSS	FEARLESS
AEEFLRST	REFLATES
AEEFLRSW	WELFARES
AEEFMNOR	FOREMEAN
	FORENAME
AEEFMNRS	ENFRAMES
AEEFMORS	FEARSOME
AEEFMRRS	REFRAMES
AEEFMRTY	FEMETARY
AEEFNRST	FASTENER
	FENESTRA

	REFASTEN
AEEFNRTT	FATTENER
AEEFNSSS	SAFENESS
AEEFORRV	OVERFEAR
AEEFOSTU	FEATEOUS
AEEFRRST	FERRATES
AEEFRSST	FEASTERS
AEEFRSTU	FEATURES
AEEFRSWY	FREEWAYS
AEEFTTUV	FAUVETTE
AEEGGHIW	WEIGHAGE
AEEGGINR	AGREEING
AEEGGIRV	AGGRIEVE
AEEGGLLS	ALLEGGES
AEEGGLOU	AEGLOGUE
AEEGGLRS	GREGALES
AEEGGNNR	GANGRENE
AEEGGNOS	GASOGENE
AEEGGNOZ	GAZOGENE
AEEGGNRS	ENGAGERS
AEEGGOPS	EPAGOGES
AEEGGPRU	PUGGAREE
AEEGGRSU	REGAUGES
AEEGHIRS	HIREAGES
AEEGHIRT	HERITAGE
AEEGHLOT	HELOTAGE
AEEGHLRS	SHEARLEG
AEEGHLRW	RAGWHEEL
AEEGHMPR	GRAPHEME
AEEGHNRS	SHAGREEN
AEEGHNST	THENAGES
AEEGHNSW	WHANGEES
AEEGHORS	GHERAOES
AEEGHRRT	GATHERER
	REGATHER
AEEGIILW	WEIGELIA
AEEGIINR	AEGIRINE
AEEGIIRT	AEGIRITE
AEEGIIST	GAIETIES
AEEGIKLM	GAMELIKE
AEEGIKLT	GATELIKE
AEEGIKLU	AGUELIKE
AEEGILLS	GALILEES
	LEGALISE
AEEGILLZ	LEGALIZE
AEEGILMN	LIEGEMAN
AEEGILMR	GLEAMIER
AEEGILMS	GELSEMIA
	MILEAGES
AEEGILNR	ALGERINE
AEEGILNS	ENSILAGE
	LINEAGES
AEEGILNT	GALENITE
	GELATINE
	LEGATINE
AEEGILNV	INVEAGLE
AEEGILOU	EULOGIAE
AEEGILPR	PERIGEAL
AEEGILRS	GASELIER
AEEGILST	EGALITES
	ELEGIAST
AEEGILSW	WEIGELAS
AEEGILTV	LEVIGATE
AEEGIMNR	GERMAINE
AEEGIMNT	GEMINATE
AEEGIMRS	GAMESIER
	REIMAGES
AEEGIMRT	EMIGRATE
	REMIGATE
AEEGINNT	ANTIGENE
AEEGINPR	PERIGEAN
AEEGINRR	REGAINER
AEEGINRS	ANERGIES
	GESNERIA
AEEGINRT	GRATINEE

	INTERAGE
AEEGINRZ	RAZEEING
AEEGINSS	AGENESIS
	ASSIGNEE
AEEGINST	SAGENITE
AEEGINSU	EUGENIAS
AEEGINSV	ENVISAGE
AEEGINSZ	AGENIZES
AEEGINTV	AGENTIVE
	NEGATIVE
AEEGINTX	EXIGEANT
AEEGIPPS	PIPEAGES
AEEGIPQU	EQUIPAGE
AEEGIPRS	PIERAGES
AEEGIRRS	GREASIER
AEEGIRSS	GREASIES
AEEGIRTT	AIGRETTE
AEEGIRTV	ERGATIVE
AEEGISSS	ASSIEGES
AEEGISTY	GAYETIES
AEEGKLLS	KLEAGLES
AEEGLLNR	ALLERGEN
AEEGLLPR	PRELEGAL
AEEGLLRS	ALLEGERS
AEEGLLSZ	GAZELLES
AEEGLMNS	MELANGES
AEEGLMNV	GAVELMEN
AEEGLMOS	MESOGLEA
AEEGLMRS	GLEAMERS
AEEGLMRT	TELEGRAM
AEEGLMRY	MEAGERLY
	MEAGRELY
AEEGLMST	MELTAGES
AEEGLNNR	ENLARGEN
AEEGLNNT	ENTANGLE
AEEGLNOS	GASOLENE
AEEGLNOT	ELONGATE
AEEGLNRR	ENLARGER
AEEGLNRS	ENLARGES
	GENERALS
	GLEANERS
AEEGLNRT	REGENTAL
AEEGLNSU	EUGLENAS
AEEGLNSV	EVANGELS
AEEGLNVY	EVANGELY
AEEGLOOZ	ZOOGLEAE
AEEGLORS	AEROGELS
AEEGLOST	SEGOLATE
AEEGLPRS	PEREGALS
AEEGLRRS	REGALERS
AEEGLRSS	EELGRASS
	GEARLESS
	LARGESSE
AEEGLRSU	LEAGUERS
AEEGLRSW	LEGWEARS
AEEGLRSZ	REGLAZES
AEEGLRTU	REGULATE
AEEGLRUX	EXERGUAL
AEEGLSST	GATELESS
AEEGLSSV	SELVAGES
AEEGLSSW	WAGELESS
AEEGLSSY	EYEGLASS
AEEGLSTT	GALETTES
AEEGLSTV	VEGETALS
AEEGLTTU	TUTELAGE
AEEGLTUV	EVULGATE
AEEGMMNR	ENGRAMME
AEEGMMNS	GAMESMEN
AEEGMMOS	GAMESOME
AEEGMMST	GEMMATES
	TAGMEMES
AEEGMNOR	ARGEMONE
AEEGMNRS	AGREMENS
AEEGMNRT	AGREMENT
AEEGMNSS	GAMENESS
	MAGNESES
AEEGMNTT	TEGMENTA
AEEGMNTZ	GAZEMENT
AEEGMOOT	OOGAMETE
AEEGMOST	SOMEGATE
AEEGMRST	GAMESTER
	MEAGREST
AEEGMRSU	REMUAGES
AEEGMSSS	MEGASSES
	MESSAGES
AEEGMSSU	MESSUAGE
AEEGNNNO	ENNEAGON
AEEGNNPS	PANGENES
AEEGNNRS	ENRANGES
AEEGNNRT	GENERANT
AEEGNNRU	ENRAUNGE
AEEGNNRV	ENGRAVEN
AEEGNOPS	PEONAGES
AEEGNPPS	GENAPPES
AEEGNRRT	ETRANGER
AEEGNRRV	ENGRAVER
AEEGNRST	ESTRANGE
	GRANTEES
	GREATENS
	NEGATERS
	REAGENTS
	SEGREANT
	SERGEANT
	STERNAGE
AEEGNRSU	RENAGUES
AEEGNRSV	AVENGERS
	ENGRAVES
AEEGNRTU	GAUNTREE
AEEGNRWY	GREENWAY
AEEGNSSS	SAGENESS
AEEGNSTT	TENTAGES
AEEGNSTV	VENTAGES
AEEGNTTV	VEGETANT
AEEGOPRV	OVERPAGE
AEEGOPSS	SAPEGOES
AEEGORSV	OVERAGES
AEEGORVV	OVERGAVE
AEEGOSTX	GEOTAXES
AEEGPRRS	ASPERGER
	PRESAGER
AEEGPRRT	PARGETER
AEEGPRSS	ASPERGES
	PRESAGES
AEEGPRSU	PUGAREES
AEEGRRRT	REGRATER
AEEGRRSS	GREASERS
AEEGRRST	REGRATES
AEEGRRSU	REARGUES
AEEGRRSW	WAGERERS
AEEGRRTT	RETARGET
AEEGRSST	RESTAGES
AEEGRSTT	GREATEST
AEEGRSTU	TREAGUES
AEEGRSTW	STREWAGE
AEEGRSUZ	GUEREZAS
AEEGSSTT	GESTATES
AEEGSTTZ	GAZETTES
AEEHHHSS	HASHEESH
AEEHHIRT	HEATHIER
AEEHHLNZ	HAZELHEN
AEEHHNST	ENSHEATH
	HEATHENS
AEEHHOOP	PAHOEHOE
AEEHHRSS	REHASHES
AEEHHRST	HEATHERS
	SHEATHER
AEEHHRTY	HEATHERY
AEEHHSST	SHEATHES
AEEHIKLR	HARELIKE
AEEHIKRS	SHIKAREE
AEEHILNP	ELAPHINE
AEEHILRS	SHIRALEE
AEEHILRT	ETHERIAL
AEEHIMNT	HEMATEIN
	HEMATINE
AEEHIMNX	HEXAMINE
AEEHIMPT	EPITHEMA
AEEHIMTT	HEMATITE
AEEHINRS	INHEARSE
AEEHINRT	ATHERINE
	HERNIATE
AEEHIPRS	PHARISEE
AEEHIPST	APHETISE
	HEAPIEST
	HEPATISE
AEEHIPTT	HEPATITE
AEEHIPTZ	APHETIZE
	HEPATIZE
AEEHIRRS	HEARSIER
AEEHIRRT	EARTHIER
	HEARTIER
AEEHIRSS	ASHERIES
AEEHIRST	HEARTIES
AEEHIRSV	SHIVAREE
AEEHIRTW	WHEATIER
AEEHISST	ATHEISES
	ESTHESIA
AEEHISTT	ATHETISE
	HESITATE
AEEHISTV	HEAVIEST
AEEHISTZ	ATHEIZES
AEEHITTZ	ATHETIZE
AEEHKLLR	RAKEHELL
AEEHKLLU	KEELHAUL
AEEHKMNS	KHAMSEEN
AEEHKNRR	HANKERER
	HARKENER
AEEHKNRS	HEARKENS
AEEHKRST	HEKTARES
AEEHKRSU	HEUREKAS
AEEHLLSS	SEASHELL
AEEHLMNW	WHALEMEN
	WHEELMAN
AEEHLMNY	HYMENEAL
AEEHLMOS	HEALSOME
AEEHLMPT	HELPMATE
AEEHLNOS	ENHALOES
AEEHLNOT	ANETHOLE
AEEHLNPT	ELEPHANT
AEEHLNRT	LEATHERN
AEEHLNSS	HALENESS
AEEHLNTX	EXHALENT
AEEHLNVY	HEAVENLY
AEEHLORS	ARSEHOLE
AEEHLORV	OVERHALE
AEEHLOSU	ALEHOUSE
AEEHLPST	HEELTAPS
	PLEASETH
AEEHLPTT	TELEPATH
AEEHLRRT	LATHERER
AEEHLRST	HALTERES
	LEATHERS
AEEHLRSV	HAVERELS
AEEHLRTT	HEARTLET
AEEHLRTY	LEATHERY
AEEHLSST	HATELESS
	HEATLESS
AEEHLSTT	ATHLETES
AEEHLTTY	ETHYLATE
AEEHMMRR	HAMMERER
	REHAMMER
AEEHMNNY	HYMENEAN
AEEHMNPS	SHEEPMAN
AEEHMNRS	SHAREMEN
	SHEARMEN
AEEHMNRT	EARTHMEN
AEEHMNST	METHANES
AEEHMNTU	ATHENEUM
AEEHMNTX	EXANTHEM
AEEHMPRR	HAMPERER
AEEHMPSS	EMPHASES
AEEHMRSS	MAHSEERS
AEEHMRST	ERATHEMS
AEEHMRTY	ERYTHEMA
AEEHMSST	MATHESES
AEEHMTUX	EXHUMATE
AEEHNNSS	SNEESHAN
AEEHNNTX	XANTHENE
AEEHNOPR	EARPHONE
AEEHNPST	HAPTENES
	HEPTANES
	PHENATES
	STEPHANE
AEEHNRSS	ARSHEENS
AEEHNRST	HASTENER
	HEARTENS
AEEHNRSU	UNHEARSE
AEEHNRSV	RESHAVEN
AEEHNRTT	HATERENT
	THREATEN
AEEHNRTU	URETHANE
AEEHNRTW	WATERHEN
	WREATHEN
AEEHNRWY	ANYWHERE
AEEHNSST	ANTHESES
AEEHNSTU	UNEATHES
AEEHNSTW	ENSWATHE
	WHEATENS
AEEHOPRT	EPHORATE
AEEHOPRV	OVERHEAP
AEEHORRV	OVERHEAR
AEEHORSS	SEAHORSE
	SEASHORE
AEEHORTV	OVERHATE
	OVERHEAT
AEEHOSTU	TEAHOUSE
AEEHPPRS	PRESHAPE
AEEHPRRS	REPHRASE
	RESHAPER
AEEHPRRT	THREAPER
AEEHPRSS	RESHAPES
	SPHAERES
	SPHEARES
AEEHPRST	PREHEATS
	SPREATHE
AEEHPRUV	UPHEAVER
AEEHPSUV	UPHEAVES
AEEHQSSU	QUASHEES
AEEHRRSS	SHEARERS
AEEHRRTU	URETHRAE
AEEHRRTW	WREATHER
AEEHRSSV	RESHAVES
AEEHRSSW	REWASHES
AEEHRSTT	EARTHSET
	THEATERS
	THEATRES
AEEHRSTV	THREAVES
AEEHRSTW	WEATHERS
	WREATHES
AEEHRTVW	WHATEVER
AEEHSTTW	SAWTEETH
AEEHSTVY	HEAVYSET
AEEIIMRT	METAIRIE
AEEIINRT	INERTIAE
AEEIISST	ASEITIES
AEEIJPRS	JAPERIES
AEEIKKLL	LAKELIKE
AEEIKKLP	PEAKLIKE
AEEIKKLW	LIKEWAKE
AEEIKLLS	SEALLIKE

AEEIKLMS	SEAMLIKE
AEEIKLMU	LEUKEMIA
AEEIKLMZ	MAZELIKE
AEEIKLPT	TAPELIKE
AEEIKLRW	WEAKLIER
AEEIKLST	LEAKIEST
AEEIKLSV	VASELIKE
AEEIKLVW	WAVELIKE
AEEIKMMR	MERIMAKE
AEEIKMNT	KETAMINE
AEEIKNRS	SNEAKIER
AEEIKNRT	ANKERITE
	KREATINE
AEEIKNSS	AKINESES
AEEIKPST	PEAKIEST
AEEIKRRS	RAKERIES
	SKEARIER
AEEIKRTW	TWEAKIER
AEEILLNT	TENAILLE
AEEILLRS	REALLIES
AEEILLRT	LAETRILE
AEEILLST	LEALTIES
AEEILMMN	MELAMINE
AEEILMMT	MEALTIME
AEEILMNT	MELANITE
AEEILMNZ	MELANIZE
AEEILMRS	ALMERIES
	MEASLIER
AEEILMRT	EREMITAL
	MATERIEL
	REALTIME
AEEILMST	MEALIEST
	METALISE
AEEILMSV	MALVESIE
AEEILMTZ	METALIZE
AEEILNNS	SELENIAN
AEEILNPR	PERINEAL
AEEILNPS	ALEPINES
	PENALISE
	SEPALINE
AEEILNPT	PETALINE
	TAPELINE
AEEILNPZ	PENALIZE
AEEILNRR	NEARLIER
AEEILNRS	ALIENERS
AEEILNRT	ELATERIN
	ENTAILER
	TREENAIL
AEEILNSS	SEALINES
AEEILNSX	ALEXINES
AEEILNTV	ELVANITE
	VENTAILE
AEEILORT	AEROLITE
AEEILOTT	ETIOLATE
AEEILPRR	PEARLIER
AEEILPRS	ESPALIER
	PEARLIES
AEEILPRT	PEARLITE
AEEILPST	EPILATES
AEEILPSW	PALEWISE
AEEILQSU	EQUALISE
AEEILQUX	EXEQUIAL
AEEILQUZ	EQUALIZE
AEEILRRS	REALISER
AEEILRRT	RETAILER
AEEILRRZ	REALIZER
AEEILRSS	REALISES
AEEILRST	ATELIERS
	EARLIEST
	LEARIEST
	REALTIES
AEEILRSV	VELARISE
AEEILRSY	YEARLIES
AEEILRSZ	REALIZES
	SLEAZIER
AEEILRTT	LATERITE
	LITERATE
AEEILRTV	LEVIRATE
	RELATIVE
AEEILRTZ	LATERIZE
AEEILRVW	LIVEWARE
	REVIEWAL
AEEILRVZ	VELARIZE
AEEILSST	ASTELIES
AEEILSTT	AILETTES
AEEILSTV	ELATIVES
	LEAVIEST
	VEALIEST
AEEILSVW	ALEWIVES
AEEILTTV	LEVITATE
AEEILTUV	ELUVIATE
AEEIMMNT	MEANTIME
AEEIMNNS	ENAMINES
AEEIMNRS	REMANIES
AEEIMNRT	ANTIMERE
AEEIMNRX	EXAMINER
AEEIMNSS	NEMESIAS
AEEIMNST	ETAMINES
	MATINEES
	MISEATEN
	SEMINATE
AEEIMNSX	EXAMINES
AEEIMNUV	MAUVEINE
AEEIMOSS	AMEIOSES
AEEIMPRS	EMPAIRES
AEEIMRRS	SMEARIER
AEEIMRSS	SERIEMAS
AEEIMRST	EMIRATES
	REAMIEST
	STEAMIER
AEEIMRTV	VIAMETER
AEEIMSSS	MISEASES
	SIAMESES
AEEIMSST	SEAMIEST
	STEAMIES
AEEIMSSZ	SIAMEZES
AEEIMSTT	ESTIMATE
	ETATISME
	MEATIEST
	TEATIMES
AEEIMSTW	TEAMWISE
AEEINNRS	ANSERINE
AEEINNTV	VENETIAN
AEEINOPS	PAEONIES
AEEINPRS	NAPERIES
AEEINPRT	APERIENT
AEEINPTT	PIANETTE
AEEINRRS	REARISEN
AEEINRRT	RETAINER
AEEINRSS	SENARIES
AEEINRST	ARENITES
	ARSENITE
	RESINATE
	STEARINE
	TRAINEES
AEEINRSU	UNEASIER
AEEINSSS	EASINESS
AEEINSST	ETESIANS
	TENIASES
AEEINSSV	VAINESSE
AEEINSTT	ANISETTE
	TETANIES
	TETANISE
AEEINSTV	NAIVETES
AEEINSVW	INWEAVES
AEEINTTZ	TETANIZE
AEEIOOPP	EPOPOEIA
AEEIORST	ETAERIOS
AEEIPPRR	PAPERIER
AEEIPPSS	APEPSIES
AEEIPPST	APPETISE
AEEIPPSU	EUPEPSIA
AEEIPPTT	APPETITE
AEEIPPTZ	APPETIZE
AEEIPRRR	RARERIPE
	REPAIRER
AEEIPRRS	PEREIRAS
	SPEARIER
AEEIPRST	PARIETES
	PETARIES
AEEIPRTV	PERVIATE
AEEIPSST	EPITASES
AEEIPSTT	PEATIEST
AEEIPSTX	EXPIATES
AEEIQRSU	QUEASIER
AEEIQRUZ	QUEAZIER
AEEIQSTU	EQUISETA
AEEIRRSS	REARISES
	RERAISES
AEEIRRST	ARTERIES
	REASTIER
AEEIRRTT	RETRAITE
AEEIRRTW	WATERIER
AEEIRRVW	WAVERIER
AEEIRSST	SERIATES
AEEIRSTT	ARIETTES
	ITERATES
	TEARIEST
	TREATIES
	TREATISE
AEEIRSTV	EVIRATES
AEEIRSTW	SWEATIER
	TAWERIES
	WASTERIE
	WEARIEST
AEEIRSTY	YEASTIER
AEEIRSVV	AVERSIVE
AEEISSTX	EXTASIES
AEEISSVW	SEAWIVES
AEEISTTT	ETATISTE
	STEATITE
AEEISTTV	AVIETTES
	ESTIVATE
	EVITATES
AEEISTUX	EUTAXIES
	EUTEXIAS
AEEITTUX	EUTAXITE
AEEITUVX	EXUVIATE
AEEJLNPT	JETPLANE
AEEJLOSU	JEALOUSE
AEEJNRST	SERJEANT
AEEJOPRT	PEJORATE
AEEKKLWY	LYKEWAKE
AEEKKNOS	KOKANEES
AEEKKPSY	KEEPSAKY
AEEKLLSS	LEAKLESS
AEEKLLST	LAKELETS
	SKELETAL
AEEKLMMU	MAMELUKE
AEEKLMRT	TELEMARK
AEEKLMRY	YARMELKE
AEEKLMSS	MAKELESS
AEEKLNST	KANTELES
AEEKLPSS	PEAKLESS
AEEKLSSW	WAKELESS
AEEKLSTY	EYESTALK
AEEKMNSS	KAMSEENS
AEEKMORV	MAKEOVER
AEEKMOTY	YOKEMATE
AEEKMRRR	REMARKER
AEEKMRRS	REMAKERS
AEEKMRRT	MARKETER
	REMARKET
AEEKMRST	MEERKATS
AEEKNNNS	NANKEENS
AEEKNNPS	KNEEPANS
AEEKNORW	REAWOKEN
AEEKNPRT	PERTAKEN
AEEKNPSU	SNEAKEUP
AEEKNPSW	NEWSPEAK
AEEKNRSS	SNEAKERS
AEEKNRSW	REWAKENS
	WAKENERS
AEEKNSSW	WEAKNESS
AEEKORRV	OVERRAKE
AEEKORST	KERATOSE
	KREASOTE
AEEKORTV	OVERTAKE
	TAKEOVER
AEEKORVW	OVERWEAK
AEEKPRSS	RESPEAKS
	SPEAKERS
AEEKPRST	PERTAKES
AEEKQRSU	SQUEAKER
AEEKRRST	RETAKERS
	STREAKER
AEEKRRSW	WREAKERS
AEEKRSST	SAKERETS
AEELLLPT	PELLETAL
AEELLLTT	TELLTALE
AEELLMMS	MAMSELLE
AEELLMSS	MEALLESS
AEELLNOV	NOVELLAE
AEELLOSV	ALVEOLES
AEELLOTT	ALLOTTEE
AEELLPRS	PARELLES
AEELLPTT	PALLETTE
	PLATELET
AEELLPTY	TELEPLAY
AEELLRRT	TERRELLA
AEELLRRV	RAVELLER
AEELLSST	SATELLES
	TESSELLA
AEELLSSZ	ZEALLESS
AEELLSTT	STELLATE
AEELLSWY	WALLEYES
	WEASELLY
AEELLTVV	VALVELET
AEELMMTU	MALEMUTE
AEELMNPS	EMPANELS
	EMPLANES
	ENSAMPLE
AEELMNPT	PLATEMEN
AEELMNRT	LAMENTER
AEELMNSS	LAMENESS
	MALENESS
	MANELESS
	NAMELESS
	SALESMEN
AEELMNST	MANTEELS
	STEELMAN
	TALESMEN
AEELMNSW	WEALSMEN
AEELMNSY	AMYLENES
AEELMNTT	MANTELET
AEELMNTV	LAVEMENT
AEELMOTT	MATELOTE
AEELMPRS	EMPALERS
	RESAMPLE
AEELMPRX	EXEMPLAR
AEELMPRY	EMPYREAL
AEELMPSX	EXAMPLES
AEELMPTT	PALMETTE
	TEMPLATE
AEELMRST	LAMETERS
AEELMSSS	SEAMLESS
AEELMSST	MATELESS
	MEATLESS
	TAMELESS
AEELMSTU	EMULATES

AEELNNPS ENPLANES
AEELNNRT LANNERET
AEELNNSS LEANNESS
AEELNOPR PERONEAL
AEELNOPT ANTELOPE
AEELNORU ALEURONE
AEELNOSS ENOLASES
AEELNPPS SPALPEEN
AEELNPRR PRERENAL
AEELNPRS REPANELS
AEELNPSS PALENESS
AEELNQSU SQUALENE
AEELNRRS LEARNERS
RELEARNS
AEELNRRT RELEARNT
AEELNRSS REALNESS
AEELNRST ALTERNES
ETERNALS
TELERANS
AEELNRSV ENSLAVER
AEELNRSW RENEWALS
AEELNRTV LEVANTER
RELEVANT
AEELNRTW TREELAWN
AEELNRTX EXTERNAL
AEELNRUU NEURULAE
AEELNRUV REVENUAL
AEELNSST LATENESS
AEELNSSV ENSLAVES
VANELESS
AEELNSTY ENTAYLES
AEELNTUV EVENTUAL
AEELNTVY VENTAYLE
AEELOPRS PAROLEES
AEELOPRV OVERLEAP
AEELOPSX POLEAXES
AEELOPTT TOEPLATE
AEELORRS RELEASOR
AEELORST OLEASTER
AEELORSU AUREOLES
AEELORSV OVERSALE
AEELORTT TOLERATE
AEELORTV ELEVATOR
OVERLATE
AEELORTW TOLEWARE
AEELORVZ OVERZEAL
AEELOSSW LEASOWES
AEELOTTT TEETOTAL
AEELPRRS PEARLERS
RELAPSER
AEELPRRT PALTERER
AEELPRRY PARLEYER
AEELPRSS PLEASERS
RELAPSES
AEELPRST PETRALES
PLEATERS
PRELATES
REPLATES
AEELPRSU PLEASURE
SERPULAE
AEELPRSV VESPERAL
AEELPRTY PTERYLAE
AEELPSST SPATLESE
TAPELESS
AEELPSTT PALETTES
AEELPSTU EPAULETS
AEELPSTV SEPTLEVA
AEELPSTZ SPAETZLE
AEELQRSU SQUEALER
AEELQSUZ QUEZALES
AEELRRST ALTERERS
REALTERS
RELATERS
AEELRRSV RAVELERS
REVERSAL
SLAVERER
AEELRRSX RELAXERS
AEELRRTU URETERAL
AEELRRTV TRAVELER
AEELRSST RESLATES
STEALERS
TEARLESS
TESSERAL
AEELRSSU LEASURES
AEELRSSV SEVERALS
AEELRSSW WARELESS
AEELRSTT ALERTEST
AEELRSTU RESALUTE
AEELRSTX EXALTERS
AEELRSTY EASTERLY
AEELRSUV REVALUES
AEELRSVY AVERSELY
AEELSSST ALTESSES
SATELESS
SEATLESS
AEELSSTU SETUALES
AEELSSTV SALVETES
AEELSSVW WAVELESS
AEELSTTY LAYETTES
AEELSTVW WAVELETS
AEEMMNRS MERESMAN
AEEMMNTZ MAZEMENT
AEEMMPSY EMPYEMAS
AEEMMRRY YAMMERER
AEEMMRST AMMETERS
METAMERS
AEEMMSST MESSMATE
AEEMNNOS ANEMONES
AEEMNNPS PENNAMES
AEEMNNRT REMANENT
AEEMNNSS MEANNESS
AEEMNORV OVERNAME
AEEMNORZ ARMOZEEN
AEEMNOSS ANEMOSES
AEEMNOSW SEAWOMEN
AEEMNOSX AXONEMES
AEEMNPRS PRENAMES
SPEARMEN
AEEMNPRT PERMEANT
PETERMAN
AEEMNPRY EMPYREAN
AEEMNPTV PAVEMENT
AEEMNRST REMANETS
AEEMNRSV VERSEMAN
AEEMNRSW MENSWEAR
AEEMNRTU NUMERATE
AEEMNRTV AVERMENT
AEEMNRTW WATERMEN
AEEMNRUV MANEUVER
AEEMNRVY EVERYMAN
AEEMNSSS SAMENESS
AEEMNSST TAMENESS
AEEMNSTU MANSUETE
AEEMORST EROTEMAS
AEEMORTV OVERTAME
AEEMPPRR PAMPERER
AEEMPRRT TAMPERER
AEEMPRRV REVAMPER
AEEMPRST TEMPERAS
AEEMPRSY EMPAYRES
AEEMPRTT ATTEMPER
AEEMPSTU AMPUTEES
AEEMQRRU REMARQUE
AEEMQRSU MARQUEES
AEEMQTTU MAQUETTE
AEEMRRSS SMEARERS
AEEMRRST REMASTER
STREAMER
AEEMRRSU MEASURER
AEEMRRTT TETRAMER
AEEMRSST MASSETER
SEAMSTER
STEAMERS
AEEMRSSU MEASURES
REASSUME
AEEMRSTT TEAMSTER
AEEMRSTW STEMWARE
AEEMRSTY METAYERS
AEEMRTWY YAWMETER
AEEMSSST SEAMSETS
AEEMSSSU MASSEUSE
AEEMSSTU MEATUSES
AEEMSTTU AMUSETTE
AEENNOST NEONATES
AEENNPST PENTANES
AEENNRRS ENSNARER
AEENNRSS ENSNARES
NEARNESS
RENNASES
AEENNRTU ENAUNTER
AEENNRTV REVENANT
AEENNRUX ANNEXURE
AEENNSSS SANENESS
AEENNSST NEATNESS
AEENNSTT SETENANT
AEENOORT AEROTONE
AEENOPRS PERAEONS
PERSONAE
AEENOPSU EUPNOEAS
AEENORRS REASONER
AEENORRV OVERNEAR
AEENORSS RESEASON
SEASONER
AEENORST EARSTONE
RESONATE
AEENORTV OVERNEAT
RENOVATE
AEENORVW OVENWARE
AEENOTTU OUTEATEN
AEENPPTT APPETENT
AEENPQTU PETANQUE
AEENPRUV PARVENUE
AEENPSSX EXPANSES
AEENPTTY ANTETYPE
AEENRRRW WARRENER
AEENRRSS RARENESS
AEENRRST TERRANES
AEENRRSV RAVENERS
AEENRRSW ANSWERER
REANSWER
AEENRRSY YEARNERS
AEENRRTT NATTERER
RATTENER
AEENRRTU RENATURE
AEENRRTV TAVERNER
AEENRSSS SEARNESS
AEENRSST ASSENTER
EARNESTS
SARSENET
AEENRSSU ANURESES
AEENRSSX XERANSES
AEENRSTT ENTREATS
RATTEENS
AEENRSTU SAUTERNE
AEENRSTV AVENTRES
VETERANS
AEENRSUV UNREAVES
AEENRTTV ANTEVERT
AEENRTTX EXTERNAT
EXTRANET
AEENRTTY ENTREATY
AEENRTUV AVENTURE
AEENSSST SENSATES
AEENSTTV NAVETTES
AEENSUVW UNWEAVES
AEEOPRRT PATERERO
PERORATE
AEEOPRST OPERATES
PROTEASE
AEEOPRTT OPERETTA
AEEOPSTZ EPAZOTES
AEEORRSU REAROUSE
AEEORRSW SOWARREE
AEEORRTV OVERRATE
AEEORRVW OVERWEAR
AEEORRVY OVERYEAR
AEEORSSV OVERSEAS
AEEORSTV OVEREATS
AEEORSVV OVERSAVE
AEEORSVW OVERAWES
AEEORSVY OVEREASY
AEEPPRRR PREPARER
AEEPPRRS PAPERERS
PREPARES
REPAPERS
AEEPPRST PREPASTE
PRETAPES
AEEPRRRT PARTERRE
AEEPRRSS ASPERSER
SPEARERS
AEEPRRST TAPERERS
AEEPRRSV PREAVERS
AEEPRRTT PATTERER
PRETREAT
AEEPRRTU APERTURE
AEEPRSSS ASPERSES
PREASSES
REPASSES
AEEPRSST TRAPESES
AEEPRSSZ SPREAZES
AEEPRSTT PEARTEST
PRETASTE
AEEPRSTU EPURATES
SUPERATE
AEEPRSTZ TRAPEZES
AEEPSSTT SPATTEES
AEEQRRUV QUAVERER
AEERRRST ARRESTER
REARREST
AEERRSST ASSERTER
REASSERT
SERRATES
TERRASES
AEERRSSU ERASURES
REASSURE
AEERRSSW SWEARERS
AEERRSTT RETRATES
RETREATS
TREATERS
AEERRSTU AUSTERER
TREASURE
AEERRSTV TRAVERSE
AEERRSTW WATERERS
AEERRSVW WAVERERS
AEERSSSS REASSESS
AEERSSSU SEASURES
AEERSSSV ASSEVERS
AEERSSSY ESSAYERS
AEERSSTT ESTREATS
RESTATES
RETASTES
AEERSSTW SWEATERS
AEERSSTZ ERSATZES
AEERSSUU URAEUSES
AEERSSUV VAREUSES
AEERSTTT ATTESTER
AEERSTTX EXTREATS
AEERSTWW WETWARES
AEERTTTZ TERZETTA
AEERVWYY EVERYWAY

AEESSSSS	ASSESSES
AEESSTTT	TESTATES
AEFFFLRS	FLAFFERS
AEFFGIIL	EFFIGIAL
AEFFGINR	FIREFANG
AEFFGIRS	GIRAFFES
AEFFGNRS	ENGRAFFS
AEFFGOST	OFFSTAGE
AEFFGRSU	GAUFFERS
	SUFFRAGE
AEFFHIKY	KAFFIYEH
AEFFHILL	HALFLIFE
AEFFILNY	AFFINELY
AEFFILRW	WAFFLIER
AEFFILUV	EFFLUVIA
AEFFIMRR	AFFIRMER
	REAFFIRM
AEFFIMRW	FARMWIFE
AEFFIPRS	PIAFFERS
AEFFIRSX	AFFIXERS
AEFFKLRU	FREAKFUL
AEFFKORS	RAKEOFFS
AEFFKOST	OFFTAKES
	TAKEOFFS
AEFFLMSW	FLAMFEWS
AEFFLNSS	SNAFFLES
AEFFLNTU	AFFLUENT
AEFFLRRS	RAFFLERS
AEFFLRSW	WAFFLERS
AEFFLSTU	FEASTFUL
	SUFFLATE
AEFFLSUX	AFFLUXES
AEFFMRSU	EARMUFFS
AEFFNNSS	NAFFNESS
AEFFNORT	AFFRONTE
AEFFORST	AFFOREST
AEFFOSVW	WAVEOFFS
AEFFQRSU	QUAFFERS
AEFFRSST	RESTAFFS
	STAFFERS
AEFFRTTU	TARTUFFE
AEFGGGOS	FOGGAGES
AEFGGILR	FLAGGIER
AEFGGINU	FEAGUING
AEFGGLRS	FLAGGERS
AEFGGMOS	MEGAFOGS
AEFGHINR	HANGFIRE
AEFGHINS	SHEAFING
AEFGHOSS	FOGASHES
AEFGHTTU	FUGHETTA
AEFGIIRS	GASIFIER
AEFGIISS	GASIFIES
AEFGIKLN	FANGLIKE
AEFGIKNR	FREAKING
AEFGILNR	FINAGLER
AEFGILNS	FINAGLES
AEFGILOS	FOLIAGES
AEFGILRR	FRAGILER
AEFGILTT	LIFTGATE
AEFGIMTU	FUMIGATE
AEFGINRW	WAFERING
AEFGINRY	AREFYING
AEFGINST	FEASTING
AEFGINTU	FANTIGUE
AEFGIRRU	ARGUFIER
AEFGIRST	FRIGATES
AEFGIRSU	ARGUFIES
AEFGIRTU	FIGURATE
	FRUITAGE
AEFGIRTW	GIFTWARE
AEFGISTU	FATIGUES
AEFGLLNO	LONGLEAF
AEFGLLOP	FLAGPOLE
AEFGLLSS	FLAGLESS
AEFGLLSU	FULLAGES
AEFGLMNU	FUGLEMAN
AEFGLMOP	MEGAFLOP
AEFGLNOX	FLEXAGON
AEFGLNRS	FLANGERS
AEFGLNSS	FANGLESS
AEFGLOOR	FLOORAGE
AEFGLOPR	LEAPFROG
AEFGLORW	GAREFOWL
AEFGLOST	FLOTAGES
AEFGLOSW	FLOWAGES
AEFGLRTU	GRATEFUL
AEFGLSTU	STAGEFUL
AEFGLTUX	FLUXGATE
AEFGMNOR	FORGEMAN
AEFGMNRT	FRAGMENT
AEFGMORS	FROMAGES
AEFGNNOT	FONTANGE
AEFGNORT	FRONTAGE
AEFGNRRS	GRANFERS
AEFGNRST	ENGRAFTS
AEFGOOPT	FOOTPAGE
AEFGOORT	FOOTGEAR
AEFGOOST	FOOTAGES
AEFGORRS	FORAGERS
AEFGORST	FAGOTERS
AEFGORTT	FROTTAGE
AEFGOSSU	FOUGASSE
AEFGRRST	GRAFTERS
	REGRAFTS
AEFHIKRS	FREAKISH
AEFHIKSW	WEAKFISH
AEFHILLN	FELLAHIN
AEFHILLR	FIREHALL
AEFHILLT	TEFILLAH
AEFHILMS	FISHMEAL
AEFHILMT	HALFTIME
AEFHILNS	SHINLEAF
AEFHILOR	FORHAILE
AEFHILOX	HEXAFOIL
AEFHILRS	FLASHIER
AEFHIMSS	FAMISHES
AEFHLMSU	SHAMEFUL
AEFHLNOT	HALFTONE
AEFHLNSS	HALFNESS
AEFHLORS	FAHLORES
AEFHLPRS	PARFLESH
AEFHLRSS	FLASHERS
AEFHLRST	FARTHELS
AEFHLRTY	FATHERLY
AEFHLSST	FLASHEST
AEFHLSTU	HASTEFUL
AEFHMNRS	FRESHMAN
AEFHNRSW	FERNSHAW
AEFHRSST	SHAFTERS
AEFHRSTT	FARTHEST
AEFIIKLW	WAIFLIKE
AEFIILMS	FAMILIES
AEFIILNS	FINALISE
AEFIILNT	ANTILIFE
AEFIILNZ	FINALIZE
AEFIILSS	SALIFIES
AEFIILST	FETIALIS
	FILIATES
AEFIIMNS	INFAMIES
	INFAMISE
AEFIIMNZ	INFAMIZE
AEFIIMRS	RAMIFIES
AEFIINRT	FAINTIER
AEFIINRV	VINIFERA
AEFIINSS	SANIFIES
AEFIINST	FAINITES
AEFIINSZ	NAZIFIES
AEFIIPRT	APERITIF
AEFIIRRS	FRIARIES
	RARIFIES
AEFIIRRT	RATIFIER
AEFIIRST	RATIFIES
AEFIIRSU	AURIFIES
AEFIITVX	FIXATIVE
AEFIJLOS	JEOFAILS
AEFIKLMO	FOAMLIKE
AEFIKLNU	FAUNLIKE
AEFIKLNW	FAWNLIKE
AEFIKLRY	FREAKILY
AEFIKLST	FLAKIEST
AEFIKMRR	FIREMARK
AEFIKRUW	WAUKRIFE
AEFILLOT	FELLATIO
AEFILLRW	FIREWALL
AEFILMNR	INFLAMER
	RIFLEMAN
AEFILMNS	FLAMINES
	INFLAMES
	MISFALNE
AEFILMNT	FILAMENT
AEFILMST	FLAMIEST
AEFILMSY	MAYFLIES
AEFILMTY	FEMALITY
AEFILNNR	INFERNAL
AEFILNOR	FORELAIN
AEFILNOT	OLEFIANT
AEFILNPS	LIFESPAN
AEFILNRT	INFLATER
AEFILNRU	FRAULEIN
AEFILNST	INFLATES
AEFILNSV	FLAVINES
AEFILNTT	ANTILEFT
AEFILOOR	AEROFOIL
AEFILORS	FORESAIL
AEFILORT	FLOATIER
AEFILOST	FOLIATES
AEFILPPR	FLAPPIER
AEFILPRX	PREFIXAL
AEFILPST	FLEAPITS
AEFILRST	FLARIEST
	FRAILEST
AEFILRSU	FAILURES
AEFILRSV	FAVRILES
AEFILRSZ	FILAZERS
AEFILRTT	FILTRATE
AEFILRTU	FAULTIER
	FILATURE
AEFILRUW	WEARIFUL
AEFILSSS	FILASSES
AEFILSSW	SAWFLIES
AEFILSTT	FLATTIES
AEFILSTU	FISTULAE
AEFILSTV	FESTIVAL
AEFILSTW	FLATWISE
	FLAWIEST
AEFILSTX	FLAXIEST
AEFILSWY	LIFEWAYS
AEFILTUU	FAUTEUIL
AEFIMMMR	MAMMIFER
AEFIMMRS	MISFRAME
AEFIMNST	MANIFEST
AEFIMORR	AERIFORM
AEFIMORT	FORMIATE
AEFIMOST	FOAMIEST
AEFIMRRS	FIREARMS
AEFIMRRW	FIRMWARE
AEFIMRSS	MISFARES
AEFINNSS	FAINNESS
AEFINNST	INFANTES
AEFINNSZ	FANZINES
AEFINOPR	PINAFORE
AEFINORS	FARINOSE
AEFINOTT	FETATION
AEFINPRS	FIREPANS
	PANFRIES
AEFINRRS	REFRAINS
AEFINRRU	UNFAIRER
AEFINRRZ	FRANZIER
AEFINRSS	FAIRNESS
	SANSERIF
	SERAFINS
AEFINRST	FAINTERS
	FENITARS
AEFINRSX	XERAFINS
AEFINSTT	FAINTEST
AEFINSTW	FAWNIEST
AEFIORTV	FAVORITE
AEFIPRRT	FIRETRAP
AEFIQRSU	AQUIFERS
AEFIRRRS	FARRIERS
AEFIRRRY	FARRIERY
AEFIRRST	FRATRIES
AEFIRSTW	WASTRIFE
AEFIRTUX	FIXATURE
AEFISTTT	FATTIEST
AEFKLLOT	FOLKTALE
AEFKLMRY	FLYMAKER
AEFKLNRS	FLANKERS
AEFKLOSS	SEAFOLKS
AEFKLRST	FARTLEKS
AEFKLRUW	WREAKFUL
AEFKLSST	FLASKETS
AEFKLSTT	TALKFEST
AEFKNORR	FORERANK
AEFKNORS	FORSAKEN
AEFKNPRR	PREFRANK
AEFKNRRS	FRANKERS
AEFKNRST	FRANKEST
AEFKOPRS	FORSPEAK
AEFKORRS	FORSAKER
AEFKORRW	WORKFARE
AEFKORSS	FORSAKES
AEFKORTU	FREAKOUT
AEFLLMMU	FLAMMULE
AEFLLNNS	FANNELLS
	FLANNELS
AEFLLNNU	UNFALLEN
AEFLLORT	FELLATOR
AEFLLORV	OVERFALL
AEFLLORW	FALLOWER
AEFLLOST	FLOATELS
AEFLLPRT	PRATFELL
AEFLLPSS	FLAPLESS
AEFLLPTU	PLATEFUL
AEFLLRUW	AWFULLER
AEFLLRUX	FLEXURAL
AEFLLSSW	FLAWLESS
AEFLLSTT	FLATLETS
AEFLLSTY	FESTALLY
AEFLMNOT	MATFELON
AEFLMORU	FORMULAE
	FUMAROLE
AEFLMORW	LEAFWORM
AEFLMOSS	FOAMLESS
AEFLMOTU	FLAMEOUT
AEFLMPRR	FRAMPLER
AEFLMSUW	WAMEFULS
AEFLNNNS	FLANNENS
AEFLNNOT	FONTANEL
AEFLNNOY	NONLEAFY
AEFLNOPR	FOREPLAN
AEFLNOPT	PANTOFLE
AEFLNORS	FARNESOL
AEFLNOSV	FLAVONES
AEFLNRSS	SALFERNS
AEFLNRSU	FLANEURS
	FUNERALS
AEFLNRTU	FLAUNTER
AEFLNSST	FLATNESS
AEFLNSTT	FLATTENS

AEFLNSUY	UNSAFELY
AEFLOORS	SEAFLOOR
AEFLOORV	FOVEOLAR
AEFLOOSV	FOVEOLAS
AEFLOPRT	TERAFLOP
AEFLOPRY	FOREPLAY
AEFLOPSW	PEAFOWLS
AEFLORRV	FLAVORER
AEFLORSS	SAFROLES
AEFLORST	FLOATERS
	FORESTAL
	REFLOATS
AEFLORSU	FUSAROLE
AEFLORSY	FORELAYS
AEFLORTW	FLEAWORT
AEFLOSSU	FOSSULAE
AEFLOSSW	SEAFOWLS
AEFLOSTT	FALSETTO
AEFLPPRS	FLAPPERS
AEFLPPRY	FLYPAPER
AEFLPRSS	FELSPARS
AEFLPRSY	PALFREYS
AEFLPSUU	PAUSEFUL
AEFLRSSU	REFUSALS
AEFLRSTT	FATTRELS
	FLATTERS
AEFLRSTU	REFUTALS
AEFLRSZZ	FRAZZLES
AEFLRTTU	AFLUTTER
AEFLRTTY	FLATTERY
AEFLSSTU	FLATUSES
	SULFATES
AEFLSTTT	FLATTEST
AEFLSTTU	TASTEFUL
AEFLSTUW	WASTEFUL
AEFMNORS	FORAMENS
AEFMNRRY	FERRYMAN
AEFMNRST	RAFTSMEN
AEFMNRSU	FRAENUMS
AEFMORRS	FOREARMS
AEFMORRT	REFORMAT
AEFMORST	FOREMAST
	FORMATES
AEFMORVW	WAVEFORM
AEFMOSSU	FAMOUSES
AEFMOSUW	WAMEFOUS
AEFNNSTU	UNFASTEN
AEFNOPRR	PROFANER
AEFNOPRS	PROFANES
AEFNOPSY	PAYFONES
AEFNORRW	FOREWARN
AEFNORST	SEAFRONT
AEFNORSU	FURANOSE
AEFNPRSU	SUPERFAN
AEFNRRST	TRANSFER
AEFNRRUY	FUNERARY
AEFNSSST	FASTNESS
AEFNSSTU	UNSAFEST
AEFNSTUY	UNSAFETY
AEFOORTW	FOOTWEAR
AEFOPRRT	FOREPART
AEFOPRST	FOREPAST
AEFOPRSW	FOREPAWS
AEFORRSV	FAVORERS
AEFORRSW	FORSWEAR
AEFORRSY	FORAYERS
AEFORRUV	FAVOURER
AEFORRWY	FORWEARY
AEFORSSY	FORESAYS
AEFORSTV	OVERFAST
AEFORSTW	FORWASTE
	SOFTWARE
AEFORSTY	FORESTAY
AEFOSTTU	OUTFEAST
AEFOSTUU	FEATUOUS
AEFOSTUV	VOUTSAFE
AEFPRSST	PRESSFAT
AEFRRSST	STRAFERS
AEFRSSTW	FRETSAWS
AEFRSTTU	TARTUFES
AEFRSTUW	WAFTURES
AEGGGILN	ALEGGING
AEGGGINN	ENGAGING
AEGGGLSU	LUGGAGES
AEGGHIRS	SHAGGIER
AEGGHISS	HAGGISES
AEGGHJRY	JAGGHERY
AEGGHLRS	HAGGLERS
AEGGHMOS	HEMAGOGS
AEGGHMSU	MESHUGGA
AEGGHOPY	GEOPHAGY
AEGGHORU	ROUGHAGE
AEGGIINV	GINGIVAE
AEGGIJST	JAGGIEST
AEGGIKNR	KNAGGIER
AEGGILLN	ALLEGING
AEGGILLR	GRILLAGE
AEGGILMN	GLEAMING
AEGGILNN	ANGELING
	GLEANING
AEGGILNR	GANGLIER
	LAGERING
	REGALING
AEGGILNS	LIGNAGES
AEGGILNT	GELATING
	LEGATING
	TEAGLING
AEGGILNU	LEAGUING
AEGGILNV	GAVELING
AEGGILRS	SLAGGIER
AEGGILRW	WAGGLIER
AEGGIMNN	MANEGING
	MENAGING
AEGGIMRT	GREGATIM
AEGGIMSU	MISGAUGE
AEGGINNR	ANGERING
	ENRAGING
AEGGINNT	AGENTING
	NEGATING
AEGGINNU	UNAGEING
AEGGINNV	AVENGING
AEGGINOS	SEAGOING
AEGGINRS	GEARINGS
	GREASING
	SNAGGIER
AEGGINRV	GREAVING
AEGGINRW	WAGERING
AEGGINSS	SIGNAGES
AEGGINST	NAGGIEST
AEGGIOPR	ARPEGGIO
	GEROPIGA
AEGGIOSS	ISAGOGES
AEGGIQRU	QUAGGIER
AEGGIRRU	GARRIGUE
AEGGIRST	RAGGIEST
	STAGGIER
AEGGIRSU	GARIGUES
AEGGIRWY	EARWIGGY
AEGGISST	SAGGIEST
	STAGGIES
AEGGISSW	SWAGGIES
AEGGISTT	TAGGIEST
AEGGLNPT	EGGPLANT
AEGGLNRS	GANGRELS
AEGGLORY	GARGOYLE
AEGGLRRS	GARGLERS
AEGGLRST	STRAGGLE
AEGGLRSY	GREYLAGS
AEGGMNNS	GANGSMEN
AEGGMORR	ERGOGRAM
AEGGMORT	MORTGAGE
AEGGNNSU	GUNNAGES
AEGGNORV	OVERGANG
AEGGNORW	WAGGONER
AEGGNRRS	GRANGERS
AEGGNRST	GANGSTER
AEGGOPRU	GROUPAGE
AEGGRSST	GAGSTERS
	STAGGERS
AEGGRSSW	SWAGGERS
AEGGRSTY	STAGGERY
AEGHHMSU	MESHUGAH
AEGHIJRS	JAGHIRES
AEGHILLM	MEGILLAH
AEGHILLS	SHIGELLA
AEGHILMT	MEGALITH
AEGHILNR	NARGHILE
	NARGILEH
AEGHILNS	HEALINGS
	LEASHING
	SHEALING
AEGHILNT	ATHELING
AEGHILNX	EXHALING
AEGHILPS	SHAGPILE
AEGHILRT	LITHARGE
	THIRLAGE
AEGHILRU	LAUGHIER
AEGHILST	LAIGHEST
AEGHIMNW	WEIGHMAN
AEGHIMPS	MAGESHIP
AEGHIMST	MEGAHITS
AEGHINNN	HENNAING
AEGHINNT	NAETHING
AEGHINNV	HAVENING
AEGHINRS	HEARINGS
	HEARSING
	SHEARING
AEGHINRT	EARTHING
	HEARTING
	INGATHER
AEGHINRV	HAVERING
AEGHINST	GAHNITES
	HEATINGS
AEGHINSV	HEAVINGS
	SHEAVING
AEGHINSZ	GENIZAHS
AEGHINTT	GNATHITE
AEGHIOPS	ESOPHAGI
AEGHIPPR	EPIGRAPH
AEGHIPRT	GRAPHITE
AEGHIRRS	GHARRIES
AEGHIRSS	GARISHES
AEGHLNOS	HALOGENS
AEGHLNOY	HYALOGEN
AEGHLOPY	HYPOGEAL
AEGHLOSS	GALOSHES
AEGHLOTX	HEXAGLOT
AEGHLRSU	LAUGHERS
AEGHLRTU	LAUGHTER
AEGHLRTY	LETHARGY
AEGHLSTW	THALWEGS
AEGHMNOP	PHENOGAM
AEGHMNOS	HOGMANES
AEGHMNOY	HOGMENAY
AEGHMOPT	APOTHEGM
AEGHMORS	HOMAGERS
AEGHNNST	HANGNEST
AEGHNOPT	HEPTAGON
	PATHOGEN
AEGHNOPY	HYPOGEAN
AEGHNORV	HANGOVER
	OVERHANG
AEGHNOSX	HEXAGONS
AEGHNPSW	SPANGHEW
AEGHNRSS	GNASHERS
AEGHNSST	STENGAHS
AEGHOPPR	PROPHAGE
AEGHOPPY	APOPHYGE
AEGHOPXY	EXOPHAGY
AEGHORST	SHORTAGE
AEGHOSST	HOSTAGES
AEGHOSSU	GASHOUSE
AEGHPRSS	SPREAGHS
AEGHPRTU	UPGATHER
AEGHRTTU	RETAUGHT
AEGIILLU	AIGUILLE
AEGIILMN	EMAILING
AEGIILMR	REMIGIAL
AEGIILNN	ALIENING
AEGIILNR	GAINLIER
AEGIILRR	GLAIRIER
AEGIILTT	LITIGATE
AEGIILTV	LIGATIVE
AEGIIMNR	IMAGINER
	MIGRAINE
AEGIIMNS	IMAGINES
AEGIIMTT	MITIGATE
AEGIINNN	NENNIGAI
AEGIINNR	ARGININE
AEGIINRR	GRAINIER
AEGIIRRT	IRRIGATE
AEGIISTV	VESTIGIA
AEGIJLNR	JANGLIER
AEGIKLNS	LINKAGES
	SNAGLIKE
AEGIKLNT	GNATLIKE
AEGIKLNW	WEAKLING
AEGIKLOT	GOATLIKE
AEGIKMNR	REMAKING
AEGIKMRW	WIGMAKER
AEGIKNNS	SNEAKING
AEGIKNNW	WAKENING
AEGIKNPS	SPEAKING
AEGIKNRS	SKEARING
AEGIKNRT	RETAKING
AEGIKNRW	REWAKING
	WREAKING
AEGIKNSS	SINKAGES
AEGIKNTW	TWEAKING
AEGIKPPS	KIPPAGES
AEGIKPRS	GARPIKES
AEGIKSTW	GAWKIEST
AEGILLLS	ILLEGALS
AEGILLMS	LEGALISM
	MILLAGES
AEGILLNR	ALLERGIN
AEGILLNS	GALLEINS
	NIGELLAS
AEGILLNU	LINGULAE
AEGILLNY	GENIALLY
AEGILLPR	PILLAGER
AEGILLPS	PILLAGES
	SPILLAGE
AEGILLRU	GUERILLA
AEGILLRV	VILLAGER
AEGILLSS	GALLISES
AEGILLST	LEGALIST
	STILLAGE
	TILLAGES
AEGILLSV	VILLAGES
AEGILLSZ	GALLIZES
AEGILLTU	LIGULATE
AEGILLTY	LEGALITY
AEGILMMR	AGLIMMER
	LAMMIGER
AEGILMNP	EMPALING
AEGILMNR	GERMINAL
	MALIGNER
	MALINGER
AEGILMNS	MEASLING

AEGILMNT	LIGAMENT
	METALING
	TEGMINAL
AEGILMNU	AEMULING
AEGILMNY	YEALMING
AEGILMRS	GREMIALS
	LAMIGERS
	REGALISM
AEGILMRX	LEXIGRAM
AEGILMTU	MULTIAGE
AEGILNNP	PANELING
AEGILNNR	LEARNING
AEGILNNS	EANLINGS
	LEANINGS
AEGILNNT	GANTLINE
	LATENING
AEGILNNU	UNGENIAL
AEGILNNW	WEANLING
AEGILNNY	YEANLING
AEGILNOR	GERANIOL
	REGIONAL
AEGILNOS	GASOLINE
AEGILNOT	GELATION
	LEGATION
AEGILNPR	GRAPLINE
	PEARLING
AEGILNPS	ELAPSING
	PLEASING
AEGILNPT	PLEATING
AEGILNQU	EQUALING
AEGILNRR	GNARLIER
AEGILNRS	ALIGNERS
	ENGRAILS
	NARGILES
	REALIGNS
	SALERING
	SANGLIER
	SIGNALER
	SLANGIER
AEGILNRT	ALERTING
	ALTERING
	INTEGRAL
	RELATING
	TANGLIER
	TRIANGLE
AEGILNRV	RAVELING
AEGILNRX	RELAXING
AEGILNRY	LAYERING
	RELAYING
	YEARLING
AEGILNSS	GAINLESS
	GLASSINE
	LEASINGS
	SEALINGS
AEGILNST	EASTLING
	GELATINS
	GENITALS
	STEALING
AEGILNSV	LEAVINGS
	SLEAVING
AEGILNSW	SWEALING
AEGILNSY	YEALINGS
AEGILNTV	VALETING
AEGILNTX	EXALTING
AEGILNTZ	TEAZLING
AEGILNUV	VAGINULE
AEGILOPS	SPOILAGE
AEGILOPT	PILOTAGE
AEGILORS	GASOLIER
	GIRASOLE
	SERAGLIO
AEGILOSS	GOLIASES
	SOILAGES
AEGILOST	LATIGOES
	OTALGIES
AEGILOSU	EULOGIAS
AEGILPPS	SLIPPAGE
AEGILPPU	PUPILAGE
AEGILPRU	PLAGUIER
AEGILRRU	GLAURIER
AEGILRSS	GLASSIER
AEGILRST	GLARIEST
	REGALIST
AEGILRSY	GREASILY
AEGILRSZ	GLAZIERS
AEGILRTT	AGLITTER
AEGILRTU	LIGATURE
AEGILRTY	REGALITY
AEGILRVW	LAWGIVER
AEGILRYZ	GLAZIERY
AEGILSSS	GLASSIES
AEGILSTZ	GLAZIEST
AEGIMMST	GAMMIEST
AEGIMNNO	NONIMAGE
AEGIMNNR	ENARMING
	RENAMING
AEGIMNNS	MEANINGS
AEGIMNNT	ENTAMING
AEGIMNPR	EMPARING
AEGIMNRR	REARMING
AEGIMNRS	GERMAINS
	SMEARING
AEGIMNRT	EMIGRANT
	REMATING
AEGIMNRU	GERANIUM
	MAUNGIER
AEGIMNSS	GAMINESS
AEGIMNST	MANGIEST
	MINTAGES
	MISAGENT
	STEAMING
	TEAMINGS
AEGIMNSV	VEGANISM
AEGIMNTU	TEGUMINA
	UMANGITE
AEGIMOOS	OOGAMIES
AEGIMORR	ARMIGERO
AEGIMORS	GORAMIES
AEGIMORW	WAGMOIRE
AEGIMPRS	EPIGRAMS
	PRIMAGES
AEGIMPRU	UMPIRAGE
AEGIMPSS	MISPAGES
AEGIMPST	PIGMEATS
AEGIMQRU	QUAGMIRE
AEGIMRRS	ARMIGERS
AEGIMRRT	RAGTIMER
AEGIMRSS	GISARMES
AEGIMRST	MAGISTER
	MIGRATES
	RAGTIMES
	STERIGMA
AEGIMSST	SIGMATES
AEGIMSSU	MISUSAGE
AEGIMSTU	GAUMIEST
AEGINNNX	ANNEXING
AEGINNOS	ANGINOSE
	GANOINES
AEGINNOT	NEGATION
AEGINNPS	SNEAPING
	SPEANING
AEGINNRS	AGINNERS
	EARNINGS
	ENGRAINS
	GRANNIES
AEGINNRV	RAVENING
AEGINNRY	RENAYING
	YEARNING
AEGINNST	ANTIGENS
	GENTIANS
	STEANING
AEGINNSU	GUANINES
	SANGUINE
AEGINORR	ORANGIER
AEGINORS	IGNAROES
	ORGANISE
	ORIGANES
AEGINORZ	ORGANIZE
AEGINOSS	AGONISES
AEGINOSZ	AGONIZES
AEGINPPR	PAPERING
AEGINPPS	GENIPAPS
AEGINPRS	PREASING
	SPEARING
AEGINPRT	RETAPING
	TAPERING
AEGINPRV	REPAVING
AEGINPRY	REPAYING
AEGINPSS	SPAEINGS
	SPINAGES
AEGINPSY	GYPSEIAN
AEGINPTY	EGYPTIAN
AEGINQTU	EQUATING
AEGINRRS	EARRINGS
	GRAINERS
AEGINRRV	AVERRING
AEGINRSS	ASSIGNER
	REASSIGN
	SEARINGS
	SERINGAS
AEGINRST	ANGRIEST
	ASTRINGE
	GANISTER
	GANTRIES
	GRANITES
	INGRATES
	RANGIEST
	REASTING
	STEARING
	TASERING
AEGINRSV	VINEGARS
AEGINRSW	RESAWING
	SWEARING
	WEARINGS
AEGINRSY	RESAYING
	SYNERGIA
AEGINRTT	ARETTING
	GNATTIER
	TREATING
AEGINRTV	AVERTING
	GRIEVANT
	TAVERING
	VINTAGER
AEGINRTW	TWANGIER
	WATERING
AEGINRTX	RETAXING
AEGINRVW	WAVERING
AEGINRVY	VINEGARY
AEGINRWX	REWAXING
AEGINRWY	WEARYING
AEGINSST	EASTINGS
	GENISTAS
	GIANTESS
	SEATINGS
	TEASINGS
	TSIGANES
AEGINSSY	ESSAYING
AEGINSTT	ESTATING
	TANGIEST
AEGINSTU	SAUTEING
	UNITAGES
AEGINSTV	VINTAGES
AEGINSTW	SWEATING
AEGINSTY	YEASTING
AEGINSTZ	TZIGANES
AEGINSVW	WEAVINGS
AEGINSVY	SAVEYING
AEGIOPRR	PROGERIA
AEGIORSS	ARGOSIES
AEGIORSV	VIRAGOES
AEGIORTV	RAVIGOTE
AEGIOSTT	GOATIEST
AEGIOSTU	AGOUTIES
AEGIOSTX	GEOTAXIS
AEGIPPRT	GRIPTAPE
AEGIPPST	GAPPIEST
AEGIPRSS	PRISAGES
	SPAIRGES
AEGIPRST	GRAPIEST
AEGIPRTY	PTERYGIA
AEGIPSST	GASPIEST
AEGIQRSU	SQUIRAGE
AEGIRRSS	GRASSIER
AEGIRRSU	SUGARIER
AEGIRRSZ	GRAZIERS
AEGIRRTY	ARGYRITE
AEGIRSST	AGISTERS
AEGIRSTT	STRIGATE
AEGIRSTV	VIRGATES
	VITRAGES
AEGIRSUU	AUGURIES
AEGISSST	GASSIEST
AEGISSTT	STAGIEST
AEGISSTW	GAWSIEST
AEGISTUZ	GAUZIEST
AEGJLNOR	JARGONEL
AEGJLNRS	JANGLERS
AEGJLTUU	JUGULATE
AEGKKKNO	ANGEKKOK
AEGKKNOS	ANGEKOKS
AEGKLOSU	KAGOULES
AEGKMNRU	GUNMAKER
AEGKMRSY	KERYGMAS
AEGLLLMU	GLUMELLA
AEGLLNNO	NONLEGAL
AEGLLNOS	ALLONGES
	GALLEONS
AEGLLNOV	LONGEVAL
AEGLLNPS	LANGSPEL
AEGLLNRS	LANGRELS
AEGLLNST	GELLANTS
AEGLLNSY	LANGLEYS
AEGLLOOZ	ZOOGLEAL
AEGLLOPR	GALLOPER
AEGLLORS	ALLEGROS
AEGLLORV	OVERGALL
AEGLLORY	ALLEGORY
AEGLLOSS	GOALLESS
AEGLLOST	TOLLAGES
AEGLLOTT	TOLLGATE
AEGLLRVY	GRAVELLY
AEGLLSSU	GALLUSES
	SEAGULLS
	SULLAGES
AEGLMNNO	MANGONEL
AEGLMNOY	AMYLOGEN
AEGLMNRS	MANGLERS
AEGLMNSS	GLASSMEN
AEGLMNTU	GUNMETAL
AEGLMOPS	MEGALOPS
AEGLMORS	GOMERALS
AEGLMOSU	MOULAGES
AEGLMOTV	MEGAVOLT
AEGLMPSU	PLUMAGES
AEGLMRSU	MAULGRES
AEGLMSSU	GAUMLESS
AEGLNNOR	NONGLARE
AEGLNNPT	PLANGENT
AEGLNNSY	LANGSYNE
AEGLNNTU	UNTANGLE

AEGLNOPT	GANTLOPE
AEGLNORY	YEARLONG
AEGLNOST	TANGELOS
AEGLNOSU	ANGULOSE
AEGLNPRS	GRAPNELS
	SPANGLER
	SPRANGLE
AEGLNPSS	PANGLESS
	SPANGLES
AEGLNPST	SPANGLET
AEGLNRRW	WRANGLER
AEGLNRSS	SLANGERS
AEGLNRST	STRANGLE
	TANGLERS
	TRANGLES
AEGLNRSU	GRANULES
AEGLNRSW	WANGLERS
	WRANGLES
AEGLNRSY	LARYNGES
AEGLNRTW	TWANGLER
AEGLNRUY	GUNLAYER
AEGLNSTT	GANTLETS
AEGLNSTU	LANGUETS
AEGLNSTW	TWANGLES
AEGLNSUW	GUNWALES
AEGLNTTU	GAUNTLET
AEGLNTUU	UNGULATE
AEGLOOOZ	ZOOGLOEA
AEGLOOPU	APOLOGUE
AEGLOORY	AEROLOGY
	AREOLOGY
AEGLOOSZ	ZOOGLEAS
AEGLOPRS	PERGOLAS
AEGLOPRY	PLAYGOER
AEGLOPTT	PLOTTAGE
AEGLORST	GLOATERS
	LEGATORS
AEGLORSU	GLAREOUS
AEGLORSV	VORLAGES
AEGLORTU	OUTGLARE
AEGLORTV	TRAVELOG
AEGLORTW	WATERLOG
AEGLORTY	GEOLATRY
AEGLOSSW	GALOWSES
AEGLOSTV	VOLTAGES
AEGLOSUY	GEALOUSY
AEGLPPRR	GRAPPLER
AEGLPPRS	GRAPPLES
AEGLPRSU	EARPLUGS
	GRAUPELS
	PLAGUERS
AEGLPSSU	PLUSAGES
	PLUSSAGE
AEGLRRSU	REGULARS
AEGLRRUV	VULGARER
AEGLRSTU	GAULTERS
	GESTURAL
	TRAGULES
AEGLRTUY	ARGUTELY
AEGLSSTT	GESTALTS
AEGLSSUV	VALGUSES
AEGLSTUU	GLUTAEUS
AEGLSTUV	VULGATES
AEGLSUUY	GUAYULES
AEGMMNOR	GAMMONER
AEGMMRRU	RUMMAGER
AEGMMRSU	RUMMAGES
AEGMNNOS	AGNOMENS
AEGMNNOT	MAGNETON
AEGMNORR	RENOGRAM
AEGMNORS	MEGARONS
AEGMNORV	MANGROVE
	VENOGRAM
AEGMNOST	GEOMANTS
	MAGNETOS
	MEGATONS
	MONTAGES
AEGMNOSX	MAGNOXES
AEGMNOXY	XENOGAMY
AEGMNRST	GARMENTS
	MARGENTS
	RAGMENTS
AEGMNRTU	ARGENTUM
	ARGUMENT
AEGMNSSW	SWAGSMEN
AEGMNSSY	GAMYNESS
AEGMNSTU	AUGMENTS
	MUTAGENS
AEGMOORS	MOORAGES
AEGMOPRW	GAPEWORM
AEGMOPST	POSTGAME
AEGMORSS	GOSSAMER
AEGMPRUZ	GAZUMPER
AEGMPSTU	STUMPAGE
AEGNNOPT	PENTAGON
AEGNNORT	NEGATRON
AEGNNOST	NEGATONS
	TONNAGES
AEGNNPRT	PREGNANT
AEGNNRSU	GUNNERAS
AEGNNRTY	GANNETRY
AEGNNSTT	TANGENTS
AEGNNSTU	TUNNAGES
AEGNNTUU	UNGUENTA
AEGNOORS	OREGANOS
AEGNOPRR	PARERGON
AEGNOPST	PONTAGES
AEGNORRS	GROANERS
AEGNORRY	ORANGERY
AEGNORST	ESTRAGON
	NEGATORS
	ORANGEST
	RAGSTONE
	STONERAG
AEGNORSW	WAGONERS
AEGNORTT	TETRAGON
AEGNORTU	OUTRANGE
AEGNORTY	NEGATORY
AEGNORUV	VARGUENO
AEGNOSSY	NOSEGAYS
AEGNOTUY	AUTOGENY
AEGNPPRU	GUNPAPER
AEGNPRRS	RESPRANG
AEGNPRSS	ENGRASPS
AEGNPRST	TREPANGS
AEGNPRSU	SPEARGUN
AEGNPRYY	PANEGYRY
AEGNRRST	GRANTERS
	REGRANTS
	STRANGER
AEGNRSSY	GRAYNESS
AEGNRSTU	STRAUNGE
AEGNRSTW	TWANGERS
AEGNRSYY	ASYNERGY
AEGNSSST	GASTNESS
AEGNSSSY	SYNGASES
AEGNSTTU	GAUNTEST
	TUTENAGS
AEGOORST	ROOTAGES
AEGOORSV	VORAGOES
AEGOOSWY	WAYGOOSE
AEGOPPRS	PROPAGES
AEGOPPST	STOPPAGE
AEGOPPSU	SUPPEAGO
AEGOPRST	PORTAGES
	POTAGERS
AEGOPRTU	PORTAGUE
AEGOPSST	GESTAPOS
	POSTAGES
AEGOPSSU	SPOUSAGE
AEGOPSTT	GATEPOST
	POTTAGES
AEGORRRT	GARROTER
	REGRATOR
AEGORRST	GARROTES
AEGORRTT	GAROTTER
	GARROTTE
AEGORSSS	SARGOSES
AEGORSST	STORAGES
AEGORSTT	GAROTTES
AEGORSTU	OUTRAGES
AEGORSUV	OUVRAGES
AEGORSVY	VOYAGERS
AEGORTTU	TUTORAGE
AEGORTUU	OUTARGUE
AEGORUVY	VOYAGEUR
AEGOSSTW	STOWAGES
AEGOSSYZ	AZYGOSES
AEGOSTTU	OUTGATES
AEGOSTTV	GAVOTTES
AEGPRRSS	GRASPERS
	SPARGERS
AEGPSSTU	UPSTAGES
AEGPSSUU	GAUPUSES
AEGPSSUW	GAWPUSES
AEGQRTUU	TRUQUAGE
AEGRRSSS	GRASSERS
AEGRRSSY	RYEGRASS
AEGRRSUU	AUGURERS
AEGRRSUV	GRAVURES
	VERRUGAS
AEGRSSSU	SARGUSES
AEGRSSUV	SEVRUGAS
AEGRSTTY	STRATEGY
AEGRSTUU	AUGUSTER
AEGSSTUU	AUGUSTES
AEGSTTTU	GUTTATES
AEHHHIST	SHEHITAH
AEHHIKSS	SHEIKHAS
AEHHIMPY	HYPHEMIA
AEHHIMTW	HAMEWITH
AEHHINST	INSHEATH
AEHHIPSW	PEISHWAH
AEHHISST	HASHIEST
	SHEHITAS
AEHHISVY	YESHIVAH
AEHHLNTU	UNHEALTH
AEHHNRSS	HARSHENS
AEHHNRSW	HERNSHAW
AEHHORST	HAROSETH
AEHHRRST	THRASHER
AEHHRSST	HARSHEST
	THRASHES
AEHIIKLR	HAIRLIKE
AEHIIKRT	TERAKIHI
AEHIIKST	SHIITAKE
AEHIILMO	HEMIOLIA
AEHIILMT	LITHEMIA
AEHIILNR	HAIRLINE
AEHIILST	HAILIEST
AEHIIMNT	THIAMINE
AEHIIMOP	HEMIOPIA
AEHIINNT	IANTHINE
AEHIINTZ	THIAZINE
AEHIIRRW	WIREHAIR
AEHIIRST	HAIRIEST
AEHIKKLW	HAWKLIKE
AEHIKLLO	HALOLIKE
AEHIKLLT	LATHLIKE
AEHIKLNP	KEPHALIN
AEHIKLRS	RASHLIKE
AEHIKMNZ	KHAZENIM
AEHIKNSS	SNEAKISH
AEHIKSST	SHAKIEST
	SHITAKES
AEHIKSSY	SAKIYEHS
AEHILLNT	THALLINE
AEHILMNY	HYMENIAL
AEHILMOS	HEMIOLAS
AEHILMOT	HALIMOTE
AEHILMQS	SHEQALIM
AEHILMRU	HAULMIER
AEHILMSW	LIMEWASH
AEHILMSY	LEHAYIMS
AEHILNOP	APHELION
	PHELONIA
AEHILNRS	INHALERS
AEHILNRU	INHAULER
AEHILNSY	HYALINES
AEHILNTX	ANTHELIX
AEHILNTZ	ZENITHAL
AEHILORS	AIRHOLES
	SHOALIER
AEHILORT	AEROLITH
AEHILOTZ	THIAZOLE
AEHILPRS	EARLSHIP
	HARELIPS
	PLASHIER
AEHILPST	HAPLITES
AEHILRSS	HAIRLESS
AEHILRSU	HAULIERS
AEHILRSV	LAVISHER
	SHRIEVAL
AEHILRTY	EARTHILY
	HEARTILY
AEHILSST	HELIASTS
	SHALIEST
AEHILSSV	LAVISHES
AEHILSSW	SHAWLIES
	WHAISLES
AEHILSTT	LATHIEST
	LITHATES
AEHILSTY	HYALITES
AEHILSUV	VIHUELAS
AEHILSWZ	WHAIZLES
AEHIMMSS	SHAMMIES
AEHIMMST	HAMMIEST
AEHIMMSW	WHAMMIES
AEHIMNNU	INHUMANE
AEHIMNRS	HARMINES
	SHIREMAN
AEHIMNSS	SHAMISEN
AEHIMNST	HEMATINS
AEHIMNSU	HUMANISE
AEHIMNTU	INHUMATE
AEHIMNUZ	HUMANIZE
AEHIMPRS	SAMPHIRE
	SERAPHIM
AEHIMPRT	TERAPHIM
AEHIMPRX	XERAPHIM
AEHIMPSS	EMPHASIS
	MISSHAPE
	PHAEISMS
AEHIMPST	MATESHIP
	SHIPMATE
AEHIMRRS	MARSHIER
AEHIMRSS	MARISHES
	MISHEARS
AEHIMSSS	MESSIAHS
AEHIMSST	ATHEISMS
	MASHIEST
	MATHESIS
AEHINNPZ	PHENAZIN
AEHINNSS	SHANNIES
AEHINNTX	XANTHEIN
	XANTHINE
AEHINOPS	APHONIES
AEHINOPU	EUPHONIA
AEHINORT	ANTIHERO
AEHINOTT	THIONATE

AEHINPPY	EPIPHANY
AEHINPRS	HEPARINS
	PARISHEN
	SERAPHIN
AEHINPRT	PERIANTH
AEHINPST	PENTHIAS
	THESPIAN
AEHINRRS	SHARNIER
AEHINRSS	ARSHINES
AEHINRST	HAIRNETS
	INEARTHS
	THERIANS
AEHINRSV	ENRAVISH
	VANISHER
AEHINRSW	SHERWANI
AEHINRTU	HAURIENT
AEHINRTW	TARWHINE
AEHINSSS	ASHINESS
	HESSIANS
AEHINSST	ANTHESIS
	SHANTIES
	SHEITANS
	STHENIAS
AEHINSSV	VANISHES
AEHINSSZ	HAZINESS
AEHINSTT	HESITANT
AEHINSTW	INSWATHE
AEHINTTT	ANTITHET
AEHIOPRS	APHORISE
AEHIOPRU	EUPHORIA
AEHIOPRZ	APHORIZE
AEHIOPTT	THIOTEPA
AEHIORRV	OVERHAIR
AEHIORST	HOARIEST
AEHIORTU	THIOUREA
AEHIPPRS	PAPISHER
	SAPPHIRE
AEHIPPSS	PAPISHES
AEHIPPST	EPITAPHS
	HAPPIEST
	PEATSHIP
AEHIPRRS	PHRASIER
AEHIPRRT	RATHRIPE
AEHIPRSS	PARISHES
	SHARPIES
AEHIPRST	TRIPHASE
AEHIPRTT	THREAPIT
AEHIPSSW	PEISHWAS
AEHIPSTZ	ZAPTIEHS
AEHIPSWW	WASHWIPE
AEHIQSSU	QUASHIES
AEHIRRRS	HARRIERS
AEHIRRSS	ARRISHES
AEHIRRST	TRASHIER
AEHIRRSV	RAVISHER
AEHIRRTW	WRATHIER
AEHIRSST	SHERIATS
AEHIRSSV	RAVISHES
AEHIRSSW	SWASHIER
AEHIRSTU	THESAURI
AEHIRSTW	SWATHIER
	WATERISH
AEHIRSTY	HYSTERIA
AEHIRSWY	HAYWIRES
AEHIRTYZ	YAHRZEIT
AEHISSST	STASHIES
AEHISSSW	SIWASHES
AEHISSSY	ESSAYISH
AEHISSTT	ATHEISTS
	HASTIEST
	STAITHES
AEHISSTU	HIATUSES
AEHISSTW	WASHIEST
AEHISSVY	YESHIVAS
AEHISTTW	THAWIEST
	THWAITES
AEHJLOSW	JAWHOLES
AEHJNNOS	JOHANNES
AEHKMOPW	MOPEHAWK
AEHKNNSU	UNSHAKEN
AEHKNOSW	HAWKNOSE
AEHKNRST	THANKERS
AEHKNSSU	ANKUSHES
AEHKNSWW	NEWSHAWK
AEHKOOPR	REAPHOOK
AEHKOSTU	SHAKEOUT
AEHKPSSU	SHAKEUPS
AEHKRRSS	SHARKERS
AEHLLLTY	LETHALLY
AEHLLMOP	LAMPHOLE
AEHLLMTY	METHYLAL
AEHLLNRT	ENTHRALL
AEHLLNTU	UNLETHAL
AEHLLORW	HALLOWER
AEHLLRSS	HERSALLS
AEHLLSST	HALTLESS
AEHLMMNS	HELMSMAN
AEHLMNOS	MANHOLES
AEHLMNOT	HOTELMAN
	METHANOL
AEHLMNUY	HUMANELY
AEHLMORS	ARMHOLES
AEHLMOSU	HAMULOSE
AEHLMPPT	PAMPHLET
AEHLMPSW	WHAMPLES
AEHLMRSS	HARMLESS
AEHLMRST	THERMALS
AEHLMRSU	HUMERALS
AEHLNOST	ANETHOLS
	ETHANOLS
AEHLNPRS	SHRAPNEL
AEHLNPTY	ENTHALPY
AEHLNRST	ENTHRALS
AEHLNSST	NATHLESS
AEHLNSSU	UNLASHES
	UNSHALES
AEHLNSTY	NAYTHLES
AEHLNTUZ	HAZELNUT
AEHLOPRT	PLETHORA
AEHLOPSS	HAPLOSES
AEHLOPST	TAPHOLES
AEHLORST	LOATHERS
	RATHOLES
AEHLORSY	HOARSELY
AEHLORUV	OVERHAUL
AEHLOSSS	ASSHOLES
AEHLOSST	SHOALEST
AEHLOSTT	LOATHEST
AEHLPPRT	THRAPPLE
AEHLPRSS	PLASHERS
	SPLASHER
AEHLPSSS	SPLASHES
AEHLPSST	PATHLESS
	PLASHETS
AEHLPSTU	SULPHATE
AEHLRRTU	URETHRAL
AEHLRSSS	SLASHERS
AEHLRSST	HARSLETS
	SLATHERS
AEHLSSTT	STEALTHS
AEHLSSTW	THAWLESS
AEHLSSWY	SHAWLEYS
AEHLSTTY	STEALTHY
AEHMMRSS	SHAMMERS
AEHMNNPY	NYMPHEAN
AEHMNOPR	MORPHEAN
AEHMNORS	HORSEMAN
	MENORAHS
	RHAMNOSE
	SHOREMAN
AEHMNOST	HOASTMEN
AEHMNOSU	HOUSEMAN
AEHMNPRU	PREHUMAN
AEHMNRST	TRASHMEN
AEHMNSTU	HUMANEST
AEHMOPRT	METAPHOR
AEHMOPST	APOTHEMS
AEHMORST	TERAOHMS
AEHMOSTT	HEMOSTAT
AEHMOSTU	OUTSHAME
AEHMOSTW	SOMEWHAT
AEHMOSTY	HOMESTAY
AEHMPRST	HAMPSTER
AEHMRSSS	SMASHERS
AEHMRSST	HAMSTERS
AEHMRSTU	MAUTHERS
AEHMRSTW	MAWTHERS
AEHMSSSU	SHAMUSES
AEHMSTTY	AMETHYST
AEHMSUZZ	MEZUZAHS
AEHNNOPT	PANTHEON
AEHNNOTX	XANTHONE
AEHNNPRU	NENUPHAR
AEHNNPSU	UNSHAPEN
AEHNNSUV	UNSHAVEN
AEHNNSUW	UNWASHEN
AEHNOOPT	HANEPOOT
AEHNOPPY	HYPOPNEA
AEHNOPRT	HAPTERON
AEHNOPST	PHAETONS
	PHONATES
	STANHOPE
AEHNOPSW	WANHOPES
AEHNOPSY	HYPONEAS
AEHNOPXY	XENOPHYA
AEHNOQTU	HAQUETON
AEHNORSS	HOARSENS
	SENHORAS
AEHNOSSX	HEXOSANS
AEHNPRSS	SHARPENS
AEHNPRST	PANTHERS
AEHNPSSU	UNSHAPES
AEHNPSTY	PHYTANES
AEHNRSSS	RASHNESS
AEHNRSTU	HAUNTERS
	UNEARTHS
	UNHEARTS
	URETHANS
AEHNRTTU	EARTHNUT
AEHNSSTT	THATNESS
AEHNSSTW	WHATNESS
AEHNSSTY	SHANTEYS
AEHNSTUW	UNSWATHE
AEHOORST	TOHEROAS
AEHOPPRS	PROPHASE
AEHOPRRY	PYORRHEA
AEHOPRSS	PHAROSES
AEHOPRST	PHORATES
	POTSHARE
AEHOPSST	PATHOSES
	POTASHES
	SPATHOSE
	TEASHOPS
AEHOPSTT	HEATSPOT
	POSTHEAT
AEHOPSTU	PHASEOUT
	TAPHOUSE
AEHOQRUU	HUAQUERO
AEHORRRW	HARROWER
AEHORRSV	OVERRASH
AEHORRSW	WARHORSE
AEHORSST	ASTHORES
	EARSHOTS
	HAROSETS
	HOARSEST
AEHORSSW	SAWHORSE
AEHORSTT	RHEOSTAT
AEHORSTU	OUTHEARS
AEHORSTX	OXHEARTS
	THORAXES
AEHORSUV	HAVEOURS
AEHORSVW	OVERWASH
AEHORSWY	HORSEWAY
AEHOSSTU	HOUSESAT
AEHPPRSW	WHAPPERS
AEHPPSSU	SHAPEUPS
AEHPRRSS	PHRASERS
	SHARPERS
AEHPRSST	SHARPEST
	SPARTHES
AEHPRSUX	HARUSPEX
AEHPRSUY	EUPHRASY
AEHPSTTT	PHATTEST
AEHQRSSU	QUASHERS
	SQUASHER
AEHQSSSU	SQUASHES
AEHRRSTU	URETHRAS
AEHRRSTY	TRASHERY
AEHRRTTW	THWARTER
AEHRSSST	SHASTERS
AEHRSSSW	SWASHERS
AEHRSSTT	SHATTERS
AEHRSSTV	HARVESTS
AEHRSSTW	SWATHERS
AEHRSTTY	SHATTERY
AEHRSTUU	HAUTEURS
AEHSSTUX	EXHAUSTS
AEIIINTT	INITIATE
AEIIIRRT	RETIARII
AEIIKLLT	TAILLIKE
AEIIKLNT	KALINITE
AEIIKNRS	KAISERIN
AEIIKNSS	AKINESIS
AEIIKNST	KAINITES
AEIIKRTY	TERIYAKI
AEIILLMR	MILLIARE
	RAMILLIE
AEIILLRS	RAILLIES
AEIILLST	TAILLIES
AEIILLTV	ILLATIVE
AEIILMNN	MAINLINE
AEIILMNS	ALIENISM
AEIILMPR	IMPERIAL
AEIILMRS	RAMILIES
AEIILMTT	MILITATE
AEIILNNS	ANILINES
AEIILNQU	AQUILINE
	QUINIELA
AEIILNRR	AIRLINER
AEIILNRS	AIRLINES
	SNAILIER
AEIILNRT	INERTIAL
AEIILNST	ALIENIST
	LITANIES
AEIILNSZ	SALINIZE
AEIILNTZ	LATINIZE
AEIILPPT	TAILPIPE
AEIILPRT	LIPARITE
AEIILQSU	SILIQUAE
AEIILRSS	LAIRISES
AEIILRST	LAIRIEST
	LISTERIA
AEIILRSV	RIVALISE
	VIRELAIS
AEIILRSZ	LAIRIZES
AEIILRTT	LITERATI
AEIILRVZ	RIVALIZE
AEIILSSS	SILESIAS
AEIILSSW	LEWISIAS
AEIILSTV	VITALISE

AEIILSTX LAXITIES
AEIILSTZ TAILZIES
AEIILTVZ VITALIZE
AEIIMMRT MARITIME
AEIIMMSX MAXIMISE
AEIIMMTX MAXIMITE
AEIIMMXZ MAXIMIZE
AEIIMNRU URINEMIA
AEIIMNST MINIATES
AEIIMNSZ SIMAZINE
AEIIMNTT INTIMATE
AEIIMNTU MINUTIAE
AEIIMNTV VITAMINE
AEIIMOSS AMEIOSIS
AEIIMPRR IMPAIRER
AEIIMPSY EPIMYSIA
AEIIMRSS MISRAISE
AEIIMRST AIRTIMES
SERIATIM
AEIIMRSV VIREMIAS
AEIIMSTT IMITATES
AEIINNRS SIRENIAN
AEIINNRT TRIENNIA
AEIINNSS INSANIES
AEIINNTV INNATIVE
AEIINOTT NOTITIAE
AEIINPRT PAINTIER
AEIINPST PIANISTE
AEIINPTZ PATINIZE
AEIINQSU EQUINIAS
AEIINRRV RIVERAIN
AEIINRSS AIRINESS
AEIINRST INERTIAS
RAINIEST
AEIINRSY YERSINIA
AEIINRTZ TRIAZINE
AEIINSST ISATINES
SANITIES
SANITISE
TENIASIS
AEIINSSX SIXAINES
AEIINSTV VANITIES
AEIINSTX AXINITES
AEIINSTZ SANITIZE
AEIINSVV INVASIVE
AEIINTTT TITANITE
AEIINTTU UINTAITE
AEIIPRRS PRAIRIES
AEIIPRST PARITIES
AEIIPRSW PAIRWISE
AEIIPRTZ TRAPEZII
AEIIPRZZ PIZZERIA
AEIIPSST EPITASIS
AEIIRRST RARITIES
AEIIRRSV RIVIERAS
AEIIRRTT IRRITATE
AEIIRSSS SIRIASES
AEIIRSST IRISATES
SATIRISE
AEIIRSTV VAIRIEST
AEIIRSTW WISTERIA
AEIIRSTX SEXTARII
AEIIRSTZ SATIRIZE
AEIIRSVV VIVARIES
AEIIRTTT TRITIATE
AEIIRTVZ VIZIRATE
AEIISTTV VITIATES
AEIISTVZ IZVESTIA
AEIITTTV TITIVATE
AEIITTVV VITATIVE
AEIJKLZZ JAZZLIKE
AEIJLMSS MAJLISES
AEIJLNSV JAVELINS
AEIJLNSW JAWLINES
AEIJLOPS JALOPIES
AEIJLOSU JALOUSIE
AEIJMMST JAMMIEST
AEIJMNSS JASMINES
AEIJNRST NARTJIES
AEIJNRTU JAUNTIER
AEIJNSTT JANTIEST
AEIJNSTU JAUNTIES
AEIJORST JAROSITE
AEIJORVZ JAROVIZE
AEIJPSSS JASPISES
AEIJSTZZ JAZZIEST
AEIKKLLW LIKEWALK
AEIKKLMS MASKLIKE
AEIKKLNT TANKLIKE
AEIKKLPR PARKLIKE
AEIKKMNO KAKIEMON
AEIKLLMP PALMLIKE
AEIKLLMS SELAMLIK
AEIKLLPY PLAYLIKE
AEIKLLSS KILLASES
AEIKLLST SALTLIKE
AEIKLMOT MOATLIKE
AEIKLMST MASTLIKE
AEIKLNNP PANNIKEL
AEIKLNOS KAOLINES
AEIKLNOV NOVALIKE
AEIKLNPS SKIPLANE
AEIKLNSS SEALSKIN
AEIKLNST LANKIEST
AEIKLNSW SWANLIKE
AEIKLNSY SNEAKILY
AEIKLNTU AUNTLIKE
AEIKLOPS SOAPLIKE
AEIKLOST KEITLOAS
AEIKLPRS SPARLIKE
AEIKLPRT TRAPLIKE
AEIKLPSS KALPISES
AEIKLPSW WASPLIKE
AEIKLQUY QUAYLIKE
AEIKLRSS SERKALIS
AEIKLRST LARKIEST
STALKIER
STARLIKE
AEIKLRSV KLAVIERS
AEIKLRTW WARTLIKE
AEIKLRVY VALKYRIE
AEIKLRWY WALKYRIE
AEIKLSSS SAIKLESS
AEIKLSTT TALKIEST
AEIKMMSS MISMAKES
AEIKMNRS RAMEKINS
AEIKMNST MANKIEST
MISTAKEN
AEIKMPRS RAMPIKES
AEIKMPSS MISSPEAK
AEIKMRST MISTAKER
AEIKMSST MISTAKES
AEIKMSTW MAWKIEST
AEIKNNTU ANTINUKE
AEIKNPRR PRANKIER
AEIKNPRS RANPIKES
AEIKNRRS SNARKIER
AEIKNRST KERATINS
NARKIEST
AEIKNRSW SWANKIER
AEIKNRTW KNITWEAR
AEIKNSST SNAKIEST
AEIKNSSW SWANKIES
AEIKNSSY KYANISES
AEIKNSTU UNAKITES
AEIKNSTV KISTVAEN
AEIKNSTW TWANKIES
WANKIEST
AEIKNSTY KYANITES
AEIKNSYZ KYANIZES
AEIKOSST STOKESIA
AEIKPRRS SPARKIER
AEIKPRSS SPARKIES
AEIKPRST PARKIEST
AEIKPSTW PAWKIEST
AEIKQSTU QUAKIEST
AEIKRSST ASTERISK
SARKIEST
AEILLLMO MALLEOLI
AEILLLMS ALLELISM
AEILLLNY LINEALLY
AEILLMNS MANILLES
AEILLMNY MENIALLY
AEILLMSS MAILLESS
AEILLMSY MESIALLY
AEILLNNO LANOLINE
AEILLNNS NAINSELL
AEILLNNU UNLINEAL
AEILLNOR ALLERION
AEILLNPS SPLENIAL
AEILLNPY ALPINELY
AEILLNQU QUINELLA
AEILLNRY LINEARLY
AEILLNSS AINSELLS
NAILLESS
SENSILLA
AEILLNVY VENIALLY
AEILLOSS LOESSIAL
AEILLOTV VOLATILE
AEILLPPR APPERILL
AEILLPRS PERILLAS
AEILLPSS ILLAPSES
AEILLPST PALLIEST
PASTILLE
AEILLQSU SQUILLAE
AEILLQTU TEQUILLA
AEILLRRS RALLIERS
AEILLRRY RAILLERY
AEILLRSS RAILLESS
SALLIERS
AEILLRST LITERALS
TALLIERS
AEILLRSU RUELLIAS
AEILLRSY SERIALLY
AEILLRTU TAILLEUR
AEILLRVX VEXILLAR
AEILLSSS SAILLESS
AEILLSST TAILLESS
AEILLSTW WALLIEST
AEILLSUV ALLUSIVE
AEILLSYZ SLEAZILY
AEILLTUZ LAZULITE
AEILMMNS MELANISM
AEILMMNT IMMANTLE
AEILMMNY IMMANELY
AEILMMOR MEMORIAL
AEILMMOT IMMOLATE
AEILMMRT TRILEMMA
AEILMMSS MELISMAS
AEILMMST MALMIEST
AEILMMTU MALEMIUT
AEILMNNO MINNEOLA
AEILMNNP IMPANNEL
AEILMNNS LINESMAN
MELANINS
AEILMNOS LAMINOSE
MINEOLAS
SEMOLINA
AEILMNPS IMPANELS
MANIPLES
AEILMNRS MARLINES
MINERALS
MISLEARN
AEILMNRT TERMINAL
TRAMLINE
AEILMNRU LEMURIAN
AEILMNSS ISLESMAN
AEILMNST AILMENTS
ALIMENTS
MANLIEST
MELANIST
SMALTINE
AEILMNSU ALUMINES
AEILMOOV MOVIEOLA
AEILMOPR PROEMIAL
AEILMOPS EPISOMAL
AEILMORS MORALISE
AEILMORT AMITROLE
ROLAMITE
AEILMORZ MORALIZE
AEILMOST LOAMIEST
AEILMOSW WAILSOME
AEILMPRS IMPALERS
IMPEARLS
LEMPIRAS
AEILMPRU PLUMERIA
AEILMPRV PRIMEVAL
AEILMPSS PESSIMAL
AEILMPST IMPLATES
PALMIEST
PALMIETS
PETALISM
SEPTIMAL
AEILMPTY PLAYTIME
AEILMQRU QUALMIER
AEILMRRS LARMIERS
AEILMRSS REALISMS
AEILMRST LAMISTER
LAMITERS
MARLIEST
MARLITES
MISALTER
AEILMRSY MISLAYER
SMEARILY
AEILMRTT REMITTAL
AEILMRUV VELARIUM
AEILMSSX SMILAXES
AEILMSTT MALTIEST
METALIST
SMALTITE
AEILMSTU SIMULATE
AEILMSTY LAYTIMES
STEAMILY
TALEYSIM
AEILMSUV MISVALUE
AEILMTTU MUTILATE
ULTIMATE
AEILNNOS SOLANINE
AEILNNPU PINNULAE
AEILNNRT INTERNAL
AEILNNSY INSANELY
AEILNNTY INNATELY
AEILNOPR PELORIAN
AEILNOPS OPALINES
AEILNOPT ANTIPOLE
AEILNOPU POULAINE
AEILNORS AILERONS
ALERIONS
ALIENORS
AEILNORT ORIENTAL
RELATION
TAILERON
AEILNORV OVERLAIN
AEILNOSS ANISOLES
AEILNOST ELATIONS
INSOLATE
TOENAILS
AEILNOSX SILOXANE
AEILNOTT TONALITE
AEILNPPT PIEPLANT

AEILNPRS	PEARLINS
	PRALINES
AEILNPRT	INTERLAP
	TRAPLINE
	TRIPLANE
AEILNPSS	PAINLESS
	SPANIELS
AEILNPST	PANELIST
	PANTILES
	PLAINEST
AEILNPSU	SPINULAE
AEILNPSW	PINWALES
AEILNPSX	EXPLAINS
AEILNPTT	TINPLATE
AEILNPTY	PENALITY
AEILNQSU	QUINELAS
AEILNQTU	QUANTILE
AEILNRRS	SNARLIER
AEILNRSS	RAINLESS
AEILNRST	ENTRAILS
	LATRINES
	RATLINES
	RETINALS
	TRENAILS
AEILNRSU	LUNARIES
AEILNRSV	RAVELINS
AEILNRSX	RELAXINS
AEILNRSY	INLAYERS
	SNAILERY
AEILNRTT	RATTLINE
AEILNRTU	AUNTLIER
	RETINULA
	TENURIAL
AEILNRTV	INTERVAL
AEILNRTY	INTERLAY
AEILNSST	EASTLINS
	ELASTINS
	NAILSETS
	SALIENTS
	SALTINES
	STANIELS
AEILNSSU	INULASES
AEILNSSZ	LAZINESS
AEILNSTU	ALUNITES
	INSULATE
AEILNSTV	VENTAILS
AEILNSTW	LAWNIEST
AEILNSUV	UNVAILES
AEILNSUW	LAUWINES
AEILNSUY	UNEASILY
AEILNTVY	NATIVELY
	VENALITY
AEILNUVV	UNIVALVE
AEILOORV	OVARIOLE
AEILOPPR	OILPAPER
AEILOPPT	OPPILATE
AEILOPRS	PELORIAS
	POLARISE
AEILOPRT	EPILATOR
	PETIOLAR
AEILOPRZ	POLARIZE
AEILOPST	SPOLIATE
AEILORRT	RETAILOR
AEILORSS	SOLARISE
AEILORST	SOTERIAL
AEILORSV	OVERSAIL
	VALORISE
	VARIOLES
	VOLARIES
AEILORSY	ROYALISE
AEILORSZ	SOLARIZE
AEILORTT	LITERATO
AEILORTV	VIOLATER
AEILORTZ	TRIAZOLE
AEILORVZ	VALORIZE

AEILORYZ	ROYALIZE
AEILOSST	ISOLATES
AEILOSSX	OXALISES
AEILOSTT	TOTALISE
AEILOSTV	VIOLATES
AEILOTTV	VOLITATE
AEILOTTZ	TOTALIZE
AEILPPQU	APPLIQUE
AEILPPRS	APPERILS
	APPLIERS
AEILPRRS	REPRISAL
AEILPRRT	PALTRIER
	PRETRIAL
AEILPRST	PILASTER
	PLAISTER
	PLAITERS
AEILPRSU	SPIRULAE
AEILPRSV	PREVAILS
AEILPRSW	SLIPWARE
AEILPRTV	LIVETRAP
AEILPRXY	PYREXIAL
AEILPSST	PALSIEST
AEILPSSY	PAISLEYS
AEILPSTT	PLATIEST
AEILPSTY	PTYALISE
AEILPSUV	PLAUSIVE
AEILPTYZ	PTYALIZE
AEILQRSU	SQUAILER
AEILQRTU	QUARTILE
	REQUITAL
AEILQSTU	LIQUATES
	TEQUILAS
AEILQSUY	QUEASILY
AEILQTUY	EQUALITY
AEILRRST	RETIRALS
	RETRIALS
	TRAILERS
AEILRRSU	RURALISE
AEILRRTT	RATTLIER
AEILRRTU	RURALITE
AEILRRTY	LITERARY
AEILRRUZ	RURALIZE
AEILRSST	REALISTS
	SALTIERS
	SALTIRES
	SLAISTER
AEILRSSV	REVISALS
	RIVALESS
AEILRSTT	TERTIALS
AEILRSTU	URALITES
AEILRSVV	REVIVALS
AEILRSVY	VIRELAYS
AEILRTTY	ALTERITY
AEILRTUV	VAULTIER
AEILRTUZ	LAZURITE
AEILRTVV	TRIVALVE
AEILRTWY	WATERILY
AEILRTXZ	ZELATRIX
AEILSSSV	VESSAILS
AEILSSTT	SALTIEST
	SLATIEST
AEILSSTW	SWALIEST
AEILSTTW	WALTIEST
AEILSTVY	VILAYETS
AEILSTWY	SWEATILY
AEILSTYY	YEASTILY
AEIMMMRZ	MAMZERIM
AEIMMNNT	IMMANENT
AEIMMNOT	AMMONITE
AEIMMNSS	MISNAMES
AEIMMPRS	SPAMMIER
AEIMMPST	PSAMMITE
AEIMMRRS	SMARMIER
AEIMMRST	MARMITES
	RAMMIEST

AEIMMRTU	IMMATURE
AEIMMSST	MISMATES
AEIMMSTT	SEMIMATT
AEIMMSZZ	MIZMAZES
AEIMNNOT	NOMINATE
AEIMNNRS	REINSMAN
AEIMNNRT	TRAINMEN
AEIMNNST	MANNITES
AEIMNOPT	PTOMAINE
AEIMNORS	MORAINES
	ROMAINES
	ROMANISE
AEIMNORW	AIRWOMEN
AEIMNORZ	ARMOZINE
	ROMANIZE
AEIMNOSS	ANEMOSIS
AEIMNOST	AMNIOTES
	MISATONE
	SOMNIATE
AEIMNOSU	MOINEAUS
AEIMNOSW	WOMANISE
AEIMNOTZ	MONAZITE
AEIMNOUX	EXONUMIA
AEIMNOWZ	WOMANIZE
AEIMNPRZ	PRIZEMAN
AEIMNPSX	PANMIXES
AEIMNQRU	RAMEQUIN
AEIMNRRS	MARINERS
AEIMNRRV	RIVERMAN
AEIMNRSS	SEMINARS
	SIRNAMES
AEIMNRST	MINARETS
	RAIMENTS
AEIMNRSU	ANEURISM
AEIMNRSY	SEMINARY
AEIMNRTT	MARTINET
AEIMNRTU	RUMINATE
AEIMNRTW	WARIMENT
AEIMNRTY	TYRAMINE
AEIMNSSS	SAMISENS
AEIMNSST	MANTISES
	MATINESS
AEIMNSSU	ANIMUSES
AEIMNSSZ	MAZINESS
AEIMNSUV	MAUVEINS
	MAUVINES
AEIMNTTU	MATUTINE
AEIMNTVZ	VIZAMENT
AEIMOOPS	IPOMOEAS
AEIMOPRS	MEROPIAS
AEIMOPSX	APOMIXES
AEIMOPTT	OPTIMATE
AEIMORRS	ARMOIRES
	ARMORIES
AEIMORST	AMORTISE
	ATOMISER
AEIMORTT	AMORETTI
AEIMORTZ	AMORTIZE
	ATOMIZER
AEIMOSST	AMITOSES
	AMOSITES
	ATOMISES
	OSMIATES
AEIMOSTX	TOXEMIAS
AEIMOSTZ	ATOMIZES
AEIMOTTV	MOTIVATE
AEIMPRRS	RAMPIRES
AEIMPRRT	IMPARTER
AEIMPRSS	IMPRESAS
	MISPARSE
	SAMPIRES
AEIMPRST	APTERISM
	PRIMATES
AEIMPRSV	VAMPIRES
AEIMPRSW	SWAMPIER

AEIMPRTU	APTERIUM
AEIMPSSS	IMPASSES
AEIMPSST	IMPASTES
	PASTIMES
AEIMQRSU	MARQUISE
AEIMRRRS	MARRIERS
AEIMRRSS	SIMARRES
AEIMRSST	ASTERISM
	MAISTERS
	MISRATES
	SEMITARS
	SMARTIES
AEIMRSSV	MISAVERS
AEIMRSSY	EMISSARY
AEIMRSTT	MISTREAT
	TERATISM
AEIMRSTU	MURIATES
	SEMITAUR
AEIMRSTV	VITAMERS
AEIMRSTW	WARTIMES
AEIMRSTX	MATRIXES
AEIMRSTY	SYMITARE
AEIMRSWW	SWIMWEAR
AEIMSSST	ASTEISMS
	MASSIEST
	MISSEATS
AEIMSSTT	ETATISMS
	MASTIEST
	MISSTATE
AEIMSSTX	MASTIXES
AEIMSSTZ	MESTIZAS
AEIMSTYZ	AZYMITES
AEIMTTUV	MUTATIVE
AEINNNOX	ANNEXION
AEINNOPS	SAPONINE
AEINNOPV	PAVONINE
AEINNORS	RAISONNE
AEINNORT	ANOINTER
	INORNATE
	REANOINT
AEINNOST	ENATIONS
	SONATINE
AEINNOTT	INTONATE
AEINNOTV	INNOVATE
	VENATION
AEINNPRS	PANNIERS
AEINNPST	PANTINES
AEINNRRS	INSNARER
AEINNRRT	INERRANT
AEINNRSS	INSNARES
AEINNRST	ENTRAINS
	TRANNIES
AEINNRSU	ANEURINS
	UNARISEN
AEINNRSW	SWANNIER
AEINNRTT	INTRANET
AEINNSST	INSANEST
	STANINES
AEINNSSV	VAINNESS
AEINNSSZ	ZANINESS
AEINNSTT	ANTIENTS
	STANNITE
AEINNTUV	UNNATIVE
AEINOPPT	ANTIPOPE
AEINOPRT	ATROPINE
AEINOPSS	SENOPIAS
AEINOPST	SAPONITE
AEINOPSZ	EPIZOANS
AEINOPTZ	TOPAZINE
AEINOQRU	AEQUORIN
AEINOQTU	EQUATION
AEINORRT	ANTERIOR
AEINORRW	IRONWARE
AEINORSS	ERASIONS
	SENSORIA

AEINORST ANOESTRI
ARSONITE
NOTARIES
NOTARISE
ROSINATE
SENORITA
AEINORSV AVERSION
AEINORTT TENTORIA
AEINORTZ NOTARIZE
AEINOSST ASSIENTO
ASTONIES
AEINOSSV EVASIONS
AEINOSSX SAXONIES
AEINOSTV STOVAINE
AEINOSTX SAXONITE
AEINOSXZ OXAZINES
AEINOTVX VEXATION
AEINPPPS PANPIPES
AEINPPRS SNAPPIER
AEINPPRY PAPYRINE
AEINPPSS PINESAPS
AEINPPST NAPPIEST
AEINPRRT PRETRAIN
TERRAPIN
AEINPRRU UNREPAIR
AEINPRST PAINTERS
PANTRIES
PERTAINS
PINASTER
PRISTANE
REPAINTS
AEINPRSU UNPRAISE
AEINPRSW SPAWNIER
AEINPRTT TRIPTANE
AEINPRTU PAINTURE
AEINPRTX EXPIRANT
AEINPSST STEAPSIN
AEINPSTT PATIENTS
AEINPSTU PETUNIAS
SUPINATE
AEINPSTY EPINASTY
AEINPTTY ANTITYPE
AEINQRTU ANTIQUER
QUAINTER
AEINQSTU ANTIQUES
QUANTISE
AEINQTTU EQUITANT
AEINQTUZ QUANTIZE
AEINRRST RESTRAIN
RETRAINS
STRAINER
TERRAINS
TRAINERS
TRANSIRE
AEINRRTT RETIRANT
AEINRRTV VERATRIN
AEINRRTW INTERWAR
AEINRRUW UNWARIER
AEINRSST ARTINESS
RESIANTS
RETSINAS
SNARIEST
STAINERS
STARNIES
STEARINS
AEINRSSU ANURESIS
SENARIUS
AEINRSSW WARINESS
AEINRSSX XERANSIS
AEINRSTT INTREATS
NITRATES
STRAITEN
TARTINES
TERTIANS
AEINRSTU RUINATES
TAURINES
URANITES
URINATES
AEINRSTW TINWARES
AEINRSUV VAURIENS
AEINRSUZ AZURINES
SUZERAIN
AEINRSVV VERVAINS
AEINRSZZ SNAZZIER
AEINRTTU TAINTURE
AEINRTUV VAUNTIER
AEINSSST SAINTESS
SESTINAS
AEINSSSV VINASSES
AEINSSTT ANTSIEST
INSTATES
NASTIEST
SATINETS
TITANESS
AEINSSTU SINUATES
AEINSSTX SEXTAINS
AEINSSVW WAVINESS
AEINSSWX WAXINESS
AEINSTTT NATTIEST
AEINSTTV TASTEVIN
AEINSTTW TAWNIEST
AEINSTUV SUIVANTE
AEINSTWY YAWNIEST
AEINSUVV VESUVIAN
AEINTTUU AUTUNITE
AEIOPPST APPOSITE
AEIOPRRT PRIORATE
AEIOPRRW AIRPOWER
AEIOPRSV VAPORISE
AEIOPRTX EXPIATOR
AEIOPRVZ VAPORIZE
AEIOPSST SOAPIEST
AEIOPTTV OPTATIVE
AEIOQSSU SEQUOIAS
AEIORRRS ARRIEROS
AEIORRSS ROSARIES
AEIORRST ROARIEST
ROTARIES
AEIORRSV SAVORIER
AEIORSSV SAVORIES
AEIORSTT TOASTIER
AEIORSTU OUTRAISE
SAUTOIRE
AEIORSTV TRAVOISE
VIATORES
VOTARIES
AEIORSVW AVOWRIES
AEIORTTV ROTATIVE
AEIOSSTT TOASTIES
AEIOSSTZ AZOTISES
AEIOSTZZ AZOTIZES
AEIPPPST PAPPIEST
AEIPPRRS APPRISER
AEIPPRRT TRAPPIER
AEIPPRRZ APPRIZER
AEIPPRSS APPRISES
AEIPPRST PERIAPTS
AEIPPRSZ APPRIZES
AEIPPSST SAPPIEST
AEIPPSTY YAPPIEST
AEIPPSTZ ZAPPIEST
AEIPQRTU PRATIQUE
AEIPRRRS SPARRIER
AEIPRRSS ASPIRERS
PRAISERS
AEIPRRST PARTIERS
AEIPRRSU UPRAISER
AEIPRRSY SPRAYIER
AEIPRRTV PRIVATER
AEIPRSST PASTRIES
PIASTERS
PIASTRES
RASPIEST
TRAIPSES
AEIPRSSU UPRAISES
AEIPRSSV PARVISES
PAVISERS
AEIPRSSX PRAXISES
AEIPRSTV PRIVATES
AEIPRSTW WIRETAPS
AEIPRSTY ASPERITY
AEIPRSVY VESPIARY
AEIPRSWW WARPWISE
AEIPRSXY PYREXIAS
AEIPSSST PASTISES
AEIPSSSV PASSIVES
AEIPSSTT PASTIEST
AEIPSSTW WASPIEST
AEIPSSTY EPISTASY
AEIPSZZZ PIZAZZES
AEIPTTUV PUTATIVE
AEIQRRRU QUARRIER
AEIQRRSU QUARRIES
AEIQRRTU QUARTIER
AEIRRRST STARRIER
TARRIERS
AEIRRRSV ARRIVERS
AEIRRSST TARSIERS
AEIRRSSY SISERARY
AEIRRSTT RETRAITS
STRAITER
TARRIEST
AEIRRSTW STRAWIER
AEIRRSVV VIVERRAS
AEIRRTTT RETRAITT
AEIRRTTY TERTIARY
AEIRRVWY RIVERWAY
AEIRSSST ASSISTER
TIRASSES
AEIRSSSZ ASSIZERS
AEIRSSTT ARTISTES
ARTSIEST
STRIATES
AEIRSSTV TRAVISES
AEIRSSTW WAISTERS
WAITRESS
WASTRIES
AEIRSTTT ATTRITES
RATTIEST
TARTIEST
TITRATES
TRISTATE
AEIRSTTW WARTIEST
AEIRSTTX EXTRAITS
AEIRSTTZ TRISTEZA
AEIRSTUZ AZURITES
AEIRSTVY VESTIARY
AEIRSWWY WAYWISER
WIREWAYS
AEIRTTTW ATWITTER
AEISSSST SASSIEST
AEISSSTW TISWASES
AEISSSTY ESSAYIST
AEISSTTT TASTIEST
AEISSTTU SITUATES
AEISSTTV STATIVES
VASTIEST
AEISSTVV SAVVIEST
AEISSTWZ TIZWASES
AEISTTTT TATTIEST
AEISTTTU ATTUITES
AEISTTTW TAWTIEST
AEJKPSTU KAJEPUTS
AEJLNSUV JUVENALS
AEJLOSSU JALOUSES
AEJLOSUY JEALOUSY
AEJLOSUZ AZULEJOS
AEJNORSZ ZANJEROS
AEKKLLWY LYKEWALK
AEKKMNOO KAKEMONO
AEKKOSSS SAKKOSES
AEKLLSTU KELLAUTS
AEKLMORS LARKSOME
AEKLMOSU LEUKOMAS
AEKLMRUW LUKEWARM
AEKLMRUY YARMULKE
AEKLNNSS LANKNESS
AEKLNOSY ANKYLOSE
AEKLNPPS KNAPPLES
AEKLNPRS PRANKLES
AEKLNPRT PLANKTER
AEKLNRSV KLAVERNS
AEKLOPRT LAKEPORT
AEKLOPRW ROPEWALK
AEKLOPTY KALOTYPE
AEKLORSY ROKELAYS
AEKLORTV OVERTALK
AEKLORVW WALKOVER
AEKLOSST SKATOLES
STALKOES
AEKLOSVZ ZELKOVAS
AEKLPRRS SPARKLER
AEKLPRSS SPARKLES
AEKLPRST SPARKLET
AEKLRSST STALKERS
AEKLRSUW WAULKERS
AEKMMNRS MARKSMEN
AEKMNRSU UNMAKERS
UNMASKER
AEKMOOST MATOOKES
AEKMOPRT TOPMAKER
AEKMORTW TEAMWORK
WORKMATE
AEKMPRRV VERKRAMP
AEKMPRSU UPMAKERS
AEKMPRTU UPMARKET
AEKNNRSS RANKNESS
AEKNORRV OVERRANK
AEKNORUY EUKARYON
AEKNOTTU OUTTAKEN
AEKNPPRS KNAPPERS
AEKNPRSS SPANKERS
AEKNPSSU UNSPEAKS
AEKNRSST STARKENS
AEKNRSSW SWANKERS
AEKNRSTZ KRANTZES
AEKNSSTW SWANKEST
AEKNSSWY SWANKEYS
AEKOORSV OVERSOAK
AEKOPRRT PARROKET
AEKOPRSS PRESOAKS
AEKOPSTU OUTSPEAK
SPEAKOUT
AEKORRSS ROSAKERS
AEKORRWW WORKWEAR
AEKORSSS KAROSSES
AEKORSTV OVERTASK
AEKORSTW SEATWORK
AEKORTUY EUKARYOT
AEKOSTTU OUTSKATE
OUTTAKES
STAKEOUT
TAKEOUTS
AEKPPSSU UPSPEAKS
AEKPRRSS SPARKERS
AEKPSSSY PASSKEYS
AEKQRSUW SQUAWKER
AEKRRSST STARKERS
AEKRSSTT STARKEST
AELLLORY LOYALLER

AELLLRTU	TELLURAL
AELLLSUV	VULSELLA
AELLMNOZ	MANZELLO
AELLMNST	STALLMEN
AELLMNTY	MENTALLY
	TALLYMEN
AELLMORR	MORALLER
AELLMORT	MARTELLO
AELLMOSS	LOAMLESS
AELLMOTY	TOMALLEY
AELLMPUU	PLUMULAE
AELLMRST	TRAMELLS
AELLMRSY	MERSALYL
AELLMSST	SMALLEST
AELLMSWX	MAXWELLS
AELLNOPS	PALLONES
AELLNOPV	VOLPLANE
AELLNORS	LLANEROS
AELLNOSV	NOVELLAS
AELLNOWW	ENWALLOW
AELLNPRU	PRUNELLA
AELLNPSS	PLANLESS
AELLNPTT	PLANTLET
AELLNPTU	PLANTULE
AELLNRUY	NEURALLY
	UNREALLY
AELLNRVY	VERNALLY
AELLNSST	TALLNESS
AELLNSTT	TALLENTS
AELLNTTY	LATENTLY
AELLNTUU	LUNULATE
AELLNTUY	LUNATELY
AELLOOPS	PALEOSOL
AELLOPPR	APPELLOR
AELLOPRS	REPOSALL
AELLOPRT	PREALLOT
AELLOPRW	WALLOPER
AELLOPTY	ALLOTYPE
AELLORRY	ROYALLER
AELLORSS	ROSELLAS
AELLORST	REALLOTS
	ROSTELLA
AELLORSV	ALLOVERS
	OVERALLS
AELLORSW	SALLOWER
AELLORTT	ALLOTTER
AELLORWW	WALLOWER
AELLOSTY	LOYALEST
AELLOSUV	ALVEOLUS
AELLPRSS	SPALLERS
AELLPSSY	PLAYLESS
AELLPSTY	PLAYLETS
AELLQRSU	SQUALLER
AELLRRSU	ALLURERS
AELLRRTY	RETRALLY
AELLRTTY	LATTERLY
AELLRTVY	TREVALLY
AELLRTYY	LYRATELY
AELLRWYY	LAWYERLY
AELLSSST	SALTLESS
	TASSELLS
AELLSSTW	SETWALLS
	SWALLETS
AELLSSTY	TASSELLY
AELLSTUU	ULULATES
AELLSTVY	VESTALLY
AELLSUVV	VALVULES
AELLSUXY	SEXUALLY
AELMMNOS	MAMELONS
AELMMORW	MEALWORM
AELMMOSY	MYELOMAS
AELMMRSS	SLAMMERS
AELMMRST	STRAMMEL
	TRAMMELS
AELMMSST	STAMMELS
AELMMSSY	MALMSEYS
AELMNNOT	NONMETAL
AELMNNOU	NOUMENAL
AELMNNRY	MANNERLY
AELMNNTU	UNMANTLE
AELMNOPS	NEOPLASM
	PLEONASM
AELMNORS	ALMONERS
AELMNOST	SALMONET
AELMNOSU	MELANOUS
AELMNOWY	LAYWOMEN
AELMNOYY	YEOMANLY
AELMNPRS	LAMPERNS
AELMNRSU	MENSURAL
	NUMERALS
AELMNSTT	MANTLETS
AELMNSTU	NUTMEALS
AELMNSTY	MESNALTY
AELMOOPT	OMOPLATE
AELMOORS	SALEROOM
AELMOPRR	PREMOLAR
	PREMORAL
AELMOPRS	PLEROMAS
	RAMPOLES
AELMOPRT	PROMETAL
	TEMPORAL
AELMOPSU	AMPOULES
AELMOPSX	EXOPLASM
AELMOPSY	MAYPOLES
	PLAYSOME
AELMOPTT	METAPLOT
	PALMETTO
AELMORST	MOLERATS
AELMORSU	RAMULOSE
AELMORSV	REMOVALS
AELMORSY	RAMOSELY
AELMORTU	EMULATOR
AELMOSSS	MOLASSES
AELMOSST	MALTOSES
AELMOSSY	AMYLOSES
AELMOSTT	MATELOTS
AELMOSTY	ATMOLYSE
AELMOTVZ	MAZELTOV
AELMOTYZ	ATMOLYZE
AELMPRRT	TRAMPLER
AELMPRSS	SAMPLERS
AELMPRST	TEMPLARS
	TRAMPLES
AELMPRSY	LAMPREYS
	SAMPLERY
AELMPSUX	AMPLEXUS
AELMQSUU	SQUAMULE
AELMRSST	LAMSTERS
	TRAMLESS
AELMRSTT	MALTSTER
	MARTLETS
AELMRSTU	STAUMREL
AELMRSTY	MASTERLY
AELMRTUY	MATURELY
AELMSSSS	MASSLESS
AELMSSST	MASTLESS
AELNNNPU	UNPANNEL
AELNNOOP	NAPOLEON
AELNNOOX	NALOXONE
AELNNOPT	PENTANOL
AELNNOQU	NONEQUAL
AELNNORU	NEURONAL
AELNNOSU	ANNULOSE
AELNNPRS	PLANNERS
AELNNPSU	UNPANELS
AELNNRSS	ENSNARLS
AELNNRST	LANTERNS
AELNNRSU	UNLEARNS
AELNNRTU	UNLEARNT
AELNNSST	STANNELS
AELNNSTU	ANNULETS
AELNOOTZ	ENTOZOAL
AELNOPPY	POLYPNEA
AELNOPRS	PERSONAL
	PSORALEN
AELNOPRV	OVERPLAN
AELNOPST	LAPSTONE
	PLEONAST
	POLENTAS
AELNOPSU	APOLUNES
AELNORSU	ALEURONS
	NEUROSAL
AELNORSV	VERONALS
AELNORTT	TETRONAL
	TOLERANT
AELNORTU	OUTLEARN
AELNORTY	ORNATELY
AELNOSSV	OVALNESS
AELNOSTV	VOLANTES
AELNOSTY	ANOLYTES
AELNPPRS	PREPLANS
AELNPPRT	PREPLANT
AELNPPSY	PLAYPENS
	SPYPLANE
AELNPRST	PANTLERS
	PLANTERS
	REPLANTS
AELNPRSU	PURSLANE
	SUPERNAL
AELNPRTY	PLENARTY
AELNPSSS	SNAPLESS
	SPANLESS
AELNPSSU	SPANSULE
AELNPSTX	EXPLANTS
AELNPTTU	PATULENT
	PETULANT
AELNPTTY	PATENTLY
AELNQSUU	UNEQUALS
AELNRRSS	SNARLERS
AELNRRTY	ERRANTLY
AELNRRUV	NERVULAR
AELNRSST	SALTERNS
AELNRSTT	SLATTERN
	TRENTALS
AELNRSTU	NEUTRALS
AELNRSTV	VENTRALS
AELNRSUU	NEURULAS
AELNRSUV	UNRAVELS
AELNRSVY	SYLVANER
AELNRSXY	LARYNXES
AELNRTTW	TRAWLNET
AELNRUWY	UNWARELY
AELNSSST	SALTNESS
AELNSSTY	STANYELS
AELNSTUV	ENVAULTS
AELNSUUX	UNSEXUAL
AELNTTUX	EXULTANT
AELOOPRZ	ZOOPERAL
AELOORRS	ROSEOLAR
AELOORSS	AEROSOLS
	ROSEOLAS
AELOORTW	WATERLOO
AELOORTZ	ZOOLATER
AELOPPRS	PROLAPSE
	PROPALES
	SAPROPEL
AELOPPSU	PAPULOSE
AELOPPTU	POPULATE
AELOPPXY	APOPLEXY
AELOPQUY	OPAQUELY
AELOPRRV	REPROVAL
AELOPRSS	REPOSALS
AELOPRST	PETROSAL
	POLESTAR
	PROLATES
AELOPRSU	LEAPROUS
AELOPRSV	OVERLAPS
AELOPRVY	OVERPLAY
AELOPSSS	SOAPLESS
AELOPSST	APOSTLES
AELOPSSU	ESPOUSAL
	SEPALOUS
AELOPSSX	EXPOSALS
AELOPSTT	PALETOTS
AELOPSTU	OUTLEAPS
	PETALOUS
AELOPTTU	OUTLEAPT
AELORRST	REALTORS
	RELATORS
	RESTORAL
AELORSSS	LASSOERS
AELORSTU	ROSULATE
AELORSTV	LEVATORS
	OVERSALT
AELORSTY	ROYALETS
AELORSTZ	ZELATORS
AELORSUU	ROULEAUS
AELORSVY	LAYOVERS
	OVERLAYS
AELORSWY	OWRELAYS
AELORTTV	VARLETTO
AELORTYZ	ZEALOTRY
AELORUUX	ROULEAUX
AELOSSTV	SOLVATES
AELOSSTY	ASYSTOLE
AELOSSVY	SAVELOYS
AELOSTTU	TOLUATES
AELOSTTW	WASTELOT
AELOSTUV	OVULATES
AELOSTUY	AUTOLYSE
AELOTUUV	OUTVALUE
AELOTUYZ	AUTOLYZE
AELPPPRU	PREPUPAL
AELPPRSS	SLAPPERS
AELPPSST	STAPPLES
AELPPSSU	APPULSES
AELPRRRU	LARRUPER
AELPRRSW	SPRAWLER
AELPRRTT	PRATTLER
AELPRSST	PERSALTS
	PLASTERS
	PSALTERS
	STAPLERS
AELPRSSU	PERUSALS
AELPRSSY	PARSLEYS
	SPARSELY
AELPRSTT	PARTLETS
	PLATTERS
	PRATTLES
	SPLATTER
	SPRATTLE
AELPRSTU	APLUSTRE
AELPRSTY	PEYTRALS
	PLASTERY
	PSALTERY
AELPRSUY	SUPERLAY
AELPSSSS	PASSLESS
AELPSSST	PASTLESS
AELPSSTT	PELTASTS
AELPSSTU	PULSATES
	SPATULES
AELPSUUV	UPVALUES
AELQRRSU	QUARRELS
AELQRSUY	SQUARELY
AELQSTTU	SQUATTLE
AELQSTUZ	QUETZALS
AELRRSSW	WARSLERS
AELRRSTT	RATTLERS
	STARTLER
AELRRSTW	TRAWLERS

	WARSTLER
AELRRTVY	VARLETRY
AELRSSST	STARLESS
AELRSSSW	WRASSLES
AELRSSTT	SLATTERS
	STARLETS
	STARTLES
AELRSSTU	SALUTERS
AELRSSTW	WARSTLES
	WARTLESS
	WASTRELS
	WRASTLES
AELRSSUW	WALRUSES
AELRSTTT	TARTLETS
	TATTLERS
AELRSTTU	LUSTRATE
	TUTELARS
AELRSTTY	SLATTERY
AELRSTUV	VAULTERS
	VESTURAL
AELRSTWY	TRAWLEYS
AELRSTWZ	WALTZERS
AELRSUVY	SURVEYAL
AELRTTTW	TWATTLER
AELRTTUX	TEXTURAL
AELRTTUY	TUTELARY
AELSSSTU	SALTUSES
AELSSSTY	STAYLESS
AELSSTTW	WATTLESS
AELSSWZZ	SWAZZLES
AELSTTTW	TWATTLES
AELSTTUU	USTULATE
AELSTTUY	ASTUTELY
AEMMMOTU	OMMATEUM
AEMMMRTY	MAMMETRY
AEMMNNOY	MONEYMAN
AEMMNPRS	RAMPSMEN
AEMMNRRY	MERRYMAN
AEMMNRTU	RAMENTUM
AEMMOORT	ROOMMATE
AEMMORSS	MARMOSES
AEMMORST	MARMOSET
AEMMORSW	WOMMERAS
AEMMPRSS	SPAMMERS
AEMMRSST	STAMMERS
AEMMRTUY	MAUMETRY
AEMMRTWY	MAWMETRY
AEMMSSTU	SUMMATES
AEMMSSUW	WAMMUSES
AEMNNOPW	PENWOMAN
AEMNNORS	MONERANS
	SONARMEN
AEMNNORT	ORNAMENT
AEMNNOSS	MANNOSES
AEMNNOST	MONTANES
AEMNNOSZ	MENAZONS
AEMNNRST	MANRENTS
	REMNANTS
AEMNOORR	MAROONER
AEMNOORT	ANTEROOM
AEMNOORY	AERONOMY
AEMNOOTZ	METAZOON
AEMNOPRS	MANROPES
	PROSEMAN
AEMNOPRT	EMPATRON
AEMNOPRW	MANPOWER
AEMNORRS	RANSOMER
AEMNORST	MONSTERA
	ONSTREAM
	STOREMAN
	TONEARMS
AEMNORSU	ENAMOURS
	NEUROMAS
AEMNORSV	OVERMANS
	OVERSMAN
AEMNORSY	ROMNEYAS
AEMNORTT	TORMENTA
AEMNORTU	ROUTEMAN
AEMNORTY	MONETARY
AEMNORVY	OVERMANY
AEMNORYY	YEOMANRY
AEMNOSTU	NOTAEUMS
	OUTNAMES
	SEAMOUNT
AEMNPRSS	PRESSMAN
AEMNPRSU	SUPERMAN
AEMNPSST	ENSTAMPS
	PASSMENT
AEMNPSTU	SPUMANTE
AEMNPSTY	PAYMENTS
AEMNQSUW	SQUAWMEN
AEMNRRSU	MANURERS
	SURNAMER
AEMNRRUY	NUMERARY
AEMNRSST	SARMENTS
	SMARTENS
AEMNRSSU	SURNAMES
AEMNRSSW	WARMNESS
AEMNRSTU	ANESTRUM
	MENSTRUA
	TRANSUME
AEMNRSTV	VARMENTS
AEMNRSTW	TRANSMEW
	TREWSMAN
AEMNRSUY	ANEURYSM
AEMNSTTU	NUTMEATS
AEMNSTWY	WAYMENTS
AEMOOPST	POMATOES
AEMOORRW	WAREROOM
AEMOORST	TEAROOMS
AEMOORSW	WOOMERAS
AEMOORTT	AMORETTO
AEMOOSST	MAESTOSO
	OSTEOMAS
AEMOOSSV	VAMOOSES
AEMOOSTT	TOMATOES
AEMOOSTU	AUTOSOME
AEMOOTTY	TOMATOEY
AEMOPPRS	PAMPEROS
AEMOPRTW	POMWATER
	TAPEWORM
AEMOQSSU	SQUAMOSE
AEMORRRS	ARMORERS
AEMORRRU	ARMOURER
AEMORRST	REARMOST
AEMORRSW	EARWORMS
AEMORRSY	ROSEMARY
AEMORRVW	OVERWARM
AEMORSSS	MORASSES
AEMORSST	MAESTROS
AEMORSSW	SEAWORMS
AEMORSSY	MAYORESS
AEMORSTV	OVERMAST
AEMORSVW	OVERSWAM
AEMORTTU	TAUTOMER
AEMOSSTT	EASTMOST
	STOMATES
AEMOSSTW	TWASOMES
AEMOSSUZ	ZAMOUSES
AEMOSSWY	SOMEWAYS
AEMOSTTZ	MOZETTAS
AEMOTTZZ	MOZZETTA
AEMPPRST	PRESTAMP
AEMPRRST	TRAMPERS
AEMPRRSW	PREWARMS
AEMPRRSY	SPERMARY
AEMPRSST	RESTAMPS
	STAMPERS
AEMPRSSW	SWAMPERS
AEMPRSTT	TRAMPETS
AEMPRSTU	TEMPURAS
	UPSTREAM
AEMPSSUW	MAWPUSES
	WAMPUSES
AEMPSTTT	ATTEMPTS
AEMQRSSU	MARQUESS
	MASQUERS
AEMRRSST	ARMRESTS
AEMRRSSW	SWARMERS
AEMRRTUV	VERATRUM
AEMRSSSU	ASSUMERS
	MASSEURS
AEMRSSTT	MATTRESS
	SMARTEST
	SMATTERS
AEMRSSTY	MAYSTERS
AEMRSTTU	MATUREST
	TESTAMUR
AEMRSTTX	MARTEXTS
AEMRTUUX	TRUMEAUX
AEMSTTTU	TESTATUM
AENNNPST	PENNANTS
AENNNTTU	UNTENANT
AENNOOTZ	ENTOZOAN
AENNOPRT	PATRONNE
AENNOPST	PENTOSAN
AENNOPUW	UNWEAPON
AENNORST	NORTENAS
	RESONANT
AENNORSU	UNREASON
AENNORSY	ANNOYERS
AENNORTU	UNORNATE
AENNORTW	WANTONER
AENNORUX	NEURAXON
AENNORVY	NOVENARY
AENNOSSU	UNSEASON
AENNOSTU	TONNEAUS
AENNOSTX	NONTAXES
AENNOTUX	TONNEAUX
AENNPRSS	SPANNERS
AENNPSSU	PANNUSES
AENNQSTU	QUANNETS
AENNRSTT	ENTRANTS
AENNRSTY	TYRANNES
AENNRSWY	SWANNERY
AENNRTTY	TENANTRY
AENOOPST	TEASPOON
AENOORRT	RATOONER
AENOOSTZ	OZONATES
AENOPPRS	PROPANES
AENOPRSS	PERSONAS
	RESPONSA
AENOPRST	OPERANTS
	PRONATES
	PROTEANS
AENOPRSY	PYRANOSE
AENOPRTT	PATENTOR
AENOPRWY	WEAPONRY
AENOPSSU	POSAUNES
AENORRRW	NARROWER
AENORRSS	SERRANOS
AENORRST	ANTRORSE
AENORSST	ASSENTOR
	SENATORS
	STARNOSE
	TREASONS
AENORSSU	ANSEROUS
	ARSENOUS
AENORSTT	ORNATEST
AENORSTU	OUTEARNS
AENORSTV	VENATORS
AENORSTW	STONERAW
AENORSUV	RAVENOUS
AENORTTX	TETRAXON
AENORTTY	ATTORNEY
AENORTWW	TOWNWEAR
AENOSSTU	SOUTANES
AENOSSTZ	STANZOES
AENOSSUU	NAUSEOUS
AENOSSVW	WAVESONS
AENPPRSS	PARSNEPS
	SNAPPERS
AENPPRST	PARPENTS
AENPPRSU	UNPAPERS
AENPRRST	PARTNERS
AENPRRSW	PRAWNERS
	PREWARNS
AENPRSST	PASTERNS
	RAPTNESS
AENPRSSW	SPAWNERS
AENPRSTT	PATTERNS
	TRANSEPT
	TRAPNEST
AENPRSTU	PERSAUNT
AENPRSUV	PARVENUS
AENPSSST	PASTNESS
AENPSSSY	SYNAPSES
AENPSSTU	PESAUNTS
AENPSSTW	STEWPANS
	WASPNEST
AENPSSTY	SYNAPTES
AENPSSTZ	SPETSNAZ
AENPSTZZ	SPETZNAZ
AENQRRTU	QUARTERN
AENQSTTU	QUESTANT
AENRRRTY	ERRANTRY
AENRRSTT	TRANTERS
AENRSSST	SARSNETS
AENRSSTT	TARTNESS
AENRSSTU	ANESTRUS
	SAUNTERS
AENRSSTV	SERVANTS
	VERSANTS
AENRSSUW	UNSWEARS
AENRSTTU	TAUNTERS
AENRSTUV	VAUNTERS
AENRSTUW	UNWATERS
AENRSTWY	STERNWAY
AENRTUVY	VAUNTERY
AENRTUWY	UNWATERY
AENRTWYY	ENTRYWAY
AENSSSTV	VASTNESS
AENSSSTW	WASTNESS
AENSSTTU	TAUTNESS
	UNSTATES
AENSSTTX	SEXTANTS
AENSSTXY	SYNTAXES
AEOOPPPS	PAPPOOSE
AEOOPPSS	PAPOOSES
AEOOPRRT	OPERATOR
AEOOPRSS	OROPESAS
AEOOPSTT	POTATOES
AEOORRST	SORORATE
AEOORTTT	TATTOOER
AEOORTTV	ROTOVATE
AEOPPRRV	APPROVER
AEOPPRSS	APPOSERS
AEOPPRST	TRAPPOSE
AEOPPRSV	APPROVES
AEOPQRTU	PAROQUET
AEOPQSTU	OPAQUEST
AEOPRRRT	PARROTER
AEOPRRSS	ASPERSOR
AEOPRRST	PRAETORS
	PRORATES
AEOPRRSV	VAPORERS
AEOPRRTV	OVERPART
AEOPRRUV	VAPOURER
AEOPRRVW	WRAPOVER
AEOPRRWW	WARPOWER

AEOPRSST	ESPARTOS
	PORTASES
	PROTASES
	SEAPORTS
AEOPRSSU	ASPEROUS
AEOPRSSV	OVERPASS
	PASSOVER
AEOPRSTT	PROSTATE
AEOPRSTU	APTEROUS
AEOPRSTV	OVERPAST
AEOPRSVY	OVERPAYS
AEOPRSWY	ROPEWAYS
AEOPRTWX	WATERPOX
AEOPSSST	POTASSES
AEOPTTUY	AUTOTYPE
AEOQRSTU	EQUATORS
	QUAESTOR
AEOQRSUV	VAQUEROS
AEOQRTTU	TORQUATE
AEOQRTUZ	QUATORZE
AEORRRST	ARRESTOR
AEORRSST	ASSERTOR
	ASSORTER
	ORATRESS
	REASSORT
	ROASTERS
AEORRSSU	AROUSERS
AEORRSSV	SAVORERS
AEORRSTT	ROSTRATE
AEORRSUV	SAVOURER
AEORRTTV	OVERTART
AEORRTUV	AVOUTRER
AEORRTZZ	TERRAZZO
AEORRVWY	OVERWARY
AEORSSSS	ASSESSOR
AEORSSTT	STRATOSE
	TOASTERS
AEORSSTV	VOTARESS
AEORSSTX	STORAXES
AEORSSUU	ROUSSEAU
AEORSTTT	ATTESTOR
	TESTATOR
AEORSTTU	OUTRATES
	OUTSTARE
AEORSTUV	OUTRAVES
AEORSTUW	OUTSWARE
	OUTSWEAR
	OUTWEARS
AEORSTVY	OVERSTAY
AEORSUVW	WAVEROUS
AEORSVWY	OVERSWAY
AEORTUWY	OUTWEARY
	ROUTEWAY
AEORTVXY	VEXATORY
AEOSTTTU	OUTSTATE
AEOSTTUW	OUTWASTE
AEPPPSSU	PAPPUSES
AEPPRRST	STRAPPER
	TRAPPERS
AEPPRRSW	PREWRAPS
	WRAPPERS
AEPPRSSU	UPSPEARS
AEPPRSSW	SWAPPERS
AEPPSSTU	PASTEUPS
AEPQRSTU	PARQUETS
AEPRRRSS	SPARRERS
AEPRRSSY	RESPRAYS
	SPRAYERS
AEPRRSTU	PARTURES
	PASTURER
	RAPTURES
AEPRRSTY	PARTYERS
AEPRSSST	SPARSEST
	TRESPASS
AEPRSSTT	SPATTERS
	TAPSTERS
AEPRSSTU	PASTURES
	UPSTARES
AEPRSSTY	YAPSTERS
AEPRSTTU	STUPRATE
	UPSTATER
AEPRSTTY	TAPESTRY
AEPRSTUX	SUPERTAX
AEPRTUVY	PYRUVATE
AEPSSSSU	PASSUSES
AEPSSTTU	UPSTATES
AEQRRSSU	SQUARERS
AEQRRSTU	QUARTERS
AEQRSSTU	SQUAREST
AEQRSTTU	QUARTETS
	SQUATTER
AEQRSTUZ	QUARTZES
AEQRTTTU	QUARTETT
AERRSSSU	ASSURERS
AERRSSTT	RESTARTS
	STARTERS
AERRSSTU	SERRATUS
AERRSSTV	STARVERS
AERRSSTY	STRAYERS
AERRSTUY	TREASURY
AERSSSST	STRASSES
AERSSSTY	SATYRESS
AERSSTTT	STRETTAS
AERSSTTU	STATURES
AERSSTTW	SWATTERS
AERSSTUX	SURTAXES
AERSSTXY	STYRAXES
AERSTTUV	VETTURAS
AERSTTVY	TRAVESTY
AERTTUXY	TEXTUARY
AESSSTTU	STATUSES
AESSTTTU	ASTUTEST
	STATUTES
AFFFFINN	NIFFNAFF
AFFFFIRR	RIFFRAFF
AFFFGILN	FLAFFING
AFFFLLOS	FALLOFFS
AFFGGINR	GRAFFING
AFFGGINS	GAFFINGS
AFFGHIRT	AFFRIGHT
AFFGIINP	PIAFFING
AFFGIINX	AFFIXING
AFFGIIRT	GRAFFITI
AFFGILMN	MAFFLING
AFFGILNR	RAFFLING
AFFGILNW	WAFFLING
AFFGIMRS	MISGRAFF
AFFGINNY	NYAFFING
AFFGINQU	QUAFFING
AFFGINST	STAFFING
AFFGINUW	WAUFFING
AFFGIORT	GRAFFITO
AFFHILLS	FALLFISH
AFFHILNS	HAFFLINS
AFFHILST	FLATFISH
AFFHILTU	FAITHFUL
AFFIINTY	AFFINITY
AFFIISTX	FIXATIFS
AFFILLMM	FLIMFLAM
AFFILMNS	MAFFLINS
AFFILSUX	SUFFIXAL
AFFIMSST	MASTIFFS
AFFINORR	FORFAIRN
AFFINOSU	AFFUSION
AFFINRSU	FUNFAIRS
	RUFFIANS
AFFIORRS	FORFAIRS
AFFIPSTT	TIPSTAFF
AFFIRRSU	FURFAIRS
AFFIRSSU	SUFFARIS
AFFLLOOT	FOOTFALL
AFFLLTUU	FAULTFUL
AFFLOOOT	FOALFOOT
AFFLOOTT	FLATFOOT
AFFLOPSY	PLAYOFFS
AFFLORTU	FORFAULT
AFFLRRUU	FURFURAL
AFFMOPRS	OFFRAMPS
AFFNORSS	SAFFRONS
AFFNORST	AFFRONTS
AFFNORSY	SAFFRONY
AFFNRRUU	FURFURAN
AFGGGILN	FLAGGING
AFGGGINR	FRAGGING
AFGGGINS	FAGGINGS
AFGGILNN	FANGLING
	FLANGING
AFGGILOP	GIGAFLOP
AFGGINOR	FORAGING
AFGGINOT	FAGOTING
AFGGINRT	GRAFTING
AFGGORTY	FAGGOTRY
AFGHIINT	FAITHING
AFGHILLN	HALFLING
AFGHILNS	FLASHING
AFGHILNT	FANLIGHT
AFGHILPS	FLAGSHIP
AFGHINRT	FARTHING
AFGHINRW	WHARFING
AFGHINST	SHAFTING
AFGHIOST	GOATFISH
AFGHIRSY	GRAYFISH
AFGHLLUU	LAUGHFUL
AFGHLNSU	FLASHGUN
AFGHLSTU	FLAUGHTS
	GHASTFUL
AFGHRSTU	FRAUGHTS
AFGIILLN	FLAILING
AFGIILNS	FAILINGS
AFGIIMNN	INFAMING
AFGIINNT	FAINTING
AFGIINRS	FAIRINGS
	FRAISING
AFGIINTX	FIXATING
AFGIKLNN	FANKLING
	FLANKING
AFGIKNNR	FRANKING
AFGIKORT	KOFTGARI
AFGILLNS	FALLINGS
AFGILLNT	FLATLING
AFGILMMN	FLAMMING
AFGILMNO	FLAMINGO
AFGILNOS	LOAFINGS
AFGILNOT	FLOATING
AFGILNPP	FLAPPING
AFGILNRU	INFRUGAL
AFGILNST	FATLINGS
AFGILNTT	FLATTING
AFGILNTU	FAULTING
AFGILORW	GAIRFOWL
AFGILSSY	GLASSIFY
AFGIMNOS	FOAMINGS
AFGIMNRS	FARMINGS
	FRAMINGS
AFGIMNTU	FUMIGANT
AFGIMORS	GASIFORM
AFGIMRST	MISGRAFT
AFGINNNS	FANNINGS
AFGINNSU	SNAFUING
AFGINNSW	FAWNINGS
AFGINORV	FAVORING
AFGINORY	FORAYING
AFGINPPR	FRAPPING
AFGINRST	INGRAFTS
	STRAFING
AFGINRSW	SWARFING
AFGINRSY	FRAYINGS
AFGINRTU	FIGURANT
AFGINSST	FASTINGS
AFGINSTW	WAFTINGS
AFGINSUY	SANGUIFY
AFGIORST	ISOGRAFT
AFGKNOPS	PAKFONGS
AFGKORST	KOFTGARS
AFGLLNOT	FLATLONG
AFGLLRUU	FULGURAL
AFGLLRUY	FRUGALLY
AFGLLSSU	GLASSFUL
AFGLLSTU	GASTFULL
AFGLNNOO	GONFALON
AFGLNORU	GROANFUL
AFGLNOUW	WAGONFUL
AFGNNNOO	GONFANON
AFGOORTZ	ZOOGRAFT
AFHIILRS	FRAILISH
AFHIILSS	SAILFISH
AFHIILST	FISHTAIL
AFHIIMST	MISFAITH
AFHIINST	FAINTISH
AFHIKSUY	KUFIYAHS
AFHILLNS	HALFLINS
AFHILLSW	WALLFISH
AFHILLSY	FLASHILY
AFHILOSY	OAFISHLY
AFHILSST	SALTFISH
AFHILSTT	FLATTISH
AFHILSTW	HALFWITS
AFHIMNST	MANSHIFT
AFHIMNSU	HAFNIUMS
AFHINOSS	FASHIONS
AFHINSTU	UNFAITHS
AFHIOSSU	FASHIOUS
AFHIRSST	STARFISH
AFHISSWY	FISHWAYS
AFHKLNTU	THANKFUL
AFHKORSX	FOXSHARK
AFHKORSY	HAYFORKS
AFHKRSTU	FUTHARKS
AFHLLOTU	LOATHFUL
AFHLNSUY	UNFLASHY
AFHLOSTU	OUTFLASH
AFHLOSTY	HAYLOFTS
AFHLRTUW	WRATHFUL
AFHNOOST	FANTOOSH
AFHOOPST	POOFTAHS
AFHOOPTT	FOOTPATH
AFHOORTT	HAFTOROT
AFHOPSTU	POUFTAHS
AFIIKMRS	FAKIRISM
AFIILLLY	FILIALLY
AFIILLNU	UNFILIAL
AFIILMMS	FAMILISM
AFIILMNS	FINALISM
AFIILNRU	UNIFILAR
AFIILNST	FINALIST
AFIILNTY	FINALITY
AFIILORS	AIRFOILS
AFIILRST	AIRLIFTS
AFIIMNPR	RIFAMPIN
AFIIMRSY	FAIRYISM
AFIINNOS	SAINFOIN
	SINFONIA
AFIINOTX	FIXATION
AFIIORRT	TRIFORIA
AFIJMNOR	JANIFORM
AFIKLNNR	FRANKLIN
AFIKLORT	FORKTAIL
AFIKLOST	FLOKATIS
AFIKMNNR	FINNMARK
AFIKMNRS	FINMARKS

AFIKNRST	RATFINKS
AFIKRSTY	KARSTIFY
AFILLLOT	FLOTILLA
AFILLMSS	MISFALLS
AFILLMUY	AIMFULLY
AFILLNPU	PLAINFUL
AFILLPST	PITFALLS
AFILLPSU	PAILFULS
	PAILSFUL
AFILLSUV	VIALFULS
AFILLTUY	FAULTILY
AFILMNOR	FORMALIN
	INFORMAL
AFILMNOS	FOILSMAN
AFILMOPR	PALIFORM
AFILMSSS	FALSISMS
AFILNNNO	NONFINAL
AFILNORT	FLATIRON
	INFLATOR
AFILNPPT	FLIPPANT
AFILNRTU	TRAINFUL
AFILNRUY	UNFAIRLY
AFILNSTU	FLUTINAS
	INFLATUS
AFILORSW	AIRFLOWS
AFILORTY	FILATORY
AFILOSTX	FOXTAILS
AFILRSTU	FISTULAR
AFILSSTU	FISTULAS
AFILSTTU	FLAUTIST
AFIMMNOR	MANIFORM
AFIMMNOY	AMMONIFY
AFIMMORR	RAMIFORM
AFIMNOPR	NAPIFORM
AFIMNORR	RANIFORM
AFIMNORT	NATIFORM
AFIMNOSU	INFAMOUS
AFIMORRU	AURIFORM
AFIMORRV	VARIFORM
AFIMORSV	VASIFORM
AFIMSSTT	FATTISMS
AFIMSSUV	FAUVISMS
AFINNORS	FRANIONS
AFINNOST	FONTINAS
AFINNOTU	FOUNTAIN
AFINNRTY	INFANTRY
AFINOPSY	SAPONIFY
AFINQTUY	QUANTIFY
AFINRSTX	TRANSFIX
AFINSSTU	FAUNISTS
	FUSTIANS
AFIOOPRR	AIRPROOF
AFIORSTU	FAITOURS
AFIORSTZ	SFORZATI
AFIRSTTY	STRATIFY
AFISSSTT	SITFASTS
AFISSTTT	FATTISTS
AFISSTUV	FAUVISTS
AFKLNOTU	OUTFLANK
AFKLNPRU	PRANKFUL
AFKLNSTU	TANKFULS
AFKLORTW	FLATWORK
AFKLOSWY	FOLKWAYS
AFKMOORT	FOOTMARK
AFKMORRW	FARMWORK
AFKRRSTU	FRAKTURS
AFLLLORY	FLORALLY
AFLLLUWY	LAWFULLY
AFLLMNUY	MANFULLY
AFLLMORY	FORMALLY
AFLLMPSU	PALMFULS
AFLLNOOV	FLAVONOL
AFLLNOSW	SNOWFALL
AFLLNUUW	UNLAWFUL
AFLLOOTW	FOOTWALL
AFLLOSTU	FALLOUTS
	OUTFALLS
AFLLRTUY	ARTFULLY
AFLLSTUW	WASTFULL
AFLMNNUU	UNMANFUL
AFLMNOPR	PLANFORM
AFLMNORU	UNFORMAL
AFLMOPRT	PLATFORM
AFLMORRU	FORMULAR
AFLMORSU	FORMULAS
AFLMORSW	WOLFRAMS
AFLMORTU	FOULMART
AFLMORTW	FLATWORM
AFLMOSST	FLOTSAMS
AFLMOSUY	FAMOUSLY
AFLNOPRU	APRONFUL
AFLNORST	FRONTALS
AFLNRTUU	UNARTFUL
AFLNTUUV	VAUNTFUL
AFLNTUUY	UNFAULTY
AFLOOSTW	WOOLFATS
AFLOPSTT	FLATTOPS
AFLORSSU	FUSAROLS
AFLORSUV	FLAVOURS
AFLORUVY	FLAVOURY
AFLOSTUU	FLATUOUS
AFLPRSTY	FLYTRAPS
AFLPSSTY	FLYPASTS
AFLRSTTU	STARTFUL
AFLRSTUY	TRAYFULS
AFMNNNUY	FUNNYMAN
AFMNNORT	FRONTMAN
AFMNORST	FORMANTS
AFMNOSUU	UNFAMOUS
AFMOOPRR	PROFORMA
AFMORSSU	AUSFORMS
AFMORSTU	FOUMARTS
AFMORTUY	FUMATORY
AFMOSSTU	SFUMATOS
AFNNOTTY	NONFATTY
AFNORRSW	FORWARNS
AFNORSTW	FANWORTS
AFNOSTUW	OUTFAWNS
AFOOPPRS	APPROOFS
AFOOPRRT	RATPROOF
AFOORSTZ	FORZATOS
	SFORZATO
AFOOSTWY	FOOTWAYS
AFORSTTW	FORSWATT
AFOSSTTU	OUTFASTS
AFOSSTUU	FASTUOUS
AGGGGILN	GAGGLING
AGGGHILN	HAGGLING
AGGGHINS	SHAGGING
AGGGILNN	GANGLING
AGGGILNR	GARGLING
	RAGGLING
AGGGILNS	LAGGINGS
	SLAGGING
AGGGILNW	WAGGLING
AGGGINNS	GANGINGS
	SNAGGING
AGGGINRS	RAGGINGS
AGGGINSS	SAGGINGS
AGGGINST	STAGGING
	TAGGINGS
AGGGINSU	GAUGINGS
AGGGINSW	SWAGGING
AGGGIYZZ	ZIGZAGGY
AGGHIILS	GHILGAIS
AGGHILNU	LAUGHING
AGGHILST	GASLIGHT
AGGHILSY	SHAGGILY
AGGHIMNO	HOMAGING
AGGHIMNS	GINGHAMS
AGGHINNP	PHANGING
AGGHINNS	GNASHING
	HANGINGS
AGGHINNW	WHANGING
AGGHINPR	GRAPHING
AGGHINST	GHASTING
AGGHINUW	WAUGHING
AGGHISTT	GASTIGHT
AGGHJMNO	MAHJONGG
AGGHLOOT	GOLGOTHA
AGGIIJJS	JIGAJIGS
AGGIILNN	ALIGNING
AGGIILNR	GLAIRING
AGGIILNS	SILAGING
AGGIILNT	LIGATING
	TAIGLING
AGGIILNV	GINGIVAL
AGGIIMNS	IMAGINGS
AGGIINNR	GRAINING
AGGIINNS	AGNISING
	GAININGS
AGGIINNZ	AGNIZING
AGGIINRS	AGRISING
AGGIINRT	TRIAGING
AGGIINRZ	AGRIZING
AGGIINST	AGISTING
AGGIINSU	AGUISING
AGGIINUZ	AGUIZING
AGGIJJOS	JIGAJOGS
AGGIJLNN	JANGLING
AGGIKNSS	GASKINGS
AGGILLNS	GINGALLS
AGGILLNU	ULLAGING
AGGILLNY	GALLYING
AGGILMNN	MANGLING
AGGILMNO	GLOAMING
AGGILMNR	MALGRING
AGGILMNU	GLAUMING
AGGILNNO	GANGLION
AGGILNNR	GNARLING
AGGILNNS	ANGLINGS
	SLANGING
AGGILNNT	GNATLING
	TANGLING
AGGILNNW	WANGLING
AGGILNOP	GALOPING
AGGILNOT	GLOATING
	GOATLING
AGGILNPU	PLAGUING
AGGILNPY	GAPINGLY
AGGILNRY	GRAYLING
	RAGINGLY
AGGILNSS	GLASSING
AGGILNSZ	GLAZINGS
AGGIMNRU	MAUGRING
AGGINNOR	GROANING
AGGINNOT	TANGOING
AGGINNOW	WAGONING
AGGINNPR	PRANGING
AGGINNPS	SPANGING
AGGINNRR	GNARRING
AGGINNRT	GRANTING
AGGINNRU	RAUNGING
AGGINNST	STANGING
AGGINNSW	GNAWINGS
AGGINNTU	GAUNTING
AGGINNTW	TWANGING
AGGINORT	GAROTING
AGGINOST	GIGATONS
AGGINOVY	VOYAGING
AGGINOWY	WAYGOING
AGGINPRS	GRASPING
	PARGINGS
	SPARGING
AGGINPSS	GASPINGS
AGGINPUZ	UPGAZING
AGGINRSS	GRASSING
	SIRGANGS
AGGINRST	GRATINGS
AGGINRSU	SUGARING
AGGINRSV	GRAVINGS
AGGINRSZ	GRAZINGS
AGGINRTY	GYRATING
AGGINRUU	AUGURING
AGGINRYZ	AGRYZING
AGGINSSS	GASSINGS
AGGINSST	STAGINGS
AGGINSWY	GAYWINGS
AGGIRTUZ	ZIGGURAT
AGGKLNNU	ANGKLUNG
AGGLLLOY	LOLLYGAG
AGGLLOOY	ALGOLOGY
AGGLMOOR	LOGOGRAM
AGGLNOPW	GANGPLOW
AGGLOORY	AGROLOGY
AGGLRSTY	STRAGGLY
AGGMORRS	GROGRAMS
AGGMOSTY	MYSTAGOG
AGGNOSSY	SYNAGOGS
AGGNUWZZ	ZUGZWANG
AGHHIILT	HIGHTAIL
AGHHINSS	SHASHING
AGHHISWY	HIGHWAYS
AGHHLOTU	ALTHOUGH
AGHIILNN	INHALING
AGHIILNS	NILGHAIS
AGHIINNS	HAININGS
AGHIINRT	AIRTHING
AGHIIPRR	HAIRGRIP
AGHIIRTT	AIRTIGHT
AGHIJNRT	NIGHTJAR
AGHIKNNS	SHANKING
AGHIKNNT	THANKING
AGHIKNRS	SHARKING
AGHIKNSS	SHAKINGS
AGHIKNSW	HAWKINGS
AGHILLNO	HALLOING
	HOLLAING
AGHILLNS	HALLINGS
AGHILLNT	ALLNIGHT
AGHILMTY	ALMIGHTY
AGHILNOO	HOOLIGAN
AGHILNOR	LONGHAIR
AGHILNOS	SHOALING
AGHILNOT	LOATHING
AGHILNPR	RALPHING
AGHILNPS	PLASHING
AGHILNRS	HARLINGS
	RINGHALS
AGHILNRY	NARGHILY
AGHILNSS	HASSLING
	LASHINGS
	SLANGISH
	SLASHING
AGHILNST	HALTINGS
	LATHINGS
AGHILNSU	LANGUISH
	NILGHAUS
	SHAULING
AGHILNSW	SHAWLING
	WHALINGS
AGHILNSY	NYLGHAIS
AGHILRSY	GARISHLY
AGHILRTY	GRAITHLY
AGHILSUY	AGUISHLY
AGHIMMNS	SHAMMING
AGHIMMNW	WHAMMING
AGHIMNSS	MASHINGS
	SMASHING
AGHIMNTY	THINGAMY

AGHIMOST	OGHAMIST
AGHIMPRU	GRAPHIUM
AGHINNOS	NIHONGAS
AGHINNOT	GNATHION
AGHINNSS	SNASHING
AGHINNST	TANGHINS
AGHINNTU	HAUNTING
AGHINNTY	ANYTHING
AGHINORS	ORANGISH
AGHINOST	HOASTING
AGHINPPW	WHAPPING
AGHINPPY	HAPPYING
AGHINPRS	HARPINGS
	PHRASING
	SHARPING
AGHINPSS	SHAPINGS
AGHINPSW	PSHAWING
AGHINQSU	QUASHING
AGHINRRU	HURRAING
AGHINRRY	HARRYING
AGHINRSS	SHARINGS
AGHINRST	TRASHING
AGHINRTW	THRAWING
	WRATHING
AGHINSST	HASTINGS
	STASHING
AGHINSSV	SHAVINGS
AGHINSSW	SWASHING
	WASHINGS
AGHINSTT	HATTINGS
AGHINSTW	SWATHING
	THAWINGS
AGHINUZZ	HUZZAING
AGHIOPRS	ISOGRAPH
AGHIPRRT	TRIGRAPH
AGHIRSTT	STRAIGHT
AGHISSTW	SIGHTSAW
AGHJMNOS	MAHJONGS
AGHKOSSW	GOSHAWKS
AGHLLMPU	GALLUMPH
AGHLMOOR	HOLOGRAM
AGHLMOOY	HOLOGAMY
AGHLMPSU	GALUMPHS
AGHLNOSU	SHOGUNAL
AGHLNSUY	NYLGHAUS
AGHLOOSS	GASOHOLS
AGHLOTUU	OUTLAUGH
AGHMMOOY	HOMOGAMY
AGHMNPSU	SPHAGNUM
AGHMOOPY	OMOPHAGY
AGHMOPRY	MYOGRAPH
AGHNNSTU	SHANTUNG
AGHNOORS	SHAGROON
AGHNOSTU	HANGOUTS
	TOHUNGAS
AGHNPRSY	SYNGRAPH
AGHNTTUU	UNTAUGHT
AGHOOPYZ	ZOOPHAGY
AGHOPSSW	SWAGSHOP
AGHORSTW	WARTHOGS
AGHRSTTU	STRAUGHT
AGIIIKMR	KIRIGAMI
AGIIILNS	LIAISING
AGIIINNS	INSIGNIA
AGIIKLNS	SKAILING
AGIIKNNT	ANTIKING
AGIIKNRT	TRAIKING
AGIILLLM	MILLIGAL
AGIILLNV	VIALLING
AGIILLOV	VILLAGIO
	VILLIAGO
AGIILMNP	IMPALING
AGIILMNS	MAILINGS
	MISALIGN
AGIILMNU	MIAULING
AGIILNNP	PLAINING
AGIILNNS	NAILINGS
	SNAILING
AGIILNNU	INGUINAL
AGIILNNV	ANVILING
AGIILNNY	INLAYING
AGIILNOP	PIGNOLIA
AGIILNOR	ORIGINAL
AGIILNOT	INTAGLIO
	LIGATION
	TAGLIONI
AGIILNOX	GLOXINIA
AGIILNPT	PLAITING
AGIILNQU	QUAILING
AGIILNRS	GLAIRINS
	RAILINGS
AGIILNRT	RINGTAIL
	TRAILING
AGIILNRV	RIVALING
	VIRGINAL
AGIILNSS	AISLINGS
	SAILINGS
AGIILNST	TAILINGS
AGIILNSW	WAILINGS
AGIILNTT	LITIGANT
AGIILNTV	VIGILANT
AGIILORU	OLIGURIA
AGIILOSV	VILIAGOS
AGIILPST	PIGTAILS
AGIILTVY	VAGILITY
AGIIMMNS	MAIMINGS
AGIIMMSS	IMAGISMS
AGIIMNNR	INARMING
AGIIMNOR	IGNORAMI
AGIIMNOU	MIAOUING
AGIIMNOW	MIAOWING
AGIIMNPV	IMPAVING
AGIIMNSS	AMISSING
AGIIMNST	GIANTISM
AGIIMNTT	MITIGANT
AGIIMORS	ORIGAMIS
AGIIMSST	IMAGISTS
AGIINNPS	SPAINING
AGIINNPT	PAINTING
	PATINING
AGIINNRS	INGRAINS
AGIINNRT	TRAINING
AGIINNRV	RAVINING
AGIINNST	SAINTING
	SATINING
	STAINING
AGIINNSW	SWAINING
AGIINNTT	TAINTING
AGIINOPT	OPIATING
AGIINORS	SIGNORIA
AGIINORT	RIGATONI
AGIINPRS	ASPIRING
	PAIRINGS
	PRAISING
AGIINPRT	PIRATING
AGIINRRV	ARRIVING
AGIINRSS	RAISINGS
AGIINRTT	ATTIRING
AGIINSSZ	ASSIZING
AGIINSTV	VISTAING
AGIINSTW	WAISTING
	WAITINGS
AGIISSTV	VISAGIST
AGIJLLNS	JINGALLS
AGIJLNPY	JAPINGLY
AGIJMNOR	MAJORING
AGIJNNSU	JAUNSING
AGIJNNTT	TJANTING
AGIJNNTU	JAUNTING
AGIJNRRS	JARRINGS
AGIKKNNS	SKANKING
AGIKLMOR	KILOGRAM
AGIKLNNP	PLANKING
AGIKLNNR	RANKLING
AGIKLNOP	POLKAING
AGIKLNOS	OAKLINGS
	SKOALING
AGIKLNST	SKLATING
	STALKING
	TALKINGS
AGIKLNSW	WALKINGS
AGIKLNTY	TAKINGLY
AGIKLNUW	WAULKING
AGIKLORY	KILOGRAY
AGIKMNNU	UNMAKING
AGIKMNPU	UPMAKING
AGIKMNRS	MARKINGS
AGIKMNSS	MASKINGS
AGIKNNPP	KNAPPING
AGIKNNPR	PRANKING
AGIKNNPS	SPANKING
AGIKNNRR	KNARRING
AGIKNNRS	RANKINGS
AGIKNNRU	UNRAKING
AGIKNNST	TANKINGS
AGIKNNSW	SWANKING
AGIKNORT	TROAKING
AGIKNOSS	SOAKINGS
AGIKNOST	GOATSKIN
AGIKNOSY	KAYOINGS
AGIKNPRS	PARKINGS
	SPARKING
AGIKNPTU	UPTAKING
AGIKNQSU	QUAKINGS
AGIKNRSS	SARKINGS
AGIKNRST	KARTINGS
	STARKING
AGIKNSST	SKATINGS
	TASKINGS
AGILLLNS	LALLINGS
AGILLMNS	SMALLING
AGILLMNU	MULLIGAN
AGILLMNY	MALIGNLY
AGILLMSU	GALLIUMS
AGILLNOW	ALLOWING
AGILLNOY	ALLOYING
AGILLNPS	SPALLING
AGILLNRU	ALLURING
	LINGULAR
AGILLNRY	NARGILLY
	RALLYING
AGILLNST	STALLING
AGILLNSU	LINGUALS
	LINGULAS
AGILLNSW	WALLINGS
AGILLNSY	SALLYING
	SIGNALLY
	SLANGILY
AGILLNTY	TALLYING
AGILLOOR	GILLAROO
AGILLOPT	GALLIPOT
AGILLORS	GORILLAS
AGILLOST	GALLIOTS
AGILLPRY	PLAYGIRL
AGILLPUY	PLAGUILY
AGILLSSU	LUGSAILS
AGILLSSY	GLASSILY
AGILMMNS	LAMMINGS
	SLAMMING
	SMALMING
AGILMNNT	MANTLING
AGILMNPS	LAMPINGS
	PSALMING
	SAMPLING
AGILMNQU	QUALMING
AGILMNRS	MARLINGS
AGILMNST	MALTINGS
AGILMOPR	LIPOGRAM
AGILMORS	ALGORISM
AGILMPSU	PLAGIUMS
AGILNNNP	PLANNING
AGILNNOP	PANGOLIN
AGILNNOS	LOANINGS
AGILNNPT	PLANTING
AGILNNRS	SNARLING
AGILNNSS	LINSANGS
AGILNNST	SLANTING
	TANLINGS
AGILNNUW	UNLAWING
AGILNNUY	UNGAINLY
	UNLAYING
AGILNOOO	OOGONIAL
AGILNOOS	ISOGONAL
AGILNOPR	PAROLING
AGILNOPS	GALOPINS
AGILNOPT	PLOATING
AGILNORS	RANGOLIS
AGILNORT	TRIGONAL
AGILNOSS	GLOSSINA
	LASSOING
AGILNOST	ANTILOGS
	SALTOING
	SOLATING
AGILNOSV	SALVOING
AGILNOTT	TOTALING
AGILNOTY	ANTILOGY
AGILNPPP	PLAPPING
AGILNPPS	LAPPINGS
	SAPPLING
	SLAPPING
AGILNPPY	APPLYING
AGILNPRS	GRAPLINS
	SPARLING
	SPRINGAL
AGILNPSS	SAPLINGS
AGILNPST	PLATINGS
	SPALTING
	STAPLING
AGILNPSW	LAPWINGS
	SPAWLING
AGILNPSY	PALSYING
	SPLAYING
AGILNPTT	PLATTING
AGILNPUY	UPLAYING
AGILNRSS	RASSLING
AGILNRST	RATLINGS
	STARLING
AGILNRSU	SINGULAR
AGILNRSW	WARLINGS
	WARSLING
AGILNRTT	RATTLING
AGILNRTW	TRAWLING
AGILNRVY	RAVINGLY
AGILNRWW	WRAWLING
AGILNRWX	WRAXLING
AGILNSST	ANGLISTS
	LASTINGS
	SALTINGS
	SLATINGS
AGILNSSV	SALVINGS
AGILNSSW	SWALINGS
AGILNSTT	SLATTING
AGILNSTU	SALUTING
AGILNSUV	AVULSING
AGILNSUW	WAULINGS
AGILNSVY	SAVINGLY
AGILNSWW	WAWLINGS
AGILNSWY	SWAYLING
AGILNTTT	TATTLING
AGILNTTW	WATTLING

AGILNTUV	VAULTING
AGILNTUX	LUXATING
AGILNTWZ	WALTZING
AGILNTXY	TAXINGLY
AGILOOPY	APIOLOGY
AGILOORS	GLORIOSA
AGILOOXY	AXIOLOGY
AGILOPST	GALIPOTS
AGILORSS	GIRASOLS
AGILORSW	AIRGLOWS
AGILOSST	SALIGOTS
AGILRSSY	GRASSILY
AGILSYYZ	SYZYGIAL
AGIMMNPS	SPAMMING
AGIMMNRS	SMARMING
AGIMMNRT	TRAMMING
AGIMMOSY	MISOGAMY
AGIMNNOS	MASONING
AGIMNNOW	WOMANING
AGIMNNRU	MANURING
	UNARMING
AGIMNNSW	SWINGMAN
AGIMNNTU	UNTAMING
AGIMNOOV	AMOOVING
AGIMNORR	ARMORING
AGIMNORS	ORGANISM
	ROAMINGS
AGIMNORU	ORIGANUM
AGIMNORY	AGRIMONY
AGIMNOST	ANTISMOG
AGIMNOSV	VAMOSING
AGIMNPPS	MAPPINGS
AGIMNPRS	RAMPINGS
AGIMNPRT	TRAMPING
AGIMNPSS	SPASMING
AGIMNPST	STAMPING
	TAMPINGS
AGIMNPSV	VAMPINGS
AGIMNPSW	SWAMPING
AGIMNRRY	MARRYING
AGIMNRST	MIGRANTS
	SMARTING
AGIMNRSW	SWARMING
	WARMINGS
AGIMNRSY	MYRINGAS
AGIMNRTU	MATURING
AGIMNSSU	ASSUMING
AGIMNSTT	MATTINGS
AGIMNTTU	MUTATING
AGIMORRT	MIGRATOR
AGIMORSS	ISOGRAMS
AGIMORSU	GOURAMIS
AGIMQRUY	QUAGMIRY
AGIMRRST	TRIGRAMS
AGINNNNY	NANNYING
AGINNNOY	ANNOYING
AGINNNPS	PANNINGS
	SPANNING
AGINNNST	TANNINGS
AGINNNSV	VANNINGS
AGINNNSW	SWANNING
AGINNNUW	UNWANING
AGINNOOP	NAPOOING
AGINNOPR	APRONING
AGINNOPT	POIGNANT
AGINNORT	IGNORANT
AGINNOST	ASTONING
AGINNOSU	ANGINOUS
AGINNOTT	NOTATING
AGINNPPS	SNAPPING
AGINNPRW	PRAWNING
AGINNPST	PANTINGS
AGINNPSW	SPAWNING
	WINGSPAN
AGINNPUY	UNPAYING
AGINNQTU	QUANTING
AGINNRRS	SNARRING
AGINNRSS	SNARINGS
AGINNRST	RANTINGS
	STARNING
AGINNRSW	WARNINGS
AGINNRTT	TRANTING
AGINNRTU	NATURING
AGINNRTY	TRAYNING
	TYRANING
AGINNSTU	SAUNTING
	UNSATING
AGINNSTW	WANTINGS
AGINNSTY	STAYNING
AGINNSUY	UNSAYING
AGINNSWY	YAWNINGS
AGINNTTU	ATTUNING
	NUTATING
	TAUNTING
AGINNTUV	VAUNTING
AGINNTUX	UNTAXING
AGINNVVY	NAVVYING
AGINOOPS	POGONIAS
AGINOORT	ROGATION
AGINOPPS	APPOSING
AGINOPQU	OPAQUING
AGINOPRV	VAPORING
AGINORRS	GARRISON
	ROARINGS
AGINORRW	ARROWING
AGINORRZ	RAZORING
AGINORSS	ASSIGNOR
	SIGNORAS
	SOARINGS
AGINORST	ORGANIST
	ROASTING
AGINORSU	AROUSING
AGINORSV	SAVORING
AGINORTT	ROTATING
	TROATING
AGINORTV	GRAVITON
AGINORTY	GYRATION
	ORGANITY
AGINOSST	AGONISTS
AGINOSSU	SAGOUINS
AGINOSTT	TANGOIST
	TOASTING
AGINOSTU	OUTGAINS
AGINPPRS	RAPPINGS
AGINPPRT	TRAPPING
AGINPPRW	WRAPPING
AGINPPST	STAPPING
	TAPPINGS
AGINPPSW	SWAPPING
AGINPPTU	PUPATING
AGINPPUY	APPUYING
AGINPRRS	SPARRING
AGINPRRY	PARRYING
AGINPRSS	PARSINGS
	PINGRASS
	RASPINGS
AGINPRST	PARTINGS
	PRATINGS
AGINPRSW	WARPINGS
AGINPRSY	PRAYINGS
	SPRAYING
AGINPRTT	PRATTING
AGINPRTU	UPRATING
AGINPRTY	PARTYING
AGINPSSS	PASSINGS
AGINPSST	PASTINGS
AGINPSSU	PAUSINGS
AGINPSTT	SPATTING
AGINPSWY	YAWPINGS
AGINPSZZ	SPAZZING
AGINQRSU	SQUARING
AGINRRST	STARRING
	TARRINGS
AGINRRTY	TARRYING
AGINRSST	GASTRINS
	STARINGS
AGINRSSU	ASSURING
AGINRSSY	SYRINGAS
AGINRSTT	RATTINGS
	STARTING
AGINRSTV	STARVING
AGINRSTW	RINGTAWS
	STRAWING
	WRASTING
AGINRSTY	STINGRAY
	STRAYING
AGINRSVW	SWARVING
AGINRSVY	VARYINGS
AGINRSWY	RINGWAYS
AGINRTYY	GYNIATRY
AGINSSTT	TASTINGS
AGINSSTW	WASTINGS
AGINSSWY	SWAYINGS
AGINSTTT	TATTINGS
AGINSTTW	SWATTING
AGINSVVY	SAVVYING
AGINSWWX	WAXWINGS
AGIOORSU	ORAGIOUS
AGIOORSZ	GRAZIOSO
AGIOORTU	AUTOGIRO
AGIOPPRT	AGITPROP
AGIOPRUY	UROPYGIA
AGIORRTT	GRATTOIR
AGIORSST	AGISTORS
	ORGIASTS
AGIRSSTU	SASTRUGI
AGIRSTUZ	ZASTRUGI
AGIRTTUY	GRATUITY
AGJLRSUU	JUGULARS
AGJNOORS	JARGOONS
AGJNOPST	JOGPANTS
AGKLNNOS	ANKLONGS
AGKLNNSU	ANKLUNGS
AGKMMORY	KYMOGRAM
AGKMNOPS	KAMPONGS
AGKMPRSU	PUGMARKS
AGKNOPST	PAKTONGS
AGKORRSW	RAGWORKS
AGKORSSW	GASWORKS
AGLLLNOW	LONGWALL
AGLLMOPW	GLOWLAMP
AGLLNOOS	GALLOONS
AGLLNSTU	GALLNUTS
	NUTGALLS
AGLLOOST	GALLOOTS
AGLLOPSU	PLUGOLAS
AGLLPRSU	SPURGALL
AGLLRUVY	VULGARLY
AGLMOOTY	ATMOLOGY
AGLMOPSY	POLYGAMS
AGLMOPYY	POLYGAMY
AGLMORSU	GLAMOURS
AGLNORSU	LANGUORS
AGLNOSST	GLASNOST
AGLNOSUU	ANGULOUS
AGLNOSWY	LONGWAYS
AGLNPSUY	GUNPLAYS
AGLNRUUV	UNVULGAR
AGLNSSSU	SUNGLASS
AGLNSTUY	YGLAUNST
AGLOOPST	GOALPOST
AGLOOTUY	AUTOLOGY
AGLOPRSS	LOPGRASS
AGLORSSY	GLOSSARY
AGLPSSSY	SPYGLASS
AGLRTTUU	GUTTURAL
AGLSTUUY	AUGUSTLY
AGMMNOOR	MONOGRAM
	NOMOGRAM
AGMMNOOY	MONOGAMY
AGMMOORT	TOMOGRAM
AGMMORSY	MYOGRAMS
AGMMORYZ	ZYMOGRAM
AGMNNOSW	GOWNSMAN
AGMNOOPR	PORNOMAG
AGMNOORS	SONOGRAM
AGMNOORY	AGRONOMY
AGMNORST	ANGSTROM
AGMNORSU	ORGANUMS
AGMNSSTU	MUSTANGS
AGMNSSTY	GYMNASTS
	SYNTAGMS
AGMOOOSU	OOGAMOUS
AGMOOPRY	POROGAMY
AGMOOTVY	VAGOTOMY
AGMOPRRS	PROGRAMS
AGMOPRSU	GOPURAMS
AGMORRSW	RAGWORMS
AGMRSSSU	GRASSUMS
AGNNNOOS	NONAGONS
AGNNOOPT	POONTANG
AGNNOORS	ORGANONS
AGNNOQTU	QUANTONG
AGNNORSU	NONSUGAR
AGNNOTUW	OUTGNAWN
AGNORRST	GRANTORS
AGNORTUY	NUGATORY
AGNOSTUW	OUTGNAWS
AGNPPRSU	UPSPRANG
AGNRSSTU	NUTGRASS
AGOORRTY	ROGATORY
AGOORTUY	AUTOGYRO
AGOPPSST	STOPGAPS
AGORRSST	GROSSART
	ROTGRASS
AGORRSTW	RAGWORTS
AGORRSTY	GYRATORS
AGORRTYY	GYRATORY
AGORSTTY	GYROSTAT
AGORSTUY	GRAYOUTS
AHHIKKRS	KHIRKAHS
AHHIKLSS	SHASHLIK
AHHILNPT	PHTHALIN
AHHILOST	HAILSHOT
AHHILPSW	WHIPLASH
AHHIMMSS	MISHMASH
AHHIMNSU	HAHNIUMS
AHHINSST	SHANTIHS
AHHIPRSS	SHARPISH
AHHISSTT	SHITTAHS
AHHKMOTW	HAWKMOTH
AHHKRSTU	KASHRUTH
AHHLMRTY	RHYTHMAL
AHHLNOPT	NAPHTHOL
AHHLNPTY	NAPHTHYL
AHHMPRRU	HARRUMPH
AHHMPRSU	HARUMPHS
AHHNORTW	HAWTHORN
AHHOPRSS	SHOPHARS
AHHOPSTU	APHTHOUS
AHHPSTUZ	HUTZPAHS
AHIIILMN	MALIHINI
AHIIKRSS	RIKISHAS
	SHIKARIS
AHIILNPS	PLAINISH
AHIILOST	HALIOTIS
AHIILPTW	WHIPTAIL
AHIILRTY	HILARITY
AHIIMNNO	HOMINIAN
AHIIMNOT	HIMATION

AHIIMNST	HISTAMIN
	ISTHMIAN
	THIAMINS
AHIIMOPX	AMPHIOXI
AHIIMRST	ISARITHM
AHIIMSSS	SASHIMIS
AHIINOPT	PHOTINIA
AHIINOTT	TITHONIA
AHIINPRS	HAIRPINS
AHIINPST	ANTISHIP
AHIINSST	SAINTISH
AHIINSSW	SWAINISH
AHIINSTU	HUITAINS
AHIINSTZ	THIAZINS
AHIIOPST	HOSPITIA
AHIIPRSS	AIRSHIPS
AHIKLNRS	RINKHALS
AHIKLRSY	RAKISHLY
AHIKLSSS	SHASLIKS
AHIKMNSS	KHAMSINS
AHIKMRSS	KASHMIRS
AHIKNPRS	PRANKISH
AHIKNPST	TANKSHIP
AHIKORRW	HAIRWORK
AHIKPRSS	SPARKISH
AHIKRSSW	RIKSHAWS
AHILLMOU	HALLOUMI
AHILLMPS	PHALLISM
AHILLMSS	SMALLISH
AHILLMTU	THALLIUM
AHILLNOS	HALLIONS
AHILLNPS	PHALLINS
AHILLNRT	INTHRALL
AHILLNST	ANTHILLS
AHILLNTW	WANTHILL
AHILLPST	PHALLIST
AHILLSTT	TALLITHS
AHILLSVY	LAVISHLY
AHILMMSS	MASHLIMS
AHILMNSS	MASHLINS
AHILMOPT	PHILAMOT
AHILMOST	HALIMOTS
	MAILSHOT
AHILMQSU	QUALMISH
AHILMTUZ	HALUTZIM
AHILNOPS	SIPHONAL
AHILNOPT	OLIPHANT
AHILNORT	HORNTAIL
AHILNRST	INTHRALS
AHILOORT	LOTHARIO
AHILOPSS	ALPHOSIS
	HAPLOSIS
AHILOPST	HOSPITAL
AHILOSTU	HALITOUS
AHILOSTZ	THIAZOLS
AHILPPSS	PALSHIPS
	SHIPLAPS
AHILPRTU	ULTRAHIP
AHILPSSY	PHYSALIS
AHILPSXY	PHYLAXIS
AHILRSTY	TRASHILY
AHILRTWY	WRATHILY
AHIMMNSU	HUMANISM
AHIMMORZ	MAHZORIM
AHIMMOSS	SHAMOSIM
AHIMMOSV	MOSHAVIM
AHIMNOST	HOISTMAN
	MANIHOTS
AHIMNOSW	WOMANISH
AHIMNSTU	HUMANIST
AHIMNTUY	HUMANITY
AHIMOOSY	YAHOOISM
AHIMOPRS	APHORISM
	MORPHIAS
AHIMOPST	OPSIMATH
AHIMORRW	HAIRWORM
AHIMPPSS	SAPPHISM
AHIMPRST	TRAMPISH
AHIMPSSW	SWAMPISH
AHIMRSST	SMARTISH
	THRIMSAS
AHIMSSTV	MITSVAHS
AHIMSTUZ	AZIMUTHS
AHIMSTVZ	MITZVAHS
AHINNNSY	NANNYISH
AHINNOPT	ANTIPHON
AHINNSTX	XANTHINS
AHINOOPY	HYPONOIA
AHINOPRU	OPHIURAN
AHINORST	TRAHISON
AHINOSST	ASTONISH
AHINOSTZ	HOATZINS
AHINPPSS	SNAPPISH
AHINPRST	TRANSHIP
AHINPRSY	SYRPHIAN
AHINPSWW	WHIPSAWN
AHINQSUV	VANQUISH
AHINRSTY	RHYTINAS
AHINRSVY	VARNISHY
AHINSSTU	INHAUSTS
AHIOOPPT	PHOTOPIA
AHIOOSST	ATISHOOS
AHIOPRST	APHORIST
AHIOPRSU	OPHIURAS
AHIOPRSV	VAPORISH
AHIOPSXY	HYPOXIAS
AHIORSST	SHORTIAS
AHIORSTV	TOVARISH
AHIORSUV	HAVIOURS
AHIOSTWY	HOISTWAY
AHIPPSST	SAPPHIST
AHIPRSST	HARPISTS
	STARSHIP
AHIPRSSW	WARSHIPS
AHIPRSWY	WHIPRAYS
AHIPSSWW	WHIPSAWS
AHIPSSWY	SHIPWAYS
AHIQRSSU	SQUARISH
AHIRRSST	STIRRAHS
AHIRSSTT	STARTISH
AHIRSSTW	TRISHAWS
AHISSSTU	SHIATSUS
AHISSTTW	WHATSITS
AHISSTUZ	SHIATZUS
AHISTTWW	WHITTAWS
AHKLOPST	SHOPTALK
AHKLORTW	LATHWORK
AHKMOORR	MARKHOOR
AHKMORRS	MARKHORS
AHKMRSTU	MUKHTARS
AHKNOTTU	OUTTHANK
AHKNOTUY	THANKYOU
AHKRSSTU	KASHRUTS
	TUSHKARS
AHLLLOOP	POOLHALL
AHLLNOOS	SHALLOON
AHLLNOSS	SHALLONS
AHLLNOSY	HALLYONS
AHLLNOUW	UNHALLOW
AHLLNRTU	TURNHALL
AHLLOPSS	SHALLOPS
AHLLOSST	SHALLOTS
AHLLOSSW	SHALLOWS
AHLLOSTU	THALLOUS
AHLLOSTY	TALLYHOS
AHLLPRYY	PHYLLARY
AHLMMOPY	LYMPHOMA
AHLMMSSU	MASHLUMS
AHLMNOOR	HORMONAL
AHLMOOPS	OMPHALOS
AHLMOPTY	POLYMATH
AHLMOSUU	HAMULOUS
AHLMSTYZ	SHMALTZY
AHLNNORT	LANTHORN
AHLNOPRS	ALPHORNS
AHLNOPST	HAPLONTS
	NAPHTOLS
AHLNORST	ALTHORNS
AHLNRTWY	THRAWNLY
AHLOOPSW	WHOOPLAS
AHLOOSTW	WOOLHATS
AHLOPSST	SLAPSHOT
AHLORRTY	HARLOTRY
AHLORTTU	ULTRAHOT
AHLOSTUU	OUTHAULS
AHLRSTUY	LATHYRUS
AHLRTTWY	THWARTLY
AHMMMOST	MAMMOTHS
AHMMMSUU	HUMMAUMS
AHMNNNOU	NONHUMAN
AHMNNSTU	HUNTSMAN
	MANHUNTS
AHMNOPST	PHANTOMS
AHMNOPTY	PHANTOMY
AHMNORRS	RAMSHORN
AHMOOPPT	PHOTOMAP
AHMOOPSS	SHAMPOOS
AHMOORSW	WASHROOM
AHMOOSSS	SAMSHOOS
AHMOPTYY	MYOPATHY
AHMORRST	SHORTARM
AHMORRSU	MORRHUAS
AHMORSST	HARMOSTS
AHMORSTY	HARMOSTY
AHMORTTW	TAMWORTH
AHMORTUW	WARMOUTH
AHMOSTTW	MOSTWHAT
AHMPSSSU	SMASHUPS
AHMPSTYY	SYMPATHY
AHMQSSUU	MUSQUASH
AHMRSSTY	THRYMSAS
AHNNSTYY	SYNANTHY
AHNOOPPY	APOPHONY
AHNOOPRS	HARPOONS
AHNOOPSU	APHONOUS
AHNOORRY	HONORARY
AHNOPPSW	PAWNSHOP
AHNOPPSY	PANSOPHY
AHNOPSST	SNAPSHOT
AHNORSSX	SAXHORNS
AHNORTWW	WANWORTH
AHNOSTTW	WHATNOTS
AHNOSTUX	XANTHOUS
AHNPPSUU	PUPUNHAS
AHOOPTYZ	ZOOPATHY
AHOOSSTY	SOOTHSAY
AHOOSTTW	SAWTOOTH
AHOPSSTW	WASHPOTS
AHOPSTTW	TOWPATHS
AHOPSTUW	SOUTHPAW
AHORTTUW	WATTHOUR
AHOSSTUW	WASHOUTS
AHOSSTUY	SOUTHSAY
AHRSTUWY	THRUWAYS
AIIILLVX	LIXIVIAL
AIIILMST	MILITIAS
AIIILNST	INITIALS
AIIILRVZ	VIZIRIAL
AIIIMRSS	SAIMIRIS
AIIIRSSS	SIRIASIS
AIIJKMOT	KOMITAJI
AIIJNRTX	JANITRIX
AIIKKSUY	SUKIYAKI
AIIKLLST	SILKTAIL
AIIKLNRR	LARRIKIN
AIIKMMSS	SKIMMIAS
AIIKMNNN	MANNIKIN
AIIKMNNS	MANIKINS
AIIKMNPR	MINIPARK
AIIKNNNP	PANNIKIN
AIIKORTY	YAKITORI
AIIKTTZZ	TZATZIKI
AIILLLMT	MILLTAIL
AIILLLUV	ILLUVIAL
AIILLMRY	MILLIARY
AIILLMST	TALLISIM
AIILLMTT	TALLITIM
AIILLNNV	VANILLIN
AIILLNOP	POLLINIA
AIILLNOT	ILLATION
AIILLNPT	ANTIPILL
AIILLNSV	VILLAINS
AIILLNVY	VILLAINY
AIILLPRS	SLIPRAIL
	SPIRILLA
AIILLQSU	QUILLAIS
AIILLUWW	WILLIWAU
AIILLWWW	WILLIWAW
AIILMMNS	MINIMALS
AIILMNOS	MONILIAS
AIILMNOT	LIMATION
	MILTONIA
AIILMNPS	ALPINISM
AIILMNPT	PALMITIN
AIILMNTT	MILITANT
AIILMNTU	MINUTIAL
AIILMPUV	IMPLUVIA
AIILMRST	MISTRIAL
	TRIALISM
AIILMRTY	LIMITARY
	MILITARY
AIILMSTV	VITALISM
AIILNOPV	PAVILION
AIILNOSS	LIAISONS
AIILNOSV	VISIONAL
AIILNPST	ALPINIST
	ANTISLIP
	PINTAILS
	TAILSPIN
AIILNSTY	SALINITY
AIILNTTY	LATINITY
AIILOPPS	PAPILIOS
AIILORSV	RAVIOLIS
AIILQSSU	SILIQUAS
AIILRSTT	TRIALIST
AIILRTTY	TRIALITY
AIILRTVY	RIVALITY
AIILSTTV	VITALIST
AIILTTVY	VITALITY
AIIMMMST	MAMMITIS
AIIMMNNY	MINYANIM
AIIMMNSS	ANIMISMS
AIIMMNSX	MAXIMINS
AIIMMNTY	IMMANITY
AIIMMSTX	MAXIMIST
AIIMNNOS	INSOMNIA
AIIMNNSV	MINIVANS
AIIMNPSS	PIANISMS
	SINAPISM
AIIMNPST	IMPAINTS
	MISPAINT
AIIMNPSX	PANMIXIS
AIIMNRST	MARTINIS
	MISTRAIN
AIIMNSST	ANIMISTS
	SAINTISM
	SAMNITIS
AIIMNSTT	IMITANTS
	TITANISM
AIIMNSTV	NATIVISM

	VITAMINS
AIIMNTTU	TITANIUM
AIIMOPSX	APOMIXIS
AIIMORTT	IMITATOR
	TIMARIOT
AIIMOSST	AMITOSIS
AIIMPPRS	PRIAPISM
AIIMPRTY	IMPARITY
AIIMRSST	SIMITARS
AIIMRSTU	TIRAMISU
AIIMRUVV	VIVARIUM
AIIMSSTT	MASTITIS
AIINNOPS	PIANINOS
AIINNOSV	INVASION
AIINNQSU	QUININAS
AIINNQTU	QUINTAIN
AIINNSTY	INSANITY
AIINOOSV	AVOISION
AIINOPSS	SINOPIAS
AIINORTT	ANTIRIOT
	TRITONIA
AIINOSTT	NOTITIAS
AIINPRSS	ASPIRINS
AIINPSST	PIANISTS
AIINRRTT	IRRITANT
AIINRSTV	VITRAINS
AIINRSTZ	TRIAZINS
AIINSTTV	NATIVIST
	VISITANT
AIINTTVY	NATIVITY
AIIORRST	SARTORII
AIIORSTT	AORTITIS
AIIORSTV	OVARITIS
AIIORTTV	VITIATOR
AIIPRRST	AIRSTRIP
AIIPRSST	PIARISTS
AIIPRVVY	VIVIPARY
AIIPSTTU	PITUITAS
AIIRSSTT	SATIRIST
	SITARIST
AIISSSTY	SYSSITIA
AIJKKNOU	KINKAJOU
AIJLLOOR	JILLAROO
AIJLLOVY	JOVIALLY
AIJLNTUY	JAUNTILY
AIJLOTVY	JOVIALTY
AIJMORTY	MAJORITY
AIJNOPPY	POPINJAY
AIJNORST	JANITORS
AIKKMOST	KOMATIKS
AIKKNOTY	KANTIKOY
AIKKRTUZ	ZIKKURAT
AIKLLLMW	WALKMILL
AIKLLMRR	RILLMARK
AIKLLMUW	WAUKMILL
AIKLLSTY	STALKILY
AIKLMNNS	LINKSMAN
AIKLMPSU	LAMPUKIS
AIKLMPTU	KALUMPIT
AIKLNPST	LANTSKIP
AIKLNSWY	SWANKILY
AIKLOSUV	SOUVLAKI
AIKLOTTW	KILOWATT
AIKLPRSY	SPARKILY
AIKLRSTT	TITLARKS
AIKLSSSY	SKYSAILS
AIKMMNOO	MAKIMONO
AIKMMRSS	MISMARKS
AIKMNOOY	YAKIMONO
AIKMORSS	KOMISSAR
AIKMRSTZ	SITZMARK
AIKNNOOS	NAINSOOK
AIKNNSSW	SWANSKIN
AIKNORST	SKIATRON
AIKNORTY	KARYOTIN
AIKNOSTT	STOTINKA
AIKRSSTY	SATYRISK
AIKRSTUZ	ZIKURATS
AILLLNOO	LINALOOL
AILLLNOS	LINALOLS
AILLLPSU	LAPILLUS
AILLMMSY	SMALMILY
AILLMNQU	QUILLMAN
AILLMNST	STILLMAN
AILLMOST	MAILLOTS
	MISALLOT
AILLMOSY	LOYALISM
AILLMOTY	MOLALITY
AILLMPRY	PRIMALLY
AILLMPSU	PALLIUMS
AILLMSSW	SAWMILLS
AILLMUUV	ALLUVIUM
AILLNNOS	LANOLINS
AILLNOPP	PAPILLON
AILLNOPS	PAILLONS
AILLNOPV	PAVILLON
AILLNORT	ANTIROLL
AILLNOST	STALLION
AILLNOSU	ALLUSION
AILLNOUV	ALLUVION
AILLNPSY	SPINALLY
AILLNPTY	PLIANTLY
AILLNSST	INSTALLS
AILLOQTU	TOQUILLA
AILLORSY	SAILORLY
AILLORSZ	ZORILLAS
AILLORTT	LITTORAL
	TORTILLA
AILLOSTY	LOYALIST
AILLPPRU	PUPILLAR
AILLPPSU	SUPPLIAL
AILLPPTU	PULPITAL
AILLPRSY	SPIRALLY
AILLPRTY	PALTRILY
AILLPSTY	PLAYLIST
AILLPSUV	PLUVIALS
AILLPSWY	SPILLWAY
AILLQSSU	SQUILLAS
AILLRSTY	RALLYIST
AILLRTUY	RITUALLY
AILLRTWY	WILLYART
AILLSTWW	WITWALLS
AILLSUVY	VISUALLY
AILLWWWY	WILLYWAW
AILMMNOO	MONOMIAL
AILMMNUU	ALUMINUM
AILMMOOR	MAILROOM
AILMMORS	MORALISM
AILMMORT	IMMORTAL
AILMMRSY	SMARMILY
AILMMSSY	MYALISMS
AILMMSTU	SUMMITAL
AILMMSUU	ALUMIUMS
AILMNNOS	NOMINALS
AILMNNOT	MANNITOL
AILMNNTU	LUMINANT
AILMNOOP	PALOMINO
AILMNOOR	MONORAIL
AILMNOOS	MOONSAIL
AILMNOOT	MOTIONAL
AILMNOPR	PROLAMIN
AILMNOPS	LAMPIONS
AILMNOPT	PILOTMAN
AILMNOPY	PALIMONY
AILMNORT	TORMINAL
AILMNOSS	MALISONS
AILMNOSU	LAMINOUS
AILMNPSS	MISPLANS
	PLASMINS
AILMNPST	IMPLANTS
	MISPLANT
AILMNPTU	PLATINUM
AILMNRSU	MURLAINS
AILMNRUY	LUMINARY
AILMNSTU	SIMULANT
AILMOORS	SAILROOM
AILMOORT	MOTORAIL
	MOTORIAL
AILMOOSV	MOVIOLAS
AILMOPRX	PROXIMAL
AILMORSS	ORALISMS
	SOLARISM
AILMORST	MORALIST
AILMORSU	SOLARIUM
AILMORSY	ROYALISM
AILMORTY	MOLARITY
	MORALITY
AILMOSTT	TOTALISM
AILMOSTU	SOLATIUM
AILMOSTV	VOLTAISM
AILMPPSY	MISAPPLY
AILMPRSU	PRIMULAS
AILMPSST	PALMISTS
	PSALMIST
AILMPSSY	MISPLAYS
AILMPSTY	PTYALISM
AILMRRSU	RURALISM
AILMRSST	MISTRALS
AILMRSSU	SIMULARS
	SURMISAL
AILMRSTU	ALTRUISM
	MURALIST
	ULTRAISM
AILNNOOT	NOTIONAL
AILNNORV	NONRIVAL
	NONVIRAL
AILNNOSS	SOLANINS
AILNNOST	ANTLIONS
AILNNOSU	UNISONAL
AILNNOTU	LUNATION
AILNNPRU	PINNULAR
AILNNPSU	PINNULAS
AILNNPTU	UNPLIANT
AILNNSTU	INSULANT
AILNOOPT	OPTIONAL
AILNOOST	SOLATION
AILNOPPT	OPPILANT
AILNOPRU	UNIPOLAR
AILNOPRV	PARVOLIN
AILNOPSY	POLYNIAS
AILNOPTV	ANVILTOP
AILNOPTY	PONYTAIL
AILNOQSU	AQUILONS
AILNORST	TONSILAR
AILNORTZ	TRIZONAL
AILNOSSS	SASSOLIN
AILNOSTY	LANOSITY
AILNOSUV	AVULSION
AILNOSVY	SYNOVIAL
AILNOTTV	VOLITANT
AILNOTTY	TONALITY
AILNOTUX	LUXATION
AILNPPSY	SNAPPILY
AILNPRSU	PURSLAIN
AILNPRSW	PRAWLINS
AILNPRUV	PULVINAR
AILNPSTU	NUPTIALS
	PATULINS
	UNPLAITS
AILNPSTY	PTYALINS
AILNPSUU	NAUPLIUS
AILNPTTU	TULIPANT
AILNQRTU	TRANQUIL
AILNQSTU	QUINTALS
AILNQTUY	QUAINTLY
AILNRSSU	INSULARS
AILNRSTT	RATTLINS
AILNRSTU	LUNARIST
AILNRTTU	RUTILANT
AILNRUWY	UNWARILY
AILNSSTU	STUNSAIL
	UNALISTS
AILNSTTU	LUTANIST
AILNSTUU	NAUTILUS
AILOOPRT	TROOPIAL
AILOORRS	SORORIAL
AILOORST	ISOLATOR
	OSTIOLAR
AILOORSW	WOORALIS
AILOORTV	VIOLATOR
AILOPRRV	PROVIRAL
AILOPRSU	PLIOSAUR
AILOPRTU	TROUPIAL
AILOPRTY	POLARITY
AILOPRUY	POLYURIA
AILOPSST	APOSTILS
	TOPSAILS
AILOPSTT	TALIPOTS
AILOQSTU	ALIQUOTS
AILORSST	ORALISTS
	SOLARIST
AILORSTU	SUTORIAL
AILORSTY	ROYALIST
	SOLITARY
AILORSUW	WOURALIS
AILORSVY	SAVORILY
AILORTTU	TUTORIAL
AILORTUV	OUTRIVAL
AILOSSTT	ALTOISTS
AILOSSTU	OUTSAILS
AILOSTTT	TOTALIST
AILOTTTY	TOTALITY
AILPPRUY	PUPILARY
AILPPSSY	PAYSLIPS
AILPQSSU	PASQUILS
AILPRSSU	SPIRULAS
	UPRISALS
AILPRSTU	STIPULAR
AILPSSWY	SLIPWAYS
AILPSTUY	PLAYSUIT
AILQSTTU	QUITTALS
AILRRSTU	RURALIST
AILRRSTY	STARRILY
AILRRTUY	RURALITY
AILRSSTU	TISSULAR
	TRISULAS
AILRSSTY	TRYSAILS
AILRSTTU	ALTRUIST
	TITULARS
	ULTRAIST
AILRSTTY	STRAITLY
AILRSUVV	SURVIVAL
AILRTTUY	TITULARY
AILSSTUW	LAWSUITS
AIMMMNOU	AMMONIUM
AIMMMSUX	MAXIMUMS
AIMMNORT	MORTMAIN
AIMMNPTU	TIMPANUM
AIMMNSTU	MANUMITS
AIMMORSS	AMORISMS
AIMMOSST	ATOMISMS
	SOMATISM
AIMMOSSU	MIASMOUS
AIMMRRSY	MISMARRY
AIMMRSUU	MASURIUM
AIMNNOPT	POINTMAN
AIMNNOSS	MANSIONS
	ONANISMS
AIMNNOTU	MOUNTAIN
AIMNNOTY	ANTIMONY

ANTINOMY
AIMNNRTU RUMINANT
AIMNOOOZ ZOONOMIA
AIMNOORV OMNIVORA
AIMNOOST AMOTIONS
AIMNOOTY MYOTONIA
AIMNOPRS RAMPIONS
AIMNOPRT PROTAMIN
AIMNOPST MAINTOPS
PTOMAINS
TAMPIONS
AIMNOPTV PIVOTMAN
AIMNOQRU MAROQUIN
AIMNORSU MAINOURS
AIMNORTY MINATORY
AIMNOSST STASIMON
AIMNOSTU MANITOUS
TINAMOUS
AIMNOTTU MUTATION
AIMNPRYY PAYNIMRY
AIMNPSTU SUMPITAN
AIMNRRSU MURRAINS
AIMNRSSU SURAMINS
URANISMS
AIMNRSTT TRANSMIT
AIMNRSTU NATRIUMS
NATURISM
AIMNRSTV VARMINTS
AIMNRSUU URANIUMS
AIMNSSTU TSUNAMIS
AIMNSSYZ ZANYISMS
AIMNSTTU ANTISMUT
AIMOPRSS PROSAISM
AIMOPRST ATROPISM
PASTROMI
AIMOPSST IMPASTOS
AIMOPSSY SYMPOSIA
AIMORRST ARMORIST
AIMORRSU ORARIUMS
ROSARIUM
AIMORRUV VARIORUM
AIMORSST AMORISTS
AIMORSSU OSSARIUM
AIMORSTT TRITOMAS
AIMORSTY RAMOSITY
AIMOSSTT ATOMISTS
SOMATIST
AIMPPRUU PUPARIUM
AIMPPSST MAPPISTS
AIMPRSST MISPARTS
AIMPRSTY PARTYISM
AIMRSSST TSARISMS
AIMRSSTT MISSTART
AIMRSSTU MATSURIS
AIMRSSTY SYMITARS
AIMRSSTZ TZARISMS
AIMRSTTU STRIATUM
AIMRTTUY MATURITY
AIMSSSTT STATISMS
AINNNOST SANTONIN
AINNOOTT NOTATION
AINNOOTV NOVATION
AINNOOTZ ZONATION
AINNOPRT ANTIPORN
AINNOPSS SAPONINS
AINNOPST PINTANOS
AINNOSST ONANISTS
AINNOTTU NUTATION
AINNPSTU UNPAINTS
AINNQSTU QUINNATS
QUINTANS
AINNRSTT INTRANTS
AINNRSTU INSURANT
AINNRSTY TYRANNIS
AINNSSTT INSTANTS

AINNSSTU UNSAINTS
AINNSTTY NYSTATIN
AINOOPTT POTATION
AINOORRS ORARIONS
AINOORST ORATIONS
AINOORTT ROTATION
AINOOSTT OSTINATO
AINOOSTV OVATIONS
AINOOTTV OTTAVINO
AINOPPRT PARPOINT
AINOPPST APPOINTS
AINOPPTU PUPATION
AINOPRSS PARISONS
AINOPRST ATROPINS
AINOPRTV PROVIANT
AINOPSSS PASSIONS
AINOPSTT POSTNATI
AINOPSTU OPUNTIAS
UTOPIANS
AINOPSTW SWAPTION
AINOPTTU OUTPAINT
AINOQRSU NARQUOIS
AINORRSW WARRISON
AINORRTT NITRATOR
AINORRTU URINATOR
AINORSST ARSONIST
AINORSSW WARISONS
AINORSTT STRONTIA
AINORSTU RAINOUTS
SUTORIAN
AINORSTX TRIAXONS
AINORTVY VANITORY
AINOSSSU SUASIONS
AINOSSTT STATIONS
AINOSSVY SYNOVIAS
AINOSTTU TITANOUS
AINPPRSS PARSNIPS
AINPPRTT TRIPPANT
AINPRSST SPIRANTS
SPRAINTS
AINPRSTU PURITANS
UPTRAINS
AINPSSST PISSANTS
AINPSSSY SYNAPSIS
AINPSSTU PUISSANT
AINPSTTU PANTSUIT
AINQRSTU QUINTARS
AINQSSSU QUASSINS
AINQTTUY QUANTITY
AINRSSTT STRAINTS
TRANSITS
AINRSTTT TITRANTS
AINRSTTU ANTIRUST
NATURIST
AINRSTTY TANISTRY
AINSSSTU SUSTAINS
AIOOORRT ORATORIO
AIOORRSW WOORARIS
AIOORSUV OVARIOUS
AIOPRRST AIRPORTS
PARITORS
AIOPRRTT PORTRAIT
AIOPRSST AIRPOSTS
AIRSTOPS
PROSAIST
PROTASIS
AIOPRSTT PATRIOTS
AIOPRSUV PAVIOURS
AIOPSTTU UTOPIAST
AIORRRSW WARRIORS
AIORRSTT TRAITORS
AIORRSTV VARISTOR
AIORRTTT TITRATOR
AIORRTWY RYOTWARI
AIORSSST ASSISTOR

AIORSSTU SAUTOIRS
AIORSSUV SAVIOURS
AIORSTTV VOTARIST
AIORSTUV VIRTUOSA
AIOSSSTY ISOSTASY
AIOSTTUW OUTWAITS
AIPPRSTY PAPISTRY
AIPRSSTU UPSTAIRS
AIPRSSTY SPARSITY
AIRRSTTY ARTISTRY
AIRRSTZZ RIZZARTS
AIRSSSTT TSARISTS
AIRSSTTT ATTRISTS
AIRSSTTU TURISTAS
AIRSSTTZ TZARISTS
AISSSTTT STATISTS
AJKMNSTU MUNTJAKS
AJKNNOOU JUNKANOO
AJLNORSU JOURNALS
AJMNNOOR NONMAJOR
AJMRSTUY JURYMAST
AJORRTUY JURATORY
AKKLRSSY SKYLARKS
AKKLSSWY SKYWALKS
AKKMOOST TOKOMAKS
AKKORSTW TASKWORK
AKKOSUVZ KUVASZOK
AKLLMRUY MULLARKY
AKLMNOOW MOONWALK
AKLNNOPT PLANKTON
AKLOPRSW LAPWORKS
AKLORSTW SALTWORK
AKLOSTTU OUTTALKS
AKLOSTUW OUTWALKS
WALKOUTS
AKLPRRSU LARKSPUR
AKMMNOOR MONOMARK
AKMNOOOT TOKONOMA
AKMNRSTU TRANKUMS
AKMOORST MOOKTARS
AKMOPRST POSTMARK
AKMORSST OSTMARKS
AKMQSTUU KUMQUATS
AKMRSSTU MUSKRATS
AKNOORST OSTRAKON
AKNOOUYZ YOKOZUNA
AKNOPSTW SWANKPOT
AKNORSTU OUTRANKS
AKOPRRTW PARTWORK
AKORRSTW ARTWORKS
AKORRSWW WARWORKS
AKORSWWX WAXWORKS
AKOSSTTU OUTTASKS
ALLLOSWY SALLOWLY
ALLLPPUY PULPALLY
ALLLPRUY PLURALLY
ALLMNORY NORMALLY
ALLMNOSY ALLONYMS
ALLMNPSU PULLMANS
ALLMOPSX SMALLPOX
ALLMORTY MORTALLY
ALLMOUWY MULLOWAY
ALLMPRUU PLUMULAR
ALLMTUUY MUTUALLY
ALLNNOUY NOUNALLY
ALLNOOPS PLANOSOL
ALLNORSS LASSLORN
ALLOOSST LATOSOLS
ALLOOSTX AXOLOTLS
ALLOPRSY PAYROLLS
ALLOPSTY POSTALLY
ALLOPTYY ALLOTYPY
ALLORSST ALLSORTS
ALLORSWY ROLLWAYS
ALLORTUW ULTRALOW

ALLORTWW WALLWORT
ALLOSSWW SWALLOWS
ALLOSTWY TOLLWAYS
ALLRUUVY UVULARLY
ALMMNRUU NUMMULAR
ALMMORTW MALTWORM
ALMNNOOR NONMORAL
ALMNOOPS LAMPOONS
ALMNOPSS PLASMONS
ALMNORTY MATRONLY
ALMNOSSU SOLANUMS
ALMNPSSU SUNLAMPS
ALMOOPRS PROSOMAL
ALMOOPRY PLAYROOM
ALMOOPSY POLYOMAS
ALMOORTU ALUMROOT
ALMOPPST LAMPPOST
PALMTOPS
ALMOPRST MARPLOTS
ALMORSUU RAMULOUS
ALMOSTTU MULATTOS
ALMPRSTU PLASTRUM
ALMPSSTY SYMPLAST
ALMRRTYY MARTYRLY
ALMRTUUY TUMULARY
ALMSSSUY ALYSSUMS
ALNNNOOT NONTONAL
ALNNOOPR NONPOLAR
ALNNOORS NONSOLAR
ALNNOORY NONROYAL
ALNNOPSY NONPLAYS
ALNNORRU NONRURAL
ALNNOTWY WANTONLY
ALNNRSSU UNSNARLS
ALNOOPPR PROPANOL
ALNOOPRS POLARONS
ALNOOPRT PORTOLAN
PRONOTAL
ALNOOPST PLATOONS
ALNOOPSV VANPOOLS
ALNOOPXY POLYAXON
ALNOOPYZ POLYZOAN
ALNOOPZZ POZZOLAN
ALNOORST ORTOLANS
ALNOPRST PLASTRON
ALNOPRTU PORTULAN
ALNOPRTY PATRONLY
ALNOPSTU OUTPLANS
ALNOPSYY POLYNYAS
ALNORRWY NARROWLY
ALNORSVY SOVRANLY
ALNPPSTU SUPPLANT
ALNRRTUU NURTURAL
ALOOPPRS PROPOSAL
ALOOPRST POSTORAL
ALOOPRTU UPROOTAL
ALOORSUV VALOROUS
ALOORTYZ ZOOLATRY
ALOPPRSU POPULARS
ALOPPRYY POLYPARY
ALOPPSSU SUPPOSAL
ALOPPSUU PAPULOUS
ALOPRRSU PARLOURS
SPORULAR
ALOPRSTT PORTLAST
ALOPRSTU POSTURAL
PULSATOR
ALOPRSTY PASTORLY
ALOPSSSU SPOUSALS
ALOPSSUV VOLUSPAS
ALOPSTUU PATULOUS
ALOPSTUY OUTPLAYS
ALOQRRSU RORQUALS
ALOQRSSU SQUALORS
ALORRSUY SURROYAL

ALORSTTW SALTWORT
ALORSTWW AWLWORTS
ALORSUVY SAVOURLY
ALORTUWY OUTLAWRY
ALOSSTTU OUTLASTS
ALOSSTXY OXYSALTS
ALPPSTUY PLATYPUS
ALPRSSUU PURSUALS
ALPRSTUU PUSTULAR
AMMNOORT MOTORMAN
AMMNOPSS PSAMMONS
AMMNPTUY TYMPANUM
AMMOORRS MAORMORS
MORMAORS
AMMOPSTU POMATUMS
AMMORRWY ARMYWORM
AMNNOOSX MONAXONS
AMNNOOTT MONTANTO
AMNNORSW MANSWORN
AMNNORSY MANSONRY
AMNNOSTT MONTANTS
AMNNOSTW TOWNSMAN
AMNNOSTY ANTONYMS
AMNNOSUW UNWOMANS
AMNNOTTU MOUNTANT
AMNNOTYY ANTONYMY
AMNNPSTU PUNTSMAN
AMNNSSTU STANNUMS
AMNNSTTU STUNTMAN
AMNOOPPS POMPANOS
AMNOOSTT OTTOMANS
AMNOOSTZ MATZOONS
AMNOOTUY AUTONOMY
AMNOOTWY TOYWOMAN
AMNOOTXY TAXONOMY
AMNOPRSW SPANWORM
AMNOPRSY PARONYMS
AMNOPRYY PARONYMY
AMNOPSTU PANTOUMS
AMNORSST TRANSOMS
AMNORSTU ROMAUNTS
AMNORSTY STRAMONY
AMNOSSYZ ZYMOSANS
AMNOSTUY AUTONYMS
AMNOTTUY TAUTONYM
AMNRSTTU TANTRUMS
AMOOORSS AMOROSOS
AMOOPRSS PROSOMAS
AMOOPRST TAPROOMS
AMOORRTY MORATORY
AMOORSTZ SMORZATO
AMOORTWY MOTORWAY
AMOOSSTU ASTOMOUS
AMOOSTVY VASOTOMY
AMOOTTUY AUTOTOMY
AMOPRRST MARSPORT
AMOPRSXY PAROXYSM
AMOPSSTT TOPMASTS
AMOQSSUU SQUAMOUS
AMORRTUY MORTUARY
AMORSTTU OUTSMART
AMORSWWX WAXWORMS
AMORTTUY MUTATORY
AMPRSSUW UPSWARMS
AMPRSTYY SYMPATRY
AMRRSSTU RASTRUMS
AMRSSTTU STRATUMS
ANNNOSSY SYNANONS
ANNOOQTU NONQUOTA
ANNOORST SONORANT
ANNOPRTY NONPARTY
ANNOPSST NONPASTS
ANNOSSTU STANNOUS
ANNPRSUY SPUNYARN
ANOOPRRT PRONATOR
ANOOPRSS SOPRANOS
ANOOPRST PATROONS
ANOORSSU ARSONOUS
ANOORSTT ARNOTTOS
RATTOONS
ANOORSUU ANOUROUS
ANOPPPRT PROPPANT
ANOPRRSS SPORRANS
ANOPRSTU STROUPAN
ANOPRTTU TRAPUNTO
ANOPSSTU OUTSPANS
ANOQRSSU SQUARSON
ANORSSTU SANTOURS
ANORSTVY SOVRANTY
ANORSUVY UNSAVORY
ANOTTUUV OUTVAUNT
ANPPSSUW SUPPAWNS
ANPRSSTU SUNTRAPS
UNSTRAPS
ANPRSTUU PURSUANT
ANRRTTUY TRUANTRY
ANRSSTYY SYNASTRY
AOOOPRST SOAPROOT
AOOOPRSZ SPOROZOA
AOOOPRTZ PROTOZOA
AOOPPRSY APOSPORY
AOOPRSSU SAPOROUS
AOOPRSTT TAPROOTS
AOOPRSTU ATROPOUS
AOOPRSTW SOAPWORT
AOOPRSUV VAPOROUS
AOOPRTTY POTATORY
AOORRSTT ROTATORS
AOORRSTU OUTROARS
AOORRTTY ROTATORY
AOORSSTU OUTSOARS
AOORSSUV SAVOROUS
AOORSTUV OUTSAVOR
AOPPRRST RAPPORTS
AOPPRSST PASSPORT
AOPPRSTU TRAPPOUS
AOPRRRTY PARROTRY
AOPRRSSW SPARROWS
AOPRRSTY PORTRAYS
AOPRRTUY POURTRAY
AOPRSSTT STARSPOT
AOPRSTTU OUTPARTS
AOPRSTTY PYROSTAT
AOPRSTUY OUTPRAYS
AOPSSSTU PASSOUTS
AOPSSTWY WAYPOSTS
AOPTTUYY AUTOTYPY
AORRSSSU ASSURORS
AORRSTTW STARWORT
AORRTTWW WARTWORT
AORSSTTU STRATOUS
AORSSTTY STAROSTY
AORSTTTU OUTSTART
AORSUVVY VOUVRAYS
AOSSTTUY OUTSTAYS
APPRRSUU PURPURAS
APRSSTTU STARTUPS
UPSTARTS
APRSSUWY SPURWAYS
ASVYYZZZ ZYZZYVAS
BBBCEOWY COBWEBBY
BBBDEEKO KEBOBBED
BBBDEEOR BEROBBED
BBBEILOR BOBBLIER
BBBEILRU BUBBLIER
BBBEILSU BUBBLIES
BBBEINOT BOBBINET
BBBELRSU BLUBBERS
BUBBLERS
BBBELRUY BLUBBERY
BBBGILNO BLOBBING
BOBBLING
BBBGILNU BLUBBING
BUBBLING
BBBHNOOY HOBNOBBY
BBBHOOUU HUBBUBOO
BBBIOSTT BOBBITTS
BBCCIKOS BIBCOCKS
BBCDEILR CRIBBLED
BBCDERSU SCRUBBED
BBCDIMOY BOMBYCID
BBCEEHOS BOBECHES
BBCEHINS NEBBICHS
BBCEHIRU CHUBBIER
BBCEILRS CRIBBLES
SCRIBBLE
BBCEILRU CLUBBIER
BBCEIOST COBBIEST
BBCEIRRS CRIBBERS
BBCEKKOS KEBBOCKS
BBCEKKSU KEBBUCKS
BBCEKLSU BLESBUCK
BBCEKLUU BLUEBUCK
BBCELORS CLOBBERS
COBBLERS
BBCELORY COBBLERY
BBCELRSU CLUBBERS
BBCEMNOU BUNCOMBE
BBCERRSU SCRUBBER
BBCGIINR CRIBBING
BBCGILNO COBBLING
BBCGILNU CLUBBING
BBCGINSU CUBBINGS
BBCHILSU CLUBBISH
BBCHILUY CHUBBILY
BBCHKOOS BOSCHBOK
BBCHKSUU BUSHBUCK
BBCILMSU CLUBBISM
BBCILRSY SCRIBBLY
BBCILSTU CLUBBIST
BBCIPSUU SUBPUBIC
BBCKLOSU SUBBLOCK
BBDDEEMO DEMOBBED
BBDDEEMU BEDUMBED
BBDDEERU REDUBBED
BBDDEILR DRIBBLED
BBDDENUU UNDUBBED
BBDEEGIR GIBBERED
BBDEEGIT GIBBETED
BBDEEIJR JIBBERED
BBDEEIST DEBBIEST
EBBTIDES
BBDEEMNU BENUMBED
BBDEENUW UNWEBBED
BBDEEOPP BEBOPPED
BBDEERRU RUBBERED
BBDEERSU SUBBREED
BBDEFILR FRIBBLED
BBDEGLRU GRUBBLED
BBDEHORT THROBBED
BBDEHRSU SHRUBBED
BBDEILLN BELLBIND
BBDEILLR BELLBIRD
BBDEILQU QUIBBLED
BBDEILRR DRIBBLER
BBDEILRS DIBBLERS
DRIBBLES
BBDEILRT DRIBBLET
BBDEILRU BLUEBIRD
BBDEIMOV DIVEBOMB
BBDEINOR RIBBONED
BBDEINRU UNRIBBED
BBDEIQSU SQUIBBED
BBDEIRRS DRIBBERS
BBDEKLNO KNOBBLED
BBDEKLNU KNUBBLED
BBDELLMU DUMBBELL
BBDELOOS BEBLOODS
BBDELOSS BOBSLEDS
BBDELSTU STUBBLED
BBDENRUU UNRUBBED
BBDERRSU DRUBBERS
BBDERSUU SUBURBED
BBDFLSUU FLUBDUBS
BBDGIILN DIBBLING
BBDGIINR DRIBBING
BBDGINRU DRUBBING
BBDGINSU DUBBINGS
BBDIIKMU DIBBUKIM
BBDIKMUY DYBBUKIM
BBDOSUYY BUSYBODY
BBEEEMSX BEMBEXES
BBEEERSU BEBEERUS
BBEEHINS NEBBISHE
BBEEHLOW BOBWHEEL
BBEEIIRR BERIBERI
BBEEILPR PEBBLIER
PLEBBIER
BBEEIMSX BEMBIXES
BBEEIMTT BIMBETTE
BBEEINRR BERBERIN
BBEEIRRS BERBERIS
BBEEISTW WEBBIEST
BBEEJLMU BEJUMBLE
BBEELLLU BLUEBELL
BBEEOPPR BEBOPPER
BBEFILRR FRIBBLER
BBEFILRS FRIBBLES
BBEFIMOR FIREBOMB
BBEFISTU FUBBIEST
BBEFLRSU FLUBBERS
BBEGIIST GIBBSITE
BBEGILNP PEBBLING
BBEGILOR GLOBBIER
BBEGILRS GRIBBLES
BBEGILRY GLIBBERY
BBEGILST GLIBBEST
BBEGINNS SNEBBING
BBEGINSW WEBBINGS
BBEGIRRU GRUBBIER
BBEGLORS GOBBLERS
BBEGLRSU GRUBBLES
BBEGRRSU GRUBBERS
BBEHINSY NEBBISHY
BBEHIOTW BOBWHITE
BBEHLORS HOBBLERS
BBEHMSTU BETHUMBS
BBEHORRT THROBBER
BBEIILRS RIBIBLES
BBEIIMRS IMBIBERS
BBEIIRST RIBBIEST
BBEIKNOR KNOBBIER
BBEIKNRU KNUBBIER
BBEILLLU BLUEBILL
BBEILLNO BONIBELL
BBEILNRS NIBBLERS
BBEILNRU NUBBLIER
BBEILORS SLOBBIER
BBEILORW WOBBLIER
BBEILOST BIBELOTS
BBEILOSW WOBBLIES
BBEILPRS PRIBBLES
BBEILQRU QUIBBLER
BBEILQSU QUIBBLES
BBEILRRU BURBLIER
RUBBLIER
BBEILRRY BILBERRY
BBEILRST STIBBLER
TRIBBLES
BBEILRSU SLUBBIER

BBEILSST	STIBBLES
BBEIMNOS	BOMBESIN
BBEIMOST	BOMBSITE
BBEIMRSU	BRUMBIES
BBEINORS	SNOBBIER
BBEINOST	NOBBIEST
BBEINRSU	SNUBBIER
BBEINSTU	NUBBIEST
BBEIORTU	OUTBRIBE
BBEIRSTU	STUBBIER
	SUBTRIBE
BBEISSTU	STUBBIES
BBEISTTU	TUBBIEST
BBEKLNOS	KNOBBLES
BBEKLNSU	KNUBBLES
BBEKLOOU	BLUEBOOK
BBEKLOSS	BLESBOKS
BBEKLSUU	BUBUKLES
BBEKNOOT	BONTEBOK
BBEKNORS	KNOBBERS
BBELLOSY	BELLBOYS
BBELLRUY	LUBBERLY
BBELLSTU	BULBLETS
BBELMOST	BOMBLETS
BBELMRSU	BUMBLERS
BBELNORS	NOBBLERS
BBELORSS	SLOBBERS
BBELORSW	WOBBLERS
BBELORSY	LOBBYERS
	SLOBBERY
BBELOTUW	BLOWTUBE
BBELRRSU	BURBLERS
BBELRSSU	SLUBBERS
BBELSSTU	STUBBLES
BBEMOSXY	BOMBYXES
BBENORSY	SNOBBERY
BBENRSSU	SNUBBERS
BBEORRXY	BOXBERRY
BBEORSSW	SWOBBERS
BBEPRSUW	BREWPUBS
BBFGILNU	FLUBBING
BBGGIILN	GLIBBING
BBGGILNO	GOBBLING
BBGGINRU	GRUBBING
BBGHILNO	HOBBLING
BBGIIIMN	IMBIBING
BBGIIJNS	JIBBINGS
BBGIIKLN	KIBBLING
BBGIILMN	BLIMBING
BBGIILNN	NIBBLING
BBGIINNS	SNIBBING
BBGIINRS	RIBBINGS
BBGIJNOS	JOBBINGS
BBGILLSU	BILLBUGS
BBGILMNO	MOBBLING
BBGILMNU	BUMBLING
BBGILNNO	NOBBLING
BBGILNNU	NUBBLING
BBGILNOW	WOBBLING
BBGILNOY	LOBBYING
BBGILNRU	BLURBING
	BURBLING
	RUBBLING
BBGILNSU	SLUBBING
BBGILRUY	GRUBBILY
BBGIMNOS	BOMBINGS
	MOBBINGS
BBGINNSU	SNUBBING
BBGINOSS	SOBBINGS
BBGINOST	STOBBING
BBGINOSW	SWOBBING
BBGINRSU	RUBBINGS
BBGINSSU	SUBBINGS
BBGINSTU	STUBBING
	TUBBINGS
BBGLOOWY	LOBBYGOW
BBHILOSS	SLOBBISH
BBHIMOSY	HOBBYISM
BBHINOSS	SNOBBISH
BBHINSSU	SNUBBISH
BBHIOOSY	BOOBYISH
BBHIORTY	HOBBITRY
BBHIOSTY	HOBBYIST
BBHIRSUY	RUBBISHY
BBHKOOSS	BOSHBOKS
BBHOOSUW	WHOOBUBS
BBHRSSUU	SUBSHRUB
BBIIILMS	BILIMBIS
BBIILLSU	SILLIBUB
BBIILSST	BIBLISTS
BBIJMOOS	JIBBOOMS
BBIKLLOO	BILLBOOK
BBIKLNOO	BOBOLINK
BBILLOYY	BILLYBOY
BBILLSUU	LULIBUBS
BBILMOSY	LOBBYISM
BBILNOSY	SNOBBILY
BBILOSTY	LOBBYIST
BBILOSUU	BIBULOUS
BBILSTUY	STUBBILY
BBIMNOSS	SNOBBISM
BBIMOOSY	BOOBYISM
BBIMOSSY	YOBBISMS
BBINORRY	RIBBONRY
BBJLOOSW	BLOWJOBS
BBKLOOSU	BLOUBOKS
BBKOOOOS	BOOBOOKS
BBLLOUYY	BULLYBOY
BBNOORSU	BOURBONS
BBNORSTU	STUBBORN
BCCCIILY	BICYCLIC
BCCDEILY	BICYCLED
BCCDHIKO	DOBCHICK
BCCDIKOR	COCKBIRD
BCCEEIRR	CEREBRIC
BCCEHIRU	CHERUBIC
BCCEHORS	BESCORCH
BCCEIIIS	CICISBEI
BCCEIILO	LIBECCIO
BCCEIIOS	CICISBEO
BCCEILOS	ECBOLICS
BCCEILOY	BIOCYCLE
BCCEILRU	CRUCIBLE
BCCEILRY	BICYCLER
BCCEILSU	CUBICLES
BCCEILSY	BICYCLES
BCCEMRUU	CUCUMBER
BCCHIKOY	BOYCHICK
BCCIIMOR	MICROBIC
BCCIISTU	CUBISTIC
BCCIITUY	CUBICITY
BCCIKLLO	COCKBILL
BCCILMOU	COLUMBIC
BCCILOOR	BROCCOLI
BCCILOSU	BUCOLICS
BCCINORR	CORNCRIB
BCCIRTUU	CUCURBIT
BCCLOOOO	COCOBOLO
BCCMOOSX	COXCOMBS
BCCMSSUU	SUCCUMBS
BCCNOORS	CORNCOBS
BCCSSUUU	SUCCUBUS
BCDDEEEK	BEDECKED
BCDDEEKU	BEDUCKED
BCDDEENU	BEDUNCED
BCDDEHIL	CHILDBED
BCDDESUU	SUBDUCED
BCDEEEHR	BREECHED
BCDEEGLU	BECUDGEL
BCDEEHLN	BLENCHED
BCDEEHNR	BEDRENCH
BCDEEHOU	DEBOUCHE
BCDEEIKN	BENEDICK
BCDEEIKR	BICKERED
BCDEEILR	CREDIBLE
BCDEEILS	DECIBELS
BCDEEILU	EDUCIBLE
BCDEEIMR	BECRIMED
BCDEEINT	BENEDICT
BCDEEIPS	BESPICED
BCDEEIRS	DESCRIBE
	ESCRIBED
BCDEEIST	BISECTED
BCDEEJOT	OBJECTED
BCDEEKMO	BEMOCKED
BCDEEKNO	BECKONED
BCDEEKRU	REEDBUCK
BCDEEKTU	BUCKETED
BCDEELNU	BEUNCLED
BCDEELOR	CORBELED
BCDEELRU	BECURLED
BCDEEMOR	RECOMBED
BCDEEMRU	CUMBERED
BCDEENSU	BEDUNCES
BCDEEORV	BEDCOVER
BCDEEOTT	OBTECTED
BCDEERSU	BECURSED
BCDEHINS	DISBENCH
BCDEHLOT	BLOTCHED
BCDEHNRU	BRUNCHED
BCDEHOOR	BROOCHED
BCDEIIOS	BIOCIDES
BCDEIIRR	RICEBIRD
BCDEIITU	DECUBITI
BCDEIKRR	REDBRICK
BCDEIKSS	SICKBEDS
BCDEIKST	BEDTICKS
BCDEILRY	CREDIBLY
BCDEIMNO	COMBINED
BCDEINOU	ICEBOUND
BCDEIRSU	CURBSIDE
BCDEKOOO	CODEBOOK
BCDEKORS	BEDROCKS
BCDEKOSS	BEDSOCKS
BCDELMRU	CRUMBLED
BCDELMSU	SCUMBLED
BCDELOSU	BECLOUDS
BCDEMNOU	UNCOMBED
BCDEMOOY	COEMBODY
BCDEMORY	CORYMBED
BCDENRUU	UNCURBED
BCDEOORT	CODEBTOR
BCDEORSU	OBSCURED
BCDEORSW	BECROWDS
BCDEOSSU	SUBCODES
BCDESSUU	SUBDUCES
BCDHIRSU	BRUCHIDS
BCDHOOSU	CUBHOODS
BCDHORSU	SUBCHORD
BCDIIMOR	BROMIDIC
BCDIIPSU	BICUSPID
BCDIKLLU	DUCKBILL
BCDILMOY	MOLYBDIC
BCDILORU	COLUBRID
BCDIMORS	SCOMBRID
BCDINOSW	COWBINDS
BCDINRUU	RUBICUND
BCDIORSW	COWBIRDS
BCDKNOOO	BOONDOCK
BCDKORSU	BURDOCKS
BCDSSTUU	SUBDUCTS
BCEEEFIN	BENEFICE
BCEEEFKN	NECKBEEF
BCEEEHIR	BEECHIER
BCEEEHRS	BREECHES
BCEEENRS	BESCREEN
BCEEERSU	BERCEUSE
BCEEFILN	FENCIBLE
BCEEFKLS	BEFLECKS
BCEEFLTU	CLUBFEET
BCEEGIRS	ICEBERGS
BCEEHKSU	BUCKSHEE
BCEEHLNR	BLENCHER
BCEEHLNS	BLENCHES
BCEEHLOT	BECLOTHE
BCEEHLRS	BELCHERS
BCEEHNRS	BENCHERS
BCEEHNRU	UNBREECH
BCEEHNTU	BEECHNUT
BCEEHOSU	BOUCHEES
BCEEIILM	IMBECILE
BCEEIKRR	BICKERER
BCEEILNR	BERNICLE
BCEEIMRS	BECRIMES
BCEEINOT	CENOBITE
BCEEIOSX	ICEBOXES
BCEEIPSS	BESPICES
	BICEPSES
BCEEIRSS	ESCRIBES
BCEEIRTT	BRETTICE
BCEEJORT	REOBJECT
BCEEKNOR	BECKONER
BCEEKNSU	BUCKEENS
BCEEKSUY	BUCKEYES
BCEELLOT	BELLCOTE
BCEELOOR	BORECOLE
BCEELRTU	TUBERCLE
BCEEMMOR	COMEMBER
BCEEMNRU	ENCUMBER
BCEEMRRU	CEREBRUM
	CUMBERER
BCEENORS	OBSCENER
BCEENRSU	CRUBEENS
BCEEPRTY	CYBERPET
BCEERSSU	BECURSES
BCEERSTU	SUBERECT
BCEERSXY	CYBERSEX
BCEERTVY	BREVETCY
BCEFFIIR	FEBRIFIC
BCEFHISU	SUBCHIEF
BCEFILOR	FORCIBLE
BCEGHILN	BELCHING
BCEGHINN	BENCHING
BCEGIINO	BIOGENIC
BCEGIMNO	BECOMING
BCEGKMSU	GEMSBUCK
BCEGLNOO	CONGLOBE
BCEHIIOT	BIOETHIC
BCEHIIRT	BITCHIER
BCEHILMY	CHIMBLEY
BCEHIMOR	BICHROME
BCEHIMRS	BESMIRCH
BCEHIMRU	CHERUBIM
BCEHINNO	CHINBONE
BCEHINRU	BUNCHIER
	CHERUBIN
BCEHINSU	SUBNICHE
BCEHIORS	BRIOCHES
BCEHIORT	BOTCHIER
BCEHIOST	BIOTECHS
BCEHIRST	BRITCHES
BCEHIRTY	BITCHERY
BCEHLOST	BLOTCHES
BCEHLRSU	BLUCHERS
BCEHMSTU	BESMUTCH
BCEHNRSU	BRUNCHES
BCEHOORS	BROOCHES
BCEHOPSU	SUBEPOCH
BCEHORRU	BROCHURE
BCEHORSS	BORSCHES

BCEHORST BOTCHERS
BCEHORSW COWHERBS
BCEHORTY BOTCHERY
BCEHRSTU BUTCHERS
BCEHRTUY BUTCHERY
BCEHSTTU BUTCHEST
BCEIIKLN ICEBLINK
BCEIIKRR BRICKIER
BCEIIKRS BRICKIES
BCEIILMS MISCIBLE
BCEIILNV VINCIBLE
BCEIILOP EPIBOLIC
BCEIIMRS IMBRICES
BCEIINRS INSCRIBE
BCEIKLMO COMBLIKE
BCEIKLMS LIMBECKS
BCEIKLOO BOOKLICE
BCEIKLOR BLOCKIER
BCEIKLRS BRICKLES
BCEIKLTU BLUETICK
BCEIKSST BESTICKS
BCEILMRS CLIMBERS
RECLIMBS
BCEILNOS BINOCLES
BCEILNRU RUNCIBLE
BCEILNYZ BENZYLIC
BCEILORS BRICOLES
CORBEILS
BCEILOSU CIBOULES
BCEILOTU TUBICOLE
BCEILPRU REPUBLIC
BCEIMNOR COMBINER
BCEIMNOS COMBINES
BCEIMNRU INCUMBER
BCEIMORS MICROBES
BCEIMOST COMBIEST
BCEIMOSW COMBWISE
BCEIMRRU CRUMBIER
BCEINORS BICORNES
BCEINORU BOUNCIER
BCEINOVX BICONVEX
BCEINRSU BRUCINES
BCEIOOPS BIOSCOPE
BCEIORRS CRIBROSE
BCEIORST BISECTOR
BCEIRRSS SCRIBERS
BCEIRSTU BRUCITES
BCEIRTTY YTTERBIC
BCEJOORT OBJECTOR
BCEJSSTU SUBJECTS
BCEKLLNU BULLNECK
BCEKLNOT BLONCKET
BCEKLNUU UNBUCKLE
BCEKLORS BLOCKERS
BCEKLRSU BUCKLERS
SUBCLERK
BCEKMSTU STEMBUCK
BCEKOORU BUCKEROO
BCEKORST BROCKETS
BCEKORSU ROEBUCKS
BCEKOSTY BYCOKETS
BCELLOSW COWBELLS
BCELLRUW WELLCURB
BCELLSSU SUBCELLS
BCELMOSS COMBLESS
BCELMRSU CLUMBERS
CRUMBLES
BCELMSSU SCUMBLES
BCELNOSW BECLOWNS
BCELORTU CLOTEBUR
BCELRSSU CURBLESS
BCEMRRSU CRUMBERS
BCEMRSSU SCUMBERS
BCENOOOX ECONOBOX
BCENORSU BOUNCERS

BCEORRSU OBSCURER
BCEORRWY COWBERRY
BCEORSSU BESCOURS
OBSCURES
BCERSSTU BECRUSTS
BCESSSTU SUBSECTS
BCESSTUU SUBCUTES
BCFIIMOR MORBIFIC
BCFIIORT FIBROTIC
BCFILORY FORCIBLY
BCFIMORU CUBIFORM
BCFLOOTU CLUBFOOT
BCFSSSUU SUBFUSCS
BCGHIINR BIRCHING
BCGHIINT BITCHING
BCGHINNU BUNCHING
BCGHINOR BROCHING
BCGHINOT BOTCHING
BCGHINPU PINCHBUG
BCGHINTU BUTCHING
BCGIIKNR BRICKING
BCGIILMN CLIMBING
BCGIILOO BIOLOGIC
BCGIINRS SCRIBING
BCGIKLNO BLOCKING
BCGIKLNU BUCKLING
BCGIKNSU BUCKINGS
BCGILMNY CYMBLING
BCGIMNOR CROMBING
BCGIMNOS COMBINGS
BCGIMNRU CRUMBING
BCGINNOU BOUNCING
BUNCOING
BCGINORU COURBING
BCGINRSU CURBINGS
BCHIILTY BITCHILY
BCHIIOPS BIOCHIPS
BCHIIOST COHIBITS
BCHIISSU HIBISCUS
BCHIKLOS BLOCKISH
BCHIKOSU CHIBOUKS
BCHIKOSY BOYCHIKS
BCHILNUY BUNCHILY
BCHILOTY BOTCHILY
BCHIOORY CHOIRBOY
BCHIOPRS PIBROCHS
BCHIORRT BIRROTCH
BCHIOTTU OUTBITCH
BCHKNORU BUCKHORN
BCHKOSTU BUCKSHOT
BCHLRSUU CLUBRUSH
BCHNOORS BRONCHOS
BCHNORSU BRONCHUS
BCHORSST BORSCHTS
BCIIILMU UMBILICI
BCIIIOTT BIOTITIC
BCIIKLNS NIBLICKS
BCIILLSY SIBYLLIC
BCIILMRU LUMBRICI
BCIILMSU BULIMICS
BCIILNVY VINCIBLY
BCIILORS COLIBRIS
BCIILOTY BIOLYTIC
BCIIMNOO BIONOMIC
BCIIMORU CIBORIUM
BCIIMRSS SCRIBISM
BCIINORV VIBRONIC
BCIIOPTY BIOTYPIC
BCIIORST BISTROIC
SORBITIC
BCIISSTU BISCUITS
BCIISTUY BISCUITY
BCIKKNSU BUCKSKIN
BCIKLOOT BOOTLICK
BCIKLOST LOBSTICK

BCIKORRW CRIBWORK
BCIKOSTT BITSTOCK
BITTOCKS
BCILLPUY PUBLICLY
BCILMOSY SYMBOLIC
BCILMOTU OUTCLIMB
BCILMPSU UPCLIMBS
BCILNOUY BOUNCILY
BCILOORS BICOLORS
BROCOLIS
BCILOORU BICOLOUR
BCIMORSU MICROBUS
BCINORSU RUBICONS
BCINOSSU SUBSONIC
BCINOSTU SUBTONIC
BCINOSUU INCUBOUS
BCINSTUU SUBTUNIC
BCIOOPSY BIOSCOPY
BCIOORST ROBOTICS
BCIOPSTU SUBOPTIC
SUBTOPIC
BCIORRSU CRIBROUS
BCIORSST CROSSBIT
BCISSTUU SUBCUTIS
BCJKMSUU JUMBUCKS
BCKKOOOO COOKBOOK
BCKLLOOS BOLLOCKS
BCKLLOSU BULLOCKS
BCKLLOUY BULLOCKY
BCKLNOSU SUNBLOCK
UNBLOCKS
BCKMMOSU BUMMOCKS
BCKNNOOS BONNOCKS
BCKOOOPY COPYBOOK
BCKOSTTU BUTTOCKS
BCLMOORU CLUBROOM
BCLMOOSU COULOMBS
BCLMOOTU OUTCLOMB
BCLOORTU CLUBROOT
BCLOOSSU SUBCOOLS
BCLORSTU CLOTBURS
BCLSSTUU SUBCULTS
BCMMRSUU CRUMBUMS
BCMORSUU CUMBROUS
BCMOSSTU COMBUSTS
BCNNOUUY UNBOUNCY
BCOOPSYY COPYBOYS
BCOORSSW CROSSBOW
BCOOSTTY BOYCOTTS
BCORSTTU OBSTRUCT
BCRSSTUU SUBCRUST
BDDDEEEM EMBEDDED
BDDDEEIM IMBEDDED
BDDDEEIR DEBRIDED
BDDDEEMU BEMUDDED
BDDDEENU UNBEDDED
BDDDENUU UNBUDDED
BDDEEELL DEBELLED
BDDEEERS REEDBEDS
BDDEEESS SEEDBEDS
BDDEEFLU BEFUDDLE
BDDEEGGU DEBUGGED
BDDEEGIL BEGILDED
BDDEEGIR BEGIRDED
BDDEEGNU BEDUNGED
BDDEEGTU BUDGETED
BDDEEHOS DEBOSHED
BDDEEIMM BEDIMMED
BDDEEIMO EMBODIED
BDDEEINR REBIDDEN
BDDEEINT INDEBTED
BDDEEINW BINDWEED
BDDEEIOR REBODIED
BDDEEIRR REEDBIRD
BDDEEIRS BIRDSEED
DEBRIDES

BDDEEISS BEDSIDES
BDDEEKNU DEBUNKED
BDDEELMU BEMUDDLE
BDDEELNO BOLDENED
BDDEENNU UNBENDED
BDDEENOT OBTENDED
BDDEENRU BURDENED
BDDEEORR BORDERED
BDDEEORS DESORBED
BDDEEOSS DEBOSSED
BDDEEOTT BEDOTTED
BDDEESSU DEBUSSED
BDDEESTU BEDUSTED
BDDEESUW SUBDEWED
BDDEFOOR FORBODED
BDDEGINS BEDDINGS
BDDEIIMO IMBODIED
BDDEILNR BRINDLED
BDDEILOO BLOODIED
BDDEINNU UNBIDDEN
BDDEINOU UNBODIED
BDDEINRU UNDERBID
BDDEIORS DISORBED
DISROBED
BDDEIOWY WIDEBODY
BDDEIRRS REDBIRDS
BDDEISSU SUBSIDED
BDDEISTU BUDDIEST
BDDELMRU DRUMBLED
BDDELOOR BLOODRED
BDDENOTU OBTUNDED
BDDENRUU UNDERBUD
BDDEORTU OBTRUDED
BDDGIINS BIDDINGS
BDDGILNU BUDDLING
BDDGINOR BRODDING
BDDGINSU BUDDINGS
BDDGINUY BUDDYING
BDDGOOSY DOGSBODY
BDDHIIRY DIHYBRID
BDDINOOW WOODBIND
BDDINOSU DISBOUND
BDDINPUU PUDIBUND
BDEEEEMS BESEEMED
BDEEEEMT BETEEMED
BDEEEGIS BESIEGED
BDEEEGMM BEGEMMED
BDEEEGNO EDGEBONE
BDEEEGRU BUDGEREE
BDEEEHST BEDSHEET
BDEEEHTU HEBETUDE
BDEEEILN BEELINED
BDEEEILV BELIEVED
BDEEEINS BENISEED
BDEEELLR REBELLED
BDEEELLV BEVELLED
BDEEELMM EMBLEMED
BDEEELPT BEPELTED
BDEEELRS BLEEDERS
BDEEELUW BLUEWEED
BDEEEMMR MEMBERED
BDEEEMNS BEDESMEN
BDEEEMRW EMBREWED
BDEEENTT BENETTED
BDEEEPSS BESPEEDS
BDEEERRS BREEDERS
REBREEDS
BDEEERRV REVERBED
BDEEERTT BETTERED
BDEEERTV BREVETED
BDEEETTW BEWETTED
BDEEFFPU BEPUFFED
BDEEFFRU BUFFERED
REBUFFED

BDEEFFTU	BUFFETED
BDEEFGGO	BEFOGGED
BDEEFGIT	BEGIFTED
BDEEFGLU	BEGULFED
BDEEFILR	BELFRIED
BDEEFINN	BEFINNED
BDEEFINR	BEFRIEND
BDEEFIRS	DEBRIEFS
BDEEFIRU	RUBEFIED
BDEEFITT	BEFITTED
BDEEFLOO	BEFOOLED
BDEEFLOU	BEFOULED
BDEEFOOR	FOREBODE
BDEEFOOW	BEEFWOOD
BDEEFSUU	SUBFEUED
BDEEGGIW	BEWIGGED
BDEEGGMO	EMBOGGED
BDEEGGNU	UNBEGGED
BDEEGGRU	BEGRUDGE
	BUGGERED
	DEBUGGER
BDEEGHIS	BESIGHED
BDEEGILN	BLEEDING
BDEEGILR	BEGIRDLE
BDEEGILU	BEGUILED
BDEEGIMR	BEGRIMED
BDEEGINR	BERINGED
	BREEDING
BDEEGINW	BEDEWING
	BEWINGED
BDEEGINY	BEDYEING
BDEEGKNU	BEGUNKED
BDEEGLNO	BELONGED
	ENGLOBED
BDEEGMOU	EMBOGUED
BDEEGMSU	BESMUDGE
BDEEGOOY	BOOGEYED
BDEEGORU	BEROUGED
BDEEGRSV	SVEDBERG
BDEEGRTU	BUDGETER
BDEEGSSU	BUGSEEDS
BDEEHLNO	BEHOLDEN
BDEEHLOR	BEHOLDER
BDEEHLOW	BEHOWLED
BDEEHLSU	BUSHELED
BDEEHMOR	HOMEBRED
BDEEHMRY	BERHYMED
BDEEHOOV	BEHOOVED
BDEEHORT	BOTHERED
BDEEHORW	BEWHORED
BDEEHOSS	DEBOSHES
BDEEIILL	ELIDIBLE
BDEEIILN	INEDIBLE
BDEEIILR	BIELDIER
BDEEIIPT	BEPITIED
BDEEIKRS	KERBSIDE
BDEEIKSS	BEKISSED
BDEEILLL	LIBELLED
BDEEILLR	REBILLED
BDEEILLT	BILLETED
BDEEILLU	ELUDIBLE
BDEEILMO	BEMOILED
	EMBOILED
BDEEILMP	BEDIMPLE
BDEEILMR	LIMBERED
BDEEILMS	BESLIMED
	BESMILED
BDEEILNR	LINEBRED
	RENDIBLE
BDEEILNU	UNEDIBLE
BDEEILNV	VENDIBLE
BDEEILOR	ERODIBLE
	REBOILED
BDEEILOS	OBELISED
BDEEILOT	BETOILED
BDEEILOZ	OBELIZED
BDEEILRV	BEDRIVEL
BDEEILRW	BEWILDER
BDEEILSV	BEDEVILS
BDEEILTT	BETITLED
BDEEIMNR	BRIDEMEN
BDEEIMOR	EMBODIER
BDEEIMOS	EMBODIES
BDEEIMRT	TIMBERED
BDEEIMST	BEDTIMES
	BEMISTED
BDEEIMSU	EMBUSIED
BDEEINOS	EBONISED
BDEEINOT	OBEDIENT
BDEEINOZ	EBONIZED
BDEEINRS	INBREEDS
BDEEINRT	INTERBED
BDEEINST	BENDIEST
BDEEINSW	BENDWISE
BDEEINSZ	BEDIZENS
BDEEIORS	REBODIES
BDEEIORU	BOUDERIE
BDEEIRRU	REBURIED
BDEEIRRV	RIVERBED
BDEEIRST	BESTRIDE
	BISTERED
BDEEIRSU	DEBRUISE
BDEEIRSY	BIRDSEYE
BDEEIRTT	BITTERED
BDEEISTU	BESUITED
BDEEKMOS	BESMOKED
	EMBOSKED
BDEEKNRU	BUNKERED
	DEBUNKER
BDEEKOOR	REBOOKED
BDEEKORR	BROKERED
BDEELLMU	UMBELLED
BDEELLOW	BELLOWED
	BOWELLED
BDEELLRU	BULLERED
BDEELLRY	REDBELLY
BDEELLTU	BULLETED
BDEELLUW	BULLWEED
BDEELMNO	EMBOLDEN
BDEELMOR	REBELDOM
BDEELMPU	BEPLUMED
BDEELMRT	TREMBLED
BDEELMRU	LUMBERED
BDEELNNO	ENNOBLED
BDEELNRS	BLENDERS
	REBLENDS
BDEELNST	BENDLETS
BDEELNTU	UNBELTED
BDEELORU	REDOUBLE
BDEELOSU	BESOULED
BDEELOSV	BELOVEDS
BDEELRTU	BUTLERED
BDEELSST	DEBTLESS
BDEEMNOT	BODEMENT
	ENTOMBED
BDEEMNOW	ENWOMBED
BDEEMNRU	NUMBERED
BDEEMORR	EMBORDER
BDEEMORS	SOMBERED
BDEEMORW	BEWORMED
BDEEMORY	REEMBODY
BDEEMOSS	EMBOSSED
BDEEMPRU	BUMPERED
BDEEMRTU	EMBRUTED
BDEEMSSU	EMBUSSED
BDEENNOT	BONNETED
BDEENORS	DEBONERS
	REDBONES
BDEENOSW	BESNOWED
BDEENOUY	UNOBEYED
BDEENPRS	PREBENDS
BDEENRRU	BURDENER
BDEENSUV	SUBVENED
BDEEOORT	REBOOTED
BDEEOPRR	REPROBED
BDEEOPRS	BEPROSED
BDEEOPRW	BEPOWDER
BDEEORRR	BORDERER
BDEEORRS	RESORBED
BDEEORRV	OVERBRED
BDEEORSS	BEDSORES
BDEEORST	BESORTED
	BESTRODE
BDEEORSV	OBSERVED
BDEEORTU	OUTBREED
BDEEORTV	OBVERTED
BDEEOSSS	DEBOSSES
	OBSESSED
BDEEOSST	BETOSSED
BDEEOSTT	BESOTTED
	OBTESTED
BDEEOSTW	BESTOWED
BDEEPRRU	PUREBRED
BDEERRTU	TRUEBRED
BDEERRWY	DEWBERRY
BDEERSSU	BURSEEDS
BDEERSUW	BURWEEDS
BDEERTTU	BUTTERED
	REBUTTED
BDEESSSU	DEBUSSES
BDEFIIRR	FIREBIRD
BDEFIIRU	RUBIFIED
BDEFIKOR	BIFORKED
BDEFILRS	FILBERDS
BDEFILSU	SUBFIELD
BDEFIMOR	BIFORMED
BDEFINRR	FERNBIRD
BDEFIORS	FIBROSED
BDEFOORS	FORBODES
BDEFOORY	FOREBODY
BDEGHHIR	HIGHBRED
BDEGHILT	BLIGHTED
BDEGHIRT	BEDRIGHT
BDEGHIST	BEDIGHTS
BDEGIILN	BIELDING
BDEGIINT	BETIDING
	DEBITING
BDEGILNN	BLENDING
BDEGILNO	INGLOBED
BDEGINNO	DEBONING
BDEGINNS	BENDINGS
BDEGINOS	OBSIGNED
BDEGINTU	DEBUTING
BDEGIOST	BODGIEST
BDEGLMRU	GRUMBLED
BDEGLNOU	BLUDGEON
BDEGLRSU	BLUDGERS
BDEGNOSW	BEDGOWNS
BDEGOOSY	GOODBYES
BDEGORRY	DOGBERRY
BDEGORSU	BUDGEROS
BDEGORUW	BUDGEROW
BDEHIKOS	KIBOSHED
BDEHILMT	THIMBLED
BDEHIOPS	BISHOPED
BDEHKOSY	KYBOSHED
BDEHLMOW	WHOMBLED
BDEHLSUV	BUSHVELD
BDEHMOOY	HOMEBODY
BDEHOOOO	BOOHOOED
BDEHORSU	BESHROUD
BDEHORSY	HERDBOYS
BDEIIIKN	BIKINIED
BDEIIKLR	BIRDLIKE
BDEIIKTZ	KIBITZED
BDEIILMR	BIRDLIME
BDEIILRU	BLUIDIER
BDEIILTY	DEBILITY
BDEIIMOS	IMBODIES
BDEIINNZ	BENZIDIN
BDEIIOPS	BIOPSIED
BDEIKMOS	IMBOSKED
BDEIKNOR	BRODEKIN
BDEIKNSU	BUSKINED
BDEILLMU	BDELLIUM
BDEILLNU	UNBILLED
BDEILLOW	BILLOWED
BDEILLOX	BOLLIXED
BDEILMNO	IMBOLDEN
BDEILMOS	SEMIBOLD
BDEILMSU	SUBLIMED
BDEILNOU	UNILOBED
BDEILNOY	BODYLINE
BDEILNRS	BLINDERS
	BRINDLES
BDEILNRU	UNBRIDLE
BDEILNST	BLINDEST
BDEILNVY	VENDIBLY
BDEILOOR	BLOODIER
BDEILOOS	BLOODIES
BDEILOPU	UPBOILED
BDEILOQU	OBLIQUED
BDEILORT	TRILOBED
BDEILORV	LOVEBIRD
BDEILOSS	BODILESS
BDEILOSW	DISBOWEL
BDEILQTU	BEDQUILT
BDEILRRS	BRIDLERS
BDEILRRY	LYREBIRD
BDEILRST	BRISTLED
	DRIBLETS
BDEILRSU	BUILDERS
	REBUILDS
BDEILRTT	BRITTLED
BDEILSST	BILSTEDS
BDEILSTU	BLUDIEST
BDEIMNOT	INTOMBED
BDEIMNSU	NIMBUSED
BDEIMNUU	UNIMBUED
BDEIMORR	IMBORDER
	MORBIDER
BDEIMORS	BROMIDES
BDEIMORY	EMBRYOID
BDEIMORZ	BROMIZED
BDEIMOSS	IMBOSSED
BDEIMRSU	IMBURSED
BDEIMRTU	IMBRUTED
BDEINOOS	NOBODIES
BDEINOOW	WOODBINE
BDEINORV	OVENBIRD
BDEINOSU	BEDOUINS
BDEINOTU	BOUNTIED
BDEINPRS	PREBINDS
BDEINRSU	BURNSIDE
BDEINRTU	TURBINED
	UNDERBIT
BDEINRUU	UNBURIED
BDEINSUX	SUBINDEX
BDEINTTU	UNBITTED
BDEIOORR	BROODIER
BDEIORRS	BROIDERS
	DISROBER
BDEIORRU	BOURRIDE
BDEIORRY	BROIDERY
BDEIORSS	DISROBES
BDEIORST	DEBITORS
	DEORBITS
BDEIORSV	OVERBIDS
BDEIORTU	TUBEROID
BDEIOSSY	DISOBEYS

BDEIOSUX	SUBOXIDE
BDEIRSSU	DISBURSE
	SUBSIDER
BDEISSSU	SUBSIDES
BDEISSTU	SUBEDITS
BDEKLMOO	BLOKEDOM
BDEKNOOS	BOOKENDS
BDEKNOOU	UNBOOKED
BDELLOOR	BORDELLO
	DOORBELL
BDELLOOX	BOLLOXED
BDELLORS	BEDROLLS
BDELLOUZ	BULLDOZE
BDELMOOS	BLOOSMED
BDELMOSY	SYMBOLED
BDELMRSU	DRUMBLES
BDELMRUU	DELUBRUM
BDELMSTU	STUMBLED
BDELNNOU	UNNOBLED
BDELNNUU	UNBUNDLE
BDELNOOS	DOBLONES
BDELNOSS	BOLDNESS
BDELNOST	BLONDEST
BDELNOTU	UNBOLTED
BDELNOUU	UNDOUBLE
BDELNOUW	UNBLOWED
BDELNRSU	BLUNDERS
	BUNDLERS
BDELOORS	BOODLERS
BDELOORV	OVERBOLD
BDELOOUW	BLUEWOOD
BDELORSU	BOULDERS
	DOUBLERS
BDELORSW	BOWLDERS
BDELORTU	TROUBLED
BDELORUU	DOUBLURE
BDELORUY	BOULDERY
BDELOSTU	DOUBLETS
BDELPSUU	SUBDUPLE
BDEMNNOS	BONDSMEN
BDEMNOSU	EMBOUNDS
BDEMNOTU	UNTOMBED
BDEMNSSU	DUMBNESS
BDEMOORS	BEDROOMS
	BOREDOMS
BDEMOOSY	SOMEBODY
BDEMOOTT	BOTTOMED
BDEMSSUU	SUBSUMED
BDENNOTU	DUBONNET
BDENNOUY	YBOUNDEN
BDENNRUU	UNBURDEN
	UNBURNED
BDENOOTU	UNBOOTED
BDENOOTW	BENTWOOD
BDENOPRU	PREBOUND
	UNPROBED
BDENORSU	BOUNDERS
	REBOUNDS
	SUBORNED
BDENOTTU	BUTTONED
BDENRSTU	SUBTREND
BDENRSUU	UNBRUSED
BDENRUUY	UNDERBUY
BDENSSTU	SUBTENDS
BDENSTUU	UNBUSTED
BDEOORRS	BROODERS
BDEOORRW	BORROWED
BDEOOTUX	OUTBOXED
BDEOOWWW	BOWWOWED
BDEOPSST	BEDPOSTS
BDEOPSTU	SUBDEPOT
BDEORRSU	BORDURES
	BOURDERS
	SUBORDER
BDEORRTU	OBTRUDER
BDEORRUW	BURROWED
BDEORSSU	ROSEBUDS
BDEORSTU	DOUBTERS
	OBTRUDES
	REDOUBTS
BDEORSUV	OVERDUBS
BDERSSUU	SUBDUERS
BDERSTUU	SUBTRUDE
BDFFIPRU	PUFFBIRD
BDFGNOOU	FOGBOUND
BDFIIITY	BIFIDITY
BDFIIORS	FIBROIDS
BDFILLLO	BILLFOLD
BDFILNOO	BLOODFIN
BDFILSUU	SUBFLUID
BDFINORU	UNFORBID
BDFINRUU	FURIBUND
BDFIRRSU	SURFBIRD
BDFLOTUU	DOUBTFUL
BDFORSUY	BODYSURF
BDGGIINR	BRIDGING
BDGGILNU	BLUDGING
BDGGLOSU	GOLDBUGS
BDGHOOUY	DOUGHBOY
BDGIIKNR	KINGBIRD
BDGIILNN	BLINDING
BDGIILNR	BRIDLING
BDGIILNU	BUILDING
BDGIINNS	BINDINGS
BDGIINRS	BIRDINGS
BDGIINRW	BIRDWING
BDGIIOOS	GOBIOIDS
BDGILNNU	BUNDLING
BDGILNOO	BLOODING
	BOODLING
BDGILNOU	DOUBLING
BDGILNOY	BODINGLY
BDGILOOS	GLOBOIDS
BDGINNOS	BONDINGS
BDGINNOU	BOUNDING
	UNBODING
BDGINOOR	BROODING
BDGINOOY	BOODYING
BDGINORS	BIRDSONG
	SONGBIRD
BDGINORU	OBDURING
BDGINOTU	DOUBTING
BDGINSUU	SUBDUING
BDGLLOSU	BULLDOGS
BDGLOOST	DOGBOLTS
BDGNRUUY	BURGUNDY
BDGOOOSW	BOGWOODS
BDHIIPRW	WHIPBIRD
BDHILNOS	BLONDISH
BDHIMOOR	RHOMBOID
BDHIMORT	BIRTHDOM
BDHIMSUU	SUBHUMID
BDHINOPS	HOPBINDS
BDHIORST	BIRDSHOT
BDHIOSSU	BUSHIDOS
BDHLOOOT	HOTBLOOD
BDHMOOOS	HOBODOMS
BDHNRSUU	UNSHRUBD
BDHOOOSY	BOYHOODS
BDIIINRS	BRINDISI
BDIIIORV	VIBRIOID
BDIIKNOS	BODIKINS
BDIILMSS	DISLIMBS
BDIILMSU	MISBUILD
BDIILOQU	OBLIQUID
BDIILORS	OILBIRDS
BDIIMNSS	MISBINDS
BDIIMRUU	RUBIDIUM
BDIKNORS	BRODKINS
BDILLOOY	BLOODILY
BDILMORY	MORBIDLY
BDILNNSU	SUNBLIND
	UNBLINDS
BDILNOOO	DIOBOLON
BDILNOWW	WINDBLOW
BDILNPRU	PURBLIND
BDILNSUU	UNBUILDS
BDILOORY	BROODILY
BDILOPRY	POLYBRID
BDILOTUU	OUTBUILD
BDILPSUU	BUILDUPS
	UPBUILDS
BDILRTUY	TURBIDLY
BDIMNORU	MORIBUND
BDIMNOSU	MISBOUND
BDIMNPSU	DUMPBINS
BDIMOOSS	DISBOSOM
BDIMOSTU	MISDOUBT
BDINNOSU	INBOUNDS
BDINNRUW	WINDBURN
BDINOORS	BRIDOONS
BDINOOSW	WOODBINS
BDINORSW	SNOWBIRD
BDINRSSU	SUNBIRDS
BDINRTUU	UNTURBID
BDINSSTU	BUNDISTS
	DUSTBINS
BDIOORSU	BOUDOIRS
BDIOORTY	BOTRYOID
BDIORSSW	WOSBIRDS
BDIOSTUY	BODYSUIT
BDIRSSTU	DISTURBS
BDKNOOOR	DOORKNOB
BDKNOOSU	BUNDOOKS
BDKOOORW	WORDBOOK
BDKOORWY	BODYWORK
BDKOOSTU	STUDBOOK
BDLLSTUU	BULLDUST
BDLNOOOU	DOUBLOON
BDLNOOUY	UNBLOODY
BDLNOOWW	BLOWDOWN
BDLOOOSX	OXBLOODS
BDLORSUW	SUBWORLD
BDMOORRS	SMORBROD
BDMOOSSS	BOSSDOMS
BDMORSUW	BUDWORMS
BDNNOOTU	BUNODONT
BDNOORSU	BOURDONS
BDNOOSUX	SOUNDBOX
BDNOOSWW	DOWNBOWS
BDNOOTUU	OUTBOUND
BDNORSTU	TURBONDS
BDNORSUW	RUBDOWNS
BDOOOSWX	BOXWOODS
BDORUWZZ	BUZZWORD
BEEEEFLN	ENFEEBLE
BEEEEFRS	FREEBEES
BEEEEKSS	BESEEKES
BEEEEMST	BETEEMES
BEEEENPS	PEEBEENS
BEEEENRT	TEREBENE
BEEEENRZ	EBENEZER
BEEEFIRS	FREEBIES
BEEEFIST	BEEFIEST
BEEEFLSS	BEEFLESS
	FEBLESSE
BEEEFLST	FEEBLEST
BEEEGILN	BELEEING
BEEEGINS	BESEEING
BEEEGIRS	BESIEGER
BEEEGISS	BESIEGES
BEEEGRRS	BERGERES
BEEEGRTT	BEGETTER
BEEEHIST	BHEESTIE
BEEEHISV	BEEHIVES
BEEEHLRT	HERBELET
BEEEHLWW	WEBWHEEL
BEEEHNOY	HONEYBEE
BEEEHNSS	SHEBEENS
BEEEILLL	LIBELLEE
BEEEILLS	LIBELEES
BEEEILNS	BEELINES
BEEEILRV	BELIEVER
BEEEILSV	BELIEVES
BEEEINST	EBENISTE
BEEEIRRZ	BREEZIER
BEEEIRST	BEERIEST
BEEEJLSW	BEJEWELS
BEEEJLSZ	JEZEBELS
BEEEJSUZ	BEJEEZUS
BEEEKLLS	BELLEEKS
BEEELLRR	REBELLER
BEEELLRT	BELLETER
BEEELLRV	BEVELLER
BEEELMNS	ENSEMBLE
BEEELMRS	RESEMBLE
BEEELMSY	BESEEMLY
BEEELMZZ	EMBEZZLE
BEEELPRS	BLEEPERS
BEEELRST	BEETLERS
BEEELRSV	BEVELERS
BEEEMMRR	REMEMBER
BEEEMNSU	UNBESEEM
BEEEMRSS	BERSEEMS
BEEEMRSW	EMBREWES
BEEENNSZ	BENZENES
BEEENSST	SEBESTEN
BEEENSTW	BETWEENS
BEEEPPPR	BEPEPPER
BEEEPRST	BEPESTER
BEEERSST	BRETESSE
BEEERSTT	BESETTER
BEEESSST	TSESSEBE
BEEFFLMU	BEMUFFLE
BEEFFRTU	BUFFETER
BEEFGILN	FEEBLING
BEEFGINR	BEFINGER
	BEFRINGE
BEEFHILS	FEEBLISH
BEEFIIRZ	FIBERIZE
BEEFILLT	LIFEBELT
BEEFILLX	FLEXIBLE
BEEFILNU	UNBELIEF
BEEFILRS	BELFRIES
BEEFINST	BENEFITS
BEEFIRRS	BRIEFERS
BEEFIRST	BRIEFEST
BEEFIRSU	RUBEFIES
BEEFLORU	BEFOULER
BEEFLORW	BEFLOWER
BEEFNORR	FREEBORN
BEEFNRTU	UNBEREFT
BEEFOORT	FREEBOOT
BEEGGNRU	GREENBUG
BEEGGNSU	GEEBUNGS
BEEGHLMR	BERGMEHL
BEEGIILL	ELIGIBLE
BEEGIILX	EXIGIBLE
BEEGILLR	GERBILLE
BEEGILMN	BEMINGLE
BEEGILNP	BLEEPING
BEEGILNT	BEETLING
BEEGILNV	BEVELING
BEEGILOS	OBLIGEES
BEEGILRU	BEGUILER
BEEGILSU	BEGUILES
BEEGIMNT	BEMETING
BEEGIMRS	BEGRIMES
BEEGINNR	BEGINNER
	BENIGNER

BEEGINNS BEGINNES
BEEGINRR BREERING
BEEGINRS BIGENERS
REBEGINS
BEEGINRZ BREEZING
BEEGINST BEIGNETS
BEEGINSU BEGUINES
BEEGINSW BEESWING
BEEGKLUY KEYBUGLE
BEEGLNOR BELONGER
BEEGLNOS ENGLOBES
BEEGMNOS GOMBEENS
BEEGMNOY BOGEYMEN
BEEGMOSU EMBOGUES
BEEGMRSU SUBMERGE
BEEGNOOW WOBEGONE
BEEGNOTT BEGOTTEN
BEEGNRSU SUBGENRE
BEEGNSTU UNBEGETS
BEEGOOPR GEOPROBE
BEEGOPSX PEGBOXES
BEEHHMOT BEHEMOTH
BEEHIKLR HERBLIKE
BEEHIMOT BOEHMITE
BEEHINSS BESHINES
NEBISHES
BEEHIRST HERBIEST
BEEHIRSV BESHIVER
BEEHISST BHISTEES
BEEHKSSU BUKSHEES
BEEHLLNT HELLBENT
BEEHLOOR BOREHOLE
BEEHLOVY BEHOVELY
BEEHLRSS HERBLESS
BEEHLRST BLETHERS
HERBLETS
BEEHLRSU BUSHELER
BEEHMRSY BERHYMES
BEEHMSTU SUBTHEME
BEEHNNOS HEBENONS
BEEHNOOP NEOPHOBE
BEEHNRRT BRETHREN
BEEHOOST BESOOTHE
BEEHOOSV BEHOOVES
BEEHORSW BEWHORES
BEEHRRST SHERBERT
BEEHRSST SHERBETS
BEEHRSSW BESHREWS
BEEIILNZ ZIBELINE
BEEIINOS EBIONISE
BEEIINOZ EBIONIZE
BEEIINRT BENITIER
BEEIIORS BOISERIE
BEEIIPST BEPITIES
BEEIIRRR BRIERIER
BEEIIRSS IBERISES
BEEIISTU UBIETIES
BEEIISTZ BITESIZE
BEEIJLSU JUBILEES
BEEIJSTU BEJESUIT
BEEIKLTU TUBELIKE
BEEIKLWY BIWEEKLY
BEEIKSSS BEKISSES
BEEILLLR LIBELLER
BEEILLNO LOBELINE
BEEILLNT BELTLINE
BEEILLNU BLUELINE
BEEILLRS LIBELERS
BEEILLRT BILLETER
BEEILLTT BELITTLE
BEEILLTU TULLIBEE
BEEILMOS EMBOLIES
BEEILMPP BEPIMPLE
BEEILMPR PERIBLEM
BEEILMRR LIMBERER
BEEILMSS BESLIMES
BESMILES
BEEILNNS BLENNIES
BEEILNRS BERLINES
BEEILNRY BERYLINE
BEEILNSS SENSIBLE
BEEILNST STILBENE
TENSIBLE
BEEILNSU NEBULISE
BEEILNUZ NEBULIZE
BEEILORS EROSIBLE
BEEILOSS OBELISES
BEEILOSZ OBELIZES
BEEILOTV LOVEBITE
BEEILRRT TERRIBLE
BEEILRSU BLUESIER
BEEILRSV VERBILES
BEEILRYZ BREEZILY
BEEILSTT BETITLES
BEEIMRRU UMBRIERE
BEEIMRST BIMESTER
BEEIMRTT EMBITTER
BEEIMSSU EMBUSIES
BEEINNSS BEINNESS
BEEINNSZ BENZINES
BEEINORT TENEBRIO
BEEINOSS EBONISES
BEEINOST BETONIES
EBONITES
BEEINOSZ EBONIZES
BEEINPRS PEBRINES
BEEINRSS NEBRISES
BEEINRTT REBITTEN
BEEINSTT BENTIEST
BEEIOQSU OBSEQUIE
BEEIORSS SOBERISE
BEEIORSW BOWERIES
BEEIORSZ SOBERIZE
BEEIORTV OVERBITE
BEEIQSUZ BEZIQUES
BEEIRRSU REBURIES
BEEIRRSV BREVIERS
BEEIRRTT BITTERER
BEEIRSSU SUBERISE
BEEIRSSW BREWISES
BEEIRSTU UBERTIES
BEEIRSUZ SUBERIZE
BEEISSTW WEBSITES
BEEKMOPR PEMBROKE
BEEKMOSS BESMOKES
BEEKNOPS BESPOKEN
BEEKNOST BETOKENS
STEENBOK
BEEKRRSS BERSERKS
BEEKRRSU REBUKERS
BEELLMTU UMBELLET
BEELLORW BELLOWER
REBELLOW
BEELLOST LOBELETS
BEELLSST BELTLESS
BEELLSUV SUBLEVEL
BEELMMOP BEPOMMEL
BEELMNNO NOBLEMEN
BEELMNSU BLUESMEN
BEELMOSW EMBOWELS
BEELMRRT TREMBLER
BEELMRRU LUMBERER
BEELMRST TREMBLES
BEELMSTU BLUESTEM
BEELMUZZ BEMUZZLE
BEELNNOR ENNOBLER
BEELNNOS ENNOBLES
BEELNOSS BONELESS
NOBLESSE
BEELNOSU BLUENOSE
NEBULOSE
BEELNOSZ BENZOLES
BEELNSSU BLUENESS
BEELNTTU BETELNUT
BEELNTUY BUTYLENE
BEELOOST OBSOLETE
BEELOQRU BRELOQUE
BEELORTT REBOTTLE
BEELORVW OVERBLEW
BEELOSTW STEELBOW
BEELOSTY EYEBOLTS
BEELPRSS PREBLESS
BEELPRUV BUPLEVER
BEELRSSS BLESSERS
BEELRSSV VERBLESS
BEELRSUZ ZEBRULES
BEELRTUU TRUEBLUE
BEELSSTU TUBELESS
BEELSTTU BLUETTES
BEEMNRRU NUMBERER
RENUMBER
BEEMOORS BORESOME
BEEMOPRT OBTEMPER
BEEMORRS SOMBERER
BEEMORSS EMBOSSER
BEEMORSW EMBOWERS
BEEMOSSS EMBOSSES
BEEMQSUU EMBUSQUE
BEEMRRSU UMBRERES
BEEMRSSU SUBMERSE
BEEMRSTU EMBRUTES
BEEMRTTU UMBRETTE
BEEMRTUZ ZERUMBET
BEEMSSSU EMBUSSES
BEENNOOS NONOBESE
BEENNOOT BOTONNEE
BEENOPTY TEENYBOP
BEENORRS ENROBERS
BEENORTU BOUNTREE
BEENORTV VERBOTEN
BEENOSST BONESETS
BEENOSTU TUBENOSE
BEENPRST BESPRENT
BEENRSTT BRENTEST
BEENRSTW BESTREWN
BEENRTTU BRUNETTE
BEENSSSU SUBSENSE
BEENSSTU SUBTEENS
SUBTENSE
BEENSSUV SUBVENES
BEEOORRT BOORTREE
BEEOORRV OVERBORE
BEEOORTT BEETROOT
BEEOPRRS REPROBES
BEEOPRSS BEPROSES
BEEOPSSU BESPOUSE
BEEORRSU BOURREES
BEEORRSV OBSERVER
VERBOSER
BEEORRTU BOURTREE
BEEORSST SOBEREST
BEEORSSU SUBEROSE
BEEORSSV OBSERVES
OBVERSES
BEEORSTU TUBEROSE
BEEORSTV OVERBETS
BEEORSTW BESTOWER
BEEORSWY EYEBROWS
BEEOSSSS OBSESSES
BEEOSSST BETOSSES
BEEPRRSU SUPERBER
BEEPRRSV PREVERBS
BEEPRSTY PRESBYTE
BEEQSSTU BEQUESTS
BEERRSTW BREWSTER
BEERRTTU REBUTTER
BEERSSSU SUBSERES
BEERSSTW BESTREWS
WEBSTERS
BEERSSUV SUBSERVE
SUBVERSE
BEERSTTU BURETTES
BEERSTTY BYSTREET
BEESTTUV BUVETTES
BEFFISTU BUFFIEST
BEFFLRSU BLUFFERS
BEFFLSTU BLUFFEST
BEFGIILL FILLIBEG
BEFGIILS FILIBEGS
BEFGIINR BRIEFING
BEFGILNU FUNGIBLE
BEFGIRSU FIREBUGS
BEFHILSU BLUEFISH
BEFHINOS BONEFISH
FISHBONE
BEFHIRSU BUSHFIRE
BEFIIRSU RUBIFIES
BEFILLXY FLEXIBLY
BEFILMOR FORELIMB
BEFILNOS LOBEFINS
BEFILNSU BLUEFINS
BEFILOST BOTFLIES
BEFILOUY LIFEBUOY
BEFILRST FILBERTS
BEFILSSU SUBFILES
BEFINORS BONFIRES
BEFIORSS FIBROSES
BEFIORTT FOREBITT
BEFIRSST FIBSTERS
BEFISSTU FUBSIEST
BEFISSUX SUBFIXES
BEFLLLUY BELLYFUL
BEFLLSTY FLYBELTS
BEFLMRSU FUMBLERS
BEFLORUW FURBELOW
BEFLSTUU TUBEFULS
BEFMOOOR FOREBOOM
BEFNOORR FORBORNE
BEFNOSSY FYNBOSES
BEFORRXY FOXBERRY
BEGGGINS BEGGINGS
BEGGIINN BINGEING
BEGGILRU BLUGGIER
BEGGINOY BOGEYING
BEGGIOST BOGGIEST
BEGGISTU BUGGIEST
BEGGLORS BOGGLERS
BEGGOOOS GOOSEGOB
BEGHHIST BEHIGHTS
BEGHIILP PHILIBEG
BEGHIKNT BEKNIGHT
BEGHILRT BLIGHTER
THERBLIG
BEGHINOR NEIGHBOR
BEGHINOT BEHOTING
BEGHINOV BEHOVING
BEGHINRT BERTHING
BRIGHTEN
BEGHINST BENIGHTS
BEGHIOST GOBSHITE
BEGHIRRT BRIGHTER
BEGHLNOU BUNGHOLE
BEGHNOTU BOUGHTEN
BEGHORTU REBOUGHT
BEGHOSTU BESOUGHT
BEGHOSUU BUGHOUSE
BEGHRRSU BURGHERS
BEGIIISS SIGISBEI
BEGIILLN LIBELING
BEGIILLY ELIGIBLY

BEGIILST	BILGIEST
BEGIIMNR	BEMIRING
	BERIMING
BEGIIMNS	MISBEGIN
BEGIIMNT	BETIMING
BEGIIMNX	BEMIXING
BEGIIMNY	BIGEMINY
BEGIINNS	INBEINGS
BEGIINRT	REBITING
BEGIINRZ	ZINGIBER
BEGIINTW	BITEWING
BEGIIOSS	SIGISBEO
BEGIKMNO	KEMBOING
BEGIKNRU	REBUKING
BEGILLLU	BLUEGILL
	GULLIBLE
BEGILLNU	BULLGINE
BEGILLNY	BELLYING
BEGILMNR	REMBLING
BEGILMNS	SEMBLING
BEGILNNY	BENIGNLY
BEGILNOR	IGNOBLER
BEGILNOS	INGLOBES
BEGILNOV	BELOVING
BEGILNOW	BOWELING
	ELBOWING
BEGILNRT	TREBLING
BEGILNSS	BLESSING
	GLIBNESS
BEGILNST	BELTINGS
BEGILNSU	BLUEINGS
	BULGINES
BEGILNTT	BLETTING
BEGILNUW	BLUEWING
BEGILNZZ	BEZZLING
BEGILORS	OBLIGERS
BEGILRST	GILBERTS
BEGILSTU	BULGIEST
BEGIMNOS	BESOMING
BEGIMNOW	EMBOWING
BEGIMNOX	EMBOXING
BEGIMNRU	EMBRUING
	UMBERING
BEGIMNSU	BEMUSING
	MISBEGUN
BEGIMOST	MISBEGOT
BEGIMOSY	BOGEYISM
BEGINNNO	NONBEING
BEGINNNR	BRENNING
BEGINNNU	UNBENIGN
BEGINNOR	ENROBING
	RINGBONE
BEGINNSU	UNBEINGS
BEGINOOS	BESOGNIO
BEGINORR	REBORING
BEGINORS	SOBERING
BEGINORW	BOWERING
BEGINRRS	BRINGERS
BEGINRRY	BERRYING
BEGINRSW	BREWINGS
BEGINRUY	REBUYING
BEGINSTT	BETTINGS
BEGKMOSS	GEMSBOKS
BEGLLORY	GORBELLY
BEGLLOSU	GLOBULES
BEGLLOTU	GLOBULET
BEGLMOOS	BEGLOOMS
BEGLMRRU	GRUMBLER
BEGLMRSU	GRUMBLES
BEGLMSUU	BLUEGUMS
BEGLNOUW	BLUEGOWN
BEGLNRSU	BLUNGERS
	BUNGLERS
BEGLOOSS	GLOBOSES
BEGLOOST	BOOTLEGS
BEGLOSUV	LOVEBUGS
BEGLRSTY	BERGYLTS
BEGMNOOY	BOOGYMEN
BEGNOORU	BOURGEON
BEGNORSU	BURGEONS
BEGNORTU	BURGONET
BEGNSSUU	SUBGENUS
BEGORRUY	BROGUERY
BEGPRSUU	SUPERBUG
BEHHKOST	KHOTBEHS
BEHIISST	BHISTIES
BEHIISTX	EXHIBITS
BEHIKLOS	BLOKEISH
BEHIKLSU	BUSHLIKE
BEHIKNST	BETHINKS
BEHIKOSS	KIBOSHES
BEHILLOS	SHOEBILL
BEHILLTY	BLITHELY
BEHILMRW	WHIMBREL
BEHILMST	THIMBLES
BEHILMTY	BIMETHYL
BEHILNPY	BIPHENYL
BEHILORR	HORRIBLE
BEHILORS	BOLSHIER
BEHILOSS	BOLSHIES
BEHILRST	BLITHERS
BEHILRTU	THURIBLE
BEHILSTT	BLITHEST
BEHIMNOO	BONHOMIE
BEHIMOOS	SEMIHOBO
BEHIMORS	BIOHERMS
BEHIMRTU	THUMBIER
BEHINNOS	SHINBONE
BEHINOPS	HIPBONES
	HOPBINES
BEHINOSW	WISHBONE
BEHIOOPR	BIOPHORE
BEHIRRST	REBIRTHS
BEHIRRSU	BRUSHIER
BEHIRSST	HERBISTS
BEHIRSSU	HUBRISES
BEHIRSSY	HYBRISES
BEHISSTU	BUSHIEST
BEHKOSSY	KYBOSHES
BEHLLOOT	BOLTHOLE
BEHLLOOW	BLOWHOLE
BEHLLOPS	BELLHOPS
BEHLLPSU	BELLPUSH
BEHLLSSU	SUBSHELL
BEHLMOSW	WHOMBLES
BEHLMRSU	HUMBLERS
BEHLMSTU	HUMBLEST
BEHLOOPY	HYPOBOLE
	LYOPHOBE
BEHLOOST	BOTHOLES
BEHLORST	BROTHELS
BEHLOSSU	SLOEBUSH
BEHLRRSU	BURRHELS
BEHLRSSU	BLUSHERS
BEHLSSSU	BUSHLESS
BEHLSSTU	BLUSHETS
BEHMNOTY	BOTHYMEN
BEHMOOOX	HOMEOBOX
BEHMOOST	BESMOOTH
BEHMOOSY	HOMEBOYS
BEHMOSTU	BEMOUTHS
BEHMPSTU	BETHUMPS
BEHNNOUY	HONEYBUN
BEHNORST	BETHORNS
BEHNRSTU	BURTHENS
BEHOOOPZ	ZOOPHOBE
BEHOOOST	BOOTHOSE
BEHOORST	THEORBOS
BEHOOSTX	HOTBOXES
BEHOOSUY	HOUSEBOY
BEHOPRST	POTHERBS
BEHORRST	BROTHERS
BEHORSSU	ROSEBUSH
BEHORSTT	BETROTHS
BEHOSSTU	BESHOUTS
BEHRRSSU	BRUSHERS
BEHRSTTU	TURBETHS
BEIIIKMN	MINIBIKE
BEIIKRST	BIRKIEST
BEIIKRTZ	KIBITZER
BEIIKSTZ	KIBITZES
BEIILLST	LIBELIST
BEIILMMO	IMMOBILE
BEIILMOS	MOBILISE
BEIILMOZ	MOBILIZE
BEIILMST	LIMBIEST
BEIILMSU	BULIMIES
BEIILNRS	RINSIBLE
BEIILOPR	PERIBOLI
BEIILRSS	RISIBLES
BEIILRST	TRILBIES
BEIILRTT	LIBRETTI
BEIILRUZ	BRUILZIE
BEIILSSV	VISIBLES
BEIILSTT	STILBITE
BEIIMNNR	RENMINBI
BEIIMNNU	BIENNIUM
BEIIMNOS	EBIONISM
BEIIMRTT	IMBITTER
BEIINORS	BRIONIES
BEIINOST	NIOBITES
BEIINQUU	BIUNIQUE
BEIINRST	BRINIEST
BEIINSST	STIBINES
BEIINSTT	STIBNITE
BEIIOPSS	BIOPSIES
BEIIORST	ORBITIES
BEIIOSTT	BIOTITES
BEIIRSST	BIRSIEST
BEIISSTT	BITSIEST
BEIISSTU	SUBITISE
BEIISTTT	BITTIEST
BEIISTUZ	SUBITIZE
BEIJLMRU	JUMBLIER
BEIJMOSU	JUMBOISE
BEIJMOUZ	JUMBOIZE
BEIJNORW	BIJWONER
BEIKKLNO	KNOBLIKE
BEIKLLOW	BOWLLIKE
BEIKLMOT	TOMBLIKE
BEIKLMOW	WOMBLIKE
BEIKLNRS	BLINKERS
BEIKLOSS	OBELISKS
BEIKLOST	BLOKIEST
BEIKLOTY	KILOBYTE
BEIKLRUY	RUBYLIKE
BEIKLSTU	BULKIEST
BEIKMNNR	BRINKMEN
BEIKNOST	STEINBOK
BEIKNRRY	INKBERRY
BEIKNRSS	BRISKENS
BEIKOORS	BOOKSIER
	BROOKIES
BEIKOORT	BROOKITE
BEIKOOST	BOOKIEST
BEIKORST	REITBOKS
BEIKOSST	BOSKIEST
BEIKRSST	BRISKEST
	BRISKETS
BEIKRSTU	BURKITES
BEILLMRY	LIMBERLY
BEILLMSS	LIMBLESS
BEILLMSU	SEMIBULL
BEILLNTU	BULLETIN
BEILLORS	BROLLIES
BEILLORV	OVERBILL
BEILLOSU	LIBELOUS
BEILLOSX	BOLLIXES
BEILLPRS	PREBILLS
BEILLRST	BRILLEST
BEILLSST	BESTILLS
BEILLSTU	BULLIEST
BEILMMOS	EMBOLISM
BEILMNOR	BROMELIN
BEILMNOU	NOBELIUM
BEILMNRU	UNLIMBER
BEILMNST	NIMBLEST
BEILMNUU	NEBULIUM
BEILMOOR	BLOOMIER
BEILMORS	EMBROILS
BEILMOSS	OBELISMS
BEILMPTU	PLUMBITE
BEILMRRU	RUMBLIER
BEILMRSS	BRIMLESS
BEILMRST	TIMBRELS
BEILMRSU	SUBLIMER
BEILMRSW	WIMBRELS
BEILMSSU	LIMBUSES
	SUBLIMES
BEILNNTU	BUNTLINE
BEILNOPS	BONSPIEL
BEILNOSU	NUBILOSE
BEILNOSW	BOWLINES
BEILNOVY	BOVINELY
BEILNRSY	BYLINERS
BEILNSSU	SUBLINES
BEILNSSY	SENSIBLY
BEILNSTU	BUSTLINE
BEILNSTY	TENSIBLY
BEILNSTZ	BLINTZES
BEILOORV	OVERBOIL
BEILOOST	LOOBIEST
BEILOPPW	BLOWPIPE
BEILOPRS	PREBOILS
BEILOPSS	POSSIBLE
BEILOQRU	BELIQUOR
	OBLIQUER
BEILOQSU	OBLIQUES
BEILORRS	BROILERS
BEILORST	STROBILE
	TRILOBES
BEILORSU	BLOUSIER
BEILORSW	BLOWSIER
BEILORTT	BLOTTIER
	LIBRETTO
BEILORWZ	BLOWZIER
BEILOSSY	BIOLYSES
BEILOSTW	BLOWIEST
BEILRRRU	BLURRIER
BEILRRTT	BRITTLER
BEILRRTY	TERRIBLY
BEILRSST	BLISTERS
	BRISTLES
BEILRSTT	BRITTLES
	TRIBLETS
BEILRSTU	BURLIEST
	SUBTILER
BEILRSTY	BLISTERY
BEILRSUY	BRULYIES
BEILRSUZ	BRULZIES
BEILRTTY	BITTERLY
BEILSTTU	SUBTITLE
BEIMMRRS	BRIMMERS
BEIMNORS	BROMINES
BEIMNRUZ	BRUNIZEM
BEIMNSSU	NIMBUSES
BEIMNSTU	BITUMENS
BEIMOORR	BROOMIER
BEIMOORS	BOSOMIER
	RIBOSOME

BEIMOOST	BOOMIEST
BEIMORRV	OVERBRIM
BEIMORSW	IMBOWERS
BEIMORSZ	BROMIZES
BEIMORTY	BIOMETRY
BEIMORYZ	RIBOZYME
BEIMOSSS	IMBOSSES
BEIMOSTV	BEVOMITS
BEIMOSTW	WOMBIEST
BEIMOSTY	SYMBIOTE
BEIMPSTU	BUMPIEST
BEIMRSSU	IMBURSES
BEIMRSTU	IMBRUTES
	RESUBMIT
	TERBIUMS
BEIMSSTU	SUBITEMS
BEINNOPS	PINBONES
BEINNOSS	BENISONS
	BONINESS
BEINNOST	BONNIEST
BEINNOSZ	BENZOINS
BEINNRYZ	ZEBRINNY
BEINNTTU	UNBITTEN
BEINOOST	BONITOES
	EOBIONTS
BEINORRW	BROWNIER
BEINORRZ	BRONZIER
BEINORST	BORNITES
	RIBSTONE
BEINORSW	BROWNIES
BEINORSY	BRYONIES
BEINORTZ	BRONZITE
BEINOSST	EBONISTS
BEINOSSX	BOXINESS
BEINOSTT	BOTTINES
BEINOSTU	BOUNTIES
BEINRRSY	NISBERRY
BEINRSSU	SUBERINS
BEINRSTT	BITTERNS
BEINRSTU	TRIBUNES
	TURBINES
BEINRSUU	UNBURIES
BEINRTTU	UNBITTER
BEINSSSU	BUSINESS
BEINSTTU	BUNTIEST
BEIOOPST	BIOTOPES
BEIOORST	ROBOTISE
BEIOORTZ	ROBOTIZE
BEIOOSSV	OVIBOSES
BEIOOSTZ	BOOZIEST
BEIOPSTY	BIOTYPES
BEIOQTUU	BOUTIQUE
BEIORRST	ORBITERS
BEIORRSU	BOURSIER
BEIORRSW	BROWSIER
BEIORRTU	ROBURITE
BEIORSST	SORBITES
BEIORSTY	SOBRIETY
BEIORSUV	BOUVIERS
BEIOSSST	BOSSIEST
BEIOSSSU	SOUBISES
BEIOSSTU	BOUSIEST
BEIOTTZZ	BOZZETTI
BEIQRSTU	BRIQUETS
BEIRRSSU	BRISURES
	BRUISERS
BEIRRSTU	BRUITERS
	BURRIEST
BEIRRTTU	TRIBUTER
BEIRSSTU	BUSTIERS
BEIRSTTU	TRIBUTES
BEIRSTTY	TREYBITS
BEISSSTU	SUBSITES
BEISSTTU	BUSTIEST
BEISTUZZ	BUZZIEST
BEJKOOST	JESTBOOK
BEJLMRSU	JUMBLERS
BEJORTTU	TURBOJET
BEKLNORY	BROKENLY
BEKLNRSU	BLUNKERS
BEKLOOOR	BOOKLORE
BEKLOORT	BROOKLET
BEKLOOSS	BOOKLESS
BEKLOOST	BOOKLETS
BEKLORUV	OVERBULK
BEKLRSSU	BURLESKS
BEKMOOPS	SPEKBOOM
BEKMOSST	STEMBOKS
BEKNNORU	UNBROKEN
BEKNOOOT	NOTEBOOK
BEKNOPRU	UPBROKEN
BEKNORSY	SKYBORNE
BEKOOORV	OVERBOOK
BEKOOPRS	PREBOOKS
BEKOORST	BOOKREST
BEKOORTU	OUTBROKE
BEKOOTTX	TEXTBOOK
BEKORSWW	WEBWORKS
BEKORTUW	TUBEWORK
BEKOSSXY	SKYBOXES
BEKRSSTU	BRUSKEST
BELLLLPU	BELLPULL
BELLLMSU	BLELLUMS
BELLMORT	MORTBELL
BELLMORU	UMBRELLO
BELLMRUY	LUMBERLY
BELLNOPS	BONSPELL
BELLNORW	WELLBORN
BELLNOSU	BULLNOSE
BELLNOSW	SNOWBELL
BELLNPSU	BULLPENS
BELLNTUY	TUNBELLY
BELLOOSU	LOBULOSE
BELLOOSX	BOLLOXES
BELLOPTY	POTBELLY
BELLORTW	BELLWORT
BELLOSST	BLOTLESS
BELLOSSU	SOLUBLES
BELLOSWY	SOWBELLY
BELLRRSU	BURRELLS
BELMMOOS	EMBLOOMS
BELMMRSU	MUMBLERS
BELMNOSU	NELUMBOS
BELMNOSY	BENOMYLS
BELMOORS	BLOOMERS
	REBLOOMS
BELMOORY	BLOOMERY
BELMOOSS	BLOOSMES
BELMOOST	BOOMLETS
BELMOPRS	PROBLEMS
BELMORST	TEMBLORS
BELMORSY	SOMBERLY
	SOMBRELY
BELMORUW	RUMBELOW
BELMOSST	TOMBLESS
BELMOSSY	SYMBOLES
BELMPRSU	PLUMBERS
	REPLUMBS
BELMPRUY	PLUMBERY
BELMRRSU	RUMBLERS
BELMRRUY	MULBERRY
BELMRSSU	SLUMBERS
BELMRSTU	STUMBLER
	TUMBLERS
	TUMBRELS
BELMRSUY	SLUMBERY
BELMSSTU	STUMBLES
BELNNOSU	UNNOBLES
BELNOORS	BORNEOLS
BELNOOSY	BOLONEYS
BELNOSTW	SNOWBELT
BELNOSUU	NEBULOUS
BELNOSYZ	BENZOYLS
BELNSSTU	SUNBELTS
BELNSTTU	BLUNTEST
BELNSTUU	UNSUBTLE
BELOOPRS	BLOOPERS
BELOOPRT	BOLTROPE
BELOORSW	ROSEBOWL
BELOORVW	OVERBLOW
BELOOSST	BOOTLESS
BELOOTUV	OBVOLUTE
BELORRTU	TROUBLER
BELORSST	BOLSTERS
	LOBSTERS
BELORSSW	BROWLESS
BELORSTT	BLOTTERS
	BOTTLERS
BELORSTU	BOULTERS
	TROUBLES
BELOSSTU	OUTBLESS
BELOSTUU	TUBULOSE
BELOSTUY	OBTUSELY
BELPRSUY	SUPERBLY
BELRRSTU	BLURTERS
BELRSSTU	BLUSTERS
	BUSTLERS
BELRSSUU	SUBRULES
BELRSTUY	BLUSTERY
BELRTUUU	TUBULURE
BELSSTTU	SUBTLEST
BELSSTUY	SUBSTYLE
BELSTTUY	SUBTLETY
BEMMOOSS	EMBOSOMS
BEMMORRS	BROMMERS
BEMMRRSU	BRUMMERS
BEMMRRUU	BEMURMUR
BEMNNSSU	NUMBNESS
BEMNOORT	TROMBONE
BEMNORSW	EMBROWNS
BEMNORSY	EMBRYONS
BEMNSSUU	SUBMENUS
BEMNSTTU	BUTMENTS
BEMNTTUY	BUTTYMEN
BEMOORRS	SOMBRERO
BEMOORTT	BOTTOMER
BEMORSST	BESTORMS
	MOBSTERS
	SOMBREST
BEMORSSU	MORBUSES
BEMORSWW	WEBWORMS
BEMOSTUX	BUXOMEST
BEMOSTUY	MYOTUBES
BEMSSSUU	SUBSUMES
BEMSSTUW	STEWBUMS
BENNNOTU	UNBONNET
BENNOOTU	BOUTONNE
BENNORSW	NEWBORNS
BENNSSSU	SNUBNESS
BENOORRV	OVERBORN
BENOORSU	BURNOOSE
BENORRSU	SUBORNER
BENORRSZ	BRONZERS
BENORRTU	TRUEBORN
BENORRUV	OVERBURN
BENORSST	SORBENTS
BENORSTU	BURSTONE
	RUBSTONE
BENORSTW	BESTROWN
	BROWNEST
BENORSUU	BURNOUSE
BENORSWY	BYWONERS
BENORTTU	BUTTONER
	REBUTTON
BENOSSTU	SUBTONES
BENOSSUZ	SUBZONES
BENOSSWY	NEWSBOYS
BENRRSUY	SUNBERRY
BENRSSTU	SUBRENTS
BENRSTUY	SUBENTRY
BENSSSUY	BUSYNESS
BEOORRRW	BORROWER
	REBORROW
BEOORRVW	OVERBROW
BEOORSSS	OBSESSOR
	SORBOSES
BEOORSST	BOOSTERS
BEOORSTY	BOTRYOSE
BEOOSTUX	OUTBOXES
BEOOTTZZ	BOZZETTO
BEOPRRSV	PROVERBS
BEOPRSST	BESPORTS
BEOPSSTU	BESPOUTS
BEOQSSTU	BOSQUETS
BEOQSTUU	BOUQUETS
BEORRRUW	BURROWER
BEORRSSW	BROWSERS
BEORRSTU	ROBUSTER
BEORSSSU	SORBUSES
BEORSSTW	BESTROWS
BEORSSUU	SUBEROUS
BEORSTUU	TUBEROUS
BEORSUVY	OVERBUSY
	OVERBUYS
BEOSSTTU	OBTUSEST
BEPRRSTU	PERTURBS
BEPSSTUY	SUBTYPES
BEQRRSUU	BRUSQUER
BERRSSTU	BURSTERS
BERRSTUU	SURREBUT
BERSSTTU	BUTTRESS
BERSSTUV	SUBVERST
	SUBVERTS
BESSSSUY	BYSSUSES
BESSSTTU	SUBTESTS
BESSTTUX	SUBTEXTS
BFFGILNU	BLUFFING
BFFGINSU	BUFFINGS
BFFHORSU	BRUSHOFF
BFFILOOS	BOILOFFS
BFFLOOSW	BLOWOFFS
BFFLOTUU	OUTBLUFF
BFFNOOSU	BUFFOONS
BFFNOSUX	SNUFFBOX
BFGILMNU	FUMBLING
BFGIOOST	BIGFOOTS
BFGIORST	FROGBITS
BFGLLORU	BULLFROG
BFHIILLS	BILLFISH
BFHILOST	FISHBOLT
BFHILOSW	BLOWFISH
	FISHBOWL
BFHIMNSU	NUMBFISH
BFHLLSUU	BLUSHFUL
BFIINORS	FIBROINS
BFIIORSS	FIBROSIS
BFILLMRU	BRIMFULL
BFILLSSU	BLISSFUL
BFIMNORU	NUBIFORM
BFIMORTU	TUBIFORM
BFINORYZ	BRONZIFY
BFIORSTT	FROSTBIT
BFKLOOSU	BOOKFULS
BFKLOOSY	FLYBOOKS
BFKSSSUU	SUBFUSKS
BFLLNOWY	FLYBLOWN
BFLLOSUW	BOWLFULS
BFLLOSWY	FLYBLOWS
BFLOORSU	SUBFLOOR
BFNOORTW	BOWFRONT

BFOOOSTY	FOOTBOYS
BGGGIINS	BIGGINGS
BGGGILNO	BOGGLING
BGGGINOR	BROGGING
BGGGINSU	BUGGINGS
BGGHIINT	BIGHTING
BGGIILNN	BINGLING
BGGIILNO	OBLIGING
BGGIILNY	GIBINGLY
BGGIINNO	BOINGING
BGGIINNR	BRINGING
BGGIINRU	BRIGUING
BGGILNNU	BLUNGING
	BUNGLING
BGGILNRU	BURGLING
BGGINOOT	TOBOGGIN
BGGINOOY	BOOGYING
BGHHHISU	HIGHBUSH
BGHHINOR	HIGHBORN
BGHHIORW	HIGHBROW
BGHHIOSY	HIGHBOYS
BGHIINRT	BIRTHING
BGHILMNU	HUMBLING
BGHILNSU	BLUSHING
BGHILRTY	BRIGHTLY
BGHIMNTU	THUMBING
BGHIMOTU	BIGMOUTH
BGHINORS	BIGHORNS
BGHINRSU	BRUSHING
BGHINRTU	UNBRIGHT
BGHINSSU	BUSHINGS
BGHIORSU	BROGUISH
BGHIPSSU	BUSHPIGS
BGHLRSUU	BULGHURS
	BURGHULS
BGHMORSU	HOMBURGS
BGHNORSU	HORNBUGS
BGHNOTUU	UNBOUGHT
BGHOOPTU	BOUGHPOT
BGHOORSU	BOROUGHS
BGIIJLNR	JIRBLING
BGIIJLNY	JIBINGLY
BGIIKLNN	BLINKING
BGIIKMNO	KIMBOING
BGIIKNNO	BOINKING
BGIIKNRS	BRISKING
BGIILLNS	BILLINGS
BGIILMNW	WIMBLING
BGIILNNN	BLINNING
BGIILNNY	BYLINING
BGIILNOR	BROILING
BGIILNOS	BOILINGS
BGIILNOX	BOLIXING
BGIILNPP	BLIPPING
BGIILNRS	BIRLINGS
	BIRSLING
	BRISLING
BGIILNSS	BLISSING
	SIBLINGS
BGIILNTY	BITINGLY
BGIILNTZ	BLITZING
BGIIMMNR	BRIMMING
BGIIMNRS	BRIMINGS
BGIIMNRU	IMBRUING
BGIINNOR	INORBING
BGIINNRS	INBRINGS
BGIINORT	ORBITING
BGIINRST	RINGBITS
BGIINRSU	BRUISING
BGIINRTU	BRUITING
BGIINSTT	BITTINGS
BGIINSTU	BUISTING
BGIINVVY	BIVVYING
BGIJLMNU	JUMBLING
BGIJNORU	OBJURING
BGIJOSUU	BIJUGOUS
BGIKLNNU	BLUNKING
BGIKLNOT	KINGBOLT
BGIKNNOU	BUNKOING
BGIKNOOR	BROOKING
BGIKNOOS	BOOKINGS
BGIKNORS	BROKINGS
BGIKNSSU	BUSKINGS
BGIKNSTU	STINKBUG
BGILLLUY	GULLIBLY
BGILLNOU	GLOBULIN
BGILLNRU	BULLRING
BGILLNSU	BULLINGS
BGILLNUY	BULLYING
BGILMMNU	BUMMLING
	MUMBLING
BGILMNOO	BLOOMING
BGILMNPU	PLUMBING
BGILMNRU	RUMBLING
BGILMNTU	TUMBLING
BGILMORY	GORBLIMY
BGILMOSU	GUMBOILS
BGILMOTU	GUMBOTIL
BGILNNOS	SNOBLING
BGILNNTU	BLUNTING
BGILNOOP	BLOOPING
BGILNORT	RINGBOLT
BGILNORY	BORINGLY
BGILNOST	BILTONGS
	BOLTINGS
BGILNOSU	BLOUSING
BGILNOSW	BOWLINGS
BGILNOTT	BLOTTING
	BOTTLING
BGILNOTU	BOULTING
BGILNOWY	BOWINGLY
BGILNRRU	BLURRING
BGILNRTU	BLURTING
BGILNSTU	BUSTLING
BGILNTTU	BUTTLING
BGILOORS	OBLIGORS
BGILRSSU	BUSGIRLS
BGIMNOOR	BROOMING
BGIMNOOS	BOOMINGS
	BOSOMING
BGIMNORS	SOMBRING
BGIMNPSU	BUMPINGS
BGIMOSSY	BOGYISMS
BGINNNOU	UNBONING
BGINNORU	UNROBING
BGINNORW	BROWNING
BGINNORZ	BRONZING
BGINNOUX	UNBOXING
BGINNRSU	BURNINGS
BGINNRTU	BRUNTING
BGINNSTU	BUNTINGS
BGINOOST	BONGOIST
	BOOSTING
BGINORST	STROBING
BGINORSW	BROWSING
BGINOSWW	WINGBOWS
BGINPRSU	UPBRINGS
BGINRSSU	SUBRINGS
BGINRSTU	BRUSTING
	BRUTINGS
	BURSTING
BGINSSSU	BUSSINGS
BGINSSTU	BUSTINGS
BGINSSWY	SWINGBYS
BGINSUZZ	BUZZINGS
BGISUWZZ	BUZZWIGS
BGKLOOOS	LOGBOOKS
BGKNOOOS	SONGBOOK
BGKORSSY	GRYSBOKS
BGLLNOOY	OBLONGLY
BGLNOOSW	LONGBOWS
BGLNOSUW	BLOWGUNS
BGLOORYY	BRYOLOGY
BGMNOOOR	GOMBROON
BGMOOSTU	GUMBOOTS
BGMORRUW	GRUBWORM
BGNOOSWY	GOWNBOYS
BGNOSSSU	SUBSONGS
BGOPRSUU	SUBGROUP
BGORSTUU	BURGOUTS
BGORSTUW	BUGWORTS
BHIIINNS	INHIBINS
BHIIINST	INHIBITS
BHIIKRSS	BRISKISH
BHIILMPS	BLIMPISH
BHIIMRST	MISBIRTH
BHIIOPRT	PROHIBIT
BHIIPSSS	SIBSHIPS
BHIKLLOO	BILLHOOK
BHIKMNTU	THUMBKIN
BHILLNOR	HORNBILL
BHILLPUW	BULLWHIP
BHILLSTU	BULLSHIT
BHILNSTU	BLUNTISH
BHILORRY	HORRIBLY
BHILORUY	BIHOURLY
BHILOSTU	HOLIBUTS
BHILOSYY	BOYISHLY
BHIMNORT	THROMBIN
BHIMOOPR	BIOMORPH
BHIMOOSS	HOBOISMS
BHIMOPRS	BIMORPHS
BHIMOPSS	PHOBISMS
BHIMORTU	BOTHRIUM
BHIMSSTU	BISMUTHS
BHINOPSU	UNBISHOP
BHINORSW	BROWNISH
BHIOOPRS	BIOPHORS
BHIOPSST	PHOBISTS
BHIRSTTU	TURBITHS
BHISSTTU	BUSHTITS
BHKLORUW	BUHLWORK
BHKMNOOY	HYMNBOOK
BHKNOOOR	HORNBOOK
BHKOOOPS	BOOKSHOP
BHLLNORU	BULLHORN
BHLLOSTU	BULLSHOT
BHLLRSUU	BULLRUSH
BHLOOOTT	TOLBOOTH
BHLOSTUU	OUTBLUSH
BHLRSUUY	BULRUSHY
BHMNTTUU	THUMBNUT
BHMOPTTU	THUMBPOT
BHMORSTU	THROMBUS
BHNOORTX	BOXTHORN
BHNOSSUW	SNOWBUSH
BHOOPSSY	SHOPBOYS
BHOORTTU	OUTTHROB
BHOOSSTW	BOWSHOTS
BHPRSSUU	BRUSHUPS
BIIKLOST	KILOBITS
BIIKNOOT	BOOTIKIN
BIILLMOR	MORBILLI
BIILLMSS	MISBILLS
BIILLNOS	BILLIONS
BIILLOSU	BOUILLIS
BIILLSTW	TWIBILLS
BIILMOTY	MOBILITY
BIILMSTU	MISBUILT
BIILNNRS	BIRLINNS
BIILNOOV	OBLIVION
BIILNOTY	NOBILITY
BIILNQSU	QUIBLINS
BIILNSTU	SUBTILIN
BIILNSVY	BIVINYLS
BIILNTUY	NUBILITY
BIILORST	STROBILI
BIILOSSU	SIBILOUS
BIILOSSY	BIOLYSIS
BIILSTTW	WITBLITS
BIIMMNSY	NIMBYISM
BIIMMOSZ	ZOMBIISM
BIIMNOSU	NIOBIUMS
BIIMSSTU	STIBIUMS
BIINOOTX	BIOTOXIN
BIINORSV	VIBRIONS
BIINOTVY	BOVINITY
BIINRSTU	BURINIST
BIIQTUUY	UBIQUITY
BIIRSSTU	BURSITIS
BIJNOSSU	SUBJOINS
BIKLLSSU	SUBSKILL
BIKLNOST	INKBLOTS
BIKLNOSY	LINKBOYS
BIKMNOOS	BOOMKINS
BIKMNPSU	BUMPKINS
BIKOOSUU	BOUSOUKI
BIKOOUUZ	BOUZOUKI
BIKORRSW	RIBWORKS
BILLMSUY	BULLYISM
BILLNOOU	BOUILLON
BILLNOSU	BULLIONS
BILLOSUY	BLOUSILY
BILLOSWY	BLOWSILY
BILLOWYZ	BLOWZILY
BILLRRUY	BLURRILY
BILLRSWY	WRYBILLS
BILMMPSU	PLUMBISM
BILMNORS	NOMBRILS
BILMOSTU	BOTULISM
BILMRSTU	TUMBRILS
BILNOSTU	BOTULINS
BILNOSUU	NUBILOUS
BILNSTUU	TUBULINS
BILOOPST	POTBOILS
BILOORST	SORBITOL
BILOPSSY	POSSIBLY
BILORSST	BRISTOLS
	STROBILS
BILOSSSU	SUBSOILS
BILOTTUU	OUTBUILT
BILSTTUY	SUBTILTY
BIMMOOSS	IMBOSOMS
BIMMORSS	BROMISMS
BIMNORSW	IMBROWNS
BIMNOSSY	SYMBIONS
BIMNOSTY	SYMBIONT
BIMNRRUU	MUIRBURN
BIMNRUUV	VIBURNUM
BIMOORST	ROBOTISM
BIMOSSSS	BOSSISMS
BIMOSSTW	MISTBOWS
BIMOSSTY	SYBOTISM
	SYMBIOTS
BIMRSSTU	BRUTISMS
BIMRSSUX	BRUXISMS
BINNORTW	TWINBORN
BINOORST	BIOTRONS
	ISOBRONT
BINORSST	RIBSTONS
BINRSSTU	INBURSTS
BINRSTUY	BUTYRINS
BINSSTUU	SUBUNITS
BIOPRRSU	SUBPRIOR
BIOPRSTW	BOWSPRIT
BIORRSTU	BURRITOS
BIORRSTW	RIBWORTS
BIORSSTT	BISTORTS
BIORSTTU	BITTOURS
BIORSTTY	BOTRYTIS

BIORSTUY BISTOURY
BIOSTTUY OBTUSITY
BIRSSTTU SUBTRIST
BISSSSTU SUBSISTS
BKKOOORW BOOKWORK
WORKBOOK
BKLOSTUU OUTBULKS
BKMOOORW BOOKWORM
BKMOORUZ ZOMBORUK
BKNNOOOS NONBOOKS
BKNOOSTW BOWKNOTS
BKORSUWY BUSYWORK
BLLLLOOY LOBLOLLY
BLLMOORW BOLLWORM
BLLOPTUU BULLPOUT
BLLOTUUY OUTBULLY
BLMMPSUU PLUMBUMS
BLMNPSUU UNPLUMBS
BLMOOOST TOMBOLOS
BLMOOOTU OUTBLOOM
BLMOOOTY LOBOTOMY
BLMOORSW LOBWORMS
BLMOOSSS BLOSSOMS
BLMOOSSY BLOSSOMY
BLMOPSUU PLUMBOUS
BLNOOSSU BLOUSONS
BLNSTUUY UNSUBTLY
BLOOPSWY PLOWBOYS
BLOORSWW LOWBROWS
BLOOSSTY SLYBOOTS
BLOOSTUW BLOWOUTS
BLOPSSTU SUBPLOTS
BLORSTUY ROBUSTLY
BLOSTUUU TUBULOUS
BLRSTUYY BUTYRYLS
BMNOOOSW MOONBOWS
BMNOOOTW BOOMTOWN
BMNOOSSU UNBOSOMS
BMNORSUW MOWBURNS
BMNORTUW MOWBURNT
BMOOORSX BOXROOMS
BMOORSSU SOMBROUS
BMOORSTU MOTORBUS
BMOORTTY BOTTOMRY
BMORSSTU STROMBUS
BNNORTUW NUTBROWN
BNNOTTUU UNBUTTON
BNNRSSUU SUNBURNS
BNNRSTUU SUNBURNT
BNOOOSTW SNOWBOOT
BNOOOSUY SONOBUOY
BNOORTUW BROWNOUT
BNOPRSTU POSTBURN
BNORRUUW UNBURROW
BNORSTUU BURNOUTS
OUTBURNS
BNORTTUU OUTBURNT
BNRSSTUU SUNBURST
BOOPSSTY POSTBOYS
BORSTTUU OUTBURST
BORSTUUY BUTYROUS
BPRSSTUU UPBURSTS
CCCDIILY DICYCLIC
CCCDIOOS COCCOIDS
CCCDKLOO COLDCOCK
CCCEEILT ECLECTIC
CCCEGOSY COCCYGES
CCCEHIOR CHOCCIER
CCCEHIOS CHOCCIES
CCCEIIRT ECCRITIC
CCCEILNY ENCYCLIC
CCCEILUY EUCYCLIC
CCCEOSXY COCCYXES
CCCHIORY CHICCORY
CCCIINSU SUCCINIC

CCCILLYY CYCLICLY
CCCILNOY CYCLONIC
CCCILOPY CYCLOPIC
CCCINSTU SUCCINCT
CCCIOORS SCIROCCO
CCCKOORW COCKCROW
CCCNOOST CONCOCTS
CCDDEENO CONCEDED
CCDDEEOT DECOCTED
CCDDELOU OCCLUDED
CCDDENOU CONDUCED
CCDEEENR CREDENCE
CCDEEHIL CLICHEED
CCDEEHLN CLENCHED
CCDEEILN LICENCED
CCDEEINS SCIENCED
CCDEEIOP CODPIECE
CCDEEIOS ECOCIDES
CCDEEIRV CREVICED
CCDEEKOR COCKERED
RECOCKED
CCDEEKOY COCKEYED
CCDEELRY RECYCLED
CCDEENOR CONCEDER
CCDEENOS CONCEDES
CCDEESSU SUCCEEDS
CCDEHHRU CHURCHED
CCDEHIKT TCHICKED
CCDEHILN CLINCHED
CCDEHIPU HICCUPED
CCDEHKLU CHUCKLED
CCDEHLTU CLUTCHED
DECLUTCH
CCDEHNRU CRUNCHED
CCDEHORS SCORCHED
CCDEHORT CROTCHED
CCDEHORU CROUCHED
CCDEHOST SCOTCHED
CCDEHRTU CRUTCHED
CCDEHSTU SCUTCHED
CCDEIILO CLEIDOIC
CCDEIINO COINCIDE
CCDEIIRT CRICETID
CCDEIIST DEICTICS
CCDEILOS SCOLECID
CCDEILYZ CYCLIZED
CCDEINOR CORNICED
CCDEINOS CONCISED
CCDEINOT OCCIDENT
CCDEIOPP COPPICED
CCDEIOPU OCCUPIED
CCDEIORT CODIRECT
CCDEKNOU UNCOCKED
CCDEKOOU CUCKOOED
CCDELNOU CONCLUDE
CCDELORU OCCLUDER
CCDELOSU OCCLUDES
CCDELOTU OCCULTED
CCDENOOO COCOONED
CCDENORU CONDUCER
CCDENOSU CONDUCES
CCDEORRU OCCURRED
CCDEORSU SUCCORED
CCDEOSTU STUCCOED
CCDHIIKP DIPCHICK
CCDHIILO CICHLOID
CCDHIILS CICHLIDS
CCDHIIOR DICHROIC
CCDHIIOT DICHOTIC
CCDHINOO CONCHOID
CCDIILNU NUCLIDIC
CCDIILOS CODICILS
CCDIILSU CULICIDS
CCDIINOO CONOIDIC
CCDIINOS SCINCOID

CCDIINST DISCINCT
CCDIIORS CRICOIDS
CCDIIORT DICROTIC
CCDILOSY CYCLOIDS
CCDINOTU CONDUCTI
CCDKLOSU CUCKOLDS
CCDKOOOW WOODCOCK
CCDNOORS CONCORDS
CCDNOSTU CONDUCTS
CCEEEILN LICENCEE
CCEEFFOT COEFFECT
CCEEGINR RECCEING
CCEEGNOS COGENCES
CCEEHIKS CHICKEES
CCEEHILN ELENCHIC
CCEEHINZ ZECCHINE
CCEEHISV CEVICHES
CCEEHKNS SCHNECKE
CCEEHKPR PRECHECK
CCEEHKRS CHECKERS
RECHECKS
CCEEHLNR CLENCHER
CCEEHLNS CLENCHES
CCEEHORS ECORCHES
CCEEHOSU COUCHEES
CCEEHRSY SCREECHY
CCEEIILS CICELIES
CCEEIIST CECITIES
CCEEILMU LEUCEMIC
CCEEILNR ENCIRCLE
LICENCER
CCEEILNS LICENCES
CCEEILNT ELENCTIC
CCEEILPY EPICYCLE
CCEEILRR RECIRCLE
CCEEILRT ELECTRIC
CCEEIMNU ECUMENIC
CCEEINOR CICERONE
CROCEINE
CCEEINOV CONCEIVE
CCEEINSS SCIENCES
CCEEIORS CICOREES
CCEEIORV COERCIVE
CCEEIPSS SPECCIES
CCEEIRSS CERCISES
ECCRISES
CCEEIRSV CERVICES
CRESCIVE
CREVICES
CCEEITTU EUTECTIC
CCEEKLOR COCKEREL
CCEEKNRW CREWNECK
CCEEKOSY COCKEYES
CCEELMNY CLEMENCY
CCEELNSU LUCENCES
CCEELOSS SCOLECES
CCEELRRY RECYCLER
CCEELRSY RECYCLES
CCEEMMNO COMMENCE
CCEEMMOR COMMERCE
CCEEMOPS COMPESCE
CCEENNOS ENSCONCE
CCEENORT CONCRETE
CCEENRST CRESCENT
CCEEORRS COERCERS
CCEEORST COERECTS
CCEFFHKO CHECKOFF
CCEFIIPS SPECIFIC
CCEFIRRU CRUCIFER
CCEFLLOU FLOCCULE
CCEFLOOS FLOCCOSE
CCEFNOST CONFECTS
CCEGHIKN CHECKING
CCEGHIOR CHOREGIC
CCEGIKLN CLECKING

CCEGILOO ECOLOGIC
CCEGILRY GLYCERIC
CCEGINNO CONGENIC
CCEGINOR COERCING
CCEGINPS SPECCING
CCEGINRY RECCYING
CCEGNOOS COGNOSCE
CCEHHINS CHINCHES
CCEHHRSU CHURCHES
CCEHIIMR CHIMERIC
CCEHIIMS ISCHEMIC
CCEHIINZ ZECCHINI
CCEHIKNP PINCHECK
CCEHIKNS CHICKENS
CCEHIKSU CHUCKIES
CCEHILNR CLINCHER
CCEHILNS CLINCHES
CCEHILOR CHOLERIC
CCEHILOY CHOICELY
CCEHILSU CULCHIES
CCEHILTY HECTICLY
CCEHINOR CORNICHE
ENCHORIC
CCEHINOS CONCHIES
CCEHINOZ ZECCHINO
CCEHINSS CHICNESS
CCEHINST TECHNICS
CCEHINSZ ZECCHINS
CCEHIORT RICOCHET
CCEHIOST CHOICEST
CCEHIRSS SCREICHS
SCRIECHS
CCEHKLRU CHUCKLER
CCEHKLSU CHUCKLES
CCEHKMSS SCHMECKS
CCEHKMSU CHECKSUM
CCEHKNSU UNCHECKS
CCEHKORW CHECKROW
CCEHKOTU CHECKOUT
CCEHKPSU CHECKUPS
CCEHLMOR CROMLECH
CCEHLNNU UNCLENCH
CCEHLNSU CLUNCHES
CCEHLRSU CLERUCHS
CCEHLRUY CLERUCHY
CCEHLSTU CLUTCHES
CULTCHES
CCEHNRRU CRUNCHER
CCEHNRSU CRUNCHES
CCEHORRS SCORCHER
CCEHORSS SCORCHES
CCEHORST CROCHETS
CROTCHES
CCEHORSU COUCHERS
CROUCHES
CCEHORTT CROTCHET
CCEHOSST SCOTCHES
CCEHRSTU CRUTCHES
SCUTCHER
CCEHRTUY CUTCHERY
CCEHSSTU SCUTCHES
CCEIIKLN NICKELIC
CCEIILNO COLICINE
CCEIILNT ENCLITIC
CCEIILNU CULICINE
CCEIILOR LICORICE
CCEIILPT ECLIPTIC
CCEIILST SCILICET
CCEIILTU LEUCITIC
CCEIINNR ENCRINIC
CCEIINOR CICERONI
CCEIIRRT CIRCITER
CCEIIRSS ECCRISIS
CCEIIRST ICTERICS
CCEIIRTT RECTITIC

CCEIIRTU	EUCRITIC
CCEIKKLO	COCKLIKE
CCEIKLRS	CLICKERS
CCEIKLRU	CLUCKIER
CCEIKLST	CLICKETS
CCEIKORS	COCKSIER
CCEIKOST	COCKIEST
CCEIKRST	CRICKETS
CCEILMOO	COELOMIC
CCEILMOP	COMPLICE
CCEILNOR	CORNICLE
CCEILNUY	UNICYCLE
CCEILOSS	SCOLICES
CCEILRRS	CIRCLERS
CCEILRRU	CURRICLE
CCEILRST	CIRCLETS
CCEILRSY	CRESYLIC
CCEILRTY	TRICYCLE
CCEILRUU	CURLICUE
CCEILSTU	CUTICLES
CCEILSYZ	CYCLIZES
CCEIMNOO	ECONOMIC
	ONCOMICE
CCEIMOPR	COPREMIC
CCEIMOST	COSMETIC
CCEIMRRU	MERCURIC
CCEINNOS	INSCONCE
CCEINNOV	CONVINCE
CCEINOOR	COERCION
CCEINOPR	COPRINCE
CCEINOPT	CONCEPTI
CCEINORS	CONCISER
	CORNICES
	CROCEINS
CCEINORT	CONCERTI
	NECROTIC
CCEINOSS	CONCISES
CCEINOST	CONCEITS
CCEINOTT	CONCETTI
	TECTONIC
CCEINOTY	CONCEITY
CCEINPRT	PRECINCT
CCEINRTU	CINCTURE
CCEINSTY	SYNECTIC
CCEIOORT	CROCOITE
CCEIOOTX	ECOTOXIC
CCEIOOTZ	ECTOZOIC
CCEIOPPS	COPPICES
CCEIOPRT	ECTROPIC
CCEIOPRU	OCCUPIER
CCEIOPSU	OCCUPIES
CCEIOPTY	ECOTYPIC
CCEIORST	CORTICES
CCEIPSST	SCEPTICS
CCEIRSSU	CIRCUSES
CCEJNOST	CONJECTS
CCEKLORS	CLOCKERS
CCEKNOST	CONTECKS
CCEKNOSY	COCKNEYS
CCEKOPST	PETCOCKS
CCEKORRY	CROCKERY
CCEKORST	CROCKETS
CCEKORSU	COCKSURE
CCELLOST	COLLECTS
CCELMOPT	COMPLECT
CCELNOSY	CYCLONES
CCELOPSY	CYCLOPES
CCELORTU	OCCULTER
CCELOSSY	CYCLOSES
CCELRUUY	CURLYCUE
CCELSSUY	CYCLUSES
CCENNORS	CONCERNS
CCENNOST	CONCENTS
	CONNECTS
CCENOORT	CONCERTO
CCENOOTT	CONCETTO
CCENOPST	CONCEPTS
CCENORST	CONCERTS
CCENORSW	CONCREWS
CCENORTY	CORNETCY
CCENOSTV	CONVECTS
CCENRRUY	CURRENCY
CCEOOORR	COROCORE
CCEOORSU	CROCEOUS
CCEOOSTT	COCOTTES
CCEOPRUY	REOCCUPY
CCEORRST	CORRECTS
CCEORRSU	REOCCURS
	SUCCORER
CCEORSSU	CROCUSES
CCEORSTU	STUCCOER
CCEORSTW	TWOCCERS
CCEOSSTU	STUCCOES
CCESSSUU	CUSCUSES
CCFGILNO	FLOCCING
CCFHKLOU	CHOCKFUL
CCFIINOR	CORNIFIC
CCFIIRUX	CRUCIFIX
CCFIKNOY	COCKNIFY
CCFILLOU	FLOCCULI
CCFILNOT	CONFLICT
CCFKLOOT	COCKLOFT
CCFLOOOO	LOCOFOCO
CCGHHIOU	HICCOUGH
CCGHIINN	CINCHING
CCGHIKNO	CHOCKING
CCGHIKNU	CHUCKING
CCGHINNO	CONCHING
CCGHINOS	GNOCCHIS
CCGHINOU	COUCHING
CCGIIKLN	CLICKING
CCGIIKNR	CRICKING
CCGIILNR	CIRCLING
CCGIILNU	GLUCINIC
CCGIKLNO	CLOCKING
	COCKLING
CCGIKLNU	CLUCKING
CCGIKNOR	CROCKING
CCGILLOY	GLYCOLIC
CCGILNOY	GLYCONIC
CCGILNSY	CYCLINGS
CCGILOSU	GLUCOSIC
CCGINNOS	SCONCING
CCGINOTW	TWOCCING
CCGKOORS	GORCOCKS
CCHHIITY	ICHTHYIC
CCHHILSS	SCHLICHS
CCHHINOT	CHTHONIC
CCHHLRUY	CHURCHLY
CCHHNRUU	UNCHURCH
CCHHOOWW	CHOWCHOW
CCHIINUZ	ZUCCHINI
CCHIIORT	ORCHITIC
CCHIKMPU	CHIPMUCK
CCHIKORY	CHICKORY
CCHIKSST	SCHTICKS
CCHILNNU	UNCLINCH
CCHILNUY	UNCHICLY
CCHINORS	CHRONICS
CCHINOSU	SCUCHION
CCHINSSU	SCUCHINS
CCHIPSSY	PSYCHICS
CCHKLOSS	SCHLOCKS
CCHKLOSY	SCHLOCKY
CCHKMOSS	SCHMOCKS
CCHKMSSU	SCHMUCKS
CCHKOOST	COCKSHOT
CCHKOPTU	PUTCHOCK
CCHKOSTU	COCKSHUT
CCHKPSUU	UPCHUCKS
CCHKSSTU	SCHTUCKS
CCHLNTUU	UNCLUTCH
CCHNRSUY	SCRUNCHY
CCHOORST	SCROOTCH
CCIIIMSV	CIVICISM
CCIIIPRT	PICRITIC
CCIIKKPW	PICKWICK
CCIIKNPY	PICNICKY
CCIILNOS	COLICINS
CCIILORT	CLITORIC
CCIILPRS	CIRCLIPS
CCIIMNSY	CYNICISM
CCIINNSU	CICINNUS
CCIINORZ	ZIRCONIC
CCIINOTY	CONICITY
CCIIRSTU	CIRCUITS
CCIIRTUY	CIRCUITY
CCIKKLOP	LOCKPICK
	PICKLOCK
CCIKKOTT	TICKTOCK
CCIKLOSW	COWLICKS
CCIKNOPR	PRINCOCK
CCIKOPRS	CROPSICK
CCIKOPST	COCKPITS
CCILLOTY	CYCLITOL
CCILNOOS	COLONICS
CCILNOSU	COUNCILS
CCILNSUY	SUCCINYL
CCILOOPS	PICCOLOS
CCILORUU	CURCULIO
CCILOSSY	CYCLOSIS
CCILSSTY	CYCLISTS
CCIMNRUU	CURCUMIN
CCINOOST	COCTIONS
CCINOPRT	PROCINCT
CCINOPSY	SYNCOPIC
CCINOPTY	PYCNOTIC
CCINORSY	CRYONICS
CCINOSTV	CONVICTS
CCIOOPST	SCOTOPIC
CCIOORSS	SIROCCOS
CCIOOTXY	OXYTOCIC
CCIOPRST	COSCRIPT
CCIOPSTU	OCCIPUTS
CCIRSSUY	CIRCUSSY
CCJNNOTU	CONJUNCT
CCKKLMUU	MUCKLUCK
CCKMMORU	CRUMMOCK
CCKMOOOR	MOORCOCK
CCKNORTU	TURNCOCK
CCKOOPST	STOPCOCK
CCKOPRSU	COCKSPUR
CCKOSSTU	CUSTOCKS
CCLLOTUY	OCCULTLY
CCLMOOPU	COCOPLUM
CCLNOOOR	CONCOLOR
CCLOOOSZ	ZOCCOLOS
CCLOORSU	OCCLUSOR
CCMOOORS	MOROCCOS
CCNOOPSU	PUCCOONS
CCNOORSU	CONCOURS
CCNOOSTU	COCONUTS
CCOOOORR	COROCORO
CCOOSSUU	COUSCOUS
CCOOTTUU	TUCOTUCO
CCORSSTU	CROSSCUT
CCORSSUU	SUCCOURS
CCOTTUUU	TUCUTUCO
CCRSUUUU	SURUCUCU
CDDDEETU	DEDUCTED
CDDDEIIS	DISCIDED
CDDDELRU	CRUDDLED
CDDDELSU	SCUDDLED
CDDDIIOY	DIDDICOY
CDDEEEEX	EXCEEDED
CDDEEEFN	DEFENCED
CDDEEEFT	DEFECTED
CDDEEEIR	REDECIDE
CDDEEEIV	DECEIVED
CDDEEEJT	DEJECTED
CDDEEENR	DECERNED
CDDEEENT	DECEDENT
CDDEEEPR	PRECEDED
CDDEEERS	SCREEDED
CDDEEERW	DECREWED
CDDEEETT	DETECTED
CDDEEFOR	DEFORCED
CDDEEGLU	CUDGELED
CDDEEHIS	DEHISCED
CDDEEHIT	CHEDDITE
CDDEEHNR	DRENCHED
CDDEEIIS	DEICIDES
CDDEEIKR	DICKERED
CDDEEIKT	DETICKED
CDDEEILN	DECLINED
CDDEEILP	PEDICLED
CDDEEINR	CINDERED
CDDEEINZ	DEZINCED
CDDEEIOT	COEDITED
CDDEEIOV	DEVOICED
CDDEEIPT	DEPICTED
CDDEEIRS	DECIDERS
	DESCRIED
CDDEEIRT	CREDITED
	DIRECTED
CDDEEKNU	UNDECKED
CDDEEKOR	REDOCKED
CDDEEKOT	DOCKETED
CDDEEKUW	DUCKWEED
CDDEELMO	COMEDDLE
CDDEELPU	DECUPLED
CDDEELSU	SCEDULED
	SECLUDED
CDDEELUX	EXCLUDED
CDDEELUY	DEUCEDLY
CDDEENOS	SECONDED
CDDEENSS	DESCENDS
CDDEEOPR	PRECODED
CDDEEORR	RECORDED
CDDEEORS	DECODERS
CDDEERUV	DECURVED
CDDEESUW	CUDWEEDS
CDDEFIIO	CODIFIED
CDDEFINO	CONFIDED
CDDEGIIN	DECIDING
CDDEGINO	DECODING
CDDEGINU	DEDUCING
CDDEHIOW	COWHIDED
CDDEHISU	CHUDDIES
CDDEHRSU	CHUDDERS
CDDEIINT	INDICTED
CDDEIISS	DISCIDES
CDDEIISU	SUICIDED
CDDEIKOS	DOCKISED
	DOCKSIDE
CDDEIKOZ	DOCKIZED
CDDEILLO	COLLIDED
CDDEILNU	INCLUDED
CDDEILOR	CLODDIER
CDDEILRU	CUDDLIER
CDDEIMOS	MISCODED
CDDEINTU	INDUCTED
CDDEIORV	DIVORCED
CDDEIRRU	CRUDDIER
CDDEIRSU	DISCURED
CDDEKNOU	UNDOCKED
CDDELLOU	COLLUDED
CDDELNOO	CONDOLED
CDDELOOR	CROODLED
CDDELORS	CODDLERS

CDDELRSU	CRUDDLES
	CUDDLERS
CDDELSSU	SCUDDLES
CDDEMNOU	DUNCEDOM
CDDENNOO	CONDONED
CDDENOOR	CORDONED
CDDENORU	UNCORDED
CDDEOORR	CORRODED
CDDEOORT	DOCTORED
CDDEOPRU	PRODUCED
CDDERSSU	SCUDDERS
CDDGHILO	GODCHILD
CDDGILNO	CLODDING
	CODDLING
CDDGILNU	CUDDLING
CDDGINRU	CRUDDING
CDDGINSU	SCUDDING
CDDHIIRY	DIHYDRIC
CDDHILOS	CLODDISH
CDDHIORS	DICHORDS
CDDIIIOS	DIDICOIS
CDDIIOSS	DISCOIDS
CDDIIOSY	DIDICOYS
CDDIISTY	DYTISCID
CDDIKOPS	PIDDOCKS
CDDIORSS	DISCORDS
CDDKOPSU	PUDDOCKS
CDDKORSU	RUDDOCKS
CDDMMOUU	MOCUDDUM
CDDOOORW	CORDWOOD
CDEEEERX	EXCEEDER
CDEEEFFT	EFFECTED
CDEEEFHL	FLEECHED
CDEEEFNR	REFENCED
CDEEEFNS	DEFENCES
CDEEEFRT	REDEFECT
	REFECTED
CDEEEHHW	WHEECHED
CDEEEHLR	CHEERLED
	LECHERED
CDEEEHMS	SMEECHED
CDEEEHOR	REECHOED
CDEEEHPS	DEPECHES
	SPEECHED
CDEEEHRS	CREESHED
CDEEEHRW	RECHEWED
CDEEEHST	TEDESCHE
CDEEEHSW	ESCHEWED
CDEEEINP	PIECENED
CDEEEINV	EVIDENCE
CDEEEIPS	EPICEDES
CDEEEIRV	DECEIVER
	RECEIVED
CDEEEISV	DECEIVES
CDEEEJRT	REJECTED
CDEEEKNW	NECKWEED
CDEEELLX	EXCELLED
CDEEELNR	CRENELED
CDEEELOS	COLESEED
CDEEELPY	YCLEEPED
CDEEELST	DESELECT
	SELECTED
CDEEELUX	EXCLUDEE
CDEEEMNT	CEMENTED
CDEEEMOR	COREDEEM
CDEEEMPR	EMPERCED
CDEEENNT	TENDENCE
CDEEENOS	SECONDEE
CDEEENRS	RECENSED
	SCREENED
	SECERNED
CDEEENRT	CENTERED
	DECENTER
	DECENTRE
CDEEEPRS	PRECEDES
CDEEEPTX	EXCEPTED
	EXPECTED
CDEEERRS	DECREERS
	SCREEDER
CDEEERSS	RECESSED
	SECEDERS
CDEEERST	DECREETS
	RESECTED
	SECRETED
CDEEERSV	SCREEVED
CDEEERTT	DETECTER
CDEEERTX	EXCRETED
CDEEESSX	EXCESSED
CDEEESTX	EXSECTED
CDEEETUX	EXECUTED
CDEEFFOR	COFFERED
	EFFORCED
CDEEFHLN	FLENCHED
CDEEFHLT	FLETCHED
CDEEFHNR	FRENCHED
CDEEFIIL	ICEFIELD
CDEEFIIS	EDIFICES
CDEEFIIT	FETICIDE
CDEEFINT	INFECTED
CDEEFKLR	FRECKLED
CDEEFKOR	FOREDECK
CDEEFLST	DEFLECTS
CDEEFNNU	UNFENCED
CDEEFNOR	ENFORCED
CDEEFORS	DEFORCES
	FRESCOED
CDEEFORT	DEFECTOR
CDEEGIIR	REGICIDE
CDEEGINO	GENOCIDE
CDEEGINR	RECEDING
CDEEGINS	SECEDING
CDEEGIOS	GEODESIC
CDEEGIOT	GEODETIC
CDEEGIRZ	GRECIZED
CDEEGLRU	CUDGELER
CDEEGNOR	CONGREED
CDEEHHSU	SHEUCHED
CDEEHHTT	THETCHED
CDEEHIKL	HELIDECK
CDEEHILN	LICHENED
CDEEHILP	CHELIPED
CDEEHILS	CHISELED
CDEEHINR	ENRICHED
	INHERCED
	NICHERED
	RICHENED
CDEEHIOS	ECHOISED
CDEEHIOZ	ECHOIZED
CDEEHIPR	CIPHERED
	DECIPHER
CDEEHIPS	CEPHEIDS
CDEEHIRR	CHERRIED
	DREICHER
CDEEHIRW	RICHWEED
CDEEHISS	DEHISCES
CDEEHIST	CHEDITES
	TEDESCHI
CDEEHITW	ITCHWEED
CDEEHKST	SKETCHED
CDEEHKTV	KVETCHED
CDEEHLMO	LEECHDOM
CDEEHLQU	QUELCHED
CDEEHLSU	SCHEDULE
CDEEHMTU	HUMECTED
CDEEHNQU	QUENCHED
CDEEHNRR	DRENCHER
CDEEHNRS	DRENCHES
CDEEHNRT	TRENCHED
CDEEHNRW	WRENCHED
CDEEHNST	STENCHED
CDEEHNUW	UNCHEWED
CDEEHORS	CHORDEES
	COSHERED
CDEEHORT	HECTORED
	TOCHERED
CDEEHPRU	CHERUPED
CDEEHPRY	CYPHERED
CDEEHQTU	QUETCHED
CDEEHRTW	WRETCHED
CDEEHSSU	DUCHESSE
CDEEIILT	ELICITED
CDEEIIMN	MEDICINE
CDEEIIMP	EPIDEMIC
CDEEIINT	INDICTEE
CDEEIIOS	DIOECIES
CDEEIIRT	DIERETIC
CDEEIIST	EIDETICS
CDEEIISV	DECISIVE
CDEEIITT	DIETETIC
CDEEIJNT	INJECTED
CDEEIJOR	REJOICED
CDEEIKLN	NICKELED
CDEEIKMY	MICKEYED
CDEEIKNR	NICKERED
CDEEIKNS	SICKENED
CDEEIKNV	INVECKED
CDEEIKPT	PICKETED
CDEEIKRR	DRECKIER
CDEEIKRT	DETICKER
CDEEIKRW	WICKEDER
	WICKERED
CDEEIKRY	YICKERED
CDEEIKST	TICKSEED
CDEEIKTT	TICKETED
CDEEILNP	PENCILED
	PENDICLE
CDEEILNR	DECLINER
	RECLINED
CDEEILNS	DECLINES
	LICENSED
	SILENCED
CDEEILNT	DENTICLE
CDEEILNU	NUCLEIDE
CDEEILOR	RECOILED
CDEEILPS	ECLIPSED
	PEDICELS
	PEDICLES
CDEEILRS	SCLEREID
CDEEILRT	DERELICT
CDEEILRU	RECUILED
CDEEIMNR	ENDERMIC
CDEEIMNS	ENDEMICS
CDEEIMOR	MEDIOCRE
CDEEIMOS	COMEDIES
CDEEIMPR	PREMEDIC
CDEEIMRS	MISCREED
CDEEIMRV	DECEMVIR
CDEEINNS	INCENSED
CDEEINNT	INDECENT
CDEEINOR	RECOINED
CDEEINOS	CODEINES
CDEEINPR	PINCERED
CDEEINPS	DISPENCE
CDEEINPT	DEPEINCT
	INCEPTED
	PEINCTED
	PENTICED
CDEEINRU	REINDUCE
CDEEINTU	INDUCTEE
CDEEINTV	INVECTED
CDEEIOPR	RECOPIED
CDEEIORV	CODERIVE
	DIVORCEE
	REVOICED
CDEEIOSS	DIOCESES
CDEEIOSV	DEVOICES
CDEEIPRR	REPRICED
CDEEIPRS	PRECISED
CDEEIPRT	DECREPIT
	DEPICTER
	PRECITED
CDEEIPRU	PEDICURE
CDEEIPST	PECTISED
CDEEIPTZ	PECTIZED
CDEEIQSU	QUIESCED
CDEEIRRS	DECRIERS
	DESCRIER
CDEEIRRT	DIRECTER
	REDIRECT
CDEEIRSS	DESCRIES
CDEEIRST	DESERTIC
	DISCREET
	DISCRETE
CDEEIRSU	DECURIES
CDEEIRSV	DESCRIVE
	SCRIEVED
	SERVICED
CDEEIRTU	CUITERED
	DEUTERIC
CDEEISUV	SEDUCIVE
CDEEITUV	EDUCTIVE
CDEEJKOY	JOCKEYED
CDEEKLNO	ENLOCKED
CDEEKLOR	RELOCKED
CDEEKLPS	SPECKLED
CDEEKMRU	MUCKERED
CDEEKNOR	RECKONED
CDEEKNRS	REDNECKS
CDEEKNRU	UNRECKED
CDEEKOOR	RECOOKED
CDEEKOPT	POCKETED
CDEEKORR	RECORKED
CDEEKORT	ROCKETED
CDEEKORV	OVERDECK
CDEEKORW	ROCKWEED
CDEEKOST	SOCKETED
CDEEKPRU	PUCKERED
CDEEKRSU	SUCKERED
CDEEKRTU	TUCKERED
CDEELLOR	CORDELLE
CDEELLOT	COLLETED
CDEELLPU	CUPELLED
CDEELMOW	WELCOMED
CDEELNOS	ENCLOSED
CDEELNPU	PEDUNCLE
CDEELNTY	DECENTLY
CDEELNUW	UNCLEWED
CDEELOOW	LOCOWEED
CDEELOPU	DECOUPLE
CDEELORS	RECLOSED
CDEELORV	CLOVERED
CDEELORY	RECOYLED
CDEELOSS	CODELESS
CDEELOST	CLOSETED
CDEELOTU	ELOCUTED
CDEELPRU	PRECLUDE
CDEELPSU	DECUPLES
CDEELRTU	LECTURED
	RELUCTED
CDEELRUX	EXCLUDER
CDEELSSU	SCEDULES
	SECLUDES
CDEELSUX	EXCLUDES
CDEEMOPR	COMPERED
CDEEMOPT	COEMPTED
	COMPETED
CDEEMORT	ECTODERM
CDEEMSTU	TUMESCED
CDEENNOS	CONDENSE
CDEENNOU	DENOUNCE

	ENOUNCED
CDEENNOV	CONVENED
CDEENNPY	PENDENCY
CDEENNTU	UNDECENT
CDEENNTY	TENDENCY
CDEENOOS	COOSENED
CDEENORR	CORNERED
CDEENORS	CENSORED
	ENCODERS
	NECROSED
	SECONDER
CDEENORT	CENTRODE
CDEENORU	COENDURE
CDEENOSS	SECONDES
CDEENOSY	ECDYSONE
CDEENOTU	DUECENTO
CDEENOTX	COEXTEND
CDEENOVX	CONVEXED
CDEENOVY	CONVEYED
CDEENPRU	PRUDENCE
CDEENRSU	CENSURED
CDEENRUV	VERECUND
CDEENSST	DESCENTS
CDEENSSU	CENSUSED
CDEENSTY	ENCYSTED
CDEEOOPR	COOPERED
CDEEOOTV	DOVECOTE
CDEEOPPR	COPPERED
CDEEOPRS	PRECODES
	PROCEEDS
CDEEOPRU	RECOUPED
CDEEORRR	RECORDER
	RERECORD
CDEEORRS	RESCORED
CDEEORRU	RECOURED
CDEEORST	CORSETED
	ESCORTED
	SECTORED
CDEEORSW	ESCROWED
CDEEORSY	DECOYERS
CDEEORTT	COTTERED
	DETECTOR
CDEEORTV	CORVETED
	VECTORED
CDEEOSST	CESTODES
	COSSETED
CDEEOSTT	ESCOTTED
CDEEPRRU	PRECURED
CDEEPRST	SCEPTRED
CDEERRRU	RECURRED
CDEERRSU	CURSEDER
	REDUCERS
CDEERRUV	RECURVED
CDEERSSU	SEDUCERS
CDEERSUV	DECURVES
CDEERSUX	EXCURSED
CDEERTTU	CURETTED
CDEERTUV	CURVETED
CDEFFINO	COFFINED
CDEFFISU	SUFFICED
CDEFFLSU	SCUFFLED
CDEFFNUU	UNCUFFED
CDEFHILN	FLINCHED
CDEFHILT	FLITCHED
CDEFHIMO	CHIEFDOM
CDEFHIRT	FRICHTED
CDEFHMOS	CHEFDOMS
CDEFIIIL	FILICIDE
CDEFIIIT	CITIFIED
CDEFIIOR	CODIFIER
CDEFIIOS	CODIFIES
CDEFIIST	DEFICITS
CDEFIITY	CITYFIED
CDEFINNO	CONFINED
CDEFINNU	INFECUND
CDEFINOR	CONFIDER
	INFORCED
CDEFINOS	CONFIDES
CDEFINOX	CONFIXED
CDEFIORY	RECODIFY
CDEFKORS	DEFROCKS
CDEFLNOU	FLOUNCED
CDEFLORY	FORCEDLY
CDEFNORU	FROUNCED
	UNFORCED
CDEFNOSU	CONFUSED
CDEFNOTU	CONFUTED
CDEFNSTU	DEFUNCTS
CDEFOSSU	FOCUSSED
CDEGHLNU	GLUNCHED
CDEGHORU	GROUCHED
CDEGHRTU	GRUTCHED
CDEGIINN	INCEDING
CDEGIINX	EXCIDING
CDEGIKNO	DECKOING
	DECOKING
CDEGIKNS	DECKINGS
CDEGILSU	CLUDGIES
CDEGINNO	ENCODING
CDEGINNS	SCENDING
CDEGINOR	RECODING
CDEGINOS	CODESIGN
	COGNISED
	COSIGNED
CDEGINOY	DECOYING
	GYNECOID
CDEGINOZ	COGNIZED
CDEGINRU	REDUCING
CDEGINRY	DECRYING
CDEGINSU	SEDUCING
CDEGINSY	DYSGENIC
CDEGKOSU	GEODUCKS
CDEGKSUW	GWEDUCKS
CDEGLNOO	COLOGNED
CDEGNORU	CONGRUED
CDEGOORS	SCROOGED
CDEGORSU	SCOURGED
	SCROUGED
CDEGORSW	SCROWDGE
CDEHHNOO	HONCHOED
CDEHIILO	HELICOID
CDEHIILS	CEILIDHS
CDEHIIMO	HOMICIDE
CDEHIIMR	CHIMERID
CDEHIINO	ECHINOID
CDEHIIVV	CHIVVIED
CDEHIKOS	HOICKSED
CDEHIKRW	HERDWICK
CDEHILMR	MERCHILD
CDEHILNR	CHILDREN
CDEHILOR	CHLORIDE
CDEHILOS	CHELOIDS
CDEHILRT	ELDRITCH
CDEHIMOR	CHROMIDE
CDEHIMOT	METHODIC
CDEHIMRS	SMIRCHED
CDEHINNR	INDRENCH
CDEHINOS	HEDONICS
CDEHINQU	QUINCHED
CDEHINST	SNITCHED
CDEHIOOR	CHOREOID
	OCHIDORE
CDEHIOSW	COWHIDES
CDEHIOTU	OUTCHIDE
CDEHIOTY	THEODICY
CDEHIQTU	QUITCHED
CDEHIRST	DITCHERS
CDEHISTT	STITCHED
CDEHISTW	SWITCHED
CDEHITTW	TWITCHED
CDEHKLSU	SHELDUCK
CDEHKNOU	UNCHOKED
CDEHKSUY	HEYDUCKS
CDEHLOOR	COHOLDER
CDEHLOOS	DESCHOOL
	SCHOOLED
CDEHLORT	CHORTLED
CDEHLOSU	SLOUCHED
CDEHMNTU	DUTCHMEN
CDEHMOOS	SMOOCHED
CDEHMOSU	SMOUCHED
CDEHMSTU	SMUTCHED
CDEHNOOP	CHENOPOD
CDEHNORS	CHONDRES
CDEHNRSU	CHUNDERS
CDEHOORR	RHEOCORD
CDEHOOST	COHOSTED
CDEHORSU	CHORUSED
CDEHORSW	CHOWDERS
	COWHERDS
CDEHOSSU	HOCUSSED
CDEHOSSW	COWSHEDS
CDEHSSSU	SCHUSSED
CDEIIILS	SILICIDE
CDEIIIMT	MITICIDE
CDEIIIOS	IDIOCIES
CDEIIIRV	VIRICIDE
CDEIIITV	VITICIDE
CDEIIKKS	SIDEKICK
CDEIIKLS	DISCLIKE
	SICKLIED
CDEIIKMM	MIMICKED
CDEIIKNR	CIDERKIN
CDEIIKNW	INWICKED
CDEIIKRS	DRICKSIE
CDEIIKRT	DICKTIER
CDEIIKST	DICKIEST
	STICKIED
CDEIILMM	DILEMMIC
CDEIILMO	DOMICILE
CDEIILNN	INCLINED
CDEIILNO	INDOCILE
CDEIILOT	IDIOLECT
CDEIILPS	DISCIPLE
CDEIILPU	PEDICULI
	PULICIDE
CDEIILRU	RIDICULE
CDEIIMOS	DIOECISM
CDEIIMRT	DIMETRIC
CDEIIMST	MISCITED
CDEIINNT	INCIDENT
CDEIINOS	DECISION
	ICONISED
CDEIINOV	INVOICED
CDEIINOZ	ICONIZED
CDEIINRT	INDICTER
	INDIRECT
	REINDICT
CDEIINTY	CYTIDINE
CDEIIOPR	PERIODIC
CDEIIOPS	EPISODIC
CDEIIOPT	EPIDOTIC
CDEIIOSU	DIECIOUS
CDEIIOSV	OVICIDES
CDEIIPPT	PEPTIDIC
CDEIIPRR	CIRRIPED
CDEIIRST	ICTERIDS
CDEIIRTU	DIURETIC
CDEIIRUV	VIRUCIDE
CDEIISSU	SUICIDES
CDEIISTT	DICTIEST
CDEIITWY	CITYWIDE
CDEIJNOO	COJOINED
CDEIJSST	DISJECTS
CDEIKLNO	INLOCKED
CDEIKLNR	CRINKLED
CDEIKLNU	UNLICKED
CDEIKLOR	CORDLIKE
CDEIKLOS	SIDELOCK
CDEIKLPR	PRICKLED
CDEIKLRT	TRICKLED
CDEIKLST	STICKLED
CDEIKLWY	WICKEDLY
CDEIKMSU	MUSICKED
CDEIKNPU	UNPICKED
CDEIKNTU	TUNICKED
CDEIKOSS	DOCKISES
CDEIKOST	DIESTOCK
CDEIKOSY	YOICKSED
CDEIKOSZ	DOCKIZES
CDEIKRRS	DERRICKS
CDEIKSTU	DUCKIEST
CDEILLOR	COLLIDER
CDEILLOS	CODILLES
	COLLIDES
CDEILLOU	LODICULE
CDEILLOY	DOCILELY
CDEILLPU	PELLUCID
CDEILMMS	SCLIMMED
CDEILMOP	COMPILED
	COMPLIED
CDEILMOS	MELODICS
CDEILMOY	MYCELOID
CDEILMPR	CRIMPLED
CDEILMRU	DULCIMER
CDEILMSY	DYSMELIC
CDEILNOS	INCLOSED
CDEILNOU	NUCLEOID
	UNCOILED
	UNDOCILE
CDEILNRY	CYLINDER
CDEILNSU	INCLUDES
	NUCLIDES
	UNSLICED
CDEILOOW	WOODLICE
CDEILOPS	SCOPELID
CDEILOPU	CLUPEOID
	UPCOILED
CDEILORS	SCLEROID
CDEILORU	CLOUDIER
CDEILORV	COVERLID
CDEILOSS	DISCLOSE
CDEILOST	DOCILEST
CDEILPPR	CRIPPLED
CDEILPSU	CLUPEIDS
CDEILRTY	DIRECTLY
CDEILSTU	DULCITES
	LUCIDEST
CDEILSXY	DYSLEXIC
CDEILTTU	CUITTLED
CDEIMMOX	COMMIXED
CDEIMOOW	WOODMICE
CDEIMORT	MORTICED
CDEIMOSS	MISCODES
CDEIMOST	DEMOTICS
	DOMESTIC
CDEIMPRS	SCRIMPED
CDEINNOU	UNCOINED
CDEINNOV	CONNIVED
CDEINOOS	COOSINED
CDEINOOZ	ENDOZOIC
CDEINORR	CORDINER
CDEINORS	CONSIDER
CDEINORT	CENTROID
	DOCTRINE
CDEINORU	DECURION
CDEINORV	CODRIVEN
CDEINOST	DEONTICS
CDEINOSU	DOUCINES
CDEINOSZ	ZINCODES

CDEINOTU	EDUCTION
CDEINOUV	UNVOICED
CDEINOVV	CONVIVED
CDEINPRS	PRESCIND
CDEINPRU	UNPRICED
CDEINPSY	DYSPNEIC
CDEINRRU	INCURRED
CDEINRSS	DISCERNS
	RESCINDS
CDEINRSU	INDUCERS
CDEINRTU	REINDUCT
CDEINRUV	INCURVED
CDEINSSX	EXSCINDS
CDEINSTY	SYNDETIC
CDEIOORS	CORODIES
CDEIOORT	COEDITOR
CDEIOPRS	PERCOIDS
CDEIOPRT	DEPICTOR
CDEIOPST	DESPOTIC
CDEIOPTY	COPYEDIT
CDEIORRT	CREDITOR
	DIRECTOR
CDEIORRV	CODRIVER
	DIVORCER
CDEIORSS	DISCOERS
CDEIORST	CORDITES
CDEIORSU	DISCOURE
CDEIORSV	CODRIVES
	DISCOVER
	DIVORCES
CDEIORSW	CROWDIES
CDEIORSY	DECISORY
CDEIORTU	OUTCRIED
CDEIOSST	CESTOIDS
CDEIOSTT	COTTISED
CDEIPRSS	DISCERPS
CDEIPRST	PREDICTS
	SCRIPTED
CDEIPRSY	CYPRIDES
CDEIPRTU	PICTURED
CDEIPSST	DISCEPTS
CDEIPSSU	CUSPIDES
CDEIRRSU	SCURRIED
CDEIRSSU	DISCURES
CDEIRSTU	CRUDITES
	CURDIEST
	CURTSIED
CDEIRSTV	VERDICTS
CDEISSST	DISSECTS
CDEISSSU	DISCUSES
CDEJNORU	CONJURED
CDEKKLNU	KNUCKLED
CDEKLMOR	CLERKDOM
CDEKLMOU	DUCKMOLE
CDEKLNOU	UNLOCKED
CDEKLNRU	CRUNKLED
CDEKLOPU	UPLOCKED
CDEKLORY	YELDROCK
CDEKLOSW	WEDLOCKS
CDEKLRTU	TRUCKLED
CDEKNOOU	UNCOOKED
CDEKNOOV	CONVOKED
CDEKNORS	DORNECKS
CDEKNORU	UNCORKED
CDEKNSSU	SUNDECKS
CDEKNSUU	UNSUCKED
CDEKNTUU	UNTUCKED
CDEKOPSY	COPYDESK
CDELLNUU	UNCULLED
CDELLOOP	CLODPOLE
CDELLORS	SCROLLED
CDELLORU	COLLUDER
CDELLOSU	COLLUDES
CDELLOTU	CLOUDLET
CDELLTUY	DULCETLY
CDELMNOO	MONOCLED
CDELMNOU	COLUMNED
CDELMPRU	CRUMPLED
CDELNOOR	CONDOLER
CDELNOOS	CONDOLES
	CONSOLED
CDELNOOU	UNCOOLED
CDELNOSS	COLDNESS
CDELNOSU	ENCLOUDS
	UNCLOSED
CDELNOSY	CONDYLES
	SECONDLY
CDELNOTU	UNCOLTED
CDELNOUW	UNCOWLED
CDELNOUY	UNCLOYED
CDELNRUU	UNCURLED
CDELNSUY	SECUNDLY
CDELOORS	COLOREDS
	CROODLES
	DECOLORS
CDELOORU	COLOURED
	DECOLOUR
CDELOORV	OVERCOLD
CDELOPSU	UPCLOSED
CDELOPTU	OCTUPLED
CDELORSS	CORDLESS
	SCOLDERS
CDELORSU	CLOSURED
CDELORSW	CLOWDERS
	SCROWLED
CDELORTU	CLOTURED
CDELOSSU	DULCOSES
CDELOSTU	COULDEST
	LOCUSTED
CDELPRSU	SCRUPLED
CDELPRUU	UPCURLED
CDELPSTU	SCULPTED
CDELRRSU	CURDLERS
CDELRSSU	SCUDLERS
CDELRSUY	CURSEDLY
CDELRTUU	CULTURED
CDELRUVY	CURVEDLY
CDELSSTU	DUCTLESS
CDELSSUY	CUSSEDLY
CDELSTTU	SCUTTLED
CDELSTUU	DUCTULES
CDEMMNOO	COMMONED
CDEMMNOS	COMMENDS
CDEMMNOU	COMMUNED
CDEMMOOS	COMMODES
CDEMMOOV	COMMOVED
CDEMMOTU	COMMUTED
CDEMMRSU	SCRUMMED
CDEMNNOS	CONDEMNS
CDEMNOOW	COMEDOWN
	DOWNCOME
CDEMNOPS	COMPENDS
CDEMNOSU	CONSUMED
CDEMNOTU	DOCUMENT
CDEMNSUU	SECUNDUM
CDEMOOPS	COMPOSED
CDEMOPTU	COMPUTED
CDEMORSU	DECORUMS
CDEMOSTU	COSTUMED
	CUSTOMED
CDEMPRSU	SCRUMPED
CDENNOOR	CONDONER
CDENNOOS	CONDONES
CDENNOOT	CONNOTED
CDENNOST	CONTENDS
CDENNOUY	UNCOYNED
CDENOORS	CONDORES
CDENOORT	CREODONT
CDENOOST	SECODONT
CDENOOTT	COTTONED
CDENOOVY	CONVOYED
CDENORSS	CORSNEDS
CDENORSU	CRUNODES
CDENORSW	DECROWNS
CDENORTU	CORNUTED
	TROUNCED
CDENOSSY	ECDYSONS
CDENOSTU	CONTUSED
CDENRSUU	UNCURSED
CDENRTUU	UNDERCUT
CDENRUUV	UNCURVED
CDEOOPPS	COPEPODS
CDEOOPRS	SCROOPED
CDEOOPST	POSTCODE
CDEOORRS	CORRODES
CDEOORSU	DECOROUS
CDEOORSV	VOCODERS
CDEOOSTV	DOVECOTS
CDEOPRRU	PROCURED
	PRODUCER
CDEOPRSU	PRODUCES
CDEOQSTU	DOCQUETS
CDEORRSW	CROWDERS
CDEORRTU	REDUCTOR
CDEORSST	DOCTRESS
CDEORSSU	SCOURSED
CDEORSSW	SCOWDERS
CDEORSTU	EDUCTORS
	SEDUCTOR
CDEORSUU	DOUCEURS
CDEOSSTU	CUSTODES
CDEPRSTY	DECRYPTS
CDEPRUUV	UPCURVED
CDERSTTU	DESTRUCT
CDFIILSU	FLUIDICS
CDFIKMNU	MINDFUCK
CDFIKORS	DISFROCK
CDFNNOOU	CONFOUND
CDFNOOSU	COFOUNDS
CDGHIILN	CHILDING
CDGHIILO	CHILIDOG
CDGHIINS	CHIDINGS
CDGHIINT	DICHTING
	DITCHING
CDGHILOS	GLOCHIDS
CDGHINNU	DUNCHING
CDGHINOR	CHORDING
CDGHINOU	DOUCHING
CDGIINNU	INDUCING
CDGIINOS	DISCOING
CDGIKLNU	DUCKLING
CDGIKLOR	GRIDLOCK
CDGIKNOS	DOCKINGS
CDGIKNSU	DUCKINGS
CDGILNOS	CODLINGS
	LINGCODS
	SCOLDING
CDGILNOU	CLOUDING
CDGILNRU	CURDLING
CDGINORS	CORDINGS
CDGINORW	CROWDING
CDGINSTU	DUCTINGS
CDGNOOOS	COONDOGS
CDHHIILS	CHILDISH
CDHIILTW	TWICHILD
CDHIINST	CHINDITS
CDHIIOOR	CHORIOID
CDHIIORT	HIDROTIC
	TRICHOID
CDHIIOSZ	SCHIZOID
CDHIISST	DISTICHS
CDHILNSU	UNCHILDS
CDHILOOP	CHILOPOD
CDHILOOS	DOLICHOS
CDHILORS	CHLORIDS
CDHIMOSU	DOCHMIUS
CDHINNOR	CHONDRIN
CDHINORY	HYDRONIC
CDHIOOPW	WOODCHIP
CDHIOORS	CHOROIDS
CDHIOORT	TROCHOID
CDHIOPRW	WHIPCORD
CDHIOPRY	HYDROPIC
CDHIOPSY	PSYCHOID
CDHIORRT	TRICHORD
CDHIOSUV	DISVOUCH
CDHIPSTY	DIPTYCHS
CDHKOORS	HORDOCKS
CDHLOOPY	COPYHOLD
CDHNORSU	CHONDRUS
CDHOORRU	UROCHORD
CDIIIMNU	INDICIUM
CDIIINSV	INVISCID
CDIIIORT	DIORITIC
CDIIKMNO	DOMINICK
CDIIKPST	DIPSTICK
CDIILMOS	DOMICILS
CDIILOPP	DIPLOPIC
CDIILOTY	DOCILITY
CDIILSVY	VISCIDLY
CDIILTUY	LUCIDITY
CDIIMNOU	CONIDIUM
	MUCINOID
	ONCIDIUM
CDIIMTUY	MUCIDITY
CDIINOOS	ISODICON
	ONISCOID
CDIINORS	CRINOIDS
CDIINORT	INDICTOR
CDIINOST	DICTIONS
CDIINOSV	VIDICONS
CDIINPRY	CYPRINID
CDIINPTU	PUNDITIC
CDIINSTT	DISTINCT
CDIIOORS	SORICOID
CDIIOOSU	DIOICOUS
CDIIOPRT	DIOPTRIC
	TRIPODIC
CDIIORSU	SCIUROID
CDIIOSSS	CISSOIDS
CDIIPTUY	CUPIDITY
	PUDICITY
CDIIRSSU	SCIURIDS
CDIIRSTT	DISTRICT
CDIJNSTU	DISJUNCT
CDIKKNOW	KICKDOWN
CDIKKOPR	DROPKICK
CDIKNNSU	NUDNICKS
CDIKNORS	DORNICKS
CDIKNOSW	WINDOCKS
	WINDSOCK
CDIKNOTW	DOWNTICK
CDIKNPSU	DUCKPINS
CDILLOOS	COLLOIDS
CDILLOTU	DULCITOL
CDILLOUY	CLOUDILY
CDILMSTU	MIDCULTS
CDILOOPS	PODSOLIC
CDILOOPZ	PODZOLIC
CDILOORS	DISCOLOR
CDILOORT	LORDOTIC
CDILOOTY	COTYLOID
CDILOSST	DISCLOST
CDILOSTY	DICOTYLS
	SCOLYTID
CDIMMOSU	MODICUMS
CDIMOORT	MICRODOT
CDINNQUU	QUIDNUNC
CDINOOOR	CORONOID
CDINOOTU	NOCTUOID

CDINOPSY	DYSPNOIC
CDINORSW	DISCROWN
CDINORTU	INDUCTOR
CDINOSTU	CONDUITS
	DISCOUNT
	NOCTUIDS
CDINOSTY	DYSTONIC
CDIOOPRS	PROSODIC
CDIOORRR	CORRIDOR
CDIOPRRS	RIPCORDS
CDIOPRSU	CUSPIDOR
CDIOSSTY	CYSTOIDS
CDIOSTUV	OVIDUCTS
CDJLNOUY	JOCUNDLY
CDKLNOOW	LOCKDOWN
CDKMMORU	DRUMMOCK
CDKMORSU	MUDROCKS
CDKNNOSU	DUNNOCKS
CDKNOORS	DORNOCKS
CDKOOORW	CORKWOOD
CDKORTUW	DUCTWORK
CDLLLOOP	CLODPOLL
CDLNOOOW	COOLDOWN
CDLNOSUU	UNCLOUDS
CDLNOUUY	UNCLOUDY
CDLOOOTW	COLTWOOD
CDLOOPSY	LYCOPODS
CDLOORTY	DOCTORLY
CDLOOSTU	OUTSCOLD
CDMNOOPU	COMPOUND
CDMNORUU	CORUNDUM
CDMOSSUW	MUDSCOWS
CDNNOOOT	CONODONT
CDNNOSTU	CONTUNDS
CDNOSTUW	CUTDOWNS
CDOOOPST	OCTOPODS
CDOOPSST	POSTDOCS
CDOORRUY	CORDUROY
CDOOSTUW	WOODCUTS
CDOPRSTU	PRODUCTS
CDORSSUW	CUSSWORD
CEEEEGHS	GEECHEES
CEEEEHLS	LEECHEES
CEEEEIPY	EYEPIECE
CEEEEJRT	REJECTEE
CEEEELST	ELECTEES
	SELECTEE
CEEEEPRS	PRECEESE
CEEEFFIR	EFFIERCE
CEEEFFRT	EFFECTER
CEEEFHLS	FLEECHES
CEEEFILR	FLEECIER
CEEEFINR	ENFIERCE
CEEEFLRS	FLEECERS
CEEEFNOR	CONFEREE
CEEEFNRS	REFENCES
CEEEGIMN	EMCEEING
CEEEGINS	EGENCIES
CEEEGINX	EXIGENCE
CEEEGITX	EXEGETIC
CEEEGMNR	MERGENCE
CEEEGNRS	REGENCES
CEEEGNRV	VERGENCE
CEEEHIKR	CHEEKIER
CEEEHIRR	CHEERIER
	REECHIER
CEEEHIRS	CHEESIER
CEEEHLLS	ECHELLES
CEEEHLRV	CHEVEREL
CEEEHLSS	SLEECHES
CEEEHMSS	SMEECHES
CEEEHNNP	PENNEECH
CEEEHNRS	ENCHEERS
CEEEHORS	REECHOES
CEEEHPRS	CHEEPERS
CEEEHPSS	SPEECHES
CEEEHRRS	CHEERERS
CEEEHRSS	CREESHES
	SECESHER
CEEEHRSW	ESCHEWER
CEEEHRVY	CHEVERYE
CEEEHSSS	SECESHES
CEEEIJTV	EJECTIVE
CEEEIKRR	CREEKIER
CEEEILNN	LENIENCE
CEEEILNS	LICENSEE
CEEEILNT	TELECINE
CEEEILRS	CELERIES
CEEEILRT	ERECTILE
CEEEILTV	CLEVEITE
	ELECTIVE
CEEEIMNN	EMINENCE
CEEEIMPR	EMPIERCE
CEEEIMRR	REREMICE
CEEEINNT	ENCEINTE
CEEEINPR	PIECENER
CEEEINPS	EPICENES
CEEEINRS	CERESINE
CEEEINSS	ESNECIES
CEEEIOPT	TOEPIECE
CEEEIPRR	CREEPIER
	CREPERIE
CEEEIPRS	CREEPIES
CEEEIPRV	PERCEIVE
CEEEIRRV	RECEIVER
CEEEIRSV	RECEIVES
CEEEIRSX	EXERCISE
CEEEIRTV	ERECTIVE
CEEEISSS	ECESISES
CEEEISTV	EVICTEES
CEEEJRRT	REJECTER
CEEEJRST	REEJECTS
CEEEKNNP	PENNEECK
CEEELLNR	CRENELLE
CEEELLSU	ECUELLES
CEEELOPR	OPERCELE
CEEELOSS	COLESSEE
CEEELPRT	PREELECT
CEEELPSY	YCLEEPES
CEEELRRV	CLEVERER
CEEELRST	REELECTS
	RESELECT
CEEELRTT	ELECTRET
	TERCELET
CEEELSST	CELESTES
CEEEMNNS	SCENEMEN
CEEEMNRT	CEMENTER
	CEREMENT
CEEEMORT	ECTOMERE
CEEEMPRS	EMPERCES
CEEEMRTY	CEMETERY
CEEENNPT	TENPENCE
CEEENNST	SENTENCE
CEEENPRS	PRESENCE
CEEENPRT	PRETENCE
CEEENQSU	SEQUENCE
CEEENRRS	RESCREEN
	SCREENER
CEEENRRT	RECENTER
	RECENTRE
CEEENRSS	RECENSES
CEEENSSS	ESSENCES
CEEENSST	CENTESES
CEEEPRRS	CREEPERS
CEEEPRRT	PREERECT
CEEEPRTX	EXPECTER
CEEERRST	ERECTERS
	REERECTS
	SECRETER
CEEERRSU	RESECURE
CEEERRSV	SCREEVER
CEEERRTX	EXCRETER
CEEERSSS	RECESSES
CEEERSST	SECRETES
	SESTERCE
CEEERSSU	CEREUSES
CEEERSSV	SCREEVES
CEEERSTX	EXCRETES
CEEERTTV	CREVETTE
CEEERTUX	EXECUTER
CEEESSSX	EXCESSES
CEEESTUX	EXECUTES
CEEFFNOS	OFFENCES
CEEFFORS	EFFORCES
CEEFFORT	EFFECTOR
CEEFGILN	FLEECING
CEEFHIKR	KERCHIEF
CEEFHIRY	CHIEFERY
CEEFHISS	CHIEFESS
CEEFHIST	CHIEFEST
	FETICHES
CEEFHKLU	CHEEKFUL
CEEFHLNS	FLENCHES
CEEFHLRT	FLETCHER
CEEFHLRU	CHEERFUL
CEEFHLST	FLETCHES
CEEFHNRS	FRENCHES
CEEFHORU	FOURCHEE
CEEFHRST	FECHTERS
	FETCHERS
CEEFIINT	INFICETE
CEEFILLY	FLEECILY
CEEFILRT	TELFERIC
CEEFILRY	FIERCELY
CEEFINPP	FIPPENCE
CEEFINRT	FRENETIC
	INFECTER
	REINFECT
CEEFIPRT	PERFECTI
CEEFIRST	FIERCEST
CEEFKLRS	FLECKERS
	FRECKLES
CEEFKLSS	FECKLESS
CEEFLNOR	FLORENCE
CEEFLNSU	FLUENCES
CEEFLNTU	FECULENT
CEEFLRST	REFLECTS
CEEFNNSU	UNFENCES
CEEFNORR	CONFRERE
	ENFORCER
	RENFORCE
CEEFNORS	ENFORCES
CEEFNORW	FENCEROW
CEEFNRVY	FERVENCY
CEEFOPRR	PERFORCE
CEEFOPRT	PERFECTO
CEEFORRS	FRESCOER
CEEFORSS	FRESCOES
CEEFORTW	CROWFEET
CEEFPRST	PERFECTS
	PREFECTS
CEEGHIKN	CHEEKING
CEEGHILN	LEECHING
CEEGHINP	CHEEPING
CEEGHINR	CHEERING
	REECHING
CEEGHINS	CHEESING
CEEGHLOW	COGWHEEL
CEEGIINP	EPIGENIC
CEEGIJNT	EJECTING
CEEGIKLN	CLEEKING
CEEGILNP	CLEEPING
CEEGILNR	CREELING
CEEGILNT	ELECTING
CEEGILOT	ECLOGITE
CEEGILRS	CLERGIES
CEEGILRT	TELERGIC
CEEGIMNS	MISCEGEN
CEEGINOO	COOEEING
CEEGINOR	EROGENIC
CEEGINPR	CREEPING
CEEGINRS	CREESING
	GENERICS
CEEGINRT	ERECTING
	GENTRICE
CEEGINST	GENETICS
CEEGINSU	EUGENICS
CEEGINXY	EXIGENCY
CEEGIORX	EXOERGIC
CEEGIRSZ	GRECIZES
CEEGLLOR	COLLEGER
CEEGLLOS	COLLEGES
CEEGLNST	NEGLECTS
CEEGLOSU	ECLOGUES
CEEGMMOR	COMMERGE
CEEGMNOY	CYMOGENE
CEEGNNOO	ONCOGENE
CEEGNNOR	CONGENER
CEEGNNPU	PUNGENCE
CEEGNORS	COGENERS
	CONGREES
CEEGNORT	CONGREET
	COREGENT
CEEGNORV	CONVERGE
CEEGNOTY	ECTOGENY
CEEGNRSU	URGENCES
CEEGNRVY	VERGENCY
CEEGORST	CORTEGES
CEEGQRSU	GRECQUES
CEEHHMNN	HENCHMEN
CEEHHSTT	THETCHES
CEEHIIST	ETHICISE
CEEHIITZ	ETHICIZE
CEEHIKLY	CHEEKILY
CEEHIKMS	KIMCHEES
CEEHIKNW	CHEEWINK
CEEHILLN	CHENILLE
CEEHILLV	CHEVILLE
CEEHILRS	CHISELER
	SCHLIERE
CEEHILRT	TELECHIR
CEEHILRV	CHEVERIL
CEEHILRW	CLERIHEW
CEEHILRY	CHEERILY
CEEHILSV	VEHICLES
CEEHILSW	SWELCHIE
CEEHILSY	CHEESILY
CEEHIMMS	CHEMMIES
CEEHIMRS	CHIMERES
CEEHIMRT	HERMETIC
CEEHIMSS	CHEMISES
CEEHINOR	COINHERE
CEEHINPR	ENCIPHER
CEEHINPT	PHENETIC
CEEHINPU	EUPHENIC
CEEHINRR	ENRICHER
CEEHINRS	ENRICHES
	INHERCES
CEEHINST	SITHENCE
CEEHINSX	CHENIXES
CEEHINTT	ENTHETIC
CEEHIORS	CHEERIOS
CEEHIOSS	ECHOISES
CEEHIOSU	ICEHOUSE
CEEHIOSV	COHESIVE
CEEHIOSZ	ECHOIZES
CEEHIPRT	HERPETIC
CEEHIRRR	CHERRIER
CEEHIRRS	CHERRIES
CEEHIRRT	CHERTIER

CEEHIRSS	RICHESSE
CEEHIRST	CHESTIER
	HERETICS
CEEHIRTT	TETCHIER
CEEHIRTU	HEURETIC
CEEHIRTV	VETCHIER
CEEHISSV	SEVICHES
CEEHISTT	ESTHETIC
	TECHIEST
CEEHISTW	CHEWIEST
CEEHKLRS	HECKLERS
CEEHKNPS	HENPECKS
CEEHKRST	RESKETCH
	SKETCHER
CEEHKRTV	KVETCHER
CEEHKSST	SKETCHES
CEEHKSTV	KVETCHES
CEEHLMOO	HEMOCOEL
CEEHLMSZ	SCHMELZE
CEEHLNOS	CHELONES
	ECHELONS
CEEHLNOT	ENCLOTHE
CEEHLNPS	PLENCHES
CEEHLNPU	PENUCHLE
CEEHLNSU	ELENCHUS
CEEHLORT	RECLOTHE
CEEHLOSS	ECHOLESS
CEEHLOSW	COWHEELS
CEEHLQSU	QUELCHES
CEEHLRSU	HERCULES
CEEHLRSW	WELCHERS
CEEHLSSS	CHESSELS
CEEHMNNS	MENSCHEN
CEEHMNOR	CHOREMEN
	CHROMENE
CEEHMNSS	CHESSMEN
	MENSCHES
CEEHMORT	COMETHER
CEEHMOTY	HEMOCYTE
CEEHMRSS	SCHEMERS
	SCHMEERS
CEEHMRST	MERCHETS
CEEHNNOW	NOWHENCE
CEEHNNRT	ENTRENCH
CEEHNOPS	PENOCHES
CEEHNORS	RECHOSEN
CEEHNORT	COHERENT
CEEHNORV	CHEVERON
CEEHNPSU	PENUCHES
CEEHNQRU	QUENCHER
CEEHNQSU	QUENCHES
CEEHNRRT	RETRENCH
	TRENCHER
CEEHNRST	TRENCHES
CEEHNRSW	WENCHERS
	WRENCHES
CEEHNSST	STENCHES
CEEHNSTU	CHUTNEES
CEEHOOPR	POECHORE
CEEHOORS	RECHOOSE
CEEHOPRY	CORYPHEE
CEEHOPST	SHEEPCOT
CEEHOPTT	POCHETTE
CEEHORRS	COHERERS
	COSHERER
CEEHORRT	HECTORER
	TORCHERE
CEEHORSS	ORCHESES
CEEHORST	TROCHEES
CEEHOSUV	VOUCHEES
CEEHPRRS	PERCHERS
CEEHPRRY	PERCHERY
CEEHPRSU	UPCHEERS
CEEHPSST	SPETCHES
CEEHQRSU	CHEQUERS
CEEHQSTU	QUETCHES
CEEHRSTW	WRETCHES
CEEHRTTU	TEUCHTER
CEEHSTTU	TEUCHEST
CEEIIKLP	EPICLIKE
CEEIIMPR	EPIMERIC
CEEIIMRT	EREMITIC
CEEIINRT	ICTERINE
	REINCITE
CEEIINST	NICETIES
CEEIINVV	EVINCIVE
CEEIIPRS	EPICIERS
CEEIIRST	SERICITE
CEEIJNOT	EJECTION
CEEIJNRT	REINJECT
CEEIJORR	REJOICER
CEEIJORS	REJOICES
CEEIJRUV	VERJUICE
CEEIKKLN	NECKLIKE
CEEIKKSS	KECKSIES
CEEIKLMU	LEUKEMIC
CEEIKLNN	NECKLINE
CEEIKLPR	PICKEREL
CEEIKNRS	SICKENER
CEEIKNST	NECKTIES
CEEIKPRS	PICKEERS
	SPECKIER
CEEIKPRT	PICKETER
CEEIKPST	PECKIEST
CEEILLLP	PELLICLE
CEEILLMS	MICELLES
CEEILLNT	LENTICEL
	LENTICLE
CEEILMOR	COMELIER
CEEILMPS	SEMPLICE
CEEILNNT	CENTINEL
CEEILNNY	LENIENCY
CEEILNOS	CINEOLES
CEEILNOT	COTELINE
	ELECTION
CEEILNOV	VIOLENCE
CEEILNPR	PENCILER
CEEILNPU	PULICENE
CEEILNPX	CINEPLEX
CEEILNRR	RECLINER
CEEILNRS	LICENSER
	RECLINES
	SILENCER
CEEILNRU	CERULEIN
CEEILNRV	VERNICLE
CEEILNSS	ENCLISES
	LICENSES
	SILENCES
CEEILNST	CENTILES
CEEILNSU	LEUCINES
CEEILORR	RECOILER
CEEILORS	CREOLISE
CEEILORZ	CREOLIZE
CEEILOSS	SOLECISE
CEEILOSZ	SOLECIZE
CEEILPRS	PRESLICE
	RESPLICE
CEEILPRY	CREEPILY
CEEILPSS	ECLIPSES
CEEILPSX	EXCIPLES
CEEILQSU	LIQUESCE
CEEILRST	RETICLES
	SCLERITE
	TIERCELS
	TRISCELE
CEEILRSU	CISELEUR
	CISELURE
	RECUILES
CEEILRSV	VERSICLE
CEEILRTU	RETICULE
CEEILRTY	CELERITY
CEEILSSV	CLEVISES
	VESICLES
	VICELESS
CEEILSTT	TELESTIC
	TESTICLE
CEEILSTU	LEUCITES
CEEIMMPY	EMPYEMIC
CEEIMMRS	MESMERIC
CEEIMNNY	EMINENCY
CEEIMNPS	SPECIMEN
CEEIMNST	CENTIMES
	TENESMIC
CEEIMORT	METEORIC
CEEIMRSX	EXCIMERS
CEEIMSTT	SMECTITE
CEEINNOP	PINECONE
CEEINNOT	NEOTENIC
CEEINNRS	INCENSER
CEEINNRT	INCENTER
	INCENTRE
CEEINNSS	INCENSES
	NICENESS
CEEINNST	NESCIENT
CEEINOPU	EUPNOEIC
CEEINORR	ENCIERRO
CEEINORT	ERECTION
	NEOTERIC
CEEINORV	OVERNICE
CEEINORX	EXOCRINE
CEEINOSS	SENECIOS
CEEINOST	ICESTONE
	SEICENTO
CEEINOTV	EVECTION
CEEINPRT	PRENTICE
	TERPENIC
CEEINPST	PECTINES
	PENTICES
CEEINPSX	SIXPENCE
CEEINQRU	QUERCINE
CEEINRRS	SINCERER
CEEINRSS	CERESINS
	SCRIENES
CEEINRST	CENTRIES
	ENTERICS
	ENTICERS
	SCIENTER
	SECRETIN
CEEINRSU	INSECURE
	SINECURE
CEEINRTT	RETICENT
CEEINRTU	CEINTURE
	ENURETIC
CEEINSST	CENTESIS
CEEINSTY	CYSTEINE
CEEIOPPR	PERICOPE
CEEIOPPS	EPISCOPE
CEEIOPRS	RECOPIES
CEEIOPST	ECTOPIES
	PICOTEES
CEEIORST	COTERIES
	ESOTERIC
CEEIORSV	REVOICES
CEEIORSX	EXORCISE
CEEIORTT	EROTETIC
CEEIORTV	ORECTIVE
CEEIORTX	EXOTERIC
CEEIORXZ	EXORCIZE
CEEIOSST	COESITES
CEEIOSTV	COVETISE
CEEIPPRR	PREPRICE
CEEIPPRS	PRECIPES
CEEIPPRT	PRECEPIT
CEEIPPTU	EUPEPTIC
CEEIPRRS	PIERCERS
	PRECISER
	REPRICES
CEEIPRSS	PRECISES
CEEIPRST	CREPIEST
	RECEIPTS
CEEIPRSU	EPICURES
CEEIPRUX	PRECIEUX
CEEIPSST	PECTISES
CEEIPSTZ	PECTIZES
CEEIQSSU	QUIESCES
CEEIRRSS	CERRISES
CEEIRRST	RECITERS
CEEIRRSV	SERVICER
CEEIRRSW	SCREWIER
CEEIRRTU	URETERIC
CEEIRSSV	SCRIEVES
	SERVICES
CEEIRSTT	TIERCETS
CEEIRSTU	CERUSITE
	CUTESIER
	EUCRITES
CEEIRSTV	VERTICES
CEEIRSTX	EXCITERS
CEEIRSVX	CERVIXES
CEEISSST	CITESSES
CEEISTTT	TECTITES
CEEISTTZ	ZETETICS
CEEISUVX	EXCUSIVE
CEEJKOTT	JOCKETTE
CEEJORRT	REJECTOR
CEEJORST	EJECTORS
CEEKKNOS	KNEESOCK
CEEKKNPS	KENSPECK
CEEKLNPU	PENUCKLE
CEEKLNSS	NECKLESS
CEEKLNST	NECKLETS
CEEKLPSS	SPECKLES
CEEKLRSS	CLERKESS
	RECKLESS
CEEKNORR	RECKONER
CEEKNRSU	SUCKENER
CEEKOPRT	POCKETER
CEEKOPRX	OXPECKER
CEEKORRT	CORKTREE
	ROCKETER
CEEKOSSY	SOCKEYES
CEEKOSTT	SOCKETTE
CEEKPRRU	PUCKERER
CEEKPRSY	RYEPECKS
CEEKRRSW	WRECKERS
CEELLLSU	CELLULES
CEELLMOU	MOLECULE
CEELLNOS	COLLEENS
CEELLNOU	NUCLEOLE
CEELLORT	RECOLLET
CEELLOSS	CELLOSES
CEELLPRU	CUPELLER
CEELLPSU	PUCELLES
CEELLRRU	CRUELLER
CEELLRVY	CLEVERLY
CEELLSSU	CLUELESS
CEELLSTY	SELECTLY
CEELMOOS	COELOMES
CEELMOPT	COMPLETE
CEELMORW	WELCOMER
CEELMOST	TELECOMS
CEELMOSW	WELCOMES
CEELMRTU	ELECTRUM
CEELNNOP	PENONCEL
CEELNNOT	CENTONEL
	NONELECT
CEELNOPU	OPULENCE
CEELNOPY	LYCOPENE
CEELNORS	ENCLOSER
	ENSORCEL

CEELNORT	ELECTRON
CEELNORU	ENCOLURE
CEELNOSS	ENCLOSES
CEELNPTU	CENTUPLE
CEELNRST	LECTERNS
CEELNRSU	LUCERNES
CEELNRTU	RELUCENT
CEELNRTY	RECENTLY
CEELNSTU	ESCULENT
CEELOOVV	COEVOLVE
CEELOPRU	OPERCULE
	RECOUPLE
CEELORSS	CORELESS
	RECLOSES
	SCLEROSE
CEELORST	CORSELET
	ELECTORS
	ELECTROS
	SELECTOR
CEELORSY	RECOYLES
CEELORTV	COVERLET
CEELOSSU	COLEUSES
CEELOSTU	ELOCUTES
CEELOSTV	COVELETS
CEELPRST	PLECTRES
	PRELECTS
CEELPRSU	CUPELERS
CEELRRTU	LECTURER
CEELRSST	LECTRESS
CEELRSSU	CURELESS
	RECLUSES
CEELRSSW	CREWLESS
CEELRSTU	CRUELEST
	LECTURES
CEELRSTY	SECRETLY
CEELRSUY	SECURELY
CEELSTTU	LETTUCES
CEEMMNTU	CEMENTUM
CEEMMORS	COMMERES
CEEMNORR	CREMORNE
CEEMNORW	NEWCOMER
CEEMNORY	CEREMONY
CEEMNOYZ	COENZYME
CEEMNRSU	CERUMENS
CEEMOORV	OVERCOME
CEEMOORW	OWRECOME
CEEMOPRS	COMPEERS
	COMPERES
CEEMOPST	COMPETES
CEEMOSSS	COSMESES
CEEMSSTU	TUMESCES
CEENNOOS	CONENOSE
CEENNORT	CRETONNE
CEENNORU	RENOUNCE
CEENNORV	CONVENER
CEENNOST	CENTONES
CEENNOSU	ENOUNCES
CEENNOSV	CONVENES
CEENNRST	CENTNERS
CEENOOST	ECOTONES
CEENOPST	POTENCES
CEENOPTW	TWOPENCE
CEENORSS	NECROSES
CEENORSU	COENURES
CEENORSV	CONSERVE
	CONVERSE
CEENORSZ	COZENERS
CEENORTT	TRECENTO
CEENORVY	CONVEYER
	RECONVEY
CEENOSVX	CONVEXES
CEENPPTU	TUPPENCE
CEENPRSS	SPENCERS
CEENPRST	PERCENTS
	PRECENTS
CEENPSSU	SUSPENCE
CEENQSUY	SEQUENCY
CEENRRSU	CENSURER
CEENRSSU	CENSURES
CEENRSTU	UNSECRET
CEENSSSU	CENSUSES
CEENSSTU	CUTENESS
CEENSTTU	CUNETTES
CEEOORRW	ORECROWE
CEEOORST	CREOSOTE
CEEOPRRS	PRESCORE
CEEOPRRT	RECEPTOR
CEEOPRTX	EXCEPTOR
CEEOPRTY	CEROTYPE
CEEOPSST	PECTOSES
CEEOPSTY	ECOTYPES
CEEOQTTU	COQUETTE
CEEORRRS	SORCERER
CEEORRSS	RESCORES
CEEORRST	ERECTORS
	SECRETOR
CEEORRSU	RECOURES
	RECOURSE
	RESOURCE
CEEORRSV	COVERERS
	RECOVERS
CEEORRSW	RECOWERS
CEEORRUV	OVERCURE
CEEORRVY	RECOVERY
CEEORSTV	COVETERS
CEEORSTW	COWTREES
CEEORSTX	COEXERTS
	CORTEXES
CEEORTTV	CORVETTE
CEEORTUX	EXECUTOR
CEEOSSST	CESTOSES
CEEOSTTT	OCTETTES
CEEPPRST	PERCEPTS
	PRECEPTS
CEEPPRSU	PREPUCES
CEEPRRSU	PRECURES
	PRECURSE
CEEPRSST	RESPECTS
	SCEPTERS
	SCEPTRES
	SPECTERS
	SPECTRES
CEEPRSSY	CYPRESES
CEEPRSTX	EXCERPTS
CEERRSST	RECTRESS
CEERRSSU	RESCUERS
	SECURERS
CEERRSSW	SCREWERS
CEERRSUV	RECURVES
CEERRTUZ	CREUTZER
CEERSSST	CRESSETS
CEERSSTU	SECUREST
CEERSSTW	SETSCREW
CEERSSUX	EXCURSES
	EXCUSERS
CEERSTTU	CURETTES
CEERTUXY	EXECUTRY
CEESSSTU	CESTUSES
CEESTTUV	CUVETTES
CEFFGHIN	CHEFFING
CEFFHIRU	CHUFFIER
CEFFHSTU	CHUFFEST
CEFFIILR	CLIFFIER
CEFFIORS	OFFICERS
CEFFIORU	COIFFEUR
	COIFFURE
CEFFIRSU	SUFFICER
CEFFISSU	SUFFICES
CEFFLORU	FORCEFUL
CEFFLRSU	SCUFFLER
CEFFLSSU	CUFFLESS
	SCUFFLES
CEFFORSS	SCOFFERS
CEFFORST	COFFRETS
CEFGHINT	FECHTING
	FETCHING
CEFGIKLN	FLECKING
CEFGILNT	CLEFTING
CEFGINNS	FENCINGS
CEFGLNUY	FULGENCY
CEFHIIMS	MISCHIEF
CEFHILNR	FLINCHER
CEFHILNS	FLINCHES
CEFHILRS	FILCHERS
CEFHILRT	FLICHTER
CEFHILST	FLITCHES
CEFHINSU	FUCHSINE
CEFHISTT	FITCHETS
CEFHISTU	FUCHSITE
CEFHISTW	FITCHEWS
CEFHLSSY	FLYSCHES
CEFHLSTU	CHESTFUL
	FUTCHELS
CEFIIIST	CITIFIES
CEFIILLM	MELLIFIC
CEFIILNO	OLEFINIC
CEFIILRT	CLIFTIER
CEFIILST	FELSITIC
CEFIILTY	FELICITY
CEFIIOPR	OPIFICER
CEFIIORS	ORIFICES
CEFIIPRT	PETRIFIC
CEFIIRRT	FERRITIC
	TERRIFIC
CEFIISTY	CITYFIES
CEFIKLOR	FIRELOCK
	FLOCKIER
CEFIKLRS	FLICKERS
CEFIKLRY	FLICKERY
CEFIKLST	FICKLEST
CEFILLLO	FOLLICLE
CEFILMRU	CRIMEFUL
	MERCIFUL
CEFILNOT	FLECTION
CEFILNST	INFLECTS
CEFILNSU	FUNICLES
CEFILOUV	VOICEFUL
CEFILRSU	FLUERICS
	LUCIFERS
CEFIMOST	COMFIEST
CEFINNOR	CONFINER
CEFINNOS	CONFINES
CEFINORS	COINFERS
	CONIFERS
	FORENSIC
	FORINSEC
	FORNICES
	INFORCES
CEFINORT	INFECTOR
CEFINOSX	CONFIXES
CEFINOTT	CONFETTI
CEFIOPRS	FORCIPES
CEFIORTY	FEROCITY
CEFIRRSU	SCURFIER
CEFIRSTU	FRUTICES
CEFIRTUV	FRUCTIVE
CEFKLLOS	ELFLOCKS
CEFKLOOR	FORELOCK
CEFKLOST	FETLOCKS
CEFKLPSY	FLYSPECK
CEFKLRUW	WRECKFUL
CEFLLOSU	FLOSCULE
CEFLNOSU	FLOUNCES
CEFLNRUU	FURUNCLE
CEFLNSTU	SCENTFUL
CEFMORSY	COMFREYS
CEFNOOTT	CONFETTO
CEFNORSU	FROUNCES
CEFNORTU	CONFUTER
CEFNOSSU	CONFUSES
CEFNOSTU	CONFUTES
CEFOPRSU	PREFOCUS
CEFORRST	CROFTERS
CEFORSSU	FOCUSERS
CEFORSTU	FRUCTOSE
CEFOSSSU	FOCUSSES
CEGGHIRS	CHIGGERS
CEGGHRSU	CHUGGERS
CEGGILOO	GEOLOGIC
CEGGILOR	CLOGGIER
	COGGLIER
CEGGILRS	SCRIGGLE
CEGGINNO	CONGEING
CEGGINOO	GEOGONIC
CEGGIORS	GEORGICS
	SCROGGIE
CEGGLNOY	GLYCOGEN
CEGGLORS	CLOGGERS
CEGHHINT	HECHTING
CEGHIINY	HYGIENIC
CEGHIKLN	HECKLING
CEGHIKNT	KETCHING
CEGHILNT	LETCHING
CEGHILNW	WELCHING
CEGHILST	GLITCHES
CEGHIMNS	SCHEMING
CEGHINNW	WENCHING
CEGHINOR	COHERING
	OCHERING
CEGHINPR	PERCHING
CEGHINRS	GRINCHES
CEGHINRT	RETCHING
CEGHINRU	EUCHRING
CEGHINST	CHESTING
	ETCHINGS
CEGHINVY	CHEVYING
CEGHIRSS	SCREIGHS
CEGHIRTU	THEURGIC
CEGHISTU	GUICHETS
CEGHLNSU	GLUNCHES
CEGHMRUY	CHEMURGY
CEGHNORS	GROSCHEN
CEGHORSU	CHOREGUS
	COUGHERS
	GROUCHES
CEGHRSTU	GRUTCHES
	GUTCHERS
CEGIILNR	CLINGIER
CEGIILNS	CEILINGS
	CIELINGS
CEGIILNT	GENTILIC
CEGIILOP	EPILOGIC
CEGIILOS	LOGICISE
CEGIILOZ	LOGICIZE
CEGIINNT	ENTICING
CEGIINNV	EVINCING
CEGIINOP	EPIGONIC
CEGIINOS	ISOGENIC
CEGIINPR	PIERCING
CEGIINPS	PIECINGS
CEGIINRT	RECITING
CEGIINSS	GNEISSIC
CEGIINSX	EXCISING
CEGIINTV	EVICTING
CEGIINTX	EXCITING
CEGIIOST	EGOISTIC
CEGIJLOU	LOGJUICE
CEGIKKLN	KECKLING
CEGIKLNR	CLERKING
	RECKLING

CEGIKNNR	RINGNECK
CEGIKNNS	NECKINGS
	SNECKING
CEGIKNPS	PECKINGS
	SPECKING
CEGIKNRT	TRECKING
CEGIKNRW	WRECKING
CEGIKSTU	GUCKIEST
CEGILMMN	CLEMMING
CEGILMNO	COMINGLE
CEGILNOO	NEOLOGIC
CEGILNOS	ECLOSING
CEGILNPU	CUPELING
CEGILNRS	CLINGERS
	CRINGLES
CEGILNRU	RECULING
	ULCERING
CEGILNRY	GLYCERIN
CEGILNSU	LUCIGENS
CEGILNSY	GLYCINES
CEGILNTU	CULTIGEN
CEGIMNOY	MYOGENIC
CEGIMNSU	MUCIGENS
CEGIMNUY	GYNECIUM
CEGINNOR	ENCORING
CEGINNOZ	COZENING
CEGINNRS	SCERNING
CEGINNRT	CENTRING
CEGINNST	SCENTING
CEGINNSY	ENSIGNCY
CEGINOOP	GEOPONIC
CEGINOOR	OROGENIC
CEGINOOY	COOEYING
CEGINOOZ	ZOOGENIC
CEGINOPR	COPERING
CEGINOPY	PYOGENIC
CEGINORS	COREIGNS
	COSIGNER
CEGINORT	GERONTIC
CEGINORV	COVERING
CEGINORW	COWERING
CEGINORZ	COGNIZER
CEGINOSS	COGNISES
CEGINOST	ESCOTING
CEGINOSZ	COGNIZES
CEGINOTV	COVETING
CEGINOXY	OXYGENIC
CEGINRRS	CRINGERS
CEGINRRU	RECURING
CEGINRST	CRESTING
CEGINRSU	RECUSING
	RESCUING
	SCUNGIER
	SECURING
CEGINRSW	SCREWING
CEGINRSY	SYNERGIC
CEGINRTU	ERUCTING
CEGINSUX	EXCUSING
CEGIRSTU	SCUTIGER
CEGKLNOS	GENLOCKS
CEGKLORS	GROCKLES
CEGLLOOU	COLLOGUE
CEGLLORY	GLYCEROL
CEGLLRYY	GLYCERYL
CEGLNOOS	COLOGNES
CEGLNOTY	COGENTLY
CEGLOOOY	OECOLOGY
CEGLOOTY	CETOLOGY
CEGLOSSU	GLUCOSES
CEGLOSSY	GLYCOSES
CEGMNNOO	COGNOMEN
CEGNNOOS	ONCOGENS
CEGNNPUY	PUNGENCY
CEGNOOTY	GONOCYTE
CEGNORSS	CONGRESS
CEGNORSU	CONGRUES
	SCROUNGE
CEGNORSY	CRYOGENS
CEGNORYY	CRYOGENY
CEGNOSST	CONGESTS
CEGNOTYY	CYTOGENY
CEGNRTUY	TURGENCY
CEGOORSS	SCROOGES
CEGORRSU	SCOURGER
	SCROUGER
CEGORSSU	SCOURGES
	SCROUGES
CEHHIIRT	HITCHIER
CEHHINPY	HYPHENIC
CEHHIRST	HITCHERS
CEHHNORU	HURCHEON
CEHHOOSS	COHOSHES
CEHHOOST	HOOTCHES
CEHHOPTY	HYPOTHEC
CEHHOSSU	CHOUSHES
CEHIIKNR	CHINKIER
CEHIIKNS	CHINKIES
CEHIILLR	CHILLIER
CEHIILLS	CHILLIES
CEHIILMO	HEMIOLIC
CEHIILMT	LITHEMIC
CEHIILNN	LICHENIN
CEHIILNT	LECITHIN
CEHIILOT	EOLITHIC
CEHIILTY	HELICITY
CEHIIMOP	HEMIOPIC
CEHIIMOS	ISOCHEIM
	ISOCHIME
CEHIIMPT	MEPHITIC
CEHIIMRT	HERMITIC
CEHIIMST	ETHICISM
CEHIINST	ICHNITES
	NITCHIES
CEHIIPPR	CHIPPIER
CEHIIPPS	CHIPPIES
CEHIIPRR	CHIRPIER
CEHIIPRT	PITCHIER
CEHIIRST	CHRISTIE
CEHIIRSZ	SCHIZIER
CEHIIRTT	CHITTIER
	TITCHIER
	TRICHITE
CEHIIRTW	WITCHIER
CEHIISTT	CHITTIES
	ETHICIST
	ITCHIEST
	THEISTIC
	TICHIEST
CEHIISVV	CHIVVIES
CEHIKLPT	KLEPHTIC
CEHIKLRS	CLERKISH
CEHIKLSU	SUCHLIKE
CEHIKMOS	HOMESICK
CEHIKNRU	CHUNKIER
CEHIKNST	CHETNIKS
	KITCHENS
	KNITCHES
	THICKENS
CEHIKNSW	CHEWINKS
CEHIKOOS	CHOOKIES
CEHIKOSS	HOICKSES
CEHIKOST	CHOKIEST
	THICKOES
CEHIKRSS	KIRSCHES
	SHICKERS
	SKRIECHS
CEHIKRST	CHIRKEST
CEHIKRSW	WHICKERS
CEHIKSST	CHEKISTS
	KITSCHES
CEHIKSTT	THICKEST
	THICKETS
	THICKSET
CEHIKTTY	THICKETY
CEHILLPR	PRECHILL
CEHILLRS	CHILLERS
	SCHILLER
CEHILLST	CHILLEST
CEHILMMS	SCHIMMEL
CEHILMSY	CHIMLEYS
CEHILMTY	METHYLIC
CEHILNOP	PHENOLIC
	PINOCHLE
CEHILNOR	CHLORINE
CEHILNOS	CHOLINES
	HELICONS
CEHILNPY	PHENYLIC
CEHILNSS	CHINLESS
CEHILNST	LINCHETS
	TINCHELS
CEHILOPT	HELICOPT
CEHILORS	CEORLISH
CEHILORT	CHLORITE
	CLOTHIER
CEHILORY	HEROICLY
CEHILPRS	PILCHERS
CEHILPTY	PHYLETIC
CEHILRSV	CHERVILS
CEHILSTT	LICHTEST
CEHILSTW	SWITCHEL
CEHILSTY	LECYTHIS
CEHILTTY	TETCHILY
CEHIMMRU	CHUMMIER
CEHIMMSS	CHEMISMS
CEHIMMSU	CHUMMIES
CEHIMNNW	WINCHMEN
CEHIMNOP	PHONEMIC
CEHIMNOR	CHOIRMEN
CEHIMNPT	PITCHMEN
CEHIMNSU	MUNCHIES
CEHIMNSY	CHIMNEYS
CEHIMOOT	HOMEOTIC
CEHIMORS	MORICHES
CEHIMORT	CHROMITE
	TRICHOME
CEHIMORZ	CHROMIZE
CEHIMOSS	ECHOISMS
CEHIMOST	MOCHIEST
CEHIMOTW	CHOWTIME
CEHIMRSS	SMIRCHES
CEHIMSST	CHEMISTS
CEHINNOS	CHINONES
CEHINNRT	INTRENCH
CEHINOOS	COHESION
CEHINOPR	PROCHEIN
CEHINOPS	CHOPINES
CEHINOPT	PHONETIC
CEHINOPU	EUPHONIC
CEHINORS	CHORINES
CEHINORT	NOTCHIER
CEHINORU	UNHEROIC
CEHINOSY	HYOSCINE
CEHINOTY	ONYCHITE
CEHINPRS	PINCHERS
	PINSCHER
CEHINPRU	PUNCHIER
	UNCIPHER
CEHINPSU	PENUCHIS
CEHINQSU	QUINCHES
CEHINRSS	RICHNESS
CEHINRST	CHRISTEN
	CITHERNS
	CITHRENS
	SNITCHER
CEHINRSW	WINCHERS
CEHINRTU	RUTHENIC
CEHINSST	CHINTSES
	SNITCHES
CEHINSTW	WITCHENS
CEHINSTZ	CHINTZES
CEHIOORS	CHOOSIER
	ISOCHORE
CEHIOPPR	CHOPPIER
CEHIOPRS	SOPHERIC
CEHIOPRU	EUPHORIC
	POUCHIER
CEHIOPSS	HOSPICES
CEHIOPST	POSTICHE
	POTICHES
CEHIOPSU	COPIHUES
CEHIOPTU	EUPHOTIC
CEHIORRT	RHETORIC
	TORCHIER
CEHIORRV	OVERRICH
CEHIORSS	CHORISES
	ORCHESIS
	ORCHISES
CEHIORST	ROTCHIES
	THEORICS
CEHIORSW	CHOWRIES
CEHIORTT	TROCHITE
CEHIORTU	COUTHIER
	TOUCHIER
CEHIOSST	ECHOISTS
	TOISECHS
CEHIOSTV	CHEVIOTS
CEHIPPRS	CHIPPERS
CEHIPRRS	CHIRPERS
CEHIPRSS	SPHERICS
CEHIPRST	PITCHERS
	SPITCHER
CEHIPSST	CHIPSETS
CEHIQSTU	QUITCHES
CEHIRSST	STRICHES
CEHIRSTT	CHITTERS
	RESTITCH
	RICHTEST
	STITCHER
CEHIRSTW	SWITCHER
CEHIRSTY	HYSTERIC
CEHIRTTW	TWITCHER
CEHIRTWY	WITCHERY
CEHISSTT	STITCHES
CEHISSTU	CUSHIEST
CEHISSTW	SWITCHES
CEHISSUW	SUCHWISE
CEHISTTW	TWITCHES
CEHKKRSU	CHUKKERS
CEHKLLOS	SKELLOCH
CEHKLMOS	HEMLOCKS
CEHKLOOS	KLOOCHES
CEHKLORS	SHERLOCK
CEHKNOSU	SUNCHOKE
	UNCHOKES
CEHKNPUY	KEYPUNCH
CEHKORSS	SHOCKERS
CEHKPSTU	KETCHUPS
CEHKRSSU	SHUCKERS
CEHKRSTU	HUCKSTER
CEHLLMOS	MOCHELLS
CEHLLMSU	MUCHELLS
	SCHELLUM
CEHLLOSY	YELLOCHS
CEHLLOUY	LOUCHELY
CEHLMNOU	HOMUNCLE
CEHLMORS	CHROMELS
CEHLMSUY	CHUMLEYS
CEHLNNOU	LUNCHEON
CEHLNNSU	CHUNNELS
CEHLNOST	CHOLENTS

	NOTCHELS
CEHLNOTU	UNCLOTHE
CEHLNPRU	PRELUNCH
CEHLNRSU	LUNCHERS
CEHLNRSY	LYNCHERS
CEHLNSTY	LYNCHETS
CEHLOORS	RESCHOOL
CEHLOOSS	SCHOOLES
CEHLORRT	CHORTLER
CEHLORST	CHORTLES
CEHLORSU	SLOUCHER
CEHLORTY	HECTORLY
CEHLOSSU	SLOUCHES
CEHLOSTU	SELCOUTH
CEHLPPSS	SCHLEPPS
CEHLPPSY	SCHLEPPY
CEHLQSUY	SQUELCHY
CEHLRRSU	LURCHERS
CEHLSTUY	LECYTHUS
CEHMNRSU	MUNCHERS
CEHMNRTU	TRUCHMEN
CEHMNSSU	MUCHNESS
CEHMOORS	MOOCHERS
CEHMOOSS	SCHMOOSE
	SMOOCHES
CEHMOOSZ	SCHMOOZE
CEHMOPRS	CHOMPERS
CEHMORSU	MOUCHERS
CEHMORUV	OVERMUCH
CEHMOSSU	SMOUCHES
CEHMRSTU	CHETRUMS
CEHMSSTU	SMUTCHES
CEHNNNOU	NUNCHEON
CEHNNOPU	PUNCHEON
CEHNNOSU	NONESUCH
	UNCHOSEN
CEHNNRSU	CHUNNERS
CEHNOOPS	HENCOOPS
CEHNOORS	COEHORNS
	SCHOONER
CEHNOPTU	PUTCHEON
CEHNORST	NOTCHERS
CEHNORSV	CHEVRONS
CEHNORTU	CHOUNTER
CEHNORVY	CHEVRONY
CEHNPPRU	PREPUNCH
CEHNPRSU	PUNCHERS
CEHNPSST	PSCHENTS
CEHNRRSU	CHURNERS
CEHNRSTU	CHUNTERS
CEHNSSSU	SUCHNESS
CEHNSSTU	CHESNUTS
CEHNSTTU	CHESTNUT
CEHNSTUY	CHUTNEYS
CEHOOORZ	ZOOCHORE
CEHOORSS	CHOOSERS
	SOROCHES
CEHOORST	CHEROOTS
CEHOORSU	OCHEROUS
	OCHREOUS
CEHOOSUW	COWHOUSE
CEHOPPRS	CHOPPERS
CEHOPPRY	PROPHECY
CEHOPRST	POTCHERS
CEHOPRSY	CORYPHES
CEHORRST	TORCHERS
CEHORSSU	CHORUSES
	CHOUSERS
CEHORSSZ	SCHERZOS
CEHORSTU	SCOUTHER
	TOUCHERS
CEHORSTW	SCOWTHER
CEHORSUV	VOUCHERS
CEHOSSSU	HOCUSSES
CEHOSTTU	COUTHEST
CEHOTTUZ	ZUCHETTO
CEHPRSTU	PUTCHERS
CEHPSSTU	PUTSCHES
CEHRRSSU	CRUSHERS
CEHRSSSU	SCHUSSER
CEHRSSTY	SCYTHERS
CEHRSTTY	STRETCHY
CEHSSSSU	SCHUSSES
CEIIILSV	CIVILISE
CEIIILVZ	CIVILIZE
CEIIIMNT	CIMINITE
CEIIINSS	SINICISE
CEIIINSV	INCISIVE
CEIIINSZ	SINICIZE
CEIIJSTU	JESUITIC
	JUICIEST
CEIIKKST	KICKIEST
CEIIKLMR	LIMERICK
CEIIKLRS	SICKLIER
CEIIKLRT	TICKLIER
CEIIKLSS	SICKLIES
CEIIKMMR	MIMICKER
CEIIKMST	KISMETIC
CEIIKNRZ	ZINCKIER
CEIIKNSS	ICKINESS
	KINESICS
CEIIKNST	KINETICS
CEIIKPRR	PRICKIER
CEIIKPST	PICKIEST
CEIIKQSU	QUICKIES
CEIIKRRT	TRICKIER
CEIIKRST	STICKIER
CEIIKSST	EKISTICS
	STICKIES
CEIIKTTT	TEKTITIC
CEIILLMT	MELLITIC
CEIILLOP	POLLICIE
CEIILLPT	ELLIPTIC
CEIILLSS	SILICLES
CEIILLSU	SILICULE
CEIILMNS	LEMNISCI
CEIILMNT	LIMNETIC
CEIILMNY	MYELINIC
CEIILMOT	CIMOLITE
CEIILNNR	INCLINER
CEIILNNS	INCLINES
CEIILNOP	PICOLINE
CEIILNOS	ISOCLINE
	SILICONE
CEIILNPS	PENICILS
CEIILNQU	CLINIQUE
CEIILNSS	ENCLISIS
CEIILOPP	EPIPLOIC
	EPIPOLIC
CEIILOPS	POLICIES
CEIILORT	ELICITOR
CEIILOTZ	ZEOLITIC
CEIILPPS	CLIPPIES
CEIILPRT	PERLITIC
CEIILPRU	PIRLICUE
CEIILPSS	ECLIPSIS
CEIILPTX	EXPLICIT
CEIILPTY	PYELITIC
CEIILQRU	CLIQUIER
CEIILRSU	SLUICIER
CEIILRSY	LYRICISE
CEIILRTV	VERTICIL
CEIILRYZ	LYRICIZE
CEIILSSS	SCISSILE
CEIIMNOT	EMICTION
CEIIMNRU	URINEMIC
CEIIMNST	MINCIEST
CEIIMOPT	EPITOMIC
CEIIMORS	ISOMERIC
CEIIMOST	COMITIES
	SEMIOTIC
CEIIMPRR	CRIMPIER
CEIIMPRS	EMPIRICS
	MISPRICE
CEIIMPSS	EPICISMS
CEIIMPTU	PUMICITE
CEIIMRRT	TRIMERIC
CEIIMRST	MERISTIC
	SCIMITER
	TRISEMIC
CEIIMRTT	TERMITIC
CEIIMSST	MISCITES
CEIINNOP	NEPIONIC
CEIINNOR	IRENICON
CEIINNOS	CONIINES
	OSCININE
CEIINNOT	NICOTINE
CEIINNRS	CINERINS
CEIINNRT	INTRINCE
CEIINNST	INSCIENT
CEIINOPR	PECORINI
CEIINOPS	EPINOSIC
CEIINOPT	EPITONIC
CEIINORS	RECISION
	SORICINE
CEIINOSS	ICONISES
CEIINOSV	INVOICES
CEIINOSX	EXCISION
CEIINOSZ	ICONIZES
CEIINOTV	EVICTION
CEIINPPR	PRINCIPE
CEIINPSS	PISCINES
CEIINRSS	SERICINS
CEIINRST	CITRINES
	CRINITES
	INCITERS
CEIINRSU	INCISURE
	SCIURINE
CEIINRTU	NEURITIC
CEIINSSU	CUISINES
CEIINSTU	CUTINISE
CEIINSTY	CYTISINE
	SYENITIC
CEIINSTZ	CITIZENS
	ZINCIEST
	ZINCITES
CEIINTUZ	CUTINIZE
CEIIOPRS	IRISCOPE
CEIIOPRT	PERIOTIC
CEIIOPSW	WICOPIES
CEIIOPTT	PICOTITE
CEIIOSTT	OSTEITIC
CEIIOSTV	SOVIETIC
CEIIPRRS	CRISPIER
CEIIPRST	PICRITES
	PRICIEST
CEIIPSST	EPICISTS
	SPICIEST
CEIIQRTU	CRITIQUE
CEIIRSST	ERISTICS
CEIIRSSU	CRUISIES
CEIIRSTT	RECTITIS
CEIIRSTV	VERISTIC
CEIISSST	CISSIEST
CEIISTVV	VIVISECT
CEIJNORT	INJECTOR
CEIJNORU	JOUNCIER
CEIJNOUV	CUNJEVOI
CEIJRSTU	JUSTICER
CEIJSSTU	JUSTICES
CEIKKLOR	CORKLIKE
	ROCKLIKE
CEIKKNRS	KNICKERS
CEIKKRRS	SKERRICK
CEIKLLTU	CULTLIKE
CEIKLMOR	CORMLIKE
CEIKLMST	MICKLEST
CEIKLMSU	SCUMLIKE
CEIKLNPS	SPICKNEL
CEIKLNRS	CLINKERS
	CRINKLES
CEIKLNRU	CLUNKIER
CEIKLNSS	SLICKENS
CEIKLOSV	LOVESICK
CEIKLOTU	LEUKOTIC
CEIKLPRS	PICKLERS
	PRICKLES
CEIKLPRU	PLUCKIER
CEIKLRSS	SLICKERS
CEIKLRST	STICKLER
	STRICKLE
	TICKLERS
	TRICKLES
CEIKLRSY	SICKERLY
CEIKLRTT	TRICKLET
CEIKLSST	SLICKEST
	STICKLES
CEIKLSTU	LUCKIEST
CEIKMNOR	MONICKER
CEIKMNST	STICKMEN
CEIKMOPT	IMPOCKET
CEIKMORS	OCKERISM
CEIKMRSS	SMICKERS
CEIKMRSU	MUSICKER
CEIKMSST	SMICKETS
CEIKMSTU	MUCKIEST
CEIKNNOT	NEKTONIC
CEIKNNSU	INSUCKEN
CEIKNOST	CONKIEST
CEIKNOTY	CYTOKINE
CEIKNQSU	QUICKENS
CEIKNRSS	SNICKERS
CEIKNRST	STRICKEN
CEIKNRSU	UNSICKER
CEIKNRSY	SNICKERY
CEIKNSSS	SICKNESS
CEIKNSST	SNICKETS
CEIKOPST	POCKIEST
CEIKORRS	ROCKIERS
CEIKORST	CORKIEST
	ROCKIEST
	STOCKIER
CEIKORSV	OVERSICK
CEIKOSSY	YOICKSES
CEIKPRRS	PRICKERS
CEIKPRST	PRICKETS
CEIKPSST	SKEPTICS
	SPICKEST
CEIKQSTU	QUICKEST
	QUICKSET
CEIKRRST	TRICKERS
CEIKRRTY	TRICKERY
CEIKRSST	STICKERS
CEIKRSTU	TRUCKIES
CEIKRTTY	RICKETTY
CEIKSTUY	YUCKIEST
CEILLMOY	COMELILY
CEILLNOS	LIONCELS
CEILLNOU	NUCLEOLI
CEILLOPS	POLLICES
CEILLOQU	COQUILLE
CEILLORS	COLLIERS
	ORSELLIC
CEILLORY	COLLIERY
CEILLOTU	COUTILLE
CEILLRTU	TELLURIC
CEILLSST	CELLISTS
CEILLSSU	CULLISES
CEILMMUY	MYCELIUM
CEILMNOP	COMPLINE

CEILMNOT	MONTICLE
CEILMOOP	PICOMOLE
CEILMOPR	COMPILER
	COMPLIER
CEILMOPS	COMPILES
	COMPLIES
	POLEMICS
CEILMOSS	SOLECISM
CEILMOSU	COLISEUM
CEILMPRS	CRIMPLES
CEILMPRU	CLUMPIER
CEILMPUU	PECULIUM
CEILMRSU	CLUMSIER
	MUSCLIER
CEILMTUU	LUTECIUM
CEILNNOT	CONTLINE
CEILNNSU	NUCLEINS
CEILNNSY	SYNCLINE
CEILNOOS	COLONIES
	COLONISE
	ECLOSION
CEILNOOZ	COLONIZE
CEILNOPR	PERCOLIN
	REPLICON
CEILNOPS	PINOCLES
CEILNOPT	LEPTONIC
CEILNOPY	POLYENIC
CEILNORS	INCLOSER
	LICENSOR
CEILNOSS	CONSEILS
	INCLOSES
CEILNOST	LECTIONS
	TELSONIC
CEILNOSU	LEUCOSIN
CEILNOSX	LEXICONS
CEILNPRY	PRINCELY
CEILNRTU	LINCTURE
CEILNRUV	CULVERIN
CEILNSST	STENCILS
CEILNSTU	CUTLINES
	LINECUTS
	TUNICLES
CEILNSUU	UNSLUICE
CEILOORZ	COLORIZE
CEILOPRT	LEPROTIC
	PETROLIC
CEILOPRV	PROCLIVE
CEILOPST	TOECLIPS
CEILOPTU	EPULOTIC
	POULTICE
CEILOPTY	EPICOTYL
	LIPOCYTE
CEILORST	CLOISTER
	COISTREL
	COSTLIER
	CREOLIST
CEILORTT	CLOTTIER
CEILORTY	CRYOLITE
CEILOSSS	OSSICLES
CEILOSST	SOLECIST
	SOLSTICE
CEILOSSU	COULISES
	COULISSE
CEILOTVY	VELOCITY
CEILPPRR	CRIPPLER
CEILPPRS	CLIPPERS
	CRIPPLES
CEILPRSS	SPLICERS
CEILPRSU	SURPLICE
CEILPRUU	PURLICUE
CEILPSSU	SPICULES
CEILRRSU	SCURRILE
CEILRSTT	CLITTERS
CEILRSTU	CURLIEST
	UTRICLES
CEILSSSS	SCISSELS
CEILSTTU	CUITTLES
CEIMMNNO	MNEMONIC
CEIMMNOU	ENCOMIUM
	MECONIUM
CEIMMORT	RECOMMIT
CEIMMORU	COREMIUM
CEIMMOSX	COMMIXES
CEIMMRRS	CRIMMERS
CEIMMRRU	CRUMMIER
CEIMMRSU	CRUMMIES
	SCUMMIER
CEIMMRSY	MERYCISM
CEIMNNOO	ENCOMION
CEIMNNOR	NONCRIME
CEIMNNOS	MECONINS
CEIMNNOY	NEOMYCIN
CEIMNOOT	EMOTICON
CEIMNOPT	PENTOMIC
CEIMNOPY	EPONYMIC
CEIMNORS	CREMOSIN
	INCOMERS
	SERMONIC
CEIMNORT	INTERCOM
CEIMNOST	CENTIMOS
CEIMNRST	CENTRISM
CEIMNRSU	NUMERICS
CEIMNSSU	MENISCUS
CEIMOOST	COOMIEST
CEIMOOUZ	ZOOECIUM
CEIMOPRS	COMPRISE
CEIMOPRX	PROXEMIC
CEIMOPRZ	COMPRIZE
CEIMOQSU	COMIQUES
CEIMORRS	MORRICES
CEIMORRT	MORTICER
CEIMORST	MORTICES
CEIMORSX	EXORCISM
CEIMORSY	ISOCRYME
CEIMORTY	EMICTORY
CEIMOSSS	COSMESIS
CEIMOSTV	VICOMTES
CEIMPRRS	CRIMPERS
	SCRIMPER
CEIMPRRU	CRUMPIER
CEIMPRSU	PUMICERS
CEIMRRSU	SCRIMURE
CEIMRRTU	TURMERIC
CEIMRSST	CRETISMS
CEIMSSTY	SYSTEMIC
CEINNNOT	INNOCENT
CEINNNOU	INCONNUE
CEINNORS	INCENSOR
CEINNORU	NEURONIC
CEINNORV	CONNIVER
CEINNORW	COWINNER
CEINNOSV	CONNIVES
CEINNOTU	CONTINUE
CEINNOTV	COINVENT
CEINOOPR	PECORINO
CEINOOSS	CONIOSES
CEINOOST	COONTIES
CEINOOTZ	ENTOZOIC
	ENZOOTIC
CEINOPPR	CORNPIPE
CEINOPPT	PEPTONIC
CEINOPRS	CONSPIRE
	INCORPSE
CEINOPRT	ENTROPIC
	INCEPTOR
CEINOPRV	PROVINCE
CEINOPST	PONCIEST
CEINOPTT	ENTOPTIC
CEINOPTU	UNPOETIC
CEINORRS	RESORCIN
CEINORRT	TRICORNE
CEINORSS	NECROSIS
	SERICONS
CEINORST	COINTERS
	CORNIEST
	NOTICERS
	RECTIONS
CEINORSU	COINSURE
	NOURICES
	ROUNCIES
CEINORTT	CONTRITE
	CORNETTI
CEINORTU	NEUROTIC
	UNEROTIC
CEINORTV	CONTRIVE
CEINOSSS	CESSIONS
	COSINESS
CEINOSST	SECTIONS
CEINOSSX	COXINESS
CEINOSSZ	COZINESS
CEINOSTT	CENTOIST
	STENOTIC
	TONETICS
CEINOSTU	COUNTIES
CEINOSTX	EXCITONS
CEINOSTY	CYTOSINE
CEINOSUV	UNVOICES
CEINOSVV	CONVIVES
CEINOTUX	UNEXOTIC
CEINPRSS	CRISPENS
	PRINCESS
CEINPSST	INSPECTS
CEINPSTY	PYCNITES
CEINRRSU	REINCURS
CEINRSST	CISTERNS
CEINRSTT	CENTRIST
	CITTERNS
CEINRSTU	CURNIEST
CEINRSUV	INCURVES
CEINRSVV	CRIVVENS
CEINRTTU	INTERCUT
	TINCTURE
CEINSSTY	CYSTEINS
	CYSTINES
CEINSTTX	EXTINCTS
CEIOOPRS	OPORICES
CEIOOTUV	OUTVOICE
CEIOOTXX	EXOTOXIC
CEIOPPRS	CROPPIES
CEIOPPSY	EPISCOPY
CEIOPRRU	CROUPIER
CEIOPRSS	PERSICOS
CEIOPRST	PERSICOT
CEIOPRSU	PRECIOUS
CEIOPRTU	EUTROPIC
	OUTPRICE
CEIOPSST	COPSIEST
CEIOPSSU	SPECIOUS
CEIORRSS	CROSIERS
CEIORRSU	COURIERS
CEIORRSZ	CROZIERS
CEIORRTU	COURTIER
CEIORRUZ	CRUZEIRO
CEIORSST	CROSSTIE
CEIORSSU	SCOURIES
CEIORSSV	CORSIVES
CEIORSSW	SCOWRIES
CEIORSSX	SIXSCORE
CEIORSTT	COTTIERS
CEIORSTU	CITREOUS
	OUTCRIES
CEIORSTV	EVICTORS
	VORTICES
CEIORSTW	COWRITES
CEIORSTX	EXCITORS
	EXORCIST
CEIORSVY	VICEROYS
CEIORTTU	TOREUTIC
CEIOSSSV	VISCOSES
CEIOSSTT	COTTISES
	SCOTTIES
CEIOSSTU	COITUSES
CEIOSSTX	COEXISTS
CEIPPSTU	CUPPIEST
CEIPQSTU	PICQUETS
CEIPRRSS	CRISPERS
CEIPRRST	RESCRIPT
	SCRIPTER
CEIPRRSU	SPRUCIER
CEIPRSST	CRISPEST
CEIPRSTU	CREPITUS
	CUPRITES
	PICTURES
	PIECRUST
CEIPSSST	CESSPITS
CEIRRRSU	CURRIERS
	SCURRIER
CEIRRRUY	CURRIERY
CEIRRSSU	CRUISERS
	SCURRIES
	SUCRIERS
CEIRRSTT	CRITTERS
	RESTRICT
	STRICTER
CEIRRSTU	CRUSTIER
	RECRUITS
CEIRRSUV	SCURVIER
CEIRSSSU	CUISSERS
	SCISSURE
CEIRSSTT	TRISECTS
CEIRSSTU	CITRUSES
	CRUSTIES
	CURTSIES
	RICTUSES
CEIRSSTV	VICTRESS
CEIRSSUV	CURSIVES
	SCURVIES
CEIRSTTU	TUTRICES
CEIRSTUV	CURVIEST
CEIRSTUY	SECURITY
CEIRSUZZ	SCUZZIER
CEISSSSU	CISSUSES
CEISSSTU	CISTUSES
CEISTTTU	CUTTIEST
CEJKNOSY	JOCKNEYS
CEJLOOSY	JOCOSELY
CEJNORRU	CONJURER
CEJNORSU	CONJURES
CEJNRTUU	JUNCTURE
CEJNSSUU	JUNCUSES
CEJOPRST	PROJECTS
CEKKLNRU	KNUCKLER
CEKKLNSU	KNUCKLES
CEKKNORS	KNOCKERS
CEKLLOOV	LOVELOCK
CEKLLOPS	PELLOCKS
CEKLLSSU	LUCKLESS
CEKLMNOS	LOCKSMEN
CEKLNOSS	SLOCKENS
CEKLNOST	STENLOCK
CEKLNRSU	CLUNKERS
	CRUNKLES
CEKLOORV	OVERLOCK
CEKLOOSS	COOKLESS
CEKLOPST	LOCKSTEP
CEKLORSS	ROCKLESS
CEKLOSSS	SOCKLESS
CEKLPRSU	PLUCKERS
CEKLRRTU	TRUCKLER
CEKLRSSU	SCULKERS

SUCKLERS
CEKLRSTU TRUCKLES
CEKLSSSU SUCKLESS
CEKMNOST STOCKMEN
CEKMNRTU TRUCKMEN
CEKNNSSU UNSNECKS
CEKNOORV CONVOKER
CEKNOOSV CONVOKES
CEKNOPST PENSTOCK
CEKNORST CRONKEST
CEKNORTU COKERNUT
CEKNOSTU UNSOCKET
CEKNPRUU UNPUCKER
CEKNRSTU STRUCKEN
CEKNRSWY WRYNECKS
CEKOOORV OVERCOOK
CEKOOPRS PRECOOKS
CEKOOPSW COWPOKES
CEKOORRS ROCKROSE
CEKOORRW COWORKER
CEKOORRY CROOKERY
CEKOORST CROOKEST
CEKOPRST SPROCKET
CEKORRTY ROCKETRY
CEKORSST RESTOCKS
STOCKERS
CEKRRSTU RESTRUCK
TRUCKERS
CEKRSSUU RUCKUSES
CELLMOSU COLUMELS
CELLNOOS COLONELS
CELLNORS ENSCROLL
CELLNSUU NUCELLUS
CELLNTUU LUCULENT
CELLNTUY LUCENTLY
CELLOOQU COLLOQUE
CELLORSS ESCROLLS
CELLOSSY CLOYLESS
CELLRRSU CRULLERS
CELLRSSU SCULLERS
CELLRSUY SCULLERY
CELMMSSU MESCLUMS
CELMNOOR COLORMEN
CELMNOOS MONOCLES
CELMNOTY CLOYMENT
CELMNOUY UNCOMELY
CELMNSSU MESCLUNS
CELMNTUU MUCULENT
CELMOOOT LOCOMOTE
CELMOOPY COEMPLOY
CELMOOSY CLOYSOME
CELMOPSU COMPULSE
CELMOPSY SYMPLOCE
CELMOSUU CUMULOSE
CELMOSYY CYMOSELY
CELMPRSU CLUMPERS
CRUMPLES
CELMPRTU PLECTRUM
CELMPSUU SPECULUM
CELMSSUU SECULUMS
CELNNOSU NUCLEONS
CELNNOTY NOCENTLY
CELNNOUV UNCLOVEN
CELNOORS CONSOLER
CORONELS
CELNOORT CONTROLE
CELNOORU ENCOLOUR
CELNOOSS CONSOLES
COOLNESS
CELNOOVV CONVOLVE
CELNOPRT PLECTRON
CELNOPUU UNCOUPLE
CELNOPUY OPULENCY
CELNORTW CROWNLET
CELNORWY CLOWNERY
CELNOSSU CLONUSES
COUNSELS
UNCLOSES
CELNOSTU NOCTULES
CELNOSUV CONVULSE
CELNOSVY SOLVENCY
CELNOVXY CONVEXLY
CELNPTUU PUNCTULE
CELNRSTU LECTURNS
CELOOORV OVERCOOL
CELOOPRS PRECOOLS
CELOOPSS CESSPOOL
CELOORRS COLORERS
RECOLORS
CELOORRU COLOURER
CELOORSS COLESSOR
CREOSOLS
CELOORTW COLEWORT
CELOORVY OVERCLOY
CELOOSTU CLOSEOUT
CELOPRSS CROPLESS
CELOPRSU COUPLERS
CELOPSSU OPUSCLES
UPCLOSES
CELOPSTU COUPLETS
OCTUPLES
CELOPSUU OPUSCULE
CELOPTTU OCTUPLET
CELOPTUX OCTUPLEX
CELORRSU CORULERS
CELORSST CORSLETS
COSTRELS
CROSSLET
CELORSSU CLOSURES
SCLEROUS
CELORSSW SCOWLERS
SCROWLES
CELORSSY SCROYLES
CELORSTT CLOTTERS
CROTTLES
CELORSTU CLOTURES
CLOUTERS
COULTERS
CELORSTY COYSTREL
CELORSUU ULCEROUS
URCEOLUS
CELORSUY CROUSELY
CELORTTU COURTLET
CELORTVY COVERTLY
CELOSSST COSTLESS
CELOSTTU CULOTTES
CELPRRSU SCRUPLER
CELPRSSU SCRUPLES
CELPRSTU RESCULPT
CELPRSUY SPRUCELY
CELRSSTU CLUSTERS
CUSTRELS
CELRSSTY CLYSTERS
CELRSTTU CLUTTERS
SCUTTLER
CELRSTUU CULTURES
CELRSTUV CULVERTS
CELRSTUY CLUSTERY
CELRTTUY CLUTTERY
CELSSTTU SCUTTLES
CELSSTUU CULTUSES
CEMMNOOR COMMONER
CEMMNOOS CONSOMME
CEMMNOOY COMMONEY
CEMMNOST COMMENTS
CEMMNOSU COMMUNES
CEMMOOST COMMOTES
CEMMOOSV COMMOVES
CEMMORTU COMMUTER
CEMMOSTU COMMUTES
CEMMRSSU SCUMMERS
CEMNNOST CONTEMNS
CEMNOORR CROMORNE
CEMNOOTY MONOCYTE
CEMNOPRS CORPSMEN
CEMNOPTT CONTEMPT
CEMNORSU CONSUMER
MUCRONES
CEMNOSSU CONSUMES
MUSCONES
CEMNRSTU CENTRUMS
CEMOOPRS COMPOSER
CEMOOPSS COMPOSES
CEMOOPST COMPOTES
CEMOOPSY MYOSCOPE
CEMOORSY SYCOMORE
CEMOOSSS COSMOSES
CEMOOSTU OUTCOMES
CEMOOSTY CYTOSOME
CEMOPRSS COMPRESS
CEMOPRST COMPTERS
CEMOPRTU COMPUTER
CEMOPSTU COMPUTES
CEMORSSU CORMUSES
CEMORSTU COSTUMER
CUSTOMER
CEMOSSTU COSTUMES
CEMOSTUY COSTUMEY
CEMOTXYY MYXOCYTE
CEMPRSTU CRUMPEST
CRUMPETS
SPECTRUM
CENNOOPR CORNPONE
CENNOORV CONVENOR
CENNOOST CONNOTES
CENNORRT CORNRENT
CENNORTU NOCTURNE
CENNOSST CONSENTS
CENNOSTT CONTENTS
CENNOSTV CONVENTS
CENNRSSU SCUNNERS
CENOOOTZ ECTOZOON
CENOORRS CORONERS
CROONERS
CENOORST CORONETS
CENOORSU CORNEOUS
CENOORTT CORNETTO
CENOORVY CONVEYOR
CENOPRSU POUNCERS
CENOPRSY NECROPSY
CENOPSSY PYCNOSES
SYNCOPES
CENOPSTU POUNCETS
CENOQRSU CONQUERS
CENOQSTU CONQUEST
CENORRSS SCORNERS
CENORRSW CROWNERS
RECROWNS
CENORRTU TROUNCER
CENORSST CONSTERS
CRESTONS
CENORSSU CORNUSES
CENORSTT CORNETTS
CENORSTU CONSTRUE
CORNUTES
COUNTERS
RECOUNTS
TROUNCES
CENORSTV CONVERTS
CENORSTW CROWNETS
CENORSUU CERNUOUS
COENURUS
CENORSUV UNCOVERS
CENORSUY CYNOSURE
CENOSSTT CONTESTS
CENOSSTU CONTUSES
COUNTESS
CENOSTTX CONTEXTS
CENPRSTY ENCRYPTS
CENPRTUU PUNCTURE
CENPSTUX EXPUNCTS
CENRRSTU CURRENTS
CENRSSTU CURTNESS
ENCRUSTS
CENRSSUU UNCURSES
CENRSSUW UNSCREWS
CEOOOPST OTOSCOPE
CEOOPRRV OVERCROP
CEOOPRSS SCOOPERS
CEOOPSWX COWPOXES
CEOORRVW OVERCROW
CEOORSST SCOOTERS
CEOORSTU OUTSCORE
CEOOSTUV COVETOUS
CEOPPRRS CROPPERS
CEOPPRST PROSPECT
CEOPPRSU SUPERCOP
CEOPRRRU PROCURER
CEOPRRSS SCORPERS
CEOPRRST PORRECTS
CEOPRRSU CROUPERS
PROCURES
CEOPRSST PROSECTS
CEOPRSTT PROTECTS
CEOPRSTW CROWSTEP
SCREWTOP
CEOPRSUU COUPURES
CUPREOUS
CEOPRSUV COVERUPS
CEOQRSTU CROQUETS
ROCQUETS
CEOQRTUY COQUETRY
CEORRSSS CROSSERS
SCORSERS
CEORRSSU COURSERS
CURSORES
SCOURERS
CEORRSSW SCOWRERS
CEORRSTU COURTERS
CEORRSTY CORSETRY
CEORSSST CROSSEST
CEORSSSU SCOURSES
SCOUSERS
SUCROSES
CEORSSTU CRUSTOSE
SCOUTERS
CEORSSUV CORVUSES
CEORSTUU COUTURES
OUTCURSE
CEORSTUV COUVERTS
CUTOVERS
OVERCUTS
CEORSTUY COURTESY
CEORTUUV OUTCURVE
CEOSSSTU COSTUSES
CEOSSTTU COTTUSES
CEPPRRSU CRUPPERS
CEPPRSSU SCUPPERS
CEPPRTUU UPPERCUT
CEPRSSTU SPRUCEST
CEPRSSUW SCREWUPS
CEPRSSUY CYPRUSES
CEPRSTUU CUTPURSE
CEPRSUUV UPCURVES
CEPSSSTU SUSPECTS
CERSSSUU RUSCUSES
CERSSTTU SCUTTERS
CERSSTUY CURTSEYS
CERSSUUX EXCURSUS
CFFGHINU CHUFFING

CFFGIINO	COIFFING
CFFGILNO	COFFLING
CFFGILNU	CUFFLING
CFFGINOS	SCOFFING
CFFGINSU	SCUFFING
CFFHINOS	CHIFFONS
CFFIKKOS	KICKOFFS
CFFIKOPS	PICKOFFS
CFFINNOU	UNCOFFIN
CFFIRTUY	FRUCTIFY
CFFKKNOO	KNOCKOFF
CFFMOSSU	OFFSCUMS
CFGHIILN	FILCHING
CFGHINOO	CHOOFING
CFGIIKLN	FICKLING
	FLICKING
CFGIKLNO	FLOCKING
CFGIKNOR	FROCKING
CFGIKNSU	FUCKINGS
CFGINORT	CROFTING
CFGINOSU	FOCUSING
CFHIINOO	FINOCHIO
CFHIIORR	HORRIFIC
CFHIKORS	ROCKFISH
CFHIKSSU	SUCKFISH
CFHILPTY	FLYPITCH
CFHIMOSS	SCOMFISH
CFHIMSSU	SCUMFISH
CFHINSSU	FUCHSINS
CFHLOPUU	POUCHFUL
CFHORSTU	FUTHORCS
CFIIIKNN	FINICKIN
CFIIILSY	SILICIFY
CFIIKNNY	FINNICKY
CFIIKNYZ	ZINCKIFY
CFIILMNU	FULMINIC
CFIILNST	INFLICTS
CFIILNUU	FUNICULI
CFIILOPR	PROLIFIC
CFIILPSU	PULSIFIC
CFIILSTU	SULFITIC
CFIIMNOS	SOMNIFIC
CFIIMOPR	PICIFORM
CFIIMORT	MORTIFIC
CFIINOPT	PONTIFIC
CFIINORT	FRICTION
CFIINOST	FICTIONS
CFIKLORY	FROLICKY
CFIKLSTU	STICKFUL
CFIKNNOS	FINNOCKS
CFIKOSSS	FOSSICKS
CFIKPSTU	PUCKFIST
CFILMOOR	COLIFORM
CFILNOSU	SULFONIC
CFILRSUU	SULFURIC
CFIMNOOR	CONIFORM
CFIMNORS	CONFIRMS
CFIMNORU	CUNIFORM
	UNCIFORM
CFIMOSSU	MISFOCUS
CFINNOTU	FUNCTION
CFIOPRUY	COPURIFY
CFKLLOSU	LOCKFULS
CFKLRTUU	TRUCKFUL
CFKNORSU	UNFROCKS
CFKOSTTU	FUTTOCKS
CFLLOORU	COLORFUL
CFLLOPRU	CROPFULL
CFLMRSUU	FULCRUMS
CFLMRUUU	FURCULUM
CFLNOORT	CORNLOFT
CFLNORSU	SCORNFUL
CFLOOPSU	SCOOPFUL
CFLOOPSW	COWFLOPS
CFLOPRSU	CROPFULS
CFMNOORS	CONFORMS
CFMOORST	COMFORTS
CFNNOORT	CONFRONT
CFNORSTU	FUNCTORS
CFOOORTW	CROWFOOT
CFRSTUUU	USUFRUCT
CGGGHINU	CHUGGING
CGGGILNO	CLOGGING
	COGGLING
CGGGINOS	COGGINGS
	SCOGGING
CGGGINSU	SCUGGING
CGGHILNU	GULCHING
CGGHINOU	COUGHING
CGGIILNN	CLINGING
CGGIINNO	COIGNING
CGGIINNR	CRINGING
CGGIINRS	GRICINGS
CGGILRSY	SCRIGGLY
CGGINNSU	SCUNGING
CGGINOOS	SCOOGING
CGGINOSU	SCOUGING
CGHHIILN	HILCHING
CGHHIINT	HITCHING
CGHHINNU	HUNCHING
CGHHINOT	HOTCHING
CGHHINTU	HUTCHING
CGHIIKNN	CHINKING
CGHIIKNO	HOICKING
CGHIIKNR	CHIRKING
CGHIIKNT	THICKING
CGHIILLN	CHILLING
CGHIILNR	CHIRLING
CGHIILNT	CHITLING
	LICHTING
CGHIIMNR	CHIRMING
CGHIIMNS	MICHINGS
CGHIIMNT	MITCHING
CGHIINNN	CHINNING
CGHIINNP	PINCHING
CGHIINNW	WINCHING
CGHIINOR	CHOIRING
CGHIINPP	CHIPPING
CGHIINPR	CHIRPING
CGHIINPT	PITCHING
CGHIINQU	QUICHING
CGHIINRR	CHIRRING
CGHIINRT	CHIRTING
	RICHTING
CGHIINST	ITCHINGS
CGHIINTT	CHITTING
CGHIINTW	WITCHING
CGHIINVV	CHIVVING
CGHIINVY	CHIVYING
CGHIINZZ	CHIZZING
CGHIKNNU	CHUNKING
CGHIKNOS	SHOCKING
CGHIKNSU	SHUCKING
CGHILMNU	MULCHING
CGHILNNU	LUNCHING
CGHILNNY	LYNCHING
CGHILNOT	CLOTHING
CGHILNRU	LURCHING
CGHIMMNU	CHUMMING
CGHIMNNU	MUNCHING
CGHIMNOO	MOOCHING
CGHIMNOP	CHOMPING
CGHIMNOR	CHROMING
CGHIMNOU	MOUCHING
CGHIMNPU	CHUMPING
CGHIMPSY	SPHYGMIC
CGHINNOS	CHIGNONS
CGHINNOT	NOTCHING
CGHINNPU	PUNCHING
CGHINNRU	CHURNING
CGHINNSY	SYNCHING
CGHINOOP	POOCHING
CGHINOOS	CHOOSING
CGHINOPP	CHOPPING
CGHINOPT	POTCHING
CGHINOPU	POUCHING
CGHINORT	TORCHING
CGHINOSU	CHOUSING
	HOCUSING
CGHINOSW	CHOWSING
CGHINOTU	TOUCHING
CGHINOUV	VOUCHING
CGHINPSY	PSYCHING
CGHINPTU	PINCHGUT
CGHINRRU	CHURRING
CGHINRSU	CRUSHING
	RUCHINGS
CGHINSTY	SCYTHING
CGHNOOOS	SOOCHONG
CGHNOOSU	SOUCHONG
CGHOORST	TORGOCHS
CGIIILNT	LIGNITIC
CGIIINNS	INCISING
CGIIINNT	INCITING
CGIIKLNN	CLINKING
	NICKLING
CGIIKLNP	PICKLING
CGIIKLNS	LICKINGS
	SICKLING
	SLICKING
CGIIKLNT	TICKLING
CGIIKMMS	GIMMICKS
CGIIKMMY	GIMMICKY
CGIIKNNS	SNICKING
CGIIKNNZ	ZINCKING
CGIIKNOY	YOICKING
CGIIKNPR	PRICKING
CGIIKNPS	PICKINGS
CGIIKNRS	SCRIKING
CGIIKNRT	TRICKING
CGIIKNRW	WRICKING
CGIIKNST	STICKING
	TICKINGS
CGIIKNSW	WICKINGS
CGIIKPST	PIGSTICK
CGIILLOS	ILLOGICS
CGIILMOS	LOGICISM
CGIILNOP	POLICING
CGIILNPP	CLIPPING
CGIILNPS	SPLICING
CGIILNQU	CLIQUING
CGIILNSS	SLICINGS
CGIILNSU	SLUICING
CGIILOST	LOGICIST
	LOGISTIC
CGIILRTU	LITURGIC
CGIIMNNO	INCOMING
CGIIMNNS	MINCINGS
CGIIMNPR	CRIMPING
CGIIMNPU	PUMICING
CGIIMNSU	MISCUING
CGIINNOS	COININGS
CGIINNOT	NOTICING
CGIINNPR	PRINCING
CGIINNSU	INCUSING
CGIINNSW	WINCINGS
CGIINNTT	TINCTING
CGIINOOS	ISOGONIC
CGIINOPT	PICOTING
CGIINORT	TRIGONIC
CGIINOST	COTISING
CGIINOSV	VOICINGS
CGIINPRS	CRISPING
CGIINRSU	CRUISING
CGIINRSV	SCRIVING
CGIJNNOU	JOUNCING
CGIKKNNO	KNOCKING
CGIKLNNO	CLONKING
CGIKLNNU	CLUNKING
CGIKLNOR	ROCKLING
CGIKLNPU	PLUCKING
CGIKLNRU	RUCKLING
CGIKLNSU	SCULKING
	SUCKLING
CGIKMNOS	MOCKINGS
	SMOCKING
CGIKNOOR	CROOKING
CGIKNOOS	COOKINGS
CGIKNORS	ROCKINGS
CGIKNORT	TROCKING
CGIKNOST	STOCKING
CGIKNPSU	KINGCUPS
CGIKNRTU	TRUCKING
CGIKNSSU	SUCKINGS
CGIKNSTU	GUNSTICK
CGILLNOS	COLLINGS
CGILLNOY	COLLYING
CGILLNSU	CULLINGS
	SCULLING
CGILLNUY	CULLYING
CGILMNOP	CLOMPING
CGILMNPU	CLUMPING
CGILMNSU	MUSCLING
CGILMNSY	CYMLINGS
CGILMNTU	MULCTING
CGILMNUU	CINGULUM
	GLUCINUM
CGILMOOY	MYOLOGIC
CGILNNNO	NONCLING
CGILNNOS	CLONINGS
CGILNNOW	CLOWNING
CGILNOOR	COLORING
CGILNOOY	COOINGLY
CGILNOPP	CLOPPING
CGILNOPU	COUPLING
CGILNORU	CLOURING
CGILNOSS	CLOSINGS
CGILNOSW	COWLINGS
	SCOWLING
CGILNOTT	CLOTTING
CGILNOTU	CLOUTING
CGILNPSU	SCULPING
CGILNRSU	CURLINGS
CGILNRYY	CRYINGLY
CGILNTTU	CUTTLING
CGILOOOZ	ZOOLOGIC
CGILOORU	UROLOGIC
CGILORSW	COWGIRLS
CGILPSTU	GILTCUPS
CGILPSTY	GLYPTICS
CGIMMNSU	SCUMMING
CGIMNNOO	GNOMONIC
	ONCOMING
CGIMNOPS	COMPINGS
CGIMNOPT	COMPTING
CGIMNOPU	UPCOMING
CGIMNPRU	CRUMPING
CGIMRRUY	MICRURGY
CGINNNOS	CONNINGS
CGINNNSU	CUNNINGS
CGINNOOR	CROONING
CGINNOPU	POUNCING
	UNCOPING
CGINNORS	SCORNING
CGINNORW	CROWNING
CGINNOSS	CONSIGNS
CGINNOTU	COUNTING
CGINOOPS	SCOOPING
CGINOOPT	COOPTING
CGINOOST	SCOOTING

CGINOOTV	COGNOVIT
CGINOPPR	CROPPING
CGINOPRS	CORPSING
CGINOPRU	CROUPING
CGINOPSU	SCOUPING
CGINOPSW	SCOWPING
CGINORSS	CROSSING
	SCORINGS
	SCORSING
CGINORSU	COURSING
	SCOURING
	SOURCING
CGINORTU	COURTING
CGINOSTU	SCOUTING
CGINPPSU	CUPPINGS
CGINPRSU	SPRUCING
CGINRRSU	SCURRING
CGINRRUY	CURRYING
CGINRSSU	CURSINGS
CGINRSSY	SCRYINGS
CGINRSTU	CRUSTING
CGINRSUZ	SCRUZING
CGINSTTU	CUTTINGS
	TUNGSTIC
CGKLNOSU	GUNLOCKS
CGKNOSTU	GUNSTOCK
CGLLOSYY	GLYCOSYL
CGLMOOYY	MYCOLOGY
CGLNOOOY	ONCOLOGY
CGLOOOTY	TOCOLOGY
CGLOOTYY	CYTOLOGY
CGMNNOOR	MONGCORN
CGMNNORU	MUNGCORN
CGNORSUY	SCROUNGY
CGOORRSW	GORCROWS
CHHIIKST	THICKISH
CHHIILTY	HITCHILY
CHHIIPST	PHTHISIC
CHHIKORS	CHIKHORS
CHHILRSU	CHURLISH
CHHIMPSU	CHUMSHIP
CHHIMRTY	RHYTHMIC
CHHKOOPS	HOCKSHOP
CHHNORSU	RHONCHUS
CHHOOPTT	HOTCHPOT
CHIIILOS	CHILIOIS
CHIIKLST	TICKLISH
CHIIKNNS	KINCHINS
CHIIKRST	TRICKISH
CHIILLLY	CHILLILY
CHIILMSY	HYLICISM
CHIILNNP	LINCHPIN
CHIILNST	CHITLINS
CHIILOPT	HOPLITIC
CHIILORT	TROCHILI
CHIILOST	HOLISTIC
CHIILPRY	CHIRPILY
CHIILPTY	PITCHILY
CHIILQSU	CLIQUISH
CHIILSTY	HYLICIST
CHIIMOPT	PHIMOTIC
CHIIMORZ	RHIZOMIC
CHIIMPRU	PICHURIM
CHIINNPS	INCHPINS
CHIINOPS	SIPHONIC
CHIINORT	ORNITHIC
CHIIORSS	CHORISIS
CHIIORST	HISTORIC
	ORCHITIS
CHIIPPRU	HIPPURIC
CHIIRSTT	TRISTICH
CHIKLLOS	HILLOCKS
CHIKLLOY	HILLOCKY
CHIKLNUY	CHUNKILY
CHIKMNNU	MUNCHKIN
CHIKMNPU	CHIPMUNK
CHIKMNTU	MUTCHKIN
CHIKNNOP	PHINNOCK
CHIKNOOS	CHINOOKS
CHIKOPTY	KYPHOTIC
CHIKORST	TROCHISK
CHIKOSST	STOCKISH
CHIKPSYY	PHYSICKY
CHILLMSU	CHILLUMS
CHILLOOT	OILCLOTH
CHILMMUY	CHUMMILY
CHILMOPS	COMPLISH
CHILMOSU	SCHOLIUM
CHILMPSU	CLUMPISH
CHILNNPY	LYNCHPIN
CHILNOOS	SCHOLION
CHILNORS	CHLORINS
CHILNOSU	ULICHONS
CHILNOSW	CLOWNISH
CHILNPUY	PUNCHILY
CHILOOOZ	HOLOZOIC
CHILOOPT	HOLOPTIC
CHILOOYZ	HYLOZOIC
CHILOPPY	CHOPPILY
CHILORST	TROCHILS
CHILOSYY	COYISHLY
CHILOTUY	TOUCHILY
CHIMMOOR	MICROMHO
CHIMMORS	MICROHMS
CHIMMORU	CHROMIUM
CHIMNNOO	NONOHMIC
CHIMNOOR	HORMONIC
CHIMNORS	CHRISMON
CHIMNORW	INCHWORM
CHIMNOSU	INSOMUCH
CHIMNOSY	CHYMOSIN
CHIMNOUY	ONYCHIUM
CHIMOORU	MOUCHOIR
CHIMORSS	CHORISMS
	CHRISOMS
CHIMORST	CHRISTOM
CHIMOSTU	MISTOUCH
CHIMPSSY	PSYCHISM
CHIMSSTY	CHYMISTS
	TYCHISMS
CHINOOPT	PHOTONIC
CHINOORS	CHORIONS
	ISOCHRON
CHINOORT	ORTHICON
CHINOPTY	HYPNOTIC
	PHYTONIC
	PYTHONIC
	TYPHONIC
CHINORTU	COTHURNI
CHINOSSU	CUSHIONS
CHINOSTZ	SCHIZONT
CHINOSUY	CUSHIONY
CHINSTTU	UNSTITCH
CHIOOPPT	PHOTOPIC
CHIOOPRS	POCHOIRS
CHIOOPTY	OOPHYTIC
CHIOORSS	ISOCHORS
CHIOORSU	ICHOROUS
CHIOORSZ	CHORIZOS
CHIOORTT	ORTHOTIC
CHIOPRST	STROPHIC
CHIOPSTY	HYPOCIST
CHIOPTTU	OUTPITCH
	PITCHOUT
CHIORSSS	CROSSISH
CHIORSST	CHORISTS
CHIPRRSU	CHIRRUPS
CHIPRRSY	PYRRHICS
CHIPRRUY	CHIRRUPY
CHIPRTTY	TRIPTYCH
CHIPSSTY	PSYCHIST
CHIRRSSU	SCIRRHUS
CHISSTTU	CHUTISTS
CHKLOOOS	HOOLOCKS
CHKLOSSY	SHYLOCKS
CHKMMOOS	HOMMOCKS
CHKMMOSU	HUMMOCKS
CHKMMOUY	HUMMOCKY
CHKNOOSS	SCHNOOKS
CHKNORSU	CORNHUSK
CHKOOOPS	COOKSHOP
CHKOOSST	SCHTOOKS
CHKOPSTU	TUCKSHOP
CHKPSTUU	PUTCHUKS
CHLMORSY	CHROMYLS
CHLMPSSU	SCHLUMPS
CHLNOOOP	COLOPHON
CHLOORSU	CHLOROUS
CHLOPSTY	SPLOTCHY
CHLORTUY	CHOULTRY
CHMNOORT	CORNMOTH
CHMNORRU	CRUMHORN
CHMOORSU	CHROMOUS
CHNNOORS	CHRONONS
CHNOOPTT	TOPNOTCH
CHNOORST	TORCHONS
CHNOPRSU	SUNPORCH
CHNOPTUU	OUTPUNCH
CHNORRSS	SCHNORRS
CHNORSSY	SYNCHROS
CHNORSTU	COTHURNS
CHOOORYZ	ZOOCHORY
CHOOPPSS	COPSHOPS
CHOOPSTU	OCTOPUSH
CHOPSTUU	TOUCHUPS
CHORSTTU	SHORTCUT
CIIIKNTU	CUITIKIN
CIIILMPT	IMPLICIT
CIIILMSU	SILICIUM
CIIILNOV	OLIVINIC
CIIILPST	SPILITIC
CIIILSTV	CIVILIST
CIIILTVY	CIVILITY
CIIIMNSV	INCIVISM
CIIINNOS	INCISION
CIIINNRT	CITRININ
CIIINOTY	IONICITY
CIIINPPR	PRINCIPI
CIIINPST	INCIPITS
CIIINTVY	VICINITY
CIIJRSTU	JURISTIC
CIIKKLLS	KILLICKS
CIIKKMSS	MISKICKS
CIIKLLSY	SICKLILY
CIIKLOPT	POLITICK
CIIKLPST	LICKSPIT
	LIPSTICK
CIIKLRTY	TRICKILY
CIIKLSTY	STICKILY
CIIKMMMS	MIMMICKS
CIIKMNNS	MINNICKS
CIIKNOOT	COOTIKIN
CIIKNPPR	PINPRICK
CIIKNPST	NITPICKS
	STICKPIN
CIIKNPTY	NITPICKY
CIIKNSTU	CUTIKINS
CIIKPSUW	WICKIUPS
CIILLNOP	POLLINIC
CIILMOPY	IMPOLICY
CIILMOSS	SCIOLISM
CIILMQSU	CLIQUISM
CIILMRSY	LYRICISM
CIILNOOT	NOCTILIO
CIILNOPS	CIPOLINS
	PICOLINS
	PSILOCIN
CIILNORT	NITROLIC
CIILNOSS	SILICONS
CIILNOST	COLISTIN
CIILOOPT	POLITICO
CIILOOTZ	ZOOLITIC
CIILOPPT	POPLITIC
CIILOPST	COLPITIS
	POLITICS
	PSILOTIC
CIILORST	CLITORIS
	COISTRIL
CIILOSST	SCIOLIST
	SOLICITS
CIILOSTY	SOLICITY
CIILOSVV	SLIVOVIC
CIILPRSY	CRISPILY
CIILRSTY	LYRICIST
CIILRTUU	UTRICULI
CIILSSSS	SCISSILS
CIILSTTY	STYLITIC
CIIMNOOS	ISONOMIC
CIIMNOSS	MISCOINS
CIIMNOST	MICTIONS
	MONISTIC
	NOMISTIC
CIIMNOVY	VIOMYCIN
CIIMORST	TRISOMIC
CIIMOSST	MISTICOS
	STOICISM
CIIMOSYZ	ISOZYMIC
CIIMPRST	SCRIMPIT
CIIMRSTY	MYRISTIC
CIIMRTTU	TRITICUM
CIINNNOO	NONIONIC
CIINNOST	NICOTINS
CIINNSTT	INSTINCT
CIINNSTU	TUNICINS
CIINOOPP	CIOPPINO
CIINOOSS	CONIOSIS
CIINOOST	COITIONS
	ISOTONIC
CIINOOTZ	ZOONITIC
CIINOPSS	PSIONICS
CIINOPSU	OPINICUS
CIINORSS	INCISORS
CIINORST	CROSTINI
CIINORSY	INCISORY
CIINOSSS	SCISSION
CIINOSTT	STICTION
CIINOTTY	TONICITY
CIINPRSS	CRISPINS
CIINPSTU	SINCIPUT
CIINQSTU	QUINTICS
CIIOOPST	ISOTOPIC
CIIOPRST	PORISTIC
CIIOPSTT	OPTICIST
CIIOPSTY	ISOTYPIC
CIIOQTUX	QUIXOTIC
CIIORRWW	WIRRICOW
CIIOTTXY	TOXICITY
CIIPRRTU	PRURITIC
CIIPRSTU	PURISTIC
CIIRSTTU	TRUISTIC
CIISSTTY	CYSTITIS
CIJKOSTY	JOYSTICK
CIJNNOOS	CONJOINS
CIJNNOOT	CONJOINT
CIJNNOTU	JUNCTION
CIJNNSTU	INJUNCTS
CIJOOSTY	JOCOSITY
CIKKLLOS	KILLOCKS
CIKKOPST	TOPKICKS
CIKKOSTU	OUTKICKS

CIKLLOPR	KILLCROP
CIKLLOPS	PILLOCKS
CIKLLORS	ROLLICKS
CIKLLORY	ROLLICKY
CIKLLOSS	SILLOCKS
CIKLLOSW	KILLCOWS
CIKLLPUY	PLUCKILY
CIKLMSSU	MISLUCKS
CIKLNOST	LINSTOCK
CIKLOPST	LOPSTICK
CIKLOSTU	OUTSLICK
CIKLOSTY	STOCKILY
CIKMNNOS	MINNOCKS
CIKMOORS	SICKROOM
CIKMOOSS	MISCOOKS
CIKMOPST	MOPSTICK
CIKMORRS	RIMROCKS
CIKMSSTU	STICKUMS
CIKNNOOS	COONSKIN
CIKNNOPS	PINNOCKS
CIKNNOST	NONSTICK
CIKNNOSW	WINNOCKS
CIKNOPTY	PYKNOTIC
CIKNOSSW	COWSKINS
CIKNPSTU	NUTPICKS
CIKNSSTU	UNSTICKS
CIKOPPST	POCKPITS
CIKOPSTT	TIPSTOCK
CIKORTTU	OUTTRICK
CIKOSSTT	STOCKIST
CIKOSSTU	SICKOUTS
CIKOSTTU	STICKOUT
CIKOSTUW	OUTWICKS
CIKPSSTU	STICKUPS
CIKPSUWY	WICKYUPS
CILLMNOR	CORNMILL
CILLMSUY	CLUMSILY
	CULLYISM
CILLNOOT	COTILLON
CILLNORS	INSCROLL
CILLNOSU	CULLIONS
	SCULLION
CILLOOOT	OCOTILLO
CILLOORS	CRIOLLOS
CILMNOPS	COMPLINS
CILMNOPU	PULMONIC
CILMNOSS	CLONISMS
CILMNOUU	INOCULUM
CILMNUUV	VINCULUM
CILMOORS	COLORISM
	MISCOLOR
CILMOOSS	LOCOISMS
CILMOPSY	OLYMPICS
CILMORUX	MICROLUX
CILMPRSY	SCRIMPLY
CILMPSUU	SPICULUM
CILMSSTU	CULTISMS
CILMSTYY	MYSTICLY
CILNOORS	ORCINOLS
CILNOORU	UNICOLOR
CILNOOSS	CLOISONS
CILNOOST	COLONIST
	STOLONIC
CILNOOTU	LOCUTION
CILNOPRS	PILCORNS
CILNOPTU	PLUTONIC
CILNORSY	LYRICONS
CILNOSTU	LINOCUTS
CILNOSUY	COUSINLY
CILNPSSU	INSCULPS
	SCULPINS
CILNPSTU	INSCULPT
CILOOPST	COPILOTS
CILOOPYZ	POLYZOIC
CILOORRT	TRICOLOR
CILOORST	COLORIST
	CORTISOL
CILOORSU	COULOIRS
CILOOSSU	SCIOLOUS
CILOPPRY	PROPYLIC
CILOPRRY	PYRROLIC
CILOPRSW	PILCROWS
CILOPRUY	CROUPILY
	POLYURIC
CILOPSSW	COWSLIPS
CILORSTY	COYSTRIL
CILOSSTU	OCULISTS
CILOSSTY	SYSTOLIC
CILOSSUU	LUSCIOUS
CILPRSTU	CULPRITS
CILPSSTU	SCULPSIT
CILRSTTY	STRICTLY
CILRSTUY	CRUSTILY
	RUSTICLY
CILRSUVY	SCURVILY
CILSSTTU	CULTISTS
CIMMOSSS	COSMISMS
CIMNNOSU	NONMUSIC
CIMNOOOZ	ZOONOMIC
CIMNOORS	OMICRONS
CIMNOORU	CORONIUM
CIMNOOTY	MYOTONIC
CIMNOPRT	COMPRINT
CIMNORSS	CRIMSONS
CIMNORSY	CRONYISM
CIMNOSTU	MISCOUNT
CIMNOSUU	MUCINOUS
CIMNOSUY	SYCONIUM
CIMOOOTZ	ZOOTOMIC
CIMOORSS	MORISCOS
CIMOPSSY	COPYISMS
CIMOSSST	COSMISTS
CIMOSTUU	MUTICOUS
CIMOSTUY	MUCOSITY
CIMOSTYZ	ZYMOTICS
CINNNOSU	INCONNUS
CINNOOSS	SCOINSON
CINNOOST	SCONTION
CINNOOTU	CONTINUO
CINNOOTX	NONTOXIC
CINNORSU	UNICORNS
CINNOSTU	UNCTIONS
CINNOSTY	SYNTONIC
CINNQUUX	QUINCUNX
CINOOOPT	COOPTION
CINOOOTZ	ZOONOTIC
CINOOPRS	SCORPION
CINOOPRT	PROTONIC
CINOOPSS	POCOSINS
CINOOSUV	COVINOUS
CINOOTXY	OXYTOCIN
CINOPSSY	PYCNOSIS
CINOPSTY	SYNOPTIC
CINORRST	TRICORNS
CINORSST	CISTRONS
	CORNISTS
CINORSTT	CONTRIST
	STRONTIC
CINORSTU	RUCTIONS
CINORSUY	COUSINRY
CINOSSST	CONSISTS
CINOSSTU	SUCTIONS
CINOSTUV	VISCOUNT
CINRSSTU	INCRUSTS
CINRSTTU	INSTRUCT
CINRSTUY	SCRUTINY
CIOOOPRS	OOSPORIC
CIOOOTTX	OTOTOXIC
CIOOPRST	PORTICOS
	PROOTICS
CIOOPTYZ	ZOOTYPIC
CIOOQSTU	COQUITOS
CIOORRWW	WORRICOW
CIOORSSU	SCORIOUS
CIOOSSTU	STOCIOUS
CIOPSSTY	COPYISTS
CIORRSTU	CURSITOR
CIORSSSS	SCISSORS
CIORSTUU	RUCTIOUS
CIPPRRUU	PURPURIC
CIPSSTTY	STYPTICS
CIRRSTTU	CRITTURS
CJNOORRU	CONJUROR
CJRSUUUU	SUCURUJU
CKKNOOTU	KNOCKOUT
CKKOORRW	ROCKWORK
CKLLMOSU	MULLOCKS
CKLLMOUY	MULLOCKY
CKLLOOPS	POLLOCKS
CKLLOORS	ROLLOCKS
CKLLORSU	RULLOCKS
CKLMMOSU	SLUMMOCK
CKLNOSTU	LOCKNUTS
CKLOOOSY	OLYCOOKS
CKLOORSW	ROWLOCKS
CKLOOSTU	LOCKOUTS
CKLOPSTU	POTLUCKS
	PUTLOCKS
CKMMMOSU	MUMMOCKS
CKMMORUW	MUCKWORM
CKMNOOOR	MOONROCK
CKMOOOOR	COOKROOM
CKNOOORS	ROCKOONS
CKNOSSTU	UNSTOCKS
CKNRSTUU	UNSTRUCK
CKOOOPST	COOKTOPS
CKOOOSTU	COOKOUTS
	OUTCOOKS
CKOOPSTT	STOCKPOT
CKOORSSU	SOUROCKS
CKOORSTU	OUTROCKS
CKOPSTTU	PUTTOCKS
CKORSTUW	CUTWORKS
CKOSSSTU	TUSSOCKS
CKOSSTUY	TUSSOCKY
CKSSSTUU	TUSSUCKS
CLLLOOPT	CLOTPOLL
CLLMOSSU	MOLLUSCS
CLLOOPSS	SCOLLOPS
CLLOOQUY	COLLOQUY
CLMMNOOY	COMMONLY
CLMOOOTY	COLOTOMY
CLMOOPST	COMPLOTS
CLMOPSTU	PLUMCOTS
CLMOSUUU	CUMULOUS
CLNNOOOR	NONCOLOR
CLNOORST	CONTROLS
CLNOORTU	CONTROUL
	COUNTROL
CLNOSSTU	CONSULTS
CLNOSTUY	UNCOSTLY
CLOOOPRT	PROTOCOL
CLOOPPSW	COWPLOPS
CLOOPSTY	POLYCOTS
CLOORTUY	LOCUTORY
CLOOSSSU	COLOSSUS
CLOOSSTY	CYTOSOLS
CLOPRSTU	SCULPTOR
CLRSSUUU	SURCULUS
CMMNNOOU	UNCOMMON
CMMOPSSY	COMSYMPS
CMNOOOST	MONOCOTS
CMNOOOTY	ONCOTOMY
CMNOORRW	CORNWORM
CMNOPSTU	CONSUMPT
CMOOPRST	COMPORTS
CMOOPSST	COMPOSTS
CMOPRSUX	SCRUMPOX
CMORSSTU	SCROTUMS
CMORSTUW	CUTWORMS
CNNOOORT	CONTORNO
CNNORSTU	NOCTURNS
CNNORSUW	UNCROWNS
CNOOOORT	OCTOROON
CNOOPPRS	POPCORNS
CNOOPRSU	CROUPONS
CNOOPSSU	SOUPCONS
CNOORRSW	CORNROWS
CNOORRTY	CRYOTRON
CNOORSST	CONSORTS
CNOORSTT	CONTORTS
CNOORSTU	CONTOURS
	CORNUTOS
	CROUTONS
	OUTSCORN
CNOOSTTW	COTTOWNS
CNOOTTUU	OUTCOUNT
CNOPRSTY	CRYPTONS
CNOPSSTY	POSTSYNC
CNOSTUUU	UNCTUOUS
COOOPSTU	OUTSCOOP
COOOPSTY	OTOSCOPY
COOOPSYZ	ZOOSCOPY
COOPPSTU	POSTCOUP
COOPRRST	PROCTORS
COOPRSST	TOPCROSS
COOPRSTU	OUTCROPS
COOPRSUU	CROUPOUS
COOPRSUY	UROSCOPY
COORRWWY	WORRYCOW
COORSSTU	OUTCROSS
COORSTUW	OUTCROWS
COOSSTTY	OTOCYSTS
COPRRSTU	CORRUPTS
DDDDEEIR	DIDDERED
DDDDEEOR	DODDERED
DDDEEEFN	DEFENDED
DDDEEENP	DEPENDED
DDDEEENR	REDDENED
DDDEEENU	UNDEEDED
DDDEEERW	REWEDDED
	WEDDERED
DDDEEFNU	DEFUNDED
DDDEEFOR	FODDERED
DDDEEGIS	DISEDGED
DDDEEHRS	SHREDDED
DDDEEIST	STEDDIED
DDDEEJRU	JUDDERED
DDDEELRT	TREDDLED
DDDEENOR	DONDERED
	REDDENDO
DDDEENOS	SODDENED
DDDEENUW	UNWEDDED
DDDEEORR	DODDERER
DDDEEORS	RESODDED
DDDEEPRU	PUDDERED
DDDEERTU	DETRUDED
DDDEGILR	GRIDDLED
DDDEGNOU	UNGODDED
DDDEHIRT	THRIDDED
DDDEIILS	DIDDLIES
DDDEIIMS	SMIDDIED
DDDEIINV	DIVIDEND
DDDEIIST	DIDDIEST
	STIDDIED
DDDEILNU	UNLIDDED
DDDEILNW	DWINDLED
DDDEILQU	QUIDDLED
DDDEILRS	DIDDLERS
DDDEILSY	DIDDLEYS

DDDEILTW TWIDDLED
DDDEIMOS DISMODED
DDDEINOR DENDROID
DDDEINRU UNDERDID
DDDEIOST DODDIEST
DDDEIQSU SQUIDDED
DDDEISTU DUDDIEST
DDDENORW DROWNDED
DDDGIILN DIDDLING
DDDIIOOR DORIDOID
DDEEEEMR REDEEMED
DDEEEENP DEEPENED
DDEEEERS RESEEDED
DDEEEERW DEERWEED
DDEEEFIR REDEFIED
DDEEEFLX DEFLEXED
DDEEEFNR DEFENDER
FENDERED
DDEEEFNS DEFENSED
DDEEEFRR DEFERRED
DDEEEGLR LEDGERED
DDEEEGMR DEGERMED
DEMERGED
DDEEEGNR DEGENDER
GENDERED
DDEEEGRR REGREDED
DDEEEGRT DETERGED
DDEEEHLW WHEEDLED
DDEEEHNU UNHEEDED
DDEEEILS DIESELED
DDEEEIMR REMEDIED
REMEIDED
DDEEEINR REDENIED
DDEEEINV DEVEINED
DDEEEIRT REEDITED
DDEEEIST DEEDIEST
STEEDIED
DDEEELLV DEVELLED
DDEEELNW WEDELNED
DDEEELPT DEPLETED
DDEEELRW REWELDED
DDEEELSS DEEDLESS
DDEEELTW TWEEDLED
DDEEEMNR REMENDED
DDEEEMNT DEMENTED
DDEEEMPR DEPERMED
DDEEEMRS DEMERSED
DDEEENNU UNNEEDED
DDEEENPX EXPENDED
DDEEENRR RENDERED
DDEEENRT TENDERED
DDEEENSU UNSEEDED
DDEEENTT DENETTED
DDEEENTX EXTENDED
DDEEENUW UNWEEDED
DDEEERRT DETERRED
DDEEERST DESERTED
DDEEERSV DESERVED
DDEEESTT DETESTED
DDEEESTV DEVESTED
DDEEESWY DYEWEEDS
DDEEFFIR DIFFERED
DDEEFFNO OFFENDED
DDEEFGGO DEFOGGED
DDEEFGIT FIDGETED
DDEEFINR FRIENDED
DDEEFINU UNDEFIDE
UNDEFIED
DDEEFLNO ENFOLDED
DDEEFLOR REFOLDED
DDEEFLOU DEFOULED
DDEEFMOR DEFORMED
DDEEFNRU REFUNDED
UNDERFED
DDEEFORR FODDERER
DDEEGGIR DERIGGED
DDEEGGOR DOGGEDER
DDEEGHNU UNHEDGED
DDEEGILN ENGILDED
DDEEGILR REGILDED
DDEEGINR ENGIRDED
ENRIDGED
DDEEGINS DESIGNED
SDEIGNED
DDEEGIRV DIVERGED
DDEEGISS DISEDGES
DDEEGIST DIGESTED
DDEEGJRU REJUDGED
DDEEGLNO GOLDENED
DDEEGMMU DEGUMMED
DDEEGOPS GODSPEED
DDEEGRRS DREDGERS
DDEEGSTU DEGUSTED
DDEEHILS SHIELDED
DDEEHINO HOIDENED
DDEEHINR HINDERED
DDEEHIRT DITHERED
DDEEHISS EDDISHES
DDEEHNOR DEHORNED
DDEEHNOY HOYDENED
DDEEHNSU DUDHEENS
DDEEHORT DEHORTED
DDEEHRRS SHREDDER
DDEEHRSS SHEDDERS
DDEEIINT INEDITED
DDEEIIRV REDIVIDE
DDEEILLV DEVILLED
DDEEILMN MILDENED
DDEEILMW MILDEWED
DDEEILNR REDLINED
DDEEILNT DENTILED
DDEEILRS DREIDELS
DDEEILRV DRIVELED
DDEEILRW WILDERED
DDEEILST DELISTED
DDEEIMNP IMPENDED
DDEEIMNR REMINDED
DDEEIMOR MOIDERED
DDEEIMSS MISDEEDS
DDEEIMST DEMISTED
DDEEIMTT DEMITTED
DDEEINNR DINNERED
DDEEINNT INDENTED
INTENDED
DDEEINNU UNDENIED
DDEEINRT DENDRITE
DDEEINRW REWINDED
DDEEINST DESTINED
DDEEINTU UNEDITED
DDEEIOPR PERIODED
DDEEIPPR REDIPPED
DDEEIPRS PRESIDED
DDEEIPRV DEPRIVED
DDEEIPSS DEPSIDES
DESPISED
DDEEIPST DESPITED
DDEEIRRS DERIDERS
DDEEIRST REDDIEST
DDEEIRSV DIVERSED
DDEEIRTV DIVERTED
DDEEISST DESISTED
STEDDIES
DDEEISTV DIVESTED
DDEEITTW DEWITTED
DDEEJLLO JODELLED
DDEEKNSU DUSKENED
DDEELLMO MODELLED
DDEELLOW DOWELLED
DDEELLOY YODELLED
DDEELMOR MOLDERED
REMOLDED
DDEELMPU DEPLUMED
DDEELMRS MEDDLERS
DDEELNOU LOUDENED
DDEELNUW UNWELDED
DDEELOOW DEWOOLED
DDEELOPR DEPLORED
POLDERED
DDEELOPX EXPLODED
DDEELOPY DEPLOYED
DDEELORS SOLDERED
DDEELOSU DELOUSED
DDEELOVV DEVOLVED
DDEELPRS PEDDLERS
DDEELPRU PRELUDED
DDEELPRY PEDDLERY
DDEELPUX DUPLEXED
DDEELRSS SLEDDERS
DDEELRST TREDDLES
DDEELRSU DELUDERS
DDEEMNNU UNMENDED
DDEEMNOR ENDODERM
DDEEMORW DEWORMED
DDEEMRRU DEMURRED
MURDERED
DDEENNOR DONNERED
REDONNED
DDEENNOY ENDODYNE
DDEENNTU UNTENDED
DDEENOPR PERDENDO
PONDERED
DDEENOPW PONDWEED
DDEENORS ENDORSED
DDEENORW WONDERED
DDEENOSS ENDOSSED
DDEENPRS SPREDDEN
DDEENRRU DURNEDER
DDEENRSU DENUDERS
SUNDERED
DDEENRTU RETUNDED
DDEEOPRT DEPORTED
DDEEOPRW POWDERED
DDEEOPSS SEEDPODS
DDEEORRW REWORDED
DDEEORTT DETORTED
DDEEORTU DETOURED
DDEEORUV DEVOURED
DDEEORVY OVERDYED
DDEEOTUX TUXEDOED
DDEEPRRU PERDURED
DDEEPRSS SPREDDES
DDEERRUV VERDURED
DDEERSTU DETRUDES
DDEERTUX EXTRUDED
DDEFFISU DIFFUSED
DDEFIIIN NIDIFIED
DDEFIILM MIDFIELD
DDEFIILR FIDDLIER
DDEFIIMO MODIFIED
DDEFIIMW MIDWIFED
DDEFILNO INFOLDED
DDEFILRS FIDDLERS
DDEFILSY FIDDLEYS
DDEFLNOU UNFOLDED
DDEFLOPU UPFOLDED
DDEFLRSU FUDDLERS
DDEFLRUU UDDERFUL
DDEFNNUU UNFUNDED
DDEGGINR DREDGING
DDEGGLOY DOGGEDLY
DDEGGNOO DOGGONED
DDEGHILN HEDDLING
DDEGHINS SHEDDING
DDEGIINR DERIDING
DDEGIIST GIDDIEST
DDEGILMN MEDDLING
DDEGILNP PEDDLING
DDEGILNR REDDLING
DDEGILNS SLEDDING
DDEGILNU DELUDING
INDULGED
UNGILDED
DDEGILOS DISLODGE
DDEGILRS GRIDDLES
DDEGILRY GLIDDERY
DDEGILST GLIDDEST
DDEGILUV DIVULGED
DDEGIMOS DEMIGODS
DDEGINNS SNEDDING
DDEGINNU DENUDING
DDEGINRS REDDINGS
DDEGINRU UNGIRDED
DDEGINST STEDDING
DDEGINSW SWINDGED
WEDDINGS
DDEGINUU UNGUIDED
DDEGIOST DODGIEST
DDEGIPRU UPGIRDED
DDEGIQSU SQUIDGED
DDEGIRRS GRIDDERS
DDEGJNUU UNJUDGED
DDEGLOPS SPLODGED
DDEGLOSS DOGSLEDS
DDEGMOOS DOGEDOMS
DDEGNORU GROUNDED
UNDERDOG
UNDERGOD
DDEGNOSS GODSENDS
DDEGNOSU DUDGEONS
DDEGOOTU OUTDODGE
DDEGORSS GORSEDDS
DDEGRRSU DRUDGERS
DDEGRRUY DRUDGERY
DDEHILNY HIDDENLY
DDEHILOO IDLEHOOD
DDEHIMOS DISHOMED
DDEHINNU UNHIDDEN
DDEHINOR DIHEDRON
DDEHIORS SHODDIER
DDEHIOSS SHODDIES
DDEHIRSS SHIDDERS
DDEHIRSW WHIDDERS
DDEHIRSY HYDRIDES
DDEHLRSU HUDDLERS
DDEHNOOU UNHOODED
DDEHNPUU UPHUDDEN
DDEHNRSU HUNDREDS
DDEHOOOO HOODOOED
DDEHOOSW WOODSHED
DDEHORSU SHROUDED
DDEHRSSU SHUDDERS
DDEHRSUY SHUDDERY
DDEIIIRS IRIDISED
DDEIIIRZ IRIDIZED
DDEIIKLS DISLIKED
DDEIIKRS KIDDIERS
SKIDDIER
DDEIILNR DIELDRIN
DDEIILOS IDOLISED
DDEIILOZ IDOLIZED
DDEIILRT TIDDLIER
DDEIILST TIDDLIES
DDEIIMSS SMIDDIES
DDEIIMSZ MIDSIZED
DDEIIMVW MIDWIVED
DDEIINRT NITRIDED
DDEIINTU UNTIDIED
DDEIIOPR PERIODID
DDEIIOPS DIOPSIDE
DIPODIES

DDEIIOST	ODDITIES
DDEIIOSX	DIOXIDES
	OXIDISED
DDEIIOXZ	OXIDIZED
DDEIIRSV	DIVIDERS
DDEIIRUV	REDUVIID
DDEIISST	STIDDIES
DDEIISTT	TIDDIEST
DDEIKNRS	KINDREDS
DDEIKOOS	SKIDOOED
DDEIKOSY	DISYOKED
DDEIKRSS	SKIDDERS
DDEIKSVY	SKYDIVED
DDEILMOP	IMPLODED
DDEILMOV	DEVILDOM
DDEILMRS	MIDDLERS
DDEILMSU	MUDSLIDE
DDEILNPS	SPINDLED
	SPLENDID
DDEILNRT	TRINDLED
DDEILNRU	UNRIDDLE
DDEILNSW	DWINDLES
	SWINDLED
DDEILOPS	DISPLODE
	LOPSIDED
DDEILOST	DELTOIDS
DDEILOSY	DYSODILE
DDEILPRS	PIDDLERS
DDEILPRU	PUDDLIER
DDEILQRU	QUIDDLER
DDEILQSU	QUIDDLES
DDEILRRS	RIDDLERS
DDEILRSS	SLIDDERS
DDEILRST	STRIDDLE
	TIDDLERS
DDEILRSY	SLIDDERY
DDEILRTW	TWIDDLER
DDEILRZZ	DRIZZLED
DDEILSTW	TWIDDLES
DDEILSTY	LYDDITES
	TIDDLEYS
DDEIMMNU	UNDIMMED
DDEIMNNU	UNMINDED
DDEIMNSU	MUEDDINS
DDEIMNUV	VIDENDUM
DDEIMORS	DERMOIDS
DDEIMOSS	DESMOIDS
DDEIMOSU	MEDUSOID
DDEIMSTU	MUDDIEST
DDEINNRU	UNRIDDEN
DDEINNTU	UNDINTED
DDEINOPS	DISPONED
DDEINORS	INDORSED
DDEINOSW	DISENDOW
	DISOWNED
	DOWNSIDE
DDEINOWW	WINDOWED
DDEINPPU	UNDIPPED
DDEINPSS	DISPENDS
DDEINRST	STRIDDEN
DDEINRTU	INTRUDED
DDEINSST	DISTENDS
DDEINSSW	SWIDDENS
DDEINSTU	DISTUNED
DDEIOORZ	ODORIZED
DDEIOPRS	DROPSIED
DDEIOPRV	PROVIDED
DDEIOPSS	DISPOSED
DDEIOPST	PODDIEST
DDEIORRS	DISORDER
	SORDIDER
DDEIOSST	SODDIEST
DDEIOSTW	DOWDIEST
DDEIPRSS	DISPREDS
DDEIPRSU	SPUDDIER
DDEIPSTU	DISPUTED
DDEIRSSU	DRUIDESS
DDEIRSTU	RUDDIEST
	STURDIED
DDEISSTU	STUDDIES
DDEKMOSU	DUKEDOMS
DDELLNUU	UNDULLED
DDELLOOP	DOLLOPED
DDELMNOU	UNMOLDED
DDELMRSU	MUDDLERS
DDELNORU	UNLORDED
DDELNOSY	SODDENLY
DDELNRTU	TRUNDLED
DDELNSUY	SUDDENLY
DDELOORS	DOODLERS
DDELOPRS	PLODDERS
DDELORST	STRODDLE
	STRODLED
	TODDLERS
DDELOSYY	DYSODYLE
DDELPRSU	PUDDLERS
DDELSSTU	STUDDLES
DDEMMSSU	SMEDDUMS
DDEMNOOU	UNDOOMED
DDEMNOST	ODDMENTS
DDEMNOUU	DUODENUM
DDEMNPUU	PUDENDUM
DDEMOOTU	OUTMODED
DDENNORS	DENDRONS
DDENNOSU	UNSODDEN
DDENOOPS	ENDOPODS
DDENOOUW	UNWOODED
DDENOPSS	DESPONDS
DDENORSU	REDOUNDS
DDENORTU	ROTUNDED
DDENORUW	UNWORDED
DDENOSST	SNODDEST
DDENOSTU	STOUNDED
DDENOSTW	STOWNDED
DDENOSUW	SWOUNDED
DDENOTTU	DONUTTED
	UNDOTTED
DDENRSTU	DURNDEST
DDENSTUY	SUDDENTY
DDEOOOOV	VOODOOED
DDEOORSW	REDWOODS
DDEOORWW	ROWDEDOW
DDEOOSWY	DYEWOODS
DDEOOUUV	VOUDOUED
DDEOPRRS	PRODDERS
DDEOPRSW	DEWDROPS
DDEORTUU	OUTDURED
DDEPRSSU	SPUDDERS
DDFGIILN	FIDDLING
DDFGILNU	FUDDLING
DDFIILSU	DISULFID
DDFIIOSU	FIDDIOUS
DDFMNOUU	DUMFOUND
DDGGIINY	GIDDYING
DDGGILNU	GUDDLING
DDGGINNO	DINGDONG
DDGGINOS	DODGINGS
DDGGINRU	DRUDGING
DDGHIINW	WHIDDING
DDGHILNO	HODDLING
DDGHILNU	HUDDLING
DDGHINTU	THUDDING
DDGHOOOS	GODHOODS
DDGIIINO	INDIGOID
DDGIIINV	DIVIDING
DDGIIKNS	SKIDDING
DDGIIKNY	KIDDYING
DDGIILMN	MIDDLING
DDGIILNN	DINDLING
DDGIILNP	PIDDLING
DDGIILNR	RIDDLING
DDGIILNT	TIDDLING
DDGIILNW	WIDDLING
DDGILMNU	MUDDLING
DDGILNNO	NODDLING
DDGILNOO	DOODLING
DDGILNOP	PLODDING
DDGILNOT	TODDLING
DDGILNPU	PUDDLING
DDGILNRU	RUDDLING
DDGIMNUY	MUDDYING
DDGIMRSU	DRUDGISM
DDGINNOS	NODDINGS
	SNODDING
DDGINOPR	PRODDING
DDGINOQU	QUODDING
DDGINORS	RODDINGS
DDGINPSU	PUDDINGS
	SPUDDING
DDGINPUY	PUDDINGY
DDGINRUY	RUDDYING
DDGINSTU	STUDDING
DDGOOOSW	DOGWOODS
DDHILOSY	SHODDILY
DDHILSUY	DUDISHLY
DDHIORSY	HYDROIDS
DDHIOSWY	DOWDYISH
DDHLLOOO	DOLLHOOD
DDIIIIVV	DIVIDIVI
DDIILOPS	DIPLOIDS
DDIILOPY	DIPLOIDY
DDIIMMUY	DIDYMIUM
DDIIMRSU	DRUIDISM
	SIDDURIM
DDIINOPU	DUPONDII
DDIIQSTU	QUIDDITS
DDIIQTUY	QUIDDITY
DDIKOOSS	SKIDDOOS
DDILOOPP	DIPLOPOD
DDILOOWW	WILDWOOD
DDILORSY	SORDIDLY
DDILOSSY	DYSODILS
DDIMOOSS	DODOISMS
DDIMOSUY	DIDYMOUS
DDIMOSWY	DOWDYISM
DDINNOWW	DOWNWIND
DDINOOOT	ODONTOID
DDINOOWW	WOODWIND
DDLLMOOS	DOLLDOMS
DDLMORSU	DOLDRUMS
DDMNOORS	DROMONDS
DDNOORTW	DOWNTROD
DDOORWWY	ROWDYDOW
DDORSSTY	DROSTDYS
DEEEEFRR	REFEREED
DEEEEFRZ	DEFREEZE
DEEEEGKR	KEDGEREE
DEEEEHLR	REHEELED
DEEEEKMN	MEEKENED
DEEEELTY	EYELETED
DEEEEMMS	MESEEMED
DEEEEMRR	REDEEMER
DEEEEMST	ESTEEMED
DEEEENPR	DEEPENER
DEEEENRV	VENEERED
DEEEERTT	TEETERED
DEEEFFIR	EFFEIRED
DEEEFHLO	FEEDHOLE
DEEEFHST	SHEETFED
DEEEFINR	FINEERED
	NEEDFIRE
	REDEFINE
DEEEFIPT	TEPEFIED
DEEEFIRS	REDEFIES
DEEEFIRW	FIREWEED
DEEEFLLR	REFELLED
DEEEFLPT	DEEPFELT
DEEEFLRR	FERRELED
DEEEFLRT	FELTERED
	TELFERED
DEEEFLRU	REFUELED
DEEEFLRX	REFLEXED
DEEEFLSX	DEFLEXES
DEEEFMNR	FREEDMEN
DEEEFNRS	ENSERFED
DEEEFNRT	DEFERENT
DEEEFNSS	DEFENSES
DEEEFNST	ENFESTED
DEEEFORV	OVERFEED
DEEEFRRR	DEFERRER
	REFERRED
DEEEFRRT	FERRETED
DEEEFRST	FESTERED
DEEEFRTT	FETTERED
DEEEFRTW	FEWTERED
DEEEGGPR	REPEGGED
DEEEGHNW	WHEENGED
DEEEGILS	ELEGISED
DEEEGILZ	ELEGIZED
DEEEGINS	DESIGNEE
DEEEGIPR	PEDIGREE
DEEEGIRR	GREEDIER
DEEEGISS	DIEGESES
DEEEGISW	EDGEWISE
DEEEGLPR	REPLEDGE
DEEEGLPS	PLEDGEES
DEEEGLSS	EDGELESS
DEEEGLSV	SELVEDGE
DEEEGMRR	DEMERGER
	REMERGED
DEEEGMRS	DEMERGES
DEEEGNNR	ENGENDER
DEEEGNRU	RENEGUED
DEEEGNRV	REVENGED
DEEEGRRS	REGREDES
DEEEGRRT	DETERGER
DEEEGRSS	EGRESSED
DEEEGRST	DETERGES
DEEEGRTT	GETTERED
DEEEHHSW	WHEESHED
DEEEHKRS	SHREEKED
DEEEHLMT	HELMETED
DEEEHLPW	WHEEPLED
DEEEHLRW	WHEEDLER
DEEEHLSS	HEEDLESS
DEEEHLSW	WHEEDLES
DEEEHLWZ	WHEEZLED
DEEEHMMR	REHEMMED
DEEEHMMS	EMMESHED
DEEEHMNS	ENMESHED
DEEEHMPS	HEMPSEED
DEEEHMPW	HEMPWEED
DEEEHPRT	THREEPED
DEEEHRTT	TETHERED
DEEEIKLR	DEERLIKE
	REEDLIKE
DEEEIKLS	SEEDLIKE
DEEEIKLW	WEEDLIKE
DEEEILNR	NEEDLIER
DEEEILNS	SELENIDE
DEEEILRV	RELIEVED
DEEEILTV	DELETIVE
DEEEILVW	WEEVILED
DEEEIMNS	INSEEMED
DEEEIMRS	REMEDIES
DEEEIMST	SEEDTIME
DEEEINNX	ENDEXINE
DEEEINRR	REINDEER
DEEEINRS	NEREIDES
	REDENIES

DEEEINST	NEEDIEST
DEEEINSX	ENDEIXES
DEEEINTV	EVENTIDE
DEEEIPRS	SPEEDIER
DEEEIPTX	EXPEDITE
DEEEIRRR	DERRIERE
DEEEIRSS	DIERESES
DEEEIRST	REEDIEST
DEEEIRSZ	RESEIZED
DEEEIRTW	TWEEDIER
DEEEIRVW	REVIEWED
DEEEISST	SEEDIEST
	STEEDIES
DEEEISSV	DEVISEES
DEEEISTW	WEEDIEST
DEEEJLLW	JEWELLED
DEEEJNRU	DEJEUNER
DEEEJNSU	DEJEUNES
DEEEJRRS	JERREEDS
DEEEJRSY	JERSEYED
DEEEKLNN	KENNELED
DEEEKLNR	KERNELED
DEEEKNSW	WEEKENDS
DEEEKOPW	POKEWEED
DEEEKORV	REEVOKED
DEEEKPRR	REPERKED
DEEEKRST	STREEKED
DEEEKRSW	RESKEWED
	SKEWERED
DEEELLLV	LEVELLED
DEEELLNT	DENTELLE
DEEELLNV	NEVELLED
DEEELLNW	NEWELLED
DEEELLPR	REPELLED
DEEELLPT	PELLETED
DEEELLPX	EXPELLED
DEEELLRT	TELLERED
DEEELLRV	REVELLED
DEEELMOS	SOMEDELE
DEEELMRT	REMELTED
DEEELNPU	UNPEELED
DEEELNRS	NEEDLERS
DEEELNRT	RELENTED
DEEELNRU	UNREELED
DEEELNSS	LESSENED
	NEEDLESS
	SELDSEEN
DEEELNSU	UNSEELED
DEEELOPV	DEVELOPE
DEEELPRT	PELTERED
	REPLETED
DEEELPST	DEPLETES
	STEEPLED
DEEELRSS	REDELESS
DEEELRST	DEERLETS
	STREELED
DEEELRTT	LETTERED
DEEELRTW	TWEEDLER
	WELTERED
DEEELSSS	SEEDLESS
DEEELSSV	VESSELED
DEEELSSW	WEEDLESS
DEEELSTW	TWEEDLES
DEEELTVV	VELVETED
DEEEMNNT	NEEDMENT
DEEEMNRS	EMENDERS
DEEEMNSS	DEMESNES
	SEEDSMEN
DEEEMPRT	TEMPERED
DEEEMPTX	EXEMPTED
DEEEMRRU	MURDEREE
DEEEMRSS	DEMERSES
DEEEMRST	DEEMSTER
DEEENNRT	ENTENDER
DEEENNUW	UNWEENED
DEEENOPR	REOPENED
DEEENORS	ENDORSEE
DEEENPRT	REPENTED
	REPETEND
DEEENPRU	UNPEERED
DEEENPRV	PREVENED
DEEENPRX	EXPENDER
DEEENPSS	DEEPNESS
DEEENPSX	EXPENSED
DEEENRRR	RENDERER
DEEENRRT	TENDERER
DEEENRRV	REVEREND
DEEENRST	RENESTED
	RESENTED
DEEENRTT	TENTERED
DEEENRTU	NEUTERED
DEEENRTX	EXTENDER
DEEENRUV	REVENUED
	UNREEVED
DEEENSSS	SEEDNESS
DEEENSSY	EYEDNESS
DEEENSTT	DETENTES
DEEENSTU	DETENUES
DEEENSTX	DENTEXES
DEEENSUV	VENDEUSE
DEEEOPRR	PEDERERO
DEEEOPRT	DEPORTEE
DEEEORST	STEREOED
DEEEORSV	OVERSEED
DEEEORSW	OREWEEDS
DEEEORVY	OVEREYED
DEEEOSTV	DEVOTEES
DEEEPPPR	PEPPERED
DEEEPRSS	SPEEDERS
DEEEPRST	ESTREPED
	PESTERED
DEEEPRSZ	SPREEZED
DEEEPRTX	EXPERTED
DEEEQRRU	REQUERED
DEEEQSUZ	SQUEEZED
DEEERRRT	DETERRER
DEEERRRV	VERDERER
DEEERRST	DESERTER
DEEERRSV	DESERVER
	RESERVED
	REVERSED
DEEERRTV	REVERTED
DEEERSSV	DESERVES
DEEERSTT	DETESTER
	RESETTED
	RETESTED
	SETTERED
	STREETED
DEEERSTV	REVESTED
DEEERSTW	WESTERED
DEEERSTX	EXSERTED
DEEERSUW	SERUEWED
DEEERSVW	SERVEWED
DEEERTTT	TETTERED
DEEERTTV	REVETTED
DEEERTTW	REWETTED
DEEESTTU	SUEDETTE
DEEESTTV	VEDETTES
DEEFFGLU	EFFULGED
DEEFFGOR	GOFFERED
DEEFFINR	NIFFERED
DEEFFINS	EFFENDIS
DEEFFINT	INFEFTED
DEEFFIRS	SERIFFED
DEEFFNOR	FOREFEND
	OFFENDER
	REOFFEND
DEEFFRSU	SUFFERED
DEEFGGOR	DEFOGGER
DEEFGILR	FLEDGIER
DEEFGINR	FINGERED
DEEFGINS	FEEDINGS
DEEFGIPS	PIGFEEDS
DEEFGIRT	FIDGETER
DEEFGIUW	GUDEWIFE
DEEFGLNU	ENGULFED
DEEFGLOO	FEELGOOD
DEEFGLUW	GULFWEED
DEEFGORR	REFORGED
DEEFGORY	FROGEYED
DEEFHIMU	HUMEFIED
DEEFHINT	HINDFEET
DEEFHLOR	FREEHOLD
DEEFHLRS	FELDSHER
DEEFHORT	FOTHERED
DEEFIILN	FEDELINI
	LENIFIED
DEEFIINT	DEFINITE
DEEFIIRS	DEIFIERS
	EDIFIERS
	FIRESIDE
DEEFIIRV	VERIFIED
DEEFILLR	REFILLED
DEEFILLT	FILLETED
DEEFILMR	REFILMED
DEEFILMS	MEDFLIES
DEEFILNX	INFLEXED
DEEFILPR	PILFERED
	PREFILED
DEEFILRS	DEFILERS
	FIELDERS
DEEFILRT	FILTERED
DEEFIMSS	MISFEEDS
DEEFIMTU	TUMEFIED
DEEFINRR	INFERRED
DEEFINRS	DEFINERS
DEEFINRZ	FRENZIED
DEEFINSS	FINESSED
DEEFINST	FENDIEST
	INFESTED
DEEFIORS	FORESIDE
DEEFIORT	FOETIDER
DEEFIPRR	PREFIRED
DEEFIPRX	PREFIXED
DEEFIRRV	FERVIDER
DEEFIRST	RESIFTED
DEEFIRTT	REFITTED
DEEFISTT	FETIDEST
DEEFLLNU	UNFELLED
DEEFLLOW	FELLOWED
DEEFLLRU	FULLERED
DEEFLNNU	FUNNELED
DEEFLNOR	ENFOLDER
	FORELEND
DEEFLNSU	NEEDFULS
	UNSELFED
DEEFLNTU	DEFLUENT
DEEFLNUX	UNFLEXED
DEEFLORW	DEFLOWER
	FLOWERED
	REFLOWED
DEEFLOST	FEEDLOTS
DEEFLPSU	SPEEDFUL
DEEFLRRU	FERRULED
DEEFLRUX	REFLUXED
DEEFMNOR	ENFORMED
DEEFMNOT	FOMENTED
DEEFMORR	DEFORMER
	REFORMED
DEEFMORS	FREEDOMS
DEEFMPRU	PERFUMED
DEEFNOOR	FOREDONE
DEEFNORZ	DEFROZEN
DEEFNOST	SOFTENED
DEEFNRRU	REFUNDER
DEEFNSST	DEFTNESS
DEEFOORR	REROOFED
DEEFOORS	FOREDOES
DEEFOORT	REFOOTED
DEEFORST	DEFOREST
	FORESTED
	FOSTERED
DEEFORTU	FOUTERED
DEEFPRSU	PERFUSED
DEEFRRTU	RETURFED
DEEGGHHO	HEDGEHOG
DEEGGHIP	HEDGEPIG
DEEGGIJR	JIGGERED
	REJIGGED
DEEGGINR	GINGERED
	NIGGERED
	RENIGGED
DEEGGIRR	DREGGIER
	RERIGGED
DEEGGLOR	DOGGEREL
DEEGGNOR	ENGORGED
DEEGGNPU	UNPEGGED
DEEGGORR	REGORGED
DEEGGORT	GORGETED
DEEGGQSU	SQUEGGED
DEEGGRRU	RUGGEDER
DEEGHHIR	HIGHERED
DEEGHHOP	HEDGEHOP
DEEGHHSU	SHEUGHED
DEEGHHUW	WHEUGHED
DEEGHILS	SLEIGHED
DEEGHINR	REHINGED
DEEGHIST	HEDGIEST
DEEGHITW	WEIGHTED
DEEGHNRU	HUNGERED
DEEGHOPR	GOPHERED
DEEGHOPS	SHEEPDOG
DEEGHORW	HEDGEROW
DEEGHOSW	HOGWEEDS
DEEGHOTT	DOGTEETH
	GHETTOED
DEEGIINN	INDIGENE
DEEGIISS	DIEGESIS
DEEGIKST	KEDGIEST
DEEGILMO	LIEGEDOM
DEEGILMP	IMPLEDGE
DEEGILMT	GIMLETED
DEEGILNN	NEEDLING
DEEGILNO	ELOIGNED
	LEGIONED
DEEGILNR	ENGIRDLE
	LINGERED
	REEDLING
DEEGILNS	SEEDLING
DEEGILNT	DELETING
DEEGILNV	DEVELING
DEEGILNW	WEDELING
DEEGILRS	LEIDGERS
DEEGILRW	WEREGILD
DEEGILRY	GREEDILY
DEEGILST	GELIDEST
	LEDGIEST
DEEGIMMR	IMMERGED
DEEGIMNN	EMENDING
DEEGIMNR	REMEDING
DEEGIMRU	DEMIURGE
DEEGINNR	ENRINGED
DEEGINNS	ENSIGNED
DEEGINNT	TEENDING
DEEGINNW	ENDEWING
DEEGINOP	PIGEONED
DEEGINPS	SPEEDING
DEEGINRR	DERINGER
DEEGINRS	DESIGNER
	ENERGIDS

	REDESIGN
	REEDINGS
	RESIGNED
DEEGINRY	REDYEING
DEEGINSS	DINGESES
	EDGINESS
	SDEIGNES
	SEEDINGS
DEEGINST	INGESTED
	SIGNETED
	STEEDING
DEEGINSW	WEEDINGS
DEEGINSX	DESEXING
DEEGINZZ	GIZZENED
DEEGIOST	EGOTISED
DEEGIOTZ	EGOTIZED
DEEGIPSW	PIGWEEDS
DEEGIRST	DIGESTER
	ESTRIDGE
	REDIGEST
DEEGIRSU	GUDESIRE
DEEGIRSV	DIVERGES
DEEGISST	SEDGIEST
DEEGISTW	WEDGIEST
DEEGJPRU	PREJUDGE
DEEGJRSU	REJUDGES
DEEGLLOR	GOLLERED
DEEGLLRU	GRUELLED
DEEGLLUY	GULLEYED
DEEGLNOR	GOLDENER
DEEGLNOU	ENGOULED
DEEGLNOZ	LOZENGED
DEEGLNRY	LEGENDRY
DEEGLOPR	PLEDGEOR
DEEGLOPS	DOGSLEEP
DEEGLORV	GROVELED
DEEGLORW	GLOWERED
	REGLOWED
DEEGLOSY	GOLDEYES
DEEGLPRS	PLEDGERS
DEEGLPST	PLEDGETS
DEEGLRSS	SLEDGERS
DEEGLRSW	WERGELDS
DEEGMNOR	MONGERED
DEEGMNRU	DUNGMERE
DEEGMSUW	GUMWEEDS
DEEGNNOS	ENDOGENS
DEEGNNOY	ENDOGENY
DEEGNOPU	GEEPOUND
DEEGNORV	GOVERNED
DEEGNPRU	REPUGNED
DEEGNPUX	EXPUGNED
	EXPUNGED
DEEGNRUY	UNGREEDY
DEEGNSTU	NUTSEDGE
DEEGOSTU	OUTEDGES
DEEGOTUW	GOUTWEED
DEEGPRUX	EXPURGED
DEEGRRSU	RESURGED
DEEGRSTU	GESTURED
DEEGRTTU	GUTTERED
DEEGSSTU	GUSSETED
DEEHHIRT	HITHERED
DEEHHNPY	HYPHENED
DEEHHPRS	SHEPHERD
DEEHHRST	THRESHED
DEEHHRSU	HUSHERED
DEEHIKLR	HERDLIKE
DEEHIKLS	SHEDLIKE
DEEHIKRS	SHREIKED
	SHRIEKED
DEEHIKSV	KHEDIVES
DEEHILNS	ENSHIELD
DEEHILRS	HIRSELED
	RELISHED
	SHIELDER
DEEHILSS	HIDELESS
DEEHILSV	DISHEVEL
DEEHIMMS	IMMESHED
DEEHIMNS	INMESHED
DEEHIMRT	MITHERED
DEEHINPR	EPHEDRIN
DEEHINRR	HINDERER
DEEHINRS	DRISHEEN
	RESHINED
DEEHINST	DISTHENE
DEEHINTW	WHITENED
DEEHIORS	HEROISED
DEEHIORZ	HEROIZED
DEEHIPRS	HESPERID
	PERISHED
DEEHIRRS	REDSHIRE
DEEHIRRT	DITHERER
DEEHIRRW	WHERRIED
DEEHIRST	DIETHERS
DEEHIRSV	SHIVERED
	SHRIEVED
DEEHIRSW	SHREWDIE
DEEHIRTW	WITHERED
DEEHIRTY	HEREDITY
DEEHKLPS	HELPDESK
DEEHKNOS	KEESHOND
DEEHKNRU	HUNKERED
DEEHKORS	KOSHERED
DEEHLLOR	HOLLERED
DEEHLLOV	HOVELLED
DEEHLMMW	WHEMMLED
DEEHLMNU	UNHELMED
DEEHLMSW	WELDMESH
DEEHLNPU	UNHELPED
DEEHLORV	OVERHELD
	VERDELHO
DEEHLOST	HOSTELED
DEEHLOSU	HOUSELED
DEEHLOSV	SHOVELED
DEEHLPPS	SHLEPPED
DEEHLSTU	SLEUTHED
DEEHMNRS	HERDSMEN
DEEHMNSU	UNMESHED
DEEHMORT	MOTHERED
DEEHNOPY	PHONEYED
DEEHNORR	DEERHORN
	DEHORNER
DEEHNORT	DETHRONE
	THRENODE
DEEHNOWY	HONEYDEW
DEEHNPRS	PREHENDS
DEEHNSTU	ENTHUSED
DEEHOORV	HOOVERED
DEEHOPRT	POTHERED
DEEHORRS	REDHORSE
DEEHORRT	DEHORTER
DEEHORSU	REHOUSED
DEEHORSW	RESHOWED
	SHOWERED
DEEHORTT	HOTTERED
DEEHORTX	EXHORTED
DEEHPRSY	SYPHERED
DEEHRRSW	SHREWDER
DEEHRTUW	WUTHERED
DEEIIKLT	TIDELIKE
DEEIILNS	SIDELINE
DEEIILRV	LIVERIED
DEEIILRW	WIELDIER
DEEIIMRS	DIMERISE
DEEIIMRZ	DIMERIZE
DEEIIMST	ITEMISED
DEEIIMTZ	ITEMIZED
DEEIINOZ	DEIONIZE
DEEIINST	DIETINES
DEEIINSX	ENDEIXIS
DEEIIPRS	EPEIRIDS
DEEIIPRU	PRIEDIEU
DEEIIRSS	DIERESIS
DEEIIRST	SIDERITE
DEEIIRSV	DERISIVE
DEEIIRSW	WEIRDIES
DEEIISSS	DISSEISE
DEEIISSW	SIDEWISE
DEEIISSX	DEIXISES
DEEIISSZ	DISSEIZE
DEEIJNNO	ENJOINED
DEEIJNOR	REJOINED
DEEIJRTT	JITTERED
DEEIKKRY	YIKKERED
DEEIKLLR	KILLDEER
DEEIKLLS	KILLDEES
	SKELLIED
DEEIKLMO	DOMELIKE
DEEIKLMW	MILKWEED
DEEIKLNN	ENKINDLE
	ENLINKED
DEEIKLNR	REKINDLE
	RELINKED
DEEIKLNS	SILKENED
DEEIKLNU	DUNELIKE
DEEIKLOV	DOVELIKE
DEEIKLSW	SILKWEED
DEEIKMSW	MIDWEEKS
DEEIKMSY	MISKEYED
DEEIKNNP	PINKENED
DEEIKNRS	DEERSKIN
DEEIKNRT	TINKERED
DEEIKNTT	KITTENED
DEEIKOSV	DOVEKIES
DEEIKPPR	KIPPERED
DEEIKRSU	DUKERIES
DEEIKRSV	SKIVERED
DEEIKSTT	DISKETTE
DEEILLMP	IMPELLED
	MILLEPED
DEEILLNO	NIELLOED
DEEILLOR	ORIELLED
DEEILLPR	PERILLED
DEEILLRT	TILLERED
	TREDILLE
DEEILLRV	RIVELLED
DEEILLVY	VEILEDLY
DEEILLWY	WILLEYED
DEEILMNU	DEMILUNE
DEEILMOS	MELODIES
	MELODISE
DEEILMOZ	MELODIZE
DEEILMPT	IMPLETED
DEEILNOS	ESLOINED
	LESIONED
DEEILNOT	DELETION
	ENTOILED
DEEILNPP	LIPPENED
DEEILNRS	REDLINES
DEEILNRU	UNDERLIE
DEEILNSS	IDLENESS
	LINSEEDS
DEEILNST	ENLISTED
	LINTSEED
	LISTENED
	TINSELED
DEEILNSV	SNIVELED
DEEILNSY	DYELINES
DEEILNTT	ENTITLED
DEEILNUV	UNLEVIED
	UNVEILED
DEEILOPT	LEPIDOTE
	PETIOLED
DEEILORT	DOLERITE
	LOITERED
DEEILORV	EVILDOER
	OVERIDLE
DEEILOSS	OILSEEDS
DEEILOTT	TOILETED
DEEILPPR	LIPPERED
DEEILPRX	DIPLEXER
DEEILPSS	SEEDLIPS
DEEILPST	EPISTLED
DEEILPSU	EPULIDES
DEEILPSY	SPEEDILY
DEEILRRV	DRIVELER
DEEILRST	RELISTED
DEEILRSU	LEISURED
DEEILRSV	DELIVERS
	DESILVER
	SILVERED
	SLIVERED
DEEILRSW	WIELDERS
DEEILRSY	YIELDERS
DEEILRTT	LITTERED
	RETITLED
DEEILRVY	DELIVERY
DEEILSSS	IDLESSES
DEEILSST	TIDELESS
DEEILSSV	DEVILESS
DEEILSTU	DILUTEES
DEEILSTV	DEVILETS
DEEILSUV	DELUSIVE
DEEILSVW	SWIVELED
DEEILTUY	YULETIDE
DEEIMMNS	ENDEMISM
DEEIMMOS	SEMIDOME
DEEIMMRS	IMMERSED
	SIMMERED
DEEIMMSS	MISDEEMS
DEEIMNOR	DOMINEER
DEEIMNOS	DEMONISE
	DOMINEES
DEEIMNOZ	DEMONIZE
DEEIMNPT	PEDIMENT
DEEIMNRR	REMINDER
	REREMIND
DEEIMNRT	REMINTED
DEEIMNRV	VERMINED
DEEIMNSS	DESMINES
	SIDESMEN
DEEIMNST	DEMENTIS
	SEDIMENT
	TIDESMEN
DEEIMNSU	SEMINUDE
DEEIMNTT	MITTENED
DEEIMORS	EMEROIDS
DEEIMOST	TEDISOME
DEEIMPRR	PERIDERM
	REPRIMED
DEEIMPRS	DEMIREPS
	EPIDERMS
	IMPEDERS
	PREMISED
	SIMPERED
DEEIMPRX	PREMIXED
DEEIMPSS	SEMIPEDS
DEEIMRSS	DERMISES
DEEIMRST	DEMERITS
	DEMISTER
	DIMETERS
	MISTERED
DEEIMRTT	REMITTED
DEEIMSSU	MEDIUSES
DEEINNPR	REPINNED
DEEINNRS	SINNERED
DEEINNRT	INDENTER
	INTENDER
	INTERNED

DEEINNRU	UNREINED
DEEINNRV	INNERVED
DEEINNST	DENTINES
	DESINENT
DEEINNSZ	DENIZENS
DEEINNTV	INVENTED
DEEINNTW	ENTWINED
DEEINNUV	UNENVIED
	UNVEINED
DEEINOPS	DISPONEE
DEEINORS	INDORSEE
	ORDINEES
DEEINORT	ORIENTED
DEEINORW	IRONWEED
DEEINOST	SIDENOTE
DEEINOSV	NOSEDIVE
DEEINOTV	DENOTIVE
DEEINPPR	NIPPERED
DEEINPSS	DISPENSE
	PIEDNESS
DEEINPST	PENTISED
DEEINPSU	UNESPIED
DEEINPSW	PINWEEDS
DEEINQRU	ENQUIRED
	INQUERED
DEEINQSU	SEQUINED
DEEINRRT	INTERRED
	TRENDIER
DEEINRRV	REDRIVEN
DEEINRRW	REWINDER
DEEINRSS	DIRENESS
DEEINRST	INSERTED
	NERDIEST
	RESIDENT
	SINTERED
	TRENDIES
DEEINRSU	UREDINES
DEEINRSW	REWIDENS
	WIDENERS
DEEINRSX	INDEXERS
DEEINRTT	RETINTED
DEEINRTU	RETINUED
	REUNITED
DEEINRTV	INVERTED
DEEINRTW	WINTERED
DEEINRTX	DEXTRINE
DEEINSST	DESTINES
DEEINSSV	VENDISES
DEEINSSW	DEWINESS
	WIDENESS
DEEINSTT	DINETTES
	INSETTED
DEEINSTU	DETINUES
DEEINSTV	EVIDENTS
	INVESTED
DEEINSUZ	UNSEIZED
DEEINTUV	DUVETINE
DEEINUVW	UNVIEWED
DEEIOPRT	PERIDOTE
	PROTEIDE
DEEIOPRX	PEROXIDE
DEEIOPSS	EPISODES
DEEIOPST	EPIDOTES
	POETISED
DEEIOPSX	EPOXIDES
DEEIOPTZ	POETIZED
DEEIORRV	OVERRIDE
DEEIORSV	OVERSIDE
DEEIORSW	DOWERIES
	WEIRDOES
DEEIORTU	ETOURDIE
DEEIORTV	OVEREDIT
DEEIORTZ	EROTIZED
DEEIORVW	OVERWIDE
DEEIOTVX	VIDEOTEX
DEEIPPQU	EQUIPPED
DEEIPPRZ	ZIPPERED
DEEIPPST	PEPTIDES
	PEPTISED
DEEIPPTT	PIPETTED
DEEIPPTZ	PEPTIZED
DEEIPQRU	REPIQUED
DEEIPQTU	PIQUETED
DEEIPRRS	PRESIDER
	REPRISED
	RESPIRED
DEEIPRRV	DEPRIVER
	REPRIVED
DEEIPRRZ	REPRIZED
DEEIPRSS	DESPISER
	DISPERSE
	PRESIDES
DEEIPRST	PREEDITS
	PRIESTED
	RESPITED
DEEIPRSU	DUPERIES
DEEIPRSV	DEPRIVES
	PREVISED
DEEIPRTT	PITTERED
	PRETTIED
DEEIPRTX	EXTIRPED
DEEIPSSS	DESPISES
DEEIPSST	DESPITES
	SIDESTEP
DEEIPSTT	TEPIDEST
DEEIPSTU	DEPUTIES
	DEPUTISE
DEEIPTUZ	DEPUTIZE
DEEIQRRU	REQUIRED
DEEIQRSU	ESQUIRED
DEEIQRTU	REQUITED
DEEIQRUV	QUIVERED
DEEIQTUU	QUIETUDE
DEEIRRSS	DERRISES
	DESIRERS
	DRESSIER
	RESIDERS
DEEIRRST	DESTRIER
DEEIRRSU	RUDERIES
DEEIRRSV	DERIVERS
	REDRIVES
DEEIRRTV	DIVERTER
	VERDITER
DEEIRRWW	WIREDREW
DEEIRRZZ	RIZZERED
DEEIRSST	DIESTERS
	EDITRESS
	RESISTED
	SISTERED
DEEIRSSU	DIURESES
	REISSUED
	RESIDUES
DEEIRSSV	DEVISERS
	DISSERVE
	DISSEVER
	DIVERSES
DEEIRSTT	TIREDEST
DEEIRSTU	ERUDITES
	SURETIED
DEEIRSTV	VERDITES
DEEIRSTW	WEIRDEST
DEEIRTTT	TITTERED
DEEIRTTV	RIVETTED
DEEIRTTW	WITTERED
DEEISSSU	DISEUSES
DEEISTTV	VIDETTES
DEEJKNTU	JUNKETED
DEEJPRRU	PERJURED
DEEJPTTU	UPJETTED
DEEKKOOY	OKEYDOKE
DEEKLNOS	SLOKENED
DEEKLNST	SKLENTED
DEEKLOOR	RELOOKED
DEEKLRSS	SKELDERS
DEEKMNOY	MONKEYED
DEEKNNNU	UNKENNED
DEEKNOTW	KNOTWEED
DEEKNOTY	KEYNOTED
DEEKORRW	REWORKED
DEEKORST	RESTOKED
DEEKOSVY	DOVEKEYS
DEEKRUVY	KURVEYED
DEELLMOR	MODELLER
DEELLMOW	MELLOWED
DEELLNOP	POLLENED
DEELLNOR	ENROLLED
	RONDELLE
DEELLOPR	REPOLLED
DEELLORR	REROLLED
DEELLORW	ROWELLED
	WELLDOER
DEELLORY	YODELLER
DEELLOTW	TOWELLED
DEELLOTX	EXTOLLED
DEELLOVW	VOWELLED
DEELLOVY	VOLLEYED
DEELLOWY	YELLOWED
DEELLPUW	UPWELLED
DEELLRSU	DUELLERS
DEELLRSW	DWELLERS
DEELLSSW	WELDLESS
DEELLSUX	DUXELLES
DEELMMOP	POMMELED
DEELMMPU	EMPLUMED
	PUMMELED
DEELMNOO	MELODEON
DEELMNOS	LODESMEN
DEELMNTU	UNMELTED
DEELMNTW	WELDMENT
DEELMOOS	DOLESOME
DEELMOPR	EMPOLDER
DEELMOPY	EMPLOYED
DEELMORS	MODELERS
	MORSELED
	REMODELS
DEELMOST	MOLESTED
DEELMOSU	DUELSOME
DEELMPPU	PEPLUMED
DEELMPSU	DEPLUMES
DEELMRUY	DEMURELY
DEELNNTU	TUNNELED
DEELNOOS	LOOSENED
DEELNORT	REDOLENT
	RONDELET
DEELNORV	OVERLEND
DEELNOSS	LESSONED
DEELNOSU	ENSOULED
DEELNOSY	ESLOYNED
DEELNPRS	RESPLEND
DEELNRTU	UNDERLET
DEELNRTY	TENDERLY
DEELNSSW	LEWDNESS
DEELNSTY	ENSTYLED
DEELNTTU	UNLETTED
DEELNWWY	NEWLYWED
DEELOORT	RETOOLED
DEELOPPR	LOPPERED
DEELOPRR	DEPLORER
DEELOPRS	DEPLORES
DEELOPRX	EXPLODER
	EXPLORED
DEELOPRY	REDEPLOY
DEELOPSV	DEVELOPS
DEELOPSX	EXPLODES
DEELORRS	RESOLDER
	SOLDERER
DEELORSU	DELOUSER
	URODELES
DEELORSV	RESOLVED
DEELORSY	YODELERS
DEELORTT	DOTTEREL
	TOLTERED
DEELORTV	REVOLTED
DEELORTW	TROWELED
DEELORTY	DELETORY
DEELORUV	LOUVERED
DEELORVV	REVOLVED
DEELORVW	OVERLEWD
DEELOSSU	DELOUSES
DEELOSTV	DOVELETS
DEELOSVV	DEVOLVES
DEELOTUV	EVOLUTED
DEELPPRU	REPULPED
DEELPRRU	PRELUDER
DEELPRSS	SPELDERS
DEELPRSU	PRELUDES
	REPULSED
DEELPRTU	DRUPELET
DEELPRUV	PULVERED
DEELPRUX	DUPLEXER
DEELPSUX	DUPLEXES
	EXPULSED
DEELPTTY	PETTEDLY
DEELRSTU	DELUSTER
	LUSTERED
	RESULTED
	ULSTERED
DEELRSTW	LEWDSTER
	WRESTLED
DEELRSTY	RESTYLED
DEELRSUV	REVULSED
DEEMMORS	MESODERM
DEEMMRRU	DUMMERER
DEEMMRSU	SUMMERED
DEEMNNRU	UNDERMEN
DEEMNNTU	TENENDUM
DEEMNOOS	ENDOSOME
	MOONSEED
DEEMNOQU	QUEENDOM
DEEMNORR	MODERNER
DEEMNORS	SERMONED
DEEMNORT	ENTODERM
	MENTORED
DEEMNOSS	DEMONESS
	ENMOSSED
DEEMNOST	DEMETONS
DEEMNOSU	EUDEMONS
DEEMOOPR	PODOMERE
DEEMOORT	ODOMETER
DEEMOPPY	POMPEYED
DEEMOPRV	PREMOVED
DEEMOPST	DEEPMOST
DEEMOQRU	QUEERDOM
DEEMORRT	TREMORED
DEEMORRW	DEWORMER
DEEMORST	MODESTER
DEEMORSW	WORMSEED
DEEMORSX	EXODERMS
DEEMORTU	MOUTERED
	UDOMETER
DEEMPPRU	REPUMPED
DEEMPRST	DEMPSTER
DEEMPRSU	PRESUMED
DEEMPRTU	PERMUTED
DEEMPSUW	SUMPWEED
DEEMRRRU	DEMURRER
	MURDERER
DEEMRSTU	DEMUREST
	MUSTERED
DEEMRTTU	MUTTERED

DEEMSSTY	SYSTEMED
DEENNNOP	PENNONED
DEENNNPU	UNPENNED
DEENNOPT	DEPONENT
DEENNOPU	UNOPENED
DEENNORS	ENDERONS
DEENNORW	RENOWNED
DEENNOSS	DONENESS
DEENNOST	ENDNOTES
	SONNETED
DEENNOSY	DOYENNES
DEENNPST	PENDENTS
DEENNRTU	UNRENTED
	UNTENDER
DEENNRUV	UNNERVED
DEENNSSU	NUDENESS
	UNSENSED
DEENNSTU	UNNESTED
DEENNTTU	UNNETTED
	UNTENTED
DEENNTUV	UNVENTED
DEENOORT	ENROOTED
DEENOORV	OVERDONE
DEENOORW	WOODENER
DEENOPPR	PREPONED
DEENOPRR	PONDERER
DEENOPSS	SPONDEES
DEENOPST	PENTODES
DEENORRS	ENDORSER
DEENORRW	WONDERER
DEENORSS	ENDORSES
DEENORST	ERODENTS
DEENORSW	ENDOWERS
	REENDOWS
	WORSENED
DEENORTU	DEUTERON
DEENOSSS	ENDOSSES
DEENOSST	STENOSED
DEENPPRS	PERPENDS
DEENPRSS	SPENDERS
DEENPRST	PRETENDS
DEENRRSU	ENDURERS
	SUNDERER
DEENRRTU	RETURNED
DEENRSSU	RUDENESS
DEENRSTU	DENTURES
	SEDERUNT
	UNDERSET
	UNDESERT
	UNRESTED
DEENRSUU	UNDERUSE
DEENRSUV	UNSERVED
	UNVERSED
DEENRTUV	VENTURED
DEENSSSY	SYNDESES
DEENSTTU	UNTESTED
DEENTTUV	UNVETTED
DEENTTUW	UNWETTED
DEENTUVY	DUVETYNE
DEEOOPPR	PEREOPOD
DEEOORRV	OVERDOER
	OVERRODE
DEEOORSV	OVERDOES
	OVERDOSE
DEEOPPRS	PREPOSED
DEEOPPST	ESTOPPED
DEEOPRRR	PREORDER
DEEOPRRS	PEDREROS
DEEOPRRT	PORTERED
	REPORTED
DEEOPRRU	REPOURED
DEEOPRRV	REPROVED
DEEOPRRW	POWDERER
DEEOPRSS	DEPOSERS
DEEOPRST	DOPESTER
	POSTERED
	REEDSTOP
	REPOSTED
DEEOPRSY	EYEDROPS
DEEOPRTT	POTTERED
	REPOTTED
DEEOPRTW	POWTERED
DEEOPRTX	EXPORTED
DEEOPRUZ	DOUZEPER
DEEOPSST	POSSETED
DEEOPSSU	ESPOUSED
DEEOPSTU	OUTSPEED
DEEOQRTU	REQUOTED
	ROQUETED
DEEORRRS	ORDERERS
	REORDERS
DEEORRRV	VERDEROR
DEEORRST	RESORTED
	RESTORED
	ROSTERED
DEEORRSV	OVERREDS
DEEORRTT	RETORTED
DEEORRTU	REROUTED
	RETOURED
DEEORRUV	DEVOURER
	OVERRUDE
DEEORRVW	OVERDREW
DEEORSST	DOSSERET
	OERSTEDS
DEEORSTT	ROSETTED
	TETRODES
DEEORSTX	DEXTROSE
DEEORSTY	OYSTERED
	STOREYED
DEEORSUV	OVERUSED
DEEORSVY	OVERDYES
DEEORTTT	TOTTERED
DEEORTTX	EXTORTED
DEEORTUV	DEVOUTER
DEEOSSUX	EXODUSES
DEEOSTUW	OUTWEEDS
DEEOSTUX	TUXEDOES
DEEPPRSU	SUPPERED
DEEPPRTY	PRETYPED
DEEPPSSU	SPEEDUPS
DEEPRRSU	PERDURES
DEEPRRVY	REPRYVED
DEEPRSTU	PERTUSED
DEEPRSUW	PURSEWED
DEEPRSUY	PSEUDERY
DEEPRTTU	PUTTERED
DEEPRUVY	PURVEYED
DEERRSSS	DRESSERS
DEERRSUV	VERDURES
DEERRTTU	TURRETED
DEERRTUX	EXTRUDER
DEERSSST	DESSERTS
	STRESSED
DEERSSSU	DURESSES
DEERSSTU	RUSSETED
DEERSSTY	DYESTERS
DEERSSUV	SUVERSED
DEERSTTU	TRUSTEED
DEERSTUV	VESTURED
DEERSTUX	EXTRUDES
DEERSUVW	SURVEWED
DEERSUVY	SURVEYED
DEERTTUX	TEXTURED
DEFFHILW	WHIFFLED
DEFFHLSU	SHUFFLED
DEFFHORS	SHROFFED
DEFFIINT	TIFFINED
DEFFIKLS	SKIFFLED
DEFFILNS	SNIFFLED
DEFFILOV	FIVEFOLD
DEFFIMOS	FIEFDOMS
DEFFIORS	OFFSIDER
DEFFIOSS	OFFSIDES
DEFFIQSU	SQUIFFED
DEFFIRSU	DIFFUSER
DEFFISSU	DIFFUSES
DEFFISUX	SUFFIXED
DEFFLNSU	SNUFFLED
DEFFLOSU	SOUFFLED
DEFFLRTU	TRUFFLED
DEFFNORS	FORFENDS
DEFFNOSS	SENDOFFS
DEFFSSUU	SUFFUSED
DEFFSTUY	DYESTUFF
DEFGGILN	FLEDGING
DEFGHILT	FLIGHTED
DEFGHIRT	FRIGHTED
DEFGIIIN	IGNIFIED
DEFGIILN	DEFILING
	FIELDING
DEFGIILU	UGLIFIED
DEFGIINN	DEFINING
DEFGIINY	DEIFYING
	EDIFYING
DEFGIIRR	FRIGIDER
DEFGILNU	INGULFED
DEFGILRU	DIRGEFUL
DEFGILTY	GIFTEDLY
DEFGINSU	DEFUSING
	FEUDINGS
DEFGINTU	UNGIFTED
DEFGINUZ	DEFUZING
DEFGIOOW	GOODWIFE
DEFGIORS	FIREDOGS
DEFGJORU	FORJUDGE
DEFGMOOY	FOGEYDOM
DEFGNORU	UNFORGED
DEFGOOSX	DOGFOXES
DEFHIIMU	HUMIFIED
DEFHIINS	FIENDISH
	FINISHED
DEFHILLO	LIFEHOLD
DEFHILSS	DISFLESH
DEFHINSU	UNFISHED
DEFHIOOW	WIFEHOOD
DEFHIRST	REDSHIFT
DEFHLOOS	ELFHOODS
	SELFHOOD
DEFHLOSU	FLOUSHED
DEFHOOOR	FORHOOED
DEFHOORS	SERFHOOD
DEFHOORW	FORHOWED
DEFIIILV	VILIFIED
DEFIIIMN	MINIFIED
DEFIIINS	NIDIFIES
DEFIIINV	VINIFIED
DEFIIIVV	VIVIFIED
DEFIILLN	INFILLED
DEFIILLO	OILFIELD
DEFIILLP	FILLIPED
DEFIILLW	WILDLIFE
DEFIILMS	MISFIELD
	MISFILED
DEFIILNO	DIOLEFIN
DEFIILNS	INFIDELS
	INFIELDS
DEFIILRW	WILDFIRE
DEFIILSU	FLUIDISE
DEFIILTY	FIDELITY
DEFIILUZ	FLUIDIZE
DEFIIMNO	OMNIFIED
DEFIIMNR	INFIRMED
DEFIIMNU	MUNIFIED
DEFIIMOR	MODIFIER
DEFIIMOS	MODIFIES
DEFIIMRS	MISFIRED
DEFIIMSS	FIDEISMS
DEFIIMSW	MIDWIFES
DEFIINOT	NOTIFIED
DEFIINTU	FINITUDE
DEFIINTY	IDENTIFY
DEFIIOSS	OSSIFIED
DEFIIOTV	VIDEOFIT
DEFIIPRU	PURIFIED
DEFIIPSS	FISSIPED
DEFIIPTY	TYPIFIED
DEFIIRRT	DRIFTIER
DEFIISST	FIDEISTS
DEFILLNU	UNFILLED
DEFILLPU	UPFILLED
DEFILMNU	FULMINED
	UNFILMED
DEFILNNO	NINEFOLD
DEFILNOR	INFOLDER
DEFILNOU	UNFOILED
DEFILNRS	FLINDERS
DEFILNRU	UNRIFLED
	URNFIELD
DEFILNRY	FRIENDLY
DEFILOPR	PROFILED
DEFILORR	FLORIDER
DEFILORU	FLUORIDE
DEFILORV	FRIVOLED
DEFILOTU	OUTFIELD
DEFILPRU	PRIDEFUL
DEFILPTU	UPLIFTED
DEFILRRU	FLURRIED
DEFILRVY	FERVIDLY
DEFILRZZ	FRIZZLED
DEFILSSU	SULFIDES
DEFIMNOR	INFORMED
DEFIMOPR	PEDIFORM
DEFIMORY	REMODIFY
DEFIMOSW	WIFEDOMS
DEFIMRRU	DRUMFIRE
DEFINNRU	REINFUND
	UNFRIEND
DEFINOPR	FORPINED
DEFINORW	FOREWIND
DEFINSTU	UNSIFTED
DEFINTTU	UNFITTED
DEFIOORW	FIREWOOD
DEFIOPRT	PIEDFORT
	PROFITED
DEFIORRU	FROIDEUR
DEFIORSU	FOUDRIES
DEFIORTU	OUTFIRED
DEFIOTXY	DETOXIFY
DEFIRRST	DRIFTERS
DEFIRSSU	FISSURED
DEFISSTU	FEUDISTS
DEFKLORY	FORKEDLY
DEFKNORU	UNFORKED
DEFLLOOR	FOLDEROL
DEFLLOOW	FOLLOWED
DEFLMOSS	SELFDOMS
DEFLMPRU	FRUMPLED
DEFLNOOU	UNFOOLED
DEFLNOPS	PENFOLDS
DEFLNORS	FONDLERS
	FORLENDS
DEFLNORU	FLOUNDER
	UNFOLDER
DEFLNOST	TENFOLDS
DEFLNRUU	UNFURLED
DEFLNSSU	FUNDLESS
DEFLOORS	FLOODERS
	FORSLOED
	REFLOODS
DEFLOORT	FORETOLD

DEFLOORV	OVERFOLD
DEFLOOSS	FOODLESS
DEFLOOUW	FUELWOOD
DEFLOPUW	UPFLOWED
DEFLORSS	FORDLESS
DEFLORST	TELFORDS
DEFLORSU	FOULDERS
DEFLPRUU	UPFURLED
DEFLRSUU	DESULFUR
	SULFURED
DEFMNORU	UNFORMED
DEFMOOOR	FOREDOOM
DEFMORSS	SERFDOMS
DEFNNORT	FRONDENT
DEFNNOSS	FONDNESS
DEFNNOUW	NEWFOUND
DEFNOOPS	SPOONFED
DEFNOORS	FRONDOSE
DEFNOORU	UNROOFED
DEFNOORV	OVERFOND
DEFNOOTU	UNFOOTED
DEFNOPRS	FORSPEND
DEFNORRU	FRONDEUR
DEFNORSU	FOUNDERS
	REFOUNDS
DEFNORTU	FORTUNED
DEFNORUV	OVERFUND
DEFNOSSW	DOWFNESS
DEFNRRUU	UNDERFUR
	UNFURRED
DEFNRTUU	UNTURFED
DEFNTTUU	UNTUFTED
DEFOORRW	FOREWORD
DEFOOSSU	DOOFUSES
DEFOOTUX	OUTFOXED
DEFORRUW	FURROWED
DEFORSST	DEFROSTS
	FROSTEDS
DEFORSTW	FROWSTED
DEGGGIIT	GIGGITED
DEGGGILN	GLEDGING
DEGGHINS	HEDGINGS
DEGGHIRS	DREGGISH
DEGGHLOS	SHOGGLED
DEGGHRSU	SHRUGGED
DEGGIINN	DEIGNING
DEGGILNP	PLEDGING
DEGGILNS	GELDINGS
	SLEDGING
	SNIGGLED
DEGGILNU	DELUGING
DEGGILRW	WRIGGLED
DEGGINNU	UNEDGING
DEGGINRU	UNRIGGED
DEGGINSW	WEDGINGS
DEGGINUW	UNWIGGED
DEGGIORS	DISGORGE
DEGGIOST	DOGGIEST
DEGGIPRS	SPRIGGED
DEGGIRRU	DRUGGIER
DEGGIRST	STRIGGED
DEGGIRSU	DRUGGIES
DEGGLMSU	SMUGGLED
DEGGLNSU	SNUGGLED
DEGGLORS	DOGGRELS
DEGGLORY	GORGEDLY
DEGGLRUY	RUGGEDLY
DEGGNOOR	DOGGONER
DEGGNOOS	DOGGONES
DEGGNORU	UNGORGED
DEGGNOSU	GUDGEONS
DEGGRRSU	DRUGGERS
	GRUDGERS
DEGGRSTU	DRUGGETS
DEGHIILL	GHILLIED
DEGHIINS	DINGHIES
DEGHIKNT	KNIGHTED
DEGHILNS	HINDLEGS
	SHINGLED
DEGHILOU	OUGHLIED
DEGHILPT	PLIGHTED
DEGHILST	DELIGHTS
	SLIGHTED
DEGHINNS	SHENDING
DEGHINNU	UNHINGED
DEGHIOOS	SHOOGIED
DEGHIOPS	DOGESHIP
DEGHIORU	DOUGHIER
DEGHIPST	DESPIGHT
	SPIGHTED
DEGHIQTU	QUIGHTED
DEGHITTW	TWIGHTED
DEGHLNOR	HORNGELD
DEGHLOOS	DOGHOLES
	GOLOSHED
	SHOOGLED
DEGHLOPU	PLOUGHED
DEGHLORY	HYDROGEL
DEGHLOSU	SLOUGHED
DEGHMOSU	GUMSHOED
DEGHMPRU	GRUMPHED
DEGHNORT	THRONGED
DEGHNORY	HYDROGEN
DEGHOOSU	DOGHOUSE
DEGHORRS	DROGHERS
DEGHPSUU	UPGUSHED
DEGIIIRS	RIGIDISE
DEGIIIRZ	RIGIDIZE
DEGIIIST	DIGITISE
DEGIIITZ	DIGITIZE
DEGIIKNS	KINGSIDE
DEGIIKST	KIDGIEST
DEGIILMN	DELIMING
DEGIILNR	GRIDELIN
DEGIILNS	EILDINGS
	SIDELING
DEGIILNT	DILIGENT
DEGIILNV	DEVILING
DEGIILNW	WIELDING
DEGIILNY	YIELDING
DEGIILTY	GELIDITY
DEGIIMNP	IMPEDING
	IMPINGED
DEGIIMNS	DEMISING
DEGIIMSU	MISGUIDE
DEGIINNR	NIDERING
DEGIINNS	DESINING
	INDIGENS
	SDEINING
DEGIINNT	ENDITING
	INDIGENT
	TEINDING
DEGIINNW	INDEWING
	WIDENING
DEGIINNX	INDEXING
DEGIINNZ	DIZENING
DEGIINOS	INDIGOES
DEGIINOV	VIDEOING
DEGIINRS	DESIRING
	RESIDING
	RINGSIDE
DEGIINRT	DIRIGENT
DEGIINRV	DERIVING
	VIRGINED
DEGIINRW	WEIRDING
DEGIINST	DINGIEST
	INDIGEST
DEGIINSV	DEVISING
DEGIIRST	RIDGIEST
	RIGIDEST
DEGIISSU	DISGUISE
DEGIJMSU	MISJUDGE
DEGIKKNO	DEKKOING
DEGIKLNU	DUKELING
DEGIKNNU	UNKINGED
DEGILLNU	DUELLING
DEGILLNW	DWELLING
DEGILMNO	MODELING
DEGILMOS	MISLODGE
DEGILMPS	GLIMPSED
DEGILNNO	OLDENING
DEGILNNS	LENDINGS
DEGILNOP	DELOPING
	DIPLOGEN
DEGILNOS	GLENOIDS
	SIDELONG
DEGILNOW	DOWELING
DEGILNOY	YODELING
DEGILNPS	SPELDING
DEGILNRU	INDULGER
DEGILNRY	YELDRING
DEGILNSU	INDULGES
DEGILNSV	DEVLINGS
DEGILNSW	SWINGLED
	WELDINGS
DEGILNWY	WINGEDLY
DEGILOOR	GOODLIER
DEGILOOY	IDEOLOGY
DEGILORV	OVERGILD
DEGILOST	GODLIEST
	GOLDIEST
DEGILOSZ	GOLDSIZE
DEGILPSU	PULSIDGE
DEGILRRS	GIRDLERS
DEGILRSU	GUILDERS
	SLUDGIER
DEGILRSW	WERGILDS
DEGILRUV	DIVULGER
DEGILRZZ	GRIZZLED
DEGILSUV	DIVULGES
DEGIMMNO	MODEMING
DEGIMNNS	MENDINGS
DEGIMNOS	MENDIGOS
	SMIDGEON
DEGIMNOT	DEMOTING
DEGIMNPU	IMPUGNED
DEGIMNRU	DEMURING
DEGIMNSS	SMIDGENS
DEGIMOOT	GOODTIME
DEGIMOOY	GEOMYOID
DEGIMRSU	SMUDGIER
DEGINNNU	UNENDING
DEGINNOP	DEPONING
DEGINNOT	DENOTING
DEGINNOV	DOVENING
DEGINNOW	ENDOWING
DEGINNOZ	DOZENING
DEGINNPS	SPENDING
DEGINNPU	UPENDING
DEGINNRT	TRENDING
DEGINNRU	ENDURING
	UNRINGED
DEGINNSS	SENDINGS
DEGINNST	STENDING
DEGINNSU	UNSIGNED
DEGINNSY	DESYNING
DEGINNTU	DETUNING
	UNTINGED
DEGINNUW	UNWINGED
DEGINOOR	RODEOING
DEGINOPR	PROIGNED
DEGINOPS	DEPOSING
	DISPONGE
	PIDGEONS
DEGINORR	ORDERING
DEGINORS	NEGROIDS
DEGINORU	GUERIDON
DEGINORV	DOVERING
	RINGDOVE
DEGINORW	DOWERING
DEGINOSW	WENDIGOS
	WIDGEONS
DEGINOTV	DEVOTING
DEGINOTX	DETOXING
DEGINPRS	SPRINGED
DEGINPRY	PREDYING
DEGINPSU	DISPUNGE
DEGINPTU	DEPUTING
DEGINRRS	GRINDERS
	REGRINDS
DEGINRRY	GRINDERY
	REDRYING
DEGINRSS	DRESSING
DEGINRST	STRINGED
DEGINRSW	REDWINGS
DEGINRSY	SYNERGID
	SYRINGED
DEGINSSU	DINGUSES
DEGINSSW	SWINDGES
DEGINSTU	DUNGIEST
DEGINTTU	DUETTING
DEGIOORS	GOODSIRE
DEGIOOST	GOODIEST
DEGIOPRR	PORRIDGE
DEGIOPSS	GOSSIPED
DEGIOPST	PODGIEST
DEGIORRU	GOURDIER
DEGIORRV	OVERGIRD
DEGIORST	DIGESTOR
	GRODIEST
	STODGIER
DEGIOTUU	OUTGUIDE
DEGIPSTU	PUDGIEST
DEGIQSSU	SQUIDGES
DEGIRRTU	TURGIDER
DEGIRSTU	DURGIEST
DEGISSST	DISGESTS
DEGJMNTU	JUDGMENT
DEGLLNOY	GOLDENLY
DEGLLOOP	GOLLOPED
DEGLLOSS	GOLDLESS
DEGLMNOT	LODGMENT
DEGLMOOY	DEMOLOGY
DEGLNOUV	UNGLOVED
DEGLNRTU	GRUNTLED
DEGLOOPR	PROLOGED
DEGLOOPY	PEDOLOGY
DEGLOOUU	DUOLOGUE
DEGLOPRS	PLEDGORS
DEGLOPSS	SPLODGES
DEGLPRSU	SPLURGED
DEGMMNUU	UNGUMMED
DEGMOOPR	POGROMED
DEGMRSSU	SMUDGERS
DEGNNORU	GROUNDEN
DEGNNOSU	DUNGEONS
DEGNNOUW	UNGOWNED
DEGNOORS	DRONGOES
DEGNOOSS	GOODNESS
DEGNOOST	STEGODON
DEGNOPPU	OPPUGNED
DEGNORRU	GROUNDER
	REGROUND
DEGNORSU	GUERDONS
DEGNORTU	TRUDGEON
DEGNORUU	UNROUGED
DEGNORYY	GYRODYNE
DEGNPRUU	UNPURGED
DEGNRSTU	TRUDGENS
DEGOORSV	OVERDOGS

DEGORSST	STODGERS
DEGORSTU	DROGUETS
DEGPRSUU	UPSURGED
DEGRRSTU	TRUDGERS
DEHHILTW	WITHHELD
DEHHISTW	WHISHTED
DEHHLSUY	HUSHEDLY
DEHHMRTY	RHYTHMED
DEHHOOSW	WHOOSHED
DEHIIKLS	DISHLIKE
DEHIILLS	HILLSIDE
	SIDEHILL
DEHIILLW	WHILLIED
DEHIILNS	LINISHED
DEHIILSV	DEVILISH
DEHIIMMS	SHIMMIED
DEHIIMNS	MINISHED
DEHIIMRU	MUDIRIEH
DEHIIMST	DITHEISM
	SMITHIED
DEHIIMSW	WHIMSIED
DEHIINNS	SHINNIED
DEHIINNW	WHINNIED
DEHIINSS	SHINDIES
DEHIIPSS	SHIPSIDE
DEHIIRRW	WHIRRIED
DEHIIRST	DISHERIT
DEHIISST	DISHIEST
DEHIISTT	DITHEIST
	STITHIED
DEHIJMNO	DEMIJOHN
DEHIKLMS	MILKSHED
DEHIKLOO	HOODLIKE
DEHIKMOS	SHEIKDOM
DEHIKPSU	DUKESHIP
DEHILLOP	PHELLOID
DEHILLRS	SHRILLED
DEHILLRT	THRILLED
DEHILMOS	DEMOLISH
DEHILMPW	WHIMPLED
DEHILMSS	DISHELMS
DEHILMTY	DIMETHYL
DEHILNOR	INHOLDER
DEHILNPY	DIPHENYL
DEHILOOR	HELIODOR
DEHILOOS	DHOOLIES
DEHILOPS	DEPOLISH
	POLISHED
DEHILOTY	HOLYTIDE
DEHILPRT	PHILTRED
DEHILPSU	SULPHIDE
DEHILPSY	SYLPHIDE
DEHILRTW	WRITHLED
DEHILSTW	WHISTLED
DEHILTTW	WHITTLED
DEHIMNOS	HEDONISM
	MONISHED
DEHIMORS	HEIRDOMS
DEHIMOSS	DISHOMES
DEHIMOST	ETHMOIDS
DEHIMPRS	SHRIMPED
DEHIMPSY	DEMYSHIP
DEHIMSTU	HUMIDEST
DEHIMSTY	MYTHISED
DEHIMTYZ	MYTHIZED
DEHINOOP	INHOOPED
DEHINOPR	NEPHROID
DEHINOPS	DIPHONES
	SIPHONED
	SPHENOID
DEHINORS	HORDEINS
DEHINOST	HEDONIST
DEHINPSS	ENDSHIPS
DEHINPSU	PUNISHED
DEHINSUW	UNWISHED

DEHIOOST	DHOOTIES
	HOODIEST
DEHIOOVW	WIVEHOOD
DEHIOPRS	SPHEROID
DEHIOPRT	TROPHIED
DEHIORRR	HORRIDER
DEHIORSS	DISHORSE
	HIDROSES
DEHIORTU	OUTHIRED
DEHIORTW	WORTHIED
DEHIORTY	THYREOID
DEHIOSSU	DISHOUSE
DEHIOSSW	SIDESHOW
DEHIOSTU	HIDEOUTS
DEHIPSSU	PSEUDISH
DEHIQSSU	SQUISHED
DEHIRRST	REDSHIRT
DEHIRRSU	DHURRIES
DEHIRSTT	THIRSTED
	THRISTED
DEHIRTWW	WITHDREW
DEHKLNOU	ELKHOUND
DEHKNOOU	UNHOOKED
DEHKNSUU	UNHUSKED
DEHKOOSS	SKOOSHED
DEHLLOOO	HOLLOOED
DEHLLOOW	HOLLOWED
DEHLLOPY	PHYLLODE
DEHLMMOW	WHOMMLED
DEHLMMUW	WHUMMLED
DEHLMOOT	HOTELDOM
DEHLMORY	HYDROMEL
DEHLMOSU	MUDHOLES
DEHLMPSU	SHLUMPED
DEHLNOOW	DOWNHOLE
DEHLNTUY	HUNTEDLY
DEHLOOOW	WOODHOLE
DEHLOOPT	POTHOLED
DEHLOORV	HOLDOVER
	OVERHOLD
DEHLOOSS	HOODLESS
	SLOOSHED
DEHLOOST	TOEHOLDS
	TOOLSHED
DEHLOOSW	WOOLSHED
DEHLOPRU	UPHOLDER
DEHLOPSS	SPLOSHED
DEHLORSU	SHOULDER
DEHLPRUU	UPHURLED
DEHLRRSU	HURDLERS
DEHLRSWY	SHREWDLY
DEHLSTTU	SHUTTLED
DEHMMRTU	THRUMMED
DEHMNOOY	HOMODYNE
DEHMNRUY	UNRHYMED
DEHMOORW	WHOREDOM
DEHMOOSS	SHMOOSED
DEHMOOST	SMOOTHED
DEHMOOSZ	SHMOOZED
DEHMOPRY	HYPODERM
DEHMORUU	HUMOURED
DEHNNTUU	UNHUNTED
DEHNOOPU	UNHOOPED
DEHNOORU	HONOURED
DEHNOOSW	HOEDOWNS
	WOODHENS
DEHNOPSY	SYPHONED
DEHNORSU	ENSHROUD
	HOUNDERS
	UNHORSED
DEHNORSY	ENHYDROS
DEHNORTY	THRENODY
DEHNOSSW	SNOWSHED
DEHNOSTZ	DOZENTHS
DEHNOSUU	UNHOUSED

DEHNRSTU	THUNDERS
DEHNRSUU	UNRUSHED
DEHNRTUY	THUNDERY
DEHOOOPP	POPEHOOD
DEHOOPRT	THEROPOD
DEHOOSSW	SWOOSHED
DEHOPRST	POTSHERD
DEHORRST	REDSHORT
DEHORTUY	OUTHYRED
DEHOSSTU	STOUSHED
DEHPPSTU	SHTUPPED
DEHPRSSU	SPRUSHED
DEHPRSUU	UPRUSHED
DEHQSSUU	SQUUSHED
DEHRRSTU	DRUTHERS
DEHRSTTU	THRUSTED
DEIIIMST	DIMITIES
DEIIINSV	DIVINISE
DEIIINVZ	DIVINIZE
DEIIIRSS	IRIDISES
DEIIIRSZ	IRIDIZES
DEIIIRTV	VIRIDITE
DEIIISVV	DIVISIVE
DEIIKKLS	DISKLIKE
DEIIKLMS	MISLIKED
DEIIKLNR	KINDLIER
DEIIKLNS	DISLIKEN
DEIIKLNV	DEVILKIN
DEIIKLRS	DISLIKER
DEIIKLSS	DISLIKES
DEIIKNST	DINKIEST
DEIIKSVV	SKIVVIED
DEIILLMP	MILLIPED
DEIILLMT	TIDEMILL
DEIILLST	DILLIEST
DEIILMNS	MIDLINES
DEIILMPR	DIMPLIER
DEIILMRU	DELIRIUM
DEIILMST	DELIMITS
	LIMITEDS
DEIILMSU	SEDILIUM
DEIILMSV	DEVILISM
	MIDLIVES
	MISLIVED
DEIILMSW	SEMIWILD
DEIILNNU	INDULINE
DEIILNOS	LIONISED
DEIILNOT	TOLIDINE
DEIILNOZ	LIONIZED
DEIILNPV	VILIPEND
DEIILNTT	INTITLED
DEIILNVY	DIVINELY
DEIILNXY	XYLIDINE
DEIILOPS	PLOIDIES
DEIILORS	IDOLISER
DEIILORZ	IDOLIZER
DEIILOSS	IDOLISES
DEIILOSZ	IDOLIZES
DEIILPRT	TRIPLIED
DEIILPSS	SIDESLIP
DEIILRST	REDISTIL
DEIILSTU	UTILISED
DEIILSTV	LIVIDEST
DEIILTUV	DILUTIVE
DEIILTUY	TUILYIED
DEIILTUZ	TUILZIED
	UTILIZED
DEIIMMRS	DIMERISM
DEIIMMST	MISTIMED
DEIIMMTT	IMMITTED
DEIIMNOS	DOMINIES
DEIIMNRT	DIRIMENT
DEIIMNTU	MUTINIED
DEIIMNUV	VENIDIUM
DEIIMPRU	PERIDIUM

DEIIMRSV	MISDRIVE
DEIIMSST	MISDIETS
	MISEDITS
DEIIMSTT	TIMIDEST
DEIIMSVW	MIDWIVES
DEIINNOP	PINIONED
DEIINNPP	PINNIPED
DEIINNTW	INTWINED
DEIINNUV	UNDIVINE
DEIINORS	DERISION
	IRONISED
	IRONSIDE
	RESINOID
DEIINORT	RETINOID
DEIINORZ	IRONIZED
DEIINOST	EDITIONS
	SEDITION
DEIINOSV	VISIONED
DEIINOTY	IDONEITY
DEIINPPW	WINDPIPE
DEIINPRS	INSPIRED
DEIINPRT	INTREPID
DEIINPRY	PYRIDINE
DEIINPSS	SIDESPIN
DEIINPTU	UNPITIED
DEIINQRU	INQUIRED
DEIINQSU	QUINSIED
	SQUINIED
DEIINRSS	INDRISES
	INSIDERS
DEIINRST	DISINTER
	INDITERS
	NITRIDES
	RINDIEST
DEIINRSU	DISINURE
	URIDINES
DEIINRSV	DIVINERS
DEIINRTU	UNTIDIER
DEIINSST	INSISTED
	TIDINESS
DEIINSTU	DISUNITE
	NUDITIES
	UNITISED
	UNTIDIES
DEIINSTV	DIVINEST
DEIINSTW	WINDIEST
DEIINTTU	INTUITED
DEIINTTY	IDENTITY
DEIINTUZ	UNITIZED
DEIIOPRS	PRESIDIO
DEIIOPRT	DIPTEROI
DEIIOPZZ	PEZIZOID
DEIIORST	DIORITES
DEIIORSX	OXIDISER
DEIIORSZ	IODIZERS
DEIIORTX	TRIOXIDE
DEIIORTY	IODYRITE
DEIIORXZ	OXIDIZER
DEIIOSSX	OXIDISES
DEIIOSTT	OTITIDES
DEIIOSXZ	OXIDIZES
DEIIPPRR	DRIPPIER
DEIIPPST	DIPPIEST
DEIIPRST	RIPTIDES
	SPIRITED
	TIDERIPS
DEIIPRSZ	DISPRIZE
DEIIPTTY	TEPIDITY
DEIIQSTU	DISQUIET
DEIIRRVV	VIVERRID
DEIIRSSU	DIURESIS
DEIIRSTT	DIRTIEST
	TRITIDES
DEIISSTT	DIETISTS
	DITSIEST

DEIISTTZ	DITZIEST
DEIISTVV	VIVIDEST
DEIISTZZ	DIZZIEST
DEIJNNOU	UNJOINED
DEIJNORS	JOINDERS
DEIJNSSU	DISJUNES
DEIJORRY	JOYRIDER
DEIJORSY	JOYRIDES
DEIKKLNO	KLONDIKE
DEIKKNNU	UNKINKED
DEIKLLOR	LORDLIKE
DEIKLLSS	DESKILLS
DEIKLMMS	SKLIMMED
DEIKLMNU	UNMILKED
DEIKLMRU	DRUMLIKE
DEIKLNNU	UNLINKED
DEIKLNRS	KINDLERS
DEIKLNRW	WRINKLED
DEIKLNSS	KINDLESS
DEIKLNTW	TWINKLED
DEIKLSSS	DISKLESS
DEIKLSTT	SKITTLED
DEIKLSTU	DUSTLIKE
DEIKMNOO	KIMONOED
DEIKMOSY	MISYOKED
DEIKMPRS	SKRIMPED
DEIKNNOR	DONNIKER
DEIKNNPU	UNPINKED
DEIKNNRU	UNKINDER
DEIKNNSS	KINDNESS
DEIKNORV	OVERKIND
DEIKNORW	INWORKED
DEIKNOSS	DOESKINS
DEIKNRRS	DRINKERS
DEIKNRSS	REDSKINS
DEIKNSSU	UNKISSED
DEIKORSS	DROSKIES
DEIKORST	DORKIEST
DEIKOSSY	DISYOKES
DEIKPRSU	PRUSIKED
	SPRUIKED
DEIKRRSU	SKURRIED
DEIKRSVY	SKYDIVER
DEIKSSTU	DUSKIEST
DEIKSSVY	SKYDIVES
DEILLMNU	UNMILLED
DEILLNSW	INDWELLS
DEILLNTU	UNTILLED
DEILLNUW	UNWILLED
DEILLOOV	LIVELOOD
DEILLOPW	PILLOWED
DEILLORR	LORDLIER
DEILLORS	DOLLIERS
DEILLORT	TROLLIED
DEILLORU	LOUDLIER
DEILLOSV	LIVELODS
DEILLOWW	WILLOWED
DEILLPRR	PREDRILL
DEILLRRS	DRILLERS
	REDRILLS
DEILLRSV	DREVILLS
DEILLSTU	DUELLIST
	DULLIEST
DEILMNOO	MELODION
DEILMNSS	MILDNESS
	MINDLESS
DEILMNSU	MUSLINED
DEILMOOT	DOLOMITE
DEILMOPR	IMPLORED
	IMPOLDER
DEILMOPS	IMPLODES
DEILMORU	LEMUROID
	MOULDIER
DEILMORV	OVERMILD
DEILMOSS	MIDSOLES
DEILMOST	MELODIST
	MODELIST
	MOLDIEST
DEILMOSU	EMULSOID
DEILMOTV	DEMIVOLT
DEILMPPU	PLUMIPED
DEILMPSU	DISPLUME
	IMPULSED
DEILMPTU	MULTIPED
DEILMRRU	DRUMLIER
DEILMRSU	MISRULED
DEILMSSY	DEMISSLY
DEILNNOT	INDOLENT
DEILNOOS	EIDOLONS
	SOLENOID
DEILNOPT	TOPLINED
DEILNORS	DISENROL
DEILNOSS	SONDELIS
DEILNOSU	DELUSION
	INSOULED
	UNSOILED
DEILNOTU	OUTLINED
DEILNOVV	INVOLVED
DEILNPRS	SPELDRIN
	SPINDLER
DEILNPRU	UNDERLIP
DEILNPSS	SPELDINS
	SPINDLES
DEILNPST	SPLINTED
DEILNRSS	RINDLESS
DEILNRST	SNIRTLED
	TENDRILS
	TRINDLES
DEILNRSW	SWINDLER
DEILNRTU	UNDERLIT
DEILNRTY	TRENDILY
DEILNSSV	VILDNESS
DEILNSSW	SWINDLES
	WILDNESS
	WINDLESS
DEILNSTU	DILUENTS
	INSULTED
	UNLISTED
DEILNTTU	UNTILTED
	UNTITLED
DEILNTUY	UNITEDLY
DEILNUWY	UNWIELDY
DEILOOPS	POOLSIDE
DEILOOPW	WOODPILE
DEILOPPY	POLYPIDE
DEILOPRS	LEPORIDS
DEILOPRU	PRELUDIO
DEILOPSS	DESPOILS
	DIPLOSES
	SOLIPEDS
DEILOPST	PISTOLED
DEILOPSU	EUPLOIDS
DEILOPUY	EUPLOIDY
DEILOQRU	LIQUORED
DEILORRW	LOWRIDER
DEILORSS	SOLDIERS
DEILORST	STOLIDER
DEILORSU	SOULDIER
DEILORSY	SOLDIERY
DEILORTY	ELYTROID
DEILOSST	SOLIDEST
DEILOSSV	DISSOLVE
DEILOSTT	DOILTEST
DEILOSTU	SOLITUDE
	TOLUIDES
DEILOSVW	OLDWIVES
DEILOTUV	OUTLIVED
DEILOTUW	OUTWILED
DEILOTUY	OUTYIELD
DEILPPRT	TRIPPLED
DEILPPST	STIPPLED
DEILPPSU	SUPPLIED
DEILPPTU	PULPITED
DEILPRSS	DRIPLESS
DEILPSTT	SPLITTED
DEILPSTU	STIPULED
DEILPSUY	SPULYIED
DEILPSUZ	SPULZIED
DEILPTTU	UPTILTED
DEILRRSU	SLURRIED
DEILRSSY	DRESSILY
DEILRSTU	DILUTERS
	LURIDEST
	STUDLIER
DEILRSVY	DIVERSLY
DEILRSZZ	DRIZZLES
DEILRTVY	DEVILTRY
DEILSSTU	DUELISTS
DEILSSTY	DISTYLES
	STYLISED
DEILSTUY	SEDULITY
DEILSTYZ	STYLIZED
DEILSWZZ	SWIZZLED
DEILTWZZ	TWIZZLED
DEIMMNOO	OMNIMODE
DEIMMNOS	DEMONISM
DEIMMOOV	MOVIEDOM
DEIMMOST	IMMODEST
DEIMMOSV	MISMOVED
DEIMMPST	MISDEMPT
DEIMMRST	MIDTERMS
DEIMMSTU	DUMMIEST
	SUMMITED
DEIMNNOS	MISDONNE
DEIMNNOU	UNMONIED
DEIMNNSU	MINUENDS
DEIMNOOS	DOMINOES
	MONODIES
DEIMNOOT	DEMOTION
	MOTIONED
DEIMNOOX	MONOXIDE
DEIMNOPT	PIEDMONT
DEIMNORT	DORMIENT
DEIMNOST	DEMONIST
DEIMNOTW	DOWNTIME
DEIMNOWW	WIDOWMEN
DEIMNPRU	UNPRIMED
DEIMNPSS	MISSPEND
DEIMNPTU	IMPUDENT
DEIMNRTU	RUDIMENT
	UNMITRED
DEIMNSSS	MISSENDS
DEIMNSST	MINDSETS
	MISTENDS
DEIMNSSU	UNMISSED
DEIMNSSW	MISWENDS
DEIMNSTU	MISTUNED
DEIMOORS	MOIDORES
DEIMOOSS	SODOMIES
	SODOMISE
DEIMOOST	DOOMIEST
	MOODIEST
	SODOMITE
DEIMOOSZ	SODOMIZE
DEIMOPRS	PROMISED
DEIMOPRT	IMPORTED
DEIMOPRV	IMPROVED
DEIMOPST	IMPOSTED
DEIMORRR	MIRRORED
DEIMORRS	MISORDER
	MORRISED
DEIMORSS	MISDOERS
DEIMORST	MORTISED
DEIMORSU	DIMEROUS
	ERODIUMS
	SOREDIUM
DEIMORSV	MISDROVE
DEIMORUX	EXORDIUM
DEIMOSST	DISTOMES
	MODISTES
DEIMOSTT	DEMOTIST
DEIMPRST	DIREMPTS
DEIMPSTU	DUMPIEST
DEIMPSTY	MISTYPED
DEIMQRSU	SQUIRMED
DEIMRSSU	SURMISED
DEIMRSTU	DIESTRUM
DEIMRSUU	RESIDUUM
DEINNNOU	INNUENDO
DEINNNPU	UNPINNED
DEINNNSU	NUNDINES
DEINNNTU	UNTINNED
DEINNOOT	NOONTIDE
DEINNOPT	ENDPOINT
DEINNORS	ENDIRONS
DEINNORT	INDENTOR
DEINNORU	UNIRONED
DEINNOWW	WINNOWED
DEINNPRU	UNDERPIN
DEINNRSU	UNRINSED
DEINNRTU	INTURNED
DEINNRUU	UNINURED
DEINNRUV	UNDRIVEN
DEINNRUW	UNWINDER
DEINNSTU	DUNNIEST
	DUNNITES
DEINNTUU	UNUNITED
DEINNTUW	UNTWINED
DEINOOPS	POISONED
DEINOOPT	OPTIONED
DEINOOPW	PINEWOOD
DEINOOSU	IDONEOUS
DEINOOSZ	OZONIDES
	OZONISED
DEINOOTV	DEVOTION
DEINOOZZ	OZONIZED
DEINOPPR	PROPINED
DEINOPPW	DOWNPIPE
DEINOPRS	DISPONER
	POINDERS
	PRISONED
DEINOPRT	DIPTERON
DEINOPRU	INPOURED
DEINOPRV	PROVINED
DEINOPRY	PYRENOID
DEINOPSS	DISPONES
	DOPINESS
	SPINODES
DEINOPSU	UNPOISED
DEINOPTW	DEWPOINT
DEINORRS	INDORSER
DEINORSS	INDORSES
	SORDINES
DEINORST	DRONIEST
DEINORSU	DOURINES
	SOURDINE
DEINORSW	DISOWNER
	WINDORES
	WINDROSE
DEINORTT	INTORTED
DEINORVW	OVERWIND
DEINOSST	DONSIEST
DEINOSSV	VOIDNESS
DEINOSSZ	DOZINESS
DEINOSTW	DOWNIEST
DEINOSWZ	DOWNSIZE
DEINOTTU	DUETTINO
DEINOTUV	INDEVOUT
DEINPPRU	UNRIPPED
DEINPPTU	UNTIPPED

DEINPPUZ	UNZIPPED
DEINPRST	SPRINTED
DEINPRTU	TURNIPED
DEINPRUZ	UNPRIZED
DEINPSST	STIPENDS
DEINPTTU	INPUTTED
DEINQSTU	SQUINTED
DEINRRTU	INTRUDER
DEINRSSU	INSUREDS
	SUNDRIES
DEINRSTT	STRIDENT
	TRIDENTS
DEINRSTU	INTRUDES
DEINRSTX	DEXTRINS
DEINRTUW	UNDERWIT
DEINSSST	DISNESTS
	DISSENTS
DEINSSSY	SYNDESIS
DEINSSTT	DENTISTS
DEINSSTU	DISTUNES
DEINSSUU	UNISSUED
DEINSTUU	UNSUITED
DEINTTUW	UNWITTED
DEIOOPRR	DROOPIER
DEIOORSW	WOODSIER
DEIOORSZ	ODORIZES
DEIOOSST	OSTEOIDS
DEIOOSTW	WOODIEST
DEIOOSVV	VOIVODES
DEIOOSWW	WOIWODES
DEIOPRRV	PROVIDER
DEIOPRSS	DISPOSER
	DROPSIES
DEIOPRST	DIOPTERS
	DIOPTRES
	DIPTEROS
	PERIDOTS
	PROTEIDS
	RIPOSTED
	TOPSIDER
DEIOPRSV	DISPROVE
	PROVIDES
DEIOPRSW	DROPWISE
DEIOPRSX	PEROXIDS
DEIOPSSS	DISPOSES
DEIOPSST	DEPOSITS
	TOPSIDES
DEIOPSTV	POSTDIVE
DEIORRRT	TORRIDER
DEIORRSS	DROSSIER
DEIORRSW	DROWSIER
DEIORRSY	DERISORY
DEIORRTU	OUTRIDER
DEIORRTW	WORRITED
DEIORRZZ	RIZZORED
DEIORSSS	DOSSIERS
DEIORSST	STEROIDS
DEIORSSU	DESIROUS
DEIORSSV	DEVISORS
DEIORSTT	DORTIEST
DEIORSTU	IODURETS
	OUTRIDES
	OUTSIDER
	SUITORED
DEIORSTW	ROWDIEST
	WORDIEST
DEIORSWW	WIDOWERS
DEIORTTX	TETROXID
DEIORTUV	OUTDRIVE
DEIOSSTU	OUTSIDES
DEIOSSTX	EXODISTS
DEIOSTTT	DOTTIEST
DEIOSTUW	WIDEOUTS
DEIOSTUZ	OUTSIZED
DEIPPRRS	DRIPPERS
DEIPPRST	STRIPPED
DEIPPTTU	TITUPPED
DEIPRRTU	IRRUPTED
	PUTRIDER
DEIPRSSU	DISPURSE
	SUSPIRED
DEIPRSTU	DISPUTER
	STUPIDER
DEIPRSTZ	SPRITZED
DEIPSSTU	DISPUTES
	PUDSIEST
DEIPTTTU	TITTUPED
DEIQRRSU	SQUIRRED
DEIQRSTU	SQUIRTED
DEIRRSST	STRIDERS
DEIRRSTU	STURDIER
DEIRSSST	DISSERTS
	DISTRESS
DEIRSSTU	DIESTRUS
	DRUSIEST
	STUDIERS
	STURDIES
DEIRSSUY	DYSURIES
DEIRSTTU	DETRITUS
DEIRSTUX	DRUXIEST
DEIRSUVV	SURVIVED
DEISSSTU	SUDSIEST
DEISSTTU	DUSTIEST
DEISTTTU	DUETTIST
DEJLOOOR	JORDELOO
DEJOOPPY	POPJOYED
DEKKLNOY	KLONDYKE
DEKKSSTT	TSKTSKED
DEKLNOOU	UNLOOKED
DEKLOOPU	UPLOOKED
DEKLRSSU	SKUDLERS
DEKLSTTU	SKUTTLED
DEKMNOSU	UNSMOKED
DEKMPRSU	SKRUMPED
DEKNNOSS	NONSKEDS
DEKNORUW	UNWORKED
DEKNRSTU	DRUNKEST
DEKNRSUY	UNDERSKY
DEKNSSSU	DUSKNESS
DEKOOPRV	PROVOKED
DEKOOTWW	KOWTOWED
DEKOPSST	DESKTOPS
DEKORSWY	KEYWORDS
DEKPRSSU	PREDUSKS
DELLLOOP	LOLLOPED
DELLMOOS	MODELLOS
DELLMOSW	SWELLDOM
DELLMOSY	SELDOMLY
DELLNOPU	UNPOLLED
DELLNORU	UNROLLED
DELLNORW	ROWNDELL
DELLNPUU	UNPULLED
DELLNSSU	DULLNESS
DELLOPRS	REDPOLLS
DELLOPRU	UPROLLED
DELLOPTU	POLLUTED
DELLORRY	DROLLERY
DELLORSS	LORDLESS
DELLORST	DROLLEST
	STROLLED
DELLOSTY	OLDSTYLE
DELLOSVW	LOWVELDS
DELLOTUW	OUTDWELL
DELMNOOV	NOVELDOM
DELMNORY	MODERNLY
DELMNOSU	UNSELDOM
DELMNOTW	MELTDOWN
DELMNPUU	PENDULUM
	UNPLUMED
DELMOOSW	ELMWOODS
DELMOPRS	PREMOLDS
DELMORSS	SMOLDERS
DELMORSU	MOULDERS
	REMOULDS
	SMOULDER
DELMOSTY	MODESTLY
DELMRTUU	MULTURED
DELMTTUU	TUMULTED
DELNOOSU	NODULOSE
	UNLOOSED
DELNOOSZ	SNOOZLED
DELNOOWY	WOODENLY
DELNOPPU	UNLOPPED
DELNOPRS	SPLENDOR
DELNOPUW	UNPLOWED
DELNORSU	LOUNDERS
	NOURSLED
	ROUNDELS
	ROUNDLES
	UNSOLDER
DELNORTU	ROUNDLET
DELNORYY	YONDERLY
DELNOSSU	LOUDNESS
DELNOSTW	LETDOWNS
DELNOSUU	UNDULOSE
	UNSOULED
DELNOSUV	UNSOLVED
DELNOTWY	WONTEDLY
DELNPRSU	PLUNDERS
DELNRRTU	TRUNDLER
DELNRSTU	RUNDLETS
	TRUNDLES
DELNSUZZ	SNUZZLED
DELOOORW	WOODLORE
DELOOPPS	PLEOPODS
DELOORRV	OVERLORD
DELOORRW	WORDLORE
DELOORSS	DOORLESS
	LORDOSES
	ODORLESS
DELOORSV	OVERSOLD
DELOORSW	WOOLDERS
DELOORTY	ROOTEDLY
DELOORUV	OVERLOUD
DELOOSSW	WOODLESS
DELOOTUV	OUTLOVED
DELOPPRS	DROPPLES
DELOPPST	STOPPLED
DELOPRST	DROPLETS
DELOPRSU	POULDERS
	POULDRES
DELOPSTU	POSTLUDE
DELORSST	OLDSTERS
	STRODLES
DELORSSW	WORDLESS
DELORSTT	DOTTRELS
DELORSUY	DELUSORY
DELOSSUU	SEDULOUS
DELOSTTT	DOTTLEST
DELOSTUU	OUTDUELS
DELOSTUW	WOULDEST
DELOTTUW	OUTDWELT
DELOTUVY	DEVOUTLY
DELPSTUU	PUSTULED
DELRSSTU	STRUDELS
DELSSSSU	SUDSLESS
DELSSSTU	DUSTLESS
DEMMNOOO	MONOMODE
DEMMNOOS	DOOMSMEN
DEMMNOSU	SUMMONED
DEMMNSUU	UNSUMMED
DEMMRRSU	DRUMMERS
DEMMRRUU	MURMURED
DEMMRSTU	STRUMMED
DEMNNOSU	SOUNDMEN
DEMNOOOP	MONOPODE
DEMNOOPT	TOMPONED
DEMNOORS	DOORSMEN
DEMNOORU	UNMOORED
DEMNOOSS	ENDOSMOS
DEMNOOSW	WOODSMEN
DEMNORST	MORDENTS
DEMNORSW	SWORDMEN
DEMNORSY	SYNDROME
DEMNORUW	UNWORMED
DEMNOSTU	DEMOUNTS
	MUDSTONE
DEMOOPPS	POPEDOMS
DEMOOPRR	PRODROME
DEMOOPRS	PREDOOMS
DEMOOPRT	PROMOTED
DEMOORST	DOOMSTER
DEMOORSU	DORMOUSE
DEMOORTY	ODOMETRY
DEMOOSTU	OUTMODES
DEMOOTUV	OUTMOVED
DEMOPPRT	PROMPTED
DEMOPSSU	POSSUMED
DEMORRUU	RUMOURED
DEMORTUY	UDOMETRY
DEMPRSTU	DUMPSTER
DENNNSUU	UNSUNNED
DENNOOOZ	ENDOZOON
DENNORST	TENDRONS
DENNORSU	ENROUNDS
DENNOSTU	UNSTONED
DENNOTUW	UNWONTED
DENNPRUU	UNPRUNED
DENNRRUU	UNDERRUN
DENNRTUU	UNTURNED
DENNRTUY	UNTRENDY
DENOOOTW	WOODNOTE
DENOOOVW	OVENWOOD
DENOOPPR	PROPONED
DENOOPRS	PRODNOSE
DENOOPSY	POYSONED
DENOORRS	ENDORSOR
DENOORTU	UNROOTED
DENOORTX	NEXTDOOR
DENOOSSW	WOODNESS
DENOOSTU	DUOTONES
DENOPPRS	PROPENDS
DENOPRSS	RESPONDS
DENOPRST	PORTENDS
	PROTENDS
DENOPRSU	POUNDERS
DENOPRSV	PROVENDS
DENOPRUV	UNPROVED
DENOPSTU	OUTSPEND
	UNPOSTED
DENOPSTW	STEWPOND
DENOPSUX	EXPOUNDS
DENOPTTU	UNPOTTED
DENOQTUU	UNQUOTED
DENORRSU	RONDURES
	ROUNDERS
	UNORDERS
DENORRSW	DROWNERS
DENORRTU	ROTUNDER
DENORRUU	ROUNDURE
DENORSSU	DOURNESS
	RESOUNDS
	SOUNDERS
DENORSTU	ROUNDEST
	TONSURED
	UNSORTED
DENORSTY	DRYSTONE
DENORSUU	UNROUSED
	UNSOURED
DENORSUW	WOUNDERS

DENORTTU	UNROTTED
DENORTUW	UNDERTOW
DENOSSTU	SOUNDEST
DENOSTUW	UNSTOWED
DENOTUUV	UNDEVOUT
DENPRSTU	UPTRENDS
DENPRSUU	UNPURSED
DENPRTUU	UPTURNED
DENPSSSU	SUSPENDS
DENRRTUU	NURTURED
DENRSSSU	SUNDRESS
DENRSTTU	STRUNTED
DENRSTUU	UNRUSTED
DENSSTTU	STUDENTS
DENSTUVY	DUVETYNS
DEOOORSW	ROSEWOOD
DEOOOSWW	WOODWOSE
DEOOPPRS	PROPOSED
DEOOPPRT	PTEROPOD
DEOOPRRV	PROVEDOR
DEOOPRST	DOORSTEP
	TORPEDOS
DEOOPRTU	UPROOTED
DEOOPWWW	POWWOWED
DEOORRST	REDROOTS
DEOORRSW	SORROWED
DEOORRVW	OVERWORD
DEOORRWW	OWREWORD
DEOORSTU	OUTDOERS
DEOORTUV	OUTDROVE
DEOORTUW	OUTROWED
DEOOTTUV	OUTVOTED
DEOPPRRS	DROPPERS
DEOPPRST	STROPPED
DEOPPRSU	PURPOSED
DEOPPSSU	SUPPOSED
DEOPRRTU	PROTRUDE
DEOPRSTU	POSTURED
	PROUDEST
	SPROUTED
DEOPRSUU	POURSUED
	UPROUSED
DEOPSSTU	UPTOSSED
DEORRSST	RODSTERS
DEORRSSW	SWORDERS
DEORRTTU	TORTURED
DEORSSTU	OUTDRESS
DEORSSTW	WORSTEDS
DEORSSTY	DESTROYS
DEORSSUV	OVERSUDS
DEORSTTU	STROUTED
DEORSTUU	OUTDURES
DEORSTUV	OVERDUST
DEORSTUX	DEXTROUS
DEOSSSYY	ODYSSEYS
DEOSSTTU	TESTUDOS
DEPPSSYY	DYSPEPSY
DEPRRTUU	RUPTURED
DEQRSUUY	SURQUEDY
DERSTTTU	STRUTTED
DFFGINSU	DUFFINGS
DFFIILUY	FLUIDIFY
DFFIIMRS	MIDRIFFS
DFFIIRST	TRIFFIDS
DFFIIRTY	TRIFFIDY
DFFIORSU	DIFFUSOR
DFFLOORU	FOURFOLD
DFFOORUW	WOODRUFF
DFFOSSTU	DUSTOFFS
DFGGHIOT	DOGFIGHT
DFGGIINR	FRIDGING
DFGHILOS	GOLDFISH
DFGIIIRY	RIGIDIFY
DFGIILRY	FRIGIDLY
DFGIINNS	FINDINGS
DFGIINRT	DRIFTING
DFGILNNO	FONDLING
DFGILNOO	FLOODING
DFGILNOS	FOLDINGS
DFGINNOU	FOUNDING
DFGINNSU	FUNDINGS
DFGINOOR	FORDOING
DFGINOSU	FUNGOIDS
DFGMOOSY	FOGYDOMS
DFHIIMUY	HUMIDIFY
DFHILSSU	DISHFULS
DFHIMRSU	DRUMFISH
DFHINOOT	HINDFOOT
DFHINOPS	FISHPOND
DFHISSTU	STUDFISH
DFHLOOOT	FOOTHOLD
DFHNOOUX	FOXHOUND
DFIIINVY	DIVINIFY
DFIILMTU	MULTIFID
DFIILOSY	SOLIDIFY
DFIILTUY	FLUIDITY
DFIINPRT	DRIFTPIN
DFIKNOOS	SKINFOOD
DFILLOOT	FLOODLIT
DFILLORY	FLORIDLY
DFILLOWW	WILDFOWL
DFILMMOS	FILMDOMS
DFILNNOU	NONFLUID
DFILNOPS	PINFOLDS
DFILORSU	FLUORIDS
DFIMOOOR	IODOFORM
DFIMOOSS	FOODISMS
DFIMORSS	DISFORMS
DFINOSTU	OUTFINDS
DFINRSUW	WINDSURF
DFIOOPRS	DISPROOF
DFKMMOPU	DUMMKOPF
DFLMOSUW	MUDFLOWS
DFLNOOWW	DOWNFLOW
DFLOORUU	ODOURFUL
DFLOOSTU	FOLDOUTS
DFLOOSTW	TWOFOLDS
DFLOPRUU	PROUDFUL
DFNOOPRU	PROFOUND
DFNOOTUU	OUTFOUND
DFOOOORW	WOODROOF
DFOOOSTW	SOFTWOOD
DGGGIINS	DIGGINGS
DGGGINOS	DOGGINGS
DGGGINRU	DRUGGING
	GRUDGING
DGGHIINT	DIGHTING
DGGIILNR	GIRDLING
	RIDGLING
DGGIILNS	GILDINGS
	GLIDINGS
DGGIINNR	GRINDING
DGGIINNW	WINGDING
DGGIINRS	GIRDINGS
	RIDGINGS
DGGIINSU	GUIDINGS
DGGILNOS	GODLINGS
	LODGINGS
DGGIMNSU	SMUDGING
DGGINNOO	NOODGING
DGGINNSU	SNUDGING
DGGINOST	STODGING
DGGINRTU	TRUDGING
DGGIRSTU	DRUGGIST
DGHHOOOS	HOGHOODS
DGHIILNS	HIDLINGS
	HILDINGS
DGHIIMNT	MIDNIGHT
DGHIIMST	MISDIGHT
DGHIINNW	HINDWING
DGHIINPS	SPHINGID
DGHIINRT	THIRDING
DGHIINSS	DISHINGS
	SHINDIGS
DGHIISST	DISSIGHT
DGHIKNOO	KINGHOOD
DGHILLNU	DUNGHILL
DGHILNNO	HONDLING
DGHILNOS	HOLDINGS
DGHILNRU	HURDLING
DGHILNSY	HYLDINGS
DGHILOOR	GIRLHOOD
DGHILPSY	DIGLYPHS
DGHINNOU	HOUNDING
DGHINNSU	DUNSHING
DGHINNUZ	NUDZHING
DGHINOWY	HOWDYING
DGHINSTU	HINDGUTS
	UNDIGHTS
DGHIOORS	DROOGISH
DGHIOPSS	DOGSHIPS
	GODSHIPS
DGHNOTUU	DOUGHNUT
DGHOOOTT	DOGTOOTH
DGHORRUY	ROUGHDRY
DGHORSTU	DROUGHTS
DGHORTUY	DROUGHTY
DGIIIMRS	DIRIGISM
DGIIINNT	INDITING
DGIIINNV	DIVINING
DGIIINOS	IODISING
DGIIINOZ	IODIZING
DGIIIRTY	RIGIDITY
DGIIKLNN	KINDLING
DGIIKLNS	KIDLINGS
DGIIKNNR	DRINKING
DGIILLNR	DRILLING
DGIILLNS	DILLINGS
DGIILLNU	ILLUDING
DGIILLNW	WILDLING
DGIILLOU	LIGULOID
DGIILMNP	DIMPLING
DGIILNNN	DINNLING
DGIILNNP	PINDLING
DGIILNNW	WINDLING
DGIILNNY	INDIGNLY
DGIILNOR	DROILING
DGIILNOS	DISLOIGN
DGIILNPS	DISPLING
DGIILNSS	SLIDINGS
DGIILNSW	WILDINGS
DGIILNTU	DILUTING
DGIIMNNS	MINDINGS
DGIIMNOS	MISDOING
DGIIMNOU	GONIDIUM
DGIIMNSS	SMIDGINS
DGIIMOSS	SIGMOIDS
DGIIMPUY	PYGIDIUM
DGIINNOP	POINDING
DGIINNOR	NONRIGID
DGIINNOW	INDOWING
DGIINNRW	WINDRING
DGIINNSS	SINDINGS
DGIINNSW	WINDINGS
DGIINORR	GRIDIRON
DGIINORS	DORISING
DGIINORZ	DORIZING
DGIINOSV	VOIDINGS
DGIINOSW	WINDIGOS
DGIINOSX	DIGOXINS
DGIINOTT	DITTOING
DGIINOWW	WIDOWING
DGIINPPR	DRIPPING
DGIINPPS	DIPPINGS
DGIINPUV	UPDIVING
DGIINRST	STRIDING
DGIINRSV	DRIVINGS
DGIINRTY	DIRTYING
DGIINSSU	DISUSING
DGIINTTY	DITTYING
DGIINVVY	DIVVYING
DGIINYZZ	DIZZYING
DGIKLOOY	KIDOLOGY
DGIKMNOS	KINGDOMS
DGIKNOOR	DROOKING
DGIKNOOW	KINGWOOD
DGIKNORU	DROUKING
DGIKNOSS	DOGSKINS
DGILLNOR	DROLLING
	LORDLING
DGILLNOY	DOLLYING
DGILLOOW	GOODWILL
DGILMNOS	MOLDINGS
DGILMNOU	MOULDING
DGILMNPU	DUMPLING
DGILMSUY	SMUDGILY
DGILNNOO	NOODLING
DGILNNOU	LOUNDING
DGILNNOW	LOWNDING
DGILNNRU	NURDLING
DGILNOOR	DROOLING
DGILNOOW	WOOLDING
DGILNORS	GIRLONDS
	LORDINGS
DGILNORY	YOLDRING
DGILNOTY	DOTINGLY
DGILNPUY	DUPLYING
DGILOOTW	GILTWOOD
DGILOPSU	SOLPUGID
DGILOSTY	STODGILY
DGILRTUY	TURGIDLY
DGIMMNRU	DRUMMING
DGIMMNUY	DUMMYING
DGIMNNOU	MOUNDING
DGIMNOOY	MOODYING
DGIMNPSU	DUMPINGS
DGINNNSU	DUNNINGS
DGINNOOS	SNOODING
DGINNOPU	POUNDING
DGINNOPW	POWNDING
DGINNORU	ROUNDING
DGINNORW	DROWNING
	ROWNDING
DGINNOSU	SOUNDING
	UNDOINGS
DGINNOSW	SOWNDING
DGINNOUW	WOUNDING
DGINNSSY	SYNDINGS
DGINNSUW	WINDGUNS
DGINOOPR	DROOPING
DGINOOPS	SPONGOID
DGINOOTU	OUTDOING
DGINOPPR	DROPPING
DGINOPPS	DOPPINGS
DGINORSV	DROVINGS
DGINORSW	DROWSING
	SWORDING
	WORDINGS
DGINOSSW	DISGOWNS
DGINOSUY	DIGYNOUS
DGINPRUY	UPDRYING
DGINSTUY	STUDYING
DGIOOPRU	GROUPOID
DGIOPRRY	PORRIDGY
DGIOSUYZ	DIZYGOUS
DGISSSTU	DISGUSTS
DGLNORSU	GOLDURNS
DGLOOOPY	PODOLOGY
DGLOOOSW	LOGWOODS
DGLOOOSY	DOSOLOGY

DGLOOOXY	DOXOLOGY
DGMNNOUU	MUNDUNGO
DGMOOSUW	GUMWOODS
DGMOPRSU	GUMDROPS
DGMOPSYY	GYPSYDOM
DGMORSUU	GURUDOMS
DGNNORUU	UNGROUND
DGNOOORS	GODROONS
DGNOOSTW	DOGTOWNS
DGNOOTYZ	ZYGODONT
DGOORSTT	DOGTROTS
DGOPRSTU	POSTDRUG
DHHILOTW	WITHHOLD
DHHIOPPS	PHOSPHID
DHIIIMNS	DIMINISH
DHIIINST	HISTIDIN
DHIIIOST	HISTIOID
	IDIOTISH
DHIILOSS	SOLIDISH
DHIIMNOO	HOMINOID
DHIIMNOS	HOMINIDS
DHIIMOST	ISTHMOID
DHIIMPSS	MIDSHIPS
DHIIMTUY	HUMIDITY
DHIINPSW	WINDSHIP
DHIINRSU	HIRUDINS
DHIINTWW	WITHWIND
DHIIOPRU	OPHIURID
DHIIOPSX	XIPHOIDS
DHIIORSS	HIDROSIS
DHIIORSZ	RHIZOIDS
DHIKNOOW	HOODWINK
DHIKORSY	HYDROSKI
DHILLNOW	DOWNHILL
DHILLOPY	PHYLLOID
DHILLORS	DROLLISH
DHILLOST	TOLLDISH
DHILMOPY	LYMPHOID
DHILMOSY	MODISHLY
DHILNOPS	DOLPHINS
DHILOPRS	LORDSHIP
DHILOPSS	SLIPSHOD
DHILORRY	HORRIDLY
DHILPSSU	LUDSHIPS
	SULPHIDS
DHILPSSY	SYLPHIDS
DHIMMNOT	MIDMONTH
DHIMNOST	HINDMOST
DHIMNOSU	UNMODISH
DHIMOOOY	OMOHYOID
DHIMOOSS	MISSHOOD
DHIMOPPY	HIPPYDOM
DHIMOPRS	DIMORPHS
DHIMORSU	HUMIDORS
	RHODIUMS
DHINNOTW	THINDOWN
DHINOOPR	PHORONID
DHINOORS	DISHONOR
DHINOPSS	DONSHIPS
DHINORSS	DISHORNS
DHINORSU	ROUNDISH
DHINOTUW	WHODUNIT
DHIOOOPR	IODOPHOR
DHIOOPRZ	RHIZOPOD
DHIOPRSU	PROUDISH
DHIOPSTY	TYPHOIDS
DHIORSTY	THYROIDS
	THYRSOID
DHIORSWY	ROWDYISH
DHIPRSSY	SYRPHIDS
DHJOPRSU	JODHPURS
DHKMNOOO	MONKHOOD
DHKMOOSU	MUDHOOKS
DHLLOPYY	PHYLLODY
DHLMOOSU	HOODLUMS
DHLOOORT	ROOTHOLD
DHLOORSY	HYDROSOL
DHLOOSTU	HOLDOUTS
DHLORXYY	HYDROXYL
DHLOSSTU	SHOULDST
DHMMRSUU	HUMDRUMS
DHMNOOOT	HOMODONT
DHMOOPPU	PUMPHOOD
DHMORTUY	DRYMOUTH
DHNNOOSU	NUNHOODS
DHNOOOSS	SONHOODS
DHNOOSWW	SHOWDOWN
DHNOPSUW	PUSHDOWN
DHNORSUU	UNSHROUD
DHNORSUW	DOWNRUSH
DHNOSTUW	SHUTDOWN
DHOOOPRT	ORTHOPOD
DHOOORTX	ORTHODOX
DHOOPRST	DROPSHOT
DHOOPRSU	UPHOORDS
DHOORSUW	WOODRUSH
DHOPRSSU	PUSHRODS
DHOPRSYY	HYDROPSY
DIIIKMNS	MINIDISK
DIIILLQU	ILLIQUID
DIIILTVY	LIVIDITY
DIIIMOST	IDIOTISM
DIIIMRSU	IRIDIUMS
DIIIMTTY	TIMIDITY
DIIINOSV	DIVISION
DIIINTVY	DIVINITY
DIIIPRST	DISPIRIT
DIIIRTVY	VIRIDITY
DIIITVVY	VIVIDITY
DIIJNOSS	DISJOINS
DIIJNOST	DISJOINT
DIIKKNSS	KIDSKINS
DIIKLLNY	KINDLILY
DIIKLNSS	DISLINKS
DIIKNOST	DOITKINS
DIILLMNR	MILLRIND
DIILLMNW	WINDMILL
DIILLMOU	LIMULOID
DIILLMPY	LIMPIDLY
DIILLQUY	LIQUIDLY
DIILLSST	DISTILLS
DIILLSTY	IDYLLIST
DIILMNSS	DISLIMNS
DIILMOSS	IDOLISMS
	SOLIDISM
DIILMOTY	MYTILOID
DIILMUUV	DILUVIUM
DIILNNSU	INDULINS
DIILNOST	TOLIDINS
DIILNOTU	DILUTION
	TOLUIDIN
DIILNOUV	DILUVION
DIILNOXY	XYLOIDIN
DIILNSXY	XYLIDINS
DIILNTUY	UNTIDILY
DIILOPRT	TRIPLOID
DIILOPSS	DIPLOSIS
DIILOPSY	YPSILOID
DIILOQSU	SOLIQUID
DIILORSU	SILUROID
DIILORTU	UTILIDOR
DIILOSST	IDOLISTS
	SOLIDIST
DIILOSTY	SOLIDITY
DIILQSUU	LIQUIDUS
DIILRSSU	SILURIDS
DIILSSTY	IDYLISTS
DIIMMNOU	DOMINIUM
DIIMNNOO	DOMINION
DIIMNNSU	UNDINISM
DIIMNOPT	MIDPOINT
DIIMNORS	MIDIRONS
DIIMNSUU	INDUSIUM
DIIMOPRS	PRISMOID
DIIMORSS	DIORISMS
DIIMPUXY	PYXIDIUM
DIIMRUUV	DUUMVIRI
DIIMTTUY	TUMIDITY
DIINNOSU	DISUNION
DIINOOPS	IODOPSIN
DIINOOPU	DOUPIONI
DIINOQSU	QUINOIDS
DIINOSSU	SINUSOID
DIINSTUY	DISUNITY
DIIOPRTY	PITYROID
DIIORSST	SISTROID
DIIORSSV	DIVISORS
DIIORSTX	TRIOXIDS
DIIPSTTY	TIDYTIPS
DIJOSSTU	JUDOISTS
DIKLMOOW	MILKWOOD
DIKLNNOW	DOWNLINK
DIKLNNUY	UNKINDLY
DIKLNORS	LORDKINS
DIKLRUUU	DURUKULI
DIKNOOSW	INKWOODS
	WOODSKIN
DIKNORSV	DVORNIKS
DIKNORTU	OUTDRINK
DIKOOSTU	DITOKOUS
DILLMNOP	MILLPOND
DILLMSSU	MUDSILLS
DILLOORS	DOORSILL
DILLOSTY	STOLIDLY
DILLPSSY	PSYLLIDS
DILMNOOS	SMILODON
DILMNORW	LINDWORM
DILMNRSU	DRUMLINS
DILMOOSU	MODIOLUS
DILMOSSU	SOLIDUMS
DILMOSSY	ODYLISMS
DILNNOOS	NONSOLID
DILNOPST	DIPLONTS
DILNOPSU	LISPOUND
DILNOQSU	QUODLINS
DILNOSXY	INDOXYLS
DILNOUWY	WOUNDILY
DILNPSSU	LISPUNDS
DILOOPPY	POLYPOID
DILOOPRY	DROOPILY
DILOORSS	LORDOSIS
DILOOSUY	ODIOUSLY
DILOOTUV	VOLUTOID
DILOPRTY	TORPIDLY
DILORRTY	TORRIDLY
DILORSTU	DILUTORS
DILORSWY	DROWSILY
DILOSSTY	STYLOIDS
DILPRTUY	PUTRIDLY
DILPSTUY	STUPIDLY
DILRSTUY	STURDILY
DIMMNORY	MYRMIDON
DIMMOOSU	ISODOMUM
DIMMOSST	MIDMOSTS
DIMNNOOS	MIDNOONS
DIMNNOSS	DONNISMS
DIMNNOST	DINMONTS
DIMNOOOS	ISODOMON
DIMNOOST	MONODIST
DIMNOPSU	IMPOUNDS
DIMNOSSU	MISSOUND
DIMNOSTU	DISMOUNT
DIMNOSTW	MIDTOWNS
DIMNOSUW	UNWISDOM
DIMOOPRR	PRODROMI
DIMOOPRY	MYRIOPOD
DIMOORTW	MODIWORT
DIMOOSST	SODOMIST
DIMOPRSU	MISPROUD
DIMOPSSU	SPODIUMS
DIMORSSW	MISWORDS
DIMORSTY	MIDSTORY
DIMORSWY	ROWDYISM
DIMOSTUY	DUMOSITY
DIMRSTUU	TRIDUUMS
DIMRSUUV	DUUMVIRS
DINNOORS	RONDINOS
DINNOOST	TONDINOS
DINNOPSW	PINDOWNS
DINOOORW	IRONWOOD
DINOOPSU	DIPNOOUS
DINOORRS	INDORSOR
DINOORST	TORDIONS
DINOORSU	NIDOROUS
DINOOSST	ISODONTS
DINOOSTT	ODONTIST
DINOOSTY	NODOSITY
DINOPRTY	DRYPOINT
DINORSTU	STURNOID
	TURDIONS
DINORSWW	WINDROWS
DINOSTUW	OUTWINDS
DINPRTUY	PUNDITRY
DINRSTUY	INDUSTRY
DIOOPRRT	PRODITOR
DIOOPRRV	PROVIDOR
DIOOPRTX	PROTOXID
DIOORSST	DISROOTS
DIOORSTT	RIDOTTOS
DIOPRSST	DISPORTS
DIOPSSST	DISPOSTS
DIORRSST	STRIDORS
DIORSSTT	DISTORTS
DIOSSTUU	STUDIOUS
DIPRSSTU	DISRUPTS
DIRSSTTU	DISTRUST
DKLNOOOW	LOOKDOWN
DKMNOOOR	KOMONDOR
DKNORTUU	OUTDRUNK
DKOOOPRW	PORKWOOD
DKOOORWW	WOODWORK
DKORSTUW	STUDWORK
DLLMORRU	DRUMROLL
DLLMORSU	SLUMLORD
DLLNORUY	UNLORDLY
DLMNOOSW	SNOWMOLD
DLMNOOSY	MYLODONS
DLMNOOTY	MYLODONT
DLMNOSUU	UNMOULDS
DLMORSUY	SMOULDRY
DLNOOPRU	POULDRON
DLNOOSUU	NODULOUS
DLNOOSWW	LOWDOWNS
	SLOWDOWN
DLNOPRSU	PULDRONS
DLNOPSSY	SPONDYLS
DLNORTUY	ROTUNDLY
DLNOSUUU	UNDULOUS
DLOOOORS	DOLOROSO
DLOOORSU	DOLOROUS
DLOOOSTW	WOODLOTS
DLOOPPSY	POLYPODS
DLOOPPUW	PULPWOOD
DLOOPPYY	POLYPODY
DLOOPSTU	OUTPLODS
DLOOPSTY	TYLOPODS
DLOOPSWY	PLYWOODS
DMMOOORT	MOTORDOM
DMMOORSU	MUDROOMS
DMNNOOOT	MONODONT

DMNOOOPS	MONOPODS
DMNOOOPY	MONOPODY
DMNOOSTU	MOONDUST
DMNOOSTW	DOWNMOST
	TOWMONDS
DMOOOQSU	QUOMODOS
DMOOORWW	WOODWORM
	WORMWOOD
DMOPPPUU	PUPPODUM
DMOPPPUY	PUPPYDOM
DMORSTUW	MUDWORTS
DMPPPUUY	MUDPUPPY
DNNOOOWY	NONWOODY
DNNOOPRU	PUNDONOR
DNNOORSW	NONWORDS
DNNOOTWW	DOWNTOWN
DNNORRUU	RUNROUND
DNNORSUU	UNROUNDS
DNNORSUW	RUNDOWNS
DNNORTUW	DOWNTURN
	TURNDOWN
DNNOSSUW	SUNDOWNS
DNNRSTUU	TURNDUNS
DNOOPPRU	PROPOUND
DNOOPRSW	SNOWDROP
DNOOPRUW	DOWNPOUR
DNOOPSUY	DUOPSONY
DNOORSUW	WONDROUS
DNOOSTUW	NUTWOODS
DNOOSTWW	STOWDOWN
DNOOTUUW	OUTWOUND
DNOPRSSU	SUNDROPS
DNOPRSUU	ROUNDUPS
DNORRSUU	SURROUND
DNORSSUY	UNDROSSY
DOOOPPRT	PROTOPOD
DOOOPRST	DOORPOST
	DOORSTOP
DOOORSTU	OUTDOORS
DOOORSUW	SOURWOOD
DOOOSTTU	OUTSTOOD
DOOPRRTW	DROPWORT
DOOPRSTU	DROPOUTS
	OUTDROPS
DOOPSWWY	POWSOWDY
DOORRSTU	DORTOURS
DOORRSUU	ORDUROUS
DOORSSUU	SUDOROUS
DOSTTUUY	OUTSTUDY
EEEEFNRZ	ENFREEZE
EEEEFRRS	REFEREES
EEEEFRRZ	REFREEZE
EEEEGGRR	GREEGREE
EEEEGMRR	REEMERGE
EEEEGQSU	SQUEEGEE
EEEEGSSX	EXEGESES
EEEEGSTX	EXEGETES
EEEEHTTY	EYETEETH
EEEELLPX	EXPELLEE
EEEELMST	TELESEME
EEEELNSV	SLEEVEEN
EEEENRRV	VENEERER
EEEEPPSW	PEESWEEP
EEEEPRRV	REPREEVE
EEEEPTTW	PEETWEET
EEEFFFOS	FEOFFEES
EEEFFLOR	FOREFEEL
EEEFFLTY	EFFETELY
EEEFFNRT	EFFERENT
EEEFFORS	OFFEREES
EEEFFORT	FOREFEET
EEEFFOTU	ETOUFFEE
EEEFFRVW	FEVERFEW
EEEFGMRR	GERMFREE
EEEFGRSU	REFUGEES
EEEFHRSS	SHEREEFS
EEEFIPRR	REPRIEFE
EEEFIPST	TEPEFIES
EEEFIRRT	FREETIER
EEEFIRST	REEFIEST
EEEFLRRS	FLEERERS
EEEFLRSX	REFLEXES
EEEFLSST	FEETLESS
EEEFLSTT	FLEETEST
EEEFNNPY	PENNYFEE
EEEFNORS	FORESEEN
EEEFNRRT	REFERENT
EEEFNRSS	FREENESS
EEEFNRSV	ENFEVERS
EEEFNRTT	ENFETTER
EEEFNRUZ	UNFREEZE
EEEFORRS	FORESEER
EEEFORRV	OVERFREE
EEEFORSS	FORESEES
EEEFRRRR	REFERRER
EEEFRRRT	FERRETER
EEEFRRSZ	FREEZERS
EEEFRRTT	FETTERER
EEEGGILN	NEGLIGEE
EEEGGIRS	EGGERIES
EEEGHINT	EIGHTEEN
EEEGHLRS	SHEERLEG
EEEGHMNU	HEGUMENE
EEEGHNSW	WHEENGES
EEEGIKST	GEEKIEST
EEEGILMN	LIEGEMEN
EEEGILNV	ENVEIGLE
	LEVEEING
EEEGILPS	ESPIEGLE
EEEGILRT	GLEETIER
EEEGILSS	ELEGISES
EEEGILSZ	ELEGIZES
EEEGIMNX	EXEEMING
EEEGINNR	ENGINEER
EEEGINRR	GREENIER
EEEGINRS	ENERGIES
	ENERGISE
	GREENIES
	RESEEING
EEEGINRV	ENGRIEVE
EEEGINRZ	ENERGIZE
EEEGIPRS	PERIGEES
EEEGIRTY	TIGEREYE
EEEGISSX	EXEGESIS
EEEGISTV	EGESTIVE
EEEGITVV	VEGETIVE
EEEGKLRS	KEGELERS
EEEGLMOS	GLEESOME
EEEGLNRT	GREENLET
EEEGMNOS	MONGEESE
EEEGMNRT	EMERGENT
EEEGMNRU	MERENGUE
EEEGMORT	GEOMETER
EEEGMRRS	REMERGES
EEEGNNRS	SENGREEN
EEEGNPRS	EPERGNES
EEEGNRRS	GREENERS
	REGREENS
	RENEGERS
EEEGNRRU	RENEGUER
EEEGNRRV	REVENGER
EEEGNRRY	GREENERY
EEEGNRST	GREENEST
EEEGNRSU	RENEGUES
EEEGNRSV	REVENGES
EEEGNSTT	GENETTES
EEEGOPRT	PROTEGEE
EEEGRRST	GREETERS
	REGREETS
EEEGRSSS	EGRESSES
EEEGRSUX	EXERGUES
EEEHHSSW	WHEESHES
EEEHILRW	EREWHILE
	WHEELIER
EEEHILSW	WHEELIES
EEEHINRS	SHEENIER
EEEHINSS	SHEENIES
EEEHIPRS	SHEEPIER
EEEHIRSS	HERESIES
EEEHIRST	ETHERISE
	SHEETIER
EEEHIRSX	HEXEREIS
EEEHIRTZ	ETHERIZE
EEEHIRWZ	WHEEZIER
EEEHKLNO	KNEEHOLE
EEEHLLSS	HEELLESS
EEEHLMNW	WHEELMEN
EEEHLMPT	HELPMEET
EEEHLNSW	ENWHEELS
EEEHLNTV	ELEVENTH
EEEHLNTY	ETHYLENE
EEEHLNXY	HEXYLENE
EEEHLOPP	PEEPHOLE
EEEHLOPW	WEEPHOLE
EEEHLOSY	EYEHOLES
EEEHLPSW	WHEEPLES
EEEHLRSW	WHEELERS
EEEHLSWZ	WHEEZLES
EEEHMMSS	EMMESHES
EEEHMNNT	MENTHENE
EEEHMNPS	SHEEPMEN
EEEHMNSS	ENMESHES
EEEHMNTV	VEHEMENT
EEEHNNPT	NEPENTHE
EEEHNNQU	HENEQUEN
EEEHNPRS	ENSPHERE
EEEHNRSS	HERENESS
EEEHNRTV	REVEHENT
EEEHNRVW	WHENEVER
EEEHNSSS	SNEESHES
EEEHNSSY	SHEENEYS
EEEHORST	SHOETREE
EEEHPRSS	HERPESES
EEEHPRST	SPREETHE
EEEHRRVW	WHEREVER
EEEHRSST	SEETHERS
	SHEEREST
	SHEETERS
EEEHRSTT	TEETHERS
EEEHRSWZ	WHEEZERS
EEEHSSST	ESTHESES
EEEHSSTT	ESTHETES
EEEIKLMS	MISLEEKE
EEEIKLRS	SKEELIER
	SLEEKIER
EEEIKLRT	TREELIKE
EEEIKLSW	WEEKLIES
EEEIKNTX	EKTEXINE
EEEIKRRS	SKEERIER
EEEIKRST	REEKIEST
EEEILLRV	REVEILLE
EEEILMRS	SEEMLIER
EEEILNNO	EOLIENNE
EEEILNPR	PELERINE
EEEILNRY	EYELINER
EEEILNST	ENLISTEE
	SELENITE
EEEILPRS	SLEEPIER
EEEILRRV	RELIEVER
EEEILRST	LEERIEST
	SLEETIER
	STEELIER
EEEILRSV	RELIEVES
EEEILRSZ	SLEEZIER
EEEILSST	SEELIEST
	STEELIES
EEEILSSW	ELSEWISE
EEEILSTV	TELEVISE
EEEILTVW	TELEVIEW
EEEIMNRU	MEUNIERE
EEEIMNST	EMETINES
EEEIMPRR	PREMIERE
EEEIMPRS	EMPERIES
	EMPERISE
	EPIMERES
	PREEMIES
EEEIMPRZ	EMPERIZE
EEEIMRRS	MISERERE
EEEIMRST	EREMITES
EEEIMRTT	REMITTEE
EEEINNNT	NINETEEN
EEEINNRT	INTERNEE
	RETINENE
EEEINQRU	QUEENIER
EEEINQSU	QUEENIES
EEEINQTU	QUEENITE
EEEINRRS	SNEERIER
EEEINRSS	EERINESS
	ESERINES
EEEINRST	ETERNISE
	TEENSIER
EEEINRSV	VENERIES
EEEINRSW	WEENSIER
EEEINRSZ	SNEEZIER
EEEINRTT	REINETTE
	TEENTIER
EEEINRTZ	ETERNIZE
EEEINSSW	SWEENIES
EEEINSTT	TEENIEST
EEEINSTW	TWEENIES
	WEENIEST
EEEINTUX	EUXENITE
EEEIPRRV	REPRIEVE
EEEIPRST	PEERIEST
	STEEPIER
EEEIPRSW	SWEEPIER
EEEIPSST	EPEEISTS
	SEEPIEST
EEEIPSTW	WEEPIEST
EEEIQSUX	EXEQUIES
EEEIRRST	REESTIER
	RETIREES
EEEIRRSV	REREVISE
	REVERIES
EEEIRRTV	RETRIEVE
EEEIRRVW	REREVIEW
	REVIEWER
EEEIRSST	STEERIES
EEEIRSSV	SEVERIES
EEEIRSSZ	RESEIZES
EEEIRTVX	EXERTIVE
EEEISSTW	SWEETIES
EEEJLLRW	JEWELLER
EEEJLRSW	JEWELERS
EEEJNPSY	JEEPNEYS
EEEKLLSS	KEELLESS
EEEKLLSU	UKELELES
EEEKLNNR	ENKERNEL
EEEKLNRS	KNEELERS
EEEKLNSS	SLEEKENS
EEEKLPSW	EKPWELES
EEEKLRSS	SLEEKERS
EEEKLSST	SLEEKEST
EEEKMNSS	MEEKNESS
EEEKMORV	OVERMEEK
EEEKMRSS	KERMESSE
EEEKNNSS	KEENNESS
EEEKNORS	KEROSENE
EEEKNORV	OVERKEEN
	OVERKNEE

EEEKNPST KEEPNETS
EEEKOPRV OVERKEEP
EEEKORSV REEVOKES
EEEKRRST STREEKER
EEEKRSST KEESTERS
SKEETERS
EEELLLRV LEVELLER
EEELLLSW SEWELLEL
EEELLNOR ENROLLEE
EEELLNQU QUENELLE
EEELLPRR REPELLER
EEELLPRX EXPELLER
EEELLRRS RESELLER
EEELLRRT RETELLER
EEELLRRV REVELLER
EEELLRSV LEVELERS
EEELMNST ELEMENTS
STEELMEN
EEELMOPP EMPEOPLE
EEELMOPY EMPLOYEE
EEELMORT TELOMERE
EEELMOTT OMELETTE
EEELMPSX EXEMPLES
EEELMRTU MULETEER
EEELMSSS SEEMLESS
EEELMSST TEEMLESS
EEELNOPV ENVELOPE
EEELNOSV NOVELESE
EEELNQTU QUEENLET
EEELNRRU UNREELER
EEELNRSW NEWSREEL
EEELNRSY SERENELY
EEELNRTV NERVELET
EEELOPPR REPEOPLE
EEELORST SLOETREE
EEELPPRS PRESLEEP
EEELPRSS PEERLESS
SLEEPERS
SPEELERS
EEELPRST REPLETES
EEELPRSX REEXPELS
EEELPRSY SLEEPERY
EEELPSST STEEPLES
EEELRRSV REVELERS
EEELRRTT LETTERER
RELETTER
EEELRSST TREELESS
EEELRSSV SLEEVERS
EEELRSTT RESETTLE
EEELRSTV LEVERETS
VERSELET
EEELRSVY SEVERELY
EEELRTVV VELVERET
EEELSSTU EUSTELES
EEELSSTW WEETLESS
EEELSTVY STEEVELY
EEELTTTX TELETEXT
EEEMMNRS MERESMEN
EEEMMORS MESOMERE
EEEMMRUZ MEZEREUM
EEEMNNTT TENEMENT
EEEMNORZ MEZEREON
EEEMNPRT PETERMEN
EEEMNRST ENTREMES
EEEMNRSV VERSEMEN
EEEMNRVY EVERYMEN
EEEMNSST MEETNESS
EEEMORRV EVERMORE
EEEMORST EROTEMES
STEREOME
EEEMORTV OVERTEEM
EEEMPRRT RETEMPER
TEMPERER
EEEMPRSS EMPRESSE
EEEMPSSY EMPYESES

EEEMRRTX EXTREMER
EEEMRSST SEMESTER
EEEMRSTX EXTREMES
EEENNOPR NEOPRENE
EEENNOSV VENENOSE
EEENNPST PENTENES
EEENNRST ETRENNES
EEENNRUV UNEVENER
EEENNSSV EVENNESS
EEENNSTT ENTENTES
EEENOPRR REOPENER
EEENORSV OVERSEEN
EEENORVW OVERWEEN
EEENORVY EVERYONE
EEENOSTY EYESTONE
EEENPPRS PREPENSE
EEENPRRS PREENERS
EEENPRRT REPENTER
EEENPRST PRETEENS
PRETENSE
TERPENES
EEENPRSV PREVENES
EEENPSST ENSTEEPS
STEEPENS
EEENPSSW ENSWEEPS
EEENPSSX EXPENSES
EEENRRSS SNEERERS
EEENRRST ENTERERS
REENTERS
RESENTER
TERREENS
TERRENES
EEENRRSV RENVERSE
VENERERS
EEENRRSW RENEWERS
EEENRRTU RETURNEE
EEENRRTV REVERENT
EEENRRUV REVENUER
EEENRSST SERENEST
EEENRSSU ENURESES
EEENRSSZ SNEEZERS
EEENRSTV EVENTERS
EEENRSTX EXTERNES
EEENRSTY YESTREEN
EEENRSUV REVENUES
UNREEVES
EEENSSTW SWEETENS
TWEENESS
EEENSSWY SWEENEYS
EEEOPRRV OVERPEER
EEEOPRSX REEXPOSE
EEEORRSV OVERSEER
EEEORRSX XEROSERE
EEEORSST EROTESES
EEEORSSV OVERSEES
EEEORSSY EYESORES
EEEORSVY OVEREYES
EEEPPPRR PEPPERER
EEEPPSTU STEEPEUP
EEEPRRST PESTERER
EEEPRRSU REPERUSE
EEEPRRSV PERVERSE
PRESERVE
EEEPRRTW PEWTERER
EEEPRSST ESTREPES
STEEPERS
EEEPRSSW SWEEPERS
EEEPRSSZ SPREEZES
EEEPSSTT STEEPEST
EEEPSTTT SEPTETTE
EEEQRRSU REQUERES
EEEQRRUV VERQUERE
EEEQRSTU QUEEREST
EEEQRSUZ SQUEEZER
EEEQSSUZ SQUEEZES

EEERRRSV RESERVER
REVERERS
REVERSER
EEERRRTV REVERTER
EEERRSST STEERERS
EEERRSSV RESERVES
REVERSES
EEERRSTT RESETTER
EEERSSTV SEVEREST
EEERSSUV REVEUSES
EEERSSUW SERUEWES
EEERSSVW SERVEWES
EEERSTTW TWEETERS
EEERSTVX VERTEXES
EEERSTWZ TWEEZERS
EEESSTTT SESTETTE
EEESSTTV STEEVEST
EEESSTTW SWEETEST
EEESTTTX SEXTETTE
EEFFFGLU GEFUFFLE
EEFFFKLU KEFUFFLE
EEFFFNOS ENFEOFFS
EEFFFORS FEOFFERS
EEFFGIIS EFFIGIES
EEFFGINR EFFERING
EEFFGIRR GREFFIER
EEFFGLSU EFFULGES
EEFFHIKY KEFFIYEH
EEFFINST FIFTEENS
EEFFISUV EFFUSIVE
EEFFLNTU EFFLUENT
EEFFLORT FOREFELT
EEFFLSUX EFFLUXES
EEFFMORR FREEFORM
EEFFMOTT MOFFETTE
EEFFNOSS OFFENSES
EEFFORRS OFFERERS
REOFFERS
EEFFORSX FORFEXES
EEFFRRSU SUFFERER
EEFFSSTU SUFFETES
EEFGIILR FILIGREE
EEFGILNR FLEERING
EEFGILNS FEELINGS
EEFGILNT FLEETING
EEFGINNP PFENNIGE
EEFGINRR FINGERER
REFRINGE
EEFGINRS FEERINGS
FEIGNERS
REEFINGS
EEFGINRV FEVERING
EEFGINRZ FREEZING
EEFGIRRU REFIGURE
EEFGLMNU FUGLEMEN
EEFGLNRY GREENFLY
EEFGLNUV VENGEFUL
EEFGLORS FORELEGS
EEFGLOSS SOLFEGES
EEFGMNOR FORGEMEN
EEFGNOOR FOREGONE
EEFGOORR FOREGOER
EEFGOORS FOREGOES
EEFGORRS REFORGES
EEFGORSY FROGEYES
EEFHILLR HELLFIRE
EEFHILRS FLESHIER
SHELFIER
EEFHIMSU HUMEFIES
EEFHIRSV FEVERISH
EEFHIRTY ETHERIFY
EEFHISST FETISHES
EEFHISSY FISHEYES
EEFHISTT HEFTIEST
EEFHLLWY FLYWHEEL

EEFHLMOT HOMEFELT
EEFHLMST THEMSELF
EEFHLNSU SHEENFUL
EEFHLRSS FLESHERS
EEFHMNRS FRESHMEN
EEFHMORR HEREFROM
EEFHNORT FOREHENT
EEFHNRSS FRESHENS
EEFHORRT THEREFOR
EEFHORRW WHEREFOR
EEFHORSW FORESHEW
EEFHRRSS FRESHERS
EEFHRRSU FUEHRERS
EEFHRSST FRESHEST
FRESHETS
EEFIIKLL LIFELIKE
EEFIIKLW WIFELIKE
EEFIIKRS FIKERIES
EEFIILLN LIFELINE
EEFIILMT LIFETIME
EEFIILNS LENIFIES
EEFIILRW WIFELIER
EEFIIMNN FEMININE
EEFIIMNS FEMINISE
EEFIIMNZ FEMINIZE
EEFIINRS FINERIES
EEFIIRRS REIFIERS
EEFIIRRT FREITIER
EEFIIRRV VERIFIER
EEFIIRST FEISTIER
FERITIES
FIERIEST
EEFIIRSV VERIFIES
EEFIKLLT FELTLIKE
EEFIKLMU FUMELIKE
EEFIKLNR FERNLIKE
EEFIKLRS SERFLIKE
EEFIKNNP PENKNIFE
EEFILLMT TELEFILM
EEFILLNY FELINELY
EEFILLRW FREEWILL
EEFILLSS LIFELESS
EEFILMNR RIFLEMEN
EEFILMOS LIFESOME
EEFILMST FISTMELE
EEFILMTX FLEXTIME
EEFILNOS FELONIES
OLEFINES
EEFILNSS FINELESS
EEFILNUV NIEVEFUL
EEFILORS FORELIES
EEFILPRR PILFERER
EEFILPRS PREFILES
EEFILRRT FERTILER
FILTERER
REFILTER
EEFILRSS FIRELESS
EEFILRST FERLIEST
EEFILRSU FUSILEER
EEFILSST FELSITES
EEFILSSW WIFELESS
EEFILSTT FELTIEST
EEFIMORT FORETIME
EEFIMRRS MISREFER
EEFIMRST FEMITERS
EEFIMSTU TUMEFIES
EEFINNSS FINENESS
EEFINNST FENNIEST
EEFINORV OVERFINE
EEFINRRR INFERRER
EEFINRRS REFINERS
EEFINRRY REFINERY
EEFINRSS FINESSER
RIFENESS
EEFINRST FERNIEST

	INFESTER
EEFINRSU	REINFUSE
EEFINRSZ	FRENZIES
EEFINSSS	FINESSES
EEFINSTT	FEINTEST
EEFIORRV	OVERRIFE
EEFIORSX	ORIFEXES
EEFIPRRS	PREFIRES
EEFIPRSX	PREFIXES
EEFIRRST	FERRITES
EEFIRRSU	SUREFIRE
EEFIRRTT	FRETTIER
EEFIRRVY	REVERIFY
EEFIRSTT	FRISETTE
EEFIRSTY	ESTERIFY
EEFIRTTZ	FRIZETTE
EEFISSSW	FESSWISE
EEFISTWW	WEFTWISE
EEFKNORW	FOREKNEW
EEFLLNSS	FELLNESS
EEFLLORT	FORETELL
EEFLLORV	OVERFELL
EEFLLRSU	FUELLERS
EEFLLRXY	REFLEXLY
EEFLLSSS	SELFLESS
EEFLMNSU	MENSEFUL
EEFLMORU	FUMEROLE
EEFLMSSU	FUMELESS
EEFLNNOS	ENFELONS
EEFLNORT	FORELENT
EEFLNORU	FLUORENE
EEFLNORW	ENFLOWER
EEFLNOST	FELSTONE
EEFLNRSS	FERNLESS
	FLENSERS
	FRESNELS
EEFLNRSU	SNEERFUL
EEFLNRTU	REFLUENT
EEFLNSSS	SELFNESS
EEFLNSSU	SENSEFUL
EEFLNTUV	EVENTFUL
EEFLOOSV	FOVEOLES
EEFLOOTV	FOVEOLET
EEFLOPTT	POLTFEET
EEFLORRW	FLOWERER
	REFLOWER
EEFLORSS	FORLESES
EEFLORTV	LEFTOVER
EEFLORTW	FLOWERET
EEFLORVW	OVERFLEW
EEFLORWW	WEREWOLF
EEFLOSTU	OUTFEELS
EEFLOSUX	FLEXUOSE
EEFLRRSU	FERRULES
EEFLRSST	FRETLESS
EEFLRSTT	FETTLERS
EEFLRSTU	FLEURETS
EEFLRSUX	FLEXURES
	REFLUXES
EEFLSSSU	FUSELESS
EEFMNORT	FOMENTER
EEFMNRRY	FERRYMEN
EEFMNRST	FERMENTS
EEFMORRR	REFORMER
EEFMORST	FRETSOME
EEFMOSTT	MOFETTES
EEFMPRRU	PERFUMER
EEFMPRSU	PERFUMES
EEFMSTTU	FUMETTES
EEFNNORS	ENFROSEN
EEFNNORZ	ENFROZEN
EEFNORRZ	REFROZEN
EEFNORST	ENFOREST
	SOFTENER
EEFNORTU	FOURTEEN
EEFNORTW	FOREWENT
EEFNOSTT	OFTENEST
EEFNQRTU	FREQUENT
EEFNRTTU	UNFETTER
EEFOORRT	ROOFTREE
EEFOPRRZ	PREFROZE
EEFORRST	FORESTER
	FOSTERER
	REFOREST
EEFORRSU	FERREOUS
EEFORRSV	FOREVERS
EEFORRTY	FERETORY
EEFORSUV	FEVEROUS
EEFOSSTT	FOSSETTE
EEFOSSTU	FOETUSES
EEFOSTTU	FOUETTES
EEFPRSSU	PERFUSES
EEFRRSSU	REFUSERS
EEFRRSTT	FRETTERS
EEFRRSTU	REFUTERS
EEGGGLST	GLEGGEST
EEGGHLLS	EGGSHELL
EEGGHLOR	HOGGEREL
EEGGHMSU	MESHUGGE
EEGGHSTU	THUGGEES
EEGGIJRR	REJIGGER
EEGGIKLN	GLEEKING
EEGGIKNR	GREEKING
EEGGILNR	LEGERING
EEGGILNS	NEGLIGES
EEGGILNT	GLEETING
EEGGILNY	GINGELEY
EEGGILOR	LEGGIERO
EEGGILST	LEGGIEST
EEGGIMNR	EMERGING
EEGGINNP	PEENGING
EEGGINNR	GREENING
	RENEGING
EEGGINRS	GREESING
EEGGINRT	GREETING
EEGGINST	EGESTING
EEGGINSU	SEGUEING
EEGGJLRU	REJUGGLE
EEGGKRSS	SKEGGERS
EEGGLNSS	GLEGNESS
EEGGLOOR	GEOLOGER
EEGGNNSS	GENSENGS
EEGGNORS	ENGORGES
EEGGORRS	REGORGES
EEGGORSU	GOUGERES
EEGGPRRS	PREGGERS
EEGGPRSU	PUGGREES
EEGGQRSU	SQUEGGER
EEGHHINT	HEIGHTEN
EEGHIIST	EIGHTIES
EEGHIKNT	THEEKING
EEGHIKRS	SKEIGHER
EEGHILNS	HEELINGS
	SHEELING
EEGHILNW	WHEELING
EEGHILRS	SLEIGHER
EEGHIMNW	WEIGHMEN
EEGHINNS	SHEENING
EEGHINPS	PHEESING
EEGHINPT	PHENGITE
EEGHINPW	WHEEPING
EEGHINPZ	PHEEZING
EEGHINRS	GREENISH
	REHINGES
	SHEERING
EEGHINST	SEETHING
	SHEETING
EEGHINSY	HYGIENES
EEGHINTT	TEETHING
EEGHINWZ	WHEEZING
EEGHIOTT	GOETHITE
EEGHIRSW	REWEIGHS
	WEIGHERS
EEGHIRTW	WEIGHTER
EEGHISST	SIGHTSEE
EEGHISTY	EYESIGHT
EEGHKRSS	SKREEGHS
EEGHLNNT	LENGTHEN
EEGHMNOY	HEGEMONY
EEGHMNSU	HEGUMENS
EEGHMNUY	HEGUMENY
EEGHNNRU	ENHUNGER
EEGHNOOP	GEOPHONE
EEGHNOPS	PHOSGENE
EEGHNOPY	HYPOGENE
EEGHNRST	GREENTHS
EEGHNRSY	GREYHENS
EEGHNSSU	HUGENESS
EEGHOPTY	GEOPHYTE
EEGHORTT	TOGETHER
EEGHOSTT	GHETTOES
EEGHSTTU	TEUGHEST
EEGIILNR	LINGERIE
EEGIILNV	INVEIGLE
EEGIIMNS	GEMINIES
EEGIINRT	REIGNITE
EEGIINTV	GENITIVE
EEGIIOST	EGOITIES
EEGIJLNW	JEWELING
EEGIJLNY	JEELYING
EEGIJNRS	JEERINGS
EEGIKLLN	GLENLIKE
EEGIKLLU	GLUELIKE
EEGIKLNN	KNEELING
EEGIKLNS	KEELINGS
	SLEEKING
EEGIKLOT	EKLOGITE
EEGIKMNS	SMEEKING
EEGIKNNS	KEENINGS
EEGIKNPS	KEEPINGS
EEGIKNRS	KREESING
	SKEERING
EEGIKNRY	REKEYING
EEGIKNST	KITENGES
	STEEKING
EEGILLNV	LEVELING
EEGILMOS	EGLOMISE
EEGILNOR	ELOIGNER
EEGILNPS	PEELINGS
	SLEEPING
	SPEELING
EEGILNRR	LINGERER
EEGILNRS	LEERINGS
	REELINGS
EEGILNRU	REGULINE
EEGILNRV	LEVERING
	REVELING
EEGILNSS	SEELINGS
EEGILNST	GENTILES
	SLEETING
	STEELING
EEGILNSV	SLEEVING
EEGILNSW	SWEELING
EEGILNTW	TWEELING
EEGILNTX	TELEXING
EEGILOPU	EPILOGUE
EEGILOSS	GELOSIES
EEGILOSU	EULOGIES
	EULOGISE
EEGILOUZ	EULOGIZE
EEGILPSS	SPIEGELS
EEGILQSU	SQUILGEE
EEGILRSU	REGULISE
EEGILRSV	VELIGERS
EEGILRTV	VERLIGTE
EEGILRTY	LEGERITY
EEGILRUZ	REGULIZE
EEGILSST	ELEGISTS
EEGIMMNW	EMMEWING
EEGIMMRS	GREMMIES
	IMMERGES
EEGIMMST	GEMMIEST
EEGIMNNS	MENINGES
EEGIMNNW	ENMEWING
EEGIMNRS	REGIMENS
EEGIMNRT	METERING
	REGIMENT
EEGIMNRU	MERINGUE
EEGIMNRY	EMERYING
EEGIMNSS	SEEMINGS
EEGIMNST	MEETINGS
	STEEMING
EEGIMNSU	EUGENISM
EEGIMRST	GERMIEST
EEGINNPR	PREENING
EEGINNQU	QUEENING
EEGINNRS	ENGINERS
	INGENERS
	SERENING
	SNEERING
EEGINNRT	ENTERING
EEGINNRV	ENERVING
EEGINNRW	RENEWING
EEGINNRY	ENGINERY
	RENEYING
EEGINNST	STEENING
EEGINNSU	INGENUES
	UNSEEING
EEGINNSV	EEVNINGS
	EVENINGS
EEGINNSW	ENSEWING
EEGINNSZ	SNEEZING
EEGINNTV	EVENTING
EEGINOOS	OOGENIES
EEGINOPR	PERIGONE
EEGINOPS	EPIGONES
EEGINORR	ERIGERON
EEGINORS	ERINGOES
EEGINORV	VIROGENE
EEGINOSS	GENOISES
EEGINOST	EGESTION
EEGINPRR	PEREGRIN
EEGINPRS	SPEERING
	SPREEING
EEGINPRT	PETERING
EEGINPRU	PUREEING
EEGINPRV	PREEVING
EEGINPST	STEEPING
EEGINPSW	SWEEPING
	WEEPINGS
EEGINQRU	QUEERING
EEGINQUU	QUEUEING
EEGINRRS	RESIGNER
EEGINRRV	REVERING
EEGINRSS	GREISENS
EEGINRST	GENTRIES
	INTEGERS
	REESTING
	STEERING
	STREIGNE
EEGINRSU	SEIGNEUR
EEGINRSV	SEVERING
	VEERINGS
EEGINRSW	RESEWING
	SEWERING
EEGINRTU	GENITURE
EEGINRTV	EVERTING
EEGINRTW	TWEERING
EEGINRTX	EXERTING
	GENETRIX

EEGINSSS	GNEISSES
EEGINSSU	GENIUSES
EEGINSTT	GENTIEST
EEGINSTU	EUGENIST
EEGINSTV	STEEVING
	VENTIGES
EEGINSTW	SWEETING
EEGINSTX	EXIGENTS
EEGINTTV	VIGNETTE
EEGINTTW	TWEETING
EEGINTUX	TEGUEXIN
EEGINTWZ	TWEEZING
EEGIOPSU	EPIGEOUS
EEGIORST	ERGOTISE
EEGIORTZ	ERGOTIZE
EEGIORVV	OVERGIVE
EEGIOSST	EGOTISES
EEGIOSTZ	EGOTIZES
EEGIPRST	PRESTIGE
EEGIRRST	REGISTER
EEGIRRSV	GRIEVERS
EEGIRSTT	GRISETTE
	TERGITES
EEGIRSTU	GUERITES
EEGISSTV	VESTIGES
EEGISTTV	VEGETIST
EEGJORSU	GOUJEERS
EEGKLNOW	WEEKLONG
EEGKNORS	KEROGENS
EEGKNRSU	GERENUKS
EEGLLRRU	GRUELLER
EEGLMMSU	GEMMULES
EEGLMNOP	EMPLONGE
EEGLMNTU	EMULGENT
EEGLMORS	GOMERELS
EEGLMOSS	GLOSSEME
EEGLNNTU	UNGENTLE
EEGLNOPY	POLYGENE
EEGLNOSU	EUGENOLS
EEGLNOSZ	LOZENGES
EEGLNOTY	TELEGONY
EEGLNPRU	REPLUNGE
EEGLNSTT	GENTLEST
EEGLOPRS	GOSPELER
EEGLORRV	GROVELER
EEGLORVY	LEVOGYRE
EEGLRRSU	GRUELERS
EEGLRSTW	WERGELTS
EEGMMOSU	GEMMEOUS
EEGMNOST	EMONGEST
	GEMSTONE
EEGMNOYZ	ZYMOGENE
EEGMNSST	SEGMENTS
EEGMNTTU	TEGUMENT
EEGMORSU	GRUESOME
EEGMORSW	GREWSOME
EEGMORTY	GEOMETRY
EEGMRSTU	GUMTREES
EEGNNNOR	NONGREEN
EEGNNORT	ROENTGEN
EEGNNOSS	GONENESS
EEGNNOSV	EVENSONG
EEGNNOXY	XENOGENY
EEGNOORV	ENGROOVE
	OVERGONE
EEGNOOST	OSTEOGEN
EEGNOPTY	GENOTYPE
EEGNORST	ESTROGEN
EEGNORSU	GENEROUS
EEGNORSY	ERYNGOES
EEGNOTYZ	ZYGOTENE
EEGNPRUX	EXPUNGER
EEGNPSUX	EXPUNGES
EEGNRSSY	GREYNESS
EEGNRSUY	GUERNSEY
EEGNSSTU	GUESTENS
EEGOOPSY	POOGYEES
EEGOORRV	REGROOVE
EEGOORSV	OVERGOES
EEGOPRST	PROTEGES
EEGOPRSU	SUPEREGO
EEGORRST	OSTREGER
EEGORRUV	OVERURGE
EEGORRVW	OVERGREW
EEGORSSS	OGRESSES
EEGORSTU	UROSTEGE
EEGORSTV	OVERGETS
EEGPPRRS	PREPREGS
EEGPRSUX	EXPURGES
EEGRRSSU	RESURGES
EEGRRSTU	GESTURER
EEGRRSUY	GRUYERES
EEGRSSSU	GUESSERS
EEGRSSTU	GESTURES
EEHHIPSS	SHEEPISH
EEHHIRST	ETHERISH
EEHHIRTW	HEREWITH
EEHHLLLO	HELLHOLE
EEHHLRST	THRESHEL
EEHHNOPT	ETHEPHON
EEHHNOSU	HENHOUSE
EEHHRRST	THRESHER
EEHHRSST	THRESHES
EEHHSSTW	WHEESHTS
EEHIIKLV	HIVELIKE
EEHIJMNR	MIJNHEER
EEHIKLLT	HELLKITE
EEHIKLMO	HOMELIKE
EEHIKLMP	HEMPLIKE
EEHIKLRW	WHELKIER
EEHIKLWY	WHEYLIKE
EEHIKRRS	SHRIEKER
EEHILLMS	SHLEMIEL
EEHILLNP	HELPLINE
EEHILLRS	HELLIERS
	SHELLIER
EEHILMNS	HEMLINES
EEHILMNU	HELENIUM
EEHILMOR	HOMELIER
EEHILNOP	NEOPHILE
EEHILNPW	PINWHEEL
EEHILNST	THEELINS
EEHILORT	HOTELIER
EEHILOSS	HELIOSES
EEHILRSS	HEIRLESS
	RELISHES
EEHILRSV	SHELVIER
EEHILSST	LEISHEST
	SHELTIES
EEHILSSV	HIVELESS
EEHILWYZ	WHEEZILY
EEHIMMSS	IMMESHES
	MISHMEES
EEHIMNOS	HEMIONES
EEHIMNRS	SHIREMEN
EEHIMNRT	THEREMIN
EEHIMNSS	INMESHES
EEHIMOST	HOMESITE
EEHIMPRS	EMPERISH
EEHIMPRT	HEMIPTER
EEHIMPST	EPITHEMS
	HEMPIEST
EEHIMQUV	VEHMIQUE
EEHIMRRU	RHEUMIER
EEHIMRST	ERETHISM
	ETHERISM
EEHIMRTT	THERMITE
EEHIMSST	MESHIEST
EEHINNQU	HENEQUIN
	HENIQUEN
EEHINNRS	ENSHRINE
EEHINNRT	INHERENT
EEHINNSS	SNEESHIN
EEHINNST	HENNIEST
EEHINORS	HEROINES
EEHINORT	ETHERION
	HEREINTO
EEHINPRS	INSPHERE
EEHINPRT	NEPHRITE
	PREHNITE
	TREPHINE
EEHINPSX	PHENIXES
EEHINRRS	ERRHINES
EEHINRSS	RESHINES
EEHINRTT	THIRTEEN
EEHINRTW	WHITENER
EEHIOPPS	HOSEPIPE
EEHIORSS	HEROISES
EEHIORST	ISOTHERE
	THEORIES
	THEORISE
EEHIORSZ	HEROIZES
EEHIORTZ	THEORIZE
EEHIOSTX	ETHOXIES
EEHIPPST	PSEPHITE
EEHIPPTY	EPIPHYTE
EEHIPRRS	PERISHER
	SPHERIER
EEHIPRSS	PERISHES
EEHIPRST	TREESHIP
EEHIPRTT	PERTHITE
	TEPHRITE
	THREEPIT
EEHIPSST	STEEPISH
EEHIPSTT	EPITHETS
EEHIPSUU	EUPHUISE
EEHIPUUZ	EUPHUIZE
EEHIQRSU	QUEERISH
EEHIRRSS	SHERRIES
EEHIRRSV	SHIVERER
EEHIRRSW	WHERRIES
EEHIRRTW	WITHERER
EEHIRRTX	HERETRIX
EEHIRSST	HEISTERS
EEHIRSSV	SHRIEVES
EEHIRSSX	RHEXISES
EEHIRSTT	ETHERIST
EEHIRTVY	THIEVERY
EEHISSST	ESTHESIS
	HESSITES
EEHISSTW	SWEETISH
EEHISTTW	THEWIEST
EEHISTWY	WHEYIEST
EEHKLOSY	KEYHOLES
EEHKOOSY	EYEHOOKS
EEHLLLOW	WELLHOLE
EEHLLMPS	PHELLEMS
EEHLLMSS	HELMLESS
EEHLLNSS	ENSHELLS
EEHLLORV	HOVELLER
EEHLLOSS	HOLELESS
EEHLLOST	THEELOLS
EEHLLPSS	HELPLESS
EEHLLRSS	SHELLERS
EEHLMMNS	HELMSMEN
EEHLMMSW	WHEMMLES
EEHLMNOT	HOTELMEN
EEHLMOOS	HOLESOME
EEHLMOSS	HOMELESS
EEHLMOYZ	HEMOLYZE
EEHLMRST	THERMELS
EEHLNOPT	PHENETOL
EEHLNOTT	TELETHON
EEHLOPSS	HOPELESS
EEHLOPST	HEELPOST
	PESTHOLE
EEHLORST	HOSTELER
EEHLORSV	SHOVELER
EEHLOSSS	SHOELESS
EEHLPPRS	SHLEPPER
EEHLPRST	TELPHERS
EEHLPRSU	SPHERULE
EEHLPSSY	PHYLESES
EEHLRSST	SHELTERS
EEHLRSSV	SHELVERS
EEHLRSSW	WELSHERS
EEHLRSTY	SHELTERY
EEHLSSTT	SHTETELS
EEHLSSTW	THEWLESS
EEHMMOPR	MORPHEME
EEHMMORT	OHMMETER
EEHMNOOS	MOONSHEE
EEHMNOPS	PHONEMES
EEHMNORS	HORSEMEN
	SHOREMEN
EEHMNOSU	HOUSEMEN
EEHMNOSW	SOMEWHEN
EEHMNRSU	ENRHEUMS
EEHMNRSY	MYNHEERS
EEHMNSSU	UNMESHES
EEHMNTTU	UMTEENTH
EEHMOORT	RHEOTOME
EEHMOOSS	HOMEOSES
EEHMORST	THEOREMS
EEHMORVW	WHOMEVER
EEHMRSUX	EXHUMERS
EEHMSSTY	METHYSES
EEHNNORT	ENTHRONE
EEHNNOSS	SHONEENS
EEHNNPPU	UNHEPPEN
EEHNNSSS	NESHNESS
EEHNNSTU	UNNETHES
EEHNOORS	HONOREES
EEHNOPRU	HEREUPON
EEHNOPST	POSHTEEN
	POTHEENS
EEHNOPTY	HYPNOTEE
	NEOPHYTE
EEHNORSS	SENHORES
EEHNORST	HONESTER
EEHNORSW	HERONSEW
	NOWHERES
EEHNORTU	HEREUNTO
EEHNORTV	OVERHENT
EEHNOSST	ETHNOSES
EEHNPRSU	UNSPHERE
EEHNRTTU	UNTETHER
EEHNSSTU	ENTHUSES
EEHNSSTV	SEVENTHS
EEHOOPRS	OOSPHERE
EEHOOPRV	OVERHOPE
EEHOOPSW	WHOOPEES
EEHOORSV	OVERSHOE
EEHOOSST	TOESHOES
EEHOOTTY	EYETOOTH
EEHOPPRY	HYPEROPE
EEHOPPSW	PEEPSHOW
EEHOPRSU	EUPHROES
EEHOPRVY	OVERHYPE
EEHOPSST	HEPTOSES
EEHORRSV	HOVERERS
EEHORRSW	SHOWERER
EEHORRTX	EXHORTER
EEHORSSU	REHOUSES
EEHORSVW	WHOSEVER
EEHORTTU	THEREOUT
EEHORTUW	WHEREOUT
EEHOSSTY	EYESHOTS
EEHPRSST	HEPSTERS
	SPERTHES

EEHPRSTY	PHYSETER
EEHRRSTW	WHERRETS
EEHRSSSU	RHESUSES
	USHERESS
EEHRSSTW	WERSHEST
EEHRSTTW	WHETTERS
EEHSSTUY	SHUTEYES
EEIIKKLT	KITELIKE
EEIIKLLN	LINELIKE
EEIIKLLR	LIKELIER
EEIIKLLT	TILELIKE
EEIIKLLV	VEILLIKE
EEIIKLNP	PINELIKE
EEIIKLNV	VEINLIKE
EEIIKLPP	PIPELIKE
EEIIKLRW	WIRELIKE
EEIIKLSV	VISELIKE
EEIIKLSW	LIKEWISE
EEIILLMM	MILLIEME
EEIILLMT	MELILITE
EEIILLOP	EOLIPILE
EEIILLRV	LIVELIER
EEIILMNT	ILMENITE
	MELINITE
	TIMELINE
EEIILMRT	TIMELIER
EEIILMSS	EMISSILE
EEIILNPP	PIPELINE
EEIILNST	LENITIES
EEIILNTV	LENITIVE
EEIILORS	OILERIES
EEIILRST	TILERIES
EEIILRSV	LIVERIES
EEIILRSW	WISELIER
EEIILSTV	LEVITIES
	VEILIEST
EEIILSTW	LEWISITE
EEIIMMTT	MIMETITE
EEIIMNOT	MEIONITE
EEIIMNST	ENMITIES
EEIIMOST	MOIETIES
EEIIMPRS	RIEMPIES
EEIIMRSS	MISERIES
EEIIMRTZ	ITEMIZER
EEIIMSST	ITEMISES
EEIIMSSV	EMISSIVE
EEIIMSTZ	ITEMIZES
EEIINNST	EINSTEIN
	NINETIES
EEIINORT	ERIONITE
EEIINPPR	PIPERINE
EEIINPRS	PINERIES
EEIINPRV	VIPERINE
EEIINRRV	RIVERINE
EEIINRSS	RESINISE
	SIRENISE
EEIINRST	ERINITES
	NITERIES
EEIINRSV	VINERIES
EEIINRSW	SINEWIER
	WINERIES
EEIINRSZ	RESINIZE
	SIRENIZE
EEIINRTT	INTERTIE
	RETINITE
EEIINRTV	REINVITE
EEIINSST	SIENITES
EEIINSSV	INESSIVE
EEIINSSW	EISWEINS
EEIINSTT	ENTITIES
EEIINSTV	INVITEES
	VEINIEST
EEIIOPTZ	EPIZOITE
EEIIORSS	OSIERIES
EEIIPRSX	EXPIRIES
EEIIPRTT	EPITRITE
EEIIQSTU	EQUITIES
EEIIQTUV	QUIETIVE
EEIIRRSV	RIVIERES
EEIIRRTV	TIRRIVEE
EEIIRSTV	VERITIES
EEIISSTV	VISITEES
EEIISTVW	VIEWIEST
EEIJKRST	JERKIEST
EEIJLMSS	MEJLISES
EEIJLNNU	JULIENNE
EEIJLNRT	JETLINER
EEIJLNUV	JUVENILE
EEIJMMST	JEMMIEST
EEIJNNOR	ENJOINER
EEIJNRRU	REINJURE
EEIJSTTT	JETTIEST
EEIKLLRS	SKELLIER
EEIKLLRY	KYRIELLE
EEIKLLSS	SKELLIES
EEIKLMST	STEMLIKE
EEIKLNOS	NOSELIKE
EEIKLNOV	OVENLIKE
EEIKLNRU	RUNELIKE
EEIKLNSS	LIKENESS
EEIKLNST	NESTLIKE
EEIKLNSY	KEYLINES
EEIKLNTT	TENTLIKE
EEIKLOPP	POPELIKE
EEIKLOPR	ROPELIKE
EEIKLOPT	POETLIKE
EEIKLORS	ROSELIKE
EEIKLORT	LORIKEET
EEIKLPST	PIKELETS
	SPIKELET
	STEPLIKE
EEIKLRST	TRISKELE
EEIKLSTV	VESTLIKE
EEIKMPSS	MISKEEPS
EEIKMRSS	KERMISES
EEIKNORS	KEROSINE
EEIKNORV	REINVOKE
EEIKNPSY	PINKEYES
EEIKNRRT	TINKERER
EEIKNRST	KERNITES
EEIKNSWY	EYEWINKS
EEIKOQUV	EQUIVOKE
EEIKORSU	EUROKIES
EEIKPPRR	KIPPERER
EEIKPRST	PERKIEST
EEIKPSST	PESKIEST
EEIKRRSS	SKERRIES
EEIKRRST	RESTRIKE
EEIKRSST	KEISTERS
	KIESTERS
EEIKSSTY	SKIEYEST
EEIKSTTT	TEKTITES
EEILLMPR	IMPELLER
EEILLMRS	SMELLIER
EEILLMRU	REILLUME
EEILLMSS	LIMELESS
EEILLMST	MELLITES
EEILLNOR	LONELIER
EEILLNPS	SPINELLE
EEILLNSS	LINELESS
EEILLNSY	SENILELY
EEILLNVV	VENVILLE
EEILLOOP	EOLOPILE
EEILLORS	ORSEILLE
EEILLORV	LOVELIER
EEILLOSV	LOVELIES
EEILLPSS	ELLIPSES
	PILELESS
EEILLPSY	SLEEPILY
EEILLRSS	LEISLERS
EEILLRST	TREILLES
EEILLSSS	ISLELESS
EEILLSSV	VEILLESS
EEILLSTV	EVILLEST
EEILLSTW	WELLSITE
EEILLTVY	VELLEITY
EEILLVWY	WEEVILLY
EEILMNNO	LIMONENE
EEILMNNS	LINESMEN
EEILMNNU	ENLUMINE
EEILMNOP	PEMOLINE
EEILMNOR	LEMONIER
EEILMNRS	ERMELINS
EEILMNRU	LEMURINE
	RELUMINE
EEILMNSS	ISLESMEN
EEILMNSU	SELENIUM
	SEMILUNE
EEILMNSY	MYELINES
EEILMOPS	POLEMISE
EEILMOPZ	POLEMIZE
EEILMORT	MOTELIER
EEILMOST	MESOLITE
	MISLETOE
EEILMPST	IMPLETES
EEILMPSX	IMPLEXES
EEILMQTU	MIQUELET
EEILMRST	TERMLIES
EEILMRSV	VERMEILS
EEILMSST	TIMELESS
EEILMSTT	MELTIEST
EEILMSUV	EMULSIVE
EEILNNOT	NONELITE
EEILNNST	LENIENTS
	SENTINEL
EEILNNSV	ENLIVENS
EEILNOPR	LEPORINE
EEILNORS	ELOINERS
EEILNOST	NOSELITE
EEILNOSV	NOVELISE
EEILNOVV	LOVEVINE
EEILNOVZ	NOVELIZE
EEILNPPZ	ZEPPELIN
EEILNPRS	PILSENER
EEILNPRU	PERILUNE
EEILNPRV	REPLEVIN
EEILNPST	PENLITES
	PLENTIES
EEILNQUY	EQUINELY
EEILNRSS	REINLESS
EEILNRST	ENLISTER
	LISTENER
	REENLIST
	SILENTER
EEILNRSV	LIVENERS
	SNIVELER
EEILNRTT	NETTLIER
EEILNRTY	ENTIRELY
	LIENTERY
EEILNRUV	UNVEILER
EEILNSST	SETLINES
EEILNSSV	EVILNESS
	LIVENESS
	VEINLESS
	VILENESS
EEILNSSW	WINELESS
EEILNSTT	ENTITLES
EEILNSTV	VEINLETS
EEILNSUV	VEINULES
EEILNTUV	VEINULET
EEILOPRS	PELORIES
EEILOPST	PETIOLES
EEILORRT	LOITERER
EEILORRV	OVERLIER
EEILORRW	LOWERIER
EEILORST	LITEROSE
	TROELIES
EEILORSV	OVERLIES
	RELIEVOS
	VOLERIES
EEILORSW	OWLERIES
EEILORVV	OVERLIVE
	OVERVEIL
EEILOSST	ESTOILES
EEILOSTW	OWELTIES
EEILOSTZ	ZEOLITES
EEILOSVW	VOWELISE
EEILOTTT	TOILETTE
EEILOVWZ	VOWELIZE
EEILPPSS	PIPELESS
EEILPPSY	EPILEPSY
EEILPRRS	REPLIERS
EEILPRSS	SPIELERS
EEILPRST	EPISTLER
	PELTRIES
	PERLITES
	REPTILES
EEILPRSU	SUPERLIE
EEILPRSV	PRELIVES
EEILPSSS	PELISSES
EEILPSST	EPISTLES
EEILPSSU	EPULISES
EEILPSSV	PELVISES
EEILPSTY	EPISTYLE
EEILQRSU	RELIQUES
EEILRRSV	RELIVERS
	RESILVER
	REVILERS
	SILVERER
	SLIVERER
EEILRRTT	LITTERER
EEILRSST	LEISTERS
	RITELESS
	TIRELESS
EEILRSSU	LEISURES
EEILRSSV	SERVILES
EEILRSSW	WIRELESS
EEILRSTT	RETITLES
EEILSSTW	WITELESS
EEILSSTX	EXITLESS
	SEXTILES
EEILSSVW	VIEWLESS
EEILSSVX	SILVEXES
EEILSTTX	TEXTILES
EEILSTUX	ULEXITES
EEILSTVY	STIEVELY
EEIMMNRS	IMMENSER
EEIMMORS	MEMORIES
	MEMORISE
EEIMMORZ	MEMORIZE
EEIMMOST	SOMETIME
EEIMMRSS	IMMERSES
EEIMMRST	MERISTEM
	MIMESTER
	MISMETRE
	STEMMIER
EEIMMRSU	EUMERISM
EEIMMRTT	TERMTIME
EEIMMSSS	MISSEEMS
EEIMMSST	MISMEETS
EEIMMSTU	SEMIMUTE
EEIMNNOS	NOMINEES
EEIMNNRS	REINSMEN
EEIMNOPS	EPISEMON
EEIMNORS	EMERSION
EEIMNORT	TIMONEER
EEIMNORV	OVERMINE
	VOMERINE
EEIMNOST	MONETISE
	SEMITONE

EEIMNOTX	XENOTIME
EEIMNOTZ	MONETIZE
	ZONETIME
EEIMNPRS	SPERMINE
EEIMNPRU	PERINEUM
EEIMNPRZ	PRIZEMEN
EEIMNPST	SEPIMENT
EEIMNQSU	MESQUINE
EEIMNRRT	TERMINER
EEIMNRRV	RIVERMEN
EEIMNRST	MISENTER
EEIMNRSV	MINEVERS
EEIMNRTU	MUTINEER
EEIMNRTV	VIREMENT
EEIMNSSS	MISSENSE
EEIMNSSW	MISWEENS
EEIMNSTT	MINETTES
EEIMNSTV	MISEVENT
EEIMOPRS	MOPERIES
	PROMISEE
	REIMPOSE
EEIMOPSS	EPISOMES
EEIMOPST	EPISTOME
	EPITOMES
	EPSOMITE
EEIMORSS	ISOMERES
EEIMORST	TIRESOME
EEIMORSZ	SIEROZEM
EEIMORTV	OVERTIME
EEIMORTX	OXIMETER
EEIMOSSS	SEMIOSES
EEIMOSSW	SOMEWISE
EEIMOSSX	EXOMISES
EEIMOTTT	TOTEMITE
EEIMPPRS	EPISPERM
EEIMPPST	PIPESTEM
EEIMPRRS	PREMIERS
	REPRIMES
	SIMPERER
EEIMPRSS	EMPRISES
	IMPRESES
	IMPRESSE
	MESPRISE
	PREMISES
	SPIREMES
EEIMPRST	EMPTIERS
EEIMPRSX	PREMIXES
EEIMPRSZ	EMPRIZES
	MESPRIZE
EEIMPSST	SEPTIMES
EEIMPSSY	EMPYESIS
EEIMPSTT	EMPTIEST
EEIMQRSU	REQUIEMS
EEIMQSTU	MESQUITE
EEIMQTUZ	MEZQUITE
EEIMRRST	MERRIEST
	MITERERS
	RIMESTER
	TRIREMES
EEIMRRTT	REMITTER
	TRIMETER
EEIMRSST	MEISTERS
	MISSTEER
	TRISEMES
EEIMRSTT	EMITTERS
	TERMITES
EEIMRSTU	EMERITUS
EEIMRTTY	TEMERITY
EEIMSSST	MESSIEST
	METISSES
EEINNNPS	PENNINES
EEINNOPS	PENSIONE
EEINNPTT	PENITENT
EEINNRST	INTENSER
	INTERNES
EEINNRSU	NEURINES
EEINNRSV	INNERVES
	NERVINES
EEINNRTT	RENITENT
EEINNRTV	INVENTER
	REINVENT
EEINNRUX	XENURINE
EEINNSST	TENNISES
EEINNSTT	SENTIENT
EEINNSTW	ENTWINES
	WENNIEST
EEINNSTZ	NETIZENS
EEINOOPT	OPTIONEE
EEINOPPR	PEPERINO
	PEPERONI
EEINOPRS	ISOPRENE
	PIONEERS
EEINOPTY	EYEPOINT
EEINORRR	ORNERIER
EEINORRT	REORIENT
EEINORSS	ESSOINER
EEINORST	ONERIEST
	SEROTINE
EEINORSV	EVERSION
EEINORTT	TENORITE
EEINORTX	EXERTION
EEINOSSS	ENOSISES
	NOESISES
EEINOSST	ESSONITE
EEINOSTT	NOISETTE
	TEOSINTE
EEINPPSS	PEPSINES
EEINPRRS	PRERINSE
	REPINERS
	RIPENERS
EEINPRSS	EREPSINS
	RIPENESS
EEINPRSU	PENURIES
	RESUPINE
EEINPRTU	PREUNITE
EEINPRTX	INEXPERT
EEINPSST	PENTISES
EEINPSTT	INEPTEST
	SPINETTE
EEINQRRU	ENQUIRER
EEINQRSU	ENQUIRES
	INQUERES
	SQUIREEN
EEINQSTU	QUIETENS
EEINQSUY	QUEYNIES
EEINRRSS	RESINERS
EEINRRST	INSERTER
	REINSERT
	REINTERS
	RENTIERS
	TERRINES
EEINRRSU	REINSURE
EEINRRSV	VERNIERS
EEINRRTU	REUNITER
EEINRRTV	INVERTER
EEINRRTW	WINTERER
EEINRRTX	INTERREX
EEINRSST	INTERESS
	SENTRIES
	TRENISES
EEINRSSU	ENURESIS
EEINRSSV	INVERSES
	VERSINES
EEINRSTT	INERTEST
	INSETTER
	INTEREST
	STERNITE
	TRIENTES
EEINRSTU	ESURIENT
	NEURITES
	RETINUES
	REUNITES
EEINRSTV	NERVIEST
	REINVEST
	SERVIENT
	SIRVENTE
EEINRSTX	INTERSEX
EEINRSTY	SERENITY
EEINRSUV	UNIVERSE
EEINRSVX	VERNIXES
EEINRSWW	NEWSWIRE
EEINRTTY	ENTIRETY
	ETERNITY
EEINSSST	SESTINES
EEINSSSW	WISENESS
EEINSSSX	SEXINESS
EEINSSTW	NEWSIEST
EEINSSTX	SIXTEENS
EEINSSTY	SYENITES
EEINSSUX	UNISEXES
EEINSTTT	NETTIEST
	TENTIEST
EEINSTTW	TENTWISE
	TWENTIES
EEINSTTX	EXISTENT
EEIOPPRS	EPISPORE
	POPERIES
EEIOPPST	EPITOPES
EEIOPRRS	ROPERIES
EEIOPRRT	PORTIERE
EEIOPRRV	OVERRIPE
EEIOPRST	POETISER
	POETRIES
EEIOPRTZ	POETIZER
EEIOPSST	POETISES
EEIOPSTZ	POETIZES
EEIORRRS	ORRERIES
EEIORRSS	ROSERIES
	ROSIERES
EEIORRTV	OVERTIRE
EEIORRTW	TOWERIER
EEIORRTX	EXTERIOR
EEIORRUV	OUVRIERE
EEIORSST	EROTESIS
EEIORSSX	OREXISES
EEIORSTZ	EROTIZES
EEIORSVW	OVERWISE
EEIORSVZ	OVERSIZE
EEIORVVW	OVERVIEW
EEIORVWW	WIREWOVE
EEIPPPRR	PREPPIER
EEIPPPRS	PREPPIES
EEIPPPST	PEPPIEST
EEIPPQRU	EQUIPPER
EEIPPRRS	PERSPIRE
EEIPPRRT	PERIPTER
EEIPPRTY	PERIPETY
EEIPPRTZ	PEPTIZER
EEIPPSST	PEPTISES
EEIPPSTT	PIPETTES
EEIPPSTZ	PEPTIZES
EEIPQRSU	PERIQUES
	REEQUIPS
	REPIQUES
EEIPRRRS	PERRIERS
EEIPRRSS	PRISERES
	REPRISES
	RESPIRES
EEIPRRSV	REPRIVES
EEIPRRSX	EXPIRERS
EEIPRRSZ	REPRIZES
EEIPRRTT	PRETERIT
	PRETTIER
EEIPRSSS	PRESSIES
EEIPRSST	RESPITES
EEIPRSSV	PREVISES
EEIPRSTT	PRETTIES
EEIPRSTX	PREEXIST
EEIPRSTY	PERSEITY
	YPERITES
EEIPRSVW	PREVIEWS
EEIPRSZZ	PREZZIES
EEIPRTUV	ERUPTIVE
EEIPSSSS	SPEISSES
EEIPSSTT	PESTIEST
EEIPSSTW	SPEWIEST
	STEPWISE
EEIPSTTT	PETTIEST
EEIQRRRU	REQUIRER
EEIQRRSU	QUERIERS
	REQUIRES
EEIQRRTU	REQUITER
EEIQRRUV	QUIVERER
	VERQUIRE
EEIQRSSU	ESQUIRES
EEIQRSTU	QUIETERS
	REQUITES
EEIQRSTW	QWERTIES
EEIQRTUY	QUEERITY
EEIQSSSU	ESQUISSE
EEIQSTTU	QUIETEST
EEIRRRST	RETIRERS
	TERRIERS
EEIRRRTW	REWRITER
EEIRRSST	RESISTER
	TRESSIER
EEIRRSSU	REISSUER
EEIRRSSV	REVERSIS
	REVISERS
EEIRRSTV	RESTRIVE
	REVERIST
	RIVERETS
	RIVETERS
EEIRRSTW	REWRITES
EEIRRSVV	REVIVERS
EEIRRTTT	TITTERER
EEIRSSSU	REISSUES
	SEISURES
EEIRSSSV	IVRESSES
EEIRSSTT	RESTIEST
EEIRSSTU	SURETIES
EEIRSSTV	SIEVERTS
	TREVISES
	VESTRIES
EEIRSSUZ	SEIZURES
EEIRSTTU	SUETTIER
EEIRSTVV	VETIVERS
EEIRSTVY	SEVERITY
EEIRTTTZ	TERZETTI
EEIRTTVV	VETIVERT
EEISSSTV	VITESSES
EEISSTTT	TESTIEST
EEISSTTU	SUETIEST
EEISSTTV	STIEVEST
EEISSTTW	STEWIEST
EEISSTTZ	ZESTIEST
EEISTTTX	TETTIXES
EEISTUXZ	ZEUXITES
EEJJLNUY	JEJUNELY
EEJKMOOS	JOKESOME
EEJKNRTU	JUNKETER
EEJKORST	JOKESTER
EEJLLMSU	JUMELLES
EEJLLORY	JOLLEYER
EEJLPSTU	PULSEJET
EEJNOORS	REJONEOS
EEJNORSY	ENJOYERS
	REENJOYS
EEJORSST	RESOJETS
EEJPRRRU	PERJURER

EEJPRRSU	PERJURES
EEJPRSTU	SUPERJET
EEJQRRSU	JERQUERS
EEKKORWW	WORKWEEK
EEKKOSTV	VETKOEKS
EEKKRRST	TREKKERS
EEKLLNRY	KERNELLY
EEKLLNSV	KNEVELLS
EEKLLSUU	UKULELES
EEKLNNNU	UNKENNEL
EEKLNOSS	KEELSONS
EEKLNOST	SKELETON
EEKLNOSV	VELSKOEN
EEKLOSSU	LEUKOSES
EEKLOSSY	YOKELESS
EEKLRSST	KESTRELS
	SKELTERS
EEKNOPRS	RESPOKEN
EEKNORTY	KEYNOTER
EEKNOSTY	KEYNOTES
	KEYSTONE
EEKNSSST	KNESSETS
EEKNSSSW	SKEWNESS
EEKNSSTU	NETSUKES
EEKOORST	KREOSOTE
EEKOPRTV	OVERKEPT
EEKOPSTU	OUTKEEPS
EEKORRSV	REVOKERS
EEKORSST	RESTOKES
EEKORSTV	OVERKEST
EEKRRSUZ	KREUZERS
EEKRRTUZ	KREUTZER
EEKRSSTY	KEYSTERS
EELLLLMP	PELLMELL
EELLMORS	MORELLES
EELLMORW	MELLOWER
EELLMPTU	PLUMELET
EELLMRSS	SMELLERS
EELLMRSV	VERMELLS
EELLNORR	ENROLLER
	REENROLL
EELLNOUV	NOUVELLE
EELLNPRU	PRUNELLE
EELLNRSU	SULLENER
EELLNSSS	LENSLESS
EELLNSST	SNELLEST
EELLNSSW	WELLNESS
EELLNSTU	ENTELLUS
EELLNSUV	UNLEVELS
EELLOPSS	ELLOPSES
	POLELESS
EELLORRR	REROLLER
EELLORSS	ROSELLES
EELLORST	SOLLERET
EELLORSV	OVERSELL
EELLORSZ	ROZELLES
EELLORTX	EXTOLLER
EELLORVY	VOLLEYER
EELLORWY	YELLOWER
EELLOSSS	SOLELESS
EELLOSSV	LOVELESS
EELLOSUV	LEVULOSE
EELLPRSS	PRESELLS
	RESPELLS
	SPELLERS
EELLQRSU	QUELLERS
EELLRSSU	RULELESS
EELLRSSW	SWELLERS
EELLSSTU	TELLUSES
EELLSSTW	SWELLEST
EELLSTVY	SVELTELY
EELMMPSU	EMPLUMES
EELMMPUX	EXEMPLUM
EELMNOOS	LONESOME
	OENOMELS
EELMNORS	SOLEMNER
EELMNSUY	UNSEEMLY
EELMNTTU	TEMULENT
EELMNTUY	UNMEETLY
EELMOOSV	LOVESOME
EELMOPRS	PLEROMES
EELMOPRY	EMPLOYER
	REEMPLOY
EELMOPST	LEPTOMES
EELMOPSY	EMPLOYES
	POLYSEME
EELMORST	MOLESTER
EELMORSW	EELWORMS
EELMORTV	OVERMELT
EELMORTY	MOTLEYER
	REMOTELY
EELMOSSV	MOVELESS
EELMOTVW	TWELVEMO
EELMPPRU	EMPURPLE
EELMPSST	SEMPLEST
	STEMPELS
	STEMPLES
EELMPSTT	TEMPLETS
EELMRRTU	MURRELET
EELMRSST	RESMELTS
	SMELTERS
	TERMLESS
EELMRSTY	SMELTERY
EELMRTUX	LUXMETER
EELMSSST	STEMLESS
EELMSSTT	STEMLETS
EELNNOSS	LONENESS
EELNNRTU	TUNNELER
EELNNUVY	UNEVENLY
EELNOORS	LOOSENER
EELNOPPU	UNPEOPLE
EELNOPRT	PETRONEL
EELNOPSV	ENVELOPS
EELNOPSY	POLYENES
EELNOPTY	POLYTENE
EELNOQTU	ELOQUENT
EELNORST	ENTRESOL
EELNORTT	TELETRON
EELNORTV	OVERLENT
EELNOSSS	NOSELESS
	SOLENESS
EELNOSST	NOTELESS
	TONELESS
EELNOSSU	SELENOUS
EELNOSSY	ESLOYNES
EELNOSSZ	ZONELESS
EELNOSTT	NOTELETS
EELNOSTU	TOLUENES
EELNOSUV	VENULOSE
EELNOTVV	EVOLVENT
EELNRSST	NESTLERS
	SLENTERS
EELNRSTT	LETTERNS
	NETTLERS
EELNRSUV	NERVULES
EELNSSSW	NEWSLESS
EELNSSTT	TENTLESS
EELNSSTU	TUNELESS
	UNSTEELS
EELNSSTV	VENTLESS
EELNSSTY	ENSTYLES
EELNSSUV	UNSELVES
EELNSTTU	LUNETTES
	UNSETTLE
EELOORVV	OVERLOVE
EELOPPRS	PEOPLERS
EELOPPSS	PEPLOSES
	POPELESS
EELOPPST	ESTOPPEL
EELOPRRX	EXPLORER
EELOPRSX	EXPLORES
EELOPRTT	TELEPORT
EELOPSST	POETLESS
EELOPSTU	EELPOUTS
	OUTSLEEP
	SLEEPOUT
EELOQRUY	REQUOYLE
EELORRSV	RESOLVER
EELORRTV	REVOLTER
EELORRTW	TROWELER
EELORRUV	OVERRULE
EELORRVV	REVOLVER
EELORSSS	ROSELESS
EELORSST	SOLERETS
EELORSSV	RESOLVES
EELORSTT	LORETTES
EELORSTU	RESOLUTE
EELORSTV	OVERLETS
EELORSVV	EVOLVERS
	REVOLVES
EELORTTU	ROULETTE
EELORTUV	REVOLUTE
	TRUELOVE
EELOSSST	OSSELETS
EELOSSSU	SOLEUSES
EELOSSTT	TELEOSTS
EELOSSTU	SETULOSE
EELOSSTV	VOTELESS
EELOSTTX	SEXTOLET
EELOSTUV	EVOLUTES
	VELOUTES
EELPPSSU	PEPLUSES
EELPPSTU	SEPTUPLE
EELPQRSU	PREQUELS
EELPRRSU	REPULSER
EELPRSST	SPELTERS
EELPRSSU	REPULSES
EELPRSTY	PEYTRELS
EELPRSTZ	PRETZELS
EELPRSUX	PLEXURES
EELPRTXY	EXPERTLY
EELPSSTZ	SPELTZES
EELPSSUX	EXPULSES
	PLEXUSES
EELPSTUX	SEXTUPLE
EELRRSTW	WRESTLER
EELRSSST	RESTLESS
	TRESSELS
EELRSSTT	SETTLERS
	STERLETS
	TRESTLES
EELRSSTU	STREUSEL
EELRSSTW	SWELTERS
	WRESTLES
EELRSSTY	RESTYLES
	TYRELESS
EELRSSTZ	SELTZERS
EELRSTWY	WESTERLY
EELSSSTV	VESTLESS
EELSSSTZ	ZESTLESS
EELSSTTV	SVELTEST
EELSSTTX	TEXTLESS
EELSSTUY	EUSTYLES
EEMMNNOY	MONEYMEN
EEMMNOOP	MENOPOME
EEMMNOST	MEMENTOS
EEMMNOTV	MOVEMENT
EEMMNRRY	MERRYMEN
EEMMOORS	MEROSOME
EEMMOOSS	MESOSOME
EEMMOSSU	MOUSMEES
EEMMRSST	STEMMERS
EEMMRSTY	STEMMERY
EEMMRTUX	EXTREMUM
EEMNNOPR	PRENOMEN
EEMNNOPW	PENWOMEN
EEMNNOSV	ENVENOMS
EEMNOOSS	SOMEONES
EEMNOOSY	MOONEYES
EEMNOPRS	PROSEMEN
EEMNORRS	SERMONER
EEMNORST	SERMONET
	STOREMEN
EEMNORSU	MOUNSEER
EEMNORSV	OVERSMEN
	VENOMERS
EEMNORSY	MONEYERS
EEMNORTU	ROUTEMEN
EEMNPRSS	PRESSMEN
EEMNPRSU	SUPERMEN
EEMNPRTU	ERUMPENT
	UNTEMPER
EEMNRSTU	MUENSTER
EEMNRSTW	TREWSMEN
EEMNSSTU	MUTENESS
	TENESMUS
EEMNSTTV	VESTMENT
EEMOORRT	OROMETER
EEMOORRV	MOREOVER
EEMOORTT	ROOMETTE
EEMOOSSX	EXOSMOSE
EEMOPRRS	EMPERORS
	PREMORSE
EEMOPRSV	PREMOVES
EEMOPRSW	EMPOWERS
EEMOQRSU	MORESQUE
EEMOQTTU	MOQUETTE
EEMORRSS	REMORSES
EEMORRSU	UROMERES
EEMORRSV	REMOVERS
EEMORRTU	MOUTERER
	OUTREMER
EEMORSST	SOMERSET
EEMORSTT	REMOTEST
EEMORSTU	TEMEROUS
EEMOSSST	MESTESOS
EEMOTTTU	TEETOTUM
EEMOTTZZ	MOZZETTE
EEMPPRST	PREEMPTS
EEMPRRSU	PRESUMER
	SUPREMER
EEMPRSST	SEMPSTER
EEMPRSSU	PRESUMES
	SUPREMES
EEMPRSTT	TEMPTERS
EEMPRSTU	PERMUTES
EEMPSSTT	TEMPESTS
EEMPSSTY	EMPTYSES
EEMRRSSU	RESUMERS
EEMRRSTU	MUSTERER
EEMRRSUU	EREMURUS
	REMUEURS
EEMRRTTU	MUTTERER
EEMSSTTU	MUSETTES
EENNNOSS	NONSENSE
EENNNOTV	NONEVENT
EENNNPTY	TENPENNY
EENNOORT	ROTENONE
EENNOPSS	OPENNESS
EENNOPTX	EXPONENT
EENNORRW	RENOWNER
EENNORST	ENTERONS
	TENONERS
EENNORSU	NEURONES
EENNOSTT	NONETTES
EENNQSUU	UNQUEENS
EENNRSUV	UNNERVES
EENNSSSU	UNSENSES
EENNSSTX	NEXTNESS
EENOORST	OESTRONE

	ROESTONE
EENOORTV	OVERTONE
EENOPPRS	PREPONES
	PROPENES
	PROPENSE
EENOPPST	PEPTONES
EENOPRSS	RESPONSE
EENOPRST	PROTENSE
EENOPRSU	PERONEUS
EENOPRTT	ENTREPOT
EENOPRTU	OUTPREEN
EENOPRXY	PYROXENE
EENOPSST	PENTOSES
	POSTEENS
EENOPSTT	POSTTEEN
	POTTEENS
EENOPSTY	NEOTYPES
EENORRSV	OVERRENS
EENORRTT	ROTTENER
EENORSSS	SORENESS
EENORSST	ESTRONES
EENORSSU	NEUROSES
EENORSTT	ONSETTER
EENORSTV	OVERNETS
EENORSTX	EXTENSOR
EENORSVW	OVERSEWN
EENORTVW	OVERWENT
EENOSSST	STENOSES
EENOSSSY	ESSOYNES
EENOSTTT	TONETTES
EENPPRST	PERPENTS
EENPRSST	PENSTERS
	PERTNESS
	PRESENTS
	SERPENTS
EENPRSSU	PURENESS
EENPRSTT	STREPENT
EENPRSTV	PREVENTS
EENPRTUX	UNEXPERT
EENPSSSU	SUSPENSE
EENPSSTY	STEPNEYS
EENPSTTU	PETUNTSE
EENPTTUZ	PETUNTZE
EENQSSTU	SEQUENTS
EENRRRTU	RETURNER
EENRRSSU	ENSURERS
EENRRSTV	RENVERST
EENRRSUV	NERVURES
EENRRTUV	VENTURER
EENRSSSU	SURENESS
EENRSSTT	STERNEST
	TESTERNS
EENRSSTU	TRUENESS
EENRSSTW	WESTERNS
EENRSSTY	STYRENES
EENRSTUV	VENTURES
EEOOPPRS	REOPPOSE
EEOOPRST	PROTEOSE
EEOOPRSX	EXOSPORE
EEOOPRTZ	ZOETROPE
EEOORRVW	OVERWORE
EEOORTVV	OVERVOTE
EEOOSSST	OSTEOSES
EEOPPRRR	PROPERER
EEOPPRSS	PORPESSE
	PREPOSES
EEOPPSTU	OUTPEEPS
EEOPRRRT	REPORTER
EEOPRRRV	REPROVER
EEOPRRSS	REPOSERS
EEOPRRSU	REPOSURE
EEOPRRSV	REPROVES
EEOPRRSW	REPOWERS
EEOPRRTT	POTTERER
EEOPRRTV	OVERPERT
EEOPRRTX	EXPORTER
	REEXPORT
EEOPRSSS	ESPRESSO
EEOPRSST	PORTESSE
EEOPRSSU	ESPOUSER
	REPOUSSE
EEOPRSSX	EXPOSERS
	EXPRESSO
EEOPRSTT	PROETTES
	TREETOPS
EEOPRSTU	OUTPEERS
EEOPRSTV	OVERSTEP
EEOPRSTY	SEROTYPE
EEOPRSUX	EXPOSURE
EEOPRTVY	OVERTYPE
EEOPSSSU	ESPOUSES
	POSEUSES
EEOPSSTW	SWEETSOP
EEOPSSTY	EYESPOTS
EEOPSTUW	OUTWEEPS
EEOQRSTU	REQUOTES
EEOQRTTU	ROQUETTE
EEORRRST	RESORTER
	RESTORER
	RETRORSE
EEORRRTT	RETORTER
EEORRSST	RESTORES
EEORRSSV	REVERSOS
EEORRSTU	REROUTES
EEORRSTV	EVERTORS
	RESTROVE
EEORRSTX	EXTRORSE
EEORRSTY	OYSTERER
EEORRSUV	OVERSURE
EEORRTTT	TOTTERER
EEORRTTX	EXTORTER
EEORRTUV	OVERTURE
	TROUVERE
EEORSSST	OSSETERS
EEORSSTT	ROSETTES
EEORSSTV	ESTOVERS
	OVERSETS
EEORSSUV	OVERUSES
EEORSSVW	OVERSEWS
EEORSTTU	OUTSTEER
EEORSTUV	OUTSERVE
EEORSTVW	OVERWETS
EEORSTVX	VORTEXES
EEORTTTZ	TERZETTO
EEOSSSVW	VOWESSES
EEOSSTTT	SESTETTO
EEPPRSST	STEPPERS
EEPPRSTY	PRETYPES
EEPPSSUW	UPSWEEPS
EEPQRRUU	PERRUQUE
EEPRRSSS	PRESSERS
EEPRRSST	PRESTERS
EEPRRSSU	PERUSERS
	PRESSURE
EEPRRSTV	PERVERTS
EEPRRSUU	REPURSUE
EEPRRSVY	REPRYVES
EEPRRTTU	PUTTERER
EEPRSSTT	PRETESTS
EEPRSSTX	SEXPERTS
EEPRSSUX	SUPERSEX
EEPRSTTU	UPSETTER
EEPRSTTX	PRETEXTS
EEPSSTTY	TYPESETS
EEQRSSTU	QUESTERS
	REQUESTS
EERRSSST	RESTRESS
EERRSSTU	TRESSURE
EERRSSTW	STREWERS
	WRESTERS
EERRSSVW	SWERVERS
EERRSTTU	REUTTERS
	UTTERERS
EERRSTUV	VESTURER
EERRSTVY	REVESTRY
EERRSUVY	RESURVEY
EERSSSST	STRESSES
EERSSSTU	ESTRUSES
EERSSSUY	SEYSURES
EERSSTTU	TRUSTEES
EERSSTUU	UTERUSES
EERSSTUV	VESTURES
EERSSUVW	SURVEWES
EERSTTTU	UTTEREST
EERSTTUX	TEXTURES
EESSSTTT	SESTETTS
EESSTTTX	SEXTETTS
EFFFGINO	FEOFFING
EFFFILRU	FLUFFIER
EFFFINOS	INFEOFFS
EFFFISTU	FUFFIEST
EFFFOORS	FEOFFORS
EFFGILRU	GRIEFFUL
EFFGINOR	OFFERING
EFFGINSU	EFFUSING
EFFGIRRU	GRUFFIER
EFFGRSTU	GRUFFEST
EFFHIILS	FILEFISH
EFFHIIRW	WHIFFIER
EFFHIISW	FISHWIFE
EFFHIITT	FIFTIETH
EFFHILRW	WHIFFLER
EFFHILSW	WHIFFLES
EFFHIRSS	SHERIFFS
EFFHIRSW	WHIFFERS
EFFHISTU	HUFFIEST
EFFHISTW	WHIFFETS
EFFHLLSU	SHELFFUL
EFFHLRSU	SHUFFLER
EFFHLSSU	SHUFFLES
EFFHOOOR	FOREHOOF
EFFHOORS	OFFSHORE
EFFIIMST	MIFFIEST
EFFIINRS	SNIFFIER
EFFIINSS	IFFINESS
EFFIINST	NIFFIEST
EFFIIPRS	SPIFFIER
EFFIISST	STIFFIES
EFFIKLLO	FOLKLIFE
EFFIKLRU	RUFFLIKE
EFFIKLSS	SKIFFLES
EFFILNRS	SNIFFLER
EFFILNSS	SNIFFLES
EFFILORT	FORELIFT
EFFILPRS	PIFFLERS
EFFILPRU	PLUFFIER
EFFILRRS	RIFFLERS
EFFILRRU	RUFFLIER
EFFILRSU	SIFFLEUR
EFFINOSU	EFFUSION
EFFINRSS	SNIFFERS
EFFINRSU	SNUFFIER
EFFINSST	STIFFENS
EFFIOPRS	PIFFEROS
EFFIORST	FORFEITS
EFFIORSX	FOXFIRES
EFFIOSTT	TOFFIEST
EFFIPSTU	PUFFIEST
EFFIQRSU	SQUIFFER
EFFIRSTT	TRIFFEST
EFFIRSTU	STUFFIER
EFFISSTT	STIFFEST
EFFISSUX	SUFFIXES
EFFLMNUU	UNMUFFLE
EFFLMRSU	MUFFLERS
EFFLNRSU	SNUFFLER
EFFLNRUU	UNRUFFLE
EFFLNSSU	SNUFFLES
EFFLOSSU	SOUFFLES
EFFLRRSU	RUFFLERS
EFFLRSTU	TRUFFLES
EFFNRSSU	SNUFFERS
EFFOOORT	FOREFOOT
EFFOORRS	OFFERORS
EFFOPRRS	PROFFERS
EFFORRST	TROFFERS
EFFORRUV	OVERRUFF
EFFRRSUU	FURFURES
EFFRSSTU	RESTUFFS
	STUFFERS
EFFSSSUU	SUFFUSES
EFGGGILN	FLEGGING
EFGGIINN	FEIGNING
EFGGILOS	SOLFEGGI
EFGGINRU	REFUGING
EFGGIORR	FROGGIER
EFGGIOST	FOGGIEST
EFGGIRRS	FRIGGERS
EFGGISTU	FUGGIEST
EFGGLORS	FLOGGERS
EFGGORRY	FROGGERY
EFGHHIIL	HIGHLIFE
EFGHIILS	FLEISHIG
EFGHILNS	FLESHING
	SHELFING
EFGHINRS	FRESHING
EFGHINRT	FRIGHTEN
EFGHIOSY	FOGEYISH
EFGHIPRT	PREFIGHT
EFGHIRST	FIGHTERS
	FREIGHTS
	REFIGHTS
EFGHNOTU	FOUGHTEN
EFGHORTU	REFOUGHT
EFGIIINS	IGNIFIES
EFGIILNR	REFILING
EFGIILNT	FILETING
EFGIILNU	FIGULINE
EFGIILRU	UGLIFIER
EFGIILSU	UGLIFIES
EFGIIMNS	MISFEIGN
EFGIINNR	ENFIRING
	INFRINGE
	REFINING
EFGIINNT	FEINTING
EFGIINNX	ENFIXING
EFGIINRR	FRINGIER
	REFIRING
EFGIINRU	FIGURINE
EFGIINRX	REFIXING
EFGIINRY	REIFYING
EFGIINRZ	FRIEZING
EFGIITUV	FUGITIVE
EFGIKLLU	GULFLIKE
EFGIKLOR	FROGLIKE
EFGIKNOR	FOREKING
EFGILLNO	LIFELONG
EFGILLNU	FUELLING
EFGILLUU	GUILEFUL
EFGILMOR	FILMGOER
EFGILNNS	FLENSING
EFGILNOR	FLORIGEN
EFGILNRS	FLINGERS
EFGILNRU	FERULING
EFGILNRY	FERLYING
	REFLYING
EFGILNSS	SELFINGS
EFGILNST	FELTINGS
EFGILNTT	FETTLING
EFGILNTW	LEFTWING

EFGILPRU	FIREPLUG
EFGILSST	GIFTLESS
EFGILSTU	GULFIEST
EFGIMNST	FIGMENTS
EFGIMOSY	FOGEYISM
EFGIMRUU	REFUGIUM
EFGINNNP	PFENNING
EFGINNPS	PFENNIGS
EFGINNRS	FERNINGS
EFGINORV	FORGIVEN
EFGINORW	FOREWING
EFGINPUY	PINGUEFY
EFGINRRY	FERRYING
	REFRYING
EFGINRSU	GUNFIRES
	REFUSING
EFGINRSW	SWERFING
EFGINRTT	FRETTING
EFGINRTU	FEUTRING
	REFUTING
EFGINRTY	GENTRIFY
EFGIOOST	GOOFIEST
EFGIOPTT	PETTIFOG
EFGIORRV	FORGIVER
EFGIORSV	FORGIVES
EFGIRRST	GRIFTERS
EFGIRRSU	FIGURERS
EFGLOOTY	FETOLOGY
EFGLOOVX	FOXGLOVE
EFGLORST	FROGLETS
EFGLRSUU	SURGEFUL
EFGLSSTU	SLUGFEST
EFGNOSST	SONGFEST
EFGNSSUU	FUNGUSES
EFGOORRS	FORGOERS
EFGORRSU	FERRUGOS
EFGORSTU	FOREGUTS
EFHHIRSS	FRESHISH
EFHIIKLS	FISHLIKE
EFHIILLT	HELILIFT
EFHIILNS	FISHLINE
EFHIILRT	FILTHIER
EFHIILST	TILEFISH
EFHIIMSU	HUMIFIES
EFHIINRS	FINISHER
	REFINISH
EFHIINSS	FINISHES
EFHIIPPS	PIPEFISH
EFHIIPRS	FIRESHIP
EFHIIRST	SHIFTIER
EFHIISST	FISHIEST
EFHIKLOO	HOOFLIKE
EFHILLSY	ELFISHLY
EFHILOPS	FISHPOLE
EFHILRSU	FLUSHIER
EFHILSSS	FISHLESS
EFHILTWY	WHITEFLY
EFHINNOT	FENTHION
EFHINSST	FISHNETS
EFHIOOOR	FORHOOIE
EFHIOPRS	FORESHIP
EFHIORRT	FROTHIER
EFHIORSS	ROSEFISH
EFHIORSV	OVERFISH
EFHIORTT	FORTIETH
EFHIPRSS	SERFSHIP
EFHIPRSU	FURPHIES
EFHIRRTU	THURIFER
EFHIRSST	SHIFTERS
EFHISSTU	SHUFTIES
EFHISSUW	HUSWIFES
EFHKLNOU	FUNKHOLE
EFHLLLSU	SHELLFUL
EFHLNORS	HORNFELS
EFHLNOUY	HONEYFUL
EFHLOOSS	HOOFLESS
EFHLOOSX	FOXHOLES
EFHLOPST	FLESHPOT
EFHLOPSU	HOPEFULS
EFHLORSY	HORSEFLY
EFHLOSSU	FLOUSHES
EFHLOSUU	HOUSEFUL
EFHLOSUY	HOUSEFLY
EFHLRSSU	FLUSHERS
EFHLSSTU	FLUSHEST
EFHLSTTW	TWELFTHS
EFHNORST	FORHENTS
EFHOORSW	FORESHOW
EFHORRTY	FROTHERY
EFHRRSTU	FURTHERS
EFHRSTTU	FURTHEST
EFIIILRV	VILIFIER
EFIIILSV	VILIFIES
EFIIIMNS	MINIFIES
EFIIINNT	INFINITE
EFIIINSV	VINIFIES
EFIIIRVV	VIVIFIER
EFIIISTX	FIXITIES
EFIIISVV	VIVIFIES
EFIIKLNT	FLINKITE
EFIIKLRS	FLISKIER
EFIIKNPR	FIREPINK
EFIIKRRS	FRISKIER
EFIILLNT	TEFILLIN
EFIILLRR	FRILLIER
EFIILLRS	FRILLIES
EFIILMRS	FLIMSIER
EFIILMSS	FLIMSIES
	MISFILES
EFIILMST	FILMIEST
EFIILNRT	FLINTIER
EFIILNTY	FELINITY
	FINITELY
EFIILOQU	FILIOQUE
EFIILRRT	FLIRTIER
EFIILRST	FILISTER
EFIILRSU	FUSILIER
EFIILSTT	FITLIEST
EFIIMMNS	FEMINISM
EFIIMNOS	FISNOMIE
	OMNIFIES
EFIIMNRR	INFIRMER
EFIIMNRS	MISINFER
EFIIMNST	FEMINIST
EFIIMNSU	MUNIFIES
EFIIMNTY	FEMINITY
EFIIMRRS	RIMFIRES
EFIIMRSS	MISFIRES
EFIINNOS	SINFONIE
EFIINNST	FINNIEST
EFIINORR	INFERIOR
EFIINORT	NOTIFIER
EFIINOST	NOTIFIES
EFIINPSV	FIVEPINS
EFIINPSX	SPINIFEX
EFIINRRT	FERRITIN
EFIINRST	SNIFTIER
EFIINRSU	UNIFIERS
EFIINRSY	RESINIFY
EFIINSTT	NIFTIEST
EFIINSUV	INFUSIVE
EFIIORSS	OSSIFIER
EFIIOSSS	OSSIFIES
EFIIPRRU	PURIFIER
EFIIPRST	SPITFIRE
EFIIPRSU	PURIFIES
EFIIPRTY	TYPIFIER
EFIIPSTY	TYPIFIES
EFIIRRST	FIRRIEST
EFIIRRTU	FRUITIER
EFIIRRZZ	FRIZZIER
EFIIRSTT	RIFTIEST
EFIIRTUV	FRUITIVE
EFIIRVVY	REVIVIFY
EFIISSTT	FISTIEST
EFIISTTW	WIFTIEST
EFIISTZZ	FIZZIEST
EFIJLORS	FRIJOLES
EFIJLOST	JETFOILS
EFIKKLLO	FOLKLIKE
EFIKKLOR	FORKLIKE
EFIKLLOT	LOFTLIKE
EFIKLLOW	WOLFLIKE
EFIKLMOR	FOREMILK
EFIKLNSU	FLUNKIES
EFIKLOOR	ROOFLIKE
EFIKLOOT	FOOTLIKE
EFIKLORS	FOLKSIER
EFIKLORW	LIFEWORK
EFIKLRSU	SURFLIKE
EFIKLRTU	TURFLIKE
EFIKLSTU	FLUKIEST
	LUTEFISK
EFIKNNOS	FINNESKO
EFIKNORS	FORESKIN
EFIKNRSU	REFUSNIK
EFIKNSTU	FUNKIEST
EFIKORRW	FIREWORK
EFIKORST	FORKIEST
EFIKRRSS	FRISKERS
EFIKRSST	FRISKETS
EFILLLNU	FLUELLIN
EFILLMSU	SMILEFUL
EFILLOOS	FOLIOLES
EFILLORV	OVERFILL
EFILLORW	LOWLIFER
EFILLOSW	LOWLIFES
EFILLRRS	FRILLERS
EFILLRUY	IREFULLY
EFILLSTY	STELLIFY
EFILLTUY	FUTILELY
EFILMNOS	FOILSMEN
EFILMNSU	FULMINES
EFILMOST	FILEMOTS
EFILMRSS	FIRMLESS
EFILMSSS	SELFISMS
EFILMSST	FILMSETS
	LEFTISMS
EFILMSUY	EMULSIFY
EFILNNTU	INFLUENT
EFILNOOR	ROOFLINE
EFILNORU	FLUORINE
EFILNOSU	NOISEFUL
EFILNOSX	FLEXIONS
EFILNRTT	FLITTERN
EFILNRYZ	FRENZILY
EFILNSUX	INFLUXES
EFILNUWY	UNWIFELY
EFILOOSS	FLOOSIES
EFILOOSZ	FLOOZIES
EFILOPPR	FLOPPIER
EFILOPPS	FLOPPIES
EFILOPRR	PROFILER
EFILOPRS	PROFILES
EFILORRU	FLOURIER
EFILORRV	FRIVOLER
EFILORSS	FLOSSIER
EFILORST	FLORIEST
	TREFOILS
EFILORTU	FLUORITE
EFILOSSS	FLOSSIES
EFILOSSX	SEXFOILS
EFILOSTT	LOFTIEST
EFILOSTU	OUTFLIES
EFILPPRS	FLIPPERS
EFILPPST	FLIPPEST
EFILPPSU	PIPEFULS
EFILPRTU	UPLIFTER
EFILPSTU	SPITEFUL
EFILRRST	FLIRTERS
	TRIFLERS
EFILRRSU	FLURRIES
EFILRRZZ	FRIZZLER
EFILRSST	RIFTLESS
	STIFLERS
EFILRSTT	FLITTERS
EFILRSTW	FEWTRILS
EFILRSTY	FLYTIERS
EFILRSVV	FLIVVERS
EFILRSZZ	FRIZZLES
EFILRTTU	FRUITLET
EFILSSST	SELFISTS
EFILSSTT	LEFTISTS
EFILSSTU	SULFITES
EFILSTTU	FLUTIEST
	FUTILEST
EFILSTTW	SWIFTLET
EFIMMRSU	FERMIUMS
EFIMNORR	INFORMER
	REINFORM
	RENIFORM
EFIMNORS	ENSIFORM
	FERMIONS
EFIMNRSS	FIRMNESS
EFIMNSTT	FITMENTS
EFIMOORR	FIREROOM
EFIMORRT	RETIFORM
EFIMORRW	FIREWORM
EFIMORST	SETIFORM
EFIMOSST	SEMISOFT
EFIMOSTT	OFTTIMES
EFIMPRRU	FRUMPIER
EFIMRSTU	FREMITUS
EFINNORS	INFERNOS
EFINNPSU	FINESPUN
EFINNSTU	FUNNIEST
EFINOPRS	FORPINES
EFINOPTX	PONTIFEX
EFINORRT	FRONTIER
EFINORSU	REFUSION
EFINORTY	RENOTIFY
EFINOSSX	FOXINESS
EFINOSSZ	FOZINESS
EFINOSTT	FISTNOTE
EFINRRRU	FURRINER
EFINRSST	SNIFTERS
EFINRSSU	INFUSERS
EFINRTTU	UNFITTER
EFIOOPST	POOFIEST
EFIOORST	ROOFIEST
EFIOOSST	FOOTSIES
EFIOOSTT	FOOTIEST
EFIOOSTW	WOOFIEST
EFIOPRRS	PORIFERS
EFIOPRRT	PROFITER
EFIOPRST	FIREPOTS
	PIEFORTS
	POSTFIRE
EFIORRST	FROSTIER
	ROTIFERS
EFIORRSW	FROWSIER
EFIORRTT	RETROFIT
EFIORRUZ	FROUZIER
EFIORRWZ	FROWZIER
EFIORSST	FOISTERS
EFIORSTU	FOUSTIER
	OUTFIRES
EFIORSTW	FROWIEST
EFIORTTU	REOUTFIT
EFIPPRRS	FRIPPERS

EFIPPRRY FRIPPERY
EFIPRRUY REPURIFY
EFIPRSST PRESIFTS
EFIPRSTU SUPERFIT
EFIPRSUX SUPERFIX
EFIPRTTY PRETTIFY
EFIRRRSU FURRIERS
EFIRRRUY FURRIERY
EFIRRSSU FRISEURS
FRISURES
EFIRRSTT FRITTERS
EFIRRSTU FRITURES
FRUITERS
FURRIEST
EFIRRSZZ FRIZZERS
EFIRRTUY FRUITERY
EFIRSSSU FISSURES
EFIRSSTU SURFEITS
SURFIEST
EFIRSSTW SWIFTERS
EFIRSTTU TURFIEST
TURFITES
EFIRSTUX FIXTURES
EFIRSTUZ FURZIEST
EFISSSTU FUSSIEST
EFISSTTU FUSTIEST
EFISSTTW SWIFTEST
EFISTTTU TUFTIEST
EFISTUZZ FUZZIEST
EFKLLOOR FOLKLORE
EFKLMNOS MENFOLKS
EFKLMOOT FOLKMOTE
EFKLMORS MERFOLKS
EFKLNRSU FLUNKERS
EFKLNSUY FLUNKEYS
EFKLOPSU POKEFULS
EFKLORSS FORKLESS
EFKLORUW FLUEWORK
EFKLPSSU SKEPFULS
EFKNOORW FOREKNOW
EFKOOPRS FORSPOKE
EFKORRTW FRETWORK
EFLLLOOW WOOLFELL
EFLLLOWY FELLOWLY
EFLLLPSU SPELLFUL
EFLLNSSU FULLNESS
EFLLNTUY FLUENTLY
EFLLOORW FOLLOWER
EFLLOOTW FOOTWELL
EFLLORUV OVERFULL
EFLLOSST LOFTLESS
EFLLOUWY WOEFULLY
EFLLRUUY RUEFULLY
EFLLSUUY USEFULLY
EFLMMRUY FLUMMERY
EFLMNOOU MONOFUEL
EFLMNRUU FRENULUM
EFLMORRY FORMERLY
EFLMORSS FORMLESS
EFLMORSU FULSOMER
EFLMPRSU FRUMPLES
EFLNOOSU FELONOUS
EFLNORSU FLEURONS
EFLNORTT FRONTLET
EFLNORYZ FROZENLY
EFLNOSSU FOULNESS
SULFONES
EFLNOSTT FLETTONS
FONTLETS
EFLNOSTY STONEFLY
EFLNSSTU NESTFULS
EFLNSSUY SYNFUELS
EFLNSTTU TENTFULS
EFLNSUUU UNUSEFUL
EFLOOPRV FLOPOVER
EFLOORRS FLOORERS
EFLOORSS FORSLOES
ROOFLESS
EFLOORST FOOTLERS
EFLOORSW FORESLOW
EFLOORSZ FOOZLERS
EFLOORTU FOOTRULE
EFLOORUV OVERFOUL
EFLOORVW OVERFLOW
EFLOOSST FOOTLESS
EFLOPPRS FLOPPERS
EFLOPRUW POWERFUL
EFLOPRUX FOURPLEX
EFLORRUY RYEFLOUR
EFLORSTT FORTLETS
EFLORSTU FLOUTERS
EFLORSTW FELWORTS
EFLORSUY YOURSELF
EFLORSVY FLYOVERS
EFLOSUUX FLEXUOUS
EFLPRSSU PRESSFUL
EFLPRSUU PURSEFUL
EFLRSSTU FLUSTERS
TURFLESS
EFLRSTTU FLUTTERS
EFLRSTUU FRUSTULE
SULFURET
EFLRSTUY FLUSTERY
EFLRTTUY FLUTTERY
EFMNNNUY FUNNYMEN
EFMNNORT FRONTMEN
EFMNORTY FROMENTY
EFMNRTUY FRUMENTY
FURMENTY
EFMOORST FOREMOST
EFMOORSU FOURSOME
EFMOPRRS PERFORMS
PREFORMS
EFMOPRST POMFRETS
EFNNOOOR FORENOON
EFNNORST FORNENST
EFNNORSU FENURONS
EFNNORUZ UNFROZEN
EFNOOOTT FOOTNOTE
EFNOOPRT PENTROOF
EFNOORRW FOREWORN
EFNOOSST EFTSOONS
FESTOONS
EFNOPRST FORSPENT
EFNORRST REFRONTS
RENFORST
EFNORRSU FORERUNS
EFNORRSW FROWNERS
EFNORSTU FORTUNES
EFNOSSST SOFTNESS
EFNRSSTU FUNSTERS
EFOOOPRT FOOTROPE
EFOOORST FOOTSORE
EFOOPRRS PROOFERS
REPROOFS
EFOOPRSS SPOOFERS
EFOOPRST FORETOPS
POOFTERS
EFOOPRSY SPOOFERY
EFOOPRTW WETPROOF
EFOOPSTT FOOTSTEP
EFOORRSW FORSWORE
EFOORSTT FOOTREST
EFOORSTV OVERSOFT
EFOORSTW WOOFTERS
EFOOSTUX OUTFOXES
EFOPRRSU PROFUSER
EFOPRSTU POUFTERS
EFORRRUW FURROWER
EFORRSST FORTRESS
EFORRSTW FROWSTER
EFORRSTY FORESTRY
EFORRSUV FERVOURS
EFORRTTU FROTTEUR
EFORSSST FOSTRESS
EGGGIILR GIGGLIER
EGGGILNS LEGGINGS
EGGGILOR GOGGLIER
EGGGILRS GIGGLERS
EGGGINPS PEGGINGS
EGGGIORR GROGGIER
EGGGLORS GOGGLERS
EGGGNNOR RONGGENG
EGGGOOOS GOOSEGOG
EGGGORRY GROGGERY
EGGHIINN NEIGHING
EGGHIINW WEIGHING
EGGHILRS HIGGLERS
EGGHINSS GHESSING
EGGHIRST THIGGERS
EGGHLORU ROUGHLEG
EGGHLOSS SHOGGLES
EGGHRTUY THUGGERY
EGGIIJLR JIGGLIER
EGGIILLN GINGELLI
EGGIILNR NIGGLIER
EGGIILNS GINGELIS
EGGIILRW WIGGLIER
EGGIINNN ENGINING
EGGIINNR GREINING
REIGNING
EGGIINNS SINGEING
EGGIINNT TINGEING
EGGIINNW WINGEING
EGGIINRV GRIEVING
REGIVING
EGGIIPST PIGGIEST
EGGIIRTW TWIGGIER
EGGIISTW WIGGIEST
EGGIKLNO GONGLIKE
EGGIKLNS KEGLINGS
EGGIKNOS GINGKOES
GINKGOES
EGGILLNY GINGELLY
EGGILMNU EMULGING
EGGILMSS LEGGISMS
EGGILNNO LONGEING
EGGILNNT GENTLING
GLENTING
EGGILNNU LUNGEING
EGGILNRS NIGGLERS
SNIGGLER
EGGILNRU GRUELING
REGLUING
EGGILNRY GINGERLY
EGGILNSS SNIGGLES
EGGILNSU LUGEINGS
EGGILNSY GLEYINGS
EGGILOOS GOOGLIES
EGGILOST LOGGIEST
EGGILQSU SQUIGGLE
EGGILRRW WRIGGLER
EGGILRSW WIGGLERS
WRIGGLES
EGGIMNNU EMUNGING
EGGIMORS SMOGGIER
EGGIMSTU MUGGIEST
EGGINNNR GRENNING
EGGINNOR ENGORING
EGGINNSS GINSENGS
EGGINORR GORGERIN
ROGERING
EGGINORU ROGUEING
EGGINOUV VOGUEING
EGGINRRU GRUNGIER
REURGING
EGGINRSS GRESSING
SERGINGS
SNIGGERS
EGGINRSY GREYINGS
EGGINSSU GUESSING
SNUGGIES
EGGINSTT GETTINGS
EGGINSTU GUESTING
GUNGIEST
EGGIOSST SOGGIEST
EGGIPRRS PRIGGERS
SPRIGGER
EGGIPRRY PRIGGERY
EGGIPRSU PUGGRIES
EGGIPSTU PUGGIEST
EGGIRRST TRIGGERS
EGGIRSSW SWIGGERS
EGGIRSTT TRIGGEST
EGGIRSTU RUGGIEST
STUGGIER
EGGIRSTW TWIGGERS
EGGISTUV VUGGIEST
EGGJLORS JOGGLERS
EGGJLRSU JUGGLERS
EGGJLRUY JUGGLERY
EGGLMOOY GEMOLOGY
EGGLMRSU SMUGGLER
EGGLMSSU SMUGGLES
EGGLNSSU SNUGGLES
EGGLORSS SLOGGERS
EGGLORST TOGGLERS
EGGLORUY GURGOYLE
EGGLPRSU PLUGGERS
EGGLRSSU SLUGGERS
EGGLRSTU GURGLETS
STRUGGLE
EGGMNTUY NUTMEGGY
EGGMSSTU SMUGGEST
EGGNOOST GEOGNOST
EGGNOOSY GEOGNOSY
EGGNORST GONGSTER
EGGNRSUY SNUGGERY
EGGNSSTU SNUGGEST
EGGOORSU GORGEOUS
EGGOPRRS PROGGERS
EGGSSSTU SUGGESTS
EGHHHIST HEIGHTHS
EGHHIIMS SEMIHIGH
EGHHILTY EIGHTHLY
EGHHINSS HIGHNESS
EGHHIORV OVERHIGH
EGHHORUW ROUGHHEW
EGHHOSSW SHOWGHES
EGHIIKLS SIGHLIKE
EGHIILLS GHILLIES
EGHIILNR HIRELING
EGHIILNS SHEILING
SHIELING
EGHIIMRT MIGHTIER
EGHIINNR INHERING
EGHIINRR REHIRING
EGHIINRT THINGIER
EGHIINST HEISTING
NIGHTIES
THINGIES
EGHIINSV INVEIGHS
EGHIINTV THIEVING
EGHIIRST RIGHTIES
TIGERISH
EGHIISTY HYGIEIST
EGHIKNRS GHERKINS
EGHIKRSS SKREIGHS
SKRIEGHS
EGHILLNO HELLOING

EGHILLNS	SHELLING
EGHILMNW	WHELMING
EGHILMPS	MEGILPHS
EGHILNNU	UNHELING
EGHILNOV	HOVELING
EGHILNPS	HELPINGS
EGHILNPT	PENLIGHT
EGHILNPW	WHELPING
EGHILNRS	HERLINGS
	SHINGLER
EGHILNSS	SHINGLES
EGHILNST	ENLIGHTS
	LIGHTENS
EGHILNSV	SHELVING
EGHILNSW	WELSHING
EGHILNUW	GLUHWEIN
EGHILORT	REGOLITH
EGHILOSU	GHOULIES
	OUGHLIES
EGHILPRT	PLIGHTER
EGHILPST	PIGHTLES
EGHILRST	LIGHTERS
	RELIGHTS
	SLIGHTER
EGHILSSS	SIGHLESS
EGHILSST	SLEIGHTS
EGHILSTT	LIGHTEST
EGHIMNNS	MENSHING
EGHIMNOR	HOMERING
EGHIMNSS	MESHINGS
EGHIMNUX	EXHUMING
EGHIMPRU	GRUMPHIE
EGHIMSTT	MIGHTEST
EGHINNOY	HONEYING
EGHINNSS	NIGHNESS
EGHINNST	SENNIGHT
EGHINNSU	UNHINGES
EGHINORT	THROEING
EGHINORV	HOVERING
EGHINOSS	SHOEINGS
EGHINOST	HISTOGEN
EGHINOSU	GINHOUSE
EGHINPRS	SPHERING
EGHINPSS	SPHINGES
EGHINQTU	QUETHING
EGHINRRS	HERRINGS
EGHINRRU	HUNGRIER
EGHINRRY	HERRYING
EGHINRST	RIGHTENS
EGHINRSU	USHERING
EGHINRSW	SHREWING
	WHINGERS
EGHINRTW	WRETHING
EGHINSTT	SHETTING
	TIGHTENS
EGHINTTW	WHETTING
EGHINTUW	UNWEIGHT
EGHIOOSS	SHOOGIES
EGHIOPSS	PISHOGES
EGHIOPSU	PISHOGUE
EGHIORST	GHOSTIER
EGHIORSU	ROUGHIES
EGHIOSTT	GOTHITES
EGHIOSTU	TOUGHIES
EGHIOSTV	EIGHTVOS
EGHIOTUW	OUTWEIGH
EGHIQRTU	REQUIGHT
EGHIRRST	RIGHTERS
EGHIRRUY	HIERURGY
EGHIRSST	RESIGHTS
	SIGHTERS
EGHIRSTT	RIGHTEST
	STREIGHT
EGHISSTU	GUSHIEST
EGHISSTY	HYGEISTS
EGHISTTT	TIGHTEST
EGHKLNOU	GUNKHOLE
EGHLLOSU	LUGHOLES
EGHLMNOP	PHLEGMON
EGHLNORS	LEGHORNS
EGHLNPSU	ENGULPHS
EGHLNRUY	HUNGERLY
EGHLOOOR	HOROLOGE
EGHLOORY	RHEOLOGY
EGHLOOSS	GOLOSHES
	SHOOGLES
EGHLOOST	THEOLOGS
EGHLOOTY	ETHOLOGY
	THEOLOGY
EGHLOPRU	PLOUGHER
EGHLOPRY	HYPERGOL
EGHMNOOY	HOMOGENY
EGHMNORS	GEMSHORN
EGHMNOSU	HUMOGENS
EGHMOPUY	HYPOGEUM
EGHMOSSU	GUMSHOES
EGHNOOPT	PHOTOGEN
EGHNOOSS	HOGNOSES
EGHNOOTY	THEOGONY
EGHNORSU	ENROUGHS
	ROUGHENS
EGHNORUV	HUNGOVER
	OVERHUNG
EGHNOSTU	TOUGHENS
EGHNOSUU	GUNHOUSE
EGHNRSTT	STRENGTH
EGHOOOSW	HOOSEGOW
EGHORRSU	ROUGHERS
EGHORRTW	REGROWTH
EGHORSTU	RESOUGHT
	ROUGHEST
EGHOSTTU	TOUGHEST
EGHPSSUU	UPGUSHES
EGIIINSV	VISIEING
EGIIJLNR	JINGLIER
EGIIKKLN	KINGLIKE
EGIIKLLO	KILLOGIE
EGIIKLNN	LIKENING
EGIIKLNR	KINGLIER
	RINGLIKE
EGIIKLNW	WINGLIKE
EGIIKLTW	TWIGLIKE
EGIIKNNR	REINKING
EGIIKNNS	SKEINING
EGIILMMN	IMMINGLE
EGIILMST	LEGITIMS
EGIILNNO	ELOINING
EGIILNNR	RELINING
EGIILNNS	ENISLING
	ENSILING
EGIILNNU	LINGUINE
EGIILNNV	LIVENING
EGIILNOR	LIGROINE
	RELIGION
	REOILING
EGIILNPR	PERILING
EGIILNPS	SPEILING
	SPIELING
EGIILNRS	RESILING
	RIESLING
EGIILNRT	GIRTLINE
	RETILING
	TINGLIER
	TIRELING
EGIILNRV	RELIVING
	REVILING
EGIILNST	LIGNITES
	LINGIEST
EGIILNSV	VEILINGS
EGIILNSW	WISELING
EGIILRRS	GRISLIER
EGIILRTU	GUILTIER
EGIILRTZ	GLITZIER
EGIIMMNO	MIMEOING
EGIIMMNW	IMMEWING
EGIIMNNU	INGENIUM
EGIIMNOS	IGNOMIES
EGIIMNPR	IMPINGER
EGIIMNPS	IMPINGES
EGIIMNRS	REMISING
EGIIMNRT	MERITING
	MITERING
	RETIMING
EGIIMNRX	REMIXING
EGIIMNST	MINGIEST
EGIIMNSV	MISGIVEN
EGIIMNTT	EMITTING
EGIIMOPT	IMPETIGO
EGIIMORR	GRIMOIRE
EGIIMPST	GIMPIEST
EGIIMRST	GRIMIEST
	TIGERISM
EGIIMSSV	MISGIVES
EGIINNPR	REPINING
	RIPENING
EGIINNRS	RESINING
EGIINNSS	SEININGS
EGIINNST	GINNIEST
	STEINING
EGIINNSV	VEININGS
EGIINNSW	SINEWING
EGIINNVW	VINEWING
EGIINNWZ	WIZENING
EGIINOPR	PEIGNOIR
EGIINORS	SEIGNIOR
EGIINPRS	SPEIRING
	SPIERING
EGIINPRV	PRIEVING
EGIINPRX	EXPIRING
EGIINPSS	PIGSNIES
EGIINQTU	QUIETING
EGIINRRS	RERISING
EGIINRRT	RETIRING
EGIINRRW	REWIRING
EGIINRST	GIRNIEST
	IGNITERS
	REISTING
	RESITING
	STINGIER
	STRIGINE
EGIINRSU	SIGNIEUR
EGIINRSV	REVISING
EGIINRSW	RINGWISE
	SWINGIER
EGIINRSZ	RESIZING
EGIINRTU	INTRIGUE
EGIINRTV	RIVETING
EGIINRTX	GENITRIX
EGIINRVV	REVIVING
EGIINSSS	SEISINGS
EGIINSSZ	SEIZINGS
EGIINSTW	WINGIEST
EGIINSTX	EXISTING
EGIINSTZ	ZINGIEST
EGIINSVW	VIEWINGS
EGIIOPRS	PIROGIES
EGIIPPRR	GRIPPIER
EGIIPRST	GRIPIEST
EGIIPRSW	PERIWIGS
EGIIPSST	PIGSTIES
EGIIRRTT	GRITTIER
EGIITUXY	EXIGUITY
EGIJKNOS	JINGKOES
EGIJKNRS	JERKINGS
EGIJLLNY	JELLYING
EGIJLNRS	JINGLERS
EGIJLNRU	JUNGLIER
EGIJLNST	JINGLETS
EGIJMMNY	JEMMYING
EGIJNNOY	ENJOYING
EGIJNQRU	JERQUING
EGIJNSST	JESTINGS
EGIJNTTY	JETTYING
EGIKKLNS	LEKKINGS
EGIKKNRT	TREKKING
EGIKLLNN	KNELLING
EGIKLNOS	SONGLIKE
EGIKLNPS	SKELPING
EGIKLNRS	ERLKINGS
EGIKLNSS	KINGLESS
EGIKLNST	KINGLETS
EGIKMNPS	KEMPINGS
EGIKMNRS	SMERKING
EGIKNNNS	KENNINGS
EGIKNNOT	TOKENING
EGIKNNRS	KERNINGS
EGIKNNSY	ENSKYING
EGIKNORV	OVERKING
	REVOKING
EGIKNPPS	SKEPPING
EGIKNRRS	SKERRING
EGIKNRSU	RESKUING
EGILLMNS	SMELLING
EGILLNNO	LONGLINE
EGILLNNS	SNELLING
EGILLNOS	LOGLINES
EGILLNOV	LIVELONG
EGILLNPS	SPELLING
EGILLNQU	QUELLING
EGILLNST	GILLNETS
	STELLING
	TELLINGS
EGILLNSW	SWELLING
	WELLINGS
EGILLNSY	YELLINGS
EGILLNTU	GLUTELIN
EGILLOOR	GLORIOLE
EGILLRRS	GRILLERS
EGILMMNS	LEMMINGS
EGILMMRS	GLIMMERS
EGILMMRY	GLIMMERY
EGILMNNO	LEMONING
EGILMNNU	UNMINGLE
EGILMNOT	LONGTIME
EGILMNPU	IMPLUNGE
EGILMNRS	GREMLINS
	MERLINGS
	MINGLERS
EGILMNRU	RELUMING
EGILMNST	MELTINGS
	SMELTING
EGILMNSU	LEGUMINS
EGILMOOR	GLOOMIER
	OLIGOMER
EGILMORS	GOMERILS
EGILMOSU	ELOGIUMS
EGILMOUU	EULOGIUM
EGILMPRS	GLIMPSER
EGILMPRU	GLUMPIER
EGILMPSS	GLIMPSES
EGILNNST	NESTLING
EGILNNTT	NETTLING
EGILNOPP	PEOPLING
	POPELING
EGILNORS	RESOLING
EGILNORW	LOWERING
	ROWELING
EGILNOSS	LIGNOSES
	LOGINESS
EGILNOSU	LIGNEOUS

EGILNOSW	LONGWISE
EGILNOTW	TOWELING
EGILNOVV	EVOLVING
EGILNPRS	PINGLERS
	SPERLING
	SPRINGLE
EGILNPRY	REPLYING
EGILNPSS	SPIGNELS
EGILNPST	PELTINGS
	PESTLING
EGILNPSY	YELPINGS
EGILNPTT	PETTLING
EGILNRRU	RULERING
EGILNRRY	ERRINGLY
EGILNRSS	RINGLESS
	SLINGERS
EGILNRST	LINGSTER
	RINGLETS
	STERLING
	TINGLERS
	TRINGLES
EGILNRSW	NEWSGIRL
EGILNRUV	VELURING
EGILNSSS	SIGNLESS
EGILNSST	GLISTENS
	SINGLETS
EGILNSSU	UGLINESS
EGILNSSW	SWINGLES
	WINGLESS
EGILNSTT	LETTINGS
	SETTLING
EGILNSTW	SWELTING
	WELTINGS
	WINGLETS
EGILNSUV	EVULSING
EGILNSUY	GUYLINES
EGILNTUX	EXULTING
EGILNVXY	VEXINGLY
EGILOOOS	OOLOGIES
EGILOOPR	GLOOPIER
EGILOORR	GROOLIER
EGILOOSU	ISOLOGUE
EGILOOTY	ETIOLOGY
EGILORRW	GROWLIER
EGILORSS	GLOSSIER
EGILORTV	OVERGILT
EGILORTY	GYROLITE
EGILOSSS	GLOSSIES
EGILOSST	ELOGISTS
EGILOSTU	EULOGIST
EGILPPRS	GRIPPLES
EGILPSTU	GULPIEST
EGILRRZZ	GRIZZLER
EGILRSST	GLISTERS
	GRISTLES
EGILRSTT	GLITTERS
EGILRSTU	GURLIEST
EGILRSUV	VIRGULES
EGILRSZZ	GRIZZLES
EGILRTTY	GLITTERY
EGILSSTW	TWIGLESS
EGIMMNOV	EMMOVING
EGIMMNST	STEMMING
EGIMMRST	GRIMMEST
EGIMMSTU	GUMMIEST
	GUMMITES
EGIMNNNO	MIGNONNE
EGIMNNOV	ENMOVING
	VENOMING
EGIMNNSW	SWINGMEN
EGIMNNUW	UNMEWING
EGIMNORS	NEGROISM
EGIMNORV	REMOVING
EGIMNOST	MITOGENS
EGIMNOSU	GEMINOUS
EGIMNOSY	MOSEYING
EGIMNPRS	IMPREGNS
EGIMNPRU	IMPUGNER
EGIMNPST	EMPTINGS
	PIGMENTS
EGIMNPTT	TEMPTING
EGIMNPTY	EMPTYING
EGIMNRSS	GRIMNESS
EGIMNRSU	RESUMING
EGIMNRUY	ERYNGIUM
EGIMORSS	OGREISMS
EGIMORST	ERGOTISM
	GORMIEST
EGIMOSST	EGOTISMS
EGIMOSTW	TWIGSOME
EGIMPRRU	GRUMPIER
EGIMSSSU	MISGUESS
EGINNNOT	TENONING
EGINNNOZ	ENZONING
EGINNNRS	RENNINGS
EGINNNST	STENNING
EGINNNUY	ENNUYING
EGINNOOR	RONEOING
EGINNOOS	IONOGENS
EGINNOPR	REPONING
EGINNOPS	OPENINGS
EGINNORS	NEGRONIS
EGINNORT	NITROGEN
EGINNORV	VIGNERON
EGINNORZ	REZONING
EGINNOSU	ENGINOUS
EGINNPRT	PRENTING
EGINNPSU	PENGUINS
EGINNRRS	GRINNERS
EGINNRRU	UNERRING
EGINNRST	STERNING
EGINNRSU	ENSURING
EGINNRSV	NERVINGS
EGINNRTU	RETUNING
EGINNRTV	VENTRING
EGINNSSS	SENSINGS
EGINNSST	NESTINGS
EGINNSTT	NETTINGS
	STENTING
	TENTINGS
EGINNSTV	VENTINGS
EGINNSUW	UNSEWING
EGINNSUX	UNSEXING
EGINNSVY	ENVYINGS
EGINOORV	INGROOVE
EGINOOSS	ISOGONES
EGINOPRS	PERIGONS
	REPOSING
	SPONGIER
EGINOPRW	POWERING
EGINOPRY	PIGEONRY
EGINOPST	PONGIEST
EGINOPSU	EPIGONUS
EGINOPSX	EXPOSING
EGINOPSY	POESYING
EGINOPXY	EPOXYING
EGINORRS	IGNORERS
EGINORSS	GORINESS
	SIGNORES
EGINORST	GENITORS
	ROSETING
EGINORSW	RESOWING
EGINORSY	SEIGNORY
EGINORTT	OTTERING
EGINORTU	OUTREIGN
	ROUTEING
EGINORTV	REVOTING
EGINORTW	TOWERING
EGINORTX	OXTERING
EGINORTZ	ROZETING
EGINORVW	OVERWING
	WINGOVER
EGINORXX	XEROXING
EGINOSTT	TENTIGOS
EGINOTUV	OUTGIVEN
EGINPPPR	PREPPING
EGINPPRS	REPPINGS
EGINPPST	STEPPING
EGINPRRS	RESPRING
	SPERRING
	SPRINGER
EGINPRRU	REPURING
EGINPRSS	PRESSING
	SPERSING
	SPRINGES
EGINPRST	PRESTING
EGINPRSU	PERSUING
	PERUSING
	SUPERING
EGINPRTU	ERUPTING
	REPUTING
EGINPRTY	RETYPING
EGINPRUV	PREVUING
EGINPRYY	PERIGYNY
EGINPSSY	PIGSNEYS
EGINPSTT	PETTINGS
	SPETTING
EGINQRUY	QUERYING
EGINQSTU	QUESTING
EGINQSUU	QUEUINGS
EGINRRST	RESTRING
	RINGSTER
	STRINGER
EGINRRSW	WRINGERS
EGINRRSY	SERRYING
EGINRRTY	RETRYING
EGINRSST	RESTINGS
	STINGERS
	TRESSING
	TRIGNESS
EGINRSSV	SERVINGS
	VERSINGS
EGINRSSW	SWINGERS
EGINRSSY	SYRINGES
EGINRSTT	GITTERNS
EGINRSTV	STERVING
EGINRSTW	STREWING
	WRESTING
EGINRSVW	SWERVING
EGINRTTU	UTTERING
EGINSSTT	SETTINGS
	TESTINGS
EGINSSTV	VESTINGS
EGINSSTW	STEWINGS
	WESTINGS
EGINSTTT	STETTING
EGINSTTW	WETTINGS
EGIOOPST	GOOPIEST
EGIOORRV	GROOVIER
EGIOOSST	GOOSIEST
EGIOPRSS	GOSSIPER
EGIOPRSU	GROUPIES
	PIROGUES
EGIOPRTU	PORTIGUE
EGIORRTT	GROTTIER
EGIORRTU	GROUTIER
EGIORRTV	OVERGIRT
EGIORSST	GORSIEST
	STRIGOSE
EGIORSSU	GRISEOUS
EGIORSTU	GOUSTIER
EGIORSTV	VERTIGOS
EGIORSTY	OYSTRIGE
EGIORSTZ	ZORGITES
EGIORSUV	GRIEVOUS
EGIOSSTT	EGOTISTS
EGIOSTTU	GOUTIEST
EGIOSTUV	OUTGIVES
	VOGUIEST
EGIOSUUX	EXIGUOUS
EGIPPRRS	GRIPPERS
EGIPRSUU	GUIPURES
EGIRRSTT	GRITTERS
EGIRRSTY	REGISTRY
EGIRSSTU	SURGIEST
EGIRSTTT	GRITTEST
EGIRSTTU	TURGITES
EGISSTTU	GUSTIEST
	GUTSIEST
EGISSYYZ	SYZYGIES
EGISTTTU	GUTTIEST
EGJLNORU	JONGLEUR
EGJLNOTU	JELUTONG
EGJOSSTT	GJETOSTS
EGKLORSW	LEGWORKS
EGLLMORW	GROMWELL
EGLLOOPY	PELOLOGY
EGLLPSSU	PLUGLESS
EGLMMSTU	GLUMMEST
EGLMNOOS	ENGLOOMS
	LONGSOME
EGLMNOOY	MENOLOGY
EGLMNORS	MONGRELS
EGLMNSSU	GLUMNESS
EGLMOORS	LEGROOMS
EGLMOPRU	PROMULGE
EGLMORSS	GORMLESS
EGLMOSSS	SMOGLESS
EGLNNOOR	LONGERON
EGLNNOSS	LONGNESS
EGLNNTUY	UNGENTLY
EGLNOOOY	OENOLOGY
EGLNOOPR	PROLONGE
EGLNOOPY	PENOLOGY
EGLNOORV	OVERLONG
EGLNOPYY	POLYGENY
EGLNORSU	LOUNGERS
EGLNORUU	LONGUEUR
EGLNOSSS	SONGLESS
EGLNOSSY	LYSOGENS
EGLNOSUV	UNGLOVES
EGLNOSXY	LOXYGENS
	XYLOGENS
EGLNOSYY	LYSOGENY
EGLNPRSU	PLUNGERS
EGLNRSSU	RUNGLESS
EGLNRSTU	GRUNTLES
EGLNRTUY	URGENTLY
EGLOOORY	OREOLOGY
EGLOOPRU	PROLOGUE
EGLOOPTY	LOGOTYPE
EGLOORSS	REGOSOLS
EGLOORSY	SEROLOGY
EGLOOSXY	SEXOLOGY
EGLOPRTU	GROUPLET
EGLOPSTU	GLUEPOTS
EGLORRSW	GROWLERS
EGLORRWY	GROWLERY
EGLORSSS	GLOSSERS
EGLORSSU	ROSESLUG
EGLORSUU	RUGULOSE
EGLORSUY	RUGOSELY
EGLPRRSU	SPLURGER
EGLPRSSU	SPLURGES
EGLPRSUY	GYPLURES
EGLRSTTU	GUTTLERS
EGLRSUZZ	GUZZLERS
EGLSSSTU	GUSTLESS
EGLSSUUV	VULGUSES
EGMMNOOR	MONOGERM

EGMMORST GROMMETS
EGMMOSSU GUMMOSES
EGMMRSTU GRUMMEST
GRUMMETS
EGMNNOOY MONOGENY
NOMOGENY
EGMNNOSW GOWNSMEN
EGMNOOOS MONGOOSE
EGMNOORY MEROGONY
EGMNOOSU MUNGOOSE
EGMNORSU MURGEONS
EGMNOSYZ ZYMOGENS
EGMNRSSU GRUMNESS
EGMNSSSU SMUGNESS
EGMOORRS GROOMERS
REGROOMS
EGMORSTU GOURMETS
EGNNOOTY ONTOGENY
EGNNORST RONTGENS
EGNNOSTU GUNSTONE
NONGUEST
EGNNOTTU UNGOTTEN
EGNNSSSU SNUGNESS
EGNNSTTU TUNGSTEN
EGNNSTUU UNGUENTS
EGNOOOPR GONOPORE
EGNOOPRS PROGNOSE
EGNOORRV GOVERNOR
EGNOOTUX OXTONGUE
EGNOPPRU OPPUGNER
EGNOPRSS SPONGERS
EGNOPRSY PYROGENS
EGNORRST STRONGER
EGNORRSW WRONGERS
EGNORSST SONGSTER
EGNORSSU SURGEONS
EGNORSTT TONGSTER
EGNORSTU STURGEON
EGNORSTW WRONGEST
EGNORSUY YOUNGERS
EGNOSTUY YOUNGEST
EGNPRRSU RESPRUNG
EGNPRSUU SUPERGUN
EGNRRSTU GRUNTERS
RESTRUNG
EGOOPRRU PROROGUE
EGOORRSV GROOVERS
EGOORRVW OVERGROW
EGOORSTT GROTTOES
EGOORSTU OUTGOERS
EGOPRRSS PROGRESS
EGOPRRSU GROUPERS
REGROUPS
EGOPSSUY GYPSEOUS
EGORRSSS GROSSERS
EGORRSST GROSERTS
EGORRSSU GROUSERS
EGORRSTU GROUTERS
EGORSSST GROSSEST
EGORSSTU GROUSEST
EGOSSTUU OUTGUESS
EGPRSSTY GYPSTERS
EGPRSSUU UPSURGES
EHHIIPRS HEIRSHIP
EHHIISTV THIEVISH
EHHILMNT HELMINTH
EHHILOPR RHEOPHIL
EHHILOST SHITHOLE
EHHINOPT THIOPHEN
EHHIOPRS HEROSHIP
EHHIORTT HITHERTO
EHHIPRSS HERSHIPS
EHHIPSST PHTHISES
EHHIRSSW SHREWISH
EHHIRSTW WHITHERS
EHHISSTU HUSHIEST
EHHLOOST SHOTHOLE
EHHNOORS SHOEHORN
EHHOOPST THEOSOPH
EHHOOSSW WHOOSHES
EHHOOSTU HOTHOUSE
EHHORSTU SHOUTHER
EHHRSSTU THRUSHES
EHIIIPSX PIXIEISH
EHIIKLPT PITHLIKE
EHIIKLPW WHIPLIKE
EHIIKSSW WHISKIES
EHIILLST HILLIEST
EHIILLSW WHILLIES
EHIILMOS HOMILIES
EHIILNPS HIPLINES
EHIILNRS LINISHER
EHIILNSS LINISHES
EHIILOSS HELIOSIS
EHIILPSU HUIPILES
EHIILRRW WHIRLIER
EHIILRSV LIVERISH
EHIILRSW WHIRLIES
EHIILSTT LITHITES
THELITIS
EHIIMMRW WHIMMIER
EHIIMMSS SHIMMIES
EHIIMNNO HOMININE
EHIIMNOS HOMINIES
EHIIMNOZ HOMINIZE
EHIIMNSS MINISHES
EHIIMPST MEPHITIS
EHIIMRSW WHIMSIER
EHIIMSST SMITHIES
EHIIMSSW WHIMSIES
EHIINNOS INHESION
EHIINNOT THIONINE
EHIINNQU HENIQUIN
EHIINNRS INSHRINE
EHIINNRW WHINNIER
EHIINNSS SHINNIES
EHIINNSW WHINNIES
EHIINRRT HIRRIENT
EHIINRST INHERITS
EHIINRSZ RHIZINES
EHIINSST SHINIEST
SHINTIES
EHIINSTW WHINIEST
EHIINSVX VIXENISH
EHIIPPRW WHIPPIER
EHIIPPST HIPPIEST
EHIIPRSV VIPERISH
EHIIPSTT PITHIEST
EHIIRRST SHIRTIER
EHIIRRSW WHIRRIES
EHIIRRTX HERITRIX
EHIIRSSU HUISSIER
EHIIRSSW SWISHIER
EHIIRSTT SHITTIER
THIRTIES
EHIISSST STISHIES
EHIISSTT STITHIES
EHIISTTW WHITIEST
WITHIEST
EHIISTTX SIXTIETH
EHIJNNOS JOHNNIES
EHIKKLOO HOOKLIKE
EHIKKLSU HUSKLIKE
EHIKKRSS SHIKKERS
EHIKLMNY HYMNLIKE
EHIKLMOT MOTHLIKE
EHIKLNOR HORNLIKE
EHIKLNOS SINKHOLE
EHIKLOOP HOOPLIKE
EHIKLOSY YOKELISH
EHIKLOTY LEKYTHOI
EHIKLRSU RUSHLIKE
EHIKLSTU HULKIEST
EHIKMNST METHINKS
EHIKNORS SHONKIER
EHIKNOSS HOKINESS
EHIKNPSU SHUNPIKE
EHIKNRRS SHRINKER
EHIKNRST RETHINKS
THINKERS
EHIKNSTU HUNKIEST
EHIKOOST HOOKIEST
EHIKOPRS POKERISH
EHIKRRSS SHIRKERS
EHIKRSSW WHISKERS
EHIKRSWY WHISKERY
EHIKSSTU HUSKIEST
EHIKSSTW WHISKETS
EHIKSSWY WHISKEYS
EHILLLMO MOLEHILL
EHILLMOP PHILOMEL
EHILLMOY HOMELILY
EHILLNOS HELLIONS
EHILLNSS INSHELLS
EHILLOOS OILHOLES
EHILLOPY LYOPHILE
EHILLPTY PHYLLITE
EHILLRRS SHRILLER
EHILLRRT THRILLER
EHILLRST THILLERS
EHILLRTY LITHERLY
EHILLSST HILTLESS
EHILLSSW SWELLISH
EHILLSTU HULLIEST
EHILLSVY ELVISHLY
EHILMNOS LEMONISH
EHILMOOR HEIRLOOM
EHILMOST HELOTISM
EHILMPSW WHIMPLES
EHILMPSY SYMPHILE
EHILMQUU UMQUHILE
EHILMSTT MELTITHS
EHILNOOP OENOPHIL
EHILNOPS PINHOLES
EHILNOPT THOLEPIN
EHILNORU UNHOLIER
EHILNOSS HOLINESS
EHILNOST HOLSTEIN
HOTLINES
NEOLITHS
EHILNOSV NOVELISH
EHILNOTX XENOLITH
EHILNPSY SYLPHINE
EHILNSTY ETHINYLS
EHILNSWY NEWISHLY
EHILOOPZ ZOOPHILE
EHILOOST HOOLIEST
EHILOPRS PILHORSE
POLISHER
REPOLISH
EHILOPRT HELIPORT
EHILOPSS POLISHES
EHILOPST HELISTOP
HOPLITES
ISOPLETH
EHILOPXY OXYPHILE
EHILORSS SLOSHIER
EHILORTY RHYOLITE
EHILOSST HOSTILES
EHILPRST PHILTERS
PHILTRES
EHILPRSU PLUSHIER
EHILPRSY SYLPHIER
EHILPSSS SHIPLESS
EHILPSST PITHLESS
THLIPSES
EHILPSSY PHYLESIS
EHILPSTU SULPHITE
EHILRRSW WHIRLERS
EHILRSST SLITHERS
THRISSEL
EHILRSSU SLUSHIER
EHILRSSV SHRIVELS
EHILRSTT THRISTLE
EHILRSTU LUTHIERS
EHILRSTW WHIRTLES
WHISTLER
EHILRSTY SLITHERY
EHILRTTW WHITTLER
EHILRTTY TRIETHYL
EHILSSSW WISHLESS
EHILSSTT THISTLES
EHILSSTU LUSHIEST
EHILSSTW WHISTLES
EHILSTTU THULITES
EHILSTTW WHITTLES
EHIMMNUY HYMENIUM
EHIMMRSS SHIMMERS
EHIMMRSY SHIMMERY
EHIMMSSY SHIMMEYS
EHIMNOPR MORPHINE
EHIMNORT THERMION
EHIMNOSS HOMINESS
MONISHES
EHIMNOST HOISTMEN
EHIMNOSU HEMIONUS
EHIMNOTT MONTEITH
EHIMNPRS NEPHRISM
PHRENISM
EHIMNPST SHIPMENT
EHIMNRRU MURRHINE
EHIMNRRY MYRRHINE
EHIMNRSU INHUMERS
RHENIUMS
EHIMNSTY THYMINES
EHIMOOSS HOMEOSIS
EHIMOOST SMOOTHIE
EHIMOPRS SOPHERIM
EHIMOPSS PHIMOSES
EHIMORSS HEROISMS
EHIMORST ISOTHERM
MOITHERS
EHIMORSZ RHIZOMES
EHIMORTU MOUTHIER
EHIMOSTT MOTHIEST
EHIMPPSS PSEPHISM
EHIMPRRS SHRIMPER
EHIMPRSU MURPHIES
EHIMPRSW WHIMPERS
EHIMPSTU HUMPIEST
HUMPTIES
TUMPHIES
EHIMPSUU EUPHUISM
EHIMPTTU UMPTIETH
EHIMRRTY HERMITRY
EHIMRSST SMITHERS
EHIMRSSU HEURISMS
EHIMRSTW MISTHREW
EHIMRSTY SMITHERY
EHIMSSTU MUSHIEST
TUMSHIES
EHIMSSTY METHYSIS
MYTHISES
EHIMSSWY WHIMSEYS
EHIMSTTY MYTHIEST
THYMIEST
EHIMSTYZ MYTHIZES
EHINNORT INTHRONE
EHINNOTW NONWHITE
EHINNRST THINNERS

EHINNRSY	SHINNERY
EHINNSST	THINNESS
EHINNSSU	SUNSHINE
EHINNSSY	SHINNEYS
EHINNSTT	THINNEST
EHINOPPR	HORNPIPE
EHINOPRT	TRIPHONE
EHINOPST	PHONIEST
	SIPHONET
EHINOPSW	WINESHOP
EHINORRT	THORNIER
EHINORSS	HERISSON
EHINORST	HORNIEST
	ORNITHES
EHINORTV	OVERTHIN
EHINORZZ	HIZZONER
EHINOSST	HISTONES
EHINOSTU	OUTSHINE
EHINPPSS	SHIPPENS
EHINPRSU	PUNISHER
EHINPSSU	PUNISHES
EHINPSSX	SPHINXES
EHINRSSU	INRUSHES
EHINRSTZ	ZITHERNS
EHINSSST	THISNESS
EHINSSUW	UNWISHES
EHIOOPST	ISOPHOTE
EHIOOPSW	WHOOPSIE
EHIOORTT	TOOTHIER
EHIOOSST	STOOSHIE
EHIOOSTT	HOOTIEST
EHIOPPPS	POPESHIP
EHIOPPRS	SHOPPIER
EHIOPPST	HOPPIEST
	POETSHIP
EHIOPPSU	EOHIPPUS
EHIOPRSS	ROSEHIPS
	SPOSHIER
EHIOPRST	TROPHIES
EHIOPTTW	WHITEPOT
EHIORRST	HERITORS
EHIORRTU	ROUTHIER
EHIORRTW	WORTHIER
EHIORSST	HOISTERS
	HORSIEST
	HOSTRIES
	SHORTIES
EHIORSTT	THEORIST
	THORITES
EHIORSTU	OUTHIRES
EHIORSTV	OVERHITS
EHIORSTW	WORTHIES
EHIORTUY	YOUTHIER
EHIORTWZ	HOWITZER
EHIOSSSW	WHOSISES
EHIOSSTT	TOSHIEST
EHIOSSTU	HOUSESIT
	HOUSIEST
EHIOSSTW	SHOWIEST
EHIOSSTY	ISOHYETS
EHIOSTVY	YESHIVOT
EHIOTTUW	WHITEOUT
EHIPPRSS	SHIPPERS
EHIPPRSW	WHIPPERS
EHIPPSSU	HIPPUSES
EHIPPSTW	WHIPPETS
EHIPQSUY	PHYSIQUE
EHIPRSST	HIPSTERS
	THRIPSES
EHIPRSSW	WHISPERS
EHIPRSTU	SUPERHIT
EHIPRSTW	WHIPSTER
EHIPRSWY	WHISPERY
EHIPSSTU	PUSHIEST
EHIPSTUU	EUPHUIST
EHIQSSSU	SQUISHES
EHIRRRSU	HURRIERS
EHIRRSSV	SHRIVERS
EHIRRSTT	THIRSTER
EHIRRSTV	THRIVERS
EHIRRSTW	WHIRRETS
	WRITHERS
EHIRRTTU	TRUTHIER
EHIRSSSW	SWISHERS
EHIRSSTU	RUSHIEST
EHIRSSTW	SWITHERS
EHIRSTTW	WHITRETS
	WHITSTER
	WHITTERS
EHIRSWZZ	WHIZZERS
EHIRTTTW	WHITTRET
EHISSSTU	STUSHIES
EHISSSTW	SWISHEST
EHISSTUW	THUSWISE
EHISSUVW	HUSWIVES
EHKLNOOT	KNOTHOLE
EHKLOOSS	HOOKLESS
EHKLOOST	HOOKLETS
EHKLOOSZ	KOLHOZES
EHKLOSTY	LEKYTHOS
EHKLSTUY	LEKYTHUS
EHKMOORW	HOMEWORK
EHKMORSU	HUMORESK
EHKMORSW	MESHWORK
EHKNNRSU	SHRUNKEN
EHKNOOOS	HOOKNOSE
EHKNORSU	UNKOSHER
EHKOOSSS	SKOOSHES
EHKOPSSY	KYPHOSES
EHKRSSTU	TUSHKERS
EHLLMOPY	PHYLLOME
EHLLNSSU	UNSHELLS
EHLLNSTU	NUTSHELL
EHLLOOOP	LOOPHOLE
EHLLOORW	HOLLOWER
EHLMMOSW	WHOMMLES
EHLMMSUW	WHUMMLES
EHLMNOST	MENTHOLS
EHLMNOSY	HOMELYNS
EHLMNOTU	MOLEHUNT
EHLMNOUY	UNHOMELY
EHLMNSSY	HYMNLESS
EHLMOORW	WORMHOLE
EHLMOOST	LOTHSOME
EHLMOPSY	MESOPHYL
EHLMORTY	MOTHERLY
EHLMOTXY	METHOXYL
EHLMPSSU	HUMPLESS
EHLNNOPU	UNHOLPEN
EHLNOPSU	SULPHONE
EHLNORSS	HORNLESS
EHLNORST	HORNLETS
EHLNOSTY	HONESTLY
EHLNRSTU	LUTHERNS
EHLNSSSU	LUSHNESS
	SHUNLESS
EHLNSTYY	ETHYNYLS
EHLOOPRT	PORTHOLE
	POTHOLER
EHLOOPSS	HOOPLESS
EHLOOPST	POSTHOLE
	POTHOLES
EHLOOPTY	HOLOTYPE
EHLOORVY	OVERHOLY
EHLOOSSS	SLOOSHES
EHLOPPRT	THROPPLE
EHLOPRTY	PROTHYLE
EHLOPSSS	SPLOSHES
EHLOPSSY	SPYHOLES
EHLORSST	HOLSTERS
	HOSTLERS
EHLORSTT	THROSTLE
EHLORSTW	WHORTLES
EHLORSTY	HOSTELRY
EHLORSUV	OVERLUSH
EHLORTTT	THROTTLE
EHLOSSTT	SHOTTLES
EHLOSSTW	THOWLESS
EHLOSSTY	THYLOSES
EHLOSTXY	ETHOXYLS
EHLPSSTU	PLUSHEST
EHLRSSTU	HURTLESS
	HUSTLERS
	RUTHLESS
EHLSSTTU	SHUTTLES
EHMMOOOR	HOMEROOM
EHMMOOSS	HOMMOSES
EHMMRRTU	THRUMMER
EHMMSSUU	HUMMUSES
EHMNNSTU	HUNTSMEN
EHMNOOPR	NEOMORPH
EHMNOORS	HORMONES
	MOORHENS
EHMNOOST	SMOOTHEN
EHMNOOTW	HOMETOWN
	TOWNHOME
EHMNOOTY	THEONOMY
EHMNOPSU	HOMESPUN
EHMNPRYY	HYPERNYM
EHMNPSTY	NYMPHETS
EHMNSTTU	HUTMENTS
EHMOOOTZ	ZOOTHOME
EHMOOPRT	HOMEPORT
EHMOOPTY	HOMOTYPE
EHMOORST	RESMOOTH
	SMOOTHER
EHMOORTU	OUTHOMER
EHMOOSSS	SHMOOSES
EHMOOSST	SMOOTHES
EHMOOSSZ	SHMOOZES
EHMOPRSW	MORPHEWS
EHMORSST	SMOTHERS
EHMORSTU	MOUTHERS
EHMORSTY	SMOTHERY
EHMORTUV	VERMOUTH
EHMOSSUU	HOUMUSES
EHMOTUZZ	MEZUZOTH
EHMPRSTU	THUMPERS
EHMRRSTU	MURTHERS
EHMRSTUV	VERMUTHS
EHMRTUYY	EURYTHMY
EHMSSTUY	THYMUSES
EHNNOPRS	NEPHRONS
EHNNOPSY	HYPNONES
EHNNORRT	NORTHERN
EHNNORTU	UNTHRONE
EHNNOSTU	UNHONEST
EHNNRSSU	SHUNNERS
EHNOOPTY	HONEYPOT
EHNOORRS	HONORERS
EHNOORRU	HONOURER
EHNOORSS	SOREHONS
EHNOORSW	WHORESON
EHNOORTW	HONEWORT
EHNOOSSW	SNOWSHOE
EHNOOSTU	OUTSHONE
EHNOPRSW	PRESHOWN
EHNOPRSY	HYPERONS
EHNOPSSS	POSHNESS
EHNOPSSY	HYPNOSES
EHNORRST	NORTHERS
EHNORRTY	ERYTHRON
EHNORSST	SHORTENS
EHNORSSU	ONRUSHES
	UNHORSES
EHNORSTT	THORNSET
EHNORSTU	SOUTHERN
EHNORTUV	OVERHUNT
EHNOSSUU	UNHOUSES
EHNOSTUU	NUTHOUSE
EHNOSTUY	YOUTHENS
EHNRSSTU	HUNTRESS
	SHUNTERS
EHNSSSTU	THUSNESS
EHOOPRST	HOOPSTER
EHOOPRSW	WHOOPERS
EHOOPRSX	HORSEPOX
EHOOPRTY	ORTHOEPY
EHOOPSTT	PHOTOSET
EHOOPSTU	HOUSETOP
	POTHOUSE
EHOOPSTY	OOPHYTES
EHOOPTYZ	ZOOPHYTE
EHOORSST	ORTHOSES
	RESHOOTS
	SHEROOTS
	SHOOTERS
	SOOTHERS
EHOORSTV	OVERSHOT
EHOOSSSW	SWOOSHES
EHOOSSTT	SOOTHEST
EHOOSTUU	OUTHOUSE
EHOPPRSS	SHOPPERS
EHOPPRST	PROPHETS
EHOPPRSW	WHOPPERS
EHOPPRSY	PROPHESY
EHOPRRSY	ORPHREYS
EHOPRSST	HOTPRESS
	STROPHES
EHOPRSSW	PRESHOWS
EHOPRSTU	POUTHERS
	SUPERHOT
EHOPRSTY	TROPHESY
EHOPRSUV	PUSHOVER
EHOPRTUY	EUTROPHY
EHOPSSTY	PHYTOSES
EHORRSTW	THROWERS
EHORRSTY	HERSTORY
EHORSSTT	SHORTEST
EHORSSTU	SHOUTERS
	SOUTHERS
EHORSTUY	OUTHYRES
EHORTTUW	OUTTHREW
EHOSSSTU	STOUSHES
EHPRSSSU	SPRUSHES
EHPRSSUU	UPRUSHES
EHPRSTTU	TURPETHS
EHPSSTUY	TYPHUSES
EHQRSSUU	QURUSHES
EHQSSSUU	SQUUSHES
EHRRSTTU	THRUSTER
EHRSSSTY	SHYSTERS
EHRSSTTU	SHUTTERS
EIIILMSS	SIMILISE
EIIILMSZ	SIMILIZE
EIIILNRV	INVIRILE
EIIILPPR	LIRIPIPE
EIIIMMNS	MINIMISE
EIIIMMNZ	MINIMIZE
EIIIRRTV	TIRRIVIE
EIIIRSST	IRITISES
EIIJKNRT	JIRKINET
EIIJMPST	JIMPIEST
EIIJNRSU	INJURIES
EIIKKLLM	MILKLIKE
EIIKKLLS	SILKLIKE
EIIKKLNS	SKINLIKE
EIIKKNST	KINKIEST
EIIKLLLY	LILYLIKE
EIIKLLMN	LIMEKILN

EIIKLLNO	LIONLIKE
EIIKLLRS	SKILLIER
EIIKLLSS	SKILLIES
EIIKLMRS	MISLIKER
EIIKLMSS	MISLIKES
EIIKLMST	MILKIEST
EIIKLNOR	IRONLIKE
EIIKLNRS	SLINKIER
EIIKLNRT	TINKLIER
EIIKLPSS	PLISKIES
EIIKLPSW	WISPLIKE
EIIKLRTT	KITTLIER
EIIKLSST	SILKIEST
EIIKLSTU	SUITLIKE
EIIKMPRS	SKIMPIER
EIIKMRRS	SMIRKIER
EIIKMRST	MIRKIEST
EIIKNNRS	SKINNIER
EIIKNNSS	INKINESS
EIIKNNST	KINETINS
EIIKNNSW	WINESKIN
EIIKNPST	PINKIEST
EIIKNRST	STINKIER
EIIKNSST	SINKIEST
EIIKNSTZ	ZINKIEST
EIIKPPRS	SKIPPIER
EIIKPSST	SPIKIEST
EIIKQRRU	QUIRKIER
EIIKRSST	RISKIEST
EIIKSSTV	SKIVIEST
EIIKSSVV	SKIVVIES
EIILLLVY	LIVELILY
EIILLMMR	MILLIREM
EIILLMMS	MILLIMES
EIILLMNR	MILLINER
EIILLMNS	MILLINES
	SLIMLINE
EIILLMNU	ILLUMINE
EIILLMRS	MILLIERS
EIILLNST	NIELLIST
EIILLNSU	SUILLINE
EIILLNSV	VILLEINS
EIILLNTV	VITELLIN
EIILLPSS	ELLIPSIS
EIILLRST	STILLIER
EIILLRVY	VIRILELY
EIILLSST	SILLIEST
EIILLSTT	TILLIEST
	TILLITES
EIILLSTW	TWILLIES
EIILLSUV	ILLUSIVE
EIILMMOS	MILESIMO
EIILMMOT	IMMOTILE
EIILMNNT	LINIMENT
EIILMNOT	LIMONITE
EIILMNSS	LIMINESS
EIILMOPT	IMPOLITE
EIILMPPR	PIMPLIER
EIILMPRS	IMPERILS
	LIMPSIER
EIILMPRT	PRELIMIT
EIILMPST	LIMEPITS
EIILMRSS	SLIMSIER
EIILMRST	LIMITERS
	MIRLIEST
EIILMRZZ	MIZZLIER
EIILMSSS	MISSILES
EIILMSST	ELITISMS
	SLIMIEST
EIILMSSV	MISLIVES
EIILMSTT	MILTIEST
	MISTITLE
EIILMSTY	MYELITIS
EIILNNOT	LENITION
EIILNORS	LIONISER
EIILNORZ	LIONIZER
EIILNOSS	ELISIONS
	ISOLINES
	LIONISES
	OILINESS
EIILNOST	ETIOLINS
EIILNOSV	OLIVINES
EIILNOSZ	LIONIZES
EIILNOTT	TOILINET
EIILNQTU	QUINTILE
EIILNRST	NIRLIEST
	NITRILES
EIILNSSW	WILINESS
EIILNSTT	INTITLES
	LINTIEST
EIILNSTY	SENILITY
EIILNSVY	SYLVIINE
EIILNTTU	INTITULE
EIILNTUV	VITULINE
EIILOPST	PISOLITE
	POLITIES
EIILORST	ROILIEST
EIILORTT	TROILITE
EIILOSST	SOILIEST
EIILOTVV	VOLITIVE
EIILPPRR	RIPPLIER
EIILPPRS	SLIPPIER
EIILPPST	LIPPIEST
EIILPRST	TRIPLIES
EIILPRSU	PLURISIE
EIILPRTT	TRIPLITE
EIILPSST	PITILESS
	SPILITES
EIILPSTY	PYELITIS
EIILPSUZ	SPUILZIE
EIILQSSU	SILIQUES
EIILRRSW	SWIRLIER
EIILRRTW	TWIRLIER
EIILRSTT	STILTIER
EIILRSTU	UTILISER
EIILRTUZ	UTILIZER
EIILSSTT	ELITISTS
	SILTIEST
EIILSSTU	ULITISES
	UTILISES
EIILSTUY	TUILYIES
EIILSTUZ	TUILZIES
	UTILIZES
EIIMMNNO	MENOMINI
EIIMMNNT	IMMINENT
	MINIMENT
EIIMMNSU	IMMUNISE
EIIMMNTU	IMMINUTE
EIIMMNUZ	IMMUNIZE
EIIMMPRU	IMPERIUM
EIIMMRSW	SWIMMIER
EIIMMSSS	SEISMISM
EIIMMSST	MIMSIEST
	MISTIMES
EIIMNOPT	PIMIENTO
EIIMNOSS	EMISSION
	SIMONIES
EIIMNOSV	VISNOMIE
EIIMNOSZ	SIMONIZE
EIIMNOTV	MONITIVE
EIIMNPRS	PRIMINES
EIIMNRSS	MIRINESS
	RIMINESS
EIIMNRST	INTERIMS
	MINISTER
	MISINTER
EIIMNRSV	MINIVERS
EIIMNRTT	INTERMIT
EIIMNRTX	INTERMIX
EIIMNSTT	MINTIEST
EIIMNSTU	MUTINIES
EIIMNSTV	MINIVETS
EIIMOPRX	MIREPOIX
EIIMOPSS	MISPOISE
EIIMOPST	OPTIMISE
EIIMOPSZ	EPIZOISM
EIIMOPTZ	OPTIMIZE
EIIMOSSS	SEMIOSIS
EIIMOSSV	OMISSIVE
EIIMOSTY	MOYITIES
EIIMOSUX	EXIMIOUS
EIIMOTVV	VOMITIVE
EIIMPRRS	PRIMSIER
EIIMPRSS	MISPRISE
	PISMIRES
EIIMPRSZ	MISPRIZE
EIIMPSST	PIETISMS
EIIMPSTW	WIMPIEST
EIIMQSTU	QUIETISM
EIIMRRRS	SMIRRIER
EIIMRSTT	METRITIS
EIIMRSTW	MISWRITE
EIIMSSSS	MISSISES
EIIMSSST	MISSIEST
EIIMSSSV	MISSIVES
EIIMSSSZ	SIZEISMS
EIIMSSTT	MISTIEST
	SEMITIST
EIINNNPS	NINEPINS
EIINNOOR	ONIONIER
EIINNOSU	UNIONISE
EIINNOSV	ENVISION
EIINNOUZ	UNIONIZE
EIINNPSS	SPINNIES
EIINNQSU	QUININES
EIINNRTV	INVERTIN
EIINNSST	TININESS
EIINNSSW	INSINEWS
EIINNSTT	TINNIEST
EIINNSTW	INTWINES
EIINOPRS	RIPIENOS
EIINOPRT	POINTIER
EIINOPST	SINOPITE
EIINOPTT	PETITION
EIINORRT	INTERIOR
EIINORSS	IONISERS
	IRONISES
EIINORST	IRONIEST
EIINORSV	REVISION
	VISIONER
EIINORSZ	IONIZERS
	IRONIZES
EIINOSST	INOSITES
	NOISIEST
EIINOSTV	NOVITIES
EIINPPRS	SNIPPIER
EIINPPSS	PIPINESS
EIINPPST	NIPPIEST
EIINPRRS	INSPIRER
EIINPRSS	INSPIRES
EIINPRST	PRISTINE
EIINPSST	SNIPIEST
	SPINIEST
EIINPSSX	PIXINESS
EIINPSTZ	PINTSIZE
EIINPTUV	PUNITIVE
EIINQRRU	INQUIRER
EIINQRSU	INQUIRES
EIINQSSU	QUINSIES
	SQUINIES
EIINQSTU	INQUIETS
EIINQTUY	EQUINITY
	INEQUITY
EIINRRTW	WINTRIER
EIINRSST	INSISTER
	SINISTER
EIINRSSW	WIRINESS
EIINRSTT	NITRITES
	STINTIER
EIINRSTU	NEURITIS
EIINRSTV	INVITERS
	VINTRIES
	VITRINES
EIINRTUZ	UNITIZER
EIINRTVY	INVERITY
EIINSSSZ	SIZINESS
EIINSSTU	UNITISES
EIINSTTT	NITTIEST
	TINTIEST
EIINSTTW	TWINIEST
EIINSTUZ	UNITIZES
EIIOPRRS	PRIORIES
EIIOPSTV	POSITIVE
EIIORRST	RIOTRIES
EIIORSST	RIOTISES
EIIORSTZ	RIOTIZES
EIIOSSTT	OSTEITIS
	OTITISES
EIIOSSTZ	ZOISITES
EIIOTTTV	TOTITIVE
EIIPPPST	PIPPIEST
EIIPPRRS	RIPPIERS
EIIPPRRT	TRIPPIER
EIIPPSTT	TIPPIEST
EIIPPSTZ	ZIPPIEST
EIIPRRSS	PRISSIER
EIIPRRST	STRIPIER
EIIPRRTW	TRIPWIRE
EIIPRSSS	PRISSIES
EIIPRSST	SPIRIEST
EIIPRSTT	RISPETTI
	TRIPIEST
EIIPRSTU	PURITIES
EIIPRSTV	PRIVIEST
EIIPRSTY	PYRITISE
EIIPRSVV	SPIVVIER
EIIPRTYZ	PYRITIZE
EIIPSSTT	PIETISTS
	STIPITES
	TIPSIEST
EIIPSSTW	SWIPIEST
	WISPIEST
EIIPSTTT	PITTITES
EIIPSTTU	PITUITES
EIIQSTTU	QUIETIST
EIIRRSTW	WRISTIER
EIIRSSTV	REVISITS
	VISITERS
EIIRSTTU	UTERITIS
EIIRSTTW	TWISTIER
EIIRSTTZ	RITZIEST
EIISSSST	SISSIEST
EIISSSTZ	SIZEISTS
EIISSTTV	STIVIEST
EIISTTTW	WITTIEST
EIJJNTUY	JEJUNITY
EIJKKSSU	JUKSKEIS
EIJKNOSS	JOKINESS
EIJKNSTU	JUNKIEST
EIJKORRS	SKIJORER
EIJLLOST	JOLLIEST
EIJLMTTU	MULTIJET
EIJLOSTT	JOLTIEST
EIJLOSTW	JOWLIEST
EIJMNPSS	JIMPNESS
EIJMPSTU	JUMPIEST
EIJNORST	JOINTERS
EIJNORTU	JOINTURE
EIJNOSTT	JETTISON
EIJNPRSU	JUNIPERS

EIJNRRSU	INJURERS
EIJNRRUY	REINJURY
EIJNSTTW	TWINJETS
EIJRSTUY	JESUITRY
EIJSSSUV	JUSSIVES
EIKKLNOO	NOOKLIKE
EIKKLNOT	KNOTLIKE
EIKKLNRS	KLINKERS
EIKKLSTU	TUSKLIKE
EIKKNRSS	SKINKERS
EIKKOOST	KOOKIEST
EIKKSTUY	YUKKIEST
EIKLLMOO	KILOMOLE
EIKLLMPU	PLUMLIKE
EIKLLMSS	MILKLESS
EIKLLNSW	INKWELLS
EIKLLNUY	UNLIKELY
EIKLLOOW	WOOLLIKE
EIKLLORV	OVERKILL
EIKLLOSS	SKOLLIES
EIKLLOSU	SOULLIKE
EIKLLRSS	RESKILLS
EIKLLSSS	SKILLESS
EIKLLSST	SKILLETS
EIKLMNNS	LINKSMEN
EIKLMNOO	MOONLIKE
EIKLMNOS	MOLESKIN
EIKLMNRS	KREMLINS
EIKLMORV	OVERMILK
EIKLMORW	WORMLIKE
EIKLMOSS	MOSSLIKE
EIKLMPPU	PUMPLIKE
EIKLNOOR	OERLIKON
EIKLNOPR	PLONKIER
EIKLNOSW	SNOWLIKE
EIKLNPRS	PLINKERS
	SPRINKLE
EIKLNRRU	KNURLIER
EIKLNRSS	SLINKERS
EIKLNRST	LINKSTER
	STRINKLE
	TINKLERS
EIKLNRSW	WINKLERS
	WRINKLES
EIKLNRTW	TWINKLER
EIKLNSSS	SKINLESS
EIKLNSST	LENTISKS
EIKLNSSY	SKYLINES
EIKLNSTT	KNITTLES
EIKLNSTW	TWINKLES
EIKLOOPR	PLOOKIER
EIKLOORT	ROOTLIKE
EIKLOPRU	PLOUKIER
EIKLOPRW	PILEWORK
EIKLORTY	KRYOLITE
EIKLOSSU	LEUKOSIS
EIKLOSTY	YOLKIEST
EIKLPSSU	PUSSLIKE
EIKLRSSS	RISKLESS
EIKLRSST	KLISTERS
EIKLRTUZ	KLUTZIER
EIKLSSTT	SKITTLES
EIKLSSTU	SULKIEST
EIKLSTTT	KITTLEST
EIKMMRRS	KRIMMERS
EIKMMRSS	SKIMMERS
EIKMNORS	MONIKERS
EIKMNOST	TOKENISM
EIKMNOSU	MOUSEKIN
EIKMOPSS	MISSPOKE
EIKMORTW	TIMEWORK
EIKMOSST	SMOKIEST
EIKMOSSU	KOUMISES
EIKMOSSY	MISYOKES
EIKMPSSU	MUSPIKES
EIKMRRSS	SMIRKERS
EIKMRSTU	MURKIEST
EIKMSSSU	KUMISSES
EIKMSSTU	MUSKIEST
EIKNNORS	EINKORNS
	NONSKIER
EIKNNOST	INKSTONE
EIKNNPSS	PINKNESS
EIKNNRSS	SKINNERS
EIKNOORS	ROOINEKS
EIKNOOST	NOOKIEST
EIKNOPSS	POKINESS
EIKNORST	INSTROKE
EIKNORSV	INVOKERS
EIKNORTT	KNOTTIER
EIKNOSTW	WONKIEST
EIKNPRRS	PRINKERS
EIKNPRSU	SPUNKIER
EIKNPRTU	TURNPIKE
EIKNPSSU	SPUNKIES
EIKNPSTU	PUNKIEST
EIKNRRTU	RETURNIK
EIKNRSST	STINKERS
EIKNRSTT	KNITTERS
	TRINKETS
EIKNSSSU	UNKISSES
EIKNSSTT	SKINTEST
EIKNSTUZ	KUNZITES
EIKOOPRS	SPOOKIER
EIKOORST	ROOKIEST
EIKOPPRS	PORKPIES
EIKOPPRW	PIPEWORK
EIKOPRST	PORKIEST
EIKOPRSV	OVERSKIP
EIKORRWW	WIREWORK
EIKPPRSS	SKIPPERS
EIKPPSST	SKIPPETS
EIKPRRSU	SPRUIKER
EIKRRSST	SKIRRETS
	SKIRTERS
	STRIKERS
EIKRRSSU	SKURRIES
EIKRSSTT	SKITTERS
EIKRSSTU	TURKISES
EIKRSTTY	SKITTERY
EIKRSTWY	SKYWRITE
EIKSSTTU	TUSKIEST
EILLLNOY	LONELILY
EILLLOVY	LOVELILY
EILLLPUV	PULVILLE
EILLMNNO	MONELLIN
EILLMNOU	LINOLEUM
EILLMNQU	QUILLMEN
EILLMNST	STILLMEN
EILLMNSU	MULLEINS
EILLMOPR	IMPELLOR
EILLMOPS	PLIMSOLE
EILLMOST	MELILOTS
EILLMPSS	MISSPELL
	PSELLISM
EILLMPTU	MULTIPLE
EILLMSST	MISTELLS
EILLMSTU	MULLITES
EILLMUVX	VEXILLUM
EILLNOPT	PLOTLINE
EILLNOPY	EPYLLION
EILLNOST	STELLION
EILLNOTU	LUTEOLIN
EILLNPUU	LUPULINE
EILLNSST	LINTLESS
EILLNSTY	SILENTLY
	TINSELLY
EILLNSUV	LEVULINS
EILLNSVY	SNIVELLY
EILLNUVY	UNLIVELY
EILLOORW	WOOLLIER
EILLOOSW	WOOLLIES
EILLOPSS	SLIPSOLE
EILLOPTY	POLITELY
EILLORST	TRILLOES
	TROLLIES
EILLORSU	ROUILLES
EILLORSZ	ZORILLES
EILLORWW	WILLOWER
EILLOSSS	SOILLESS
EILLOSST	TOILLESS
EILLOSTW	LOWLIEST
EILLOSVW	LOWLIVES
EILLPRSS	SPILLERS
EILLPSSS	SLIPLESS
EILLQSTU	QUILLETS
EILLRRST	TRILLERS
EILLRSST	STILLERS
EILLRSSW	SWILLERS
EILLRSTT	TESTRILL
EILLRSVY	SILVERLY
EILLSSST	LISTLESS
	SLITLESS
EILLSSTT	STILLEST
EILLSTTT	LITTLEST
EILLSTUV	VITELLUS
EILMMNOS	MOLIMENS
EILMMPRU	PLUMMIER
EILMMRSS	SLIMMERS
EILMMRSU	SLUMMIER
EILMMSST	SLIMMEST
EILMMSTU	LUMMIEST
EILMNOOS	OINOMELS
	SIMOLEON
EILMNOPT	PILOTMEN
EILMNORS	MISENROL
EILMNOST	MOLINETS
EILMNOSU	EMULSION
EILMNOSV	NOVELISM
EILMNOTU	MOULINET
EILMNOTY	MYLONITE
EILMNPSS	LIMPNESS
	PLENISMS
EILMNPSU	SPLENIUM
EILMNPTU	TUMPLINE
EILMNRST	MINSTREL
EILMNSSS	SLIMNESS
EILMNSSU	EMULSINS
EILMNSTU	MUSLINET
EILMNTUY	MINUTELY
	UNTIMELY
EILMOOPS	LIPOSOME
EILMOORS	SLOOMIER
EILMOOST	TOILSOME
EILMOPRR	IMPLORER
EILMOPRS	IMPLORES
	PELORISM
EILMOPST	MILEPOST
	POLEMIST
EILMORRS	LORIMERS
EILMORSY	RIMOSELY
EILMOSTT	MOTLIEST
EILMOSTU	OUTSMILE
EILMOSUV	VOLUMISE
EILMOUVZ	VOLUMIZE
EILMPPRU	IMPURPLE
	PLUMPIER
EILMPRRU	RUMPLIER
EILMPRSS	SIMPLERS
EILMPRSU	SLUMPIER
EILMPRUY	IMPURELY
EILMPSST	MISSPELT
	SIMPLEST
EILMPSSU	IMPULSES
EILMPSTU	LUMPIEST
	PLUMIEST
EILMRSSU	MISRULES
EILMRSSY	REMISSLY
EILMRSTU	MURLIEST
EILMRSTY	LYMITERS
EILMSSTU	LITMUSES
EILMSSTY	MISSTYLE
EILMSTUU	MULTIUSE
EILMSUUV	ELUVIUMS
EILMTTUU	LUTETIUM
EILMTTUY	MULTEITY
EILNNOST	INSOLENT
EILNNOSV	NONLIVES
EILNNOSW	SNOWLINE
EILNNOTT	NONTITLE
EILNNOTV	VINOLENT
EILNNPSU	PINNULES
EILNNSTU	UNSILENT
EILNNTTY	INTENTLY
EILNOOPP	EPIPLOON
EILNOOPS	POLONIES
	POLONISE
EILNOOPZ	POLONIZE
EILNOOST	LOONIEST
	OILSTONE
EILNOOSV	VIOLONES
EILNOPPS	PLENIPOS
EILNOPPY	POLYPINE
EILNOPRS	PROLINES
EILNOPRT	TERPINOL
	TOPLINER
EILNOPRU	NEUROPIL
EILNOPSS	EPSILONS
EILNOPST	POINTELS
	PONTILES
	POTLINES
	TOPLINES
EILNOPTU	UNPOLITE
EILNORRS	LORINERS
EILNORRT	RITORNEL
EILNORST	RETINOLS
EILNORTT	TROTLINE
EILNORTU	OUTLINER
EILNORTW	TOWNLIER
EILNORVV	INVOLVER
EILNOSSU	ELUSIONS
EILNOSSW	LEWISSON
EILNOSTU	ELUTIONS
	OUTLINES
EILNOSTV	NOVELIST
	VIOLENTS
EILNOSTW	TOWLINES
EILNOSUV	EVULSION
EILNOSVV	INVOLVES
EILNOTUV	INVOLUTE
EILNOTXY	XYLONITE
EILNOTYZ	ZYLONITE
EILNPRSS	PILSNERS
EILNPRST	SPLINTER
EILNPRSU	PURLINES
EILNPRUY	UNRIPELY
EILNPSSS	SPINLESS
EILNPSST	PLENISTS
EILNPSSU	SPINULES
	SPLENIUS
EILNPSUY	SUPINELY
EILNQUUY	UNIQUELY
EILNRRUU	UNRULIER
EILNRSST	SLINTERS
	SNIRTLES
EILNRSTU	INSULTER
	LUSTRINE
EILNRSTY	TINSELRY
EILNRTUV	VIRULENT
EILNRTWY	WINTERLY

EILNSSTT	TINTLESS
EILNSSTU	UTENSILS
EILNSSTW	WESTLINS
EILNSSVY	SYLVINES
EILNSTTU	LUTENIST
EILNSUWY	UNWISELY
EILOOPRR	POORLIER
EILOOPST	LOOPIEST
EILOOPTZ	ZOPILOTE
EILOORST	OESTRIOL, TROOLIES
EILOORTV	OVERTOIL
EILOOSST	OSTIOLES, STOOLIES
EILOOSTW	WOOLIEST
EILOOSTY	OTIOSELY
EILOOSTZ	ZOOLITES
EILOPPPR	POPPLIER
EILOPPRS	SLOPPIER
EILOPPST	LOPPIEST
EILOPPTY	POLYPITE
EILOPRRT	PORTLIER
EILOPRSS	SPOILERS
EILOPRST	POITRELS
EILOPRSU	PERILOUS
EILOPRSV	OVERSLIP, SLIPOVER
EILOPRTT	PLOTTIER
EILOPRTW	PILEWORT
EILOPRYZ	PYROLIZE
EILOPSSS	PSILOSES
EILOPSST	PISTOLES, PTILOSES, SLOPIEST
EILOPSSV	PLOSIVES
EILOPSTT	PISTOLET, PLOTTIES, POLITEST
EILOPSTX	EXPLOITS
EILOPSUV	PLUVIOSE
EILORRTU	ULTERIOR
EILORSSS	RISSOLES
EILORSST	ESTRIOLS
EILORSSU	SOILURES
EILORSTT	TRIOLETS
EILORSTU	LOURIEST, OUTLIERS
EILORSUV	RIVULOSE
EILORSZZ	SOZZLIER
EILORTTY	TOILETRY
EILORTUV	OUTLIVER
EILORVWY	OVERWILY
EILOSSST	LOSSIEST
EILOSSTU	LOUSIEST
EILOSTTT	STILETTO
EILOSTUV	OUTLIVES, SOLUTIVE
EILOSTUW	OUTWILES
EILOTVVY	VOTIVELY
EILPPPRY	PREPPILY
EILPPRRS	RIPPLERS
EILPPRRT	TRIPPLER
EILPPRRU	PURPLIER
EILPPRSS	SLIPPERS
EILPPRST	PRESPLIT, RIPPLETS, STIPPLER, TIPPLERS, TRIPPLES
EILPPRSU	PERIPLUS, SUPPLIER
EILPPRSY	SLIPPERY
EILPPRTU	PULPITER
EILPPSST	STIPPLES
EILPPSSU	SUPPLIES
EILPPSSW	SWIPPLES
EILPPSTU	PULPIEST
EILPRSST	RESPLITS, SPIRTLES
EILPRSTT	SPLITTER, TRIPLETS
EILPRSTY	PRIESTLY, SPRITELY
EILPRSUU	PURLIEUS
EILPRSUY	PLEURISY
EILPRTTY	PRETTILY
EILPSSSU	PUSSLIES
EILPSSTT	SPITTLES
EILPSSTU	STIPULES
EILPSSUY	SPULYIES
EILPSSUZ	SPULZIES
EILQRRSU	SQUIRREL
EILQRSTU	QUILTERS
EILQRSUU	LIQUEURS
EILQRSUY	SQUIRELY
EILQSTUU	LUSTIQUE
EILRRSSU	SLURRIES
EILRRSTU	SULTRIER
EILRRSTW	TWIRLERS
EILRRTWY	WRITERLY
EILRSSST	STIRLESS
EILRSSTT	SLITTERS, STILTERS, TESTRILS
EILRSSTU	SURLIEST
EILRSSTY	SISTERLY, STYLISER
EILRSSUV	SURVEILS
EILRSSZZ	SIZZLERS
EILRSTTU	SLUTTIER, SURTITLE
EILRSTTW	WRISTLET
EILRSTTZ	STRELITZ
EILRSTUV	RIVULETS
EILRSTYZ	STYLIZER
EILRSUUX	LUXURIES
EILRSWZZ	SWIZZLER
EILSSSTY	STYLISES
EILSSTTU	LUSTIEST
EILSSTTY	STYLITES
EILSSTUU	LITUUSES
EILSSTVY	SYLVITES
EILSSTYZ	STYLIZES
EILSSWZZ	SWIZZLES
EILSTWZZ	TWIZZLES
EIMMMNOT	IMMOMENT
EIMMMORZ	MOMZERIM
EIMMNNOT	MONIMENT
EIMMNNTU	MUNIMENT
EIMMNORS	MISNOMER
EIMMOPRU	EMPORIUM
EIMMOPST	METOPISM
EIMMOSSV	MISMOVES
EIMMOSTT	TOTEMISM
EIMMPRRS	PRIMMERS
EIMMPRST	PRIMMEST
EIMMPRSU	PREMIUMS
EIMMPSSU	PESSIMUM
EIMMRRST	TRIMMERS
EIMMRSST	MISTERMS
EIMMRSSW	SWIMMERS
EIMMRSTT	TRIMMEST
EIMMRSTU	RUMMIEST
EIMMSSTU	MUMSIEST
EIMMSTUY	YUMMIEST
EIMNNOOT	NOONTIME
EIMNNOPT	IMPONENT, POINTMEN
EIMNNOST	MENTIONS
EIMNNOTT	OINTMENT
EIMNNOUY	EUONYMIN
EIMNOOPS	EMPOISON
EIMNOORS	IONOMERS, MOONRISE
EIMNOORT	MOTIONER, REMOTION
EIMNOORV	OMNIVORE
EIMNOOSS	MONOSIES
EIMNOOST	EMOTIONS, MOONIEST
EIMNOOSX	EXOMIONS
EIMNOPPU	PEPONIUM
EIMNOPRS	PROMINES
EIMNOPRT	ORPIMENT
EIMNOPSS	PEONISMS
EIMNOPST	EMPTIONS, NEPOTISM, PIMENTOS
EIMNOPTT	IMPOTENT
EIMNOPTV	PIVOTMEN
EIMNORSS	MERSIONS
EIMNORSU	INERMOUS, MONSIEUR
EIMNORSW	WINSOMER
EIMNORTW	TIMEWORN
EIMNORTY	ENORMITY
EIMNOSST	MESTINOS, MOISTENS, SENTIMOS
EIMNPRSS	PRIMNESS
EIMNPSST	MISSPENT
EIMNPSTU	NUMPTIES
EIMNRSST	ENTRISMS, MINSTERS, TRIMNESS
EIMNRSSU	NEURISMS
EIMNRSTU	TERMINUS, UNMITERS, UNMITRES
EIMNRSTY	ENTRYISM, MISENTRY
EIMNSSSS	SENSISMS
EIMNSSTU	MISTUNES
EIMNSTTU	MINUTEST
EIMNSUZZ	MUEZZINS
EIMOORST	MOORIEST, MOTORISE, ROOMIEST
EIMOORTZ	MOTORIZE
EIMOOSST	OSTOMIES
EIMOPPRR	IMPROPER
EIMOPPST	MOPPIEST
EIMOPRRS	PRIMEROS, PRIMROSE, PROMISER
EIMOPRRT	IMPORTER, REIMPORT
EIMOPRRV	IMPROVER
EIMOPRSS	IMPOSERS, PROMISES, SEMIPROS
EIMOPRST	IMPOSTER
EIMOPRSV	IMPROVES
EIMOPRSW	IMPOWERS
EIMOPRUU	EUROPIUM
EIMOPSTY	PEYOTISM
EIMOQSTU	MISQUOTE
EIMORRSS	MORRISES
EIMORRST	MORTISER, STORMIER
EIMORRTT	REMITTOR
EIMORRTV	OVERTRIM
EIMORRWW	WIREWORM
EIMORSST	EROTISMS, MORTISES, TRISOMES
EIMORSSV	VERISMOS
EIMORSTT	OMITTERS
EIMORSTU	MISROUTE, MOISTURE
EIMORSTV	VOMITERS
EIMORSTW	MISWROTE, WORMIEST
EIMORSTY	ISOMETRY
EIMORSVW	OVERSWIM
EIMOSSST	MOSSIEST
EIMOSSTT	MOISTEST
EIMOSSTU	MOUSIEST
EIMOSSTX	EXOTISMS
EIMOSSTZ	MESTIZOS
EIMOSSYZ	ISOZYMES
EIMOSTTT	MOTTIEST, TOTEMIST
EIMOSTTU	TIMEOUTS, TITMOUSE
EIMPRRST	PRETRIMS
EIMPRRSU	PRIMEURS
EIMPRSST	IMPRESTS
EIMPRSSU	PRIMUSES
EIMPRSTU	IMPUREST, IMPUTERS, STUMPIER
EIMPSSST	MISSTEPS
EIMPSSTU	SPUMIEST, STUMPIES
EIMPSSTY	EMPTYSIS, MISTYPES
EIMPSTTU	TUMPIEST
EIMQRRSU	SQUIRMER
EIMQSSTU	MESQUITS
EIMQSTUY	MYSTIQUE
EIMQSTUZ	MEZQUITS
EIMRRRSU	SMURRIER
EIMRRSSU	SURMISER
EIMRSSST	MISTRESS
EIMRSSSU	MISUSERS, SURMISES
EIMRSSTT	METRISTS
EIMRSSTY	SMYTRIES
EIMRSSUU	MIURUSES
EIMRSTTU	SMUTTIER
EIMRSTUV	VITREUMS
EIMRSTUX	MIXTURES
EIMSSSSU	MISSUSES
EIMSSSTU	MUSSIEST
EIMSSTTU	MUSTIEST
EIMSTUZZ	MUZZIEST
EINNOOTX	NEOTOXIN
EINNOPPT	PENPOINT
EINNOPRU	PREUNION
EINNOPRY	PYRONINE
EINNOPSS	PENSIONS
EINNOQSU	QUINONES
EINNORSS	IRONNESS
EINNORST	INTONERS, TERNIONS
EINNORSU	REUNIONS
EINNORSV	ENVIRONS
EINNORTT	TONTINER
EINNORTU	NEUTRINO
EINNORTV	INVENTOR, NOVERINT
EINNORWW	WINNOWER
EINNOSSS	NOSINESS
EINNOSST	TENSIONS
EINNOSSU	NONISSUE, UNSONSIE
EINNOSSV	VENISONS
EINNOSTT	TINSTONE, TONTINES

EINNOSTU NOUNIEST
EINNPRSS SPINNERS
EINNPRST ENPRINTS
EINNPRSY SPINNERY
EINNPSST SPINNETS
EINNPSSU PUNINESS
EINNPSSY SPINNEYS
EINNPSTU PUNNIEST
EINNPSXY SIXPENNY
EINNRSTU RUNNIEST STURNINE
EINNRSTV VINTNERS
EINNRTTU NUTRIENT
EINNSSTT TENNISTS
EINNSSTU SUNNIEST
EINNSSUW UNSINEWS
EINNSSWY SWINNEYS
EINNSTUW UNTWINES
EINOOPRS POISONER SNOOPIER SPOONIER
EINOOPSS SPOONIES
EINOOPSZ OPSONIZE
EINOORSS EROSIONS
EINOORST SNOOTIER
EINOORSZ OZONISER SNOOZIER
EINOORZZ OZONIZER
EINOOSST ISOTONES
EINOOSSZ OOZINESS OZONISES
EINOOSTZ ZOONITES
EINOOSZZ OZONIZES
EINOOTXX EXOTOXIN
EINOPPRS POPERINS PROPINES
EINOPRRS PRISONER
EINOPRSS PORINESS PRESSION ROPINESS
EINOPRST POINTERS PORNIEST PROTEINS REPOINTS TROPINES
EINOPRSU PRUINOSE
EINOPRSV OVERSPIN PROVINES
EINOPRTU ERUPTION
EINOPSSW WINESOPS
EINOPSTT NEPOTIST
EINOPSWX SWINEPOX
EINOQSTU QUESTION
EINOQTTU QUOTIENT
EINORRST INTRORSE SNORTIER
EINORRTV INVERTOR
EINORRTW INTERROW
EINORSSS ROSINESS
EINORSST OESTRINS TERSIONS
EINORSSU NEUROSIS RESINOUS
EINORSSV VERSIONS
EINORSTT SNOTTIER TENORIST TRITONES
EINORSTU ROUTINES SNOUTIER
EINORSTV INVESTOR
EINORSTY TYROSINE
EINORSTZ TRIZONES
EINORSUV SOUVENIR
EINORTTU RITENUTO
EINOSSSS SESSIONS
EINOSSST SONSIEST STENOSIS
EINOSSTT SNOTTIES STONIEST
EINOSSTW SNOWIEST
EINOSTTT TOTIENTS
EINOSTTW TOWNIEST
EINOSTUU TENUIOUS
EINOSTVY VENOSITY
EINPPRRT PREPRINT
EINPPRSS SNIPPERS
EINPPSST SNIPPETS
EINPPSTY SNIPPETY
EINPRRST PRINTERS REPRINTS SPRINTER
EINPRRTU PRURIENT
EINPRRTY PRINTERY
EINPRSST SPINSTER
EINPRSTU REPUNITS UNPRIEST UNRIPEST
EINPRTTU INPUTTER
EINPSTTX SPINTEXT
EINPSTTY TINTYPES
EINQRSTU SQUINTER
EINQRTTU QUITRENT
EINQSSTU INQUESTS
EINQSTTU QUINTETS
EINQSTUU UNIQUEST UNQUIETS
EINQTTTU QUINTETT
EINRRSSU INSURERS
EINRSSST INSTRESS
EINRSSSU SUNRISES
EINRSSTT ENTRISTS STINTERS
EINRSSXY SYRINXES
EINRSTTU RUNTIEST
EINRSTTW TWINTERS
EINRSTTY ENTRYIST
EINRSTUV UNRIVETS VENTURIS
EINRSTUW UNWRITES
EINRTUUV UNVIRTUE
EINSSSST SENSISTS
EINSSTTU NUTSIEST
EINSSTTW ENTWISTS TWINSETS
EINSSTUW UNWISEST
EINSSTUX UNSEXIST
EINSSTXY SYNTEXIS
EINSTTTU NUTTIEST
EINSTTTW TWITTENS
EIOOPPRS PORPOISE
EIOOPPST OPPOSITE
EIOOPRST PORTOISE ROOPIEST
EIOOPSST ISOTOPES
EIOOPSTV POOVIEST
EIOOPTYZ EPIZOOTY
EIOORRSS SORORISE
EIOORRST ROOTSIER
EIOORRSZ SORORIZE
EIOORSTT ROOTIEST TORTOISE
EIOOSSST OSTEOSIS
EIOOSSTT SOOTIEST TOOTSIES
EIOOSTTZ ZOOTIEST
EIOOSTWZ WOOZIEST
EIOPPPST POPPIEST
EIOPPRTW PIPEWORT
EIOPPSST SOPPIEST
EIOPPTTY TIPPYTOE
EIOPQRSU PIROQUES
EIOPQSTU POSTIQUE
EIOPRRSS PRIORESS
EIOPRRST PIERROTS SPORTIER
EIOPRRSU SUPERIOR
EIOPRRSV PREVISOR
EIOPRRTV OVERTRIP
EIOPRSSS PROSSIES
EIOPRSST PERIOSTS PROSIEST PROSTIES REPOSITS RIPOSTES TRIPOSES
EIOPRSTT PORTIEST RISPETTO SPOTTIER
EIOPRSTU ROUPIEST SPOUTIER
EIOPRSTV OVERTIPS PIVOTERS SORPTIVE SPORTIVE
EIOPRSUV PERVIOUS PREVIOUS VIPEROUS
EIOPRTTT TRIPTOTE
EIOPRTTY PETITORY
EIOPRTUZ OUTPRIZE
EIOPSSST SEPIOSTS
EIOPSSSU POUSSIES
EIOPSSTU SOUPIEST
EIOPSSTX EXPOSITS
EIOPSSTY ISOTYPES
EIOPSTTT POTTIEST
EIOPSTTU POUTIEST
EIOPSTTY PEYOTIST
EIOPSTUW WIPEOUTS
EIOQRSTU QUOITERS
EIOQSTUX QUIXOTES
EIORRRST ERRORIST
EIORRRSW WORRIERS
EIORRRTU ROTURIER
EIORRSST RESISTOR ROISTERS SORRIEST
EIORRSSV REVISORS
EIORRSTT RORTIEST
EIORRSTU STOURIER
EIORRSTV OVERSTIR SERVITOR
EIORRSUV OUVRIERS REOVIRUS
EIORRSVV REVIVORS
EIORRSVY REVISORY
EIORRTTU TROUTIER
EIORSSTT STOITERS
EIORSSTY SEROSITY
EIORSTTU TOUSTIER TUTORISE
EIORSTTV VIRETOTS
EIORSTUV VIRTUOSE VITREOUS VOITURES
EIORTTUW OUTWRITE
EIORTTUZ TUTORIZE
EIOSSSTT TOSSIEST
EIOSSTTU TOUSIEST
EIOSSTTW TOWSIEST
EIOSSTUZ OUTSIZES
EIOSTTTT TOTTIEST
EIOSTTTU TOUTIEST
EIOSTTUZ TOUZIEST
EIOSTTWZ TOWZIEST
EIPPQRSU QUIPPERS
EIPPRRST STRIPPER TRIPPERS
EIPPRRSY PERSPIRY
EIPPRRTY TRIPPERY
EIPPRSTT TRIPPETS
EIPQRSTU QUIPSTER
EIPRRRSU SPURRIER
EIPRRSST STRIPERS
EIPRRSSU SPURRIES SURPRISE UPRISERS
EIPRRSTZ SPRITZER
EIPRRSUV UPRIVERS
EIPRRSUY SYRUPIER
EIPRRSUZ SURPRIZE
EIPRSSST PERSISTS
EIPRSSSU SUSPIRES
EIPRSSTT SPITTERS TIPSTERS
EIPRSSTU PURSIEST
EIPRSSTZ SPRITZES
EIPRSTTU PURTIEST PUTTIERS
EIPRSUVW PURVIEWS
EIPRSVVY SPIVVERY
EIPSSSTU PUSSIEST
EIPSSTXY PTYXISES
EIQRRSTU SQUIRTER
EIQRSSSU SQUIRESS
EIQRSSTU QUERISTS
EIQRSTTU QUITTERS
EIQRSTUU SEQUITUR
EIQRSUZZ QUIZZERS
EIQRUYZZ QUIZZERY
EIQSSUZZ SQUIZZES
EIRRRSST STIRRERS
EIRRSSTV STRIVERS
EIRRSTTU TRUSTIER
EIRRSUVV SURVIVER
EIRSSSTU SUITRESS TSURISES
EIRSSTTU RUSTIEST TRUSTIES
EIRSSTTW RETWISTS TWISTERS
EIRSSTUV REVUISTS STUIVERS
EIRSSUVV SURVIVES
EIRSSUVW SURVIEWS
EIRSTTTU RUTTIEST
EIRSTTTW TWITTERS
EIRSTTUX TUTRIXES
EIRTTTWY TWITTERY
EIRTTUWZ WURTZITE
EISSSSTU TUSSISES
EISSSTUW WUSSIEST
EJLLORSY JOLLYERS
EJLOPSTU PULSOJET
EJLORSST JOSTLERS
EJMOPRUV OVERJUMP
EJNORRSU REJOURNS
EJNORSUY JOURNEYS
EJNRSTUU UNJUSTER
EJNSSSTU JUSTNESS
EJOORSVY OVERJOYS
EJOPPRST PROPJETS
EJOPRSTT JETPORTS
EJORSSTU JOUSTERS
EJORSTUV OVERJUST
EJOSSTTU OUTJESTS
EKKLNPRU KERPLUNK
EKKLOOSY OLYKOEKS
EKKLOOSZ KOLKOZES
EKKLRSSU SKULKERS

EKKMORSY	KROMESKY
EKLLMSSU	SKELLUMS
EKLLNORS	KNOLLERS
EKLLOSSY	KYLLOSES
EKLLRRSU	KRULLERS
EKLNOOOR	ONLOOKER
EKLNOPRS	PLONKERS
EKLNORSS	SNORKELS
EKLNOSST	KNOTLESS
EKLNPRSU	PLUNKERS
EKLNPSSU	SPELUNKS
EKLOOORV	OVERLOOK
EKLOOPSW	SLOWPOKE
EKLORSSW	WORKLESS
EKLSSSTU	TUSKLESS
EKLSSTTU	SKUTTLES
EKMMORSU	MURKSOME
EKMMRSSU	SKUMMERS
EKMNOSSU	MUSKONES
EKMOOPRR	MOREPORK
EKMOOPST	SMOKEPOT
EKMOORSW	WORKSOME
EKMOOSSS	KOSMOSES
EKMOOSTU	OUTSMOKE
EKMOSSUY	KOUMYSES
EKMRSTUY	MUSKETRY
EKNNOORT	KENOTRON
EKNNOPSU	UNSPOKEN
EKNOOPRW	OPENWORK
EKNOORSS	SNOOKERS
EKNOORST	STROOKEN
EKNOPPSU	UPSPOKEN
EKNOPSSY	PYKNOSES
EKNORSST	STONKERS
EKNORSTT	KNOTTERS
EKNORSTW	NETWORKS
EKNORSUY	YOUNKERS
EKNRSTUY	TURNKEYS
EKOOOPRT	POKEROOT
EKOOORTV	OVERTOOK
EKOOPRRV	PROVOKER
EKOOPRRW	ROPEWORK
EKOOPRSV	PROVOKES
EKOOPRSY	SPOOKERY
EKOOPSTU	OUTSPOKE
EKOORRVW	OVERWORK
EKOORSST	STOOKERS
	STROOKES
EKOORSTW	KOTOWERS
EKOORSUU	EUROKOUS
EKOORTWW	KOWTOWER
EKOPRSTU	UPSTROKE
EKOPRSUY	KOUPREYS
EKORRSST	STROKERS
EKORRUVY	KURVEYOR
EKORSSTU	KURTOSES
EKORSTWY	SKYWROTE
EKPPSSUU	SEPPUKUS
ELLLMOWY	MELLOWLY
ELLLNSUY	SULLENLY
ELLLORRS	LORRELLS
ELLLOWYY	YELLOWLY
ELLMNOOS	MOELLONS
ELLMNOSY	SOLEMNLY
ELLMNOTY	MOLTENLY
ELLMNOUW	UNMELLOW
ELLMNPUY	LUMPENLY
ELLMOORS	MORELLOS
ELLMPSUU	PLUMULES
ELLNNOST	TONNELLS
ELLNNSSU	NULLNESS
ELLNOORV	LOVELORN
ELLNOOSW	WOOLLENS
ELLNOPRU	PRUNELLO
ELLNOSST	STOLLENS
ELLNOSSU	NOUSELLS
ELLNOSVY	SLOVENLY
ELLNOSXY	XYLENOLS
ELLNOUVY	UNLOVELY
ELLNPSSU	UNSPELLS
ELLOORRV	ROLLOVER
ELLOOSST	TOOLLESS
ELLOOSSW	WOOSELLS
ELLOOSTU	TOLUOLES
ELLOPRRS	PROLLERS
ELLOPRST	POLLSTER
ELLOPRTU	POLLUTER
ELLOPRUV	PULLOVER
ELLOPSST	PLOTLESS
ELLOPSTU	OUTSPELL
	POLLUTES
ELLORRST	STROLLER
	TROLLERS
ELLORSTY	TROLLEYS
ELLOSSSU	SOULLESS
ELLOSSTU	OUTSELLS
	SELLOUTS
ELLOSTTU	OUTTELLS
ELLOSTUW	OUTSWELL
	OUTWELLS
ELLOSTUY	OUTYELLS
ELLPPSSU	PULPLESS
ELLPPSUY	SUPPLELY
ELLPSSUW	UPSWELLS
ELLSSSTU	LUSTLESS
ELMMNOTU	LOMENTUM
ELMMNOTY	MOMENTLY
ELMMOPSU	PUMMELOS
ELMMORST	TROMMELS
ELMMOSUX	LUMMOXES
ELMMPSTU	PLUMMETS
ELMMRSSU	SLUMMERS
ELMMRSTU	STRUMMEL
	TUMMLERS
ELMMRSUY	SUMMERLY
ELMMSSTU	STUMMELS
ELMNNOSU	UNSOLEMN
ELMNNOTU	UNMOLTEN
ELMNOOOP	MONOPOLE
ELMNOOSS	MOONLESS
ELMNOOST	MOONLETS
ELMNOPSU	PULMONES
ELMNORSS	NORMLESS
ELMNOSTW	SNOWMELT
ELMNPPSU	PLUMPENS
ELMNPSUU	UNPLUMES
ELMNUUZZ	UNMUZZLE
ELMOOPPS	POMPELOS
ELMOOPSY	POLYSOME
ELMOORST	TREMOLOS
ELMOORSY	MOROSELY
ELMOOSSY	LYSOSOME
ELMOPRSY	POLYMERS
ELMOPRTY	METOPRYL
ELMOPRYY	POLYMERY
ELMOPSYY	POLYSEMY
ELMORSSU	EMULSORS
ELMORSTT	MOTTLERS
ELMORSTU	MOULTERS
ELMORUUV	VERMOULU
ELMOSTUU	TUMULOSE
ELMOSYYZ	LYSOZYME
ELMPPRSU	PLUMPERS
ELMPPSSU	PUMPLESS
ELMPPSTU	PLUMPEST
ELMPRSSU	RUMPLESS
ELMRRTUU	MULTURER
ELMRSTUU	MULTURES
ELMRSUZZ	MUZZLERS
ELNNNOOV	NONNOVEL
ELNNOOSU	UNLOOSEN
ELNNOPSU	NONUPLES
ELNNOPTU	NONUPLET
ELNNORSS	LORNNESS
ELNNOSSU	NOUNLESS
ELNNOSTY	NONSTYLE
ELNNRSTU	TRUNNELS
ELNOOPPR	PROPENOL
ELNOOSST	SOLONETS
ELNOOSSU	UNLOOSES
ELNOOSSZ	SNOOZLES
ELNOOSTZ	SOLONETZ
ELNOPPRY	PROPENYL
ELNOPRVY	PROVENLY
ELNOPSTU	PLEUSTON
ELNOPTTY	POTENTLY
ELNOPTYY	POLYTENY
ELNORSSU	NOURSLES
ELNORSTU	TURNSOLE
ELNORSVY	SLOVENRY
ELNORTTY	ROTTENLY
ELNOSSST	LOSTNESS
ELNOSSSW	SLOWNESS
	SNOWLESS
ELNOSSTV	SOLVENTS
ELNOSSTW	TOWNLESS
	WONTLESS
ELNOSTTW	TOWNLETS
ELNOSTUZ	ZONULETS
ELNOSUUV	VENULOUS
ELNOSUVY	VENOUSLY
ELNPPSUU	UNSUPPLE
ELNPRTUU	PURULENT
ELNPUUZZ	UNPUZZLE
ELNRSUUY	UNSURELY
ELNRSUZZ	NUZZLERS
ELNSSUZZ	SNUZZLES
ELOOPPRY	POLYPORE
ELOOPRSS	SPOOLERS
ELOOPRSU	SUPERLOO
ELOOPRTV	OVERPLOT
ELOOPRUW	OWERLOUP
ELOOPSSS	SESSPOOL
ELOORSST	ROOTLESS
ELOORSTT	ROOTLETS
	TOOTLERS
ELOORSTU	TORULOSE
ELOORSUV	OVERSOUL
ELOORSVW	OVERSLOW
ELOOSSST	SOOTLESS
ELOOSSTU	OUTSOLES
ELOOSSWY	WOOLSEYS
ELOOSTUV	OUTLOVES
ELOOSVVX	VOLVOXES
ELOPPRRY	PROPERLY
ELOPPSST	STOPPLES
ELOPPTYY	POLYTYPE
ELOPRRSU	PROULERS
ELOPRRSW	PROWLERS
ELOPRRSY	PYRROLES
ELOPRRTY	PORTERLY
ELOPRSSS	PLESSORS
ELOPRSST	PORTLESS
ELOPRSSU	SPORULES
ELOPRSTT	PLOTTERS
ELOPRSTU	PLOUTERS
	POULTERS
ELOPRSTW	PLOWTERS
ELOPRSTY	PROSTYLE
	PROTYLES
ELOPRSUV	OVERPLUS
ELOPRSYY	PYROLYSE
ELOPRXYY	PYROXYLE
ELOPRYYZ	PYROLYZE
ELOPSSST	SPOTLESS
	STOPLESS
ELOPSSUU	OPULUSES
ELOPSTTU	OUTSLEPT
	OUTSPELT
ELOPSTUY	OUTYELPS
ELORSSTT	SETTLORS
	SLOTTERS
ELORSTUY	ELYTROUS
	SOUTERLY
	UROSTYLE
ELORTTTU	TROUTLET
ELOSSSTY	SYSTOLES
ELOSSTUU	SETULOUS
ELOSSWZZ	SWOZZLES
ELPPRSTU	PURPLEST
ELPPRSUY	RESUPPLY
ELPPSSTU	SUPPLEST
ELPRRSSU	SLURPERS
ELPRSSSU	SPURLESS
ELPRSSTU	SPURTLES
ELPRSTTU	SPLUTTER
ELPRSTUU	PULTURES
ELPRSUZZ	PUZZLERS
ELPSSSUY	PUSSLEYS
ELPSSTUU	PUSTULES
ELPSTUXY	SEXTUPLY
ELRRSSTU	RUSTLERS
ELRRSTTU	TURTLERS
ELRSSSTU	RUSTLESS
ELRSTTUY	SLUTTERY
ELRSTUUV	VULTURES
ELSSSTUY	STYLUSES
ELSSSTYY	SYSTYLES
EMMMNOTU	MOMENTUM
EMMNNOTU	MONUMENT
EMMNOOOS	MONOSOME
EMMNOORS	MONOMERS
EMMNOORT	MOTORMEN
EMMNOOST	MOMENTOS
EMMNORSU	RESUMMON
	SUMMONER
EMMNORSY	MERONYMS
EMMNORYY	MERONYMY
EMMNOSTU	OMENTUMS
EMMNOSTY	METONYMS
EMMNOTTU	TOMENTUM
EMMNOTYY	METONYMY
EMMOOORS	ROOMSOME
EMMOOSTY	MYOTOMES
EMMOPRRS	PROMMERS
EMMOPRSU	SUPERMOM
EMMOPTTY	POMMETTY
EMMRRRUU	MURMURER
	REMURMUR
EMMRRSTU	STRUMMER
EMMRSTYY	SYMMETRY
EMNNNOOU	NOUMENON
EMNNNOOY	NONMONEY
EMNNOOOT	MONOTONE
EMNNOORT	NONMETRO
EMNNOPTY	NONEMPTY
EMNNOSTW	TOWNSMEN
EMNNOSYY	SYNONYME
EMNNPSTU	PUNTSMEN
EMNNSTTU	STUNTMEN
EMNOOPST	METOPONS
EMNOOPTY	MONOTYPE
EMNOORST	MESOTRON
	MONTEROS
EMNOORSU	ENORMOUS
	NEMOROUS
EMNOORSW	NEWSROOM
EMNOORTY	NOOMETRY
EMNOOSST	MOONSETS
EMNOOSUV	VENOMOUS

Letters	Anagrams
EMNOOTTY	TENOTOMY
EMNOOTUV	OUTVENOM
EMNOOTWY	TOYWOMEN
EMNOPSSU	SPUMONES
EMNORRSU	MOURNERS
EMNORSST	MONSTERS
EMNORSTT	SORTMENT
	TORMENTS
EMNORSTU	MONTURES
	MOUNTERS
	REMOUNTS
EMNORSUU	NUMEROUS
EMNOSSST	STEMSONS
EMNOSUUY	EUONYMUS
EMNOSUVY	EVONYMUS
EMNRSSTU	MUNSTERS
	STERNUMS
EMOOPRRT	PROMOTER
EMOOPRSS	OOSPERMS
EMOOPRST	PROMOTES
EMOOPRSY	POMEROYS
	PYROSOME
EMOOPRSZ	ZOOSPERM
EMOOPSSU	ESPUMOSO
EMOORRST	RESTROOM
EMOORSST	MOROSEST
EMOORSSU	UROSOMES
EMOORTYZ	ZOOMETRY
EMOOSSTW	TWOSOMES
EMOOSSTY	MYOSOTES
EMOOSSXY	OXYSOMES
EMOOSTUV	OUTMOVES
EMOPPRRT	PROMPTER
EMOPPRUV	OVERPUMP
EMOPRSST	STOMPERS
EMOPRSSU	SPERMOUS
	SUPREMOS
EMORRRUU	RUMOURER
EMORRSSU	MORSURES
EMORSSSU	SMOUSERS
EMORSSTU	OESTRUMS
	STRUMOSE
EMORSUVW	OVERSWUM
EMOSSSTT	MOSTESTS
EMOSSTTW	WESTMOST
EMOSSTVZ	ZEMSTVOS
EMOSTTTU	TETOTUMS
EMPRRTUY	TRUMPERY
EMPRSSTU	STUMPERS
	SUMPTERS
EMPRSSUU	RUMPUSES
EMPRSTTU	STRUMPET
	TRUMPETS
EMRRSSTU	STURMERS
ENNNOORW	NONOWNER
ENNNOOVW	NONWOVEN
ENNNORTY	NONENTRY
ENNOOORT	TENOROON
ENNOOOTZ	ENTOZOON
ENNOOPPT	OPPONENT
ENNOORST	NORTENOS
ENNOORTV	NONVOTER
ENNOOSTT	NONETTOS
ENNOPRSU	UNPERSON
ENNOPRUV	UNPROVEN
ENNOPTWY	TWOPENNY
ENNORSST	STERNSON
ENNORSSU	NONUSERS
ENNORSSW	WORNNESS
ENNORSTU	NEUTRONS
ENNORTTU	UNROTTEN
ENNOSSTU	NEUSTONS
	SUNSTONE
ENNPPTUY	TUPPENNY
ENNRSSTU	STUNNERS
ENOOORSV	OVERSOON
ENOOOSSZ	ZOONOSES
ENOOPPRS	PROPONES
ENOOPPST	POSTPONE
ENOOPRSS	POORNESS
	SNOOPERS
ENOOPSSY	SPOONEYS
ENOOPSTT	POTSTONE
	TOPSTONE
ENOORRVW	OVERWORN
ENOORSSW	SWOONERS
ENOORSSZ	SNOOZERS
ENOORSTU	OUTSNORE
ENOORSVW	OVERSOWN
ENOOSSTT	TESTOONS
ENOOSTXY	OXYTONES
ENOPPRRU	UNPROPER
ENOPRRSU	PRONEURS
ENOPRSST	POSTERNS
ENOPRSTT	PORTENTS
ENOPRTUW	UPTOWNER
ENOPSSST	STEPSONS
ENOPSSSY	SYNOPSES
ENOPSTTU	OUTSPENT
ENOQSTUU	UNQUOTES
ENORRSST	SNORTERS
ENORRSTT	TORRENTS
ENORRSUV	OVERRUNS
	RUNOVERS
ENORRTUU	TOURNURE
ENORRTUV	OVERTURN
	TURNOVER
ENORSSSU	SOURNESS
ENORSSTT	SNOTTERS
	STENTORS
ENORSSTU	TONSURES
ENORSTTU	STENTOUR
ENORSTTY	SNOTTERY
ENORSTUV	VENTROUS
ENORSTUY	TOURNEYS
ENOSSSUU	SENSUOUS
ENOSSTTU	STOUTENS
ENPRRSSU	PRESSRUN
	SPURNERS
ENPRSSSY	SPRYNESS
ENPRSSTU	PUNSTERS
ENPRSSUU	PRUNUSES
	UNPURSES
ENPRTTUY	UNPRETTY
ENRRRTUU	NURTURER
ENRRSTUU	NURTURES
ENRSSSTU	UNSTRESS
ENRSSTTU	ENTRUSTS
ENRSSTUU	UNSUREST
ENRSTTUU	UNTRUEST
EOOOPRSS	OOSPORES
	SOPOROSE
EOOOPRSZ	ZOOSPORE
EOOOPRTZ	ZOOTROPE
EOOORRST	ROSEROOT
EOOPPRRS	PROPOSER
EOOPPRSS	OPPOSERS
	PROPOSES
EOOPPRSV	POPOVERS
EOOPPSST	POSTPOSE
EOOPPTTY	TOPOTYPE
EOOPRRSS	SPOORERS
EOOPRRST	PROTORES
	TROOPERS
EOOPRRTU	OUTROPER
	UPROOTER
EOOPRSST	STOOPERS
EOOPRSSW	SWOOPERS
EOOPRSTU	OUTROPES
	PORTEOUS
EOOPRSTV	OVERPOST
	OVERTOPS
	STOPOVER
EOOPRSTW	TOWROPES
EOOPRTUW	OUTPOWER
EOOPSTYZ	ZOOTYPES
EOOQTTUU	OUTQUOTE
EOORRRSW	SORROWER
EOORRSST	ROOSTERS
EOORSSTU	OESTROUS
EOORSSVW	OVERSOWS
EOORSTUW	OUTSWORE
EOORTTUV	OUTVOTER
EOORTTUW	OUTTOWER
	OUTWROTE
EOOSTTUV	OUTVOTES
EOPPRRSS	PROSPERS
EOPPRRST	STROPPER
EOPPRRSU	SUPERPRO
EOPPRRTY	PROPERTY
EOPPRSST	STOPPERS
EOPPRSSU	PURPOSES
	SUPPOSER
EOPPRSSW	SWOPPERS
EOPPSSSU	SUPPOSES
EOPRRSSS	PRESSORS
EOPRRSST	PORTRESS
	PRESORTS
	SPORTERS
EOPRRSTU	POSTURER
	RESPROUT
	TROUPERS
EOPRRUVY	PURVEYOR
EOPRSSTT	PROTESTS
	SPOTTERS
EOPRSSTU	OUTPRESS
	POSTURES
	SEPTUORS
	SPOUTERS
EOPRSSUU	POURSUES
	UPROUSES
EOPRSSUV	OVERSUPS
EOPRSSUW	POURSEWS
EOPSSSTU	UPTOSSES
EOPSSTTT	POSTTEST
EOPSSTTU	OUTSTEPS
EOPSSTTW	STEWPOTS
EOQRRSTU	TORQUERS
EOQRSSTU	QUESTORS
EORRRTTU	TORTURER
EORRSSST	STRESSOR
	TROSSERS
EORRSSTT	STERTORS
EORRSSTU	ROUSTERS
	TRESSOUR
	TROUSERS
EORRSSTW	STROWERS
	TROWSERS
EORRSSTY	ROYSTERS
	STROYERS
EORRSTTT	TROTTERS
EORRSTTU	TORTURES
	TROUTERS
EORRSUVY	SURVEYOR
EORRTUUV	TROUVEUR
EORSSSTU	TUSSORES
EORSSTTT	STOTTERS
	STRETTOS
EORSSTTU	OUTSERTS
	TUTORESS
EORSSTTW	SWOTTERS
EORSSTUX	SEXTUORS
EORSTTUW	OUTWREST
EORSTTUY	TUTOYERS
EORSTUUV	VERTUOUS
EOSSTTTU	STOUTEST
EPPPRTUY	PUPPETRY
EPPRRSUU	PURPURES
EPPRSSSU	SUPPRESS
EPPRSSUY	SUPERSPY
EPRRRSSU	SPURRERS
EPRRSSUU	PURSUERS
	USURPERS
EPRRSSUY	SPURREYS
EPRRSTUU	RUPTURES
EPRSSTTU	SPUTTERS
EPRSTTUY	SPUTTERY
EQRRTUUU	TRUQUEUR
ERRSSSTU	TRUSSERS
ERRSSTTU	TRUSTERS
ERRSSTTY	TRYSTERS
ERRSTTTU	STRUTTER
ERSSTTTU	STUTTERS
FFFGILNU	FLUFFING
FFFILLUY	FLUFFILY
FFFILOST	LIFTOFFS
FFFMOOTU	FOOTMUFF
FFGGIILN	GLIFFING
FFGGINRU	GRUFFING
FFGHIINW	WHIFFING
FFGHINOU	HOUFFING
FFGHINOW	HOWFFING
FFGHIORS	FROGFISH
FFGHIRSU	GRUFFISH
FFGIIKNS	SKIFFING
FFGIILNP	PIFFLING
FFGIILNR	RIFFLING
FFGIILNS	SIFFLING
FFGIINNS	SNIFFING
FFGIINPS	SPIFFING
FFGIINRS	GRIFFINS
FFGIINST	STIFFING
	TIFFINGS
FFGIKNOS	SKOFFING
FFGILMNU	MUFFLING
FFGILNPU	PLUFFING
FFGILNRU	RUFFLING
FFGILNSU	SLUFFING
FFGILRUY	GRUFFILY
FFGINNSU	SNUFFING
FFGINOPU	POUFFING
FFGINORS	GRIFFONS
FFGINOSW	SOWFFING
FFGINPSU	PUFFINGS
FFGINSTU	STUFFING
FFGIORTU	FOGFRUIT
FFHIINSS	SNIFFISH
FFHIISST	STIFFISH
FFHIISTY	FIFTYISH
FFHIKNSU	HUFFKINS
FFHILOOS	FOOLFISH
FFHILOSW	WOLFFISH
FFHILOSY	OFFISHLY
FFHIOPSS	SPOFFISH
FFHIRSSU	SURFFISH
FFHOOOST	OFFSHOOT
FFHOOSSW	SHOWOFFS
FFHOSSTU	SHUTOFFS
FFIILMOR	FILIFORM
FFIILNSY	SNIFFILY
FFIILNTY	FLINTIFY
FFIILPSY	SPIFFILY
FFIINOOS	SOFFIONI
FFIKLORT	FORKLIFT
FFIKLRSU	FRISKFUL
FFILLLSU	FULFILLS
FFILLTUY	FITFULLY
FFILNSUY	SNUFFILY
FFILRTUU	FRUITFUL
FFILSSTU	FISTFULS

FFILSTUY	STUFFILY
FFIMORSU	FUSIFORM
FFINOOST	FINFOOTS
FFINOPRT	OFFPRINT
FFINOPSS	SPINOFFS
FFINOPST	PONTIFFS
FFJMOPSU	JUMPOFFS
FFKLORSU	FORKFULS
	FORKSFUL
FFLLOOSU	LOOFFULS
FFLMNOOU	MOUFFLON
FFLNOTUU	FOUNTFUL
FFLORRUU	FURFUROL
FFNORSTU	TURNOFFS
FFNSTUUY	UNSTUFFY
FFOOPSST	STOPOFFS
FFOORRUU	FROUFROU
FGGGIINR	FRIGGING
FGGGILNO	FLOGGING
FGGGINOR	FROGGING
FGGGINRU	FRUGGING
FGGHIINT	FIGHTING
FGGHIISS	FISHGIGS
FGGHINTU	GUNFIGHT
FGGIILNN	FLINGING
FGGIINNR	FRINGING
FGGIINRT	GRIFTING
FGGIINRU	FIGURING
FGGIISZZ	FIZZGIGS
FGGILNOR	FROGLING
FGGILNOS	GOLFINGS
FGGINOOR	FORGOING
FGGINORS	FORGINGS
FGHIIKNS	KINGFISH
FGHIILNT	INFLIGHT
FGHIINSS	FISHINGS
FGHIINST	INFIGHTS
	SHIFTING
FGHILLTU	LIGHTFUL
FGHILMTU	MIGHTFUL
FGHILNSU	FLUSHING
	LUNGFISH
FGHILRTU	RIGHTFUL
FGHINOOW	WHOOFING
FGHINORT	FROTHING
FGHINOTU	INFOUGHT
FGHINRSU	FRUSHING
FGHIOPST	GIFTSHOP
FGHIOTTU	OUTFIGHT
FGHLORUU	FURLOUGH
FGHNOORS	FOGHORNS
FGHNOTUU	UNFOUGHT
FGIIIKNN	FINIKING
FGIIINNX	INFIXING
FGIIKLNS	FLISKING
FGIIKNNS	KNIFINGS
FGIIKNRS	FRISKING
FGIILLNR	FRILLING
FGIILLNS	FILLINGS
FGIILMNP	FLIMPING
FGIILNNT	FLINTING
FGIILNOO	FOLIOING
FGIILNOS	FOILINGS
FGIILNPP	FLIPPING
FGIILNRS	RIFLINGS
FGIILNRT	FLIRTING
	TRIFLING
FGIILNSS	FISSLING
FGIILNST	STIFLING
FGIILNTT	FLITTING
FGIILNZZ	FIZZLING
FGIINNST	SNIFTING
FGIINNSU	INFUSING
FGIINNUX	UNFIXING
FGIINNUY	UNIFYING
FGIINOQU	QUOIFING
FGIINOST	FOISTING
FGIINRRS	FIRRINGS
FGIINRST	FRISTING
FGIINRTT	FRITTING
FGIINRTU	FRUITING
FGIINRZZ	FRIZZING
FGIINSST	SIFTINGS
FGIINSTT	FITTINGS
FGIINSTW	SWIFTING
FGIINSZZ	FIZZINGS
FGIIRSTU	FIGURIST
FGIKLNNU	FLUNKING
FGILLNOW	WOLFLING
FGILLNOY	FOLLYING
FGILMNPU	FLUMPING
FGILMNUY	FUMINGLY
FGILNNTU	GUNFLINT
FGILNOOR	FLOORING
FGILNOOS	FOOLINGS
FGILNOOT	FOOTLING
FGILNOOZ	FOOZLING
FGILNOPP	FLOPPING
FGILNOPS	FOPLINGS
FGILNORS	ROLFINGS
FGILNORU	FLOURING
FGILNOSS	FLOSSING
FGILNOST	SOFTLING
FGILNOSU	FLOUSING
	FOULINGS
FGILNOSW	FOWLINGS
	WOLFINGS
FGILNOTU	FLOUTING
	OUTFLING
FGILNPRU	PURFLING
FGILNPSU	UPFLINGS
FGILNRRU	FLURRING
FGILNSTU	FLUTINGS
FGILNSTY	FLYTINGS
FGILNUZZ	FUZZLING
FGIMNORS	FORMINGS
FGIMNPRU	FRUMPING
FGIMORRU	GRUIFORM
FGIMOSSY	FOGYISMS
FGINNORT	FRONTING
FGINNORW	FROWNING
FGINOOPR	PROOFING
FGINOOPS	SPOOFING
FGINOORS	ROOFINGS
FGINOOST	FOOTINGS
FGINORST	FROSTING
FGINORTU	FOUTRING
FGINRRSU	FURRINGS
FGINRSSU	SURFINGS
FGINRSTU	TURFINGS
FGINSTTU	TUFTINGS
FGIORSTW	FIGWORTS
FGISSTUU	FUGUISTS
FGLLMOOU	GLOOMFUL
FGLLNSUU	LUNGFULS
FGLNORSU	FURLONGS
FGLNORUW	WRONGFUL
FGLOOOST	FOOTSLOG
FGLORSUU	FULGOURS
FGLSSTUU	GUTSFULS
FGNOORSU	FOURGONS
FGNOORTU	UNFORGOT
FHHIKOOS	FISHHOOK
FHHOORST	SHOFROTH
FHIIKLMS	MILKFISH
FHIIKNSS	FISHSKIN
FHIILLTY	FILTHILY
FHIILNOS	LIONFISH
FHIILRST	FLIRTISH
FHIILSTY	SHIFTILY
FHIKLLLO	HILLFOLK
FHIKMNOS	MONKFISH
FHIKNORT	FORTHINK
FHILLOOT	FOOTHILL
FHILMPSU	LUMPFISH
FHILMRTU	MIRTHFUL
FHILOPST	SHOPLIFT
FHILORSU	FLOURISH
FHILORTY	FROTHILY
FHILPSSU	SHIPFULS
FHIMNOOS	MOONFISH
FHIMORSW	FISHWORM
FHIMPRSU	FRUMPISH
FHINOSSU	FUSHIONS
FHINRTTU	UNTHRIFT
FHINSSTU	UNSHIFTS
FHIOOPTT	PHOTOFIT
FHIOPSSX	FOXSHIPS
FHIORSTY	FORTYISH
FHIPSSTU	UPSHIFTS
FHKORSTU	FUTHORKS
FHLLLOTU	LOTHFULL
FHLLOSTU	SLOTHFUL
FHLMORUU	HUMORFUL
FHLMOTUU	MOUTHFUL
FHLNORSU	HORNFULS
FHLOOSTU	SOOTHFUL
FHLOOTTU	TOOTHFUL
FHLOPSSU	SHOPFULS
FHLORTTU	TROTHFUL
FHLORTUW	WORTHFUL
	WROTHFUL
FHLORTUY	FOURTHLY
FHLOSTUU	OUTFLUSH
FHLOTUUY	YOUTHFUL
FHLRTTUU	TRUTHFUL
FHNOSTUX	FOXHUNTS
FHOOORST	FORSOOTH
	HOOFROTS
FHOOOSTT	HOTFOOTS
FIIINNOX	INFIXION
FIIINNTY	INFINITY
FIIKLRSY	FRISKILY
FIILLMOS	MILFOILS
FIILLMSY	FLIMSILY
FIILLMTU	MULTIFIL
FIILLNTY	FLINTILY
FIILLSSU	FUSILLIS
FIILMNRY	INFIRMLY
FIILMOPR	PILIFORM
FIILMPSY	SIMPLIFY
FIILNOST	TINFOILS
FIILRTUY	FRUITILY
FIILRYZZ	FRIZZILY
FIILTTUY	FUTILITY
FIIMMNSU	INFIMUMS
FIIMOPRR	PIRIFORM
FIIMOPRS	PISIFORM
FIIMOSTY	MOISTIFY
FIINNOSU	INFUSION
FIINORTU	FRUITION
FIINOSSS	FISSIONS
FIINTUXY	UNFIXITY
FIIQUYZZ	QUIZZIFY
FIKKLNOS	KINFOLKS
	KINSFOLK
FIKLLLSU	SKILLFUL
FIKLLOSY	FOLKSILY
FIKLNOSW	WOLFKINS
	WOLFSKIN
FIKLNSSU	SKINFULS
FIKLSSTU	KISTFULS
FIKNORSW	FORSWINK
FIKNOSSX	FOXSKINS
FIKRSSTU	TURFSKIS
FILLLUWY	WILFULLY
FILLNSUY	SINFULLY
	SULFINYL
FILLNUUW	UNWILFUL
FILLOPPY	FLOPPILY
FILLOPSU	SPOILFUL
FILLOSSY	FLOSSILY
FILMNOOS	MONOFILS
FILMOPRS	SLIPFORM
FILMORRY	LYRIFORM
FILMOSSU	MOFUSSIL
FILMOSTU	MOISTFUL
FILMPRUY	FRUMPILY
FILNNSUU	UNSINFUL
FILNORSU	FLUORINS
FILNOSUX	FLUXIONS
FILOOOPR	OILPROOF
FILOOSTW	WITLOOFS
FILORSST	FLORISTS
FILORSTU	FLORUITS
FILORSTY	FROSTILY
FILORWYZ	FROWZILY
FILRSTTU	TRISTFUL
FILSSTTU	FLUTISTS
FILSTTUY	STULTIFY
FIMMNOOR	OMNIFORM
FIMMORRU	MURIFORM
FIMMORSS	MISFORMS
FIMNORSU	UNIFORMS
FIMOORRT	ROTIFORM
FIMOPRRY	PYRIFORM
FIMORRSU	URSIFORM
FIMORTUY	FUMITORY
FIMOSTUY	FUMOSITY
FIMRSTUU	FUTURISM
FINOOPSY	OPSONIFY
FINORSSS	FRISSONS
FINORSUY	INFUSORY
FIOORSSU	FURIOSOS
FIORTTUY	FORTUITY
FIRSTTUU	FUTURIST
FIRTTUUY	FUTURITY
FJLLOUYY	JOYFULLY
FJLNOUUY	UNJOYFUL
FKKLOORW	WORKFOLK
FKKOORTW	KOFTWORK
FKLMOOOT	FOLKMOOT
FKLMOOST	FOLKMOTS
FKLNOOTW	TOWNFOLK
FKLNRTUU	TRUNKFUL
FKMOORRW	FORMWORK
FKNORSUW	FORSWUNK
FKOOORTW	FOOTWORK
FLLNOSUY	SULFONYL
FLLOOPUW	UPFOLLOW
FLLRSUUY	SULFURYL
FLMNOOSU	MOUFLONS
FLMNORUU	MOURNFUL
FLMOOORW	MOORFOWL
FLMOOOST	TOMFOOLS
FLMOORSU	ROOMFULS
FLMORSTU	STORMFUL
FLNOOPSU	SPOONFUL
FLNOORRS	FORLORNS
FLNOOSTU	SNOOTFUL
FLNOOTUW	OUTFLOWN
FLOOOPTT	POLTFOOT
FLOOOSTU	OUTFOOLS
FLOOPTTY	TOPLOFTY
FLOORSSW	FORSLOWS
FLOOSTUW	OUTFLOWS
FLOPRSTU	SPORTFUL
FLORTTUU	TROUTFUL
FLRSTTUU	TRUSTFUL
FMNOOOOR	MOONROOF

FMOOPRST	POSTFORM
FMRSSTUU	FRUSTUMS
FNNOOORT	FRONTOON
FNNOORST	FRONTONS
FNOOORTW	FOOTWORN
FNOOPRSU	SUNPROOF
FNOORRSW	FORSWORN
FNOORSSU	SUNROOFS
FNOORTUW	OUTFROWN
FOOOPRST	ROOFTOPS
FOOOPSTT	FOOTPOST
FOOORSTT	FOOTROTS
FOOOSTTU	OUTFOOTS
FOORSTTX	FOXTROTS
FOPSSSTU	FUSSPOTS
GGGGIILN	GIGGLING
GGGGIINR	GRIGGING
GGGGILNO	GOGGLING
GGGGILNU	GLUGGING GUGGLING
GGGGINOR	GROGGING
GGGHIILN	HIGGLING
GGGHIINT	THIGGING
GGGHIINW	WHIGGING
GGGHINOS	HOGGINGS SHOGGING
GGGIIJLN	JIGGLING
GGGIIJNS	JIGGINGS
GGGIILNN	NIGGLING
GGGIILNS	LIGGINGS
GGGIILNW	WIGGLING
GGGIINNS	SNIGGING
GGGIINPR	PRIGGING
GGGIINPS	PIGGINGS
GGGIINRS	RIGGINGS
GGGIINRT	TRIGGING
GGGIINSW	SWIGGING WIGGINGS
GGGIINTW	TWIGGING
GGGIJLNO	JOGGLING
GGGIJLNU	JUGGLING
GGGIJNOS	JOGGINGS
GGGIJNSU	JUGGINGS
GGGIKNSU	SKUGGING
GGGILNOO	GOOGLING
GGGILNOS	LOGGINGS SLOGGING
GGGILNOT	TOGGLING
GGGILNPU	PLUGGING PUGGLING
GGGILNRU	GURGLING
GGGILNSU	SLUGGING
GGGILORY	GROGGILY
GGGIMNSU	MUGGINGS SMUGGING
GGGINNOS	NOGGINGS SNOGGING
GGGINNSU	SNUGGING
GGGINOPR	PROGGING
GGGINORT	TROGGING
GGGINOSS	SOGGINGS
GGGINPSU	PUGGINGS
GGGINRSU	RUGGINGS
GGGINSSU	SUGGINGS
GGGINSTU	TUGGINGS
GGHHIINT	HIGHTING
GGHHINOU	HOUGHING
GGHHISTU	THUGGISH
GGHIILNT	LIGHTING
GGHIINNW	WHINGING
GGHIINPT	PIGHTING
GGHIINRT	GIRTHING RIGHTING
GGHIINST	SIGHTING
GGHIINTW	WIGHTING
GGHIIPRS	PRIGGISH
GGHILSSU	SLUGGISH
GGHIMSTU	THUGGISM
GGHINORU	ROUGHING
GGHINOST	GHOSTING
GGHINOSU	SOUGHING
GGHINOTU	OUGHTING TOUGHING
GGHINOTY	HOGTYING
GGHOOPRS	GROGSHOP
GGIIILLN	GINGILLI
GGIIILNS	GINGILIS
GGIIINNT	IGNITING
GGIIJLNN	JINGLING
GGIIKLNN	KINGLING
GGIILLNR	GRILLING
GGIILLNY	GILLYING
GGIILMNN	MINGLING
GGIILMNY	GINGLYMI
GGIILNNP	PINGLING
GGIILNNS	SINGLING SLINGING
GGIILNNT	GLINTING TINGLING
GGIILNPS	PIGLINGS
GGIILNRS	RIGLINGS
GGIIMNOS	MISGOING
GGIIMNPU	GUIMPING
GGIIMPRS	PRIGGISM
GGIINNNR	GRINNING
GGIINNNS	GINNINGS
GGIINNOR	GROINING IGNORING
GGIINNOS	INGOINGS
GGIINNOT	INGOTING
GGIINNOW	WONGIING
GGIINNRS	RINGINGS
GGIINNRW	WRINGING
GGIINNSS	SIGNINGS SINGINGS
GGIINNST	STINGING
GGIINNSW	SWINGING
GGIINNTW	TWINGING
GGIINNUV	UNGIVING
GGIINPPR	GRIPPING
GGIINPSY	GIPSYING
GGIINRST	RINGGITS
GGIINRTT	GRITTING
GGIINSSU	GUISINGS
GGIINSTU	GIUSTING
GGIIRRSS	GRISGRIS
GGIITTUU	GUITGUIT
GGILLNUY	GULLYING
GGILLOOW	GOLLIWOG
GGILMMNO	GLOMMING
GGILMNOO	GLOOMING
GGILNNOP	PLONGING
GGILNNOS	LONGINGS
GGILNNOU	LOUNGING
GGILNNPU	PLUNGING PUNGLING
GGILNNUU	UNGLUING
GGILNOOP	GLOOPING
GGILNOPP	GLOPPING
GGILNORW	GROWLING
GGILNORY	GLORYING
GGILNOSS	GLOSSING GOSLINGS
GGILNOSV	GLOVINGS
GGILNOSZ	GLOZINGS
GGILNOTU	GLOUTING
GGILNRUY	URGINGLY
GGILNTTU	GLUTTING GUTTLING
GGILNUZZ	GUZZLING
GGILQSUY	SQUIGGLY
GGIMMNSU	GUMMINGS
GGIMNOOR	GROOMING
GGIMNPRU	GRUMPING
GGINNNSU	GUNNINGS
GGINNOOS	ONGOINGS
GGINNOPR	PRONGING
GGINNOPS	SPONGING
GGINNORW	WRONGING
GGINNOSS	SINGSONG
GGINNOTU	TONGUING
GGINNRTU	GRUNTING
GGINNUVY	UNGYVING
GGINOORV	GROOVING
GGINOOST	STOOGING
GGINOOTU	OUTGOING
GGINOPRS	PROGGINS
GGINOPRU	GROUPING
GGINOPSU	UPGOINGS
GGINORSS	GROSSING
GGINORSU	GROUSING
GGINORSW	GROWINGS
GGINORTU	GROUTING
GGINOSUV	VOGUINGS
GGINPRSU	PURGINGS
GGINPSYY	GYPSYING
GGINRSSU	SURGINGS
GGINSSUY	GUSSYING
GGLLOOWY	GOLLYWOG
GGLLPUUY	PLUGUGLY
GHHIILST	LIGHTISH
GHHIINSW	WHISHING
GHHIIRST	RIGHTISH
GHHIISTT	TIGHTISH
GHHILOSU	GHOULISH
GHHIMNPU	HUMPHING
GHHIMOST	HIGHMOST
GHHINOOS	HOOSHING
GHHINSSU	SHUSHING
GHHIOPST	HIGHSPOT
GHHIORSU	ROUGHISH
GHHIOSTU	TOUGHISH
GHHIRSST	SHRIGHTS
GHHOORTU	THOROUGH
GHHOSTTU	THOUGHTS
GHIIILNS	SHILINGI
GHIIJNOS	JINGOISH
GHIIKNNT	THINKING
GHIIKNPS	KINGSHIP
GHIIKNRS	SHIRKING SHRIKING
GHIIKNSW	WHISKING
GHIILLNO	HILLOING
GHIILLNS	SHILLING
GHIILMST	MISLIGHT
GHIILMTY	MIGHTILY
GHIILNOT	LITHOING
GHIILNPR	HIRPLING
GHIILNRS	HIRLINGS HIRSLING
GHIILNRT	THIRLING
GHIILNRW	WHIRLING
GHIILNST	TINGLISH
GHIILNTW	WHITLING
GHIILOTT	OILTIGHT
GHIILTTW	TWILIGHT
GHIIMMNS	SHIMMING
GHIIMMNW	WHIMMING
GHIIMNNU	INHUMING
GHIIMNST	SMITHING
GHIIMRST	RIGHTISM
GHIINNNS	SHINNING
GHIINNNT	THINNING
GHIINNNY	HINNYING
GHIINNRS	SHRINING
GHIINNST	NITHINGS
GHIINNSW	WHININGS
GHIINNUV	UNHIVING
GHIINOST	HOISTING
GHIINPPS	HIPPINGS SHIPPING
GHIINPPW	WHIPPING
GHIINRRS	SHIRRING
GHIINRRW	WHIRRING
GHIINRST	SHIRTING
GHIINRSV	SHRIVING
GHIINRTT	TRITHING
GHIINRTV	THRIVING
GHIINRTW	WRITHING
GHIINSSS	HISSINGS
GHIINSST	INSIGHTS
GHIINSSW	SWISHING WHISSING WISHINGS
GHIINSTT	SHITTING TITHINGS
GHIINSTW	WHISTING WHITINGS
GHIINSVV	SHIVVING
GHIINTTW	TWINIGHT
GHIINWZZ	WHIZZING
GHIIORSV	VIGORISH
GHIIRSTT	RIGHTIST
GHIKLNTY	KNIGHTLY
GHIKLSTY	SKYLIGHT
GHIKNNTU	THUNKING UNKNIGHT
GHIKNSSU	HUSKINGS
GHIKRSTU	TUGHRIKS
GHILLNOO	HOLLOING
GHILLNOU	HULLOING
GHILLOTW	LOWLIGHT
GHILLSTY	SLIGHTLY
GHILMNSU	MULSHING
GHILMPSU	GLUMPISH
GHILNOOS	SHOOLING
GHILNOPP	HOPPLING
GHILNOPS	LONGSHIP
GHILNOPY	HOPINGLY
GHILNOSS	SLOSHING
GHILNOST	SLOTHING
GHILNOSU	HOUSLING
GHILNOSW	HOWLINGS
GHILNPSU	INGULPHS
GHILNRSU	HURLINGS
GHILNRTU	HURTLING
GHILNRUY	HUNGRILY
GHILNSSU	SLUSHING
GHILNSTU	HUSTLING SUNLIGHT
GHILOPRS	SHOPGIRL
GHILORSW	SHOWGIRL
GHILORSY	OGRISHLY
GHILPRTY	TRIGLYPH
GHILPSTU	UPLIGHTS
GHIMMNSU	HUMMINGS
GHIMNOPR	MORPHING
GHIMNOPU	GUMPHION
GHIMNOPW	WHOMPING
GHIMNORU	HUMORING
GHIMNOSS	MOSHINGS
GHIMNOTU	MOUTHING
GHIMNPTU	THUMPING
GHIMNPUW	WHUMPING
GHIMNSTU	GUNSMITH
GHIMPRSU	GRUMPISH
GHIMPSYY	PYGMYISH
GHIMRSSU	SIMURGHS
GHINNNSU	SHUNNING
GHINNOOR	HONORING

GHINNOPY PHONYING
GHINNORS HORNINGS
GHINNORT NORTHING
THORNING
THRONING
GHINNOST NOTHINGS
GHINNSSU SNUSHING
GHINNSTU HUNTINGS
SHUNTING
GHINOOPT PHOTOING
GHINOOPW WHOOPING
GHINOOST SHOOTING
SOOTHING
GHINOOSW WOOSHING
GHINOOTT TOOTHING
GHINOOTW WHOOTING
GHINOPPS HOPPINGS
SHOPPING
GHINOPPW WHOPPING
GHINOPSS GINSHOPS
GHINORSS HORSINGS
SHORINGS
GHINORST SHORTING
GHINORSV SHROVING
GHINORSW SHOWRING
SHROWING
GHINORTT TROTHING
GHINORTW INGROWTH
THROWING
WORTHING
GHINOSST HOSTINGS
GHINOSSU HOUSINGS
GHINOSSW SHOWINGS
GHINOSTT HOTTINGS
SHOTTING
TONIGHTS
GHINOSTU HOUTINGS
SHOUTING
SOUTHING
GHINOSTW SOWTHING
GHINOSUY YOUNGISH
GHINOTTU OUTNIGHT
GHINPSSU GUNSHIPS
GHINPTTU PHUTTING
GHINRRUY HURRYING
GHINRSSU RUSHINGS
GHINRSTU UNGIRTHS
UNRIGHTS
GHINSSTU HUSTINGS
UNSIGHTS
GHINSTTU HUTTINGS
SHUTTING
GHIORTTU OUTRIGHT
GHIOSTTU OUTSIGHT
GHIPRSST SPRIGHTS
GHIPRSTU UPRIGHTS
GHIPRSUU GURUSHIP
GHIPSSYY GYPSYISH
GHLMOOOS HOMOLOGS
GHLMOOOY HOMOLOGY
GHLNNOOR LONGHORN
GHLNOORU HOURLONG
GHLNOOYY HOLOGYNY
GHLNORSU SLUGHORN
GHLNOTYY YONGTHLY
GHLOOORY HOROLOGY
GHLORTUU TURLOUGH
GHMNOOOY HOMOGONY
GHMORSSU SORGHUMS
GHMOSSTU MUGSHOTS
GHMPSSUY SPHYGMUS
GHNOPRSY GRYPHONS
GHNOPYYY HYPOGYNY
GHNOSSTU GUNSHOTS
SHOTGUNS
GHNOSTUU UNSOUGHT
GHNOSTUY YOUNGTHS
GHOOOSSW HOOSGOWS
GHOORTUY YOGHOURT
GHOPRTUW UPGROWTH
GHORSTUY YOGHURTS
GIIILMNT LIMITING
GIIILNNS INISLING
GIIILNNU LINGUINI
GIIILOTV VITILIGO
GIIIMMNX IMMIXING
GIIINNOS IONISING
GIIINNOT IGNITION
GIIINNOZ IONIZING
GIIINNTV INVITING
GIIINORS SIGNIORI
GIIINSTV VISITING
GIIJMMNY JIMMYING
GIIJMNOS JINGOISM
GIIJNNOS JOININGS
GIIJNNOT JOINTING
GIIJNNRU INJURING
GIIJNOST JINGOIST
JOISTING
GIIKKLNP KINGKLIP
GIIKKNNS SKINKING
GIIKKNRS KIRKINGS
GIIKLLNS KILLINGS
SKILLING
GIIKLMNS MILKINGS
GIIKLNNP PLINKING
GIIKLNNS INKLINGS
SLINKING
GIIKLNNT TINKLING
GIIKLNNW WINKLING
GIIKLNRS SKIRLING
GIIKLNST KILTINGS
KITLINGS
GIIKLNTT KITTLING
GIIKMMNS SKIMMING
GIIKMNPS SKIMPING
GIIKMNRS SMIRKING
GIIKNNNS SKINNING
GIIKNNOV INVOKING
GIIKNNPR PRINKING
GIIKNNPS KINGPINS
PINKINGS
GIIKNNSS SINKINGS
GIIKNNST STINKING
GIIKNNSW SWINKING
WINKINGS
GIIKNNTT KNITTING
GIIKNNTW TWINKING
GIIKNORS SKIORING
GIIKNPPS SKIPPING
GIIKNPSS PIGSKINS
GIIKNQRU QUIRKING
GIIKNRRS SKIRRING
GIIKNRSS GRISKINS
GIIKNRST SKIRTING
STRIKING
GIIKNSSV SKIVINGS
GIILLMNS MILLINGS
GIILLMNU ILLUMING
GIILLNOS GILLIONS
GIILLNPR PRILLING
GIILLNPS PILLINGS
SPILLING
GIILLNQU QUILLING
GIILLNRT TRILLING
GIILLNST STILLING
TILLINGS
GIILLNSW SWILLING
GIILLNTT LITTLING
GIILLNTW TWILLING
GIILLNVY LIVINGLY
GIILLNWY WILLYING
GIILLOPW POLLIWIG
GIILLPSW PIGSWILL
GIILLTUY GUILTILY
GIILLTYZ GLITZILY
GIILMMNP PLIMMING
GIILMMNS SLIMMING
GIILMNNU LUMINING
UNLIMING
GIILMNOS SMOILING
GIILMNPR RIMPLING
GIILMNPS LIMPINGS
SIMPLING
GIILMNPW WIMPLING
GIILMNPY IMPLYING
GIILMNSS SMILINGS
GIILMNST MISTLING
GIILMNSY MISLYING
GIILMNZZ MIZZLING
GIILMPRS PILGRIMS
GIILMPSU PUGILISM
GIILNNNU UNLINING
GIILNNPP NIPPLING
GIILNNPS SPLINING
GIILNNPU UNPILING
GIILNNTU UNTILING
GIILNNTW TWINLING
WINTLING
GIILNNUV UNLIVING
GIILNOPS PIGNOLIS
SPOILING
GIILNOPT PILOTING
GIILNORS LIGROINS
GIILNOSS SOILINGS
GIILNOST TOILINGS
GIILNPPR RIPPLING
GIILNPPS LIPPINGS
SIPPLING
SLIPPING
GIILNPPT TIPPLING
GIILNPPU UPPILING
GIILNPPY PIPINGLY
GIILNPRS SPIRLING
GIILNPRT TRIPLING
GIILNPSS LISPINGS
SPILINGS
GIILNQSU QUISLING
GIILNQTU QUILTING
GIILNRSW SWIRLING
GIILNRTW TWIRLING
GIILNRVY VIRGINLY
GIILNSST LISTINGS
GIILNSTT SLITTING
STILTING
TILTINGS
TITLINGS
GIILNSTU LINGUIST
GIILNSTW WITLINGS
GIILNSTY STINGILY
GIILNSZZ SIZZLING
GIILNTTT TITTLING
GIILNTTU TITULING
GIILNTTV VITTLING
GIILNTTW TWILTING
GIILNZZZ ZIZZLING
GIILOSST OLIGISTS
GIILPSTU PUGILIST
GIILRSST STRIGILS
GIILRTTY GRITTILY
GIIMMNPR PRIMMING
GIIMMNRS RIMMINGS
GIIMMNRT TRIMMING
GIIMMNRU IMMURING
GIIMMNSW SWIMMING
GIIMNNOP IMPONING
GIIMNNOR MINORING
GIIMNNOY IGNOMINY
GIIMNNTU MINUTING
MUNITING
MUTINING
GIIMNNUX UNMIXING
GIIMNOPS IMPOSING
GIIMNOST MOISTING
GIIMNOTT OMITTING
GIIMNOTV MOTIVING
VOMITING
GIIMNPPR PRIMPING
GIIMNPRS PRIMINGS
GIIMNPRU UMPIRING
GIIMNPTU IMPUTING
GIIMNRRS SMIRRING
GIIMNSST MISTINGS
GIIMNSSU MISUSING
GIIMNSSW SWINGISM
GIIMNSTT SMITTING
GIIMNSTU MUISTING
GIIMNSTY STIMYING
GIIMORRS RIGORISM
GIINNNOO ONIONING
GIINNNOT INTONING
NOINTING
GIINNNPS PINNINGS
SPINNING
GIINNNRU INURNING
GIINNNST TINNINGS
GIINNNSW WINNINGS
GIINNNTW TWINNING
GIINNOPR PROINING
GIINNOPS PIONINGS
GIINNOPT POINTING
GIINNOQU QUOINING
GIINNORS IRONINGS
NIGROSIN
ROSINING
GIINNORT IGNITRON
GIINNPPS SNIPPING
GIINNPRT PRINTING
GIINNPSS SNIPINGS
GIINNPSU PINGUINS
GIINNRSS RINSINGS
GIINNRSU INSURING
RUININGS
GIINNRTU UNTIRING
GIINNRUW UNWIRING
GIINNSSW INSWINGS
GIINNSTT STINTING
TINTINGS
GIINNSTU UNITINGS
GIINNSTW TWININGS
GIINNUVW UNWIVING
GIINOPST POSITING
SOPITING
GIINOPTV PIVOTING
GIINOQTU QUOITING
GIINORSS SIGNIORS
GIINORST IGNITORS
RIOTINGS
ROISTING
ROSITING
GIINORSV VISORING
GIINORSY SIGNIORY
GIINORTZ ROZITING
GIINORVZ VIZORING
GIINOSTT STOITING
GIINPPQU QUIPPING
GIINPPRT TRIPPING
GIINPPST TIPPINGS
GIINPRSS PRISSING
RISPINGS

GIINPRST	SPIRTING
	STRIPING
GIINPRSU	SIRUPING
	UPRISING
GIINPSTT	PITTINGS
	SPITTING
GIINPSTW	WINGTIPS
GIINPTTU	TITUPING
GIINQRSU	SQUIRING
GIINQRTU	QUIRTING
GIINQTTU	QUITTING
GIINQUZZ	QUIZZING
GIINRRST	STIRRING
GIINRSTV	STRIVING
GIINRSTW	WRITINGS
GIINSSSW	SWISSING
GIINSSTT	SITTINGS
GIINSSTU	SUITINGS
	TISSUING
GIINSTTW	TWISTING
	WITTINGS
GIINSWZZ	SWIZZING
GIINTTTW	TWITTING
GIIORRST	RIGORIST
GIIORSSV	ISOGRIVS
GIIPRSTZ	SPRITZIG
GIJKLNOY	JOKINGLY
GIJLLNOY	JOLLYING
GIJLNOST	JOSTLING
GIJLNSTU	JUNGLIST
	JUSTLING
GIJNOSTT	JOTTINGS
GIJNOSTU	JOUSTING
GIJNTTUY	JUTTYING
GIKKLNSU	SKULKING
GIKKNNSU	SKUNKING
GIKLLNNO	KNOLLING
GIKLNNOP	PLONKING
GIKLNNPU	PLUNKING
GIKLNNRU	KNURLING
	RUNKLING
GIKLNNUY	UNKINGLY
GIKLNOPR	PORKLING
GIKLNRSU	LURKINGS
GIKLORRW	WORKGIRL
GIKMNOSS	SMOKINGS
GIKNNOOS	SNOOKING
GIKNNOPR	PRONKING
GIKNNOQU	QUONKING
GIKNNOST	STONKING
GIKNNOSW	KNOWINGS
	SNOWKING
GIKNNOTT	KNOTTING
GIKNNOTU	KNOUTING
GIKNNOUY	UNYOKING
GIKNNPSU	SPUNKING
GIKNNRTU	TRUNKING
GIKNOOPS	SPOOKING
GIKNOOST	STOOKING
GIKNOOTW	KOTOWING
GIKNOPST	KINGPOST
GIKNORRW	RINGWORK
GIKNORST	STROKING
GIKNORSW	WORKINGS
GIKNSSTU	TUSKINGS
GILLMOOY	GLOOMILY
GILLMPUY	GLUMPILY
GILLNNSU	NULLINGS
GILLNOPR	PROLLING
GILLNOPS	POLLINGS
GILLNORS	ROLLINGS
GILLNORT	TROLLING
GILLNOST	TOLLINGS
GILLNOSY	LOSINGLY
GILLNOVY	LOVINGLY
GILLNPUY	PULINGLY
GILLNPYY	PLYINGLY
GILLNSUY	SULLYING
GILLOOPW	POLLIWOG
GILLOPWY	POLLYWIG
GILLORVY	GILLYVOR
GILLOSSY	GLOSSILY
GILMMNSU	SLUMMING
GILMMTUY	MULTIGYM
GILMNOOS	SLOOMING
GILMNOPY	MOPINGLY
GILMNORS	MORLINGS
GILMNORT	MORTLING
GILMNOSS	MOSLINGS
GILMNOSU	MOUSLING
GILMNOSY	SMOYLING
GILMNOTT	MOTTLING
GILMNOTU	MOULTING
GILMNOUV	VOLUMING
GILMNOVY	MOVINGLY
GILMNPPU	PLUMPING
GILMNPRU	RUMPLING
GILMNPSU	SLUMPING
GILMNSUY	MUSINGLY
GILMNUZZ	MUZZLING
GILMOOSY	MISOLOGY
GILMOOXY	MIXOLOGY
GILMPRUY	GRUMPILY
GILNNOOS	GLONOINS
	LOONINGS
	SNOOLING
GILNNOSU	NOUSLING
GILNNOTU	NONGUILT
GILNNOTW	TOWNLING
GILNNOUV	UNLOVING
GILNNRSU	NURSLING
GILNNSSU	UNSLINGS
GILNNUZZ	NUZZLING
GILNOOOY	OINOLOGY
GILNOOPS	LOOPINGS
	SPOOLING
GILNOORT	ROOTLING
GILNOOST	LOOTINGS
	STOOLING
	TOOLINGS
GILNOOSY	SINOLOGY
GILNOOTT	TOOTLING
GILNOOVY	VINOLOGY
GILNOOWY	WOOINGLY
GILNOPPP	PLOPPING
	POPPLING
GILNOPPS	LOPPINGS
	SLOPPING
GILNOPPT	TOPPLING
GILNOPRU	PROULING
GILNOPRW	PROWLING
GILNOPSU	SOUPLING
GILNOPSY	POSINGLY
	SPONGILY
GILNOPTT	PLOTTING
GILNOPTZ	PLOTZING
GILNORSU	LOURINGS
GILNORTU	TROULING
GILNORVY	ROVINGLY
GILNOSSW	SLOWINGS
GILNOSTT	SLOTTING
GILNOSTU	TOUSLING
GILNOSVW	WOLVINGS
GILNOSWY	YOWLINGS
GILNOSZZ	SOZZLING
GILNOTUY	OUTLYING
GILNOTUZ	TOUZLING
GILNPPRU	PURPLING
GILNPPSU	SUPPLING
GILNPRSU	PURLINGS
	SLURPING
	SPURLING
GILNPRYY	PRYINGLY
GILNPSSU	PLUSSING
GILNPUZZ	PUZZLING
GILNRRSU	SLURRING
GILNRSTU	LUSTRING
	RUSTLING
GILNRTTU	TURTLING
GILNRTYY	TRYINGLY
GILNSSTU	SINGULTS
	TUSSLING
GILNSSTY	STYLINGS
GILNSTTU	SUTTLING
GILNTUUY	UNGUILTY
GILNUWZZ	WUZZLING
GILOOORS	ROSOGLIO
GILOOOST	OOLOGIST
GILOORSS	GIROSOLS
GILOORSU	GLORIOUS
GILOORVY	VIROLOGY
GILOOSSS	ISOGLOSS
GILOOSST	OLOGISTS
GILOOSTW	TWIGLOOS
GILOOSTY	SITOLOGY
GILORSTT	TRIGLOTS
GILOSTUY	GULOSITY
GIMMMNSU	MUMMINGS
GIMMMNUY	MUMMYING
GIMMNOTY	TOMMYING
GIMMNSSU	SUMMINGS
GIMMNSTU	STUMMING
GIMMOSSU	GUMMOSIS
GIMMPSYY	PYGMYISM
GIMNNORS	MORNINGS
GIMNNORU	MOURNING
GIMNNOTU	MOUNTING
GIMNNOUV	UNMOVING
GIMNNSTU	MUNTINGS
GIMNOOOU	OOGONIUM
GIMNOOPS	SPOOMING
GIMNOORS	MOORINGS
	SMOORING
GIMNOORT	MOTORING
GIMNOORV	VROOMING
GIMNOOSS	OSMOSING
GIMNOOST	MOOTINGS
	SMOOTING
GIMNOPRT	TROMPING
GIMNOPST	STOMPING
GIMNOPTU	GUMPTION
GIMNORRU	RUMORING
GIMNORRW	RINGWORM
GIMNORST	STORMING
GIMNORSU	ROUMINGS
GIMNORSW	MISGROWN
GIMNOSST	GNOMISTS
GIMNOSSU	MOUSINGS
	MOUSSING
	SMOUSING
	SOUMINGS
GIMNOSTU	MOUSTING
	SMOUTING
GIMNOSYY	MISOGYNY
GIMNPRTU	TRUMPING
GIMNPSTU	STUMPING
GIMNRRSU	SMURRING
GIMNSTTU	SMUTTING
GIMNSTYY	STYMYING
GIMORSSW	MISGROWS
GIMPSSYY	GYPSYISM
GIMRSSUU	GURUISMS
GINNNOOS	NOONINGS
GINNNOST	STONNING
GINNNOSU	NONUSING
GINNNOSW	WONNINGS
GINNNPSU	PUNNINGS
GINNNRSU	RUNNINGS
GINNNSTU	STUNNING
	TUNNINGS
GINNNTUU	UNTUNING
GINNOOPS	SNOOPING
	SPOONING
GINNOOST	SNOOTING
GINNOOSW	SWOONING
GINNOOSZ	SNOOZING
GINNOPPU	UNPOPING
GINNOPRU	UNROPING
GINNOPRY	PROYNING
GINNOPSS	SPONGINS
	SPONSING
GINNOPSY	PYONINGS
GINNOPTU	GUNPOINT
GINNOPTY	POYNTING
GINNORSS	SNORINGS
	SORNINGS
GINNORST	SNORTING
GINNORSU	GRUNIONS
GINNOSST	STONINGS
GINNOSTT	SNOTTING
GINNOSTU	SNOUTING
	STOUNING
GINNOSTY	STONYING
GINNOSUW	SWOUNING
GINNPRSU	PRUNINGS
	SPURNING
GINNRSSU	NURSINGS
GINNRSTU	TURNINGS
	UNSTRING
GINNSTTU	NUTTINGS
	STUNTING
GINNSTUY	UNTYINGS
GINOOPPS	OPPOSING
	POGONIPS
GINOOPRS	SPOORING
GINOOPRT	TROOPING
GINOOPSS	SOOPINGS
GINOOPST	STOOPING
GINOOPSW	SWOOPING
	WOOPSING
GINOORST	ROOSTING
	ROOTINGS
GINOORTW	WROOTING
GINOOSTT	TOOTSING
GINOPPPR	PROPPING
GINOPPQU	QUOPPING
GINOPPSS	SOPPINGS
GINOPPST	STOPPING
	TOPPINGS
GINOPPSW	SWOPPING
GINOPRSS	PROSINGS
GINOPRST	SPORTING
GINOPRSU	INGROUPS
	POURINGS
GINOPRSV	PROVINGS
GINOPRTU	TROUPING
GINOPSST	POSTINGS
	SIGNPOST
	STOPINGS
GINOPSSU	SPOUSING
GINOPSTT	SPOTTING
GINOPSTU	POUTINGS
	SPOUTING
GINOPTTY	TYPTOING
GINOQRTU	TORQUING
GINORRWY	WORRYING
GINORSST	RINGTOSS
	SORTINGS
GINORSSU	SOURINGS
GINORSTU	OUTGRINS

	OUTRINGS
	ROUSTING
	ROUTINGS
	TOURINGS
GINORSTW	STROWING
	WORSTING
GINORSTY	ROYSTING
	STORYING
	STROYING
GINORTTT	TROTTING
GINORTTU	TROUTING
	TUTORING
GINOSSSS	SOSSINGS
GINOSSST	TOSSINGS
GINOSSSU	SOUSINGS
GINOSSSW	SOWSSING
GINOSSTT	SOTTINGS
GINOSSTU	OUTSINGS
	TOUSINGS
GINOSSTV	STOVINGS
GINOSSTW	STOWINGS
GINOSTTT	STOTTING
	TOTTINGS
GINOSTTW	SWOTTING
GINOSTUW	OUTSWING
	OUTWINGS
GINOTUVY	OUTVYING
GINPPPUY	PUPPYING
GINPPRSU	UPSPRING
GINPRRSU	PURRINGS
	SPURRING
GINPRSTU	SPURTING
GINPRSUU	PURSUING
	USURPING
GINPRSUY	SYRUPING
GINPSSUW	UPSWINGS
GINPSTTU	PUTTINGS
GINPTTUY	PUTTYING
GINRSSTU	RUSTINGS
	TRUSSING
GINRSTTU	RUTTINGS
	STURTING
	TRUSTING
GINRSTTY	TRYSTING
GINRSTUU	SUTURING
GINSTTTU	TUTTINGS
GIOOORSV	VIGOROSO
GIOOPRRS	PORRIGOS
GIOORRSU	RIGOROUS
GIOORSTU	GOITROUS
GIOORSUV	VIGOROUS
GIOPRRSU	PRURIGOS
GIOPRSSY	GOSSIPRY
GIOPRSTU	GROUPIST
GIORSTUY	RUGOSITY
GIOSTYYZ	ZYGOSITY
GJOORSTT	JOGTROTS
GKLOOOTY	TOKOLOGY
GLLLOORS	LOGROLLS
GLLOOPTY	POLYGLOT
GLLOOPWY	POLLYWOG
GLLOOXYY	XYLOLOGY
GLMMSSUU	SLUMGUMS
GLMNOOOS	MONOLOGS
GLMNOOOT	MONOGLOT
GLMNOOOY	MONOLOGY
	NOMOLOGY
GLMNORUW	LUNGWORM
GLMNRTUU	NGULTRUM
GLMOOOPY	POMOLOGY
GLMOOORS	MOORLOGS
GLMOORWW	GLOWWORM
GLMOOYYZ	ZYMOLOGY
GLMORSUW	LUGWORMS
GLNNOORS	LORGNONS
GLNOOOSY	NOSOLOGY
GLNOOOTY	ONTOLOGY
GLNOOPRS	PROLONGS
GLNOOPSY	POLYGONS
GLNOOPYY	POLYGONY
GLNOPRSU	LONGSPUR
GLNOPYYY	POLYGYNY
GLNORSTY	STRONGLY
	STRONGYL
GLNORTUW	LUNGWORT
GLNOSSUW	SUNGLOWS
GLNOSTTU	GLUTTONS
GLNOTTUY	GLUTTONY
GLOOOPSY	POSOLOGY
GLOOOPTY	OPTOLOGY
	TOPOLOGY
GLOOORUY	OUROLOGY
GLOOPRYY	PYROLOGY
GLOOPSSY	GOSSYPOL
GLOOPTYY	LOGOTYPY
	TYPOLOGY
GLOORSUU	ORGULOUS
GLOOSTUW	OUTGLOWS
GMMPSUUW	MUGWUMPS
GMNNOOOY	MONOGONY
GMNNOOYY	MONOGYNY
GMNOORSU	GUNROOMS
GMNOORSW	MORWONGS
GMORSTUW	MUGWORTS
GNNPRSUU	UNSPRUNG
GNNRSTUU	UNSTRUNG
GNOOORSS	GORSOONS
GNOOOSSS	GOSSOONS
GNOORSUW	WRONGOUS
GNOORTUW	OUTGROWN
GNOPRSTU	GUNPORTS
GNOPRSUW	GROWNUPS
GNPPRSUU	UPSPRUNG
GOOPRSST	GOSPORTS
GOOPRTUU	OUTGROUP
GOORSSTU	OUTGROSS
GOORSTUW	OUTGROWS
GOORTTUW	GOUTWORT
HHIILOPT	THIOPHIL
HHIINNST	THINNISH
HHIIPSST	PHTHISIS
HHILPSSY	SYLPHISH
HHIMMOSS	MISHMOSH
HHIMNPSY	NYMPHISH
HHIMPSSU	SUMPHISH
HHINOOSW	NOHOWISH
HHINOPPS	PHOSPHIN
HHIORSST	SHORTISH
HHKKSSUU	KHUSKHUS
HHMRSTUY	RHYTHMUS
HHOOPPRS	PHOSPHOR
HHOOSSTT	HOTSHOTS
HIIILMNS	NIHILISM
HIIILNST	NIHILIST
HIIILNTY	NIHILITY
HIIINRST	RHINITIS
HIIKMNST	MISTHINK
HIIKMRSS	SKIRMISH
HIIKNPSS	KINSHIPS
HIIKOPRS	PIROSHKI
HIIKOPRZ	PIROZHKI
HIIKQRSU	QUIRKISH
HIIKSSTT	SKITTISH
HIILLMMO	MILLIMHO
	MILLIOHM
HIILLSTT	LITTLISH
HIILMMSS	SLIMMISH
HIILMOST	HOMILIST
HIILMPSU	SILPHIUM
HIILMPSY	IMPISHLY
HIILMSTU	LITHIUMS
HIILMSWY	WHIMSILY
HIILMTUY	HUMILITY
HIILPSST	THLIPSIS
HIILPSSY	SYPHILIS
HIILRSTT	TRILITHS
HIILRSTY	SHIRTILY
HIILSSTT	STILTISH
HIIMNSTT	TINSMITH
HIIMOPSS	PHIMOSIS
HIIMSSTT	SHITTIMS
HIINNNSY	NINNYISH
HIINNOST	THIONINS
HIINORST	HISTRION
HIINPSTW	TWINSHIP
HIIORSST	HISTRIOS
HIIPPQSU	QUIPPISH
HIIQRSSU	SQUIRISH
HIISSSSY	SISSYISH
HIISSTXY	SIXTYISH
HIITTTZZ	TZITZITH
HIKLORTY	KRYOLITH
HIKMNSUU	MINSHUKU
HIKMOSTZ	SHKOTZIM
HIKNNORS	INKHORNS
HIKNNSTU	UNTHINKS
HIKNOTTU	OUTTHINK
HIKOOPRZ	PIROZHOK
HIKOOPSS	SPOOKISH
HIKOPSSY	KYPHOSIS
HILLMSUY	MULISHLY
HILLNOUY	UNHOLILY
HILLOOST	LITHOSOL
HILLOPST	HILLTOPS
HILLOSWY	OWLISHLY
HILLPSUY	PLUSHILY
HILLSSUY	SLUSHILY
HILMMOSU	HOLMIUMS
HILMNOOT	MONOLITH
HILMOOPT	PHILOMOT
HILMOPSY	MOPISHLY
HILMOSSW	WHOLISMS
HILMOTUY	MOUTHILY
HILMPPSU	PLUMPISH
HILMPRTU	PHILTRUM
HILMPSYY	SYMPHILY
HILMSTUU	THULIUMS
HILNOPSU	UNPOLISH
HILNORTY	THORNILY
HILNOSTY	THIONYLS
	TONISHLY
HILOOPYZ	ZOOPHILY
HILOOSTT	OTOLITHS
HILOOSTZ	ZOOLITHS
HILOOTTY	TOOTHILY
HILOPPSY	POPISHLY
HILOPSXY	OXYPHILS
HILORSTU	UROLITHS
HILORSUU	URUSHIOL
HILORTUW	OUTWHIRL
HILORTWY	WORTHILY
HILOSSTW	WHOLISTS
HILOSSTY	HYLOISTS
	THYLOSIS
HILOSTWW	WHITLOWS
HILOSTYY	TOYISHLY
HILPPRSU	PURPLISH
HILPPSUY	UPPISHLY
HILPRSUW	UPWHIRLS
HILSSTTU	SLUTTISH
HIMMOPRU	PHORMIUM
HIMMSSTY	MYTHISMS
HIMNOPRS	MORPHINS
HIMNOPRX	PHORMINX
HIMNOPSY	PHISNOMY
HIMNOSTY	THYMOSIN
HIMNSSTY	HYMNISTS
HIMOOPRS	ISOMORPH
HIMOPRRT	TRIMORPH
HIMOPRSW	SHIPWORM
HIMOPRWW	WHIPWORM
HIMOPSSS	SOPHISMS
HIMOPSST	PHOTISMS
HIMORSTU	HUMORIST
	THORIUMS
HIMORSTW	MISTHROW
HIMOSTTV	MITSVOTH
HIMOTTVZ	MITZVOTH
HIMPRSTU	TRIUMPHS
HIMPSTUY	PYTHIUMS
HIMRSSTY	RHYMISTS
HIMRSTTU	MISTRUTH
HIMSSTTY	MYTHISTS
HINNORST	TINHORNS
HINNPSSU	NUNSHIPS
HINNSSUY	SUNSHINY
HINOORST	HORNITOS
HINOORSZ	HORIZONS
HINOPPSS	SHIPPONS
HINOPSSS	SONSHIPS
HINOPSSY	HYPNOSIS
HINOPSTW	TOWNSHIP
HINORSST	HORNISTS
HINORTXY	THYROXIN
HINOSSTU	SNOUTISH
HINPPSSU	PUSHPINS
HIOOOPRZ	ZOOPHORI
HIOOPRTT	POORTITH
HIOORSST	ORTHOSIS
HIOOSSTT	SHOOTIST
HIOPRSSW	WORSHIPS
HIOPRSUZ	RHIZOPUS
HIOPSSST	SOPHISTS
HIOPSSTU	UPHOISTS
HIOPSSTY	PHYTOSIS
HIORRSSY	SORRYISH
HIOSSTTU	STOUTISH
HIOSTTUW	WITHOUTS
HIPPPSUY	PUPPYISH
HIPSUYZZ	ZIZYPHUS
HKKLOOSY	KOLKHOSY
HKKLOOYZ	KOLKHOZY
HKKOOPYY	HOKYPOKY
HKKOOSSY	SKYHOOKS
HKMNORRU	KRUMHORN
HKMOOORW	HOOKWORM
HKNNRSUU	UNSHRUNK
HKNOORRW	HORNWORK
HKNOOSWW	KNOWHOWS
HKOOOPST	POTHOOKS
HKOOPRSW	WORKSHOP
HKOOSVYZ	SOVKHOZY
HLLLOOWY	HOLLOWLY
HLLMNOOU	MONOHULL
HLLOPPRY	PROPHYLL
HLMOOSTY	SMOOTHLY
HLMORRSY	MYRRHOLS
HLNOOPPY	POLYPHON
HLOOSTUW	OUTHOWLS
HLOPRSTY	PROTHYLS
HLPRSSUU	SULPHURS
HLPRSUUY	SULPHURY
HMMNOOSY	HOMONYMS
HMMNOOYY	HOMONYMY
HMMOORSU	MUSHROOM
HMMRSTUU	HUMSTRUM
HMNOOOST	MOONSHOT
HMNOOOTY	HOMOTONY
HMNOORRW	HORNWORM
HMNOOSTU	UNSMOOTH

HMNOPSYY	HYPONYMS
	SYMPHONY
HMNOPYYY	HYPONYMY
HMOOOPRZ	ZOOMORPH
HMOOORSW	SHOWROOM
HMOOPTYY	HOMOTYPY
HMOORSUU	HUMOROUS
HMOORTUU	OUTHUMOR
HNNORTTU	NONTRUTH
HNNOSSTY	SYNTHONS
HNOOOOPR	OOPHORON
HNOOPPYY	HYPOPYON
HNOOPRSW	SHOPWORN
HNOOPRTU	HORNPOUT
HNOOPSTY	TYPHOONS
HNOORRTW	HORNWORT
HNOORSTU	SOUTHRON
HNOOSSTU	UNSHOOTS
HNOPRTUW	UPTHROWN
HNORSTUW	UNWORTHS
HNORTUWY	UNWORTHY
HNOSSTUU	UNSHOUTS
HNOSTTUU	OUTHUNTS
HNRSTTUU	UNTRUTHS
HOOOSTTU	OUTSHOOT
	SHOOTOUT
HOOPPSST	POTSHOPS
HOOPPSTY	PHOTOPSY
HOOPRRST	PORTHORS
HOOPSSTT	POTSHOTS
HOOPSSTU	UPSHOOTS
HOOPSSTW	POSTSHOW
HOOPSSTY	TOYSHOPS
HOOQSSUY	SQUOOSHY
HOORTTUW	OUTTHROW
	OUTWORTH
HOOSSTTU	OUTSHOTS
HOOSTTUU	OUTSHOUT
HOPPRRYY	PORPHYRY
HOPRRSUY	PYRRHOUS
HOPRSSTU	HOTSPURS
HOPRSTUW	UPTHROWS
HOPSSTTU	SHOTPUTS
HORRSTTU	THRUSTOR
HOSSTTUU	SHUTOUTS
HPRSTTUU	THRUPUTS
	UPTHRUST
IIIJJLNS	JINJILIS
IIIKLNPS	SPILIKIN
IIIKMNNS	MINIKINS
IIIKMNSS	MINISKIS
IIILLMMN	MINIMILL
IIILLMNP	MINIPILL
IIILLMNU	ILLINIUM
IIILLNOS	ILLISION
IIILMRSV	VIRILISM
IIILMUVX	LIXIVIUM
IIILRTVY	VIRILITY
IIIMMMNS	MINIMISM
IIIMMNST	INTIMISM
	MINIMIST
IIIMMPRS	IMPRIMIS
IIIMNSTT	INTIMIST
IIIMNTTY	INTIMITY
IIINORRS	IRRISION
IIINPRST	INSPIRIT
IIINQTUY	INIQUITY
IIINSSTU	SINUITIS
IIIOSTTU	OUISTITI
IIISSTTW	WISTITIS
IIJJSTUU	JIUJITSU
IIJLLNOS	JILLIONS
IIJMNOSS	MISJOINS
IIJNNOST	INJOINTS
IIJNNSTU	NINJITSU
IIKKLNOS	KOLINSKI
IIKKNPSS	KIPSKINS
IIKLLNOS	SKILLION
IIKLLNSY	SLINKILY
IIKLMNPS	LIMPKINS
IIKLMPSY	SKIMPILY
IIKLNOSS	OILSKINS
IIKLQRUY	QUIRKILY
IIKMNNOO	MONOKINI
IIKMNORS	KIRIMONS
IIKMNPSS	SIMPKINS
IIKNOSTT	STOTINKI
IILLLMUX	MILLILUX
IILLLPTU	LILLIPUT
IILLLPUV	PULVILLI
IILLMNOS	MILLIONS
IILLMRTU	TRILLIUM
IILLMUUV	ILLUVIUM
IILLNOOR	ORILLION
IILLNOPS	PILLIONS
IILLNORT	TRILLION
IILLNOST	STILLION
IILLNOSU	ILLUSION
IILLNOSZ	ZILLIONS
IILLNSST	INSTILLS
IILLNSTT	LITTLINS
IILLOPUV	PULVILIO
IILMMNSU	LUMINISM
IILMMPSS	SIMPLISM
IILMMSUU	SIMULIUM
IILMMSWY	SWIMMILY
IILMNORT	MIRLITON
IILMNOSS	LIONISMS
IILMNSTU	LUMINIST
IILMORSS	SIMILORS
IILMORST	TROILISM
IILMOTTY	MOTILITY
IILMPSST	SIMPLIST
IILMRSSY	MISSILRY
IILNNOOT	NOLITION
IILNNOQU	QUINOLIN
IILNNOST	NITINOLS
IILNNSSU	INSULINS
IILNOOST	INOSITOL
IILNOOTV	VOLITION
IILNOPST	PINITOLS
IILNORSS	SIRLOINS
IILNPPSY	SNIPPILY
IILNRTWY	WINTRILY
IILOOPPR	LIRIPOOP
IILOPRST	TRIPOLIS
IILOPSSS	PSILOSIS
IILOPSST	PTILOSIS
IILOPSTY	PILOSITY
IILORSTT	TROILIST
IILORSTV	VITRIOLS
IILOSSTV	VIOLISTS
IILPRSSY	PRISSILY
IILRSSTU	SILURIST
IILSSTTT	TITLISTS
IILSTUUV	UVULITIS
IILSTUVV	VULVITIS
IIMMMNSU	MINIMUMS
IIMMNTUY	IMMUNITY
IIMMOPST	OPTIMISM
IIMMOPSU	OPIUMISM
IIMMSTTU	MITTIMUS
IIMNNOOT	MONITION
IIMNNOSU	MISUNION
	UNIONISM
IIMNNOTU	MUNITION
IIMNOOSS	OMISSION
IIMNOPRS	IMPRISON
IIMNOPST	MISPOINT
IIMNORTT	INTROMIT
IIMNORTY	MINORITY
IIMNOSSS	MISSIONS
IIMNOSST	SIMONIST
IIMNOSTX	MIXTIONS
IIMNPRST	IMPRINTS
	MISPRINT
IIMNPTUY	IMPUNITY
IIMNRSTY	MINISTRY
IIMOPSTT	OPTIMIST
IIMORSTY	RIMOSITY
IIMOSSTY	MYOSITIS
IIMOTTVY	MOTIVITY
IIMPRTUY	IMPURITY
IIMRRTUV	TRIUMVIR
IIMRSTTU	TRITIUMS
IIMRSTUV	TRIVIUMS
IIMSSSTU	MISSUITS
IIMSSTUW	SWIMSUIT
IINNOOPS	OPINIONS
IINNOPPT	PINPOINT
IINNOPTU	PUNITION
IINNOSTU	INUSTION
	UNIONIST
	UNITIONS
IINNPSST	TINSNIPS
IINNQSTU	QUINTINS
IINNSTTU	TINNITUS
IINOOPST	POSITION
IINOPSSS	ISOSPINS
IINORSST	IRONISTS
IINORSTT	INTROITS
IINOSTTU	TUITIONS
IINOSTVY	VINOSITY
IINRTTUY	TRIUNITY
IINSSTTW	INTWISTS
IIOOPSTV	OVIPOSIT
IIOOSTTY	OTIOSITY
IIOPRRTY	PRIORITY
IIOPRSSS	PISSOIRS
IIORRRSY	IRRISORY
IIORSSTV	IVORISTS
	VISITORS
IIORSTUV	VIRTUOSI
IIOSSTTU	OUSTITIS
IIPRSSTU	SPIRITUS
IJJMSSUU	JUJUISMS
IJJSSTUU	JUJITSUS
	JUJUISTS
IJJSTUUU	JIUJUTSU
IJKLLOSY	KILLJOYS
IJLNOQSU	JONQUILS
IJMPSTUU	JUMPSUIT
IJNNOSTU	UNJOINTS
IJNNSTUU	NINJUTSU
IKKLNORW	LINKWORK
IKKLNOSY	KOLINSKY
IKKMNOSU	KIKUMONS
IKKNORST	KIRKTONS
IKKORSSY	SIKORSKY
IKLLMORW	MILLWORK
IKLLOOTV	KILOVOLT
IKLLOSSY	KYLLOSIS
IKLLOSTU	OUTKILLS
IKLMNPSU	LUMPKINS
IKLMOOSS	LOOKISMS
IKLMOPSS	MILKSOPS
IKLMORSW	SILKWORM
IKLMORTW	MILKWORT
IKLMOSSY	SOYMILKS
IKLNOOST	KILOTONS
IKLNOOSW	WOOLSKIN
IKLNOPST	SLIPKNOT
IKLNOTTY	KNOTTILY
IKLNPSSU	SKULPINS
IKLNPSUY	SPUNKILY
IKLOOPSY	SPOOKILY
IKLOOSTT	TOOLKITS
IKLOSSSU	SOUSLIKS
IKMNNOSW	MISKNOWN
IKMNOOOS	OKIMONOS
IKMNOORS	OMIKRONS
IKMNOSSW	MISKNOWS
IKMNPPSU	PUMPKINS
IKMNRSTU	TRINKUMS
IKNNOPSY	PONYSKIN
IKNNRSTU	TURNSKIN
IKNOOPRT	PINKROOT
IKNOORRW	IRONWORK
IKNOOSST	ISOKONTS
IKNOPRSW	PINWORKS
IKNOPSST	INKSPOTS
IKNOPSSY	PYKNOSIS
IKNOPSTT	STINKPOT
IKNOPSTW	TOWNSKIP
IKNORSTW	TINWORKS
IKNPSSTU	SPUTNIKS
IKORSSTU	KURTOSIS
IKORSTTU	OUTSKIRT
ILLLMOPS	PLIMSOLL
ILLLMPPU	PULPMILL
ILLLOOPP	LOLLIPOP
ILLLOOWY	WOOLLILY
ILLMNOSU	MULLIONS
ILLMNRSU	MILLRUNS
ILLMOORS	MOORILLS
ILLMOOST	TIMOLOLS
ILLMOPRW	PILLWORM
ILLMOPSS	PLIMSOLS
ILLMOSSY	LISSOMLY
ILLMPSUY	PSYLLIUM
ILLMPTUY	MULTIPLY
ILLNOORT	TORNILLO
ILLNOQSU	QUILLONS
ILLNORSU	RULLIONS
ILLNPSUU	LUPULINS
ILLOOPRW	POORWILL
ILLOORSZ	ZORILLOS
ILLOORTT	ROTOTILL
ILLOPPSS	SLIPSLOP
ILLOPPSY	SLOPPILY
ILLOPRTW	PILLWORT
ILLOPRXY	PROLIXLY
ILLOPSST	POLLISTS
ILLORSTU	TROLLIUS
ILLORSUY	ILLUSORY
ILLOSTUW	OUTWILLS
ILLOSTXY	XYLITOLS
ILLOTTWY	WITTOLLY
ILLRSTUY	SULTRILY
ILMMSSSU	SLUMISMS
ILMNOOPS	POLONISM
ILMNOOPU	POLONIUM
ILMNOSUU	LUMINOUS
ILMNOTTU	MULTITON
ILMOPPSU	POPULISM
ILMORSTU	TURMOILS
ILMORSTY	STORMILY
ILMOSTUV	VOLUMIST
ILMOSTUY	TIMOUSLY
ILMPPTUU	PULPITUM
ILMPSSTU	PLUMISTS
ILMPSTUY	STUMPILY
ILMSSTUU	STIMULUS
ILMSTTUY	SMUTTILY
ILNNORSU	LINURONS
ILNOOPRT	PLIOTRON
ILNOOPSS	PLOSIONS
ILNOOPSV	VOLPINOS
ILNOOPSY	SNOOPILY
	SPOONILY

ILNOORSS	ROSINOLS
ILNOORTW	TOILWORN
ILNOOSST	SOLITONS
ILNOOSTU	SOLUTION
ILNOOSTY	SNOOTILY
ILNOOTUV	VOLUTION
ILNOPRSU	PURLOINS
ILNOPSSU	PULSIONS
	UPSILONS
ILNOPSSW	SNOWSLIP
ILNOPSSY	YPSILONS
ILNOPSTU	UNSPOILT
ILNORSST	NOSTRILS
ILNORSSU	SURLOINS
ILNORSTU	TORULINS
ILNORSTY	NITROSYL
ILNORTXY	NITROXYL
ILNOSSTW	STOWLINS
ILNOSSTY	TYLOSINS
ILNOSTTY	SNOTTILY
ILNOSTUV	VOLUTINS
ILNOSUVY	VINOUSLY
ILNPSUUV	PULVINUS
ILOOORSS	ROSOLIOS
ILOOPPRS	PROPOLIS
ILOOPSST	POLOISTS
	TOPSOILS
ILOORSTU	RISOLUTO
ILOOSSST	SOLOISTS
ILOPPSTU	POPULIST
ILOPRSTY	SPORTILY
ILOPSSTU	SLIPOUTS
ILOPSTTY	SPOTTILY
ILOPSUUV	PLUVIOUS
ILOQRTUU	LOQUITUR
ILPPRTUY	PULPITRY
ILRSTTUY	TRUSTILY
ILRSTUUX	LUXURIST
ILSSSTTY	STYLISTS
IMMNOORS	MORONISM
IMMNOSSU	MUSIMONS
IMMNOSUU	MUONIUMS
IMMOORTU	MOTORIUM
IMMOPSTU	OPTIMUMS
IMMRSTUY	SUMMITRY
IMMSSSTU	SUMMISTS
IMNNNOSU	MUNNIONS
IMNNOORS	NORIMONS
IMNNOOTT	MONOTINT
IMNNOSUU	NUMINOUS
IMNOOPPS	POMPIONS
IMNOOPST	TOMPIONS
IMNOOPSU	OPSONIUM
IMNOORRS	MORRIONS
IMNOORST	MONITORS
	TROMINOS
IMNOORTY	MONITORY
	MORONITY
IMNOORVY	OMNIVORY
IMNOOSUX	OXONIUMS
IMNOPPSU	PUMPIONS
IMNOPRSW	PINWORMS
IMNOPSSU	SPUMONIS
IMNORRSU	MURRIONS
IMNORSTY	TRIONYMS
IMNOSTUU	MUTINOUS
IMNRSTUU	UNTRUISM
IMOOPRRS	PROMISOR
IMOOPRST	IMPOSTOR
IMOOPRSU	IMPOROUS
IMOOQSTU	MOSQUITO
IMOORRTT	TRIMOTOR
IMOORSTT	MOTORIST
IMOORSTU	SUMOTORI
	TIMOROUS
IMOORSTY	MOROSITY
IMOORTVY	VOMITORY
IMOOSSTY	MYOSOTIS
IMOOSTUV	VOMITOUS
IMOPRRSY	PRIMROSY
IMOPRSST	TROPISMS
IMOPRSTU	PROTIUMS
IMOPSSST	MISSTOPS
IMOPSSTU	UTOPISMS
IMORSSST	MISSORTS
IMORSSTU	TOURISMS
IMORSTTU	MISTUTOR
	TUTORISM
IMOSSSTU	MISSOUTS
IMOSSTUW	OUTSWIMS
IMPPPSUY	PUPPYISM
IMRSSSTU	SISTRUMS
IMRSSTTU	MISTRUST
IMRSSTTY	MISTRYST
IMRSTTUY	YTTRIUMS
INNNNOOU	NONUNION
INNNOOPT	NONPOINT
INNNOPRT	NONPRINT
INNNORSU	RUNNIONS
INNNORTU	TRUNNION
INNNOSTY	SYNTONIN
INNOOPRT	TROPONIN
INNOOPRU	PROUNION
INNOOPSS	OPSONINS
	SPONSION
INNOOPSU	UNPOISON
INNOORST	NOTORNIS
INNOPRSU	UNPRISON
INNORTTU	NOTTURNI
INNOSSTU	NONSUITS
INOOOSSZ	ZOONOSIS
INOOOTXZ	ZOOTOXIN
INOOPRST	PORTIONS
	POSITRON
	SORPTION
INOOPSSS	POISSONS
INOOPSST	POSITONS
INOOPSTT	SPITTOON
INOOPTTU	OUTPOINT
INOORSST	ISOTRONS
	TORSIONS
INOORSSU	ROSINOUS
INOORSTT	TORTONIS
INOORSTY	SONORITY
INOPPSST	TOPSPINS
INOPRTTU	PRINTOUT
INOPRTUY	PUNITORY
INOPSSSU	POUSSINS
INOPSSSY	SYNOPSIS
INOPSSTU	SPINOUTS
INORSSUV	UNVISORS
INOSSTUW	SNOWSUIT
INPPRRUU	PURPURIN
INPRRSTU	SURPRINT
INPRSSTU	UNSTRIPS
INPRSSTY	TRYPSINS
INPRSTTU	TURNSPIT
INRSSTTU	INTRUSTS
INRSTTUU	UNITRUST
INSSSTUU	SUNSUITS
INSSTTUW	UNTWISTS
IOOPRRSV	PROVISOR
IOOPRSSV	PROVISOS
IOOPRSSY	ISOSPORY
IOOPRSTT	POSTRIOT
IOOPRSTY	ISOTROPY
	POROSITY
IOORRSTY	SORORITY
IOORRTTT	TROTTOIR
IOORSSTT	RISOTTOS
IOORSSUV	VOUSSOIR
IOORSTTU	TORTIOUS
IOORSTTY	TOROSITY
IOORSTUV	VIRTUOSO
IOORSUUX	UXORIOUS
IOOSSTTU	STOTIOUS
IOPPPRST	PITPROPS
IOPPRSST	RIPSTOPS
IOPRRSUV	PROVIRUS
IOPRSSTT	PROTISTS
	TROPISTS
IOPRSSUU	SPURIOUS
IOPRSTTU	OUTSTRIP
IOPRSTUU	POURSUIT
IOPRSTUY	PYRITOUS
IOPRSUVX	POXVIRUS
IOPSSTTU	UTOPISTS
IOQRSTTU	QUITTORS
IOQRSTUU	TURQUOIS
IOQRTUXY	QUIXOTRY
IORRSSST	TSORRISS
IORRSUVV	SURVIVOR
IORSSTTU	TOURISTS
IORSSTTW	TWISTORS
IORSSUUU	USURIOUS
IORSTTUY	TOURISTY
	YTTRIOUS
IORSTUUV	VIRTUOUS
IPPTTTUY	TITTUPPY
IPRRSSTU	STIRRUPS
IPRRSTUU	PRURITUS
IPRSSTUU	PURSUITS
JJSSTUUU	JUJUTSUS
JLNSTUUY	UNJUSTLY
JLOOSUYY	JOYOUSLY
JMOPSTUU	OUTJUMPS
JNNOORRU	NONJUROR
JNOORSSU	SOJOURNS
JNOOSUUY	UNJOYOUS
KKNOORTW	KNOTWORK
KKOOSSUU	KOUSKOUS
KLLMNSUU	NUMSKULL
KLLMOSSU	MOLLUSKS
KLNORSTY	KLYSTRON
KLOOORWW	WOOLWORK
KLOOOSTU	LOOKOUTS
	OUTLOOKS
KLOOPRSW	SLOPWORK
KLOSSTUU	OUTSULKS
KMOOORRW	WORKROOM
KNNNOSUW	UNKNOWNS
KNOOPSTT	TOPKNOTS
KNOPRSTY	KRYPTONS
KNORRSTY	KRYTRONS
KOOPRSTW	TOPWORKS
	WORKTOPS
KOORSTUW	OUTWORKS
	WORKOUTS
KORRSTWY	TRYWORKS
KORSTTUW	TUTWORKS
LLLMMSUU	MULMULLS
LLLOOPPY	LOLLYPOP
LLMOOPRS	ROLLMOPS
LLOOPRST	TROLLOPS
LLOOPRTY	TROLLOPY
LLOOPSTU	OUTPOLLS
LLOORSTU	OUTROLLS
	ROLLOUTS
LLOPSTUU	OUTPULLS
	PULLOUTS
LLOSUUVV	VOLVULUS
LMNOOOPY	MONOPOLY
LMNOOPYY	POLYONYM
LMOOOOPR	POOLROOM
LMOOOORT	TOOLROOM
LMOOPRTU	PULMOTOR
LMOOPSYY	POLYSOMY
LMOORSWW	SLOWWORM
LMOOSSSU	MOLOSSUS
LMOOTXYY	XYLOTOMY
LMOPPRTY	PROMPTLY
LMOSTUUU	TUMULOUS
LMRSSTUU	LUSTRUMS
LNOOOPRT	POLTROON
LNOOOPYZ	POLYZOON
LNOOPPRY	PROPYLON
LNOOPSTU	PULTOONS
LNOOPSWW	SNOWPLOW
LNRSTUUV	VULTURNS
LOOOORSS	OLOROSOS
LOOPPSUU	POPULOUS
LOOPPSUY	POLYPOUS
LOOPRSTT	STOLPORT
LOOPRSUY	POROUSLY
LOOPSTTU	OUTPLOTS
LORSSTUU	LUSTROUS
MMNOOOSY	MONOSOMY
MMOORTTY	TOMMYROT
MMOPSSTY	SYMPTOMS
MNNOOOSS	MONSOONS
MNNOOOTY	MONOTONY
MNNOORSU	MONURONS
MNNOPRTU	NONTRUMP
MNNOSSYY	SYNONYMS
MNNOSTUU	UNMOUNTS
MNNOSYYY	SYNONYMY
MNOOOPPS	POMPOONS
MNOOOPRT	MOONPORT
MNOOORTW	MOONWORT
MNOOORXY	OXYMORON
MNOOPRTU	PRONOTUM
MNOOPSTY	TOPONYMS
MNOOPTYY	TOPONYMY
MNOORSSU	SUNROOMS
MNOOSTTW	TOWMONTS
MNORSSTU	NOSTRUMS
MNORSTUU	SURMOUNT
MOOOPRRT	PROMOTOR
MOOORRTW	MOORWORT
	TOMORROW
	WORMROOT
MOOPSSSU	OPOSSUMS
MOORRSUU	RUMOROUS
MOORSTUU	TUMOROUS
MOORSTUY	UROSTOMY
MOPRTTUU	OUTTRUMP
MORRSSTU	ROSTRUMS
MORSSTUU	STRUMOUS
MSSTTUUU	TSUTSUMU
NNOOOPST	PONTOONS
	SPONTOON
NNOOPRSU	PRONOUNS
NNOOPSSS	SPONSONS
NNOORSTY	NONSTORY
NNOORTTU	NOTTURNO
NOOOPPRS	PROSOPON
NOOORSSU	SONOROUS
NOOPRSSS	SPONSORS
NOORSSTU	UNROOSTS
NOORSTUW	OUTSWORN
NOPSSSTU	SUNSPOTS
NORSTTUU	OUTTURNS
	TURNOUTS
NOSTTTUU	OUTSTUNT
NRSSTTUU	UNTRUSTS
NRSTTUUY	UNTRUSTY
OOOOPRST	POTOROOS
OOOPRSSU	SOPOROUS
OOOPRSTU	OUTROOPS
OOORSTTU	OUTROOTS

OOPRSSSU SOURSOPS
OOPRSSTV PROVOSTS
OOPRSTTU OUTPORTS
OUTSPORT
OOPRSTUU OUTPOURS
OOPSSSTT TOSSPOTS
OOPSSTTU OUTPOSTS
OORSTTTU OUTTROTS
OORSTTUU TORTUOUS
OPPRRSTU PURPORTS
OPPRSSTU SUPPORTS
OPRSSSUU SOURPUSS
ORRSSTTU TRUSTORS
ORSSTTUU SURTOUTS
RRSSSUUU SUSURRUS

Other Scrabble titles from Chambers:

Official Scrabble® Words International

The book which combines the word lists of *Official Scrabble® Words* and the *Official Scrabble® Tournament and Club Word List*. Essential for people who compete at an international level or who wish to play with the increased vocabulary.

ISBN: 0550 10058 X
Hardback
Price: £14.99

Family Scrabble® Dictionary

Ideal for families and recreational players: inflections are shown in full, an example definition is given for each headword, and vulgar, obsolete and offensive words have been omitted.

ISBN: 0550 12011 4
Hardback
Price: £14.99

Top Scrabble® Tips by Allan Simmons

Tips on Scrabble strategy for beginners and more advanced players, with puzzles to test Scrabble play.

ISBN: 0550 12002 5
Paperback
Price: £5.99

Titles of further interest:

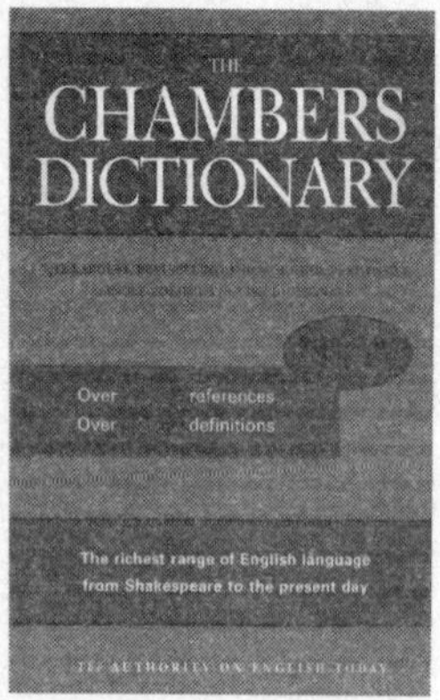

The Chambers Dictionary

The most comprehensive and authoritative single-volume dictionary of English available, and the official dictionary for Scrabble®. With over 215,000 references and 300,000 definitions.

ISBN: 0550 14000 X
Hardback
Price: £30

ISBN: 0550 14000 5
Thumb-indexed
Price: £35

The Chambers Encyclopedia

A unique single-volume encyclopedia. Over 200,000 facts and figures arranged in tables, diagrams and lists and organized into fourteen thematic sections.

ISBN: 0550 13001 2
Hardback
Price: £25

Chambers Book of Facts

The most reliable source of up-to-date facts and figures available, with over 160,000 facts covering 280 fields of interest.

ISBN: 0550 10057 1
Hardback
Price: £14.99